THE LITTLE WAY ASSOCIATION

Helps the Missions under the Patronage of St Therese

St Therese is calling on generous souls to adopt her method of spirituality which she called "The Little Way of Spiritual Childhood", and it was to promote this Little Way and to help missionaries spread the Gospel all over the world that The Little Way Association came into being. Its aims are:

1) **To help missionaries make Christ known and loved.**
2) **To follow the Little Way by imitating St Therese, Patroness of the Missions, in her love of God and mankind; in her childlike simplicity and perfect confidence in God.**
3) **To help all priests and missionaries by prayer and sacrifice.**

ST THERESE – OUR MODEL

Our inspiration in all our Mission endeavours is St Therese, who, during her short life in Carmel, spiritually adopted two missionaries. Realising how much missionaries need the support of the prayers of the faithful, The Little Way helps to fulfil this need as follows: daily Mass and Adoration of the Blessed Sacrament, the distribution of prayer leaflets, the publication of three Mission magazines annually, by organising pilgrimages and by encouraging prayer at our Shrine Centres. In Lourdes we have a chapel dedicated to St Therese, in the St Pius X Basilica, and pilgrims are welcome to visit it as well as our centre at 46 rue de la Grotte. Here, as at our Centres in Walsingham, Knock and Fatima, videos are shown and a range of spiritual books is available. Pilgrims visiting these Centres are encouraged to pray for the Missions and for all missionaries throughout the world. For these same intentions pilgrimages are organised each month from May to October to Our Lady's Shrine in Fatima, and annually to Lisieux.

FINANCIAL HELP

In the last financial year our benefactors again enabled us to send over four million pounds to the Missions. This is used to roof mission chapels (£900 stg), to build dispensaries (£2,500 stg) and small houses (£600stg), to support native sisters and catechists, to relieve hunger, to help needy and starving children, lepers and victims of natural disasters, to support self-help projects and to provide Mass Offerings for needy priests. We make no deduction for expenses from Mission donations and rely upon our friends to help us meet our administrative expenses.

St Therese of the Child Jesus, draw us along your Little Way of confidence and love and lead us to God, our Father.

THE LITTLE WAY ASSOCIATION (CD/2009)
Sacred Heart House, 119 Cedars Road, Clapham Common, London SW4 0PR. Tel: 020 7622 0466 / 500

074694412

Society of St Peter the Apostle

Mission . Today . Tomorrow . Forever

SPA-sponsored seminarians in Burma (Myanmar)

The SPA funds the training of EVERY seminarian in mission dioceses worldwide.

We need your help to make sure that seminaries stay open and that vocations are not turned away for lack of funds.

Please consider sharing your faith by including the SPA in your Will.

Thanks to you, future seminarians will be able to train for the priesthood and serve their communities – who long to live by faith and the sacraments.

The SPA is the Pope's official charity for training seminarians and Religious. Mass is offered daily in St Peter's Basilica for all SPA benefactors.

Support the training of priests Help build the Church of the future

Name (PRINT) ....

Address ....

.... Postcode ....

I enclose my donation of £ ....

☐ I wish to Gift Aid this and any future donations I make to the Pontifical Mission Societies

and/or

☐ Please send me information about how to leave a gift to the SPA in my Will

YB CD 09

Pontifical Mission Societies
Reg Charity No. 1056651

To: Mgr John Dale, National Director, SPA, 23 Eccleston Square, London SW1V 1NU
tel (020) 7821 9755 (office hours) spa@missio.org.uk www.missio.org.uk

London & Capital
intelligent investors

Catholic Bible School

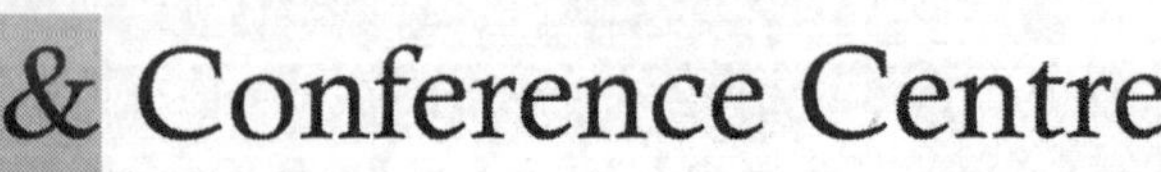

& Conference Centre

www.catholic-bible-school.org

The Living Word - a living experience

Catholic Bible School
Nutbourne House
Farm Lane
Nutbourne
Chichester, PO18 8SD
Tel 01243 371766
Fax 01243 371459
info@catholic-bible-school.org
www.catholic-bible-school.org

This Georgian farmhouse with Tudor origins, together with its newly appointed Conference Facilities in the adjacent barn conversion can accommodate groups from 5 to 80 people in a peaceful setting and provides an ideal venue for awaydays, retreats, meetings and conferences.

The Catholic Bible School provides a wide range of Scripture based courses as well as training in Spiritual Direction and other pastoral skills. Distance Learning programmes are also available.

Contact Course Administrator for a copy of our current programme.

Need Prayer Support ? S.O.S. Prayer Line 7.30pm - midnight
Telephone 01243 377331

073193221

RATCLIFFE COLLEGE

HMC Roman Catholic Co-educational Day and Boarding School for Students aged 3 to 18

Senior School (11-18 year-olds),
Junior Department (5-11 year-olds), Nursery School (3-5 year-olds)

- **Impressive** teaching resources and very good academic standards
- Pastoral care a **top priority**
- Full, weekly and occasional boarding in **high quality** accommodation
- Drama, Music, Sport and **many** other extra-curricular activities
- **School buses** from Leicester, Loughborough and Nottingham
- **State-of-the-art** Sixth Form Centre opened January 2007

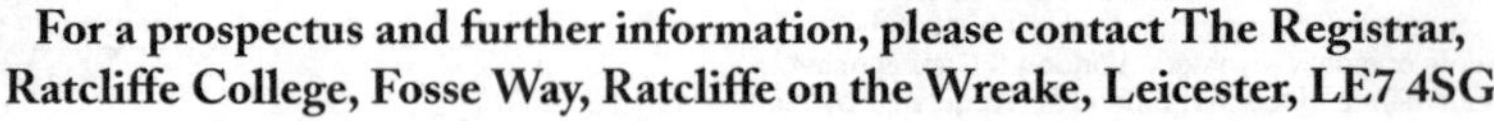

For a prospectus and further information, please contact The Registrar, Ratcliffe College, Fosse Way, Ratcliffe on the Wreake, Leicester, LE7 4SG

Telephone: 01509 817000 Fax: 01509 817004
registrar@ratcliffe.leics.sch.uk www.ratcliffecollege.com

Registered as a Charity No. 1115975

073193222

Bellerive FCJ Catholic College

(A school specialising in the Sciences, Maths and computing)

Windermere Terrace, Sefton Park, Liverpool L8 3SB
email: bhalligan@btconnect.com
Tel: (0151) 727 2064
Fax: (0151) 727 8242
www.bellerive.liverpool.sch.uk

Bellerive FCJ is located in the Archdiocese of Liverpool and admits Catholic pupils from schools across Merseyside. It is nationally recognised as a high performing specialist school. It aims to implement the mission of the Church in line with the Bishops' Conference of England and Wales.

"Schooling has been, and remains, an important part of the mission of the church. The aims of our schools are to help everyone within the school community to grow in faith; to make the most of every ability they have been given; to achieve academic excellence and to prepare well for adult life in a modern and diverse society."

073693646

AMPLEFORTH
COLLEGE
Telephone
01439 766863
EMail
admissions@
ampleforth.org.uk
www.ampleforth
college.york.
sch.uk

Society of Our Lady of Lourdes

President: Cardinal Cormac Murphy-O'Connor,
Archbishop of Westminster

The Society is a company limited by guarantee and a Registered Charity
Company Registration No. 4156243, Charity Registration No.1086419

The Society, which is under the patronage of the Archbishops of England and Wales and the Bishop of Tarbes and Lourdes, has been caring for pilgrims for 97 years.

Principal activities in 2009:

- Annual Mass for the Feast in February;
- Day of Recollection at Ealing Abbey in April,
- Pilgrimage to Lourdes 22 May to 29 May,
- Annual weekend retreat at Buckden Towers in July,
- Pilgrimage of the Sick to Aylesford – 17th August,

Benefits of Membership:

- Opportunity of making a real contribution to the work of Our Lady,
- Two Masses are offered each week, one for living Friends and the other for deceased Friends of the Society.
- A monthly Mass is also offered for deceased Friends on the Society's Obituary List.
- Members' magazine 'Pilgrims' Way' published twice yearly,

For further information, please contact the Secretary, ***Society of Our Lady of Lourdes***,
Church of the Immaculate Heart of Mary, Botwell Lane, Hayes, Middlesex, UB3 2AB
Tel 020 8848 9833, Email enquiries@soll-lourdes.com quoting reference CD09.

www.soll-lourdes.com **"More than a pilgrimage……."**

Next Pilgrimage 22 – 29 May 2009

074694415

Daughters Of The Heart Of Mary

International Religious Congregation

We are committed to working for a more human future through Education, Healthcare, Social and Cultural activities

We wear no distinguishing sign, and live either alone, in our families or in a community.

Is God calling you to this vocation?

Further information from:
Daughters of The Heart of Mary
41 Murray Road, Wimbledon, London SW19 4PD

Tel: No. 208 946 3564

073693644

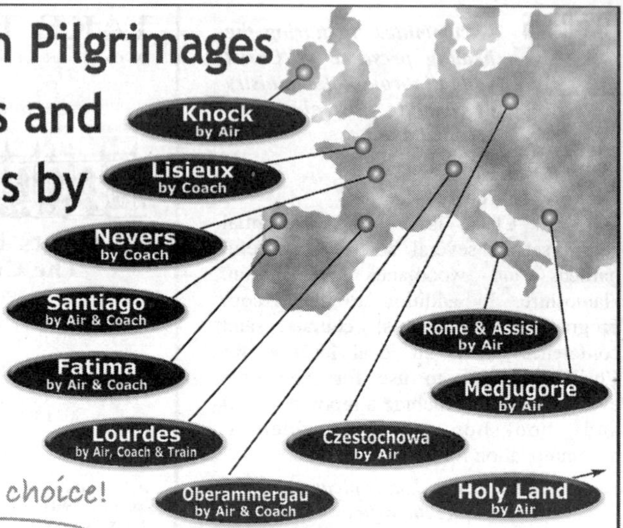

THE CATHOLIC DIRECTORY

OF ENGLAND AND WALES

FOR THE YEAR OF OUR LORD

2009

ONE HUNDRED AND SEVENTIETH
YEAR OF ISSUE

Published for the Bishops' Conference of England and Wales by

Gabriel Communications Limited

Published annually, on behalf of the Bishops' Conference of England and Wales,
by Gabriel Communications Limited,
4th Floor, Landmark House, Station Road, Cheadle Hulme, Cheshire SK8 7JH

Enquiries regarding this publication should be addressed to the publisher.

Editorial amendments and enquiries to:

D. Catherine Wybourne (Editor),
The Catholic Directory, Gabriel Communications Limited,
4th Floor, Landmark House, Station Road, Cheadle Hulme, Cheshire SK8 7JH
Tel: 0161- 488 1700 Fax: 0161- 488 1701
E-mail: ecd@totalcatholic.com

ISBN 978-1-904657-44-6

Printed & bound in Great Britain by:
William Clowes Limited, Beccles, Suffolk

Cover illustration is a window in St Peter's Cathedral, commemorating St Edmund Arrowsmith.

It shows St Edmund, with Lancaster Castle in the background. As one of the Forty Martyrs of England and Wales, St Edmund was martyred at Lancaster on August 28th 1628.

The window, which was given anonymously to the cathedral, was executed by Charles Lightfoot Ltd, and was blessed on Pentecost Sunday, May 19th 2002, by the Bishop of Lancaster, The Rt Rev Patrick O'Donoghue.

Photo: © Lancaster Cathedral

CONTENTS

NOTES ON THE USE OF THIS DIRECTORY

- A full Contents page appears at the beginning of the book. This list has been categorised, which enables the user to to see at a glance the various segments into which each section is divided and the pages on which they appear.
- A General Index, an Index of Places and one for the Advertisers is provided at the back of the directory.
- In each Diocesan section the Cathedral Church is placed first but the town in which it is situated is to be found in its alphabetical position.
- When two dates are given in a parish entry, the first, generally, is that of the foundation of the parish; the second is the date of the existing church or chapel.
- A list of Catholic Schools in each Diocese is to be found at the end of each Diocesan section together with their addresses, telephone/fax numbers, e-mail addresses (if available) and the name of the parish in which they are situated.
- The academic qualifications of the clergy are not given in the parish entries – they are given (if known) in the Clergy lists towards the end of the Directory.

Key to Symbols used in this Directory

†	In the parish entries, denotes that the church is registered for marriages.
A	Access only (ramps, etc)
	Full Facilities (access plus suitable toilet)
	Loop System for hearing-aid users
S	Mass celebrated regularly in Word and Sign and/or Confession in Sign Language. Enquire for details and times.
L	Denotes Listed Building (all Grades)

FOREWORD

The 170th edition of the Catholic Directory for England and Wales is a remarkable testament to the vitality and creativity of the Church in the 21st century. Compared with its 19th century predecessors, the Directory is now a much bigger book, reflecting not only growth in numbers but also increased involvement of Catholics in every aspect of national and social life. In education, caring and healthcare and the multiplicity of interests represented by Catholic Societies, the Catholic Church in England and Wales contributes largely to the common good. This book is an invaluable record of what has been done and is being done not just by individuals but by all the many organizations which make up the Church. It is also a record of diversity. No two dioceses are the same, and the differing ways in which they are trying to meet the challenges of our time is demonstrated in these pages.

The existence of such a complex work of reference depends entirely on the willingness of many people to be chivvied into making contributions, checking them for accuracy, typesetting, revising, correcting, searching out additional information and finally seeing the Directory through to the press. To all our contributors, our critics, our advertisers and the team at Gabriel, whose efforts go far beyond what might reasonably be expected of them, my thanks for making the 2009 Directory possible.

D. Catherine Wybourne

HIS HOLINESS POPE BENEDICT XVI

Bishop of Rome
Vicar of Jesus Christ

**SUCCESSOR OF ST. PETER, PRINCE OF THE APOSTLES,
SUPREME PASTOR OF THE UNIVERSAL CHURCH,
PRIMATE OF ITALY,
ARCHBISHOP AND METROPOLITAN OF THE ROMAN PROVINCE,
SOVEREIGN OF THE STATE OF THE VATICAN CITY.**

His Holiness POPE BENEDICT XVI (JOSEPH RATZINGER), Roman Pontiff; born in Marktl Am Inn, Germany, 16 April, 1927; ordained priest 29 June, 1951; appointed Archbishop of Munich 28 May, 1977; appointed Cardinal-Priest of Santa Maria Consolatrice al Tiburtino, 27 June, 1977; appointed Prefect of the Congregation for the Doctrine of Faith, 25 November, 1981; appointed Titular Cardinal-Bishop of Velletri-Segni, 5 April 1993; appointed Cardinal-Bishop of Ostia, 30 Nov, 2002; elected Pope, 19 April, 2005; inaugurated 24 April, 2005.

THE COLLEGE OF CARDINALS

Cardinals are priests of outstanding learning, piety, judgement and ability, chosen by the Pope (who alone has power to create Cardinals) to assist and to advise him in the government of the Church. They rank as Princes of royal blood, have the title of Eminence and take precedence over bishops and all other prelates. Since the 12th century they have been constituted as the Sacred College; they form the Senate of the Supreme Pontiff and on his death it is they who elect his successor.

Before the Sacred College was established in its present form, the Pope had his body of advisers composed of the neighbouring bishops and representatives of the priests and deacons of the City of Rome. These three divisions or Orders are still retained in the Sacred College.

A: Cardinal Bishops are the bishops of the seven 'Titular suburbicarian Sees', viz., the dioceses which adjoin the City of Rome. The Titular See of Ostia is always assigned to the senior Cardinal Bishop (who is also Dean of the Sacred College) in addition to that diocese which he already holds.

B: Cardinal Priests, formerly the rectors of the ancient 'titular churches' of Rome, are now in fact archbishops or bishops, mostly with dioceses outside Rome and thus not resident in Curia.

C: Cardinal Deacons, formerly the deacons in charge of the regional divisions of Rome, are now bishops holding important posts in the Roman Curia.

By the decree Ingravescentem Aetatem, which became operative on 1 January, 1971, Pope Paul VI ruled that Cardinals over the age of 80 may not vote in the election of a Pope or retain office in the Roman Curia.

■ CARDINAL BISHOPS OF THE HOLY ROMAN CHURCH

Arinze, Francis, b Eziowelle, Nigeria 1 Nov 1932; Cardinal Deacon 25 May 1985; Prefect of the Congregation for the Sacraments and Divine Worship. Created Cardinal Bishop April 2005.

Bertone, Tarcisio, b Romano Canavese, Italy, 2 Dec 1934; Cardinal Priest 21 Oct, 2003; Camerlengo 4 April 2007; Cardinal BP of Frascati 10 May 2008.

Etchegaray, Roger, b Espelette, France 25 Sept 1922; Cardinal Priest 30 June 1979; President emeritus of the Commission for Justice and Peace and of the Pontifical Council "Cor Unum". Created Cardinal Bishop. President of the Committee for The Great Jubilee of AD2000.

Re, Giovanni Battista, b Borno, Italy, 30 Jan 1934, Cardinal Priest 21 Feb 2001, Prefect of Congregation of Bishops, titular Abp of Vescovia, Forum Novum. Cardinal Bishop, 2002.

Sodano, Angelo, b. Isola d'Asti, Piedmont, Italy, 23 Nov. 1927; Cardinal Priest 28th June 1991; Secretary of State, retired. Created Cardinal Bishop 1994; Dean of the College of Cardinals.

■ CARDINAL PATRIARCHS OF ORIENTAL RITE

Daoud, Moussa I Ignace, b Meskane, Syria 18 Sept 1930, Cardinal Bishop 21 Feb 2001, Prefect of the Congregation for the Oriental Churches, retired; Patriarch Emeritus of Antioch.

Delly, Emmanuel III (Emmanuel-Karim), b Telkaif Iraq 6 Oct 1927; Cardinal 24 Nov, 2007; Abp of Baghdad (Chaldean); Patriarch of Babylon.

Ghattas, Stephanos II, b Cheikh Zein-el-Dine, 16 June 1920, Cardinal Bishop 21 Feb, 2001, Coptic Patriarch of Alexandria. Retired.

Sfeir, Nasrallah Pierre, b. Reyfoun, Lebanon 15 May 1920; Cardinal Priest 26 November 1994, Maronite Patriarch of Antioch.

■ CARDINAL PRIESTS

Agnelo, Geraldo Majella, b Juiz de Fora, 19 Oct 1933, Cardinal Priest 21 Feb 2001, Abp of São Salvador da Bahia, Brazil.

Agré, Bernard, b Monga, Ivory Coast, 2 March 1926, created Cardinal Priest 21 Feb 2001, Abp of Adidjan, Ivory Coast. Retired

Agustoni, Gilberto, b Shaffhausen, Switzerland, 26 July 1922; Cardinal Deacon 26 Nov 1994; titular Abp of Caorle; former Prefect of the Supreme Tribunal of the Apostolic Segnatura. Cardinal Priest, 24 Feb, 2005.

Alvarez Martinez, Francisco, b Santa Eulalia de Ferrones Llanera, 14 July 1925, Cardinal Priest 21 Feb 2001, former Abp of Toledo, Spain. Retired, 2002.

Ambrozic, Aloysius Matthew, b Toronto, Canada, 27 Jan 1930; Cardinal Priest 21 Feb 1998. Abp of Toronto.

Amigo Vallejo, Carlos (OFM), b Medina de Rioseco, Spain, 23 Aug, 1934, Cardinal Priest 21 Oct 2003; Abp of Seville, Spain.

Angelini, Fiorenzo, b Rome 1 Aug 1916; Cardinal Deacon 28 June 1991; Cardinal Priest 26 Feb 2002; President of the Pontifical Council for Pastoral Care of Health Care Workers, Retired.

Antonelli, Ennio; b Todi, Italy, 18 Nov 1936; Cardinal Priest 21 Oct, 2003. Abp of Florence.

Antonnetti, Lorenzo; b. Romagnano Sesia 31 Jul 1922; Cardinal Deacon 21 Feb 1998; former administrator of the Patrimony of the Apostolic See; Cardinal Priest 1 Mar 2008.

Aponte Martinez, Luis, b Lajas, Puerto Rico 4 Aug 1922; Cardinal Priest 5 Mar 1973; Abp of San Juan de Puerto Rico. Retired.

Araujo, Serafim Fernandes de, b Minas Novas, Brazil, 13 Aug 1924; Cardinal Priest 21 Feb 1998. Abp emeritus of Belo Horizonte, Brazil.

Arns, Paulo Evaristo (OFM), b Forquilhinha, Brazil 14 Sept 1921; Cardinal Priest 5 Mar 1973; former Abp of São Paulo.

Backis Audrys Juazos, b Kaunas, 1 Feb 1937, Cardinal Priest, 21 Feb 2001, Abp of Vilnius, Lithuania

Bagnasco, Angelo; b. Pontevico, Italy, 14 Jan 1943; Cardinal Priest 24 Nov 2007; Abp of Genoa.

Barbarin, Philippe Xavier, b Rabat, Morroco, 17 Oct, 1950; Cardinal Priest 21 Oct, 2003. Abp of Lyon.

Baum, William Wakefield, b Dallas, Texas 21 Nov 1926; Cardinal Priest 24 May 1976.

Bergoglio, Jorge Mario (SJ), b Buenos Aires, 17 Dec 1936, Cardinal Priest 21 Feb 2001, Abp of Buenos Aires, Argentina

Bevilacqua, Anthony Joseph, b Brooklyn, USA, 17 June 1923; Cardinal Priest 28 June 1991; Abp Philadelphia. Retired.

Biffi, Giacomo, b Milan, Italy, 13 June 1928; Cardinal Priest 25 May 1985; Abp of Bologna.

Bozanic, Josip, b Rijeka, Jogoslavia (now Croatia), 20 March 1949; Cardinal Priest 21 Oct 2003; Abp of Zabreb, Croatia.

Brady, Sean Baptist; b. Drumcalpin, Ireland, 16 Aug 1939; Cardinal Priest 24 Nov 2007; Abp of Armagh.

Caffarra, Carlo, b Samboseto di Busseto, Italy 1 June 1938; Cardinal Priest 24 March 2006; Abp of Bologna

Canestri, Giovanni, b Castelspina, Italy, 30 Sept 1918; Cardinal Priest 28 June 1988; former Abp of Genoa.

Canizares Llovera, Antonio b. Utiel 15 Oct 1945, Cardinal Priest 24 Mar 2006, Abp of Toledo, Spain.

Cheong Jin-Suk, Nicholas, b Seoul, Korea 7 December 1931; Cardinal Priest 24 March 2006; Abp of Seoul & Apostolic Administrator of P'yŏng-yang

Carles Gordo, Ricardo Maria, b 24 Sept 1926; Cardinal Priest 26 Nov 1994; Abp of Barcelona, Spain. Retired.

Cassidy, Edward Idris. b Sydney, 5 July 1924; Cardinal Deacon 28 June 1991. President of the Pontifical Council for the Promotion of Christian Unity. Cardinal Priest 2002. Retired.

Castrillon Hoyos, Darío, b. Medellín 4 Jul 1929; Cardinal Deacon 21 Feb 1998; Prefect Emeritus Congregation for Clergy; Cardinal Priest 1 Mar 2008.

Ce, Marco, b Izano, Italy 8 July 1925; Cardinal Priest 30 June 1979; Patriarch of Venice. Retired.

Cheli, Giovanni, b. Turin, Italy, 4 Oct 1918; Cardinal Deacon 21 Feb 1998; former President Pontifical Council for pastoral care of Migrants; Cardinal Priest 1 Mar 2008.

Cipriani Thorne, Juan Luis, b Lima, 28 Dec 1943, Cardinal Priest 21 Feb 2001, Abp of Lima, Peru.

Clancy, Edward Bede, b Lithgow, Australia, 13 Dec 1923; Cardinal Priest 28 June 1988; Abp of Sydney. Retired.

Connell, Desmond, b Dublin, 24 March 1926, Cardinal Priest, 21 Feb 2001, Abp of Dublin, Ireland. Retired.

da Cruz Policarpo, José, b Alvonrninha, 26 Feb 1936, Cardinal Priest 21 Feb 2001, Patriarch of Lisbon, Portugal.

Daly, Cahal Brendan, b. Loughguile, Ireland, 1 Oct 1917; Cardinal Priest 28 June 1991; former Abp of Armagh, Ireland.

Danneels, Godfried, b Kanegem, Belgium, 4 June 1933; Cardinal Priest 2 Feb 1983; Abp of Malines-Brussels.

Darmaatmadja, Julius Riyadi (SJ), b. Muntilan, Indonesia, 20 Dec. 1934; Cardinal Priest 26 Nov. 1994; Abp of Jakarta.

De Giorgi, Salvatore, b Palermo, Italy, 6 Sep 1930; Abp of Palermo; Cardinal Priest 21 Feb 1998; Abp Emeritus of Palermo, Italy.

Deskur, Andrzej Maria, b Sancygniow, Poland, 29 Feb 1924; Cardinal Deacon 25 May 1985; former President of the Pontifical Council for Social Communications; Cardinal Priest.

Dias, Ivan, b 14 April 1936, Cardinal Priest 21 Feb 2001, Abp of Bombay, India; Prefect of the Congregation for Evangelisation of Peoples.

DiNardo, Daniel Nicholas, b. Steubenville, OH, 23 May 1949; Cardinal Priest 24 Nov 2007; Abp of Galveston-Houston.

do Nascimento, Alexandre, b Malanje, Angola, 1 March 1925; Cardinal Priest 2 Feb 1983; Abp of Luanda, Retired.

Dziwisz, Stanislaw, b Raba Wyzna, Poland 27 April 1939; Cardinal Priest 24 March 2006; Abp of Krakow

Egan, Edward Michael, b Oak Park, Chicago, 2 April 1932, Cardinal Priest, 21 Feb 2001, Abp of New York.

Erdo, Peter, b Budapest, Hungary, 25 June 1952; Cardinal Priest 21 Oct 2003; Abp of Exztergom-Budapest.

Errázuriz Ossa, Francisco Javier, b Santiago de Chile, 5 Sept 1933, Cardinal Priest 21 Feb 2001, Abp of Santiago, Chile.

Falcao Freire, José, b Erere, Brazil 23 October 1925; Cardinal Priest 28 June 1988; Abp of Brasilia. Retired 28 Jan, 2004.

Furno, Carlo, b Bairo Canavese, Italy, 2 Dec 1921; Cardinal Deacon 26 Nov 1994; titular Abp of Abari; Cardinal Priest 24 Feb 2005.

García-Gasco y Vicente, Agustín; b. Corral de Almaguer, Spain, 12 Feb 1931; Cardinal Priest 24 Nov 2007; Abp of Valencia.

George, Francis Eugene (OMI), b Chicago, USA, 16 Jan 1937; Cardinal Priest 21 Feb 1998. Abp of Chicago.

Giordano, Michele, b S. Arcangelo, Italy, 26 September 1930; Cardinal Priest 28 June 1988; Abp of Naples, Italy, Retired.

Glemp, Jozef, b Inowroclaw, Poland, 18 Dec 1928; Cardinal Priest 2 Feb 1983; Abp of Warsaw.

González Zumárraga Antonia José, b Pujili, 18 March 1925, Cardinal Priest 21 Feb 2001, Abp of Quito, Ecuador. Retired.

Gracias, Oswald, b. Mumbai, India, 24 Dec 1944, Cardinal Priest 24 Nov 2007; Abp of Mumbai (Bombay).

Gulbinowicz, Henryk Roman, b Szukiszki, Poland, 17 Oct 1923; Cardinal Priest 25 May 1985; Abp of Wroclaw. Retired.

Honore Jean, b Saint-Brice-en-Cogles, 13 Aug 1920, Cardinal Priest 21 Feb 2001, Abp emeritus of Tours, France.

Hummes, Claudio (OFM), b Montenegro, 8 Aug 1934, Cardinal Priest 21 Feb 2001, Abp of São Paulo, Brazil; Prefect of the Congregation for Clergy.

Husar Lubomyr (MSU), b Lviv, 26 Feb 1933, Cardinal Priest 21 Feb 2001, Major Abp of Lviv, Ukraine.

Jaworski Marian, b Lviv, 21 Aug 1926, Cardinal Priest 21 Feb 2001, Bp of Lviv, Ukraine.

Karlic, Estanislao Esteban, b. Oliva, Argentina 7 Feb 1926; Cardinal Priest 24 Nov 2007; Abp of Paraná.

Keeler, William Henry, b San Antonio, 4 March 1931; Cardinal Priest 26 Nov 1994; Abp of Baltimore, USA, Retired.

Kim Sou-Hwan, Stephen, b Tae Gu, 8 May 1922; Cardinal Priest 28 April 1969; former Abp of Seoul.

Kitbunchu, Michael Michai, b Samphran, Thailand 25 Jan 1929; Cardinal Priest 2 Feb 1983; Abp of Bangkok.

Korec, Jan Chrystostom (SJ). Bosany, Czechoslovakia, b 22 Jan 1924; Cardinal Priest 28 June 1991; Bp of Nitra, Czechoslovakia, Retired.

Laghi Pio, b Castiglione, Italy, 21 May 1922; Cardinal Deacon 28 June 1991; Prefect of the Congregation for Catholic Education. Cardinal Priest 2002. Retired.

Law, Bernard F, b Torreon, Mexico, 4 Nov 1931; Cardinal Priest 25 May 1985; former Abp of Boston. Retired 2002; Archpriest of St Mary Major Basilica

Lehman Karl, b Sigmaringen, 16 May 1936, Cardinal Priest 21 Feb 2001, Bp of Mainz, Germany.

López Rodríguez, Nicolas de Jesus, b Barranca, Dominican Republic, 31 Oct 1936; Cardinal Priest 28 June 1991; Abp of Santo Domingo.

Lourdusamy, Simon D, b Kalleri, India 5 Feb 1924; Cardinal Deacon 25 May 1985; Cardinal Priest.

McCarrick Theodore Edgar, b New York, 7 July 1930, Cardinal Priest 21 Feb 2001, Abp of Washington DC, USA, Retired.

Macharski, Franciszek, b Cracow, Poland 20 May 1927; Cardinal Priest 30 June 1979; Abp of Cracow, Retired.

Mahoney, Roger Michael, b. Hollywood, USA, 27 Feb 1936; Cardinal Priest 28 June 1991; Abp Los Angeles.

Maida, Adam Joseph, b East Vandergrift, U.S.A. 18 March 1930; Cardinal Priest 26 Nov 1994; Abp of Detroit, U.S.A.

Margéot, Jean b Quatre-Bornes, Mauritius 3 Feb 1916; Cardinal Priest 28 June 1988; former Bp of Port Louis, Mauritius.

Martínez Sistach, LLuís, b. Barcelona, Spain, 29 Apr 1937, Cardinal Priest 24 Nov 2007; Abp of Barcelona.

Martínez Somalo, Eduardo, b Banos de Rio Tobia, Spain, 31 March 1927; Cardinal Deacon 28 June 1988; former Prefect of the Sacred Congregation for Institutes of Consecrated Life and

Societies of Apostolic Life. Cardinal Priest. Retired Feb 11 2004; Camerlengo of the Holy Roman Church, Retired.

Martini, Paul Carlo Maria, SJ, b Turin, Italy, 15 Feb 1927; Cardinal Priest 2 Feb 1983; former Abp of Milan. Retired 2002.

Mayer, Augustin (OSB), b Altotting, Germany, 23 May 1911; Cardinal Deacon 25 May 1985; Created Cardinal Priest.

Medina Estévz, Jorge Arturo Augustin, b. Santiago, Chile, 23 Dec 1926; Cardinal Deacon 21 Feb1998; Prefect Emeritus Congregation for Divine Worship; Cardinal Priest 1 Mar 2008.

Meisner, Joachim, b Wroclaw, Poland, 25 Dec 1933; Cardinal Priest 2 Feb 1983; Abp of Cologne.

Murphy-O'Connor, Cormac, b Reading, 24 Aug 1932, Cardinal Priest 21 Feb 2001, Abp of Westminster, England.

Napier, Wilfred Fox (OFM), b Swartberg, 8 March 1941, Cardinal Priest 21 Feb 2001, Abp of Durban, South Africa.

Njue, John, b. Embu, Kenya 1944, Cardinal Priest 24 Nov 2007; Abp of Nairobi.

Noe, Virgilio, b Zelata di Berequardo, Italy, 30 March 1922; Cardinal Deacon 28 June 1991; Cardinal Archpriest of the Vatican Basilica. Cardinal Priest 2002. Retired.

Obando Bravo, Miguel (SDB), b La Libertad, Nicaragua 2 Feb 1926; Cardinal Priest 25 May 1985; Abp of Managua. Retired.

O'Brien, Keith Michael Patrick, b Ballycastle, Ireland, 17 March, 1938; Cardinal Priest 21 Oct 2003; Abp of Edinburgh and St Andrews; former Apostolic Administrator, Argyll and the Isles.

O'Malley, O.F.M. Cap, Seán Patrick, b Lakewood, U.S.A. 29 June 1944; Cardinal Priest 24 March 2006; Abp of Boston

Okogie, Anthony Olumbunmi, b Lagos, Nigeria, 16 June, 1936; Cardinal Priest 21 Oct 2003; Abp of Lagos.

Ortega y Alamino, Jaime Lucas, b Jaguey Grande, Cuba, 18 Oct 1936; Cardinal Priest 26 Nov 1994; Abp of San Cristobal de la Habana, Cuba.

Ouellet, Marc, PSS, b Lamotte, Canada, 8 June, 1944; Cardinal Priest 21 Oct 2003; Abp of Quebec.

Panafieu, Bernard Louis Auguste Paul, b Chatellerault, Poitiers, France, 26 Jan, 1931; Cardinal Priest 21 Oct 2003; Abp of Marseille, Retired.

Paskai, Laszlo (OFM), b Szegad, Hungary 8 May 1927; Cardinal Priest 28 June 1988; former Abp of Esztergom, Hungary. Retired 2002.

Pell, George, b Ballarat, Australia, 8 April, 1941; Cardinal Priest 21 Oct 2003; Abp of Sydney.

Pengo, Polycarp, b Mwazye, Tanzania, 5 Aug 1944; Cardinal Priest 21 Feb 1998. Abp of Dar-es-Salaam.

Pham Dinh Tung, Paul Joseph, b 15 June 1919, Viêtnam; Cardinal Priest 26 Nov 1994; Apostolic Administrator, sede vacante et ad nutum Sanctae Sedis, of Lan Són et Cao Bang, Viêtnam, 1998; Abp of Hanoi. Retired.

Pham Minh Man, Jean-Baptiste, b Ca Mau, Vietnam, 1934; Cardinal Priest 21 Oct, 2003; Abp of Ho Chi Mihn Ville.

Pimenta, Simon Ignatius, b Marol, India, 1 March 1920; Cardinal Priest 28 June 1988; former Abp of Bombay.

Piovanelli, Silvano, b Ronta di Mugello, Italy 21 Feb 1924; Cardinal Priest 25 May 1985; Abp of Florence. Retired.

Poggi, Luigi, b Piacenza, Italy, 25 Nov 1917; Cardinal Deacon 26 Nov 1994; titular Abp of Forontoniana, Archivist and Librarian of the Holy See; Cardinal Priest 24 Feb 2005. Retired.

Poletto Severino, b Salgareda, 18 March 1933, Cardinal Priest 21 Feb 2001, Abp of Turin, Italy.

Poupard, Paul, b Bouzille, France, 30 Aug 1930; Cardinal Deacon 25 May 1985; Cardinal Priest 29 Jan 1996; President of pontifical Council for Dialogue with Non-Believers and of Pontifical Council for Culture, Retired.

Pujats, Janis, b Nautreni, Riga, 14 Nov 1930, Cardinal Priest 21 Feb 2001, Abp of Riga, Latvia.

Puljic, Vinko, b Prijecani, Bosnia Herzegovina, 8 Sept 1945; Cardinal Priest 26 Nov 1994; Abp of Vrhbosna-Sarajevo, Bosnia Herzegovina.

Quezada Toruño, Rodolfo, b Ciudad de Guatemala, Guatemala, 8 March, 1932; Cardinal Priest 21 Oct 2003; Abp of Guatemala.

Razafindratandra, Armand Geatan, b Ambohimalaza, Madagascar, 7 Aug 1925; Cardinal Priest, 26 Nov 1994; Abp of Antananarivo, Madagascar. Retired.

Ricard, Jean-Pierre; b Marseille, France 25 September 1944; Cardinal Priest 24 March 2006; Abp Bordeaux et Bazes.

Rigali, Justin Francis; b Los Angeles, USA, 19 April, 1935; Cardinal Priest 21 Oct 2003; Abp of St Louis, USA; Abp of Philadelphia, USA

Rivera, Carrera Norberto, b La Purisima, Mexico, 6 June 1942; Cardinal Priest 21 Feb 1998. Abp of Mexico.

Robles Ortega, Francisco, b. Mascota, Mexico, 2 Mar 1949, Cardinal Priest 24 Nov 2007; Abp of Monterrey.

Rodriguez Madariaga, Oscar Andrés (SDB), b Tegucigalpa, 29 Dec 1942, Cardinal Priest 21 Feb 2001, Abp of Tegucigalpa, Honduras.

Rosales, Gaudencio Borbon, b Batangas City, Philippines 10 August 1932; Cardinal Priest 24 March 2006; Apostolic Administrator of Lipa; Abp of Manila, Philippines

Rouco Verela, Anthonio Maria, b Villalba, Spain, 24 Aug 1936; Cardinal Priest 21 Feb 1998. Abp of Madrid.

Rubiano Saenz Pedro, b Cartago, 13 Sept 1932, Cardinal Priest 21 Feb 2001, Abp of Bogata, Colombia.

Ruini, Camillo, b Sassuolo, Italy, 19 Feb 1931; Cardinal Priest 28 June 1991; Cardinal Priest 28 June 1991; Vicar General for the Diocese of Rome.

Saldarini, Giovanni, b Cantu', Italy, 11 Dec 1924; Cardinal Priest 28 June 1991; Abp of Turin, Italy. Retired.

Sales, Eugenio de Araujo, b Acari, Brazil, 8 Nov 1920; Cardinal Priest 28 April 1969; Abp of Sao Sebastiao do Rio de Janeiro. Retired.

Sanchez, Jose, T, b Pandan, Philippines, 17 March 1920; Cardinal Deacon 28 June 1991; former Prefect of the Congregation for the Clergy. Cardinal Priest 2002.

Sandoval Iniguez, Juan, b Yahualica, Mexico, 28 March 1933; Cardinal Priest 26 Nov 1994; Abp of Guadulajara, Mexico.

Santos, Alexandre José Maria dos (OFM), b Zavala, Mozambique, 18 March 1924; Cardinal Priest 28 June 1988; Abp of Maputo, Mozambique. Retired.

Sarr, Théodore-Adrien, b. Fadiouth, Senegal, Cardinal Priest 24 Nov 2007; Abp of Dakar.

Scheid, Eusebio Oscar (SCI), b Luzerna, Brazil, 8 Dec, 1932; Cardinal Priest 21 Oct 2003; Abp of Rio de Janeiro.

Scherer, Odilo Pedro, b. São Paulo, Brazil, 21 Sep 1949; Cardinal Priest 24 Nov 2007; Abp of São Paulo.

Schonborn, Christoph (OP). b Skalsko, Czech Rep. 22 Jan 1945; Cardinal Priest 21 Feb 1998. Abp of Vienna.

Schwery, Henri, b Saint Leonard, Switzerland, 14 June 1932. Cardinal Priest 28 June 1991; former Bp of Sion, Switzerland.

Scola, Angelo, b Milan, Italy, 7 Nov 1941; Cardinal Priest 21 Oct 2003; Patriarch of Venice.

Sepe, Crescenzio, b Carinaro, Italy, 2 July 1943, Cardinal Deacon 21 Feb 2001, secretary-general of the Great Jubilee Committee, titular Abp of Grado; Prefect of the Congregation for the Evangelisation of the Peoples. Retired.

Shan Kuo-hsi, Paul, SJ, b Puyang, China, 2 Dec 1923; Bp of Kaohsiong. Cardinal Priest 21 Feb 1998. Retired.

Shirayanagi, Peter Seiichi, b Hachioji, Japan, 17 June 1928; Cardinal Priest, 26 Nov 1994; Abp of Tokyo. Retired.

Silvestrini, Achille, b Brisighella, Italy, 25 October 1923; Cardinal Deacon 28 June 1988; Prefect of the Congregation for the Eastern Churches. Created Cardinal Priest. Retired.

Simonis, Adrianus J, b Lisse, Netherlands 26 Nov 1931; Cardinal Priest 25 May 1985; Abp of Utrecht. Retired.

Stafford, James Francis, b. Baltimore, USA 26 Jul 1932; Cardinal Deacon 21 Feb 1998; Cardinal Priest 1 Mar 2008: major Penitentiary

Sterzinsky, Georg Maximilian, b Warlack, Poland, 9 Feb 1936; Cardinal Priest 28 June 1991; Abp of Berlin.

Swiatek, Kasimierz, b Walga, Estonia 21st Oct 1914; Cardinal Priest 26 Nov 1994; Abp of Minsk-Mohilev, Belarus. Retired.

Szoka, Edmund Casimir, b Grand Rapids, USA, 14 Sept 1927; Cardinal Priest 28 June 1988; former Abp of Detroit.

Terrazas Sandoval Julio (CSsR), b Vallegrande, 7 March 1936, Cardinal Priest 21 Feb 2001, Apb of Santa Cruz de la Sierra, Bolivia.

Tettamanzi, Dionigi, b Renate, Italy, 14 March 1934; Cardinal Priest 21 Feb 1998. former Abp of Genoa; Abp of Milan 2002.

Tomko, Jozef, b Udavske, Czechoslovakia, 11 Mar 1924; Cardinal Deacon 25 May 1985; President of the Congregation for the Evangelization of the Peoples; Created Cardinal Priest. Retired.

Tonini, Ersilio, b Centovera di San Giorgio Piacentino, Italy, 20 July 1914; Cardinal Priest 26 Nov 1994; Abp emeritus of Ravenna-Cervia, Italy.

Toppo, Telesphore Placidus, b Chainpur, India, 15 Oct, 1939; Cardinal Priest 21 Oct 2003; Abp of Ranchi, India.

Tumi, Christian Wiyghari, b Kikai Kelaki, Cameroon, 15 Oct 1930; Cardinal Priest 28 June 1988; Abp of Douala.

Turcotte, Jean-Claude, b Montreal, Canada 26 June 1936; Cardinal Priest, 26 Nov 1994; Abp of Montreal, Canada.

Turkson, Peter Kodwo Appiah, b Wassaw Nauta, Ghana, 11 Oct, 1948; Cardinal Priest 21 Oct 2003; Abp of Cape Coast, Ghana.

Urosa Savino, Jorge Liberato; b Caracas, Venezuela 28 August 1942; Cardinal Priest 24 March 2006; Abp of Caracas.

Vidal, Ricardo, b Mogpoc, Philippines, 6 Feb 1931; Cardinal Priest 25 May 1985; Abp of Cebu.

Ving-Trois, André Armand; b. Paris 7 Nov 1942; Cardinal Priest 24 Nov 2007; Ordinary of France for Faithful of Eastern Rites.

Vithayathil, Varkey (CSsR), b Parur, 29 May 1927, Cardinal Priest 21 Feb 2001, Abp of Ernakulam-Angemaly of the Siro-Malabaresi, India.

Vlk, Miloslav, b Lisnice-Sepekov, Czech Republic, 17 May 1932; Cardinal Priest 26 Nov 1994; Abp of Prague.

Wamala, Emmanuel, b Kamaggwa, Uganda, 15 Dec 1926; Cardinal Priest 26 Nov 1994; Abp of Kampala, Uganda. Retired.

Wetter, Friedrich, b Landau, Germany 20 Feb 1928; Cardinal Priest 25 May 1985; Abp of Munich and Freising. Retired.

Williams, Thomas Stafford, b Wellington, New Zealand, 20 Mar 1930; Cardinal Priest 2 Feb 1983; Abp of Wellington, New Zealand. Retired.

Zen Ze-Kiun, S.D.B., Joseph, b Shanghai, China 13 January 1932; Cardinal Priest 24 March 2006; Bishop of Hong Kong

Zubeir Wako, Gabriel, b Mboro, Sudan, 27 Feb, 1941; Cardinal Priest 21 Oct 2003; Abp of Khartoum, Sudan.

■ CARDINAL DEACONS

Betti, Umberto (OFM), b. Pieve S. Stefano, Italy, 7 Mar 1922; Cardinal Deacon 24 Nov 2007.

Cacciavillan, Agostino, b Novale, Italy, 14 Aug 1926, Cardinal Deacon 21 Feb 2001, President of Administration of the Patrimony of the Apostolic See, retired, titular Abp of Amiterno.

Comastri, Angelo, b. Sorano Italy, 17 Sep 1943; Cardinal Deacon 24 Nov 2007; Archpriest of St Peter's.

Coppa, Giovanni, b. Alba, Italy, 9 Nov 1925, Cardinal Deacon 24 Nov 2007; Apostolic Nuncio Emeritus to Czech Republic.

Cordero Lanza di Montezemolo, Andrea, b Turin, Italy 27 August 1925; created Cardinal Deacon 24 March 2006; Retired Papal nuncio; Archpriest of St Paul's-outside-the-Walls.

Cordes, Paul Josef, b. Kirchhundem, Germany 5 Sep 1934, Cardinal Deacon 24 Nov 2007; President of Pontifical Council Cor Unum.

Cottier, Georges Marie Martin (OP), b Cligny, Switzerland, 25 April 1922; Cardinal Deacon 21 Oct 2003; titular Abp of Tullia.

Dulles, Avery (SJ), b 24 Aug 1818; Cardinal Deacon 21 Feb 2001, theologian, Professor at Fordham University, New York, USA.

Farina, Raffaele (SDB), b. Buonalbergo, Italy 24 Sep 1933, Cardinal Deacon 24 Nov 2007; Archivist of Vatican Secret Archives.

Foley, John Patrick, b. Darby, PA. 11 Nov 1935; Cardinal Deacon 24 Nov 2007; Grand Master of Equestrian Order of the Holy Sepulchre.

Grocholewski, Zenon, b Brodki, Poland, 11 Oct 1939, Cardinal Deacon 21 Feb 2001, prefect of the Congregation for Catholic Education, titular Abp of Agropoli.

Herranz Casado, Julian, b Baena, Cordoba, Spain, 31 March 1930; Cardinal Deacon 21 Oct 2003; Abp of Vertara; President of the Council for the Interpretation of Law, Retired.

Kasper, Walter, b Heidenheim/Brenz 5 March 1933, Cardinal Deacon 21 Feb 2001, secretary of the Pontifical Council for the Promotion of Christian Unity. Bp Emeritus of Rottenburg-Stuttgart, Germany.

Lajolo, Giovanni, b. Novara, Italy 3 Jan 1935; Cardinal Deacon 24 Nov 2007; President Pontifical Commission for Vatican City State.

Levada, William Joseph, b Long Beach, U.S.A. 15 June 1936; created Cardinal Deacon 24 March 2006; Prefect of the Congregation for the Doctrine of the Faith 13 May 2005

Lozano Barragan, Javier, b Toluca, Mexico, 26 Jan 1933; Cardinal Deacon 21 Oct 2003; former Bp of Zacatecas, Mexico; Abp ad personam; President of the Council for Pastoral Care of Health Workers.

Marchisano, Francesco, b Racconigi, Turin, Italy, 25 June, 1929; Cardinal Deacon 21 Oct 2003; Vicar General for the State of the Vatican City. Retired.

Martino, Renato Raffaele, b Salerno, Italy, 23 Nov 1932; Cardinal Deacon 21 Oct 2003; titular Abp of Segerme; President of the Council for Justice and Peace.

Mejia, Jorge Maria, b Buenos Aires, Argentina, 31 Jan 1923, Cardinal Deacon 21 Feb 2001, archivist and librarian of the Holy Roman Church, titular Abp of Apollonia. Retired.

Nagy, Stanislaw Kazimierz (SCI), b Bierruniu Starym, Wadowice, Poland, 30 Sept, 1921; Cardinal Deacon 21 Oct 2003; titular Abp of Hular.

Navarrete Cortés, Urbano, (SJ), b. Camarena de la Sierra, Spain 25 May 1920; Cardinal Deacon 24 Nov 2007.

Nicora, Attilio, b Varese, Milan, Italy, 16 March 1937; Cardinal Deacon 21 Oct 2003; Abp, President, Patrimony of the Apostolic See.

Rode, Franc, C.M., b Rodica, Yugoslavia (now Slovenia) 23 September 1934; created Cardinal Deacon 24 March 2006; Prefect of the Congregation for the Institutes of Consecrated Life and the Societies of Apostolic Life, 11 February, 2004.

Rylko, Stanislaw, b. Andrychów, Poland 4 Jul 1945, Cardinal Deacon 24 Nov 2007; President of Pontifical Council for Laity.

Sandri, Leonardo, b. Buenos Aires, Argentina, 18 Nov 1943; Cardinal Deacon 24 Nov 2007; Prefect of Congregation for Oriental Churches.

Saraiva Martins, José, b Gagos, Portugal, 6 Jan 1932, Cardinal Deacon 21 Feb 2001, Prefect of the Congregation for the Causes of the Saints, titular Abp of Tuburnica.

Sebastiani, Sergio, b Montemonaco, Italy, 11 April 1931, Cardinal Deacon 21 Feb 2001, President of the Prefecture of the Holy See's Economic Affairs, titular Abp Cesarea di Mauritania.

Spidlek, Tomas (SJ), b Boskovice, Moravia, Czechoslovakia (now Czech Republic), 17 Dec, 1919; Cardinal Deacon 21 Oct 2003.

Tauran, Jean-Louis, b Bordeaux, France, 3 April, 1943; Cardinal Deacon 21 Oct 2003; titular Abp of Telepte; Archivist and Librarian of the Holy See. President of Pontifical Council for Interreligious Dialogue.

Tucci, Roberto, (SJ), b 21 April 1921, Vatican Radio official, Cardinal Deacon 21 Feb 2001.

Vallini, Agostino, b Poli, Italy 17 April, 1940; created Cardinal Deacon 24 March 2006; Prefect of the Supreme Tribunal of the Apostolic Signature 27 May 2004.

Vanhoye, S.J., Albert, b Hazebrouck Nord, France 24 July 1923; created Cardinal Deacon 24 March 2006; biblical scholar

■ PATRIARCHS OF THE ORIENTAL RITE (Other than Cardinals) IN FULL COMMUNION WITH THE HOLY SEE

Abdel-Ahad, His Beatitude Ignace Pierre Patriarch of Antiochia {Antioch} (Syrian), Lebanon

Delly, (Emmanuel) His Beatitude Karim III, Chaldean Patriarch of Babylon (Iraq).

Laham, His Beatitude Gregory III, Greek-Melkite Patriarch of Antioch.

Naguib, Archbishop Antonios, Coptic Patriarch of Alexandria

Sabbah, His Beatitude Michel, Latin Patriarch of Jerusalem.

Tarmouni, His Beatitude Nersés Bedros XIX, Armenian-Catholic Patriarch of Cilicia

THE ROMAN CURIA

SECRETARIAT OF STATE

Secretary of State: Cardinal Tarciso Bertone, S.D.B.
First section (General Affairs) Mgr Fernando Filoni, Titular Abp of Volturnum
Second Section (Relations with States) Mgr Dominique François Joseph Mamberti, Titular Abp of Sagona
Office: Palazzo Apostolico, 00120 Vatican City

■ THE CONGREGATIONS

The Congregations are permanent commissions for conducting the affairs of the Church. Each Congregation is composed of Cardinals, one of whom occupies the office of Prefect.

1. Congregation for the Doctrine of Faith
Prefect: **Cardinal William F Levada,** Abp of San Francisco.
Secretary: **Abp Luis Francisco Ladaria Ferrer SJ,** Titular Abp of Thibica.
Office: Piazza del S. Uffizio 11, 00193 Roma.

2. Congregation for the Eastern Churches
Prefect: **Cardinal Leonardo Sandi,** Titular Abp of Aemona
Secretary: **Mgr Antonio Maria Veglio,** Titular Abp of Eclano.
Office: Palazzo del Bramante, Via della Conciliazione 34, 00193 Roma.

3. Congregation for the Divine Worship and the Sacraments
Prefect: **Cardinal Francis Arinze.**
Secretary: **Mgr Albert Malcolm Ranjith Patabendige Don,** Titular Abp of Umbriatico.
Office: Palazzo delle Congregazioni, Piazza Pio XII 10, 00193 Roma.

4. Congregation for the Causes of Saints
Prefect: **Abp Angelo Amato SDB,** Titluar Abp of Sila.
Secretary: **Mgr Michele Di Ruberto,** Titluar Abp of Biccari.
Office: Palazzo delle Congregazioni, Piazza Pio XII 10, 00193 Roma.

5. Congregation for Bishops
Prefect: **Cardinal Giovanni Battista Re.**
Secretary: **Mgr Francesco Monterisi,** Titular Abp of Alba Maritimmo.
Office: Palazzo delle Congregazioni, Piazza Pio XII 10, 00193 Roma.

6. Congregation for the Evangelisation of the Peoples
Prefect: **Cardinal Ivan Dias**
Secretary: **Mgr Robert Sarah,** former Abp of Conakry.
Office: Palazzo di Propaganda Fide, Piazza di Spagna 48, 00187 Roma.

7. Congregation for Clergy
Prefect: **Cardinal Claudio Hummes, OFM**
Secretary: **Mgr Mauro Piacenza,** Titular Archbishop of Victoriana.
Office: Palazzo delle Congregazioni, Piazza Pio XII 3 00193 Roma.

8. Congregation for Institutes of Consecrated Life and Societies of Apostolic Life.
Prefect: **Cardinal Franc Rodé, CM**
Secretary: **Mgr Gianfranco Agostino Gardin, OFM Conv.,** Titular Abp of Cissa.
Office: Palazzo delle Congregazioni, Piazza Pio XII 3, 00193 Roma.

9. Congregation for Catholic Education in Seminaries and Institutes of Studies
Prefect: **Cardinal Zenon Grocholewski.**
Secretary: **Abp Jean-Louis Brugués OP.**
Office: Palazzo delle Congregazione, Piazza Pio XII 3, 00193 Roma.

■ THE TRIBUNALS

1. The Apostolic Penitentiary
Penitentiary: **Cardinal James Francis Stafford.**
Regent: **Rev Gianfranco Girotti OFMConv.**
Office: Palazzo della Cancelleria, Piazza della Cancelleria 1, 00186 Roma.

2. The Apostolic Segnatura
Prefect: **Abp Raymond Leo Burke.**
Secretary: **Bp Frans Daneels O.Praem,** Titular Bp of Bita.
Office: Palazzo della Cancelleria Apostolica, Piazza della Cancelleria 1, 00186, Roma.

3. The Roman Rota
Dean: **Bp Antoni Stankiewicz,** Titular Bp of Nova Petra.
Office: Palazzo della Cancelleria Apostolica, Piazza della Cancelleria 1, 00186, Roma

■ THE OFFICES

1. The Apostolic Camera
Camerlengo: **Cardinal Tarcisio Bertone, SDB.**
Vice-*Camerlengo:* **Mgr Paolo Sardi,** Titular Abp of Sutri.
Secretary & Chancellor: **Enrico Serafini.**
Office: Palazzo Apostolico, 00120 Vatican City.

2. Prefecture for the Economic Affairs of the Holy See
President: **Abp Velasio De Paolis,** Titular Abp of Thelepte
Secretary General: **Mgr Vincenzo Di Mauro,** Titular Bp of Arpi.
Office: Palazzo delle Congregazioni, Largo del Colonnato 300193 Roma.

3. Administration of the Patrimony of the Holy See
President: **Cardinal Attilio Nicora,** Abp Emeritus of Verona.
Secretary: **Abp Domenico Calcagno.**
Office: Palazzo Apostolico, 00120 Vatican City

4. Prefecture of the Papal Household
Prefect: **Mgr James Michael Harvey.** Titular Abp of Memfi.
Regent: Mgr Paolo de Nicolo
Office: Via Monte della Farina, 64 00186 Roma

5. The Statistical Office of the Church
Office: Palazzo Apostolico, 00120 Vatican City.

■ PONTIFICAL COUNCILS

1. Pontifical Council for the Laity
President: **Mgr Stanislaw Rylko,** Titular Abp of Novica.
Secretary: **Mgr Josef Clemens,** Titular Bp of Segerme.
Under-Secretary: **Prof. Avv. Guzman Carriquiry.**
Office: Piazza S. Calisto 16, 00153 Roma.

2. Pontifica Council for the Promotion of Christian Unity
President: **Cardinal Walter Kasper.**
Secretary: **Mgr Brian Farrell LC,** Titular Bp of Abitine.
Office: Via dell' Erba 1, 00193 Roma.
President Emeritus: **Cardinal Johannes Willebrands.**

3. Pontifical Council for the Family
President: **Cardinal Ennio Antonelli.**
Secretary: **Mgr Karl Josef Romer,** Titular Bp of Colonnata.
Office: Piazza S. Calisto 16, 00153 Roma.

4. Pontifical Commission for Justice and Peace with Pontifical Council for Pastoral Care for Migrants & Itinerants
President: **Cardinal Renato Raffaele Martino,** Titular Abp of Segerme.
Secretary: **Mgr Giampaolo Crepaldi,** Titular Bp of Bisarcio.
Secretary for Migrants: **Abp Agostino Marchetto**
Office: Piazza S. Calisto 16, 00153 Roma.

5. Pontifical Council 'Cor Unum'
President: **Mgr Paul Josef Cordes,** Titular Abp of Naisso.
Secretary: **Mgr Karel Kasteel.**
Office: Piazza S. Calisto 16, 00153 Roma.

6. Pontifical Council for Pastoral Care of Health Workers
President: **Cardinal Javier Barragán Lozano,** Abp Emeritus of Zacatecas.
Secretary: **Rev José Luis Redrado Marchite,** Titular Bp of Ofena.
Office: Via della Conciliazione 3, 000193 Roma

7. Pontifical Council for the Interpretation of Law
President: **Mgr Francesco Coccopalmerio,** Titular Abp of Coeliana.
Vice-President: **Mgr Bruno Bertagna,** Titular Bp of Drivasto.
Secretary: **Bp Juan Ignacio Arrieta Ochoa de Chinchetru,** Titular Bp of Civitate.
Office: Palazzo delle Congregazioni, Piazza Pio XII, 10, 00193 Roma.

8. Pontifical Council for Inter-Religious Dialogue
President: **Cardinal Jean-Louis Pierre Tauran.**
Secretary: **Mgr Pier Luigi Celata,** Titular Abp of Doclea.
Office: Via dell' Erba 1, 00193 Roma.

9. Pontifical Council for Culture
President: **Mgr Gianfranco Ravasi,** Titular Abp of Villamagna in Proconsulari.
Secretary: **Rev Bernard Ardura O.Praem.**
Office: Piazza S. Calisto 16, 00153 Roma.

10. Pontifical Council for Social Communication
President: **Mgr Claudio Maria Celli,** Titular Abp of Cluentum
Secretary: Post is currently vacant.
Office: Palazzo S. Carlo, 00120 Vatican City

■ SYNOD OF BISHOPS

Secretary General: **Mgr Nikola Eterovic,** Titular Abp of Sisak.
Office: Piazzo Pio XII 3, 00193 Roma.

■ VATICAN PRESS OFFICE

Director: **Fr Federico Lombardi, SJ,** Via della Conciliazione 54, 00193 Roma.
Tel. 0039 06 698921 **Telex:** 2017 Press VA
Fax 0039 06 69885178

■ APOSTOLIC NUNCIATURE TO THE EUROPEAN UNION

Nuncio: **His Excellency Archbishop André Pierre Louis Dupuy,** Titular Abp of Selsea.
Mailing Address: B-1180 Bruxelles, Avenue Brugmann 289
Tel: (32-2)3407700/3407711; **Fax:** 3407704

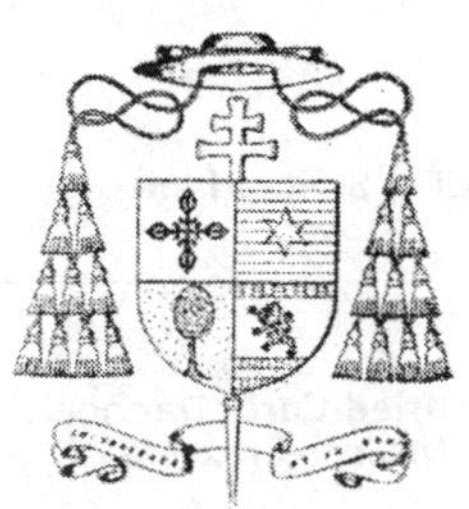

In veritate et in spe
(In truth and in hope)

THE APOSTOLIC NUNCIATURE

Established 17 January 1982

Formerly the Apostolic Delegation (established 21 November 1938)

The Apostolic Nuncio

His Excellency

Archbishop Faustino Sainz Muñoz

Born Almadén, Spain, 5th June, 1937; ordained priest for the Diocese of Madrid, 19th Dec 1964.
Studied at the Pontifical Gregorian University, obtaining Doctorate in Canon Law.
Entered Diplomatic Service of the Holy See in 1970; Service in: Senegal, Scandinavia, Council of Public Affairs of the Church of the Secretariat of State of His Holiness in the Vatican.
Apostolic Pro-Nuncio to Cuba, 29th Oct, 1988; Consecrated Titular Archbishop of Novaliciana, 18th Dec, 1988; Apostolic Pro-Nuncio in Zaire, 7th Oct, 1992; Apostolic Nuncio to the European Communities in Brussels, 21st Jan 1999;
Apostolic Nuncio to Great Britain from 2004.

His Excellency Archbishop Faustino Sainz Muñoz, Apostolic Nuncio to Great Britain

First Counsellor: **Mgr Brian Udaigwe**

Private Secretary: **Mgr Vincent G Brady**

Address: 54 Parkside, London SW19 5NE
Tel: 020-8944 7189 **Fax:** 020-8947 2494

Telegraphic Address: (Overseas) Nuntius, London SW19

Former Apostolic Delegates to Great Britain:
Archbishop (later Cardinal) William Godfrey (1938-1954)
Archbishop Gerald Patrick O'Hara (1954-1963)
Archbishop Hyginus Cardinale (1963-1969)
Archbishop Domenico Enrici (1969-1973)
Archbishop Bruno Bernard Heim (1973-1982)

Former Pro-Nuncios to Great Britain
Archbishop Bruno Bernard Heim (1982-1985)
Archbishop Luigi Barbarito (1986-1993)

Former Apostolic Nuncios to Great Britain
Archbishop Luigi Barbarito (1994-1997)
Archbishop Pablo Puente (1997-2004)

Biographical information of the above may be found in the Historical Interest section

BRITISH EMBASSY TO THE HOLY SEE

Ambassador Extraordinary and Plenipotentiary:
His Excellency Mr Francis Campbell
Via XX Settembre 80A, 00187 Rome
Tel: (39) 06 4220 4000 **Fax:** (39) 06 4220 4205
Email: holysee@fco.gov.uk **Website:** www.britishembassy.gov.uk/holysee

PRESIDENTS & SECRETARIES OF THE EPISCOPAL CONFERENCES OF EUROPE

The following information is supplied by the office of the CCEE, Switzerland

■ ALBANIA

President: **S E Mgr Angelo Massafra OFM**
Arcivescovo Metropolita di Shkodra
Sheshi Gjon Pali II
Hof 19AL-Shkodra, Albania
Tel: 00 355 22 427 44
Fax: 00 355 22 436 73
E-mail: curiashkoder@hotmail.com

Secretary: **Mgr Dodé Gjergji**
Amministratore Apostolico di Sapa
Kisha Katolike
La vau i dejës 2950 AL-Tirana, Albania
Tel/Fax: 00 355 424 71 59
E-mail: cealbania@albnet.net

■ AUSTRIA

President: **S E Dr Christoph Card Schönborn**.
Erzbischof von Wien
Erzbischöfliches Ordinariat
Wollzeile 2.
A-1010 Wien.
Tel: 0043 1 515 523 724
Fax: 0043 1 515 52 3728
E-mail: ebs@edw.or.at

Secretary: **Mgr Dr Agidius Zsifkovics**
Sekretarär der Bischofskonferenz,
Rotenturmstr 2
A-1010 Wien.
Tel: 0043 1 516 113 425
Fax: 0043 1 516 113 436
Email: Sekreariat@bischofskonferenz.at

Assistant Secretary: **Herr Dr Paul Wuthe**
Rotenturmnstr. 2
A-1010 Wien
Tel: 0043 1 516 113 495
Fax: 0043 1 516 113 436
E-mail: paul.wuthe@bischofskonferenz.at

■ BELARUS

President: **S E Kazimierz Card. Swiatek**.
Arcivescovo di Minsk et Pinsk
Praeses CE Bielorussia
ul. Szewczenki 12/1
BY-225710 Pinsk, Belarus
Tel/Fax: 00 375 165 359 278
E-mail: maria@maria.belpak.minsk.by

Secretary: **S E Mgr Anton Dzimyanka**
Vescovo ausiliare di Minsk-Mohilev
pl. Sowietskaja 4,
BY-230025 Grodno, Belarus
Tel: 00 375 152 244 51 38
Fax: 00 375 152 75 64 36
E-mail: gsekrecb@mail.grodno.by

■ BELGIUM

President: **S E Godfried Card. Danneels**.
Archevêque de Malines-Bruxelles,
Wollemarkt 15
B-2800 Mechelen.
Tel: 00 32 15 21 65 01
Fax: 00 32 15 20 94 85
E-mail: secretariaat.aarsbisdom@kerknet.be

Secretary: **Rev Chan Etienne Quintiens**.
Guimardstraat 1
B-1040 Bruxelles.
Tel: 00 32 2 509 96 93
Fax: 00 32 2 509 96 95
E-mail: ce.belgica@catho.kerknet.be

■ BOSNIA HERZEGOVINA

President: **S E Mgr Franjo Komarica**
Bisckup von Banja Luka
Biskupski Ordinarijat
Kralja Petra 1, 80-pp.93
BA-78101 Banja Luka
Bosnia Herzegovina
Tel: 00 387 51 305 984
Fax: 00 387 51 304 993
E-mail: tajnbisk@inecco.net

Secretary: **Mgr ivo Tomasevic**
Biskupska Konferencije BiH
Kaptol 32
BA-71000 Sarajevo
Bosnia Herzegovina
Tel/Fax: 00 387 33 666 867
E-mail: bkbih@bih.net.ba

■ BULGARIA

President: **S E Mgr Christo Proykov**.
Esarca Apostolico di Sofia,
Ul Liulin Planina n. 5,
BG-1606, Sofia, Bulgaria
Tel: 00 359 2 953 04 06
Fax: 00 359 2 952 61 86
E-mail: proykov@techno-link.com

Secretary: **Rev Srecko Rimac**
Ul. Liulin Planina n. 5
BG-1606 Sofia, Bulgaria
Tel: 00 359 2 944 40 29
Fax: 00 359 2 952 61 86
E-mail: proykov@techno-link.com

■ CROATIA

President: **S E Josip Card. Bozanic**.
Arcivescovo di Zagrabria
Vice-presidente CCEE
Kaptol 31,
HR-10000 Zagreb, Kroatia.
Tel: 00 385 1 489 48 02
Fax: 00 385 1 481 60 94
E-mail: jbozanic@zg.hinet.hr

uzgnadb@zg.htnet.hr
Secretary: **Mgr Vjekoslav Huzjak**
Tajnistvo HBK
Kaptol 22 HR-10000 Zagreb, Kroatia
Tel: 00 385 1 481 18 93
Fax: 00 385 1481 18 94

■ **CZECH REPUBLIC**
President: **S E Mgr Jan Graubner**.
Arcivescovo di Olomouc
Wurmova, 9
CZ-771 01 Olomouc, Czeska Republica
Tel: 00 420 587 405 401
Fax: 00 420 585 224 840
E-mail: gatnarp@arcibol.cz
Secretary: **Mgr Ladislav Hucko, CSc**.
Press Secretary, Czech Bish Conf
Thákurova 3
CZ-16000 Praha 6, Czeska Republica
Tel: 00 420 220 181 618
Fax: 00 420 220 181 200
E-mail: herman@cirkev.cz

■ **ENGLAND & WALES**
President:
S E Cormac Card. Murphy-O'Connor.
Archbishop of Westminster
Archbishop's House
Ambrosden Avenue, Westminster,
London SW1P 1QJ, England
Tel: 020-7798 9033
Fax: 020-7798 9077
E-mail: archbishop@rcdow.org.uk
Secretary: **Mgr Andrew Summersgill**.
39 Eccleston Square,
London. SW1V 1BX.
Tel: 020-7901 4810
Fax: 020-7901 4819
E-mails: gensec@cbcew.org.uk
secretariat@cbcew.org.uk

■ **FRANCE**
President: **Mgr André Vingt-Trois,**
Abp of Paris. 7 Rue St Vincent, 75018
Paris, Cedex 08, France
Tel: 0033 1 492 411 11
Fax: 0033 1 192 410 98
Secretary: **Père Antoine Herouard (Interim)**.
106, rue de Bac
F-75341 Paris cedex 07, France
Tel: 0033 1 454 969 70
Fax: 0033 1 454 813 39
E-mails: secretariat.general@cef.fr
sg@ced.fr

■ **GERMANY**
President: **President Abp Dr Robert Zollitsch**. Erzbischofliches Ordinariat
Schoferstr 2, D-79098 Frieburg im
Breisgau, Bundesrepublick Deutschland
Tel: 0049 0761 2188-0
Fax: 0049 0761 2188-505
Secretaries: **Pralat Dr Hans Langendörfer SJ**.
Kaiserstrasse 161
D-53113, Bonn
Tel: 0 49 228 10 32 90
Fax: 0049 228 10 32 99
E-mail: sekretaer@dbk.de
Herr Dr Rainer Ilgner,
Stellvetreter des Sekreters der
Deutschen, Bischofskonferenz
Kaiserstrasse 161
D 53113, Bonn.
Tel: 0049 228 10 32 90
Fax: 0049228 10 32 99

■ **GREECE**
President: **S E Mgr Franghoskos Papamanalis OFMCap**.
Vescovo di Syros e Santorini
Katholiki Episkopi
GR-84100 Syros.
Tel: 0030 22810 82768
Fax: 0030 22810 83924
E-mail: srensis@otenet.gr
Secretary: **S E Mgr Nikolaos Printezis**.
Katholiki Archiepiskopi Náxou-Tinou,
Genikós Grammatéas
Tis Ierás Synódou
GR-842 00 Tinos.
Tel: 0030 28330 022 382
Fax: 0030 22830 024 769
E-mail: iskietin@thn.forthnet.gr

■ **NETHERLANDS**
President:
S E Adrianus Joannes Card. Simonis.
Aartsbisschop van Utrecht
Maliebaan 40, P.B. 14019,
NL-3581 Utrecht CR.
Tel: 0031 30 231 69 56
Fax: 0031 30 231 19 62
E-mail: secretariaat@aartsbisdom.nl
Secretary: **Rev Prof Eduard J J M Kimman SJ**.
PB 13049
NL-3507 Utrecht LA.
Tel: 0031 30 232 69 03
Fax: 0031 30 230 70 95
E-mail: SecrSG@rkk.nl

■ **HUNGARY**
President: **Cardinal Péter Erdo**.
Primate, Abp of Esztergom-Budapest
H-1014 Budapest, Úri u. 62.
Tel: 00-36-1 225-2590
Fax: 00-36-1 202-5458
Secretary: **Rev P. László Nemet SVD**.
Magyar Katolikus Püspöki Konferencia
Titkársága H -1071 Budapest,
Városligeti fasor 45. P.O. Box H-1406
Budapest, Pf. 79.
Tel: (00-36-30) 742-4441, (00-36-30) 742-4443, (00-36-1) 342-6959,
Fax: 342-6957
E-mails: pkt@katolikus.hu

■ **IRELAND**
President: **His Grace, Seán Brady**,
Archbishop of Armagh
Ara Coeli, Cathedral Road

Armagh Northern Ireland BT61 7QY.
Tel: 0044 28 375220 45
Fax: 0044 28 375261 82
E-mail: admin@aracoeli.com

Secretaries: **Bishop William Lee**.
Bishop of Waterford and Lismore
Bishop's House, John's Hill,
Co. Waterford, Ireland.
Tel: 00353 51 874 463
Fax: 00353 51 852 703
E-mails: waterfordlismore@eircom.net
ex-sec@iecon.ie

Rev Dr Aidan O'Boyle.
Executive Secretary. of the Irish Bishops' Conf.
Columba Centre, Maynooth
Co. Kildare, Ireland.
Tel: 00353 1 505 30 20
Fax: 00353 1 629 23 60
E-mail: Ex.sec@iecon.ie

■ ITALY

President: **Mgr Angelo Bagnasco,**
Abp of Genoa.
Piazza Matteotti, 4 16123 Genova (GE).
Tel: 010 27001
Fax: 010 2700220
E-mail: curia@diocesi.genova.it

Secretary: **S E Mgr Giuseppe Betori**.
Circonvallazione Aurelia, 50
I-00165, Roma.
Tel: 0039 06 663 983 03
Fax: 0039 06 663 982 22
E-mail: segrgen@chiesacattolica.it

■ LATVIA

President: **S E Joannes Card. Pujats**.
Archiepiscopus Rigensis
M. Pils iela, 2a
LV-1050 Riga, Latvia.
Tel/Fax: 00371 7 220 775

Secretary: **Rev Juris Skapars**
Klostera iela 4
LV-1050 Riga
Tel: 00371 7 14 82 39
Fax: 0037 9 12 74 56
E-mail: jskapars@yahoo.com

■ LITHUANIA

President: **Rt Rev Sigitas Tamkevicius**.
SJ Abp of Kaunas, Rotuses a. 14a
LT-44279 Kaunas.
Tel: (370-37) 40 90 26
Fax: (370-37) 32 00 90
E-mails: ordinaras@kn.lcn.lt

Secretary: **Rev Gintarus Grusas**.
S Skapo 4
LT-2001 Vilnius, Lietuva.
Tel: 00370 5 212 54 55
Fax: 00370 5 212 09 72
E-mail: lvk@takas.lt

■ LUXEMBURG

President: **S E Mgr Ferdinand Franck**.
Archiveque du Luxemburg
4 rue Génistre
B.P. 419
L-2014 Luxemburg.
Tel: 00352 451 60 31
Fax: 00352 455 680
E-mails: fernand.franck@cathol.lu
archeveche@cathol.lu

Secretary: **Rev Dr Georges Hellinghausen**.
Bischofsvikar Luxemburg
Priesterseminar
52 rue Jules Wilhelmstrasse
L-2728 Luxemburg
Tel: 00352 436 051 325
Fax: 00352 423 103
E-mail: georges.hellinghausen@ci.educ.lu

■ MALTA

President: **Mgr Paul Cremona OP**.
Archbishop of Malta
Archbishop's Curia, PO Box 29
MT-Floriana, Malta.
Tel: 00356 2123 4317
Fax: 00356 2122 3307

Secretary: **Rev Joseph Magro**.
7 Triq Carlo Flamingo
MT-Tal-Virtu, Rabat, Malta
Tel: 00356 2590 6135
Fax: 00356 2145 32 78
E-mail: joe.magro@maltadiocese.org

■ POLAND

President: **S E Mgr Jozef Michalik**.
Skwer Ks. Kard S. Wyszynskiego 6
PL-01-015 Warszawa, Polen.
Tel: 0048 22 53 04 800
Fax: 0048 22 838 09 67
E-mail: skep@episkopat.pl

Secretary: **S E Mgr Piotr Libera**.
Skwer Ks.Kard. S. Wyszynskiego 6
PL-01 015 Warszawa.
Tel: 0048 22 838 92 51-4
Fax: 0048 22 838 09 67
E-mail: skep@episkopal.pl

■ PORTUGAL

President: **D. Jorge Ortiga**.
Abp of Braga
Rua Sao Domingos 94B, 4710-435
Braga CODEX, Portugal.
Tel: 00351 253.20.31.80
Fax: 00351 253.20.31.90
E-mail:gab.patriarca@patriacard.o-lisboa.pt

Secretary: **P. Manuel Morujao**.
Quinta do Cabeço, Porta D
1885-076 MOSCAVIDE.
Tel: 00351 218855460
Fax: 00351 218855461

■ ROMANIA

President: **S E Mgr Lucian Murecan**.
Arcivescovo e Metropolita di Alba Iulia e Fig.
Str Petru Pavel Aron nr 2
RO-515400 Blaj

Rumanien.
Tel: 0040 258 710 608
Fax: 0040 258 710 855
Secretary: **Rev Cazimir Budáu-Surchea.**
Str. Popa Tatu 68
RO-70772 Bucuresti.
Tel: 0040 21 311 12 89
Fax: 0040 21 311 15 91
E-mail: b_cazimir@pcnet.ro

■ RUSSIA
President: **S E Mgr Tadeusz Kondrusiewicz.**
Arcivescovo Metropolita
dell'Arcidiocesi
della Madre di Dio a Mosca
Novoya Basmannayastr.16-31
Rus-107078 Mosca
Tel/Fax: 007 095 261 67 14
E-mail: cathmos@dol.ru
Secretary: **Rev Igor Kowalewski**
Ul.F. Engelsa, 46, str, 4
RU-107005 Mosca
Tel: 007 095 265 41 90
Fax: 007 095 265 47 35
E-mail: cecr@rambler.ru

■ SCANDINAVIA
President: **S E Mgr Gerhard Schwenzer.**
Bishop of Oslo.
Akersveien 5
N-0177 Oslo
Tel: 0047 232 195 00
Fax: 0047 232 195 01
E-mail: gerhardschwenzer@
katolsk.no
Secretary: **S E Mgr William Kenney.**
Auxiliary Bishop of Stockholm
Box 135
S-421 22 Västra Frölunda, Sweden.
Tel: 0046 31 709 57 15
Fax: 0046 31 492 170
E-mails: nbk@bishopsoffice.org
william.kenney@bishopsoffice.org

■ SCOTLAND
President: **S E Keith Patrick Card. O'Brien.**
Archbishop of St Andrews and
Edinburgh
Archbishop's House
42 Greenhill Gardens
Edinburgh EH10 4BJ.
Tel: 0131 447 3337
Fax: 0131-447 0816
E-mails*:* archkp@lineone.net
card.inal@staned.org.uk
Secretary: **Rev Paul M Conroy**
Bishops' Conference of Scotland
64 Aitken Street, Airdrie ML6 6LT
Tel: 01236 764061
Fax: 01236 762489
E-mail: gensec@bpsconfscot.com

■ SERBIA & MONTENEGRO
President: **SE Mgr Stanislav Hocevar.**
Arcivescovo Metropolita Belgrado
Svetozara Markovica 20
YU-11000 Belgrad, Serbia.
Tel: 00381 11 303 22 46
Fax: 00381 11 303 22 48
E-mail: nadbisbg@eunet.yu
Secretary: **Rev P Leopoldo Marko.**
Rochmes OFM
Nadbiskupsi Ordinarijat
Svetozara Markovici 20
YU-11000 Belgrad, Serbia.
Tel: 00381 11 303 44 46
Fax: 00381 11 303 22 48
E-mail: nadbisbg@eunet.yu

■ SLOVAKIA
President: **S E Mgr Frantisek Tondra.**
Vescovo di Spis
Spisská Kapitula
SK-053 04 Spisské Podhradie
Slovakia.
Tel: 00421 53 454 11 36
Fax: 00421 53 450 22 08
E-mails: predseda.kbs@kbs.sk
tondra@kbs.sk
Secretaries: **Mgr Marián Chovanec.**
Rimskokatolicky biskupsk úrad
PO Box 46 A
SK-950 50 Nitra
Slovakia.
Tel: 00421 37 651 55 72
Fax: 00421 37 772 17 49
E-mail: chovanec@kbs.sk
Rev Cyril Jancisin.
Kapitulsk 11
PO Box 113
SK-814 99 Bratislava
Slovakia.
Tel: 00421 2 544 352 34
Fax: 0421 2 544 359 13
E-mail: cjancisin@kbs.sk

■ SLOVENIA
President: **S E Mgr Franc Kramberger.**
Bischof von Maribor
Slomoskov trg 19.
SI-2000 Maribor
Slovenia.
Tel: 00 386 2 229 04 01
Fax: 00 386 2 252 30 92
E-mails: ordinariat@slomsek.net
skofija.maribor@rkc.si
Secretary: **Mr Andrej Saje.**
Tiskovni urad SSK
Krekov trg 1 p.p. 95
SL-1001 Ljubljana.
Tel: 00 386 1 438 48 00
Fax: 00 386 1 231 56 43
E-mail: andrej.saje@rkc.si

■ SPAIN
President: **S E Antonio Maria Card. Rouco Varela**, Arzobispo de Madrid
San Justo 2
E-28033, Madrid.
Tel: 0034 91 366 56 01
Fax: 0034 91 366 77 39

E-mail: arzmadrid@planalfa.es
Secretary: **Rev Dr Juan Antonio Camino SJ**.
C/Añastro, 1
E-28033 Madrid.
Tel: 0034 91 343 96 15
Fax: 0034 91 343 97 30
E-mail: secretaria.cee@planalfa.es

■ **SWITZERLAND**
President: **Mgr Kurt Koch**.
Bp of Basel
Bischöfliches Ordinariat
Baselstr. 58
Case postale 216
4500 Solothurn
Tel: 0041 32 625 58 25
Fax: 0041 32 625 58 45
E-mails: generalvikariat@bistum-basel.ch
Secretary: **Abbé Felix Gmür**.
Av. du Moléson 21,
Case postale 22
CH-1706 Fribourg.
Tel: 0041 26 322 47 94
Fax: 0041 26 322 49 93
E-mail: sbk-ces@gmx.ch

■ **TURKEY**
President: **S E Mgr Ruggero Franceschini**.
Arcivescovo di Izmir
Necat be Blv No. 2
P.K. 267
TR-35210 Izmir, Turkei.
Tel: 0090 232 484 84 36
Fax: 0090 232 484 53 58
E-mail: curiaves@yahoo.it
Secretary: **Rev Mauro Pesce**.
Secretarius ce Turchia
Kurtulus Cad. No 197-201/D14
TR-34375 Istanbul Turkey
Tel: 0090 212 219 7810
Fax: 0090 212 219 1548
E-mail: mauropesce2807@yahoo.it

■ **UKRAINE (BYZANTINE RITE)**
President: **S E Lubomyr Card. Husar**.
Arcivescovo Maggiore di Kiev
Chiesa cattolica ucraina
pl Sviatoho Yura, 5
UA-79000 Lviv.
Tel: 00380 322 971 121
Fax: 00380 322 971 404
E-mail: lhusa@ugcc.org.ua
Secretaries: **Mgr Dr Iwan Dacko**.
Mitred Protopresbyter
Birkenweg 3
D-83629 Weyarn (Naring).
Tel: 0049 8063 80 99 90
Fax: 0049 8063 92 21
S E Mgr Wasyl Ihor Medwit.
Sekretär der Synode (Byzantine)
vul.Riznytcka 11-b/28-29
UA-01011 Kyiv-Ucraina.
Tel/Fax: 00380 44 290 68 49
E-mail: synod@i.com.ua

■ **UKRAINE (LATIN RITE)**
President: **S E Mgr Marian, Card. Jaworski**.
Erzbischof von Lemberg
Pl. Katedralna 1
UA-79008 Lviv, Ukraina.
Tel: 00 380 322 76 94 15
Fax: 00 380 322 96 61 14
E-mail: jaworski@rkc.lviv.ua
Secretary: **Mgr Marian Buczek**.
Sekretär der Bischofskonferenz
Pl. Katedralny 1
UA-79008 Lviv.
Tel: 00380 322 769 415
Fax: 00380 322 966 114
E-mail: k@rkc.lviv.ua

COUNCIL OF THE EPISCOPAL CONFERENCES OF EUROPE

President: **Cardinal Peter Erdö**, Abp of Esztergom-Budapest and Primate of Hungary.
Vice-Presidents: **Cardinal Josip Bozanic**, Abp of Zagreb; **Cardinal Jean-Pierre Ricard**, Abp of Bordeaux.
Secretary: **Rev Mgr Aldo Giordano**. Cura Secretariatus Consilii, Gallusstr. 24, CH-9000. St Gallen, Switzerland.
Tel: 00 41 71 227 6040 **Fax:** 0041 71 227 604 **E-mail:** ccee@ccee.ch

STRUCTURE AND HIERARCHY OF THE CHURCH

COMECE – COMMISSION OF THE BISHOPS' CONFERENCES OF THE EUROPEAN COMMUNITY

COMECE is the Commission of the Bishops' Conferences of the European Community. It is made up of bishops delegated by the Catholic Bishops' Conferences of the European Union and it has a permanent Secretariat in Brussels. COMECE was launched in 1980 and its primary objectives are: To monitor and analyse the political process of the European Union; to inform and raise awareness within the Church of the development of EU policy and legislation; to promote reflection, based on the Church's social teaching, on the challenges facing a united Europe.

Secretariat Address: **COMECE**, 42 Rue Stévin, B-1000 Brussels.
Tel: +32 (2) 235 05 10, **Fax:** +32 (2) 230 33 34, **E-mail:** comece@comece.org

President: **Rt Rev Adrianus van Luyn SDB,** Bishop of Rotterdam, Netherlands.

Vice-Presidents: **Most Rev Diarmuid Martin,** Archbishop of Dublin, Ireland.
Rt Rev Piotr Jarecki, Bishop of Warsaw, Poland.

Secretary General: **Rev Piotr Mazurkiewicz**

Assistant to the Secretary General: **Stefan Lunte**

Administration: **Agnes Paillard; Maud Oger.**

Secretariat Members: **Monique Baujard** (Migration and Asylum; Relations with European Parliament); **Michael Kuhn** (Seconded by the Austrian Bishops' Conference); **Vincent Legrand** (International Relations; Interreligious Dialogue –Islam); **Alessandro Calcagno** (Seconded by the Italian Bishops' Conference); **Joanna Lopatowska** (Human Rights; Legal Affairs); **Katharina Schauer** (Bio-ethical Issues); **Johanna Touzel** (Public Relations)

Bishop Delegates to COMECE

Rt Rev Czeslaw Kozon,
Bp of Copenhagen (Scandinavia)

Rt Rev Virgil Bercea,
Bp of Oradea Mare/Gran Varadino (Romania)

Most Rev Nikólaos Fóscolos,
Abp of Athens (Greece)

Rt Rev Adolfo Gonzalez Montes,
Bp of Almeria (Spain)

Rt Rev Rimantas Norvila,
Bp of Vilkaviskis (Lithuania)

Rt Rev Christo Proykov,
Apostolic Echarch of Sofia, President of the Bishops' Conference (Bulgaria)

Most Rev Hippolyte Simon,
Abp of Clermont, France

Rt Rev Reinhard Marx,
Bp of Trier, Germany

Abp Fernand Franck,
Abp of Luxembourg

Rt Rev Egon Kapellari,
Bp of Graz-Seckau, Austria

Rt Rev William Kenney C.P.,
Auxiliary Bp of Birmingham (England & Wales)

Rt Rev Giuseppe Merisi,
Bp of Lodi, Italy

Rt Rev Peter Moran,
Bp of Aberdeen, Scotland

Rt Rev Vaclav Maly,
Auxiliary Bp of Prague, Czech Republic

Rt Rev Mario Grech,
Bp of Gozo (Malta)

Rt Rev Frantisek Rábek,
Bp of the Armed Forces, Slovakia

Rt Rev Anton Stres C.M.,
Bp of Celje, Slovenia

Rt Rev Jozef De Kesel,
Auxiliary Bp of the Archdiocese of Malines, Brussels

Rt Rev Antons Justs,
Bp of Jelgava, Latvia

THE HIERARCHY OF THE UNITED KINGDOM AND IRELAND AT THE PRESENT TIME

The Province of Westminster consists of the Archiepiscopal See of Westminster, with the four Suffragan Sees of Brentwood, East Anglia, Northampton and Nottingham.
The Province of Birmingham consists of the Archiepiscopal See of Birmingham, with the two Suffragan Sees of Clifton and Shrewsbury.
The Province of Liverpool consists of the Archiepiscopal See of Liverpool with the six Suffragan Sees of Hallam, Hexham and Newcastle, Lancaster, Leeds, Middlesbrough and Salford.
The Province of Cardiff consists of the Archiepiscopal See of Cardiff with the Suffragan Sees of Menevia and Wrexham.
The Province of Southwark consists of the Archiepiscopal See of Southwark with the three Suffragan Sees of Arundel and Brighton, Plymouth, and Portsmouth.

■ PROVINCE OF WESTMINSTER

His Eminence Cardinal Cormac Murphy-O'Connor, Archbishop of Westminster: ord Bp 21 Dec 1977; installed as Archbp 22 March 2000.

Auxiliaries:
Right Rev George Stack, Bishop of Gemellae: ord 10 May 2001.
Right Rev Bernard Longley, Bishop of Zama: ord Bp 23 Jan 2003.
Right Rev Alan Hopes, Bishop of Cuncacestre: ord Bp 23 Jan 2003.
Right Rev John Arnold, Bishop of Lindisfarne: ord Bp 2 Feb 2006.

Suffragans:
Right Rev Peter Doyle, Bishop of Northampton: ord 28 June 2005.
Right Rev Thomas McMahon OP, Bishop of Brentwood: ord 17 July 1980.
Right Rev Malcolm McMahon Bishop of Nottingham: ord Bishop 8 Dec 2000.
Right Rev Michael Evans, Bishop of East Anglia: ord Bishop 27 May 1995.

■ PROVINCE OF BIRMINGHAM

Most Rev Vincent Nichols, Archbishop of Birmingham: ord Bp 24 Jan 1992; installed Archbp 29 March 2000.

Auxiliary:
Right Rev William Kenney CP, Bishop of Midica: ord Bp 24 Aug 1987.
Right Rev Philip Pargeter, Bishop of Valentiniana: ord 21 Feb 1990.
Right Rev David Christopher McGough, Bishop of Chunavia: ord Bp 8 Dec 2005.

Suffragans:
Right Rev Brian M Noble, Bishop of Shrewsbury: ord Bishop 30 Aug 1995.
Right Rev Declan R Lang, Bishop of Clifton: ord Bishop 28 March 2001.

■ PROVINCE OF LIVERPOOL

Most Rev Patrick Altham Kelly, Archbishop of Liverpool: ord Bishop 3 April 1984; trans as Archbp 3 July 1996.

Auxiliaries:
Right Rev Vincent Malone, Bishop of Abora: ord 3 July 1989.
Right Rev Thomas Williams, Bishop of Mageó: ord Bishop 27 May 2003.

Suffragans:
Right Rev Arthur Roche, Bishop of Leeds: ord April 7, 2004.
Right Rev Terence Drainey, Bishop of Middlesbrough: ord 25 Jan 2008.
Bishop of Hexham and Newcastle: Sede Vacante.
Right Rev John Rawsthorne, Bishop of Hallam: ord Bishop 16 Dec 1981; trans 3 July 1997.
Right Rev Terence Brain, Bishop of Salford: ord Bishop 22nd May 1991; trans 8th Oct 1997.
Right Rev Patrick O'Donoghue, Bishop of Lancaster: ord Bishop 29 June 1993; trans Lancaster 4 July 2001.
Right Rev Michael Campbell OSA, Coadjutor Bishop of Lancaster: ord Bishop 31 March 2008

Attached to the Diplomatic Service of the Holy See

Most Rev Paul Richard Gallagher, Titular Archbishop of Hodelm: Apostolic Nuncio to Burundi, formerly Special Envoy and

Permanent Observer of the Holy See to the Council of Europe; ord Archbishop 13 March 2004.

■ PROVINCE OF CARDIFF

Most Rev Peter D Smith LLB, JCD ord 27 May, 1995; trans to Cardiff 26 October, 2001.

Suffragan:

Right Rev Mark Jabalé OSB, Bishop of Menevia: ord Co-adjutor Bishop 7 Dec 2000; inst as Bishop 12 June 2001.

Right Rev Edwin Regan, Bishop of Wrexham: ord Bishop 13 Dec 1994.

■ PROVINCE OF SOUTHWARK

Most Rev Kevin McDonald, Archbishop of Southwark: ord 2 May 2001; trans to Southwark 2004.

Auxiliary:

Right Rev Paul Hendricks, Bishop of Rossmarkaeum, ord 14 Feb 2006.

Right Rev John Hine, Bishop of Beverley, ord 27 Feb 2001.

Right Rev Patrick Lynch SSCC, Bishop of Castrum, ord 14 Feb 2006.

Suffragans:

Right Rev Christopher Budd, Bishop of Plymouth: ord 15 Jan 1986.

Right Rev Crispian Hollis, Bishop of Portsmouth: ord 5 May 1987; trans 6 Dec 1988.

Right Rev Kieran Thomas Conry, Bishop of Arundel & Brighton: ord Bp 9 June 2001.

■ BISHOPRIC OF THE FORCES

Right Rev Thomas Matthew Burns, ord **Bishop-in-Ordinary to HM Forces:** 18 June, 2002.

By Apostolic Constitution Spirituali Militum Curae of 21 April 1986, Forces Ordinariates replaced Forces Vicariates. Bishop-in-Ordinary to Her Majesty's Forces 20 Nov 97 making the Military Ordinary equivalent to a Diocesan Ordinary.

■ II. SCOTLAND

THE HIERARCHY AT THE PRESENT TIME

The Province of St Andrews and Edinburgh consists of the Archiepiscopal See of St Andrews and Edinburgh, and the Suffragan Sees of Aberdeen, Argyll and the Isles, Dunkeld, and Galloway.

The Province of Glasgow consists of the Archiepiscopal See of Glasgow, and the Suffragan Sees of Motherwell and Paisley.

■ PROVINCE OF ST ANDREWS AND EDINBURGH

His Eminence Cardinal Keith Patrick O'Brien, Archbishop of St Andrews and Edinburgh: ord 5 Aug 1985.

Suffragans:

Aberdeen: Right Rev Peter Moran, Bishop of Aberdeen: ord 1 Dec 2003.

Right Rev Vincent Logan, Bishop of Dunkeld: ord 26 Feb 1981.

Right Rev John Cunningham, Bishop of Galloway: ord 28 May 2004.

Right Rev Ian Murray, Bishop of Argyll and the Isles: ord 7 Dec 1999.

■ PROVINCE OF GLASGOW

Most Rev Mario Joseph Conti, Archbishop of Glasgow: ord Bishop of Aberdeen 3 May 1977; trans 22 Feb 2002.

Suffragans:

Right Rev Joseph Devine, Bishop of Motherwell: ord Auxiliary in Glasgow 31 May 1977; trans 13 May 1983.

Right Rev Philip Tartaglia, Bishop of Paisley: ord November 2005.

■ THE BISHOPS' CONFERENCE OF SCOTLAND

General Secretary: Rev Paul M Conroy, Bishops' Conference of Scotland, 64 Aitken Street, Airdrie, Lanarkshire ML6 6LT

Tel: 01236-764061 **Fax:** 01236-762489

E-mail: gensec@bpsconfscot.com

III. IRELAND

THE HIERARCHY AT THE PRESENT TIME

PROVINCE OF ARMAGH

His Eminence Cardinal Sean Brady, Archbishop of Armagh: cons 19 Feb 1995, installed 3 November 1996.

Auxiliary:
Most Rev Gerard Clifford, Bishop of Geron: cons 21 April 1991
Suffragans:
Most Rev John McAreavey, Bishop of Dromore cons Sept. 19th, 1999).
Most Rev Patrick Walsh, Bishop of Down and Connor: cons 15 May 1983, transl: 28 April 1991.
Auxiliary:
Most Rev Anthony Farquhar, Bishop of Ermiana: cons 15 May 1983.
Most Rev Donal McKeown, Bishop of Cell Ausaille, cons 29 April 2001
Most Rev Seamus Hegarty, Bishop of Derry: cons 1982, trans 1994.
Auxiliary: **Most Rev Francis Lagan, Titular Bishop of Sidnacestra:** cons 20 March 1988.
Most Rev Colm O'Reilly, Bishop of Ardagh and Clonmacnois: cons 10 April 1983.
Most Rev Michael Smith, Bishop of Meath: cons 29 Jan 1984.
Most Rev Joseph Duffy, Bishop of Clogher: cons 2 Sept 1979.
Most Rev Leo O'Reilly, Bishop of Kilmore: cons 10 Dec 1972.
Most Rev Philip Boyce, Bishop of Raphoe: cons 1 Oct 1995.

PROVINCE OF DUBLIN

Most Rev Diarmuid Martin, Archbishop of Dublin: cons 6 January 1999, transl. May 2003.

Emeritus Archbishop, Desmond Cardinal Connell, cons 6 March 1988.

Auxiliaries:
Most Rev Raymond Field, Bishop of Ard Mor: cons 21 Sept 1997
Most Rev Eamonn Walsh, Bishop of Elmhama: cons 22 Apr 1990.
Most Rev Fiachra O Ceallaigh, cons 17 September 1994.

Suffragans:
Most Rev Séamus Freeman SAC, Bishop of Ossory: apptd Bp 14 Sept 2007.
Most Rev James Moriarty, Bishop of Kildare and Leighlin: cons 1991. trans 2002.
Most Rev Denis Brennan, Bishop of Ferns; ord Bp 23 April 2006.

PROVINCE OF CASHEL

Most Rev Dermot Clifford, Archbishop of Cashel and Emly: cons 9 Mar 1986; trans 12 Sept 1988.
Suffragans:
Most Rev William Lee, Bishop of Waterford and Lismore: cons 25 July 1993
Most Rev John Buckley, Bishop of Cork and Ross: cons 29 April 1984.
Most Rev John Magee, Bishop of Cloyne: cons 1987.
Most Rev William Walsh, Bishop of Killaloe: cons 2 Oct 1994.
Most Rev William Murphy, Bishop of Kerry: cons 10 Sept 1995.
Most Rev Donal Murray, Bishop of Limerick: cons 18 April 1982; trans 1996.

PROVINCE OF TUAM

Most Rev Michael Neary, Archbishop of Tuam: cons 13 Sept 1992; trans 1995.

Suffragans:
Most Rev Brendan Kelly, Bishop of Achonry: cons 20 Nov 2007.
Most Rev John Kirby, Bishop of Clonfert: cons 9 April 1988.
Most Rev Christopher Jones, Bishop of Elphin: cons 15 August 1994.
Most Rev Martin Drennan, Bishop of Galway and Kilmacduagh: Ord Bp 21 Sept 1997; trans 23 May 2005.
Most Rev John Fleming, Bishop of Killala: cons 7 April 2002.

THE IRISH EPISCOPAL CONFERENCE

Executive Secretary: Rev Aidan O'Boyle, The Columba Centre, Maynooth, Co Kildare, **Tel:** 00353 505 3000 **Fax:** 00353 629 2360

THE CATHOLIC BISHOPS' CONFERENCE OF ENGLAND AND WALES

President: **Cardinal Cormac Murphy-O'Connor**

Vice-President: **Archbishop Patrick Kelly**

Membership: Diocesan, Auxiliary and Emeritus Bishops of England and Wales, the Apostolic Exarch for the Ukrainians and the Catholic Bishop of HM Forces

Standing Committee: The Metropolitans and the Chairmen of Conference Departments

Departments: Christian Life and Worship; Dialogue and Unity; Evangelisation and Catechesis, Catholic Education and Formation; Christian Responsibility and Citizenship; International Affairs

■ GENERAL SECRETARIAT

39 Eccleston Square, London SW1V 1BX
Tel: 020-7630 8220 **Fax:** 020-7901 4821
E-mail: secretariat@cbcew.org.uk
Internet: www.catholicchurch.org.uk

■ General Secretary
Mgr Andrew Summersgill
Tel: 020-7901 4810, **Fax:** 020-7901 4819
E-mail: gensec@cbcew.org.uk

■ Assistant General Secretaries
Mr Charles Wookey, for Christian Responsibility and Citizenship,
Tel: 020-7901 4812
E-mail: charles.wookey@cbcew.org.uk
Mr David Ryall, with responsibility for International Affairs, **Tel:** 020-7901 4861
E-mail: david.ryall@cbcew.org.uk
Mgr Andrew Faley, for Ecumenical Affairs,Interfaith Relations, Evangelisation, Catechesis and Catholic Education and Formation, **Tel:** 020-7901 4811
E-mail: andrew.faley@cbcew.org.uk
Mr Laurence Fenton, with responsibility for Operations, **Tel:** 020-7901 4826
E-mail: laurence.fenton@cbcew.org.uk

Assistant to the General Secretary:
Miss Lorraine Welch, Tel: 020-7901 4815
E-mail: lorraine.welch@cbcew.org.uk

■ CATHOLIC COMMUNICATIONS NETWORK

39 Eccleston Square, London SW1V 1BX
Tel: 020-7901 4800. **Fax:** 020-7901 4820
E-mail: ccn@cbcew.org.uk
Website: www.catholicchurch.org.uk
Out of Hours: 0789 3707043

Head of News and Information:
Alexander DesForges
Senior Media Officer: **Maggie Doherty**
Webmaster: **James Abbot**
E-mail: james.abbott@cbcew.org.uk
Office Manager/Media Assistant:
Johanna van den Broeke

Unless otherwise stated, the following Committees may be contacted at 39 Eccleston Square, London, SW1V 1BX

■ DEPARTMENT OF CHRISTIAN LIFE AND WORSHIP

Chairman: **Rt Rev Arthur Roche.**

Bishop Members:
Rt Rev Alan Hopes
Rt Rev David McGough
Rt Rev Thomas McMahon,
Rt Rev Brian Noble,
Rt Rev Michael Campbell.

Acting Secretary: **Mr Martin Foster.**
Tel: 020-7901 4851
E-mail: martin.foster@cbcew.org.uk

Department Administrator:
Mrs Grace Applewaithe.

■ The Committee for Liturgy advises the bishops on matters relating to liturgy, liturgical music, art and architecture. It has a Subcommittee for Formation that works with diocesan Liturgy Commissions.
Chairman: **Rt Rev Alan Hopes.**
Chairman of Formation Subcommittee:
Rev Peter McGrail.

■ The Committee for Patrimony encourages an understanding and appreciation of the patrimony of the Catholic Church in England and Wales as a record of the past, witness of a living tradition and tool of the 'new evangelisation'. The Subcommittee for patrimony works with diocesan Historic Churches Committees in the care and conservation of church building and to maintain the exemption from listed building control.
Chairman: **Rt Rev Thomas McMahon.**
Chairman of Subcommittee:
Miss Sophie Andreae.
Hon Sec to Patrimony:
Mrs Tricia Brooking,
Tel: 01628-637759
E-mail: triciabrooking@dsl.pipex.com

■ The Committee for Spirituality brings matters relating to Spirituality to the attention of the Bishops' Conference. It gathers information about provision in England and Wales and encourages good practice.
Chairman: **Rt Rev Brian Noble**
Secretary: **Mgr Kevin McGinnell**

■ DEPARTMENT OF DIALOGUE AND UNITY

Chairman: **Most Rev Kevin McDonald**

Bishop Members:
Rt Rev Michael Evans, Rt Rev Declan Lang, Rt Rev Philip Pargeter, Rt Rev Hugh Lindsay, Rt Rev Paul Hendricks.

Secretary: **Mgr Andrew Faley**
Tel: 020-7901 4811
E-mail: andrew.faley@cbcew.org.uk

General Email Enquiries:
E-mail: dialunity@cbcew.org.uk

■ Committee for Christian Unity
Purpose: To monitor ecumenical progress in England and Wales; to represent the Conference on various ecumenical committees and, through the Department of Dialogue and Unity, to provide the Conference with background information with regard to all matters of ecumenical concern.
Chairman: **Rt Rev Michael Evans.**
Secretary: **Rev David Bulmer**
Tel: 020 7901 4842 **Fax:** 020 7901 4821
E-mail: dialunity@cbcew.org.uk

■ Committee for Catholic/Jewish Relations
Purpose: To foster the relationship between the Church and the Jewish people, thus implementing the official teaching of the Church; to promote an understanding of the living faith of Judaism and the Jewish roots of Christianity; to encourage dialogue and reconciliation; and to eradicate anti-semitism wherever it is found.
Chairman: **Most Rev Kevin McDonald.**
Secretary: **Sr Clare Jardine.** c/o 39 Eccleston Square, London SW1V 1BX
Tel: 020-7901 4842 **Fax:** 020 7901 4821
E-mail: dialunity@cbcew.org.uk

■ Committee for Other Faiths
Purpose: To help Catholics deepen their faith by promoting a greater awareness and understanding of other faiths, through dialogue, prayer and action in the light of the Church's teaching.
Chairman: **Most Rev Kevin McDonald**
Acting Secretary: **Mgr Andrew Faley.**
Tel: 020-7901 4841

■ DEPARTMENT OF EVANGELISATION AND CATECHESIS

Chairman: **Bishop Malcolm McMahon OP**

Bishop Members:
Rt Rev Ambrose Griffiths OSB, Rt Rev

Kieran Conry, Rt Rev Edwin Regan, Rt Rev John Arnold.

Assistant General Secretary for Evengalisation and Catechesis: **Mgr Andrew Faley.**
Tel: 020-7901 4811
Fax: 020-7901 4821
E-mail: andrew.faley@cbcew.org.uk

Department Secretary: **Mrs Veronica Murphy,** 13 Snipewood, Eccleston, Chorley PR7 5RQ **Tel:** 0771 426 426 1883
E-mail: veronica.murphy@cbcew.org.uk

Department Administrator:
Mrs Grace Applewaithe,
Tel: 020-7901 4842 **Fax:** 020-7901 4821
E-mail: grace.applethwaite@cbcew.org.uk

■ **Living and Sharing Our Faith**
Purpose: A national project of Catechetics and religious education.
Chairman: **Rt Rev Edwin Regan.**
Secretary: **Sr Vicky Hummell,** 39 Eccleston Square, London SW1V 1BX
Tel: 020-7901 4884 **Fax:** 020-7901 4893
E-mail: vhummell@cesew.org.uk

■ **Catholic Youth Ministry**
Chairman: **Rt Rev Kieran Conry**

The Bishops' Conference of England and Wales seeks to add guidance, value and support to the work of Catholic Youth Ministry by working in partnership with all those committed to enabling young people and young adults to enjoy the fullness of life and to be an integral part of Church and society.

National Youth Co-ordinator: to be appointed
E-mail: youth@cbcew.org.uk
39 Eccleston Square, London, SW1V 1BX
Tel: 020-7901 4872 **Fax:** 020 7901 4821

See also CASE under agencies of the Bishops' Conference.

■ **DEPARTMENT OF CATHOLIC EDUCATION AND FORMATION**

Chairman: **Most Rev Vincent Nichols**

Bishop Members:
Rt Rev Mark Jabalé, Rt Rev Vincent Malone, Rt Rev George Stack, Rt Rev Kevin Dunn, Rt Rev Peter Doyle.

Assistant General Secretary for Catholic Education and Formation:
Mgr Andrew Faley.

Department Secretary: **Rev Michael Cooke**, St John's Presbytery, The Crescent, Bromley Cross, Bolton BL7 9JP
Tel: 01204 301927
E-mail: michael.cooke@cbcew.org.uk

Department Administrator:
Mrs Grace Applewaithe,
Tel: 020-7901 4842 **Fax:** 020-7901 4821
E-mail: grace.applethwaite@cbcew.org.uk

■ **Committee for Ministerial Formation**
Purpose: To serve the Church's mission, by advising the Bishops' Conference from within the Department of Catholic Education and Formation, to foster and facilitate initial and ongoing formation for formally authorised pastoral ministries, ordained and lay.
Chairman: **Rt Rev George Stack.**
Secretary: **Fr Paul Embery** (See National Office for Vocation).

See also Catholic Education Service under Agencies of the Bishops' Conference and National Office for Vocation under Offices of the Bishops' Conference.

■ **DEPARTMENT OF CHRISTIAN RESPONSIBILITY AND CITIZENSHIP**

Department Chairman:
Most Rev Peter Smith

Episcopal members: **Rt Rev Terence Brain, Rt Rev Christopher Budd, Rt Rev John Hine, Rt Rev Bernard Longley, Rt Rev Thomas Williams, Rt Rev Declan Lang.**
Staff: **Charles Wookey** (*Department Secretary*); **Richard Zipfel** (*Senior Adviser on Community Relations*); **Elizabeth Davies** (*Marriage and Family Life Project Officer*).

Department Administrator:
Tel: 020-7901 4828
E-mail: crc.admin@cbcew.org.uk
The Department and its associated agencies exist to assist both diocesan bishops and the Bishops' Conference collectively in promoting Catholic social action and in contributing to domestic public policy (excluding international affairs). The Department has three strategic priorities:

- marriage and family life;
- the support of marginalised and vulnerable people;
- 'life' issues and the dignity of the person;

In addition, at any one time a number of discrete public policy issues outside these strategic priorities are being addressed by time-limited, ad-hoc working groups chaired by one of the Department Bishops and involving lay experts.

From 2008 CSAS also forms part of the department's work.

Catholic Safeguarding Advisory Service
CSAS, 43 Temple Row, Birmingham B3 1RB **Tel:** 0121 237 6076
Website: www.csas.uk.net
Director: **Mr Adrian Child**
E-mail: adrian.child@csas.uk.net
PA to Director: **Claire Johnson**
E-mail: claire.johnson@csas.uk.net
National Safeguarding Systems Adviser: **Sally Robinson**
E-mail: sally.robinson@csas.uk.net
Team Secretary: **Sophie Robbins**
E-mail: sophie.robbins@csas.uk.net
National Learning & Development Adviser: Awaiting Appointment

Following the acceptance of the Cumberlege Commission's report "Safeguarding with Confidence" a new body, the National Catholic Safeguarding Commission (NCSC) was established to set the strategic direction of the Church's safeguarding policy.

In support of this the Catholic Safeguarding Advisory Service (CSAS) is established to be responsible for driving and supporting improvements in safeguarding practice. Its primary role is one of co-ordination, advice and support in respect of the wider job of safeguarding children, young people and vulnerable adults.

Caritas Social Action Network and the Catholic Association for Racial Justice, Agencies of the Bishops' Conference also relate to the Bishops through the Department.

STRUCTURE AND HIERARCHY OF THE CHURCH

■ Marriage and Family Life

Chairman of the Committee for Marriage and Family Life: **Rt Rev John Hine.**
Believing that marriage is the cornerstone of family life, the Committee:

- Develops informed reflection on the issues concerning marriage and the family;
- Advises on and responds to issues concerning marriage and family life within the Church, ecumenical, state and inter-faith areas as appropriate;
- Fosters and encourages pastoral services for families across the dioceses.

The **Marriage and Family Life Project Office** supports dioceses implementing the plan of collaborative action approved by the Bishops in April 2005, arising from the priorities identified in Listening 2004:'

- A need for welcoming, family-sensitive, friendly parishes where Christian community thrives and sustains the lives of those both at its heart and on the margins;
- A need to deepen and share among laity and clergy alike a much wider understanding of marital and family spirituality as the heart of the domestic church;
- A need to explore and better understand what we mean by passing on faith in God, the primary role of parents and to equip them accordingly.

See www.celebratingfamily.org.uk

Marriage and Family Life Project Officer: **Elizabeth Davies. Tel:** 01902-621594
E-mail: elizabeth.davies@cbcew.org.uk
Project Support Worker: To be Appointed
Project Office Administrator: Annabelle Williams **Tel:** 020 7901 4823
E-mail: annabelle.williams@cbcew.org.uk

■ Support for marginalised and vulnerable people

Senior Advisor on Community Relations: **Richard Zipfel Tel:** 020-7901 4831
E-mail: richard.zipfel@cbcew.org.uk
The Community Relations Advisor addresses issues of race relations, urban poverty and community development with special emphasis on new equality regulations.

■ Healthcare Reference Group

Purpose: To advise the Bishops' Conference on healthcare issues and liaise with the Bishops' advisors on Healthcare Chaplaincy.
Chairman: **Rt Rev Thomas Williams**
National Chaplaincy Liaison Officers: **Revv Paul Mason, Peter Michael Scott**
Tel: 020-7901 4828
E-mail: crc.admin@cbcew.org.uk

■ Travellers' Issues Working Group

To support Catholics involved in the ministry or services to Travellers and to address issues related to the welfare of Travellers.
Episcopal Liaison: **Rt Rev Bernard Longley**
Co-ordinator: **Richard Zipfel**
Tel: 020-7901 4828
E-mail: richard.zipfel@cbcew.org.uk

■ DEPARTMENT OF INTERNATIONAL AFFAIRS

Chairman: **Rt Rev Crispian Hollis**

Bishop Members:
Rt Rev Tom Burns, Rt Rev John Crowley, Most Rev Patrick Kelly, Rt Rev William Kenney, Rt Rev David Konstant, Rt Rev Patrick Lynch, Rt Rev Patrick O'Donoghue, Rt Rev John Rawsthorne, Rt Rev Charles Caruana, Mgr Michael McPartland SMA.

Secretary: **Dr David Ryall**
Tel: 020-7901 4861
General email enquiries:
E-mail: international@cbcew.org.uk

■ International Justice and Peace

Purpose: To brief and represent the bishops on issues relating to international justice and development in the light of the Church's social teaching, particularly on issues of world poverty, peace, human rights and security.
Bishop Responsible:
Rt Rev Crispian Hollis.
Secretary: **Dr David Ryall**
Tel: 020-7901 4861
E-mail: david.ryall@cbcew.org.uk

■ Environmental Justice

Purpose: To brief and represent the bishops on issues of environmental responsibility and justice in the light of the Church's teaching on the gift of Creation and our care and respect for it.
Chairman: **Rt Rev Declan Lang**
Contact: **Dr David Ryall.**

■ European Affairs

Purpose: To advise and inform the bishops on issues relating to Europe in the light of the Church's social teaching.
Bishop Responsible: **Rt Rev William Kenney CP.** *Secretary:* **Dr David Ryall.**

■ Office for Refugee Policy

Purpose: Monitors information and prepares briefs on migration to enable bishops to develop policy and respond to debates. The ORP represents bishops on the migration issue nationally and internationally and acts as a catalyst for lay engagement in refugee work.
Bishop Responsible:
Rt Rev Patrick Lynch.
Policy Advisor:
Mr John Joseet. Tel: 020-7901 4862
E-mail: john.joseet@cbcew.org.uk
General email enquiries:
E-mail: refugees@cbcew.org.uk

■ Committee for Overseas Mission

Purpose: The Committee for Overseas Mission supports the bishops in the promotion and implementation of the Church's contemporary missionary vision in England and Wales. This committee comes under the remit of the Pontifical Mission Societies, which comprise the Association for the Propagation of the Faith, the Pontifical Missionary Union, the Society of St Peter the Apostle and Mission Together.
Chairman: **Rt Rev Crispian Hollis.**
Secretary: **Mgr John Dale.** 23 Eccleston Square, London SW1V 1NU
Tel: 020-7821 9755 **Fax:** 020-7630 8466
E-mail: frjohndale@missionsocieties.org.uk
Website: www.missionsocieties.org.uk

In addition, other public policy issues are addressed by time-limited, ad-hoc working groups chaired by one of the department bishops and involving lay experts.
The current work of the department can be found on the Bishops' Conference website under:
www.catholic-ew.org.uk/international

See also the Apostleship of the Sea and CAFOD under Agencies of the Bishops' Conference.

■ AGENCIES OF THE BISHOPS' CONFERENCE

Agencies, established by and directly answerable to the Bishops' Conference, exercise executive functions in the name of the Conference. Each Agency has a bishop as President, Chairman or Episcopal Assistant.

■ Apostleship of the Sea

Apostleship of the Sea (AOS) is the official maritime welfare and mission agency of both Bishops' Conferences in Great Britain and a registered charity, wholly reliant on voluntary contributions. It deploys port chaplains and ship visitors who welcome international merchant seafarers to our shores in the name of the Catholic Church, regardless of their creed or nationality. One million international seafarers visit each year. They work away from home for up to 12 months facing loneliness, danger and exploitation as they deliver the goods and resources we consume. Our task is to address the spiritual, social and material well-being of seafarers. We do this through practical expressions of Mission, Solidarity, Welfare and Hosptitality.

- Mission: We reach out to seafarers in the name of Christ;
- Solidarity: We stand alongside seafarers when their rights are ignored;
- Welfare: We look after seafarers who are abandoned in port and those who are sick or injured;
- Hospitality: We welcome seafarers to ecumenical centres.

Through port based and sea-going chaplaincy AOS seeks to identify and empower crew members to be light and life on board their ships, supporting other seafarers in their faith and their daily life and tasks.

Bishop Promoter:
Rt Rev Thomas Burns SM.
Chairman: **Mr Eamonn Delaney.**
National Director: **Captain Paul Quinn OBE.** Herald House, Lamb's Passage, Bunhill Row, London EC1Y 8LE **Tel:** 020-7588 8285
Fax: 020-7588 8280
E-mail:
londonoffice@apostleshipofthesea.org.uk
Website: www.apostleshipofthe sea.org.uk

■ Caritas – social action

Caritas is an official agency of the Catholic Bishops' Conference of England and Wales and also part of Caritas Internationalis Federation. There are many professional Catholic organisations providing social care (working with the homeless, adoption services, care for vulnerable adults etc) with England and Wales. These organisations together represent the Catholic Voluntary Sector and it is for these organisations that Caritas exists. Caritas is a network agency for this sector and works to provide these organisations with three key services:

Co-ordination: facilitation and servicing of Special Interest Forums as determined by the member agencies, or by the Catholic Bishops' Conference of England and Wales.

Theological Reflection: on Catholic social action in order to inform practical action.
Advocacy: on behalf of member agencies on matters which affect them as Catholic agencies, and advocacy on behalf of, and at the request of, the Bishops' Conference on specific issues relating to social exclusion.

Chair of Trustees: **Bishop Terence Brain**
Vice-Chair: **Margaret Dight**
Director: **Mrs Philippa Gitlin**
Tel: 020-7901 4875
E-mail: caritas@cbcew.org.uk
Website: www.caritas-socialaction.org.uk

■ Catholic Association for Racial Justice (CARJ)

CARJ is an Agency of the Bishops' Conference, linked to the Department of Christian Responsibility and Citizenship.

Episcopal Chairman of CARJ:
Rt Rev Kieran Conry
Chair: **Margaret-Ann Fisken**
National Co-ordinator: **Mrs Cecilia Taylor-Camara.** CARJ, 9 Henry Road, Manor House, London N4 2LH
Tel: 020-8802 8080 **Fax:** 020 8211 0808
E-mail: carj@btconnect.com
Website: www.carj.org

■ Catholic Education Service

Chairman: **Most Rev Vincent Nichols**
Chief Executive: **Ms Oona Stannard.**

The Catholic Education Service was established as an agency of the Bishops' Conference following the recommendations of the committee chaired by Bishop Hugh Lindsay in 1988. The Catholic Education Service's role is to support, defend and promote the educational work of the Church in England and Wales. It does this primarily by working at policy level and at the statutory interface with government, its agencies and NGOs. The CES also works in close partnership with diocesan officers and national organisations include NBRIA, ACVIC and CATSC. It manages a number of projects and forums including the National Project; Living and Sharing Our Faith, and the Further and Higher Education panel. The CES's remit in education extends from cradle to grave including Further and Higher Education.
There are over 2,000 maintained Catholic primary and secondary schools, over 150 independent Catholic schools, and 12 non-maintained Catholic special schools, which together educate in excess of three-quarters of a million pupils. There are 17 Catholic sixth-form Colleges in England and Wales, as well as five colleges of higher education or university colleges.
E-mail: general@cesew.org.uk
Website: www.cesew.org.uk
CES is a Registered Charity No 313147

■ Further and Higher Education Panel

Purpose: To discern opportunities and obligations in the sphere of Further and Higher Education which should be addressed by the Catholic community at a national level. The Panel is managed from within the CES.

Chairman: **Rt Rev Vincent Malone.**

■ Catholic Agency for Overseas Development (CAFOD)

CAFOD is the Catholic Agency for Overseas Development, the official international development and relief agency of the Catholic Church in England and Wales. It is a member of the worldwide Caritas

Internationalis federation.
Together with local partner organisations in more than 50 countries, CAFOD works to build a better world for people living in poverty. In emergency situations, CAFOD also provides immediate relief and stays on to help people rebuild their lives.
CAFOD and its partners put pressure on governments and institutions to tackle the causes of poverty. In UK schools and parishes, CAFOD raises awareness of these issues and encourages people to fundraise and campaign.
Chairman: **Rt Rev John Rawsthorne.**
Director: **Mr Chris Bain.** 2 Romero Close, Stockwell Road, London SW9 9TY
Tel: 020-7733 7900 **Fax:** 020-7274 9630
E-mail: cafod@cafod.org.uk
Website: www.cafod.org.uk
CAFOD is a Registered Charity No. 285776

■ Catholic Agency to Support Evangelisation (CASE)
Purpose: To engage and equip Catholics in England and Wales in proclaiming the Gospel; to promote dialogue between gospel and culture; and to offer information on the Catholic faith to seekers through the Catholic Enquiry Office.
Chair of Advisory Board:
Rt Rev Malcolm McMahon OP
Director: **Mgr Keith Barltrop**
Team: **Ms Clare Ward, Ms Clare Ford, Ms Emily Davis.**
39 Eccleston Square, London SW1V 1BX
Tel: 020-7901 4863 **Fax:** 020-7901 4863
E-mail: info@caseresources.org.uk
Websites: www.caseresources.org.uk
www.life4seekers.co.uk
www.comehomeforchristmas.co.uk
www.yfaith.co.uk

■ OFFICES OF THE BISHOPS' CONFERENCE

■ National Office for Vocation
Chairman: **Rt Rev George Stack**
Director: **Rev E Clare,** 39 Eccleston Square, London SW1V 1BX **Tel:** 020-7901 4829
E-mail: enquiries@ukvocation.org
Websites: www.ukvocation.org
www.ukpriest.org

The National Office for Vocation works collaboratively with local and national agencies in order to support the promotion of 'vocation' within the Catholic community. This includes the calling to marriage, to single life, to the diaconate as well as priesthood and consecrated life.The office was opened in September 2002 in direct response to the 1997 Church Document "New Vocations for a New Europe". This Vatican document highlights the heart of all pastoral work in the Church as that of creating a stronger "culture of vocation" within which every member has a stronger sense of being personally called by God.

■ THE CONSULTATIVE BODIES

The Bishops' Conference undertakes, whenever practical, to enter into formal consultation with these bodies on matters of particular concern to them. Review Report, para (50) (vii).

■ Canon Law Society of Gt Britain and Ireland
President: **Mgr David Hogan.**
General Secretary: **Rev James O'Kane,** Scottish National Tribunal, 22 Woodrow Road, Glasgow G41 5PN
E-mail: nationaltribunal@hotmail.com
Website: www.clsgbi.org

■ Catholic Missionary Union
President: **Rev John Dale**
Secretary: **Mr Seamus Crowe,** 13 Coventry Road, Bulkington, Warks CV12 9LY
Website: www.cmu.org.uk
Episcopal Liaison: **Rt Rev Declan Lang.**

■ Catholic Union of Great Britain
Purpose: Founded in 1871, the Catholic Union is the principle lay forum dedicated to the defence of Catholic values and the promotion of the common good in Parliament and public life. The Union draws upon the broad expertise of its members to scrutinise new legislation with a view to collating and providing an expert response in cooperation with parliamentarians and the hierarchy. The Catholic Union seeks to promote the role of faith in citizenship, through educational activities, conferences and the media.
President: **The Lord Brennan, QC**
Secretary: **Emilia Klepacka,** The Catholic Union, St Maximilian Kolbe House, 63 Jeddo Road, London W12 9EE
Tel: 020-8749 1321
E-mail: info@catholicunion.org
Episcopal Liaison: **Rt Rev John Arnold.**
Website: www.catholicunion.org

■ Conference of Religious
President: **Sr Kathleen McGhee SND.**
Vice-President: **Abbot Martin Shipperlee OSB.** *General Secretary:* **Ms Connie Burke.**
3 Montpelier, Ealing London W5 2XP
E-mail: gensec@corew.org
Website: www.corew.org
Episcopal Members of the Mixed Commission: **Rt Rev Kieran Conry, Rt Rev Declan Lang, Rt Rev Bernard Longley, Rt Rev Patrick Lynch.**

■ National Board of Catholic Women

The Board consists of representatives of national Catholic organisations with diocesan links appointed by the local bishop. It serves as a forum for Catholic women to exchange views and concerns about the status of women in the Church and in the world, and make recommendations. It has consultative status with the United Nations (ECOSOC); is a member of the World Union of Catholic Women's Organisations and the European Alliance of Catholic Women in Europe. Through its representation on these and other national, ecumenical and interfaith groups, the NBCW is able to put forward the issues of concern to Catholic women.

President: **Mrs Yogi Sutton**
E-mail: patyogisutton@hotmail.com
Hon Secretary: **Jean Horan.**
Episcopal Liaison: **Most Rev Patrick Kelly**
Development Officer: **Mrs Angela Perkins.**
E-mail: enquiries@nbcw.org

■ National Conference of Priests

Chairman: **Rev Fr Tom Jordan**
Tel: 01708 740308
E-mail: taj.jordan@ntlworld.com
Executive Secretary: **Rev David Mills**
Tel: 01249 813131
E-mail: calne@cliftondiocese.com
Press Enquiries: **Rev Tony Slingo**
Tel: 01695 622001
E-mail: tony.slingo@btinternet.com

See Clergy Life and Formation Page 609

■ National Council for Lay Associations

Purpose: Delegates from 25 lay apostolic associations, nine liaison representatives, Episcopal Advisor, Chaplain, four officers and three advisors, form the Council. Ideas, insights and experiences are shared during two day conferences on major issues of national concern, raised by the diverse network of organisations or by the Bishops' Conference so that recommendations can be made as one of its consultative bodies. The Council fosters co-operation between member associations to strengthen their apostolate, is a member of the European Forum of National Laity Committees and has links with the Pontifical Council for Laity.

President: **Mr Malcolm Forster**, 21 Bassett Crescent West, Southampton, Hampshire SO16 7EB **Tel:** 023-8079 0942
E-mail: malcolmandrita@btinternet.com
Hon Secretary: **Mrs Rita Forster.** (See details above).
Episcopal Liaison: **Rt Rev Thomas Williams.**
Chaplain: **Canon Joseph Carter**
Bishops' Conference Liaison:
Mr Charles Wookey.

■ FINANCE AND LEGAL ORGANISATIONS

■ Catholic Trust for England and Wales

(Charity No 1097482)
Established in April 2003 to bring together the National Catholic Fund, the Catholic Media Trust and the Lisbon Trust Fund, to be the charitable trust for the administration of the Bishops' Conference Secretariat and some agencies and offices of the Bishops' Conference.
CaTEW is a charitable company limited by guarantee (No 4734592). The bishops are the members and appoint Trustees to administer the Trust.

Chairman of Trustees: **Rt Rev Malcolm McMahon OP.**
Vice-Chairman: **Mgr Michael McKenna.**
Other Trustees: **Ms Alison Cowdall, Mr John Gibbs, Mr Peter Lomas, Mr Ben Andradi, Mgr Canon Nicholas Rothon, Mr Robin Smith, Dr James Whiston.**
Secretary: **Mgr Andrew Summersgill,** 39 Eccleston Square, London SW1V 1BX
Tel: 020-7901 4810

■ Catholic Church Insurance Association

The Insurance Committee of the Roman Catholic Dioceses in England, Wales and Scotland. Established to meet the insurance needs of Catholic Dioceses, Religious Orders and other Catholic Organisations, largely based on the Catholic National Mutual Limited, an insurance company domiciled in Guernsey and wholly owned by its Catholic Member Organisations.

Insurance Manager:
John Rogers, LLB FCII,
Oakley House, Mill Street, Aylesbury, Bucks HP20 1BN
Tel: 01296-422030
Fax: 01296-428049
E-mail: enquiries@ccia.org.uk
Website: www.ccia.org.uk

■ Colloquium (CaTEW) Ltd

Company Number: 4735081
VAT Registration Number: 223547084

Directors: **Mr John Gibbs, Mgr Michael McKenna, Mr David Morgan, Mr Michael Phelan.**
The principal activity is to initiate the development of a comprehensive publishing strategy for the Bishops' Conference. It will continue to consider publishing projects from the Bishops' Conference departments, agencies and offices according to established criteria.

■ Historic Churches Committees
Under the ecclesiastical exemption provision of the Town and Country Planning Act, listed churches are exempt from the requirement to obtain from their local authority Listed Building Consent for works of repair and refurbishment, providing they obtain approval from the diocesan Historic Churches Committee.
Regulations for these Committees have been confirmed by the Catholic Bishops' Conference of England and Wales in its 1999 Directory on the Ecclesiastical Exemption from Listed Building Control. These regulations are monitored by the Patrimony Committee of the Department of Christian Life and Worship.

Birmingham: *Secretary:* **Rev Brian Doolan,** Cathedral House, St Chad's Queensway, Birmingham B4 6EU
Tel: 0121-2130 6209 **Fax:** 0121-236 2699
E-mail: hcc@rc-birmingham.org

Brentwood: *Minutes Secretary:* **Helen Barwell,** *Secretary:* **Rev Paul Keane,** Clergy House, 28 Ingrave Road, Brentwood Essex CM15 8AT
Tel: 01277 265235
E-mail: frpaulkeane@yahoo.com

East Anglia: Rev Edmund Eggleston, The Presbytery, 17 Howdale Road, Downham Market, Norfolk PE38 9AB
Tel: 01366-382353
E-mail: edeggleston@hotmail.com

Hallam: Mr Philip Jones, Diocesan Pastoral Centre, St Charles Street, Sheffield S9 2WU **Tel:** 0114 2566405
E-mail:philjones68@bluyonder.co.uk.

Hexham & Newcastle: Prof John J Murray, *HCC Sec*: St Vincent's Diocesan Offices, St Cuthbert's House, West Road, Newcastle upon Tyne NE15 7PY
Tel: 0191-243 3303 **Fax:** 0191-243 3309
E-mail: julia.herron@edurcdhn.org.uk

Leeds: Mr David Damant, Hinsley Hall, 62 Headingly Lane, Leeds LS6 2BX
Tel: 0113-261 8023 **Fax:** 0113-261 8035
E-mail: david.damant@dioceseofleeds.org.uk

Middlesbrough: Miss Jenny Dowson, Curial Offices, 50a The Avenue, Linthorpe, Middlesbrough TS5 6QT
Tel: 01642-850505 ext 237
Fax: 01642-851404
E-mail:hcc@dioceseofmiddlesbrough.co.uk

Northampton: Mrs Barbara Nicholson, St Teresa's Presbytery, New Road, Princes Risborough, Bucks HP27 0JN
Tel: 01844-345578 **Fax:** 01844-274503
E-mail: barbara_prisborough@hotmail.com

North-West (Lancaster, Liverpool, Salford and Shrewsbury): Mr John Cowdall, 47 Southport Road, Chorley, Lancashire PR7 1LF
Tel/Fax: 01257-277128,
E-mail: johncowdall@jcachorley.freeserve.co.uk

Nottingham: Mr Howard Walters, Diocesan Property Department, Willson House, Derby Road, Nottingham NG1 5AW
Tel: 0115-953 9802 **Fax:** 0115-953 9805
E-mail: property@nrcdt.org.uk

Southern (A&B, Clifton, Plymouth, Portsmouth, Southwark): Mr Mike State, 9 Preston Avenue, Rustington, West Sussex BN16 2DE
Tel/Fax: 01903-856018
E-mail: m.state@btinternet.com

Wales & Hereford (Cardiff, Menevia, Wrexham): Mr Philip King, Archbishop's House, 41-43 Cathedral House, Cardiff CF11 9HD
Tel: 029-2037 4148 **Fax:** 029-2034 5950
E-mail:philipking@supanet.com

Westminster: Mr Chris Fanning, St Joseph's Chapel Entrance, Catherine Close, off Joseph's Grove, London NW4 4TY
Tel: 020-8202 2695 **Fax:** 020-8202 1459
E-mail: cfanning@rcdow.org.uk
historicchurches@rcdow.org.uk
Please send E-mails to both addresses.

ECUMENICAL RELATIONS

The Bishops' Conference of England and Wales is a full member of the ecumenical instruments – known as 'Churches Together' – established in 1990 to enable the various Christian Churches and ecclesial communities to collaborate with each other and undertake joint work when appropriate. There are different expressions of the Churches Together for each of the nations of England, Wales, Scotland and Ireland, and for the four nations together. At national level, the Bishops' Conference is a member of Churches Together in England and of CYTÛN (Churches Together in Wales). At four-nations level, it is a member of Churches Together in Britain and Ireland, through which the Churches throughout these islands can share in conversation together and tackle issues which need the wider canvas.

Through these ecumenical bodies the Churches are engaged in a process of growing together and exploring new forms of partnership. Currently work is undertaken on international affairs, Church and society, local ecumenism, Church life, inter-faith relations, mission and racial justice, international students, spirituality, youth work and the community of women and men.

■ CHURCHES TOGETHER IN BRITAIN AND IRELAND

General Secretary: **Rev Robert Fyffe,**
3rd Floor, Bastille Court, 2 Paris Gardens, London SE1 8ND
Tel: 020-7654 7211 **Fax:** 020-7654 7222.
E-mail: bob.fyffe@ctbi.org.uk
Internet: www.ctbi.org.uk

NAMES AND ADDRESSES OF MEMBER CHURCHES, BODIES IN ASSOCIATION AND AGENCIES

■ FULL MEMBERS

Antiochian Orthodox Society of Britain: Fr Michael Harper, 3 West View, Newnham, Cambridge CB3 9JB **Tel:** 01223 362933 **E-mail:** aslanharper@clara.co.uk

Baptist Union of Great Britain: Rev Jonathan Edwards (*Gen Sec*), Baptist House, 129 Broadway, Didcot, Oxon. OX11 8RT **Tel:** 01235-517700 **Fax:** 01235-517715 **E-mail:** info@baptist.org.uk

Cherubim and Seraphim Council of Churches (UK): *Senior Apostle*, **Richard Fasunloye,** 25 Seymour Gardens, Ilford, Essex IG1 3LN **Tel:** 07957 296338

Church in Wales: Mr John Richfield *(Admin. Assist. to the Governing Body)*. 39 Cathedral Road, Cardiff CF11 9XL **Tel:** 029-2034 8200 **Fax:** 029-2038 7835 **E-mail:** johrichfield@churchinwales.org.uk

Church of England: Mr William Fittall, Church House, Great Smith Street, London SWIP 3NZ **Tel:** 020-7898 1360 **Fax:** 020-7898 1369 **E-mail:** cofe.comms@c-of-e.org.uk

Church of God of Prophecy: Bishop Wilton R Powell OBE, *(National Overseer)* 6 Beacon Court, Birmingham Road, Great Barr, Birmingham B43 6NN **Tel:** 0121 358 2231 **Fax:** 0121 358 8617 **E-mail:** admin@cogop.org.uk

Church of Ireland: Mrs Janet Maxwell, *(Head of Synod Services and Communications)* Church of Ireland House, Church Avenue, Rathmines, Dublin 6, RoI **Tel:** 00 353 1 412 5621 **Fax:** 00 353 1 412 8821 **E-mail:** janet.maxwell@rcbdub.org

Church of Scotland: VRev Dr Finlay MacDonald. 121 George Street, Edinburgh EH2 4YN **Tel:** 0131-240 2240 **Fax:** 0131 240 2239 **E-mail:** pracproc@cofscotland.org.uk

Congregational Federation: Rev Michael Heaney, 4 Castle Gate, Nottingham NGI 7AS **Tel:** 0115-911 1460 **Fax:** 0115-911 1462 **Email:** admin@congregational.org.uk

Coptic Orthodox Church: Bishop Angaelos, Coptic Orthodox Church Centre, Shephalbury Manor, Broadhall Way, Stevenage SG2 8RH **Tel:** 01438-745232 **Fax:** 01438-313879 **Email:** admin@copticcentre.com

Council of African and Afro/Caribbean Churches: Most Rev Fr Olu Abiola 31 Norton House, Sidney Road, London SW9 OJJ **Tel:** 020-7274 5589

Council of the Oriental, Orthodox Christian Churches: Bishop Angaelos, Coptic Orthodox Church Centre,

Shephalbury Manor, Broadhall Way, Stevenage SG2 8RH **Tel:** 01438-745232 **Fax:** 01438-313879 **Email:** admin@copticcentre.com

German-speaking Congregation: Pastor Christoph Hellmich (Chairman). Council for German Church Work, 35 Craven Terrace, London W2 3EL **Tel:** 020-7706 8589 **Fax:** 020-7707 2870 **E-mail:** office@ev-synode.org.uk

Greek Orthodox Church: His Eminence Archbishop Gregorios, Oecumenical Patriarch (Archdiocese of Thyateira & GB), 5 Craven Hill, London. W2 3EN **Tel:** 020-7723 4787 **Fax:** 020-7224 9301 **E-mail:** thyateiragb@yahoo.com

Independent Methodist Churches: Mr William C Gabb, 66 Kirkstone Drive, Loughborough LE11 3RW **Tel:** 01509-268566 **Fax:** 01509-227014 **E-mail:** gensec@imcgb.org.uk

International Ministerial Council of Great Britain: Rt Rev Sheila Douglas MA *(International Moderator)*, 217 Langhedge Lane, London N18 2TG **Tel:** 020-8345 5376 **E-mail:** imcgb@aol.com

Joint Council for Anglo-Caribbean Churches: Rev Esme Beswick, 141 Railton Road, London SE24 0LT **Tel:** 020-8539 4931

Lutheran Council of Great Britain: Rev Thomas Bruch *(Gen Sec)*, 30 Thanet Street, London WC1H 9QH **Tel:** 020-7554 2900 **Fax:** 020-7383 3081 **E-mail:** enquiries@lutheran.org.uk

Methodist Church: Rev David G Deeks *(Gen Sec)*, Methodist Church House, 25 Marylebone Road, London NW1 5JR **Tel:** 020-7486 5502 **Fax:** 020-7224 1510 **E-mail:** generalsecretary@methodist.org.uk **Website:** www.Methodist.org.uk

Methodist Church in Ireland: Rev Donald Ker, 1 Fountainville Avenue, Belfast BT9 6AN **Tel:** 028-9032 4554 **Fax:** 028-9023 9467 **E-mail:** secretary@irishmethodist.org

Moravian Church: Jackie Morten, Moravian Church Ho, 5 Muswell Hill, London N10 3TJ **Tel:** 020 8365 3371 **Email:** office@moravian.org.uk

New Testament Assembly: Rev Nezlin Sterling, 5 Woodstock Avenue, London W13 3VQ **Tel:** 020-8579 3841 **Fax:** 020 8537 9253 **E-mail:** njsterinta@aol.com

Presbyterian Church of Wales: Rev Ifan Roberts *(Gen Sec)*, Tabernacle Church, 81 Merthyr Road, Whitchurch, Cardiff CF14 1DD **Tel:** 029-2062 7465 **Fax:** 029-2061 6188 **E-mail:** swyddfa.office@ebcpcw.org.uk

Religious Society of Friends: Gillian, *Chief Recording Clerk:* **Ashmore** Friends House, Euston Road, London NW1 2BJ **Tel:** 020-7663 1000 **Fax:** 020-7663 1001 **E-mail:** enquiries@quaker.org.uk

Roman Catholic Church in England and Wales: Mgr Andrew Summersgill *(Gen Sec)*, 39 Eccleston Square, Victoria, London SW1V 1BX **Tel:** 020-7630 8220 **Fax:** 020-7901 4821 **E-mail:** secretariat@cbcew.org.uk **Website:** www.catholic-ew.org.uk

Roman Catholic Church in Scotland: Rev Fr Paul Conroy *(Gen Sec)*, 64 Aitken Street, Airdrie, Lanarkshire ML6 6LT **Tel:** 01236-764061 **Fax:** 01236-762489 **E-mail:** gensec@bpsconfscot.com

Russian Orthodox Church: Gillian Crow, 6 Maiden Place, London NW5 1HZ **Tel:** 020 7272 9898 **E-mail:** gillian@crow.co.uk

Salvation Army: Commissioner John Matear *(Territorial Commander UK & RoI)*, 101 Newington Causeway, London SE1 6BN **Tel:** 020 7367 4500 **Fax:** 020-7367 4728 **E-mail:** info@salvationarmy.org.uk **Website:** www.salvationarmy.org.uk

Scottish Episcopal Church: Mr John Stuart, 21 Grosvenor Crescent, Edinburgh EH12 5EE **Tel:** 0131-225 6357 **Fax:** 0131-346 7247 **E-mail:** office@scotland.anglican.org

Trans-Atlantic & Pacific Alliance of Churches: Archbishop Paul Hackman *(President)*, 281-283 Rye Lane, Peckham, London SE15 4UA **Tel/Fax:** 020 7639 4058 **E-mail:** tapacglobal@aol.com

Union of Welsh Independents: Rev Dr Geraint Tudor, Ty John Penri, 5 Axis Court, Riverside Business Park, Swansea Vale, Swansea SA7 0AJ **Tel:** 01792-795888 **Fax:** 01792-795376 **E-mail:** undeb@annibynwyr.org

United Free Church of Scotland: Rev John O. Fulton. 11 Newton Place, Glasgow, G3 7PR **Tel:** 0141 332 3435 **Fax:** 0141 333 1973 **E-mail:** office@ufcos.org.uk

United Reformed Church: Rev Dr David Cornick, 86 Tavistock Place, London WC1H 9RT **Tel:** 020-7916 2020 **Fax:** 020-7916 2021 **E-mail:** urc@urc.org.uk

■ BODIES IN ASSOCIATION

Action of Christians Against Torture: Mr Terry Newland. ACAT UK, 8 Southfield, Saltash PL12 4LX **Tel:** 01752 210389 **E-mail:** uk.acat@googlemail.com

Association of Interchurch Families: Mr Keith Lander *(Exec Officer)*, 3rd Floor, Bastille Court, 2 Paris Gardens, London SE1 8ND **Tel:** 020-7654 7251 **Fax:** 020-7654 7222 **E-mail:** info@interchurchfamilies.org.uk

Bible Society: Rev Dr David Spriggs, 7 Frankpledge Road, Cheylesmore, Coventry CV3 5GT **Tel/Fax:** 02476 506320 **E-mail:** david.spriggs@biblesociety.org.uk

Christian Council on Ageing: Mrs Christine Hodgeson, 6 The Ridgeway, Market Harborough, Leics LE16 7HQ **Tel:** 01858-432771 **E-mail:** info@ccoa.org.uk

Christian Education: Peter Fishpool *(Chief Exec)*, 1020 Bristol Road, Selly Oak, Birmingham B29 6LB **Tel:** 0121-472 4242 **Fax:** 0121 472 7575 **E-mail:** admin@christianeducation.org.uk

Christian Aware: Mrs Barbara Butler, 2 Saxby Street, Leicester LE2 0ND **Tel/Fax:** 0116 254 0770 **E-mail:** barbarabutler@christiansaware.co.uk

Church Action on Poverty: Mr Niall Cooper *(Nat Co-ord)*. Central Buildings, Oldham Street, Manchester M1 1JQ **Tel:** 0161-236 9321 **Fax:** 0161-237 5359 **E-mail:** info@church-poverty.org.uk

Church Alert to Sex Trafficking across Europe: Jane Martin *(Trustee)*. PO Box 983, Cambridge CB3 8WY **Tel:** 0845 456 9335 **E-mail:** contact@chaste.org.uk

College of Preachers: Ms Marfa Jones *(Admin)*. 14A North Street, Bourne, PE10 9AB **Tel:** 01778 422929 **Fax:** 01778 422929 **E-mail:** administrator@collegeofpreachers.org.uk

Community of Aidan and Hilda: Rev Ray Simpson *(Guardian)* Lindisfarne Retreat, The Open Gate, Berwick-upon-Tweed TD15 2SD **Tel:** 01289 389222 **E-mail:** ca-and-h@deman.co.uk

Corrymeela Community: David Stephens, Corrymeela House, 8 Upper Crescent, Belfast BT7 1NT **Tel:** 028 90 508080 **Fax:** 028 90 508070 **E-mail:** belfast@corrymeela.org

Ecumenical Committee for Corporate Responsibility: Miles Litvinoff *(Co-ord)*, PO Box 500, Oxford OX1 1ZL **Tel:** 020 8965 9682 **E-mail:** info@eccr.org.uk

Faith in Europe: Dr Philip Walters *(Gen Sec)*, 81 Thorney Leys, Witney OX28 5BY **Tel:** 01993 771 778 **E-mail:** philip.walters@waltfam.freeserve.co.uk

Feed the Minds: Ms Rachel Searle *(Dir)*, 36 Causton Road, London SW1P 4ST **Tel:** 020 7592 3900 **Fax:** 020 7592 3939 **E-mail:** info@feedtheminds.org.uk

Fellowship of Reconciliation: Chris Cole *(Dir)*, St James Church Centre, Beauchamp Lane, Oxford OX4 3LF **Tel:** 01865 748 796 **E-mail:** office@for.org.uk

Fellowship of St Alban and St Sergius: Rev Stephen Platt. 1 Canterbury Road, Oxford OX2 6LU **Tel:** 01865-552991 **Fax:** 01865 316700 **E-mail:** gensec@sobornost

Focolare Movement: Celia Blackden *(Dir)*, 16 Parkfields, Welwyn Garden City, Herts AL8 6ED **Tel:** 01707 339706 **Fax:** 01707 696413 **E-mail:** celiablackden@yahoo.co.uk

Housing Justice: Rev Judith Maizel-Long *(Dir. of External Affairs)* 209 Old Marylebone Rd, London NW1 5QT **Tel:** 020 7723 7273 **Tel:** 020 7723 5943 **E-mail:** info@housingjustice.org.uk

The Industrial Mission Association: Rev Stephn Hazlett *(Sec)*, 14 The Oaks West, Sunderland SR2 8HZ **Tel:** 0191 565 4121 **E-mail:** stephen.hazlett@lineone.net

International Ecumenical Fellowship: Jill Freston, 59 Old High Street, Headington, Oxford OX3 9HT **Tel:** 01865 762247 **E-mail:** jillfreston@tiscali.co.uk

Iona Community: Rev Kathy Galloway *(Leader)*, 4th Floor, Savoy House, 140 Sauchiehall Street, Glasgow G2 3DH **Tel:** 0141-332 6343 **Fax:** 0141-332 1090 E-mail: admin@iona.org.uk

Irish School of Ecumenics: Dennis Anderson *(Dir)*. 683 Antrim Rd, Belfast BT15 4EG (Also at: Bea House, Milltown Park, Dublin 6, RoL) **Tel:** 028 9077 5010 **Fax:** 028 9037 3986 **E-mail:** danderso@tcd.ie

L'Arche: Ms Lal Keenan, L'Arche Community, 15 Norwood High Street, London SE27 9JU **Tel:** 020 8670 6714 **Fax:** 020 8670 0818 **E-mail:** info@larche.org.uk

Living Stones: Mr Colin South, *(Trust Administrator)* 22 Ebenezer Close, Witham Essex CM8 2HX **Tel:** 01376 510391 **E-mail:** colinsouth@aol.com

MODEM: John Nelson, *(Nat. Sec.)*, 24 Rostron Crescent, Formby, Merseyside L37 2ET **Tel:** 01704-873973

Retreat Association: Paddy Lane *(Exec Officer)*, The Central Hall, 256 Bermondsey Street, London SE1 3UJ **Tel:** 020 7357 7736 **Fax:** 020 7357 7724 **E-mail:** info@retreats.org.uk

Student Christian Movement: Liam

Purcell *(Co-ord)*, Unit 308F, The Big Peg, 120 Vyse Street, Birmingham B18 6NF **Tel:** 0121-200 3355 **E-mail:** scm@movement.org.uk

The Society of Ecumenical Studies: Rev Mark Woodruff *(Sec)*, 26 Daysbrook Road, London SW2 3TD **Tel:** 020 8678 8195 **E-mail:** ecumenicalstudies@btinternet.com

WWDP (Women's World Day of Prayer Movement): National Office: Commercial Road, Tunbridge Wells, Kent TN1 2RR **Tel:** 01892-541411 **Fax:** 01892 541745 **E-mail:** office@wwdp-natcomm.org

YMCA: Ms Helen Dennis *(Policy & Parliamentary Officer)*. 53 Parker Street, London WC2B 5PT **Tel:** 0845 873 663 **E-mail:** enquiries@ymca.org.uk

■ ASSOCIATE MEMBER

Roman Catholic Church in Ireland: Rev Fr Aidan O'Boyle. Irish Episcopal Conference, St Patrick's College, Maynooth, Co Kildare. **Tel:** 00353 1 505 3020 **Fax:** 00353 1 629 2360 **E-mail:** ex.sec@iecon.ie

■ NETWORKS

Churches Network for Racial Justice: Rev Andy Bruce, 2 Bastille Court, 2 Paris Gardens, London SE1 8ND **Tel:** 020-7654 7241 **Fax:** 020-7654 7222 **E-mail:** info@ctbi.org.uk

Global Mission Network: Canon Janice Price, 2 Bastille Court, 2 Paris Gardens, London SE1 8ND **Tel:** 020-7654 7232 **Fax:** 020-7654 7222 **E-mail:** info@ctbi.org.uk

Churches Network for Inter Faith Relations: Rev Peter Colwell, 2 Bastille Court, 2 Paris Gardens, London SE1 8ND **Tel:** 020-7654 7254 **Fax:** 020-7654 7222 **E-mail:** ccifr@ctbi.org.uk

Churches Network for International Students: Ms Gilian Court, 2 Bastille Court, 2 Paris Gardens, London SE1 8ND **Tel:** 020-7654 7234 **Fax:** 020-7654 7222 **E-mail:** info@ctbi.org.uk

■ AGENCIES

Cafod: Mr Chris Bain, 2 Romero Close, Stockwell Road, London SW9 9TY **Tel:** 020-7733 7900 **Fax:** 020-7274 9630 **E-mail:** hqcafod@cafod.org.uk

Christian Aid: Dr Daleep Mukarji. Inter-Church House, 35-41 Lower Marsh, London SE1 7RL **Tel:** 020-7620 4444 **E-mail:** info@christian-aid.org

Christians Abroad: Mr Philip Wetherell, Bon Marche Centre, Suite 223, 242-251 Ferndale Road, London SW9 8BJ **Tel:** 0870 770 7990 **Fax:** 0870 770 7991 **E-mail:** director@cabroad.org.uk

Christian Enquiry Agency: Mr Gareth Squire *(Dir)*, 27 Tavistock Square, London WC1H 9HH **Tel:** 020 7387 3659 **Fax:** 020 7529 8134 **E-mail:** cea@christianity.org.uk

Churches Agency for Safeguarding: Ron Ludgate *(Dir)*, Methodist Church House, 25 Marylebone Road, London NW1 5JR **Tel:** 020 7467 5216 **Fax:** 020 7467 3763 **E-mail:** cas@methodistchurch.org.uk

Churches' Media Council: Andrew Graystone, PO Box 149, Manchester M19 2AX **Tel:** 0845 652 0027 **E-mail:** info@churchesmediacouncil.org.uk

One World Week: Kevin Fray *(CEO)*, PO Box 2555, Reading RG1 4XW. **Tel:** 0118-939 4933 **Fax:** 0118-939 4936 **E-mail:** enquiries@oneworldweek.org

ROOTS. Rosemay Nixon *(Dir)*, Bastille Court, 2 Paris Gardens, London SE1 8ND **Tel:** 020-7654 7215 **Fax:** 020-7654 7222 **E-mail:** info@rootsontheweb.com

SCIAF: Mr Paul Chitnis. 19 Park Circus, Glasgow G1 6BE **Tel:** 0141-354 5555 **Fax:** 0141-354 5533 **Email:** sciaf@scaif.org.uk

Christian Youth Work Training Network: Peter Fishpool, 1020 Bristol Road, Selly Oak, Birmingham B29 6LB **Tel:** 0121-472 4242 **Fax:** 0121-472 7575

Churches Community Work Alliance: Nils Chittenden, St Chad's College, North Bailey, Durham DH1 3RH **Tel:** 0191-334 3346 **Fax:** 0191-334 3371 **E-mail:** nilsc@ccwa.org.uk

Churches' Criminal Justice Forum: c/o Caritas-Social Action, 39 Eccleston Square, Victoria, London SW1V 1BX **Tel:** 020-7901 4878 **Fax:** 020-7901 4821 **E-mail:** info@ccjf.org.uk

Churches' Stewardship Network: Major Derek Jones, The Salvation Army, 101 Newington Causeway, London SE1 6BN **Tel:** 020 7367 4931 **Fax:** 020 7367 4711 **E-mail:** Christine.ord@salavationarmy.org.uk

Consultative Group for Ministry Among Children: Doug Swanney *(Sec)*, The Methodist Church, Methodist Church House, 25 Marylebone Road, London NW1 5JR **Tel:** 020-7467 3791 **Fax:** 020-7367 5281 **E-mail:** secretary@cgmcontheweb

Eco-congregation: Jo Rathbone *(Co-ord)*. The Arthur Rank Centre, Stoneleigh Park, Warks CV8 2LZ **Tel:** 024 7669 2491 **Fax:** 024 7641 4808

E-mail: ecocongregation@aroca.org.uk

Environment Issues Network: Ken Austin *(Sec)*, 16 Meades Lane, Chesham Bucks HP5 1ND **E-mail:** kencaustin2@aol,com

Joint Liturgical Group of Great Britain: Mgr Kevin McGinnell, Our Lady of Lourdes, 40 Lloyds Coffee Hall, Milton Keynes MK6 5EB **Tel:** 01908 233121 **Fax:** 01908 233131 **E-mail:** mcginnell.nores@btconnect.com

Spectrum: Ms Mary McGinty *(Sec)*, Wesley College, College Park Drive, Henbury Rd, Bristol BS10 7QD **E-mail:** mary.mcginty@ctbi.org.uk

CHURCHES TOGETHER IN ENGLAND

General Secretary:
The Rev Bill Snelson, Churches Together in England, 27 Tavistock Square, London WC1H 9HH
Tel: 020-7529 8141 **Fax:** 020-7529 8134 **E-mail:** bill.snelson@cte.org.uk
Website: www.cte.org.uk

Executive Officer (Healthcare): **Rev Debbie Hedge** (London address); *Executive Officer (Youth):* **John Baxter Brown** (London address); *Education Officer:* **Sarah Lane** (London address) *Interfaith Officer:* **Celia Blackden** (London address)

Free Churches Group: Rev Mark Fisher (London address)

Set all free – Abolition of Slave Trade: Richard Reddie (London address)

Field Officer North/Midlands: **Jenny Bond,** Churches Together in England, (London address) **Tel:** 07805 380 699
Field Officer South: **Rev John Bradley** (London address)

The basis of Churches Together in England is as follows:
Churches Together in England unites in pilgrimage those Churches in England which acknowledging God's revelation in Christ, confess the Lord Jesus Christ as God and Saviour according to the Scriptures, and, in obedience to God's will and in the power of the Holy Spirit commit themselves:

- To seek a deepening of their communion with Christ and with one another in the Church, which is his body;
- to fulfil their mission to proclaim the Gospel by common witness and service in the world
- to the glory of the one God, Father, Son and Holy Spirit

■ THE PRESIDENTS OF THE CHURCHES, TOGETHER IN ENGLAND ARE:

The Archbishop of Canterbury
The Cardinal Archbishop of Westminster
Bishop Nathan Hovhannissian
Commissioner Elizabeth Matear

■ THERE ARE 29 FULL MEMBERS:

Antiochian Orthordox Church
The Baptist Union of Great Britain
Cherubim and Seraphim Council of Churches
Church of England
Church of God of Prophecy
Church of Scotland
Congregational Federation
Coptic Orthodox Church
Council of African and Caribbean Churches
Council of Oriental Orthodox Christian Churches
Evangelische Synod Deutscher Sprache in Große Britannien
Greek Orthodox Church
Ichthus Christian Fellowship
Independent Methodist Churches
International Ministerial Council of Great Britain
Joint Council for Anglo-Caribbean Churches
Lutheran Council of Great Britain
Methodist Church
Moravian Church
New Testament Assembly
New Testament Church of God
Religious Society of Friends
Roman Catholic Church
Russian Orthodox Church
Salvation Army
Transatlantic and Pacific Alliance of Churches
United Reformed Church
Wesleyan Holiness Church
Seventh Day Adventists - Observers

■ BODIES IN ASSOCIATION:

Action by Christians Against Torture (ACATE)
Association of Centres Adult Theological Education
Association of Interchurch Families

Bible Society
Council on Christian Approaches to Defence and Disarmament (CCADD)
Church Alert to Sex Trafficking Across Europe (CHASTE)
Churches East West European Relations Network (CEWERN)
Church Action on Disability (CHAD)
Churches Criminal Justice Forum (CCJF)
Christian Council on Ageing
Christian Education
Christians Aware
Church Action on Poverty
Church Community Work Alliance
College of Preachers
Community of Aidan and Hilda
Corrymeela
Ecumenical Council for Corporate Responsibility
Faith in Europe
Feed the Minds
Fellowship of St Alban and St Sergius
Fellowship of Reconciliation
Housing Justice
Industrial Mission Association
International Ecumenical Fellowship
Iona Community
L'Arche
Living Stones
MODEM
Society for Ecumenical Studies
Student Christian Movement
William Temple Foundation
The Focolare Movement
Retreat Association
Y Care International
Young Men's Christian Association England
Women's World Day of Prayer

■ **AGENCIES**

Churches Media Council
Christian Enquiry Agency
Christian Aid
CAFOD

CYTÛN: CHURCHES TOGETHER IN WALES

CYTÛN: Eglwysi Ynghyd yng Nghymru/Churches Together in Wales

58 Richmond Road, Cardiff CF24 3UR
Tel: 029-2046 4204
E-mail: post@cytun.org.uk
Website: www.cytun.org.uk

Chief Executive: **Rev Aled Edwards OBE**
Bilingual Personal Assistant/Office Manager to the Chief Executive: **Mrs Sasha Perriam**
Assistant Chief Executive: **Mr Siôn Rhys Evans**
National Assembly Policy Officer: **Mr Andrew P Connell**

The objects of CYTÛN are the advancement of the Christian religion and of any other purposes which are charitable according to the law of England and Wales.

CYTÛN shall seek to further its objects by:

1 Gathering together the churches in Wales in all the richness of their present diversity so that they can learn from and value each others' traditions in a parity of esteem.
2 Offering the churches the opportunity to enter into a new commitment to reflect together theologically on matters of faith, order and ethics; to pray together and to learn to appreciate each others' pattern of prayer; to work together, sharing resources and presenting the Gospel in word and action.
3 Seeking to help the churches to arrive at a common mind so that they might become more fully united in faith, communion, pastoral care and mission.
4 Acting as a body which enables the churches themselves to reach their decisions in the context of common study, prayer and worship.
5 Enabling the churches to do together whatever they can.

■ **Member Denominations:**

The Baptist Union of Wales, 94 Mansel Street, Swansea SA1 5TZ
The Catholic Church, the Church in Wales, 39 Cathedral Road, Cardiff CF11 9XF
Congregational Federation, Crosslyn, Spittal, Haverfordwest, Dyfed SA62 5QT
Convenanted Baptists (BUGB), 3 Edith Road, Dinas Powys DV6 4AD
German Speaking Lutheran Church, Cardiff.
The Reformed and United Congregations Methodist Churches, 58 Richmond Road, Cardiff CF24 3UR; and 20-22 North Road, Cardiff

STRUCTURE AND HIERARCHY OF THE CHURCH

Presbyterian Church of Wales Tabernacle Chapel, 81 Merthyr Road, Cardiff CF14 1DD
Religious Society of Friends, Hafan Dawel, Llangoedmor, Cardigan SA43 2LD
Salvation Army, East Moors Road, Ocean Park, Cardiff CF1 5SA
Union of Welsh Independents, Ty John Penri, 5 Axis Court, Riverside Business Park, Swansea Vale SA7 0AJ
United Reformed Church, Minster Road, Roath Park, Cardiff CF23 5AS

■ Aligned Groupings
The Covenanted Churches in Wales, The Free Church Council of Wales

■ Observers
Black Majority Churches
Churches Together in Britain & Ireland (CTBI)
Free Church Council of Wales
German Speaking Lutheran Church
Lutheran Council of Great Britain
Orthodox Churches
Seventh Day Adventists

■ Agencies
CAFOD
Christians Against Torture
Christian Aid
Churches National Housing Coalition
Wales Council on Alcohol and other drugs

■ Bodies in Associaton:
In addition to those registered by CTBI, the following are listed only by CYTÛN:

Cardiff Adult Christian Education Centre
Council for Sunday Schools and Christian Education in Wales
Covenanted Churches in Wales
Christian Education Movement, Wales
Churches' Tourism Network, Wales
Fellowship of Reconciliation
Free Churches of Wales
Welsh Committee for Women's World Day of Prayer

STRUCTURE AND HIERARCHY OF THE CHURCH

ENGLISH ANGLICAN / ROMAN CATHOLIC COMMITTEE

■ ROMAN CATHOLIC MEMBERS:

Co-Chairman: **Rt Rev Declan Lang, Bishop of Clifton,** St Ambrose, North Road, Leigh Woods, Bristol BS8 3PW **Tel:** 0117-973 8850 **Fax:** 0116-973 5913 **E-mail:** declan.lang@cliftondiocese.com

Co-Secretary: **Sr M Cecily Boulding OP.** St Dominic's Convent, Stone Staffs HP4 2BE **Fax:** 01785 812091

Co-Secretary: **Rev John O'Toole,** Becket House, Santos Road, Wandsworth, London SW18 1NT **Tel:** 020-8874 3348 (H) **or** 020-8684 7682(W) **Fax:** 020-8684 6626 **E-mail:** jotoole@cectootingbec.org.uk

Castle, Anthony P, 36 St John's Road, Great Wakering, Essex SS3 0AL **Tel:** 01702-218660 **E-mail:** ant_castle@hotmail.com

Evans, Canon David, Immaculate Conception, Causeway, Bicester Oxon OX26 1AW **Tel:** 07957 712 972 **E-mail:** davidecevans@beeb.net

Evans, Rt Rev Michael, Bishop of East Anglia, The White House, 21 Upgate, Poringland, Norwich NR14 7SH **Tel:** 01508-492202 **Fax:** 01508-495358 **E-mail:** offices@east angliadiocese. org.uk

Faley, Rev Andrew, *AGS for Ecumenical Affairs and Interfaith Relations*, 39 Eccleston Square, Victoria, London SW1V 1BX **Tel:** 020-7901 4811 **Fax:** 020-7901 4821 **E-mail:** andrew.faley@cbcew.org.uk

Harris, Ms Alana Wadham College, Oxford OX1 3PN

Harvey, Peter, 15 Wingfield Street, Bungay, Suffolk NR35 1EZ **Tel:** 01986-894401 **E-mail:** peter.harvey@tiscali

Rowlands, Mrs Anna, 2 Leys Avenue, Cambridge CB4 2AW **Tel:** 01223 303535 **E-mail:** afr26@cam.ac.uk

Steele Mgr William J, Ashlea, 62 Headingley Lane, Leeds LS6 2BU **Tel:** 0113-261 8049 **E-mail:** william.steele@doceseofleeds.org.uk

Tyler, Peter, Sarum College, 19 The Close, Salisbury, Wilts SP1 2EH **Tel:** 01722-424836 **E-mail:** pmtyler@sarum.ac.uk

Walsh, Stephen, 29 Orchard Grove, Orpington, Kent BR6 0RX **Tel/Fax:** 01698 825355(H) 020-7782 8931(W) **E-mail:** walshfamily4@msn.com

Walton, Mrs Louise. 31 Churston Close, 162-164 Tulse Hill, London SW2 3BX **Tel:** 020 8671 0517 **Mbl:** 07855 142 787 **E-mail:** louisewalton1980@yahoo.co.uk

■ **ANGLICAN MEMBERS:**

Co-Chairman: **Rt Rev Michael Scott-Joynt.** Bishop of Winchester, Wolvesey, Winchester, Hants SO23 9ND **Tel:** 01962-854050 **Fax:** 01962-897088 **E-mail:** michael.scott-joynt@dial.pipex.com

Co-Secretary: **Rev Prebendary, Dr Paul Avis,** Council for Christian Unity, Church House, Great Smith Street, London SW1P 3NZ **Tel:** 020-7898 1470 **Fax:** 020-7898 1483 **E-mail:** paul.avis@c-of-e.org.uk

Mr Francis Bassett, Council for Christian Unity, Church House, Great Smith Street, London SW1P 3NZ **Tel:** 020-7898 1481 **Fax:** 020-7989 1483 **E-mail:** francis.bassett@c-of-e.org.uk

Dyer, Canon Anne, St John's College, South Bailey, Durham DH1 3RJ **Tel:** 0191 334 3866 **E-mail:** a.c.dyer@durham.ac.uk

Faull, V. Rev Vivienne, The cathedral Centre, 21 St Martin's, Leicester LE1 5DE **Tel:** 0116 248 7456 **E-mail:** viv.faull@leccofe.org

Forster, Rt Rev Dr Peter, Bishop of Chester, Bishop's House, Abbey Square, Chester CH1 2JD **Tel:** 01244-350864 **Fax:** 01244-3148187 **E-mail:** bpchester@chester.anglican.org

Goodall, Rev Canon Jonathan, Lambeth Palace, London SE1 7JU **Tel:** 020 7898 1273 **Fax:** 0207898 1221 **E-mail:** jonathan.goodall@c-of-e.org.uk

Hannaford, Rev Canon Prof, The Vicarage, Church Lane, Tunstall, Carnforth LA6 2RQ **Tel:** 01524 274 376 **E-mail:** rhannaford@ucsm.ac.uk

Jones, Prof Gareth. Dept of Theology and Religious Studies, Canterbury Christ Church University College, Canterbury, Kent CT1 1QU **Tel:** 01227 782 910 **E-mail:** gj7@canterbury.ac.uk

Pettersen, Rev Canon Alvyn, 2 College Green, Worcester WR1 2LH **Tel:** 01905-729487 **E-mail:** alvynpettersen@worcestercathedral.org.uk

Richards, Mr Dennis, c/o St Aidan's Church of England High School, Oatlands Drive, Harrogate Nth Yorks HG2 8JR **E-mail:** dennisrichards@btconnect.com

Ruddock, Rev Canon Bruce. The Precintor's Lodging, 14a Minster Precints, Peterborough PE1 1XX **Tel:** 01905-21961 **E-mail:** bruceruddock@peterborough-cathedral.org.uk

Scott, Mr Jonathan, Merton Grange, Wheeler's Lane, Bearwood, Bournmouth, Dorset BH11 9QJ **Tel:** 01202 573 218 **E-mail:** joffawoofa@hotmail.com

Seymour, Rev Dr John, 6 Mountague Place, London E14 0EX **Tel:** 020 7093 1452 **E-mail:** drjohnseymour@hotmail.com

Swinson, Mrs Margaret, 46 Glenmore Ave, Liverpool L18 4QF **Tel/Fax:** 0151 724 3533 **E-mail:** margaret.swinson@tiscali

Worthen, Rev Dr Jeremy. Vice-Principal SEITE, SECL, Cornwallis NW, University of Kent at Canterbury, Kent CT2 7NF **Tel:** 01227-764000 ext 7406 **E-mail:** j.worthen@seite.co.uk

Methodist Observer: Rev David Chapman. 23 Ryecroft Drive, Horsham, West Sussex RH12 2AW **Tel:** 01403-253915 **E-mail:** davidm.chapman@btinternat.com

Church of Wales Observer: Dr Sue Huyton. The Vicarage, Old Mold Road, Gwersyllt, Wrexham LL11 4SB **Tel:** 01978 756 391 **E-mail:** suehuyton@aol.com

CTE Observer on the English ARC: Rev Bill Snelson, Churches Together in England, 27 Tavistock Square, London WC1H 9HH **Tel:** 020-7529 8141 **Fax:** 020-7529 8134 **E-mail:** bill.snelson@cte.org.uk

BRITISH METHODIST / ROMAN CATHOLIC COMMITTEE

■ **ROMAN CATHOLIC MEMBERS:**

Co-Chairman: Rt Rev Michael Evans, The White House, 21 Upgate, Poringland, Norwich NR14 7SH **Tel:** 01508-492202 **Fax:** 01508-495358, **E-mail:** bishop@east-angliadiocese.org.uk

Co-Secretary: Rev Dr Adrian Graffy. Clergy House, 28 Ingrave Road, Brentwood, Essex CM15 8AT **Tel/Fax:** 01277 265423 **E-mail:** adriangraffy@dioceseofbrentwood.org

Faley, Mgr Andrew, AGS for Ecumenical Affairs and Interfaith Relations, 39 Eccleston Square, Victoria, London SW1V 1BX **Tel:** 020-7901 4811 **Fax:** 020-7901 4821 **E-mail:** andrew.faley@cbcew.org.uk

Griffiths, Rt Rev Ambrose, St Mary, Broadfield, Leyland, Preston PR5 1PD **Tel:** 01772 421183 **Fax:** 01772 621183 **E-mail:** ambroseg@btconnect.com

McFadden, Rev William, Scotus College, 2 Chesters Road, Bearsden, Glasgow G61 4AG **Tel:** 0141-942 8384 **E-mail:** WRMCF299@aol.com

Murray, Dr Paul, Dept of Theology, University of Durham, Abbey House, Palace Green, Durham DH1 3RS **Tel:** 0191-334 3947 **E-mail:** paul.murray@durham.ac.uk

Noakes, Rev Dr Kenneth, Parish of St Catherine, 4 Lewens Lane, Wimborne, Dorset BH21 1LE **Tel:** 01202-693336 **E-mail:** office@stcatherines.plus.com

O'Donnell, Sr Denise, Llantarnam Abbey, Cwmbran, Torfaen NP44 3YJ **Tel:** 01633-483232 **E-mail:** denise@ssjoseph.fsnet.co.uk

Philips, Rev Dr Peter, St Mary of the Angels, Chester Road, Childer Thornton, Ellesmere Port, Cheshrie CH66 1OJ **Tel:** 0151-327 6158 **E-mail:** p.phillips@firenet.ws.

Preston, Mrs Sheilagh, National Board of Catholic Women, 286 Abbeydale Road South, Totley Rise, Sheffield S17 3LN **Tel:** 0114-236 9521 **E-mail:** jackpreston@onetel.com

Sherrington, Rev John, 36 Uttoxeter Road, Mickleover, Derby DE3 5GE **Tel:** 01322 514107 **E-mail:** john-sherrington@btinternet.com

Watkins, Dr Clare, Vice-Principal and Director of Studies, Margaret Beaufort Institute, 12 Grange Road, Cambridge CB3 9DX **Tel:** 01223-741040 **E-mail:** clare@drwatkins.co.uk

■ **METHODIST MEMBERS:**

Co-Chairman: Rev Dr Richard G Jones. 35 Davies Road, West Bridgford, Nottingham NG2 5JE **Tel:** 0115-914 2352

Co-Secretary: Rev David Chapman. 23 Ryecroft Drive, Horsham West Sussex RH12 2AW **Tel/Fax:** 01403-253915 **Mbl:** 07720 661 257 **E-mail:** davidm.chapman@btinternet.com

Ball, Mr Edward. Dept of Theology, University of Nottingham, University Park, Nottingham NG7 2RD **Tel:** 0115-951 5854 **E-mail:** ed.ball@nottingham.ac.uk

Geary, Rev Alison, 89 Halifax Road, Nelson BB9 0EG **Tel/Fax:** 01282 615 716 **E-mail:** amgeary@aol.com

Hoggard, Dr Trevor, Via del Blanco di Santo Spirito 3, 00186 Roma, Italy **Tel:** 0039 06 686 8314 **Fax:** 0039 06 689 6981 **E-mail:** methodistchurchrome@virgilio.it

Jones, Rev Margaret, 44 Belmont Road, Bushey, Herts WD23 2JP **Tel:** 01923-460941 **Fax:** 01923-223906, **E-mail:** margaret.jones945@ntlworld.com

Lieu, Prof Judith, Dept of Theology and Religious Studies, King's College London, Strand, London WC2 2LS **Tel:** 020-7828 2336 **Fax:** 020-7848 2255 **E-mail:** judith.lieu@kcl.ac.uk

Powell, Rev Gareth J. University Chaplaincy, 20-22 North Road, Cardiff CF10 3DY **Tel:** 029-2034 4791 **E-mail:** Powellg1@cardiff.ac.uk

Sulston, Rev Peter, Methodist Church House, 25 Marylebone Road, London NW1 5JR **Tel:** 020-7486 5502 **E-mail:** uim@methodistchurch.org.uk

Walsh, Mrs Gillian. 29 Orchard Grove, Orpington, Kent BR6 0RX **Tel:** 01689-825355 **E-mail:** walshfamily4@msn.com

Wellings, Rev Dr Martin. 53 Oxford Road, Kidlington, Oxford OX5 2BP **Tel:** 01865 373958 **E-mail:** martin@wellingsmethodist.fsnet.co.uk

English ARC Observer: Rev Canon Alvyn Pettersen, 2 College Green, Worcester WR1 2LH **Tel:** 01905-28854 **E-mail:** alvynpettersen@worcestercathedral.org.uk

THE DIOCESES
OF ENGLAND AND WALES

COUNTIES SHOWING THE DIOCESES TO WHICH THEY BELONG

COUNTY	DIOCESE
Aberconwy	Wrexham
Anglesey	Wrexham
Avon	Clifton
Bedfordshire	Northampton
Berkshire	Northampton Portsmouth
Bristol	Clifton
Buckinghamshire	Northampton
Cambridgeshire	East Anglia
Channel Islands	Portsmouth
Carmarthenshire	Menevia
Ceredigion	Menevia
Cheshire	Shrewsbury Liverpool
Cleveland	Middlesbrough Hexham & Newcastle
Colwyn	Wrexham
Cornwall	Plymouth
Cumbria	Lancaster Leeds
Denbighshire	Wrexham
Derbyshire	Nottingham, Shrewsbury, Hallam
Devonshire	Plymouth
Dorset	Plymouth, Portsmouth
Durham	Hexham & Newcastle
Dyfed	Menevia
Essex	Brentwood
Flintshire	Wrexham
Glamorgan, Mid	Cardiff
Glamorgan, South	Cardiff
Glamorgan, West	Menevia
Gloucestershire	Clifton
Greater Manchester	Salford Shrewsbury Leeds Liverpool
Gwent	Cardiff
Gwynedd	Wrexham
Hampshire	Portsmouth
Herefordshire	Cardiff
Hertfordshire	Westminster
Isles of Scilly	Plymouth
Kent	Southwark

COUNTY	DIOCESE
Lancashire	Lancaster, Liverpool, Salford
Leicestershire	Nottingham
Lincolnshire	Nottingham
London	Westminster Brentwood Southwark
Man, Isle of	Liverpool
Merseyside	Liverpool Shrewsbury
Midlands, West	Birmingham
Norfolk	East Anglia
Northamptonshire	Northampton
North East Lincolnshire	Nottingham
North Lincolnshire	Nottingham
Northumberland	Hexham & Newcastle
Nottinghamshire	Nottingham, Hallam
Oxfordshire	Birmingham, Portsmouth
Pembrokeshire	Menevia
Powys	Menevia Wrexham
Rutland	Nottingham
Shropshire	Shrewsbury
Somerset	Clifton
Staffordshire	Birmingham
Suffolk	East Anglia
Surrey	Arundel & Brighton, Southwark
Sussex, East	Arundel & Brighton
Sussex, West	Arundel & Brighton
Swansea	Menevia
Tyne & Wear	Hexham & Newcastle
Warwickshire	Birmingham
West Midlands	Birmingham
Wight, Isle of	Portsmouth
Wiltshire	Clifton
Worcestershire	Birmingham
Yorkshire, North & East	Leeds, Middlesbrough
Yorkshire, South	Hallam
Yorkshire, West	Leeds/Salford

ARCHDIOCESE OF WESTMINSTER

Comprising the Greater London Boroughs north of the Thames and west of Waltham Forest and Newham,
plus the districts of Staines and Sunbury-on-Thames, and the county of Hertfordshire.

Diocesan Website: www.rcdow.org.uk

Patrons of the Diocese
Our Blessed Lady Immaculate, 8 Dec; and St Joseph, 19 Mar;
St Peter, Prince of the Apostles, 29 June; and St Edward, 13 Oct.
Consecrated to the Sacred Heart of Jesus, 17 June 1873.

Suffragan Sees
Brentwood, East Anglia, Northampton, Nottingham

HE Cardinal Cormac Murphy-O'Connor, Archbishop of Westminster

Archbishop
HE Cardinal Cormac Murphy-O'Connor STL, PhL
born Reading, Berks 24th August 1932; ordained priest 28th October 1956; ordained Bishop of Arundel & Brighton 21st December 1977; appointed Archbishop of Westminster March 22nd 2000; created Cardinal-Priest of the title Santa Maria Sopra Minerva, February 21, 2001.

Residence:
Archbishop's House, Ambrosden Avenue, London SW1P 1QJ.
Tel: 020-7798 9033. **Fax:** 020-7798 9077
E-mail: archbishop@rcdow.org.uk

Private Secretary:
Rev Martin Hayes BA, BD.
Tel: 020-7798 9041.
E-mail: martinhayes@rcdow.org.uk

Personal Secretary to the Archbishop:
Sr Damian McGrath RSM, Tel: 020-7798 9039

Press Secretary to the Cardinal:
Alexander DesForges Tel: 020-7798 9045/7901 4807
E-mail: alexander.desforges@cbcew.org.uk

Diocesan Communications Office:
Tel: 020-7798 9031

■ Auxiliary Bishops

Rt Rev John Arnold, titular Bishop of Lindisfarne. Born 12th June 1953 in Sheffield. Episcopal ordination 2nd February 2006 by Cardinal Cormac Murphy-O'Connor. Office: Archbishop's House, Ambrosden Avenue, London SW1P 1QJ **Tel:** 020-7931 6062
E-mail: johnarnold@rcdow.org.uk
(Moderator of the Curia, Pastoral responsibility for Department of Inter faith).

Rt Rev George Stack, titular Bishop of Gemellae in Numidia. Born 9th May 1946 in Cork, Ireland. Ordained 21st May 1972; Episcopal ordination 10th May 2001 by Cardinal Cormac Murphy-O'Connor. Office: Archbishop's House, Ambrosden Avenue, London SW1P 1QJ **Tel:** 020-7798 9060
Fax: 020-7798 9077 (Pastoral responsibility for Department of Education and Formation, Ecumenism, and Justice & Peace).
E-mail: georgestack@rcdow.org.uk

Rt Rev Alan Hopes, titular Bishop of Cuncacestre. Born 17 March, 1944, Oxford. Ordained 4 December 1995;
Episcopal ordination 24 January 2003 by Cardinal Cormac Murphy-O'Connor. Office: Archbishop's House, Ambrosden Avenue, London SW1P 1QJ **Tel:** 020-7798 9043
(Pastoral responsibility for Department for Clergy and Consecrated Life).
E-mail: alanhopes@rcdow.org.uk

Rt Rev Bernard Longley, titular Bishop of Zarna. Born 5 April, 1955, Manchester. Ordained 12 December 1981; Episcopal ordination 24 January 2003 by Cardinal Cormac Murphy-O'Connor. Office: Archbishop's House, Ambrosden Avenue, London SW1P 1QJ **Tel:** 020-7931 6061 (Pastoral Responsibility for Department for Pastoral Affairs).
E-mail: bernardlongley@rcdow.org.uk

■ ADMINISTRATION

■ Vicars General
Mgr Seamus O'Boyle, Archbishop's House, Ambrosden Avenue, London SW1P 1QJ **Tel:** 020-7931 6076

■ Safeguarding Service
Mgr Canon Henry Turner,
Tel: 01582-712245

■ Safeguarding Advisor
Mr Peter Turner, Tel: 020-7798 9350

■ Chancellor
Rt Rev John Arnold, Archbishop's House, Ambrosden Avenue, London SW1P 1QJ
Tel: 020-7931 6062.

■ Financial Secretary
Mr Paolo Camoletto. *Office*: Vaughan House, 46 Francis Street, London SW1P 1QN
Tel: 020-7798 9036 **Fax:** 020-7798 9077
E-mail: paolocamoletto@rcdow.org.uk

■ Diocesan Planned Giving and Gift Aid
Manager: **Charles Donington**;
Co-ordinators: **Mary Harrington** and **Anne Rimell**. *Office:* Vaughan House, 46 Francis Street, London SW1P 1QN
Tel: 020-7798 9004 **Fax:** 020-7798 9011

■ Episcopal Vicar for Religious
Rev Michael Campbell OSA

■ Vicar for Religious
Sr Amadeus Bulger CJ

■ Registrar for Deceased Clergy
Archbishop's House, Ambrosden Avenue, London SW1P 1QJ **Tel:** 020-7798 9035

■ Westminster Diocesan Archives
16a Abingdon Road, London W8 6AF
Tel: 020-7938 3580

■ Data Protection Officer
Rev John Conneely

■ Agency for Evangelisation
Director: **Fr Michael O'Boy,** Vaughan House, 46 Francis Street, London SW1P 1QN. **Fax:** 020-7798 9157

■ EDUCATION AND FORMATION

■ Westminster Diocese Education Service
Director: **Paul Barber**, Vaughan House, 46 Francis Street, London SW1P 1QN.
Tel: 020-7798 9005 **Fax:** 020-7798 9013

■ Co-Ordinator School Chaplains
Mgr Vladimir Felzmann, KCHS, DD, MSc(Eng), All Saints Pastoral Centre, London Colney, Herts AL2 1AF
Tel: 01727-829206
E-mail: vladimirf@compuserve.com

■ University Chaplain
Senior Chaplain: **Rev Peter Wilson**, Newman House, 111 Gower Street, London WC1E 6AR **Tel:** 020-7387 6370

■ All Saints Pastoral Centre
Shenley Lane, London Colney, St Albans, Herts AL2 1AF *Director:* **Mgr Vladimir Felzmann**.
Conference and Retreat Centre:
Tel: 01727-822010 **Fax:** 01727-822880

■ SPEC CENTRE
Part of the Agency for Evangelisation (Retreat and Resource Centre for ages 16 to 30), *Co-Directors:* Sandra and David Satchell, **Tel:** 01727-828888
Bookshop: *McCrimmons at All Saints* (open daily 11am to 5pm), **Tel & Fax:** 01727-827612

■ Vocations
Director of Vocations: **Rev Christopher Vipers**. **Tel:** 020-7798 9083

■ Liturgical Commission
Chair: **Rev Allen Morris**.

■ ECUMENISM

Clergy House, 47 Francis Street, London SW1P 1QR

■ DEPARTMENT FOR PASTORAL AFFAIRS

Director: **Edmund Adamus**, Vaughan House, 46 Francis Street, SW1P 1QN **Tel:** 020-7798 9363 **Fax:** 020-7798 9077
Services for Deaf and Hard of Hearing People: **Tel:** 020-8202 3611
Textphone: 020 8732 8340
Services for People with Physical Disability: **Rev Tad Tokarski Tel:** 020-8366 9843

■ St Joseph's Pastoral Centre
For children with special needs and adults with learning disabilities, their families, friends, advocates and staff. St Joseph's Pastoral Centre, St Joseph's Grove, The Burroughs, Hendon, NW4 4TY.
Tel: 020-8202 3999 **Fax:** 020-8202 1418

■ **Catholic Children's Society (Westminster)**
Chief Executive: **Mr Jim Richards,** 73 St Charles Square, London W10 6EJ **Tel:** 020-8969 5305 **Fax:** 020-8960 1464 **Website:** www.cathchild.org.uk

■ **The Cardinal Hume Centre**
Enabling homeless people to fulfil their potential. *Director:* **Cathy Corcoran MBE,** 3-7 Arneway Street, Horseferry Road SW1P 2BG **Tel:** 020-7222 1602

■ **The Passage** (Helping homeless people)
Chief Executive: **Sr Ellen Flynn DC,** St Vincent's, Carlisle Place SW1P 1NL **Tel:** 020-7595 1850 **Fax:** 020-7592 1870

■ **Committee for the Welfare of Sick and Retired Clergy**
Chair: **Rt Rev Alan Hopes**

■ **Hospital Chaplains**
Chaplaincy Co-ordinator: **Rev Peter Scott,** **Tel:** 020-7349 5609

■ **CONSULTATIVE BODIES**

■ **Metropolitan Cathedral Chapter**
(erected 19 June 1852)
Members of the Chapter: **Canon Michael Brockie** (*Provost*), **Canon Vincent Berry, Canon Bernard Scholes, Canon Daniel Cronin, Canon Patrick Davies, Canon Colin Davies, Canon Christopher Tuckwell, Canon Stuart Wilson, Canon Edward Matthews, Canon Michael Munnelly, Canon Paul McGinn, Mgr Canon Henry Turner, Canon Philip Cross, Canon Charles Acton, Canon Patrick Browne, Mgr Canon Thomas Egan, Canon Robert Plourde, Canon Digby Samuels.** *Canons Emeriti:* **Mgr Canon Frederick Miles, Canon John McDonald, Canon John Formby, Canon Richard Marriott; Mgr Canon Adrian Arrowsmith, Canon Peter Gilburt, Canon Peter Phillips, Canon Louis Thomas.** *Honorary Canons:* **Canon Reginald Fuller.**

■ **COUNCIL OF PRIESTS**
Cardinal and Auxiliary Bishops, Private Secretary, Vicars General, and others representing priestly work of the diocese.

■ **WESTMINSTER MATRIMONIAL TRIBUNAL**
(For the Diocese of Westminster, and the Tribunals of the Falkland Islands, Ascension Island, St Helena, Tristan da Cunha; and for the Bishopric of the Forces).
Tribunal Office: Vaughan House, 46 Francis Street, London SW1P 1QN **Tel:** 020-7798 9003 *Judical Vicar:* **Rev John Conneely**; *Personal Assistant:* **Mrs Maureen Scammell.** *Assistant Judicial Vicar:* **Canon Michael Brockie,** *Canonical Assistants:* **Rev Nicholas Kavanagh, Mrs Alicia Sloan.** *Tribunal Assistants:* **Mr Matthew Gillespie, Miss Marilyn Smith.**

■ **WESTMINSTER CATHEDRAL**
Metropolitan Cathedral of the Most Precious Blood. *Administrator:* **Canon Christopher Tuckwell.** *Sub Administrator:* **Rev Slawomir Witon.** *College of Cathedral Chaplains:* **Revv Michael Archer, Denis Sarsfield, Sr Bridget Cullen DC. Rev Michael Dunne, Rev Thevakingsley Arulananthem, Rev Anthony Brunning.**
Address: Cathedral Clergy House, 42 Francis Street, SW1P 1QW **Tel:** 020-7798 9055 **Fax:** 020-7798 9090
Also in residence: **Rev Michael Durand.**
Cathedral Communications:
Rev Timothy Dean.
Cathedral Website:
www.westminstercathedral.org.uk

■ **Cathedral Choir School**
Ambrosden Avenue, SW1P 1QH
Tel: 020-7798 9081.
Head: **Mr Neil McLaughlan.**

■ **Diocesan Seminary**
Allen Hall, 28 Beaufort Street, London SW3 5AA **Tel:** 020-7349 5600
Rector: **Mgr Mark O'Toole.**
See entry under Chelsea 2

■ WESTMINSTER

1. † Metropolitan Cathedral of the Most Precious Blood.
(1903; cons 28 June, 1910)
Victoria Street and Ambrosden Avenue.
For clergy, see above.
M: *Sat 1st M of Sun 6pm. Sun 8am, 9am (CW monthly), 10.30am (Sung), 12noon, 5.30pm, 7pm Hds* (vigil *5.30pm*). *7am, 8am, 10.30am, 12.30pm, 1.05pm, 5.30pm*

- ***Cardinal Hume Centre***, 3-7 Arneway Street, SW1P 2BG **Tel:** 020-7222 1602 *Director*: **Cathy Corcoran MBE**.
- Franciscan Friars of the Atonement (SA): St Francis Friary, 47 Francis Street, London SW1P 1QR **Rev Michael Seed, Br Denis Burgelin**
- ***The Passage***, Day Centre and Night-Shelter for Homeless People, St Vincent's, Carlisle Place, SW1P 1NL **Tel:** 020-75921850
- ***Daughters of Charity (SVP)***, St Vincent's, Carlisle Place, SW1P 1NL **Tel:** 020-7834 4004 Also 94a Horseferry Road, SW1P 2EE **Tel:** 020-7222 6485
- ***Franciscan Sisters of Our Lady of Victories***, Cathedral Clergy House. **Tel:** 020-7798 9067
- ***Augustinian Sisters***, Archbishop's House.

2. Sacred Heart.
Chapel of Ease, Horseferry Road, SW1P 2EF
Served from the Cathedral.
M: *Sun 11am.*

■ ABBOTS LANGLEY

† St Saviour. (1928; 1963)
96 The Crescent, Abbots Langley, Watford, Herts WD5 0DS **Tel:** 01923-265646
Fax: 01923-291146

- ***Salvatorian Fathers (SDS)***: **Rev Henry Nevin.**
  M: *Sat 1st M of Sun 6pm, Sun 9am, 11am, 6pm. Hds 6pm* (vigil), *10am, 8pm.*

■ ACTON

† Our Lady of Lourdes
(1878; 1902; cons 17 May 1961)
High Street.

- ***Picpus Fathers (SSCC)***: **Revv John Leahy** *(Parish Priest)*, **Fintan Crotty, Kieran Murtha, Dcn Tito Pereira,** 5 Berrymead Gardens, Acton W3 8AA
  Tel: 020-8992 2014 **Fax:** 020-8993 9940
  E-mail: acton@rcdow.org.uk
  Website: www.olol-acton.com
  M: *Sat 1st M of Sun 7pm. Sun 9am, 10.30am, 12noon, 6pm. Hds 7am, 10am, 8pm.*
- ***Emmaus House (Acton Homeless Concern)***, 1 Berrymead Gardens W3 **Tel:** 020-8992 5768
- ***Medical Mission Sisters (SCMM)***, Generalate, 41 Chatsworth Gardens, Acton W3 9LP **Tel:** 020-8992 6444
- ***IBVM (Loreto Sisters)***, 4 Buxton Gardens, W3 9LQ **Tel:** 020-8993 6931
- ***Religious Sisters of Charity***, 9 Rosemont Road W3 9LU **Tel:** 020-8992 4461

■ ACTON (EAST)

† St Aidan of Lindisfarne.
(1922; 1961; cons 31 Oct 1972)
24 Sunningdale Avenue, Acton W3 7NS
Tel: 020-8743 5732
Rev Danny Horan.
M: *Sat 1st M of Sun 6.30pm. Sun 9am 11am. Hds 10am, 7.30pm.*

- ***Sisters of the Infant Jesus***, 16 East Acton Lane, London W3 7EG **Tel:** 020-8248 9458. Also 30 Sunningdale Avenue, W3 7NS **Tel:** 020-8743 0116
- ***Sisters of Mercy***, 39 Ashfield Road, W3 7JF **Tel:** 020-8740 6168.

■ ACTON (WEST)

† The Holy Family. (1967)
The Presbytery, Vale Lane, Acton W3 0DY
Tel: 020-8992 1308 **Fax:** 020-8896 9393
Rev John Wiley.
M: *Sat 1st M of Sun 6pm. Sun 9am, 11am, 12.30pm (Iraqi Chaldean Rite). Hds 10am, 7pm (Polish).*

- ***Sacred Hearts Community (SS.CC)***, 372 Uxbridge Road, W5 3LH **Revv Kenneth Barnes, Derek Laverty, Fr Christopher McEneny**. **Tel:** 020-8992 5941
- ***Franciscan Missionaries of Mary***, 26 Inglis Road, W5 3RL. **Tel:** 020-8992 0802

■ ARNOS GROVE N11

See New Southgate.

■ ASHFORD

† St Michael (1906; 1928; cons 19.11.2006)
Fordbridge Road.
Mgr James Overton, 112 Clarendon Road, Ashford, Middx TW15 2QD
Tel: 01784-252230 **Fax:** 01784-247090
E-mail: ashford@rcdow.org.uk
M: *Sat 1st M of Sun 6pm. Sun 9.30am, 11.30am, 6pm. Hds 9.30am, 8pm.*

■ BALDOCK

† Holy Trinity and St Augustine of Canterbury
(1913; 1926; new church 1977; cons 17 Dec 1977)
Holy Trinity Church, London Road, Baldock, Herts SG7 6LQ **Tel:** 01462-893127
Rev Michael Lambert, Resident at Hitchin.
M: *Sat 1st M of Sun 6.30pm. Sun 8.30am, 10.30am* (*Sung*) *Hds 10am, 7.30pm.*

■ BARNET

† Mary Immaculate and St Gregory the Great (1849; 1860; cons 15 Dec 1931; new church 1975)
82 Union Street, Barnet, Herts EN5 4HZ
Tel: 020-8449 3338 **Fax:** 020-8449 4761
Rev Jeremy Davies; *In Residence:* **Rev Fred de L'orme.**

M: *Sat 1st M of Sun 6.30pm. Sun 8am, 9.30am, 11.15am, 6.30pm. Hds* (vigil *7.30pm*), *10am, 7.30pm.*

- ***Poor Clares***, Poor Clare Monastery, Galley Lane, Arkley, Barnet, EN5 4AN *Chaplain:* **Rev John Ball Tel:** 020-8449 8815
- ***Sisters of St Martha***, 124 Wood Street, Barnet EN5 4AY **Tel:** 020-8449 6759
- ***Sisters of Christian Instruction***, Summerhill, Leecroft Road, Barnet, Herts EN5 2TH **Tel:** 020-8440 1853

■ BAYSWATER

† St Mary of the Angels (1857)
The Parish House, Moorhouse Road, Bayswater W2 5DJ **Tel:** 020-7229 0487
Fax: 020-7229 3223
Rev Alan Robinson.
Also in residence: **Rev Nizar Samaan.**

M: *Sat 1st M of Sun 6.30pm. Sun 8am, 9.30am* (*Folk*), *11am* (*Portuguese*), *12noon* (*Sung*), *6pm. Hds 8am, 10am, 7.30pm*

- ***Spanish Catholic Chaplaincy***, 47 Palace Court, London, W2 4LS. ***Vincentians (CM):*** **Revv Ernesto Atanes, Segundo Pena, Benito Fraile, José Lopez, Jorgelouis Rodriguez.**
  Tel: 020-7229 8815
  M: *Sun 10.30am, 6pm.*
- ***Czech Centre***, Velehrad House, 22 Ladbroke Square, W11 3NA
  Tel: 020-7727 7849
  M: *Sun 8pm.*
- ***Comboni Missionaries (Mccj)***, Comboni House, 16 Dawson Place, W2 4TJ **Revv Benito de Marchi, Franco Mastromauro. Tel:** 020-7229 7059
- ***Sisters of Sion,*** 34 Chepstow Villas, W11 2QZ **Tel:** 020-7229 6266.
- ***Sion Centre for Encounter and Dialogue***. **Tel:** 020-7727 3597. The Centre, with its library and publications, provides a place for the study of Judaism and the Jewish roots of Christianity.
- ***Society of the Holy Child Jesus***, 10 Holland Park Avenue, W11 3QU
  Tel: 020-7727 7440
- ***Servants of the Mother of God***, 7 Pembridge Square, W2 4EQ
  Tel: 020-7229 1424
- ***Pembridge House***, 29 Pembridge Square, W2 4DS Pastoral care entrusted to the Prelature of Opus Dei.
  Tel: 020-7229 3584

■ BERKHAMSTED

† Sacred Heart Church (1909; 1967)
Park Street, Berkhamsted HP4 1HX
Tel: 01442-863845
Rev John Boland.

M: *Sat 1st M of Sun 6pm. Sun 8.30am, 10.30am. Hds as announced.*

■ BETHNAL GREEN

† Our Lady of the Assumption (1902; 1912)
Our Lady of the Assumption,Victoria Park Square E2 9PB **Tel:** 020-8980 1968
Fax: 020-8983 7713
E-mail: assumption.bg@lineone.net
Assumptionists (AA): **Revv Tom O'Brien** (*Regional Superior*) **Tel:** 020-8709 5280
E-mail: assumptionists@freeuk.com
Revv Andrew O'Dell *(Parish Priest)*, **Brendan O'Malley, Joachim Duy Nguyth Khnong, Jean-Marie Nguyen Paluku.**

M: *Sat 1st M of Sun 7pm. Sun 9.30am, 11.30am. Hds 8am, 12.15pm, 6.30pm.*

- ***Canonesses of St Augustine (Congregation of Our Lady)***, 44 Stafford Cripps House, Globe Road, E2 0LN **Tel:** 020-8981 6221

■ BISHOP'S STORTFORD

† St Joseph and the English Martyrs (1900; 1906; cons 19 June 1906)
3 Windhill, Bishop's Stortford, Herts CM23 2ND **Tel:** 01279-654063
Canon Edward Matthews.

M: *Sat 1st M of Sun 6pm. Sun 9am, 11am, 6pm. Hds* (vigil *7.30pm*), *9.30am, 7.30pm.*

■ BOREHAMWOOD

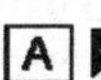

† St Teresa of the Child Jesus (1925; 1962; cons 27 Oct 1978)
291 Shenley Road, Borehamwood, Herts WD6 1TG **Tel:** 020-8953 1294
Rev Peter Lyness.
Administrator: **Fr Michael Daly**

M: *Sat 1st M of Sun 6pm. Sun 9.30am* (*Family*), *11am* (*Sung*). *Hds 9.30am, 7.30pm.*

■ BOREHAMWOOD (NORTH)

† SS John Fisher and Thomas More (1955; 1958; cons 27 October 1992)
Presbytery, 28 Rossington Avenue, Borehamwood, Herts WD6 4LA
Tel: 020-8953 0715
Revv Frans Azzopardi, Michael Daly.

M: Sat 1st M of Sun 6pm. Sun 10.30am, 6.30pm. Hds (As announced).

- ***Scalabrini Fathers (CS)***, Villa Scalabrini, Green Street, Shenley, Herts **Tel:** 020-8207 5713 **Rev Alberto Vico.**
- ***Sisters of the Angels.*** Villa Scalabrini. **Tel:** 020-8236 8592

■ **BOW**

† Our Lady and St Catherine of Siena
(1868; 1870)
177 Bow Road, Bow E3 2SG
Tel: 020-8980 3961
Rev Donald Graham.
M: *Sat 1st M of Sun 6pm. Sun 9.30am (Sung), 11.30am. Hds 10am, 6pm.*
- ***Sisters of Charity of Jesus and Mary,*** 23 Bow Road, London E3 2AD **Tel:** 020-8983 4335
- ***Columban Sisters***, 8 Ridgdale Street E3 2PW **Tel:** 020-8980 3017
- ***Sisters of Mercy,*** 152 Bruce Road, E3 3EU **Tel:** 020-8980 0044

■ **BOW COMMON**

† The Holy Name and Our Lady of the Sacred Heart
(1892; 1894; cons June 30, 1894)
117 Bow Common Lane E3 4AU
Served from Poplar
Rev Aidan Rossitter CJ. Tel: 020-7987 3477
M: *Sun 9.15am. Hds As announced.*
- ***Vietnamese Chaplaincy:*** **Rev Paul Huynh Chanh. Tel/Fax:** 020-7987 3477 **Website:** www.lavang.co.uk **M:** *Sun 9.30am (English), 12noon, 3.15pm (Vietnamese).*

■ **BOXMOOR**

See Hemel Hempstead

■ **BRENTFORD**

† St John the Evangelist (1856; 1866)
44 Boston Park Road, Brentford, Middx TW8 9JF **Tel:** 020-8560 1671
Fax: 020-8568 8806
Rev Gerard Quinn.
M: *Sat 1st M of Sun 6.30pm 9.30, 11.30, Hds 9am, 7.30pm.*
- ***Servants of the Mother of God,*** St Mary's Convent, 2 The Butts, Brentford, Middx TW8 8BQ **Tel:** 020-8847 4800

■ BROOK GREEN

† Holy Trinity
(1851; 1853; cons 2 June 1866)
41 Brook Green, W6 7BL
Tel: 020-7603 3832 **Fax:** 020-7603 0511
Revv Terry Tastard, James Neal.
Also in residence: **Fr Nizar Semaan** (Syrian Catholic Chaplain)
M: *Sat 1st M of Sun 6pm. Sun 8.30am, 10am 11.30am (Sung), 6pm. Hds 9.30am, 12.30pm, 6pm.*
- ***Poor Sisters of Nazareth,*** Nazareth House, Hammersmith Road, W6 8DB **Tel:** 020-8748 3549
- ***Society of the Sacred Heart,*** Provincial House, 3 Bute Gardens, W6 7DR **Tel:** 020-8748 9353; 9 Bute Gardens W6 7DR **Tel:** 020-8741 8457; 121 Blythe Road W14 0HL **Tel:** 020-7603 2787
- ***Spanish Sisters of Santa Ana,*** 93 Addison Gardens W14 **Tel:** 020-7603 0018
- ***Austrian Catholic Centre,*** 29 Brook Green, W6 **Tel:** 020-7603 2697

■ **BUNHILL ROW**

† St Joseph (1856; 1901)
St Joseph's Presbytery, 15 Lamb's Passage, Bunhill Row EC1Y 8LE **Tel:** 020-7628 0326
Rev Peter Newby (resident at Moorfields).
M: *Sun 11.30am. Hds 12.05pm, 6pm.*

■ **BUNTINGFORD**

† St Richard of Chichester
(1912; 1914; cons June 5, 1940)
3 Station Road, Buntingford, Herts SG9 9HT **Tel:** 01763-271471
Rev Ian Dickie.
M: *Sun 9.30am, 6.30pm. Hds 10am, 8pm.*

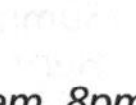

■ **BURNT OAK**

† The Annunciation (1928)
The Presbytery, 4 Thirleby Road, Burnt Oak, Edgware, Middlesex HA8 0HQ
Tel: 020-8959 1971
Canon Colin Davies.
Also in residence: **Fr Frank McGuire.**
M: *Sat 1st M of Sun 6.30pm. Sun 9am, 10.30am, 12noon. Hds 9am, 7.30pm (2pm Annunciation Junior School).*

■ **BUSHEY AND OXHEY**

† The Sacred Heart of Jesus and St John the Evangelist (1863; 1959; cons 20 Sept 1977)
Sacred Heart Presbytery, London Road, Bushey, Watford, Herts WD23 1BA
Tel: 020-8950 2077
Rev Michael Markey.
M: *Sat 1st M of Sun 6pm. Sun 8.30am, 10.30am (sung), 6pm. Hds (vigil 7.30pm), 10am, 8pm.*
- ***Dominican Sisters,*** Rosary Priory, 93 Elstree Road, Bushey, Watford, Herts WD2 3RJ **Tel:** 020-8950 1148 *Chaplain:* **Rev Michael Platts OP.**

■ **CAMDEN TOWN**

† Our Lady of Hal (1921; 1933)
165 Arlington Road, Camden Town, NW1 7EX **Tel:** 020-7485 2727
Fax: 020-7485 1213
Revv Dominic McKenna, John Conneely.
M: *Sat 1st M of Sun 7.30pm. Sun 8.30am, 10am, 12noon, 6pm (Portuguese). Hds 12noon.*
- ***Helpers of the Holy Souls,*** Holy Rood House, 3 Gloucester Avenue, NW1 7AS **Tel:** 020-7485 1745
- ***Alexian Brothers,*** 28 Delancey Street NW1 7NH **Tel:** 020-7482 4199

■ **CARPENDERS PARK AND SOUTH OXHEY**
† St Joseph (1952; 1960)
St Joseph's Church, Oxhey Drive, South Oxhey, Watford, Herts WD19 7SW
Tel: 020-8428 2774 **Fax:** 020-8421 5840
Rev Aidan Sharratt.
M: *Sat 1st M of Sun 6pm, Sun 8.30am, 10.30am. Hds 9.15am, 7pm.*

■ **CHELSEA**
1. **† St Mary**
(1798; 1811; 1879; cons June 12, 1882)
Cadogan Street, St Mary's Rectory, Draycott Terrace, Chelsea, London SW3 2QR
Tel: 020-7589 5487 **Fax:** 020-7581 5727
Canon Stuart Wilson, Rev Paul McDermott
M: *Sat 1st M of Sun 6.30pm. Sun 10am* (*Family*), *11.30pm* (*Sung Latin*), *6.30pm. Hds* (vigil *6.30pm*), *7.30am, 12noon, 6.30pm.*
- ***Daughters of the Cross,*** St. Wilfrid's Convent, 29 Tite Street, SW3 4JX
Tel: 020-7351 5339 (Convent);
Tel: 020-7352 8712 (Residents);
Tel: 020-7351 2117 (Provincialate).
Chaplain: **Rev William Wilby.**
- ***Dawliffe Hall,*** 2 Chelsea Embankment SW3 4LG. **Tel:** 020-7352 1545. (Pastoral care entrusted to the Prelature of Opus Dei).

2. **† Our Most Holy Redeemer and St Thomas More**
(1892; 1895; cons June 21, 1905)
7 Cheyne Row, Chelsea, London SW3 5HS
Tel: 020-7352 0777 **Fax:** 020-7352 4223
Canon Michael Brockie.
M: *Sat 1st M of Sun 6.30pm. Sun 10am, 11am* (*Sung Latin*), *12.15pm, 6.30pm. Hds 8am, 10am, 6.30pm.*
- ***Allen Hall,*** Diocesan Seminary, 28 Beaufort Street, Chelsea, SW3 5AA
Tel: 020-7349 5600 **Fax:** 020-7349 5601
E-mail: allenhall@rcdow.org.uk

Rector: **Mgr Mark O'Toole** BSc, BD, MPhil, STL **Tel:** 020-7349 5605;
Vice-Rector: **Fr Roger Taylor**, MA, STB
Tel: 020-7349 5627;
PA to Rector: **Mrs Helena Duckett**
Tel: 020-7349 5786

Formation Team:
Canon Charles Acton STL (Dean of Studies) **Tel:** 020-7349 5611 **Sr Bernadette Hunston** SCJA, BA, MTh *(Formation Advisor)* **Tel:** 020-7349 5622 **Fr John Hemer** MHM STB, MA, LSS *(Formation Advisor)* **Tel:** 020-7349 5600 **Miss Sally McAllister** MA, *(Formation Advisor)*
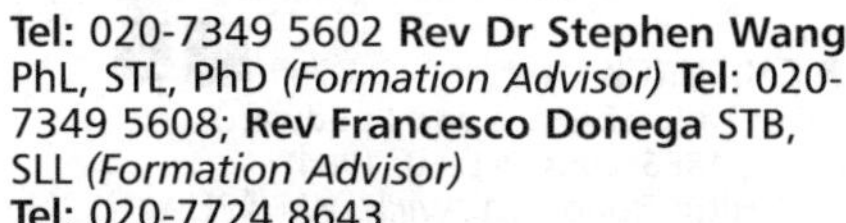
Tel: 020-7349 5612 **Rev Dr Dermot Power** BA, BD, STL, STD *(Spiritual Director)* **Tel:** 020-7349 5602 **Rev Dr Stephen Wang** PhL, STL, PhD *(Formation Advisor)* **Tel:** 020-7349 5608; **Rev Francesco Donega** STB, SLL *(Formation Advisor)*
Tel: 020-7724 8643

Academic Staff:
Canon Charles Acton STL (Dean of Theology, Systematic Theology) **Rev Dr Francis Selman** MA, MTh, PhD, PhL *(Dean of Philosophy)* * **Rev John Conneely** JCL *(Canon Law)* **Rev Francesco Donega** STB, SLL *(Liturgy, Systematic Theology)* **Rev Peter Harris** BEd, MTh *(Church History)* **Rev John Hemer** MHM, STB, LSS *(Scripture, Biblical Greek)* **Sr Bernadette Hunston** SCJA, BA, MTh *(Spiritual Theology)* **Miss Sally McAllister** *(Pastoral Co-ordinator & Pastoral Theology), 020 7349 5612* **Rev Dr Anthony Meredith** SJ, MA, DPhil *(Patristics)* **Miss Letitia Nicoll** LGSM, DipCE, FESB *(Vocal Communications)* **Rev Dr Joseph O'Hanlon** BA, BD, MTh, LSS, PhD *(Scripture)* **Rev Dom Alexander Bevan OSB** *(Latin)* **Rev Dr Dermot Power** BA, BD, STL, STD *Spirituality, Systematic Theology)* **Fr Roger Taylor** MA, STB, MA *(Liturgy)* **Prof Clemens Sedmak** PhD *(Moral Theology)* **Rev Dr Stephen Wang** PhL, STL, PhD *(Philosophy, Systematic Theology)*; **Dr Clare Watkins** *(Pastoral Theology);* **Sr Petronia Williams** OSM, DipEd *(Pastoral Supervisor)*

Administration:
Administrator: **Mr Gerald Daly** BA,
Tel: 020-7349 5606; *Receptionist/ Conference Co-ordinator:* **Miss Mary Aldridge Tel:** 020-7349 5600; *Librarian:* **Rev Dr Francis Selman** MA, MTh, PhD, STL

■ **CHESHUNT**
St Paul (1998)
17 Churchfield Park, Cheshunt, Herts EN8 9EG
Tel: 01992-629878 **Fax:** 01992-621741
Rev Anton Cowan (*Secretary, Council of Censorship*).
M: *Sun* (*5pm Sat*) *9am, 11am. Hds 9.30am, 8pm.*

■ **CHINESE CATHOLIC CHAPLAINCY**
See under Soho Square Parish.

■ **CHIPPERFIELD,** Kings Langley
Our Lady, Mother of the Saviour (1989)
Catholic Church, Dunny Lane, Chipperfield, Kings Langley WD4 9DB
Tel: 01923-265327
- ***Salvatorians*** (***SDS***)*:* **Rev Desmond Cantwell.**
M: *Sat 1st M of Sun 6pm. Sun 9am, 11am. Hds 7.30pm.*

■ CHISWICK 

† Our Lady of Grace and St Edward
(1852; 1886; cons Oct. 10, 1904)
247 High Road, Chiswick, W4 4PU
Tel: 020-8994 2877 **Fax:** 020-8987 8332
Revv Tony Dwyer, Edward Houghton.
M: *Sat 1st M of Sun 6.30pm. Sun 8.30am, 9.45am (Family), 11am, 12.15pm, 6.30pm. Hds, 10am, 12.30pm, 7.30pm.*

- ***Religious Sisters of Charity,*** Provincial House, 55 Barrowgate Road, Chiswick W4 4QT **Tel:** 020-8995 1963
- ***Missionary Sisters of Mary Immaculate (PIME),*** Regina Pacis Convent, 10 Chiswick Lane, W4.
  Tel: 020-8994 2053
  Fax: 020-8747 9354
  House of Studies and Kindergarten.
- ***Comboni Missionary Sisters (Verona Sisters),*** 2 Chiswick Lane, W4 2JF House for student Sisters and elderly Sisters. **Tel:** 020-8994 0449.

■ CHORLEYWOOD

† St John Fisher (1955)
Hill Cottage, Shire Lane, Chorleywood, Rickmansworth, Herts WD3 5NH
Tel: 01923-283616
Rev James Duffy, (resident at Rickmansworth).
M: *Sat 1st M of Sun 5pm. Sun 9.15am.*

■ CLAPTON

† St Scholastica
(1862; 1962; cons Feb 15, 1987)
17 Kenninghall Road, Clapton, E5 8BS
Tel: 020-8985 2178
Rev David Barrow.
M: *Sat 1st M of Sun 6pm. Sun 10am, 11.45am. 6pm. Hds 9.30am, 7.30pm.*

- ***Servite Sisters,*** Flat 1 Brownsea Court, 161 Clarence Road E5 8EF
  Tel: 020-8985 3489

■ CLAPTON PARK 

† St Jude (1964)
Blurton Road.
131 Glenarm Road, Clapton Park, E5 0NB
Tel: 020-8525 1929
Rev Neil Hannigan.
M: *Sat 1st M of Sun 6.30pm. Sun 9.30am, 11.30am (Sung), 6pm. Hds 10am (Sung), 7pm.*

- ***Sisters of Mercy,*** 4 Hilsea Street, Clapton E5 0SG. **Tel:** 020-8986 3196
- ***Columban Sisters,*** 148 Glenarm Road, E5 0NB. **Tel:** 020-8986 4435

■ CLERKENWELL 

† SS Peter and Paul (1842; 1847)
5 Amwell Street, Roseberry Avenue, Clerkenwell, EC1R 1UL **Tel:** 020-7837 2094

- ***Pallottine Fathers (SCA):***
  Rev George Ranahan.
  M: *Sat 1st M of Sun 6.30pm. Sun 10am, 12noon. Hds 12noon, 7.30pm.*
- ***Pallottine Missionary Sisters,*** 35 Wilmington Square, WC1X 0EG
  Tel: 020-7837 3010
- † ***St Peter*** (See Italian Church)

■ COCKFOSTERS 

† Christ the King (1936; 1940)
Monastery of Christ the King, Bramley Road, Cockfosters N14 4HE
Tel: 020-8440 7769 (*Monastery*);
020-8449 6648 (*Parish*)
Fax: 020-8440 2296

- ***Benedictines (Olivetan) (OSB):*** **Bernard de Smet; Revv Doms Benedict M Heron, Paschal M Pennington, Bernard M Akoeso** (Priest in charge & *Superior*), **Felician M Roux, Emmanuel Boateng**.
  M: *Sat 1st M of Sun 5.30pm. Sun 8.30am (CW), 10am (CW), 12noon, 6.30pm (with Group 2nd, 4th, 5th Sun). Hds 8am, 11am, 7.30pm.*
- ***Benedictine Centre for Spirituality,*** Day and residential courses.
  Tel: 020-8449 2499

■ COMMERCIAL ROAD 

† St Mary and St Michael
(1856; cons Dec. 4, 1929)
2 Lukin Street, Commercial Road, E1 0AA
Tel: 020-7790 5911 **Fax:** 020-7265 9795
Revv James Mulligan, Christiano Braz.
M: *Sat 1st M of Sun 7pm. Sun 9.30am, 11am. Hds 9.30am, 12.30pm, 7pm.*

- ***Sisters of Mercy,*** 88 Hardinge Street E1 0EB **Tel:** 020-7790 1459

■ COPENHAGEN STREET 

† The Blessed Sacrament (1916)
157 Copenhagen Street, Kings Cross N1 0SR **Tel:** 020-7837 4841
Fax: 020-7837 7591
Revv Jim Kennedy, Celestine Chigboa.
M: *Sat 1st M of Sun 7pm. Sun 9am, 11am, 6.30pm. 1st Sun M for Lesbian & Gay Community. Hds 8am, 10am (school), 12.30pm, 7pm.*

- ***Sisters of Mercy***
  E-mail: kingscross@ourladyofmercy.co.uk

■ CRANFORD 

† Our Lady and St Christopher (1967; 1970)
32 High Street, Cranford, Hounslow TW5 9RG **Tel:** 020-8759 2160
Rev Paschal Ryan.
M: *Sat 1st M of Sun 6pm. Sun 8.30am, 10.30am. Hds 9.30am, 7.30pm.*

■ CRICKLEWOOD 

† St Agnes (1883; 1930)

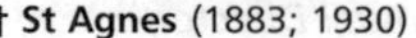

35 Cricklewood Lane, Cricklewood NW2 1HR **Tel:** 020-8452 2475
Rev Paul McDermott.
M: *Sat 1st M of Sun 6.30pm. Sun 9am, 10.30am, 12noon,6.30pm. Hds As announced.*

- ***Sisters of St Joseph of Peace,*** 157 Walm Lane, NW2 3AY **Tel:** 020-8450 8859
- ***Sisters of Mercy,*** 149 Walm Lane, NW2 3AU **Tel:** 020-8450 7472
- ***Dominican Sisters:*** St Rose's Convent, 160 Anson Road NW2 6BH **Tel:** 020-8830 7465

■ CROXLEY GREEN

† St Bede (1958; cons 1975)
185 Baldwins Lane, Croxley Green, Rickmansworth, Herts WD3 3LL
Tel: 01923-231969 **Fax:** 01923-211089
Canon Philip Cross.
M: *Sat 1st M of Sun 6pm. Sun 10am, 6pm.Hds 10am, 7.30pm.*

■ CUFFLEY

† St Martin de Porres
4 Church Close, Cuffley, Herts EN6 4LS.
Tel: 01707-873308
Rev Patrick Carroll.
M: *Sat 1st M of Sun 5.30pm. Sun 9am, 11am. Hds 9.30am, 8pm.*

■ CZECH CENTRE See Bayswater

■ DOLLIS HILL

† St Mary and St Andrew (1915; 1933)
216 Dollis Hill Lane, Dollis Hill, London NW2 6HE **Tel:** 020-8452 6158
Fax: 020-8450 3350
Rev Eugene Fitzpatrick.
M: *Sat 1st M of Sun 7pm. Sun 8.30am, 10.30am, 12noon. Hds 9.30am, 7.30pm.*

- ***Sisters of St Louis,*** 119 Dollis Hill Lane, Dollis Hill, London NW2 6HS **Tel:** 020-8208 0696

■ EALING

1. † Abbey Church of St Benedict (1897; 1899)
Ealing Abbey, Charlbury Grove, Ealing, London W5 2DY **Tel:** 0208-862 2160 (*Parish*)
Fax: 020-8862 2166 (*Parish*)
Fax: 0208-862 2206 (*Monastery*).
E-mail: ealingmonk@ealingabbey.co.uk
Web: www.ealingabbey.org.uk

- ***Benedictines (OSB);*** **Father Peter Burns** (*Parish Priest*), **Abbot Francis Rossiter** (*Prior*), **Fr Timothy Gorham** (Sub *Prior*), **Robin Burgess** *(Diocesan Priest)*, **Gordon Nunn** *(permanent deacon)*,**Rt Rev Martin Shipperlee** (*Abbot*), **Gregory Chillman, Stanislaus Hobbs, Dunstan Watkins, Vincent Cooper, Andrew Hughes, Thomas Stapleford, Alban Nunn, Alexander Bevan, Dominic Taylor, Matthew Freeman**.
M: *Sat 1st M of Sun 6pm. Sun 8am, 9am, 10.15am (Family M in Parish Centre), 10.30am (Sung), 12noon, 7pm. Hds 7am, 9.15am, 6pm, 8pm.*
- ***Benedictine Study and Arts Centre,*** 74 Castlebar Road, London W5 2DD **Tel:** 020-8862 2156 **Fax:** 020-8862 2206
- ***Capitanio Sisters,*** Nile Lodge, Queen's Walk, W5 1TJ **Tel:** 020-8997 3933
- ***Little Company of Mary,*** 12 Blakesley Avenue, Ealing W5 2DW **Tel:** 020-8997 1833
- ***Dominican Sisters,*** 7-8 Montpelier Avenue, W5 2XP **Tel:** 020-8997 8850
- ***Medical Missionaries of Mary,*** 2 Denbigh Road, W13 8PX **Tel:** 020-8998 1725
- ***Sisters of Charity (of St Jeanne Antide),*** 6 Woodfield Road, W5 1SJ **Tel:** 020-8 998 9549
- ***Brothers of St Gabriel,*** 11 Longfield Road, W5 **Tel:** 020-8998 9182
- ***Sisters of the Holy Cross,*** 82 The Avenue, W13 **Tel:** 020-8997 2858
- ***Missionaries of Africa (White Fathers) (MAfr),*** 15 Corfton Road, W5 2HP House for elderly and visitors
Tel: 020-8998 2920
Tel: 020-8998 2920 (*Superior*)
E-mail: wfcorfton@ntlworld.com
Fr Chris Wallbank (*Superior*), **Fr Patrick Fitzgerald, Br Joseph Mullen, Br Patrick O'Reilly.**
- ***Missionary Sisters of Our Lady of Africa (White Sisters),*** 5 Charlbury Grove, Ealing, W5 2D **Tel:** 020-8998 5017
- ***Sisters of the Resurrection,*** 18 Carlton Road, W5 2AW **Tel:** 020-8810 6241 Also: **Sr Joanna Maria Szponka,** 84 Gordon Road W5 2AR **Tel:** 020-8998 8954

2. † Our Lady Mother of the Church (1986)
Windsor Road. See Polish Church.

■ EARLS COURT. See Kensington

■ EASTCOTE

† St Thomas More
(1935; 1977; cons Feb 6, 1978)
32 Field End Road, Eastcote, Pinner, Middx HA5 2QT
Tel: 020-8866 6581 **Fax:** 020-8429 2346
M: *Sat 1st M of Sun 6.30pm. Sun 9.30am, 11.30am. Hds 9.30am, 7.30pm.*

■ EDGWARE

† St Anthony of Padua
(1913; 1931; 1958)
5 Garratt Road, Edgware, Middx HA8 9AN
Tel: 020-8952 0663

Rev Patrick Sammon.
M: *Sat 1st M of Sun 6.30pm. Sun 10am, 12noon, 6.30pm. Hds 10am, 12pm, 8pm.*

- ***Daughters of Mary, Mother of Mercy,*** 16 St Margaret's Road, Edgware, Middlesex, HA8 9UP **Tel:** 020-8958 8316
- ***Dominican Sisters,*** 267 Hale Lane, Edgware, Middlesex HA8 8NW **Tel:** 020-8958 5622

■ EDMONTON

† The Most Precious Blood and St Edmund, KM (1903; cons May 17, 1907)
115 Hertford Road, Edmonton, N9 7EN
Tel: 020-8803 6631 **Fax:** 020-8345 6495
Rev Sean Carroll.
M: *Sat 1st M of Sun 7pm. Sun 8am, 9.15am, 10.30am, 12noon, 6.30pm. Hds 9.15am, 12noon, 7.30pm.*

■ ELSTREE See Borehamwood

■ ELY PLACE

† St Etheldreda
(1252-1290; 1297; crypt re-opened 1876; ch. re-opened 1879)
Tel: 020-7405 1061 **Fax:** 020-7405 7440

- ***Institute of Charity (IC):*** **Fr Tom Deidun, Fr Denis Labartette.**
  M: *Sun 9am, 11am* (*Sung Lat*). *Hds 8am, 12.10pm, 1pm, 6pm* (*Sung Latin*).
- ***Rosminian Sisters,*** 13 Ely Place, Holborn Circus, EC1N 6RY **Tel:** 020-7405 1588

■ ENFIELD

A S

† Our Lady of Mount Carmel and St George (1862; 1958; cons 16 July 1967)
Revv Richard Andrew, Jim Byrne. 45 London Road, Enfield, EN2 6DS
Tel: 020-8363 2569 **Fax:** 020-8342 0159
M: *Sat 1st M of Sun 7pm. Sun 8am, 9.15am* (*Sung*), *10.30am* (*Sung*), *12noon, 6.30pm. Hds 12.30pm, 8pm.*

- ***Sisters of the Holy Family of Nazareth,*** 52 London Road, Enfield, Middx EN2 6EN **Tel:** 020-8363 4483

† Chapel of Ease: Our Lady of Walsingham and The English Martyrs
Holtwhites Hill.
M: *Sun 9am* (*Sung*), *10.30am* (*Sung*). *Hds* (vigil *7.30pm*), *10am.*

■ EUSTON NW1

See Somers Town

■ FARM STREET

A

† The Immaculate Conception (1849)
Berkeley Square.

- ***Jesuits (SJ):*** *Parish Staff:* **Revv William Pearsall** (*Parish Priest*), **Anthony Meredith.** Also in residence: **Revv Hugh Duffy** (*Superior*), **John Edwards, Vincent Hawe, Francis Laishley, William MacCurtain, Thomas McCoog, Paul O'Reilly, Joseph Raybould, David Stewart, Anthony Horan, Br William Jordan.** 114 Mount Street, W1K 3AH **Tel:** 020-7493 7811 **Fax:** 020-7495 6685
  M: *Sat 1st M of Sun 6pm. Sun 8am, 9.30am, 11am* (*Sung Latin*), *12.30pm, 4.15pm, 6.15pm. Hds* (vigil *6pm*), *8am, 1.05pm, 6.pm.*
- ***Jesuit Provincial Offices,*** 114 Mount Street, London W1K 3AH **Tel:** 020-7499 0285. **Fax:** 020-7408 7111 **Rev Michael Holman** (*Provincial*), **Rev Paul Hamill, Br Stephen Power.**

■ FELTHAM

† St Lawrence (1910; 1934)
St Lawrence's Presbytery, The Green, Feltham, Middx TW13 4AF
Tel: 020-8890 2367
Fr Gerard Burke, Rev Emmanuel Ogunnaike MSP.
M: *Sat 1st M of Sun 6pm. Sun 9am* (*Sung*), *11am, 6pm. Hds 9.30am, 12.15pm, 8pm.*

- ***Sisters of Mercy,*** 35 Ruscombe Way, Feltham, Middlesex TW14 9NY **Tel:** 020-8751 0862

■ FINCHLEY (CHURCH END)

† St Philip the Apostle
(1918; 1933; cons May 1975)
Regent's Park Road.
Rev John P Dermody. Also in residence: **Rev Gerard Balinnya, Rev Krzysztof Kawczynski.** The Priest's House, Gravel Hill, Finchley N3 3RJ **Tel:** 020-8346 2459 **Fax:** 020-8349 1392
M: *Sat 1st M of Sun 6.30pm. Sun 8.30am, 10am (Sung), 12noon (Family), 6.30pm (Polish) . Hds 12noon, 7.30pm.*

- ***Consolata Fathers (IMC),*** 3 Salisbury Avenue, N3 3AJ **Tel:** 020-8346 5498 **Revv Luis Tomas, Giuseppe Giovanetti.**
- ***Xaverian Missionaries, (SX),*** House of Studies: 260 Nether Street, London N3 1HT **Tel:** 020-8346 0428 **Revv Ennio Casalucci, Yulius Bandaso, Kevin Ryan** *(Superior)*, **Sahr Ndomaina.**

■ FINCHLEY (EAST)

† St Mary (1898; 1953)
279 High Road, Finchley, N2 8HG
Tel: 020-8883 4234 **Fax:** 020-8365 3738
Rev Anthony Pellegrini.
Parish Sister: **Sr Avis.**
M: *Sat 1st M of Sun 6.30pm. Sun 8.30am, 10am, 12 noon (Sung in Latin). Hds 10am, 8pm.*

- ***Carmelite Friars (OCarm),*** 63 East End Road, East Finchley, London N2 0SE **Tel:** 020-8346 1458 **Fax:** 020-8349 8828

Website: www.carmelite.org
Revv James Moran (*Prior*), **Richard Copsey** (*Provincial Bursar*), **Robert Puthussery** (*Sub-Prior*), **Sean Ford, Michael Cox.**

- ***Good Shepherd Sisters,*** 61 East End Road, East Finchley, N2 0SE **Tel:** 020-8346 8100
- ***Poor Sisters of Nazareth,*** Nazareth House, 162 East End Road, N2 0RU **Tel:** 020-8883 1104 **Fax:** 020-8444 3691 *Chaplain:* **Rev Austin Hart**.
- ***Daughters of Wisdom (La Sagesse),*** 1 King Street, East Finchley, N2 8EA **Tel:** 020-8 365 2924

■ **FINCHLEY (NORTH)**
† St Alban (1903; new church 1909)
51 Nether Street, Finchley, N12 7NN
Tel: 020-8446 0224 **Fax:** 020-8343 7400
Rev Bernard McCumiskey.
M: *Sat 1st M of Sun 6pm. Sun 9am, 10.15am, 12noon, 6pm. Hds* (vigil *6pm*), *10am, 6pm.*

- ***Belarusian Catholic Mission,*** Marian House, Holden Avenue, N12 8HY **Tel:** 020-8445 5358 **Mitred Archpriest Alexander Nadson** (*Rector*). Services (*Byzantine-Slavonic Rite*). **M:** *Sun 10.30am.*
- ***Sisters of the Poor Child Jesus,*** 56 King's Lodge, Kingsway N12 0EW **Tel:** 020-8446 6230

■ **FRENCH CHURCH**
† Notre Dame de France (1865; 1868; 1955)
5 Leicester Place, Leicester Square WC2H 7BX
Tel: 020-7437 9363 **Fax:** 020-7440 2645

- ***Marist Fathers (SM):*** **Revv Martin McAnaney, Paul Walsh** (*Rector*), **Jean-Marie Bloqueau, Christian Andraud, Edmund Duffy.**
M: *Sat 1st M of Sun 6pm. Sun 10am, 11.30am.* (*All in French*). *Hds 12.15pm* (*English*), *6pm* (*English*), *7.30pm* (*French*).

■ **FULHAM**
1. † St Thomas of Canterbury (1847; 1969)
60 Rylston Road, Fulham, SW6 7HW
Tel: 020-7385 4040 **Fax:** 020-7610 2506
Rev Canon Paul McGinn, Revv Anthony O'Gorman, Pedro Luís Pereira Rodrigues (*Chaplain to Portugese Community*)
M: *Sat 1st M of Sun 6.30pm. Sun 9am, 10.30am* (*Children*), *12noon, 3pm* (*Portugese*), *6pm. Hds* (vigil *6.30pm*) *9.30am, 8pm.*

2. † Our Lady (of Perpetual Help) (1922)
2 Tynemouth Street, Fulham, SW6 2QT
See Stephendale Road Parish.

3. † Holy Cross
(1843-48; 1884; 1924; cons Oct 11, 1928)
Ashington Road, Parson's Green.
See Parson's Green Parish

■ **FULHAM ROAD**
† Our Lady of Dolours
(1864; 1875; cons Nov 4, 1953)
St Mary's Priory, 264 Fulham Road, Kensington, SW10 9EL
Tel: 020-7352 6965 **Fax:** 020-7351 9749

- ***Servites (OSM):*** **Revv Patrick Ryall** (*Prior/Provincial*), **Dermot MacNeice** (*Parish Priest*), **Thomas Robinson, James Mulherin, Philip Allen, Gnana Pragasam.**
M: *Sat 1st M of Sun 6.30pm. Sun 8.30am, 10am* (*Sung*), *11.15am* (*Span*), *12.15pm, 7pm. Hds* (vigil *6.30pm*), *10am, 7pm.*
- ***Sisters Hospitallers of the Sacred Heart (Spanish),*** 46 Roland Gardens, SW7 3PW **Tel:** 020-7373 5820; *Provincialate* **Tel:** 020-7373 3054
- ***Sisters of the Cross and Passion,*** 7 Stadium Street, London SW10 0PU **Tel:** 020-7352 6013

■ **FURNEUX PELHAM**
See Buntingford

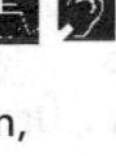

■ **GARSTON**
† Our Lady and St Michael (1954)
Catholic Church, Crown Rise, Garston, Watford, Herts WD2 6NE
Tel: 01923-673239 **Fax:** 01923-677869
Rev William Klowl IMC.
M: *Sat 1st M of Sun 6pm. Sun 8.30am, 10am, 12noon. Hds* (vigil *7.30pm*), *9.30am, 7.30pm.*

■ **GERMAN CHURCH**
† St Boniface
(1809; 1875; cons Oct 4, 1925; 1960)
47 Adler Street, E1 1EE **Tel:** 020-7247 9529
Rev Heinz Medoch. Also in residence: **Rev Victor Camilleri OFM**.
M: *Sun 11am* (*2nd, 4th, 5th Sun*).

■ **GOLDERS GREEN**
† St Edward the Confessor
(1909; 1915; cons Sept 30, 1931)
700 Finchley Road, Golders Green, NW11 7NE **Tel/Fax:** 020-8455 1300
Rev John Helm.
Parish Deacon: **Rev Anthony Clark**
M: *Sat 1st M of Sun 6.30pm. Sun 9am, 10.30am, 12.15pm, 6pm. Hds* (vigil *7.30pm, Thurs 7pm*), *12noon, 7.30pm* (*Thurs 7pm*).

- ***National Office for Vocation:*** The Chase Centre, 114 West Heath Road NW3 7TX **Tel:** 020-8458 6017 **Email:** enquires@ukvocation.org

ARCHDIOCESE OF WESTMINSTER

■ GRAHAME PARK

† St Margaret Clitherow (1970; 1973)
The Presbytery, Everglade Strand, Grahame Park, London NW9 5PX **Tel:** 020-8205 6830.
Rev John Hai Pham.
M: *Sat 1st M of Sun 6.30pm. Sun 9am, 12noon. Hds 9.15am, 11am (term-time), 7pm.*

■ GREENFORD

A S

† Our Lady of the Visitation (1928; 1937)
358 Greenford Road, Greenford, Middx UB6 9AN. **Tel:** 020-8578 1363
Fax: 020-8813 2230

- ***Pallottine Fathers (SCA):*** **Revv Thomas Daly, Kevin Ward, William Hanly, Seamus Stapleton**
  M: *Sat 1st M of Sun 7pm. Sun 8am, 9am, 10.30am, 12noon, 7pm. Hds 8.30am, 12noon, 7.30pm.*

■ GROVE PARK

† St Joseph (1964, cons 23 Feb 1973)
1 Bolton Road, Grove Park, W4 3TE
Tel: 020-8994 6861
Rev John Seabrook.
M: *Sat 1st M of Sun 6.30pm. Sun 9am, 11am. Hds* (vigil *7.30pm*), *10am, 7.30pm.*

■ GUNNERSBURY

† St Dunstan (1931)
141 Gunnersbury Avenue, Gunnersbury W3 8LE **Tel:** 020-8992 5037
In pastoral care of Chiswick. Also in residence: **Revv Richard Price, Mgr George Tütto**.
M: *Sun 10am.*

- **Westpark,** 1 Leopold Road, W5 3PB. Pastoral care entrusted to the Prelature of Opus Dei. **Tel:** 020-8992 3954.
- ***Woodlands,*** 12 Gunnersbury Avenue, W5 3NJ Pastoral care entrusted to the Prelature of Opus Dei. **Tel:** 020-8992 4025
- ***Little Company of Mary,*** 93 Gunnersby Avenue W5 4LR **Tel:** 020-8752 1373

■ HACKNEY

† St John the Baptist
(1847; 1956; cons June 14, 1972)
3 King Edward's Road, Hackney E9 7SF
Tel: 020-8985 2496 **Rev David Evans**.
M: *Sat 1st M of Sun 6pm. Sun 9.30am, 11.30am. Hds 9.30am, 7.30pm.*

- ***Religious Sisters of Charity,*** St Joseph's Hospice, Mare Street, E8 4SA
  Tel: 020-8525 6000
  Chaplain: **Rev Brian Griffiths** (OSCam)
  Tel: 020 3076 1313
- ***Sisters of Charity of St Paul,*** 28 Warneford Street, Hackney, E9 7NG
  Tel: 020-8 986 2346;
  also at 4 Queensgate Villas E9 7BU
  Tel: 020-8986 2386

■ HAMMERSMITH

† St Augustine's Priory
(1903; 1916; cons June 20, 1933)
55 Fulham Palace Road, Hammersmith, W6 8AU
Tel: 020-8748 3788 **Fax:** 020-8846 9574

- ***Augustinians (OSA):*** **Revv Barry Clifford, John Murphy** (*Sub-Prior*), **George Stibbles, Gianni Notarianni, Richard Piatt.**
  M: *Sat 1st M of Sun 6pm. Sun 9am, 11am, 12.15pm, 6.30pm. Hds 8am, 10am, 12.15pm, 6.30pm.*

■ HAMPSTEAD

† St Mary (1796; 1816; cons 1977)
4 Holly Place, Church Row, Hampstead, NW3 6QU **Tel:** 020-7435 6678
Mgr Phelim Rowland
M: *Sat 1st M of Sun 6.30pm. Sun 8.30am, 10am, 11.30am, 6.30pm. Hds 10am, 6.30pm.*

- ***Columban Missionaries (SSC),*** St Columban's, 28 Redington Road, Hampstead, London NW3 7RB
  Tel: 020-7794 8131
  Fax: 020-7794 7074
  Revv Peter Hughes, Thomas O'Reilly, Frank Nally *(Superior)*, **Eamonn O'Brien, Parig Digan, Thomas Ryan, Aodh O'Halpin**.
- ***Institute of St Marcellina,*** Hampstead Towers, 6 Ellerdale Road, NW3 6BD
  Tel: 020-7435 0181
- ***Sisters of St Dorothy,*** 99 Frognal, NW3 6XR **Tel:** 020-7794 6893

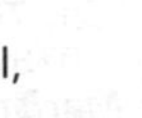
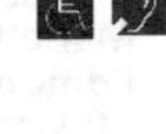

■ HAMPTON HILL AND UPPER TEDDINGTON

† St Francis De Sales
(1920; 1928; 1966, cons 18 Dec 1976)

- ***Fransalians (MSFS):*** **Revv Huebert Miranda, Martin Griffin, Andrezej Marzewski,** 16 Wellington Road, Hampton Hill, Middx TW12 1JR
  Tel: 020-8977 1415 **Fax:** 020-8943 9593
  M: *Sat 1st M of Sun 6pm. Sun 9am (Sung), 11am. Hds* (vigil *8pm*), *9.30am, 8pm.*

■ HAMPTON-ON-THAMES

† St Theodore of Canterbury
(1927; 1986; cons. March 22, 1987)
110 Station Road, Hampton-on-Thames, Middx TW12 2AS
Tel: 020-8979 3596 **Fax:** 020-8979 8854
Rev Bernard Boylan.
M: Sat 1st M of Sun 6.30pm. Sun 8.30am, 10.30am, 5pm. Hds 9.30am, 7.30pm.

- ***Servants of the Mother of God,*** 112 Station Road. **Tel:** 020-8255 4997

■ HANWELL

† Our Lady and St Joseph (1853; 1967)
52 Uxbridge Road, Hanwell W7 3SU
Tel: 020-8567 4056 **Fax:** 020-8810 0219
Canon Bernard Scholes, Rev Richard Nesbitt.

M: *Sat 1st M of Sun 6.30pm. Sun 8am, 10am (sung Family), 12noon, 6pm. Hds (vigil 6pm), 9.15am, 12.15pm, 7.30pm.*

- ***Sisters of St Joseph of Peace,*** St Mary's Convent, 50 Uxbridge Road, W7 3PP **Tel:** 020-8567 8635
- ***Medical Mission Sisters (SCMM),*** 8 Springfield Road W7 3JP **Tel:** 020-8566 0547

■ HAREFIELD

† St Paul Merle Avenue
Rev Cedric Stanley. 1 Dunster Close, Park Lane, Harefield, Middx UB9 6BS
Tel: 01895-822365

M: *Sat 1st M of Sun 6.30pm. Sun 9am, 11am. Hds 9.15am, 7pm.*

■ HARPENDEN

† Our Lady of Lourdes
(1905; 1929; cons May 28, 1936)
Rothamsted Avenue.
Mgr Canon Henry Turner.
Tel: 01582-712245 **Fax:** 01582-460601

M: *Sat 1st M of Sun 6pm. Sun 8.30am, 9.45am, 11.30am. Hds 9.15am, 8pm.*

- ***Dominican Sisters,*** Dominican Convent, 18 Kirkdale Road, Harpenden, Herts AL5 2PT **Tel:** 01582-712814

■ HARRINGAY

† St Augustine of Canterbury (1963)
49 Mattison Road, Harringay, N4 1BG
Tel: 020-8348 1378
Rev James Noctor.

M: *Sat 1st M of Sun 6.30pm. Sun 10.30am. Hds 10am.*

- ***Sisters of St Louis,*** 161 Wightman Road, N8 0BB **Tel:** 020-8341 5606

■ HARROW (NORTH)

† St John Fisher (1939)
Imperial Drive.
Rev Kevin Jordan. 80 Imperial Close, North Harrow, Middlesex HA2 7LW
Tel: 020-8868 7531

M: *Sat 1st M of Sun 6pm. Sun 8.30am, 10am (CW), 11.30am (sung). Hds 9am (School), 10am, 7.30pm.*

■ HARROW (SOUTH) & NORTHOLT

1. † St Gabriel (1933)
390b Northolt Road, South Harrow HA2 8EX **Tel:** 020-8864 5455
Rev Gerard Skinner

M: *Sat 1st M of Sun 6pm. Sun 8.30am, 10am, 12noon. Hds 10am.*

- ***Sisters of St Louis,*** 67 Parkfield Road, South Harrow, Middx HA2 8LA **Tel:** 020-8 248 3838

2. † St Bernard's Church (1965)
Mandeville Road, Northolt UB5 5HE
Served from No 1.

M: *Sun 9am, 11am. Hds 7.30pm*

■ HARROW-ON-THE-HILL

† Our Lady and St Thomas of Canterbury (1873; 1894)
22 Roxborough Park, Harrow-on-the-Hill, Middlesex HA1 3BE
Tel: 020-8422 2513 **Fax:** 020-8869 6896
Rev Guy Sawyer.

M: *Sat 1st M of Sun 6pm. Sun 8.30am, 10am, 11.15am, 6.30pm. Hds 9.30am, 8pm.*

- ***Sisters of St Louis,*** 85 Bessborough Road, Harrow HA1 3DB **Tel:** 020-8422 2158

■ HARROW ROAD

† Our Lady of Lourdes and St Vincent de Paul (1876; 1912; 1975)
Rev Francis Antwi-Darkwah
337 Harrow Road W9 3RB
Tel: 020-7286 2170 **Fax:** 020-7266 3506

M: *Sat 1st M of Sun 6.30pm. Sun 10am (Fam), 12noon (Sung), 6.30pm. Hds 10am, 7.30pm.*

■ HARROW WEALD See Wealdstone

■ HATFIELD

† Marychurch (1930, 1971)
26 Salisbury Square, Hatfield, Herts AL9 5JD **Tel:** 01707-262439
Rev Philip Knights.

M: *Sat 1st M of Sun 6pm. Sun 11am, 6pm.*

- ***Chapel of Ease,*** St Thomas More, Station Road, Welham Green. **M:** *Sun 9.30am. Hds eve, 7.30pm.*

■ HATFIELD SOUTH

† St Peter (1959; 1961)
St Peter's Presbytery, Bishop's Rise, Hatfield, Herts AL10 9HN
Tel: 01707-262121
Rev Mark Vickers.

M: *Sat 1st M of Sun 6pm. Sun 9.15am, 11am (CW). Hds 9.30am, 7.30pm.*

■ HAVERSTOCK HILL

† Our Lady of the Rosary and St Dominic (1867; 1874; cons Aug 1, 1923)
St Dominic's Priory, Southampton Road, NW5 4LB (at top of Malden Road, nearest tubes Chalk Farm and BelsizePark)
Tel: 020-7482 9210 **Fax:** 020-7482 9239

- ***Dominicans (OP):*** **Revv Anthony**

Rattigan (*Prior and Parish Priest*), **Tel:** 020-7482 9224; **John Farrell** (*Provincial*) **Tel/Fax:** 020-7485 2760; **Columba Ryan, Bede Bailey, Michael Dunn, Denis Geraghty, Peter Harries** (*Hospital Chaplain to University College London Hospitals)* **Tel:** 020-7482 9216; Dermot Morrin, **Rudolf Loewenstein, Timothy Gardner** (*Hospital Chaplain to Royal Free Hospital)* **Tel:** 020-7482 9217; **Dominic White, Alistair Jones.**
M: *Sat 1st M of Sun 6pm. Sun 8.30am, 10am, 12pm, 6pm. Hds* (vigil *6pm*). *7.30am, 9.30am, 7.15pm.*

- ***Dominican Sisters,*** 97 Constantine Road. NW3 2LP **Tel:** 020-7267 1579
- ***Sisters of Providence,*** Bartrams Hostel, Rowland Hill Street, Haverstock Hill, NW3 **Tel:** 020-7794 4504

■ HAYES

† The Immaculate Heart of Mary
(1912; 1954; 1961; cons Oct. 24, 1972)
Botwell House, Botwell Lane, Hayes, Middlesex UB3 2AB **Tel:** 020-8573 2065, **Fax:** 020-8561 6748
E-mail: Botwell@claret.org.uk

- ***Claretian Missionaries (CMF):*** **Revv Martin Stone, John O'Byrne, James D Fischer, Paul Smyth** (*Provincial*).
M: *Sat 1st M of Sun 6.30pm. Sun 8.30am, 10am* (*Sung*), *12noon* (*Sung*), *5pm. Hds* (vigil *7.30pm*), *12.15pm, 7.30pm.*
- ***Society of the Sacred Heart,*** St Mary's Convent, 208 Botwell Lane, Hayes, Middx UB3 2AJ **Tel:** 020-8573 8658

■ HEADSTONE LANE

† St Theresa of the Child Jesus (1953)
22 Boniface Walk, Harrow, Middx HA3 6PU **Tel:** 020-8428 3260
Rev Richard Parsons (*Administrator*).
M: *Sat 1st M of Sun 5pm. Sun 10am, 6pm. Hds 10am, 7.30pm.*

■ HEATHROW See London Airport

■ HEMEL HEMPSTEAD (BOXMOOR)

† SS Mary and Joseph (1890; 1938; 1951)
186 St John's Road, Boxmoor, Herts HP1 1NR **Tel:** 01442-391759
Rev John Byrne (also serves Hemel West/North)
Parish Sister: **Sr Teresa O'Donovan OP.**
M: *Sun 9am, 11.30am. Hds 10am, 7.30pm.*

- ***Dominican Sisters,*** St Mary's Convent, Green End Road, Boxmoor, Herts HP1 1QW **Tel:** 01442-255577

■ HEMEL HEMPSTEAD (EAST)

† Our Lady Queen of all Creation
(1955; 1987; cons Nov 13, 1987) St Albans Road. **Rev Raymond Legge.** The Presbytery, Rant Meadow, Hemel Hempstead, Herts HP3 8PG **Tel:** 01442-255471
M: *Sat 1st M of Sun 5.30pm. Sun 9.30am, 11am. Hds* (vigil *7.30pm*), *9.30am, 7.30pm.*

■ HEMEL HEMPSTEAD (NORTH)

† Highfield and Grovehill (1971)
299 St Agnell's Lane, Grovehill, Hemel Hempstead HP2 6EQ **Tel:** 01442-259141
Rev John Byrne

1. Grove Hill: Church of the Resurrection
(Shared Church: June 1977)
Henry Wells Square.
M: *Sat 1st M of Sun 5pm. Sun 9.30am. Hds 7.30pm.*

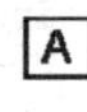

2. Highfield: St Paul
(Shared Church: 1971)
Solway.
M: *Sun 11.30am. Hds 11am.*

■ HEMEL HEMPSTEAD (WEST)

St Mark (1977)
Gadebridge and Warners End.
186 St John's Road, Boxmoor, Herts HP1 1NR. **Tel:** 01442-391759
Rev John Byrne
Deacon: **Rev Simon Wright**
M: *Sat 1st M of Sun 5.30pm. Sun 10.15am.*

■ HENDON

† Our Lady of Dolours
(1849; 1863; reconst 1927; cons March 25, 1966)
4/6 Egerton Gardens, Hendon, NW4 4BA
Tel: 020-8202 0560 **Fax:** 020-8201 5707
Rev Dominic Byrne.
M: *Sat 1st M of Sun 6pm. Sun 10am, 12noon, Hds As announced.*

- ***Poor Handmaids of Jesus Christ,*** St Joseph's Convent, Watford Way, NW4 4TY. **Tel:** 020-8202 7626.

■ HENDON (WEST)

St Patrick (1964)
Hendon Broadway.
Rev John White. St Patrick's, 167 The Broadway, West Hendon, NW9 7EB
Tel: 020-8202 5143 **Fax:** 020-8203 7895
M: *Sat 1st M of Sun 7pm. Sun 9.30am, 12noon, 6.30pm. Hds 10am, 8pm.*

■ HERTFORD

† The Immaculate Conception and St Joseph
(Priory 1087-1539; 1848; 1858; cons Oct. 1866)
23 St John's Street, Hertford, Herts SG14 1RX **Tel:** 01992-582109
Rev Gladstone Liddle, Dcn Timothy Marsh
M: *Sat 1st M of Sun 6pm. Sun 8.30am, 10.30am* (*Sung, CW*), *6pm. Hds 7.30am, 10am* (*in school during term*), *8pm.*

■ **HESTON**

† **Our Lady Queen of Apostles**
(1928; 1929; 1964; cons May 19, 1974)
15 The Green, Heston Road, Heston, Middlesex TW5 0RL
Tel: 020-8570 1818 **Fax:** 020-8572 7861
Rev Simon Nguyen Duc Tang, Dcn James Richards, Benedict Vuong Thuat OP, Paul Rout OFM, Peter Hung Phuoc Lam OP.
M: *Sat 1st M of Sun 7pm. Sun 8am, 9.30am, 11.30am, 5.30pm. Hds (vigil 7pm), 10am, 7pm.*

■ **HIGHBURY**

† **St Joan of Arc** (1920; 1962, cons 2001)
60 Highbury Park, Highbury N5 2XH
Tel: 020-7226 0257
Rev Gerard King. Also in residence: **Rev Voytek Przyjalkowski**.
M: *Sat 1st M of Sun 6.30pm. Sun 9am, 11am, 2.30pm (Congolese Community Mass). Hds 7.15am, 9.15am, 7.30pm.*
- ***Sisters of St Paul of Chartres,*** 30 Aberdeen Park, N5 2BL **Tel:** 020-7359 1712
- ***Sisters of Mercy,*** 40 Aberdeen Road N5 2XD **Tel:** 020-7359 3897

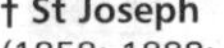

■ **HIGHGATE**

† **St Joseph**
(1858; 1888; cons April 28, 1932)
St Joseph's Retreat, Highgate Hill, N19 5NE
Tel: 020-7272 2320 **Fax:** 020-7281 9433
- ***Passionists (CP):*** *Parish Team:* **Revv Mark White, Daniel Donovan, Christopher Kelly, Charles Owen**. *Community:* **Revv Theodore Davey, Aidan Baker, Timothy Cullen, Malachy Steenson, Conleth O'Hara, Joseph Ward, Francis Welsh, Bernard Connolly, Peter Aspin.**
M: *Sat 1st M of Sun 7pm. Sun 8am, 10am, 12noon (Folk), 5pm, 1.30pm (Polish), 5pm. Hds (vigil 6.30pm), 9.30am, 11am, 12noon (Pol), 6.30pm.*
- ***Missionaries of Africa (White Fathers) (MAfr),*** 42 Stormont Road, Highgate, London N6 4NP **Tel:** 020-8342 8447 **Fax:** 020-8347 8147 **Revv Paul Walsh** (*Sector Superior*), **David Goergan** (*Secretary*) **Tel:** 020-8348 7799 **E-mail:** mafrgb@blueyonder.co.uk **Rev Jack Thora** (*Treasurer*), **Tel:** 020-8340 5036 **E-mail:** mafrukpt@blueyonder.co.uk
- ***Augustinian Sisters of Meaux,*** 'Bethanie' Convent, 54 Highgate Hill, N19 5NQ **Tel:** 020-7272 3696

■ **HILLINGDON**

† **St Bernadette**
(1937; 1961; cons Oct 7, 1978)
160 Long Lane, Hillingdon, Middlesex UB10 0EH **Tel:** 01895-234577
Fax: 01895-274154
Rev James Garvey
M: *Sat 1st M of Sun 6pm. Sun 9am, 11am, 6pm. Hds 9.30am, 7.30pm.*
- ***Sisters of Mercy,*** St Raphael's Convent, Court Drive, Hillingdon UB10 0BW **Tel:** 01895-233771

■ **HITCHIN**

† **Our Lady Immaculate and St Andrew**
(1890; 1902; cons 1977)
Our Lady Immaculate and St Andrew, 16 Nightingale Road SG5 1QS
Tel: 01462-459126 **Fax:** 01462-432043
- ***Assumptionists (AA);*** **Revv Michael Lambert** (*Superior and Parish Priest*) **Tel:** 01462-457673; **Christopher Burgess, Robert Henshaw** (*Superior & Parish Priest*).
M: *Sat 1st M of Sun 6pm. Sun 8.30am, 10.30am (Sung), 5pm. Hds 7.30am, 10am (term-time), 7.30pm.*

■ **HODDESDON**

† **St Augustine** (1932; 1962)
Presbytery, Esdaile Lane, Hoddesdon, Herts EN11 8DS **Tel:** 01992-440986
Administrator: **Rev Philip Miller.** Also in residence. **John Panakkaran CMI**
M: *Sat 1st M of Sun 6.30pm. Sun 9.15am (CW), 11.15am (CW), 4pm (Ital), 1st Sun only 5.30pm (Latin). Hds 9.30am, 12noon, 8pm.*

■ **HOLBORN (CIRCUS), EC1** See Ely Place

■ **HOLBORN (HIGH),** WC1
See Lincoln's Inn Fields

■ **HOLLOWAY**

† **Sacred Heart of Jesus**
(1855; cons May 29, 1928)
62 Eden Grove, Holloway, N7 8EN
Tel: 020-7607 3594
Rev Gideon Wagay.
M: *Sat 1st M of Sun 6pm. Sun 8.30am, 10.15am (Sung), 12noon (Folk). Hds 9.15am, 7.30pm.*
- ***Sisters of La Sainte Union,*** 51 Freegrove Road, N7 9RG **Tel:** 020-7609 7160

■ **HOLLOWAY (UPPER),** N19
See Upper Holloway

■ **HOMERTON**

† **Immaculate Heart of Mary and St Dominic**
(1873; cons June 30, 1884)
Kenworthy Road.
Rev Tony Doyle, Presbytery, Ballance Road, Homerton, E9 5SR **Tel:** 020-8985 1495
M: *Sat 1st M of Sun 6.30pm. Sun 9am, 11am. Hds 9.30am, 7.30pm.*

■ **HORNSEY,** N8
See Stroud Green

■ **HOUNSLOW**
† **SS Michael and Martin**
(1884; 1929; cons Oct 12, 1938)
94 Bath Road, Hounslow, Middx. TW3 3EH
Tel: 020-8570 1693. **Fax:** 020-8570 8059
Revv Anthony Convery, Anthony Psaila.
M: *Sat 1st M of Sun 6.15pm. Sun 9am, 10.30am, 12noon, 6pm. Hds* (vigil *8pm*), *9am, 12noon, 6pm.*

■ **HOXTON**
† **St Monica's Priory** (1863; 1864)
19 Hoxton Square, Hoxton N1 6NT
Tel: 020-7739 5006 **Fax:** 020-7613 0394
- ***Augustinians (OSA):*** **Revv Paul Graham** (*Parish Priest*), **Mark Minihane**. *Parish Sisters:* **Srs Assumpta, Kathleen**. **M:** *Sat 1st M of Sun 6.30pm. Sun 9am, 11am, 7pm. Hds* (vigil *7pm*) *10.30am, 12noon.*
- ***Ashwell House,*** Shepherdess Walk, N1 7NA. Hall of Residence for Women University Students. Pastoral care entrusted to the Prelature of Opus Dei. **Tel:** 020-7490 5021.
- ***Little Sisters of Jesus,*** 148 Fellows Court, Weymouth Terrace, E2 8LW **Tel:** 020-7729 3605
- ***Ursulines of Jesus,*** 150 Kingsland Road, E2 8EB **Tel:** 020-7739 8036

■ **HUNGARIAN CHAPLAINCY**
See Gunnersbury

■ **ISLE OF DOGS**
See Millwall

■ **ISLEWORTH**
† **Our Lady of Sorrows and St Bridget**
(1675; 1910; cons Oct. 6, 1910)
112 Twickenham Road, Isleworth, Middlesex TW7 6DL.
Tel: 020-8560 1431 **Fax:** 020-8568 7371
Rev Stewart Hasker (*Administrator*).
M: *Sat 1st M of Sun 6pm. Sun 8am, 10am, 12noon. Hds* (vigil *7pm*), *9am, 7pm.*
- ***Faithful Companions of Jesus,*** Gumley House Convent, Twickenham Road, Isleworth TW7 6DN **Tel:** 020-8560 1428

■ **ISLINGTON**
† **St John the Evangelist**
(1839; 1843; cons. June 26, 1873)
39 Duncan Terrace, Islington, N1 8AL
Tel: 020-7226 3277 **Fax:** 020-8568 7371
Rev Shaun Lennard. Also in residence: **Rev Raphael Zernoff OSA**.
M: *Sat 1st M of Sun 6pm. Sun 9am, 10.30am* (*Fam*), *12noon, 6pm. Hds 7.30am. 10am, 12.30pm, 7.30pm.*
- ***Sisters of the Cross and Passion,*** 40 Duncan Terrace, N1 8AL **Tel:** 020-7359 8719

■ **ITALIAN CHURCH**
† **St Peter** (1863)
(Personal Parish for Italians)
136 Clerkenwell Road, EC1R 5EN
Tel: 020-7837 1528 **Fax:** 020-7837 9071
E-mail: chiesaitaliana@aol.com
Website: chiesaitaliana.org.uk
- ***Pallottine Fathers (SAC):*** **Rev Carmelo Di Giovanni, Ryszard Wrobel**. **M:** *Sat 1st M of Sun 7pm. Sun 9.30am, 11am, 12.30pm, 7pm. Hds 10am, 12.15pm, 8pm.*

■ **KENSAL NEW TOWN**
† **Our Lady of the Holy Souls** (1862; 1882)
Bosworth Road, Kensal Town.
Rev Shaun Church, 68 Hazlewood Crescent, Kensal Road, W10 5DJ
Tel: 020-8969 2660 *Parish Sister:* **Sr Margarita Cunningham RSM**.
M: *Sat 1st M of Sun 6pm. Sun 9am, 11am. Hds 9.30am, 7.30pm,*
- ***Missionaries of Charity,*** 177 Bravington Road, W9 3AR **Tel:** 020-8960 2644
- ***Sisters of Mercy,*** 76 Fifth Avenue, W10 4DP **Tel:** 020-8960 2505

■ **KENSAL RISE**

† **Church of the Transfiguration** (1977)
1 Wrentham Avenue NW10 3HT
Tel: 020-8964 4040.
Rev Sean Thornton.
M: *Sat 1st M of Sun 6pm. Sun 9am, 11am, 12.30pm* (*Italian*), *5pm. Hds 10am, 7.30pm.*
- ***Stigmatine Fathers (CSS),*** **Rev Natalino Mignolli**, 2 Leigh Gardens NW10 5HP **Tel:** 020 8969 1414
- ***Religious of Jesus and Mary,*** 200 Chamberlayne Road NW10 3JX **Tel:** 020-8451 1957
- ***Daughters of Charity (SVP),*** 58 Wrentham Avenue NW10 3HG **Tel:** 020-8964 9796

■ **KENSINGTON**
1. † **Our Lady of Victories**
(1794; 1812; 1869; 1958)
235a Kensington High Street.
Tel: 020-7937 4778
Mgr Jim Curry, Revv Frederick Jackson, Hector Rouco Gutierrez.
Also in residence: **Rt Rev Alan Hopes,** 16 Abingdon Road, Kensington, W8 6AF
Tel: 020-7798 9023 **Fax:** 020-7937 4221
M: *Sat 1st M of Sun 6.30pm. Sun 8.30am, 10am* (*Fam*), *11.30am* (*Sung Lat*), *12.45pm, 6.30pm. Hds 10am, 12.30pm, 7.30pm.*

- ***Augustinian Recollects (OAR),*** 18 Cheniston Gardens, W8 6TQ **Revv Patrick O'Hagan** (*Prior*), **Roberto Riezu, Jesus Frances** **Tel/Fax:** 020-7937 7681
- ***Daughters of St Paul,*** Pauline Books and Media, 199 Kensington High Street, W8 6BS **Tel:** 020-7937 9591
- ***Society of the Holy Child Jesus,*** 10 Holland Villas Road, Kensington W14 8BU **Tel:** 020-7603 7450

2. † Our Lady of Mount Carmel and St Simon Stock (1862; 1959)
41 Kensington Church Street, Kensington W8 4BB **Tel:** 020-7937 9866
Fax: 020-7938 1470

- ***Discalced Carmelites (OCD),*** **Rev Matthew Blake** (*Prior and Parish Priest*), **Revv Fabian McCormick, Michael McGoldrick, Iain Matthew.** **M:** *Sat 1st M of Sun 6pm. Sun 8.30am, 10am* (*Family*), *11am* (*Sung Lat*), *12.15pm, 6pm* (*Folk*). *Hds* (vigil *6pm*), *8am, 12.15pm, 6pm.*
- ***Religious of the Assumption,*** Maria Assumpta Pastoral and Education Centre, 23 Kensington Square W8 5HN **Tel:** 020-7361 4700
- ***Adoratrices, Handmaids of the Blessed Sacrament and of Charity,*** 38 Kensington Square, London W8 5HP **Tel:** 020-7937 5237
- ***Religious of Mary Immaculate,*** 41 Kensington Church Street, W8 4BB Hostel and Club for working girls and students of all nationalities. Social Centre for Spanish **Tel:** 020-7373 3869
- ***Heythrop College (University of London)*** Kensington Square, London W8 5HQ **Tel:** 020-7795 6600 **Fax:** 020-7795 4200 *Principal:* **Rev John McDade(SJ).**

■ KENSINGTON (NORTH)
See Kensal New Town, Notting Hill, St Charles' Square

■ KENSINGTON (SOUTH)
See Fulham Road and Oratory

■ KENTISH TOWN
† Our Lady Help of Christians
(1859; cons June 2, 1925)
4 Lady Margaret Road, Kentish Town NW5 2XT
Tel: 020-7485 4023 **Fax:** 020-7267 3118
Rev Tom Forde. Also in residence:
Rev Eddie Woo MAfr
M: *Sat 1st M of Sun 7pm. Sun 8.30am, 10am* (*Sung*), *12noon* (*Family*), *1.15pm* (*Spanish*), *6.30pm* (*Folk*). *Hds 10am, 7pm.*

- ***The Irish Centre,*** St Oliver Plunket House, 52 Camden Square, NW1 9XB **Tel:** 020-7916 2222
- ***Sisters of La Sainte Union,*** Croft Lodge, Highgate Road, NW5 1RP **Tel:** 020-7485 6169
- ***Daughters of Charity (SVP) (Spanish Province),*** 95 Huddleston Road, N7 0AE *Social Service for Spanish Immigrants* **Tel:** 020-7607 3974
- ***Congregation of Jesus (CJ),*** Mary Ward House, 39 St George's Avenue N7 0HB **Tel:** 020-7700 3256

■ KENTON
† All Saints (1932; 1963)
The Presbytery, 2a Salehurst Close, Harrow, Middlesex HA3 0UG **Tel:** 020-8204 3550
Rev Dermot O'Neill.
M: *Sat 1st M of Sun 6.30pm. Sun 8.30am, 10am, 11.30am. Hds As announced.*

■ KILBURN

† Sacred Heart of Jesus
(1864; 1879; cons June 18, 1909)
New Priory, Quex Road, Kilburn, NW6 4PS
Tel: 020-7624 1701 **Fax:** 020-7328 8176
E-mail: parish@omiquex.org.uk.

- ***Oblates of Mary Immaculate (OMI):*** **Revv Liam Griffin Anjelo Wijewickrama, Eugene Ford.** *Parish Sister:* **Sr Maria Margaret LSU.** **Tel:** 020-7624 9170 **M:** *Sat 1st M of Sun 6pm. Sun 9am, 11am, 12.30pm, 7pm. Hds* (vigil *7pm*), *7.30am, 10am, 12.15pm, 7.30pm.*
- ***Jesuits (SJ),*** Copleston House, 221 Goldhurst Terrace, London NW6 3EP **Tel:** 020-7604 5860 **Fax:** 020-7604 5850 **Revv John McDade, Robert Carty, James Hanvey, Robert Murray, Patrick Riordan, Paul Hamill** (*Superior*), **Kizito Kiyimba, Bro James Hodkinson, Revv Brendan Callaghan.**
- ***Sisters of the Holy Family of Bordeaux,*** 2 Aberdare Gardens, NW6 3PX **Tel:** 020-7624 7573
- ***Sisters of La Sainte Union,*** 14 Quex Road, NW6 4PL **Tel:** 020-7624 9865
- ***Daughters of Charity***, 119 Victoria Road, Kilburn, NW6 6TD **Tel:** 020-7624 3587
- ***The Missionary Association of Mary Immaculate (OMI),*** 237 Goldhurst Terrace NW6 3EP **Tel:** 020-7328 8610 **Revv Paschal Dillon.**

■ KILBURN WEST
† Immaculate Heart of Mary (1948)
1 Stafford Road, Kilburn West NW6 5RS
Tel: 020-7624 2188

- ***Oblates of Mary Immaculate (OMI):*** **Rev Francis Ryan.** **M:** *Sun 9am, 11.30am. Hds 9am, 7pm.*

■ KING'S CROSS, N1
See Copenhagen Street

■ KINGS LANGLEY See Chipperfield

■ KINGSBURY GREEN
† St Sebastian and St Pancras (1926; 2001)
Hay Lane, Kingsbury Green.
Revv David Williamson, Robert Matau *(Romanian Chaplain)*, Presbytery, Hay Lane, Kingsbury Green, NW9 0NG
Tel: 020-8204 2834/2117
Pastoral Assistant: **Mrs Liz Wilson**.
Romanian Chaplaincy: **Tel:** 020 8204 4392
M: *Sat 1st M of Sun 6.30pm. Sun 8am, 10am, 11am (Romanian), 12noon, 6.30pm. Hds 9.30am, 7.30pm.*

■ KINGSLAND
† Our Lady and St Joseph (1854; 1964)
100a Balls Pond Road, Kingsland N1 4AG
Tel: 020-7254 4378
Revv Christopher Colven, Nicholas Schofield. Also in residence: **Rev Albert Ovie Ofere**. *Parish Sister:* **Sr Winefred UJ**.
M: *Sat 1st M of Sun 7pm. Sun 8am, 9.30am, 11am* (*Sung*), *12.15pm, 6.30pm. Hds* (vigil *6pm*), *9am, 12noon, 6pm, 8pm.*
- ***Ursulines of Jesus,*** 8 King Henry's Walk, N1 4PB **Tel:** 020-7254 8321
- ***Loreto Sisters (IBVM),*** 57 Parkholme Road E8 3AQ **Tel:** 020-7254 4345

■ KINGSWAY, WC2
See Lincoln's Inn Fields

■ KNEBWORTH
† St Thomas More (1929; 1936)
72 London Road, Knebworth, Herts SG3 6HB **Tel:** 01438-813303
Canon Danny Cronin.
M: *Sat 1st M of Sun 6pm. Sun 8am, 10am* (*Sung*). *Hds 9.30am, 7.30pm.*

■ LAXTON PLACE
† St Anne (1853; 1857; 1938; 1970)
Priest's House, Laxton Place, Longford Street, Regent's Park NW1 3PT
Tel: 020-7387 3833
Rev Mark Coningsby.
M: *Sat 1st M of Sun 6.30pm. Sun 9.30am, 11am. Hds 12.30pm, 7pm.*

■ LEBANESE MARONITE CENTRE
Our Lady of Lebanon
6 Dobson Close, Swiss Cottage NW6 4RS
Tel: 020-7586 1801 **Fax:** 020-7722 0436
- ***Lebanese Maronite Order (LMO): Rev* Adel El Alam** (*Prior & Parish Priest*).
M: (*Maronite Rite*) *Sat 1st M of Sun 7pm. Sun 12.30pm, 7pm at Our Lady of Sorrows, 17 Cirencester Street, W2 5SR*

■ LEICESTER SQUARE, WC2
See French Church

■ LETCHWORTH
† St Hugh of Lincoln (1907; 1963)
Broadway.
Rev Seamus Murphy. 84 Pixmore Way, Letchworth, Herts SG6 3TP
Tel: 01462-683504
M: *Sat 1st M of Sun 7pm. Sun 8am, 9.30am, 11am, 12.30pm* (*Pol*). *Hds 9.30am, 7.30pm.*
- ***Sisters of Charity of Jesus and Mary,*** Provincial House, 108 Spring Road, Letchworth, Herts SG6 3SL **Tel:** 01462-682153

■ LIMEHOUSE
† Our Lady Immaculate
(1881; 1934; cons Oct 17, 1945)
636 Commercial Road, E14 7HS
Tel: 020-7987 3563 **Fax:** 020-7536 9043
Served from Millwall. **Rev Peter Harris**
M: *Sun 11.45am. Hds As announced.*
- ***Daughters of Charity (SVP),*** 63/64 Island Row, E14 7HU **Tel:** 020-7987 3336
- ***Young Christian Workers Community,*** 5 Island Row, E14 7HS **Tel:** 020-7515 0168

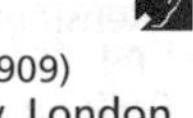

■ LINCOLN'S INN FIELDS
† St Anselm and St Cecilia (1687; 1909)
70 Lincoln's Inn Fields, Kingsway, London WC2A 3JA **Tel:** 020-7405 0376
Rev David Barnes.
M: *Sat 1st M of Sun 6pm. Sun 10am (Family), 12noon, 2nd Sun 6pm (Filipino). Hds (vigil 6pm), 8.30am, 12.30pm, 6pm sung (Latin).*

■ LITHUANIAN CHURCH
† St Casimir (1901; 1912)
21 The Oval, Hackney Road, E2 9DT
Tel: 020-7739 8735
Rev Petras Tverijonas.
M: *Sun 10am (Lithuanian/English), 12noon (Lithuanian), 6pm (Lithuanian). Hds 7pm.*

■ LONDON AIRPORT (HEATHROW)
St George's Interdenominational Chapel Opposite Car Park No. 2.
Rev Paschal Ryan (*Airport Chaplain*). St George's Chapel, Heathrow Airport, Hounslow, Middlesex TW6 1JH **Tel/Fax:** 020-8745 4261 (home 020-8759 2160).
Pastoral Assistants: **Deacon Robert Levett (Mbl:** 07882 491127**), Shaun Loader**. **Tel:** 020-8759 1351 **Mbl:** 0956-524147; **Sr Margaret Byrnes**, **Tel:** 020-8561 3923
M: *Sun 12.30pm. Hds 7.30am, 12.30pm, 6pm.*

■ **LONDON COLNEY**
† **Our Lady, St Mary of Walsingham** (1959)
Haseldine Road.
Rev Mark Anwyll. 189 High Street, London Colney, Herts AL2 1RP
Tel: 01727-822218
M: *Sat 1st M of Sun 6pm. Sun 9.30am, 11am, 5pm, Hds 9am, 7.30pm.*
• ***All Saints Pastoral Centre,*** Shenley Lane, London Colney, Herts AL2 1AP **Tel:** 01727-822010 **Fax:** 01727-822880

■ **MAIDA VALE** See St John's Wood

■ **MAIDEN LANE** (Covent Garden)
† **Corpus Christi** (1873; cons Oct 18, 1956)
Corpus Christi Presbytery, Maiden Lane, WC2E 7NB **Tel:** 020-7836 4700
Rev Christopher Vipers *(Vocation Director).*
M: *Sat 1st M of Sun 6pm. Sun 9.30am, 11.30am. Hds 12.05pm, 1.05pm, 6.30pm* (*Tridentine*).

■ **MALTESE CHAPLAINCY** See Pimlico

■ **MANOR HOUSE**
† **St Thomas More** (1969; 1975)
9 Henry Road, Manor House, N4 2LH
Tel: 020-8802 9910 **Rev Clive Lee**.
M: *Sat 1st M of Sun 6pm (Sung), 7.30pm (Portuguese). Sun 10am (Sung), 12noon (Sung). Hds 7.15pm.*
• ***Ursuline Sisters of Malta,*** 36 Adolphus Road, N4 2AY **Tel:** 020-8800 5228

■ **MARYLEBONE**
† **Our Lady of the Rosary**
(1855; new Church 1963)
211 Old Marylebone Road, Marylebone, NW1 5QT
Tel: 020-7723 5101 **Fax:** 020-7258 0307
Rev Duncan Adamson. Also in residence: **Austin Garvey, Antony Brunning**.
Tel: 020-7723 7757
M: *Sat 1st M of Sun 6pm. Sun 8.30am, 10am, 11.30am, 7pm. Hds 8am, 12.30pm, 6pm.*
• ***Tyburn Convent (Adorers of the Sacred Heart, OSB),*** 8 Hyde Park Place, W2 2LJ **Tel:** 020-7723 7262 *Chaplain:* **Rev David Clark Tel:** 020-7706 2842

■ **MILE END**
† **The Guardian Angels**
(1869; 1901; cons Oct. 20, 1927)
377 Mile End Road, E3 4QS
Tel: 020-8980 1845
Rev Anthony H Sacré. Also in residence: **Revv Stephen Delany, Brian Nash**.
M: *Sat 1st M of Sun 5.30pm* (*Latin American*). *Sun 9am, 10.30am, 6pm. Hds 9.30am, 7.30pm.*

■ **MILL END & MAPLE CROSS** 
† **St John the Evangelist** (1969)
St John's Presbytery, Berry Lane, Mill End, Rickmansworth, Herts WD3 2HG
Tel: 01923-779890
Rev Desmond Baker.
M: *Sat 1st M of Sun 6pm. Sun 10am, 6pm. Hds 10am, 8pm.*

■ **MILL HILL**
1. † **Sacred Heart and Mary Immaculate**
(1889; 1922; 1995)
The Broadway.
• ***Vincentians (CM):*** **Revv Kevin O'Shea** (*Superior & Parish Priest*), **Jack Harris, Hugh McMahon, Fergus Kelly, Joel Bernardo**. 2 Flower Lane, Mill Hill NW7 2JB **Tel:** 020-8959 1021
E-mail: parishoffice@shmi.info
M: *Sat 1st M of Sun 6pm. Sun 8.30am, 10am* (*Folk*), *11.30am, 6pm. Hds 7am, 10am, 12.15pm, 7.30pm.*
• ***Daughters of Charity (SVP),*** Provincial House, The Ridgeway, NW7 1EH **Tel:** 020-8906 3777 *Director:* **Rev Fergus Kelly**. **Tel:** 0208 959 1021
• ***Franciscan Sisters of Mill Hill,*** St Mary's Abbey, The Ridgeway NW7 4HX **Tel:** 020-8959 1364
Generalate: **Tel:** 020-8959 4854

■ **MILLWALL**  
† **St Edmund** (1846; 1874, 2000)
297 West Ferry Road E14 3RS
Rev Peter Harris.
Tel: 020-7987 4114
Also serves Limehouse
M: *Sat 1st M of Sun 6pm. Sun 10am. Hds As Announced.*

■ **MOORFIELDS**
† **St Mary Moorfields** (1710; 1903)
4/5 Eldon Street, EC2M 7LS
Tel: 020-7247 8390 **Fax:** 020-7247 2537
Rev Peter Newby. (Also serves Bunhill Row)
M: *Sun 10am.Hds Eve 7pm, 8.05am, 12noon, 12.30pm, 1.05pm, 5.30pm.*

■ **MUCH HADHAM**
† **Holy Cross** (1939)
The Priest House, Malting Lane, Much Hadham, Herts SG10 6AW
Tel/Fax: 01279-842354
Rev Bob Styles SJ.
Also Serves Sawbridgeworth.
M: (*in Shared Church of St Andrew and Holy Cross*) *Sun 11am. Hds 9.30am, 12.30pm.*
• ***Daughters of the Holy Cross,*** St Elizabeth's Centre (School, College and Home for Adults with Epilepsy and Autism, and other medical conditions), South End, Much Hadham, Herts SG10 6EW **Tel:** 01279-843541 *Chaplain:* **Rev Paul Arnold**. **Tel:** 01279-842145 **M:** *Sun 11am. Hds 5.30pm.*

ARCHDIOCESE OF WESTMINSTER

■ MUSWELL HILL
† Our Lady of Muswell
(1917; 1938; cons Sept. 23, 1959)
1 Colney Hatch Lane, Muswell Hill, N10 1PN
Tel: 020-8883 5607 **Fax:** 020-8444 3464
Rev Charles Cahill, Also in residence: **Rev Jan Swagemakers MHM.**
M: *Sat 1st M of Sun 6.30pm. Sun 8.30am, 10am, 11.45am. Hds 10am, 12.30pm, 7.30pm.*
- ***Sisters of Marie Auxiliatrice,*** 20 Elgin Road N22 7UE. **Tel:** 020-8881 8547
- ***Sisters of St Louis,*** 11 Dukes Avenue N10 2PS

■ NEASDEN
† St Patrick (1981)
The Presbytery, Hardie Close, Neasden, NW10 0UH
Tel: 020-8451 0367 **Fax:** 020-8830 3022
Rev Patrick McLaughin.
M: *Sat 1st M of Sun 6.30pm. Sun 9.30am, 11.30am. Hds 9.30am, 7.30pm.*

■ NEW BARNET
† Mary Immaculate and St Peter (1912; 1938)
63 Somerset Road, New Barnet, Herts EN5 1RF
Tel: 020-8449 1961 **Fax:** 020-8441 1331
- ***Holy Ghost Fathers (CSSp):*** **Revv Derek McCartney** (*Parish Priest*), **Nicodemus MMasi.** **M:** *Sat 1st M of Sun 6pm. Sun 9.30am, 11am, 7pm. Hds 9.30am, 7.30pm.*
- ***African Missions (SMA),*** 33 Lyonsdown Road **Tel:** 020-8440 4715 **Revv Rob Morland** (*Superior*), **Anthony Cussen, Martin Walsh, Tom McNamara, Peter Burrows.**

■ NEW SOUTHGATE
† Our Lady of Lourdes (1923; 1935)
373 Bowes Road, New Southgate, N11 1AA **Tel:** 020-8368 1638
Fax: 020-8361 3172
Mgr Canon Tom Egan, Rev Damian Cassidy O.Carm, Petros Gebremichael CM.
Pastoral Assistant: **Mrs Aileen Adams.**
M: *Sat 1st M of Sun 6.30pm. Sun 8.30am, 9.45am (Choir), 11.15am (Fam), 12.30pm, 6.30pm. Hds 8am, 10am, 7.30pm.*
- ***Sisters of Our Lady of the Missions,*** 2 Brookdale, London N11 1BL **Tel:** 020-8361 6848
- ***Sisters of St Louis,*** 16 Chaucer Close, London N11 1AV **Tel:** 020-8361 1935

■ NORTHFIELDS (WEST EALING)
† SS Peter and Paul
(1926; 1931; cons Oct 29, 1959)
38 Camborne Avenue, Northfields W13 9QZ
Tel: 020-8567 5421
Rev Jim Duffy.
M: *Sat 1st M of Sun 6.30pm. Sun 8.30am, 10am (Family), 11.30am (Sung), 6.30pm. Hds 9.30am, 8pm.*
- ***Little Company of Mary,*** 33 Mattock Lane, W5 5BH **Tel:** 020-8567 1464
- ***Medical Mission Sisters (SCMM),*** 109 Clitherow Avenue, W7 2BL **Tel:** 020-8567 1504
- ***Religious of the Sacred Heart of Mary,*** 54 Grange Road, W5 5BX **Tel:** 020-8567 7228

■ NORTHOLT See Harrow (South)

■ NORTHWOOD
† St Matthew (1924; cons Oct 12, 1954)
32 Hallowell Road, Northwood, Middlesex HA6 1DW
Tel: 01923-835330 **Fax:** 01923-840736
Rev Timothy Hutton; *Also in residence* **Rev Geoffrey Eneh.**
M: *Sat 1st M of Sun 6pm. Sun 9am, 11am (Sung), 6pm. Hds 10am.*
- ***Daughters of Charity (SVP)***; 32 Norwich Road, Northwood HA6 1NB **Tel:** 020 8866 4442

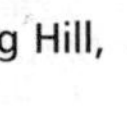

■ NOTTING HILL
† St Francis of Assisi (1860)
The Presbytery, Pottery Lane, Notting Hill, W11 4NQ **Tel:** 020-7727 7968
Rev Shaun Middleton.
M: *Sat 1st M of Sun 6pm. Sun 10am, 11.30am, 1pm (Gheez Rite), 6pm. Hds 8am, 7.30pm.*
- ***Sisters of St Mary of Namur,*** 47 Cornwall Crescent, W11 1PG **Tel:** 020-7221 4160
- ***Sisters of the Temple:*** 28 Penzance Street W11 4OX **Tel:** 020-7602 8782

■ OGLE STREET
† St Charles Borromeo
(1862; cons Oct. 4, 1921)
8 Ogle Street, W1W 6HS
Tel: 020-7636 2883
Rev Alan J Fudge.
Parish Assistant: **Sr Pauline Forde DC.**
M: *Sat 1st M of Sun 6pm. Sun 9am, 11am, 6pm. Hds 8am, 12.30pm, 6pm.*
- ***University Chaplaincy,*** 111 Gower Street, WC1. See under University Chaplaincy.

■ OLD HALL GREEN & PUCKERIDGE
(c.1660)
Both served from Buntingford
Rev Ian Dickie, Resident at Buntingford

1. Old Hall Green
† St Edmund of Canterbury and the English Martyrs

(1769; 1818; new church cons Dec. 2, 1911)
Deacon: **Rev Ronald Saunders.**
M: *Sun 11am. Hds as announced.*

2. Puckeridge
† St Thomas of Canterbury (1926)
M: *Sat 1st M of Sun 6pm. Hds as announced.*

• ***St Edmund's College,*** (1793; 1853) Old Hall Green, Ware, Herts SG11 1DS **Tel:** 01920-821504 *Chaplain:* **Rev Michael Pinot de Moira. Tel:** 01920-821334

■ ORATORY

† Immaculate Heart of Mary
(1854; 1884; cons April 16, 1884)
The Oratory, Brompton Road SW7 2R
Tel: 020-7808 0900 **Fax:** 020-7584 1095

• ***Fathers of the Oratory of St Philip Neri (Oratorians):*** **Revv Ignatius Harrison** (*Provost*), **George Bowen, Charles Dilke** (*Parish Priest*), **John Fordham, Ronald Creighton-Jobe; Patrick Doyle, Julian Large, Rupert McHardy.**
M: *Sat 1st M of Sun 6pm. Sun 7am, 8am, 9am (Trid), 10am* (*Sung Eng*), *11am* (*Solemn Lat*), *12.30pm, 4.30pm, 7pm. Hds* (vigil *6.30pm*), *7am, 8am, 9am (Trid)10am, 12.30pm, 5.30pm, 6.30pm* (*Solemn Latin*).

• ***Canonesses of St Augustine,*** More House, 53 Cromwell Road, SW7 2EH **Tel:** 020-7584 2040 **Fax:** 020-7581 5748

■ OSTERLEY

† St Vincent de Paul (1934; 1936)
2 Witham Road, Osterley, Middlesex TW7 4AJ **Tel:** 020-8560 4737
Fax: 020-8569 7422
Rev Mark Leenane. Also in residence: **Rev Roger Reader, Fr Thomas Paradyil MST.**
Tel: 020-8560 4213
M: *Sun 9.30am* (*CW*), *11.30am, 6pm. Hds* (vigil *7.30pm*), *9.30am, 7.30pm.*

• ***Vincentians (CM),*** St Vincent's, 29 Eversley Crescent, Isleworth, Middlesex TW7 4LR **Tel:** 020-8560 7021 **Fax:** 020-8568 8677 **Revv Noel Travers, Austin Mbelu, Chacko Panathara, Cirino Potrido.**

• ***The Lillie Road Centre,*** More House, 28 The Grove, Isleworth, Middx TW7 4JU **Tel:** 020-8568 9487/2079 **Rev Ken McCabe** (*Director*).

• ***Dominican Sisters (Cong of Newcastle, Natal),*** 121 Thornbury Road, Isleworth TW7 4HD **Tel:** 020-8560 9438

■ OXHEY, HERTS See Bushey

■ OXHEY (SOUTH) See Carpenders Park.

■ PADDINGTON

1. † Our Lady of Sorrows (1912)
17 Cirencester Street, Paddington W2 5SR
Tel: 020-7286 2672
Rev Stephen Bartlett (*Administrator*).
M: *Sat 1st M of Sun 6pm. Sun 9.30am, 11am. Hds 10am, 5.30pm.*

2. Our Lady of Lourdes See Harrow Road

■ PALMERS GREEN

† St Monica (1910; 1914)
The Presbytery, Stonard Road, Green Lanes, Palmers Green, London N13 4DJ
Tel: 020-8886 9568
Revv Sean Leonard, Philip Dyer-Perry.
Parish Sister: **Sr Joyce.** *Catechetical Co-ordinator:* **Sr Eileen Toomey.**
M: *Sat 1st M of Sun 6pm. Sun 8am, 9am, 10.30am* (*Family*), *12noon, 5.30pm. Hds* (vigil *7pm*), *9.30am, 10.30am, 7pm.*

• ***Daughters of Providence,*** 8 Oakthorpe Road, Palmers Green N13 5UH **Tel:** 020-8886 8186

■ PARSONS GREEN

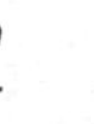

† Holy Cross
(1843-48; 1884; 1924; cons Oct 11, 1928)
Ashington Road.
Rev Michael Lowry. 22 Cortayne Road, SW6 3QA **Tel:** 020-7736 1068
Fax: 020-7371 8144
M: *Sat 1st M of Sun 6.30pm. Sun 9.30am* (*Family*), *11.30am* (*Sung*). *Hds 10am, 7.30pm.*

■ PERIVALE

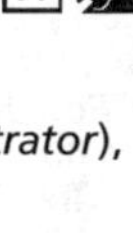

† St John Fisher (1936; 1970)
Western Avenue.
Rev Anthony Sammarco (*Administrator*), 41/42 Langdale Gardens, Perivale, Greenford, Middlesex UB6 8DQ
Tel: 020-8997 3164 **Fax:** *020-8997 1919*
M: *Sat 1st M of Sun 6.30pm. Sun 8am, 9.30am (CW), 11.30am, 8pm 1st Sun M Sri Lankan, 2nd Filipino, 3rd Portuguese, 4th Polish, 5th Arabic. Hds 7am, 10am, 7.30pm.*

■ PIMLICO

1. † Holy Apostles
(1917; 1957; cons May 10, 1974)
Winchester Street. **Canon Patrick Browne.** *(Albanian Chaplain)*, Also in residence: **Rev Gary Walsh,** 47 Cumberland Street, SW1V 4LY **Tel:** 020-7834 6965 **Fax:** 020-7821 8609
M: *Sat 1st M of Sun 6pm. Sun 9am, 10.30am* (*Family*), *12.30pm* (*Spanish*). *Hds* (vigil *7pm*), *10am, 7pm.*

• ***The Maltese Mission,*** 1 Balniel Gate, Lindsay Square, London SW1V 3SD

• ***Franciscans (OFM),*** **Revv Charles Diacono, Stephen Sciberras. Tel/Fax:** 020-7834 9512

• ***Franciscan Sisters of the Heart of Jesus,*** 9 St George's Drive, SW1V 4DJ **Tel:** 020-7834 4020 (*Convent*)

Tel: 020-7834 5356 (*Hostel*)
- ***Sisters of Notre Dame,*** 5 Westmoreland Terrace, SW1V 4GT **Tel:** 020-7828 5221

2. St John Chrysostom, Pimlico,
Melkite Greek Catholic Church Based at St Barnabas CofE Church, see page 119.

■ PINNER

† St Luke (1914; 1957)
28 Love Lane, Pinner, Middlesex HA5 3EX
Tel: 020-8866 0098 **Fax:** 020-8866 7869
Canon Robert Plourde.
Pastoral Assistant: **Winnie Brady.**
M: *Sat 1st M of Sun 6pm. Sun 9am, 11am. Hds* (vigil *7.30pm*), *10am.*
- ***Dominican Sisters,*** 34 Love Lane, Pinner, Middx HA5 3EX **Tel:** 020-8866 5460
- ***The Grail:*** 125 Waxwell Lane, Pinner, Middx HA5 3ER **Tel:** 020-8866 2195 **Fax:** 020-8866 1408
- ***Daughters of Charity (SVP),*** Farmside, 43 High Street, Pinner HA5 5PJ **Tel:** 020-8866 4442

■ POLISH CHURCH

1. † Our Lady of Czestochowa and St Casimir (1905; 1930)
2 Devonia Road, Islington, N1 8JJ
Tel: 020-7226 9944 **Fax:** 020-7359 8042
Revv Stanislaw Wachala, Krzysztof Kawczynski.
M: *Sat 1st M of Sun 6pm. Sun 9am, 11am, 12.30pm, 3.30pm, 7pm. Hds 9am,11am, 7pm.*
- ***Polish Catholic Mission,*** 2 Devonia Road, Islington, London N1 8JJ **Tel:** 020-7226 3439 **Fax:** 020-7226 7677 **Mgr Tadeusz Kukla** (*Vicar Delegate for Poles in England and Wales*).

2. † St Andrew Bobola (1961)
1 Leysfield Road, Shepherds Bush, W12 9JF
Tel: 020-8740 5862 and 743 8848
Mgr Bronislaw Gostomski,
M: *Sat 1st M of Sun 6pm. Sun 9am, 10.30am, 12noon* (*Sung*), *5pm. Hds 10am, 7pm.*

3. † Our Lady Mother of the Church (1986)
2 Windsor Road, Ealing W5 5PD
- ***Marian Fathers (MIC):*** **Revv Dariusz Kwiatowski, Pawel Nawalaniec** (*Superior*), **Tadeusz Wyszomierski, Krzysztof Wojcieszak** (*Parish Priest*), **Mariusz Jarzabak. Tel:** 020-8567 1746 **Fax:** 020-8810 0185
M: *Sat 1st M of Sun, 7.30pm; Sun 9am, 10.15am, 11.30am, 1pm,5.15pm, 7pm.*
- ***Polish Catholic Centre (POK),*** 1 Courtfield Gardens, W13 0EY **Tel:** 020-8810 9035
- ***Sisters of the Resurrection,*** 84 Gordon Road, W5 2AR **Tel:** 020-8998 8954 **M:** *Mon-Fri 7.30am.*
- ***Sisters of the Holy Name of Jesus,*** 57 Mount Park, Ealing W5 2PU **Tel:** 020-8997 2030 **M:** *Sat 5pm.*
- ***Kolbe House (for elderly people),*** 18 Hunger Lane W5 3HH **Tel:** 020-8992 4978 **M:** *Sun 10am.*

■ PONDERS END

† Church of Mary, Mother of God
(1912; 1921; cons 8 Sept 1985)
192 Nags Head Road, Ponders End, Enfield, Middlesex EN3 7AR
Tel: 020-8804 2149 **Fax:** 020-8804 2749
Rev John Shewring, Mbl: 07973-539907
Mrs Cora Coman (*Catechetical co-ordinator*).
M: *Sat 1st M of Sun 6pm. Sun 8am, 9.30am* (*Family*), *11am* (*Sung*), *12.30pm* (*Italian*), *6pm. Hds 9.30am, 12.30pm, 8pm.*
- ***Italian Catholic Centre,*** 197 Durants Road, Enfield, Middx EN3 7DE **Tel:** 020-8804 2307 **Mgr Agostino Gonella.**
- ***Suore Collegine della Sacra Famiglia,*** 197 Durants Road, Enfield, Middx EN3 7DE **Tel:** 020-8804 2307

■ POPLAR

† SS Mary and Joseph
(1816; 1856; 1954; new church cons 12 Oct, 1960)
Canton Street.
Clergy House, 9 Pekin Street, Poplar, E14 6EZ
Tel: 020-7987 4523 **Fax:** 020-7538 4810
Rev Aidan Rossiter.
M: *Sat 1st M of Sun 6pm. Sun 9.15am (Bow Common), 11am (Poplar). Hds 9.30am (10am if with school), 8pm. 6.30pm (Bow Common).*
- ***Faithful Companions of Jesus,*** Pope John House, Hale Street, E14 0BS **Tel:** 020-7517 9599
- ***Religious of the Assumption,*** 47 Bazely Street, E14 0ES **Tel:** 020-7515 8944
- ***Sisters of Mercy,*** 9 Mountague Place, E14 0EX **Tel:** 020-7987 2275

■ POTTERS BAR

† Our Lady and St Vincent (1962, 1969)
243 Mutton Lane, Potters Bar, Herts EN6 2AT
Tel: 01707-654359
Rev Timothy O'Connor.
M: *Sat 1st M of Sun 6pm. Sun 9am, 11am.*
- ***Sisters of St Martha,*** 1A The Avenue, EN6 1EG **Tel:** 01703 645901

■ PUCKERIDGE See Old Hall Green

■ QUEENSWAY

† Our Lady, Queen of Heaven (1954; 1973)
4a Inverness Place, London W2 3JF
Tel: 020-7229 8153
Rev Terence McGuckin.

M: *Sat 1st M of Sun 5.30pm, Sun 10am, 11.30am, 1pm* (*Ethiopian, Gheez Rite*), *4.30pm. Hds 9.30am, 6.30pm.*

- ***Prelature of Opus Dei,*** 4 Orme Court, W2 4RL **Mgr Nicholas Morrish** (*Regional Vicar*), **Revv Bernard Marsh, Paul Hayward, Stefan Hnylycia, Joseph Gabiola. Tel:** 020-7229 7574

RADLETT

† St Anthony of Padua
(1905; new church 1910)
22 The Crosspath, Radlett, Herts WD7 8HN
Tel/Fax: 01923-856165

M: *Sat 1st M of Sun 6pm. Sun 8.30am, 10.30am* (*Sung*), *6pm. Hds 10am, 8pm.*

REDBOURN

† St John Fisher (1936; 1967)
1 Peppard Close, Redbourn, St Albans, Herts AL3 7EB **Tel:** 01582-792270
Rev Neil Reynolds.

M: *Sat 1st M of Sun 6.30pm. Sun 10.15am, 6.30pm. Hds 9.15am, 7.30pm.*

REGENTS PARK, NW1 See Laxton Place

RICKMANSWORTH

† 1 Our Lady Help of Christians (1886; 1909)
5 Park Road, Rickmansworth, Herts WD3 1HU **Tel:** 01923-773387
Rev James Duffy.

M: *Sat 1st M of Sun 6.30pm. Sun 8.30am, 10.30am* (*Sung*), *6.30pm* (*Folk*). *Hds* (*vigil 8pm*), *9.30am, 8pm.*

- ***Daughters of Jesus,*** 55 Nightingale Rd, Rickmansworth **Tel:** 01923-773948
- ***Housetop Centre:*** 111a High Street WD3 1AN. **Tel:** 01923-779446

2. St John the Evangelist Mill End
See Mill End

ROYSTON

† St Thomas of Canterbury and the English Martyrs (1911; 1917)
6 Melbourn Road, Royston, Herts SG8 7DB
Tel: 01763-243117
Rev Seamus McGeoghan.

M: *Sat 1st M of Sun 6.30pm. Sun 9am. 10.30am. Hds 9.15am, 8pm.*

RUISLIP

† Most Sacred Heart (1921; 1939)
73 Pembroke Road, Ruislip, Middlesex HA4 8NN **Tel:** 01895-632739
Revv Michael Johnston, Agustin Conesa.

M: *Sat 1st M of Sun 6pm. Sun 8.30am, 10am* (*Family*), *11.30am* (*Sung*), *6pm. Hds* (*vigil 8pm*), *10am, 8pm.*

RUISLIP (SOUTH)

† St Gregory the Great
(1958; 1967; cons 1 Nov 1975)
447 Victoria Road, South Ruislip, Middlesex HA4 0EG **Tel:** 020-8845 2186
Rev Dennis Touw.

M: *Sat 1st M of Sun 5.30pm. Sun 10am* (*Sung*), *6pm. Hds 10am, 8pm.*

ST ALBANS

† SS Alban and Stephen
(1840; 1904; cons 1977)
14 Beaconsfield Rd, St Albans, Herts, AL1 3RB
Tel: 01727-853585 **Fax:** 01727-855410

- ***Missionaries of the Sacred Heart (MSC):*** **Revv Charles Sweeney** (*Parish Priest*), **Jerry Daly, Thomas Hewitt**.
  M: *Sat 1st M of Sun 6pm. Sun 9.30am, 11.30pm, 7pm. Hds 9am, 10am, 7.30pm.*
- ***Mass Centre,*** Marshalswick (St John Fisher School).
  M: *Sun 9am. Hds 2.40pm* (*In School Term*).
- ***Sisters of Mercy,*** Maryland, Townsend Drive **Tel:** 01727-858745 Home for Elderly Ladies **Tel:** 01727-865568
  M: *Sun 9am. Hds 9am.*
- ***Loreto Sisters (IBVM),*** 5 Bedford Park Road AL1 3RS **Tel:** 01727-858266
  3/4 Bedford Park Road AL1 3RS
  Tel: 01727-853144

ST ALBANS (SOUTH)

† St Bartholomew (1959; cons 1985)
47 Vesta Avenue, St Albans, Herts AL1 2PE
Tel: 01727-850066 **Fax:** 01727-812191
Rev Timothy Edgar (*Administrator*)

M: *Sat 1st M of Sun 6pm. Sun 8.30am, 10.30am. Hds As advertised.*

- ***Brothers of the Sacred Heart,*** Watling House, King Harry Lane AL3 4AW
  Tel: 01727-861969

ST CHARLES' SQUARE, W10 (North Kensington)

† St Pius X (1937; 1955)
Rev Marcus Winter. 79 St Charles' Square, W10 6EB **Tel:** 020-8969 6844. Also in residence: **Rev Anthony Baxter** (*Heythrop College*) **Tel:** 020-8968 6446. **Rev Brian Creak Tel:** 020 8968 3373

M: *Sat 1st M of Sun 6pm. Sun 8am, 10am, 12noon. Hds 8.20am, 12.30pm.*

- ***Carmelite Nuns,*** Monastery of the Most Holy Trinity, St Charles' Square W10 6EA
  Tel: 020-8969 8702
- ***Society of the Sacred Heart,*** 16 Lawrence Terrace, W10 5SX
  Tel: 020-8969 4160
- ***Little Sisters of Jesus,*** 13 Wheatstone House, Telford Road, London W10 5XT
  Tel: 020-8960 0440
- ***Holy Family Sisters of the Needy,*** 17 Highlever Road W10 6PP
  Tel: 020 8960 6743

■ ST JOHN'S WOOD
† Our Lady
(1833; 1836; cons May 14, 1925)
Lisson Grove.
Rev Allen Morris, *Also in residence:* **Revv Alexander Master, William Ochojia, Canon John McDonald** (*Chaplain:* Hospital of St John & St Elizabeth) 54 Lodge Road, St John's Wood, NW8 8LA **Tel:** 020-7286 3214 **Fax:** 020-7266 5859

M: *Sat 1st M of Sun 6pm. Sun 8am, 9.30am* (*Family*), *10.45am* (*Sung Lat*), *12noon, 6pm* (*Folk*). *Hds* (vigil *6pm*), *10am, 7.30pm.*

- ***Order of Malta,*** (Grand Priory of England), Brampton House. 60 Grove End Road, NW8 9NH **Tel:** 020-7586 3179.
- ***Sisters of Mercy,*** 54 Lodge Road, NW8 8LA **Tel:** 020-7286 6387; Also 39 Alma Square, NW8 9PY **Tel:** 020-7289 3657
- ***Handmaids of the Sacred Heart of Jesus,*** 25 St Edmund's Terrace, NW8 7PY **Tel:** 020-7722 2756
- ***Carmelite Missionaries,*** 189 Gloucester Place, NW1 **Tel:** 020-7262 4737; Hostel 020-7723 1919
- ***Redemptorist Mater House of Formation,*** 11 Harewood Avenue NW1 6LD **Tel:** 020-7723 9364 **Rev Francesco Donega**.

■ ST MARGARETS-ON-THAMES
† St Margaret of Scotland (1930; 1969)
130 St Margaret's Road, East Twickenham, Middlesex TW1 1RL **Tel:** 020-8892 3902
Rev Jeremy Trood.

M: *Sat 1st M of Sun 6.30pm. Sun 8.30am, 10.30am, 6.30pm. Hds 7.15am, 10am, 8pm.*

■ SAWBRIDGEWORTH, Herts
Most Holy Redeemer
Sayesbury Road. **Tel:** 01279-842354

M: *Sun 9.30am. Hds 12.30am, 8pm.*

Served from Much Hadham.

■ SHENLEY
† The Good Shepherd (1969; 1976)
Catholic Church, Black Lion Hill, Shenley, Herts WD7 9DH **Tel:** 01923-857005
Rev John Elliott.
In the pastoral care of Radlett

M: *Sun 8.30am, 11.30am. Hds 8pm.*

■ SHEPHERDS BUSH
1. † The Holy Ghost and St Stephen
(1889; 1904; cons April 24, 1936)
44 Ashchurch Grove, Shepherd's Bush, W12 9BU **Tel:** 020-8743 5196
Rev John Whooley; Sr Joanne Whooley.

M: *Sat 1st M of Sun 6pm. Sun 9.15 am, 11am* (*Family*), *12.30pm. Hds 9.30am, 8pm.*

- ***Augustinians:*** Provincial Office, 15 Dorville Crescent, Hammersmith W6 0HH **Tel/Fax:** 020-8748 1529 (*Provincial Office*), **Tel/Fax:** 020-741 7586 (*Community*). **Revv David Middleton** (*Provincial*), **Fionan C Heffernan**.
- ***Franciscan Missionaries of Mary,*** Provincialate, 5 Vaughan Avenue W6 0XS **Tel:** 020-8748 4077
- ***Sisters of Our Lady of Charity,*** 14 Dorville Crescent, Hammersmith W6 0MJ **Tel:** 020-8748 4793

2. † St Andrew Bobola (1961)
Leysfield Road. See Polish Church.

■ SHEPPERTON
† St John Fisher (1936; 1965)
Wood Road.
Rev Peter Scott. 15 Wood Road, Shepperton, Middlesex TW17 0DH
Tel: 01932-563116

M: *Sat 1st M of Sun 6pm. Sun 8.30am, 10.30am. Hds As announced*

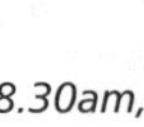

■ SOHO SQUARE
† St Patrick (1792; 1893)
21a Soho Square, W1D 4NR
Tel: 020-7437 2010
Rev Alexander Sherbrooke. *Parish Sister:* **Sr Dympna Bermingham SMG**.

M: *Sat 4pm (Portuguese), 1st M of Sun 6pm. Sun11am, 2.15pm* (*Cantonese*), *5pm, 6pm* (*Span*). *Hds 8am, 12.30pm, 1.05pm, 6pm.*

- ***Chinese Catholic Centre,*** 21a Soho Square **Tel:** 020-7439 1878 *Director:* **Rev Eddie Woo**. SOS Prayerline: **Tel:** 020-7434 9211

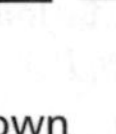

■ SOMERS TOWN
† St Aloysius
(1798; 1808; 1968; cons 24 May 1992)
20 Phoenix Road, Euston, Somers Town NW1 1TA **Tel:** 020-7387 1971
Rev James McNicholas.
Parish Sister: **Sr Ambrose Stafford SMG.**

M: *Sat 1st M of Sun 6pm. Sun 8.30am, 10.30am, 12.15pm, 6pm. Hds 9.30am, 12.30pm, 6pm.*

- ***Faithful Companions of Jesus,*** St Aloysius Convent, 32 Phoenix Road, NW1 1TA **Tel:** 020-7387 7174
- ***Servants of the Mother of God,*** 70-71 Euston Square, NW1 1DJ **Tel:** 020-7387 5855
- ***Consolata Missionary Sisters,*** 11 Regent Square, WC1H 8HZ **Tel:** 020-7837 2256

■ SOUTHALL
† St Anselm (1906; 1930; 1968)
St Anselm's Rectory, The Green, Southall, Middlesex UB2 4BE **Tel:** 020-8574 3300

Revv James Crampsey SJ, Gerard Hassay SJ.
M: *Sat 1st M of Sun 6.30pm. Sun 9am, 11am, 6.30pm. Hds 9.15am, 12.15pm, 7.30pm.*

• ***Missionaries of Charity,*** 41 Villiers Road, Southall, Middx UB1 3BS **Tel:** 020-8574 1892
• ***Brothers of St Gabriel,*** 2 Church Avenue, Southall, Middx UB2 4DH **Tel:** 020-8843 0690
• ***Society of Jesus,*** Di Nobili House, 6 Osterley Park Road UB2 4BL **Tel:** 020-8571 1833. **Revv Michael Kirwan, Michael Barnes.**

■ **SPANISH CENTRE** See under Bayswater

■ **SPANISH PLACE**
† **St James** (1791; 1890; cons April 28, 1949)
George Street/Blandford Street.
Rev Terence Phipps.
Also in residence: **Rev Nicholas Kavanagh.**
22 George Street, W1U 3QY
Tel: 020-7935 0943
M: *Sat 1st M of Sun 6pm. Sun 8.30am, 9.30am* (*Trid*), *10.30am,* (*Sung Lat*), *12noon, 4pm, 7pm Hds 7.15am, 11am* (*Trid*), *12.30pm, 6pm* (*Sat 10am*).

• ***Society of the Holy Child Jesus,*** 8 Deans Mews, Cavendish Square, W1G 9EE **Tel:** 020-7580 4102

■ **SPITALFIELDS, E1.** See Underwood Road

■ **STAINES**
† **Our Lady of the Rosary** (1890; 1932)
59 Gresham Road, Staines, Middlesex TW18 2BD **Tel:** 01784-452381
Rev Saviour Grech.
M: *Sat 1st M of Sun 6.30pm. Sun 9am, 11am* (*Family*). *Hds 9.15am, 7pm.*

■ **STAMFORD HILL**
† **St Ignatius** (1894; 1903)
27 High Road, Stamford Hill N15 6ND
Tel: 020-8800 2121 or 020-8802 5303
Fax: 020-8802 8102
• ***Jesuits (SJ):*** **Peter Randall** (*Parish Priest*). Also in residence: **Revv Bernard Parkin, Michael Bossy, Paul Fletcher, Bernard Charles, James Conway, Peter Scally, Kevin Fox, Rafel Hazarski** 27 High Road, South Tottenham N15 6ND
M: *Sat 1st M of Sun 7pm. Sun 8.30am, 10am* (*Fam*), *11.30am* (*Sung*), *4.30* (*Spanish*), *7pm. Hds 10am, 7.30pm.*
• ***Servite Sisters,*** St Mary's Convent, 90 Suffolk Road, N15 5RL **Tel:** 020-8800 2940
• ***Ursulines of Jesus,*** 11 Amhurst Park, N16 5DH **Tel:** 020-8800 4486 Provincialate **Tel:** 020-8802 0256 Also 149 Bethune Road, N16 5DY **Tel:** 020-8800 4623

■ **STANMORE**
† **St William of York** (1938; 1960)
1 Du Cros Drive, Stanmore, Middlesex HA7 4TJ **Tel:** 020-8954 1299
Rev Daniel Magnier.
M: *Sat 1st M of Sun 6pm. Sun 8am, 10am. Hds 9am, 7pm.*

■ **STANWELL**
† **St David** (1964; 1967)
Everest Road.
Rev Ken Rimini (*Administrator*). St David's, Everest Road, Stanwell, Staines, Middlesex TW19 7EE **Tel:** 01784-255973
M: *Sat 1st M of Sun 6pm. Sun 10am. Hds* (vigil *7.30pm*), *9.30am.*

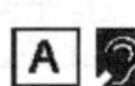

■ **STEPHENDALE ROAD**

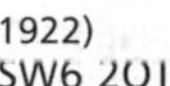

† **Our Lady (of Perpetual Help)** (1922)
2 Tynemouth Street, Fulham, SW6 2QT
Tel: 020-7736 4864
Rev Roger Kirinich.
Administrator: **Mrs Margaret McMahon.**
M: *Sat 1st M of Sun 6.30pm. Sun 9am, 11am. Hds 9am, 7.30pm.*

■ **STEVENAGE**
Bedwell and Pin Green
Rev Denis Watters. St Joseph's Presbytery, Bedwell Crescent, Stevenage, Herts SG1 1NJ **Tel:** 01438-351243 **Fax:** 01438-367372
Parish Sister: **Sr Geraldine (OP).**
Tel: 01438-351243

1. St Joseph
Bedwell Crescent, Bedwell.
M: *Sun 10am, 6pm. Hds 9.15am.*

2. All Saints
The Oval, Pin Green. (Shared Church).
M: *Sat 1st M of Sun 6pm. Sun 12noon. Hds 11am.*

■ **STEVENAGE**
Old Town and Symonds Green
Rev Francis Leonard. 4 Basil's Road, Stevenage, Herts SG1 3PX
Tel: 01438-226857 **Fax:** 01438-226095
Parish Sister: **Sr Loretta Dooley OP.**

1. Transfiguration of Our Lord
Grove Road, Old Town (1912; 1914)
M: *1st M of Sun 6pm. Sun 11am. Hds 10.30am.*

2. Christ the King
Filey Close, Symonds Green (Shared Church).
M: *Sun 9am. Hds* (vigil) *7.30pm.*
Lister Hosp Chaplain: **Bernadette Cassidy.**
Tel: 01438-314333, Ext 5518
• ***Sisters of Charity of Jesus and Mary,*** 3 Hitchen Road, Stevenage, Herts SG1 3BJ **Tel:** 01438-354247

■ **STEVENAGE**
† **St Hilda (Shephall)** (1958)
9 Breakspear, Stevenage, Herts SG2 9SQ
Tel: 01438-352182
Rev John Ablewhite.
M: *Sat 1st M of Sun 6.30pm; 9.30am (Sung), 11am (CW). Hds 9.30am, 8pm.*

■ **STOKE NEWINGTON**
† **Our Lady of Good Counsel**
(1882; 1936; 1976)
Presbytery, Bouverie Road, Stoke Newington N16 0AJ **Tel:** 020-8800 5250
Rev Michael Mannion.
Also in residence: **Rev Athanasio Dzadagu**.
M: *Sat 1st M of Sun 6.30pm. Sun 9am, 11am, 6.30pm. Hds 10am, 7.30pm.*
- ***Sisters of Charity of St Jeanne Antide,*** 'Bethany', 53 Bethune Road, N16 5EE **Tel:** 020-8802 3430

■ **STONEBRIDGE**
† **The Five Precious Wounds** (1926; 1957)
The Presbytery, Brentfield Road, Stonebridge Park, NW10 8ER
Tel/Fax: 020-8965 3313
Revv James Mallon, Andrew O'Connell
M: *Sat 1st M of Sun 6pm. Sun 10am (Sung), 12noon (Fam). Hds 10am, 7pm.*

■ **STROUD GREEN**
† **St Peter-in-Chains** (1894; 1896)
12 Womersley Road, Hornsey, N8 9AE
Tel: 020-8340 3394
Rev David Irwin.
M: *Sat 1st M of Sun 6.30pm. Sun 9.45am (Sung), 11.15am (Family), 7pm. Hds (vigil 7.30pm), 9.15am, 12noon, 7.30pm.*
- ***Sisters of Christian Instruction,*** St Gildas Convent, 36 Dickinson Road N8 9ET **Tel:** 020-8340 7203
- ***Sisters of Our Lady of Sion,*** 63 Mount View Road, N4 4SR **Tel:** 020-8340 0303
- ***Sisters of Providence,*** 78 Oakfield Road, N4 4LB **Tel:** 020-8340 1088

■ **SUDBURY**
† **St George**
(1924; 1926; cons April 18, 1928)
970 Harrow Road, Sudbury, Wembley, Middlesex HA0 2QE
Tel: 020-8904 2552 **Fax:** 020-8904 0744
Rev Anthony Seeldrayers.
M: *Sat 1st M of Sun 6.15pm. Sun 8.30am, 9.45am (Fam), 11.15am (Sung), 5.30pm. Hds 9.30am, 8pm.*

■ **SUNBURY-ON-THAMES**
† **St Ignatius of Loyola**
(1862; 1869; cons May 22, 1984)
The Rectory, Green Street, Sunbury-on-Thames, Middx TW16 6QB
Tel: 01932-783507 **Fax:** 01932-779134
Rev Michael Tuck.
Parish Sister: **Sr Liza Randall**
M: *Sat 1st M of Sun 6pm. Sun 9.30am, 11.30am. Hds 9am, 11.30am, 8pm.*

■ **SWISS COTTAGE**
† **St Thomas More** (1938; 1968)
Presbytery, Maresfield Gardens, Swiss Cottage, NW3 5SU
Tel: 020-7435 1388
Rev Gerard Sheehan. Also in residence: **Canon Peter Phillips Tel:** 020-7431 6192
M: *Sun 10am, 12noon (Sung), 6.30pm. Hds 7am, 10am, 7pm.*
- ***Jesuits (SJ),*** Southwell House. 39 Fitzjohn's Avenue, London NW3 5JT *Youth Project:* **Tel:** 020-7435 8534. *Community:* **Tel:** 020-7435 9794 **Fax:** 020-7435 9133 **Revv Michael Smith, Christopher Pedley, Bro Alan Harrison.**
- ***Netherhall House,*** Nutley Terrace, NW3 5SA **Tel:** 020-7435 8888 Hall of Residence for male University Students. Pastoral Care entrusted to the Prelature of Opus Dei.
Mgri Richard Stork, Joseph Evans, Rev Laurence Richardson
- ***Congregation of Jesus (CJ),*** 49 Fitzjohn's Avenue, NW3 6PG **Tel:** 020-7794 4972 **Fax:** 020-7431 6118

■ **TEDDINGTON and HAMPTON WICK**
† **The Sacred Heart**
(1882; 1893; cons June 14, 1944)
262 Kingston Road, Teddington, Middlesex TW11 9JQ **Tel:** 020-8977 2986
M: *Sat 1st M of Sun 6.30pm. Sun 9.30am (Fam), 11.15am (Sung), 6.30pm. Hds 9.30am, 7.30pm.*
- ***Sons of Divine Providence (FDP),*** House of Our Lady of Westminster, 13 Lower Teddington Road, Hampton Wick, Kingston-on-Thames, KT1 4EU **Tel:** 020-8977 5130 **Fax:** 020-8977 0105
Rev Stephen Beale
Website:
www.sonsofdivineprovidence.org
Also Orione House, 12 Station Road, Hampton Wick, Kingston-upon-Thames, KT1 4HG **Tel:** 020-8977 0754 (*residential care home for the elderly*); Columbo House (*residential care home for those with learning disabilities*); St John's Ho (*Supported living for those with learning disabilities*); Both at 1 Ferry Road, Teddington TW11 9NN

■ **TEDDINGTON (UPPER)** See Hampton Hill

■ **TOLLINGTON PARK**
† **St Mellitus** (1925; 1959)
The Presbytery, St Mellitus Church, Tollington Park, N4 3AG
Tel: 020-7272 3415

ARCHDIOCESE OF WESTMINSTER

Rev David Ardagh-Walter.
M: *Sat 1st M of Sun 6.30pm. Sun 9.30am, 11.30am, 6.30pm, 2nd Sun 2pm (Igbo), 6.30pm. Hds* (vigil 6.30pm), *9.30am, 6.30pm.*

■ TOTTENHAM

† St Francis de Sales (1793; 1895)
729 High Road, Tottenham, N17 8AG
Tel: 020-8808 3554 **Fax:** 020-8365 9709
Revv John Buckley, Lamont Phillips.
M: *Sat 1st M of Sun 7pm. Sun 8.30am, 10.30am* (*Fam*), *12noon, 7pm. Hds 9.30am, 7.30pm.*

- ***Sisters of Marie Auxiliatrice,*** 93 Mount Pleasant Road N17 8NG
  Tel: 020-8801 9883

■ TOTTENHAM (SOUTH), N15

See Stamford Hill

■ TOTTENHAM (WEST), N15

See West Green

■ TOTTERIDGE, N20 See Whetstone

■ TOWER HILL

† The English Martyrs (1865; 1876)
30 Prescot Street, E1 8BB
Tel: 020-7488 4654 **Fax:** 020-7488 1418

- ***Oblates of Mary Immaculate (OMI),*** **Rev Terence Williams-Keogh OMI.**
  M: *Sat 1st M of Sun 6.30pm. Sun 9am, 11am. Hds* (*6.30pm Eve*) *9.30am, 12noon, 1pm.*

■ TRING

† Corpus Christi (1910; 1913; 2001)
51 Langdon Street, Tring, Herts HP23 6BA
Tel: 01442-823161
Canon Vincent Berry, *Pastoral Assistant:* **Mrs Wendy Hinds Tel:** 01442-824369
M: *Sat 1st M of Sun 6pm. Sun 8.30am, 10.30am. Hds (vigil 7.30pm), 12noon.*

■ TWICKENHAM

† St James (1883; 1885; cons July 23, 1887) 61 Pope's Grove, Twickenham, Middlesex TW1 4JZ **Tel:** 020-8892 4578
Rev Ulrick Loring.
M: *Sat 1st M of Sun 6pm. Sun 8am, 10.30am* (*Sung*), *12.15pm. Hds 9am, 7.30pm.*

- ***Wellspring Community*** *(Christian Brothers, Presentation Brothers, Presentation Sisters),* 7 Waldegrave Gardens, Twickenham TW1 4PQ
  Tel: 020-8892 2870
- ***Christian Brothers,*** 38 Strawberry Hill Road, Twickenham, Middlesex TW1 4PU
  Tel: 020-8892 7472
- ***Sisters of Mercy,*** 88 Pope's Grove, Twickenham, Middlesex TW1 4JX
  Tel: 020-8744 2812
- ***Xaverian Brothers,*** 58 Bonser Road, Twickenham TW1 4RG
  Tel: 020-8287 3008

■ TWICKENHAM (EAST)

See St Margaret's-on-Thames

■ TYBURN CONVENT See Marylebone

■ UKRAINIAN CATHEDRAL

† Cathedral Church of the Holy Family in Exile (1968)
Duke Street (off Oxford Street).
Revv Benjmin Lysykanch, Ireneu Kraiczyi, Pedro Navochadia, Athanasius McVay.
Tel: 020-7629 1574
M: (*Ukrainian Rite, Julian Calendar*). *Sun 10.30am* (*High*). *Hds 6pm.*

■ UNDERWOOD ROAD

† St Anne (1850; 1855; cons Sept 27, 1905)
St Anne's Church, Underwood Road, E1 5AW **Tel:** 020-7247 7833
Rev José Maria Ribeiro, Carlos Salinos, Oswaldo Arujo.
M: *Sat 1st M of Sun 6pm (English), 7pm* (*Portugese*). *Sun 10.30am* (*English*), *12noon, 4pm, 7pm* (*Brazilian*). *Hds 9.30am, 7.30pm.*

- ***Sisters of Mercy,*** McAuley House, 1 Gunthorpe Street, E1 7RG
  Tel: 020-7247 4958

■ UNIVERSITY CHAPLAINCIES:

1. † Central London, Newman House, 111 Gower Street, WC1E 6AR
Tel: 020-7387 6370 **Fax:** 020-7388 6431
E-mail: pjw@universitycatholic.net
Website: www.universitycatholic.net
Chaplains: (*Senior Chaplain*); **Revv Peter Wilson, Brian Creak, Paul Graham (OSA); Mark Barrett (OSB), Joseph Evans, (SMG)**; *Administrator:* **Mrs Petronella Philips-Devaney**; *Receptionist:* **Sr Brid Mily LSU.**
M: *Term only – Sun 10.30am, 7.30pm. Hds 12.30pm, 5.30pm, 9pm.*

2. West London
More House, 53 Cromwell Road, SW7 2EH
Tel: 020-7584 2040 (Chaplains)
Tel: 020-7589 8433 (Students)
Rev Geoff Wheaton SJ.
M: *Sun 11am, 6pm* (*Term time only*).

3. Heythrop College
Kensington Square W8 5HQ
Tel: 020-7795 4215
Sr Bernie Devine.

4. Goodenough College Chaplaincy
Mecklenburgh Square WC1 2AB
Tel: 020-7837 4147 **Rev Casimir Adjo.**

5. St Mary's College
Waldegrave Road, Strawberry Hill, Twickenham TW1 4SX
Chaplain: **Rev Gerald Devlin,**

Tel: 020-8240 4006
E-mail: devling@smuc.ac.uk
Assistant Chaplain: **Rebecca Walker, Tel:** 020-8240 4002, *Chaplaincy Administrator:* **Mrs Kerry Anzollito. Tel:** 020-8240 4331
E-mail: anzolitk@smuc.ac.uk
Website: www.smuc.ac.uk

M: *11am (all year), 6pm (term-time only). Hds: 1pm.*

■ UPPER HOLLOWAY

† St Gabriel (1928; 1967)
Holloway Road. **Rev Kevin McDevitt,** 17 St John's Villas, N19 3EE **Tel:** 0207-272 8195
Also in residence: **Rev Nigel Charles.**
Parish Sisters: **Srs Pauline Cogan.**

M: *Sat 1st M of Sun 6pm. Sun 9am, 10.30am, 12noon, 6pm. Hds 12noon, 7.30pm.*

- ***Marist Sisters,*** 17 St John's Villas N19 3EE **Tel:** 020-7272 1079
- ***Servants of the Mother of God,*** 15 Goddard Place, Monnery Road N19 5GS **Tel:** 020-7281 0429

■ UXBRIDGE

† Our Lady of Lourdes and St Michael
(1891; 1931; cons May 14, 1936)
Presbytery, Osborn Road, Uxbridge, Middlesex UB8 1UE **Tel:** 01895-233193
Rev Matthew Heslin.

M: *Sat 1st M of Sun 6.30pm. Sun 8.30am, 10.30am (Family), 5pm. Hds 10am, 7pm.*

- ***Sisters of the Sacred Hearts of Jesus and Mary,*** Pield Heath House, Hillingdon, Middx UB8 3NW - Special School. **Tel:** 01895-233092 (Convent), 258507 (School). Also (For retired Sisters) Marian House, 100 Kingston Lane, Uxbridge, Middlesex UB8 3PW **Tel:** 01895 253299 Chaplain: **Rev Joe Carter, Tel:** 01895-232719

■ VICTORIA See Westminster and Pimlico

■ WALTHAM CROSS

† The Immaculate Conception and St Joseph
(1859; 1931; cons July 3, 1971)
204 High Street, Waltham Cross, Herts EN8 7D **Tel:** 01992-623156
Fax: 01992-640196
Rev John Cunningham.

M: *Sat 1st M of Sun 6.30pm. Sun 8.30am, 10.45am, 12.15pm, 6.30pm. Hds 10am, 8pm.*

- ***Canossian Daughters of Charity,*** Holy Cross Convent, 3 Longlands Close, Cheshunt, Herts EN8 8LW **Tel:** 01992-621168

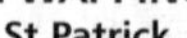

■ WAPPING

† St Patrick
(1871; 1892; cons May 22, 1902)
The Presbytery, Dundee Street, Green Bank, Wapping E1 9PH **Tel:** 020-7481 2202
Canon Digby Samuels.

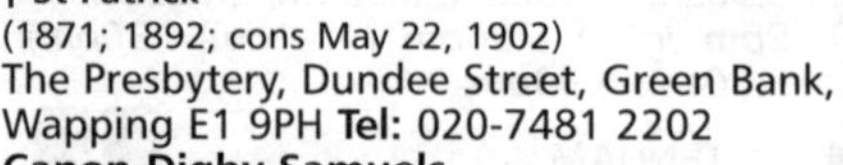

M: *Sat 1st M of Sun 7pm. Sun 10am, 6.30pm. Hds 10am, 8pm.*

- ***SPECeast.*** *Director:* **Cleo Gammon, Tel:** 020-7680 7600 **E-mail:** speceast@btconnect.com

■ WARE

† Sacred Heart of Jesus and St Joseph
(1870; 1921; 1939)
The Presbytery, King Edward's Road, Ware, Herts SG12 7EJ **Tel:** 01920-462140
Rev John Gray.

M: *Sat 1st M of Sun 6.30pm. Sun 8.30am, 10.30am (Sung). Hds 10am, 8pm.*

- ***Carmelite Monastery,*** Ware Park, SG12 0DT. Tel: 01920-462154 *Chaplain:* **Rev Bernard Crowe,** The Lodge, Ware Park, Herts SG12 0DS **Tel:** 01920-460396

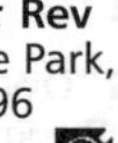

■ WARWICK STREET

† Our Lady of the Assumption and St Gregory
(1730; 1790; cons July 24, 1928)
24 Golden Square, Warwick Street W1F 9JR
Tel: 020-7437 1525 **Fax:** 020-7025 1598
Canon Patrick Davies, Mgr Seamus O'Boyle.

M: *Sat 1st M of Sun 6pm. Sun 10.30am 5pm. Hds 8am, 12.15pm, 12.45pm, 5.45pm.*

■ WATFORD

† Holy Rood (1883; 1890; cons July 5, 1900)
Market Street.
Revv Paul McAleenan, John Elliott. Holy Rood House, Exchange Road, Watford, Herts WD18 0QA **Tel:** 01923-224085
Deacon: **Neville Dyckhoff**

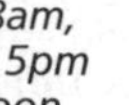

M: *Sat 1st M of Sun 7pm. Sun 8am, 9.30am (Sung), 11am (Folk), 2.15pm (Polish), 6.30pm. Hds 8am, 12noon, 7.30pm.*

- ***Adoration Sisters,*** 18 Percy Road, Watford WD18 0QA **Tel:** 01923-222505

■ WATFORD (NORTH)

† St Helen (1925; 1935)
Church of St Helen, The Harebreaks, Watford, Herts WD24 6NJ
Tel: 01923-223175
Rev Patrick Foley.

M: *Sun 9am, 11am, 6pm. Hds 10am, 8pm.*

■ WEALDSTONE and HARROW WEALD

† **St Joseph** (1898; 1901; 1931)
St Joseph's Presbytery, 191 High Road, Harrow Weald, Middx, HA3 5EA
Tel: 020-8427 1955 **Fax:** 020-8863 0543
E-mail: st.joseph.weald@btconnect.com

- ***Salvatorians (SDS):*** **Rev Michael Doherty** (*Parish Priest*), **Revv Noel Keane, Frank Waters**.
  M: *Sat 1st M of Sun 6pm. Sun 8.15am, 9.30am* (*Folk/Children alt Sun*), *11am* (*Sung*), *12.30pm, 6pm. Hds 7.30am, 10am, 7.15pm.*
- ***Salvatorians (SDS)***, Salvatorian Community House, High Road, Harrow Weald, Middx HA3 5DY **Tel:** 020-8427 2808 **Revv Michael Doherty** (*Superior*), **Peter Preston** (*Provincial Superior*), **John Murray, Bernard Finan, Thomas Hennessey.** Also Provincial Residence, 129 Spencer Road, Harrow Weald, Middlesex HA3 7UA
  Tel: 0208-426 0495 **Fax:** 0208-426 0927
- ***Sisters of Our Lady of the Missions,*** 192 High Street, HA3 7AY
  Tel: 020-8427 1541; 108 Spencer Road, Wealdstone HA3 7AR
  Tel: 020-8861 4174 (Provincial House)

■ WELHAM GREEN See under Hatfield

■ WELWYN GARDEN CITY

† **St Bonaventure** (1925; 1926; cons Sept 14 1974)
81 Parkway, Welwyn Garden City, Herts AL8 6JF **Tel:** 01707-322579
Served from Welwyn Garden City East.
In residence: **Rev Joe Boward** (retired).
M: *Sun 8am, 10.30am* (*Lat on 1st Sun*). *Hds 10am, 7pm.*

- ***Focolare Movement,*** Focolare Centre for Unity (Residential Conference Centre), 69 Parkway, Welwyn Garden City, Herts AL8 6HH **Tel:** 01707-323620

■ WELWYN GARDEN CITY (Digswell)

† **Holy Family** (1967)
194 Knightsfield, Welwyn Garden City, Herts AL8 7RQ **Tel:** 01707-327434
Rev William McConalogue.
M: *Sat 1st M of Sun 6.30pm. Sun 10am, 7pm. Hds 9.30am, 11am, 8pm.*

■ WELWYN GARDEN CITY (EAST)

† **Our Lady, Queen of Apostles.**
(1961; cons 18 Dec 1973)
141 Woodhall Lane, Welwyn Garden City, Herts AL7 3TP **Tel:** 01707-323234
Rev Norbert Fernandes.
M: *Sat 1st M of Sun 5.30pm. Sun 9.30am, 11.30am. Hds 9.30am, 7pm.*

- ***Hospitaller Order of St John of God (OH)***, **Br John O'Neill.** 97 Great Gannett, Welwyn Garden City AL7 3DD
  Tel: 01707-336587

■ WEMBLEY

1. † **St Joseph** (1901; 1957)
Presbytery, High Road, Wembley, Middx HA9 6AG
Tel: 020-8902 0081 **Fax:** 020-8795 0392
Revv John Menonkari (CMI), Joseph Kuzhichalil (CMI).
M: *Sat 1st M of Sun 6.30pm. Sun 9am, 12. Hds* (*vigil 7.30pm*), *9.30am, 12.30pm.*

2. † **English Martyrs (Wembley Park)**
(1930; 1970)
The Presbytery, Chalkhill Road, Wembley Park, Middx, HA9 9EW **Tel:** 020-8904 2306
- ***Augustinian Recollects (OAR):*** **Revv John Docherty, Julio Espinosa.**
  M: *Sat 1st M of Sun 6pm. Sun 9am, 11am, 6pm. Hds 9.30am, 7.30pm.*

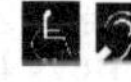

3. † **St Erconwald (Preston Road)**
(1932; 1970)
112 Carlton Avenue East, Wembley, Middlesex HA9 8NB
Tel: 020-8904 6031 **Fax:** 020-8385 1493
Rev Alan Ashton.
M: *Sat 1st M of Sun 5.30pm. Sun 9am, 11.30am. Hds 9.30am, 8pm.*

■ WEST DRAYTON and YIEWSLEY

† **St Catherine**
(1867; 1869; cons Sept. 29, 1893)
20 The Green, West Drayton, Middx UB7 7PJ
Tel: 01895-442777
Rev Brian Smith.
M: *Sat 1st M of Sun 7pm. Sun 9am, 11am* (*Sung/CW*), *6pm. Hds 9am, 11am, 7.30pm.*

■ WEST GREEN

† **St John Vianney**
(1927; 1959; cons June 20, 1964)
4 Vincent Road, West Green, Tottenham N15 3QH **Tel:** 020-8888 5518
Fax: 020-8888 5554 **Rev Joe Ryan,** *Parish Sister:* **Sr Stephanie Greene (OLA).**
Tel: 020-8888 9036
M: *Sat 1st M of Sun 6pm. Sun 8.30am, 10am, 11.30am. Hds 10am, 7.30pm.*

- ***Sisters of Our Lady of the Apostles,*** 10 Vincent Road, West Green, N15 3QH
  Tel: 020-8888 9036
- ***Comboni Missionary Sisters:*** 26 Black Boy Lane N15 3AR (Provincial House).
  Tel: 020-8809 4069 **Fax:** 020-8809 2893
- ***Sisters of St John of God,*** 103 Black Boy Lane N15 3AS **Tel:** 020-8374 1693

■ WESTMINSTER, SW1.

See Cathedral entry at beginning of this section, also Pimlico

■ WHEATHAMPSTEAD

† St Thomas More (1936; 1938; 1978)
7 Marford Road, Wheathampstead, Herts AL4 8AY **Tel:** 01582-832114
Rev Brian Reynolds.
M: *Sun 8.30am, 10am, 5pm. Hds 10am, 8pm.*

■ WHETSTONE

† St Mary Magdalen (1926; 1958; cons 1979)
6 Athenaeum Road, Whetstone N20 9AE
Tel: 020-8445 0838 **Rev Philip Law**.
M: *Sat 1st M of Sun 5.30pm. Sun 8.30am, 10am (Childrens Lit), 12noon (Sung), 7pm (Folk). Hds* (vigil *8pm*), *9.30am, 8pm.*

- ***Missionaries of Africa, (White Fathers) (MAfr),*** Oak Lodge, 48 Totteridge Common, London N20 8LZ **Tel:** 020-8959 1515 **Fax:** 020-8959 742 **Revv Hans Schrenk** (*Superior*), **Richard Calcutt, Patrick Shanahan, Joseph Cummins, Aylward Shorter**.
- ***Sisters of the Sacred Heart of Jesus, (St Jacut),*** 4 Oakleigh Park South, Whetstone, N20 9JU **Tel:** 020-8445 3743 Provincial House, 6 Oakleigh Park South. **Tel:** 020-8445 4655

■ WHITE CITY

† Our Lady of Fatima
(1951; 1965; cons May 17, 1980)
Catholic Church, Commonwealth Avenue, White City, W12 7QR
Tel: 020-8743 8334
Revv Keith Stoakes, Ephrem Andom.
M: *Sat 1st M of Sun 7pm. Sun 9am, 11am, 6pm. Hds 9.30am, 7.30pm.*

- ***Marist Sisters,*** 22 Bloemfontein Road, W12 7BX. **Tel:** 020-8749 4850
- ***Religious Sisters of Charity***, 13 Arminger Road, W12 **Tel:** 020-8749 5918

■ WHITECHAPEL, E1

See Commercial Road, German Church and Underwood Road.

■ WHITTON

† St Edmund of Canterbury
(1934; 1935; 1963)
Presbytery, St Edmund's Lane, 213 Nelson Road, Whitton, Middx TW2 7BB
Tel: 020-8894 9923
In Residence: **Rev Brendan Carmondy SJ**
M: *Sat 1st M of Sun 6.30pm. Sun 9.30am* (*Family*), *11.15am* (*Sung*), *6pm. Hds 9.30am, 7.30pm.*

■ WILLESDEN

† Our Lady of Willesden (1886; 1931)
Shrine of Our Lady of Willesden, Acton Lane.
Revv Stephen Willis, Edward Burton.
The Presbytery, Nicoll Road, Willesden, NW10 9AX
Tel: 020-8965 4935 **Fax:** 020-8961 0928
M: *Sat 1st M of Sun 6pm. Sun 9am, 11am, 5.30pm. Hds* (vigil *7pm*), *10am, 12.30pm, 7.30pm (sung). Brazilian Chaplaincy Mass in Shrine Church: Sat 1st M Sun 7.30pm, Sun 2pm.*

■ WILLESDEN GREEN

† St Mary Magdalen (1901; 1939)
Harlesden Road.
Rev Hugh MacKenzie, Clergy House, Peter Avenue, NW10 2DD **Tel:** 020-8451 4677
Fax: 020-8451 0288
In residence: **Rev Anthony Ponweera.**
Parish Sister: **Sr Lily DC.**
M: *Sat 1st M of Sun 6.30pm. Sun 9am, 10.30am, 12noon, 6.30pm. Hds* (vigil *6.30pm*), *9.30am, 12noon, 7pm.*

- ***Jesuits (SJ), Polish Jesuits,*** House of Our Lady of Mercy, 182 Walm Lane, London NW2 3AX. **Revv Tadeusz Sporny, Leszek Golebewski, Jerzy Bialek, Tomas Rakowski, Artur Wyzima. Br Boleshaw Krol**. **Tel:** 0208-452 4304
- ***Divine Word Missionaries (SVD),*** 8 Teignmouth Road, NW2 4HN **Tel:** 020-8452 8430 **Revv Michael Egan** *(Superior)*, **Martin McPake, Kieran Fitzharris, Kevin O'Toole.**
- ***Sisters of the Holy Family of Bordeaux,*** 83 St Gabriel's Road, NW2 4DU **Tel:** 020-8452 3844
- ***Little Sisters of the Assumption,*** 52 Kenneth Crescent, NW2 4PN **Tel:** 020-8452 1687 **Fax:** 020-8208 3625
- ***Montfort Missionaries (SMM),*** 27 St Gabriel's Road, Cricklewood, London NW2 4DS **Tel:** 020-8450 4291 **Rev Kieran Flynn.**
- ***De Paul Trust,*** 247 Willesden Lane, NW2 5RY **Tel:** 020-8830 1093
- ***Daughters of Wisdom (La Sagesse),*** 9 The Oaks, 25 Brondesbury Park NW6 7BY **Tel:** 020-8830 2530

■ WOOD GREEN

† St Paul the Apostle (1882; 1904; 1970)
22 Bradley Road, Wood Green, N22 7SZ
Tel: 020-8888 2390
Canon Michael Munnelly, Rev John McKenna.
M: *Sat 1st M of Sun 6.30pm. Sun 8am, 10am (Fam), 11.30am (Sung), 6pm (Folk). Hds 9.30am, 8pm.*

- ***Daughters of Providence,*** 82 Sylvan Avenue, N22 5HY **Tel:** 020-8888 6923
- ***Daughters of Divine Love,*** 84 Sylvan Avenue N22 5HY **Tel:** 020-8888 1898

■ **YEADING** 

† **St Raphael** (1957; 1961; cons 4 May, 1975)
St Raphael's House, Morrison Road,
Yeading, Middlesex UB4 9JP
Tel: 020-8845 1919 **Fax:** 020-8845 1215
Revv John Welsh, Sean O'Toole *(Chaplain Hillingdon Hosp).*
M: *Sat 1st M of Sun 7pm. Sun 9am, 10.30am (Sung), 12noon, 7pm. Hds 9.30am, 7.30pm.*

■ Catholic Churches of the Eastern Rite

■ **BELARUSIAN CATHOLIC CHURCH**
Marian House, Holden Avenue N12 8HY
Tel: 020-8445 5358
M: *Marian House, Sun 10.30am.*

■ **CHALDEAN CATHOLIC CHURCH**
38 Cavendish Avenue, W13 0JQ
Tel: 020-8997 0370
Fr Habib J Jaujou
M: *West Acton, Sun 12.30pm.*

■ **ERITREAN CATHOLIC CHURCH,**
(Gheez Rite)
1 Commonwealth Avenue W12 7QR
Tel: 020-8743 8315
M: *Notting Hill, Sun 1pm.*

■ **ETHIOPIAN CATHOLIC CHURCH,**
(Gheez Rite)
29 Eversley Crescent, Isleworth TW7 4LR
Tel: 020-78560 8416
M: *Queensway, Sun 1pm.*

■ **MARONITE CATHOLIC CHURCH**
6 Dobson Close, London NW6 4RS
Tel: 020-7586 1801
M: *For Lebanese: Paddington, Sun 12noon. For Cypriots: Convent of Daughters of Providence, Palmers Green, Sun 10.30am.*

■ **MELKITE CATHOLIC CHURCH**
46 Sunderland Avenue, Oxford OX2 3AT
Rev Fr Shafiq Abouzayd
Tel: 01865 514041
M: *Sun 11.30am. St Barnabas Anglican Church, St. Barnabas Street, Off Pimlico Road, London SW1W 8PF*

■ **SYRIAC CATHOLIC CHURCH**
The Parish House, Moorhouse Road W2 5DJ
M: *Brook Green, Sun 1pm.*

■ **SYRO-MALABAR CHURCH**
373 Bowes Road N11 1AA (New Southgate)
Tel: 020-8368 1638
M: *Hounslow, 1st Sun 3pm. Southall, 3rd Sun 3pm. Wembley 1, 4th Sun 4pm. paddington, Last Sun 5pm.*

■ **UKRAINIAN CATHOLIC CHURCH**
Cathedral of the Holy Family in Exile
Duke Street (off Oxford Street)
Tel: 020-7629 1534
M: *Sun 10.30am.*

■ **ORDERS OR CONGREGATIONS, ETC**

■ **Men**
African Missions, Society of: New Barnet.
Alexian Brothers: Camden Town.
Assumptionists: Bethnal Green, Hitchin.
Augustinians: Hammersmith, Hoxton, Shepherd's Bush, Islington.
Augustinian Recollects: Kensington (1), Wembley.
Benedictines (English Cong): Ealing.
Benedictines (Olivetan): Cockfosters.
Camillians: Homerton.
Carmelites: Finchley East.
Carmelites, Discalced: Kensington (2).
Charity, Institute of (Rosminians): Ely Place.
Christian Brothers: Twickenham.
Claretian Missionaries: Hayes.
Columban Fathers: Hampstead.
Comboni Missionaries: Bayswater.
Consolata Fathers: Finchley Church End, Garston.
Divine Providence, Sons of: Teddington.
Divine Word Missionaries: Willesden Green.
Dominicans: Haverstock Hill.
Franciscans: Pimlico.
Franciscan Friars of the Atonement: Westminster.
Fransalians: Hampton Hill.
Gabriel, Brothers of St: Ealing.
Holy Ghost Fathers: New Barnet.
Hospitaller Order of Saint John of God, Brothers of the: Welwyn Garden City East.
Jesuits: Farm Street, Kensington (2), Kilburn, Southall, Stamford Hill, Swiss Cottage, Willesden Green.
Josephites: Poplar
Lebanese Maronite Order: Lebanese Centre.
Malta, Order of: St John's Wood.
Marian Fathers: Polish Church (3).
Marist Fathers: French Church.
Missionaries of Africa (MAfr) (White Fathers): Ealing, Highgate, Whetstone.
Montfort Missionaries: Willesden Green.
Oblates of Mary Immaculate: Kilburn, Kilburn West, Tower Hill.
Oratorians: Oratory.
Pallottine Fathers: Clerkenwell, Greenford, Italian Church.
Passionists: Highgate.
Presentation Brothers: Twickenham.
Sacred Heart, Brothers of the: St Albans.
Sacred Heart, Missionaries of the: St Albans.

Sacred Hearts Community: Acton West, Acton.
Salvatorians: Abbots Langley, Chipperfield, Harrow Weald.
Scalabrini Fathers: Borehamwood.
Servites (Servants of Mary) OSM: Fulham Road.
Stigmatine Fathers: Kensal Rise.
Vincentians: Mill Hill (1), Osterley, Bayswater.
Xaverian Brothers: Twickenham.
Xaverian Missionaries: Finchley Church End.

■ Women

Adoration Sisters, Watford.
Adoratrices, Handmaids of the Blessed Sacrament and of Charity: Kensington (2).
Adorers of the Sacred Heart (Contemplative Benedictines): Marylebone.
Assumption, Religious of the: Kensington (2), Poplar.
Assumption, Little Sisters of the: Willesden Green, Homerton.
Augustinian Sisters: Westminster.
Canonesses of St Augustine (Congregation of Our Lady): Bethnal Green, Oratory.
Canossian Daughters of Charity: Waltham Cross.
Capitanio Sisters: Ealing.
Carmelites: St Charles' Square.
Carmelite Missionaries: St John's Wood.
Cenacle, Sisters of Our Lady of the: Cockfosters.
Charity (of Jesus and Mary), Sisters of: Bow, Letchworth, Stevenage.
Charity (of St Jeanne Antide), Sisters of: Ealing, Stoke Newington.
Charity of St Paul (Selly Park), Sisters of: Hackney, Hounslow.
Charity, Religious Sisters of: Acton, Chiswick, Hackney, White City.
Christian Instruction (St Gildas), Sisters of: Barnet, Stroud Green.
Columban Sisters: Bow, Clapton Park.
Comboni Missionary Sisters (Verona Sisters): Chiswick, West Green.
Congregation of Jesus: Kentish Town, Swiss Cottage.
Consolata Missionary Sisters: Somers Town.
Cross (Liege), Daughters of the: Chelsea, Much Hadham.
Cross and Passion, Sisters of the: Fulham Road, Islington.
Cross, Sisters of the Holy: Ealing.
Daughters of Charity (of St Vincent de Paul): Cathedral, Kensal Rise, Kentish Town, Kilburn, Limehouse, Mill Hill, Northwood, Pinner.
Divine Love, Daughters of: Wood Green.
Dominican Sisters (Congregation. of Newcastle, Natal): Bushey, Cricklewood, Edgware, Harpenden, Haverstock Hill, Hemel Hempstead, Osterley, Stevenage.
Dominican Sisters (Congregation. of Oakford, Natal): Pinner
Dominican Sisters (Congregation of Stone): Ealing.
Dorothy, Sisters of St: Hampstead.
Faithful Companions of Jesus: Isleworth, Poplar, Somers Town.
Franciscan Missionaries of Mary: Acton West, Shepherds Bush.
Franciscan Sisters (Mill Hill): Mill Hill.
Franciscan Sisters of the Heart of Jesus: Pimlico.
Franciscan Sisters of Our Lady of Victories: Cathedral.
Good Shepherd Sisters: Finchley East.
Grail (English Society of the): Pinner.
Handmaids of the Sacred Heart of Jesus (Rome): St John's Wood.
Helpers of the Holy Souls, Society of: Camden Town.
Holy Child Jesus, Society of the: Bayswater, Edmonton, Kensington, Spanish Place.
Holy Family of Bordeaux, Sisters of the: Kilburn, Willesden Green.
Holy Family of Nazareth, Sisters of the: Enfield.
Holy Family Sisters of the Needy: St Charles Square
Holy Name of Jesus, Sisters of the: Polish Church (3).
Institute of BVM (Loreto Sisters): Acton, Kingsland, St Albans.
Jesus, Daughters of: Rickmansworth.
Jesus, Little Sisters of: Hoxton, St Charles' Square.
Jesus, Sisters of the Infant: Acton East.
Jesus and Mary, Religous of: Kensal Rise.
John of God, Sisters of: West Green.
Joseph of Peace, Sisters of St: Cricklewood, Hanwell.
Louis, Sisters of St: Dollis Hill, Harringay, Harrow South, Harrow-on-the-Hill, Muswell Hill, New Southgate.
Marcellina, Institute of St: Hampstead.
Marie Auxiliatrice, Society of: Muswell Hill, Tottenham.
Marist Sisters: Upper Holloway, White City.
Martha, Sisters of St: Barnet.
Mary Immaculate, Missionary Sisters of (PIME): Chiswick.
Mary Immaculate, Religious of: Kensington (2).
Mary of Namur, Sisters of St: Notting Hill, Watford.

Mary, Handmaidens of (Spanish Nursing Sisters): Kensington (1).
Mary, Little Company of: Ealing, Gunnersbury, Northfields.
Mary Mother of Mercy, Daughters of: Edgware.
Medical Mission Sisters (Society of Catholic Medical Missionaries): Acton, Brentford, Hanwell, Northfields.
Medical Missionaries of Mary: Ealing.
Mercy, Institute of Our Lady: Highbury, Poplar.
Mercy Sisters (Union): Cathedral, Acton East, Bethnal Green, Bow, Clapton Park, Commercial Road, Cricklewood, Feltham, Hillingdon, Kensal, New Town, St Albans, St Albans South, St John's Wood, Underwood Road.
Missionaries of Charity: Kensal New Town, Southall.
Missionary Sisters of Our Lady of Africa (White Sisters): Ealing.
Nazareth, Poor Sisters of: Brook Green, Finchley East.
Notre Dame, Sisters of: Pimlico.
Our Lady of the Apostles, Sisters of: West Green.
Our Lady of Charity, Sisters of: Shepherd's Bush.
Our Lady of the Missions, Sisters of: New Southgate, Wapping, Wealdstone.
Pallottine Missionary Sisters: Clerkenwell.
Paul of Chartres, Sisters of St: Highbury.
Paul, Daughters of St: Kensington (1).
Poor Child Jesus, Sisters of the: Finchley North.
Poor Clares: Barnet.
Poor Handmaids of Jesus Christ: Hendon.
Poor, Little Sisters of the: Stoke Newington.
Providence (of the Immaculate Conception, Champion), Sisters of: Haverstock Hill.
Providence (Ruille-sur-Loire), Sisters of: Stroud Green.
Providence (St Brieuc), Daughters of: Palmers Green, Wood Green.
Resurrection, Sisters of the: Ealing, Polish Church (3).
Rosminian Sisters: Ely Place.
Sacred Heart of Jesus (St Jacut), Sisters of the: Whetstone.
Sacred Heart of Mary (Beziers), Religious of the: Northfields.
Sacred Heart, Sisters Hospitallers of the: Fulham Road.
Sacred Heart, Society of the: Brook Green, Hayes, St Charles' Square.
Sacred Hearts of Jesus and Mary (Chigwell), Sisters of the: Uxbridge.
Sainte Union des Sacrés Coeurs, Congregation of the: Holloway, Kentish Town, Kilburn.
Santa Ana, Spanish Sisters of: Brook Green.
Servants of the Mother of God: Bayswater, Brentford, Hampton on Thames. Somers Town, Upper Holloway.
Servite Sisters: Clapton, Stamford Hill.
Sion, Sisters of Our Lady of: Bayswater, Stroud Green.
Suore Collegine della Sacra Famiglia: Ponders End.
Sisters of the Temple: Notting Hill.
Ursulines of Jesus: Hoxton, Kingsland, Stamford Hill.
Ursulines of St Angela Merici: Manor House.
Wisdom (La Sagesse) Daughters of: Finchley East, Willesden Green.

■ SOCIETIES AND ORGANISATIONS

For Societies and Organisations without representation in the diocese please see the main Societies and Organisations section.

Aid to the Church in Need. Benhill House, 12-14 Benhill Road, Sutton SM1 4DA **Tel:** 020 8642 8668 **Fax:** 020 8661 6293 *National Director (UK):* **Neville Kyrke-Smith**. *Area Secretaries manager:* **Margaret Regan**. Westminster Area *Secretaries:* **Dr David Black**, 11 The Wick, Hertford SG14 3HN **Tel:** 01992 587285 **E-mail:** drblack@btopenworld.com **Dr Seamus O'Brien**, 9 Wilby Mews, W11 3NP **Tel:** 020 7727 9568 **E-mail:** jjob@waitrose.com **Website:** acnuk.org

Apostleship of the Sea. Apostleship of the Sea (AOS) is the official maritime welfare and mission agency of the Catholic Church in Great Britain. For more information see the entry in 'Ecclesial Organisations and Chaplaincies' Section. AOS, Herald House, Lamb's Passage EC1Y 8LE **E-mail:** londonoffice@apostleshipofthesea.org.uk **Website:** www.apostleshipofthe sea.org.uk

Archconfraternity of St Stephen. The Archconfraternity of St Stephen exists to promote and encourge high standards of altar serving. For more information see the entry in 'Catholic Societies' Section. *National Director:* **Fr Dennis Touw** *President:* **Mr Michael Chute**, PO Box 568, London WC1A 1YT. *Secretary:* **Mr Michael O'Leary**, PO Box 568, London WC1A 1YT. **E-mail:** secretary@guildofststephen.org

ARCHDIOCESE OF WESTMINSTER

Website: www.guildofststephen.org

Ascent Movement. For Christians in their middle and later years in their spiritual growth, to encourage them to take up their responsibilities as members of the Church through Friendship, Spirituality and Mission. *National President:* **Miss Margaret Snowdon;** *National Secretary:* **Mrs Marie Ryde,** 63 Dartmouth Road, Hendon, London NW4 3HY **Tel:** 020-8202 4930 **E-mail:** marieryde@btinternet.com **Website:** www.ascentmovement.org.uk

Association for Latin Liturgy. To promote the use of Latin texts and music in the approved rites of the Church. *Diocesan Representative:* **Mr E M Barrett,** 14 Connaught Mansions, Prince of Wales Drive, SW11 4SA **Tel:** 020-7978 5676

Association of Separated and Divorced Catholics. A federation of lay support groups to provide mutual help and spiritual support to those who have experienced the pain of marriage breakdown. **Frank Hacklett,** 164 Whitmore Road, Harrow, HA1 4AQ **E-mail:** frankhacklett@btinternet.com

Association for the Propagation of the Faith (APF) The APF ensures that every bishop in the new churches has funds to build churches/schools. For more information see the entry in 'Catholic Societies' Section. *Diocesan Director:* **Rev Kevin McDevitt** **Tel:** 020 7272 8195 *Mill Hill Missionaries:* 58 Cookham Road, Maidenhead SL6 7HT **Website:** www.missionsocieties.org.uk

Association for Priests of African or Asian Descent. Sponsored by Catholic Association for Racial Justice. *Secretary:* **Cecilia Taylor-Camara,** 9 Henry Road N4 2LH Tel: 020 8802 8080

Association of Blind Catholics. To enable blind Catholics to participate more fully in the life of the Church. *Hon Sec:* **Paul Questier,** 58 Oakwood Road, Horley, Surrey RH6 7BU **Tel:** 01293-772104

Association of Catholic Women. Under the patronage of Our Lady and St Joseph, the ACW unites women from all parts of the country who find happiness and fulfilment in giving glad assent to the Church's teachings as proclaimed by the magisterium. *Chairman:* **Mrs Josephine Robinson,** *Secretary:* **Mrs Ruth Real,** 22 Surbiton Hill Park, Surbiton, Surrey KT5 8ET **Tel** 0208-399 1459 **E-mail:** acwreview@aol.com

Association of Mary Help of Christians. To promote personal devotion to, and public honour of Our Lady under the title 'Help of Christians'. A prayer meeting is held on the fourth Saturday of each month at 4pm at 36 Adolphus Road N4 2AY. Contact: **Mother Eugenia Pantalleresco** Tel: 020 8800 5228

Assumption Lay Volunteer Programme. Offers young people over 20 the opportunity to share their lives for a year with poor and marginalised communities connected with Assumption Sisters around the world. Openness to others and a willingness to do anything required. *Volunteer Co-ordinator:* 23 Kensington Sq, W8 5HN **Tel:** 020 7361 4752 **E-mail:** alvpccoordinator@hotmail.com **Website:** www.alvp.org.uk

Banneux ND International Union of Prayer. Promulgates the message given by Our Lady at Banneux, under the title 'Virgin of the Poor' by films, all-night vigils, retreats and pilgrimages. **Website:** banneux-nd.org.uk *Secretary:* Mrs Maria Hare, 10 Bramble Close, Hillingdon UB8 3QE **Tel:** 01895 420753

CAFOD Official agency of the Church, Works through organisations in the developing world, and supports over 500 long-term self-help projects in 50 countries. For more information see the entry in 'Catholic Bishop's Conference' Section. *Regional organiser:* **Tony Sheen.** CAFOD Westminster, 29 Bramley Road, N14 4HE **Tel:** 020-8449 6970

Carmelite Secular Institute (The Leaven), A secular institute for women, single or widowed. Contact: **Miss Patricia Edwards,** 17 Pioneer Way W12 0EZ **Tel:** 020 8749 1919 **Website:** www.carmelite.org/leaven

Carmelite Third Order, Offers lay people and diocesan clergy the opportunity of deepening their relationship with Jesus Christ, within one of the most ancient traditions of the Church. For more information see the entry in 'Catholic Societies' Section. For details of monthly meetings through the diocese, and more information about Carmelite spirituality please contact **Maureen Beck** Tel: 020 7834 9684 or **Sylvia Lucas,** 0788 9436165 **Website:** www.carmelite.org

Catenian Association. International organisation for practising Catholic men founded in 1908 with world-wide membership of over 10,000 and over 290 groups in the UK. Groups meet monthly. **Head Office:** 2nd Floor, 1 Copthall House, Station Square, Coventry CU1 2FY **Tel:** 024 7622 4533

Website: www.thecatenianassociation.org.uk *Province No 2 (City and East London):* **B Noakes Tel:** 01245 441247 *Province No 8 (West London, West Herts):* **N Lamb Tel:** 0118 958 1597 *Province No 2 (Central & North London, Herts):* **R Pyper Tel:** 01992 460596

Catholic Agency to Support Evangelisation. To support and resource Catholic communties and individuals in England and Wales to offer the Gospel to promote dialogue betweeen gospel and culture and to offer information on the Catholic Faith through the Catholic Enquiry Office. 114 West Heath Road London NW3 7TX *Chair of Exec Committee:* **Br Malcolm McMahon** *Director:* **Mgr Keith Barltrop** *Team:* **Clare Ford, Clare Ward, Emily Davis**
E-mail: info@caseresources.org.uk

Catholic Archive Society. The Catholic Archive Society promotes and advises on listing, management and preservation of records of diocese, religious foundations and institutions of the Catholic Church. It does not collect or store archives. *Chair:* **Judith Smeaton**, 33 Middlethorpe Drive, Dringhouses, York YO24 1NA *Secretary:* **Margaret Harcourt Williams**, Innyngs House, Hatfield Park, Hatfield, Herts AL9 5PL
Website: www.catholic-history.org

Catholic Evangelisation Services Equipping the parish through the production of Catholic Teaching resources on video and DVD for Sacramental Preparation, Parish Renewal, Youth Work and Small group use. **David Payne** PO Box 333, St Albans, Herts AL2 1EL
Tel: 01727-822837

Catholic Evidence Guild, (Westminster Diocesan Catechists). For the training and provision of public speakers on the Catholic Faith. Meets near Westminster Cathedral. Enquiries to: **Mr Phil Gough,** Catholic Evidence Guild, 84 Grove Green Road, Leytonstone, London E11 4EL

Catholic Charismatic Renewal. Information and resource centre for the National Service Committee: contacts with prayer groups and communities in Britain and abroad. Bi-monthly magazine, 'Goodnews'.
Allen Hall, 28 Beaufort Street, SW3 5AA
Tel: 020 7352 5298 **Fax:** 020 7351 4486
Email: ccruk@ontel.com
Website: www.ccr.org.uk

Catholic Education Service for England and Wales Represents Hierarchy and Catholic bodies in Educational Matters. *Chairman:* **Archbishop Vincent Nichols Director: Mrs Oona Stannard**, 39 Eccleston Square, SW1V 1BK
Tel: 020 7901 4880 **Fax:** 020 7901 4893
Email: general@cesew.org.uk
Website: www.cesew.org.uk

Catholic Enquiry Office
To interest non-Catholics in the belief and practice of Catholics and to reach out to those who no longer practise their Faith by means of advertising and the distribution of free literature.
Tel: 020 8458 3316
Website: www.life4seekers.co.uk
Email: enquiries@life4seekers.co.uk

Catholic Medical Association. *Master of Westminster Branch:* **Dr Michael Jarmulowicz**, 6 St Andrew's Road, NW10 2QS **Tel:** 020-8459 8572

Catholic Record Society To publish the historical sources for post-Reformation Catholic History in England and Wales. ***President:*** **Bishop Daniel Mullins** *(Menevia-Emeritus Bishop)*. Chairman Professor V A McClelland. *Hon Secretary:* **Dr L Gooch**, 12 Melbourne Place, Wolsingham, Co Durham DL13 3EH
Website: www.catholic-history.org.uk

Catholic Stage Guild To cater for the spiritual and temporal needs of Catholics engaged in the Theatre, Films, Television, Radio and allied arts including performers, writers and technicians. Associate Membership open to all. *Chaplain:* **Canon J McDonald**. *Secretary:* **Molly Steele** 1 Maiden Lane WC2E 7NB
Tel: 020 7240 1221
E-mail: info@catholicstageguild.org.uk

Catholic Truth Society To explain the faith, teaching and life of the Catholic Church. For more information see the entry in 'Catholic Societies' Section. *Chair:* **Rt Rev Paul Hendricks MA, PhL, VG** *(Southwark); General Secretary:* **Fergal Martin LLB, LLM** Offices, 40-46 Harleyford Road, London SE11 5AY
Tel: 020 7640 0042
E-mail: info@cts-online.org.uk
Website: www.cts.org.uk

Catholic Fund for Homeless and Destitute People. c/o St Martin of Tours HA, 318-320 St Paul's Road N1 2LF
Tel: 020-7704 3850

Catholic Union of Great Britain. A non-political association of members of the Catholic laity to watch over Catholic interests. For more information see the entry in 'Catholic Societies' Section. *Secretary:* **Ms Emilia Iclepacka**, St

Maximilian Kolbe House, 63 Jeddo Road, W12 9EE **Tel:** 020 8749 1321 **Fax:** 020 8735 0861 **E-mail:** info@catholicunion.org **Website:** www.catholicunion.org

Catholic Women's League. *Westminster Branch President:* **Mrs Christine Pugh**, 8 Thornton Road, Little Heath, Potters Bar EN6 1JH

Christian Life Community Small groups of Christians who meet regularly to help each other deepen their life of prayer. CLC's special characteristic is the spirituality of St Ignatius, helping members to integrate prayer with action in their daily lives. *National Chaplain:* **Br Alan Harrison** *Diocesan Representative:* **Michael Dorey**, 13c Peabody Estate, Old Pye St SW1P 2LG

Dominican Laity Men and women called to spread the Gospel in the tradition of St Dominic. London Fraternity meets monthly at Haverstock Hill. *Chaplain:* **Fr Denis Geraghty OP** *Secretary:* **Stephen White**, 10 St Simon's Avenue, SW15 6DU **E-mail:** stephenwhite@lycos.com

Emmanuel Community An association of the Faithful, recognised by the Holy See, for lay people, priests and consecrated men and women. *Contact:* **David & Alice Boyles**, 5 Finch Close, Knaphill, Woking GU21 2LF **Tel:** 01483 480740 **E-mail:** dboyles@ukonline.co.uk **Website:** www.emmanuel.info

Focolare Movement An international ecclesial movement which engages in dialogue with those who want to work for peace and unity. Residential Conference Centre, 69 Parkway, Welwyn Garden City, Herts AL8 6JG **Tel:** 01707 323620 **Website:** www.focolare.org

Friends of the Holy Father To pray for the Holy Father's intentions, study and promote his teaching. Supports a fund assisting in defraying the expenses of his Apostolic Ministry. *Chairman:* **John Dean Dip Law; Dip lP** *Secretary:* **Dr Michael Straiton MB, KCSG**, Vaughan House, 46 Francis St SW1P

Good Counsel Network Catholic pregnancy counselling organisation. For more information see the entry in 'Catholic Societies' Section. *Director:* **Clare McCullough**, PO Box 46679 NW9 8ZT **Tel:** 020 7723 1740 **E-mail:** info@goodcounselnetwork.freeserve.co.uk

Grail, The. ***The Grail Centre:*** The Grail Centre, 125 Waxwell Lane, Pinner, Middlesex HA5 3ER **Tel:** 020-8866 2195 **E-mail:** grailcentre@compuserve.com

Guild of Our Lady of Ransom For the Conversion of England and Wales by prayer; appreciation of our Catholic Heritage by publications, historical pilgrimages and rambles; financial support for poor rural and inner-city parishes, including those in Westminster. *Master:* **Mgr Anthony Stark KCHS**, 31 Southdown Road, Wimbledon SW20 8QJ **Tel:** 020 8947 2598 **Fax:** 020 8944 6355 **E-mail:** mgr.ags@btinternet.com

Guild of St Agatha Catholic Association of Bellringers. Guild Office, 1 Albert Road, Bournemouth, Dorset BH1 1BZ *Diocesan Representative:* **Fr Shaun Lennard**, 39 Duncan Terrace N1 8AL **Tel:** 020 7226 3277

Heralds of the Gospel Association of Pontifical right formed mainly for young people who alternate a life of recollection, study and prayer with evangelizing activities. Their spirituality is based on devotion to the Holy Eucharist, love for Mary and fidelity to the Pope. *Contact:* 29 Lower Teddington Road, Hampton Wick KT1 4HQ **Tel:** 020 8943 4159 **E-mail:** LumenMaria@aol.com **Website:** www.arautos.org

Holy Childhood One of the Pontifical Mission Societies, it is the Church's official overseas charity for children. Through its project **Mission Together** it encourages children to be concerned with Mission through prayer, learning activities and fund-raising. For free materials or to arrange a school assembly please contact: *National Co-ordinator:* **Monika Chmelova** **Tel:** 020 7821 9755 **Website:** www.missiontogether.org.uk

Housing Justice (Formally Catholic Housing Aid Society). Information, campaigning and advice. **Website:** www.housingjustice.org.uk *Chief Executive:* **Alison Gelder**, 209 Old Marylebone Road, London NW1 5QT *Project Administrator:* **Guy Cruls** (Guide Neighbourhood Programme) **Tel:** 020 7723 7273 ext 229 **Fax:** 020 7723 5943 **E-mail:** info@housingjustice.org.uk

Knights of St Columba A fraternal order of Catholic men, supporting the mission of the Church and the spiritual, intellectual and material welfare of its members and their families. **Provincial Grand Knights:** *Province 11:* **Dr Gilbert Igboaka**, 91 Brownlow Road N11 2BN *Province 29:* **Andy McKie**, 218 Knella Road, Welwyn Garden City, Herts AL7 3NW *Province 30:* **Martin D'Cuhna** 17

Shakespeare Rd W7 1LT

Latin Mass Society For the preservation of the traditional Roman Rite and the continuing use of Latin and Gregorian chant in the life and worship of the Church. 11-13 Macklin Street WC2B 5NH **Tel:** 020 7404 7284 **Fax:** 020 7831 5585 **E-mail:** thelatinmasssociety@snmail.co.uk **Website:** www.latin-mass-society.org

Lay Missionary and Volunteer Network A partnership of several missionary and volunteer groups which send lay volunteers overseas. each has its own Charism and we meet to share ideas, resources and training, organising an 8 day pre-departure training course for volunteers each summer. *Contact:* LMVN, 23 Kensington Square W8 5HN **E-mail:** admin@lmvn.org

Linacre Centre for Healthcare Ethics A research and education centre established in 1977 under a charitable trust formed by the Catholic Archbishops of England and Wales. *Director:* **Dr Helen Watt**, 38 Circus Road NW8 9SE **Tel:** 020 7266 7410 **Fax:** 020 7266 5424 **E-mail:** admin@linacre.org **Website:** www.linacre.org

Malta, Order of (British Association) A religious order of the Church, supporting the Hospital of St John and St Elizabeth in London and other hospitaller work including pilgrimages to Lourdes and Walsingham. *President:* **Charles Weld Esq** *Chancellor:* **Hugh van Cutsem Esq**, 58 Grove End Road, London NW8 9NE **Tel:** 020 7296 1414 **Fax:** 020 7289 3243

Marriage Care Professionally trained marriage counsellors offer help to those with marital difficulties, and courses for engaged couples. Resource for teachers and others who are responsible for delivering personal health and social education to young people. **Helpline:** 0845 660 6000 Mon - Fri 10am - 4pm. **Website:** www.marriagecare.org.uk National Office, Clitherow House, 1 Blythe Mews, Blythe Road, London W14 0NW **Tel:** 020 7371 1341 **Fax:** 020 7371 4921 **E-mail:** info@marriagecare.org.uk

Marriage Encounter Provides weekends where couples and priests can enrich their lives through improving communication. *Priest:* **Canon John Naughton Tel:** 020 8946 2091 *Contact:* **Tony & Margaret Hunt**, 213 Chambersbury Lane, Hemel Hempstead HP3 8BQ **Tel:** 01442 393838 **Website:** www.wwme.org.uk

Mary Potter Centre Offering counselling, talks, courses and workshops to build self-understanding, confidence, deal with stress, difficult relationships, loss, bereavement, anxiety, distress. *Director:* **Sr Josephine Bugeja LCM**, 33 Mattock Lane, London W5 5BH **Tel:** 020 8840 4313 **E-mail:** jbugeja@aol.com **Website:** http://members.aol.com/jbugeja

Ming Ai A lifelong education centre having close links with Caritas-Hong Kong with a wide range of leisure, cookery, health, business and oriental language classes. It promotes links between our diocese and the Church of Hong Kong and China. *Director:* **Dr Therese Shak**, Denver House, 1 Cline Road, Bounds Green N11 2LX **Tel:** 020 8361 7161 **Fax:** 020 8361 4207 **Website:** www.mingai.org.uk

Newman Association. *Circle Secretaries, London:* **Therese & Anthony Havery**, 27 Southfields, NW4 4LX; **Mrs Anne Riley**, 17 Mount Pleasant Road W5 1SG

Our Lady's Catechists: Association of men and women who are qualified to give religious instruction. For more information see the entry in 'Catholic Societies' Section. *Diocesan Representative:* **Mrs Charmaine Jayasuriya**, 21 Charlesworth Close, Hemel Hempstead, Herts HP3 9EC **Tel:** 01422-267035 **E-mail:** dcharmainej@aol.com **Website:** www.ourladycatechists.co.uk

Pax Christi International Catholic Movement for Peace, promoting a greater sense of Christian responsibility on the issues of war and peace. **Website:** www.paxchristi.org.uk *National President:* **Bishop Malcolm McMahon** *General Secretary:* **Patricia Gaffney**, St Joseph's, Watford Way, London NW4 4TY **Tel:** 020 8203 4884 **Fax:** 020 8203 5234 **E-mail:** paxchristi@gn.apc.org

Pontifical Missionary Union Through its quarterly magazine, 'Mission Outlook', encourages the interest of priests, religious and laity in the overseas missions of the Church and developments in the younger churches. *Contact:* **Mgr John Dale** *(National Director)*, Pontifical Mission Societies, 23 Eccleston Square SW1V 1NU **Tel:** 020 7821 9755 **Website:** www.missio.org.uk

Prison Advice and Care Trust (formerly the Bourne Trust). Provides advice, support to prisoners and families.

Website: www.prisonadvice.org.uk *Director:* **Andy Keen-Downs**, Suite C5, City Cloisters, 196 Old Street, London EC1V 9FR **Tel:** 020-7490 3139 **E-mail:** info@prisonadvice.org.uk **Website:** www.prisonadvice.org.uk

Pioneer Total Abstinence Association of the Sacred Heart. 20 Parkfields Avenue NW9 7PE

Radiant Light Encouraging people to grow in the Catholic faith and share it with others. *Contact:* Radiant Light, 25 Rothamsted Avenue, Harpenden, Herts AL5 2DN **E-mail:** mail@radiantlight.org.uk **Website:** www.radiantlight.org.uk

St Joseph's Society (formerly the Aged Poor). To provide sheltered accommodation for elderly Catholics of limited means. *Secretary:* **S Dolan**. St Joseph's House, 42 Brook Green, W6 7BW **Tel:** 020-7603 9817

St Vincent De Paul Society is an international Christian voluntary organization dedicated to tackling poverty and disadvantage by providing direct practical assistance to anyone in need. *Westminster Central Council President:* **Siobhan Garibaldi**, The St Vincent de Paul Society, 5th Floor, 291-299 Borough High Street, London SE1 1JG

Servite Secular Institute A life of service to God and his people through consecration lived by vows of chastity, poverty and obedience. In union with others of like mind, remaining in their own circumstances. Women of prayer living in the world as Servants of Mary. **Eileen Healy,** 39 Wellington Row, London E2 7BB **Tel:** 020 7729 5183 **E-mail:** eileen.healy@tiscali.co.uk **Website:** www.ssi.org.uk

Sion Centre for Dialogue & Encounter For the study of other faiths and for inter-religious dialogue focussing on the relationship between Christianity and Judaism. Resources, library, day conference facilities, regular study programme, outreach staff. *Contact:* 34 Chepstow Villas, London W11 2QZ **Tel:** 020 7727 3597/7313 8286 **Fax:** 020 7313 8281 **E-mail:** sioncde@yahoo.co.uk **Website:** www.sistersofsion.org

Society of Catholic Artists Aims to encourage high Standards in Church art, to assist propective patrons in the selection of suitable artists and craftsmen and to provide fellowship to those who have the arts and Catholicism in common *Chair:* **Mary Davey.** *Sec:* **Patrick Pike,** 46 Waterloo Road, N19 5NH **E-mail:** ralderson@ukonline.co.uk **Website:** www.catholicartisits.co.uk

Society of Our Lady of Lourdes To promote devotion to Our Lady, organise services and pilgrimages to Lourdes, and assist sick pilgrims, financially and otherwise, to go there. Church of the Immaculate Heart of Mary, Botwell Lane Hayes, Middx UB3 2AB **Tel:** 020 8848 9833 **Fax:** 020 8848 9844

Society of St Augustine of Canterbury. To help maintain the official residence of the Archbishop of Westminster. *Secretary:* **M Milbourn**, The River House, St Mary's Lane, Hertingfordbury SG14 2LF

Society of St Gregory. *Diocesan Representative:* **John Ainslie**, 76 Great Bushey Drive, London N20 8QL **E-mail:** westminster@ssg.org.uk

Teams of Our Lady. An international Catholic Movement for Christian married couples that aims to deepen the couples' spirituality. For more information see the entry in 'Catholic Societies' Section. *Contact couple:* **Michael & Kay Vadon**, 162 Popes Lane, Ealing W5 4NJ **Tel:** 020 8840 2592 **E-mail:** kayvadon@hotmail.com **Website:** teamsofourlady.org.uk

Union of Catholic Mothers. *Diocesan President:* **Mrs Norrie Fox**. *Secretary:* **B Hegarty**, 6a Rutland Park Gardens NW2 4RG *Spiritual Director:* **Rev David Irwin**.

Westminster Ecclesiastical Education Fund. (Fund for the Training of Candidates for the Priesthood). *Contact:* **Rt Rev John Arnold,** Archbishop's House, London SW1P 1QJ

Young Christian Workers and Impact! A movement for young people between the ages of 16-30 Through a programme of enquiry in small groups the YCW educates and trains young people for their mission of Christian service and apostolate in everyday life. YCW HQ, St Joseph's, Watford Way, London NW4 4TY **Tel:** 020 8203 6290 **E-mail:** info@ycwimpact.com **Website:** www.ycwimpact.com

Youth 2000 Seeks to draw young people, between 15-35, into the heart of the Church through a programme of prayer festivals and regular prayer groups. Westminster group meets every Wednesday at 7.00pm in Corpus Christi, Maiden Lane, WC2 **Tel:** 020 7370 0211 **E-mail:** info@youth2000.org **Website:** www.youth200.org

■ HOSPITALS

To contact the Catholic Chaplain of a particular hospital we suggest you contact the hospital reception directly.

■ CATHOLIC SCHOOLS - Maintained

Each Primary School entry ends with an indication of the parish within which the school is situated.
All schools with websites are to be found listed at www.westminsterdiocese.org.uk
ND = not in the Trusteeship of the Diocese. All Schools are Voluntary Aided unless otherwise stated.

■ CITY OF WESTMINSTER

▲ Primary Schools

(Junior & Infant unless stated, +N=Nursery)

Our Lady of Dolours: (+N) 19 Cirencester St, London W2 5SR **Tel:** 020 7641 4326 **Fax:** 020 7641 4389 (*Paddington*)

St Edward: (+N) Lisson Grove, London NW1 6LH **Tel:** 020 7723 5911 **Fax:** 020 7723 5250 (*St John's Wood*) ND

St Joseph: (+N) Lanark Rd, Sutherland Ave, London W9 1DF **Tel:** 020 7286 3518 **Fax:** 020 7286 2303 (*St John's Wood*)

St Mary of the Angels: (+N) Shrewsbury Rd, London W2 5PR **Tel:** 020 7641 6110 **Fax:** 020 7641 4484 (*Bayswater*)

St Vincent: (+N) St. Vincent St, Marylebone, London W1U 4DF **Tel:** 020 7641 6110 **Fax:** 020 7641 6116 (Spanish Place) ND

St Vincent de Paul: (+N) Primary School, Morpeth Terrace, London SW1P 1EP **Tel:** 020 7641 5990 **Fax:** 020 7641 5901 (*Cathedral*)

Westminster Cathedral: Bessborough Place, London SW1V 3SE **Tel:** 020 7641 5915 **Fax:** 020 7821 9349 (*Pimlico*)

▲ Secondary School

St. George: Lanark Rd, Maida Vale, London W9 1RB **Tel:** 020 7328 0904 **Fax:** 020 7624 6083

■ LONDON BOROUGH OF BARNET

▲ Primary Schools

(Junior & Infant unless stated, +N=Nursery)

The Annunciation: (Infants +N) Thirleby Rd, Burnt Oak, Edgware, Middx HA8 0HQ **Tel:** 020 8959 2325 **Fax:** 020 8906 4116 (*Burnt Oak*)

The Annunciation: (Junior) The Meads, Burnt Oak, Middx HA8 9HQ **Tel:** 020 8906 0723 **E-mail:** head.annunciationjnr.barnet@lgfl.net (*Burnt Oak*)

Blessed Dominic: (+N) Lanacre Ave, Grahame Park, London NW9 5FN **Tel:** 020 8205 3790 **Fax:** 020 8205 9341 (*Grahame Park*)

Our Lady of Lourdes: (+N) Bow Ln, North Finchley, London N12 0JP **Tel:** 020 8346 1681 **Fax:** 020 8346 0579 (*Finchley East*)

Sacred Heart: 2 Oakleigh Park South, Whetstone, London N20 9JU **Tel:** 020 8445 3854 **Fax:** 020 8445 0862 (*Whetstone*) ND

St Agnes: (+N) Thorverton Rd, Cricklewood, London NW2 1RG **Tel:** 020 8452 4565 **Fax:** 020 8830 6709 (*Cricklewood*)

St Catherine: (+N) Vale Drive, Barnet, Herts EN5 2ED **Tel:** 020 8440 4946 (*Barnet*)

St Joseph: (Infants +N) Watford Way, Hendon, London NW4 4TY **Tel:** 020 8202 9852 **Fax:** 020 8201 5787 (*Hendon*)

St Joseph: (Junior) Watford Way, Hendon, London NW4 4TY **Tel:** 020 8202 5229 **Fax:** 020 8202 5530 (*Hendon*)

St Theresa: 80 East End Rd, Finchley, London N3 2TD **Tel:** 020 8346 8826 **Fax:** 020 8346 0215 (*Finchley Church End*) ND

St Vincent: The Ridgeway, Mill Hill, London NW7 1EJ **Tel:** 020 8959 3417 **Fax:** 020 8906 9733 (*Mill Hill*)

▲ Secondary Schools

Bishop Douglass Catholic High: Hamilton Rd, Finchley, London N2 0SQ **Tel:** 020 8444 5211/3 **Fax:** 020 8444 0416

Finchley Catholic High: (Boys) Woodside Ln, Finchley, London, N12 8TA **Tel:** 020 8445 0105 **Fax:** 020 8446 0691

St James Catholic High: Great Strand, Grahame Park, Colindale, Middx NW9 5PE **Tel:** 020 8358 2800 **Fax:** 020 8358 2801

St Michael Catholic Grammar: (Girls) Nether St, North Finchley, London N12 7NJ **Tel:** 020 8446 2256 **Fax:** 020 8343 9598 **E-mail:** stmichael@rmplc.co.uk

■ LONDON BOROUGH OF BRENT

▲ Primary Schools

(Junior & Infant unless stated, +N=Nursery)

The Convent of Jesus & Mary: (Infant +N) 21 Park Ave, Willesden Green, London NW2 5AN **Tel:** 020 8459 5890 **Fax:** 020 8451 9499 (*Willesden Green*) ND

Our Lady of Grace: (Infants +N) Dollis Hill Ave, London NW2 6EU **Tel:** 020 8450 6757 **Fax:** 020 8452 1501 (*Dollis Hill*)

Our Lady of Grace: (Junior) Dollis Hill Ln, London NW2 6HS **Tel:** 020 8450 6002 **Fax:** 020 8208 3430 (*Dollis Hill*)

Our Lady of Lourdes: (+N) Wesley Rd, Stonebridge, London NW10 8PP **Tel:** 020 8961 5037 **Fax:** 020 8963 1197

(*Stonebridge*)
St Joseph: (Infants +N) Waverley Ave, Wembley, Middx HA9 6TA **Tel:** 020 8903 6032 **Fax:** 020 8903 5263 (*Wembley*)
St Joseph: (Junior) Chatsworth Ave, Wembley, Middx HA9 6BE **Tel:** 020 8902 3438 **Fax:** 020 8903 5482 (*Wembley*)
St Joseph: (+N) Goodson Rd, Willesden, London NW10 9LS **Tel:** 020 8965 5651 (*Wembley*)
St Margaret Clitherow: (+N) Quainton St, Neasden, London NW10 0BG **Tel:** 020 8450 3631 **Fax:** 020 8450 3729 (*Wembley Park*)
St Mary: (+N) Canterbury Rd, Kilburn, London NW6 5ST **Tel:** 020 7624 3830 **Fax:** 020 7372 4932 (*Kilburn*)
St Mary Magdalen: (Junior) Linacre Rd, Willesden Green, London NW2 5BB **Tel:** 020 8459 3159 **Fax:** 020 8459 0108 (*Willesden Green*)
St Robert Southwell: (+N) Slough Ln, Kingsbury Green, London NW9 8YD **Tel:** 020 8204 6148 **Fax:** 020 8905 0287 **E-mail:** admin@robsouth.brent.sch.uk (*Kingsbury Green*)

▲ Secondary Schools

Cardinal Hinsley Mathematics & Computing College: (Boys) Harlesden Rd, London NW10 3RN **Tel:** 020 8965 3947 **Fax:** 020 8965 3430
Convent of Jesus & Mary Language College: (Girls) Language College, Crownhill Rd, Willesden, London NW10 4EP **Tel:** 020 8965 2986 **Fax:** 020 8838 0071
St Gregory: Donnington Rd, Kenton Rd, Harrow, Middx HA3 0NB **Tel:** 020 8907 8828 **Fax:** 020 8909 1161

■ LONDON BOROUGH OF CAMDEN

▲ **Primary Schools**

(Junior & Infant unless stated,+N=Nursery)
Our Lady: (+N) Pratt St, London NW1 0DP **Tel:** 020 7485 7997 **Fax:** 020 7428 9426
Rosary: (+N) 238 Haverstock Hill, London NW3 2AE **Tel:** 020 7794 6292 **Fax:** 020 7794 6292
St Aloysius: (Infants +N) 28 Phoenix Rd, London NW1 1TA **Tel:** 020 7387 3551 **Fax:** 020 7255 9719 (*Somers Town*)
St Aloysius: (Junior) Aldenham St, London NW1 1PS **Tel:** 020 7387 9591 (*Somers Town*)
St Dominic: (+N) Southampton Rd, London NW5 4JS **Tel:** 020 7485 5918 **Fax:** 020 7284 0961 (*Haverstock Hill*) ND
St Eugene de Mazenod: Mazenod Ave, Quex Rd, London NW6 4LS **Tel:** 020 7624 4837 **Fax:** 020 7328 2880 (*Kilburn*)
St Joseph: (+N) Macklin St, Drury Ln, London WC2B 5NA **Tel:** 020 7242 7712 **Fax:** 020 7430 1834 (*Lincoln's Inn Fields*)
St Patrick: Holmes Rd, Kentish Town, London NW5 3AH **Tel:** 020 7267 1200 **Fax:** 020 7485 4691 (*Kentish Town*)

▲ Secondary Schools

La Sainte Union: (Girls) Highgate Rd, London NW5 1RP **Tel:** 020 7428 4600 **Fax:** 020 7267 7647 ND
Maria Fidelis: (Girls) 34 Phoenix Rd, Euston, London NW1 1TA **Tel:** 020 7387 3856 **Fax:** 020 7388 9558 ND

■ LONDON BOROUGH OF EALING

▲ **Primary Schools**

(Junior & Infant unless stated, +N=Nursery)
Mount Carmel: (+N) Little Ealing Ln, Ealing, London W5 4EA **Tel:** 020 8567 4646 **Fax:** 020 8579 5362 (*Northfields*)
Our Lady of the Visitation: Greenford Rd, Greenford, Middx UB6 9AN **Tel:** 020 8575 5344 **Fax:** 020 8575 6734 (*Greenford*)
St Anselm: Church Ave, Southall, Middx UB2 4BH **Tel:** 020 8574 3906 (*Southall*)
St Gregory: Woodfield Rd, London W5 1SL **Tel:** 020 8997 7550 **Fax:** 020 8810 6506 (*Ealing*)
St John Fisher: (+N) Thirlmere Ave, Rydal Crescent, Perivale, Greenford UB6 7AF **Tel:** 020 8998 4426 **Fax:** 020 8810 9131; Infant & Nursery Dept: **Tel.** 020 8998 9830 (*Perivale*)
St Joseph: (+N) York Ave, Hanwell, London W7 3HU **Tel:** 020 8567 6293 **Fax:** 020 8840 0278 (*Hanwell*)
St Raphael: Hartfield Ave, Northolt, Middx UB5 6NL **Tel:** 020 8841 0848 **Fax:** 020 8842 4617 (*Yeading*)
St Vincent: 1 Pierrepoint Rd, London W3 9JR **Tel:** 020 8992 6625 **Fax:** 020 8896 0623 **E-mail:** admin@st-vincents.ealing.sch.uk (*Acton*)

▲ **Secondary School**

Cardinal Wiseman School: Greenford Rd, Greenford, Middx UB6 9AW **Tel:** 020 8575 8222 **Fax:** 020 8575 9963

■ LONDON BOROUGH OF ENFIELD

▲ **Primary Schools**

(Junior & Infant unless stated, +N=Nursery)
Our Lady of Lourdes: The Limes Ave, New Southgate, London N11 1RD **Tel:** 020 8361 0767 **Fax:** 020 8361 6682 (*New Southgate*)
St Edmund: Hertford Rd, London N9 7HS **Tel:** 020 8807 2664 **Fax:** 020 8807 8877 **E-mail:** office@

st-edmunds.enfield.sch.uk (*Edmonton*)
St George: Gordon Rd, Enfield, Middx EN2 0QA **Tel:** 020 8363 3729 (*Enfield*)
St Mary: (+N) Durants Rd, Ponders End, Enfield, Middx EN3 7DE **Tel:** 020 8804 2396 **Fax:** 020 8805 8847 (*Ponders End*)
St Monica: Cannon Rd, Southgate, London N14 7HE **Tel:** 020 8886 4647 **Fax:** 020 8882 8424 (*Palmers Green*)

▲ Secondary Schools
St Anne Catholic High: (Girls) Oakthorpe Rd, Palmers Green, London N13 5TY **Tel:** 020 8886 2165
St Ignatius College: (Boys) Turkey St, Enfield, Middx EN1 4NP. **Tel:** 01992 717835/760520 **Fax:** 01992 652070

■ LONDON BOROUGH OF HACKNEY

▲ Primary Schools
(Junior & Infant unless stated, +N=Nursery)
Our Lady and St Joseph (+N) Buckingham Rd, London N1 4DG **Tel:** 020 7254 7353 **Fax:** 020 7249 3870 **E-mail:** seanjflood@yahoo.co.uk
St Dominic: (Infants +N) Ballance Rd, Homerton, London E9 5SR **Tel:** 020 8985 0995 (*Tower Hamlets*)
St Dominic: (Junior) Ballance Rd, Homerton, London E9 5SR **Tel:** 020 8985 6438 **Fax:** 020 8986 5092 (*Homerton*)
St Monica: (+N) Hoxton Square, London N1 6NT **Tel:** 020 7739 582 **Fax:** 020 7613 4465 (*Hoxton*)
St Scholastica (+N) Kenninghall Rd, London E5 8BS **Tel:** 020 8985 3466 **Fax:** 020 8533 0014 (*Clapton*)

▲ Secondary Schools
Cardinal Pole: Kenworthy Rd, Homerton, London E9 5RB **Tel:** 020 8985 5150 **Fax:** 020 8533 7325
Our Lady's Convent High: (Girls) 6-16 Amhurst Park, London N16 5AF **Tel:** 020 8800 2158 **Fax:** 020 8809 1518 ND

■ LONDON BOROUGH OF HAMMERSMITH & FULHAM

▲ Primary Schools
(Junior & Infant unless stated, +N=Nursery)
Holy Cross: (+N) Basuto Rd, Fulham, London SW6 4BL **Tel:** 020 7736 1447 **Fax:** 020 7371 9954 (*Parsons Green*)
The Good Shepherd: (+N) Gayford Rd W12 9BY **Tel:** 020 8743 5060 (*Shepherds Bush*)
Larmenier & Sacred Heart: (Infants +N) Great Church Ln, London W6 8DH **Tel:** 020 8748 9444 **Fax:** 020 8748 2387 (*Brook Green*) ND
Pope John: (+N) Commonwealth Ave, London W12 7QR **Tel:** 020 8743 9428 **Fax:** 020 8749 7117 (*White City*)
St Augustine: Disbrowe Rd, London W6 8QE **Tel:** 020 7385 4333 **Fax:** 020 7386 7751 (*Hammersmith*)
St Mary: (+N) Masbro Rd, London W14 0CT **Tel:** 020 7603 7717 **Fax:** 020 7602 7432 (*Brook Green*)
St Thomas of Canterbury: Estcourt Rd, London SW6 7HB **Tel:** 020 7385 8165 **Fax:** 020 7385 0918 (*Fulham*)

▲ Secondary Schools
Sacred Heart High: (Girls) 212 Hammersmith Rd, London W6 7DG **Tel:** 020 8748 7600 **Fax:** 020 8748 0392 (ND)
The London Oratory: (Boys) Seagrave Rd, London SW6 1RX **Tel:** 020 7385 0102 **Fax:** 020 7381 3836 (ND)

■ LONDON BOROUGH OF HARINGEY

▲ Primary Schools
(Junior & Infant unless stated, +N=Nursery)
Our Lady of Muswell: (+N) Pages Ln, London N10 1PS **Tel:** 020 8444 6894 **Fax:** 020 8356 4620 (*Muswell Hill*)
St Francis de Sales: (Infants +N) Brereton Rd, Tottenham, London N17 8DA **Tel:** 020 8808 4432 (*Tottenham*)
St Francis de Sales: (Junior) Brereton Rd, Tottenham, London N17 8DA **Tel:** 020 8808 2923 **Fax:** 020 8801 7438 (*Tottenham*)
St Gildas: (Junior) 1 Oakington Way, Crouch End, London N8 9EP **Tel:** 020 8348 1902 **Fax:** 020 8340 7805 (*Stroud Green*)
St Ignatius: (+N) St Annes Rd, Stamford Hill, London N15 6ND **Tel:** 020 8800 2771 **E-mail:** admin@st-igs.haringey.sch.uk (*Stamford Hill*)
St John Vianney: (+N) Stanley Rd, West Green, London N15 3HD **Tel:** 020 8889 8421. **Fax:** 020 8881 2528 (*West Green*)
St Martin de Porres: (+N) Blake Rd, Wood Green, London N11 2AF **Tel:** 020 8361 1445 **Fax:** 020 8361 5849 **E-mail:** admin@stmartinporres.haringey.sch.uk (*Wood Green*)
St Mary Priory: (Infants +N) Hermitage Rd, London N15 5RE **Tel:** 020 8800 9229 **Fax:** 020 8800 1375 **E-mail:** infants@stmarysrcpriory.haringey.sch.uk (*Stamford Hill*) ND
St Mary Priory: (Junior) Hermitage Rd, Stamford Hill, London N15 5RE **Tel:** 020 8800 9305 **Fax:** 020 8880 1142 **E-mail:** admin@stmarysrcpriory.haringey.sch.uk (*Stamford Hill*) ND

St Paul: Bradley Rd, Wood Green, London, N22 4SZ **Tel:** 020 8888 7081 **Fax:** 020 8889 1397 (*Wood Green*)
St Peter-in-Chains: (Infants) 3 Elm Grove, London N8 9AJ **Tel:** 020 8340 6789 **Fax:** 020 8340 3653 (*Stroud Green*)

▲ **Secondary School**

St Thomas More: Glendale Ave, Wood Green, London N22 5HN **Tel:** 020 8888 7122 **Fax:** 020 8889 8496

■ LONDON BOROUGH OF HARROW

▲ **Primary Schools**

(Junior & Infant unless stated, +N=Nursery)
St Anselm: Roxborough Park, Harrow HA1 3BE **Tel:** 020 8422 1600 **Fax:** 020 8422 3564 (*Harrow-on-the-Hill*)
St Bernadette: Clifton Rd, Kenton, Harrow Middx HA3 9NS **Tel:** 020 8204 8902 **Fax:** 020 8905 0738 (*Kenton*)
St George: Sudbury Hill, Harrow, Middx HA1 3SB **Tel:** 020 8422 1272 **Fax:** 020 8864 5540 (*Sudbury*)
St John Fisher: Melrose Rd, Pinner, Middx HA5 5RA **Tel:** 020 8868 2961 **Fax:** 020 8866 5882 (*Harrow North*)
St Joseph: Dobbin Close, Belmont, Harrow, Middx HA3 7LT **Tel:** 020 8863 8531 **Fax:** 020 8863 3341 (*Wealdstone*)
St Teresa: (+N) Long Elmes, Harrow Weald, Middx HA3 6LE **Tel:** 020 8428 8640 **Fax:** 020 8420 1571 (*Headstone Ln*)

▲ **Seconday Schools**

Sacred Heart Language College: (Girls) 186 High St, Wealdstone, Harrow, Middx HA3 7AY **Tel:** 020 8863 9922 **Fax:** 020 8861 5051
Salvatorian College: (Boys) High Rd, Harrow Weald, Middx HA3 5DY **Tel:** 020 8863 2706 **Fax:** 020 8863 3435

▲ **Sixth Form College**

St Dominic: Mount Park Ave, Harrow-on-the-Hill, Middx HA1 3HX **Tel:** 020 8422 8084 **Fax:** 020 8422 3759 **Email:** stdoms@stdoms.ac.uk

■ LONDON BOROUGH OF HILLINGDON

▲ **Primary Schools**

(Junior & Infant unless stated, +N=Nursery)
Botwell House: (+N) Botwell Ln, Hayes, Middx UB3 2AB **Tel:** 020 8573 2229 **Fax:** 020 8569 0286 (*Hayes*)
Sacred Heart: (+N) Herlwyn Ave, Ruislip, Middx HA4 6EZ **Tel:** 01895 633240 **Fax:** 01895 625 772 (*Ruislip*)
St Bernadette: (+N) 160 Long Ln, Hillingdon, Middx UB10 0EH **Tel:** 01895 232298 **Fax:** 01895 230086 (*Hillingdon*)
St Catherine: (+N) Money Ln, West Drayton, Middx UB7 7NX **Tel:** 01895 442839 **Fax:** 01895 442631 (*West Drayton*)
St Mary: (+N) Rockingham Close, Uxbridge, Middx UB8 2UA **Tel:** 01895 232814 (*Uxbridge*)
St Swithun Wells: (+N) Hunters Hill, South Ruislip, Middx HA4 9HS **Tel:** 020 8845 2604 **Fax:** 020 8845 1611 (*Ruislip South*)

▲ **Secondary School**

The Douay Martrys: Edinburgh Drive, Ickenham, Uxbridge, Middx UB10 8QY **Tel:** 01895 635371 **Fax:** 01895 678953

■ LONDON BOROUGH OF HOUNSLOW

▲ **Primary Schools**

(Junior & Infant unless stated, +N=Nursery)
Our Lady & St John: (+N) Boston Park Rd, Brentford, Middx TW8 9JF **Tel:** 020 8560 7477 **Fax:** 020 8568 8806 (*Brentford*)
St Lawrence: (+N) Victoria Rd, Feltham, Middx TW13 4AF. **Tel:** 020 8890 3878. (*Feltham*)
St Mary: (+N) South St, Isleworth, Middx TW7 6DL **Tel:** 020 8560 7166 **Fax:** 020 8232 8820 (*Isleworth*)
St Mary: (+N) Duke Rd, Chiswick, London, W4 2DF **Tel:** 020 8994 5606 **Fax:** 020 8742 7630 (*Chiswick*)
St Michael's & St Martin's: (+N) Belgrave Rd, Hounslow, Middx TW4 7AG **Tel:** 020 8572 9658 **Fax:** 020 8572 1982 (*Hounslow*)
The Rosary: (+N) 10 The Green, Heston, Middx TW5 0RL **Tel:** Key Stage 1: 020 8570 4942 Key Stage 2: 020 8581 0066 **Fax:** 020 8581 0065 **E-mail:** head.rosary.hounslow@igfl.net (*Heston*)

▲ **Secondary Schools**

Gumley House: (Girls) Twickenham Rd, Isleworth, Middx TW7 6PN **Tel:** 020 8568 8692 **Fax:** 020 8758 2674 (ND)
Gunnersbury: (Boys) The Ride, Boston Manor Rd, Brentford, Middx TW8 9LB **Tel:** 020 8568 7281 **Fax:** 020 8569 7946
St Mark: 106 Bath Rd, Hounslow, Middx TW3 3EJ **Tel:** 020 8577 3600 **Fax:** 020 8577 0559

■ LONDON BOROUGH OF ISLINGTON

▲ **Primary Schools**

(Junior & Infant unless stated, +N=Nursery)
Blessed Sacrament: (+N) Boadicea St, London N1 0UF **Tel:** 020 7278 2187 **Fax:** 020 7278 0015
Christ the King: (+N) 55 Tollington Park, London N4 3QW **Tel:** 020 7272 5987

Fax: 020 7272 7780 (*Tollington Park*)
Sacred Heart: Eden Grove, London N7 8EN **Tel:** 020 7607 3407 (*Holloway*)
St Joan of Arc: (+N) Northolme Rd, Highbury Park, London N5 2UX **Tel:** 020 7226 3920 **Fax:** 020 7704 9220 (*Highbury*)
St John the Evangelist: (+N) Duncan St, Islington, London N1 8LB **Tel:** 020 7226 1314 **Fax:** 020 7226 5563
St Joseph: (+N) Highgate Hill, London N19 5NE **Tel:** 020 7272 1270 **Fax:** 020 7272 9728 (*Highgate*) ND
St Peter & St Paul: (+N) Compton St, Goswell Rd, London EC1V 0EU **Tel:** 020 7253 0839 **Fax:** 020 7336 7226 (*Clerkenwell*)

▲ **Secondary Schools**
Mount Carmel Technology College: (Girls) Holland Walk, Duncombe Rd, London N19 3EU **Tel:** 020 7281 3536 **Fax:** 020 7281 0420
St Aloysius: (Boys) Hornsey Ln, Highgate, London N6 5LY **Tel:** 020 7263 1391 **Fax:** 020 7263 5963

■ ROYAL BOROUGH OF KENSINGTON & CHELSEA

▲ **Primary Schools**
(Junior & Infant unless stated, +N=Nursery)
Oratory: Bury Walk, Cale St, London SW3 6QH **Tel:** 020 7589 5900 **Fax:** 020 7581 5220 (ND)
Our Lady of Victories: (+N) Clareville St, London SW7 5AQ **Tel:** 020 7373 4491 **Fax:** 020 7244 0591 (*Kensington*)
The Servite: (+N) 252 Fulham Rd, London SW10 9NA **Tel:** 020 7352 2588 **Fax:** 020-7351 4024 (*Fulham Rd*) ND
St Charles: (+N) St Charles Square, London W10 6EB **Tel:** 020 8969 5566 **Fax:** 020 8960 4338 (*St Charles Square*)
St Francis of Assisi: (+N) Treadgold St, London W11 4BJ **Tel:** 020 7727 8523 **Fax:** 020 7229 2174 (*Notting Hill*)
St Joseph: (+N) Cadogan St, London SW3 2QT **Tel:** 020 7589 2438 **Fax:** 020 7581 2438 (*Chelsea*)
St Mary: (+N) East Row, London W10 5AW **Tel:** 020 8969 0321 **Fax:** 020 8964 3122. (*Kensal New Town*)

▲ **Secondary Schools**
The Cardinal Vaughan: (Boys) 89 Addison Rd, Kensington, London W14 8BZ **Tel:** 020 7603 8478 **Fax:** 020 7602 3124 **E-mail:** mail@cvms.co.uk
Sion-Manning: (Girls) St Charles Square, North Kensington, London W10 6EL **Tel:** 020 8969 7111 **Fax:** 020 8969 5119
St Thomas More Language College: Cadogan St, Chelsea, London SW3 2QS **Tel:** 020 7589 9734 **Fax:** 020 7823 7868
St Charles Catholic Sixth Form College: St Charles Square, London W10 6EY **Tel:** 020 8968 7755 **Fax:** 020 8968 1061

■ LONDON BOROUGH OF RICHMOND

▲ **Primary Schools**
(Junior & Infant unless stated, +N=Nursery)
The Sacred Heart: St Mark's Rd, Teddington, Middx TW11 9DO **Tel:** 020 8977 6591 (*Teddington*)
St Edmund: St Edmunds Ln, Nelson Rd, Whitton, Middx TW2 7BB **Tel:** 020 8894 7898 **Fax:** 020 8898 3032 (*Whitton*)
St James: (+N) 260 Stanley Rd, Twickenham, Middx TW2 5NP **Tel:** 020 8898 4670 **Fax:** 020 8893 3038 (*Twickenham*)

■ LONDON BOROUGH OF TOWER HAMLETS

▲ **Primary Schools**
(Junior & Infant unless stated, +N=Nursery)
English Martyrs: (+N) St Mark St, London E1 8DJ **Tel:** 020 7709 0182 **Fax:** 020 7680 9395 (*Tower Hill*)
Guardian Angels: Whitman Rd, Mile End, London E3 4RB **Tel:** 020 8980 3939 **Fax:** 020 8983 4210 (*Mile End*)
Holy Family: (+N) Wade's Place, London E14 0DE **Tel:** 020 7987 3066 (*Poplar*)
Our Lady: (+N) Copenhagen Place, Limehouse, London E14 7DA **Tel:** 020 7987 1798 **Fax:** 020 7538 2682 (*Limehouse*)
St Elizabeth: (Infants +N) Bonner Rd, London E2 9JY **Tel:** 020 8980 3964 (*Bethnal Green*)
St Agnes: (+N) Rainhill Way, Bow, London E3 3ES **Tel:** 020 8980 3076 (*Bow*)
St Anne: (+N) Underwood Rd, London E1 5AW **Tel:** 020 7247 6327 **Fax:** 020 7377 5024 (*Underwood Rd*)
St Edmund: (+N) 297 West Ferry Rd, Millwall, London E14 8RS **Tel:** 020 7987 2546 **Fax:** 020 7538 0332 (*Millwall*)
St Mary & St Michael: (+N) Sutton St, Commercial Rd, London E1 0BD **Tel:** 020 7790 4986 **Fax:** 020 7790 9343 (*Commercial Rd*)

▲ **Secondary School**
Bishop Challoner: Hardinge St, London, E1 0AB **Tel:** 020 7790 3634 **Fax:** 020 7702 7398

■ COUNTY OF SURREY

▲ **Primary Schools**
(Junior & Infant unless otherwise stated)
Our Lady of the Rosary: Park Ave, Staines, Middx TW18 2EF **Tel:** 01784-453539

Fax: 01784-449485 (*Staines*).
St Ignatius: Green St, Sunbury-on-Thames, Middx TW16 6QG **Tel:** 01932-785396 (*Sunbury*).
St Michael: Feltham Hill Rd, Ashford, Middx **Tel:** 01784-253333 **Fax:** 01784-240834 (*Ashford*).

▲ Secondary School
St Paul: The Ridings, Green St, Sunbury-on-Thames, Middx TW16 6NX **Tel:** 01932-783811 **Fax:** 01932-786485

■ HERTFORDSHIRE

▲ Primary Schools - St Albans Deanery
(Junior & Infant unless stated, +N=Nursery)
St Adrian: Watling View, St Albans, Herts AL1 2PB **Tel:** 01727-852687 **Fax:** 01727-850822 (*St Albans South*)
St Alban & St Stephen: (Infants + N) Vanda Crescent, St Albans, Herts AL1 5EX. **Tel:** 01727-854643. (*St Albans*)
St Alban & St Stephen: (Juniors) Cecil Rd, St Albans, Herts AL1 5LG **Tel:** 01727-866668 **Fax:** 01727-810710 (*St Albans*)
St Albert the Great: Acorn Rd, Rant Meadow, Hemel Hempstead, Herts HP3 8DW **Tel:** 01442-64835 **Fax:** 01442-246418 (*Hemel Hempstead East*)
St Bernadette: (+N) Walsingham Way, London Colney, Herts AL2 1NL **Tel:** 01727-822489 (*London Colney*)
St Cuthbert Mayne: (Juniors) Clover Way, Gadebridge, Hemel Hempstead, Herts IP1 3EA **Tel:** 01442-253347 **Fax:** 01442-230320 (*Hemel Hempstead*)
St Dominic: Southdown Rd, Harpenden, Herts AL5 1PF **Tel:** 01582-760047 **Fax:** 01582-760047 (*Harpenden*)
St John Fisher: Hazelmere Rd, Marshalwick, St Albans, Herts AL4 9RW. **Tel:** 01727-861077 **Fax:** 01727-831163 (*St Albans*)
St Rose: (Infants +N) Green End Rd, Boxmoor, Hemel Hempstead, Herts HP1 1QW **Tel:** 01442-398855 **Fax:** 01442-398835 (*Hemel Hempstead*)
St Teresa: (+N) Brook End, Borehamwood, Herts WD6 5HL **Tel:** 020-8953 3753 **Fax:** 020-8381 5273 (*Borehamwood*).
St Thomas More: Greenway, Berkhamsted, Herts HP4 3LF **Tel:** 01442-865074 (*Berkhamsted*)

▲ Primary Schools - Watford Deanery
(Junior & Infant unless stated, +N=Nursery)
Divine Saviour: (+N) Broomfield Rise, Abbots Langley, Herts WD5 OHW. **Tel:** 01923-265607 (*Abbots Langley*)
The Holy Rood: Greenbank Rd, Watford, Herts WD17 4FS **Tel:** 01923-481340 **Fax:** 01923-481342 (*Watford*)
Sacred Heart: Merryhill Rd, Bushey, Herts WD2 1DU **Tel:** 020-8950 6417 **Fax:** 020-8421 8768 (*Bushey*)
St Anthony: (+N) Croxley View, Watford, Herts WD1 8BW **Tel:** 01923-226987 (*Watford*)
St Catherine of Siena: Horseshoe Ln, Garston, Watford, Herts WD2 7HP **Tel:** 01923-676022 **Fax:** 01923-893497 (*Garston*)
St John: Berry Ln, Mill End, Rickmansworth, Herts WD3 2H. **Tel:** 01923-774004 **Fax:** 01923-710915 (*Mill End*)
St Joseph: Ainsdale Rd, South Oxhey, Watford, Herts WD1 6DW **Tel:** 020-8428 5371 **Fax:** 020-8421 0568 (*Carpenders Park*)

▲ Primary Schools - Hatfield Deanery
(Junior & Infant unless stated, +N=Nursery)
Holy Family: (+N) Crookhams, Welwyn Garden City, Herts AL7 1PG **Tel:** 01707-320308 **Fax:** 01707-327419 (*Welwyn Garden City/Digswell*)
Our Lady: (+N) Woodhall Ln, Welwyn Garden City, Herts AL7 3TF **Tel:** 01707 324408 **Fax:** 01707 391005 (*Welwyn Garden City*[*East*])
Pope Paul: Baker St, Potters Bar, Herts EN6 2ES **Tel:** 01707 659755 (Potters Bar)
St Philip Howard: Woods Ave, Hatfield, Herts AL10 8NN **Tel:** 01707 263969 **Fax:** 01707 263969 (*Hatfield*)

▲ Primary Schools - Stevenage Deanery
(Junior & Infant unless stated, +N=Nursery)
Our Lady: Old Hale Way, Hitchin, Herts SG5 1XT **Tel:** 01462 622555 **Fax:** 01462 622777 (*Hitchin*)
St John: (+N) Providence Way, Baldock, Herts SG7 6TT **Tel:** 01462 892478 **Fax:** 01462 892478. (*Baldock*)
St Margaret Clitherow: Broadhall Way, Stevenage, Herts SG2 8RH **Tel:** 01438 352863 **Fax:** 01438 352553 (*Stevenage/Shephall*)
St Mary: (+N) Melbourn Rd, Royston, Herts SG8 7DB **Tel:** 01763 242875 **Fax:** 01763 248825 (*Royston*)
St Thomas More: Highfield, Letchworth, Herts SG6 3QB **Tel:** 01462 620670 (*Letchworth*)
St Vincent de Paul: (+N) Bedwell Crescent, Stevenage, Herts SG1 1NJ **Tel:** 01438 729555 **Fax:** 01438 358122 (*Stevenage*)

▲ Primary Schools - Lea Valley Deanery
(Junior & Infant unless stated, +N=Nursery)
Sacred Heart: Broadmeads, Ware, Herts SG12 9HY **Tel:** 01920 461678 (*Ware*)
St Augustine: (+N) Riversmead, Hoddesdon, Herts EN11 8DP **Tel:** 01992 463549 (*Hoddesdon*)

St Cross: Upper Marsh Ln, Hoddesdon, Herts EN11 8BN **Tel:** 01992 467309 **Fax:** 01992 450362 (*Hoddesdon*)

St Joseph: (+N) North Rd, Hertford, Herts SG14 2BY **Tel:** 01992 583148 **Fax:** 01992 550503 (*Hertford*)

St Joseph: (+N) Royal Ave, Waltham Cross, Herts EN8 7EN **Tel:** 01992 629503 **Fax:** 01992 628824 (*Waltham Cross*)

St Joseph: (+N) Great Hadham Rd, Bishops Stortford, Herts CM23 2NL **Tel:** 01279 652576 **Fax:** 01279 466519 (*Bishop's Stortford*)

St Paul: Park Ln, Cheshunt, Herts EN7 6LR **Tel:** 01992 635060 **Fax:** 01992 625215 (*Waltham Cross*)

St Thomas of Canterbury: High St, Puckeridge, nr Ware, Herts SG11 1RZ **Tel:** 01920 821450 **Fax:** 01920 822534 (*Old Hall Green/Puckeridge*)

▲ Secondary Schools

John F Kennedy: Hollybush Ln, Hemel Hempstead, Herts HP1 2PJ **Tel:** 01442 266150 **Fax:** 01442 250014

John Henry Newman: Hitchin Rd, Stevenage, Herts SG1 4AE **Tel:** 01438-314643 **Fax:** 01438-747882

Loreto College: Hatfield Rd, St Albans, Herts AL1 3RQ **Tel:** 01727-856206 **Fax:** 01727-833794

Nicholas Breakspear: Colney Heath Ln, St Albans, Herts AL4 0TT **Tel:** 01727-860079 **Fax:** 01727-848912

St Joan of Arc: High St, Rickmansworth, Herts WD3 1HG **Tel:** 01923-773881 **Fax:** 01923-897545.

St Mary: Windhill, Bishop's Stortford, Herts CM23 2NQ **Tel:** 01279-654901 **Fax:** 01279-653889 **E-mail:** info@stmarys.net

St Michael: High Elms Ln, Garston, Watford, Herts WD2 7JT **Tel:** 01923-673760 **Fax:** 01923-680511 **Fax:** 020-8421 0568. (*Carpenders Park*).

■ Independent Schools

St Christina Girls School (Girls) 25 St Edmund's Terrace, NW8 7PY **Tel:** 020 7722 8784 **Fax:** 020 7586 4961

St Columba College: (Boys) Preparatory School, 8 King Harry Ln, St Albans, Herts AL3 4AW **Tel:** 01727 862616 **Fax:** 01727 863997

St Anthony Preparatory: (Boys) 90 Fitzjohn's Ave, London NW3 6AA **Tel:** 020-7435 0316 **Fax:** 020-7435 9223

St Benedict Junior School: (Boys). 5 Montpellier Ave, Ealing, London W5 2XP **Tel:** 020-8862 2050

St Martha Convent Junior School: (Girls) 5B Union St, Barnet, Herts EN5 4HY **Tel:** 020 8449 4346 **E-mail:** mail@stmarthasjunior.co.uk

St Mary Preparatory: (Girls) 47 Fitzjohn's Ave, London NW3 6PG **Tel:** 020 7435 1868 **Fax:** 020 7794 7922 **E-mail:** enquiries@stmh.co.uk

St Philip Preparatory: (Boys) 6 Wetherby Place, London SW7 4ND **Tel:** 020 7373 3944 **Fax:** 020 7244 9766

The Cavendish School: 179 Arlington Rd, London NW1 7EY **Tel:** 020 7485 1958 **Fax:** 020 7267 0098

Vita et Pax Preparatory School: Priory Close, Green Rd, Southgate, London N14 4AT **Tel:** 020 8449 8336 **Fax:** 020 8440 0483

Westminster Cathedral Choir School: (Boys) Ambrosden Ave, London SW1P 1QH **Tel:** 020 7798 9081 **Fax:** 020 7798 9090

▲ Secondary

More House School: (Girls) 22 Pont St, London SW1X 0AA **Tel:** 020 7235 2855 **Fax:** 020 7259 6782

St Benedict School: (Boys) 54 Eaton Rise, London W5 2ES **Tel:** 020 8862 2010 **Fax:** 020 8862 2199 **E-mail:** headmaster@stbenedicts.org.uk

St Columba College: (Boys) King Harry Ln, St Albans, Herts, AL3 4AW **Tel:** 01727 855185 **Fax:** 01727 863997

St Martha Convent School: (Girls) The Mount, Camlet Way, Barnet, Herts EN5 5PX **Tel:** 020 8449 6889 **Fax:** 020 8441 5632

▲ Primary and Secondary

St Augustine Priory School: (Girls) Hillcrest Rd, Ealing, W5 2JL **Tel:** 020 8997 2022 **Fax:** 020 8810 6501

St Catherine Catholic School: (Girls) Cross Deep, Twickenham, Middx, TW1 4QJ **Tel:** 020 8891 2898 **Fax:** 020 8744 9629

St Edmund College: Old Hall Green, Ware, Herts, SG11 1DS **Tel:** 01920 821504 **Fax:** 01920 823011

■ Non-maintained Special Schools

Pield Heath House: Pield Heath Rd, Hillingdon, Middx UB8 3NW **Tel:** 01895 258507 **Fax:** 01895 256497

St Elizabeth School: Much Hadham, Hertfordshire, SG10 6EW **Tel:** 01279 843451 **Fax:** 01279 843903

DIOCESE OF ARUNDEL AND BRIGHTON

(Province of Southwark)

Formed 28 May 1965, by the Division of the Diocese of Southwark. Consisting of the Counties of East Sussex and West Sussex and the County of Surrey outside the Greater London Boroughs.

Patrons of the Diocese
Our Lady, 15 August
St Philip Howard, 19 October

Bishop 
Rt Rev Kieran Thomas Conry PhB, STB;
born Coventry, Feb 1st, 1951; ordained priest July 19th, 1975; cons Bishop of Arundel & Brighton by Cardinal Cormac Murphy O'Connor June 9th, 2001

Residence:
High Oaks, Old Brighton Road North, Pease Pottage, West Sussex RH11 9AJ.

Tel: 01293-526428 **Fax:** 01293-614714
E-mail: bishop@dabnet.org

Bishop's Secretary:
Mrs Elizabeth Hembrey
E-mail: elizabeth.hembrey@dabnet.org.

Secretary:
Mrs Sue Jennings
E-mail: sue.jennings@dabnet.org

Rt Rev Kieran Thomas Conry
Bishop of Arundel & Brighton

■ ADMINISTRATION

■ Diocesan Curia
Bishop's House, The Upper Drive, Hove, East Sussex BN3 6NB **Tel:** 01273-506387
Fax: 01273-501527

■ The Vicars General
Mgr Canon John Hull (*Chancellor*).
Tel: 01273-859701
E-mail: vg@dabnet.org
Mgr Benny O'Shea.
Tel: 01372-462451
E-mail: thebenny@talk21.com

■ Diocesan Matrimonial Tribunal
Tribunal Administrator: **Mrs Angela Fishenden.**
Tel: 01273-859703 **Fax:** 01273-859713
E-mail: tribunal@dabnet.org

■ Finance Department
Financial Secretary: **Mr J Brotherton.**
Tel/Fax: 01273-859705
E-mail: finance@dabnet.org

■ Safeguarding Office
Safeguarding Co-ordinator: **Rev Kieron O'Brien**; *Safeguarding Officer:* **Rosemarie Clerkin.** **Tel:** 01273-241203
Fax: 01273-859717
E-mail: rosemarie.clerkin@dabnet.org

■ Mission and Unity
Episcopal Vicar: **Rev Anthony Churchill STL**
Specialist Advisor: **John Roberts**

■ THE CHRISTIAN EDUCATION CENTRE
4 Southgate Drive, Crawley, West Sussex RH10 6RP
Tel: 01293-515666 **Fax:** 01293-616945

■ The Catholic Schools Service
Director: **Mrs Mary Reynolds BA, CertEd;**
Tel: 01293-511130
Fax: 01293-616945
E-mail: schools@dabnet.org

■ The Pastoral Services Team
Episcopal Vicar for Pastoral Affairs: **Rev Mgr Tony Barry;** *Co-ordinator of the Pastoral Services Team:* **Katherine Avery;** *Adult Formation:* **David Wills, Rev Robert Esdaile;** *Justice & Peace:* Awaiting Appointment; *Liturgy:* **Ms Barbara Hopper;** *Marriage and Family Life:* **Mrs Liz James, Rev Tom Treherne;** *Mission and Unity:* **Mr John Roberts, Rev Anthony Churchill;** *Youth:* **Ray Mooney, Rev Con Foley;** *Social Action:* **Susan O'Brien**
Tel: 01293-515666
Fax: 01293-616945

■ **Communications and Information**
Office: **Tel:** 01293-511130
Fax: 01293-616945
E-mail: mark.woods@dabnet.org

■ **A&B News**
Editor: **Mrs Pauline Groves.**

■ **VOCATIONS**

Religious Life: *Episcopal Vicar:* **Rt Rev Dom Stephen Ortiger OSB;**

Ministry to Priests: *Director:* **Rev Tony Bridson**

Priesthood:
Vocations Director: **Rev Paul Turner**

Permanent Diaconate:
Director: **Rev Paul Scholey,**

Retreat House:
St Cuthmans, Coolham
Director: **Denise Mitchell**
E-mail: stcuthmans@dabnet.org

■ **CONSULTATIVE BODIES**

■ **The Council of Priests**
Secretary: **Mrs Elizabeth Hembrey**

■ **The College of Consultors**
Rev Tony Barry, Rev Tony Bridson, Mgr John Hull, Rev David Parmiter, Mgr Benny O'Shea, Mgr Jeff Scott, Rev Paul Turner.

■ **Cathedral Chapter**
(erected 21 October, 1967)
Rev Provost Bernard Thom, Rev Canon Anthony Whale, Mgr Canon John Hull, Canon Peter Humfrey, Canon Seamus Hester, Canon Gerald Coates, Canon Dennis Barry, Canon Timohty Madeley, Canon Eric Flood, Mgr Canon Jeff Scott. *Canons Emeriti:* **Canon Dermod Fogarty, Canon John Stapleton, Mgr Provost Emeritus Terence Stonehill. Canon Richard Incledon, Canon Michael Reynell,** *Honorary Canons:* **Canon Brendan MacCarthy, Canon Geoffrey Burke, Canon Brian O'Sullivan, Canon Michael Spelman.**

DIOCESE OF ARUNDEL AND BRIGHTON

■ **ARUNDEL AND BRIGHTON**
† CATHEDRAL CHURCH OF OUR LADY AND ST PHILIP HOWARD
(1748; 1873; cons 14 May 1952)
Cathedral House, Parsons Hill, Arundel
W. Sussex BN18 9AY
Tel: 01903-882297 **Fax:** 01903-885335
E-mail: aruncath1@aol.com
Website: www.arundelcathedral.org
Rev Timothy Madeley (*Cathedral Dean*), **Revv Malcolm King, David Clifton** (*Deacon*).
M: *Sun 9.30am, 11.15am.*
• ***Poor Clares,*** Crossbush, Arundel, W. Sussex BN18 9PJ **Tel:** 01903-882536
• ***Chapel of Our Lady Help of Christians*** **M:** *Sat 1st M of Sun 6.15pm.*

■ **ADDLESTONE,** Weybridge
The Holy Family (1976; cons 1977)
Ongar Hill, Spinney Oak, Ongar Hill, Addlestone, Weybridge, Surrey KT15 1BP
Tel: 01932-848616
E-mail:holyfamilyaddlestone@yahoo.co.uk
Rev Emmanuel Agius.
M: *Sat 1st M of Sun 6pm. Sun 9.30am, 11am, (5.30pm at St George's College). Hds 9.15am, 8pm.*
• ***St George's College (Josephites, CJ),*** Weybridge Road, KT15 2QS
Tel: (Community): 01932-839444
(Senior School): 01932-839300
Junior School: 01932-839400
Fax: (Community): 01932-842268;
(Senior School): 01932-839301;
(Junior School): 01932-839401
E-mail: info@st-georges-college.co.uk
Websites:
www.st-georges-college.co.uk
www.josephiteworld.org
Bro Michael Powell PhD, MPhil, MEd (*Administrator & Bursar*)
Tel: 01932-839457 **E-mail:** brmichael@st-georges-college.co.uk
Rev Francis Owen, Tel: 01932-839450
E-mail: owenoga@aol.com
Rev Andrew Alexander, BSc
Tel: 01932-839449;
Rev Christopher Hunting, MA
Tel: 01932-839452
Rev Adrian Cadwallader
Tel: 01932-839451
Rev Martin Ashcroft, STB, MA
Tel: 01932-839454
E-mail: frmartin@st-georges-college.co.uk
Bro Patrick Matthews
Tel: 01932-839456
E-mail: pmatthews@st-georges-college.co.uk
• ***Hospitaller Sisters of the Sacred Heart,*** Firfield House, Simplemarsh Road, Addlestone, Surrey KT15 1QR
Tel: 01932-842254

■ **ADUR VALLEY,** West Sussex
Our Lady, Queen of Peace
45 Johns Street, Shoreham-by-Sea, West Sussex BN43 5DL **Tel:** 01273-452654
Rev Sean Finnegan
M: Sun 9am, 6pm. Hds 8pm.

■ **ANGMERING,** West Sussex
See East Preston

■ **ASH,** Surrey
† **The Holy Angels** (1934; cons 8 July 1959)
65 Ash Church Road, Ash, Aldershot, Hants GU12 6LU **Tel:** 01252-321422
See Farnham (3).

■ **ASHTEAD,** Surrey
† **St Michael** (1944; 1967; cons 1976)
The Priest's House, The Marld, Ashtead, Surrey KT21 1RS
Tel: 01372-272267 **Fax:** 01372-279029
Rev Brian Lowden.
Deacon: **Rev Peter Andrews.**
M: *Sat 1st M of Sun 6pm. Sun 8.30am, 10.30am. Hds 9.30am, 8pm.*

■ **BAGSHOT,** Surrey
† **Christ the King** (1927)
11 Bell Place, Guildford Road, Bagshot, Surrey GU19 5NE
Tel: 01276-473525 (Parish Office) for Bagshot and Camberley North.
Parish office **E-mail:** cb@dabnet.org
Rev Mgr Richard Madders
Tel: 01276-476678
M: *Sat 1st M of Sun 6.30pm. Sun 11am. Hds 10am.*

■ **BANSTEAD,** Surrey
† **St Ann (1931)**
4 Brighton Road, Banstead, Surrey SM7 1BS.
Tel: 01737-353724 **Fax:** 01737-379910
E-mail: stannbanstead@tiscali.co.uk
Rev Miceál Beatty.
Deacon: **Rev Kevin O'Brien**
M: *Sun 8.30am, 10am, 6pm. Hds (vigil 8pm), 9.30am.*

■ **BATTLE,** East Sussex
† **Our Lady Immaculate and St Michael** (1882; 1888)
14 Mount Street, Battle, East Sussex TN33 0EG **Tel:** 01424-773125
Rev Anthony White
M: *Sat 1st M of Sun 6pm. Sun 10.30am. Hds 10am.*
• ***Mass Centre:*** Northiam.

■ **BEXHILL,** East Sussex
1. † St Mary Magdalene
(1893; 1907; cons 10 September 1913)
Sea Road, Bexhill-on-Sea,
East Sussex TN40 1RH
Tel: 01424-210263 **Fax:** 01424-731077
E-mail: bexhill@dabnet.org
Website: www.stmm.co.uk
Rev Christopher Spain.
M: *Sat 1st M of Sun 6pm. Sun 11am, 6pm. Hds 10am.*
• ***Sisters of Providence (Rosminians),*** 8 Rotherfield Avenue, Bexhill-on-Sea, East Sussex TN40 1SY **Tel:** 01424-214818

2. St Martha, Little Common
Cooden Sea Road. Served from Bexhill (1).
M: *Sun 9am. Hds 9am.*

3. Our Lady of the Rosary, Sidley
Southlands Road. Served from Bexhill (1).
M: *Sun 10am. Hds 7pm.*

■ **BILLINGSHURST,** West Sussex
† **St Gabriel** (1925; 1962)
18 East Street, Billingshurst, West Sussex RH14 9QH **Tel:** 01403-782128
Served from Storrington
Deacon: **Rev Roger Stone**
M: *Sun 10.30am. Hds 9.30am, 8pm.*

■ **BOGNOR REGIS,** West Sussex A
† **Our Lady Of Sorrows**
(1880; 1882; cons 11 May 1965)
Parish Centre, Clarence Road, Bognor Regis, West Sussex PO21 1JX
Tel: 01243-823619 **Fax:** 01243-842718
E-mail: pp@olos.fsnet.co.uk
Website: bognorcartholicparish.co.uk
Revv Anthony Churchill STL, Dominic O'Hara.
M: *Sat 1st M of Sun 5.15pm. Sun 8am, 10am, 6pm. Hds (Vigil 7.30pm), 7am, 10am, 6.30pm.*
• ***Servite Sisters of the Third Order,*** St Juliana's Convent, Marian Way, High Street, Bognor Regis, PO21 1PA
Tel: 01243-821734 **Fax:** 01243-824896
Villa Maria, Campbell Road, Bognor Regis, West Sussex PO21 1NA **Tel:** 01243-823721
• ***Benedictine Sisters of Our Lady of Grace and Compassion,*** St Joseph's, Albert Road, PO21 1NJ
Tel: 01243-864051 **Fax:** 01243-841954
Chaplain: **Canon Dermod Fogarty,**
Tel: 01243-840689 **Fax:** 01243-841954
Tel: 01243- 864490 (residents)

■ **BOSHAM,** West Sussex A
Our Lady of the Assumption
Bosham Lane. Served from Chichester.
M: *Sun 11am. Hds 7.30pm.*

■ **BRAMLEY,** Surrey
† **St Thomas More** (1943)
High Street, Bramley, Surrey GU5 0HG
Served from Cranleigh
M: *Sun 9am.*

■ BRIGHTON

1. † St John the Baptist (1779; cons. 7 July 1835)
2 Bristol Road, Brighton, East Sussex BN2 1AP
Tel: 01273-681587 **Fax:** 01273-692686
Rev David Foley.
M: *Sat 1st M of Sun 6.30pm. Sun 9am, 11am. Hds 10am, 8pm.*
- ***Sisters of Mercy,*** 13 Bristol Road, Brighton BN2 1AP **Tel:** 01273-626150 **Fax:** 01273 600530

2. † St Mary Magdalen
(1858; 1961; cons 27 June 1956)
55 Upper North Street, Brighton, East Sussex BN1 3FH
Tel: 01273-326793 **Fax:** 01273-735070
Rev Raymond Blake.
M: *Sat 1st M of Sun 6pm. Sun 10.30am, 12noon (Pol), 5pm. Hds (vigil 6pm). 9.30am (in the School during term time), 12.15pm, 8pm.*
- ***Poor Servants of the Mother of God,*** St Anne's Convent, 3 Lansdowne Road, Hove, East Sussex BN3 1DN **Tel:** 01273-733871

3. † St Joseph (1879; 1979)
Tel: 01273-386159 **Fax:** 01273-380595
E-mail: st.josephsbrighton@btinternet.com
Website: stjosephsbrighton.co.uk
Rev John Inglis. 6 Wellington Road, Brighton, BN2 3AA
M: *Sun 9.30am, 11.30am, 5.30pm. Hds 12pm, 7pm.*

4. St Francis (1957; cons. 1978)
Moulsecoomb Way, Moulsecoomb, Brighton, East Sussex BN2 4PB
Tel: 01273-601606
Served from Brighton, St Josephs
M: *Sun 9.30am.*

5. † St Mary
(1906; 1912, cons 7 Dec 1979)
5 Surrenden Road, Preston Park, Brighton, East Sussex BN1 6PA **Tel:** 01273-554509
Rev Oliver Heaney
M: *Sat 1st M of Sun 7pm. Sun 10am, 12noon. Hds 10am, 7.30pm.*
- ***Benedictine Sisters of Our Lady of Grace and Compassion,*** St Mary's House, 38/39 Preston Park Avenue, Brighton BN1 6HG Home for the Aged. **Tel:** 01273-556035 *Chaplain:* **Rev Hugh O'Sullivan SDB. Tel:** 01273-501891 Grace & Compassion Convent: 57 Surrenden Road, Brighton East Sussex BN1 6PQ **Tel:** 01273-502129 **Fax:** 01273-552540
- ***Sisters of Charity of Nevers,*** 29 Harrington Road, Preston Park, Brighton, East Sussex BN1 6RF **Tel:** 01273-550488 **Fax:** 01273-555958

6. St Thomas More
(1963; 1973; Cons 10 July, 1983)
Braybon Avenue, Patcham, Brighton, East Sussex BN1 8HG
Tel/Fax: 01273-563017/859701
E-mail: vg@dabnet.org
Website: www.sttm.com
Rev Mgr Canon John Hull. 14 Church Close, Patcham BN1 8HS.
M: *Sat 1st M of Sun 6pm. Sun 9am, 11am. Hds 9.30am, 7.30pm.*

7. Chaplaincy to Sussex and Brighton Universities
Sunday Mass at the Meeting House, University of Sussex.
Chaplain Sussex University: **Rev Paul Wilkinson**. Howard House, 2 Station Approach, Falmer, Brighton, East Sussex BN1 9SD **Tel:** 01273-698032/873879
Fax: 01273-642955
Chaplain Brighton University: **Sr Blanaid McCauley (SSL),** c/o Howard House, 2 Station Approach, Falmer, Brighton, East Sussex BN1 9SD
Tel: 01273-698032 **Fax:** 01273-642955
M: *Sun 6pm during term time at Meeting House, University of Sussex.*

■ BROADFIELD, Crawley, West Sussex
See Crawley (4).

■ BURGESS HILL, East Sussex
† St Wilfrid (1922; 1940; cons 29 May 1984)
Station Road, Burgess Hill, East Sussex RH15 9EN **Tel:** 01444-232358
E-mail: stwilfrids.bh@freeuk.com
Website: http//home.freeuk.net/stwilfridss/
Rev Richard McGrath.
M: *Sat 1st M of Sun 6pm. Sun 9.30am. Hds (vigil 7.30pm) 9.15am.*
- ***Augustinian Sisters,*** St George's Retreat, RH15 0SQ **Tel:** 01444-235874 **M:** *Sun 11am. Hds 11am.*
- ***Franciscan Missionaries of Littlehampton,*** 92 Mill Road, RH15 8EL **Tel:** 01444-233179 **M:** *Sat 1st M of Sun 5pm.*

■ BURWASH, East Sussex >
Christ the King (1969)
High Street. Served from Heathfield.

M: *Sun 9am, Hds 9.30am.*

■ CAMBERLEY, SURREY
† St Tarcisius
(1874; 1924; cons 24 June 1926)
London Road, Camberley, Surrey GU15 3EY Parish office: **Tel:** 01276-473525
E-mail: cb@dabnet.org
Rev Mgr Richard Madders MBE

M: *Sun 10am, 6pm. Hds 10am, 8pm.*

■ **CAMBERLEY (NORTH),** Surrey
† **St Peter and St John** (1963)
Caesar's Camp Road, Camberley, Surrey GU15 4ED **Tel:** 01276-473525
Parish office **E-mail:** cb@dabnet.org
Rev Mgr Richard Madders.
M: *Sun 9.30am. Hds 7am, 8pm.*

■ **CATERHAM,** Surrey
† **The Sacred Heart of Jesus**
(1878; 1881; cons 6 July 1897)
Essendene Road, Caterham, Surrey.
Tel: 01883-343241 **Fax:** 01883-330304
E-mail: priest@sacredheart.junglelink.co.uk
Website: www.sacred-heart.co.uk
Rev Kieran Gardiner.
37 Whyteleafe Road, CR3 5EG
M: *Sat 1st M of Sun 6pm. Sun 10.30am. Hds 10am, 8pm.*
- ***Society of the Sacred Heart,*** Marden Lodge, Marden Park, Woldingham, Surrey CR3 7YA **Tel:** 01883-650264

■ **CHERTSEY,** Surrey
† **St Anne** (1898; 1920; 1930)
10 Highfield Road, Chertsey, Surrey KT16 8BU
Tel: 01932-562375 **Fax:** 01932-564810
E-mail: pp@st-annes-chertsey.org.uk
Website: www.st-annes-chertsey.org.uk
Rev Peter Brealey SDB (*Rector & Parish Priest*).
- ***Salesians (SDB):*** Salesian House, 1 Salesian Gardns, off Eastworth Road, Chertsey KT16 8SG **Tel:** 01932-579050 **Fax:** 01932-579051 **Revv Andrew Ebrahim, Adam Gliwinski, Michael Hynes.**
M: *Sat 1st M of Sun 6.30pm. Sun 8.30am, 10.30am. Hds 9.30am, 7.30pm.*

■ **CHICHESTER,** West Sussex
† **St Richard** (1846; 1859; 1958)
Market Avenue, Chichester, West Sussex.
Tel: 01243-782343, **Fax:** 01243-782332
E-mail: kieron@chicathchurch.prestel.co.uk
Revv Kieron O'Brien, Royston Pegley, Malcolm King, The Presbytery, Cawley Road, PO19 1XB
M: *Sat 1st M of Sun 6pm. Sun 8.30am, 10am. Hds Eve 7.30pm, 9.15am, 12.15pm.*

■ **CHIDDINGFOLD,** Surrey
St Teresa of Avila (1959)
Woodside Road. Served from Haslemere.
M: *Sun 9am. Hds 10am.*

■ **CHILWORTH,** Guildford, Surrey
† **The Holy Ghost** (1890; cons 18 June 1892)
Franciscan Friary, Sample Oak Lane GU4 8QR
Tel: 01483-898071
- **Franciscans (Friars Minor) (OFM):** Franciscan Friary, Sample Oak Lane GU4 8QR **Tel:** 01483 893168
E-mail: austin@friar.org
Revv Austin McCormack *(Guardian & Parish Priest)*, **Patrick Lonsdale** *(Vicar & Vocations Director)*, **Brs Peter Hall, Ignatius Kelly, Alberic Torrens, George Smulski, John Forest OFM**
Deacon: **Rev Roy Waters**. 1 Malthouse Cottages, Goose Green, Gomshall, Guildford, GU5 9LW.
M: *Sat 1st M of Sun 6pm. Sun 10.45am. Hds 7.45am, 10am.*

■ **COBHAM,** Surrey
† **Sacred Heart**
(1912; 1958; cons 13 September 1961)
25 Between Streets, Cobham, Surrey KT11 1AA **Tel:** 01932-862518
Parish Office: **Tel:** 01932-865992
Fax: 01932-865023
E-mail: sacredheartcobham@talk21.com
Rev James Maguire.
M: *Sat 1st M of Sun 6pm. Sun 9am, 11am. Hds 10am, 8pm.*
- ***Company of Mary,*** Notre Dame Convent, Burwood House, Burwood Park, KT11 1HA **Tel:** 01932-868331 "Lestonnal", 27 Between Streets, Cobham, Surrey. KT11 1AA **Tel:** 01932-866450 **Fax:** 01932-865023

■ **COOLHAM,** West Sussex
- ***The Retreat Centre of St Cuthman,*** Coolham, Horsham, West Sussex RH13 8QL *Director:* **Mrs Denise Mitchell Tel:** 01403-741220 **Fax:** 01403-741026 **E-mail:** stcuthmans@dabnet.org

■ **COPTHORNE,** Crawley, East Sussex
See Crawley (7).

■ **COULSDON (SPLIT DIOCESE),** Surrey
Archdiocese of Southwark, part Diocese of Arundel & Brighton
† **St Aidan** Chipstead Road
The Presbytery, 1 Portnalls Road, Coulsdon, Surrey CR3 3DD **Tel:** 020-8660 2452
M: *Sat 1st Mass of Sun 6pm. Sun 9am, 11am. Hds (vigil 7pm), 10am, 8pm.*

■ **CRANLEIGH,** Surrey
† **Christ the Redeemer of Mankind**
(1929; 1933; cons 12 September 1963)
The Presbytery, 2 St Nicolas Avenue, Cranleigh, Surrey GU6 7AQ
Tel: 01483-272075
E-mail: jcrom@netcomuk.co.uk
Rev Kenneth Freeman.
M: *Sat 1st M of Sun 6pm. 11am. Hds 10am, 8pm.*

■ **CRAWLEY,** West Sussex
1. † **St Francis and St Anthony** (1861; 1959)
14 Haslett Avenue West, Crawley, West Sussex RH10 1HR

Tel: 01293-524176 **Fax:** 01293-511675
Revv Anthony Barry, Simon Hall, Christopher Bergin.
Also resident: **Paul Turner**
Deacon: **Rev Andrew Bayes.**
Parish Sister: **Sr Hannah Murray IJS**
M: *Sat 1st M of Sun 6pm. Sun 9.30am, 11.30am, 5.30pm. Hds As announced.*
- ***Sisters of Notre Dame,*** 107 Gales Drive, Three Bridges **Tel:** 01293-527393

2. St Bernadette
Tilgate Way, Crawley, RH10 5BS
Served by Crawley Team.
M: *Sun 9am. Hds As announced.*
- ***Sisters of the Infant Jesus,*** The Presbytery, Tilgate Way, Crawley RH10 5BS **Tel:** 01293-523796

3. Our Lady, Queen of Heaven
Served by Crawley Team.
M: *Sun 11.15am. First Sun of Month 9.30am (Pol). Hds As announced.*

4. Christ the Lord
(Ecumenical and Shared) Broadfield Barton, Broadfield. Served by Crawley Team.
M: *Sun 9.30am. Hds As announced.*

5. St Theodore of Canterbury
Gossops Green Lane.
Served by Crawley Team.
M: *Sat 1st M of Sun, 6.30pm. Hds As announced.*
- ***Dominican Missionary Sisters,*** The Convent, 4 Gossops Green Lane, Gossops Green, Crawley, West Sussex RH11 8BJ **Tel:** 01293-524067 **Fax:** 01293-527140

6. St Edward the Confessor
Hillcrest Close, Pound Hill, Worth, Crawley, West Sussex RH10 7EQ
Served by Crawley Team.
M: *Sun 11am. Hds As announced.*
- ***Sisters of the Infant Jesus,*** 22 Hexham Close, Pound Hill, Crawley, West Sussex RH10 7TZ **Tel:** 01293-881874

7. Copthorne
- ***Franciscan Missionaries of Littlehampton,*** Bankside Lodge, Borers Arms Road, RH10 3LN **Tel:** 01342-712088

■ CROWBOROUGH, East Sussex
† St Mary, Mother of Christ
(1910; 1923; 1936)
The Green.
Tel: 01892-654608 **Fax:** 01892-611519
Rev Kevin Griffin. Priest's Cottage, Queen's Road, Chapel Green, Crowborough, East Sussex TN6 2LB
M: *Sat 1st M of Sun 6pm. Sun 9.30am, Hds 9.30am, 7.30pm.*

■ DORKING, Surrey
† St Joseph (1871; 1895)
2 Falkland Grove, Dorking, Surrey RH4 3DL
Tel: 01306-882433,
E-mail: stjosephs@tiscali.co.uk
Website: sjcc.org.uk.
Rev Dominic Rolls. *Deacon:* **Rev Tony Kinal**
Also in residence: **Rev Victor Cook**
M: *Sat 1st M of Sun 6pm. Sun 9am, 11am. Hds 7.30am, 9.30am, 8pm.*
- ***Servite Sisters,*** St Joseph's Priory, Harrow Road, West Dorking RH4 3BG **Tel:** 01306-882824

■ DUNCTON, West Sussex
† SS Anthony and George
(1866; cons 18 August 1869)
Served from Petworth. **Tel:** 01798-42169
M: *Sun 8.30am.*

■ DURRINGTON, West Sussex
See Worthing (3).

■ EAST GRINSTEAD, West Sussex
† Our Lady and St Peter
(1879; 1898; cons 1 August 1899)
London Road
Tel: 01342-325705 **Fax:** 01342-302507
Rev Steven Purnell. 17 St James Road, RH19 1DL *Deacon:* **Rev Ted Darlison**.
M: *Sat 1st M of Sun 6.15pm. Sun 10.30am. Hds (vigil 8pm), 9.30am.*

■ EAST PRESTON WITH ANGMERING, West Sussex.
Our Lady of the Sea
Vermont Drive, East Preston.
Rev David Rea. Priest's House, Vermont Drive, East Preston, Littlehampton, West Sussex BN16 1JU
Tel: 01903-785091 **Fax:** 01903-770490
M: *Sat 1st M of Sun 6pm. Sun 10am. Hds 10am, Vigil Mass 6pm.*

■ EAST WITTERING
See The Witterings

■ EASTBOURNE, East Sussex
1. † Our Lady of Ransom & St Gregory with St Agnes (1867; 1890; 1904; cons 8 July 1926)
2 Grange Road, Eastbourne, East Sussex BN21 4EU
Tel: 01323-723222 **Fax:** 01323-645605
E-mail: ransomagnes@mistral.co.uk
Canon Seamus Hester, Rev Tim Hunting.
M: *Sat 1st M of Sun 6pm. Sun 10.30am, 5.30pm. Hds 12noon, 7pm.*
- ***Dominican Sisters,*** Holy Rosary Convent, 34 The Goffs BN21 1HD **Tel:** 01323-722435

2. St Gregory (1934; 1967)
Victoria Drive, Old Town.
Served from Eastbourne (1).
M: *Sun 9.15am. Hds 7.30am.*

3. † St Agnes
(1906; cons 28 Sept 1909)

10 Whitley Road, BN22 8NJ
Tel/Fax: 01323-725684
Served from Eastbourne (1).
M: *Sat 1st M of Sun 5pm. Sun 11.15am; Hds 10am.*

• ***Sisters of Our Lady of the Missions:*** 66 Whitley Road, BN22 8NE
Tel: 01323-730277

4. Christ the King (1967)
3 Princes Road, Langney Village, Eastbourne BN23 6HT
Tel: 01323-760048
Website: www.christ-the-king.org.uk
Rev Barry Anderson.
Deacon: **Rev Eugene Adams**
M: *Sat 1st M of Sun 6pm. Sun 11.30am. Hds 12noon.*

A

5. Holy Rood
Castle Drive, Pevensey Bay.
Served from Eastbourne (4).
M: *Sat 4pm.*

■ **EFFINGHAM,** Leatherhead, Surrey
† Our Lady of Sorrows
(1897; 1913; cons 8 Oct 1913)
Lower Road, Effingham, Leatherhead KT24 5JP **Tel:** 01372-458263
M: *Sat 1st M of Sun 6.30pm. Sun 9am, 11am, 6.30pm. Hds 9.15am, 8pm.*

• ***Religious of Christian Instruction,*** St Teresa's Convent, Effingham Hill, Dorking RH5 6ST **Tel:** 01372-453810

■ **EGHAM PARISH,** Surrey
1. † The Assumption of Our Lady
(1906; 1931; cons 26 Sept 1936)
Harvest Road, Englefield Green TW20 0QR
Rev David Maskell.
91 Harvest Road, Englefield Green, Surrey TW20 0QR **Tel:** 01784-434280/452756
Fax: 01784-470289
Email: churchoftheassumption@yahoo.co.uk
Deacon: **Rev Aidan Lynch**
M: *Sat 1st M of Sun 6pm. Sun 9.30am, 11am.*

2. † St John of Rochester (1961)
Rochester Road, Egham Hythe, Middx TW18 3HN **Tel:** 01784-452756
M: *Sun 10am, 6pm.*

3. † University of London
Royal Holloway College. **Tel:** 01784-452756
Chaplain: **Rev Vladimir Nikiforov,** Founders Building West, Room FW173, Royal Holloway, Egham, Surrey TW20 0EK
Tel: 01784-414358 or 07742 582923
Email: vladimir.nikiforov@rhul.ac.uk

■ **EPSOM,** Surrey
† St Joseph
(1864-66; 1930; cons 19 March 1974; new Church cons 1 May 2001)
Church & Parish Office: St Margaret Drive, Epsom, Surrey KT18 7JQ
Tel: 01372-723573 **Fax:** 01372-730933
E-mail: sjcparishoffice@aol.com
Website: www.st-josephs-epsom.org.uk
Priests' House, 1 St Margaret Drive, Epsom, Surrey KT18 7LB
Revs William Davern, Bruno Witchalls.
M: *Sat 1st M of Sun 6pm. Sun 9.30am, 11.30am, 6pm. Hds 10am, 7.30pm.*

Sisters of Charity of Jesus and Mary, Triest House, 5 St Margaret Drive, Epsom, Surrey KT18 7LB. **Tel:** 01372-745297

Sisters of the Sacred Hearts of Jesus and Mary, Aymer House, 49 Woodcote Hurst, Epsom, Surrey KT18 7DS
Tel: 01372-729829 **Fax:** 01372-729870

■ **ESHER,** Surrey
† The Holy Name (1923; 1961)
42 Arbrook Lane, Esher, Surrey KT10 9EE
Tel: 01372-462451 **Fax:** 01372-463887
Mgr Benny O'Shea.
M: *Sat 1st Mass of Sun 6pm. Sun 9.30am, 11am. Hds 10am, 8pm.*

■ **EWELL,** Surrey
† St Clement (1937; 1962)
307 Kingston Road, Ewell, Surrey KT19 0BW
Tel: 020-8393 5572 **Fax:** 020-8393 4151
Rev Graham Bamford.
M: *Sat 1st M of Sun 6pm. Sun 8.30am, 10.30am, 6pm. Hds 10am, 8pm.*

■ **FARNCOMBE,** Surrey
Served from Godalming.
M: *Sun 8.45am in St John's Parish Church (C of E), St John's Street.*

■ **FARNHAM,** Surrey
1. † St Joan of Arc
(1890; 1930; cons 30 May 1956)
19 Tilford Road, Farnham, Surrey GU9 8DJ
Tel: 01252-716711 **Fax:** 01252-716733

Website: www.stjoanofarcfarnham.co.uk
Canon Anthony Whale.
M: *Sat 1st M of Sun 6.30pm. Sun 9.15am, 11.15am, 6.30pm. Hds 8am, 10am, 8pm.*

• ***Missionary Sister Servants of the Holy Spirit:*** 78 Firgrove Hill, Farnham GU9 8LW **Tel:** 01252-722329
Fax: 01252-721809

2. The Holy Family (1956)
Alma Lane, Heath End, Farnham, Surrey GU9 0LH Served from Ash (3).
M: *Sun 9.15am. Hds 10am.*

3. The Holy Angels
65 Ash Church Road, Ash, Aldershot, Hants GU12 6LU **Tel:** 01252-321422
Rev David Osborne

Deacon: **Rev John Edwards**
M: *Sat 1st M of Sun 6pm, Sun 11am. Hds: 8pm.*

■ **FETCHAM,** Surrey
Holy Spirit (1968)
5 Bell Lane, Fetcham, Surrey KT22 9ND
Tel/Fax: 01372-373387
E-mail: holyspiritchurch@supanet.com
Rev Hugh Flower.
Deacon: **Rev Ian Wells**
M: *Sat 1st M of Sun 6pm. Sun 8.30am, 10.30am. Hds 9.30am, 8pm.*

■ **FOREST ROW,** East Sussex
Our Lady of the Forest
88 Hartfield Road, Forest Row, East Sussex RH18 5BZ Served from East Grinstead.
M: *Sun 9am.*

■ **FRIMLEY,** Surrey
† Our Lady Queen of Heaven (1954)
Rev John O'Sullivan. 111 Portsmouth Road, Frimley, Camberley. GU16 7AA
Tel: 01276-504876 **Fax:** 01276-500070
E-mail: olqh@ntlworld.com
Website: www.olqh.com
M: *Sat 1st M of Sun 6pm. Sun 8.30am, 10.30am, 5.30pm. Hds 7.15am, 10am.*

■ **GATWICK AIRPORT CHAPLAINCY**
London Gatwick Airport, West Sussex.
Chaplaincy Team: **Rev Richard Wilson OSB, Dcn Chris Dobson, Sr Jo Threlfall SND**
Tel: 01293-503851

■ **GODALMING,** Surrey
† St Edmund, King and Martyr
(1899; 1906; cons 3 Oct 1923)
19 Croft Road, Godalming, Surrey GU7 1DB
Tel: 01483-416880
Rev Michael J Perry.
Charterhouse School Chaplaincy is served from Sutton Park.
M: *Sun 6pm. Hds 12.15pm, 6.45pm (Pol), 8pm.*
• ***Franciscan Missionaries of the Divine Motherhood,*** Ladywell Convent, Ashstead Lane, GU7 1ST
Mother House and Novitiate:
Tel: 01483-425775 **Fax:** 01483-419265
St Clare's Community: 01483-423764
La Verna Community: 01483-419267
Retreat Centre: 01483-419269
Fermain, Tuesley lane, Godalming, Surrey GU7 1SS **Tel:** 01483-416636

■ **GOMSHALL,** Surrey
St Mary of the Angels (1948)
near Station Approach.
Served from Chilworth.
M: *Sun 9am. Hds 8pm.*

■ **GORING-BY-SEA,** West Sussex 
† English Martyrs
(1937; 1968; cons 5 May 1970)
Goring Way, Goring-by-Sea, West Sussex.
Tel: 01903-242624 **Fax:** 01903-249697
E-mail: emgoring@talktalk.net
Rev Liam O'Connor. 37 Compton Avenue, BN12 4UE
M: *Sat 1st M of Sun 6pm. Sun 8.15am, 10.30am, First Sun of month 6pm (Pol). Hds 9.30am, 7.30pm.*
• ***Franciscan Missionaries of the Divine Motherhood,*** Maryfield, 78 Langbury Lane, Ferring, West Sussex. BN12 6QE
Tel: 01903-700695

■ **GOSSOPS GREEN,** Crawley, East Sussex
St Theodore (1959)
Gossops Green Lane, Gossops.
Served by Crawley Team.

■ **GUILDFORD,** Surrey
1. † St Joseph
Tel: 01483-562704 **Fax:** 01483-452206
Website: www.stjo-guildford.co.uk
Revv Colin Wolczak, John Horn, Aaron Spinelli. *Deacons:* **Revv John Lamb, Charles Parker**
12 Eastgate Gardens, GU1 4AZ
M: *Sun 8am, 10.30am, 6.30pm. Hds 7.30am, 10am, 7.30pm.*
• ***Franciscan Missionaries of the Divine Motherhood,*** Marymount, 26 Jenner Road, Guildford, Surrey GU1 3PP
Tel: (Convent) 01483-563939

2. St Mary
157 Aldershot Road, Guildford, Surrey GU2 8BP **Tel:** 01483-573279
M: *Sat 1st M of Sun 7pm. Sun 10.30am. Hds 9am (School term only), 10am, 8pm.*

3. St Pius X (1973)
Tel: 01483-572605
Laustan Close, Merrow. Served from Guildford
M: *Sun 9.45am. Hds 10am.*

4. University of Surrey Chaplaincy of St Thomas More
More House, 12 Queen Eleanor's Road, Onslow Village, Guildford, Surrey GU2 5SL
Chaplain: **Mr John McCarthy.**
Tel: 01483-571091
Fax: 01483-453314 (*Students*)
Tel: 01483-821977 **Fax:** 01483-453314
M: *5.15pm in University Quiet Room. Hds As advertised.*

■ **HAILSHAM,** East Sussex
1. † St Wilfrid (1922; 1955)
South Road, Hailsham, East Sussex BN27 3JG **Tel:** 01323-841504
Fax: 01323-441688
Rev Rory Kelly.
Deacon: **Rev John Truman**
M: *Sat 1st M of Sun 6pm. Sun 10.30am. Hds 10am, 7pm.*

2. † St George
Polegate, East Sussex. Served from Hailsham.

■ **HAMPDEN PARK,** East Sussex [A]
St Joachim (1960)
106 Brodrick Road, Hampden Park, East Sussex BN22 9NY
Served from Eastbourne (4).
M: *Sun 9.30am; Hds Eve 7.30pm.*
- **Sisters of the Infant Jesus:** 106 Brodrick Road, Hampden Park, Eastbourne, E. Sussex, BN22 9NY
Tel/Fax: 01323 501793

■ **HANGLETON,** East Sussex
See Hove (3).

■ **HASLEMERE,** Surrey
† Our Lady of Lourdes
(1908; 1924; cons 28 September 1932)
Weydown Road, Haslemere, Surrey.
Tel: 01428-643877
Website: www.oll.haslemere.com
Rev Stephen Hardaker,
21 Derby Road, GU27 1BS
M: *Sat 1st M of Sun 6pm. Sun 10.45am. Hds 8pm.*
- ***Daughters of the Cross,*** Holy Cross Hospital, Hindhead Road, GU27 1NQ
Tel: 01428-643311
Chaplain: **Rev Phelim McGowan SJ.**
M: *Sun 9am. Hds 9.30am.*

■ **HASSOCKS,** See Keymer

■ **HASTINGS,** East Sussex
† St Mary Star of the Sea
(1880; con 15 May 1922)
1 High Street, Hastings, East Sussex TN34 3EY **Tel:** 01424-421263
Fax: 01424-460893
Pallottine Fathers (SCA): **Revv John O'Brien SCA, John Sweeney SCA.**
M: *Sat 1st M of Sun 6pm. Sun 10am, 11.30am. Every 2nd Sun of month 3pm (Pol). Hds 10am, 7.30pm.*

■ **HAYWARDS HEATH** [A] [S]
West Sussex.
1. † St Paul (1886; 1930)
Hazelgrove Road, Haywards Heath, West Sussex RH16 3PQ
Tel: 01444-450139 **Fax:** 01444-441439
Rev Martin Jakubas.
Deacon: **Rev Gerard Irwin**
M: *Sun 8.30am, 10.30am, 5pm. Hds 7am, 11am, 8pm.*
- ***Augustinian Sisters,*** St Raphael's Nursing Home, Church Lane, Danehill, RH17 7EZ **Tel:** 01825-790485

2. See Staplefield.

3. See Horsted Keynes.

■ **HEATH END,** Surrey
See Farnham, (2).

■ **HEATHFIELD WITH BURWASH,** East Sussex.
St Catherine (1953)
Presbytery, Mutton Hall, Heathfield, East Sussex TN21 8NX **Tel:** 01435-862191
Rev Michael Creech CSSR.
Deacon: **Rev Michael Thoms**
M: *Sun 11am. Hds 7.30pm.*
- ***Benedictine Sisters of Our Lady Grace and Compassion,*** Holy Cross Priory, Cross in Hand, TN21 0TS **Tel:** 01435-863298 Home for the Elderly. *Chaplain:* **Dom Illtud Barrett (OSB),**
Tel: 01435-867239 **Fax:** 01435-867843

■ **HENFIELD,** West Sussex
† Corpus Christi (1959)
Tanyard, Henfield, West Sussex BN5 9PE
Tel: 01273-492974 **Fax:** 01273-491173
Deacon: **Seamus Mahon.**
Served from West Grinstead
M: *Sat 1st M of Sun 6pm. Hds 10.30am, 8pm.*
- ***Sisters of the Blessed Sacrament,*** Golden Square, BN5 9DP
Tel: 01273-493435

■ **HERON'S GHYLL,** 
Uckfield, East Sussex
† St John the Evangelist
(1879; 1897; cons 7 Sept 1904)
Served from Uckfield.
M: *Sun 11.30am.*

■ **HERSHAM,** Surrey 
† All Saints (1957)
13 Queen's Road, Hersham, Walton-on-Thames, Surrey KT12 5LU
Tel: 01932-221007
Canon Brendan MacCarthy.
M: *Sun 9am, 11am, 6pm. Hds (vigil 8pm), 9.30am.*

■ **HIGH SALVINGTON,** Worthing, East Sussex
See Worthing (3).

■ **HINDHEAD AND BEACON HILL,** Surrey 
† St Anselm (1951)
Churt Road, Hindhead, Surrey GU26 6PD
Served from Haslemere.
M: *Sun 10.30am. Hds (vigil) 8pm.*

■ **HOLLINGTON,** East Sussex 
Served from St Leonard's.
† Holy Redeemer (1834)
31 Upper Church Road, Hollington, St Leonards-on-Sea TN37 7AS
Tel: 01424-751543
M: *Sat 1st M of Sun 7pm. Sun 9am, 10.30am. Hds - see newsletter.*

- ***Sisters of Our Lady of the Missions,*** 18 Old Roar Road, St Leonards-on-Sea, E. Sussex TN37 7HA **Tel:** 01424-751331
- ***The Poor Clares,*** Hollingdene, 22 Upper Church Road, Hollington, St Leonard's-on-Sea, East Sussex TN37 7AS
- ***Capuchin Franciscans (OFMCap),*** 31 Upper Church Road, Hollington, St Leonard's-on-Sea, East Sussex TN37 7AS **Tel:** 01424-752665 **Bros Prins Casinader, Patrick Mulligan**

■ **HORLEY,** Surrey
† The English Martyrs (1929; 1935; 1962)
Vicarage Lane. Horley, Surrey RH6 8AR
Tel: 01293-431703
Rev Paul Jennings.
M: *Sat 1st M of Sun 6.30am. Sun 9am, 10.30am. Hds (vigil 7.30pm), 10am.*

■ **HORNS CROSS,** East Sussex
See Northiam.

■ **HORSHAM,** West Sussex
1. † St John the Evangelist
(1845; 1923; cons 25 Oct 1927)
The Presbytery, 3 Springfield Road, Horsham, West Sussex. RH12 2PJ
Tel: 01403-253667 **Fax:** 01403-271509
Rev Terry Martin.
Deacon: **Rev Tom Murray.**
M: *Sat 1st M of Sun 6.15pm. Sun 9am, 11am, 1pm (Pol), 5pm (Italian). Hds, 10am, 7.30pm.*
- ***Holy Family Sisters,*** Bedford Road, Horsham RH13 5BL **Tel:** 01403-241070

2. Roffey, All Saints (C of E)
Crawley Road. Served from Horsham (1).
M: *Sun 9am. Hds 12.30pm.*

■ **HORSTED KEYNES,**
Haywards Heath, E. Sussex
St Stephen (1970)
Hamsland. Served from Haywards Heath.

■ **HOVE,** East Sussex
1. † The Sacred Heart
(1879; 1881; cons 25 Oct 1887)
39 Norton Road, Hove, E. Sussex BN3 3BF
Tel: 01273-732843 **Fax:** 01273-735179
Rev Carl Davies
Deacon: **Rev Paul Scholey.**
M: *Sat 1st M of Sun 6pm. Sun 9.30am, 11.30am, 5.30pm. Hds 8am, 12noon, 7pm.*

2. † St Peter
(1902; 1915; cons 28 June 1927)
Portland Road. **Tel:** 01273-733840
Rev Jeremiah O'Brien. St Peters, Shelley Road, BN3 5GD
M: *Sat 1st M of Sun 6pm. Sun 8.30am, 10am (Fam), 11.15am, 6pm. Hds (vigil 6pm), 8am, 10am, 8pm.*

3. † St George
West Blatchington. **Tel:** 01273-503647
Rev David Weston, *Deacon:* **Rev Richard Harvey.** The Chantry, 13 Court Farm Road, Hove, East Sussex BN3 7QR
M: *Sun 10am, 6.30pm. Hds 11am, 8pm.*

■ **HURSTPIERPOINT,** East Sussex
† St Luke (1925)
121 Cuckfield Road, Hurstpierpoint, West Sussex. Served from Keymer.
M: *Sun 8.30am. Hds 8pm.*

■ **KEYMER,** Hassocks, East Sussex A
† St Edward the Confessor (1920; 1922)
Priests House, 2 Lodge Lane, BN6 8NA
Tel: 01273-845384 **Fax:** 01273-846874
Rev Anthony Collins.
M: *Sat 1st M of Sun 6pm. Sun 10.30am. Hds 9.30am.*

■ **KNAPHILL,** Surrey
† St Hugh (1908; 1971; cons 1978)
95 Victoria Road, Knaphill, Woking, Surrey GU21 2AA **Tel:** 01483-472404
Email: sthugh.priest@ntlworld.com
Website: www.sthughoflincoln.org
Mgr Canon Jeffrey H Scott
M: *Sat 1st M of Sun 6.15pm. Sun 9.30am, 11.30am. Hds 9.05am (School), 11am.*

■ **LANCING,** West Sussex
† The Holy Family
(1970; cons 30 May 1972)
Monks Farm Presbytery, 127 North Road, Lancing, West Sussex BN15 9BB
Tel/Fax: 01903-752293
Rev Daryl George. *Deacon:* **Rev John Body**
M: *Sun 10.30am.*

■ **LANGLEY GREEN,** Crawley, East Sussex
† See Crawley (3).

■ **LANGNEY,** Eastbourne, East Sussex
See Eastbourne (4).

■ **LEATHERHEAD,** Surrey
† Our Lady and St Peter
(1915; 1923; cons 8 September 1964)
Garlands Road, Leatherhead, KT22 7EZ
Tel: 01372-372278 **Fax:** 01372-813384
Rev Michael Masterson.
M: *Sun 8.30am, 10am, 6pm. Hds 7am, 12.30pm, 8pm.*

■ **LEWES,** East Sussex
† St Pancras
(1865; 1870; 1939; cons 4 July 1962)

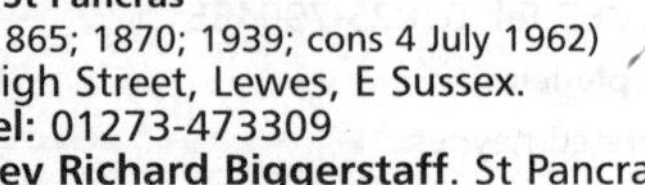

High Street, Lewes, E Sussex.
Tel: 01273-473309
Rev Richard Biggerstaff. St Pancras, Irelands Lane, BN7 1QX

M: *Sat 1st M of Sun 6pm. Sun 9am, 10.30am. Hds 9.15am, 12.30pm, 8pm.*

• ***Priory of Our Lady of Good Counsel, Canonesses of St Augustine,*** Dove Cottage, Kingston Ridge, Kingston near Lewes, East Sussex BN7 3JX **Tel:** 01273-486677 *Chaplain:* **Rev Joesph Cummins MAfr** White Gates, Church Lane, Kingston near Lewes, East Sussex BN7 3LN **Tel:** 01273 483775 **M:** *Sun 9am. Hds 9am.*

■ **LINGFIELD,** Surrey
† **St Bernard** (1940)
Vicarage Road, Lingfield, Surrey RH7 6EZ
Tel: 01342-325705
Served from East Grinstead.
Deacon: **Rev Ted Rider.**
M: *Sun 9am. Hds 9.30am.*

■ **LITTLE COMMON,** Bexhill-on-Sea
St Martha (1940)
Cooden Road. Served from Bexhill-on-Sea.
M: *Sun 9am.*

■ **LITTLEHAMPTON,** West Sussex
† **St Catherine, VM**
(1859; 1883; 1903; cons 8 May 1962)
Beach Road, Littlehampton, West Sussex BN17 5JH **Tel:** 01903-731171
Fax: 01903-731813
Rev Albert Van Der Most.
M: *Sat 1st M of Sun 6.30pm. Sun 10.30am. Hds (vigil 6.30pm), 10am.*

• ***Franciscan Missionaries of Littlehampton,*** St Joseph's Nursing Home, East Street BN17 6AU **Tel:** 01903-721053; Community **Tel:** 01903-715589 **M:** *Sun 10.30am. Hds 10.30am.*

■ **MAYFIELD,** East Sussex
1. † **St Thomas of Canterbury** (1932; 1957)
Priest's House, Station Road TN20 6BU
Tel: 01435-872381
Rev Mario Sanderson.
M: *Sat 1st M of Sun 6pm. Sun 10am. Hds 7.30pm.*

• ***Society of the Holy Child Jesus.*** The Old Palace, High Street, TN20 6PH Boarding and Day School for Girls: **Tel:** 01435-874600 (School Switchboard); 01435-874619 (Community) **Website:** www.shcj.org

■ **MERSTHAM,** Surrey
† **St Teresa of the Child Jesus** (1959)
Weldon Way, Merstham, Redhill, Surrey RH1 3QA **Tel/Fax:** 01737-643399
Rev Charles Howell
M: *Sat 1st M of Sun 5.30pm. Sun 10.30am. Hds 7.30am, 12.15pm, 8pm.*

■ **MIDHURST,** West Sussex
† **The Divine Motherhood and St Francis**
(1230-1767; 1869; 1958; cons 25 May 1966)
Bepton Road. **Tel:** 01730-813167
Rev Peter Johnstone. St Mary's Presbytery, Bepton Road, GU29 9HD
M: *Sat 1st M of Sun 6.pm. Sun 8am, 10.30am. Hds 12noon, 7.30pm.*

• ***Sisters of Mercy,*** The Convent of Mercy, Little Ashfield, Midhurst, W. Sussex GU29 9JP **Tel:** 01730-816600 (Convent); 01730-813956 (Junior School). **Fax:** 01730-810788

• ***De La Salle Brothers,*** Clayton Court, Hill Brow, Liss, Hants GU33 7QP **Tel:** 01730-893130

■ **MILFORD,** Surrey
St Joseph (1967)
Portsmouth Road. Served from Godalming.
M: *Sat 1st M of Sun 6pm. Sun 8.30am (Pol), 10.15am. Hds (vigil 7pm), 9am, 6.45pm (Polish).*

■ **MOLESEY,** Surrey
† **St Barnabas** (1905; 1931; cons June 11, 1981)
28 Vine Road, Molesey, Surrey KT8 9LF
Tel: 020-8979 1176
Rev Richard Brennan SPS.
M: *Sat 1st M of Sun 6pm. Sun 10am, 6pm. Hds 9.30am, 8pm.*

• ***St Patrick's Missionary Society (Kiltegan Fathers).*** 20 Beauchamp Road, East Molesey, Surrey KT8 0PA **Tel:** 020-8979 1890 **Fax:** 020-8941 8221 **E-mail:** spsuk@aol.com **Revv Patrick McCallion (*Director of Promotion*), John Collins, Patrick Kelleher.**

• ***Missionaries of St Paul (of Nigeria).*** Address above: **Fr Joseph Udoh MSP.**

• ***Sisters of the Christian Retreat,*** House of Prayer, 35 Seymour Road, East Molesey, Surrey KT8 0PB **Tel:** 020-8941 2313

■ **MOULSECOOMB,** Brighton
See Brighton, (4).

■ **NEWHAVEN,** East Sussex
† **Sacred Heart** (1895; 1898; cons 6 June 1975)
36 Fort Road, Newhaven, E Sussex BN9 9EJ
Tel: 01273-515254
Rev Cyril Cravos.
M: *Sat 1st M of Sun 6pm. Sun 10am. Hds 10am, 7.30pm.*

■ **NORTHIAM,** East Sussex
† **St Teresa of Lisieux** (1930; 1935, 1986)
Horn's Cross (between Northiam and Brede).
Served from Battle
M: *Sun 10am. Hds 7pm.*

■ **OXTED,** Surrey
† **All Saints** (1914; 1920; cons 6 July 1927)
Priest's House, 17 Bluehouse Lane, Oxted Surrey RH8 0AA **Tel:** 01883-713776
Website: www.allsaints.oxted.btinternet.co.uk
Rev John Olliver.
Deacon: **Rev Stuart Geary**.
M: *Sat 1st M of Sun 5.30. Sun 11am.*

■ **PARKMINSTER,** West Sussex
St Hugh's Charterhouse
Henfield Road, Partridge Green, Horsham, W Sussex RH13 8EB **Tel:** 01403-864231
• ***Carthusians (OCart):*** (*Prior*) **Rev John Babeau**.
M: *Sun 10.30am. Hds 10.30am.*

■ **PATCHAM,** Brighton
See Brighton, (6).

■ **PEACEHAVEN,** East Sussex
† **Immaculate Conception** (1924)
Edith Avenue. **Tel:** 01273-583600
Website: www.peacehavenchurch.org.uk
Rev Tom Ryan SPS. 218 Arundel Road Central, Peacehaven, East Sussex BN10 8BJ
M: *Sat 1st M of Sun 6.30pm. Sun 9.30am, 10.30am. Hds 9.30am,7.30pm.*

■ **PETWORTH,** West Sussex
† **The Sacred Heart** (1869; cons 19 June 1901)
The Presbytery, Angel Street, Petworth, W. Sussex GU28 0BG **Tel/Fax:** 01798-342169
Rev Peter Newsam.
M: *Sat 1st M of Sun 5.30pm. Sun 10.30am. Hds 10am, 7pm.*

■ **PEVENSEY BAY,** East Sussex
The Holy Rood (1964; cons 4 May 1966)
Castle Drive. Served from Eastbourne (4).
M: *1st M of Sun Sat 4pm.*

■ **POLEGATE,** East Sussex
† **St George** (1938)
Served from Hailsham.
M: *Sun 8.45am.*

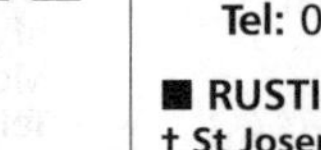

■ **PORTSLADE,** See Southwick

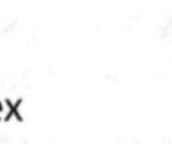

■ **POUND HILL,** Crawley, W. Sussex
St Edward the Confessor
See Crawley (6).

■ **PRESTON PARK,** Sussex
See Brighton (5).

■ **PULBOROUGH,** W. Sussex
† **St Crispin and St Crispinian** (1925; 1953)
Church Place.
M: *Sun 11am (Served from Storrington)*

■ **REDHILL,** Surrey
† **St Joseph**
122 Ladbroke Road, Redhill, Surrey, RH1 1LF
Tel: 01737-761017 **Fax:** 01737-763061
Revv Laurence Quin-Morris, Kevin Dring.
Deacon: **Rev Tim Murrill**
M: *Sat 1st M of Sun 6pm. Sun 8am, 10.30am 5.30. Hds 10am, 8pm.*
• ***Sisters of St Dorothy,*** "Rosebank" 10 Linkfield Lane, Redhill RH1 1JL
Tel: 01737-771487

■ **REIGATE,** Surrey
† **The Holy Family** (1938; cons 9 May 1951)
Yorke Road. Reigate, Surrey RH2 9HF
Tel: 01737-243781 **Fax:** 01737-216804
E-mail: holyfamily.reigate@dabnet.org
Adminstrator: **Rev Charles Howell**
M: *Sat 1st M of Sun 6pm; Sun 10am. Hds Vigil 7pm, 9.30am*

■ **ROFFEY,** West Sussex
Served from Horsham (1).

■ **ROSE GREEN,** West Sussex
St Anthony of Viareggio
Gossamer Lane, Aldwick.
Served from Bognor Regis.
M: *Sun 11am. Hds 6.30pm*

■ **ROTHERFIELD,** East Sussex
† **St Peter, Prince of the Apostles** (1963)
Meadow View, off South Street.
Served from Wadhurst.
M: *Sun 9am. Hds (vigil 7.30pm).*

■ **ROTTINGDEAN,** Brighton & Hove
† **Our Lady of Lourdes, Queen of Peace** (1925; 1957; cons 10 Sept 1958)
Whiteway Lane.
Tel: 01273-302903
Rev Graham Ricketts. Eastfield, Steyning Road, BN2 7GA
M: *Sat 1st M of Sun 6.30pm. Sun 10.30am. Hds 10am, 8pm.*
• ***Sisters of St Martha,*** St Martha's Convent, The Green BN2 7HA
Tel: 01273-302354 /305401

■ **RUSTINGTON,** West Sussex
† **St Joseph** (1951)
Station Road, Rustington, W Sussex BN16 3BE **Tel:** 01903-783973
Rev Brendan Burke.
M: *Sat 1st M of Sun 6.30pm. Sun 10am.*

■ **RYDES HILL,** Surrey
See Guildford, No 2.

■ **RYE,** E. Sussex
† **St Anthony of Padua**
(1900; 1930; cons 28 September 1933)
Watchbell Street, Rye, East Sussex TN31 7HB
Tel: 01797-222173 **Fax:** 01797-223066
• ***Franciscans (Friars Minor Conventual) (OFM Conv):*** **Rev Joseph Aylookunnel** (*Parish Priest*).

M: *Sat 1st M of Sun 6pm. Sun 8am, 10.45am. Hds 9am, 7pm.*

■ **ST LEONARDS,** E. Sussex
† **St Thomas of Canterbury and English Martyrs**
(1834; 1889; cons 28 September 1907)
The Presbytery, Magdalen Road, St Leonards, East Sussex TN37 6ET
Tel: 01424-420815 **Fax:** 01424-203688
E-mail: engmartyrs@stleonards99.fsnet.co.uk
Website: www.stocrec.org.uk
Rev Ian Byrnes.
M: *Sun 11am, 6pm. Hds - see newsletter.*
- ***Canonesses of St Augustine,*** Alix Lodge, 118 Filsham Road, St Leonards-on-Sea, E. Sussex TN38 0PE
Tel: Hastings 01424-420678. Filsham Lodge120 Filsham Road, TN38 0PE
Tel: 01424-434532

■ **SEAFORD,** East Sussex
† **St Thomas More** (1900; 1936)
54 Sutton Road, Seaford, East Sussex BN25 1SS **Tel:** 01323-892427.
Website: www.st-thomas-more.co.uk
Rev Niven Richardson
M: *Sat 1st M of Sun 6pm. Sun 8am, 10.30am. Hds 10am, 7.30pm.*
- ***Sisters of Providence,*** Annecy, Sutton Avenue, BN25 4LA **Tel:** 01323-892178 Shalom, 10a Sutton Avenue, Seaford, East Sussex BN25 4LA
Tel: 01323-896954

■ **SELSEY,** West Sussex
Our Lady of Mount Carmel and St Wilfrid
(1920; 1961)
Church Road, Selsey, W Sussex PO20 0LS
Tel: 01243-602312 Served from Chichester.
M: *Sat 1st M of Sun 5.30pm. Sun 10am. Hds 9.30am, 8pm.*

■ **SHOREHAM-BY-SEA,**West Sussex
† **St Peter**
West Street, Shoreham-by-Sea, W. Sussex BN43 5DL See Adur Valley.

■ **SIDLEY,** East Sussex
Our Lady of the Rosary
Southlands Road. Served from Bexhill on Sea.
M: *Sun 10am. Hds 7pm.*

■ **SLINDON,** Arundel, West Sussex
† **St Richard**
(Pre-Reformation; 1865; cons 5 May 1953)
Served from Bognor Regis
M: *Sun 9am. Hds 7.30pm*

■ **SOUTHWICK with PORTSLADE,** West and East Sussex
1. St Theresa of Lisieux (1942; 1955; cons 1980)
Old Shoreham Road, Southwick, W. Sussex.
Rev Alistair Simmons, The Priest's House, 92 Downland Avenue, Southwick, West Sussex BN42 4RY
Tel: 01273-708227 **Fax:** 01273-239946
Parish Sister: **Sr Pauline Hannon IJS**
M: *Sat 1st M of Sun 6pm. Sun 10.30am. Hds 7.30pm.*
2. † Star of the Sea Hall (1912; cons 17 Sept 1958)
Church Road, Portslade, BN41 1LB
M: *Sun 9am. Hds 9.30am in the School Hall, during term.*

■ **STAPLEFIELD,** East Sussex
† **Our Lady of Fatima** (1966)
See Hayard's Heath, (1).
M: *Sat 1st M of Sun 5pm. Hds Eve. 7.30pm.*

■ **STEYNING,** West Sussex
† **Christ the King** (1951)
Bramber Road. **Tel:** 01903-812658
Parish Office, Penlands Way, BN44 3PN
Served from Shoreham.

■ **STORRINGTON,** Pulborough
† **Our Lady of England**
(1882; 1904; cons 19 June 1959)
School Lane, Storrington, Pulborough RH20 4LN
Tel: 01903-742150 **Fax:** 01903-740821
Website: norbertines.co.uk
E-mail: Whitecanons.storrington@btinternet.com
- ***Canons Regular of Premontre (O Praem):*** **Right Rev Paul MacMahon** (*Prior*), **Revv Andrew H Smith** (*Sub-prior & Parish Priest*), **Ian McClean, Martin Gosling** (*Bursar & Assistant Priest*).
M: *Sat 1st M of Sun 6pm. Sun 8am, 10am. Hds 9am, 7.30pm.*
- ***Merrywood House,*** Merrywood Lane, Thakeham, Pulborough, RH20 3HD
Tel: 01903-743349

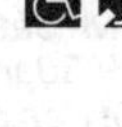

■ **SUNNINGDALE,** Berks
The Sacred Heart
London Road, Sunningdale, Ascot, Berks SL5 0JY
Tel: 01344-621238/621267
Fax: 01344-874175
Email: sacredheart.sunningdale@yahoo.com
- ***Verona Fathers, Comboni Missionaries (MCCJ),*** **Revv Paul Felix** (*Provincial Superior*), **John Troy** (*Priest in Charge*), **Robert Hicks** (*Provincial Bursar*).
M: *Sat 1st M of Sun 6pm. Sun 10am, 11.30am. Hds 10am, 7pm.*

■ **SUTTON PARK,** Guildford, Surrey
† **St Edward**
(Pre-Reformation: 1876; cons 31 May 1950)
Rev Brian Taylor. Sutton Park, Guildford, Surrey, GU4 7QN
Tel: 01483-504630 **Fax:** 01483-457187

M: Sun 9.30am. Hds 9.30am, 8pm.

■ **TADWORTH,** Surrey
† **St John the Evangelist** (1958; 1966; cons 1978)
59 The Avenue, Tadworth, Surrey KT20 5AB
Tel: 01737-813102 **Fax:** 01737-819598
Email: stjohnstadworth@hotmail.com
Website: www.stjohnstadworth.org.uk
Rev Martin Breen.
M: *Sat 1st M of Sun 6pm. Sun 8.30am, 10.30am. Hds 7.15am, 10am, 7.30pm.*

■ **TATSFIELD,** Surrey
Served from Oxted.
M: *Second Friday of Month, 7.30pm.*

■ **THAMES DITTON,** Surrey
† **Our Lady of Lourdes** (1952; 1965)
Hampton Court Way, Thames Ditton, Surrey KT7 0LP **Tel:** 020-8398 6127
Parish Office: **Tel:** 020-8398 2191
Rev Rob Esdaile.
E-mail: rob_esdaile@yahoo.co.uk
M: *Sat 1st M of Sun 6pm. Sun 8.15am, 11am. Hds 9.30am, 8pm.*
• ***Sons of Divine Providence (FDP),*** Sundial House, The Molesey Venture, Orchard Lane, East Molesey, Surrey KT8 0BN **Tel:** 020-8398 1140
Web: www.sonsofdivineprovidence.org
Residential Care and Horticultural Training Centre for Adults with Learning Disabilities.

■ **TILGATE,** Crawley, West Sussex
See Crawley (2).

■ **UCKFIELD,** East Sussex
† **Our Lady Immaculate and St Philip Neri** (1885; 1945; 1958; cons 21 September 1961)
The Priest's House, High Street, Newtown, Uckfield, E Sussex TN22 5DJ
Tel: 01825-762221 **Rev David A Buckley**
Deacon: **Rev David Tutt**
M: *Sat 1st M of Sun 5.30pm. Sun 9.30am. Hds 9.30am, 7.30pm.*
• ***Order of the Visitation,*** Foxhunt Green, Waldron, Heathfield TN21 0RX
Tel: 01435-812619 **M:** *Sun 8am.*

■ **UPPER BEEDING,** Steyning
The Towers (1929)
Upper Beeding, Steyning, West Sussex BN44 3TF See Steyning
• ***Sisters of the Blessed Sacrament,*** The Towers, Upper Beeding, Steyning, W. Sussex BN44 3TF **Tel:** 01903-812185

■ **WADHURST,** East Sussex
† **Sacred Heart** (1929)
The Priest's Cottage, Mayfield Lane, Wadhurst, East Sussex TN5 6DQ
Tel: 01892-782470
Website: www.sacredheartwadhurst.org.uk
Rev Kevin Gaskin.
M: *Sat 1st M of Sun 6pm. Sun 8am, 10.30am. Hds 10am, 8pm.*

■ **WALTON-ON-THAMES,** Surrey
† **St Erconwald** (1906; 1937)
22 Esher Avenue, Walton-on-Thames, Surrey KT12 2TA
Tel/Fax: 01932-221101
Rev John Pearson.
M: *Sat 1st M of Sun 6pm. Sun 9.30am, 11am. Hds 9.30am, 8pm.*
Italian Mass: 12 noon
• ***The Company of Mary,*** 48 Churchfield Road, KT12 2SY **Tel:** 01932-221030

■ **WARLINGHAM,** Surrey
† **St Ambrose** (1936; 1958; cons 1978)
2 Warren Park, off Chapel Road, Warlingham, Surrey CR6 9LD
Tel: 01883-622142 **Fax:** 01883-627762
Served from Oxted
M: *Sun 9am.*

■ **WEST BLATCHINGTON,** East Sussex
See Hove, No 3.

■ **WEST BYFLEET,** Surrey
† **Our Lady Help of Christians** (1917)
Madeira Road, West Byfleet, Surrey KT14 6DH **Tel:** 01932-342892
Fax: 01932-354523
E-mail: ourladyswb@aol.com
Rev Anthony Hale CP.
M: *Sat 1st M of Sun 6pm. Sun 9.30am, 11am, 6.30pm. Hds 10.30am.*

■ **WEST GRINSTEAD,** West Sussex
† **Our Lady of Consolation and St Francis** (Pre-Reformation; 1876; cons 27 September 1899)
Priest's House, Park Lane, West Grinstead, Horsham, W Sussex RH13 8LT
Tel: 01403-710273 **Fax:** 01403-712512
Website: www.consolation.org.uk
E-mail: revdavidgoddard@ukonlinw.co.uk
Rev David Goddard.
Deacon: **Rev Seamus Mahon**
M: *Sat 1st M of Sun 6pm. Sun 9.30am. Hds 12noon, 8pm. Pilgrimage enquiries to the Parish Priest.*

■ **WEST HOATHLY,** West Sussex A
St Dunstan (1958)
North Lane. Served from Worth Abbey.
Contact: **Rev James Cutts OSB.**
Tel: 01342-710313
M: *Sun 11.30am; Hds Vigil 7.30pm.*

■ **WEYBRIDGE,** Surrey
Christ the Prince of Peace (1750; cons. 30 July 1881)
Priest's House, Portmore Way, Weybridge, Surrey KT13 8JD **Tel:** 01932-842643
Fax: 01932-854648 **E-mail:** parishpriest@cpp.org.uk **Website:** www.cpp.org.uk
Rev Thomas Treherne.

Sr Mary Murphy SIJ, 78 Thames Street, Weybridge, Surrey KT13 8NH
Tel: 01932-848843

M: *Sat 1st M of Sun 6pm. Sun 9am, 10.30am, 6pm. Hds 8am, 10am, 8pm.*

- ***St George's College:*** See Addlestone

■ **WHYTELEAFE,** Surrey
St Thomas of Canterbury (1961)
Station Road, CR3 0EP
Served from Caterham.

M: *Sun 9am, 5pm. Hds 6pm.*

■ **WITLEY,** Surrey See under Godalming.

■ **THE WITTERINGS,** West Sussex
St Peter
Church Road, East Wittering W. Sussex PO20 8PS
Tel: 01243-782343 Served from Chichester.

M: *Sun 9am. Hds 10.30am.*

■ **WOKING,** Surrey
† **St Dunstan** (1898: 1925; cons 9 June 1937)
Shaftsbury Road, Woking, Surrey GU22 7DT
Tel: 01483-760652
E-mail: st.dunstan@ntlworld.com
Website: www.st-dunstans.org
Revv Francis Harrington, David Palmiter. *Deacon:* **Rev Russell Young.**
The Priests House, St Pauls Road, Woking, Surrey GU22 7DZ

M: *Sat 1st M of Sun 6pm. Sun 9am, 10.30am, 12noon (Italian), 5.30pm. Hds 9.30am, 12.15pm, 8pm.*

- ***Scalabrini Fathers (CS),*** 14 Oriental Road, GU22 7AW **Tel:** 01483-714440

■ **WONERSH,** Guildford, Surrey
St John's Seminary
(1891; Chapel cons 4 May 1896)
Wonersh, Guildford Surrey GU5 0QX
Tel: 01483-892217 (staff);
Fax: 01483-894531
Website: www.wonersh.org
E-mail: rector.wonersh@dial.pipex.com
Rector: **Rev Mgr Canon Jeremy Garratt** Ph B, MA, STL; *Rector's Secretary:* **Ms Melissa Kingdon** BSc **Tel:** 01483 891024 *Bursar:* **Mr Tony Lee; Tel:** 01483 891020 *Finance Assistant:* **Mrs Bernie Minchella; Tel:** 01483 891029; *Bursar's Secretary:* **Mrs Nina Segrove;** *Director of Studies:* **Rev Jonathan How** BSc, BTh, PhL, PGCE(A), ARCS, FHEA, **Tel:** 01483 891023; *Academic's Secretary:* **Mrs Rebecca Teller** BSc **Tel:** 01483 891028; *Director of Spirituality:* **Rev Gerard Bradley,** BMus, BTh, AKC; **Tel:** 01483 891021; *Pastoral Director:* **Sr M Finbarr Coffey** HC, BA, HDipEd, CertTh, **Tel:** 01483 891025; *Human Development Director:* **Rev Paul Lyons** MLitt, MA. *Other Full-time Staff: Senior Lecturer in Divinity, Librarian:* **Rev Stephen Dingley** MA, PhD, STL, **Tel:** 01483 891027; *Spiritual Director:* **Michael Woodgate** BA, **Tel:** 01483 891026.

M: *Please enquire.*

- ***Franciscan Missionaries of the Divine Motherhood:*** St John's Seminary, Wonersh, Guildford, Surrey GU5 0QX **Tel:** 01483-894233
- ***Institute of Charity, St Mary's,*** Derryswood, Wonersh, Surrey GU5 0RA **Tel:** 01483-893196

■ **WOODINGDEAN,** Brighton & Hove
St Patrick
Served from Rottingdean.
Tel: 01273-302903

M: *Sun 9am.*

■ **WORCESTER PARK,** Surrey
St Matthias
Cheam Common Road.
Archdiocese of Southwark, part Diocese of Arundel and Brighton.
Tel: 020-8337 1782

■ **WORTH ABBEY,** Crawley
(1933; cons 13 July 1975)
The Abbey of Our Lady Help of Christians
Paddockhurst Road, Turners Hill, Crawley, West Sussex RH10 4SB
Website: www.worthabbey.net
Community: **Tel:** 01342-710310
Fax: 01342-710311
Bursar: 01342-710225 **Fax:** 01342-710291
Head: 01342-710222 **Fax:** 01342-710230
E-mail: school@worth.org.uk
Church Administrator:
01342-710316 **Fax:** 01342-710311
E-mail: church@worthabbey.net

- ***Benedictines (OSB);*** **Rt Rev Dom Christopher Jamison (Abbot),** **Tel:** 01342-710320 **E-mail:** cjamison@worth.org.uk. **Very Rev Dom Kevin Taggart** (*Prior*), **Rev Dom Aidan Murray** (*Subprior & Bursar*), **Rt Rev Dom Stephen Ortiger, Rev Dom Charles Hallinan, Rev Dom Ian Condon, Rev Dom Bede Hill, Rev Dom Philip Gaisford, Rev Dom Richard Wilson, Rev Dom Patrick Fludder** (*Co-ordinator, The Open Cloister*), **Rev Dom Alexander da Costa Fernandes, Rev Dom James Cutts** (*Parish Priest*), **Rev Dom Paul Fleetwood, Rev Dom Mark Barrett, Rev Dom Luke Jolly, Rev Dom Roderick Jones** (*Church Administrator*), **Rev Dom Thomas Haynes** (*Guestmaster*), **Rev Dom Martin McGee** (*School Chaplain*), **Rev Dom Peter Williams, Br Anthony Brockman, Br Gabriel Dobson** *c/o Worth Abbey:* **Rev Doms Andrew Brenninkmeyer, John Bolton, Blane Maxwell, Francis Edwards, Gregory**

Mitchell. *Permanent Deacon on the Parish:* **Rev Chris Dobson**.
E-mail: abbey@worth.org.uk
Website: www.worth.org.uk
M: *Sat 1st M of Sun 5.15pm. Sun 9.30am. Hds (Vigil 7.30pm), 8am, 5.30pm W. Hoathly Sun 11.30am.*

- ***The Open Cloister,*** Worth Abbey, Paddockhurst Road, Turners Hill, Crawley, West Sussex RH10 4SB
Tel: 01342-710318 **Fax:** 01342-710311
E-mail: toc@worthabbey.net

■ **WORTHING,** West Sussex

1. † St Mary of the Angels (1864)
Richmond Road, Worthing.
Tel: 01903-200416 **Fax:** 01903-532332
Rev Christopher Benyon. 68 Gratwicke Road, BN11 4BJ
M: *Sat 1st M of Sun 6pm. Sun 8.30am, 10.30am, 5pm (Ital). Hds 7am, 10.30am.*

- ***Sisters of Our Lady of Sion,*** 60 Gratwicke Road, Worthing, BN11 4BR
Tel: 01903-200322
- ***Sisters of Mercy,*** St Mary's Care Home, 14 Westbrooke, BN11 1RF

Tel: 01903-233530. Convent, 19/21 Salisbury Road, Worthing, West Sussex BN11 1RD **Tel:** 01903-233904

2. † St Charles (1958; 1962)
Chesswood Road, Worthing, Sussex BN11 2AE **Tel:** 01903-239611
Rev Daryl George. *Deacon:* **Rev Patrick Moloney.**
M: *Sat 6pm.*

3. St Michael (1927, 1938)
19 Hayling Rise, High Salvington, Worthing, Sussex BN13 3AL
Tel: 01903-264770
Rev Christopher Ingle.
Deacon: **Rev Mark Woods**
M: *Sat 1st M of Sun 6pm. Sun 8.30am, 10.30am. Hds 9.30am, 7.30pm.*

■ **ORDERS OR CONGREGATIONS, ETC**

■ **Men**

Benedictines (English Congregation): Worth.
Carthusians: Parkminster.
Charity, Institute of (Rosminians): Wonersh.
Comboni Missionaries (Verona Fathers): Sunningdale.
De La Salle Brothers: Midhurst.
Franciscans (Capuchins): Hollington.
Franciscans (Conventual): Rye.
Franciscans (Friars Minor): Chilworth.
Josephites: Weybridge.
Kiltegan Fathers (St Patrick's Missionary Society) SPS: Molesey, Peacehaven.
Missionaries of St Paul (of Nigeria) MSP: Molesey.
Norbertine Canons: Storrington.
Pallottine Fathers: Hastings.
Salesians: Chertsey.
Scalabrini Fathers: Woking.

■ **Women**

+ denotes Secular Institute
Augustinian Sisters (Bruges): Burgess Hill, Haywards Heath.
Our Lady of Grace and Compassion, Benedictine Sisters of: Bognor, Brighton (5), Heathfield.
Blessed Sacrament, Sisters of the: Upper Beeding. Henfield.
Canonesses Regular of St Augustine (of Windesheim): Lewes.
Canonesses of St Augustine (Congr of Our Lady): St Leonards (1).
Charity, Sisters of (Nevers): Brighton (5).
Charity, Sisters of Jesus and Mary: Epsom.
Christian Instruction (Ghent), Religious of: Effingham.
Christian Retreat, Sisters of the: Molesey.
Cross, Daughters of the : Haslemere.
Dominican Sisters (Third Order) (Congr of Newcastle, Natal): Eastbourne (1).
Dominican Missionary Sisters, Crawley.
Dorothy, Sisters of St: Redhill.
Franciscan Missionaries of the Divine Motherhood: Ferring, Godalming, Guildford, Wonersh.
Franciscan Missionaries of Littlehampton: Burgess Hill, Copthorne, Littlehampton.
Holy Child Jesus, Society of the: Mayfield.
Holy Family (of Villefranche-de-Rouergue), Sisters of the: Horsham.
Holy Spirit, Missionary Sister Servants of: Farnham.
Infant Jesus, Sisters of the: Crawley (2, 6), Weybridge, Hampden Park, Eastbourne.
Martha, Sisters of St: Rottingdean.
Mary, Sisters of the Company of: Cobham, Hersham, Walton-on-Thames.
Mercy Sisters Institute of Our Lady of Mercy: Brighton (1), Worthing.
Mercy Sisters of: Midhurst.
Notre Dame (Namur), Sisters of: Crawley (1).
Picpus Sisters: (See Sacred Hearts, Sisters of the). Epsom
Poor Clares: Arundel. Hollington.
Poor Servants of the Mother of God: Hove (2).
Providence (Rosminian) Sisters of: Bexhill.
Providence (Rouen), Sisters of: Seaford.
Sacred Heart (Madrid), Hospitaller Sisters of the: Addlestone.
Sacred Heart (Paris), Society of the: Caterham.

Sacred Hearts of Jesus and Mary (Picpus), Congregation of the: Epsom.
Servite Sisters: Bognor Regis, Dorking.
Sion, Sisters of Our Lady of: Worthing,
Visitation, Order of the: Waldron.
Vocation Sisters: Guildford.

■ Cabrini Children's Society

49 Russell Hill Road, Purley, Surrey CR8 2XB **Tel:** 020-8668 2181

■ Diocesan Institutions,Societies

For Societies and Organisations without representation in the diocese please see the main Societies and Organisations section.

Apostleship of the Sea. *Port Chaplain,* Newhaven: **Rev Cyril Cravos.** Shoreham, *Ships visitors:* **Patrick Byrne, John Boyden.**

Archconfraternity of St Stephen for Altar Servers. *Diocesan Director:* **Rev David Parmiter.**

Association of Separated and Divorced Catholics. A federation of self help groups to provide mutual help and spiritual support to those who have experienced the pain of marriage breakdown. *Diocesan Contact:* **Margaret Tel:** 01444 412196.

Association of Priests and Laity of St Thérèse of the Child Jesus. *Secretary:* **Mrs Marjorie Davis.** 68 Northdown Park Road, Cliftonville, Margate, Kent CT9 3PT

Association for the Propagation of the Faith. *Diocesan Director*: **Rev Richard Biggerstaff**

CAFOD, Catholic Agency for Overseas Development. *Manager:* CAFOD, St John's Seminary, Wonersh, Guildford, Surrey GU5 0QX **Tel/Fax:** 01483-898866

Catenian Association. Syssex Residents: *Provincial Secretary*: **Martin Klust,** 23 Neville Road, Peacehaven, East Sussex BN10 8PE **Tel:** 01273-584204 **Fax:** 01273-583294 **Surrey Residents:** *Provincial Secretary*: **Mr Terry McCarthy,** High Pines, Bishop's Walk, Croydon CR0 8DA **Hants Residents:** *Provincial President:* **Adrian Koehurst** 22 Ashdown, 1 Chine Crescent Road, Bournemouth BH2 5LJ

Catholic Nurses Guild. *National Secretary:* **Mrs N McCarthy.** 91 Beverscone Road, Thornton Heath, Surrey CR7 7LX

Catholic Police Guild. *Secretary* (Brighton): **John Goulding,** 8 Pembury Close, Haywards Heath, RH16 3RZ **Tel:** 01444-454574

Catholic Study Circle for Animal Welfare. Contact: **Miss M Ragge,** 32 Chester Avenue, Lancing BN15 8PQ

Catholic Women's League. *Diocesan Secretary:* **Miss Brenda Hilliam,** 19 Bermuda Place, Sovereign Harbour, Eastbourne, East Sussex BN23 5YE.

Christian Life Communities. Linking whole human life with fullness of Christian faith: Contact: **Miss J Gill,** 45 Firswood Avenue, Ewell, Epsom, Surrey KT19 0PO **Tel:** 020-8393 2764

Dominican Secular Institute: *Moderator:* **Miss Ann Hamilton,** Hope Cottage, 3 Hylands Yard, Rye, East Sussex TN31 7EP.

Ecumenical Society of the Blessed Virgin Mary: A Society to advance the study of the Blessed Virgin Mary in the Church under Christ and of related theological questions, and in the light of such studies to promote ecumenical action. *London Area Secretary:* **Mr J P Farrelly KCSG,** 11 Belmont Road, Wallington, Surrey SM6 8TE **Tel:** 020-8647 5992

Grail, The. *Diocesan Representative:* **Mary Low.** 35 Coombe Lee, Hove BN3 2ND **Tel:** 01273-772596 Grail Headquarters: *President,* **Mrs Judith O'Grady,** The Grail Centre, 125 Waxwell Lane, Pinner, Middlesex HA5 3ER **Tel:** 020-8866 2195 **Fax:** 020-8866 1408 **E-mail:** waxwell@compuserve.com

Knights of St Columba. Prov 35 (Surrey) covers the areas of Epsom, Guildford, Redhill, Weybridge and Woking Deaneries: *Provincial Grand Knight:* **Michael Steele,** 19 Merrow Woods, Guildford, Surrey GU1 2LQ **Tel:** 01483 503875 *Provincial Secretary:* **John Walters,** 9 Highview Road, Woking, Surrey GU22 9NU **Tel:** 01483 832323 *Provincial Youth Officer:* **Colin Swan,** 165b Merton Road, Wimbledon, London SW19 1EE **Tel:** 020-8241 7497 *Provincial Chaplain:* **Rev Mr F Carter (Deacon),** 331 Cannon Hill Lane, London SW20 9HQ **Tel:** 020-8540 6234
Prov 34 (Sussex) covers Brighton, Crawley Eastbourne, Lewes, St Leonards-on-Sea and Worthing Deaneries: *Provincial Grand Knight*: **Geoffrey Breeze,** 8 Coney Road, East Wittering, Chichester, West Sussex PO20 8DA **Tel:** 01243-671082 **E-mail:** geoffreybreeze@btinternet.com; *Provincial Secretary:* **John Dyker,** 94 Beaumont Park, Littlehampton, West Sussex BN17 6PH **Tel:** 01903 717783 **E-mail:** johndyker@tiscali.co.uk
Provincial Youth Officer: **Tony Herbert,** Torton House, Hollybrook Road, Northgate, Crawley, West Sussex RH10 2DU **Tel:** 01293-416474 *Provincial Chaplain:* **Canon Dennis Barry,** **Tel:** 01243-823619

Leaven Carmelite Secular Institute, The: Contact: **R Kinman**, 1 The Enterdent, Godstone, Surrey RH9 8EG **Tel:** 01883-742488

Marriage Care. *Headquarters:* Clitherow House, 1 Blythe Mews, Blythe Road, London W14 0NW **Tel:** 0171-371 1341 **Fax:** 020-7371 4921 Established in 1946 to support Marriage and Family Life, Marriage Care provides a free confidential counselling service for adults in 80 centres throughout England and Wales. For an appointment or futher details contact your local centre at:
Brighton: **Tel:** 01273-220111
Eastbourne: **Tel:** 01323-417460
West Surrey: **Tel:** 01483-860616
Crawley: **Tel:** 0800 389 3801

Our Lady's Catechists. *Catechetical Secretary:* **Mrs A P O'Rorke**, Denstone, Wadhurst, East Sussex TN5 6SX **Tel:** 01892-782282

Society of St Gregory. *Diocesan Representative:* **Gill Ness-Collins**, 13 De Braose Way, Steyning, West Sussex BN44 3FD **Tel:** 01903-812480 **E-mail:** gill.ness-collins@ssg.org.uk

Society of St Peter Apostle for Native Clergy. *Diocesan Director*: **Rev Richard Biggerstaff.**

Society of St Vincent de Paul. Arundel and Brighton *Central Council President*: Mr Peter Wells, 8 Highcroft Road, Sharpthorne, West Sussex RH19 8NK **Tel:** 01342-811543 **E-mail:** pww.pkw@virgin.net
Secretary: **Mr P Bush**, 23 Trumpsgreen Avenue, Virginia Water, Surrey GU25 4EP **Tel:** 01344 843483

Society of the Holy Childhood. *Diocesan Director:* **Rev Richard Biggerstaff**.

Teams of Our Lady. An international Catholic Movement for Christian married couples that aims to deepen the couples' spirituality. A 'Team' consists of four or five couples and a priest or religious as spiritual advisor meeting monthly to share the journey of faith, guided by the Holy Spirit. *Contact couple:* **Graham and Zofia Stott**, 6 Queen Eleanor's Road, Guildford, Surrey GU2 7SL **Tel:** 01483-576944 **E-mail:** stott.family@ntlworld.com

Union of Catholic Mothers. *Diocesan Branch President:* **Mrs Marilyn Simmonds**, 74 Wish Hill, Willingdon, East Sussex BN20 9HA **Tel:** 01323-502673
Diocesan Secretary: **Mrs Mary Hogan**, The Pines, WIndermere Road, Hayward's Heath, West Sussex RH16 3JK **Tel:** 01444-452746
Spiritual Adviser: To be appointed.

Walsingham Association. *St Leonards Deanery:* **Mrs S M Coleman**, 8 Crowborough Road, Hastings, Sussex. TN35 5EF **Tel:** 01424-422128

■ HOSPITALS

To contact the Catholic Chaplain of a particular hospital we suggest you contact the hospital reception directly.

■ CATHOLIC SCHOOLS - Maintained

■ BRIGHTON & HOVE

▲ Primary

St Bernadette's, Preston Road BN1 6UT **Tel:** 01273-553813 **Fax:** 01273-563213 **E-mail:** mail@st-berns.brighton-hove.sch.uk (*Brighton 5*)

St John the Baptist, Whitehawk Hill Road BN2 0AH **Tel:** 01273-607924 **Fax:** 01273-603450 **E-mail:** admin@stjohn.brighton-hove.sch.uk (*Brighton 1*)

St Joseph's, Davey Drive, Hollingdean BN1 7BF **Tel:** 01273-556607 **Fax:** 01273-504007 **E-mail:** admin@st-josephs.brighton-hove.sch.uk (*Brighton 3*).

St Mary Magdalen, Spring Street BN1 3EF **Tel:** 01273-327533 **Fax:** 01273-327259 **E-mail:** office@stmarymags.brighton-hove.sch.uk (*Brighton 2*)

Cottesmore St Mary's, The Upper Drive BN3 6NB **Tel:** 01273-555811 **Fax:** 01273-555423 **E-mail:** admin@cottesmore.brighton-hove.sch.uk (*Hove*)

St Mary's, Church Road BN41 1LB **Tel:** 01273-418416 **Fax:** 01273-421680 **E-mail:** office@stmarys.brighton-hove.sch.uk (*Portslade*)

Our Lady of Lourdes, The Green, High Street BN2 7HA **Tel:** 01273-306980 **Fax:** 01273-308809. **E-mail:** admin@lourdes.brighton-hove.sch.uk (*Rottingdean*)

▲ Secondary

Cardinal Newman School The Upper Drive, Hove BN3 6ND **Tel:** 01273-558551 **Fax:** 01273-508778 **E-Mail:** cncs@newman.brighton-hove.sch.uk (*Hove 1*)

■ EAST SUSSEX

▲ Primary

(Junior & Infant unless stated. +N=Nursery)

St Mary Magdalene's, Hastings Road, Bexhill TN40 2ND **Tel:** 01424-735810 **Fax:** 01424-733664 **E-mail:** office@stmarymagsbex.e-sussex.sch.uk (*Bexhill-on-Sea*)

DIOCESE OF ARUNDEL AND BRIGHTON

St Mary's, Chapel Green, Crowborough TN6 2LB **Tel:** 01892-655291 **Fax:** 01892-661365 **E-mail:** office@stmarysrc.e-sussex.sch.uk (*Crowborough*)
St Thomas a Becket Infants, Tutt's Barn Lane BN22 8XT **Tel:** 01323-726004 **Fax:** 01323-733634 **E-mail:**office@stthomasbecket.inf.e-sussex.sch.uk (*Eastbourne*)
St Thomas a Becket Junior, Tutt's Barn Lane BN22 8XT **Tel:** 01323-737221 **Fax:** 01323-738580 **E-mail:** office@stthomasbecket.e-sussex.sch.uk (*Eastbourne*)
Sacred Heart, Old London Road TN35 5NA **Tel:** 01424-429494 **Fax:** 01424-715594 **E-mail:** g-office@sacred-heart.e-sussex.sch.uk (*Hastings*)
St Pancras, De Montford Road BN7 1SR **Tel:** 01273-473017 **Fax:** 01273-486559 **E-mail:** office@st-pancras.e-sussex.sch.uk (*Lewes*)
St Mary Star of the Sea, Magdalen Road TN37 6EU **Tel:** 01424-427801 **Fax:** 01424-200868 **E-mail:** office@st-mary-star.e-sussex.sch.uk (*St Leonards-on-Sea*)
Annecy Catholic Primary School, Sutton Avenue BN25 4LF **Tel:** 01323-894892 **Fax:** 01323-894171 **E-mail:** head@annecy.e-sussex.sch.uk (*Seaford*)
St Philip's, New Town TN22 5DJ **Tel:** 01825-762032 **Fax:** 01825-748706 **E-mail:** office@stphilips.e-sussex.sch.uk (*Uckfield*).

▲ Secondary
St Richard's College, Ashdown Road TN40 1SE **Tel:** 01424-731070 **Fax:** 01424-215623 **E-mail:** admin@st-richards.e-sussex.sch.uk (*Bexhill-on-Sea*) (*11-16*)

■ WEST SUSSEX

▲ Primary
(Junior & Infant unless stated. +N=Nursery)
Our Lady Queen of Heaven, Hare Lane, Langley Green RH11 7PZ **Tel:** 01293-526057 **Fax:** 01293-538341. **E-mail:** office@olqoh.w-sussex.sch.uk (*Langley Green*)
St Francis of Assisi, Southgate Drive RH10 6HD **Tel:** 01293-521009 **Fax:** 01293-521041 (*Crawley 1*) **E-mail:** office@st-francisassisi.w-sussex.sch.uk
St Robert Southwell, Lamb's Farm Road, Roffey, Horsham RH12 4LP **Tel:** 01403-252357 **Fax:** 01403-252394 **E-mail:** office@st-robertsouthwell.w-sussex.sch.uk (*Roffey*)
St Wilfrid's, Arundel Road BN16 4JR **Tel:** 01903-782188 **Fax:** 01903-850751 **E-mail:** office@st-wilfrids-angmering.w-sussex.sch.uk (*Angmering*)
St Philip's, London Road BN18 9BA **Tel:** 01903-882115 **Fax:** 01903-883038 **E-mail:** office@st-philips.w-sussex.sch.uk (*Arundel*)
St Mary's, Glamis Street PO21 1DJ **Tel:** 01243-822287 **Fax:** 01243-841588 **E-mail:** office@st-marys-bognor.w-sussex.sch.uk (*Bognor Regis*)
St Wilfrid's, School Close, Queen Elizabeth Avenue RH15 9RJ **Tel:** 01444-235254 **Fax:** 01444-230048 **E-mail:** office@st-wilfrids-burgesshill.w-sussex.sch.uk (*Burgess Hill*)
St Richard's, Cawley Road PO19 1XB **Tel:** 01243-784549 **Fax:** 01243-530646 **E-mail:** office@st-richards.w-sussex.sch.uk (*Chichester*)
St Peter's, Chapman's Lane RH19 1JB **Tel:** 01342-321985 **Fax:** 01342-300679 **E-mail:** office@st-peters-eastgrinstead.w-sussex.sch.uk (*East Grinstead*)
The English Martyrs, Derwent Drive, The Boulevard, Worthing BN12 6LA **Tel:** 01903-502868 **Fax:** 01903-503149 **E-mail:** bursar@englishmartyrs.w-sussex.sch.uk (*Goring*)
St Joseph's, Hazelgrove Road RH16 3PQ. **Tel:** 01444-452584 **Fax:** 01444-414760 **E-mail:** office@st-josephs.w-sussex.sch.uk **Website:** www.st-josephs.w-sussex.sch.uk (*Haywards Heath*)
St John's, Blackbridge Lane RH12 1RR **Tel:** 01403-265447 **Fax:** 01403-252458 **E-mail:** office@stjohnsp-hor.w-sussex.sch.uk (*Horsham*)
St Catherine's, Highdown Drive BN17 6HL **Tel:** 01903-716039 **Fax:** 01903-722521 **E-mail:** office@st-catherines.w-sussex.sch.uk (*Littlehampton*)
St Peter's, Sullington Way, Shoreham BN43 6PJ **Tel:** 01273-454066 **Fax:** 01273-440257 **E-mail:** office@-st-petersrc.shoreham.w-sussex.sch.uk (*Shoreham-by-Sea*)
St Mary's, Cobden Road BN11 4BD **Tel:** 01903-234115 **Fax:** 01903-215034 **E-mail:** office@st-marysrc.w-sussex.sch.uk (*Worthing*)

▲ Secondary
St Philip Howard High School, Elm Grove South, Barnham PO22 0EN **Tel:** 01243-552055 **Fax:** 01243-552900 **E-mail:** office@st-philiphoward.w-sussex.sch.uk (*Barnham*)
St Wilfrid's, Old Horsham Road, Southgate RH11 8PG

Tel: 01293-421421 **Fax:** 01293-421429 **E-mail:** office@stwilfrids-crawley.w-sussex.sch.uk **Website:** www.stwilfrids.com (*Crawley 1*)

St Paul's College, Jane Murray Way, Burgess Hill, West Sussex RH15 8GA **Tel:** 01444-873898 **Fax:** 01444-873899 **E-mail:** office@st-pauls.w-sussex.sch.uk (*Burgess Hill*)

Chatsmore Catholic High School, Goring Street, Goring-by-Sea BN12 5AF **Tel:** 01903-241368. **Fax:** 01903-240183 **E-mail:** office@chatsmore.w-sussex.sch.uk (Worthing) (11-16)

■ SURREY

▲ Primary

(Junior & Infant unless otherwise stated. +N = Nursery)

St Anne's, Free Prae Road, Chertsey, Surrey KT16 8ET **Tel:** 01932-562251 **Fax:** 01932-562366 **E-mail:** office@stannes-chertsey.surrey.sch.uk (*Chertsey*)

St Augustine's, Tomlinscote Way, Frimley, Surrey GU16 8PY **Tel:** 01276-709099 **Fax:** 01276-709098 **E-mail:** info@staugustine.surrey.sch.uk (*Frimley*)

St Joseph's, Aldershot Road, Guildford GU2 8YH **Tel:** 01483-888401 **Fax:** 01483-888402 **E-mail:** info@st-josephs-guildford.surrey.sch.uk (*Guildford*)

Cardinal Newman, Arch Road, Walton-on-Thames KT12 4QT **Tel:** 01932-222536 **Fax:** 01932-232638 **E-mail:** office@cardinal-newman.surrey.sch.uk (*Hersham*)

St Dunstan's, Onslow Crescent, Woking GU22 7AX **Tel:** 01483-715190 **Fax:** 01483-722866. **E-mail:** reception@stdunstans.surrey.sch.uk (*Woking*)

Holy Family, Ongar Hill, Weybridge KT15 1BP **Tel:** 01932-846366 **Fax:** 01932-830093 **E-mail:** info@holy-family.surrey.sch.uk (*Addlestone*)

St Cuthbert Mayne, St Nicolas Avenue, Cranleigh GU6 7AQ **Tel:** 01483-274961 **Fax:** 01483-273683 **E-mail:** info@stcuthbert-mayne.surrey.sch.uk **Website:** www.stcuthbert-mayne.surrey.sch.uk (*Cranleigh*)

St Joseph's, Norfolk Road, Dorking RH4 3JA **Tel:** 01306-883934 **Fax:** 01306-500286 **E-mail:** info@stjosephs-dorking.surrey.sch.uk (*Dorking*)

St Clement's, Fennells Mead, Ewell KT17 1TX **Tel/Fax:** 020-8393 8789 **E-mail:** info@stclements.surrey.sch.uk (*Ewell*)

St Edmund's, The Drive, Godalming GU7 1PF **Tel/Fax:** 01483-414497 **E-mail:** info@stedmunds.surrey.sch.uk (*Godalming*)

St Hugh of Lincoln, Five Oaks Close, St John's, Woking GU21 8TU **Tel:** 01483-480441 **Fax:** 01483-799593 **E-mail:** info@sthugh-of-lincoln.surrey.sch.uk (*Knaphill*)

St Paul's, Hampton Court Way, Thames Ditton KT7 0LP **Tel:** 020-8398 6791 **Fax:** 020-8398 4275 **E-mail:** info@stpauls-thamesditton.surrey.sch.uk (*Thames Ditton*)

Marist Catholic Primary, Old Woking Road, Weybridge KT14 6HS **Tel:** 01932-344477 **Fax:** 01932-352642 **E-mail:** info@marist.surrey.sch.uk (*West Byfleet*)

St Charles Borromeo, Portmore Way, Weybridge KT13 8JD **Tel:** 01932-842617 **Fax:** 01932-830362 **E-mail:** info@stcharlesb.surrey.sch.uk (*Weybridge*)

St Cuthbert's, Bagshot Road, Englefield Green TW20 0RY **Tel:** 01784-434128 **Fax:** 01784-477270 **E-mail:** head@stcuthberts.surrey.sch.uk (*Englefield Green*)

St Anne's, Court House, Court Road, Burgh Heath, Banstead SM7 2PH **Tel:** 01737-350012 **Fax:** 01737-373589 **E-mail:** info@stannes-banstead.surrey.sch.uk (*Banstead*)

St Francis, Whyteleafe Road, Caterham CR3 5ED **Tel:** 01883-342005 **Fax:** 01883-340724 **E-mail:** info@stfrancis.surrey.sch.uk **Website:** www.stfrancis.surrey.sch.uk (*Caterham*)

St Joseph's, Rosebank, West Street, Epsom KT18 7RT **Tel:** 01372-727850 **Fax:** 01372-725609 **E-mail:** info@stjosephs-epsom.surrey.sch.uk (*Epsom*)

St Polycarp's, Waverley Lane, Farnham GU9 8BQ **Tel:** 01252-716307 **Fax:** 01252-717842 **E-mail:** info@stpolycarps.surrey.sch.uk **Website:** www.stpolycarps.surrey.sch.uk (*Farnham*)

St Thomas of Canterbury, Horseshoe Lane West, Merrow, Guildford GU1 2SX **Tel:** 01483-888388/9 **Fax:** 01483-888385 **E-mail:** head@st-thomas.surrey.sch.uk (*Guildford*)

St Peter's, Grange Road, Leatherhead KT22 7JN. **Tel:** 01372-274913 **Fax:** 01372-279913 **E-mail:** office@stpeters-leatherhead.surrey.sch.uk (*Leatherhead*)

St Joseph's, Linkfield Lane, Redhill RH1 1DU **Tel:** 01737-765373 **Fax:** 01737-768557 **E-mail:** secretary@stjosephs-redhill.surrey.sch.uk (*Redhill*)

St Alban's, Beauchamp Road, KT8 2PG **Tel:** 020-8979 5893 **Fax:** 020-8941 4527 **E-mail:** admin@stalbans.surrey.sch.uk (*East Molesey*)

▲ Secondary

All Hallows, Weybourne Road GU9 9HF **Tel:** 01252-319211 **Fax:** 01252-328649 **E-mail:** admin@allhallows.net (*Farnham*)

St Peter's Catholic Comprehensive, Horseshoe Lane East, Merrow, Guildford GU1 2TN **Tel:** 01483-534654 **Fax:** 01483-306571 **E-mail:** info@ st-peters.surrey.sch.uk (*Guildford, Merrow*)

St Andrew's Grange Road, Leatherhead KT22 7JP **Tel:** 01372-277881 **Fax:** 01372-279135 **E-mail:** enquiries@st-andrews. surrey.sch.uk (*Ashtead*)

St Bede's, (C. of E. and Catholic), 64 Carlton Road, Redhill. RH1 2LQ **Tel:** 01737-212108 **Fax:** 01737-212118 **E-mail:** info@st-bedes.surrey.sch.uk (*Redhill*)

St John the Baptist, Elmbridge Lane, Rydens Way, Kingfield GU22 9AL **Tel:** 01483-729343 **Fax:** 01483-727578 **E-mail:** info@sjb.surrey.sch.uk (*Woking*)

Salesian School, Guildford Road, Chertsey KT16 9LU **Tel:** 01932-582520 **Fax:** 01932-582521 **E-mail:** headteacher@salesian. surrey.sch.uk (*Chertsey*)

■ Catholic Schools - Independent

▲ Primary

Sacred Heart School, Mayfield Lane, Wadhurst TN5 6DQ **Tel:** 01892-783414 **Fax:** 01892-783510 **E-mail:** admin@ sacredheartwadhurst.org.uk **Website:** www.sacredheartwadhurst. org.uk (*Wadhurst*)

St John's Beaumont College, Old Windsor, Berks SL4 2JN **Tel:** 01784-432428 **Email:** admissions@ stjohnsbeaumont.co.uk (*Englefield Green*)

Rydes Hill Prep. School, Rydes Hill House, Aldershot Road GU2 8BP **Tel:** 01483-563160 **Fax:** 01483-306714 **Email:** enquiries@rydeshill.com (*Guildford*)

Cranmore Preparatory School Epsom Road, West Horsley, Leatherhead KT24 6AT **Tel:** 01483-280340 **Fax:** 01483-280341 **E-mail:** office@cranmoreprep.co.uk (*West Horsley*)

St George's College Junior School, Thames Street, Weybridge KT13 8NL **Tel:** 01932-839400 **Fax:** 01932-839401 (Co-educational 3-11) (Weybridge) **E-mail:** (initial.surname)@st-georges-college.co.uk

Barrow Hills Preparatory School, Roke Lane, Godalming GU8 5NY **Tel:** 01428-682634 **Fax:** 01428 861906 info@barrowhills.org.uk (Witley)

St Margaret's School, Convent of Mercy GU29 9JN **Tel:** 01730-813956 **Fax:** 01730-810829 **E-mail:** smsadmin@ conventofmercy.org (*Midhurst*)

▲ Primary & Secondary

The Towers, Upper Beeding, Steyning BN44 3TF **Tel:** 01903-812185 **Fax:** 01903-813858 (5-16 yrs) **E-mail:** admin@towers.w-sussex.sch.uk (*Steyning*)

St George's College, Weybridge Road, Addlestone, Surrey KT15 2QS **Tel:** 01932-839300 **Fax:** 01932-839301 **E-mail:** contact@st-georges-college.co.uk **Website:** www.st-georges-college.co.uk

Worth School, Paddockhurst Road, Turners Hill, Crawley RH10 4SD **Tel:** 01342-710200 **Fax:** 01342-710230 Junior House: **Tel:** 01342-715442 *Bursar:* **Tel:** 01342-710225 **Fax:** 01342-710291 Austin House: **Tel:** 01342-710254 **Email:** information@worth.org.uk (*Worth*)

Notre Dame School, Burwood House KT11 1HA **Tel:** 01932-869990 (Snr) 01932-869991 (Jnr) **Fax:** 01932-589480 **Senior School E-mail:** headmistress@notredame.co.uk **Prep School E-mail:** headmaster@notredame.co.uk (*Cobham*)

St Teresa's School, Effingham Hill, Dorking, RH5 6ST **Tel:** 01372-452037 **Fax:** 01372-450311 **Email:** info@stteresas.surrey.sch.uk (*Dorking*)

St Teresa's Prep School, (Grove House), Guildford Road, Effingham KT24 5QA **Tel:** 01372-453456 **Fax:** 01372-451562 **Email:** info@stteresasprep.co.uk (*Effingham*)

Our Lady of Sion School, Gratwicke Road BN11 4BL **Tel:** 01903-204063 **E-mail:** enquiries@sionschool.org.uk (*Worthing*)

■ Secondary

St Leonard's–Mayfield School, The Old Palace TN20 6PH **Tel:** 01435-874600 **Fax:** 01435-872627 **E-mail:** enquiry@stlm.e-sussex.sch.uk **Website:** stlm.e-sussex.sch.uk (*Mayfield*)

More House School, Moons Hill, Frensham GU10 3AP **Tel:** 01252-792303 (9-18 yrs) **Email:** schooloffice@morehouseschool.co.uk (*Frensham*)

Woldingham School, Marden Park CR3 7YA **Tel:** 01883-654206/349431 **Fax:** 01883-348653 (11-18 yrs) **Email:** registrar@woldingham.surrey.sch.uk **Website:** www.woldinghamschool.co.uk (*Woldingham*)

■ Catholic Schools - Special

St Joseph's, Amlet's Lane, Cranleigh, Surrey GU6 7DH **Tel:** 01483-272449 **Fax:** 01483-276003 **E-mail:** office@st-josephcranleigh.surrey.sch.uk (*Cranleigh*). *Learning difficulties.*

St Dominic's, Hambledon, Godalming, Surrey GU8 4DX **Tel:** 01428-684693/682741 **Fax:** 01428-685018 office@stdominicsschool.org.uk (*Godalming*) *Boys and Girls with specific learning difficulties resulting from impaired physical health and/or an emotional disorder. Weekly boarding and day pupils.*

ARCHDIOCESE OF BIRMINGHAM

Consisting of the Counties of Warwickshire, those parts of the county of Oxfordshire which belonged to the former County of Oxfordshire north of the Thames, Staffordshire, West Midlands and Worcestershire
(**Suffragan Sees:** Clifton, Shrewsbury)

Patrons of the Diocese
Our Blessed Lady, Conceived Without Sin, 8 December
St Chad, 2 March.

Most Rev Vincent Nichols, Archbishop of Birimgham

Archbishop
Most Rev Vincent Nichols, PhL, MA, MEd, STL
born Crosby, Liverpool 8th November 1945; ordained priest 21st December 1969; Episcopal ordination 24th January 1992; installed Archbishop of Birmingham 29th March 2000.

Residence:
Archbishop's House, 8 Shadwell Street, Birmingham B4 6EY
Tel: 0121-236 9090 **Fax:** 0121-212 0171
E-mail: archbishop@rc-birmingham.org

Secretary:
Rev Martin Pratt c/o Archbishop's House
Tel: 0121-236 9090 **Fax:** 0121-212 0171

Translated to Westminster

■ AUXILIARY BISHOPS

Rt Rev Philip Pargeter, Bishop of Valentiniana, born in Wolverhampton, 13 June 1933, ordained 21 February 1959, cons by Archbishop Couve de Murville, 21 February 1990. Residence: Grove House, College Road, Sutton Coldfield B73 5AH

Rt Rev David McGough, Titular Bishop of Chunavia, born in Tunstall, 20 November 1944, ordained Priest 14 March 1970, ordained Bishop 8 December 2005.
Residence: The Rocks, 106 Draycott Road, Tean, Staffs ST10 4JF
Tel/Fax: 01538 722433
E-mail dmcgough@btinternet.com

Rt Rev William Kenney CP, Titular Bishop of Midica, born 7 May 1946, ordained Priest 29 June 1969, ordained Bishop 24 August 1987 (Auxiliary Bishop of Stockholm). Transfered to Birmingham 17 October 2006.
Residence: St Hugh's House, 27 Hensington road, Woodstock, Oxon
Tel/Fax: 01993 812234
E-mail: wk@sthughs.plus.com

■ ADMINISTRATION

■ Diocesan Curia
Cathedral House, St Chad's Queensway, Birmingham, B4 6EX **Tel:** 0121-230 6237 **Fax:** 0121-236 2699 Office Hours: Monday to Friday 8.30am -12noon.

■ Vicar General
Rt Rev Mgr Canon John Moran VG. Catherdral House, St Chad's Queensway, Birmingham B4 6EX **Tel:** 0121-230 6237
E-mail: john.moran@rc-birmingham.org
Residence: 14 Spring Road, Edgbaston B15 2HG **Tel:** 0121 440 3487

■ Episcopal Vicar for Religious
Rev Michael Ho-Huu-Nghia. 650 Tile Hill Lane, Coventry CV4 9TA
Tel: 02476-466834

■ Diocesan Boundary Commission
Secretary: **Canon David Goodwin**. St John the Evangelist, Loomer Road, Chesterton, Staffs ST5 7JS **Tel:** 01782 561600

■ Diocesan Archivist
Rev John Sharp, Cathedral House, St Chad's Queensway, Birmingham B4 6EX
Tel: 0121-230 6252

■ Diocesan Treasurer
Rev John Carlyle

■ Registrar for Deceased Clergy
c/o Cathedral House.

EDUCATION AND FORMATION

Diocesan Schools Commission
61 Coventry Road, Coleshill, Birmingham B46 3EA **Tel:** 01675-430230 (3 lines)
Fax: 01675-430321
E-mail: bdsc@bdsc.org.uk
Website: bdsc.org.uk
Director of Schools: **Rev Marcus Stock STL, MA**

Department of Religious Education (Schools)
Don Bosco House, Coventry Road, Coleshill B46 3EA
Tel: 01675-464755 **Fax:** 01675-464448
Website: theredepartment.com
Director: **Rev Jonathan Veasey STL.**

Department for Adult and Family Catechetics
Maryvale Institute, Maryvale House, Old Oscott Hill, Birmingham B44 9AG
Tel: 0121-360 8118 **Fax:** 0121-366 6786
E-mail: director@maryvale.ac.uk
Website: maryvale.ac.uk
Director: **Rev Paul Watson.**

Vocations Director
Rev Eddie Clare. Vocations Office, Oscott College, Chester Road, Oscott, Sutton Coldfield, West Midlands B73 5AA
Tel: 0121-355 4163
E-mail: eddie@vocations.org.uk

Diocesan Youth Service
The Youth Office, Coleshill B46 3EA
Tel: 01675-466912
E-mail: jackie.craig@bcys.co.uk

Youth Retreats
Rev Bill Wilton, Soli House, Mill Lane, Stratford-on-Avon **Tel:** 01789-267011
Rev Philip Gay. Alton Castle, Alton, Staffs **Tel:** 01538-703224 (9-13Yrs)

LITURGY AND ECUMENISM

Diocesan Ecumenical Commission
Chairman: **Rev Kevin Kavanagh.**
Secretary: **Sister Teresa Burke**. St Paul's Convent, Selly Park, Birmingham B29 7LL
Tel: 0121-415 6100

Diocesan Liturgical Commission
Chairman: **Rev Paul McNally.**
c/o Oscott College

CHRISTIAN RESPONSIBILITY
Commission for Social and Racial Justice
Chairman: **Mgr T Fallon PhD**, 101 Hunters Road, Handsworth, Birmingham B19 1EB

Diocesan Commission for Justice, Peace and Overseas Aid
Chairman: **Rev Gerry Murray**, The Presbytery, Our Lady, Stratford Road, Shirley B90 4AY **Tel:** 0121 744 1967

Diocesan Pastoral Service for the Deaf
Rev Gerard Lennon. Ozanam House, 40 Gravelly Hill North, Birmingham B23 6BQ **Tel:** 0121-382 5834

Diocesan Advisor on Disability
Mr Sean O'Donnell, c/o Cathedral House, St Chad's, Queensway Birmingham B4 6EX
Tel: 07882 128997
Email: sean.odonnell@rc-birmingham.org

CONSULTATIVE BODIES

Metropolitan Cathedral Chapter
(erected 24 June 1852)
Provost: **Rt Rev David McGough**. *Canons:* **John Moran, Patrick McKinney, Patrick Browne, Gary Byrne, David Evans, Gerard Hanlon, Thomas Farrell, Sean Grady, Peter Gilsenan, John Gunn, Daniel McHugh, David Cousins, William Kenney**. *Canons Emeriti:* **Peter Taylor, T J Gavin, Kevin Good, Edward Stewart, Philip Pargeter, David Goodwin.**
Honorary Canons: **Sean McTernan, Anthony Piercy.**

DIOCESAN MATRIMONIAL TRIBUNAL
Officialis: **Rt Rev Mgr David Cousins JCL.** Cathedral House, St Chad's Queensway, Birmingham B4 6EU **Tel:** 0121 236 5535
Contact E-mail addresses:
Mgr Cousins/Kay McGinley:
kay.mcginley@rc-birmingham.org
Mary Boylan:
mary.boylan@rc-birmingham.org
Trish Kennedy:
patricia.kennedy@rc-birmingham.org

■ BIRMINGHAM
Metropolitan Cathedral Church of St Chad
(1808; 1941; cons 21 June 1841;
Minor Basilica 11 June 1941)
Cathedral House, St Chad's Queensway,
B4 6EU
Tel: 0121-236 2251 **Fax:** 0121-230 6279
Website: www.stchadscathedral.org.uk
Canon Pat Browne *(Cathedral Dean)*,
Tel: 0121-230 6209 **Email:**
canon_pat.browne@rc-birmingham.org
M: *Sat 1st M of Sun 4.30pm. Sun 9am, 11am (Sung). Hds 8am. 12noon, 6pm.*

■ ABBEY HULTON
See Stoke-on-Trent (4).

■ ABBOTS BROMLEY, Staffs [A]
† Sacred Heart (1915, 1938)
Church Lane, Abbots Bromley WS15 3DD
Served from Uttoxeter.
M: *Sun 11.30am. Hds (eve 8pm).*

■ ACOCKS GREEN
See Birmingham (6).

■ ADDERBURY, Oxon [A]
St George
Round Close Road, West Adderbury,
Nr Banbury Served from Hethe
M: *Sun 8.30am. Hds eve 7pm.*

■ ALCESTER
† Our Lady and St Joseph (1889)
Priory Road, Alcester, Warwicks B49 5DY
Tel: 01789-762573
Website: www.olsj.org.uk
• ***Benedictines (OSB)*: Rev Richard Jones**
Deacon: **Rev Peter Griffiths**
M: *Sun 8.30am, 10.30am. Hds 9.15am, 7.30pm.*

■ ALDRIDGE, Walsall
† St Mary of the Angels (1939; 1949; 1963)
39 Whetstone Lane, Aldridge, Walsall
WS9 0JD **Tel:** 01922-452316
Rev Canon Gerard Hanlon,
Deacon: **Rev John Higgins.**
M: *Sat 1st M of Sun 6pm. Sun 10am. Hds 9.45am, 7.30pm.*

■ ALTON, Stoke-on-Trent, Staffs
† St John Baptist (1840; cons 5 July 1930)
Castle Hill, Alton, Stoke-on-Trent
ST10 4AH. Served from Alton Castle.
Rev Philip Gay
M: *Sun 6pm. Hds 6.30pm.*
• ***Alton Castle***, Diocesan Youth Retreat.
Tel: 01538-703224

■ ALVECHURCH, Worcs [A]
St Mary (1971)
School Lane. Served from Redditch.
M: *Sun 9.45am.*

■ ARLEY, nr Nuneaton
† St Joseph (1926, 1996)
Spring Hill. Served from Nuneaton (2).
M: *Sun 11am. Hds (eve 7.30pm).*

■ ASHLEY, North Staffs [A]
† Our Blessed Lady and St John the Baptist
(1791; 1825)
Presbytery, 75 Church Road, Ashley,
Market Drayton, Shropshire TF9 4JY
Tel: 01630-672219 Served from Clayton.
M: *Sat 1st M of Sun 6pm. Sun 10.30am. Hds eve 7.15pm.*

■ ASTON, Staffs
† Holy Michael, Archangel (1882)
Aston, Stone, Staffs ST15 0BJ
Tel: 01785-815453
Served from Stone.
M: *Sun 9.30am. Hds 8am (in the hall).*
• ***Sisters of Charity of St Paul*, Thomas Morris (SVD)** (Retired). Aston Hall, ST15 0BJ Retirement Home for Priests
Tel: 01785-812001

■ ATHERSTONE, Warks
† St Benedict (1839; 1859)
Owen Street, Atherstone, Warks CV9 1DG
Tel: 01827-713177
Rev Peter Gallagher.
M: *Sat 1st M of Sun 6pm. Sun 9.30am. Hds (eve 7pm). 10.30am.*

■ AVON DASSETT, Leamington
† St Joseph (1855; cons. 4 July 1855)
Served from St Francis of Assisi, Kineton.
M: *Sun 11am.*

■ BADDESLEY CLINTON, [A]
West Midlands
† St Francis of Assisi
(1755; 1870; cons 5 Sept 1894)
Rising Lane, Baddesley Clinton,
Knowle, Solihull, W. Midlands B93 0DD
Tel: 01564-782498
Website: www.sfachurch.co.uk
Rev John Sharp.
M: Sat 1st M of Sun 6pm. Sun 9.30am. Hds 9am, 7.30pm.
• ***Poor Clares,*** Rising Lane, Knowle
B93 0DD **Tel:** 01564-783269

■ BALSALL COMMON, [A]
West Midlands
Blessed Robert Grissold, St Philomena
(1942; 1948)
Meeting House Lane.
48 Oxhayes Close, Balsall Common,
Coventry CF17 7PS **Tel:** 01564-772098
Rev Sebastian Arikat
Served from Baddesley Clinton.
M: *Sun 9.30am. Hds 7.30pm.*

■ **BAMPTON,** Oxon
Served from Carterton.
M: *Sun 9pm (in CofE Church of St Mary the Virgin).*

■ **BANBURY,** Oxon
1. † St John
(1828; 1838: cons 17 June 1938)
25 South Bar Street, Banbury, Oxon OX16 9AE **Tel:** 01295-262073
Rev Mervyn Tower.
M: *Sun 9am, 10.40am, Vigil 4pm, 5.30pm. Hds Vigil 4pm. (Vigil 6.30pm eve), 10am, 7.30pm.*
• ***Sisters of Charity of St Paul,*** The Coach House, 6 St John's Road OX16 5AX
Tel: 01295-279420

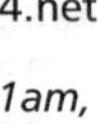

2. † St Joseph the Worker (1968)
Edmunds Road, Banbury, Oxon OX16 0PP
Tel: 01295-264661
Rev David Gnosill.
M: *Sun 9am, Vigil 6 pm (St Thomas, Wroxton), 10am (St Francis, Hardwick), 11.15am (St Joseph's). Hds 9.30am, 7pm.*

■ **BARTON UNDER NEEDWOOD,** Staffs
† Our Lady of Perpetual Succour
(1946; 1963)
16 Wales Lane, Barton Under Needwood, Burton-on-Trent, Staffs DE13 8JF
Tel: 01283-713104
Rev Arul Samy.
M: *Sun 10.45am. Hds 9.30am.*

■ **BEARWOOD,** Warley, West Midlands
† Our Lady of Good Counsel and St Gregory the Great (1900; 1934)
Three Shires Oak Road, Smethwick, Warley B67 5BT
Tel: 0121-429 1743
Rev Edwin Cownley.
M: *Sat 1st M of Sun 5pm. Sun 9am, 11am. Hds 10am, 7.30pm.*

■ **BEDWORTH,** Nuneaton
† St Francis of Assisi (1881; cons 1923)
Rye Piece Ringway CV12 8JH
Tel: 024-7631 2102
Rev David Lacy.
M: *Sat 1st M of Sun 4pm. Sun 9.30am. Hds 9.30am, 7pm.*

■ **BENSON,** Oxon, RAF Station
St Stephen
Served from Dorchester-on-Thames.
Tel: 01491-825529
M: *Sat 6.30pm. Sun 11am.*

■ **BENTLEY,** Staffs
Mary Immaculate (1962)
Everest Road. Served from Darlaston.
M: *Sun 11am. Hds 6.30pm.*

■ **BERINSFIELD,** Oxon
Served from Dorchester.
M: *Sun 9.30am. Hds 6.30pm.*

■ **BEWDLEY,** Worcs
The Holy Family (1953)
High Street. Served from Stourport.
M: *Sun 8am. Hds 12noon.*

■ **BICESTER,** Oxon
1. † The Immaculate Conception
(1883; 1920; 1963)
The Causeway, Bicester, Oxon OX26 6AW
Tel: 01869-253277 **Fax:** 01869-249530
E-mail: immaculateconception@ic24.net
Revv Paul Martin, Bernard Garrett.
M: *Sat 1st M of Sun 6pm. Sun 11am, Hds 10.30am, 7.30pm.*
• ***Presentation Sisters,*** Provincialate, Kings End, Bicester, Oxon.
Tel: 01869-323660 **Fax:** 01869-323659

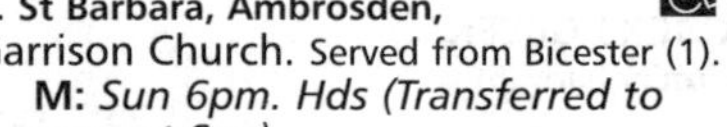

2. St Barbara, Ambrosden,
Garrison Church. Served from Bicester (1).
M: *Sun 6pm. Hds (Transferred to nearest Sun).*

■ **BIDDULPH,** Staffs
† English Martyrs (1952; 1955)
The Priests' House, Church Road, Biddulph, Staffs ST8 6JG **Tel:** 01782-513130
Rev Julian Booth,
Deacon: **Rev Dr David Child.**
M: *Sat 1st M of Sun 6.30pm. Sun 10.30am. Hds (eve 7.30pm), 10am.*

■ **BIDFORD-ON-AVON,** Alcester, Warks
† St Joseph the Worker (1960)
Quinney's Lane, Bidford-on-Avon, Alcester B50 4JL **Tel:** 01789-773291
Website: www.stjosephs-bidford.co.uk
Rev John Moore.
M: *Sat 1st M of Sun 5.30pm. Sun 11am. Hds 9.15am, 7.30pm.*

■ **BILSTON,** West Midlands
† Holy Trinity (1832; 1834)
Oxford Street, Bilston, W. Midlands.
Tel: 01902-493459
Rev Geoffrey Hargreaves. Presbytery, Tame Street, WV14 7EL
M: *Sat 1st M of Sun 6.30pm. Sun 11am. Hds 9.30am, 7.30pm.*

■ **BIRCHES HEAD,** Hanley
See Stoke-on-Trent (10).

■ **BIRMINGHAM**
1. (See start of parish list)

2. Oscott College
Chester Road, Sutton Coldfield, West Midlands, B73 5AA
St Mary's Seminary

(1794; 1838; church cons 29 May 1838)
Tel: 0121-321 5000 (Staff);
Fax: 0121-321 5002
Tel: 0121-3321 5026 (Bursar);
Tel: 0121-321 5000 (Students).
Rector: **V. Rev Mark Crisp**
E-mail: rector@oscott.org
Revv Hugh Sinclair *(Spiritual Director)*; **Kenneth W Collins, Paul McNally** *(Pastoral Director),* **Philip Egan, Harry Curtis, Zbigniew Zieba, Richard Walker, Paul Fitzpatrick** *(Estates Director & Pastoral Co-ordinator)*.

3. † Christ the King
(1932; 1963, 1994)
124 Warren Farm Road, Kingstanding B44 0QN **Tel:** 0121-373 0988
Rev Michael White.
E-mail: Michael@christ-theking.org.uk
M: *Sat 1st M of Sun 6.30pm. Sun 10am, 12noon, (evening M as announced). Hds 9am, 12noon, 7.30pm.*

4. † Corpus Christi
(1919; 1971; cons 1976)
Lyttleton Road, Stechford.
Rev Paul Devaney. 139 Albert Road, Stechford B33 8UR **Tel:** 0121-783 2792
E-mail: pauldevaney2@btopenworld.com
M: *Sat 1st M of Sun 6pm. Sun 9.30am, 11.30am, 6pm. Hds (eve 7.30pm), 9.30am, 7.30pm.*
- ***Sisters of Mercy,*** 133 Albert Road, Stechford B33 8UB **Tel:** 0121-784 2090

5. † Holy Family (1901; 1928; 1976)
763 Coventry Road, Small Heath, B10 0HT
Tel: 0121-772 0059 **Fax:** 0121-773 1485
E-mail: fra.rohan@googlemail.com
Revv Anthony Rohan.
M: *Sat 1st M of Sun 6.30pm. Sun 9.30am, 11.30am, 6.30pm. Hds 9.30am, 1pm, 7pm.*

6. † Sacred Heart and the Holy Souls
(1905; 1940; cons. 24 Oct 1945)
1151 Warwick Road, Acocks Gr, B27 6RG
Tel: 0121-706 0800 **Fax:** 0121-707 5734
Rev David Tams.
M: *Sat 1st M of Sun 5pm. Sun 8.30am, 10am, 12noon. Hds 10am, 12.30pm, 7.45pm.*
- ***Presentation Sisters,*** 40 Victoria Road, B27 7YA **Tel:** 0121-706 0446
- ***Religious Sisters of Charity,*** St Anne's Convent, 3 Elmdon Road, Acock's Green B27 6LT **Tel:** 0121-707 9366

7. † Sacred Heart and St Margaret Mary
(1897; 1922; cons 22 June 1933)
Witton Road, Aston B6 6EG
Tel: 0121-327 0505
Rev Peter Jones.
M: *Sat 1st M of Sun 12.30pm. Sun 10.30am. Hds As announced.*
- ***Daughters of Divine Love,*** 46 Little Oaks Road, Aston, Birmingham B6 6JX **Tel:** 0121-326 6964

8. † The Oratory, The Immaculate Conception
(1851; 1909; cons 23 June 1920)
141 Hagley Road, Edgbaston B16 8UE
Tel: 0121-454 0496 **Fax:** 0121-455 8160
E-mail: oratory@globalnet.co.uk
- ***Fathers of the Oratory of St Philip Neri (Cong Orat):*** **Very Rev Paul Chavasse** (*Superior*); **Revv Guy Nicholls** (*Parish Priest*), **Dermot Fenlon, Gregory Winterton, Philip Cleevely, Bro Lewis Berry**.
  M: *Sat 1st M of Sun 5.45pm. Sun 8.30, 10.30am (Latin), 12noon, 5.30pm. Hds (eve 5.45pm). 7.30am, 11am, 12.45pm, 5.45pm, 8pm.*
- ***Sisters of Charity of St Paul***, Vernon Road, B16 9SL **Tel:** 0121-454 1797
- ***Sisters of Charity of St Paul,*** Annie Bright Weston House, 6 Norfolk Road, Edgbaston B15 3QD **Tel:** 0121-454 1289

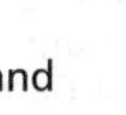

9. † The Mother of God and Guardian Angels (1947; 1955, 1997)
Hurst Lane, Castle Bromwich.
Tel: 0121-747 2873
Rev Peter Conley. Presbytery, Kitsland Road, B34 7NA
M: *Sat 1st M of Sun 6.30pm. Sun 10am. Hds 10am, 7pm.*

10. † Our Lady of the Assumption
(1679; 1778; 1957)
82 Old Oscott Hill, Maryvale, B44 9SP
Tel: 0121-360 7141
Rev David Oakley.
M: *Sat 1st M of Sun 6pm. Sun 9.30am, 11.30am. Hds 9.30am, 7.30pm.*
- ***Maryvale Institute of Further and Higher Education,*** Maryvale House, Old Oscott Hill, B44 9AG **Tel:** 0121-360 8118 Director: Rev Paul Watson.
- ***Bridgettine Sisters (OSsS)***, Convent, Maryvale Institute, Old Oscott Hill, Kingstanding B44 9AG **Tel:** 0121-325 2414 **Fax:** 0121 325 2411 **E-mail:** bridgettine.maryvale@ dsl.pipex.com
- ***Little Sisters of the Assumption (LSA)***, Convent, 99 Old Oscott Hill, Birmingham B44 9SR **Tel:** 0121-360 8072

ARCHDIOCESE OF BIRMINGHAM

11. † Our Lady Help of Christians
(1950; 1967)
57 East Meadway, Kitts Green B33 0AU
Tel: 0121-783 3537
E-mail: oloh783537@btconnect.com
Rev Paul Haines.
M: *Sun 10am, 6pm. Hds 9am, 6.30pm.*

12. † Our Lady of Lourdes
(1931, 1935, 1966, 1980)
222 Trittiford Road, Yardley Wood, B13 0EU
Tel: 0121-444 5106 **Fax:** 0121-444 0662
Canon Sean Grady.
Deacon: **Rev Peter Seeney**.
M: *Sat 1st M of Sun 6pm. Sun 9am, 11am, 6pm. Hds Vigil 7pm; 9.15am, 7pm.*

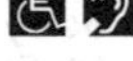

13. † Our Lady of Perpetual Succour
(1956; 1960)
Leach Green Lane, Rednal.
Tel: 0121-453 3452
Rev Nicholas Latham, 1 Quarry Walk, Rednal B45 9BQ
E-mail: johnlatham1@virgin.net
Deacon: **Rev Pat Linthwaite**.
M: *Sat 1st M of Sun 6.45pm. Sun 11am, Hds 11am. 7.30pm.*

14. † Our Lady of the Rosary and St Teresa of Lisieux
(1914; 1933; cons 8 June 1934)
141 Parkfield Road, Saltley, B8 3BB
Tel: 0121-327 0585 **Fax:** 0121-328 814
E-mail: rosary@btinternet.com
Rev Bernard Kelly.
M: *Sat 1st M of Sun 5.30pm. Sun 9.30am, 12noon. Hds: As announced.*

15. † Our Lady and St Brigid
(1918; 1936)
Frankley Beeches Road, Northfield, B31 5AB
Tel: 0121-475 1252
Rev Noel Breslin.
M: *Sat 1st M of Sun 5pm. Sun 9am, 11.30am. Hds 9.30am, 11am, 7.30pm.*
- ***Sisters of Charity of St Paul,*** St Brigid's Convent, 65 Frankley Beeches Rd; B31 5AB **Tel:** 0121-475 3178
- ***Sisters of Our Lady of Charity,*** The Priory; 2 Maryland Drive, B31 2AR **Tel:** 0121-475 6232
- ***Sisters of Our Lady of Charity,*** 4 St Laurence Road, Northfield B31 2AR **Tel:** 0121-475 4949

16. † Our Lady and St Rose of Lima
(1933; 1961)
Gregory Avenue, Weoley Castle, B29 5DY
Tel: 0121-475 1634
Web: www.strose.org.uk
Rev David Standen.
M: *Sat 1st M of Sun 5.30pm. Sun 9.30am, 11am. Hds 10am, 7pm.*

17. † St Mary
(1870; 1876; cons 13 Apr 1932, 1977)
Vivian Road, Harborne B17 0DN
Tel: 0121-427 2538 **Fax:** 0121-428 3656
Website: www.stmarysharborne.org.uk
- ***Augustinians (Austin Friars) (OSA);*** **Revv George Donaghy** (*Prior & Parish Priest*), **Michael Roche** (*Sub-Prior*), **Jacob Choi, Bernard O'Connor, Michael Power,** St Mary's Priory, 111 Vivian Road, Harborne, Birmingham B17 0DN *Deacon:* **Rev John Leach**, 160 Knightlow Road, Harborne B17 8QA **Tel:** 0121-684 1469 **M:** *Sat 1st M of Sun 6pm. Sun 8am, 9.30am, 11am, 12.20pm, 5pm. Hds 6.45am, 8am, 10am, 12noon, 6pm.*
- ***Little Sisters of the Poor,*** St Joseph's Home, 71 Queen's Park Road, B32 2LB **Tel:** 0121-427 2486
- ***Jesuits (SJ):*** Manresa House, 10 Albert Road, Harborne B17 0AN (1939) **Tel:** 0121-427 2628 **Fax:** 0121-428 1833 **E-mail:** manresa@btinternet.com **Rev Paul Nicho°lson** (*Superior & Novice Director*), 10 Albert Road, Harborne, Birmingham B17 0AN **Tel:** 0121-428 4993 **E-mail:** pauln@jesuits.net. **John McCabe, Joseph Munitiz, Damian Howard, R Darwen, D Mansfield.**
- ***Sisters of Sion,*** 49 St Peter's Road B17 0AV **Tel:** 0121-426 6679

18. † St Mary and St John
(1922; 1937; cons. 2 July 1953)
20 Gravelly Hill North, Erdington B23 6BQ
Tel: 0121-373 0263
Revv Patrick Kevin Joyce, Gerard Lennon
M: *Sat 1st M of Sun 7pm. Sun 9.30am, 11am, 6pm. Hds 9am, 12.15pm, 7.30pm.*

19. † English Martyrs
(1908; 1923; cons 11 July 1946)
Evelyn Road, Sparkhill, B11 3JN
Tel: 0121-722 1272
Rev Patrick Gilsenan.
M: *Sat 1st M of Sun 6pm. Sun 9.30am, 11am. Hds (eve 7.30pm). 9.15am, 10.30am (school), 7pm.*

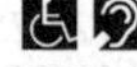

20. St Ambrose Barlow
(1979, 1981, 1986)
Lakey Lane, Hall Green. B28 8QU
Tel: 0121-777 4524 **Canon John Gunn**.
E-mail: ja.gunn@btinternet.com
Rev Neil Bayliss. *Deacon:* **Rev John Stark**.
M: *Sat 1st M of Sun 5.30pm. Sun 9am, 11am, 5.30pm. Hds (eve 7pm). 9.15am, 7pm.*

- ***Sisters of Charity of St Paul:*** 191 Lakey Lane, Hall Green B28 8RX. **Tel:** 0121-778 2760

21. † St Anne
(1849; 1884; cons. 16 April 1936)
Alcester Street, Birmingham B12 0PD
Tel: 0121-772 2780
E-mail: sabham@btopenworld.com
- ***Oblates of Mary Immaculate (OMI):*** **Revv Leo Philomin, Peter Cluas, Michael Ryan**. 96 Bradford Street B12 0PB
  M: *Sat Vigil 1.00pm, Sun 11am, 6.30pm. Hds 1pm, 7pm.*

A

22. † St Anne (1968)
Chelmsley Wood.
Tel: 0121-770 3283
Rev Gerardo Fabrizio. *Deacon:* **Rev Stuart Hill**, Presbytery: 281A Bosworth Drive, B37 5DP **Tel:** 0121-770 3283
M: *Sat 1st M of Sun 6.30pm. Sun 9.30am, 11.30am. Hds (eve 7.30pm). 9am, 11am.*
- ***Sisters of the Poor Child Jesus,*** Fey House, 236 Coleshill Heath Road A37 7HU **Tel:** 0121-779 2234

A

23. † St Augustine of England
(1913; 1939, 1978)
Avenue Road, Handsworth, B21 8ED
Tel: 0121-554 2662
Rev Peter Smith. *Deacon:* **Rev John Green**.
M: *Sun 9am, 11am. Hds 9.15am, 7.30pm.*
- ***Sisters of Charity of St Paul,*** 153 Church Lane, Handsworth, Birmingham. **Tel:** 0121-551 7041 Also 164 Uplands Road B21 8BS **Tel:** 0121-681 9308

24. † St Catherine of Siena
(1858; 1875; 1965, 1971)
Bristol Street, B5 7BE **Tel:** 0121-622 4049
Rev James Fleming (SCC), Columban Missionary Outreach Team
M: *Sat 1st M of Sun 5.30pm. Sun 11am, 12.20pm (Latin Tridentine Mass). Hds 12.45pm, 6pm. Ukranian Rite 2nd Sun 3pm.*
- ***St Catherine's Mission Centre.*** *Team leader:* **Mauricio Silva**, *Team Members:* **Nathalie Silva, Jane Trainor, Begonia Leguina.**
  E-mail: stcatherines@bupanet.com
- ***Society of the Holy Child Jesus,*** 203 Bristol Road, B5 7UB **Tel:** 0121-440 8669
- ***Missionaries of Charity,*** 13 Spring Road B15 2HG **Tel:** 0121-440 8637

25. † St Dunstan (1896; 1968)
Kingsfield Road, Kings Heath, B14 7JN
Tel: 0121-444 1386
E-mail: stdunstan.rc.net
Rev Christopher Fitzpatrick.
M: *Sat 1st M of Sun 5.30pm. Sun 9am, 10.30am, 12noon, 6.30pm. Hds (eve 7pm). 8am, 9.30am, 12.30pm, 8pm.*
- ***Sisters of St. Mary Madeleine Postel,*** Provincial House, 236 Alcester Road, Kings Heath B14 6DR
  Tel: 0121-444 7463

26. † St Edward (1889; 1904, 1989)
93 Raddlebarn Road, Selly Park, B29 7DB
Tel: 0121-472 0190
Rev Denis McGillicuddy.
M: *Sat 1st M of Sun 6pm. Sun 10.15am, 6pm. Hds (eve 7pm), 9.15am, 7pm.*
- ***Sisters of Charity of St Paul,*** St Paul's Convent, 94 Selly Park, B29 7LL
  Tel: 0121-415 6100/6105 Mother House

27. † St Francis
(1840; 1894; cons. 21 June, 1900)
101 Hunters Road, Handsworth B19 1EB
Tel: 0121-554 0905
Mgr Thomas Fallon.
M: *Sat 1st M of Sun 7pm. Sun 9.30am, 11.30am, 12.45pm, 2.30pm (in Vietnamese), 6.30pm. Hds 9.30am, 11am, 6pm (in Vietnamese), 7.30pm.*
- **Sisters of Mercy,** St Mary's, 98 Hunters Road, B19 1EB **Tel:** 0121-554 3271
- **Columban Sisters,** 55 Thornhill Road, B21 9BT **Tel:** 0121-523 6090
- **Missionary Sisters Servants of the Holy Spirit,** 14 Wye Cliff Road, Handsworth, Birmingham B20 3TB
  Tel: 0121-515 2341

28. Vietnamese Pastoral Centre
10-12 Wye Cliff Road, Handsworth, Birmingham B20 3TB
Tel: 0121-554 8082 **Fax:** 0121-523 6258
Website: www.vietmartyrs.org.uk
Rev Peter Nguyen Tien Dac, IDD.
E-mail: tiendac@amserve.net

29. St Gerard (1967, 1981, 2001)
Yatesbury Avenue, Castle Vale.
Tel: 0121-747 7390 **Fax:** 0121-749 1057
Rev Michael G Knight. Presbytery, 2 Renfrew Square, Castle Vale, B35 6JT
M: *Sun 9am, 11am, 5pm. Hds 10am, 7.30pm.*

30. † St John the Evangelist and St Martin
(1896, 1966, 1977)
31 George Street, Balsall Heath, B12 9RG
Tel: 0121-440 3025
E-mail: info@stjohnandmartin.org.uk
Website: www.stjohnandmartin.org.uk
Rev Dominic Innamorati SCJ.
M: *Sat 1st M of Sun 6pm. Sun 10am. Hds 9.30am, 7.30pm.*
- ***Society of the Holy Child Jesus,*** 35 Hampden Retreat, Balsall Heath
  Tel: 0121-440 2523

- ***Sisters of St Joseph of Lyon,*** 103 Anderton Park Road, Moseley B13 9DS **Tel:** 0121-449 3854.
- ***Sisters of Our Lady of Charity,*** 91 Salisbury Road, Moseley B13 9DP **Tel/Fax:** 0121-449 5108

31. † St John Fisher (1956; 1964; 1972)
1 Cofton Road, West Heath, B31 3QT
Tel: 0121-475 3194
E-mail: father@stjohnfisher.fsnet.co.uk
Rev George Gryowski.
M: *Sat 1st M of Sun 6.15pm. Sun 9.30am, 6.30pm. Hds (eve 7.30pm), 9.15am, 6pm.*

A
32. † St Joseph (1867; 1872)
182 Thimblemill Lane, Nechells B7 5HT
Tel: 0121-327 0235
E-mail: stjosephs@smartemail.co.uk
M: *Sat 1st M of Sun 6pm. Sun 9.15am, 11.15am. Hds 9.30am, 7.30pm.*
- ***Sisters of Charity of St Paul,*** 79 Medway Tower (13th Floor), Cromwell Street, Nechells, Birmingham B7 5BQ **Tel:** 0121-359 2953

33. SS Joseph and Helen(1902; 1933)
Station Road, King's Norton.
Tel: 0121-458 1236
Rev David Barry. 84 Northfield Road B30 1JG
Deacon: **Rev Paul Russell.**
M: *Sat 1st M of Sun 6pm. Sun 9am, 11am. Hds 9am, 7pm.*

A
34. † St Jude (1966)
St Jude's Close, Maypole B14 5PE
Tel: 0121-430 6932
Rev Frank Rowe.
M: *Sat 1st M of Sun 6.30pm. Sun 10am. Hds 10am, 7pm.*

S A
35. † St Margaret Mary
(1926; 1937; cons 1966)
59 Perry Common Road B23 7AB
Tel: 0121-373 0069
Rev Richard Sharples.
M: *Sat 1st M of Sun 6.30pm; Sun 9am, 11am. Hds 9.15am.*

36. † St Michael *(1846; 1862)*
Moor Street, B4 7UG **Tel:** 0121-643 0940
Rev John O'Brien.
M: *Sun 9.30am, (11am, 12.15pm for Poles). Hds 12.10pm, 1.10pm, (10.15am, 7.30pm for Poles).*
- ***Polish Catholic Centre,*** Bordesley Street, B5 5PH **Tel:** 0121-358 7102 **Revv Zygfryd Zastocki (CRL), Appolinary Zawistowski (CRL).**

37. † St Patrick
(1876; 1895; cons. 19 June 1902)
106 Dudley Road, B18 7QN
Tel: 0121-454 0418
Revv Eddie Clare, John Peyton.
M: *Sat 1st M of Sun 6pm. Sun 9.30am, 11.30am, 7pm. Hds 9.15am, 12.30pm, 7pm.*

38. St Paul (1966; 1977)
Sisefield Road, Kings Norton B38 9JB
Tel: 0121-458 1139
Rev Stefan Laszczyk.
M: *Sat 1st M of Sun 6pm. Sun 10am. Hds 9am, (Term time 11am), 7pm.*

40. St Peter (1969; 1976)
42 Adams Hill, Bartley Green, B32 3QG
Tel: 0121-476 1799
Website: www.strose.org.uk
Rev David Standen.
Deacon: **Rev Bill Baines.**
M: *Sun 9am, 11am. Hds 9.15am, 7pm.*
- ***Newman College of Higher Education,*** Genners Lane, B32 3NT **Tel:** 0121-476 1181 ext 2266 *Principal:* **Dr Pamela Taylor.** *Chaplain:* **Sr Margaret Holland IJS.** **M:** *(St Mary's Chapel) Sun 7pm. Hds 12.30pm.*

41. † SS Peter and Paul (1929; 1971)
552 Kingsbury Road, Erdington. B24 9ND
Tel: 0121-373 1437
Rev John Batthula.
Deacon: **Rev Adrian Davies.**
M: *Sat 1st M of Sun 6.30pm. Sun 9am, 11am. Hds 9.15am, 7.30pm.*

42. † St Teresa (1940)
273 Wellington Road, Perry Barr, B20 2QQ
Tel: 0121-356 4402
Rev Simon Hall.
Deacon: **Rev Anthony Hewitt.**
M: *Sat 1st M of Sun 5pm. Sun 10am, 12noon. Hds 10am, 7pm.*

43. † Erdington Abbey
SS Thomas and Edmund of Canterbury
(1846; cons. 1850)
Sutton Road, B23 6QN
Tel: 0121-373 0143
Fax: 0121-382 6854
Mbl: 097901-638164
E-mail: ppabbeyerdington@aol.com

- ***Redemptorists (CSsR):*** **Revv Gabriel Maguire** (*Rector and Parish Priest*), **Francis Dickinson. Fax:** 0121-384 2285 **M:** *Sat 1st M of Sun 6pm. Sun 8am, 9.15am (Childrens), 10.30am (Sung), 12pm, 6pm. Hds (eve 7.30pm). 7am, 10am, 12noon, 7.30pm.*
- ***Daughters of the Holy Spirit,*** 174 Orphanage Road, B24 0AA **Tel:** 0121-373 1110

44. † St Thomas More
(1936; 1969; 1978)
130 Horse Shoes Lane, Sheldon B26 3HU
Tel: 0121-743 2367
Canon Peter Gilsenan.
M: *Sat 1st M of Sun 5.30pm. Sun 8.30am, 10.30am. Hds 9am, 12noon, 7pm.*

45. † St Vincent de Paul (1883; 1968)
Nechells Parkway, B7 4JY
Tel: 0121-359 3305
Rev John Carlyle.
M: *Sun 10am, 12noon. Hds 9.30am, 7.30pm.*
• ***Little Sisters of the Assumption (LSA),*** Convent, 2 Heneage Place, Barrack Street, Birmingham B7 4ER
Tel: 0121-333 4824

46. † St Wilfrid (1959; 1965)
Shawsdale Road, Castle Bromwich B36 8LL
Tel: 0121-747 2146
Rev George Bennett.
M: *Sat 1st M of Sun 6pm. Sun 8.30am, 10.30am. Hds As announced.*

47. University of Birmingham
Catholic Chaplaincy. Newman House, 29 Harrisons Road, Edgbaston B15 3QR
Chaplain: **Rev Julian Green.**
Tel: 0121-454 4395 (*Chaplain and Warden*)
Tel: 0121-454 2508 (*Resident Students*)
M: *Sun 10.30am, 6.30pm (in term). Hds As announced.*

47a Newman College of Higher Education
Genners Lane, Bartley Green B32 3NT
Tel: 0121-476 1181
Principal: **Dr Pamela Taylor,**
Chaplain: **Sr Margaret Holland.**
M: *St Mary's Chapel Sun 7pm. Hds 12.30pm Term time.*

48. University of Aston
Catholic Chaplain: **Rev John O'Brien**
Office: Chaplaincy, Lawrence Tower, Aston B4 7ET
M: *Sun 7pm in Martin Luther King Centre on the University Campus. Hds, as announced.*

49. University of Central England.
Chaplain: **Sr Christina McCann (CSJ),**
UCE Ecumenical Chaplaincy: c/o Student Services, Baker Building, Perry Barr, Birmingham B42 2SU **Tel:** 0121-331 5345
E-mail: christina.mccann@uce.ac.uk
M: *Sun 5.45pm. Hds 5.45pm.*

50. Our Lady of the Caribbean
West Indian Chaplaincy, Chapel Centre, Bayswater Road, Birchfield B20.
Served from Smethwick.

Chaplain: **Rev John O'Brien.**
Tel: 0121-515 2084
M: *Sun 11.30pm. Hds 7.45pm.*
• ***Sisters of Charity of St Paul,*** St Paul's Convent, 50 Little Oaks Road, Aston, Birmingham B6 6JX **Tel:** 0121-328 9626

■ **BLACKHEATH,** Birmingham
† English Martyrs (1961)
297 Oldbury Road, Rowley Regis, Warley, W. Midlands B65 0PR
Tel: 0121-559 1677
Rev Christopher Handforth.
M: *Sat 1st M of Sun 5pm. Sun 9.30am. Hds Vigil 6.30pm.*

■ **BLACKMORE PARK,** Worcester
† Our Blessed Lady and St Alphonsus
(1846; cons 19 Aug 1846)
Hanley Swan, Worcester WR8 0EA
Tel: 01684-310317
Served from Upton on Severn.
M: *Sat 1st M of Sun 6.30pm. Hds 10am.*

■ **BLOXWICH,** Walsall
† St Peter (1798; 1869)
208 High Street, Bloxwich, Walsall WS3 3LA **Tel:** 01922-476765
Rev Robert Murphy.
M: *Sat 1st M of Sun 5.30pm. Sun 9.30am. Hds 10am, 7pm.*

■ **BOLDMERE,** Birmingham
See Sutton Coldfield (2).

■ **BRAILES,** Warks
† SS Peter and Paul (1726)
Tel: 01608-685259
Rev Brian Doolan
Friars lane, Lower Brailes, Oxon OX15 5HU
Tel: 01608 685259
Serves Ilmington and Shipston
M: *Sun 11.30am. Hds 11.30am.*

■ **BREWOOD,** Stafford
† St Mary (1844; cons 21 June 1924)
Kiddemore Green Road, Brewood, Stafford ST19 9BG **Tel:** 01902-850394
E-mail: father@stmarybrewood.org.uk
Rev Michael Miners.
Deacon: **Rev Stephen Gee**
M: *Sat 1st M of Sun 6pm. Sun 10.30am. Hds 9am, 7.30pm.*

■ **BRIERLEY HILL,** West Midlands
† St Mary (1873; 1983)
High Street, DY5 3AE **Tel:** 01384-823445
Rev John Darley.
M: *Sun 10.30am, 5.30pm. Hds, as announced.*

■ **BRIZE NORTON,** Oxon, RAF Station
The Holy Family
Brize Norton, Carterton OX18 3LX
Chaplaincy: **Tel:** 01993-897529 ext 7529

Mass Chaplain (Supply) **Rev James Caulfield**
M: *Sun 11.15am.*

■ **BROADWAY,** Worcs
† **St Saviour** (1828; 1928)
Leamington Road, WR12 7EA
Tel: 01386-853753
Rev Peter Rogers
M: *Sat 1st M of Sun 6.30pm. Sun 8am, 10am. Hds 10.30am, 7pm.*

■ **BROMSGROVE,** Worcs
† **St Peter** (1858; cons 29 September 1910)
Rock Hill. **Tel:** 01527-832530
Mgr Graham Wilkinson. The Presbytery, 2a Charford Road, Bromsgrove B60 3LU
M: *Sat 1st M of Sun 6pm. Sun 8.30am, 10.30am. Hds (eve 6pm). 9am.*

■ **BROWNHILLS,** Walsall
† **St Bernadette** (1935)
High Street. **Tel:** 01543-372759
E-mail: davidmell@aol.com
Rev David Mellor. 40 Warren Place, WS8 6BY
M: *Sat 1st M of S 6.30pm. Sun 10am. Hds 9.30am, 7.30pm.*

■ **BUCKNALL,** Stoke-on-trent
See Stoke-on-Trent (13).

■ **BULKINGTON,** Warks
Our Lady of the Sacred Heart (1849.1869)
Weston Lane, Bulkington, Nuneaton, Warwicks CV12 9RU **Tel:** 02476-312293
E-mail: michaelgamble@olsh.fsnet.co.uk
Website: www.olsh.fsnet.co.uk
Rev Michael Gamble.
M: *Sat 1st M of Sun 6pm. Sun 10am. Hds 9.30am, 7.30pm.*

■ **BURFORD,** Oxon
† **SS John Fisher and Thomas More** (1939)
171 The Hill, Burford, Oxon OX18 4RE
Tel/Fax: 01993-823219
Rev Ian Ker.
M: *Sun 9.15am, 11am. Hds 10am, 7pm.*

■ **BURNTWOOD,** Walsall
† **St Joseph** (1876; 2003)
Cannock Road, Burntwood, Staffs. WS7 8XY **Tel:** 01543-686266
E-mail: stjosephschurch@postmaster.co.uk
Rev Patrick Mileham.
Deacon: **Rev Thomas Deaville**
M: *Sat 1st M of Sun 6pm. Sun 10am. Hds (eve 7.30pm). 9.15am, 7.30pm.*

■ **BURSLEM,** Stoke-on-Trent
See Stoke-on-Trent (11).

■ **BURTON-ON-TRENT,** Staffs
† **SS Mary and Modwen** (1851; 1879)
78A Guild Street, DE14 1NB
Tel: 01283-63246
E-mail: modwenrc@aol.com
Revv Stephen Wright, Michael Crumpton. *Deacon:* **Rev: Henry Atkinson**.
M: *Sun 9am, 11am, 6pm, 2pm. Hds 9.15am (at St Modwen's School, during term). 12.30pm, 7.30pm.*

■ **CANNOCK,** Staffs
† **St Mary and St Thomas More** (1873; 1924)
2 Hallcourt Cresent, Walsall Road, Cannock, Staffs WS11 3AB **Tel:** 01543-503149
Rev Patrick Brennan.
Deacon: **Rev Paul Hender.**
M: *Sat 1st M of Sun 6.15pm. Sun 10.30am. (1st Sun of month, Pol Mass 12.45pm). Hds (eve 7.15pm). 9.15am.*

■ **CARTERTON,** Oxon
† **St Joseph** (1914; 1940)
Arkell Avenue, Carterton, Oxon OX8 3BS
Tel: 01993-842463
Rev Andrew Foster.
Deacon: **Rev Bernard Curtin**.
M: *Sun 11am. Hds 9.30am, 7pm.*

■ **CASTLE BROMWICH**
See Birmingham, Nos (10) and (46).

■ **CASTLE VALE**
See Birmingham (30).

■ **CAVERSHAM,** Reading, Berks
1. † **Our Lady and St Anne**
(1896; 1903; cons 26 July 1933)
2 South View Avenue, Caversham, Reading, Berks RG4 5AB
Tel: 0118-947 1787 **Fax:** 0118-947 7625
E-mail: st.anne@virgin.net
Rev Giles Goward.
Deacon: **Rev Michael Walker.**
M: *Sat 1st M of Sun 5.30pm. Sun 10am, 6.30pm. Hds 7am, 9.15am, 7.30pm.*

■ **CAVERSWALL**
† **St Filumena** (1811; 1853; 1864)
Caverswall, Stoke-on-Trent ST11 9EA
Tel: 01782-393161
Rev James Edward McInerney.
Deacon: **Rev Peter Bowyer**.
M: *Sun 8.30am, 11am. Hds 9.15am, 7.30pm.*

■ **CHARLBURY,** Oxon
† **St Teresa of Lisieux** (1931)
5 Enstone Road, Charlbury, Oxon OX7 3QR **Tel:** 01608-810576
Mgr V. Rev David Evans.
M: *Sun 11am. Hds 9.30am, 7.30pm.*

■ **CHEADLE,** Staffs
† **St Giles** (1823; 1846; cons 31 August 1846)
Bank Street, Cheadle, Stoke-on-Trent.
Tel/Fax: 01538-753130 or
Tel: 01850-592307

Rev Alexander Brown.
M: *Sat 1st M of Sun 5.30pm. Sun 10am. Hds (eve 6.30pm). 10am, 6.30pm.*
Also serving Tean and Cotton.

■ **CHESTERTON,** Newcastle, Staffs
† **St John The Evangelist** (1923; 1926; 1957)
Loomer Road, Chesterton, Newcastle, Staffs ST5 7JS **Tel:** 01782-561600
Served from Wolstanton
In Residence: **Very Rev Canon David Goodwin** (retired).
M: *Sun 9.30am, 5pm. Hds 10.00am.*

■ **CHIPPING NORTON,** Oxon
† **Holy Trinity** (1836)
London Road, Chipping Norton, Oxon OX7 5AX **Tel:** 01608-642703
Rev Francis Hull SJ.
M: *Sat 1st M of Sun 6pm. Sun 10.30am. Hds 9am, 7pm.*

■ **CLAYTON,** Newcastle, Staffs
† **Our Lady and St Werburgh** (1957; 1958)
Seabridge Lane, Clayton, Newcastle, Staffs ST5 4AG **Tel:** 01782-613023
Rev Stephen Fawcett.
M: *Sun 8.15am, 10am. Hds 2.15pm, 7.15pm.*

■ **CLENT,** Worcs
SS Oswald and Wulstan, Holy Cross. (1926)
Served from Stourbridge (1).
M: *Sun 9.30am.*

■ **CODSALL,** Wolverhampton
† **St Christopher** (1934: 2000)
115 Wolverhampton Road, Codsall, Wolverhampton WV8 1PF
Tel: 01902-842891 **Fax:** 01902-843332
Website: www.stchristopherscodshill.org.uk
Rev Dominic Chukka.
M: *Sat 1st M of Sun 5.30pm. Sun 9.30am. Hds 11am, 7pm.*

■ **COLESHILL,** Birmingham
Sacred Heart and St Teresa of the Child Jesus (1882; 1941, 2002)
67 Coventry Road, Coleshill, Birmingham B46 3EA
Tel: 01675-463939 **Fax:** 01675-430325
E-mail: mstock@btinternet.co.uk
Revv Marcus Stock, Edgard Dizon
M: *Sat 1st M of Sun 5.30pm. Sun 10.30am. Hds 10am, 7.30pm.*
- ***Sisters of Charity of St Paul,*** 11 Brendan Close, Coleshill B46 3EF
Tel: 01675-430093

■ **COLWICH,** Staffs
St Mary's Abbey (1836; 1928)
Colwich ST18 0UF
Tel: 01889-881282
E-mail: stmarysabbey@btopenworld.com
- ***Benedictine Nuns,*** St Mary's Abbey, Colwich, Little Haywood, Stafford ST18 0UF . **Tel:** 01889-88128 *Chaplain:* **V Rev Dom Luke Waring OSB**.
Tel/Fax: 01889-881173

■ **COSELEY,** Staffs
St John Fisher (1960)
Yew Tree Lane. Served from Bilston.
M: *Sun 9.30am. Hds 6.30am.*

■ **COTTON,** Staffs
† **St Wilfrid's** (1848; cons 21 Sept 1900)
Cotton Lane, Oakamoor, ST10 3DP
Served from Cheadle.
M: *Sun 8.30am.*

■ **COUGHTON,** Alcester, Warks
† **SS Peter and Paul and St Elizabeth** (1857)
B49 5JA Served from Alcester.
M: *Sat 1st M of Sun 6pm.*

■ **COVENTRY,** West Midlands
1. † **Christ the King and Our Lady of Lourdes** (1932; 1933)
14 Westhill Road, Coventry, West Midlands CV6 2AA **Tel:** 024-7659 1618
V Rev Tom Farrell, Rev Richard Scott.
Deacons: **Revv Patrick Flanagan, Gerard O'Reilly**.
M: *Sat 1st M of Sun 6pm. Sun 9am, 12noon. Hds 9.15am, 7pm*

2. † **Corpus Christi** (1956)
Ernesford Grange, Coventry, West Midlands
Tel: 024-7644 8170
E-mail: corpuschristicov@catholic.org
Rev Adrian MacNamara. Presbytery, Langbank Avenue, CV3 2QP
M: *Sat 1st M of Sun 6.30pm. Sun 9.30am, 11.30am. Hds 9.30am, 7.30pm.*
- ***Sisters of Charity of St Paul,*** Corpus Christi Convent, Ernesford Grange, Langbank Avenue, CV3 3BS
Tel: 024-7633 3881

3. † **The Most Holy Sacrament and St Osburg** (1766; cons 9 Sept 1845)
Upper Hill Street, Coventry, W Midlands
Tel: 024-7622 0402
Rev Garry Byrne, St Osburg's, Barras Lane, CV1 4AQ.
M: *Sat 1st M of Sun 5.30pm. Sun 8.30am, 10.30am, 12.15pm. Hds 9am, 12.15pm, 6pm.*
- ***Presentation Sisters,*** 14 Stoney Road, Cheylesmore CV1 2NP
Tel: 024-7663 0381 **Fax:** 024-7655 5543

4. † **The Precious Blood of Our Lord and All Souls** (1924; cons 28 June 1963)
Kingsland Avenue, Earlsdon CV5 8DX
Tel: 024-766 74161

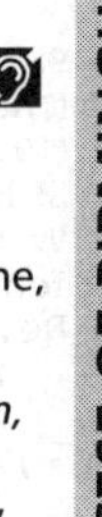

Rev Michael Brandon.
M: *Sat 1st M of Sun 5.30pm. Sun 9.30am, 11.15am. Hds (eve 7pm). 9.30am, 7pm.*

5. † The Sacred Heart (1924; 1934)
Harefield Road, Coventry CV2 4BT
Tel: 024-7645 6214 **Fax:** 024-7665 1308
E-mail: sacred-heart@btconnect.com
Rev Anthony Norton.
M: *Sat 1st M of Sun 5pm. Sun 9am, 10.30am. Hds 9.30am, 7pm.*

6. † St Mary and St Benedict
(New Church 1893; cons 7 June 1932)
52a Raglan Street, Coventry, W Midlands CV1 5QF **Tel:** 024-7625 8901
Rev Jimmy Lutwama AJ
M: *Sat 1st M of Sun 6pm. Sun 9.30am, 11.30am. Hds 9.30am, 6.30pm.*
- ***Daughters of Our Lady of the Sacred Heart,*** The Convent, Raglan Street, Coventry CV1 5QA **Tel:** 024-7622 239

7. † Our Lady of the Assumption
(1950; 1952)
Tile Hill Lane, Coventry, W Midlands CV4 9TA **Tel:** 024-7646 6834
E-mail: michaelho@tiscali.co.uk
Rev Michael Ho-Huu-Nghia.
M: *Sat 1st M of Sun 5pm. Sun 9am, 11am. Hds 10am, 7pm.*

8. † Holy Family (1951; 1967)
177 Parkgate Road, Holbrooks, Coventry, W Midlands CV6 4GF **Tel:** 024-7633 3128
E-mail: des56@hotmail.com
Rev Desmond Devenney.
Deacon: **Rev Patrick Oldman.**
M: *Sat 1st M of Sun 6pm. Sun 9am, 11am. Hds 9.15am, 7pm.*
- ***Sisters of Charity of St Paul,*** 13 Penny Park Lane. **Tel:** 024-7633 3941

9. † St Elizabeth
(The Good Shepherd, Ss Elizabeth & Helen)
(1912; 1916; cons 8 September 1962)
St Elizabeth's Road, Great Heath, Coventry, W Midlands CV6 5BX
Tel: 024-7668 8536 **Fax:** 024-7665 4561
Revv John Wairagu AJ, Moses Pityal AJ.
M: *Sat 1st M of Sun 6.30pm. Sun 8.30am, 11am. Hds 9.15am, 6.30pm*
- ***Franciscan Missionaries of Mary***, 61/3 Blackwell Road, Coventry CV6 5JS. **Tel:** 024-7666 4983

10 † St Anne (1970, 1979)
2 Dunsmore Avenue, Coventry, West Midlands CV3 3HJ **Tel:** 024-7630 3389
Rev Joseph Vu-Duc-Yen.
M: *Sat 1st M of Sun 6pm. Sun 10am, Hds 9.30am, 6.30pm.*

11. † St John Fisher (1964. 1972)
Presbytery, Tiverton Road, Wyken, Coventry, West Midlands CV2 3DL
Tel: 024-7644 3459 **Fax:** 024-7665 9554
Rev Robert Wright.
M: *Sat 1st M of Sun 6.30pm. Sun 9am, 11am, 5.30pm. Hds 9am, 7pm. (At Walsgrave Hospital, Sun 11am).*

12. † St John Vianney (1959; 1962)
Mount Nod Way, Coventry CV5 7GX
Tel: 024-7646 6332
E-mail: jonathan.veasey@tiscali.co.uk
Rev Jonathan Veasey.
Deacon: **Rev Thomas Rooke.**
M: *Sat 1st M of Sun 6pm. Sun 10am. Hds 9.15am, 7.30pm.*

13. † St Joseph the Worker (1962, 1981)
1 De Montfort Way, Coventry, W Midlands CV4 7DU
Tel: 024-7641 9111
Rev Michael F Jordan.
M: *Sun 9am, 5pm. Hds 10am.*

14. † St Patrick (1950; 1956; 1971; 1983)
Deedmore Road, Bell Green, Coventry, W Midlands CV2 1EQ **Tel:** 024-7661 2193
Revv Bob Wright *(Parish Priest)*, **Paul Moss.** Served from Coventry (11)
M: *Sat 1st M of Sun 5.30pm. Sun 9am, 11am. Hds 9.30am, 11am (SS Peter & Paul, in term time), 7.30pm.*

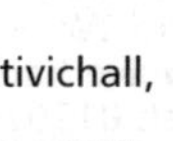

15. † St Thomas More
(1943; 1946, 1968)
The Presbytery, 112 Knoll Drive, Stivichall, Coventry, CV3 5DE
Tel: 024-7641 1900 **Fax:** 024-7641 7935
E-mail: tmenezes@thomasmore.plus.com
Website: www.stmcov.org
Rev Timothy Menezes.
Tel/Fax: 024-7669 3086 *Deacons:* **Revv Patrick Jeary, Anthony Colby.**
M: *Sun 9am, 11am, 6pm. Hds 6.45am, 9am, 6pm, 7.30pm.*

16. St Augustine, Radford
Served from Coventry (1).
M: *Sun 10am. Hds 11am.*

17. University of Warwick.
Catholic Chaplaincy: **Rev Prem Fernando**
Aquinas House, 6 Gibbet Hill Road, Coventry CV4 7AJ **Tel:** 024-7641 9369
M: *See Chaplaincy Noticeboard.*

18. St Stanislaus Kostka, Polish Church (1961)
Springfield Road, Coventry, W. Midlands CV1 4GR **Tel:** 024-7622 2455
M: *Sat 1st M of Sun 5pm. Sun 9am, 11am. Hds 7.30pm.*

19. St Vladimir the Great, Ukrainian Church. Broad Street CB6 5TR **Tel:** 024-7663 8598 **Rev Mykhajlo Onatsko**.
See Apostolic Exarchate for Ukrainians.
M: *Sun 10.30am.*

20. University of Coventry
University of Coventry Catholic Chaplaincy. *Chaplain:* **Rev John Nolan**, Upper Hill Street, Coventry CV1 4AQ
Tel: 02476-258901
M: *Sun 7pm in term time.*

■ **CRADLEY HEATH,**
Warley, West Midlands
† **Our Lady of Lourdes** (1968)
228 Halesowen Road, Old Hill, B64 6HN
Tel: 01384-410516
Rev Anthony Pham-Tri-Van.
M: *Sun 11am, 5pm. Hds 10am, 8pm.*

■ **CRESSWELL,** Staffs
† **Ss Mary and Thomas** (1816)
Tel: 01538-722433
Served from St Augustine's, Stoke-on-Trent (7).
M: *Sun 10.30am. Hds (7.30pm eve).*

■ **DARLASTON,** Staffs A
† **St Joseph** (1865; 1874; 1978; 1983)
Church Street, Darlaston, Staffs WS10 8DY
Tel/ Fax: 0121-526 2287
Rev Ron Cosslett
M: *Sat 1st M of Sun 6.30pm. Sun 9am. Hds 9am.*

■ **DORCHESTER-ON-THAMES**
† **St Birinus** (1849)
Tel: 01865-340417
E-mail: johnosman@birinus.fsnet.co.uk
Rev John Osman. Bridge House, OX9 8JR
M: *Sat 1st M of Sun 6.30pm. Sun 11am. Hds 9.30am, 6.30pm.*

■ **DORRIDGE, SOLIHULL** A
† **St George and St Teresa of the Child Jesus** (1917; 1935, 1985)
337 Station Road, Dorridge, Solihull, West Midlands B93 8EZ
Tel: 01564-772098 **Fax:** 01564-739779
E-mail: catholic-church@dorridge.fslife.co.uk
Mgr Canon J Daniel McHugh;
M: *Sat 1st M of Sun 5.30pm. Sun 8.45am, 10.30am. Hds 10am, 7.30pm.*
- ***Columban Fathers (SSC),*** St Columban's Widney Manor Road, Knowle, Solihull. West Midlands, B93 9AB **Tel:** 01564-772096/776202 **Fax** 01564-770500 **Rev Denis Carter** (*Director*), **Revv Joseph Flanagan, Liam Griffiths, Bernard O'Connor, Cyril Murphy.**

■ **DROITWICH,** Worcs A
† **Sacred Heart and St Catherine of Alexandria** (1909; 1921; cons. 29 Sept 1932)
208 Worcester Road, Droitwich, Worcs
Tel: 01905-773258
- ***Priests of the Sacred Heart (of Betharram) (SCJ):*** The Presbytery, 8 Clifford Close, Droitwich, Worcs WR9 8UT **Tel:** 01905-773258 **Rev T Kelly** (*Superior and Parish Priest*), *Deacon:* **Rev Peter Tibke**.
M: *Sun 8.30am, 10.30am, 6pm. Hds 9.15am, 7.15pm.*

■ **DUDLEY,** West Midlands A
† **Our Blessed Lady and St Thomas of Canterbury**
(1835; cons 29 May, 1842)
10 St Joseph Street, Dudley, West Midlands DY2 7AX **Tel:** 01384-255611
Deacon: **Rev James Fantham.**
Served from Tipton.
M: *Sat 1st M of Sun 6pm. Sun 11am. Hds As announced.*
- ***Daughters of Divine Love,*** The Convent, 10 St Joseph Street, Dudley DY2 7AZ **Tel:** 01384-212636

■ **ECCLESHALL,** Staffs A
† **Sacred Heart** (1904)
45 Stone Road, Eccleshall, Staffs ST21 6DL
Tel: 01785-850302
Rev Stephen Cochrane
Deacon: **Rev Mark Carter**.
M: *Sun 10am. Hds 10am.*

■ **EDGBASTON**
See Birmingham (8).

■ **ENSTONE,** Oxon
Served from Charlbury.
M: *Sun 9.30am. (In Youth Hall).*

■ **ERDINGTON**
See Birmingham, (20, 42, 43)

■ **EVESHAM,** Worcs A
† **St Mary and St Egwin**
(1887; 1912; cons 18 Sept 1913)
High Street, Evesham, Worcs WR11 4EJ
Tel: 01386-442468
Rev Christopher Draycott.
M: *Sun 8am, 10am, 6.30pm. Hds 7.30am, 10am, 7pm.*

■ **EYNSHAM,** Oxon
† **St Peter** (1929; 1940; 1986)
Abbey Street, Eynsham, Oxon OX29 1HR
Tel: 01865-881613
E-mail: meflatman@brookes.ac.uk
Rev Martin Flatman.
Deacon: **Rev Christopher Blackman**
M: *Sat 1st M of Sun 7.30pm. Sun 10am. Hds 9.30am, 7.30pm.*

■ **FEATHERSTONE,** Staffs
Church of the Holy Family
HM Prison. Served from Wolverhampton (8).
M: *Sat 1st M of Sun 10am.*

■ **FECKENHAM,** Worcs
SS John Fisher and Thomas More (1935)
High Street. Served from Redditch.
M: *Sun 10.15am.*

■ **FEGG HAYES**
See Stoke (9).

■ **FENTON.**
See Stoke (6).

■ **FOUR OAKS**
See Sutton Coldfield (4).

■ **GLASCOTE HEATH**
Sacred Heart
Silver Link Road, Glascote Heath B77 2EA
Served from Tamworth.
M: *Sun 9am, 12noon. Hds 7pm.*

■ **GNOSALL,** Staffs
Served from Stafford (1).
Deacon: **Rev Louis Livesey.**
M: *Sun 8.45am (in St Laurence Anglican Parish Church).*

■ **GOLDENHILL**
See Stoke (13).

■ **GORING-ON-THAMES,** Reading
† **Our Lady and St John** (1897; 1938)
Ferry Lane, Goring-on-Thames, Reading RG8 9DX
Rev Thomas E Williams.
Tel: 01491-872181
Also in parish: **Rev Jacob Lewis**, The Beeches, Compton, Berks RG20 6RE
Tel: 01635-578714
M: *Sat 1st M of Sun 6pm. Sun 10am. Hds 6pm.*

■ **GREAT BARR,** Birmingham [A]
† **The Holy Name of Jesus**
(1935; 1938; cons 7 Sept 1965)
Birmingham Road, Great Barr, Birmingham **Tel:** 0121-357 1351
Fax: 0121-357 2863
E-mail: info@holyname.org.uk
Rev Colin Fortune
Deacon: **Rev Terence Charles.**
- ***Priests of the Sacred Heart (of Betharram) (SCJ);* Rev Anton Madej SCJ, Br Liam Finucane.** 9 Cross Lane, Birmingham B43 6LN
  M: *Sat 1st M of Sun 12.30pm (at St Mark's School). Sun 8.30am, 10.30am, 5.30pm. Hds, as announced.*
- ***Marist Sisters,*** 26 Cross Lane, Birmingham B43 6LN
  Tel: 0121-357 6341

■ **GREAT HAYWOOD,** Stafford
† **St John the Baptist** (1845, 1983)
Presbytery, Main Road, Great Haywood, Stafford ST18 0SW **Tel:** 01889-881324
Rev Michael Doyle.
M: *Sat 1st M of Sun 6pm. Sun 9.30am. Hds 10am, 7.30pm.*

■ **GREAT WYRLEY AND CHESLYN HAY**
St Thomas More
Huthill Lane. Served from Cannock.
M: *As announced.*

■ **HADZOR,** Droitwich [A]
Hereford and Worcs
† **SS Richard and Hubert** (1878)
Hadzor Lane, WR9 7DS
Served from Redditch.
M: *Sat 1st M of Sun 5pm.*
- ***Chez Nous: House of Prayer & Hospitality.* Revv Denis Labartette IC, John Moss IC. Tel:** 01905-772790
  E-mail: cheznous@rosmini.org

■ **HALESOWEN,** West Midlands
† **Our Lady and St Kenelm** (1927; 1962)
22 Cobham Road, Halesowen, W. Midlands B63 3JZ **Tel:** 0121-602 1972
Rev Bruce M Dutson.
M: *Sat 1st M of Sun 6.30pm. Sun 10am. Hds 9.15am, 7.30pm.*

■ **HAMPTON-ON-THE-HILL,** Warks
† **St Charles Borromeo** (1808; 1819)
Presbytery, Hampton-on-the-Hill, Warwick CV35 8QR **Tel:** 01926-492263
Rev Joseph Quigley.
M: *Sun 9.30am, 11am. Hds 10am, 7.30am.*

■ **HANDSWORTH**
See Birmingham (24, 28 and 29).

■ **HANLEY**
See Stoke-on-Trent (1, 10).

■ **HARBORNE**
See Birmingham (19).

■ **HARTLEBURY,** Worcs
See Harvington.

■ **HARVINGTON,** Kidderminster, Worcs [A]
† **St Mary** (circa 1580; 1825)
Priest's House, Harvington Hall Lane, Harvington, Kidderminster DY10 4LR
Tel: 01562-777319
E-mail: dh.stmarys@tiscali.co.uk
Rev David Anthony Higham.
M: *Sun 8.30am, 10.30am. Hds 8am, 7pm, (Corpus Christi 6pm).*
- ***Harvington Hall,*** DY10 4LR Centre of Pilgrimage to the English Martyrs.
  Tel: 01562-777846 **Fax:** 01562-777190

■ **HAUNTON,** Nr Tamworth, Staffs [A]
† **SS Michael and James** (1845; 1902; cons 1907)
Haunton, Nr Tamworth, Staffs B79 9HL
Tel: 01827-373241 **Fax:** 01827-373628

ARCHDIOCESE OF BIRMINGHAM

E-mail: sean@home4u83.freeserve.co.uk
Website: measevalley.org.uk
Rev Sean Turley.
M: *Sat 1st M of Sun 6.30pm. Sun 10.30am. Hds 10.30am, 7.30pm.*

- ***Sisters of St Joseph of Lyon,*** St Joseph's Convent, Haunton Hall B79 9HW **Tel:** 01827-373453

■ **HEDNESFORD,** Staffs
† **Our Lady of Lourdes** (1898; 1934)
Uxbridge Street, Hednesford, Staffs WS12 5DB **Tel:** 01543-422576
Fax: 01543-871022 **E-mail:** frhogan@ourladyhednesford.com
Website: www.ourladyhednesford.com
Rev Philip Newbold.
M: *Sun 9.30am, 5.30pm. Hds 8am, 7pm.*

■ **HENLEY-IN-ARDEN,** Warks
St Mary's (1961)
School Chapel, Arden Road
Served from Wootton Wawen.
M: *Sat 1st M of Sun 5.30pm. (in St Nicholas' Anglican Church, Beaudesert Lane). Hds 9.15am (St Mary's School, Arden Road).*

■ **HENLEY-ON-THAMES,** Oxon
† **The Sacred Heart**
(1884; 1936; cons 24 June 1949)
31 Vicarage Road, Henley-on-Thames, Oxon RG9 1HT
Tel: 01491-573258 **Fax:** 01491-576885
Website: www.sacredhearthenley.co.uk
Rev Anthony Wilcox.
E-mail: anthony.wilcox@ukonline.co.uk
M: *Sat 1st M of Sun 6pm. Sun 8.30am, 10.30am. Hds (eve 7pm), 9.30am, 7pm.*

■ **HETHE WITH ADDERBURY**
† **Holy Trinity** (1832)
Hethe, Bicester, Oxon OX6 9AW
Tel: 01869-277396
Rev John Burns.
M: *Sun 8.30am (at Adderbury) 10am, (at Hethe). Hds (eve 7pm at Adderbury), 10am, 7.30pm, (at Hethe).*

■ **HILLMORTON.**
See Rugby (3).

■ **ILMINGTON,** Shipston-on-Stour, Warks.
† **St Philip, Apostle** (1935)
Crabmill Lane, Ilmington, Shipston-on-Stour, CV36 4LE **Tel:** 01608-682241
Served from Brailes
Rev Anthony Sims (retired). Grump Street, Ilmington CV36 4LE
M: *Sat 1st M of Sun 6.30pm. Hds, 9pm.*

■ **KEELE,** Newcastle, Staffs
University of Keele. The Cottage, 12 The Village, ST5 5AR **Tel:** 01782-628352 or (University) 01782-621111 (Ext 7162)
Chaplains: **Rev Stephen Cochrane, Mr Ray Bayliss**.
M: *Sun 12noon.*

■ **KENILWORTH,** Warks
1. † **St Augustine of England**
(1842; 1852; cons 1 Sept 1904)
Beehive Hill, Kenilworth, Warks.
Tel: 01926-852943
In Residence: **Rev Eamon Clarke** (Retired).
Served from St Francis, Kenilworth (2).
M: *Sun 8am.*

2. † **St Francis of Assisi** (1964, 1993)
110 Warwick Road, Kenilworth, Warks CV8 1HL **Tel:** 01926-55224
Rev Kevin J. Hooper.
M: *Sat 1st M of Sun 6.30pm. Sun 9.30am, 11.15pm. Hds 9.30am, 7.30pm.*

■ **KIDDERMINSTER,** Worcs
1. † **St Ambrose**
(1831; 1856; cons 5 Aug 1902)
Birmingham Road, Kidderminster, Worcs DY10 2BY **Tel:** 01562-822839
Revv Douglas Lamb, Derek Edwards.
Deacons: **Revv Peter Mason, Peter Hesketh, Thomas Ashcroft**.
M: *Sat 1st M of Sun 6.30pm. Sun 10.30am. Hds 9.30am.*

2. † **Our Lady and St Pius X** (1956; 1971)
Canterbury Road.
Served from Kidderminster (1).
M: *Sun 9am. Hds 7.30pm.*

3. † **Our Lady of Ostra Brama, Polish Church** (1963)
"Nasz Dom", 50 Pitt Street, Kidderminster DY10 2UN **Tel:** 01562-745914
Rev Jan Gora
M: *Sun 10am. Hds 10am.*

■ **KIDLINGTON,** Oxon
† **St Thomas More** (1934; 1968; cons 1976)
142 Oxford Road, Kidlington, Oxon OX5 1DZ
Tel: 01865-377093 **E-mail:** parish@stthomandsthugh.free-online.co.uk
Rev Christopher Greaney.
M: *Sat 1st M of Sun 6pm. Sun 8.15am, 11am. Hds 9.15am, 7.30pm.*

■ **KIDSGROVE,** Stoke-on-Trent
† **St John the Evangelist** (1891; 1892)
The Avenue, Kidsgrove, Stoke-on-Trent ST7 1AE **Tel:** 01782-782912
Rev David Newell.
M: *Sat 1st M of Sun 6.30pm. Sun 9am. Hds (eve 7pm), 1pm.*

- ***Daughters of Divine Love,*** The Avenue, Kidsgrove, Staffs ST7 1AT **Tel:** 01782-782912

■ **KINETON,** Warks
† **St Francis of Assisi** (1971, 1976)
Southam Street, Kineton, Warwicks.
Tel: 01926-640275
E-mail: david@saint-francis.freeserve.co.uk
Website: www.stfrancis-kineton.co.uk
Rev David P Condron. The Presbytery, Anvil House, Southam Street, CV35 0LL
Deacon: **Rev Ralph Watkins**.
M: *Sat 1st M of Sun 5pm (in St Peter's Anglican Church, Wellesbourne). Sun 10am (St Francis), 11am (St Joseph's, Avon Dassett). Hds Kineton, 10am, 7.30pm.*

■ **KINGSHURST,** Birmingham
† **SS Anthony and John the Baptist** (1964)
Oakthorpe Drive, Kingshurst, Birmingham B37 6HY **Tel/Fax:** 0121-770 3023
Rev Stephen Goodman
Deacon: **Rev Stuart Hill.**
M: *Sat 1st M of Sun 6pm (St John's Water Orton). Sun 9.30am, 6pm (St Anthony's, Kingshurst), 11pm (St John the Baptist Church, Arran Way). Hds 9.30am, 7.30pm (St Anthony's), 11pm (St John the Baptist's).*
• ***Sisters of Christian Instruction,*** St Gildas Convent, 422 Chester Road, B36 0LF **Tel:** 0121-770 3518

■ **KINGSTANDING**
See Birmingham (4).

■ **KINGSWINFORD,** W. Midlands
† **Our Lady of Lourdes** (1943; 1951; 1983)
Summerhill, Kingswinford, W Midlands. DY6 9JG **Tel:** 01384-274520
Rev James Ward.
Deacon: **Rev John Brindley.**
M: *Sat 1st M of Sun 5.30pm. Sun 10.30am. Hds 9.30am, 7.30pm.*

■ **KNUTTON,** Staffs
Our Lady of Sorrows (1953)
Cotswold Avenue, Knutton, Staffs ST5 6HP
Served from Wolstanton.
M: *Sun 9am.*

■ **LEAMINGTON SPA,** Warks
† **St Peter** (1822; 1864; cons 21 Aug 1864)
Dormer Place, Leamington Spa, Warks CV32 5AA **Tel:** 01926-423824
Revv John Cross, Christopher Miller.
M: *Sat 1st M of Sun 6.30pm. Sun 9am, 11am, 5.30pm. Hds 9.30am, 12.30pm, 7.30pm.*

■ **LEEK,** Staffs
† **St Mary** (1828; 1887)
Compton, Leek, Staffs ST13 5NH
Tel/Fax: 01538-382385
E-mail: father@stmaryleek.org.uk
Rev Michael Bonaccorsi.
M: *Sat 1st M of Sun 6pm; Sun 10am. Hds 9am, 7pm.*

■ **LICHFIELD,** Staffs
1. † **Holy Cross** (1801; 1803)
St John Street, Lichfield, Staffs WS14 9DX
Tel: 01543-263234
Mgr Michael Sharkey, Rev Bernard Maddox.
M: *Sun 8.30am. Hds 8am.*

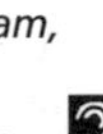

2. **SS Peter and Paul** (1967)
The Dimbles. Served from Lichfield (1).
M: *Sat 1st M of Sun 6pm. Sun 11am. Hds 7.30pm.*

■ **LILLINGTON,** Warks
† **Our Lady** (1958; 1963)
170 Valley Road, Lillington, Warwicks CV32 8SJ **Tel:** 01926-423552
Rev Laurence Crowe.
M: *Sat 1st M of Sun 6pm. Sun 8am, 10am. Hds 9am.*

■ **LITTLE MALVERN,** Malvern, Worcs
† **St Wulstan** (1862)
Priest's House, Ledbury Road, Little Malvern WR14 4JL
Tel: 01684-574658
Dom Christopher Calascione OSB.
M: *Sat 1st M of Sun 5pm. Sun 10.30am. Hds 7pm.*

■ **LITTLEMORE**
See Oxford (7).

■ **LONGTON**
See Stoke-on-Trent (11).

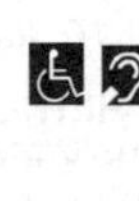

■ **LOWER GORNAL**
Dudley, West Midlands.
† **St Peter and the English Martyrs** (1863; 1928; 1967)
Temple Street, Lower Gornal, Dudley, W Midlands DY3 2PE **Tel:** 01384-252254
Rev David J Lloyd.
M: *Sun 9am, 6.30pm. Hds 9.30am, 7.30pm.*

■ **MALVERN,** Worcs
† **St Joseph** (1866; 1876)
Newtown Road, Malvern, Worcs.
Tel: 01684-574250
E-mail: rc@stjosephsmalvern.fsnet.co.uk
Rev Mgr Patrick Kilgarriff. 125 Newtown Road, WR14 1PF. *Deacon:* **Rev Louis Kelly.**
M: *Sat 1st M of Sun 6pm. Sun 9am, 10.30am. Hds 9am, 10.30am, 7.30pm.*

■ **MARCHINGTON,** Uttoxeter, Staffs
St Thomas a Becket
(1939; 1956; cons 14 Aug 1965)
Presbytery, Hall Road, Marchington, Uttoxeter, Staffs ST14 8LG

ARCHDIOCESE OF BIRMINGHAM

Tel: 01283-820323
Rev Vincent Royles
Tel: 01283-820323
M: *Sun 10.30am. Hds 6.30pm.*

■ **MARYVALE**
Institute of Further and Higher Education.
See Birmingham (10).

■ **MEIR**
See Stoke-on-Trent, (8).

■ **MONKS KIRBY,** Rugby, Warks
St Joseph's (1869. New Church 1992)
Brockhurst Lane, Monks Kirby, Rugby, Warks CV23 0RA **Tel:** 01788-832471
Served from Rugby (3)
M: *Sun 9.15am. Hds 7.30pm.*

■ **NEW INVENTION,** W. Midlands
St Edmund Gennings
Forest Gate, New Invention, W. Midlands.
Served from Willenhall.
M: *Sun 9am. Hds 7.30pm,*

■ **NEWCASTLE-UNDER-LYME.**
† Holy Trinity
(1825; 1834; cons 3 Sept 1889)
London Road, Newcastle-under-Lyme, Staffs ST5 1LQ **Tel:** 01782-616483
Revv Philip Griffin, Eric Kemball.
Deacon: **Rev Neil Adlington.**
M: *Sat 1st M of Sun 5.15pm. Sun 9.30am, 11.45am, 5.15pm. Hds (eve 7.30pm). 10am, 7.30pm.*
- ***Sisters of Mercy,*** St Bernard's Convent, London Road, ST5 1LH **Tel:** 01782-614459

■ **NUNEATON,** Warks
1. **† Our Lady of the Angels** (1829; 1936)
Coton Road, Nuneaton CV11 5UA
Tel: 02476-382139
E-mail: olannuneaton@aol.com
Rev Philip Harrop; *Deacons:* **Revv Michael Skidmore, Trevor Smith.**
M: *Sat 1st M of Sun 6pm. Sun 9.30am, 11am. Hds 9.30am, 8pm.*
- ***Presentation Sisters,*** 129 Manor Court Road, Nuneaton. CV11 5HG **Tel:** 024-7635 0615

2. **† St Anne** (1949, 2000)
93 Camp Hill Road, Nuneaton CV10 0JP
Tel: 024-7639 2365
Rev Stephen Day.
M: *Sat 1st M of Sun 5pm. Sun 9am. Hds 10am, 7pm.*

■ **OLDBURY,**
Warley, West Midlands
† St Francis Xavier (1865; 1965)
10 Simpson Street, Oldbury, Warley, W. Midlands B69 4AL **Tel:** 0121-559 1677
Served from Blackheath.
M: *Sun 11am. Hds 11am.*
- ***Daughters of St Francis de Sales,*** 10 Simpson Street, Oldbury, Warley, W. Midlands B69 4AL **Tel:** 0121-552 9528

■ **OLTON,** Solihull, West Midlands A
1. **† The Holy Ghost and Mary Immaculate**
(1889; 1929, 1990)
St Bernard's Road, Olton, Solihull, W Midlands B92 7BL
Tel: 0121-706 0505 **Fax:** 0121-706 8105
- ***Priests of the Sacred Heart (Betharram) (SCJ):*** **Revv Edward W Simpson** (*Parish Priest*), ***Austin Hughes. Bros Liam Finucane, Gerard Sutherland.***
M: *Sun 9am, 11am, 6pm. Hds 7am, 10.15am, 7.30pm.*
- ***Servite Sisters,*** Convent of Our Lady of Compassion, 89 St Bernard's Road, B92 7DG **Tel:** 0121-706 1912

■ **OSCOTT**
See Birmingham (2).

■ **OULTON,** Stone, Staffs
St Mary's Abbey (1853; cons 24 Nov 1854)
Kibblestone Road, Oulton, Stone, Staffs ST15 8UP
Rev David Charlesworth.
- ***Benedictine Nuns*** **Tel:** 01785-812049
M: *Sun 11am. Hds 10am.*

■ **OXFORD**
1. **† The Oxford Oratory, (Parish of St Aloysius)**
(1793; 1875)
25 Woodstock Road, Oxford OX2 6HA
Tel: 01865-315800 **Fax:** 01865-310470
E-mail: parish@oxfordoratory.org.uk
Website: www.oxford.oratory.org.uk
- ***Oratorians (Cong Orat):*** **Very Rev Provost Robert Byrne, Revv Dominic Jacob, Richard Duffield, Jerome Bertram, Daniel Seward** *(parish priest),* **Anton Webb, Joseph Welch, Br Nicholas Edmonds-Smith.**
M: *Sat 1st M of Sun 6.30pm. Sun 9.30am, 11am (Sung Latin), 6.30pm. Hds (vigil 6pm), 7.30am, 10am, 6pm.*
- ***Benedictines (OSB):*** St Benet's Hall, 38 St Giles, Oxford OX1 3LN (1897). House of Studies (Ampleforth Abbey). **Tel/Fax:** 01865-280556 **Rev Leo Chamberlain** MA, OSB (*Master*), **Very Rev Adrian Convery** MA, OSB (*Chaplain*).
- ***Dominicans (OP):*** Blackfriars, Priory of the Holy Spirit, 64 St Giles, Oxford OX1 3LY. House of Studies. (First Founded 1221; restored 1921; cons 20 May 1929). Community **Tel:** 01865-278400 **Fax:** 01865-278403. **Revv Denis Minns** (*Prior*), **Kevin Lloyd, Felix Watts, Vincent Cook, Piers Linley, Timothy**

Radcliffe, David Sanders, Vivian Boland, Brian Davies, Richard Finn (*Regent*), **Mark Edney, Simon Gaine**.

- ***Jesuits (SJ):*** Campion Hall (1896), Brewer Street, Oxford OX1 1QS **Tel:** 01865-286100 **Fax:** 01865-286148 **Revv Ian Brayley** 286105; **Charles Rodger** 286107; **Clarence Gallagher** 286115; **William Hewett** 286118; **Nicholas King** 286119; **Richard Randolph** 286129. **John Moffatt, Philip Endean, Peter L'Estrange.**
- **Winton** (Pastoral care entrusted to the Prelature of Opus Dei), 4 Canterbury Road OX2 6LU **Tel:** 01865-513410
- ***Society of the Holy Child Jesus,*** The Cherwell Centre, 14/16 Norham Gardens, OX2 6QB **Tel:** 01865-552106
- ***Society of the Sacred Heart,*** 11 Norham Gdns, OX2 6PS **Tel:** 01865-554906
- ***Sisters of Notre Dame,*** 145-147 Woodstock Road, OX2 7LZ **Tel:** 01865-557987
- ***Dominican Sisters,*** 9/10 Tackley Place OX2 6RR **Tel:** 01865-513051

2. † Corpus Christi (1935; 1937,1983)
Margaret Road, Headington, Oxford.
Tel: 01865-762433, **Fax:** 01865-742494.
Also serves Wheatley.
Revv John Baggley, Anthony de Vere. 88 Wharton Road, Headington Oxford OX3 8AJ *Deacon:* **Rev Michael Walsh.**
M: *Sun 9am, 11am, 6.30pm. Hds 9.15am, 7.30pm.*

- ***Sisters of the Sacred Heart,*** 85 Old High Street, Headington, OX3 9HT **Tel:** 01865-761389

3. † Greyfriars

- ***St Edmund of Abingdon and St Frideswide*** (1793; 1911; 1931) Iffley Road, Oxford OX4 1SB **Tel:** 01865-243694 (Parish & University Hall); **Tel:** 01865-248972/728519 (Students) **Fax:** 01865-727027
- ***Capuchin Franciscans (OFMCap);*** **Rev Bros Charles Serignat** (*Guardian*), **Ambrose May** (*Parish Priest*), **Thomas More Mann, Anthony McDowell, Martin Mikuskiewicz, Martin Sanderson, Paul Coleman.**
  M: *Sat 1st M of Sun 6.30pm. Sun 9am, 11am, 5.30pm. Hds 7.30am, 10am, 7.30pm.*
- ***Centre for Travelling Mission to the Travelling People***, 18 Leopold Street, OX4 1PS **Tel:** 01865-240325 *Director:* **Sr Margaret Begley.**

4. † St Anthony of Padua
(1956; 1960, 2000)
115 Headley Way, Oxford OX3 7SS
Tel: 01865-762964
E-mail: stanthonyofpaduaoxford@yahoo.co.uk
Rev Aldo Tapparo.
M: *Sat 1st M of Sun 6.30pm. Sun 10am. Hds 9.30am, 7pm.*

- ***Religious of the Assumption,*** St Catherine's, 2 Harberton Mead, OX3 0DB **Tel:** 01865-764293 (Convent), 763796 (Students). Residence for students attending Oxford College of Technology.

5. † Our Lady Help of Christians
(1906; 1962, 1967)
Hollow Way, Cowley, Oxford OX4 2ND
Tel: 01865-770910
E-mail: Kier65000@aol.com

- ***Salesians (SDB):*** **Revv Kieran Patrick Anderson** (*Parish Priest*), **John Ashton.**
  M: *Sat 1st M of Sun 5.30pm. Sun 10am. Hds 7pm.*
- ***Salesian Sisters of St John Bosco (FMA):*** Elmthorpe, Oxford Road, Cowley, OX4 2LF **Tel:** 01865-775349

6. † SS. Gregory and Augustine (1912)
322 Woodstock Road, Oxford OX2 7NS
Tel: 01865-515138
Rev John Saward.
M: *Sat 1st M of Sun 6.30pm. Sun 8am, 10.30pm. Hds (eve 6pm), 7.30am, 10am.*

- ***De La Salle Brothers.*** Great Britain Provincialate **Tel:** 01865-311332 140 Banbury Road, Oxford OX2 7BP *Provincial:* **Br Sean Sellors**; *Auxiliary Provincial:* **Br Owen Smith**; *Director:* **Br Dominic Green.** Second Community Residence: 130 Banbury Road, **Tel:** 01865-556874

7. † Blessed Dominic Barberi
(1960; 1968, 1993)
The Barberi Rectory, 2 St Mary's Close, Littlemore, Oxford OX4 4PJ
Tel/Fax: 01865-778454 Office
Tel: 01865-775591
Revv John Hancock; John Nightingale, 20 Beaumont Buildings, Oxford OX1 2LL
Tel: 01865-553536
M: *Sat 1st M of Sun 6pm. Sun 11am. Hds 9am, 7.30pm.*

- ***Sisters of the Spiritual Family The Work,*** The Work, International Centre of Newman Friends, Ambrose Cottage, 9 College Lane, Littlemore, Oxford OX4 4LQ **Tel:** 01865-779743 **Fax:** 01865-773397 **E-mail:** thework@uk2.net **Website:** www.thework-fso.org
- ***Society of the Holy Child Jesus,*** 89 Rose Hill, Oxford OX4 4HT **Tel:** 01865-774561

8. University Catholic Chaplaincy
(for members of University only)
The Old Palace, St Aldate's, Oxford OX1 1RD **Tel:** 01865-276993
Chaplains: **Revv John Moffatt SJ, Roger Dawson SJ**.
Assistant Chaplain: **Sr Nora Coughlan**.
M: *(In term); Sun 9am, 11am, 5.45pm. Hds 7.45am, 12.15pm, 6pm. (Times out of term, as announced).*

A

9. Oxford Brookes University
Chaplain: **Rev Martin Flatman**, 62 London Road, Headington, Oxford OX3 7PD
Tel: 01865-750463
Assistant: **Sr Veronica Ann**, St Catherine's, 2 Harberton Mead, Oxford OX3 0BD
Tel: 01865-764293
M: *(in term) Sun 6pm.*

10. Sacred Heart (1955)
Tel: 01865-779658
Presbytery, Sawpit Road, Blackbird Leys, OX4 5BD
Rev David Hartley.
M: *Sun 9.30am, 6pm. Hds 9am, 7pm.*
(See also Diocese of Portsmouth).

■ **PACKMOOR,** Stoke-on-Trent
See Stoke-on-Trent (15).

■ **PENKRIDGE,** Staffs
Served from Brewood.
In St Michael's Anglican Church.
M: *Sun 9am. Hds 6.30am.*

■ **PERRY BARR**
See Birmingham (42).

■ **PERSHORE,** Worcs
† Holy Redeemer St Wulstan and St Eadburga (1913; 1959)
14 Priest Lane, Pershore, Worcs WR10 1EB
Tel: 01386-552737
Rev John Walsh.
Deacon: **Rev James Gilligan**.
M: *Sat 1st M of Sun 6.30pm. Sun 9.30am. Hds 9.15am, 7.30pm.*

■ **PRINCETHORPE,** Rugby, Warks
† Our Lady of the Angels
(1835; 1837; cons 17 Oct 1843)
Served from Wappenbury.
M: *Sun 10am. Hds As Announced.*
- ***Missionaries of the Sacred Heart (MSC):*** Princethorpe College, Leamington Road, CV23 9PX (Chapel cons 8 May 1901).
Tel: 01926-634200 **Fax:** 01926-633365
Revv Carl Tranter, Alan J Whelan, Mr John Shinkwin (*Headmaster*).

■ **QUINTON,** West Midlands
Our Lady of Fatima (1952)

Higgins Lane, Quinton, B32 1LL
Tel: 0121-422 4865 **Fax:** 0121-422 9552
Rev Seamus Hetherton, The Presbytery, 23 Upper Meadow Road, Quinton B32 1NT
M: *Sat 1st M of Sun 6pm. Sun 8.30am, 10.30am, 12noon. Hds 10am, 7pm.*
- ***Cross and Passion Sisters,*** 39 Higgins Lane, Birmingham. B32 1LL
Tel: 0121-422 7811

■ **REDDITCH,** Worcs
1. † Our Lady of Mount Carmel (1834)
Beoley Road West, Redditch, Worcs B98 8LT
Tel: 01527-63096
Fax: 01527-591966
E-mail: office@mtcarmel.fsnet.co.uk
Revv Anthony Joyce, Paul Smith, Joseph Nguyen Van Tien.
Deacon: **Rev Desmond Chilton**.
M: *Sat 1st M of Sun 5pm. Sun 8.30am, 9.45am (Pol), 11am, 6pm. Hds (eve 7pm), 9.30am 12.30pm, 7pm, (11am & 4pm Polish).*
- ***Presentation Sisters,*** 13 Shakespeare Avenue, Lodge Park, Redditch.
Tel: 01527-525820 Also at: 27 Bushley Close, Woodrow, Redditch
Tel: 01527-501565

2. St Benedict (1957)
Rowan Road, Batchley.
Served from Redditch (1).
M: *Sun 9am.*

3. Woodrow
Served from Redditch (1).
St Thomas More Parish Centre, Woodrow.
M: *Sun 11.30am.*

4. St Gregory's, Winyates
M: *Sat 1st M of Sun 6pm.*

■ **REDNAL**
See Birmingham (13).

■ **RUGBY**
1. † The Sacred Heart (1953, 1959, 1998)
Alwyn Road, Bilton.
Tel/ Fax: 01788-813263
17 Lime Tree Avenue, Bilton CV22 7QT
Rev PW (Ted) Mullen IC, 22 Dalkeith Avenue, Bilton CV22 7NH **Tel:** 01788-812540
E-mail: sacredatbilton@tiscali.co.uk
Deacon: **Rev John Burrows**.
M: *Sat 1st M of Sun 6pm. Sun 9.30am. Hds 9.30am, 7pm.*

2. † St Marie
(1847; 1872; cons 8 Sept 1882)
Dunchurch Road, Rugby.
Tel: 01788-542703
- ***Institute of Charity (IC):*** **Revv Philip Sainter** (*Parish Priest*), **Anthony Baxter, Anthony Primavesi, Paul Nellculam,**

John Buckner. Presbytery, Oak Street, CV22 5EL
M: *Sat 1st M of Sun 6pm. Sun 9am, 11am (Sung), 12.30pm (Pol), 6pm. Hds (eve 7pm). 10am, 7pm.*
- ***Sisters of Providence (Rosminians),*** St Marie's Convent, Oak Street, CV22 5EL **Tel:** 01788-543604

3. **† English Martyrs** (1955; 1966)
30 High Street, Hillmorton, CV21 4EE (near Canal Marina).
Tel: 01788-565016
Rev Malcolm Glaze.
M: *Sat 1st M of Sun 6pm. Sun 11am. Hds (eve 7pm), 9.15am.*

■ RUGELEY, Staffs
† SS Joseph and Etheldreda
(1850; 1851; cons 12 June 1951)
Lichfield Street, Rugeley, Staffs.
Tel/Fax: 01889-582586
E-mail: frpeterstonier@stjosephsrugeley.co.uk
Rev Peter Stonier, 34 Heron Street, WS15 2DZ
Deacons: **Revv Peter Kilgallon, Jim Rowe**
M: *Sat 1st M of Sun 7pm. Sun 11am, 6.30pm. Hds as announced.*

■ SALTLEY
See Birmingham (16).

■ SEDGLEY, Dudley
† St Chad and All Saints
(1786; 1823; cons 2 Sept 1891)
High Holborn, Sedgley, Dudley, W. Midlands.
Tel: 01902-882215
Rev Joseph Narikuzhi. 2 Catholic Lane, Dudley DY3 3UE
M: *Sun 10.30am (2nd & 4th Sun Sung Latin), 6.30pm. Hds 9.30am, 7.30pm.*

■ SELLY PARK
See Birmingham (26).

■ SHELDON
See Birmingham (44).

■ SHELFIELD, Walsall
† St Francis of Assisi (1890; 1932)
Mill Road, Shelfield, Walsall WS4 1RH
Tel/Fax: 01922-682542
Rev Thomas Walton.
M: *Sat 1st M of Sun 7pm. Sun 11am. Hds 11am, 7pm.*

■ SHIPSTON-ON-STOUR, Warks
Our Lady and St Michael
Darlingscote Road, Shipston-on-Stour
Served from Brailes.
M: *Sun 10am. Hds 7.30pm.*

■ SHIRLEY, Solihull
† Our Lady of the Wayside (1934; 1937, 1967)
566 Stratford Road, Shirley, Solihull B90 4AY
Tel: 0121-744 1967 **Fax:** 0121-733 6998
E-mail: gerard@olwayside.fsnet.co.uk
Rev Gerard Murray. *Deacon:* **Rev Sean Loone**. Also in residence: **Mgr Louis McRaye**.
M: *Sun 9am, 11am, 5.15pm. Hds 7am, 11am, 8pm.*
- ***Sisters of Charity of St Paul,*** St Paul's, 35 Hollington Way, Monks Path, Solihull, B90 4YD **Tel:** 0121-704 1282

■ SHOTTERY, Stratford-upon-Avon
Our Lady of Peace & Blessed Robert Dibdale
(1973)
Church Lane. Served from Stratford-upon-Avon.
M: *Sun 9.30am. Hds Vigil 7pm.*

■ SILVERDALE, Staffs
† Sacred Heart (1891; 1915; 1925)
1 High Street, Silverdale, Staffs ST5 6NG
Served from Newcastle-under-Lyme.
Deacon in residence: **Rev Neil Adlington**.
M: *Sun 10.30am. Hds as announced.*

■ SMALL HEATH
See Birmingham (5).

■ SMETHWICK, West Midlands
† St Philip (1862; 1893; cons 25 June 1936)
Messenger Road, Smethwick, W. Midlands B66 3DU
Tel/Fax: 0121-558 1065
Revv Uchenna Njoku, Ugochukwu Ikwuka CSSp
M: *Sat 1st M of Sun 5pm. Sun 10am.*
- ***Sisters of the Infant Jesus,*** 28 Bush Avenue, Smethwick B66 3LD **Tel:** 0121-565-0369

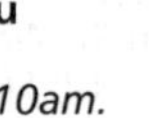

■ SOLIHULL, West Midlands
† St Augustine of England
(1760; 1839; cons 12 July 1932)
Station Road, Solihull, W. Midlands B91 3TG
Tel/Fax: 0121-705 0228
E-mail: admin@staugustinesolihull.org.uk
Website: staugustinesolihull.org.uk
Revv Dominic Kavanagh, Andrew McCann. Also in residence: **Rev Sean McTernan** (retired), The Presbytery, 1 Herbert Road, Solihull B91 3QE
Deacon: **Rev Ernest Titchmarsh**.
M: *Sat 1st M of Sun 12.30pm, 6pm. Sun 9am, 11am. Hds 12noon, 7.30pm.*

■ SONNING COMMON, Reading
† St Michael (1947; 1963)
18 Peppard Road, Sonning Common, Reading RG4 9SU **Tel:** 0118-972 3418
Rev Chris Bester.
Deacon: **Rev Dr Francis Andrews**.
M: *Sat 1st M of Sun 5.30pm. Sun 9am (St Martin's School), 10.30am. Hds 7pm.*

■ **SOUTHAM,** Warks
† Our Lady and St Wulstan
(1876; 1925; cons 14 May 1956)
Wood Street, Southam, Leamington Spa, Warwicks CV33 0PP **Tel:** 01926-812351
Rev John Laybourn.
Deacon: **Rev Walter Terence Hum.**
M: *Sat 1st M of Sun 5.30pm. Sun 10am. Hds 9.15am, 7.30pm.*
- ***Sisters of the Poor Child Jesus,*** Our Lady's Convent, Wood Street CV47 1PP **Tel:** 01926-8112338 Provincial Administration: 1 The Cloisters, Daventry Road, Southam CV47 1FE **Tel/Fax:** 01926-811903 Old House Retreat: **Tel/Fax:** 01926-815765

■ **SPARKHILL.**
See Birmingham (21).

■ **SPETCHLEY PARK,** Worcs
† St John the Baptist (1681; 1921)
Spetchley Park, Worcester.
Served from Worcester (1),
M: *Sat 1st Mass Sun 4.30pm. Hds 6pm.*

■ **STAFFORD**
1 † St Austin (1813; 1862; cons 26 July 1911)
82 Wolverhampton Road, Stafford ST17 4AW **Tel\Fax:** 01785-223553
E-mail: staustinrc@aol.com
Revv Michael Neylon, Robert Devaney, Brian Whatmore 26 Knightley Way, Gnosall, Stafford ST20 0HX
Tel: 01786-823726
Deacon: **Revv David McCarroll, Louis Livesey**
M: *Sat 1st M of Sun 5.20pm. Sun 10.30am, 6pm. Hds (eve 7.30pm). 10am, 7.30pm.*
- ***Sisters of St Joseph (Cluny),*** St Joseph's Convent, Lichfield Road, ST17 4LG **Tel:** 01785-251577 *Chaplain:* **Rev Petroc Howell. Tel:** 01785-225679

2. † St Patrick
(1895; 1930; 1953; cons 3 Sept 1966)
48 Sandon Road, Stafford ST16 3HF
Tel: 01785-252393
E-mail: stpatrick.stafford@virgin.net
Website: www.stpatrickstafford.co.uk
Rev Walter T Bance.
M: *Sat 1st M of Sun 5.30pm. Sun 9.30am. Hds 9am, 7.30pm.*

3. † St Anne (1964)
Lynton Avenue, Weeping Cross, Baswich, ST17 0EA **Tel:** 01785-661012
E-mail: father21pat@yahoo.com
Rev Patrick Broun.
M: *Sat 1st M of Sun 6pm. Sun 10am, 5.30pm. Hds (eve 7pm), 9.10am, 7pm.*

■ **STANBROOK,** Worcs
St Mary's Abbey (Benedictine nuns)
(1838; cons 6 Sept 1871)
Stanbrook, Callow End, Worcester WR2 4TD
Tel: 01905-830209
E-mail: secretary@stanbrookabbey.org.uk
M: *Sun 8.45am. Hds 8.45am.*

■ **STECHFORD**
See Birmingham (4).

■ **STOKE-ON-TRENT**
1. † Sacred Heart (1860; 1891; cons 13 July 1911)
Jasper Street, Hanley, Stoke-on-Trent
Tel: 01782-215217 **Fax:** 01782-283272
Website: sacredhearthanley.co.uk
Rev Peter Weatherby. Presbytery, 1 Eastwood Place, ST1 3DB
M: *Sat 1st M of Sun 5.45pm. Sun 10.30am. Hds 1.05pm, 7pm.*

2. † Sacred Heart (1853; 1930; 1977)
13 Queen's Avenue, Tunstall ST6 6EE
Tel: 01782-838357
Rev Patrick Farrelly.
M: *Sun 9.15am, 6.30pm. Hds 10am, 7.30pm.*
- ***Society of Jesus (SJ),*** **Brian Wall** (Chaplain to Staffordshire University).

3. † Our Lady and St Benedict
(1938; 1962; cons 28 May 1966)
Abbey Lane, Abbey Hulton ST2 8AU
Tel: 01782-534545 **Fax:** 01782-545052
E-mail: revmichaelvaughan@supanet.com
Rev Michael Vaughan
M: *Sat 1st M of Sun 6pm. Sun 10.30am. Hds As Announced.*

3a St Bernards (1967)
Field Avenue. Served from Lady and St Benedict.
M: *Sun 9am. Hds As Announced.*

4. † Our Lady of the Angels and St Peter in Chains
(1838; 1857; cons 19 Aug 1885)
Hartshill Road, Stoke-on-Trent, Staffs.
Tel: 01782-844308
E-mail: ppourlady.stoke@tiscali.co.uk
Rev Joseph Nguyen The-Quang.
Deacon: **Rev Anthony Bradshaw.**
M: *Sat 1st M of Sun 5.45pm. Sun 10am. Hds 9.30am, 7pm.*

5. † Our Lady of Perpetual Succour
(1922)
Masterson Street, Fenton, Stoke-on-Trent, Staffs. **Tel:** 01782-414071.
Rev Kazimierz Budzinski.
Deacon: **Rev William A Davies.**
M: *Sat 1st M of Sun 6.30pm. Sun 9.30am. Hds 10am, 7.30pm.*

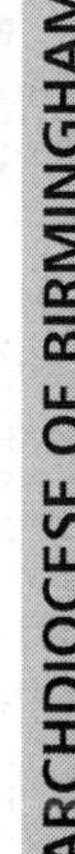

6. † St Mary (1923; 1969)
Ford Green Road, Norton-le-Moors, Stoke-on-Trent, Staffs ST6 8LT
Tel: 01782-257371
Rev Simon Stephens.
Deacon: **Rev Dr Paul Mayland.**
M: *Sat 1st M of Sun 6pm. Sun 10.30am. Hds 9.30am, 7pm.*

7. † St Augustine of Canterbury (1934; 1957; 1971)
Sandon Road, Meir, Stoke-on-Trent ST3 7DF
Tel: 01782-313734 **Fax:** 01782-315034
E-mail: staugustinesmeir@aol.com
Rev Jan Nowotnik. *Deacon:* **Rev Trevor Borthwick.**
M: *Sat 1st M of Sun 6pm. Sun 10am. Hds 9.30am, 7.30pm.*

8. St Bernadette (1962)
Fegg Hayes Road, Fegg Hayes, Stoke-on-Trent, Staffs
Tel: 01782-835287
Served from Sacred Heart, Stoke-on-Trent (2).
M: *Sat 1st M of Sun 6am. Hds Vigil 7pm.*

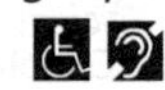

9. † St George and St Martin (1923; 1928; cons 6 June 1935)
Boulton Street, Birches Head, Stoke-on-Trent ST1 2LS **Tel:** 01782-212217
Rev Nazarius Mgungwe. Presbytery, Gibbins Street, ST1 2LS
Deacon: **Rev Richard Pemberton.**
M: *Sun 9.45am, 5pm. Hds 9.15am, 7pm.*

10. † St Gregory (1820; 1869; 1887; 1970; cons 1978)
Heathcote Road, Longton, Stoke-on-Trent ST3 2JU **Tel:** 01782-313796
Rev John Gilbert.
M: *Sat 1st M of Sun 5.45pm. Sun 10am. Hds (eve 5.45pm). 10am.*
- ***Sisters of Charity of St Paul,*** 25 Nashe Drive, Stoke-on-Trent, ST3 2HD **Tel:** 01782-313736

11. † St Joseph (1895; 1927; cons 22 June 1937)
Hall Street, Burslem, Stoke-on-Trent ST6 4BB **Tel:** 01782-837602
Rev M Amalados.
M: *Sat 1st M of Sun 5.45pm. Sun 10am. Hds 10am, 6pm.*

12. † St Joseph (1870; 1883; 1953; cons 16 May 1968)
High Street, Goldenhill, Stoke-on-Trent ST6 5RD **Tel:** 01782-782121
Rev David Newell.
M: *Sun 11am. Hds 10am, 7pm.*

13. † St Maria Goretti (1956; 1960)
Presbytery, 137 Aylesbury Road, Bentilee, Stoke-on-Trent ST2 0LU
Tel: 01782-281970 **Fax:** 01782-210518
E-mail: priest@stmariagoretti.org.uk
Rev Brian Wall.
M: *Sat 1st M of Sun 6pm. Sun 10.45am. Hds 10am, 7pm.*

14. † St Patrick (1920; 1936)
Mellor Street, Packmoor.
Served from Biddulph.
M: *Sun 9am. Hds Vigil 7.30pm.*

15. † St Peter (1760; 1937)
Waterloo Road, Cobridge, Stoke-on-Trent ST6 3HP **Tel:** 01782-837602
Served from Stoke (11).
M: *Sun 8.30am. Hds 6pm.*

16. † St Teresa of the Child Jesus (1926)
100 Stone Road, Trent Vale, Stoke-on-Trent ST4 6SP **Tel:** 01782-658063
E-mail: trentvaleteresa@btinternet.com
Rev Robert Taylerson.
M: *Sat 1st M of Sun 5.30pm. Sun 9.30am, 5.30pm. Hds (eve 7.30pm). 9am, 7.30pm.*

■ STONE, Staffs

† The Immaculate Conception and St Dominic (1842; 1854; cons 4 Feb 1863)
Margaret Street, Stone, Staffs.
Tel: 01785-813951
E-mail: parish@stdominics.plus.net
Rev Gerard Doyle. Presbytery, Station Road, ST15 8EW
Deacon: **Rev M McCormack.**
M: *1st M of Sun 6pm; Sun 8.15am, 10.45am. Hds 9am, 6pm.*
- ***Dominican Sisters,*** St Dominic's Convent, 21 Station Road, ST15 8ER **Tel:** 01785-812091 *Chaplain:* **Rev Jonathan Fleetwood OP.**

■ STONOR, Henley-on-Thames Oxon

† Holy Trinity (1351)
Tel: 01491-638587 Served from Watlington.
M: *Sun 10.30am. Hds 10.30am.*

■ STOURBRIDGE, W. Midlands

1. † Our Lady and All Saints (1816; 1864; cons 9 July 1891)
13 New Road, Stourbridge, West Midlands DY8 1PQ **Tel:** 01384-395308
Rt Rev Patrick McKinney, Rev Peter Norton
M: *Sat 1st M of Sun 5pm. Sun 8.30am, 10.30am. Hds (eve 7.30pm). 8am, 12.30pm, 7.30pm.*

2. SS Oswald and Wulstan.
See Clent.

■ STOURPORT, Worcs
† St Wulstan and St Thomas of Canterbury (1935; 1973; 1983)
32 Vale Road, Stourport, Worcs DY13 8YL
Tel: 01299-822633
E-mail: parish.stwulstan@dsl.pipex.com
Rev Stephen Pimlott.
Deacons: **Revv Patrick Duffy, John O'Brien.**
M: *Sat 1st M of Sun 5.30pm. Sun 10am, 6pm. Hds 9.15am, 7.30pm.*

■ STRATFORD-UPON-AVON
† St Gregory the Great (1852; 1866; cons 22 Oct 1966)
Warwick Road, Stratford-upon-Avon, Warwicks CV37 6UJ
Tel: 01789-292439 **Fax:** 01789-267852
E-mail: stgregoryssua@aol.com
Website: st-gregorys.org
• ***Benedictines (OSB):*** **Dom Austin Gurr**, St Gregory's Priory, Welcombe Road, CV37 6UJ
M: *Sat 1st M of Sun 5.30pm. Sun 815am, 11.15am. Hds 9am, 7pm.*
• ***Catholic Youth Training Centre,*** Soli House, Mill Lane, CV37 6BJ
Tel: 01789-267011

■ STREETLY, Sutton Coldfield
† St Anne (1958; 1959)
Bridle Lane, Streetly, Sutton Coldfield B74 3HB **Tel:** 0121-353 3778
Fax: 01121-352 0826
E-mail: frgwil@st-anne-streetly.fsnet.co.uk
Rev Gwilym Lloyd, 24 Grosvenor Avenue, Streetly, Sutton Coldfield B74 3PE
Tel: 0121-353 4493
M: *Sat 1st M of Sun 6pm. Sun 8.30am, 11am. Hds 9am, 7.30pm.*

■ STUDLEY, Warks
† St Mary (1851; 1853)
St Mary, 103 Alcester Road, Studley, Warks B80 7NW **Tel:** 01527 852524
Rev Doms Alexander Austin OSB, Augustine Stickland OSB
• ***Benedictines (OSB):***
M: *Sat 1st M of Sun 5pm, Sun 10.30am. Hds 9am, 7.30pm.*

■ SUTTON COLDFIELD, West Midlands
1. † Holy Trinity (1834; 1934)
69 Lichfield Road, Sutton Coldfield, B74 2NU
Tel: 0121-354 1211 **Fax:** 0121-354 5549
E-mail: holy.trinity@htc.org.uk
Revv Gerald Breen, Ray Corbett.
M: *Sat 1st M of Sun 6pm. Sun 9am, 10.30am, 7pm. Hds (eve 7.30pm). 10am, 7.30pm.*
• ***Missionaries of Africa (White Fathers) (MAfr),*** 129 Lichfield Road, Sutton Coldfield, West Midlands B74 2SA
Tel: 0121-308 0226 **Fax:** 0121-323 2476
Revv Thomas Cummins (*Superior*), **Peter Kelly, Angus Shelton, Francis Nolan**.

2. † St Nicholas (1922; 1953; 1980)
243 Jockey Road, Boldmere, Sutton Coldfield, West Midlands B73 5US
Tel: 0121-354 1763
E-mail: stnicholasrc@btinternet.com
Rev Timothy Ford.
M: *Sat 1st M of Sun 6. Sun 9am, 11am. Hds 9.15am, 7.30pm.*
• ***Crusaders of the Holy Spirit,*** 464 Chester Road, Sutton Coldfield B73 5BP
Rector: **Rev Francis Barrett,**
Tel: 0121-384 4280

3 † Holy Cross and St Francis (1951; 1975)
Springfield Road, Walmley, Sutton Coldfield, W. Midlands.
Tel: 0121-351 2161 **Fax:** 0121-313 0899
Rev Michael Dolman, 1 Signal Hayes Road, B76 8RS
M: *Sat 1st M of Sun 6pm. Sun 8.30am, 10.30am. Hds (eve 7.30pm). 9am, 7.30pm.*

4. † Sacred Heart (1953; 1986)
534 Lichfield Road, Four Oaks, Sutton Coldfield, W. Midlands B74 4EH
Tel: 0121-308 2560
Mgr David A Cousins.
M: *Sat 1st M of Sun 5pm (at Convent, Footherley Hall). Sun 8.30am, 10.30am. Hds 10am, (5pm at Convent), 8pm.*
• ***Hospitaller Sisters of the Sacred Heart,*** Footherley Hall, Shenstone, Lichfield WS14 0HG **Tel:** 01543-480253

■ SWYNNERTON, Staffs
Our Lady of the Assumption (1825, 1871)
8 Weaver's Walk, Swynnerton, Staffs ST15 0QZ **Tel:** 01782-796677
E-mail: assumption@btinternet.co.uk
Rev Bernard Anwyl.
M: *Sat 1st M of Sun 5.30pm. Sun 10am. Hds 9am, 7.30pm.*

■ TAMWORTH, Staffs 
1. † St John Baptist (1815; 1829)
8 St John Street, Tamworth, Staffs B79 7EX
Tel: 01827-62161/2 **Fax:** 01827-313162
E-mail: stjohnrctamworth@tiscali.co.uk
• ***Missionaries of the Sacred Heart (MSC):*** **Revv John Finn** (*Parish Priest*); **Manus Ferry. Bro Donal Hallissey.**
Deacon: **Rev Brian Cox.**
M: *Sat 1st M of Sun 6.30pm. Sun 8.30am, 10.30am. Hds 10am, 7.30pm.*

2. † Sacred Heart
Silver Link Road, Glascote Heath, Tamworth, Staffs. **Tel:** 01827-288226
Served from Tamworth (1).
M: *Sun 9am, 12noon. Hds 11am 7pm.*

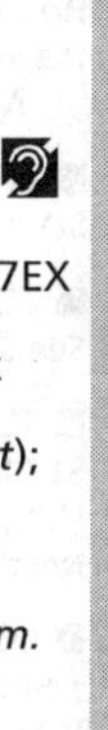

■ **TEAN,** Stoke-on-Trent A
† St Thomas of Canterbury
(1889; 1938; cons 20 June 1956)
St Thomas' Road, Tean, Stoke-on-Trent
ST10 4DS **Tel:** 01538-722433
Served from Cheadle.
M: *Sun 5.30pm. Hds As announced*

■ **TENBURY WELLS,** Worcs
The Sacred Heart and Our Lady
(1936; 1939; 1974)
Berrington Road. Served from Kidderminster.
M: *Sun 10.30am. Hds 10.30am.*

■ **TETTENHALL,** Wolverhampton
† St Thomas of Canterbury (1931; 1965,1972)
Haywood Drive, Tettenhall, Wolverhampton
WV6 8RF **Tel:** 01902-751025
Deacon: **Rev Brian Dockerty.**
M: *Sat 1st M of Sun 5.15pm. Sun 11am. Hds 10am, 7pm.*

■ **THAME,** Oxon
† St Joseph (1913; 1922, 1997)
Brook Lane, Thame, Oxon OX9 2AB
Tel: 01844-212860 **Fax:** 01844-218773
E-mail: stjosephsthame@btinternet.com
Website: www.stjosephsthame.org
Rev Mark Lagorio.
M: *Sat 1st M of Sun 6pm. Sun 9am, 11am. Hds as announced.*
• ***Daughters of Providence,*** Providence Convent, St Joseph's Brook Lane, OX9 2AB **Tel/Fax:** 01844-214314

■ **TILE CROSS**
See Birmingham (13).

■ **TIPTON,** West Midlands A
† Sacred Heart and Holy Souls (1920; 1940)
31 Victoria Road, Tipton, W Midlands
DY4 8SN **Tel:** 0121-557 1321
Revv Bengt Jakobson, Emmanuel Gill-Hammett.
M: *Sun 9.30am. Hds as announced.*

■ **TRENT VALE**
See Stoke-on-Trent (17).

■ **TUNSTALL**
See Stoke-on-Trent (2).

■ **TUTBURY,** Burton-on-Trent
St Christopher (1960)
Wakefield Avenue. Served from Barton under Needwood. **M:** *Sun 9am. Hds (eve 6pm).*

■ **UPTON-ON-SEVERN,** Worcs
† St Joseph (1850; 1983)
9 School Lane, Upton-on-Severn WR8 0LA
Tel: 01684-592602
Rev Dominic Round.
M: *Sun 10.30am. Hds 7.30pm.*

■ **UTTOXETER,** Staffs
† St Mary (1835; 1839)
11 Balance Street, Uttoxeter, Staffs ST14 8JB
Tel: 01889-562082
Website: catholicchurch@uttoxeter.org.uk
Rev Frederick Sheldon.
M: *Sun 9.30am. Hds 7.30pm.*

■ **WALMLEY,** Sutton Coldfield, Warks
See Sutton Coldfield (3).

■ **WALSALL,** West Midlands
1. † St Mary (1822; 1825; cons 25 July 1891)
The Mount, Vicarage Walk, Walsall WS1 3NF
Tel/Fax: 01922-622633
Canon Peter Taylor, Rev Michael J Leadbeater, 21 New College Close
WS1 3TF **Tel:** 01922-628645.
M: *Sat 1st M of Sun 7pm. Sun 9am, 11am. Hds (eve 7.30pm). 10am.*
• ***Sisters of Mercy,*** Maryvale Court, Glebe Street, Walsall. **Tel:** 01922-641819

2. St Catherine with St Chad (1962)
Edison Road, Beechdale Estate.
Served from Walsall (3).
M: *Sat 1st M of Sun 6.30pm. Hds (vigil 7.30pm).*

3. † St Patrick (1856; 1966; cons 17 March 1979)
Blue Lane East, Walsall WS2 8HN
Tel: 01922-623823
Rev John B Harrington.
M: *Sun 10am, 7pm. Hds 9.30am, 1pm.*

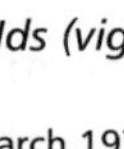
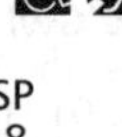
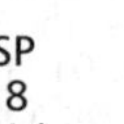

4. † St Thomas of Canterbury
(1958; 1960; 1967)
Dartmouth Avenue, Walsall WS3 1SP
Tel: 01922-26923 **Fax:** 01922-36118
Deacon: **Rev Michael McGrail** (*Parish Administrator*).
M: *Sun 10.45am. Hds, as announced.*
• ***Marist Sisters,*** 79 Dartmouth Avenue, Walsall WS3 1ST **Tel:** 01922-611986

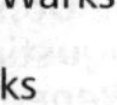

■ **WAPPENBURY,** Leamington Spa, Warks
† St Anne (1734; 1849)
Wappenbury, Leamington Spa, Warks
CV33 9DW
Tel: 01926-632214
Rev Timothy O'Brien.
Also serves Our Lady of the Angels, Princethorpe.
M: *Sun 8.30. Hds 7pm.*

■ **WARLEY,** West Midlands
† Our Lady and St Hubert
(1934; cons 18 June 1935)
Wolverhampton Road, Oldbury, Warley, W. Midlands.
Tel: 0121-422 2388 **Fax:** 0121-421 8216
E-mail: plblundell@btinternet.com
Rev Peter Blundell. Presbytery, Bleakhouse Road, Oldbury B68 0TQ
M: *Sun 9am, 10.30am. Hds 9.15am, 7pm.*

■ **WARNDON**, Worcs
See Worcester (3).

■ **WARSTOCK**
See Birmingham (35).

■ **WARWICK**
† **St Mary Immaculate** (1860; cons 15 June 1939)
45 West Street, Warks CV34 6AB
Tel/Fax: 01926-492913
Website: www.stmaryimmaculate.org.uk
Canon Edward M Stewart.
M: *Sat 1st M of Sun 6.30pm. Sun 8.30am, 10.30am (Sung). Hds 10am, 7.30pm.*

■ **WATER ORTON**, Warks
See Coleshill

■ **WATLINGTON**, Oxon
† **St Edmund Campion** (1928; 1930; 1989)
2 Watcombe Road, Watlington, Oxon OX49 5QJ **Tel:** 01491-612431
Rev Gerard Egan (CSSp).
M: *Sun 9am. Hds 9.15am, 7.30pm.*

■ **WEDNESBURY**, West Midlands
† **St Mary on the Hill** (1850; 1874; 1979)
St Mary's Road, Wednesbury, W. Midlands WS10 9DL **Tel:** 0121-556 0414
Rev Peter Madden.
M: *Sat 1st M of Sun 6pm. Sun 10am. Hds 9am, 7pm.*

■ **WELLESBOURNE**, Warks
Served from Kineton.
M: *Sat 1st M of Sun 5pm (in St Peter's Anglican Church).*

■ **WEOLEY CASTLE**
See Birmingham (16).

■ **WEST BROMWICH**, W. Midlands
1. † **St Michael and the Holy Angels** (1832; 1877; cons 27 Sept 1917)
260 High Street, West Bromwich, W. Midlands B70 8AQ **Tel:** 0121-553 2278
Rev Louis Le-Van-Hong.
M: *Sat 1st M of Sun 6pm. Sun 10.30am. Hds (eve 7.30pm). 10am.*

2. † **Holy Cross** (1948; 1951)
40 Hall Green Road, Stone Cross, West Bromwich, West Midlands B71 3LA
Tel: 0121-588 2743
Rev Timothy Burke.
M: *Sat 1st M of Sun 5.30pm. Sun 10.30am. Hds (eve 7pm), 7pm.*

3. † **St Joseph** (1958)
Birchfield Way, Yew Tree Estate.
Served from West Bromwich (2).
M: *Sun 9am. Hds 10am.*

■ **WEST HEATH**
See Birmingham (32).

■ **WHEATLEY**, Oxon
Our Lady of Lourdes (1962)
Crown Road. Served from Oxford (2).
M: *Sun 10am.*

■ **WHITNASH**, Warks
† **St Joseph** (1957; 1963; 1980)
Murcott Road, Whitnash, Leamington Spa, Warwicks CV31 2JJ
Tel: 01926-772712 **Fax:** 01926-74139
Email: brian.boyle7@ntlworld.com
Website: www.stjosephswhitnash.co.uk
• ***Sacred Heart Fathers of Betharram (SCJ):*** **Rev Brian Boyle. Br M Richards**.
M: *Sat 1st M of Sun 6.30pm. Sun 10am, 5pm. Hds 9.30am, 7pm.*
• ***Sisters of Charity of St Paul,*** 16 The Seekings, Whitnash, Leamington Spa, Warwickshire CV31 2SH
Tel: 01926-888257

■ **WILLENHALL**, West Midlands
† **St Mary** (1864; 1907)
Leveson Street, Willenhall, West Midlands WV13 1DA **Tel:** 01902-605043
Rev Paul Edwards
M: *Sat 1st M of Sun 6pm. Sun 10.30am. Hds (eve 7pm), 10am.*

■ **WITNEY**, Oxon
† **Our Lady and St Hugh of Lincoln** (1914; 1933; 1976)
Presbytery, Tower Hill, Witney, Oxon OX8 5YA **Tel:** 01993-702661
Website: www.ourladyandsthugh.org.uk
Rev Patrick Armstrong.
Deacon: **Rev Frank Ryan**.
M: *Sat 1st M of Sun 6.30pm. Sun 8.30am, 10am. Hds 9.15am, 7pm.*

■ **WOLSTANTON**, Newcastle, Staffs
† **St Wulstan** (1927; 1959; cons 1969)
Church Lane, Wolstanton, Newcastle, Staffs ST5 0EF **Tel:** 01782-626611
Revv Anthony Dykes, Anthony Davies.
M: *Sat 1st M of Sun 6pm. Sun 10.30am. Hds 9.30am, 7.30pm.*

■ **WOLVECOTE**, Oxon
See Oxford (6).

■ **WOLVERHAMPTON**
1. † **Corpus Christi** (1958; 1959, 1991)
Griffiths Drive, Ashmore Park, Wolverhampton WV11 2LH
Tel/Fax: 01902-732713
Rev Patrick Udoma.
Deacon: **Rev Frank Lockett.**
M: *Sat 1st M of Sun 6pm. Sun 11am. Hds 9.30am, 7pm.*

2. † **SS Mary and John** (1855; cons 8 June 1905)
Snowhill, Wolverhampton WV2 4AD

Tel: 01902-421676 **Fax:** 01902-311622
Revv Kazimierz Stefek, Bazyli Cendrowicz, Br Rafal Smaga.
M: *Sat 1st M of Sun 6.30pm. Sun 10am, 11.30am. Hds (eve 6.30pm), 10am.*

- ***Little Brothers of the Good Shepherd,*** Montini House, 2 Richmond Road, Wolverhampton WV3 9HY **Tel:** 01902-422218; Overnight Shelter, Thornley Street. **Tel:** 01902-773721

3. † Our Lady of Perpetual Succour (1923; 1934)
Presbytery, Cannock Road, Old Fallings, Wolverhampton WV10 8PG
Tel/Fax: 01902-731189
Rev Gerard Kelly.
Deacon: **Rev Steven Tuck.**
M: *Sat 1st M of Sun 7pm. Sun 10am. Hds 9am, 7.30pm.*

4. † St Anthony of Padua (1938; 1939; 1976, 1988)
Bee Lane, Ford-houses, Wolverhampton WV10 6LE
Tel: 01902-782144 **Fax:** 01902-788145
E-mail: st-anthony-wolves@supanet.com
Rev Brendan Carrick.
M: *Sat 1st M of Sun 6pm. Sun 10am. Hds 9.15am, 7pm..*

- ***Sisters of St Joseph of Lyon,*** St Joseph's Convent, 5 Wealden Hatch, Moseley Parklands. **Tel:** 01902-784851

5. † St Joseph (1903, 1925; 1967; 1984)
'The Island', Willenhall Road, Wolverhampton WV1 2QN
Tel: 01902-452841
Rev James Mealy.
M: *Sat 1st M of Sun 7pm. Sun 10.30am. Hds 10am, 7.30pm.*

6. † St Michael (1923; 1929; 1968; 1976)
173 Coalway Road, Merry Hill, Wolverhampton WV3 7ND
Tel: 01902-341343
Rev Stephen Squires.
M: *Sun 9am, 10.30am. Hds (Carmel Chapel 9am), 10am, 7.30pm.*

- ***Carmelites,*** Monastery of the Magnificat, Poplar Road, Penn Fields, WV3 7LE **Tel:** 01902-342660 *Chaplain:* **Rev Jimmy Lutwana AJ**, 2 Riley Crescent, Wolverhampton WV3 7DR **Tel:** 01902-683814
- ***Sisters of Mercy,*** St Joseph's Convent of Mercy, Poplar Road, Penn Fields, Wolverhampton. **Tel:** 01902-332617

6a St Plus X
Castlecroft Avenue.
M: *Sun 9.45am. Hds 7.30am*

7. † St Patrick (1865; 1972, 1976)
Wolverhampton Road, New Cross, Wolverhampton WV10 0QQ
Tel: 01902-736440
Rev Eamon Corduff;
Deacon: **Rev Michael Ainsworth.**
M: *Sat 1st M of Sun 6pm. Sun 9.30am, 6pm. Hds (eve 7.30pm). 9.30am, 6pm.*

- **Hope Community, Sisters of the Infant Jesus,** 122 Clover Ley, Heath Town W10 0AD **Tel:** 01902-453590

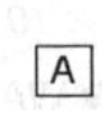

8. † SS Peter and Paul (1725; cons 13 Nov 1885)
North Street, Wolverhampton WV1 1RJ
Tel: 01902-23005
E-mail: phdaly@pacelli.fsnet.co.uk
Rev Patrick H Daly.
M: *Sat 1st M of Sun 5.30pm. Sun 10.15am, 6.45pm. Hds 12.30pm, 7.30pm.*

- ***Sisters of the Infant Jesus,*** 24 Merridale Road, WV3 9SB **Tel:** 01902-426672

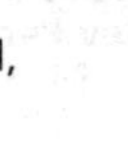

9. † St Teresa of the Infant Jesus (1933; cons 1969)
23 Birmingham New Road, Parkfield, Wolverhampton WV4 6BL
Tel: 01902-421676
Served from SS Mary and John, Wolverhampton (2).
M: *Sat 1st M of Sun 5pm. Sun 9am. Hds 9.30am, 7.30pm.*

10. † Polish Church: Holy Trinity.
Stafford Road, Oxley, Wolverhampton.
Tel: 01902-422833
Rev Edward Pondel (CSSp). 74 Green Drive. Wolverhampton WV10 6DW
M: *Sat 1st Mass of Sun 6pm. Sun 9.30am, 11.15am. Hds 11am, 6pm.*

11. Ukrainian Church
See Apostolic Exarchate for Ukrainians.

12. Wolverhampton University
Chaplain: **Rev Patrick Daly.** *Chaplaincy Centre,* University of Wolverhampton, Molineux Street, Wolverhampton WV1 1SB
Tel: 01902-322903
M: *Sun 6pm.*

■ **WOLVEY,** Warks
† St James the Less (1889; 1925)
Coventry Road. Served from Bulkington.

■ **WOMBOURNE,** Wolverhampton
† St Bernadette (1961)
9 Rennison Drive, Wombourne, Wolverhampton WV5 9HW
Tel: 01902-893434
Rev Andrew McGann.
M: *Sat 1st M of Sun 6.30pm). Sun 10am. Hds 10am, 7pm.*

ARCHDIOCESE OF BIRMINGHAM

■ **WOODCOTE,** Oxon
† **Christ the King** (1958; 1966)
South Stoke Road, Woodcote, Reading RG8 0PL
Served from Goring-on-Thames.
M: *Sun 12noon. Hds 8am.*

■ **WOODLANE,** Yoxall, Burton-on-Trent A
† **St Francis of Sales** (1793)
Tel: 01543-472802
Served from Barton under Needwood.
M: *Sat 1st M of Sun 6.15. Hds 7.30pm.*

■ **WOODSTOCK,** Oxon.
† **St Hugh of Lincoln,** Hensington Road. (1934). Served from Kidlington.
M: *Sun 9.30am. Hds (eve 6pm at Spencer Court).*

■ **WOOTTON WAWEN** A
Solihull, West Midlands
† **Our Lady and St Benedict** (1814; 1904)
Alcester Road, Wootton Wawen, Solihull, W. Midlands B95 6BQ **Tel:** 01564-792647
Rev Patrick Sayles.
M: *Sun 10pm. Hds 7.30pm.*

■ **WORCESTER**
1. † **St George** (1685; 1829)
1 Sansome Place, Worcester WR1 1UG
Tel: 01905-22574 **Fax:** 01905-22635
Revv Brian McGinley, Keith Enston.
Deacon: **Rev Reginald Lewis.**
M: *Sat 1st M of Sun 6pm. Sun 9.30am, 11am, 12.30pm (Polish), 7pm. Hds (eve 6pm). 12noon.*

• ***Sisters of St Marie Madeleine Postel,*** St Mary's Convent, The Grange, Battenhall Avenue WR5 2NP
Tel: 01905- 358231

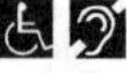

2. † **Our Lady Queen of Peace** (1948; 1951; 1984)
10 Bransford Road, St John's WR2 4EN
Tel: 01905-423633 **Fax:** 01905-339399
Website: www.olqp-worcester.org.uk
Rev Paul Whieldon.
M: *Sat 1st M of Sun 7pm. Sun 9am, 11am. Hds 10am, 7.30pm.*

3. **St Joseph** (1963, 1976) A
Presbytery, Chedworth Drive, Warndon WR4 9PG **Tel:** 01905-454352
Rev Kevin Kavanagh.
Deacon: **Rev Anthony Hartshorn.**
M: *Sat 1st M of Sun 6pm. Sun 10am. Hds 9.15am, 7.30pm.*

■ **WROXTON,** Banbury, Oxon A
† **St Thomas of Canterbury** (1894)
Stratford Road. Served from Banbury (2).
M: *Sun 9am.*

■ **WYTHALL,** Warks
St Aidan (1950)
Station Road. Served from Shirley.
M: *Sat 1st M of Sun 6pm.*

■ **YARDLEY WOOD**
See Birmingham (12).

■ **YOXALL,** Staffs
See Woodlane.

■ **ORDERS OR CONGREGATIONS, ETC.**

■ **Men**
Augustinians: Birmingham (17).
Benedictines (English Congregation): Alcester, Oxford (1), Stratford-upon-Avon, Studley.
Charity, Institute of (Rosminians): Hadzor, Rugby (2).
Columban Missionaries: Dorridge.
De La Salle Brothers: Oxford (6).
Dominicans: Oxford (1).
Franciscans (Capuchin): Oxford (3).
Good Shepherd, Little Brothers of the: Wolverhampton (2).
Holy Spirit, Crusaders of, Sutton Coldfield (2)).
Jesuits: Birmingham (17), Oxford (1).
Missionaries of Africa (White Fathers): Sutton Coldfield (1).
Oblates of Mary Immaculate: Birmingham (21), Kingshurst.
Oratory, Congregation of: Birmingham (8), Oxford (1).
Redemptorists: Birmingham (43).
Sacred Heart, Missionaries of the: Princethorpe, Tamworth.
Sacred Heart (Betharram), Priests of the: Droitwich, Great Barr, Olton, Whitnash, Worcester (1).
Salesians: Oxford (5).

■ **Women**
The symbol † is used to distinguish Secular Institutes
Assumption, Little Sisters of the: Birmingham (10).
Assumption, Religious of the: Oxford (4).
Benedictine Nuns (English Congregation): Stanbrook.
Benedictine Nuns (Independent Community): Oulton.
Bridgettine Sisters: Birmingham (10).
Carmelites: Wolverhampton (6).
Charity, Missionaries of: Birmingham (24).
Charity, Religious Sisters of: Birmingham (6).
Charity (of St Paul, Selly Park), Sisters of: Birmingham (8, 15, 20, 23, 26, 32), Aston-by-Stone, Banbury (2), Coleshill, Coventry (2), Shirley, Stoke-on-Trent (10), Whitnash.

Christian Instruction, Sisters of: Kingshurst.
Columban Missionary Sisters: Birmingham (27).
Cross and Passion, Sisters of: Quinton.
Divine Love, Daughters of: Birmingham (7), Dudley, Kidsgrove.
Dominican Sisters (Congregation of Newcastle, Natal): Oxford (1).
Dominican Sisters (3rd Order): Congr of Stone (St Catherine of Siena): Stone.
Franciscan Missionaries of Mary: Coventry (9).
Holy Child Jesus, Society of the: Birmingham (24, 30), Oxford (1, 7).
Holy Spirit, Daughters of the: Birmingham (43).
Holy Spirit, Missionary Sister Servants: Birmingham (27).
Hospitaller Sisters of the Sacred Heart, Sutton Coldfield (4)
Infant Jesus, Sisters of the: Wolverhampton (7, 8), Smethwick.
Joseph (Lyon), Sisters of St: Haunton, Birmingham (30), Wolverhampton (4).
Joseph (Cluny), Sisters of St: Stafford (1).
Marist Sisters: Great Barr, Walsall (4).
Marie Madeleine Postel, Sisters of: Birmingham (25), Worcester (1).
Mercy Sisters Institute of Our Lady of Mercy: Newcastle under Lyme.
Mercy, Sisters of (Union): Birmingham (4, 27), Newcastle, Walsall (1), Wolverhampton (6).
Notre Dame (Namur), Sisters of: Oxford (1).
Our Lady of Charity, Sisters of: Birmingham (15, 30).
Poor Child Jesus, Sisters of the: Birmingham (22), Southam.
Poor Clares (Colettines): Baddesley Clinton.
Poor, Little Sisters of the: Birmingham (17).
Presentation Sisters: Birmingham (6), Bicester (1), Coventry (3), Nuneaton (1), Redditch (1).
Providence, Daughters of: Thame.
Providence, Sisters of (Rosminians): Rugby (2).
Sacred Heart, Daughters of Our Lady of The: Coventry (6).
Sacred Heart Society of the: Oxford (1).
Sacred Heart (St Aubin), Sisters of the: Oxford (2).
Salesian Sisters of St John Bosco: Oxford (5).
Servite Sisters: Olton.
Sion (Sisters of) Birmingham (17).
St Francis de Sales, Daughters of: Oldbury
Work, Sisters of the Spiritual Family The Work: Oxford (7).

■ DIOCESAN INSTITUTIONS, SOCIETIES, ETC

For Societies and Organisations without representation in the diocese please see the main Societies and Organisations section.

Archconfraternity of St Stephen for Altar Servers, *Secretary:* **Mr P. Rollason**, 25 Max Road, B32 1LD

Birmingham Catholic Rambling Club. *Secretary*: **Mary Gibbons**, Flat 25, Wilsford Green, 4 Oakhill Drive, Birmingham B15 9NN **Tel:** 0121-772 6744

Birmingham Diocesan Catholic Scout Guild. *Chairman*: **Mr D Hurley**, 222 Hobs Moat Road, Solihull, W.Midlands. B92 8JY **Tel:** 0121-743 4969

Calix: To interest Catholic men and women with an alcoholic problem in the virtue of total abstinence, and to promote the spiritual development of alcoholics. **J M Stone**, 70 Boleyn Road, Rednal B45 0NR **Tel:** 0121-453 9628 Meetings at Olton Friary, 1st Sunday of month.

Catholic Family History Society: Meets regularly at St Chad's Cathedral. Local contact: **Mr J A Duffy**, 153 Broadway North, Walsall WS1 2QB

Cardinal Newman (Friends of): c/o Oratory House, Hagley Road, Birmingham B16 8UE **Tel:** 0121-454 0496

Catenian Association. Contact: **Bill Johnson**. 94 St Bernards Road, Solihull B92 7BW **Tel:** 0121 706 2359

Catholic Housing Aid Society. *Director:* **E Pearse**, 44- 46 Coventry Road, Bordesley, Birmingham. B10 ORX Case referrals to **Miss K Dunne**. **Tel:** 0121-766 5072

Marriage Care. For Diocesan centres at Birmingham, Coventry, Oxford, Stoke-on-Trent. **Tel:** 0800 389 3801

Catholic Men's Society. Birmingham Archdiocesan Council. *Secretary*: **P Young**, 3 Eider Close, Spennells, Kidderminster DY10 4TE **Tel:** 01562-639068

Catholic Nurses Guild. Birmingham Diocesan Branch. *Hon Secretary*: **Miss Anita Hall**, 5 The Congreaves, Shard End, Birmingham B34 6TR.

Catholic Study Circle for Animal Welfare, For information write to: **Deborah Jones,** 2 Lower Barns, Chipping Norton OX7 5YP

Catholic Teachers' Federation. Birmingham. *Archdiocesan Hon Secretary*: **Miss M D Dunne, BEd,** 31 Walmley Ash Road, Walmley, Sutton Coldfield B76 8JA **Tel:** (Home) 0121-351 3121 (School) 0121-772 5037

Catholic Women's League. Birmingham

Archdiocesan Branch. *Secretary*: **Mrs R Slater**, 19 Arden Vale, Knowle B92 9NS

Catholic Youth Centre. *Director:* **Rev Bill Wilton**. Soli House, Mill Lane, Stratford-upon-Avon, Warwicks, CV37 6BJ **Tel:** 01789-67011

Catholic Youth Centre – Alton Castle, Castle Hill, Alton, Staffs ST10 4AH **Tel:** 01538-703224.

City of Birmingham Pastoral Council. *Secretary*: **Ms Winifred Flanagan**, Ladywell, 69 Groveley Lane, West Heath B31 4QQ **Tel:** 0121-477 8557

Civil Service Catholic Guild. *Secretary:* **Mrs J Whittaker**, 183 Barrows Lane, Yardley, Birmingham B26 1QS

Friends of the Holy Father. *Promoter:* **Mrs P Van Der Valk,** 84 Shenstone Court, Coalway Road, Penn, Wolverhampton WV3 7LZ **Tel:** 01902-342646

Grail, The. *Diocesan Representatives:* **Pete and Teresa Singleton**, 7 Beech Road, Bourneville B30 1LL **Tel:** 0121-458 1657

Guild of Catholic Doctors. Midland Branch. *Master:* **Mr J Kelly**, 58 Hintlesham Avenue B15 2PH. *Secretary:* **Dr J F Leahy,** 5 Winsford Green, 10 Oak Hill Drive, Edgbaston B15 3UG **Tel:** 0121-456 4114

Knights of St Columba. Prov 18 (Birmingham). *Prov Grand Knight:* **Mr Michael Mason**, 9 Jubilee Close, Walsall WS3 7SS **Tel:** 01922 639560

Leaven Carmelite Secular Institute, The: *Contact:* **A Emery**, 13 Parkway, Dairyfields, Trentham, Staffs ST4 8AJ

Legion of Mary. Senatus of Birmingham. Legion HQ. St Francis' Presbytery, 101 Hunters Road, Birmingham B19 1EB. *Secretary:* **Mrs P Sheehan,** 6 Morfa Gardens, Coventry CV6 1PX **Tel:** 92476-593039.

Newman Association. *Birmingham Circle. Secretary:* **Miss W Flanagan**, 123 Groveley Lane, West Heath B31 4QQ *Coventry Circle. Secretary:* **Tel:** 01926-859675 *North Staffs Circle. Secretary:* **Mr V Owen**, 14 Lower Oxford Road, Newcastle-under-Lyme, Staffs ST4 5LD **Tel:** 01762-619698 *Worcester Circle. Secretary:* **Mr David Taylor**, 49 Meadow Road, Malvern WR14 2RZ **Tel:** 01684 573994

North Staffs Association of Christian Management. *Secretary:* **L Cooke**, 10 Spinney Close, Endon, Stoke-on-Trent, Staffs. **Tel:** 01782-502073

Our Lady's Catechists. *Diocesan Organiser:* **Mrs A Bayley**, St Bede's, Finchfield Gardens, Wolverhampton WV3 9L7 **Tel:** 01902-421567

St Barnabas Society. *Secretary:* **Rev Robin Sanders**, 4 First Turn, Wolvercote, Oxford OX2 8AH **Tel:** 01865-513377

Society of St Gregory. *Diocesan Representative:* **Anne Tibke**, 3 Grosvenor Way, Droitwich Spa, Worcestershire WR9 7SR **Tel:** 01905-776224 **E-mail:** birmingham@ssg.org.uk

Society of St Vincent de Paul. Birmingham Central Council. *President:* **Mr Michael Gould**, 17 Woodlands Avenue, Wolstanton ST6 1PD **Tel:** 01782-611012

Staffordshire Catholic History Society. *Chairman:* **J May**. *Secretary:* **Mr John Tams,** 55 Stafford Road, Store, Staffs ST15 0HE **Tel:** 01785-812735

Teams of Our Lady. An international Catholic Movement for Christian married couples that aims to deepen the couples' spirituality. A 'Team' consists of four or five couples and a priest or religious as spiritual advisor meeting monthly to share the journey of faith, guided by the Holy Spirit. *Contact couple:* **Nick and Clare St John**, 23 Scampton Close, Bicester, Oxon OX26 4FF **Tel:** 01869-246787 **E-mail:** nick.f.stjohn@btinternet.com

Trade Unionists, Christian Association of. Clive Robinson. 31 Daventry Road, Coventry CV3 5DJ. **Tel:** 0246 501579

Union of Catholic Mothers, Diocesan Branch. *Secretary:* **Mrs M Smith**, 31 Juliet Drive, Bilton, Rugby CV22 6LY **Tel:** 01788-815894

University of Birmingham Newman Catholic Society. *Secretary:* c/o The Chaplaincy, 29 Harrisons Road, Birmingham B15 3QS **E-mail:** newmancath@bham.ac.uk Web: www.bugs.bham.ac.uk//newmancath

Walsingham Association. *Birmingham:* **Mrs A Roebuck**, 35 Greening Rd, Birmingham B15 2XA **Tel:** 0121-454 0130 *Oxford:* **Rev J Welch**, The Oratory House, 25 Woodstock Road, Oxford OX2 6HA **Tel:** 01865-315800 *Shirley:* **Miss R Simcox**, 503 Stratford Road, Shirley, Solihull B90 4AJ *Solihull:* **Mrs K Toole**, 10 Ulverley Court, Ulverley Green, Solihull B92 8BP **Tel:** 0121-706 8589 *Wolverhampton:* **Miss K Raby**, 26 Northfield Grove, Finchfield, Wolverhampton WV3 8DW

■ CHURCHES IN THE BIRMINGHAM POSTAL DISTRICT AREA

(Arranged according to their districts)

4: St Chad's Cathedral; Chapel-of-Ease, Brearley Street; St Michael.
5: St Catherine.
6: Sacred Heart and St Margaret Mary.

7: St Joseph; St Vincent de Paul.
8: Our Lady of the Rosary and St Teresa of Lisieux.
10: Holy Family.
11: English Martyrs.
12: St Anne; St John the Evangelist.
13: St Martin de Porres.
14: St Dunstan.
16: The Oratory.
17: St Mary (Harborne).
18: St Patrick.
19: St Francis.
20: St Teresa.
21: St Augustine.
23: SS Mary and John; St Margaret Mary; SS Thomas and Edmund of Canterbury.
24: SS Peter and Paul.
26: St Thomas More.
27: Sacred Heart and Holy Souls.
28: St Ambrose Barlow.
29: Our Lady and St Rose of Lima; St Edward
30: SS Joseph and Helen; St Paul.
31: Our Lady and St Brigid; St John Fisher.
32: Our Lady of Fatima (Quinton); St Peter.
33: Corpus Christi; Our Lady Help of Christians.
34: Mother of God.
35: St Gerard.
36: St John the Baptist; St Wilfrid.
37: St Anne (Chelmsley Wood); St Anthony (Kingshurst).
44: Christ the King; Our Lady (Maryvale).
45: Our Lady of Perpetual Succour.
46: Sacred Heart and St Teresa of the Child Jesus (Coleshill).
47: St Jude.

■ **HOSPITALS**

To contact the Catholic Chaplain of a particular hospital we suggest you contact the hospital reception directly.

■ **CATHOLIC SCHOOLS - Maintained**

■ **BIRMINGHAM**

▲ **Junior and Infant**

St Chad, Hospital Street, B19 3XD **Tel:** 0121-464 6554 *(Birmingham)*

St Anne, Lowe Street B12 0ER **Tel:** 0121-772 5037 *(Birmingham 23)*

St Catherine, Great Colmore Street, B15 2AY **Tel:** 0121-692 1051 *(Birmingham 26)*

St Patrick, Dudley Road, B18 7QW **Tel:** 0121-454 0767 *(Birmingham 38)*

St Edmund, Roseberry Street, Spring Hill B18 7PA. **Tel:** 0121-523 7274 *(Birmingham 38)*

St Vincent, Vauxhall Grove, B7 4HP **Tel:** 0121-359 2359 *(Birmingham 45)*

Sacred Heart, Earlsbury Gardens, Birchfield B20 3AE **Tel:** 0121-356 4721 *(Birmingham 8)*

Holy Souls, Mallard Close, Acocks Green, B27 6RG **Tel:** 0121-464 6780 *(Birmingham 7)*

St John and St Monica (Balsall Heath), Chantry Road, Moseley B13 8DW **Tel:** 0121-464-5868 *(Birmingham 31)*

St Wilfrid (Castle Bromwich), Shawsdale Road, Firs Estate B36 8LY **Tel:** 0121-675 3319*(Birmingham 46)*

Guardian Angels (Castle Bromwich), Hurst Lane, Shard End B34 7HN **Tel:** 0121-747 2782 *(Birmingham 10)*

St Gerard, Yatesbury Avenue, Castle Vale, B35 6LB **Tel:** 0121-464 2613 *(Birmingham 30)*

The Oratory, Oliver Road, Ladywood, B16 9ER **Tel:** 0121-454 0600 *(Birmingham 9)*

The Abbey, Sutton Road, Erdington, B23 6QL **Tel:** 0121-373 1793 *(Birmingham 43)*

SS Mary and John, Beaufort Road, Hunton Hill, Erdington B23 7NR **Tel:** 0121-382 3522 *(Birmingham 20)*

St Mark, Almond Croft, Off Old Walsall Road, Great Barr B42 1NU **Tel:** 0121-357 9892 *(Great Barr)*

St Francis, Brougham Street B19 1PH **Tel:** 0121-464-5072 *(Birmingham 29)*

St Clare, Robert Road, Handsworth B20 3RT **Tel:** 0121-554 3289 *(Birmingham 29)*

St Augustine, Avenue Road, Handsworth B21 8ED **Tel:** 0121-554 5069 *(Birmingham 25)*

St Mary, Vivian Road, Harborne B17 0DN **Tel:** 0121-464 2141 *(Birmingham 19)*

St Dunstan, Drayton Road, Kings Heath B14 7LP **Tel:** 0121-464 4648 *(Birmingham 27)*

St Alban, Broad Lane, Kings Heath B14 5AL **Tel:** 0121-444 6530 *(Birmingham 27)*

St Joseph, Station Road, King's Norton B30 1DD **Tel:** 0121-458 2458 *(Birmingham 34)*

St Paul, Sisfield Road, King's Norton B38 9JB **Tel:** 0121-464 1546 *(Birmingham 39)*

Christ the King, Warren Farm Road, Kingstanding B44 0QN **Tel:** 0121-464 9800 *(Birmingham 4)*

Maryvale RC Primary, Old Oscott Hill, Maryvale B44 9AG **Tel:** 0121- 675 1434 *(Birmingham 11)*

St Martin de Porres, Oakland Road, Moseley B13 9DN **Tel:** 0121-464 5500 *(Birmingham 31)*

St Joseph, Rocky Lane, Nechells B7 5HA **Tel:** 0121-464 8140 *(Birmingham 33)*

St Brigid, Frankley Beeches Road, Northfield B31 5AB **Tel:** 0121-464 2364 *(Birmingham 17)*

St Teresa (Perry Barr), Butlers Road, Handsworth Wood B20 **Tel:** 0121-554 9581*(Birmingham 42)*

St Margaret Mary, Perry Common Road, Erdington B23 7AB **Tel:** 0121-464 6355 *(Birmingham 36)*
SS Peter and Paul, Kingsbury Road, Pype Hayes B24 9ND **Tel:** 0121-373 6028 *(Birmingham 41)*
Our Lady of Fatima, Winchfield Drive, Harborne B17 8TR **Tel:** 0121-429 2900 *(Birmingham 12)*
St James, Leach Heath Lane, Rednal, Birmingham B45 9BN **Tel:** 0121-453 2638 *(Birmingham 15)*
St Columba, Lickey Road, Rednal, Birmingham B45 8TD **Tel:** 0121-453 4841 *(Birmingham 15)*
Holy Rosary, Bridge Road, Saltley B8 3SF **Tel:** 0121-464 4519 **Fax:** 0121-464 1637 *(Birmingham 16)*
St Edward, Greenland Road, Selly Park B29 7PN **Tel:** 0121-464 1730 *(Birmingham 28)*
St Thomas More, Horse Shoes Lane, Sheldon B26 3HU **Tel:** 0121-743 3289 *(Birmingham 44)*
Holy Family, Coventry Road, Small Heath, B10 0HT **Tel:** 0121-772 2670 *(Birmingham 6)*
St Bernadette, Hobmoor Road, Yardley B25 8QL **Tel:** 0121-783 7232 *(Birmingham 6)*
English Martyrs, Evelyn Road, Sparkhill B11 3JW **Tel:** 0121-464 3150 *(Birmingham 21)*
St Bernard, Wake Green Road, Moseley, B13 9QE **Tel:** 0121-464 3795 *(Birmingham 21)*
Corpus Christi, Lyttelton Road, Stechford B33 8BL **Tel:** 0121-675 2784 *(Birmingham 5)*
St Joseph, Little Sutton Lane, Sutton Coldfield B75 6PB **Tel:** 0121-354 6270 *(Sutton Coldfield 1)*
St Nicholas, Jockey Road, Boldmere, Sutton Coldfield B73 5US **Tel:** 0121-355 2649 *(Sutton Coldfield 2)*
Holy Cross, Laburnum Drive, Walmley, Sutton Coldfield B76 8SP **Tel:** 0121-675 2158 *(Sutton Coldfield 3)*
Our Lady, East Meadway, Tile Cross B33 0AU **Tel:** 0121-464 4459 *(Birmingham 13)*
St Jude (Warstock), Baverstock Road, Maypole B14 5PD **Tel:** 0121-464 5069 *(Birmingham 35)*
Our Lady and St Rose, Gregory Avenue, Weoley Castle, B29 5DY **Tel:** 0121-464 2283 *(Birmingham 18)*
St John Fisher, Alvechurch Road, West Heath, B31 3PN **Tel:** 0121-475 3489 *(Birmingham 32)*
Our Lady of Lourdes, Trittiford Road, Yardley Wood B13 0EU **Tel:** 0121-444 2684 *(Birmingham 14)*
St Ambrose Barlow, Shirley Road, Hall Green B28 9JJ **Tel:** 0121-464 2791 *(Birmingham 22)*
St Peter, Adams Hill, Bartley Green B32 3QD **Tel:** 0121-464 6921 *(Birmingham 40)*
St Cuthbert, Gumbleberrys Close, Stechford B8 2PS **Tel:** 0121-675 2205 *(Birmingham 5)*

▲ Secondary Comprehensive

Archbishop Ilsley, Victoria Road, Acocks Green B27 7XY **Tel:** 0121-706 4200 /8960/8523 *(Birmingham)*
St Edmund Campion, Sutton Road, Erdington B23 5AX **Tel:** 0121-464 7700 and 0121-250 7731 *(Birmingham)*
St John Wall, Oxhill Road, Handsworth B21 8HH **Tel:** 0121-554 1825 *(Birmingham)*
Bishop Challoner, Institute Road, Kings Heath B14 7EG **Tel:** 0121-444 4161 *(Birmingham)*
Cardinal Wiseman, Old Oscott Hill, Great Barr B44 9SR **Tel:** 0121-360 6383 *(Birmingham)*
Bishop Walsh, Wylde Green Road, Sutton Coldfield B76 8QT **Tel:** 0121-351 3215/6 *(Birmingham)*
St Paul (Girls), Vernon Road, Edgbaston B16 9SL **Tel:** 0121-454 0895
St Thomas Aquinas, Wychall Lane, King's Norton B38 8AP **Tel:** 0121-464 4643
Holy Trinity, Oakley Road, Small Heath B10 0AX **Tel:** 0121-772 0184

■ BERKSHIRE

▲ Secondary

Blessed Hugh Farringdon, Fawley Road, Southcote, Reading, Berks RG30 3EP. **Tel:** 0118-957 4730, **Fax:** 0118-956 8150 *(Reading).*

▲ Primary

St Anne, Washington Road, Caversham Reading RG4 0AA **Tel:** 0118-901 5537 *(Caversham)*
St Martin, 10 Pendennis Avenue RG4 0SS **Tel:** 0118-901 5544 *(Caversham)*

■ COVENTRY

▲ Primary

Christ the King, Infants, Westhill Road CV6 2AA **Tel:** 024 76 592047 *(Coventry 1)*
Holy Family, Penny Park Lane, Holbrook CV6 2GU **Tel:** 024 76 333631 *(Coventry 8)*
Corpus Christi, Langbank Avenue, Ernesford Grange CV3 3BS **Tel:** 024 76 454931 *(Coventry 2)*
St Osburg, Upper Hill Street CV1 4AP **Tel:** 024 76 227165 *(Coventry 3)*
St Mary & St Benedict, Leigh Street, Hillfields CV1 5HG **Tel:** 024 76 229486 *(Coventry 6)*

St Elizabeth, St Elizabeth's Road, Foleshill CV6 5BX **Tel:** 024 76 687527 *(Coventry 9)*
Good Shepherd, Spring Road CV6 7FN **Tel:** 024 76 689392 *(Coventry 9)*
All Souls, Avercorn Road CV5 8ED **Tel:** 024 76 675836 *(Coventry 4)*
Sacred Heart, Brays Lane CV2 4BT **Tel:** 024 76 453314 *(Coventry 5)*
St Augustine, Heathcote Street, Radford CV6 3BL **Tel:** 024 76 596988 *(Coventry 1)*
St Thomas More, Watercall Avenue, Stivichall CV3 5QD **Tel:** 024 76 412619 *(Coventry 15)*
Our Lady of the Assumption, Hawthorne Lane, Tile Hill CV4 9LB **Tel:** 024 76 466655 *(Coventry 7)*
St Patrick, Deedmore Road, Bell Green CV1 1EQ **Tel:** 024 76 612671 *(Coventry 14)*
SS Peter and Paul, Arkle Drive, Walsgrave CV2 2E **Tel:** 024 76 615665 *(Coventry 14)*
St Anne, Chace Avenue, Willenhall CV3 3AD **Tel:** 024 76 30 2882 *(Coventry 10)*
St John Vianney, Mount Nod Way, CV5 7GX **Tel:** 024 76 4 64088 *(Coventry 12)*
St John Fisher, Kineton Road, Wyken CV2 3NR **Tel.** 024 76 443333 *(Coventry 11)*
St Gregory (Binley), Harry Rose Road, Wyken CV2 5AT **Tel:** 024 76 445900 *(Coventry 5 & 11)*
Holy Family, Penny Park Lane, Holbrook CV6 2GU **Tel:** 024 76 33 2724 *(Coventry 8)*
Corpus Christi, Langbank Avenue, Ernesford Grange CV3 3BS **Tel:** 024 76 454241 *(Coventry 2)*
Christ The King, Junior, Scots Lane CV6 2DJ **Tel:** 024 76 335790 *(Coventry 1)*

▲ Secondary Comprehensive

Bishop Ullathorne, Leasowes Avenue, Green Lane CV3 6BH **Tel:** 024 76 414515 *(Coventry)*
Cardinal Wiseman, Potters Green Road, Walsgrave CV2 2AJ **Tel:** 024 76 617231/616237 *(Coventry)*
Cardinal Newman, Sandpits Lane, Keresley CV6 3FR **Tel:** 024 76 33 2382 *(Coventry)*

■ DUDLEY

▲ Junior and Infant

St Mary's, Mill Street, Brierley Hill, W. Midlands DY5 2TH **Tel:** 01384-818435 *(Brierley Hill)*
St Joseph, Hillcrest Road, Dudley DY2 7PW **Tel:** 01384-818925 *(Dudley)*
St Chad, Catholic Lane, Sedgley, Dudley DY3 1SS **Tel:** 01902-818720 *(Sedgley)*
Our Lady, Bundle Hill, Halesowen B63 4AR **Tel:** 01384-816880 *(Halesowen)*
St Joseph, Leavale Road, Norton, Stourbridge Worcs **Tel:** 01384-818325 *(Stourbridge)*

▲ Secondary Comprehensive

Bishop Milner, Burton Road, Dudley DY1 3BY **Tel:** 01384-816600 *(Dudley)*

■ OXFORDSHIRE

▲ Primary

St Aloysius, 143 Woodstock Road, Oxford OX2 7PH **Tel:** 01865-515094 *(Oxford)*
St Joseph, Headley Way, Headington, Oxford OX3 7SX **Tel:** 01865-763357 *(Oxford)*
Our Lady, Oxford Road, Cowley, Oxford OX4 2LE **Tel:** 01865-779176 *(Oxford)*
St John Fisher, Sandy Lane, West Blackbird Leys OX4 5LD **Tel:** 01865-779676 *(Oxford)*
St John, Avocet Way, Chatsworth Drive, Bodicote Chase OX16 9HA **Tel:** 01295-263740 *(Banbury)*
St Joseph, Fiennes Road, Neithrop OX10 0ET **Tel:** 01295-264284 *(Banbury)*
St Mary, Queen's Avenue, Kingsend OX6 8NX **Tel:** 01869-252035 *(Bicester)*
St Joseph, Lawton Avenue, Carterton OX8 3JY **Tel:** 01993-841240 *(Carterton)*
Holy Trinity, 24 London Road OX7 5AX **Tel:** 01608-643487 *(Chipping Norton)*
Sacred Heart, Greys Hill RG9 1SL **Tel:** 01491-572796 *(Henley-on-Thames)*
St Thomas More, Oxford Road OX5 1EA **Tel:** 01865-373674 *(Kidlington)*
Our Lady of Lourdes, Curbridge Road, Witney OX8 7JZ **Tel:** 01993-702480 *(Witney)*
St Joseph, Brook Lane, Thame OX9 2AB **Tel:** 01844-214278 *(Thame)*

▲ Secondary Comprehensive

Blessed George Napier, Addison Road, Banbury **Tel:** 01295-264216
St Gregory the Great, Cricket Road, Oxford. OX4 3DR **Tel:** 01865-749933

■ SANDWELL

▲ Junior and Infant

St Gregory, Park Road, Smethwick, Sandwell W. Midlands B67 5HX **Tel:** 0121-429 4609
St Francis Xavier, McKean Road, Oldbury, Warley, W Midlands B69 4BA **Tel:** 0121-552 1485 *(Oldbury)*
St Philip, Messenger Road, Smethwick, Sandwell, W Midlands B66 3DU **Tel:** 0121-558 1643 *(Smethwick)*
St Hubert, Wolverhampton Road, Oldbury, Warley, W. Midlands B96 0LP **Tel:** 0121-422 2629 *(Warley)*
Holy Name, Cross Lane, Great Barr, Birmingham B43 6LN **Tel:** 0121-357 3216
St Mary, Manor House Road, Wednesbury, W Midlands WS10 9PN **Tel:** 0121-505 3595 *(Wednesbury)*
St John Bosco, Monmouth Drive, Hateley Heath B71 2ST **Tel:** 0121-556 0228 *(West Bromwich)*

▲ **Secondary Comprehensive**

Stuart Bathurst, Wood Green Road, Wednesbury, W Midlands WS10 9QS **Tel:** 0121-556 1488/4358

■ **SOLIHULL**

▲ **Junior and Infant**

St George and St Teresa, Mill Lane, Dorridge, Solihull B93 8PA **Tel:** 01564-774906 *(Dorridge)*

St Andrew, Windrush Close, Olton, Solihull B92 8QL **Tel:** 0121-743 5675 *(Birmingham 44)*

Our Lady of the Wayside, Stratford Road, Shirley, Solihull B90 4AY **Tel:** 0121-744 6852 *(Shirley)*

St Augustine, Herbert Road, Solihull B91 3QE **Tel:** 0121-705 4355 *(Solihull)*

Our Lady of Compassion, Kineton Green Road, Olton B92 7DG **Tel:** 0121-706 9508 *(Olton)*

St Anne, Nine Acres Drive, Chelmsley Wood B37 5DD **Tel:** 0121-770 3878 *(Birmingham 24)*

St Patrick, Dunster Road, Chelmsley Wood B37 7UU **Tel:** 0121-770 1227 *(Birmingham 24)*

St John the Baptist, Arran Way, Chelmsley Wood B36 0QE **Tel:** 0121-770 1892 *(Kingshurst)*

St Anthony, Forbridge Road, Kingshurst, Chelmsley Wood B37 6NY **Tel:** 0121-770 3168

▲ **Secondary Comprehensive**

St Peter, Whitefields Road, Solihull B91 3NE **Tel:** 0121-705 3988

Archbishop Grimshaw, Kew Close, Cook's Lane B37 0NY **Tel:** 0121-770 5331/2/3

■ **STAFFORDSHIRE**

▲ **Junior and Infant**

English Martyrs, Woodland Street, Biddulph, Stoke-on-Trent ST8 6LW **Tel:** 01782-512644 *(Biddulph)*

St Mary, Wharf Lane ST19 9BG **Tel:** 01902-850261 *(Brewood)*

St Modwen, Belvoir Road DE13 0RA **Tel:** 01283-239050 *(Burton)*

St Mary, Hunter Road WS11 3AE **Tel:** 01543-510380 *(Cannock)*

St Filumena, Caverswall, Stoke-on-Trent ST11 9EA **Tel:** 01782-392367 *(Caverswall)*

St Joseph, High Street, Chasetown, Nr Walsall WS7 8XL **Tel:** 01543-510485 *(Chasetown)*

St Giles, Charles Street, Cheadle, Staffs ST10 1ED **Tel:** 01538-753220 *(Cheadle)*

Our Lady and St Werburgh, Seabridge Lane, Clayton, Newcastle, Staffs ST5 4AG **Tel:** 01782-297451 *(Clayton)*

St Christopher, Wolverhampton Road, Codsall, Staffs WV8 1PF **Tel:** 01902-434310 *(Codsall)*

The Faber, C P Cotton, Oakamoor, Stoke-on-Trent ST10 3DN **Tel:** 01538-702324 *(Cotton)*

St John, Main Street, Great Haywood, Staffs ST18 0SL **Tel:** 01889-808190 *(Great Haywood)*

St Thomas More, Huthill Lane **Tel:** 01922-857075 *(Great Wyrley)*

St Joseph, Hill Top WS12 5DE **Tel:** 01543-512230 *(Hednesford)*

St John the Evangelist, Gloucester Road, Kidsgrove, Stoke-on-Trent ST7 1AE **Tel:** 01782-296736 *(Kidsgrove)*

St Mary, Cruso Street, Leek ST13 8BW **Tel:** 01538-483190 *(Leek)*

St Joseph, Cherry Orchard, Lichfield WS14 9AN **Tel:** 01543-263505 *(Lichfield)*

SS Peter and Paul, Dimbles Hill **Tel:** 01543-510748 *(Lichfield)*

St Mary, Stanier Street, Newcastle, Staffs ST5 2SU **Tel:** 01782-619685 *(Newcastle-under-Lyme)*

St Joseph, Newman Grove WS15 1BN. **Tel:** 01889-256120 *(Rugeley)*

St Anne, Lynton Avenue, Weeping Cross ST17 0EA **Tel:** 01785-663128 *(Stafford 3)*

St Austin, Garden Street ST17 4BT **Tel:** 01785-356769 *(Stafford 1)*

Blessed Mother Teresa of Calcutta, Somerset Road, Highfields, Stafford ST17 9UZ **Tel:** 01785-356405 *(Stafford)*

St Patrick, Marston Road ST16 3BT **Tel:** 01785-356685 *(Stafford 2)*

St Dominic, Newcastle Street, Stone ST15 8TJ **Tel:** 01785-812038 *(Stone)*

St Elizabeth, Claremont Road, Coton Lane, Estate B79 8EN **Tel:** 01827-475860 *(Tamworth)*

St Gabriel, Wilncote Lane, Belgrave B77 2LF **Tel:** 01827-475045 *(Tamworth)*

St Thomas, Parklands Road, Tean, Stoke-on-Trent ST10 4DS **Tel:** 01538-722378 *(Tean)*

St Joseph, Springfield Road, Uttoxeter, Staffs ST14 7JX **Tel:** 01889-562702 *(Uttoxeter)*

St Wulstan, Church Lane, Wolstanton, Newcastle, Staffs ST5 0EF **Tel:** 01782-296140 *(Wolstanton)*

St Bernadette, Lindale Drive, Wombourne, Wolverhampton WV5 8DU **Tel:** 01902-894787 *(Wombourne)*

▲ **Secondary Comprehensive**

Cardinal Griffin, Stafford Road, Cannock WS11 2AW **Tel:** 01543-502215 *(Cannock)*

Painsley RC High School, Station Road, Cheadle, Staffs ST10 1LH **Tel:** 01538-483944 *(Cheadle)*

St John Fisher RC High School, Ashfields New Road, Newcastle-under-Lyme ST5 2SJ **Tel:** 01782-615636 *(Newcastle-under-Lyme)*
St Joseph's College, Trent Vale ST4 5NT **Tel:** 01782-848008 *(Stoke-on-Trent)*
Blessed William Howard, Rowley Avenue, Stafford ST17 9AB **Tel:** 01785-244236 *(Stafford)*

■ STOKE-ON-TRENT

▲ Primary

St Thomas, North Street, Stoke-on-Trent ST4 7NA **Tel:** 01782-234919 *(Stoke-on-Trent)*
Our Lady and St Benedict, Abbey Lane, Abbey Hulton, Stoke-on-Trent ST2 8AU **Tel:** 01782-234646 *(Stoke-on-Trent 4)*
St Maria Goretti, Aylesbury Road, Bucknall ST2 0LY **Tel:** 01782-234747 *(Stoke-on-Trent (14)*
St George, Boulton Street, Birches Head ST1 2NQ **Tel:** 01782-234384 *(Stoke-on-Trent 10)*
St Peter, Waterloo Road, Cobridge, Burslem ST6 3HL **Tel:** 01782-236415 *Stoke-on-Trent 16)*
Our Lady's, Watkin Street, Fenton ST4 4NP **Tel:** 01782-235385 *(Stoke-on-Trent 6)*
St Joseph, Colclough Lane, Goldenhill ST6 5RG **Tel:** 01782-235393 *(Stoke-on-Trent 12)*
St Gregory, Spring Garden Road, Longton ST3 2QN **Tel:** 01782-235045
St Augustine, Sandon Road, Meir ST3 7DF **Tel:** 01782-319504 *(Stoke-on-Trent 8)*
St Mary, Ford Green Rd, Norton, Smallthorne ST6 8EZ **Tel:** 01782-234820 *(Stoke-on-Trent 7)*
St Teresa, 98 Stone Road, Trent Vale ST4 6SP **Tel:** 01782-235676 *(Stoke-on-Trent 17)*
St Wilfred's, Queens Avenue, Tunstall, Stoke-on-Trent. **Tel:** 01782-838496 *(Stoke-on-Trent)*

▲ Secondary Comprehensive

St Thomas More RC High School, Hall Road, Longton, Stoke-on-Trent ST3 2NJ **Tel:** 01782-315188 *(Stoke-on-Trent)*
St Margaret Ward RC High School Little Chell Lane, Tunstall Stoke-on-Trent ST6 6LZ **Tel:** 01782-234483 *(Stoke-on-Trent)*

■ WALSALL

▲ Junior and Infant

St Peter, Lichfield Road, Bloxwich, Walsall WS3 3LY **Tel:** 01922-710872
St Joseph, Rough Hay Road, Darlaston, Wednesbury WS10 8HN **Tel:** 0121-568 6496 *(Darlaston)*
St Mary, Jesson Road, Walsall WS1 3AY **Tel:** 01922-720711 *(Walsall)*
St Patrick, Blue Lane, East Walsall WS2 8HN. **Tel:** 01902-720063 *(Walsall)*
St Thomas of Canterbury, Dartmouth Avenue WS3 1SP **Tel:** 01922-720712 *(Walsall)*
St Mary of the Angels, Weston Crescent, Aldridge WS9 0HA **Tel:** 01922-743411 *(Aldridge)*
St Bernadette, Narrow Lane, Brownhills WS8 6HX **Tel:** 01543-452921 *(Brownhills)*
St Francis, Mill Road, Shelfield Nr Walsall WS4 1RH **Tel:** 01922-682583 *(Shelfield)*
St Anne, Blackwood Road, Streetly B74 3PL **Tel:** 0121-353 5114 *(Streetly)*

▲ Secondary Comprehensive

St Thomas More, Bilston Road, Willenhall, W Midlands WV13 2JY **Tel:** 01902-368798 *(Willenhall)*
St Francis of Assisi, Erdington Road, Aldridge WS9 0RN **Tel:** 01922-740300 *(Aldridge)*

■ WARWICKSHIRE

▲ Infant

Our Lady of the Angels, Coton Road, Riversley Park CV11 5TY **Tel:** 024 76 326080 *(Nuneaton)*
St Marie, Dunchurch Road, Rugby CV22 6AQ **Tel:** 01788-542203 *(Rugby)*

▲ Junior and Infant

Our Lady of the Angels, Coton Road, Riversley Park CV11 5TY **Tel:** 024 76 326080 *(Nuneaton)*
Our Lady, St Faith's Road B49 6AG **Tel:** 01789-762555 (Alcester)
St Edwards, Packington Lane, Coleshill, Birmingham B46 3EJ **Tel:** 01675-463249 *(Coleshill)*
St Mary, Arden Road, Henley-in-Arden, Solihull B95 5LT **Tel:** 015642-792316 *(Henley-in-Arden)*
Our Lady, Leamington Road, Princethorpe, Rugby CV23 9PU **Tel:** 01926-632385 *(Princethorpe)*
St Gregory, Avenue Road CV37 6UZ **Tel:** 01789-204517 *(Stratford-upon-Avon)*
St Mary, Pool Road, Studley B80 7QU Tel: 01527-852140 (Studley)
St Benedict, Church Walk CV9 1PS **Tel:** 01827-712320 *(Atherstone)*
St Francis RC, Rye Piece Ringway, Bedworth CV12 8JH **Tel:** 024 76 315279 (Bedworth)
St Patrick, Cashmore Avenue CV31 3EU **Tel:** 01926-425958 *(Leamington)*
St Anthony, Sydenham Drive CV31 1NJ **Tel:** 01926-428800 *(Leamington)*
Our Lady and St Teresa, Windmill Hill,

Cubbington, Leamington CV32 7LN
Tel: 01926-424420 *(Lillington)*
St. Joseph's Junior, Coton Road, Riversley Park, Nuneaton. CV11 5TY
Tel: 024 76 383807
St. Marie's Junior, Merttens Drive, Rugby. CV22 7AF **Tel:** 01788-543636
English Martyrs, High Street, Hillmorton, Rugby CV21 4EE
Tel: 01788-543423 *(Hillmorton)*
St Mary, Daventry Road, Southam CV47 1PS **Tel:** 01926 812512 *(Southam)*
St Mary, Priory Pools, off Wathen Road.
Tel: 01926-493959 *(Warwick)*
St Joseph, Rowley Road, Whitnash, Leamington Spa CV31 2LJ
Tel: 01926-427552 *(Whitnash)*

▲ Secondary Comprehensive
St Benedict, Kinwarton Road B49 6PX
Tel: 0178976-2888 *(Alcester)*
St Thomas More, Greenmore Road CV10 7EX **Tel:** 024 76 642400 *(Nuneaton)*
Trinity Catholic Technology College, Guy's Cliffe Avenue CV32 6NB **Tel:** 01926-428416 *(Leamington Spa)*

■ WOLVERHAMPTON

▲ Junior and Infant
Holy Trinity, Fraser Street, Bilston, W Midlands WV14 7PD
Tel: 01902-558977 *(Bilston)*
The Giffard School, Hordern Road, Whitmore Reans, Tettenhall WV6 0HR
Tel: 01902-556447 *(Whitmore Reans)*
Corpus Christi, Ashmore Avenue, Ashmore Park, Wolverhampton WV11 2LT
Tel: 01902-558725 *(Wolverhampton 1)*
St Anthony, Stafford Road, Fordhouses WV10 6NW **Tel:** 01902-558935 *(Wolverhampton 4)*
Holy Rosary, Hickman Avenue WV1 2BS
Tel: 01902-558874 *(Wolverhampton 8)*
SS Mary and John, Caledonia Road WV2 1HZ **Tel:** 01902-558780 *(Wolverhampton 2)*
St Michael, Telford Gardens, Merry Hill, WV3 7LE **Tel:** 01902-556368 *(Wolverhampton 6)*
St Mary, Cannock Road WV10 8PG
Tel: 01902-556355 *(Wolverhampton 3)*
St Teresa, Malins Road, Parkfield WV4 6AW **Tel:** 01902-558862 *(Wolverhampton 9)*
St Patrick, Graiseley Lane, Wednesfield WV11 1PG **Tel:** 01902-556451 *(Wolverhampton 7)*

▲ Secondary Comprehensive
St Edmund, Compton Road West WV3 9DU
Tel: 01902-558888
Our Lady and St Chad's School, Old Fallings Lane WV10 8BL
Tel: 01902-558250

■ WORCESTERSHIRE

▲ Junior and Infant
Mount Carmel, Downsell Road, Webheath, Redditch B97 5RR
Tel: 01527-546398 *(Redditch)*
St Thomas More, Woodrow Centre, Studley Road, Redditch B98 7RT
Tel: 01527-525821 *(Redditch)*
St Peter, Rock Hill, Bromsgrove B61 7LH
Tel: 01527-831872 *(Bromsgrove)*
St George, Thornloe Walk WR1 3JX
Tel: 01905-25841 *(Worcester)*
St Joseph, Chedworth Drive, Warndon WR4 9PG **Tel:** 01905-452772 *(Worcester 3)*
Our Lady Queen of Peace, Bransford Road, St John's WR2 4EN
Tel: 01905-421409 *(Worcester 2)*
St Mary, Leamington Road, Broadway WR12 7EA **Tel:** 01386-853337 *(Broadway)*
St Joseph, Ombersley Way, Droitwich WR9 0RY **Tel:** 01905-773572 *(Droitwich)*
St Mary, High Street, Evesham W11 4EJ
Tel: 01386-446748 *(Evesham)*
St Joseph, Newtown Road, Malvern WR14 1PF **Tel:** 01684-573016 *(Great Malvern)*
Holy Redeemer, Priest Lane, Pershore WR10 1EB **Tel:** 013865-552518 *(Pershore)*
St Wulstan, Elmfield Walk, Stourport on Severn, Worcs DY13 8TX **Tel:** 01299-877808 *(Stourport on Severn)*
St Ambrose, Leswell Street, Kidderminster DY10 1RP **Tel:** 01562-823568 *(Kidderminster)*

▲ Secondary Comprehensive
St Bede, Holloway Lane, Redditch B98 7HA
Tel: 01527-52591 *(Redditch)*
Hagley RC High School, Brake Lane, Hagley, Stourbridge DY8 2XL
Tel: 01562-883193 *(Stourbridge)*
St Augustine High, Stonepits Lane, Hunt End, Redditch B97 5LX
Tel: 01527-550400 *(Redditch)*
Blessed Edward Oldcorne, Timberdine Avenue, Worcester WR5 2BE
Tel: 01905-352615/360111 *(Worcester)*

■ CATHOLIC SCHOOLS - INDEPENDENT

■ OXFORDSHIRE

▲ Primary
St John's Priory St John's Road.
Tel: 01295-2427 *(Banbury)*
Oratory Prep School Goring Heath Great Oaks Reading RG8 7SF
Tel: 017357-4511

▲ Primary and Secondary
Rye St Antony, Pullen's Lane, Headington

Hill, Oxford OX3 0BY **Tel:** 01865-762802 **Fax:** 01865-763611

▲ **Secondary**

Oratory School, Woodcaote, nr Reading RG8 0PJ **Tel:** 01491-680207

■ **STAFFORDSHIRE**

▲ **Primary**

St Bede's, Bishton Hall, Wolseley Bridge near Stafford ST17 0XN **Tel:** 01889-881226/881277 *(Great Haywood)*

▲ **Primary and Secondary**

St Dominic's Priory School, ST15 8EN **Tel:** 01785-814181 *(Stone)*

St Dominic's Junior School, Hartshill Road, Stoke-on-Trent ST4 7LY **Tel:** 01782-48588 *(Stoke-on-Trent)*

■ **WARWICKSHIRE**

▲ **Junior**

Crackley Hall School, St Joseph's Park, Kenilworth CV8 2FT **Tel:** 01926-514444 **Website:** www.crackleyhall.co.uk

▲ **Secondary**

Princethorpe College, Near Rugby, Warwicks CV23 9PX **Tel:** 01926-632147 **Website:** www.princethorpe.co.uk (Princethorpe)

■ **WORCESTERSHIRE**

▲ **Primary**

Penrhyn School, Winterfold House, Chaddesley Corbett. Prep school for boys. **Tel:** 01562-777234

▲ **Primary and Secondary**

Holy Trinity High School (for Girls), Birmingham Road, Kidderminster, DY10 2BY **Tel:** 01562-822929

St Mary's Convent School, Mount Battenhall, Worcester WR5 2HP **Tel:** 01905-357786

DIOCESE OF BRENTWOOD

Formed on 22nd March 1917 by the division of the Archdiocese of Westminster, consists of the Geographical County of Essex, comprising the London Boroughs of Barking & Dagenham, Havering, Newham, Redbridge and Waltham Forest, the Unitary Authorities of Southend-on-Sea and Thurrock and the Administrative County of Essex.

Patrons of the Diocese
Our Lady of Lourdes (11th February),
St Edmund of Canterbury (16th November),
St Erconwald (13th May), St Cedd (26th October).

Bishop
Rt Rev Thomas McMahon, Bishop of Brentwood. Born in Dorking, Surrey, 17th June 1936; ordained 28th November 1959; ordained bishop by Cardinal Hume, 17th July 1980.

Residence:
Bishop's House, Stock, Ingatestone, Essex, CM4 9BU
Tel: 01277-840268

Office:
Cathedral House, Ingrave Road, Brentwood, Essex CM15 8AT.
Tel: 01277-232266 **Fax:** 01277-261152
E-mail: bishopthomas@dioceseofbrentwood.org

Bishop's Secretary:
Mrs Janet Steele,
Cathedral House, Ingrave Road, Brentwood, Essex CM15 8AT **Tel:** 01277-232266

Rt Rev Thomas McMahon, Bishop of Brentwood.

■ ADMINISTRATION

Except where another number is given, fax communications for Cathedral House should be sent to:
Fax: 01277-265264

■ The Vicars General

Mgr John Armitage, The Presbtery, 1 Berwick Road, Custom House, London E16 3DR **Tel:** 020-7476 2084
E-mail: vgbrentwood@hotmail.co.uk
Office: Tel: 01277-232266
Mgr David Manson, St John's Presbytery, Roman Road, Ingatestone, Essex CM4 9AA
Tel: 01277-353193
E-mail:
ingatestone@dioceseofbrentwood.org
Office: Tel: 01277-232266

■ Moderator of the Curia

Mgr Gordon Read, The Presbytery, Church Street, Kelvedon, Colchester, Essex CO5 9AH **Tel/Fax:** 01376-570348
E-mail:
kelvedon@dioceseofbrentwood.org

■ Vicars for Religious

Rev Adam Sowa, MS, 4 Blytheswood Road, Goodmayes, Ilford, Essex IG3 8SH
Tel: 020-8590 9026
Email: goodmayes@dioceseofbrentwood.org
Sr Josephine Canny, OA, 20 Higham Station Avenue, South Chingford, London E4 9AY **Tel:** 020-8531 0466
E-mail: mnicannaid@yahoo.ie

■ Chancellor

Mgr Gordon Read. Cathedral House, Ingrave Road, Brentwood, Essex CM15 8AT
Tel: 01277-265283 **Fax:** 01277-265273
E-mail: tribunal@dioceseofbrentwood.org
Secretary: **Mrs Karen Avery**. *Archivist and Historian:* **Rev Stewart Foster**; *Assistant Archivist:* **Miss Jane Neely**,
Tel: 01277-265283

■ FINANCE

■ Finance Office

Cathedral House, Ingrave Road, Brentwood, Essex CM15 8AT
Director of Finance: **Mr Gerald P Curran**.
Secretary: **Mrs Mary Gajewska**
Tel: 01277-265280 **Fax:** 01277-202163
E-mail: finance@dioceseofbrentwood.org

■ **Diocesan Gift Aid Office**
Diocesan Co-ordinator for Offertory Giving and Gift Aid: **Mr Michael Boultard**. *Gift Aid Secretary:* **Mrs Elizabeth Bukenya**. *Assistant:* **Mrs Teresa Edwards**. Cathedral House, Ingrave Road, Brentwood, Essex CM15 8AT **Tel:** 01277-265282
E-mail: giftaid@dioceseofbrentwood.org

■ **COMMUNICATIONS & PRESS OFFICERS**
Diocesan Communications Officer: **Rev John J Harvey**, 9 Trap's Hill, Loughton, Essex IG10 1SZ **Tel:** 020-8508 3492
Fax: 020-8532 0138
E-mail: loughton@dioceseofbrentwood.org
Diocesan Press Officer: **Mrs Mary Huntington**, **Tel:** 01245-227518
E-mail: mary@huntingtonm.freeserve.co.uk

■ **Registrar for Deceased Clergy**
Rev Brian McWilliams. Nazareth House, 111 London Road, Westcliff-on-Sea, Essex SS1 1PP **Tel:** 01702-345627

■ **EDUCATION AND FORMATION**

■ **Education**
Director: **Mgr George Stokes**. *Assistant Director:* **Miss Aileen Donnelly**. Education Department, Cathedral House, Ingrave Road, Brentwood, Essex CM15 8AT
Tel: 01277-265284 **Fax:** 01277-265260
E-mail: education@dioceseofbrentwood.org
Secretary: **Mrs Janet Simmons.**

■ **Brentwood Religious Education Service**
Director: **Mgr George Stokes**. **Mr Anthony Castle** (*Co-ordinator for CCRS*); **Sr Jude Groden, RSM** (*Primary RE Adviser*); **Miss Colette Dawson** (*Secondary RE Adviser/Co-ordinator of Inspections*). **Miss Mary Cronin** (*Secretary*). Cathedral House, Ingrave Road, Brentwood, Essex CM15 8AT **Tel:** 01277-265285
E-mail: bres@dioceseofbrentwood.org

■ **Primary Headteachers' Association**
Secretary: Vacant

■ **HIGHER EDUCATION**
Chaplain to the University of Essex: **Rev Martin Boland**. Catholic Chaplaincy, University of Essex, Wivenhoe Park, Colchester CO4 3SQ **Tel:** 01206-872018
E-mail: brightlingsea@ dioceseofbrentwood.org
Website: www.essex.ac.uk/cathchap
Chaplain to Anglia Ruskin University/ Chelmsford Campus: **Rev Frank Jackson**, The Presbytery, Beardsley Drive, Springfield, Chelmsford, Essex CM1 6GQ
Tel: 01245-465333 **E-mail:** springfield@dioceseofbrentwood.org
Chaplain to East London University: **Dcn Thomas Dunston CSJ**, 79 Barking Road, Canning Town, London E16 4HB
Tel/Fax: 020 7476 4129 **Email:** canningtown@ dioceseofbrentwood.org

■ **Priestly Formation**
Diocesan Director of Vocations: **Rev Joseph Silver**, St Vincent's Presbytery, Waldegrave Road, Daganham, Essex RM8 2QB **Tel/Fax:** 020-8590 7222
E-mail: bdvocations@aol.com
Promotor of Vocations: **Rev Dominic Howarth**, Walsingham House, Lionel Road, Canvey Island, Essex SS8 9DE
Tel: 01268-696610
Email: frdominic@bcys.net

■ **Permanent Diaconate**
Diocesan Director: **Rev Brian O'Shea**, 16 East Thurrock Road, Grays, Essex RM17 6SR **Tel:** 01375-372306
Fax: 01375-371702
E-mail: grays@ dioceseofbrentwood.org

■ **LITURGY AND ECUMENISM**

■ **Diocesan Liturgy Commission**
Executive Committee: *President:* **Bishop Thomas McMahon**. *Chairman:* **Rev Michael Butler**. (Liturgy Office, Cathedral House). *Secretary:* **Mrs Helen Barwell**. Liturgy Office, Cathedral House, Ingrave Road, Brentwood, Essex CM15 8AT
Tel: 01277-265287
E-mail: liturgy@dioceseofbrentwood.org

■ **Ecumenism**
Ecumenical Officer: **Mr Michael Malone-Lee**. Marshalls House, Marshalls Drive, London Road, Braintree, Essex CM7 2LN
Tel: 01376-551012
E-mail: malonelee@btinternet.com

■ **CHRISTIAN RESPONSIBILITY**

■ **Diocesan Commission for Justice and Social Responsibility**
President: **Bishop Thomas McMahon;** *Director:* **Mr Phil Butcher;** *Assistant Director:* **Mrs Davina Bolt;** *Administrative Secretary:* **Mrs Elizabeth Abbott,** Cathedral House, Ingrave Road, Brentwood, Essex CM15 8AT
Tel: 01277-265290
E-mail: cjsr@dioceseofbrentwood.org

■ **Diocesan Commission for the Safeguarding of Children and Vulnerable Adults**
Chairman: **Mrs Linda Ransom;** *Safeguarding Co-ordinator:* **Mr Simon Moules**; Childcare House, Little Wheatley Chase, Rayleigh, Essex SS6 9EH

Tel: 01268-784564 **Fax:** 01268-784664
Emergency Mbl: 07800 790217
E-mail: childprotection@dioceseofbrentwood.org

■ **Catholic Children's Society**
Director: **Mr Dick Madden**, Childcare House, Little Wheatley Chase, Rayleigh, Essex SS6 9EH
Tel: 01268-784544 **Fax:** 01268-784540
E-mail: director.childcarebccs@virgin.net

■ **Diocesan Youth Commission**
Youth Office, Cathedral House, Ingrave Road, Brentwood, Essex CM15 8AT
Tel: 01277-265286 **E-mail:** info@bcys.net
Administrator: **Mrs Suzanne Reeves**
Youth Chaplain and Youth Service Director: **Rev Dominic Howarth**.
Residence: 21 Eastfield Road, Brentwood, Essex CM14 4HB **Tel:** 01277 201427

■ **Ministry to Priests**
Diocesan Director: **Rev Adrian Graffy**, Clergy House, 28 Ingrave Road, Brentwood, Essex CM15 8AT **Tel:** 01277-265243
E-mail: adriangraffy@dioceseofbrentwood.org

■ **Supporting Ministry**
Diocesan Director: **Rev Adrlan Graffy**, Clergy House, 28 Ingrave Road, Brentwood, Essex CM15 8AT
Tel: 01277-265243
E-mail: adriangraffy@dioceseofbrentwood.org

■ **CONSULTATIVE BODIES**

■ **Canons of the Diocese**
Mgr J David Donnelly, Mgr D Michael Corley.

■ **College of Consultors**
The College of Consultors consists of the Deans of the 12 Deaneries in the Diocese, viz: Brentwood (**Rev John McGrath**): Barking (**Rev William Young**); Colchester (**Mgr Gordon Read**); Havering (**Rev John Hayes**); Mid-Essex (Vacant); Newham (**Rev John King**); North Essex (**Rev Anthony McKentey**); Redbridge (**Rev Paul Bruxby**); Southend-on-Sea (**Rev Kevin Hale**); South Essex (**Rev Philip Denton**); Waltham Forest (Vacant); West Essex (**Rev James Hawes**).

■ **Council of Priests**
Chairman: **Rev Michael Stokes**, 114 Connaught Avenue, Frinton-on-Sea, Essex CO13 9AD **Tel/Fax:** 01255-674475
E-mail: frinton@dioceseofbrentwood.org
Secretary: **Rev Daniel Mason**, 56 St Antony's Road, Forest Gate, London E7 9QB **Tel:** 020-8472 0433
Fax: 020-8503 5797
E-mail: forestgate@dioceseofbrentwood.org

■ **Commission for Evangelisation and Formation**
Director: **Rev Dr Adrian Graffy**
Members: **Mrs Lucy Studham**, *Co-ordinator of the Diocesan Pastoral Council and Pastoral Support Team.* **Sr Margaret Duffy RSM**, *Advisor for people who are Deaf and Hard of Hearing. Secretary,* **Mr Clive Dewi Thomas**, Cathedral House, Ingrave Road, Brentwood, Essex CM15 8AT
Tel: 01277-265289
Email: cef@dioceseofbrentwood.org
Consultors to the commission: **Revv Martin Boland, Paul Keane, Mrs Michelle Moran**.

■ **Diocesan Pastoral Council**
President: **Bishop Thomas McMahon**. *Co-ordinator:* **Mrs Lucy Studham**. *Secretary:* **Mr Clive Dewi Thomas**. Cathedral House, Ingrave Road, Brentwood, Essex CM15 8AT
Tel: 01277-265289 **E-mail:** bdpc@dioceseofbrentwood.org

■ **DIOCESAN MATRIMONIAL TRIBUNAL**

Judicial Vicar: **Mgr Gordon Read**. Cathedral House, Ingrave Road, Brentwood, Essex CM15 8AT
Tel: 01277-265283 **Fax:** 01277-265273
E-mail: tribunal@dioceseofbrentwood.org
Judges: **Mgr Gordon Read, Revv Joseph White, Paul Bruxby, John Harvey, Mrs Karen Avery.** *Defender of the Bond:* **Rev James Cassidy, CRIC.** *Advocates:* **Mgr Gordon Read, Rev Paul Bruxby, Rev John Harvey.** *Administrator:* **Mrs Karen Avery.**

■ **BRENTWOOD**
† Cathedral Church of St Mary and St Helen (1814; 1861; cons 15 June 1869; Dedication 31 May 1991)
Clergy House, 28 Ingrave Road, Brentwood, Essex CM15 8AT **Tel:** 01277-265235
E-mail: cathedral@dioceseofbrentwood.org
Website: www.brentwood-cathedral.co.uk
Mgr William Nix (*Cathedral Dean*), **Rev Paul Keane**. Also in Residence: **Rev Adrian Graffy.** *Deacon:* **Rev Paul Conrad**.
Also serves Holy Cross and All Saints, Warley
M: *Sun 8am, 9.30am, 11.30am, 6.30pm. Hds 9.15am, 1.10pm, 8pm.*

- ***Sisters of Mercy,*** 41 Priest's Lane, CM15 8BU **Tel:** 01277-220455
- ***Ursulines,*** Ursuline Generalate, 93 Queens Road, CM14 4EY **Tel:** 01277-260156 (office hours). **Fax:** 01277-263618 **Tel:** 01277-263886 (outside office hours). The Grange Community, 93 Queens Road, CM14 4EY **Tel:** 01277-216840
- ***Institute of the Blessed Virgin Mary, Loreto Sisters,*** 54 Cromwell Road, CM14 5DZ **Tel:** 01277-214027
- ***Sion Evangelisation Centre for National Training,*** Sawyers Hall Lane, CM15 9BY **Tel:** 01277-215011
- ***Community of Our Lady of Walsingham;*** Diocesan House of Prayer, Abbotswick, Navestock Side, Brentwood, Essex CM14 5SH **Tel:** 01277-373959 (House of Prayer) **Tel:** 01277-373848 (Community) **E-mail:**houseofprayer@dioceseofbrentwood.org **Website:** www.dioceseofbrentwood.net/houseofprayer

■ **ABRIDGE,** Essex
See Hainault.

■ **ARDLEIGH**
See Greenstead (2).

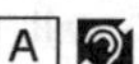

■ **AVELEY,** Essex
† The Holy Cross
(1952; 1953; 1961; cons 23 March 1971)
The Presbytery, Easington Way, South Ockendon, RM15 5EJ **Tel:** 01708-853130
Fax: 01708-670590
E-mail: aveley@dioceseofbrentwood.org
Website: www.holycross.aveley.org.uk
Rev Philip Denton.
M: *Sat 1st M of Sun 5.30pm, Sun 9am, 11am. Hds 9.30am, 7.30pm.*

- ***La Sainte Union Sisters,*** 20 Little Belhus Close, South Ockendon, Essex RM15 5BG **Tel/Fax:** 01708-852707

St Paul (1964)
Mill Road - Closed all services at The Holy Cross

■ **BARKING,** Essex
1. † St Mary and St Ethelburga (1858; 1869; cons 10 Oct 1957; new church cons 11 Oct 1979)
Linton Road, Barking
Tel: 020-8594 2849 **Fax:** 020-8262 5898
E-mail: barkingssm&e@dioceseofbrentwood.org
Rev William Young, The Presbytery, 41 Linton Road, Barking, Essex IG11 8HG
M: *Sun 8am, 11am. Hds 11am, 7.30pm.*
See also Ilford (3).

2. † St Thomas More
(1935, 1991, ded 22 June 1992)
514 Longbridge Road, Barking, IG11 9BY
Tel: 020-8590 2191 **E-mail:** barkingstm@dioceseofbrentwood.org
Pallottine Fathers (SCA): **Rev Michael Coen**, (Parish Priest), **Mgr Anthony Harris**.
M: *Sun 9am, 11.30am, 6.30pm. Hds 9am, 7.30pm.*
See also Dagenham (3).

■ **BARKINGSIDE,** Ilford, Essex
† St Augustine of Canterbury
(1928; 1954; cons Apr 29, 1980)
Cranbrook Road North.
Tel: 020-8554 3568 **Fax:** 0870 705 9323
E-mail: barkingside@dioceseofbrentwood.org
Website: staugustinescatholicchurch.co.uk
Rev Paul Bruxby. St Augustine's Presbytery, Loudoun Avenue IG6 1AU
M: *Sat 1st M of Sun 6.30pm. Sun 9am, 11am. Hds 8.30am, 10am, 7.30pm.*

■ **BASILDON**
The Basildon Catholic Team Ministry serving the parishes of:

1. † St Basil the Great, Luncies Road (1953; 1956, cons 6 Oct 1981).
M: *Sat 1st M of Sun 5pm; Sun 11am. Hds 9.30am, 7pm.*

2. † The Most Holy Trinity, Wickhay (21 Sept 1958; 1972; new church 1980)
M: *Sat 1st M of Sun 6pm; Sun 10am. Hds (vigil 8pm); 11am.*

3. † St Therese of Lisieux, Florence Way (1926; 1954; new church opened 8 Dec 1991, dedicated 21 May 1992).
M: *Sun 9am; 5pm. Hds 9.30am.*

Team Members: **Revv Julian Wiener, Paul Dynan; Sister Clare Kane, OSU, Sister Anne Spilberg, OSU, and Mr & Mrs Brian & Maureen Devine.**
The Team Office – The Priest's House, Luncies Road, Basildon, Essex SS14 1SD
Tel: 01268-553425 **Fax:** 01268-551836
Email: basildonstb@dioceseofbrentwood.org

Website: www.basildoncatholics.com
Also resident: **Rev Richard Ashton**, (retired), Evelyn May House, Florence Way, Laindon SS16 6AJ

■ **BECKTON, E6**
† **St Mark's Church** (1987)
Tollgate Road, Beckton E6 **Tel:** 020-7511 3024
Mgr John Armitage VG (*Parish Priest*), resident at Custom House.
Office Tel: 020-7476 2084
E-mail: customhouse@dioceseofbrentwood.org
M: *Sat 1st M of Sun 6pm. Sun 12 noon. Hds 8pm.*
See also Custom House and Silvertown & North Woolwich.

■ **BECONTREE,** Essex
† **St Vincent** (1923; 1927; 1931; cons 4 Dec 1973)
Waldegrave Road, Dagenham, RM8 2QB
Tel/Fax: 020-8590 7222
E-mail: becontree@dioceseofbrentwood.org
Rev Joseph Silver.
M: *Sun 9am, 12noon, 7pm. Hds 9.30am, 8pm.*
- ***La Sainte Union Sisters***, 54 Dunkeld Road, Dagenham, Essex RM8 2PR
Tel: 020-8270 3291

■ **BENFLEET,** Essex
† **Holy Family**
(1949; new church cons 14 May 1975)
661 High Road, South Benfleet, SS7 5SF
Tel: 01268-792082
Office **Tel/Fax:** 01268-799649
E-mail: benfleet@dioceseofbrentwood.org
Website: www.holyfamily-church.org
Rev William Newton (*Priest in Charge*).
M: *Sat 1st M of Sun 6pm. Sun 11am. Hds 9.30am.*
See also Hadleigh.

■ **BILLERICAY,** Essex
† **The Most Holy Redeemer**
(1911; 1918, dedicated 29 Nov 1985)
21 Laindon Road, Billericay, Essex CM12 9LL
Tel: 01277-624891 **Fax:** 01277-632071
E-mail: billericay@dioceseofbrentwood.org
Website: www:mostholyredeemer.org.uk
Rev John McGrath.
M: *Sat 1st M of Sun 6pm. Sun 9am, 11am, 5pm. Hds (vigil 8pm), 9.15am (School), 10.30am, 8pm.*

■ **BLACK NOTLEY,** Essex
See Braintree.

■ **BOREHAM,** Chelmsford
See Springfield (3).

■ **BRAINTREE,** Essex
† **Our Lady Queen of Peace**
(1897; 1939; cons 8 September 1954)
The Avenue, Braintree, Essex CM7 3HY
Tel: 01376-326779
E-mail: braintree@dioceseofbrentwood.org
Website: www.olqp.co.uk
Rev Anthony McKentey.
M: *Sat 1st M of Sun 6pm. Sun 9am, 11am. Hds 9.30am (School), 11am, 7.30pm.*
- ***Missionary Franciscan Sisters of the Immaculate Conception,*** 2 Broad Road, Bocking CM7 9RS
Tel: 01376-326654 **Fax:** 01376-340401
Residential Home. **Tel:** 01376-345503
M: *Sun 5pm.*

■ **BRIGHTLINGSEA-WITH-WIVENHOE,** Essex
1. † St Sabina (1904, 1958; 1964)
Richard Avenue.
Rev Martin Boland *(Chaplain to University of Essex).* 1 Recreation Way, Brightlingsea, Essex CO7 0NJ **Tel/Fax:** 01206-302485
E-mail: brightlingsea@dioceseofbrentwood.org
Website: www.b-a-wparish.org.uk
M: *Sat 1st M of Sun 6pm. Hds 9am.*

2. † St Monica, Wivenhoe (1958; 1967)
De Vere Lane, Wivenhoe.
M: *Sun 10am. Hds Either on the eve or on the day 7.30pm.*

■ **BUCKHURST HILL,** Essex
Served from Woodford Green.
M: *Sun 9am (in St James' URC, Palmerston Road).*

■ **BURNHAM-ON-CROUCH,** Essex
† **St Cuthbert** (1908; 1910; cons 12 April 1967)
Western Road, Burnham-on-Crouch, Essex.
Tel: 01621-782034 **Fax:** 01621-786576
E-mail: burnham@dioceseofbrentwood.org
Rev Peter Connor. (Linked with Maldon - **Tel:** 01621-852259)
M: *Sun 11.15am. Hds (vigil 7.30pm)*

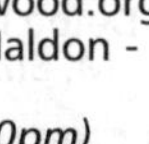

■ **CANNING TOWN, E16**
† **St Margaret and All Saints**
(1859; 1876; cons 4 February 1919; restored October 1951)
79 Barking Road, Canning Town E16 4HB
Tel/Fax: 020-7476 4129 **E-mail:** canningtown@dioceseofbrentwood.org
***Community of St John (CSJ):* Revv Martin Sabathé** (Prior and *Parish Priest*), **Peter Pitre**. *Deacon:* **Rev Thomas Dunton** *(Chaplain to University of East London)*, **Br Maire Sean O'Leary**
M: *Sat 1st M of Sun 6.30pm. Sun 9am, 11.30am. Hds 9.30am, 7.30pm.*
- ***Anchor House*** 'Working at the heart of homelessness', 81 Barking Road, E16 4HB
Tel: 020-7476 6062 **Fax:** 020-7511 5078
E-mail: keith@anchorhouseuk.org
Director: **Keith Fernett**.
- ***Franciscan Friars of the Renewal (CFR),***

St Fidelis Friary, Killip Close, E16 1LX **Tel:** 020-7474 0766 **Fax:** 020-7411 5225 **Revv Emmanuel Mansford** (*Superior*), **Raphaël Chilou, Angelus Houle. Bros Dominic Bormauns, John Bosco Mills, Barnabas Leonard, Umile Aiello**
- ***Franciscan Missionaries of Mary,*** St Margaret's Convent, Bethell Avenue E16 4JU **Tel:** 020-7511 3463
- ***Sisters of Charity,*** 11 Ruscoe Road, E16 1JA **Tel:** 020-7476 4525

■ CANVEY ISLAND, Essex A

† Our Lady of Canvey and the English Martyrs
(1938; 1953; dedicated 15 May 1998)
224 Long Road, Canvey Island, Essex SS8 0JS
Tel: 01268-682599 **Fax:** 01268-696908
E-mail: canveyisland@dioceseofbrentwood.org
Rev John D Meehan.
M: *Sat 1st M of Sun 6pm. Sun 9am, 11am. Hds 9.30am, 7.30pm.*
- ***Sisters of Mercy,*** The Convent, 60 Lionel Road, SS8 9DQ **Tel/Fax:** 01268-683630
- ***Diocesan Youth Retreat House,*** Walsingham House, Lionel Road, SS8 9DE **Tel/Fax:** 01268-515970

■ CHADWELL HEATH S

† St Bede (1935; 1949; 1963)
Bishop's Avenue, Chadwell Heath, Romford, Essex RM6 5RS **Tel/Fax:** 020-8590 8818
E-mail: chadwellheath@dioceseofbrentwood.org
Rev Martin O'Connor.
M: *Sat 1st M of Sun 6pm. Sun 9am, 11am. Hds 9.05am, 8pm.*

■ CHADWELL ST MARY, Grays, Essex

† St Joseph (1968; 1975)
1 Defoe Parade. Served from Tilbury.
M: *Sun 9am. Hds (vigil 7pm).*

■ CHELMER VILLAGE

See Springfield (2).

■ CHELMSFORD

1. † Our Lady Immaculate
Linked with **The Holy Name**
178 New London Road, Chelmsford CM2 0AR
Tel: 01245-352898 **Fax:** 01245-600043
E-mail: chelmsfordoli@dioceseofbrentwood.org
Website: www.olichurch.co.uk
Norbertine Canons (OPraem): **V. Rev Hugh Allan** *(Superior and Parish Priest)*, **Revv Stephen Cansse, Michael Gallagher, Cadoc Leighton, Richard Saksons, John Wisdom**. **Br Rupert Allen, James Foley**

A

† Our Lady Immaculate
(1845; 1847, cons 20 Oct 1866)
New London Road
M: *Sun 9am, 12noon, 7pm. Hds, 7am, 9.30am, 12.30pm.*

- ***Servite Sisters,*** 1a Moulsham Drive, CM2 9PX **Tel:** 01245-260446 **Fax:** 01245-345572

A

† The Holy Name (1965; 1970)
Lucas Avenue.
M: *Sat 1st M of Sun 6pm. Sun 10.30am. Hds 7.30pm.*

2. † The Blessed Sacrament
(1952; 1953; 1962; ded 7 July 2005)
116 Melbourne Avenue, Chelmsford CM1 2DU **Tel:** 01245-354256
E-mail: chelmsfordbs@dioceseofbrentwood.org
Rev Niall Harrington.
M: *Sat 1st M of Sun 7pm. Sun 9.30am, 11.30am. Hds (vigil 8pm), 9.30am (in term time in St Pius X School).*
- ***Canonesses of the Holy Sepulchre,*** 43 Anderson Avenue, CM1 2DA **Tel:** 01245-604108 **E-mail:** anderson2003@blueyonder.co.uk and at 22 Anderson Avenue CM1 2QB **Tel:** 01245-604128

See also Springfield.

■ CHIGWELL, Essex

† Chigwell Convent (cons. 5 Nov 1925)
803 Chigwell Road, Woodford Bridge, Chigwell, Essex IG8 8AU
- ***Sisters of the Sacred Hearts of Jesus and Mary:*** **Tel:** 020-8504 1624 **Email:** shjmgensec@aol.com (Generalate): **Tel:** 020-8506 0329 **Email:** shjmcomsec@aol.com (Community) **Tel:** 020 8505 8180 **Fax:** 020-8559 2149
Served from Woodford Green.
M: *Sun 10am. Hds 10am.*
Domus Mariae Conference and Retreat Centre, **Tel/Fax:** 020 8506 0359
JPIC Office and Resource Centre: **Tel/Fax:** 020 8559 1629

■ CHINGFORD, E4

1. † Our Lady of Grace and St Teresa of Avila
(1919; 1931; cons 13 May 1949)
Kings Road, Chingford
Tel: 020-8529 1804
E-mail: chingfordolg&sta@dioceseofbrentwood.org
Mgr Christopher Brooks, 1 Kings Road, E4 7HP
M: *Sat 1st M of Sun 6pm. Sun 8.30am, 10.30am. Hds 9.15am, 8pm.*
- ***Franciscan Missionaries of the Divine Motherhood,*** Assisi, 2 Brodie Road, Chingford, Loudon E4 7HE **Tel:** 020-8524 9908

Gilwell Park, Scout Training Centre and Campsite. See Waltham Abbey.

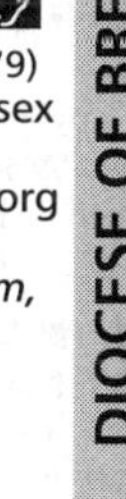

2. † Christ the King
(1932, new church dedicated 5 Sept 1997)
455 Chingford Road, Chingford E4 8SP
Tel: 020-8527 3087 **Fax:** 020-8527 0125
E-mail:chingfordctk@
dioceseofbrentwood.org
Rev Britto Belvendran.
M: *Sat 1st M of Sun 6pm. Sun 9am, 11am. Hds 10am, 8pm.*

- ***Oblates of the Assumption,*** 20 Higham Station Avenue E4 9AY
Tel: 020-8531 0466

■ CLACTON-ON-SEA, Essex
† Our Lady of Light and St Osyth
(1894; 1903; 1918; ded 15 Oct 2004)
1 Church Road, Clacton-on-Sea, CO15 6AG
Tel: 01255-423319
E-mail: clacton@dioceseofbrentwood.org
Website: www.ourladyoflight.co.uk
Rev James McCormack.
M: *Sat 1st M of Sun 6pm. Sun 11am. Hds 7.30pm. For other times see bulletin.*

- ***Missionary Franciscan Sisters of the Immaculate Conception,*** St Clares, 16 Russell Road CO15 6BE
Tel/Fax: 01255-421236
- ***Sisters of Mercy (Westminster),*** St Michael's Convent, 93 Marine Parade East, CO15 6JW Care Home;
Tel: 01255-423688 *Chaplain:* **Rev Bernard Caszo, MSFS.** Also: Convent of Mercy, 97 Marine Parade East CO15 6JW
Tel: 01255-426136

See also Holland-on-Sea and Jaywick.

■ CLAYHALL, Essex
† St John Vianney
(1944; 1966; cons 27 July 1983)
1 Stoneleigh Road, Clayhall, Ilford IG5 0JB
Tel: 020-8550 4540 **Fax:** 020-8551 9935
E-mail: clayhall@dioceseofbrentwood.org
Rev Jeba Marshall.
M: *Sun 10.30am, 5pm. Hds 9.15am, 8pm.*

■ COGGESHALL, Essex
St Bernard (1928)
Stoneham Street. Served from Kelvedon.
M: *Sun 9am. Hds 6pm.*

■ COLCHESTER
1. † St James the Less and St Helen
(1837; cons 9 May 1933)
51 Priory Street, Colchester CO1 2QB
Tel: 01206-866317 **Fax:** 01206-791213
E-mail: colchester@dioceseofbrentwood.org
Revv Joseph Whisstock, Philip Willenbrock, Brett Adams.
M: *Sat 1st M of Sun 6.15pm. Sun 8am, 10.30am, 6.30pm. Hds 9.15am, 12.15pm, 7.30pm.*

- ***Canonesses of the Holy Sepulchre:*** 48 Priory Street, CO1 2QB.
Tel: 01206-867296 (Community)
Tel: 01206-869479 (Prioress)
E-mail: teresalenahan@
hotmail.co.uk
- ***Colchester Garrison and MCTC:*** **Rev Bernard (Brian) McGilloway,** *Officiating Chaplain.*

2. St Joseph
Mill Road, Mile End.
Served from Colchester (1).
M: *Sun 9.15am.*

3. † St Cedd and St Gregory, West Mersea
(1962)
Served from Colchester (1).
M: *Sun 8.30am. Hds (vigil 7.30pm).*

4. † St Theodore of Canterbury, Monkwick
(1964).
Prince Philip Road.
Served from Colchester (1).
M: *Sun 10.15am.*

■ COLLIER ROW
† Corpus Christi (1952; 1965; cons 6 Dec 1979)
Lowshoe Lane, Collier Row, Romford, Essex RM5 2AP **Tel/Fax:** 01708-749050
E-mail: collierrow@dioceseofbrentwood.org
Rev Sean F Sheils.
M: *Sat 1st M of Sun 6.30pm. Sun 9am, 11.30am. Hds 9am, 7.30pm.*

■ CORRINGHAM, Essex
See Stanford-le-Hope.

■ CRANHAM, Essex
St Peter's Catholic Centre (1977)
Front Lane. Served from Upminster.
M: *Sun 12.15pm.*

■ CUSTOM HOUSE, E16
† St Anne (1899; 1981)
1 Berwick Road, Custom House, London E16 3DR **Tel:** 020-7476 2084
E-mail: customhouse@
dioceseofbrentwood.org
Mgr John Armitage, VG.
E-mail: vgbrentwood@hotmail.co.uk
M: *Sun 10.30am, 6pm.*
Hds 9.15am, 7.30pm.

See also Beckton and Silvertown & North Woolwich.

- ***Canonesses of the Holy Sepulchre,*** 71 Cundy Road, Custom House, London E16 3DJ Tel: 020-7476 5490
- ***Holy Family Sisters of the Needy,*** 14 Berwick Road, Custom House, London E16 3DR Tel: 020-7476 6501

■ DAGENHAM, Essex
1 † St Peter (1926; 1928; 1937)
52 Goresbrook Road, Dagenham RM9 6UR
Tel/Fax: 020-8595 1227. **E-mail:**
dagenhamstp@dioceseofbrentwood.org
Missionaries of La Salette (MS): **Revv**

Augustyn Hamielec (*Parish Priest*); **Leszek Gamracy**.
M: *Sat 1st M of Sun 5.30pm. Sun 9am, 11am. Hds 9am, 7.30pm.*
- ***Sisters of the Sacred Hearts of Jesus and Mary,*** Sacred Heart Convent, Goresbrook Road, RM9 6XP **Tel:** 020-8592 3835

2. † Holy Family
(1930; 1934; cons 13 Nov 1958)
Oxlow Lane, Dagenham, Essex RM9 5XJ
Tel: 020-8592 1634 **Fax:** 0870-706 1496
E-mail:dagenhamhf@dioceseofbrentwood.org
Rev Stephen Myers. Also in residence: **Rev John McKeon**
M: *Sat 1st M of Sun 6pm. Sun 9.30am, 11am. Hds 9.30am, 7.30pm.*
- ***Holy Family Sisters of the Needy,*** 14 Berwick Road, Custom House, London E16 3DR Tel: 020-7474 6501
- ***Ursulines (Brentwood),*** 147 Halbutt Street, RM9 5AH **Tel:** 020-8924 4640

3 † St Anne (1958)
Woodward Road. Served from Barking (2).
M: *Sat 1st M of Sun 5pm. Hds (vigil 7.30pm).*

■ DANBURY
† English Martyrs (1962)
Maldon Road, Danbury, Chelmsford, Essex
Tel: 01245-324138
E-mail: danbury@dioceseofbrentwood.org
Rev Paul Fox. 36 Inchbonnie Road, South Woodham Ferrers, Essex CM3 5FG
M: *Sat 1st M of Sun 6pm. Sun 10.45am. Hds 8pm.*
See also South Woodham Ferrers.

■ DEBDEN
† St Thomas More (1953; 1963)
Willingale Road, Loughton, Essex.
Served from Loughton.
M: *Sat 1st M of Sun 6pm. Hds 9am.*

■ DODDINGHURST, Essex
St Margaret of Scotland (1970)
Doddinghurst Road, Brentwood.
Served from Ongar.
M: *Sun 10am. Hds See Newsletter.*

■ DOVERCOURT, Essex
See Harwich.

■ DUNMOW, Essex

† Our Lady and St Anne Line (1853; 1971)
Mill Lane, Dunmow, Essex CM6 1BG
Tel: 01371-872550
E-mail: dunmow@dioceseofbrentwood.org
Rev Martin Nott
M: *Sat 1st M of Sun 5.30pm. Sun 11am. Hds 9am, 8pm.*
See also Hatfield Broad Oak.

■ EAST HAM, E6

† St Michael (1925; 1928; 1959; cons 25 June 1969)
21 Tilbury Road, East Ham, London E6 6ED
Tel: 020-8472 2557 **Fax:** 020-8586 2189
E-mail: eastham@dioceseofbrentwood.org
Rev Brian O'Higgins.
M: *Sun 9am, 11am, 6.30pm. Hds 9.30am, 7.30pm.*
- ***Sisters of Mercy,*** 7 Tilbury Road, E6 4ED **Tel:** 020-8552 4729
- ***Sisters of the Immaculate Heart of Mary,*** 36 Chesley Gardens, E6 3LN **Tel:** 020-8472 9634

■ EAST TILBURY, Essex
See Linford.

■ EASTWOOD

† St Peter (1955; 1973; 1968; cons 10 Nov 1983)
59 Eastwood Road North, Eastwood, Leigh-on-Sea, Essex SS9 4BX
Tel: 01702-522879 **Fax:** 01702-525323
E-mail: eastwood@dioceseofbrentwood.org
Website: www.saint-peters.co.uk
Rev Robert Mortimer-Anderson.
M: *Sun 8.30am, 10am, 6pm. Hds am see newsletter, 7.30pm.*

■ ELM PARK,
Hornchurch, Essex
† St Alban (1939; 1960, Cons 31 Jan 1978)
Langdale Gardens.
Tel: 01708-451449 **Fax:** 01708-456151
E-mail: elmpark@dioceseofbrentwood.org
Rev Bob Hamill. 1 Ullswater Way, RM12 5JX
M: *Sat 1st M of Sun 6.30pm. Sun 9am, 11am. Hds (vigil 7.30pm), 10am, 7.30pm.*

■ EPPING, Essex
† The Immaculate Conception
(1932; 1934; 1954; Ded 8 Dec 1993)
11 Church Hill, Epping, Essex CM16 4RA
Tel: 01992-572516 **Fax:** 01992-570096
E-mail: epping@dioceseofbrentwood.org
Rev James Hawes.
Deacon: **Rev Duncan J Whitehouse**.
M: *Sat 1st M of Sun 6pm. Sun 9am, 11am. Hds 10am, 8pm.*

■ FOREST GATE, E7

† St Antony of Padua (1884; 1891)
56 St Antony's Road, Forest Gate E7 9QB
Tel: 020-8472 0433 **Fax:** 020-8503 5797
E-mail: forestgate@dioceseofbrentwood.org
Revv Denis Hall, Daniel Mason.
Also in residence: **Revv John Duckett, Stewart Foster**.
M: *Sat 1st M of Sun 6.30pm. Sun 8.30am, 10am, 11.30am, 6.30pm (Latin, Extraordinary Form), 1st and 3rd Sun of the month 3pm (Spanish), 4th Sun of the Month 5pm (Tamil). Hds*

8am, 10am, 7.30pm.
- ***Sisters of St Joseph of Tarbes,*** 20 Lancaster Road, Forest Gate, London E7 9PW **Tel:** 020-8472 2713
- ***Society of the Sacred Heart,*** 159 Boleyn Road, E7 9QH **Tel:** 020-8472 2859
- ***Ursulines (Roman Union),*** Ursuline Convent, 38 Grosvenor Road, E7 8JA **Tel:** 020-8471 6644 **Fax:** 020-8548 1012
- ***Durning Hall Community Centre,*** Earlham Grove, E7
  Served from Forest Gate.
  M: *Sun 10.30am.*

■ FRINTON-ON-SEA
† Sacred Heart and St Francis. (1923)
114 Connaught Avenue, Frinton-on-Sea Essex CO13 9AD **Tel:** 01255-674475
E-mail: frinton@dioceseofbrentwood.org
Rev Michael W Stokes.
M: *Sat 1st M of Sun 6pm, Sun 8.30am. Hds (vigil 7.30pm), 9.15am.*
- ***Sisters of Mercy,*** 12 Cambridge Road, CO13 9HN **Tel:** 01255-674479

■ GALLEYWOOD
See Chelmsford (1).

■ GIDEA PARK
† Christ the Eternal High Priest (1963; 1974)
410 Brentwood Road, Gidea Park, Romford, Essex RM2 6DH
Tel: 01708-449914 **E-mail:** gideapark@dioceseofbrentwood.org
Rev Gerard Hughes.
M: *Sun 9am, 11am, 6.30pm. Hds 9am, 8pm.*
- ***Sisters of Mercy,*** St Mary's Convent, 13 Burntwood Avenue, Hornchurch RM11 3JD **Tel:** 01708-437711

■ GOODMAYES
† St Cedd (1966; cons 1 Dec 1983)
High Road, Goodmayes, Ilford, Essex.
Tel/Fax: 020-8590 9026
E-mail: goodmayes@dioceseofbrentwood.org
Missionaries of La Salette (MS): **Revv Adam Sowa** (*Parish Priest*), **Edward Tredota**. 4 Blythswood Road, IG3 8SH
M: *Sat 1st M of Sun 7.30pm. Sun 9.30am, 11am, 12.30pm (Polish), 6.30pm. Hds (vigil 7.30pm), 10am, 7.30pm.*
- ***Sisters of the Immaculate Heart of Mary, Mother of Christ,*** 5 Ashgrove Road, IG3 9XE **Tel:** 020-8590 3955

■ GRAYS, Essex
† St Thomas of Canterbury
(1886; 1918; con 12 Oct 1986)
16 East Thurrock Road, Grays, RM17 6SR
Tel: 01375-372306 **Fax:** 01375-371702
E-mail: grays@dioceseofbrentwood.org
Revv Brian O'Shea, also in residence **Mgr George Stokes**.
M: *Sat 1st M of Sun 6.30pm. Sun 8.30am, 11am, 6.30pm. Hds (vigil 8pm), 12noon, 8pm.*
- ***La Sainte Union Sisters,*** 25 College Avenue, RM17 5UN **Tel:** 01375-372339

See also Stifford Clays.

■ GREAT BADDOW, Essex
See Chelmsford (1)

■ GREAT BARDFIELD, Essex
† The Holy Spirit (1955; 1985)
Church House, Braintree Road, CM7 4RN
Tel: 01371-810428 **E-mail:** greatbardfield@dioceseofbrentwood.org
Rev John Timmins.
M: *Sun 9.30am. Hds 7pm.*
See also Thaxted

■ GREAT WAKERING, Essex
St Edmund of Canterbury (1962)
Little Wakering Road.
Chapel of Witness, Shoeburyness parish.

■ GREENSTEAD with ARDLEIGH and MISTLEY (1982)
Priest's House, 21 Blackthorn Avenue, Greenstead, Colchester, Essex CO4 3QD
Tel/Fax: 01206-870460
E-mail: greenstead@dioceseofbrentwood.org
Rev Conrad Smith.

Greenstead
† St John Payne (1972; ded 1 Oct 2004)
Blackthorn Avenue.
M: *Sun 10.30am. Hds 7.30pm.*

Ardleigh
M: *Sun 8.50am. Hds 8.15am. In St Mary the Virgin, C-of-E Parish Church.*

Mistley
M: *Sat 1st M of Sun 6.30pm. Hds 9.45am. In St Mary & St Michael C of E Parish Church.*

■ HADLEIGH, Essex
† St Thomas More (1982)
14 High Street. Served from Benfleet.
M: *Sun 9am. Hds (vigil 7.30pm).*

■ HAINAULT, Essex

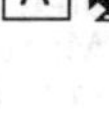

† The Assumption
(1952; 1953; cons 11 Feb 1983)
98 Manford Way, Chigwell, Essex IG7 4DF
Tel/Fax: 020-8500 3953
E-mail: hainault@dioceseofbrentwood.org
Rev Jean-Claude Selvini.
M: *Sat 1st M of Sun 6pm. Sun 10am, 12noon. Hds 10am, 8pm.*

■ HALSTEAD, Essex

† St Francis of Assisi (1928; 1955)
90 Colchester Road, Halstead, Essex

CO9 2EW **Tel/Fax:** 01787-472477
E-mail: halstead@dioceseofbrentwood.org
• ***Pallottine Fathers (SCA):***
Rev Liam Sweeney
M: *Sat 1st M of Sun 6pm. Sun 11am. Hds 11am, 8pm.*

See also Sible Hedingham.

■ **HARLOW,** Essex

1. † Church of the Assumption
(1894; 1951; Cons 29 Nov 1991)
Church House, Mulberry Green, Old Harlow, Essex CM17 0HA **Tel:** 01279-429388
E-mail: harlowold@dioceseofbrentwood.org
Rev Michael Butler.
M: *Sat 1st M of Sun 6pm. Sun 9am, 11am. Hds 10am, 8pm.*

2. Our Lady of Fatima & St Thomas More
The Presbytery, Howard Way, Harlow, Essex CM20 2NS **Tel:** 01279-426017
E-mail: harlowolf@dioceseofbrentwood.org
• ***Missionaries of La Salette (MS).*** **Revv Boguslow Kot** *(Parish Priest)*, **Slawomir Jedrych,** also in residence: **Andrzej Forys**

† Our Lady of Fatima
(1894; 1955;cons 25 March 1985)
Howard Way
M: *Sun 8am, 11am. Hds 9.30am.*

† St Thomas More
(1957; 1965; cons 28 Sept 1984)
Hodings Road
M: *Sat 1st M of Sun 6.30pm. Sun 9.30am, 1st & 3rd Sun 4pm (Polish). Hds 7.30pm.*
• ***Sisters of the Sacred Hearts of Jesus and Mary,*** The Convent, 6 The Gowers, CM20 2JP **Tel:** 01279-436512
• ***Sion Community,*** 1 Upper Park, CM20 1TN **Tel:** 01279-427980

3. St Luke's and Holy Cross
The Presbytery, Tracyes Road, Harlow, Essex CM18 6JJ **Tel:** 01279-425776
E-mail: harlowhc@dioceseofbrentwood.org
Rev Bernard Soley.

† St Luke (1962, 1966)
Perry Road, Staple Tye, Great Parndon (Shared with C of E and Methodists)
M: *Sun 9am. Hds 9.15am (in term time in St Luke's School).*

† Holy Cross (1957; 1958; 1963)
Tracys Road
M: *Sat 1st M of Sun 5.30pm. Sun 11am. Hds, 11.15am (term time only), 7.30pm.*

■ **HAROLD HILL**

1. † Most Holy Redeemer
(1952; 1953; 1964; cons 18 June 1982)
Petersfield Avenue, Harold Hill, Romford, Essex RM3 9PB **Tel:** 01708-343492
Fax: 01708-343306 **E-mail:** haroldhillmhr@dioceseofbrentwood.org
Rev Joseph Tan
M: *Sun 9am, 11am, 6pm. Hds 9.30am, 7.30pm.*

2. † St Dominic (1954; 1956)
281 Straight Road, Harold Hill, Romford, Essex RM3 7JS **Tel:** 01708-342127
E-mail: haroldhillstd@dioceseofbrentwood.org
Rev David Papworth
M: *Sat 1st M of Sun 6.30pm. Sun 10.30am. Hds 10am, 7.30pm.*

■ **HARWICH and DOVERCOURT,** Essex

† Our Lady Queen of Heaven
(1864; 1955)
129 Fronks Road, Dovercourt, Harwich, Essex CO12 4EF **Tel:** 01255-503383
E-mail: harwich@dioceseofbrentwood.org
Rev Michael W Stokes
M: *Sun 10.45am. Hds 11.30am, 7.30pm.*

■ **HATFIELD BROAD OAK,** Essex

Our Lady of Lourdes (1952)
High Street. Served from Dunmow.
M: *Sun 9am.*

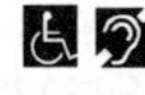

■ **HEYBRIDGE,** Maldon, Essex

See Maldon

■ **HOCKLEY,** Essex

St Pius X (1956)
Southend Road. Served from Rochford.
M: *Sun 9am. Hds 11am.*

■ **HOLLAND-ON-SEA,** Essex

All Souls (1970)
Brighton Road. Served from Clacton-on-Sea.
M: *Sun 9.30am. Hds See weekly bulletin.*

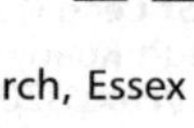

■ **HORNCHURCH,** Essex

1. † St Mary Mother of God
(1931; cons 27 June 1933)
213 Hornchurch Road, Hornchurch, Essex RM12 4TL **Tel:** 01708-447761
Fax: 01708-449267

E-mail: hornchurchstmmg@dioceseofbrentwood.org
Website: stmaryshornchurch.org.uk
Revv John F Hayes, Mark Swires
M: *Sat 1st M of Sun 6.30pm. Sun 8am, 9.30am, 11.30am. Hds (vigil 7.30pm), 8.30am, 11am, 7.30pm.*

2. † English Martyrs (1955)
240 Alma Avenue, Hornchurch, Essex RM12 6BJ
Tel: 01708-507020 **Fax:** 01708-441825
E-mail: hornchurchem@dioceseofbrentwood.org
Rev Joseph Farrell.
M: *Sun 10am, 6.30pm. Hds 9.30am, 7.30pm.*

■ **HULLBRIDGE,** Essex
See Rayleigh.

■ **HUTTON AND SHENFIELD,** Essex
† St Joseph the Worker
(1959; 1969; cons 30 April 1976)
Highview Crescent, Hutton, Brentwood CM13 1BJ **Tel:** 01277-221917
E-mail: hutton@dioceseofbrentwood.org
Rev Leslie Knight.
M: *Sat 1st M of Sun 6pm. Sun 8.30am, 10.30am. Hds 9.15am, 8pm.*

ILFORD, Essex
1. † SS Peter and Paul
(1896; 1899; dedicated 28 June 1996)
342 High Road, Ilford, Essex IG1 1QP
Tel: 020-8478 0583 **Fax:** 020-8553 3097
E-mail: ilfordssp&p@dioceseofbrentwood.org
Website: www.ssppilford.org.uk
Revv Thomas Lavin, Patrick Okoye.
M: *Sat 1st M of Sun 6pm. Sun 9.30am, 11am, 6pm. Hds 10am, 12.30pm, 8pm.*
- ***Ursulines (Roman Union),*** 8 Coventry Road, IG1 4QS **Tel:** 020-8554 8178 **Fax:** 020-8518 0155
- ***Ursulines (Desenzano),*** 10 Coventry Road, IG1 4QR **Tel:** 020-8518 3947. **E-mail:** ursdes@aol.com

2. † St John the Baptist
(1967; cons 2 May 1976)
349 Wanstead Park Road, Cranbrook, Ilford, Essex IG1 3TS **Tel:** 020-8554 3763
Email: ilfordstjtb@dioceseofbrentwood.org
Rev John Tuohy.
M: *Sat 1st M of Sun 6pm. Sun 8.30am, 10.30am. Hds 9am, 7.30pm.*

† St Mary and St Erconwald
(1953; 1972; cons 4 May 1979)
387 Ilford Lane, Ilford, Essex IG1 2SL
Served from St Mary and St Ethelburga, Barking
M: *Sat 1st M of Sun 6pm. Sun 9.30am, Hds (vigil 7pm), 9.30am.*

■ **INGATESTONE,** Essex
† St John the Evangelist and St Erconwald
(circa 1703; 1932; cons 4 June 1932)
Roman Road, Ingatestone, Essex CM4 9AA
Tel: 01277-353193 **E-mail:** ingatestone@dioceseofbrentwood.org
Website: www.ingatestoneparish.org.uk
Mgr David Manson, VG.
M: *Sat 1st M of Sun 6pm, Sun 11am. Hds 9am, 8pm (on SS Peter and Paul and All Saints this Mass is usually celebrated in the C-of-E Church at Buttsbury).*

■ **JAYWICK,** Essex
All Saints (1973)
Union Road. Served from Clacton-on-Sea.
M: *Sun 8am. Hds See weekly bulletin.*

■ **KELVEDON,** Colchester, Essex
† St Mary Immaculate and the Holy Archangels
(1875; cons 24th Oct 1891)
Church Street, Kelvedon, Colchester, Essex CO5 9AH **Tel/Fax:** 01376-570348
E-mail: kelvedon@dioceseofbrentwood.org
Website: www.rc.net/uk/brentwood/stmaryimmac
Mgr Gordon Read.
M: *Sun 11am. Hds 10am.*
See also Coggeshall and Tiptree.

■ **LAINDON,** Basildon, Essex
See Basildon

■ **LEIGH-ON-SEA,** Essex
† Our Lady of Lourdes and St Joseph
(1912; 1925; cons 6 Sept 1929)
161-181 Leigh Road.
Tel: 01702-478078 **Fax:** 01702-475285
E-mail: leighonsea@dioceseofbrentwood.org
Website: www.ourladyoflourdeschurch.co.uk
Rev Kevin Hale. 1 Cliffsea Grove, SS9 1NG
Also: **Rev Cornelius Joyce (Retired)**, 11A Woodfield Park Drive SS9 1LN
Tel: 01702-712562; **Rev Basil Pearson**, c/o 1 Cliffsea Grove, SS9 1NG
M: *Sat 1st M of Sun 5.30pm. Sun 8am, 9.30am, 11.30am, 1st Sun of month 4pm (Latin, Extraordinary Form). Hds 12noon, 8pm.*

■ **LEXDEN,** Colchester, Essex
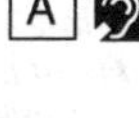
1. † St Teresa of Lisieux
(1937; 1960; 1971; con 10 Nov 1989)
16 Clairmont Road, Lexden, Colchester, Essex CO3 5BE
Tel: 01206-576898 **Fax:** 01206-368226
E-mail: lexden@dioceseofbrentwood.org
Website: www.stteresa.co.uk
Mgr Arthur Barrow.
M: *Sun 9am, 11am. Hds 10.30am, 8pm.*

2. St John the Baptist (1961)
Iceni Way, Shrub End. Served from Lexden No 1.
M: *Sat 1st M of Sun 6.30pm.*

■ **LEYTON, E10**
† St Joseph
(24 July 1884; 1918; 1924; cons 23 Oct 1930)
68 Grange Park Road, Leyton E10 5ES
Tel: 020-8539 2908 **Fax:** 020-8928 1057
E-mail: leyton@dioceseofbrentwood.org
Website: joseph.claret.org.uk
Claretian Missionaries (CMF): **Revv James Boothman** (*Parish Priest*), **Philip Blandford**
M: *Sat 1st M of Sun 6pm. Sun 8am, 10am, 12noon, 6pm. Hds 8am, 9am, 7.30pm.*
- ***Marian Missionary Sister of the Poor:*** 1 Colchester Road, Leyton, London E10 6HA **Tel:** 020-8518 7499

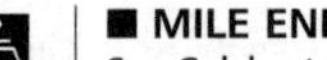

■ **LEYTONSTONE, E11**
Served from Stratford.
M: *Sun 9am. In Holy Trinity & St Augustine C of E Church, Holloway Rd.*

■ **LINFORD,** Stanford-le-Hope, Essex
Served from Stanford-le Hope
Information: **Albert and May Dass**
Tel: 01375-361235
M: *Sun 9am, in Linford Methodist Church.*

■ **LOUGHTON,** Essex
† St Edmund of Canterbury
(1927; 1958; cons 24 Oct 1976)
9 Trap's Hill, Loughton, Essex IG10 1SZ
Tel: 020-8508 3492 **Fax:** 020-8532 0138
E-mail: loughton@dioceseofbrentwood.org
Rev John J Harvey.
M: *Sun 9am, 11am. Hds 12.15pm, 8pm.*
See also Debden.

■ **MALDON,** Essex
† Assumption of Our Lady
(1897; 1925; con 14th Jan 1975)
60a Victoria Road, Maldon, Essex CM9 5HF
Tel: 01621-852259
E-mail: maldon@dioceseofbrentwood.org
Rev Peter Connor. (Linked with Burnham on Crouch - **Tel:** 01621 782034)
M: *Sat 1st M of Sun 5pm. Sun 9am. Hds 9.30am (in the school in term time), otherwise 12noon, 7.30pm*
• ***Franciscan Minoresses,*** Franciscan Convent, Mount View, West Chase, London Road, CM9 6HN
Tel: 01621-852780

■ **MANNINGTREE**
See Mistley, Greenstead (3).

■ **MANOR PARK, E12**
1. † St Stephen
(1918; 1924; 1959; cons 1 Jun 1978)
Church Road, Manor Park.
Tel/Fax: 020-8478 1895
E-mail: manorpark@dioceseofbrentwood.org
Rev Sean Connolly. 146 Little Ilford Lane, Manor Park E12 5PJ
M: *Sat 1st M of Sun 6.30pm. Sun 8.30am, 11.30am. Hds 10am, 7.30pm.*

2. † St Nicholas (1869; 1918)
Gladding Road. Served from Manor Park (1).
M: *Sun 10am.*
• ***Religious of the Sacred Heart of Mary, (Béziers),*** 21 Gladding Road, E12 5DD
Tel: 020-8478 0809

■ **MAYLANDSEA,** Essex
See Burnham-on-Crouch.

■ **MELBOURNE ESTATE**
See Chelmsford (2).

■ **MILE END**
See Colchester (2).

■ **MISTLEY**
See Greenstead (3).

■ **MONKWICK**
See Colchester (4).

■ **MOULSHAM**
See Chelmsford (1).

■ **MULBERRY GREEN**
See Harlow (1).

■ **NAZEING,** Essex
Served from Waltham Abbey.
M: *Sun 8.30pm in St Giles Church Hall.*

■ **NEW HALL SCHOOL**
Boreham, Chelmsford CM3 3HT
See Springfield (3).

■ **NEWBURY PARK,** Ilford, Essex
† St Teresa (1952; 1954; con 1st Oct 1985)
Eastern Avenue. **Tel/Fax:** 020-8590 2414
E-mail:newburypark@dioceseofbrentwood.org
Rev Eamonn Power (*Priest in Charge*), The Presbytery, Brook Road, IG2 7JA
M: *Sat 1st M of Sun 6pm. Sun 8am, 10.30am. Hds 9.30am, 7.30pm.*

■ **NORTH WOOLWICH, E16**
See Silvertown and North Woolwich.

■ **ONGAR,** Essex
† St Helen (1869; 1918)
87 High Street, Ongar, Essex CM5 9DX
Tel: 01277-362645
E-mail: ongar@dioceseofbrentwood.org
Rev Andrew Hurley (*Priest in Charge*).
M: *Sat 1st M of Sun 5.30pm. Sun 8.30am. Hds See Newsletter.*
See also Doddinghurst.

■ **ORSETT,** Essex
See Tilbury.

■ **PARNDON,** Essex
See Harlow (3).

■ **PILGRIMS HATCH,** Essex
See Brentwood

■ **PITSEA,** Essex
See Basildon.

■ **PRITTLEWELL,** Essex
See Southend-on-Sea.

■ **PURFLEET,** Essex.
See Grays.

■ **RAINHAM,** Essex
† Our Lady of La Salette
(1938; 1967; cons 19 Sept 1984)

1 Rainham Road, Rainham, Essex RM13 8SP
Tel/Fax: 01708-552897
E-mail: rainham@dioceseofbrentwood.org
Missionaries of La Salette (MS): **Revv Mariusz Fura** (*Parish Priest*), **Waldemar Smialek**.
M: *Sat 1st M of Sun 6pm. Sun 9am, 11am. Hds 9.30am, 7.30pm.*

■ **RAYLEIGH,** Essex
† Our Lady of Ransom
(1931; 1934; 1965; cons 1 June 1967)
50 London Hill, Rayleigh, Essex SS6 7HP
Tel: 01268-742229
E-mail: rayleigh@dioceseofbrentwood.org
Website: www.olor.org.uk
Rev Martin Joyce.
Also resident:
Rev Andrew G A Dorricott *(retired)*, 25 Homeregal House, Bellingham Lane SS6 7HN **Tel:** 01268 774552
Rev Derek Powney *(Retired)*, 1 Eastview Drive SS6 9NY **Tel:** 01268 780622
M: *Sat 1st M of Sun 6pm. Sun 8am, 10am. Hds 7.30am, 9.30am, 8pm.*

■ **ROCHFORD,** Essex
† St Teresa of the Child Jesus
(1950; 1977; cons 2 Feb 1977)
'Sweynes', 109 Ashingdon Road, Rochford, Essex SS4 1RF **Tel:** 01702-544334
E-mail: rochford@dioceseofbrentwood.org
Rev Gerry Drummond (*Priest in Charge*).
M: *Sat 1st M of Sun 5.30pm. Sun 10.30am. Hds 9.30am, 8pm.*
See also Hockley

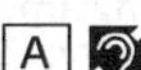

■ **ROMFORD,** Essex
† St Edward the Confessor
(1854; 1856; 1918; cons 6 May 1856)
5 Park End Road, Romford, Essex RM1 4AT
Tel/Fax: 01708-740308
E-mail: romford@dioceseofbrentwood.org
Website: www.stedwards-romford.org.uk
Rev Tom Jordan.
M: *Sat 1st M of Sun 6.30pm. Sun 9.30am, 11.30am. Hds 9.15am (in the school in term time), 12.15pm, 8pm.*

■ **ROYAL DOCKS**
Comprises the parishes of: Beckton, **St Mark's**, Custom House, **St Anne's**, Silvertown & North Woolwich, **St Mary and St Edward with St John**.
Mgr John Armitage, VG (*Parish Priest*)
Resident at Custom House.

■ **RUSH GREEN**
See Hornchurch (1).

■ **SAFFRON WALDEN,** Essex
† Our Lady of Compassion (1906; 1918)
Castle Street, Saffron Walden, Essex CB10 1BP
Tel: 01799-527011 **Fax:** 01799-516827
E-mail: saffronwalden@dioceseofbrentwood.org
Website: www.rc.net/brentwood/olc
Rev John Garrett.
M: *Sat 1st M of Sun 6pm. Sun 8.30am, 10.30am. Hds 9.30am in church or school, 8pm.*

■ **SHENFIELD,** Essex
See Hutton.

■ **SHOEBURYNESS,** Essex
† St George and the English Martyrs
(1862; 1891; 1939, cons 23 April 1990)
96 Ness Road, Shoeburyness, Essex SS3 9DH **Tel/Fax:** 01702-292726
E-mail: shoeburyness@dioceseofbrentwood.org
Rev Graham Smith.
M: *Sat 1st M of Sun 6pm. Sun 10.30am. Hds 9.30am, 8pm.*
See also Thorpe Bay.

■ **SHRUB END,** Colchester
See Lexden (2).

■ **SIBLE HEDINGHAM,** Essex
Served from Halstead.
M: *Sun 9am. Hds 6pm. In St Peter's C of E Church.*

■ **SILVER END,** Essex
St Mary (1966)
Sheepcotes Lane. Served from Witham.
M: *Sun 9am. Hds (vigil 8pm).*

■ **SILVERTOWN AND NORTH WOOLWICH, E16**
† St Mary and St Edward with St John
(1887; 1922; cons 17 June 1937)
Newland Street, Silvertown.
Mgr John Armitage, VG (*Parish Priest*)
Resident at Custom House.
M: *Sun 9am. Hds (vigil 7.30pm).*
See also Beckton and Custom House.

■ **SNARESBROOK**
See Wanstead.

■ **SOUTH CHINGFORD**
See Chingford (2).

■ **SOUTH OCKENDON**
See Aveley.

■ **<SOUTH WOODFORD, E18**
† St Anne Line (1966)
7 Grove Crescent, South Woodford E18 2JR
Tel: 020-8989 5242
E-mail: southwoodford@dioceseofbrentwood.org
Rev Francis Coveney.
M: *Sat 1st M of Sun 6.30pm. Sun 9.30am, 11am. Hds 9.30am, 8pm.*

■ **SOUTH WOODHAM FERRERS** Essex
† **Holy Trinity** (1982)
(Church shared with C of E and Methodists). Trinity Square. **Tel:** 01245-324138
E-mail: danbury@dioceseofbrentwood.org
Rev Paul Fox. 36 Inchbonnie Road, CM3 5FG
M: *Sun 8.45am, 5.30pm. Hds 10am.*
See also Danbury.

■ **SOUTHEND-ON-SEA**
Linked with Prittlewell, Essex
418 Southchurch Road, Southend-on-Sea, Essex SS1 2QB **Tel:** 01702-465720
E-mail: southend@dioceseofbrentwood.org
Rev Tom Saunders.

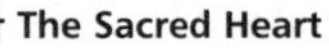

† **The Sacred Heart**
(1909; 1910; 1918; cons 13 Sept 1955)
Southchurch Road, Southend-on-Sea.
M: *Sat 1st M of Sun 5.30pm. Sun 11am. Hds 9.30am.*

† **St John Fisher**
(1939; 1955; 1964; cons 1 Mar 1974)
Manners Way, Prittlewell.
M: *Sun 9am. Hds 7.30pm*

■ **SPRINGFIELD**, Chelmsford
1. † **St Augustine of Canterbury** (1983)
Shared with CofE, URC and Methodists.
New Bowers Way. **Tel:** 01245-465333
E-mail: springfield@dioceseofbrentwood.org
Website: www.staugustine-springfield.com
Rev Frank James Jackson.
The Presbytery, Beardsley Drive, Springfield, Chelmsford, Essex CM1 6GQ
Deacon: **Rev Kevin Lyons**.
M: *Sun 9am. Hds 8pm.*

2. **The Church of Our Saviour, Chelmer Village** (1985)
Ashton Place, Chelmer Village,
Shared with CofE, URC and Methodists.
Served from Springfield (1).
M: *Sun 12noon.*

3. **New Hall School**
Boreham, off White Hart Lane, Springfield.
Served from Springfield (1).
M: *Sun 10.30am in school chapel.*

■ **STANFORD-LE-HOPE**, Essex.
† **Our Lady and St Joseph**
(1909; 1913; Rebuilt 1992; ded 11 Feb 1993)
30 Southend Road, Stanford-le-Hope, Essex SS17 0PF **Tel:** 01375-672167.
E-mail: stanfordlehope@dioceseofbrentwood.org
Rev David Clemens.
M: *Sat 1st M of Sun 5.30pm. Sun 11am. Hds 9.15am, 8pm (or eve 8pm).*
See also Linford.

■ **STANSTED**, Essex
† **St Theresa of Lisieux**
(1970; 2002; dedicated 3 Oct 2003)
High Lane, Stansted, Essex CM24 8LQ
Tel: 01279-814349
E-mail: stansted@dioceseofbrentwood.org
Rev Joseph White.
M: *Sat 1st M of Sun 6pm. Sun 9am, 10.30am. Hds 8am, 8pm.*

■ **STIFFORD CLAYS**, Essex A
St Peter (1958)
Whitmore Avenue. Served from Grays.
M: *Sun 9.30am. Hds 7pm.*

■ **STOCK**, Ingatestone, Essex A
† **Our Lady and St Joseph**
(1744; 1852; 1937; cons 3 Jun 1971)
Mill Road, Stock, Ingatestone, Essex.
Tel: 01277-840268
Rt Rev Thomas McMahon (*Parish Priest*) (Bishop's House, CM4 9BU); **Mgr David Manson, VG** (*Priest in Charge*). St John's Presbytery, Roman Road, Ingatestone, CM4 9AA **Tel:** 01277-353193
E-mail: ingatestone@dioceseofbrentwood.org
M: *Sun 9am. Hds 10.30am.*

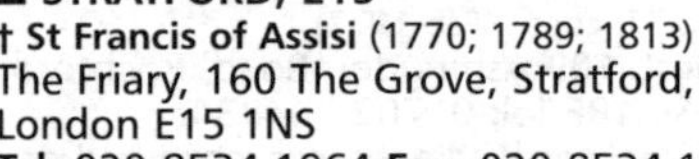

■ **STRATFORD, E15**
† **St Francis of Assisi** (1770; 1789; 1813)
The Friary, 160 The Grove, Stratford, London E15 1NS
Tel: 020-8534 1964 **Fax:** 020-8534 1119
E-mail: stratford@dioceseofbrentwood.org
Franciscans (Friars Minor) (OFM):
Revv Francis Conway (*Guardian*) **Kieran Fitzsimons** (*Parish Priest*), **Daniel Couvery** (*Vicar*), **Simon Simmonds**,
Deacon: **Christopher Dyczek**.
M: *Sat 1st M of Sun 6pm. Sun 10.15am 12 noon. Hds 8am, 12.15pm, 8pm.*
See also Leytonstone.

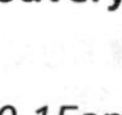

■ **THAXTED**, Essex A
† **The English Martyrs** (1952)
Church Lane, Park Street.
Served from Great Bardfield.
M: *Sun 11am. Hds 8.30am.*

■ **THEYDON BOIS**, Essex
See Epping.

■ **THORPE BAY**, Essex
† **St Gregory** (1928)
The Broadway. Served from Shoeburyness.
M: *Sun 9am.*

TILBURY, Essex
† **Our Lady Star of the Sea**
(1887; 1907; cons 8 June 1954)
96 Dock Road, Tilbury, Essex RM18 7BT
Tel: 01375-842309 **Fax:** 01375-855306
E-mail: tilbury@dioceseofbrentwood.org
Rev James McShane. Also in residence: **Rev Pat Foley SPS** (*Port Chaplain*).

M: *Sat 1st M of Sun 6.30pm. Sun 11am. Hds 10am.*

• ***Sisters of Mercy,*** Convent of Mercy, Malta Road, RM18 7BU **Tel:** 01375-856965

See also Chadwell St Mary.

■ **TIPTREE,** Essex
† St John Houghton
Church Road. Served from Kelvedon.
M: *Sun 6pm. Hds 7.30pm.*

■ **UNIVERSITY OF ESSEX**
† Catholic Chaplaincy
Wivenhoe Park, Colchester, CO4 3SQ
Tel: 01206-872018 **E-mail:** brightlingsea@dioceseofbrentwood.org
Website: www.essex.ac.uk/cathchap
Chaplain: **Rev Martin Boland**.
M: *Sun 12.10pm in term time and as announced.*

■ **UPMINSTER,** Essex
† St Joseph (1923; 1939)
The Presbytery, Champion Road, Upminster, Essex RM14 2SY
Tel: 01708-222432 **Fax:** 01708-640553
E-mail: upminster@dioceseofbrentwood.org
Website: www.stjos.net
Rev John Taylor.
M: *Sat 1st M of Sun 6.30pm. Sun 9am, 10.30am. Hds 7am, 10am, 8pm.*

• ***Religious of the Sacred Heart of Mary,*** 70 St Mary's Lane, RM14 2QR **Tel:** 01708-224096 **E-mail:** rshmupminster@care4free.net

See also Cranham.

■ **UPTON PARK, E13**
† Our Lady of Compassion
(1902; 1911; cons 24 Oct 1929. Re-dedicated after re-ordering 5 Feb 1993)
Green Street, Upton Park E13 9AX
Tel: 020-8472 1181 **Fax:** 0870 7062755
E-mail: uptonpark@dioceseofbrentwood.org
Rev John King.
M: *Sun 9am, 11am, 7.30pm. Hds 8am, 10am, 8pm.*

■ **VICTORIA DOCKS, E16**
See Custom House.

■ **WALTHAM ABBEY,** Essex
† St Thomas More and St Edward (1951; 1973)
The Presbytery, 5 Monkswood Avenue, Waltham Abbey, Essex EN9 1LA
Tel: 01992-711051
E-mail: walthamabbey@dioceseofbrentwood.org
Rev Anthony Onuoha (*Priest in Charge*).
M: *Sat 1st M of Sun 6.30pm. Sun 9.45am, 11.15am. Hds 10am, 8pm.*

See also Nazeing.

• ***Gilwell Park***, E4. Scout Training Centre and Campsite. **Tel:** 020-8433 7100 Information Centre: 0845-300 1818
M: *RC Chapel as announced.*

■ **WALTHAMSTOW, E17**
1. † Our Lady and St George
(1847; 1849; 1901; cons 7 Oct 1925; new church 1996; dedicated 23 April 1997)
132 Shernhall Street, Walthamstow E17 9HU
Tel: 020-8520 5877 **Fax:** 020-8520 4805
E-mail: walthamstowol&stg@dioceseofbrentwood.org
Revv Maurice Gordon, Lambert Basabose, WF, Sergio Magbanua SSP.
Deacon: **Rev Joseph Baffour-Awuah**.
M: *Sat 1st M of Sun 6pm. Sun 8.30am, 10am, 12 noon, 4.30pm at Whipps Cross University NHS Hospital. Hds (vigil 7.30pm), 9.15am, 7.30pm.*

2. † Our Lady of the Rosary and St Patrick (1908; 1919; cons 6 March 1985)
61 Blackhorse Road, Walthamstow E17 7AS
Tel: 020-8520 3647
E-mail: walthamstowolr&stp@dioceseofbrentwood.org
Society of African Missions, (SMA): **Revv John F. Brown, Eddie Deeney**.
M: *Sat 1st M of Sun 7pm. Sun 9am, 11.30am, 6pm. Hds 9.30am, 7.30pm.*

• ***Canonesses of St Augustine,*** Congregation of Our Lady, 35 Maude Terrace, E17 7DG **Tel:** 020-8521 0231

• ***Daughters of Mary Mother of Mercy,*** 1 Brettenham Avenue E17 5DG **Tel:** 020-8523 4243

■ **WALTON-ON-THE-NAZE,** Essex
See Frinton-on-Sea.

■ **WANSTEAD, E11**
† Our Lady of Lourdes (1919; 1928)
51 Cambridge Park, Wanstead E11 2PR
Tel: 020-8989 2074 **Fax:** 020-8532 9091
E-mail: wanstead@dioceseofbrentwood.org
Website: www.ourladyoflourdeswanstead.com
Rev Patrick J Sammon.
Also in residence: **Rev Keiran Dodd, Tel:** 020-8530 0333, **Rt Rev Bishop John Crowley, Tel:** 020-8530 5512
M: *Sat 1st M of Sun 6.30pm. Sun 9.30am, 11.30am, 6.30pm. Hds (vigil 8pm), 7am, 9.15am, 8pm.*

• ***Sisters of Mercy,*** St Joseph's Convent, 57 Cambridge Park, E11 2PR **Tel:** 020-8989 3142

■ **WARLEY,** Brentwood, Essex
† Holy Cross and All Saints
(1881; cons 2 July 1919)
135 Warley Hill. Served from the Cathedral.
M: *Sat 1st M of Sun 6.30pm. Sun 11am.*

• ***Daughters of Charity of St Vincent de***

Paul: **Rev Philip Walshe CM**, Marillac Hospital, Eagle Way, CM13 3BL
Tel: 01277-220276

■ **WEST HORDON, Essex**
See Upminster.

■ **WEST MERSEA**
See Colchester (3).

■ **WESTCLIFF-ON-SEA,** Essex 
† Our Lady Help of Christians and St Helen
(1862; 1869-1902; cons 12 August 1919)
27 Milton Road, Westcliff-on-Sea, SS0 7JP
Tel: 01702-342324 **Fax:** 01702-352686
E-mail: westcliff@dioceseofbrentwood.org
Website: www.shwos.com
Rev Jean-Laurent Marie.
M: *Sun 9.30am, 11.15am, 6pm. Hds 10am (in St Helen's School), 12.15pm, 8pm.*
- ***Poor Sisters of Nazareth,*** Nazareth House, 111 London Road, Southend-on-Sea, SS1 1PP **Tel:** 01702-345627 **Fax:** 01702-430352
- ***Little Company of Mary,*** 11/13 Grosvenor Road SS0 8EP **Tel:** 01702-341537
- ***Sisters of Mercy (Westminster),*** 48-50 Ditton Court Road, SS0 7HF **Tel/Fax:** 01702-304931

■ **WICKFORD,** Essex  
† Our Lady of Good Counsel
(1926; 1951; cons 8 Dec 1976)
61 London Road, Wickford, Essex SS12 0AW
Tel: 01268-733219
E-mail: wickford@dioceseofbrentwood.org
Website: www.wickfordcatholic.net
Rev John Glynn.
M: *Sat 1st M of Sun 6pm. Sun 9am, 11am. Hds 9.15am, 8pm.*

■ **WITHAM,** Essex 
† The Holy Family and All Saints
(1774; 1851; Dedicated 1 Nov 1989)
14 Guithavon Street, Witham, Essex CM8 1BN
Tel/Fax: 01376-512219
E-mail: witham@dioceseofbrentwood.org
Website: holyfamily-witham.org
Rev David H Prior (*Priest in Charge*).
M: *Sat 1st M of Sun 6pm. Sun 11am. Hds 10am (in term time in Holy Family School), 12.15pm, 8pm.*
See also Silver End.

■ **WIVENHOE,** Essex
See Brightlingsea (2).

■ **WOODFORD GREEN,** Essex 
† St Thomas of Canterbury (1894; 1896)
557-559 High Road, Woodford Green, Essex IG8 0RB
Tel: 020-8504 1686 **Fax:** 020-8504 1844
E-mail: woodfordgreen@dioceseofbrentwood.org
Franciscans (Friars Minor) (OFM):
Rev Roger Barralet (*Guardian, Parish Priest and Provincial Bursar*), **Brian McGrath** (*Vicar Provincial and Vicar*),
Tel: 020-8504 1688
Provincialate: **Tel:** 020-8504 7540
Fax: 020-8504 7541
E-mail: curia@friar.org
Revv Michael Copps *(Provincial)*, **Boniface Kruger** (*Provincial Secretary*),
Tel/Fax: 020-8498 9994 Franciscan Community: **Tel:** 020-8504 1688
Fax: 020-8504 1844
E-mail: Woodford@friar.org.
Revv Walter Hobson, Gervase Leyden, Austin Kinsella, Anthony McNeill, Darious Kaczharczyk, John Dougan. Bros Malachy Seymour, Raymond Hynes (*Vice-Commissary of the Holy Land*).
M: *Sat 1st M of Sun 6pm. Sun 8.30am, 10am, 11.30am. Hds (vigil 7.30pm), 10am, 8pm.*
- ***Sisters of the Holy Family of Bordeaux,*** Holy Family Convent, 5 The Green, IG8 0NF **Tel:** 020-8505 2265

See also Buckhurst Hill and Chigwell.

■ **WRITTLE,** Essex
See Chelmsford (1).

■ ORDERS OR CONGREGATIONS

■ Men

Claretian Missionaries of Mary: Leyton.
Community of St John: Canning Town
Franciscans (Friars Minor): Stratford, Woodford Green.
Franciscan Friars of the Renewal: Canning Town.
Missionaries of La Salette: Dagenham (1), Goodmayes, Harlow (2), Rainham.
Norbertines Canons (OPraem), Chelmsford (1).
Pallottine Fathers (Society of Catholic Apostolate): Barking (2), Halstead.
Society of African Missions: Walthamstow (2).

■ Women

Canonesses of the Holy Sepulchre: Chelmsford (2), Colchester, Custom House.
Canonesses of St Augustine: Walthamstow (2).
Charity (of St. Vincent de Paul), Daughters of: Warley.
Community of Our Lady of Walsingham: Brentwood.
Daughters of Mary Mother of Mercy: Walthamstow (2).
Franciscan Minoresses: Maldon.
Franciscan Missionaries of Mary: Canning Town.
Franciscan Missionaries of the Divine

Motherhood: Chingford (1).
Holy Family (of Bordeaux), Sisters of the: Woodford Green.
Holy Family Sisters of the Needy: Custom House.
Immaculate Heart of Mary, Sisters of the: East Ham, Goodmayes.
Institute of the Blessed Virgin Mary, Loreto Sisters: Brentwood.
La Sainte Union Sisters: Aveley, Becontree, Grays.
Little Company of Mary: Westcliff-on-Sea.
Marian Missionary Sisters of the Poor: Leyton.
Mercy, (The Institute), Sisters of: Brentwood, Canvey Island, East Ham, Frinton-on-Sea, Gidea Park, Tilbury, Wanstead.
Mercy Sisters of (Union): Clacton-on-Sea, Westcliff-on-Sea.
Missionary Franciscan Sisters of the Immaculate Conception: Braintree, Clacton-on-Sea.
Nazareth, Poor Sisters of: Westcliff-on-Sea.
Oblates of the Assumption: Chingford (2).
Sacred Heart of Mary (Béziers), Religious of the: Manor Park (2), Upminster.
Sacred Hearts of Jesus and Mary (Chigwell), Sisters of The: Chigwell, Dagenham (1), Harlow (2).
Servite Sisters (Third Order): Chelmsford (1).
Sisters of Charity: Canning Town.
Sisters of St Joseph of Tarbes: Forest Gate
Society of the Scared Heart: Forest Gate.
Ursulines (Brentwood): Basildon, Brentwood, Dagenham (2).
Ursulines (Roman Union): Forest Gate, Ilford (1).

■ DIOCESAN ASSOCIATIONS AND SOCIETIES

For Societies and Organisations without representation in the diocese please see the main Societies and Organisations section.

Association for the Propagation of the Faith: *Diocesan Director:* **Rev Joseph Farrell**. 240 Alma Avenue, Hornchurch, Essex RM12 6BJ **Tel:** 01708-507020 **Fax:** 01708-441825 **E-mail:** hornchurchem@dioceseofbrentwood.org

Brentwood Diocese Sick and Retired Clergy Fund: *Joint Administrators*: **Revv Kevin Hale, Leslie Knight, Brian O'Higgins**. All correspondence to: The Joint Administrators, c/o 1 Cliffsea Grove, Leigh-on-Sea, Essex SS9 1NG

Brentwood Ecclesiastical Education Fund: *Secretary/Treasurer*: **Rev Anthony McKentey**, The Presbytery, The Avenue, Braintree, Essex CM7 3H **Tel:** 01376-326779 **E-mail:** braintree@dioceseofbrentwood.org

Catenian Association, Province No 2 (East Anglia and London). *Contact:* **Mr Bernard Noakes**, 24 Petersfield, Broomfield, Chelmsford CM1 4EP **Tel:** 01245-441247 **Email:** b.noakes@virgin.net

Catholic Clothing Guild: *Hon Secretary:* **Mrs M Doherty**, 3 The Chapel, The Mall, Hornchurch, Essex RM11 1EP **Tel/Fax:** 01708-479476 **E-mail:** mondo@mondo.free-online.co.uk

Catholic Handicapped Fellowship: *Diocesan Chaplain*: **Rev Bob Hamill**. *Chairman*: **Mrs T McHale**, 120 Hamilton Avenue, Barkingside, Ilford, Essex IG6 1AB **Tel:** 020-8554 7605 *Secretary:* **Mrs A Kyndt**, 6 The High Road, South Woodford, London E18 2QL **Tel:** 020-8989 9032

Catholic Women's League: Brentwood Diocesan Branch: *Hon. Secretary:* **Mrs A T Evans**, 36 Empress Avenue, Manor Park, London E12 5ES **Tel:** 020 8989 0857 **E-mail:** angela.evans18@btopenworld.com **Website:** www.catholicwomensleague.org.uk Sheltered housing for the elderly: *Registered Office:* 594 Rayleigh Road, Eastwood, Leigh-on-Sea, Essex SS9 5HU **Tel:** 01702-510523

Grail, The: *Diocesan Representatives:* **Christopher & Christine Robinson**, 85 Westbourne Grove, Westcliff-on-Sea, Essex SS0 9TT **Tel:** 01702-346291 **E-mail:** seachange@talktalk.net ***Grail Headquarters:*** The Grail Centre, 125 Waxwell Lane, Pinner, Middlesex HA5 3ER **Tel:** 020-8866 2195 **E-mails:** Grail community: waxwell@compuserve.com Business & centre: grailcentre@compuserve.com

Guild of St Stephen for Altar Servers: *Diocesan Director*: **Rev Jean-Laurent Marie**. *Chairman:* **John McCormack**. 21 Docklands Avenue, Ingatestone, Essex CM4 9DS **Tel:** 01277-355264 **E-mail:** wjp_innes@btopenworld.com **Website:** www.guildofststephenbrentwood.org.uk

Knights of St Columba: Brentwood Province No. 10. *Provincial Grand Knight*: **Mr Brian Dillon**. *Provincial Secretary:* **Geoffrey Pugh**, 38 Mayflower Drive, Maldon, Essex CM9 6XX **Tel:** 01621 843297 **E-mail:** geoffreypugh@btinternet.com *Provincial Chaplain:* **Rev Leslie Knight**. **Tel:** 01277-221917

Our Lady's Catechists: *Diocesan Representative:* **Mrs M Francis**, 34 Woodcote Road, London E11 2QA **Tel:** 020-8989 4814 **Email:** isabel@poppy34.freeserve.co.uk

Pioneer Total Abstinence Association of the Sacred Heart of Jesus: *Hon Secretary:* **Thomas Mahon**, 38 Hunts Close, Writtle, Chelmsford, Essex CM1 3HJ **Tel:** 01245-420011 Meetings 3rd Sunday of month 3pm.

Society of St Gregory. *Diocesan Representative:* **Julie-Ann Gylaitis**, 38 Robert Road, Exhall, Coventry CV7 9GU **Tel:** 02476-316252 **E-mail:** brentwood@ssg.org.uk

St Vincent de Paul Society: Brentwood Central Council. *President*: **George Hasberry**, Minsmere, Pump Street, Hordon-on-the-Hill, Stanford-le-Hope, Essex SS17 8PG **Tel:** 01375-641060 **E-mail:** ghasberry@btinternet.com *Chaplain: Deacon:* **Rev Dwight N Hayter**.

Secular Clergy Common Fund: *Diocesan Representative:* **Rev George Towler**. Appledore, Stock Road, Stock, Ingatestone, Essex CM4 9PN **Tel:** 01277-829915 **E-mail:** gtowruss@hotmail.co.uk

Secular Clergy New Common Fund: *Diocesan Representative:* **Rev Kevin Hale**. 1 Cliffsea Grove, Leigh-on-Sea, Essex SS9 1NG **Tel:** 01702-478078 **Fax:** 01702-475285 **E-mail:** leighonsea@dioceseofbrentwood.org

Serviam Lay Association: Ursuline Convent, 38 Grosvenor Road, Forest Gate, London E7 8JA **Tel:** 020-8471 6644; Ursuline Convent, 8 Coventry Road, Ilford, Essex IG1 4QS **Tel:** 0208 554 8178

Teams of Our Lady. An international Catholic Movement for Christian married couples that aims to deepen the couples' spirituality. A 'Team' consists of four or five couples and a priest or religious as spiritual advisor meeting monthly to share the journey of faith, guided by the Holy Spirit. *Contact couple:* **David and Sue Moncaster**, 'Thatchers', Great Waltham, Chelmsford CM3 1DE **Tel:** 01245-362778 **E-mail:** gw-thatchers@tiscali.co.uk

■ HOSPITALS

To contact the Catholic Chaplain of a particular hospital we suggest you contact the hospital reception directly.

■ CATHOLIC SCHOOLS - MAINTAINED

■ ESSEX COUNTY COUNCIL

1. North West Area (Uttlesford and Braintree)

▲ Primary

St Francis Primary School, Gilchrist Way, Braintree, Essex CM7 7S **Tel:** 01376-320440 **Fax:** 01376-322498 **E-mail:** braintreestfrancisprimary@dioceseofbrentwood.org *(Braintree)*

St Thomas More Primary School, South Road, Saffron Walden, Essex CB11 3DW **Tel:** 01799-523248 **E-mail:** saffronwaldenstthomasmoreprimary@dioceseofbrentwood.org *(Saffron Waldron)*

Holy Family Primary School, Maltings Lane, Witham, Essex CM8 1DX **Tel:** 01376-513418 **Fax:** 01376-502239 **E-mail:** withamholyfamilyprimary@dioceseofbrentwood.org *(Witham)*

2. North East Area (Colchester and Tendring)

▲ Primary

St Clare's Primary School, Cloes Lane, Clacton-on-Sea, Essex CO16 8AG **Tel:** 01255-425344 **Fax:** 01255-473026 **E-mail:**clactonstclaresprimary@dioceseofbrentwood.org *(Clacton-on-Sea)*

St Clare's Nursery School, St James Church Hall, Tower Road, Clacton-on-Sea, Essex. **Tel/Fax:** 01255-427629 **E-mail:** clactonstclaresnursery@dioceseofbrentwood.org *(Clacton-on-Sea)*

St Thomas More's Primary School, Priory Street, Colchester CO1 2QB **Tel:** 01206-865722 **Fax:** 01206-868745 **E-mail:** colchesterstthomasmoreprimary@dioceseofbrentwood.org *(Colchester)*

St Joseph's Primary School, The Drive, Dovercourt, Harwich, Essex CO12 3SU **Tel:** 01255-503493. **Fax:** 01255-508958. **E-mail:** harwichstjosephsprimary@dioceseofbrentwood.org *(Harwich)*

St Teresa's Primary School, Clairmont Road, Lexden, Colchester CO3 5BE **Tel:** 01206-508445 **Fax:** 01206-500929 **E-mail:** lexdenstteresasprimary@dioceseofbrentwood.org *(Lexden)*

▲ Secondary Comprehensive

St Benedict's College, Norman Way, Colchester CO3 3US **Tel:** 01206-549222. **Fax:** 01206-579342 **E-mail:** colchesterstbenedictscollege@dioceseofbrentwood.org *(Colchester)*

3. West Area (Epping and Harlow)

▲ **Primary**

St Alban's Primary School, First Avenue, Harlow, Essex CM20 2NP **Tel:** 01279-425383 **Fax:** 01279-431320 **E-mail:** harlowstalbansprimary@dioceseofbrentwood.org *(Harlow 2)*

Holy Cross Primary School, Tracyes Road, Harlow, Essex CM18 6JJ **Tel:** 01279-424452 **E-mail:** harlowholycrossprimary@dioceseofbrentwood.org *(Harlow 3)*

St Luke's Primary School, Pyenest Road, Harlow, Essex CM19 4LU **Tel/Fax:** 01279-423499 **E-mail:** harlowstlukesprimary@dioceseofbrentwood.org *(Harlow 3)*

St John Fisher Primary School, Burney Drive, Loughton, Essex IG10 2DY **Tel:** 020-8508 6315 **E-mail:** loughtonstjohnfisher@dioceseofbrentwood.org *(Loughton)*

▲ **Secondary Comprehensive**

St Mark's West Essex Catholic School, Tripton Road, Harlow, Essex CM18 6AA **Tel:** 01279-421267/8 **Fax:** 01279-418220 **E-mail:** harlowstmarks@dioceseofbrentwood.org *(Harlow)*

4. Central Area (Brentwood, Chelmsford and Maldon)

▲ **Primary**

St Helen's Infant School, Queens Road, Brentwood, Essex CM14 4EY **Tel:** 01277-215626 **E-mail:** brentwoodsthelensinfant@dioceseofbrentwood.org *(Brentwood)*

St Helen's Junior School, Sawyers Hall Lane, Brentwood, Essex CM15 9BX **Tel:** 01277-213962. **E-mail:** brentwoodsthelensjunior@dioceseofbrentwood.org *(Brentwood)*

St Joseph the Worker Primary School, Highview Crescent, Hutton, Brentwood, Essex CM13 1BJ **Tel/Fax:** 01277-227282 **E-mail:** huttonstjosephprimary@dioceseofbrentwood.org *(Hutton)*

Our Lady Immaculate Primary School, New London Road, Chelmsford, CM2 0RG **Tel:** 01245-353755 **Fax:** 01245-344292 **E-mail:** chelmsfordOLIprimary@dioceseofbrentwood.org *(Chelmsford 1)*

St Pius X Primary School, Tennyson Road, Chelmsford, CM1 4HY **Tel:** 01245-354875 **Fax:** 01245-358926 **E-mail:** chelmsfordstpiusxprimary@dioceseofbrentwood.org *(Chelmsford)*

St Joseph's Primary School, Trinity Square, South Woodham Ferrers, Essex CM3 5JX **Tel:** 01245-321828 **Fax:** 01245-321795 **E-mail:** SWFstjosephsprimary@dioceseofbrentwood.org *(Danbury)*

St Francis Primary School, Mount View, West Chase, London Road, Maldon, Essex CM9 6HN **Tel:** 01621-856698 **Fax:** 01621-859225 **E-mail:** maldonstfrancisprimary@dioceseofbrentwood.org *(Maldon)*

The Bishops' Primary School, Beardsley Drive, North Springfield, Chelmsford, Essex CM1 6ZQ **Tel:** 01245-460107 **Fax:** 01245-464377 **E-mail:** springfieldthebishopsprimary@dioceseofbrentwood.org *(Springfield)*

▲ **Secondary Comprehensive**

Ursuline Convent High School, Queens Road, Brentwood, Essex CM14 4EX **Tel:** 01277-227156 **Fax:** 01277-229454 **E-mail:** brentwoodursulineconventhigh@dioceseofbrentwood.org *(Brentwood)*

St John Payne Comprehensive School, Patching Hall Lane, Chelmsford, CM1 4DJ **Tel:** 01245-256030 **Fax:** 01245-352337 **E-mail:** chelmsfordstjohnpayne@dioceseofbrentwood.org *(Chelmsford)*

5. South West Area (Basildon)

▲ **Primary**

St Anne Line Infant School, Wickhay, Basildon, Essex SS15 5AF **Tel:** 01268-524263 **Fax:** 01268-273187 **E-mail:** basildonstannelineinfant@dioceseofbrentwood.org *(Basildon 2)*

St Anne Line Junior School, Wickhay, Basildon, Essex SS15 5AF **Tel:** 01268-470444 **Fax:** 01268-273187 **E-mail:** basildonstannelinejunior@dioceseofbrentwood.org *(Basildon 2)*

St Teresa's Primary School, Elsenham Crescent, Basildon, Essex SS14 1UE **Tel:** 01268-553502 **Fax:** 01268-581425 **E-mail:** basildonstteresasprimary@dioceseofbrentwood.org *(Basildon 1)*

St Peter's Primary School, Coxes Farm Road, Billericay, Essex CM11 2UB **Tel:** 01277-653770 **Fax:** 01277-633146 **E-mail:** billericaystpetersprimary@dioceseofbrentwood.org *(Billericay)*

▲ **Secondary Comprehensive**

De La Salle School, Ghyllgrove, Basildon, Essex SS14 2LA **Tel:** 01268-281234 Fax: 01268-288710 **E-mail:** basildondelasalle@dioceseofbrentwood.org *(Basildon)*

6. South East Area (Castle Point and Rochford)

▲ **Primary**

Holy Family Primary School, Kents Hill Road, South Benfleet, Essex SS7 5PX

DIOCESE OF BRENTWOOD

Tel: 01268-792231
E-mail: benfleetholyfamilyprimary@dioceseofbrentwood.org *(Benfleet)*

St Joseph's Primary School, Vaagen Road, Canvey Island, Essex SS8 9DP **Tel:** 01268-683903 **Fax:** 01268-683903 **E-mail:** canveystjosephsprimary@dioceseofbrentwood.org *(Canvey Island)*

Our Lady of Ransom Primary School, Little Wheatley Chase, Rayleigh, Essex SS6 9EH **Tel:** 01268-785741 **Fax:** 01268-785167 **E-mail:** rayleighOLransomprimary@dioceseofbrentwood.org *(Rayleigh)*

St Teresa's Primary School, Ashingdon Road, Rochford, Essex SS4 1RF **Tel:** 01702-547918 **Fax:** 01702-530193 **E-mail:** rochfordstteresasprimary@dioceseofbrentwood.org *(Rochford)*

■ Southend-on-Sea Unitary Authority

▲ Primary

Our Lady of Lourdes Primary School, Manchester Drive, Leigh-on-Sea, Essex SS9 3HS **Tel:** 01702-475689 **E-mail:** leighOLLprimary@dioceseofbrentwood.org *(Leigh-on-Sea)*

St George's Primary School, Eagle Way, Shoeburyness, Essex SS3 9RX **Tel:** 01702-293522, **Fax:** 01702-716481 **E-mail:**shoeburynessstgeorgesprimary@dioceseofbrentwood.org *(Shoeburyness)*

Sacred Heart Primary School, Windermere Road, Southend-on-Sea, Essex SS1 2RF **Tel:** 01702-468052 **Fax:** 01702-603061 **E-mail:** southendsacredheartprimary@dioceseofbrentwood.org *(Southend-on-Sea)*

St Helen's Primary School, North Road, Westcliff-on-Sea, Essex SS0 7AH **Tel:** 01702-343823 **Fax:** 01702-437065 **E-mail:** westcliffsthelensprimary@dioceseofbrentwood.org *(Westcliff-on-Sea)*

▲ Secondary Comprehensive

St Bernard's High School, Milton Road, Westcliff-on-Sea, Essex SS0 7JS **Tel:** 01702-343583/352447 **Fax:** 01702-390201. **E-mail:** westcliffstbernardshigh@dioceseofbrentwood.org *(Westcliff-on-Sea)*

St Thomas More High School for Boys, Kenilworth Gardens, Westcliff-on-Sea, Essex SS0 0BW **Tel:** 01702-344933 **Fax:** 01702-436990 **E-mail:**westcliffstthomasmoreboyshigh@dioceseofbrentwood.org *(Westcliff-on-Sea)*

■ Thurrock Unitary Authority

▲ Primary

Holy Cross Primary School. Daiglen Drive, South Ockendon, Essex RM15 5RP **Tel:** 01708-853000 **Fax:** 01708-856337 **E-mail:** aveleyholycrossprimary@dioceseofbrentwood.org *(Aveley)*.

St Thomas of Canterbury Primary School, Ward Avenue, Grays, Essex RM17 5RW. **Tel:** 01375-375826. **Fax:** 01375-392188. **E-mail:** grayssttthomasofcanterbury@dioceseofbrentwood.org *(Grays)*

St Joseph's Primary School, Scratton Road, Stanford-le-Hope, Essex SS17 0PA **Tel:** 01375-672217 **Fax:** 01375-640095 **E-mail:** stanfordlehopestjosephsprimary@dioceseofbrentwood.org *(Stanford-le-Hope)*

St Mary's Primary School, Calcutta Road, Tilbury, Essex RM18 2QH **Tel:** 01375-843254 **E-mail:** tilburystmarysprimary@dioceseofbrentwood.org *(Tilbury)*

▲ Secondary Comprehensive

Convent High School for Girls, College Avenue, Grays, Essex RM17 5UX **Tel:** 01375-376173 **Fax:** 01375-394724 **E-mail:** graysconventhighschool@dioceseofbrentwood.org *(Grays)*

■ LONDON BOROUGH OF BARKING & DAGENHAM

▲ Primary

St Joseph's Primary School, The Broadway, Barking, Essex IG11 7AR **Tel:** 020-8270 6474 **Fax:** 020-8270 6478 **E-mail:** barkingstjosephsprimary@dioceseofbrentwood.org *(Barking)*

St Vincent's Primary School, Burnside Road, Dagenham, Essex RM8 2JN **Tel:** 020-8270 6695 **Fax:** 020-8270 6696 **E-mail:** becontreestvincentsprimary@dioceseofbrentwood.org *(Becontree)*

The St Teresa Primary School, Bowes Road, Dagenham, Essex RM8 2XJ **Tel:** 020-8270 4757 **Fax:** 020-8270 4756 **E-mail:** dagenhamstteresasprimary@dioceseofbrentwood.org *(Dagenham)*

St Joseph's Primary School, Connor Road, Dagenham, Essex RM9 5UL **Tel:** 020-8270 6480 **Fax:** 020-8595 5061 **E-mail:** dagenhamstjosephsprimary@dioceseofbrentwood.org *(Dagenham)*

St Peter's Primary School, Goresbrook Road, Dagenham, Essex RM9 6UU **Tel:** 020-8270 6524 **Fax:** 020-8270 6525 **E-mail:** dagenhamstpetersprimary@dioceseofbrentwood.org *(Dagenham 1)*

▲ Secondary Comprehensive

All Saints Catholic Comprehensive

Technology College, Terling Road, off Wood Lane, Dagenham, Essex RM8 1JT
Tel: 020-8270 4242 **Fax:** 020-8595 4024
E-mail: dagenhamallsaints@dioceseofbrentwood.org *(Dagenham 2)*

■ LONDON BOROUGH OF HAVERING

▲ Primary

St Patrick's Primary School, Lowshoe Lane, Collier Row, Romford, Essex RM5 2AP
Tel: 01708-745655 **Fax:** 01708-731696
E-mail: collierrowstpatricksprimary@dioceseofbrentwood.org *(Collier Row)*

St Alban's Primary School, Heron Flight Avenue, Hornchurch, Essex RM12 5LN
Tel: 01708-555644 **Fax:** 01708-555160
E-mail: elmparkstalbansprimary@dioceseofbrentwood.org *(Elm Park)*

St Ursula's Infant School, Straight Road, Romford, Essex RM3 7JS
Tel: 01708-345200
E-mail: haroldhillstursulasinfant@dioceseofbrentwood.org *(Harold Hill 2).*

St Ursula's Junior School, Straight Road, Romford, Essex RM3 7JS
Tel: 01708-343170 **Fax:** 01708-379590
E-mail: haroldhillstursulasjunior@dioceseofbrentwood.org *(Harold Hill 2).*

St Mary's Primary School, Hornchurch Road, Hornchurch, Essex RM12 4TL
Tel: 01708-448430 **Fax:** 01708-449807
E-mail: hornchurchstmarysprimary@dioceseofbrentwood.org *(Hornchurch)*

La Salette Primary School, Dunedin Road, Rainham, Essex RM13 8SP
Tel: 01708-555554 **Fax:** 01708-521861
E-mail: rainhamlasaletteprimary@dioceseofbrentwood.org *(Rainham)*

St Peter's Primary School, Dorset Avenue, Romford, Essex RM1 4JA
Tel: 01708-745506 **Fax:** 01708-730699
E-mail: romfordstpetersprimary@dioceseofbrentwood.org *(Romford)*

St Joseph's Primary School, 115 St Mary's Lane, Upminster, Essex RM14 2QB
Tel: 01708-220277 **Fax:** 01708-640605
E-mail: upminsterstjosehsprimary@dioceseofbrentwood.org *(Upminster)*

▲ Secondary Comprehensive

The Campion School, Wingletye Lane, Hornchurch, Essex RM11 3BX
Tel: 01708-452332 **Fax:** 01708-456995
E-mail: hornchurchthecampion@dioceseofbrentwood.org *(Gidea Park)*

Sacred Heart of Mary Girls' School, 70 St Mary's Lane, Upminster, Essex RM14 2QR **Tel:** 01708-222660/228590
Fax: 01708-226686
E-mail: upminstersacredheart@dioceseofbrentwood.org *(Upminster)*

■ LONDON BOROUGH OF NEWHAM

▲ Primary

St Helen's Primary School, Falcon Street, London E13 8DD **Tel:** 020-7476 1785
Fax: 020-7476 7907
E-mail: canningtownsthelensprimary@dioceseofbrentwood.org *(Canning Town)*

St Joachim's Primary School, Shipman Road, Custom House, London E16 3DT
Tel: 020-7476 1658 **Fax:** 020-7511 4209
E-mail: customhousestjoachimsprimary@dioceseofbrentwood.org *(Custom House)*

St Michael's Primary School, Arthur Road, East Ham, London E6 6EF
Tel: 020-8472 3964
E-mail: easthamstmichaelsprimary@dioceseofbrentwood.org *(East Ham)*

St Antony's Primary School, Upton Avenue, Forest Gate, London E7 9QB
Tel: 020-8552 3670 **Fax:** 020-8470 2580
E-mail: forestgatestantonysprimary@dioceseofbrentwood.org *(Forest Gate)*

St Winefride's Primary School, Church Road, Manor Park, London E12 6HB
Tel: 020-8478 0510
E-mail: manorparkstwinefridesprimary@dioceseofbrentwood.org *(Manor Park).*

St Francis Primary School, Maryland Park, Stratford, London E15 1HB
Tel: 020-8534 0476 **Fax:** 020-8555 3068
E-mail: stratfordstfrancisprimary@dioceseofbrentwood.org *(Stratford)*

St Edward's Primary School, Green Street, Upton Park, London E13 9AX
Tel: 020-8472 4337 **Fax:** 020-8470 4522
E-mail: uptonparkstedwardsprimary@dioceseofbrentwood.org *(Upton Park)*

▲ Secondary Comprehensive

St Bonaventure's Comprehensive School, Boleyn Road, Forest Gate, London E7 9QD
Tel: 020-8472 3844 **Fax:** 020-8471 2749
E-mail: forestgatestbonaventure@dioceseofbrentwood.org *(Forest Gate)*

St Angela's Ursuline Convent School, St George's Road, Forest Gate, London E7 8HX **Tel:** 020-8472 6022
Fax: 020-8475 0245
E-mail: forestgatestangelasursuline@dioceseofbrentwood.org (*Forest Gate)*

■ LONDON BOROUGH OF REDBRIDGE

▲ Primary

St Augustine's Primary School, Cranbrook Road, Gants Hill, Ilford, Essex IG2 6RG **Tel:** Infants: 020-8554 1919 Juniors: 020-8554 3453
E-mail: barkingsidestaugustinesprimary@dioceseofbrentwood.org *(Barkingside)*

St Bede's Primary School, Canon Avenue, Chadwell Heath, Romford, Essex RM6 5RR

Tel: 020-8590 1376 **Fax:** 020-8597 7440 **E-mail:** chadwellheathstbedesprimary@dioceseofbrentwood.org *(Chadwell Heath)*

St Aidan's Primary School, Benton Road East, Ilford, Essex IG1 4AS **Tel:** 020-8590 5223 **E-mail:** ilfordstaidansprimary@dioceseofbrentwood.org. *(Ilford)*

SS Peter & Paul's Primary School, Gordon Road, Ilford, Essex IG1 1SA **Tel:** 020-8478 1267 **Fax:** 020-8478 0575 **E-mail:** ilfordssppprimary@dioceseofbrentwood.org *(Ilford)*

Our Lady of Lourdes Primary School, Chestnut Drive, Wanstead, London E11 2TA **Tel:** 020-8989 9521 **E-mail:** wansteadOLLprimary@dioceseofbrentwood.org *(Wanstead)*

St Antony's Primary School, Mornington Road, Woodford Green, Essex IG8 0TX **Tel:** 020-8504 4706 **Fax:** 020-8559 2824. **E-mail:** woodfordgreenstantonys primary@dioceseofbrentwood.org *(Woodford Green)*

▲ Secondary Comprehensive

Canon Palmer Comprehensive School, Aldborough Road South, Seven Kings, Ilford, Essex IG3 8EU **Tel:** 020-8590 3808 **E-mail:** ilfordcanonpalmer@dioceseofbrentwood.org

Trinity Catholic High School, Mornington Road, Woodford Green, Essex IG8 0TP **Tel:** 020-8504 3419 **Fax:** 020-8505 7546 **E-mail:** woodfordgreentrinityhigh@dioceseofbrentwood.org *(Woodford Green)*

■ LONDON BOROUGH OF WALTHAM FOREST

▲ Primary

St Mary's Primary School, Station Road, Chingford, London E4 7BJ. **Tel:** 020-8529 4723 **Fax:** 020-8529 1012 **E-mail:** chingfordstmarysprimary@dioceseofbrentwood.org *(Chingford)*

St Joseph's Junior School, Vicarage Road, Leyton, London E10 5DX **Tel:** 020-8539 5971 **Fax:** 020-8556 9668 **E-mail:** leytonstjosephsjuniore@dioceseofbrentwood.org *(Leyton)*

St Joseph's Infant School, Marsh Lane, Leyton, London E10 7BL **Tel:** 020-8539 3000 **Fax:** 020-8558 1049 **E-mail:** leytonstjosephsinfant@dioceseofbrentwood.org *(Leyton)*

St Mary's Junior School, Shernhall Street, Walthamstow, London E17 3EA **Tel:** 020-8520 3552 **Fax:** 020-8520 3092 **E-mail:** walthamstowstmarysjunior@dioceseofbrentwood.org *(Walthamstow 1)*

St Helen's Infant School, Shernhall Street, Walthamstow, London E17 3EA **Tel:** 020-8520 8500 **Fax:** 020-8520 6500 **E-mail:** walthamstowsthelensinfant@dioceseofbrentwood.org *(Walthamstow 1)*

St Patrick's Primary School, Longfield Avenue, Walthamstow, London E17 7DP. **Tel:** 020-8923 7711 **Fax:** 020-8509 3261 **E-mail:** walthamstowstpatricksprimary@dioceseofbrentwood.org *(Walthamstow 2)*

▲ Secondary Comprehensive

Holy Family Catholic College, *Walthamstow House Site:* 1 Shernhall Street, Walthamstow, London E17 3EA **Tel:** 020-8520 0482 **Fax:** 020-8521 0364 *Wiseman House Site:* Shernhall Street, Walthamstow, London E17 9RT **Tel:** 020-8520 3587 **E-mail:** walthamstowholyfamilycollege@dioceseofbrentwood.org *(Walthamstow)*

■ CATHOLIC SCHOOLS - INDEPENDENT

■ ESSEX

▲ Primary

St Philomena's Catholic Preparatory School, 53 Hadleigh Road, Frinton-on-Sea, Essex CO13 9HQ **Tel:** 01255-674492 **Fax:** 01255-674459 **E-mail:**frintonstphilomenaspreparatory@dioceseofbrentwood.org *(Frinton-on-Sea)*

Loyola Preparatory School, 103 Palmerston Road, Buckhurst Hill, Essex IG9 5NH **Tel/Fax:** 020-8504 7372 **E-mail:**buckhursthillloyolapreparatory@dioceseofbrentwood.org *(Woodford Green)*

Ursuline Preparatory School, Old Great Ropers, Great Ropers Lane, Warley, Brentwood, Essex CM13 3HR **Tel:** 01277-227152 **Fax:** 01277-202559 **E-mail:** brentwoodursulinepreparatory@dioceseofbrentwood.org *(Brentwood)*

New Hall Preparatory School, Boreham, Chelmsford, CM3 3HT **Tel:** 01245-467588 **Fax:** 01245-464348 **E-mail:** chelmsfordnewhallpreparatory@dioceseofbrentwood.org *(Springfield).*

▲ Secondary

New Hall School, Boreham, Chelmsford, CM3 3HT **Tel:** 01245-467588 **Fax:** 01245-464348 **E-mail:** chelmsfordnewhallschool@dioceseofbrentwood.org *(Springfield)*

■ LONDON BOROUGH OF HAVERING

▲ Primary

St Mary's Hare Park Independent

Primary School, South Drive, Gidea Park, Romford, Essex RM2 6HH
Tel: 01708-761220
E-mail: gideaparkstmarysharepark@dioceseofbrentwood.org *(Gidea Park)*

■ LONDON BOROUGH OF REDBRIDGE

▲ Primary

Ilford Ursuline Preparatory School, 2 Coventry Road, Ilford, Essex IG1 4QR
Tel: 020-8518 4050 **Fax:** 020-8518 2060
E-mail: ilfordursulinepreparatory@dioceseofbrentwood.org *(Ilford).*

St Joseph's Convent Independent Primary School for Girls, 59 Cambridge Park, Wanstead, London E11 2PR
Tel/Fax: 020-8989 4700
E-mail: wansteadstjosephsconvent@dioceseofbrentwood.org *(Wanstead)*

▲ Secondary

Ilford Ursuline High School, Moreland Road, Ilford, Essex IG1 4JU
Tel: 020-8554 1995 **Fax:** 020-8554 9537
E-mail: ilfordursulinehighschool@dioceseofbrentwood.org *(Ilford)*

■ CATHOLIC SCHOOL - SPECIAL

St John's School, Turpin's Lane, Woodford Bridge, Essex IG8 8BA
Tel: 020-8504 1818
E-mail: woodfordbridgestjohnsschool@dioceseofbrentwood.org *(Woodford Green)*

ARCHDIOCESE OF CARDIFF

Name changed from "Diocese of Newport and Menevia", 1896; from Newport, 7 February 1916 when erected into an Archdiocese. Consisting of the counties of Cardiff, Bridgend, Vale of Glamorgan, Newport, Torfaen, Blaenau Gwent, Monmouthshire, Merthyr Tydfil; Rhondda Cynon Taff; Caerphilly, Hereford and Worcester. Restructuring of Archdiocese 19th March 1987, old County of West Glamorgan taken into new Diocese of Menevia.

Patron of the Archdiocese
Our Lady of the Immaculate Conception, 8 Dec

Archbishop
Most Rev Peter D Smith LLB, JCD, Archbishop of Cardiff. Born Battersea, South London 21 October, 1943; ordained priest 15 July, 1972. Bishop of East Anglia 27 May 1995 transferred to Cardiff 26 October, 2001.

Residence:
Archbishop's House, 41-43 Cathedral Road, Cardiff CF11 9HD
Tel: 029-2022 0411 **Fax:** 029-2037 9036
E-mail: arch@rcadc.org

Personal Assistant:
Mrs Gill Healey
E-mail: p.a@rcadc.org

Most Rev Peter D Smith, Archbishop of Cardiff

■ ADMINISTRATION

■ Diocesan Curia
Archbishop's House, 41-43 Cathedral Road, Cardiff, CF11 9HD
Tel: 029-2022 0411 **Fax:** 029-2037 9036
E-mail: arch@rcadc.org

■ Vicar General
Mgr Canon Robert Reardon, Archbishop's House, 41-43 Cathedral Road, Cardiff, CF11 9HD
Tel: 029-2037 9494 **Fax:** 029-2037 9036
E-mail: v.g@rcadc.org

■ Chancellor
Awaiting appointment

■ Episcopal Vicar for Religious
Rev Christopher Fuse I.C. St Joseph's Presbytery, New Zealand Road, Cardiff, CF14 4BR
Tel: 029-2041 1819
E-mail: chrisfuse@mac.com

■ Archdiocesan Treasurer
Mr Anthony Hurley FCA. Archbishop's House, 43 Cathedral Road, Cardiff CF11 9HD
Tel: 029-2037 4148 **Fax:** 029-2037 9036
E-mail: finance@rcadc.org

■ Archdiocesan Information Officer
Rev John Owen. 62 Park Place, Cardiff CF10 3AS **Tel:** 029-2022 9785

■ Archdiocesan Projects Manager
Mr Michael Bamber. Archbishop's House, 41-43 Cathedral Road, Cardiff, CF11 9HD
Tel: 029-2037 4148 **Fax:** 029-2037 9036
E-mail: property@rcadc.org

■ Registrar for Deceased Clergy
Archbishop's House,
41-43 Cathedral Road, Cardiff CF11 9HD
Tel: 029-2022 0411 **Fax:** 029-2037 9036

■ CONSULTATIVE BODIES

■ Metropolitan Cathedral Chapter
(Erected 12 March 1920)
Provost: **Canon Patrick Daly**.
Canons: **Revv Patrick Kerrisk, John Maguire, Robert Reardon, John Griffiths, Peter Collins, Mathew Jones, Edward O'Connell, Joseph Boardman, Patrick O'Gorman**
Canons Emeritus: **Revv Philip Dwyer, Sean Kearney, Thomas Keane, Paul Chidgey**.
Honorary Canons: **Revv John O'Regan, James Mulvihill, Francis Mulvey, Francis O'Donnell, Ieuan Wyn Jones.**

■ **College of Consultors**
Mgr Canon Robert Reardon, Mgr Canon John Maguire, Rt Rev Paul Stonham, Revv Allan Davies-Hale, John Kelly, William Isaac, John Meredith, Canon John Griffiths, Canon Peter Collins, Michael Hagerty.

■ **Council of Priests**
Chairman: **Rev Canon Matthew Jones**.
Secretary: **Rev David Hayman**.

■ **EDUCATION AND FORMATION**
Diocesan Director for Schools & Colleges: **Mrs Anne Robertson**, Archbishop's House, 41/43 Cathedral Road, Cardiff CF11 9HD **Tel:** 029-2023 3838
Fax: 029-2037 9036
E-mail: schools@rcadc.org
Diocesan Director for Religious Education: **Mrs Anne Manghan**. Pastoral Resources Centre, 910 Newport Road, Cardiff CF3 4LL
Tel: 029-2036 2599 **Fax:** 029-2079 3172
E-mail: r.e@rcadc.org
Diocesan Director for Adult Education: **Rev Allan Davies-Hale**. St John Lloyd Presbytery, Glan-y-Mor Road, Cardiff CF3 1RQ **Tel/Fax:** 029-2077 8631
E-mail: davies-hale.allen@rcadc.org
Director of CCRS: **Mr James Siemens**, St David's Catholic College, Ty Gwyn Road, Penylan, Cardiff CF23 5QD
Tel: 029-2049 8555
E-mail: jsiemens@st-davids-coll-ac.uk

■ **Vocations**
Director: **Rev Paul Millar**, 201 New Road, Porthcawl CF36 5NN **Tel:** 01656-782789
E-mail: starofthesea201-vocations @yahoo.co.uk
Promoter: **Rev William Isaac**, St Mary's Presbytery, 39 Ewenny Road, Bridgend CF31 3HS
Tel: 01656-652034
E-mail: w.isaac@btconnect.com

■ **Permanent Diaconate**
Director Formation: **Rev Canon Peter Collins**, St David's Cathedral, Clergy House, Charles Street, Cardiff CF10 2SF
Tel: 029-2023 1407

■ **LITURGY AND ECUMENISM**

■ **Diocesan Liturgical Commission**
Chairman: **Rev John Meredith**. Our Lady of the Angels, Oak Street, Cwmbran.
Tel: 01633-482346 **Fax:** 01683-876288
E-mail: j.meredith10@ntlworld.com

■ **Commission for Christian Unity**
Chair: **Mrs Carys Whelan DSG**, Cae'r Delyn, St Hilary, Cowbridge CF71 7DP
Tel: 01446-772888
E-mail: carys@caerdelyn.com

■ **OTHER DIOCESAN COMMISSIONS**

■ **Safeguarding Advisors Commission**
Contact: **Canon Peter Collins**,
Tel: 029-2033 1407
Rachel McMullen, Archbishop's House, 43 Cathederal Road, Cardiff CF11 9HD
Tel: 029-2037 9480
E-mail: cpo@rcada.org

■ **Family Life Commission**
Convenor: **Mrs Anne Ballard**, DSG, 408 Western Avenue, Llandaff, Cardiff CF5 2BL
Tel: 029-2021 2821
E-mail: annejim98@yahoo.com
Parenting Support Officer: **Mrs Joanne Hinds,** Pastoral Resources Centre, 910 Newport Road, Rumney, Cardiff CF3 4LL
Tel: 029-2079 5241
E-mail: parenting@rcadc.org

■ **Forum for Women**
Convenor: **Mrs Ann Callus**, 7 Cycoed Avenue, Cardiff. **Tel:** 029-2075 2499
E-mail: avcallus@aol.com

■ **Justice & Peace and Intergrity of Creation (JPIC).** *Network Co-ordinator*: **Pauline Lawrence,** 4 Beech Grove, Denygraig, Porthcawl CF36 5DP
Tel: 01656-771016
E-mail: lawrencecymru@aol.com

■ **NATIONAL MARRIAGE TRIBUNAL FOR WALES**
(erected 18 June 2007) Archbishop's House, 43 Cathedral Road, Cardiff CF11 9HD
Administrator: **Rev David Hayman**, The Priest's House, Conway Road, Pontypool NP4 6HL **Tel:** 01495-762280

■ CARDIFF

† Metropolitan Cathedral Church of St David
(1842; 1887; 1959)
Clergy House, St David's Cathedral, Charles Street, Cardiff CF10 2SF **Tel:** 029-2023 1407
Rev Canon Peter Collins *(Cathedral Dean)*. Also in residence: **Rev Raymond O'Shea (retired)**.
E-mail: cardiff.met.cath@btinternet.com
Website: cardiffmetropolitancathedral.org.uk
M: *Sat 1st M of Sun 5.45pm. Sun 11am, 5.45pm. Hds (vigil 5.15pm), 11am, 12.30pm.*

- ***Sisters of Nazareth,*** Colum Road, Cardiff CF10 3UN **Tel:** 029-2022 0943 Chaplain: **Rev Gerard Mackrell (SMM)** **Tel:** 029-2023 1809
  M: *Sun 10am, 11am (Polish).*

■ ABERCYNON

† St Thomas (1925; 1927)
Cardiff Road, Abercynon, Rhondda Cynon Taff County Borough CF45 4RR
Tel/Fax: 01443-740353
Rev Gregory Matus, The Presbytery, Cardiff Road, Abercynon CF45 4RR
Tel: 01443 740353
E-mail: g.matus@btconnect.com
M: *Sun 9.30pm. Hds 10am.*

■ ABERDARE

Served from Mountain Ash

■ ABERGAVENNY

† Our Lady and St Michael (1687; 1860)
Priory of Our Lady & St Michael, 10 Pen-y-Pound, Abergavenny NP7 5UD
Tel: 01873-856660
Rev Dom Thomas Regan (OSB).
Permanent Deacon: **Rev Dr Andreas Erhardt,** 226 Underhill Crescent, Abergavenny NP7 6DU
Tel: 01873-855078
E-mail: erhardt.andreas@rcadc.org
M: *Sat 1st M of Sun 6.30pm, Sun 10am, 6.30pm. Hds (Vigil) 7pm, 9.15am, 7pm.*

- ***Daughters of the Holy Spirit,*** 151 Park Crescent, Abergavenny NP7 5TN **Tel:** 01873-853370

■ ABERKENFIG

† St Robert of Newminster (1879; 1924)
Bridgend Road, Aberkenfig, Bridgend CF32 9PS **Tel/Fax:** 01656-720256
Served from Maesteg
M: *Sun 11am. Hds Vigil 6.30pm, 11am (school in term-time).*

■ ABERTILLERY

† 1 St Mary (1877)
Hill Street, Abertillery, Blaenau Gwent County Borough
Tel: 01495-212339
Rev Dom Aidan Doyle (OSB). 2 Queen Street, NP13 1AN. See also Brynmawr.
M: *Sun 9.30am. Hds, See Newsletter.*

■ BARGOED

† St Peter (1916)
Usk Road, Bargoed, Caerphilly County Borough **Tel:** 01443-831949
E-mail: stpeters.bargoed@btopenworld.com
Deacon: **Rev Philip Gummett (retired)**. 11 Glyn March Street, Deri, Bargoed CF81 9HZ **Tel:** 01443-831488
E-mail: papapgumme@aol.com
Served from Abercynon
M: *Sun 11.15am. Hds See Newsletter.*

■ BARRY

† St Helen (New church 1892; 1907)
Wyndham Street, Barry, Vale of Glamorgan County Borough
Tel: 01446-735051 **Fax:** 01446-740133
Rev Canon Patrick O'Gorman. The Presbytery, Court Road, Barry CF63 4ET
M: *Sat 1st M of Sun, 6.30pm; Sun 8.30am. 10.30am. Hds, See Newsletter.*

■ BELMONT, Hereford

† Abbey of St Michael & All Angels
(1854; 1959)
Belmont, Hereford HR2 9RZ
Monastery: **Tel:** 01432-374710
Abbot: **Tel:** 01432-374718
E-mail: abbot@belmontabbey.org.uk
Prior: **Tel:** 01432-374780
E-mail: peterbrady@belmontabbey.org.uk
Parish Priest: **Tel:** 01432-277319
E-mail: pp@belmontparish.plus.com
Bursar: **Tel:** 01432 374749
E-mail: bursar@belmontabbey.org.uk
Guest Master: **Tel:** 01432 374727
E-mail: fathercadfan@belmontabbey.org.uk
Retreats: **Tel:** 01432 374727
E-mail: retreats@belmontabbey.org.uk
Hedley Lodge: **Tel:** 01432 374747
E-mail: hedley@belmontabbey.org.uk
Dom Nicholas Wetz OSB
Fax: 01432-374711

- ***Benedictines (OSB):*** **Rt Rev Dom Paul Stonham** (*Abbot*), **Very Rev Dom Peter Brady** (*Prior*), **Rt Rev Dom Jerome Hodkinson** (*Titular Abbot of Shrewsbury*); **Dom Peter Madden** (*Sub-Prior*); **Rev Dom Dominic Blaney, The Very Rev Dom Wulstan Probert** *(Cathederal Prior of Worcester)*, **Rev Dom Lawrence Beer, Rev Dom Dyfrig Harris, Rev Dom Francis McKenna, Dom Bernard Wassell, Rev Dom Nicholas Wetz** *(Parish Priest)*, **Rev Dom Brendan Thomas** *(Novice Master)*, **Rev Dom James Norris, Rev Dom Cenydd Marrison, Rev Dom Richard Simons,**

Rev Dom Cadfan Williams *(Guest Master)*, **Dom Raphael Aspinwall, Dom Andrew Berry, Dom Paul Lyons**
M: *Sun 8.30am, 9.30am (Sung), 11am. Hds 7.30 8.30 12noon (sung).*

- ***Hedley Lodge.*** Belmont Abbey, Hereford, HR2 9RZ *Permanent Deacon:* **Rev Eddie Wyman 1** Bridle Road, Hereford HR4 0PP **Tel:** 01432-263575 **E-mail:** redjag@tiscali.co.uk
Retreat and Conference Centre. **Tel:** 01432-374712 *Guest Master* **Tel:** 01432-374727 **E-mail:** retreats@belmontabbey.org.uk
- ***Passionist Nuns.*** 19/21 Woodfield Gardens, Belmont, Hereford HR2 9RN

■ BLAENAVON

† The Sacred Heart and St Felix (1868)
Ellick Street, Blaenavon, Torfaen County Borough NP4 9RA
Served from Pontypool.
M: *Sun 9am. Hds 7pm.*

■ BRIDGEND

† St Mary (1856)
39 Ewenny Road, Bridgend CF31 3HS
Tel/Fax: 01656-652034
E-mail: w.isaac@btconnect.com
Revv William Isaac, Timothy McGrath, *Permanent Deacon:* **Rev Dr Philip Manghan,** 25 Lark Rise, Brackla, Bridgend CF31 2NU
Tel: 01656-663747
E-mail: philipmanghan@lineone.net
M: *Sat 1st M of Sun 6pm. Sun, 10.30am, 6pm. Hds 9.30am, 12noon, 7pm.*

■ BROMYARD, Herefordshire

† St Joseph (1908; 1957)
21 Old Road, Bromyard, HR7 4BQ
Served from Belmont Abbey.
Rev Dom James Norris (OSB).
Tel: 01432-374739
M: *Sun 11am. Hds midday and 7.30pm.*

■ BRYNMAWR

† St Mary (1863)
Catholic Road, Blaenau Gwent County Borough NP23 4EF **Tel:** 01495-212339
Served from Abertillery.
M: *Sun 11am. Hds as arranged.*

■ CAERLEON

† SS Julius, Aaron and David (1884)
High Street, Newport NP18 1AG
Tel: 01633 272144
Served from Newport (2).
M: *Sat 1st M of Sun 6.30pm. Hds See Newsletter.*

† St Julius The Martyr
Beaufort Road, St Julian's Est, Beaufort
Served from Caerleon
M: *Sun 11.15am. Hds See Newsletter.*

■ CAERPHILLY

† St Helen (1912; 1964)
Nantgarw Road, Caerphilly CF83 3FB
Tel: 029-2088 3192 (Parish Centre)
Fax: 029-2088 2444
E-mail: johngwynfor@btconnect.com
Rev Canon John Griffiths. St Helen's Church, Nantgarw Road, Caerphilly, CF83 3FB
Permanent Deacons: **Rev Geoffrey Beach,** 97 Van Road, Caerphilly CF83 1LA
Tel: 029-2086 1850
E-mail: geoff@beachfamily.plus.com
Rev Melvyn Morrisey, Carmel, Corbetts Lane, Caerphilly CF83 3HX
Tel: 029-2086 4960
E-mail: mel_morissey@tiscali.co.uk
M: *Sat 1st M of Sun 6.30pm. Sun 10am. Hds 7pm.*

■ CALDICOT

† St Paul (1961)
Longcroft Road, Monmouthshire.
Served from Chepstow.
M: *Sun 9am. Hds 7pm.*

■ CARDIFF

1. † Metropolitan Cathedral.
See start of Parish Section

2. † The Blessed Sacrament (1931; 1960)
151 Wentloog Road, Rumney, Cardiff CF3 8HE **Tel:** 029-2079 7872
Canon Francis Mulvey.
M: *Sat 1st M of Sun 7pm. Sun 10am. Hds 10am, 7pm.*

3. † Christ the King (1955; 1978)
Newborough Avenue, Llanishen, Cardiff.
Tel: 029-2075 3945 **Fax:** 029-2076 3727
E-mail: ckadmin@inspiron.co.uk
Served from Cardiff (8).
M: *Sat 1st M of Sun 6.30pm. Sun 8.30am, 10.30am. Hds 12.45pm, 7.30pm.*

4. † The Holy Family
(1955; New church 1980)
Carter Pl, Fairwater, Cardiff CF5 3NP
Tel: 029-2056 3871 **Canon Patrick Kerrisk.**
M: *Sat 1st M of Sun 6pm. Sun 11am. Hds (vigil 7.30pm), 9am.*

5. † Our Lady of Lourdes (1957)
Gabalfa Avenue, Gabalfa, Cardiff.
Served from Cardiff (2).
M: Sat 1st M of Sun 6pm; Hds As announced.

6. † Sacred Heart (1937)
Broad Street, Leckwith, Cardiff CF11 8BY
Tel: 029-2038 3187 **Fax:** 029-2037 3258
Rev Liam Hennessy.
M: *Sun 9.30am. Hds 9.30am.*

7. † St Alban-on-the-Moors
(1891; 1911; cons 1949)
Swinton Street, Splottlands, Cardiff
Tel: 029-2046 3219 **Fax:** 029-2048 8308
- ***Institute of Charity (IC):*** **Revv Polycarp Shayo** *(Parish Priest)*, **Graham Venn, Br Francis Belt**.
  St Alban's, Cameron Street, CF24 2NX
  E-mail: graham@rosmini.org & fbelt@globalnet.co.uk
  M: *Sat 1st M of Sun 7pm. Sun 10am, Hds (vigil 7pm), 12 noon.*

8. † St Brigid (1952; 1964; cons 1977)
Crystal Glen, Cardiff CF14 5QN
Tel/Fax: 029-2075 2389
E-mail: pp@3churches.org
Revv Canon Matthew Jones, James Kaniparampil (CMI).
M: *Sun 10.30am, 6pm. Hds (vigil 7.30pm), See also St Paul & Christ the King.*

9. † St Cadoc (1957)
Barnstaple Road, Llanrumney.
Tel: 029-2077 8038
E-mail: brigcardiff@aol.com
Rev Brian Gray, Parracombe Crescent, Llanrumney, Cardiff CF3 5LT
M: *Sat 1st M of Sun 5.30pm. Sun 9am, 11am. Hds (Vigil 7.30pm), 9am.*

10. † St Clare (1932)
Mill Road, Ely, Cardiff CF5 4AE
Served from Cardiff (12).
M: *Sat 1st M of Sun 6pm. Sun 9am. Hds Vigil 7pm.*

11. † St Cuthbert
Pomeroy Street, The Docks, Cardiff.
Tel: 029-2048 0147
Served from Cardiff (6).
M: *Sun 11am. Hds 7pm.*

12. † St Francis of Assisi
(1927; 1960; cons 1977)
Cowbridge Road West, Ely.
Tel/Fax: 029-2059 1503
E-mail: frmstfrancis@aol.com
Rev Martin Donnelly. St Francis Presbytery, 277 Cowbridge Road West, Cardiff CF5 1JB **Tel:** 029-2059 1503
Permanent Deacon: **Rev Mauriel Scanlon,** 117 Pencisely Road, Llandaff, Cardiff
Tel: 029-2021 2651
E-mail: conorcarter@hotmail.com
M: *Sun 10.30am, 6pm. Hds 9.30am.*
- ***Daughters of Charity of St Vincent de Paul,*** 200 Grand Avenue, Ely, Cardiff CF5 4HX **Tel:** 029-2067 9594

13 † St John Lloyd. (1966; 1975).
Glan-y-Mór Road, Trowbridge, Cardiff CF3 1RQ
Tel/Fax: 029-2077 8631
E-mail: davies-hale.allan@rcadc.org
Rev Allan Davies-Hale.
M: *Sat 1st M of Sun 6.30pm. Sun 10.30am, 5pm. Hds (vigil) 7pm, 10am.*

14 † St Joseph (1913; 1936)
New Zealand Road, Cathays, CF14 3BR
Tel: 029-2041 1819 **Fax:** 029-2041 1820
E-mail: chrisfuse@mac.com
- ***Institute of Charity (IC):*** **Revv Christopher Fuse** (*Rector and Parish Priest*), **Edward J Cody, Bro Brian Butler**.
  M: *Sat 1st M of Sun 6pm. Sun 9.15am, 11am. Hds 12noon, 7pm.*
- ***Sisters of St Joseph of Annecy***, The Convent, 200 North Road, Cardiff CF14 3BL **Tel**: 029-2061 9619

15. † St Mary of the Angels
(1865; 1907)
Kings Road, Canton, Cardiff.
Tel: 029-2023 0492 **Fax:** 029-2033 2239
Mgr Canon John Maguire, Revv Michael Christopher Delaney (OSB). Andrea Bord
67 Talbot Street, CF11 9BX
M: *Sun 10am, 12noon, 6pm. Hds 9.30am, 12.15pm, 7.30pm.*

16. † St Patrick (1866; 1930)
Grange Gardens, Grangetown CF11 7LJ
Tel: 029-2025 3514
E-mail: johnfahy67@ntlworld.com
Rev John Fahy.
M: *Sat 1st M of Sun 6.30pm. Sun 9am, 11am. Hds 10am, 7pm.*

17. St Paul (1975)
Cyncoed Road, Cardiff CF2 6AD
Served from Cardiff (8).
M: *Sat 1st M of Sun 6pm. Sun 9am. Hds 9.30am.*

18. † St Peter.
(1861; cons 28 June 1948)
St Peter's Street, Roath, Cardiff CF24 3BA
Tel: 029-2048 3394 **Fax:** 029-2045 1535
E-mail: stpeters@rosmini.org
- ***Institute of Charity (IC):*** **Revv David J Myers** (*Rector and Parish Priest*), **Peter Reynolds, James McKnight, Michael McCarthy**.
  M: *Sat 1st M of Sun 6pm. Sun 9.30am, 11am (Sung), 12.15pm. Hds 8am, 5.30pm.*

19. St Philip Evans (1975)
Llanedeyrn Drive, Llanedeyrn, Cardiff CF23 9UL **Tel:** 029-2073 1061
E-mail: pevansparish@aol.com
Rev Wayne Anthony Hodges.
M: *Sat 1st M of Sun 6.30pm. Sun 10am, 11.30am (Welsh). Hds See Newsletter.*

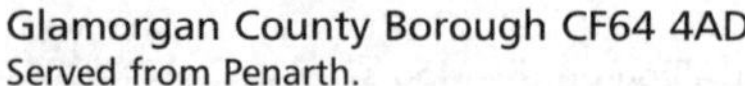

20. † St Teilo (1925)
Old Church Road, Whitchurch, Cardiff CF14 1AD **Tel:** 029-2062 3444
Rev Canon Edward O'Connell *(Parish Priest).*
M: *Sun 9am, 11am, 6.30pm. Hds (vigil 7.30pm), 10am, 6pm.*

21. University Chaplaincy.
62 Park Place, Cardiff CF10 3AS
For Students of Cardiff University.
Chaplain: **Rev John Owen.**
Tel: 029-2022 9785
E-mail: r-c-chaplaincy@cf.ac.uk
M: *Sun 6.15pm.*

■ CHEPSTOW
† St Mary (1975)
Bulwark Road, Chepstow, NP16 5JE
Tel: 01291-622649 **Fax:** 01291-627938
E-mail: stmarychepstow@btopenworld.com
Rev Barry English.
M: *Sat 1st M of Sun 6pm. Sun 11am. Hds 9.30am.*

■ COWBRIDGE
† St Cadoc (1955)
Townmill Road, Cowbridge, Vale of Glamorgan CF71 7BE.
Served from Llantwit Major.
Rev Pierce Maher
M: *Sat 1st M of Sun, 5.30pm.*

■ CWMBRAN
1. † Our Lady of the Angels (1864; 1882)
Wesley Street, Cwmbran, Torfaen County Borough. **Tel/Fax:** 01633-482346
E-mail: j.meredith10@ntlworld.com
Rev John Meredith. Presbytery, Oak Street, Cwmbran NP44 3LT
Permanent Deacon: **Rev Peter McLaren,** 1 Wiston Path, Fairwater, Cwmbran NP44 4PZ **Tel:** 01633-770754
E-mail: peter.mclaren@ntlworld.com
M: *Sat 1st M of Sun 6pm. Sun 9.30am (1st Sun of month 4pm Pol), 6pm. Hds 9.30am, 7.30pm.*
- ***Sisters of Joseph of Annecy,*** Abbey Community: St Joseph's Convent, Llantarnam Abbey, Cwmbran NP44 3YJ **Tel:** 01633-483232/873368

2. † St David (1961; 1963)
Avondale Road, Pontnewydd, Torfaen County Borough NP44 1TT
Tel: 01633-484401
Served from Our Lady of Angels.
M: *Sat 1st M of Sun 5pm. Sun 11.15am. Hds (Vigil) 6.30pm,10am.*

■ DINAS POWYS
† St Mary (1922)
Edith Road, Dinas Powys, Vale of Glamorgan County Borough CF64 4AD
Served from Penarth.
M: *Sun 11.15am, 6.30pm. Hds (vigil) 7.30pm.*

■ EBBW VALE
† All Saints (1865; 1905; 1924)
Tredegar Road NP23 6JQ
Tel: 01495-302243 **Rev Michael Hagerty.**
M: *Sat 1st M of Sun 7pm. Sun 11am. Hds 10am, 7pm.*

■ FERNDALE
† Our Lady of Penrhys (1910; 1912)
Oakland Terrace, Ferndale, Rhondda Cynon Taff County Borough.
Served from Tonypandy.
M: *Sun 11am. Hds 7pm.*
- ***Shrine of Our Lady of Penrhys:*** **Website:** www.catholicwales.org

■ GLAMORGAN UNIVERSITY
Catholic Chaplaincy, 20 Llantwit Road, Treforest, Pontypridd CF37 1TR
Catholic Chaplain: **Rev Gareth Leyshon**
E-mail: gleyshon@glam.ac.uk
Tel/Fax: 01443-491514
M: *See St Dyfrig's, Treforest for Mass times.*

■ HEREFORD
1. † St Francis Xavier
(1684; 1837; cons 5 Oct 1922)
19 Broad Street, Hereford HR4 9AP
Tel: 01432-273485
Rev Dom Michael Evans OSB
M: *Sat 1st M of Sun 6pm. Sun 9am. Hds 1pm, 6pm.*

2. † Our Lady Queen of Martyrs (1954)
101 Belmont Road, Hereford HR2 7JR
Tel: 01432-265177
Rev Dom Cenydd Marrison OSB
M: *Sun 9.30am, 11.30am, 6.30pm. Hds 9.30am, 7pm.*
- ***Poor Clares (Colettines) Convent***, Much Birch, Hereford HR2 8PS **Tel:** 01981-540546 *Chaplain:* **Rev Dom Antony Tumelty** *(OSB)* **Tel:** 01981-540051

■ HIRWAUN
See Mountain Ash.

■ KINGTON, Herefordshire
St Bede the Venerable (1939)
Bridge Street.
Served from Weobley.
M: *Sat 1st Mass Sun 6pm. Hds 12 noon.*

■ LEDBURY, Herefordshire
† The Most Holy Trinity (1926; 1976)
Served from Ross-on-Wye
New Street, Ledbury, Hereford HR8 2EE
Tel/Fax: 01531-635354
M: *Sun (vigil 6pm Sat) 9.15am. Hds See Newsletter.*

■ **LEOMINSTER,** Herefordshire
† **St Ethelbert** (1879; New church 1888)
86 The Bargates, Leominster, Herefordshire HR6 8QS **Tel:** 01568-612238
Rev Francis X Slater.
M: *Sat 1st M of Sun 6pm (at Leintwardine). Sun 9am, 6.30pm. Hds 12noon, 7.30pm.*

■ **LLANARTH**
St Mary and St Michael (1750)
Served from Monmouth.
M: *Sun 11am. Hds (Vigil 7.30pm).*

■ **LLANTRISANT**
† **All Hallows** (1969; 1974; 1995)
School Road, Miskin, Pontyclun, Rhondda, Cynon, Taff County Borough CF72 8PG
Tel: 01443-228866
E-mail: all_hallows@btinternet.com
Provost: **Canon Patrick Daly.**
M: *Sat 1st M of Sun 6.30pm. Sun 10am. Hds 9.30am, 7.30pm.*

■ **LLANTWIT MAJOR**
† **Our Lady and St Illtyd** (1950; 1966)
Ham Lane East, Llantwit Major, Vale of Glamorgan CF61 1TQ
Tel: 01446-792381
Rev Pierce Maher
M: *Sun 9am. Hds See Newsletter.*

■ **MAESTEG**
† **Our Lady and St Patrick** (1872)
Monica Street, Bridgend County Borough CF34 9AY **Tel:** 01656-733282
E-mail: sec@ourladyandstpatrick.org.uk
Rev David L Smith.
M: *Sun 9.30am, 5pm. Hds 8am, 9.30am (School), 7pm.*

■ **MERTHYR TYDFIL**
1. † **St Mary's** (1829)
Rev Michael St Clair. St Mary's Priory, Pontmorlais West, Merthyr Tydfil CF47 8RG
Tel: 01685-723336
Permanent Deacon: **Rev David O'Keefe,** 17 Gwendoline Street, Merthyr Tydfil CF47 9AD **Tel:** 01685 375761
E-mail: dave@@okeefemerthyr.fsnet.co.uk
M: *Sat 1st M of Sun 5.30pm. Sun 11am. Hds See Newsletter.*
• ***Sisters of St Joseph of Annecy,*** Glen Thorne, The Grove, Merthyr Tydfil. **Tel:** 01685-722205

2. † **St Aloysius** (Cons 1978)
The Presbytery, Chestnut Way, Gurnos Est, Merthyr Tydfil CF47 9SB **Tel:** 01685-722672
Mbl: 07711 804733
Rev Silvio Briffa.
M: *Sun 10am, 6.30pm. Hds 10am, 7pm.*

3. † **St Illtyd** (1844; 1846)
Rev Michael P Evans. Presbytery, Dowlais, Merthyr Tydfil CF48 3BT
Tel: 01685-723600
Permanent Deacon: **Rev Garth Tasker,** 63 Perybryn Estate, Penydarren, Merthyr Tydfil CF47 9YY
Tel: 07939 310176
E-mail: garth.tasker@tiscali.co.uk
M: *Sat 1st M of Sun 6.30pm. Sun 11am. Hds (vigil) 7pm, 10am.*
• ***Convent of the Missionaries of Charity,*** Balaclava Road, Dowlais, Merthyr Tydfil CF48 3BS **Tel:** 01685-376232

■ **MERTHYR VALE**
† **St Benedict** (New church 1932)
Nixonville Road, Merthyr Tydfil CF48 4RG
Tel: 01443-690244
Served from Merthyr Tydfil (1).
M: *Sun 9am. Hds see newsletter.*

■ **MONMOUTH**
† **St Mary** (1787; 1893)
3 Charist Rise, Monmouth NP25 5GA
Tel: 01600-712029
E-mail: stmaryrc@gotadsl.co.uk
Rev Nicholas James, 55 Cornpoppy Ave, Monmouth NP25 5SD
Tel: 01600 712029
E-mail: stmaryrc@gotadsl.co.uk
M: *Sat 1st M of Sun 6pm. Sun 9.15am. Hds 9.15am, 7pm.*

■ **MOUNTAIN ASH, ABERDARE, HIRWAUN,** Rhondda Cynon Taff County Borough
Parish of Mary Immaculate
Rev Mark Rowles, The Presbytery, Miskin Road, Mountain Ash CF45 3UA
Tel: 01443 473710
E-mail: ourladyoflourdes_ma@yahoo.co.uk

1. **St Joseph** (1868)
Monk Street, Aberdare
M: *Sun 11am. Hds See Newsletter.*
• ***Dominican Sisters:*** 54 Monk Street, Aberdare CF44 7RF **Tel:** 01685 872299

2. **St Therese of Lisieux** (1880)
High Street, Hirwaun
M: *Sun 9am. Hds See Newsletter.*

3. **Our Lady of Lourdes** (1874-1899)
Miskin Road, Mountain Ash
M: *Sat 1st Mass of Sun 5.30pm. Hds See Newsletter.*

■ **NEWBRIDGE**
† **Our Lady of Peace** (1926; 1939)
Ashfield Road, Caerphilly County Borough NP11 4RB
Tel: 01495-243304 **Mbl:** 07980-236936
E-mail: catholicchurch@byinternet.com
Rev Kevin Paine.
M: *Sun 6pm. Hds as announced.*

■ **NEWPORT**
All Saints Parish:

Revv John Kelly, VF, BA, (*Moderator*), **George Areekuzhy CMI**, The Presbytery, 9 Stow Hill, Newport, NP20 1TP
Tel: 01633-265533
E-mail: stmarynpt@hotmail.co.uk
Revv Richard Reardon, Adrian Wiltshire, The Presbytery, St Michael Street, Newport NP20 2BZ **Tel:** 01633-676876
Permanent Deacon: **Rev Noel Williams,** 8 Llanwern Street, Newport NP19 OBZ
Tel: 01633-665428
E-mail: mrnoelwilliams@yahoo.co.uk

1. St Anne (1959)
Oliphant Circle, Malpas
M: *Sun 9.30am Hds: 7pm*
• ***Sisters of St Joseph of Annecy***, St Joseph's Convent, Harding Avenue, Newport NP20 6ZE **Tel:** 01633- 858539

2. St Basil & St Gwladys (1882)
Tregwilym Road, Rogerstone
M: *Sun 9.30am Hds: (Vigil 7pm).*

3. St David (1934-1963)
Park Crescent, Maesglas, Newport
M: *Sat 1st Mass of Sun 6pm, Sun 11am Hds: 9.30am*
• ***Sisters of St Joseph of Annecy***, St David's Presbytery, Park Crescent, Newport NP20 3AQ **Tel:** 01633- 815922

4. St David Lewis (1967)
Monnow Way, Bettws Estate, Newport
M: *Sat 1st Mass of Sun 6pm Sun 10.30am Hds: 10am 7pm*

5. St Mary (1812-1840)
Stow Hill, Newport
M: *Sun 9am 11.15am 6pm Hds: (Vigil 7pm), 12.15pm*
• **Sisters of St Joseph of Annecy,** St Joseph's Convent, Stow Park Circle, Newport NP20 4HN **Tel:** 01633- 252321

6. St Michael (1872-1889)
Clarence Street, Pillgwenlly, Newport
M: *Sat 1st Mass of Sun 6pm, Sun 10.30am Hds: 9.30am in term time, 7pm*

St Gabriel's Parish:
7. St Gabriel (1963)
Ringland Circle, Ringlands,
Rev Michael Ronan, St Gabriel's Presbytery,141 Ringland Circle, Newport NP19 9PQ **Tel:** 01633- 272144
M: *Sat 1st Mass of Sun 5.30pm, Sun 10am Hds: See Newsletter*

St Patricks's Parish:
8. St Patrick (1909-1925)
Cromwell Road, Newport
Revv Brian E. Cuddihy, IC, (Rector), **Raymund J. Bunting, IC, Douglas Rayner, IC,** The Presbytery, 151 Cromwell Road, Newport, NP19 OHS **Tel:** 01633- 672334
E-mail: spn.cromwellroad@ntlworld.com
M: *Sat 1st Mass of Sun 6pm, Sun 10am Hds: Vigil 7pm, 10am*
• ***Sisters of St Joseph of Annecy,*** Provincialate, 173 Chepstow Road, Newport NP19 8GH **Tel:** 01633-245075

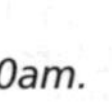

■ **PENARTH,** Vale of Glamorgan
† **St Joseph** (1860; 1915)
Wordsworth Avenue, Penarth, Newport CF64 2RL
Tel: 029-2070 8247 **Fax:** 029-2070 6014
E-mail: priesthouse@aol.com
Rev Canon Joseph Boardman.
Permanent Deacon: **Rev Elfed Jones,** 179 Stanwell Road, Penarth CF64 3LN
Tel: 029-2021 5158
E-mail: elfed179@ntlworld.com
M: *Sat 1st M of Sun 5pm. Sun 9.30am. Hds 10am, 7.30pm.*

■ **PONTLLANFRAITH**
† **Sacred Heart** (1853; 1873; 1926)
Blackwood Road, Pontllanfraith, Caerphilly County Borough. **Tel:** 01495-224828
Served from Newbridge.
M: *Sat 1st M of Sun 6pm. Sun 9.30am. Hds See Newsletter.*

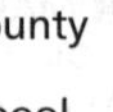

■ **PONTYPOOL**
† **St Alban** (1884)
George Street, Pontypool, Torfaen County Borough. **Rev David Hayman,** The Presbytery, Conway Road, Pontypool, NP4 6HL **Tel:** 01495-762280
E-mail: priest@pontypoolparish.co.uk
Permanent Deacon: **Rev Patrick Maloney,** 87 Golf Road, New Inn, Pontypool, Torfaen NP4 OQW GAD **Tel:** 01495-756695
E-mail: mrpatmaloney@yahoo.co.uk
M: *Sat 1st M of Sun 6pm. Sun 11am. Hds 9.30am.*

■ **PONTYPRIDD**
See Treforest

■ **PORTH**
See Ynyshir

■ **PORTHCAWL**
† **Our Lady Star of the Sea**
(1913; 1969; cons June 1975)
201 New Road, Porthcawl, Bridgend County Borough CF36 5NN
Tel/Fax: 01656-782789
E-mail: olsots@btinternet.com
Rev Paul Millar.
Permanent Deacons: **Rev Robert Coyne,** 14 Austin Avenue, Newton, Porthcawl CF36 5RS GAD **Tel:** 01656-783540
E-mail: robert@thecoynes.plus.com
Rev Anthony Martin, 27 Wellfield Avenue, Porthcawl CF36 5TP **Tel:** 01656-772270
E-mail: anthony@smartin27.fsnet.co.uk

M: *Sat 1st M of Sun 6pm. Sun 10.30am. Hds See Newsletter.*

- ***Sisters of St Clare,*** St Clare Convent, The Clevis, Newton, Porthcawl CF36 5NR **Tel:** 01656-784553

■ **PYLE** 

† **St Joseph of Arimathea** (1929)
Pisgah Street, Kenfig Hill, Pyle, Bridgend County Borough CF33 6DA
Served from Porthcawl.
M: *Sun 9am. Hds See Newsletter.*

■ **RHYMNEY**

† **St John** (1861)
Hill Street, Rhymney, Tredegar NP22 5JD
Served from Tredegar.
M: *Sun 10.30am. Hds (Vigil 7pm).*

■ **RISCA**

† **St Anthony of Padua and St Clare** (1868)
Lyne Road, Risca, Blaenau Gwent County Borough. **Tel:** 01633-613697
Served from Newbridge.
M: *Sun 11am. Hds as announced.*

■ **ROGERSTONE, BASSALEG AND RHIWDERIN**

See Newport (1)

■ **ROSS-ON-WYE**

† **St Frances of Rome** (1841; 1869; 1930)
Sussex Avenue, Hereford HR9 5AL
Tel: 01989-562186
Served from Belmont Abbey
M: *Sat 1st M of Sun 6.30pm. Sun 11am. Hds 9.15am, 7pm.*

■ **TONYPANDY**

† **SS Gabriel and Raphael** (1886)
Primrose Street, Tonypandy, Rhondda, Cynon, Taff County Borough.
Tel/Fax: 01443-432142
Rev David O'Donnell, Presbytery, Trinity Road, Tonypandy CF40 1DG
M: *Sat 1st M of Sun 6.30pm. Hds 10am.*

■ **TONYREFAIL**

Rhondda, Cynon, Taff County Borough.
Served from Ynyshir.
M: *Sun 11am. Hds, See Newsletter.*

■ **TREDEGAR**

† **The Immaculate Conception** (1852; 1860)
Dukestown, Blaenau Gwent County Borough.
Rev John Cole, The Immaculate Conception, Dukestown, Scwrfa Road, Tredegar NP22 4AT **Tel:** 01495-717224
M: *Sun 9am, 5.30pm. Hds 9am or 7pm as announced.*

■ **TREFOREST**

† **St Dyfrig R.C. Church** (1857; 1927)
Broadway, Pontypridd Rhondda, Cynon, Taff County Borough CF37 1DB
Tel: 01443-402439
E-mail: stdyfrig@tiscali.co.uk
Rev Gareth Leyshon.
Also resident: **Rev Michael Cronin,** retired.
M: *Sat 1st M of Sun, 6.30pm; Sun 10am. Hds 9.30am, 7.30pm.*

■ **TREORCHY**

† **The Immaculate Conception** (1915)
Glyncoli Road, Rhondda Cynon Taff County Borough CF42 6SB
Served from Tonypandy.
M: *Sun 9am. Hds (vigil 7pm).*

- ***The Sisters of St Joseph,*** 14 Glyncoli Road, Treorchy CF42 6SB **Tel:** 01443-773474

■ **USK**

† **St David Lewis and St Francis Xavier** (1806; 1847)
5 Porth-y-Carne Street, Usk, Monmouthshire NP15 1RY
Tel: 01291-672594
Rev Francis Lynch.
M: *Sat 1st M of Sun 6.30pm. Sun 10am. Hds (Vigil 7pm), 10am.*

■ **WEOBLEY**

† **St Thomas of Hereford** (1834)
Kington Road, Weobley, Hereford HR4 8QS
Tel: 01544-318325
Dom Stephen Holdsworth OSB.
M: *Sun 11am. Hds 7pm.*

■ **YNYSHIR**

St Mary Magdalene (1929)
Gaynor Avenue, Rhondda, Cynon, Taff County Borough.
Tel: 01443-682689
Canon John O'Regan. Presbytery, Turberville Road, Porth, CF39 0NF
M: *Sun 6.30pm. Hds 8am, 7pm.*

■ **ORDERS OR CONGREGATIONS, ETC**

■ **Men**

Benedictines (English Congregation): Abergavenny, Belmont, Bromyard, Hereford (1, 2), Weobley.
Charity, Institute of (Rosminians): Cardiff (7, 14, 18), Newport (3).

■ **Women**

Charity, Missionaries of, Dowlais.
Charity (SVP), Daughters of: Cardiff (12).
Clare, Sisters of St: Porthcawl.
Dominican Sisters: Aberdare.
Holy Spirit, Daughters of the: Abergavenny.
Joseph (Annecy), Sisters of St: Cardiff (14), Cwmbran, Merthyr Tydfil (1), Newport (1,3), Treorchy.

Nazareth, Sisters of: Cardiff (1).
Passionists: Belmont, Hereford.
Poor Clares (Colettines): Hereford (2).

■ DIOCESAN INSTITUTIONS, SOCIETIES

For Societies and Organisations without representation in the diocese please see the main Societies and Organisations section.

Apostleship of the Sea. *Lay Port Chaplain:* **Richard Withers**

Association for the Propagation of the Faith: *Contact:* **Margaret Buckley** c/o Our Lady and St Patrick Presbytery, Monica Street, Maesteg CF34 9AY

Association of Separated and Divorced Catholics: Contacts: **Tony and Pat Capron, Tel:** 01656 789446

Cardiff Archdiocesan Music Resources Group (CAMRG): Belmont Abbey, Hereford. **Tel:** 01432-277388

Cardiff Catholic Association of Corfiots: St Spiridion. *President*: **Mr T Cuschieri**. 7 Hendy Street, Roath Park, Cardiff CF2 5EU. **Tel:** 029-2049 2026

Catholic Deaf Service: *Contact*: **Miss Mary Chisholm**, Catholic Deaf Service, St Philip Evans, Llanedeyrn Drive, Cardiff CF23 9UL

Catholic Charismatic Renewal, Wales: *Information & Enquiries*: **Pat Williams**. **Tel:** 029-2061 7374

Catenian Association. *Grand Director:* **Mr J D Hall**, 33 Cherry Orchard, Lisvane, Cardiff CF4 5UE **Tel:** 029-2076 6492

Catholic Clothing Guild, *Hon Secretary & Treasurer*: **Mrs T Mitchell**, 11 Mallards, Haven, Penarth CF64 5RF

Catholic People's Weeks. *Contact:* **Mrs P Quinn**, 59 Station Road, Llanishen, Cardiff CF4 5UT **Tel:** 029-2075 3108

Catholic Association of Teachers, Schools and Colleges (CATSC) (formerly Catholic Teachers Federation). South Glamorgan Association: *Chairman:* **Mr R Jeffries** (*Headteacher*) St Mary's Primary School, Wyndham Crescent, Cardiff CF11 9BF **Tel:** 029-2022 5680

Catholic Truth Society. Welsh Province Branch, Cathedral Bookshop, Charles Street, Cardiff CF10 2GE **Tel:** 029-2039 7174 *President*: **The Archbishop of Cardiff**; *Manager*: **Miss Mary Joseph**.

Catholic Women's League. Cardiff Province Branch. *Liaison Officer*: **Mrs Julia James,** 20 Lodge Drive, Baglan, Port Talbot

Covenant Scheme, Archdiocesan. *Gift Aid Organiser*: **Mr Tony Hurley**, FCA. Archbishop's House, 43 Cathedral Road, Cardiff, CF11 9HD **Tel:** 029-2037 4148

Glamorgan University, Catholic Chaplaincy – Glamorgan. *Chaplain:* **Rev Gareth Leyshon**, St Dyfrig's Presbytery, Broadway, Treforest, Pontypridd CF37 1DB **Tel:** 01443-302439 **E-mail:** chaplaincy@glam.ac.uk

Guild of Catholic Guiders. *Chaplain:* **Rev Canon Peter Collins**. St David's Cathedral, Clergy House, Charles Street, Cardiff CF10 2SF **Tel:** 029-2023 1407 *Chair:* **Mrs Geraldine Dorman,** 147 Stanwell Road, Penarth CF64 3LL **Tel:** 029-2070 7402 **E-mail:** gmdorman@hotmail.com

HCPT, The Pilgrimage Trust. Regional *Secretary*: **Miss Helen Williams.** 38 Parcwern Road, Sketty, Swansea, SA2 0SF **Tel:** 01792-208540

Knights of St Columba. Prov 20 (South Wales). *Provincial Secretary*: **Mr Peter Sims-Coomber**, 14 Llangorse Road, Cyncoed, Cardiff CF23 6PF **Tel:** 029-2075 1285

Legion of Mary. Cardiff Comitium. *Secretary*: **Mrs Muriel Reece**. 52 Ty Mawr Avenue, Runmey, Cardiff.

Marriage Care (Formerly CMAC – Catholic Marriage Advisory Council). Supports Family life through Marriage Preparation, Education and Counselling. Cardiff Centre: Bishop Brown House, Durham Street, Grangetown, Cardiff CF1 7PD For appointments: **Tel:** 029-2022 4238/2075 3912. *President:* **His Grace the Archbishop of Cardiff**. *Chairman:* **Mr Simon James LLB**. **Tel:** 02920-233081 *Secretary:* **Mrs Val Call. Tel:** 029-2070 0335 Marriage Preparation and Education Enquiries: **Mrs Bonny Harvey, Tel:** 01446-738738

Natural Family Planning Centre. Contact: **Mrs C Norman**, 218 Heathwood Road, Cardiff, CF4 4BS **Tel:** 029-2075 4628

Our Lady's Catechists. *Diocesan Contact:* **Mrs Theresa Plunkett**, 83 Owls Lodge Lane, Mayals, Swansea SA3 5DP

St David's Metropolitan Cathedral Choir: *Organist & Master of the Music*: **Dr David Neville**. St David's Cathedral, Charles Street, Cardiff CF10 2SF

St Jude Society. *Secretary*: **John Massey**. 18 Homelands Road, Rhiwbina, Cardiff. **Tel:** 02920-627870

Society of St Vincent de Paul. Cardiff Central Council. *President*: **Mr Joe Kemble**, 33 Hamilton Street, Canton, Cardiff CF11 9BP **Tel:** 029-2025 8024

Society of St Gregory, The. *Diocesan*

Contact: **Miss Frances M Bibey**. 27 Manor Street, Heath, Cardiff CF4 3PU **Tel:** 02920-619575 **E-mail:** cardiff@ssg.org.uk

Union of Catholic Mothers - Wales. Archdiocese of Cardiff Branch: *President:* **Mrs Val Dart**, 2 Heol Mabon, Rhiwbina, Cardiff CF14 6RL **Tel:** 029-2061 1851 *Archdiocesan Secretary*: **Mrs Mary Jeans**, 5 Banastre Avenue, Cardiff CF14 3NR **Tel:** 029-2040 1293

University Catholic Chaplaincy. Cardiff: *Chaplain*: **Rev John Owen**. 62 Park Place, Cardiff CF10 3AS **Tel:** 029-2022 9785

Welsh National Catholic Men's Society. *President*: **Mr Michael O'Hea**, 60 Alexander Road, Rhyddings, Neath SA10 8EG **Tel:** 01639-636971

Y Cylch Catholig Aim: to help Welsh-speaking Catholics to live a full spiritual life through the medium of their own language, by offering opportunities for worship in Welsh and by promoting the work of providing books and essential resources to this end. (Under the patronage of the Bishops of Wales.) *President*: **Bishop Daniel Mullins**. *Chairman:* **Bishop Edwin Regan**; *Vice-Chairman*: **Rev John Fitzgerald**, Aberystwyth. *Treasurer*: **Harri Pritchard Jones**, *Secretary*: **Miranda Richards**, Bryn Hyfryd, Longford Road, Caergybi LL65 1TR **Tel:** 01407-762084

Young Christian Workers & Impact. For young people aged between 13-30. Headquarters: St Joseph's, off St Joseph's Grove, London NW4 4TY **Tel:** 0208 203 6290 **E-mail:** info@ycwimpact.com **Website:** www.ycwimpact.com

■ HOSPITALS

To contact the Catholic Chaplain of a particular hospital we suggest you contact the hospital reception directly.

■ CATHOLIC SCHOOLS - MAINTAINED

■ CARDIFF

▲ Primary Schools

St Francis Primary School, Wilson Road, Ely, Cardiff CF5 4JL

Christ the King RC Primary School, Everest Avenue, Llanishen, Cardiff CF14 5AS

Holy Family RC Primary School, Beechley Drive, Fairwater, Cardiff CF5 3SN

St Alban's RC Primary School, Mona Place, Tremorfa, Cardiff CF24 2TG

St Bernadette's RC Primary School, Bryn Heulog, Pentwyn, Cardiff CF23 7JB

St Cadoc's RC Primary School, Shaw Close, Llanrumney, Cardiff CF3 5NX

St Cuthbert's RC Primary School, Letton Road, off Lloyd George Avenue, Atlantic Wharf, Cardiff CF10 4AB

St John Lloyd RC Primary School, Cemaes Crescent, Trowbridge, Cardiff CF3 8TA

St Joseph's RC Primary School, 204 North Road, Cardiff CF14 3BL

St Mary's RC Primary School, Wyndham Crescent, Canton, Cardiff CF11 9EF

St Patrick's RC Primary School, Durham Street, Grangetown, Cardiff CF11 6GA

St Peter's RC Primary School, Southey Street, Roath, Cardiff CF24 3SP

St Philip Evans RC Primary School, Coed y Gores, Llanedeyrn, Cardiff CF23 9NX

▲ Secondary Schools

Corpus Christi RC High School, Tydraw Road, Lisvane, Cardiff CF23 6XL

St Illtyd's RC High School, Newport Road, Rumney, Cardiff CF3 1XQ

Mary Immaculate High School, Caerau Lane, Wenvoe, Cardiff CF5 5QZ

St David's Catholic College, Ty Gwyn Road, Penylan, Cardiff CF23 5QD

■ VALE OF GLAMORGAN

▲ Infant School

St Helen's RC Infant School, Maesycwm Street, Barry CF63 4EH

▲ Primary School

St Joseph's RC Primary School, Sully Road, Penarth CF64 2TQ

▲ Junior School

St Helen's RC Junior School, Ty-Newydd Road, Barry, Vale of Glamorgan CF63 8BB

▲ Secondary Schools

St Richard Gwyn RC High School, Argae Lane, Cadoxton, Barry CF63 1BL

■ BLAENAU GWENT

▲ Primary School

All Saints RC Primary School, Heol yr Ysgol, Ebbw Vale NP23 6QP

St Joseph's RC Primary School, Ashvale, Tredegar NP22 4AQ.

St Mary's RC Primary School, Catholic Road, Brynmawr NP23 4EF

■ NEWPORT

▲ Primary School

St David's RC Primary School, Park Crescent, Maesglas, Newport NP20 3AQ

St David's Lewis RC Primary School, Meon Close, Bettws, Newport NP20 7DU
St Gabriel's RC Primary School, Ringland Circle, Ringland, Newport NP19 9PQ
St Joseph's RC Primary School, Fairoak Avenue, Maindee, Newport NP19 8FW
St Mary's RC Primary School, Queen's Hill, Newport NP20 5HJ
St Michael's RC Primary School, Baldwin Close, Pill, Newport NP20 2LW
St Patrick's RC Primary School, Fairfax Road, Somerton, Newport NP19 0HR

▲ Secondary Schools
St Joseph's RC High School, Pencarn Way, Tredegar Park, Newport NP10 8XH

■ TORFAEN

▲ Primary School
Our Lady of the Angels RC Primary School, Victoria Street, Cwmbran NP44 3JR.
St David's RC Primary School, Caldicot Way, Pontnewydd, Cwmbran NP44 1UF
Padre Pio RC Primary School, Conway Road, Pontypool NP4 6HL

▲ Secondary Schools
St Alban's RC High School, The Park, Pontypool NP4 6XG

■ MONMOUTHSHIRE

▲ Primary School
St Mary's RC Primary School, Bulwark Road, Chepstow NP16 5JE
Our Lady & St Michael's RC Primary School, Pen-y-Pound, Abergavenny NP7 5UD

■ BRIDGEND

▲ Primary School
St Robert's RC Primary School, Day-y-Lan Road, Aberkenfig CF32 9AB
St Mary's RC Primary School, Llangewydd Road, Bridgend CF31 4JW
St Mary & St Patrick's RC Primary School, Monica Street, Maesteg CF34 9AY

▲ Secondary School
Archbishop McGrath RC High School, Tondu, Bridgend CF32 9EH

■ MERTHYR TYDFIL

▲ Primary School
St Illtyd's RC Primary School, Rocky Road, Dowlais, Merthyr Tydfil CF48 3BT
St Mary's RC Primary School, Caedraw Road, Merthyr Tydfil CF47 8HA
St Aloysius' RC Primary School, Cedar Way, Gurnos, Merthyr Tydfil CF47 9PA

▲ Secondary School
Bishop Hedley RC High School, Pen-y-Darren, Merthyr Tydfil CF47 9AN

■ CAERPHILLY

▲ Primary School
St Helen's RC Primary School, Lansbury Park, Caerphilly CF83 1QH

■ RHONDDA/CYNON/TAFF

▲ Primary School
St Margaret's RC Primary School, Ty Fry, Aberdare CF44 7PP
Our Lady's RC Primary School, Miskin Road, Mountain Ash CF45 3UA
St Michael's RC Primary School, John Place, Treforest, Pontypridd CF37 1SP
SS Gabriel & Raphael RC Primary School, Primrose Street, Tonypandy CF40 1BJ

▲ Secondary School
Cardinal Newman RC High School, Dynea Road, Rhydfelin, Pontypridd CF37 5DP

■ HEREFORDSHIRE

▲ Primary School
Our Lady's RC Primary School, Boycott Road, The Poole, Hereford HR2 7RN
St Francis Xavier RC Primary School, Venn's Lane, Hereford HR1 1DT
St Joseph's RC Primary School, The Avenue, Ross-on-Wye HR9 5AW

▲ Secondary School
St Mary's RC High School, Lugwardine, Hereford HR1 4DR

■ CATHOLIC SCHOOLS - INDEPENDENT

■ CARDIFF

▲ Primary and Secondary
St John's College, Old St Mellons, Cardiff
Tel: 02920-778936.

■ HEREFORDHSIRE

▲ Primary School
(Prep School for Girls and Boys),
St Richard's, Bredenbury Court, Bromyard, Herefordshire HR7 4TD
Tel: 01885-482491

DIOCESE OF CLIFTON

Province of Birmingham

Consisting of the City and County of Bristol, the Counties of Gloucestershire, Somerset, Wiltshire, South Gloucestershire, North Somerset, Bath and North East Somerset.

Patrons of the Diocese:
Our Blessed Lady Conceived Without Sin, December 8th
SS. Peter & Paul, Apostles, June 29th

Bishop

Rt Rev Declan R Lang BA, Bishop of Clifton.
Born in Cowes, Isle of Wight, April 15th, 1950; ordained priest June 7th 1975, ordained Bishop of Clifton by Rt Rev Mervyn Alexander, March 28th 2001

Address:
St Ambrose, North Road, Leigh Woods, Bristol BS8 3PW
Tel: 0117-973 3072 **Fax:** 0117-973 5913
E-mail: declan.lang@cliftondiocese.com
Website: www.cliftondiocese.com

Bishop's Private Secretary:
Mr Chris Jelly.
E-mail: chris.jelly@cliftondiocese.com

Retired Bishop

Rt Rev Mervyn A Alexander DD, LLD, retired Bishop of Clifton. Born in London, June 29th, 1925; ordained July 18th 1948; ordained Bishop by Bishop Rudderham April 25th, 1972; trans to Clifton December 20th 1974.
Residence: St Joseph's Presbytery, Camp Road, Weston-super-Mare BS23 2EN **Tel:** 01934-629865

Rt Rev Declan R Lang BA, Bishop of Clifton

■ ADMINISTRATION

■ Vicars General

Mgr Canon P Gabriel Leyden. Corpus Christi Presbytery, 14 Ellenborough Park South, Weston-super-Mare, North Somerset BS23 1XW **Tel:** 01934-621929
E-mail: CorpusChristi.Weston@virgin.net

Mgr Canon Jeremy H Rigden. Holy Family Presbytery, Marlowe Avenue, Park North, Swindon SN3 2PT **Tel:** 01793-52793

■ Diocesan Financial Administrator

Ms Margaret Marshall. Alexander House, 160 Pennywell Road, Bristol BS5 0TX
Tel: 0117-902 5591 **Fax:** 0117-902 5520
E-mail: Finance.Office@CliftonDiocese.com

■ Diocesan Archivist

Rev Canon Dr J Anthony Harding.
Flat D, St John's Road, South Parade, Bath, BA2 4AF

■ Diocesan Episcopal Vicar for Religious

Dom Alexander George OSB. Downside Abbey, Stratton-on-the-Fosse, Radstock BA3 4RH **Tel:** 01761-235114

■ Diocesan Trustees

Chairman: **Rt Rev Declan Lang**, Bishop of Clifton.

■ Priests' Retirement Fund Committee

Chairman: **Rev Canon Alan Finley.**
Secretary of Infirm Priests' Society: **Rev Patrick Auger.**

■ Chancellor

Rev Robert King. 103 Queens Road, Clifton, Bristol BS8 1LL
Tel: 0117-914 0003 **Email:**
robert.king@cliftondiocese.com

■ Communications Officer

Mr Tom Bigwood, St Ambrose, North Road, Leigh Woods, Bristol BS8 3PW
Tel: 0117-973 3072
E-mail: tom.bigwood@cliftondiocese.com

■ EDUCATION AND FORMATION

■ Department for Schools & Colleges

Director: **Mr Ian McNiff.** *Secretary:* **Mrs Jenny Fitzgerald;** *Primary Schools Adviser:* **Mrs Patricia Antolik;** *Secondary Schools Adviser:* **Mrs Ann Fowler.** Alexander House, Pennywell Road, Bristol BS5 0TX

Tel: 0117-902 5593 **Fax:** 0117-902 5520
E-mail: Schoolsandcolleges@cliftondiocese.com

■ **Department for Adult Education & Evangelisation**
Department Head: **Rev Michael McAndrew**. Alexander House, 160 Pennywell Road, Bristol BS5 0TX
Tel: 0117-902 5593 **Fax:** 0117-902 5520
E-mail: adult.education@cliftondiocese.com

■ **LITURGY AND ECUMENISM**

■ **Department for Liturgy**
Department Head: **Rev Michael Fountaine**, St Dunstan's Presbytery, 20A Bristol Road, Keynsham BS31 2BQ
Tel: 0117-983 3930

■ **Diocesan Ecumenical Commission**
Diocesan Ecumenical Officer: **Rev Michael Robertson**, St Bonaventure's Presbytery, Egerton Road, Bishopston, Bristol BS7 8HP
Tel: 0117 942 4448 **Fax:** 01249-816392
Chairman: **Miss Ann Doyle**. 16 Sherwood Avenue, Melksham SN12 7HJ
Tel: 01225-707486

■ **Diocesan Pastoral Council**
Information from the Department for Adult Education & Evangelisation.

■ **Vocations Director**
Rev Robert King, 103 Queens Road, Clifton, Bristol BS8 1LL **Tel:** 0117 914003
Email: robert.king@cliftondiocese.com

■ **CHRISTIAN RESPONSIBILITY**

■ **Ministry to Priests**
Director of Ongoing Formation: **Rev Christopher Whitehead,** St Bernadette's Presbytery, Wells Road, Bristol BS14 9NU
Tel: 01275 833699

■ **CONSULTATIVE BODIES**

■ **Cathedral Chapter and College of Consultors**
(erected June 28th, 1852)
Provost: **Mgr Provost Richard Twomey.**
Canons: **Mgr P G Leyden, Mgr W Mitchell, Mgr J H Rigden, Revv L O'Driscoll** (*Canon Penitentiary*), **T Atthill, M Fitzpatrick, B McEvoy, A Finley.**
Honorary Canons: **Revv A P Cotter, G Rodgers, J A Supple, W Roche, M Hayes, E P Murphy, T P Barry, R Corrigan, M English, JA Harding, D Millett.**

■ **COUNCIL OF PRIESTS**
Secretary: **Rev Robert King**, 103 Queen's Road, Clifton Bristol BS8 1LL.
Tel: 0117-914 0003
E-mail: robert.king@cliftondiocese.com

■ **DIOCESAN MATRIMONIAL TRIBUNAL**
Office: Clifton Diocesan Tribunal, Diocesan Offices, Egerton Road, Bishopston, Bristol, BS7 8HU **Tel:** 0117-983 3907 **Fax** 0117-983 3915. *Judicial Vicar (Officialis):* **Rev Richard Dwyer JV, JCL, Adv Dip Ed.**

■ **CLIFTON**
† Cathedral Church of SS Peter and Paul (1973)
Clifton Cathedral House, Clifton Park, Bristol BS8 3BX
Tel: 0117-973 8411 **Fax:** 0117-974 4897
E-mail: Cathedral@Clifton.Diocese.com
Website: www.cliftoncathedral.org.uk
Rev Canon Alan Finley (*Cathedral Dean*); *Deacons:* **Rev Kevin Moloney, John Colling**.
M: *Sat 1st M of Sun 6pm. Sun 8am, 9.30am (Fam), 11am (Sol), 6pm. Hds 7.30am, 12noon, 7.30pm.*

- ***Sisters of La Retraite***, Emmaus House, Pastoral Retreat Centre, Clifton Hill, Bristol BS8 4PD **Tel:** 0117-907 9950 **Fax:** 0117-907 9952
- ***Little Sisters of the Poor,*** 66 Cotham Hill, Bristol BS6 6JT Residential Home and Day Centre for Men and Women. **Tel:** 0117-973 3815 **Fax:** 0117-970 6086
- ***Sisters of the Temple,*** St Angela's Convent, 5 Litfield Place, Clifton, Bristol BS8 3LU Nursing Sisters. Home for Invalided or Retired Priests. Home for Ladies. **Tel:** 0117-973 5436 **Fax:** 0117-970 6844

■ **AMESBURY,** Wilts
† Christ the King (1934, 1985)
The Presbytery, 4 Lords Croft, SP4 7EP
Tel: 01980-622177
Rev Mark Moran.
The Presbytery, 4 Lords Croft.
M: *Sat 1st M of Sun 6pm. Sun 10.30am. Hds 9.30am, 7pm.*

■ **BATH**
1. † Our Lady and St Alphege
(1929; cons. 1954)
St Alphege's Presbytery, Oldfield Lane, Bath BA2 3NR
Tel: 01225-424894
Rev Richard Burton.
M: *Sun 10am, 6pm. Hds 9.30am, 7pm.*

1a † St Joseph (1969)
Sladebrook Road, Southdown.
Served from Bath (1).
M: *Sat 1st M of 6pm. Hds 7pm.*

2. † St John the Evangelist
(1685; 1861; cons. Oct 6th, 1863)
St John's Presbytery, South Parade, Bath BA2 4AF
Tel: 01225-464471 **Fax:** 01225-462614
Rev Thomas Gunning.
M: *Sat 1st M of Sun 5.45pm. Sun 10am, 6.30pm. Hds (vigil 5.45pm), 7.45am, 10am, 5.45pm.*

- ***Sisters of La Sainte Union,*** 29 Pulteney Road. BA2 4EZ Chapel No. 28. **Tel:** 01225-461984

3. † St Mary's
(1832; 1881, cons. 1981)
Julian Road, Bath BA1 2SF
Canon Brian McEvoy. 4 Harley Street, Bath BA1 2SF **Tel:** 01225-311715
Also attached: **Rev John Foster.**
Deacon: **Rev Richard Hayward**.
M: *Sun 9am, 10.30am, 5pm. Hds (vigil 7.30pm). 10am, 6.30pm.*
Serves Weston and Batheaston.

A

4. † SS Peter and Paul
(1919, 1965 cons. 1976)
112 Entry Hill, Combe Down, BA2 5LS
Rev William McLoughlin OSM.
Tel/Fax: 01225-832096
M: *Sat 1st M of Sun 6pm. Sun 9.30am. Hds (vigil 7.15pm).*

5. Bath University & Bath Spa University College (1967)
Chaplaincy Centre.
Tel: 01225-826458
Chaplain: **Rev William McLoughlin OSM**.
SS Peter & Paul, 112 Entry Hill BS2 5LS
Tel/Fax: 01225-832096
M: *Sun 12noon. Hds 1.20pm (at The University Chaplaincy Centre, Bath, term time only).*

A

■ **BATHEASTON**
† The Good Shepherd (1967)
2 North End, Batheaston.
Parish Office: Tel: 01225 858845
In residence: **Canon Edmond P Murphy,** (retired).
Served from Bath (3).
M: *Sun 10am. Hds 7pm.*

■ **BEDMINSTER**
See Bristol (3).

■ **BERKELEY,** Glos
At Berkeley Castle.
Served from Thornbury.
M: *Sun 10am.*

■ **BISHOP'S CLEEVE,** Glos
St Michael's & All Angels C of E Church, School Road.
Served from Winchcombe.
M: *Sat 5.30pm.*

■ **BISHOPS LYDEARD,** Som
Served from Taunton.
Bishops Lydeard Parish Church, Church Street.
M: *Sat 5pm, (at Bishops Lydeard Parish Church, Church St). 1st Sun of the month.*

■ **BISHOPSTON**
See Bristol (4).

■ **BISHOPSWORTH**
See Bristol (16).

■ **BISLEY,** Glos
St Mary of the Angels (1930)
Served from Stroud.
M: *Sun 8.30am.*

■ **BLAISDON,** Longhope, Glos A
† Served from Newent.
• ***Salesians (SDB):*** **Rev Aidan Murray**. Drumlanrig, Ross Road, Newent, Glos GL18 1BG **Tel/Fax:** 01531-821647
M: *Sun 11am Blaisdon Village Hall. Hds 7.30pm.*

■ **BOURTON-ON-THE-WATER,** Glos
† Our Lady Help of Christians
Station Road.
Served from Stow-on-the-Wold.
M: *Sun 8.30am. Hds (vigil 7pm).*

■ **BRADFORD-ON-AVON,** Wilts
† St Thomas More (1955)
3 Market Street, Bradford-on-Avon BA15 1LH **Tel/Fax:** 01225-862739
Rev Conrad Lowry.
M: *Sat 1st M of Sun 6pm. Sun 10.30am. Hds (vigil 6pm). 10am.*

■ **BRIDGWATER,** Som
† St Joseph (1849, 1882; cons. 1907)
9 Binford Place TA6 3NJ **Tel:** 01278-422703
Rev Thomas Kelly.
Deacon: **Rev Robert Cornell.**
M: *Sun 5pm. Sun 9.30am (vigil). Hds 9.30am, 7.30pm.*

■ **BRISTOL**
1. † St Mary-on-the-Quay
(1730; 1790; 1843)
St Mary-on-the-Quay Presbytery, 20 Colston Street, Bristol BS1 5AE
Tel: 0117 926 4702 **Fax:** 0117-927 6917
Revv Michael Cleary SVD (*Parish Priest*) **Nicodemus Lobo Ratu SVD,**
Tel: 0117 926 4702
M: *Sun 9.30am, 11am, 5.15pm, 6.15pm. Hds 12.15pm, 1.15pm, 5.30pm.*

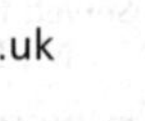

2. † St Nicholas of Tolentino
(1848; cons. 1895)
Lawford's Gate, Bristol BS5 0RE
Tel: 0117-983 3920
E-mail: stnick.bristol@blueyonder.co.uk
Rev Richard McKay.
Deacon: **Rev Jack Brannigan.**
M: *Sun 10.30am. Hds 9.30am, 8pm.*

St Maximilian Kolbe with St Edith Stein and the Holocaust Martyrs
Alfoxton Road, Bristol BS7 9NH
Served from Bristol (2).
M: *Sun 9am. Hds 6.30pm.*

3. † Holy Cross (1872; 1922)
Dean Lane, Bedminster, Bristol BS3 1DB
Tel: 0117-983 3927
Rev Francis Bermingham.
Parish Sister: **Sr Margaret Maher.**
M: *Sat 6.30pm. Sun 10am. Hds 9.30am, 7.30pm.*
• ***Sisters of St Joseph of Annecy,*** St Joseph's Convent, 68 Coronation Road, Southville, BS3 1AS
Tel: 0117-966 3879

4. † St Bonaventure A
(1890; 1907; cons. June 13th, 1936)
Egerton Road, Bishopston, Bristol BS7 8HP
Tel: 0117-942 4448 **Fax:** 0117-907 4921
Rev Michael Roberts.
Deacon: **Rev Robert James.**
M: *Sun 9.30am, 11am, 7pm. Hds 9.15am, 7pm.*
• ***Daughters of Charity (SVP),*** 135 Chesterfield Road, St Andrew's, Bristol BS5 5DU **Tel:** 0117 924 8230

5. † St Bernard
(1902 cons. June 24th 1982)
Pembroke Avenue, Shirehampton.
Rev Vincent Ryan. 43 Station Road, Shirehampton, Bristol BS11 9TU
Tel: 0117-983 3929
M: *Sun 10am, 6.30pm. Hds 10am, 7.30pm.*

6. † St Gerard Majella A
(1909; Cons. April 29th, 1959)
69 Talbot Road, Knowle, Bristol BS4 2NP
Tel: 0117-983 3924
Rev George Henwood.
M: *Sun 9am, 5pm. Hds 10am, (vigil 7.30pm).*

7. † St Patrick (1923; cons. 1995)
St Patrick's Presbytery, Dillon Court, Redfield, Bristol BS5 9PF
Tel: 0117-955 7662
Rev Gregory A Grant.
Parish Sister: **Sr Maria Comerford.**
M: *Sat 1st M of Sun 6.30pm. Sun 8.30am, 10am (Fam). Hds 9.15am, 7.30pm.*
• ***Salvatorian Sisters,*** The Convent, Dillon Court, Netham Road, Redfield, Bristol BS5 9PF **Tel:** 0117-941 3774

8. † St Joseph (1925) A
232 Forest Road, Fishponds, Bristol BS16 3QT
Rev Eric E Foxwell. Tel: 0117-983 3912
M: *Sat 1st M of Sun 6pm. Sun 10am, 6pm. Hds (vigil vigil 7.30pm), 9.30am.*

9. † St Teresa of the Child Jesus A
(1927; 1960)
71 Gloucester Road North, Filton, Bristol BS34 7PL **Tel:** 0117-983 3938

Rev Tom Finnegan.
Deacon: **Rev Tom Douglas**
M: *Sat 1st M of Sun 6pm. Sun 8.15am, 10am. Hds (vigil 7pm), 10am.*

10. † Our Lady of Lourdes and St Bernadette (1937; 1938)
Hanham Road, Kingswood.
Rev Patrick Auger. 2 Court Road, Kingswood, Bristol. BS15 9QB
Tel: 0117-949 8743 **Fax:** 0117-967 3188
M: *Sat 1st Mass of Sun 6 pm, Sun 10am, 6.30pm. Hds 11am, 7pm.*

11. † Sacred Heart
(1939: cons. June 20th, 1950)
Grange Court Road, Westbury-on-Trym, Bristol BS9 4DR **Tel:** 0117-983 3926
Rev Kevin Mortimer.
M: *Sat 1st M of Sun 6.30pm. Sun 9.30am, 11am. Hds (vigil 7pm), 8am, 10am, 7pm.*
- ***Sisters of Mercy,*** 139 Westbury Road, Westbury-on-Trym, BS9 4AN **Tel:** 0117-962 0203

12. † St John Fisher (1951)
56 Begbrook Park, Frenchay, Bristol BS16 1NF **Tel:** 0117-983 3939
M: *Sun 6.30pm. Hds (vigil 7.30pm).*

13. † Christ the King (1952)
The Presbytery, Filwood Broadway, Bristol BS4 1JN
Tel: 0117-966 4843 **Fax:** 0117-953 7198
E-mail: ChristtheKing.Knowle@CliftonDiocese.com
Rev Michael Derrick D'Mello. *Parish Sister:* **Sr Joanna Brennan**. **Tel:** 0117-966 4854
M: *Sun 10am, 6.30pm. Hds 7pm.*
- ***Religious Sisters of Charity,*** 2 Filwood Broadway, BS4 1HD **Tel:** 0117-966 4854

14. † Our Lady of the Rosary
(1953; Cons. Oct. 7th, 1978)
12 Kingsweston Lane, Lawrence Weston, BS11 0QU **Tel:** 0117-982 3380
Rev Cosmas Ikirodah MSP.
M: *Sun 9.30am, 6.30pm. Hds 9.30am, 7pm.*
- ***Servants of the Holy Spirit,*** Kingsweston Lane, BS11 0QU **Tel:** 0117-982 2431

15. † St Vincent de Paul (1955)
Glencoyne Square, Southmead.
Rev George Batten, The Presbytery, St Vincent de Paul, Embleton Road, Southmead, Bristol BS10 6DS
Tel: 0117-983 3916 **Fax:** 0117-983 3911
Parish Sisters: **Sr M Cecilia, Sr M Margaret.**
M: *Sat 1st M of Sun 4.30pm. Sun 10.30am. Hds 9.30am, 6.30pm.*

16. † St Pius X (1956)
The Presbytery, Gatehouse Avenue, Withywood, BS13 9AB
Tel: 0117-964 6922 **Fax:** 0117-964 6907
Rev Michael Healey
M: *Sun 10.30am, 5pm. Hds 9.30am (10.45am in term time), 7pm.*

17. † St Antony (1957)
Keinton Walk, Henbury, BS10 7BE
St Antony's Presbytery, Satchfield Crescent, Henbury, Bristol BS10 7BE
Tel: 0117-983 3906 **Fax:** 0117-983 3934
Rev Michael Walsh.
M: *Sat 1st M of Sun 6.30pm. Sun 9.30am. Hds 9.30am, 7.30pm.*

18. † St Augustine of Canterbury
(1959; 1975)
St Augustine's Presbytery, Boscombe Crescent, Downend, Bristol BS16 6QR
Tel: 0117-983 3939 **Fax:** 0117-983 3909
E-mail: info@staugustinebristol.com
Deacons: **Revv Peter Hinchey, Michael Belt.**
M: *Sat 1st M of Sun 6pm. Sun 9.30am. Hds 9.15am.*

19. † Holy Family (1966)
Holy Family Presbytery, Southsea Road, Patchway, Bristol BS34 5BP
Tel: 0117-908 1247
Rev Eugene Campbell. *Deacon:* **Revv Donald Cramer-Barnicoat, Michael Roberts.**
M: *Sat 1st M of Sun 6pm. Sun 9.30am, 11am. Hds 9am, 7pm.*

20. † St Bernadette (1968)
Wells Road, Whitchurch, Bristol BS14 9HU
Tel: 01275-833699
Rev Christopher Whitehead.
M: *Sat 1st M of Sun 5.45pm. Sun 10.15am Hds 10.30am, 7.30pm.*

21. Polish Church of Our Lady of Ostrobrama (1968)
Polish Catholic Church, Cheltenham Road, Bristol BS6 5RH **Tel/Fax:** 0117-924 3056
Rev Zygmunt Fraczek.
M: *Sat 7pm, Sun 10am, 7pm. Hds 8.30am, 7pm.*

22. † University Catholic Chaplaincy. St Catherine of Sienna and St Thomas Aquinas (1964)
103 Queen's Road, Clifton, Bristol BS8 1LL
Tel: 0117-914 0003 *Chaplain:* **Rev Robert King. E-mail:** Robert.King@bristol.ac.uk
M: *During Term Time, Sun 6pm. Out of Term as advertised. Hds 8.15am.*

23. University of the West of England, Bristol
Chaplain: **Rev Tom Finnegan.**
Tel: 0117-983 3938

24. St James Priory
Whitson Street, Bristol BS2 3NZ
Tel: 0117-929 9100
M: *Sun 8am. Hds 8am.*

A

■ **BROCKWORTH**
† **St Patrick** (1968 dedication June 12th 1981)
The Priest's House, 24 Ermin Street, Brockworth, Glos. GL3 4HL
Tel: 01452-862709 **Fax:** 01452-863794
E-mail: presbytery@msn.com
Rev Christopher Hickey.
M: *Sat 1st M of Sun 6.30pm. Sun 10am. Hds 9.15 am, 6.30pm.*
• ***Presentation Sisters,*** The Convent, Court Road, Brockworth GL3 4QT
Tel: 01452-863820

■ **BRUTON,** Som
Anglican Parish Church.
Served from Shepton Mallet.
M: *Sun 6.30pm.*

A

■ **BURNHAM-ON-SEA,** Som
† **Our Lady and the English Martyrs** (1967)
Highbridge Road, Burnham-on-Sea, Somerset **Tel/Fax:** 01934 742564
Rev Tibor Szende OSB.
M: *Sat 1st M of Sun 5.30pm. Sun 11am. Hds (vigil 7.30pm), 10am.*
• ***Sisters of La Retraite,*** Jaycroft Road, TA8 1LB **Tel:** 01278-782968 and at 14 The Grove, Burnham-on-Sea, Somerset TA8 2PA **Tel:** 01278-788007

A

■ **CALNE,** Wilts
† **St Edmund** (1948)
65 Oxford Road, Calne, Wilts SN11 8AQ
Tel: 01249-813131. **Fax:** 01249-816392.
E-mail: calne@cliftondiocese.com
Rev David Mills.
M: *Sat 1st M of Sun 6pm. Sun 10am. Hds 10am, 7.30pm.*

■ **CASTLE CARY,** Som
St Andrews (CofE) Ansford
Served from Wincanton.
M: *Sun 6.30pm. (1st & 3rd Sat of the M).*

■ **CHARD,** Som
† **English Martyrs**
(1919; 1926; cons. Sept. 27th, 1966)
2 East Street TA20 1EP **Tel:** 01460-62197
Canon James F O'Brien.
M: *Sun 8am, 11am. Hds (vigil 7.30pm) 9am.*

A

■ **CHEDDAR,** Som
† **Our Lady Queen of the Apostles**
(1945; 1966; cons. June, 1977)
The Presbytery, Tweentown, Cheddar, BS27 3HU **Tel:** 01934-742564.
E-mail: cheddarparish@aol.com
Rev Tibor Szende OSB
M: *9am. Hds 7pm.*

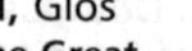

A

■ **CHELTENHAM,** Glos
1. † St Gregory The Great
(1809; 1857; cons. Nov. 6, 1877)
St Gregory's, 10 St James Square, Cheltenham GL50 3PR
Tel: 01242-523737 **Fax:** 01242-518194
E-mail: gregchurch.cheltenham@cliftondiocese.com
Also serves Prestbury.
Revv Bosco McDonald (*Parish Priest*), **Tom Smith**. *Deacons:* **Revv David McDonald, Robin Littlewood.**
M: *Sun 9.30am, 11.15am, 6pm. Hds 7.30am, 9.30am, 1pm, 7.30pm*

2. † Sacred Hearts (1957)
Moorend Road, Charlton Kings, Cheltenham GL53 9AU
Tel: 01242-524932
E-mail: sacredhearts@btopenworld.com
Rev Paul Brandon
M: *Sat 1st M of Sun 5.30pm. Sun 8.30am, 10.30am, 4pm (Pol). Hds 7am, 9.30am, 7.30pm.*
• ***Poor Sisters of Nazareth,*** Nazareth House, London Road, Charlton Kings GL52 6YJ **Tel:** 01242-516361 *Chaplain:* **Rev Joseph Kelly OCarm.**

A

3. † St Thomas More (1967)
Princess Elizabeth Way, Cheltenham GL51 7RA **Tel:** 01242-523737
Rev Bosco McDonald.
M: *Sat 1st M of Sun 6.30pm. Sun 9.30am, Hds 11am, 7pm.*

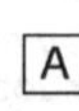

■ **CHEW MAGNA**
The Sacred Heart Parish, Chew Valley
The Sacred Heart, 49 High Street, Chew Magna, Bristol BS40 8PR
Tel: 01275-833699
Rev Christopher Whitehead
Deacon: **Rev Mark Forge**
M: *Sat 1st M of Sun 6pm. Hds 10am.*

■ **CHILCOMPTON,** Bath
† **St Aldhelm** (1939)
Tel: 01761-235114
Served from Downside.
M: *Sun 9.30am.*

■ **CHIPPENHAM,** Wilts
† **The Assumption of The Blessed Virgin Mary**
(1855; 1936)
20 Station Hill, Chippenham, Wilts. SN15 1EG **Tel:** 01249-652404
E-mail: maeve.opie@virgin.net
Rev Canon Desmond Millett,
20 Station Hill, Chippenham.
M: *Sat 1st M of Sun 6.30pm. Sun 9.30am, 6.30pm. Hds 12.10pm, 7.30pm.*

■ **CHIPPING CAMPDEN,** Glos A

† **St Catharine**
(1854; 1891; cons. May 10th, 1954)
The Priest's House, Lower High Street, Chipping Campden, Glos GL55 6DZ
Tel: 01386-840261
Rev John Brennan.
M: *Sat 1st M of Sun 6pm. Sun 10.30am. Hds (vigil vigil 6pm), 10am.*
- ***Sisters of Charity of St Paul,*** St Paul's Convent, Leyesbourne, GL55 2AD **Tel:** 01386-840510

■ **CHIPPING SODBURY,** South Glos

† **St Lawrence** (1838)
71 Broad Street, Chipping Sodbury, Bristol BS37 6AD
Tel: 01454-312161 **Fax:** 01454-316787
Website: www.stlawrenceandstpaul.co.uk
Rev James Williams.
Deacon: **Vincent Calder**
M: *Sun 9am.*
- ***Salvatorian Sisters,*** 62 Station Road, Yate, South Gloucestershire BS37 4PW **Tel:** 01454-327105

■ **CHURCHDOWN,** Glos

† **Our Lady of Perpetual Succour** (1954, 1992)
Cheltenham Road East, Gloucester GL3 1HU
Tel: 01452-713254
Deacon: **Rev Luis Navarro.**
M: *Sun 8.30am, 10.30am. Hds 9.15am, 7.30pm.*

■ **CINDERFORD,** Glos

† **Our Lady of Victories** (1939)
Flaxley Street, Cinderford, Glos
Tel: 01594-822167
Rev Barnabas Page
M: *Sun 9am, 6pm. Hds 9.30am, 8pm.*
- ***Franciscan Sisters of the Immaculate Conception,*** 93 Belle Vue Road GL14 2AA **Tel:** 01594-822310

■ **CIRENCESTER,** Glos A

† **St Peter** (1855; 1861; 1896; 1996)
7 St Peter's Road, Cirencester, Glos GL7 1RE **Tel/Fax:** 01285-652087
Rev Michael Davies. *Deacon:* **Rev John Fothergill**
M: *Sat 1st M of Sun 6pm. Sun 9.30am, 11am. Hds 10am, 6pm.*

■ **CLEVEDON** A

† **The Immaculate Conception**
(1882; cons. 1887)
Marine Hill, Clevedon BS21 7PP
- ***Franciscans (Friars Minor) (OFM):*** **Rev Reg Gray** (*Parish Priest and Guardian*), **Roger Barralet (Vicar), Rev Maurice Ryan. Tel:** 01275-873205 **Fax:** 01275-349001 **E-mail:** clevedon@friar.org

Deacon: **Rev John Woodcock.**
M: *Sat 1st M of Sun 6.30pm. Sun 10 (family Mass). Hds 7am, 10.30am, 8pm.*
- ***Sisters of Mercy,*** Marine Hill, Clevedon, BS21 7PW **Tel:** 01275-872261

■ **COLEFORD,** Glos

† **St Margaret Mary** (1930; 1933)
4 High Nash, Coleford, Glos GL16 8HN
Tel: 01594-833173
Rev Barnabas Page
M: *Sat 1st M of Sun 6pm. Sun 9am. Hds 10am, 8.30pm.*

■ **COMBE DOWN**

See Bath (4).

■ **CORSHAM,** Wilts

† **St Patrick**
Bath Road, Corsham, Wilts.
- ***Kiltegan Fathers (SPS):*** **Rev John O'Brien,** St Patrick's Presbytery, 30 Park Lane, Corsham, Wilts SN13 9LG **Tel:** 01249-712136 **Fax:** 01249-714698 **M:** *Sat 1st M of Sun 5.30pm. Sun 8.30am, 10.30am. Hds 9.30am (in school in term time), 7.30pm (in Church).*

■ **CREWKERNE,** Som

St Peter (1935)
South Street. Served from Chard.
M: *Sun 9.30am. Hds 7pm.*

■ **CRICKLADE,** Wilts

† **St Mary's** (1984)
High Street. Served from Fairford.
M: *Sun 9.30am. Hds 7pm.*

■ **DEVIZES,** Wilts A

† **Our Lady, The Immaculate Conception** (1861)
St Joseph's Presbytery, St Joseph's Place, SN10 1DD
Tel: 01380-723572 **Fax:** 01380 723377
E-mail: devizes@catholic.org
Website: www.devizesrc.com
- ***Fransalians (MSFS):*** **Rev E Philip Baptiste.** *Assistant Priest:* **Rev Saji Mathew** **M:** *Sat 1st M of Sun 6pm. Sun 10.30am, 5pm . Hds (vigil 7.30pm), 9.30am.*
- ***Sisters of St Joseph of Annecy,*** St Joseph's Place, Devizes SN10 0DD **Tel:** 01380-722543

■ **DOWNEND**

See Bristol (18).

■ **DOWNSIDE ABBEY**

St Gregory's Abbey
Stratton on the Fosse, Radstock BA3 4RH
Abbey: **Tel:** 01761-235161 **Fax:** 01761-235124 *Abbot:* **Tel:** 01761-235121 **Fax:** 01761-235156; *Prior:* **Tel:** 01761-235119; *Bursar:* **Tel:** 01761-235122; *School:* **Tel:** 01761-235100 **Fax:** 01761-235105

Headmaster: **Tel:** 01761-235101
E-mail: monks@downside.co.uk
Website: www.downside.co.uk
- ***Benedictines (OSB).*** **Rt Rev Dom Aidan Bellenger** (*Abbot*); **V Rev David Foster** (*Prior*), **Dom James Hood** (*Sub-Prior*), **V Rev Philip Jebb, Doms Sebastian Moore, Laurence Kelly, Gervase Murray-Bligh, Bede Maitland, Cyprian Stockford, Columba Thorne, Ambrose Lambert, Dominic Mansi, Michael Clothier, Alexander George** (*Director, St Bede Centre*), **Leo Maidlow-Davis** (*Headmaster*), **Boniface Hill, Anselm Brumwell, Martin Gowman** (*Guestmaster*).
  M: *Weekdays 8.35am, Sun 11am.*

■ **DOWNTON,** Wilts
† **Good Shepherd and Our Blessed Lady Queen of Angels** (1950)
Barford Lane. Served from Salisbury (1).
M: *Sun 11am.*

■ **DULVERTON,** Som [A]
† **St Stanislaus** (1955)
High Street, Dulverton, Som TA22 9HB
Rev Robert Miller. Bridge House, 2 High Street, Dulverton, TA22 9HB
Tel: 01398-324217
M: *Sat 1st M of Sun 5.30pm. Sun 10am. Hds 7.30pm*

■ **DURSLEY,** Glos [A]
† **St Dominic** (1939)
St Dominc's Presbytery, Jubilee Road, Dursley, Glos. GL11 4ES
Tel: 01453-542039 **Fax:** 01453 548762
Rev Vincent Curtis.
M: *Sun 8.30am, 10.30am. Hds 7.30pm.*

■ **FAIRFORD,** Glos [A]
St Thomas of Canterbury
Norcott Road, GL7 4BX **Tel:** 01285-712586
Rev Phillip Beisly.
M: *Sat 6pm. Sun (vigil 7pm), 10am.*

■ **FISHPONDS**
See Bristol (8).

■ **FRENCHAY**
See Bristol (12).

■ **FROME,** Som [A]
† **St Catharine** (1851; 1928; 1968)
4 Park Road, Frome, Som. BA11 1EU
Tel: 01373-462705
Rev Joseph O'Brien.
M: *Sat 1st M of Sun 7pm. Sun 9.30am, 5.30pm. Hds 9.30am, 7.30pm.*

■ **GLASTONBURY,** Som
† **Our Lady** (1926; 1940; cons. July 2nd, 1941)
St Mary's Presbytery, Magdalene Street, Glastonbury BA6 9EJ **Tel:** 01458-832203
Fax: 01458-835931 (Office)
Rev P J Kevin Knox-Lecky.
E-mail: pjkevin.knoxlecky@cliftondiocese.com
Website: www.glastonburyshrine.co.uk
M: *Sat 1st M of Sun 6pm (except 1st Sun of month). Sun 8.30am, 10.30am, 12.15pm. Hds 10am, 7.30pm.*

■ **GLOUCESTER**
1. † **St Peter** (About 1789; cons, Oct. 8th 1868)
London Road, Gloucester GL1 3EX
Tel: 01452-523603 **Fax:** 01452-541130
Rev Bernard Massey
Deacons: **Revv Colm Robinson, James Jenkinson, Timothy Medows**.
M: *Sat 1st M of Sun 6pm. Sun 9am, 10.30am, 5.30pm. Hds 8am, 12noon, 7pm.*
- ***Poor Servants of the Mother of God,*** St Michael's Convent, 16 Tewkesbury Road, Longford, Glos GL2 9DT
  Tel: 01452-525118

2. † **The Good Shepherd, Ukrainan Church** (Cons 18 Dec 1977, Ukrainian Rite)
The Presbytery, Derby Road, Gloucester GL1 4AE **Tel:** 01452-529069
Very Rev Stephen Wiwcharuk STD (*Mitred Archpriest*).
M: *Sun 11am.*

■ **GLOUCESTER**
See Brockworth, Churchdown, Matson and Tuffley.

■ **HENBURY**
See Bristol (17).

■ **HIGHWORTH,** Swindon
Served from Swindon, No 3.
M: *Sun 12.15, in St Michael's Parish Church (CofE).*

■ **HOLCOMBE,** Som
† **St Cuthbert**
Served from Downside Abbey
Dom Gervase Murray-Bligh (OSB).
Tel: 01761-235144
M: *Sun 9am. Hds 9am.*

■ **ILMINSTER,** Som
† **St Joseph** (1953)
Station Road. Served from Chard.
M: *Sat 1st M of Sun 5.30pm. Hds 6pm.*

■ **KEMERTON,** Tewkesbury, Glos
† **St Benet** (1843)
St Benet's Presbytery, Evesham Road, Kemerton, Tewkesbury, Glos GL20 7JE
Tel: 01386-725286
- ***Benedictines (OSB):*** **Rev Dom Francis Hughes**
  M: *Sat 1st M of Sun 6pm. Sun 10am. Hds 10am, 7pm.*

■ **KEYNSHAM,** Bath & N E Som
† **St Dunstan** (1935)
20A Bristol Road, Keynsham BS31 2BQ
Tel: 0117-983 3930 **Rev Michael Fountaine**
M: *Sat 1st M of Sun 6pm. Sun 10.30am. Hds (vigil 7.30pm), 10am.*
• ***Poor Servants of the Mother of God,*** Convent & St Teresa's Nursing Home. See Corston.

■ **KINGSWOOD**
See Bristol (10).

■ **KNOWLE**
See Bristol (6).

■ **KNOWLE WEST**
See Bristol (13).

■ **LANGPORT,** Som
† **St Joseph** (1905; 1929)
The Hill, TA10 9QF
Served from Somerton.
• ***Fransalians: (MSFS)*** **Rev Francis Stephen. Tel:** 01458-272824
M: *Sun 10.30am. Hds 9.30am.*

■ **LAVINGTON,** Wilts
St Joseph (1932; 1945; 1971)
Littleton Panell. Served from Devizes (1).
Tel: 01380-723572
M: *Sun 9am. Hds 7.30pm.*

■ **LAWRENCE WESTON**
See Bristol (14).

■ **LYDNEY,** Glos A
† **St Joseph** Naas Lane
Served from Cinderford.
Tel: 01594-822167
M: *Sun 11am. Hds 6.30pm.*

■ **MALMESBURY,** Wilts
† **St Aldhelm** (1867; 1875)
26 Cross Hayes, Malmesbury, Wilts. SN16 9BG **Tel:** 01666-822195
• ***Fransalians. (MSFS):*** **Rev George O'Sullivan.**
M: *Sat 1st M of Sun 6.30pm. Sun 8.30am, 10.30am. Hds 10am, 7.30pm.*

■ **MARLBOROUGH,** Wilts
† **St Thomas More**
(1937; 1948; Cons. Sept 6th 1985)
George Lane, Marlborough, Wilts.
Rev John Blacker, Priest's House, 3 Priorsfield, Marlborough SN8 4AQ
Tel: 01672-513267
M: *Sat 1st M of Sun 6pm. Sun 11am. Hds 10am.*

■ **MATSON,** Glos
† **St Augustine of Canterbury**
(1962; 27 May 1988)
Matson Lane, Matson, Glos.

Rev Gary Brassington, St Augustines Presbytery, 256 Painswick Road GL4 4BS
Tel/Fax: 01452-412702
M: Sat 1st M of Sun 6.30pm. Sun 10am. Hds 10am, 7.30pm.

■ **MELKSHAM,** Wilts
† **St Anthony of Padua** (1939)
The Avenue, West End, Melksham, Wilts. **Rev Richard Northey**. 22 West End, Melksham, Wilts SN12 6HJ
Tel: 01225-702128
M: *Sat 1st M of Sun 5.30pm. Sun 9.30am. Hds (vigil vigil 7pm), 9.30am.*

■ **MELLS,** Som
St Dominic's
The Manor House. Served from Frome.
M: *Sun 11.30am.*

■ **MERE,** Wilts
† **St Mary** (1949)
Pettridge Lane. Served from Warminster.
M: *Sun 10am.*

■ **MIDSOMER NORTON**
† **Holy Ghost** (1913)
High Street. Served from Downside Abbey **Dom Michael Clothier (OSB).**
Tel: 01761-235111
M: *Sun 11am. Hds 9.30am.*

■ **MILBORNE PORT,** Som
St John the Evangelist (C of E)
Served from Wincanton.
M: *Sun 9am.*

■ **MILTON,** Weston-super-Mare
See Weston-super-Mare (3).

■ **MINEHEAD,** Som A
† **Sacred Heart** (1895; 1898)
8 Townsend Road, Minehead, Som TA24 5RG **Tel:** 01643-702201
Rev Michael Thomas.
Deacon: **Rev Vincent Woods.**
Serves also Watchet.
M: *Sat 1st M of Sun 5pm. Sun 11am. Hds 10am, 7pm.*

■ **MORETON-IN-MARSH,** Glos
Congregational Church
Oxford Street. Served from Chipping Campden.
M: *Sun 9am.*

■ **NAILSEA,** Bristol
† **St Francis**
Ash Hayes Road, Nailsea, Bristol BS48 2LP **Tel/Fax:** 01275-851530
Rev Michael McAndrew. *Deacons:* **Revv Paul Reddington Tel:** 01275-858485 **Ivan Reynolds.**
M: *Sat 1st M of Sun 6.30pm. Sun 9.30am, 10.30am.*

■ **NEWENT,** Glos
† **Our Lady of Lourdes** (1960)
Ross Road. Serves also Blaisdon.
• ***Salesians (SDB),*** **Rev Aidan Murray (SDB).** (*Parish Priest*), Drumlanrig, Ross Road, Newent, Glos GL18 1BG
Tel/Fax: 01531-821647
E-mail: aidansdb@newentbb.co.uk
M: *Sat 1st M of Sun 5.30pm; Sun 9am. Hds (vigil vigil 7pm), 10am.*

■ **NORTON ST PHILIP,** Som
† **Our Lady** (1923; 1961)
Served from Downside Abbey
Dom Gervase Murray-Bligh (OSB),
Tel: 01761-235144
M: *Sun 10.30am. Hds 6.30pm.*

■ **NYMPSFIELD,** Glos
† **St Joseph**
(1847; 1923; cons. Oct. 19th, 1932)
Tinkley Lane, Nympsfield GL10 3UH
Tel: 01453-860408
Served from Dursley.
M: *Sat 1st M of Sun 5.30pm. Hds 9.30am, 7.30pm.*
• ***Marist Sisters.*** 'Our Lady's Homestead', Nympsfield, Stonehouse, GL10 3TY
Tel: 01453-860228

■ **PAINSWICK,** Glos
† **Our Lady and St Thérèse**
Friday Street. Served from Stroud.
M: *Sun 8.30am.*

■ **PATCHWAY**
See Bristol (19).

■ **PAULTON**
† **Methodist Chapel**
Park Road. Served from Downside Abbey
Dom Michael Clothier (OSB).
Tel: 01761-235111 or 01761-235161 (recorded message)
M: *Sat 1st M of Sun 6pm.*

■ **PEASEDOWN ST JOHN**
† **St Joseph**
(1926; 1959; 1989 New Mass Centre)
Served from Bath (4).
Tel: 01225-420809.
M: *Sun 9am. Hd 7pm.*

■ **PEWSEY,** Wilts
† **Holy Family** (1964)
Broadfields. Served from Marlborough.
M: *Sun 9am. Hds (vigil 7.30pm).*

■ **PORTISHEAD**
† **St Joseph** (1887)
87 West Hill, Portishead BS20 6LN
Tel: 01275-842912
Rev Gerard Walsh.
Deacon: **Rev Peter Rose.**
M: *Sat 1st M of Sun 6pm. Sun 10.30am. Hds (Vigil 8.45pm), 12.00 pm.*

■ **POSTLIP,** Glos
St James (12th century; Restored 1891)
In the parish of Winchcombe.
For information contact **Rev John Brennan, Tel:** 01386-840261

■ **PRESTBURY,** Glos
Holy Name Hall
Pennine Road, Lynworth, Cheltenham, Glos. GL4 8EX
Served from Cheltenham (1).
M: *Sun 8am.*

■ **PRINKNASH ABBEY**
Our Lady and St Peter (1928; 1937)
Cranham, Gloucester, GL4 8EX
Abbey: **Tel:** 01452-812455
Fax: 01452-813305
E-mail: prinknash@waitrose.com
Website: www.prinknashabbey.org.uk
• ***Benedictines (OSB).***
Rt Rev Francis Baird (*Abbot*)
E-mail: abbotfrancis@waitrose.com
Very Rev Stephen Horton *(Prior, Novice Master)*, **Rt Rev Aldhelm Cameron-Brown** *(Abbot Emeritus/Oblate Master)*, **Rt Rev Mark Hargreaves** *(Abbot Emeritus, Director of Music, Abbot's Secretary)*, **Revv Alphege Stebbens** *(Subprior)*, **Fabian Binyon, Aelred Baker, Damian Sturdy** *(Sacristan, Cellarer, Pastoral Secretary, Master of Ceremonies)*, **Martin McLaughlin** *(Bursar/Vocations Promoter)*, **William Harwood** *(Deacon & Guestmaster)*.
M: *Sun 8.15am, 10.30am. Hds 10.30am.*

■ **RADSTOCK**
† **St Hugh** *(1913)*
Wells Hill. Served from Downside Abbey
Dom Michael Clothier (OSB)
Tel: 01761-235148 or messages on
Tel: 01761-235161
M: *Sun 9.30am. Hds 6pm.*
• ***Sisters of Our Lady of Sion,*** The Gate House, Ammerdown, Radstock.
Tel: 01761-432756 Ammerdown Conference Centre, **Tel:** 01761-433709

■ **RANDWICK**
Stroud, GL6 6EP
Convent Chapel. Served from Stroud.
M: *Sun 11am.*
• ***Benedictine Sisters of Our Lady of Grace and Compassion***
Tel: 01453-764486

■ **REDFIELD**
See Bristol (7).

■ SALISBURY, Wilts
1. † St Osmund
(1790; cons. Sept. 6th, 1848)
95 Exeter Street, Salisbury, Wilts. SP1 2SF
Tel/ Fax: 01722-333581
E-mail: st.osmund@talk21.com
Rev Canon Michael Fitzpatrick.
M: *Sun 9am, 11am, 7.15pm. Hds (vigil 7pm), 7.30am, 9.45am-term time, 12.40pm, 7pm.*
• ***Sisters of La Retraite,*** 16 Belle Vue Road, Salisbury, SP1 3VF
Tel: 01722-322785

2. † St Gregory and the English Martyrs (1938)
44 St Gregory's Avenue, Salisbury, Wilts. SP2 7JP **Tel:** 01722-334496
Rev Andrew Goodman. *Deacons:* **Revv John Proctor, John Detain.**
M: *Sun 9.30am. Hds 7.30pm.*

3. † Most Holy Redeemer (1964)
Bishopdown, Salisbury, Wilts.
Tel: 01722-327354 Served from Salisbury (1).
M: *Sat 1st M of Sun 7pm. Sun 9.45am. Hds 7pm.*

■ SEDBURY, Glos
† Sacred Heart Chapel
Grahamstown Road, Sedbury.
Served from Coleford.
M: *Sun 10.30am. Hds 7pm.*

■ SHEPTON MALLET, Som
† St Michael (1804; 1967)
6 Park Road, BA4 5BP **Tel:** 01749-342587
Served from Wells.
Pastoral Assistant: **Sr Anne Martin.**
M: *Sun 11.00am. Hds 7.30pm.*

■ SHIREHAMPTON.
See Bristol (5).

■ SOMERTON, Som
St Dunstan (1965)
St Dunstan's Presbytery, Langport Road, TA11 6RS **Tel/Fax:** 01458-272824
Fransalians (MSFS): **Rev Francis Stephen.**
M: *Sat 1st M of Sun 6pm. Sun 9am. Hds 7pm.*

■ SOUTH PETHERTON, Som
St Michael, (1961).
Lightgate Road. Served from Yeovil.
M: *Sun 9.30am. Hds 7.30pm.*

■ SOUTHDOWN
See Bath (1a).

■ STONEHOUSE, Glos
† St Joseph (1966; cons. 1976)
St Joseph's Presbytery, Oldends Lane, Stonehouse GL10 2DG
Tel/Fax: 01453-822121
Rev William Watson.
M: *Sun 10am. Hds (vigil 7.30pm), 10am.*

■ STOW-ON-THE-WOLD, Glos
† Our Lady and St Kenelm (1918)
Back Walls, GL54 1DR
Tel/Fax: 01451-830431
Rev Ian McCarthy.
Mobile: 07941-232246
E-mail: icm52@aol.com
M: *Sun 10am, 6.30pm. Hds 10am,7.30pm.*

■ STRATTON ON THE FOSSE, Som
† St Benedict (1856; cons. 1957)
Served from Downside Abbey
Dom Aidan Bellenger (OSB).
Tel: 01761-235112
M: *Sun 8am, 6pm. Hds 7.30am.*

■ STROUD, Glos
† The Immaculate Conception
(1857; cons. Dec. 8th 1982)
Beeches Green, Stroud, Glos GL5 4AA
Tel: 01453-762442
Fax: 01453-755314
E-mail: immac.concept@tiscali.co.uk
Rev David Ryan. *Deacon:* **Rev Stephen Bentley. Tel:** 01453-751101
M: *Sat 1st M of Sun 6.30pm. Sun 10am (Sung). Hds 9.30am, 7.30pm.*
• ***Dominican Sisters,*** St Rose's Convent, Beeches Green GL5 4AB
Tel: 01453-762449

■ SWINDON, Wilts
1. † Holy Rood
(1848; 1851; 1905; cons. 1971)
2 Groundwell Road, Swindon, Wilts. SN1 2LU
Tel: 01793-522062 **Fax:** 01793-432619
Mgr Canon Richard J Twomey, Rev James Finan. *Deacons:* **Rev Dennis Sutton. Anthony Guilfoyle.** *Parish Sister:* **Sr Cecelia Jennings (SMG).**
M: *Sat 1st M of Sun 6.30pm. Sun 8am, 9.30am, 11am (Sung), 5.30pm. Hds (vigil 6.30pm), 8am, 9.30am, 12.45pm, 7.30pm.*
• ***Poor Servants of the Mother of God.*** St Mary's Convent, Groundwell Road SN1 2LU **Tel:** 01793- 535775

2. † Holy Family (1962)
Holy Family Presbytery, Marlowe Avenue, Park North, SN3 2PT **Tel:** 01793-527931
Mgr Canon Jeremy Rigden VG. *Deacons:* **Rev Thomas McLaughlin.**
M: *Sat 1st M of Sun 6pm. Sun 10am, 6pm. Hds (vigil 7.30pm), 9.30am, 7.30pm.*
• ***Presentation Sisters,*** St Michael's Convent, Marlowe Avenue, Park North, SN3 2PT **Tel:** 01793-535708

3. † St Mary (1953)
St Mary's Presbytery, Tovey Road, Swindon SN2 1LQ
Tel: 01793-535089 **Fax:** 01793 480560
E-mail: toveyroad@aol.com
Rev Liam Slattery. *Deacons:* **Revv Shaun Murphy, Hugh Anscombe.**
M: *Sat 1st M of Sun 6.30pm. Sun 9am, 10.30am, 6.30pm. Hds 9am, 7pm.*

4. Polish Catholic Centre
Whitbourne Avenue, Swindon, Wilts.
Tel: 01793-523184
Rev Stefan Orzel, 27 Groundwell Road, Swindon SN2 1LT **Tel:** 01793-531257
M: *Sun 9am, 10.45am. Hds 9am, 7pm. (Holy Rood Church).*

5. † St Peter
St Peter, Carronbridge Road, Westlea, Swindon SN5 7ES **Tel/Fax:** 01793-874400
Rev Dr Michael Saunders. St Peter, Carronbridge Road.
M: *Sat 1st M of Sun 6pm. Sun 10am. Hds (vigil 7.30pm), 10am.*
- ***Sisters of The Saviour and The Blessed Virgin,*** 61 New Road, Chisledon, Swindon SN4 0PE **Tel:** 01793-740606

■ TAUNTON, Som
† St George (1790; 1860; cons. 1912)
Billet Street, Taunton, Somerset TA1 3NN
Tel: 01823-272700
Rev John Cunningham (*Parish Priest*), *Deacon:* **Rev Trevor Jones.**
M: *Sun 8am, 9.30am, 6.30pm. Hds 9.30am, 12.30pm, 9.30pm.*
- ***Sisters of St Joseph of Annecy,*** 19 South Road, Taunton, TA1 3DT **Tel:** 01823-333810

2. St Teresa of Lisieux (1959)
Eastwick Road, Taunton, Somerset TA2 7HF
Served from Taunton (1).
Tel: 01823-333608
Parish Sister: **Sr Margaret Mary.** (Franciscan Sisters of Mill Hill).
M: *Sat 1st M of Sun 6.30pm. Sun 11am. Hds (vigil 7pm), 10am.*

■ TETBURY, Glos
† St Michael (1936; 1942)
The Green, Tetbury, Glos.
Mgr Canon William Mitchell. 31 Silver Street, GL8 8DH **Tel:** 01666-502367
Fax: 01666 503910 *Deacon:* **Rev James Bradley**. **Tel:** 01666-502981
M: *Sat 1st M of Sun 5.30pm. Sun 9.30am. Hds 9.30am, 7pm.*

■ TEWKESBURY, Glos
† St Joseph (1870)
Chance Street, Tewkesbury, Glos. GL20 5RF
Rev Richard Dwyer. Tel: 01684-293273
Fax: 01684 291667 *Deacon:* **Rev John Torr.**
M: *Sat 1st M of Sun 6pm. Sun 8.30am, 10.30am. Hds 9.30am, 7.30pm.*

■ THORNBURY, nr Bristol
† Christ the King (1941; 1951; 1964)
11 Castle Street, Thornbury, Bristol. BS35 1HA
Tel: (Office) 01454-412223
Tel: (Presbytery) 01454-854586
Fax: 01454-412427
E-mail: mcallister@sds.org
Website: www.ctk-thornbury.org.uk
- ***Salvatorians (SDS):*** **Revv Alexander McAllister, Charles Reddan**.
Deacons: **Revv Kingsley Fulbrook, Lawrence McCarthy**
Parish Sister: **Sr Josephine O'Malley**.
Tel: 01454-327105
M: *Sun 8.30am, 11am, 6.30pm. Hds 7.45am, 10am (9.15am term time), 7.45pm.*

■ TISBURY, Wilts
† The Sacred Heart
(1898; cons. Sept. 12th 1934)
Trellis House, Station Road, Tisbury, Salisbury, Wiltshire. SP3 6JR
Tel: 01747-870228 **Fax:** 01474-870159
Canon Thomas Atthill.
M: *Sun 9am, 6.30pm. Hds 7.30pm.*

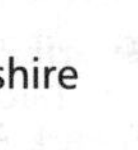

■ TROWBRIDGE, Wilts
† St John the Baptist (1876)
2 Wingfield Road, Trowbridge, Wiltshire BA14 9EA **Tel:** 01225-752152
Canon Liam O'Driscoll. *Parish Sisters:* **Srs Anne Power, M Leonard**.
Tel: 01225-753112
M: *Sat 1st M of Sun 6pm. Sun 10.30am, 6pm. Hds (vigil 6pm), 9am, 7.30pm.*
- ***Polish Centre*, Rev Andrzej Budzynski**. 6 Waterworks Road, BA14 0AL **Tel:** 01225-752930 **M:** *Sun 11am.*
- ***Sisters of St John of God,*** The Convent, 23 Avenue Road BA14 0AQ **Tel:** 01225-753112

■ TUFFLEY, Glos
† English Martyrs
English Martyrs Presbytery, Tuffley Lane, Tuffley, Glos GL4 0NX **Tel:** 01452-504997
Rev Keith Miles.
M: *Sat 1st M of Sun 6pm. Sun 10am. Hds 9am, 7.30pm.*

■ WARDOUR, Tisbury, Wilts
† All Saints (16th Cent.; 1776)
Served from Tisbury.
M: *Sun 11am. Hds 10am.*

■ **WARMINSTER,** Wilts
† St George
(1922; 1938; cons. 23 April 1978)
31 Boreham Road, Warminster, Wilts BA12 9JP
Tel: 01985-212329
Rev Bede Rowe.
Also attached **Rev Raymond Hayne.**
M: *Sat 1st M of Sun 6pm. Sun 8.30am, 10.30am. Hds 10am, 7.30pm.*
• ***Salvatorian Sisters***, 9c Boreham Road BA12 9JP **Tel:** 01985-217647

■ **WATCHET,** Som
Knights Templar School, Liddymore Road.
Served from Minehead.
M: *Sun 9.30am. Hds (vigil 7pm).*

■ **WELLINGTON,** Som
† St John Fisher (1937)
57 Mantle Street, Wellington, Somerset TA21 8AX **Tel:** 01823-662283
Rev Robert Rainbow.
M: *Sat 1st M of Sun 5pm. Sun 11am. Hds 9.15am.*

■ **WELLS,** Som
† SS Joseph and Teresa
(1875; 1888; cons. 1890)
16 Chamberlain Street, Wells, BA5 2PF
Tel/Fax: 01749-673183
E-mail: ssjosephteresa@cliftondiocese.com
Also serves Shepton Mallett.
Rev Philip Thomas.
Mbl: 07768-360879
M: *Sat 1st M of Sun 6pm. Sun 9am. Hds (vigil 7.30pm), 10am.*

■ **WEST HARPTREE**
† St Mary, C of E
Served from Chew Magna.
M: *Sun 9am. Hds 7pm. (In St Michael's, East Harptree).*

■ **WESTBURY,** Wilts
† St Bernadette, West End (1938)
Served from Trowbridge.
M: *Sun 9am. Hds 6pm.*

■ **WESTBURY-ON-TRYM**
See Bristol (11).

■ **WESTON-SUPER-MARE**
1. † Corpus Christi
(1929; cons. June 6th 1934)
Corpus Christi Presbytery, 14 Ellenborough Park South, BS23 1XW
Tel: 01934-621929 **Fax:** 01934-642415
E-mail: corpuschristi.weston@virgin.net
Mgr Canon P Gabriel Leyden VG. Also in Residence: **Canon Timothy Barry (Retired), Tel:** 01934-415969 *Deacons:* **Revv Stephen Munday, Peter Gregory.**
M: *Sat 1st M of Sun 6.30pm. Sun 10.30am. Hds 10am, 7.30pm.*
• ***Sisters of La Retraite,*** 13 Walliscote Road, BS23 1XE **Tel:** 01934-621982

2. † St Joseph
(1851; 1858; cons. 1958)
St Joseph's Presbytery, Camp Road, Weston-super-Mare BS23 2EN
Tel: 01934-629865
Deacon: **Rev Thomas Moffatt.**
M: *Sun 10.30am, 6.30pm. Hds 10.30am, 6.30pm.*

3. † Our Lady of Lourdes
(1938; cons. Feb. 11th, 1978)
28 Baytree Road, Milton, Weston-super-Mare BS22 8HQ **Tel:** 01934-627137
Rev Martin Queenan.
M: *Sat 1st M of Sun 5.30pm. Sun 9.30am. Hds (vigil 7.30pm), 11am.*

■ **WHADDON,** Wilts
† The Holy Family
Southampton Road, Whaddon
Served from Salisbury (1).
M: *Sun 6pm.*

■ **WINCANTON,** Som
† SS Luke and Teresa (1881; cons. 1908)
St Luke's Presbytery, South Street, Wincanton, Somerset BA9 9DH
Tel: 01963-34408
E-mail: stlukes@nascr.net
Rev Louis Beasley-Suffolk.
M: *Sat 1st M of Sun 6.30pm (except 3rd Sun of month). Sun 11am. Hds (vigil 7.30pm), 9.30am.*
• ***Sisters of Christian Instruction,*** Sisters of St Gilda's, 8 Elm Drive, Wincanton, Somerset BA9 9EZ

■ **WINCHCOMBE,** Glos
† St Nicholas (1915)
St Nicholas, Chandos Street, Winchcombe GL54 5HX

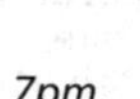
Tel: 01242-602412
Rev Peter Slocombe.

M: *Sun 8.30am, 10.30am. Hds 7pm.*

■ **WITHYWOOD**
See Bristol, (16a).

■ **WIVELISCOMBE,** Som
St Richard (1967)
Church Street. Served from Wellington.
M: *Hds 7.30pm.*

■ **WOODCHESTER,** Stroud, Glos
† The Annunciation
(1846; cons. Oct. 10th 1849)
St Mary's Hill House, St Mary's Hill, Inchbrook, Woodchester, Stroud GL5 5HP
Tel: 01453-832120
Rev Piers Linley OP.
M: *Sat 1st M of Sun 6pm. Sun*

DIOCESE OF CLIFTON

10.30am, Hds 8am (Convent Chapel), 10am (Priory Church), 7pm (Priory Church).
- ***Poor Clares,*** Convent of the Immaculate Conception, Convent Lane, Woodchester GL5 5HS
  Tel: 01453-832250

■ WOOTTON BASSETT, Wilts
† The Sacred Heart
Sacred Heart Presbytery, High Street, Wootton Bassett, Swindon SN4 7AH
Tel/Fax: 01793-852366.
Rev John Reville.
M: *Sat 1st M of Sun 6pm. Sun 10am. Hds (vigil 7pm). 9.30am.*

■ WOTTON-UNDER-EDGE, Glos
† Holy Cross (1952)
13 Old Town, GL12 7DH
Tel/Fax: 01453-842281
E-mail: aelredsds@aol.com
- ***Salvatorians (SDS)*** **Rev Aelred Dobson.**
  M: *Sun 10.30am, 5.30pm. Hds 9.15am, 7.30pm.*

■ WROUGHTON, Wilts
A

† St Joseph (1954)
St Joseph's Presbytery, Devizes Road, Wroughton SN4 0RZ
Tel: 01793-812330
Rev Nicholas Tranter.
Deacon: **Rev Laurence Moss.**
M: *Sun 9.30am, 5.30pm. Hds 7.30pm.*

■ YATE
St Paul *(1981)*
Sundridge Park, Yate, South Gloucestershire BS37 4EP
Rev James Williams
Served from Chipping Sodbury.
Website: www.stlawrenceandstpaul.co.uk
M: *Sat 1st M of Sun, 5pm. Sun 11am. Hds 9.30am.*
- ***Salvatorian Sisters,*** 62 Station Road, Yate, South Gloucestershire BS37 4PW
  Tel: 01454-327105

■ YATTON
SS Dunstan and Antony
Claverham Road. Served from Clevedon.
M: *Sun 8.30am. Hds 8pm on eve of Feast.*

■ YEOVIL, Som
† The Holy Ghost (1887; cons. May 17th, 1899)
The Avenue
- ***Fransalians (MSFS):*** **Revv Sunny Paul** (*Parish Priest*), **Alan James Blackford, Andrezej Marszewski.** 73 Higher Kingston BA21 4AR. **Tel:** 01935-423549.
  M: *Sat 1st M of Sun 6.15pm. Sun 9am, 10.30am. Hds (vigil 7.30pm), 8am, 10am, 7.30pm.*

■ YEOVILTON
Our Lady and St Augustine, Catholic Church
HMS Heron, RNAS Yeovilton, Ilchester BA22 8HT
M: *Sun 9.30am.*

■ ORDERS OR CONGREGATIONS, ETC

■ Men
Benedictines (English Congregation): Downside, Kemerton.
Benedictines (Congregation of Subiaco): Prinknash.
Carmelites (O.Carm): Cheltenham (2)
Divine Word, Society of: St Mary on the Quay, Bristol.
Dominicans: Woodchester.
Franciscans (Friars Minor): Clevedon.
Fransalians: Devizes (1), Malmesbury, Somerton, Yeovil.
Kiltegan Fathers: Corsham.
Missionaries of St Paul (of Nigeria): Bristol 14.
Salesians: Blaisdon, Newent.
Salvatorians: Thornbury, Wootton.

■ Women
Charity, Religious Sisters of: Bristol (13).
Charity (of St Paul), Sisters of: Chipping Campden.
Christian Instruction (St Gildas), Sisters of: Wincanton.
Daughters of Charity (SVP): Bristol (4).
Dominican Sisters (Third Order), Franciscan Sisters (of the Immaculate Conception): Cinderford.
Francisan Sisters of Mill Hill: Taunton (1).
Grace & Compassion, Benedictine Sisters of Our Lady of: More Hall.
Holy Spirit (Steyl), Sister Servants of the: Bristol (14).
John of God, Sisters of St: Trowbridge.
Joseph (Annecy), Sisters of St: Bristol (3), Devizes (1), Taunton (1).
Marist Sisters: Nympsfield.
Mercy, Sisters of (Union): Bristol (11,19), Clevedon.
Nazareth, Poor Sisters of: Cheltenham (2).
Poor, Little Sisters of the: Clifton.
Poor Clares: Woodchester.
Poor Servants of the Mother of God: Clifton, Corston, Gloucester, Swindon (1).
Presentation Sisters (of the Blessed Virgin Mary): Brockworth, Corsham, Swindon (2).
Retraite, Sisters of La: Clifton, Salisbury (1), Weston-super-Mare (1), Shepton Mallet.
Sainte-Union des Sacres Coeurs, Congregation of la: Bath (2), Cheltenham (2), Portishead.
Salvatorian Sisters: Warminster, Bristol (7), Yate.
Saviour and the Blessed Virgin, Sisters of: Swindon.

Sion, Sisters of Our Lady of: Radstock.
Temple, Sisters of the: Clifton.

■ ASSOCIATIONS AND SOCIETIES

ADVENT. Information contact: **Mr Peter Harrison**, 34 Clayfield Road, Brislington, Bristol BS4 4NH **Tel:** 0117-983 4888

Association of Our Lady of Mount Carmel. *Secretary:* (Bristol Centre), **Mrs Elizabeth Dillon**, 'Steppings', Ladye Bay, Clevedon, BS21 7BU **Tel:** 01275-794094

Association of Separated and Divorced Catholics. A federation of self help groups to provide mutual help and spiritual support to those who have experienced the pain of marriage breakdown. *Diocesan Representative:* **Rev Dcn Dennis Sutton,** 4 Wardour Cl, Lawn, Swindon SN3 1JZ. **Tel:** 01793 520753

Association of Sisters in Pastoral Ministry. *Secretary:* **Sr Mary Riordan**. 29 Pulteney Road, Bath BA2 4EZ **Tel:** 01225-461984

Catenian Association. *Press Secretary:* **Mr Tony Kay**, Upper Seagry, Chippenham SN15 5EX **Tel:** 01249-443377

Catholic Fund for Overseas Development (CAFOD). *Manager:* **Tony Vassallo.** CAFOD Clifton, The Mount, Taunton, Somerset, TA1 3NR **Tel:** 01823-338903

Catholic Women's League. *Branch Secretary:* **Margaret Richards,** 28 Church Road, Chelthenham GL53 0PR **Tel:** 01242-241745

CHAS (Bristol). *Advice Service Manager:* **Mr Mike Mills**, PO Box 2219, Bristol BS99 7HH **Tel:** 0117-935 1260

Christian Life Community. *Representative in the Diocese:* **Mrs Judith Collin,** 21 Eggshill Lane, Yate, Bristol BS37 4BH **Tel:** 01454-318972

Clifton Diocesan Pilgrimage to Lourdes. *Director:* Awaiting Appointment

Consecrated Women. *Liaison Person:* **Elizabeth Rees**, 2 Parkfields, High Street, Butleigh, Glastonbury BA6 78SZ **Tel:** 01458-851561

Days of Recollection. *Hon Sec:* **Mrs Peggy Found**, 138 Charlton Park, Midsomer Norton, Bath BA3 4PP **Tel:** 01761-414458

English Catholic History Association. *Secretary:* **Mrs Toni Eccles,** 6 Townside, Church Street, Tisbury, Salisbury SP3 6AX **Tel:** 01747-871070

Friends of St Mary's Church, Cricklade. *Secretary:* **Mrs Gerry Dudley,** 4 Playdells, Cricklade, Wiltshire SN6 6NG **Tel:** 01793-750107

Glastonbury Pilgrimage Committee. *Secretary:* **Mrs Geraldine Forbes,** 2 Woods Batch, Street BA16 0BH **Tel:** 01458-841418

Holy Souls Cemetery. *Registrar:* **Mrs Carol Fackrell**. 4 Edward Road, Brislington, Bristol, BS4 3ES **Tel:** 0117-977 2386

Infirm Priests Society. *Secretary:* **Rev Patrick Auger**. 2 Court Road, Kingswood, Bristol BS15 9QB **Tel:** 0117-949 8743 **Fax:** 0117-967 3188

Knights of Our Lady (Militia Sanctae Mariae). Contact: **Martin A A Blake**. 4 Dunkerton Close, Glastonbury, Somerset BA6 8LZ **Tel:** 01458-833726

Knights of St Columba. *Provincial Grand Knight:* **Mr Richard Purdon**, 37 Anglesey Mead, Chippenham SN15 3UB **Tel:** 01249-655366

Latin Mass Society. Representative in Diocese: **Nigel Taylor,** 29 Camden Road, Bristol BS3 1QA Tel: 0117 9669976

Legion of Mary. *Secretary:* **Mrs Mary Belt**, 148 Northcote Road, Downend, Bristol BS16 6AR **Tel:** 0117-940 0799

Marriage Care.
Gloucestershire: *Secretary:* **Mrs Anne Fry**, 4 New Court Park, Charlton Kings, Cheltenham GL53 9AY **Tel:** 01242-234882 **Wiltshire:** *Centre Manager:* **Mr David Bourne**, 23 Webb Close, Chippenham, Wiltshire SN15 3XF **Tel:** 01249-444034

Newman Association. Miss Clare Haynes, 9 The Croft, Painswick, Stroud GL6 6QP **Tel:** 01452-812514

Secular Franciscan Order. *Regional Secretary:* **Mrs Joan Woollard**. Flat 9, Drake Court, 264 Citadel Road, Plymouth PL1 2PY **Tel:** 01752-254131

Serra Club of the Cotswolds: *Hon Secretary:* **Mr John Westlake**, 49 Collum End Rise, Cheltenham GL53 0PA **Tel:** 01242-521711

Servite Secular Institute. *Secretary:* **John Kyffin**. 2 Meadow Close, Cheltenham GL51 0TZ **Tel:** 01242 239680

Teams of Our Lady. *Contact couple:* **John and Jane Andrews**, 17 Oakbrook Drive, Cheltenham, Gloucs GL51 6SB **Tel:** 01452 713330

Union of Catholic Mothers, *Sec:* **Mrs Pat Uglow,** 11 Stanhill Drive, Dursley GL11 4PP **Tel:** 01453-542179

■ HOSPITALS

To contact the Catholic Chaplain of a particular hospital we suggest you contact the hospital reception directly.

■ CATHOLIC SCHOOLS—MAINTAINED

■ BATH

▲ Primary

St John's, Pulteney Road, BA2 4EZ **Tel:** 01225-461887 **Fax:** 01225-442306 (Bath 2)

St Mary's School, Penn Hill Road, Weston, BA1 4EH **Tel:** 01225-429030 **Fax:** 01225-319012 (Bath 3)

▲ Secondary

St Gregory's Catholic College, Combe Hay Lane, Odd Down, BA2 8PA **Tel:** 01225-832873 **Fax:** 01225-835848 (Bath)

■ THE GREATER BRISTOL AREA

▲ Primary

SS Peter & Paul (Cathedral), Aberdeen Road, Redland, BS6 6HY **Tel:** 0117-903 0070 **Fax:** 0117-903 0071 (Bristol)

Our Lady of the Rosary, Tide Grove, Lawrence Weston, BS11 OPA **Tel:** 0117-903 0025 **Fax:** 0117-903 0026 (Bristol 14)

St Bernard's, Station Road, Shirehampton BS11 9TU **Tel:** 0117-903 0352 (Bristol 5)

St Bonaventure's, Egerton Road, Bishopston, BS7 8HP **Tel:** 0117-924 7212 **Fax:** 0117-942 8127 (Bristol 4)

The School of Christ the King, Hartcliffe Road, BS4 1HD **Tel:** 0117-966 4844, **Fax:** 0117-963 1849 (Bristol 13)

Holy Cross, Dean Lane, Bedminster, BS3 1DB **Tel:** 0117-377 2199 **Fax:** 0117-377 2375 (Bristol 3)

St Joseph's, Chatsworth Road, Fishponds, BS16 3QR **Tel:** 0117-377 2160 **Fax:** 0117-377 2161 (Bristol 8)

St Nicholas of Tolentine Primary School, Pennywell Road, BS5 0TJ **Tel:** 0117-377 2260 (Bristol 2)

St Patrick's, Blackswarth Road, Redfield, BS5 8AS **Tel:** 0117-377 2387 **Fax:** 0117-377 2388 (Bristol 7)

St Pius X, Gatehouse Avenue, Withywood, BS13 9AB **Tel:** 0117-377 2165 **Fax:** 0117-377 2166 (Bristol 16)

St Teresa's, Luckington Road, Monks Park, BS7 0UP **Tel:** 0117-903 0412 **Fax:** 0117-903 0413 (Bristol 9)

St Bernadette Primary School, Gladstone Road, Hengrove, BS14 9LP **Tel:** 0117-377 2373 (Bristol 20)

▲ Secondary

St Brendan's Sixth Form College, Broomhill Road, Bristol, BS4 5RQ **Tel:** 0117-977 7766 **Fax:** 0117-972 3351(Bristol)

St Bernadette Colege, Fossdale Avenue, BS14 9LS **Tel:** 0117-377 2050 **Fax:** 0117-377 2054 (Bristol 3,4,6,7,13,16)

St Bede's Catholic College, Lawrence Weston, BS11 OSU **Tel:** 0117-377 2200 **Fax:** 0117-377 2201 (Bristol)

■ SOUTH GLOUCESTERSHIRE LEA

▲ Primary

St Mary, Webbs Wood Road, Bradley Stoke, Bristol BS32 8EJ **Tel:** 01454-866930 **Fax:** 01454-866391

Our Lady of Lourdes, Hanham Road, Kingswood, BS15 8PX **Tel:** 01454-867160 **Fax:** 01454-867161 (Bristol 10)

Holy Family, Amberley Road, Patchway, BS34 6BY. **Tel:** 01454-866786 **Fax:** 01454-866788 (Bristol 19)

St Augustine of Canterbury, Boscombe Crescent, Downend, BS16 6QR **Tel:** 01454-866690 **Fax:** 01454-866694 (Bristol 18)

Christ the King, Easton Hill Road, Bristol, BS35 1AW. **Tel:** 01454-866680 **Fax:** 01454-866681 (Thornbury)

St Paul's, Sundridge Park, Yate, Bristol, BS37 5SB **Tel:** 01454-866790 **Fax:** 01454-866792 (Yate)

■ SWINDON LEA

▲ Primary

Holy Rood Junior School, Upham Road, Swindon, Wiltshire, SN3 1DH **Tel:** 01793-527679 **Fax:** 01793-491647 (Swindon 1)

Holy Rood Infant School, Groundwell Road, Swindon, Wiltshire, SN1 2LU **Tel:** 01793-523802 **Fax:** 01793-491647 (Swindon 1)

Holy Family Catholic Primary School, Marlowe Avenue, Swindon, Wiltshire, SN3 2PT **Tel:** 01793-521933 **Fax:** 01793-521932 (Swindon 2)

St Mary's, Bessemer Road East, Swindon, Wiltshire, SN2 1PE **Tel:** 01793-523850 **Fax:** 01793-523506 (Swindon 3)

St Catherine's, Davenwood, Stratton St Margaret, Wiltshire, SN2 7LL **Tel:** 01793-822699 **Fax:** 01793-332021 (Swindon 3)

▲ Secondary

St Joseph's Catholic College, Ocotal way, Swindon SN3 3LR **Tel:** 01793-825999 **Fax:** 01793-820148 (Swindon 1)

■ SOMERSET

▲ Primary

St Joseph's, Park Avenue, Somerset TA6 7EE **Tel:** 01278-422786 **Fax:** 01278-429791 (Bridgwater)

St Joseph's, Oxford Street, Somerset TA8 1LG **Tel:** 01278-784641 **Fax:** 01278-794403 (Burnham-on-Sea)

St Louis First School, Welshmill Lane, Somerset, BA11 3AP **Tel:** 01373-463728 **Fax:** 01373-453565 (Frome)
St Benedict's, Charlton Lane, Bath, BA3 4BD **Tel:** 01761-418594 **Fax:** 01761-411810 (Midsomer Norton)
St George's, The Mount, Somerset, TA1 3NR. **Tel:** 01823-284130 **Fax:** 01823-325947 (Taunton)
St Joseph's & St. Teresa's, Lovers Walk, Somerset, BA5 2QL **Tel:** 01749-678791 **Fax:** 01749-670682 (Wells)
Our Lady's, Tout Hill, Somerset, BA9 9DH **Tel:** 01963-32660 **Fax:** 01963-31653 (Wincanton)
St Gildas Primary, Mary Street, Somerset, BA21 4BJ **Tel:** 01935-423630 **Fax:** 01935-411048 (Yeovil)

▲ Secondary
St Augustine of Canterbury (Joint Church School), Lyngford Road, Priorswood TA2 7EF **Tel:** 01823-337128 **Fax:** 01373-453565 (Taunton 1)

■ NORTH SOMERSET LEA

▲ Primary
St Francis, Station Road, Bristol, BS48 4PD **Tel:** 01275-855373 **Fax:** 01275-798466 (Nailsea)
St Joseph's, Bristol Road, Portishead, Bristol BS20 6QB **Tel:** 01275-848367 **Fax:** 01275-845638 (Portishead)
Corpus Christi, Ellenborough Park South, BS23 1XW **Tel:** 01934-621919 **Fax:** 01934-621590 (Weston-super-Mare)

■ WILTSHIRE

▲ Primary
Christ the King, Earls Court Road, Amesbury, Wiltshire, SP4 7LX **Tel:** 01980-622039 (Amesbury)
St Edmund's, Duncan Street, Calne, Wiltshire, SN11 9BX **Tel:** 01249-813821 **Fax:** 01249-822127 (Calne)
St Mary's, Rowden Hill, Chippenham, Wiltshire, SN15 2AH **Tel:** 01249-653469 **Fax:** 01249-460232 (Chippenham)
St Patrick's, Lacock Road, Corsham, Wiltshire, SN13 9HS **Tel:** 01249-713125 **Fax:** 01249-701670 (Corsham)
St Joseph's, Bath Road, Devizes, Wiltshire, SN10 1DD **Tel:** 01380-723084 **Fax:** 01380-723546 (Devizes)
St Joseph's, Holloway Hill, Malmesbury, Wiltshire, SN16 9BB **Tel:** 01666-822331 **Fax:** 01666-829328 (Malmesbury)
St Osmund's, Exeter Street, Salisbury, Wiltshire, SP1 2SG **Tel:** 01722-322632 (Salisbury)
St John's, Wingfield Road, Trowbridge, Wiltshire, BA14 9EA **Tel:** 01225-752006 **Fax:** 01225-769606 (Trowbridge)
Wardour Roman Catholic School, Tisbury, Wardour, Wiltshire, SP3 6RF **Tel:** 01747-870537 (Wardour)
St George's, Woodcock Road, Warminster, Wiltshire, BA12 9EZ **Tel:** 01985-218284 **Fax:** 01985-212797 (Warminster)

▲ Secondary
St Joseph's Secondary, Church Road, Salisbury, Wiltshire, SP1 1QY **Tel:** 01722-335380 **Fax:** 01722-410741 (Salisbury)
St Augustine's R.C. Comprehensive Wingfield Road, Trowbridge, Wiltshire, BA14 9EN **Tel:** 01225-350001 **Fax:** 01225-350002 (Trowbridge)

■ GLOUCESTERSHIRE

▲ Primary
Catholic School of St Gregory the Great, Knapp Road, Cheltenham, Gloucestershire, GL50 3QH **Tel:** 01242-513659 **Fax:** 01242-237870 (Cheltenham 1)
St Thomas More, Lewis Road, Hester's Way, Cheltenham, Gloucestershire, GL51 0HZ **Tel:** 01242-513339 **Fax:** 01242-257402 (Cheltenham 3)
St Catharine's, Lower High Street, Chipping Campden, Gloucestershire, GL55 6DZ **Tel:** 01386-840677 (Chipping Campden)
St Mary's, Cheltenham Road East, Churchdown, Gloucestershire GL53 1HU **Tel:** 01452-714053 **Fax:** 01452-714207 (Churchdown)
St Peter's School, Horton Road, Gloucester GL1 3PY **Tel:** 01452-524792 (Gloucester)
St Joseph's, Nympsfield, Front Street, Glos GL10 3TY **Tel:** 01453-860311 (Nympsfield)
Rosary, Beeches Green, Stroud, Glos, GL5 4AB **Tel:** 01453-762774 (Stroud)
St Dominic, St Mary's Hill, Inchbrook, Stroud, Glos GL5 5HP **Tel:** 01453-832682 (Woodchester)

▲ Secondary
Christ College, Arle Road, Cheltenham, Gloucestershire, GL51 8LE **Tel:** 01242-702220 (Cheltenham)
St Peter's High School & XI Form Centre, Stroud Road, Gloucester, GL4 0DD **Tel:** 01452-520594 **Fax:** 01452-509209 (Gloucester)

■ CATHOLIC SCHOOLS - INDEPENDENT

■ THE GREATER BRISTOL AREA

▲ Secondary
St Ursula's High, Brecon Road, Westbury-

on-Trym, BS9 4DT **Tel:** 0117-962 2616 **Fax:** 0117-962 2616 (Bristol)

■ BATH

▲ Secondary

Prior Park College, Ralph Allen Drive, Combe Down, BA2 5AH **Tel:** 01225-835353 **Fax:** 01225-835753 (Bath)

■ SOMERSET

▲ Primary

All Hallows, Cranmore Hall, Somerset, Shepton Mallet, BA4 4SF **Tel:** 01749-880227 **Fax:** 01749-880709 (Shepton Mallet)

▲ Primary & Secondary

Downside School, Stratton on the Fosse, Radstock BA3 4RJ **Tel:** 01761-235100 **Fax:** 01761-235105 (Stratton-on-the-Fosse)

■ WILTSHIRE

▲ Primary

Prior Park Preparatory, Calcutt Street, Swindon SN6 6BB **Tel:** 01793-750275 **Fax:** 01793-750910 (Cricklade)

■ DORSET

▲ Primary & Secondary

St Mary's, Shaftesbury, Dorset, SP7 9LP **Tel:** 01747-854005 **Fax:** 01747-851557

■ GLOUCESTERSHIRE

▲ Primary & Secondary

St Anthony's Convent, 91 Belle Vue Road, Cinderford, Glos. GL14 2AA. **Tel:** 01594-823558, **Fax:** 01594-824799 (Cinderford)

▲ Secondary

St Edward's School, Cirencester Road, Charlton Kings, Cheltenham, GL52 8EY **Tel:** 01242-538600 **Fax:** 01242-538610 (Cheltenham)

St Edward's Junior School, London Road, Cheltenham GL52 6NR **Tel:** 01242-538900 **Fax:** 01242-538901

■ CATHOLIC SCHOOLS - SPECIAL

St Rose's Special School Stratford Lawn, Stroud, Glos. GL5 4AP **Tel:** 01453-763793 **Fax:** 01453 752617 (Stroud). School for physically handicapped boys and girls (Approved by the DES and DHSS)

St Edward's School, Melchett Court, Sherfield English, Romsey, Hants SO5 6ZR **Tel:** 01794-884271 **Fax:** 01794-884902 (Sherfield English) Residential special school for boys (Approved by the DES and DHSS)

DIOCESE OF EAST ANGLIA

Province of Westminster

Formed on March 13th, 1976 by the decree Quod Ecumenicum. Pope Paul VI formed the Diocese of East Anglia for the counties of Cambridge, Norfolk and Suffolk, from the Diocese of Northampton. In 1998 the Unitary Authority of Peterborough was established from part of North Cambridgeshire.

Patrons of the Diocese
Our Lady of Walsingham, 24 September;
St Felix ,8 March; St Edmund, 20 November

Bishop
Rt Rev Michael Evans MTh; R.I.P
born in South London, 10 Aug, 1951; ordained priest 22 June, 1975; ordained Bishop 19 March 2003.

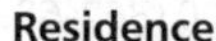

Residence:
The White House, 21 Upgate, Poringland, Norwich, Norfolk NR14 7SH.
Tel: 01508-492202, **Fax:** 01508-495358
E-mail: office@east-angliadiocese.org.uk

Bishop's Private Secretary:
Rev Mark Hackeson.

Rt Rev Michael Evans, Bishop of East Anglia

■ ADMINISTRATION

■ The Diocesan Curia
The White House, 21 Upgate, Poringland, Norwich NR14 7SH **Tel:** 01508-492202.
Fax: 01508-495358
Office hours 9am-5pm Monday-Friday.
E-mail: office@east-angliadiocese.org.uk

■ Vicar General
Rev Mgr Anthony Rogers. The Catholic Rectory, Hills Road, Cambridge CB2 1JR
Tel: 01223-350787
E-mail: tr@olem.org.uk

■ Chancellor
Rev Peter Brown. 16 Park Road, Wells-Next-The-Sea, Norfolk NR23 1DQ
E-mail: eachancellor@ntlworld.com

■ Vice-Chancellor
Rev Mark Hackeson. The White House, 21 Upgate, Poringland, Norwich, NR14 7SH
Tel: 01508-492202 **Fax:** 01508-495358
E-mail: office@east-angliadiocese.org.uk

■ FINANCE

Diocesan Finance Office: The White House, 21 Upgate, Poringland, Norwich, NR14 7SH
Tel: 01508-492540 **Fax:** 01508-495358
E-mail: finance@east-angliadiocese.org.uk

■ Vicar for Finance
Rev Mgr Philip Shryane.

■ Financial Administrator
Lt Col John Pitt. The White House, 21 Upgate, Poringland, Norwich NR14 7SH
Tel: 01508-492540

■ Registrar for Deceased Clergy
Rev Mark Hackeson. The White House, 21 Upgate, Poringland, Norwich NR14 7SH
Tel: 01508-492202 **Fax:** 01508-495358
E-mail: office@east-angliaciocese.org.uk

■ Diocesan Communications Officer
Awaiting Appointment

■ Bishop's Press Officer
Rev Mark Hackeson, The White House, 21 Upgate, Poringland, Norwich NR14 7SH
Tel: 01508-492202 **Fax:** 01508-495358
E-mail: office@east-angliadiocese.org.uk

■ DIOCESAN COMMISSIONS

■ Diocesan Schools Service Commission:
Chairman: **Deacon Rev Roger Sparks**.
Director: **Mrs Julie O'Connor**, The White House, 21 Upgate, Poringland, Norwich NR14 7SH **Tel:** 01508-495509 **Fax:** 01508-494833
E-mail: joschools@eastangliadiocese.org.uk

■ **Diocesan Commission for Evangelisation**
Chairman: **Deacon Rev Dr John Morrill,** Commission for Evangelisation, 47 Lisburn Road, Newmarket, Suffolk CB8 8HS
Tel: 01638-688688 (mornings)
E-mail: deacert_programme@yahoo.com

■ **Diocesan Youth Service**
Director: **Mr Hamish McQueen**, The White House, 21 Upgate, Poringland, Norwich NR14 7SH **Tel:** 01508-494833
Fax: 01508-495358 **Mbl:** 0781 2004934
Email: dys@east-angliadiocese.org.uk

■ **Vocations - Priestly Formation**
Vocations Director: **Rev David Bagstaff**. Catholic Presbytery, 4 Norwich Road, North Walsham, Norfolk NR28 9JA
Tel: 01692 403258
E-mail: david.bagstaff@boltblue.com

■ **Vocations - Permanent Diaconate**
Director: Awaiting Appointment. c/o The White House, 21 Upgate, Poringland, Norwich NR14 7SH
E-mail: martinhardy@yahoo.co.uk

■ **Diocesan Liturgical Commission**
Chairman: **Rev James Walsh**. Cathedral House, Unthank Road, Norwich NR2 2PA
Tel: 01603-624615 **Fax:** 01603-762512
E-mail: enq@stjohncathedral.co.uk

■ **Commission for Dialogue & Unity**
Chairman: **Rev Geoffrey Cook**. 20 Brierley Walk, Cambridge CB4 3NH
Tel: 01223-351650
E-mail: gmwc@mole.bio.cam.ac.uk
Secretary: **Mrs Elizabeth Barker.** St Andrew's, 6 Van Gogh Place, St Ives, Cambs PE17 6HE **Tel:** 01480-383608
E-mail: elizabeth.barker@ntlworld.com

■ **Commission for Marriage and Family Life**
Chairman: **Mrs Mary Mustoe-Arthur.**
Tel: 01263 514642

■ **Commission for Social Concern**
Chairman: **Mr Bernard Segrave-Daly,** Woodbine Cottage, Uggeshall, Beccles, Suffolk NR34 8BH **Tel:** 01502-578649
Fax: 01502-727201

■ **Child Protection Commission**
Chairman: **Mr Denis White,** The White House, 21 Upgate, Poringland, Norwich NR14 7SH
Diocesan Co-ordinator: **Mrs Barbara Warwick,** The White House, 21 Upgate, Poringland, Norwich NR14 7SH
Tel: 01362-699015

■ **Pastoral Service for Deaf and Hearing Impaired**
Rev Mgr Philip Shryane, 21 Westgate Street, Bury St. Edmunds Suffolk IP33 1QE
Tel: 01284-754358 **Fax:** 01284-700198

■ **Justice and Peace Commission**
Chairman: **Sr Pat Robb CJ,** 19 Rackham Close, Cambridge CB4 3HX
Tel: 01223-473806
E-mail: pr.cj@ntlworld.com

■ **Diocesan Matrimonial Tribunal**
Tribunal Office: The White House, 21 Upgate, Poringland, Norwich NR14 7SH
Tel: 01508-495168 **Fax:** 01508-495358
E-mail: tribunal@east-angliadiocese.org.uk
Judicial Vicar: **Rev Simon Blakesley**.
Tribunal Administrator: **Mrs Rosemarie Mingay**. Office Hours: 9am - 1pm Mon - Thurs. Address all correspondence to the Tribunal Administrator.

■ **EAST ANGLIA**
1. † Cathedral of St John the Baptist
(1722; 1894; 1910; cons 26 June 1957)
St Giles' Gate, Norwich.
Tel: 01603-624615 **Fax:** 01603-623684
E-mail: enq@stjohncathedral.co.uk
Website: www.stjohncathedral.co.uk
Rev James Walsh *(Cathedral Dean);*
Revv Anthony Seely, David Ward.
Also in residence: **Rev Laurie Locke.**
Cathedral House, Unthank Road, NR2 2PA
M: *Sat 1st M of Sun 6pm. Sun 9am, 11am. Hds 7.30am, 10am, 12.15pm, 7.30pm.*

■ **ACLE,** Norfolk
Served from Gt Yarmouth.
M: *Sun 9.15am (St Edmund's Anglican Church). Hds See Gt Yarmouth.*

■ **ALCONBURY,** Huntingdon, Cambs
USAF Chaplain. **Tel:** 01480-823343
M: *Sun 11.30am, 5.15pm.*

■ **ALDEBURGH,** Suffolk.
† Our Lady and St Peter (1906; 1924)
15 The Terrace, Aldeburgh, Suffolk IP15 5HJ
Tel: 01728-452782
E-mail: aldeburghrc@btinternet.com
Rev Christopher Smith.
M: *Sat 1st M of Sun 6pm. Sun 11am. Hds 10am.*

■ **ATTLEBOROUGH,** Norfolk
Served from Wymondham Parish.
M: *Sun 8.30am in the Methodist Church*

■ **AYLSHAM,** Norfolk
† **St John of the Cross** (1899; 1961)
White Hart Street. **Tel:** 01692 403258
Served from North Walsham.
M: *Sun 9am. Hds 9am.*

■ **BAR HILL,** Cambs
Served from Cambridge (1).
M: *Sat 1st M of Sun 6pm. (in Church Centre).*

■ **BECCLES,** Suffolk
† **St Benet Minster**
(1898; 1901; cons 10 July 1908).
St Mary's Road, Beccles NR34 9NQ
Tel: 01502-713179
Email: antonysutch@yahoo.co.uk
Dom Antony Sutch OSB. The Presbytery, 2 Grange Road, NR34 9NR. *Deacons:* **Revv Michael Wells, Anthony Felton.**
M: *Sun 10.30am, 6pm. Hds 9am, 7pm.*

■ **BLAKENEY,** Holt, Norfolk
(Chapel of Ease of Walsingham Parish).
† **St Peter** (1962)
Back Lane, Blakeney, Norfolk
NR25 7NP **Tel:** 01263 741519
Resident Priest: **Rev William Wells.**
M: *Sat 1st M of Sun 6pm. Sun 11am. Hds 9,30am*

■ **BRANDON,** Suffolk
St Thomas of Canterbury (1923; 1976, cons 1993)
Weeting Road. **Tel:** 01842-812200
E-mail: martinrichardfears@hotmail.com
Rev Martin Fears. 18 Stuart Close Brandon, IP27 0HP
M: *Sun 9am (Pol), 11am. Hds 10am.*

■ **BRANTHAM,** Suffolk
† **Holy Family** (1920)
Served from Ipswich (5).
M: *Sun 9am. Hds 7.30pm.*

■ **BUCKDEN,** Huntingdon, Cambs
St Hugh of Lincoln (1957)
The Towers, Buckden, Huntingdon, Cambs. PE19 9TA **Tel:** 01480-810344
E-mail: jim@claret.org
Website: www.sthughs.claret.org.uk
- ***Claretian Missionaries (CMF):*** **Rev James Kennedy** (*Parish Priest*), **Chris Newman** (*director of Claret Centre*). **Peter Waring** (*in residence*), **Br Billy Wilkes.**
  M: *Sat 1st M of Sun 6.30pm. Sun 9am, 10.30am. Hds 12noon, 8pm..*
- ***Claret Youth Centre,*** (Retreats etc.).
  Tel: 01480-810344

■ **BUNGAY,** Suffolk
† **St Edmund, King and Martyr**
(1657; 1823; 1891; cons 6 September 1910)
St Mary's Street, Bungay, Suffolk NR35 1AX
Tel: 01986-893355
E-mail: Charles177@btinternet.com
- ***Benedictines (OSB):*** **Rt Rev Dom Charles Fitzgerald-Lombard OSB.**
  M: *Sat 1st M of Sun 6.30pm. Sun 10.30am. Hds 9.15am.*

■ **BURNHAM MARKET,** Norfolk
St Henry Walpole (1959)
The Green, Burnham Market, Norfolk PE31 8HD.
Served from Walsingham (2).
M: *Sun 9.30am Hds 10am.*

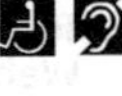

■ **BURY ST EDMUNDS,** Suffolk
† **St Edmund King & Martyr**
(1685; 1791; 1837)
21 Westgate Street, Bury St Edmunds, Suffolk IP33 1QG **Tel:** 01284-754358
Email: st.edmunds@btinternet.com
Website: stedmundkm.org.uk
Mgr Philip Shryane. *Deacon:* **Revv Chris Heath, Alan McMahon.**
M: *Sat 1st M of Sun 6.30pm. Sun 8.30am, 10am, 6pm. Hds 12noon, 7.30pm.*

■ **CAISTER-ON-SEA,** Norfolk
St Ignatius Loyola
Ormesby Road. Served from Yarmouth.
M: *Sat 1st M of Sun 6pm. Hds See Gt. Yarmouth.*

■ **CAMBOURNE,** Cambs
The Ark Ecumenical Church
Served from Cambridge 1.
M: *Sat 1st M of Sun 5pm Hds See Cambridge (1).*

■ **CAMBRIDGE**
1. † **Our Lady and the English Martyrs**
(1841; 1890; cons 8 Oct 1890)
The Catholic Rectory, Hills Road, Cambridge CB2 1JR
Tel: 01223-350787 **Fax:** 01223-224860
E-mail: office@olem.org.uk
Website: www.olem.org.uk
Mgr Anthony Rogers VG. Revv Richard Healey, Rafael Esteban M.Afr.
Also in residence: **Rev Christopher Back.** *Deacons:* **Revv Robert Joyce, Anthony Northrop, Anthony Sutton, Andrew Neate.**
M: *Sat 1st M of Sun 6pm. Sun 8am, 9.30am, 10.45am, 12.15pm (Polish), 5pm, 6.15pm (Latin). Hds Vigil 7.30pm, M 8am, 10am, 12.15pm, 7.30pm (Sung).*

St Edmund's College (1896; 1916)
Mount Pleasant, Cambridge, CB3 0BN
College in the University of Cambridge.
Visitor: **Archbishop of Westminster.**

DIOCESE OF EAST ANGLIA

Master: **Prof Paul Luzio, Tel:** 01223-336120 **Rev Dr Michael Robson (OFMConv) BA, PhD, FRHistS, Tel:** 01223-336123, **Email:** majpr100@cam.ac.uk (*Dean*) **Rev James McSweeney CP, Tel:** 01763-246110, **Rev Dr Geoffrey Cook, MSc, PhD,** (*life fellow*) **M:** *Sun 10.30am. Hds 6.30pm.*

Anglia Ruskin University
Our Lady & The English Martyrs, Hills Road, Cambridge CF2 1JR **Tel:** 01223-353730
Chaplain: **Ms Antoinette Askin**

- ***Dominicans (OP):*** Blackfriars, Buckingham Road, Cambridge CB3 0DD **Tel:** 01223 741251 **Fax:** 01223-741054 **Website:** www.chez.com/ blackfriarscambridge/
  Priory of St Michael. (First founded 1238; destroyed 1538; restored 1938). **Revv Martin Robindra Ganeri** *(Prior),* **Edmund Hill, John Orme Mills, Aidan Nichols, Richard Conrad, Paul White, John Patrick Kenrick** *(Novice-master),* **Thomas Crean, Dominic Ryan.**
  M: *Sun 8.15am. 11am, 6pm. Hds 7.30am.*
- ***Dominican Sisters (Stone):*** St Catherine's, 155 Huntingdon Road, Cambridge CB3 0DH **Tel:** 01223-353253
- ***Congregation of Jesus (CJ Community),*** 8 Brookside, Cambridge CB2 1JE **Tel:** 01223-353913
- ***Sisters of the Holy Family of Bordeaux,*** Hope House, Brooklands Avenue, Cambridge CB2 2BQ **Tel:** 01223-368792
- ***Margaret Beaufort Institute of Theology.*** 12 Grange Road, Cambridge CB3 9DU Roman Catholic member body of the Cambridge Theological Federation. *Principal:* **Dr Susan O'Brien.** **Tel:** 01223-741039 **Fax:** 01223-741054

2. † St Laurence (1938; 1958, cons 2006)
91 Milton Road, Cambridge CB4 1XB
Tel: 01223-704640
E-mail: pp@saintlaurence.org.uk
Rev David Paul. *Deacon:* **Rev Geoffrey Cook.**
M: *Sat 1st M of Sun 6pm. Sun 8am, 9.30am (in St Laurence's School, Arbury Rd), 11am. Hds 8.30am, 9.30am, 7.30pm.*

3. † St Vincent de Paul (1960)
Ditton Lane. Served from Cambridge (1).
M: *Sun 10.15am.*

4. Cambridge University Catholic Chaplaincy
Fisher House, Guildhall Street, Cambridge CB2 3NH **Tel:** 01223-742192
Fax: 01223-329180
Chaplains: **Rev Alban McCoy (OFMConv) Tel:** 01233 742190; **Sr Mirjam Magyar (OP) MPHil (Cantab) Tel:** 01223-742193
M: *Sun 9.30am (Latin), 11.15am (sung), 5.30pm.*

5 † St Philip Howard
33 Walpole Road, Cherry Hinton, Cambridge CB1 3TH **Tel:** 01223-211235
E-mail: sphcc@btinternet.com
Website: www.sphcc.btinternet.co.uk
Mgr Eugene Harkness, Tel: 01223-211235; **Rev Peter Edwards, Tel:** 01223-240757
M: Sat 1st M of Sun 5.30pm, *Sun 10am, 12noon. Hds 9.30am, 5.30pm.*

6. Our Lady Queen of Poland
231 Chesterton Road, Cambridge CB4 1AS
Tel/Fax: 01223-350787
Rev Piotr Kisiel.
M: Sun 7.30pm also see Cambridge (1).

■ CAVENDISH, Suffolk
Served from Clare.
M: *Sun11.45am (in URC Church).*

■ CHATTERIS, Cambs
Served from March.
M: *Sun 9am (at the Anglican Church of St Peter and St Paul, High St, Chatteris).*

■ CLARE, Suffolk
† Mother of Good Counsel
(Founded 1248; restored 1953)
Clare Priory, Clare, Sudbury, Suffolk CO10 8NX
Tel: 01787-277326 **Fax:** 01787-278688
Fr Benignus O'Rourke (OSA)
Email: clare.priory@virgin.net
Website: www.clarepriory.org.uk
House of Prayer and Reconciliation.

- ***Augustinians (OSA):*** **Revv David Middleton** (*Provincial*), **Bernard Rolls** (*Prior*). Non-residents: **Revv Gabriel McDonagh, Christopher Marsden, Derek McGuire.**
  M: *Weekdays 10am (Priory Oratory), Sun 8am, 10am (Priory Church). Hds (vigil 7.30pm), 10am.*

■ COLDHAM COTTAGE, Lawshall, near Bury St Edmunds.
† Our Lady Immaculate and St Joseph (1574; 1870), Bury Road.
Rev Gerard Quigley. Coldham Cottage, Bury Road, Lawshall, Suffolk IP29 4PL
Tel/Fax: 01284-830393
M: *Sat 1st M of Sun 5pm. Sun 10.30am. Hds Vigil 7pm.*

■ COSTESSEY, Norfolk
† Our Lady and St Walstan (1564; 1841)
Tel: 01603-742812
Presbytery, Town House Road, NR8 5AA
Deacon: **Rev William Dimelow.**
M: *Sat 1st M of Sun 6pm. Sun 10am. Hds 9.15am, 7.30pm.*

■ CROMER, Norfolk
† Our Lady of Refuge (1890; 1906)
147 Overstand Road, Cromer, Norfolk

NR27 OJH Served from Sheringham
M: Sat 1st M of Sun 6pm; Sun 9am. Hds 9am

■ **DEREHAM,** Norfolk
† Sacred Heart and St Margaret Mary (1912; 1925; 1951)
Commercial Road, East Dereham, Norfolk NR19 1AS **Tel/Fax:** 01362-694066
E-mail: derehamrc@tiscali.co.uk
Rev John Barnes. 35 London Road, NR19 1AS
M: *Sat 1st M of Sun 6pm. Sun 9am, 11am. Hds 10am, 7.30pm.*

■ **DERSINGHAM,** Norfolk
St Cecilia's (cons. 22nd March 1991)
Rev James Fyfe. 81, Mountbatten Road, Dersingham, King's Lynn, Norfolk PE31 6YE
Tel: 01485-453818
M: *Sun 9am. Hds (Vigil 7.30pm).*

■ **DISS,** Norfolk
† The Most Holy Trinity (1912; 1925; 1999)
Stanley Road, Diss, Norfolk.
Tel: 01379-642914
Rev Simon Blakesley, VJ,
Changes to parish planned, all correspondence to: The Diocesan Tribunal, The White House, 21 Upgate, Poringland, Norwich NR14 7SH
M: *Sun 9.30am, 11.30am, 6pm. Hds 10am, 8pm.*

■ **DOWNHAM MARKET,** Norfolk
St Dominic (1937; 1941, cons 28th Nov 2006)
Howdale Road, Downham Market, Norfolk.
Tel: 01366-382353
E-mail: office@saintdominics.org.uk
Website: www.saintdominics.org.uk
Rev Edmund Eggleston. The Presbytery, 17 Howdale Road PE38 9AB
M: *Sat 1st M of Sun 6pm. Sun 9.30am. Hds 9.30am, 7pm.*

■ **ELY,** Cambs
† St Etheldreda
(1890; 1903; Cons. 22nd May 1987)
19 Egremont Street, Ely, Cambs CB6 1AE
Tel: 01353-662759 **Fax:** 01353-662759
Email: anthony.shryane@tiscali.uk
Rev Anthony Shryane.
M: *Sat 1st M of Sun 6.30pm. Sun 9am, 11am. Hds 9.30am, eve 7.30pm*

■ **FAKENHAM,** Norfolk
† St Anthony of Padua (1905; 1909)
29 Wells Road, Fakenham, Norfolk NR21 9EG **Tel:** 01328-853481
E-mail: stanthonyschurch@tiscali.co.uk
Rev Anthony Webb *Deacon:* **Rev Paul Hirons**
M: *Sat 1st M of Sun 6pm. Sun 10.45am. Hds 10am, 7pm.*

■ **FELIXSTOWE,** Suffolk
1. † St Felix (1899; 1912; 1958)
8 Gainsborough Road, Felixstowe IP11 7HT
Tel: 01394-282561
E-mail: office@saintfelix.co.uk
Website: www.saintfelix.co.uk
Rev David Hennessy.
M: *Sat 1st M of Sun 6pm. Sun 9am. Hds 10am.*
• ***Religious of Jesus and Mary,*** 63 Orwell Road, Felixstowe IP11 7PP. St Felix Convent for retired Sisters.
Tel: 01394-282386

2. St Cecilia
Trimley St Mary, Suffolk.
M: *Sun 11.30am, Hds (vigil 7pm).*

■ **FRAMLINGHAM,** Suffolk
St Clare (1953; 2003)
Fore Street, Framlingham.
Served from Woodbridge.
Deacon: **Rev Michael Vipond**. 8 The Scrum, Danforth Drive, Framlingham, Suffolk, IP13 9HH **Tel:** 01728-724646
M: *Sun 9am. Hds 6.30pm.*

■ **GILLINGHAM,** Beccles, Suffolk
Our Lady of Perpetual Succour (1898)
Norwich Road. Served from Beccles.
M: *Sun 8am. Hds 8am.*

■ **GORLESTON,** Great Yarmouth, Norfolk
† St Peter (1889; 1939; cons 5 May 1964)
Lowestoft Road, Gorleston, Great Yarmouth, Norfolk **Tel:** 01493-662239
E-mail: rev_mccarthy@ntlworld.com
Rev Henry MacCarthy, 17a Sussex Road, Great Yarmouth NR31 6PF
M: *Sat 1st M of Sun 6.30pm. Sun 9.30am. Hds 9.30am, 7.30pm.*

■ **GREAT BARTON**
Montana, East Barton Road, Great Barton, Bury St Edmunds IP31 2RF
• ***Benedictine Sisters of Our Lady of Grace and Compassion.***
Superior: **Sr Thaya Moses**
Chaplain: **Rev Paul Mercer**
Tel: 01284-787321 **E-mail:** superior@montanagtbarton.wanadoo.co.uk
M: *Sun 10.30am. Hds 10.30am.*

■ **GREAT YARMOUTH**
† St Mary
(1827; 1850; cons 22 Aug 1950)
79 Regent Road, Yarmouth NR30 2AJ
Tel: 01493-842001 **Fax:** 01493-844968
E-mail: stmarysrcgy@btinternet.com
Rev Gordon Williams.
Deacon: **Rev Peter Glanville.**
M: *Sun 11am. Hds 10am, 7.30pm.*

■ **HADLEIGH,** Suffolk
† St Joseph (1966)

Presbytery, 12 Long Bessels, Hadleigh IP7 5DB **Tel:** 01473-823989
Fax: 01473-810095
Rev Michael Vulliamy.
Deacon: **Rev Andrew Morton**
M: *Sun 11am. Hds 7pm.*

■ **HALESWORTH,** Suffolk
St Edmund, King and Martyr (1950; 1957)
Church Farm Lane. Served from Southwold.
M: *Sun 9am. Hds 7pm.*

■ **HARLESTON,** Norfolk
St Thomas More
Jay's Green. Served from Bungay.
M: *Sun 9am. Hds 7.30pm.*

■ **HAVERHILL,** Suffolk
† **St Felix** (1938; 1964)
Princess Way, Haverhill, Suffolk.
Tel: 01440-702754/704923
E-mail: frteader@aol.com
Rev Michael Teader. 3 Wentworth Terrace, Haverhill CB9 9BP
M: *Sat 1st M of Sun 6.30pm. Sun 10am. Hds 9.30am, 7.30pm.*
- ***Sisters of Mercy,*** 5 Wratting Road, Haverhill. **Tel:** 01440-710711

■ **HOVETON,** Norfolk
See Wroxham.

■ **HUNSTANTON,** Norfolk
† **Our Lady of Perpetual Succour and St Edmund, King and Martyr**
(1903; 1905; 1958)
30 Sandringham Road, Hunstanton, Norfolk PE36 5DR **Tel:** 01485-532110
Served from Desingham
Rev James Fyfe.
M: *Sat 1st M of Sun 6pm (Pentecost - End Sept). Sun 11am. Hds 10am.*
- ***Daughters of Divine Charity,*** Provincialate, 27 Sandringham Road, PE36 5DP **Tel:** 01485-532837

■ **HUNTINGDON,** Cambs
† **St Michael Archangel** (1872; 1900, cons 2000)
82 Hartford Road, Huntingdon, Cambs PE29 1XG **Tel:** 01480-453257
E-mail: michaelarch@tesco.net
Rev Nicholas Kearney.
M: *Sun 9am, 11am. 4.30pm (Polish).*

■ **IPSWICH,** Suffolk
1. † **St Pancras** (1861; cons 12 October 1961)
1 Orwell Pl, Ipswich, Suffolk IP4 1BD
Tel: 01473-252596
E-mail: stpancras.parishpriest@btinternet.com
Website: www.stpancras.rcchurch.uk.net
Rev Francis A Leeder.
M: *Sat 1st M of Sun 6pm. Sun 9.30am, 11am.*

2. † **St Mary** *(1827; 1838; 1960)*
322 Woodbridge Road, Ipswich, Suffolk IP4 4BD **Tel:** 01473-728115
E-mail: secretary@st-mary.org.uk
Website: www.st-mary.org.uk
Mgr Peter Leeming.
Deacon: **Rev Christopher Brighten.**
M: *Sun 9am, 10.30am, 12noon (Pol), 6pm. Hds 9.15am. 12noon (Polish), 7.30pm.*
- ***Religious of Jesus and Mary,*** 320 Woodbridge Road, Ipswich, IP4 4BB **Tel:** 01473-713162 **Fax:** 01473-727297

3. † **St James** (1949; 1952, 1999)
482 Landseer Road, Ipswich IP3 9LU
Tel: 01470-726701 **Rev Adrian Gates.**
M: *Sat 1st M of Sun 6.30pm. Sun 9.30am. Hds 10am, 7.30pm.*

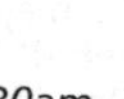

4. † **St Mary Magdalen** (1954; 1956)
468 Norwich Road, Ipswich IP1 6JS
Tel: 01473-741975
Revv Russell Frost, Martin Orme.
Deacon: **Rev Clive Brooks**
M: *Sun 8am, 10am, 6pm. Hds 9.30am (School or Church) 7.30pm.*

5. † **St Mark's** (1959)
180 Hawthorn Drive, Chantry Est., Ipswich IP2 0QQ **Tel:** 01473-684963
E-mail: stmarks@iaconnect.co.uk
Website: stmarksparish.org.uk
Rev Michael Ryan. St Mark's, 180 Hawthorn Drive, Ipswich, IP2 0QQ
M: *Sat 1st M of Sun 6.30pm. Sun 11am. Hds 8am (except during term time 9.15am St Mark's School), 7.30pm.*

■ **KESGRAVE,** Suffolk
† **Holy Family and St Michael** (1931)
Main Road, Kesgrave.
Served from Ipswich (2).
M: *Sat 1st M of Sun 6pm. Sun 9.15am. Hds Vigil 6pm.*

■ **KING'S LYNN,** Norfolk
1. † **Our Lady of the Annunciation**
(1778; 1897; cons 6 August 1947)
London Road, King's Lynn, Norfolk.
Tel: 01553-772220 **Fax:** 01553-772220
Revv Peter Rollings, David Baker.
Presbytery, North Everard Street, PE30 5HQ
Deacon: **Rev John Belfield.**
M: *Sat 1st M of Sun 6pm. Sun 8am, 11.15am. Hds 10.30am.*

2. Church of the Holy Family
(April 22nd 1985)
Field Lane, Gaywood.
Served from King's Lynn (1).
M: *Sun 9.45am, 6.30pm. Hds 9.15am, 7.30pm.*

■ **KIRTLING,** Newmarket
† Our Lady Immaculate and St Philip
(1872; 1877)
Newmarket Road, Kirtling CB8 9PA
Tel: 01638-730603
Served from Newmarket.
M: *Sun 8am (please phone to confirm).*

■ **LAKENHAM**
St Mark's C of E Church
Hall Road. See Norwich (1).
M: *Sun 5.30am*

■ **LAKENHEATH,** Suffolk
US Air Force Base Chapel.
Chaplain: **Tel:** 01638-523711
M: *Sat 1st M of Sun 5pm. Sun 9.30am, Hds As Announced).*

■ **LEISTON,** Suffolk
† All Saints **(1919; 1964)**
Seaward Avenue. Served from Aldeburgh.
M: *Sun 9.15am. Hds 7pm.*

■ **LODDON,** Norfolk
Served from Poringland.
M: *Sat 1st M of Sun 6pm at St. John's Methodist Church, George Lane, Loddon.*

■ **LOWESTOFT,** Suffolk
1. † Our Lady Star of the Sea
(1880; 1902; cons 22 October 1952)
Gordon Road, Lowestoft, Suffolk NR32 1NL
Tel: 01502-572453 **E-mail:**
brendanmoffat@yahoo.co.uk
Rev Brendan Moffatt.
M: *Sat 1st M of Sun 5pm. Sun 10.30am. Hds 10.30am, 7.30pm.*

2. St Nicholas (1996)
Morton Rd, Pakefield.
Served from Lowestoft (1).
M: *Sun 9am. Hds 9.15am.*

■ **LYNFORD,** Thetford, Norfolk.
† Our Lady of Consolation and St Stephen. (1878; cons 7 Oct 1884).
Served from Thetford.
M: *No regular services.*

■ **MARCH,** Cambs.
† Our Lady of Good Counsel and St Peter
(1911; 1953)
The Presbytery, 8 St John's Road, March, Cambs. PE15 8RJ **Tel:** 01354-653268

- ***Institute of Charity (IC):* Rev Eric Willett,** *Deacon:* **Rev Martin Wells.**
  M: *Sat 1st M of Sun 6pm. Sun 11am. Hds 10am, 7pm.*
- ***Franciscan Missionaries of Mary*,** Assisi Convent, 11 Princes Walk, March, P15 8AH **Tel:** 01354-652266

■ **MARHAM,** Norfolk
St George
RAF Station, King's Lynn, PE33 9NP
Chaplain: **Rev John Walsh**, Church Centre, RAF Marham, King's Lynn, Norfolk PE33 9NP **Tel:** 01760-337261 ext 7244
M: *No Sun Mass. Weekdays as announced.*

■ **MILDENHALL,** Suffolk
1. St John the Evangelist
St John's Close. Served from Brandon.
M: *Sun 9am. Hds 7.30pm.*

2. US Air Force Base Chapel
Tel: 01638-542822 **Fax:** 01638 545401
Chaplain: **Rev Patrick Beck**
M: *Sun 9.30pm, 5pm.*

■ **NAYLAND,** Suffolk
† The Sacred Heart (1902)
Tel: 01473-823989 Served from Hadleigh.
M: *Sun 9.15am. Hds 9.30am.*

■ **NEWMARKET,** Suffolk S
† Our Lady Immaculate and St Etheldreda
(1857; 1863; 1966)
14 Exeter Road, Newmarket, Suffolk CB8 8LT
Tel: 01638-662492 (office hours), 01638-730603 (outside office hours)
E-mail: stetheldreda@btinternet.com
Website: www.olise.co.uk
Rev Michael Griffin.
Deacon: **Rev John Morrill.**
M: *Sat 1st M of Sun 6.30pm. Sun 10.30am. Hds 9.30am, 7.30pm.*

- ***Sisters of St Louis,*** St Louis Convent, Fordham Road, CB8 7AA
  Tel: 01638-663616

■ **NORTH WALSHAM,** Norfolk
† The Sacred Heart (1925; 1935, 1990)
King's Arms Street, North Walsham, Norfolk. **Tel:** 01692-403258
E-mail: david.bagstaff@boltblue.com
Website:
www.sacredheartnorthwalsham.com
Rev David Bagstaff. 4 Norwich Road, NR28 9JP
M: *Sun 11am. Hds 10.30.*

■ **NORWICH,** Norfolk
1. See start of Parish list

2. Lakenham
Served from Cathedral of St John the Baptist (Norwich (1)
M: *Sun 5.30pm in St Marks Anglican Church.*

3. † Holy Apostles (1953, 1996)
41 Earlham West Centre, Norwich NR5 8AD **Tel:** 01603-624615
Rev Laurie Locke (*Priest-in-Charge*).
M: *Sun 9.30am. Hds 9.30pm.*

4. † St George
(1869; 1964; cons 24 May 1966)
223 Sprowston Road, Norwich NR3 4HZ
Tel: 01603-426971 **Fax:** 01603-418378
E-mail: stgeorgenorwich@fsmail.net
Rev Tony McSweeney; *Deacons:* **Ian Hatfield, Nicholas Greef, Rev Francis Hanley**.
M: *Sun 10.30am, eves 5.30pm. Hds eves 8pm.*
- ***Congregation of Jesus (CJ),*** Mary Ward House, 30 Constitution Hill, Norwich, NR3 4BU **Tel:** 01603-484901

5. St Boniface (1950, 2001)
Brabazon Road, Hellesdon.
Served from Norwich (4).
M: *Sun 8am. Hds (Vigil 7.30pm)*

6. Our Lady, Mother of God
St William's Way, Thorpe St Andrew.
Served from Norwich (4).
M: *Sat 1st M of Sun 5.30pm. Hds 10am.*

7. University of East Anglia Chaplaincy
The Chaplaincy, University Plain, NR4 7TJ
Tel: 01603-592168
E-mail: catholiccommunity@uea.ac.uk
Website:
www.uea.ac.uk/chaplaincy/catholic.htm
Awaiting Appointment at time of editing.
Mrs Marion Houssart, MA.
M: *Sun 6pm (term-time only).*

■ **OXBURGH,** King's Lynn, Norfolk
† The Immaculate Conception and St Margaret
(1835)
Served from Swaffham.
M: *12noon, quarterly 1st Sat of month, March, June, September, December.*

■ **PAPWORTH,** Cambs
Served from Huntingdon
M: *Sat 1st M of Sun 6pm at Papworth Methodist Church, Church Lane.*

■ **PETERBOROUGH,** Cambs
1. † St Peter and All Souls
(1847; 1896; cons 24 Oct 1961)
Park Road, Peterborough, Cambs.
Revv David Jennings, Nguyen Minh Hoan (John Minh), Joseph Cuanam CssR
The Presbytery, Geneva Street, PE1 2RS
Deacons: **Revv Claudio Chiappinelli, John Bedford. Tel:** 01733-562528
Fax: 01733-346933 **E-mail:** parishoffice@stpeterandallsouls.org.uk
Website: www.stpeterandallsouls.org.uk
M: *Sat 1st M of Sun 6pm. Sun 8.30am, 10.30am, 12.30pm (Pol), 6pm, 7.30pm (Polish) Hds 9.30am, 12.30pm, 7.30pm (Polish). 1st Sat M 7.15pm (Lithuanian) Monthly M in Portuguese - please call.*
- ***Daughters of Jesus,*** 93 Lincoln Road, Peterborough PE1 2SH **Tel:** 01733-315038
- ***Sisters of Mercy,*** 3 Park Crescent, Peterborough PE1 2TJ **Tel:** 01733-554424

2. † Sacred Heart & St Oswald
(1959, 1965, 2003)
933 Lincoln Road, Walton, Peterborough PE4 6AE **Tel:** 01733-322750
E-mail: parishpriest@sacredheartandstoswald.org
Website: www.sacredheartandstoswalds.org
Rev Bruce Burbidge.
M: *Sat 1st M of Sun 6pm, Sun 10am Hds (Vigil) 7.30pm, 7.30pm.*

3. Our Lady of Lourdes (1965), Welland Road, Dogsthorpe, Peterborough PE1 3SP
Tel: 01733-562528
Served from Peterborough (1).
M: *Sun 9.15am. Hds 6pm. 2nd Sat M 4.30pm (Syro-Malabar Rite).*

4. St Luke's
Benyon Grove, Orton Malborne, Peterborough PE2 0XS **Tel:** 01733-370877
Email: saintlukesparish@yahoo.co.uk
Website: www.saintlukesparish.org.uk
Rev John Warrington. St Luke's Presbytery, 14 Sellers Grange, Orton Goldhay, Peterborough PE2 5XX
M: *Sat 1st M of Sun 6pm. Sun 11am. Hds 10am, 7.30pm.*

5. Sacred Heart School
Bretton, Peterborough
M: *Sun 12noon. Hds 9.15am.*

6. St Anthony, Italian Mission
3 Fairfield Road, Fletton PE2 8BD
Tel: 01733-565527 Served from London.
- ***Scalabrini Fathers (SC):*** For Pastoral Matters see Peterborough (1). **M:** *Sat 1st M of Sun 7.30pm. Sun 10am.*
- ***Working Sisters of the Holy House of Nazareth,*** 275 Gladstone Street, Peterborough PE1 2BX **Tel:** 01733-561314

7. Polish Mission
Rev Andrzej Szczepaniak SChr. 189 Fletton Avenue, PE2 8DE
Tel: 01733-552726
Polish Club, 63 Church Street, Stanground
Tel: 01733-552726
M: *Sun 10.30am (Polish), See also Peterborough (1).*

8. St Olga, Ukrainian Mission (1964)
67 New Road, Woodston, PE2 9HD
Ukrainian Catholic Church of Byzantine Rite.
Tel: 01733-561400 **Mbl:** 07970 309262

■ **PORINGLAND,** Norwich
Our Lady of the Annunciation
(1950; 1966; 1973, cons 7th June 2003)
17 Upgate, Poringland, Norwich NR14 7SH
Tel: 01508-492202 (office hours)

Tel: 01508-493919 (other times)
Fax: 01508-495358
E-mail: mhackeson@eastangliadiocese.org.uk
Website:
ourladyoftheannunciation-poringland.org.uk
Rev Mark Hackeson.
M: *Sun 9am. Hds 8am. 7.30pm.*

■ **QUIDENHAM,** Norwich
Our Lady of Mount Carmel
(1949; cons 24 Sept 1957)
Convent Chapel. Carmelite Sisters:
Tel: 01953-887202 (Monastery).
Chaplain: **Rev Richard Zang CSC**.
Chaplain's Residence, Camelite Monastery, Quidenham NR16 2PH
Tel: 01953-887302
M: *Sun 10.30am. Hds 8am.*

■ **RAMSEY,** Cambs
† **The Sacred Heart of Jesus** (1863)
37 Newtown Road, Ramsey, PE26 1EQ
Tel: 01733-203411 Served from Whittlesey
M: *Sun 9am. Hds 7.30pm.*

■ **ST IVES,** Cambs
† **The Sacred Heart** (1902)
Park Road. **Tel:** 01480-462192
E-mail: office@sacredheart-stives.org
Website: www.sacredheart-stives.org
Rev Paul Maddison. 19 Needingworth Road, PE27 5JT
M: *Sat 1st M Sun 5pm. Sun 8am, 11am. Hds 10am, 8pm.*

■ **ST NEOTS,** Cambs
† **St Joseph** (1918; 1931)
39 East Street, St Neots, Cambs. PE19 1JU
Tel: 01480-472587
E-mail: frpatstneots@aol.com
Website: www.stjosephsparish.org.uk
Rev Patrick Cleary VF.
Mbl: 07989 353193
M: *Sun 8am, 11am, 5.30pm. Hds 10am, 8pm.*

■ **SAWSTON,** Cambs
† **Our Lady of Lourdes** (1958)
135 High Street, Sawston, Cambs. CB2 4HJ
Served from Cambridge (1).
Tel: 01223-350787
E-mail: sawston.olem@hotmail.co.uk
Website: ololsawston.com
Rev Rafael Esteban Mafr, *(Priest in Charge)*
M: *Sun 8.45am, 11.15am.*

■ **SAWTRY,** Cambs
Women's Institute Hall
Gidding Road, Sawtry PE28 5TS
Tel: 01773-370877
Served from St Luke's, Peterborough (4).
M: *Sun 9.15am.*

■ **SHERINGHAM,** Norfolk
† **St Joseph** (1908; cons 2 Aug 1936)
Cromer Road, Sheringham, Norfolk NR26 8RT
Tel: 01263-822036
Email: st_joseph@tiscali.co.uk
Website:
www.stjosephscatholicchurch.org.uk
Rev Denys Loyd, *Deacon:* **Rev Ron O'Toole Tel:** 01263-512065
M: *Sun 10.30am. Hds M 10.30am.*

■ **SOUTHWOLD,** Suffolk
† **The Sacred Heart**
(1897; 1916; cons 7 June 1956)
Wymering Road, Southwold, Suffolk.
Tel: 01502-723207 **Rev Roger Spencer VF,** Presbytery, The Common, Southwold IP18 6AH
M: *Sun 11am, Sats Easter - end Sept 1st M of Sun 6pm. Hds 10am.*

■ **STOKE-BY-NAYLAND,** Suffolk
† **Our Lady Immaculate and St Edmund, King and Martyr** (Pre-Reformation: 1823)
Withermarsh Green, CO6 4TA
M: *No regular Services*

■ **STOWMARKET,** Suffolk
† **Our Lady** (1878; 1884)
Stricklands Road, Stowmarket, Suffolk
Tel: 01449-612946 (*Parish Priest*)
Tel: 01449-771703 (*Parish Office*)
E-mail:
ourlady.stowmarket@btinternet.com
Website: www.ourladys-stowmarket.co.uk
Rev David Finegan. 29 Lockington Road IP14 1BQ
M: *Sun 8.30am, 10.15am. Hds 8am, 10am, 7.30pm.*

■ **SUDBURY,** Suffolk
† **Our Lady and St John the Evangelist**
(1876; 1893, cons 9th December 1993)
The Croft, Sudbury, Suffolk CO10 1HW
Tel: 01787-372703
E-mail: ourlady@stjohntheevengelist.fsnet.uk
E-mail: www.ourladyofsudbury.co.uk
Rev Peter Brett.
Deacon: **Rev Anthony Ranzetta**.
M: *Sat 1st M of Sun 5pm. Sun 9.30am. Hds 6.30am, 9.30am, 7.30pm.*

■ **SWAFFHAM,** Norfolk
† **Our Lady of Pity** (1911; 1920; 1960)
33 Station Street, Swaffham, Norfolk PE37 7HP
Tel: 01760-721418 **Fax:** 01760-720529
E-mail: fr.mcjohnstone@tesco.net
Website: www.catholicparish-swaffham.org.uk
Rev Michael Johnstone, 31 Station Street, PE37 7HP
M: *Sun 8.30am, 10.30am. Hds 9.30am, 7.30pm.*

• ***Daughters of Divine Charity,*** Sacred Heart Convent, Mangate Street. **Tel:** 01760-724577

■ **THETFORD,** Norfolk
† **St Mary** (1820; 1826)
73 Newtown, Thetford, Norfolk IP24 3AU
Tel: 01842-752266
E-mail: office@stmarysthetford.org.uk
Website: www.stmarysthetford.org.uk
Rev Mathew George.
M: *Sun 8am, 10am, 6.30pm. Hds 10am, 7.30pm.*

■ **TRIMLEY,** St Mary, Suffolk
See Felixstowe (1).

■ **WALSINGHAM,** Norfolk
1. **National Shrine of Our Lady**
(14th century; cons 8 Sept 1938)
Slipper Chapel, Houghton St Giles.
Revv Noel Wynn (*Director of the Shrine*), **Peter Murray (SM).** Pilgrim Bureau, Friday Market, NR22 6EG **Tel:** 01328-820217 **Fax:** 01328-821087 **E-mail:** rcnationalshrine@walsingham.org.uk
Website: www.walsingham.org.uk
Resident at Slipper Chapel Cottage: **Rev Paul Trinder.**
M: *Daily 12noon, Sun 12noon, (& 5pm Easter to end of Sept). (Also as arranged, for details please consult website).*

2. † **The Church of the Annunciation**
(1935; 1950; cons 26th March 2007)
Friday Market, Little Walsingham NR22 6BZ
Tel: 01328-821353
• ***Marist Fathers (SM):*** **Revv Michael Simison SM** (***Parish Priest***), **John McAllister.** *Deacon:* **Stephen Leeder.**
M: *Sun 10.30am. Hds 9.30am, 7pm.*
• ***Marist Sisters,*** 57 High Street, Little Walsingham NR22 6BZ
Tel: 01328-820246
• ***Little Sisters of Jesus,*** 7-8 Egmere Road, Little Walsingham, Norfolk NR22 6BT **Tel:** 01328-820422
M: *Daily 8am, Vespers 4.30pm, Sun 8am*
• ***Marist Fathers (1):*** Half Moon House, 12 Hindringham Road, Gt. Walsingham, Norfolk NR22 6DR **Tel:** 01328-820588
Revv Peter Murray (*Superior*), **Philip Graystone, Michael Simison** *(Parish Priest)*, **Noel Wynn** *(Shrine Director)*.

■ **WATTON,** Thetford, Norfolk
Methodist Church
High St, Watton. Served from Swaffham.
M: *Sun 1st M of Sun 5.30pm.*

■ **WELLS-NEXT-THE-SEA, Norfolk**
† **Our Lady Star of the Sea** (1928)
The Buttlands, Wells-next-the-Sea, Norfolk. NR23 1EY
• ***Marist Fathers:*** **Rev Michael Simison SM**
Served from Walsingham.
M: *Sat 1st M of Sun 6pm. Sun 9.15am. Hds 9.30am*

■ **WHITTLESEY,** Cambs
St Jude the Apostle (1963)
3 Station Road, Whittlesey, Cambs PE7 1SA
Tel: 01733-203411
• ***Institute of Charity (IC).***
Rev Anthony Slack
M: *Sun 10.30am. Hds (vigil 7.30pm), 10am.*

■ **WISBECH,** Cambs.

† **Our Lady and St Charles Borromeo**
(1840; 1854; 1962)
69 Queen's Road, Wisbech, Cambs PE13 2PH
Tel: 01945-583466
E-mail: doman@mac.com
• ***Institute of Charity (IC).*** **Rev John Doman.** *Deacon:* **Rev Michael Jordan.**
M: *Sat 1st M of Sun 6pm. Sun 10am. Hds 7pm.*

■ **WOODBRIDGE,** Suffolk
† **St Thomas of Canterbury**
(1851; 1930; cons June 1984)
21a St John's Street, Woodbridge, IP12 1ED
Tel: 01394-383551
E-mail: admin@stthomas-woodbridbe.co.uk
Rev Ivan Rudkin.
M: *Sat 1st M of Sun 6pm. Sun 11am. Hds (vigil 7.30pm).*

■ **WOOLPIT,** Suffolk
Served from Stowmarket. **Tel:** 01449-612946
M: *Sat 1st M of Sun 6pm (in St Mary's CofE church).*

■ **WROXHAM,** Norfolk
St Helen
Horning Road, Hoveton St John.
Served from North Walsham.
Tel: 01692-403258
M: *Sat 1st M of Sun 5.30pm. Hds 6pm.*

■ **WYMONDHAM,** Norfolk
† **Our Lady and St Thomas of Canterbury**
(1912; 1952)
1 Norwich Road, Wymondham, NR18 0QE
Tel: 01953-603104 **Rev Richard White;**
M: *Sat 1st M of Sun 6pm. Sun 10am. Hds 10am, 7pm.*

■ **ORDERS OR CONGREGATIONS ETC**

■ **Men**
Augustinians: Clare.
Benedictines (English Congregation): Beccles, Bungay.
Claretians: Buckden.
Dominicans: Cambridge (1, 4).
Institute of Charity: March, Whittlesey, Wisbech.
Marist Fathers: Walsingham (1, 2).

Scalabrini Fathers: Peterborough (5).

■ Women

Canonesses Regular of St Augustine (Congregation of Our Lady): Walsingham.
Carmelites: Quidenham, (2).
Congregation of Jesus: Norwich (4), Cambridge (1).
Divine Charity, Daughters of: Hunstanton, Swaffham.
Dominican Sisters (Stone): Cambridge.
Franciscan Missionaries of Mary: March.
Grace and Compassion, Benedictine Sisters of Our Lady of: Great Barton.
Holy Family of Bordeaux, Sisters of the: Cambridge (1).
Holy House of Nazareth, Sisters of the: Peterborough (6).
Jesus, Daughters of: Peterborough (1).
Jesus, Little Sisters of: Walsingham (2).
Jesus and Mary, Religious of: Felixstowe, Ipswich (2).
Louis, Sisters of St: Newmarket.
Marist Sisters: Walsingham (2).
Mercy, Sisters of Institute of Our Lady of Mercy: Haverhill, Peterborough (1).

■ ORGANISATIONS AND SOCIETIES

For Societies and Organisations without representation in the diocese please see the main Societies and Organisations section.

Catholic Agency for Overseas Development. (CAFOD) The CAFOD East Anglia Office is responsible for promotion and liaison with Parishes, Youth, Schools and Religious in the Diocese of East Anglia. CAFOD is the official overseas aid agency of the Catholic Church in England and Wales. One of the major relief and development agencies in the UK, helping people throughout the Third World to help themselves. If you, your parish or school would like to know how to help, please contact:
John Malley, Tel: 01603 624714
Email: jmalley@cafod.org.uk

Aid to the Church in Need. For further information please contact the Area Secretary **Michael Keaveney** at: Pilgrim's Rest, Station Road, Walsingham, Norfolk NR22 6EB
Tel: 01328 820781
The National UK Director **Neville Kyrke-Smith** can be contacted at: Aid to the Church in Need, 1 Times Square, Sutton, Surrey SM1 1LF
Tel: 0208 642 8668 **Fax:** 0208 861 6293
E-mail: acn@accnuk.org.

Benedictine Life North Norfolk Oblates of Douai Abbey meet at the "Mother Julian Chapter" every second Thursday at Our Lady & St Walstan, Costessey, Norwich at 2pm. For information contact: **Francis Buxton**
Tel: 01328 701793

Catenian Association The Catenian Association is an international brotherhood of Catholic business and professional men who meet socially once a month to offer mutual support and to encourage friendship among Catholic families.
Norwich and District Circle (86)
Secretary: **John McClean**, 5 Cranleigh Rise, Eaton, Norwich NR4 6PQ
Tel: 01603-456176
E-mail: jmclean44@aol.com
Cambridge Circle (52)
Secretary: **John Bishop**, 27 High Street, Needingworth, St Ives, Cambs PE27 4SA
Tel: 01480 300666
Ipswich Circle (123)
Membership officer: **Gerry Elliot**, 5, Milnrow, Pinewood, Ipswich, Suffolk, IP2 0SN **Tel:** 01473-684159
E-mail: gerrye@lineone.net
Peterborough Circle (184)
Secretary: **Gerry Prendergast**, 2, Gildale, Werrington, Peterborough PE4 6QY **Tel:** 01733-575018
West Norfolk Circle:
Secretary: **Joe Reynolds**, Postgate Cottage, Station Road, Walsingham, Norfolk NR22 6EB.
Tel: 01328 821677
E-mail: jreynolds_38@yahoo.co.uk

Catholic Clothing Guild
President: **Mrs. D. Stanley**, 20 Baxter Close, Fakenham, Norfolk NR21 8LE
Vice President: **Mrs. P Bright**, 2 Cage Lane, Stretham, Ely, Cambs CB6 3LB.
Secretary: **Mrs F Ripper**, 3 Spring Way, Sible Hedingham, Halstead, Essex CO9 3SB. **Tel:** 01787 460234.

Catholic Women's League
We are a national organisation of over 5,000 members, encouraging women to use their skills in charitable and educational work in the service of the Church.
Diocesan President: **Mrs Janet Scally**, 7 Banham Close, Cambridge CB4 1HX
Tel: 10223-365330
E-mail: jj.scally@ntlworld.com
Diocesan Secretary: **Mrs Margaret Cianni**, 45 Foxcovert Rd, Peterborough PE6 7HF **Tel:** 01733-252195
E-mail: cianni@tours.freeserve.co.uk
There are local groups in Buckden, Cromer, Cambridge, Fakenham, Ipswich, Lowestoft, Norwich, Peterborough, Southwold and Wymondham, as well as individual members throughout the Diocese.

Diocesan Service Team for Charismatic Renewal
The Diocesan Service team for Charismatic Renewal exists to co-ordinate and support prayer groups in the Diocese. They also organise days of renewal at intervals. It is part of a network which is led by the National Service Committee at Allen Hall. Information regarding Renewal prayer groups or other events may be obtained from the regional contact:
Mrs Pat Welling, 20 East Anglian Way, Gorleston, Norfolk NR31 6QY
Tel: 01493 287001
Website: www.ccr-eastanglia.org.uk

Friends of the Holy Father
Secretary: **Mrs. Mary Purves,** 2 Victoria Street, Southwold, Suffolk IP18 6HZ
Tel: 01502 723261

Friends of the Roman Catholic Cathedral of East Anglia
Aims, broadly, to raise funds in order to preserve the cathedral and so enhance its standing as the cathedral church of East Anglia thus furthering interest in its activities and history.
Subscriptions are £10 pa Ordinary member; £100 for Life membership.
Fuller information is available from the *Secretary:* **The Secretary**, Friends of the Cathedral, Cathedral House, Unthank Road, Norwich NR2 2PA
E-mail: friends@stjohncathedral.co.uk

Guild of Catholic Doctors
Hon Secretary (England & Wales):
Dr. C. Walker, 42, Charlock Road, Thetford, Norfolk. IP24 2TR

Guild of Our Lady of Ipswich
Secretary: **Miss Jean Johnson**, 14, Ashmere Grove, Ipswich, Suffolk.

Knights of St Columba
Provincial Grand Knight: **Nigel Gorham**, 65, Roman Way, Felixstowe, Suffolk. IP11 9NR **Tel:** 01394-284015
E-mail: ksceastanglia@aol.com
Provincial Secretary: **Joseph Rodriguez**, 29 Sutton Court, Werrington, Peterborough PE4 6GG
Tel: 01733-327633
E-mail: kscpeterborough@btinternet.com
The following Councils function in the Diocese:
Cambridge (287)
Joe Coyle, Beggars Roost, Station Approach, Newmarket, Suffolk CB8 9BB
Great Yarmouth (534)
Alan Skoyles, 34 Victoria Road, Gorleston, Great Yarmouth, Norfolk. NR31 6EF **Tel:** 01493-661863
Ipswich (206)
Vernon Watts, 23 Drovers Court, Trimley St. Mary, Suffolk IP11 OHJ
Tel: 01394-278739
King's Lynn (319)
Michel Charles Prentice, Doric Cottage, 1 Low Road, Wretton, King's Lynn, Norfolk. PE33 9QN
Tel: 01366-500210
E-mail: francispmartin@btinternet.com
Lowestoft (518)
Don Blakeman, 59 Breydon Way, Lowestoft, Suffolk NR33 9AS
Tel: 01502-531043
E-mail: jennifer_08_44@yahoo.co.uk
Norwich (286)
Brian Lafferty, 14, Kitchener Road, Great Yarmouth, Norfolk. NR30 4HU
Tel: 01493-855583
E-mail: brian.laff@btinternet.com
Peterborough (313)
Peter O'Connor, 41 Somersby Garth, Welland, Peterborough PE1 4AU
Tel: 07944 292814
E-mail: kscpeterborough@btinternet.com

Lay Fraternity of St Charles De Foucauld
An association whose members help each other to love God more and to know Him in the Gospels, to adore Him more in the Blessed Sacrament and to love all people without exception.
Contact: **Mr. Roger Borthwick**, 7 St. George's Drive, Toftwood, Dereham, Norfolk NR19 1LQ **Tel:** 01362-693886

Lay Dominican Fraternities
Members of two lay Domincian Fraternities in East Anglia, located at Cambridge and Walsingham, strive to live our baptismal vocation as lay members in the Order of Preachers. Inquirers are invited to contact:
Secretary: **Mrs. Mary Winning,** 3, Collingwood Road, Downham Market, Norfolk PE38 9SB **Tel:** 01366-383464
Mrs. Daphne Tinsley, 12 Knights Street, Walsingham, Norfolk NR22 6BT
Tel: 01328-820507

Marriage Care
Website: www.marriagecare.org.uk
Marriage Care provides a free confidential counselling service throughout England and Wales. For an appointment or further details contact your local centre at:
Newmarket & Cambridge
Tel: 01638-560580
Norwich & Peterborough
Tel: 0800-389-3801

National Board of Catholic Women
Diocesan Contact: **Mrs Ita Flack**, 87 Longsands Road, St. Neots, Cambs PE19 1TW **Tel:** 01480-473252

Natural Family Planning
A natural family planning service is available in Norfolk taught by a Catholic female teacher who is NANFPT qualified. For further information contact:
Mrs. Debbie Bool, 8 Angel Road, Norwich NR3 3HP **Tel:** 01603-219308,
Mrs. Elizabeth Hoey, 7 Bedford Row, Foul Anchor, Tydd, Wisbech, Norfolk PE13 5RF **Tel:** 01945-420618
E-mail: TonyHoey@aol.com

Our Lady's Catechists
Diocesan representative:
Angela Ashby, 45 Seaton Road, Felixtowe, Suffolk IP11 9BS
Tel: 01394-276907
E-mail: angela@ashbysoft.com

Secular Discalced Carmalite Order
Following in the footsteps of the great Carmelite reformers St. Teresa of Jesus and St. John of the Cross, generations of Carmelites have discovered in the Carmelite way of life a means of developing a close relationship with God and a wonderful foundation for serving God's people. We have a Rule of Life supported by a formation programme and meet monthly as a community.
Jane Nicholson, Magazine Farm, Sedgeford, Hunstanton, Norfolk PE36 5LW **Tel:** 01485-570082
E-mail: jnicholson@taracharity.org

Secular Franciscan Order
St. Francis of Assisi left us 'a dream to dream and a journey to challenge everyone'. All Franciscans are inspired by him to follow Christ. The secular Franciscan Order belongs to this family. Gathering in fraternities, they strive to grow in the love of God and in peace with each other. In this way, they aspire to be faithful disciples of Christ. Your diocesan contact for further information is: **Mr. Stuart Leishman SFO**, 113 Cumberland House, St. Mary's Court, Peterborough PE1 1UN
Tel: 01733-569427
E-mail: sleish218@btinternet.com

Society of St Gregory
The national Catholic society promoting understanding, active participation and good practice in the celebration of the Liturgy. The Society organises summer schools, lectures and study days for all who are engaged in Liturgy and music. The Society's quarterly journal, 'Music and Liturgy' (available by subscription), contains articles, news, reviews and a practical liturgy planner. The Society is a registered charity. *Diocesan Contact:* **Rosemary Muntus**, Old Mill House, The Causeway, Hitcham, Suffolk IP7 7NF
Website: www.ssg.org.uk

SPICMA (Special Projects in Christian Missionary Areas). *Director:* **P J Phelan**, 49 Gainsborough Street, Sudbury, Suffolk CO10 6UE
Tel: 01787-312093 **Fax:** 01787-312093

St Vincent De Paul Society
East Anglia central Council
Central Council Board:
President: **Mr Chris Burton**, 79 Tennison Road, Cambridge CB1 2DG
Tel: 01223-352327
Spiritual Director: **Rev Henry MacCarthy**, 17A, Sussex Road, Gorleston, Norfolk NR31 6PF
Treasurer: **Mr Bernard Shaw**, 98, Brampton Road, Cambridge CB1 3HL
Secretary: **Mr. Tim Bushell**, 10 Bernard Road, Gorleston, Norfolk NR31 6EG
Tel: 01493-657592
E-mail: t.bushell@ntlworld.com

Union of Catholic Mothers. *Diocesian President*: **Mrs Marguerite Wayling**, Red Lodge, 8 Windmill Lane, Old Costessey, Norwich, NR8 5ED
Tel: 01603-742161
Secretary: **Mrs Beryl Stock**, 49 Lovelace Road, Norwich, Norfolk NR4 7AE
Tel: 01603-501644
Spiritual Advisor: **Rev Henry MacCarthy,** 17A Sussex Rd, Gorleston, Norfolk NR31 6PF
There are foundations at: Aldeburgh & Leiston, Costessey, East Dereham, Haverhill, St James' Ipswich, St Neots, West Earlham & Norwich.

Walsingham Association.
The Association exists primarily to spread devotion to Our Lady of Walsingham and encourage pilgrimage to her Shrine. Branches throughout the country meet regularly with members seeking to deepen their devotion to Our Lady and to support prayerfully the growth and development of the shrine.
Bury St Edmunds: **Mrs M Kirby**, 158 Westley Rd, Bury St Edmunds, Suffolk IP33 3SE **Tel:** 01284-754962
Cambridge: **Miss M Plumb**. 44 Belvoir Road, Cambridge CB4 1JJ
Tel: 01223-356863
East Dereham: **Mrs T Sanderson,** 7 Homestead, Daffy Green, Shipdham, Dereham, Norfolk NR25 7QQ
Tel: 01362-822590
Gorleston: **Mrs M K Bean**, Brow Lodge, 12 Yallop Ave, Gorleston, Norfolk NR31 6HA **Tel:** 01493-665573
Ipswich: **Mrs E M Smith**. 25 Gressland Court, Mead Drive, Kesgrave, Ipswich,

Suffolk IP5 2HJ **Tel:** 01473-712691
Kings Lynn: Mr A D Athey, 2 Castleacre Close, South Wooton, Kings Lynn, Norfolk PE30 3TD **Tel:** 01553-671791
Norwich: **Mrs Barbara Scrutton**, 19, Albury Walk, EATON, Norwich NR4 6JE **Tel:** 01603-458851
Peterborough: **Mrs S Myszka**. 53 Tollgate, Bretton, Peterborough PE3 9XA **Tel:** 01733-263573
Swaffham: **Mrs N Doran**. Iona, Norwich Road, Swaffham, Norfolk PE37 8DE **Tel:** 01760-725220
National Secretary: **Miss Anne Milton**, Walsingham Association, Pilgrim Bureau, Friday Market, Walsingham, Norfolk NR22 6DB **Tel:** 01328-820217
Fax: 01328 821087
E-mail: walsinghamassociation@walsingham.org.uk
Website: www.walsingham.org.uk

■ HOSPITALS

To contact the Catholic Chaplain of a particular hospital we suggest you contact the hospital reception directly

■ CATHOLIC SCHOOLS - MAINTAINED

■ Peterborough

▲ Junior and Infants (4-11)

St Thomas More, Park Lane, Peterborough PE1 5JW *(Peterborough 3)*
Tel: 01733-566005 **Fax:** 01733 312350
Email: office@st-thomasmore.peterborough.sch.uk

Sacred Heart, Tollgate, Bretton, Peterborough PE3 6XD *(Peterborough 5)*
Tel/Fax: 01733-262449
Email: sacred@peterborough.gov.uk

▲ Secondary Comprehensive (11-18)

St John Fisher, Reeves Way, Peterborough PE1 5JN *(Peterborough 1)*
Tel: 01733-343646 **Fax:** 01733 347983
Email: enquiries@st-johnfisher.peterborough.sch.uk

■ CAMBRIDGESHIRE

▲ Junior and Infants (4-11)

St Alban's Primary School, Lensfield Road, Cambridge CB2 1LS *(Cambridge 1)*
Tel: 01223-712148 **Fax:** 01223 461286
E-mail: office@stalbans.cambs.sch.uk

St Laurence, Arbury Road, Cambs CB4 2JX *(Cambridge 2)* **Tel/Fax:** 01223-712227
E-mail: office@stlaurence.cambs.sch.uk

All Saints Inter-Church Primary School, County Road, March PE15 8ND *(March)*
Tel: 01354-658770 **Tel:** 01354-658870
E-mail: office@allsaints.cambs.sch.uk

▲ Secondary Comprehensive (11-18)

St Bede's Inter-Church, Birdwood Road, Cambridge CB1 3TD *(Cambridge 5)*
Tel: 01223-568816 **Fax:** 01223-576482
E-mail: office@stbedes.cambs.sch.uk

■ NORFOLK

▲ Junior and Infants (5-11)

St John's, Heigham Road, Norwich NR2 3AT *(Norwich 1)* **Tel:** 01603-626025
Fax: 01603-619454
E-mail: office@st-johns.norfolk.sch.uk

St Augustine's, West End, Costessey, Norwich NR8 5AH *(Costessey)*
Tel: 01603-743833 **E-mail:** office@st-augustines.norfolk.sch.uk

St Mary's Primary School, East Anglian Way, Church Road, Gorleston *(Gorleston)*
Tel: 01493-445117 **Fax:** 01493-445118
E-mail: office@st-marys-pri.norfolk.sch.uk

St Martha's, Field Lane, Gaywood, King's Lynn PE30 4AY *(King's Lynn)*
Tel: 01553-774829 **Fax:** 01553-763381
E-mail: office@st-marthas.norfolk.sch.uk

▲ Middle (8-12)

St Thomas More Junior, Jessop Road, Norwich NR2 3QB *(Norwich 4)*
Tel: 01603-441484 **Fax:** 01603-441483
E-mail: office@st-thomasmore.norfolk.sch.uk

▲ Secondary Comprehensive (11-18)

Notre Dame High, Surrey Street, Norwich NR1 3PB *(Great Yarmouth)*
Tel: 01603-611431 **Fax:** 01603-763381
E-mail: office@notredamehigh.norfolk.sch.uk

■ SUFFOLK

▲ First (5-9)

St Edmund's Primary School, Westgate Street, Bury St. Edmunds IP33 1QG *(Bury St. Edmunds)*
Tel: 01284-755141 **Fax:** 01284-762425
E-mail: office@st-edmunds.suffolk.sch.uk

St Felix, School Lane, Haverhill CB9 9DE *(Haverhill)* **Tel:** 01440-703775
Fax: 01440-710768 **E-mail:** ad.st.felix@talk21.com

St Joseph's, Beaconsfield Road, Sudbury CO10 6JP *(Sudbury)* **Tel:** 01787-373365
Fax: 01787-882195 **E-mail:** office@stjosephs.p@talk21.com

St Louis, Fordham Road, Newmarket CB8 7AA *(Newmarket)*
Tel: 01638-662719 **Fax:** 01638-660572
E-mail: ad.st.louis.p@talk21.com

▲ **Junior and Infant (5-11)**
St Benet's, Ringsfield Road, Beccles NR34 9PQ *(Beccles)* **Tel:** 01502-712012 **Fax:** 01502 710902 **E-mail:** ad.stbenets.p@talk21.com
St Edmund's, St. Mary Street, Bungay NR35 1AY *(Bungay)* **Tel:** 01986-892502 **Fax:** 01986-892502 **E-mail:** ad.stedmundsbungay.p@ talk21.com
St Mark's, Stonelodge Lane West, Ipswich IP2 9HN *(Ipswich 5)* **Tel:** 01473-601748 **Fax:** 01473-684588 **E-mail:** ad.stmarks.p@talk21.com
St Mary's, Woodbridge Road, Ipswich IP4 4BA *(Ipswich 2)* **Tel:** 01473-728372 **Fax:** 01473-716893 **E-mail:** ad.stmarys.p@talk21.com
St Pancras, Stratford Road, Ipswich IP1 6EF (Ipswich 4) **Tel:** 01473-742074 **Fax:** 01502-585807 **E-mail:** admin.kex @c2bn.net
St Mary's, Kirkley Cliff, Lowestoft NR33 0DG *(Lowestoft)* **Tel:** 01502-565384 **E-mail:** office.stmarylt@talk21.com

▲ **Middle (9-13)**
St Louis, St Andrew's Street South, Bury St. Edmunds IP33 3PH *(Bury St. Edmunds)* **Tel:** 01284-753495 **Fax:** 01284-729387 **E-mail:** ad.stlouismiddle.p@talk21.com

▲ **Secondary Comprehensive**
St Benedict's (13-18), Beeton's Way, Bury St Edmunds IP32 6HR (13-18) *(Bury St. Edmunds)* **Tel:** 01284-753512 **Fax:** 01284-701927 **E-mail:** office@ st-benedicts.suffolk.sch.uk
St Albans's (11-16), Digby Road, Ipswich IP4 3NJ *(Ipswich 2)* **Tel:** 01473-726178 **Fax:** 01473-718628 **E-mail:** office@stalbans.suffolk.sch.uk

■ **CATHOLIC SCHOOLS -INDEPENDENT**

■ **CAMBRIDGESHIRE**

▲ **Primary and Secondary**
St Mary's Junior Independent School. 2 Brookside, Cambridge CB2 1JE *(Cambridge 1)* **Tel:** 01223-353253 **Fax:** 01223-357451 **E-mail:**juniorschool@ stmaryscambridge.co.uk
St Mary's Senior, Bateman Street, Cambridge CB2 1LY *(Cambridge 1)* **Tel:** 01223-353253 **E-mail:** enquiries@ stmaryscambridge.co.uk

■ **NORFOLK**

▲ **Primary (2¾ - 12)**
Notre Dame Preparatory School, 147 Dereham Road, Norwich NR2 3TA *(Norwich 1)* **Tel:** 01603-625593 **Fax:** 01603-444139 **E-mail:** info@ notredameprepschool.co.uk

▲ **Primary and Secondary (4-17)**
Sacred Heart, 17 Mangate Street, Swaffham PE37 7WQ *(Swaffham)* **Tel:** 01760-721330/24577 **E-mail:** info@sacredheartschool.co.uk

■ **SUFFOLK**

▲ **Primary (3-11)**
Moreton Hall, Mount Road, Bury St Edmund's, Suffolk. IP32 7BJ **Tel:** 01284-753532 **Fax:** 01284 769197 **E-mail:** office@moretonhall.net

DIOCESE OF HALLAM

Province of Liverpool
Formed 30 May 1980 by the division of the dioceses of Leeds and Nottingham. Consisting of the County of South Yorkshire, parts of the High Peak and Chesterfield districts of Derbyshire and the district of Bassetlaw in Nottinghamshire.

Patroness of the Diocese:
Our Lady of Perpetual Succour, 27 June.

Bishop
Rt Rev John Rawsthorne;
born in Crosby 12th November, 1936.
Ordained 16th June, 1962.
Consecrated by Archbishop Worlock 16th December, 1981.
Installed as second Bishop of Hallam 3rd July, 1997.

Residence:
75 Norfolk Road, Sheffield S2 2SZ
Tel/Fax: 0114-278 7988
E-mail: bishopofhallam@btinternet.com

Secretary:
Mrs Sheila Parden.

Rt Rev John Rawsthorne, Bishop of Hallam

■ ADMINISTRATION

■ Vicar General:
Mgr William Kilgannon. St Wilfrid's Presbytery, St Ronan's Road, Sheffield S7 1DX
Tel: 0114-255 0827

■ Diocesan Contact Details:
Website: www.hallam-diocese.com
Fax: 0114-256 2673

■ Chancellor
Mgr David Kirkwood.

■ Vice-Chancellor
Rev John Metcalfe.

■ Director of Finance
Mr Ed Whittaker
Tel: 0114-256 6430
E-mail: finance@hallam-diocese.com

■ Diocesan Finance Board
Bishop John Rawsthorne, Mgr William Kilgannon, Mgr David Kirkwood, Revv Gerard Harney, John McNamee, Mr Peter McKinney, Mrs Sheilagh Preston.

■ Penitentiary
Rev Martin Clayton VF, St Mary's Presbytery, Mortomley Lane, High Green, Sheffield S35 3HS

■ Episcopal Vicar for Religious
Rev Leonard May. 13 Stag Lane, Rotherham S60 3NR **Tel:** 01709-305891

■ Associate Vicar for Religious
Sr Mary Bernadette Ward.

■ Diocesan Schools Commission
Chairman: **Rev John McNamee**; Co *Directors of Schools; Primary:* **Mr John Cape** *Secondary:* **Mr Jim Conway**. Hallam Diocesan Pastoral Centre, St Charles Street, Sheffield S9 3WU
Tel: 0114-256 6440 **Fax:** 0114-256 2673
Education Officer: **Mrs Clare Thorpe**.
E-mail: schools@hallam-diocese.com

■ Diocesan Property Department
Property Manager: **Mr Tom Garrud BSc, MRICS**; *Secretary:* **Mrs Kathleen Reeves**.
Tel: 0114-256 6420
E-mail: property@hallam-diocese.com

■ Diocesan Safeguarding Co-ordinator
Rev Peter D McGuire, Tel/Fax: 01246-432289 **E-mail:** pdmcg@btopenworld.com

■ Diocesan Archivist
Diocesan Archivist: **Mr Tony Haigh**, Hallam Pastoral Centre, St Charles Street, Sheffield S9 3WU **Tel:** 0114-256 6404 (voice mail only)
E-mail: archives@hallam-diocese.com

■ EDUCATION AND FORMATION

■ Director of Adult Education:
Miss Mary Dolan. **Tel:** 0114-256 6410
Fax: 0114-256 2673
Secretary: **Miss Pat Travis**.
E-mail: adulteducation@hallam-diocese.com

■ VOCATIONS PROMOTION TEAM

Director: **Rev Mark McManus**. The Presbytery, 2 Spencer Street, Chesterfield S40 4DS **Tel:** 01246-232 686 *Vocations Promoter:* **Rev Craig Fitzpatrick**, Cathedral House, Norfolk Street, Sheffield S1 2JB **Tel:** 0114 272 2522

■ Diocesan Youth Service

Director of Youth Services: **Mrs Judi Shimmell**, Hallam CYS, St Charles Street, Sheffield, S9 3WU
Tel: 0114-256 6464 **Fax** 0114-256 2673
E-mail: jshimmell@hallam-diocese.com
Web: www.hallam-diocese.com/youth

■ LITURGY AND ECUMENISM

■ Commission for Mission and Unity

Ecumenical Officer: **Rev Gerard Harney. Rt Rev John Rawsthorne, Rev Terence Tolan, Sr Patricia Montgomery SND, Ann Brown, Ann Callaghan, William Callaghan, Maureen Cunningham, Roy Dyson;** *Representative to the Council of Christians and Jews:* **Rev Peter Cullen**.

■ Council for Liturgy

Membership: **Rt Rev John Rawsthorne, Rev Peter McGuire, Dr Christine Dodd, Dr Frank Neal, Mr Philip Jakob, Mr Frank McDermott, Rev Augustine O'Reilly**
Contact: **Rev Peter McGuire**, 28 College Road, Spinkhill, Sheffield S21 3XB
Tel/Fax: 01246-432289
E-mail: pdmcg@btopenworld.com

■ CONSULTATIVE BODIES

■ Council of Priests

Chairman: **Mgr William Kilgannon VG**, *Secretary:* **Rev John Metcalfe**.

■ Hallam Religous Core Group

Episcopal Vicar: **Rev Leonard May**. *Treasurer:* **Sr Etheldreda Henbrough**. *Secretary:* **Sr Patricia Montgomery**

■ COLLEGE OF CONSULTORS

Mgr W Kilgannon VG, D Kirkwood JCD, VF Revv Peter Cullen, G Harney, P D McGuire, D Sexton, D Stoker, John McNamee.

■ DIOCESAN MATRIMONAL TRIBUNAL

Chancellor: **Mgr David Kirkwood**. *Vice-Chancellor:* **John Metcalfe**. *Judicial Vicar:* **Mgr David Kirkwood**. *Associate Judicial Vicar:* **Rev Mark McManus.** *Tribunal Administrator:* **Mrs Anne Ashton**. Hallam Pastoral Centre, St Charles Street, Attercliffe, Sheffield, S9 3WU
Tel: 0114-256 6450 **Fax:** 0114-256 2673
E-mail: tribunal@hallam-diocese.com

■ HISTORIC CHURCHES COMMITTEE

Chairman: **Rev John Metcalfe**; *Secretary:* **Mr Philip Jones**, Hallam Pastoral Centre, St Charles' Street, Sheffield S9 3WU
Tel: 0114-256 6405 (Voice Mail only) 0114-249 7674

■ SHEFFIELD

L A

1. The Cathedral Church Of St Marie (1816, 1850; cons 1889)
Norfolk Row, Sheffield. Cathedral House: Norfolk Street, Sheffield S1 2JB
Tel: 0114-272 2522 **Fax:** 0114 276 3861
E-mail: office@stmariecathedral.org
Web: www.stmariecathedral.org
Rev Christopher Posluszny (*Cathedral Dean*); **Rev Craig Fitzpatrick**.
M: *Sat 1st M of Sun 6.30pm. Sun 8.30am, 10.30am, 12.30pm (Pol), 6.30pm, Hds 8am, 11.30am, 12.45pm, 5.30pm.*

■ ARMTHORPE

A

Our Lady of Sorrows and St Francis (1935, 1959; cons 1984)
Mere Lane, Armthorpe, Doncaster DN3 2DB **Tel:** 01302-831395
E-mail: armthorpe@catholicweb.com
Website: www.armthorpe.catholicweb.com
Rev Darren Reid, *Deacon:* **Rev Peter Marshall.**
M: *Sun 10am. Hds, 9.30am.*

■ ASKERN

A

Blessed English Martyrs (1953)
2 Wood View, Moss Road, High Street, Askern, Doncaster DN6 0ND
Tel: 01302-700564
E-mail: office@askourlady.co.uk
Website: www.askourlady.co.uk
Served from Doncaster, Our Lady of Perpetual Help.
• ***Marist Sisters*** in residence.
M: *Sat 1st M of Sun 6pm. Hds as announced*

■ BAMFORD, Derbyshire

L 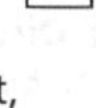

Our Lady of Sorrows
Ashopton Road, Bamford, Sheffield S33 0DB
Tel: 01433-651431
Rev W Anthony Burke.
M: *Sun 9am. Hds 7pm.*

DIOCESE OF HALLAM

■ **BARNSLEY**

1. Blessed Sacrament (1956)
Presbytery, Matlock Road, Athersley, Barnsley S71 3SG **Tel:** 01226-205447

- ***School Sisters of Notre Dame*** in residence. **Email:** ssnd27@yahoo.co.uk
  Served from Darton.
  M: *11am. Hds as announced.*

2. Holy Rood
The Rectory: George Street, Barnsley S70 1AX **Tel:** 01226-203730
E-mail: barnsley@catholicweb.com
Website: www.barnsley.catholicweb.com
Rev Terence Boyle (*Rector*).
M: *Sun 8am, 9.30am, 11.15am, (1st & 3rd Sun 4pm Pol). Hds 12.30pm, 7pm.*

- ***Sisters of Mercy,*** Princess Street, Barnsley S70 1PR
  Tel: 01226-282716

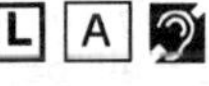

5. Our Lady and St James
(1964, 1976)
70 West Street, Worsbrough, Barnsley S70 5DJ **Tel:** 01226-284961
E-mail: worsbrough@catholicweb.com
Website: www.worsbrough.catholicweb.com
Rev Anthony Attree,
Deacon: **Rev Richard Booker**
M: *Sat 1st M of Sun 6pm. Sun 10am. Hds (vigil 7pm), 10am.*

■ **BRINSWORTH**

St Edward the Confessor (1967)
Closed 2005. Records held at St Bede's, Rotherham.

■ **CARCROFT**

St George and the English Martyrs
Skellow Road, Carcroft, Doncaster DN6.
Served from Woodlands.
M: *Sat 1st M of Sun 6pm. Hds as announced*

■ **CHESTERFIELD,** Derbyshire

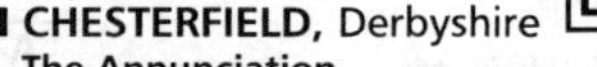

1. The Annunciation
2 Spencer Street, Chesterfield, Derbyshire S40 4SD **Tel:** 01246-232686
Fax: 01246-558034.
Website: www.annunciation.org
Rev Mark McManus.
M: *Sun 8am, 9.30am, 11am, 7pm, (9.30am Pol in convent). Hds As announced.*

- ***Daughters of Divine Charity,*** St Joseph's Convent, Newbold Road, Chesterfield **Tel:** 01246-230321

2. The Holy Family (1942; cons 1998)
Derby Road, Chesterfield, Derbyshire S40 2EP **Tel:** 01246-273753.
Rev Francis Paul Flynn.
M: *Sat 1st M of Sun 6.30am. Sun 10am. Hds 9am.*

3. St Hugh of Lincoln (1963)

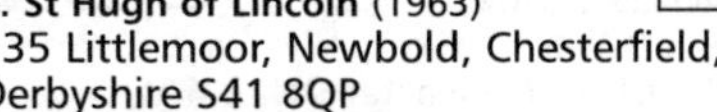

135 Littlemoor, Newbold, Chesterfield, Derbyshire S41 8QP
Tel: 01246-277635
Rev Terence Doherty VF.
M: *Sat 1st M of Sun 6pm. Sun 10.30am. Hds, as announced.*

■ **CLOWNE,** Derbyshire

The Sacred Heart (1968)
Cresswell Road, Clowne, Chesterfield, Derbyshire S43 4NB **Tel:** 01246-810812
E-mail: pdmcg@btopenworld.com
Rev Peter D McGuire.
M: *Sun 9.30am; Hds 7pm.*

■ **CUDWORTH**

St Mary Magdalene (1961)
Prospect Street, Cudworth, Barnsley S72 8JS **Tel:** 01226-710320
E-mail: stmarymagdalenes@btinternet.com
Rev Andrew Browne.
M: *Sun 10am. Hds as announced.*

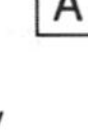

■ **DARTON**

St Teresa (1948)
19 Bloomfield Road, Darton, Barnsley S75 5AP **Tel:** 01226-382240
Website: www.darton.catholicweb.com
Rev Thomas Durkin.
M: *Sun 9.30am. Hds 9.30am.*

■ **DEARNE VALLEY>**

1. Corpus Christi
The Presbytery, 23 Park Street, Wombwell, Barnsley S73 OHQ **Tel:** 01226 752 372
Email: bjdaviesrev@hotmail.com
Website: www.corpuschristiparish.co.uk
Rev Brian Davies

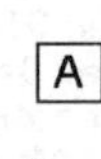
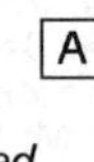

2. Sacred Heart
Lockwood Road, Goldthorpe
M: *Sun 9.30am. Hds as announced.*

3. Sacred Heart & St Helen
West Street, Hoyland
M: *Sun 11.15am. Hds as announced.*

4. St Michael & All Angels
Park Street, Wombwell
M: *Sat 11.15am. Hds as announced.*

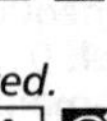

■ **DEEPCAR**

St Ann
Deepcar, Sheffield S30 5QE
Tel: 0114-288 2187
Fax: 0114-253 1553
Rev Gerard Harney.
M: *Sun 9.15am, 6.30pm. Hds 10am, 7.30pm.*

- ***Carmelites,*** Carmelite Monastery, Kirk Edge S6 6LJ

■ **DENABY MAIN**
St Alban (1895)
Denaby Main, Doncaster DN12 4AQ
Tel: 01709-862177
Rev John Cooke.
M: *Sat 1st M of Sun 6.30pm. Sun 10.30am. Hds 9.15am, 12noon, 7.30pm.*

■ **DINNINGTON**
St Joseph (1915)
1 Swinston Hill Road, Dinnington, Sheffield S31 7RX **Tel:** 01909-562664
Rev Andy Greydon.
Also in residence: **Rev Brian Green**
M: *Sun 9.30am. Hds 9.30am, 7.30pm.*

■ **DONCASTER**
1. Our Lady of Mount Carmel and St Mary Magdalene (1948; cons 1985)
134 Armthorpe Road, Wheatley Hills, Doncaster DN2 5JN **Tel:** 01302-323936
E-mail: parish@olmc.org.uk
Website: www.olmc.org.uk
Rev Craig Elliott.
Deacon: **Rev Lloyd Edwards**
M: *Sat 1st M of Sun 6.30pm. Sun 10am. Hds As announced.*

2. Our Lady of Perpetual Help (1946; cons 1977)
54 High Street, Bentley, Doncaster DN5 0AT **Tel:** 01302-874337
E-mail: office@askourlady.co.uk
Website: www.askourlady.co.uk
Rev James Kennedy.
M: *Sun 10am. Hds 9.30am.*

3. St Paul *(1959,1973)*
21 Goodison Boulevard, Cantley Estate, Cantley, Doncaster DN4 6BT
Tel: 01302-535800
Rev Bernard O'Brien;
Deacon: **Rev William Taylor.**
M: *Sat 1st M of Sun 6pm. Sun 9.30am. Hds As announced.*
• ***Sisters of Mercy,*** Convent of Mercy, Warning Tongue Lane, Cantley, Doncaster DN3 3QU **Tel:** 01302-538518

4. St Peter in Chains (cons 1988)
Chequer Road, Doncaster DN1 2AA
Tel: 01302-342068
E-mail: doncaster@catholicweb.com
Website: www.doncaster.catholicweb.com
Rev Augustine O'Reilly.
M: *Sun 10am, 1.15pm (Pol), 6pm. Hds 12.15pm, 7.30pm.*
• ***Marist Sisters,*** 33 Chequer Road, Doncaster DN1 2AA **Tel:** 01302-329783

5. Polish Chaplain
Polish Church of Our Lady, Windmill Lane, Mansfield NG 18 2AL **Rev Stefan Bober.**
M: *Sun 1.15pm at St Peter's. Hds 10am.*

6. Sacred Heart (1953, 1955)
44 Warmsworth Road, Balby, Doncaster DN4 0RR **Tel:** 01302-853937
Fax: 01302-768404
E-mail: oconnor@father.fslife.co.uk
Rev Patrick O'Connor.
M: *Sun 9am, 1st & 3rd Sun 3pm (Ukrainian Rite).*

■ **DRONFIELD,** Derbyshire
Holy Spirit (1961; cons 1992)
4 Stonelow Road, Dronfield, Derbyshire via Sheffield S18 6EP **Tel:** 01246-413094
Rev J Martin Williams.
M: *Sat 1st M of Sun 6pm. Sun 10am. Hds 9.30am, 7.30pm.*

■ **EDLINGTON**
St Mary (1933)
Bungalow Road, Edlington, Doncaster DN12 1BL **Tel:** 01302-853937
E-mail: oconnor@father.fslife.co.uk
Website: www.stmaryschurch.org.uk
Rev Patrick O'Connor.
M: *Sat 1st M of Sun 6.30pm. Sun 11am. Hds As announced.*

■ **FINNINGLEY**
Holy Family
Served from Rossington.
M: *Sat 1st M of Sun 6pm.*

■ **GOLDTHORPE**
Sacred Heart
Served from Dearne Valley

■ **GRIMETHORPE**
St Paul (1952)
70 Brierley Road, Grimethorpe, Barnsley S72 7EN **Tel:** 01226-711377
E-mail: grimethorpe2766@aol.com
• ***Marist Sisters in residence.***
M: *Sat 1st M of Sun 6pm. Hds As announced.*

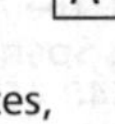

■ **HARWORTH,** Notts
St Patrick (1947)
16 Grosvenor Road, Harworth-Bircotes, Notts DN11 8EX **Tel:** 01302-742489
Rev T. Gerald White.
M: *Sun 10.30am. Hds 9.30am.*

■ **HATHERSAGE**
St Michael the Archangel
Main Road, Hathersage, Derbyshire, S32 1BB **Tel:** 01433-650352
Rev W Anthony Burke.
M: *Sun 10.30am. Hds 9am..*

■ **HIGH GREEN,** Sheffield
St Mary
Presbytery: Mortomley Lane, High Green, Sheffield S35 3HS **Tel:** 0114-284 8344
Rev Martin Clayton VF,

Deacon: **Rev Bill Burleigh.**
Email: martinclayton@wanadoo.co.uk
M: *Sat 1st M of Sun 6.30pm. Sun 9am, 11.20am. Hds 10am, 7.30pm.*

- ***Servite Sisters,*** The Convent, Pack Horse Lane, High Green, Sheffield S35 3HY **Tel:** 0114-2844 4956

■ HOYLAND
Sacred Heart and St Helen
Served from Dearne Valley

■ KIRK EDGE

- ***Carmelite Monastery of the Holy Spirit. (Carmelites)*** Kirk Edge Road, High Bradfield, Sheffield S6 6JL
M: *Sun 8am.*

■ KIRK SANDALL
St Thomas of Canterbury (1935; cons 1980)
(Chapel of Ease to Armthorpe).
M: *Sat 1st M of Sun 6pm. Hds As announced.*

■ KIVETON PARK
St Augustine of Canterbury
(Chapel of Ease to Dinnington)
M: *Sat 1st M of Sun 6.30pm.*

■ MALTBY
St Mary Magdalene (cons 1974)
Morrell Street, Maltby, Rotherham S66 7LH
Tel: 01709-812883
Rev Antony Hayne VF, Rev Geoffrey Hurst
Deacon: **Rev Geoffrey Spark.**
M: *Sat 1st M of Sun 6pm. Sun 10.30am. Hds 9am, 7.30pm.*

■ MEXBOROUGH
English Martyrs (1947)
Cemetery Road, Mexborough S64 9PM
Tel: 01709 862 177
E-mail: johncooke@hotmail.co.uk
Website: emchurch@netfirms.com
Rev John Cooke, St Alban's Presbytery, Denaby Main, Doncaster DN12 4AQ
M: *Sun 10am. Hds 7.30pm vigil.*

■ MOORENDS
St Joseph and St Nicholas
Bloomhill Road, Moorends, Doncaster DN8 4SS **Tel:** 01405-812248
Website: ourjo.org.uk
Rev Roy Pannell.
M: *Sun 11am, 6pm. Hds As announced.*

■ MOUNT ST MARY'S COLLEGE, Spinkhill, Derbyshire
See Spinkhill (2).

■ NEW WHITTINGTON, Chesterfield
St Patrick.
Chapel closed. Records kept at St Hugh's, Chesterfield.

■ OLDCOTES, Notts
St Helen
Main Street, Oldcotes, Worksop, Notts, S81 8JF **Tel:** 01909-730315
Rev T Gerald White.
Deacon: **Rev Peter Hunt**
M: *Sun 9am, 6pm. Hds 7pm.*

■ PENISTONE
St Mary
(Chapel of Ease to Deepcar).
M: *Sun 10.30am. Hds (vigil 7.30pm).*

■ RAWMARSH
St Joseph
Green Lane, Rawmarsh, Rotherham S62 6JY **Tel:** 01709-522537
Website: www.rawmarsh.catholicweb.com
Rev Kieran O'Connell.
M: *Sun 9.30am. Hds (vigil 7pm), 9am.*

■ RETFORD
St Joseph (cons 1970)
Babworth Road, Retford, Notts DN22 7BP
Tel: 01777-703373
Rev Bill Bergin
M: *Sat 1st M of Sun 6pm. Sun 10am. Hds 10am, 7.30pm.*

■ ROCHE ABBEY
Maltby, Roche Abbey
Served from Maltby.
M: *On Trinity Sunday 11am.*

■ ROSSINGTON
Christ the King (1931; cons 1979)
Skipwith Gardens, Rossington, Doncaster DN11 0TU
Tel: 01302-868231 **Fax:** 01302-867398,
E-mail: christtheking@doncaster.co.uk
Rev John McNamee
Deacon: **Rev Henry Meahan**
M: *Sun 11am, 6pm. Hds 9.15am, 7pm.*

■ ROTHERHAM
1. St Bede (cons 1992)
Station Road, Rotherham S60 1HF
Tel: 01709-562012
Mgr John Ryan.
E-mail: john@stbedeschurch.com
M: *Sun 9.30am, 6.15pm, (2nd & 4th Sun of month 5pm Pol). Hds 9.30am, 7.30pm.*

2. The Forty Martyrs (1971)
Kimberworth Park, Wingfield Road.
Tel: 01709-551271
Mgr John Ryan, St Bede's Presbytery, Station Road, Rotherham S60 1HF
Tel: 01709 562012
M: *Sun 11.30am. Hds (Vigil 7.30pm).*

3. The Immaculate Conception (St Mary's) (1946)

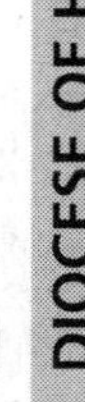

Herringthorpe. Herringthorpe Valley Road, Rotherham S65 3BA **Tel:** 01709-363753
Rev Desmond Sexton.
M: *Sat 1st M of Sun 6pm. Sun 10.30am. Hds 9.15am, 7pm.*

A

■ ROYSTON
Our Lady and St Joseph
Midland Road. Served from St Teresa's, Darton.
M: *Sun 6pm. Hds as announced.*

■ SHEFFIELD
1. (See start of Parish List)

A

2. St Anthony
Sandby Drive, Gleadless S8.
(Chapel of Ease to Sheffield (21), St Theresa).
M: *Sun 9.15am. Hds (vigil 7.30pm).*

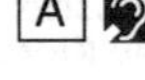

3. St Catherine of Alexandria
(cons 1951)
23 Melrose Road, Burngreave, Sheffield S3 9DN **Tel:** 0114-249 8225
Rev Albert Savaille.
E-mail: albertsavaille@hotmail.com
M: *Sat 1st M of Sun 5pm. Sun 9.15am.Hds As announced .*

A

4. St Charles Borromeo
Presbytery, St Charles' Street, Attercliffe, Sheffield S9 3WU **Tel:** 0114-244 1794
M: *Sun 9.15am. Hds as announced*

A

5. Claremont Hospital Chapel
Sandygate Road, Sheffield S10 5UB
Tel: 0114-263 0330.
M: *Wed 10am (except solemnities).*

6. English Martyrs
Baslow Road, Totley S17 4DR
(Chapel of Ease to Sheffield (14), Our Lady and St Thomas).
M: *Sat 1st M of Sun 6.30pm. Hds (vigil 7.30pm).*

7. St Francis of Assisi
(1968; cons 1989)
277 Sandygate Road, Sheffield, S10 5SD
Tel: 0114-263 0383
E-mail: stfrancis@frkevin.f9.co.uk
Website: www.stfrancisrc-sheffield.org.uk
Rev Kevin Thornton.
M: *Sat 1st M of Sun 6.15pm. Sun 9am, 11am. Hds 12noon, 7.30pm.*
- ***Sisters of Mercy,*** 'Highbury' 411 Sandygate Road, Sheffield S10 5UB **Tel:** Convent 0114-263 0842

A

8. Holy Family (1953)
Presbytery, 20 Eastern Drive, Arbourthorne, Sheffield S2 3WP **Tel:** 0114-239 9376
E-mail: EBKeating@aol.com
- ***Sisters of the Presentation (PBVM):***
M: *Sun 10.30am. Hds 11.30am.*

L A

10. St Joseph
St Joseph's Road, Handsworth, Sheffield S13 9AT **Tel:** 0114-269 3175
Mgr David Kirkwood JCD.
M: *Sat 1st M of Sun 6.30pm. Sun 10.30am. Hds 9.30am, 7.30pm.*

A

11. St Vincent
40 Pickmere Road, Crookes, Sheffield S10 1GV **Tel:** 0114-266 1988
E-mail: crookes@catholicweb.com
Website: www.crookes.catholicweb.com
Rev Patrick Walsh.
M: *Sat Vigil 6pm. Sun 10am, 6pm. Hds 9.30am, 7.30pm.*

L

12. St Michael's Cemetery Chapel
Rivelin Valley Road Served from St Vincent's.
M: *1st Mon and Bank Holidays 10.30am.*

A

13. Mother of God and St Wilfrid
St Wilfrid's Presbytery, St Ronan's Road, Sheffield S7 1DX **Tel:** 0114-255 0827
Mgr William Kilgannon.
M: *Sat 1st M of Sun 6.30pm. Sun 8.30am, 10am. Hds (vigil 7.30pm), 10am (12noon if on Thurs), 7.30pm.*
- ***Daughters of Charity (SVP),*** 43 St Ronans Road, Sheffield S7 1DX **Tel:** 0114-258 6456

L A

14. Our Lady of Beauchief and St Thomas of Canterbury (cons 1989)
Meadowhead, Sheffield S8 7UD
Tel: 0114-274 7257
Rev John Metcalfe.
M: *Sun 9.15am, 11.15am. Hds 10am, 7.30pm.*

A

15. Our Lady of Lourdes (1954)
30 Springwater Avenue, Hackenthorpe, Sheffield S12 4HU **Tel:** 0114-248 6102
Rev Paul O'Hara.
M: *Sat 1st M of Sun 6.30pm. Sun 11am. Hds 9.30am, 7.30pm.*

A

17. St Oswald (1948)
Southend Road, Wybourn, Sheffield S2 5FT
Tel: 0114-272 3881 **Fax:** 0114-272 5760
- ***Marist (SM):*** **Rev Thomas Goonan.**
M: *Sat 1st M of Sun 6pm. Sun 9.15am. Hds 9.15am, 7.30pm.*

A

18. St Patrick (1930)
Barnsley Road, Sheffield S5 0QF
Tel: 0114-245 6160
Rev Peter Hurley. *Deacon:* **Rev Andrew Crowley**
M: *Sat 1st M of Sun 6.30pm. Sun 10.30am. Hds 9.15am, 7pm.*
- ***Sisters of Mercy,*** 16 Swanbourne Road, Sheffield S5 7TL **Tel:** 0114-245 6472

19. Polish Catholic Centre
518-520 Ecclesall Road, Sheffield S11 8RL
Tel: 0114-266 5425
Rev Andrzej Pyster. 32 Bristol Road, Sheffield S11 8RL **Tel:** 0114-266 3952
M: *Sun At Centre 10.30am, at Cathedral 12.30pm. 1st & 3rd Sunday Holyrood, Barnsley 4pm; 2nd & 4th Sunday, St Bede, Rotherham 5pm. Hds 10.30am.*

20. The Sacred Heart
(1920; cons 1947)
479 Langsett Road, Hillsborough. Sheffield S6 2LN **Tel:** 0114-234 3580
E-mail: sacredheart479@btinternet.com
Rev Shaun Smith.
M: *Sat 1st M of Sun 6.30pm. Sun 10.30am. Hds (vigil 7.30pm). 9am.*

21. St Theresa (1934; cons 1967)
Prince of Wales Road, Manor.
Tel: 0114-239 7191
Rev Adrian Tomlinson, Presbytery, 311 Queen Mary Road, Sheffield S2 1EA
M: *Sat 1st M of Sun 5pm. Sun 11am. Hds 9.30am.*

22. St Thomas More (1948)
Wordsworth Avenue, Sheffield S5 9JE
Tel: 0114-232 1441
Rev Martin Trask, 477 Wordsworth Avenue, Sheffield S5 9JE
M: *Sat 1st M of Sun 5pm. Sun 9am. Hds 9.45am, 7.30pm.*

23. University of Sheffield Chaplaincy.
Padley House, Wellesley Road, Sheffield S10 2SY **Tel:** 0114-268 1197
Fax: 0114-266 0178
E-mail: p.j.cullen@sheffield.ac.uk
Website: www.shef.ac.uk/ccf
Chaplain: **Rev Peter Cullen**.
M: *Sun 11am (Chaplaincy), 6.30pm (in Earnshaw Hall, Heathcote Room). Hds 1.15pm, 5.15pm.*

24. Sheffield Hallam University Chaplaincy
18 Broomhall Road, Sheffield S10 2DR
Tel: 0114-266 4228
Chaplain: **Sr Anne Lee**
M: *As announced.*

26. St William of York
Ecclesall Road, Sheffield S11 8TL
Tel: 0114-266 2034
E-mail: www.stwilliams@care4free.net
Rev Terence Tolan.
M: *Sat 1st M of Sun 6.30pm. Sun 9.30am, 11.15am. Hds 10am, 7.30pm.*

■ SPINKHILL, Derbyshire

Immaculate Conception
28 College Road, Spinkhill, Sheffield S21 3YB **Tel/Fax:** 01246-432289
E-mail: pdmcg@btopenworld.com
Rev Peter McGuire.
M: *Sat 1st M of Sun 6pm. Sun 11am, 7pm. Hds (vigil 7pm), 9.30am.*

Mount St Mary's College
College Road, Spinkhill, Sheffield S21 3YL
Tel: 01246-434111 *(Community).*
Fax: 01246-435511
Tel: 01246-433388 **Fax:** 01246-435511
- ***Jesuits (SJ):*** **Revv Michael Beattie, Peter Knott**. 11 College Road, Spinkhill, Sheffield S31 9YB **Tel:** 01246-437127

Barlborough Hall School
Barlborough, Derbyshire S43 4TJ
- ***Society of Jesus.*** **Tel:** 01240-810511 **Fax:** 01246-570605

■ STAINFORTH

Our Lady of the Assumption
East Lane, Stainforth, Doncaster.
Tel: 01302-841278 (Church Office)
Tel: 01302-812248 (Presbytery)
Website: www.ourjo.org.uk
Rev Roy Pannell, The Presbytery, Bloomhill Road, Moorends, Doncaster DN8 4SS
M: *Sat 1st M of Sun 6pm. Hds As announced.*

■ STAVELEY, Derbyshire

St Joseph (1983)
The Mount, Chesterfield Road, Staveley, Chesterfield, Derbyshire S43 3QF
Tel: 01246-277635
Rev Terence Doherty, St Hugh's Presbytery, Littlemoor, Newbold, Chesterfield S41 8QP **Tel:** 01246-277635
E-mail: terrydoherty@littlemoor.fslife.co.uk
M: *Sun 9am. Hds As announced.*

■ SWALLOWNEST, Rotherham

Mass Centre, Christ Church Anglican Church Swallownest **Tel:** 0114 269 3175
Served from St Joseph, Handsworth
M: *Sun 9am. Hds (vigil 7pm).*

■ THRYBERGH

St Gerard (1911; cons 1983)
Doncaster Road, Thrybergh, Rotherham S65 4AD **Tel:** 01709-850381 (Parish Office).
Rev Desmond Sexton, The Presbytery, Immaculate Conseption, Herringthorpe, Valley Road, Rotherham S65 3BA
Tel: 01709 363 573
M: *Sun 10.45am.*

■ TICKHILL

The Parish Rooms (Mass Centre)
Northgate. Served from Maltby.
M: *As announced.*

■ WATH-UPON-DEARNE

St Joseph (cons 1982)
Doncaster Road, Wath-upon-Dearne,

Rotherham S63 7AA **Tel:** 01709 522 537
Rev Kieran O'Connell, The Presbytery, 131 Green Lane, Rawmarsh, Rotherham S62 6JY
M: *Sun 8.30am, 11am. Hds 8.30am, (9.30am in School), 7pm. (In school holidays 9am, 7pm)*

A

■ WICKERSLEY
Blessed Trinity (1960; cons 1990)
Northfield Lane, Wickersley, Rotherham S66 0HF **Tel:** 01709-812883
E-mail: hayne@priory9.fsnet.co.uk
Rev Antony Hayne, The Presbytery, Morrell Street, Maltby, Rotherham S66 7LH
M: *Sun 9.30am. Hds (vigil 7pm).*

A

■ WOMBWELL
St Michael and all the Angels (cons 1968)
23 Park Street, Wombwell, Barnsley S73 0HQ **Tel:** 01226-752372
E-mail: bjdaviesrev@hotmail.com
Website: www.sacredheartandstmichaels.co.uk
Rev Brian Davies VF.
M: *M Sat 1st M of Sun; 5.30pm Hds. As announced*

A

■ WOODLANDS
St Joseph and St Teresa (1927)
Welfare Road, Woodlands, Doncaster DN6 7QG **Tel:** 01302-330205
Rev D Norman.
M: *Sun 9.am. Hds 9.15am.*

A

■ WORKSOP, Notts
St Mary and St Joseph the Worker
Rev Peter Kirkham, The Presbytery, 101 Wingfield Ave, Worksop S81 OSF
Tel: 01909 473 373
1. St Joseph the Worker
Wingfield Ave, Worksop S81 OSF
M: *M Sat 1st M of Sun 6pm, Sun 4pm (Polish). Hds 10am.*
2. St Mary
Park Street, Worksop
M: *Sun 11am. Hds (vigil 7pm).*
• ***Sisters of the Sacred Hearts of Joseph and Mary***, St Mary's Convent, Park Street, Worksop S80 1HH
Tel: 01709 476 045

■ ORDERS AND CONGREGATIONS ETC

■ Men
Jesuits: Barlborough, Spinkhill.
Marists: Sheffield (17).

■ Women
Carmelites: Kirk Edge.
Charity, Daughters of (SVP): Sheffield (13).
Divine Charity, Daughters of: Chesterfield (1).
La Sainte Union Sisters: Sheffield (3).
Marist Sisters: Askern, Doncaster (4), Goldthorpe, Grimethorpe.
Mercy, Sisters of Institute of Our Lady of Mercy: Doncaster (3), Sheffield (7, 11, 18).
Sisters of Charity of St. Paul the Apostle, Sheffield (20 14).
Mercy Sisters (Union), Barnsley (2).
Notre Dame, School Sisters: Barnsley (1).
Presentation Sisters: Sheffield (8), Bamford.
Servite Sisters: Sheffield, High Green.
Sisters of the Heart of Jesus and Mary: Sheffield (4), Worksop.

■ SOCIETIES AND ORGANISATIONS
For Societies and Organisations without representation in the diocese please see the main Societies and Organisations section.

Aid to the Church in Need. *Northern Appeals Manager:* **Dr Heather Ward,** 11 Deepdale Road, Wollaton, Nottingham NG8 2FU
Tel: 0115-928 3603

Ascent Movement
Contacts: **Mrs Veronica Sowerby Tel:** 0114-230 6797, **Sr Clare Smith Tel:** 0114-255 1540

Association of the Ladies of Charity of St Vincent de Paul. *President:* **Mrs Brenda Murphy, Tel:** 0114-268 6271; *Treasurer:* **Mrs Briege Russell;** *Secretary:* **Miss Joan Gillham.**

Association of Interchurch Families. *Contact:* **Andrew Crowley,** 219 Abbeyfield Road, Sheffield S4 7AW

Carmel Care Centre*:*
172 Dykes Hall Road, Sheffield S6 4GS
Tel: 0114-233 5727

CAFOD. (Catholic Fund for Overseas Development) *Diocesan representative:* Awaiting Appointment. St William's Presbytery Office, Ecclesall Road, Sheffield S11 8TL
Tel/Fax: 0114-268 7817

The Catenian Association *Provincial President:* **Mr Colin Croxall, Tel:** 01924 366540; *Vice-President:* **Mr David Brinkley;** *Provincial Secretary:* **Malcolm Walker,** The Cottage, Tow Lane, Fenton, Gratham NG32 2LE

Catholic Deaf Association *Secretary*: **Mrs Angela Rowan**. 91 Hallam Grange Rise, Sheffield S10 4BE **Tel:** 0114-230 4061 *Chaplains*: **Rev Dan Harrison** at Boston Spa & **Rev Peter Hurley** at St Patrick, Sheffield.

Catholic Men's Society *President*: **John Dempsey**. *Secretary*: Awaiting appointment. *Treasurer*: Awaiting appointment.

Charistmatic Renewal. Contact: **Yvonne and Tony Lazenby, Tel:** 01302-742368; *Spiritual Director:* **Rev Antony Hayne.**

Cor Unum. *Diocesan Representative:* **Rev Michael Killeen.**

Cursillos in Christianity. Contact: **Mrs Elizabeth Corcoran**, 85 Grove Road, Sheffield S7 2GY **Tel:** 0114-236 9675

De La Salle Association Club. Address: Beauchief Hall Estate, Beauchief Drive, Sheffield S8 7BA. *Chair:* **Mr Bernard Kelly**; *Membership Secretary:* **Mr Terence Green Tel:** 0114 249 9588

Diocese of Hallam University Chaplaincy Association. *President:* **Rt Rev John Rawsthorne**. *Vice-President:* **Prof M F Lynch**. Diocesan Officers: *Chairman:* **Mr J J McNally**; *Secretary:* **John Booth**, 34 Hallamshire Rd, Sheffield S10 4FP **Tel:** 0114 263 0913 *Treasurer:* **Mr T A Conneely**.

Diocesan Records Office. Sheffield Archives, 52 Shoreham Street, Sheffield S1 4SP **Tel:** 0114-255 1121 **E-mail:** archives@sheffield.go.uk

Ecumenical Society of the Blessed Virgin Mary. *Secretary:* **Mr Dennis Gerard, Tel:** 0114-236 0244

English Catholic History Association (formerly English Catholic History Group). *Secretary:* **Miss Toni Eccles**, 6 Townside, Church Street, Tisbury, Salisbury, Wiltshire. **Tel:** 01747-871971; *Regional Co-ordinator:* **Mrs Barbara Smith**, Apartment 6, Ladybower Lodge, Asopton Road, Bamford, Hope Valley S33 0BY **Tel:** 01433-651048

Guardians of the Shrine of Our Lady of Doncaster. Contact: **Mr Walter Whitman Tel:** 01709-894 851

Guild of Catholic Doctors. *Master:* **Mr Andrew Raftery**, Carnbrea, 280 Ecclesall Road South, Sheffield S11 9PS **Tel:** 0114-235 2666; *Secretary:* **Dr Stephen Brennan**, Winhill House, Aston Lane, Thornhill, Bamford S33 0BR **Tel:** 01433-651423

HCPT (Handicapped Children's Pilgrimage Trust). *Sheffield Leader:* **Miss Karina McGann**, 145 Narborough Road, South Leicester LE43 2LH **Tel:** 0116-291 9615; *Doncaster Leader:* **Mr Philip Hall**, 7 Willow Lane, Rossington, Doncaster DN11 0EQ

Knights of St Columba *District Deputy Hallam:* **Terence A Conneely**. 43 Durlstone Drive, Sheffield S12 2TT **Tel:** 0114-239 0947

Marriage Care Hallam *Appointments:* **Tel:** 0800 839 3801 *Councelling and Correspondence Address:* 524 Queen's Road, Sheffield S2 4TD. *National Helpline:* **Tel:** 0845 660 6000

Society of St Vincent de Paul. *President:* **Mr Kevin McCready**. *Secretary:* **Paddy McGloin**, 941, Abbedale Road, Sheffield S7 2QD **Tel:** 0114-236 0244

Survive-Miva. Head Office: Survive-Miva, 5 Park Vale Road, Aintree, Liverpool L9 2DG **Tel:** 0151-523 3878 **Fax:** 0151-523 3841 **E-mail:** info@survive-miva.org

The Walsingham Association. Sheffield Branch. *Chairman:* **Mrs Peggy McGloin, Tel:** 0114-236 0244; *Secretary:* **Miss Joan Duggan, Tel:** 0114-264 5694; *Treasurer:* **Mrs Mary Steel, Tel:** 0114-275 9440

Union of Catholic Mothers. *Diocesan President*: **Mrs Angela Mellors Tel:** 01909-720707; *Secretary:* **Mrs Delia Fox, Tel:** 01709 373493; *Treasurer:* **Mrs Rosemary Spence, Tel:** 01246 822895 *Spiritual Adviser:* **Rev Andrew Browne.**

■ HOSPITALS

To contact the Catholic Chaplain of a particular hospital we suggest you contact the hospital reception directly.

■ CATHOLIC SCHOOLS - MAINTAINED

■ BARNSLEY M.B.

▲ Junior and Infant

St Dominic, Carlton Road, Barnsley S71 2BE **Tel:** 01226-282085 **E-mail:** f.nelis@barnsley.org

St Helen, West Street, Hoyland S74 9DL **Tel:** 01226-742172 **E-mail:** head@st.helens.barnsley.sch.uk

Holy Rood Shaw Street, Barnsley S70 6JL **Tel:** 01226-281219 **E-mail:** jexley@catholicweb.com

St Michael, Stonyford Road, Wombwell, Barnsley S73 8AF **Tel:** 01226-752120 **E-mail:** jill.marieshaw@barnsley.org Catchment area: Brampton, Darfield, Great Houghton, Little Houghton, Middlecliffe, Wombwell. *(Wombwell)*

Sacred Heart, Lockwood Road, Goldthorpe, Rotherham S63 9JY **Tel:** 01709-892385 **E-mail:** sacredheart.primary@barnsley.org

▲ Secondary

St Michael's Catholic and Church of England High School, Carlton Road, Barnsley S71 2BT **Tel:** 01226-282845 **E-mail:** SMH@barnsley.org

■ DERBYSHIRE C.C.

▲ Junior and Infant

Immaculate Conception, College Road, Spinkhill, Sheffield S31 9YB **Tel:** 01246-432916 **E-mail:** stephenowen@ immaculate.derbyshire.sch.uk

Catchment area: Barlborough, Clowne, Creswell, Eckington, Halfway, Killamarsh, Marsh Lane, Mosborough, Renishaw, Spinkhill, Whitwell.

St Joseph, Calver Crescent, Staveley. S43 3LY **Tel:** 01246-472798 **E-mail:** janeeburke@ st-josephsrc.sch.derbyshire.com *Catchment area:* Barrow Hill, Brimington, Duckmanton, Hollingwood, Inkersall, Mastin Moor, New Whittington, Old Whittington, Poolsbrook, Staveley, Woodthorpe.*)*

St Mary, Cross Street, Chesterfield, Derbyshire S40 4ST **Tel:** 01246-232170 **E-mail:** info@stmarys.derbyshire.sch.uk

▲ **Secondary**

St Mary's Catholic High School, Newbold Road, Upper Newbold, Chesterfield, Derbyshire S41 8AG **Tel:** 01246-201191 **E-mail:** tmoore@stmaryschesterfield.org.uk

■ **DONCASTER M.B.**

▲ **Junior and Infant**

St Alban, Wadworth Street, Denaby Main, Doncaster DN12 4AQ **Tel:** 01709-862298 **E-mail:** admin@stalbans.doncaster.sch.uk *Catchment area:* Conisborough, Denaby Main, Mexborough, Old Denaby. Denaby Main.

Holy Family, Kirton Lane, Stainforth, Doncaster DN7 5BL **Tel:** 01302-841283 **E-mail:** head@holyfamily.doncaster.sch.uk *Catchment area:* The parishes of Moorends and Stainforth.

Our Lady of Perpetual Help, Arksey Lane, Bentley, Doncaster DN5 0RR **Tel:** 01302-874291 **E-mail:** admin@ourladys.sch.uk *Catchment area:* Arksey, Bentley, Cusworth, Scawsby, Scawthorpe, Sprotborough.

Our Lady of Sorrows, Mere Lane, Armthorpe, Doncaster DN3 2DB **Tel:** 01302-833941 **E-mail:** admin@ ourladysorrows.doncaster.sch.uk *Catchment area:* Armthorpe, Barnby Dun, Edenthorpe, Kirk Sandal.

Our Lady of Mount Carmel, Sandringham Road, Intake, Doncaster DN2 5JG **Tel:** 01302-349743 **E-mail:** head@ ourladyofmountcarmel.doncaster.sch.uk *Catchment area:* Clay Lane, Intake, Wheatley Hills, Wheatley Park.

St Francis Xavier, Roberts Road, Doncaster DN4 0JN. **Tel:** 01302-344678, **E-mail:** admin@xavier.doncaster.sch.uk *Catchment area:* The parishes of the Sacred Heart and St Peter.

St Joseph Catholic, Bevan Avenue, Rossington, Doncaster DN11 0NB **Tel:** 01302-868098 **E-mail:** jba@st-josephs.doncaster.sch.uk *Catchment area:* Auckley, Bawtry, Blaxton, Branton, Finningley, Rossington, Tickhill.

St Joseph and St Theresa, Doncaster Lane, Woodlands, Doncaster DN6 7QN **Tel:** 01302-723320 **E-mail:** admin@ st-joseph-st-theresa.doncaster.sch.uk *Catchment area:* Adwick le Street, Askern, Campsall, Carcroft, Highfields, Norton, Skellow, Woodlands.

St Peter Sandy Lane, Doncaster DN4 5EP **Tel:** 01302-369143 **E-mail:** admin@stpeter.doncaster.sch.uk *Catchment area:* Parishes of St Peter and St Paul.

St Mary, Bungalow Road, Edlington, Doncaster DN12 1DL **Tel:** 01709-863280 **E-mail:** admin@ st-marys-pri.doncaster.sch.uk *Catchment area:* Edlington, Warmsworth.

▲ **Secondary**

The McAuley Catholic High School, Doncaster Lower School (I-III forms), Acacia Road, Cantley, Doncaster DN4 6NU Upper School (IV-VI), Cantley Lane, Cantley, Doncaster DN3 3QF **Tel:** 01302-537396 **E-mail:** head@mcauley.org.uk

■ **NOTTINGHAMSHIRE C.C.**

▲ **Junior and Infant**

Holy Family, Netherton Road, Worksop, Notts S80 2SF **Tel:** 01909-473917 **E-mail:** headteacher@ holyfamily.notts.sch.gov.uk

St Joseph, Babworth Road, Retford, Notts DN22 7BP **Tel:** 01777-702850 **E-mail:** office@ st-josephs.notts.sch.uk *Catchment area:* Retford and the surrounding villages.

St Patrick, Whitehouse Road, Harworth-Bircotes, Notts DN11 8EF **Tel:** 01302-743145 **E-mail:** susan.christian@ stpatricks.notts.sch.uk *Catchment area:* Bircotes, Haworth, Styrrup.

■ **ROTHERHAM M.B.**

▲ **Junior and Infant**

St Bede Wortley Road, Rotherham S61 1PD **Tel:** 01709-740101

E-mail: st.bedesRCJunior-Infant@rotherham.gov.uk
Catchment area: Parishes of St Bede and the Forty Martyrs.

St Gerard, "Park Nook", Doncaster Road, Thrybergh, Rotherham S65 4AZ **Tel:** 01709-850568 **E-mail:** sgcpahollinghurst@rgft.org *Catchment area:* Dalton, Hooton, Roberts, Ravenfield, Thrybergh.

St Joseph, Lidgett Lane, Dinnington S31 7QD **Tel:** 01909-550123 **E-mail:**Dinnington-St.Josephs.Primary@rotherham.gov.uk *Catchment area:* Brampton, Dinnington, Gildingwells, Harthill, Kiveton Park, Langton Brookhouse, Laughton Common, Letwell, North Anston, Slade Hooton, South Anston, Thorpe Salvin, Thurcroft, Todwick, Wales, Woodsetts.

St Joseph, Green Lane, Rawmarsh, Rotherham S62 6JR **Tel:** 01709-710270 **E-mail:**Rawmarsh-St.JosephsRCJunior-Infant@rotherham.gov.uk

St Mary, Herringthorpe Valley Road, Rotherham S65 2NU **Tel:** 01709-361502 **E-mail:** stmarysherringthorpe@rotherham.gov.uk *Catchment area:* Eastwood, East Dene, Herringthorpe, Broom, Brecks, Wickersley, Broom Valley.

St Mary Magdalene, Muglet Lane, Maltby, Rotherham S66 7JU **Tel:** 01709-812611 **E-mail:** maltbystmarys.primary@rotherham.gov.uk *Catchment area:* Bramley, Maltby, Wickersley.

Our Lady and St Joseph, Fitzwilliam Street, Wath-upon-Dearne, Rotherham S63 7HG **Tel:** 01709-760084 **E-mail:** school@olsjwath.force9.co.uk *Catchment area:* Brampton, Swinton, Wath.

▲ Secondary

St Bernard Catholic High School, Herringthorpe Valley Road, Rotherham S65 3BE **Tel:** 01709-828183 **E-mail:** st.bernards-catholic-high-school@rotherham.gov.uk

Pope Pius X Catholic High School, Wath Wood Road, Wath-upon-Dearne, Rotherham S63 7PQ **Tel:** 01709-760218 **E-mail:** papa-pius.x-comprehensive@rotherham.gov.uk

■ SHEFFIELD M.B.

▲ Junior and Infant

Emmaus Catholic & Church of England Primary School, Southend Road, Sheffield S2 5FT

St Ann Stockbridge, McIntyre Road, Stocksbridge, Sheffield S30 5DG **Tel:** 0114-288 4281 **E-mail:** enquiries@st-anns.sheffield.sch.uk *Catchment area:* Deepcar, Penistone, Stocksbridge.

St Catherine Firshill Crescent, Sheffield S3 7BX **Tel:** 0114-242 1177 **E-mail:** stcatherines@totalise.co.uk

St John Fisher, Springwater Avenue, Hackenthorpe, Sheffield S12 4HJ **Tel:** 0114-248 5009 **E-mail:** fisher@rmplc.co.uk *Catchment area:* Base Green, Beighton, Frecheville, Gleadless, Hackenthorpe, Waterthorpe and parts of Westfield.

St Joseph, St Joseph's Road, Handsworth, Sheffield S13 9AT **Tel:** 0114-269 2773 **E-mail:** enquiries@st-josephs-sheffield.sch.uk *Catchment area:* St Joseph's parish, Darnall, Swallownest, Treeton.

St Marie Fulwood Road, Sheffield S10 3DQ **Tel:** 0114-230 1904 **E-mail:** enquiries@st-maries-sheffield.sch.uk *Catchment area:* Parishes of St Francis, Holy Family, St Marie and part of St William's.

St Mary, Pack Horse Lane, High Green, Sheffield S35 4HY **Tel:** 0114-284 8488 **E-mail:** headteacher@st-marysgreen.sheffield.sch.uk

St Patrick Barnsley Road, Sheffield S5 0QF **Tel:** 0114-245 6183 **E-mail:** enquiries@st-patricks.sheffield.sch.uk

Sacred Heart, Ripley Street, Hillsborough, Sheffield S6 2NU **Tel:** 0114-234 4362 **E-mail:** enquiries@sacredheart.sheffield.sch.uk

St Theresa Prince of Wales Road, Sheffield S2 1EY **Tel:** 0114-239 7251 **E-mail:** manager@st-theresas.sheffield.sch.uk

St Thomas of Canterbury Chancet Wood Drive, Sheffield S8 7TR **Tel:** 0114-274 5597 **E-mail:** enquiries@st-thomascanterbury.sheffield.sch.uk *Catchment area:* south-east Sheffield.

St Thomas More Creswick Lane, Grenoside, Sheffield S30 3NN **Tel:** 0114-246 8020 **E-mail:** enquiries@st-thomasmore.sheffield.sch.uk

St Wilfrid Millhouses Lane, Sheffield S7 2HE **Tel:** 0114-236 5529 **E-mail:** enquiries@st-wilfrids.sheffield.sch.uk *Catchment area:* The parishes of the Mother of God and St Wilfrid and St William.

▲ Secondary

All Saints Catholic High School, Granville Road, Sheffield S2 2RJ **Tel:** 0114-272 4851 **E-mail:** allsheff@aol.com

Notre Dame Catholic High School, Oakbrook, Fulwood Road, Sheffield S10 3BT **Tel:** 0114-230 2536
E-mail: school@notredamehigh.co.uk

■ CATHOLIC SCHOOLS - INDEPENDENT

■ DERBYSHIRE C.C.

▲ Primary

Barlborough Hall School Barlborough, Derbyshire via Chesterfield S43 4TJ
Tel: 01246-810511
E-mail: barlborough.hall@virginnet.co.uk
Catchment area: Boarders are taken from the U.K. and overseas; day-boys and girls attend from Sheffield, Rotherham, Chesterfield and Worksop areas (8-13 years).

▲ Secondary

Mount St Mary's College, Spinkhill, Derbyshire, via Sheffield S21 3YL
Tel: 01246-433388
E-mail: headmaster@msmcollege.com

■ SHEFFIELD M.B.

▲ Primary

Mylnhurst School, Sheffield Button Hill, Ecclesall, Sheffield S11 9HJ
Tel: 0114-236 1411
E-mail: christopher_emmott@hotmail.com
Catchment area: Sheffield, Rotherham, Derbyshire.

DIOCESE OF HEXHAM AND NEWCASTLE

Province of Liverpool
Comprising the counties of Northumberland, Tyne and Wear, Durham and that part of Cleveland north of the River Tees.

Patrons of the Diocese
Our Blessed Lady Immaculate, 8 December
St Cuthbert, Bishop and Confessor, 20 March.

Bishop
Sede Vacante

Administrator:
Canon Seamus Cunningham
St Mary's Presbytery, Farringdon Road,
Cullercoats, North Shields NE30 3EY
Tel/Fax: 0191-251 3770 **Email:** office@rcdnh.org.uk

Retired Bishops
Rt Rev Hugh Lindsay, born in Newcastle upon Tyne, 20 June, 1927; ordained 19 July 1953; ordained Bishop of Chester-le-Street (Cuncacestre) and Auxiliary for Hexham and Newcastle by Archbishop Beck 11 December 1969; trans 12 December 1974; Retired 11 January 1992. **Residence:** Boarbank Hall, Grange Over Sands, Cumbria LA11 7NH. **Tel/Fax:** 01539-535591.

Rt Rev Ambrose Griffiths, born in London, 4 December, 1928; ordained 21 July 1957; ordained Bishop of Hexham and Newcastle by Archbishop Worlock, 20 March, 1992; Retired 25 May, 2004. **Residence:** St Mary's, Broadfield Walk, Leyland, Preston, Lancs PR25 1PD. **Tel:** 01772-422339
E-mail: ambroseg@btconnect.com

Bishop's Secretaries
Rev Peter Stott and Mrs Paula Henley
Bishop's House, 800 West Road, Newcastle upon Tyne NE5 2BJ
Tel: 0191 228 0003 **Fax:** (0191) 274 0432
Email: office@rcdhn.org.uk.
Diocesan website: www.rcdhn.org.uk
Registered Charity Number: 235 686

■ Area Episcopal Vicars

1. **Mgr Gerard Lavender**, Holy Family, 60 Cockerton Green, Darlington DL3 9EU **Tel:** 01325 464848
2. **Rev James O'Keefe**, 233 Whickham View, Newcastle upon Tyne, NE15 7HP **Tel:** 0191-274 6147
3. **Rev Philip Quinn**, St Wilfrids, 128 Bondicar Terrace, Blyth, Northumberland, NE24 2JZ **Tel:** 01670352513
4. **Rev Martin Stempczyk**, St Bede's Chapel Road, Jarrow, Tyne and Wear NE32 3LX **Tel:** 0191-489 7364
5. **Rev Christopher Jackson**, St Mary's, 27 Bridge Street, Sunderland SR1 1TQ **Tel:** 0191-274 6147

■ Consultors

Canon Seamus Cunningham, Mgr. Gerard Lavender, Revv James O'Keefe, Philip Quinn, Christopher Jackson, Martin Stempczyk, Michael Corbett, John James, Henry O'Reilly, Dennis Tindall, Gerard Lee, Peter Leighton.

■ Diocesan Pastoral Council

Chairman: **Mr. John Hardy, MA, Dip. Arch, RABA.**
Vice-Chairman: **Sr. Barbara Carroll**
Clerk to the Council: **Mrs. Pat Kennedy MPS**, 42 Southwood Gardens, Newcastle upon Tyne NE3 3BU **Tel/Fax:** 0191-284 1690
Email: pat@limexhex.freeserve.co.uk
Members: **A. Evens, C. Baker, S. Cunningham, G. Lee, P. Simpson, M. Doyle, A. McCarthy, S. Watson, C. Grady, E. Shuttleworth, C. Simcox, Barbara Carroll**

■ Council of Priests

Chairman: **Rev Gerard Lee**
Secretary: **Rev Shaun O'Neill**
Tel: 01642-676799

■ **Council of Laity**
Clerk to the Council: **Mrs P. Kennedy, MPS, Tel/Fax:** 0191-284 1690
Email: pat@limexhex.freeserve.co.uk

■ **Diocesan Matrimonial Tribunal**
Judicial Vicar: **Very Rev Paul J. Zielinski, B.D., J.C.L., J.V.**
Associate Judicial Vicar: **Rev Michael Brown, MA, BA, JCL.**
Assistant Judges: **Canon Francis Kearney, STD., Revv. John Butters, BA, STD, Michael McCoy, JCL, Brian McNamara, STL, David Tanner, JCJ, John Cooper, JCL.**
Defender of the Bond: **Mr Julian Moffatt, Mr Michael Rowell**
Notary: **Mrs Sheila Winter,** St Vincent's Diocesan Offices, St Cuthbert's House West Road, Newcastle upon Tyne NE15 7PY
Tel: 0191-243 3308 **Fax:** 0191-243 3309
Emails: tribunal@edurcdhn.org.uk
paul.zielinski@edurcdhn.org.uk

■ **Co-ordinator for Marriage and Family Life**
Mr Eddie Donkin, Our Lady, Queen of Peace, Penshaw DH4 7JZ **Tel:** 0191-385 6438

■ **Child Protection Office**
Child Protection Co-ordinator: **Rev. Dennis Tindall, MPS.** *Child Protection Officer:* **Mr Vincent Rice** *Secretary:* **Ms Julia Frees**
Tel: 0191-243 3305
Email: childprotection@edurchdn.org.uk

■ **Diocesan Education Service**
Director: **Dr Harry O'Neill**
Deputy Director: **Miss J Pate**
Adult RE Advisor: **Mrs Sharon O'Donnell**
Schools RE Advisor: **Sr Sheila McNamara**
Schools Support Officer: awaiting appointment. *Chair of Diocesan Education Board:* **Rev Sean Hall Tel:** 0191-416 3805
Secretarial Support: **Miss Louise Graham, Mrs Joan Laidler, Mrs Graziella Laughran**
Web Manager: **Miss Karen Burbridge**
Administrator of Courses: **Mrs Terry Harris**
St Vincent's Diocesan Offices, St Cuthbert's House, West Road, Newcastle upon Tyne NE15 7PY **Tel:** 0191-243 3310/243 3313
Fax: 0191-243 3309
Email: schools@edurcdhn.org.uk or re@edurcdhn.org.uk

CROSSROAD: Adult Education Programme
LIMEX: Home-based Theology and Pastoral Ministry Course
Liaison: **Mrs P. Kennedy, MPS.**
Tel/Fax: 0191-284 1690
Email: pat@limexhex.freeserve.co.uk

■ **Commission for Christian Unity & Interfaith Relations**
Chairman: **Rev Gordon Ryan**
Ecumenical Officer: **Andrea Murray**

■ **Liturgical Commission**
Chairman: **Rev Peter Leighton**
Executive Secretary: **Rev Adrian Dixon,** St Joseph's, High West Street, Gateshead NE8 1LX **Tel:** 0191-477 1524
Arts & Architecture Sub-Committee
Chairman: **Rev Martin Deegan**
Children's Liturgy of the Word
Co-ordinator: **Mrs Angela Joyce**
Tel: 0191-285 2651
Liturgical Formation Sub-Committee
Chairman: **Mrs Angela Joyce**

■ **Historic Churches Committee**
Chairman: **Rev Adrian Dixon**
For information and advice, consult
Mr Tim Dillon (*Property Manager*)
Tel: 0191-243 3300 **Fax:** 0191-243 3309

■ **Justice and Peace Co-ordinating Council**
Chairman: **Mr John Marshall**, 34 Netherby Drive, Newcastle-upon-Tyne NE5 2RS
Tel: 0191-245 2840 **Email:** john.marshall@justiceandpeace.co.uk
Secretary: **Mrs Jill Oliver**, 1 Osprey Close, Esh Winning, Durham DH7 9JP
Asylum Seekers and Refugees Worker: **Mr Michael McHugh**, Our Lady & St Vincent Presbytery, Monkchester Road, Newcastle upon Tyne NE6 2TX **Tel:** 0191-275 9815
Email: hnasylum@aol.com
Website: www.justiceandpeace.co.uk

■ **Director of Vocations**
Rev Andrew Downie, Catholic Chaplaincy, 14 Windsor Terrace, Jesmond, Newcastle Upon Tyne NE2 4HE **Tel:** 0191 239 9527
Promoter of Vocations: **Rev Michael McCoy Tel:** 0191-219 3810 (day), 385 2434 (evening)

■ **Permanent Diaconate Formation Team**
Director: **Rev Michael Whalen**
Tel: 0191-281 0940 *Director of Deacons:*
Rev Bill Rooke Tel: 0191-256 5217
Rev John Gibbons Tel: 0191-426 0426
Tel: 0191-581 3249 **Mrs Pat Kennedy**
Tel: 0191-284 1690
Email: mwhalen@genie.co.uk

■ **Diocesan Trustees**
The Bishop, The Vicar General, The Area Episcopal Vicars
Secretary to the Trustees: **Mrs Kathleen M Smith, BSc, FCA**

■ **Diocesan Chancellor**
Rev Peter Stott, St Joseph's Wallsend Road, North Shields NE29 7AA
Tel: 0191-257 5801

■ **Episcopal Vicar for Religious**
Rev John Cooper, St Robert's Oldgate, Morpeth, Northumberland NE61 1QF

DIOCESE OF HEXHAM AND NEWCASTLE

Tel: 01670-513410
Vicar for Religious: **Sr. Barbara Carroll**, 50 Turnberry, West Monkseaton NE25 9NZ
Tel: 0191-251 1783

■ Diocesan Finance Office

Financial Secretary: **Mrs Kathleen M. Smith, BSc, FCA**
Secretary: **Mrs Lynne Matthews**
Schools Grants Officer: **Mr Denis McNally**
Accountant: **Mr Jeffrey Ledger**
Human Resources Officer: **Mr Jim Hughes, BSc, MA.**
Property Manager: **Mr Tim Dillon, BSc (Hons), ARICS**.
Clerk of Works: **Mr Bill Martin.**
Secretary: **Mrs Julia Herron.** *Parish Support/Internal Audit:* **Mrs Dorothy Dent**
Tel: 07796 175041 St Vincent's Diocesan Offices, St Cuthbert's House. West Road, Newcastle upon Tyne NE15 7PY
Tel: 0191-243 3300 **Fax:** 0191-243 3309
Email: finance@edurcdhn.org.uk

■ Gift Aid Office

Gift Aid Organiser: **Mr Jim Hughes, BSc, MA.** *Assistant:* **Mrs Maureen Wilson**
St Vincent's Diocesan Offices, St Cuthbert's House. West Road, Newcastle upon Tyne NE15 7PY
Tel: 0191-243 3306 **Fax:** 0191-243 3309
Email: gift.aid@edurcdhn.org.uk

■ Diocesan Finance Committee

Chairman:
Secretary: **Rev. Richard B. Harriott**, St John the Baptist, Annitsford, Cramlington, Northumberland NE23 7QR
Tel: 0191-250 0200
Members: Council of Priest's representative (to be announced), **Tim Dillon, Austin Donohoe, Michael Hogan, Jeff Ledger, Bill Martin, Kathleen Smith**

■ St Cuthbert's Care

Executive Director: **Mr Austin Donohoe,** St Cuthbert's House, West Road, Newcastle upon Tyne NE15 7PY
Tel: 0191-228 0111 **Fax:** 0191-228 0177

■ Youth Services

Diocesan Director: **Rev Dermott Donnelly,** Youth Ministry Team (YMT)
Tel: 01207-592244 **Fax:** 01207-592245
Email: admin@ymt.org **Website:** www.ymt.org
Youth Support & Management Team: Chairman: **Rev Philip Quinn**, *Secretary:* **Mrs Pat Kennedy**
Co-ordinator of School Chaplains and Retreats:
Rev Michael McCoy Tel: 0191-219 3810/385 2434 (evening)

■ HEXHAM AND NEWCASTLE

A

1. Cathedral Church of St Mary
(1844; cons. 21 Aug 1860)
Clayton Street West,
NE1 5HH **Tel:** 0191-232 6953
Fax: 0191-232 0913
E-mail: office@stmaryscathedral.org.uk
Website: www.stmaryscathedral.org.uk
Rev Peter Leighton (*Dean*); **Rev Christopher Warren**
M: *Sat 1st M of Sun 6.30pm. Sun 8am, 10am, 11.30am, 6.30pm. Hds. (vigil 5.30pm) 8am, 12.05pm, 5.30 pm.*

- ***Sisters of Mercy,*** St Anne's Convent, 9 Summerhill Gr, NE4 6HQ **Tel:** 0191-232 0942

■ ALNWICK, Northd

† St Paul
Percy Street, Alnwick, North.
Tel/Fax: 01665-602012
Rev Desmond McGivern.
3 Prudhoe Villas, NE66 1UP
M: *Sat 1st M of Sun 6.30pm. Sun 9.30am. Hds 10am, 7.30pm.*

- ***Sisters of Mercy,*** St Mary's Convent, Bailiffgate NE66 1LX **Tel:** 01665-602148

■ AMBLE, Morpeth, Northd

† The Sacred Heart and St Cuthbert
(1913; 1987)
37 High Street, NE65 0LE
Tel: 01665-710252 **Fax:** 01665-714224
Rev John Clohosey.
M: *Sat 1st M of Sun 6.30pm. Sun 10am. Hds 9am, 7pm.*

■ ANNFIELD PLAIN, Co Durham

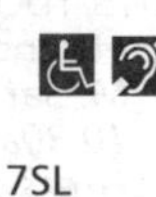

† St Teresa (1953)
James Street, Annfield Plain, DH9 7SL
Tel: 01207-234388 **Fax:** 01207-237947
Rev Bernard Pitt (in residence).
M: *Sun 9am. Hds (vigil 7pm), 9.30am.*

■ ANNITSFORD, Northd

A

† St John the Baptist
(1863; 1866; new church cons. 22 June 1906)
Annitsford, Cramlington, Northd NE23 7QR
Tel: 0191-250 0200
Rev Richard Harriott.
M: *Sat 1st M of Sun 6.30pm. Sun 9am, 11am. Hds 9.15am, 7pm.*

■ **ASHINGTON,** Northd
† **St Aidan** (1893; 1905)
Station Road, Ashington, Northd NE63 8AD
Tel: 01670-812200 **Fax:** 01670-857463
Rev Ian Jackson.
M: *Sat 1st M of Sun 5.30pm. Sun 10.30am. Hds Vigil 7pm 10am.*

■ **BACKWORTH**
See Newcastle upon Tyne (7).

■ **BARNARD CASTLE**
† **St Mary**
(1847; new church cons 29 Sept 1928)
Birch Road, Barnard Castle, Co Durham DL12 8NR **Tel:** 01833-638133
Rev Wilfrid Elkin.
M: *Sat 1st M of Sun 6.30pm. Sun 9am (Latin), 10.30am. Hds 10am.*

■ **BEDLINGTON,** Northd
† **St Bede** (1992)
Catholic Row, Bedlington, Northd NE22 6HS
Tel: 01640-823258
Rev Neil Fitzpatrick.
M: *Sat 1st M of Sun 6.30pm. Sun 9am, 11am. Hds (vigil 7.30pm), 9.30am.*

■ **BELLINGHAM,** Hexham, Northd
† **St Oswald** (1749; 1839; cons. 10 May 1950)
Bellingham, Hexham, Northd. NE48 2JT
Tel: 01434-220262 Also 01434-220319
Rev Michael McKenna.
M: *Sun 10.45am. Hds 7.15pm.*

■ **BELL'S CLOSE**
See Newcastle upon Tyne (8).

■ **BENTON**
See Newcastle upon Tyne (9).

■ **BERWICK-UPON-TWEED,** Northd
† **Our Lady and St Cuthbert**
(1829; cons 9 Oct 1948)
64 Ravensdowne, Berwick-upon-Tweed, TD15 1DQ **Tel:** 01289-307297
Rev Brendan Kelly.
M: *Sat 1st M of Sun 6.30pm. Sun 9am 10.30am, Hds 10am, 6.30pm.*
• ***Sisters of Mercy,*** Convent of Mercy, 72 Ravensdowne, TD15 1DQ
Tel: 01289-307706

■ **BILLINGHAM**
1. † **St John the Evangelist** (1922; 1931; 1960)
Central Avenue, Billingham, Cleveland S23 1LR **Tel/Fax:** 01642-553153
Rev John Butters.
M: *Sat Vigil 5.30pm. Hds 9am.*

2. † **Our Lady of the Most Holy Rosary** (1949; 1960)
Sidlaw Road, Billingham, Cleveland.
Tel/Fax: 01642-553118
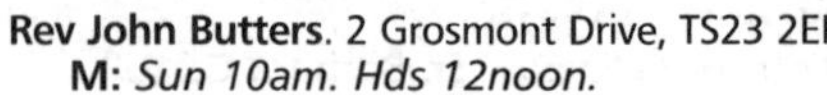
Rev John Butters. 2 Grosmont Drive, TS23 2EP
M: *Sun 10am. Hds 12noon.*

3. † **St Joseph** (1962)
Rev John Butters, Low Grange Avenue, Billingham, Cleveland.
Tel: 01642-560048 **Fax:** 01642 566006
M: *Sun 8am, 6.30pm. Hds 7pm.*

■ **BIRTLEY,** Tyne and Wear
† **St Joseph** (1696; 1843)
Birtley Lane, Birtley, Tyne and Wear DH3 1LJ
Tel: 0191-410 2923 **Fax:** 0191-410 5843
Rev Anthony Duffy, Rev Deacon Peter Lavery
M: *Sat 1st M of Sun 6pm. Sun 8.15am, 10.45am. Hds (vigil 7pm). 12.05pm, 7pm.*
• ***Daughters of Jesus,*** 9 Egton Terrace, DH3 1LX **Tel:** 0191-410 8658

■ **BISHOP AUCKLAND,** Co Durham
1 † **St Wilfrid** (1845-46)
Hexham Street, Bishop Auckland, Co Durham DL14 7PU
Tel/Fax: 01388-603541
Rev Jonathan Rose.
M: *Sun 9.30am. Hds 12.10pm.*

2. † **St Mary** (1956)
Vart Road, Woodhouse Close Estate, Bishop Auckland DL14 6PQ
Tel: 01388-603431
Rev Jonathan Rose.
M: *Sun 11am, 6pm. Hds 9.15am, 7pm.*

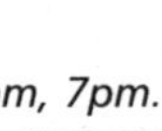
3. † **St Paulinus** (1938; 1953)
Manor Road, St Helen's, Bishop Auckland DL14 9ER **Tel:** 01388-604169
Rev Henry Ryan (In residence)
M: *Sat 1st M of Sun 6.30pm. Hds (vigil 6.30pm).*

■ **BLACKHALL,** Hartlepool, Cleveland
† **St Joseph** (1950; cons 13 Nov 1952)
Coast Road, Blackhall, Hartlepool, Cleveland TS27 4HW **Tel:** 0191-586 4319
Rev Malcolm Cairns.
M: *Sun 6pm (vigil), 10am. Hds 9.15am, 7pm.*

■ **BLACKHILL,** Co. Durham
† **Our Blessed Lady Immaculate**
(1857; cons 11 July 1934)
Derwent Street, DH8 8LP
Tel/Fax: 01207-502320
Rev Seamus Doyle.
M: *Sat 1st M of Sun 5.30pm. Sun 11am. Hds 10am, 7pm.*

■ **BLAYDON-ON-TYNE,** Tyne and Wear
See Gateshead (9).

■ **BLYTH,** Northd
† **Our Lady and St Wilfrid** (1861; 1862)
Waterloo Road, Blyth, Northd NE24 1EA
Tel: 01670-352513 **Rev Philip Quinn**.
M: *Sat 1st M of Sun 7pm. Sun 11am, 6pm. Hds 10am, 6pm.*
• ***Sisters for Christian Community,*** 27, Grange Close, South Beach Close, South Beach Manor, Blyth, Northumberland NE24 3HS **Tel:** 01670-352398

■ **BOLDON,** Tyne and Wear
† **The Sacred Heart** (1896; 1936)
New Road, NE35 9DR
Served from St Oswald's, South Shields
Rev John Gibbons.
M: *Sat 1st M of Sun 6.30pm. Sun 9am. Hds 12noon, 7.05pm.*

■ **BROOMS,** Co Durham
† **Our Blessed Lady and St Joseph** (1748; 1802; 1869; cons 14 Sept 1932)
Brooms, Leadgate, Co Durham DH8 6RS
Tel: 01207-503550
Rev Michael Keoghan.
M: *Sat 1st M of Sun 6pm. Sun 10am. Hds (vigil 7pm St Joseph's Hall), 10am in Church.*

■ **BYERMOOR,** Burnopfield
† **Sacred Heart** (1869; 1876; cons 9 Oct 1948)
Byermoor, Burnopfield, Newcastle upon Tyne NE16 6NU **Tel:** 01207-270226
Rev John Taggart.
M: *Sat 1st M of Sun 6pm. Sun 10am. Hds 10am, 7.15pm.*

■ **CHEESEBURN GRANGE,** Stamfordham, Newcastle upon Tyne
† **St Francis Xavier** (abt 1725)
Served from Ponteland.
M: *Sun 8.45am.*

■ **CHESTER LE STREET**
† **St Cuthbert** (1881; 1910)
Ropery Lane, Chester le Street, Co Durham DH3 3PH **Tel/Fax:** 0191-388 2302

Rev Peter Carr.
M: *Sat 1st M of Sun 6.30pm. Sun 9am, 10.30am. Hds (vigil 7.30pm), 9am, 10.30am, 7.30pm.*

■ **CHILTON**
See Windlestone.

■ **CHOPWELL,** Newcastle upon Tyne
See Gateshead (10).

■ **COCKERTON**
See Darlington (2).

■ **CONSETT,** Co Durham
1. † **St Patrick** (1926; 1959)
Victoria Road, Consett, Co Durham DH8 5AX **Tel:** 01207-502196
Rev Jeffrey Dodds.
M: *Sat 1st M of Sun 6.30pm. Sun 9.30am, 6pm. Hds 7.30pm (vigil), 10am, 12.05pm.*

2. † **St Pius X** (1931; 1954)
Sussex Road, Moorside DH8 8HH
Tel: 01207-508236 Served from Blackhill.
M: *Sun 11am. Hds 9am.*

■ **CORBRIDGE,** Northd
St Andrew's Parish Church.
Served from Hexham.
M: *Sat 1st M of Sun 6pm. Hds 6pm.*

■ **COUNDON,** Bishop Auckland
† **St Joseph** (1926; 1932; cons 3 Oct 1946)
Victoria Lane, Coundon, Bishop Auckland, Co Durham DL14 8NL **Tel:** 01388-602030
Rev Peter Kelly
M: *Sun 9am. Hds 10am.*

■ **COWPEN,** Blyth, Northd
† **St Cuthbert** (1838; 1841)
292 Cowpen Road, Cowpen, Blyth, Northd. NE24 5JN Served from Blyth.
Rev Robert Kinlen.
M: *Sun 9am. Hds (vigil 7pm).*

■ **COXHOE,** Durham
† **SS Joseph, Patrick and Cuthbert**
(1839 at Sedgefield; 1966)
Church Street, Coxhoe, Durham DH6 4DA
Tel: 0191-377 0542
Rev Shaun Swales, Rev Deacon Vincent Purcell.
M: *Sat 1st M of Sun 6pm. Hds (vigil 7pm).*

■ **CRAMLINGTON,** Northd
† **St Paul** (1969; 1970)
St Paul's Parish House, Dewley, Cramlington, Northd. NE23 6EF
Tel/Fax: 01670-712476
Rev Simon Lerche (*Parish Priest*).
M: *Sat 1st M of Sun 6pm. Sun 9am.*

■ **CRAWCROOK**
See Gateshead (11).

■ **CROOK,** Co Durham
† **Our Lady Immaculate and St Cuthbert** (1853; cons 7 Sept 1926)
Church Hill, Crook, Co Durham DL15 9DN
Tel/Fax: 01388-762724
Rev Edward Gibbons.
M: *Sun 10am, 6pm. Hds 9.30am, 7.30pm.*
• ***Faithful Companions of Jesus (FCJ),*** Convent of Mercy, Crook, Co Durham DL15 9DN **Tel:** 01388-768516

■ **CROXDALE,** Durham
† **St Herbert, Croxdale Hall** (15th cent; 1807)
Served from Tudhoe.

■ **CULLERCOATS,** North Shields
St Mary
Farringdon Road NE30 3EY
Tel/Fax: 0191-251 3770
Canon Seamus Cunningham VG.
M: *Sat 1st M of Sun 5.30pm. Sun 11am. Hds Vigil 7pm, 9am.*

■ **DARLINGTON,** Co Durham
1. † **St Augustine** (1783; 1826)
30 Coniscliffe Road, Darlington, Co Durham DL3 7RG
Tel: 01325-266602 **Fax:** 01325-253363
Rev Michael Higginbottom.
M: *Sat 1st M of Sun 6.30pm. Sun 9.15am, 11am. Hds 10am, 12.05pm.*
- ***Hospitaller Order of Saint John of God (OH),*** Provincial House, 235 Carmel Road North, Darlington DL3 9TF **Tel:** 01325-357695

2. † **Holy Family** (1928; 1960)
Prior Street, Cockerton.
Tel: 01325-464848 **Fax:** 01325-382534
Mgr Gerard Lavender, Rev Clement Lee CSsR. 60 Cockerton Green DL3 9EU
M: *Sun 9.30am, 6.30pm. Hds 9.30am, 7.00pm.*
- ***Carmelites,*** Carmelite Convent, Nunnery Lane, DL3 9PN **Tel:** 01325-481666 **Fax:** 01325-481303
M: *Sun 8am Hds 8am.*

3. † **St Anne** (1956)
Welbeck Avenue, Haughton-le-Skerne, DL1 2DR **Tel:** 01325-464547
M: *Sat 1st M of Sun 6pm. Sun 10.30am. Hds 9.30am, 7pm.*
- ***Cross and Passion Sisters,*** St Anne's Presbytery, Welbeck Avenue DL1 2DR **Tel:** 01325-464547

4. † **St Teresa** (1945; 1970)
Harris Street, Darlington, Co Durham. DL1 4NL **Tel/Fax:** 01325-257681
Rev Greg Price.
M: *Sat 1st M of Sun 5.30pm, Sun 10.30a.m. Hds 9.30am, 7pm.*

5. † **St Thomas Aquinas** (1927; 1929)
North Road, Darlington, Co Durham DL1 2PU **Tel:** 01325-463636
M: *Sun 11am. Hds 10am, 7pm.*
- ***Daughters of Charity (SVP):*** St Thomas Aquinas Prestbytery, North Road, Darlington DL1 2PU **Tel:** 01325 381086

6. † **SS William and Francis de Sales** (1870)
Barton Street. Served from Darlington (3).
M: *Sun 9am. Hds 7pm.*

■ **DIPTON,** Stanley, Co Durham
† **St Patrick** (1907; 1934; 1968)
North Road, Dipton, Stanley, Co Durham DH9 9BB Served from Southmoor
Tel: 01207-570209 **Fax:** 01207-571455
M: *Sun 10.30am. Hds 9.15am, 7pm.*

■ **DUNSTON** See Gateshead (20).

■ **DURHAM**
1. † **St Cuthbert**
(1685; 1827; cons 20 July 1910)
Old Elvet, Durham DH1 3HL
Tel: 0191-384 3442 **Fax:** 0191-375 0442
Rev Anthony Currer.
E-mail: a.t.currer@durham.ac.uk
M: *Sun 8.30am, 11am. Hds 12.15pm, 6.15pm.*
- University Chaplaincy.
M: *Sun 6.30pm (during Uni. term only)*

2. † **St Godric**
(1863; 1864; 1909; cons 23 Sept 1959)
Castle Chare, Durham. Served from St Joseph's
M: *Sun 9.15am, 6pm. Hds 10.30am.*
- ***Institute of Charity,*** Rosmini House, Woodbine Road, Pity Me, Durham DH1 5DR **Tel:** 0191-384 9268.
Rev Terence Watson.
- ***Mill Hill Missionaries,*** Tenter House, 17 Tenter Terrace, Durham City DH1 4RD
Tel: 0191-384 5626 **Fax:** 0191-383 0351
Revv Francis Graham, David Bingham.

3. † **St Joseph** (1937; 1948)
Mill Lane, Gilesgate, DH1 2JG
Tel: 0191-384 3810 **Fax:** 0191-384 3706
Rev Colm Hayden, Rev Andrew Shaw
M: *Sat 1st M of Sun 5.30pm. Sun 9am, 11am. Hds (vigil 5.30pm), 10am, 7pm.*

■ **EASINGTON COLLIERY**
† **Our Lady.** (1923; 1978)
Cemetery Road, Easington Colliery, Peterlee Co Durham SR8 3SP **Tel:** 0191-527 0454
M: *Sat 1st M of Sun 6.30pm. Sun 10am. Hds 10am, 7pm.*

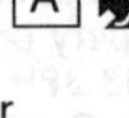

■ **EASINGTON LANE**
† **St Mary** (1921; 1939)
South Hetton Road, Tyne and Wear DH5 0LG **Tel:** 0191-526 2136
Rev Paul Tully
M: *Sat 1st M of Sun 6pm. Hds (vigil 7pm).*

■ **EBCHESTER**
See Gateshead (10).

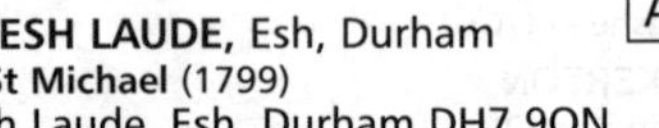

■ **ESH LAUDE,** Esh, Durham
† **St Michael** (1799)
Esh Laude, Esh, Durham DH7 9QN
Tel: 0191-373 4349
Served from Ushaw Moor.
M: *Sun 8am. Hds 9am.*
- ***Sisters of Mercy,*** St Michael's Convent, DH7 9QY **Tel:** 0191-373 1217

■ ESH WINNING
See Newhouse.

■ FELLING
See Gateshead (12, 13).

■ FERRYHILL, Co Durham
† All Saints (1925; 1927)
Dean Road, Ferryhill, Co Durham
DL17 8ET **Tel:** 01740-651343
Rev Brian Murphy.
M: *Sun 10am. Hds (vigil 7pm), 10am.*

■ FOREST HALL Newcastle upon Tyne (13).

■ FRAMWELLGATE MOOR
St Bede
Carr House Drive, Framwellgate Moor,
Co Durham DH1 5LZ Served from Durham (3).
M: *Sat 1st M of Sun 6.30pm. Sun 10.45am. Hds 9.15am, 7pm.*

■ GAINFORD, Co Durham
† St Osmund (1852; cons 27 May 1936)
Eden Crest, DL2 3DE
Tel/Fax: 01325-730191
Rev Michael Melia.
M: *Sun 9am. Hds 7pm.*

■ GATESHEAD, Tyne and Wear
1. † St Joseph (1851; 1859; cons 20 May 1959)
High West Street, Gateshead, Tyne and Wear NE8 1LX **Tel:** 0191-477 1524
Rev Adrian Dixon.
M: *Sun 10.30am. Hds 9am, 12noon (Latin), 7.30pm.*

2. St Anne (1976)
Rokeby View, Harlow Green, Gateshead, Tyne and Wear NE9 7UD
Tel: 0191-491 3722
Rev Graham Williams
M: *Sat 1st M of Sun 6pm. Sun 10.30am, 6pm. Hds 10am, 7pm.*

3. † Our Lady of the Annunciation (1938; 1953)
Millway, Gateshead, Tyne and Wear NE9 5PQ **Tel:** 0191-487 4237
Rev Sean Conaty (*Retired*) in residence.
Served from St Peter's, Gateshead.
M: *Sun 10am. Hds 10am, 7.30pm.*

4. † Corpus Christi
(1927; 1936; cons 20 May 1959)
Kelvin Grove, Gateshead, Tyne and Wear NE8 4QP **Tel/Fax:** 0191-477 1428
Rev Michael C Purtill.
M: *Sun 10am, 6pm. Hds 9am, 7pm.*

5. † The Holy Rosary
Mass in Teams Community Centre.
In the Pastoral Care of **Rev Kevin Daly**
M: *Sun 10am. Hds 10am.*

6. † Immaculate Heart of Mary
(1949; 1960)
Malvern Gdns, Lobley Hill, Gateshead, Tyne and Wear NE11 9LL **Tel:** 0191-460 4274
Rev Michael Humble
M: *Sat 1st M of Sun 5.30pm. Sun 9.45am. Hds 7pm.*

7. † St Peter (1929; 1932; 1962)
Kells Lane, Low Fell, Gateshead, Tyne and Wear NE9 5HY **Tel/Fax:** 0191-487 6505
Rev David Taylor.
M: *Sat 1st M of Sun 6pm. Sun 8.30am, 10.30am. Hds (vigil 7.30pm), 10pm.*

8. † St Wilfrid (1903; 1955)
Sunderland Road, Gateshead, Tyne and Wear NE8 3QR **Tel/Fax:** 0191-477 1524
M: *Sat 1st M of Sun 6pm. Hds 10am, 7.30pm.*
• ***Sisters of Divine Love:*** (in residence)

9. † St Joseph
(1898; 1905; cons 31 May 1930)
Shibdon Road, Blaydon-on-Tyne, Gateshead, Tyne and Wear NE21 5AE
Tel: 0191-414 3115
Rev Keith Walker.
M: *Sat 1st M of Sun 6.30pm. Sun 10.45am. Hds (vigil 7.30pm).*

10. † Our Lady of Lourdes (1914)
Hall Road, Chopwell, Gateshead, Tyne and Wear NE17 7AD Served from Highfield.
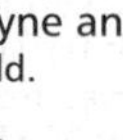
Tel/Fax: 01207-542339
M: *Sun 9am. Hds (vigil 7.30pm).*
• ***Sisters of Our Lady of Good and Perpetual Succour,*** St Mary's Convent, Ebchester, Consett, Co Durham, DH8 0QD **Tel:** 01207-560288 *Chaplain:* **Rev James Donnelly**. Chaplain's Cottage, The Convent, Ebchester, Consett DH8 0QD **Tel/Fax:** 01207-562304
M: *Sat 1st M of Sun 5pm. Sun 8am. Hds 5pm.*

11. † St Agnes (1892; 1905; 1959; 1983)
Westburn, Ryton, Gateshead, Tyne and Wear. NE40 4ET **Tel:** 0191-413 2766
Canon Francis Kearney.
M: *Sat 1st M of Sun 6.30pm. Sun 9.30am. Hds (vigil 7.30pm), 10.15am.*

12. † St Patrick
(1841; 1895; cons 24 May 1950)
9 High Street, Felling Gateshead, Tyne and Wear NE10 9LT
Tel: 0191-495 2277 **Fax:** 0191-495 2675
Rev Ian Patterson
M: *Sun 10.05am. Hds 10am.*

13. † St Augustine (1956; 1962)
Wealcroft, Leam Lane Estate, Gateshead, Tyne and Wear NE10 8QS
Tel: 0191-469 3042 **Fax:** 0191-469 0375
Rev Ciaran McDonnell.

M: *Sat 1st M of Sun 6pm. Sun 10am, 6pm. Hds (vigil 7.30pm), 10am, 7.30pm.*

14. † St Joseph (1912; 1914; 1929)
Smailes Lane, Highfield, Rowlands Gill, Tyne and Wear NE39 2DB
Rev Derek Peel
Tel/Fax: 01207-542339
M: *Sat 1st M of Sun 6.30pm. Sun 10.45am. Hds 10.45am, 7pm.*

15. † St Alban (1935; 1937)
Queen Victoria Street, Pelaw, Tyne and Wear NE10 0QN **Tel:** 0191-469 2168
Served from St Patrick's, Felling.
M: *Sat 1st M of Sun 6.30pm. Sun 10am. Hds (7pm vigil).*

16. † St Mary and St Thomas Aquinas (From Stella Hall 1700; 1831)
Stella Road, Blaydon-on-Tyne, Tyne and Wear NE21 4LR **Tel:** 0191-414 2749
Rev David Phillips.
M: *Sat 1st M of Sun 5pm. Sun 11am. Hds 9.15am, 7pm.*

17. † St Mary (1948)
Dockendale Lane, Whickham NE16 4EN
Tel: 0191-460 4274
Served from Immaculate Heart of Mary (6), **Rev Michael Humble**.
Also resident: **Rev Joseph Travers,** retired
M: *Sun 930am, 6.15pm. Hds 9.30am, 7.30pm.*

18. † St Anne (1962)
Half Fields Road, Winlaton, Tyne and Wear NE21 5RN **Tel:** 0191-414 2654
Rev Keith Walker.
M: *Sun 9.15am. Hds 9.30am.*

19. † St Oswald (1884; 1903)
High Street, Wrekenton, Tyne and Wear NE9 7JQ **Tel/Fax:** 0191-487 6227
Rev Kevin Cummins.
M: *Sat 1st M of Sun 6pm. Sun 9am, 11am. Hds 7.30pm.*

20. † St Philip Neri (1880; 1895; 1934)
Ellison Road, Tyne and Wear. NE8 2QU
Tel: 0191-460 4122
Rev Michael Humble, Tel: 0191-460 4274
M: *Sun 11am. Hds (7pm vigil).*

■ GOSFORTH
See Newcastle upon Tyne (14).

■ HALTWHISTLE, Northd
† St Wilfrid
Served from Haydon Bridge.
Tel: 01434-684265
Masses in The Two Churches, Main Street.
M: *Sun 11am. Hds (vigil 7pm).*

■ HARTLEPOOL, Cleveland
1. † St Joseph
(1867; 1895; cons 18 March 1936)
Hutton Avenue, Hartlepool, Cleveland TS26 9PN **Tel:** 01429-272985
Rev David Coxon, The Presbytery, St Paul's Road, TS26 9EY
M: *Sun 8am, 10am, 6.30pm. Hds 12.05pm, 6.30pm.*

2. † St Cuthbert (1928; 1932; 1955)
130 Stockton Road, Hartlepool, Cleveland TS25 5AX **Tel/Fax:** 01429-272925
Rev James Angus.
M: *Sat 1st M of Sun 6pm. Sun 9am, 10.30am. Hds 8am, 12noon.*

3. † St John Vianney (1961)
King Oswy Drive, Hartlepool, Cleveland TS24 9LX **Tel/Fax:** 01429-267457
Rev David Coxon also **Rev Deacon Thomas Rooke** (in residence).
M: *Sat 1st M of Sun 6.30pm. Sun 9.30am. Hds 8am, 10am, 7.15pm.*
- ***Faithful Companions of Jesus,*** 19 Brus Corner, West View, Hartlepool TS24 9LA **Tel:** 01429-268284

4. † The Immaculate Conception (1834; 1851; cons 5 Sept 1934)
Durham Street, Hartlepool, Cleveland
Tel: 01429-266080
M: *Sun 10am. Hds 6.30pm.*

5. † St Patrick (1961)
Owton Manor Lane, Hartlepool, Cleveland TS25 3QC **Tel:** 01429-266734
Rev Adrian Tuckwell.
M: *Sun 8.30am, 10.30am, 6.30pm. Hds 9am, 6.30pm.*

6. † St Teresa (1949; 1952)
Stockton Road, Owton Manor, Hartlepool, Cleveland **Tel:** 01429-266734
Presbytery, Braemar Road, TS25 3AS
Served from St Patricks.
M: *Sat 1st M of Sun 6.15pm. Sun 10am. Hds 9am, 7pm.*

7. † St Thomas More (1950; 1953)
Easington Road, Hartlepool, Cleveland TS24 8JZ **Tel:** 01429-274775
Rev Hugh McCann.
M: *Sat 1st M of Sun 6pm. Sun 8.30am, 10.30pm. Hds (vigil 6.30pm), 10am.*

■ HAYDON BRIDGE, Hexham
† St John of Beverley (1862; 1873)
North Bank, Haydon Bridge, Hexham, Northd NE47 6LP **Tel:** 0434-684265
Rev Leo Pyle.
M: *Sun 9.30am. Hds 7pm.*

■ **HEBBURN,** Tyne and Wear
1. † St Aloysius (1871; 1888)
Bell Street, Hebburn, Tyne and Wear.
Rev Martin Morris, Rev Dcn Peter Jones
Tel: 0191-483 2165; **Rev Ernest Donnelly** (in residence), **Tel:** 0191-483 4322 Prince Consort Road, NE31 1BE
M: *Sat 1st M of Sun 6pm. Sun 11am. Hds (vigil 7pm). 10am.*

2. † St James (1967)
Mill Lane, Hebburn, Tyne and Wear
NE31 2ET **Tel:** 0191-420 0526
M: *Sun 9.30am. Hds 7pm.*

■ **HEXHAM,** Northd
† St Mary (1721; 1830; cons 21 Dec 1979)
Hencotes, Hexham, Northd. NE46 2EB
Tel: 01434-603119
Rev Martin Deegan.
M: *Sun 10am, 7.30pm. Hds 10am,7.30pm.*

■ **HIGHFIELD**
See Gateshead (14).

■ **HOLY ISLAND,** Northd
St Aidan's Chapel
Served from Seahouses.
M: *Last Sun in June - First Sun in Sept. Usually 6pm, depending on tides. See notice on Church door, or* **Tel:** *01665-720427.*

■ **HORDEN,** Co Durham A
† Our Lady Star of the Sea
(1921; 1925; new church opened and cons 12 June 1980)
South Terrace, Horden, Co Durham SR8 4NQ
Tel: 0191-586 4221
Rev Kevin Gallagher.
M: *Sat 1st M of Sun 6pm. Sun 11am. Hds (vigil 7pm), 10am.*

■ **HOUGHTON-LE-SPRING** A
† St Michael (1832; 1837)
Durham Road, Houghton-le-Spring, Tyne and Wear DH5 8NF
Tel: 0191-584 2142 **Fax:** 0191-512 0849
Rev William O'Gorman.
M: *Sun Vigil (Sat) 6pm, 9am, 11am. Hds 9.30am, 7.30pm.*

■ **HUTTON HENRY**
† SS Peter and Paul
(1825; 1895; cons 27 June 1911)
Hutton Henry, Hartlepool, Cleveland
TS27 4RQ **Tel/Fax:** 0191-586 2526
Served from Blackhall.
M: *Sun 8.30am. Hds As announced.*

■ **JARROW,** Tyne and Wear
1. † St Bede (1861)
Chapel Road, Jarrow, Tyne and Wear
NE32 3LX **Tel:** 0191-489 7364
Fax: 0191-430 1351
Rev Martin Stempcyzyk.
M: *Sat 1st M of Sun 6.15pm. Sun 10am. Hds (vigil 7pm), 12.15pm.*

2. † St Matthew (1935; 1958)
York Avenue, Jarrow, Tyne and Wear
NE32 5LP **Tel:** 0191-489 7295
Rev Peter V Martin.
M: *Sun 9am, 11am, 6pm. Hds 9.30am, 7pm.*

3. † St Mary (1952)
Glasgow Road, Jarrow, Tyne and Wear
NE32 4AU **Tel:** 0191-489 7907
M: *Sat 1st M of Sun 5.30pm. Sun 9am, 10.30am. Hds (vigil 7.30pm), 9.30am.*

4. † St Joseph (1962; 1972) A
St Joseph's Way, Hedworth Est, Jarrow, Tyne and Wear NE32 4PJ
Tel: 0191-536 2954
M: *Sat 1st M of Sun 6.30pm. Sun 10am. Hds 9.15am, 7.30pm.*
- ***Daughters of Mary and Joseph,*** 4 Green Bank Villas, Jarrow NE32 3NA **Tel:** 0191-489 8726

■ **KILLINGWORTH**
See Newcastle upon Tyne (18).

■ **LANCHESTER,** Durham
† All Saints (1901; 1926)
Kitswell Road, Lanchester, Durham
DH7 0JH
Tel: 01207-520374 **Fax:** 01207-521875
Canon Robert Spence.
M: *Sat 1st M of Sun 6.30pm. Sun 10am. Hds 10am, 7pm.*

■ **LANGLEY MOOR,** Durham
† St Patrick (1876; 1911; cons 10 Oct 1933)
High Street, Langley Moor, Durham
DH7 8JN **Tel:** 0191-373 0219
Rev Alan MacKnight (In residence).
M: *Sat 1st M of Sun 6pm. Sun 10am. Hds (vigil 7pm), 10am.*

■ **LANGLEY PARK,** Durham
St Joseph (1920)
Served from Langley Moor.
M: *Sun 9.30am, 6pm. Hds (vigil 7pm), 8am.*

■ **LONGBENTON**
See Newcastle upon Tyne (19).

■ **LONGHORSLEY,** Morpeth, Northd
† St Thomas of Canterbury (About 1700; 1841)
Longhorsley, Morpeth, Northd NE65 8UY
Tel: 01670-788344
Rev Ian Hoskins
M: *Sun 10.30am. Hds 10am.*

■ **LYNEMOUTH,** Northd
Served from Ashington.

■ **METRO CENTRE**
Gateshead, NE11 9XG
Oasis of Peace, Blessed Sacrament Chapel. 31 The Boulevard.
Rev D Phillips. Tel: 0191-460 1196

■ **MIDDLETON-IN-TEESDALE,** Co Durham
† St Aidan (1957)
Served from Barnard Castle.
M: *(Easter to October - Time to be announced)*

■ **MINSTERACRES,** Consett
Retreat of the Immaculate Heart of Mary and Church of St Elizabeth (1756; 1854)
Minsteracres, Consett, Co. Durham DH8 9RT
Tel: 01434-673248 **Fax:** 01434-673540
- ***Passionists (CP):*** **Rev Jeroen Hoogland** (*Rector*); **Revv Luke Magee** (*Parish Priest*); **Mark Whelehan, Richard Appleyard,** *Deacon:* **Rev Andrew O'Connor**.
  M: *Sun 8.30am, 10.30am. Hds 8.30am, 7.30pm.*
- ***Retreat and Conference Centre,*** and Residential Youth Centre. **Tel:** 01434-673248.

■ **MORPETH,** Northd
† St Robert of Newminister (1778; 1849)
Oldgate Street, Morpeth, Northd NE61 1QF
Tel: 01670-513410
Rev John Cooper. In residence: **Rev James Doherty, Tel:** 01670-505063
M: *Sun 9am, 11am, 7pm. Hds 9.15am, 12.30pm, 7.30pm.*

■ **MURTON,** Seaham, Co Durham
† St Joseph (1900; 1964)
Church Lane, Murton, Seaham, Co Durham SR7 9RD **Tel/Fax:** 0191-581 2221
Mobile: 0780 1071738
Rev Anthony Hastie. (In Residence): **Rev Ronald Richmond, Tel:** 0191-526 1116
M: *Sun 9.30am. Hds 9.30am.*

■ **NEWBIGGIN-BY-THE-SEA,** Northd
† St Mary (1926; 1954)
Front Street. Served from Ashington.
M: *Sun 9am. Hds 6.30pm.*

■ **NEWCASTLE**
1. See start of the parish list.

2. † St Andrew
(1798; 1875; cons 27th Sept 1921)
9 Worswick Street, Newcastle NE1 6UW
Tel: 0191-2321892
Rev Michael Corbett.
M: *Sat 1st M of Sun 6pm. Sun 10.30am, 6pm. Hds 8am, 12.15pm, 6pm.*

3. † St Bede (1937; 1952)
233 Whickham View, Denton, Newcastle NE15 7HP
Tel: 0191-274 6147 **Fax:** 0191-275 3591
Rev James O'Keefe.
M: *Sun 9am, 11am. Hds 10am, 7pm.*
- ***Good Shepherd Sisters.*** St Bede's Convent, 4 Brignall Gdns, NE15 7AA **Tel:** 0191-274 5570

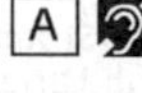

4. † St Dominic's
(1860; 1873; cons. 6 June 1935)
St Dominic's Priory, 41a Red Barns, Newcastle NE1 2TP (On Bridge Street)
Tel: 0191-232 5939 **Fax:** 0191-261 1026
- ***Dominicans (OP):*** **Revv Leo Edgar** (*Superior and Parish Priest*), **Colin Carr, Rev Dcn John Baptist Watson, Bro Columba Rabbett.**
  M: *Sat 1st M of Sun 5.30pm. Sun 8.30am, 10am, 7pm. Hds (vigil 5.30pm), 7.30am, 10am, 7.30pm.*

5. † English Martyrs (1929; 1963)
176 Stamfordham Road, Newcastle NE5 3JR **Tel:** 0191-286 9246
Rev Paul McCourt.
M: *Sat 1st M of Sun 5.30pm. Sun 10am. Hds 9.30am, 7pm.*

6. † St Michael (1873; 1891; cons 23 July 1931)
Westmorland Road, Elswick, Newcastle NE4 5RD **Tel:** 0191-273 3582
Rev William Bellamy. 115 Clumber Street, NE4 7RD
M: *Sun 10.15am, 6.30pm. Hds 9am, 10am, 8pm.*
- ***Little Sisters of the Poor,*** St Joseph's Home, Westmorland Road NE4 7QA **Tel:** 0191-273 1279
- ***Missionaries of Charity,*** Durham Street, NE4 **Tel:** 0191-273 0026

7. † Our Lady and St Edmund
(1883; 1903; 1954)
Station Road, Backworth, Newcastle NE27 0RU **Tel:** 0191-268 4332
M: *Sun 9.30am. Hds 9.30am.*

8. † St George (1868; 1869)
Bell's Close, Newcastle NE15 6XX
Tel: 0191-267 4120
Rev James Keane.
M: *Sat 1st M of Sun 6.30pm. Sun 10am. Hds 10am.*

9. † St Aidan (1887; 1906)
Coach Lane, Benton, Newcastle NE12 8AD
Tel: 0191-266 2112
M: *Sat 1st M of Sun 5pm. Sun 9.30am. Hds (vigil 5pm), 6.30pm.*
- ***Sisters of La Sagesse,*** Coach Lane, Benton, Newcastle NE12 8AD
  Tel: 0191-266 2112

10. † St Joseph
(1903-5; 1931; cons 22 March 1938)
South Benwell Road, Benwell, Newcastle NE15 6JL **Tel:** 0191-273 4402
Served from Newcastle (3).
M: *Sun 9am. Hds As announced.*

11. † St Lawrence (1878; 1898)
Byker Crescent, Byker, Newcastle NE6 2JT
Served from Newcastle (25).
M: *Sat 1st M of Sun 6.30pm. Sun 9.30am. Hds As announced.*

12. † St Robert
(1930; 1955; cons June 1963)
Cedar Road, Fenham, Newcastle NE4 9PH
Tel: 0191-273 3903 **Fax:** 0191 273 7430
Rev Michael Hickey.
M: *Sat 1st M of Sun 6.30pm. Sun 8.30am, 10.30am. Hds 10am, 7.30pm.*
- ***Society of the Sacred Heart***, 129 Cedar Road, NE4 9PE **Tel:** 0191-272 3000

13. † St Mary of the Rosary
(1928; 1952; 1961)
Forest Hall, Clousden Hill, Newcastle NE12 7AB **Tel/Fax:** 0191-268 4222
Rev Michael Brown.
M: *Sat 1st M of Sun 6pm. Sun 10am. Hds 10am, 7pm.*

14. † St Charles
(1896; 1911; cons 1986)
Church Road, Gosforth, Newcastle NE3 1TX **Tel:** 0191 285 1370
Rev Cornelius O'Connor.
M: *Sat 1st M of Sun 6.30pm. Sun 8.30am, 10am, 11.30am. Hds (Vigil 7pm), 10am, 7pm.*
- ***Sisters of Mercy,*** Moor Road South, NE3 1NN **Tel:** 0191-285 1056

15. † St Teresa of the Child Jesus
(1927)
Heaton Road, Newcastle NE6 5HN
Tel: 0191-265 5290
Revv Denis Kellett, Patrick McMahon.
M: *Sat 1st M of Sun 6.30pm. Sun 9am, 11am. Hds (7.00pm vigil), 10am.*
- ***Sisters of Mercy,*** Parkhead Road, Heaton, NE7 7DH **Tel:** 0191-281 3887

16. † The Holy Name
(1901; 1903; 1929; cons. 27 Sept 1979)
7 North Jesmond Avenue, Newcastle NE2 3JX **Tel:** 0191-281 0940
Rev Michael Whelan.
M: *Sun 10.15am, 7pm. Hds 10am, 7.30pm.*
- ***Sisters of Marie Reparatrice,*** 194 Osborne Road, Jesmond, NE2 3LD **Tel:** 0191-281 7261

17. † St Cuthbert (1861; 1939; 1960)
Hillsview Avenue, North Kenton, Newcastle
Tel: 0191-286 9673
Rev Laurence Jones, Rev Dcn Neil Munro.
Presbytery, Balmain Road, NE3 3QR
M: *Sat 1st M of Sun 6.30pm. 915am, 10.45am. Hds 9.30am, 7pm.*

18. Killingworth, Northd
Served from Forest Hall.
M: *Sun As announced.*

19. SS Peter and Paul (1960)
Bardsey Place, Longbenton, Newcastle NE12 8PB **Tel:** 0191-266 1533
Served from Forest Hall (13).
Rev David Milburn (in residence).
M: *Sat 1st M of Sun 6pm. Sun 10am. Hds 9am, 12noon, 7pm.*

20. † Sacred Heart
(1912; cons 9 June 1986)
Great North Road, North Gosforth, Newcastle **Tel:** 0191-236 3182
Rev James Dunne. Sacred Heart Presbytery, NE3 5EB
M: *Sat 1st M of Sun 6.30pm. Sun 9.30am, Hds (vigil 6.30pm), 10am, 6.30pm.*

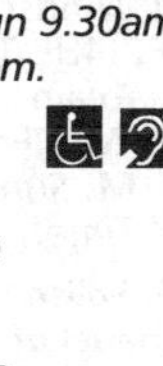

21. † St Matthew
(1884; 1949; 1978)
West Road, Ponteland, Newcastle NE20 9SX **Tel:** 01661 822767
Rev Vincent Melia.
M: *Sat 1st M Sun 6pm. Sun 10am, 6.30pm. Hds 8am, 10am, 7.30pm.*

22. St Cuthbert (1935; 1969)
Hexham Road, Throckley, Newcastle NE15 9DZ **Tel:** 0191-267 4389
In Residence: **Rev Patrick Laydon.**
M: *Sun 10am, 5.30pm. Hds 10am, 6pm.*

23. † St Anthony of Padua (1860)
Church Street, Walker, Newcastle NE6 3BT
Tel: 0191-262 3817 **Fax:** 0191-263 8692
Rev Michael Conaty.
M: *Sat 1st M of Sun 6pm. Sun 10.45am. Hds 10am.*
- ***De la Salle Brothers,*** 24-26 Hexham Avenue NE6 3UW **Tel:** 0191-234 1132/295 3202
- ***Religious of the Assumption.*** 24-26 Hexham Avenue NE6 3UW **Tel:** 0191-263 8229/295 3202

24. † St Francis of Assisi (1935; 1938; 1967)
Stotts Road, Walkergate, Newcastle NE6 4UH **Tel:** 0191-262 3669 also 0191-262 3817 **Fax:** 0191-263 8692
Rev Michael Conaty.
M: *Sun 9.15am. Hds 7pm.*

25. † Our Lady and St Vincent
(1932; 1951; 1953)
Monkchester Road, Newcastle NE6 2TX
Tel/Fax: 0191-265 5217
Rev William Rooke.
M: *Sun 10.45am. Hds As announced.*

26. † St John Vianney
(1959; 1965)
Hillhead Parkway, West Denton, Newcastle NE5 1DP **Tel:** 0191-267 6063
Rev Anthony Cornforth.
M: *Sat 1st M of Sun 6pm. Sun 8.30am, 10.30am. Hds 10.45am, 7pm.*

A

27. St Mark (1963; 1965)
Trevelyan Drive, Westerhope, Newcastle NE5 4BT **Tel:** 0191-286 0596
Rev Seamus O'Kane
M: *Sun 8.30am, 10am. Hds (vigil 7pm) 8.30am.*

28. Catholic Chaplaincy to University of Newcastle, University of Northumbria and Newcastle College
14 Windsor Terrace, Jesmond, Newcastle NE2 4HE **Tel:** 0191-281 1053
Chaplains: **Rev Andrew Downie, Ms Mia Fox.**
M: *Sun 11am, 6.45pm. During Term Time.*

29. Polish Catholic Centre (Chapel of Our Lady of Czestochowa).
2 Maple Terrace, Newcastle NE4 7SF
Tel: 0191-273 3575
Rev Robert Mazurouski.
M: *Sat 1st M of Sun 6pm. Sun 10am, 11.15am, 6pm.*

■ **NEW HARTLEY,** Whitley Bay
† Our Lady and St Joseph (1895)
New Hartley, Whitley Bay, Tyne and Wear NE25 0RT **Tel:** 0191-237 0455
Served from Cramlington.
Rev J Brian Malia (in residence).
M: *Sun 9am. Hds 7pm.*

■ **NEW SEAHAM,** Co Durham
† St Cuthbert (1934; 1966)
St Cuthbert's, Park House, Stockton Road, SR7 0HR **Tel/Fax:** 0191-581 2221
Mbl: 0789 1071783
Rev Anthony Hastie.
M: *Sat 1st M of Sun 6pm. Sun 10.30am. Hds 7pm (vigil), 10.30am.*

■ **NEW SILKSWORTH,** Sunderland A
† St Leonard (1873; cons 12 Oct 1875)
Silksworth Terrace, Sunderland, Tyne and Wear SR3 2BB **Tel:** 0191-521 0355
• ***Redemptorist Fathers (CSsR):*** **Rev Brian Russell.**
M: *Sat 1st M of Sun 6pm.*
Hds As Announced.

■ **NEWHOUSE,** Esh Winning A
Queen of Martyrs
(1871; 1883; cons 27 Sept 1894)
Newhouse Road, DH7 9LF
Served from Ushaw Moor.
Tel: 0191-373 4340/373 0219
M: *Sun 9.30am. Hds (vigil 7pm), 11am.*

■ **NEWTON AYCLIFFE,** Co Durham. A

1. † St Mary (1954; 1960)
Central Avenue, Newton Aycliffe, Co Durham DL5 5NP **Tel/Fax:** 01325-313611
Rev Michael Campion
M: *Sat 1st M of Sun 6.30pm. Sun 11am. Hds 11am, 7pm.*

2. St Joseph (1968; New Church 1984)
Served from St Mary's.
Tel: 01325-313611
M: *Sun 9.30am. Hds 9.30am.*

■ **NORTH GOSFORTH**
See Newcastle upon Tyne (20).

■ **NORTH SHIELDS**
1. † St Cuthbert (1821; 1975)
Albion Road West, North Shields, Tyne and Wear NE29 0JB **Tel:** 0191-257 3408
Rev Gerard Lee
M: *Sat 1st M of Sun 6pm. Sun 10.45am. Hds (vigil 7pm), 12.10pm.*

2. † St Joseph (1935; 1955)
Wallsend Road, North Shields, Tyne and Wear NE29 7AA **Tel:** 0191-257 5801
Fax: 0191-259 2589
Rev Peter J Stott.
M: *Sun 9.30am Hds 9.30am, 5.30pm.*
• ***Sisters of Mercy,*** 17 Cartington Road, North Shields, NE29 7BL
Tel: 0191-257 8165

■ **OTTERBURN,** Northd
St Peter (1936; 1953; cons 20 May 1980)
Served from Bellingham.
M: *Sun 9am. Hds (vigil 7.15pm).*

■ **PELAW** See Gateshead (15).

■ **PENSHAW,** Tyne and Wear
† Our Lady Queen of Peace (1919; 1865)
Penshaw, Tyne and Wear DH4 7JZ
Tel: 0191-385 2434
Rev Michael McCoy.
M: *Sat 1st M of Sun 6.30pm. Sun 10am, 6pm. Hds (vigil 7pm), 10am.*

■ **PETERLEE,** Co Durham
Our Lady of the Rosary (1954; 1966)
Passfield Way, Peterlee, Co Durham SR8 1DE **Tel/Fax:** 0191-586 2526
Revv Francis McCullagh, John Massedar.

M: *Sat 1st M of Sun 6pm, Sun 10am. Hds As announced*

■ PONTELAND
See Newcastle upon Tyne (21).

■ PRUDHOE, Northd
† Our Lady and St Cuthbert
(1870; 1905; cons 4 Oct 1951)
Highfield Lane, Prudhoe, Northd. NE42 6EY
Tel: 01661-832298
Very Rev Paul Zielinski.
M: *Sat 1st M of Sun 6.30pm. Sun 10am. Hds 9am, 7.30pm.*

■ ROTHBURY, Northd A
St Agnes 1922; New church 1959
Served from Longhorsley.
M: *Sun 10am. Hds 7pm.*

■ RYHOPE, Sunderland A
† St Patrick (1897; 1915; cons 3 Oct 1956)
Smith Street, Ryhope, Sunderland, Tyne and Wear SR2 0RG **Tel:** 0191-521 0340
Rev Alban Walker (in residence)
M: *Sun 10am. Hds As Announced*

■ SACRISTON, Durham A
† St Bede (1867; 1881; cons 17 July 1929)
Front Street, Sacriston, Durham DH7 6AB
Tel: 0191-371 0257
E-mail: regionalbursar@mhmdurham.sagehost.co.uk
Rev James Cronin MHM.
M: *Sat 1st M of Sun 7pm. Sun 10am. Hds 9am, 7pm.*

■ SEAHAM HARBOUR A
† St Mary Magdalen
Harbour Walk, Seaham Harbour, Co Durham SR7 7DS
Tel: 0191-581 2368
Revv Thomas Burke, Edward Wilkinson (in residence).
M: *Sun 8.30am, 10.30am. Hds 9.30am, 7pm.*
• ***Sisters of Mercy,*** 1 Antrim Gardens, Dene House Road. **Tel:** 0191-581 3249

■ SEAHOUSES, Northd
† St Aidan (1962; 1973)
18 King Street, Seahouses, Northumberland NE68 7XP **Tel:** 01665-602012
Rev Anthony Owens
M: *Oct 1st to Sunday before Easter: Sat 1st M of Sun 6pm. Sun 10am. Easter to End Sept: Sat 1st M of Sun 6pm. Sun 9am, 11am. Hds 10am, 7pm.*

■ SEDGEFIELD, Stockton, Cleveland
† St John Fisher (1935; 1950)
Front Street, Sedgefield, Stockton, Cleveland. **Tel/Fax:** 01740-620405
Served from Coxhoe.
Rev John Caden (retired priest in residence), Presbytery, West Park Lane, TS21 2BX
M: *Sun 10.30am, 6pm. Hds (vigil 7pm), 10am.*

■ SHILDON, Co Durham
† St Thomas Apostle (1905; 1934)
Tel: 01388-602030. Served from Coundon.
Rev Peter Kelly.
M: *Sun 10.30am. Hds 7pm.*

■ SHOTLEY BRIDGE, Co Durham
† Our Lady of the Rosary (1949; 1952)
43 Snows Green Road, Shotley Bridge, Co Durham DH8 0HD **Tel:** 01207-504196
Served from Blackhill.
M: *Sun 9.30am. Hds (vigil 7pm).*

■ SHOTTON, Durham A
† Our Lady of Lourdes (1921; 1940)
Flemingfield, Shotton Colliery, Shotton, Durham DH6 2JQ **Tel:** 0191-526 1150
In Residence: **Rev Desmond Meagher**
M: *Sun 10am only. Hds 9am, 7pm.*

■ SILKSWORTH
See New Silksworth.

■ SOUTH MOOR, Stanley A
† St Mary (1912; 1932)
South Moor, Stanley, Co Durham DH9 6NR
Tel: 01207-232798 **Fax:** 01207-239013
Rev Dennis Tindall.
M: *Sat 1st M of Sun 6.30pm. Sun 10.30am. Hds (vigil 7.30pm), 9.30am.*

■ SOUTH SHIELDS, Tyne and Wear
1. † St Bede (1849; 1876; cons 14 Sept 1949)
Westoe Road, South Shields, Tyne and Wear NE33 4LZ **Tel:** 0191-456 3536
Fax: 0191-420 0099 **Mbl:** 0411 826250
Rev Michael Weymes.
M: *Sun 9.30am, 5pm. Hds 12 noon.*

2. † St Gregory (1929)
The Parish House, 20 St Gregory's Court, South Shields NE34 6NR
Tel: 0191-456 0724 **Fax:** 0191-427 6482
Rev Patrick Kennedy (in residence).
M: *Sat 7pm (at St Vincent's, Whitburn). Sun 9.30am, 6pm. Hds 10am, 7pm, (vigil 7pm at St Vincent's, Whitburn).*

3. † Holy Rosary (1955; 1968)
Horsley Hill Square, South Shields NE34 7SA **Tel:** 0191-456 2495
Fax: 0191-420 0099 **Mbl:** 0411-826250
M: *Sat 1st M of Sun 5.30pm. Hds 6pm.*

4. † SS Peter and Paul A
(14 Dec 1884; 8 July 1906; cons 23 Oct 1930)
Boldon Lane, Tyne Dock, South Shields
Tel: 0191-456 1858

Rev John James. St Peter and St Paul's Presbytery, Belle Vue Crescent, NE33 4RE
M: *Sun 10.30am. Hds 7pm.*

5. † St Oswald (1965)
Gainsborough Avenue, Whiteleas, South Shields NE34 8JN **Tel:** 0191-536 7447
Rev John Gibbons.
M: *Sun 11am, 6pm. Hds (vigil 7pm), 9.30am.*

■ STANLEY, Co Durham
† St Joseph (1872; 1902; cons 21 Aug 1929)
Thorneyholme Tce, Stanley, Co Durham DH9 0BL
Tel: 01207-299012 **Fax:** 01207-283173
Rev Joseph Park.
M: *Sun 10am, 6pm. Hds (Vigil 7pm), 9.30am, 7pm.*

■ STELLA See Gateshead (16).

■ STOCKTON-ON-TEES
1. † St Mary (1783; 1842; cons 7 July 1942)
2 Major Street, Stockton-on-Tees, Cleveland TS18 2DD
Tel: 01642-676164 **Fax:** 01642-672329
Rev Patrick McKenna.
M: *Sat 1st M of Sun 5.30pm. Sun 11am. Hds 12.05pm.*
- ***Sacred Heart, Society of (Paris),*** 510 Yarm Road, Stockton on Tees TS16 0BG **Tel:** 01642-6480904

2. † St Bede (1951; cons 5 Dec 1951)
Bishopton Road, Stockton-on-Tees, Cleveland TS18 4PA
Tel: 01642-676164 **Fax:** 01642-672329
Rev Patrick McKenna (in residence).
M: *Sun 9.45am, 6.30pm. Hds 10am, 7.30pm.*

3. † St Cuthbert
(1884; 1906; 1920; cons 2 July 1958)
Yarm Road, Stockton-on-Tees, Cleveland
Tel: 01642-674321
Rev Simon Weymes
Presbytery, Spring Street, TS18 3NR
M: *Sat 1st M of Sun 5.15pm. Sun 9am, 11am. Hds 10am, 12noon, 7pm.*

4. † St Joseph (1933; 1935)
Ragworth Road, Norton, Stockton-on-Tees, Cleveland TS20 1EW **Tel:** 01642-553816
Served from SS Peter & Paul.
M: *Sat 1st M of Sun 6.30pm. Sun 10am. Hds 10am, 7pm.*

5. English Martyrs and SS Peter and Paul (1956)
Redhill Road, Stockton-on-Tees, Cleveland TS19 9BY **Tel/Fax:** 01642-676799
Rev Shaun O'Neill.
M: *Sat 1st M of Sun 6pm. Sun 9.15am. Hds 9.30am, 7.30pm.*

7. † St Patrick (1967)
Presbytery, Glenfield Road, Fairfield, Stockton-on-Tees, Cleveland TS19 7PJ
Tel/Fax: 01642-580171
Rev Nicholas Jennings.
M: *Sat 1st M of Sun 6pm. Sun 10am. Hds 7.30am, 10.30am.*

■ SUNDERLAND, Tyne and Wear
1. † St Mary (1743; 1835; cons 24 Sept 1947)
27 Bridge Street, Sunderland, Tyne and Wear SR1 1TQ **Tel:** 0191-567 5354
Rev Christopher W Jackson, Canon Alexander Barrass (in residence).
M: *Sun 8am (at Oaklea Convent), 11am, 6.30pm. Hds 12.05pm, 6.05pm, 7.30am (at Oaklea Convent).*
- ***Sisters of Mercy,*** St Anthony's Convent, Tunstall Road, SR2 7JR **Tel:** 0191-567 4653 Somerleyton Convent. **Tel:** 0191-565 9740.
- ***Sunderland University:*** *Chaplain:* **Rev Kevin Dixon.**

2. † St Anne (1957; 1959)
Hylton Road, Pennywell, Sunderland, Tyne and Wear SR4 9AA **Tel:** 0191-534 2346
Rev Kevin T Dixon.
M: *Sun 10am, 5.30pm. Hds 6.30pm.*

3. † St Benet
(1865; 1889; cons. 4 May 1960)
The Causeway, Monkwearmouth, Sunderland, Tyne and Wear SR6 0BH
Tel: 0191-567 2965
- ***Redemptorists (CSsR):*** **Revv Oliver Keyes** (*Rector & Parish Priest*), **Jan Milcz, Terence Creech, Stephen Wetherall** (Holy Cross House).
M: *Sat 1st M of Sun 6.30pm. Sun 9am, 10.30am. Hds 8am, 10am, 7pm.*

4. † St Cecilia and St Patrick
(1927; 1957)
Ryhope Road, Sunderland, Tyne and Wear SR2 7TG **Tel:** 0191-567 2718
Rev Denis O'Mahoney.
M: *Sat 1st M of Sun 6.30pm. Su 10am. Hds (vigil 7pm), 9am, 7pm.*

5. † St Hilda (1905)
The King's Road, Southwick, Sunderland, Tyne and Wear SR5 2JD **Tel:** 0191-548 6839
Rev Noel Colahan.
M: *Sun 10am, 6.30pm. Hds 10am, 6.30pm.*

6. † The Holy Family (1960; 1968)
Presbytery, Gardiner Road, Grindon, Sunderland, Tyne and Wear SR4 9PS

Tel: 0191-534 2460
Rev George Dolan (in residence).
M: *Sun 11am. Hds 9.30am.*

7. Holy Rosary
(1949; 1953; cons. 22 June 1960)
Arbroath Road, Farringdon, Sunderland, Tyne and Wear SR3 3LD **Tel:** 0191-528 1992
Rev Stephen Watson.
M: *Sat 1st M of Sun 6pm. Sun 11am. Hds (vigil 6.30pm), 6.30pm.*

8. † Immaculate Heart of Mary
(1949; 1954)
Durham Road, Springwell, Sunderland, Tyne and Wear SR3 4DF
Tel: 0191-528 3779 **Fax:** 0191-551 3831
Served from Sunderland (7)
In residence: **Rev Philip O'Brien (retired)**
M: *Sun 9.30am, 6pm. Hds 10am.*

9. † St Joseph
(1872; 1907; cons 28 Sept 1938)
Paxton Terrace, Millfield, Sunderland, Tyne and Wear SR4 6HP **Tel:** 0191-567 4574
Rev Gordon Ryan.
M: *Sat 1st M of Sun 6.30pm. Sun 9.30am, Hds 9.30am, 7.30pm.*
- ***Little Sisters of the Poor,*** Holy Cross Home, Ettrick Grove, High Barnes, SR4 8QA **Tel:** 0191-567 0862
  M. *Sun 10.15am.*

10. † Sacred Heart (1955; 1958)
Chiswick Road, Hylton Castle Estate, Sunderland, Tyne and Wear SR5 3PY
Tel: 0191-548 0177
Served from St Hilda's
M: *Sat 1st M of Sun 6.30pm. Sun 10.30am. Hds 10am, 7pm.*

■ **SWINBURNE,** Barrasford, Hexham
† St Mary (1841; 1960)
Barrasford, Hexham, Northd. NE48 4DE
Tel: 01434-603736
In residence: **Rev John Campbell**.
Served from St Mary's, Hexham.
M: *Sun 10.15am. Hds 8.30am.*

■ **THORNLEY,** Durham
† Sacred Heart and English Martyrs
(1850; 1900)
Dunelm Road, Thornley, Durham DH6 3HA **Tel/Fax:** 01429-820255
Rev Gary Dickson.
M: *Sat 1st M of Sun 6pm. Sun 9am. Hds 9am, 7pm.*

■ **THROCKLEY**
See Newcastle upon Tyne (22).

■ **THROPTON,** Morpeth. Northd
† All Saints (bef. 1702; 1753)
Thropton, Morpeth, Northd NE65 7ND
Tel: 01669-620288
Served from Longhorsley.
In residence: **Rev Deacon Jude Newton**
M: *Sun 8am. Hds 10am.*

■ **TOW LAW,** Bishop Auckland
† St Joseph
26 Castle Bank, Co Durham DL13 4AF
Served from Willington.
Tel: 01388-746220 **Fax:** 01388 747440
M: *Sun 9am. Hds 7pm.*

■ **TRIMDON,** Co Durham
† St William (1864)
Front Street, Trimdon, Co Durham TS29 6LZ **Tel:** 01429-880238
Served from Coxhoe.
In residence: **Rev Barrie McKenzie**.
M: *Sun 9.30am, 5pm. Hds 10am, 7pm.*

■ **TUDHOE,** Spennymoor, Co Durham
† St Charles (1858; 1870)
St Charles Road, Tudhoe Village, DL16 6JY
Tel: 01388-814713
Rev Henry O'Reilly.
M: *Sat 1st M of Sun 6pm. Sun 10am. Hds (vigil 7pm), 10am, 7pm.*

■ **TYNE DOCK** See South Shields (4).

■ **TYNEMOUTH,** North Tyneside
† Our Lady and St Oswin (1871; 1890)
Front Street, Tynemouth.
Canon Seamus Cunningham VG, St Mary's, Farringdon Road, Cullercoats, North Shields NE30 3EY
Tel/Fax: 0191-251 3770
M: *Sun 9.30am, 6pm. Hds 10am, 7.30pm.*

■ **USHAW,** Durham
St Cuthbert's College
(1808; 1881; chapel cons 19 June 1897)
Durham DH7 9RH
President: **Rev John Marsland,**
Tel: 0191-373 8501
E-mail: president@ushaw.ac.uk
President's Secretary: **Mrs Marjorie Towers Tel:** 0191-373 8510
E-mail: marjorie.towers@ushaw.ac.uk
Director of Teaching and Learning: **Sr Patricia McDonald** SHCJ, BA, PGCE, MA, BD, MPhil, LSS, PhD (Scripture).
Tel: 0191-373 8530
E-mail: p.mcdonald@ushaw.ac.uk
Director of Educational Outreach: **Mrs Ros Stuart-Buttle** BA, MA, PGCE
Tel: 0191-373 855
E-mail: Ros.Stuart-Buttle@ushaw.ac.uk
Course Administrator: **Mrs Ann Scott**
Tel: 0191-373 8517
E-mail: ann.scott@ushaw.ac.uk
Director of Finance and Communications: **Mr John Mortimer Tel:** 0191-373 8511
E-mail: john.mortimer@ushaw.ac.uk

Director of Estates and Facilities: **Mr Peter Seed Tel:** 0191-373 8505
E-mail: peter.seed@ushaw.ac.uk
Conference Centre Manager: **Ms Angie George Tel:** 0191-373 518
E-mail: angie.george@ushaw.ac.uk
Finance Manager: **Mr Denis D'Ugo**
Tel: 0191-373 506
E-mail: dendugo@ushaw.ac.uk

Teaching Staff:
Sr Helen Bamber SHCJ, (Assistant to Director of Education Outreach),
Tel: 0191 373 8569
E-mail: helen.bamber@ushaw.ac.uk
Rev Bernard Barlow (OSM) PhB, MA, DRS, MS, STL, PhD, PGCE (Church History)
Tel: 0191 373 8535
E-mail: Bernard.Barlow@ushaw.ac.uk
Rev Philip Caldwell BA, PGCE, STB, STL, STD, (Systematic Theology)
Tel: 0191 373 8533
E-mail: philip.caldwell@ushaw.ac.uk
Rev Jeremy Corley BA, MA, PhD (Scripture), **Tel:** 0191 373 8521
E-mail: jeremy.corley@ushaw.ac.uk
Peter Cullen, BA, MA, (Spiritual Director), **Tel:** 0191 373 8576 **E-mail:** peter.cullen@ushaw.ac.uk
Bro Brendan Geary (FMS), PhD, (Human Development) **Tel:** 0191-373 8507
E-mail: Brendan.Geary@ushaw.ac.uk
Rev Philip Gillespie PhB, STB, SLL, (Liturgy), **Tel:** 0191-373 8524
E-mail: p.gillespie@ushaw.ac.uk
Mr Timothy Harrison BA, MMus, LTCL, (Director of Music) **Tel:** 0191-373 8607,
E-mail: timothy.harrison@ushaw.ac.uk
Rev Chris Hughes BA, LLB (Pastoral Director), **Tel:** 0191-373 8525
E-mail: chris.hughes@ushaw.ac.uk
Mr Scott Opperman BA, MA, (Systematic Theology), **Tel:** 0191-373 8531
E-mail: scott.opperman@ushaw.ac.uk
Rev Vincent Purcell BA (hons), CPS, (Pastoral Director), **Tel:** 0191-373 8560
E-mail: vincent.purcell@ushaw.ac.uk
Rev Dr Michael Sharratt STL, PhD
Tel: 0191-373 8536
E-mail: michael.sharratt@ushaw.ac.uk
Rev James Sheehy, (Spiritual Director), **Tel:** 0191-373 8528,
E-mail: jim.sheehy@ushaw.ac.uk

Visiting Lecturers: **Revv Steven Billington** BSc, STB, PhL; **Michael McCoy** MA, JCL; **Rev David Potter** MA, STL, PhD

■ **USHAW MOOR,** Durham
† St Joseph (1909; 1931; cons 17 May 1938)
Durham Road, Ushaw Moor, Durham DH7 7LF **Tel:** 0191-373 0219
Rev Michael Griffiths.
M: *Sat 1st M of Sun 6pm. Sun 10.45am. Hds 10am.*

■ **WALBOTTLE**
See Newcastle upon Tyne (22).

■ **WALLSEND,** Tyne and Wear
1. † Our Lady and St Columba (1885; 1904; 1957)
Carville Road, Wallsend, Tyne and Wear NE28 6RQ **Tel:** 0191-262 3882
Rev Anthony Donaghue.
M: *Sat 1st M of Sun 6pm. Sun 9.30am. Hds (vigil 7pm), 10am.*

2. † St Bernadette (1958)
Station Road North, Wallsend, Tyne and Wear NE28 8AE
Tel/Fax: 0191-262 8488
Rev Anthony Donaghue.
In residence: **Rev Patrick O'Connell**
M: *Sun 11am, 6.30pm. Hds 9am, 7pm.*

3. † Our Lady and St Aidan (1865)
Coniston Road, Wallsend, Northd NE28 0EP
Tel: 0191-262 3820
Rev John McElhone. The Presbytery, Coniston Road, NE28 0EP
M: *Sun 9.30am. Hds 10am.*

■ **WASHINGTON,** Tyne and Wear
1. † Our Blessed Lady Immaculate (1861; 1878; cons 27 Sept 1933)
Village Lane, Washington, Tyne and Wear NE38 7HS **Tel/Fax:** 0191-416 3583
Rev Mark Millward.
M: *Sat 1st M of Sun 5pm. Sun, 10.30am, 6.30pm. Hds. (vigil 6.30pm). 12 noon.*

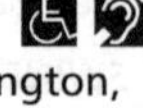

2. † St Bede (1965)
New Road, Coach Road Est, Washington, Tyne and Wear NE37 2HE
Tel: 0191-416 3805 **Fax:** 0191-417 7394
Rev Sean Hall, Rev Deacon Frank O'Neill.
M: *Sat 1st M of Sun 6pm. Sun 10.30am. Hds 9.15am, 7pm.*

3. St John Boste (Cons June 1983)
3 Crighton, Oxclose, Washington, Tyne and Wear NE38 0LB **Tel/Fax:** 0191-417 9834
M: *Sun 9am, 5pm. Hds 7pm (vigil), 9am.*

■ **WEST AUCKLAND**
See Bishop Auckland (3).

■ **WEST CORNFORTH.**
See Coxhoe.

■ **WEST DENTON**
See Newcastle upon Tyne (26).

■ **WEST MONKSEATON**
Immaculate Heart of Mary (1961; 1962)
Served from Backworth. **Tel:** 0191-265 4332

The Presbytery, Church Close, West Monkseaton, Whitley Bay, Tyne and Wear. NE25 9PG. **Rev Thomas Cunningham** (retired: in residence)

M: *Sat 1st M of Sun 6pm. Sun 11am. Hds 10am, 7.30pm.*

■ **WESTERHOPE**
See Newcastle-upon-Tyne (27).

■ **WHICKHAM**
See Gateshead (17).

■ **WHITBURN,** Sunderland
St Vincent (1950)
Mill Lane, Sunderland, Tyne and Wear
Served from South Shields (2).

M: *Sat 1st M of Sun 7pm. Hds (vigil 7pm)*

■ **WHITLEY BAY,** Tyne and Wear
† **St Edward** (1911; 1928)
Coquet Avenue, Whitley Bay, Tyne and Wear NE26 1EE **Tel:** 0191-252 8021
Rev David Russell.

M: *Sat 1st M of Sun 6.30pm. Sun 9am,11am, Hds (vigil 7.30pm), 10am, 7.30pm.*

■ **WHITTINGHAM,** Alnwick, Northd
† **Our Lady Immaculate**
(Callally Castle, 16th cent; 1881; cons 6 Sept 1933)
Whittingham, Alnwick, Northd. NE66 4SY
Tel: 01665-574240
Rev David Tanner.

M: *Sun 11am. Hds (vigil 6.30pm).*

■ **WIDDRINGTON,** Northd
St Joseph (1937)
Served from Amble.

M: *Sat 1st M of Sun. Hds (as announced).*

■ **WILLINGTON,** Co Durham
† **Our Lady of Perpetual Succour and St Thomas of Canterbury** (1877; 1905)
Cumberland Tce, Willington, Co Durham DL15 0PB
Tel: 01388-746220
Fax: 01388 747440
Rev John Reid.

M: *Sat 1st M of Sun 6pm. Sun 10.30am. Hds (vigil 7pm).*

■ **WINDLESTONE,** Ferryhill
† **Sacred Heart** (1948)
South View, Chilton DL17 0PU
Tel: 01325-313611
Served from All Saints, Ferryhill.

M: *Sat 1st M of Sun 6pm. Hds 7pm.*

■ **WINLATON**
See Gateshead 18.

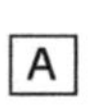

■ **WOLSINGHAM,** Bishop Auckland
† **St Thomas of Canterbury** (1849; 1954)

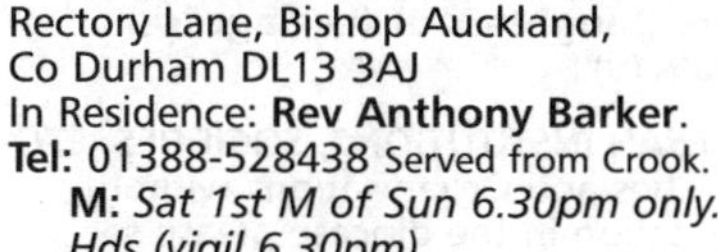

Rectory Lane, Bishop Auckland, Co Durham DL13 3AJ
In Residence: **Rev Anthony Barker.**
Tel: 01388-528438 Served from Crook.

M: *Sat 1st M of Sun 6.30pm only. Hds (vigil 6.30pm).*

• ***Sisters of Mercy,*** Mill Race, 19a West End, Wolsingham DL13 3AS
Tel: 01388-527194

■ **WOOLER,** Northd
† **St Ninian** (1854)
Burnhouse Road, Wooler, Northd.
Tel: 01665 574240
Served from Whittingham.

M: *Sun 9.00am. Hds 7pm.*

■ **WREKENTON** See Gateshead (19).

■ **ORDERS OR CONGREGATIONS, ETC**

■ **Men**
Charity, Institute of: Durham (2).
De la Salle Brothers: Newcastle (23).
Dominicans: Newcastle (4).
Hospitaller Order of Saint John of God: Darlington (1).
Mill Hill Missionaries: Durham (2).
Passionists: Minsteracres.
Redemptorists: Sunderland (3), New Silksworth.

■ **Women**
Assumption, Religious of the: Newcastle (23).
Carmelites: Darlington (2).
Christian Community, Sisters for: Blyth: New Hartley
Cross and Passion, Sisters of the: Darlington (3).
Daughters of Charity (SVP): Darlington (5)
Sisters of Divine Love: St Wilfrid, Gateshead (8)
Faithful Companions of Jesus: Crook, Hartlepool (1).
Good Shepherd Sisters: Newcastle (3).
Jesus, Daughters of: Birtley.
Marie Reparatrice Sisters of: Newcastle (16)
Mary and Joseph, Daughters of: Jarrow.
Mercy Sisters of Institute of Our Lady of Mercy: Alnwick, Esh Laude, Heaton, Newcastle (14), North Shields.
Mercy, Sisters of: Newcastle (1, 15) Seaham Harbour, (2), Sunderland (1), Wolsingham.
Mercy Sisters of (Union): Morpeth.
Missionaries of Charity: Newcastle (6).
Our Lady of Good and Perpetual Succour, Sisters of: Chopwell.
Poor, Little Sisters of the: Newcastle (6), Sunderland (9).
Sacred Heart (Paris), Society of the: Newcastle (12).

Wisdom, Daughters of (La Sagesse): Newcastle (9).

■ DIOCESAN INSTITUTIONS, SOCIETIES, ETC

For Societies and Organisations without representation in the diocese please see the main Societies and Organisations section.

Apostleship of the Sea. Contact: **Mr Tony McAvoy, Tel: (mobile)** 07703-781546

Archconfraternity of St Stephen for Altar Servers. *Diocesan Director:* **Rev M Anthony Hastie.**

Association of Missionary Children. Contact: **Rev W. Rooke.**

Association for the Propagation of the Faith. *Diocesan Director*: **Rev W. Rooke.**

Association of Inter-Church Families: *Regional Secretaries:* **Tony and Barbara Bone, Tel:** 0191-477 5746

Catenian Association. Province No 5. *Secretary:* **Ian Fairhurst**, 51 Woodside, Ponteland NE20 9JD **Tel:** 01661-824646

Catholic Men's Society. Hexham and Newcastle Diocesan Council. Contact: St Joseph's Parish Centre, Birtley DH3 1LJ **Tel:** 0191-410 2541

Catholic Nurses Guild: *Chaplain:* Awaiting Appointment. *Secretary:* **Mrs J Hall, Tel:** 01670-732661

Catholic Teachers' Federation. *Secretary:* **Mr J Mullen**. 6 Ravensdale Crescent, Low Fell, Gateshead, Tyne and Wear.

Catholic Truth Society, Upper Level, Princess Square, Newcastle upon Tyne, **Tel:** 0191-232 1169. *Secretary:* **Rev W Elkin.**

Catholic Women's League. *President*: **Mrs Kathleen Lucas**, 167 Sherburn Way, Wardley, Gateshead NE10 8TZ **Tel:** 0191-469 3538 *Vice President*: **Mrs Nancy Anderson,** 7 Gullane Close, Bill Quay, Gateshead NE10 0TQ **Tel:** 0191-469 5062 *Treasurer:* **Mrs Pat Biagioni,** 27 Burnside Grove, Stockton TS18 4ET **Tel:** 01642 615660 *Secretary*: **Mrs Rosemary Duffy,** 7 The Bungalows, Mount Pleasant, Birtley, Co. Durham DH3 1LW **Tel:** 0191 492 0531

Charismatic Renewal (Hexham & Newcastle): *Secretary:* **Mrs Karen Burbridge,** 72 Eddrington Grove, Newcastle-upon-Tyne NE5 1LA **Tel:** 0191-267 4289

Diocese of Hexham and Newcastle Catholic Handicapped Children's Fellowship. *Secretary:* **Mrs Ann Lowe**. 44 Doncrest Road, Donwell Village, Washington, Tyne and Wear. NE37 1ED **Tel:** 0191-416 2086

Durham University Catholic Society. *Chaplain:* **Rev Anthony Currer**. St Cuthbert's, Old Elvet, Durham DH1 3HL **Tel:** 0191-384 3442

Family and Social Action. *Diocesan Organiser:* **Rev Brendan Kelly**. St Cuthberts, 64 Ravensdowne, Berwick TD15 1DQ **Tel:** 01289 307297

Handicapped Children's Pilgrimage Trust. *North-East Representative:* **Mrs M Rathbone.** 57 Birchwood Avenue, North Gosforth, Newcastle-upon-Tyne. NE13 6QA **Tel:** 0191-236 6508

Hexham and Newcastle Diocesan Deaf Service. *Director and Chaplain:* **Rev R. Kinleen**, St Cuthbert's, Cowpen, Blyth **Tel:** (Text) 0191-233 0160; (Voice): 0191-232 6953 *Club:* Our Lady of Lourdes Deaf Club, 2 Summerhill Gr, Newcastle upon Tyne NE4 6EE

Knights of St Columba. Province No 4 (Northumberland): *Provincial Grand Knight:* **Mr A E Semens,** 16 Cheviot Road, Jarrow NE32 5NT **Tel:** 0191-421 9611 **E-mail:** aes@blueyonder.co.uk

Leaven Carmelite Secular Institute, The: *Contact:* A Harrison, 30 Sedley Road, Wallsend, Tyne & Wear NE28 6AU.

Legion of Mary. *President*: **Mrs Emma Hindes** 6 Julian Road, Wardley, Gateshead NE10 8AB **Tel:** 0191-266 5111

Marriage Care. For local diocesan centres **Tel:** 0800 839 3801.

Marriage Encounter. World Wide Marriage Encounter, **Bill and Josie Devlin**, 15 Cranbourne Grove, Tynemouth NE30 3NB **Tel:** 0191-252 7008

Northern Brethren's Fund. *Secretary:* **Rev James Angus**; *Treasurer:* **Rev Peter Carr**, St Cuthbert's, Ropery Lane, Chester le Street DH3 3PH **Tel:** 0191-388 2302

Our Lady's Catechists: *Diocesan Reprsentative:* **Sr Agnes Sheldon,** 38 Hexham Avenue, Walker, Newcastle upon Tyne NE6 3AL **Tel:** 0191-263 9229

Society of St Peter the Apostle. *Diocesan Director:* **Rev W Rooke. Tel:** 0191-265 5217

Society of St Vincent de Paul. Tyne Central Council. *President:* **Mr Joseph Gilfillan, SVP**, Blackfriars, New Bridge Street NE1 2TP

Teams of Our Lady. An international Catholic Movement for Christian married couples that aims to deepen the couples' spirituality. A 'Team' consists of four or five couples and a priest or religious as spiritual advisor meeting monthly to share the journey of faith, guided by the Holy Spirit. *Contact couple:* **Mike & Anne Duffy**, 4 Gill Burn, Rowlands Gill, Tyne & Wear

NE39 2PT **Tel:** 01207-542443

Walsingham Association. Tyneside Association: *All enquiries to:* **Mrs M Greaves**, 2 Langholm Road, Gosforth, Newcastle upon Tyne NE3 5JY **Tel:** 0191-285 5095

■ CHURCHES IN THE NEWCASTLE AND GATESHEAD POSTAL DISTRICT AREAS (arranged according to their districts).

■ NEWCASTLE

NE1: Cathedral; St Andrew; St Dominic.
NE2: Holy Name.
NE3: St Cuthbert; (Kenton) St Charles; (Gosforth) Sacred Heart (North Gosforth).
NE4: St Michael; St Robert.
NE5: English Martyrs; St John Vianney; (West Denton) St Mark (Westerhorpe).
NE6: Our Lady and St Vincent; St Anthony; St Francis; St Lawrence; St Teresa.
NE12: (Benton) St Aidan; (Forest Hall) St Mary; (Longbenton) SS Peter and Paul.
NE15: St Bede; St Joseph; (Bell's Cl) St George; (Throckley) St Cuthbert.
NE16: (Byermoor) Sacred Heart; (Whickham) St Mary.
NE17: (Chopwell) Our Lady of Lourdes.

■ GATESHEAD

NE8: Corpus Christi; Holy Rosary; Our Lady and St Wilfrid; St Joseph; (Dunston) St Philip Neri.
NE9: Our Lady of the Annunciation; St Anne; St Peter; (Wrekenton) St Oswald.
NE10: (Felling) St Patrick; St Augustine; (Pelaw) St Alban.
NE11: Immaculate Heart of Mary.

■ HOSPITALS

To contact the Catholic Chaplain of a particular hospital we suggest you contact the hospital reception directly.

■ CATHOLIC SCHOOLS - MAINTAINED

■ DURHAM

▲ Primary

St Bede's, Kingsway, Darlington **Tel:** 01325-466411

St Mary's Birch Road DL12 8JR **Tel:** 01833-690222 *(Barnard Castle)*

St Wilfrid's Murphy Crescent DL14 6QH **Tel:** 01388-603451 *(Bishop Auckland)*

Our Lady & St Thomas, Cumberland Terrace, Willington DL15 0PB **Tel:** 01388-746336 *(Bishop Auckland)*

St Joseph's Coast Road, Hartlepool TS27 4HE **Tel:** 0191-5864308 *(Blackhall)*

Our Lady & St Joseph's St Ives Road, Leadgate DH8 7SN **Tel:** 01207-503979 *(Brooms)*

St Cuthbert's Ropery Lane DH3 3PH **Tel:** 0191-388 2305 *(Chester-le-Street)*

St Patrick's Stanley Road DH8 6LN **Tel:** 01207-503982 *(Consett 1)*

St Pius X Thornfield Road, The Grove DH8 8AX **Tel:** 01207-503604 *(Consett 2)*

St Joseph's Victoria Lane, Bishop Auckland DL14 8NN **Tel:** 01388-602608 *(Coundon)*

St Cuthbert's Church Hill DL15 9DN **Tel:** 01388-762889 *(Crook)*

St Patrick's North Road, Dipton DH9 9BB **Tel:** 01207-570316 *(Dipton)*

St Godric's Castle Chare DH1 4RA **Tel:** 0191-384 7452 *(Durham)*

St Joseph's Mill Lane, Gilesgate DH1 2JQ **Tel:** 0191-386 5611 *(Durham 3)*

St Thomas More Thorndale Road, Belmont DH1 2AQ **Tel:** 0191-386 4761 *(Durham)*

St Michael's Esh Laude DH7 9QY **Tel:** 0191-373 1205 *(Esh Village)*

Our Lady Queen of Martyrs, Durham Road DH7 9PA **Tel:** 0191-373 4343 *(Esh Winning)*

Our Lady Star of the Sea Thorpe Road, Peterlee SR8 4AB **Tel:** 0191-586 3895 *(Horden)*

All Saints, Kitswell Road DH7 0JG **Tel:** 01207-520435 *(Lanchester)*

St Patrick's Goatbeck Terrace DH7 8JJ **Tel:** 0191-378 0552 *(Langley Moor)*

St Joseph's Church Lane, Seaham SR7 9RD **Tel:** 0191-526 1795 *(Murton)*

St Cuthbert's Mill Road SR7 0HW **Tel:** 0191-581 3090 *(New Seaham)*

St Joseph's Garburn Place DL5 7DE **Tel:** 01325-300337 *(Newton Aycliff)*

St Mary's Central Avenue DL5 5NP **Tel:** 01325-300339 *(Newton Aycliffe)*

St Benet's St Benet's Way, Ouston, Chester-le-Street Co Durham DH2 1QX **Tel:** 0191-410 5857 *(Ouston)*

Our Lady of the Rosary Westway SR8 1DE **Tel:** 0191-586 2264 *(Peterlee)*

St Bede's Front Street DH7 6AB **Tel:** 0191-371 0272 *(Sacriston)*

Seaham Harbour Denehouse Road SR7 7BJ **Tel:** 0191-581 3055 *(Seaham)*

Our Lady of Lourdes Fleming Field DH6 2JQ **Tel:** 0191-526 1531 *(Shotton)*

St Mary's, Southmoor, Hustledown Stanley DH9 6PH **Tel:** 01207-232189 *(Southmoor)*

Tudhoe St Charles Durham Road DL16 6SL **Tel:** 01388-814285 *(Spennymoor)*

St Joseph's Front Street, Stanley DH9 0NP **Tel:** 01207-232624 *(Stanley)*

St Godric's Wheatley Hill DH6 3NR **Tel:** 01429-820333 *(Thornley)*

Blessed John Ducket, Smith Street, Tow

Law DL13 4AU **Tel:** 01388-731082 *(Tow Law)*

St William's Elwick View, Trimdon Village TS29 6JU **Tel:** 01419-880348 *(Trimdon Station)*

St Joseph's Durham Road DH7 7LF **Tel:** 0191-373 0355 *(Ushaw Moor)*

St Mary's TS28 5AN **Tel:** 01429-838294 *(Wingate)*

St Chad's Baltic Road, Bishop Auckland DL14 0EP **Tel:** 01388-603632 *(WittonPark)*

St Mary's Pemberton Road, Consett DH8 8JD **Tel:** 01207-502657 *(Blackhill)*

St Mary Magdalen, Denehouse Road, Seaham SR7 7BJ **Tel:** 0191-581 3055

▲ **Secondary Comprehensive**

St John's RC Woodhouse Lane DL14 6JT **Tel:** 01388-603246 *(Bishop Auckland)*

Carmel Technology College, The Headlands DL3 8RW **Tel:** 01325-463009 *(Darlington)*

St Leonard's North End DH1 4NG **Tel:** 0191-384 8575 *(Durham)*

St Bede's Consett Road DH7 0RD **Tel:** 01207-520424 *(Lanchester)*

St Bede's West Way SR8 1DE **Tel:** 0191-586 2291 *(Peterlee)*

■ **GATESHEAD**

▲ **Infant**

St Joseph's Mitchell Street, Co Durham DH3 1LU **Tel:** 0191-410 2324 *(Birtley)*

▲ **Primary**

St Joseph's Croftdale Road NE21 4BG **Tel:** 0191-414 3108 *(Blaydon)*

Sacred Heart Burnopfield, Newcastle-upon-Tyne NE16 6NU **Tel:** 01207-270396 *(Byermoor)*

St Agnes Ryton Main Street, Tyne and Wear NE40 4NF **Tel:** 0191-413 2184 *(Crawcrook)*

St Philip Neri Ellison Road NE8 2QU **Tel:** 0191-460 4378 *(Dunston)*

St Augustine's Colegate Leam Lane Estate NE10 8PP **Tel:** 0191-469 2949 *(Felling)*

St John the Baptist Willow Grove NE10 9PQ **Tel:** 0191-469 2969 *(Felling)*

Corpus Christi Dunsmuir Grove NE8 4QL **Tel:** 0191-477 2175 *(Gateshead 1)*

St Joseph's Prince Consort Road NE8 1LR **Tel:** 0191-490 1517 *(Gateshead 7)*

St Wilfrid's Carville Street NE10 0EP **Tel:** 0191-477 1909 *(Gateshead 5)*

St Joseph's Smailes Lane, Rowlands Gill NE39 2DB **Tel:** 01207-542647 *(Highfields)*

St Anne's Pickering Green, Harlow Green NE9 7HX **Tel:** 0191-420 1688 *(Low Fell)*

St Peter's Dryden Road NE9 5TU **Tel:** 0191-487 8233 *(Low Fell)*

St Alban's Rothbury Avenue NE10 0RY **Tel:** 0191-469 3251 *(Pelaw)*

SS Mary & Thomas Aquinas Stella Lane, Blaydon-on-Tyne NE21 4NE **Tel:** 0191-414 3116 *(Stella)*

St Mary's Duckpool Lane NE16 4HB **Tel:** 0191-420 5828 *(Whickham)*

St Oswald's Easington Avenue NE9 7L **Tel:** 0191-487 8641 *(Wrekenton)*

▲ **Junior**

St Joseph's School Street, Co Durham DH3 2PN **Tel:** 0191-410 2231 *(Birtley)*

▲ **Secondary Comprehensive**

St Thomas More Croftdale Road, Tyne and Wear NE21 4BQ **Tel:** 0191-499 0111 *(Blaydon)*

St Edmund Campion Rugby Gardens NE9 7JX **Tel:** 0191-487 7638 *(Wrekenton)*

■ **HARTLEPOOL**

▲ **Primary**

St Cuthbert's Streatford Road TS25 5AJ **Tel:** 01429-275040 *(Hartlepool 2)*

St Joseph's Musgrave Street TS24 7HT **Tel:** 01429-272747. *(Hartlepool 4)*

St Teresa's Callander Road TS25 3BG **Tel:** 01429-274936 *(Hartlepool 6)*

St Bega's Thorpe Street TS24 0DX **Tel:** 01429-267768 *(Hartlepool (1)*

St John Vianney King Owsy Drive TS24 9PA **Tel:** 01429-273273 *(Hartlepool 3)*

Sacred Heart Hart Lane TS26 8NL **Tel:** 01429-272684 *(Hartlepool 4)*

▲ **Secondary**

English Martyrs School and Sixth Form College, Catcote Road TS25 4HA **Tel:** 01429-273790 *(Hartlepool 4)*

■ **STOCKTON**

▲ **Primary**

St Cuthbert's Parkfield TS18 3SY **Tel:** 01642-393532 *(Stockton-on-Tees 3)*

St Patrick's Lingfield Road, Fairfield TS19 7PL **Tel:** 01642-580850 *(Stockton-on-Tees 7)*

St Gregory's RC Ragpath Lane TS19 9AD **Tel:** 01642-393582 *(Stockton-on-Tees 5)*

St John the Evangelist, Cowpen Lane TS23 1LJ **Tel:** 01642-643400 *(Billingham 1)*

St Joseph's Low Grange Avenue TS23 3NN. **Tel:** 01642-560056. *(Billingham 3)*

St Paul's Wolviston Mill Lane TS22 5LU. **Tel:** 01642-360022 *(Billingham 2)*

Our Lady of the Most Holy Rosary, Rievaulx Avenue TS23 2BS **Tel:** 01642-552274 **Fax:** 01642-551135 *(Billingham 2)*

St Bede's Green Lane, Stockton-on-Tees TS19 0DW **Tel:** 01642-678071 *(Stockton-on-Tees 2)*

▲ **Secondary Comprehensive**
Our Lady and St Bede's Bishopton Road West TS19 0QH **Tel:** 01642-890800 *(Stockton-onTees)*
St Michael's Beamish Road TS23 3DX **Tel:** 01642-560612 *(Billingham)*

■ DARLINGTON

▲ **Primary**
Holy Family Prior Street DL3 9EN **Tel:** 01325-380821 *(Darlington)*
St Augustine's Beechwood Avenue DL3 7HP **Tel:** 01325-380819 *(Darlington 1)*
St Teresa's Harris Street DL1 4NL **Tel:** 01325-380754 *(Darlington 4)*

■ NEWCASTLE-UPON-TYNE

▲ **Primary**
St Michael's Clumber Street NE4 7RD **Tel:** 0191-273 9383 *(Elswick)*
St George's NE15 6XX **Tel:** 0191-267 5677 *(Bell's Close)*
St Joseph's Armstrong Road NE15 6JB **Tel:** 0191-273 9063 *(Benwell)*
St Lawrence's Headlam Street NE6 2JX **Tel:** 0191-265 9881 *(Byker)*
St Bede's Howlett Hall Road NE15 7HS **Tel:** 0191-274 3430 *(Denton Burn)*
The English Martyrs Netherby Drive, Fenham NE5 2RT **Tel:** 0191-274 7463 *(Fenham)*
Sacred Heart Convent Road, NE4 9XZ **Tel:** 0191-274 6695 *(Fenham)*
St Charles' Regent Farm Road, Gosforth NE3 3HE **Tel:** 0191-285 2553 *(Gosforth)*
St Oswald's Hartford Road NE3 5LE **Tel:** 0191-285 2437 *(Gosforth)*
St Teresa's Heaton Road NE6 5HN **Tel:** 0191-265 5076 *(Heaton)*
St Cuthbert's Balmain Road, NE3 3QR **Tel:** 0191-286 0129 *(Kenton)*
Our Lady & St Anne's Primary School Summerhill Terrace, NE4 6EB **Tel:** 0191-232 5496
St Cuthbert's Walbottle Village NE15 8JL **Tel:** 0191-267 5956 *(Walbottle)*
St Alban's Westbourne Avenue NE6 4HQ **Tel:** 0191-262 5552 *(Walker)*
St Vincent's Monkchester Road NE6 2TX **Tel:** 0191-265 5049 *(Walker)*
St John Vianney Hillhead Road NE5 1DN **Tel:** 0191-267 2233 *(West Denton)*
St Mark's Bardon Close, Newbiggin Hall Estate NE5 4BT **Tel:** 0191-286 9349 *(Westerhope)*
St Catherine's Prmary School, Greystoke Gate, Sandyford, Newcastle upon Tyne NE2 1PS **Tel:** 0191-232 6803

▲ **Secondary Comprehensive**
St Cuthbert's High Gretna Road NE15 6PH **Tel:** 0191-274 4510 *(Benwell)*
St Mary's Benton Park Road NE7 7PE **Tel:** 0191-266 8813 *(Benton)*
Sacred Heart Fenham Hall Drive NE4 9YH **Tel:** 0191-274 7373 *(Fenham)*

■ NORTH TYNESIDE

▲ **Primary**
St Mary's Farringdon Road, North Shields NE30 3EY **Tel:** 0191-252 4066 *(Cullercoats)*
St Mary's, Great Lime Road, Forest Hall NE12 0AB **Tel:** 0191-200 8381 *(Forest Hall)*
St Stephen Bardsey Place NE12 8NU **Tel:** 0191-200 7425 *(Longbenton)*
St Cuthbert's Lovaine Place NE29 0BU **Tel:** 0191-200 5620 *(North Shields)*
St Joseph's Wallsend Road NE29 7BT **Tel:** 0191-200 5077 *(North Shields)*
St Columba's Station Road NE28 8EN **Tel:** 0191-200 7235 *(Wallsend 1)*
St Bernadette's Rising Sun Cottages, NE28 9EW **Tel:** 0191-262 2161 *(Wallsend 2)*
Holy Cross Coniston Road NE28 0EP **Tel:** 0191-262 5176 *(Wallsend)*
Star of the Sea Arcot Avenue Whitley Bay NE25 9DY **Tel:** 0191-200 8728 *(West Monkseaton)*

▲ **Secondary Comprehensive**
St Thomas More Lynn Road, North Shields, NE 29 8LF **Tel:** 0191-257 2869

■ NORTHUMBERLAND

▲ **First**
St Cuthbert's Links Avenue, Morpeth NE65 0SA **Tel:** 01665-710413 *(Amble)*
St John's Lisburn Street NE66 1UR **Tel:** 01665-602547 *(Alnwick)*
St Aidan's Norham Road NE63 0LF **Tel:** 01670-813308 *(Ashington)*
St Bede's Ridge Terrace NE22 6EQ **Tel:** 01670-822389 *(Bedlington)*
St Cuthbert's Tweedmouth TD15 2EX **Tel:** 01289-307785 *(Berwick-on-Tweed)*
St Andrew's Albion Way NE24 5BL **Tel:** 01670-352606 *(Blyth)*
St Paul's Doddington Drive NE23 6DF **Tel:** 01670-713553 *(Cramlington)*
St Mary's Hencotes, NE46 2EE **Tel:** 01434-603791 *(Hexham)*
St Robert's Old Gate NE61 1QF **Tel:** 01670-512031 *(Morpeth)*
St Matthew's Highfield Lane NE42 6EY **Tel:** 01661-835484 *(Prudhoe)*

▲ **Middle**
Thomas Percy Blakelaw Road NE66 1AZ **Tel:** 01665-602650 *(Alnwick)*
St Benedict's Moorhouse Lane NE63 9LR

Tel: 01670-813658 *(Ashington)*
St Wilfrid's Claremont Terrace NE24 2LE **Tel:** 01670-352919 *(Blyth)*
St Peter's Northumberian Road NE23 6DB **Tel:** 01670-716343 *(Cramlington)*
St Joseph's Highford Lane NE46 2DD **Tel:** 01434-605124 (Hexham)

▲ Secondary Comprehensive
St Benet Biscop High Ridge Terrace NE22 6ED **Tel:** 01670-822795 *(Bedlington)*

■ SOUTH TYNESIDE

▲ Infants
St Aloysius Argyle Street NE31 1RZ **Tel:** 0191-483 2845 *(Hebburn)*

▲ Primary
St James' Solway Road NE31 2BP **Tel:** 0191-483 2672 *(Hebburn)*
St Joseph's, St Joseph's Way, Jarrow, Tyne and Wear NE32 4PJ **Tel:** 0191-536 4311
St Mary's Ayr Drive NE32 4AW **Tel:** 0191-489 8336 *(Jarrow)*
St Matthew's Alnwick Grove NE32 5YT **Tel:** 0191-489 8355 *(Jarrow)*
St Bede's Claypath Lane NE33 4PG **Tel:** 0191-456 0108 *(South Shields 1)*
St Gregory's Harton House Road East NE34 6DZ **Tel:** 0191-455 2909 *(South Shields 2)*
St Oswald's Nash Avenue NE34 8NS **Tel:** 0191-536 7922 *(South Shields 5)*
SS Peter and Paul Olive Street NE33 4RD **Tel:** 0191-455 2862 *(South Shields 4)*

▲ Junior
St Aloysius Argyle Street NE31 1BQ **Tel:** 0191-483 2274 *(Hebburn)*
St Bede's Harold Stret NE32 3AJ **Tel:** 0191-489 8218 *(Jarrow)*

▲ Secondary Comprehensive
St Joseph's Mill Lane NE31 2ET **Tel:** 0191-421 2828 *(Hebburn)*
St Wilfrid Marton Lane, NE34 0PH **Tel:** 0191-456 9121

■ SUNDERLAND

▲ PRIMARY
St Michael's Durham Road DH5 8NF **Tel:** 0191-553 6535 *(Houghton-le-Spring)*
St Leonard's Tunstall Village Road SR3 2BB **Tel:** 0191-553 6288 *(New Silksworth)*
Our Lady Queen of Peace Station Road DH4 7JZ **Tel:** 0191-385 2585 *(Penshaw)*
St Patrick's Smith Street SR2 0RQ **Tel:** 0191-553 6256 *(Ryhope)*
English Martyrs Redcar Road, Southwick SR5 5AU **Tel:** 0191-553 5540 *(Sunderland 9)*
St Anne's Hylton Road, Pennywell SR4 9AA **Tel:** 0191-553 6860 *(Sunderland 6)*
St Benet's Fulwell Road, Sunderland, SR6 9QU **Tel:** 0191-516 9516 *(Sunderland 7)*
St Cuthbert's Grindon Lane SR4 8H. **Tel:** 0191-528 4043 *(Sunderland 4)*
St John Bosco Bradford Avenue SR5 4JW **Tel:** 0191-536 4149 *(Sunderland 10)*
St Joseph's Rutland Street SR4 6HY. **Tel:** 0191-553 7725 *(Sunderland 11)*
St Mary's Meadowside, Thornholme Road SR2 7QN **Tel:** 0191-553 6087 *(Sunderland 5)*
St Bede's Hampshire Place NE37 2NP **Tel:** 0191-416 2979 *(Washington)*
St John Boste Castle Road, Oxclose Village NE38 0HL **Tel:** 0191-416 5871 *(Washington)*
St Joseph's Village Lane NE38 7HU **Tel:** 0191-219 3805 *(Washington)*

▲ Secondary Comprehensive
St Aidan's Willow Bank Road, Ashbrook SR2 7HJ **Tel:** 0191-553 6073 *(Sunderland)*
St Anthony's Thornhill Terrace SR2 7JN **Tel:** 0191-553 7700 *(Sunderland)*
St Robert of Newminster Biddick Lane NE38 8AF **Tel:** 0191-219 3810 *(Washington)*

DIOCESE OF LANCASTER

Province of Liverpool

Founded 22 November 1924 by the division of the Archdiocese of Liverpool and the Diocese of Hexham and Newcastle, consisting of the counties of Lancashire (The Hundreds of Amounderness and Lonsdale) and the County of Cumbria.

Patrons Of The Diocese
Our Blessed Lady of Lourdes, 11 February
St Cuthbert, 20 March

Bishop
Rt Rev Patrick O'Donoghue;
born at Mourne Abbey, Co Cork, Ireland 4th May 1934, ordained priest 25th May 1957, ordained Auxiliary Bishop of Westminster by Cardinal Hume 29th June 1993, installed as fifth Bishop of Lancaster 4th July 2001.

Rt Rev Patrick O'Donoghue, Bishop of Lancaster

Residence:
Bishop's Apartment, Cathedral House, Balmoral Road, Lancaster LA1 3BT
Tel: 01524-596050

Coadjutor Bishop:
Rt Rev Michael G Campbell OSA
Pastoral Centre, Balmoral Road, Lancaster LA1 3BT
Tel: 01524-596050 and 01229 820210

Bishop's Chaplain:
Rev Robert Billing
Tel: 01524-596050
E-mail: robertbilling@yahoo.co.uk

Personal Assistant:
Miss Elizabeth Hendry
Tel: 01524-596050 (9am-5pm Mon-Fri)
E-mail: liz.hendry@lancasterdiocese.org.uk

■ ADMINISTRATION

All addresses Pastoral Centre, Balmoral Road, Lancaster LA1 3BT unless otherwise stated.

■ Vicars General

Rev Mgr Canon Patrick Mulvany. St Patrick's Presbytery, 51 St John's Road, Morecambe LA3 1EX **Tel:** 01524-410322

Rev Mgr Canon Aiden J Turner. Our Lady Star of the Sea, 2 St Annes Road East, Lytham St Annes FY8 1UL
Tel: 01772-856229

■ Diocesan Chancellor

Rev Mgr Michael Tully, SS Mary and James, Snow Hill, Scorton, Preston PR3 1AY **Tel:** 01524-791268 **Fax:** 01524-729868

■ Diocesan Communications Officer

Canon Stephen Shield, Cathedral House, Balmoral Road, Lancaster LA1 3BT **Tel:** 01524-384820 **Fax:** 01524-384831
E-mail: clergy@lancastercathedral.org.uk

■ Episcopal Vicar for Religious

For Lancashire: **Rev Mgr Michael Kirkham**, 42 Oxford Court, Oxford Road, Ansdell, Lythem St Annes FY8 4EB **Tel:** 01253-737038; For Cumbria: **Rev Mgr Provost Francis Slattery**, St Herbert's, Lake Road, Windermere LA23 2EQ **Tel:** 015394-43402

■ Episcopal Vicar for Ecumenism

Rev Mgr Canon A J Turner

■ Diocesan Trustees

Chairman: **The Bishop; Rev Canon AJ Turner; Rev P Draper; Miss E Gillet; Mr J Bolton; Mr S Moore, Mr H Cameron, Mr A MacPhie, Mgr P Mulvany, Mr B Flood, Mrs L Lofthouse**
Rev R Dewhurst, Rev S Hawksworth.
Secretary: **Rev R Billing**. *Financial Administrator:* **Mr Stephen Moore**.
Tel: 01524-596059 **Fax:** 01524-596058

■ EDUCATION AND FORMATION

Tel: 01524 841190 **Fax:** 01524 846258

■ **Diocesan Education Service**
Chairman: **Rev L Ruscillo**
Assistant Education Advisers: **Mr A Scott**, (*Schools Management Service*), *Adviser RE*: **Mr Adrian Dempsey**.
Office: The Education Centre, Balmoral Road, Lancaster LA1 3BT
Tel: 01524-841190 **Fax:** 01524-846258
E-mail: doles@netcomuk.co.uk
Secretaries: **Miss Lynn Tomlinson, Mrs Heather Watts, Mrs Mavis Long**.

■ **Representatives on Education Committee**
Lancashire: **Mr E J Fox.**
Blackpool: Awaiting appointment.
Cumbria: **Mr A Scott.**

■ **Consultants to Schools Management Service**
Mr E J Fox.

■ **Diocesan Representative to Catholic Education services.**
Mr A Scott. The Education Centre, Balmoral Road, Lancaster LA1 3BT
Tel: 01524-841190
Fax: 01524-846258.
E-mail: doles@netcomuk.co.uk

■ **Permanent Diaconate Director**
Rev Adrian Towers, St Andrew and Blessed George Haydock, 114 Hoyles Lane, Cottam, Preston PR4 0NB
Tel: 01772-726166. **Rev C Barwise** (*Director for ordained Deacons*), 16 Fairfield Drive, Ashton, Preston PR2 1JJ
Tel: 01772-760045.

■ **Diocesan Youth Service**
Youth Service Management Group Chair, The Bishop, Rev. Mgr P. Mulvany *(Vice Chair)*, **Rev R Billing, P Conner, S Ashton, Mrs M Donnelly, Mrs M Machin, Mr S Hornshaw.**
Diocesan Youth Service Director:
Rev Phillip Conner, 18 Blyne Road, Torrisholme, Morecambe LA4 6NU
Tel: 01524-412250

■ **LITURGY AND ECUMENISM**

■ **Liturgical Formation**
Rev Geoffrey Steel, St Augustine's, 10 Waverley Road, Carlisle, Cumbria CA3 9JU,
Tel: 01228-526765; **Rev G Paul Johnstone,** St Mary's Church, St Bridget's Lane, Egremont C22 2BD
Tel: 01946-820251.

■ **Commission for Christian Unity**
Chairman: **Rev Mgr Canon A J Turner. Rev M Lakeland, Rev C Cousens, Rev S Pearson, Mr C Ginns, Mr G Stappard, Mrs S Doherty, Dr D Sawyer, PhD, Mgr M Molyneux, Rev Terry Marley** *(for Lancashire),* **R Wordsworth, Rev S Pearson. Dr Michael Mullett, Rev Andrew Dodd** (for Cumbria)
Secretary: **Mr Tony Parrini**

■ **CONSULTATIVE BODIES**

■ **Cathedral Chapter**
Erected February 16th. 1925.
Canons: **Rt Rev Michael Campbell, Mgr Aiden Turner, Rev Robert Dewhurst, John X Gibson, T Dakin** (*Penitentiary*), **James Flannery, P Mulvany, Gregory Turner, S Shield, Dunstan Cooper, Mgr Peter Verity, A Hayes.** *Honorary Canons:* **Mgri S Monaghan, Francis Cookson**.

■ **Council of Priests**
Chairman: The Bishop *Vice-chairman:* TBA; *Secretary:* **Rev P Smith.** *Ex-Officio Members:* **Mgr P Mulvany, Edward Gould**. *Vicars for Religious:* **Mgr Canon F Slattery, Mgr M Kirkham**; *Diocesan Communications Officer:* **Canon Stephen Shield,** *Vocations Director:* **E Gribben.**

■ **College of Consultors**
The Cathedral Chapter.

■ **Diocesan Matrimonial Tribunal**
Judicial Vicar: **Mgr M Tully**. SS Mary & James, Snow Hill, Scorton PR3 1AY
Tel: 01524-791268 **Fax:** 01524-844212
Associate Judicial Vicar: **Canon N McArdle**. *Members:* **Rev Deacon James Woods, Canon N McArdle, Rev T P Forster, Mrs C M Foster**. *Medical Expert:* **Dr A D'Souza**. *Treasurer: All rogatory commissions should be sent for the attention of the Tribunal Administrator,* **Mrs C E Horn**.

■ **Diocesan Faith & Justice Commission**
President: **Rt Rev P O'Donoghue, Bishop of Lancaster.** *Chair:* **Mr T Mattinson**, 20 Oakfield, Fulwood, Preston PR2 9RJ
Tel: 01772-862158 *Development Worker:* Awaiting appointment. St Bernadette's Presbytery, Bowerham Road, Lancaster LA1 4HT **Tel/Fax:** 01524-383081

■ **LANCASTER**
1. Cathedral Church of St Peter A 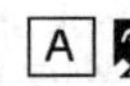 
(1736; 1799; cons 4 Oct 1859; Cathedral 1924)
East Road, Lancaster.
Tel: 01524-384820 **Fax:** 01524-384831
E-mail: clergy@lancastercathedral.org.uk.
Website: lancastercathedral.org.uk
Canon Stephen Shield *(Cathedral Dean)*: **Rev Andrew Allman,** Cathedral House Presbytery, Balmoral Road, Lancaster LA1 3BT *Deacon:* **Rev James Woods**.
M: *Sat 1st M of Sun 6.30pm. Sun 10.30am, 6.30pm. Hds (vigil 6.30pm), 12.15pm, 7.30pm.*

- ***Poor Sisters of Nazareth,*** Nazareth House, Ashton Road, LA1 5AQ **Tel:** 01524-32074 **Fax:** 01524-841344 **E-mail:** nazareth.house@virgin.net *Chaplain:* **Rev Mgr Canon Patrick O'Dea PA**
- ***Polish Parish of Our Lady,*** Queen of Poland, Nelson Street, LA1 1PY **Tel:** 01524-39820 **Mbl:** 0961-369284 **Rev Marian Jachym SChr**, Polish Chaplain.

■ **ALSTON,** Cumbria
St Wulstan (1953)
King's Arms Lane CA9 3JF Served from Carlisle (2). **Tel:** 01228-21509
M: *Sat 1st M of Sun 6pm. Hds 6pm.*

■ **ALSTON LANE,** Longridge A
† Our Lady and St Michael
(1765; 1856; cons 26 September 1957)
Alston Lane, Longridge, Preston PR3 3BN
Tel: 01772-782244
Rev Thomas H Doyle.
M: *Sat 1st M of Sun 7pm. Sun 8.30am, 10.30am. Hds (vigil 7.30pm). 7.30am, 9am, 7.30pm.*

■ **AMBLESIDE,** Cumbria A
† Mater Amabilis (1886; 1933)
Wansfell Road, Ambleside, Cumbria, LA22 0EG
Tel: 01539-432283 **Fax:** 01539-434412
E-mail: parishpriest@materamabilis.org.uk
Website: www.materamabilis.ic24.net
Rev Anthony Gaskin.
M: *Sat 1st M of Sun 7.30pm. Sun 10am. Hds 10am, 7.30pm.*

■ **ANSDELL,** Lancs
† St Joseph (1908; 1914; cons 1964)
Woodlands Road, Ansdell, Lytham St Annes, Lancs FY8 4EP
Tel/Fax: 01253-737037
E-mail: stjosephs-ansdell@hotmail.com
Website: www.stjosephsansdell.net
Rev Henry Holden.
M: *Sat 1st M of Sun 6pm. Sun 9.30am, 5.05pm. Hds 9am, 12noon, 7.30pm.*

- ***Sisters of Charity of Jesus and Mary,*** Stella Matutina Convent, 16 Clifton Drive, FY8 5RQ **Tel:** 01253-734834 **Fax:** 01253-795356 *Chaplain:* **Rev Mgr Michael Kirkham,** 42 Oxford Court, Oxford Road, Ansdell, Lytham St Anne's FY8 4EB **Tel:** 01253-737038

■ **APPLEBY,** Cumbria A
† Our Lady of Appleby (1958; cons 8 Sep 1959)
Tel: 01768-351474
Rev Peter Chappell, The Presbytery, Garth Head's Road, Appleby, Cumbria CA16 6UA
Deacon: **Rev Eric Wooff,**
Tel: 017683-52317
M: *Sat 1st M of Sun 6pm. Sun 11am. Hds 7pm.*

■ **ARNSIDE,** Cumbria A
† Our Lady of Lourdes (1926; 1977)
Silverdale Road. Served from Milnthorpe.
M: *Sun 10.45am. Hds 10am.*

■ **ASKAM-IN-FURNESS,** Cumbria
† St Anthony (1956)
Crossley Street. Served from Dalton-in-Furness.
M: *Sun 10.30am.*

■ **BARROW-IN-FURNESS,** Cumbria A
1. † Sacred Heart (1902; 1930)
Lumley Street, Barrow-in-Furness, Cumbria LA14 2BA
Tel: 01229-821498 **Fax:** 01229 833862
E-mail: sheart@tiscali.co.uk
Rev Francis Osman. The Presbytery, Pottery Street. LA14 2AX
M: *Sat 1st M of Sun 6.30pm. Sun 8am, 10.30am. Hds (vigil 6.30pm), 10.30am, 6.30pm.*

2. † Holy Family (1951) A
Ostley Bank, Newbarns.
25 Harrel Lane, Barrow-in-Furness, Cumbria LA13 9LN **Tel:** 01229-824429
Rev John Heaney.
M: *Sat 1st M of Sun 6.30pm Sun 9am, 11am. Hds (vigil 6.30pm). 9.10am.*

3. † St Mary of Furness A S
(1865; 1867; cons 28 May 1931)
Duke Street, Barrow-in-Furness, Cumbria LA14 1XW **Tel:** 01229-820210
Rev John Watson.
Deacon: **Rev Nick Donnelly.**
M: *Sat 1st M of Sun 6pm. Sun 10.30am, 6.30pm. Hds (vigil 5.45pm). 12.10pm, 7pm.*

- ***Religious of the Sacred Heart of Mary,*** 245 Abbey Road, LA14 5JY **Tel:** 01229-820284.

4 † **St Columba** (1916; 1923-1958)
Church Lane, Walney, Barrow-in-Furness, Cumbria. **Tel:** 01229-471405
Rev Joseph O'Connor. The Presbytery, 13 Margate Street, Walney, LA14 3AF.
Website: www.walneychurches.cbj.net
M: *Sat 1st M of Sun 5.30pm. Sun 11am. Hds 9.30am, 6.30pm.*

5. † **St Patrick** (1885; 1901; 1933)
Michaelson Road, Barrow Island, Barrow-in-Furness, Cumbria LA14 2RJ
Tel/Fax: 01229-820621
E-mail: stpatrickscumbria@yahoo.co.uk
Website: www.stpatrickscumbria.org
Rev Paul Harrison
Served from St Columba's.
M: *Sat 1st M of Sun 7pm. Sun 9.30am. Hds 12.05pm.*

6. † **St Pius X** (1955, 1957) A
Schneider Road, Ormsgill, Barrow-in-Furness, Cumbria LA14 4AA
Tel: 01229-820283
Rev John Hawkins.
M: *Sat 1st M of Sun 6pm. Sun 10.30am, 5.30pm. Hds (vigil 6.30pm). 9am.*

■ BLACKPOOL

1. † **Christ the King** (1949) A
Chepstow Road, Grange Park, Blackpool
Tel/Fax: 01253-391002
E-mail: robert@hornr.freeserve.co.uk
Rev Robert Horn, Christ the King Presbytery, Gateside Drive, Grange Park, FY3 7PL
M: *Sat 1st M of Sun 6pm. Sun 10.30am. Hds 10am, 7.30pm.*
• ***Society of the Holy Child Jesus***, 195 Newton Drive, Blackpool FY3 8NY
Tel: 01253-392047

2. † **Sacred Heart Church** (1854) A
Church House, 17 Talbot Road, Blackpool FY1 1LB
Tel: 01253-620964
Rev Canon Robert Dewhurst, Rev John Winstanley.
Also in residence: **Canon Edmond Carey**
M: *Sat 1st M of Sun 5.45pm. Sun 8am, 10am, 12noon, 4pm. Hds (vigil 5.45pm), 10am, 12.05pm, 5.45pm.*

3. † **Holy Family** (1929) A S
Links Road, North Shore, Blackpool FY1 2RU
Tel: 01253-351258 **Fax:** 01253-590018
E-mail: vjf@holyfamily.org.uk
Website: holy-family.org.uk
Rev Valentine Farrell.
M: *Sat 1st M of Sun 7pm. Sun 10.30am. Hds 10am, 7.30pm.*

• ***Religious Sisters of Charity of Jesus and Mary Bethany,*** 10 Argyle Road, Blackpool FY2 9UE **Tel:** 01253-356215

4. † **Our Lady of the Assumption** (1947; 1961)
125 Common Edge Road, Blackpool FY4 5DF
Tel: 01253-832958, **Fax:** 01253-792967
E-mail: gdbbpl2004@aol.com
Rev Geoffrey Bottoms
M: *Sat 1st M of Sun 6pm. Sun 10.30am. Hds 10am, 7.30pm.*

5. † **St Bernadette** (1949) A
Devonshire Road, Bispham, Blackpool
Tel: 01253-352587
E-mail: subirous@fsmail.net
Revv Stephen Pearson, Stewart Keeley. 26 All Hallows Road, Bispham, Blackpool FY2 0AS
M: *Sat 1st M of Sun 6.30pm. Sun 9.30am, 11am, 6.30pm. Hds (vigil 7pm). 9.30am, 7pm.*
• ***St Winefride's House,*** Low Moor Road, Bispham, Blackpool. (Administration) **Tel:** 01253-351142.

6. † **St Cuthbert** A
(1880; con 21 June 1923)
Lytham Road, South Shore, Blackpool
Tel: 01253-346471 **Fax:** 01253-401258
Rev Bernard Woods. *Deacon:* **Rev Paul Marley**. 53 Crystal Road, South Shore, FY1 6BS
M: *Sat 1st M of Sun 7pm. Sun 10.30am. Hds 9am (10am in School during term)*

7. † **St John Vianney** (1934; 1959) A
Glastonbury Avenue, Marton, Blackpool FY1 6RD **Tel/Fax:** 01253-762227
E-mail: frjoe@btinternet.com
Website: www.sjv.org.uk
Revv Joseph Connor, Kevin Dorgan.
Deacon: **Rev Tom Bland**. Also in residence: **Rev Brendan Monaghan.**
M: *Sat 1st M of Sun 5.30pm. Sun 9am, 11am, 5.30pm. Hds 9am, 7pm.*

9. † **St Kentigern** (1904; 1932) A
25a Newton Drive, Blackpool FY3 8BT
Tel/Fax: 01253-393439
Email: stkents@aol.com
Rev John C Foulkes.
Also in residence: **Rev Edward Gannon**
Website: www.st.kentigerns.cd.uk
M: *Sat 1st M of Sun 6pm. Sun 10.30am, 6pm. Hds (vigil 7pm) 10am.*
• ***Polish Chaplain:*** **Rev Mariusz Gutowski,** Polish Centre, Lancaster LA1 1PT
Tel: 01524-39820
M: *Sun 12.30pm.*

10. St Margaret, Clitherow A
(cons 3 Nov 1993)
Chapel-of-Ease to St Cuthbert's
575 Lytham Road, Clitherow, Blackpool.
M: *Sun 9am. Hds 7pm.*

11. St Monica Merseyside
2 St Monica's Way, Little Marton, Blackpool, FY4 4FA **Tel:** 01253-761623
Rev Joseph O'Connor
M: *Sat 1st M of Sun 6pm. Sun 10.30am. Hds (vigil 7pm). 9.30am.*

■ **BOARBANK HALL**
See Grange-over-Sands.

■ **BOLTON-LE-SANDS,** Carnforth
† St Mary of the Angels
(1844; 1869; cons 6 May 1884)
Main Road, Bolton-le-Sands, Carnforth, Lancs LA5 8DN **Tel:** 01524-822353
Served from Carnforth.
M: *Sat 1st M of Sun 6.30pm. Sun 10am. Hds 10am, 7.30pm.*

■ **BRAMPTON,** Cumbria
St Ninian's Chapel, Craw Hall (1895; 1957)
Served from Warwick Bridge.
Tel: 01228-560273
M: *Sun 9am. Hds 12noon.*

■ **CALDER VALE,** Garstang
Served from Garstang.
M: *Sun 8.30am (in the Misson Room).*

■ **CARLISLE,** Cumbria
1. † Christ the King
Edgehill Road, Harraby, Carlisle, Cumbria.
Tel: 01228-525632
E-mail: jfbctk@aol.com
Rev John F Baron. Winton Crescent, Harraby, CA1 3JX
Tel: 01228 521530
M: *Sat 1st M of Sun 6.30pm. Sun 9.30am. Hds Vigil, 7pm, 10am.*
- ***Sisters of the Sacred Hearts of Jesus and Mary***, 45 Edgehill Road, Harraby, Carlisle, Cumbria CA1 3PF **Tel/Fax:** 01228-5415411

2. † Our Lady and St Joseph A
(1798; 1825; 1893; cons 5 Aug 1952)
Warwick Square, Carlisle, Cumbria CA1 1LB
Tel: 01228-521509 **Fax:** 01228-599193
E-mail: olsjcarlisle@easicom.com
Mgr Canon Gregory Turner,
E-mail: tgregoryturner@aol.com
Deacons: **Revv Gibson Harrison, John Constable, Kevin Hickey** (retired).
M: *Sat 1st M of Sun 6pm (Alston) Sun 10am, 4.30pm. Hds 8am, 12.10pm, 7pm.*
- ***Religious of the Sacred Heart of Mary***, St Gabriel's Convent, 52 Victoria Place, CA1 1HP **Tel:** 01228-522239 **Fax:** 01228-598228 **Email:** carlisleshm@tiscali.co.uk

3. † St Augustine (cons 15 July 1979) A
10 Waverley Road, Carlisle, Cumbria CA3 9JU **Tel:** 01228-526765
Rev Geoffrey Steel.
M: *Sat 1st M of Sun 6.30pm. Sun 10.15am. Hds (vigil 7.30pm). 9am.*

4. † St Bede (1866; 1959) A
120 Wigton Road, Carlisle, Cumbria CA2 7ES **Tel/Fax:** 01228-521704
Rev James Leon Allen.
Website: www.saintbedes.church.co.uk
M: *Sat 1st M of Sun 6pm. Sun 11am. Hds (vigil 7pm). 9.30am, 7pm.*

5. St Edmund (1970) A
Orton Road, Carlisle, Cumbria CA2 6TS
Tel: 01228 535233
E-mail: stedmund1950@byinternet.com
Website: www.saint-edmunds.co.uk
The Rectory, St Edmund's Park, Orton Road CA2 6TS *Deacon:* **Rev Frank Bell**
Served from Wigton
M: *Sun 11am.*

6. † St Margaret Mary
(1933; 1962; cons 15 May 1983)
Scalegate Road, Carlisle, Cumbria CA2 4JX
Tel: 01228-522137 **Fax:** 01228-599052
Rev John Walsh.
M: *Sat 1st M of Sun 5.15pm. Sun 10.45am. Hds 9am, 7pm.*

■ **CARNFORTH,** Lancs
† Our Lady of Lourdes (1926; 1967)
Kellet Road, Carnforth, Lancs LA5 9LR
Tel: 01524-732940
Canon John X Gibson.
M: *Sun 8.30am, 11am. Hds 9.30am, 7.30pm.*
- ***Monastery of Our Lady of Hyning*** Please see Yealand

■ **CATFORTH,** Preston
† St Robert of Newminster (1876)
Benson Lane, Catforth, Preston PR4 0HY
Tel: 01772-690425
Resident Priest: **Rev Robert Swan**.
M: *Sun 10.30am. Hds 8am, 7pm.*

■ **CATON,** Lancaster
Our Lady Immaculate (1963)
Station Road. Served from Hornby.
M: *Sat 1st M of Sun 6pm. Hds (vigil 6pm).*

■ **CLAUGHTON-ON-BROCK,** Preston
† St Thomas Apostle (1358; 1596; 1794)
Tel: 01995-640208
Rev Anthony Keefe MA. Rectory, Smithy

Lane, Claughton-on-Brock, Preston PR3 0PN
M: *Sat 1st M of Sun 6.30pm. Sun 9am. Hds (Vigil 7.30pm), 9.30am, 7.30pm.*

■ **CLEATOR,** Cumbria
† **St Mary** (1853; 1872; cons 17 Aug 1907)
Cleator, Cumbria CA23 3AB
Tel: 01946-810324 **Fax:** 01946-810614
Revv Emmanuel Gribben, James Burns,
Deacon: **Rev John Kennedy.**
M: *Sat 1st M of Sun 7pm. Sun 10.30am, 5.30pm. Hds (vigil 7pm). 9.15am.*
• ***House of Formation & Diocesan Vocations Centre:*** St Mary's Priory, **Tel:** 01946-810324

■ **CLEATOR MOOR,** Cumbria
St Bega's Chapel, and Social Centre.
Served from Cleator.
M: *Sun 9am. Hds 7pm.*

■ **CLEVELEYS,** Blackpool
1. † **St Teresa** (1937; cons 1977)
St George's Avenue, Cleveleys, Blackpool.
Tel: 01253-853340
E-mail: frj26@hotmail.com
Rev Christopher Cousens. Presbytery, St Teresa's Avenue, FY5 3JT
Deacons: **Revv J B Collier, B Ward.**
M: *Sat 1st M of Sun 6.30pm. Sun 9am, 10.30am. Hds (vigil 6.30pm). 9.30am, 6.30pm*
2. † **St John Southworth** (1971)
Chapel-Hall, Northumberland Avenue, Blackpool. **Tel:** 01253-822154
Rev Gerard Dunn. 4 Ripon Close, FY5 2LQ
M: *Sat 1st M of Sun 6pm. Sun 10am, 5pm. Hds 10am, 7.30pm.*

■ **COCKERMOUTH,** Cumbria
† **St Joseph** (1848; 1856; cons 16 Dec 1962)
Crown Street, Cockermouth CA13 0EJ
Tel: 01900-822121 **Rev James McElroy.**
M: *Sat 1st M of Sun 6.30pm. Sun 10.30am. Hds 9am, 7.30pm.*

■ **CONISTON,** Cumbria
† **Sacred Heart** (1866; 1872)
Haws Bank, Torver Road, Coniston, Cumbria LA21 8AW **Tel:** 01539-441351
Rev Peter Houghton.
M: *Sun 10am. Hds eve 7pm, 10am.*

■ **COTTAM,** Preston
† **St Andrew and Blessed George**
(1793; cons 25 October 1894)
Presbytery, Hoyle's Lane, Haydock, Cottam, Preston. PR4 0NB **Tel:** 01772-726166
E-mail: parishpriest@standrewscotham.org
Website: www.standrewscotham.org
Rev Adrian J Towers.
Deacon: **Rev John Cliffe**
M: *Sat 1st M of Sun 6pm. Sun 10am, 6pm. Hds 9.15am, 7pm.*

■ **DALTON-IN-FURNESS,** Cumbria
† **Our Lady of the Rosary and St Margaret of Scotland** (1879; 1893; cons 22 May 1981)
Tel: 01229-462513
Rev William Glasswell. 101 Ulverston Road, Dalton-in-Furness, Cumbria LA15 8EY
M: *Sat 1st M of Sun 6.30pm. Sun 9am, 6.30pm. Hds 9am, 6.30pm.*

■ **DODDING GREEN,** Mealbank
SS Robert and Alice, (1723)
Dodding Green, Mealbank, Kendal LA8 9DH **Tel:** 01539-720063
Served from Kendal.

■ **EGREMONT,** Cumbria
† **St Mary** (1878; 1907; 1960; cons 1978)
St Bridget's Lane, Egremont, Cumbria CA22 2BD **Tel:** 01946-820251
Rev Peter Sayer.
Deacon: **Rev Thomas Davy.**
M: *Sat 1st M of Sun 5.45pm. Sun, 10.30am. Hds (vigil 7pm). 9.15am.*

■ **FERNYHALGH,** Preston
† **Our Lady of the Well**
(11th Cent; 1348; cons 12 Aug 1795)
Fernyhalgh Lane, Fernyhalgh, Preston PR2 5RR **Tel:** 01772-862231
Rev Thomas Hoole. St Mary's, Fernyhalgh Lane, Fulwood, Preston PR2 5RR
M: *Sat 1st M of Sun 6.30pm. Sun 10am, 3pm. Hds 9am, 7.30pm.*
• ***Ladyewell House and shrine,*** Fernyhalgh Lane, PR2 5ST
Tel: 01772-700181
E-mail: ladyewell@ladyewell.freeserve.co.uk
Website: www.ladyewell.freeserve.co.uk
Rev Thomas Hoole.

■ **FLEETWOOD,** Lancs
1. † **St Mary** (1841; 1866; cons 21 April 1937)
Lord Street, Fleetwood, Lancs FY7 6DT
Tel: 01253-873331
Website: www.stmarys-fleetwood.org.uk
Rev Peter Draper. Presbytery, 34 Kemp Street, FY7 6JX.
Deacon: **Rev William C Wright.**
M: *Sat 1st M of Sun 6.30pm. Sun 8.30am, 10.30am. Hds (vigil 7pm). 10am, 12.10pm.*
2. † **St Edmund of Canterbury**
(1952; 1956)
4 Melbourne Avenue, Fleetwood, Lancs FY7 8AY **Tel:** 01253-873129
E-mail: stedmundsparish@btinternet.com
Priest in charge: **Rev David Burns.**
M: *Sat 1st M of Sun 6pm. Sun 10.30am. Hds As announced.*

3. † **St Wulstan**
(1925; 1926; cons 1976)
Poulton Road, Fleetwood, Lancs FY7 7JY
Tel: 01253-873609 **Fax:** 01253-772567
Rev David Burns. *Deacon:* **Rev Paul Conneely.**
M: *Sat 1st M of Sun 6pm. Sun 9am, 10.30am. Hds (vigil 7pm). 10am, 7pm.*

■ **FLOOKBURGH,** Cumbria
St Cuthbert (1935; 1988)
Served from Grange-over-Sands.
M: *Sun 9am. Hds 6.45pm.*

■ **FRECKLETON AND WARTON,** Preston
† **Holy Family** (1899)
1 Lytham Road, Preston PR4 1AD
Tel: 01772-632254 **Fax:** 01772-631975
Rev Peter Burns.
M: *Sat 1st M of Sun 6.30pm. Sun 8.30am, 10.30am. Hds (vigil 7pm). 10am.*

■ **FRIZINGTON,** Cumbria
† **St Joseph** (1875; 1890)
The Priory, Yeathouse Road, Frizington, Cumbria CA26 3PX **Tel:** 01946-810284
Rev Bernard Hearty.
M: *Sat 1st M of Sun 6pm. Sun 11.30am. Hds 9am, 7pm.*

■ **GALGATE,** Lancaster
St Joseph
Main Road. Served from University.
M: *Sat 1st M of Sun 6.30pm.*

■ **GARSTANG,** Lancs
† **St Mary and St Michael**
(1778; 1858; cons 19 June 1968)
Bonds Lane, Garstang, Preston, Lancs PR3 1ZB
Tel: 01995-602164 **Fax:** 01995-602548
Rev David Elder. *Deacon:* **Rev D'Arcy Ryan.**
M: *Sat 1st M of Sun 6.30pm. Sun 10.30am, (8.30am at Calder Vale). Hds (vigil 7.30pm), 7.15am, 9.30am.*

■ **GLENRIDDING,** Cumbria
† **St Philip Howard** (cons 8 Dec 1979)
Penrith, Glenridding, Cumbria CA11 0PD
Tel: 015394-34569 Served from Grasmere.
M: *Sat 1st M of Sun 5pm summer, 4pm winter. Hds 5pm summer, 4pm winter.*

■ **GOOSNARGH,** Preston
† **St Francis**
(1755; 1802; 1835; cons 23 July 1936)
Hill Chapel, Goosnargh, Preston PR3 2FJ
Tel: 01772-865229 **Fax:** 01772-861169
Website: www.stfrancishillchapel.org
Rev Michael Lakeland. Horns Lane PR3 2FJ
M: *Sat 1st M of Sun 6.30pm. Sun 8.30am, 10.30am. Hds (vigil 7.30pm) 9.15am.*

■ **GRANGE-OVER-SANDS,** Cumbria
† **St Charles** (1882; 1884; cons 3 Sep 1983)
Tel: 01539-532731
Rev W Alfred Parker, *Deacon:* **Rev George Bissett.**
M: *Sat 1st M of Sun 6pm. Sun 10.30am. Hds (vigil 6.45pm). 10am.*

■ **Canonesses of St Augustine of the Mercy of Jesus;** Convent of Our Lady of Lourdes, Boarbank Hall, LA11 7NH
Nursing Home & Guest House
Tel: 01539-532288 **Fax:** 01539-535386
E-mail: mail@boarbankhall.org.uk
Website: www.boarbankhall.org.uk
Chaplain: **Rt Rev Hugh Lindsay,** former Bishop of Hexham and Newcastle.
Tel: 01539-535591 **Website:** www.boarbank@freenetname.co.uk
M: *Sun 11am*

■ **GRASMERE,** Cumbria
Our Lady of the Wayside (1965)
Keswick Road, Ambleside, Grasmere, Cumbria LA22 9RX **Tel:** 015394-35469
Rev David Duane.
M: *Sat 1st M of Sun 6pm. Sun 11am. Hds 8am, 6pm.*

■ **GREAT ECCLESTON,** Preston
† **St Mary**
(1688; 1760; 1835; cons 26 Sept 1985)
Tel: 01995-670268
Rev Stephen Ashton. St Mary's, Hall Lane, Great Eccleston, Preston PR3 0XN
M: *Sat 1st M of Sun 6.30pm. Sun 8am, 10.45am. Hds 9am, 7.30pm.*

■ **HALTON,** Lancaster
St Robert Bellarmine.
Served from Lancaster (3).
M: *Sun 9.30am.*

■ **HAMBLETON,** Blackpool, Lancs
St Francis of Assisi
Church Lane.
Served from St Mary's, Great Eccleston.
M: *Sun 9.15am. Hds (vigil 7pm).*

■ **HARRINGTON,** Cumbria
† **St Mary** (1872; 1893)
22 Church Road, Harrington, Cumbria CA14 5QA **Tel:** 01946-830234
• ***(OSB):*** (Belmont): **Rev Dom Bede Moore.**
M: *Sat 1st M of Sun 6pm. Sun 9.15am. Hds (vigil 6pm), 9.30am.*

■ **HAWKSHEAD,** Cumbria
Tel: 01539-441351 Served from Coniston.
M: *Sat 1st M of Sun 6pm. (In St Michael and All Angels Anglican Church).*

■ **HORNBY**
† **St Mary** (1762; 1820)
59 Main Street, Hornby, Lancaster LA2 8JT

Tel: 01524-221246
E-mail: hornbyclergy@yahoo.co.uk
Rev Luiz Ruscillo.
M: *Sun 10.45am. Hds 9am.*

■ **KENDAL,** Cumbria
† Holy Trinity and St George
(About 1750; 1791; 1837)
New Road, Kendal, Cumbria.
Tel/Fax: 01539-720063
E-mail: kendalrcl@aol.com
Rev Paul Embery. *Deacon:* **Rev John Selby**, Presbytery, 33 Blackhall Road, Kendal, Cumbria LA9 4BW
Tel: 015396-20690 *Deacons:* **Revv Bernard Loveland**. **Tel:** 015239-563391; **Keith Armstrong**, Cornerstones, 4 Arches Meadow, Kendal, **Tel:** 01539-739806
M: *Sat 1st M of Sun 6pm. Sun 10am, 6pm. Hds (vigil 7pm) 9.30am, 12.15pm.*
- ***Salesian Sisters of St John Bosco***, (FMA), Brettargh Holt, Kendal LA8 8EA
Tel: 01539-560340
E-mail: bretta.fma@ukonline.co.uk
Retreat and Conference Centre. Residential Youth Centre.

■ **KESWICK,** Cumbria
† Our Lady of the Lakes and St Charles
(1928; cons 4 November 1972)
High Hill, Keswick, Cumbria CA12 5PB
Tel: 01768-772928
Rev Peter J Sharrock.
M: *Sat 1st M of Sun 5.30pm. Sun 8am, 10.45am. Hds (vigil 7pm), 10am.*
- ***Diocese of Lancaster Catholic Youth Service,*** Diocesan Residential Youth Centre, Castlerigg Manor, CA12 4AR *Chaplain:* **Rev Peter J Sharrock**. *Director:* **Rev Peter Stanton**
Tel: 01768-772711 (Visitors 772129)
Fax: 01768-775302

■ **KIRKBY LONSDALE,** Cumbria
St Joseph (1966)
Back Lane, Kirkby Lonsdale, Cumbria LA6 2AP Served from Hornby.
Tel/Fax: 015242-71725/015242-73737
Deacon: **Rev Paul Broadbent.**
M: *Sun 9am. Hds 7pm.*

■ **KIRKBY STEPHEN,** Cumbria
Tel: 01768-351474 Served from Appleby.
M: *Sun 9am. Hds 10am (services at the Anglican Parish Church).*

■ **KIRKHAM,** Lancs
† St John the Evangelist
(1762; cons 22 April 1845)
The Willows, Ribby Road, Kirkham, Lancs PR4 2BE **Tel/Fax:** 01772-683664
Rev G Paul Johnstone.
M: *Sat 1st M of Sun 6.30pm. Sun 10.30am, 6.30pm. Hds 9.15am, 7pm.*

■ **KNOTT END,** Blackpool, Lancs
† St Bernard
(1920; 1922; 1975; cons 23 Mar 1985)
Hackensall Road, Knott End, Blackpool FY6 0AX **Tel:** 01253-790264
Served from St William's, Pilling.
M: *Sat 1st M of Sun 6pm. Sun 11am. Hds (vigil 7.30pm). 11am.*

■ **LANCASTER**
2. † St Bernadette
(1948; 1958; cons 15 June 1980)
Bowerham Road, Lancaster LA1 4HT
Tel: 01524-63000
E-mail: peter.foulkes@talktalk.net
Website: www.st-bernadettes.org.uk
Rev Peter Foulkes. *Deacon:* **Rev Paul Wawszczyk.** *Also in residence:* **Rev Canon Nicholas McArdle.**
M: *Sat 1st M of Sun 6.30pm. Sun 11am. Hds (vigil 7.30pm). 9am.*
- ***St Martin's College:*** *Chaplain:* **Rev Peter Foulkes.**

3. † St Joseph (1896; cons 1901)
Slyne Road, Lancaster LA1 3HU
Tel: 01524-32493
Website: www.stjoseph.fsnet.co.uk
Rev Andrew Broster. *Deacon:* **Rev Stephen Pendlebury.**
M: *Sat 1st M of Sun 6.30pm. Sun 11am, Hds 10am, 7pm.*

4. St Thomas More (1937)
Willow Lane, Lancaster LA1 5PT
Tel: 01524-32616
Served from the Cathedral.
M: *Sun 9.30am. Hds 9am.*
- ***Ursuline Sisters,*** Ursuline Convent, St Thomas More Walk, Lancaster LA1 5PT

5. Lancaster University Chaplaincy
Bailrigg, Lancaster LA1 4YW
Rev Hugh Pollock *(Chaplain),*
Tel: 01524-594079
E-mail: h.f.pollock@lancaster.ac.uk
Tel: 01524-594080
Website: www.lancs.ac.uk;/vsevs/chap-cen
M: *Sun 11.30pm. Hds times vary over the year.*

■ **LEA TOWN,** Preston
† St Mary (1800)
Tel: 01772-726425 Served from Our Lady and St Bernard's, Preston
In residence: **Rev M Joseph Diskin,** Presbytery, Darkinson Lane, Lea Town, Preston PR4 0RJ
M: *Sat 1st M of Sun 7pm. Sun 9am. Hds 9am, 7pm.*

■ **LONGTOWN,** Carlisle
Our Lady of Good Counsel (1953)
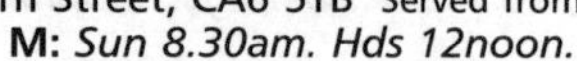
Burn Street, CA6 5TB Served from Carlisle (3).
M: *Sun 8.30am. Hds 12noon.*

■ **LYTHAM,** Lancs
† **St Peter** (1199; 1839; cons 21 Aug 1924)
4 Clifton Street, Lytham, Lancs FY8 5EP
Tel/Fax: 01253-736721
Rev Francis Flynn. *Deacon:* **Rev William Riley.**
M: *Sat 1st M of Sun 6.30pm. Sun 10am. Hds 12noon, 7.30pm.*
• ***Sisters of the Cross and Passion,*** St Paul's Convent and Nursing Home, 19 East Beach FY8 5EU **Tel:** 01253-736913 (Nursing Home); **Tel:** 01253-794601 (Community). **Fax:** 01253-732623
• ***Sisters of the Holy Child Jesus,*** 2 Clifton Street, Lytham, Lancs FY8 5EP **Tel/Fax:** 01253 732019

■ **MARYPORT,** Cumbria
† **Our Lady and St Patrick** (1838; 1847)
Crosby Street, Maryport, Cumbria.
Tel: 01900-812157 **E-mail:** frdavidburns @maryportolsp.fsnet.co.uk
Rev Bryan Irvine. The Priory, Eaglesfield Street, CA15 6EU
M: *Sat 1st M of Sun 6.15pm. Sun 10.30am. Hds (vigil 6pm), 9.15am.*
• ***Sisters of Mercy,*** Kirkby Street, CA15 6EX **Tel:** 01900-812339

A

■ **MILLOM,** Cumbria
† **Our Lady and St James** (1867; 1888)
Queen Street, Millom, Cumbria.
Tel: 01229-772479
Rev Mark Houston. Presbytery, Lonsdale Road, Millom LA18 4AS
M: *Sat 1st M of Sun 6pm. Sun 10.30am. Hds. 7pm, 10am.*

A

■ **MILNTHORPE,** Cumbria
Christ the King (1946; 1970)
15 Haverflatts Lane, Milnthorpe LA7 7PS
Tel: 015395-62387
Canon Alf Hayes.
M: *Sat 1st M of Sun 5.30pm. Sun 9am. Hds 7am. See also under Arnside.*

■ **MORECAMBE,** Lancs
1. † **The Good Shepherd** (1962)
The Square, Torrisholme, Morecambe, Lancs LA4 6NJ **Tel:** 01524-412250
Served from St Mary's, Morecambe.
M: *Sun 8.30am, 11.30am. Hds 7pm.*

2. **Holy Family** (1979)
Holy Family Presbytery, Westgate, Morecambe, Lancs LA4 4TL
Tel: 01524-422555
Priest in Charge: **Mgr Canon P. Mulvany.**
Deacon: **Rev Brian Burns.**
25a Deanpoint, Morecambe.
Tel: 01524-422555
Served from St Patrick's, Morecambe.
M: *Sat 1st M of Sun 6.45pm. Sun 10am. Hds 10am, 7.30pm.*

3. † **St Mary** (1895; cons 1975)
Matthias Street, Morecambe, Lancs LA4 5JR **Tel:** 01524-410501
E-mail: revdooper@ stmarysmorecambe.wanadoo.co.uk
Rev Canon Dunstan Cooper, *Deacons:* **Revv T Fagan**, 43 Tarnbrook Court, Euston Road, Morecambe LA4 5LA **Tel:** 01524-421070; **John McCann**, 15 Stuart Avenue, Morecambe LA4 6EB **Tel:** 01524-421795
M: *Sat 1st M of Sun 6pm. Sun 10am. Hds 9.30am, 12.10pm.*

4. † **St Patrick** (1925; cons 7 June 1981)
Fairfield Road, Sandylands, Morecambe, Lancs. **Tel/Fax:** 01524-410322
Mgr Canon Patrick Mulvany VG, 22 St John's Road, LA3 1EX *Deacon:* **Rev James Murphy.**
M: *Sat 1st M of Sun 5.45pm. Sun 11am. Hds (vigil 6.30pm), 10.30am, 2pm in school.*

■ **NEWHOUSE,** Barton, Preston
† **St Mary** (1721; 1806; cons 1906)
St Mary's, Station Lane, Barton, Newhouse, Preston PR3 5DY **Tel:** 01772-862831
Rev John J Marsh.
M: *Sat 1st M of Sun 6.30pm. Sun 10.30am. Hds (vigil 7.30pm). 9.15am.*

■ **PENRITH,** Cumbria
† **St Catherine** (1833; 1850)
Virgin and Martyr.
Drovers Lane, Penrith, Cumbria CA11 9EL
Tel: 01768-862273
Website: www.st-catherines-penrith.org.uk
Rev Jerome Ainsworth.
M: *Sat 1st M of Sun 6.30pm. 8.30am, 10.30am. Hds 9.15am, 7pm.*

■ **PILLING,** Preston, Lancs
† **St William of York** (1891; cons 8 Sept 1991)
St William's, Garstang Road, Pilling, Preston, PR3 6AL **Tel:** 01252-790264
Rev Bernard Partington.
M: *Sun 9.30am. Hds 9.30am.*

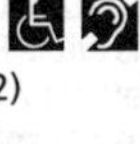

■ **POULTON-LE-FYLDE,** Lancs
1. † **St John the Evangelist** (1813; 1912)
Breck Road, Poulton-le-Fylde, Lancs FY6 7HT
Tel: 01253-883110 **Fax:** 01253-880273
Rev Gerald A C Muir.
Deacon: **Rev Bill Milton**
M: *Sat 1st M of Sun 6pm. Sun 11am. Hds (vigil 7.30pm). 9.15am.*

2. † **English Martyrs**
(1962, cons 1986)
154 High Cross Road, High Cross, Poulton-le-Fylde, Lancs FY6 8DA
Tel/Fax: 01253-882497
Rev John D G Colllins.

M: *Sat 1st M of Sun 6pm. Sun 9.30am, 11.15am. Hds (vigil 7pm). 10am.*

3. St Martin de Porres (1964)
Fleetwood Road, Carleton.
Tel: 01253-791782
Served from St John's, Poulton.
M: *Sun 9.30am. Hds 7.30am.*

■ PRESTON

1. † The Blessed Sacrament
(1928; 1956; cons 25 Sept 1962)
The Rectory, Farringdon Lane, Ribbleton, Preston PR2 6LX
Tel: 01772-791782 **Fax:** 01772-798091
E-mail: norman.johnston@btinternet.com
Rev Norman Johnston. *Deacon:* **Rev Michael Dolan, Tel:** 01772-791778
M: *Sat 1st M of Sun 6.30pm. Sun 8.30am, 10am. Hds (vigil 7.30pm). 9.30am, 12.05pm.*
- ***Xaverian Missionaries,*** 179 Ribbleton Avenue, PR2 6AA **Tel:** 01772-792292 **Fax:** 01772-793723 **Mob:** 07967-713688 E-mail: prestonxav@aol.com **Revv Emilio Paloschi, James Clarke**.

2. † Sacred Heart
(1903; 1938; cons 9 Sept 1953)
44 Beech Grove, Ashton-on-Ribble, Preston PR2 1DU
Tel: 01772-726674 **Fax:** 01772-722006
E-mail: sashton@open4free.co.uk
Rev Paul Swarbrick. *Deacon:* **Rev Christopher Barwise.**
M: *Sat 1st M of Sun 6.30pm. Sun 9.30am, 11am. Hds 9.30am, 6.30pm.*

3. † Holy Family (1964)
The Church House, Whitby Avenue, Ingol, Preston PR2 3YP
Tel: 01772-729992 **Fax:** 01772-735993
Rev Peter Dolan.
M: *Sat 1st M of Sun 7pm. Sun 8am, 10am. Hds 9.15am, 7.30pm.*

4. † Our Lady and St Bernard (1953)
Elswick Road, Larches Estate, Preston.
Tel: 01772-726336
Rev Simon Hawksworth. 64 Larches Lane, Preston PR2 1PP *Deacon:* **Rev M. Green**.
M: *Sat 1st M of Sun 6.30pm. Sun 10.45am. Hds (vigil 6.30pm) 9am.*

5. † Our Lady and St Edward (1943)
St Edward's, 4 Marlborough Drive, Fulwood, Preston PR2 9UE
Tel: 01772-862437 **Fax:** 01772-865889
E-mail: olse@fulwood4.fsnet.co.uk
Website: www.fulwood4.fsnet.co.uk
Rev Patrick McMahon.
Deacon: **Rev J Peter Williams**
M: *Sat 1st M of Sun 6pm, Sun 8.30am, 10.30am. Hds 9.15am, 7.30pm.*

6. † St Anthony of Padua (1960)
Cadley Causeway, Cadley, Preston PR2 3RX
Tel: 01772-725193 **Fax:** 01772-732304
Website: www.saintanthony.freeserve.co.uk
Rev Richard Kinlen.
Deacons: **Revv Thomas Butler, John Monk, John Kilshaw.**
M: *Sat 1st M of Sun 6.30pm. Sun 10.15am. Hds (vigil 7.30pm) 9.15am, 4pm.*
- ***Little Sisters of the Poor,*** Rest Home and Day Centre of Men and Women, Garstang Road, PR2 4RB **Tel:** 01772-717454 **Fax:** 01772-712368 *Chaplain:* **Rev Bernard Anthony Ashcroft**.
- ***Carmelites,*** St Vincent's Road, PR2 4QA **Tel:** 01772-717194 Served from Carmelite centre.

7. St Augustine of Canterbury
(1838; 1840; cons 9 July 1931)
St Austin's Place, Preston PR1 3YJ
Tel: 01772-555547
Rev Michael Murphy.
M: *Sat 1st M of Sun 6.30pm. Sun (1st in Month, in sign language, 6pm). Sun 8.30am, 10.30am. Hds 9.15am, 7pm.*
- ***Society of the Holy Child Jesus,*** 42 St Austin's Place, PR1 3YJ **Tel:** 01772-202812
- ***Religious of the Sacred Heart of Mary,*** The Parish House, St Austin's Place, Preston PR1 3YJ **Tel:** 01772-822358

8. St Clare (1971; 1979)
Sharoe Green Lane North, Fulwood, Preston PR2 4HH
Tel/Fax: 01772-719604
E-mail: enquiries@stclares.co.uk
Website: www.saintclares.co.uk
Revv Christopher Loughton, Philip Smith. *Deacon:* **Rev Frederick Sanderson**.
M: *Sat 1st M of Sun 6.30pm. Sun 9.30am, 6pm. Hds (vigil 7.15pm). 9.30am, 7.15pm.*
- ***Discalced Carmelites (OCD):*** Tabor, Carmelite Centre, 169 Sharoe Green Lane, Fulwood, Preston PR2 8HE **Tel:** 01772-717122 Community: **Rev Eugene McCaffery** (*Prior*), **Revv John Hughes, William Moran**
- ***Sisters of Charity of Nevers:*** 17-19 Oakengate, Fulwood, Preston PR2 6RB **Tel:** 01772-793519 **Fax:** 01772-793494

9. † St Gregory the Great
(1924; 1936; cons 24 June 1936)
Blackpool Road, Preston PR1 6HQ
Tel: 01772-795328

Rev Joseph Maley. *Deacon:* **Rev James Maguire.**
M: *Sat 1st M of Sun 6.30pm. Sun 10am. Hds (Vigil 7.30pm) 9am.*

10. † St Ignatius
(1833-1836; cons 31 July 1929)
Meadow Street, Preston PR1 1TT
Tel/Fax: 01772-253920
Served from St Thomas of Canterbury & English Martyrs.
M: *Sun10am (family), 8pm. Hds 10.30am.*

11. † St Joseph
(1860; 1874; cons 19 March 1974)
Skeffington Road, Preston.
Tel/Fax: 01772- 796053
E-mail: rectory@stjosephspreston.org.uk
Rev Anthony Walsh. Presbytery, Caroline Street, Preston PR1 5UY
M: *Sun 10.30am. Hds 9.15am, 7pm.*
- ***Dominican Sisters,*** 150 Fletcher Road, PR1 5HE **Tel:** 01772-792747

12. † St Maria Goretti
(1953; cons 18 Oct 1984)
Gamull Lane, Ribbleton, Preston PR2 6SJ
Tel: 01772-700231 **Fax:** 01772-702635
Web: www.smgpreston.org.uk
Rev Timothy Sullivan.
Deacon: **Rev Graham Lavery**.
M: *Sat 1st M of Sun 7pm. Sun 9am, 10.30am. Hds 9.30am, 7pm.*

14. † SS Peter and Paul (1964; 1972)
Lea Road, Ashton, Preston.
Tel: 01772-726811
Rev Simon Hawksworth, 64 Larches Lane, Preston PR2 1PP **Tel:** 01772 726336
Deacon: **Rev James Slater**.
M: *Sun 10.30am. Hds 7pm.*

15. † St Teresa (1932)
Church Avenue, Fishwick, Preston
PR1 4UD. **Tel/Fax:** 01772-794506
Rev Anthony Walsh, resident at St Joseph, Preston (11).
M: *Sat 1st M of Sun 6.30pm. Sun 10.00am. Hds 9.15am, 7pm.*

16. † St Thomas of Canterbury and the English Martyrs
(1863; 1867; cons 14 Sept 1921)
18 Garstang Road, Preston, Lancs
PR1 1NA
Tel: 01772-257878 **Fax:** 01772-252578
Rev Thomas Singleton.
E-mail:
presbytery@englishmartyrspreston.org.uk
Website: www.englishmartyrspreston.org.uk
M: *Sat 1st M of Sun 7pm. Sun 11am (Children's Liturgy of Word), 4pm. Hds (vigil 7pm). 9am.*

17. † St Walburge
(1850; 1854; cons 23 Sept 1936)
Weston Street, Preston PR2 2QE
Tel: 01772-726370
Served from Sacred Heart, Ashton, Preston
Rev Paul Swarbrick. Tel: 01772-722006
M: *Sat 1st M of Sun 6.30pm. Sun 11am, 12noon. Hds 12.15pm.*
- ***The Talbot Library,*** **Rev Michael Dolan Tel:** 01772-760186
- ***Capuchin Franciscans (OFM Cap),*** St Walburge's Presbytery, Weston Street, Preston PR2 2QE **Brs Mark Elvins** (Guardian), **Francis Maple, John Delaney. Tel:** 01772-73449 **E-mail:** capuchin.preston@btinternet.com

18. † St Wilfrid
(1793;1843; cons 17 Sept 1952)
1 Winckley Square, Preston PR1 3JJ
Tel: 01772-253402/555244
Fax: 01772-251955
- ***Jesuits (SJ):*** *Parish Staff:* **Revv James Langan, Thomas Lakeland.** *Deacon:* **Rev William Adams, Revv Christopher Dyckhoff** (*Superior*), **Gerard Marsden, Frederick Lane, Clifford Taunton, Alexander Welsh, Hilary Thomas, Kifle Wansamo, Gerard Gallen, Peter Orr. Bros Michael Hayward, Andrew Atkinson.**
M: *Sat 1st M of Sun 5.35pm. Sun 7am, 9.30am, 11am, 4.30pm, 6pm Trid 1st Sun. Hds (vigil 5.35pm). 7am, 8.30am, 12.15pm, 1pm, 5.35pm.*
- ***Sisters of Charity of Our Lady of Mercy,*** 4 Bethany, Mount Street, PR1 8BS **Tel:** 01772-250031

19. University of Central Lancashire
Chaplain: **Rev Peter Stanton**. *Assistant:* **Sr Shelagh Duggan**. Multi-Faith Centre, St Peter's Square, Preston.
Tel: 01772-892615

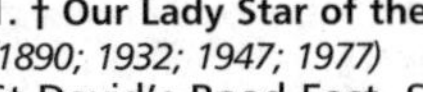

■ ST ANNES-ON-THE-SEA, Lancs

1. † Our Lady Star of the Sea
(1890; 1932; 1947; 1977)
St David's Road East, St Annes-on-the-Sea, Lancs. **Tel:** 01253-723661
E-mail: info@ourladystarofthesea.co.uk
Website: ourladystarofthesea.co.uk
Mgr Canon Aidan J Turner. MA, VG, Rev Michael Docherty. 2 St Annes Road East, FY8 1UL *Deacon:* **Rev William Gillan**, 19 Salcombe Road, Lytham St Annes FY8 2RD
Tel: 01253-725997
M: *Sat 1st M of Sun 6.30pm. Sun 9.30am, 11am, 6.30pm. Hds (vigil 7pm). 10am, 4pm, 7pm.*
- ***Daughters of Wisdom,*** 3 Balmoral Road, FY8 1ER **Tel:** 01253-724189

2. St Alban (1964)
64 Kilnhouse Lane, St Annes-on-the-Sea FY8 3AA **Tel:** 01253-725557
Rev Patrick Hibbert.
M: *Sat 1st M of Sun 7.15pm. Sun 8.30am, 10.30am. Hds (vigil 7.30pm), 10am.*

■ **SCORTON,** Preston, Lancs
† **SS Mary and James** (1713; 1861; 1961)
Snow Hill, Scorton, Preston, Lancs PR3 1AY
Tel: 01524-791268 **Fax:** 01524-7792868
E-mail: lancaster@lancstrib.co.uk
Mgr Michael J Tully.
M: *Sat 1st M of Sun 6.30pm. Sun 9am, 11am. Hds 9am, 7pm.*

■ **SEASCALE,** Cumbria
St Joseph (1960)
Gosforth Road, Seascale, Cumbria CA20 1PS
Tel: 01946-820251
E-mail: seascale.rc@ukonline.co.uk
Website:
http://web.ukonline.co.uk/seascale.rc
Served from Egremont.
Rev Peter Sayer
M: *Sun 9am. Hds 12noon.*

■ **SEDBERGH,** Cumbria
Served from Kendal.
M: *Sun 12pm (in Parish Church) Hds 7.30pm.*

■ **SHAP,** Cumbria
Served from Penrith.
M: *Sun 12.30pm in Methodist Church Schoolroom, on main road opposite bowling green.*

■ **SILLOTH,** Cumbria
† **Our Lady of the Assumption**
(1932; New Church 1950)
Wampool Street. **Tel:** 01697-812157
Rev Bryan Irving
Served from Maryport.
Parish Sister: **Sr Clare McNamara.**
M: *Sun 8.30am. Hds 11am.*

■ **STAVELEY,** Cumbria
Chapel of the Sacred Heart
Off Station Road. Served from Windermere.
Tel: 015394-43402
M: *Sat 1st M of Sun 6pm.*

■ **THORNTON-LE-FYLDE,** Blackpool
1. † Sacred Heart (1898; cons 14 Jan 1973)
Heys Street, Thornton-le-Fylde, Blackpool FY5 4HL **Tel:** 01253-821637
Rev Peter Clarke.
Deacon: **Rev Anthony Edwards.**
M: *Sat 1st M of Sun 6.30pm. Sun 10am. Hds (vigil 7.30pm), 11am (during term-time).*

2. St Nicholas Owen (1974)
Little Thornton, Thornton-le-Fylde, Blackpool.
Canon Thomas Dakin. *Deacon:* **Rev Dominic Hyland**. Presbytery, Raikes Road, Thornton Cleveleys FY5 5LS
E-mail: dakinlanc@btopenworld.com
M: *Sun 10am. Hds 9am.*

■ **THURNHAM,** Lancaster
† **SS Thomas and Elizabeth**
(1785; 1847; cons 29 Aug 1848)
Thurnham, Lancaster LA2 0DT
Tel: 01524-751363
Served from St Bernadette's, Lancaster.
Rev Peter Foulkes
M: *Sun 9am. Hds 7pm.*

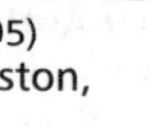

■ **ULVERSTON,** Cumbria
† **St Mary of Furness** (1678; 1822; 1895)
Victoria Road, Brogden Park, Ulverston, Cumbria LA12 0BY
Tel: 01229-582205
Canon James Flannery.
M: *Sat 1st M of Sun 7pm. Sun 10am, 6.30pm. Hds (vigil 7pm). 10am.*

■ **WARWICK BRIDGE,** Carlisle
† **Our Lady and St Wilfrid** (Before 1720; 1842)
The Presbytery, Warwick Bridge, Carlisle, Cumbria CA14 8RL
Tel: 01228-560273 **Fax:** 01228-560284
• ***Benedictines (OSB):***
Rev Stephen Wright. *Deacons:* **Revv Francis Bell, William J Kirkley.**
M: *Sat 1st M of Sun 6pm. Sun 10.30am. Hds 6pm.*

■ **WEETON,** Lancs
St Joseph
Army Barracks.
Rev David Smith
M: *As Announced.*

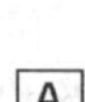

■ **WESHAM,** Preston, Lancs
† **St Joseph** (1885; cons 18 March 1886)
Fleetwood Road, Wesham, Preston, Lancs PR4 3HA **Tel:** 01772-683593/495219
Rev Joseph W Bootle. The Presbytery, Mowbreck Lane, Wesham, Preston, Lancs.
M: *Sat 1st M of Sun 7pm. Sun 10am. Hds 9.15am, 7pm.*

■ **WESTBY,** Kirkham, Lancs
† **St Anne** (1752; 1860; cons 8 Nov 1900)
Westby Mills, Westby, Kirkham, PR4 3PL
Tel: 01772-683664 Served from Kirkham.
Rev G Paul Johnstone
Deacon in residence: **Rev David Done.**
M: *Sun 9am. Hds eve 7pm.*

■ **WHITEHAVEN,** Cumbria
1 † St Mary (1927; 1961; cons 1982)
High Road, Kells, Whitehaven, Cumbria CA28 9PG **Tel:** 01946-692757

Rev Aelred Grugan.
M: *Sat 1st M of Sun 6.30pm. Sun 10am, 9pm. Hds (vigil 7.30pm), 9pm.*

2. † St Begh (1706; 1868; cons 1907)
St Begh's Priory, Coach Road, Whitehaven, Cumbria CA28 7TE
Tel: 01946-692342 **Fax:** 01946-591831
E-mail: m.carney@tiscali.co.uk
- ***Benedictines, (OSB):*** **Dom Matthew Carney** (*Parish Priest*), **Very Rev Hugh Menken.**
  M: *Sat 1st M of Sun 6pm. Sun 10am (Children), 6pm. Hds (vigil 7pm), 7pm.*

A

3. St Benedict (1961)
Mirehouse, Whitehaven, Cumbria.
Tel: 01946-692083 **Fax:** 01946-692213
Rev Kevin Lowry.
Presbytery, Whinlatter Road, CA28 8BN.
M: *Sat 1st M of Sun 5.30pm. Sun 9am, 11am, 6pm. Hds 9am, 7pm.*

4. St Michael
Moresby Parks. Served from Whitehaven (2).
M: *Sun 11am. Hds (vigil 6.30pm).*

5. SS Gregory and Patrick
Quay Street. Served from Whitehaven, (2).
M: *Sun 8am. Hds 10.30am.*

■ **WIGTON,** Cumbria
† St Cuthbert (1837; 1857)
Burnfoot, Wigton, Cumbria CA7 9HU
Tel: 016973-42379
Rev Peter Hart. Tel: 016973-42154.
M: *Sun 10am, 6pm. Hds 9.15am, 7pm.*

■ **WINDERMERE,** Cumbria
† Our Lady of Windermere and St Herbert (1883; 1964)
Lake Road, Windermere, Cumbria LA23 2EQ **Tel:** 015394-43402
Mgr Canon Francis Slattery.
Deacon: **Rev Robert B Wordsworth.**
M: *Sun 10am, 5.15pm.*
- ***Daughters of Wisdom,*** The Convent, Queen's Drive. LA23 2DE
  Tel: 015394-42104

A

■ **WORKINGTON,** Cumbria
1. † Our Lady Star of the Sea and St Michael (1810; 1876; cons 1921)
The Priory, Banklands, Workington, Cumbria CA14 3EP
Tel: 01900-602114 **Fax:** 01900-871797
E-mail: mphill0207@aol.com
Web: www.olsmworkington@btinternet.com
- ***Benedictines (OSB):*** **Revv Michael Phillips, Paul Browne, Paschal Tran.**
  M: *Sat 1st M of Sun 6.30pm. Sun 9.30am, 6.30pm. Hds (vigil 6.30pm). 12.10pm, 6.30pm.*
- ***Sisters of Charity of St Paul,*** Derwent Meadows, Stainbarn, CA14 3EP
  Tel: 01900-602028

2. St Gregory
(1965; new church cons Oct 13, 1982)
Furness Road, Workington, Cumbria CA14 3PD **Tel:** 01900-603800
Rev Edmund Gornall.
M: *Sat 1st M of Sun 6pm. Sun 10am. Hds (vigil 6pm). 9.30am.*

■ **YEALAND,** Carnforth
† St Mary (1782; cons 4 Aug 1852)
2 Yealand Road, Yealand Conyers, Nr Carnforth, Lancs, LA5 9SF
Tel: 01524-732943
Rev Joseph L Bamber.
M: *Sat 6pm, Sun 9am. Hds 8.30am.*
- ***Bernardines,*** Monastery of Our Lady of Hyning, Hyning Hall, Carnforth, Lancs LA5 9SE **Tel:** 01524-732684 *Chaplain:* **Rev Michael McKenna (MHM). Tel:** 01524-733383/734208 (Guests) **Fax:** 01524-720287
  Web: www.bernadine.org

■ **ORDERS OR CONGREGATIONS, ETC**

■ **Men**
Benedictines *(English Congregation):* Harrington, Warwick Bridge, Whitehaven (2), Workington (1).
Order of Friars Minor Capuchin: Preston (18)
Discalced Carmelites: Preston (8).
Jesuits: Preston (18).
Mill Hill Missionaries: Yealand.
Xaverian Missionaries: Preston (1).

■ **Women**
Canonesses of St Augustine of the Mercy of Jesus: Grange-over-Sands.
Benardine Cistercians: Yealand.
Carmelites: Preston (6).
Charity *(of Jesus and Mary),* Sisters of: Ansdell, Blackpool (3).
Charity *(of Our Lady of Mercy),* Sisters of: Preston (18).
Charity *(of St Paul),* Sisters of: Workington (1).
Charity *(Nevers)* Sisters of: Preston (8).
Cross and Passion, Sisters of the: Lytham.
Dominican Sisters *(Third Order; Congregation of Oakford):* Preston (11).
Holy Child Jesus, Society of the: Blackpool (1), Preston (7), Lytham.
Mercy, Sisters of Institute of Our Lady of: Maryport.
Nazareth, Poor Sisters of: Lancaster (1).
Poor, Little Sisters of the: Preston (6).
Sacred Heart of Mary, Religious of the:

DIOCESE OF LANCASTER

Barrow-in-Furness (3), Preston (7).
Sacred Hearts of Jesus and Mary, Sisters of the: Carlisle (1).
Salesian Sisters of St John Bosco: Kendal.
Ursuline Sisters: Lancaster (4).
Wisdom, Daughters of (La Sagesse): Preston (6), St Annes (1), Windermere.

■ ORGANISATIONS AND SOCIETIES

For Societies and Organisations without representation in the diocese please see the main Societies and Organisations section.

Achille Ratti Climbing Club Under the Patronage of the Bishop of Lancaster and the Bishop of Wrexham, The Achille Ratti Climbing Club is open to all, Catholic and non-Catholic, young and old, who have a genuine love of the hills. Further information from the Secretary. *Chairman:* **David Ogden**. *Hon Secretary:* **Mr David Armstrong**, 18 Aviemore Close, Garswood, Wigan WN4 0RY

Archconfraternity of St Stephen. *Director:* **Rev R Billing**.

Apostleship Of The Sea Port *Chaplain:* Fleetwood: **Rev B McMahon**.

Association Of Interchurch Families. *Local Co-ordinators:* **John and Kate Bates**. 14 Rosedale Drive, Longridge, Preston. **Tel:** Longridge 2492

Association for the Propagation of the Faith *Director:* **Rev N Johnston**. St Teresa's, Cleveleys, FY5 3JT

Carmelite Secular Order (OCDS). *Contact:* **Morag Ketley**, **Tel:** 01695-556548

Catenian Association. *Provincial Membership Officer:* **Mr Des Stevenson**, 1 Park Road, Thornton Cleveleys, Blackpool FY5 5HG **Tel:** 01253-860188

Catholic Caring Services to Children & Community Head Office; 218 Tulketh Road, Preston, PR2 1ES
Tel: 01772-732313/4 or 735632
Fax: 01772-768726 *Director:* **Mr J Cullen**. *Treasurer: Deacon:* **Mr Mark Belderbos**. Barrow Office: 2 Rodney Street, Barrow-in-Furness LA14 1ND
Tel: 01226-870349

Society of St Vincent de Paul Lancaster Central Council. *President:* **Mr Paul Hammond**, 21 Regent Park, Morecambe, LA4 4QP *Treasurer:* **Mr Derek Bates;** *Secretary:* **Mr Paul Desborough**, 4 Brearwood Way, Thornton-Clevelys FY5 4FP.

Handicapped Children's Area Representative: Mrs Margaret Miller. 7 Dunbar Drive, Fulwood, Preston, PR2 3JJ **Tel:** 01772-718007

Broughton Catholic Charitable Society. Founded in 1787 for Lancashire born Catholic priests or laypersons, or resident in Lancashire, or of Lancashire parentage the society aims to bring spiritual benefits of its members, both living and dead, and the relief of hardship, wherever it is encountered, by making grants
Secretary: **Mr Leo Casey**. 16, Norwood Close, Worsley, Manchester, M28 7ES.
Tel: 0161 790 5758
Email: leocasey@bulldoghome.com

Catholic Clothing Guild: *Hon Secretary:* **Mrs H Walters**, 40 Oxenholme Road, Kendal, Cumbria LA9 7HH

Catholic Family History Society meets regularly in Preston. *North-West Group Secretary:* **Mrs Jean Smith**, 10 Irving Close, Woodsmoor, Stockport, Cheshire SK2 7DX

Catholic Men's Society of Great Britain. Lancaster Diocesan Council. *Secretary:* **Joseph Murphy**. 37 Ribble Road, Fleetwood, Lancs FY7 7BX
Tel: 01253-874083

Catholic Nurses Guild *Diocesan Chaplain*: **Rev M Lakeland**. St Clare's, Sharoe Green North, Fulwood, Preston PR2 4HH *Secretary:* **Mrs M Thorne**. 23 Albion Mews, Lancaster LA1 1GE
Tel: 01524-32316

Catholic Scouts Priest Chaplain to the Scout County of West Lancashire: **Rev N Johnston**. **Tel:** 01772-791782.

Catholic Women's League *Secretary:* **Mrs P Nichols**, 8 Albany Avenue, Blackpool FY4 1QB **Tel:** 01253-347325

Cursillos in Christianity. *Secretary:* **Mrs V Callaghan**, 51 Lower Bank Road, Fulwood, Preston PR2 4NT
Tel: 01772-717506

Knights of St Columba Province 6, *(Cumbria). Provincial Grand Knight:* **Mr J M Carter**, Ritson House, The Square, Allithwaite, Grange over Sands LA11 7QF **Tel/Fax:** 01539-534200 *Secretary:* **Mr Peter Hamilton**. Cavalier Cottage, Newton-in-Furness, Cumbria.
Province 7, *(Lancaster). Provincial Grand Knight:* **Mr E J GIlleade**, 9 Hindley Close, Fulwood, Preston PR2 9UG
Tel: 01772-653897 *Secretary:* Awaiting appointment.

L'Arche Community 1/3 Moor Park Avenue, Preston PR1 6AS

Our Lady's Catechists: *Diocesan Representative:* **Mrs Freda Collinge**, 39 Eldon Court, Glen Eldon Road, St Anne's FY8 2BH **Tel:** 01253-725369

Union of Catholic Mothers *Secretary:* **Mrs M C Strain**, Broadfield, Egremont, Cumbria CA22 2NG **Tel:** 01946-820300

■ HOSPITALS

To contact the Catholic Chaplain of a particular hospital we suggest you contact the hospital reception directly.

■ CATHOLIC SCHOOLS – VOLUNTARY AIDED

■ CUMBRIA

▲ Infant

SS Gregory and Patrick's Catholic Infants School, Esk Avenue, CA28 8AJ **Tel:** 01946-852666 *(Whitehaven).*

▲ Primary

Sacred Heart Catholic Primary School, Lumley Street, LA14 2BA **Tel:** 01229-894635 *(Barrow-in-Furness).*

Holy Family Catholic Primary School, Ostley Bank, LA13 9LR **Tel:** 01229-89462 *(Barrow-in-Furness).*

St Columba's Catholic Primary School, Church Lane, Walney LA14 3AD **Tel:** 01229-471522 *(Barrow-in-Furness).*

St Pius X Catholic Primary School, Schneider Road, LA14 4AA **Tel:** 01229-894651 *(Barrow-in-Furness).*

St Cuthbert's Catholic Primary School, Victoria Road, CA1 2UE **Tel:** 01228-607505 *(Carlisle).*

St Bede's Catholic Primary School, Strathclyde, Avenue, CA2 7DS **Tel:** 01228-607550 *(Carlisle).*

St Margaret Mary's Catholic Primary School, Kirklands Road, Upperby Read CA2 4JD **Tel:** 01228-607540 *(Carlisle).*

St Patrick's Catholic Primary School, Todholes Road CA25 5DG **Tel:** 01946-855011 *(Cleator Moor).*

St Joseph's Catholic School, Mountain View CA13 0DG **Tel:** 01900-325932 *(Cockermouth).*

Our Lady of the Rosary Catholic Primary School, Crooklands Brow, LA15 8JH **Tel:** 01229-897923 *(Dalton-in-Furness).*

St Bridget's Catholic Primary School, St Bridget's Lane, CA22 2BS **Tel:** 01946-820320 *(Egremont).*

St Joseph's Catholic Primary School, Yeathouse Road, CA26 3PX **Tel:** 01946-810702. *(Frizington).*

Dean Gibson Catholic Primary School, Hawesmead Avenue, LA9 5HB **Tel:** 01539-773630 *(Kendal).*

St Patrick's Catholic Primary School, Ennerdale Road, CA15 8HN **Tel:** 01900-812582 (Maryport).

St James' Catholic Primary School, Lonsdale Road, LA18 4AS **Tel:** 01229-772731 *(Millom).*

St Catherine's Catholic Primary School, Drovers Lane, CA11 7RQ **Tel:** 01768-242170 *(Penrith).*

St Mary's Catholic Primary School, Springfield Road, LA12 0EA **Tel:** 01229-894132 *(Ulverston).*

St Mary's Catholic School, High Road Kells CA28 9PG **Tel:** 01946-852685 *(Whitehaven).*

St Mary's Catholic Primary School, Holden Road, Salterbeck, Workington CA14 5LN **Tel:** 01946-830433 *(Harrington).*

St Cuthbert's Catholic Primary School, Wigton CA7 9HZ **Tel:** 016973-43119 *(Wigton).*

St Cuthbert's Catholic Primary School, Princes Road, LA23 2DD **Tel:** 015394-62480 *(Windermere).*

St Patrick's Catholic Primary School, Derwent Street, CA14 2DS **Tel:** 01900-325237 *(Workington).*

St Gregory's Catholic Primary School, Furness Road, Westfield, CA14 3PD **Tel:** 01900-325248 *(Workington).*

▲ Junior

St Begh's Catholic Junior School, Coach Road, CA28 7TE **Tel:** 01946-852663 *(Whitehaven).*

▲ Comprehensive High Schools

St Bernard's Catholic High School, Rating Lane, LA13 9LE **Tel:** 01229-894620 *(Barrow-in-Furness).*

Newman School, Lismore Place, Carlisle CA1 1NA **Tel:** 01228-607470 *(Carlisle).*

St Benedict's Catholic High School, Red Lonnine, Kensingham, CA28 8UG **Tel:** 01946-852680 *(Whitehaven).*

St Joseph's RC High School, Harrington Road, CA14 3EE **Tel:** 01900-325240 *(Workington).*

■ LANCASHIRE

▲ Primary

Alston Lane Catholic Primary School, Preston Road, Longridge, Preston PR3 3BJ **Tel:** 01772-783661 *(Alston Lane).*

Our Lady of Lourdes Catholic Primary School, Kellet Road, LA5 9LS **Tel:** 01524-732289 *(Carnforth).*

St Mary's Catholic Primary School, Smithy Lane, Preston PR3 0PN **Tel:** 01995-640258 *(Claughton-on-Brock).*

St Mary's Catholic Primary School, London Street, FY7 6EU **Tel:** 01253-878445 *(Fleetwood).*

St Edmund's Catholic Primary School, Melbourne Avenue, FY7 8AY **Tel:** 01253-872886 *(Fleetwood).*

St Wulstan's Catholic Primary School, Poulton Road, FY7 7JY **Tel:** 01253-874785 *(Fleetwood).*

St Mary and St. Michael Catholic Primary School, Castle Lane, Garstang, Preston PR3 1RB **Tel:** 01955-603023 *(Garstang).*

St Francis Catholic Primary School, The Hill, Horns Lane, Preston PR3 2FJ **Tel:** 01772-865369 *(Goosnargh).*

St Mary's Catholic Primary School, St Mary's Road, Preston PR3 0ZH **Tel:** 01995-670364 *(Great Eccleston).*

The Willows Catholic Primary School, Victoria Road, Preston PR4 2BT **Tel:** 01772-684371 *(Kirkham).*

Cathedral Catholic Primary School, Balmoral Road, LA1 3BT **Tel:** 01524-64686 *(Lancaster).*

St Bernadette's Catholic Primary School, Bowerham Road, LA1 4HT **Tel:** 01524-63934 *(Lancaster).*

St Joseph's Catholic Primary School, Aldren's Lane, LA1 2DU **Tel:** 01524-65576 *(Lancaster).*

St Mary's Catholic Primary School, Darkinson Lane, Lea Town PR4 0RJ **Tel:** 01772-729881 *(Lea Town).*

St Peter's Catholic School, Norfolk Road, Lytham, FY8 4JG **Tel:** 01253-734658 *(Lytham).*

St Mary's Catholic Primary School, Coniston Road, LA4 5PS **Tel:** 01524-413032 *(Morecambe).*

St Patrick's Catholic Primary School, Littledale Avenue, Heysham LA3 2ER. **Tel:** 01524-51766 *(Morecambe).*

St Mary and St Andrew's Catholic Primary School, Station Lane, Barton, Preston. PR3 5DY **Tel:** 01772-862335 *(Newhouse).*

St William's Catholic School, Garstang Road, Preston PR3 6AL **Tel:** 01253-790389 *(Pilling).*

St John's Catholic Primary School, Breck Road, FY6 7HT **Tel:** 01253-883690 *(Poulton-le-Fylde).*

Blessed Sacrament Catholic Primary School, Farrington Lane, Ribbleton, PR2 6LX **Tel:** 01772-792572 *(Preston).*

Sacred Heart Catholic Primary School, Poulton Street, PR2 2SA **Tel:** 01772-726937 *(Preston).*

Holy Family Catholic School, Whitby Avenue, Ingol PR2 3YP **Tel:** 01772-727471 *(Preston).*

Our Lady and St Edward's Catholic Primary School, Lightfoot Lane, Fulwood PR2 3LP **Tel:** 01772-862305 *(Preston).*

St Anthony's Catholic Primary School, St Anthony's Drive, Fulwood, Preston PR2 3SQ **Tel:** 01772-726621 *(Preston).*

St Augustine's Catholic Primary School, St Austin's Place, PR1 3YJ **Tel:** 01772-253851 *(Preston).*

St Bernard's Catholic Primary School, Victoria Park Avenue, Lea PR2 1RP **Tel:** 01772-728153 *(Preston).*

St Clare's Catholic Primary School, Sharoe Green Lane North, Fulwood, PR2 9HH **Tel:** 01772-787037 *(Preston).*

St Gregory's Catholic Primary School, Blackpool Road, Deepdale PR1 6QH **Tel:** 01772-795415 *(Preston).*

St Ignatius Catholic Primary School, St Ignatius Square, PR1 1TT **Tel:** 01772-555252 *(Preston).*

St Joseph's Catholic Primary School Caroline Street, PR1 5XL **Tel:** 01772-796112 *(Preston).*

St Maria Goretti Catholic Primary School Gamull Lane, Ribbleton PR2 6SJ **Tel:** 01772-700052 *(Preston).*

St Teresa's Catholic Primary School, Downing Street, Fishwick PR1 4RH **Tel:** 01772-797397 *(Preston).*

English Martyrs Catholic Primary School, Sizer Street, PR1 7DR **Tel:** 01772-556092 *(Preston).*

Our Lady Star of the Sea Catholic Primary School, Kenilworth Road, FY8 1LB **Tel:** 01253-726015 *(St Annes on Sea).*

Sacred Heart Catholic School, Heys Street, FY5 4HL **Tel:** 01253-821392 *(Thornton-le-Fylde).*

Holy Family Catholic Primary School, Lytham Road, Warton, Preston PR4 1AH **Tel:** 01772-633623 *(Warton).*

St Joseph's Catholic Primary School, Garstang Road North, Preston PR4 3HA **Tel:** 01772-683009 (Wesham).

Cardinal Allen Catholic High School, Melbourne Avenue FY7 8AY **Tel:** 01253-872659 *(Fleetwood).*

Our Lady's High School, Morecambe Road, LA1 2RX **Tel:** 01524-66689 *(Lancaster).*

St Bede's Catholic High School, Talbot Road, FY8 4JL **Tel:** 01253-737174 *(Lytham).*

Our Lady's Catholic High School, St Anthony's Drive, Fulwood PR2 3SQ **Tel:** 01772-726441 *(Preston).*

Corpus Christi Catholic High School, St Vincent's Road, Fulwood PR2 8QY **Tel:** 01772-716912 *(Preston).*

Christ the King Catholic High School, Lawrence Avenue, Frenchwood PR1 4LX **Tel:** 01772-252072 *(Preston).*

■ BLACKPOOL LEA

▲ Primary

Christ the King Catholic Primary School, Bathurst Avenue, Grange Park FY3 7PL **Tel:** 01253-35985 *(Blackpool).*

Holy Family Primary School, Seacrest Avenue, FY1 2SD **Tel:** 01253-354496 *(Blackpool).*

Our Lady of the Assumption School, Catholic Primary School, Common Edge

Road, FY4 5DF **Tel:** 01253-762833 *(Blackpool).*
St Bernadette's Catholic Primary School, Devonshire Road, Bispham FY2 0AJ **Tel:** 01253-353641 *(Blackpool).*
St Cuthbert's Catholic Primary School, Lightwood Avenue FY4 2AU **Tel:** 01253-403232 *(Blackpool).*
St John Vianney's Catholic Primary School, Glastonbury Avenue, Marton FY1 6RD **Tel:** 01253-312098 *(Blackpool).*
St Kentigern's Catholic Primary School, Newton Drive, FY3 8BT **Tel:** 01253-393302 *(Blackpool).*
St Teresa's Catholic Primary School, St Teresa's Avenue FY3 3JT **Tel:** 01253-852457 *(Cleveleys)*

▲ Comprehensive High Schools
St Mary's Comprehensive High School, St Walburga's Road, FY3 7EQ **Tel:** 01253-396286 *(Blackpool)*

■ SIXTH-FORM COLLEGE IN THE FURTHER EDUCATION SECTOR
Cardinal Newman College, Lark Hill, Frenchwood, Preston PR1 4HD **Tel:** 01772-460181 *(Preston).*

■ CATHOLIC SCHOOLS - INDEPENDENT

■ CUMBRIA

▲ Secondary
Austin Friars School, Etterby Scaur CA3 9PB **Tel:** 01228-528042 *(Carlisle).*

■ LANCASHIRE

▲ Primary
St Pius X Preparatory School, 200 Garstang Road, Fulwood PR2 8RD **Tel:** 01772-719937 *(Preston).*

DIOCESE OF LEEDS

Province of Liverpool

The Diocese of Leeds consists of the County of West Yorkshire and parts of North Yorkshire, parts of North Humberside, Cumbria, Greater Manchester and Lancashire. It is within the Ecclesiastical Province of Liverpool.

It was formed on 20th December 1878, by division of the Diocese of Beverley into the Diocese of Leeds and Middlesbrough. On 30th May 1980, fifty parishes from South Yorkshire were taken away to form the greater part of the new Diocese of Hallam. In 1982 the two York parishes were ceded to the diocese of Middlesbrough to unite the city of York under one bishop.

Patrons of the Diocese

Our Lady of Perpetual Succour, June 27th;
Saint Wilfrid, October 12th

Rt Rev Arthur Roche, Bishop of Leeds

Bishop

Rt Rev Arthur Roche, born in Batley Carr, 6th March 1950, ordained Priest 19th July 1975 by Bishop William Gordon Wheeler; ordained Auxiliary Bishop of Westminster by Cardinal Cormac Murphy-O'Connor, 10th May 2001; appointed Coadjutor Bishop of Leeds 16th July 2002; appointed ninth Bishop of Leeds, 7th April 2004.

Residence:
Bishop's House, 13 North Grange Road, Leeds LS6 2BR.
Tel: 0113-230 4533 **Fax:** 0113-278 9890
E-mail: bishop@dioceseofleeds.org.uk

Bishop's Secretary:
Rev Martin Kelly.
E-mail: dolsec@aol,com
Diocesan Website: www.dioceseofleeds.org.uk

DIOCESE OF LEEDS

■ BISHOP EMERITUS
Rt Rev David Konstant MA.
Residence: Ashlea, 62 Headingley Lane, Leeds LS6 2BU
Tel: 0113-261 8002 **Fax:** 0113-261 8058
E-mail: dakons@aol.com

■ CURIA
All diocesan offices and agencies are based in Hinsley Hall unless otherwise stated.

■ Diocesan Pastoral Centre
Hinsley Hall, Diocese of Leeds Pastoral Centre, 62 Headingley Lane, Leeds LS6 2BX
Tel: 0113-261 8000 **Fax:** 0113-224 2406
Director: **Mgr Kieran Heskin VG**.
General Manager: **Mr Austin Smith.**

■ Diocesan Curial Offices
Finance & Property Offices: Hinsley Hall, 62 Headingley Lane, Leeds LS6 2BX **Tel:** 0113-261 8023 **Fax:** 0113-261 8035 *Moderator of the Curia:* **Mgr Kieran Heskin VG**, *Chancellor:* **Very Rev Mgr Canon J Bryan Sharp VCL LLB**, *Vice-Chancellor:* **Rev Martin Kelly**.

■ Vicars General:
Mgr Kieran Heskin BA PhD, Mgr Michael McQuinn BAC(Hons), Hinsley Hall, 62 Headingley Lane, Leeds LS6 2BX **Tel:** 0113-261 8023

■ Bishop's Presbyteral Council
Chairman: **Bishop Arthur Roche.**
Secretary: **Rev Kevin Gleeson**.

■ Finance & Property Administration
(Finance Board and Directors of the Diocese of Leeds Trustee)
Chairman: **Bishop Arthur Roche;**
Secretary: **Mr David Herd;** *Members:* **Mr Terence Forbes, Mgr Kieran Heskin, Mgr Michael McQuinn, Mr Robin Smith, Ms Ann O'Brien, Mr Tony Hester, Mr Peter Lomas, Mrs Trina Hagerty.**

■ Financial Administration
Director of Finance: **Mr David Herd.**
Accounts Supervisor: Awaiting Appointment.

■ Property Administration
Property Administrator: **Mr David Damant.**

■ Finance & Property Committee
Chairman: **Mgr Kieran Heskin VG.**

■ Finance Sub-Committee
Chairman: **Mgr Kieran Heskin VG.**

■ Historic Churches Committee.
Chairman: **Mgr Kieran Heskin VG.**
Secretary: **Mr David Damant.**

■ Media and Communications
Diocesan Communications Officer: **Mr John Grady, Tel:** 0113-261 8022 **Fax:** 0113-261 8035 **Mobile:** 0770-334 1527
E-mail: john.grady@dioceseofleeds.org.uk
Diocesan Newspaper: Catholic Post.

■ Diocesan Archives
Archivist: **Mr Robert Finnigan.**
Tel: 0113 261 8031

■ Liturgy Commission
Chairman: **Mgr Philip Moger**, Cathedral Church of St Anne, Great George Street, Leeds LS2 8BC **Tel:** 0113 245 4545
E-mail: Prmoger@aol.com
Diocesan Director of Liturgical Music: **Mr Benjamin Saunders**. Cathedral House, Great George Street, Leeds LS2 8BE
Tel: 0113-244 8634 **Fax:** 0113-245 3626

■ Safeguarding Officer
Safeguarding Office, Diocese of Leeds, Hinsley Hall, 62 Headingley Lane, Leeds LS6 2BX **Tel:** 0113-261 8046 (office)

■ Bishop's Adviser on Healthcare
V. Rev Canon Christopher Irving;
Tel: 0113-392 3527
E-mail: christopher.irving@dioceseofleeds.org.uk

■ Diocesan Council for Education
Episcopal Delegate: **Mrs Trina Hagerty**
Principal Officer: **Ms Deirdre Rowe**
Administration Assistant: **Mrs Beverley Sice**
Tel: 0113 261 8034

■ Chancery
Chancellor: **V. Mgr Canon Rev J Byran Sharp,** Hinsley Hall, 62 Headingley Lane, Leeds LS6 2BX
Vice-Chancellor: **Rev Martin Kelly.**

■ Tribunal
All correspondence to the Tribunal Administrator. **Tel:** 0113-261 8029
Judicial Vicar: **Mgr Patrick Hennessy**.
Associate Judicial Vicar: **Rev John Aveyard.** *Tribunal Administrator:* **Mrs Pauline Place**. *Notary:* **Mrs Helen Abrahams.** *Defender of the Bond:*
Judges: **V Rev Canon Martin Forde, Revv David Drake-Brockman, Anthony Fenton, Mr Anthony Kerr.**

■ Chapter of Canons
Rev Mgr Canon J Bryan Sharp *(Provost),* **Revv Canons Joseph Finan, Sean Gilligan, Lawrence Hulme, Christopher Irving, Peter Maguire, John Nunan, Thomas O'Connor, Vincent O'Hara, Francis Robinson, Joseph Smith, Joseph Taylor, Martin Forde** *(Canon Penitentiary).*
Honorary Canons: **Revv Canons Hugh Barr, John Kelly, Michael McCreadie, Peter McGuire, Edward McSweeney, John Murphy, Denis Tangney.**

■ VICARIATE FOR CLERGY
Episcopal Vicar: Awaiting Appointment..

■ Diocesan Vocations Service
Vocations Director: **Rev Paul Grogan**. Leeds Trinity College, Brownberrie Lane, Horsforth, Leeds LS18 5HD
Tel: 0113-283 7199
E-mail: Dolvocs@aol.com

■ Permanent Diaconate Programme
Director: **Rev Kevin Firth**, St Patrick's Presbytery, Bolton Brow, Sowerby Bridge HX6 2BA **Tel:** 01484-653225

■ Vicariate for Christian LIFE
Episcopal Vicar: **Mgr Peter Rosser,** 5 St Mark's Avenue, Leeds LS2 9BN
Tel: 0113-244 6070
Vicar for Religious: **Sr Gemma,** "Thorneycroft", St Joseph's Convent, 918 Bradford Road, Birstall, Batley WF17 9PH

■ Justice & Peace Commission
Fieldworker: **Ms Sheelagh Fawcett.** Hinsley Hall, 62 Headingley Lane, Leeds LS6 2BX
Tel: 0113-261 8055

■ Race Relations Commission
Chairman: **Mr Philip Francis**. *Secretary:* **Mrs Philomena Fernandez.** 60 Upper Rushton Road, Bradford BD3 7EU

■ Peru Commission
Chairman: **Rev Canon Vincent O'Hara**.
Secretary: **Mrs Shirley Poland**. 3 Henley Crescent, Rawdon, Leeds LS19 6PA **Tel:** 0113-250 3804

■ Family Life Ministry
Co-ordinator: **Mrs Breda Theakston,**
Tel: 0113-261 8050

■ Catholic Care
Director: **Mr Mark Wiggin,** 11 North Grange Road, Leeds LS6 2BR
E-mail: info@catholic-care.org.uk
Website: www.catholic-care.org.uk

■ VICARIATE FOR EVANGELISATION
Episcopal Vicar: **Rev Dr John Wilson**.
Tel: 0113 261 8001

■ **Myddleton Grange**
Office: Langbar Road, Ilkley, West Yorkshire LS29 0EB. *Director:* **Rev Simon Lodge**, **Tel:** 01943-607887 **Fax:** 01943-885470 **E-mail:** myddeltonlodge@compuserve.com.

■ **Youth**
Youth Chaplains: **Revv Martin Kelly, Stephen Webb. Tel:** 0113 261 8058 *Youth Officer:* **Anna Cowell.**

■ **VICARIATE FOR OUTREACH**
Episcopal Vicar: **Rev Paul Fisher**. **Tel:** 01942-465531

■ **Commission for Christian Unity**
All correspondence to: **Rev Paul Fisher**, St Joseph's Presbytery, 25 Naylor Street, Batley Carr, Dewsbury WF13 2DF **Tel:** 01924-465531 *Secretary:* **Sr Baptista CP**.

■ **Interfaith Group**
Convenor & Interfaith Officer: **Mr David Jackson**, 55 Kirkgate, Shipley BD18 3LU **Tel:** 01274-581094 **E-mail:** dandt@kirkgate.triom.net

■ **West Yorkshire Ecumenical Council**
62 Headingley Lane, Leeds LS6 2BX *County Ecumenical Officer:* **Rev Paul Fisher**. **Tel:** 0113-261 8053

■ **LEEDS** L A
1. † Cathedral Church of St Anne
(1786; 1794, 1838; 1904; 1924)
Cookridge Street, Leeds.
Cathedral House, Great George Street, LS2 8BE **Tel:** 0113-245 4545
Website: www.leedscathedral.org.uk
E-mail: cathedral@dioceseofleeds.org.uk
Rev Mgr Philip Moger *(Dean of Cathedral)*, **Revv Michael McLaughlin, Samuel Ofia MSP**; *Priest in Residence:* **Mgr Michael McQuinn VG**, **Tel:** 0113-245 6339 *Deacons:* **Revv John Lythe, Michael Mkpadi**. *Chaplain to Leeds Hospital Trust:* **V Rev Canon Christopher Irving**. *Director of Music:* **Benjamin Saunders**. **Tel:** 0113-244 8634. **E-mail:** music@leedscathedral.org.uk
M: *Sat 1st M of Sun 6pm. Sun 9.30am, 11am, 6pm. Hds (vigil 5.30pm). 8am, 10am, 12.30, 1pm, 5.30pm.*

■ **ADDINGHAM,** Ilkley, West Yorks A
† Our Lady and the English Martyrs
(1923; 1927)
Bolton Road, Addingham, Ilkley, West Yorkshire LS29 0NQ **Tel:** 01943-830259
Rev Jeremiah O'Mahony.
M: *Sun 10.15am. Hds 7.30pm.*

■ **ARDSLEY,** West Yorks A
Our Lady of the Nativity (1958)
Westerton Road, West Ardsley
Served from Morley. **Tel:** 0113 253 4881
M: *Sun 9.30am. Hds As announced.*

■ **BAILDON,** West Yorks A
† St Aidan (1929; 1933; 1945)
Baildon Road, Baildon, Shipley, West Yorkshire BD17 6AQ **Tel:** 01274-583032
Rev Richard Carter. Also in residence: **Rev Mark Knowles (Retired)**
M: *Sat 1st M of Sun 6.30pm. Sun 10am. Hds 12noon, 7.30pm.*

■ **BARDSEY,** East Keswick, West Yorks
The Blessed Sacrament (1935)
Served from Wetherby. **Tel:** 01937 582283
M: *As announced.*

■ **BARNOLDSWICK,** Colne, Lancs
† St Joseph (1898; 1907; 1929; 1979)
22 Gisburn Road, Barnoldswick, Colne, Lancs. BB8 5HA **Tel:** 01282-812204
Deacon: **Rev Simon Winn STL**.
M: *Sat 1st M of Sun 6.30pm. Sun 10am. Hds 10am, 7.30pm.*

■ **BATLEY,** West Yorks L
† St Mary of the Angels
(1853; 1870; 1915; 1929)
Upton Street, Batley, West Yorkshire.
Rev Timothy Wiley. Presbytery, Cross Bank Road, WF17 8PQ **Tel:** 01924-474650
M: *Sat 1st M of Sun 6pm. Sun 8.30am, 11am. Hds (vigil 7.30pm). 9am, 7.30pm.*
- ***Franciscan Missionaries of the Divine Motherhood (FMDM)*** 6 Staincliffe View, Staincliffe, Dewsbury WF13 4JN **Tel:** 01924 403368

■ **BATLEY CARR, West Yorks**
† St Joseph (1881)
25 Naylor Street, Batley Carr, Dewsbury, West Yorkshire WF13 2DF
Tel: 01924-465531
Rev Paul Fisher. *Deacon:* **Rev Patrick Kelly**.
M: *Sat 1st M of Sun 6.30pm, Sun 10.30pm.*
- ***Sisters of the Cross and Passion,*** Dewsbury WF13 3TQ **Tel:** 01924-461455

■ **BENTHAM,** Lancaster
† **St Boniface** (1866; 1959)
31 Robin Lane, High Bentham, Lancaster LA2 7AB **Tel:** 01524-261315
Rev Mgr A B Boylan

■ **BINGLEY,** West Yorks
1. † The Sacred Heart (1873)
Crownest Road, Bingley **Tel:** 01274-567639
Served from St Mary's, Cottingley
M: *Sat 1st M of Sun 6pm, Sun 11am Hds As Announced.*

■ **BIRSTALL,** Batley
† **St Patrick** (1876-1906; 1909)
Low Lane, Birstall, Batley WF17 9HD
Rev Anthony Wilson.
Tel: 01924-472257 **Fax:** 01924-471958
M: *Sat 1st M of Sun 6pm. Sun 10am. Hds 9am, 7.30pm.*
- ***Sisters of Charity of St Paul,*** The Convent Birstall WF17 9PH **Tel:** 01924-474640

■ **BISHOP THORNTON,** Ripley
† **St Joseph** (Penal Days; 1809)
St Joseph's Presbytery, Cobler Lane, Bishop Thornton, Ripley, Harrogate HG3 3JR
Tel: 01423-770036
Rev Patrick Waldron.
M: *Sat 1st M of Sun 6pm. Sun 10am. Hds As Announced.*

■ **BRADFORD**
1. † St Anthony of Padua
(1940; 1954; 1961; 2 Oct 1974)
Bradford Road, Bradford BD14 6HW
Rev Maurice Pearce.Tel: 01274-574720
M: *Sat 1st M of Sun 6.30pm. Sun 10am. Hds 9am, 7.30pm.*
- ***Franciscan Sisters,*** St Anthony's, Bradford Road, BD14 6HW **Tel:** 01274-882167

2. † St Columba (1929; 1940; 1958)
The Presbytery, 229 Tong Street, Dudley Hill, Bradford BD4 9PY
Tel/Fax: 01274-682284
Also serves St Peters, Bradford (15)
Rev Frank Smith
M: *Sat 1st m of Sun 5.30pm. Sun 11am.*

3. † St Cuthbert's
(1878; 1891; 1953)
Wilmer Road, Heaton, Bradford BD9 4RX
Tel: 01274-543789
Served from St Cuthbert and First Martyrs, Bradford (10).
M: *Sat 1st m of Sun 5.30pm. Hds 9.15am.*

4. Holy Trinity (Ukrainian Rite),
Park View Road, Heaton. BD9 4PA
Rev Irineu Kraiczyi.
The Presbytery, 10 Park View Road, Heaton BD9 4PA **Tel:** 01274-542307
M: *Sun 9am, 10.30am.*

5. † The Immaculate Conception.
(1932; 1955; 1960)
Leeds Road, Idle, Bradford BD10 9SS
Served from St Francis, Bradford (13).
Tel: 01274-637937
M: *Sun 9am. Hds As Announced*

6. † St John the Evangelist
(1954; 1955)
Cooper Lane, Buttershaw, Bradford BD6 3NS **Tel/Fax:** 01274-679026
Website: www.stjohnsbuttershaw.co.uk
Joint Parish with St Winefride, Bradford (17)
M: *Sun 9.15am, 11am. Hds (vigil 7pm), 11am.*

7. † St Joseph
(1868; 1887; 14 Sept 1937)
Pakington Street, Bradford BD5 7LD
Rev John Newman.
Deacon: **Rev Nick Baggio.**
Tel/Fax: 01274-720299
M: *Sat 1st M of Sun 5pm. Sun 10am, 6pm. Hds 9.15am, 12noon, 7.30pm.*
- ***Sisters of the Cross and Passion,*** 2 St Luke's Close, Little Horton, Bradford BD5 0XA **Tel:** 01274-308120
- ***Daugthers Of Mary, Mother Of Mercy,*** 74 Little Horton Lane, Bradford BD5 0HU **Tel:** 01274-724085

8. † St Matthew
(1957; 1959; 1980)
The Presbytery, Saffron Drive, Allerton, Bradford BD15 7NQ **Tel:** 01274-542431
Rev Canice McGinn.
M: *Sat 1st M of Sun 6.30pm. Sun 10am. Hds 10am, 7.30pm.*
- ***Sisters of the Holy Family of Bordeaux,*** Holy Family Convent, 79 Grange Road, Allerton, Bradford, BD15 7RS **Tel:** 01274-498843

9. Our Lady of Czestochowa and St Maximilian Kolbe (Polish Church) (1960)
29 Edmund Street, Bradford BD5 0BH
Tel: 01274-720848
Revv Andrzej Marcak, Wieslaw Duracz.
M: *Sat 1st M of Sun 6pm. Sun 10am, 11.15am. Hds 10.30am, 7.30pm.*

10. † St Cuthbert and the First Martyrs (1935; 1936)
The Presbytery, Heights Lane, Heaton, Bradford BD9 6HQ **Tel:** 01274-543789
Rev Eamonn Hegerty BA
Also serves St Cuthberts, Bradford (3).
M: *Sun 10.30am, 6pm. Hds 11am (term time) 7.30pm.*

11. † Our Lady of Lourdes and St William (1882; 1909; 1926; 1952)
26 Duncombe Street, Ingleby Road, Bradford BD8 9AJ **Tel:** 01274-542534
Rev James Callaghan.
M: *Sat 1st M of Sun 6pm. Sun 11.30am. Hds 10am, 7.30pm.*

A

12. † Our Lady of Perpetual Succour and St Clare
(1917; 1944; 1956; 1968)
Moorside Road, Fagley, Bradford BD2 3JE
Rev William Finnegan. Tel: 01274-637438
M: *Sun 10am, 5.30pm.*
• ***Sisters of St. Joseph of Peace,*** 30 Loxley Close, Fagley, Bradford BD2 3HX

A

13. † Our Lady and St Francis of Assisi (1938)
St Francis Presbytery, 144 Norman Lane, Eccleshill, Bradford BD2 2JU
Tel: 01274-637937
Rev Patrick Wall
Also serves The Immaculate Conception, Bradford (5)
M: *Sat 1st M of Sun 6.30pm. Sun 11am. Hds 9.30am, 7.30pm.*

L

14. † St Patrick (1852; 11 July 1903)
Sedgfield Terrace, Bradford BD1 2RU
Tel: 01274-724941
Rev Jeremiah Murphy.
M: *Sun 10am (May - Sept), 11am (Oct - Apr). 6pm. Hds (vigil 7.30pm). 12.15pm.*
• ***Franciscan Friars of Renewal (CFR),*** **Rev Anelus Houle CFR.** St Pio Friary, 1 Sedgfield Terrace, Bradford BD1 2RU **Tel:** 01274-721989

15. † St Peter (1921; 1952)
651 Leeds Road, Bradford BD3 8EL
Served from St Columba, Bradford (2)
M: *Sun 9am Hds As Announced.*

A

16. † The Sacred Heart
(1922; 1930; 1938)
Old Road, Thornton, West Yorkshire BD13 3DR Served from St Williams.

A

17. † St Theresa and St Winefride (1933; 1947)
54 St Paul's Avenue, Wibsey, Bradford BD6 1ST **Tel:** 01274-677992
Joint Parish with St John, Bradford (6)
Revv Keiron Walker, Kenneth Hawley.
M: *Sat 1st M of Sun 6.15pm. Sun 8.15am, 10.15am. Hds 9am, 7.30pm.*

18. University of Bradford.
Chaplaincy, 1 Ashgrove, Bradford BD7 1BN
Tel: 01274-721636 **Fax:** 01274-740125
Rev Stephen Brown
M: *Sun 11am, 5.30pm (during term time). Hds As Announced.*

19. Italian Catholic Mission
68 Little Horton Lane, Bradford BD5 0HU
Tel: 01274-721612
M: *Sun 10.30am.*

A

■ **BRIGHOUSE,** West Yorks
† St Joseph (1867)
Martin Street, Brighouse, West Yorkshire HD6 1DA **Tel:** 01484-712679
Rev Philip Fitzgerald.
M: *Sat 1st M of Sun 6pm. Sun 8.30am, 11am. Hds 9am (School term time), 11.30am, 7.30pm.*

■ **BROUGHTON HALL,** Skipton
† The Sacred Heart (1453)
Rev Geoffrey M Parfitt. The Manse, Broughton, BD23 3AE **Tel:** 01756-793794
M: *Sun 9am, (1st Sun 11.30am Trid), Hds 11.30am.*

■ **BURLEY-IN-WHARFEDALE**
† SS John Fisher and Thomas More (1932)
Bradford Road, Burley-in-Wharfedale, Ilkley LS29 7PX **Tel:** 01943-863179
V. Rev Canon Joseph Smith.
M: *Sat 1st M of Sun 6pm. Sun 9am, 11am (August only 6pm, 10.30am). Hds 10am, 7.30pm.*

■ **CARLTON,** Goole, N. Humberside L A
† St Mary (1380; 1842)
Station Road, Carlton **Tel:** 01757 703345
Served from St Mary's, Selby
M: *Sun 11.15am Hds As Announced.*

A

■ **CASTLEFORD,** West Yorks
† St Joseph (1877; 11 July 1906)
Pontefract Road, Castleford, W. Yorkshire WF10 4JB **Tel:** 01977-552753
Rev Sean Durcan.
M: *Sat 1st M of Sun 6pm. Sun 10am, 6pm. Hds 9.30am, 7.30pm.*

A

■ **CLECKHEATON,** West Yorks
† Our Lady of Unfailing Help and St Paul of the Cross (1925; 1946; 1953)
57 Dewsbury Road, Cleckheaton, West Yorkshire BD19 5BT **Tel:** 01274-872984
Rev Peter Smith.
M: *Sat 1st M of Sun 6.30pm. Sun 9 am, 11.15am. Hds 10am, 7pm.*

L

■ **CLIFFORD,** West Yorks
† St Edward, King and Confessor
(1841; 1848; 1859)
Chapel Lane, Clifford, West Yorkshire LS23 6HU **Tel:** 01937-842318
Fax: 01937-842916 **Rev Michael Ingwell.**
M: *Sat 1st M of Sun 6pm. Sun 10am. Hds 9am, 7.30pm.*

■ **COTTINGLEY**
St Mary and St Monica (1970)
Opened 1998

DIOCESE OF LEEDS

The Presbytery, Bradford Old Road, Cottingley, BD16 1SA **Tel:** 01274-567639
Also Serves Bingley
Rev Sean Molloy
M: *Sat 1st M of Sun 6.30pm. Sun 11am. Hds As Announced.*

■ **DEWSBURY,** West Yorks
1. † Our Lady and St Paulinus (1841; 1871, 1921)
Cemetery Road, Dewsbury, West Yorkshire WF13 2SE **Tel:** 01924-465638
Rev Nicholas Hird
M: *Sat 1st M of Sun 6.30pm. Sun 9am, 11am. Hds 10am, 7pm.*

2. † St Thomas More (1952; 1954; 1956)
Maple Road, Dewsbury, West Yorkshire.
Rev Kevin Gleeson. Greengates House, Chickenley Lane, WF12 8QD
Tel: 01924-465073
M: *Sat 1st M Sun 6pm, Sun 11am. Hds 10am, 7.30pm.*

■ **EARBY,** Colne, Lancs
† St Patrick (1925; 1928)
Salterforth Road. Served from Broughton Hall.
Tel: 01756-793794
Deacon: **Rev Malcolm King**.
M: *Sun 10.30am. Hds 7pm.*

■ **ELLAND,** West Yorks
† St Patrick (1902; 1960)
Victoria Road, Elland, West Yorkshire HX5 0PU **Tel:** 01422-373734
Rev Sean Leonard.
M: *Sat 1st M of Sun 5.30pm. Sun 10am. Hds (vigil 7.30pm), 10am, .*

■ **GARFORTH,** Leeds
† St Benedict (1883; 1998)
Completed 1998.
Aberford Road, Garforth LS25 1PX
Tel: 0113-286 3224
Rev Gerard Kearney
M: *Sat 1st M of Sun 6.30pm. Sun 8.30am, 10am. Hds 9.30am, 7.30pm.*

■ **GARGRAVE,** North Yorks
Served from Broughton Hall.
Tel: 01756 793794
M: *Sat 1st M of Sun 6pm (summer), 4.30pm (winter). Hds As Announced.*

■ **GOOLE,** East Yorks
† St Joseph & St Thomas of Canterbury
Pasture Road, Goole DN14 6DP
Tel: 01405-430245
Served from Howden
Rev Neville Atkinson.
M: *Sat 1st M of Sun 7pm. Sun 10am. Hds 10am, 7pm.*

■ **HALIFAX,** West Yorks
1. † St Albans (1946; 1956)
Huddersfield Road, Halifax, West Yorkshire HX3 0AP **Tel:** 01422-352141
Served from St Marie, Halifax (3)
M: *Sun 9.30am, 6pm. Hds 9am, 7.30pm.*

2. † St Columba (1941)
Highroad Well Lane, Halifax, West Yorkshire HX2 0QF **Tel:** 01422-361682
Rev Michael Mahady.
M: *Sat 1st M of Sun 7pm. Sun 9am, 11am. Hds 10am, 7.30pm.*

3. † St Marie (1827; 1836; 1934)
Gibbet Street, Halifax, West Yorkshire.
Rev David Smith, St Marie's Presbytery, 2 Clarence Street, Halifax HX1 5DH
Tel: 01422-352141
M: *Sun 11am, 12.45pm, 12.30pm (Pol), 3rd Sun 3pm (Ital), Hds 10am (term time), 12.15pm, 5.45pm.*

- ***Polish Chaplain:*** **Rev Wieslaw Duracz.** 29 Edmund Street, Bradford BD5 0BH **Tel:** 01274 720848.
- ***Brothers of the Hospitaller Order of Saint John of God:*** Genil, 27 Savile Row, Halifax, West Yorkshire HX1 2BA **Tel:** 01422-329038 **Tel:** 01422-381534

4. † Our Lady of Lourdes and St Malachy (1921; 1933)
Nursery Lane, Ovenden, Halifax, West Yorkshire HX3 5NS **Tel:** 01422-352382
Rev Peter Nealon.
M: *Sat 1st M of Sun 6.30pm. Sun 9am, 11am. Hds 9.30am, 7.30pm.*

- ***Cross and Passion,*** Sisters, 5a Nursery Close, Halifax HX3 5NT **Tel:** 01422-360894

5. † The Sacred Heart and St Bernard (1893; 1898; 1986)
Presbytery, Range Lane, Halifax HX3 6DL
Tel: 01422-353690 **Fax:** 01422-254684
V. Rev Canon Joseph Taylor.
M: *Sat 1st M of Sun 7pm. Sun 10am. Hds 10am, 7.30pm.*

■ **HARROGATE,** North Yorks
1. † St Aelred of Rievaulx (1912; 1957; 1978)
71 Woodlands Drive, HG2 7BE
Tel: 01423-889442
Rev James Leavy.
Deacon: **Rev David Arblaster**
Tel: 01423-560279
M: *Sat 1st M of Sun 6.30pm. Sun 10am. Hds 9.30am, 7.30pm.*

2. St John Fisher
High School. Served from St Robert, Harrogate.
M: *Sun 10.15am.*

3. † St Joseph (1925; 1929)
281 Skipton Road, Harrogate, North Yorkshire HG1 3HD **Tel:** 01423-504124
Rev Neil Byrne.

M: *Sat 1st M of Sun 6.30pm. Sun 8am, 11am. Hds 12noon, 6.30pm.*

4. † Our Lady Immaculate and St Robert L A
(1861; 1873; 10 May 1930; 1980)
Robert Street, Harrogate, North Yorkshire HG1 1HP **Tel:** 01423-504988
Rev Mgr Donal Lucey, Rev Christopher Angel.
M: *Sat 1st M of Sun 6.15pm. Sun 9am, 11.30am, 6pm. Hds (vigil 7pm), 12noon, 7pm.*
- ***Society of the Holy Child Jesus,*** Oatlands Drive, HG2 8PU **Tel:** 01423-885101

■ HAWORTH, Keighley, West Yorks
† Our Lady of Lourdes (1922; 1925)
Ebor Lane, Haworth, Keighley, West Yorkshire BD22 8HR **Tel:** 01535-643240
Rev Benjamin Griffiths.
M: *Sun 10am. Hds 9.30am, 7.30pm.*

■ HECKMONDWIKE, West Yorks L
† The Holy Spirit (1915; 1964)
Bath Road, Heckmondwike WF16 9EA
Rev John Abberton. Presbytery, 18 Cemetery Road, Heckmondwike WF16 9EB
Tel: 01924-402579
M: *Sat 1st M of Sun 6pm. Sun 10am. Hds (vigil 7.30pm) 9.30am.*

■ HEMSWORTH, Pontefract
† The Sacred Heart (1891; 1994)
The Presbytery, Market Street, Hemsworth, Pontefract, West Yorkshire WF9 4LB
Tel: 01977-610733
Rev Anthony Fenton.
M: *Sun 10.30am. Hds 10am.*

■ HORSFORTH, Leeds A
1. † St Mary (1896; 1928; 1972)
Broadgate Lane, Horsforth, Leeds LS18 4AG
Tel: 0113-258 2607 **Fax:** 0113-258 1567
Rev Daniel Harrison.
M: *Sat 1st M of Sun 6.30pm. Sun 8.30am, 10.45am. Hds 9.30am, 7.30pm.*

2. Leeds Trinity College A
Brownberrie Lane, Horsforth, Leeds LS18 5HD **Tel:** 0113-283 7199
Chaplain: **Rev Paul Grogan.**
M: *Sun 6pm (term time). Hds As Announced.*
- ***Comboni Missionaries,*** Verona Fathers (MCCJ), Brownberrie Manor, Brownberrie Lane (opposite TASC), Horsforth, LS18 5HE **Rev Robert Staton. Tel:** 0113-258 2658

■ HOWDEN
Sacred Heart
Sacred Heart Presbytery, 1 Buttfield Road, Howden, Goole DN14 7DW
Tel: 01430-430245
Also serves St Joseph's, Goole.
M: *Sat 1st M of Sun 6.30pm. Sun 9.30am. Hds 7.30pm.*

■ HUDDERSFIELD, West Yorks
1. English Martyrs (1970)
Teddington Avenue, Dalton, Huddersfield, HD5 9HS **Tel:** 01484-536357
Served from St Joseph's, Huddersfield (2)
M: *Sat 1st M of Sun 6.30pm. Sun 10.45am. Hds 9.10am, 7.30pm.*

2. † St Joseph (1895; 1896; 1913; 1954) A
Somerset Road, Huddersfield.
Tel/Fax: 01484-536357
Revv John Aveyard, Michael Hall.
Also Serves English Martyrs, Huddersfield (1) and Meltham.
M: *Sat 1st M of Sun 6.30pm. Sun 11am, Hds 9.30am, 7.30pm.*

3. Our Lady of Czestochowa (Polish Church) (1962)
88 Fitzwilliam Street, Huddersfield, West Yorkshire HD1 5BB
Tel: 01484-420474
Rev Eugeniusz Trojnar.
M: *Sun 9.30am, 11.15am. Hds 10am, 7.30pm.*

4. † Our Lady of Lourdes (1938; 1961)
Sheepridge Road, Huddersfield
Served from St Patricks, Huddersfield (5)
M: *Sat 1st M of Sun 6pm. Sun 10.30am. Hds 9.30am, 7pm.*
- ***Sisters of the Presentation,*** Ashbrow Road. HD2 1DX **Tel:** 01484-534530.

5. † St Patrick (1828; 1832) L A
34 New North Road, Huddersfield, West Yorkshire HD1 5JY **Tel:** 01484-531483
Serves Our Lady of Lourdes, Huddersfield and Holy Family, Slaithwaite
Revv Ian Smith, Vitalis Kondo MSP
M: *Sat 1st M of Sun 6pm. Sun 9am, 11am, 6.30pm. Hds (vigil 7.30pm). 9.30am, 12.15pm.*

6. Huddersfield University
Ecumenical Chaplaincy, Queensgate, Huddersfield, West Yorkshire HD1 3DH
Rev Peter Clarke Tel: 01484-472090

■ ILKLEY, West Yorks
1. † Sacred Heart of Jesus (1897)
Stockeld Road, Ilkley, West Yorkshire LS29 9HD **Tel:** 01943-607690
Rev Mgr Kieran Heskin.
M: *Sat 1st M of Sun 6.30pm. Sun 8.30am, 10.30am. Hds 9.30am, 7.30pm.*

• ***Sisters of the Cross and Passion,*** 'Elmleigh', 42 King's Road, LS29 9AT **Tel:** 01943-607003 The Briery Retreat House, 38 Victoria Avenue, Ilkley LS29 9BW **Tel:** 01943-607287

2. † Myddelton Grange (1922)
Langbar Road, Ilkley, West Yorkshire LS29 0EB **Tel:** 01943-607887
Fax: 01943-885470
E-mail: info@myddeltongrange.org.uk
Director: **Rev Simon Lodge.**
M: *As Announced.*

■ KEIGHLEY, West Yorks L A

1. † St Anne (1835; 1838)
North Street, Keighley, West Yorkshire BD21 3AD **Tel:** 01535-603356
V. Rev Canon Sean Gilligan
M: *Sat 1st M of Sun 6.30pm, Sun 9.30am, 11am. Hds 9.10am, 12.10pm, 7.30pm.*

2. † St Joseph (1922; 1934; 1941; 1973)
Queens Road, Ingrow, Keighley, West Yorkshire BD21 1AT **Tel:** 01535-603931
Rev John O'Keeffe.
M: *Sat 1st M of Sun 6.30pm. Sun 9am, 11am. Hds (vigil 7.30pm), 10am.*

L
3. † Our Lady of Victories (1939; 1945)
West Lane, Guard House, Keighley, West Yorkshire BD22 6ES **Tel:** 01535-603819
Rev Patrick Mungovin.
M: *Sat 1st M of Sun 6.30pm. Sun 10am. Hds 9.30am, 7.30pm.*

■ KNARESBOROUGH, North Yorks L A

† St Mary (1693; 1831)
25 Bond End, Knaresborough HG5 9EW
Tel: 01423-862388 **Fax:** 01423-869631
Rev George Corrie OSB.
M: *Sat 1st M of Sun 6pm. Sun 10am (Family), 5pm. Hds 9.15am, 7.30pm.*

■ KNOTTINGLEY, West Yorks

† St Michael (1939; 1962; 1964, 1999)
Hill Top, Knottingley, West Yorkshire WF11 9AQ **Tel:** 01977-672800
M: *Sat 1st M of Sun 6pm. Sun 9.30am. Hds 9am, 7pm.*

■ LEEDS

1. Please see start of diocese list.

A
2. † St Anthony (1904; 1905; 1934)
19 Old Lane, Beeston, Leeds LS11 7AA
Tel: 0113-271 6597 **Fax:** 0113-277 4998
Rev Robert Owens.
M: *Sat 1st M of Sun, 6.30pm. Sun 9am, 11am. Hds 7.30am, 9.30am, 7.30pm.*

A
3. † The Assumption *(1954; 1957)*
Spen Lane, Leeds 16
Served from Our Lady of Lourdes (22).
M: *Sat 1st M of Sun, 6pm. Sun 9.30am. Hds 12.30pm.*

A
4. † St Augustine
(1898; 1908; 1936; 19 June 1952)
Harehills Road, Leeds LS8 5HR
Tel: 0113-249 0762 **Fax:** 0113-240 0076
Rev Michael Kelly.
M: *Sat 1st M of Sun 6.30pm. Sun 10am, 6.30pm. Hds 9.45am 7.30pm.*

A
5. St Brigid (1929; 1954; 1984)
Elland Road, Churwell, Leeds LS27 7QR
Tel: 0113-253 4894
M: *Sun 9.30am, 6pm. Hds 9.30am, 7.30pm.*

A
7. † Christ the King (1928)
Houghley Lane, Bramley, Leeds LS13 2DX
Tel: 0113-257 4740
Rev Dennis Cassidy
Serves Holy Spirit, Leeds (14).
M: *Sun 9.30am, 6.30pm. Hds 9am, 7pm.*

8. † Corpus Christi (1933; 1962)
Neville Road, Osmondthorpe, Leeds LS9 0HD **Tel:** 0113-294 7305
Fax: 0113-248 6064
Rev Paul Redmond STL
M: *Sat 1st M of Sun 6pm. Sun 8.30am, 10.30am, 6.30pm. Hds (vigil 7.15pm). 8am, 10am.*

9. † St Francis of Assisi
(1882; New Church +16 March 1985)
Bismarck Street, Leeds LS11 6TN
Tel: 0113-270 6962 **Fax:** 0113-270 1771
Rev Mgr Canon Francis Robinson.
Pastoral Assistant: **Sr Damien (CP).**
M: *Sun 8.30am, 10.30am. Hds 12noon, 7.30pm.*
• ***Society of the Sacred Heart,*** 1 Crossland Terrace, Leeds LS11 6EU **Tel:** 0113-226 2406

A
10. † St Gregory the Great
(1954; 1970)
Swarcliffe Drive, Leeds LS14 5AW
Tel: 0113-293 0288 **Fax:** 0113-232 8101
Rev John Kelly.
Pastoral Assistant: **Sr Nora Dowd RSM.**
M: *Sat 1st M of Sun 6.30pm. Sun 10am. Hds 9.30am, 7.30pm.*
• ***Sisters of Mercy,*** 9 Swarcliffe Drive, Leeds LS14 5JW **Tel:** 0113-232 3932

A
11. † Holy Family (1872; 1923)
12 Green Lane, New Wortley, Leeds LS12 1HU **Tel/Fax:** 0113-263 7484
Rev Francis McGrath.
M: *Sat 1st M of Sun 6.30pm. Sun 10am, 11am. Hds 9.30am, 7.30pm.*

DIOCESE OF LEEDS

12. † Holy Name of Jesus
(1943; 1951; 1953; 1979)
52 Otley Old Road, Leeds LS16 6HW
Tel: 0113-267 8257
Rev Patrick Smythe
M: *Sat 1st M of Sun 6.30pm, Sun 9am, 11am. Hds 9.30am, 7.30pm*

13. † Holy Rosary (1936, 1937)
Chapeltown Road **Tel:** 0113-262 3624
Rev Gerald Thornton, Parish House, 3 Cross Francis Street, Leeds LS7 4BZ
M: *Sun 9am, 11am. Hds 10am, 7.30pm.*

14. Holy Spirit (1970)
Bradford Road, Stanningley, Leeds LS28 6NE
Served from Christ the King, Leeds (7).
Tel: 0113-257 4740
M: *Sun 10.45am. Hds 10.30am.*

15. † The Immaculate Heart of Mary
(1945; 1946; 1956; 1959)
294 Harrogate Road, Leeds LS17 6LE
Tel/Fax: 0113-268 1373
Revv Nigel Polland, Stephen Webb.
Deacon: **Rev Michael Leahy.**
M: *Sat 1st M of Sun 6.30pm. Sun 8am, 9.30am, 11am, 6.30pm. Hds 9.15am, 11am, 7.30pm.*

- ***Sisters of the Cross and Passion,*** St Gemma's Convent, 329 Harrogate Road, Leeds LS17 6QD
  Tel: 0113-268 1719
  St Gemma's Hospice. **Tel:** 0113-218 5500 *Chaplain:* **Rev Paul Williment.**

16. St John
Halton. Served from St Theresa, Leeds (25)
M: *Sun 9.30am. Hds 9.30am.*

17. † St Nicholas (1938; 1961; 1975)
Oakwood Lane, Gipton, Leeds LS9 6QY
Tel: 0113-249 5131 **Fax:** 0113-216 1934
Rev Eugene McGillycuddy.
M: *Sat 1st M of Sun 6.30pm. Sun 10am. Hds 9.30am, 7pm.*

18. † Our Lady of Good Counsel
(1954; 1960; 1975)
Presbytery, Rosgill Drive, Kentmere Avenue, Seacroft, Leeds LS14 6QY
Tel: 0113-273 5917 **Tel:** 0113-265 7274
Rev Steven Billington.
M: *Sat 1st M of Sun 6pm. Sun 10am. Hds 9.15am, 7pm.*

19. † Our Lady of Lourdes (1930; 1954)
130 Cardigan Road, Leeds LS6 3BJ
Tel: 0113-275 2093
Rev Anthony Jackson,
Priest in residence: **Rev Michael Hughes.**
M: *Sun 11am Hds 7.30pm*

20. † St Patrick
(1883; 1891; 22 April 1926)
Torre Road, Leeds LS9 7QL
Tel: 0113-248 2851
Rev John Carter.
M: *Sat 1st M of Sun 6pm. Sun 9am, 11am. Hds 9am, 12.15pm, 7.30pm.*

21. † St Paul (1953; 1954; 1996)
Buckstone Crescent, Leeds LS17 5ES
Tel: 0113-268 2942
V Rev Canon Michael McCreadie
M: *Sat 1st M of Sun 6.30pm. Sun 9am, 11am. Hds 9.30am, 7.30pm.*

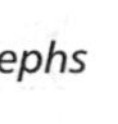

22. † St Peter with St Joseph (1948; 1953)
Petersfield Avenue, Belle Isle Road, LS10 3QN **Tel:** 0113-271 2378
Rev Eamon McGeough.
M: *Sun 10.30am. Hds (vigil St Josephs School 5pm), 12 noon, 7.30pm.*

- ***Sisters of Mercy,*** St Joseph's Convent , Joseph Street, Hunslet, Leeds LS10 2AD
  Tel: 0113 270 5677

23. † St Philip (1934; 1996)
Church House, St Philip's Ave, Middleton, Leeds LS10 3TR **Tel:** 0113-270 5157
Rev Barrie Cummins.
M: *Sat 1st M of Sun 6.30pm. Sun 10am. Hds 10am, 7.30pm.*

24. Polish Catholic Centre
Church of Our Lady of Czestochowa.
Newton Hill Road.
Mgr Jozef Matysik, Rev Miroslaw Slawicki. SChr. 6a Harehills Lane, Leeds LS7 4EY **Tel:** 0113-262 3220
M: *Sat 1st M of Sun 6.30pm, Sun 9.30am, 11am. Hds 10am, 7pm*

25. † St Theresa of the Child Jesus
(1930; 1953)
Station Road, Cross Gates, Leeds LS15 7JY
Tel: 0113-264 5260
Rev Mgr Philip Holroyd.
Deacon: **Rev Thomas Marshall**
M: *Sat 1st M of Sun 6.30pm. Sun 8am, 10.30am, 6pm. Hds 9.30am (St Theresa's School), 12.15pm.*

- ***Sisters of the Holy Family of Bordeaux,*** Holy Family Convent, 393 Selby Road, Leeds LS15 7AY **Tel:** 0113-264 6669

26. Leeds Universities Catholic Chaplaincy
5 St Mark's Avenue, Leeds LS2 9BN
Tel: 0113 - 243 8263
Rev Peter Kravos,
Priest in residence: **Rev Peter Rosser**
Tel: 0113-245 6070
M: *Sun 10am, 5pm (during term time). Hds 8.30am, 1.15pm.*

27. † St Urban
(1902; 1951; 1963; +1988)
2 Moor Park Drive, Leeds LS6 4BX
Tel: 0113-228 8550
Rev Michael Krychiwskyi
M: *Sat 1st M of Sun 6pm. Sun 8.30am, 10.30am. Hds 9.15am, 7.30pm.*

- ***Little Sisters of the Poor,*** Mount St Joseph's, Shire Oak Road, leeds LS6 2DE **Tel:** 0113-278 4101 *Chaplain:* **Rev Gerald Creasey.**
- ***Sisters of Charity of St Paul,*** St Paul's Convent, 11 Moor Drive, Leeds LS6 4BY **Tel:** 0113-275 8852

28. † St Wilfrid (1958; 1960)
2a Whincover Bank, Leeds LS12 5JW
Tel: 0113-263 9531
Rev Frank Carroll.
M: *Sat 1st M of Sun 6.30pm. Sun 9.30am. Hds 7pm.*

■ MELTHAM A
Served from St Joseph's, Hudderfield (2).
M: *Sun 11am. (Masses in St Bartholomew Anglican Parish Church)*

■ MENWITH HILL STATION
Menwith Hill Station, Harrogate, North Yorkshire HG3 2RF **Tel:** 01423-777855
M: *Sat 1st M of Sun 5pm. Sun 9.15am Hds 12 noon, 5pm*

■ MIRFIELD
St Aidan (1927; 1968)
33 Fenton Street, Mirfield WF14 8DG
Tel: 01924-494950
Rev Gregory Knowles.
M: *Sat 1st M Sun 6.30pm, Sun 9.30am. Hds As Announced.*

■ MOORTHORPE A
† St Joseph (1904; 1912; 1928; 1984)
Barnsley Road, Moorthorpe, South Elmsall, Nr Pontefract WF9 2BP
Tel/Fax: 01977-642762
M: *Sat 1st M of Sun 6pm. Sun 9.30am. Hds (vigil 7pm), 9.30am.*

■ MORLEY A
† St Francis of Assisi (1890; 1980)
Corporation Street, Morley, Leeds.
Rev John Galvin. Presbytery, Westfield Road, LS27 9NF **Tel:** 0113-253 4881
M: *Sat 1st M of Sun 6.30pm. Sun 11.15am. Hds (vigil 7.30pm). 12noon.*

■ MYTHOLMROYD

Church of the Good Shepherd (1966; 1992)
Royal Fold, New Road, HX7 5EA
Tel: 01422-886189 **Rev John Gott.**
Deacon: **Rev Nigel Bavidge.**
M: *Sat 1st M of Sun 6pm. Sun 8.45am, 10.45am. Hds (vigil 7pm), 10am, 7pm.*

■ NORMANTON
† St John the Baptist (1871; 1885; 1904)
Newland Lane, Normanton WF6 1BA
Tel: 01924-892172
V Rev Canon Peter Maguire.
M: *Sat 1st M of Sun 7pm. Sun 10am. Hds 9.15am (in school), 12.30pm, 7.30pm.*

■ OSSETT
† St Ignatius (1878; 1910; 1933; 1978)
Storr's Hill Road, Ossett WF5 0DQ
Tel: 01924-273517
Rev Mark Naughton.
M: *Sun 9am, 11am. Hds 9.30am, 7.30pm.*

■ OTLEY

† Our Lady and All Saints (1851; 11 May 1970)
4 Bridge Street, Otley LS21 3AZ
Tel/Fax: 01943-462146
V. Rev Canon Thomas O'Connor.
M: *Sat 1st M of Sun 6:30pm, Sun 9:30am (not August), 10am (August), 11:15am (not August). Hds 8am, 9.15am (Not School Hols), 7.30pm.*

■ PATELEY BRIDGE, Harrogate
† Our Lady Immaculate (1928; 1935; 1984)
Priest's House, Panorama Way, Ripon Road, Pateley Bridge, Harrogate HG3 5NJ
Tel: 01423-711277
V. Rev Canon Vincent O'Hara.
M: *Sat 1st M of Sun 6.30pm. Sun 10.30am Hds 7.30pm.*

■ PONTEFRACT

† St Joseph (1800)
Back Street, Pontefract WF8 1NL
Tel: 01977-702297
Deacon: **Rev Anthony Winn.**
M: *Sun 8.30am, 11am, 6.30pm. Hds 9am, 12 noon, 7pm.*

■ PUDSEY A
† St Joseph (1883, 1901; 1933; 1983)
Mount Pleasant Road, Pudsey LS28 7AZ
Tel/Fax: 0113-257 0803
Rev Michael O'Reilly.
M: *Sat 1st M of Sun 6.30pm. Sun 9.30am, 11.15am. Hds 9.15am, 7.30pm.*

■ QUEENSBURY
† St Theresa of the Child Jesus (1934; 1949)
Russell Road, Queensbury BD13 2AN
Tel: 01274-880119
Rev Michael Nealon.
M: *Sat 1st M of Sun 6.30pm. Sun 10am. Hds 10am, 7.30pm.*

■ RIPON, N Yorks
† St Wilfrid (1850; 1862; 1912)
Coltsgate Hill, Ripon, North Yorkshire HG4 2AB **Tel:** 01765-603614
Rev Paul Moxon.

M: *Sat 1st M of Sun 6.30pm. Sun 10am. Hds 9.30am, 7.30pm.*

■ **ROTHWELL,** Leeds
† **St Mary (1915; 1937; 1948)**
40 Park Lane, Rothwell, Leeds LS26 0ES
Tel: 0113-282 4453
Rev Carlos Carvallo.
M: *Sat 1st M of Sun 6pm. Sun 9.30am, 11am. Hds 10am, 7pm.*

■ **SCARTHINGWELL,**
Tadcaster, North Yorks
† **The Immaculate Conception** (1854)
Served from Sherburn-in-Elmet.
Tel: 01977 685226
M: *Sun 11am. Hds 9.30am.*

■ **SELBY,** North Yorks
1. † **St Mary** (1822; 1854; 1856; 1952)
St Mary's Presbytery, Leeds Road, Gowthorpe, Selby YO8 4HS
Tel: 01757-703345 **Fax:** 01757-290038
E-mail: stmarys.selby@virgin.net
Rev Mgr Bernard W Bickers.
M: *Sat 1st M of Sun 6pm. Sun 9am, & 10.30am. Hds 9am, 7.30pm.*

■ **SETTLE,** North Yorks
† **St Mary and St Michael** (1864; 1974)
Tillman Close, Craven Terrace, Settle, North Yorkshire BD24 9RA
Served from Bentham
Tel: 01729 822525
M: *Sat 1st M of Sun 6pm. Sun 11.15am Aug 31st to Easter, 11am Easter to Aug 31st. Hds 10am.*

■ **SHERBURN-IN-ELMET**
St Joseph the Worker (1958; 1984)
Presbytery, Church View, Low Street, Sherburn-in-Elmet LS25 6BG
Tel: 01977-685226
Rev Michael McCarthy.
M: *Sun 9am. Hds 7.30pm.*

■ **SHIPLEY**
† **St Mary and St Walburga**
(1863; 1867; 1962)
Kirkgate, Shipley BD18 3LU
Tel: 01274-583708
Rev Nigel Barr. *Deacon:* **Rev Barry Barton**
M: *Sat 1st M of Sun 5.30pm. Sun 9.30am. Hds 9.10am (9.30am term time), 7.30pm.*

■ **SICKLINGHALL,** Wetherby, W. Yorks
† **Mary Immaculate** (1854)
Served from Wetherby. **Tel:** 01937-582283
In residence: **Rev John Murphy (OMI).**
M: *Sat 1st M of Sun 6pm. Hds 7pm.*
• ***Sisters of the Holy Family of Bordeaux,*** Main Street, LS22 4BD
Tel: 01937-582076

■ **SILSDEN**
† **Our Lady of Mount Carmel**
(1916; 1920; 1957)
7 Wesley Place, Silsden BD20 0PH
Tel: 01535-653153
Rev Malachy Larkin
M: *Sat 1st M of Sun 6.30pm, (Airdale Hospital). Sun 11am. Hds 7.30pm.*

■ **SKIPTON**
† **St Stephen's** (1836; 1842; 1853; 1923)
Castle View Terace, Skipton BD23 1NV
Tel: 01756-793000
E-mail: peterdawber@aol.com
Website: www.st-stephens-church.info
Rev Peter Dawber.
M: *Sat 1st M of Sun 6pm, Sun 9am, 6pm. Hds 9.15am, 10.30am, 7.30pm.*

■ **SLAITHWAITE**
† **Holy Family** (1915)
60 Commercial Street, Slaithwaite HD7 5JZ
Tel: 01484-842146 **Fax:** 01484-842124
Served from St Patrick's, Huddersfield (5)
Rev Barry Farmer IC.
M: *Sat 1st M of Sun 5.45pm. Sun 9.30am. Hds 10am, 7pm.*

■ **SOWERBY BRIDGE,** West Yorks
† **Sacred Heart and St Patrick** (1920; 1924)
Bolton Brow, Sowerby Bridge HX6 2BA
Tel: 01422-832085
Rev Kevin Firth.
Deacon: **Rev David Marshall**
M: *Sat 1st M of Sun 6.30pm. Sun 11am. Hds 7.30pm.*

■ **TADCASTER,** North Yorks
† **St Joseph** (1866; 1869)
St Joseph's Street, Tadcaster, North Yorkshire LS24 9HA **Tel:** 01937-833105
Rev Michael Walsh
M: *Sat 1st M of Sun 6pm. Sun 10am. Hds 11am, 7.30pm.*

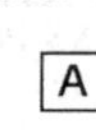

■ **THRESHFIELD,** nr Grassington
St Margaret Clitherow (Chapel of Ease)
Served from Skipton.
M: *Sun 10.30am. Hds (vigil 7.30pm).*

■ **UPPERMILL,** Oldham, Lancs
Sacred Heart and St William (1943; 1952; 1967)
31 High Street, Uppermill, Odlham, Lancs. OL3 6HS **Tel:** 01457-872603
Rev Joseph Falloon MSC.
M: *Sat 1st M of Sun 6pm. Sun 8.30am, 10am. Hds 9.30am, 7.30pm.*

■ **WAKEFIELD,** West Yorks
1. † **St Austin** (1828; 15 Dec 1990)
6 Wentworth Tce, Wakefield, West Yorkshire WF1 3QN
Tel: 01924-372080 **Fax:** 01924-215723
Revv Timothy Swinglehurst, Matthew Habron.

M: *Sat 1st M of Sun 6.30pm. Sun 9am, 11am, 6pm. Hds 7.45am, 12 noon, 7.30pm.*

2. † English Martyrs (1932; 1957)
313 Dewsbury Road, Lupset, Wakefield, West Yorkshire WF2 9DD
Tel: 01924-373290
M: *Sat 1st M of Sun 6.30pm. Sun 10am.Hds 10am (School), 7.30pm.*

3. † SS Peter and Paul
(1926; 1954; 16 Oct 1992)
St George's Walk, Kettlethorpe, Wakefield, West Yorkshire WF2 7NR
Tel: 01924-240240
Rev Barrie Senior.
Deacon: **Rev Nicholas Shields**.
Tel: 01924-377921
M: *Sat 1st M of Sun 6.30pm. Sun 9am, 11.30am. Hds 12 noon, 7.30pm.*

■ **WETHERBY,** West Yorks
† St Joseph (1882; 1927; 1986)
Presbytery, 20 Westgate, Wetherby, West Yorkshire LS22 6LL **Tel/Fax:** 01937-582283
V Rev Canon John Nunan. *Deacons:* **Revv Dougal MacDougall, Charles Commer**
M: *Sun 10am, 6pm. Hds 11am, 8pm.*

■ **WINDHILL,** Shipley
St Anthony of Padua (1948; 1967)
Crag Road. Served from Shipley.
M: *Sun 11am. Hds As announced.*

■ **WOOD HALL**
Linton, Wetherby LS22 4HZ
• ***The Carmelite Monastery***:
Tel: 01937-583734 **Fax:** 01937-582486
M: *Sun (please enquire). Weekdays 8am.*

■ **YEADON,** Leeds
† SS Peter and Paul
(1907; 1909 Cragwood; 1956; 1959 Yeadon).
New Road, Yeadon LS19 7HW
Tel: 0113-250 2192
V. Rev Canon Martin Forde.
M: *Sun 8.30am, 11am, 6.30pm. Hds 9.30am, 7.30pm.*
• ***Sisters of Mercy,*** Maria Regina Convent, Cemetery Road, LS19 7UR
Tel: 0113-250 3458.

■ **ORDERS OR CONGREGATIONS, ETC**

■ **Men**
Benedictines (English Congregation): Knaresborough.
Charity, Institute of: Slaithwaite.
Oblates of Mary Immaculate: Sicklinghall.
Sacred Heart, Missionaries of the: Uppermill.
Verona Fathers: Horsforth (2).

■ **WOMEN**
Carmelites: Wood Hall.
Charity (of St Paul), Sisters of: Leeds (27), Birstall.
Cross and Passion, Sisters of the: Leeds (15), Batley Carr, Bradford (7), Halifax (4), Ilkley (1).
Franciscan Missionaries of the Divine Motherhood: Batley
Franciscan Missionaries Sisters of Littlehampton: Bradford (1)
Holy Child Jesus, Society of the: Harrogate (4).
Holy Family of Bordeaux, Sisters of the: Bradford (8), Leeds (8, 25), Sicklinghall.
Mercy, Sisters of Institute of Our Lady of Mercy: Leeds (10, 22), Yeadon.
Poor, Little Sisters of the: Leeds (28).
Presentation, Sisters of the: Huddersfield (4).
Sisters of St Joseph of Peace: Bradford (12).
Society of the Sacred Heart, Leeds (9).

■ **DIOCESAN INSTITUTIONS, SOCIETIES, ETC**
For Societies and Organisations without representation in the diocese please see the main Societies and Organisations section.
Archconfraternity of St Stephen for Altar Servers. *Diocesan Director:* **Frank Sheriden.**
Association of Separated and Divorced Catholics. Contacts: **Marie & Ken Wright.** Providence Cottage, 9 Sycamore Avenue, Halton, Leeds LS15 7RB
Tel: 0113-264 0638
Association of Single Catholics *Chaplain*: **Rev Eugene McGillycuddy,**
Tel: 0113 249 5131
Beginning Experience. Enquiries: **Maria Sinclair Tel:** 0113 261 2732
Bradford Catholic Players *Chairman:* **Mr Simon Carroll Tel:** 01274-371713
Secretary: **Mrs Jeanette Leach**
Tel: 01274-687346
Catenian Association The Provincial No. 3 (North), *Secretary*: **Paul Bareham**. 50 Green Park Road, Skircoat Green, Halifax HX3 0SN **Tel:** 01422-350057
Catholic Clothing Guild *Hon Secretary:* **Mrs Irene de Tute**. 36 Blenheim Road, Wakefield WF1 3JZ **Tel:** 01924 372623
Catholic Women's League *President*: **Mrs Sally Hamp Tel:** 01535 632664
Secretary: **Mrs Joan D Cheetham**
Tel: 01484-518537
Charismatic Renewal. *Secretary:* **Tony Hackett Tel:** 01274 824203
Dominican Secular Institute. *Regional Representative:* **A Mollan.** 131 Croslands Road, Huddersfield, HD3 3PW **Tel:** 01484-651385

Focolare Contact: Focolare Comm. 11 Drummond Avenue, Leeds LS16 5JZ **Tel:** 0113-274 2808

Grail, The. *Diocesan Representative:* **Tony & Sheelagh Pickles**. 20 The Avenue, Leeds L15 8JN **Tel:** 0113 2600844

Housing Aid Centres (CHAS)
Bradford: City House 21-27 Cheapside Road, Bradford BD1 4HR **Tel:** 01274 726790
Dewsbury: Units 8 & 9, Empire House, Wakefield Old Road, Dewsbury WF12 8DJ **Tel:** 01924 324990
Huddersfield: 1st Floor, Standard House, Half Moon Street, Huddersfield HD1 2JF **Tel:** 01484 223922

Knights of Saint Columba Leeds Province No. 5: *Provincial Grand Knight:* **Colin Spiller Tel:** 01274 566332

Lay Associatesof Holy Family. Enquiries: **Mr Alan Dinsdale**. 33 Barleyfields Road, Wetherby **Tel:** 01937-583709

Leeds Diocesan Lourdes Association. *Secretary & Treasurer*: **Sheila Ambler**, 12 Springfield, Clifford, Weatherby LS23 6HQ **Tel:** 01937-845835

Leeds Schola Gregoriana. Details: **Sylvia Noble**. 3 Uplands, Skipton BD23 1BJ **Tel:** 01756-795222

Legion of Mary, *Leeds Comitium Secretary:* **Dennis Lackey** 8 Ladywood Mead, Leeds LS8 2LZ **Tel:** 0113 265 8429

Our Lady's Catechists: *Diocesan Representative:* **Mrs B Stitt**, 2 Hereford Road, Harrogate HG1 2NP **Tel:** 01423-563846

Pontifical Mission Aid Societies *Diocesan Director:* **Rev K Walker**. 54, St Paul's Avenue, Wibsey, Bradford BD6 1ST

Society of St Vincent de Paul *President*: **Mrs Marie Atherton.** 15 Prestwich Drive, Hudderfield HD2 2NU **Tel:** 01484-541990

Teams of Our Lady. An international Catholic Movement for Christian married couples that aims to deepen the couples' spirituality. A 'Team' consists of four or five couples and a priest or religious as spiritual advisor meeting monthly to share the journey of faith, guided by the Holy Spirit. *Contact couple:* **Sue and David Walsh**, St Wilfrid's, Hillcrest, Collingham, Wetherby, West Yorkshire LS22 5DN **Tel:** 01937-574831 **E-mail:** saintwilfrids@openworld.com

The Third Order of Discalced Carmelites Enquiries to: **Mrs J Wyatt,** 2 Sulphur Wells, Broughton BD23 3AL

Union of Catholic Mothers *Secretary*: **Mrs E Millin, Tel:** 01484 653584

Walsingham Association:
Bradford: **Mr W Smith.** 26 Windermere Road, Great Horton, Bradford. BD7 4RQ **Tel:** 01274-571209
Leeds: **Mrs M Mercer**, 4 New Adel Gardens, Leeds LS16 6DB.

■ HOSPITALS

To contact the Catholic Chaplain of a particular hospital we suggest you contact the hospital reception directly.

■ CATHOLIC SCHOOLS - MAINTAINED

Further information can be obtained from the Schools. In case of difficulty, consult the Diocesan Council for Education. **Tel:** 0113-261 8034 **Fax:** 0113-261 8035

■ WEST YORKSHIRE

■ BRADFORD M.B.

▲ Primary

Our Lady & St. Brendan The Bank, Idle, Bradford BD10 0QA **Tel:** 01274-611992 *(Bradford 3)*

Our Lady of Victories Guard House Road, Keighley BD22 6JP **Tel:** 01535-607149 *(Keighley 3)*

Sacred Heart, Valley Drive, Ilkley LS29 8NL **Tel:** 01943-609578 *(Ilkley)*

St Anne Skipton Road, Keighley BD21 3AD **Tel:** 01535-210600 *(Keighley 1)*

St Anthony, Bradford Road, Clayton, Bradford BD14 6HW **Tel:** 01274-414761 **Fax:** 01274-414762 *(Bradford 2).*

St Anthony, High Busy Lane, Shipley BD18 1HD **Tel:** 01274-592738 *(Shipley 2)*

St Clare Fagley Road, Fagley, Bradford BD2 3JD **Tel:** 01274-637841 *(Bradford 15)*

St Columba Tong Street, Bradford BD4 9PY **Tel:** 01274-681961 *(Bradford 3)*

St Cuthbert & First Martyrs Scotchman Road, Bradford BD9 5AT **Tel:** 01274-543445 *(Bradford 4)*

St Francis Myers Lane, Bradford BD2 4ES **Tel:** 01274-638520 *(Bradford 16)*

St John the Evangelist Beacon Road, Bradford BD6 3DQ **Tel:** 01274-679030. *(Bradford 7)*

St Joseph Park Lane, Bradford BD5 0RB **Tel:** 01274-727970 **Fax:** 01274-393458 *(Bradford 8)*

St Joseph, Crownest Road, Bingley, Bradford BD16 4HQ **Tel:** 01274-564883 *(Bingley)*

St Joseph Queen's Road, Keighley BD21 1AR **Tel:** 01535-605880 **Fax:** 01535-690419 *(Keighley 2)*

St Matthew Saffron Drive, Bradford BD15 7NE **Tel:** 01274-541737 *(Bradford 11)*

St Mary and St. Peter Federated School Upper Nidd Street, Leeds Road, Bradford BD3 9ND **Tel:** 01274-73977 *(Bradford 18)*

St Walburga Victoria Park, Shipley BD18 4RL **Tel:** 01274-531102 *(Shipley 1)*

St William Young Street, Bradford BD8 9RG **Tel:** 01274-545743 *(Bradford 14, 17)*

St Winefride St Paul's Avenue, Bradford BD6 1SR **Tel:** 01274-677705 *(Bradford (20)*

▲ Secondary Comprehensive

St Bede's Grammar School (Boys) (11-18), Highgate, Bradford BD9 4BQ **Tel:** 01274-541221 **Fax:** 01274-498290 *(Bradford)*

Yorkshire Martyrs College (11-18), Westgate Hill Street, Bradford BD4 6NR **Tel:** 01274-681262. **Fax:** 01274-689747 *(Bradford)*

St Joseph's College (Girls) (11-18) Cunliffe Road, Bradford BD8 7AP **Tel:** 01274-401500 *(Bradford)*

Holy Family School (Mixed) (11-18), Spring Gardens Lane, Keighley BD20 6LH **Tel:** 01535-210212 *(Keighley)*

■ CALDERDALE M.B.

▲ Primary

St Joseph, Finkil Street, Hove Edge, Brighouse HD6 2NT **Tel:** 01484-713037 **Fax:** 01484-400496 *(Brighouse)*

St Joseph, Portland Road, Halifax HX3 6LA **Tel:** 01422-360646 *(Halifax 6)*

St Malachy Furness Place, Illingworth, Halifax HX2 8JY **Tel:** 01422-244628 **Fax:** 01422-242088 *(Halifax 5)*

St Mary Swires Road, Halifax HX1 2ER **Tel:** 01422-362365 **Fax:** 01422-255116 *(Halifax 4)*

St Patrick, Hullenedge Road, Elland, Halifax HX4 0QX **Tel:** 01422-373104 *(Elland)*

Sacred Heart, St Peter's Avenue, Sowerby Bridge HX6 1BL **Tel:** 01422-831360 *(Sowerby Bridge)*

▲ Secondary Comprehensive

St Catherine's Catholic High (GM) Holdsworth Road, Holmfield, Halifax HX2 9TH **Tel:** 01422-245411 **Fax:** 01422-240008 *(Halifax 5)*

■ KIRKLEES M.B.

▲ Primary

Holy Spirit, Bath Road, Heckmondwike WF16 9EA **Tel:** 01924-325712 *(Heckmondwike)*

Our Lady of Lourdes Bradley Boulevard, Sheepridge, Huddersfield HD2 1EA **Tel:** 01484-310700 *(Bradley)*

St Joseph, Healds Road, Dewsbury WF13 4HY **Tel:** 01924-325327 *(Batley Carr)*

St Joseph, Grosvenor Road, Dalton, Huddersfield HD5 9HU **Tel:** 01484-531669 *(Huddersfield 6)*

St Mary's Upton Street, Batley WF17 8PH **Tel:** 01924-326740 *(Batley)*

St Patrick, Nova Lane, Birstall, Batley WF17 9LQ **Tel:** 01924-326747 *(Birstall)*

St Patrick, Clayton Fields, George Avenue, Birkby, Huddersfield HD2 2BJ **Tel:** 01484-300800 **Fax:** 01484-300808. *(Clayton Fields)*

St Paulinus, Temple Road, Dewsbury WF13 3QE **Tel:** 01924-325330 *(Dewsbury)*

▲ Secondary Comprehensive

St John Fisher High Oxford Road, Dewsbury WF13 4LL **Tel:** 01924-527000 **Fax:** 01924-527004. *(Dewsbury)*

All Saints High Bradley Bar, Huddersfield HD2 2JT **Tel:** 01484-426466 **Fax:** 01484-456452 *(Huddersfield 10)*

■ LEEDS M.B.

▲ Primary (5-11) "Inner Leeds"

Christ the King, Kings Approach, Bramley, Leeds LS13 2DX **Tel:** 0113-214 6106

Corpus Christi, Halton Moor Avenue, Leeds LS9 0HA **Tel:** 0113-248 3095

Holy Family, Parliament Road, Leeds LS12 2LH **Tel:** 0113-214 3565

Holy Name, Otley Old Road, Leeds LS16 6NF **Tel:** 0113-293 6444

Holy Rosary & St Anne, Leopold Street, Leeds LS7 4AW **Tel:** 0113-262 1287 **Fax:** 0113-262 3305

Immaculate Heart of Mary, Harrogate Road, Leeds LS17 6SX **Tel:** 0113-293 0294

Mount St Mary, Raincliffe Road, Leeds LS9 9LR **Tel:** 0113-293 0336

Our Lady of Good Counsel, Pigeon Cote Road, Leeds LS14 1EP **Tel:** 0113-214 4123 **Fax:** 0113-225 6006

Sacred Heart, Eden Way, Leeds LS4 2TF **Tel:** 0113-214 4560 **Fax:** 0113-214 4561

St Anthony, Barkly Road, Leeds LS11 7JS. **Tel:** 0113-214 1700 **Fax:** 0113-277 2633

St Augustine, St Wilfrid's Circus, Leeds LS8 3PF **Tel:** 0113-293 0350 **Fax:** 0113-293 0655

St Francis of Assisi, Lady Pit Lane, Leeds LS11 6RX **Tel:** 0113-270 0978

St Joseph, Joseph Street, Leeds LS10 2AD **Tel:** 0113-271 2093

St Nicholas, Oakwood Lane, Leeds LS9 6QY **Tel:** 0113-293 0318

St Patrick, Torre Road, Leeds LS9 7QL **Tel:** 0113-248 0380

St Paul, Buckstone Crescent, Leeds LS17 5ES **Tel:** 0113-293 9901

St Philip, St Philip's Avenue, Leeds LS10 3SL **Tel:** 0113-271 6763
St Theresa, Barwick Road, Leeds LS15 8RQ **Tel:** 0113-293 0240 **Fax:** 0113-293-0242
St Urban, Tongue Lane, Leeds LS6 4QE **Tel:** 0113-293 4477

▲ Primary (5-11) "Outer Leeds"
St Benedict, Station Fields, Garforth, Leeds LS25 1PS **Tel:** 0113-214 6821 **Fax:** 0113-287 7138
St Edward, Westwood Way, Boston Spa, Wetherby LS23 6DJ **Tel:** 01937-843946
St Francis, Highcliffe Road, Morley, Leeds LS27 9LZ **Tel:** 0113-214 5424
St Joseph, Manor Square, Otley, Leeds LS21 3AP **Tel:** 01943-463840 **Fax:** 01943-464191
St Joseph, Mount Pleasant Road, Pudsey LS28 7AZ **Tel:** 0113-256 5407
St Joseph, Barley Fields Road, Wetherby LS22 6PR **Tel:** 01937-582163
St Mary, Broadgate Ln, Horsforth, Leeds LS18 5AB **Tel:** 0113-258 4593
St Mary, Royds Lane, Rothwell, Leeds LS26 0BJ **Tel:** 0113-214 6313
SS Peter & Paul, New Road, Yeadon, Leeds LS19 7HW **Tel:** 0113-250 3540

▲ Secondary School (11-16)
Cardinal Heenan, Tongue Lane, Leeds LS6 4QE **Tel:** 0113-294 1166 **Fax:** 0113-294 0320
Corpus Christi, Neville Road, Leeds LS9 0TT **Tel:** 0113-248 2666
Mount St Mary, Elleby Road, Leeds LS9 8LA **Tel:** 0113-245 5248

▲ Secondary School (11-18)
St Mary's Comprehensive School, Bradford Road, Menston, Ilkley LS29 6AE **Tel:** 01943-883000 **Fax:** 01943-870242

▲ Sixth Form College
Notre Dame Sixth Form College St Mark's Avenue, Leeds LS2 9BL **Tel:** 0113-294 6644 **Fax:** 0113-294 6006 *(Leeds)*

■ WAKEFIELD M.B.

▲ Primary
English Martyrs, Dewsbury Road, Lupset, Wakefield WF2 9DD **Tel:** 01924-303635 **Fax:** 01924-303639 *(Wakefield)*
Holy Family, Cobblers Lane, Pontefract WF8 2HN **Tel:** 01977-7722840 *(Pontefract)*
Sacred Heart, Highfield Road, Hemsworth, Pontefract WF9 4LJ **Tel:** 01977-723140 *(Hemsworth)*
St Austin, Duke of York Street, Wakefield WF1 3PF **Tel:** 01924-303710 *(Wakefield)*
St Ignatius, Storrs Hill Road, Ossett WF5 0DQ **Tel:** 01924-302895 *(Ossett)*
St John the Baptist, Beckbridge Lane, Normanton WF6 2HZ **Tel:** 01924-302580 (Normanton)
St Joseph, Pontefract Road, Castleford WF10 4JB **Tel:** 01977-723060 **Fax:** 01977-723140 *(Castleford)*
St Joseph, Barnsley Road, Moorthorpe, Pontefract WF9 2BP **Tel:** 01977-723830 *(Moorthorpe)*
St Joseph, Newgate, Pontefract WF8 4AA **Tel:** 01977-723555 *(Pontefract)*

▲ Secondary Comprehensive
St Thomas a Becket Comprehensive School (11-16) Barnsley Road, Sandal, Wakefield WF2 6EQ **Tel:** 01924-303545 **Fax:** 01924-303548 *(Wakefield)*
St Wilfrid's High School (11-18) Cutsyke Road, Featherstone, Pontefract WF7 6BD **Tel:** 01977-691000 **Fax:** 01977-723569 *(Pontefract 1)*

■ NORTH YORKSHIRE COUNTY

▲ Primary
Barkston Ash R.C. Primary London Road, Barkston Ash, Tadcaster LS24 9PS **Tel:** 01937-557373 *(Sherburn-in-Elmet)*
St Joseph, Bishop Thornton, Harrogate HG3 3JR **Tel:** 01423-770083 *(Bishop Thornton)*
St Joseph, Coppice Rise, Harrogate HG1 2DP. **Tel:** 01423-562650 *(Harrogate)*
St Joseph, Station Road, Tadcaster LS24 9JG **Tel:** 01937-832344 *(Tadcaster)*
St Mary, Tentergate Road, Knaresborough HG5 9BG **Tel:** 01423-864631 *(Knaresborough)*
St Mary, Baffam Lane, Selby YO8 9AX **Tel:** 01757-706616 **Fax:** 01757-290793 *(Selby)*
St Robert, Ainsty Road, Harrogate HG1 4AP **Tel:** 01423-504730 *(Harrogate)*
St Stephen, Gargrave Road, Skipton BD23 1PJ **Tel:** 01756-793787 *(Skipton)*
St Wilfrid, Church Lane, Ripon HG4 2ES **Tel:** 01765-603232 *(Ripon)*

▲ Secondary Comprehensive
Holy Family School (11-16), Carlton, Longhedge Lane, Carlton, Snaith, Nr Goole DN14 9NS **Tel:** 01405-860276 *(Carlton)*
St John Fisher High School (11-18) Hookstone Drive, Harrogate HG2 8PT **Tel:** 01423-887254 **Fax:** 01423-881056 *(Harrogate)*

■ EAST RIDING OF YORKSHIRE

▲ Primary (5-11)

St Joseph, Kennedy Drive, Goole DN14 6HQ **Tel:** 01405-762607 *(Goole)*

■ LANCASHIRE COUNTY

▲ Primary (5-11)

St Joseph, West Close Road, Barnoldswick, Nr Colne BB18 5EN **Tel:** 01282-813045 *(Barnoldswick)*

■ CATHOLIC SCHOOL - SPECIAL - INDEPENDENT

St John's School for the Deaf & Partially Hearing, Church Street, Boston Spa, Wetherby LS23 6DF **Tel:** 01937-842144 **Fax:** 01937-541471 *(Clifford)*

ARCHDIOCESE OF LIVERPOOL

Extending from the Mersey to the Ribble, encompassing Merseyside, parts of Lancashire, Cheshire and Greater Manchester, and the Isle of Man

Suffragan Sees
Hallam, Hexham and Newcastle, Lancaster, Leeds, Middlesbrough, Salford

Patrons of the Archdiocese
Our Blessed Lady Immaculate, 8 December;
St Joseph, 19 March; St Kentigern, 14 January

Most Rev Patrick Kelly, Archbishop of Liverpool

Archbishop
Most Rev Patrick Kelly KC*HS STL PhL,
Archbishop of Liverpool; born in Morecambe, Lancs, 23 November 1938; ordained priest 18 February 1962; ordained bishop by Bishop Holland, 3 April 1984; trans to Liverpool 21 May 1996.

Residence:
Archbishop's House, Lowood, Carnatic Road, Liverpool L18 8BY
Tel: 0151-724 6398 **Fax:** 0151-724 6405
E-mail: archbishop.liverpool@rcaolp.co.uk

Auxiliary Bishop
Rt Rev Thomas Anthony Williams, Bishop of Mageo;
Born in Liverpool 10 Feb 1948;ordained priest 27 May 1972, ordained bishop by Archbishop Kelly 27 May 2003
Office: Liverpool Archdiocesan Centre for Evangelisation,
Tel: 01511-522 1000

Former Auxiliary Bishop
Rt Rev Vincent Malone BSc DipEd FCollP Bishop of Abora;
Born in Liverpool 11 Sept 1931; ordained priest 18 Sept 1955, ordained bishop by Archbishop Worlock 3 July 1989.
Residence: 17 West Oakhill Park, Liverpool L13 4BN
Tel: 0151-228 7637 **Fax:** 0151-475 0841
E-mail: vmalone@rcaolp.co.uk

Attached to the Diplomatic Service of the Holy See
Most Rev Paul Richard Gallagher, Titular Archbishop of Hodelm: Apostolic Nuncio to Burundi, born 23 Jan 1954; ord priest 31 July 1977; ord Archbishop 13 March 2004.
Address: Nunciature Apostolique, Chaussée Prince Louis Rwagasore, BP1068, Bujumbura, Burundi.
Tel: 00257 22 23 26, **Fax:** 00257 22 31 76
E-mail: nonciat@cbinf.com

■ ADMINISTRATION

Unless otherwise noted the address for all departments listed below is: Archdiocese of Liverpool, Centre for Evangelisation, Croxteth Drive, Sefton Park, Liverpool L17 1AA
Tel: 0151-522 1000
E-mail: (initial).(surname)@rcaol.co.uk

■ Diocesan Curia
Tel: 0151-522 1012 (*Vicars General, Chancellor*) **Fax:** 0151-522 1014

■ Vicars General
Rt Rev Vincent Malone, *Bishop of Abora*.
Rt Rev Thomas Williams, *Bishop of Mageo*
Rev Mgri John Butchard and John Furnival, Rev Thomas Neylon.

■ Chancellor
Mrs Joan Davis

■ Episcopal Vicar for Religious
Rev Godric Timney OSB, St Anne's Priory, 23 Prescot Road. Ormskirk L39 4TG
Tel: 01695 572168 **Fax:** 01695 571136
E-mail: paxorm@aol.com

■ VICARIATE FOR FINANCE AND DEVELOPMENT
Tel: 0151-522 1020 **Fax:** 0151-522 1021
Episcopal Vicar: **Rev Sean Kirwin**. *Finance:*

Mr John McMahon BA ACA, Mrs Sandra Hesketh, Mr Stephen Kevins, Miss Elena Stopforth, Miss Jeanette Adamson, Mr Terry Finnegan, Miss Carly Watts, Mr Darren Melling, Miss Clare Willmitt, Mrs Rose Jesson, Mr Andrew Davis, Miss Claire Moa. *Administration:* **Mr Aaron Kiely KHS BA FRSA, Mrs Marje Gornall,** *Catholic Cemeteries:* **Mrs Sandra Brennan. Tel/Fax:** 0151-522 1017 *Solicitor & Property Manager:* **Mrs Veronica Clarke LLB.** *Gift Aid Co-ordinator:* **Mrs Pauline Beirnes.** *Parish Clubs Team:* **Mr Andrew Thomas, Mr George Davies, Mrs Cathy Sampson.** *Building Projects:* **Mr Terry Gawne, Mr David Chesser, Mr Brian Dunn, Mr Peter Downs.** *IT Co-ordinator:* **Mr James Bainbridge.** *Human Resources Support Officer:*
Mrs Louise Simms Tel: 0151 522 1090
Human Resources Administrator:
Mrs Gillian Sener

■ **Diocesan Communications Officer**
Peter Heneghan, BEd(Hons),
Tel: 0151-522 1007 **Fax:** 0151-522 1008
E-mail: p.heneghan@rcaol.co.uk

■ **EDUCATION AND FORMATION**

■ **Vicariate for Schools and Colleges**
Tel: 0151-522 1071 **Fax:** 0151-522 1082. *Episcopal Vicar:* **Rev Michael O'Dowd.** *Director:* **Mr Frank Cogley.** *Senior Development Officer:* **Mr Chris Williams;** *Diocesan Schools Officers:* **Mr Alan Bell, Miss Madeleine Haines, Mr Stephen Roberts, Miss Catherine O'Leary, Miss Teresa Jones, Mr Anthony Ford.** *Administration:* **Mrs Frances Coldicutt, Mrs Michelle Underwood, Miss Rosa Dover.**

■ **Episcopal Vicar for Formation**
Rev John McLoughlin
Tel: 0151 522 1041 **Fax:** 0151 522 1060

■ **Department for Christian Education**
Tel: 0151-522 1050 **Fax:** 0151-522 1060
Director: **Rev Desmond Seddon.**
Assistants: **Rev David Melly, Ms Nora Finnegan, Mrs Marie Connolly, Mr Paul Mannings, Mrs Denises Hegarty.**

■ **Department for Pastoral Formation**
Tel: 0151-522 1040 **Fax:** 0151-522 1060
Parish and Adult Formation Advisors: **Mrs Maureen Knight,** 33 Litherland Park, Litherland, Liverpool L21 9HP
Tel: 0151-522 1046 **Mr John Biggins, Tel:** 01744 740463, **Mrs Veronica Murphy, Tel:** 0151 522 1048
Administrative Assistant: **Mrs Julie Cassidy**
Tel: 0151 522 1040
Rainbow Group Co-ordinator: c/o Department of Pastoral Formation.

■ **Safeguarding Department**
Safeguarding Co-ordinator: **Rev Dcn Desmond Bill, Tel:** 0151- 522 1043
E-mail: d.bill@rcaol.co.uk
Safeguarding Support Staff: **Mrs Jean Robbins, Mrs Sylvia Cawley**

■ **Chaplaincy to the Deaf**
Contact: **Sr Dorothy,** Nugent Care, 99 Edge Lane, Liverpool L7 2PE **Tel:** 0151-261 2000 **Textphone:** 0151-707 8216

■ **Permanent Diaconate**
Director: **Mgr Austin W Hunt.** Liverpool Archdiocesan Centre for Evangelisation, Croxteth Drive, Sefton Park, Liverpool L17 1AA
Tel: 0151-522 1042 **Fax:** 0151-522 1060
E-mail: a.hunt@talktalk.net
Vocations Director: **Rev Stephen J Maloney,** All Saints Presbytery, 3 Oakfield, Anfield, Liverpool L4 2QG
Tel: 0151 287 8787 *Episcopal Vicar for Evangelisation:* **Rev Philip Inch,** Our Lady's Presbytery, Hedgefield Road, Gateacre, Liverpool L25 2RW **Tel:** 0151 487 9372
Fax: 0151 283 4735
Email: 4ccv@rcaolp.co.uk
Assistant to the Episcopal Vicar: **Rev Michael Crilly,** St Basil's Presbytery, Hough Green Road, Widnes WA8 4SZ
Tel/Fax: 0151 424 6641

■ **LITURGY AND ECUMENISM**

■ **Diocesan Liturgical Commission**
Chairman: **Rev John McLoughlin.**

■ **Diocesan Ecumenism Commission**
Chairman: **Miss Claire Davidson,** 205 Utting Avenue East, Liverpool L11 1DF. **Tel:** 0151-226 9821.

■ **CHRISTIAN RESPONSIBILITY**

■ **Justice and Peace Commission**
Fieldworker: **Mr Stephen Atherton,**
Tel: 0151-522 1080 **Fax:** 0151-522 1060

■ **Nugent Care**
(Formerly Catholic Social Services)
99 Edge Lane, Liverpool L7 2PE
Tel: 0151-261 2000
Chief Executive: **Miss Kathleen Pitt.**

■ **CONSULTATIVE BODIES**

■ **Metropolitan Cathedral Chapter**
(erected 13 September 1851)
Provost: **Mgr Peter Cookson.** *Canons:* **Bishop Vincent Malone, Bishop Thomas**

Williams, Mgr James Commins, Michael O'Connor, Vincent Burrowes, Thomas Neylon, Christopher Cunningham, Kevin Mullen (*Secretary*), **Brian Mullan, Joseph D'Arcy, Michael Culhane, John Gaine, Albert Shaw, Leo Stoker, Gerard Wharton.** *Honorary Canons:* **Brendan Alger, James Collins, Roger Daley, William O'Sullivan, John Short, Peter Cronin.**

■ **Archbishop's Council**
The Vicars General, **Canon Joseph Kelly, Revv Anthony O'Brien, Michael O'Dowd, Sean Kirwin, Philip Inch, John McLoughlin, Mr John Cowdall, Miss Carol Chapman.** *Secretary:* **Mrs Veronica Clarke**

■ **METROPOLITAN TRIBUNAL**
Tel: 0151-522 1061 *Officialis:* **Rev Brian Murphy** *Vice-Officialis:* **Rev Thomas Wood.** *Assistant to the Officialis:* **Revv Paul Benbow, Atli Gunnar Jonnsson, Sr Martine Neill, Sr Patricia Redgrave, Mr Paul Robbins.**
Defender of the Bond: **Rev Aidan Prescott**; *Promoter of Justice:* **Mgr George Mooney**; *Tribunal Administrator:* **Miss Maureen Stigberg**

■ **LIVERPOOL**
1. † Metropolitan Cathedral of Christ the King (1933; 1959; cons 14 May 1967).
Mount Pleasant, Liverpool L3 5TQ
Tel: 0151-709 9222 **Fax:** 0151-708 7274
E-mail: enquiries@metcathedral.org.uk
Golden Book Office: **Tel:** 0151-707 2107
Visitors Centre: **Tel:** 0151-707 3525
Music Office: **Tel:** 0151-708 7283
Rev Anthony O'Brien (*Dean*), **Revv Michael Williams, Ian O'Shea, Andrew Robinson Noel Abbott, Don Campion** (Cathedral House, Mount Pleasant, Liverpool L3 5TQ).
M: *Sat 1st M of Sun 6.30pm (Crypt). Sun 8.30am, 10am (Crypt), 11am (Solemn Mass), 4pm (Royal Liverpool Hospital Chapel), 1pm (Polish, Crypt), 7pm (Crypt). Hds (vigil 5.15pm), 8am, 12.15pm (Crypt), 5.15pm.*
Director of Music: **Mr Timothy Noon, Tel:** 0151-708 7283. *Artistic Director:* **Sr Anthony Wilson SND MBE NDD ATD.**
Tel: 0151-709 9222
- ***Daughters of Charity of St Vincent de Paul***, Mount Pleasant, L3 5TQ **Tel:** 0151-709 1903
- ***Catholic Chaplaincy to Liverpool University,*** See Liverpool No 59.

■ **AINSDALE**
See Southport (3).

■ **ANDERTON,** Chorley
† St Joseph (1862; 1863)
28 Bolton Road, Adlington, Chorley, Lancs PR6 9NA **Tel/ Fax:** 01257-480237
Rev Francis Marsden
M: *Sat 1st M of Sun 5.30pm. Sun 9.30am. Hds (vigil 7.30pm), 9am.*

■ **APPLETON**
See Widnes (3).

■ **ASHTON-IN-MAKERFIELD**
1. † St Oswald and St Edmund Arrowsmith (1822; 1930; cons 12 September 1951)
Liverpool Road, Ashton-in-Makerfield, Wigan, Lancs WN4 9NP
Tel/Fax: 01942-727249
E-mail: bnewns9671@aol.com
Rev Brian Newns.
Deacon: **Rev John O'Brien.**
M: *Sun 8.30am, 10.30am (Sung). Hds 12.10pm, 7.30pm.*

2. St Wilfrid (1972)
Bolton Road, Ashton-in- Makerfield, Wigan, Lancs WN4 8TH
Tel: 01942-866102 **Fax:** 01942-865901
Rev Anthony Mangnall (resident at Holy Family, Platt Bridge). *Deacons:* **Revv Michael Swift, Roy Moore.**
M: *Sat 1st M of Sun 5.30pm. Sun 10am. Hds As announced.*

■ **ASTLEY,** Tyldesley, Manchester
St Ambrose Barlow (1965;1981)
Astley, Tyldesley, Manchester.
Tel: 01942-883845
Served from Atherton (1).
Deacon: **Rev Robert Hewerton.**
M: *9am, 11am. Hds As Announced.*

■ **ATHERTON,** Manchester
1. † St Richard (1894; 1928)
Mayfield Street, Atherton, Manchester M46 0AQ
Tel: 01942-883395 **Fax:** 01942-871163
Rev Paul Seddon.
M: Sat 6pm, *Sun 9.30am, 6.30pm. Hds 12noon, 7pm.*

2. † Sacred Heart (1865; 1869)
Church closed 2004. Registers at St Richard, Atherton.

■ **AUGHTON,** Ormskirk, Lancs A
† **St Mary** (1784; 1822)
Prescot Road, Aughton, Ormskirk L39 6TA
Tel: 0151-547 3397 **Rev Desmond Seddon.**
Deacon: **Rev Grahame Appleyard.**
M: *Sat 1st M of Sun 5.30pm. Sun 9am, Hds As announced.*

■ **BIRCHLEY,** Billinge, Wigan A
† **St Mary** (1618; 1828)
Birchley Road, Birchley, Billinge, Wigan WN5 7QJ **Tel:** 01744-892227
Rev Bernard Jackson.
Deacon: **Rev Michael McGlynn.**
M: *Sat 1st M of Sun 6pm. Sun 8am, 11am. Hds 9am, 7.30pm.*

■ **BLUNDELLSANDS,** Liverpool
† **St Joseph** (1886; cons 22 September 1938)
Warren Road, Blundellsands, Liverpool L23 6UE **Tel:** 0151-924 2101
Mgr Peter Fleetwood.
M: *Sat 1st M of Sun 6.30pm. Sun 11.15am. Hds 10am, 7.30pm.*
- ***Company of Mary (Montfort Missionaries),*** (SMM), Montfort House, 28 Burbo Bank Road, L23 6TH **Tel:** 0151-924 5250 **Very Rev Frederick Scragg,** (*Provincial*) **Tel:** 0151-287 6865 **Revv Robert Douglas** (*Rector*); **James Cree, Robert Ellwood, Daniel Hogan; Bros Anselm Thompson, Stanley Williams**
Tel: 0151-287 6862 **Fax:** 0151-287 0410
E-mail: smml@nildram.co.uk
- ***Sandymount Retreat House,*** Sandymount, 16 Burbo Bank Road L23 6TH (Company of Mary and Emmaus House of Prayer). *Co-directors:* **Rev Frederick Matthews SMM, Mr Archie Cameron** (Emmaus Family of Prayer).
Tel: 0151-924 4850 **Fax:** 0151-924 4439
E-mail: admin@emmaus.ukfreedom.com
Web: www.emmaus.uk.com
- ***Religious of the Sacred Heart of Mary,*** Seafield, 24 Warren Road, Blundellsands, Liverpool L23 6UE **Tel:** 0151-924 6268 Arrowsmith House, 26 Warren Road, Blundellsands, Liverpool L23 6UE
Tel: 0151-931 2881
- ***Sisters of Notre Dame,*** 8 Warrenhurst Court, Warren Road, Blundellsands L23 6TY **Tel:** 0151-924 7303

■ **BOOTHSTOWN,** Manchester A
† **Holy Family** (1897; 1930)
208 Chaddock Lane, Boothstown, Worsley Manchester M28 1DN
Tel: 0161-790 2390 **Fax:** 0161-799 0417
Rev David P Heywood.
Deacon: **Rev James Melia.**
M: *Sun 9am, 11am. Hds 9.15am, 7pm.*

■ **BOOTLE,** Merseyside A
1. † **St James**
(1845; 1885; cons 23 July 1947)
2 Chestnut Grove, Bootle, Merseyside L20 4LX
- ***Salesians (SDB):*** Presbytery,
Tel: 0151-944 1039 **Fax:** 0151-922 3263
Revv Thomas Williams (*Rector*), **Gerard O'Shaughnessy** (*Parish Priest*), **John Booth, James Gerard Briody, Michael Cunningham, Michael Duggan, Sean Murray.**
M: *Sun 10.30am. Hds (vigil 7.30pm).*

2. † **St Joan of Arc** (1926; 1961) A
Peel Road, Bootle, Merseyside L20 4RW
Tel: 0151-922 1498 **Fax:** 0151-933 4254
Rev Michael de Felice.
M: *Sun 10am, 6.30pm. Hds 9am, 7pm.*

3. † **St Monica** (1923; 1960)
Fernhill Road, Bootle, Merseyside L20 9HQ
Tel: 0151-922 4819
Rev Patrick Sexton. *Deacons:* **Revv John Chegwin, Anthony Sinnott.**
M: *Sat 1st M of Sun 6pm. Sun 9.30am. Hds 9am, 7pm*
- ***Sisters of Our Lady of the Missions,*** 36 Oxford Road, L20 9HW
Tel: 0151-525 1744

4. † **St Richard of Chichester and St Alexander** (1938; 1952)
Miranda Road, Bootle, Merseyside.
Tel: 0151-922 4819
Rev Patrick Sexton (Resident at Bootle (3).
M: *Sun 11am. Hds 12.05pm.*

5. † **St Robert Bellarmine**
(1932; 1993)
52 Orrell Road, Bootle, Merseyside L20 6DZ
Tel: 0151-922 1352
- ***Sacred Heart Fathers (SCJ)***
Rev Patrick Harnett.
M: *Sat 1st M of Sun 6.30pm. Sun 8.30am, 10.30am, 6.30pm. Hds (vigil 7.30pm), 9am, 7.30pm*

6. † **St Winefride** (1895) A
Parish Closed 2008. Registers at St James.
- ***Sisters of Marie Auxiliatrice,*** 57 Merton Road L20 7AP **Tel:** 0151-922 5100 Centre of Adoration.

■ **BRINDLE,** Hoghton, Preston
† **St Joseph** (1677; 1786; 1977)
St Joseph's Presbytery, Chapel Fold, Brindle, Hoghton, Preston PR5 0DE
Tel: 01254-852026 **Fax:** 01254-851258
- ***Benedictines (OSB):***
M: *Sat 1st M of Sun 6.30pm. Sun 8am, 10.30am. Hds 9.15am, 7.30pm.*

■ **BRINSCALL,** Chorley
† **St Joseph** (1884)
Bury Lane, Brinscall, Chorley, Lancs
PR6 8SD **Tel:** 01254-830229
Rev Peter C Crowther.
Deacons: **Revv Simon Gilbertson, John Hogan**
M: *Sun 10.45am. Hds (vigil 7.30pm).*

■ **BRYN,** Wigan
† **Our Lady Immaculate**
(1896; 1903; cons 8 Sept 1955)
Downall Green Road, Bryn, Wigan
WN4 0LZ **Tel:** 01942-727271
Rev Anthony Reynolds KHS,
Deacon: **Rev Malcolm Cunliffe**
M: *Sat 1st M of Sun 7pm. Sun 10am. Hds 9am, 7.30pm.*

A

■ **BURSCOUGH,** Ormskirk
† **St John the Evangelist** (1700; 1815)
Chapel Lane, Lathom, Burscough,
Ormskirk, Lancs L40 7RA
Tel: 01704-892205
Rev Joseph A Robinson.
Deacon: **Rev Kenneth Breen.**
M: *Sat 1st M of Sun 6.30pm. Sun 9.30am, 6.30pm. Hds (vigil 7.30pm). 9.30am.*

A

■ **BURTONWOOD,** Warrington
† **St Paul of the Cross** (1886; 1902; cons 1972)
Clay Lane, Burtonwood, Warrington
WA5 4HW **Tel:** 01925-226184
Rev John Schofield.
M: *Sat 1st M of Sun 6pm. Sun 9.30am. Hds (vigil 7pm). 9.30am.*

A

■ **CASTLETOWN,** Isle of Man
† **St Mary** (1826; 1921)
24 Bowling Green Road, Castletown,
Isle of Man IM9 1EB
Tel: 01624-822272
Rev Gerald Hurst.
M: *Sun 9am. Hds 7.30pm.*

A

■ **CHORLEY,** Lancs
1 † Sacred Heart (1875; 1894)
Brooke Street, Chorley, Lancs PR6 0NG
Tel: 01257-410588 **Rev Francis Ball.**
M: *Sat 1st M of Sun 7pm. Sun 11am, Hds 9.30am, 7.30pm.*

2. † St Gregory (1774; 1815)
Weld Bank, Chorley, Lancs PR7 3NW
Tel: 01257-262462
Mgr Michael McKenna.
M: *Sun 9.30am, 11am, 6.30pm. Hds 9.30am, 7.30pm.*

A

3. † St Joseph (1910; 1960)
Harper's Lane, Chorley, Lancs PR6 0HR
Tel: 01257-262713 **Fax:** 01257-270749
Rev Peter Stanley.
M: *Sat 1st M of Sun 6pm. Sun 8.30am, 10.30am, 4.30pm. Hds (vigil 6.30pm), 8.30am, 7.30pm.*

A

4. † St Mary
(1847; 1854; cons 25 Aug 1927)
Mount Pleasant, Chorley, Lancs PR7 2SR
Tel: 01257-262537 **Fax:** 01257-276553
Rev Francis Marsden
M: *Sat 1st M of Sun 7pm. Sun 8am, 11am, 4.30pm. Hds (vigil 7.30pm), 9am, 12noon.*
• ***Daughters of Wisdom,*** (La Sagesse), 7 Southport Road, Chorley. PR7 1LB
Tel: 01257-262706

■ **CLAYTON GREEN,** Chorley, Lancs
† **St Bede** (1822; 1824)
598 Preston Road, Clayton-le-Woods,
Clayton Green, Chorley PR6 7EB
Tel/Fax: 01772-335209
E-mail: maoneille@mara.freeserve.co.uk
Rev Michael O'Neill MHM.
M: *Sat 1st M of Sun 6.30pm. Sun 8.30am, 10.30am, Hds 9.15am, 7pm.*

A

■ **COPPULL,** Chorley, Lancs
† **St Oswald** (1904; 1927)
Tansley Avenue, Coppull, Chorley, Lancs
PR7 5DJ **Tel/Fax:** 01257-791208
Rev Laurence J Mayne.
M: *Sat 1st M Sun 6.30pm. Sun 9.30am. Hds 9am, 7.30pm.*

A

■ **CROFT,** Warrington
† **St Lewis** (1827)
Mustard Lane, Croft, Warrington WA3 7BD
Tel: 01925-763171
Rev Bernard Eager
M: *Sun 8.30, 11am. Hds As announced*

■ **CRONTON,** Widnes
† **The Holy Family** (1910)
Hall Lane, Cronton, Widnes WA8 9DP
Tel: 0151-424 2129
Served from Widnes (3).
M: *Sat 1st M of Sun 7pm. Sun 10am. Hds (vigil 7pm). 10am, 7pm.*

A

■ **CROSBY,** Liverpool
1. † St Helen (1930)
Alexandra Road, Crosby, Liverpool
L23 7TQ **Tel:** 0151-924 3417
Rev Mgr Peter Fleetwood; *Deacons:* **Revv Peter Deary, William Douglas.**
M: *Sun 9am, 10.30am, 6.30pm. Hds 9am, 12noon, 7.30pm.*

A

2. † SS Peter and Paul (1826; 1894)
161 Liverpool Road, Crosby, Liverpool
L23 5TE **Tel:** 0151-928 3456
Office: **Tel/Fax:** 0151-943 1930
E-mail: ssppaul@aol.com
Mgr John Furnival VG. Also resident: **Rev**

John Seddon (National Chaplain to the Scout Movement) 165 Liverpool Road, Crosby L23 0QN
Tel/Fax: 0151-949 1782 *Deacons:* **Revv Anthony R Johnson, Ernest Diggory, Terence Rimmer.**
M: *Sat 1st M of Sun 5.30pm. Sun 9.30am, 11.30am (Sung), 5.30pm. Hds (vigil 7.30pm), 9.30am, 7.30pm.*
• ***Poor Sisters of Nazareth,*** Nazareth House, Liverpool Road, L23 0QT
Tel: 0151-928 3254 Home for the Elderly.

■ **CROSTON,** Lancs
Holy Cross
Served from Mawdesley.
M: *Sun 9am. Hds 7.30pm.*

■ **DOUGLAS,** Isle of Man
† St Mary (1814; 1859; cons 1906)
Hill Street, Douglas, Isle of Man IM1 1EG
Tel: 01624-675509 **Fax:** 01624-674359
E-mail: bjpalgen@yahoo.co.uk
Canon Brendan Alger, Rev Brian Dougherty.
M: *Sun 11am, 7pm. Hds 7.30pm.*

■ **EARLESTOWN,** Lancs
See Newton-le-Willows (3).

■ **ECCLESTON,** Chorley, Lancs
St Agnes
The Green, Eccleston, Chorley, Lancs PR7 5PH
Tel: 01257-451337 **Fax:** 01257-452150
E-mail: odowd@btinternet.com
Rev Michael O'Dowd.
M: *Sat 1st M of Sun 6pm. Sun 10am. Hds 12.15pm, 7.30pm.*

■ **EUXTON,** Chorley, Lancs
† St Mary (12th cent; 1735; 1865)
Wigan Road, Euxton, Chorley, Lancs PR7 6JW **Tel:** 01257-262665
Rev Gerald McCusker
Deacon: **Rev Gerard Fishwick**
M: *Sun 10am. Hds 9.15am, 7pm.*

■ **FARINGTON,** Preston
† St Catherine Labouré (1948; 1949)
Stanifield Lane, Farington, Preston PR5 2QA **Tel/Fax:** 01772-421174
Served from Leyland.
M: *Sun 8.30am, 10am, 6pm. Hds 9.10am, 7pm.*
• **Sisters of Our Lady of the Missions,** Moss Lane, Leyland PR5 2JS
Tel: 01772-421388

■ **FORD,** Liverpool
The Holy Spirit (1953)
68 Sterrix Lane, Litherland, Ford, Liverpool L21 0DA **Tel/Fax:** 0151-928 0040
Rev John Harris. *Deacon:* **Rev John Murphy.**
M: *Sat 1st M of Sun 5.15pm. Sun 9.45am, 11.30am. Hds (vigil 7.30pm). 7.30pm.*

■ **FORMBY,** Liverpool
1. † Our Lady of Compassion (1686; 1864)
18 School Lane, Formby, Liverpool L37 3LW **Tel/Fax:** 01704-873230
Rev Bernard Higham. *Deacons:* **Revv Fred Cooke, Paul Collins.**
M: *Sun 9am, 11am. Hds 12noon, 8pm.*

2. St Jerome (1968)
Greenloons Drive, Formby, Liverpool L37 2LX **Tel:** 01704-875935
Rev Bernard Higham, resident at Formby (1), In residence: **Very Rev J Frederick Matthews SMM** (*Episcopal Vicar for Religious*), **Tel:** 01704-830784
Deacons: **Revv Terence Cunningham, Joseph P Moreland.**
M: *Sat 1st M of Sun 6.30pm. Sun 9.30am. Hds As announced.*
• ***Mill Hill Missionaries (MHM).*** Regional Office and APF: St Peter's House, College Avenue, Freshfield, Liverpool L37 1LE (1884). **Tel:** 01704-875048
Charles N. Cammack (*Administrator*).
Tel: 01704-834962 **Fax:** 01704-834963
• ***Mill Hill Missionaries (MHM).*** Herbert House. 41 Victoria Road, Freshfield, L37 1LW **Tel:** 01704-875833
Fax: 01704-832960. **Revv Francis Downs** (*Rector*), **James Dalziel** (*Vice Rector*), **Joseph Burton, William Dowds, Edmund Slowey, Brendan Sullivan, Frederick Moss, John McClorey, David Staples.**
• **Poor Servants of the Mother of God,** St Joseph's Nursing Home, Blundell Avenue, Freshfield. L37 1PI
Tel: 01704-872132

■ **FRESHFIELD,** Liverpool 
† St Anne (1816; 1933)
Timms Lane, Freshfield, Liverpool L37 7DW **Tel:** 01704-872467
Rev John P Bradley.
M: *Sat 1st M of Sun 5.30pm. Sun 10am. Hds (vigil 7pm), 10am.*

■ **GOLBORNE,** Warrington
† All Saints (1863; 1928; New church cons 1992)
High Street, Golborne, Warrington WA3 3BG **Tel:** 01942-728962
Rev John Joyce.
M: *Sat 1st M of Sun 5.30pm. Sun 10.30am. Hds 9.15am, 12noon, 7.30pm.*

■ **HARESFINCH.**
See St Helens, No 10.

■ **HAYDOCK,** St Helens
† The Blessed English Martyrs (1879; 1905)
Piele Road, Haydock, St Helens WA11 0JY
Tel: 01942-727005
Rev Thomas J Kennedy. *Deacons:* **Revv**

Peter Barr, Frank Murray.
M: *Sat 1st M of Sun 6pm. Sun 10.30am. Hds (vigil 7pm). 10am, 7pm.*

■ **HIGHER FOLDS**
See Leigh (5).

■ **HIGHTOWN,** Liverpool
† **Our Lady of Victories** (1916)
Sandy Lane, Hightown, Liverpool L38 3RP
Tel: 0151-929 2149
Rev David A Gamble.
M: *Sun 10am. Hds 9.15am, 12noon.*

■ **HINDLEY,** Wigan
† **St Benedict**
(1650; 1869; cons 10 October 1929)
Market Street, Hindley, Wigan WN2 3AA
Tel: 01942-255306.
Rev Joseph Weston.
M: *Sat 1st M of Sun 7pm. Sun 11am. Hds (vigil 7pm), 12noon.*

■ **HINDLEY GREEN,** Wigan
† **Sacred Heart** (1901; 1932)
96 Swan Lane, Hindley Green, Wigan, Lancs WN2 4HD
Tel: 01942-255834
Rev Joseph Weston
Deacon: **Rev Kenneth A Holding**.
M: *Sat 1st M of Sun 5.30pm. Sun 9.30am. Hds, As announced.*

■ **HOGHTON**
See Brindle.

■ **HUYTON,** Liverpool
1. † **St Agnes** (1856; 1870)
Huyton Hey Road, Huyton, Liverpool.
Tel: 0151-489 1296 **Fax:** 0151-482 1010
Served from Huyton (2).
M: *Sat 1st M of Sun 7pm. Sun 10am, 4.30pm. Hds as announced.*
• ***Helpers of the Holy Souls,*** 32 St Agnes Road, Huyton L36 5TA
Tel: 0151-480 7904

2. † **St Aidan** (1992)
Adswood Road, Huyton, Liverpool L36 7XR **Tel:** 0151-489 3085
Rev Anton Fernandopalle
Deacons: **Revv Anthony Whelan, Michael Whelan**.
M: *Sat 1st M of Sun 5pm. Sun 11am. Hds As announced.*
• ***School Sisters of Notre Dame,*** St Aidan's Convent, 92 Adswood Road. L36 7XR.
Tel: 0151-481 0324.

3. † **St Columba** (1938; 1939)
Hillside Avenue, Huyton, Liverpool L36 8DL **Tel:** 0151-489 1802
Rev Michael Lee. *Deacons:* **Revv Patrick Meaney, Christopher Pearson**.
M: *Sun 10am. Hds 12noon, 7.30pm.*

4. † **St Dominic** (1934; 1938)
Southdean Road, Huyton, Liverpool L14 8UL
Tel: 0151-489 1684 **Fax:** 0151-482 6053
E-mail: sdb-huyton@msn.com
• ***Salesians (SDB):*** **Revv George Robson** (*Parish Priest*), **Peter Dooley. James Gallagher, Anthony Frain.**
M: *Sat 1st M of Sun 6.30pm. Sun 10.45am. Hds (vigil 7.30pm). 9.30am.*
• ***Sisters of Mercy,*** The Convent, 72 Finch Lea Drive, Huyton, Liverpool L14 9QN
Tel: 0151-228 8064

■ **INCE,** Wigan
† **St William** (1873; 1908)
Ince Green Lane, Ince, Wigan WN2 2DG.
Tel: 01942 512815 **Fax:** 01942-517914
Rev Ronald McGivern
M: *Sat 1st M of Sun 6pm (Jan, Mar, May, Jul, Sep, Nov). Sun 9.30am. Hds (vigil as announced), 10.15am.*

■ **INCE BLUNDELL,** Liverpool
† **Holy Family** (1701; 1860)
Back o' th' Town Lane, Ince Blundell
Tel: 0151-929 2177
Rev David A Gamble, Resident at Hightown.
M: *Sun 9am. Hds As announced*
• ***Augustinian Nursing Sisters of the Mercy of Jesus,*** Ince Blundell Hall, Back 'o'th' Town Lane, Ince Blundell, Liverpool L38 6JL Nursing Home.
Tel: 0151-929 2596. Retired Priests in residence: **Rev Canon Peter Cronin, Revv David Bullen, James Clarkson, Francis Goulbourn.**
Ince Benet, Cross Barn Lane, Ince Blundell, Liverpool L38 6JD **Rev Thomas Cullinan**
• ***Parish Mission Sisters***, 8 Carr House Lane, Ince Blundell, Liverpool L38 1QG
Tel: 0151-929 2053

■ **KIRKBY,** Liverpool
1. † **Holy Angels** (1955)
Sidney Powell Avenue, Kirkby, Liverpool L32 0TP **Tel:** 0151-546 5300
Rev Andrew Rowlands,
resident at Kirkby (5).
M: *Sat 1st M of Sun 7pm. Sun 11am. Hds 9am, 7pm.*

2. † **St Joseph the Worker** (1963)
Bewley Drive, Southdene, Kirkby, Liverpool L32 7PZ
Tel: 0151-546 3674. **Fax:** 0151-546 9857.
E-mail: stjosephs.kirkby@rcaolp.co.uk
Rev Nicholas Wilde.
M: *Sat 1st M of Sun 6pm Sun 11am. Hds 9am.*
• ***Sisters of Our Lady of the Missions,*** 35 Dalry Crescent, Kirkby, Liverpool L32 7QF

3. † St Laurence (1952)
Closed 2007, Registers at St Joseph the Worker, Kirkby
- ***Daughters of the Heart of Mary***, 8 Cherryfield Drive, Southdene, Kirkby, Liverpool L32 9PA **Tel:** 0151 546 5892

4. † St Mary Mother of God (1958)
Bigdale Drive, Kirkby, Liverpool
Tel: 0151-546 3838 **Fax:** 0151-548 6509
E-mail: parishmaterdei@yahoo.co.uk
- ***Missionaries of the Sacred Heart (MSC)***. **Rev Kevin Blade**. St Mary's, Kennelwood Avenue, Kirkby, Liverpool L33 6UF
  M: *Sat 1st M of Sun 7.30pm. Sun 10am. Hds (vigil 7.30pm), 10am.*

5. † St Michael (1965)
Oatlands Road, Westvale, Kirkby, Liverpool L32 4UH
Tel: 0151-546 9687 **Fax:** 0151-549 2399
E-mail: arowlands@stmichaels.co.uk
Rev Andrew Rowlands.
M: *Sun 9.30am, Hds 10am.*

6. SS Peter and Paul (1966; 1977)
Apostles Way, Kirkby, Liverpool L33 1XL
Tel: 0151-548 4644
Fax: 0151-547 5047
Rev Kevin Blade MSC
M: *Sat 1st M of Sun 6pm. Sun 11am. Hds As announced.*

■ **KNOWSLEY,** Liverpool
St John Fisher (1964)
37 Tithebarn Road, Knowsley, Liverpool L34 0EU **Tel:** 0151-546 4489
Rev Paul Benbow
E-mail: sjf.knowsley@blueyonder.co.uk
M: *Sat 1st M of Sun 5.30pm. Sun 10am. Hds 9.10am, 7.30pm.*

■ **LEIGH,** Lancs
1. † Our Lady of the Rosary (1879; 1939)
Plank Lane, Leigh.
Tel/Fax: 01942-673320
E-mail: ourlady@rcdeanery.org
Rev John Finch, resident at Leigh (2).
Deacon: **Rev Dennis Vint**, 33 Urmston Street, Leigh WN7 4SF **Tel:** 01942-746217
M: *Sun 11am. Hds As announced.*

2. † Sacred Heart
(1904; 1929; cons June 1951)
Walmesley Road, Leigh WN7 1YE
Tel/Fax: 01942-673753
E-mail: shleigh@blueyonder.co.uk
Rev John Finch;
Deacon: **Rev Anthony Arrowsmith.**
M: *Sun 9.30am. Hds As announced.*

3. † St Joseph
(1670; 1778; 1855; cons 31 July 1931)
Chapel Street, Leigh
Tel: 01942-673517 **Fax:** 01942-269094
Rev Stephen Cooper, Presbytery, Mather Lane, WN7 2PR *Deacons:* **Revv William Parr, Bernard Worden.**
M: *Sun 8.30am, 10.30am. Hds (vigil 7.30pm). 9.15am, 12.05pm.*

4. † The Twelve Apostles
(1879; 1902; 1929)
Nel Pan Lane, Leigh, Lancs WN7 5JS
Tel/Fax: 01942-673320
E-mail: twelveapostles@rcdeanery.org
Rev John Finch. (resident at Leigh No.2)
M: *Sat 1st M of Sun 6.30pm (with Children's Liturgy). Hds As announced.*

5. St Gabriel Archangel
(1956; cons 1977)
Kensington Drive, Higher Folds, Leigh, Lancs WN7 2XW
Tel: 0161-790 2390 **Fax:** 0161-799 0417
E-mail: dpathfb@aol.com
Rev David P Heywood, resident at Boothstown.
M: *Sat 1st M of Sun 6pm. Hds (vigil 7pm), 2.45pm.*

■ **LEYLAND,** Preston
† St Mary (1845; 1954; 1964)
Broadfield Walk, Leyland, Preston PR5 1PD
Tel: 01772-421183 **Fax:** 01772-621183
E-mail: ppstmarysleyland@btconnect.com
Also resident: **Rt Rev Ambrose Griffiths**
- ***Benedictines (OSB):***
  Rev Jonathan Cotton.
  M: *Sat 1st M of Sun 6pm. Sun 9.30am, 11am. Hds (vigil 7.15pm). 12.15pm, 7.15pm.*
- ***Franciscan Missionary Sisters of St Joseph,*** "Alverna", 35 Westgate, Leyland. **Tel:** 01772-424665

■ **LITHERLAND,** Liverpool
1. † English Martyrs (1861; 1935)
School Lane, Litherland, Liverpool. L21 7LX **Tel:** 0151-928 3697
Rev William Simpson (resident at Litherland No. 2).
M: *Sat 1st M of Sun 6.15pm. Sun 10.45am. Hds As announced.*

2. † Our Lady Queen of Peace
(1959, cons 1977)
Presbytery, Kirkstone Road West, Litherland, Liverpool L21 0EQ
Tel/Fax: 0151-928 3697
Rev F William Simpson.
M: *Sat 1st M of Sun 5pm. Sun 9.30am. Hds As announced.*

3. † St Elizabeth of Hungary
(1904; 1912)
Presbytery, Webster Street, Litherland, Liverpool L21 8JH
Tel: 0151-922 3820 **Fax:** 0151-933 7941
Rev Barry McAllister.
M: *Sat 1st M of Sun 6pm. Sun 10am. Hds 9am, 7pm.*

■ LITTLE CROSBY

† St Mary (1660; 1847; cons 7 Sept 1847)
St Mary's, Back Lane, Little Crosby, Liverpool L23 4UA
Tel: 0151-924 1783
Rev Dunstan Harrington
M: *Sun 11.15am. Hds 9.15am.*

■ LIVERPOOL

1. See start of parish list.

2. † Blessed Sacrament (1872; 1878)
Walton Vale, Aintree, Liverpool.
Tel: 0151-474 2682 **Fax:** 0151-474 2569
E-mail: blessed@locall.net
Parish Office: *Mon-Fri: 10.00am - 3.00pm.*
Rev William Murphy *Deacon:* **Rev Charles Hegarty** 9 Park Vale Road, L9 2DG
M: *Sun 10.30am, 5pm. Hds 9.15am, 12noon, eve Mass as announced.*

2a Blessed Sacrament Shrine
4 Dawson Street, Liverpool L1 1LE
Tel: 0151-709 5528 **Fax:** 0151-709 5977
E-mail: pjcostello@aol.com
- ***Blessed Sacrament Congregation (SSS):*** **Very Rev Gary P Walsh** (*Superior*), **Revv Patrick Walsh, Melville Wright, Bro John Bartaby, Bro Francis Barker.**
  M: *Sat 1st M of Sun 5.40pm. Sun 11.30am, 5pm. Hds (vigil 5.40pm). 8.10am, 10.50am, 11.30am, 12.10pm, 12.20pm (Hall), 12.40pm, 1.10pm, 5.40pm.*

3. † Christ the King (1926; cons 1993)
78 Queens Drive, Wavertree, Liverpool L15 6YQ **Tel:** 0151-722 2231
Fax: 0151-722 2755
Revv Grant Maddock, Michael Fitzsimons, Jean Ilunga.
M: *Sat 1st M of Sun 6pm. Sun 9.30am. Hds as announced*

4. † Holy Cross Great Crosshall Street
Parish closed 2001.
Registers at Liverpool (26).

5. † Holy Family (1965)
Mackets Lane, Halewood, Liverpool L25 8TG
Tel: 0151-486 9883 **Fax:** 0151-486 9885
Rev Vincent McShane.
M: *Sat 1st M of Sun 5.15pm. Hds 7.30pm.*

6. † Holy Name (1929; 1966)
Moss Pits Lane, Fazakerley, Liverpool L10 9LG **Tel:** 0151-476 0289 **Fax:** 0151-476 0285 **Rev M Beattie OCD**
Deacon: **Rev George Hamer.**
M: *Sat 1st M of Sun 6pm. Sun 10am. Hds As announced.*

7. † Holy Trinity (1926; 1940)
Banks Road, Garston, Liverpool L19 8JY
Tel: 0151-427 7518
E-mail: ht@rcal.fsnet.co.uk
Rev Ronald Johnson (resident at St Francis of Assisi).
M: *Sun 11.15am. Hds 9.15am.*

8. † Sacred Heart and St Michael
(1857; 1886; cons 1 July 1909)
Parish Office: 2 Hall Lane, Liverpool L7 8TG. 2 Hall Lane, L7 8TG
Tel: 0151-709 1824
Rev Arthur FitzGerald. St Michael's Presbytery, Horne Street, Liverpool L6 5GH
Tel: 0151-263 6578
M: *Sat 1st M of Sun 6.30pm. Hds As announced.*

9. † Our Lady of the Annunciation
(1851-1858; 1962)
Bishop Eton, Woolton Road, Wavertree, Liverpool L16 8NQ
Tel: 0151-737 4110 **Fax:** 0151-738 0834
- **Redemptorists (CSsR); Revv Desmond Keegan** (*Parish Priest*), **Anthony Foy, James Corrigan, James Smale.**
  Deacon: **Rev John Keeley.**
  Monastery: **Tel:** 0151-722 1108
  M: *Sat 1st M of Sun 6.30pm. Sun 8.30am, 10am, 11.30am, 6pm. Hds 7am, 9am, 12noon, 7.30pm.*
- **Liverpool Hope University,** Hope Park, L16 8ND
  Tel: 0151-737 3000 **Fax:** 737 3100
- ***Sisters of Notre Dame,*** Convent of Notre Dame, 285 Woolton Road, L16 8NB **Tel:** 0151-722 1501

10. † Our Lady of the Assumption
(1949)
Hartsbourne Avenue, Gateacre, Liverpool. The Presbytery, Hedgefield Road, L25 2RW
Tel: 0151-487 9372 **Fax:** 0151-283 4735
E-mail: philipinch@btinternet.com
Rev Philip Inch
M: *Sun, 11am, Hds 9.30am.*

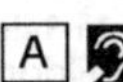

11. † Our Lady of Good Help
(1871; 1887)
Chestnut Grove, Wavertree, Liverpool L15 8HS **Tel:** 0151-722 2231 **Fax:** 0151-722 2755 **Rev Grant Maddock,** resident at

Liverpool (3). *Deacon:* **Rev Paul G Farrell.**
M: *Sun 11.15am, 4.30pm.*
Hds As announced.

- ***Sisters of Our Lady of the Cenacle,*** Lance Lane, L15 6TW Retreat House. **Tel:** 0151-722 2271
- ***Sisters of the Cross and Passion,*** 33 North Drive, Victoria Park, L15 8JE **Tel:** 0151-722 4212

A

12. † Our Lady of the Immaculate Conception (1856; New church 1986)
York Terrace, Everton, Liverpool.
Tel: 0151-207 0177 **Fax:** 0151-298 2112
Rev Graeme Dunne, resident at Liverpool (28). *Deacon:* **Rev Gerard Fitzpatrick.**
M: *Sun 11.30am. Hds 7pm.*

13. † St Anne and St Bernard (1884; 1901)
95a Kingsley Road, Liverpool L8 2TY
Tel: 0151-709 4434 **Fax:** 0151-708 0317
E-mail: stbsliv@yahoo.co.uk
Rev Peter Morgan.
Deacon: **Rev Francis Bowman.**
M: *Sun 10am. Hds 12noon.*

- ***Passionists (CP)***, Inner City Mission. **Rev Austin Smith.** 9 Steve Biko Close, Liverpool L8 0QB **Tel:** 0151-734 4308

A

14. † Our Lady of Mount Carmel
(1865; 1878; cons 5 Sept 1951)
27 High Park Street, Liverpool L8 8DX
Tel: 0151-727 1463 **Fax:** 0151-727 1463
E-mail: olmc@btinternet.com
Rev John Southworth.
M: *Sat 1st M of Sun 5.30pm. Sun 11am. Hds 7pm.*

15. † Our Lady Queen of Martyrs and St Swithin (1963)
Stonebridge Lane, Croxteth, Liverpool L11 9AZ **Tel:** 0151-546 3574
Revv Kenneth Hyde, Andrew Unsworth.
Deacon: **Revv Malcolm Fletcher, Leonard Barton (retired).** *Parish Sister:* **Sr Sara Hynes.**
M: *Sat 1st M of Sun 6pm. Sun 8.30am, 11.15am. Hds (vigil 7.30pm), 9.45am.*

- ***Salesian Sisters of St John Bosco (FMA),*** St John Bosco High School, Stonebridge Lane, L11 9BB **Tel:** 0151-546 3136; Convent: 0151-546 4820
- ***Redemptoristine Monastery,*** Back Gillmoss Lane, L11 0AY **Tel:** 0151-546 3968

16. † Our Lady of Reconciliation de la Salette (1854; 1860; cons 1910)
39 Eldon Place, Liverpool L3 6HE
Tel: 0151-207 0177 **Fax:** 0151-298 2112
Rev Graeme Dunne, resident at Liverpool (28).
M: *Sat 1st M of Sun 6pm. Hds 9.15am.*

17. † St Mary
Highfield Street. Parish closed 2000.
Registers at Liverpool (26).

A

18. † St Mary
(1776; 1860; cons 1950)
Church Road, Woolton, Liverpool L25 6DA
Tel: 0151-428 2256 **Fax:** 0151-428 9936
Rev Patrick O'Brien.
Deacon: **Rev Adrian Dickinson.**
M: *Sat 1st M of Sun 5.30pm. Sun 9am, 11am. Hds (vigil 7.30pm) 12noon.*

- ***De La Mennais Brothers,*** St Francis Xavier's College, Beaconsfield Road, Liverpool, L25 6EG **Tel:** 0151-428 6341 (Community), **Tel:** 0151-288 1000 (College).
- ***Divine Word Missionaries (SVD),*** 10 Blackwood Avenue, Liverpool L25 3PH **Tel:** 0151-428 2860 **Revv Oliver O'Connor,** retired, **Brian Gilmore.**
- ***Poor Servants of the Mother of God,*** St Gabriel's Convent, Knolle Park, L25 6HT **Tel:** 0151-421 0717
- ***Sisters of Notre Dame,*** 120 School Lane, Woolton, Liverpool L25 7UD

A

19. † St Mary of the Angels
Fox Street. Parish closed 2001.
Registers at Liverpool (26).

20. † All Saints & Diaconate Centre
(1899; cons 6 Oct 1921)
3 Oakfield, Anfield, Liverpool L4 2QG
Tel: 0151-287 8787 **Fax:** 0151-287 8788
Rev Stephen Maloney *(Vocations Director),* **Rev Francis Ferns.**
Deacon: **Rev James Armstrong.**
Tel: 0151-287 8787 **Fax:** 0151-287 8788
M: *Sat 1st M of Sun 6pm. Sun 9am, 10.30am. Hds 11.15am, 7.30pm.*

21. St Albert (1966, 1976, cons 1977)
31 Hollow Croft, Cantril Farm/Stockbridge Village, L28 4EA
Tel: 0151-228 7126 **Fax:** 0151-259 6743
Missionaries of the Sacred Heart (MSC): **Rev Fintan O'Driscoll.**
M: *Sat 1st M of Sun 6.30pm. Sun 9am, 11am. Hds, 9.15am, 7.30pm.*

22. † St Alphonsus
Great Mersey Street. Parish closed 2001.
Registers at Liverpool (26).

23. † St Ambrose (1953)
Heathgate Avenue, Speke, Liverpool L24 7RS **Tel:** 0151-425 2289
Fax: 0151-425 3600 **Rev Edward Cain.**
M: *Sat 1st M of Sun 7pm. Sun 11am. Hds As announced.*

Hale Mass Centre
M: *Sun 9.30am.*

24. † St Andrew the Apostle (1952)
Portway, Hunts Cross, Liverpool L25 0QD
Tel: 0151-486 9883 **Fax:** 0151-486 9885
Rev Vincent McShane, resident at Liverpool (5).
M: *Sat 1st M of Sun 6.45pm. Sun 11am. Hds As announced.*

25. † St Anne
(1840; 1846; cons 24 May 1916)
Overbury Street, Edge Hill, Liverpool L7 3HJ
Tel: 0151-709 4434 **Fax:** 0151-708 0317
E-mail: stbsliv@yahoo.co.uk
Rev Peter Morgan, 95a Kingsley Road, Liverpool L8 2TY
M: *Sat 1st M of Sun 5.30pm. Sun 11.15am. Hds (vigil 6pm).*
- ***Sisters of the Infant Jesus:*** 16 Grinfield Street, L7 3EQ **Tel:** 0151-707 0903
- ***Congregation of Christian Brothers***: 16 Grinfield Street, L7 3EQ **Tel:** 0151-708 5077

26. † St Anthony (1804; 1833)
St Anthony's Presbytery, Scotland Road, Liverpool L5 5BD
Tel: 0151-207 0177 **Fax:** 0151-298 2112
Rev Graeme Dunne. *Deacon:* **Rev Gerard Fitzpatrick.**
M: *Sun 9.30am, 3pm (Latin Tridentine Mass). Hds 12noon, 6.30pm (Latin Tridentine Mass).*

27. † St Anthony of Padua
(1926; 1932; 1967)
Queens Drive, Mossley Hill, Liverpool.
Tel: 0151-724 2109 **Fax:** 0151-724 2553
- ***Franciscans (Friars Minor Conventual) (OFMConv):*** **Revv Vincent Kennedy, Gerald Hicks** (*Guardian & Parish Priest*), **E-mail:** hicksfriar@aol.com; Greyfriars, 1 Elmsley Road, L18 8AY
  M: *Sat 1st M of Sun 6pm. Sun 9.30am, 11am, 6pm. Hds 9.30am, 12noon, 7.30pm.*
- ***Sisters of Charity of Notre Dame d'Evron,*** Marymount, North Mossley Hill Road, L18 8BS **Tel:** 0151 724 2203

28 † St Austin. (1838).
561 Aigburth Road, Grassendale L19 0NU
Tel: 0151-427 3033 **Fax:** 0151-494 0600
E-mail: www.saintaustins.org
- ***Benedictines (OSB):*** **Revv David Morland, Theodore Young, Gerald Hughes.**
  M: *Sat 1st M of Sun 7pm. Sun 8am, 9.30am, 11am, 4pm, 6pm. Hds 7am, 9am, 4.30pm, 7pm.*
- ***Daughters of St Paul,*** Thecla House, 16 Darby Road, Liverpool L19 9DX **Tel:** 0151-494 3828

29. † St Bernadette (1936)
Mather Avenue, Allerton, Liverpool.
Tel: 0151-427 7648
Rev Joseph Keller. St Bernadette's, Heath Road, Liverpool L19 4TW
M: *Sat 1st M of Sun 6.30pm. Sun 10.30am. Hds (vigil 4.30pm), 10am.*

30. † St Brendan (1962)
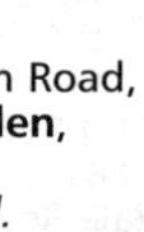
Prescot Road, Old Swan, Liverpool.
Tel: 0151-228 3327
St Brendan's Church House, Crofton Road, Liverpool L13 5UJ. **Rev Mark Madden,** resident at Liverpool (54).
M: *Sun 8am. Hds As announced.*

31. † St Cecilia (1905; 1930)
21 Green Lane, Tuebrook, Liverpool L13 7DT
Tel: 0151-228 1310 **Fax:** 0151-259 6061
Email: ceciliatuebrook@aol.com
Rev Mark Madden.
M: *Sat 1st M of Sun 5.30pm. Sun 11.30am. Hds (vigil 7pm), 10am.*

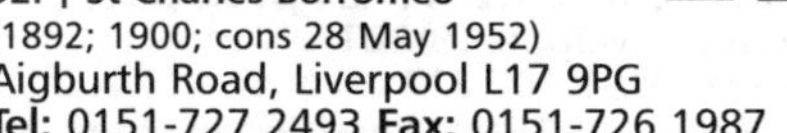

32. † St Charles Borromeo
(1892; 1900; cons 28 May 1952)
Aigburth Road, Liverpool L17 9PG
Tel: 0151-727 2493 **Fax:** 0151-726 1987
Rev George Russell.
M: *Sat 1st M of Sun 6pm. Sun 11.30am, Hds As announced.*

33. † St Christopher (1940)
47 Stapleton Avenue, Speke, Liverpool L24 0SF **Tel:** 0151-486 1874
Fax: 0151-486 3963 **E-mail:** stchristopher@amserve.com
Rev Denis J Cunningham.
M: *Sat 1st M of Sun 7pm. Sun 9.30am, 11am. Hds 9am, 6pm.*

34. † St Clare (Cons 3 June 1890)
Arundel Avenue, Sefton Park, Liverpool L17 2AU
Tel: 0151-733 2374 **Fax:** 0151-280 6062
Rev Aidan Prescott.
M: *Sun 8.30am, 10.30am. Hds 12.10pm, 7.30pm.*

35. † St Cuthbert (1928)
Aviemore Road, Stanley, Liverpool. Parish closed 2002. Registers at Liverpool (30).

36. St Cyril of Jerusalem (1967)
Southbrook Road, Netherley, Liverpool.
Rev Philip Inch.
Tel: 0151-487 3755 **Fax:** 0151-487 9335
M: *Sun 9.30pm, Hds 12noon.*
- ***Sisters of St Mary of Namur.*** St Cyril's Parish House, Southbrook Road, Netherley, L27 1YW **Tel:** 0151-487 3755

37. St Finbar
Dingle Mount. Parish closed 2001.
Registers at Liverpool (14).

38. † St Francis of Assisi
(1883; 1904; cons 3 July 1930)
Earp Street, Garston, Liverpool L19 1RT
Rev Ronald Johnson, Holy Trinity, Banks Road, Garston, Liverpool L19 8JY
Tel: 0151-427 7518
M: *Sat 1st M of Sun 5.30pm. Sun 9.15am. Hds (7pm), 11am.*

39. † St Francis de Sales
(1883; 1917; cons 9 June 1938)
Hale Road, Walton, Liverpool L4 3RL
Tel: 0151-525 3483 **Fax:** 0151-525 2449
Rev John B Thompson.
M: *Sat 1st M of Sun 7pm. Sun 10.30am Hds (vigil 7pm), 12noon.*

40. † St Francis Xavier (1845; 1848)
2 Salisbury Street, Liverpool L3 8DR
Tel: 0151-298 1911
Rev Patrick Connors SJ *(Parish Priest),* **Br Kenneth Vance.** 11 Langsdale Street, Everton, Liverpool L3 8DT
Tel/Fax: 0151-207 2271
M: *Sun 10.15am, Hds 12noon, 7pm.*

41. St Gregory (1970)
Damson Road, Netherley, Liverpool L27 8XR
Rev Philip Inch, Tel: 0151-487 7993
M: *Sat 1st M of Sun 5pm. Hds 7pm.*
- ***Daughters of Charity (SVP),*** St Gregory's Presbytery, Damson Road, Netherley, L27 8XR **Tel:** 0151-487 7993

42. † St Hugh of Lincoln (1904)
Cranborne Road, Wavertree, Liverpool L15 2HY Served from Liverpool (37).
M: *Sat 1st M of Sun 6pm. Hds 9.05am.*

43. † St John the Evangelist (1871; 1885)
70 Fountains Road, Kirkdale, Liverpool L4 1QL **Tel:** 0151-922 3604
Rev Terence McSweeney.
M: *Sat 1st M of Sun 7pm. Sun 11.15am, 6pm. Hds (vigil 7pm). 12noon, 7pm.*

44. † St Joseph
Grosvenor Street. Parish closed 2001.
Registers at Liverpool (26).

45. † St Malachy
Beaufort Street. Parish closed 2001.
Registers at 281 Beaufort Street, Liverpool L8 6UA

46. † St Margaret Mary (1931; 1932)
Pilch Lane, Knotty Ash, Liverpool L14 0JG
Tel: 0151-228 1332 **Fax:** 0151-259 6019
Rev Mark Moran. *Deacon:* **Rev William Cummings.** *Parish Visitor Co-ordinator:* **Maureen McKnight**. **Tel:** 0151-228 3970
M: *Sun 9.30am, 11am, 6pm. Hds 11am, 7.30pm.*
- ***Daughters of Charity (SVP),*** Adult Blind Residential and Rehabilitation Centre, Christopher Grange, Youens Way, East Prescot Road, L14 2EW
Tel: 0151-220 2525 **Fax:** 0151-220 1972
- ***Sisters of St Mary of Namur,*** St Mary's Convent, 55-57 Swanside Road, L14 7NJ
Tel: 0151-228 3970

47. St Mark (1965)
Penmann Crescent, Halewood, Liverpool L26 0UG **Tel:** 0151-486 9883
Fax: 0151 486 9885
Rev Vincent McShane, resident at Liverpool (5).
M: *Sun 9.30am, 6pm. Hds (vigil 7.30pm).*

48. † St Matthew
(1922; 1930; cons 24 Jun 1950)
Queen's Drive, Clubmoor, Liverpool.
Tel: 0151-226 1828
Rev Conor Stainton Polland. St Matthew's, 19 Townsend Avenue, Liverpool L13 9DL
M: *Sat 1st M of Sun 6.30pm. Sun 10am. Hds (vigil 7.30pm) 9.10am.*

49. † St Michael
(1861; 1865; cons 19 May 1932)
West Derby Road, Liverpool
Tel: 0151-263 6578
Rev Arthur FitzGerald, Horne Street, Liverpool L6 5EH
M: *Sun 10.30am. Hds As announced.*
- ***Sisters of St Mary of Namur,*** 25 Newsham Drive, Liverpool L6 7UG
Tel: 0151-263 1492

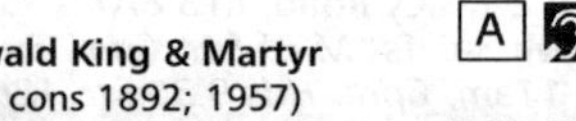

50. † St Oswald King & Martyr
(1839; 1842; cons 1892; 1957)
St Oswald Street, Old Swan, Liverpool L13 5SB
Tel: 0151-228 3327 **Fax:** 0151-259 0859
Rev Mark Madden Tel: 0151-254 2979
Fax: 0151-254 2980.
M: *Sun 10am. Hds, As announced.*
- ***Sisters of Mercy, St Oswald Street,*** L13 5SB. **Tel:** 0151-228 5056.
- ***Sisters of St Joseph of the Apparition,*** Oakhill Park, Old Swan, Liverpool L13 4BP
Tel: (Convent) 0151-228 8849
Fax: 0151-259 7471

51. St Paschal Baylon (1964)
Chelwood Avenue, Liverpool L16 2LN
Tel: 0151-722 1988
E-mail: paschal@freeuk.com
Rev Grant Maddock.
M: *Sun 10am. Hds As announced.*

52. † St Patrick (1821; 1827)
Park Place, Liverpool L8 5RA
Tel: 0151-709 2635
Served from Liverpool (14).
Rev John Southworth
M: *Sun 10am. Hds 9am.*

53. † St Paul (1879; 1914; cons 1915)
Spring Grove, West Derby, Liverpool
L12 8SJ **Tel:** 0151-228 3405
Revv Sean Kirwin, Kieran O'Grady
Deacon: **Rev Joseph McGunigle.**
M: *Sun 8.30am, 11.15am, 5pm. Hds As Announced.*
- ***Carmelites,*** Honeysgreen Lane, L12 9HY **Tel:** 0151-228 6105
- ***Little Company of Mary,*** 409 Eaton Road, L12 2AJ **Tel:** 0151-228 0342
- ***Sisters of Mercy***, Broughton Hall Convent, Yew Tree Lane, L12 9HH **Tel:** 0151- 228 9232

54. † University Church of St Philip Neri
(1853; 1920)
30 Catharine Street, Liverpool L8 7NL
Parish closed 2001. **Tel:** 0151-709 3858.
University Chaplain: **Rev Ian McParland.**
M: *Sun 12noon.*

55. † St Philomena (1937; 1940; 1971)
Sparrow Hall Road, Liverpool L9 6BU
Tel: 0151-525 6191
Served from Liverpool (15).
Deacon: **Rev Terence Gilvin (retired).**
In Residence: **Revv Christopher Fallon; Babu Appadan** *(Asst Chaplain University Hospital Aintree & Keralan Community Spiritual Director).*
M: *Sun 9.45am. Hds 11am.*
- ***Religious of the Sacred Heart of Mary:*** 2 Martinhall Road, Liverpool 9, **Tel:** 0151-526 3106

56. † St Sebastian (1904; 1914)
Lockerby Road, Fairfield, Liverpool.
Tel: 0151-263 1755
Rev Patrick A Kelly. 18 Lilley Road, L7 0LR
M: *Sat 1st M of Sun 6.30pm. Sun 10am. Hds 9.30am, 12noon.*
- ***Poor Servants of the Mother of God,*** Rosemont Convent, 70 Laurel Road, L7 9LE Home for Women. **Tel:** 0151- 263 3694
- ***Sisters of the Little Ones***, 14 Holly Road, L7 0LH Short-stay Home for Mentally Handicapped,

Tel: 0151-263 2412
- ***L'Arche Community,*** The Ark Workshop, Lockerby Road, Liverpool L7 0HG Care of Mentally Handicapped. **Tel:** 0151-260 0422 **Fax:** 0151-263 2260

57. † St Swithin
(1425; 1768; 1824; 1959)
Parish closed 2004.

58. † St Sylvester (1875; 1889)
27 Silvester Street, Liverpool L5 8SE
Tel: 0151-207 0161 **Fax:** 0151-298 2616
Rev Frederick Rose.
M: *Sun 11am. Hds 9am.*

59. † St Teresa of the Child Jesus
(1928; 1937)
Utting Avenue East, Norris Green, Liverpool L11 3BW
Tel: 0151-226 1354 **Fax:** 0151-270 2665
E-mail: oblate@norris3.freeserve.co.uk
- ***Oblates of Mary Immaculate, (OMI):*** **Revv Dennis Connor** (*Parish Priest*), **Francis Gormley, Michael Phelan.** *Deacon:* **Rev Donagh McKillop**. St Teresa's, Utting Avenue East, Liverpool L11 3BW
  M: *Sat 1st M of Sun 6pm. Sun 9.30am, 11.15am, 6pm. Hds (vigil 8pm), 9am, 12noon, 6pm.*

60. St Thomas More (1964)
Rundle Road, Aigburth, Liverpool.
Tel: 0151-726 0627 **Fax:** 0151-291 7095
Rev George Russell (resident at Liverpool 35) *Deacons:* **Revv Paul McNicholl, Jeremy Mitchinson, Paul Mannings.**
Tel: 0151-427 2850
M: *Sun 9.45am. Hds 7.30pm.*

61. † St Timothy (1957)
Rockwell Road, West Derby, Liverpool
L12 4XY **Tel:** 0151-228 0088
Served from Liverpool (53).

M: *Sun 9.45am. Hds As announced.*
- ***Little Servant Sisters of Blessed Virgin Mary,*** resident in Presbytery.

62. † St Vincent de Paul (1852; 1857)
St James Street, Liverpool.
Served from Liverpool (14).
Rev John Southworth
M: *Sat 1st M of Sun 6.30pm. Hds (vigil 6.30pm)*
- ***Missionaries of Charity***, 55 Seel Street, L1 4AZ **Tel:** 0151-709 0628
- ***Congregation of Christian Brothers,*** 55 Parr Street L1 4JN **Tel:** 0151-709 5344
- ***Sisters of the Sacred Hearts of Jesus and Mary,*** 9b Cookson Street L1 5EU **Tel:** 0151-708 8215

■ **LONGTON,** Preston
† St Oswald (1894)
Chapel Lane, Longton, Preston PR4 5EB
Tel: 01772-612136

Rev Leo Cooper.
Deacon: **Rev Leo McNicholas.**
M: *Sat 1st M of Sun 6pm. Sun 8.45am, 10.30am. Hds* 9.15am,7pm.

■ **LOWTON,** Warrington
† St Catherine of Siena (1933; 1959)
Tel: 01942-206030 **Fax:** 01942-746243
Rev Bernard Eager. *Deacons:* **Revv Derek Morris, Francis Newton** (retired).
Presbytery, Newton Road, WA3 1LB
E-mail: stcatherines@freeuk.com
M: *Sat 1st M of Sun 6.30pm, Sun 10am.*

■ **LYDIATE,** Liverpool
1. † Our Lady (1681; 1854; cons 1892)
Southport Road, Lydiate, Liverpool L31 4HH **Tel:** 0151-526 0362
Rev John Smith, resident at Lydiate (2).
M: *Sun 9.30am. Hds As announced.*

2. † St Gregory the Great (1958; 1959)
Liverpool Road, Lydiate, Liverpool L31 2NA
Tel: 0151-526 3843 **Fax:** 0151-520 0602
Rev John Smith.
M: *Sat 1st M of Sun 6.30pm. Sun 8am, 11am. Hds (vigil 7.30pm). 9am.*
• ***Sisters of St Clare,*** St Clare's Convent, 197 Green Lane, Maghull, Liverpool L31 8BD **Tel:** 0151-531 6675

■ **MAGHULL,** Liverpool
† St George (1887; 1929)
Station Road, Maghull, Liverpool L31 3D.
Tel: 0151-526 1071 **Fax:** 0151-526 9660
Canon Joseph Kelly.
Deacon: **Rev Stephen Crowther**
M: *Sat 1st M of Sun 6.30pm. Sun 9.30am, 11.30am, 6.30pm. Hds 9am, 7.30pm.*
• ***Sisters of Mercy:*** 'Maricourt', Hall Lane, Maghull, Liverpool L31 3DZ
Tel: 0151-526 1803
Chaplain: **Rev John Booth SDB.**

■ **MAWDESLEY,** Ormskirk, Lancs
† SS Peter and Paul (1831)
Ridley Lane, Mawdesley, Ormskirk, Lancs L40 2RE Served from Tarleton.
M: *Sat 1st M of Sun 6pm. Sun 11am. Hds 9am.*
• ***Sons of Divine Providence***, Gradwell Farm, Moor Road, Croston, Lancs
Tel: 01772- 600915 Holiday home especially for people with disabilities

■ **MELLING,** Liverpool
† Most Holy Redeemer and St Kentigern (1897; 1900; 1938)
Waddicar Lane, Melling, Liverpool.
Tel/Fax: 0151-547 3397
Rev Desmond Seddon, resident at Aughton
M: *Sun 10.30am. Hds As Announced.*

■ **NETHERTON,** Liverpool
1. † Our Lady of Walsingham (1956)
Stand Park Avenue, Netherton, Liverpool L30 3SA **Tel:** 0151-525 4812
Rev Anthony Eagleton,
Deacon: **Rev Gerard Fitzpatrick.**
M: *Sat 1st M of Sun 6.30pm. Sun 10am. Hds 9.15am, 7.30pm.*

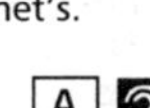

2. † St Benet (1742; 1793)
Copy Lane, Netherton, Liverpool L30 7PE
Tel: 0151-520 2600 **Fax:** 0151-531 8836
E-mail: benets2@tiscali.co.uk
Rev Sean O'Connor.
M: *Sat 1st M of Sun 6.30pm. Sun 11am. Hds (vigil 7pm), 9am.*

2a St Raymond's Chapel-of-Ease.
Higher End Park. Served from St Benet's.
M: *Sun 9.30am. Hds 12noon.*

■ **NEWTON-LE-WILLOWS,** Merseyside
1. St David (1968)
Park Road South, Newton-le-Willows, Merseyside WA12 8JW
Tel: 01925-226578 **Fax:** 01925-225432
Rev Vincent Fedigan.
M: *Sat 1st M of Sun 6.30pm. Sun 11am. Hds (vigil 6.30pm).*

2. † SS Mary and John (1861; 1864)
Crow Lane East, Newton-le-Willows, Merseyside WA12 9UD **Tel:** 01925-226106
Served from Newton-le-Willows (1).
M: *Sun 9.30am, 4.30pm. Hds 7.30am, 12noon.*

3. † St Patrick (1932; 1958)
111 Common Road, Newton-le-Willows, Merseyside WA12 9JH
Tel: 01925-225884 **Fax:** 01925-290625
Rev Francis Smith.
M: *Sun 11am. Hds, 10.30am.*

■ **OLD ROAN,** Aintree, Liverpool
† Holy Rosary (1947; 1956)
Altway, Old Roan, Aintree, Liverpool L10 2LG
Tel: 0151-526 8468 **Fax:** 0151-286 8597
Mgr John Butchard VG.
Deacon: **Rev Anthony Grayston, Bernard Rigby**
M: *Sat 1st M of Sun 6pm. Sun 10.30am, 6pm. Hds 9am, 12noon, 7.30pm.*

■ **ONCHAN,** Douglas, Isle of Man
† St Anthony (1923; cons 1988)
Onchan, Douglas, Isle of Man.
Tel: 01624-674891
Served from Douglas.
M: *Sat 1st M of Sun 5pm. Sun 9.30am. Hds 7pm.*

■ **ORMSKIRK,** Lancs
† **St Anne** (1732; 1850)
23 Prescot Road, Ormskirk, Lancs L39 4TG
Tel: 01695-572168 **Fax:** 01695-571136
E-mail: paxorm@aol.com
• ***Benedictines (OSB):*** **Rev Doms Godric Timney** (*Parish Priest*), **Benjamin Standish**. *Deacons:* **Revv Desmond Bill, Philip McDermott.**
M: *Sat 1st M of Sun 7pm. Sun 9am, 10.30am, 4.30pm. Hds 12noon, 8pm.*
• ***Sisters of Our Lady of Charity,*** 133 Prescot Road, Aughton, Ormskirk L39 4SN
Tel: 01695-572216

■ **ORRELL,** Wigan
† **St James** (1699; 1805)
St James Road, Orrell, Wigan, Lancs WN5 7AA **Tel:** 01695-622476
E-mail: gerry54@hotmail.com
Rev Gerard Tuite FDP.
Deacon: **Rev Joseph Lloyd.**
M: *Sat 1st M of Sun 6pm. Sun 8.30am, 10.30am. Hds 7.30am, 9am, 7.30pm.*

■ **PADGATE**
See Warrington, No 5.

■ **PARBOLD,** Wigan
† **Our Lady and All Saints**
(1883; cons 24 May 1884)
Lancaster Lane, Parbold, Wigan, Lancs WN8 7HS **Tel:** 01257-463248 **Fax:** 01257-462495
E-mail: parbold@hotmail.com
• ***Benedictines (OSB):*** **Rev Gordon Beattie**. *Deacons:* **Revv David Bennett, Brian Norman**
M: *Sat 1st M of Sun 6pm. Sun 10am. Hds 9.30am, 7pm.*
• ***Sisters of Notre Dame,*** Lancaster House, Lancaster Lane, Parbold WN8 7HT **Tel:** 01257-465000
Fax: 01257-464065 *Chaplain:* **Mgr peter McGuire, Tel:** 01257-465017

■ **PEEL,** Isle of Man
† **St Patrick** (1865)
Patrick Street, Peel, Isle of Man.
Tel: 01624-813181 Served from Ramsey.
Rev Brian O'Mahony (CSSp).
Deacon: **Rev Eric Moore.**
M: *Sun 9am. Hds 7.30pm.*

■ **PENKETH,** Warrington
† **St Joseph** (1923)
Meeting Lane, Penketh, Warrington, Cheshire WA5 2BB
Tel: 01925-722105 **Fax:** 01925-726055
Rev Richard Ebo. *Deacons:* **Revv John McClure, John Traynor.**
M: *Sat 1st M of Sun 6.45pm. Sun 10.30am, 4pm. Hds As announced.*
• ***Sisters of Charity of St Paul,*** St Joseph's Convent, 99 Westbrook Crescent WA5 2TE **Tel:** 01925-230657

■ **PENWORTHAM,** Preston
1. † **St Mary Magdalen** (1912)
Leyland Road, Penwortham.
Tel: 01772-742085
Rev Austin Griffin. 1 Windsor Avenue, Penwortham, Preston, Lancashire PR1 9AY
M: *Sat 1st M of Sun 6pm. Sun 10.30am. Hds As announced.*

2. † **St Teresa** (1933; 1959)
34 Queensway, Penwortham, Preston, Lancs PR1 0DS **Tel/Fax:** 01772-743337
Rev Austin Griffin.
M: *Sat 1st M of Sun 7.15pm. Sun 9.10am, 5pm. Hds As announced.*

■ **PLATT BRIDGE,** Wigan
† **Holy Family** (1893; 1895; 1960)
Lily Lane, Platt Bridge, Wigan, WN2 5LL **Tel:** 01942-866102

Rev Anthony Mangnall,
Deacon: **Rev Terence Rose**
M: *Sat 1st M of Sun 6.30pm. Sun 11.30am. Hds, as announced.*

■ **PORT ERIN AND PORT ST MARY,** Isle of Man
St Columba (1903; 1923)
Castletown Road, Port Erin, Isle of Man.
Tel: 01624-822272 Served from Castletown.
M: *Sun 11am. Hds 10am.*

■ **PORTICO,** Prescot, Merseyside
† **Our Lady Help of Christians** (1790; 1792)
Portico Lane, Portico, Prescot, Merseyside L34 2QT **Tel:** 0151-426 6251
Rev David J Melly. *Deacons:* **Revv Gerald Marsh, Vincent Anderson.**
M: *Sat 1st M of Sun 6.30pm. Sun 9am, 10.30am. Hds As announced.*

■ **PRESCOT,** Merseyside
† **Our Lady Immaculate and St Joseph**
(1848; 1857)
Vicarage Place, Prescot, Merseyside.
Tel: 0151-426 6462
E-mail: olisj.prescot@rcaolp.co.uk
Mgr Anthony Dennick. 1 West Street, L34 1LE
M: *Sat 1st M of Sun 6.15pm. Sun 11am. Hds (vigil 7.15pm), 12noon.*

■ **PULROSE,** Douglas, Isle of Man
† **Sacred Heart**
Parish closed 2001. Registers at Douglas.

■ **RAINFORD,** St Helens, Merseyside
† **Corpus Christi** (1875)
Chapel Street, Rainford, St Helens, Merseyside WA11 8BY **Tel:** 01744-882157
Canon Leo P. Stoker.
M: *Sat 1st M of Sun 6pm. Sun 10am. Hds 9am, 7pm.*

■ **RAINHILL,** Liverpool
† **St Bartholomew** (1838; 1840)
Warrington Road, Rainhill, Liverpool L35 6NY
Tel: 0151-426 4638 **Fax:** 0151-430 8873
Revv Philip Swanson (Resident at Sutton Manor), **Luke Dumbill** (Resident in Presbytery). *Deacons:* **Revv Bernard Smith, Francis Wright**.
M: *Sat 1st M of Sun 5.15pm. Sun 9.30am. Hds 9.15am, 7.30pm.*
• ***Jesuits (SJ),*** Loyola Hall, Warrington Road, Rainhill, Merseyside, L35 6NZ **Tel:** 0151-426 4137 **Fax:** 0151-431 0115 **E-mail:** loyola@clara.net. **Website:** www.loyolahall.co.uk Retreat Centre. *Director:* **Ruth Holgate**; **Rev Ian Tomlinson** (*Superior*), **Revv Gerald O'Mahony, Gerald Fitzgibbon, Robert Marsh. Br Norman Smith.**
• ***Institute of the Blessed Virgin Mary,*** Loreto Sisters (IBVM).

■ **RAMSEY,** Isle of Man
† **Our Lady Star of the Sea and St Maughold** (1863; 1910)
Priest's House, Queens Promenade, Ramsey, Isle of Man IM8 1BH
Tel: 01624-813181
Rev Brian O'Mahony CSSp.
M: *Sat 1st M of Sun 6.30pm. Sun 11am. Hds (vigil 7.30pm). 11am.*

■ **ROBY,** Liverpool
† **St Aloysius** (1934; cons 23 April 1952)
Twig Lane, Roby, Liverpool L36 2LF
Tel: 0151-4477 0250 **Fax:** 0151-477 0254
E-mail: pp@st-aloysius.org.uk
Rev John Ealey. *Deacon:* **Rev Kevin Dunn; Mr Peter Thomas** (*Pastoral Assistant*).
M: *Sat 1st M of Sun 6pm. Sun 9am. Hds 10am, 7pm.*

■ **ST. HELENS,** Merseyside
1. † **Holy Cross and St Helen** (1862)
Corporation Street, St Helens, Merseyside WA10 1EF **Tel:** 01744-22077
Rev Paul Glover. Also resident: **Rev James Matthews**. *Deacon:* **Rev Arthur Willcock.**
M: *Sat 1st M of Sun 6.45pm. Sun 9.30am. Hds (vigil 7pm). 12.15am.*

2. † **Our Lady Mother of God** (1962)
219 Fleet Lane, Parr. Parish closed 2004. Registers at St Helens (14).

3. † **Sacred Heart** (1876; 1878)
Borough Road, St Helens.
Parish closed 2003. Registers St Helens (8).

4. † **St Anne and Bl Dominic** (1845; 1850; 1973)
Monastery Lane, Sutton, St Helens, Merseyside WA9 3SP
Tel: 01744-811935 **Fax:** 01744-820557
Rev Peter Hannah (*Parish Priest, resident at St Helens No. 14*)
Deacon: **Rev John Philip McLoughlin**
M: *Sat 1st M of Sun 6.30pm. Sun 11am. Hds As announced.*
• ***Sisters of the Cross and Passion,*** 17 Tillbrook Drive, Sutton, St Helens WA9 3WP **Tel:** 01744-811601

5. † **St Austin** (1895; 1906)
Heath Street, St Helens, Merseyside WA9 5NN **Tel:** 01744-812115
Rev Martin Kershaw. *Deacon:* **Rev Kevin Taylor**
M: *Sat 1st M of Sun 6.30. Sun 8.30am, 10.30am. Hds (vigil 7.15pm). 9.15am, 12 noon.*

6. † **St Joseph** (1875; 1878)
Sutton Road. Parish closed 2004. Registers at St Helens (14).

7. † **St Julie** (1964; cons 12 July 1969)
Howards Lane, Eccleston, St Helens, Merseyside WA10 5HJ **Tel:** 01744-28196
Rev Thomas Neylon.
M: *Sun 9.45am, 6.30pm. Hds 9.10am.*
• ***Carmelites,*** Green Lane, Eccleston, St Helens, WA10 5HH **Tel:** 01744-28132
M: *Daily 8am.*

8. † **St Mary and Vocations Centre** 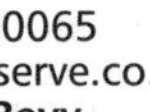
(1743; 1915; 1929)
Lowe House, St Helens, Merseyside WA10 2BE
Tel: 01744-22167 **Fax:** 01744-730065
E-mail: clerygy@lowehouse.freeserve.co.uk
Rev Paul Glover. Also resident: **Revv Stephen Pritchard** (*Youth Chaplain*), **Brendan Rice.**
M: *Sun 11am, 4.30pm. Hds 12.10pm, 7.30pm.*

9. † **St Mary Immaculate**
(1674; cons 8 Dec 1845)
Blackbrook Road, St Helens, Merseyside WA11 9RJ **Tel:** 01744-23079
Rev Terence Dooley.
M: *Sat 1st M of Sun 6pm. Sun 8am, 9.30am, 11am, 4.30pm. Hds (vigil 7.30pm). 9.30am, 7.30pm.*
• ***Sisters of Mercy,*** Blackbrook Road, St Helens, WA11 9RJ **Tel:** 01744-22345

10. † **St Patrick** (1964)
Loughrigg Avenue, Clinkham Wood, St Helens, Merseyside WA11 7AP
Tel: 01744-21748
Rev Kevan O'Brien, resident at St Helens (11).
M: *Sat 1st M of Sun 5pm. Sun 11am. Hds 10.30am.*

11. † SS Peter and Paul
(1938; 1939; cons 25 June 1992)
Woodlands Road, Haresfinch, St Helens, Merseyside WA11 9AQ **Tel:** 01744-23837
Rev Kevin O'Brien STB.
M: *Sun 9.30am. Hds 12.30pm, 7.30pm.*

12. † St Teresa (1925; 1927; 1965)
Devon Street, St Helens, Merseyside WA10 4HX **Tel/Fax:** 01744-23128
Rev Thomas Neylon, resident at St Helens (7).
M: *Sat 1st M of Sun 6.30pm. Sun 11.15am. Hds 2.15pm.*
- ***De La Salle High School,*** Mill Brow, Eccleston WA10 5JU **Tel:** 01744-201511

13. † St Thomas of Canterbury
(1892; 1911)
Dentons Green Lane, Windleshaw, St Helens, Merseyside WA10 6SE **Tel:** 01744-23973
Rev Thomas Gagie.
M: *Sat 1st M of Sun 5.30pm. Sun 9am, 10.30am. Hds 9am, 12noon.*
- ***De La Salle Brothers,*** St John's House, 7 Wokefield Way, Eccleston WA10 4QP **Tel:** 01744-22275 **Fax:** 01744-25255

14. † St Vincent de Paul (1902; 1904)
Derbyshire Hill Road, St Helens, Merseyside WA9 2LS **Tel:** 01744-22972
Rev Peter Hannah. *Deacon:* **Rev Edward Kane**
M: *Sun 9.30am. Hds, 9am.*

■ **SCARISBRICK,** Ormskirk, Lancs
† St Elizabeth (1732; 1812; 1888)
Hall Road, Ormskirk, Lancs L40 9QE
Tel: 01704-880226
Served from Ormskirk
M: *Sun 9.30am. Hds7pm.*

■ **SEAFORTH VILLAGE,** Liverpool
† Our Lady Star of the Sea
(1884; 1901; cons 1906)
Church Road, Seaforth Village, Liverpool.
Tel: 0151-928 2338 (Tribunal) 0151-522 1070
Rev Thomas Wood. 1 Crescent Road, Seaforth Village, Liverpool L21 4LJ
M: *Sat 1st M of Sun 5pm. Sun 11am. Hds (vigil 7pm), 10am.*

■ **SHEVINGTON,** Wigan
† St Bernadette (1965)
Wigan Road, Shevington, Wigan, Lancs.
Tel/Fax: 01257-423675
Rev John Hindley.
M: *Sat 1st M of Sun 6.30pm. Sun 10am. Hds As announced.*

■ **SKELMERSDALE,** Lancs
Priests' House, 184 Liverpool Road, Skelmersdale, Lancs WN8 8BX
Tel: 01695-724476
Team Ministry: **Revv Michael Thompson, James Causey**. *Deacons:* **Revv Desmond P L Alger, Anthony Callaghan.**
M: *(Times in all centres in Skelmersdale subject to alteration. Mass in Skelmersdale Ecumenical Centre Sat 11am).*

1. St Francis of Assisi (1967)
Beechtrees, Digmoor, Skelmersdale, Lancs.
M: *Sat 1st M of Sun 6.30pm. Sun 10am. Hds 9.30pm.*
- ***Sisters of the Holy Family of Bordeaux,*** 157 Beechtrees, Digmoor WN8 9EZ **Tel:** 01695-724916
- ***Congregation of La Sainte Union des Sacrés Coeurs,*** 146 Egerton, Tanhouse, Skelmersdale, WN8 6AE **Tel:** 01695-723245

2. St Mary Queen of Apostles (1993)
Maryvale, Ashurst Road, Skelmersdale, Lancs. **Tel:** 01695-556595
M: *Sat 1st M of Sun 5pm. Sun 11am. Hds 10am.*

3. St Richard (1865)
Parish Centre, Liverpool Road, Skelmersdale, Lancs WN8 8BX
Tel: 01695-729449
M: *Sun 9am. Hds (vigil 7.30pm).*

■ **SOUTH HILL,** Chorley, Lancs
† St Chad (1670; 1791)
Town Lane, Whittle-le-Woods, South Hill, Chorley, Lancs PR6 8AJ **Tel:** 01257-263969
Rev Peter Crowther (Resident at St Joseph, Brinscall). *Deacons:* **Revv Simon Gilbertson, John Hogan.**
M: *Sat 1st M of Sun 5.30pm. Sun 9.15am. Hds 9am, 9pm.*
- ***Brothers of Charity (FC),*** Lisieux Hall, Whittle-le-Woods, Chorley, PR6 7DX **Tel:** 01257-266311

■ **SOUTHPORT,** Merseyside
1. † Holy Family (1893; 1912; cons 8 June 1932)
1 Brompton Road, Southport, Merseyside PR8 6AS **Tel:** 01704-532613
Mgr J Kennedy, Rev Philip Gregory.
M: *Sat 1st M of Sun 6.30pm. Sun 9.30am, 11am. Hds 9.30am, 12.15pm, 7pm.*

2. † Our Lady of Lourdes (1931; 1956)
Waterloo Road, Hillside, Southport, Merseyside. **Tel:** 01704-568286
Rev Atli Jónsson (Resident at St Joseph, Southport). *Deacon:* **Rev William Ball**.
Tel: 01704-551306
M: *Sat 1st M of Sun 5.30pm. Sun 11am. Hds 7.30pm.*

3. † Sacred Heart
(1878; 1907; cons 1961)
483 Liverpool Road, Ainsdale, Southport, Merseyside PR8 3BP **Tel:** 01704-577527
Rev Brian Lawlor OSA. (Resident at St John Stone).
M: *Sat 1st M of Sun 5.30pm. Sun 9.15am. Hds 9am, 6pm.*

4. † St John Stone
Sandbrook Way, Southport, Merseyside PR8 3RN
Tel: 01704-577722 **Fax:** 01704-570647
- ***Augustinians (OSA):*** **Revv Sean Quinlan** (*Prior*), **Brian Lawlor** (*Parish Priest*), **Killian O'Mahoney**.
M: *Sat 1st M of Sun 6.30pm. Sun 10.30am, 5pm. Hds 10am, 7.30pm.*

5. † St Joseph (1867; cons. 1914)
Saxon Road, Birkdale, Southport, PR8 2AY
Tel: 01704-568313
Web: http://mysite.freeserve.com/olstj
Rev Atli Jonsson, St Joseph's Rectory, 40 York Road, Birkdale, Southport PR8 2AY
Deacon: **Rev William Ball**.
M: *Sat 1st M of Sun 7pm. Sun 9.30am. Hds 10am.*
- ***Sisters of Notre Dame,*** 21 Weld Road, PR8 2AZ **Tel:** 01704-568361

6. † St Marie on the Sands
(1839; 1875; cons. 18 Oct 1911)
Seabank Road, Southport, Merseyside.
Tel/Fax: 01704-531229
Rev John Heneghan. *Deacon:* **Rev Peter Fehrenbach**. 25 Seabank Road PR9 0EJ
M: *Sat 1st M of Sun 6pm. Sun 9am, 11am. Hds 12noon.*
- ***Resident at 27 Seabrook Road,*** Southport PR9 0EJ **Mgr Anthony Stringfellow, Tel:** 01704-537783; **Rev Gerard Britt (retired), Tel:** 01704-547201
- ***Daughters of Charity (SVP),*** 'Santa Barbara', 99 Leyland Avenue, Southport PR9 0JQ **Tel:** 01704-549548
Also at: St Vincent's, 33 - 35 Leicester Street, Southport PR9 0EX
Tel: 01704 546386

7. † St Patrick (1912; 1934)
35 Marshside Road, Churchtown, Southport, Merseyside PR9 9TJ
Tel: 01704-228943 **Fax:** 01704-233386
Rev Thomas Leigh.
M: *Sat 1st M of Sun 6.30pm. Sun 9am, 10.30am. Hds 9.15am, 7.30pm.*
- ***Sisters of Charity of St Paul,*** St Patrick's Convent, 13 Marshside Road.
Tel: 01704-21451

8. † St Teresa of Avila
(1883; 1898; cons 9 Sept 1910)
27 Everton Road, Birkdale, Merseyside PR8 4BT **Tel:** 01704-566865
Canon John J Gaine.
M: *Sun 9am, 10.30am, 6pm. Hds 9am, 6pm, 8pm.*

■ STANDISH, Wigan
† St Marie of the Annunciation
(1574; 1884; cons. 1924)
Almond Brook Road, Standish, Wigan WN6 0TB **Tel:** 01257-423291
Rev John Hindley.
M: *Sat 1st M of Sun 7pm. Sun 11am. Hds As announced.*

■ SUTTON MANOR, St Helens
† St Theresa of the Child Jesus (1923; 1924)
Gartons Lane, Sutton Manor St Helens WA9 4RR **Tel:** 01744-812127
Fax: 01744-812327 **Rev Philip Swanson,** *Deacon:* **Rev Terence Alcock.**
M: *Sat 1st M of Sun 6.45pm. Sun 11am. Hds 7.30pm.*

■ TARLETON, Preston
† Our Lady Help of Christians (1925)
Hesketh Lane, Tarleton, Preston PR4 6AS
Tel: 01772-812242 **Rev Gerald Anders**
M: *Sat 1st M of Sun 5.30pm. Sun 10am. Hds (vigil 6.45pm), 11am.*

■ THORNTON, Liverpool
† St William of York (1955)
Edge Lane, Thornton, Liverpool L23 4TG
Tel: 0151-931 4993 **Fax:** 0151-932 0413
Rev Dunstan Harrington, The Presbytery, 74 Edge Lane, Thornton, Liverpool L23 4TG
M: *Sat 1st M of Sun 6.15pm. Sun 8am, 9.30am. Hds 10.30am, 7.30pm.*

■ UPHOLLAND, Skelmersdale
† St Teresa
(1917; 1940; cons 1955)
College Road, Upholland, Skelmersdale WN8 0PY **Tel:** 01695-622001
Rev Anthony Sligo.
M: *Sat 1st M of Sun 6pm. Sun 10am. Hds (vigil 7.30pm), 9.15am, 12noon.*
- ***Sons of Divine Providence (FDP),*** Roby Mill, Upholland, Skelmersdale WN8 0QT
Tel/Fax: 01695-622516
E-mail: cperratta2002@yahoo.co.uk
Cardinal Heenan House – Residential Care for Elderly People.
Tel: 01695-622885 **Fax:** 01695-627609
St Gabriel's Bungalows (10). Upholland, Skelmersdale, Lancs WN8 0QS (Independent accommodation for older people).
Retreat House for Small Groups. 2 Walthew Green Farm, Upholland,

Skelmersdale, Lancs WN8 0QT
Tel/Fax: 01695-622516

- ***Sisters of Notre Dame,*** Ayrefield Road, Roby Mill, Skelmersdale WN8 0QP **Tel:** 01257-252207
- ***Carmelite Monastery,*** Stoney Brow, Upholland, Skelmersdale WN8 0QE. **Tel:** 01695-622988

■ **WARRINGTON,** Cheshire [A]
(See also Diocese of Shrewsbury).

1. † Sacred Heart (1892; 1894)
7 Liverpool Road, Warrington WA5 1AE
Parish Office: **Tel:** 01925-630928
Served from Warrington (2).
M: *Sat 1st M of Sun 5.30pm. Sun 11.30am. Hds (vigil 7.30pm), 1.10pm.*

- ***Sisters of Charity of St Paul,*** 7 Liverpool Road, WA5 1AE **Tel:** 01925-633732

[A]
2. † St Alban
(1776; 1823; cons 25 Sept 1951)
Bewsey Street, Warrington WA2 7JQ
Tel: 01925-630928 **Fax:** 01925-245256
E-mail: stalabanspriory@tiscali.co.uk
Rev Christopher Cunningham.
Deacons: **Revv Paul Cooper, Terence Dolan**
M: *Sun 9.30am. Hds 9.30am.*

2a St Anselm, Chapel-of-Ease.
Hawleys Lane, Dallam, Warrington.
M: *Sun 8.30am.*

[A]
3. † St Benedict
(1902; 1915; cons 1943)
Rhodes Street, Warrington WA2 7QE
Tel/Fax: 01925-630127 **E-mail:** stbenedicts.warrington@rcaolp.co.uk
Mgr John Devine.
M: *Sun 9.30am. Hds As announced.*

[A]
4. † St Mary
(1877; cons 30 Aug 1927)
Buttermarket Street, Warrington WA1 2NS
Tel: 01925-635664 **Fax:** 01925-411830
E-mail: william@ampleforth.org.uk

- ***Benedictines (OSB):*** **Rev William Wright.**
M: *Sat 1st M of Sun 6pm. Sun 9am, 11am (Sung Latin), 5pm. Hds 12.10pm.*
- ***Poor Servants of the Mother of God,*** St Joseph's Welfare Centre, 9 Museum Street, WA1 1JA **Tel:** 01925-635448

4a St Ambrose Chapel-of-Ease
Irwell Road.
M: *Sun 9am. Hds (vigil 7pm).*

[A]
5. † St Oswald (1929)
Padgate Lane, Warrington WA1 3LB
Tel: 01925-813248
Rev Charles Canning. *Deacons:* **Revv Anthony Kerrigan, Michael Oxley.**
M: *Sun 8.30am, 10am. Hds 9am, 6.30pm.*

- ***Sisters of the Cross and Passion,*** St Benedict's Convent, Bruche Avenue, South Manchester Road, WA1 3JD **Tel:** 01925-812597

6. † St Stephen the First Martyr (1952)
Sandy Lane, Orford, Warrington WA2 9HS
Tel: 01925-632849 **Fax:** 01925-415224
Rev Gordon Abbs.
M: *Sun 10am. Hds 9.15am.*

7. The Resurrection & St Bridget
St Bridget's Close, Cinnamon Brow.
Tel: 01925-831900
Served from Warrington (6).
M: *Sun 11.15am. Hds (vigil 7pm), 10am.*

■ **WATERLOO,** Liverpool [A]

1. † St Edmund of Canterbury (1906; 1933; 1955)
62 Oxford Road, Waterloo, Liverpool L22 8QF **Tel/Fax:** 0151-928 3629
E-mail: fr.john@virgin.net
Rev John Cullen.
M: *Sat 1st M of Sun 5.15pm. Sun 9.45pm. Hds (vigil 7pm), 12noon.*

[A]
2. † St Thomas of Canterbury
(1868; 1877; cons 14 Sept 1982)
32 Great Georges Road, Waterloo, Liverpool L22 1RD **Tel:** 0151-928 2645
Rev John Cullen, resident at Waterloo (1).
M: *Sun 11.15am, 4.30pm. Hds 7pm.*

- ***Augustinian Sisters of the Mercy of Jesus,*** Augustinian Convent, Park House, Waterloo, Liverpool L22 3XS **Tel:** 0151-928 4343. *Chaplain:* **Rev Brian Murphy. Tel:** 0151-928 1436

■ **WHISTON,** Prescot [A]

1. † St Luke the Evangelist (1937; 1940)
Shaw Lane, Whiston, Prescot L35 5AT
Tel: 0151-426 6795 **Fax:** 0151-426 5755
E-mail: stlukeswhiston.org.uk
Revv Malcolm Prince, Colin Fealey, Sean Riley. *Deacons:* **Revv Anthony Green, John Woodruff.**
M: *Sat 1st M of Sun 6.30pm. Sun 10am, 11am (Hospital), 5pm. Hds (vigil 7.30pm), 12noon.*

[A]
2. St Leo (1975; 1978)
Lickers Lane, Whiston, Prescot L35 3PN
Tel: 0151-426 6482
Rev Michael McCormick.
M: *Sat 1st M of Sun 6.30pm. Sun 10am. Hds 9am, 7.30pm.*

■ **WIDNES,** Cheshire

1. † Our Lady of Perpetual Succour (1958)
Mayfield Avenue, Hough Green, Widnes, Cheshire WA8 8PH **Tel:** 0151-424 4021
Rev William Redmond.
M: *Sat 1st M of Sun 6.30pm. Sun 11am. Hds 9am, 7.30pm.*

2. St Basil and All Saints (1968)
Hough Green Road, Widnes, Cheshire WA8 4SZ **Tel/Fax:** 0151-424 6641
Rev Michael Crilly.
M: *Sat 1st M of Sun 6pm. Sun 11.15am. Hds 8.30am, 7.30pm.*

3. † St Bede (1750; 1847; cons 1847)
Leigh Avenue, Widnes, Cheshire WA8 6EL **Tel:** 0151-424 2738 **Rev Philip Reece.**
Also in residence: **Revv Matthew Nunes, James Preston.**
M: *Sat 1st M of Sun 6pm. Sun 8.30am, 10.30am, 5.30pm. Hds (vigil 7.30pm), 10.30am, 7pm.*

4. † St John Fisher (1951; 1952)
55 Moorfield Road, Widnes, Cheshire WA8 3JA **Tel/Fax:** 0151-424 3841
Rev Peter Fox. *Deacon:* **Rev John Williams**. *Parish Sister:* **Sr Eileen Moore.**
M: *Sat 1st M of Sun 6pm. Sun 10.30am. Hds 9.15am, 7.30pm.*
- ***Sisters of St Clare,*** 6 Eltham Walk, Widnes, Cheshire WA8 3RX **Tel:** 0151-423 3888

5. † St Marie (1865)
Lugsdale Road, Widnes, Cheshire WA8 6DB Served from Widnes (4).
Tel: 0151-424 2738
M: *Sun 9am (parish hall). Hds 12noon (School).*

6. † St Michael's (1879)
St Michael's Road, Ditton, Widnes, Cheshire WA8 8TF
Tel: 0151-424 2827 **Fax:** 0151-424 2837
Rev William Redmond.
M: *Sat 1st M of Sun 6pm. Sun 10am. Hds (vigil 7pm). 9am.*

7. † St Pius X (1959)
154 Birchfield Road, Widnes, Cheshire WA8 9EF **Tel/Fax:** 0151-424 2970
Served from Widnes (3).
M: *Sun 9.30am. Hds 9am, 7.30pm.*

8. † St Raphael the Archangel (1959)
Liverpool Road, Widnes, Cheshire WA8 7ER **Tel/Fax:** 0151-424 2498
Served from Widnes (3).
M: *Sun 10am. Hds 9.15am.*

■ **WIGAN,** Lancs

1. † Sacred Heart
(1903; new church cons 13 July 1938)
Throstlenest Avenue, Wigan, Lancs.
Tel: 01942-745689
Revv John Birchall, Andrew Jolly. Sacred Heart Presbytery, Springfield Road, Wigan, WN6 7AT
M: *Sat 1st M of Sun 6.30pm. Sun 9am, 11am. Hds (vigil 7.30pm). 9am, 7.30pm.*

2. St Aidan (1972)
Holmes House Avenue, Winstanley, Wigan, Lancs. WN3 6EE **Tel:** 01942-511630
Rev Francis W Tillotson.
Deacon: **Rev James Cardy.**
M: *Sat 1st M of Sun 6pm. Sun 9.15am, 10.45am. Hds 9.30am, 7.30pm.*

3. † St Cuthbert (1872; 1887)
Sherwood Drive, Wigan, Lancs.
Tel: 01942-203583 **Fax:** 01942-732151
E-mail: stcuthbert@blueyonder.co.uk
Rev Edward O'Toole
M: *Sun 10am, Hds 10am.*

4. † St Edward (1927)
Scot Lane, Newtown, Wigan, Lancs WN5 0UA **Tel:** 01942-244175
E-mail: stedwards@rcal177.freeserve.co.uk
Rev Edward O'Toole.
Deacon: **Rev Paul Blinston.**
M: *Sat 1st M of Sun 5.30pm. Sun 11.30am. Hds (vigil 6.30pm).*

4a Precious Blood Chapel-of-Ease
Marsh Green. Closed 2007

5. † St John
(1696; 1819; cons 17 June 1959)
13 Powell Street, Standishgate, Wigan, Lancs WN1 1XD **Tel:** 01942-242325
Served from St Mary's.
Resident in Presbytery: **Rev John Kearns**
M: *Sat 1st M of Sun 7pm. Sun 11am. Hds (vigil 7pm), 10am.*

6. † St Jude (1871; 1966)
Poolstock Lane, Worsley Mesnes, Wigan, Lancs. WN3 5JE **Tel:** 01942-244864
Revv Patrick MacNally, Simon Gore.
Deacon: **Rev Robert Smith**
M: *Sat 1st M of Sun 7pm. Sun 10.30am, 6.30pm. Hds 10.30am, 7.30pm.*

7. † St Mary (1818; cons 1969)
Standishgate, Wigan, Lancs. WN1 1XL
Tel: 01942-242066
Rev John Johnson. Tel: 01942-493420
M: *Sun 9.30am, 4.30pm. Hds 7.30am, 12.05pm, 5.30pm.*

8. † St Patrick (1847, 1880)
67 Hardybutts, Wigan, Lancs. WN1 3RZ
Tel: 01942-512815
Served from St William, Ince.
Rev Ronald McGivern
M: *Sat 1st M of Sun 6pm. Sun 10.45am. Hds 9.15am.*

■ **WILLASTON,** Douglas, Isle of Man A

† **St Joseph** (1954; 1955)
Fenella Avenue, Willaston, Douglas, Isle of Man
Tel: 01624-676062
Served from St Mary of the Isle, Douglas.
Deacon: **Rev Graham Priest**
M: *Sat 1st M of Sun 6.30pm. Hds (vigil 6.30pm).*

■ **WOOLSTON,** Warrington A

† **St Peter and St Michael** (1677; 1835)
Weir Lane, Woolston, Warrington WA1 4QQ
Tel: 01925-812443
Rev John Gildea. *Deacons:* **Revv Thomas Washington, James McGraw.**
M: *Sat 1st M of Sun 6.30pm. Sun 8.30am, 11.15am. Hds 9.15am (St Peter's School), 7.30pm (in Church).*

■ **WRIGHTINGTON,** Wigan

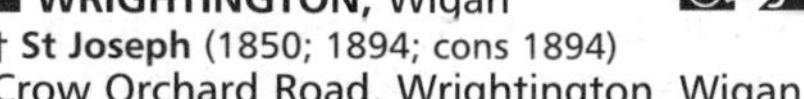

† **St Joseph** (1850; 1894; cons 1894)
Crow Orchard Road, Wrightington, Wigan.
Tel: 01257-422879
Rev Kevin Mulhearn. St Joseph's Presbytery, High Moor, Wrightington, Wigan WN6 9PA
M: *Sun 8.30am, 10.45am, 6pm. Hds 7am, 9am, 7pm.*
Shrine to St John Rigby.

■ **ORDERS AND CONGREGATIONS, ETC**

■ **Men**
Augustinians: Southport (4).
Benedictines (English Congregation): Liverpool (28), Brindle, Leyland, Ormskirk, Parbold, Warrington (4).
Blessed Sacrament Fathers: Liverpool (2a).
Charity, Brothers of: South Hill.
Christian Brothers, Congregation of: Liverpool (25, 62).
De La Mennais Brothers: Liverpool (18).
De La Salle Brothers: St Helens (13).
Divine Providence, Sons of: Mawdesley, Upholland.
Divine Word Missionaries: Liverpool (18).
Franciscans (Friars Minor Conventual): Liverpool (27).
Jesuits: Rainhill.
Mill Hill Missionaries: Formby (2), Clayton Green.
Oblates of Mary Immaculate: Liverpool (58).
Montfort Missionaries: Blundellsands.
Passionists: Liverpool (13).
Redemptorists: Liverpool (9).
Sacred Heart Fathers: Bootle (5)
Sacred Heart Missionaries: Liverpool (21), Kirkby (4).
Salesians: Bootle (1).

■ **Women**
The symbol + is used to distinguish Secular Institutes
Augustinian Canonesses of the Mercy of Jesus: Ince Blundell, Waterloo (2).
Carmelites: Liverpool (53), St Helens (7), Upholland.
Cenacle, Sisters of Our Lady of the: Liverpool (11).
Charity (of Notre Dame d'Evron), Sisters of: Liverpool (27).
Charity (of St Paul, Selly Park), Sisters of: Penketh, Southport (7), Warrington (1).
Charity (of St Vincent de Paul), Daughters of: Liverpool (1, 41, 46), Southport (6).
Charity, Missionaries of: Liverpool (61).
Cross and Passion, Sisters of the: Liverpool (11), St Helens (4), Warrington (5).
Franciscan Missionaries of St Joseph: Leyland.
Holy Family of Bordeaux, Sisters of the: Skelmersdale (1).
Holy Souls, Helpers of the: Huyton (1),
Infant Jesus, Sisters of the: Liverpool (25).
Institute of the Blessed Virgin Mary, Loreto Sisters: Rainhill.
Joseph (of the Apparition), Sisters of St: Liverpool (50).
Little Ones, Sisters of the: Liverpool (56).
Little Servant Sisters of the Blessed Virgin Mary Conceived Immaculate (of Stara Wies): Liverpool (60).
Marie Auxiliatrice, Society of: Bootle (6).
Mary, Little Company of: Liverpool (53).
Mary, Sisters of St (Namur): Liverpool (36, 46, 49).
Mercy, Sisters of Institute of Our Lady of Mercy: Huyton (4), Liverpool (50, 53), Maghull, St Helens (9).
Nazareth, Poor Sisters of: Crosby (2).
Notre Dame (Namur), Sisters of: Blundellsands, Liverpool (9, 18), Parbold, Southport (5), Upholland.
Our Lady of Charity, Sisters of: Ormskirk.
Our Lady of the Missions, Sisters of: Bootle (3), Farington, Kirkby (2).
Parish Mission Sisters: Ince Blundell.
Paul, Daughters of St: Liverpool (28).
Poor Servants of the Mother of God: Liverpool (18, 56), Formby (2) Warrington (4).
Redemptoristines: Liverpool (15).
Sacred Heart of Mary, Religious of the: Blundellsands, Liverpool (55).
Sacred Hearts of Jesus and Mary, Sisters of the: Liverpool (62).
Sainte Union des Sacrés Coeurs, Congregation of La: Skelmersdale (1).
Salesian Sisters of St John Bosco: Liverpool (15).
School Sisters of Notre Dame, Huyton (2).
Sisters of St Clare (Cong of Newry):

Lydiate (2), Widnes (4).
Wisdom, Daughters of (La Sagesse): Chorley (4).

■ NUGENT CARE

(formerly Catholic Social Services)
Director: **Miss Kathleen Pitt.**
Office: 99 Edge Lane, Liverpool L7 2PE
Tel: 0151-261 2000
Community Homes: These provide for boys and girls from age 0 to 18 years.
Family Placement Services.
Advice and Information Service.
Service for the Deaf.
Community Care of the Elderly.
Services for the Mentally Handicapped: (Community and Residential).

■ DIOCESAN INSTITUTIONS, SOCIETIES, ETC

For Societies and Organisations without representation in the diocese please see the main Societies and Organisations section.

Apostleship of the Sea. *Port Chaplain:* **Rev Patrick Harnett SCJ.** St Robert's Presbytery, 52 Orrel Road, Bootle L20 6DZ **Tel:** 0151-922 6161

Association of Our Lady of Mount Carmel *Chairman:* **Mr R V Doyle.** 25 Netherby Street, Liverpool L8 4RX **Tel:** 0151-727 1451

Association for the Propagation of the Faith. *Archdiocesan Director:* **Rev Deacon William Ball.**

Broughton Catholic Charitable Society. Founded in 1787 for Lancashire born Catholic priests or laypersons, or resident in Lancashire, or of Lancashire parentage the society aims to bring spiritual benefits of its members, both living and dead, and the relief of hardship, wherever it is encountered, by making grants
Secretary: **Mr Leo Casey.** 16 Norwood Close, Worsley, Manchester M28 7ES **Tel:** 0161 790 5758
Email: leocasey@bulldoghome.com

Catenian Association. *Provincial Secretary:* **Mr Stephen Cooper.** 14 Abbots Way, Penwortham, Preston PR1 0BD **Tel:** 01772 742173

Cathedral Cantata Choir. *Membership Secretary:* **Mrs Mary Hartley,** c/o Metropolitan Cathedral, Liverpool.

Cathedral Choir Association. *Secretary:* **Mrs Aileen Dobbins,** 60 Palmerston Road, Liverpool L18 8AJ **Tel:** 0151 724 6644

Cathedral Concerts Society *Hon Secretary:* **Philip Dobbins.** Metropolitan Cathedral, Liverpool L3 5TQ **Tel:** 0151-708 7283

Cathedral Orchestra For information and details of auditions write to Orchestra Manager, Cathedral Orchestra, Metropolitan Cathedral, Liverpool L3 5TQ **Tel:** 0151-708 7283

Cathedral Guild of Guides *Head of Guild:* **Mr P A Mannings.** 32 North Sudley Road, Aigburth, Liverpool L17 0BG **Tel:** 0151-727 2749

Cathedral Education Service: *Organiser:* c/o Metropolitan Cathedral.

Catholic Blind Institute: Christopher Grange. Youens Way, East Prescot Road, Liverpool L14 2EW **Tel:** 0151-220 2525

Catholic Engaged Encounter: *Contact:* **Tom & Anne Hemingway,** 36 Wadeson Way, Croft, Warrington WA3 7JS **Tel:** 01925-762681

Cafod (Catholic Fund for Overseas Development). *Liverpool Organiser:* **Chris Lappine**

Catholic Men's Society. *Secretary:* **Mr P Ludley,** Flat 2, Haldane Court, Haldane Road, Liverpool L4 4UB

Catholic Pictorial The official monthly magazine of the Archdiocese of Liverpool. *Editor:* **Mr Peter Heneghan.** Press Office, Archdiocese of Liverpool, Croxteth Drive, Sefton Park, Liverpool L17 1AA **Tel:** 0151-522 1007 **Fax:** 0151-522 1008
E-mail: catholicpictorial@rcaol.co.uk

Catholic Society for Welfare (Warrington & District). Contact: **Sr Margaret,** St Joseph's Centre, 9 Museum Street, Warrington, WA1 1JA

Christian Life Communities: *Regional Representative:* **Jack Woodruff.** 22 Cyprus Street, Prescot, Merseyside L34 5RY

Cursillo Movement. *Spiritual Director:* **Canon J Collins. Tel:** 0151-531 9859

Divorced and Separated Catholics: Rainbow Groups: Spiritual and personal support for victims of marriage breakdown. Contact: Department of Pastoral Formation, Centre for Evangelisation, Croxteth Drive, Liverpool L17 1AA **Tel:** 0151-522 1040

English Catholic History Association. *Regional Co-ordinator:* **Mrs Rose Mary Foster.** 139a Seaview Road, Wallasey, Wirral, Merseyside L45 4NZ **Tel:** 0151-639 0325

Focolare Movement. Contact: Men's House: **Rev Frank Johnson.** 14 Sinclair Drive, Liverpool L18 0HN **Tel:** 0151-722 3981 **Fax:** 0151-475 1033

Friends of Blessed Dominic. Contact: St Anne's Presbytery, Sutton, St Helens, WA9 3SP

Friends of Liverpool Metropolitan Cathedral. *Hon Secretary:* **Claire Hanlon**, Metropolitan Cathedral

Grail, The. *Diocesan Representative:* **Miss Claire Davidson**. 309 Utting Avenue East, Liverpool, L11 1DF **Tel:** 0151-226 9821 More information: The Grail Centre, 125 Waxwell Lane, Pinner, Middlesex. HA5 3ER **Tel:** 020-8866 2195 **Fax:** 020-8866 1408

Guild of Catholic Doctors. *Hon Secretaries:* **Drs Vincent Donnelly & Lelia Jennings**. 77 Dowhills Road, Liverpool L23 8SL **Tel:** 0151-924 1016

Handicapped Children's Pilgrimage Trust *Regional Chairman*: **Chris Sheekey**, 13 Kingfisher House, Pighue Lane, Liverpool L13 1DQ

Jospice International - St Joseph's Hospice Association. *Headquarters:* La Casa De San José, Ince Road, Thornton, Liverpool, L23 4UE **Tel:** 0151-924 7871 or 0151-924 3812/3 also: Hettinga House, Dark Lane, Ormskirk, Lancs. **Tel:** 01695-578713/572942

Knights of St Columba. Area 2 (Liverpool): *Provincial Grand Knight*: **Stephen Laffan**, 57 Wandsworth Road, Liverpool L11 1DR *Provincial Secretary:* **Desmond E Byrne**, 15 Oxbrow Road, Liverpool L23 0AF *Provincial Chaplain:* **Rev Thomas Wood.**

Latin Mass Society. *Representative:* **Mr James Pennington**, 3 Alder Road, Prescot, Merseyside L34 2SG **Tel:** 0151-426 0361

Legion of Mary. Headquarters: 32 Derby Lane, Liverpool L13 3DL **Tel:** 0151-228 1451 (eve only) *Secretary:* **Mrs Ursula Donnelly**, 6 Southbank Road, Liverpool L7 9LP

Liverpool Catholic Ramblers' Association. *Contact:* **Mr T Reilly**. 1 Stanmore Road, Wavertree, Liverpool L15 9ER **Tel:** 0151-737 1041

Lourdes Pilgrimage Association. *Secretary:* **Rev V A Anderson.** 6 Willoughby Drive, Eccleston Hill, St Helens WA10 3AY **Tel:** 01744-758088

Marriage Care. Headquarters: Clitherow House, 18 Lythe Mews, Blythe Road, London W14 0NW **Tel:** 0171-371 1341 **Fax:** 0171-371 4921 Liverpool Centre: **Tel:** 0151-261 2003

Marriage Encounter *Diocesan Contact*: **Deryck & Mary Whitehouse**, 43 Grasmere Avenue, Warrington WA2 0SU **Tel:** 01925-819176

North West Catholic History Society *Representative:* **Mr B T Farrimond**, 1 Tower Hill, Ormskirk L39 2EE **Tel:** 01695-575038

Notre Dame Association, for details: **Norah Burns**. 41 Newsham Drive, Newsham Park, Liverpool L6 7UJ **Tel:** 0151-263 1684

Our Lady's Catechists. *Diocesan Representative:* **Sr Joyce Barnes SND**, 4 Herm Road, Liverpool L5 8YP **Tel:** 0151-297 0962

Rainbow Groups. The groups offer spiritual and personal support to those Catholics who have suffered marriage breakdown. *Contact:* Department of Pastoral Formation, Centre for Evangelisation, Croxteth Drive, Liverpool L17 1AA **Tel:** 0151-522 1040

St Barnabas Society. *Diocesan Representative:* **Jonathan Brown**, 66 Chester Road, Anfield Liverpool L6 4DZ **Tel:** 0151 260 1186 **Mbl:** 0798 334 2006 **E-mail:** j.a.i.brown@bigfoot.com

St Joseph's Society. For membership and information, contact: **Rev C J Cunningham**, St Alban's, Bewsey Street, Warrington, WA2 7JQ

School for the Blind and Partially Sighted; Yew Tree Lane, Liverpool L12 9HN Under the care of the Daughters of Charity **Tel:** 0151-228 3433

Scout Association. *National Scout Chaplain:* **Rev John Seddon**. 165 Liverpool Road, Crosby, Liverpool L23 5TE **Tel:** 0151-949 1782

Secular Franciscan Order. *Contact:* **Gerard McCormick**, 8 Coed Onn Road, Flint, Clywd CH6 5NE **Tel:** 01352-734405

Serra Clubs in the Archdiocese (forming part of Serra International: District 60). *Secretary*: **Mr D C Wall.** 17 The Calders, Liverpool L18 3LN **Tel:** 0151-724 6249

Simmarian Club - Liverpool. For social and benevolent activities among students of St Mary's College of Higher Education *(Strawberry Hill)* and among Catholic teachers. *Chaplain:* **Rev Alexander Fleming**. *Secretary:* **Mr Geoff Farrell**, 123 Manor Road, Crosby, Liverpool L23 7TJ

Society of St Gregory. *Diocesan Representative:* **Clare Orrell**, 14 Stanley Park, Litherland, Liverpool L21 9JT **Tel:** 0151-280 5213 **E-mail:** liverpool@ssg.org.uk

Survive-MIVA. 5 park Vale Road, Aintree, Liverpool L9 2DG **Tel:** 0151-523 3878 **Fax:** 0151-523 3841 **E-mail:** info@survive-miva.org

Union of Catholic Mothers. Liverpool Archdiocesan Branch. *Secretary*: **Mrs Kathy Davies**, 18 Sydenham Avenue, Liverpool L18 3AX

University Chaplaincy. *Chaplain:* **Rev Ian McParland**, Philip Neri House, 30

Catharine Street, Liverpool L8 7NL
Tel: 0151-709 3858

Walsingham Association. *Federation Secretary:* **Mrs J Graham**. 44 St Mary's Avenue, Birchley, Billinge, Wigan, Lancs WN5 7QL **Tel:** 01744-892601

■ CHURCHES IN THE LIVERPOOL POSTAL DISTRICT AREA

(arranged according to their districts)

L1: St Vincent; Blessed Sacrament Shrine.
L3: Cathedral; Our Lady of Reconciliation; St Francis Xavier.
L4: All Saints; St Francis de Sales; St John.
L5: Our Lady Immaculate; St Anthony; St Sylvester.
L6: St Michael.
L7: Sacred Heart; St Anne; St Sebastian.
L8: St Anne & St Bernard; Our Lady of Mount Carmel; St Patrick; University Church of St Philip Neri.
L9: Blessed Sacrament; St Philomena.
L10: Holy Name; Holy Rosary (Old Roan).
L11: Our Lady Queen of Martyrs; St Teresa.
L12: St Paul; St Timothy.
L13: St Cecilia; St Matthew; St Oswald.
L14: St Margaret Mary; St Dominic (Huyton).
L15: Christ the King; Our Lady of Good Help; St Hugh.
L16: Our Lady of the Annunciation; St Paschal Baylon.
L17: St Charles Borromeo; St Clare; St Thomas More.
L18: St Anthony of Padua.
L19: Holy Trinity; St Austin; St Bernadette; St Francis of Assisi.
L20: Bootle: St James; St Joan; St Monica; St Richard; St Robert.
L21: Litherland: St Elizabeth; English Martyrs; Our Lady; Seaforth: Our Lady.
L22: Waterloo: St Edmund; St Thomas.
L23: Blundellsands: St Joseph. Crosby: St Helen; St Mary; SS Peter and Paul; Thornton: St William.
L24: St Ambrose; St Christopher.
L25: Our Lady of the Assumption; St Mary; St Andrew; Holy Family.
L26: St Mark.
L27: St Cyril; St Gregory.
L28: St Albert.

■ HOSPITALS

To contact the Catholic Chaplain of a particular hospital we suggest you contact the hospital reception directly.

■ CATHOLIC SCHOOLS - MAINTAINED

■ LIVERPOOL LEA

▲ Primary and Infant

All Saints' Primary School, Oakfield, Anfield L4 2QG
Tel: 0151 263 7732 **Fax:** 0151 263 5570
E-mail: allsaints-ao@allsaints-inf.liverpool.sch.uk

Blessed Sacrament Infant School Hunslet Road, Walton L9 9JQ
Tel: 0151-525 3528 **Fax:** 0151-525 2998
E-mail: blessedi-ao@blessedsacrament-inf.liverpool.sch.uk

Christ the King Primary Meadway L15 7LZ
Tel: 0151-722 3462 **Fax:** 0151-722 2980
E-mail: christ-ao@christtheking.liverpool.sch.uk

Emmaus C of E & RC Primary School Fir Tree Drive, South Croxteth Park, L12 0JE
Tel: 0151-233 1414 **Fax:** 0151-233 1416
E-mail: emmaus-ao@emmaus.liverpool.sch.uk

Faith CofE and RC Primary Bute Street, Liverpool L5 3LA
Tel: 0151-207 1083 **Fax:** 0151-207 4993
E-mail: faith-ao@faith.liverpool.sch.uk

Holy Cross Primary Fontenoy Street L3 2DU
Tel: 0151- 236 9505 **Fax:** 0151-233 4237
E-mail: holycross-ao@holycross-st-marys.liverpool.sch.uk

Holy Name Primary Moss Pits Lane L10 9LG
Tel: 0151-525 3545 **Fax:** 0151-525 6292
E-mail: holyname-ao@holyname.liverpool.sch.uk

Holy Trinity Primary Banks Road L19 8JY
Tel: 0151-427 7466 **Fax:** 0151-494 1946
E-mail: holytrinity-ao@holytrinity.liverpool.sch.uk

The Trinity Primary Titchfield Street L5 8UT **Tel:** 0151-298 2917
Fax: 0151-207 0840 **E-mail:** trinity-ao@ thetrinity.liverpool.sch.uk

Much Woolton RC (St Mary's) Primary Watergate Lane, L25 8QH
Tel: 0151-428 6114 **Fax:** 0151-428 7753
E-mail: muchwoolton-ao@muchwoolton.liverpool.sch.uk.

Our Lady Immaculate Primary Northumberland Terrace, L5 3QF
Tel: 0151-260 8957 **Fax:** 0151-260 6786
E-mail: immaculate-ao@ourladyimmaculate.liverpool.sch.uk

Our Lady of the Assumption Primary Hartsbourne Avenue, Gateacre, L25 2RY.
Tel: 0151-487 9301 **Fax:** 0151-487-0024
E-mail: ourladyp-ao@ourlady-pri.liverpool.sch.uk

Our Lady of Good Help Primary South Drive, Wavertree, L15 8JL
Tel: 0151-733 6937 **Fax:** 0151-280-0430

E-mail: goodhelp-ao@ ourladyofgoodhelp.liverpool.sch.uk

Our Lady of Mt Carmel Primary North Hill Street, L8 8BQ
Tel: 0151-727 5336 **Fax:** 0151-727 3196
E-mail: carmel-ao@ ourladymountcarmel.liverpool.sch.uk

Our Lady's Bishop Eton Primary Green Lane, L18 2EP
Tel: 0151-722 2982 **Fax:** 0151-737 2503
E-mail: bishopeton-ao@ ourladybishopeton.liverpool.sch.uk

Sacred Heart Primary Hall Lane, L7 8TQ
Tel: 0151-709 1782 **Fax:** 0151-709 5646
E-mail: sacred-ao@ sacredheart.liverpool.sch.uk

St Ambrose's Primary School Alderfield Drive, L24 7SF
Tel: 0151-425 2306 **Fax:** 0151-425 2167
E-mail: ambrose-ao@ st-ambrose.liverpool.sch.uk

St Anne's Primary Overbury Street, L7 3HJ
Tel: 0151-709 1698 **Fax:** 0151-708 9619
E-mail: annes-ao@st-annes. liverpool.sch.uk

St Anthony of Padua Primary, Sands Road, Mossley Hill, L18 8BD
Tel: 0151-724 3233 **Fax:** 0151-724 6911
E-mail: padua-ao@ st-anthonypadua.liverpool.sch.uk

St Austin's Primary Riverbank Road, L19 9DH
Tel: 0151-427 1800 **Fax:** 0151-494 9804
E-mail: austins-ao@ st-austins.liverpool.sch.uk

St Cecilia's Junior School, Green Lane, L13 7EA
Tel: 0151-228 1760 **Fax:** 0151-230 0232
E-mail: cecilasj-ao@ st-cecilias-jun.liverpool.sch.uk

St Cecilia's Infants School, Snaefell Avenue, L13 7HB
Tel: 0151-220 2153 **Fax:** 0151-259 0365
E-mail:ceciliasi-ao@ st-cecilias-inf.liverpool.sch.uk

St Charles' Primary Tramway Road, L17 7JA
Tel: 0151-727 5830 **Fax:** 0151-475 3436
E-mail: charles-ao@ st-charles.liverpool.sch.uk

St Christopher's Primary, Tarbock Road, Speke, L24 0SN
Tel: 0151-486 2835 **Fax:** 0151-448 0778
E-mail: christopherj-ao@ st-christophers-jun.liverpool.sch.uk

St Clare's Primary Garmoyle Close, L15 0DW
Tel: 0151-733 4318 **Fax:** 0151-735 0172
E-mail: clares-ao@ st-clares.liverpool.sch.uk

St Cuthbert's Primary Aviemore Road, L13 3BB **Tel/Fax:** 0151-228 4137
E-mail: cuthberts-ao@ st-cuthberts.liverpool.sch.uk

St Finbar's Primary South Hill Road, L8 9RY
Tel: 0151-727 3963 **Fax:** 0151-726 9950
E-mail: finbars-ao@ st-finbars.liverpool.sch.uk

St Frances de Sales Catholic Infant School. Margaret Road, Walton, L4 3RX
Tel: 0151-525 8489 **Fax:** 0151-525 9345
E-mail: desalesi-ao@ st-francisdesales-inf.liverpool.sch.uk

St Gregory's Primary Montreal Road, Netherley, L27 7AG
Tel: 0151-498 4313 **Fax:** 0151-487 3794
E-mail: gregory-ao@ st-gregorys.liverpool.sch.uk

St Hugh's Primary Earle Road, L7 6HE
Tel: 0151-733 2899 **Fax:** 0151-280 0184
E-mail: hughs-ao@ st-hughs.liverpool.sch.uk

St John's Catholic Primary Sessions Road, L4 1SR **Tel:** 0151-922 1924 **Fax:** 0151-933 0915 **E-mail:** johnsi-ao@ st-johns-inf.liverpool.sch.uk

St Malachy's Primary Park Street L8 6XJ
Tel: 0151-709 3682 **Fax:** 0151-709 7842

St Michael's Primary Guion Street, L6 9DU
Tel: 0151-263 8460 **Fax:** 0151 260 5308

St Nicholas' Primary Orthes Street L3 5XF
Tel: 0151-709 5532 **Fax:** 0151-708 8330

St Oswald's Infant School, St Oswald Street L13 5SB **Tel:** 0151-228 8436
Fax: 0151-280 3760
E-mail: oswaldsi-ao@ st-oswalds.liverpool.sch.uk

St Matthew's Primary School, Queens Drive L4 8UA
Tel: 0151-226 1871 **Fax:** 0151-226 5921
E-mail: matthewsj-ao@ st-matthews-jun.liverpool.sch.uk

St Paschal Baylon Primary, Chelwood Avenue, L16 2LN **Tel:** 0151-722 0464
Fax: 0151-722 1712

St Patrick's Primary Upper Hill Street, L8 5UX
Tel: 0151-709 1062 **Fax:** 0151-707 9367
E-mail: patricks-ao@ st-patricks.liverpool.sch.uk

St Paul's and St Timothy's Infants South Parkside Drive, West Derby L12 8RP **Tel:** 0151-228 2114 **Fax:** 0151-254 1743
E-mail: paultimothy-ao@ st-pauls-st-timothys.liverpool.sch.uk

Our Lady's and St Philomena's Primary Sparrow Hall Road, L9 6BU
Tel: 0151-525 8552 **Fax:** 0151-523 2499

St Sebastian's Primary Holly Road L7 0LH
Tel: 0151-260 9697 **Fax:** 0151-260 5679
E-mail: sebastians-ao@ st-sebastians.liverpool.sch.uk

St Teresa of Lisieux Infant Utting Avenue East, L11 1DD
Tel: 0151-226 5018 **Fax:** 0151-233 2302
E-mail: stol-ao@ st-teresaoflisieux.liverpool.sch.uk

St Vincent de Paul Primary Pitt Street, L1 5BY **Tel:** 0151-709 2572 **Fax:** 0151-707 8942 **E-mail:** vincent-ao@st-vincentdepaul.liverpool.sch.uk

▲ **Junior**

Blessed Sacrament Junior School Cedar Road, L9 9AF **Tel:** 0151-525 9600 **Fax:** 0151-523 7618

St Frances de Sales' Junior School. Hale Road, Walton, L4 3RL **Tel:** 0151-525 7602 **Fax:** 0151-527 3380

St Oswald's Junior School Montague Road, Old Swan, L13 5TE **Tel:** 0151-259 4580 **Fax:** 0151-228 4512

St Paul's Junior Mixed Spring Grove, L12 8SJ **Tel:** 0151-228 1159 **Fax:** 0151-259 3045

St Teresa's Catholic Junior School, Utting Avenue East, L11 1DD **Tel:** 0151-226 5020 Inf Dept: **Tel:** 0151-226 5018 **Fax:** 0151-270 3100

▲ **Secondary**

Archbishop Beck High School Cedar Road, Liverpool, L9 9AF **Tel:** 0151-525 6326 **Fax:** 0151-524 2465

Bellerive FCJ Catholic College Windermere Terrace, Sefton Park, Liverpool, L8 3SB **Tel:** 0151-727 2064 **Fax:** 0151-727 8242

Broughton Hall High School Yew Tree Lane, Liverpool, L12 9HJ **Tel:** 0151-228 3622 **Fax:** 0151-228 1980

Cardinal Heenan High School Honeysgreen Lane, Liverpool, L12 9HZ **Tel:** 0151-228 3472 **Fax:** 0151-252 1246

De La Salle High School Carr Lane East, Liverpool, L11 4SG **Tel:** 0151-546 3134 **Fax:** 0151-548 4146

Notre Dame Catholic College Everton Valley, Liverpool, L4 4EZ **Tel:** 0151-263 3104 **Fax:** 0151-260 1849

Academy of St Francis of Assisi, Gardeners Drive, Liverpool, L6 7AR **Tel:** 0151-260 7600 **Fax:** 0151-260 9222

St Edward's College North Drive, Sandfield Park, L12 1LF **Tel:** 0151-281 1999 **Fax:** 0151-281 1909

St Francis Xavier's College, Beaconsfield Road, Liverpool, L25 6EG **Tel:** 0151-288 1000 **Fax:** 0151-288 1001

St Benedict's College, Horrocks Avenue, Liverpool, L19 5PF **Tel:** 0151-427 5302 **Fax:** 0151-494 3244

St John Bosco Arts College Stonedale Crescent, Liverpool, L11 9DQ **Tel:** 0151-546 6360 **Fax:** 0151-548 5949

St Julie's High School Speke Road, Woolton, Liverpool, L25 7TN **Tel:** 0151-428 6421 **Fax:** 0151-421 1399

■ **HALTON LA**

▲ **Primary**

St Basil's Primary Hough Green Road, WA8 4SZ **Tel:** 0151-424 7839 **Fax:** 0151-420 8973

St Bede's Junior School Appleton Village, WA8 6EL **Tel:** 0151-424 3386 **Fax:** 0151-495 1886

St Bede's Infant School, Leigh Avenue, Appleton Village WA8 6EL **Tel:** 0151-424 3112 **Fax:** 0151-423 3521

St John Fisher Primary Edward Street, WA8 0BW **Tel:** 0151-424 7794 **Fax:** 0151-422 2135

St Gerard's Primary Lugsdale Road, WA8 6DD **Tel:** 0151-424 2879 **Fax:** 0151-424 4461

St Michael's Primary St Michael's Road, WA8 8TD **Tel:** 0151-424 4468 **Fax:** 0151-424 3063

Our Lady of Perpetual Succour Primary, Clincton View, Hough Green WA8 8JW **Tel:** 0151-424 6130 **Fax:** 0151-420 6214

▲ **Secondary**

Saints Peter & Paul Catholic College & City Learning Centre Highfield Road, Widnes WA8 7DW **Tel:** 0151-424 2139 **Fax:** 0151-495 1889

■ **LANCASHIRE LA**

▲ **Primary**

St Joseph's Primary Rothwell Road, Anderton, Lancs, PR6 9LZ **Tel:** 01257-480598 **Fax:** 01257-485886 *(Anderton)*

St Joseph's Primary Bournes Row, Hoghton, Preston, Lancs PR5 0DQ **Tel:** 01254-853473 **Fax:** 01254-851536 *(Brindle)*

St Joseph's Primary Bury Lane, Withnell, Chorley PR6 8SD **Tel:** 01254-830400 **Fax:** 01254-832317 *(Brinscall)*

St John the Evangelist Catholic Primary School, Chapel Lane, Lathom, Ormskirk L40 7RA **Tel:** 01704-893523 **Fax:** 01704-897381 *(Burscough)*

St Bede's Primary Preston Road, Clayton Green, Chorley PR6 7EB **Tel/Fax:** 01772-335861 *(Chorley)*

Sacred Heart Primary Brooke Street, Chorley PR6 0LB **Tel:** 01257-262659 **Fax:** 01257-271412 *(Chorley)*

St Chad's RC Primary Blackburn Road, Whittle-le-Woods PR6 8LL **Tel:** 01257-264480 **Fax:** 01257-232152 *(Chorley)*

St Gregory's Primary Eaves Green Road, PR7 3QG **Tel:** 01257-263865 **Fax:** 01257-234181 *(Chorley)*

St Joseph's Primary Cedar Road, Chorley PR6 0JF **Tel:** 012572-65998 **Fax:** 01257-233107 *(Chorley)*

St Mary's RC Primary Hornchurch Drive, Chorley PR7 2RJ **Tel:** 01257-262811 **Fax:** 01257-268263 *(Chorley)*

St Oswald's Primary Spendmore Lane, Coppull, Chorley PR7 5DH *(Coppull)* **Tel:** 01257-791379 **Fax:** 01257-795516

St Mary's Primary Wigan Road, Euxton, Chorley PR7 6JW **Tel:** 01257-262049 **Fax:** 01257-234324 *(Euxton)*

St Catherine's Primary Moss Lane, Leyland, Preston PR25 4SJ **Tel:** 01772-423767 **Fax:** 01772-457656 *(Farington)*

St Mary's RC Primary Haig Avenue, Leyland, Preston PR25 2QA **Tel:** 01772-422431 **Fax:** 01772-455133 *(Leyland)*

St Anne's Primary Slater Lane, Leyland PR25 1TL **Tel:** 01772-422769 **Fax:** 01772-455188 *(Leyland)*

St Oswald's Primary Chapel Lane, Longton, Preston, PR4 5EB **Tel:** 01772-613402 **Fax:** 01772-613440 *(Longton)*

SS Peter and Paul Primary Ridley Lane, Mawdesley, Lancs L40 3PP **Tel/Fax:** 01704-822216 *(Mawdesley)*

St Anne's Primary Aughton Street, Ormskirk L39 3LQ **Tel:** 01695-574697 **Fax:** 01695-578275 *(Ormskirk)*

Our Lady & All Saints Primary Brandreth Drive, Parbold, Lancs WN8 7HD **Tel/Fax:** 01257-462466 *(Parbold)*

St Mary Magdalen's Primary Buller Avenue, Penwortham, Preston PR1 9QQ **Tel:** 01772-742351 **Fax:** 01772-750351 *(Penwortham)*

St Teresa's Primary Stanley Grove, Penwortham, Preston PR1 0JH **Tel:** 01772-742331 **Fax:** 01772-752491 *(Penwortham)*

St Mary's Primary Hall Road, Scarisbrick L40 9QE **Tel/Fax:** 01704-880626 *(Scarisbrick)*

St Richard's Primary Sandy Lane, Skelmersdale, WN8 8LQ **Tel/Fax:** 01695-722346 *(Skelmersdale and Upholland)*

St Francis of Assisi Primary Blakehall, Skelmersdale, WN8 9AZ **Tel/Fax:** 01695-558560 *(Skelmersdale and Upholland)*

St Edmund's Primary Windrows, New Church Farm, Skelmersdale, Lancs WN8 8NP **Tel/Fax:** 01695-724798 *(Skelmersdale and Upholland)*

St Teresa's Primary College Road, Upholland, nr Wigan WN8 0PY **Tel/Fax:** 01695-623842 *(Skelmersdale and Upholland)*

St John's Primary Flamstead, Birch Green, Skelmersdale, WN8 6PF **Tel:** 01695-721323 **Fax:** 01695-727589 *(Skelmersdale and Upholland)*

St James' Primary Ashurst Road, Ashurst, WN8 6TN **Tel/Fax:** 01695-728989 *(Skelmersdale and Upholland)*

St Joseph's Primary Mossy Lea Road, Wrightington, Wigan, WN6 9RE **Tel:** 01257-423092 **Fax:** 01257-423357 *(Wrightington)*

▲ Secondary

Leyland St Mary's Technology College *(Grant Maintained School).* Royal Avenue, Leyland, PR25 1BS **Tel:** 01772-421909 **Fax:** 01772-424705 *(Leyland)*

All Hallows High School Crabtree Avenue, (from Central Drive), Penwortham PR1 0LN **Tel:** 01772-746121 **Fax:** 01772-908502 *(Penwortham)*

St Bede's High School St Anne's Road, Ormskirk, L39 4TA **Tel:** 01695-570335 **Fax:** 01695-571686 *(Ormskirk)*

Our Lady Queen of Peace High School Glenburn Road, Skelmersdale, Lancs WN8 6JW **Tel:** 01695-725635 **Fax:** 01695-556046 *(Skelmersdale)*

Holy Cross High School Burgh Lane, Chorley, Lancs, PR7 3NT **Tel:** 01257-262093 **Fax:** 01257-232878 *(Chorley)*

■ WIGAN LEA

▲ Primary

St Oswald's Primary Council Avenue, Ashton-in-Makerfield WN4 9AZ **Tel:** 01942-724820 **Fax:** 01942-726874 *(Ashton-in-Makerfield)*

St Wilfrid's Primary, Golborne Road, Ashton-in-Makerfield WN4 8SJ **Tel:** 01942-707101 **Fax:** 01942-204597 *(Ashton-in-Makerfield)*

St Ambrose Barlow Primary Manchester Road, Astley M29 7DY **Tel:** 01942-883912 **Fax:** 01942-776498 *(Astley)*

St Richard's Primary Flapper Fold Lane, Atherton, Manchester M46 0HA **Tel:** 01942-882980 **Fax:** 01942-894830 *(Atherton)*

Holy Family RC Primary, Kendal Road, Boothstown, Worsley, Manchester M28 1AG **Tel:** 0161-790 2123 **Fax:** 0161-703 8378 *(Boothstown)*

Our Lady Immaculate (Downall Green RC) Primary, Downall Green Road, Bryn, Wigan WN4 0LZ **Tel:** 01942-727067 *(Bryn)* **Fax:** 01942 776614

All Saints' Primary Hazel Grove, Golborne Warrington, WA3 3LU *(Golborne)* **Tel:** 01942-747655 **Fax:** 01942-747654

St Benedict's Primary Abbott Street, Hindley, WN2 3DG
JM Dept: **Tel/Fax:** 01942-253522

Sacred Heart Primary Swan Lane, Hindley Green, WN2 4HD **Tel:** 01942-767768 **Fax:** 01942-521742 *(Hindley Green)*

Sacred Heart Primary Lodge Lane, Hindsford, Atherton M46 9BN **Tel/Fax:** 01942-883429 *(Atherton)*

St William's Primary Ince Green Lane, Ince, Wigan, WN2 2DG **Tel:** 01942-235782 **Fax:** 01942-824185 *(Ince)*

Sacred Heart Primary Windermere Road, Leigh, WN7 1UX **Tel:** 01942-674226 **Fax:** 01942-262684 *(Leigh)*

St Joseph's Primary Mather Lane, Leigh, Lancs, WN7 2PR **Tel:** 01942-606395 **Fax:** 01942-766682 *(Leigh)*

Twelve Apostles' Primary Nel Pan Lane, Leigh, WN7 5JS **Tel:** 01942-674312 *(Leigh)*

St Gabriel's Primary Kensington Drive, Higher Folds, Leigh WN7 2YG **Tel:** 01942-673603 **Fax:** 01942-681637 *(Leigh)*

St Catherine of Siena Primary Cranham Avenue, Lowton, Warrington, WA3 2PQ **Tel/Fax:** 01942-671528 *(Lowton)*

St James Catholic Primary School, St James Road, Orrell, Wigan, WN5 7AA **Tel/Fax:** 01942-748455. *(Orrell)*

Holy Family Wigan Street, Platt Bridge, Wigan, WN2 5JF **Tel:** 01942-704148 **Fax:** 01942-704149 *(Platt Bridge)*

St Marie's Avondale Street, Standish WN7 0LF **Tel:** 01257-422975 **Fax:** 01257-401117 *(Standish)*

St Bernadette's Primary Church Lane, Shevington, Appley Bridge, Wigan WN6 8BD **Tel/Fax:** 01257-401125 *(Shevington)*

Sacred Heart Primary Springfield Road, Wigan WN6 7RH **Tel:** 01942-231478 **Fax:** 01942-323641 *(Wigan)*

St Aidan's Primary Holmes House Avenue, Winstanley, Wigan, WN3 6EE **Tel:** 01942-223544 **Fax:** 01942-222634 *(Wigan)*

St Cuthbert's Primary Thorburn Road, Norley Hall WN5 9LW **Tel:** 01942-222721 **Fax:** 01942-700694 *(Wigan)*

St Jude's Primary Worsley Mesnes Drive, Worsley Mesnes, Wigan WN3 5AN **Tel:** 01942-204091 **Fax:** 01942-513364 *(Wigan)*

St Mary and St John Primary, Standishgate, Wigan, WN1 1XL **Tel:** 01942-206733 **Fax:** 01942-513869 *(Wigan)*

St Patrick's Primary Hardybutts, Wigan, WN1 3RZ **Tel:** 01942-244361 **Fax:** 01942-244363 *(Wigan)*

▲ Secondary

St Edmund Arrowsmith High School Rookery Avenue, Ashton-in-Makerfield Wigan WN4 9PF **Tel:** 01942-728651 **Fax:** 01942-730035 *(Ashton-in-Makerfield)*

St Mary's RC High School Manchester Road, Astley, Manchester, M29 7EE **Tel:** 01942-884144 **Fax:** 01942 884357 (Astley)

St Peter's High School Howard's Lane, Orrell, Wigan WN5 8NU **Tel:** 01942-747693 **Fax:** 01942-747694 *(Orrell)*

St John Fisher High School Baytree Road, Springfield, Wigan WN6 7RN *(Wigan)* **Tel:** 01942-510715 **Fax:** 01942-519039

▲ Sixth Form College

St John Rigby RC Sixth Form College Orrell, Wigan WN5 0LJ **Tel:** 01942-214797 **Fax:** 01942-216514 (Wigan)

■ SEFTON LEA

▲ Primary

Our Lady, Star of the Sea Primary, Kepler Street, Seaforth, Liverpool L21 3TR **Tel:** 0151-928 3158 **Fax:** 0151-949 0221 *(Crosby)*.

All Saints Primary Chesnut Grove, Bootle L20 4LX **Tel:** 0151-922 2440 **Fax:** 0151-933 7883 *(Bootle)*

St Monica's Primary Aintree Road, L20 9EB **Tel:** 0151-525 1245 **Fax:** 0151-525 1865

St Robert Bellarmine's Primary Harris Drive, L20 6ED **Tel:** 0151-922 1216 **Fax:** 0151-922 2282*(Bootle)*

St Mary's (Little Crosby RC) Primary Back Lane, Little Crosby, L23 4TS **Tel:** 0151-924 4447 **Fax:** 0151-932 0844 *(Crosby)*

Great Crosby RC Primary (SS Peter and Paul and St Helen) The Northern Road, Great Crosby, Liverpool L23 2RQ **Tel:** 0151-924 8661 **Fax:** 0151-924 1331 *(Crosby)*

St William of York Primary St William Road, Crosby, Liverpool L23 9XH **Tel:** 0151-924 7280 **Fax:** 0151-931 4558 *(Crosby)*

Ursuline RC Primary Nicholas Road, Blundellsands, Liverpool L23 6TT **Tel:** 0151-924 1704 **Fax:** 0151-924 2158 *(Crosby)*

Holy Spirit Primary Poulsom Drive, Bootle, L30 2NR **Tel:** 0151-525 7497 **Fax:** 0151-525 2206 *(Ford)*

Our Lady of Compassion Primary, Bull Cop, Formby, Liverpool L37 8BZ **Tel:** 01704-877281 **Fax:** 01704 873345 *(Formby)*

St Jerome's Primary Greenloons Drive, Formby, Liverpool L37 2LX **Tel:** 0151-288 6003 **Fax:** 01704-831724 *(Formby)*

English Martyrs' Primary School Lane, Liverpool, L21 7LX **Tel:** 0151-928 5601 **Fax:** 0151-928 3570 *(Litherland)*

Our Lady Queen of Peace Primary Ford Close, Litherland, Liverpool L21 0EP **Tel.** 0151-928 3676 **Fax:** 0151-949 0769 *(Litherland)*

St Elizabeth's Primary: Webster Street, Litherland, Liverpool L21 8JH
Junior: **Tel:** 0151-922 5752
Infant: **Tel:** 0151-922 7480
Fax: 0151-922 2236 *(Litherland)*

St Gregory's Primary Sandy Lane, Lydiate, L31 2LB **Tel:** 0151-526 5856 **Fax:** 0151-228 6583 *(Lydiate)*

St John Bosco Primary Green Lane, Maghull, Liverpool L31 8BW **Tel/Fax:** 0151-520 2628 *(Lydiate)*

St George's Primary Dennett Close, Liverpool L31 5PD **Tel:** 0151-526 1624 **Fax:** 0151-288 6560 *(Maghull)*

Our Lady of Walsingham Primary Stand Park Avenue, Netherton, Bootle, L30 3SA **Tel:** 0151-525 0395 **Fax:** 0151-523 3362 *(Netherton)*

St Benedict's Primary, Copy Lane, Netherton, Bootle, L30 7PG **Tel:** 0151-526 6423 **Fax:** 0151-531 9530 *(Netherton)*

Holy Rosary Primary Aintree Lane, Old Roan, Liverpool, L10 2JD **Tel:** 0151-288 6206 **Fax:** 0151-288 6207 *(Old Roan)*

Holy Family Primary Norwood Crescent, Southport, PR9 7DU **Tel:** 01704-213084 **Fax:** 01704-211951 *(Southport)*

Our Lady of Lourdes Primary Grantham Road, Southport, PR8 4LT **Tel:** 01704-568375 **Fax:** 01704-565779 *(Southport)*

St Teresa's Infants Everton Road, Southport, PR8 4BT **Tel/Fax:** 01704-567528 *(Southport)*

St Patrick's Primary Radnor Drive, Southport, PR9 9RR **Tel:** 01704-225906 **Fax:** 01704-507180 *(Southport)*

St Edmund's and St Thomas' Primary Oxford Road, Liverpool, L22 8QF **Tel:** 0151-928 5586 **Fax:** 0151-928 4352 *(Waterloo)*

▲ Secondary

Savio High School Netherton Way, Bootle, L30 2NA **Tel:** 0151-521 3088 **Fax:** 0151-525 8435 *(Bootle)*

St Ambrose Barlow Catholic College Copy Lane, Bootle, L30 7PQ **Tel:** 0151-526 7044 **Fax:** 0151-527 2153 *(Bootle)*

Holy Family High School Virgins Lane, Thornton, Crosby, Liverpool, L23 4UL **Tel:** 0151-924 6451 **Fax:** 0151-932 1417 *(Crosby)*

Sacred Heart Catholic College Liverpool Road, Crosby. L23 5TF **Tel:** 0151-931 2971 **Fax:** 0151-924 8715 *(Crosby)*

St Wilfrid's High School Orrell Road, Litherland, L21 8NU **Tel:** 0151-928 4543 **Fax:** 0151-928 9921 *(Litherland)*

Maricourt High School Hall Lane, Maghull, L31 3DZ **Tel:** 0151-330 3366 **Fax:** 0151-284 6631 *(Maghull)*

Christ the King High School and Sixth Form Centre, Stamford Road, Southport, PR8 4EX **Tel:** 01704-565121 **Fax:** 01704-550447

■ ST HELENS LA

▲ Primary

St Mary's Primary Birchley Road, Billinge, Wigan, WN5 7QJ **Tel:** 01744-678610 **Fax:** 01744-678611 *(Birchley)*

St Julie's Primary Brooklands Road, Eccleston, St Helens, WA10 5HG **Tel/Fax:** 01744-25032 *(Eccleston)*

English Martyrs' Primary Piele Road, Haydock, St Helens, WA11 0JY **Tel:** 01942-723552 **Fax:** 01942-273706 *(Haydock)*

St Mary's Junior, Barn Way, Cross Lane, Newton-le-Willows, WA12 9QQ **Tel:** 01744-678603 **Fax:** 01744-678605

St Mary's Infant, Victoria Road, Newton-le-Willows WA12 9RX **Tel/Fax:** 01925-224927 *(Newton-le-Willows)*

Corpus Christi Primary Old Lane, Rainford, St Helens, WA11 8JF **Tel:** 01744-678102 **Fax:** 01744-678103

St Bartholomew's Primary School Lane, Rainhill, L35 6NN **Tel:** 01744-678550 **Fax:** 01744-678554 *(Rainhill)*

St Mary's (Blackbrook) RC Primary Chain Lane, St Helens, WA11 9QY **Tel:** 01744-678161 **Fax:** 01744-678164

Holy Cross Primary, Charles Street, St Helens, WA10 1LN **Tel:** 01744-678319 **Fax:** 01744 678320

Holy Spirit Primary, Brunswick Street, Parr, St Helens WA9 2JE **Tel:** 01744-757727 **Fax:** 01744-678672 *(St Helens)*

St Austin's Primary School Heath Street, St Helens WA9 5NJ **Tel:** 01744-606598 **Fax:** 01744-678005 *(St Helens)*

St John Vianney Primary Elton Head Road, Sutton Heath, St Helens WA9 5BT **Tel/Fax:** 01744-678750 *(St Helens)*

St Anne's Primary Monastery Lane, Sutton, St Helens WA9 3SP **Tel:** 01744-811670 **Fax:** 01744-817471

St Theresa's Primary Cannon Street, Sutton Manor, St Helens WA9 4XU **Tel:** 01744-678652 **Fax:** 01744-678653 *(St Helens)*

St Teresa's Primary Devon Street, St Helens WA10 4HX **Tel/Fax:** 01744-678667 *(St Helens)*

SS Peter and Paul Primary Derwent Road, Haresfinch, St Helens WA11 9AT **Tel:** 01744-678640 **Fax:** 01744-678642 *(St Helens)*

St Thomas of Canterbury Primary (Windleshaw) Rainford Road, St Helens WA10 6BX **Tel:** 01744-621380 **Fax:** 01744-621381 *(St Helens)*

▲ **Secondary**

St Aelred's Catholic Technology College Birley Street, Newton-le-Willows, Merseyside, WA12 9UW **Tel:** 01925-225974 **Fax:** 01925-290759

De La Salle High School Mill Brow, Eccleston, St Helens, WA10 4QH **Tel:** 01744-20511 **Fax:** 01744-20543 *(St Helens)*

St Augustine of Canterbury High School Boardman's Lane, St Helens, WA11 9BB **Tel:** 01744-678112 **Fax:** 01744-678113 *(St Helens)*

St Cuthbert's Catholic College for Business & Enterprise Berry's Lane, St Helens, WA9 3HE **Tel:** 01744-678123 **Fax:** 01744-678127 *(St Helens)*

Carmel College (RC Sixth Form College) Prescot Road, St Helens, WA10 3AG **Tel:** 01744-452200 **Fax:** 01744-452222 *(St Helens)*

■ **WARRINGTON LEA**

▲ **Primary**

St Paul of the Cross Primary Milnthorpe Road, Burtonwood, Warrington WA5 4PN **Tel:** 01925-224686 **Fax:** 01925-221259 *(Burtonwood)*

St Lewis' Primary Mustard Lane, Croft, Warrington WA3 7BD **Tel:** 01925-762268 **Fax:** 01925-767784 *(Croft)*

St Joseph's Primary Walton Avenue, Penketh, Warrington, Cheshire, WA5 2AU **Tel:** 01925-723340 **Fax:** 01925-721402 *(Penketh)*

St Vincent's Primary Finlay Avenue, Penketh, Warrington, Cheshire, WA5 2PN **Tel:** 01925-726544 **Fax:** 01925-721770 *(Penketh)*

Sacred Heart Primary Selby Street, WA5 1NS **Tel:** 01925-636235 **Fax:** 01925-230971 *(Warrington)*

St Alban's Primary Bewsey Road, WA5 0JS **Tel:** 01925-632128 **Fax:** 01925-241269 *(Warrington)*

St. Benedict's Primary Quebec Road WA2 7SB **Tel:** 01925-234699 **Fax:** 01925-234701 *(Warrington)*

St Bridget's Primary Capesthorne Road, WA2 0ER **Tel:** 01925-811873 **Fax:** 01925-816498 *(Warrington)*

St Oswald's Padgate Lane, Padgate, WA1 3LB **Tel:** 01925-813015 **Fax:** 01925-820545 *(Warrington)*

St Stephen's Primary Sandy Lane, Orford, Warrington, WA2 9HS **Tel:** 01925-630100 **Fax:** 01925-243396 *(Warrington)*

St Peter's Primary Hillock Lane, Woolston, Warrington, WA1 4PQ **Tel:** 01925-815314 **Fax:** 01925-851702 *(Woolston)*

▲ **Secondary**

St Gregory's High Cromwell Avenue, Westbrook, Warrington, WA5 1HG **Tel:** 01925-574888 **Fax:** 01925-243816 *(Warrington)*

■ **KNOWSLEY LA**

▲ **Primary**

St Albert's Primary Steers Croft, Stockbridge Village, Liverpool L28 8AJ **Tel:** 0151-477 8560 **Fax:** 0151-477 8561 *(Stockbridge Village)*

St Brigid's Primary Waterpark Drive, Stockbridge Village, Liverpool, L28 7RE **Tel:** 0151-477 8150 **Fax:** 0151-477 8151 *(Stockbridge Village)*

Holy Family Primary Hall Lane, Cronton, Widnes, WA8 5DW **Tel:** 0151-424 3926 **Fax:** 0151-420 3177 *(Cronton)*

St Andrew the Apostle Primary Higher Road, Halewood, Liverpool L26 1TD **Tel:** 0151-288 8940 **Fax:** 0151-288 8941 *(Halewood)*

St Mark's Primary Fir Avenue, Halewood, Liverpool L26 0XR **Tel:** 0151-288 8910 **Fax:** 0151-288 8912 *(Halewood)*

Holy Family Primary Arncliffe Road, Halewood, Liverpool L25 9PA **Tel:** 0151-282 8971 **Fax:** 0151-282 8972 *(Halewood)*

St Aidan's Primary Adswood Road, Huyton, Liverpool L36 7XR **Tel:** 0151-477 8370 **Fax:** 0151-477 8371 *(Huyton)*

St Agnes's Primary St John's Road, Huyton, Liverpool L36 0UX **Tel:** 0151-477 8530 **Fax:** 0151-477 8531 *(Huyton)*

St Anne's Primary Marina Crescent, Huyton, Liverpool L36 5XL **Tel:** 0151-477 8260 **Fax:** 0151-477 8261 *(Huyton)*

St Columba's Primary Hillside Road, Huyton, Liverpool L36 8BL

Tel: 0151-477 8360
Fax: 0151-477 8361 *(Huyton)*
St Dominic's Southdean Road, Liverpool, L14 8UL **Tel:** 0151-477 8300
Fax: 0151-477 8301
Inf Dept **Tel:** 0151-477 8280
Fax: 0151-477 8281 *(Huyton)*
St Joseph's Primary Edenfield Crescent, Huyton, Liverpool L36 6DS
Tel: 0151-489 4072 **Fax:** 0151-449 0135 *(Huyton)*
St Margaret Mary's Junior School Pilch Lane, Liverpool L14 0JG
Tel: 0151-477 8490 **Fax:** 0151-477 8491
St Margaret Mary's Infant School Pilch Lane, Liverpool L14 0JG
Tel: 0151-228 4024 **Fax:** 0151-228 0073
St Laurence's Primary Leeside Avenue, Kirkby, Liverpool L32 9QX
Tel: 0151-546 4733
Fax: 0151-547 4218 *(Kirkby)*
St Joseph the Worker Primary Bewley Drive, Kirkby, Liverpool L32 9PF
Dept **Tel:** 0151-477 8173
Fax: 0151-477 8172. *(Kirkby)*
SS Peter and Paul Primary Moorfield, Tower Hill, Kirkby, Liverpool L33 1DZ
Tel: 0151- 548 6890 **Fax:** 0151-548 0179
Holy Angels' Primary, Kirkby Row, Kirkby, Liverpool L32 0TQ **Tel:** 0151-477 8400
Fax: 0151-477 8401 *(Kirkby)*
St Marie's Primary Bigdale Drive, Northwood, Kirkby, Liverpool L33 6XL
Tel: 0151-477 8480
Fax: 0151-477 8481
St John Fisher Primary Tithebarn Road, Knowsley Village, L34 0HA
Tel: 0151-546 8742
Fax: 0151-549 1274 *(Knowsley)*
Our Lady's Catholic Primary Ward Street, Prescot, L34 6JJ
Tel: 0151-477 8280
Fax: 0151-477 8221 *(Prescot)*
St Aloysius' Primary Twig Lane, Huyton, L36 2LF **Tel:** 0151-489 5083
Tel: 0151-489 6354 *(Roby)*
St Luke's Primary Shaw Lane, Prescot, L35 5AT **Tel:** 0151-477 8580
Fax: 0151-477 8581
St Leo's Primary Lickers Lane, Whiston, Prescot L35 3SR **Tel:** 0151-477 8580
Fax: 0151-477 8581 *(Whiston)*

▲ SECONDARY

St Edmund of Canterbury High School, Lordens Road, Huyton, Liverpool, L14 8UD **Tel:** 0151-489 5911
Fax: 0151-489 3058 *(Huyton)*
All Saints' High Bewley Drive, Kirkby, Liverpool L32 9PQ **Tel:** 0151-546 6881
Fax: 0151-545 4512 *(Kirkby)*
St Edmund Arrowsmith Scotchbarn Lane, Whiston, Prescot, L35 7JD **Tel:** 0151-477 8520 **Fax:** 0151-477 8521 *(Prescot)*

■ ISLE OF MAN

▲ Primary

St Mary's Primary St Mary's Road, Douglas **Tel:** 01624-673807
Fax: 01624-615404

■ Extra-Diocesan Schools Serving the Archdiocese

Brownedge St Mary's High Station Road, Bamber Bridge, Preston, PR5 6PB
Tel: 01772-39813 **Fax:** 01772-629236
St Joseph's High School and Sports College Chorley New Road, Horwich, Bolton BL6 6HW **Tel:** 01204-697456
Fax: 01204-669018
Cardinal Newman Catholic High School Bridgewater Avenue, Latchford, Warrington WA4 1RX
Tel: 01925-635556 **Fax:** 01925-628600
Cardinal Newman College Larkhill Road, Preston, PR1 4HD
Tel: 01772-460181/460183
Fax: 01772-204671

■ CATHOLIC SCHOOLS – INDEPENDENT

St Mary's College Everest Road, Great Crosby, Liverpool, L23 5TW
Tel: 0151-924 3926 **Fax:** 0151-932 0363
Carleton House Preparatory School Lyndhurst Road, Mossley Hill, Liverpool, L18 8AQ **Tel:** 0151-724 4880
Fax: 0151-724 6086
Runnymede St Edward's Preparatory Dept North Drive, Sandfield Park, Liverpool, L12 1LE **Tel:** 0151-281 2300
Fax: 0151-281 4900
St Mary's College Preparatory School (co-educational) The Mount, Blundellsands Road West, Liverpool, L23 6TF **Tel:** 0151-924 6302 **Fax:** 0151 932 0450

■ Higher Education

Liverpool Hope University Hope Park, Liverpool L16 9JD **Tel:** 0151-291 3000
Fax: 0151-291 3100

DIOCESE OF MENEVIA

Province of Cardiff

Separated from the former Diocese of Newport and Menevia, and from the Diocese of Shrewsbury, and formed into the Vicariate of Wales, by Pope Leo XIII, 4 March 1895. The Vicariate was erected into the Diocese of Menevia, 12 May 1898. Restructured, with its Cathedral Church at Swansea, 12 February 1987. Consisting of the City and County of Swansea. The Counties of Carmarthenshire, Ceredigion, Pembrokeshire. The Southern Half of the County of Powys and The County Borough of Neath Port Talbot.

Patron of the Diocese
St Joseph

Bishop
Rt Rev Thomas Matthew Burns SM BA BD
born 3 June, 1944
Ordained priest 16 Dec, 1971; Ordained Bishop of the Forces 18 June, 2002; Announced as Bishop 16 October 2008

Rt Rev Thomas Matthew Burns SM, BA, BD
Bishop of Menevia

Residence:
'Bryn Rhos', 79 Walter Road, Swansea SA1 4PS
Tel: 01792-650534 **Fax:** 01792-518786

Bishop's Personal Secretary:
Mrs Helen Mitchell. Curial Offices, 27 Convent Street, Greenhill, Swansea SA1 2BX
Tel: 01792-644017 **Fax:** 01792-458641
E-mail: curia@meneviacurialoffice.org

Bishop Emeritus
Rt Rev Daniel J Mullins, BA. born in Kilfinane, Co Limerick, 10 July 1929; ordained 12 April 1953; cons Bishop of Stowe and Auxiliary in Cardiff by Archbishop Murphy, 1 April 1970; trans to Menevia 12 February 1987; retired 12 June 2001. Address: 8 Rhodfa Gwendraeth, Kidwelly SA17 4SR **Tel:** 01554-890142

■ ADMINISTRATION

■ Diocesan Curia
Curial Offices, 27 Convent Street, Greenhill, Swansea SA1 2BX
Tel: 01792-644017 **Fax:** 01792-458641
E-mail: curia@meneviacurialoffices.org

■ Vicars General
Mgr Provost David Bottrill. "Maes-Gwyn", Our Lady of Margam, 63 Margam Road, Port Talbot SA13 2HR **Tel:** 01639-883323; **Mgr Canon Brian Kinrade**, The Presbytery, 9 Promenade Ter. Mumbles, Swansea SA3 4DS **Tel:** 01792 366305

■ Cathedral Dean
Rev Canon Michael Flook
Diocesan Communications Officer:
Rev Michael Burke. The Presbytery, School Road, Morriston, Swansea SA6 6HZ
Tel/Fax: 01792-771053

■ Chancellor
Mgr Canon Clyde Hughes Johnson. The Presbytery, Vergam Terrace, Fishguard, Pembs SA65 9DF **Tel:** 01348-873865

■ EDUCATION AND FORMATION
Sr Angela Murray OSU. Education Office, 27 Convent Street, Greenhill, Swansea SA1 2BX
Tel: 01782-652757 **Fax:** 01792-458641
E-mail: educationmenevia@aol.com

■ Diocesan Finance Committee
Mgr Canon Clyde H Johnson, Mr Tony Phillips, Mr Michael Cronin, Mr Bob Watts, Mr Keith Thomas. Curial Offices, 27 Convent Street, Greenhill, Swansea SA1 2BX

■ Financial Secretary
Mr Tony Phillips. Diocesan Finance Office, Curial Offices, 27 Convent Street, Greenhill, Swansea SA1 2BX
Tel: 01792-650883 **Fax:** 01792-460675

■ **Episcopal Vicar for Religious**
Rev Michael Fewell CMF. Claret House, 99 Alexandra Road, Gorseinon, Swansea SA4 4NX **Tel:** 01792-892722

■ **Diocesan Secretary**
Sister Mary Carr (UJ). 27 Convent Street, Greenhill, Swansea SA1 2BX
Tel: 01792-644017

■ **Registrar for Deceased Clergy**
Sr Mary Carr UJ.

■ **Diocesan Director of Vocations**
Canon Michael Flook. 27 Convent Street, Greenhill, Swansea SA1 2BX
Tel: 01792-652683

■ **Diocesan Director of Diaconal Vocations**
Canon Michael Lewis, The Presbytery, Ithon Road, Llandrindod Wells, Powys LD1 6AS **Tel:** 01597-822353
Fax: 01597-824380

■ **CONSULTATIVE BODIES**

■ **Cathedral Chapter**
Canons: **Mgri David Bottrill, Clyde H Johnson, Brian Kinrade, Canons Revv Michael Flook, James Morrissey, Michael Lewis.** *Honorary Canons:* **Sylvester O'Donnell, Nicholas Jenkins.**
Canons Emeriti: **Seamus Cunnane, Edmund Mullins, Richard Byron.**

■ **Council of Priests**
Secretary: **Rev John Patrick Thomas**. The Presbytery, 9 Fountain Row, Haverfordwest, Pembrokeshire SA61 15X **Tel:** 01437 762284

■ **DIOCESAN MATRIMONIAL TRIBUNAL**
Judicial Vicar: **Rev Michael Burke**.
The Presbytery, School Road, Morriston, Swansea SA6 6HZ **Tel:** 01792-771053

■ **Diocesan Youth Development Director**
Rev Teyrnon Williams, 41 Pontardawe Road, Clydach, Swansea SA6 5NS
Tel: 01792-842244

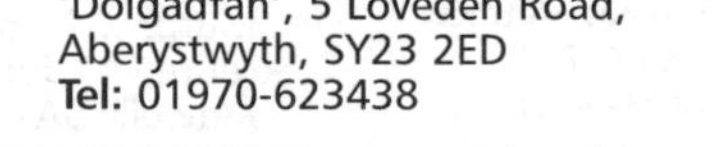

■ **SWANSEA**
1. Cathedral Church of St Joseph
(1875; 1888)
Convent Street, Greenhill, Swansea SA1 2BX **Tel:** 01792-652683
E-mail: philips3@ntlworld.com
Canon Michael Flook.
M: *Sat 1st M of Sun 5.30pm. Sun 8am, 10am. Hds 7.45am, 9.30am, 7pm.*
- ***Ursulines of Jesus,*** St Mary's Convent, 28 Convent Street, Greenhill, Swansea SA1 2BX **Tel:** 01792-461837

■ **ABERAERON,** Ceredigion
Holy Cross (1958)
Victoria Street. Served from Lampeter.
M: *Sat 6pm. Hds 7pm.*

■ **ABERYSTWYTH,** Ceredigion
† **Our Lady of the Angels and St Winefride** (1874)
Queen's Road, Aberystwyth, Ceredigion SY23 2HS **Tel:** 01970-612549
E-mail: parishofaberystwyth@btinternet.com
Rev Paul Watson VF (*Parish Priest*),
Rev Phillip Harris
M: *Sat 1st M of Sun 6pm. Sun 11am. Hds Vigil Mass 7pm, 10am, 12.15pm.*
- ***University Chaplaincy,***
Tel: 01970-612549.
Chaplain: **Rev Paul Watson.**
- ***Daughters of the Holy Spirit,*** 'Dolgadfan', 5 Loveden Road, Aberystwyth, SY23 2ED
Tel: 01970-623438

■ **AMMANFORD,** Carmarthenshire
† **Our Lady of the Rosary** (1914)
35 Margaret Street, Ammanford, SA18 2NP
Tel: 01269-592533
Rev Carlito Reyes.
M: *Vigil 6pm. Sun 9.30am. Hds 7pm*

■ **BRECON,** Powys
† **St Michael** (1642; 1851)
11 St Michael's Street, Brecon, LD3 9AB
Tel: 01874-622046
Rev Ross Patterson.
M: *Sun 8.30am, 11am. Hds 10am.*
- ***Irish Ursuline Union,*** The Convent, Glam-organ Street, LD3 7DN
Tel: 01874-622080.
- ***Society of the Sacred Heart,*** Llannerchwen, Llandefaelog Fach, Brecon, LD3 9PP House of Prayer
Tel: 01874-622902
(Nearest Mass Centre for Sennybridge Brecon Beacons, National Park Mountain Centre, Llangorse and Talybont-on-Usk).

■ BRITON FERRY, Neath Port Talbot County Borough [A]
† Our Lady of the Assumption (1958)
Neath Road, Briton Ferry, Neath Port Talbot County Borough SA11 2YR
E-mail: neath@rosmini.org
Website: www.catholicneath .co.uk
Served from Neath.
M: *Sun 9.30am. Hds 7pm.*

■ BUILTH WELLS, Powys [A]
† Christ the King (1953)
Garth Road. Served from Llandrindod Wells.
M: *Sun 9am. Hds 10am.*

■ BURRY PORT, Carmarthenshire
† Our Lady Star of the Sea (1918; 1964)
Pencoed Road, Burry Port, Carmarthenshire SA16 0PN **Tel:** 01554-832520
Fax: 01554-833339
Rev Thomas Kochalumchuvattil MSFS
M: *Sat 1st M of Sun 6.30pm. Sun 9.30am. Hds 7pm.*

■ CALDEY ISLAND, off Tenby
1. Abbey of Our Lady and St Samson (1913; cons 23 July 1960)
Caldey Island, off Tenby, SA70 7UH
Tel: 01834-842632 **Fax:** 01834-845942
E-mail: brotherdaniel@tiscali.co.ku
- ***Cistercians of the Strict Observance (OCSO):*** **Rev Daniel Van Santvoort** (*Abbot*); **Rev Robert O'Brien** (*Prior*), **Br Gildas Gage** (*Prior*), **Revv Stephen Peate, Rev Senan Mahony; Bros Paul Cushieri, Dominic Maria Morgan, Gabriel Collins, David Hodges; Teilo Rees, Michael Strode, Br Titus Keet, Br Luca Cestaro** (Sub *Prior*)
  M: *Sun 10.45am. Hds 10.45 (Winter), 9am (Summer).*

2. † St David (6th cent)
Number 2 Cottage, Caldey Island, off Tenby
Tel: 01834-842632
M: *Sun 9.30am. Hds (Winter) 9am.*

■ CARDIGAN, Ceredigion
† Our Lady of the Taper (1904; 1930; 1970)
Welsh National Shrine of Our Lady, North Road, Cardigan, Ceredigion SA43 1LT
Tel: 01239-612615 **Fax:** 01239-612757
E-mail: mair@tapyer.orangehome.co.uk
Rev Jason Jones.
M: *Sun 10.30am, Welsh Mass 1st Sun 5pm. Hds 9.30am, 7pm. Latin Mass Extraordinary Rite as announced*
- ***Irish Ursuline Union:*** 'Ty Mair', 74 North Road, Cardigan SA43 1AA
  Tel: 01239-612436

Shrine Website: www.cardigantaper.org

■ CARMARTHEN, Carmarthenshire

† St Mary's (1851; 1889)
St Mary's Retreat, Union Street, Carmarthen SA31 3DE
Tel/Fax: 01267-237205
- *Parish Priest:* **Fr Morty O'Shea, SOLT**
  Parish Sisters: **Srs Mary Trinity, Mary Immaculate SOLT**

M: *Sat 1st M of Sun 5.30pm. Sun 10.30am. Hds (Vigil 7.30pm), 9.15am.*

■ CLYDACH & PONTARDAWE, Swansea [A]
† St Benedict (1908; 1915)
41 Pontardawe Road, Clydach, Swansea SA6 5NS **Tel:** 01792-842244
E-mail: benedictclydach@aol.com
Website: home.catholicweb.com/stbenedictclydach
Rev Teyrnon Williams.
M: *Sat 1st M of Sun 6pm. Sun 10am. Hds Vigil 7pm, 9.30am.*

■ CRICKHOWELL, Powys
† St Joseph (1934)
Brecon Road, Crickhowell, Powys
Served from Brecon.
M: *See notices for Brecon.*

■ CWMAVON, Neath Port Talbot County Borough
St Philip Evans
Served from Port Talbot (2).
M: *Sun 8.45am. Hds 9am.*
- ***Ursulines of Jesus,*** 45 Salem Road, Cwmavon, Port Talbot SA12 9EL
  Tel: 01639-888302

■ CYMER, nr Port Talbot
St Joseph Served from Our Lady of Margam.
M: *Sun 8.45am. Hds 5.30pm.*

■ FISHGUARD, Pembrokeshire
† The Holy Name (1900; 1921)
Vergam Terrace, Fishguard, Pembrokeshire SA65 9DF **Tel:** 01348-873865
Rev Mgr Canon Clyde Hughes Johnson
M: *Sat 1st M of Sun 6pm. Sun 11am. Hds 10am, 6.30pm.*
- ***Sisters of Mercy,*** 15 Heol Emrys, Pen-yr-Aber, Fishguard, Pembrokeshire SA65 9EE
  Tel: 01348-872821
  Also: Rose Cottage, 18 Ropeyard Close, Penbank, Fishguard, Pembrokeshire SA65 9BJ **Tel:** 01348-873312.
  Chaplain: **Rev E J Mullins.**
  M: *11.45am Daily*

■ GLYNNEATH, Neath Port Talbot County Borough
St John Kemble (1986)
Llewellyn Street. Served from Neath.
M: *Sun 11.30am. Hds Vigil 6pm.*

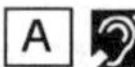

■ **GORSEINON,** Swansea

1. † Blessed Sacrament (1926; 1967)
99 Alexandra Road, Gorseinon, Swansea SA4 4NX **Tel:** 01792-892722
E-mail: blessedsacrament@claret.org.uk
Website: blessedsacrament@claret.org.uk
- ***Claretian Missionaries (CMF)* Rev Michael Fewell** (*Parish Priest*), Claret House, 99 Alexandra Road, Gorseinon, SA4 4NX.
  In residence: **Rev Bernard Guest**.
  M: *Sun 10am, 6pm. Hds (Vigil 7pm), 9.30am.*

3. Penclawdd Community Centre.
Served from Dunvant, Swansea (8).
M: *Sat 1st M of Sun 5.30pm.*

■ **HAVERFORDWEST,** Pembrokeshire

† St David and St Patrick
(1872; cons 29 Oct 1949)
Dew Street, Haverfordwest, Pembrokeshire
Tel: 01437-762284
Rev John Patrick Thomas Priest's House, 9 Fountain Row, SA61 1SX
M: *Sat 1st M of Sun 6.30pm. Sun 10am. Hds (Vigil 7.30pm) 10am.*
- ***Cistercian Sisters,*** Holy Cross Abbey, Whitland, Pembrokeshire SA34 0QX **Tel:** 01994-240725 *Resident Chaplain:* **Rt Rev John Moakler OCSO.**

■ **HAY-ON-WYE,** Hereford

† St Joseph (1929; 1967)
The Presbytery, 4 Belmont Road, Hay-on-Wye, Hereford HR3 5DA
Tel: 01497-820452
Rev Timothy Maloney (IC).
M: *Sun 10am. Hds 10am.*

■ **KIDWELLY,** Carmarthenshire

Our Lady and St Cadoc (1975)
Priory Street. Served from Burry Port.
M: *Sun 11am.*

■ **KNIGHTON,** Powys

† Our Lady of Perpetual Succour and St Nicholas (1975)
Market Square. Served from Presteigne.
M: *Sun 11am; Hds 11am.*

■ **LAMPETER,** Ceredigion

† Our Lady of Mount Carmel (1940)
"Carmel", Pontfaen Road, Lampeter, Ceredigion SA48 7BS **Tel:** 01570-422437
M: *10am. Hds (Vigil 7pm), 10am. Polish Mass, 2nd Sunday of month, 2.30pm (**Rev Edward Sopala, Tel:** 02920-230427); Polska Msza Swieta: W Kazda druga Niezdielé Miésiacá 2.30pm.*

■ **LLANDEILO,** Ammanford

St David (New church opened 7 July 1987)
Carmarthen Road, Llandeilo, Carmarthenshire. Served from Ammanford.
M: *Sun 11am. Hds 6pm.*
- ***Sisters of the Cross and Passion,*** The Lodge, Rhosmaen, Llandeilo SA19 7AS **Tel:** 01558-823791

■ **LLANDOVERY,** Carmarthenshire

† Our Lady (1934; 1935; 1980)
College View, Llandovery, Carmarthenshire SA20 0BD Served from Brecon.
M: *Sat 1st M of Sun 5pm. Hds 7pm.*

■ **LLANDRINDOD WELLS,** Powys

† Our Lady of Ransom and the Holy Souls (1900; 1911; 1971)
The Presbytery, Ithon Road, Llandrindod Wells, Powys LD1 6AS
Tel: 01597-822353 **Fax:** 01597-824380
E-mail: mrflewis@aol.com
Canon Michael Lewis.
M: *Sun 11am. Hds 7pm.*

■ **LLANELLI,** Carmarthenshire

† Our Lady, Queen of Peace (1862; 1938; 1995)
Waun-lan-yr-afon Road, Llanelli, Carmarthenshire SA15 3AA
Tel: 01554-774070
E-mail: olqpllanelli@btinternet.com
- ***Carmelites (OCarm),*** **Revv Michael Manning** (*Prior & Parish Priest*), **Patrick Fitzgerald-Lombard, Bro Anthony O'Donnell.** The Presbytery, Waun-lan-yr-afon Road, Llanelli SA15 3AB
  M: *Sat 1st M of Sun 6pm. Sun 10am, 5.30pm. Hds 10am, 7pm.*
- ***Sisters of Mercy,*** 6 Union Buildings, Llanelli SA15 1JW **Tel:** 01554-752768

■ **LLANGENNITH**

See Gower (1).

■ **MILFORD HAVEN,** Pembrokeshire

† St Francis of Assisi (1903; 1929)
128 Priory Road, Milford Haven, Pembrokeshire SA73 2EE
Tel/Fax: 01646-693371
Email: milfordhavenparish@hotmail.co.uk
Rev Dominic Joseph Kochu Purakkal, OSB.
M: *Sun 11am, 6pm. Hds 9.30am, 7pm.*

■ **NARBERTH,** Pembrokeshire

† Immaculate Conception (1981)
Served from Haverfordwest.
M: *Sun 5pm (Christmas and Easter, 11.30am). Hds 7pm.*

■ **NEATH,** Neath Port Talbot County Borough

† St Joseph (1888; 1934; cons 13 Dec 1962)
Presbytery, Westernmoor, Neath, Neath Port Talbot County Borough SA11 1TP
Tel: 01639-643323
E-mail: neath@rosmini.org
Website: www.catholicneath.co.uk

- ***Rosminians (IC):*** **Revv Eugene Monaghan, William Curran, Eddie Murphy.**
  M: *Sat 1st M of Sun 7pm. Sun 11am. Hds (vigil 7pm), 10.30am.*

■ **NEWCASTLE EMLYN,** Carmarthenshire
† Our Lady Queen of Peace
(1960; 1967; cons 1977)
Served from Cardigan.
M: *Vigil Mass 6.30pm. Hds, (vigil 7pm).*

■ **PEMBROKE,** Pembrokeshire
† St Joseph, Monkton (1978)
Served from Pembroke Dock.
M: *Sat 1st M of Sun 6.30pm. Hds (vigil 7pm).*

■ **PEMBROKE DOCK,** Pembrokeshire
† St Mary (1843; 1846)
Catholic Rectory, Meyrick Street, Pembroke Dock, Pembrokeshire SA72 6AL
Tel: 01646-682079.
E-mail: johnd72@aol.com
Rev Patrick Fitzgerald-Lombard, O Carm.
M: *Sun 11am, 6.30pm. Hds 7pm.*
- ***Sisters of the Sacred Hearts of Jesus and Mary,*** The Convent, 4 Park Street, SA72 6JG **Tel:** 01646-682837

■ **PENPARCAU,** Near Aberystwyth
The Welsh Martyrs (1970)
Pierciefield Lane. Served from Aberystwyth.
M: *Sun 9am.*

■ **PONTARDULAIS,** Swansea
† St Bride (1924; 1994)
4 Cross Street, Pontardulais, Swansea SA4 1LR **Tel:** 01792-882512
Served from Gorseinon.
M: *Sat 1st M of Sun 5.30pm. Sun 8.30am. Hds 7pm.*
- ***Sisters of the Cross and Passion,*** St Bride's House, 4 Cross Street, Pontardulais, Swansea SA4 1LR
  Tel: 01267-221116

■ **PONTYBEREM**
Eglwys y Groes (Holy Cross) (1966; 1991)
Heol y Bryn. Served from Carmarthen.
Tel: 01267-237205
M: *Sun 8.30am. Hds 6.30pm.*

■ **PORT TALBOT,**
Neath Port Talbot County Borough
1. Our Lady of Margam (1973)
Margam Road, Margam, Port Talbot SA13 2HR **Tel:** 01639-883323
E-mail: sylvester.odonnell1@virgin.net
Canon A S O'Donnell. (Priest in residence): **Mgr Provost David Bottrill,** "Maes-Gwyn", 63 Margam Road, Port Talbot. SA13 2HR
M: *Sat 1st M of Sun 6pm. Sun 10am. Hds 9am, 7pm.*

2. † St Joseph (1852; 1931)
Presbytery, Water Street, Port Talbot SA12 6LE **Tel:** 01639-882846
Rev Joseph Cefai.
M: *Sat 1st M of Sun 6pm. Sun 10am, 6.30pm. Hds 10am, 6.30pm.*

3. † St Therese of Lisieux
Southdown Road, Port Talbot SA12 7HL
Tel: 01639-884791 **Rev Paul Brophy.**
M: *Sat 1st M of Sun 5pm. Sun 11am. Hds 9.30am, 7pm.*

■ **PRESTEIGNE,** Powys
Chapel of the Assumption of Our Lady and St Therese
Rev Mark Byrne, SOLT, Ty Mair, Kings Turning Road, Presteigne LD8 2LD
Tel: 01544-262188
M: *Sun 9am. Hds 7pm.*

■ **RHAYADER,** Powys
† St Francis of Assisi (1957)
Served from Presteigne.
M: *Sat 1st M of Sun 6pm. Hds (vigil 7pm).*

■ **ST DAVIDS,** Pembrokeshire
† St Michael
Town Hall Lane. Served from Fishguard.
M: *Sun 9am. Hds Vigil 6pm.*
- ***Sisters of Mercy,*** St Non's Retreat Centre, St Non's, St David's, Pembrokeshire SA62 6BN
  Tel: 01437-720224/720161
  E-mail: stnonsretreat@aol.com
  Website: st.nonsretreat.org.uk
- ***Daughters of Charity of SVP***, 19 Maes-Yr-Hedydd, St David's, Pembrokeshire SA62 6QW **Tel/Fax:** 01437-721808

■ **SAUNDERSFOOT**
St Bride (1966)
The Ridgeway. Served from Tenby.
M: *Sun 9.30am. Hds 9.30am.*

■ **SWANSEA**
1. (See start of Parish List)

2. † Our Lady of Lourdes (1925; 1968)
136 Penygraig Road, Townhill, Swansea SA1 6LA **Tel/Fax:** 01792-655336
E-mail: ourladyofloudres@hotmail.co.uk
Rev Pius Augustine, M.A ,M.Ph, Holy Cross Church, Upper King's Head Road, Gendros SA5 8BR **Tel:** 01792 586454
Mob: 07796 107241
M: *Sun 11am. Hds 11am.*

3. † Our Lady Star of the Sea (1909; 1916)
9 Promenade Terrace, Mumbles, Swansea SA3 4DS **Tel:** 01792-366305
Rt. Rev. Mgr Brian Kinrade, M.A, VG.
Website: www.geocities.com/catholicchurchmumbles

M: *Sat 1st M of Sun 6.30pm. Sun 8.30am, 10.30am. Hds 9am, 7.30pm.*
- ***Sisters of St Joseph of Annecy,*** 22 Devon Place, Mumbles. **Tel:** 01792-363549

4. † Holy Cross (1954)
Upper Kings Head Road, Gendros, Swansea SA5 8BR **Tel:** 01792-586454
Email: holycrossmenevia@hotmail.co.uk
Website: www.rc.net/uk/menevia/holycross
Rev Cyril Thadathil, M.A, MTh
M: *Sat 1st M of Sun 5.30pm. Sun 10.30am. Hds 9.30am, 7.30pm.*
- ***Sisters of the Cross and Passion:*** 88 Ravenhill Road, Ravenhill, S. Wales SA5 5AN **Tel:** 01792-581277

5. † St Benedict
(1928; 1936; 1961; cons 1975)
Llythrid Avenue, Sketty Road, Swansea SA2 0JJ **Tel:** 01792-298412
Rev Neil Evans.
Tel: 01792-466709
M: *Sat 1st M of Sun 6pm. Sun 8.30am, 11am. (Mass 3rd Sun 1.30pm for Pol). Hds 9.30am, 7.30pm.*
- ***Ursulines of Jesus,*** Stella Maris Convent, Eaton Crescent (Retired sisters), SA1 4QR **Tel:** 01792-473453. Also at: 39 Eaton Crescent SA1 6QL **Tel:** 01792-472243. *Chaplain:* **Canon (Emeritus) Richard Byron**, **Tel:** 01792-369651

6. † St David's Priory (1813; 1847)
St David's Place, Swansea SA1 3NG
Tel: 01792-653343
- ***Benedictines (OSB):***
  M: *Sun 11am, 6pm. Hds 12.30am, 7pm.*
- ***Ursulines of Jesus:*** 115 Walter Road, **Tel:** 01792-473180
- ***Missionaries of Charities:*** 235-6 The Strand, SA1 2AW **Tel:** 01792-463107

7. † St Illtyd (1913; 1927; cons 1977)
St Illtyd's Cres, St Thomas, Swansea SA1 8HS **Tel:** 01792-424107
Rev Pius Augustine, M.A, M.Ph. Holy Cross Church, Upper King's Head Road, Gendros SAS 8BR **Tel:** 01792 586454
Mob: 07796 107241
Parish Sisters*:* **Srs Carmel Reynolds, Lily Kelly SM** Resident at presbytery.
M: *Sat 1st M of Sun 6.30pm. Sun 9.30am. Hds 9.30am.*

8. St Joachim and St Anne (1966)
Llysteg, Dunvant, Swansea SA2 7QQ
Tel: 01792-201046 **Rev Peter Kelly.**
M: *Sun 10.30am, 6.30pm. Hds 7.30am, 10am, 7.30pm.*

9. † St Peter (1927)
Cwm Level Road, Landore, Swansea.
Tel: 01792-771840 **Fax:** 01792-771916
Served from Gendros
M: *Sun 9am. Hds 10.30am.*

10. † The Sacred Heart (1889; 1955) A
School Road, Morriston Swansea SA6 6HZ
Tel: 01792-771053
E-mail: michael@w-burke.freeserve.co.uk
Website: www.home.catholicweb.com/ sacredheartmorriston
Rev Michael Burke.
M: *Sun 8.45am, 10.30am, 6.30pm (March-Oct); 9.30am, 11am, 6.30pm (Oct-March). Hds 9.30am, 7.30pm.*

11. University Chaplaincy
Chaplain: **Rev Neil Evans**
M: *At University College (During term time). Friday M 1.30pm.*

■ **TENBY,** Pembrokeshire A
† Holyrood and St Teilo (1888; 1893)
St Florence Parade, Tenby, Pembrokeshire SA70 7DT
Tel: 01834-842692 **Fax:** 01834-849147
Website: www.saint-teilos-tenby.co.uk
Rev Owen Mc Greal.
M: *Sat 1st M of Sun 5.30pm. Sun 11am. Hds (vigil 7pm), 11am,.*

■ **WHITLAND**
Holy Cross Abbey
Velfry Road, Whitland, Carmarthenshire SA34 0QX **Tel/Fax:** 01994-240725
Rt Rev Dom John Moakler OCSO.
M: *Sun 9am.*

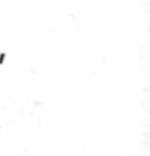

■ **YSTRADGYNLAIS,** Swansea
† Sacred Heart (1910; 1939)
Catholic Church, Pantyffynon Road, Ystradgynlais, Swansea SA9 1EU
Tel: 01639-842202
E-mail: selva.raj@mailcitycom
Rev Selva Raj Mallavarappu SDS.
M: *Sat 1st M of Sun 6pm. Sun 10.30am. Hds 10.30am, 7pm.*

■ **ORDERS OR CONGREGATIONS, ETC**

■ **Men**
Benedictines: Milford Haven, Swansea (4, 6)
Carmelites: Llanelli, Pembroke Dock.
Cistercians: Caldey Island, Whitland.
Claretian Missionaries: Gorseinon.
Rosminians: Hay-on-Wye, Neath.
Missionaries of St Francis de Sales: Burry Port.
Missionaries of the Sacred Heart of Jesus and Mary: Swansea
Society of Our Lady of the Most Holy Trinity: Carmarthen, Presteigne.
Salvatorians: Ystradgynlais.

■ **Women**
Cistercians: Whitland.

Cross and Passion, Sisters of the: Pontarddulais, Llandeilo, Swansea (4).
Daughters of Charity of S.V.P: St David's.
Holy Spirit, Daughters of the: Aberystwyth.
Mercy, Sisters of: Fishguard, St Davids (1), Llanelli (1).
Missionaries of Charity: Swansea.
Sacred Heart, Society of the: Brecon.
Sacred Hearts of Jesus and Mary, Sisters of the: Pembroke Dock.
St Joseph of Annecy, Sisters of: Swansea (3).
Society of Our Lady of the Most Holy Trinity: Carmarthen.
Ursulines (Union of Irish Ursulines): Brecon, Cardigan
Ursulines of Jesus: Swansea (1,5,6), Cwmavon.

■ DIOCESAN INSTITUTIONS, SOCIETIES ETC

For Societies and Organisations without representation in the diocese please see the main Societies and Organisations section.

Apostleship of the Sea. *Port Chaplains*: The Parish Priest. St Francis Presbytery, 128 Priory Road, Milford Haven, Dyfed SA73 2EE **Tel:** 016462-3371 **Rev Teyrnon Williams**, 41 Pontardawe Road, Clydach, Swansea SA6 5NS **Tel:** 01792-842244

Catholic Deaf Service. *Director:* **Sr Mary Chisholm DC**. *Chaplin:* **Fr Tony Hodges** Welsh Deaf Association: 200 Grand Avenue, Ely, Cardiff CF5 4HX. **Tel/Fax:** 02920-679594 **Email:** dcself@talktalk.net

Archconfraternity of St Stephen for Altar Servers. *Spiritual Director:* **Fr Jason Jones STB,** The Presbytery, North Road, Cardigan SA43 1LT **Tel:** 01239-612615

Association for the Propagation of the Faith. Menevia. *Diocesan Director:* **Rev Paul Watson,** The Presbytery, Queen's Road, Aberystwyth SY23 2HS **Tel:** 01970-612549

Association of Our Lady of Mount Carmel. *Diocesan Representative*: Awaiting appointment

Association of Separated and Divorced Catholics, Menevia. *Contact:* **Mrs Bernadette Harris**. 12 Golf Road, Port Talbot, West Glamorgan SA12 6RH *Chaplain:* **Mgr Canon Brian Kinrade**. **Tel:** 01597-822353

CAFOD The Catholic Fund for Overseas Development – *Wales and Hereford National Office:* 11 Richmond Road, Cardiff CF24 3AQ **E-mail:** southwales@cafod.org.uk

Catenian Association. The Association of Catholic Professional and Business Men – *Secretary:* **P Maunder**, 222 Albany Road, Cardiff CF24 3RZ *Swansea Circle Secretary:* **M E O'Rouke**, 21 Glanyrafon Rd, Sketty SA2 9JE

Catholic Charismatic Renewal in Wales. is served by a National Service Committee with members drawn from the three dioceses in Wales. Its main activity is the planning of an annual Wales National Conference held in August. Members are also available to organise retreats, healing services, seminars and days of prayer. *Chairperson:* **Mrs Fran Graham, Tel:** 01792 535987 *Secretary:* **Mrs Penny Cavill, Tel:** 01291 621342

Catholic Charismatic Renewal in Menevia. A group meets on the first Saturday of each month at the Diocesan Pastoral Centre in Carmarthen. Members organise days of renewal and seminars. For further information *Contact:* **Fran Graham, Tel:** 01792-535987

Catholic Women's League. A National Non-Political Organisation for the Promotion of Religious and Intellectual Interests and for the Formation and Collective Expression of Catholic Public Opinion. Section in the Parish of Our Lady, Briton Ferry.

Civil Service Catholic Guild: Swansea Branch. *Secretary*: **Mrs J Burridge**. 1 Mount Pleasant, Felindre, Swansea. **Tel:** 01792-75598

Faith and Light. An international Christian Association of people with a learning disability, their families and friends. *National Co-ordinator Wales:* **Mrs Angela Glover**, 20 Ravenhill Rd Fforestfach, Swansea **Tel:** 01792 581331

Grail, The. *For information.* The President, The Grail Centre, 125 Waxwell Lane, Pinner, Middx HA5 3ER or **E-mail:** waxwell@compuserve.com *Diocesan Representative:* **Bob and Cess Hughes**, Fernhill, 24 Chapel Street, Mumbles, Swansea SA3 4NH **Tel:** 01792-363875

Handicapped Children's Pilgrimage Trust. (Welsh Region). *Chairman*: **Mr Roger Thomas,** 18 Main Avenue, Peterston-Super-Ely, Cardiff.

Knights of St Columba. *Prov Secretary*: **Mr Peter Sims-Coomer,** 14 Llangorse Road, Cyncoed, Cardiff CF23 6PF **Tel:** 029-2075 1285

Latin Mass Society. For the preservation and frequent use of the Tridentine Rite. All Masses celebrated in the Extraordinary Rite are in accordance with the Missale Romanum (1926)

under the Motu Proprio "Summorum Pontificum" of Pope Benedict XVI July 2007. Local representative for Menevia is **Mr S Mazzeo, Tel:** 07816 771877.

Legion of Mary. Enquiries; Consult local Parish Priest. *Diocesan Contact:* **Mrs P O'Connell.** 63 Dan-y-Graig Road, Neath. **Tel:** 01639-760498

Marriage Care. *Swansea Centre:* c/o 63 Margam Road, Port Talbot S12 2HR **Tel:** 0845 3801

National Network of Pastoral Musicians. The NNPM is a network of people active in liturgy and music who wish to be in touch with others doing similar things. For further information contact *Area Secretary:* **Jennifer Burridge.** 1 Mount Pleasant, Felindre, Swansea SA5 7PH **Tel:** 01792-775598 **E-mail:** jennifer.burridge@ssg.org.uk **Website:** www.nnpm.org.uk

Secular Franciscan Order. Saint Francis of Assisi left us *'a Dream to dream and a Journey to challenge everyone'. All* Franciscans are inspired by him to follow Christ. The Secular Franciscan Order belongs to this family. Your contact for further information is: *Diocesan Contact:* **A Bradley**. 3 Western Avenue, Port Talbot, West Glamorgan, SA12 7LS **Tel:** 01639-883855.

Our Lady's Catechists. *Contact:* **Mrs Teresa Plunkett**, 53 Owls Lodge Lane, Mayals, Swansea SA3 5DP **Tel:** 01792-403266 **E-mail:** g.plunkett888@btinternet.com

Society of St Gregory, The. The national Society which works to assist priests and people to celebrate the liturgy worthily. *Contact:* **Jennifer Burridge**. 1 Mount Pleasant, Felindre, Swansea SA5 7PH **Tel:** 01792-775598 **E-mail:** jennifer.burridge@ssg.org.uk

St David's Children Society (formerly Catholic Children's and Family Care Society – Wales). *Administrator:* **Mr Gerry Cooney**, Bishop Brown House, Durham Street, Grangetown, Cardiff CF1 7PD **Tel:** 029-2066 7007

St Vincent de Paul Society. Menevia Central Council. *President*: **Peter Royds,** 10 Llewellyn Street, Glynneath, Neath SA11 5AE **Tel:** 01639-720793

Union of Catholic Mothers (Wales). Menevia Diocesan Branch. *President*: **Mrs Rose Maunder**, 5 Lee Street, St Thomas, Swansea **Tel:** 01792-642470 *Secretary:* **Awaiting appointment,** *Treasurer:* **Mrs Carole Chichester**. 1 Hawthorns, 20 Grove Hill, Pembroke **Tel:** 01646 680436 *Chaplain:* **Rev Paul Watson**, The Presbytery, Queen's Road, Aberystwyth SY23 2HS **Tel:** 01970-612549

Teams of Our Lady. An international Catholic Movement for Christian married couples that aims to deepen the couples' spirituality. A 'Team' consists of four or five couples and a priest or religious as spiritual advisor meeting monthly to share the journey of faith, guided by the Holy Spirit. *Contact couple:* **John and Dolores Hoskins. Tel:** 01554-758091 **E-mail:** doloreshoskins@lineone.net

University Catholic Chaplaincy. *Chaplain* (non-resident): **Rev Neil Evans** c/o St Benedicts, Llythrid Ave, Swansea SA2 0JJ **Tel:** 01792-298412

Y Cylch Catholig. Aim: To help Welsh speaking Catholics to live a full spiritual life through the medium of their own language, by offering opportunities for worship in Welsh, and by promoting the work of providing books and essential resources to this end. *Secretary:* **Sue Roberts**. Delfryn, Yr Ala, Pwllheli, Gwynedd. **Tel:** 01758-614977

Young Christian Workers & Impact. For young people aged between 13-30. *Headquarters:* St Joseph's, off St Joseph's Grove, London NW4 4TY **Tel:** 0208 203 6290 **E-mail:** info@ycwimpact.com **Website:** www.ycwimpact.com

■ HOSPITALS

To contact the Catholic Chaplain of a particular hospital we suggest you contact the hospital reception directly.

■ CATHOLIC SCHOOLS - MAINTAINED

■ CARMARTHENSHIRE

▲ Aided Secondary Schools

St John Lloyd Havard Road, Llanelli. **Tel:** 01554-772 589 *(Llanelli)* **E-mail:** office@stlloydscarms.sch.uk

▲ Aided Primary Schools

St Mary's Union Street, Carmarthen. **Tel:** 01267-234297 *(Carmarthen)* **E-mail:** staff.stmarysc@ysgolccc.org.uk

St Mary's Havard Road, Llanelli. **Tel:** 01554-759178 *(Llanelli)* **E-mail:** atmin.stmarysc@ysgolccc.org.uk

■ CEREDIGION

▲ Aided Primary Schools

St Padarn's Llanbadarn Road, Aberystwyth SY23 1EZ **Tel:** 01970-630632 **E-mail:** prif@stpadarnsrcp.ceredigion.sch.uk *(Aberystwyth)*

■ PEMBROKESHIRE

▲ Aided Primary Schools

Holy Name Vergam Terrace, Fishguard. **Tel:** 01348-872506 **E-mail:** head.holyname@pembrokeshire.gov.uk *(Fishguard)*

Mary Immaculate Merlin's Hill, Haverfordwest. **Tel:** 01437-762324 **E-mail:** head.maryimmaculate@pembrokeshire.gov.uk *(Haverfordwest)*

St Francis' Priory Road, Milford Haven. **Tel:** 01646-694830 **E-mail:** stfrancis@pembrokeshire.gov.uk *(Milford Haven)*

St Mary's Britannia Road, Pembroke Dock. **Tel:** 01646-682879 *(Pembroke Dock)*

St Teilo Greenhill, Tenby. **Tel:** 01834-843995 **E-mail:** head.sttelios@pembrokeshire.gov.uk *(Tenby)*

■ POWYS

▲ Aided Primary Schools

St Joseph's Silver Street, Brecon. **Tel:** 01874-624488 *(Brecon)* **E-mail:** office@st-josephs.powys.sch.uk

■ SWANSEA

▲ Aided Infant Schools

St Joseph's Caepistyll Street, Swansea SA1 2BE **Tel:** 01792-653609 **E-mail:** stjosephs.infants@swansea-edunet.gov.uk

▲ Aided Primary Schools

St Joseph's Caepistyll Street, Swansea SA1 2BE **Tel:** 01792-653609 **E-mail:** st.josephs.rcjuniorschool@swansea-edunet.gov.uk

St David's West Cross Avenue, West Cross, Swansea. **Tel:** 01792-512212 *(Swansea 6)* **E-mail:** st.davids.primaryschool@swansea-edunet.gov.uk

St Illtyd's Jersey Road, Bonymaen, Swansea SA1 8HR **Tel:** 01792-462104 **E-mail:** st.illtyds.school@swansea-edunet.gov.uk *(Swansea 7)*

St Joseph's Clydach, Swansea SA6 5NX **Tel:** 01792-842494 **E-mail:** St.joseph.RCPrimary.School@swansea-edunetgov.uk *(Clydach)*

▲ Aided Secondary Schools

Bishop Vaughan Catholic Comprehensive School Mynydd Garnlwyd Road, Morriston, Swansea SA6 7QC **Tel:** 01792-772006 **E-mail:** bishop.vaughan.school@swansea-edunet.gov.uk *(Swansea)*

■ NEATH PORT TALBOT County Borough

▲ Aided Secondary Schools

St Joseph's RC Comprehensive School Newton Avenue, Aberavon, Port Talbot SA12 6EY **Tel:** 01639-884305 **E-mail:** m.a.callus@neath-porttalbot.gov.uk

▲ Aided Infants Schools

St Joseph's Water Street, Port Talbot SA12 6LE **Tel:** 01639-882579 **E-mail:** stjosephs.inf@neath-porttalbot.gov.uk

▲ Aided Junior Schools

St Joseph's Nobel Avenue, Aberavon, Port Talbot SA12 6YN **Tel:** 01639-769743 **E-mail:** stjosephs.jnr@neath-porttalbot.gov.uk

St Therese's Southdown Road, Sandfields Port, Talbot SA12 7HL **Tel:** 01639-882797 **E-mail:** stthereses.pri@npt.gov.uk *(Port Talbot)*

St Joseph's Cook Rees Avenue, Neath SA11 1BW. **Tel:** 01639-635099. **E-mail:** stjosephs.pri@npt.gov.uk *(Neath)*

DIOCESE OF MIDDLESBROUGH

(Province of Liverpool)
Consists of Boroughs of Middlesbrough, Redcar and Cleveland, Stockton on Tees (South of the River Tees), cities of Kingston upon Hull and York, East Yorkshire and most of North Yorkshire

Patrons of the Diocese
Our Lady of Perpetual Help, 27th June. St Wilfrid, 12th October. St John of Beverley, 7th May.

Rt Rev Terence Drainey, Bishop of Middlesbrough.

Bishop
Rt Rev Terence Patrick Drainey STB, born Manchester, 1st August 1949; ordained priest 12th July 1975; ordained Bishop of Middlesbrough 25th January 2008.

Residence:
16 Cambridge Road, Middlesbrough TS5 5NN
Tel: 01642-818253
Email: bishop@dioceseofmiddlesbrough.co.uk

Bishop's Secretary:
Mrs Judy Coates Tel: 01642 850505
E-mail: bishopsecretary@dioceseofmiddlesbrough.co.uk

Bishop Emeritus
Rt Rev John Crowley, Our Lady of Lourdes, 51 Cambridge Park, Wanstead, London E11 2PR

■ **ADMINISTRATION**

■ **Diocesan Curia**
50a The Avenue, Linthorpe, Middlesbrough TS5 6QT
Tel: 01642-850505 **Fax:** 01642-851404
E-mail: reception@dioceseofmiddlesbrough.co.uk
Website: www.middlesbrough-diocese.org.uk

■ **Vicar General**
Rt Rev Mgr Canon Gerard Dasey, St Bede, 17 Mount Pleasant Avenue, Marske-by-the-Sea, Redcar TS11 7BW
Tel: 01642-485722 **Fax:** 01642-481362
E-mail: vicargeneral@dioceseofmiddlesbrough.co.uk

■ **Episcopal Vicars**
Canon Michael Loughlin *(South)*, **Canon Jerry Twomey** *(Central)*, **Rev John Paul Leonard** *(North)*.

■ **Episcopal Vicar for Religious**
V Rev Adrian Convery OSB, MA.
Ampleforth Abbey, York YO62 4EN
Tel: 01439-766774

■ **Bishop's Council**
Rt Rev Terence Patrick Drainey, Mgr Canon Gerard Dasey VG, Canons Michael Loughlin EV, Jerry Twomey EV, Revv John Paul Leonard EV, Derek Turnham *(Secretary)*.

■ **Chancellery**
Chancellor: **V Rev Canon Alan Sheridan JCL, BA.**
E-mail: chancellor.jv@dioceseofmiddlesbrough.co.uk

■ **The Diocesan Schools' Service**
Director of Schools: Vacancy.
Religious Education Adviser: Vacancy.
Education Administrator: **Mrs Jackie Green.**

■ **Bishop's Advisor on Prisons**
Rev Patrick Cope. HMYOI Deerbolt, Bowes Road, Barnard Castle, Co Durham DL12 9BG
Tel: 01833-633326 **Mbl:** 07860 108431
E-mail: patrick.cope01@hmps.gsi.gov.uk

■ **Diocesan Tribunal**
Judicial Vicar: **V Rev Canon Alan Sheridan JCL, BA.**
E-mail: chancellor.jv@dioceseofmiddlesbrough.co.uk
Tribunal Administrator:
Mrs Maureen Raine.
E-mail: tribsec@dioceseofmiddlesbrough.co.uk

■ **Diocesan Finance & Property Department**
Financial Secretary: **Dr Jim Whiston KSG, OBE, BSc, PhD, CChem, FRSC.**
E-mail: financialsecretary@dioceseofmiddlesbrough.co.uk/jim.whiston@btinternet.com
Secretary: **Mrs Pat Wilson.**
E-mail: sectofinancialsecretary@dioceseofmiddlesbrough.co.uk
Finance Manager: **Mr Anthony McKenna** (am only); *Finance Assistants:* **Mr Daniel Woodgate, Miss Francesca Rossi.**
E-mail: finance@dioceseofmiddlesbrough.co.uk
Buildings Manager: **Miss Sharon Westcough.**
E-mail: propertymanager@dioceseofmiddlesbrough.co.uk
Gift Aid & Legacy Promotions Officer: **Mr Martin Russell. E-mail:** giftaid.legacy@dioceseofmiddlesbrough.co.uk

■ **Diocesan Trustee**
The Middlesbrough Diocesan Trust is a registered charity, administered by the Diocese of Middlesbrough Trustee, a private company. Offices: 50a The Avenue, Linthorpe, Middlesbrough TS5 6QT
The Directors of the Company are:
Rt Rev TP Drainey, Rt Mgr Canon G Dasey, Mgr Canon R Morgan, Canon M Ryan, Mr P Fulton, Mrs M V Walmsley, Mr J N Hinman, Mr A R I Iveson, Sr A M Conway RSM, Mgr Canon G Dasey, Dr J Whiston (*Director & Secretary*).

■ **Council of Priests**
President: **Rt Rev Terence Patrick Drainey**
Chairman: **V Rev John Loughlin VF.**
Secretary: **Mgr David Hogan JCL, KCHS.**
Mgr Canon Gerard Dasey VG; Rev John Paul Leonard EV (North); **Canon Jerry Twomey** (Central); **Canon Michael Loughlin EV** (South); **V Rev Adrian Convery OSB, MA EV Religious; Canon Alan Sheridan JCL, BA; Rev Derek Turnham.**
Six members elected by diocesan clergy: Northern Vicariate: **Mgr David Hogan JCL KCHS, Rev P Cope.** Central Vicariate: **Rev Kevin Trehy, V Rev John Loughlin.** Southern Vicariate: **Revv David Hynes, William Massie.**

■ **Ecumenical Officer**
Rev T J Bywater, SS Leonard & Mary, The Presbytery, Church Hill, Malton YO17 7EJ

■ **Bishop's Council for Evangelisation and Adult Formation**
Chair: **Mr Roger Iveson**; *Director of Adult Formation:* **Rev John Lumley MTh, BA, BD, PGCE;** *Adult Formation Adviser:* **Mrs Jane Cook LLB(Hons), BA(Hons) Theology (Dunelm).**
Council Members: **Mrs Caroline Dollard, Mr Kit Dollard, Canon Edmund Gubbins, Rev Michael Keogh, Mr Mike McCann, Miss Fian Moffat, Rev James O'Brien, Rev Gerard Robinson MBA, MTh, MALit, Sr Catherine Ryan RSM.**

■ **Bishop's Council for Social Concern**
President: **Rt Rev Terence Patrick Drainey;** *Chair:* **Rev John Steel** (Catholic Child Care); *Secretary:* **c/o Rev John Steel;** *Members:* **Rev John Paul Leonard** (Youth), Vacancy (Homeless), **Rev Patrick Cope** (Prison Service), **Mrs Jan O'Neill** (Educational Psychologist), **Mrs Jane Cook** (Adult Formation),
Mrs Bernadette Smallwood (Deaf/Hearing Impaired). Contact through **Jenny Dowson,** Curial Offices. **Tel:** 01642-850505
E-mail: socialconcern@dioceseofmiddlesbrough.co.uk

■ **Retired Priests' Welfare Committee**
Chairman: **Mgr Canon G Dasey;**
Secretary: **Dr J Whiston; Mgr D C Hogan JCL, KCHS; Canon M Davern, Miss K Crossen, Revv C Larwood, M Sellers, D Turnham.**

■ **Historic Churches Committee**
Chairman & Convenor: **Mgr D C Hogan JCL, KCHS, Mrs P Brown MCD, BArch, FRIBA, MRTPI(retired); Mgr Canon G Dasey VG; Mr M Desmond BA(Hons), DipArch, RIBA; Dr Diane Green BA Hons DPhil (Oxon), Dr J M Hargreaves MBE, DUniv(York), DipTP, MRTPI(retired); Mr K Knight BA(Hons), DipArch(Sheffield), MA(York), APMP, IHBC, RIBA; Rev B Leach OSB, ARICS; Rev R Lovatt; Mr J V Taylor MA; Rev D Turnham; Miss S Westcough BEng(Hons), ICIOB; Miss S Weston GRSM(Lond), LRAM, ARCO; Dr J Whiston KSG, OBE, BSc, PhD, CChem, FRSC; Miss J Dowson** (*Secretary*). **Tel:** 01642-850505
E-mail: hcc@dioceseofmiddlesbrough.co.uk

■ **Diocesan Women's Commission**
Chairperson: **Christine Clarke,** 5 Arras Drive, Cottingham East Yorks HU16 5LE
Tel: 01482-844128 Contacts:
Middlesbrough: **Catherine Rowland**
Tel: 01642-813522; York: **Pamela Ellis**
Tel: 01904-793391; Scarborough & Coast: **Christine Clarke Tel:** 01482 844128;
Whitby & Eskdale: **Alison Pattinson**
Tel: 01287-660298; Hull: **Sr Anna Hawke**
Tel: 01482-374396; Richmond & Dales: **Christine Clarke Tel:** 01482-844128

■ **Diocesan Archives**
Held at Curial Offices, 50a The Avenue, Linthorpe, Middlesbrough TS5 6QT All enquiries in writing to: **Mr D Smallwood**

(*Diocesan Archivist*). **E-mail:** archives@dioceseofmiddlesbrough.co.uk

■ **Diocesan Youth Service: "Life to the Full"**
Youth Office, Curial Offices, 50a The Avenue, Linthorpe, Middlesbrough TS5 6QT **E-mails:** youthmanager@dioceseofmiddlesbrough.co.uk youthoffice@dioceseofmiddlesbrough.co.uk **Website:** www.middlesbrough-diocese.org.uk/youthservice
Line Manager: **Dr Jim Whiston**; *Diocesan Youth Officer:* **Rev John Paul Leonard**, St Clare of Assisi, 102 Low Lane, Brookfield, Middlesbrough TS5 8EB **Tel/Fax:** 01642-593686 **Mbl:** 07809 110518 *Youth Manager:* **Miss Fiona Moffat** *Youth Worker:* Vacancy *School Chaplaincy Co-ordinator:* **Rev John Paul Leonard**.

■ **Diocesan Justice & Peace Commission**
Chair: **Barbara Hungin**, 4 Butts Lane, Egglescliffe, Stockton on Tees TS16 9BT **Tel:** 01642-784398 *Secretary:* **Kate Ward**, 2 The Glen, Egglescliffe, Stockton on Tees TS16 9BX **Tel:** 01642-781676 *Treasurer:* **Nan Saeki**, 55 Moorgate, York YO24 4HP *Newsletter Editor:* **Chris Dove**, 22 Blackburn Yard, Whitby YO22 4DS **Tel:** 01947-825043

■ **Liaison for Handicapped**
Rev T O'Neill, St Gabriel, Allendale Road, Ormesby, Middlesbrough TS7 9LF **Tel:** 01642-314501

■ **Chaplains to Higher Education**
University of Hull: **Rev James O'Brien**, Chaplaincy, 115 Cottingham Road, Hull HU5 2DS **Tel:** 01482-343216 University of York: **V Rev Antony Lester**, More House, Heslington, York YO10 5DX **Tel:** 01904-410249 **E-mail:** yorkuniversity@middlesbrough-diocese.org.uk University of Humberside: **Rev James O'Brien**, Chaplaincy, 115 Cottingham Road, Hull HU5 2DS. **Tel:** 01482-343216 Chaplains Office: **Tel:** 01482-440550, Ext. 3291 University of Teesside: **Rev Gerard Robinson**, Sacred Heart Presbytery, 1 Park Road South, Middlesbrough TS5 6LD **Tel:** 01642-850113

■ **National Conference of Priests' Delegates**
V Rev John Loughlin

■ **Pontifical Missions**
Society of St Peter Apostle, APF & Holy Childhood: *Diocesan Director:* **Rev Michael Marsden**, Our Lady of Lourdes, 56 Swanland Road, Hessle HU13 0LY **Tel:** 01482-648802

■ **College of Consultors**
Rt Rev Terence Patrick Drainey, Mgr Canon Gerard Dasey, Canons Michael Loughlin, Jerry Twomey, Rev John Paul Leonard, V Rev Adrian Convery OSB, MA, EV Religious, Canon Alan Sheridan JCL, BA, Mgr David Hogan JCL, KCHS

■ **The Cathedral Chapter**
(Erected 15th February, 1881)
Provost: **Canon William Madden, Mgr Canon Ricardo Morgan, Mgr Canon Gerard Dasey, Canons Gerald Cox, Daniel Spaight, Edmond Gubbins, Michael Ryan, Michael Bayldon, Michael Loughlin, Jerry Twomey, Alan Sheridan.**

■ **Honorary Canons**
Canons J R Charlton, L Collingwood, K Coughlan, M Davern, P Harney.

■ **Ministry to Priests**
Contact: **Canon Edmond Gubbins**.

■ **Safeguarding**
Co-ordinator: **Rev John B Steel**, *Office:* Safeguarding Office, Curial Offices, 50a The Avenue, Linthorpe, Middlesbrough TS5 6QT; **Tel:** 01642-850505 ext237 *Home:* St Mary's House, High Street, Yarm TS15 9AA **Tel:** 01642-781800 **Fax:** 01642-656148 **E-mail:** safeguarding@dioceseofmiddlesbrough.co.uk
Deputy: **Rev Ken Senior**
Secretary: **Miss Jenny Dowson**
Administration Assistant: **Ms Patti Wieczorek**

■ **Bishop's Council for Liturgy**
President: **Rt Rev Terence Patrick Drainey**; *Chairman:* **Rev Gerard Robinson**; *Secretary:* **Mrs Kath Gallagher**.
Council Members: **Rev John Wood, Mgr David Hogan JCL, KCHS, Revv Damian Humphries OSB, MA, BD, John Lumley MTh, BA, BD, PGCE, Stephen Maughan JCL, BA, Mr Kit Dollard, Mrs Caroline Dollard, Mrs Val Goldsack, Mrs Sue Westmacott.**
E-mail: liturgy@dioceseofmiddlesbrough.co.uk

■ **Diocesan Master of Ceremonies**
Rev Gerard Robinson, Sacred Heart Presbytery, 1 Park Road South, Middlesbrough TS5 6LD
Tel: 01642-850113 **Fax:** 01642-852122
E-mail: stpatrickmbro@middlesbrough-diocese.org.uk

■ **Diocesan Vocations Director for Priesthood and Permanent Diaconate**
Rev Gerard Robinson MBA, MTh, MALit, Sacred Heart Presbytery, 1 Park Road South, Middlesbrough TS5 6LD

Tel: 01642-850113 **Fax:** 01642-852122
E-mail: stpatrickmbro@
middlesbrough-diocese.org.uk
Co-ordinator for the Permanent Diaconate:
Rev John Wood

■ **Diocesan Vocations Team**
Revv Gerard Robinson *(Chairman)*, **Bede Leach, John Paul Leonard, Neil McNicholas, John Wood, John Steel, Sr Maria Varley CP, Mrs Sarah Conway, Mr Sean Conway, Mr Andrew Gardner, Mr Gary Norris, Mrs Kathleen Stead, Mr Mick Thorpe, Mrs Kath Gallagher** *(Secretary)*.

■ **Diocesan Communications Team**
The Communications Team, which meets four times each year to co-ordinate all aspects of communication throughout the diocese, is made up of the following people and areas of responsibility:
Diocesan Communications Officers: **Dr Jim Whiston**, Curial Offices, 50a The Avenue, Linthorpe, Middlesbrough TS5 6QT **Tel:** 01642-850505 (evenings **Tel:** 01325-374870).
E-mail: jim.whiston@btinternet.com
Rev Derek Turnham, St Joseph, 1 Tanton Road, Stokesley, Middlesbrough TS9 5HN
Tel: 01642-710239
E-mail: moderatorofthecuria@
dioceseofmiddlesbrough.co.uk
Secretary: **Miss Jenny Dowson**, Administrative Support for Communications.
Catholic Voice: Free Diocesan Newspaper available in every parish on first Sunday of each month
E-mail: catholicvoice@
dioceseofmiddlesbrough.co.uk
Copy to be submitted to Editor at Curial Offices by first Friday of each preceding month. *Editor:* **Mr Brian Dowd**
Catholic Voice Distribution Manager:
Mr Denis Dorgan,
E-mail: d.dorgan@ntlworld.com
Photographer: **Mr Les Clark**
Liaison with Local Radio: **Mr Tom Timpson**, BBC Radio Humberside; **Rev Gerard Robinson**, BBC Radio Tees; **Mrs Veronica Walmsley**, BBC Radio North Yorkshire
Diocesan Website: www.middlesbrough-diocese.org.uk
Webmaster: **Mr Brian Dowd**
Bishop's Secretary: **Mrs Judy Coates**
Year Book Editors: **Dr Jim Whiston and Rev Derek Turnham**. Contact with the Team can be made through either of the Communications Officers or **Miss Jenny Dowson** at the Curial Office or
E-mail: catholicvoice@
dioceseofmiddlesbrough.co.uk

■ **MIDDLESBROUGH**
The Cathedral Church of St Mary
(1986)
Dalby Way, Coulby Newham, Middlesbrough TS8 0TW
Tel: 01642-597750 **Fax:** 01642-576971
Email: stmaryscathedral@
middlesbrough-diocese.org.uk
Website:
www.middlesbroughrccathedral.org
Mgr Canon Ricardo Morgan, Rev Simon Broughton *(Assistant Priest)*. *Deacons:* **Revv L Collings, K Senior**. Cathedral House, Dalby Way, Coulby Newham, Middlesbrough TS8 0TW
M: *Sat 1st M of Sun 6.30pm. Sun 10am, 5pm. Hds 9.30am, 7pm.*

■ **AMPLEFORTH ABBEY**, York

St Laurence's Abbey (1608; 1802; church cons 6 Sept 1961)
York YO62 4EN
Tel: 01439-766000 (Reception)
Tel: 01439-766714 **Fax:** 01439-766724 (Monastery)
E-mail: stlaurencesabbey@
middlesbrough-diocese.org.uk
Website: www.abbey.ampleforth.org.uk
• ***Benedictines (OSB):*** *Abbot:* **Rt Rev Cuthbert Madden, Tel:** 01439-766700 **Fax:** 01439-788132; *Prior:* **V Rev Colin Battell, Tel:** 01439-766712 **Fax:** 01439-788132; *Sub-Prior:* **Rev Bede Leach, Tel:** 01439 766819; *Titular Prior of Durham:* **V Rev Benet Perceval**. *Titular Prior of Chester:* **V Rev Dominic Milroy**. *Titular Prior of Norwich:* **V Rev Henry Wansbrough** *Episcopal Vicar for Religious:* **V Rev Adrian Convery, Tel:** 01439-766774 *Headmaster:* **Rev Gabriel Everitt, Tel:** 01439-766800. *Housemasters:* St John's: **Rev Wulstan Peterburs, Tel:** 01439-766751; St Oswald's: **Rev Chad Boulton, Tel:** 01439-766752; St Bede's: **Rev Oswald McBride, Tel:** 01439-766758.
Other Resident Priests of the Community: **Revv Martin Haigh, Edmund Hatton, Benedict Webb, Justin Caldwell, Aidan Gilman,**

Geoffrey Lynch, Rupert Everest, Mark Butlin, Edward Corbould, Dunstan Adams, Anselm Cramer, Francis Davidson, Gregory Carroll, Alberic Stacpoole, Leo Chamberlain, Bonaventure Knollys, Matthew Burns, Edgar Miller, Francis Dobson, Christopher Gorst, Alexander McCabe, Peter James, Cyprian Smith, Antony Hain, Hugh Lewis-Vivas, Jeremy Sierla, Bernard McInulty, James Callaghan, Kentigern Hagan, Edwin Cook, Kieran Monahan, Sebastian Jobbins, John Fairhurst, Rainer Verborg. Hospitality & Pastoral Office, **Tel:** 01439-766889
Fax: 01439-766755
E-mail: pastoral@ampleforth.org.uk
Secretary: **Mrs Yvonne Wall.**

- **The Grange Retreat & Conference Centre, Tel:** 01439-766874
Procurator: **Mr Peter Bryan**, Ampleforth College, York YO62 4ER
Tel: 01439-766857

■ AMPLEFORTH VILLAGE, North Yorks
Our Lady & St Benedict (1802; 1907)
East End, Ampleforth, York YO62 4DA
Tel: 01439-788596/766472
E-mail: bonaventure@ampleforth.org.uk
Served from Ampleforth Abbey.

- ***Benedictines (OSB)*: Revv Bonaventure Knollys, Rainer Verborg.**
M: *Sat 1st M of Sun 6pm. Sun 10am. Hds 11.15am, 7.30pm.*

■ BEDALE, North Yorks
SS Mary & Joseph (1812; 1878)
Tel: 01969-623141
Served from Leyburn.
M: *Sun 11.15am. Hds 9.15am.*

■ BEVERLEY, East Yorks
St John of Beverley (1846; 1898; cons 1999)
North Bar Without, Beverley.
Tel: 01482-882321 **Fax:** 01482-871833
E-mail: stjohnofbeverley@middlesbrough-diocese.org.uk
Rev Roy Lovatt (*Parish Administrator*).
5 North Bar Without HU17 7AG
M: *Sat 1st M of Sun 6.30pm. Sun 9am, 10.30am. Hds 9.30am, 7pm.*

■ BRIDLINGTON, East Yorks
Our Lady & St Peter (1867; new church 1894; cons 29 June 2005)
Victoria Road, Bridlington.
Tel: 01262-673696
E-mail: ourladyandstpeter@middlesbrough-diocese.org.uk
Website: www.ourladysbrid.co.uk
V Rev David Grant VF. 32 Victoria Road YO15 2AT
Deacon: **Rev Brian Morgan.**
M: *Sat 1st M of Sun 6pm. Sun 8.30am, 10.30am. Hds 9.30am, 7pm.*

- ***Sisters of Mercy,*** St Mary's Convent, High Street YO16 4PU **Tel:** 01262-674550
- ***Canonesses of St Augustine,*** 91 Cardigan Road, YO15 3JU **Tel:** 01262-609116

■ BROTTON
St Anthony of Padua (1905; 1968)
High Street, Brotton. **Tel:** 01287-623619
Served from Saltburn.
M: *Sun 9.45am. Hds 10.15am, 7pm.*

■ CATTERICK, North Yorks
St Bede
Marne Barracks. **Tel:** 01748-872309
Served from Catterick Garrison.
M: *Sun 9am.*

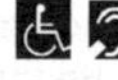

■ CATTERICK GARRISON, N. Yorks
St Joan of Arc
Community Chaplain (RC): **Rev T J Forbes-Turner,** Baden-Powell House, Scotton Road, Catterick Garrison, North Yorkshire DL9 3JS
Tel: 01748-872309 (office)
Tel: 01748-872258 (church)
E-mail: timbo.forbesturner190@mod.uk
Website: www.army.mod.uk/garrisons/catterick_garrison/welfare/church_activities/index.htm *or* www.armychaplains.com
M: *Sun 9am St Bede's, Marne Barracks, Catterick Village. 10.30am, St Joan of Arc, Catterick Garrison.*

■ COTTINGHAM, East Yorks
Holy Cross (1917; 1928)
Carrington Avenue, Cottingham.
Tel: 01482-847763 **Fax:** 01482-845225
E-mail: holycross@middlesbrough-diocese.org.uk
Website: www.holycrosscottingham.org.uk
Rev Patrick Day. 3 Carrington Avenue HU16 4DU
M: *Sat 1st M of Sun 6.30pm. Sun 10am. Hds 7pm.*

■ CRATHORNE, North Yorks
St Mary (1777)
Tel: 01609-883308 **Fax:** 01609-884014
E-mail: stmarycrathorne@middlesbrough-diocese.org.uk
Served from Osmotherley.
M: *Sun 9am. Hds 9.30am.*

■ DORMANSTOWN, Redcar
St William (1939)
Ramsey Road.
Tel: 01642-484047 **Fax:** 01642-492563
Served from Redcar (Sacred Heart).
M: *Sun 9am. Hds 9am.*

■ DRIFFIELD, East Yorks
Our Lady & St Edward (1880; 1886)
Westgate, Driffield YO25 6TD

Tel: 01377-253362
Rev David Hynes.
M: *Sat 1st M of Sun 6.30pm. Sun 10.30am. Hds (vigil 7pm), 8.30am.*

■ **EASINGWOLD,** York
St John the Evangelist (1794; 1830)
St John's Priory, Long Street, Easingwold, York YO61 3JB
Tel: 01347-821295 **Fax:** 01347-823524
E-mail: stjohntheevangelist@ middlesbrough-diocese.org.uk
• ***Benedictines (OSB):***
V Rev Leo Chamberlain, Rev Edwin Cook
M: *Sat 1st M of Sun 6pm. Sun 8.30am, 10.30am. Hds (vigil 7pm), 12noon, 7pm.*

■ **EGTON BRIDGE,** North Yorks
St Hedda (1790; 1867; cons 14 July 1885)
Egton Bridge, Whitby, North Yorkshire.
Tel: 01947-897937
Rev Peter Ryan (Parish Priest), Island Cottage, Lealholm, Whitby, N. Yorkshire YO21 2AQ
M: *Sun 10.30am. Hds as announced.*

■ **FILEY,** North Yorks
St Mary (1904; 1906)
Tel: 01723-513139
Rev Sean O'Donnell. 23 Brooklands, Filey, North Yorkshire YO14 9BA
M: *Sat 1st M of Sun 6pm (Apr-Oct), 4pm (Nov-Mar). Sun 9am (July/Aug only) 10.30am. Hds 10.30am, 6.30pm.*
• ***Sisters of Mercy,*** Endsleigh Convent, South Crescent Road YO15 9JL
Tel: 01723-512058

■ **GILLING EAST,** York
Our Lady & The Holy Angels
Tel: 01439-766873
E-mail: matthew@ampleforth.org.uk
Served from Ampleforth Abbey.
• ***Benedictines (OSB):*** **Rev Matthew Burns**.
M: *Sun 9am. Hds 7.30pm.*
• ***St Martin's, Ampleforth***. Gilling Castle, Gilling East, York YO62 4HP
Tel: 01439-766600 **Fax:** 01439-788538
Mr Nicholas Higham (Headmaster), **Rev John Fairhurst OSB** (Chaplain).
Served from Ampleforth.

■ **GREAT AYTON,** North Yorks
St Margaret Clitherow (2004)
Sunnyfield. **Tel:** 01642-710239
Served from Stokesley.
M: *Sun 10.30am. Hds (vigil 7pm).*

■ **GREEN HAMMERTON,** York
St Joseph
Tel: 01904-791242 **Fax:** 01904-780072
E-mail: stjosephgreenhammerton@ middlesbrough-diocese.org.uk
Website: www.ourladysyork.org.uk
Served from Our Lady, York
M: *Sat 1st M of Sun 5.30pm Hds (vigil 6.30pm).*

■ **GUISBOROUGH**
St Paulinus (1927; 1959)
150 Park Lane, Guisborough TS14 6EP
Tel: 01287-638233 **Fax:** 01287-637173
Canon Michael Bayldon VF, St Paulinus' Presbytery, 13 Grafton Close, Guisborough TS14 7BP
M: *Sat 1st M of Sun 6pm. Sun 8.30am, 10am. Hds 10am.*

■ **HAWES,** North Yorks
St Margaret's CofE Church
Tel: 01969-623141
Served from Leyburn.
M: *Sat 1st M of Sun 6.30pm (from 3rd Sun of May until end of August).*

■ **HEDON**
SS Mary & Joseph (1803)
Baxtergate, Hedon HU12 8JN
Tel: 01482-898338
E-mail: ssmaryandjosephhedon@ middlesbrough-diocese.org.uk
Rev William Ryan.
M: *Sat 1st M of Sun 6pm. Sun 11am. Hds 9.30am, 7pm.*

■ **HELMSLEY,** York
St Mary (1894)
High Street. **Tel:** 01439-766877
Served from Ampleforth Abbey.
Rev Alberic Stacpoole OSB.
M: *Sun 9am. Hds As announced.*

■ **HESSLE**
Our Lady of Lourdes (1928; 1951)
56 Swanland Road, Hessle HU13 0LY
Tel: 01482-648802 **Fax:** 01482-641254
E-mail: ourladyoflourdeshessle@ middlesbrough-diocese.org.uk
V Rev Michael Marsden VF.
Deacon: **Rev Chris Larwood.**
M: *Sun 8.30am, 10.30am, 5.30pm. Hds (vigil 7.30pm), 10am, 7.30pm.*

■ **HOLME-ON-SPALDING-MOOR**
St John The Baptist (1670; 1743; 1766)
Served from Market Weighton.
Tel: 01430-873202
M: *Sun 9am.*

■ **HORNSEA,** (See also Marton)
Sacred Heart (1928; 1956; cons 6 May 1959)
25 Southgate, Hornsea HU18 1RE
Tel: 01964-532918
V Rev Peter Egan VF.
M: *Sat 1st M of Sun 6pm. Sun 9.30am. Hds (vigil 7pm), 9.30am.*

• ***Sisters of Mercy,*** 57 Eastgate, Hornsea HU18 1NB **Tel:** 01964-536473

■ HULL

1. St Charles Borromeo (1779; 1829)
12 Jarratt Street, Hull HU1 3HB
Tel: 01482-329100 **Fax:** 01482-219671
E-mail: stcharlesborromeo@middlesbrough-diocese.org.uk
Canon Michael Loughlin EV, Rev Stephen Maughan JCL (Assistant Priest).
M: *Sat 1st M of Sun 5pm, Sun 10am, 6.30pm. Hds (vigil 6.30pm) 12.10pm.*

2. Holy Name (1933, cons 7 June 1933)
Hall Road, Hull HU6 8AT
Tel: 01482-847763 **Fax:** 01482-845225
E-mail: holynamehull@middlesbrough-diocese.org.uk
Rev Patrick Day *(Parish Administrator)*, 3 Carrington Avenue, Cottingham HU16 4DU
M: *Sun 11am. Hds 9.30am*

3. St Anthony and Our Lady of Mercy (1976)
Beverley Road, Hull.
Tel: 01482-850767 **Fax:** 01482-801253
Email: stanthonyandourladyofmercy@middlesbrough-diocese.org.uk
Rev Norman Jacobson *(Parish Administrator)*, 28 Inglemire Lane, Hull HU6 7TA
Deacon: **Rev Ray Leahy**, 124 Stanbury Road, Haworth Park, Hull HU6 7BX
M: *Sun 9.30am. Hds 7pm. On schooldaysan additional Mass will be arranged.*

4. Our Lady of Lourdes and St Peter Chanel (1925; 1957; cons 1976)
119 Cottingham Road, Hull HU5 2DH
Tel: 01482-342519 (Parish)
E-mail: ourladyoflourdesandstpeterchanel@middlesbrough-diocese.org.uk
Rev John O'Gara SM *(Superior & Parish Priest)*
• ***Marist Fathers (SM):*** 117 Cottingham Road, Hull HU5 2DH **Tel:** 01482-444180 **Fax:** 01482-470811 **Revv Gerard Burns** *(Assistant Priest);* **Michael Coleman Tel:** 01482-446448 **Clive Birch, Tel:** 07985 630463 (residing at St Catherine's, 146 Southcoates Lane, Hull HU9 3AJ).
M: *Sat 1st M of Sun 6.30pm. Sun 8.30am, 10.30am. Hds as arranged*
Also: Newman House, 729 Beverley Road, Hull HU6 7ER **Revv Austin Horsley** *(Bursar)*; **Peter Corcoran** (*Hospital Chaplain),* **Tel:** 01482-440396*;* **Paul Sacco, Robin Duckworth.**
Tel: 01482 856884

5. Sacred Heart
(1926; 1928; 1955; cons 3 May 1961)
Southcoates Lane, Hull HU9 3AS
Tel: 01482-376332
Rev Michael Sellers (*Parish Administrator*). 280 Southcoates Lane, Hull HU9 3AS
M: *9.30am. Hds 7pm.*
• ***Sisters of Mercy,*** behind St Catherine's Home, 146 Southcoates Lane HU9 3AJ **Tel:** 01482-703443

6. St Bede (1952)
94 Staveley Road, Bilton Grange, Hull HU9 4SJ **Tel:** 01482-376332
Rev Michael Sellers.
M: *Sat 1st M of Sun 5.30pm. Sun 11am. Hds 10.30am.*

7. St Francis of Assisi (1973; 1997)
45 Wembley Park Avenue, Hull HU8 0ND
Tel/Fax: 01482-835707
E-mail: stfrancis@middlesbrough-diocese.org.uk
Rev Bill Serplus (*Parish Administrator*). St Mary Queen of Martyrs Presbytery, 200 Nidderdale, Bransholme, Hull HU7 4BS
M: *Sun 9.30am. Hds (vigil 7pm).*

8. St Mary, Queen of Martyrs
Holwell Road, Hull HU7 4BS
Tel/Fax: 01482-835707
E-mail: stmaryqueenofmartyrs@middlesbrough-diocese.org.uk
Rev Bill Serplus (*Parish Administrator*).
M: *Sat 1st M of Sun 6.30pm. Sun 11am. Hds 9.15am.*

9. St Stephen
Annandale Road, Greatfield, Hull
Parish Co-ordinator: **Sr Anna Hawke CJ**
96 Annandale Road, Greatfield, Hull HU9 4LA **Tel:** 01482-374396
E-mail: ststephenhull@middlesbrough-diocese.org.uk
Website: www.ststephen.org.uk
M: *Fri 6pm, Hds as advertised.*
• ***Congregation of Jesus (CJ),*** 96 Annandale Road, Greatfield, Hull HU9 4LA

10. St Vincent de Paul (1896; 1933)
Queen's Road, Hull
Tel: 01482-343017
Rev Michael White. 2 Victoria Avenue, Hull HU5 3DR
M: *Sun 9am, 11am. Hds 9.30am, 7.30pm.*

11. WEST HULL PARISHES
Parishes of St Joseph, Corpus Christi and St Wilfrid.
Rev William Massie, 187 Pickering Road, Hull HU4 6TD **Tel/Fax:** 01482-351012

E-mail: westhullparishes@middlesbrough-diocese.org.uk
Website: www.westhullparishes.co.uk

St Joseph (1926; 1952)
Boothferry Road
M: *Sun 11am. Hds (vigil 7pm).*

Corpus Christi (1932)
Spring Bank West
M: *Sat 1st M of Sun 5pm. Hds 9.30am.*

St Wilfrid's (1896; 1956)
The Boulevard
M: *Sun 9.30am. Hds 11am.*
- ***Daughters of Charity (SVP),*** St Wilfrids, 200 The Boulivard, Hull HU3 3EL

12. St Willibrord (1962)
University Chaplaincy.
Tel: 01482-343216 **Fax:** 01482-494104
E-mail: stwillibrord@middlesbrough-diocese.org.uk
Web: www.hull.ac.uk/cathchap
Chaplain: **Rev James O'Brien**.
115 Cottingham Road, Hull HU5 2DH
M: *Sun 12noon, 6.30pm. Hds 12.30pm, 5.30pm.*

■ **INGLEBY BARWICK,** Stockton on Tees
St Thérèse of Lisieux (1994)
Canon Alan Sheridan (Parish Priest). 9 Holystone Drive, Ingleby Barwick TS17 0PW
Tel/Fax: 01642-750480
E-mail: sttherese@middlesbrough-diocese.org.uk
Deacon: **Rev John B Steel**, St Mary's House, High Street, Yarm TS15 9AA
Tel: 01642-781800 **Fax:** 01642-656148
E-mail: johnsteel@middlesbrough-diocese.org.uk
M: *Sat 1st M of Sun 7pm. Sun 11am in St Thérèse of Lisieux School, Lamb Lane, TS17 0QP* ***Tel:*** *01642-763623*

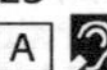

■ **KIRKBYMOORSIDE,** York
St Chad (1858; 1897; cons 15 June 1947)
Piercy End, Kirkbymoorside
Tel: 01751-431468
E-mail: kentigern@ampleforth.org.uk
Served from Ampleforth Abbey.
- ***Benedictines (OSB):*** Pastoral Team: **Revv Kentigern Hagan, Alexander McCabe.**
  M: *Sat 1st M of Sun 6.30pm. Sun 10.30am. Hds 7.30pm.*

■ **LEALHOLM,** Whitby, North Yorks
Our Lady of the Sacred Heart (1932; 1948)
Lealholm Bank, Whitby, North Yorkshire
Tel: 01947-897937
Rev Peter Ryan (*Parish Administrator*). Island Cottage, Lealholm, Whitby, North Yorkshire YO21 2AQ
M: *Sun 9am. Hds 9am.*

■ **LEYBURN,** North Yorks
SS Peter & Paul (1742; 1835)
Richmond Road, Leyburn, North Yorkshire DL8 5DL **Tel:** 01969-623141
Rev Patrick O'Neill.
M: *Sun 9.45am. Hds 10.30am.*

■ **LOFTUS**
SS Joseph & Cuthbert
(1876; 1883; cons 9 June 1949)
39 High Street, Loftus TS13 4HA
Tel: 01287-640278
Rev John McKeever.
M: *Sat 1st M of Sun 6.45pm. Sun 9am. Hds 8am, 7pm.*

■ **MALTON,** North Yorks
SS Leonard & Mary (12th Century, 1972)
Tel/Fax: 01653-692128
E-mail: stleonardandmary@middlesbrough-diocese.org.uk
Rev Timothy Bywater. The Presbytery, Church Hill, Malton YO17 7EJ
M: *Sat 1st M of Sun 6.30pm. Sun 9.30am. Hds (vigil 7pm), 9.30am.*

■ **MARKET WEIGHTON,** York
Our Lady of Perpetual Help (1841; 1905; 1960)
2 Sancton Road, Market Weighton, York YO43 3DB **Tel:** 01430-873202
Canon Gerald Cox.
Deacon: **Rev William Adlington**, 1 Sandfield Close, Market Weighton, York YO43 3ET **Tel:** 01430-873362
M: *Sat 1st M of Sun 6pm. Sun 10.30am. Hds 9.15am (term time only), 7pm.*

■ **MARSKE-BY-THE-SEA,** Redcar
St Bede (1936; 1964)
17 Mount Pleasant Avenue, Marske-by-the-Sea TS11 7BW
Tel: 01642-485722 **Fax:** 01642-481362
Mgr Canon Gerard M Dasey VG (*Parish Priest*)
M: *Sun 8.30am, 10.30am, 6.30pm. Hds 8.30am, 9.30am (school term time), 7pm.*

■ **MARTON,** Skirlaugh
Most Holy Sacrament (1774; 1789)
Tel: 01964-532918 Served from Hornsea.
M: *Sun 11am.*

■ **MIDDLESBROUGH**
1. See start of Parish list

2. Corpus Christi (1949; 1958)
The Greenway, Thorntree, Middlesbrough. Served from Ormesby. **Tel:** 01642-314501
E-mail: corpuschristimbro@middlesbrough-diocese.org.uk
M: *9.30am. Hds 11am.*

3. Holy Name of Mary
(1904; 1938; cons 30 Oct 1957)
The Avenue, Linthorpe, Middlesbrough TS5 6QT **Tel:** 01642-814794
E-mail: holynameofmary@middlesbrough-diocese.org.uk
Website: www.holynameandstthomasmore.org.uk
Rev Paul Farrer (*Parish Administrator*), St Thomas More Presbytery, Kirkham Row, Beechwood, Middlesbrough TS4 3EE
M: *Sat 1st M of Sun 7pm. Sun 10.30am. Hds 9.15am.*

4. St Patrick
(2000; 1932; cons 25 May 1954)
Sacred Heart Church, Linthorpe Road, Middlesbrough.
Tel: 01642-850113 **Fax:** 01642-852122
Tel: 07787 961033 *(Hospital Chaplain)*
E-mail: stpatrickmbro@middlesbrough diocese.org.uk
Website: www.sacredheartandstpatrick.com
Rev Gerard Robinson *(Parish Priest)*, **Rev Paul Dowling** *(Assistant Priest & Hospital Chaplain)*, 1 Park Road South, TS5 6LD
Parish Sister: **Sr Mary Condron FCJ**.
M: *Sun 10am, 6.30pm. Hds 9am, 7pm.*
- ***Redemptorist Community* (CSsR),** The John Paul Centre, 49/55 Grange Road, Middlesbrough TS1 5AU **Tel:** 01642-247831 or 251800 **Fax:** 01642-221003 Community: **Revv Andrew Burns, Barrie O'Toole, Br Michael Duxbury**.
- ***Chaplaincy:*** Teesside University, Middlesbrough.

5. St Alphonsus
(1885; 1960; cons 1 Dec 1960)
95 Westbourne Grove, North Ormesby, Middlesbrough TS3 6EW
Tel: 01642-245043 **Fax:** 01642-240561
V Rev David White VF.
M: Sat 1st M of Sun 6pm. *Sun 10am. Hds (vigil 7pm), 10am (in St Alphonsus School in term time), 7pm.*
- ***Sisters of the Cross and Passion,*** The Presbytery, Chantry Close, Park End, Middlesbrough TS3 7LZ **Tel:** 01642-314305

6. St Clare of Assisi (1967)
102 Low Lane, Brookfield, Middlesbrough TS5 8EB **Tel/Fax:** 01642-593686
Rev John Paul Leonard EV
E-mail: stclares@middlesbrough-diocese.org.uk
Website: www.stclare.org.uk
M: *Sat 1st M of Sun 6pm. Sun 9.30am. Hds (vigil 7pm), 9am.*

7. St Francis of Assisi
(1934; 1935; cons 4 Oct 1952)
5 Levick Crescent, Acklam, Middlesbrough TS5 4RL **Tel:** 01642-818190
E-mail: stfrancismbro@middlesbrough-diocese.org.uk
Rev Peter Keeling.
M: *Sat 1st M of Sun 7pm. Sun 10.30am. Hds 10am, 7pm.*
- ***Faithful Companions of Jesus,*** 4 Thornfield Road, Middlesbrough TS5 5LB **Tel:** 01642-813501

8. St Joseph
(1926; 1934; cons 29 Oct 1958)
Marton Road, Middlesbrough
St Joseph's Presbytery, Park Road South, Middlesbrough TS4 2RB
Tel: 01642-818203
Rev Patrick Keogh.
M: *Sat 1st M of Sun 6.30pm. Sun 10.15am. Hds (vigil 7pm), 10am.*

9. St Thomas More
Beechwood (1962; 1974)
Kirkham Row, Beechwood, Middlesbrough TS4 3EE **Tel/Fax:** 01642-814794
E-mail: stthomasmore@middlesbrough-diocese.org.uk
Website: www.holynameandstthomasmore.org.uk
Rev Paul Farrer STB.
M: *Sat 1st M of Sun 6pm. Sun 9.15am, Hds (vigil 7pm).*
- ***Daughters of Mary & Joseph,*** St Thomas More's Convent, Beechwood TS4 3EE **Tel:** 01642-850167

■ **NORTHALLERTON,** North Yorks 
Sacred Heart (1871; 1934)
41 Thirsk Road, Northallerton, North Yorkshire DL6 1PJ **Tel:** 01609-773323
E-mail: sacredheartnorthallerton@middlesbrough-diocese.org.uk
Website: www.members.aol.com/sacredheartna
Rev James Blenkinsopp *(Parish Administrator).*
M: *Sat 1st M of Sun 6pm. Sun 10am. Hds (vigil 7pm), 9.30am.*

■ **NUNTHORPE,** Middlesbrough 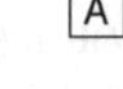
St Bernadette (1963)
Gypsy Lane, Nunthorpe, Middlesbrough TS7 0EB **Tel/Fax:** 01642-316171
E-mail: stbernadette@middlesbrough-diocese.org.uk
Mgr David Hogan VF, JCL, KCHS.
M: *Sat 1st M of Sun 6.30pm. Sun 8.30am, 10.30am. Hds (vigil 7pm), 9.15am, 12noon.*

■ **ORMESBY,** Middlesbrough
St Gabriel (1968; 1975)
Allendale Road, Ormesby, Middlesbrough TS7 9LF **Tel:** 01642-314501
E-mail: stgabriel@middlesbrough-diocese.org.uk
Rev Thomas O'Neill
M: *Sat 1st M of Sun 7pm. Sun 11am. Hds (vigil 7pm), 10am.*

■ **OSMOTHERLEY,** North Yorks
Our Lady of Mount Grace (1655)
The Monastery of Our Lady of Mount Grace, 18 North End, Osmotherley, Northallerton, North Yorkshire DL6 3BB
Tel: 01609-883308 **Fax:** 01609-884014
E-mail: ourladyofmountgrace@middlesbrough-diocese.org.uk
Website: www.ladychapel.org.uk
Benedictines (OSB): **V Rev Dom Damian Humphries** *(Prior).*
M: *Sat 1st M of Sun 3.30pm (at the Lady Chapel). Sun 10.30am. Hds 7.30pm.*

■ **PICKERING,** North Yorks
St Joseph (1904; 1911)
41 Potter Hill, Pickering, North Yorkshire YO18 8AD **Tel:** 01751-472727
E-mail: stjosephpickering@middlesbrough-diocese.org.uk
Website: www.stjopickering.org
V Rev William East VF *(Parish Administrator)*
M: *Sun (Oct-Mar) 8.30am, 11am. (Apr-Sept) 8am, 11am. Hds 10am, 7.30pm.*

■ **POCKLINGTON,** East Yorks
SS Mary & Joseph (1807; 1863)
48 Union Street, Pocklington, York YO42 2JN
Tel: 01759-303126
Rev Francis Gallagher.
M: *Sat 1st M of Sun 6.30pm. Sun 9.30am. Hds 9.30am, 7pm.*

■ **REDCAR**
1. Sacred Heart (1874; 1914; cons 4 June 1948)
7 Lobster Road, Redcar TS10 1SH
Tel: 01642-484047 **Fax:** 01642-492563
Rev Dermot Nunan.
Deacon: **Rev Ken Flanagan.**
M: *Sat 1st M of Sun 6.30pm. Sun 10.30am, Exposition 9.30am-10.30am. Hds (vigil 7pm), 10am.*

2. St Alban (1968; 1972)
3 Yew Tree Avenue, Redcar TS10 4QN
Tel/Fax: 01642-485901
Rev Roger Guiver *(Parish Administrator).*
M: *Sun 9am, 11am. Hds (vigil 7pm), 9am.*

3. St Augustine (1937; 1955)
10 Warwick Road, Redcar TS10 2ER
Tel: 01642-482738.
Rev John Lumley.
M: *Sat 1st M of Sun 6.30pm. Sun 10am. Hds 10am, 7pm.*

■ **RICHMOND,** North Yorks
SS Joseph & Francis Xavier (1784; 1868)
Newbiggin, Richmond, North Yorkshire.
Tel: 01748-822175
Website: www.stjosephsfx.co.uk
Rev Daniel O'Neill. Loyola Lodge, 25 Victoria Road, Richmond DL10 4AS
M: *Sat 1st M of Sun 6.30pm. Sun 9.30am. Hds 9.30am, 7pm.*

■ **SALTBURN**
Our Lady of Lourdes (1928; 1936)
Milton Street, Saltburn-by-Sea TS12 1DE
Tel: 01287-623619
Canon William Madden.
M: *Sat 1st M of Sun 6pm. Sun 11am. Hds (vigil 7pm), 9.30am.*

■ **SCARBOROUGH,** North Yorks
V Rev John Loughlin VF *(Moderator)*
St Peter's Rectory, Castle Road, Scarborough, North Yorkshire YO11 1TH
Tel: 01723-360358
E-mail: scarboroughparishes@middlesbrough-diocese.org.uk
Also in residence: **Rev James Twist**
Rev John Bane *(Co-pastor)*, St Joseph's Presbytery, 1 Greylands Park Grove, Newby, Scarborough YO12 6HY **Tel:** 01723-362632
Also in residence: **Rev Tom O'Connell** (retired), Link Walk, Eastfield, Scarborough YO11 3LR **Tel:** 01723-582205
E-mail: tom.oconnell@btopenworld.com
Incorporating the churches of:

St Joseph (1949; 1960)
Green Lane, Newby
M: *Sun 10am. Hds 10.30am.*

St George (1957; 1965)
Moor Lane, Eastfield, Scarborough YO11 3LW
M: *Sun 8.30am. Hds 9.30am.*
• ***Daughters of Mary & Joseph,*** Moor Lane, Eastfield, YO11 3LW
Tel: 01723-584255

St Peter
(1835; 1858; cons 2 July 1908)
Castle Road, Scarborough.
M: *Sun 11.30am. Hds (Vigil Mass) 7pm.*

St Edward the Confessor
(1913; 1969)
Avenue Victoria.
M: *(Vigil Mass) 6.30pm. Hds 7pm.*

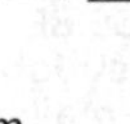

■ **STAITHES,** North Yorks
Our Lady Star of the Sea (1885)
Tel: 01947-840218

Rev Peter Mulholland. 32 Staithes Lane, Staithes, North Yorkshire TS13 5AD
M: *Sun 9.30am. Hds 9.30am.*

■ STOKESLEY
St Joseph (1860; 1873; 1975)
1 Tanton Road, Stokesley TS9 5HN
Tel: 01642-710239
E-mail: stjosephstokesley@middlesbrough-diocese.org.uk
Rev Derek Turnham *(Parish Administrator)*
M: *Sat 1st M Sun 6pm. Sun 9am. Hds 9am.*

■ TEESVILLE, Middlesbrough
Parish of St Andrew's (2002)
Tel: 01642-453556 **Fax:** 01642-455441
Email: standrews@middlesbrough-diocese.org.uk
Website: www.standrewsteesville.org.uk
Incorporating the churches of:

St Andrew's (1962)
Fabian Road, Teesville

St Anne's (1970)
Birchington Avenue, Eston

St Peter's (1874; 1905)
Middlesbrough Road, South Bank

Canon Edmond Gubbins. 1 Bondfield Road, Teesville, Middlesbrough TS6 9BA
Deacon: **Rev Patrick Thomas.**
Parish Sisters: **Srs Maria Varley CP, Cecilia Wilkinson CP.**
Parish Worker: **Mr Joseph Gallagher.**
M: *Sat 1st M of Sun 6.30pm (St Andrew's); 9.30am (St Andrew's); 11am (St Anne's); 12.15pm (St Peter's 2nd & 4th Sun of month). Emergency and Holiday Mass times - St Andrew's, Sat 1st M of Sun 5pm, 11am. Hds 9am (St Peter's); 10.30am (St Anne's); 7pm (St Andrew's).*

■ THIRSK, North Yorks
All Saints (1839; 1867)
5 Castlegate, Thirsk, North Yorkshire YO7 1HL
Tel: 01845-523113 **Fax:** 01845-527323
Rev Colman Ryan.
M: *Sun 8.30am, 10.30am. Hds 9am, 7.15pm.*

■ THORNABY
1. Christ the King (1968)
Trenchard Avenue, Thornaby TS17 0EG
Tel: 01642-659008
Canon Daniel Spaight.
Deacon: **Rev Richard Hall**
M: *Sat 1st M of Sun 7pm. Sun 9.30am. Hds 12noon, 7.30pm.*

2. St Patrick (1872; 1891)
39 Westbury Street, Thornaby TS17 6NW
Tel: 01642-674140
Rev Michael Keogh.
Deacon: **Rev Richard Hall**
M: *Sun 10.30am, 6.30pm. Hds 10am, 7pm.*

■ UGTHORPE, North Yorks
St Anne (1679; 1855; cons 15 May 1955)
Tel: 01947-840218
Rev Peter Mulholland (Parish Administrator). 32 Staithes Lane, Staithes, North Yorkshire TS13 5AD
M: *Sun 11.15am. Hds 7pm.*

■ ULSHAW BRIDGE,
Middleham, North Yorks
SS Simon & Jude (1733; 1788; 1867)
Served from Leyburn. **Tel:** 01969-623141
M: *Sun 8.30am. Hds (Vigil) 6.30pm*

■ WHITBY, North Yorks
St Hilda (1805; 1876; cons 24 Sept 1925)
27 Bagdale, Whitby, North Yorks YO21 1QS
Tel: 01947-602476
Website: www.sthildaswhitby.org.uk
M: *Sat 1st M of Sun 7pm. Sun 10.30am. Hds 9.30am.*
Incorporating the church:

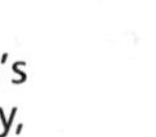

English Martyrs (1950; 1998)
Sleights, Whitby, North Yorks
Served from St Hilda.
M: *Sun 9am. Hds 7pm.*

Rev Neil McNicholas BA. St Hilda's Presbytery, 1 Walker Street, Whitby, YO21 1QT **E-mail:** sthilda@middlesbrough-diocese.org.uk
• ***Sisters of Mercy,*** St Joseph's Convent, West Cliff YO21 3HT **Tel:** 01947-604532

■ WITHERNSEA
SS Peter & John Fisher (1906; 1936)
91 Bannister Street, Withernsea HU19 2DT
Tel: 01964-612204
Rev John Wood.
M: *Sat 1st M of Sun 6.30pm. Sun 9am. Hds 12.30pm, 7pm.*

■ WYCLIFFE, Nr Hutton Magna, Co Durham
St Mary (1743; 1849)
Wycliffe, Barnard Castle, DL12 9TT
Tel/Fax: 01833-627227
E-mail: stmarywycliffe@middlesbrough-diocese.org.uk
Served from Richmond.
M: *Sun 11.30am. Hds (vigil 7pm).*

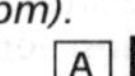

■ YARM
SS Mary & Romuald (1795; 1860; cons 1960)
Canon Alan Sheridan *(Parish Administrator)*, 9 Holystone Drive, Ingleby Barwick, Stockton on Tees TS17 0PW
Tel: 01642-750480

Deacon in Residence: **Rev John B Steel**. St Mary's House, High Street, Yarm TS15 9AA
Tel: 01642-781800 **Fax:** 01642-656148
E-mail: ssmaryandromuald@middlesbrough-diocese.org.uk

M: *Sat 1st M of Sun 5.30pm. Sun 9.30am. Hds as announced in Newsletter.*

■ YORK

1. English Martyrs (1882; 1932; cons 9 July 1940)
Dalton Terrace, York YO24 4DA
Tel: 01904-623783
E-mail: englishmartyrs@middlesbrough-diocese.org.uk
Website: www.englishmartyrsyork.org.uk
Rev Dominique Minskip.
Also in residence: **Rev William Charlton**

M: *Sat 1st M of Sun 6.30pm. Sun 10.30am. Hds 9.30am, 6pm.*

- ***Congregation of Jesus (CJ Community),*** The Bar Convent, 17 Blossom Street, York YO24 1AQ **Tel:** 01904-464917. Accommodation – cafe-museum-gift shop. *Business Manager:* **Miss Jo Dodd**. **Tel:** 01904-643238 **Fax:** 01904-631792 **E-mail:** info@bar-convent.org.uk **Website:** www.bar-convent.org.uk
- ***St Bede's CJ Community:*** 23 Blossom Street, York YO24 1AQ **Tel:** 01904-464950
- ***St Bede's Pastoral Centre:*** 21 Blossom Street, York YO24 1AQ **Tel:** 01904-464900 **E-mail:** admin@stbedes.org.uk **Website:** www.stbedes.org.uk
- ***St Joseph's Infirmary Community (CJ):*** 27 Blossom Street, York YO24 1AQ **Tel:** 01904-658335

2. Our Lady (1955)
Gale Lane, Acomb, York YO24 3AE
Tel: 01904-791242 **Fax:** 01904-780072
E-mail: ourlady@middlesbrough-diocese.org.uk
Website: www.ourladysyork.org.uk
Rev Patrick Smith.

M: *Sun 9.30am, 5pm. Hds 9.15am, 7pm.*

3. St Aelred (1932; 1956)
216 Fifth Avenue, Tang Hall, York YO31 0PN
Tel/Fax: 01904-426446
E-mail: staelred@middlesbrough-diocese.org.uk
Website: www.aelred.com
Canon Jerry Twomey EV

M: *Sat 1st M of Sun 6pm. Sun 9.30am. Hds (Vigil 7.30pm), 9am.*

4. St George
(1849; 1850; cons 1991)
Peel Street, York.
Tel: 01904-623728
E-mail: stgeorgeyork@middlesbrough-diocese.org.uk
Website: www.stgeorgeschurch-york.org.uk
V Rev Patrick Hartnett VF. Rectory, 7 Peel Street, York YO1 9PZ

M: *Sun 10.30am, 6.30pm. Hds 10am, 7.30pm.*

- ***Carmelites, (ODC),*** Carmelite Monastery, Thicket Priory, YO19 6DE **Tel:** 01904-448277
- ***Poor Clare, (Colettines),*** St Joseph's Monastery, Lawrence Street, York YO10 3EB **Tel:** 01904-410936
- ***Sisters of Mercy,*** The Convent, 102 Lawrence Street, York YO10 3EB **Tel:** 01904-414588
- ***Carmelite Friars,*** University Chaplaincy, More House, Heslington, York YO10 5DX **V Rev Antony Lester** *(Prior and University Chaplain),* **Rev Pat O'Keeffe** *(Vocations Co-ordinator and Hospital Chaplain)*, **Tel:** 01904-410446; **Brs Gerard Walsh, Neil Scott.** University Chaplain's Office: **Tel:** 01904-410249. Provincial Office: **Tel:** 01904-410998 **Fax:** 01904 410664 **E-mail:** provincial@carmelite.org **Website:** www.carmelite.org Projects Office: **Tel:** 01904 410521 **E-mail:** projects@carmelite.org
- ***Carmelite Sisters of Corpus Christi (O.Carm),*** 110 Lawrence Street, York YO10 3EB **Tel:** 01904-410900

5. St Joseph (1941; 1942)
Kingsway North, Clifton, York.
Tel/Fax: 01904-622448
E-mail: stjosephyork@middlesbrough-diocese.org.uk
Website: www.stjosephs-york.org.uk
Rev Ross Thompson *(Parish Administrator)*. 169 Burdyke Avenue, Clifton, York YO30 6JX

M: *Sat 1st M of Sun 5.15pm. Sun 9.30am. Hds 9am, 7pm.*

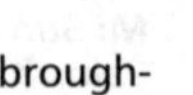

6. St Paulinus (1968)
Monkton Road YO31 9AX
Tel: 01904-768931
E-mail: stpaulinusyork@middlesbrough-diocese.org.uk
Rev Kevin Trehy (Parish Administrator)
3 Holly Tree Lane, Haxby, York YO32 3YJ

M: *Sun 11am. Hds 9.30am.*

7. St Wilfrid
(1742; 1864; cons 14 July 1945)
Duncombe Place, York.
Tel: 01904-624767 **Fax:** 01904-629161
E-mail: stwilfrid@middlesbrough-diocese.org.uk
Website: www.stwilfridsyork.org.uk

Canon Michael Ryan. Rectory, Petergate House, 11 High Petergate YO1 7EN.
M: *Sun (Vigil 6.15pm), 8.30am, 11am. Hds (Vigil 6.30pm), 10am, 12.10pm.*
- ***Shrine of St Margaret Clitherow,*** The Shambles. **Tel:** 01904-624767
M: *Sat 10am*

8. St Margaret Clitherow (1985) A
Holly Tree Lane, Haxby, York YO32 3YJ
Tel: 01904-768931
E-mail: stmargaretclitherowhaxby@middlesbrough-diocese.org.uk
Rev Kevin Trehy.
M: *Sat 1st M of Sun 6pm. Sun 9am. Hds 7pm.*

9. University Chaplaincy
More House, Heslington, York YO10 5DX
V Rev Antony Lester O.Carm *(University Chaplain and Prior)*
Tel: 01904-410249
E-mail: yorkuniversity@middlesbrough-diocese.org.uk
Website: www.york.ac.uk/chap
M: *Sun 11am. Derwent College 056 (during university term). Hds 5.30pm More House (during university term).*

■ RELIGIOUS COMMUNITIES

■ Men
Benedictines: Ampleforth, Osmotherley.
Carmelite O.Carm: York (4).
Redemptorists: Middlesbrough (4).
The Society of Mary (Marist Fathers): Hull (4).

■ Women
Congregation of Our Lady (Canonesses of St Augustine): Beverley, Bridlington.
Carmelites York (4).
Congregation of Jesus (CJ): York (1), Hull (9).
Corpus Christi Carmelites: York (4).
Daughters of Charity (SVP): Hull (11).
Daughters of Mary and Joseph: Middlesbrough (9), Scarborough.
Faithful Companions of Jesus: Middlesbrough (7).
Poor Clare Colettines: York (4).
Sisters of the Cross and Passion: Middlesbrough (5).
Sisters of Mercy: Bridlington, Filey, Hull (5), Hornsea, Whitby, York (4).

■ DIOCESAN INSTITUTIONS AND SOCIETIES

For Societies and Organisations without representation in the diocese please see the main Societies and Organisations section.

Apostleship of the Sea *Diocesan Port Chaplains:* **Rev Michael Sellers, Tel:** 01482 376332 (Hull); Local priests assist on Rota basis (Tees South); *Lay Chaplains:* **Mr Tony McAvoy** (Middlesbrough), **Ms Anne Mclaren** (Hull).

Archconfraternity of St Stephen for Altar Servers *Diocesan Director*: **Rev William Massie,** West Hull Parishes, 187 Pickering Road, Hull HU4 6TD **Tel:** 01482-351012

Association for the Propagation of the Faith *Diocesan Director*: **Rev Michael Marsden,** Our Lady of Lourdes, 56 Swanland Road, Hessle HU13 0LY **Tel:** 01482-648802

The Catholic Agency for Overseas Development *Diocesan Manager:* **Mr David Cross,** CAFOD, Middlesbrough Diocesan Office, 54 Blossom Street, York YO24 1AP **Tel:** 01904-671767 **Fax:** 01904-658054

Catenian Association *Secretary Prov. No. 5:* **I. Oliver**, 5 Long Meadows, Darras Hall, Ponteland, Newcastle-upon-Tyne NE20 9DX **Tel:** 01661-821575 (For Middlesbrough/Redcar/Yarm circles). *Secretary Prov. No. 3N:* **P A Bareham,** 50 Green Park Road, Shircoat Green, Halifax HX3 0SN **Tel:** 01422-350057 **E-mail:** paulbareham@btopenworld.com (For Hull/Scarborough/York circles).

Catholic Child Care – Diocese of Middlesbrough *Administrator:* **Rev John Steel**, Curial Offices, 50a The Avenue, Linthorpe, Middlesbrough TS5 6QT **Tel:** 01642-850505 **Fax:** 01642-851404

Catholic Association of Teachers, Schools & Colleges: *Cleveland*: **Miss R Morris,** 8 Braemar Road, Linthorpe, Middlesbrough TS5 5HU **Tel:** 01642-821579 **E-mail:** ritamorris@hotmail.com

Catholic Women's League *President:* **Mrs Mary Durcan**, 92 Legard Dr, Anlaby, East Yorkshire HU10 7TD **Tel:** 01482-650954

Catholic Women's Luncheon Club *Hon Sec:* **Mrs Margaret Flood,** 'Rosedene', 1 Inglemire Lane, Beverley High Road, Hull HU6 6UH **Tel:** 01482-345353 *Hon Treasurer:* **Miss Susan Goodfellow,** 40 Etherington Drive, Hull HU6 7JU **Tel:** 01482-806769

Council of the Marist Way. The Marist Way is the lay branch of the Marist Family. It brings together people who wish to participate in the life and mission of the Church in the "Spirit of Mary" - a way of living the gospel envisaged by Jean-Claude Colin, founder of the Society of Mary. For

more information, please contact: **Mrs Agnes McGrogan**, 15 Daleston Avenue, Linthorpe, Middlesbrough TS5 5PA
Tel: 01642-817504
E-mail: ammway.mcgrogan@talktalk.net

Knights of St Columba Middlesbrough: **Michael McGeary**, 41 Queens Road, Linthorpe, Middlesbrough TS5 6EF

Legion of Mary *President:* **Mrs Maria Crawford**, 511 Normanby Road, Normanby, Middlesbrough TS6 0DX
Tel: 01642-454781

Marriage Care *Middlesbrough:* 55 Grange Road, Middlesbrough. All enquiries and appointments by arrangement.
Tel: 0191-232 0342
Mon - Fri. 10am to 4.30pm.
E-mail: angela@marriagecare.org.uk

Newman Association Cleveland Circle: *Secretary:* **Mrs Judith Brown**, 12 Orchard Road, Linthorpe, Middlesbrough TS5 5PL **Tel:** 01642-814977

Our Lady's Catechists: *Diocesan Representative*: **Miss Elizabeth Rodgers**, 102 Finkle Street, Cottingham, East Yorkshire HU16 4AZ **Tel:** 01482-849085

Pontifical Society of the Holy Childhood *Treasurer*: **Rev Michael Marsden**, Our Lady of Lourdes, 56 Swanland Road, Hessle HU13 0LY **Tel:** 01482-648802

Postgate Society *Secretary:* **Rev D Minskip**, English Martyrs Presbytery. Dalton Terrace, York YO24 4DA
Tel: 01904-623783
Website:
www.catholic-history.org.uk/postgate.htm

Priests' Training Fund *Diocesan Treasurer*, 50a The Avenue, Linthorpe, Middlesbrough TS5 6QT
Tel: 01642-850505 **Fax:** 01642-851404

Society of St Peter Apostle for Native Clergy *Diocesan Director*: **Rev Michael Marsden**, Our Lady of Lourdes, 56 Swanland Road, Hessle HU13 0LY
Tel: 01482-648802

Survive-Miva *Director:* **Mr S P Foran**.
Tel: 0151-523 3878 **Fax:** 0151-523 3841

Society of St Gregory. *Diocesan Representative:* **Val Goldsack**, 3 Poplars Road, Linthorpe, Middlesbrough TS5 6RL
E-mail: middlesbrough@ssg.org.uk

Society for the Protection of the Unborn Child Tel: 01642-604545
E-mail: eileenbrydon@spuc.org.uk

Society of St Vincent De Paul *Central Council Contact:* **Mr M Walmsley**, 35 Danebury Drive, Acomb, York YO26 5EQ
Tel: 01904-791289

Teams of Our Lady (Equipes Notre-Dame). An international movement for married couples who value Christian married life. Teams usually consist of about five couples plus a chaplain. Each team meets once a month to eat a simple meal and discuss, share and pray together. It is NOT necessary for both partners to be Catholic or churchgoers. *Contact couple:* **Peter and Di Wordsworth**, 61 The Avenue, Linthorpe, Middlesbrough TS5 6QU
Tel: 01642-827993
E-mail: pdwordsworth@yahoo.co.uk

Union of Catholic Mothers *Diocesan Secretary:* **Miss Elizabeth Dunn**, 25 The Leyes, Osbaldwick York YO10 3PR
Tel: 01904-411689

Walsingham Association. *East Yorkshire:* **Mrs B Curtis**, 33 Calder Grove, Longhill Estate, Hull HU8 9NU
Tel: 01482-782477

Yorkshire Brethren Fund Infirm and Retired Clergy Fund *Hon. Secretary*: **Rev Michael Ingwell**. St Edward's Presbytery, 2 Chapel Lane, Clifford LS23 6HU **Tel:** 01937-842318

■ HOSPITALS

To contact the Catholic Chaplain of a particular hospital we suggest you contact the hospital reception directly.

■ CATHOLIC SCHOOLS - MAINTAINED

■ MIDDLESBROUGH & EAST CLEVELAND

▲ Junior and Infants

St Mary's RC Primary Tennyson Avenue, TS6 7AD **Tel:** 01642-455309
Fax: 01642-458078 *(Grangetown)*

St Paulinus Primary The Avenue, TS14 8DN **Tel:** 01287-637978
Fax: 01287-635976 *(Guisborough)*

St Joseph's Primary Rosecroft Lane, Loftus, Saltburn, TS13 4PZ **Tel:** 01287-640613
Fax: 01287-643121 *(Loftus)*

St Bede's Primary Redcar Road, TS11 6AE
Tel: 01642-485217 **Fax:** 01642-490359 *(Marske)*

St Alphonsus' RC Primary Cadogan Street, North Ormesby, TS3 6PX
Tel/Fax: 01642-243400 *(Middlesbrough)*

St Augustine's Primary Gunnergate Lane, Coulby Newham, TS8 0TE
Tel: 01642-599001 **Fax:** 01642-579100 *(Middlesbrough)*

St Bernadette's Primary Cookgate, Nunthorpe, TS7 0PZ
Tel: 01642-310198
Fax: 01642 314801 *(Middlesbrough)*

St Clare's Primary Trimdon Avenue, Acklam, TS5 8RZ **Tel:** 01642-815412
Fax: 01642-815525 *(Middlesbrough)*

Corpus Christi Primary Cargo Fleet Lane, TS3 8NL **Tel:** 01642-211597
Fax: 01642-231916 *(Middlesbrough)*

St Edward's Primary Eastbourne Road, TS5 6QS **Tel:** 01642-819507 **Fax:** 01642-811902 *(Middlesbrough)*
St Gabriel's Primary Allendale Road, Ormesby, TS7 9LF **Tel:** 01642-315538 Fax: 01642-304420 *(Middlesbrough)*
St Gerard's Primary Avalon Court, Hemlington, TS8 9HU **Tel:** 01642-591820 **Fax:** 01642-594069 *(Middlesbrough)*
St Joseph's Primary Marton Road, TS4 2NT **Tel/Fax:** 01642-819252 *(Middlesbrough)*
St Pius X Primary Amersham Road, TS3 7HD **Tel:** 01642-314453 **Fax:** 01642-287287 *(Middlesbrough)*
St Thomas More Primary Erith Grove, TS4 3QH **Tel:** 01642-317350 **Fax:** 01642-300597 *(Middlesbrough)*
Sacred Heart Primary Ayresome Street, TS1 4NP **Tel:** 01642-816083 **Fax:** 01642-645899 *(Middlesbrough)*
St Benedict's Catholic VA Primary Mersey Road, TS10 1LS **Tel:** 01642-495770 **Fax:** 01642-495779 *(Redcar)*
St Margaret Clitherow's Catholic Primary St Margaret's Grove, TS6 6TA **Tel:** 01642-835370 **Fax:** 01642-453103 *(South Bank)*
Christ the King Primary Tedder Avenue, Thornaby, TS17 9JP **Tel/Fax:** 01642-761252 *(Thornaby)*
St Patrick's Primary Westbury Street, TS17 6NE **Tel:** 01642-676724 **Fax:** 01642-679454 *(Thornaby)*
St Thérèse of Lisieux RC Primary Lamb Lane, TS17 0QP **Tel:** 01642-763623 **Fax:** 01642-763892 *(Ingleby Barwick)*

▲ Secondary Comprehensive

St David's RC Technology College St David's Way, TS5 7EY **Tel:** 01642-298100 **Fax:** 01642-298101 *(Middlesbrough)*
The Newlands Catholic School FCJ Saltersgill Avenue, TS4 3JW **Tel:** 01642-825311 **Fax:** 01642-812709 *(Middlesbrough)*
Sacred Heart Comprehensive Mersey Road, TS10 1PJ **Tel:** 01642-487100 **Fax:** 01642-771470 *(Redcar)*
St Peter's Catholic College of Maths & Computing Normanby Road, TS6 6SP **Tel:** 01642-453462 **Fax:** 01642-455010 *(South Bank)*
St Patrick's Comprehensive Baysdale Road, TS17 9DE **Tel:** 01642-613327 **Fax:** 01642-618227 *(Thornaby)*

▲ Sixth Form College

St Mary's Saltersgill Avenue, TS4 3JP **Tel:** 01642-814680 **Fax:** 01642-819624 *(Middlesbrough)*

■ EAST YORKSHIRE

▲ Primary

St Charles' Primary Norfolk Street, HU2 9AA **Tel:** 01482-326610 **Fax:** 01482-616446 *(Hull)*
Endsleigh Holy Child RC Primary Inglemire Avenue, HU6 7TE **Tel:** 01482-853203 **Fax:** 01482-851102 *(Hull)*
Holy Name Primary Danepark Road, HU6 9AA **Tel/Fax:** 01482-850286 *(Hull)*
St Mary Queen of Martyrs Primary Nidderdale, Sutton Park, HU7 4BS **Tel:** 01482-825625 **Fax:** 01482-820276 *(Hull)*
St Vincent's RC Primary Queens Road, HU5 2QR **Tel:** 01482-342645 **Fax:** 01482-342462 *(Hull)*
St Thomas More Primary Elgar Road, HU4 7NP **Tel:** 01482-354093 **Fax:** 01482-507657 *(Hull)*
St Richard's Primary Marfleet Lane, HU9 5TE **Tel:** 01482-781928 **Fax:** 01482-787327 *(Hull)*

▲ Junior and Infant

St John of Beverley Primary Wilberforce Crescent, HU17 0BU **Tel:** 01482-882487 **Fax:** 01482-475242 *(Beverley)*
St Mary's RC Primary George Street, YO15 3PS **Tel:** 01262-670138 **Fax:** 01262-670838 *(Bridlington)*
St Mary's RC Primary Sancton Road, YO43 3DB **Tel:** 01430-872330 *(Market Weighton)*
St Mary & St Joseph Primary Maxwell Road, YO42 2HE **Tel/Fax:** 01759-303287 *(Pocklington)*

▲ Secondary Comprehensive

St Mary's College (11-18) Cranbrook Avenue, Hull, HU6 7TN **Tel:** 01482-851136 **Fax:** 01482-804522 *(Hull)*

■ NORTH YORKSHIRE

▲ Junior and Infant

Sacred Heart RC Primary Broomfield Avenue, Northallerton, DL7 8UL **Tel/Fax:** 01609-780971 *(Northallerton)*
St Benedict's RC Primary Back Lane, Ampleforth, York, YO62 4DE **Tel:** 01439-788340 *(Ampleforth)*
St Hedda's RC Primary Egton Bridge, Whitby, YO21 1UX **Tel/Fax:** 01947-895361 *(Egton Bridge)*
St Peter & St Paul RC Primary Richmond Road, Leyburn, DL8 5DL **Tel:** 01969-622351 *(Leyburn)*
St Mary's RC Primary Highfield Road, YO17 7DB **Tel:** 01653-692274 **Fax:** 01653-698702 *(Malton)*
St Joseph's Primary Swainsea Lane,

YO18 8AR **Tel:** 01751-473102 *(Pickering)*

St Mary's RC Primary Cross Lanes, DL10 7DZ **Tel:** 01748-822365 **Fax:** 01748-821124 *(Richmond)*

St George's Primary Overdale, Eastfield, YO11 3RE **Tel:** 01723-583535 **Fax:** 01723-586679 *(Scarborough)*

St Peter's RC Primary North Leas Avenue, YO12 6LX **Tel:** 01723-372720 **Fax:** 01723-501812 *(Scarborough)*

All Saints Primary Green Lane East, Sowerby, YO7 1NB **Tel:** 01845-523058 *(Thirsk)*

St Hilda's Primary Waterstead Lane, YO21 1PZ **Tel:** 01947-603901 **Fax:** 01947-605874 *(Whitby)*

St Aelred's Primary Fifth Avenue, YO31 0QQ **Tel:** 01904-422800 **Fax:** 01904-415234 *(York)*

English Martyrs RC VA Primary Hamilton Drive, Acomb, YO24 4JW **Tel:** 01904-791370 **Fax:** 01904-789204 *(York)*

St George's RC Primary Winterscale Street, YO10 4BT **Tel:** 01904-636427 **Fax:** 01904-610994 *(York)*

Our Lady's RC Primary Windsor Garth, Acomb, YO24 4QW **Tel:** 01904-791646 **Fax:** 01904-789200 *(York)*

St Wilfrid's Primary Monkgate, YO31 7PB **Tel:** 01904-659726 **Fax:** 01904-673879 *(York)*

▲ Secondary Comprehensive

St Augustine's Catholic High School Sandybed Lane, YO12 5LH **Tel:** 01723-363280 **Fax:** 01723-500490 *(Scarborough)*

All Saints Mill Mount, YO24 1BJ **Tel:** 01904-647877 **Fax:** 01904-545220 *(York)*

■ CATHOLIC SCHOOLS - INDEPENDENT

■ NORTH YORKSHIRE

▲ Primary

St Martin's Ampleforth Gilling Castle, Gilling East, York, YO62 4HP **Tel:** 01439-766600 **Fax:** 01439-788538 **E-mail:** headmaster@stmartins.ampleforth.org.uk

▲ Secondary

Ampleforth College York, YO62 4ER **Tel:** 01439-766800 **Fax:** 01439-788330 **E-mail:** headmaster@ampleforth.org.uk

▲ Joint RC/CofE School

St Francis Xavier Darlington Road, DL10 7DA **Tel:** 01748-823414 **Fax:** 01748-823946 *(Richmond)*

DIOCESE OF NORTHAMPTON

(Province of Westminster)

Consisting of the counties of Bedford, Buckingham and Northampton and that part of Berkshire (formerly in Buckinghamshire) lying between the River Thames and the boundary with Buckinghamshire.

Patrons of the Diocese

Our Blessed Lady Immaculate, 8 Dec.
St Thomas of Canterbury, 29 Dec.

Bishop

Rt Rev Peter Doyle, Bishop of Northampton. Born at Wilpshire, near Blackburn on 3 May 1944; ordained priest 8 June 1968; consecrated Bishop of Northampton on 28 June 2005 by Cardinal Cormac Murphy O'Connor.

The Rt Rev Peter Doyle, Bishop of Northampton

Residence:
Bishop's House, Marriott Street, Northampton, NN2 6AW
Tel: 01604-715635 **Fax:** 01604-792186
E-mail: admin@northamptondiocese.com
Website: www.northamptondiocese.org

Bishop's Personal Assistant:
Miss Tricia Elliott.
E-mail: admin@northamptondiocese.com

Bishop Emeritus

Rt Rev Patrick Leo McCartie, born Sept 5 1925 in West Hartlepool, Co. Durham; ordained priest at Oscott College, July 17, 1949; ordained Auxiliary Bishop of Birmingham May 20, 1977; installed Bishop of Northampton March 19, 1990. Residence: Aston Hall, Aston by Stone, Staffordshire ST15 0BJ **Tel:** 01785-286715.
E-mail: leo.mccartie@btinternet.com

DIOCESE OF NORTHAMPTON

■ ADMINISTRATION

■ Diocesan Curia

Bishop's House, Marriott Street, Northampton NN2 6AW
Tel: 01604-715635 **Fax:** 01604-792186
E-mail: admin@northamptondiocese.com

■ Vicar General

Mgr Provost Sean Healy, St Augustine, 32 London Road, Daventry, Northants NN11 4BZ **Tel:** 01327-300248

■ Diocesan Finance Board

President: **The Bishop of Northampton**
Members: **The Bishop of Northampton, Rev Mgr Provost Séan Healy, Rev Mgr Peter Wilson, Rev Mgr Kevin McGinnell, Rev Brendan Killeen, Mr Peter Haddon.**
Secretary to the Trustees and Assistant to the Financial Secretary: **Mrs Barbara Nicholson,** St Teresa's Presbytery, New Road, Princes Risborough, Bucks HP27 OJN
Tel: 01844345578; **Fax:** 01844 274503
E-mail: barbara_prisborough@hotmail.com

■ Diocesan Finance Office

Bishop's House, Marriott Street, Northampton NN2 6AW
Tel: 01604 712065 **Fax:** 01604 711641
Office Hours: Mon to Fri: 9am to 5pm.
Director of Finance and Development:
Rev Michael Phelan OBE, MA.
E-mail: MikePhelan@aol.com
Financial Secretary: **Mr Tim Redding BSc (Hons), ACA. Mbl:** 07766234527
E-mail: tim@nrcdfinance.com
Bookkeeper: **Mrs Wendy Wilson**.
E-mail: wendy@nrcdfinance.com
Accounts Assistants: **Mrs Vivien Carroll and Mr Frank Sutcliffe**
Planned Giving & Gift Aid Officer:
Mr Brin Dunsire, 'Ker Anna', Aylesbury Road, Princes Risborough, Bucks HP27 0JN
Tel: 01844 273337 **Fax:** 01844 273338
E-mail: brin@nrcdfinance.com

■ Communications

Diocesan Communications Officer: **Rev Paul Hardy**. St Edward's Presbytery, Burchard Crescent, Shenley Church End,

Milton Keynes MK5 6DX
Tel: 01980 504771

■ **The Vine (Diocesan monthly)**
Editor: **Rev Paul Hardy**, St Edward's Presbytery, Burchard Crescent, Shenley Church End, Milton Keynes MK5 6DX
Tel/Fax: 01908-504771
E-mail: vine01@btopenworld.com
News Editor & Vine for the Blind*:* **Mrs Margaret Busby**, 1 Bewcastle Close, Bedford MK41 8BQ **Tel:** 01234-267016
E-mail: vine02@globalnet.co.uk

■ **Diocesan Archivist**
Mrs Margaret Osborne. Please write to: Bishop's House, Marriott Street, Northants.

■ **Diocean Registrar for Deceased Clergy**
Rev Bernard Hughes, 16 Bedford Road, Wilstead, Beds MK45 3HW
Tel: 01234-743748

■ **PASTORAL SERVICES**

■ **Safeguarding Commission**
Child Protection Co-ordinator: **Kay-Marie Taylor-Duke**, Bishop's House, Marriott Street, Northampton NN2 6AW
Tel: 07799 888855

■ **Deaf and Hearing Impaired Pastoral Services**
Co-ordinator: **Mr Martin Redmond**, Kings Corner, 9 Main Road, Biddenham, Bedford MK40 4BB
Tel: 01234-218036 **Mbl:** 07889-015610
E-mail: martinredmond@btopenworld.com
Chaplain: **Rev Gerard Byrne**, St Brendan, Beanfield, Corby NN18 0AZ
Tel: 01536 202879 *Pastoral Worker:* **Sr Marie Power**, 40 Lloyds, Coffee Hall, Milton Keynes MK6 5EB **Tel:** 07976 726585

■ **Bishop's Hospital Advisor**
Rev Jonathan Hill, 366 Leagrave High St, Luton, Beds LU4 0NG **Tel:** 01582-663706
E-mail: FrJohnhill@aol.com

■ **Catholic Handicapped Children's Fellowship**
Priest with responsibility for those with special needs: **Canon Kevin O'Driscoll**, 226 Trelawney Avenue, Langley, Slough SL3 7UD **Tel:** 01753-543770
Secretary: **Andrea Leather**, 34 Mendip Way, Sundon Park, Luton Beds LU3 3JL
Tel: 01582-503533

■ **Diocesan Pilgrimage to Lourdes**
Director: **Rev Damien Walne**, 1 Elwes Way, Great Billing, Northampton NN3 9EA
Tel: 01604-406410 *Secretary:* **Mr Michael Carter**, 6 Gilletts Lane, High Wycombe, Bucks HP12 4BB. **Tel:** 01494 534429

■ **EDUCATION AND FORMATION**

■ **Diocesan Vocations Team**
Chairman: **The Bishop**. *Director:* **Rev Mark Floody**. *Other members:* **Rev Mgr Provost Sean Healy, Rev Canon John Udris, Revv Seamus Keenan, Mark Floody, Jonathan Hill.**

■ **Episcopal Vicar for Education and Formation Mgr Kevin KcGinnell**, The Holy Ghost, 33 Westbourne Road, Luton LU4 8JD **Tel:** 01582-728849
Fax: 01582-704298
Mbl: 07889-762005
E-mail: mcginnell.nores@btconnect.com

■ **NORES – The office for Religious Education, Catechesis and Schools**
Director: **Mgr Kevin KcGinnell**, The Holy Ghost, 33 Westbourne Road, Luton LU4 8JD
Tel: 01582-728849 **Fax:** 01582-704298
Mbl: 07889-762005
E-mail: admin.nores@btconnect.co.uk
Website: www.nores.co.uk

■ **Pastoral and Religious Education Centre** *Secretary:* Mrs Jackie McCarthy.
Tel: 01908 233121 **Fax:** 01908 233131
Our Lady of Lourdes, Lloyds Coffee Hall, Milton Keynes MK6 5EB
Tel: 01908-233121 **Fax:** 01908-233131
E-mail: admin.nores@btconnect.co.uk
Website: www.nores.co.uk

■ **Diocesan Youth Service**
Northampton Youth Ministry Office (NYMO) Ker Anna, Aylesbury Road, Princes Risborough, Bucks HP27 0JN
Tel: 01844-273337 **Fax:** 01844-273338
E-mail: info@nymo.org
Website: www.nymo.org
Chaplain: **Rev Tony Brennan**. Holy Cross Presbytery, 2 Severn Way, Bedford MK41 7BX **Tel:** 01234-352607
E-mail: holycross.bedford@tiscali.co.uk
Diocesan Youth Ministry Co-ordinator: **Avril Baigent, E-mail:** avril@nymo.org
Ezekiel Project: Northampton: 16 St Michael's Avenue, Northampton NN1 4JQ
Tel: 01604 47527 **Beccy Burke**
E-mail: beccy@nymo.org
Website: www.ezekielproject.com

■ **Diocesan Vocations**
Diocesan Vocations Director:
Rev Mark Floody, 24 Freshwater Close, Marsh Farm, Luton LU3 3TA
Tel: 01582-502400
E-mail: mark.floody@btinternet.com
Diocesan Promotor of Vocations:
Rev Jonathan Hill Tel: 01582-663706
E-mail: FrJohnhill@aol.com

■ **LITURGY**

■ **Liturgy Commission**
President: **The Bishop**. *Chair:* **Mgr Kevin McGinnell,** The Holy Ghost, 33 Westbourne Road, Luton LU4 8JD
Tel: 01582-728849 **Fax:** 01582-704298
Mbl: 07889-762005
E-mail: mcginnell.nores@btconnect.com
Department Chairs: *Pastoral Rites:* **Rev Canon John Udris**; *Music:* **Sr Avril OP**; *Liturgical Formation:* **Rev Andy Ollard**; *RCIA Co-ordinator:* **Mgr Kevin MgGinnell**.

■ **ECUMENISM**

■ **Diocesan Ecumenical Commission**
President: The Bishop. *Chairman:* **Rev Deacon Paul Lipscomb**, Crane House, Rowanhurst Drive, Farnham Common, Bucks SL2 3HG
Tel: 01753-645349 *Secretary:* **Sr Helen Haigh**, Convent of Jesus and Mary, Thornton MK17 OHJ **Tel:** 01280 813254
Ecumenical Officer: **Rev Dr James Cassidy CRIC**, 30 Langcliffe Drive, Heelands MK13 7PL **Tel/Fax:** 01908-221228

■ **HISTORIC CHURCHES COMMITTEE**
Chairman: **Rev Mgr Sean Healy** *Secretary:* **Mrs Barbara Nicholson**, St Theresa's Presbytery, New Road, Princes Risborough, Bucks HP27 0JN
Tel: 01884-345578 *Other Members:* **Revv John McCardle, Robert Preece, Mr Stephen Foster, Mr Anthony New, Mr Paul Flood, Miss Liz Clark, Mr Tim Redding**. Representatives from English Heritage, the Joint Amenities and the Local Planning Authorities.

■ **CONSULTATIVE BODIES**

■ **Cathedral Chapter**
(erected 24 June 1852)
Provost: **Rev Mgr Sean Healy** *Canons:* **McAleenan, Daniel Kiely, Stanislaus Condon, John Koenig** (*Canon Penitentiary*), **Timothy Russ** (*Canon Theologian*), **Denis McSweeney** (*Canon Precentor*), **Bosco Clarke, Kevin O'Driscoll, Canon John Udris, Bennie Noonan**. *Honorary Canons:* **Canon Norman Smith, Mgr Edward McBride, Brian Frost, Patrick Carey, Daniel Cronin, Antony Griffiths, Michael Griffiths, Michael Hazell**.

■ **College of Consultors**
Mgr Sean Healy VG, Canon John Udris, Mgri Kevin McGinnel, Anthony McDermott, Revv Seamus Keenan, Francis Higgins.

■ **Diocesan Council of Priests**
President: **The Bishop of Northampton. Revv Brendan Killeen, Andrew Behrens, Tony Brennan, John Danford, James Evans, Paul Hardy, Michael Harrison, Francis Higgins, Jonathan Hill, Tom Kenny, Richard Moroney, Bennie Noonan, Anthony Parsons, Robert Reece, Phillip Swingler, Joe Walsh, Leszek Wisniewski. Rev Canons John Koenig, John Udris, Kevin O'Driscoll.**
Rev Mgr Anthony, McDermott, Kevin McGinnell, Gerald Moorcraft, Peter Wilson.
Rev Mgr Provost Sean Healy.

■ **Diocesan Council of Deacons**
President: **The Bishop of Northampton. Rev Fr Francis Higgins, Paul Lipscomb, John Lovelock, John Crowshaw, John Derbyshire, Noel Guina, Joanna Hale.**

■ **Diocesan Pastoral Council**
President: **The Bishop**. *Chairman:* **Mrs Mary Bull**, 29 Southfield Drive, Hazelmere, Bucks HP15 7HB
Tel: 01494-712556
E-mail: marybull@waitrose.com
Secretary: **Rev Paul Hardy**, St Edwards Presbytery, Burchard Crescent, Shenley Church End, Milton Keynes MK5 6DX
Tel/Fax: 01908-504771
E-mail: vine01@btopenworld.com

■ **DIOCESAN MATRIMONIAL TRIBUNAL**
Officialis: **Rev Dr Brendan Killeen**. Bishop's House, Marriott Street, Northampton, NN2 6AW **Tel:** 01604-710743
Fax: 01604-792186 *Vice-Officiales:* **Canon John Koenig**. *Judges:* **Mgr Patrick McAleenan, Revv Seamus Keenan, John McCardle**. *Defenders of the Bond:* **Revv Dr Richard Barrett, Dr James Cassidy CRIC, Sr Ellen Burke DHS, Mr Paul Sefton**. *Promoter of Justice:* **Canon Timothy Russ**. *Tribunal Secretary:* **Mrs Margaret Lacken**

■ **NORTHAMPTON**

1. Cathedral of Our Lady and St Thomas
(1825; 1864; 1959; cons 22 June 1960)
Cathedral House, Kingsthorpe Road Northampton NN2 6AG **Tel:** 01604-714556
E-mail: info@northamptoncathedral.org
Website: www.northamptoncathedral.org
Rev John Udris (*Cathedral Dean*). **Revv Benny Joseph, Simon Penhalagon**. *Parish Sister:* **Sr Brenda Moore DHS.** *Deacons:* **Rev Philip Nash**. 5 Vicarage Close, Northampton NN2 6GH **Tel:** 01604-714938
M: *Sat 1st M of Sun 7pm. Sun 8.30am, 10.30am, 5.15pm. Hds (vigil 7pm). 9.30am, 8pm.*

- ***Daughters of the Holy Spirit:*** Provincial House, 103 Halestone Road, Northampton NN5 7AQ **Tel:** 01604-755296

■ **AMPTHILL,** Bedford.
Mass in St Andrew's (C of E) Church. Served from Flitwick.
M: *Sat 1st M of Sun 6pm. Hds 9am.*

■ **ASTON-LE-WALLS,** Northants A
† The Sacred Heart (1688; 1827; 1859)
Aston-le-Walls, Daventry, Northants.
Tel: 01295-660221 **Fax:** 01295-660043
E-mail: gpmadams@yahoo.co.uk
Mgr Graham Adams. The Presbytery, Aston-le-Walls, Northampton NN11 6UF
M: *Sun 10.45am. Hds 10am.*

■ **AYLESBURY,** Bucks A
1. † St Joseph (1888; 1937)
56 High Street, Aylesbury, Bucks HP20 1SE
Tel/Fax: 01296-482267
E-mail: jpbeirne.stjoseph@btinternet.com
Rev John Beirne.
M: *Sat 1st M of Sun 6pm. Sun 10am, 11.30am. Hds (vigil 7pm), 10am, 12.30pm.*

2. † Our Lady of Lourdes
69 Camborne Avenue, Bedgrove HP21 7UE
Tel/Fax: 01296-427881
E-mail: ourladyoflourdes@talktalk.net
Rev: Joseph Pham Ngoc Dung, Presbytery, 13 Pevensey Close, Bedgrove, Aylesbury HP21 9UB
Parish Sister: **Sr Bernadette Larkin.**
M: *Sat 1st M of Sun 6.30. Sun 10am. Hds 9.30am, 8pm.*

- ***Daughters of Providence:*** 45 Kerr Place, Old Brewery Close, Walton Street, Aylesbury HP21 7BB **Tel:** 01296-487368

3. † The Guardian Angels (1964; 1967) A
6 Chaloner Road, Southcourt HP21 8NN
Tel: 01296-421826
Rev John Fleming.
M: *Sun 9.30am, 6pm. Hds 10am, 8pm.*

4 † St Clare (1966)
Elmhurst Road. **Tel/Fax:** 01296-482267
All correspondence to Aylesbury (1).
M: *Sun 8.45am, 6.30pm. Hds 7.30pm.*

■ **BEACONSFIELD,** Bucks
† St Teresa of the Child Jesus and SS John Fisher and Thomas More
(1920; 1927; cons 30 Sept 1947)
40 Warwick Road, Beaconsfield, HP9 2PL **Tel:** 01494-673018
E-mail: office@littleflower.co.uk
Website: www.littleflower.co.uk
Rev Francis P Higgins, *Deacon:* **Rev Michael Phelan, Tel:** 01494 675259. *Parish Sisters:* **Sr Anne Campbell. Sr Winifred McCahill,** Bon Secours Convent, Cores End Road, Bourne End **Tel:** 01628-522956
E-mail: office@saintdunstans.co.uk
M: *Sat 1st M of Sun 6pm. Sun 8.45am, 11.30am. Hds 10.30am, 8pm.*

■ **BEDFORD** A
1. † St Joseph and the Holy Child
(1863; 1874; 1912; cons 19 Aug 1964)
Midland Road, Bedford.
Tel/Fax: 01234-352569
E-mail: stjosephsbedford@yahoo.co.uk
Revv Seamus Keenan, Joseph Thoppil. 2 Brereton Road, MK40 1HU
M: *Sun 8.15am, 9.30am, 11am, 6.30pm. Hds 7.30am, 10.45am, 7.30pm.*

2. † Christ the King (1953; 1960)
London Road. **Tel/Fax:** 01234-267714
E-mail: brendang@btinternet.com
Rev Brendan Gorman MA. Presbytery, Harrowden Road, Bedford MK42 0SP
M: *Sat 1st M of Sun 6pm. Sun 8.30am, 11am. Hds 10am, 7.30pm.*

- ***Daughters of the Holy Spirit,*** 188 London Road, Bedford, MK42 0PS **Tel:** 01234-350794

3. † Holy Cross (1957)
355 Goldington Road, Bedford MK41 0DP
Tel: 01234-353116
E-mail: holycrossbedford@tiscali.co.uk
Website: www.holycrossbedford.co.uk
Rev Anthony Brennan, 2 Severn Way, Brickhill, Bedford MK41 7BX; *Pastoral Worker & Chaplain to De Montfort University, Bedford:* **Elizabeth Ridley MA, BMus, HDip RE.** 355 Goldington Road, Bedford MK41 0DP
M: *Sat 1st M of Sun 6pm. Sun 9.15am, Hds 9.30am, 7.30pm.*

- ***Daughters of the Holy Spirit,*** 24 Bradgate Road, MK40 3DE **Tel:** 01234-214662

4. † St Frances Cabrini (Italian Church) A
10 Woburn Road, Bedford MK40 1EG
Tel: 01234-359515 **Fax:** 01234-340626

E-mail: info@italianmission.co.uk
- ***Scalabrini Fathers (CS):*** **Rev Pietro Celotto.**
  M: *Sun 10.15am, 11.30 (English), 6pm. Hds 10.30am, 7.30pm.*

5. † SS Philip and James (1967)
2 Severn Way, Brickhill, Bedford MK41 7BX **Tel:** 01234-352607
Email: holycrosschurch@btinternet.com
Rev Anthony Brennan
M: *Sun 8am, 11am. Hds 7pm.*

6. St Josaphat
York Street. Ukrainian Church of Byzantine Rite. Served by The Ukrainian Catholic Cathedral, London. **Rev Mykola Martynyuk**
M: *On 2nd & 4th Sun of month at 11am.*

7. Sacred Heart of Jesus and St Cuthbert (Polish Church)
The Presbytery, Sacred Heart of Jesus & St Cuthbert, 8 Mill Street, Bedford, MK40 3EU
Tel/Fax: 01234-266901
E-mail: grzegorz@btinternet.com
Rev Grzegorz Aleksandrowicz.
M: *Sun 10am, 7pm. Hds 10am.*

8. Our Lady of Ransom,
Kempston, Bedford. See Kempston.

■ **BIGGLESWADE,** Beds
† St Peter (1905; 1924; 1973)
7a Station Road, Biggleswade SG18 8AL
Tel: 01767-312013
Website: www.st-peter.eu
Rev Canon Michael Griffiths
M: *Sat 1st M of Sun 6.30pm. Sun 8.30am, 10am. Hds 9.30am, 7.30pm.*

■ **BILLING,** Northants
See Great Billing.

■ **BLETCHLEY,** Milton Keynes
See Milton Keynes, (4).

■ **BOURNE END,** Bucks
† St Dunstan (1956)
Cores End Road, Bourne End, Bucks SL8 5AR
Email: office@saintdunstans.co.uk
Website: www.stdunstans.co.uk
Fr Francis P Higgins (*Parish Priest*), 40 Warwick Road, Beaconsfield.
M: *Sun 10am. Hds 9.30am.*
- ***Bon Secours Sisters:*** The Presbytery, Cores End Road, Bourne End, Bucks SL8 5AR
  Tel/Fax: 01628-522956

■ **BRACKLEY,** Northants
† St Martin (1957)
Halls Lane. Served from Buckingham.
M: *Sun 9am. Hds (vigil 7.30pm).*

■ **BUCKINGHAM**
† St Bernardine of Siena (1892; 1974)
Chandos Road, Buckingham MK18 1AL
Tel: 01280-813105
E-mail: dankiely@tiscali.co.uk
Website: www.stbernardines.org.uk
Canon Daniel Kiely. *Deacon:* **Rev John Lovelock,** 40 Gilbert Scott Road, Bucks MK18 1PS **Tel:** 01280-812997
M: *Sat 1st M of Sun 5.30pm. Sun 11am. Hds 9am, 7.30pm.*
- ***Religious of Jesus and Mary***, Thornton, Milton Keynes MK17 0HT
  Tel: 01280-813254 (See Thornton)

■ **BURNHAM,** Bucks
† Our Lady of Peace
(1935; 1958; cons 12 Sept 1962)
Lower Britwell Road, Burnham, Slough SL2 2NL **Tel:** 01628-605764
Fax: 01628-663901
E-mail: fathermlt@btopenworld.com
Rev Michael Turner,
Deacons: **Rev George Brooker**. 56 Lower Cippenham Lane, Slough, SL1 5DF
Tel: 01753-524100 **Rev Edward Connelly** (Retired). 54 Hogfair Lane, Burnham SL1 7HQ **Tel:** 01628-661615
M: *Sat 1st M of Sun 6pm. Sun 9.45am, 6pm. Hds 9.30am.*

■ **BURTON LATIMER,** Northants
† St Nicholas Owen (1971)
Kettering Road. Served from Kettering (1)
E-mail: john.koenig@ntlworld.com
M: *Sun 9am. Hds 7pm.*

■ **CADDINGTON,** Beds
St Thomas, Apostle, (1964)
Manor Road. Served from Luton (6)
E-mail: stmargaret@freeuk.com
M: *Sat 1st M of Sun 6pm.*

■ **CHALFONT ST GILES,** Bucks
† The Divine Child of Prague (1940)
Tripps Hill. Served from Gerrards Cross.
E-mail: st.joseph@btconnect.com
M: *Sun 9am.*

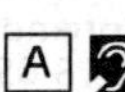

■ **CHESHAM,** Bucks
† St Columba (1909; 1960)
432 Berkhamstead Road, Chesham, Bucks HP5 3HQ **Tel/Fax:** 01494-785269
Mbl: 07976-839535
E-mail: webcolumba@yahoo.co.uk
Website: www.rc.net/northampton/stcolumba
Rev Patrick Bailey.
M: *Sun 10am, 6pm. Hds 9.15am, 8pm.*

■ **CHESHAM BOIS,** Bucks
† Our Lady of Perpetual Succour (1915; 1953)
30 Amersham Road, Chesham Bois, Bucks HP6 5PE **Tel:** 01494-727469
E-mail: bdavenport@talktalk.net
Rev Bernard Davenport.
M: *Sat 1st M of Sun 6pm. Sun 9am, 10.30am (Tridentine). Hds 8.30am, 8pm.*

■ **CIPPENHAM,** Bucks
St Andrew, Washington Drive, SL1 5RE
Served from Burnham.
M: *Sun 11.30am. Hds 7.30pm.*

■ **CORBY,** Northants
1. † Our Lady of Walsingham
(1934; 1938; cons 11 June 1963)
71 Occupation Road, Corby, Northants NN17 1EE **Tel/Fax:** 01536-203121
E-mail: ourlady.corby@virgin.net
Mgr Patrick McAleenan, Rev Robert Preece. *Deacon:* **Rev Gerard Lee,** 5 Chestnut Avenue, Corby, Northants NN17 2ER **Tel:** 01536-399421
M: *Sat 1st M of Sun 6.30pm. Sun 9.30am, 11am, 7pm. Hds (vigil 6.30pm), 10am (9am in school term), 7pm.*

2. † St Brendan A
(1956; 1962; cons 1976)
Beanfield Avenue, Corby, Northants NN18 0AZ **Tel/Fax:** 01536-202879
Email: stbrendans@uwclub.net
Rev Gerard Byrne.
M: *Sat 1st M of Sun 6pm. Sun 9am, 11am. Hds 10am, 7pm.*
• ***Sisters of St Clare,*** St Clare's Convent, 15 Glyndebourne Gardens, NN18 0QA **Tel:** 01536-741425

3. St John Ogilvie
(1980 Cons 17 October 1991)
1 Copenhagen Road, Danesholme, Corby, Northants. NN18 9BX **Tel:** 01536-745545
Rev Stephen McGuinness *Deacon:* **Rev Shaun Howard,** 17 St Dunstan's Close, Kettering, Northants NN15 5JE
Tel: 01536-516005
M: *Sun 11.15am, 5pm. Hds 7pm.*

4. † St Patrick (1962; cons 17 March 1981)
Morland Road, Corby, Northampton NN18 0SP **Tel:** 01536-202323
Rev John Osborne. Catholic Presbytery, Millais Road, NN18 0SP
M: *Sat 1st M of Sun 6pm. Sun 10am, 6pm. Hds 10am (St Patrick's School during term), 7pm.*

■ **CRANFIELD,** Beds
Cranfield University
In Central Library Building, Cranfield, MK43 0LA Served from Woburn Sands.
Deacon: **Philip Pugh,** 66 Westoning Road, Harlington, Beds LU5 6PD St Mary's, Aspley Hill, Woburn Sands, Beds MK17 8NN
Tel: 01908-583195
M: *Sun Chaplaincy: 6pm.*

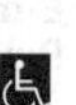

■ **CROUGHTON,** Northants
RAF Croughton, Northampton NN13 5XP
Tel: 01280-708287/708700
Fax: 01280-708703
E-mail: ricardito.salditos@croughton.af.mil (Access by permit only).
Chaplain: Office of the Chaplain, 422 ABG/HC, RAF Croughton, Brackley, Northampton NN13 5XP
M: *Sun 9.30am*

■ **DATCHET,** Slough, Berks A
† St Augustine (1923; 1928)
70 Eton Road, Datchet, Slough, Berks SL3 9AY **Tel:** 01753-542862
• ***Kiltegan Fathers (SPS),*** **Rev Sean Rynn**
M: *Sat 1st M of Sun 6pm. Sun 11am. Hds 9.30am.*

■ **DAVENTRY,** Northants
1. † St Augustine (1880; 1916; 1972)
32 London Road, Daventry, Northampton NN11 4BZ **Tel:** 01327-300248
E-mail: staugustinedav@aol.com
Mgr Canon Sean Healy VG,
Deacon: **Rev David Franklyn,** 20 Oriel Road, Daventry NW11 4SP
Tel: 01327 878897
M: *Sat 1st M of Sun 5pm. Sun 10.30am. Hds 9.15am, 8pm.*

■ **DENHAM,** Bucks A
The Most Holy Name (1961)
Old Mill Road. Served from Gerrards Cross.
M: *Sun 9.30am.*

■ **DESBOROUGH,** Northants A
Holy Trinity (1972)
Victoria Street. Served from Kettering.
M: *Sun 9am. Hds (vigil 7pm).*

■ **DOWNLEY,** Bucks
See High Wycombe, No 4.

■ **DUNSTABLE,** Beds
1. † St Mary (1927; 1935; 1964)
82 West Street, Dunstable, Beds LU6 1NY
Tel: 01582-662710 **Fax:** 01582-670968
Email: stmary82w@aol.com
Website: www.stmarys-dunstable.co.uk
• ***Vincentians (CM):*** **Rev Kieran Magovern** (*Superior and Parish Priest*); **Revv Cornelius Curtin, James Sheil, Eamon Raftery.** *Permanent Deacon:* Phillip Pugh, 46 Westoning Road, Harlington, Beds LU5 6PD. **Tel:** 01525 875445
M: *Sat 1st M of Sun 6pm. Sun 8.30am, 10.30am. Hds 9.30am, 7.30pm.*

2. Our Lady of Czestochowa (Polish Church)
17 Victoria Street, Dunstable, Beds LU6 3AZ **Tel/Fax:** 01582-662807
Website: www.ppld.co.uk
Rev Czeslaw Osika (SChr).
M: *Sun 9am, 11am. Hds 10am, 7.30pm.*

■ **DUSTON**
See Northampton (5).

■ **EARLS BARTON,** Northants
St Anselm (1968)
Churchill Road, NN6 0PQ
Served from Great Billing.
M: *Sun 9.15am. Hds 6.30pm.*

■ **ETON,** Berks A
† Our Lady of Sorrows (1911; 1914)
Eton Court. Served from Datchet.
M: *Sun 9.30am. Hds 6.30pm.*

■ **ETON COLLEGE,** Berks
Eton College, Windsor, SL4 6DW
Tel: 01753-671409
Chaplain: **Rev Nicholas Heap.**
M: *Sun As announced.*

■ **ETON WICK,** Berks
St Gilbert (1964)
Eton Wick Road. Served from Burnham.
M: *Sun 9am. Hds (vigil 7.30pm).*

■ **FAWLEY COURT**
St Anne's Church (Divine Mercy Shrine) (1973)
St Joseph's Chapel (1953)
Marlow Road, Henley-on-Thames, Oxon RG9 3AE **Tel:** 01491-574917/574506 **Fax:** 01491-411587 **E-mails:** marian-f@dircon.co.uk ***or*** fcoffice@dircon.co.uk
Website: www.marians-uk.org
• ***Marian Fathers (MIC):*** **Revv Wojciech Jasinski STM** (*Delegate of the Polish Provincial in Great Britain*), **Stanislaw Drozdowski STM, Andrzej Gowkeilewicz, Andrzej Janicki, Aleksander Karpinski, Jan Przbysz, Bros Piotr Jagodzinski, Waldemar Karpuk, Bronislaw Swistak, Franciszek Zaborowski, Jacek Branka.**
M: *Sat 7.30pm (Polish), Sun 12noon (St Anne's, Polish); St Joseph's: 8.30am (English), 7.30pm (Polish).*

■ **FLITWICK,** Beds
Sacred Heart (1983)
Tel: 01525-715109 **Fax:** 01525-721752
Email: webadmin@sacredheartflitwick.co.uk
Website: www.sacredheartflitwick.co.uk
Canon Denis McSweeney
M: *Sun 9am, 11am. Hds 7.30pm.*

■ **GERRARDS CROSS,** Bucks
† St Joseph (1913; 1915; 1963; cons 1976)
Austenwood Common, Chalfont St Peter Gerrards Cross, Bucks SL9 8RY
Tel: 01753-886581 **Fax:** 01753-892371
E-mail: office@stjosephs.org.uk
Website: www.stjosephs.org.uk
• ***Discalced Carmelites (ODC):*** **Revv Anthony Parsons,** (*Superior & Parish Priest*): **Martin McDonald, Maurice Flynn.**
M: *Sat 1st M of Sun 6.30pm. Sun 7.45am, 9am, 5.30pm. Hds (vigil 8pm), 7am, 9am, 11am, 8pm.*

• ***Sisters of the Holy Cross.*** Holy Cross Convent, The Grange, Gold Hill East, SL9 9DW Day School **Tel:** 01753-890108 School **Tel:** 01753-895600.

■ **GOLDINGTON.**
See Bedford (3).

■ **GREAT BILLING,** Northants A
† Our Lady of Perpetual Succour & St Anselm "Diocesan Shrine" (1874; 1878)
High Street, Great Billing, Northants.
Tel/Fax: 01604-406410
E-mail: ourladysparish@aol.com
Website: www.ourladyandstanselm.org
Rector & Parish Priest: **Rev Damien Walne.**
1 Elwes Way, Great Billing, Northants NN3 9EA
M: *Sun 8am, 10.30am (Sung). Hds 9am, 7.30pm.*

■ **GREAT HARROWDEN,** Northants
St Hubert's Chapel
Served from Wellingborough.
M: *Last Sun of month, 11am.*

■ **GREAT MISSENDEN,** Bucks
Immaculate Heart of Mary (1954; 1964)
Damien House, 23 High Street, Great Missenden Bucks HP16 9AA
Tel: 01494-862049
Email: info@ihmissenden.org.uk
Website: www.ihmissenden.org.uk
Canon Timothy Russ. *Deacon:* **Rev John Crowshaw,** Hammerswood, 64 Long Park, Chesham Bois, Amersham, Bucks HP6 5LF
Tel: 01494-726931 **Fax:** 01494-434209
M: *Sat 1st M of Sun 6pm. Sun 11am. Hds 9.30am, 8pm.*

■ **HADDENHAM,** Bucks
The Good Shepherd (1956; 1990)
45 The Croft, Haddenham, Bucks HP17 8AS **Tel:** 01844-290178
Website: www.haddenhamrc.co.uk
Rev Leszek Wisniewski
M: *Sat 1st M of Sun 5pm. Sun 9.30am, 6pm. Hds (vigil 5pm), 9.30am, 8pm.*

■ **HALTON,** Aylesbury, Bucks
The Holy Family (1919; 1962)
RAF Station. *Office:* **Tel:** 01296-623535 Ext 6414 **Fax:** 01296-624768
Email: prcc@halton.raf.mod.uk
RC Principal Chaplain: **Rev Mgr John Walsh.** *Permanent Deacon:* **Rev Peter Swindlehurst,** 181b Aylesbury Road, Wendover, Aylesbury HP22 6AA
M: *Sun 10.30am.*

■ **HAZLEMERE,** Bucks
See High Wycombe (5).

■ **HENLOW,** Beds
St Andrew
RAF Station, SG16 6DN

Served from Shefford.
M: *Sat 1st M of Sun 6pm.*

■ **HIGH WYCOMBE,** Bucks
1. † St Augustine, Apostle of England (1889; 1894; 1957)
24 Amersham Hill, High Wycombe, Bucks HP13 6NZ **Tel/Fax:** 01494-523969
Website: www.st-augustines-church.org.uk
Revv William Strain, Thomas Feighan, Innocent Abonyi (MSP).
M: *Sat 1st M of Sun 7pm. Sun 8am, 9.30am, 11am (Sung), 7pm. Hds 8am, 10am, 6.30pm.*

2. St Wulstan (1970)
Presbytery, Hollis Road, Totteridge HP13 7UN **Tel/Fax:** 01494-438300
E-mail: stwulstans@clara.co.uk
Website: www.stwulstanschurch.org
Rev Stanislaus Maciuszek.
M: *Sun 9am, 10.45am (Polish), 12noon. Hds 10am, 8pm.*

3. Our Lady of Grace (1981)
Squirrel Lane, Booker, High Wycombe HP12 4RY **Tel:** 01494-438300
Served from High Wycombe (2)
M: *Sun 10.30am. Hds 7pm.*

4. St James
Plomer Hill, Downley.
Served from High Wycombe, No 1.
M: *Sun 9.15am. Hds See Newsletter.*

5. St Edmund Campion (1982)
Cedar Avenue, Hazlemere
Served from High Wycombe No. 1.
M: *Sun 11am. Hds See Newsletter.*

■ **HOUGHTON REGIS,** Beds
St Vincent de Paul (1963; 1979)
Hammersmith Gardens, LU5 5RG
Served from Dunstable (1)
M: *Sat 1st M of Sun 6.30pm. Sun 11am. Hds 10am, 7.30pm.*

■ **IVER HEATH,** Bucks
Bridgettine Convent (1931)
Chaplain: **Rev Richard Dangerfield,** The Presbytery, Fulmer Common Road, Iver Heath, Bucks SL0 0NR **Tel:** 01753-662296
M: *Sat 1st M of Sun 5pm, 10am. Hds 8am, 8pm.*
• ***Bridgettine Sisters,*** Fulmer Common Road SL0 0NR
Tel: 01753-662073 **Fax:** 01753-662172
E-mail: sbriggitae@iverconvent.fsnet.co.uk

■ **KEMPSTON,** Bedford
Our Lady of Ransom
307 Bedford Road, Kempston, Bedford MK42 8QB **Tel:** 01234-352569
Served from Bedford (1).
M: *Sun 9.30am Hds 7.30pm.*

■ **KETTERING,** Northants
† St Edward (1891; 1940; cons 24 Sept 1946)
London Road, Kettering, Northants.
Tel: 01536-512497
E-mail: john.koenig@ntlworld.com
Website: www.stedwardskettering.org.uk
Revv Canon John Koenig, Andrew Richardson, 2 The Grove, NN15 7QQ
M: *Sat 1st M of Sun 6pm. Sun 8am, 10.30am, 7pm. Hds (vigil 7.30pm), 10am, 7.30pm. Permanent Deacons:* **Rev Leslie Allday, Rev Keith Watson,** 17 Rushton Road, Rothwell, Kettering NN14 6HG.
• ***Sisters of Our Lady,*** Crossway, 131 Hawthorne Road, Kettering NN15 7JU.
Tel: 01536-513711 **Fax:** 01536-392599

■ **KING'S SUTTON,** Northants
Served from Aston-le-Walls.
M: *Sun 9am (C of E Church).*

■ **LANGLEY**
See Slough (3).

■ **LAXTON HALL,** near Corby
Dedicated to Mary Immaculate, Mother of the Church and her Crusade (7 Dec 1970)
Laxton Hall, Northants NN17 3AU
Tel: 01780-444242 **Fax:** 01780-444574
M: *Sun 10am, 12noon (Pol). Hds 7am*
• ***Franciscans (Friars Minor Conventual) (OFM Conv):*** **Rev George Tyc.**

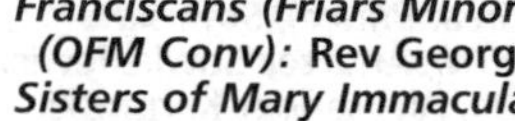

• ***Sisters of Mary Immaculate,***
Tel: 01780-444292

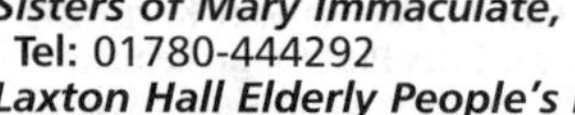

• ***Laxton Hall Elderly People's Home,***
Tel: 01780-444649

■ **LEIGHTON BUZZARD,** Beds
† The Sacred Heart
5 Beaudesert, Leighton Buzzard, Beds LU7 8HZ **Tel/Fax:** 01525-372321
Rev John Danford.
E-mail: sacredheart.lb@tiscali.co.uk
Website: www.rc.net/northampton/sacredheart
M: *Sat 1st M of Sun 6pm; Sun 9am, 10.30am. Hds: 9.30am, 8pm.*

■ **LITTLE CHALFONT,** Bucks
† St Aidan (1964)
Finch Lane, Little Chalfont, Bucks. HP7 9NE
Tel: 01494-763518
E-mail: kjp2906@yahoo.com
Website: www.rc.net/northampton/staidan
Rev Kenneth J Payne.
M: *Sat 1st M of Sun 6pm. Sun 10.30am. Hds 9.30am, 8pm.*

■ **LONG BUCKBY,** Northants
† St Joseph (1943)
Station Road. Served from Daventry.
M: *Sat 1st M of Sun 6.30pm. Hds 7pm.*

■ **LONG CRENDON,** Bucks
Our Lady of Light (1971)
Presbytery, Long Crendon, Bucks HP18 9BS
Tel: 01844-208754
E-mail: fr.eric@tiscali.co.uk
Website: www.ourladyoflight.org.uk
Rev Eric Manley-Harris.
M: *Sun 10am. Hds 9.30am.*

■ **LUTON,** Beds
1. † Our Lady Help of Christians
(1884; 1910; 1959)
52 Castle Street, Luton, Beds. LU1 3AG
Tel: 01582-723254 **Fax:** 01582-451840
E-mail: ourladysluton@googlemail.com
Rev Dariusz Bialowas, *Deacon:* **Rev Gerry McGrogan**. 272 Stockingstone Road, Luton LU7DE **Tel:** 01592 728544
M: *Sat 1st M of Sun 6pm. Sun 9.30am. 11.30am, 5pm. Hds 9am, 12.45pm, 7pm.*
- ***Sisters of St Clare,*** 3 Abigail Close, Luton, LU3 1ND **Tel:** 01582-424518

2. † The Holy Ghost (1964; 1965)
Beech Hill.
Tel: 01582-728849 **Fax:** 01582-704298
E-mail: mcginnell.nores@btconnect.com
Website: www.holyghostparish.co.uk
Mgr Kevin McGinnell. 33 Westbourne Road, Luton, Beds. LU4 8JD
Deacon: **Rev Paul Wyer**
M: *Sat 1st M of Sun 6.30pm. Sun 8.30am, 10am, 11.30am. Hds 10am, 7.30pm.*
- ***Daughters of the Holy Spirit:*** 106 Dorrington Close, Luton LU3 1XR **Tel:** 01582-755917

3. † Sacred Heart of Jesus (1948; 1950)
148 Ashcroft Road, Stopsley, Luton, Beds. LU2 9AY **Tel:** 01582-723099
E-mail: sacredheartluton@yahoo.co.uk
Rev Christopher Whitehouse.
M: *Sat 1st M of Sun 6.30pm. Sun 8.30am, 10am, 11.30am. Hds 9am, 10.45am, 7.30pm.*

4. † Holy Family (1976)
24 Freshwater Close, Marsh Farm, Luton LU3 3TA **Tel:** 01582-502400
E-mail: mark.floody@btinternet.com
Rev Mark Floody.
M: *Sat 1st M of Sun 6pm. Sun 9am, 11.45am. Hds, (vigil) 7.30pm.*

4a † St John the Apostle (1966)
296 Sundon Park Road, Luton, Beds. LU3 3AL **Tel:** 01582-582032
Rev Mark Floody (*Parish Priest*). *Deacon in residence*: **Rev John Derbyshire**.
M: *Sun 10.15am. Hds 10am.*

5. † St Joseph (1937; 1960)
Gardenia Avenue, Limbury, Luton, Beds. LU3 2NS **Tel:** 01582-571187
Fax: 01582-561506
E-mail: johnmcardle@sky.com
Website: www.stjosephsrc.org.uk
Rev John McArdle, *Deacon*: **Rev James Grennell**, 39 Blandford Avenue, Luton LU2 7AY **Tel:** 01582-580877
M: *Sat 1st M of Sun 6.30pm. Sun 9am, 11am, 7pm. Hds 9.30am, 7.30pm.*
- ***Daughters of the Holy Spirit,*** 8 Marsh Road, LU3 2NH. **Tel:** 01582-573149.
- ***Sisters of the Sacred Heart (St Jacut):*** 55 Kingsdown Avenue, Luton LU2 5BA **Tel:** 01582-897378
- ***Sisters of St Clare,*** 3 Abigail Close, Luton LU3 1ND **Tel:** 01582-424518

6. † St Margaret of Scotland (1946)
22a Bolingbroke Road, Farley Hill, Luton, Beds LU1 5JD **Tel:** 01582-720966
E-mail: stmargaret@freeuk.com
Rev Eamon Murray, *Also in Residence:* **Rev Pat Branagan.**
M: *Sun 9am, 11am. Hds 9am, 7.30pm.*

7. † St Martin de Porres (1962)
366 Leagrave High Street, Luton, Beds. LU4 0NG **Tel:** 01582-663706
E-mail: frjonhill@orangehome.co.uk
Rev Jonathan Hill.
M: *Sat 1st M of Sun 6.30pm. Sun 9am, 11am, 6.30pm. Hds (vigil 6.30pm), 9am, 7.30pm.*

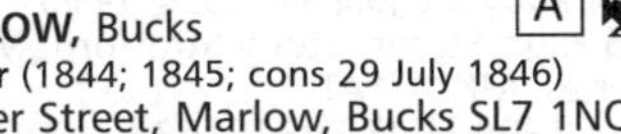

■ **MARLOW,** Bucks
† St Peter (1844; 1845; cons 29 July 1846)
7 St Peter Street, Marlow, Bucks SL7 1NQ
Tel: 01628-483696
Canon Bosco Clark.
E-mail: bosco.clarke@googlemail.com
M: *Sun 9am, 11am, 5.30pm. Hds 7.30am, 7.30pm.*

■ **MILTON KEYNES,** Bucks
1. Our Lady of Lourdes (1974, 1976)
40 Lloyds, Coffee Hall, Milton Keynes, Bucks MK6 5EB **Tel/Fax:** 01908-670850
Website: www.ourladyoflourdes.org.uk
Rev Joseph Williams.
M: *Sun 10am, 6.30pm; Malayalam Group, 6.30pm 1st Sat of month. Hds 9.30am, 7.30pm.*
- ***Diocesan Pastoral & Religious Education Centre,*** 40 Lloyds, Coffee Hall, Milton Keynes, Bucks MK6 5EB **Tel:** 01908-233121 **Fax:** 01908-233131

1a Ecumenical Church of Christ the Cornerstone (1987; 1992)
300 Saxon Gate West, Milton Keynes MK9 2ES
Tel: 01908-237777 **Fax:** 01908-200216
E-mail: citychurchmk@aol.com
Website: www.cornerstonemk.org.uk
Served from Milton Keynes (1).

M: *Sat 1st M of Sun 5.30pm; Hds: 12.30pm.*
Catholic Member of Ministerial Team: **Rev Joseph Williams.**

2. St Augustine (1981)
Langcliffe Drive, Heelands, Milton Keynes, MK13 7PL **Tel/Fax:** 01908-221228
E-mail: james.cassidy@zetnet.co.uk
- ***Canons Regular of the Immaculate Conception (CRIC)*. Fr James M Cassidy (CRIC),** Langcliffe Drive, Heelands, Milton Keynes, Bucks MK13 7PL
  M: *Sat 1st M of Sun 6pm. Sun 11am, 5pm. Hds (enquire at Presbytery).*
- ***Society of the Holy Child Jesus,*** 25 Bradwell Road, Bradville, MK13 7AX **Tel:** 01908-314448

2a The Cross, Stable Church and Community Centre
Downs Barn Blvd, Downs Barn.
Served from Milton Keynes (2).
M: *Sun 9am.*

3. St Francis of Sales
(1865; 1867; cons Jan 24 1981)
Radcliffe Street, Wolverton, Milton Keynes.
Tel/Fax: 01908-313162/564363
E-mail: bernard.barrett15@diginet.co.uk
Website: saints-francis-and-mary.org.uk
Rev Bernard Barrett. 22 Stratford Road, Milton Keynes MK12 5LJ
M: *Sun 11am, 5.30pm.*

3a St Mary Magdalene (1954; 1958)
105 High Street, Stony Stratford, Milton Keynes, MK11 1AT
Tel: 01908-564363/313162
Served from Milton Keynes (3).
Resident: **Rev Richard Barrett**
M: *Sat 1st M of Sun, 6.30pm. Sun 9.15am. Hds 7.30pm.*

4. St Thomas Aquinas (1903; 1956)
1 Sycamore Avenue, Bletchley, Milton Keynes MK2 2JE **Tel:** 01908-372315
E-mail: staq@uwclub.net
Rev Michael Harrison. *Deacon:* **Rev Noel Guina**, 3 Penina Close, Bletchley MK3 7TL **Tel:** 01908-649356
E-mail: guina@btinternet.com
M: *Sat 1st M of Sun, 6pm Sun 7.30am, 8.30am (Italian). Hds Please ring for details.*

A

4a All Saints (1965)
Shenley Road, Bletchley.
Served from Milton Keynes No 4.
M: *Sun 9am, 11am, 6.30pm. Hds Please ring for details.*

5. St Edward the Confessor Shenley
Rev Paul Hardy. Burchard Crescent, Shenley Church End, Milton Keynes MK5 6DX **Tel/ Fax:** 01908-504771
E-mail: vine01@btopenworld.com
M: *Sat 1st M of Sun 6pm. Sun 8.30am, (July/August - check time), 10.30am. Hds (vigil 7.30pm), 7.30am.*
- ***Sisters of the Holy Family, (Bordeaux),*** 61 Engaine Drive, Shenley Church End MK5 6BA **Tel:** 01908-505720

6. Christ the King (1993)
Kents Hill. Part of the Ecumenical Project.
1 Frithwood Crescent, Kents Hill MK7 6HG
Tel: 01908-671342 **Rev James Evans.**
M: *Sun 11.30am (Anglican/Free Church worship 9.30am). Hds 7.30pm.*
- ***De Montfort University,*** Milton Keynes Campus. *Ecumenical Chaplain:* **Rev Susan Chapman.**

■ MISSENDEN, Bucks
See Great Missenden.

■ NEWPORT PAGNELL, Bucks
† St Bede (1953; 1987)
High Street, Newport Pagnell, Milton Keynes **Tel:** 01908-671342
Served from Milton Keynes No6.
Rev James Evans.
M: *Sat 1st M of Sun 6.30pm. Sun 9am, Hds (vigil 7.30pm). 10am.*
NB. *(Full facilities only on Sat evng Vigil Mass, Holy days & Week day Masses).*

■ NORTHAMPTON
1. See start of the parish list

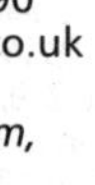

2. † St Aidan (1957; 1964)
Manor House, 10 Manor Road, Kingsthorpe NN2 6QJ
Tel: 01604-715661 **Fax:** 01604-713590
E-mail: tonymcdstaidan@tinyworld.co.uk
Mgr Anthony McDermott.
M: *Sat 1st M of Sun 6pm. Sun 7am, 9am, 7pm. Hds 9.15am, 7.30pm.*

3. † St Gregory the Great (1947; 1954)
Park Avenue North. **Tel:** 01604-713015
E-mail: andrew.behrens@ntlworld.com
Rev Andrew Behrens. 22 Park Avenue North, NN3 2HS. *Deacons:* **Rev Michael Fleming**. 22 Lavant Walk, Parklands, Northampton NN3 6EL **Tel:** 01604-647750
E-mail: mvf@btinternet.com
Rev Rory Stewart. 39 Bush Hill, Northampton NN3 2PD **Tel:** 01604-408407
Rev Michael Graney, 16 Ledaig Way, Northants NN3 6DA **Tel:** 01604-452327
M: *Sat 1st M of Sun 6pm. Sun 9am, 11am. Hds 7am, 9am, 7pm.*
- ***Daughters of the Holy Spirit:*** 255 Abington Avenue, Northampton NN3 2BU **Tel:** 01604-720437

A

4. The Sacred Heart (1974; 1976)
Pyramid Close, Weston Favell, Northampton NN3 8DP **Tel:** 01604-402301

- ***Sacred Heart Fathers (SCJ):*** **Rev Francis Calnan** (*Superior and Parish Priest*). **M:** *Sun 9am, 10.30am, 6pm. Hds 9.30am, 7.30pm.*

5. † St Patrick (1953; 1994)
Ashwood Road, Duston
Tel: 01604-751071
Website: www.duston.org.uk
Rev Phillip Swingler. 28 Peveril Road, Duston. NN5 6JW
M: *Sat 1st M of Sun 6pm. Sun 9.30am, 11am. Hds 9.30am, 7pm.*
- ***Sisters of Nazareth,*** Nazareth House, 116/120 Harlestone Road, NN5 6AD Old People's Home. **Tel:** 01604-751385
- ***Daughters of the Holy Spirit,*** 22 Holyrood Road, Northampton NN5 7AH **Tel:** 01604-756192

A

6. SS Stanislaus and Lawrence
(Polish Church), Duke Street.
Tel/Fax: 01604-631623
Rev Bogdan Cisek, Flat 2, St Lawrence House, Duke Street, Northants NN1 3BA
M: *Sun 10.30am. Hds 7pm.*
- ***Sisters of the Holy Family of Nazareth,*** 437 Wellingborough Road, Northampton NN1 4EZ **Tel:** 01604-629328

7. SS Francis and Therese
Overslade Close, Clannell Road, Hunsbury Heath NN4 0RZ **Rev Brendan Killeen**; *Deacon:* **Rev Peter Found**, 123 Bouverie Road, Hardingstone NN4 6EG
Tel: 01604-768483
M: *Sat 1st M of Sun 7pm. Sun 9.30am. Hds 10am, 7.30pm.*

8. Our Lady of Perpetual Succour
Great Billing, Northants. See Great Billing.

■ OLNEY, Bucks
† Our Lady Help of Christians and St Lawrence
(1899; 1900; cons 26 Aug 1952)
West Street, Olney, Bucks MK46 5HJ
Tel: 01234-711212 **Fax:** 01234-241349
Parish Co-ordinator: **Sr Rita Scott DHS**.
Rev Malcolm Bull, 27 Cardington Road, Bedford MK42 0BN
Tel: 01234 350628
M: *Sat 6.30pm. Sun 10.30am. Hds 7pm.*
- ***Daughters of the Holy Spirit:*** St Joseph's Convent, 33 West Street, Olney, MK46 5HH **Tel:** 01234-711267 13 Aspreys, Olney, MK46 5LN **Tel:** 01234-712162

■ OUNDLE, Northants
† The Most Holy Name of Jesus (1971)
West Street, Oundle, Northants.
Mgr Peter Wilson. The Priest's House, 10 Stoke Hill, PE8 4BH **Tel:** 01832-272615
Website: www.oundlechurch.freeserve.co.uk
M: *Sat 1st M of Sun 6.15pm (Oundle School Chapel). 10am. Hds 12.50pm, 7pm.*

■ PRINCES RISBOROUGH, Bucks
† St Teresa of the Child Jesus
(1922; 1938; cons 3 Oct 1945)
New Road, Princes Risborough, Bucks. HP27 0JN
Tel: 01844-345578
Fax: 01844-274503
E-mail: Geraldmoorcraft85@hotmail.com
Mgr Gerald Moorcraft.
M: *Sat 1st M of Sun 6.30pm. Sun 8am, 10am. Hds 9am, 8pm.*

A

■ RAUNDS, Northants
St Thomas More (1967)
Marshalls Road. Served from Thrapston.
M: *Sun 11am, 6.30pm. Hds 10am.*

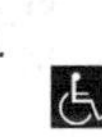

■ ROTHWELL, Northants
St Bernadette (1959)
Rock Hill, NN14 2BY Served from Kettering.
M: *Sun 10.30am. Hds 7pm.*

■ RUSHDEN, Northants
† St Peter (1902; 1904; 1956)
Higham Road, Rushden, Northants.
Tel: 01933-353649
E-mail: fjw.stpeters@ukonline.co.uk
Website: www.catholicrushden.org.uk
Rev Joe Walsh. 1 Hayway, NN10 6AG
M: *Sat 1st M of Sun 6.30pm. Sun 9am, 10.30am. Hds 9.30am, 7.30pm, at Sharnbrook; Vigil 7.30pm.*

■ SHEFFORD, Beds
† St Francis of Assisi
(1728; 1884; cons 3 July 1884)
High Street, Shefford, Beds.
Tel: 01462-813436
E-mail: frbennie@ontel.com
Rev Benjamin Noonan. 25 High Street, SG17 5DD *Deacon:* **Rev Peter Hyde**. 63 Hillfoot Road, Shillington, Hitchin, Herts SG5 3NS **Tel:** 01462-711702
M: *Sun 9am, 5.15pm, Hds 9.30am, 7.30pm.*

A

■ SLOUGH, Berks
1. † Our Lady Immaculate and St Ethelbert
(1885; new church cons 19 April 1910).
Wellington Street, Slough, Berks SL1 1XU
Tel: 01753-523147
E-mail: saintethelberts@ukgateway.net
Revv Raymond Abuga MSP, Patrick Feeney SPS.
M: *Sun 9am, 11am, 6.30pm. Hds 9.30am, 12.30pm.*

2. The Holy Redeemer (1968; 1990)
Presbytery, Wrexham Road, Slough SL2 5QR
Tel: 01753-578328
E-mail: noeltconnolly@yahoo.com
Rev Noel Connolly SPS.

M: *Sat 1st M of Sun 6.30 pm. Sun 9.30am, 11am. Hds 7.30pm.*

- ***Brigidine Sisters,*** 47 The Cherries, Wexham, Slough, Berks SL2 5TS **Tel:** 01753-575827

3. † The Holy Family
(1955; 1957; cons 8 May 1968)
Trelawney Ave, Langley
Tel: 01753-543770
E-mail: holyfamily@freeuk.com
Website: www.holyfamily.co.uk
Canon Kevin O'Driscoll, 226 Trelawney Avenue, Langley, SL3 7UD

M: *Sat 1st M of Sun 5.30pm. Sun 9.30am, 11am, 6.30pm. Hds 9.30am, 7.30pm.*

- ***Daughters of St Paul,*** Convent of Our Lady Queen of Apostles, Middle Green, SL3 6BT **Tel:** 01753-557629 **M:** *Sun 8.45am*

4. † St Anthony (1934; 1964) A S
Presbytery, Farnham Road, Slough, Berks SL2 3AE **Tel/Fax:** 01753-643320
E-mail: rich.mor@btopenworld.com
Rev Richard Moroney, Farnham Road. *Deacons*: **Rev Frank Shepherd**. Broom House, Stoke Poges Lane, Stoke Poges, Slough SL2 4NP **Tel:** 01753-529456 **Rev Paul Lipscomb,** Crane House, Rowanhurst Drive, Farnham Common, Slough SL2 3HG
Tel: 01753-645349
E-mail: paullipscomb@btinternet.com
Rev Marek Gajdus, 3 Hadlow Court, Slough SL2 3XQ **Tel:** 01753-733582

M: *Sat 1st M of Sun 6.30pm. Sun 8am, 10.15am. Hds eve 7.30pm, 7am, 9.15am, 12noon.*

5. † Divine Mercy (Polish Church)
48 Pitts Road, Slough, Berks SL1 3XH
Tel: 01753-533861
E-mails: parafiaslough@btinternet.com darek.kuwaczka@btinternet.com

- ***Marian Fathers (MIC):*** **Revv Dariusz Kuwaczka, Krzysztof Nowak**. *M: Sat 1st M of Sun 6pm. Sun 8.30am, 10am, 11.30am, 6pm. Hds 10.15am, 7pm.*

■ STONY STRATFORD
See Milton Keynes (3b).

■ SUNDON PARK
See Luton (4b).

■ THORNTON A
Thornton College, Milton Keynes, MK17 0HJ

- ***Religious of Jesus and Mary (RJM)***. **Tel:** 01280-813254 **Fax:** 01280-814004 *Chaplain:* **Rev Jim McCormick**. The Villa, Thornton College. MK17 0HH **Tel:** 01280-813466 **M:** *Sun & Hds 9am.*

■ THRAPSTON, Northants A
† St Paul the Apostle (1949; 1964; 1968)
2 Sackville Street, Thrapston, Northampton NN14 4NZ **Tel:** 01832-732772
Rev Brian Leatherland, 102 Finedon Road, Irthlingborough NN9 5TZ

M: *Sat 1st M of Sun 6.30pm. Sun 9am. Hds 7pm.*

■ TODDINGTON, Beds
St Elizabeth's Chapel.
Park Road, LU5 6HB
Served from Dunstable (1).
Tel: 01582-662710 **Fax:** 01582-670968
E-mail: stmary82@aol.com

M: *Sun 9am.*

■ TOTTERIDGE, Bucks
See High Wycombe (2).

■ TOWCESTER, Northants A
† St Thomas More
The Presbytery, 1 Meeting Lane, Towcester, Northampton NN12 6JX
Tel: 01327 359151
Rev Brendan Killeen.
All correspondence to Northampton (7).

M: *Sat 1st M of Sun 5.30pm. Sun 11am. Hds (vigil 7.30pm).*

■ TURVEY, Bedford
1. Monastery of Christ Our Saviour
Turvey Mews, Turvey, Bedford MK43 8DH
Tel: 01234-88121 **Fax:** 01234 881742
E-mail: turveymonks@yahoo.co.uk

- ***Benedictines (Olivetan Congregation) (OSB)***, **Rev John Mayhead** (*Superior*).

2. Priory of Our Lady of Peace
Turvey Abbey, Turvey, Bedford MK43 8DE
Tel: 01234-881432
E-mail: info@turveyabbey.org.uk
Website: www.turveyabbey.org.uk

■ WELLINGBOROUGH, Northants
1. † Our Lady of the Sacred Heart
(1868; 1886; cons 4 May 1954)
Ranelagh Road, Wellingborough, Northants.
Tel/Fax: 01933-222780
E-mail: edmundworthty@yahoo.co.uk
Rev Edmund Worthy. 82 Knox Road, NN8 1JA *Deacon:* **Rev Peter Griffin,** 178 London Road, Wollaston, Northants NN9 2QS **Tel:** 01933-664611

M: *Sat 1st M of Sun 6pm. Sun 9am, 12.30pm (Polish). Hds 7pm.*

- ***Poor Handmaids of Jesus Christ,*** St Catherine's Convent, 49 Grove Street, Wellingborough NN8 3HW **Tel:** 01933-227978

2. St Edmund Campion
Henshaw Road, NN8 2BE
Served from Wellingborough (1).

Tel/Fax: 01933-222780
E-mail: edmundworthty@yahoo.co.uk
M: *Sun 10.30am, 5.30pm. Hds 9.15am.*

■ **WENDOVER,** Bucks
† **St Anne** (1950; 1961)
Aylesbury Street.
Tel: 01296-623404
Served from Great Missenden.
M: *Sun 9.15am. Hds (vigil 8pm). 10.30am.*

■ **WESTCOTT,** Bucks
† **St Edmund of Canterbury** (1949)
Lower Green. **Tel:** 01844-208754
Served from Long Crendon.
M: *Sun 8.30am. Hds 7.30pm.*

■ **WINSLOW,** Buckingham
† **St Alban's Chapel** (1941; 1948)
Sheep Street, Winslow, Buckingham MK18 3HL **Tel:** 01296-712615
E-mail: kevinoconnell168@aol.com
Rev Kevin O'Connell.
M: *Sat 1st M of Sun 6pm. Sun 11am Hds 10am, 8pm.*

■ **WOBURN SANDS,** Milton Keynes
† **St Mary** (1926; 1956; cons 8 May 1957)
Aspley Hill, Woburn Sands, Milton Keynes MK17 8NN **Tel/Fax:** 01908-583195
E-mail: stmarys.church@zen.co.uk
Rev Kenneth Bowen.
M: *Sat 1st M of Sun 6.30pm. Sun 8am, 10.30am. Hds 10am, 7.30pm.*

■ **WOLVERTON**
See Milton Keynes (3a).

■ **YELVERTOFT,** Northants
Our Lady of the Most Holy Rosary (1957)
Served from Daventry.
E-mail: staugustinedav@aol.com
M: *Sun 9am. Hds 6pm.*

■ **ORDERS AND CONGREGATIONS, ETC**

■ **Men**
Benedictines (Olivetan): Turvey (1).
Canons Regular of the Immaculate Conception: Milton Keynes (2).
Carmelites (Discalced): Gerrards Cross.
Marian Fathers: Fawley Court, Slough (5).
Sacred Heart Fathers (St Quentin): Northampton (4).
Scalabrini Fathers: Bedford (4).
Society of Christ (Polish): Dunstable (2).
Vincentians: Dunstable (1).

■ **Women**
Benedictines (Olivetan): Turvey (2).
Bon Secours Sisters (of Paris): Bourne End.
Bridgettine Sisters (Rome): Iver Heath.
Brigidine Sisters: Slough (2).
Clare, Sisters of St: Corby (2), Luton (5).
Holy Child Jesus, Society of the: Milton Keynes (2).
Holy Cross, Sisters of the: Gerrards Cross.
Holy Family (Bordeaux), Sisters of: Milton Keynes (5).
Holy Family of Nazareth, Sisters of the: Northampton (6) (Polish).
Holy Name of Jesus, Sisters of the: (Polish)
Holy Spirit, Daughters of the: Northampton (1, 3, 5), Bedford (2, 3), Luton (2, 5), Olney.
Jesus and Mary, Religious of: Thornton, Buckingham.
Mary Immaculate, Sisters of: Laxton Hall (Polish).
Nazareth, Sisters of: Northampton (5).
Our Lady, Sisters of: Kettering.
Paul, Daughters of St: Slough (3).
Poor Handmaids of Jesus Christ: Wellingborough (1).
Providence, Daughters of: Aylesbury (2).
Sacred Heart of Jesus, Sisters of the (St Jacut): Luton (5).
Sacred Heart, Sisters of the: Great Missenden.

■ **SOCIETIES AND ORGANISATIONS**
For Societies and Organisations without representation in the diocese please see the main Societies and Organisations section.

Advent. A support group of priests and religious who have resigned active ministry. *Chair:* **Maura Potter. National web:** www.adventgroup.org.uk *Local contacts:* **Maura Potter,** 14 Lawrence Way, Burnham, Slough, Berks SL1 6HQ **Tel:** 01628-666278 **Web:** maurapotter@hotmail.com

Aid to the Church in Need. A charity supporting Christians who are persecuted and in pastoral need. *Nat. Director:* **Neville Kyrke-Smith,** *Area Sec:* **Heather Ward,** 11 Deepdale Road, Wollaton, Nottinghamshire NG8 2FU **Tel:** 01159-283603 **E-mail:** Heatherward@tinyworld.co.uk

Archconfraternity of St Stephen for Altar Servers. *Diocesan Director:* **Rev Peter Griffin,** 82 Knox Rd, Wellingborough NN8 1JA *Diocesan Contact:* **Ken de Boize,** c/o 82 Knox Rd, Wellingbrough NN8 1JA

Association of Blind Catholics. The Association produces a monthly cassette tape for members of extracts from Catholic newspapers. It also sends members, on request, tapes of various religious books on a "lending library" system. This Association caters not only for the totally blind but for those who are visually impaired. *Secretary:* **Mr Paul Questier,** 58 Oakwood Rd, Horley,

Surrey RH6 7BU **Tel:** 01293-772104 *Chairman & Diocesan Representative:* **Mr David Tinkler Tel:** 01536-485490

Association of Interchurch Families. *Bedfordshire Contact:* **Elaine and Leslie Leach**, 58 Aylesbury Road, Bedford MK41 9RE **Tel:** 01234-401842 **E-mail:** les.elaine.leach@ntlworld.com *Milton Keynes contact:* **Beverley** and **Paul Hollins**, 3 Castle Meadow Close, Newport Pagnell MK16 9EJ **Tel:** 01908 312043 **Email:** info@interchurch-families.org.uk *Berkshire contact:* **Rita and Mike Courthold**, 23 Hillside Road, Hungerford RG17 0BH **Tel:** 01488-684232 **E-mail:** j.j.d.courthold@rl.ac.uk *Buckinghamshire contact:* **Amanda and Cris Johnson**, 328 Berkhampstead Road, Chesham, Bucks HP5 3HF **Tel:** 01494-786648

Association of Our Lady of Mount Carmel. A worldwide lay apostolate, dedicated to increasing adoration of Our Eucharistic Lord through Rosary Circles, regular vigils of prayer and Holy Hours. *Spiritual Director* **Rev Brendan Grady, OCarm**. *Secretary*: (Leicester Centre) **Mr Des O'Reilly**, 32 Hilary Crescent, Whitwick, Coalville, Leicester LE67 5PL **Tel:** 01530-834446

Association of Separated and Divorced Catholics. *Diocesan Representative:* **Mr Henry Worthy**, 52 Teesdale, Northampton NN3 5DH **Tel:** 01604-513032 **Website:** www.asdcengland.org.uk

Beginning Experience. Lay ministry for people experiencing loss through bereavement, separation or divorce. *Contact:* **Felicity Harrison**. 16 Mapperley Drive, Northampton NN3 9UF **Tel:** 01604-403869

Catenian Association. Aylesbury Circle (169), *Secretary:* **TMB Kirwan**, Plumtree Cottage, Duck Lane, Ludgershall, Nr Aylesbury Bucks HP18 9XZ (177), *Secretary:* **Mr Mike Norton,** 179b Kimbolton Road, Bedford MK41 8DR. Luton Circle (216) *Secretary:* **Mr Oliver Bloor**, 2 George St, Markyate, St Albans, Herts AL3 8JX. Milton Keynes Circle (293) *Secretary:* **Mr P M Cywinski**, 10 Wood Lane, Great Linford ,Milton Keynes MK14 5AZ. Northampton Circle (35), *Secretary:* **Mr Frank Sudlow**, 3 Aspen Close, Berrydale, Northampton NN3 5HS **Tel:** 01604 406777 **E-mail:** sudlow@compuserve.com South Bucks Circle (124), *Secretary:* **Mr G B Cox**, 1 Kelvin Close, High Wycombe HP13 5ST.

Catholic Agency for Overseas Development (CAFOD). The Official Overseas Development and Relief Agency of the Catholic Church in England and Wales, member of the Caritas International Federation. *Diocesan Manager:* **Mr Frank Sudlow,** Cafod Northampton, St Gregory's Catholic Primary School, Grange Road, Northampton NN3 2AX **Tel:** 01604 785254. **E-mail:** northampton@cafod.org.uk. **Website:** www.cafod.org.uk/northampton

Catholic Charismatic Renewal: For information contact: *Northampton Diocesan Service Committee:* **John and Veronica Murphy**, 78 Sundon Road, Harlington, Beds LU5 6LS **Tel:** 01525-873366

Catholic Clothing Guild. Northampton Diocesan Division. *President*: Awaiting Appointment. *Hon Secretary/Treasurer:* **Mrs Freda Sidebotham**. 6 Alwyn Close, Luton, Beds. LU2 7JX **Tel:** 01582-721922

Catholic Handicapped Children's Fellowship. *Priest with responsibility for handicapped:* **Rev Canon K O'Driscoll**. **Tel:** 01753-543770 *Chairman*: **Judith Beare**, 26 Bunyans Close, Leagrave, Luton LU3 2PX **Tel:** 01582-571943 *Secretary*: **Andrea Leather**, 34 Mendip Way, Sundon Park, Luton **Tel:** 01582-503533 *Treasurer*: **Ted Leather**, 34 Mendip Way, Sundon Park, Luton. **Tel:** 01582-503533 *Booking Officer for chalet at Hemsby:* **Mrs. Kath Scott**, 4 Cotswold Gardens, Sundon Park, Luton. **Tel:** 01582-574051 Luton Deanery Mass 1st Sun of month (see local bulletins).

Catholic Women's League. *President*: **Mrs Eileen Carkelt,** 'Grey Squirrels' 9 Ashlea Road, Gerrards Cross, Bucks SL9 8NY. **Tel:** 01753 888969. *Vice President:* **Mrs Cherry-Anne Evans,** 38 Lionel Ave, Wendover, Bucks HP22 6LP. **Tel:** 01296 622097. *Secretary:* **Mrs Jane Dawson,** 16 Sefton Paddock, Stoke Poges, Bucks SL2 4PT **Tel:** 01753-663892 *Chaplain:* Awaiting Appointment

Christian Campaign for Nuclear Dis-Armament. *South Midlands Regional Representative:* **Barbara Sunderland,** 13 Park Lane, Henlow, Beds SG16 6AT **Tel:** 01462-814186

Christian Life Community. *Contact for Midlands Region:* **John and Margaret Partridge**, 129 Windmill Road, Oxford OX3 7DN **Tel:** 01865 764919 **E-mail:** partridge700@btinternet.com

Christian Mediation Centre. *Regional contact:* **William Neeson**, 5 Hillside

Way, Weston Favell, Northampton NN3 3AW **Tel:** 01604 411581 **E-mail:** bill@ananda96.fsnet.co.uk

The Grail *Diocesan Representative:* **Mrs Chris Drysdale**, 99 Huntley Grove, Peterborough, Cambs PE1 2QW

Jesus Caritas Priests' Fraternity. *Contact:* **Rev John Danford Tel:** 01525-372321 or **Rev Derek Lance Tel:** 01604-491759

Knights of St Columba. Prov 38 (Northampton). *Prov Grand Knight*: **Mr Michael Smith**, 24 Lambourn Court, Emerson Valley, Milton Keynes MK4 2DA. **Tel:** 01908-507184 *Prov Secretary:* **Peter Dellar**, 10 Miletree Crescent, Dunstable, Beds LU6 BLS **Tel:** 01582 SL1969. Province 23 (Thames Valley), *Prov Grand Knight:* **John Johnson**, 9 Tancred Road, High Wycombe HP13 5EQ **Tel:** 01494 438941

Legion of Mary. *President, Northampton Curia:* **Mrs Catherine Stratten**, 9 Cranmere Avenue, Northampton NN1 5SF **Tel:** 01604-471755 *Secretary:* **Joyce Gilsenan**, 8 Cook Close, Walton Park, Milton Keynes MK7 7JA **Tel:** 01908 550189

Life. *Aylesbury*: Office **Tel:** 01296-428651. *High Wycombe:* Office 01494-448544. *Northamptonshire*: *Chairperson:* **Mrs Margaret Refoy, Tel:** 01536-483903 *National office:* **Tel:** 01926-421587 **E-mail:** info@lifeuk.org **Website:** www.lifeuk.org **Helpline Tel:** 0800 915 4600

Latin Mass Society *Northamptonshire Representative:* **Paul Beardsmore,** 4 Sandringham Way, Market Harborough, Leicestershire LE16 8EP **Tel:** 01858 434037 **E-mail:** pbeardsmore@btinternet.com

Luton Good Counsel. An agency providing pro-life pregnancy counselling from a Catholic perspective, including free pregnancy testing, counselling, practical help, moral support, post-abortion counselling and training for Natural Fertility Awareness. *Contacts:* **Mrs Emanuela Coy**, 18 West Hill Rd, Luton LU1 3LY **Tel:** 01582-655246; **Mrs Margaret Langley**, 16 West Hill Road, Luton LU1 3LY **Tel:** 01582-411155

Maranatha Community. An inter-denominational Christian Community dedicated to Unity, Renewal and Healing. *Contact:* **Sr Bernadette Larkin**, 41 Plested Court, Stoke Mandeville, Aylesbury, Bucks HP22 5UB **Tel:** 01296-615169

Marriage Care (Formerly CMAC). *Headquarters:* Clitherow House, 1 Blythe Mews, Blythe Road, London W14 0NW **Tel:** 0207-371 1341 **Fax:** 0207-371 4921 Professionally trained marriage counsellors offer counselling for those with marital and relationship difficulties. Appointments: Watford/Luton: **Tel:** 0207-243 1898 Milton Keynes: **Tel:** 01908-696606 Northampton: **Tel:** 0800-389 3801 South Bucks: **Tel:** 01494-525875

Missionaries of the Poor Supporters Association (MoSPA). Based in the Diocese this organisation, a registered charity, supports the Missionaries of the Poor by raising funds for the poor and destitute who are living in parts of the world where there are insufficient resources. *Chairman:* **Rev Ken Payne,** St Aidan's, Little Chalfont, Bucks HP7 9NE *Secretary:* **Mrs Judith Bentley,** 6 High Street, Great Billing NN3 9DT *Treasurer:* **Miss Caroline Loftus,** 85 Broadway East, Northampton NN3 2PP **E-mail:** kenpayne@post.com **Website:** www.mopsa.org.uk

National Board of Catholic Women. *Diocesan Link:* **Mrs Maura Potter**, 14 Lawrence Way, Burnham, Slough Berks SL1 6HQ **Tel:** 01628 666278 **E-mail:** maurapotter.nbcw@hotmail.co.uk

NOAH Enterprise. Provides support for homeless and socially excluded people in Luton through day-care, training and work experience. Welfare Services: 141 Park Street, Luton LU1 3HG **Tel:** 01582-728416 **Fax:** 01582-486757 Training Services: 11-15 High Town Road, Luton LU2 0BW **Tel:** 01582-736751 Furniture Link: 54 Church Street, Luton LU1 3JG **Tel:** 01582-484001

Northampton Notre Dame Association. An association of former Notre Dame High School pupils. *Contact:* **Mrs Jose Sear** *(President).* 23 Penfold Close, Northampton NN2 8AP **Tel:** 01604-843161 or **Mrs Mary March** *(Secretary)* 418 Kettering Road, Northampton NN3 6QL **Tel:** 01604-642857

Our Lady's Catechists. For details, *Please Contact:* **Mrs Jean White**, Pixie Cottage, Ellesborough Road, Wendover, Bucks HP22 6EL **Tel:** 01296-583280

Pax Christi. *Diocesan Representative:* **Mr Graham Ryan**, 75 London Road, Luton, Beds LU1 3UG **Tel:** 01582-618926 **E-mail:** g.ryan93@ntlworld.com

Priest's Eucharistic League, The purpose of the League is renewal in Christian life and ministry. Though originally intended for priests, the League in Britain now welcomes into associate membership students of the priesthood, permanent deacons, religious and special ministers of the Eucharist. *Diocesan Director:* **Rev Frank McDermott**, 13 Pevensey Close, Bedgrove, Aylesbury Bucks HP21 9UB **Tel:** 01296 427881

Pro Labore Dei, (In aid of the destitute). An ecclesial movement with a radical fundamental option for the poorest of the poor. *Contact:* **Sr Theresa**. 2 Pembroke Ave, Luton LU4 9BH **Tel:** 01582-593741 **Mbl:** 07949-124364 **E-mail:** theresa@pro-labore-dei.org **Website:** www.prolaboredei.org

Rainbows for all God's Children. Rainbows is an international organisation which helps children and adults through the grieving process following the loss of a parent through death or through family separation. Rainbows National Office and Resource Centre: Unit 7, High Town Enterprise Park, York Street, Luton LU2 0HA **Tel:** 01582-724106 **Fax:** 01582-728102 *Contact:* **Mr Bill Danaher.** **E-mail:** rainbows.dc@virgin.net **Website:** www.rainbowsgb.org *Diocesan Contacts:* **Sr Brenda Moore, Tel:** 01604-720437; **Mrs Carole Behrens, Tel:** 01604 713015 **E-mail:** carole.behrens@ntlworld.com **Miss Christine Cornwell, Tel:** 01753 887243 **E-mail:** christine@cornwell-charitydays.co.uk **Mrs Carole Shoreland, Tel:** 01604 494236 **E-mail:** carole_shoreland@hotmail.com **Mrs Helen Finkenrath, Tel:** 01234 824435 **E-mail:** helen@finkenrath.freeserve.co.uk

Secular Franciscan Order. *Contact:* **Mr Michael J Mortimer, SFO** 40 The Ridgeway, Bedford MK41 8ES

Secular Order of Discalced Carmelites. A group meets regularly at St Joseph's Priory, Gerrards Cross. Please ring for further details. **Rosemary Hill, Tel:** 01844-346438

Society of St Gregory. Works to foster knowledge and understanding of the liturgy and music of the Church and to improve standards. *Diocesan Contact:* **Maureen Hicks**, Westways, 15 Burkes Road, Beaconsfield **Tel:** 01494 673178 **E-mail:** membership@ssg.org.uk

Society for the Protection of Unborn Children (SPUC). Leighton Buzzard Branch. *Contact*: **Mr Jim Rueth**, 6 Lime Grove, Linslade, Beds. LU7 7SU **Tel:** 01525-757830 *Northampton Contact:* **Alan Eccles**, 45 Westrising, Northampton NN4 0TR **Tel:** 01604 674049

St Barnabas Society. *Regional Representative:* **Dr Cyprian Blamires**, The Mount, Burnmill Road, Market Harborough, Leics LE16 7JG **Tel/Fax:** 01858-468224 **E-mail:** cpblamires@aol.com

St Francis' Children's Society. The registered adoption and fostering agency of the Diocese. We find families for children with special needs, support birth parents and counsel adopted children and adults. *Office:* Collis House, 48 Newport Road, Woolstone, Milton Keynes MK15 0AA **Tel:** 01908-572700 **Fax:** 01908-572701 **E-mail:** enquiries@sfcs.org.uk **Website:** www.sfcs.org.uk *Directors:* **Mrs Christine Smith, Mr Richard Gordon**

St Thomas a Becket Foundation. The Foundation is a registered charity. Through the work of its pastoral workers it strives to be of pastoral support to people with disabilities in the Diocese of Northampton. Furthermore the Foundation offers help to parishes as they put in place the requirements of the Disability Discrimination Act. *Chairman of Trustees:* **Rev Kevin O'Driscoll**. 226 Trelawney Ave, Langley, Slough SL3 7UD **Tel:** 01753-543770 *Pastoral Worker:* **Mr John Bonner**.

St Vincent de Paul Society. Northampton Central Council. *President:* **Richard Massey**, 10 Magnolia Drive, Rushden, Northants NN10 0XD **Tel:** 01933-313456 **E-mail:** richardem@hotmail.co.uk

Teams of Our Lady. An international Catholic Movement for Christian married couples that aims to deepen the couples' spirituality. A 'Team' consists of four or five couples and a priest or religious as spiritual advisor meeting monthly to share the journey of faith, guided by the Holy Spirit. *Contact couple:* **Paul and Clare Callaghan**, 4 Butlers Close, Aston-le-Walls, Daventry, Northants NN11 6UH **Tel:** 01295-660652 **E-mail:** pauljcallaghan@onetel,com *Chaplain:* **Rev James Evans**, 1 Frithwood Crescent, Kents Hill MK7 6HG **Tel:** 01908-671342 **Website:** www.teamsofourlady.org.uk

Union of Catholic Mothers. *President*: Appointment Pending, *Deputy President:* **Mrs Linda Lawless, Tel:** 01933 359395 *Secretary:* **Mrs Adrianne Hutchins, Tel:** 01494-775326 *Treasurer:* **Mrs Valerie Brierley, Tel:** 01933-319166 *Media Officer:* **Mrs Jenny Hyde, Tel:** 01462-711702 *Chaplain:* **Rev Gerard Byrne**, St Brendan, Beanfield Ave, Corby NN18 0AZ **Tel:** 01536 202879

Walsingham Association. *National Secretary:* **Miss Anne Milton**. Pilgrim Bureau, Friday Market, Walsingham, Norfolk. NR22 6EG **Tel:** 01328-820217 **Fax:** 01328-821087 **E-mail:** rcnatshrine@aol.com **Website:** www.walsingham.org.uk *Local Contact and Diocesan Pilgrimage Director:* **Rev Mr Michael Fleming**. 22 Lavant Walk, Parklands, Northampton NN3 6EL **Tel:** 01604-647750 **E-mail:** mvf@btinternet.com

Worldwide Marriage Encounter (includes Marriage Encounter and Engaged Encounter Weekends). Worldwide Marriage Encounter has helped thousands of couples in the UK to bring new joy to their marriages and strengthen their foundations. *Diocesan Contacts:* **Chris and Pru Hill**, 4 Crediton Close, Northampton NN3 3AJ **Tel:** 01604 639697 **E-mail:** hill@chrisandpru.net **Website:** www.wwme.org.uk

Youth 2000 - Midland Region. *Contact:* **Francis Hooper, Tel:** 01604 636033 **E-mail:** francishooper@btinternet.com

■ HOSPITALS

To contact the Catholic Chaplain of a particular hospital we suggest you contact the hospital reception directly.

■ CATHOLIC SCHOOLS - MAINTAINED

■ BEDFORDSHIRE

▲ Lower

St John Rigby Lower, Polehill Avenue, MK41 9DQ **Tel:** 01234-401900 **Fax:** 01234-401661 **E-mail:** stjohnrig@deal.bedfordshire.gov.uk *(Bedford)*

St Joseph's Lower, Chester Road, MK40 4HN **Tel:** 01234-352062 **Fax:** 01234-00420 **E-mail:**stjolow@deal.bedfordshire.gov.uk *(Bedford 1)*

St Mary's Lower, Dunstable Road LU1 4BB **Tel:** 01582-602420 **Fax:** 01582-63974 **E-mail:** stmaryscaddington@schools.bedfordshire.gov.uk *(Caddington)*

St Vincent's Lower, Hammersmith Gardens, Dunstable, LU5 5RG **Tel/Fax:** 01582-862456 **E-mail:** stvincent@deal.bedfordshire.gov.uk *(Houghton Regis)*

▲ Infant/Primary

Sacred Heart Primary, Langford Drive, LU2 9AJ **Tel:** 01582-730704 **Fax:** 01582-451877 **E-mail:** sacred.heart.infants.admin@luton.go.uk *(Luton 3)*

St Joseph's Infant, Gardenia Avenue, LU3 2NS **Tel:** 01582-573446 **Fax:** 01582-561555 **E-mail:** st.josephs.infants.head@luton.gov.uk *(Luton 5)*

St Margaret of Scotland Infant, Rotherham Avenue, Farley Hill, LU1 5PP **Tel:** 01582-729590 **Fax:** 01582-481289 **E-mail:** st.margaret.of.scotland.infants.admin@luton.gov.uk *(Luton 7)*

St Martin de Porres Primary, Pastures Way, LU4 0PF **Tel:** 01582-617600 **Fax:** 01582 617601 **E-mail:** st.martin.de.porres.primary.admin@luton.gov.uk *(Luton 8)*

▲ Junior

St Joseph's Junior, Gardenia Avenue, LU3 2NS **Tel:** 01582-572964 **Fax:** 01582-565845 **E-mail:** st.josephs.junior@luton.gov.uk *(Luton 5)*

St Margaret of Scotland Junior, Rotherham Avenue, Farley Hill, LU1 5PP **Tel:** 01582-723430 **Fax:** 01582-655440 **E-mail:** st.margaret.of.scotland.junior.admin@luton.gov.uk *(Luton 7)*

▲ Middle

St Gregory's Middle, Biddenham Turn, MK40 4AT **Tel/Fax:** 01234-268649 **E-mail:** stgreg@deal.bedfordshire.gov.uk *(Bedford)*

▲ Upper Comprehensive

St Thomas More Upper, Tyne Crescent, Brickhill, MK41 7UL (13-18) **Tel:** 01234-400222 **Fax:** 01234-400223 **E-mail:** email@stm.bed.sch.uk *(Bedford)*

Cardinal Newman Comprehensive, Warden Hill Road, LU2 7AE **Tel:** 01582-597125 **Fax:** 01582-503088. **E-mail:** cardinal.newman.head@luton.gov.uk *(Luton)*

■ BERKSHIRE

▲ Infant & Nursery

Our Lady of Peace Infant & Nursery, Derwent Drive, SL1 6HW **Tel:** 01628-661886 **Fax:** 01628-660130 **E-mail:** post@ourlady-inf.slough.sch.uk *(Burnham)*

▲ Junior

Our Lady of Peace Junior, Derwent Drive, SL1 6HW **Tel:** 01628-666715 **Fax:** 01628-666950 **E-mail:** post@ourlady-jun-slough.sch.uk *(Burnham)*

▲ Primary

St Anthony Primary, Farnham Road, SL2 3AA **Tel:** 01753-645828 **Fax:** 01753-645011

E-mail: post@stanthonys.slough.sch.uk *(Slough)*

St Ethelbert's Primary, Wexham Road SL2 5QR **Tel:** 01753-522048 **Fax:** 01753-552613 **E-mail:** post@stethelberts.slough.sch.uk *(Slough)*

Holy Family Primary, (Grant Maintained), High Street, SL3 8NF **Tel:** 01753-541442 **Fax:** 01753-549721 **E-mail:** school.admin@ holyfamilycatholicschool.org.uk *(Langley)*

▲ Secondary School

St Joseph's High, Shaggy Calf Lane, SL2 5HW **Tel:** 01753-524713 **Fax:** 01753-579128 **E-mail:** office@st-josephs.slough.sch.uk *(Slough)*

▲ Secondary Grammar

St Bernard's Convent, Langley Road, SL3 7AF **Tel:** 01753-527020 **Fax:** 01753-576919 **E-mail:** secretary@ st-bernards.slough.sch.uk *(Slough)*

■ BUCKINGHAMSHIRE

▲ Infant/Primary Combined

St Joseph's Infant, Hazell Avenue, HP21 7JF **Tel:** 01296-484618 **Fax:** 01296-719748 **E-mail:** office@ stjosephsrcinfant.bucks.sch.uk *(Aylesbury)*

Our Lady's Primary, Amersham Road, Amersham HP6 5PL **Tel:** 01494-726390 **Fax:** 01494-726795 **E-mail:** headteacher@ ourladys.bucks.sch.uk *(Amersham)*

St Louis Primary, Harris Court, HP20 2XZ **Tel:** 01296-488915 **Fax:** 01296-486754 **E-mail:** office@stlouisrcc.bucks.sch.uk *(Aylesbury)*

St Joseph's Primary, Priory Road, SL9 8SB **Tel:** 01753-887743 **Fax:** 01753-892971 **E-mail:**office@ st-josephscombined.bucks.sch.uk *(Chalfont St Peter)*

St Augustine's Primary, Daw's Hill Lane, HP11 1PW **Tel:** 01494-522338 **Fax:** 01494-443098 **E-mail:** ekennedy@staugustines.bucks.sch.uk *(High Wycombe)*

St Peter's Primary, Prospect Road, SL7 2PJ **Tel:** 01628-472116 **Fax:** 01628-488123 **E-mail:** office@stpetersrc.bucks.sch.uk *(Marlow)*

St Thomas Aquinas Primary, St Mary's Avenue, Bletchley, Milton Keynes, MK3 5DT **Tel/Fax:** 01908-373977 **E-mail:** stthomascombined@milton-keynes.gov.uk *(Milton Keynes)*

Bishop Parker Primary, Barton Road, Bletchley, Milton Keynes. MK2 3BT **Tel:** 01908-372129 **Fax:** 01908-645031 **E-mail:** bishopcombined@milton-keynes.gov.uk *(Milton Keynes)*

St Monica's Primary, Currier Drive, Neath Hill, MK14 6HB **Tel:** 01908-606966 **Fax:** 01908-608486 **E-mail:** stmonicas@milton-keynes.gov.uk *(Milton Keynes)*

St Mary Magdalene Primary, Ardwell Lane, Greenleys, Milton Keynes MK12 6AY **Tel:** 01908-321746 **Fax:** 01908-220533 **E-mail:** stmarymagdalenec@ milton-keynes.gov.uk *(Milton Keynes)*

St Bernadette's Primary, Tewksbury Lane, Monkston Park, Milton Keynes MK10 9PH **Tel:** 01908-692438 **Fax:** 01908-691739 **E-mail:** stbernadettes@ milton-keynes.gov.uk *(Milton Keynes)*

▲ Junior & Secondary

St Edward's Junior, Hazell Avenue, HP21 7JF **Tel:** 01296-424544 **Fax:** 01296-381509 **E-mail:** office@stedwards.bucks.sch.uk *(Aylesbury)*

St Paul's Comprehensive, Phoenix Drive, Woughton Campus, MK6 5EN **Tel:** 01908-669735 **Fax:** 01908-676206 **E-mail:** enquiries@st-pauls.org.uk *(Milton Keynes)*

St Bernards Secondary, Daws Hill Lane, HP11 1PW **Tel:** 01494-535196 **Fax:** 01494-446523 **E-mail:** office@st-bernards.bucks.sch.uk *(High Wycombe)*

■ NORTHAMPTONSHIRE

▲ Infant & Primary

Our Lady of Walsingham Primary, Occupation Road, NN17 1EE **Tel:** 01536-203805 **Fax:** 01536-200702 **E-mail:** head@ ourladys-pri-corby.northants-ecl.gov.uk *(Corby)*

St Brendan's Primary, Beanfield Avenue, Corby NN18 0AZ **Tel:** 01536-202491 **Fax:** 01536-407912 **E-mail:** head@ stbrendans-pri.northants-ecl.gov.uk *(Corby)*

Our Lady's Infant, Henshaw Road, Wellingborough NN8 2BE **Tel:** 01933-224900 **Fax:** 01933-224902 **E-mail:** head@ ourladys-inf.northants.ecl.gov.uk *(Wellingborough)*

St Gregory's Primary, Grange Road, Northampton NN3 2AX **Tel:** 01604-403511 **Fax:** 01604-403606 **E-mail:** head@ stgregorys.northants.ecl.gov.uk *(Northampton)*

St Mary's Primary, Woodside Way, King's Heath, Northampton NN5 7HX

Tel: 01604-581011 **Fax:** 01604-581397 **E-mail:** bursar@stmarys.northants-ecl.gov.uk *(Northampton)*

Good Shepherd Primary, Kingsland Gardens, Kingsthope, Northampton NN2 7BH **Tel:** 01604-714399 **Fax:** 01604-714672 **E-mail:** head@thegoodshepherd.northants-ecl.gov.uk *(Northampton)*

St Mary's Primary, Aston-le-Walls, Nr. Daventry, NN11 6UF **Tel** 01295-660258 **E-mail:** head@stmarys-pri.northants-ecl.gov.uk *(Aston-le-Walls)*

St Patrick's Primary, Patrick Road, Corby NN18 9NT **Tel:** 01536-744447 **Fax:** 01536-461374 **E-mail:** head@stpatricks.northants-ecl.gov.uk *(Corby)*

St Edward's Primary, Eastleigh Road, Kettering NN15 6PT **Tel:** 01536-481430 **Fax:** 01536 522354 **E-mail:** head@stedwards.northants-ecl.gov.uk *(Kettering)*

St Thomas More Primary, Northampton Road, Kettering NN15 7JZ **Tel/Fax:** 01536-512112 **E-mail:** head@stthomasmore.northants-ecl.gov.uk *(Kettering)*

▲ Junior

Our Lady's Junior, Henshaw Road, Wellingborough NN8 2BE **Tel:** 01933-222396 **E-mail:** head@ourladys-jun.northants-ecl.gov.uk *(Wellingborough)*

▲ Secondary

Thomas Becket RC Upper, Becket Way, Kettering Road North, Northampton NN3 6HT **Tel:** 01604-493211 **Fax:** 01604-497300 **E-mail:** admin@thomasbecket.northants.ecl.gov.uk *(Northampton)*

■ CATHOLIC SCHOOLS - INDEPENDENT

■ BERKSHIRE

▲ Primary

St Bernard's Prep. Hawtry Close, Slough, SL1 1TB **Tel:** 01753-521821 **Fax:** 01753-552364 **E-mail:** info@stbernardsprep.org *(Slough)*

■ BUCKINGHAMSHIRE

▲ Primary

St Teresa's, Aylesbury Road, Princes Risborough HP17 0JW **Tel:** 01844-345005 **Fax:** 01844-345131 **E-mail:** office@stteresas.bucks.sch.uk *(Princes Risborough)*

▲ Primary and Secondary

Thornton College, Convent of Jesus and Mary, Thornton, Milton Keynes, MK17 0HJ **Tel:** 01280-812610 **Fax:** 01280-824042 **E-mail:** head@thorntoncollege.com *(Thornton)*

DIOCESE OF NOTTINGHAM

Province of Westminster

Consisting of the Counties of Derbyshire, Leicestershire, Lincolnshire, Nottinghamshire and Rutland except parts of the High Peak and Chesterfield districts of Derbyshire and the district of Bassetlaw in Nottinghamshire

Patrons of the Diocese

Our Blessed Lady Immaculate, 8 December

St Hugh of Lincoln, 17 November

Bishop

Rt Rev Malcolm McMahon OP, Bishop of Nottingham: Born in London 14 June 1949; ordained 26 June 1982; consecrated Bishop of Nottingham 8 December 2000

Residence:
Bishop's House, 27 Cavendish Road East,
The Park, Nottingham NG7 1BB
Tel: 0115-947 4786 **Fax:** 0115-947 5235
Website: www.nottingham-diocese.org.uk

Rt Rev Malcolm McMahon OP, Bishop of Nottingham

■ **ADMINISTRATION**

■ **Diocesan Curia**
Willson House, Derby Road, Nottingham NG1 5AW **Tel:** 0115-953 9800

■ **Vicars General**
Mgr Canon Thomas McGovern, St Joseph's Presbytery, Station Road, Oakham, Rutland LE15 6QU
Tel: 01572 722308
Rev John Guest 23 Belle Vue Road, Ashbourne Derbyshire DE6 1AT
Tel: 01335 342236

■ **Episcopal Vicars**
Nottinghamshire: **Rev Eamonn O'Hara,** Sacred Heart Presbytery, 99 Carlton Hill, Carlton, Notts NG4 1FP
Tel: 0115-9118266 **Fax:** 0115-9100684
Derbyshire: **Rev John Sherrington,** 36 Uttoxeter Road, Mickleover, Derby DE3 9GE
Tel: 01332-514107
Leicestershire & Rutland: **Rev John J Maloney**, Blessed Sacrament, Gooding Avenue, Braunstone, Leicester LE3 1JS
Tel: 0116-285 8795
Lincolnshire: **Rev Michael Moore**, The Presbytery, Ashby Road, Scunthorpe, North Lincolnshire DN16 2RS
Tel: 01724-844895 **Fax:** 01724-844895

■ **Vicar for Religious**
Sr Madeleine Campion CSJP, St Joseph's Convent, 134 Ratcliffe Road, West Bridgford, Nottingham NG2 5HG
Tel: 0115-982 5355

■ **Trusteees and Finance Committee**
The Bishop, The Vicars General, Rev Mgr Canon David Forde, Rev Canon Edward Jarosz, Rev Ka Fai Lee, Rev Michael Moore, *Financial Secretary and Secretary to the Trustees:* **Mr Edward Poyser**, Willson House, Derby Road, Nottingham, NG1 5AW
Tel: 0115-953 9800
Fax: 0115-953 9805 (Secretary)

■ **Diocesan Archives**
Rev Canon Anthony Dolan. Willson House, Derby Road, Nottingham NG1 5AW
Tel: 0115-953 9803

■ **Diocesan Secretaries**
Bishop's Secretary: **Miss Catherine Campbell.**

■ **Chancery**
Mgr John Hadley. Willson House, Derby Road, Nottingham NG1 5AW **Tel:** 0115-953 9804 **Fax:** 0115-953 9808

■ **Bishop's Chaplain**
Rev Geoffrey Hunton. Bishop's House, 27 Cavendish Road East,
The Park, Nottingham NG7 1BB
Tel: 0115-947 4786 **Fax:** 0115-947 5235
E-mail: bishop-chaplain@nrcdt.org.uk

■ **Diocesan Safeguarding Co-ordinator**
Mr John Creedon, Family Care, Warren House, 2 Pelham Court, Pelham Road, Nottingham NG5 1AP **Tel:** 0115-960 3010 **Fax:** 0115-960 8374

■ **Registrar for Deceased Clergy**
Rev Canon O O'Neill. Our Lady of Victories, 1 Fairfield Road, Market Harborough, Leicestershire LE16 9QQ **Tel:** 01858-462359 **Fax:** 01858-464211

■ **Diocesan Communications Officer**
Awaiting Appointment, Bishop's House, 27 Cavendish Road East, The Park, Nottingham NG7 1BB
Tel: 0115-947 4786 **Fax:** 0115-947 5235

■ **Diocesan Property Department**
Consultant: **Mr Howard Walters MBIAT**. Willson House, Derby Road, Nottingham NG1 5AW
Tel: 0115-953 9802 **Fax:** 0115-953 9805

■ **Historic Churches Committee**
Chairman: **Mgr Thomas McGovern**. *Secretary:* **Mr Howard Walters MBIAT**. Willson House, Derby Road, Nottingham NG1 5AW
Tel: 0115-953 9802 **Fax:** 0115-953 9805

■ **EDUCATION AND FORMATION**

■ **Diocesan Education Service**
Director: **Mr Edward Hayes,** Diocesan Centre, Mornington Crescent, Mackworth, Derby DE22 4BD **Tel:** 01332-293833 **Fax:** 01332-293305 Willson House, Derby Road, Nottingham NG1 5AW
Tel: 0115-953 9801 **Fax:** 0115-953 9806

■ **Diocesan Youth Officer**
Rev Joseph Wheat. The Briars Residential Youth Centre, Crich Common, Crich, Matlock, Derbyshire DE4 5BW
Tel: 01773-852044
E-mail: wheatJ75@hotmail.com

■ **Diocesan Director of Vocations**
Rev David Cain. 21 Hinkley Road, Leicester LE3 OTA. **Tel:** 0116-251 9370

■ **LITURGY AND ECUMENISM**

■ **Diocesan Liturgical Commission**
President: **The Bishop**. *Chairman:* **Rev Paul Chipchase,** The Presbytery, Laughton Way, Ermine Estate, Lincoln LN2 2HE
Tel: 001522-522971 **Fax:** 01522-539008

■ **Diocesan Master of Ceremonies**
Rev Philip McBrien. The Presbytery, New Street, Oadby, Leicester LE2 4LJ
Tel: 0116-271 5139
Assistant: **Rev John Cairns**.

■ **Diocesan Ecumenical Commission**
Chairman: **Rev Kevin Clark**.
Secretary: **Mrs Monica Purdue**, 114 Cross Street, Arnold, Nottingham NG5 7BY
Tel: 0115-993 9235

■ **Diocesan Ecumenical Officers**
CT in all Lincolnshire: Awaiting Appointment. Nottinghamshire & Derbyshire; **Philip Webb.** Leicestershire: **John Downing.**

■ **CONSULTATIVE BODIES**

■ **Cathedral Chapter**
(erected 2 July 1852)
Provost: **Mgr Brian Dazeley.** *Canons:* **Mgri T McGovern VG, David Forde, Jonathan Moore, Joseph Phelan, Edward Walker, Rev Canons Bernard Needham, Owen O'Neill, Timothy O'Sullivan, Brendan O'Sullivan, Edward Jarosz.** *Canons Emeriti:* **Mgri Martin Cummins, Peter Dooling, Rev Canons Owen O'Neill, Patrick Snee.** *Honorary Canons:* **Roger Maher, Michael Bell, Anthony Dolan, John Berry, George Woodall.**

■ **College of Consultors**
The Bishop's Council.

■ **Council of Priests**
Chairman: **The Bishop.**
Minutes Secretary: **Rev Geoffrey Hunton.**

■ **DIOCESAN MATRIMONIAL TRIBUNAL**
Tribunal Office: Willson House, Derby Road, Nottingham NG1 5AW **Tel:** 0115-953 9804 **Fax:** 0115-953 9808 **Mgr Edward Walker** (*Vicar Judicial*), **Mgr John Hadley, Revv Peter Ingman, Canon George Woodall, Rev Keith Frisby. Mgr Provost Brian M Dazeley, Rev Peter Vellacott.**

■ **Justice and Peace Commission**
Priest with Responsibility: **Rev Alan Burbidge.** *Worker:* **Mr Paul Scola.** Diocesan Centre, Mornington Crescent, Mackworth, Derby DE22 4BD
Tel: 01332-293305

■ **NOTTINGHAM**
1. Cathedral Church of St Barnabas
(1842; cons 27 Aug 1844)
Derby Road, Nottingham NG1 5AE
Tel: 0115-953 9839 **Fax:** 0115-959 8112
Dean: **Revv Michael Brown, Bosco Lobo MSFS, Robert O'Callaghan, James Anthony (Deacon).**
M: *Sat 1st M of Sun 6.30pm. Sun 8am, 10am (Sung), 11.15am (Choral), 6pm. Hds (vigil 1st M) 6.30pm, 7.30am, 1pm, 6.30pm.*
Cathedral House, North Circus Street, Nottingham NG1 5AE **Tel:** 0115-947 4758
• ***Little Company of Mary,*** Cathedral Ho, North Circus Street, Nottingham NG1 5AE **Tel:** 0115-947 4758

■ **ALFRETON,** Derbyshire
† **Christ the King** (1883; 1927)
104 Nottingham Road, Alfreton, DE55 7GL
Tel: 01773-833174
Rev Cornellus Moynihan.
Deacon: **Rev Les Lemon.**
M: *Sat 1st M of Sun, 6.30pm, Sun 10.30am. Hds, as announced.*
• ***Franciscan Minoresses:*** San Damiano Convent. 1 Hall Street, Alfreton, Derby. DE56 7BT **Tel:** 01773-833168

■ **ALLESTREE,** Derby
See Derby (7).

■ **ALVASTON,** Derby
See Derby (4).

■ **ARNOLD**
See Nottingham (4).

■ **ASHBOURNE,** Derbyshire
† **All Saints** (1861; 1888)
23 Belle Vue Road, Ashbourne, Derbyshire DE6 1AT **Tel:** 01335-342236
Rev John Guest VG.
M: *Sun 9.30am. Hds, 7.30pm.*
• ***Sisters of Mercy,*** St Mary's Nursing Home, Ednaston, Brailsford, Derby DE6 3BY **Tel:** 01335-360753

■ **ASHBY,** Scunthorpe, North Lincs
See Scunthorpe (1).

■ **ASHBY-DE-LA-ZOUCH,** Leics
† **Our Lady of Lourdes** (1908; 1915)
Station Road, Ashby-de-la-Zouch, Leicestershire LE65 2GL **Tel:** 01530-412237
Mgr Canon Joseph Phelan.
M: *Sat 1st M of Sun 5.30pm. Sun 10am. Hds 9am, (Vigil) 7pm.*

■ **ASPLEY**
See Nottingham (16).

■ **AYLESTONE**
See Leicester (7).

■ **BAKEWELL,** Derbyshire
The English Martyrs (1890; 1948)
Buxton Road, Bakewell, Derbyshire DE45 1NS Served from Hassop.
M: *Sat 1st M of Sun 6.15pm. Sun 9am. Hds 7.30pm.*

■ **BARDNEY,** Lincolnshire
St Francis
Station Road. Served from Lincoln (1).

■ **BARTON-UPON-HUMBER,** North Lincs.
† **St Augustine Webster** (1842; 1848; 1938)
White Cross Street, Barton-upon-Humber, DN18 5DF **Tel:** 01652-632180
Served from Scunthorpe (2).
M: *Sun 11.15am. Hds (vigil) 7pm.*

■ **BEESTON**
See Nottingham (6).

■ **BELPER,** Derbyshire [A]
| **Our Lady of Perpetual Succour** (1909; 1919)
12 Gibfield Lane, Belper, Derbyshire DE56 1WA **Tel:** 01773-822182
Rev Michael Kirkham.
M: *Sat 1st M of Sun 6.30pm. Sun 11am. Hds As announced.*
• ***Franciscan Minoresses***, St Elizabeth's Convent, 19 Cherry Tree Avenue, Belper DE56 2JD **Tel:** 01773-823129

■ **BILBOROUGH**
See Nottingham (14).

■ **BINGHAM,** Notts
Served from Radcliffe-on-Trent.
M: *Bingham Methodist Church Sun 9am. Hds, 7pm.*

■ **BIRSTALL,** Leics
† **St Teresa of Lisieux**
(1938; 1941; cons 1942; 1989)
Front Street, Birstall, Leicester.
Tel: 0116-292 9939
Rev Keith Tomlinson IC.
• ***Institute of Charity (IC):*** 53 Front Street, Birstall, LE4 4DQ
M: *Sat 1st M of Sun 6.30pm, Sun 9.30am. Hds 7pm.*

■ **BOLSOVER,** Derbyshire
St Bernadette (1943; 1944)
High Street, Bolsover, Chesterfield.
Served from Shirebrook.
M: *Sat 1st M of Sun 6pm. Hds 7pm.*

■ **BORROWASH,** Derbyshire
† **St Hugh** (1959)
Derby Road, Borrowash DE72 3HB
Tel: 01332-673562
Rev John Mack. 68 Derby Road, DE72 3HB
M: *Sun 9.15am, 11am, 6.30pm. Hds 9.30am, 7.15pm.*

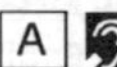

■ **BOSTON,** Lincs
† **St Mary** (1827; cons 3 October 1946)
24 Horncastle Road, Boston PE21 9BU
Tel: 01205-362056
Rev Chris Hogan. *Deacons:* **Revv David Baccas, David Witherick.**
M: *Sat 1st M of Sun 4pm. Sun 9.30am. Hds 9am, 7.30pm.*

■ **BOURNE,** Lincs
† **St Gilbert**
3 St Gilbert's Road, Bourne, PE10 9XB
Tel: 01778-423593
Rev Clement Orango MCCJ.
Deacons: **Revv Robert Dawson, Joseph Rogan.** *Also in residence:* **Rev Patrick O'Doherty** 18 Rosehip Road, Moreton, Bourne, Lincolnshire PE10 OPD
M: *Sat 1st M of Sun 6pm. Sun 8.45am. Hds 10am.*

■ **BRAUNSTONE**
See Leicester (2).

■ **BRIGG,** North Lincs
† **St Mary** (1770; 1873)
Barnard Avenue, Brigg DN20 8AS
Tel: 01652-652221
Rev Dominic O'Connor.
M: *Sat 1st M of Sun 6pm. Sun 10am. Hds (vigil 7.30pm), 9am.*

■ **BULWELL**
See Nottingham (9).

■ **BURTON-ON-TRENT,** Staffs
1. † **Holy Rosary** (1955)
Main Street, Stapenhill, Burton-on-Trent.
Tel: 01283-564814 **Fax:** 01283 530371
Rev Matthew Jakes. 125 Alexandra Road, Burton-on-Trent, DE15 0JD
M: *Sat 1st M of Sun 6.30pm. Hds 9.30am (school), 7.30pm.*

2. **St Joseph the Worker**
Mount Street, Winshill, Burton-on-Trent.
Served from Burton-on-Trent (1).
M: *Sun 9.30am, 6.30pm.*

■ **BUXTON,** Derbyshire
† **St Anne** (1850; cons 26 July 1897)
Terrace Road, Buxton SK17 6DU
Tel: 01298-23777 **Rev Dennis Higgins.**
M: *Sat 1st M of Sun 7pm. Sun 8.30am, 11am. Hds 10am, 7pm.*
• ***Presentation Sisters,*** Hardwick Square West SK17 6PX **Tel:** 01298-23653

■ **CAISTOR,** Lincolnshire
St Thomas More (1960)
Bank Lane, Caistor
Served from Market Rasen.
M: *Sun 9.15am.*

■ **CALVERTON,** Notts
St Anthony (1957)
Mansfield Lane, Calverton, Nottingham.
Served from Southwell.
M: *Sun 10.45am. Hds As announced.*

■ **CARLTON,** Nottingham
See Nottingham (5).

■ **CASTLE DONINGTON,** Leics
† **Church of The Risen Lord**
Hillside, Castle Donnington, Leics.
Served from Melbourne.
M: *Sat 1st M of Sun 6pm. Sun 9am. Hds As announced.*

■ **CHAPEL-EN-LE-FRITH,** Derbyshire
† **St John Fisher & St Thomas More** (1935; 1937)
The Presbytery, 2 Horderns Road, Chapel-en-le-Frith, High Peak, Derbyshire SK23 9ST **Tel:** 01298-813491
Rev Robert Thacker.
M: *Sat 1st M of Sun 6.30pm. Sun 11am. Hds 9.30am, 7.30pm.*

■ **CHELLASTON,** Derby
St Ralph Sherwin
Swarkstone Road, Derby.
Served from Derby (4).
M: *Sun 9am. Hds as announced.*

■ **CLAY CROSS,** Derbyshire
† **St Patrick and St Bridget** (1862; 1882)
Thanet Street, Clay Cross, Chesterfield.
Served from Alfreton.
M: *Sun 9pm. Hds as announced.*
• ***Franciscan Minoresses,*** St Clare's Convent, Stretton Road, Clay Cross S45 9AQ **Tel:** 01246-862621

■ **CLEETHORPES,** North East Lincs
† **Corpus Christi** (1914; 1930)
Grimsby Road, Cleethorpes.
Tel/Fax: 01472-692370
E-mail: corpuschristirc@connectfree.co.uk
Rev Anthony Colebrook.
M: *Sat 1st M of Sun 7pm. Sun 9.30am. Hds 7pm.*
• ***Sisters of St Joseph of Peace:*** 2 Machray Place, Grimsby Road, Cleethorpes DN35 7LJ

■ **CLIFTON,** Nottingham
See Nottingham, (2).

■ **COALVILLE,** Leics
† **St Wilfrid of York** (1887; 1900; 1961)
53 London Road, Coalville, LE67 3JB
Tel: 01530-832098 **Rev Peter Harvey.**
M: *Sat 1st M of Sun 6pm. Sun 10am. Hds 9.45am (School), 7.30pm.*

■ **CORBY GLEN,** Lincs
† **Our Lady of Mount Carmel** (Circa 1600; 1856)
High Street, Corby Glen, Grantham

NG33 4LU Served from Grantham.
M: *As Announced*

■ **COTGRAVE,** Notts
† Our Lady of Grace
12 Candleby Lane, Cotgrave, Nottingham NG12 3JG
Tel: 0115-989 2071
Served from Holy Spirit, West Bridgford.
M: *Sun 11am. Hds 7pm.*
- ***Sisters of Life,*** 22 Tollerton Park, Tollerton Lane, Tollerton.

■ **CRICH,** Derbyshire
'The Briars' Residential Youth Centre, Crich Common, Matlock, DE4 5BW
Tel: 01773-852044 **Fax:** 01773-852968
Tel: 01773-852439/852403/857936 *(Guests).*
Rev Joseph Wheat (*Director & Diocesan Youth Officer*),
M: *Sat 1st M of Sun 7.30pm. Sun As Announced. Hds As Announced.*

■ **CROWLE,** North Lincs
† St Norbert (1871; 1872)
Fieldside, Crowle, Scunthorpe, DN17 4HL
Tel: 01724-710260
Served from Gainsborough.
M: *Sun 11.15am. Hds 2pm, 7.30pm.*

■ **DEEPING ST JAMES,** Lincs
† Our Lady of Lincoln and St Guthlac
Hereward Way, Deeping St James.
Served from Bourne.
Tel: 01778-423593
M: *Sun 10.30am. Hds (Vigil) 7pm.*

■ **DERBY**
1. † St Mary (1750; cons 9 Oct 1839)
17 Bridge Gate, Derby DE1 3AU
Tel: 01332-346126
Rev Canon Timothy O'Sullivan VF.
Rev Peter Ingman.
M: *Sat 1st M of Sun 6.30pm. Sun 9am, 11am (Sung), 6.30pm. Hds (Vigil) 6.30pm, 1pm, 6.30pm.*
- ***Sisters of Mercy,*** Bridge Gate, DE1 3AU **Tel:** 01332-346920 St Philomena's Convent, Highfields, Broadway, DE3 1AU **Tel:** 01332-550122 Beechwood Convent, Broadway. **Tel:** 01332-558043

2. † St Joseph (1878; 1897; 1986)
Burton Road, Derby DE1 1TJ
Tel: 01332-343777 **Fax:** 01332-202074
Rev William Naylor.
M: *Sat 1st M of Sun 6.30pm. Sun 9am, 10.15am. Hds (vigil) 7pm, 9.30am.*

3. † St George and All Soldier Saints (1920; cons 23 April 1948)
Village Street, Old Normanton, Derby.
Tel: 01332-767038 **Revv Alan Burbidge, Gabriel Offor**, 40 Village Street, DE23 8SZ
M: *Sat 1st M of Sun 6.30pm. Sun 9.45am, 7pm. Hds 9.30am.*

4. † English Martyrs (1909; 1953)
Hollis Street, Alvaston, Derby DE24 8QU
Tel: 01332-574474
Rev Mark Brentnall.
M: *Sat 1st M of Sun 6.30pm. Sun 10.30am, Hds As Announced.*
- ***Sisters of Mercy,*** St John Fisher's Convent, Alvaston Street, DE24 0PA **Tel:** 01332-571506

5. † St Alban (1948; 1955; cons. 1976)
Roe Farm Lane, Chaddesden, Derby DE21 6ET **Tel:** 01332-672914
Rev Gerry Murphy.
M: *Sat 1st M of Sun 6.30pm. Sun 10am (Sung). Hds 9.30am, (St Alban's School in term time), 7.30pm.*
Ecumenical Church
on Oakwood, Bishop's Drive.
M: *Sun 5.30pm.*

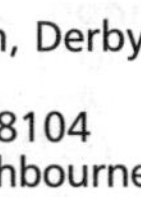

6. † Christ the King
(1960; 1972; cons 1978)
Prince Charles Avenue, Mackworth, Derby DE22 4BD
Tel: 01332-340161 **Fax:** 01332-348104
Rev John Guest VG (resident in Ashbourne).
M: *Sat 1st M of Sun 6pm. Sun 11am. Hds 9.30am.*

7. Holy Family (1971)
Blenheim Drive, Allestree, Derby.
Served from St Mary's, Derby (1).
M: *Sun 9.30am. Hds 7.30pm.*

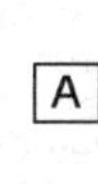

8. † Holy Spirit (1979)
Redwood Road, Sinfin, Derby.
Served from St George's, Derby (3).
M: *Sat 1st M of Sun 5.30pm. Sun 11.15am.*

9. † Our Lady of Lourdes
36 Uttoxeter Road, Mickleover, DE3 9GE
Tel: 01332-514107
Rev John Sherrington.
M: *Sat 1st M of Sun 6.30pm. Sun 8am, 10am. Hds 9.30am, 6.30pm.*

10. Polish Church of St Maximilian Kolbe (1897)
9 Gordon Road, Derby DE23 6WR
Tel: 01332-364078 **Fax:** 01332-343950
Rev Wojciech Rozdzenski.
M: *Sat 1st M of Sun 5pm. Sun 9.30am, 11am. Hds 11am, 7pm.*

■ **DUFFIELD,** Derbyshire
St Margaret Clitherow (ded 1981)
Hall Farm Road, Duffield, Derbyshire.
Served from Belper.
M: *Sun 9am. Hds As announced.*

■ **EARL SHILTON,** Leics
† St Peter and St Paul (1908)
Wood Street, Earl Shilton, Leicester.
Tel: 01455-842202
Rev Terence Fellows. 7 Melton Street, LE9 7FP
M: *Sat 1st M of Sun 6pm. Sun 11am. Hds 9.30am (at St Peter's School during term time), 7.30pm.*

■ **EAST LEAKE,** Notts
† Our Lady of the Angels (1955)
Main Street, East Leake, Loughborough, Leics. LE12 6LB
Tel/Fax: 01509-852147
Deacon: **Rev Peter Swarbrick.**
Rev Peter Vallacott. 19 De Ferrers Close, East Leake, Loughborough, Leics LE12 6QD
M: *Sat 1st M of Sun 6pm. Sun 10.30am. Hds (vigil) 7.30pm, 10am.*

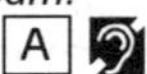

■ **EASTWOOD,** Notts
† Our Lady of Good Counsel
(1890; 1897; cons 24 April 1947)
280 Nottingham Road, Eastwood, Nottingham NG16 2AQ **Tel:** 01773-713532
Canon John Berry VF,
Deacon: **Rev Stephen Doona**
M: *Sat 1st M of Sun 5.30pm. Sun 10.15am. Hds (Vigil) 6.30pm, 9.30am.*

■ **EXTON,** Rutland
† St Thomas of Canterbury (1867)
Served from Oakham.
M: *Sun 9am.*

■ **GAINSBOROUGH,** Lincs
† St Thomas of Canterbury (1832; 1866)
Cross Street, Gainsborough DN21 2AX
Tel: 01427-612427
Rev Christopher O'Connor.
M: *Sat 1st M of Sun 7pm. Sun 9.15am. Hds (Vigil) 7.30pm, 9.30am.*

■ **GAMESLEY,** Derbyshire
† The Immaculate Conception
Long Lane, Broadbottom, Derbyshire.
Tel: 01457-852965 Served from Hadfield.
Priest in Residence: **Rev J Paul Entwistle,** 126 Glossop Road, Gamesley, Glossop, Derbyshire SK13 5HB
M: *Sun 9.15am. Hds as announced.*
• *Mass Centre:* St Margaret's School, Gamesley
M: *Sat 5pm. Hds as announced.*

■ **GLOSSOP,** Derbyshire
1. † St Mary Crowned
(1882; 1887; cons 16 August 1887)
Sumner Street, Glossop, Derbys SK13 8DP
Tel/Fax: 01457-852113
Served from Glossop (2).
M: *Sun 9.30am. Hds 9.30am, 7pm.*

2. † All Saints
(1803; 1836; cons 11 July 1936)
Church Street, Glossop, Derbys
Tel/Fax: 01457-852113
Mgr Canon Jonathan Moore.
M: *Sat 1st M of Sun 6pm. Sun 11am. Hds (Vigil) 7pm, 9.15am.*

■ **GRACE DIEU MANOR,** Coalville, Leics
Preparatory School, LE67 5UG
Tel: 01530-222276
• *Institute of Charity (IC):* **Rev Dennis Hare** (*Rector*) **Tel/Fax:** 01530-224140
E-mail: dennis.ic@btinternet.com

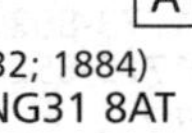

■ **GRANTHAM,** Lincs
† St Mary the Immaculate (1832; 1884)
1 North Parade, Grantham NG31 8AT
Tel: 01476-563935
Rev Canon Anthony Dolan.
M: *Sat 1st M of Sun 6pm. Sun 8am, 10am. Hds (vigil 7.30pm). 9am, 9.15am (in school term time), 7.30pm.*

■ **GRIMSBY,** North East Lincs
1. † St Mary on the Sea (1848; 1883)
Heneage Road, Grimsby, DN32 9DZ
Tel: 01472-342301 **Rev John Younger**
M: *Sun 9am. Hds 9.30am.*
• *Sisters of St Joseph of Peace,* St Francis Xavier's, 97 Abbey Road, DN32 0HN
Tel: 01472-343474

2. St John Fisher
Waltham Road, Scartho, Grimsby.
Served from Grimsby (1).
M: *Sat 1st M of Sun 6pm. Hds (vigil 7pm).*

3. St Pius X & St Peter (1960, 1993)
Chelmsford Avenue, Grimsby, North East Lincolnshire DN34 5DD
Tel: 01472-871632
Rev James Early VF (*Port Chaplain to Grimsby and Immingham*).
M: *Sun 11am. Hds 10am.*

■ **HADFIELD,** Derbyshire
† St Charles Borromeo
(1858; cons 28 May 1926)
Woolley Bridge Road, Hadfield SK13 1PQ
Tel: 01457-852351
Canon Daniel Bowdren VF.
M: *Sun 11am. Hds 9.30am.*

■ **HAINTON,** Lincs
St Francis de Sales (1736; 1836)
Served from Market Rasen.
M: *5.30pm.*

■ **HASSOP,** Derbyshire
† All Saints (1818)
Hassop, Bakewell, Derbys DE45 1NS
Tel: 01629 640241

• ***Holy Ghost Fathers (CSSp):*** **Rev Hugh Davoren** *Deacon:* **Rev John Hague.**
M: *Sun 10.30am. Hds 10am.*

■ HINCKLEY, Leics
† St Peter's (1756; 1824; 1835; 1960)
Priory Walk, Leicester Road, Hinckley LE10 1LW **Tel:** 01455-634443
Rev Frank Daly.
Deacon: **Rev Robin Pollard**
M: *Sat 1st M of Sun 6.30pm. Sun 8am, 10am. Hds 9am, 6.30pm.*

■ HOLBEACH, Lincs
† Holy Trinity (1956; 1966)
Foxes Lowe Road, Holbeach PE12 7PA
Tel: 01406-423034 **Fax:** 01406-423034
Served from Spalding.
M: *Sat 1st M of Sun 6.30pm. Sun 9.30am. Hds 7.30pm.*
• ***Sisters of Providence of the Immaculate Conception,*** Foxes Lowe Road, Holbeach. (*Parish Sisters*).

■ HORNCASTLE, Lincs
Parish Church of St Mary
Served from Woodhall Spa.
M: *Sat 1st M of Sun 6pm. Hds (vigil 6pm).*

■ HUCKNALL, Notts
† Holy Cross (1879; 1960)
Watnall Road, Hucknall, Notts. NG15 7NJ
Tel: 0115-953 9997 **Fax:** 0115-986 0880
Rev Frank Carvill.
M: *Sat 1st M of Sun 6.30pm. Sun 9.30am. Hds 9.30am, 6.30pm.*

■ HUSBANDS BOSWORTH, Leics
† St Mary (circa 1600; 1873)
Bosworth Hall, Husbands Bosworth.
Served from Market Harborough.
M: *Sun 8.15am.*

■ ILKESTON, Derbyshire
† Our Lady and St Thomas of Hereford (1858; cons 24 May 1930)
Regent Street, Ilkeston, Derbys.
Tel: 0115-932 5642
Rev Colin Taylor, 17 Nottingham Road DE7 5RF *Deacon:* **Rev Ray Faghy.**
M: *Sat 1st M of Sun 6.30pm. Sun 10.45am. Hds (Vigil) 7.30pm, 9.15am.*

■ IMMINGHAM, North East Lincs
Our Lady Star of the Sea
Allerton Drive, Immingham, DN40 2HP
Tel: 01469-573503
Rev Anthony Colebrook.
M: *Sun 10.30am. Hds As Announced.*
• ***Stella Maris,*** Seafarers' Centre.
Served from Grimsby (3).

■ KEYWORTH, Notts 
St Margaret Clitherow
Willow Brook. Served from East Leake.
Deacon: **Rev Peter Swarbrick.**
Sr M Beuno OP. 8 Elm Close, Keyworth. NG12 5AP **Tel:** 0115-937 2234
M: *Sun 9am.*

■ KIRBY MUXLOE, Leicester
St Andrew's
Hinckley Road. Served from Leicester (2).
M: *Sun 8.45am.*

■ KIRKBY-IN-ASHFIELD, Notts
Our Lady Help of Christians (1923)
Tel: 01623-754495 **Rev Frank Higgins.**
Presbytery, School Street, NG17 7BT
M: *Sat 1st M of Sun 6.30pm. Sun 10am, 6pm. Hds (Vigil 7.30pm), 9.30am, 7.30pm.*

■ LANGWITH JUNCTION
See Shirebrook.

■ LEICESTER A
1. † Holy Cross Priory (1777; 1824-5; 1951)
45 Wellington Street, Leicester LE1 6HW
Tel: 0116-255 6902 **Fax:** 0116-255 5552
• ***Dominicans (OP):*** **Revv Leon Pereira** (*Prior & Parish Priest*), **Duncan Campbell, Isidore Clarke, Fabian Radcliffe, Simon-Sebastian Robson, Euan Marley.**
M: *Sat 1st M of Sun 7.30pm. Sun 8am, 9.30am (Family Mass), 11am (Sung), 5pm (for students in term-time), 7pm. Hds (vigil 6.15pm). 10am, 12.40pm, 7.30pm.*

1a University Chaplaincies
Leicester University.
Chaplain: **Rev Peter Hunter,** Holy Cross Priory, 45 Wellington Street, Leicester LE1 6HW **Tel:** 0116-255 3856 (Priory) 0116-255 1212 (Chaplaincy)
De Montfort University.
Chaplain: As above
M: *Sun* 5pm *(term time at the Chaplaincy, Wellington Street).*

2. † The Most Blessed Sacrament (1935; 1938; 1957) A
Gooding Avenue, Leicester LE3 1JS
Tel/Fax: 0116-285 8795
Revv John J Maloney, Gi Hong Choi, Joel Nwalozie
M: *Sat 1st M of Sun 6pm. Sun 9am, 10.30am. Hds 9.30am, 7.30pm.*

3. † The Sacred Heart & St Margaret Mary (1883; 1890; 1924) A
Mere Road, Leicester.
Tel: 0116-262 4645 **Fax:** 0116-251 1437
Mgr John Lally, 25 Mere Road, LE5 3HS
M: *Sat 1st M of Sun 6pm. Sun 11.15am. Hds 9.15am, 7.30pm.*

DIOCESE OF NOTTINGHAM

4. † Mother of God (1957)
Greencoat Road, New Parks, Leicester.
Tel: 0116-287 2229
M: *Sun 10am. Hds 6.30pm.*
• ***Institute of Charity (IC),*** **Revv Paul Nellikulam, Joseph Pooavathumkal.**
Parish Sister: **Sr Anna Patricia Pereira IC**

5. † Our Lady of Good Counsel
(1845; 1922; 1975)
Gleneagles Avenue, Leicester.
Tel: 0116-266 1621
Rev Marcel Fangoo CSSp. 15 Peebles Way, Leicester LE4 7ZB
M: *Sat 1st M of Sun 6pm. Sun 10.15am. Hds 9am, 7.30pm.*

6. Our Lady of the Rosary
Armadale Drive, Nether Hall.
Served from Leicester (9).
M: *Sun 9am.*

7. † St Edward the Confessor (1915; 1921)
633 Aylestone Road, Leicester LE2 8TF
Tel: 0116-299 7231 **Fax:** 0116-291 0281
Rev P Coyle. *Deacon:* **Rev John Parker.**
M: *Sun 9.30am. Hds (Vigil) 7pm, 10am.*

8. † St John Bosco
Pasley Road, Eyres Monsell, Leicester
Tel: 0116-278 6134
Served from South Wigston.
M: *Sat Vigil 6pm, Sun 11.15am. Hds 7.30pm.*

9. † St Joseph (1938; 1942; 1968)
Uppingham Road, Leicester.
Tel: 0116-241 5159 **Fax:** 0116-241 5293
Rev John Daley IC.
12 Goodwood Road, LE5 6SG
M: *Sat 1st M of Sun 6pm. Sun 10.30am, 6pm. Hds 10am, 7pm.*
• ***Sisters of St Joseph of Peace,*** 411 Uppingham Road, LE5 6RA
Tel: 0116-241 6255

10. † St Patrick (1959)
100 Beaumont Leys Lane, Leicester LE4 2BD
Tel: 0116-235 3329 **Fax:** 0116-235 4599
Rev Jimmy Browne.
M: *Sat 1st M of Sun 6.30pm. Sun 8.30am, 10.30am. Hds (Vigil 7pm), 9.30am.*

11. † St Peter (1896; 1950)
21 Hinckley Road, Leicester LE3 0TA
Tel: 0116-251 9802 **Fax:** 0116-262 8608
Rev Canon Edward Jarosz.
In Residence: **Rev David Cain**
M: *Sat 1st M of Sun 6.30pm. Sun 8.45am, 11.15am. Hds (Vigil 6.30pm) 10am, 7pm.*
• ***Dominican Sisters,*** St Catherine's, 188 Glenfield Road, LE3 6DG
Tel/Fax: 0116-285 5575
• ***Servitium Christi,*** (Secular Institute), 11 Brampton Avenue, LE3 6DA
Tel: 0116-285 8057

12. † St Thomas More (1947; 1952)
75 Knighton Road, Knighton, Leicester LE2 3HN
Tel: 0116-221 8385 **Fax:** 0116-221 8514
Rev Malachy Brett VF.
M: *Sat 1st M of Sun 6pm. Sun 9am, 11am. Hds 10am, 7.30pm.*
• ***Carmelite Sisters (Corpus Christi)***. 15 Southernhay Close, Knighton, Leicester LE2 3TW **Tel:** 0116-270 4564

13. St Paul's Polish Church
Wakerley Road Extension, Leicester.
Rev Slawomir Jakubiec
M: *Sat 1sts M of Sun, 6pm, Sun 8.45am, 9.45am. Hds 10am, 7pm.*

14. Nether Hall
Rosary Chapel of Ease, Armadale Drive.
Served from Leicester (9).
M: *Sun 9am.*

15. † The Immaculate Conception
(1967; cons 1976)
New Street, Oadby, Leicester LE2 4LJ
Tel: 0116-271 5139
Rev Philip McBrien.
Deacon: **Rev Vincent Kelly**
M: *Sat 1st M of Sun 5.30pm. Sun 10am. Hds 10am, 7pm.*

16. † St Mary (1905)
Countesthorpe Road, South Wigston, LE8 2PG
Tel: 0116-278 3863 **Fax:** 0116-278 5546
Revv Stephan Foster, Richard Hardstaff.
Deacon: **Rev Kevin O'Connor.**
M: *Sun 8am, 10am, 6pm. Hds 9am (In St John Fisher School during term time), 12.30pm, 7.30pm.*

■ LINCOLN

1. † St Hugh (1799; 1893; cons 27 Jan 1927)
Monks Road.
Tel: 01522-528961 **Fax:** 01522-537685
Rev John Kyne. *Deacons:* **Revv Peter Brogan, John Wilford,**
34 Broadgate LN2 5AQ
M: *Sun 8.30am, 10am, 12.15pm (Pol), 7pm. Hds 10am, 7pm.*
• ***Sisters of Providence (of Ruillé-sur-Loire),*** St Joseph's Convent, The Mount, 16 Wragby Road, LN2 5SL
Tel: 01522-540894

2. † Our Lady of Lincoln (1933; 1964)
Laughton Way, Ermine Estate, Lincoln LN2 2HE

DIOCESE OF NOTTINGHAM

Tel: 01522-522971 **Fax:** 01522-539008
Rev Paul Chipchase,
Deacons: **Rev Peter Allen.**
M: *Sat 1st M of Sun 6.30pm. Sun 9.30am, 11am. Hds (Vigil 6.30pm), 9.45am.*

3. Ss Peter and Paul (1968)
Skellingthorpe Road, Lincoln LN6 7RB
Tel: 01522-682278 **Fax:** 01522-696838
Rev Kevin Clark.
M: *Sat 1st M of Sun 6pm. Sun 9am, 11am. Hds c.f. Newsletter.*

■ **LONG EATON,** Derbyshire
† St Francis of Assisi (1884; 1930)
199 Tamworth Road, Long Eaton NG10 1DH **Tel:** 0115-973 4816
Rev Sean Hanratty.
M: *Sat 1st M of Sun 6pm. Sun 10.30am. Hds 7.30pm.*

■ **LOUGHBOROUGH,** Leics
1. † St Mary (1833; 1836; 1925)
97 Ashby Road, Loughborough LE11 3AB
Tel: 01509-262123
- ***Institute of Charity (IC):*** **Rev Philip Scanlan IC, VF** (*Rector and Parish Priest*), **Rev Charles Sormany.**
  M: *Sat 1st M of Sun 6.30pm. Sun 9am, 11am. Hds (vigil 7.30pm). 9.15am, 7.30pm.*
- **Loughborough University Chaplaincy:** Served from Loughborough (2).
  M: *Sun 6pm.*

2. † Sacred Heart (1956)
203 Park Road, Shelthorpe, Loughborough LE11 2HE **Tel:** 01509-822646
Rev Peter Wade.
M: *Sat 1st M of Sun 5.30pm. Sun 10am. Hds 9.30am, 7pm.*
- ***Sisters of Providence,*** (Rosminians) Our Lady's Convent, Park Road, LE11 2EF Day School. Provincial House. **Tel:** 01509-212054

■ **LOUTH,** Lincs
† St Mary (1819; 1938)
69 Upgate, Louth, Lincs LN11 9HD
Tel/Fax: 01507-603277
Rev Paul Lloyd.
M: *Sat 1st M of Sun 6pm. Sun 10am. Hds 10am, 7pm.*

■ **LUDDINGTON,** North Lincs
† St Joseph and St Dympna (1872; 1877)
High Street, Luddington, Crowle.
Served from Gainsborough.
M: *1st Fri of M 7pm.*

■ **LUTTERWORTH,** Leics
† Our Lady of Victories and St Alphonsus (1880)
28 Bitteswell Road, Lutterworth LE17 4EY
Tel: 01455-552523 **Rev John Feeley.**
M: *Sat 1st M of Sun 5.30pm. Sun 10.15am. Hds (Vigil 7pm), 10.30am.*

■ **MABLETHORPE,** Lincs
† St Joseph (1913; 1938)
Seaholme Road, Mablethorpe, Lincs.
Tel: 01507-472300
Rev James Lynch. 2 Newstead Road, LN12 2PA
M: *Sat 1st M of Sun 7.30pm. Sun 9am. Hds 9.30am, 7.30pm.*
- ***Sisters of Notre Dame:*** 139 Victoria Road, Mablethorpe, Lincolnshire LN12 2AL **Tel:** 01507-478884

■ **MACKWORTH**
See Derby (6).

■ **MANSFIELD,** Notts
1. † St Philip Neri
(1862; 1878; 1925; cons 24 Mar 1925)
3 Chesterfield Road South, Mansfield NG19 7AB
Tel: 01623-623458 **Fax:** 01623-423363
Revv Philip Ziomek, Joseph Nnabblugwa,
Deacon: **Rev Barry Dickinson**
M: *Sat 1st M of Sun 6pm. Sun 8am, 10am, 6pm. Hds (Vigil 7.30pm), 8am, 12.10pm.*

2. † St Patrick (1958; 1989)
Clipstone Road West, Forest Town, Mansfield NG19 0BU **Tel:** 01623-622705
Rev Philip Holland.
M: *Sat 1st M of Sun 6.30pm. Sun 10.30am. Hds (vigil 7pm). 9am (in school during term time).*

3. Polish Church of Our Lady of Ostrobrama and St Barbara
Windmill Lane, Mansfield NG18 2AL
Tel: 01623-626470
Rev Szczepan Bober SAC. 38 Nursery Street, Mansfield NG18 2AG.
M: *Sun 11am. Hds 6pm (Winter), 7pm (Summer).*

■ **MARKET BOSWORTH,** Leics
Our Lady and St Gregory (1931)
Station Road, Market Bosworth.
Served from Earl Shilton.
M: *Sun 9.15am. Hds (vigil 7.30pm).*

■ **MARKET HARBOROUGH,** Leics
† Our Lady of Victories (1859; 1877, 2005)
Coventry Road, Market Harborough.
Tel: 01858-462359 **Fax:** 01858-464211
Rev Canon Owen O'Neill. 1 Fairfield Road, LE16 9QQ
M: *Sat 1st M of Sun 6.30pm. Sun 10am. Hds (vigil see News Letter).*
- ***Presentation Sisters,*** 60 Coventry Road, LE16 9BZ **Tel:** 01858-462432

■ **MARKET RASEN,** Lincs
† **Holy Rood** (1782; 1824; 1868)
King Street, Market Rasen LN8 3BB
Tel: 01673-842455 **Fax:** 01673-842455
Rev Thomas Breslin
Deacon: **Rev Stephen Boulter**
M: *Sun 11am. Hds 7.30pm.*

■ **MARPLE BRIDGE,** Cheshire
† **St Mary** (1859; cons 17 May 1946)
Hollins Lane, Marple Bridge, Cheshire
SK6 5BB **Tel:** 0161-427 2408
Rev John Cairns.
M: *Sat 1st M of Sun 6.30pm. Sun 11.15am. Hds See newsletter.*

■ **MATLOCK,** Derbyshire
† **Our Lady and St Joseph**
(1883; cons 22 June 1935)
Bank Road, Matlock, Derbyshire.
Tel/Fax: 01629-582804
Canon Bernard Needham VF. 1 St Joseph Street, Matlock, Derbyshire DE4 3NG
Deacon: **Rev Richard Walsh**.
M: *Sat 1st M of Sun 6pm. Sun 8.30am, 10.30am. Hds 9.30am, 7pm.*
• ***Presentation Sisters,*** Chesterfield Road, DE4 3FT **Tel:** 01629-582416 Chaplain: **Rev Trevor Clarke, Michael Tutcher Tel:** 01629-582703

■ **MEASHAM,** Derbyshire
† **St Charles Borromeo** (1881)
72 Bosworth Road, Measham, Swadlincote, DE12 7LQ **Tel:** 01530-270284
Served from Ashby-de-la-Zouch.
M: *Sat 1st M of Sun 6.45pm. Hds 10.30am.*

■ **MELBOURNE,** Derby
† **Our Lady of Mercy and St Philip Neri** (1906)
Church Street, Melbourne, Derby DE73 1EJ
Tel: 01332-862631
Rev Anthony Axe OP.
Deacon: **Rev Paul Boshell.**
M: *Sun 10.30am. Hds As Announced.*

■ **MELTON MOWBRAY,** Leics
1. † St John the Baptist (1840; cons 6 Apr 1842)
Thorpe End, Melton Mowbray, Leics.
Tel: 01664-562274
Rev James O'Hanlon, St Peter's Presbytery, 77 Welby Lane LE13 0ST.
M: *Sat 1st M of Sun 6pm (Convent). Sun 9am. Hds 7.30pm (School 9.15am).*
• ***St Francis' Convent,*** 52 Dalby Road, LE13 0BP **Tel:** 01664-562422

2. St Peter (1964)
Welby Lane, Melton Mowbray, Leics.
Served from Melton Mowbray (1).
M: *Sun 10.30am. Hds (vigil 7.30pm).*

3. Our Lady of Czestochowa
(Polish Church) (1963)
Sandy Lane, Melton Mowbray, Leics.
Tel: 01664-622101
Canon Stanislaw Tylka (119 Sandy Lane, LE13 0AW)
M: *Sat 1st M of Sun 7pm. Sun 11am. Hds 9am, 7pm.*

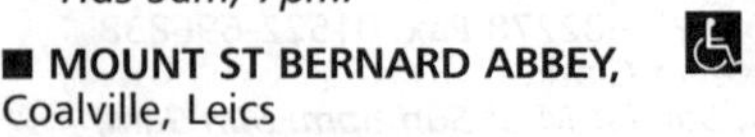

■ **MOUNT ST BERNARD ABBEY,**
Coalville, Leics
Our Lady and St Bernard
(1835-44; cons 20 Aug 1945)
Coalville, Leics LE67 5UL
Tel: 01530 832298/832022
Fax: 01530 814608
E-mail: mountstbernardabbey@btinternet.com
• ***Cistercians of Strict Observance (OCSO)***: **Rt Rev Dom Joseph Delargy** (*Abbot*), **Rt Rev Dom Ambrose Southey** (*Retired Abbot General*), **Revv Denis Geoghegan** (*Prior & Bursar*), **Peter Logue, Paul Diemer, Hilary Costello, Luke Harris, Andrew Henson, Richard Adam, Theodore Berkeley, Justin Barr, Anselm Stark, Mark Hartley, Matthew Dunn, Stephen Gowers, Peter Claver Craddy, Terence Wilson** (*Novice Master*), **Laurence Ezeilo** (*Guest Master,* **Tel:** 01530-839162), **Rufus Pound, John Paul Sanderson. Revv Bros Paul Greaves** (*Subprior*), **Gabriel Manogue, Thomas Taylor, Jonathan Gell, George Lord, Martin Horwath, David Howells, William Foster, Michael Burleigh, Erik Varden, Adam Suvit, Andrew Stojanovic.**
M: *Sun 8am, 9am (Sung, concelebrated). Hds 8am, 9am (Sung, concelebrated).*

■ **NARBOROUGH,** Leics
† **St Pius X** (1965)
52 Leicester Road, Narborough LE19 2DF
Tel: 0116-286 3676
Mgr John Hadley VF.
M: *Sat 1st M of Sun 6pm. Sun 9am, 10.30am. Hds 11am, 7.30pm.*

■ **NEW MILLS,** Derbyshire
† **The Annunciation** (1843; 1845)
St Mary's Road, New Mills SK22 3BW
Tel: 01663-743182 **Fax:** 01663-749412
Served from Marple Bridge.
M: *Sun 9.30am, 6pm. Hds See newsletter.*

■ **NEW OLLERTON,** Notts
† **St Joseph** (1929, 1995)
Sherwood Drive, New Ollerton NG22 9PP
Tel: 01623-860238
Rev John Tavares.
M: *Sat 1st M of Sun 6.30pm. Sun 10am. Hds (vigil 7pm), 10am, 7.30pm.*

■ **NEWARK,** Notts
† **Holy Trinity** (1802; 1836)
Boundary Road, Newark NG24 4AU
Tel: 01636-704936
Fax: 01636-704936
Rev Michael O'Donoghue.
Also in residence: **Rev Derl Daly.**
Rev Michael Mason, 5 Boundary Court;
Rev Brian Welsh, 9 Fell Croft, Farndon, Newark Notts NG24 3TB
Tel: 01636 676765
M: *Sat 1st M of Sun 7pm. Sun 10am, 6.30pm. Hds 7.30am, 9.30am, 7pm.*

■ **NOTTINGHAM**
1. See start of the parish list.

2. † **Corpus Christi**
Southchurch Drive, Clifton.
Tel: 0115-921 2964
Rev Christopher P Thomas, Presbytery, Listowel Crescent, Clifton NG11 9BP
M: *Sat 1st M of Sun 6pm. Sun 9.15am. Hds (Vigil) 7.30pm, 9.10am, 7.30pm.*

3. † **The Holy Spirit** (1879; 1930)
Melton Road, West Bridgford.
Tel: 0115-981 4271
Revv Gregory Tobin VF, Rev Christopher A Thomas. 29 Charnwood Grove, NG2 7NT
M: *Sat 1st M of Sun 6.30pm. Sun 9am, 10.30am. Hds 9.15am, 7.30pm.*
- ***Sisters of St Joseph of Peace,*** 134 Radcliffe Road, West Bridgford, NG2 5HG **Tel:** 0115-981 4068
- ***Lithuanian Catholic Centre,*** 16 Hound Road, West Bridgford, NG2 6AH **Tel:** 0115-982 1892 **Rev P Tverijonas.**

4. † **The Good Shepherd**
(1923; 1929; cons 22 June 1950; 1964; cons 27 Oct 1983)
3 Thackeray's Lane, Woodthorpe NG5 4HT
Tel: 0115-926 8288
Revv Frank McLaughlin, Ka Fai Lee, *Deacon:* **Rev John Wakeling**
M: *Sat 1st M of Sun 6.30pm. Sun 10am, 11.30am, 5.30pm, Hds, eve 7.30pm, 10am, 7.30pm.*
- ***Little Company of Mary,*** 3 Egerton Road, Woodthorpe, Nottingham NG5 4FF **Tel:** 0115-920 3383

5. † **The Sacred Heart of Jesus & St Bernadette**
(1877; 1883; 1931; cons 21 May 1945)
99 Carlton Hill, NG4 1FP
Tel: 0115-911 8266 **Fax:** 0115-910 0684
Rev Eamonn O'Hara
M: *Sat 1st M of Sun 6.30pm. Sun 10.30am. Hds 9.15am, 7.30pm.*

6. † **The Assumption**
(1884; 1898; 1954)
Foster Avenue, Beeston.
Tel: 0115-922 8145 **Fax:** 0115-925 5324
Rev Ephraim Nwachukwu. The Priest's House, 25 Foster Avenue, NG9 1AE
M: *St 1st M of Sun 5.30pm. Sun 9am. Hds (vigil 7.30pm), 1pm.*

7. † **Our Lady and St Edward**
(1885; 1956)
Gordon Road, Nottingham NG3 2LG
Tel: 0115-950 1064
- ***Franciscans (Friars Minor) (OFM):*** **Revv Quentin Jackson** (Vicar & *Parish Priest*), **John Forest Holden** (*Guardian*), **John McCaffery, Bro Didacus Pierce** Gordon Road, NG3 2LG
M: *Sat 1st M of Sun 6.30pm, Sun 9.30am, 11.15am. Hds 7.30am, 10am, 7.30pm.*

8. † **Our Lady of Perpetual Succour (Ukrainian Church)**
Sneinton Road, Nottingham.
Tel: 0115-950 5313 **Rev Mykola Martynyuk.** Thorneywood House, 575 Carlton Road, Nottingham NG3 7AF
M: *Sun 10am. Hds 10am, 7.30pm.*

9. † **Our Lady of Perpetual Succour**
(1890; 1920; 1955; cons 8 May 1951)
Brooklyn Road, Bulwell, Nottingham NG6 9ES
Tel: 0115-927 8403 **Fax:** 0115-975 0883
Rev Paul Newman.

M: *Sat 1st M of Sun 4.30pm. Sun 10.15am. Hds 9.30am, 7pm.*
- ***Poor Clares (Colettines),*** Brooklyn Road, NG6 9ET **Tel:** 0115-927 8489

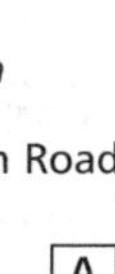

10. **The Infant of Prague**
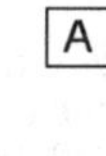
Cherry Orchard Mount, Nottingham NG5 5TQ Served from Nottingham (9).
M: *Sat 1st M of Sun 6pm. Hds (vigil) 7pm.*

11. **Our Lady and St Patrick in the Meadows**
(1867; 1883; closed in 1979; New church, 1981)
Launder Street, The Meadows, Nottingham NG2 1JH
Served from the Cathedral, Nottingham, (1)
M: *Sun 9.30am. Hds 9.30am.*

12. † **St Mary** (1880; 1910; cons 2 Feb 1931)
Goodliffe Street, Hyson Green, Nottingham
Tel: 0115-978 6473
Parish Sisters. 35 Belton Street, Hyson Green, Nottingham NG7 6FY
Served from Nottingham (15).
M: *Sun As announced.*

- ***Sisters of St Francis*** Reconciliation Centre, St Francis House, 20 Leslie Road, Forest Fields, Nottingham NG7 6PD. **Tel:** 0115-978 3889.
- ***Little Company of Mary,*** The Sanctuary, 588 Radford Road, Basford, Nottingham NG7 7EX **Tel:** 0115-979 1088

13. † St Augustine, Apostle of England (1879; 1923; cons 21 Sept 1940) A
Woodborough Road, Nottingham.
Served from Cathedral, Nottingham (1).
M: *Sat 1st M of Sun 6pm. Sun 11am. Hds 10am.*

- ***Sisters of the Presentation (IPBVM),*** St Augustine's House, Westville Gardens, Woodborough Road, Nottingham NG3 4QF **Tel:** 0115-950 6963

14. † St Hugh of Lincoln (1950) A
90 Staverton Road, Bilborough, Nottingham, NG8 4EX
Tel: 0115-929 3633
Mgr Canon Edward Walker.
M: *Sun 9.30am, 5.30pm. Hds 9.30am, 7.30pm.*

15. † St Paul (1898; 1929)
Lenton Boulevard, Lenton, Nottingham, NG7 2BY **Tel:** 0115-978 6236
Rev John McCay.
M: *Sat 1st M of Sun 6pm. Sun 10.30am. Hds As announced.*

16. † St Teresa of Lisieux (1947; 1966) A
8 Kingsbury Dr, Aspley, Nottingham, NG8 3EP **Tel:** 0115-929 2022
Rev Michael Gallagher.
M: *Sat 1st M of Sun 6.30pm. Sun 10.30am. Hds (vigil) 7.30pm, 9.20am.*

17. † St John the Evangelist (1933; 1952) A
Midland Avenue, Stapleford, Nottingham NG9 7BT
Tel: 0115-939 7339 **Fax:** 0115-939 1785
Served from Ilkeston.
Deacon: **Rev Ray Faghy**. St John's, Midland Avenue, Stapleford, Nottingham NG9 7BT
M: *Sun 9am, Hds 7.30pm.*

18. St Thomas More (1971) A
Glenwood Avenue, Wollaton, Nottingham.
Tel: 0115-928 6271
Served from Nottingham 6.
Deacon: **Rev Anthony Cordes.**
In residence: **Rev John Abbott**
M: *Sun 10.45am. Hds 7.30pm.*

- ***Sisters of St Joseph of Peace.*** 749 Wollaton Road, Wollaton Village, Nottingham NG8 2AN **Tel:** 0115-928 0919

19. University of Nottingham Catholic Chaplaincy
10 Broadgate, Beeston, Nottingham NG9 2HF Office: **Tel:** 0115-951 3929/3930
Fax: 0115-951 4376 *and marked 'Chaplains'*
E-mail: christopher.thomas@nottingham.ac.uk
Chaplain: **Rev Christopher P Thomas, Tel:** 0115-928 6271
M: *Sun 11am, Great Hall, Trent Building. Hds phone for details.*

20. Polish Church of Our Lady of Czestochowa
2 Sherwood Rise, Nottingham NG7 6JN
Revv Wlodzimierz Skoczen, Tel: 0115-960 8831
Wladyslaw Wlodarczyk Tel: 0115-962 3713
M: *Sun 9.30am, 11am, 6.30pm. Hds 11am, 7.30pm.*

21. St Bernadettes
Sneinton Dale, Sneinton. Served from Nottingham (5).
M: *Sun 8.30am. Hds 7pm (Vigil).*

■ OAKHAM, Rutland

† St Joseph. (1883; 1975)
Station Road, Oakham, Rutland LE15 6QU
Tel: 01572-722308
Mgr Canon Thomas McGovern VG.
Deacon: **Rev Raymond Keogh**
M: *Sat 1st M of Sun 6.30pm. Sun 10.30am. Hds 9.30am, 7.30pm.*

■ OAKWOOD.

See Derby (5).

■ OLD NORMANTON.

See Derby (3).

■ OLLERTON

See New Ollerton.

■ OSGODBY, Lincs

Our Lady and St Joseph
Main Street, Osgodby, Lincolnshire LN8 3TA Served from Market Rasen
M: *Sat 1st M of Sun 1st Sat of Month 5.30pm.*

■ RADCLIFFE-ON-TRENT, Notts A

† St Anne (1938, 2002)
6 New Road, Radcliffe-on-Trent NG12 2AJ
Tel: 0115-933 2738
Rev Anthony Franey.
M: *Sat 1st M of Sun 6.30pm. Sun 10.30am. Hds 10am.*

- ***Mass Centre:*** Bingham Methodist Church **M:** *Sun 9am. Hds 7pm (on the day).*

■ RAINWORTH, Notts

† St George (1960)
Warsop Lane, Rainworth, Notts NG21 0AG.
Served from Mansfield (2).
M: *Sun 9am. Hds 7pm.*

DIOCESE OF NOTTINGHAM

■ **RATCLIFFE COLLEGE,** Leics
The Immaculate Conception (1844; 1867; 1961)
Fosse Way, Ratcliffe-on-the-Wreake, Leicestershire LE7 8SG **Tel:** 01509-817000
• ***Institute of Charity (IC):*** **Rev Simon Giles**

■ **RIPLEY,** Derbyshire
† **St Joseph** (1930)
94 Butterley Hill, Ripley, Derbys DE5 3LW
Tel: 01773-743336 **Fax:** 01773-512908
Rev Joseph Keogh.
M: *Sat 1st M of Sun 6pm. Sun 10.30am. Hds 9am, 7pm.*

■ **ROTHLEY,** Leics
Sacred Heart
Mountsorrel Lane, Rothley, Leicestershire.
Served from Birstall.
M: *Sun 11am. Hds (vigil 7pm)*

■ **SCUNTHORPE,** North Lincs
1. † **St Bernadette**
(1939; 1950; new Church cons Dec 1980)
Ashby Road, Scunthorpe DN16 2RS
Tel: 01724-844895 **Fax:** 01724-844895
Rev Michael Moore.
Deacon: **Rev Harry Tompkinson.**
M: *Sat 1st M of Sun 6.30pm. Sun 8.30am, 10.30am, 6.30pm. Hds (vigil 7pm). 9.10am (10.30 in school during term time).*

2. † **The Holy Souls** (1897; 1911)
Frodingham Road, Scunthorpe DN15 7TA
Tel: 01724-842197
Rev John Cahill VF.
Deacon: **Rev Bernard Croft.**
M: *Sat 1st M of Sun 5.30pm, Sun 9.30am, 6.30pm, 3pm (Traditional Latin Mass). Hds 9am, 7pm.*

■ **SHEPSHED,** Leics
† **St Winefride** (1842; 1928; cons 4 May 1945)
50 Charnwood Road, Shepshed LE12 9QF
Tel: 01509-502313
Rev Michael Eastwood.
Deacon: **Rev William Hutchinson.**
M: *Sat 1st M of Sun 6pm. Sun 10.15am. Hds 9.30am, 7.30pm.*

■ **SHIREBROOK,** Derbyshire
† **St Joseph** (1904;1907)
120 Langwith Road, Shirebrook, Derbyshire NG20 9RP **Tel:** 01623-742349
Rev Jonathan Cotton.
M: *Sun 10am. Hds 9am.*

■ **SILEBY,** Leics
† **St Gregory and St Alban** (1842)
24 The Banks, Sileby, Leics LE12 7RE
Tel: 01509-813801 Served from Syston.
Deacons: **Revv Brendan Campbell, Brian Ratcliffe**

M: *Sun 9am. Hds (vigil 7.30pm).*

■ **SKEGNESS,** Lincs
† **The Sacred Heart** (1898; 1950)
22 Grosvenor Road, Skegness, Lincolnshire PE25 2DB **Tel:** 01754-762528
Rev Mgr Canon Peter Dooling.
M: *Sat 1st M of Sun 6pm, Sun 11am. Hds 10am 7pm.*

■ **SLEAFORD,** Lincs
† **Our Lady of Good Counsel**
27 Jermyn Street, Sleaford, Lincs NG34 7RU
Tel: 01529-302529 **Fax:** 01529-302529
Canon Michael Bell VF.
M: *Sat 1st M of Sun 6pm. Sun 10am. Hds (Vigil) 7.30pm, 9am.*

■ **SOUTHWELL,** Notts
† **Our Lady of Victories** (1962)
Halam Road, Southwell, Notts NG25 0AD
Tel: 01636-812686 **Fax:** 01636-819063
Mgr Provost Brian Dazeley.
M: *Sat 1st M of Sun 6pm. Sun 9am. Hds As announced.*

■ **SPALDING,** Lincs
† **The Immaculate Conception and St Norbert**
(1875; 1878; cons 1904, closed 2002; New Church 2004)
52 St Thomas Road, Spalding, Lincs PE11 2XX
Tel: 01775-722056, **Fax:** 01775-710227
Rev Jim Burke.
M: *Sat 1st M of Sun 4.45pm, Sun 8am, 11am; Hds (vigil) 7.30pm, 9.30am.*

■ **SPILSBY,** Lincs
† **Our Lady and the English Martyrs**
(1896; 1900; cons 1925)
3 Church Street, Spilsby, Lincs.
Tel: 01526-52245
Served from Skegness.
M: *Sun 9am. Hds (Vigil) 7.30pm*

■ **STAMFORD,** Lincs
† **St Mary and St Augustine**
(1800; 1864; cons 5 July 1952)
13 Broad Street, PE9 1PG
Tel: 01780-762010
Rev Stephen Dye.
M: *Sat 1st M of Sun 6pm. Sun 9am, 11am. Hds (vigil 7.30pm), 9am, 12pm.*

■ **STOKE GOLDING,** Leics
St Martin
Stoke Golding Lodge, Stoke Golding, Nuneaton, CV13 6HT
Tel: 01455-212207
Served from Hinckley.

■ **SUTTON-IN-ASHFIELD,** Notts
† **St Joseph the Worker** (1931; 1961)
Forest Street, Sutton-in-Asfield, Notts. NG17 1DA **Tel:** 01623-554200

Deacon: **Rev Paul Wilson**
Served from Kirkby-in-Ashfield.
M: *Sat 1st M of Sun 6pm. Sun 9.30am. Hds (vigil) 7.30pm, 10am, 7.30pm.*

A

■ **SWADLINCOTE,** Derbyshire
† **Ss Peter and Paul.** (1921; 1958; cons 1978)
Newhall Road, Swadlincote, Derbyshire
Tel: 01283-217169 **Fax:** 01283-819975
Rev Martin Sylvester. 70 Newhall Road, Swadlincote, DE11 0BD
M: *Sat 1st M of Sun 6pm. Sun 9.30am. Hds vigil 7pm), 9.30am.*

■ **SYSTON,** Leics
† **Divine Infant of Prague** (1940; 1948)
63 Broad Street, Syston, Leicester LE7 1GH
Tel: 0116-260 8476
Rev Anthony Pateman.
M: *Sat 1st M of Sun 6.30pm. Sun 11am. Hds 7.30pm.*
• ***Sisters of St Joseph of Peace,*** Sacred Heart Convent, Station Road, Rearsby, LE7 4YY
Tel: 01664-424251

■ **TIDESWELL,** Derbyshire
† **The Immaculate Heart of Mary** (1885)
Queen Street, Tideswell, Derby.
Served from Chapel-en-le-Frith.
M: *Sun 9.30am. Hds 12am.*

■ **WADDINGTON,** Lincs
Our Lady of Victories,
RAF Station. **Rev Paul Owens.**
M: *Sun 11am.*

■ **WARSOP,** Notts
St Teresa of the Child Jesus (1956; 1974)
High Street, Warsop, Mansfield NG29 0LX
Served from Mansfield No 1.
M: *Sun 9.30am. Hds 7pm.*
• ***Presentation Sisters (Parish Sisters).*** Parish House, Clumber Street, Warsop, Mansfield NG20 0LX
Tel: 01623-845091

■ **WEST BRIDGFORD,** Notts
See Nottingham (3).

■ **WHITWICK,** Leics
† **Holy Cross** (1837; 1905; cons 3 May 1924)
Parsonwood Hill, Whitwick, Leicestershire. LE67 5AT
Tel: 01530-832326 **Fax:** 01530-817515
Rev James Cahill.
M: *Sat 1st M of Sun 6pm. Sun 9am. Hds (vigil 7.30pm). 10am.*

■ **WIRKSWORTH,** Derbyshire
Our Lady and St Teresa of Lisieux (1931)
Gorsey Bank, Wirksworth, Derbyshire.
Served from Ripley.
M: *Sun 9am. Hds (vigil 7pm).*

■ **WOODHALL SPA,** Lincs
† **Our Lady and St Peter** (1896)
15 Cromwell Avenue, Woodhall Spa LN10 6TH **Tel:** 01256-352245
Fax: 01256-352245 **Rev John O'Donnell.**
M: *Sun 10am. Hds 11am, 7pm.*

■ **WOODHOUSE,** Leics
Served from Leicester (1).
M: *Sun 9am.*

■ ORDERS OR CONGREGATIONS, ETC

■ Men

Augustinians of the Assumption: Leicester (15)
Charity, Institute of (Rosminians): Birstall, Grace Dieu, Loughborough, Leicester (9), Ratcliffe College.
Cistercians: Mount St Bernard Abbey.
Dominicans: Leicester (1, 1a).
Franciscans (Friars Minor): Nottingham (7).
Holy Ghost Fathers: Hassop, Leicester (5).

■ WOMEN

The Symbol + denotes a Secular Institute.
Corpus Christi Carmelites: Leicester (12).
Dominican Sisters (Congr of Stone, St Catherine of Siena): Keyworth, Leicester (11).
Franciscan Minoresses: Alfreton, Belper, Clay Cross, Melton Mowbray (1).
Francis, Sisters of St: Nottingham (12)
Joseph of Peace, Sisters of St: Nottingham (3, 18), Cleethorpes, Grimsby (1), Leicester (9), Syston.
Little Company of Mary: Nottingham (4, 12)
Mercy, Sisters of Institute of Our Lady of Mercy: Ashbourne, Derby (1, 4).
Notre Dame, Sisters of: Mablethorpe.
Poor Clares (Colettines): Nottingham (9).
Sisters of Life: Cotgrave.
Presentation Sisters: Derby (1), Market Harborough, Matlock, Nottingham (13), Warsop.
Providence (of Ruillé-sur-Loire), Sisters of: Lincoln (1).
Providence, Sisters of (Rosminians): Loughborough (2).
+ Servitium Christi: Leicester (2).
Sisters of Providence of the Immaculate Conception: Holbeach.

■ DIOCESAN INSTITUTIONS, SOCIETIES, ETC

For Societies and Organisations without representation in the diocese please see the main Societies and Organisations section.

Apostleship of the Sea. *Port Chaplain for Grimsby and Immingham:* **Rev James Earley**, St Pius X Presbytery, Chelmsford Avenue, Grimsby, North East Lincolnshire DN32 9DZ

Tel: 01427-871632 **Fax:** 01427-753543 Seafarers' Centre: **Tel:** 01469-574195

Association for Interchurch Families. *Local contact:* **Mr and Mrs J Durney**, 213 London Road, Balderton, Newark, Nottinghamshire NG24 3HB **Tel:** 01636-677398

Association for Latin Liturgy. *Chairman:* **Mr B Marriott**, 47 Western Park Road, Leicester LE3 6HQ.

Association of Our Lady of Mount Carmel. Enquiries to: **Mr D O'Reilly**, 32 Hilary Crescent, Whitwick, Leicestershire LE67 5PL **Tel:** 01530-834446

Beauvale Society, The. *Contact:* **Rev Stephen Doona**, 52A, Derby Rd, Eastwood, Notts NG16 3NX **Tel:** 0115-938 2946

Catenian Association. Province No 15. *Secretary:* **Mr J E Simcock**. 48 Woodhall Road, Wollaton, Nottingham NG8 1LE **Tel:** 01773 785196

Catholic Clothing Guild. (Nottingham Division) *Diocesan Secretary:* **Mrs Teresa Birkin**, 146 Dale Road, Spondon, Derby **Tel:** 01332-670159

Catholic Guide Guild. *Secretary:* **Mrs Clare Spencer**, 49 Carnarvon Road, West Bridgford, Nottingham NG2 6DG **Tel:** 0115-914 2508

Catholic Marriage Care. Nottingham Centre *Secretary:* **Mrs F Reville**, 4 Stiles Road, Arnold, Nottingham. **Tel:** 0115-966 1301 Derby Centre. *Appointments Secretary:* **Mrs A Allen, Tel:** 01332-294940 Leicester Centre. *Secretary:* **Mrs A Cook**. 59 Knighton Road, Leicester. **Tel:** 0116-270 8704 Leicester Appts Office: 83 Aylestone Road, or Pastoral Centre, Loughborough. **Tel:** 0116-254 5485. *Lincolnshire Appointments:* **Tel:** 01472-821090, 01652-658407 or 01522-501674

Catholic Men's Society. Diocesan Council. *Secretary:* **Rev W B Hutchinson**, 59 Garendon Road, Shepshed, Loughborough, Leicestershire LE12 9NU **Tel:** 01509-505260

Catholic Nurses' Guild. *Diocesan Representative:* **Mrs M Lalloo**, 59a Lockton Avenue, Heanor, Derbyshire DE75 7ES **Tel:** 01773-717605

Catholic Women's League. Diocesan Branch. *Hon. Secretary:* **Mrs G Ellis**, 100 Burton Road, Carlton, Nottingham NG4 3GB **Tel:** 0115-956 2823

Couple to Couple League – for Natural Family Planning. *Contact:* **Mr and Mrs David Aldred**, 44 Park Street, Beeston, Nottinghamshire NG9 1DF **Tel:** 0115-877 8310

Diocesan Director for Mission *Diocesan Director:* **Canon D Bowdren VF**. St Charles Presbytery, Woolley Bridge Road, Hadfield, Hyde SK13 1PQ.

Grail, The. *Diocesan Representative:* **Jim and Pearl Clarke**. 6 College Road, Cranwell, Sleaford, Lincs NG34 8DJ **Tel:** 01400-261224

Guild of Catholic Doctors. Lincoln Branch: *Secretary:* **Dr J Carty**. 18 St Edward's Drive, Sudbrook, Lincoln LN2 2QR Nottingham Branch: *Secretary:* **Dr M von Fragstein**. 18 Grafton Street, Derby DE23 6PB **Tel:** 01332-290771

Guild of St Barnabas. To provide an annual income for the maintenance of the Bishop. *Secretary and Treasurer:* **Mgr Canon Jonathan Moore**, Finance Office, Willson House, Derby Road, Nottingham NG1 5AW

Guild of St Stephen for Altar Servers. *Diocesan Director:* **Mr R Bird**

HCPT The Pilgrimage Trust. *Chairman:* **Dr A Jarvis**, 17 The Huntings, Kirby Muxloe, Leicestershire LE9 2BX **Tel:** 0116-239 4653

Intercare – Medical Aid for Africa. *Chairman:* **Dr A Jarvis**, 46 The Halcroft, Syston, Leicestershire LE7 1LD **Tel:** 0116-269 5925 **Fax:** 0116-269 6805

Knights of St Columba. Province 9 (Nottingham). *Prov Grand Knight:* Awaiting appointment. Province 17 (Lincoln), *Prov Grand Knight:* **Mr P Balfe**, 3 Whattons Close, Sedgebrook, Grantham, Lincolnshire NG32 2EX **Tel:** 01949-842155

Lay Dominican Fraternity. *Secretary:* **Mr Patrick Doyle**, Forge Cottage, Long hend Lane, Swaby, Alford, Lincolnshire LN13 0BJ **Tel:** 01507-481072

Nottingham Secular Clergy Association Fund or 'Johnson Fund', for Superannuated, sick, and disabled priests. *Secretary:* **Rev Canon Edward Jarosz**, 21 Hinkley Road, LE3 0TA

Oblates of St Gilbert. *Contact:* **Rev Hillary Costello OCSO**, Mount St Bernard Abbey, Coalville, Leicestershire LE67 5UL **Tel:** 01530-832298

Our Lady's Catechists. *Diocesan Organiser:* Awaiting Appointment

Pax Christi. *President:* **Bishop Malcolm McMahon OP**.

Secular Franciscan Order. *Local Contact:* **Mrs A Hambleton**, 2 Cherry Tree Avenue, Belper, Derbyshire DE56 1FR **Tel/Fax:** 01773-823449

Secular Order of Discalced (Teresian) Carmelites. *Contact:* **Mrs Heather Ward**, 11 Deepdale Road, Wollaton, Nottingham NG8 2FU **Tel:** 0115-928 3603

Society of the Holy Childhood (Mission Together). *Director:* **Mrs Kate Tippen**, Diocesan Centre, Mornington Crescent, Derby DE22 4BD **Tel:** 01332 293833

SPANNED: *Director:* **Rev Frank Daly**, 36 Uttoxeter Road, Mickleover, Derby DE3 9GE **Tel:** 01332-514107

Sherwin Society. *Secretary:* **Mr Redfern**, 26 Penrhyn Avenue, Littleover, Derbyshire DE23 6LA

Society of St Gregory. *Diocesan Representative:* **Alison Kennedy**, St Joseph's, 12 Goodwood Road, Leicester LE5 6SG **Tel:** 0116-220 7881/241 5159 **E-mail:** nottingham@ssg.org.uk

Society of St Peter Apostle for Native Clergy. *Diocesan Director:* **Canon D Bowdren VF, Tel:** 01457-852381

Society of St Vincent de Paul. Nottingham Central Council. *President:* **Mrs M Mitchell**, 132 Saffron Road, South Wigston, Leicester LE18 4UP **Tel:** 0116-277 7669

St Barnabas Society. *Diocesan Representative:* **Mr Glyn Roberts**, 97 Handsworth Crescent, Sheffield S9 4BQ **Tel:** 0114 243 4931 **E-mail:** glyn@glynward.wanadoo.co.uk

Third Order (Secular) of the Blessed Virgin Mary of Mount Carmel. *Leader:* **Mrs T Gaydecki**, 85 Broadway Road, Leicester LE5 5TE

Union of Catholic Mothers. (Nottingham diocese). *President:* **Mrs M Jones**, 83 Roman Road, Birstall, Leicester LE4 4BF **Tel:** 0116-267 3923

University of Nottingham Catholic Chaplaincy. *Chaplain:* **Rev Christopher Thomas MEng PhD, STL, Tel:** 0115-928 6271 *Assistant Chaplain* **Tel:** 0115-922 2484 Chaplaincy Office, University Campus **Tel:** 0115-951 3926/3929 Chaplaincy House, 10 Broadgate, Beeston, Nottingham NG9 2HF **Tel:** 0115-922 2484/922 9939

Walsingham Association. *Nottingham:* **Mrs Kathleen Cheatle**, 15 Harvest Close, Top Valley, Nottingham NG5 9BW **Tel:** 0115-955 3847 *North East Lincolnshire:* **Mrs M Waters**, 433 Louth Road, New Waltham, Grimsby, North East Lincolnshire DN36 4PP **Tel:** 01472-824370

Worldwide Marriage Encounter. *Regional Co-ordinators:* **Mr and Mrs R Leek**, 2 Aston Green, Toton, Nottingham NG9 6LG **Tel:** 0115-919 8486

■ HOSPITALS

To contact the Catholic Chaplain of a particular hospital we suggest you contact the hospital reception directly.

■ CATHOLIC SCHOOLS - MAINTAINED

■ METROPOLITAN BOROUGH OF STOCKPORT (CHESTER)

▲ Infant and Junior

St Mary's, Lowry Drive, Marple Bridge, Stockport SK6 5BR **Tel:** 0161-427 7498 *(Marple Bridge)*

■ DERBYSHIRE COUNTY COUNCIL (MATLOCK)

▲ Infant and Junior

Christ the King, Firs Estate, Alfreton DE5 7EN **Tel:** 01773-832919 *(Alfreton)*

St John Fisher, Greenhill House, Alvaston Derby DE2 0PA **Tel:** 01322-572154 *(Alvaston)*

St Elizabeth's, Matlock Road, Belper Derbys, DE5 2JD **Tel:** 01773-822278 *(Belper)*

St Anne's, Lightwood Road, Buxton, SK17 7AW **Tel:** 01298-23589 *(Buxton)*

St Alban's, Newstead Avenue, Chaddesden, DE3 6NG **Tel:** 01332-673823 *(Derby 5)*

St George's, Uplands Avenue, Littleover, Derby, DE3 7GE **Tel:** 01332-766815 *(Derby 3)*

St Mary's, Edward Street, Derby DE1 3AX **Tel:** 01332-347369 *(Derby 1)*

St Joseph's, Mill Hill Lane, Derby DE3 6SB **Tel:** 01332-361660 *(Derby 2)*

St Margaret's School, Glossop Road, Charlesworth via Hyde SK14 6HB **Tel:** 01457-855818 *(Gamesley)*.

All Saints, Church Street, Old Glossop SK13 9RN **Tel:** 01457-852756 *(Glossop 2)*

St Mary's, Gladstone Street, Glossop SK13 8DN **Tel:** 01457-854473 *(Glossop 1)*

St Charles, The Carriageway, Hadfield, near Manchester SK14 7PQ **Tel:** 01457-852692 *(Hadfield)*

St Thomas, Church View, Allendale, Ilkeston DE7 4LF **Tel:** 0115-932 0550 *(Ilkeston)*

English Martyrs, Bracken Road, Long Eaton NG10 4DA **Tel:** 0115-973 3209 *(Long Eaton)*.

St Mary's, Longland's Road, New Mills, Stockport, SK12 3BW **Tel:** 01663-742412 *(New Mills)*.

St Joseph's, Chesterfield Road, Matlock, Derbys, DE4 3FT **Tel:** 01629-583616 *(Matlock)*

St Joseph's, Langwith Road, Langwith Junction Nr Mansfield NG20 9RA **Tel:** 01623-742609 *(Shirebrook)*

St Edward's, Newhall Road, Swadlincote DE11 0BD **Tel:** 01283-216721 *(Swadlincote)*

▲ **Secondary Comprehensive**

St Thomas More, Palace Fields, Buxton. **Tel:** 01298-23167 *(Buxton)*

St Benedict, Duffield Road, Darley Abbey, Derby DE22 1JO **Tel:** 01332-557032 and 01332-557485 *(Derby 1)*

St Philip Howard, St Mary's Road, Glossop SK13 8DR **Tel:** 01457-853611 *(Glossop 2)*

St John Houghton, Abbot Road, Kirk Hallam, Ilkeston. **Tel:** 0115-932 2896 *(Ilkeston)*

■ **NORTH EAST LINCOLNSHIRE DISTRICT COUNCIL**

▲ **First and Middle**

St Joseph's, Philip Avenue, Cleethorpes, North East Lincs **Tel:** 01472-690672 *(Cleethorpes)*

St Mary's, Wellington Street, Grimsby, North East Lincs DN32 7JX **Tel:** 01472-357982 *(Grimsby 1)*

▲ **Secondary Comprehensive**

St Mary's, Wooton Road, Grimsby. **Tel:** 01472-878869 *(Grimsby 1)*

■ **NORTH LINCOLNSHIRE DISTRICT COUNCIL**

▲ **Junior and Infant**

St Mary's, Grammar School Road, Brigg DN20 8BB **Tel:** 01652-653355 *(Brigg)*

St Norbert's, Fieldside, Crowle, Scunthorpe DN17 4HL **Tel:** 01724-710249 *(Crowle)*

St Bernadettes's, Annes Crescent, Ashby, Scunthorpe DN16 2LW **Tel:** 01724-842382 *(Scunthorpe 1)*

St Augustine Webster, Baildon Road, Scunthorpe DN15 8BU **Tel:** 01724-843722 *(Scunthorpe 2)*

▲ **Secondary Comprehensive**

St Bede's, Collum Avenue, Scunthorpe DN16 2TF **Tel:** 01724-861371 *(Scunthorpe 1)*

■ **LEICESTERSHIRE COUNTY COUNCIL (GLENFIELD)**

▲ **Junior and Infant**

St Peter's, Mill Lane, Earl Shilton LE9 7AW **Tel:** 01455-843840 *(Earl Shilton)*.

St Clare's, Convent Drive, Coalville LE67 3SF **Tel:** 01530-837747 *(Coalville)*

St Peter's, London Road, Hinckley LE10 1LW **Tel:** 01455-634087 *(Hinckley)*.

Christ the King, Glenfield Road, Leicester LE3 6DF **Tel:** 0116-285 7261. *(Leicester 11)*

Holy Cross, Stonesby Avenue, Leicester LE2 6TY. **Tel:** 0116-283 3135 *(Leicester 1)*

Sacred Heart, Mere Close, Mere Road, Leicester LE5 3HH **Tel:** 0116-262 4418 *(Leicester 3)*

St Patrick's, Harrison Road, Leicester LE4 6BS **Tel:** 0116-266 1149 *(Leicester 10)*

St Joseph's, Armadale Drive, Nether Hall, Leicester LE5 1HF **Tel:** 0116-241 6197 *(Leicester 9)*

St Thomas More, Newstead Road, Leicester LE2 3TA **Tel:** 0116-270 6365 *(Leicester 12)*

Sacred Heart, Beacon Road, Loughborough LE11 2BG **Tel:** 01509-822646 *(Loughborough 2)*

St Mary's, Hastings Street, Loughbrough LE11 5AX **Tel:** 01509-212204 *(Loughborough 1)*

St Joseph's, Coventry Road, Market Harborough LE16 9BZ **Tel:** 01858-465359 *(Market Harborough)*

St Charles, Bosworth Road, Measham, Swadlincote, Derbyshire DE12 7LQ **Tel:** 01530-270572 *(Measham)*

St Francis, Dalby Road, Melton Mowbray LE13 0BD **Tel:** 01664-562891 *(Melton Mowbray)*

English Martyrs, Primary Willow Crescent, Oakham LE15 6EH **Tel:** 01572-722400 *(Oakham)*

St Winefride's, Britannia Street, Shepshed LE12 9AE **Tel:** 01509-503353 *(Shepshed)*.

Bishop Ellis, Barkby Thorpe Lane, Thurmaston LE4 8GP **Tel:** 0116-269 5510 *(Syston)*

Holy Cross, Parsonwood Hill, Whitwick, Coalville LE67 5AT **Tel:** 01530-832799 *(Whitwick)*

St John Fisher, Shenley Road, Wigston LE8 1QL **Tel:** 0116-288 2203 *(Wigston)*

▲ **Secondary Comprehensive**

English Martyrs, Anstey Lane, Leicester LE4 0FE **Tel:** 0116-251 7740 *(Leicester 10)*

St Paul's, Spencefield Lane, Leicester LE5 6HN **Tel:** 0116-241 4057 *(Leicester 9)*

De Lisle, Thorpe Hill, Loughborough LE11 4SQ **Tel:** 01509-268739 *(Loughborough)*

St Martin's High School, Stoke Golding, Nuneaton CV13 6HT **Tel:** 01455-212386 *(Hinckley)*.

■ **LINCOLNSHIRE COUNTY COUNCIL (LINCOLN)**

▲ **Junior and Infant**

St Mary's, Ashlawn Drive, Boston PE21 9PX **Tel:** 01205-362092 *(Boston)*

St Mary's, Sandon Close, Grantham NG31 9AX **Tel:** 01476-562017 *(Grantham)*

St Hugh's, Woodfield Avenue, Lincoln LN6 0SH **Tel:** 01522-501137 *(Lincoln 3)*

Our Lady of Lincoln, Laughton Way, Lincoln LN2 2HYE **Tel:** 01522-527500 *(Lincoln 2)*

Our Lady of Good Counsel, The Drove, Sleaford NG34 7AT **Tel:** 01529-304373 *(Sleaford)*
St Norbert's Tollgate off Pennygate, Spalding PE11 1NJ **Tel:** 01775-722889 *(Spalding)*
St Augustine's, Kesteven Road, Stamford PE9 1SR **Tel:** 01780-762094 *(Stamford)*

▲ Secondary
St Bede's, Tollfield Road, Boston PE21 9PN **Tel:** 01205-365873 *(Boston)*

▲ Secondary Comprehensive
SS Peter and Paul, Western Avenue, Lincoln LN6 7SX **Tel:** 01522-681101 *(Lincoln)*

■ NOTTINGHAMSHIRE COUNTY COUNCIL (WEST BRIDGFORD)

▲ Junior and Infant
St Margaret Clitherow, Mildenhall Crescent, Bestwood Estate, Nottingham NG5 5RS **Tel:** 0115-926 6439 *(Nottingham 10)*
Blessed Robert Widmerpool, Listowel Crescent, Clifton, Nottingham NG11 9BH **Tel:** 0115-921 1875 *(Nottingham 2)*
Our Lady of Perpetual Succour, Piccadilly Bulwell, Nottingham NG6 9FN **Tel:** 0115-915 0500 *(Nottingham 9)*
St Augustine's, Park Avenue, Mapperly, Nottingham NG3 4JS **Tel:** 0115-960 4714 *(Nottingham 13)*
Our Lady and St Edward's, Gordon Road, Nottingham NG3 2LG **Tel:** 0115-950 3340 *(Nottingham 7)*
St Mary's, Beaconsfield Street, Hyson Green, Nottingham NG7 6FL **Tel:** 0115-970 8514 *(Nottingham 12)*
St Patrick's, Coronation Avenue, Wilford, Nottingham NG11 7AB **Tel:** 0115-915 2961 *(Nottingham 11)*
St Teresa's, Kingsbury Drive, Aspley, Nottingham NG3 7HR **Tel:** 0115-929 2017 *(Nottingham 17)*
Good Shepherd, Somersby Road, Woodthorpe. NG5 4LW **Tel:** 0115-926 2983 *(Nottingham 4)*
Sacred Heart, Southcliffe Road, Carlton, Nottingham NG4 1EO **Tel:** 0115-911 2117 *(Nottingham 5)*
The Priory, Raglan Street, Hill Top, Eastwood, Nottingham NG16 3GT **Tel:** 01773-713731 *(Eastwood)*
Holy Cross, Leen Mills Lane, Linby, Nottingham NG15 8BZ **Tel:** 0115-963 4291 *(Hucknall)*
St Philip Neri with **St Bede,** Rosemary Street, Mansfield, Nottingham NG19 6AA **Tel:** 01623-623033 *(Mansfield 1)*
St Patrick's, Lingforest Road, Mansfield, Nottintgham NG18 3NJ **Tel:** 01623-478090 *(Mansfield 2)*
Holy Trinity, Boundary Road, Newark, Nottingham NG24 4AU **Tel:** 01636-789117 *(Newark)*
St Joseph's, Main Road, Boughton, Newark, Nottingham NG22 9JE **Tel:** 01623-860392 *(New Ollerton)*
St Edmund Campion, Burleigh Road, West Bridgford, Nottingham NG2 5ND **Tel:** 0115-923 4715 *(West Bridgford)*

▲ Secondary Comprehensive
The Becket, Ruddington Lane, Wilford, Nottingham NG11 7DL **Tel:** 0115-981 7742 *(West Bridgford)*
All Saints School, Broomhill Lane, Mansfield, Nottingham NG19 6BW **Tel:** 01623-474700 *(Mansfield)*
The Trinity School, Beechdale Road, Aspley, Nottingham NG8 3EZ **Tel:** 0115-929 6251 *(Upper School)* **Tel:** 0115-929 6252 *(Lower School)* *(Nottingham 16)*
Christ The King, Darlton Drive, Arnold, Nottingham NG5 7JZ **Tel:** 0115-955 6262 *(Nottingham 4)*

■ STAFFORDSHIRE COUNTY COUNCIL (STOKE-ON-TRENT)

■ EASTERN AREA (BURTON)

▲ Junior and Infant
Holy Rosary, Alexandra Road, Stapenhill, DE15 0JE **Tel:** 01283-239030 *(Burton-on-Trent)*

▲ Secondary Comprehensive
Robert Sutton, Bluestone Lane, Stapenhill DE15 9SD **Tel:** 01283-565015 *(Burton-on-Trent)*

■ CATHOLIC SCHOOLS - INDEPENDENT

▲ Primary
Grace Dieu Manor School, Coalville, Leicester LE67 5UG (Institute of Charity) **Tel:** 01530-222276
St Joseph's Preparatory School, 33 Derby Road Nottingham NG1 5AW **Tel:** 0115-941 8356 *(Nottingham 1).*

▲ Primary and Secondary
Our Lady's Convent School, Burton Street, Loughborough, Leicester LE11 2DT (Rosminian Sisters) **Tel:** 01509-263901 *(Loughborough 2)*

▲ Secondary
Ratcliffe College, Fosse Way, Ratcliffe on the Wreake, Leicester LE7 4SG (Institute of Charity) **Tel:** 01509-817000

DIOCESE OF PLYMOUTH

(Province of Southwark)
Consisting of the Counties of Cornwall, Devon, and Dorset (west of the original county border) and the Isles of Scilly

Patron of the Diocese
St Boniface, Bishop and Martyr, 5 June

Bishop
Rt Rev Christopher Budd, Bishop of Plymouth: Born in Romford, 27 May 1937; ordained 8 July 1962; consecrated by Bishop Restieaux, 15 January 1986.

Residence:
Bishop's House, 31 Wyndham Street West, Plymouth, Devon PL1 5RZ
Tel: 01752-224414 **Fax:** 01752-223750
E-mail: bishop@plymouth-diocese.org.uk

Bishop's PA/Secretary:
Mrs Sue King.
E-mail: sue@plymouth-diocese.org.uk

Rt Rev Christopher Budd,
Bishop of Plymouth

■ ADMINISTRATION

■ Diocesan Curia
Bishop's House, 31 Wyndham Street West, Plymouth, Devon PL1 5RZ

■ Diocesan Chancellor
Canon Kevin Rea. *Vice-Chancellor:* **Rev M. Kirkpatrick**. Bishop's House, 31 Wyndham Street West, Plymouth, Devon PL1 5RZ

■ Vicar General
Mgr Robert Draper, VG. The Priest's House, Woodland Road, St Austell, Cornwall PL25 4RA **Tel:** 01726-73838

■ Episcopal Vicar for Finance and Administration
Mgr Canon Harry Doyle.

■ Diocesan Finance Committee
Secretary: **Mr John Cunningham**

■ Diocesan Financial Secretary
Mr John Cunningham. *Office:* Rosary House, 27 Fore Street, Heavitree, Exeter EX1 2QJ
Tel: 01392-255046
Fax: 01392-255109
E-mail: info@prcdtr.org.uk

■ Diocesan Solicitors
Mr Richard King, Tozers, Broadwalk House, Southernhay West, Exeter EX1 1UA
Tel: 01392 207020
E-mail: r.king@tozers.co.uk

■ Episcopal Vicar for Religious
Rev Gerald Wilson OAR, St Rita's, Ottery Moor Lane, Honiton, Devon EX14 1AP
Tel: 01404-42601

■ Diocesan Communication Officer
Mr Michael Fay. 106 Steed Close, Paignton, Devon TQ4 7SP

■ Diocesan Archivist
c/o Stoodley Knowle Convent, Anstey's Cove Road, Torquay TQ1 2JB
Email: benignus@stoodley.fsbusiness.co.uk

■ Registrar for Deceased Clergy
Mrs Sue King, Bishop's House, 31 Wyndham Street West, Plymouth, Devon PL1 5RZ

■ DEPARTMENT FOR FORMATION

■ Episcopal Vicar for Formation
Mgr Adrian Toffolo

■ Co-ordinator for Parish Services
Mr David Wells, E-mail: david@plymouth-diocesan-office.org.uk

■ Co-ordinator for Schools Services
Mr John Mannix. Cardinal Newman House, Wonford Road, Exexter EX2 4PF
Tel: 01392-671320 **Fax:** 01392-671319
E-mail: johnmannix@plymouth-diocesan-office.org.uk

■ Episcopal Vicar for Clergy
Canon Peter Webb. The Presbytery, 35a Brixey Road, Upper Parkstone, Poole Dorset

BH12 3PB **Tel:** 01202-748166

■ **Director of Vocations**
Canon Paul Cummins, Boniface House, Glenthorne Road, Exeter EX4 4QU
Tel: 01392-271191

■ **Vocations Promoter**
Rev Trevor Jordan. Christ the King, Armada Way Plymouth PL1 2EN

■ **Directors of Vocations for Permanent Diaconate**
Rev Michael Koppel, The Presbytery, Lyme Road, Axminster, Devon EX13 5BE
Rev Deacon Michael Hughes, Holy Name of Jesus and St Edward, Salisbury Street, Shaftsbury, Dorset SP7 8EL

■ **Co-ordinator for Youth Ministry**
Mrs Rebecca Barber

■ **LITURGY AND ECUMENISM**

■ **Diocesan Commission for Liturgy**
Chairman: **Rt Rev Christopher Budd**.
Secretary: **Rev Gerard Wilberforce**. Dutch Court, Topsham, Exeter EX3 0JD
Tel: 01392-876953

■ **Ecumenical Officer - Devon**
Mrs Mary Ann James, 70 Broadpark Road, Torquay, Devon TQ2 6UJ
Tel: 01803-605718
E-mail: majames.csjames@virgin.net

■ **BISHOP'S ADVISOR FOR JUSTICE AND PEACE**
Adviser: **Mrs Mary Conway**, Bishop's House, 31 Wyndham Street West, Plymouth PL1 5RZ **Tel:** 01752-260856,
E-mail: j&P@plymouth-diocese.org.uk

■ **CONSULTATIVE BODIES**

■ **Cathedral Chapter**
(Erected 26 November 1853)
Provost: Vacant. *Canons:* **Mgri Robert Draper VG, Harry Doyle. Bartholomew Nannery, Patrick Costello VF, Paul Cummins, Kenneth Noakes, Keith Mitchell, Seamus Flynn, Patrick Chrystal, John Deeny** *Canons Emeriti:* **Mgri Anthony Gilby, George Hay, Revv Kevin Rea, Bernard Jaffa;** *Honorary Canons:* **Revv Conrad Meyer, Richard Rutt, Michael Howard.**

■ **College of Consultors**
(established 1st January 1985)
Mgr Robert Draper; Anthony Cornish, Keith Mitchell, Michael Koppel, Mark Skelton.

■ **Diocesan Council of Priests:**
Chairman: **Canon Patrick Costello**
Vice-chairman: Awaiting Appointment
Secretary: **Rev Peter Coxe**

■ **Diocesan Representatives to the National Council of Priests: Revv Michael Downey, John Rice. Peter Coxe.**

■ **DIOCESAN MARRIAGE TRIBUNAL**
Diocesan Tribunal: *Judicial Vicar:* **Rev Kristian Paver JCL, Rev David Gassor JCL.**
Administrator: **Sr Sheila McCarthy,** Rosary House, Fore Street, Exeter, EX1 2QJ
Tel: 01392-271123

■ **SOCIAL CARE**
Adviser for People with Special Needs: **Mrs Sue King**, Bishop's House, 31 Wyndham Street West, Plymouth PL1 5RZ
Tel: 01752-224414 *Episcopal Vicar for Safeguarding:* **Rev Brian Kenwrick**, The Presbytery, 76 Abbey Road, Torquay, Devon TQ2 2NJ **Tel:** 01803-294142
Safeguarding Co-ordinator: **Mr Chris Jarvis**. *Child Protection Officer:* **Annette Burkinstow** *Office Administrator:* **Mary England**. St Joseph's Offices, Raglan Road, Plymouth PG1 4NA **Tel:** 01752 560792
E-mail: chris@safeguardingplymouth.co.uk
E-mail: annette@ safeguardingplymouth.co.uk
E-mail: mary@ safeguardingplymouth.co.uk

■ **PLYMOUTH**
1. Cathedral Church of St Mary and St Boniface (St Mary's Chapel, Stonehouse 1801; The Cathedral 1858, cons 22Sept, 1880)
Wyndham Street, Plymouth PL1 5HW
Canon Bartholomew Nannery (*Cathedral Dean*); **Rev Michael Kirkpatrick VF**; Retired clergy: **Revv Bryan Legg, John Bolland, Terence Clune, Daniel Donagher**. The Cathedral House, 45 Cecil Street, Plymouth PL1 5HW **Tel:** 01752-662537

M: *Sun 8am, 10am (Sung), 6pm. Hds 9.15am, 7pm (Sung).*

■ **ASHBURTON,** Devon
† Our Lady of Lourdes and St Petrok
(1912; 1914; 1935)
East Street. Served from Buckfast Abbey.
M: *Sat 1st M of Sun 9am. Sun 9.40am. Hds 10am.*

■ **AXMINSTER,** Devon
† St Mary (1831; 1862)
Lyme Road, Axminster, Devon EX13 5BE
Tel: 01297-32135
Rev Michael Koppel.
M: *Sun 9am. Hds 10am.*

■ **BARNSTAPLE,** Devon
† St Mary, Immaculate Mother of God
(Old Church 1855; New Church 31 May 1985)
The Presbytery, Higher Church Street, Barnstaple, Devon EX32 8JE
Tel: 01271-343312
Mgr Adrian Toffolo.
Deacon: **Rev John Connors.**
M: *Sun 9.30am, 6.30pm. Hds 10am, 7.30pm.*

■ **BEAMINSTER,** Devon
† St John (1967)
Shortmoor, Beaminster, Dorset DT8 3EL
Tel: 01308-422594
Served from Bridport
M: *Sat 1st M of Sun 6pm. Hds Contact Parish Office at Bridport.*

■ **BIDEFORD,** Devon
The Sacred Heart (1892)
North Road, Bideford, Devon EX39 2NW
Tel: 01237-472519
Rev Terry O'Donovan,
M: *Sat 1st M of Sun 6.30pm. Sun 11am. Hds 10am, 7.30pm.*

■ **BLANDFORD FORUM,** Dorset
† Our Lady of Lourdes and St Cecilia (1926; 1934)
Presbytery, White Cliff Mill Street, DT11 7BN
Tel: 01258-452051
Rev Ciaran McGuinness
Deacon: **Rev Michael Hughes**
M: *Sat 1st M of Sun 5.30pm, Sun 9am. Hds 10am, 7pm.*

■ **BODMIN,** Cornwall
† St Mary's Catholic Church (1846; 1886; 1965)
St Mary's Road, Bodmin, Cornwall PL31 1NF
Tel/Fax: 01208-72833
Vacant. The Presbytery, St Mary's Parish Centre, St Mary's Road, Bodmin PL31 1NF
Tel: 01208-72833
M: *Sun 10.30am. Hds 10am.*

■ **BOURNEMOUTH,** Dorset
(See also under Diocese of Portsmouth).
1. † Christ the King (1940; 1966; 1979)
46 Durdells Avenue, Kinson, Bournemouth BH11 9EH
Tel: 01202-572939 **Fax:** 01202-578334
Revv Jude McHugo CJ, William Muir CJ, (*Parish Priest*).
M: *Sun 9.30am, 6.30pm. Hds 9am.*
• ***La Sainte Union,*** 79 Rochester Road, West Howe. **Tel:** 01202-383016

2. † Our Lady of Victories and St Bernadette
(1926; 1934)
46 Draycott Road, Ensbury Park, Bournemouth BH10 5AR **Tel:** 01202-529202
Parish Co-ordinator: **Sr Paul Snell.**
M: *Sat 1st M of Sun 6pm. Sun 11am. Hds (vigil 7pm). 10am.*
• ***Poor Handmaids of Jesus Christ,*** 46 Draycott, Ensbury Park, Bournemouth. **Tel:** 01202-513555

■ **BOVEY TRACEY,** Devon
† Holy Spirit (1904; 1936; cons 1 June 1936)
Ashburton Road, Bovey Tracey TQ13 9BY
Tel/Fax: 01626-833432
Mgr George Hay.
M: *Sun 10.30am. Hds (vigil 7pm), 10am.*

■ **BRAUNTON,** Devon
St Brannoc (1958; cons June 1978)
Frog Lane, Braunton, Devon EX33 1BB
Served from Ilfracombe
M: *Sat 1st M of Sun 6.15pm (RMB Chivenor).*

■ **BRIDPORT,** Dorset
† SS Mary and Catherine (1846; 1978)
Victoria Grove, Bridport, Dorset DT6 3AD
Tel: 01308-422594
Rev Jonathan Shaddock
Also Serves Beaminster and Chideock
M: *Sun 10am. Hds, contact office*

■ **BRIXHAM,** South Devon
† Our Lady Star of the Sea
(1967; cons 8 March 1972)
43 New Road, Brixham, Devon TQ5 8NB
Tel: 01803-853406
Rev Paul Connor CJ.
M: *Sat 1st M of Sun 7pm, Sun 10am, Hds 10am, 7pm.*

■ **BROADSTONE**
See Poole (4).

■ **BUCKFASTLEIGH,** Devon
1. Buckfast Abbey,
† St Mary (1882; 1902; cons 25 Aug 1932)
Buckfastleigh, TQ11 0EE
Abbey: **Tel:** 01364-645500
Fax: 01364-643891
Monastery: **Tel:** 01364-645550
Bursar's Office: **Tel:** 01364-645590
Book Shop: **Tel:** 01364-645506
Parish Priests: **Tel:** 01364-645526
Education: **Tel:** 01364-645517
Conferences: **Tel:** 01364-645530
Southgate Retreat House:
Tel: 01364-645521
Website: www.buckfast.org.uk
• ***Benedictines (OSB):*** **Rt Rev Richard Yeo** (*Administrator*); **Very Rev Francis Straw** (*Prior/Novice Master*), **Rt Rev David Charlesworth, Very Rev**

Sebastian Wolff,; Revv Benet Conlon (*Sub-Prior*), **Paulinus Angold, Gabriel Arnold** (*Parish Priest*), **Anscar Cawley, Richard Rotter, James Courtney** (*Bursar*), **Luke Humphrey, Nicholas Marsh, Dominic May, Bros Gregory Miller, Stephen Croft, Hilarion Durkin, Daniel Smyth** (*Guestmaster*), **Nicholas Marsh, Columba Kimber, Fergus Dougherty.**
M: *Sun 9am, 10.30am (Conventual). Hds 8am, 12.05pm, 7.15pm.*

• ***Benedictine Sister,*** St Mary's Convent, 7 Buckfast Road, Buckfastleigh, Devon TQ11 0EA **Tel:** 01364-643280

2. Buckfastleigh St Benedict
(1939; cons 13 Nov 1945)
Chapel Street.
Served from Buckfast Abbey.
M: *Sun 5pm. Hds 9.30am.*

■ **BUDE,** Cornwall [A]
St Peter (1926)
Bencoolen Road, Bude, Cornwall EX23 8PJ
Tel: 01288-353415
Served from Launceston
M: *Sun 9am. Hds 10am.*

■ **BUDLEIGH SALTERTON,** Devon [A]
† St Peter, Prince of Apostles
(1923; 1927; cons 4 July 1938)
20 Clinton Terrace, Budleigh Salterton, Devon EX9 6RZ **Tel:** 01395-443339
Rev George Gerry.
M: *Sun 10am. Hds 10.30am, 7pm.*

■ **CALLINGTON,** Cornwall
Our Lady of Victories (1931; 1954)
Lower Coronation Terrace.
Served from Tavistock.
M: *Sat 1st M of Sun 6pm*

■ **CAMBORNE,** Cornwall
Our Lady of All Nations Parish
† St John the Baptist (1859)
Trevu Road, Camborne, Cornwall TR14 7AE
Tel: 01209-713143
Rev Christopher Findlay-Wilson.
Deacons: **Revv Adrian Dyer, Peter Gahan.**
M: *Sun 9.30am (Solemn), 6pm. Hds (vigil 7pm). 10am.*
Also serves Redruth

■ **CHAGFORD,** Lower Street, Devon
The Holy Family (1963)
Served from Okehampton.
M: *Sun 9am. Hds 6.30pm.*

■ **CHELSTON,** Torquay, Devon
See Torquay (3).

■ **CHIDEOCK,** Devon
† Our Lady Queen of Martyrs and St Ignatius
(1645; 1815; 1874)
Chideock, Shrine of the Dorset Martyrs.
Tel: 01308-422594
Served from Bridport
M: *Hds, Contact Parish Office at Bridport*

■ **CHUDLEIGH**
St Cyprian (1671)
Ugbrooke House. Served from Bovey Tracey.
M: *Sun 8.45am. Hds 6pm.*

■ **COMBE MARTIN,** Devon
St Mary (1946; 1968)
Castle Street. Served from Ilfracombe.
M: *Sun 9am. Hds (vigil 7pm).*

■ **CREDITON,** Devon
† St Boniface (1969)
Park Road. National Shrine of St Boniface.
Served from Exeter (4).
M: *Sun 9.30am. Hds As advertised.*

■ **CULLOMPTON,** Devon
† St Boniface (1929)
The Presbytery, Shortlands, Cullompton. EX15 1EW **Tel:** 01884-32253
Rev William Kiely.
Deacon: **Rev Edward Channing**
M: *Sat 1st M of Sun 6pm. Sun 10.30am. Hds 7pm.*

■ **DARTMOUTH,** Devon
† St John the Baptist (1868)
20 Newcomen Road, Dartmouth, TQ6 9BN
Tel: 01803-832860
Served from Brixham
M: *Sat 1st M of Sun 5pm. Hds 10am, 6pm.*

■ **DAWLISH,** Devon
† St Agatha (1907)
27 Exeter Road, Dawlish, Devon EX7 0BU
Tel: 01626-863279 Served from Teignmouth
In residence: **Mgr Anthony Gilby.**
M: *Sat 1st M of Sun 6pm. Sun 10.30am. Hds 10am, 7pm.*

■ **DEVONPORT.**
See Plymouth, Cathedral Parish.

■ **DORCHESTER,** Dorset [A]
Holy Trinity (1867; 1907; 1976)
High West Street, Dorchester, Dorset.
Rev John Rice.
Deacon: **Rev Nicholas Thompson**
Tel: 01305-251976 **Fax:** 01305-259122
The Presbytery, Holy Trinity Parish Centre, Culliford Road North, Dorchester DT1 1QG
M: *Sat 1st M of Sun 6.30pm. Sun 8.30am, 10.30am. Hds 10am, 7.30pm.*

■ **EFFORD**
See Plymouth, Efford Parish.

■ **ENSBURY PARK**
See Bournemouth (2).

DIOCESE OF PLYMOUTH

■ **EXETER**

1. † Sacred Heart
(1790; 1884; cons 30 May 1913)
25 South Street, Exeter EX1 1EB
Tel: 01392-272815
Mgr Canon Harry Doyle, Revv Michael Wheaton, David Williams (retired).
Deacon: **Rev Delian Bower**.
M: *Sat 1st M of Sun 5.30pm. Sun 9.30am, 11am. Hds 10am, 7.30pm.*

2. † The Blessed Sacrament (1930; 1932)
29 Fore Street, Heavitree, Exeter EX1 2QJ
Tel: 01392-272596
Rev Canon John Deeny VF, Rev John Watkins
M: *Sun 9am, 10.30am, 6pm. Hds 9am, 7.30pm.*
• ***Sisters of the Presentation of Mary,*** Mount St Mary's Convent, Wonford Road, EX2 4PF **Tel:** 01392-433301

3. † Holy Cross (1920; 1925; 1936)
Station Road, Topsham, Exeter EX3 0EE
Tel: 01392-873898 **Rev Michael Wheaton**.
M: *Sat 1st M of Sun 6pm. Sun 11am. Hds (vigil) 7pm, 10am.*

4. University Chaplaincy
St Boniface House, Glenthorne Road, Exeter EX4 4QU
Chaplain: **Canon Paul Cummins**.
Tel: 01392-271191
Residents: **Tel:** 01392-273692
M: *Sun 11.30am (None in University Holidays).*

■ **EXMOUTH,** Devon

1. † The Holy Ghost (1885; 1912)
Raddenstile Lane, Exmouth, Devon EX8 2JH
Tel: 01395-263384
Rev Philip Austen OSB.
Deacon: **Rev Terry Enright.**
M: *Sat 1st M of Sun 6pm. Sun 9am, 11am. Hds (vigil 7.30pm), 9.15am.*
• ***Sisters of the Holy Family,*** 2 Long Causeway. **Tel:** 01395-272702

■ **FALMOUTH,** Cornwall

† St Mary Immaculate
St Mary's Falmouth and Helston Parish
(1819; 1896; cons 8 Sept 1948)
Killigrew Street, Falmouth, Cornwall TR11 3PR Also serves Helston, Mawnan Smith, Mullion and Culdrose.
Tel: 01326-312763
Rev J Bielawski VF. Also in residence: **Canon Richard Rutt** (retired), **Rev Peter Stone** (retired).
M: *Sat 1st M of Sun 6.30pm. Sun 10.45am. Hds (vigil 7.30pm). 10.30am.*
• ***Daughters of the Cross,*** "Bethany", 33 Wood Lane, Falmouth TR11 4RA
Tel: 01326-317036

■ **GILLINGHAM,** Dorset

† St Benedict (1907; 1930)
Rolls Bridge. Served from Marnhull.
M: *Sun 10am. Hds 10am.*

■ **HARTLAND,** Devon

Our Lady and St Nectan (1964)
Well Lane, Served from Bideford.
M: *Sun 5pm.*

■ **HAYLE,** Cornwall

St Joseph (1958)
Commercial Road, Hayle, Cornwall.
Tel: 01736-796412 Served from Penzance.
M: *Sat 1st M of Sun 6pm. Hds (vigil 7pm).*
• ***Daughters of the Cross,*** St Mary's Convent, Foundry Hill, Hayle, Cornwall TR27 4JA **Tel:** 01736-759431

■ **HEAVITREE**

See Exeter (2).

■ **HELSTON,** Cornwall

1. St Mary (1968)
Clodgey Lane, Helston, Cornwall TR13 8PJ
Tel: 01326-572378
Rev John Richardson *(Assistant in Residence)*
M: *Sun 9am. Hds 7.30pm.*

■ **HOLSWORTHY,** Devon

Served from Launceston.
M: *Sat 1st M of Sun 6.30pm. In the Anglican Church*

■ **HONITON,** Devon

† The Holy Family
(1877; 1935; 1937; cons 11 Sept 1969)
Exeter Road, Honiton, Devon EX14 8AP
Tel/Fax: 01404-45349
• ***Augustinian Recollects (OAR):*** St Rita's Centre, Ottery Moor Lane, Honiton EX14 1AP **Tel/Fax:** 01404-42601 **Revv Denis Caddle** *(Parish Priest),* **Gerald Wilson** *(Vicar Provincial),* **Gabino Areitio, Marcelino Mayor, Sean Flannery, Br Terry Mulvey.**
M: *Sun 8.30am, 11am. Hds 9.30am (St Rita's), 7.30pm (Holy Family).*

■ **ILFRACOMBE,** Devon

† Our Lady of Ilfracombe, Star of the Sea
(1874; 1929; cons 12 Sept 1939)
Runnacleave Road, Ilfracombe, Devon EX34 8AQ **Tel:** 01272-863563
Rev Kieran Kirby.
M: *Sun 10.30am Hds 7pm.*

■ **ISLES OF SCILLY**

† Our Lady Star of the Sea (1930)
The Strand, St Mary's Isle.
Tel: 01720-22356 Served from Penzance.
Contact Person: **Mr Bill Dean** *(Eucharistic Minister),* **Tel:** 01720-422014
M: *See Church notice board.*

A

■ **IVYBRIDGE,** Devon
† **St Austin's Priory** (1910; 1913; 1932)
Cadleigh, Ivybridge, Devon PL21 9HW
• ***Augustinian Recollects (OAR).*** **Tel:** 01752-892606 **Rev Hugh Corrigan** (*Prior and Parish Priest*), **Rev Bro Patrick Diviny**.
M: *Sat 1st M of Sun 6pm. Sun 10.30am. Hds 10.30am, 7.30pm.*
• ***Sisters of Notre Dame,*** 37 Julian Road. **Tel:** 01752-897064

■ **KEYHAM**
See Plymouth, Holy Trinity Parish.

■ **KINGSBRIDGE,** Devon
† **Sacred Heart** (1902; 1903)
Fore Street, Kingsbridge, Devon.
Tel: 01548-852670 **Fax:** 01548-856971
Rev Anthony Cornish. The Presbytery, 19 Fosse Road, TQ7 1NG *Deacon:* **Rev Anthony Irwin.**
M: *Sat 1st M of Sun 6.15pm, Sun 10.15am. Hds 10.15am.*

■ **KINGSKERSWELL,** Devon
St Gregory (1961)
Coles Lane. Served from Newton Abbot.
M: *Sun 9am. Hds (vigil 7pm).*

■ **KINSON,** Bournemouth, Dorset
See Bournemouth (1).

A

■ **LAUNCESTON,** Cornwall
† **St Cuthbert Mayne**
(1886; 1911; cons 19 Aug 1935)
National Shrine of St Cuthbert Mayne.
21 Mayne Close, St Stephen's Hill, Launceston, Cornwall PL15 8XQ
Tel: 01566-773166
Rev David Gassor.
M: *Sun 11am. Hds 7.30pm.*

A

■ **LISKEARD,** Cornwall
† **Our Lady and St Neot** (1863)
West Street, Liskeard, Cornwall PL14 6BW
Tel: 01579-344906 Served from Saltash
Rev Michael J Lock
M: *Sun 11am.*

■ **LOOE,** Cornwall
Our Lady and St Nicholas,
West Looe. (1923). Served from Sclerder.
M: *Sun 11am (Easter - January).*

■ **LULWORTH CASTLE,** Wareham, Dorset
† **St Mary** (1780)
Castle Grounds. Served from Wool.
M: *Sat 1st M of Sun 6.30pm; Hds 8am.*

■ **LYME REGIS,** Dorset
† **SS Michael and George** (1837)
Silver Street, DT7 3HS Served from Axminster.
M: *Sun 11am. Hds (vigil 7pm).*

■ **LYNTON,** Devon
† **The Most Holy Saviour**
(1904; 1910; cons 8 Sept 1931)
45 Lee Road, Lynton, Devon EX35 6BS
M: *Sun 11am. Hds 6.30pm (weekdays 8am in the Poor Clares Convent).*
• ***Poor Clares (Colettines),*** Lee Road, EX35 6BX **Tel:** 01598-753373

■ **MARNHULL,** Dorset
† **Our Lady** (1651; 1832)
Old Mill Lane, Marnhull, Sturminster Newton, DT10 1JX **Tel:** 01258-820388
Rev Martin Budge VF. Also in residence: **Rev David Walford** (retired).
M: *Sun 9am, 6pm. Hds 7pm.*

■ **MAWNAN SMITH,** Cornwall
St Edward (New Church 1966)
Old Church Road. Served from Falmouth.
Tel: 01326-312763
M: *Thu 10am. Hds 6pm.*

■ **MODBURY,** Devon
St Monica (1962)
Palm Cross Green. Served from Ivybridge.
M: *Sun 9am.*

■ **MULLION,** Cornwall
St Michael the Archangel (1925; 1935)
Meaver Road. Served from Falmouth.
M: *Sat 1st M of Sun 4pm. Hds 10am.*

A

■ **NEWQUAY,** Cornwall
† **Most Holy Trinity** (1901; 1902; 1930)
3 Tower Road, Newquay, Cornwall TR7 1LS
Tel/Fax: 01637-851697 (Parish Office)
Tel/Fax: 01637-851176 (Presbytery)
Rev Mark O'Keeffe, Canon Conrad Meyer (retired).
M: *Sat 1st M of Sun 7pm. Sun 8.30am (July & Aug Only), 10.30am. Hds 9.30am, 7pm.*

■ **NEWTON ABBOT,** Devon
† **St Joseph** (1871; 1915)
96 Queen Street, Newton Abbot, Devon TQ12 2ET **Tel:** 01626-365231
Canon Patrick Costello VF.
M: *Sat 1st M of Sun, 6pm, Sun 10.30am, 6pm. Hds 10am, 7pm.*
• ***Polish Home Chaplain:*** **Edward Stachorski (SCJ)**. Polish House, Ilford Park, Nr Newton Abbot TQ12 6QH
Tel: 01626-332043
M: *Sun 10.30am.*
• ***Daughters of the Holy Spirit,*** 11 Devon Square, TQ12 4HN **Tel:** 01626-353423

A

■ **OKEHAMPTON,** Devon
† **St Boniface** (1906)
95 Station Road, Okehampton EX20 1ED
Tel: 01837 52229
Rev Peter Morgan OSB.

M: Sat 1st M of Sun 7pm. Sun 11am. Hds (vigil 7.30pm), 10am.

■ **OTTERY ST MARY,** Devon
† **St Anthony** (1935)
Mill Street. Served from Honiton.
Deacon: **Rev John Park.**
M: *Sat 1st M of Sun 6pm. Sun 9.30pm. Hds 9.30am, 7pm.*

■ **PADSTOW,** Cornwall
† **St Saviour and St Petroc** (1909; 1913; 1974)
Place Hill. Served from Bodmin.
M: *Sat 1st M of Sun 5.30pm. Hds 7.30pm.*
- ***Daughters of Mary and Joseph,*** 'Coloma', Boyd Avenue PL28 8ER **Tel:** 01841-533010

■ **PAIGNTON,** Devon
† **Sacred Heart and St Teresa of the Child Jesus** (1880; 1901; new Church 1931; cons 29 Sept 1959)
24 Cecil Road, Paignton, Devon TQ3 2SH
Tel/Fax: 01803-557518
Revv Canon Seamus Flynn, John M B Smethurst. *Deacon:* **Rev Joe Owen**
M: *Sat 1st M of Sun 7pm. Sun 8.30am, 10.30am. Hds 9.30am, (11am in term time), 7pm.*

■ **PARKSTONE,** Poole, Dorset
See Poole (2, 3).

■ **PENZANCE,** Cornwall
Holy Family Parish
† **The Immaculate Conception of Our Lady** (1837; 1843)
Rosevean Road, Penzance, Cornwall TR18 2DX Also serves St Ives and Hayle
Tel: 01736-362619
Rev Philip Dyson.
M: *Sun 9am, 11am. Hds 10am, 7.30pm.*
- ***St Mary's Haven,*** day care and residential centre, St Mary's Street, Penzance TR18 2DH

■ **PERRANPORTH**
Christ the King (1931)
Wheal Leisure Road, Perranporth TR6 0EZ
Rev Brian Stevens, 22 Hillgrove Road, Newquay, Cornwall TR7 2QZ
Tel: 01637-874188 or 07970-670007
M: *Sun 4pm. Hds 7pm.*

■ **PEVERELL**
See Plymouth, Peverell Parish.

■ **PLYMOUTH**
The parishes in the city of Plymouth and its neighbours have been gathered into three groups, each sharing personel and resources.

Cathedral Parish:
1. Cathedral Church See start of parish list.

Christ the King (1962)
Armada Way, Plymouth PL1 2EN City Centre & University Church. **Tel:** 01752-266523
Rev Trevor Jordan *(University Chaplain)*
M: *Sat 1st M of Sun 6pm. Students' Mass 6.30pm in term-time.*

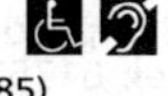

† **St Joseph's**
(1860: new Church 1985; Cons Nov 1985)
Raglan Road, Devonport, Plymouth, PL1 5HW
Tel: 01752-562976
M: *Sun 11am. Hds 11am.*
Convents which serve the Group:
- ***Sisters of St Anne.*** 32 Wyndham Square PL1 5EG **Tel:** 01752-662754.
- ***Poor Sisters of Nazareth.*** Nazareth House, Durnford Street, Stonehouse PL1 3QR **Tel:** 01752-660943
- ***Daughters of the Cross.*** 26 Wyndham Street West, PL1 5ER **Tel:** 01752-255213

Peverell Parish:
2. † St Edward the Confessor
(1910, 1933, cons 6 June 1949)
Home Park Avenue, Peverell, PL3 4PG
Tel: 01752-665406.
Rev Bernard Hahesy.
M: *Sun 10am, 5pm. Hds 10am.*

Plymstock Parish:

3. St Margaret Mary
(1933; 1961; cons 16 Oct 1981)
20 Radford Park Road, Plymstock, Plymouth PL9 9DW
Tel: 01752-401281 **Rev Terence Fleming.**
M: *Sun 10am. Hds 9.30am, 7.30pm.*

Holy Trinity Parish:

4. St Paul's (1933)
6 Pemros Road, St Budeaux, Plymouth PL5 1NE **Tel:** 01752-361161
Rev Timothy Lewis.
M: *Sat 1st M of Sun 5.30pm.*

The Holy Family (1939; new Church 1955)
70 Westeria Terrace, Beacon Park, Plymouth. **Tel:** 01752-772181
In residence: **Rev John Webb.**
M: *Sun 9am.*

Our Most Holy Redeemer
(1902; 1950, cons 10 Apr 1957)
Ocean Street, Keyham PL2 2DL
M: *Sun 10.30am. Hds 10.30am.*
Convent which serves the Parish:
- ***Sisters of Charity of St Paul.*** 60 Ocean Street, Keyham PL2 2LD **Tel:** 01752-562931

St Peters Parish:

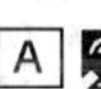

5. St Peter's
(1937; new church 1970, cons June 1987)
Tavistock Road, Crownhill, PL5 3AX
Tel: 01752-701660

Rev Canon Keith Mitchell.
M: *Sat 1st M of Sun 6.30pm. Sun 10.30am. Hds (vigil 7pm) 9.15am.*

St Thomas More (1964) A
Bampfylde Way, Southway, PL6 6SP
Tel: 01752-778269.
M: *Sun 9am. Hds 10.30am.*

Christ Church, Estover
Shared Christian Church.
Served by an Ecumenical team of Ministers.
M: *Wed, 9.30am.*

Convents which serve the Parish:
- ***Sisters of Notre Dame.*** 12 Holtwood Road, Glenholt **Tel:** 01752-768183 Also at: 15 Yeates Close, Crownhill PL5 3SD **Tel:** 01752-296662; 24 Carrisbrooke Road, Crownhill PL6 5PW **Tel:** 01752-317504
- ***Augustinian Sisters,*** St Peter's Convent, George Lane, Plympton St Maurice, PL7 2LL **Tel:** 01752-337202

Efford Parish:

6. Church Our Lady of Mount Carmel & St Teresa (1964) A
Stott Close, Pike Road, Efford PL3 6HA.
Tel: 01752-667433
M: *Sat 1st M of Sun 5pm. Hds (vigil 7pm).*

Plympton Parish:

7. † Church of Our Lady of Lourdes
(1932; cons 25 Sept 1935)
17 Vicarage Road, Plympton PL7 4JX
Tel: 01752-331288
Rev Martin Rossman
M: *Sun 10am. Hds 7pm.*

■ **POOLE,** Dorset
1. † St Mary (1839; 1973)
211a Wimborne Road, Poole, BH15 2EG
Tel: 01202-675412 **Fax:** 01202-668901
Rev Mark Skelton. *Deacons:* **Rev Peter Reeves, Rev Declan McConville.**
M: *Sun 8.30am, 10.30am, 5.30pm. Hds (vigil 7.30pm), 7.30am, 10am.*
- ***Sisters of Mercy,*** St Joseph's Convent, Parkstone Road, Poole BH15 2NU **Tel:** 01202-674515

2. † St Joseph and St Walburga
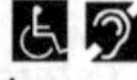
(1895; 1962)
Bournemouth Road, Parkstone, Poole.
Tel: 01202-746539
Rev Barry Hallett. The Presbytery, 2A Archway Road, Poole, BH14 9AZ
M: *Sat 1st M of Sun 5.30pm. Sun 9.45am. Hds 10.30am, 7.30pm.*
Sr. Marion Gormley *(Pastoral Assistant and RC Chaplain to University of Bournemouth)*

3. † Our Lady of Fatima (1950) A
35a Brixey Road, Upper Parkstone, Poole BH12 3PB **Tel:** 01202-748166
Canon Peter Webb.
M: *Sun 8am, 10.30am. Hds 10am.*

4. † St Anthony of Padua (1959)
135 York Road, Broadstone, Poole
BH18 8ER **Tel:** 01202-693336
Rev Keith Collins.
M: *Sat 1st M of Sun 5.30pm. Sun 10am. Hds 10.30am, 7pm.*

■ **REDRUTH,** Cornwall
The Assumption *(1936)*
Served from Camborne.
M: *Sun 11am. Hds 7pm.*
- ***Sisters of St Joseph,*** St Joseph's Convent, "Parkhenver", West End, TR15 3AA **Tel:** 01209-215806

■ **ST AGNES,** Cornwall
Our Lady, Star of the Sea (1958)
Trevaunance Road.
Tel: 01637-874188 or 07970-670007
Served from Perranporth.
M: *Sat 1st M of Sun 6pm. Hds 9.30am.*

■ **ST AUSTELL,** Cornwall
St Augustine (1913; 1937; 1990)
Woodland Road, St Austell, Cornwall
PL25 4RA **Tel:** 01726-73838
Mgr Canon Robert Draper VG.
Deacon: **Rev John Sanders.**
M: *Sat 1st M of Sun 6pm. Sun 8.30am, 10.30am. Hds 10.30am, 7pm.*

■ **ST BUDEAUX,** Plymouth
See Plymouth, Holy Trinity Parish.

■ **ST IVES,** Cornwall
† Sacred Heart and St Ita
(1902; 1908; cons 8 May, 1946)
Tregenna Hill, St Ives, Cornwall TR26 1SE
Deacon: **Rev Leo Pilley**.
M: *Sun 9.15am. Hds (vigil 6pm). 9.30am.*
Served from Penzance

■ **ST MARYCHURCH,** Devon
See Torquay (2).

■ **ST MARY'S ISLE.**
See Isles of Scilly.

■ **ST MAWES,** Cornwall
Our Lady Star of the Sea and St Anthony (1937)
Grove Hill TR2 5BJ **Tel:** 01326-270457
In residence: **Rev Terence Perkins,** (Retired).
M: *Sun 10.30am. Hds 10.30am.*

■ **SALCOMBE,** Devon
† Our Lady Star of the Sea (1959)
Devon Road. **Tel:** 01548-852670

Served from Kingsbridge.
M: *Sun 8.45am. Hds 7.15pm.*

■ **SALTASH,** Cornwall
Our Lady of the Angels
Bishop's Close, New Road, Saltash
Tel: 01752 844455
Also serves Liskeard and Torpoint.
Rev Michael J Lock, West Street, Liskeard, Cornwall PL14 6BW **Tel:** 01579-344906
M: *Sun 9am. Hds 7pm*

■ **SCLERDER,** Looe, Cornwall
† **Our Lady of Light** (1843)
The Presbytery, Sclerder, Looe, Cornwall PL13 2JD **Tel:** 01503-272627
Rev David Annear.
Deacon: **Rev Peter Skoyles.**
M: *Sun 9.15am Hds 9am.*
• ***Carmelite Convent,*** Sclerder.
Tel: 01503-272238.

■ **SEATON,** Devon
† **St Augustine**
(1910; 1920; 1937 cons 18 June 1981)
Manor Road, Seaton, Devon EX12 2AJ
Tel: 01297-20476
Rev Michael Koppel. Also in residence: **Canon Bernard Jaffa,** (*Retired*).
M: *Sat 1st M of Sun 5.30pm. Hds 5.30pm.*

■ **SHAFTESBURY,** Dorset
† **The Holy Name and St Edward the Martyr**
(1898; 1910; Cons 18th June 1994)
55 Salisbury Street, Shaftesbury, Dorset SP7 8EL **Tel:** 01747-852125
Rev Dylan James *Deacon:* **Michael Hughes**
M: *Sat 5.00pm Sun 11.00. Hds enquire Presbytery*

■ **SHALDON,** Devon
† **St Ignatius of Loyola** (1931)
42 Fore Street, Shaldon, Devon TQ14 0EA
Tel: 01626-873410 Served from Teignmouth
M: *Sun 9am.*

■ **SHERBORNE,** Dorset
† **Sacred Heart and St Aldhelm** (1894)
The Parish House, Westbury, Sherborne DT9 3EL **Tel:** 01935-812021
Rev Rev. Rodney Schofield, *Deacon:* **Rev Jonathan Simon; Revv David O'Driscoll, Michael Downey,** (*retired priests*).
M: *Sat 1st M of Sun 6pm. Sun 10.30am. Hds 10am, 6.30pm.*

■ **SIDMOUTH,** Devon
Most Precious Blood (1935)
Radway, Sidmouth, Devon EX10 8TW
Tel: 01395-513340
Revv Daniel Longland; Patrick Kilgarriff (*retired*).
M: *Sat 1st M of Sun 5.30pm. Sun 10am; Hds (vigil 7pm), 10am.*

■ **SOUTH BRENT AND TORPOINT,** Devon
1. St Dunstan, New Park (1937)
Served from Buckfast Abbey.
M: *Sun 8.30am. Hds 7.15pm.*

2. † St Saviour, Our Blessed Lady and St Bridget of Sweden (1929)
Syon Abbey, Marley Head, South Brent, Devon TQ10 9JX **Tel:** 01364-72256
M: *Sun 9am. Hds, 9am.*
• ***Bridgettine Nuns (Order of Our Most Holy Saviour).*** **Tel:** 01364-72256

■ **SOUTH MOLTON,** Devon
St Joseph (1957)
East Street. Served from Barnstaple.
M: *Sat 1st M of Sun 5.30pm. Hds (vigil 5.30pm).*

■ **SOUTHWAY,** Devon
See Plymouth, St Peter's Parish.

■ **SWANAGE,** Dorset
† **The Holy Spirit and St Edward (1902; 1904; cons 24 May 1934)**
The Presbytery, 1 Victoria Avenue, Swanage, Dorset BH19 1AH **Tel:** 01929-422491
Rev Tony Delsink.
M: *Sat 1st M of Sun 7pm (June - Aug). Sun 8am, 10am. Hds 9.15am, 7pm.*

■ **SYON ABBEY.**
See South Brent.

■ **TAVISTOCK,** Devon
Our Lady of the Assumption (1951)
Callington Road, Tavistock, Devon PL19 8EH **Tel:** 01822-612645
Rev Denis O'Gorman CRL
M: *Sun 9.15am. Hds 10am.*

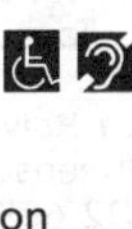

■ **TEIGNMOUTH,** Devon
† **Our Lady and St Patrick**
(1854; 1878; cons 7 Oct 1937)
Glendaragh Road, Teignmouth, Devon TQ14 8PH **Tel:** 01626-774640
Rev Jonathan Stewart.
M: *Sun 10.30am. Hds See newsletter.*

■ **TINTAGEL,** Cornwall
† **St Paul the Apostle** (1934; 1968)
Bossiney Road, Tintagel, Cornwall PL34 0AQ
Tel/Fax: 01840-770663
E-mail: bryan_s@onetel.net.uk
Rev Bryan Storey, Chy An Pronter, Bossiney Road, Tintagel PL34 0AQ
M: *Sat 1st M of Sun 6pm. Sun 10am. Hds (vigil 6pm). 10am.*

■ **TIVERTON,** Devon
St James (1967)
Old Road, (off Canal Hill), Tiverton, Devon.
Tel: 01884-252292
Revv Paul Rea CRL, Royston Davis.
40 Old Road, EX16 4HJ
M: *Sun 8.30am, 10.30am. Hds 9am, 7pm.*

• ***Sisters of the Presentation of Mary.*** The Convent, 3 Old Road, Tiverton, EX16 4HQ **Tel:** 01884-254212

■ TOPSHAM
See Exeter (3).

■ TORPOINT
St Joan of Arc (1933)
Moor View, Torpoint PL11 2LH
Tel: 01752-812347
Served from Saltash.
Canon Kevin Rea (Retired priest in residence).
M: *Sat 1st M of Sun 6pm. Hds 9am.*

■ TORQUAY, Devon
1. † Our Lady of the Assumption
(1644; 1853; cons Feb 1854)
76 Abbey Road, Torquay, Devon TQ2 5NJ
Tel/Fax: 01803-294142
Rev Brian Kenwrick.
M: *Sat 1st M of Sun 6pm. Sun 9am, 10.30am, Hds 10am, 7pm.*

2. † Our Lady Help of Christians and St Denis (1865; 1869; cons 4 Oct 1917)
Priory Road, St Marychurch, Torquay, Devon TQ1 4NY
Tel: 01803-327612 **Fax:** 01803-316226
Rev George Carrick.
M: *Sat 1st M of Sun 6pm. Sun 10am. Hds 10am, 7pm.*
• ***Daughters of the Cross,*** Stoodley Knowle Convent, Ansteys Cove Road, TQ1 2JB **Tel:** 01803-215865
• ***Margaret Clitherow CWL,*** Residential House, Priory Road, St Marychurch, Torquay TQ1 4NY **Tel:** 01803-326056

3. † Holy Angels (1938)
Queensway, Chelston, Torquay, Devon TQ2 6BP **Tel:** 01803-607116
Served from Paignton
Rev John Smethhurst
M: *Sun 9.30am, 5pm. Hds 9.30am, 7pm.*

■ TORRINGTON, Devon
The Holy Family (1965)
Gas Lane. Served from Bideford.
M: *Sun 9.30am. Hds 6.30pm.*

■ TOTNES, Devon
† St Mary and St George (1902; 1986)
Station Road, Totnes, Devon TQ9 5HW
Tel: 01803-862126
Rev Kristian Paver. Also in residence: **Rev Edward Buckley,** (retired).
M: *Sat 1st M of Sun 6.30pm. Sun 10.30am. Hds 10am, 7pm.*

■ TRURO, Cornwall
† Our Lady of the Portal and St Piran
(1885; 1973)
St Austell Street, Truro, Cornwall TR1 1SE
Tel: 01872-272291 **Rev Gilmour McDermott**
Deacon: **Rev Andrew Shute**
M: *Sat 1st M of Sun 6.15pm. Sun 9.30am, 11am. Hds 10am, 7pm.*
• ***Sisters of Notre Dame,*** The Granary, Tresilian, Truro TR2 4BN
Tel: 01872-520279

■ UGBROOKE, Chudleigh, Devon
† St Cyprian (1671)
Served from Bovey Tracey.
M: *Sun 9am. Hds 6pm.*

■ WADEBRIDGE, Cornwall
† St Michael (1948)
Trevanson Street, Wadebridge, Cornwall.
Served from Bodmin.
M: *Sun 8.30am. Hds 6pm.*

■ WAREHAM, Dorset
† St Edward the Martyr (1933)
Shatters Hill, Wareham.
Tel: 01929-552820 Served from Wool.
M: *Sun 11am. Hds (vigil 7pm).*
• ***Sisters of Mercy,*** Shatter's Hill, Wareham BH20 4QP

■ WEST MOORS, Dorset
St Anthony (1928; 1976; 1980; cons 8 Dec 1980)
Pinehurst Road, West Moors, Dorset BH22 0AP **Tel:** 01202-874811
Rev Canon Patrick Chrystal
M: *Sat 1st M of Sun 6.30pm. Sun 8.15am, 11am. Hds 8.15am, 7pm.*

■ <$IWEYMOUTH, Dorset
Parish of Our Lady, Star of the Sea
1. † St Joseph (1934)
Westham Road, Weymouth, Dorset.
Tel: 01305-786033
Parish Office: 1 Stavordale Road, Weymouth DT4 0AB
Rev Stephen Geddes,
Deacon: **Rev Geoffrey Carey**
Parish Sister: **Sr Maria Cooke** (Portland).
M: *Sat 1st M of Sun 6pm. Sun 9am. Hds 7pm.*

2. † St Augustine of Canterbury (1835)
38 Dorchester Road, Weymouth DT4 7JX
Tel: 01305-786886
M: *Sun 11am. Hds 9.30am.*

■ WIMBORNE, Dorset
† St Catherine (1926; 1933)
Lewens Lane, Wimborne, Dorset.
Tel: 01202-883312 **E-mail:** stcath@wimborne.enterprise-plc.com **Canon Kenneth Noakes.** 4 Lewens Lane, BH21 1LE
M: *Sat 1st M of Sun 5pm. Sun 9am, 11am, Hds 10.30am, 7.30pm.*

A

■ **WOOL,** Dorset
St Joseph (1973)
The Square, Wool, Dorset.
Rev Geoffrey Watts, The Priest's House, The Square BH20 6DU **Tel:** 01929 463334
M: *Sun 9am. Hds 10am.*

■ **YELVERTON,** Devon
† **Holy Cross** (1917; 1928; Extended 1979)
Dousland Road, Yelverton, Devon PL20 6AZ **Tel:** 01822-853171
Rev Michael Cole.
M: *Sun 9am, 10.30. Hds 10am, 7pm.*

■ **NAVAL ESTABLISHMENTS**
(a) Devonport
HMS Drake, for RN Personnel and Families and Fleet in HM Naval Base.
Chapel of Our Lady of the Ships
The RC Chaplain, The Chaplaincy Centre, Fisher Block, HM Naval Base, Devonport, Devon PL2 2BG
Tel: 01752-555424
M: *No Mass on Sunday*

(b) Dartmouth
Britannia Royal Naval College.
Chapel of St Philip Howard
The RC Chaplain, BRNC, Dartmouth TQ6 0HJ **Tel:** 01803-677116
M: *Sun 10am.*

(c) Torpoint
HMS Raleigh
Chapel of Our Lady, Star of the Sea.
The Chaplaincy, HMS Raleigh, Torpoint, East Cornwall, PL11 2PD
Tel: 01752-811259
M: *Sun 10am.*

(d) Lympstone
Royal Marines Commando Training Centre,
Tel: 01392-873898 Served from Exeter (3).
M: *No Mass on Sunday*

(e) Helston
HMS Seahawk, RN Air Station, Culdrose.
Tel: 01326-572378 Served from Helston
M: *No Mass on Sunday. Wed 12noon.*
Catholic Chapel of the Holy Redeemer
M: *Weds 12.15pm*

■ **ORDERS OR CONGREGATIONS, ETC**

■ **Men**
Augustinian Recollects: Honiton, Ivybridge.
Benedictines (English Congregation): Buckfast.
Carmelites (O.Carm): Lynton.
Franciscans of the Immaculate, Lanherne.
Josephites: Brixham, Kinson.

■ **Women**
Anne, Sisters of St: Plymouth (1).
Augustinian Sisters (Bruges): Plymouth (15).
Benedictine: Buckfastleigh
Bridgettine Nuns: South Brent (2).
Carmelites: Sclerder.
Charity (of St Paul), Sisters of: Plymouth (9).
Christian Instruction, Religious of: Sherborne.
Cross (of Liége), Daughters of the: Hayle.
Cross (of Torquay). Daughters of the: Plymouth (1), Torquay (2), Falmouth.
Franciscans of the Immaculate: Lanherne.
Holy Family (of Villefranche-de-Rouergue), Sisters of the: Exmouth (1).
Holy Spirit, Daughters of the: Newton Abbot.
Joseph (of Annécy), Sisters of St: Redruth.
La Sainte Union: Bournemouth (1).
Marist Sisters: Ottery St Mary.
Mary and Joseph. Daughters of: Padstow.
Mercy, Sisters of: Poole (1), Wareham, Weymouth (2).
Nazareth, Poor Sisters of: Plymouth (1).
Notre Dame (Namur), Sisters of: Plymouth (6, 11, 13), Truro.
Poor Clares (Colettines): Lynton.
Poor Handmaids of Jesus Christ: Bournemouth (2).
Presentation of Mary (of Bourg-St-Andéol), Sisters of: Exeter (2).

■ **DIOCESAN INSTITUTIONS, SOCIETIES**
For Societies and Organisations without representation in the diocese please see the main Societies and Organisations section.

Apostleship of the Sea. *Co-ordinating Port Chaplain:* **Mrs Louise Carter,** Victoria Wharf, Coxside, Plymouth PL4 0RF **Tel:** 01752 228544 *Port Chaplains:* **Rev T O'Donovan** North Road, Bideford EX39 2NW **Tel:** 01237-472519 Cathedral Clergy, 45 Cecil Street, Plymouth PL1 5HW **Tel:** 01752-662537 **Rev J Bielawski,** St Mary's Killigrew Street, Falmouth, Cornwall TR11 3PR **Tel:** 01326-312763 **Rev Jonathan Stewart**, Our Lady and St Patrick, Glendaragh Road, Teignmouth, Devon TQ14 8PH **Tel:** 01626-774640 **Rev Robert Draper**, St Augustine's Woodland Road, St Austell, Cornwall PL25 4RA **Tel:** 01726-73838
Archconfraternity of St Stephen for Altar Servers. *Diocesan Director:* **Rev Michael Lock**, Our Lady and St Neot, West Street, Liskeard, Cornwall PL14 6BW **Tel:** 01572 344906

Association of Missionary Children. *Diocesan Director:* **Rev Christopher Findlay-Wilson**, The Presbytery, 15 Trevu Road, Camborne, Cornwall TR14 7AE **Tel:** 01209-713143

Association for the Propagation of the Faith. *Diocesan Director:* **Rev Michael Kirkpatrick**. *Mill Hill Organiser:* **Rev Frank Thompson**, 23 Eccleston Square, London SW1V 1NU

Caritas Christi. For information write to: **Miss J Poole**, 50 Tarrant Close, Poole, BH17 9DN

Catenian Association. Province No. 13 (Cornwall & Devon) *Secretary*: **Robert Paice, Tel:** 01626-364888 Province 11 (Dorset) *Secretary:* **Faris Bashoo, Tel:** 01250-873733

(CAFOD) Catholic Fund for Overseas Development *Organiser covering the Plymouth Diocese* **Simon Giarche,** St Joseph's Church, Raglan Road, Plymouth PL1 2EN **Tel:** 01823-338903

Catholic People's Weeks. New programme each January from, **Mr Colin Stockford**, 18 St Leonard's Avenue, Blandford, Dorset. DT11 7NZ **Tel:** 01258-452183

Catholic Women's League. *Cornwall Branch Secretary:* **Mrs Eileen Martin, Tel:** 01579-321080 *Devon Branch Secretary:* **Mrs Mary Derry, Tel:** 01803-324219 *Dorset Branch Secretary:* **Miss D Jennings, Tel:** 01202-732119

Our Lady's Catechists. *Diocesan Representative:* **Claire Gatehouse**, 11 Winchester Close, Feniton, Exeter EX14 3EX **Tel:** 01626-773461

Co-Workers of Mother Teresa. Regional Link (Devon): **Mr & Mrs J Cronin**, 41A Shelley Avenue, St Marychurch, Torquay, Devon TQ1 4PF **Tel:** 01803-328355 Dorset: Sherborne, Dorset DT9 4EP. Cornwall: **Mrs Rita Heggie,** Trevispen, Trispen, Truro, Cornwall TR4 9B.

Exeter and District Catholic Teachers Association. *President*: **F Carty,** 8 Oak Park Road, Newton Abbot. **Tel:** 01626-66314 Catholic Teachers Federation Council, *Teacher Accounts Representative*: **P Wilmot**, Queensway School, Torquay TQ2 6DB

Guild of St Agatha, Catholic Association of Bellringers. *Diocesan Representative*: **Patrick Matthews,** 2 Norman Gdns, Branksome, Poole, Dorset, BH12 1JG **Tel:** 01202-721287

Guild of St Boniface. For expenses of Bishop's maintenance and administration of diocese. *Warden*: **Rev G Carrick**, The Presbytery, Priory Road, St Marychurch, Torquay TQ1 4NY **Tel:** 01803-316226

Knights of St Columba. Province 19 (Plymouth). *Secretary*: **Anthony Smith,** 42 Dunclair Park, Laira, Plymouth PL3 6DE Province 14 (Hants and Dorset): *Secretary:* **Robert Weston**, 180 Fairmile Road, Christchurch, Dorset BY23 2LW

Jesus Caritas Priests' Fraternity: Devon & Cornwall: **Mgr Adrian Toffolo**, The Presbytery, Higher Church Street, Barnstaple, Devon EX32 8JE **Tel:** 01271-343312 Dorset: **Rev Jude McHugo CJ**, The Presbytery, 46 Durdells Avenue, Kinson, Bournemouth BH11 9EH **Tel:** 01202-572939

Lay Dominicans. *Secretary:* **Mrs Sylvia Spice OPL**, Rock Cottage, 24 North View Road, Brixham, Devon TQ5 9TS **Tel:** 01803-851423

Legion of Mary. Contacts: Cornwall: **Mrs Gillian Jolley, Tel:** 01840-212978 Devon: **Roger John Hannaford Tel:** 01752-673269 Dorset: **Mrs Olive Gasson, Tel:** 01202-675773

Marriage Care. For Appointments: Exeter & North Devon: **Tel:** 0800 389-3801 Torbay: **Tel:** 01803-200830

Marriage Encounter England and Wales. Details obtainable from **Peter and Maureen Watson, Tel:** 01752-405183, or **Maurice and Margaret Magee, Tel:** 01803-407359

National Board of Catholic Women. *Diocesan Contact:* **Sue Walsh.**

Notre Dame Association. *Secretary*: **Mrs Bernie Holder**, 29 Langstone Road, Peverell, Plymouth PL2 3LY **Tel:** 01752-704112

Plymouth Diocesan Catholic Children's Society Ltd. *Chair:* **Peter McWilliams.** Familes for Children, Buckfast Abbey **Tel:** 01364 645499 *Office*: Rosary House, 27 Fore Street, Heavietree, Exeter EX1 2QJ **Tel:** 01392-55046 **Fax:** 01392-55109

Plymouth Diocesan Lourdes Pilgrimage. *Director:* **Mrs Sue King,** Bishop's House, 31 Wyndham Street, West Plymouth PL1 5RZ

The Pilgrimage Trust - HCPT. *Chair*: **Mr Christopher Woodman.**

Plymouth Diocesan Housekeepers' Fund. For further details please contact *Secretary*: **Rev Christopher Findlay-Wilson**, The Presbytery, 15 Trevu Road, Camborne, Cornwall TR14 7AE **Tel:** 01209-713413

Plymouth Diocesan Service Committee for Charismatic Renewal. *Chaplain:* **Rev T Fleming**, The Presbytery, 20 Redford Park Road, Plymstock,

Plymouth PL9 9DW *Secretary*: **Mrs Christine Durrant**, 4 Tarraway Road, Paignton, Devon TQ3 2DU **Tel:** 01803-527072

Plymouth Diocesan Special Needs Service: *Adviser:* **Mrs Sue King,** Bishop's House, 31 Wyndham Street West, Plymouth PL1 3RZ **Tel:** 01752-224414

Plymouth Diocesan Youth Service. *Co-ordinator for Youth Ministry:* **Rebecca Barter.**

Plymouth Diocese Catechetical Camps. *Secretary:* **Ben Barter**, Flat 2, 6 Church Road, Exeter EX2 9AX **Tel:** 01392-433295

Plymouth Justice and Peace Commission. *Chairman:* **Mrs Monica Evans.** *Adviser:* **Mary Conway,** Bishop's House, 31 Wyndham Street West, Plymouth PL1 5RZ **Tel:** 01752-224414 **E-mail:** j&p@plymouth-diocese.org.uk

Plymouth Catholic Students' Chaplaincy: *Chaplain*: **Rev Trevor Jordan,** The Presbytery, Armada Way, Plymouth PL1 2EN

Plymouth Secular Clergy Fund. For retired and infirm clergy. *Secretary*: **Rev Terry O'Donovan**, The Presbytery, North Road, Bideford, EX39 2NW

Secular Franciscan Order Further information from: *President*: **Vincent Calder**, 9 Mallard Close, Chipping, Sudbury, Bristol, Avon. *Vice President: Secretary:* **Joan Woollard**. Flat 9, Drake Court, 264 Citadel Road, Plymouth PL1 2P **Tel:** 01752-254131 *Treasurer:* **Neville Simpson**. 29 Swallowfield Road, Countesswear, Exeter. *National Assistant SFO:* **Rev Patrick Lonsdale, OFM**. Franciscan Friary, 56 St Antony's Road, Forest Gate, London E7 9QB **Tel:** 0181-472 3900

Secular Order of Discalced Carmelites: *Secretary:* **Mrs Pam Murray,** 37 Vicarage Meadow, Fowey, Cornwall PL23 1EA **Tel:** 01726-832606

Society of St Gregory. *Diocesan Representative:* **Benedict Davis**, St Joseph's, Kimberley Place, Falmouth TR11 3QL **Tel:** 013626-312683

Society of St Peter Apostle for Native Clergy. *Diocesan Director:* **Rev John Rice**, The Presbytery, White Cliff Mill Street, Blandford Forum, Dorset DT11 7BN **Tel:** 01258-452051

Society of St Vincent de Paul. Plymouth Central Council. *Secretary*: **John Jebb,** 24 Cherry Tree Drive, Brixton, Plymouth PL8 2DD **Tel:** 01752-880533

Teams of Our Lady. An international Catholic Movement for Christian married couples that aims to deepen the couples' spirituality. A 'Team' consists of four or five couples and a priest or religious as spiritual advisor meeting monthly to share the journey of faith, guided by the Holy Spirit. *Contact couple:* **Richard and Maggie Acres**, 'Greenbanks' Lower Rowe, Holt, Wimborne, Dorset BH21 7DZ **Tel:** 01202-885913 **E-mail:** richard@acres99.freeserve.co.uk

Union of Catholic Mothers. Foundations in the Diocese: Cathedral, Devonport, St Budeaux, Plymstock, Exmouth, Bournemouth (Kinson and Ensbury Park). Officers: *President:* **Maureen Downes**, *Secretary:* **Diana Holan**, 44 Shapley's Gardens, Staddiscombe, Plymouth PL9 9TY. **Tel:** 01752-401394

Walsingham Association. *Paignton:* **Mrs P Jelfs**, 246 Roselands Drive, Paignton, Devon TQ4 7RW **Tel:** 01803-552570

■ HOSPITALS

To contact the Catholic Chaplain of a particular hospital we suggest you contact the hospital reception directly.

■ CATHOLIC SCHOOLS - MAINTAINED

■ CORNWALL

▲ Junior and Infant

St Mary, Barn Lane, Bodmin PL31 1LW **Tel:** 01208-73218 *(Bodmin)*

St John, Trevu Road, Camborne TR14 7AE **Tel:** 01209-713944 *(Camborne)*

St Mary, Mongleath Road, Falmouth TR11 4PW **Tel:** 01326-314540 *(Falmouth)*

St Mary, Peverell Road, Penzance TR18 2AT **Tel:** 01736-64385 *(Penzance)*

■ DEVON

▲ Junior and Infant

St Mary, Lyme Road, Axminster EX13 5BE **Tel:** 01297-32785 *(Axminster)*

Our Lady, Chanters Hill, Barnstaple EX32 8DN **Tel:** 01271-345164 *(Barnstaple)*

St Margaret Clitherow, Polhearne Way, Brixham, TQ5 0EE **Tel:** 01803-851647 *(Brixham)*

St Mary, Buckfast, Buckfastleigh TQ11 0EA **Tel:** 01364-642389 *(Buckfast)*

St John the Baptist, Milton Lane, Dartmouth TQ6 9HW **Tel:** 01803-832495 *(Dartmouth)*

St Joseph, Regent's Gate, Long Causeway, Exmouth EX8 2JP **Tel:** 01395-264875 *(Exmouth)*

St Joseph, Coombeshead Road, Newton Abbot TQ12 1PT **Tel:** 01626-352559
St Nicholas, Ringswell Ave, Exeter EX1 3EG **Tel:** 01392-445403 *(Exeter)*
Sacred Heart, Cecil Road, Paignton TQ3 2SH **Tel:** 01803-558298 *(Paignton)*
Holy Cross, Beaumont Road, Plymouth PL4 9BE **Tel:** 01752-225420 *(Plymouth)*
Keyham Barton, Renown Street, Keyham, Plymouth PL2 2DE **Tel:** 01752-567684 *(Plymouth)*
The Cathedral School of St Mary, Cecil Street, Plymouth PL1 5HW **Tel:** 01752-265270 *(Plymouth)*
St Joseph, Chapel Street, Devonport Plymouth PL1 4DJ **Tel:** 01752-563185 *(Plymouth)*
St Paul, Pemros Road, St Budeaux, Plymouth PL5 1NE **Tel:** 01752-365459 *(Plymouth)*
St Peter, Brentford Avenue, Whitleigh, Plymouth PL5 4HD **Tel:** 01752-774176 *(Plymouth)*
Our Lady and St Patrick, Fourth Avenue, Teignmouth TQ14 9DT **Tel:** 01626-773905 *(Teignmouth)*
St John, Melbourne Street, Tiverton EX16 5LA **Tel:** 01884-253630 *(Tiverton)*
Priory RC, St Catherine's Road, Torquay TQ1 4NZ **Tel:** 01803-328480 *(Torquay)*
Queensway Catholic, Queensway, Torquay TQ2 6DB **Tel:** 01803-613095 *(Torquay)*

▲ Secondary Comprehensive
Notre Dame, Looseleigh Lane, Derriford, Plymouth PL6 5HN **Tel:** 01752-775101 *(Plymouth)*
St Boniface's College, 21 Boniface Lane, Crownhill, Plymouth PL5 3AG **Tel:** 01752-779051 *(Plymouth)*
St Cuthbert Mayne, RC/ C of E, Trumlands Road, Torquay TQ1 4RN **Tel:** 01803-328725 *(Torquay)*

■ DORSET

▲ First
St Mary, Barnes Way, Dorchester DT1 2DD **Tel:** 01305-262258 *(Dorchester)*
St Mary, Manor Road, Swanage BH19 2BH **Tel:** 01929-424909 *(Swanage)*
St Mary, Folly Lane, Wool, Wareham BH20 6DS **Tel:** 01929-462565 *(Wool)*

▲ Junior and Infant
St Catherine, Pymore Road, Bridport DT6 3TR **Tel:** 01308-423568 *(Bridport)*
Christ the King, Durdells Avenue, Kinson, Bournemouth BH11 9EH **Tel:** 01202-574277 *(Kinson)*
St Mary, Old Mill Lane, Marnhull DT10 1JX **Tel:** 01258-820417 *(Marnhull)*
St Augustine, Hardy Avenue, Weymouth DT4 0RH **Tel:** 01305-782600 *(Weymouth)*
St Catherine, Cutlers Place, Colehill, Wimborne BH21 2HN **Tel:** 01202-883763 *(Wimborne)*

▲ Combined First and Middle
St Joseph, Newlyn Way, Parkstone, Poole BH12 4EA **Tel:** 01202-741932 *(Poole)*
St Mary, Devon Road, Poole BH15 3QQ **Tel:** 01202-676207 *(Poole)*

▲ Secondary Comprehensive
St Edward, RC/ C of E, Dale Valley Road, Poole BH15 3HY **Tel:** 01202-740950 *(Poole)*

■ CATHOLIC SCHOOLS - INDEPENDENT
■ CORNWALL
St Michael's Catholic Small School, St George's Road, Truro TR1 3JD **Tel:** 01872-242123

■ DEVON

▲ Primary and Secondary
Trinity School, Ecumenical, Buckeridge Road, Teignmouth TQ14 8LY **Tel:** 01626-774138 *(Teignmouth)*
Stoodley Knowle Convent, Anstey's Cove Road, Torquay TQ1 2JB **Tel:** 01803-293160 *(Torquay)*

■ DORSET

▲ Nursery
St Joseph, 37 Parkstone Road, Poole BH15 2NU **Tel:** 01202-674515 *(Poole)*

▲ Primary and Secondary
St Antony's-Leweston Preparatory School, Sherborne, Dorset DT9 6EN **Tel/Fax:** 01963-210790 *(Sherborne)*
St Antony's-Leweston School, Sherborne DT9 6EN **Tel:** 01963-210691 *(Sherborne)*

DIOCESE OF PORTSMOUTH

(Province of Southwark)

Formed 19 May 1882, by division of the diocese of Southwark into the diocese of Southwark and Portsmouth

Comprising the counties of Hampshire, Berkshire (south of the Thames), Oxfordshire (south of the Thames), Dorset (east of the original county boundary), the Isle of Wight and the Channel Islands.

Patrons of the Diocese
Our Blessed Lady, conceived without sin, 8 December
St Edmund of Abingdon, 16 November

Rt Rev Crispian Hollis, Bishop of Portsmouth

Bishop
Rt Rev Crispian Hollis MA, STL, Bishop of Portsmouth: born Bristol 17 November 1936; ordained 11 July 1965; cons 5 May 1987 Bishop of Cincari: Auxiliary Bishop in Birmingham; app to Portsmouth 6 Dec 1988; inst 27 Jan 1989

Bishop's Residence:
Bishop's House, Edinburgh Road, Portsmouth, Hants, PO1 3HG
Tel: 023-9282 0894 **Fax:** 023-9286 3086
E-mail: bishop@portsmouthdiocese.org.uk

Bishop's Secretary:
Mrs Yvonne Archer
E-mail: bishopspa@portsmouthdiocese.org.uk

■ THE BISHOP'S COUNCIL

Mgr Vincent Harvey VG, The Presbytery, St Bedes, Popley Way, Basingstoke, Hants RG24 9DX **Tel:** 01256-819772 **Fax:** 01256-469605

Mgr Thomas McGrath VG, 36 Cookham Road, Maidenhead, Berks SL6 7EG **Tel:** 01628-783988 **Fax:** 01628-776863

Mgr John Nelson VG, 64 Liebenrood Road, Reading, Berks RG30 2EB **Tel:** 0118 957 2149 **Fax:** 0118 957 5241 **E-mail:** nelsonjohnF@aol.com

Rev Canon Paul Townsend EpV, Peterhouse, St Peter Street, Winchester, Hants SO23 8BW **Tel:** 01962-852804 **Fax:** 01962-893691 **E-mail:** canonpaul@stpeterswinchester.org.uk

■ Episcopal Vicar for the Formation of the Clergy

Rev Canon Paul Townsend EpV, **E-mail:** canonpaul@stpeterswinchester.org.uk

■ Vocations

Rev Gerard Flynn, 96 Pyle Street, Newport PO30 1UH **Tel:** 01983 522027 **E-mail:** gerarddominic@waitrose.com

Director of Formation for Permanent Deacons: **Rev Steve Melhuish,** 33 Hilland Rise, Headley, Hants GU35 8LZ **Tel:** 01428-713555 **Fax:** 01424-712387 **E-mail:** steve-melhuish@btinternet.com

■ Episcopal Vicar for Religious

Rev Thomas Taaffe, 1 Radley Road, Abingdon, Oxon OX14 3PL **Tel:** 011235 520375

■ College of Consultors

Mgr John Nelson VG, Mgr Vincent Harvey, Mgr Thomas McGrath, Canons John O'Shea, Revv Paul Townsend EpV, John Catlin, Tom Taaffe, Dominic Golding JDV.

■ Diocesan Council of Priests

Chair: **Rev John Humphreys.**

■ Pastoral Council of the Diocese

Eileen Baird, Francis Connolly, Marie Crispin, Doreen Drake, Joy Ellis, Jan Guidoboni, Paul Inwood, Nina Lake, Julie Lazarus, Jean Le Breuilly, Jim McGovern, Christine McGrew, Harry McSoley, Stephen Morgan, Anne Owen, Cath Pickles, Fran Ross, Peter Ryder, Nicky Stevens, Mary Stone, Bridie Stringer, Martin Stubbs, Kathryn Turner, Colin Warburg, Anthony Whelan, Francis Williamson, Angela Wills, and the members of the Diocesan Council of Priests.

■ **Child Protection Co-ordinator**
Tel: 023 9281 6396 **Fax:** 023 9287 2424
E-mail: amcgrory@portsmouthdiocese.org.uk

■ **The Chancellor**
Canon Richard Hind, Bishop's House, Edinburgh Road, Portsmouth PO1 3HG
Tel: 023-9282 6019 **Fax:** 023-9286 3086, **E-mail:** chancellor@portsmouthdiocese.org.uk

■ **The Diocesan Tribunal**
Judicial Vicar: **Rev Dominic Golding MCL, JCL**; *Associate Judicial Vicar:* **Mgr John Nelson STL, JCL, VG**, Portsmouth Diocesan Tribunal, 61a Yorktown Road, Sandhurst, Berks GU47 9BS

■ **CATHEDRAL CHAPTER**
(Erected 1st October 1882)
Provost: **Provost Emeritus Mgr Cyril Murtagh. Rev Canon Gerard Hetherington KCHS**. *Canons:* **Revv Mgri David Mahy, Nicholas France** (*Secretary*), **Richard Hind, Mgr Jeremy Garratt, David Hopgood, John O'Shea, Alan Griffiths, Terence Healy, Peter Turbitt** (*Penitentiary*), **Paul Townsend.** *Canons Emeriti:* **Revv Dermot MacDermot-Roe, Henry Murphy, Brian Murphy-O'Connor, Peter Wilkie.** *Honorary Canons:* **Revv Terence K Walsh.**

■ **THE DIOCESAN CURIA**
Moderator: **Mgr John Nelson**, St Edmund House, Edinburgh Road, Portsmouth PO1 3QA **Tel:** 023-9282 5430
E-mail: NelsonJohnF@aol.com

■ **Department for Pastoral Formation**
Head of Department: **Nicky Stevens,** Park Place Pastoral Centre, Winchester Road, Wickham PO17 5HA **Tel:** 01329-835583
Fax: 01329-833452
E-mail: nstevens@portsmouthdiocese.org.uk
Website: www.portsmouthdiocese.org.uk/pastoral_formation/index.htm
Director of Liturgy: **Paul Inwood,** Park Place Pastoral Centre, Winchester Road, Wickham PO17 5HA
Tel: 01329-835521 **Fax:** 01329-833092
E-mails:
pinwood@portsmouthdiocese.org.uk
paul@prcdtr-parkplace.org
Advisers for Catechesis: **Kate Harris,** kharris@portsmouthdiocese.org.uk
Youth Ministry: **David Hill.**
E-mails: dhill@portsmouthdiocese.org.uk
Advisers for Collaborative Ministry: **Angela Wills, Fran Ross.**
E-mails: awills@portsmouthdiocese.org.uk fross@portsmouthdiocese.org.uk
Adviser for Justice and Peace: **Catherine Waters-Clark. E-mails:** cwaters-clark@portsmouthdiocese.org.uk
Administrators: **Eileen Stephenson,** estephenson@portsmouthdiocese.org.uk
Nancy Robinson.

■ **Department for Schools**
Head of Department & Director of Schools: **Mr Chris Richardson**, Park Place Pastoral Centre, Winchester Road, Wickham PO17 5HA **E-mail:** crichardson@portsmouthdiocese.org.uk
Tel: 01329-835363 **Fax:** 01329-835347
E-mail: schools@portsmouthdiocese.org.uk
Deputy Directors: **Urszula Topp**
E-mail: utopp@portsmouthdiocese.org.uk

■ **Department for Finance and Property**
Head of Department: **Dcn Stephen Morgan**, St Edmund House, Edinburgh Road, Portsmouth PO1 3QA
Tel: 023-9282 5430 **Fax:** 023-9287 2424
E-mail: smorgan@portsmouthdiocese.org.uk
Diocesan Surveyor: **Sean Hayes,** St Edmund House, Edinburgh Road, Portsmouth PO1 3QA **Mbl:** 07831-165700

■ **The Diocesan Trustees**
The Rt Rev Crispian Hollis, Mgr John Nelson VG; Rev Canons Nicholas France, Gerard Hetherington, David Hopgood, Richard Hind, Kevin Ryan, Mr Peter Burns, Revv Mgr Vincent Harvey VG, Tom McGrath VG, Mrs Sheila Hughes, Peter Hancock, Iain McGrory, Mrs Elizabeth Slinn, David Morgan, Francis Davis, Miss Catherine Hargaden.
Secretary to the Trustees: **Dcn Stephen Morgan**, St Edmund House, Edinburgh Road, Portsmouth PO1 3QA
Tel: 02392 825430 **Fax:** 02392 872424

■ **Liturgical Buildings & Historic Churches**
Liturgical Buildings Officer: **Canon Alan Griffiths,** 1 Grange Road, Alresford, Hants SO24 9HD

■ **Communications Officer**
Mr Barry Hudd, Tel: 01635-44326
E-mail: bhudd@portsmouthdiocese.org.uk

■ **Diocesan Archivist**
Rev Brian Croughan, BA, MA, MTh, 20 Beaumont Road, Totton, Hants SO40 3AL
Tel: 023-8086 2270
E-mail: archives@portsmouthdiocese.org.uk

■ PORTSMOUTH
† Cathedral Church of St John the Evangelist (1882; cons 1 Jul 1971)
Bishop's House, Edinburgh Road, Portsmouth PO1 3HG
Tel: 02392-826170
Fax: 02392-839143
E-mail: stjcath@portsmouthdiocese.org.uk
Canon David Hopgood (*Cathedral Dean*), **Rev Steven Restori**.
M: *Sun 10am, 12noon, 6pm. Hds (vigil 7.30pm), 12.15pm.*

■ ABINGDON, Oxon
1. † Our Lady and St Edmund of Abingdon (1857; 1865; cons 8 May 1957)
1 Radley Road. Abingdon, Oxon OX14 3PL
Tel: 01235-520375
E-mail: stedmundabingdon@tiscali.co.uk
Rev Tom Taaffe EpV.
M: *Sun 8am, 9.30am, 11.30am, 7pm. Hds 9am, 7pm*
- ***Sisters of Mercy,*** Lismore Lodge, 34 St John's Road, Abingdon OX14 2HB **Tel:** 01235-539504

2. Our Lady Help of Christians, Chapel of Ease
Dalton Army Barracksgate, Cholswell Drive (North Side) Abingdon, Oxon OX13
Served from Abingdon.

■ ALDERNEY, Channel Islands
† St Anne and St Mary Magdalen (1845; 1945; 1958; cons 22 June 1973)
The Catholic Presbytery, Braye Road, St Anne's, Alderney, C. I. GY9 3XJ
Tel: 01481-822105
Rev Martin Laker.
M: *Sat 1st M of Sun 6pm. Sun 10am. Hds 9.15am, 6pm.*
- ***Sisters of Mercy.*** The Convent, Braye Road, St Anne's, Alderney CI GY9 3XJ **Tel:** 01481-822314

■ ALDERSHOT, Hants
1. † St Joseph (1869; 1913. Cons 22.9.1982)
Queen's Road, Aldershot, Hants GU11 3JB
Tel: 01252-320956
Fax: 01252-323030
E-mail: dmahy@stjosephs.datanet.co.uk
Canon David Mahy. *Deacon:* **Antonio D'Mello**, 3 Pool Road, Aldershot, Hants GU11 3SN **Tel:** 01252-651747
E-mail: antoniodmello@hotmail.com
Pastoral Assistant: **Sr Athanasius (FMDM).**
M: *Sun 10.30am. Hds 9.30am.*
- ***Franciscan Missionaries of the Divine Motherhood***, St Anthony's Convent, 3 Northbrook Road, Aldershot, Hants GU11 3HE **Tel:** 01252-342105

2. † St Mary
Belle Vue Road North Town.
M: *Sat 1st M of Sun 4.45pm.*

3. † St Michael and St George (1892)
St Michael's House, Queen's Avenue, GU11 2BY
Tel: 01252-347061
(Served by Army Chaplain).
M: *Sun 8am, 11am.*

■ ALRESFORD, Hants 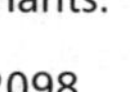
1. † St Gregory the Great (1968; cons 11 July 1975)
1 Grange Road, Alresford, Hants SO24 9HD
Tel/Fax: 01962-732262 Served from Winchester.
Canon Alan Griffiths
Deacon: **Rev Nick Reynolds**, Hall Place Cottage, Petersfield Road, Ropley, Hants. SO24 0EJ
Tel: 01962-772393 **Fax:** 01962-772098
E-mail: nickreynolds@freeuk.com
M: *Sun 11am. Hds As advertised.*

2. † St Margaret of Scotland.
Tichborne Park, Alresford, Hants.
M: *Occasional Mass only.*

■ ALTON, Hants
1. † St Mary (1911; 1938; 1966; Cons 25.6.1982)
59 Normandy Street, Alton, Hants GU34 1DN
Tel: 01420-82030
Fax: 01420-85821
Rev Peter Hart. 59 Normandy Street, GU34 1DN
E-mail: stmarysalton@waitrose.com
M: *Sat 1st M of Sun 6pm. Sun 8.30am, 11am. Hds 9.30am, 8pm.*
- ***Redemptorists (CSsR)***, Alphonsus House, Wolf Lane, Chawton, GU34 3HQ **Tel:** 01420-88222 (House) 01420-88805 (Publications Office) **Fax:** 01420-88805 **E-mail:** enquiries@rpbooks.co.uk **Revv Michael McGreevy** (*Publishing Director*).
- ***Sisters of St Marie de la Providence***, Anstey Lane, GU34 2NG **Tel:** 01420-82070 **Fax:** 01420-541711

2. St Lucy Convent Chapel
Medstead Manor, Medstead.
Served from Alton (1).
M: *Sun 10am. Hds 5.45pm.*
- ***Religious Teachers Filippini,*** Medstead Manor, Medstead, Hants GU34 5LL **Tel:** 01420-563562

■ ANDOVER, Hants
1. † St John the Baptist (1913; 1921; 1958)
Alexandra Road, Andover, Hants SP10 3AD
Tel: 01264-352829 **Fax:** 01264-357107
E-mail: office_stjohntb@btinternet.com
Website: www.catholic-andover.org.uk
Rev Peter Codd, Rev Michael Short, 37 Corunna Main, Andover, Hants SP10 1SD
M: *Sat 1st M of Sun 6pm. Sun 11am. Hds 10am, 7pm*

2. St John Fisher (1985)
Whitchurch
M: *2nd, 4th, 5th Sun of month, 9am.*

3. St Thomas More
Stockbridge.
M: *1st & 3rd Sun of month, 9am.*

■ **ARBORFIELD,** Berks
St Eligius
Garrison Church, Army Apprentice College.
Served from RMAS Camberley.
M: *Sun 9am.*

■ **ASCOT,** Berks A
† **St Francis** (1887; cons 4 July 1889)
Ascot, Berks.
Tel: 01344-620591 **Fax:** 01344-623565
E-mail: stfrancis@btinternet.com
Rev Charles McCloskey, The Friary, Coronation Road, Ascot SL5 9HG
M: *Sat 1st M of Sun 5.30pm. Sun 10am. Hds 10am, 8pm.*
- ***Marist Sisters,*** The Rosary, London Road, Sunninghill, SL5 7PS **Tel:** 01344-620009
- ***Sisters of Our Lady of Charity,*** Fairlight, The Avenue, North Ascot, SL5 7LY **Tel:** 01344-626622

■ **ASHURST,** Hants
See Totton.

■ **BASINGSTOKE,** Hants
1. † The Holy Ghost (1875; 1903)
Sherborne Road, Basingstoke, Hants RG21 5TD
Tel: 01256-465214 **Fax:** 01256-469605
E-mail: office@holyghost.org.uk
Website: www.vinntec.co.uk/hg
Rev Mgr Vincent Harvey VG.
The Presbytery, St Bedes, Popley Way, Basingstoke, Hants RG24 9DX
Tel: 01256-819772
M: *Sun 9am, 11am, 6.30pm. Hds vigil 8pm, 9.30am, 12.15pm.*
- ***Sisters of St Marie de la Providence,*** The Convent, 12 Burgess Road RG21 2NP **Tel:** 01256-321276

2. St Bede
Popley Way, Basingstoke, Hants RG24 9DX
Tel: 01256 465214 **Fax:** 01256 469605
M: *Sun 10.30am. Hds 9.30am in term time.*

3. † St Joseph A
St Michael's Road, Basingstoke, Hants RG22 6TY
Tel: 01256-323595 **Fax:** 01256-814569
E-mail: stjosephs@btinternet.com
Website: www.btinternet.com/~stjosephs
Rev Mark Hogan, Canon Brian Murphy-O'Connor (retired). *Deacons:* **Rev Patrick Taylor,** Lymington House, Parklands, Ashcombe House, Oakley Hall.
Tel: 01256-326726; **Rev Patrick O'Connell,** 33 Beechway, Basingstoke RG23 8LR.
M: *Sat 1st M of Sun 6pm. Sun 11am, Hds 10am, 8pm.*

4. St Mary
Overton. CofE Church.
M: *2nd Sun of month, 9am..*

5. Christ the King
Brighton Hill. Shared Church.
M: *3rd Sun of month 11am.*

■ **BISHOP'S WALTHAM,** Hants A
† **Our Lady, Queen of Apostles** (1912; 1977)
The Presbytery, Martin Street, Bishop's Waltham, Hants SO32 1DN
Tel/Fax: 01489-895889 **E-mail:** rev.jbuckley@bishopswaltham23.fsnet.co.uk
Rev John Buckley.
M: *Sat 1st M of Sun 6pm. Sun 9am, Hds (vigil 7.30pm), 10am, 6.30pm.*

■ **BOARS HILL,** Oxford
See North Hinksey (3).

■ **BORDON,** Hants
† **The Sacred Heart** (Con 21/6/1990)
High Street, Bordon, Hants GU35 0AU
Tel: 01420-472415
Rev Edward Richer. *Deacon:* **Rev Steve Melhuish,** 33 Hilland Rise, Headley, Hants GU35 8LZ **Tel:** 01428-713555
E-mails: ericher@bordonparish.org.uk steve.melhuish@btinternet.com
M: *Sat 1st, 3rd & 5th in month 5.30pm. Sun 11.15am. Hds 7.30pm.*

■ **BOSCOMBE**
See Bournemouth (2).

■ **BOURNEMOUTH,** Dorset
(See also under Diocese of Plymouth).
1. † The Sacred Heart
(1875; 1900; cons Feb 1975)
Albert Road, Richmond Hill, Bournemouth.
Tel: 01202-551013 **Fax:** 01202-557991
E-mail: office.sacredheart@btinternet.com
Website: www.sacredheartchurch-bournemouth.co.uk
1 Albert Road, BH1 1BZ
Rev Anthony Pennicott, Rev Jacomo Ferreira (Portuguese Language Chaplain).
M: *Sat 1st M of Sun 6pm. Sun 8am, 10.30am, 1pm (Polish), 4pm. Hds 8am, 12.15pm, 6pm.*

2. † Corpus Christi A
(1887; 1896; cons 18 July 1974)
17/18 St James Square, Boscombe, Bournemouth BH5 2BX **Tel:** 01202-425286
E-mail: web@jesuits.com
- ***Corpus Christi Jesuit Centre:*** 757 Christchurch Road, Boscombe,

Bournemouth BH7 6AN
Tel: 01202 436700

- ***Society of Jesus (SJ):*** **Rev Dennis Blackledge** (*Superior and Parish Priest*). Also in residence: **Revv Peter Hackett, Michael Barrow, Michael Beattie, Peter Knott, Robert Bulbeck, Robert Carty, Joseph Dooley, Charles Edwards, Michael Flannery, James Harkness, Geoffrey Holt, Patrick Purnell, Clifford Taunton, William Crooks, Derrick Maitland, Anthony Parish, Stanley Maxwell, Charles Praeger**.
  M: *Sat 1st M of Sun 6pm. Sun 9.30am, 11am 5pm. Hds (vigil 7pm), 7.15am, 10am, 7pm.*
- ***Handmaids of the Sacred Heart (Rome)***, 6 Parkwood Road, Bournemouth BH5 2BH
  Tel: 01202-421854 **Fax:** 01202-430927

3. The Annunciation with St Edmund Campion
Presbytery, 218 Charminster Road, Bournemouth BH8 9RW
Tel: 01202-513369 **Fax:** 01202-518192
E-mail: theannunciation@tiscali.co.uk
Website: www.annunciation.bournemouth.org.uk
Rev Marcus Brisley. *Deacon:* **Rev Barry Jennings.**

4. † The Annunciation (1906)
M: *Sun 11am, 6.30pm. Hds 8am, 7pm.*

5. † St Edmund Campion
(1955; cons 30 Nov 1981)
Castle Lane West, Strouden Park, Bournemouth.
M: *Sat 1st M of Sun 6.30pm. Sun 9.30am. Hds 10am.*

6. † Our Lady Immaculate (1927)
Seamoor Road, Westbourne, Bournemouth.
Tel: 01202-764027
Rev James McAuliffe SPS. 32 Alum Chine Road, Bournemouth BH4 8DZ
M: *Sun 9am, 11am. Hds 11am, 7pm.*

7. † Our Lady Queen of Peace and Blessed Margaret Pole
(1920; 1939; cons 27 May 1964)
Douglas Road, Southbourne, Bournemouth.
Tel: 01202-424960 **E-mail:** olqpsouthbourne@hotmail.co.uk
Rev John Dunne. 18 Douglas Road, Southbourne, Bournemouth BH6 3ER
M: *Sun 8am, 10.30am, 6.30pm. Hds 7.30am, 10am, 7.30pm.*

- ***De La Salle Brothers,*** 61 St Catherine's Road, Bournemouth, Dorset BH6 4AD
  Tel: 01202-426430

8. † St Thomas More
(1939; cons 9 July 1957)
Exton Road, Boscombe East, Bournemouth.
Tel: 01202-485588
E-mail: admin@stthomasmore.fs.net.co.uk
Rev Shaun Budden, 42 Exton Road, Boscombe East, Bournemouth BH6 5QG
M: *Sat 1st M of Sun 6pm. Sun 10am. Hds 9.30am, 6.30pm.*

9. University of Bournemouth
(Diocese of Plymouth)
Chaplain: **Rev Bill Muir CJ**, 46 Durdells Avenue, Kinson, Bournemouth BH11 9EH
Tel: 01202-572939

10. Bournemouth Hospital Chaplaincy
Chaplain: **Mgr Ron Hishon**.
Tel: 07963617031

■ BRACKNELL, Berks
1. † St Joseph (1894; 1962)
Stanley Walk, Bracknell, Berks RG12 1HA
Tel: 01344-425729 **Fax:** 01344-420842
E-mail: bracknellsj@yahoo.co.uk
Rev Christopher Rutledge.
M: *Sat 1st M Sun 6pm. Sun 10.30am. Hds 12.10pm. (Also in term time 9.15am at School).*

2. † St Margaret Clitherow (1973)
Hanworth, Bracknell, Berks.
Tel: 01344-423093 **Fax:** 01344-867445
E-mail: bracknellmc@yahoo.com
Deacon: **Anthony Cunningham.**
M: *Sun 9am, 11am. Hds (vigil 8pm), 9.10am.*

■ BRIDGEMARY
See Gosport.

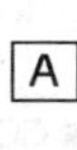

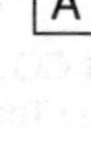

■ BROCKENHURST, Hants
See Lymington
Deacon: **Rev Stephen Morgan,** The Presbytery, 14 Empress Road, Lyndhurst, Hants SO43 7AE. **Tel:** 023 8028 2612
E-mail: smorgan@portsmouthdiocese.org.uk

■ BUCKLAND, Faringdon, Oxon
See Faringdon

■ BURGHFIELD COMMON, Berks
See Woolhampton (2).

■ CHANDLERS FORD, Hants
† St Edward the Confessor
(1938; cons 8/10/89)
Winchester Road, Chandlers Ford
Office: 191-193 Winchester Road, Chandlers Ford, Hants SO53 2DU
Tel/Fax: 023-8027 3882
E-mail: 3rivers@portsmouthdiocese.org.uk
Rev Michael Dennehy, 53 Leigh Road,

Eastleigh, Hants SO50 9DF
Tel: 023-8061 2430
E-mail: mdennehy@portsmouthdiocese.org.uk
Deacon: **Rev Paul Owen**, 34 Foyle Road, Chandlers Ford, Eastleigh SO53 4QP
Tel: 023-8025 4806 **E-mail:** deaconpaul@catholics-in-eastleigh.org.uk
M: *Sat 1st M of Sun 6.30pm. Sun 9am. Hds 7.30pm.*

■ **CHAWTON,** Hants
See Alton.

■ **CHRISTCHURCH,** Dorset
† Immaculate Conception and St Joseph (1866, 19 March 1993)
67 Purewell, Christchurch, Dorset BH23 1EH **Tel:** 01202-483340
E-mail: icsjoffice@portsmouthdiocese.org.uk
Website: www.stjosephchristchurch.org.uk
• ***Oblates of Mary Immaculate (OMI)***; **Rev John Lee** (*Parish Priest*).
M: *Sat 1st M of Sun 6.30pm. Sun 9am, 10.45am. Hds 9am, 7.30pm.*

■ **CHURCH CROOKHAM,** Hants A
† The Holy Trinity (1920; 1968; cons July 1975)
Presbytery, Aldershot Road, Church Crookham, Aldershot, Hants GU52 8JU
Tel: 01252-617811 **Fax:** 01252-625806
E-mail: p.gillen@btinternet.com
Web: www.portsmouthdiocese.org.uk/churchcrookham
Rev Patrick Gillen SDB (*Parish Priest*).
Deacon: **Rev John Cumpsty**, 17 Ridgeway Parade. The Verne, Church Crookham GU52 6NY **Tel:** 01252-683606
E-mail: deacon.john@ntlworld.com
M: *Sat 1st M of Sun 6pm. Sun 9.30am. Hds 9.30am, 8pm.*

■ **COLD ASH,** Berks
See Thatcham (2).

■ **COOKHAM,** Berks
See Maidenhead (3).

■ **COSHAM**
See Portsmouth (4).

■ **COVE,** Hants
See Farnborough (3).

■ **COWES,** Isle of Wight
† St Thomas of Canterbury (1796)
22 Terminus Road, Cowes, Isle of Wight PO31 7TJ **Tel:** 01983-292739
Rev Michael Purbrick.
M: *Sun 9.30am, 6.30pm. Hds 10am, 7pm.*

■ **CROWTHORNE AND SANDHURST,** Berks A
1. **† Holy Ghost** (1906; 1909; 1962)
51 New Wokingham Road, Crowthorne RG45 6JG Served from Sandhurst (see below)
M: *Sun 11am. Hds 10am.*

2. **St Luke's Chapel**
Broadmoor Hospital
M: *Thurs 6pm.*

3. **† The Immaculate Conception** (1959; cons 8 Dec 1985)
63-67 Yorktown Road, Sandhurst, Berks GU47 9BS
Tel/Fax: 01252-876820
E-mail: crowsand@btinternet.com
Website: www.users.zetnet.co.uk/tempusfugit/holy-ghost
Rev Kevin Jones
M*: Sat 1st M of Sun 6pm, Sun 9am. Hds (vigil 7pm).*

■ **DEDWORTH,** Berks
See Windsor (3).

■ **DIDCOT,** Oxon A
† English Martyrs (1934: 1967)
15 Manor Cres, Didcot, Oxon OX11 7AJ
Tel: 01235-812338 **Fax:** 01235-819305
E-mail: didcot@portsmouthdiocese.org.uk
Website: www.emsj.org.uk
Rev David O'Sullivan.
M: *Sat 1st M of Sun 6.30pm. Sun 10am. Hds 9am, 7pm.*

■ **DOUAI ABBEY,** Berks
† Abbey Church of St Edmund King and Martyr (Douai Abbey) (1933; cons 9 July 1993)
Upper Woolhampton, Reading, Berks RG7 5TQ **E-mail:** info@douaiabbey.org.uk
Abbey: **Tel:** 0118-971 5300
Fax: 0118-971 5303;
Bursar: **Tel:** 0118-971 5319,
E-mail: bursar@douaiabbey.org.uk;
Guestmaster: **Tel:** 0118-971-5399,
E-mail: Guestmaster@douaiabbey.org.uk;
Parish Priest: **Tel:** 0118-971 5350,
E-mail: parish@douaiabbey.org.uk;
Pastoral Director: **Tel:** 0118-971 5333
E-mail: douaiabbey@aol.com
• ***Benedictines (OSB):*** **Rt Rev Dom Geoffrey Scott** (*Abbot*), **Very Rev Dom Boniface Moran MA, Very Revv Romuald Simpson** (*Subprior*), **Robert Richardson, Augustine Stickland, Leo Arkwright, Bernard Swinhoe, Louis O'Dwyer, Terence FitzPatrick, Gervase Holdaway** (*Director of Pastoral Programme*), **Nicholas Broadbridge, Oliver Holt** (*Bursar*), **Dermot Tredget, Alban Hood** (*Novice Master/Vocations Director*), **Benedict Thompson** (*Parish Priest*), **Christopher Greener** (*Guest Master*), **Simon Hill, Hugh Somerville-Knapman.**
M: *Sun 11am. Hds 7.45am.*

Pastoral Programme (Retreats, Meditation Workshops, Conferences at Douai Abbey). Enquiries: **The Director**, **Tel:** 0118-971 5333 **E-mail:** douaiabbey@aol.com

The Cottages, (Informal accommodation) Bookings: **Dom Alban Hood** **Tel:** 0118-971 5335 **E-mail:** cottagesatdouai@hotmail.com;

■ **EARLEY,** Berks
See Reading (3).

■ **EAST COWES,** Isle of Wight
† St David (1906; 1923; 1952)
9 Connaught Road, East Cowes, Isle of Wight PO32 6DP **Tel:** 01983-292726
Rev Brian Coogan (MHM).
M: *Sun 10.30am. Hds 7pm.*
- ***Sisters of Christ,*** Millfield Avenue, PO32 6AT **Tel:** 01983-293902

■ **EAST HENDRED,** Wantage, Oxon A
1. † St Mary (cons 17 Aug 1865)
East Hendred, Wantage, Oxon OX12 8LF
Website: www.catholichendredandilsley.org.uk
Served from Douai Abbey.
M: *Sun 9.30am. Hds 7.30pm.*

2. St Amand (13th Century)
Served from East Hendred (1).
M: *Friday 8.30am.*

3. St Patrick
East Ilsley.
M: *Sun 11.15am.*

4. Milton Manor House Chapel (18th C)
Milton, Oxon
M: *As announced.*
- ***Benedictine Nuns,*** Holy Trinity Monastery, St Mary's Road, East Hendred, Oxon OX12 8LF **Tel:** 01235 833269

■ **EASTLEIGH,** Hants. A
1. † The Holy Cross (1887; cons 13 Aug 1902)
53 Leigh Road, Eastleigh, Hants SO50 9DD
Tel: 02380-612430
E-mail: mdennehey@portsmouthdiocese.org.uk
Website: www.3rivers.org.uk
Rev Michael Dennehy
Deacon: **Rev Robert Birtles**. 3 Shorts Road, Fair Oak, Eastleigh, Hants SO50 7EJ **Tel:** 02380-692416 **E-mail:** deaconbob@catholics-in-eastleigh.org.uk
Pastoral Care: **Elizabeth Nash**.
M: *Sun 11am, (Pol Mass 9am). Hds 10am.*

2. St Swithun Wells (1978)
Allington Lane, Fair Oak.
M: *Sat 1st M of Sun 5pm.*

■ **EMSWORTH,** Hants
See Havant (2).

■ **FAIR OAK,** Hants
See Eastleigh (1).

■ **FAREHAM & PORTCHESTER,** Hants A 
1. † The Sacred Heart (1873; cons 4 Oct 1978)
Hartlands Road, Fareham, Hants.
Tel: 01329-318869 **Fax:** 01329-318868
E-mail: sacred-heart@tregalic.co.uk
Rev Joseph McNerney, 43 Portland Street, PO16 0NF *Deacons:* **Revv Langford Vincent**. 29 Park Lane, Fareham PO16 7LE **Tel:** 01329-280058; **Pat Madden**, 43 Portland Street, Fareham, Hants PO16 0NF **E-mail:** langford.vincent@ntlworld.com
M: *Sun 9am. Hds 9.30am, 7pm.*

2. St Philip Howard (1980)
Bishopsfield Road.
M: *Sun 11am. Hds (vigil 7.30pm).*

3. † Our Lady of Walsingham
White Hart Lane, Portchester
M: *Sat 9pm.*

4. St Thomas More (1970)
Park Place Pastoral Centre, Winchester Road, Wickham PO17 5HA
Tel: 01329-833043 **Fax:** 01329-832226
M: *Sun 9am. (No Sun Mass in Aug).*
- ***Franciscan Missionary Sisters of St Mary of the Angels***, Winchester Road, PO17 5HA *Chaplain:* **Rev Andrew McMahon OFM. Tel:** 01329-833805 **E-mail:** parkplace@aol.com

■ **FARINGDON,** Oxon
† Blessed Hugh Faringdon
9 Marlborough Street, Faringdon, SN7 7JE
Rev Leslie Adams, 1 Coxwell Road, Faringdon, Oxon SN7 7EB
Tel: 01367 241474
Deacon: **Rev Kevin McKevitt,** 3 Hawthorne Cresent, Grove, Wantage, Oxon OX12 7JB
Tel: 01235 764168
Email: kjmck@freeuk.com
M: *Sun 9.30am, Hds 12 noon.*

■ **FARNBOROUGH,** Hants A 
1. † Our Lady Help of Christians (1898; 1902)
Queen's Road, Farnborough, Hants.
Tel/Fax: 01252-545364
E-mail: olhc@btinternet.com
- ***Salesians (SDB):*** **Rev Daniel Donohoe**. 1a Sherborne Road, Farnborough GU14 6JS *Deacon:* **Rev P. Page-Tickell,** 116 Reading Road, Farnborough, Hants, GU14 6NY **Tel:** 01252 413043 **E-mail:** deaconpaul@pagetickell.me.uk **M:** *Sat 1st M of Sun 6pm. Sun 8.30am, 10.30am. Hds 9am, 8pm.*
- ***Salesians (SDB)*** St John Bosco House, 121a Reading Road, Farnborough, Hants GU14 6NZ **Tel:** 01252-554300 **Fax:** 01252-375395

E-mail: sdb_farnborough@msn.com. **Revv Brian McGraw** *(Rector)*, **Peter Burns, Willian Carroll, John Gilheney, Laurence Martin, Brendan McGuinness, Peter Quinn, Francis Sutherland.**

2 † St Michael's Abbey
(1888; cons 12 Oct 1908)
Farnborough Road, Farnborough, Hants GU14 7NQ
Tel: 01252-546105 **Fax:** 01252-372822
E-mail: info@farnboroughabbey.org
Website: www.farnboroughabbey.org
• ***Benedictines (OSB):*** **Rt. Rev Abbot Cuthbert Brogan, Revv Doms Magnus Wilson, Wulstan Hibberd, Thomas Harper**.
M: *Sun 10am. Hds 7.15am (Low Mass), 10am (Conventual Mass).*

3. † Our Lady & St Dominic
(1949; 1975) (formerly the parishes of Our Lady of Lourdes and St Dominic Savio)
The Presbytery, 71 Highview Road, Cove, Farnborough GU14 7PT
Tel: 01252-546897 **Fax:** 01252-514578
E-mail: office@olsd.org.uk
Website: www.olsd.org.uk
Rev Anthony Sultana SDB. *Deacons:* **Rev Paul Evans**. Glebe House, 9 The Birches, Cove, Farnborough, Hants GU14 9RP
E-mail: paul-evans@deacons-online.org.uk
Rev Paul Pole-Baker. 2 Belville Close, Southwood, Farnborough GU14 0PY
Tel: 01252-544152
E-mail: paul.pole-baker@ntlworld.com
M: *Sat 1st M of Sun 6pm. Sun 8.30am, 10am. Hds (vigil 8pm), 9.15am.*
• ***Religious of Christian Education***, Lafosse House, 129 Ship Lane GU14 8BH **Tel:** 01252-511229
Orchard Rise, 127 Ship Lane, GU14 8BH **Tel:** 01252-543460 **Fax:** 01252-375309

■ **FLEET,** Aldershot, Hants
† Our Lady (1908; 1934; cons 1977)
King's Road, Fleet, Aldershot, Hants.
Tel: 01252-616963 **Fax:** 01252-615667
E-mail: ourladyfleet@tiscali.co.uk
Website: ourladyfleet.org.uk
Rev Michael Stanier, The Presbytery, 2 Connaught Road, GU51 3RA *Deacon:* **Rev Peter Lattey**, 38a Elms Road, Fleet, Hants GU51 3EQ **Tel:** 01252-621295 **Fax:** 01252-815882 **E-mail:** peter-lattey@which.net
M: *Sat 1st M of Sun 6.30pm. Sun 10.30am. Hds 9.30am, 8pm.*

2. St Thomas More (1959)
Mildmay Terrace, Hartley Wintney.
Served from Yateley
M: *Sun 9.15am.*

■ **FORDINGBRIDGE,** Hants 
† St Mary and St Philip (1872)
15 Salisbury Road, Fordingbridge SP6 1EG
Tel: 01425-653131
Fr Des Connolly, St Joseph's House of Prayer, Lyndhurst Road, Ashurst, Hants, SO40 7DU
M: *Sat 1st M of Sun 6pm. Sun 9am. Hds As announced.*

■ **GOSPORT,** Hants
1. † St Mary (1759)
High Street, Gosport. **Tel:** 02392-580119 **Fax:** 02392-526954 **E-Mail:** gosport@portsmouthdiocese.org.uk **Rev David Adams**. Maryhouse, 32 High Street, Gosport, Hants PO12 1DF
M: *Sun 11am. Hds 12noon.*

2. St Joseph
Ann's Hill Road, Gosport.
M: *Sun 9am. Hds 9.15am. (term-time).*

3. † St Columba
Nobes Avenue, Bridgemary.
M: *Sat 1st M of Sun 6pm. Hds 7.30pm.*

■ **GRAYSHOTT,** Surrey
† St Joseph (cons 26 July 1911)
St Joseph's, Headley Road, Grayshott, Hindhead, Surrey GU26 6DP
Tel: 01420-472415 **Fax:** 01420-475672
Served from Bordon.
In residence: **Rev Patrick O'Donnell** *(retired)*. St Joseph's, Headley Road, Grayshott, Hindhead, Surrey GU26 6DP, **Tel/Fax:** 01428-608223 *Deacon:* **Rev Steve Melhuish**, 33 Hilland Rise, Headly, Hants GU35 8LZ
Tel: 01428-713555 **Fax:** 01428-712387
E-mail: steve.melhuish@btinternet.com
M: *2nd & 4th Sat 5.30pm; Sun 9.30am. Hds 10am..*

■ **GUERNSEY,** Channel Islands
1. Our Lady and the Saints of Guernsey
Ampthill House, Cordier Hill, St Peter Port, Guernsey GY1 1JH
Tel: 01481-720196 **Fax:** 01481-711247
E-mail: sjoss.guernsey@virgin.net
Website: www.catholicgsy.org.uk
Revv Michael Hore, Paul James Smith, Stanislaw Gibinski.

2. † St Joseph and St Mary
(1802, 1851, cons 27 Aug 1885)
La Couperderie, St Peter Port
M: *Sun 8am, 10.30am, 6.30pm. Hds 9.30am, 7pm.*

3. † Notre Dame du Rosaire
(1792; 1829; 1962; cons 4 July 1968)
Burnt Lane, St Peter Port
M: *Sat 1st M of Sun 5.30pm. Hds (vigil 5.30pm), 11am, 5.30pm.*

4. † Our Lady Star of the Sea (1879)
Rue des Monts, St Sampson, Guernsey GY2 4HU
M: *2nd & 4th Sat 1st M of Sun 6pm. Sun 9.30am. Hds (vigil 7pm).*
- ***Sisters of Mercy,*** Cordier Hill, St Peter Port. **Tel:** 01481-720729
- ***Hospitaller Sisters of the Sacred Heart***, Le Platon Home, Clifton, St Peter Port. **Tel:** 01481-723640

5. Sark Island
In St Peter's CoE Church
M: *As announced.*

■ **HARTLEY WINTNEY,** Hants
See Fleet

■ **HAVANT,** Hants
1. † St Joseph
(1733; 1875; cons 18 April 1907)
134 West Street, Havant, Hants PO9 1LP
Tel: 023-92484 520
E-mail: tom.grufferty@ntlworld.com
Website: www.rc-havant.org.uk
Rev Tom Grufferty.
M: *Sat 1st M of Sun 6.30pm. Sun 11am. Hds 9.30am.*

2. SS Thomas of Canterbury and Thomas More (1959)
24 New Brighton Road, Emsworth.
M: *Sun 9am, 6pm. Hds 7.30pm.*

■ **HAYLING ISLAND,** Hants
† St Patrick.
(1914; 1925; cons 28 Sept 1984).
The Parish House, Manor Road PO11 0QU
Tel: 02392-463854
Email: stpathi@portsmouthdiocese.co.uk
Rev Andrew Chandler.
M: *Sat 1st M of Sun 6pm. Sun 10.30am. Hds 9am, 7.30pm.*

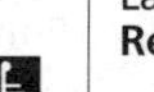

■ **HEDGE END,** Southampton
1. † Our Lady of the Assumption
(1964; 1975; Cons 23.3.1984)
Freegrounds Road, Hedge End, Southampton SO30 0HG
Tel: 01489-782555
Served from Christ the King, Southampton.
M: *Sun 10.45am. Hds 7.30pm.*

2. † St Brigid (1968)
Woodlea Gardens, West End, Hedge End, Southampton.
M: *Sun 6.30am. Hds 9.30am.*

■ **HIGHCLIFFE,** Christchurch, Dorset
† Holy Redeemer (1969)
15 Kilmington Way, Highcliffe, Christchurch, Dorset BH23 5BL **Tel/Fax:** 01425-274838
Rev David Quarmby.
E-mail: djquarmby@hotmail.com
M: *Sun 8am, 10am. Hds 10am, 7.30pm.*

■ **HOLBURY,** Hants
† St Bernard
See Waterside.

■ **HOOK,** Hants
1. † Sacred Heart (1955)
London Road, Hook, Hants RG27 9LA
Tel: 01256-762351
E-mail: office@sacredhearthook.fsnet.co.uk
Website: www.sacredhearthook.fsnet.co.uk
Rev Daniel Burns SDS *(Priest-in-Charge)*, Priest's House, London Road, Hook, Hants.
M: *Sat 1st M of Sun 6pm. Sun 10am. Hds 10am, 8pm.*
- ***Dominican Sisters of Malta,*** Maryfield Convent, London Road RG27 9LA **Tel:** 01256-762394 **E-mail:** sisters@maryfieldhook.fsnet.co.uk **Website:** www.maryfieldhook.fsnet.co.uk In residence: **Canon Anthony Zollo. Tel:** 01256-769011

■ **HORNDEAN,** Waterlooville
† St Edmund
Napier Road, Horndean.
Rev Canon Terence Healy, 5 Orchard Close, Horndean, Hants PO8 9LL
Tel: 023-9259 3010
M: *Sun 8.30am, 10.30am. Hds 9.30am, 7.30pm.*

■ **HUNGERFORD,** Berks
See Lambourn (2).

■ **HYTHE,** Southampton
See Waterside.

■ **JERSEY,** Channel Islands
West of Jersey Catholic Parish:
1. † Sacred Heart (1900; 1947)
Tel/Fax: 01534-863149
La Neuve Route, St Aubin, Jersey JE3 8BS
Rev Kevin Hoiles.
M: *Sat 1st M of Sun 6.30pm. Hds As announced.*

2. St Bernadette (1972)
Les Quennevais, Airport Road, St Brelade.
Tel: 01534-741974
M: *Sun 11.15am. Hds, As announced.*

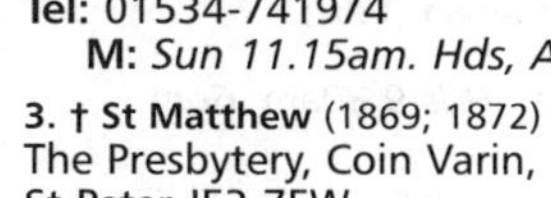

3. † St Matthew (1869; 1872)
The Presbytery, Coin Varin, St Peter JE3 7EW
Tel/Fax: 01534-863149
M: *Sun 9.30am. Hds, As announced.*

Catholic Parish in St Helier:
(United in 1999)
Parish Office: **Rev Mgr Nicholas France.**
17 Val Plaisant, St Helier, Jersey C.I. JE2 4TA
Tel: 01534-720235 **Fax:** 01534-607991
E-mail: centreparish@jerseymail.co.uk
Deacons: **Revv Iain MacFirbhisigh**, 47 Stopford Road, St Helier, Jersey JE 2 4LB

Tel: 01534-725963
E-mail: blessings@jerseymail.co.uk
Louis Omer, Leyton, Green Street, St Helier, Jersey JE2 4UH
Tel: 01534-738592

1. † St Thomas
(1804; cons 5 Sept 1893)
17 Val Plaisant, St Helier, JE2 4TA
Tel: 01534-720235 **Fax:** 01534-607991
M: *Sat 1st M of Sun 6pm. Sun 9.30am, 6pm, 3.30pm (Portuguese), 7.30pm (Polish). Hds 12.30pm, 6pm.*

2. † St Mary and St Peter
(1811; 1826; 1867; cons 28 Sept 1985)
Wellington Road, St Helier.
M: *11.15am, 7.30am (Polish); Hds As announced*
- ***Little Sisters of the Poor***, **Jeanne Jugan** Residence: New St John's Road, St Helier, Jersey JE2 3LE **Tel:** 01534-875960
- ***Jersey Catholic Pastoral Services***. **Tel:** 01534-732583 **Fax:** 01534-618833 **E-mail:** pastoralservices@localdial.com
- ***St Thomas' Welcome Centre*** (for Portuguese, Polish and others), 19 Val Plaisant, St Helier, Jersey JE2 4TA
- ***Sisters of the Immaculate Conception***, Sunnydown, 65 Jardin du Soleil, Mont Millais, St Helier JE2 4RD **Tel:** 01534-780518
- ***Sisters of the Holy Family,*** Elmsfield, 34 Clubley Estate, St Helier JE2 3LF **Tel:** 01534-875151

■ **Combined Parish of East Jersey**
Parish Office: St Patrick's Presbytery, La Grande Route de St Clement, Samares, St Clement JE2 6QN
Tel/Fax: 01534-736912
E-mail: east.parish@jerseymail.co.uk
Rev Marein Drabek MA
Deacon: **Rev Tony Ward**, Le Perchoir, Le Bourg, St Clement, Jersey JE2 6SQ
Tel: 01534-853804
E-mail: tonyandmaureen@jerseymail.co.uk

1. † Our Lady of the Annunciation and the Martyrs of Japan (1857)
St Martin
M: *Sun 9.15am. Hds 9.30am, 6pm (check venue).*

2. † The Assumption (1903)
Gorey
M: *Sun 6pm. Hds 9.30am (check venue), 6pm.*

3. St Patrick (1949)
St Clement
M: *Sat 1st M of Sun 6pm. Sun 11am. Hds 9.30am, 6pm (check venue)*
- ***Sisters of the Immaculate Conception:*** Straven Convent, Plat Douet Road, St Clement JE2 6PN **Tel:** 01534-734997

4. Portugese Chaplaincy
M: *Sun 3.30pm at St Thomas*

4. Hospital Chaplain
Rev Brian Sandeman, 26 St Clement Gardens (La Grande Route de St Clement), St Clement JE2 6QT **Tel:** 01534-722909

■ **KENNINGTON,** Oxon
See North Hinksey (4).

■ **KILN GREEN,** Reading
See Twyford (3).

■ **KINGSCLERE,** Hants
See Tadley (2).

■ **KINTBURY,** Berks
See Lambourn (3).

■ **LAMBOURN,** Berks [A]
1. † Sacred Heart
(1955; 1976; cons 15 June 1980)
Baydon Road, Lambourn, Berks RG17 8NU
Served from Wantage.
Rev Canon Peter Turbitt
M: *Sun 11.30am. Hds (vigil 8pm).*

[A]
2. † Our Lady of Lourdes (1939)
Priory Road, Hungerford, Berks.
M: *Sat 1st M of Sun 6.30pm. Sun 9.30am. Hds 10am, 7pm.*
- ***De La Salle Brothers Retreat and Pastoral Centre for Young People***. **Tel:** 01488-658267 **Fax:** 01488-657292
- ***St Cassian,*** Wallingtons Road, Kintbury, Hungerford RG17 9SR

■ **LEE-ON-THE-SOLENT AND STUBBINGTON,** Hants [A] 
1. † St John the Evangelist (1918; 1980)
South Place, Lee-on-the-Solent, Hants.
Tel/Fax: 01329-663435.
E-mail: fatherjohn@onetel.com
Rev John Humpheys. The Presbytery, Bells Lane, Stubbington PO14 12PL
M: *Sun 8am. Hds 9.30am.*

2. † Immaculate Conception (1976; 1985)
Bells Lane, Stubbington, Fareham, Hants PO14 2PL **Tel/Fax:** 01329-663435
E-mail: fatherjohn@onetel.net.uk
M: Sat 1st M of Sun 6pm. *Sun 10am, Hds (vigil 7pm).*

■ **LEIGH PARK,** Havant, Hants [A] 
† St Michael and All Angels (1955; 1970)
Dunsbury Way, Leigh Park, Havant, Hants PO9 5BD **Tel/Fax:** 023-9248 4323
E-mail:frjoe@btopenworld.com
Rev Jozef Gruszkiewicz. 83 Bramdeau Drive, Havant, Hants PO9 4RR
M: *Sat 1st M of Sun 6pm. Sun 9am, 11am. Hds 12noon, 7.30pm.*
- ***Sisters of the Immaculate Conception,*** Merriemead, Riders Lane, Stockheath,

Havant, Hants PO9 3BJ
Tel: 023-9247 7127

■ **LIPHOOK,** Hants

† **The Immaculate Conception** (1911)
108 Headley Road, Liphook, Hants GU30 7PT **Tel:** 01428-722151
Mgr Cyril Murtagh, *Provost Emeritus.*
E-mail: cmurtagh@portsmouthdiocese.org.uk
Deacon: **Rev Andrew Carter,** 41 Birchcroft Road, Liphook, Hants GU30 7PQ
Tel: 01428-724171
E-mail: ancyandnic@ancyandnics.freeserve.co.uk
M: *Sun 10.15am, 6pm. Hds (vigil 8pm) 10am.*

■ **LISS,** Hants
See Petersfield (2).

■ **LYMINGTON,** Hants

1. † **Our Lady of Mercy and St Joseph** (1800; 1911; cons 18 May 1979)
132 High Street, Lymington, Hants SO41 9AQ **Tel:** 01590-676696
E-mail: lymbrocklyn@aol.com
Rev Jamie McGrath.
M: *Sat 1st M of Sun 6.30pm. Sun 8.30am, 10.30am. Hds 11am, 7.30pm.*

2. † **St Anne** (1939, cons 26 July 1944)
Rhinefield Road, Brockenhurst, Hants SO42 7SR **Tel/Fax:** 01590-622107
M: *Sun 9.30am. Hds 9.30am.*

• ***Dominican Sisters of St Joseph:*** St Dominic's Priory, Shirley Holms Road, Lymington SO41 8HN
Tel: 01590-681874 **Fax:** 01590-681875

■ **LYNDHURST,** New Forest, Hants

† **Our Lady of the Assumption and St Edward the Confessor** (1895; cons 28 July 1896)
14 Empress Road, Lyndhurst, New Forest, Hants SO43 7AE **Tel:** 023-8028 2612
Served from Waterside.
Deacons: **Rev Stephen Short,** Furzey Lawn, Romsey Road, Lyndhurst SO43 7FL
Tel: 023-8028 0211
M: *Sun 9am. Hds Vigil 7.30pm.*

■ **MAIDENHEAD,** Berks

1. † **St Joseph** (1867; 1884; cons 26 May 1914)
36 Cookham Road, Maidenhead, SL6 7EG
Tel: 01628-783988 **Fax:** 01628-776863
E-mail: presbytery@stjosephs-mh-freeserve.co.uk
Rev Mgr Thomas McGrath VG, Rev Paul Mooney MHM.
M: *Sat 1st M of Sun 6.30pm. Sun 8am, 10.45am. Hds 10am, 7.30pm.*

• ***Mill Hill Missionaries:*** 6 Colby Gardens, Cookham Road, Maidenhead, SL6 7GZ
Revv Anthony Chantry (General Superior), **Brendan Mulhall** (Vicar General), **Michael Corcoran** & **Br Jos Boerkamp** (General Council Members), **Wim van de Salm** (Secretary General), **Ivan Fang** (Webmaster), **Br John Smith** (Rector), **Paul Mooney, Dan O'Connell, Brian Oswald** (APF).

2. † **St Elizabeth** (1963)
Lower Road, Cookham Rise.
Served from Maidenhead (1).
M: *Sun 9.15am.*

3. † **St Edmund Campion**
Maidenhead, Berks.
E-mail: st-edmundcampion@ukonline.co.uk
Web: www.st.edmundcampion-mh.co.uk
M: *Sat 1st M of Sun 6.15pm. Sun 9.30am, 11.15am. Hds 9.30am, 7.30pm.*

■ **MEDSTEAD**
See Alton (2).

■ **MILFORD-ON-SEA,** Hants 

† **St Francis of Assisi** (1967)
Park Lane, Milford-on-Sea, Hants.
Rev Gerrit Vervenne, 15 Mount Avenue, New Milton, Hants BH25 6NT
Tel: 01425-614968
M: *Sun 9.15pm. Hds 9am.*

■ **MILTON,** Oxon
See East Hendred (4).

■ **NETLEY ABBEY,** Hants

† **The Annunciation** (1956)
Station Road, Netley Abbey
Served from St Patrick's, Southampton.
M: *Sun 9am. Hds 7.30pm.*

• ***Sisters of the Cenacle,*** 48 Victoria Road, Netley Abbey SO31 5DQ
Tel/Fax: 023-8045 3718
E-mail: eastside@portsmouthdiocese.org.uk

■ **NEW MILTON,** Hants. 

† **Our Lady of Lourdes.**
(1927; 1951; cons 25 May 1955).
15 Mount Avenue, New Milton, Hants BH25 6NT. **Tel:** 01425-614968
E-mail: revmwelch@tiscali.co.uk
Rev Gerrit Vervenne. *Deacon:* **Rev Michael Welch,** 5 Grove Gardens, Barton-on-Sea, New Milton, Hants BH25 7HT
Tel: 01425-614206
M: *Sat 1st M of Sun 6pm. Sun 8am, 10.30am. Hds (vigil 7pm), 10am.*

■ **NEWBURY,** Berks

1. † **St Joseph**
(1855; 1928; cons 13 Sep 1949)
105 London Road, Newbury, Berks RG14 1JP
Tel: 01635-40167 **Fax:** 01635-30855
E-mail: parishpriest@stjosephsnewbury.org.uk
Rev Padraig Faughnan.

M: *Sun 8.30am, 11am. Hds 9.30am, 7.30pm.*

- ***Society of Franciscan Pilgrims:*** "Greccio", 8 Majendie Close, Pound Lane, Speen, Newbury RG14 1QX **Tel:** 01635-552240

2. † St Francis de Sales (1968; 1971)
Warren Lodge, Warren Road, Wash Common, RG14 6NH
Tel: 01635-40332 **Fax:** 01635-582588
E-mail: st-francis-de-sales@hotmail.co.uk
Website: stfrancisdesales.org.uk
Rev Eamon Walsh
M: *Sat 1st M of Sun 5.30pm. Sun 10am. Hds (vigil 7.30pm), 9.30am.*

■ NEWPORT, Isle of Wight

† St Thomas of Canterbury (1791)
Newport, Isle of Wight.
Tel: 01983-752317 **Fax:** 01983-522027
Website: www.stthomaschurchiow.co.uk
Rev Gerard Flynn. 96 Pyle Street, PO30 1UH
Deacons: **Revv Robert Vincent Jones**, 50 Bellcroft Drive, PO30 2JH
Tel: 01983-524694 **David Croucher**, Chalkhills, Whitwell Road, Ventnor, Isle of Wight PO38 1LJ **Tel:** 01983-853029
M: *Sat 1st M of Sun 6.30pm. Sun 11am. Hds As announced.*

- ***Verbum Dei Community***, Rosary Cottage, Nunnery Lane, Carisbrooke PO30 1YR **Tel:** 01983-529554
- ***Sisters of Mercy,*** Convent: 69 Quarry View, Camp Hill, Newport PO30 5PJ **Tel/Fax:** 01983-522710

■ NORTH BADDESLEY, Hants

See Romsey (2).

■ NORTH HINKSEY, Oxon

1. † Our Lady of the Rosary (1954)
Yarnells Hill, North Hinksey, Oxford.
Tel/Fax: 01865-247986
Rev Paul King. 60 Abingdon Road, Oxford OX1 4PE **Tel/Fax:** 01865-437066
E-mail: nhinkseyolor@portsmouth-dio.org.uk
Website: www.communigake.co.uk/oxford/hinkseycatholicparish
Deacon: **Rev Richard Budgen**. 16 Pottle Close, Cumnor, Oxford OX2 9SN
Tel: 01865-864191
E-mail: richardbudgen50@hotmail.com
M: *Sat 1st M of Sun 6.30pm. Sun 9.15am. Hds as announced.*

2. † Holy Rood (1961)
Folly Bridge, Oxford OX1 4LD
Tel: 01865-249703
M: *Sat 7.30pm (Portuguese), Sun 3pm (Portuguese) . Hds As announced.*

- ***Grandpont House,*** Abingdon Road, Oxford, OX1 4LD (Pastoral care entrusted to the Opus Dei Prelature). **Tel:** 01865-244150 *Chaplain:* **Rev James Pereiro**.

3. † St Thomas More (1945)
Boars Hill.

- ***Carmelite Priory (ODC),*** Boars Hill, OX1 5HB **Tel:** 01865-735133 **Fax:** 01865-326478
- ***Discalced Carmelites (ODC),*** **Revv Revv Vincent O'Hara** *(Prior)*, **Michael Maclaifearbigh, Edmond Smythe, Livinus Donohoe, Raphael O'Connell**.

4. The Good Shepherd (1965)
Bagley Wood Road, Kennington.
M: *Hds 7.30pm.*

5. Chapel of St Thomas
Foxcombe Road, Boars Hill.
M: *No Sun Mass.*

■ OAKLEY, Hants

See Basingstoke (7).

■ OVERTON, Hants

See Basingstoke (8).

■ PANGBOURNE, Berks

See Woolhampton (3).

■ PARK GATE, Southampton

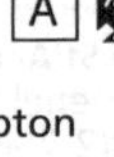

† St Margaret Mary (1965)
Middle Road, Park Gate, Southampton SO31 7GH
Tel: 01489-572797 **Fax:** 01489-572797
E-mail: stmgtmary@talktalk.net
Website: www.stmm.org.uk
Rev John Cooke. *Deacon:* **Rev Anthony Strike**, 46 Trevose Way, Fareham, Hants PO14 4NQ **Tel:** 01489-583602
M: *Sun 8am, 10.15am, 6.30pm. Hds (During term time) 10am, 2.15pm (in the School), 7.30pm. (During school holidays), 10am, 7.30pm.*

■ PARK PLACE

See Fareham (3).

■ PAULSGROVE, Hants

See Portsmouth (7).

■ PETERSFIELD, Hants

1. † St Laurence (1890; cons 1933)
12 Station Road, Petersfield, Hants GU32 2ED
Tel: 01730-262290 **Fax:** 01730-233499
E-mail: office@petersfieldparish.org.uk
Website: www.petersfieldparish.org.uk
Rev Canon Provost Gerard Hetherington.
M: *Sun 10.45am, 6pm. Hds (vigil 7pm), 10am.*

2. † St Agnes
Plantation Lane, Hill Brow, Liss.
M: *Sun 9am. Hds 7.30am.*

■ PORTCHESTER

See Farnham and Portchester.

■ PORTSMOUTH

1. See the start of parish list.

2. † Corpus Christi with St Joseph
(1893; cons 10 June 1982)
Rev Simon Thomson
21 Gladys Avenue, North End, Portsmouth PO2 9AZ **Tel/Fax:** 02392-660927
E-mail: ccsj@portsmouthdiocese.org.uk
M: *Sun 11am. Hds 9.30am.*

3. † Our Lady of Lourdes with St Swithun (1937; 1956)
105 Waverley Road, Southsea, Portsmouth PO5 2PL **Tel:** 023-9282 8305
Fax: 023-9264 4848 **Rev Peter Hollins**
M: *Sat 1st M of Sun 6pm. Hds 7.30pm.*

4. † St Swithun
(1886; 1901; cons 15 July 1908)
Waverley Road, Southsea, Portsmouth
Tel: 023-9282 8305 **Fax:** 023-9264 8498
E-mail: olow.stsw@atlworld.com
M: *Sun 8.30am, 10.15am (Pol M 7pm most 4th Sun of Month, please check). Hds 11.30am.*

- ***De La Salle Brothers,*** St John's College for Boys, Grove Road South, Southsea PO5 3QW **Tel:** 02392-815118
- ***Franciscan Missionaries of the Divine Motherhood,*** Havelock Road, Southsea PO5 1RU **Tel:** 023-9287 6246

5. † St Colman with St Paul
(1928; cons 9 June 1953)
Presbytery, St Colman's Avenue, Cosham Portsmouth PO6 2JJ
Tel: 02392-376151 **Fax:** 023-9238 4381
E-mail: stcolmanstpaul@aol.com
Rev Sean Tobin STB.
M: *Sat 1st M of Sun 6pm. Sun 9.15am. Hds 7.30pm.*

6. † St Paul (1970)
Allaway Avenue, Paulsgrove.
Served from Portsmouth (4).
M: *Sun 11am.*

7. † St Joseph
(1908; 1914; cons 6 May 1924)
Tangier Road, Copnor Bridge, Portsmouth.
Tel: 02392-822166 **Fax:** 02392-829208
E-mail: stjosephs@copnor1908.fsnet.co.uk
M: *Sat 1st M of Sun 6pm. Sun 9.30am. Hds 7pm.*

- ***Franciscan Missionaries of the Divine Motherhood,*** 1 Milton Road, Copnor Bridge, Portsmouth PO3 6AN **Tel:** 023-9287 6246

8. Portsmouth Hospital Chaplaincy
Chaplain: **Rev Andrew Chandler.**
QA **Tel:** 02392-286408
SM **Tel:** 02392-866080

Queen Alexandra Hospital
M: *Tues 5pm.*

9. Portsmouth University Chaplaincy
Catholic Chaplaincy – Student Services: Nuffield Centre, University of Portsmouth, St Michael's Road PO1 2ED
Tel: 02392-843167/832905
Fax: 02392-843430
Ms Jordan James. *Catholic Chaplaincy:* 24 Lion House, Lion Terrace, Portsmouth PO1 3AB **Tel:** 023-9283 2905

■ QUARR, Ryde, Isle of Wight

St Mary's Abbey
Quarr, Ryde, Isle of Wight. PO33 4ES
Tel: 01983-882420 **Fax:** 01983-884402
E-mail: quarr@portsmouthdiocese.org.uk
Benedictines (*Congregation of Solesmes*)
Rt Rev Dom Finbar Kealy *(Administrator);* **V Rev Nicholas Spencer** *(Prior & Novice Master),* **Rev Doms Francis Verry** (*SubPrior*), **Luke Bell, Gregory Corcoran, Duncan Smith, Tibor Szende, David Benedict McCulloch** (*Procurator*), **Alexander Tingay, David Hayes, Petroc Cobb, Anthony Okoronkwo, Brian Gerard Kelly, Michael Bernard Stevens, Paul Davern, Charles Gilman, Victor Mileham.**
M: *Sun 10am. Hds 10am. Wkds 9am*

■ READING, Berks

St James with St William of York
Forbury Road, Reading, Berks RG1 3HW
Tel: 0118-957 4171 **Fax:** 0118-956 1171
E-mail: parish@ jameswilliam-reading.org.uk
Rev Dominic Golding JV.

1. † St James (1780; 1837-40)
M: *Sat 1st M of Sun 6pm. Sun 11am, (2nd and 4th Sun Mass in Ukrainian Rite at 1pm). Hds 12.15pm.*

2. † St William of York (1904; 1906)
Upper Redlands Road, Reading RG1 5JT
M: *Sun 9am, 12noon (Latin: Extraordinary Rite), (quarterly Mass in Hungarian 3pm).*

- ***Sisters of St Marie Madeleine Postel,*** St Joseph's Convent, 64 Upper Redlands Road, RG1 5JT **Tel:** 0118-926 1711
- ***Verbum Dei Community,*** 54 Donnington Gardens, Reading RG1 5LX **Tel:** 0118-926 8825

3. † Sacred Heart (Polish Church)
Watlington Street, Reading, Berks.
Rev Jerzy Januszkiewicz. 83 London Road, Reading RG1 5BY **Tel:** 0118-957 3647
M: *Sun 9am, 10.30am. Hds 10.30am, 7pm.*

4. † Christ the King (1928; 1946; 1959)
Rev Bruce Barnes, 408 Northumberland Avenue, Whitley, Reading RG2 8NR
Tel: 0118-931 4469
E-mail: ctk.parish@btopenworld.com
Website: http://ctkpcuk.org
M: *Sat 1st M of Sun 6.30pm. Sun 10am. Hds 10am, 7.30pm.*

5. † Our Lady of Peace and Blessed Dominic Barberi (1976)
338 Wokingham Road, Earley, Reading, Berks, RG6 7DA
Tel: 0118-966 3711 **Fax:** 0118-926 1160
E-mail: parish@olop.org.uk
Deacon: **Rev Anthony Cairns**, 8 St Clement Close, Lower Earley, Reading RG6 4BT
Mbl: 07768-244033
E-mail: cainrs1@totalserve.co.uk
Pastoral Assistant: **Mrs Ann Woolley**.
Tel: 0118-969 8836 (home)
M: *Sat 1st M of Sun 6.30pm. Sun 9.30am, 11.30am, 5pm. Hds 7am, 9.45am, 7.30pm.*

6. † The English Martyrs (1926; 1935)
Tilehurst Road, Reading, Berks
Tel: 0118-957 2149 **Fax:** 0118-957 5241
E-mails: admin@englishmartyrs.org.uk
Mgr John Nelson VG, Rev Richard Maniak. 64 Liebenrood Road, Reading, Berks RG30 2EB
M: *Sat 1st M of Sun 6.30pm. Sun 9am, 11am, 5pm. Hds 9.30am, 7.30pm.*

7. † St Joseph
Park Lane, Tilehurst, Reading, Berks.
Tel/Fax: 0118-942 8632.
E-mail: office@st-josephs-tilehurst.org.uk
Fr Joseph Awoh St Joseph's Presbytery, Berkshire Drive, Reading, Berks RG31 5JJ
M: *Sun 8.30am, 10.30am. Hds 9am, 7.30pm.*

8. Reading University Chaplaincy
Chaplain: **Sabine Schwartz**
29 Upper Redlands Road, Reading RG1 5JP
Tel: 0118-926 8869 **Fax:** 0118-926 8869
E-mail: t.l.burke@reading.ac.uk
M: *Sun 6pm at St William of York. Hds 7.30pm.*

9. Reading Hospitals Chaplaincy
Chaplain: **Rev Richard Maniak**,
Tel: 0118 322 7105 (office)

■ **RINGWOOD,** Hants
† Sacred Heart and St Thérèse of Lisieux (1930; 1937)
The Close, Ringwood, Hants BH24 1LA
Tel: 01425-473728
E-mail: s.atha@uwclub.net
Rev Desmond Connolly SMM.
M: *10.30am. Hds 10am.*

■ **ROMSEY,** Hants
1. † St Joseph (1891; 1913)
The parish office, 26 Abbey Water, Romsey SP51 8EJ **Tel:** 01794-513646
Email: sasj@portsmouthdiocese.org.uk
Rev George Lyons.
M: *Sat 1st M of Sun 6pm. Sun 11am. Hds 7pm.*

- ***Daughters of Wisdom, Provincialate:*** Abbeyside, 10 The Abbey, SO51 8YB. **Tel:** 01794-516129. Convent: Abbey House, SO51 8YB. **Tel:** 01794-522320.

2. St Andrew (1975)
Fleming Avenue, North Baddesley, Romsey, Hants **Tel:** 02380-735261
M: *Sun 9.15am. Hds 10am.*

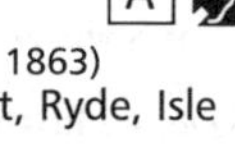

■ **RYDE,** Isle of Wight
1. † St Mary (1846; cons 21 May 1863)
St Mary's Passage, High Street, Ryde, Isle of Wight PO33 2RG
Tel: 01983-562171
E-mail: Stmarysryde@aol.com
Website: stmarysryde.co.uk
Rev Anthony Glaysher.
M: *Sat 1st M of Sun 6pm. Sun 8am, 11am. Hds 12noon, 7pm.*

2. † St Michael (1956)
Walls Road, Bembridge, Ryde, Isle of Wight.
M: *Sun 9.30am. Hds 9.30am.*

3. Holy Cross (1957)
Seafield Road, Seaview, Ryde, Isle of Wight
M: *As Announced.*

- ***Presentation Sisters,*** Presentation Convent, High Street, PO33 2RE **Tel:** 01983-562191

4. St Cecilia's Abbey (1882; 1907)
Appley Rise, Ryde, Isle of Wight PO33 1LH
Served from Quarr Abbey.

- ***Benedictine Nuns.*** PO33 1LH (Solesmes Congregation) **Tel:** 01983-562602

■ **<$ISANDHURST,** Berks
See Crowthorne and Sandhurst

■ **SANDOWN,** Isle of Wight
See South Wight.

■ **SARK,** Channel Islands
See Guernsey (4).

■ **SEAVIEW,** Isle of Wight
See Ryde (3).

■ **SHANKLIN,** Isle of Wight
See South Wight.

■ **SOLENT BISHOPRIC OF THE FORCES**
Naval Chaplaincies:
St Mary (HMS Nelson)

RC Chaplain, HMS Nelson, Edinburgh Road, Portsmouth PO1 3HH
Tel: 02392-724233 **Fax:** 023-9272 4901

A

■ **SOUTH WIGHT - SANDOWN & SHANKLIN,** Isle of Wight

1. † Sacred Heart
(1888; 1908; 1949; 1957; cons 10.6.1988)
7 Atherley Road, Shanklin, Isle of Wight PO37 7AT **Tel/Fax:** 01983-862446
E-mail: swightcatholicp@tiscali.co.uk
Rev Claro Conde.
M: *Sat 1st M of Sun 5pm. Sun 11am. Hds 7pm.*

2. † St Patrick
(1894; 1907; 1929; cons 15 Sept 1938)
Beachfield Road, Sandown.
M: *Sun 9.15am, 5pm. Hds 10am.*

- ***Sisters of Mercy,*** St Anthony's Convent, Beatrice Avenue, Shanklin, Isle of Wight. PO37 6EP
Tel: 01983-866555 **Fax:** 01983-862062.
E-mail: mercyiw@aol.com

A

■ **SOUTHAMPTON**, Hants.
St Joseph and St Edmund
14 Rockstone Place, Soton SO15 2EQ
Tel: 023-8033 3589 **Fax:** 023-8063 5153
E-mail: city@sotoncentre.fsnet.co.uk
Website: www.catholic.co.uk
Canon John O'Shea, Rev PJ Smith.

1. † St Joseph (1792; 1830; cons 23 Sept 1911)
Bugle Street, Southampton
M: *Sat 1st M of Sun 6pm. Sun 10am. Hds 12.15pm.*

A

2. † St Edmund (1884; 1889)
The Avenue, Southampton.
M: *Sun 9am, 11am, 7pm. Hds 7am, 7.30pm.*

- ***Congregation of the Sainte Union des Sacres Coeurs***, St Anne's Convent, Rockstone Place, SO15 2WZ
Tel: 023-8033 3678
- ***Verbum Dei Community***, Old All Saints Hall, 425 Winchester Road, Southampton, SO16 7DE
Tel/Fax: 02380-399301
E-mail: verbum-dei@hotmail.com
- ***Sisters of St Joseph of Annecy,*** Medaille Community, Marina Court, 23 Landguard Road, Southampton SO15 5DL **Tel:** 02380-233572

A

3. † Christ the King & St Colman (1903; 1944; 1960)
Bitterne Road East, Bitterne, Southampton SO18 5EG **Tel:** 023-8044 9088
Fax: 023-8042 1531
E-mail: ckscsoton@portsmouth-dio.org.uk
Rev James Carling, 2 Dean Road, Bitterne, Southampton SO18 6AP
M: *Sun 10.15am. Hds (vigil 7.30pm), 10am.*

- ***De La Mennais Brothers,*** St Mary's College, 57 Midanbury Lane, SO18 4DJ
Tel: 02380-558425
- ***Sisters of Our Lady of Charity,*** Redcote Convent, Bitterne SO18 5SU
Tel: 02380-463535
- ***Sisters of Our Lady of Charity,*** 'Shalom', 27 Shales Road, Bitterne SO18 6NQ.

A

4. † Holy Family
(1957; 1966; cons 19 Jan 1983)
Redbridge Hill, Millbrook, Southampton SO16 4PL **Tel:** 02380-775199
Fax: 02380-347088
E-mail: louis.mcdermott@btopenworld.com
Rev Louis McDermott OMI.
M: *Sat 1st M of Sun 6.30pm. Sun 11am. Hds 7pm.*

5. † The Immaculate Conception
(1923; 1955)
346 Portswood Road, Portswood, Southampton SO17 3SB
Tel: 02380-555470 **E-mail:** portswood@portsmouth-dio.org.uk
Rev Anthony Gatt.
M: *Sun 8.30am, 10.30am, 6.30pm. Hds 10am, 7pm.*

6. † St Boniface
(1925; cons 17 June 1947)
413 Shirley Road, Southampton SO15 3JD
Tel: 02380-771231 **Fax:** 02380-5283236
E-mail: secretary@st-boniface.org.uk
Website: www.st-boniface.org.uk
Rev David Sillince.
M: *Sat 1st M of Sun 6.30pm. Sun 8.30am, 10.30am. Hds 10am, 8pm.*

6 † St Patrick
(1879; 1939; 1950; cons 20 Apr 1963)
St Patrick's House, 45 Portsmouth Road, Woolston, Southampton SO19 9BD
Tel: 02380-448671
Rev William Wilson.
E-mail: eastside@portsmouth-dio.org.uk
M: *Sat 1st M of Sun 6pm. Sun 11am.*

A

7. † St Vincent de Paul (1975)
Coxford Road, Lordswood, Southampton SO16 5LL Served from Holy Family.
Tel: 02380-775199 **Fax:** 02380-778203
M: *Sun 9.15am. Hds 10am.*

8. Sacred Heart (Convent Chapel)
Bracken Lane, Southampton SO16 6UZ
Poor Clares (Collettines) **Tel:** 02380-772035
Chaplain: **Rev Krzysztof Kosciolek SChr.**
M *Sun 10.45am (Polish). Hds 7.30am.*

9. Southampton University Chaplaincy
52 University Road, Southampton SO17 1BJ
Tel: 02380-594622 **Fax:** 02380-594625
E-mail: mjryan_98@yahoo.com
Chaplain: **Sr Catherine Cruz**, 33 Elmsleigh Gardens, Bassett, Southampton SO16 3GE

10. Polish Chaplaincy
15 Landguard Road, Southampton SO17 5DL **Tel:** 023 8022 4418
Rev Krzysztof Kosciolek SChr.
Polish Catholic Centre, 507 Portswood Road.
Tel: 023 8055 7849

11. Southampton University Hospitals NHS Trust Chaplaincy
Mailpoint 201, Southampton General Hospital SO16 6YD
Tel: 02380-796745 - Chaplain's office
Chaplain: **Rev Michael Cronin.**
M: *Sun 4.30pm (General Hospital)*

12. Solent University of Southampton
East Park Terrace, Southampton SO14 0YN
Chaplain: **Sr Liliana Gonzalez Castenada.**
Tel: 02380-319819 **Fax:** 02380-399301

13. Port Chaplaincy
E-mail: southampton@stellamarisf.totalserve.co.uk
Chaplain: **Rev Patsy Foley SPS**, 12-14 Queen's Terrace, Southampton SO14 3BP
Tel: 023-8071 4081
Ships' Visitor: **Mr John Robinson**

■ **SOUTHBOURNE**
See Bournemouth (5).

■ **SOUTHSEA**
See Portsmouth (7).

■ **STOCKBRIDGE,** Hants
See Winchester.

■ **STUBBINGTON,** Fareham, Hants 
See Lee-on-the-Solent.

■ **TADLEY,** Hants
1. † St Michael (1959)
Bishopswood Road, Tadley, Hants RG26 4HG **Tel:** 0118-981 4572
Patrick Tansey. *Deacon:* **Rev Anthony Cairns,** 17 Blackthorn Close, Baughurst, Tadley, Hants RG26 5GW
Tel: 0118 982 1511
E-mail: anthony.cairns@googlemail.com
M: *Sat 1st M of Sun 6pm. Sun 9.40am. Hds 7.30pm.*

2. SS Peter and Paul (1969)
Swan Street, Kingsclere, Hants.
M: *Sun 11.15am.*

■ **THATCHAM,** Newbury, Berks
† Our Lady of the Assumption
(1954; 1978; cons 4.11.1982)
Bath Road, Thatcham, Berks. RG18 4AG
Tel: 01635-864416 **Fax:** 01635-864111
Rev Ignatious Maddeneni. 7 Bath Road, RG18 4AG
M: *Sat 1st M of Sun 6.15pm. Sun 10am. Hds As advertised.*

- ***Franciscan Missionaries of Mary, St Gabriel's Convent,*** Cold Ash, Thatcham Berks RG18 9HU
Tel: 01635-864161
- ***Cold Ash Centre for Retreats and Conferences,*** 
Address as above. **Tel:** 01635-865353

■ **THEALE,** Berks
See Woolhampton (4).

■ **TICHBORNE,** Alresford, Hants
See Alresford (2).

■ **TIDWORTH,** Hants
St Patrick and St George (1912)
Tel: 01980-842284/602328
Served by: Army Chaplain, St Patrick's House, St Patrick's Avenue, Tidworth SP9 7BP
M: *Sun 11.30am.*

■ **TILEHURST,** Berks
See Reading (5).

■ **TOTLAND BAY,** Isle of Wight
† St Saviour (1871; 1923; cons 1954)
Weston Lane, Totland Bay, Isle of Wight PO39 0HE **Tel:** 01983-752317
E-mail: saintsaviour1@btinternet.com
M: *Sat 1st M of Sun 6pm. Sun 9am. Hds As announced.*

- ***Companions of Martin de Porres,*** Weston Manor, Totland Bay PO39 0HF
Tel: 01983-753031

■ **TOTTON,** Southampton, Hants
† St Therese of the Child Jesus (1924)
Commercial Road, Totton, Southampton.
Tel: 02380-862270 **Fax:** 02380-571363
E-mail: kathleen@montfort.org.uk
Rev Kevin O'Brien. 20 Beaumont Road, SO40 3AL *Deacon:* **Rev Andrew Philpott,** 31 Filton Close, Calmore, Southampton, Hants SO40 2UW **Tel:** 023-8086 9853
M: *Sat 1st M of Sun 6pm. Sun 11am. Hds 9.30am.*

- ***Company of Mary (Montfort Missionaries) (SMM):*** Montfort Missionaries, St Joseph's House of Prayer & Mission, Lyndhurst Road, Ashurst, Southampton, SO40 7DU
Tel: 02380-292337 **Fax:** 02380-292346
E-mail: smm63@zoom.co.uk
Rev Ronnie Mitchell (*Superior*), **Bros Paul Allerton, Bob Ellwood, Anthony Hanley, Owen Cannon.**
M: *Sun 9am. Hds 7.30pm.*

- ***Daughters of Wisdom,***
  Tel: 023-8029 2771 **Fax:** 023-8029 2346
  M: *Sun 9am. Hds 7.30.*

■ **TWYFORD,** Berks
1. † St Thomas More (1978)
London Road, Twyford, Berks RG10 9EL
Office Tel: 0118-934 0854
E-mail: email.stthomasmore@virgin.net
Website: stthomasmore-twyford.org.uk
Rev Vincent Flanagan, 105 London Road, Twyford, Berks RG10 9EL **Rev Michael Jackson,** 4 Broadwater Road, Twyford, Reading, Berks RG10 OFX
Tel: 0118-934 0223 *Deacon:* **Rev Jerome Morland**. 11 Wetherby Close Emmer Green, Reading RG4 8UD
Tel: 0118-947 7467
M: *Sat 1st M of Sun 6.30pm. Sun 10.30am. Hds (vigil 7.30pm, 12noon, 7.30pm.*

2. † Our Lady of Peace (1963)
Braybrook Road, Wargrave, Twyford, Berks.
M: *Sun 9am.*
- ***Sisters of Our Lady of Pity;*** Home for Sick and Retired Priests, St John's Convent, Linden Hill Lane, Kiln Green, Reading, Berks RG10 9XP
  Tel: 0118-940 2964 (Convent)
  M: *Sun 10am. Hds 10am.*

■ **VENTNOR,** Isle of Wight
1. † Our Lady and St Wilfrid
(1866; 1871; cons 1972)
Trinity Road, Ventnor, Isle of Wight PO38 1NL
Tel: 01983-852297 Served from Shanklin.
M: *Sun 5pm. Hds As announced.*

2. St Joseph (1969)
Rectory Road, Niton, Ventnor, Isle of Wight.
M: *Sun 8.30am.*

■ **WALLINGFORD,** Oxon
† St John the Evangelist (1925; 1958)
St John's, Wood Street, Wallingford, Oxon OX10 0BD **Tel:** 01491-836814
E-mail: didcot@portsmouthdiocese.org.uk
Served from Didcot.
M: 1st M of Sun 5.30pm, *Sun 10am. Hds 9am, 7.30pm.*

■ **WANTAGE,** Oxon
† St John Vianney
(1927; 1961; cons 24 July 1966)
Charlton Road, Wantage, Oxon
Tel: 01235-762374 **Fax:** 01235-772881
E-mail: canonpturbitt@aol.com
Rev Canon Peter Turbitt. Marian House, Charlton Road, OX12 8ER
M: *Sat 1st M of Sun 6pm. Sun 8am, 10am. Hds 10am, 8pm.*

■ **WARGRAVE,** Berks
See Twyford (2).

■ **WASH COMMON,** Berks
See Newbury (2)

■ **WATERLOOVILLE,** Portsmouth, Hants
† The Sacred Heart (1900; 1925)
London Road, Waterlooville, Portsmouth, Hants. **Tel/Fax:** 02392-262289
Website: www.waterlooville-catholic.org.uk
Rev Kevin Bidgood. The Presbytery, 140 Stakes Hill Road, Waterlooville, Portsmouth PO7 7SR **E-mail:** frkbidgood@hotmail.com
M: *Sat 1st M of Sun 6.15pm. Sun 9.30am, 11am, 6.30pm. Hds (vigil 8pm), 7.30am, 9am, 7.30pm.*
- ***Sisters of Our Lady of Charity,*** The Mount, 358 London Road, Waterlooville PO7 7SR **Tel:** 023-9226 2105

■ **WATERSIDE,** Hants
1. † St Bernard & St Michael.
St Bernard's House, Southbourne Avenue, Holbury, Hants SO45 2NT
Tel: 023-8089 2656 **Fax:** 023-8089 4031
E-mail: admin@watersidecp.org.uk
Priest-in-charge **Rev Patrick Foley SPS;** *Deacons:* **Revv Steven Bowler,** 17 Windrush Way, Hythe SO45 6JF
Tel: 023-8020 7449; **Ian Tobin,** Trolls End, The Lane, Fawley, Hants SO45 1EY
Tel: 023-8089 7354

2. St Bernard (1939; 1971; cons Oct 1984)
M: *Sun 9am. Hds 7.30pm.*

3. St Michael (1965)
Langdown Lawn, Hythe.
M: *Sun 11am, 7pm. Hds 9.30am.*

■ **WEEKE**
See Winchester (2).

■ **WEST END,** Hants
See Hedge End (2).

■ **WESTBOURNE.**
See Bournemouth (4).

■ **WHITCHURCH,** Hants
See Andover (3).

■ **WICKHAM**
See Fareham (3).

■ **WINCHESTER,** Hants
1. † St Peter
(1674; 1792; 1926; cons 22 Sept 1938)
Jewry Street, Winchester, Hants.
Tel: 01962-852804 **Fax:** 01962-843691
E-mail: stpeterswinchester@btopenworld.com
Rev Canons Paul Townsend EpV, Alan Griffiths. St Peter Street, Winchester SO23 8BW
Deacon: **Rev Nick Reynolds,** Hall Place Cottage, Petersfield Road, Ropley, Hants

SO24 0EJ **Tel:** 01962 772393
Fax: 01962 772098
E-mail: nickreynolds@freeuk.com
M: *Sat 1st M of Sun 6pm. Sun 8am, 10.30am, 7pm. Hds 7.30am, 12.15pm, 7.30pm*

- ***Religious Teachers Filippini,*** White House, St Peter Street SO23 8BW Kindergarten School. **Tel:** 01962-854040

2. † St Thomas More
'Morestead', 53 Stoney Lane, Weeke SO22 6DR **Tel:** 01962-882711
M: *Hds 10am.*

3. St Stephen (1969)
Oliver's Battery Road North.
Served from Winchester (1).
M: *Sun 9.15am. Hds 9.30am.*

■ WINDSOR, Berks
A

1. † St Edward (1830; 1868; cons 21 Nov 1910)
Alma Road, Windsor, Berks.
Tel: 01753-865163 **Fax:** 01753-730018
E-mail: frmichael@catholicwindsor.org
Website: www.catholicwindsor.org
Rev Michael Morrissey. 44 Alma Road, Windsor, Berks SL4 3HJ *Deacon:* **Rev George Young**, 2 Carter Close, Windsor SL4 4QX **Tel:** 01753-842343
M: *Sat 1st M of Sun 6pm. Sun 11am. Hds 12noon.*

- ***Sisters of St Brigid,*** 48 Springfield Road, Windsor SL4 3PO **Tel:** 01753-859529

2. † St Mark (1968)
A

Dedworth Road, Dedworth.
M: *Sun 9.30am. Hds 7.30pm.*

3. Our Lady of Lourdes (1956)
St Luke's Road, Old Windsor
M: *Hds As announced.*

■ WINKLEBURY, Hants
See Basingstoke (3).

■ WOKINGHAM, Berks
A

† Corpus Christi (1902; 1911; 1970)
Sturges Road, Wokingham, Berks.
Tel: 0118-978 0348 **Fax:** 0118-979 5825
E-mail: corpuschristi@ntlworld.com
Website: www.corpuschristi-wokingham.org
Rev Mgr James Joyce. 60 Sturges Road, Wokingham, Berks RG40 2HE
M: *Sat 1st M of Sun 6.30pm. Sun 9am, 11am. Hds 9.30am, 8pm.*

- ***Dominican Sisters (of the Presentation of Our Lady),*** 71 Easthampstead Road, RG40 2ED **Tel:** 0118-978 2553

■ WOODLEY, Berks
A

† St John Bosco (1937; 1948)
56 Western Avenue, Woodley, Berks RG5 3BH **Tel:** 0118-969 3423
E-mail: st.john-bosco_01@tiscali.co.uk
Website: www.stjohnbosco.co.uk
Rev Christopher Whelan.
M: *Sat 1st M of Sun 6.30pm. Sun 10am. Hds 9am.*

- ***Sisters of Mercy,*** 16 Silver Fox Crescent, Woodley RG5 3JA

■ WOOLHAMPTON, Berks

1. † St Mary (1786; 1848; cons. 21.6.1995)
Douai Abbey,Upper Woolhampton, Reading, Berks RG7 5TQ
Tel: 0118-971 5350 **Fax:** 0118-971 5303
E-mail: parish@douaiabbey.org.uk
Rev Dom Benedict Thompson OSB, *Deacon:* **Rev John Foley,** 70 West End Road, Mortimer Common, Berks RG7 3TS
M: *Sun 8.30am. Hds as announced.*

2. † St Oswald (1976)
A

Abbey Park, Clay Hill, Burghfield Common, Berks. **Tel:** 0118-971 5350
M: *Sun 11am. Hds as announced.*

3. † Our Lady and St Bernadette (1958)
A

Horseshoe Road, Pangbourne, Berks.
Tel: 0118-971 5350
M: *Sun 9am. Hds as announced.*

4. † St Luke (1969)
A

Englefield Road, Theale, Berks.
Tel: 0118-971 5350
M: *Sat 1st M of Sun 5.30pm. Hds As announced.*

5. † Abbey Church of Our Lady and St Edmund King & Martyr (1933)
Upper Woolhampton, Reading RG7 5TQ
Tel: 0118-971 5300 **Fax:** 0118-971 5303
E-mail: douaiabbey@aol.com
M: *Sun 11am. Hds 7.45am.*

■ WOOTTON, Oxford
See North Hinksey (5).

■ YATELEY, Hants

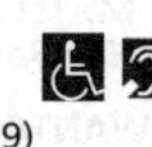

† St Swithun (1969; cons 15 July 1979)
St Swithun's Presbytery, Firgrove Road, Yateley, Hampshire, GU46 6NH

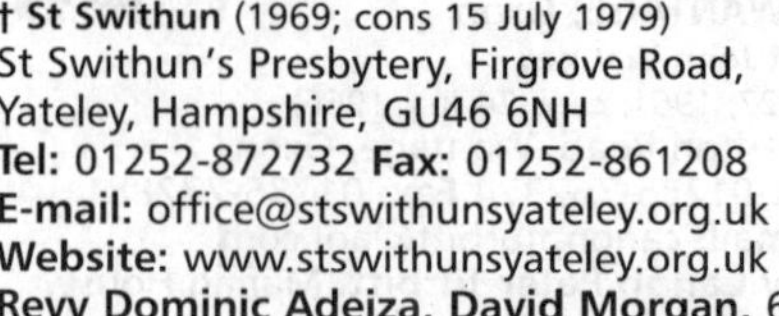

Tel: 01252-872732 **Fax:** 01252-861208
E-mail: office@stswithunsyateley.org.uk
Website: www.stswithunsyateley.org.uk
Revv Dominic Adeiza, David Morgan, 63 Maple Gardens, Yateley, Hants GU46 6JQ.
M: *Sat 1st M of Sun 6.30pm. Sun 9am, 10.30am. Hds 10am, 8pm.*

DIOCESE OF PORTSMOUTH

■ ORDERS OR CONGREGATIONS, ETC

■ Men

Benedictines Congr of Subiaco: Farnborough (2).
Benedictines Congr of Solesmes: Quarr.
Benedictines English Congr: Woolhampton.
Carmelites (Discalced): North Hinksey.
De La Mennais Brothers: Southampton (2).
De La Salle Brothers: Portsmouth (6), Bournemouth (5), Lambourn.
Franciscans (Friars Minor): Fareham.
Jesuits: Bournemouth (2).
Mill Hill Missionaries: East Cowes, Park Gate.
Martin de Porres, Companions of: Totland Bay.
Montfort Missionaries: Ashurst.
Oblates of Mary Immaculate: Christchurch, Southampton (3, 8).
Redemptorists: Alton.
Salesians: Crookham, Farnborough (1), Guernsey (2).
Salvatorians (SDS): Hook.
Society of Christ: Southampton (9).
Society of St Patrick (Kiltegan Fathers): Bournemouth (4).

■ Women

Benedictine Nuns: Ryde (4).
Benedictines Nuns: Holy Trinity, East Hendred.
Brigid, Sisters of St: Windsor.
Cenacle, Sisters of Our Lady of the: Netley Abbey.
Christ, Sisters of: East Cowes,
Christian Education, Religious of: Farnborough (3).
Dominican Sisters (Third Order) (of the Presentation of Our Lady, Tours): Wokingham.
Dominican Sisters of Malta: Hook.
Dominican Sisters of St Joseph: Brockenhurst.
Franciscan Missionaries of Mary: Thatcham.
Franciscan Missionaries of the Divine Motherhood: Aldershot, Portsmouth (6).
Franciscan Sisters (of St Mary of the Angels, Angers): Fareham.
Holy Family (of Amiens), Sisters of the: Jersey (3).
Immaculate Conception, Sisters of the: Jersey (3, 4), Leigh Park.
Marist Sisters: Ascot.
Mercy, Sisters of Institute of Our Lady of Mercy: Alderney, Guernsey (1), Newport. Shanklin, Woodley,
Our Lady of Charity, Sisters of: Ascot, Southampton (2), Waterlooville.
Our Lady of Pity, Sisters of: Twyford.
Poor Clares (Colletines): Southampton (7)
Poor, Little Sisters of the: Jersey (3).
Presentation Sisters: Ryde.
Providence, Sisters of St Marie de la: Alton Basingstoke (1).
Religious Teachers Filippini: Alton (2), Winchester.
Sacred Heart (Madrid), Hospitaller Sisters of the: Guernsey (1).
Sacred Heart (Rome), Handmaids of the: Bournemouth (2).
Sisters of Ste Marie Madeleine Postel: Reading (1).
Sainte Union des Sacrés Coeurs, Congr of the: Southampton (1).
St Joseph of Annecy, Sisters of (Medaille Community), Southampton (1).
Verbum Dei: Newport, Reading, Southampton (1).
Wisdom Daughters of (La Sagesse): Romsey.

■ DIOCESAN INSTITUTIONS, SOCIETIES

For Societies and Organisations without representation in the diocese please see the main Societies and Organisations section.

Apostleship of the Sea. *Port Chaplain at Southampton:* 48 Bugle Street, Southampton SO14 2AH **Tel:** 023-8023 1007 **Fax:** 023-8023 5308

Catenian Association. Province No 8: *Secretary:* **Mr L C Sims**, 85 Courtington Lane, Bloxham, Banbury, Oxfordshire OX15 4HS **Tel:** 01295-720414 Prov No 11: *Secretary:* **Mr L G Bill**, 2 Lambourne Court, Wadham Park, Crewkerne, Somerset TA18 7OF **Tel:** 01460-78069 Prov No 19: *Secretary:* **Mr R M S Allanson**, 4 Brokes Crescent, Reigate, Surrey RH2 9PS **Tel:** 01737-245683

Catholic Association of Widows. *Chairperson* **Mrs D B Broomhead**, 52 St Ronan's Road, Flat 2, Southsea, Hants PO4 0LU

Catholic Children's Society. *Director:* **Mr Terence Connor MA**, 49 Russell Hill Road, Purley, Surrrey CR8 2XB Family Makers, 50 Mount Pleasant, Reading RG1 2TD **Tel:** 0118-987 5121 **Mrs Wendy Inman**, 7 Bridge Street, Winchester SO23 8HM **Tel:** 01962-842024

Catholic Caring Fellowship. *Chairman:* **Dr John Weaver**, Old Chilterns, Lower Assendon, Henley on Thames RG9 6AN **Tel:** 01491-578793

Catholic HR. The National Network for people managers in Catholic organisations exists to be part of the Church's witness through encouraging, developing and supporting best practice in the management of people working in dioceses and Catholic organisations in England and Wales, and through working with the Bishops' Conference of England and Wales and other Catholic bodies to influence public policy. *Chair and Diocesan Contact:* **Sheila Hughes**, 14 Castlemews, Ringwood BH24 2BG

Catholic Nurses' Guild. *Diocesan Chaplain:* To be appointed.

Catholic Women's League. Diocesan Branch. *Secretary:* **Mrs Pat McGrath**, 38 Nightingale Road, Southsea, Hants PO5 3JN **Tel:** 023-9264 0408

Christian Life Communities. *Diocesan Representative:* **Mr J Clifford**. 21a Meadow Way, Priestwood, Bracknell, Berks RG42 1UE **Tel:** 01344-425179

Dominican Secular Institute. *Moderator:* **Miss Ann Hamilton**, 19 Lion Street, Rye, East Sussex TN31 7LB

Grail, The. *Diocesan Representative:* **Chris and Sandra Baker**, Long Acre, East Hanney, Nr Wantage, Oxon OX12 0HP **Tel:** 01235-868262

Knights of St Columba, Prov 14 (Portsmouth). *Provincial Grand Knight:* **M Carey**, 11 Cheshire Close, Whiteley, Fareham, Hants PO15 7JJ **Tel:** 01489-881510 **E-mail:** pfcarey@aol.com. Prov 23 (Thames Valley); *Provincial Grand Knight:* **John Lynn**, 52 Hemsdale, Maidenhead, Berks SL6 6SL **Tel:** 01628-636668 Prov 39 (Channel Islands) *Provincial Grand Knight:* **Mr D B Troy**, La Salette, Rue des Raisies, St Martin, Jersey JE3 6AT **Tel:** 01534-853247

Marriage Care. For Diocesan Centres in North-East Hants, Portsmouth, Reading, Southampton, See Index.

Our Lady's Catechists. *Diocesan Secretary:* **Mrs C Taylor**. 36 Ingledene Close, Bedhampton PO9 1DG **Tel:** 023-9247 9846

Pontifical Mission Societies. The Association for the Propogation of the Faith, The Holy Childhood/Mission Together; Society of St Peter the Apostle, The Missionary Union. Further information: **Rev Peter Codd**, St Joseph's, Berkshire Drive, Tilehurst, Reading RG31 5JJ **Tel:** 0118-942 8632

Portsmouth Diocesan Pilgrimage to Lourdes. *Director:* **Rev V Harvey**, Holy Ghost Presbytery, Sherbourne Road, Basingstoke RG21 5TD **Tel:** 01256-465214

Scouts. *Hon. Secretary of the Catholic Scout Advisory Council:* **Mrs K Cleary**, 36 Winchester Road, Dukinfield, Cheshire SK16 5DQ **Tel:** 0161-338 2978

Society of St Gregory. *Diocesan Representative:* **Monica Taylor**, 13 Durford Road, Petersfield, Hants GU31 4EW **E-mail:** portsmouth@ssg.org.uk

Society of St Vincent de Paul. Portsmouth Central Council. *President:* **Mr Kevin McDermott** **Tel/Fax:** 01202-418354

Teams of Our Lady. An international Catholic Movement for Christian married couples that aims to deepen the couples' spirituality. A 'Team' consists of four or five couples and a priest or religious as spiritual advisor meeting monthly to share the journey of faith, guided by the Holy Spirit. *Contact couple:* **Chris and Frankie Lane**, 50 Hill Park Road, Fareham, Hants PO15 6HT **Tel:** 01329-310785 **E-mail:** c-f.lane@ntlworld.com

Union of Catholic Mothers. Portsmouth Diocesan Foundation. *Secretary:* **Mrs Angela Brench**, 44 Lowther Road, Emmbrook, Wokingham RG41 1JD **Tel:** 0118-978 4496

Walsingham Association. *Bournemouth:* **Mrs L Arblaster**, 8 Fountain Court, 13 The Avenue, Poole BH13 6EZ **Tel:** 01202-290069 *Windsor:* **Mrs L Mullan**, 25b Straight Road, Old Windsor SL4 2RW

■ HOSPITALS

To contact the Catholic Chaplain of a particular hospital we suggest you contact the hospital reception directly.

■ CATHOLIC SCHOOLS - MAINTAINED

■ BERKSHIRE LEA

▲ Primary

St Teresa's Primary School, Easthampstead Road, Wokingham, Berks RG40 2EB **Tel:** 0118-978 4310 **Fax:** 0118-977 0032 *(Wokingham)*

St Dominic Savio Primary School, Western Avenue, Woodley, Berks RG5 3BH **Tel:** 0118-969 3893 **Fax:** 0118-969 3765 *(Woodley)*

■ WEST BERKSHIRE LEA

▲ Primary

St Finian's Primary School, The Ridge, Cold Ash, Newbury, Berks RG18 9HU **Tel:** 01635-865925 **Fax:** 01635-874892 *(Thatcham)*

St Joseph's Primary School, Newport Road, Newbury, Berks RG14 2AW **Tel:** 01635-43455 **Fax:** 01635-552859

St Paul's Primary School, City Road, Tilehurst, Reading, Berks RG31 4SZ

Tel: 0118-942 2003 **Fax:** 0118-945 4924 *(Reading 5)*

■ **WINDSOR & MAIDENHEAD LEA**

▲ **First**

St Edward's First School, Parsonage Lane, Windsor, Berks SL4 5EN **Tel/Fax:** 01753-860607 *(Windsor)*

▲ **Primary**

St Edmund Campion Primary School, Altwood Road, Maidenhead, Berks SL6 4PX **Tel:** 01628-620183 **Fax:** 01628-624010 *(Maidenhead 2)*

St Francis Catholic Primary School, Coronation Road, South Ascot SL5 9HG **Tel:** 01344-622840 **Fax:** 01344-873574 *(Ascot)*

St Mary's Primary School, Cookham Road, Maidenhead, Berks SL6 7EG **Tel:** 01628-622570 **Fax:** 01628-680017 *(Maidenhead)*

▲ **Middle**

St Edward's Royal Free Ecumenical Middle School, Parsonage Lane, Windsor, Berks SL4 5EN **Tel:** 01753-867809 **Fax:** 01753-869001 *(Windsor)*

■ **SURREY LEA**

▲ **Secondary Comprehensive**

All Hallows, Weybourne Road, Farnham, Surrey GU9 9HF **Tel:** 01252-319211 **Fax:** 01252-328649 *(Aldershot)*

■ **READING LEA**

▲ **Primary**

Christ the King Primary School, Lulworth Road, Reading, Berks RG2 8LX **Tel:** 0118-901 5434 **Fax:** 0118-901 5435 *(Reading 2)*

English Martyrs Primary School, Dee Road, Reading, Berks RG30 4BE **Tel:** 0118-901 5466 **Fax:** 0118-901 5467 *(Reading 4)*

▲ **Secondary Comprehensive**

Bl Hugh Faringdon, Fawley Road, Southcote, Reading, Berks RG30 3EP **Tel:** 0118-957 4730 **Fax:** 0118-956 8150 *(Reading)*

■ **DORSET LEA**

▲ **Primary**

St Joseph's Primary School, Dorset Road, Somerford, Christchurch, Dorset BH23 3DA **Tel:** 01202-485976 **Fax:** 01202-483092 *(Christchurch)*

■ **BOURNEMOUTH LEA**

▲ **Primary**

Corpus Christi Primary School, St James's Square, Boscombe, Bournemouth BH5 2BX **Tel:** 01202-427544 **Fax:** 01202-425592 *(Bournemouth 2)*

St Walburga's Primary School, Malvern Road, Moordown, Bournemouth, Dorset BH9 3BY **Tel:** 01202-528811 **Fax:** 01202-532875 *(Bournemouth 3)*

▲ **Secondary Comprehensive**

St Peter's, St Catherine's Road, Bournemouth, Dorset BH6 4AH **Tel:** 01202-421141 **Fax:** 01202-418886 *(Bournemouth)*

■ **BRACKNELL FOREST LEA**

▲ **Primary**

St Joseph's Primary School, Gipsy Lane, Bracknell, Berks RG12 9AP **Tel:** 01344-425246 **Fax:** 01344-305463 *(Bracknell)*

St Margaret Clitherow Primary School, Pembroke, Hanworth, Bracknell RG12 4RD. **Tel:** 01344-424030 **Fax:** 01344-304041 *(Bracknell)*

■ **PORTSMOUTH LEA**

▲ **Primary**

Corpus Christi Primary School, Gladys Avenue, North End, Portsmouth PO2 9AX **Tel:** 023-9266 1818 **Fax:** 023-9266 4780 *(Portsmouth 2)*

St John's Cathedral Catholic Primary School, Cottage View, off Arundel Street, Portsmouth PO1 1PX **Tel:** 02392-82105 **Fax:** 023-9281 5065 *(Portsmouth 1)*

St Paul's Primary School, Bourne Road, Paulsgrove, Portsmouth PO6 4JD **Tel:** 02392-375488 **Fax:** 023-9221 4067 *(Portsmouth 5)*

St Swithun's Primary School, Taswell Road, Southsea, Portsmouth PO5 2RG **Tel:** 02392-829339 **Fax:** 02392-297690 *(Portsmouth 7)*

▲ **Secondary Comprehensive**

St Edmund's, Arundel Street, Portsmouth, Hants PO1 1RX **Tel:** 02392-823766 **Fax:** 02392-871874 *(Portsmouth)*

■ **CHANNEL ISLANDS**

▲ **Junior and Infant**

Notre Dame du Rosaire Primary School, Burnt Lane, St Peter Port, Guernsey, Channel Islands GY1 1HL **Tel:** 01481-722412 **Fax:** 01481-714453 *(Guernsey)*

St Mary and St Michael Primary School, Rue des Monts, St Sampson, Guernsey, Channel Islands GY2 4HU **Tel:** 01481-245020 **Fax:** 01481-247051 *(Guernsey)*

■ **HAMPSHIRE LEA**

▲ **Primary**

St Anne's Primary School, Pinkerton Road, South Ham, Basingstoke, Hants RG22 6RE **Tel:** 01256-464165 **Fax:** 01256-842083 *(Basingstoke)*

St Joseph's Primary School, Bridge Road, Aldershot, Hants GU11 3DD **Tel:** 01252-350583 **Fax:** 01252-341158 *(Aldershot)*

St John the Baptist Primary School, Floral Way, Andover, Hants SP10 3PF **Tel:** 01264-361806 **Fax:** 01264-355211 *(Andover)*

St Bede's Primary School, Popley Way, Basingstoke, Hants RG24 9DX **Tel:** 01256-473379 **Fax:** 01256-463860 *(Basingstoke)*

St Jude's Primary School, Bishopsfield Road, Fareham, Hants PO14 1ND **Tel:** 01329-235131 **Fax:** 01329-827939 *(Fareham)*

St Patrick's Primary School, Whitefriars Avenue Road, Farnborough, Hants GU14 7BW **Tel:** 01252-542511 **Fax:** 01252-371020 *(Farnborough)*

St Bernadette's Primary School, Tile Barn Close, Cove, Farnborough, Hants GU14 8LS **Tel:** 01252-548123 **Fax:** 01252-511816 *(Farnborough 3)*

St Swithun Wells Catholic Primary School, Hillcrest Avenue, Chandlers Ford, Hants SO53 2JP **Tel:** 02380-266210 **Fax:** 02380-265273 *(Chandlers Ford)*

St Mary's Primary School, Ann's Hill Road, Gosport, Hants PO12 3NB **Tel:** 02392-583979 **Fax:** 02392-584514 *(Gosport)*

St Thomas More's Primary School, Hooks Lane, Bedhampton, Havant, Hants PO9 3DR **Tel:** 02392-475909 **Fax:** 02392-472050 *(Havant)*

Our Lady and St Joseph Primary School, Ramley Road, Pennington, Lymington, Hants SO41 8GY **Tel:** 01590-672711 **Fax:** 01590-671934 *(Lymington)*

St Anthonys Primary School, Primate Road, Titchfield Common, Fareham, PO14 4RP **Tel:** 01489-579100 **Fax:** 01489-579299 *(Park Gate)*

St Peter's Primary School, Stakes Hill Road, Waterlooville, Portsmouth, Hants PO7 7BP **Tel:** 02392-262599 **Fax:** 02392-230375 *(Waterlooville)*

St Peter's Primary School, Oliver's Battery Road North, Winchester, Hants SO22 4JB **Tel:** 01962-852820 **Fax:** 01962-855445 *(Winchester)*

▲ **Secondary Comprehensive**

Bishop Challoner, St Michael's Road, Basingstoke, Hants RG22 6SR **Tel:** 01256-462661 **Fax:** 01256-810359 *(Basingstoke)*

Oaklands RC Comprehensive School (11-18), Stakes Hill Road, Waterlooville, Hants PO7 7BW **Tel:** 02392-259214 **Fax:** 02392-230317 *(Waterlooville)*

■ **SOUTHAMPTON LEA**

▲ **Primary**

Springhill Primary School, Milton Road, Southampton, Hants SO15 2HW **Tel:** 02380-333954 **Fax:** 02380-399971 *(Southampton)*

Holy Family Primary School, Mansel Road, West Millbrook, Southampton, Hants SO16 9LP **Tel:** 02380-773264 **Fax:** 02380-512497 *(Southampton 4)*

St Patrick's Primary School, Fort Road, Woolston, Southampton, Hants SO19 7JE **Tel:** 02380-448502 **Fax:** 023-8043 8823 *(Southampton 8)*

▲ **Secondary Comprehensive**

St Anne's Convent School, Rockstone Place, Southampton, Hants SO15 2WZ **Tel:** 023-8032 8200 **Fax:** 023-8033 1767 *(Southampton)*

St George Catholic School for Boys, Leaside Way, Swaythling, Southampton, Hants SO16 3DQ **Tel:** 02380-322603 **Fax:** 02380-322606 *(Southampton)*

■ **ISLE OF WIGHT**

▲ **Primary**

Holy Cross Primary School, Springhill, East Cowes, Isle of Wight PO32 6AS **Tel:** 01983-292885 **Fax:** 01983-292885 *(East Cowes)*

St Thomas of Canterbury First School, Carisbrooke, Newport, Isle of Wight PO30 1NR **Tel:** 01983-522747 **Fax:** 01983-521050 *(Newport)*

St Mary's Primary School, Ampthill Road, Ryde, Isle of Wight PO33 1LJ **Tel:** 01983-562000 **Fax:** 01983-810681 *(Ryde)*

St Saviour's First School, Summers Lane, Totland Bay, Isle of Wight PO39 0HQ **Tel:** 01983-752175 **Fax:** 01983-759129 *(Totland Bay)*

St Wilfrid's Primary School, Trinity Road, Ventnor, Isle of Wight PO38 1NL **Tel:** 01983-852669 **Fax:** 01983-852669 *(Ventnor)*

▲ **Secondary Middle**

Archbishop King Middle School, Wellington Road, Carisbrooke, Newport, Isle of Wight PO30 5QT **Tel:** 01983-523275 **Fax:** 01983-523341 *(Newport)*

■ **OXFORDSHIRE LEA**

▲ **Junior and Infant**

St Edmund's Primary School, Radley Road, Abingdon, Oxon OX14 3PP **Tel:** 01235-521558 **Fax:** 01235-532778 *(Abingdon)*

St Amand's Primary School, St Mary's Road, East Hendred, Wantage, Oxon OX12 8LF **Tel/Fax:** 01235-833342 *(East Hendred)*

■ **CATHOLIC SCHOOLS-INDEPENDENT**

■ **BERKSHIRE**

▲ **Primary**

Marist Convent Preparatory School, Sunninghill, Ascot, Berks SL5 7PS **Tel:** 01344-626137 **Fax:** 01344-621566 *(Ascot)*

Our Lady's School, The Avenue, Crowthorne, Berks RG45 6PB **Tel/Fax:** 01344-773394 *(Crowthorne)*

▲ **Primary and Secondary**

Presentation College, 63 Bath Road, Reading, Berks RG30 2BB **Tel:** 0118-957 2861 **Fax:** 0118-957 2220 *(Reading)*

The Brigidine School, King's Road, Windsor, Berks SL4 2AX **Tel:** 01753-863779 **Fax:** 01753-850278 *(Windsor)*

▲ **Secondary**

Marist Convent, Sunninghill, Ascot, Berks SL5 7PS **Tel:** 01344-624291 **Fax:** 01344-874963 *(Ascot)*

St Mary's School, Ascot, Berks SL5 9JF **Tel:** 01344-623721 **Fax:** 01344-873281 *(Ascot)*

St Joseph's Convent School, Upper Redlands Road, Reading, Berks RG1 5JT **Tel:** 0118-966 1000 **Fax:** 0118-926 9932 *(Reading)*

■ **GUERNSEY**

▲ **Primary**

Convent of Mercy (Prep School), Cordier Hill, St Peter Port, Guernsey, Channel Islands GY1 1JH **Tel:** 01481-720729 **Fax:** 01481-716339 *(Guernsey)*

▲ **Secondary**

Blanchelande Girls' College, Les Vauxbelets, St Andrew, Guernsey GY6 8XY **Tel:** 01481-237200 **Fax:** 01481-232857

■ **JERSEY**

▲ **Primary and Secondary**

FCJ Primary School, Deloraine Road, St Saviour, Jersey, C.I. **Tel:** 01534-723063 **Fax:** 01534-880353 *(Jersey 1)*

Beaulieu Convent, Wellington Road, St Helier, Jersey, Channel Islands JE2 4RJ **Tel:** 01534-731280 **Fax:** 01534-8886077 *(Jersey 2)*

▲ **Secondary**

De la Salle College, Wellington Road, St Saviour, Jersey JE2 7TH **Tel:** 01534-726548 **Fax:** 01534-734126 *(Jersey 1)*

■ **DORSET**

▲ **Primary**

St Thomas Garnet's School, Parkwood Road, Boscombe Road, Boscombe, Bournemouth, Dorset BH5 2DE **Tel:** 01202-420172 *(Main School)* **Tel:** 01202-431286 *(Nursery)* **Fax:** 01202-773060 *(Bournemouth)*

■ **HAMPSHIRE**

▲ **Primary**

Farleigh School, Red Rice, Andover, Hants SP11 7PW **Tel:** 01264-710766 **Fax:** 01264-710070 *(Andover)*

Charlton' House School, 55 Midanbury Lane, Bitterne Park, Southampton SO18 4HE **Tel:** 02380-677575 **Fax:** 02380-344344 *(Southampton)*

▲ **Primary and Secondary**

Convent of Our Lady of Providence, Anstey Manor, Alton, Hants GU34 2NG **Tel:** 01420-82070/83878 **Fax:** 01420-541711 *(Alton)*

St John's College Lower School, Albany Road, Southsea, Hants PO5 3QW **Tel:** 02392-820237 **Fax:** 02392-873603 *(Portsmouth)*

▲ **Secondary**

Farnborough Hill Trust, Farnborough Hants GU14 8AT **Tel:** 01252-545197 **Fax:** 01252-513037 *(Farnborough 2)*

Salesian College, Reading Road, Farnborough, Hants GU14 6PA **Tel:** 01252-893000 **Fax:** 01252-893032

St John's College, Grove Road South, Southsea, Hants PO5 3QW **Tel:** 02392-815118 **Fax:** 02392-873603 *(Portsmouth 7)*

St Mary's College, 57 Midanbury Lane, Bitterne Park, Southampton, Hants SO18 4DJ **Tel:** 02380-671267 **Fax:** 023-8067 1268 *(Southampton)*

■ **OXFORDSHIRE**

▲ **Primary**

Our Lady's Convent Junior School,
Abingdon, Oxon OX14 2HB
Tel: 01235-523147 **Fax:** 01235-530387
(Abingdon)

▲ **Secondary**

Our Lady's Convent Senior School,
Radley Road, Abingdon, Oxon OX14 3PS
Tel: 01235-524658 **Fax:** 01235-535829
(Abingdon)

DIOCESE OF SALFORD

(Province of Liverpool)
Consisting of the Hundreds of Salford and Blackburn in the old County of Lancashire and Dunsop Bridge.

Patrons of the Diocese
Our Lady of Mount Carmel, 16 July; St Joseph, 19 March St John Apostle, 27 December; St Augustine, Apostle of England, 28 May; Consecrated to the Sacred Heart of Jesus, 21 September 1873 and to the Immaculate Heart of Mary, 16 July 1943

Bishop
Rt Rev Terence Brain, Bishop of Salford; born in Coventry, 19 Dec 1938; ordained Auxiliary Bishop of Birmingham 25 April 1991; installed as Bishop of Salford 7 Oct 1997.

Residence:
Wardley Hall, Worsley, Manchester M28 2ND
Tel: 0161-794 2825 **Fax:** 0161-727 8592
E-mail: bishop@wardleyhall.org.uk

Bishop's Secretary
Rev Simon Stamp
E-mail: revsec@wardleyhall.org.uk

Bishop's Secretary:
Mrs Kathleen Rowen
E-mail: kathleenrowen@wardleyhall.org.uk

Rt Rev Terence Brain, Bishop of Salford

■ ADMINISTRATION

■ Vicar General
Mgr Canon Mark Davies VG. Cathedral House, 250 Chapel Street, Salford M3 5LL
Tel: 0161-839 9299 **Fax:** 0161-832 6643
Email: vicargeneral@salforddiocese.org
Office E-mail: vg-office@salforddiocese.org

■ Bishop's Council
Rev Mgr Mark Davies VG, Rev Mgr Austin Bulfin, Rev Mgr Thomas Mulheran. Revv Paul Cannon, Ian Farrell, David Glover, Canon T Anthony McBride, *Secretary:* **Rev Simon Stamp**

■ Cathedral Chapter
(Erected 24 June 1852)
Provost: **Rev Mgr Canon Michael Quinlan**
Canons: **Rev Canons Maurice O'Connell, Eugene Dolan, J Jude Harrison, William Byrne, Thomas Anthony McBride, Mark Davies, Liam Houlihan, Paul Mitcheson.**
Honorary Canons: **Valentine Kamaitis, Charles A Dorran, Francis Deeney, Kevin O'Connor, Joseph Carter, Denis Clinch.**

■ Council of Clergy
(Reconvened 10 December 1997)
Chairman: **Rev Philip Sumner** St Mary with St Patrick, 40 Union Street West, Oldham OL8 1DL **Tel:** 0161-624 4834
Mbl: 07976 230919
E-mail: philip_sumner@tiscali.com
Secretary: **Rev Kieren Mullarkey,** St Peter's, Taylor Street, Middleton M24 1BL
Tel: 0161-643 2168
E-mail: kierenmullarkey@btopenworld.com
Membership: elected ex officio and appointed members.

■ Diocesan Curia
Cathedral House, 250 Chapel Street, Salford, M3 5LL
Tel: 0161-834 0005 **Fax:** 0161-839 5259
E-mail: curia@salforddiocese.org

■ Diocesan Chancery
Chancellor: **Rev Robert Lasia.**

■ Registrar for Deceased Clergy
Diocesan Chancery, **Tel:** 0161-834 0005

■ Diocesan Tribunal
Judicial Vicar: **Rev Christopher Dawson**
Defender of the Bond: **Diana Sliwka**
Notaries: **Sr Bridget O'Hare, Mrs Catherine Clarke, Sr Winefride Mulroy, Mrs Lynda Reynolds.**
Tribunal Administrator: **Mrs Catherine Clarke,** Cathedral House, 250 Chapel Street, Salford M3 5LL
Tel: 0161-834 0005 **Fax:** 0161-839 5259
E-mail: tribunal@salforddiocese.org

■ **Salford Roman Catholic Diocesan Trustees**
Registered Office: Wardley Hall, Worsley, Manchester M28 2ND
Secretary: **Rev Monsignor Thomas Mulheran**.
Tel: 0161-736 1421 **Fax:** 0161-745 9708

■ **Finance**
Financial Secretary: **Rev Monsignor Thomas Mulheran,** 5 Gerald Road, Pendleton, Salford M6 6DL **Tel:** 0161-736 1421 **Fax:** 0161-745 9708
E-mail: finsec@salforddiocese.org
Assistant Financial Secretary: **Rev Anthony J Kay**. *Financial Director:* **Mr Noel Loughrey** (See address above),
E-mail: noel.loughrey@salforddiocese.org
Gift Aid Co-ordinator: **Mrs Denise Walsh** (See address above)
E-mail: giftaid@salforddiocese.org

■ **Department for Administration**

Episcopal Vicar: **Rev Mgr Austin Bulfin,** Salford Diocesan Administration Offices, 5 Gerald Road, Salford M6 6DL
Tel: 0161-736 1421 **Fax:** 0161-745 9708

■ **Board of Administration**
Chairman: **Rev Mgr Austin Bulfin** (*Episcopal Vicar*). *Members:* **Mgr Canon Mark Davies; Revv Henry Jones, David Lupton, Michael Walsh**. *Financial Advisers:* **Rev Mgr Thomas Mulheran, Rev Anthony J Kay, Mr Noel Loughrey**. *Technical Adviser:* **Mr Ed McNally LL.B.**

■ **Department of Evangelisation**
Episcopal Vicar: **Rev Paul Cannon,** Our Good Lady of Counsel and Guardian Angels, Harvey Street, Elton, Bury BL8 2RD
Tel/Fax: 0161-764 1630
E-mail: olgcga@btinternet.com

■ **Office of Ecumenism**
Responsibility for Gtr Manchester: **Rev Mgr Paul F Smith,** St Charles, Moorside Road, Swinton, Manchester M27 3PD
Tel: 0161-794 1089 **Fax:** 0161-727 8077
E-mail: paulsmith@saintcharles.freeserve.co.uk
Responsibility for Lancashire: **Rev Peter Hopkinson,** St John the Baptist, St Johns Road, Padiham BB12 7BN
Tel: 01282 772200
The Diocese is also served by County Ecumenical Officers: Gtr Manchester: **Rev Graham R Kent,** St Peter's House, The Precinct Centre, Oxford Road, Manchester M13 9GH **Tel:** 0161-273 5508 **Fax:** 0161-272 7172 Lancashire: **Terry Garley,** Churches Together in Lancashire Centre-Peace, Fielden Street, Blackburn BB2 1LQ

■ **Office for Liturgy**
Rev James Manock, St Mary 129 Spring Lane, Radcliffe, Manchester M26 2QX,
Tel: 0161-723 2340
E-mail: salfordliturgyoffice@tiscali.co.uk

■ **Department for Formation**
Episcopal Vicar: **Rev Canon T Anthony McBride,** Cathedral House, 250 Chapel Street, Salford M3 5LL
Tel: 0161-834 0333 **Fax:** 0161 834 9596
E-mail: salfordcathedral@aol.com

■ **Religious Education**
Religious Education Centre, Plymouth Grove, Longsight, Manchester M13 0AS
Tel: 0161-256 6200 **Fax:** 0161-256 6201
E-mail: rec@salforddiocese.org
Primary RE Advisers: **Mrs Anne Darby**
Tel: 0161-256 6205
E-mail: adarby@salforddiocese.org
Mrs Margaret Doyle, Tel: 0161-256 6206
E-mail: mdoyle@salforddiocese.org
Secondary RE Adviser: **Mr Bernard Stuart**
RE Inspectors Organiser: **Mr Peter Foley**
Tel: 0161 494 2914

■ **Schools**
Chairman: **Rt Rev Terence J Brain;** *Members:* **Rev Mgr Austin Bulfin, Canon T Anthony McBride, Mr Martin Lochery, Mr David Rushton, Mr Bernard Stuart, Mr David Watson.** *Chair of Primary Heads Executive,* **Mr Michael O'Hare.** *Financial Adviser:* **Rev Martin Saunders**. Diocesan Schools Commission: 5 Gerald Road, Pendleton, Salford M6 6DL
Tel: 0161-736 1421 **Fax:** 0161-745 9708
E-mail: sdc@csss.unet.com

■ **Office for Youth**
Contact through: **Rev Anthony McBride,** Salford Cathedral
Diocesan Youth Ministry Co-ordinator: **Ms Lorraine Leonard,** Youth Office, Religious Education Centre, Plymouth Grove, Longsight, Manchester M13 0AS
Tel: 0161 256 6204 **Fax:** 0161 256 6201
E-mail: youth.worker@salforddiocese.org
Lancashire Youth Officer: **Mr Robert Beardsworth,** Mount Carmel High School, Wordsworth Road, Accrington BB5 0LU
Tel/Fax: 01254-395650
E-mail: bobbeardsworth@netscapeonline.co.uk
Part-time Chaplains: **Revv Kieren Mullarkey, Michael Johonnett;**

■ **Department for Social Responsibility**
Episcopal Vicar: **Rev David Glover,** 67 Kearsley Rd, Higher Crumpsall, Manchester M8 4QJ **Tel:** 0161-720 9626
E-mail: epvicsocresp@salforddiocese.org.uk

■ Faith & Justice

President: **Rev Peter Kinsella**, St Boniface, St Boniface Road, Salford M7 2GE
Tel: 0161-708 9456 **Fax:** 01204-596930
Vice-President: **Ann McGough**, Cathedral House, 250 Chapel Street, Salford M3 5LL
Tel/Fax: 0161-832 1363
E-mail: faith-and-justice@talk21.com
Website: www.salforddiocese.org.uk/faithandjustice
Diocesan Director: **Rev John Sullivan**, St Joseph, 81, Bolton Street, Ramsbottom, Bury BL0 9HY **Tel/Fax:** 01706-823200
Secretary: **Jean Raymond**, 5 Newmarket Mews, Bury New Road, Salford M7 2BX
Tel: 0161-792 9771
Editor of Harambee: **Chris George**, 80 Canada Street, Miles Platting, Manchester M40 8AE *Diocesan Co-ordinator for Asylum Seekers and Refugees:* **Peter Fell**, St Boniface Presbytery, St Boniface Road, Salford
M7 2GE **Tel/Fax:** 0161-792 0282
E-mail: revive01uk@yahoo.co.uk

■ Racial Justice

Chairman: **Rev Michael Waters**, St John's Presbytery, Bracewell Street, Burnley BB10 1TB **Tel:** 01282-423824
E-mail: fr.m.waters@tesco.net

■ Department for Vocation

Episcopal Vicar: **Rev Ian Farrell**, St Joseph's Presbytery, Portland Crescent, Longsight, Manchester M13 0BU
Tel: 0161-224 4035 **Fax:** 0161-256 1781

■ Office for Priestly Vocation

Vocations Director: **Rev David Featherstone**, St Dunstan's Presbytery, Moston Lane, Moston, Manchester M40 9PA
Tel: 0161-681 1410 **Fax:** 0161-682 9045
E-mail: stdunstanmoston@aol.com

■ OTHER DIOCESAN SERVICES

■ Archivist

Rev David Lannon PhD, St Mary, 3 Todmorden Road, Burnley BB10 4AU
Tel: 01282-422007 **Fax:** 01282-424622
E-mail: davelennon@aol.com
Website: www.churches-online.org.uk/salfordarchives
Access to these private archives may be arranged by bona-fide researchers by previous appointment. Please contact the archivist. No genealogical work will be undertaken.

■ Boundaries Board

Chairman: **Mgr John Corcoran**
Officers: **Revv Timothy Hopkins, Michael Waters**; *Consultant:* **Rev David Lannon.**

■ Cemeteries Board

Chairman: **Mr Noel Loughrey**; Cemeteries: St Mary's Cemetery, Manchester Road, Wardley, Worsley, Manchester M28 4UJ
Tel: 0161-794 2194
Fax: 0161-794 9811
St Joseph's Cemetery, Moston Lane, Manchester M40 9QL
Tel: 0161-681 1582 **Fax:** 0161-688 6366

■ Communications & Media

Diocesan Communications Officer: **Rev Michael Walsh RD, Tel:** 0161-330 2777
Fax: 0161-343 5595
E-mail: mwalsh1042@aol.com

■ Child Protection

Chairman: **Mr Michael Devlin**; *Child Protection Co-ordinator:* **Rev Barry O'Sullivan**; *Media Advisor:* **Rev Michael Walsh**; *Ex-officio:* **Rev Dr Gerard Fieldhouse Byrne**; *Secretary:* **Pam Jones.**
Office: Child Protection Commission, Cathedral House, 250 Chapel Street, Salford M3 5LL **Tel/Fax:** 0161-832 8317
E-mail: salford@copca.org.uk

■ **SALFORD**

1. † CATHEDRAL CHURCH OF ST JOHN THE EVANGELIST
(1844; 1848; ded 14 June 1890)
Chapel Street, Salford, Manchester.
Tel: 0161-834 0333 **Fax:** 0161-834 9596
E-mail: cathedral@salforddiocese.org
Canon T Anthony McBride (*Cathedral Dean*); **Rev Francis Webster MHM.** Cathedral House, 250 Chapel Street, Salford M3 5LL *Parish Sister:* **Sr Anne O'Shea**
Tel: 0161-792 9721
M: *Sun 11am, 5.30pm. Hds 8am, 12.10pm, 7.30pm.*
• ***Society of the Holy Child Jesus.*** 21 Canon Hussey Court, Islington Way, Salford M3 5HZ **Tel:** 0161-832 1326
• ***Sisters of the Holy Family,*** 12 Trinity Court, Cleminson Street, Salford M3 6DX **Tel:** 0161-835 3706

■ **ABBEY HILLS**
See Oldham (7).

■ **ACCRINGTON,** Lancs [A]

1. † St Anne
(1897; 1925; ded 26 July 1944)
Cobham Road, Accrington, Lancs BB5 2AD
Tel: 01254-232920
Rev Seamus Quigley.
M: *Sat 1st M of Sun 7pm. Sun 9am, 11am. Hds (vigil 7pm). 9am, 12.15pm.*

2. † St Joseph (1949; 1954)
Belgarth Road, Accrington, Lancs BB5 6AH
Tel: 01254-231754
E-mail: joseph@martinsaunders.org.uk
Rev Martin Saunders.
M: *Sun 8am, 10am. Hds 9.30am.*

■ **ASHTON-UNDER-LYNE,** Lancs

1. † St Ann (1852; 1859)
Burlington Street, Ashton-under-Lyne, Lancs OL6 7DG
Rev Francis Wadsworth (*Chaplain:* Tameside Gen. Hospital). **Rev Josef Wozniak** (*Polish Chaplain:* 01706-642649).
Tel: 0161-330 1194
M: *Sat 1st M of Sun 5.30pm. Sun 9am (Polish) 10.30am. Hds 12.15pm, 6.30pm.*

2. † St Christopher (1951; 1955)
Lees Road, Hurst Cross, Ashton-under-Lyne, Lancs OL6 8BA **Tel:** 0161-330 3262
Rev Myles Sheahan.
M: *Sun 9am, 11am, 6.30pm. Hds (vigil 7pm) 9.15am, 12.15pm.*

3. † St Paul (1962; 1966)
285 Stockport Road, Guide Bridge, Ashton-under-Lyne, Lancs OL7 0NT
Tel: 0161-330 2777 **Fax:** 0161-343 5595
E-mail: mwalsh1402@aol.com

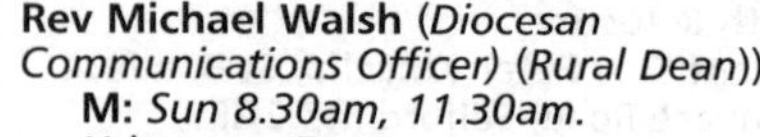

Rev Michael Walsh (*Diocesan Communications Officer*) (*Rural Dean*)).
M: *Sun 8.30am, 11.30am. Hds noon, 7pm.*
• ***Presentation Sisters,*** 111 Audenshaw Road, Audenshaw, Manchester M34 5NL
Tel: 0161-370 2733

■ **BACUP,** Lancs

† St Mary (1852-57; ded 2 July 1929)
Dale Street, Bacup, Lancs OL13 8AP.
Tel: 01706-873243
Rev Michael Twomey.
M: *Sat 1st M of Sun 7pm. Sun 9am. Hds 10am, 8pm.*

■ **BAMBER BRIDGE,** Preston [A]

1. † St Mary (1780; 1820; 1892)
Brownedge Lane, Bamber Bridge, Preston PR5 6SP
Tel: 01772-335168 **Fax:** 01772-332054
Rev Dom Terence Richardson. *Pastoral Assistant:* **Sr Mary Higney.**
M: *Sat 1st M of Sun 7pm. Sun 9.30am, 11am, 6.30pm. Hds 9.30am, 4.30pm, 7.30pm.*

2. † St Benedict's Monastery (1999)
Convent Close, Duddle Lane, Bamber Bridge, Preston PR5 6US
Tel: 01772-902201 **Fax:** 01772-902214
• ***Benedictines (OSB):*** **V.Rev Cassian Dickie** (*Prior*) **Revv Augustine Measures, David O'Brien, Stephen Wright, Francis Davidson, Aelred Burrows, Matthew Burns, Raphael Jones, Terence Richardson.**

■ **BARTON**
All Saints Friary
See Patricroft.

■ **BLACKBURN** [A]

1. † Sacred Heart & St Anne (1900; 1905; 1938)
313 Preston New Road, Blackburn BB2 6PL
Tel: 01254-51808
Rev Michael Lavin.
E-mail: mlavin@sacredheartblackburn.org.uk
Website: sacredheartblackburn.org.uk
M: *Sat 1st M of Sun 6.15pm. Sun 10.30am. Hds 7.30pm, 9am, 12noon.*
Poor Sisters of Nazareth, Nazareth House, Preston New Road, BB2 7AL
Tel: 01254-53000

2. † St Anne's (1849; 1926)
France Street, Blackburn BB2 1LX
Tel: 01254-667150
Rev James Mc Cartney (*Priest-in-Charge*).
Served from Sabden, St Mary
M: *Sun 12.15pm. Hds 12.15pm.*

3. † Christ the King and St Antony (1959; 1962)
North Road, Shadsworth, Blackburn BB1 1PY **Tel:** 01254-55888
Served from St Joseph's, Audley.

M: Sun 10.30am (6.30pm during August). Hds 9.15am.

4. † Our Lady of Perpetual Succour (1955)
Longshaw, Blackburn. **Tel:** 01254-54900
Rev Edmund Willoughby SJ. Our Lady's Presbytery, Pilmuir Road, Blackburn BB2 3JB
M: *Sat 1st M of Sun 5.30pm. Sun 10am. Hds (vigil 6.15pm), 10am.*

5. † St Alban & Good Shepherd
St Alban (1773; 1901; ded 2 Oct 1946)
Larkhill, Blackburn, Lancs BB1 6HY
Tel: 01254-59331
Fax: 01254-668102
E-mail: jude@stalbansrc.freeserve.co.uk
Canon Jude Harrison, Revv Joseph B O'Carroll, Frederick Heptonstall MHM.
M: *Sat 1st M of Sun 7.30pm. Sun 9.15am, 11.15am. Hds 9.30am 12.10pm, 7.30pm.*

6. The Good Shepherd
(1968; con 17th April 1994)
Northfield Road/Earl Street, Blackburn BB1 7ND **Tel:** 01254-661244
M: *Sat 1st M of Sun 6.30pm. Sun 10.15am. Hds 9.30am.*

- ***Marists (SM),*** St Mary's Sixth Form College, Shear Brow, BB1 8AZ (1925; 1931). **Tel:** 01254-580464 **Revv Myles Moriarty** (*Superior*), **Reginald Riley** (*Bursar*). Marists Residence, 40 Columbia Way, Lammack, Blackburn BB2 7DT **Tel:** 01254-57197
- ***Franciscan Missionaries of St Joseph,*** Franciscan Convent, East Park Road, BB1 8BB **Tel:** 01254-53962

7. † St John Vianney (1959; 1969; 1981)
Livesey, Blackburn. **Tel:** 01254-201430
Rev Kevin Griffin. St John's Presbytery, 335 Livesey Branch Road, Blackburn BB2 4QJ
M: *Sat 1st M of Sun 6pm. Sun 9.30am. Hds (vigil 7pm). 9am.*

8. † St Joseph (1869; 1877)
Audley, Blackburn.
Tel: 01254-675534 **Fax:** 01254-279581
Rev Francis Parkinson, St Joseph's Presbytery, 99 Audley Range, Blackburn BB1 1TG
M: *Sun 11am, 6.30pm (No evening mass in August). Hds 7pm.*

8a Blackburn Catholic Hospital Chaplaincy
Tel: 01254-56026
Rev David Chinnery. 149 Bolton Road, Darwen BB3 2PG **Tel/Fax:** 01254-702026

9. † St Peter in Chains
(1889; 1896; 1957)
Mill Hill, Blackburn.
Tel: 01254-51417
E-mail: stpetermillhill@aol.com
Rev Anthony Dutton. St Peter's, Presbytery, Jessel Street, Blackburn BB2 2RQ
M: *Sat 1st M of Sun 7pm. Sun 10.30am. Hds (vigil 7pm). 9am.*

12. † St Teresa of the Child Jesus (1937; 1940)
Bentley Street, Blackburn BB1 3TT
Tel: 01254-56059
Rev Paul Taylor OMI.
M: *Sat 1st M of Sun 6.30pm. Sun 9.30am. Hds 10am.*

13. † Holy Souls (1924; 1925; 1969)
Whalley New Road, Brownhill, Blackburn BB1 9BE **Tel:** 01254-248047
Rev Peter Knowles
E-mail: the parish@holysouls.freeserve.co.uk
M: *Sun 10am, 5pm. Hds (vigil 7pm), 10am.*

■ BLACKROD, Lancs

St Andrew
Hill Lane, Blackrod, Bolton
Tel: 01942-831267 Served from Haigh.

■ BOLTON

1. † The Holy Infant and St Anthony (1877)
Baxendale Street, Astley Bridge, Bolton BL1 6QH **Tel:** 01204-303871
Rev J Colin Wright.
M: *Sat 1st M of Sun 6.30pm. Sun 8.45am, 10.30am, 6.30pm. Hds (vigil 6.30pm). 9am, 11am, 6.30pm.*

- ***Salesians (SDB):*** Thornleigh Salesian House, Sharples Park, BL1 6PQ (1925). **Tel:** 01204-591144 **Revv Anthony Bailey** (*Rector*), **E-mail:** a.bailey@alesians.co.uk; **Ivor Netto, David O'Malley, Hugh Preston, Patrick Sherlock, Andrew Waller, Mervyn Williams, Michael Winstanley.**
- ***Elderly Residence: (SDB):*** St Joseph's, 10 Oldhams Lane, Bolton BL1 6PN **Tel:** 01204-590600 **Revv Terence Aylward, John Bennett, Albert Carette, Robert Coupe, Bernard Higgins, Michael Lindsay, Austin Malloy, George Williams.**

3. † St Brendan (1971 ded 1983)
Harwood, Bolton.
Tel: 01204-301927
Served from St John the Evangelist, Bromley Cross
M: *Sat 1st M of Sun 6.30pm. Sun 9.15am, 11.15am. Hds 9.30am, 7.30pm.*

4. † St Columba
(1931; 1956; ded 12 Dec 1956)
Ripley Street, Tonge Moor, Bolton BL2 3AR
Tel: 01204-303232 **Fax:** 01204-596930
E-mail: frank@prometheus1.demon.co.uk
Rev Francis McCauley.
M: *Sat 1st M of Sun 6pm. Sun 10.15am. Hds 10am, 7.30pm.*

5. † St Edmund (1861)
St Edmund Street, Bolton.
Tel: 01204-525716
Rev David Foster. St Edmund's Presbytery, 14 St Edmund Street, Bolton BL1 2JR
E-mail: anthonygrimshaw@btconnect.com
M: *Sat 1st M of Sun 7pm. Sun 10am. Hds (vigil 5.30pm), 12.15pm.*

6. † St Ethelbert
(1905; 1925; ded 3 May 1960)
Hawthorne Street, Deane, Bolton.
Tel: 01204-62653
Rev Alan Swift, St Ethelbert's Presbytery, 67 Wigan Road, Deane, BL3 5QJ
M: *Sun 9.30am, 11am, 7pm. Hds 9am, 7pm.*
• ***Sisters of the Cross & Passion:*** 3 Cairngorm Drive, Ladybridge, Bolton BL3 4UF **Tel:** 01204-655714

7. † St James the Great (1954)
St James' Presbytery, 58 Bowland Drive, Montserrat, Bolton BL1 5TX
Tel: 01204-840030
E-mail: frpattansey@aol.com
Rev Patrick Tansey.
M: *Sun 10.45am. Hds 10am, 7pm.*
Parish registers at Bolton (12).

8. † St Joseph.
(1879; 1900; ded 19 Mar 1960).
71 Horace Street, Halliwell, Bolton BL1 3PU
Tel/Fax: 01204-524597
Served from Bolton (7).
M: *Sat 1st M of Sun 6pm. Sun 9.15am, Hds 10am, 7pm.*

9. † St Osmund
(1923; 1925; 1961; ded 12 Oct 1967)
Long Lane, Breightmet, Bolton BL2 6EB
Tel: 01204-522770
Rev Geoffrey Hilton.
M: *Sat 1st M of Sun 6.30pm. Sun 8.30am, 11am. Hds 10.00am, 7.15pm (Tridentine Mass)* .

10 † St Patrick (1861)
Great Moor Street, Bolton BL1 1NS
Served from Bolton (5).
M: *Sun 11.15am. Hds 10am.*

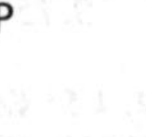

11. † SS Peter and Paul (1800; 1897)
61 Pilkington Street, Bolton BL3 6HP
Tel: 01204-522744
Rev John F McNamara.
M: *Sat 1st M of Sun 6pm. Sun 10.15am. Hds 10am (term-time), 12noon, 7pm (outside term-time).*

12. † St Thomas of Canterbury
(1958; ded 22 Nov 1968)
Lonsdale Road, Heaton, Bolton.
Tel/Fax: 01204-840042
E-mail: wb@stoc.org.uk
Website: www.stoc.org.uk
Canon William Byrne. St Thomas's Presbytery, 132 Lonsdale Road, Bolton BL1 4PN
M: *Sat 1st M of Sun 5pm. Sun 9am, 11am. Hds 9.15am (term-time), 12noon, 7pm.*

13. St Vincent de Paul
(1972; new church ded. 20 Dec 1985)
Rutherford Drive, Over Hulton, Bolton.
Tel: 01204-651695
Rev John Rigby. St Vincent's Presbytery, 40 Newbrook Road, Bolton BL5 1ER
M: *Sat 1st M of Sun 6pm. Sun 10am. Hds 10am, 7pm.*

14. † St William of York
(1936; ded 8 Dec 1954)
Lever Edge Lane, Great Lever, Bolton.
Tel: 01204-62316 **Fax:** 01204-63947
Rev John Mackie. St William's Presbytery, 76a Lever Edge Lane, Bolton BL3 3EN
M: *Sat 1st M of Sun 6.30pm. Sun 10.30am. Hds 9.30am, 7pm.*

14a Royal Bolton Hospital
Chaplain: **Rev Richard Aspden**. 33 Walker Avenue, Great Lever, Bolton BL2 3DY
Tel: 01204-528080

15. The Good Shepherd (Polish)
180 High Street, Bolton BL3 6PL
Tel: 01204-523563
E-mail: darek.kuwaczkadinternet.com
Rev Dariusz Kuwaczka.
M: *Sun 12noon. Hds 3pm.*

16. All Saints (Ukrainian) (1967)
All Saints Presbytery, 104 Lonsdale Road, Bolton BL1 4PN
Tel: 01204-840087
Rev Andrij Bohdon Choma.
M: *Sun 10.30am. Hds 10.30am.*

■ BROMLEY CROSS, Bolton

St John the Evangelist (1967)
The Crescent, Bromley Cross, Bolton BL7 9JP **Tel:** 01204-301927
Rev Michael Cooke (almanac editor),
E-mail: mcooke@salforddiocese.org
Also serves St Brendan, Bolton (3)
M: *Sat 1st M of Sun 6.30pm. Sun 9.30am, 11.15am. Hds 9.30am, 7pm.*

■ BURNLEY, Lancs

1. † Christ the King (1930)
9 Healey Court, Burnley, Lancs BB11 2QJ
Tel: 01282-423270
Rev Brian Kealey.
M: *Sat 1st M of Sun 6.30pm. Sun 10.15am. Hds 7pm.*

2. † St Mary
(Pre-1824; 1849; ded 12 Sept 1929)
Yorkshire Street, Burnley, Lancs.
Tel: 01282-422007 **Fax:** 01282-424622
E-mail: davelannon@aol.com
Website: www.churchesonline.org.uk/stmarysburnley/
Rev David Lannon (*Diocesan Archivist*). St Mary's Presbytery, 3 Todmorden Road, Burnley BB10 4AU
M: *Sat 1st M of Sun 6pm. Sun 9.45am, 11.45am. Hds (vigil 7.30pm). 9am, 12.35pm.*
- ***Franciscan Missionaries of St Joseph,*** Yorkshire Street, Burnley, Lancs BB11 3BS Chaplain: **Rev Gerard Dunne** **Tel:** 01282-833117

3. † St Augustine
(1896; 1963; ded 24 Sept 1980)
Lowerhouse Lane, Burnley, Lancs.
Served from Burnley (4).
M: *Sat 1st M of Sun 6.30pm. Sun 9.30am. Hds 11am, 7.15pm.*
- ***Sisters of Mercy,*** Park Hill Convent School, Padiham Road, BB12 6TG **Tel:** 01282-455622 Convent: **Tel:** 01282-422083 Bishopwood, 54d, Colne Road, Burnley BB10 2LD **Tel:** 01282-39200

4. † St Mary Magdalene
(1887; 1904; new church ded 23 July, 1980)
Gawthorpe Road, Burnley, Lancs BB12 0JP
Tel/Fax: 01282-422502
Rev Michael Haworth
M: *Sat 1st M of Sun 5.30pm. Sun 10.30am. Hds (vigil 7pm). 9.30am.*

4a St Teresa of the Infant Jesus (1980)
Barracks Road, Burnley, Lancs BB11 4SB
Tel: 01282-457100 Served from Burnley (1).
M: *Sun 9am.*

5. † St John the Baptist
(1891; 1908; ded 23 July 1974)
Bracewell Street, Burnley, Lancs BB10 1TB
Tel: 01282-423824
Revv Michael Waters *(Chairman; Racial Justice Commission)*, **Morrough O'Brien**
Pastoral Assistant: **Sister Godric FMSJ**
M: *Sat 1st M of Sun 6.30pm. Sun 9.30am, 11am. Hds (vigil 7pm). 9.15am, 12noon.*

■ **BURY,** Lancs
1. † Our Lady of Good Counsel and Guardian Angels (1886; 1957, ded 21 Oct 1966)
Harvey Street, Elton, Bury, Lancs BL8 2RD
Tel/Fax: 0161-764 1630
E-mail: olgcga@btinternet.com
Website: www.guardianangels-parish.org
Rev Paul Cannon RD (Head of Dept for Evangelisation. Also in residence: **Rev Francis Fitzpatrick** (retired).
M: *Sat 1st M of Sun 7pm. Sun 8.45am, 10.15am. Hds 9am, 7.30pm.*

2. † St Marie (1825; 1842)
Manchester Road, Bury, Lancs BL9 0DR
Tel: 0161-764 1048
E-mail: stmarie@bury34.freeserve.co.uk
Rev Paul Carr.
M: *Sun 9.30am, 11.15am, 5pm. Hds (vigil 7pm). 9am, 12.15pm.*
- ***Daughters of the Cross,*** 184 Manchester Road, Bury, Lancs BL9 9BD **Tel:** 0161-764 1875

3. St Joseph and St Bede (1861)
Peter Street, Bury, Lancs BL9 6AB
Tel: 0161-764 4240
E-mail: romorrow@btinternet.com
Rev Robert Morrow.
M: *Sat 1st M of Sun 6pm. Sun 10am. Hds 12.15pm, 8pm.*

■ **CASTLETON,** Rochdale
† St Gabriel and The Angels (1879; 1953)
Milne Street, Castleton, Rochdale.
Tel: 01706-631973 **Fax:** 01706-861101
E-mail: gabriels@globalnet.co.uk
Rev Barry Lomax. St Gabriel's Presbytery, Smalley Street, OL11 3EB
M: *Sat 1st M of Sun 6.30pm. Sun 11am. Hds 9am, 7.30pm.*

■ **CHADDERTON,** Oldham
† St Herbert (1916; 1917; 1957)
148 Broadway, Chadderton, Oldham OL9 0JY
Tel/Fax: 0161-624 2258
Rev Peter McKie (Rural Dean).
Email: peter@pmckie.wanadoo.co.uk
M: *Sat 1st M of Sun 6.30pm. Sun 9.30am, 11am. Hds 9.30, 7pm.*

■ **CHIPPING,** Preston
† St Mary (1828; 1928; ded 12 Mar 1928)
School Lane, Chipping, Preston.
Tel/Fax: 01995-61238
Rev Anthony Grimshaw. St Mary's Presbytery, Longridge Road, PR3 2QD
Email: bosullibe@aol.com
M: *Sun 10.30am. Hds 10am.*

■ **CLAYTON-LE-MOORS,** Accrington
† St Mary
(1819; ded 23 June 1948; new church 1958)
Devonshire Drive, Clayton-le-Moors, Accringtion BB5 5RJ
Tel: 01254-232348 **Fax:** 01254-392583
Email: clergy@stmarys-c-l-m.org.uk
Website: www.stmarys-c-l-m.org.uk
Rev Peter Tierney.
M: *Sat 1st M of Sun 7pm. Sun 10am. Hds 9.15am, 8pm.*

■ **CLITHEROE,** Lancs
† St Michael and St John the Evangelist (1797; 1850)
Lowergate, Clitheroe, Lancs BB7 1AG
Tel: 01200-423307 **Mbl:** 07791 692610
E-mail: news@smjchurch.fsnet.co.uk
Mgr John Corcoran
• ***Jesuits (SJ)****: Parish Sister:*
Eileen Pollard SND
M: *Sat 1st M of Sun 6.30pm. Sun 10am, Hds (vigil 7.30pm), 11am.*

■ **COLNE,** Lancs
† The Sacred Heart (1871; 1897)
Queen Street, Colne, Lancs BB8 9NB
Tel: 01282-863135
Rev James Tubman.
M: *Sat 1st M of Sun 6.30pm. Sun 10.30am. Hds 9am, 7pm.*
• ***Daughters of Jesus,*** Southworth, 6 Netherheys Close, Colne, Lancs BB8 9QY
Tel: 01282-859622

■ **DARWEN,** Lancs
1. † St Joseph (1856; ded 1 May 1975)
149 Bolton Road, Darwen, Lancs BB3 2PG
Tel: 01254-702026
E-mail: stjosephdarwen@btinternat.co.uk
Mgr Peter Wilkinson.
M: *Sat 1st M of Sun 6.15pm. Sun 9am. Hds (vigil 7pm). 9am.*

2. † The Sacred Heart and St Edward (1878; 1883; ded 6 Dec 1950)
370 Blackburn Road, Darwen, Lancs BB3 0AA **Tel:** 01254-702525
E-mail: sacredheartandstedward@btinternat.co.uk
Website: www.stedwards.tk
Rev John Dugdale.
M: *Sun 11am, 5.30pm. Hds 11am, 7pm.*

■ **DAVYHULME,** Urmston
† Our Lady of the Rosary (1961)
Davyhulme Road, Davyhulme, Urmston.
Served from English Martyrs, Urmston.
M: *Sun 9.30am. Hds 9.30am.*

■ **DENTON,** Manchester
1. † St Mary, (Our Lady of Sorrows) (1889; 1963)
Market Street, Denton, Manchester.
Tel: 0161-336 2358
Rev Vincent Cavey. St Mary's Presbytery, Duke Street, Denton M34 2AN.
M: *Sun 10.30am, 6pm. Hds 9.15am, 12.35pm, 8pm.*

2. † Holy Family (1954; 1955)
Wainwright Avenue, Denton.
Tel: 0161-223 2930
Rev Anthony Petty. Holy Family Presbytery, Thornley Lane North, Reddish, Stockport SK5 6QR
M: *Sat 1st M of Sun 6.30pm. Sun 10am. Hds 9.30am, 6.30pm.*

3. St John Fisher
(1965; New Church Dec 1983)
Haughton Green, Denton.
Tel: 0161-336 2625 Fax: 0161-336 2964
Rev Peter Gooden. St John Fisher's Presbytery, Mancunian Road, Haughton Green, Denton M34 7WN
M: *Sat 1st M of Sun 6pm. Sun 9.30am. Hds (vigil 7.30pm), 9.15am.*

■ **DROYLSDEN,** Manchester
† St Stephen
(1935; 1938; 1959; ded 12 May 1960)
38 Chappell Road, Droylsden, Manchester M43 7NA **Tel:** 0161-370 1505
E-mail: william@dilis.demon.co.uk
Website: dilis.demon.co.uk/index.htm
Rev William Fallon.
M: *Sun 9am, 11.30am. Hds (vigil 8pm). 12noon.*

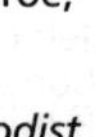

■ **DUNSOP BRIDGE,** Clitheroe, Lancs
† St Hubert (1864)
Trough Road, Dunsop Bridge, Clitheroe, BB7 3BG **Tel:** 01200-448231
Rev John Chaloner.
M: *Sat 1st M of Sun 6pm (Methodist Church, West Bradford). Sun 9am. Hds As announced.*

■ **ECCLES,** Manchester
1. † St Mary (1879; 1898; ded 29 Oct 1952)
Church Street, Eccles, Manchester M30 0LU
Tel: 0161-789 3236 **Fax:** 0161-707 5044
E-mail: stmaryeccles@cwcom.net
Rev Robert Livesey, St Mary's Presbytery, Oxford Street, Manchester M30 0LU
Tel: 0161-789 3236
M: *Sun 10.15am, 6pm. Hds (vigil 6.30pm). 10am (term time only), 12noon.*
• ***De La Salle Brothers (Elancio English School),*** St John's, 19 Ellesmere Road, M30 9HP **Tel:** 0161-789 2550
Hospital Chaplaincy: **Rev Francis Waterworth. Tel:** 0161-787 5167 (office), 0161-789 4470 (home)
E-mail: frank.waterworth@srht.nhs.uk
M: *Hope Hospital; Sun 4pm; Ladywell Hospital; Sat 1st M of Sun 4pm. Hds 12.10pm (Hope).*

2. † St Gilbert (1959)
Brookhouse, Peel Green, Eccles, Manchester M30 7PQ **Tel:** 0161-799 0144
Rev Terence McCann, 3 Highfield Avenue, Mossley Common, Worsley, Manchester M28 1AL **Tel:** 0161-799 0144
M: *Sun 10am. Hds 9am, 7pm.*

■ **FAILSWORTH,** Manchester
† Immaculate Conception (St Mary)
(1845; 1964; ded 8 Dec 1973)
Clive Road, Failsworth, Manchester M35 0NN **Tel:** 0161-681 1835
E-mail: pjnmck@aol.com
Rev Patrick J McKeown.
M: *Sun 10.15am, 6pm. Hds 9.30am, 7.30pm.*

■ **FARNWORTH,** Bolton
1. **† Our Lady of Lourdes** (1931; 1957)
Highfield, Farnworth, Bolton.
Tel/Fax: 01204-572380
Mobile: 07713-640816
E-mail: olol.stgreg@btinternet.com
Rev Gerald Murphy. Our Lady's Presbytery, 275 Plodder Lane, Farnworth, Bolton BL4 0BR
M: *Sat 1st M of Sun 6.30pm. Sun 9.30am. Hds am as announced, 7.15pm.*

2. **† St Gregory the Great.**
(1853; 1875; ded 12 June 1946)
Church Street, Farnworth, Bolton BL4 8AQ
Served from Our Lady of Lourdes, Farnworth.
M: *Sun 11.15am. Hds As announced*

■ **FENISCOWLES,** Blackburn
St Paul's
Church Hall. Served from Pleasington.
M: *Sat 1st M of Sun 7pm. Hds (vigil 7pm).*

■ **FLIXTON,** Manchester
St Monica (1953; 1968)
Woodsend Road South, Flixton M41 6QB
Tel: 0161-748 4590
Rev Bernard Charnock.
M: *Sat 1st M of Sun 5.30pm Sun 10am. Hds 10am, 7pm.*

■ **GREAT HARWOOD,** Blackburn
1. **† Our Lady and St Hubert** (ded 1 Nov 1859)
St Hubert Street, Great Harwood, Blackburn BB6 7BE
Served from St Wulstan's.
M: *Sun 9am. Hds (vigil 7pm).*

2. **† St Wulstan** (1912; 1937)
Rushton Street, Great Harwood, Blackburn BB6 7JQ **Tel/Fax:** 01254-884211
E-mail: aclarke@ntlworld.com
Rev Anthony Clarke.
M: *Sat 1st M of Sun 6.30pm. Sun 11am 6.30pm. Hds 9.30am.*

■ **HAIGH,** Wigan
1. **† Our Lady of the Immaculate Conception**
(1854; ded 25 Apr 1958)
Haigh Road, Aspull, Haigh, Wigan WN2 1YA **Tel:** 01942-516732
Rev Kevin Foulkes.
M: *Sat 1st M of Sun 6pm. Sun 9am. Hds 9am, 11am (in school in term time).*

2. **St Andrew**
Hill Lane, Blackrod, Lancs (Chapel of Ease).
M: *Sun 11am. Hds 7pm.*

■ **HASLINGDEN,** Lancs
1. **† The Immaculate Conception**
(1854; 1859; ded 17 May 1958)
Bury Road, Haslingden, Lancs BB4 5PG
Tel: 01706-215642 **Rev Richard O'Connor.**
Email: ichaslingden@boltblue.com
M: *Sat 1st M of 6.30pm. Sun 9.30am. Hds (vigil 7pm), 11am.*

2. **† St Veronica** (1959)
Helmshore, Rossendale, Haslingden, Lancs.
Served from Immaculate Conception, Haslingden.
M: *Sun 11am. Hds 9.15am.*

■ **HEATON MERSEY,** Stockport
St Winifred (1911; 1940; 1951)
Mauldeth Road, Heaton Mersey, Stockport SK4 3NB
Tel: 0161-432 4412 **Fax:** 0161-975 0120
E-mail: mrq@mrquinlan.me.uk
Rev Mgr Provost Michael R Quinlan, Rev William Foley.
M: *Sun 8.30am, 10am, 11.30am, 6.30pm. Hds (vigil 7.30pm), 9.15am, 7.30pm.*
• ***Sisters of Charity of St Paul,*** St Winifred's Convent, 1 Thornhill Road, SK4 3HJ. **Tel:** 0161-432 1722

■ **HEATON NORRIS,** Stockport
† St Mary (1867; 1897; ded 22 Aug 1952)
Roman Road, Heaton Norris, Stockport SK4 1RF
Served from St Winfred's, Heaton Mersey
M: *Sun 10am.Hds 9.30am, 7.30pm.*
• ***Sacred Heart Fathers (SCJ):*** St John's, 266 Wellington Rd North, Stockport SK4 2QR **Tel:** 0161 442 4117
Fax: 0161 282 6334
Email: prov@heartscj.fsnet.co.uk
Revv Hugh Hanley, *(Provincial & Superior),* **Gerard Jordan, Seamus Jones, Michael Walshe, Br Richard Moran, Br Joseph Tormey.**

■ **HEYWOOD,** Lancs
1. **† Our Lady and St Paul**
(1963; 1969; ded 2 Feb 1985)
Argyle Street, Heywood, Lancs OL10 3PB
Tel: 01706-360774 **Fax:** 01706-361189
Rev James Ryan.
M: *Sat 1st M of Sun 6.30pm. Sun 10am. Hds (vigil 6.30pm). 9.30am.*

2. **† St Joseph**
(1856; 1915; ded 17 May 1934)
Mary Street, Heywood, Lancs OL10 1EG
Tel/Fax: 01706-369777
Rev Paul Daly

E-mail: pdaly@salforddiocese.org
M: *Sun 9am, 11am, 6.30pm. Hds 9.15am (in primary school). 12.30pm, 6.30pm.*

■ **HOLLINWOOD,** Oldham
1. † Corpus Christi (1878; 1904; 1933)
8 Derby Street, Chadderton, Hollinwood, OL9 7HX **Tel:** 0161-624 2008
Rev Dermot Heakin.
M: *Sat 1st M of Sun 5.30pm. Sun 10am. Hds 10am, 7pm.*
• ***Polish Catholic Centre,*** "Sunnyside", Chamber Road, OL8 4NZ
Tel: 0161-624 5505
• ***Sisters of Mercy,*** 5 Werneth Grange, Grange Avenue OL8 4EN
Tel: 0161-624 1933
2. † Holy Family
(1957; 1958; ded 4 March 1988)
407 Roman Road, Limeside, Hollinwood OL8 3PY **Tel:** 0161-681 3872
Fax: 0161-681 9731 **E-mail:** holyfamily@limeside.freeserve.co.uk
Rev William Molloy.
M: *Sat 1st M of Sun 5.30pm. Sun 11am. Hds (vigil 7pm). 10am.*
• ***Missionary Sisters of Christ the King.*** Montgomery House, Hawthorn Road OL8 4NZ **Tel:** 0161-688 5829

■ **HORWICH,** Bolton, Lancs
1. † St Mary (1886; 1906)
86 Chorley New Road, Horwich, Bolton BL6 5QJ **Tel:** 01204-468209
Email: henryjones4@hotmail.com
Rev Henry Jones RD.
M: *Sun 8.30am, 11am, 6.30pm. Hds (vigil 7.30pm). 12noon.*

2. † St Anthony
Chorley New Road, Chapel-of-Ease.
Served from Horwich (1).
M: *Sun 9.45am. Hds 9.30am.*

■ **HUNCOAT,** Accrington
Our Lady's (1931)
Served from Accrington (3).
M: *Sat 1st M of Sun 6pm. Hds (vigil 7pm).*

■ **HURST GREEN,** Nr Blackburn
St Joseph
Served from Stonyhurst College.
Tel: 01254-826268.
M: *Sun 10am, 7pm. Hds 10am, 7pm.*

■ **IRLAM,** Manchester
1. † St Joseph the Worker
(1963; ded 24 June 1965)
Tel: 0161-775 3788
Rev Lionel Devany. St Joseph's Presbytery, Cutnook Lane, M44 6JX
M: *Sat 1st M of Sun 6pm. Sun 8.30am, 10.30am. Hds 9am, 6.30pm.*

2. † St Teresa (1874; 1902)
Liverpool Road, Irlam, Manchester.
Tel: 0161-775 2469
Revv Desmond O'Driscoll, Joseph Corcoran. The Presbytery, 65 Baines Ave, Irlam, Manchester M44 6AB
M: *Sun 10am, 7.15pm. Hds (vigil 7pm). 9am (9.15am during school term).*
• ***Sacred Heart,*** Lord's Street, Cadishead (Chapel of Ease).
M: *Sat 1st M of Sun 6.30pm, Sun 3.30pm. Hds 7pm.*

■ **KEARSLEY,** Bolton, Lancs
† St John Fisher (1961)
Manchester Road, Kearsley, Bolton BL4 8QQ
Rev Duncan McVicar (*Priest-in-Charge*).
Tel: 01204-572077/796090
Fax: 01204-573809
E-mail: fathers@schoenstatt.org.uk
M: *Sun 9am. Hds 7.30pm.*

■ **LANGHO,** Blackburn
† St Mary (1836; 1959; ded 10 Oct 1984)
York Lane, Langho, Blackburn BB6 8DW
Tel/Fax: 01254-248186 **Rev Sean Horgan.**
M: *Sat 1st M of Sun 6pm. Sun 10am. Hds (vigil 7.30pm). 9.30am.*

■ **LEES,** Oldham
1. † St Edward (1872; 1901; 1950)
Spring Lane, Lees, Oldham OL4 5AJ
Tel: 0161-624 3762 **Canon Eugene Dolan**
E-mail: edolan@tiscali.co.uk
Website: www.saintedwards.co.uk
M: *Sun 9.30am, 11.30am, 7pm. Hds 9.30am, 12noon, 7.30pm.*

■ **LITTLE HULTON,** Worsley, Manchester
1. † Our Lady and the Lancashire Martyrs (1959)
Kenyon Way, Little Hulton, Worsley, Manchester. **Tel:** 0161-790 5221
Parish Sister: **Sr Anne** Served from St Edmund's.
M: *Sun 11.30am. Hds (vigil 7pm).*
• ***Daughters of Charity (SVP),*** Our Lady's Presbytery, Hallstead Avenue M38 0DL
Tel: 0161-790 5765
2. † St Edmund, King and Martyr (1876; 1900)
Bridgewater Street, Little Hulton, Manchester M38 9ND **Tel:** 0161-790 2104
Rev Leo Heakin.
M: *Sun 10.30am, 6pm. Hds 9.15am, 7.15pm.*
3. † St Joseph (1961)
Tel: 0161-790 4648
Rev Kevin Tierney. St Joseph's Presbytery, Old Lane, Manchester M38 9RU
Email: kierenmullarkey@btopenworld.com
M: *Sat 1st M of Sun 6pm. Sun 9.30am. Hds 9.15am, 7pm.*

■ **LITTLE LEVER,** Bolton, Lancs
St Teresa (1963; 1975)
Redcar Road, Little Lever, Bolton BL3 1EN
Served from St Mary's Radcliffe.
M: *Sun 10.15am. Hds (vigil 7pm), 9.15am.*

■ **LITTLEBOROUGH,** Lancs A
† St Mary of the Annunciation
(1879; 1910; 1930; ded Oct 16, 1979)
40 Featherstall Road, Littleborough, Lancs OL15 8DW **Tel:** 01706-378261
E-mail: stmarys@annunciation.co.uk
Website: www.annunciation.co.uk
Rev Arthur C Nearey.
M: *Sun 8.30am, 11.15am. Hds 9.30am, 7pm.*

■ **LONGRIDGE,** Preston A
† St Wilfrid
(1869; 1909; ded 14 Aug 1926; 1st May 1991)
44 Derby Road, Longridge, Preston PR3 3JT
Tel/Fax: 01772-782641
E-mail: stwilfridlong@aol.com
Very Rev Canon Paul Mitcheson RD.
M: *Sat 1st M of Sun 5.30pm. Sun 9.30am. Hds (vigil 7.30pm), 9.30am.*
- ***St William Centre for Mission Awareness,*** Lee House, Chipping Road, Thornley, Preston PR3 2TB
Tel: 01772-782381

■ **LOSTOCK HALL,** Preston A
† Our Lady of Lourdes and St Gerard Majella
(1891; 1913 - cons 1995)
Lourdes Avenue, Lostock Hall, Preston.
Linked to St Benedict's Monastery.
Rev Dom Xavier Ho OSB.
- ***Benedictines (OSB):*** St Gerard's, Brownedge Road, Lostock Hall, Preston PR5 5AA **Tel/Fax:** 01772-335387

E-mail: saintgerards.org.uk
M: *Sat 1st M of Sun 6pm. Sun 10am, 6pm. Hds (vigil 7pm). 9.15am, 7pm (Christmas excepted).*

■ **MANCHESTER** A
1. † Christ the King
(1937; 1939; ded 25 Feb 1975)
Amos Avenue, Newton Heath, Manchester M40 2RS **Tel:** 0161-681 3055
Fax: 0161-681 1183
Email: a.denneny@btinternet.com
Rev E Alan Denneny RD.
M: *Sun 9am, 11.30am. Hds Eve 7.30pm, 12noon.*

3. † The Holy Name
(1868; 1871; ded 6 June 1923)
Oxford Road, Chorlton-on-Medlock, Manchester M13 3PG **Tel:** 0161-273 2435
Website: www.holyname.co.uk
Revv Raymond Matus *(Clifton),* **Christopher Hilton.**
M: *Sun 7.30am, 11am (Sol), 4pm (Latin Trid). Hds (vigil 5.15pm), 7am, 12.30pm, 5.15pm (sung).*
- ***Manchester University Catholic Chaplaincy,*** 338-339 Oxford Road Manchester M13 9PG
Tel: 0161-273 1456;
E-mail: info@rc-chaplaincy-um.org.uk
Website: www.rc-chaplaincy-um.org.uk
Chaplain: **Rev Ian G Kelly MPhil.**
Chaplaincy Team: **Sr Kevina Byrne FMSJ, Monica Zuniga Cobos MCR Karina Bohorquez MCR**; *Librarian:* **Miss Naomi Young MA;** *Administer:* **Mr James Crowley** BA(Hons)
M: *Sun (for UM, MMU & RNCM) 9.15am, 7pm.*

4. † Sacred Heart and St Francis of Assisi (1901; 1926; 1962)
Levenshulme Road, Gorton, Manchester. M18 7WJ
Tel: 0161-223 0338, **Fax:** 0161-230 8414
E-mail: andrewstringfellow@yahoo.com
Website: sacredheartandstfrancis.co.uk
Rev Andrew Stringfellow,
Parish Sisters: **Sr Rosario, Sr Teresa.**
M: *Sun 10.30am. Hds 11am.*
- ***Congregation of Christian Brothers:*** 47 Knutsford Road, Gorton, Manchester M18 7NJ **Tel:** 0161-223 3187
- ***Presentation Sisters,*** 47 Brookhurst Road, Gorton, Manchester M18 7ND **Tel:** 0161-220 9554

5. † Our Lady of Mount Carmel
(1885; 1908; ded 16 July 1945)
Old Road, Blackley, Manchester.
Tel: 0161-740 2071 **Fax:** 0161-740 6269
E-mail: fr.bryan@schoenstatt.org.uk
Website: www.schoenstatt.co.uk
Mount Carmel Presbytery, Wilson Road, Manchester. M9 8BG
Clergy: **Revv Bryan Cunningham, Anbuthurai Thomas, Raymond Paprakkada** (Schoenstatt Fathers).
M: *Sat 1st M of Sun 6.30pm. Sun 9am, 10.30am. Hds 9.15am, 7pm.*
- ***Daughters of the Cross,*** Convent, 2 Levedale Road, Blackley, M9 2JA
Tel: 0161-795 8919

6. † Our Lady and St John
(1892; 1927; ded 1929)
Chorlton-cum-Hardy, Manchester M21 9EE
Tel: 0161-881 3558 **Fax:** 0161-860 0158
Rev Patrick McMahon.
M: *Sat 1st M of Sun 6pm. Sun 9am, 12noon. Hds 10am, 7.30pm.*

6a † St Theresa's
Bedford Road, Firswood M16 See Stretford.
M: *Sun 10.30am, Wkd 10am, Hds 10am.*

7. † Our Lady, St Wilfrid and St Lawrence
Moss Side, Old Trafford, Hulme.
Rev Patrick Deegan, Our Lady's Presbytery, Raby Street, Mossside, Manchester M16 7JQ
Tel/Fax: 0161-226 1730
E-mail: ourladys.innercity@zoom.co.uk
M: *Sun 11.30am. Hds (vigil 7.30pm).*

- ***Sisters of St Joseph of the Apparition,*** 26 Barnhill Street, Moss Side, M14 4S. **Tel:** 0161-226 5805.
- ***Institute of the Blessed Virgin Mary, Loreto Sisters,*** 15 St Mary's Street, Hulme, Manchester M15 5WB; also 26 Blanchard Street, Hulme, Manchester M15 7PQ
- ***Sisters of Our Lady of the Cenacle,*** 4 Old Birley Street, Hulme, Manchester M15 5RG **Tel:** 0161-226 1241 **E-mail:** cenacle.centre@virgin.net
- ***The Jericho Benedictine Society,*** Morning Star Hostel, 104 Denmark Road, Manchester M15 6JS **Tel:** 0161-686 0606. **Bros Brian Quinn and Peter Petkevicius**
- ***Daughters of Charity (SVP),*** St Wilfrid's, 4 Birchvale Close, Hulme, Manchester M15 5BJ **Tel:** 0161-226 9561

7a St Alphonsus
Powell Street, Old Trafford M16
See Stretford.
M: *Sun 10.15am, Wkd 9.30am, Hds 9.30am.*

8. † St Mary (The Hidden Gem)
(1794; 1848; ded 5 apr 1926)
17 Mulberry Street, Manchester. M2 6LN
Tel: 0161-834 3547 **Fax:** 0161-257 0036
Rev Canon Denis Clinch.
Website: www.hiddengem.papalnet.co.uk
M: *Sat 1st M of Sun 5.15pm. Sun 10.15am, 12noon. Hds (vigil 5.05pm). 12noon, 1.05pm.*

9. † St Mary of the Angels and St Clare
(1853; 1883; 1957; 1975; ded 25 May, 1983)
Stockport Road, Levenshulme, Manchester.
Tel: 0161-248 8836 **Fax:** 0161-257 0026
E-mail: stmaryslevenshulme@yahoo.co.uk
Rev John Ahern. St Mary's Presbytery, Elbow Street, Manchester. M19 3PY
M: *Sat 1st M of Sun 6.30pm. Sun 11am. Hds 9.30am, 7.30pm.*

10. † St Ambrose
(1932; 1958: ded 10 Sept 1982)
Princess Road, Chorlton, Manchester M21 7QA **Tel:** 0161-445 1653
E-mail: pearley@pearley.plus.com
Rev Patrick Earley.
M: *Sat 1st M of Sun 7pm. Sun 9am, 11am. Hds 12noon, 6pm.*

- ***Franciscan Missionaries of St Joseph,*** Franciscourt, 45 Manor Drive M21 2QG. **Tel:** 0161-445 9368

11. † St Anne with St Brigid (1848; 1978)
Carruthers Street, Ancoats, Manchester M4 7EQ
Tel: 0161-273 2813 **Fax:** 0161-273 2813
E-mail: tim@vincents.fslife.co.uk
Website: www.stanne-stbrigid.co.uk
Rev Timothy Hopkins.
M: *Sun 11.45am, 6.30pm. Hds 9.30am, 7pm.*

A

11a † St Brigid
(1879; 1901; new church ded 10 May 1996)
Grey Mare Lane, Manchester M11 3DR
Served from Manchester (11).
M: *Sat 1st M of Sun 6.30pm, Sun 10.30am.*

A

12. † St Anne
(1917; 1921; 1957. ded 26 July 1975)
Crescent Road, Crumpsall, Manchester.
Tel: 0161-740 2448
Revv David Glover (Bishop's Advisor in Health Care, Chaplaincy: Head of Dept. for Social Responsibilty) **Simon Firth.** St Anne's Presbytery, 1 Crumpsall Crescent, Manchester M8 5UD
M: *Sun 10.30am, 6pm. Hds 8am, 9.15am, 7pm.*

A

13. † St Anne (1849; 1883)
Fairfield, Higher Openshaw, Manchester.
Tel: 0161-370 1615
Rev James Clarke. St Anne's Presbytery, 1537 Ashton Old Road, Manchester M11 1GR
Email: revjimclarke@yahoo.co.uk
M: *Sat 1st M of Sun 6.30pm. Sun 10.30am. Hds 9.30am, 7pm.*

14. † St Augustine & Catholic Chaplaincy Centre (1820; 1908; 1940; 1968)
Metropolitan University/Royal Northern College of Music, Grosvenor Square, All Saints, Manchester M15 6BW
Tel: 0161-236 6762 **Fax:** 0161-228 1516
Tel: 247 3496 (MMU Chaplaincy)
E-mail: augustines@eggconnect.net
Website: saintaugustines.org.uk
Rev Christopher Dawson (*Priest-in-Charge*); *Chaplain:* **Mr Bernard Burke;** *Pastoral Assistant:* **Miss Naomi Young MA.**
M: *Sun 11am, 5pm. Hds 8.30pm, 12.30pm.*

15. † St Bernard (1941; 1959)
Burnage Lane, Manchester M19 1DR
Tel: 0161-432 3628 **Fax:** 0161-432 8502
Email: stbernardsburnage@aol.com
Awaiting Appointment
M: *Sun 10am, 6pm. Hds 9.30am, 7pm.*

16. † St Bernadette (1958; 1960)
Princess Road, Withington, Manchester M20 1HH
Tel: 0161-445 7911
Email: stbernadette2004@aol.com
Served from St Cuthberts, Manchester (20)
M: *Sat 1st M of Sun 5pm (In Marist convent). Sun 10am, 4pm. Hds 12noon, 7.30pm*
- ***Marist Sisters,*** 113 Nell Lane, Chorlton-cum-Hardy, Manchester M21 2SW **Tel:** 0161-881 4528 **M:** *Sat 1st M of Sun 5pm.*

17. † St Catherine of Siena
(1928; 1929; 1957 ded 6 Oct 1988)
School Lane, Didsbury, Manchester M20 6HS
Tel: 0161- 445 2079 or 446 2069
Fax: 0161- 613 2851
E-mail: parish@stcaths.org.uk
Website: www.stcaths.org.uk
Revv Bernard Wilson, David McGarry *(Pastor Emeritus).*
M: *Sat 1st M of Sun 7pm. Sun 8am, 9.30am, 11am. Hds 8am, 10am, 12noon, 8pm.*
- ***Franciscan Missionaries of St Joseph,*** Convent of Our Lady of Lourdes, 44 Ruabon Road, Didsbury, Manchester M20 0LN **Tel:** 0161-445 4720
- ***Xaverian Brothers,*** 20 Bellfield Road, Didsbury. M20 0BH **Tel:** 0161-445 5273
- ***Opus Dei Prelature:*** 1 Pine Road, M20 6UY. **Tel:** 0161-445 6480 **Revv Peter Haverty, Peter Bristow**; also at Rydalwood, 43 Pine Road M20 0UZ **Tel:** 0161-445 1168

18. † St Chad
(1773; 1776; ded 3 Aug 1847)
7 Stock Street, Cheetham Hill, Manchester M8 8GG **Tel:** 0161-834 4699
Rev John Wisdom *(Priest in Charge).*
M: *Sun 9.45am, 11.30am. Hds 12.20pm, 8pm.*

19. † St Clare's (1929; 1938; 1958)
186 Victoria Avenue, Higher Blackley, Manchester M9 0RR
Tel: 0161-740 4161 **Fax:** 0161-740 1261
- ***Franciscans (Friars Minor Conventual) (OFM Conv):*** **Revv David Young** (*Parish Priest, Guardian*), **Andrew Fraser, Colmcille Murphy.** **M:** *Sat 1st M of Sun 6pm. Sun 8am, 10.30am. Hds 9.30am, 12noon, 7.30pm.*
- ***Good Shepherd Sisters,*** Convent of the Good Shepherd, 114 Chain Road, Blackley, Manchester M9 6QP **Tel:** 0161-643 2610 *Chaplain:* **Rev Mgr Austin Bulfin.** Presbytery, 1 Chain Road M9 6GN **Tel:** 0161-643 2595
- ***St Euphrasia's Nursing Home,*** 116 Chain Road, Blackley, Manchester M9 2GN **Tel:** 0161-643 2010
- ***Contemplative Sisters of the Good Shepherd,*** St Mary's, 114 Chain Road, Blackley, Manchester M9 6QP **Tel:** 0161-643 7656
- ***Marian Community of Reconciliation,*** Holy Mother of Faith Formation House, 112 Chain Road, Blackley, Manchester M9 6GN **Tel:** 0161-653 9777

20. † St Cuthbert (1874; 1881; 1902)
3 Palatine Road, Withington, Manchester M20 3LH **Tel/Fax:** 0161-445 1080
E-mail: brendan.curley@ntlworld.com
E-mail: timewarp.co.uk/personal/stcuthbert
Revv Brendan Curley, Robin Colpman.
M: *Sat 1st M of Sun 6pm. Sun 10am, 12noon, 5.30pm. Hds 12noon, 8pm.*

21. † St Dunstan
(1912-13; 1937, ded 23 Aug 1950)
Moston Lane, Moston, Manchester M40 9PA
Tel: 0161-681 1410 **Fax:** 0161-682 9045
E-mail: stdunstanmoston@aol.com
Rev David Featherstone (Vocations Director).
M: *Sat 1st M of Sun 7pm. Sun 10.15am. Hds (vigil 7.30pm), 9.30am (term time only), 12noon.*

22. † St Edward
(1861; 1862; ded 10 May 1981)
Thurloe Street, Rusholme, Manchester M14 5SG **Tel:** 0161-224 2589
Served from Manchester (28).
Pastoral Assistant:
Maria del Pilar Jensson MCR
M: *Sun 10am, 6.30pm. Hds 10am.*
- ***Marian Community of Reconciliation.,*** St Edward's Presbytery, 13 Thurloe Street, Rusholme, Manchester M14 5SG **Tel:** 0161-224 2589 **Email:** stedwards7924348@aol.com
- ***African Missions Society (SMA):*** Provincialate: 378 Upper Brook Street, Manchester M13 0EP **Tel:** 0161-224 4949 **Fax:** 0161-248 0241 **E-mail:** thomasjryan@compuserve.com **Rev Thomas Ryan** (*Provincial*). St Augustine's, 2 Anson Road, Victoria Park, Manchester M14 5BG **Tel:** 0161-224 7409 **Revv Patrick Connolly, Wacklaw Dominik.**
- ***Sisters of the Cross and Passion,*** St Gabriel's Hall for University Students (Women), 1 Oxford Place, Victoria Park, Manchester M14 5RP **Tel:** 0161-224 7061
- ***Greygarth Hall,*** (University Hall of Residence for men whose pastoral care is entrusted to the Opus Dei Prelature), 1 Lower Park Road, Victoria Park,

Manchester M14 5RS
Tel: 0161-224 2582 *Chaplain:* **Rev Michael Lowenthall**. Also resident: **Rev Robert Farrell.**

23. St Francis of Assisi
(1861; 1872; ded 22 June 1938; New Church ded. 21 Nov 1992)
Textile Street, Gorton, Manchester M18 8BT
Served from Sacred Heart, Gorton
M: *Sat 1st M of Sun 5.30pm. Hds (vigil 7.30pm), 9.15am (term time only).*

A

24. † St John Bosco
(1940; 1960; cons 31 Jan 1974)
197 Charlestown Road, Blackley, Manchester M9 7BD
Tel: 0161-740 5087 **Fax:** 0161-492 0718
E-mail: pjbrady9@aol.com
Website: www.jbosco.co.uk
Rev Philip Brady
M: *Sat 1st M of Sun 6pm. Sun 10am. Hds 10am, 7pm.*

25. St John Vianney (1968)
Poynter Street, Moston, Manchester M40 0DH **Tel:** 0161-681 6844
Rev Brian Seale.
M: *Sun 9am, 11.30am. Hds 10.30am.*
- ***Alexian Brothers:*** Alexian Brothers Care Centre, St Mary's Road, Moston M40 0BL **Tel:** 0161-681 1929

A

26. † St Joseph (1888; 1915)
Plymouth Grove, Longsight, Manchester.
Tel: 0161-224 4035 **Fax:** 0161-256 1781
E-Mail: stjoseph_longsight@msn.com
St Joseph's Presbytery, Portland Crescent, M13 0BU **Rev Ian Farrell**
M: *Sat 1st M of Sun 6.30pm. Sun 11am. Hds (Vigil 6.30pm). 9.30am.*
- ***Little Sisters of the Poor,*** 52 Plymouth Grove West, M13 0AR **Tel:** 0161-273 4147 *Chaplain:* **Rev James Austin.** **Tel:** 0161-273 2722
- ***Congregation of Christian Brothers:*** 35 Carmoor Road, Longsight, Manchester M13 0EA **Tel:** 0161-273 1434
- ***Manchester Hospitals,*** *Chaplain:* **Rev David Egan, Tel:** 0161-224 1895 (Home) 0161 273 4247 (Office) **M:** *Sun 3pm. Hds 12.30pm (Mass in MRI Chapel)*
- ***Coniston Hall*** (Residence for Women University Students) and ***Langsett*** (Catering and Hospitality Centre), 67-77 Hathersage Road M13 0EW **Tel:** 0161-248 5585 Pastoral Care entrusted to the Prelature of Opus Dei.

27. † St Kentigern and St Edwards

(1926; 1939)
Hart Road, Fallowfield, Manchester.
Tel/Fax: 0161-224 4664
Mbl: 07789-715899
E-Mail: stkentigerns@homecall.co.uk
Website: www.stkentigern.co.uk
Revv Thomas Connolly *(Rural Dean)*, **John Flynn.** St Kentigern's Presbytery, 36 Wilbraham Road, Manchester M14 7DW.
M: *Sat 1st M of Sun 6.30pm. Sun 9am, 11am, 6.30pm. Hds (vigil 6.30pm). 9.30am, 7pm.*

28. † St Margaret Mary
(1935; 1957; ded 9 Nov 1960)
34 St Margaret's Road, New Moston, Manchester M40 0JE **Tel:** 0161-681 1651
Canon Kevin O'Connor.
M: *Sat 1st M of Sun 6pm. Sun 10.30am, Hds 9.15am, 7.30pm.*
- ***Presentation Sisters,*** Presentation Convent, St Margaret's Road, M10 0JE **Tel:** 0161-681 1617

29. † St Patrick.
(1832: 1936: Ded. 17 March 1937)
Livesey Street, Collyhurst, Manchester M4 5EJ **Tel/Fax:** 0161-839 1020
Rev Michael Buckley, 28 Park View, Harpurhey, Manchester M9 5TF
M: *Sun 9.30am. Hds 9.30am, 7.30pm.*
- ***Presentation Sisters,*** Presentation Convent, Livesey Street, Manchester M4 5HF. Tel: 0161-832 2221.

† St Malachy's Church (1922: 1930: 1972)
Egginton Street, Collyhurst, Manchester M40 7RG. Served from St Patrick's 29.
M: *Sat 1st M of 6.30pm Sun. Sun 11.30am. Hds 10.45am.*
- ***Brother Missionaries of Charity,*** St Malachy's House, Egginton Street, Collyhurst, Manchester M40 7RG **Tel:** 0161-205 2055
- ***Daughters of Charity of St Vincent de Paul,*** St Michael's 40 George Leigh Street, Ancoats, Manchester M4 5DG

† St Joseph's Service to Deaf People (1929)
Sudell Street, Collyhurst, Manchester M4 4JF
Tel: 0161-834 8828. **Rev Peter McDonough,** (*Director of Deaf Services,* Hollywood House).
M: *Sun 11.30am. Hds 7.30pm.*
- ***Sisters of Our Lady of Evron,*** Sudell Street, Collyhurst, Manchester M4 4JF Provincialate: Emmaus, Sudell Street, Collyhurst, Manchester M4 4JF **Tel:** 0161-832 6954
- ***Henesy House;*** Norlands Nursing Home; Deanside APH; Annie Derby Court.

30. † St Richard (1936)
10/20 Sutcliffe Avenue, Longsight, Manchester M12 5TN **Tel:** 0161-224 1498
Rev Michael Dever.
M: *Sat 1st M of Sun 5.30pm (Vigil). Sun 9.30am. Hds 7pm (Vigil) 9.30am.*
- ***Franciscan Missionary Sisters of St Joseph,*** 2a Montgomery Road, Longsight, Manchester M13 9PW **Tel:** 0161-224 3024 **Fax:** 0161-225 0640

31. † St Vincent de Paul
(1896; 1908; 1955)
Craydon Street, Openshaw, Manchester.
Served from St Anne's, Manchester (11).

33. † St Willibrord (1906; 1938)
North Road, Clayton, Manchester M11 4WQ
Tel: 0161-223 0861 **Fax:** 0161-223 0722
E-mail: stwillibrords@talk21.com
Rev Stewart Ansbro.
M: *Sat 1st M of Sun 6pm. Sun 10am. Hds 10am, 7.30pm.*

34. † English Martyrs
(1876; 1896; ded 4 May 1922)
Alexandra Park, Whalley Range, Manchester.
Tel: 0161-226 1980 **Fax:** 0161-227 8788
E-mail: engmart1@hotmail.com
Rev Geoffrey Marlor. English Martyrs Presbytery, Ralph Sherwin House, 68 Alexandra Road South, Whalley Range, Manchester M16 8QT
M: *Sat 1st M of Sun 6.30pm. Sun 9.15am. Hds 7.30pm (Vigil), 9.15am.*
- ***St Bede's College,*** Alexandra Park, Whalley Range M16 8HX **Tel:** 0161-226 3323 **Mgr Terence Dodgeon** (*Rector*); **Rev Richard A Dearman, MA, STL**.
- ***St Luke's Centre***, Whalley Road, Whalley Range, Manchester M16 8BT **Tel:** 0161-226 4563 *Director:* **Rev Gerald Fieldhouse Bryne** **E-mail:** geraldbryne@stlukescentre.org.uk
- ***Sisters of Loreto,*** 165 Kingsbrook Road, M16 8NR **Tel:** 0161-881 1951

35. Polish Mission, Church of Divine Mercy
Moss Lane East, Moss Side, Manchester.
Tel: 0161-226 1588 **Fax:** 0161-232 0450
Rev Jan Wojzynski (SChr).
- ***Society of Christ Fathers,*** (Soc Chr). **Revv Andrzej Zuziak** (*Parish Priest*), **Czeslaw Osika** (*Provincial*), **Krzysztof Kosciolek**. Divine Mercy Presbytery, 196 Lloyd Street North, M14 4QB
- ***Albertine Sisters Dom Polski,*** 18 Carlton Road, Manchester M16 8B3 **M:** *Sat 1st M of Sun 7pm. Sun 10am, 12noon, 7pm. Hds (vigil 7.30pm), 8.30am, 12noon, 7pm.*
- ***Polish Circle:*** Cheetham Hill Road, Manchester. M8 7PF **M:** *Sun 9.30, Hds 9.30.*

Catholic Chaplains to Higher Education in Manchester
Catholic Chaplaincy Centre, Avila House, 337 Oxford Road, Manchester M13 9GB
Tel: 0161-273 1456
Chaplains:
- ***University of Manchester:*** **Rev Ian Kelly**. **Tel:** 0161-273 1456 ***UMIST:*** **Tel:** 0161-273 1456; *General Chaplaincy Work:* **Sr Breeda Long (FMSJ)**. **Tel:** 0161-273 1456
- ***Catholic Chaplaincy Centre,*** St Augustines, Grosvenor Square, All Saints, Manchester M15 6BW **Tel:** 0161-236 6762
- ***Manchester Metropolitan University:*** **Mr Bernard Burke**. **Tel:** 0161-236 6762.
- ***Royal Northern College of Music:*** **Mr Bernard Burke**. Tel: 0161-236 6762 **M:** *Sun 11am, 5pm. Hds 12noon.*

■ MIDDLETON, Manchester

1. † Our Lady of the Assumption
(1953; 1954; 1961; ded 8 Dec 1971)
Wood Street, Langley, Middleton, Manchester. **Tel:** 0161-643 4210
E-mail: revmullins@btinternet.com
Rev Tadgh Mullins. Our Lady's Presbytery, Bowness Road, M24 4HN
M: *Sat 1st M of Sun 6.30pm. Sun 10.30am. Hds 9.30am.*
- ***Sisters of Charity of St Paul,*** St Paul's Convent, Wood Street, Langley, M24 5QA **Tel:** 0161-643 3803.

2. † St Agnes and St John Fisher
(1966; 1968)
Boarshaw Road, Boarshaw.
Served from Our Lady of the Assumption, Langley, Middleton.
M: *Sat 1st M of Sun 5.15pm. Sun 9.15am. Hds, 7pm.*
- ***Sisters of the Cross and Passion,*** 299 Boarshaw Road, M24 2PF **Tel:** 0161-643 5179

3. † St Peter (1867; 1911)
Taylor Street, Middleton, Manchester M24 1BL **Tel:** 0161-643 2168
Rev Kieran Mullarkey *(Priest in Charge)*.
M: *Sun 9.30am, 11am, 6.30pm. Hds 9.15am (term time only), noon, 7.30pm.*

4. † St Thomas More
(1960; 1972; ded 20 June, 1980)
Mainway, Alkrington, Middleton, Manchester. **Tel:** 0161-643 3847
Parish Priest: **Rev Peter McGiveron**, St Thomas More's Presbytery, 102 Mainway,

DIOCESE OF SALFORD

Alkrington, Middleton, Manchester M24 1PP
M: Sat 1st M of Sun 6.30pm. Sun 9.15am, 11am. Hds (vigil 7pm), 9am.

■ MOSSLEY, Ashton-under-Lyne
† St Joseph (1865; 1962; 1965)
24 Curzon Street, Mossley, Ashton-under-Lyne, Lancs. OL5 0HB
Rev Michael Fleming.
E-mail: frmikefleming@aol.com
Tel: 01457-832505 **Fax:** 01457-835649
M: Sat 1st M of Sun 6.30pm. Sun 9.30am. Hds 9am, 7pm.

■ NELSON, Lancs
1. † Holy Saviour (1896; 1905)
2 Vulcan Street, Nelson, Lancs BB9 8HE
Tel/Fax: 01282-614143
Website: www.holysaviour.org.uk
Rev Christopher Gorton.
M: Sun 10.30am, 6pm. Hds (vigil 7pm). 12.05.

2. † St John Southworth
(1883; 1897; 1964)
5 Park Drive, Nelson, Lancs BB9 0TY
Tel/Fax: 01282-614859
E-mail: johnprice1000@btinternet.com
Rev John Price.
M: Sat 1st M of Sun 6.30pm. Sun 11am. Hds As announced
- ***Christ Church** (shared with the Methodist Community),* Carr Road, Nelson
M: Sun 9.30am. Hds As announced

3. † SS Peter and Paul (1897; 1914)
Gisburn Road, Barrowford, Nelson, Lancs.
Tel: 01282-613023.
E-Mail: peterandpaul@tiscali.co.uk
Rev Martin Magee. SS Peter and Paul's Presbytery, 3 Barleydale Road, Nelson, Lancs BB9 6AD
M: Sun 9.30am. Hds 7.00pm.

■ NEW SPRINGS, Wigan
† The Holy Family (1898; ded 10 Oct 1959)
24 Cale Lane, New Springs, Wigan WN2 1HA
Tel: 01942-242542
Email: holy.fam@btconnect.com
Rev Gerard Haugh.
M: Sat 1st M of Sun 7pm. Sun 9am, 11am. Hds 9.30am, 7.30pm.

■ NEWCHURCH-IN-ROSSENDALE
† St Peter (1915; 1928)
Newchurch-in-Rossendale, Lancs BB4 9EE
Tel: 01706-213410
M: Sun 9.30am. Hds 10am, 7pm.

■ OLDHAM
1. † Sacred Heart (1952; 1957)
Whetstone Hill, Derker, Oldham OL1 4NA
Served from SS Peter and Paul, Barrowford
M: Sun 10am. Hds 9am, 7.30pm.

2 † St Mary with St Patrick
(1858; 1870; ded 11 Oct 1958)
40 Union Street West, Oldham OL8 1DL
Tel: 0161-624 4834 **Mbl:** 07976 230919
E-mail: phil.sumner@telinco.com
Website:
www.saintpatrickschurch-oldham.co.uk
Rev Philip Sumner.
M: Sun 10am, 12.30pm (Pol), 6pm. Hds 12noon, 6.30pm.

3. † Our Lady (1959; 1970)
Moorside, Oldham. **Tel:** 0161-624 9039
Rev Raymond McKee. Our Lady's Presbytery, Turf Pit Lane, Moorside, Oldham OL4 2NE
M: Sat 1st M of Sun 6.30pm. Sun 11.10am. Hds (vigil 7pm). 10am.

4. † St Mary (1828; 1839)
Shaw Street, Oldham. Served from St Patrick's.
M: Sun 11.30am. Hds 10.30am.

5. † The Holy Rosary
(1952; 1955; ded 23 July, 1980).
Fir Tree Avenue, Fitton Hill, Oldham OL8 2SR
Tel: 0161-624 7925
Served from Holy Family, Hollinwood
M: Sun 9.30am. Hds 9.15am, 7pm.
- ***Sisters of St Louis,*** 85 Rosary Road, Fitton Hill, OL8 2SB **Tel:** 0161-620 9361

6. † St Anne (1878; 1901; 1935)
Rev Derek Woodhead (Chaplain to Oldham Royal Hospital).
Cook Street, Greenacres, Oldham OL4 1PB
Tel: 0161-678 7282
E-mail: st.annesoldham@btopenworld.com
M: Sat 1st M of Sun 6. Sun 11am. Hds 10.30am, 7.30pm.

7. † St Michael (1948)
Abbey Hills Road, Abbey Hills, Oldham.
Served from St Anne's, Oldham
M: Sun 9.30am Hds 9am.
- ***Franciscan Missionaries of St Joseph,*** Warren Lane, Oldham OL8 2JE **Tel:** 0161-624 6841

8. † SS Peter and Paul (Ukrainian) (1963)
Stanfield Street, Oldham.
Rev Benjamin B Lysykanych (*Vicar General*). SS Peter and Paul's Presbytery, 19 Boundary Gardens, Oldham OL1 2LP
Tel: 0161-633 5636 **Fax:** 0161-627 0250
M: Sun 11.15am. Hds 9.30.

■ OSBALDESTON, Blackburn
† St Mary (1832; 1836)
Longsight Road, Osbaldeston
Blackburn BB2 7HX **Tel:** 01254-812242
Canon Charles Anthony Dorran.
M: Sat 1st M of Sun 6.30pm. Sun 10am. Hds 10.30am, 6.30pm.

■ **OSWALDTWISTLE,** Lancs
† **St Mary** (1894; 1897; ded 8 Sept 1948)
Catlow Hall Street, Oswaldtwistle, Lancs BB5 3EZ **Tel:** 01254-232433
Mbl: 07976 391153
E-mail: pbsm@btopenworld.com
Mgr John Daly
M: *Sat 1st M of Sun 6.30pm. Sun 10am. Hds 7.30am, 9.30am, 8pm.*

■ **PADIHAM,** Lancs
1. † St John the Baptist (1864; 1881)
St John's Road, Padiham, Burnley BB12 7BN **Tel:** 01282-772200
E-mail: thepriest@stjohnspadiham.org.uk
Website: www.stjohnspadiham.org.uk
Rev Peter Hopkinson *(Rural Dean and Diocesan Ecumenical Officer, Lancashire Churches Together).*
M: *Sun 11am, 6pm. Hds (vigil 7pm). 9.15am.*

2. † St Philip the Apostle
(1953; ded 18 Dec 1955)
Slade Lane, Padiham, Burnley BB12 8NS
Tel: 01282-771494 **Rev Denis P Dwyer.**
M: *Sat 1st M of Sun 6.30pm. Sun 10am. Hds 10am, 7.30pm.*

■ **PATRICROFT,** Eccles
† **Holy Cross.** (1961)
Liverpool Road, Patricroft, Eccles, Manchester. **Tel/Fax:** 0161-789 4424
E-mail: hcsmeccles@yahoo.co.uk
Rev Michael Ryan. Holy Cross Presbytery, 370 Liverpool Road, Patricroft, Eccles, Manchester M30 8QD
M: *Sat 1st M of Sun 6.30pm. Sun 11.30am. Hds 11am, 7pm.*
• ***Franciscans (OFMConv),*** All Saints Friary, Redclyffe Road, Dumplington, Urmston, Manchester M41 7LG
Tel: 0161-202 9896 **Fax:** 0161-749 9860
Rev Brendan Blundell (*Guardian*), **E-mail:** guardian@maculimited.net
Rev Christopher Lazar (Crusade Press), **E-mail:** press@crusade.dircon.co.uk

■ **PENDLEBURY,** Manchester
† **St Mark** (1923; 1926)
Station Road, Pendlebury, Manchester.
Tel: 0161-794 1099
Fax: 0161-281 1268
Rev Robert Lasia (*Chancellor & Chaplain to HMP Forest Bank*) **E-mail:** robert@lasia.wanadoo.co.uk
St Mark's Presbytery, 184 Station Road, Pendlebury, Manchester M27 6BY
M: *Sun 10.15am, 6.30pm. Hds 12.05pm, 7.30pm.*

■ **PLEASINGTON,** Blackburn
1. † St Mary and St John the Baptist (1819)
Pleasington Priory, Pleasington Blackburn BB2 6RF **Tel:** 01254-201173
Rev Canon J Kevin Kenny RD. Priory Cottage, Sandy Lane, Pleasington, Blackburn BB2 6RF
M: *Sun 10am.*

2. St Paul
Feniscowles, Blackburn.
Served from Pleasington Priory
M: *Sat 1st M of Sun 7pm. Hds (vigil 7pm), 11.30am.*

■ **PRESTWICH,** Manchester
† **Our Lady of Grace**
(1889; 1931; ded 30 May 1956)
11 Fairfax Road, Prestwich, Manchester M25 1AS **Tel/Fax:** 0161-773 2324
E-mail: jaourladyofgrace@aol.com
Website: www.ourladyofgrace.org.uk
Mgr John Allen.
M: *Sat 1st M of Sun 7pm. Sun 9am, 11am. Hds (vigil 7.00pm). 9.30am, 12noon.*

■ **RADCLIFFE,** Manchester
† **St Mary and St Philip Neri**
(1863; 1894; 1976)
129 Spring Lane, Radcliffe, Manchester M26 2QX
Tel: 0161 723 2340 **Fax:** 0161-724 6376
E-mail: stmary.radcliffe@tiscali.co.uk
Rev James Manock. (Liturgical Formation)
M: *Sat 1st M of Sun 6.30pm. Sun 9am, 11.30am. Hds 9.30am, 7pm.*

■ **RAMSBOTTOM,** Bury, Lancs
† **St Joseph** (1862; 1880)
81 Bolton Street, Ramsbottom, Bury, Lancs BL0 9HY **Tel/Fax:** 01706-823200
Rev John Sullivan. (Director, Overseas Mission) **Email:** juansullivan@tiscali.co.uk
M: *Sat 1st M of Sun 6pm. Sun 9.30am, 11am. Hds (vigil 6pm). 9.30am, 7pm.*

■ **RAWTENSTALL,** Rossendale, Lancs
† **St James the Less**. (1828; 1844)
Burnley Road, Rawtenstall, Rossendale, Lancs BB4 8HH
Tel: 01706-215634
E-mail: stjamestheless@btinternet.com
Website: www.stjamestheless.org.uk
Rev David Lupton RD.
M: *Sat 1st M of Sun 6.30pm. Sun 8.30am, 10.30am. Hds (vigil 7pm). 9am.*

■ **REDDISH,** Stockport, Cheshire
† **St Joseph** (1882)
23 Gorton Road, Reddish, Stockport, SK5 6AZ **Tel:** 0161-432 2168
Canon Maurice O'Connell.
M: *Sat 1st M of Sun 5pm. Sun 9am, 11am. Hds 10am, 12noon, 8pm.*

■ **RIBCHESTER,** Preston
† **SS Peter and Paul** (1789)
Stydd Lodge, Ribchester, Preston PR3 3YQ
Tel/Fax: 01254-878314
Canon Francis Deeney.
M: *Sat 1st M of Sun 7pm. Sun 11am. Hds 9am, 7pm*

■ **RISHTON,** Blackburn
† **St Charles Borromeo**
(1886; 1896; 1938 ded Dec 1986)
Rishton, Blackburn. **Tel/Fax:** 01254-886243
E-mail: martin@dowd2626.fsnet.co.uk
Rev Martin C Dowd. St Charles' Presbytery, St Charles Road, BB1 4HR
M: *Sat 1st M of Sun 5.45pm. Sun 10am. Hds 11am, 7.30pm.*

■ **ROCHDALE,** Lancs
1. † Sacred Heart (1948; 1957)
Kingsway, Rochdale OL16 5BX
Tel: 01706-645603 **Fax:** 01706-340150
E-mail: dokane@sacredheartchurchrochdale.org.uk
Website: www.sacredheartchurchrochdale.org.uk
Rev David O'Kane.
M: *Sat 1st M of Sun 6pm. Sun 9.30am, 11am. Hds 9.30am, 12noon, 6.30pm.*

2. † The Holy Family (1954; 1955)
Mornington Road, Kirkholt, Rochdale OL11 2DG
Tel: 01706-649230 **Fax:** 01706-713985
E-mail: frmartin@holyfamily.fsnet.co.uk
Website: www.holyfamily.fsnet.co.uk
Rev Martin Collins.
M: *Sat 1st M of Sun 6.30pm. Sun 10am. Hds (vigil 7pm), 9.30am.*

3. † St John the Baptist
(1830; 1925; ded 24 Sept 1940)
Dowling Street, Rochdale OL11 1EX
Tel: 01706-646877 **Fax:** 01706-638398
E-mail: office.stjohnthebaptist@btinternet.com Served from Castleton.
M: *Sat 1st M of Sun 5.30pm. Sun 9.30am, Hds (vigil 7pm), 12noon (Holidays).*
- ***Polish Chapel,*** "Westfield", Manchester Road, OL11 4LX **Tel:** 01706-48450 **Rev Edward Jopala.** 31 Cheltenham Street, Rochdale OL11 3QJ **Tel:** 01706-642649 **M:** *Sun 10.45am, Hds 6.30am.*
- ***Franciscan Missionaries of St Joseph,*** Franciscan House, 37/39 Sussex Street, Rochdale OL11 1EL **Tel:** 01706-345363
- ***Pallottine Missionary Sisters,*** 29 Holstein Avenue, Rochdale OL12 6DL

4. † St Patrick (1856; 1861; 1968)
2 Watts Street, Rochdale OL12 0HE
Tel: 01706-645710 **Fax:** 01706-640424
E-mail: stpatricksrc@btinternet.com
Website: www.stpatricksrc.btinternet.co.uk
Rev Joseph F Sweeney (Rural Dean)
M: *Sun 10am, 7pm. Hds 9.30am, 7.30pm.*

5. † St Vincent de Paul
(1940; ded 25 Sept 1981)
Caldershaw Road, Norden, Rochdale OL12 6BU **Tel:** 01706-645361
E-mail: st.vincent@tiscali.co.uk
Rev Paul Brindle (Director of Junior Clergy).
M: *Sat 1st M of Sun 6.30pm. Sun 9am, 11am. Hds (vigil 6.30pm), 9.30am.*

6. St Mary and St James
(Ukrainian Church) (1976)
John Street, Rochdale. **Tel:** 01706-31241
Rev Benjamin B Lysykanych. Woodville, 328 Yorkshire Street, Rochdale OL16 2DS
M: *Sun 10am. Hds 11am.*

■ **ROYTON,** Oldham
† **SS Aidan and Oswald**
(1874; 1880; 1966; ded 28 Sept 1977)
Oldham Road, Dryclough, Royton, Oldham.
Tel: 0161-624 1322 **Fax:** 0161-287 8911
E-mail: ssaidanandoswald@ssao.wanadoo.co.uk
Website: www.aidanandoswalds.org
Rev Stephen Doyle. SS Aidan and Oswald's Presbytery, Vaughan Street, Royton, Oldham OL2 5DL
M: *Sat 1st M of Sun 5.30pm, 10am. Hds (vigil 7.30pm). 9.30am (school), 12.15pm.*
- ***Oldham and District General Hospital,*** *Chaplain:* **Rev Derek Woodhead.** St Anne's Church, 2 Cook Street, Oldham. **Tel:** 0161-678 7282 **M:** *Sat 1st M of Sun 5pm. Sun 3am. Hds (vigil 5pm), 5pm.*

■ **SABDEN,** Clitheroe
† **St Mary** (1873; ded 17 Oct 1937)
49 Whalley Road, Sabden, Clitheroe BB7 9DZ **Tel:** 01282-771517
E-mail: stmarysabden@aol.com
Website: www.stmarysabden.vze.com
Served from English Martyrs, Whalley
M: *Sat 1st M of Sun 6pm. Sun 10.30am. Hds 9.30am, 7.30pm.*

■ **SALFORD**
1. See start of the parish list.

2. Mother of God and St James
(1854; 1875; 1975)
Pendleton Way, Pendleton, Salford M6 5JA
Tel: 0161-736 1935
E-mail: s.k.braiden@btinternet.com
Rev Shaun Braiden.
M: *Sat 1st Mass of Sun 6pm. Sun 10am. Hds (vigil 6pm), 9.30am (term time only), 12.05pm.*

3. † Our Lady of Dolours (1923; 1924; 1964)
Servite Priory, 500 Bury New Road, Kersal, Salford M7 4ND
Tel: 0161-792 2152 **Fax:** 0161-792 7943
E-mail: p.conniffe@virgin.net
- ***Servites (OSM):*** **Revv Peter M Conniffe** (*Prior and Parish Priest*), **Basil M Prior, Michael M Rogers, John Knowles, Kevin Donaghey**.
  M: *Sat 1st M of Sun 6.30pm. Sun 9.15am, 11.15am, 5.30pm. Hds (vigil 7pm). 9.15am, 7pm.*
- ***Poor Sisters of Nazareth,*** Nazareth House, Scholes Lane, Prestwich M25 0NU **Tel:** 0161-773 2111
  M: *9.15am Daily.*
- ***Faithful Companions of Jesus,*** Kersal Hill Convent, 22 Singleton Road, M7 4WL
  Tel: 0161-792 2362 Provincialate: 24 Singleton Road, Salford M7 4WL
  Tel: 0161-792 2267 **Fax:** 0161 708 9683
  27 Park Lane, Salford M7 4JE
  Tel: 0161-792 4557
- ***Sisters of Our Lady of Sion,*** Flat 3, Hollyrood House, Bury Old Road, Prestwich M25 1PQ **Tel:** 0161-798 9470
- ***Nazareth House,*** Claremont, Redcliffe Holt House, Kersal Vale.
- ***Sisters of the Cross and Passion,*** 10 Tuscany View, Vine Street, Salford M7 3TX **Tel:** 0161-705 0335

4. † All Souls and St John Vianney
(1892; 1923; ded 22 May 1946)
Weaste Lane, Weaste, Salford.
Tel: 0161-736 5432
Served from St James's, Pendleton.
- ***Mill Hill Missionaries (MHM):*** *Mission Team and APF:* **Revv Jan Klaver** (*Team Leader*), **Liam Armour, Louis Purcell, Gerard Hamill**, 622 Liverpool Street, Salford M5 2HQ. **Tel:** 0161-737 9742
  M: *Sun 11.30am. Hds 9am.*

5. † St Boniface and St Joseph
(1895; 1921; 1961)
Lower Broughton, Salford.
Tel: 0161-708 9456.
E-mail: stboniface@salford7.freeserve.co.uk
Rev Peter Kinsella (President-Faith and Justice Commission) St Boniface Presbytery, Boniface Road, Salford M7 2GE
  M: *Sat 1st M of Sun 6.30pm. Sun 11.30am 12.45am (French). Hds 9am, 7pm.*

6. † St Luke (1922-1924; 1969)
Swinton Park Road, Irlams-o'th'-Height, Pendleton, Salford M6 7WR
Tel: 0161-736 2696
Website: www.stlukessalford.org.uk
Rev John Williams.
  M: *Sat 1st M of Sun 6.30pm. Sun 9.15am, 11am. Hds (vigil 7pm). 9am, 7pm.*

7. † St Joseph (1871; 1902)
St Joseph's Drive, Salford M5 3JP
Tel: 0161-872 0534
Served from St Boniface, Lower Broughton.
  M: *Sun 9.30am. Hds 10.30.*
- ***Franciscan Missionaries of St Joseph,*** 170 Tatton Street, Ordsall.
  Tel: 0161-877 3122
- ***Sion Community,*** St Joseph's Presbytery, St Joseph's Drive, Salford M5 3JP
  Tel: 0161-872 0534

8. † SS Peter and Paul (1956)
Park Road, Pendleton, Salford M6 8JR
Tel: 0161-789 4555
Rev Stephen Parkinson.
  M: *Sat 1st M of Sun 6.30pm. Sun 8.30am, 10am. Hds 9am, 6.30pm.*

9. † St Sebastian (1892; 1973)
Gerald Road, Pendleton, Salford M6 6DW
Tel: 0161-736 1774
Rev Canon Liam Houlihan (*Episcopal Vicar for Religious*).
  M: *Sun 9am, 11am. Hds 10am, 8pm.*
- ***Sisters of the Cross and Passion,*** 62 Gerald Road, Pendleton M6 6DN.
  Tel: 0161-736 5057

10. † St Thomas of Canterbury
(1879; 1901; ded 24 June 1953)
327 Gt Cheetham Street East, Higher Broughton, Salford M7 4UE
Tel: 0161-792 2108
E-mail: drjmac@tiscali.co.uk
Rev David Macfarlane.
  M: *Sat 1st M of Sun 6.30pm. Sun 10.30am, 5pm. Hds 9.15am, 6.30pm.*
- ***Holy Ghost Fathers (CSSp).*** Community: **Revv Philip Marsh** (*Director*), **Peter Ward, Sixtus Adejo, Fr. Nicodemus Mmasi, Odenigbo Uchenna**. "Just Youth", **Mr Kevin Buchanan** (*Youth Ministry Co-ordinator*). 61 Leicester Rd, Higher Broughton, Salford M7 4LH
  Tel: 0161-792 1714 **Fax:** 0161-792 0435
  E-mail: spiritan.salford@tesco.net
- ***Sisters of the Cross and Passion,*** Park Mount, 458 Bury New Road, M7 0LJ
  Tel: 0161-792 1574

11. Our Lady of the Assumption (Ukrainian), Bury Old Road.
Rev Jaroslav Rij, 36 Cardinal Street, Cheetham, Manchester M8 0PS
Tel: 0161-205 7050
  M: *Sun 9am, 10.30am (Ukranian sung). Hds 9am.*

■ **SAMLESBURY**
† St Mary and St John Southworth (1690; 1818)
Preston New Road, Preston PR5 0UL
Tel: 01772-877241
Rev Frederick Watson.
M: *Sun 10am. Hds 9.15am, 7.30pm.*

■ **SHAW**
† St Joseph (1874; 1896; 1984)
Oldham Road, Shaw, Oldham OL2 8SZ
Tel: 01706-847489
Rev John B Scanlan.
M: *Sat 1st M of Sun 6.30pm. Sun 11am, Hds 11am, 7.30pm.*

■ **STOCKPORT,** Cheshire
See Heaton Mersey, Heaton Norris, Reddish & Denton (2). (See also Diocese of Shrewsbury).

■ **STONYHURST,** Blackburn
† St Peter (1832; ded 26 June 1835)
Stonyhurst College, Stonyhurst, Blackburn, Lancs, BB7 9PZ **Tel:** 01254-826268
• ***Jesuits (SJ):*** **Revv Adrian Howell, Ronald Hull.**
M: *Sat 1st M of Sun 5.30pm. Sun 8.30am. Hds 8.30am.*

■ **STONYHURST COLLEGE**
Clitheroe, Lancs, BB7 9PZ
Tel: 01254-826345 **Fax:** 01254-826732
• ***Jesuits (SJ):*** St Mary's Hall, Stonyhurst, Clitheroe, Lancs BB7 9PU
Prep School. **Tel:** 01254-826242
Chaplain: **Rev John Twist.**

■ **STRETFORD,** Manchester
1. † St Alphonsus
(1903; 1904; 1936; ded 11 June 1947)
Ayres Road, Old Trafford, Stretford, Manchester.
M: *Sun 10.30am. Hds 9.30am.*
Served from Our Lady's, Moss Side.

2. † St Ann (1863; ded 18 June 1867)
1043 Chester Road, Stretford, Manchester M32 8LF
Tel: 0161-865 2079 **Fax:** 0161-865 4013
Revv John Hitchen *(Rural Dean)*, **Patrick Greasley** (*Assistant Priest*).
M: *Sun 9.30am, 11.30am, 6.30pm. Hds (vigil 7pm). 9.15am, 11am (in school term only).*
• ***Faithful Companions of Jesus,*** 214 Barton Road, Stretford, Manchester M32 8DP **Tel:** 0161-864 3368

3. † St Hugh of Lincoln (1938)
110 Glastonbury Road, Stretford, Manchester M32 9PD **Tel:** 0161-748 3426
Email: cleary777@aol.com
Rev Michael Cleary.
M: *Sat 1st M of Sun 7pm. Sun 10.30am. Hds 9.30am, 7pm.*
• ***Trafford General Hospital,*** Davyhulme, Chaplains Office: **Tel:** 0161-746 2624 or contact **Rev John Hitchen,** St Annes, Stretford **Tel:** 0161-865 2079
M: *Tue 12noon.*

4. † St Teresa (1928)
St Teresa's Road, Firswood, Stretford, Manchester. Served from Our lady and St John, Chorlton-cum-Hardy.
M: *Sun 10.30am. Hds 9am.*

■ **SWINTON,** Manchester
2. † St Mary of the Immaculate Conception
(1852; 1959; 1964; ded 8 Sept 1977)
Park Street, Swinton, Manchester M27 4UR
Tel: 0161-281 1818
Rev Brian Murphy (*Chaplain to Royal Manchester Children's Hospital*). *Parish Worker:* **Miss A M Bardell.**
M: *Sat 1st M of Sun 6.30pm. Sun 11am. Hds 9.30am, 7pm.*

2. † St Charles (1923; 1955)
Moorside Road, Swinton, Manchester M27 3PD
Tel: 0161-794 1089 **Fax:** 0161-727 8077
E-mail: paulsmith@saintcharles.freeserve.co.uk
Mgr Paul Smith (STL) (Rural Dean, Diocesan Ecumenical Officer, GMCT).
M: *Sat 1st M of Sun 6pm. Sun 8.45am, 11am. Hds (vigil 7.30pm). 8.30am, 7.30pm.*
• ***Franciscan Missionaries of St Joseph.*** Generalate: St Joseph's Convent, 150 Greenleach Lane, Worsley, Manchester, M28 4TD **Tel:** 0161-794 1062 Wardley Hall, Worsley, Manchester, M28 2ND **Tel:** 0161-727 8710

■ **TODMORDEN,** Lancs
† St Joseph (1868; 1929)
The Presbytery, Wellington Road, Todmorden, Lancs OL14 5HL
Tel: 01706-813676 **Fax:** 01706-810423
E-mail: stjosephintod@aol.com
Rev Anthony Gallagher.
M: *Sat 1st M of Sun 6.15pm. Sun 10am. Hds 9.15am, 7.30pm.*
• ***Residential Homes:*** Ferny Lee; Milreed Lodge, Pennine Lodge, Stanley Cryer Court, Waterside.

■ **TOTTINGTON,** Bury, Lancs
† St Hilda (1916; 1963)
Turton Road, Tottington, Bury BL8 4AW
Tel: 01204-882908 **Fax:** 01204-880360
E-mail: sthildas@tottington.freeserve.co.uk
Rev Gabriel O'Donoghue.
M: *Sat 1st M of Sun 6pm. Sun 10am, 6pm. Hds 9.15am, 7pm.*

■ **TRAFFORD PARK,** Manchester
† St Antony of Padua (1904)

Eleventh Street, Trafford Park, Manchester M17 1JF
Tel: 0161-872 0311 **Fax:** 0161-872 2764
E-mail: jelge@ukonline.co.uk
V. Rev Canon Joseph Carter. St Antony Centre for Church and Industry, Eleventh Street, Trafford Park, Manchester M17 1JF
Tel: 0161-848 9173
M: *Sun 10.30am. Hds 12.10pm.*

■ **URMSTON,** Manchester
† **English Martyrs** (1891; 1913. 5 Oct 1991)
Flixton Road, Urmston, Manchester M41 5AX
Tel: 0161-748 2328
Fax: 0161 755 3473
E-mail: mdjones@btconnect.com
Rev Michael Jones, English Martyrs Presbytery, 5 Roseneath Road, Urmston, Manchester M41 5AX
M: *Sat 1st M of Sun 6.30pm. Sun 11.15am, 5pm. Hds (vigil 7pm) 11.30am.*

- ***Franciscans (Friars Minor Conventual) (OFM Com):*** All Saints Friary (1868: ded 9 June 1868), Redclyffe Road, Dumplington, Urmston, Manchester M41 7LG **Tel:** 0161-202 9896 **Fax:** 0161-749 9860 **Revv Brendan Blundell** (*Guardian*), **Philip Doherty** (*Vocations Director*). National Centre of Crusade of Mary Immaculate; Novitiate of English Province.

■ **WALKDEN,** Worsley, Manchester [A] [hearing loop]
† **Christ the King** (1952; 1962)
Manchester Road, Walkden, Worsley, Manchester M28 3LN
Tel/Fax: 0161-790 2855
Website: www.ctkwalkden.freeserve.co.uk
Rev Martin J Broadley PhD.
M: *Sat 1st M of Sun 5pm. Sun 9am, 11.15am. Hds 12noon, 7.30pm.*

■ **WALTON-LE-DALE,** Preston
† **Our Lady and St Patrick** (1855; 1857; 1880)
Higher Walton Road, Walton-le-Dale, Preston PR5 4HD
Tel/Fax: 01772-253709
E-mail: stpsn3@aol.com
Rev John Cribben.
M: *Sat 1st M of Sun 6.30pm. Sun 9.30. Hds (vigil 7.30pm), 9.15am.*

■ **WESTHOUGHTON,** Bolton [wheelchair] [hearing loop]
† **Sacred Heart of Jesus** (1873; 1894; ded 1976)
8 Lord Street, Westhoughton, Bolton BL5 3SE
Tel: 01942-812174
Rev Michael Johonnett.
M: *Sat 1st M of Sun 6pm. Sun 9.30am, 11am. Hds (vigil 7pm), 10am.*

■ **WHALLEY,** Blackburn [A] [hearing loop]
† **English Martyrs** (1921; 1926)
The Sands, Whalley, Blackburn.
Tel/Fax: 01254-823283
Rev Philip Price. English Martyrs Presbytery, The Sands, Whalley, Blackburn BB6 9TN
M: *Sat 1st M of Sun 5pm. Sun 11am. Hds 10am, 7.30pm.*

■ **WHITEFIELD,** Manchester [A] [hearing loop]
1. † St Bernadette
(1952; 1956; ded 12 June 1973)
436 Bury New Road, Whitefield, Manchester M25 7SX
Tel: 0161-766 2356 **Fax:** 0161-796 7877
E-mail: info@saintbernadettes.org
Website: www.saintbernadettes.org
Rev Christopher Lough.
M: *Sat 1st M of Sun 6.30pm. Sun 9am, 11am. Hds 9am (term time only), 12.05pm, 7.30pm.*

2. St Michael (1966)
Whitefield, Manchester.
Tel/Fax: 0161-766 5961
E-mail: john.rowan@tiscali.co.uk
Rev Christopher McGrane. St Michael's Presbytery, Albert Road, M45 8NH
M: *Sat 1st M of Sun 6pm. Sun 10am. Hds 9.15am, 7.30pm.*

■ **WHITWORTH,** Rochdale
† **Our Immaculate Mother and St Anselm**
(1860; 1867; 1869; 1985)
John Street, Whitworth, Rochdale OL12 8DB
Tel/Fax: 01706-853562
Rev Frank Thorpe.
M: *Sat 1st M of Sun 5.30pm. Sun 10.30am. Hds10am, 7pm.*

■ **WINTON,** Eccles, Manchester [A] [hearing loop]
† **St Matthew** (1958)
Worsley Road, Winton, Eccles, Manchester M30 8BL **Tel:** 0161-789 4944.
Served from Patricroft Holy Cross.
M: *Sun 10am. Hds 9.30am.*

■ ORDERS OR CONGREGATIONS, ETC

■ Men

African Missions Society: Manchester (23).
Alexian Brothers: Manchester (26).
Benedictines (English Congregation): Bamber Bridge, Lostock Hall.
Brother Missionaries of Charity: Manchester (30).
Christian Brothers: Manchester (4, 27).
De la Salle Brothers: Eccles (1).
Franciscans (Friars Minor Conventual): Manchester (20), Patricroft.
Holy Ghost Fathers: Salford (10).
Marists: Blackburn (6).
Mill Hill Missionaries: Salford (4),

Haslingden (2), Royton, Burnley (2).
Norbertine Canons (OPraem): Manchester (18).
Salesians: Bolton (1), Heaton Norris.
Servites: Salford (3).
Schönstatt: Manchester (5), Kearsley.
Society of Christ (for Polish Emigrants) Manchester (36).

■ **Women**

Albertine Sisters: Manchester (36).
Cenacle, Sisters of Our Lady of the: Manchester (7).
Charity (of St Paul) Sisters of: Heaton Mersey, Middleton (1).
Charity (of Jesus and Mary) Sisters of: Bury.
Daughters of Charity (SVP): Little Hulton (1) Manchester (7).
Christ the King, Missionary Sisters of: Hollinwood (2).
Cross and Passion, Sisters of the: Bolton (5), Middleton (2), Manchester (23), Salford (3, 9, 10).
Cross, Daughters of the (Liege): Bury (2), Manchester (5).
Faithful Companions of Jesus: Salford (3), Stretford (2).
Franciscan Missionaries of St Joseph: Blackburn (6), Burnley (2), Heaton Mersey, Manchester (10, 18) Rochdale (3), Salford (7, 32), Swinton (2).
Good Shepherd Sisters: Manchester (20).
Holy Child Jesus, Sisters of the: Salford (1).
Holy Family, Sisters of: Salford (1).
Jesus, Daughters of: Colne (1).
Loreto, Sisters of: Manchester (7, 35).
Marian Community of Reconciliation: Manchester (19, 23).
Marist Sisters: Manchester (16).
Mercy, Sisters of: Burnley (3, 4), Hollinwood (1).
Missions, Sisters of Our Lady of the: Bamber Bridge.
Nazareth, Poor Sisters of: Blackburn (1), Salford (3).
Our Lady of Evron, Sisters of: Manchester (30).
Our Lady of Sion: Salford (3).
Pallottine Missionary Sisters: Rochdale (3).
Poor, Little Sisters of the: Manchester (27)
Presentation Sisters (Irish): Manchester (4, 29, 30), Ashton under Lyne (4).
St Louis, Sisters of: Oldham (5).
St Joseph (of the Apparition) Sisters of: Manchester (7, 35).

■ **DIOCESAN INSTITUTIONS, SOCIETIES**

For Societies and Organisations without representation in the diocese please see the main Societies and Organisations section.

Apostleship of Prayer. *Diocesan Director:* **Rev P Tansey,** St James, 58 Bowland Drive, Montserrat, Bolton BL1 5TX **Tel:** 01204-840030 **E-mail:** frpattansey@aol.com

Association for the Propagation of the Faith. *Diocesan Co-ordinator:* **Rev Jan Klaver MHM**. All Souls and St John Vianney, 622 Liverpool Street, Salford M5 5HQ **Tel:** 0161-736 5432 **E-mail:** regional@millhill17.freeserve.uk

Association of Interchurch Families. *Local Contact:* **Margaret and John Crossman,** 18 Shawclough Drive, Rochdale OL12 7HG **Tel:** 01706-650709 **Fax:** 01706-665671 **E-mail:** margaret.crossman@ukonline.co.uk. **Website:** aifw.org/aif.htm

Association of Nursing Religious *Co-ordinator:* **Sr Maureen Francis O'Driscoll,** 44 Ruabon Road, Didsbury, Manchester M20 01LN **Tel:**0161-445 4420

Association of Separated and Divorced Catholics (A.S.D.C). Ecclesiastical Adviser, **Rt Rev Mgr Canon Michael Quinlan. Tel:** 0161-432 4412

Broughton Catholic Charitable Society. Founded in 1787, for Lancashire born Catholic priests or laypersons, or resident in Lancashire, or of Lancashire parentage, the society aims to bring spiritual benefits of its members, both living and dead, and the relief of hardship, wherever it is encountered, by making grants
Secretary: **Mr Leo Casey**. 16, Norwood Close, Worsley, Manchester, M28 7ES. **Tel:** 0161 790 5758 **Email:** leocasey@bulldoghome.com

CAFOD NW Regional Office and Research Centre: St Walburge's Centre, St Walburge's Gardens, Preston PR2 2QJ **Tel:/Fax:** 01772-733310 **E-mail:** northwest@cafod.org.uk *Regional Organiser:* **Peter Grimshaw.**

"Christian Family Weeks" *Chairman*: **Mr A Holt,** 10 Stanley Road, Whitefield. **Tel:** 0161-766 3930

Calix Society. To promote total abstinence for alcoholics, and assist them in their spiritual development. *Chaplain:* **Rev Canon E Dolan. Tel:** 0161-624 3762

Catenian Association. Province No 1: *Secretary*: **D Green,** 3 Chatsworth Avenue, Culcheth, Warrington, Cheshire, **Tel:** 0192576-3454 *Membership Secretary:* **Robert Dunbar,** 4 Conway Drive, Bury BL9 7PQ **Tel:** 0161-797 2546

Catholic Children's Rescue Society, (Diocese of Salford) Inc. 390 Parrs

Wood Road, Didsbury, Manchester M20 0NA *Chairman*: **The Bishop of Salford**; *Secretary*: **Rev. Bernard Wilson**. **Tel:** 0161-445 7741 (Mon - Fri 9 -5) 0161-445 8017 (All other times)

Catholic Charismatic Renewal. *Diocesan Liaison Officer:* **Rev Arthur Nearey**, St Mary's Presbytery, 40 Featherstall Road, Littleborough OL15 8DW **Tel:** 01706-378261

Catholic Family Care. *Hon. Secretary:* **Mrs M Dyson**, c/o All Souls Primary School, Kintyre Avenue, Weaste, Salford M5 2NR **Tel:** 07949-356503

Catholic Deaf Association: An association of Deaf, Hard of Hearing and Hearing People, offering support and promoting services for Deaf People within the community. *Secretary:* **Rev P McDonough,** Hollywood House, Sudell Street, Collyhurst, Manchester M4 4JF

Catholic Family History Society. *North West Group Secretary:* **Mrs J Smith**, 10 Irving Close, Woodsmoor, Stockport SK2 7DK

Catholic Fellowship for the Handicapped, Mrs Jean Rutherford Davies, Tel: 0161-787 7688 Deanery groups in Accrington, Blackburn, Bolton, Bury, Burnley, Manchester North, Manchester South, Middleton, Oldham, Rochdale, Salford.

Catholic Social Workers' Guild. *Secretary*: To be appointed.

Catholic Stage Guild. Northern Representative: **Jack Wilby Tel:** 0208-643 4103 *Chaplain:* **Rev Denis Clinch**. **Tel:** 0161-834 3547 **Fax:** 0161-834 4207

Catholic Teachers' Association. *Diocesan Secretary:* **Mr M Bourke**, 23 Greengate, Hale Barns, Cheshire WA15 0SH **Tel:** 0161-980 4507

Catholic Truth Society. (Diocese of Salford). Bookshop: Brazennose House West, Brazennose Street, Manchester M2 5AS **Tel:** 0161-834 5115 **Fax:** 0161-834 5665

Catholic Welfare Societies (Diocese of Salford) Ltd. *Rev Secretary*: St Joseph's Welfare Centre. **Tel:** 0161-839 7492 **Rev B Wilson Tel:** 0161-432 0762

Catholic Women's League. Diocesan Branch. *President:* **Mrs Margaret Murray**; *Secretary:* **Mrs Pauline Lifford**, 22 Great Hall Close, Radcliffe M26 0DA **Tel:** 0161-724 7567 **E-mail:** pmlifford@lineone.net

Christian Life Communities (formerly Sodalities of Our Lady/Cell Movement). *Diocesan Representative:* **Jenny Bond**. 31 Dalton Drive, Swinton, Manchester M27 8UD **Tel:** 0161-743 0724

Co-Workers of Mother Teresa. *Link*: **Miss Ita Mulligan**, 25 Dene Brow, Denton, Manchester M34 1PX *Secretary*: **Mrs M Gavaghan**, 12 Norris Road, Sale Cheshire M33 3GN **Tel:** 0161-962 2429

Crusade of Mary Immaculate. *National Director:* **Rev Brendan Blundell (OFM Conv)**. All Saints, Redclyffe Road, Urmston, Manchester M31 2LE **Tel:** 0161-202 9896 Fax: 0161-749 8283 **E-mail:** editor@crusade.dircon.co.uk **Website:** www.crusade.dircon.co.uk

Crux. *Regional Officer*: **Maurice Taylor**, 2 Balmoral Avenue, Stretford, Manchester, M32 0DG **Tel:** 0161-865 2613

Dominican Secular Institute. Manchester *Regional Representative:* **Annette Mollan,** 131 Crosland Road, Lindley, Huddersfield HD3 3PW

Family and Social Action. *Diocesan Office:* St Antony's Centre, Eleventh Street, Trafford Park, Manchester M17 1JF **Tel:** 0161-848 9173 *Parish Groups Co-ordinator:* **Mr E Taylor**, **Tel:** 0161-796 6373; *Christian Family Weeks Organiser*: **Mr A Holts**, **Tel:** 0161-766 3930

Francis House Children's Hospice. 390 Parrs Wood Road, Didsbury, Manchester M20 0NA **Tel:** 0161-434 4118

Guild of Catholic Doctors. Manchester Branch. *Hon Secretary:* **Mr R H L Brown MB, ChB, FRCS (Eng)**, The Noup, 5 Ridge Avenue, Marple, Cheshire SK6 7HJ **Tel/Fax:** 0161-427 4433 **E-mail:** rhlbrown@hotmail.com *Chaplain*: **Mgr Michael Quinlan**.

Handicapped Children's Pilgrimage Trust, (Manchester Region): For more information: **Brian Harrison**, **Tel:** 01204-398431

Industrial Centre, St Antony's. For those trying to apply the Church's social thinking to their lives at work, at home and in the community; study circles, seminars and discussion groups throughout the year. Services to individuals, parish and deanery groups and schools. Meetings and conference facilities on subjects related to industrial and working life. *Contact:* **Rev J Carter** or **Mr K W Flanagan** at St Antony's Centre, Eleventh Street, Trafford Park, Manchester M17 1JF **Tel:** 0161-848 9173 **Fax:** 0161-872 9480

Knights of St Columba. Prov 8 (Salford). *Secretary*: **Mr J Regan**, 48 Willow Way, Withington M20 0JB **Tel:** 0161-445 4575 Prov 21 (East Lancs): *Secretary*: **J M Kilburn**, 12 Roetti Avenue, Burnley, Lancs BB11 2NP **Tel:** 01282-427693: Prov 33 (Central

Lancs): *Secretary:* **J Burns**, 21 Glenway, Penwortham, Preston PR1 9AJ **Tel:** 01772-743981

Legion of Mary. Manchester Comitium: *President:* **Mr Tony Kirsten**. 14 Astor Road, Manchester M19 1NP **Tel:** 0161-236 1089

Little Sisters of the Poor Flag Days Committee. *Chairman*: **Mrs Eileen Davies**. 31 Graysands Road, Hale, Altrincham, Cheshire WA15 8RY **Tel:** 0161-941 6205

Lourdes Pilgrimage Committee. *Office*: Wardley Hall, Worsley, Manchester M28 2ND **Tel:** 0161-643 3847 *Director:* **Rev Anthony Kay**.

Manchester Metropolitan University Catholic Society For details contact: All Saints, Manchester M15 6BH **Tel:** 0161-247 3496

Manchester University Catholic Society. Offers a wide variety of activities throughout the academic year Avila House, (*Catholic Chaplaincy*) 337 Oxford Road, Manchester, M13 9PG **Tel:** 0161-273 1456. **Rev Ian Kelly**.

Marriage Care. Manchester Centre: Clitherow House, Lower Chatham Street, Manchester M15 6BY **Tel:** 0161-236 5426

Blackburn Centre: *Secretary* **Mrs M Wilcock**: **Tel:** 01254-265945

Bollington Sub Centre, **Tel:** 01625-522232

Bolton Centre: *Secretary* **Mrs L Brennan** 01204-706050 **Fax:** 01204-361884

Manchester Centre: Clitherow House, Lower Chatham Street, Manchester, M15 6BY **Tel:** 0161-236 5426

Oldham Centre: **Tel:** 0161-624 0514

Rochdale Centre: *Secretary* **Mrs A O'Brien**: **Tel:** 01706-46368

Salford Centre: *Chairman:* **Mr Leo Brooks** **Tel:** 0161-773 5911 Appointments: **Tel:** 0161-773 1773

Stockport Centre: *Secretary:* **Mrs M Lee**, **Tel:** 0161-432 1730

Tameside: *Secretary:* **Mrs B Taylor**, **Tel:** 0161-339 5744

Trafford Centre: *Secretary* **Mr D G Baker**, **Tel:** 0161-980 6423 Wigan Centre: *Secretary* **Mrs T Nuttall**, **Tel:** 01695-24087

Mount Carmel, Third Order (Secular) of Our Lady of. St Mary's, Mulberry Street, Manchester, *Chapter Leader:* **F Gatley**. *Secretary:* **G Dillon**, 892 Wilmslow Road, Didsbury, Manchester, M20 5PG **Tel:** 0161-445 2106 Blackburn Chapter: Mount Carmel Convent, 11 Meins Road, Blackburn BB2 6QQ *Leader*: **Doris Wilson**, 44 Willows Lane, Accrington, BB5 0RT

Newman Association: North Cheshire Circle: Loreto Convent, Altrincham. *Secretary*: **Mrs P Havard**, 36 Windermere Drive, Alderley Edge, Cheshire, SK9 7UP **Tel:** 01625-585474

Our Lady's Catechists. An association of lay men and women who are qualified to give religious instruction. Parents, adults and Parish Priests are invited to contact the diocesan representative: **Miss B Wakefield**, 10 Bootham Court, Half Edge Lane, Eccles M30 9ET **Tel:** 0161-707 8790 **Fax:** 0161-707 9663 **E-mail:** beryl.wakefield@lineone.net **Website:**http://website.lineone.net /~beryl.wakefield/

Pax Christi. *Contact:* **Chris McKnight**, 28 Gore Crescent, Salford M5 2NT **Tel:** 0161-288 3649

Priests' and People's Eucharistic League. *Diocesan Director*: **Rev David Ryder**, 9 Crumpsall Lane, Higher Crumpsall, Manchester M8 6ED **Tel:** 0161-740 1095

St Joseph's Catholic Mission to Deaf People. *Chaplains*: **Rev Peter McDonough**, with the Sisters of Our Lady of Evron. Hollywood House, Sudell Street, Collyhurst, Manchester M4 4JF **Tel:** 0161-834 8828 **Fax:** 0161-833 3674 **E-mail:** peter.mcdonough2@ bitinternet.com

St Vincent's Housing Association Ltd, Ozanam House, 171 Upper Chorlton Road, Manchester, M16 9RA *Secretary*: **H Barrett. Tel:** 0161-881 01256

Salford Diocesan Catholic Primary School Headteachers: *Chair:* **Miss P J Jones**, Our Lady of Grace Primary School, Highfield Road, Prestwich M25 5AS **Tel:** 0161-796 7254 **Fax:** 0161-253 7398

Salford Diocesan Catholic Secondary Headteachers: *Chair*: **Mr M O'Hare**, Holy Cross College, Manchester Road, Bury BL9 9BB **Tel:** 0161-762 4500 **Fax:** 0161-762 4501 *Secretary:* **Mr Peter Donnelly**, Ss John Fisher and Thomas More High School, Gibfield Road, Colne, Lancs BB8 8JT

Salford Diocesan Scout Guild. *Diocesan Chaplain*: **Rev David Lannon. Tel:** 0161-624 8760 *Chairman*: **Mr D Cleary, Tel:** 0161-338 2978. *Secretary:* **Mr Frank Smith**, 1 The Crescents, Moss Lane, Timperley, Altrincham WA15 6JH **Tel:** 0161-973 5902

Salford Diocesan Scholarship Council (Plater College, Oxford). *Secretary*: **A Burns**, 39 Paulden Avenue, Baguley M28 9PH **Tel:** 0161-998 5784

Salford Diocesan Walsingham Pilgrimage Committee. *Chairman*: **John Martin**, 39 Glenwood Drive, Middleton, Manchester M24 2TH **Tel:** 0161-653 7284 **E-mail:** smartin817@aol.com

Schoenstatt. A Marian Movement of spiritual renewal for people in every walk of life, especially families and youth. *Chaplain*: **Rev Duncan McVicar SI** **Tel:** 01204 572077and 01204 796090

Secular Franciscan Order, *Enquiries:* **Mr Edward Roberts**. 20 Knowle Street, Hollinwood, Oldham OL8 3DG **Tel:** 0161-628 5931

Serra International, Great Britain: Manchester Club. *Secretary*: **F P Oberle**, 866 Wilmslow Road, Manchester M20 0NE **Tel:** 0161-445 5127

Society of St Gregory. Society which works to assist priests and people to celebrate the liturgy worthily, by organising summer schools, study days and conferences. The Magazine "Music & Liturgy" is published regularly. Advice is available on care and installation of organs. **Tel:** 01322-338984 **Fax:** 402694 **Website:** www.ssg-online. demon.co.uk *Secretary:* **Martin Barry**, 13 Carlton Road, Heaton Mersey, Stockport SK4 3LA **Tel:** 0161-431 0653 **E-mail:** salford@ssg.org.uk

Society of St John Chrysostom, c/o **Stefan Moroz**, 34 Holly Grove, Oldham, Lancs. OL4 3JL **Tel:** 0161-678 9082

Society of St Vincent de Paul. *Diocesan President*: **Hugh Barrett (SVP)**. *Secretary*: **Philip Cusack**, 14 Newlands Avenue, Peel Green, Eccles, Manchester. M30 7LL **Tel:** 0161-789 1786

Society of the Holy Childhood. *Director:* **Rev John Sullivan**. St Joseph, 81 Bolton Street, Ramsbottom BL10 9HY **Tel:** 01706-823200

Union of Catholic Mothers. *President*: **Mrs I Riley**. *Secretary*: **Mrs Jean Kehoe**, 11 Clarendon Road, Irlam M44 5ZA **Tel:** 0161-775 6351

Walsingham Association. *Accrington:* **Mrs S Gabrazach**. 28 Primrose Street, Accrington, Lancs BB5 0HU **Tel:** 01254-301266 *Blackburn:* **Mr F Greenwood**, 8 The Evergreens, Livesey, Blackburn BB2 5AA. **Tel:** 01254-209064. *Bolton:* **Mr P Eckersley**, 17 Charles Court, Bolton BL1 2SS. **Tel:** 01942-382768; *Burnley:* **Mrs R Singleton**. 48 Causey Foot, Nelson, Lancs BB9 0DR **Tel:** 01282-693927; *Bury:* **Mrs M Corrigan**, 14 Blackburn Street, Prestwich, Manchester M25 5FT **Tel:** 0161-798 8075; *Bury, Guardian Angels:* **Mrs M Rogers**, 23 Croft Drive, Tottington, Bury, Lancs BL8 3HT **Tel:** 01204-883949; *Bury, St Bede's:* **Mrs B Pope-More**. 507 Rochdale Old Road, Jericho, Bury, Lancs BL9 7TE **Tel:** 0161-764 6025; *North Manchester:* **Mrs I Sidorczuk**. 3 Bloomfield Crescent, Middleton, Manchester. M24 4EP **Tel:** 0161-643 8124; *Oldham:* **Mrs M Chadwick**. 41 Lindale Avenue, Chadderton, Oldham, Lancs OL9 9DW **Tel:** 0161-633 2449; *South Manchester:* **Mr B Caine**. 121 Sale Road, Northern Moor, Manchester M23 0EF **Tel:** 0161-613 5662

World-Wide Marriage Encounter: *Contact*: **Harry and Kath Gillett**. **Tel:** 01204-303540

Young Christian Workers. *Area Organiser*: YCW, Office, St Antony's Centre, Eleventh Street, Trafford Park, Manchester M17 1JF **Tel:** 0161-848 8873 *Diocesan Chaplain:* **Rev Joseph Carter**. **Tel:** 0161-872 0311

■ HOSPITALS

To contact the Catholic Chaplain of a particular hospital we suggest you contact the hospital reception directly.

■ CATHOLIC SCHOOLS - MAINTAINED

■ METROPOLITAN BOROUGH OF BOLTON

▲ Junior and Infant

St Mary Victoria Road, Horwich BL6 6EP **Tel:** 01204-333625 *(Horwich)*

Holy Infants and St Anthony Mitre Street, Bolton BL1 6QJ **Tel:** 01204-333111 *(Bolton)*

Our Lady of Lourdes Beech Avenue Farnworth BL4 0BP **Tel:** 01204-333181 *(Farnworth)*

Sacred Heart Central Drive, Westhoughton BL5 3DU **Tel:** 01942-634681 *(Westhoughton)*

St Bernard Wendover Drive, Ladybridge BL3 4RX **Tel:** 01204-652147 *(Bolton)*

St Brendan Brookfold Lane, Harwood BL2 4DZ **Tel:** 01204-333133 *(Harwood)*

St Columba Ripley Street, Bolton BL2 3AR **Tel:** 01204-333421 *(Bolton)*

St Ethelbert, Melbourne Road, Deane, Bolton BL3 5RL *(L14)* **Tel:** 01204-333036

St Gregory Presto Street, Farnworth BL4 8AJ **Tel:** 01204-332658 *(Farnworth)*

St John the Evangelist Darwen Road, Bromley Cross, Bolton BL7 9HT **Tel:** 01204-333440 *(Bolton)*

St Joseph Shepherd Cross Street, Bolton BL1 3EJ **Tel:** 01204-333055 *(Bolton)*

St Osmund and St Andrew, Blenheim Road, Breightmet, Bolton BL2 6EL and

Withins Drive, Breightmet, Bolton BL2 5LF **Tel:** 01204-333070 and 01204-333729 *(Bolton)*
SS Peter and Paul Pilkington Street, Bolton BL3 6HP **Tel:** 01204-1333030 *(Bolton)*
St Teresa Redcar Road, Little Lever, Bolton BL3 1EN **Tel:** 01204-333163 *(Little Lever)*
St Thomas of Canterbury Eastbourne Grove, Bolton BL1 5LH **Tel:** 01204-333131 *(Bolton)*
St William Nugent Road, Bolton BL3 3DE **Tel:** 01204-333522 *(Bolton)*

▲ Secondary Comprehensive
Mount St Joseph Business & Enterprise College Greenland Road, Farnworth, Bolton BL4 0HU **Tel:** 01204-391800 *(Bolton)*
St Joseph Sports College Chorley New Road Horwich BL6 6HW **Tel:** 01204-697456 *(Horwich)*
Thornleigh Salesian College Sharples Park Bolton BL1 6PQ **Tel:** 01204-301351 *(Bolton)*

■ METROPOLITAN BOROUGH OF BURY

▲ Junior and Infant
Guardian Angels Leigh Lane, Bury BL8 2RH **Tel:** 0161-764 4014 *(Bury)*
Holly Mount Holcombe Road, Greenmount, Bury BL8 4HS **Tel:** 01204-882770 *(Greenmount)*
Our Lady of Grace Highfield Road, Prestwich M25 3AS **Tel:** 0161-796 7254 *(Prestwich)*
Our Lady of Lourdes Rudgwick Drive, Bury BL8 1YA **Tel:** 0161-761 2026 *(Bury)*
St Bernadette Abingdon Avenue, Whitefield M25 8PT **Tel:** 0161-766 6098 *(Whitefield)*
St Joseph and St Bede Danesmoor Drive, Bury BL9 6ER **Tel:** 0161-764 3781 *(Bury)*
St Joseph Queen Street, Ramsbottom. **Tel:** 01706-823645 *(Ramsbottom)*
St Marie Edward Street, The Mosses, Bury BL9 0RZ **Tel:** 0161-764 3204 *(Bury)*
St Mary Belgrave Street, Radcliffe M26 4DG **Tel:** 0161-723 4210
St Michael Ribble Drive, Whitefield M45 8NJ **Tel:** 0161-766 6628 *(Whitefield)*

▲ Secondary Comprehensive
St Gabriel High Bridge Road, Bury BL9 0TZ **Tel:** 0161-764 3186 *(Bury)*
St Monica High Bury Old Road, Prestwich, Manchester M25 1JA **Tel:** 0161-773 6436 *(Prestwich)*

▲ Sixth Form College
Holy Cross Manchester Road, Bury BL9 9BB **Tel:** 0161-762 4500 *(Bury)*

■ METROPOLITAN BOROUGH OF CALDERDALE

▲ Junior and Infant
St Joseph Wellington Road, Todmorden, Lancs OL14 5HP. **Tel:** 01706-812948.

■ LANCASHIRE COUNTY COUNCIL

■ PRESTON

▲ Junior and Infant
St Mary Club Lane, Chipping, Preston PR3 2QH **Tel:** 01995-61367 *(Chipping)*
St Wilfrid St Wilfrid's Terrace, Longridge, Preston PR3 3WQ **Tel:** 01772-782394 *(Longridge)*

▲ Secondary Comprehensive
St Cecilia High Chapel Hill, Longridge, Preston PR3 2XA **Tel:** 01772-783074 *(Longridge)*

■ SOUTH RIBBLE

▲ Junior and Infant
Our Lady and St Gerard Lourdes Avenue, Lostock Hall, Preston PR5 5TB **Tel:** 01772-335025 *(Lostock Hall)*
St Mary and St Benedict Brownedge Lane, Bamber Bridge, Preston PR5 6TA **Tel:** 01772-336650 *(Bamber Bridge)*
St Patrick Higher Walton Road, Walton-le-Dale, Preston PR5 4HD **Tel:** 01772-555436 *(Walton-le-Dale)*

▲ Secondary Comprehensive
St Mary Catholic Sports College, Station Road, Bamber Bridge, Preston PR5 6PB **Tel:** 01772-339813 *(Bamber Bridge)*

■ BLACKBURN

▲ Infant
St Peter Hawkins Street, Blackburn BB2 2RY **Tel:** 01254-260318 *(Blackburn)*

▲ Junior and Infant
Holy Souls Wilworth Crescent, Blackburn BB1 8QN **Tel:** 01254-249892 *(Blackburn 10)*
Our Lady of Perpetual Succour Holmbrook Close, Blackburn BB2 3UG **Tel:** 01254-59420 *(Blackburn 3)*
Sacred Heart Lynwood Road, Blackburn BB2 6HQ **Tel:** 01254-54851 *(Blackburn 1)*
St Alban Trinity Street, Blackburn BB1 5BN **Tel:** 01254-57582 *(Blackburn 4)*
St Anne Feilden Street, Blackburn BB2 1LQ **Tel:** 01254-580462 *(Blackburn 5)*
St Antony Shadsworth Road, Blackburn BB1 2HP **Tel:** 01254-54686 *(Blackburn)*
St Mary & St Joseph Bennington Street, Blackburn BB2 3HP **Tel:** 01254-698301 *(Blackburn)*
St Edward Blackburn Road, Darwen

BB3 0AA **Tel:** 01254-701616 *(Darwen)*
St Joseph Limes Avenue, Darwen BB3 2SG **Tel:** 01254-706264 *(Darwen)*
St Paul off Preston Old Road, Feniscowles, Blackburn BB2 5HZ **Tel:** 01254-201495 *(Feniscowles)*

▲ Junior
St Peter Watson Street, Blackburn BB2 2RH **Tel:** 01254-57841

▲ Secondary Comprehensive
Our Lady and St John Catholic Arts College, North Road, Blackburn BB1 1PY **Tel:** 01254-59055 *(Blackburn)*
St Bede Catholic Sports College, Livesey Branch Road, Blackburn BB2 5BU **Tel:** 01254-202519 *(Blackburn)*

▲ Sixth Form College
St Mary's College Shear Brow, Blackburn BB1 8DX **Tel:** 01254-580464 *(Darwen)*

■ HYNDBURN

▲ Junior and Infant
St Anne and St Joseph, Sandy Lane, Accrington BB5 2AN **Tel:** 01254-233019 *(Accrington 2&3)*
St Oswald Hartley Avenue, Accrington BB5 0NN **Tel:** 01254-234924 *(Accrington 1)*
St Joseph Whalley Road, Hurst Green, Blackburn BB7 9QJ **Tel:** 01254-826246 *(Hurst Green)*
St Mary Whalley Road, Langho, Blackburn BB6 8EQ **Tel:** 01254-247157 *(Billington)*
Sacred Heart Bradshaw Row Church, Accrington BB5 4HG **Tel:** 01254-233382 *(Church)*
St Mary Devonshire Drive, Clayton-le-Moors, Accrington BB5 5RJ **Tel:** 01254-231277 *(Clayton-le-Moors)*
St Michael and St John Lowergate, Clitheroe BB7 1AG **Tel:** 01254-422560 *(Clitheroe)*
Our Lady and St Hubert Hallfield Road, Great Harwood, Blackburn BB6 7SN **Tel:** 01254-885778 *(Great Harwood)*
St Wulstan Rushton Street, Great Harwood, Blackburn BB6 7JQ **Tel:** 01254-884533 *(Great Harwood)*
St Mary Mayfield Avenue, Oswaldtwistle, Accrington BB5 3AA **Tel:** 01254-231278 *(Oswaldtwistle)*
St Charles Knowles Street, Rishton, Blackburn BB1 4HT **Tel:** 01254-886110 *(Rishton)*
St Mary Watt Street, East Sabden, Blackburn BB6 9ED **Tel:** 01282-771009 *(Sabden)*
St Mary Longsight Road, Osbaldston, Blackburn BB2 7HX **Tel:** 01282-812543 *(Osbaldston)*
Thorneyholme Catholic Primary School, Trough Road, Dunsop Bridge, Clitheroe BB7 3BG **Tel:** 01200-448276 *(Dunsop Bridge)*

▲ Sixth Form College
Blessed Trinity RC College Coal Clough Lane, Burnley, Lancs BB11 5BT **Tel:** 01282-436314 *(Burnley)*

■ PENDLE

▲ Junior and Infant
Holy Trinity Halifax Road, Brierfield, Nelson, Lancs BB9 5BL **Tel:** 01282-613709 *(Brierfield)*
Holy Saviour Holland Place, off Reedyford Road, Nelson, Lancs BB9 8HD **Tel:** 01282-612319 *(Nelson 4)*
Sacred Heart Red Lane, Colne, Lancs BB8 7JR **Tel:** 01282-864362 *(Colne)*
St John Southworth Lomeshaye Road, Nelson, Lancs BB9 0DQ **Tel:** 01282-613906 *(Nelson 1)*

▲ Secondary Comprehensive
SS John Fisher and Thomas More High Gibfield Road, Colne, Lancs BB8 8JT **Tel:** 01282-865299 or 865349 *(Colne)*

■ ROSSENDALE

▲ Junior and Infant
St Veronica Raven Avenue, Helmshore, Rossendale, Lancs BB4 4EZ **Tel:** 01706-226315 *(Haslingden)*

▲ Junior and Infant
St Joseph Huttock End Lane, Bacup, Lancs OL13 8LD **Tel:** 01706-873177 *(Bacup)*
St Mary Tong Lane, Bacup, Lancs OL13 9LJ **Tel:** 01706-873123 *(Bacup)*
St Mary Lime Road, Haslingden, Rossendale, Lancs BB4 5NP. **Tel:** 01706-214747 *(Haslingden)*
St James-the-Less Unity Way, off Haslingden Old Road, Rawtenstall, Rossendale, Lancs BB4 8SU **Tel:** 01706-216190 *(Rawtenstall)*
St Peter St Peter's Road, Newchurch, Rossendale, Lancs BB4 9EZ **Tel:** 01706-229972 *(Rawtenstall)*
Our Lady & St Anselm John Street, Whitworth, Rochdale, Lancs OL12 8DB **Tel:** 01706-853545 *(Whitworth)*

▲ Secondary Comprehensive
All Saints Catholic Language College, Haslingden Road, Rawtenstall, Rossendale, Lancs BB4 6SJ **Tel:** 01706-213693 *(Rossendale)*

■ METROPOLITAN BOROUGH OF MANCHESTER

▲ Infant

Mount Carmel Hunt Street, Blackley M9 8BL **Tel:** 0161-205 7131 *(Blackley)*

Sacred Heart Glencastle Road, Gorton M18 7NE **Tel:** 0161-223 8685 *(Gorton)*

▲ Junior and Infant

Bishop Bilsborrow Memorial Princess Road, M14 7LS **Tel:** 0161-226 3649

Christ the King Culcheth Lane, Newton Heath, M40 1LU **Tel:** 0161-681 2779 *(Newton Heath)*

Holy Name Denmark Road, M15 6JS **Tel:** 0161-226 6303 *(Moss Side)*

Our Lady's Whalley Road, M16 8AW **Tel:** 0161-226 2767 *(Manchester)*

St Ambrose Princess Road, Chorlton M21 7QA **Tel:** 0161-445 3299 *(Chorlton-cum-Hardy)*

St Anne, Carruthers Street, Ancoats M4 6EQ **Tel:** 0161-273 2417 *(Ancoats)*

St Anne Moss Bank, Crumpsall, M8 5AB. **Tel:** 0161-740 5995. *(Crumpsall)*

St Bernard Burnage Lane, M19 1DR **Tel:** 0161-432 7635 *(Burnage)*

St Brigid Grey Mare Lane, M11 3DR **Tel:** 0161-223 5538 *(Manchester)*

St Catherine School Lane, Didsbury M20 6HS **Tel:** 0161-445 6359 *(Didsbury)*

St Chad Balmfield Street, Cheetham M8 0SP **Tel:** 0161-205 6965 *(Cheetham)*

St Clare Victoria Avenue, Blackley M9 0RR **Tel:** 0161-740 4993 *(Blackley)*

St Dunstan Edale Avenue, Moston M40 9HU **Tel:** 0161-681 5665

St Edmund Upper Monsall Street, M40 8NG **Tel:** 0161-205 1700

St Edward Yew Tree Road, M14 7PW **Tel:** 0161-224 6608

St Francis Ellenbrook Street, Manchester M12 5LZ **Tel:** 0161-223 3457

St John Chepstow Road, Chorlton-cum-Hardy M21 9SN **Tel:** 0161-881 1040 *(Chorlton-cum-Hardy)*

St John Bosco Hall Moss Road, Blackley M9 7AT **Tel:** 0161-740 7094 *(Blackley)*

St Joseph Richmond Grove, Longsight M13 0BT **Tel:** 0161-224 5347 *(Longsight)*

St Kentigern Bethnall Drive, M14 7ED **Tel:** 0161-224 6842 *(Fallowfield)*

St Malachy Erasmus Street, Collyhurst M40 7RG **Tel:** 0161-205 3496 *(Collyhurst)*

St Margaret's Mary St Margaret Road, New Moston, M40 0JE **Tel:** 0161-681 1504 *(New Moston)*

St Mary's Clare Road, Levenshulme M19 2QW **Tel:** 0161-224 5995 *(Levenshulme)*

St Patrick Livesey Street, M4 5HF **Tel:** 0161-834 9004 *(Collyhurst)*

St Richard Wilpshire Avenue M12 5TL **Tel:** 0161-224 5552 *(Manchester)*

St Wilfrid Birchvale Close, M15 5BJ **Tel:** 0161-226 3339 *(Hulme)*

St Willibrord Vale Street, Clayton M11 4WR **Tel:** 0161-223 9345 *(Clayton)*

▲ Junior

Mount Carmel Wilson Road, Blackley M9 8BG **Tel:** 0161-740 4696 *(Blackley)*

Sacred Heart Knutsford Road, Gorton M18 7HS **Tel:** 0161-223 0231 *(Gorton)*

St Cuthbert Junior & Infant Hyescroft Road, M20 4UZ **Tel:** 0161-445 6079 *(Withington)*

▲ Secondary Comprehensive

Our Lady Catholic Sports College, Alworth Road, Blackley M9 0RP **Tel:** 0161-795 0711

St Matthew RC Technology College, Nuthurst Road, New Moston M40 0EW **Tel:** 0161-681 6178

St Peter RC High School - Specialist College for Business and Enterprise, Kirkmanshulme Lane, Manchester M12 4WB **Tel:** 0161-248 1550

St Thomas Aquinas, Nell Lane, Chorlton-cum-Hardy M21 7SW **Tel:** 0161-882 3142

The Barlow RC High School and Specialist Science College, Parrs Wood Road, East Didsbury M20 6BX **Tel:** 0161-445 8053

▲ Sixth Form Colleges

Loreto College Chichester Road, Hulme M15 5PB **Tel:** 0161-226 5156

Xaverian College, Lower Park Road, Victoria Park M14 5RB **Tel:** 0161-224 1781

■ METROPOLITAN BOROUGH OF OLDHAM

▲ Infant and Junior

Corpus Christi Stanley Road OL9 7HA **Tel:** 0161-652 1275 *(Chadderton)*

St Herbert Edward Street OL9 9SN **Tel:** 0161-633 1318 *(Chadderton)*

St Edward Rowland Way OL4 3LQ **Tel:** 0161-624 1377 *(Lees)*

Holy Family Limegreen Road, Limeside OL8 3NG **Tel:** 0161-652 2400 *(Oldham)*

Holy Rosary Fir Tree Avenue, OL8 2SR **Tel:** 0161-624 3035 *(Oldham 5)*

Our Lady Turf Pit Lane OL4 2NE **Tel:** 0161-652 0244 *(Oldham 3)*

Sacred Heart Whetstone Hill Road OL1 4NA **Tel:** 0161-911 3173 *(Oldham 1)*

St Anne Greenacres Road OL4 1HP **Tel:** 0161-624 4179 *(Oldham 6)*
St Patrick Lee Street OL8 1EF. **Tel:** 0161-633 0527 *(Oldham 2)*
SS Aidan and Oswald Roman Road OL2 5PQ **Tel:** 0161-652 2558 *(Royton)*
St Joseph Oldham Road, Shaw, Oldham OL2 8SZ **Tel:** 01706-847218 (Shaw)

▲ Junior
St Mary Clive Road M35 0NW **Tel:** 0161-681 6663 *(Failsworth)*

▲ Secondary Comprehensive
St Augustine of Canterbury Grange Aveune, OL8 4ED **Tel:** 0161-911 3225/8055 *(Oldham)*
Our Lady's RC High School Specialist in Maths and Computing, Vaughan Street OL2 5DL **Tel:** 0161-624 9974 *(Royton)*

■ METROPOLITAN BOROUGH OF ROCHDALE

▲ Infant and Junior
St Mary Whitelees Road, Featherstall, Littleborough, Lancs OL15 8DU **Tel:** 01706-378032 *(Littleborough)*
Alice Ingham Millgate, Halifax Road, Rochdale, Lancs OL16 2NU **Tel:** 01706-341560 *(Rochdale 3)*
St Gabriel Vicarage Road, South Castleton, Rochdale, Lancs OL11 2TN **Tel:** 01706-650280. *(Castleton)*
St Patrick Foxholes Road, Rochdale OL12 0ET **Tel:** 01706-648089 *(Rochdale 3)*
St Vincent de Paul Edenfield Road, Rochdale, Lancs OL12 7QL **Tel:** 01706-642469 *(Rochdale 4)*
Our Lady and St Paul Sutherland Road, Darnhill, Heywood, Lancs OL10 3PD **Tel:** 01706-360827 *(Heywood)*
St Joseph Pot Hall, Heywood, Lancs OL10 2AA **Tel:** 01706-369340 *(Heywood)*
St John Fisher Stanycliffe Lane, Middleton, Manchester M24 2PB **Tel:** 0161-643 3271 *(Middleton)*
St Peter Kirkway, Middleton, Manchester M24 1FL **Tel:** 0161-643 3946 *(Middleton)*
St Thomas More, Evesham Road, Alkrington, Middleton, Manchester M24 1PY **Tel:** 0161-643 7132 *(Middleton)*
Holy Family Great Gates Road, Rochdale, Lancs OL11 2DA **Tel:** 01706-640480 *(Rochdale 5)*
Sacred Heart Kingsway, Rochdale, Lancs OL16 4AW **Tel:** 01706-649981 *(Rochdale 2)*
St John the Baptist, Anne Street, Rochdale, Lancs OL11 1EZ **Tel:** 01706-647195 *(Rochdale 1)*
St Mary Wood Street, Langley, Middleton Manchester M24 5GL **Tel:** 0161-643 7594 *(Middleton)*

▲ Secondary Comprehensive
Cardinal Langley RC High School and Sports College, Rochdale Road, Middleton, Manchester M24 2GL **Tel:** 0161-643 4009
St Cuthbert's Shaw Road, Rochdale, Lancs OL16 4RX **Tel:** 01706-647761
St Joseph's Maths and Computing College, Pot Hall, Wilton Grove, Heywood OL10 2AA **Tel:** 01706-360607

■ METROPOLITAN BOROUGH OF SALFORD

▲ Junior and Infant
Holy Cross and All Saints Trafford Road, Eccles M30 0JA **Tel:** 0161-789 4386 *(Eccles)*
All Souls Kintyre Avenue, Salford M5 2NR **Tel:** 0161-921 2260 *(Salford)*
Cathedral School of St Peter and St John, Mount Street, Salford M3 6LU **Tel:** 0161-834 4150 *(Salford)*
Christ the King Holly Avenue, Worsley M28 3DW **Tel:** 0161-790 4329 *(Worsley)*
Our Lady and Lancs Martyrs Wicheaves Crescent, Little Hulton M28 0HF **Tel:** 0161-790 5089 *(Little Hulton)*
St Boniface Yew Street, Salford M7 2HL **Tel:** 0161-792 5659 *(Salford)*
St Charles Emlyn Street, Swinton M27 9PD **Tel:** 0161-794 4536 *(Swinton)*
St Edmund Bridgewater Street, Little Hulton, Worsley M38 9ND **Tel:** 0161-790 2329 *(Little Hulton)*
St Gilbert Cambell Road, Winton, Eccles M30 8LZ **Tel:** 0161-789 5035 *(Winton)*
St James Colwyn Street, Salford M6 5JG **Tel:** 0161-736 1455 *(Salford)*
St Joseph Old Lane, Little Hulton, Worsley M38 6RU **Tel:** 0161-790 5278 *(Worsley)*
St Joseph St Joseph's Drive, Salford M5 3JP **Tel:** 0161-872 1062 *(Salford)*
St Joseph the Worker, Cutnook Lane, Higher Irlam M44 6GX **Tel:** 0161-775 4548 *(Higher Irlam)*
St Luke Swinton Park Road, Salford M6 7WR **Tel:** 0161-736 6874 *(Salford)*
St Mark Queensway, Clifton, Swinton M27 8QE **Tel:** 0161-794 3876 *(Swinton)*
St Mary Milner Street, Swinton M27 4AS **Tel:** 0161-794 4028 *(Swinton)*
St Mary Hemming Drive, Eccles M30 0FJ **Tel:** 0161-789 4532 *(Eccles)*
St Philip Cavendish Road, Salford M7 4WP **Tel:** 0161-792 4595 *(Salford)*
St Sebastian Douglas Green, Salford M6 6ET **Tel:** 0161-736 6875 *(Salford)*

St Teresa Clarendon Road, Irlam, Manchester M44 5ZA **Tel:** 0161-777 8203 *(Irlam)*

St Thomas of Canterbury Hadfield Street, Salford M7 4XG **Tel:** 0161-792 3973 *(Salford)*

▲ Secondary Comprehensive

All Hallows Rc Business and Enterprise College, Weaste Lane, Salford M5 5JH **Tel:** 0161-736 4117 *(Salford)*

St Ambrose Barlow Shaftesbury Road, Swinton M27 5SZ **Tel:** 0161-794 3521 or 793 0331 *(Swinton)*

St George's RC High School and Technology College, Parsonage Drive, Little Hulton, Worsley M28 3SH **Tel:** 0161-790 4420 or 5156 *(Worsley)*

St Patrick's RC High School and Arts College Guilford Road, Winton, Eccles M30 7JF **Tel:** 0161-789 4678 *(Winton)*

■ METROPOLITAN BOROUGH OF STOCKPORT

▲ Infant

St Joseph Higginson Road, Reddish, Stockport, Cheshire SK5 6BG **Tel:** 0161-432 2155 *(Reddish)*

▲ Junior and Infant

St Winifred Didsbury Road, Stockport Cheshire SK4 3JH **Tel:** 0161-432 5782 *(Heaton Mersey)*

St Mary Roman Road, Stockport Cheshire SK4 1RF **Tel:** 0161-480 5319 *(Stockport)*

▲ Junior

St Joseph Higginson Road, Reddish, Stockport, Cheshire SK5 6BG **Tel:** 0161-432 5689 *(Reddish)*

▲ Secondary Comprehensive

St Anne Glenfield Road, Heaton Chapel, Stockport, Cheshire SK4 2QP **Tel:** 0161-432 8162 *(Heaton Chapel)*

■ METROPOLITAN BOROUGH OF TAMESIDE

▲ Junior and Infant

Our Lady of Mount Carmel, Holden Street, Ashton-under-Lyne, Lancs OL6 9JJ **Tel:** 0161-330 9521 *(Ashton-under-Lyne)*

St Christopher St Christopher's Road, Ashton-under-Lyne, Lancs OL6 9DP **Tel:** 0161-330 5880 *(Ashton-under-Lyne)*

St Anne Booth Road, Audenshaw, Manchester M34 5QA **Tel:** 0161-370 8698 *(Audenshaw)*

St John Fisher Manor Road, Denton, Manchester M34 7SW **Tel:** 0161-336 5308 *(Denton)*

St Mary Kynder Street, Denton, Manchester M34 2AR **Tel:** 0161-336 3322 *(Denton)*

St Stephen Chappell Road, Droylsden, Manchester M43 7NA **Tel:** 0161-370 2071 *(Droylsden)*

St Joseph Market Street, Mossley, Ashton-under-Lyne, Lancs OL5 0ES **Tel:** 01457-832360 *(Mossley)*

▲ SECONDARY COMPREHENSIVE

St Damian RC Science College, Lees Road, Ashton-under-Lyne OL6 8BH **Tel:** 0161-330 5974 *(Ashton-under-Lyne)*

St Thomas More RC College Specialising in Maths and Computing, Town Lane, Denton, Manchester M34 6AF **Tel:** 0161-336 2743 *(Denton)*

■ METROPOLITAN BOROUGH OF TRAFFORD

▲ Primary

St Ann Primary School, Derbyshire Lane, Stretford, Manchester M32 8HS **Tel:** 0161-865 7705 *(Stretford)*

▲ Junior and Infant

St Alphonsus, Hamilton Street, Old Trafford, Manchester M16 7PT **Tel:** 0161-872 5239 *(Stretford)*

St Hugh of Lincoln Glastonbury Road, Stretford, Manchester M32 9PD **Tel:** 0161-912 2906 *(Stretford)*

St Teresa St Teresa's Road, Firswood, Stretford, Manchester M16 0GQ **Tel:** 0161-881 3163 *(Stretford)*

Our Lady of the Rosary Davyhulme Road, Urmston, Manchester M41 7DS **Tel:** 0161-748 4626 *(Urmston)*

St Monica Woodsend Road South, Flixton, Urmston, Manchester M41 6QB **Tel:** 0161-748 3353 *(Flixton)*

English Martyrs Wycliffe Road, Urmston, Manchester M41 5AH **Tel:** 0161-748 7257 *(Urmston)*

■ STRETFORD / URMSTON

▲ Secondary Modern

St Antony's Catholic College, Bradfield Road, Urmston, Manchester M41 9PD **Tel:** 0161-911 8001 *(Urmston)*

■ METROPOLITAN BOROUGH OF WIGAN

▲ Junior and Infant

Our Lady Holly Road, Aspull, Wigan WN2 1RU **Tel:** 01942-832299 *(Aspull)*

Holy Family Longfield Street, Aspull, Wigan WN2 1EL **Tel:** 01942-246376 *(New Springs)*

■ CATHOLIC SCHOOLS - INDEPENDENT

■ BURY

▲ Primary

Bury Catholic Preparatory Arden House, 173 Manchester Road, Bury, Lancs BL9 9BH **Tel:** 0161-764 2346 *(Bury)*

■ LANCASHIRE

▲ Primary

St Joseph's Convent Primary Park Hill, Padiham Road, Burnley BB12 6TG **Tel:** 01282-455622 *(Burnley)*

St Mary's Hall Preparatory Stonyhurst, Clitheroe, Lancs BB6 9PU **Tel:** 01254-826242 *(Stonyhurst)*

▲ Secondary

Stonyhurst College Stonyhurst, Clitheroe, Lancs BB7 9PZ **Tel:** 01254-826345/826346 *(Stonyhurst)*

Oakhill College Wiswell Lane, Whalley BB7 9AF **Tel:** 01254-823546 *(Whalley)*

■ MANCHESTER

▲ Primary

St Bede's Preparatory Alexandra Park, M16 8HZ **Tel:** 0161-226 7156

▲ Secondary

St Bede's College Alexandra Park, M16 8HX **Tel:** 0161-226 3323 *(Manchester)*

■ ROCHDALE

▲ Primary

Beechwood Primary Manchester, Rochdale, OL11 4LU **Tel:** 01706-46627 *(Rochdale)*

■ STOCKPORT

Stella Maris St John's Road, Heaton Mersey, Stockport Cheshire SK4 3BR **Tel:** 0161-432 0532

■ CATHOLIC SCHOOLS - SPECIAL

St John Vianney School (age 5-19) Rye Bank Road, Firswood, Stretford, M16 0EX **Tel:** 0161-881 7843

DIOCESE OF SHREWSBURY

(Province of Birmingham)
Consisting of the Counties of Cheshire (except parts of Warrington and Widnes) and Shropshire, with parts of Derbyshire, Merseyside and Greater Manchester.

Patrons of the Diocese
Our Lady, Help of Christians, 24 May.
St Winefride, 3 November.

Bishop
Rt Rev Brian M Noble, born in Lancaster 11 April 1936; ordained 11 June 1960; ordained Bishop of Shrewsbury by Archbishop Couve de Murville 30 August 1995.

Residence:
Laburnum Cottage, 97 Barnston Road, Barnston, Heswall, Wirral CH61 1BW.
Tel: 0151-648 0623
E-mail: bishop@dioceseofshrewsbury.org

Personal Assistant:
Miss Margaret Lightbound,
Curial Offices, 2 Park Road South, Prenton, Wirral CH43 4UX
Tel: 0151-652 9855
Fax: 08701-659288
E-mail: curia@dioceseofshrewsbury.org

Rt Rev Brian M Noble, Bishop of Shrewsbury

■ **DIOCESAN CURIA & ADMINISTRATION**
Curial Offices, 2 Park Road South, Prenton, Wirral CH43 4UX
Reception: 9am to 5pm, Monday to Friday.
Tel: 0151-652 9855
Fax: 08701-671935/0151-653 5172
(Unless otherwise stated, the people below may be contacted through the Curial Offices)

■ **Bishop's Office**
Bishop's Personal Assistant:
Miss Margaret Lightbound
Fax: 08701-659288
E-mail: curia@dioceseofshrewsbury.org

■ **Vicar General & Moderator of the Curia**
Mgr John McManus VG
Personal Assistant: **Mrs Mary Passey**
E-mail: admin@dioceseofshrewsbury.org

■ **Chancery**
Chancellor: **Rev Peter C Montgomery LCL**
Tel: 08701 659288
E-mail: chancellor@dioceseofshrewsbury.org

■ **Cathedral Chapter**
Provost: **Canon Harry Stratton**
Canons: **George Browne, Paschal Byrne, Stephen Coonan, John F Gordon, Brendan Hoban, John McManus VG, Peter O'Neill, John Rafferty, Vincent Whelan**. *Honorary Canons:* **Joseph Cahill, Christopher Dwyer, Timothy Harrington, Patrick Healey, Christopher Lightbound, John Marmion, Christopher Walsh, Peter Walton.**

■ **Board of Trustees**
The Bishop (*Chair*), **Mr Austin Atkinson, Canon George Browne, Mrs Veronica Clarke, Miss Catherine Jones, Dr James Keaton, Mgr John McManus VG, Mr John Mulholland, Rev Anthony Myers, Canon Vincent Whelan.**
Registered Offices: Curial Office, 2 Park Road South, Prenton, Wirral CH43 4UX
Secretary: **Mgr John McManus VG**.

■ **Bishop's College of Consultors**
The Bishop (*Chair*), **Canon Stephen Coonan, Revv Russell Cook, John Daly, Michael Gannon, John Joyce, Nicholas Kern, Mgr John McManus VG, Revv Peter Montgomery, John O'Reilly, Canon John Rafferty, Rev David Roberts, Canon Vincent Whelan.**

■ **Council of Priests**
Chair: **Canon George Browne**, St Monica's, Appleton; *Secretary:* **Canon Brendan Hoban**, Sacred Heart, Moreton.

■ **Vicars for Religious**
Rev Maurice O'Mahony CSsR, Hawkstone Hall, Marchamley, Shrewsbury SY4 5LG.
Tel: 01630 685242
E-mail: mpomahoney48@aol.com
Sr Monica SND, 5 Marina Court, Hoscote Park, West Kirby, Wirral CH48 0QR
Tel: 0151 625 2077
E-mail: monicasnd@talktalk.net

■ **Communications**
Communications and Press Officer: **Rev John Joyce**, St Vincent's, Tatton Street, Knutsford WA16 6HR **Tel:** 01565 633040
E-mail: jjoycespat@aol.com
Editors of Catholic Voice: **Deacons Basil Stephens, Anthony Crisp,** Address for articles: 55 Church Road, West Kirby, Wirral CH48 0RN **Tel:** 0151 625 9963
E-mail: bms@pctrain.demon.co.uk

■ **Diocesan Website**
www.dioceseofshrewsbury.org

■ **Marriage Tribunal**
Our Lady's, Cavendish Street, Birkenhead CH41 8AQ **Tel:** 0151-670 0097
Fax: 0151-652 5595
E-mail: shrewsbury.tribunal@tesco.net
Officialis: **Rev John F Gordon**

■ **Boundaries Commission**
Chair: **Mgr John McManus VG**

■ **Other Appointments**
Diocesan Master of Liturgical Ceremonies: **Rev Jerome Fagan**, Our Lady & St Joseph's, Seacombe; *Diocesan Archives:* Kept in St Joseph's Primary School, Birkenhead. Available by prior appointment from the *Diocesan Archivist:* **Rev Peter Phillips**, St Mary of the Angels, Hooton. *Diocesan Register for Deceased Clergy:* **Rev David Craig**, 42 Cromwell Court, Beam Street, Nantwich CW5 5NZ; *Diocesan Director for Aid to Foreign Missions:* **Rev Frederick Robinson**, 26 Winstanley Road, Little Neston, Neston CH64 0UZ.

■ **Finance Department**
E-mail: finance@dioceseofshrewsbury.org
Financial Secretary: **Mr Frank Roche**; *Accounts Dept.:* **Nicholas Dutton, Mrs Colette Thomas, Miss Stacey Melia, Ms Linda Keys**; *Internal Auditors:* **Mr Peter Fogg, Mr Tony Martin, Mr Derek Pearce**; *Solicitor:* **Mr Philip Horton**; *Property Manager:* **Mr Peter O'Brien**; *Consultant:* **Dr James Keaton.**

■ **Diocesan Board for Finance & Planning**
Mgr John McManus VG (*Chair*), **Rev John G Feeney, Mr Paul Heitzman, Mr James Keaton, Rev Philip Moor, Rev David Roberts, Mr Frank Roche** (*Secretary*).

■ **Planned Giving & Gift Aid**
Director: **Mr Michael Russell**
E-mail: mike.russell@dioceseofshrewsbury.org

■ **Shrewsbury Diocese Commercial Company Limited**
Registered Company No. 02848927
Board of Directors: **Rev Canon Brendan Hoban, Mr James Keaton** (Chair), **Mgr John McManus VG, Mr Frank Roche** (*Company Secretary).*
E-mail: commco@dioceseofshrewsbury.org
Director of Parish Centres: **Mr Mark Hale**
E-mail: parishcentres@dioceseofshrewsbury.org
Financial Accountant: **Mrs Julie Birks**
E-mail: julie.birks@dioceseofshrewsbury

■ **VICARIATE FOR CHRISTIAN RESPONSIBILITY**
(Children's Society; Justice & Peace Commission; Family Life Commission; Child Protection Issues; The Deaf Service; Special Needs; Prison & Hospital Chaplaincy, etc.)

■ **Episcopal Vicar**
Fr Michael Gannon, St Aidans & St Hildas, Wythenshawe. **Tel:** 0161 998 2895

■ **Catholic Children's Society**
Chair: **The Bishop**; *Director:* **Mr Ged Flynn**.
Head Office: St Paul's House, Farmfield Drive, Beechwood, Prenton, Wirral CH43 7ZT **Tel:** 0151-652 1281
Fax: 0151-652 5002
E-mail: info@cathchildsoc.org.uk
Website: www.cathchildsoc.org.uk
There are also offices in Runcorn, Telford, and Wythenshawe.

■ **Justice & Peace Commission**
Chair: **Tony Walsh**, 54 Underwood Drive, Ellesmere Port CH65 9BL **Tel:** 0151-355 6419; *Secretary:* **Mike Simpson**, 2 The Rookery, South Crofts, Nantwich CW5 5SJ **Tel:** 01270-626366; *Diocesan Co-ordinator:* **Joan Sharples**, 16 Wellington Road, Nantwich CW5 7BH **Tel:** 01270-620584
E-mail: joansharples620@btinternet.com
Website: www.jp-shrewsburydiocese.org.uk
Editor of 'MouthPeace': **Marian Thompson**, 37 Dale Road, Marple, Stockport SK6 6EZ **Tel:** 0161-427 7254
E-mail: marian@tiscali.co.uk

■ **Marriage and Family Life Commission**
Chair: **Rev Michael Gannon**, St Hilda's

and St Aidan's, Wythenshawe.

■ **Marriage & Family Life Ministry**
Diocesan Co-ordinator: **Mrs Clara Donnelly**, 64 Grosvenor Street, Wallasey CH44 1AQ **Tel/Fax:** 0151-691 2811 **E-mail:**cc.donn@talktalk.net
Project Development Worker for 'Everyone is Welcome' and 'Home is a Holy Place', **Mrs Helen Bassirat**, Marriage & Family Life Office, St Anthony's, Wythenshawe. **Tel:** 0161 436 4939 **E-mail** helen.mfl@googlemail.com

■ **Child Protection**
Diocesan Safeguarding Co-ordinator: **Pauline Butterfield**, c/o Curial Offices, **Mobile:** 07715-120518 (emergency only at weekends and after 6pm). *Personal Assistants:* **Miss Alison Brady, Miss Jane Brady, Miss Anna Wise**. **E-mail:** cpva@dioceseofshrewsbury.org

■ **Pastoral Service to Deaf People**
Pastoral Worker for the Deaf: **Sr Maura Considine SCE**. Office: St Bernadette's, 22 The Drive, Brinnington, Stockport SK5 8AH **Voice & Minicom:** 0161-430 4167 **Fax:** 0161-406 7551

■ **CAFOD**
Shrewsbury Diocesan Manager: **Sue Bownas**, CAFOD Shrewsbury Office 27A Downsfield Road, Chester CH4 8HH **Tel:** 07920-232936 **E-mail:** sbownas@cafod.org.uk

■ **Manchester Airport**
Board Member: **Rev Deacon Alan Morris**. *Part-time Chaplain:* **Deacon Terence Simms**.

■ **VICARIATE FOR CLERGY**
(Junior and Newly Ordained Clergy; On-going Formation; Vocations; Retreats; Diaconate; Appraisal: Sick and Retired Priests and Deacons, etc).

■ **Episcopal Vicar**
Canon John Rafferty. St Vincent's, Altrincham. **Tel:** 0161-928 1689 **E-mail:** johnarafferty@btconnect.com

■ **Junior Clergy Group**
Contact: **Rev Jonathan Mitchell**, Holy Spirit, Runcorn.

■ **Newly Ordained Clergy Group**
Chaplain to Newly Ordained Clergy: **Rev David Long**, St Alban's, Liscard.

■ **Ministry to Priests – On-going Formation**
Director: **Canon John Rafferty**, St Vincent's, Altrincham. *Team:* **Revv Michael Lester, David Long, David Roberts**.

■ **Clergy Retreats**
Co-ordinator: **Rev Peter Robertson**, St Joseph's, Upton

■ **Vocations to the Priesthood**
Director and Co-ordinator for Promotion: **Rev Jonathan Mitchell,** Holy Spirit, Runcorn
E-mail: rjonmitchell@cantab.net

■ **Representatives to the National Conference of Priests**
Representatives: **Revv Russell Cooke, Jonathan Mitchell, Simon O'Connor.**

■ **Diaconate**
Director for Permanent Diaconate: **Rev Geoffrey O'Grady**, St Ambrose, Stockport; *Assistant Director for Permanent Diaconate:* **Deacon Peter Jackson**, 36 Arborn Drive, Upton, Wirral CH49 6JS **Tel:** 0151 677 8598

■ **VICARIATE FOR EDUCATION & FORMATION**
(Commission for Schools and Colleges; Adult Education; Youth; Schools' Administration & RE; School Chaplaincy).

■ **Episcopal Vicar**
Rev David Roberts. Holy Angels, Hale Barns **Tel:** 0161-980 4784
E-mail: robertdm@talk21.com

■ **Education Service**
E-mail: education@dioceseofshrewsbury.org
Director of Education: **Rev David Roberts;** *Director of Schools:* **Mr Michael Clarke;** *Assistant Director of Schools (Primary):* **Miss Margaret Lillis;** *Assistant Director of Schools (Secondary):* **Sr Patricia Goodstadt IBVM**; *Assistant Director of Schools (Secondary):* **Mr Ged Roper;** *Assistant Director of Schools (Secondary-Religious Dimensions),* **Rev Jim Gallagher SDB;** *Co-ordinator of School Chaplaincy:* **Mr Peter Siney,** Ellesmere Port Catholic High School; *Advisers for Parish & Adult Formation:* **Miss Paddy Rylands, Rev David Roberts; Mrs Ann Welsh,** *Catechetical Secretary:* **Mrs Rowena Nield,** *Co-ordinator of the CCRS Course:* **Rev Jonathan Brandon,** *Course Administrator:* **Mrs Philomena Fletcher;** *LIMEX Administrator:* **Mrs Dinah Davis;** *Theological Formation:* **Rev David Long;** *Research and Information Officer:* **Mrs Sue Blackwell;** *Administrative Staff:* **Mrs Kay O'Rourke, Mrs Pauline McCulloch.**

■ **Commission for Adult Education**
Chair: **Miss Paddy Rylands.**

■ **Commission for Schools & Colleges**
Chair: **Rev David Roberts,** Holy Angels, Hale Barns

■ **Diocesan Association of Primary Headteachers (DAPH)**
Mr James Gallogly, St Benedict's Catholic Primary School, Handforth (*Chair*)

■ **Diocesan Association of Secondary Headteachers (DASH)**
Mr John Cornally, Blessed Thomas Holford Catholic College, Altrincham (*Chair*).

■ **School Chaplaincy**
Diocesan Co-ordinator: **Mr Peter Siney,** Ellesmere Port Catholic High School.

■ **Youth Service**
Director: **Mr David Fitton,** St Ambrose's Parish Church, Clover Avenue, Stockport SK3 8QA. **Tel:** 0161-480 8065
Mbl: 07973 118896
E-mail: youth@dioceseofshrewsbury.org
Website: www.dioceseofshrewsbury.org

Project 2030: **Rev Hugh Hanley SCJ**, **Tel:** 0161 282 6334
E-mail: hugh@project2030.fsnet.co.uk
Website: project2030.fsnet.co.uk

■ **Disabilities Research & Development Officer**
Mrs Stella Elliott, Curial Offices, 2 Park Road South, Prenton, Wirral CH43 4UX
Tel: 0151-625 9855

■ **VICARIATE FOR EVANGELISATION, CHRISTIAN UNITY & INTERFAITH DIALOGUE**
(Ecumenical Commission; Evangelisation Issues; Shared Churches; Interfaith Issues).

■ **Episcopal Vicar**
Rev John O'Reilly. St Mary's, Crewe **Tel:** 01270-212533 **E-mail:** smc@pob-uk.net

■ **Christian Unity Commission**
Chair: **Rev John O'Reilly**, Crewe.

■ **VICARIATE FOR LITURGY & SPIRITUALITY**
(Liturgy Commission; Historic Churches Business; Re-ordering of Churches; Spiritual Development; Prayer Guiding etc.).

■ **Episcopal Vicar**
Rev Peter C Montgomery, Our Lady & St Augustine's, Latchford. **Tel:** 01925-634849
E-mail: olsa@amionline.co.uk

■ **Liturgy Commission**
Chair: **Rev Peter Dutton**, St Mary's, Middlewich.

■ **Art and Architecture Committee**
Chair: **Rev Peter C Montgomery.** Our Lady & St Augustine's, Latchford.

■ **Spiritual Formation**
Co-ordinator: **Sr Josephine Bird RC**, St Clares, 27 Downsfield Rd, Chester CH4 8HH **Tel:** 01244-680379
E-mail: josephinebird08@btinternet.com

■ **Historic Churches Committee**
Secretary to the RC Dioceses of Lancaster, Liverpool, Salford & Shrewsbury: **Mr John Cowdall**, 47 Southport Road, Chorley, Lancashire PR7 1LF **E-mail:** johncowdall@jca-chorley.freeserve.co.uk

■ **SHREWSBURY** A

1. Cathedral Church of Our Lady Help of Christians and St Peter of Alcantara
(Before 1720; 1856; cons 21 May 1891)
Town Walls, Shrewsbury.
Tel: 01743-362366
E-mail: shrewsbury.cathedral@btinternet.com
Website: www.shrewsburycathedral.org
Also serves Shrewsbury (2 & 3)
Canon Stephen Coonan (*Cathedral Dean*), **Rev Christopher Matthews.** Holy Spirit & St Martin's Parish Office, Fenhurst, Halton Brook, Runcorn WA7 2NJ **Tel:** 01928 564492 *Deacon:* **Rev Frederick Beddow**, 84 Corndon Crescent, Harlescott, Shrewsbury SY1 4LQ
Tel: 01734-462510
M: *Sun 8.30am, 10.45am, 6pm. Hds 12.15pm (plus a Mass in School), 7.30pm.*

Serves HM Prison, Shrewsbury.
• ***Sisters of Mercy,*** St Winefride's Convent, College Hill, Shrewsbury SY1 1LS **Tel:** 01743-362425

■ **ALBRIGHTON**
See Shifnal (2).

■ **ALDERLEY EDGE,** Cheshire A

† **St Pius X** (1946; 1954; 1969)
Stamford Road, Alderley Edge.
Tel: 01625-582386
E-mail: stpius@tiscali.co.uk
Rev David Peters. Stamford House, Stamford Road, Alderley Edge SK9 7NS
M: *Sat 1st M of Sun 6pm. Sun 8.30am, 10am. Hds (vigil 7.30pm), 9.15am.*
• ***Sisters of St Joseph of the Apparition,*** Provincial House, Ryleys Lane, Alderley Edge SK9 7UU
Sisters: **Tel:** 01625-584871;
Provincial: **Tel/Fax:** 01625-585655

Ecclesiastical Art by
Art Studio Demetz
- Stations of
the Cross -
-Statuary -
- Carvings -
- Mosaics -
- Crucifixes -
Metal Castings -
- Altars -
Baptismal Fonts -
-Lecterns -
Founded in 1872, The
Demetz Art Studio is
one of the worldwide
leading studios
that manufactures
ecclesiastical art. For
over 3 generations, the
Demetz family have
supplied the finest
carvings and castings to
churches, schools, and
cathedrals worldwide.
Please contact us
today to discuss your
project or to receive our
full colour catalogue
depicting their beautiful
creations.
F. A. DUMONT
CHURCH SUPPLIES
ART·STUDIO
DEMETZ®
FAD
High Street, Lyminge, Folkestone, Kent CT18 8EL
Sales: Freephone 0800 413401 Fax: 01303 863700
View online at www.fadumont.co.uk

■ **ALSAGER,** Cheshire
† **St Gabriel** (1953; 1958)
140 Lawton Road, Alsager, Cheshire ST7 2DE **Tel:** 01270-872542
Rev Anthony Grace.
Deacon: **Rev Edward Miller,** 17 Heath Avenue, Rode Heath, Stoke-on-Trent ST7 3RY
M: *Sat 1st M of Sun 6.30pm. Sun 9.30am, 11.15am. Hds. 10am (School), 7.30pm.*

■ **ALTRINCHAM,** Cheshire
1. † St Hugh of Lincoln. (1930; 1931; 1981)
314 Manchester Road, West Timperley, Altrincham WA14 5NB
Tel: 0161-973 1694
E-mail: shol.westtimp@talktalk.net
Also serves Altrincham (2).
Rev Anthony Myers.
M: *Sat 1st M of Sun 6.30pm. Sun 8.30am, 10.30am. Hds 12.15pm.*

A

2. † St John the Baptist (1957; 1960)
26 Thorley Lane, Timperley, Altrincham WA15 7AZ **Tel:** 0161-980 2635
Rev Anthony Myers.
314 Manchester Road, West Timperley, Altrincham WA14 5NB
Tel: 0161 973 1694
Email: shol.westtimp@talktalk.net
M: *Sun 5am. Hds 7.30pm.*
- ***Sisters of Loreto,*** 299/301 Stockport Road, Timperley, Altrincham WA15 7SP **Tel:** 0161-980 4164
- ***Sisters of Loreto,*** 12 Goodwood Crescent, Timperley, Altrincham WA15 7BD **Tel:** 0161-980 3709

3. † St Vincent de Paul
(1847; 1905; cons 17 July 1941)
2 Bentinck Road, Altrincham WA14 2BP
Tel: 0161-928 1689
E-mail: stvincentdepaul@btconnect.com
Website: www.stvincentsaltrincham.org.uk
Canon John Rafferty, Rev David Charters.
Deacon: **Rev John Penny**, 25 West Vale Road, Timperley, Altrincham WA15 7RL
Tel: 0161-941 1411
M: *Sat 1st M of Sun 7pm. Sun 8.30am, 9.30am (Bowdon Vale), 10am, 11.15am, 6.30pm. Hds 10am, 12.15pm, 8pm. (Bowdon Vale 11am).*
- ***Sisters of Loreto***, Loreto Convent, 28 Hartley Road, Altrincham WA14 4AY **Tel:** 0161-928 1440 **Fax:** 0161-941 3583
- ***Sisters of St Joseph of the Apparition***, Convent of St Emilie, Grange Road, Bowdon Vale, Altrincham WA14 3HA **Tel/Fax:** 0161-928 2119 (Convent) **Tel:** 0161-928 2567 (Nursing Home) **E-mail:** sja@ladyofthevale.co.uk **Website:** www.ladyofthevale.co.uk

■ **APPLETON,** Warrington
† **St Monica** (1965)
38 Dingleway, Appleton, Warrington WA4 3AB **Tel:** 01925-264695
E-mail: george@georgebrowne.wanadoo.co.uk
Website: www.stmonicas.info
Rev George Browne.
M: *Sat 1st M of Sun 6pm. Sun 8.30am, 10.15am, 5pm. Hds (vigil 7pm), 11am, 7pm.*
- ***HMYOI, Thorn Cross***, Appleton Thorn. *Chaplain:* **Rev Dcn Stephen McKevitt.**

■ **ASHTON-ON-MERSEY,** Sale
See Sale (1).

■ **BARNTON,** Northwich
† **Our Lady of Fatima** (1953; Cons 29 Jan 1983)
Churchfields, Barnton CW8 4UR
Tel: 01606-853339 Served from Weaverham
Rev James Farrell, 25 Church Lane, Weaverham, Northwich CW8 3NP
M: *Sun 9am. Hds 7.30pm.*

■ **BEBINGTON,** Wirral

A

St Luke the Physician (1987)
76 Church Road, Bebington, Wirral CH63 3EB **Tel:** 0151-644 7530
E-mail: mail@stlukethephysician.co.uk
Website: www.stlukethephysician.co.uk
Rev Peter Hooper.
Parish Sister: **Sr Brigid Kelly**
M: *Sun 9.30am (Lower Bebington Methodist Church), 11am (Poulton Lancelyn Primary School, Venables Drive), Hds. 9am or 12 noon, 7.30pm.*

■ **BIRKENHEAD,** Wirral

A 

1. † Holy Name of Jesus, Oxton
(1899; cons 13 Oct 1921)
60 Beresford Road, Oxton, Prenton CH43 2JD **Tel:** 0151-652 3034
E-mail: johnhovington@btopenworld.com
Also serves Birkenhead (7)
Rev John Hovington. *Deacon:* **Rev Philip White,** 19 Templemore Road, Oxton, Prenton CH43 2HB **Tel:** 0151-652 2330
E-mail: crumpawn@ntlworld.com
M: *Sat 1st M of Sun 5.30pm. Sun 11.30am. Hds 9.30am, 7pm.*
- ***Congregation of Christian Brothers,*** St Anselm's College, Manor Hill, Prenton, CH43 1UF **Tel:** 0151-651 1695 (Community), **Tel:** 0151-652 1408 (College). Preparatory Dept. "Redcourt", 7 Devonshire Place, Prenton CH43 1TX **Tel:** 0151-652 5228 **Fax:** 0151-653 5883
- ***Carmelites,*** Carmelite Monastery, 12 Grosvenor Place, Prenton CH43 1UA. **M:** *Sun 8am, Hds 7.45am*

2. Our lady and Holy Cross & St Paul
Parish office: Cavendish Street, Birkenhead CH41 8AQ
Tel: 0151-652 1074 **Fax:** 0151-652 5595
E-mail: ol.hc.sp@btinternet.com
Rev Philip Moor. *Deacon:* **Rev Bernard McConnell**, Flat 2, 'Intabene', 192 Upton Road, Bidston, Prenton CH43 7QQ **Tel:** 0151 653 2257 *Parish Sisters:* **Sr Francis Pollard** *(Our Lady's),* **Sr Pauline Smith RSC** *(Holy Cross & St Paul's).*

† Our Lady of the Immaculate Conception (1854; 1862; cons 8 May 1912)
Cavendish Street, Birkenhead CH41 8AQ
M: *Sat 1st M of Sun 6pm. Sun 11am. Hds. 9.30am.*
- ***Sisters of Charity,*** 137 Park Road North, Birkenhead CH41 8AA **Tel:** 0151-652 5655 **E-mail:** rscbirkenhead@tiscali.co.uk
- ***Sisters of Charity,*** St Elizabeth's Convent, 139 Park Road North, Birkenhead CH41 8AA **Tel:** 0151-651 1379 **E-mail:** rscparkrd@tiscali.co.uk
- ***Sisters of Nazareth,*** Nazareth House, Manor Hill, Prenton CH43 1UG **Tel:** 0151-652 1256 **Fax:** 0151-653 0816 (Convent), **Tel:** 0151-653 4003 (Nursing Home); 0151-652 7811 (Residential Floor). **Tel:** 0151-670 0800 (Special Needs) **Email:** nazbirkenhead@hotmail.co.uk *Non-resident Chaplain:* **Rev Raymund Burke. Tel:** 0151-648 6422

Holy Cross & St Paul (Holy Cross 1928; 1930; 1959) (St Paul 1978, 1981)
Farm Field Drive, Beechwood, Birkenhead.
M: *Sun 9.30am. Hds 11am, 2pm (Holy Cross School term time only).*

3. † St Anne, Rock Ferry (1862; 1877; cons 26 July 1962)
Highfield Road, Rock Ferry, Birkenhead CH42 2BY
Tel: 0151-645 3996
E-mail: stanne.rf@ntlworld.com
Website: www.stannesrockferry.co.uk
- ***Oblates of Mary Immaculate (OMI):*** **Revv Edward Quinn** (*Superior and Parish Priest*), **Michael Phelan**. *Deacon:* **Rev John Boggan,** 14 Woodland Grove, Rock Ferry, Birkenhead CH42 2BY **Tel:** 0151 645 4910 **E-mail:** j.boggan@merseymail.com **M:** *Sat 1st M of Sun 6.30pm. Sun 11am. Hds (vigil 7.30pm), 12.10pm, 7.30pm.*
- ***Sisters of the Holy Family of Bordeaux,*** Highfield Road, Birkenhead CH42 2BY **Tel:** 0151-645 9482

4. † St Joseph (1900)
North Road, Birkenhead.
Tel: 0151-652 5767 **Fax:** 0151-201 7956
E-mail: stjosephsbh1@hotmail.com
Website: www.stjosephsbirkenhead.co.uk
Rev Nicholas Kern. 10 Willowbank Road, Birkenhead CH42 7JY *Deacon:* **Rev Gerard Boyle**, 9 Elm Road, Birkenhead CH42 9NY **Tel:** 0151-608 1214 *Deacon:* **Rev Leslie Arch**, 106 Woodchurch Lane, Prenton CH42 2PD **Tel:** 0151-608 7585
E-mail: les.arch@btinternet.com
M: *Sat 1st M of Sun 6pm. Sun 10am, 5pm. Hds 9.15am (in school during term time), 7.30pm.*
- ***Faithful Companions of Jesus,*** 14 Heathbank Road, Birkenhead CH42 7LD **Tel:** 0151-652 3715 **E-mail:** fcjsisters@aol.com **Website:** fcjsisters.org

5. † St Michael and All Angels, Woodchurch (1952; 1965)
New Hey Road, Woodchurch, Wirral CH49 5LE **Tel:** 0151-677 4915
Fax: 0151-522 0231
E-mail: stmichael.aaa@tiscali.co.uk
Website: www.stmaaa.co.uk
Rev Simon O'Connor, *Deacon:* **Rev Patrick Regan,** 8 Ledbury Close, Prenton CH43 0UJ **Tel:** 0151-608 6146
M: *Sat 1st M of Sun 6pm. Sun 10am. Hds 9.15am, 7.30pm.*

6. † St Peter, Noctorum (1967; 1976)
St Peter's Way, Noctorum, Prenton CH43 9QR
Rev John Hovington, Presbytery, 60 Beresford Road, Oxton, Prenton CH43 2JD
Tel: 0151-652 3034
E-mail: johnhovington@btopenworld.com
M: *Sun 9.30am. Hds 9.30am (in school during term time).*

7. St Werburgh & St Laurence
† St Werburgh (1834; 1837; 2002)
St Werburgh's Square, Birkenhead CH41 2XZ
St Laurence (1864, 1890, 1978, 1995; 2002)
Beckwith Street, Birkenhead.
Tel: 0151-647 9124 **Fax:** 0151-647 9125
E-mail: werlau@btinternet.com
Rev Michael Hartley, 5 St Werburgh's Square, Birkenhead CH41 2XZ
Parish Sister: **Sr Frances Guiney**
M: *Sat 1st M of Sun 5pm (St Werburgh's), Sun 9am (St Laurence), 10.30am (St Werburgh's). Hds 9.30am (St Laurence Chapel term time only), 12.10pm (St Werburgh's), 2.30pm (St Werburgh's School term time only).*

■ BOLLINGTON, Macclesfield
† St Gregory (1830; 1834; 1957; 1972)
38 Wellington Road, Bollington,

Macclesfield SK10 5JR **Tel:** 01625-572108
E-mail: jfmsdb@gmail.com
Website: www.stgregorysbollington.co.uk
• ***Salesians (SDB).*** **Rev James Francis Mageean**, *Deacon:* **Rev John Lomas**, 49 Cedarway, Bollington, Macclesfield SK10 5HR. **Tel:** 01625-572876
M: *Sat 1st M of Sun 6pm. Sun 8.30am, 10.30am. Hds 9am, (9.15am in school in term time), 7.30pm.*
• ***Salesians (SDB):*** Savio House, Ingersley Road, Bollington, Macclesfield SK10 5RW
Tel: 01625-575405 **Fax:** 01625-560221
E-mail: saviooffice@saviohouse.org.uk
Website: www.salesians.org.uk
Youth Retreat Centre & Conference Centre. **Revv Martin Coyle** (*Rector*), **Graham Forristalle, James Robert Gardner, Bernard Parkes.**

■ **BRAMHALL,** Stockport
St Vincent de Paul (1968; 1978)
Handley Road, Bramhall, Stockport SK7 3EX *Parish Co-ordinator:* **Rowena Nield**
Tel: 0161-440 8619; *Parish Office*
Tel: 0161-440 0889. **Revv Peter Sharrocks, Jonathan Brandon.** St Peter's, 16 Green Lane, Hazel Grove, Stockport SK7 4EA
Tel: 0161-483 3476 **E mail:** stvincent@madasafish.com
M: *Sun 10am. Hds (vigil 7.30pm) 10am.*

■ **BRIDGNORTH,** Shropshire
† St John the Evangelist (1855; 1896)
13 Northgate, Bridgnorth WV16 4ER
Tel: 01746-762348
E-mail: iaingriffiths@hotmail.com
Rev Iain Griffiths.
M: *Sat 1st M of Sun 6.30pm. Sun 9am, 11am. Hds (vigil 7pm), 9.15am (in school) 12.30pm.*

■ **BROMBOROUGH,** Wirral
† Christ the King (1928; 1933; 1964)
890 New Chester Road, Bromborough, Wirral CH62 6AT **Tel:** 0151-334 1657
E-mail: mbyrne7@sky.com
Website: www.fairpromise.fsnet.co.uk
Revv Paschal Byrne, Lawrence Watson.
M: *Sat 1st M of Sun 6pm. Sun 9am, 11am, 6pm. Hds 9.15am, 12noon, 7.30pm.*

■ **BROSELEY,** Shropshire
See Telford (1)

■ **CHEADLE,** Cheshire
1. † St Ann (1952; cons 1977)
29 Vicarage Avenue, Cheadle Hulme, Cheadle SK8 7JW **Tel:** 0161-485 1685
E-mail: chris.mccurry@virgin.net
Website: www.st-anns-church.org.uk
Rev Christopher McCurry.
M: *Sat 1st M of Sun 6pm. Sun 8.30am, 10.30am. Hds 10am, 8pm.*

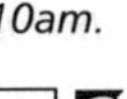

2. † St Chad (1900; 1931)
Stockport Road, Cheadle SK8 2AF
Tel: 0161-428 2480
E-mail: chads248@btinternet.com
Canon John F Gordon. *Deacon:* **Joseph Norbury** 57 Saville Road, Gatley, Cheadle SK8 4BY **Tel:** 0161 286 8965
M: *Sat 1st M of Sun 6pm. Sun 10am. Hds 9.30am, 7.30pm.*

■ **CHESTER**
1. † St Clare (1960; 1969)
27 Downsfield Road, Lache, Chester CH4 8HH
Tel: 01244-671015, **Fax:** 01244-659503
E-mail: office@stclarescatholicchurch.wanadoo.co.uk
Rev Francis Doyle. (Wrexham)
St Anthony's, 54 High Street, Saltney, Flintshire CH4 8SF **Tel:** 01244 671581
M: *Sat 1st M of Sun 6pm. Sun 9.30am. Hds as announced.*
• ***Benedictine Nuns,*** Benedictine Abbey, 10 Curzon Park South, Chester CH4 8AB
Tel: 01244-671323 **Fax:** 01244-676016
E-mail: curzonpark@benedictines.org.uk
• ***Our Lady of the Cenacle, Sisters of,*** 12 Dryersfield, off Heath Lane, Chester CH3 5RQ **Tel:** 01244-345829
• ***Our Lady of the Cenacle and Office for Spiritual Formation:*** 27 Downsfield Road, Chester CH4 8HH
Tel: 01244-680379
E-mail: josephinebird08@btinternet.com

2. † St Columba (1939; 1965; 1967)
Plas Newton Lane, Plas Newton, Chester.
Tel: 01244-400873 **Fax:** 01244-409407
E-mail: st.columba@btopenworld.com
Rev Russell Cooke. 1 Newhall Road, Plas Newton, Chester CH2 1SA *Deacon:* **Rev Lawrence Hordley**, 23 Chatsworth Drive, Newton, Chester CH2 2NB
Tel: 01244-342048
M: *Sat 1st M of Sun 7.15pm. Sun 9.15am, 11am. Hds 9.15am, 7.15pm.*

3. † St Francis (1858; 1875; cons 1900)
Grosvenor Street, Chester.
Tel: 01244-351331
Website: www.capuchinfriars.co.uk
• ***Franciscans (Capuchin) (OFMCap):*** **Fr Gordon Pesterfield** (*Parish Priest*), **Fr Adrian Marsh** (*Vicar*), **Bro Michael Welch** (*Guardian*), **Fr Lawrence Pozzuoli, Fr Andrzej Tomkiel.**
Franciscan Friary, 15 Cuppin Street, Chester CH1 2BN
M: *Sat 1st M of Sun 6.30pm. Sun 8am, 9.30am, 11am. Hds 8am, 12noon, 7pm.*

4. † St Theresa (1956; 1959)
Blacon Avenue, Blacon, Chester CH1 5BU
Tel: 01244-371660 **Fax:** 01244-390976
Rev James Kenny. *Deacon:* **Rev Charles Woods**, 36 Dyserth Road, Blacon, Chester CH1 5QF **Tel:** 01244-375634
M: *Sat 1st M of Sun 6.30pm. Sun 10am, 5.30pm. Hds (vigil 7pm), 9.30am (during term time), 9am (school holidays).*

5. † St Werburgh
(1757; 1799; 1875; cons 28 May 1936; re-ordered 14 May, 2002)
Grosvenor Park Road, Chester CH1 1QJ
Tel: 01244-350236
E-mail: werburgh465@btinternet.com
Website: www.stwerburghchester.co.uk
Rev Paul Shaw.
M: *Sun 9am, 10.45am, 6pm, Indian Syro-Malabar M 3rd Fri 7pm. Hds (vigil 7.30pm), 7.30am, 12.15pm, 7.30pm.*
- ***Armed Services:*** The Dale Army Camp. *Chaplain:* **Rev Colin Wilson**.

Waverton Mass Centre
Rowton Methodist Church, Moor Lane, Waverton CH3 7QW.
M: *Sat 1st M of Sun 6pm.*

■ **CHURCH STRETTON,** Shropshire
† St Milburga (1907; 1923; 1929)
Watling St North, Church Stretton, SY6 7AR **Tel/Fax:** 01694-722897
E-mail: milburga@care4free.net
Rev Ambrose Nicholson.
M: *Sat 1st M of Sun 6.30pm. Sun 9.15am. Hds 12noon.*

† St Walburga's Mass Centre, Lydbury North, Plowden (1862)
Incorporated into the parish of Church Stretton in 1990.
M: *Sun 11am.*

■ **CLEOBURY MORTIMER,** Kidderminster, Worcs
† St Elizabeth (1776; 1962)
Station Road, Cleobury Mortimer.
Served from Ludlow.
M: *Sun 9am. Hds (vigil 8pm).*

■ **CONGLETON,** Cheshire
† St Mary (1821; 1826)
30 West Road, Congleton CW12 4ES
Tel: 01260-273314
E-mail: stmaryscongleton@btinternet.com
Rev William Kilkenny. *Deacon:* **Rev Stephen McKevitt**, 25 Meakin Close, Congleton CW12 3TG **Tel:** 01260-271362
M: *Sat 1st M of Sun 6.30pm. Sun 8.35am, 10.30am. Hds 9.15am, 12noon, 7pm.*

- ***Thornycroft Hall***, Pexhill Road, Siddington SK11 9JN **Tel:** 01260-224219 (Conference Centre under the direction of the Opus Dei Prelature).

■ **COSFORD,** Wolverhampton
† Christ the King
RAF Station. **Tel:** 01902-377062
Rev Paul Owens (Leeds), Defence College of Aeronautical Engineering, Chaplaincy, Cosford, Wolverhampton WV7 3EX

■ **CREWE**
1. † St Mary of the Immaculate Conception
(1844; 1891; cons 14 June 1939)
13 Gatefield Street, Crewe CW1 2JP
Tel: 01270-212533 **Fax:** 01270-216407
E-mail: smc@pob-uk.net
- **Rev John O'Reilly**. *Deacon:* **Rev Peter Bravey**, 3 Blake Close, Crewe CW2 8EB **Tel:** 01270-569957
  M: *Sat 1st M of Sun 5.30pm, 7pm (Pol). Sun 9am, 11am, 12.45pm (Pol), 6.30pm. Hds 12noon, 6pm (Pol), 7.30pm.*
- ***Oblates of Mary Immaculate (OMI):*** Oblate Retreat Centre, Wistaston Hall, 89 Broughton Lane, Crewe CW2 8JS **Tel:** 01270-568653 **Fax:** 01270-650776 **E-mail:** director@oblateretreatcentre.org.uk **Website:** www.oblateretreatcentre.org.uk *Director:* **Rev Oliver Barry**. Retreat House, open to all.

2. Our Lady of Ostra Brama
Polish Catholic Centre, 71 West Street, Crewe CW1 3HF **Tel:** 01270 256284
Rev Grzegorz Januszewski (Schr).
M: *Sat 1st M of Snu 7pm (St Mary's, Crewe) Sun 12.45pm (St Mary's, Crewe). Hds 10am, (Polish Centre), 6pm (St Mary's, Crewe).*

■ **DISLEY,** Stockport
See Whaley Bridge.

■ **DUKINFIELD,** Cheshire
† St Mary (1825; 1854; cons 18 Mar 1952)
29 Zetland Street, Dukinfield SK16 4EJ
Tel: 0161-330 2424
E-mail: o.odoherty@ntlworld.com
Website: www.stmaryscatholicchurch.co.uk
Rev J Oliver O'Doherty.
M: *Sun 9.30am, 11am, 6.30pm. Hds (vigil 7.30pm), 9am (in school term time only), 12noon.*

■ **ELLESMERE,** Shropshire
† St Michael (1947; 1960)
Convent Chapel, Ellesmere.
Tel: 01691-622283
Rev Patrick English. St Michael's, 80

Scotland Street, Ellesmere SY12 0ED
Also serves Wem.
M: *Sun 11am. Hds (vigil 7pm), 9.15am.*
- ***Poor Clares (Colettines)***. Convent of Poor Clares, Ellesmere SY12 OPA
Tel/Fax: 01691-622270

■ ELLESMERE PORT
Team Ministry: **Revv Philip Atkinson, Niall Mullaley, Peter Phillips.** *Deacons:* **Revv Anthony Hunt, Paul Sutton** *(Administrator).*
Four Parishes office: St Saviours, Tarporley Road, Great Sutton, Ellesmere Port CH66 3JY
Tel: 0151 347 9342
E-mail: parishesoff@rcchep.co.uk
Website: www.rcchep.co.uk

1. † St Saviour (1959; 1960)
Tarporley Road, Great Sutton, Ellesmere Port CH66 3JY **Tel:** 0151-339 6588
E-mail: parishsts@rcchep.co.uk
Website: www.rcchep.co.uk
Rev Philip Atkinson. *Deacon:*
Rev Anthony Hunt, 1 Skipton Drive, Little Sutton, Ellesmere Port CH66 4SP
Tel: 0151-339 9684 (residence),
Tel: 0151 347 9342 (office)
M: *Sat 1st M of Sun 5pm. Sun 10am. Hds as announced.*

2. † St Mary of the Angels
(1866; cons 10 July 1883)
Chester Road, Childer Thornton, Ellesmere Port CH66 1QJ **Tel:** 0151-327 6158
E-mail: parishstm@rcchep.co.uk
Rev Peter Phillips.
M: *Sat 1st M of Sun 6pm. Sun 9.30am. Hds 9am, 7.30pm.*

3. † Our Lady Star of the Sea (1909; 1931)
2a Enfield Road, Ellesmere Port CH65 8BY
Tel: 0151-355 1255
E-mail: parishol@rcchep.co.uk
Rev Niall Mullaley. *Deacon:* **Paul Sutton**
M: *Sat 1st M of Sun 6.30pm Sun 11am. Hds (vigil 7.30pm), 12noon and as announced.*

4. † St Bernard (1968)
Sherbourne Road, Ellesmere Port.
Tel: 0151-347 9342
E-mail: parishstb@rcchep.co.uk
Rev Niall Mullaley, *Deacon:* **Rev Paul Sutton.**
M: *Sun 9am. Hds As announced.*

■ FARNDON, Cheshire
See Malpas.

■ FRODSHAM, Cheshire
† St Luke (1949; 1981)
61 High Street, Frodsham WA6 7AN
Tel/Fax: 01928-733127
E-mail: parish@stlukesparish.org.uk
Website: www.stlukesparish.org.uk
Mgr Canon Peter O'Neill.
Tel: 01928-733127

M: *Sat 1st M of Sun 6pm. Sun 9am, 11am. Hds 10am, 7pm.*

■ GREASBY, Wirral
† Our Lady of Pity (1940; 1952; 1975)
24 Mill Lane, Greasby, Wirral CH49 3NN
Tel/Fax: 0151-677 2585
E-mail: mlolopgreasby@yahoo.co.uk
Website: olopgreasby.co.uk
Rev Michael Lester.
M: *Sat 1st M of Sun 6pm. Sun 9am, 11am. Hds (vigil 7.30pm), 9.30am with school, 12noon.*

■ GREAT SUTTON
See Ellesmere Port (1).

■ HALE BARNS, Altrincham
† Holy Angels (1958; 1964)
Wicker Lane, Hale Barns, Altrincham WA15 0HF **Tel:** 0161-980 4784
E-mail: secretaryholyangels@hotmail.com
Website: www.holyangels.org.uk
Rev David Roberts.
Deacon: **Rev Alan Morris,** 35 Rivington Road, Hale, Altrincham WA15 9PJ
Tel: 0161-941 1422
M: *Sat 1st M of Sun 6pm. Sun 8.30am, 10.30am. Hds As announced.*
- ***Congregation of Christian Brothers,*** Woodeaves, Wicker Lane, Hale Barns, Altrincham WA15 0HF
Tel: 0161-904 0786 (community)
Fax: 0161-903 9182
E-mail: gb.cfc@virgin.net
St Ambrose College **Tel:** 0161-980 2711

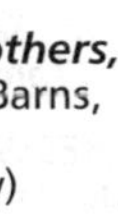

■ HANDFORTH, Wilmslow
† St Benedict (1962; 1967; 1968)
Tel: 01625-522776
Rev William O'Riordan. 10 Hall Road, Handforth, Wilmslow SK9 3AD
Deacon: **Rev Thomas Chrisp,** 41 Windemere Road, Handforth, Wilmslow SK9 3NJ **Tel:** 01625 251 047
M: *Sun 9am, 10.30am, 5.30pm. Hds 9.30am, 7.30pm.*
Serves Styal Prison.

■ HATTERSLEY, Hyde
† St James the Great
(1964; 1965; new church 1982)
40 Underwood Road, Hattersley, Hyde SK14 3DH **Tel:** 0161-338 3260
Served from Stalybridge (2).
E-mail: maccpaul@aol.com
Rev Paul Hughes.
M: *Sun 11am. Hds As announced.*

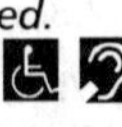

■ HAWKSTONE HALL
Marchamley, Shrewsbury SY4 5LG
Tel: 01630-685242 **Fax:** 01630-685565
E-mail: hawkhall@aol.com
Website: www.hawkstone-hall.com

- *Redemptorists (CSsR):* **Revv Maurice O'Mahony** (*Rector*), **Kevin Callaghan, William Lavery, Bro Richard Golding**.
  M: *Sun 10am. Hds As Arranged.*

■ **HAZEL GROVE,** Stockport
† **St Peter** (1897; 1931)
16 Green Lane, Hazel Grove, Stockport SK7 4EA **Tel:** 0161-483 3476
Fax: 0161-419 9592
E-mail: admin@stpetershazelgrove.org.uk
Website: www.stpetershazelgrove.org.uk
Also serves Bramhall.
Revv Peter Sharrocks, Jonathan Brandon.
M: *Sun 8.30am, 10am, 11.30am, 6pm. Mass in sign language 1st Sun of month, 3pm (except July, Aug), 3rd Sun of month Mass in Syro-Malabar Rite, 7.30pm. Hds 12noon, 7.30pm.*

■ **HEALD GREEN,** Cheadle
† **Christ Church** (1959; 1962)
Finney Lane, Heald Green, Cheadle SK8 3DY **Tel:** 0161-437 5042
E-mail: christchurchhg@yahoo.co.uk
Website: christchurchhealdgreen.co.uk
Rev Paul Lomas.
M: *Sat 1st M of Sun 6pm. Sun 9am, 11am. Hds (vigil 7.30pm), 10am.*

■ **HESWALL,** Wirral
† **Our Lady and St John**
(1919; 1928; 1939; cons 5 Nov 1958)
Telegraph Road, Heswall
Tel: 0151-342 6581
Rev Terence Boylan. 1 Boundary Lane, Heswall, Wirral CH60 5RP
M: *Sat 1st M of Sun 7pm. Sun 8.30am, 11.15am. Hds (vigil 7pm). 10am.*

■ **HOLMES CHAPEL,** Crewe
St Margaret Ward
Macclesfield Road, CW4 7MQ
See Middlewich.

■ **HOOTON**
See Ellesmere Port (1).

■ **HOYLAKE,** Wirral
† **SS Catherine and Martina** (1928)
Birkenhead Road, Hoylake, Wirral CH47 5AF
Tel: 0151-632 4388 **Fax:** 0151-633 2613
Canon Christopher Walsh. *Deacon:* **Rev Anthony Crisp**, 126 Birkenhead Road, Meols, Wirral CH47 0LE **Tel:** 0151-632 6617
M: *Sun 8.30am, 11.15am. Hds 9.30am, 7.30pm.*

■ **HYDE,** Cheshire
† **St Paul** (1848; 1854; cons 30 June 1954)
St Paul's Street, Hyde SK14 2JU
Tel/Fax: 0161-367 8326
E-mail: dionysios2003@yahoo.co.uk
Rev Denis Maher.
M: *Sat 1st M of Sun 6pm. Sun 9am, 11am. Hds 9.30am, 7.30pm.*

■ **KNUTSFORD,** Cheshire
† **St Vincent de Paul** (1866; 1927; 1983)
Tatton Street, Knutsford WA16 6HR
Tel: 01565-633040
E-mail: jjoycespat@aol.com
Website: www.stvincentsknutsford.org
Rev John Joyce.
M: *Sun 9am, 11am, 5.30pm. Hds (vigil 7pm), 9.30am (in school-term time), 12noon.*

■ **LATCHFORD, GRAPPENHALL & THELWALL,** Warrington
† **Our Lady & St Augustine of Canterbury**
(1869; 1902; cons. 10 May 1950; 2005)
26 St Mary Street, Latchford, Warrington WA4 1BN
Tel: 01925-634849
E-mail: olsa@amionline.co.uk
Rev Peter Montgomery. *Deacon:* **Rev John Clowes**, 51 Higher Lane, Lymm WA13 0BE **Tel:** 01925-752557
M: *Sat 1st M of Sun 5.30pm. Sun 9am, 11am. Hds As Announced.*

■ **LUDLOW,** Shropshire
† **St Peter** (1908; 1936; cons. 2 July 1936)
Henley Road, Ludlow SY8 1QZ
Tel: 01584-872906
Website: www.stpetersludlow.org
(Also serves Cleobury Mortimer).
Rev James Robinson.
M: *Sat 1st M of Sun 6pm. Sun 11am, 5.30pm (Moor Park School as announced). Hds 10am, 7pm.*

■ **LYMM,** Cheshire
† **St Winefride** (1902; 1928; 1933)
Booths Hill Road, Lymm WA13 0DL
Tel: 01925-752224.
Rev Anthony Elder, 18 Booths Hill Road
M: *Sat 1st M of Sun 5.45pm. Sun 9am, 10.30am. Hds 9.15am, 7.30pm.*

■ **MACCLESFIELD,** Cheshire
1. † **St Alban**
(1792, 1811; 1841; cons. 22 Oct 1931)
37a Chester Road, Macclesfield SK11 8DJ
Tel: 01625-423446 **Fax:** 01625-421867
E-mail: stalbanmacc@aol.com **Website:** http://members.aol.com/stalbanmacc
Rev Peter Burke. *Deacon:* **Rev Michael Ullmann**, 34 Ivy Road, Macclesfield SK11 8QB **Tel:** 01625-425651
M: *Sat 1st M of Sun 6.30pm. Sun 9.30am, 11am, 6.30pm. Hds (vigil 7.30pm), 9.15am in Primary School, in term time, 12.15pm.*

- ***Sisters of Charity,*** 117 Prestbury Road, Macclesfield SK10 3BU

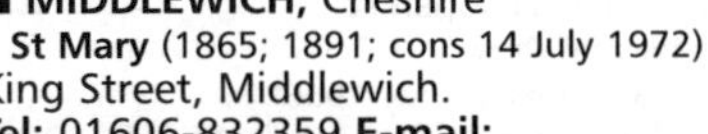

Tel: 01625-423034
E-mail: rscmacc@btinternet.com

• ***Pallottine Missionary Sisters.*** Park Mount, 52 Park Mount Drive, Macclesfield SK11 8NT
Tel: 01625-616459
Chaplain: **Rev John Woods**
Tel: 01625 420075

2. † St Edward the Confessor A
(Cons. 26 April 1939)
145 London Road, Macclesfield SK11 7RL
Tel: 01625-423576 **Fax:** 01625-424460
E-mail: st.edwardmacc@btconnect.com
Website: www.stedwardschurch.org.uk
Rev Peter Cryan. *Parish Sister:* **Sr Carmel.**
M: *Sat 1st M of Sun 5.30pm. Sun 10.30am. Hds 9.30am (in School), 7pm.*

■ **MALPAS,** Cheshire A
St Joseph's
Tilston Road, Malpas.
Also serves Farndon & Tattenhall
Tel: 01948-861327

• ***Sacred Heart Fathers (SCJ):*** **Rev John Gaul** (*Parish Priest*), St Joseph's Presbytery, Tilston Road, Malpas SY14 7DD
M: *Sun 9am. Hds: (Vigil) 7.30pm, 10am*

Farndon Mass Centre
In United Reformed Church, Church Street CH3 6QU.
M: *Sat 1st M of Sun 4.30pm*

Tatton Hall Mass Centre (1971)
St Plegmund, Tattenhall Rd, Tattenhall CH3 9RT
M: *Sun 11am. Hds 7pm.*

■ **MARKET DRAYTON,** Shropshire A
† SS Thomas Aquinas and Stephen Harding
(1884; cons 17 Aug 1887)
53 Gt Hales Street, Market Drayton TF9 1JL
Tel: 01630-652568 **Fax:** 01630-656351
E-mail: priest.greathales@btinternet.com
Website: www.ss-thomas-stephen.org.uk
Rev John McLeish.
Also serves HMYOI Stoke Heath and Tern Hill army barracks.
M: *Sat 1st M of Sun 6pm. Sun 8am, 11am. Hds 10am, 7.30pm.*

■ **MARPLE,** Stockport
The Holy Spirit (1967; 1972)
Leigh Avenue, Marple, Stockport SK6 6DF
Tel: 0161-427 4922. **Rev Marianus Kullu** (Diocese of Dibrugarh).
Deacon: **Rev Stuart Adlington**, 36 Hogarth Road, Marple Bridge, Stockport SK6 5BP
Tel: 0161-449 8427
M: *Sat 1st M of Sun 6pm. Sun 9am, 11am. Hds 10am, 7.30pm.*

■ **MIDDLEWICH,** Cheshire
† St Mary (1865; 1891; cons 14 July 1972)
King Street, Middlewich.
Tel: 01606-832359 **E-mail:** pad.st.marys@btinternet.com **Website:** www.stmarysparishmiddlewich.org.uk
Rev Peter Dutton. Presbytery, 2 New King Street, Middlewich CW10 9EB
Deacon: **Rev Anthony Ford**, 23 Hadrian Way, Middlewich CW10 9RB
Tel: 01606-237875
M: *Sat 1st M of Sun 6.30pm. Sun 10.30am. Hds (vigil 7.30pm). 9am.*

St Margaret Ward Mass Centre
Macclesfield Rd, Holmes Chapel CW4 7MQ
M: *Sun 9am. Hds 7.30pm.*

■ **MOULDSWORTH,** Cheshire
† St Cuthbert (1955)
Station Road, CH3 8AJ. Served from Tarporley.
Website: www.saintcuthbert.org.uk
Rev Joseph Carney, St Thomas Becket, 3 Nantwich Road, Tarporley CW6 9UN
Tel/Fax: 01829 732511
M: *Sun 9am. Hds As announced.*

■ **MUCH WENLOCK,** Shropshire
† St Mary Magdalene (1955, Closed Feb 2008)
Mass celebrated in Broseley, Telford (1).
Rev William Dukes Also resident: **Rev Thomas Rock** (Retired, Birmingham)

■ **NANTWICH,** Cheshire
† St Anne (1856; 1936)
Pillory Street, Nantwich CW5 5SS
Tel/Fax: 01270-625494
E-mail: stannesnantwich@btinternet.com
Website: www.stannesnantwich.org.uk
Rev John P Daly. *Deacon:* **Rev Peter Mascarenhas**, 'Roszel', 43 Audlem Road, Nantwich CW5 7DT **Tel:** 01270-624865
M: *Sat 1st M of Sun 6.30pm. Sun 10.30am. Hds as announced.*

■ **NESTON,** Wirral A
† St Winefride (1843; cons 2 Aug 1939, 1996)
5 Burton Road, Little Neston, Neston CH64 9RF **Tel:** 0151-336 4189
Rev Gerald T Courell.
M: *Sat 1st M of Sun 6.30pm. Sun 8.45am, 10.45am. Hds 9am, 10am, 7.30pm.*

■ **NEW FERRY,** Wirral
† St John Evangelist
(1902; 1934; cons 4 Aug 1943)
128 Bebington Road, New Ferry, Wirral CH62 5BJ **Tel:** 0151-645 3314
E-mail: stjohntheevangelist@gmail.com
Website: www.stjohnevang.co.uk
Rev Francis Rice.
M: *Sat 1st M of Sun 5.30pm. Sun 10am. Hds, 10am, 7.30pm.*

DIOCESE OF SHREWSBURY

■ NEWPORT, Shropshire A
† SS Peter and Paul
(1650; 1832; cons 11 July 1906)
Salter's Lane, Newport. **Tel:** 01952-811299
Website: www.sspeter-paul.co.uk
Rev Anthony Wild. Salter's Hall, Newport, Shropshire TF10 7LB
M: *Sat 1st M of Sun 6.15pm. Sun 9.45am, 6.30pm. Hds as announced.*

■ NORTHWICH, Cheshire
1. † St Wilfrid (1865)
Witton Street, Northwich CW9 5NP
Tel: 01606-42440
Rev Patrick Munroe. *Deacon:* **Rev David Harrison,** 31 Danebank Road, Witton Park, Northwich CW9 5PL. **Tel:** 01606-41518
M: *Sat 1st M of Sun 7pm. Sun 9.30am, 11am, 6.30pm. Hds (vigil 7pm), 10am, 7.30pm*

2. Polish Church, Our Lady of Czestochowa
107 London Road, Northwich CW9 8AT
Tel: 01606-42877
E-mail: edward@soska.freeserve.co.uk
Rev Edward Soska (SChr).
M: *Sun 10am. Hds 11am, 7pm.*

■ OSWESTRY, Shropshire
1. † Our Lady Help of Christians and St Oswald
(1865; cons 10 June 1890)
Upper Brook Street, Oswestry
Tel: 01691-652248 **E-mail:** philip.mcgovern2@btinternet.com
Rev Philip McGovern
Presbytery: Cae Nef, Upper Brook Street, Oswestry SY11 2TG *Deacon:* **Rev Stephen McKenna,** 23 Thornhurst Avenue, Oswestry SY11 1NF **Tel:** 01691-654983 *Deacon:* **Rev Joseph Stafanazzi,** 5 Moors Bank, St Martins, Oswestry SY10 7BE
Tel: 01691 770158
M: *Sat 1st M of Sun 6.30pm. Sun 9am, 11am. Hds (vigil 7.30pm), 9.30am.*
• ***Sisters of Charity of St Paul***, Upper Brook Street, Oswestry SY11 2TG
Tel: 01691-652849

■ PARTINGTON, Manchester A
† Our Lady of Lourdes (1957; 1964)
Chapel Lane, Partington, Manchester M31 4EZ Served from Sale (1).
Tel: 0161-775 2905 **Fax:** 0161-929 8972
E-mail: parish@olpart.fsnet.co.uk
Website: www.olpart.fsnet.co.uk
Rev Edward Wall, 164 Carrington Lane, Ashton on Mersey, Sale M33 5WL
Tel: 0161 962 4444 *Deacons:* **Rev Anthony Caffrey,** 26 Avonlea Road, Sale M33 4HZ **Tel:** 0161 973 3606, **Rev John Conway,** 58 Norris Road, Sale M33 3QR
Tel: 0161 962 6983
M: *11am. Hds 12noon (or in school 2.30pm) 7pm and as announced.*
• ***Sisters of Loreto:*** Chapel House, Partington, Manchester M31 4EZ

■ PENSBY, Wirral
† Holy Family (1968; 1977, 1998)
Pensby Road, Pensby. **Tel:** 0151-648 0137
E-mail: parishoffice@holyfamilypensby.com
Website: www.holyfamilypensby.com
Rev Patrick O'Brien. 74 Kylemore Drive, Pensby, Wirral CH61 6XZ *Deacon:* **Rev Jeffrey Telford**, 69 Nelson Drive, Pensby, Wirral CH61 5UP **Tel:** 0151-342 3859
M: *Sun 9.15am, 10.30am, Hds as announced.*

■ PLOWDEN, Lydbury North, Shropshire
See Church Stretton.

■ POYNTON, Stockport
† St Paul (1940; 1957)
Clumber Road, Poynton.
Tel/Fax: 01625-872606
E-mail: jhstratton@aol.com
Website: www.stpaulspoynton.org.uk
Canon Henry Stratton. 33 Bulkeley Road, Poynton, Stockport SK12 1NR. *Deacon:* **Rev Gerard Turnbull**, 135 Vernon Road, Poynton, Stockport SK12 1YS
Tel: 01625-879932
M: *Sat 1st M of Sun 6.30pm. Sun 9am, 11am. Hds, 9.30am, 7.30pm.*

■ ROMILEY, Stockport
† Our Lady and St Christopher (1912; 1932)
52 Barrack Hill, Romiley, Stockport SK6 3BA
Tel: 0161-430 2704 **Fax:** 0161-494 6461
E-mail: stchrisromiley@aol.com
Rev Philip Egan.
M: *Sat 1st M of Sun 6.30pm. Sun 9am, 11am. Hds (vigil 7.30pm), 9.15am, 12 noon.*
• ***Medical Missionaries of Mary***, 10 Metcalf Court, 79 Stockport Road, Romiley, Stockport SK6 3BF
Tel: 0161-494 0026.

■ RUNCORN A
1. † Holy Spirit (1968; 1971)
Fernhurst, Halton Brook, Runcorn WA7 2NJ
Parish Office: **Tel:** 01928-591216
Mbl: 07590 196795
Email: parish@holyspiritruncorn.fsnet.co.uk
Rev Jonathan Mitchell, Holy Spirit & St Martin's Parish Office, Fernhurst, Halton Brook, Runcorn WA7 2NJ. Also serves Runcorn (5).
M: *Sun 11am.*
• ***Shrewsbury Diocesan Children's Society*** - Runcorn Family Advice Centre: Holy Spirit Church.
Tel/Fax: 01928-581459

2. Our Lady, Mother of the Saviour (1974)
Lapwing Grove, Palace Fields, Runcorn WA7 2TP **Tel/Fax:** 01928-717114
Email: ourladys@btconnect.com
Website: www.doslpa12.co.uk
- ***Salvatorians (SDS):*** **Rev William Harrison SDS**. *Deacon:* **Rev Deryck Sankey**, 50 Acton Avenue, Appleton, Warrington WA4 5PT
  Tel: 01925-266459
  M: *Sat 1st M of Sun 5.30pm. Sun 10.30am. Hds (vigil 7.30pm), 9.15am, 12noon.*

3. St Augustine (1969; 1977)
Castlefields Avenue North, Castlefields, Runcorn WA7 2HT **Tel:** 01928-566068
E-mail: staugustines@sdsruncorn.fsnet.co.uk
- ***Salvatorians (SDS):*** **Rev George Malecki** (*Parish Priest*).
  M: *Sat 1st M of Sun 5pm. Sun 9.30am. Hds 9am, (in school term 9.30am), 6.30pm.*

4. † St Edward (1842; 1888; 1956)
Ivy Street, Runcorn WA7 5NZ
Tel: 01928-577755
E-mail: pw@stedwardsrc.co.uk
Rev Peter Wright.
M: *Sat 1st M of Sun 6pm. Sun 9.30am, 6pm. Hds Mass in church and schools as announced.*
- ***Sisters of Charity of Our Lady of Evron,*** 19 Park Road, Runcorn WA7 4PU
  Tel: 01928-576308

5. St Martin de Porres (1975)
St Martin's Lane, Murdishaw, Runcorn WA7 6HZ
Rev Jonathan Mitchell Holy Spirit & St Martin's Parish Office, Fernhurst, Halton Brook, Runcorn WA7 2NJ
Tel: 01928 591216 **Mbl:** 07590 196795
Served from Runcorn (1).
M: *Sun 9.30am.*

■ SALE, Cheshire

1. † All Saints (1959; 1966)
164 Carrington Lane, Ashton-on-Mersey, Sale M33 5WL **Tel:** 0161-962 4444
Email: felix_raypa@yahoo.com
Rev Edward Wall. Also in residence: **Rev Moses Igba** (Diocese of Makurdi, Nigeria). *Parish Deacons:* **Rev Anthony Caffrey**, 26 Avonlea Road, Sale M33 4HZ **Tel:** 0161 973 3606, **Rev John Conway**, 58 Norris Road, Sale M33 3QR **Tel:** 0161 962 6983
Also serves Partington & Sale (3).
M: *Sun 9.30am, 5pm. Hds (vigil 7.30pm), 9.15am.*

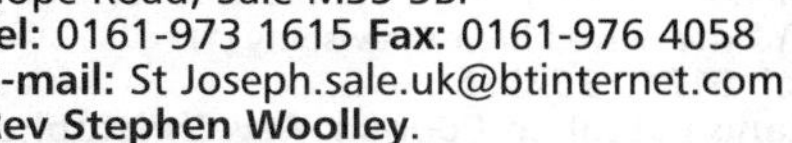

2. † St Joseph
(1866; 1884; cons 10 July 1930)
Hope Road, Sale M33 3BF
Tel: 0161-973 1615 **Fax:** 0161-976 4058
E-mail: St Joseph.sale.uk@btinternet.com
Rev Stephen Woolley.
M: *Sat 1st M of Sun 6.30pm. Sun 9am, 11am, 5.30pm. Hds 9.30am, 12.10pm, 7.30pm.*
- ***Sisters of Loreto***: 23d Roebuck Road, Sale M33 7SY **Tel:** 0161-973 3695

3. † St Margaret Ward (1983)
Cherry Lane, Sale. **Tel:** 0161-962 4444
Served from Sale (1).
M: *Sat 1st M of Sun 6.30pm. Sun 11.30am. Hds 9.15am, 7.30pm.*

■ SALE MOOR, Cheshire

Holy Family (1975)
65 Old Hall Road, Sale Moor, Sale M33 2HT
Tel: 0161-969 7800
Rev Keith Butterworth.
M: *Sat 1st M of Sun 6pm. Sun 8.45am, 10.30am. Hds 9.30am, 12noon, 7.30pm.*

■ SANDBACH, Cheshire

† St Winefride (1865; 1914; 1933)
Middlewich Road, Sandbach CW11 1HU
Tel: 01270-762198 **Fax:** 01270-750038
E-mail: stw_sandbach@btinternet.com
Rev Michael Morton.
M: *Sat 1st M of Sun 6.30pm. Sun 9am, 10.30am. Hds 7.30pm.*

■ SAVIO HOUSE

See Bollington.

■ SHAWBURY, Shrewsbury

See Whitchurch.

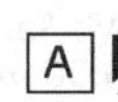

■ SHIFNAL, Shropshire

† St Mary (1860)
Shrewsbury Road, Shifnal.
Tel: 01952-460643
Email: stmarys@fatherjohnpascoe.co.uk
Website: www.shifnal66.fsnet.co.uk
Rev John Pascoe, 24 Victoria Road, Shifnal TF11 8AE Also resident: **Rev John Wright**. Danesford, High Street, Albrighton WV7 3LA **Tel:** 01902-374109; **Rev David Duggan** (Birmingham, rtrd), 5 Grange Park, Albrighton WV7 3EN
Tel: 01902-372983
M: *Sat 1st M of Sun 6.30pm. Sun 9am. Hds 7.30pm.*

† St Joseph Mass Centre (1974)
Bushfield Road, Albrighton, Shropshire WV7 3PE
M: *Sun 10.30am. Hds 10am.*

■ SHREWSBURY

1. See start of the parish list.

2. † Our Lady of Pity
(1961; 1971; 15 Sept 1992)
Meadow Farm Drive, Harlescott, Shrewsbury SY1 4JY Served from Shrewsbury (1).
Tel: 01743 362366
Canon Stephen Coonan, Rev Christopher Matthews, Cathedral House, 11 Belmont, Shrewsbury SY1 1TE. *Deacon:* **Rev Bernard Tomnay**. 71 White Lodge Park, Shawbury, Shropshire SY4 4NU **Tel:** 01939 250031
M: *Sat 1st M Sun 6pm. Hds As announced.*

3. † St Winefride (1956)
Crowmere Road, Monkmoor, Shrewsbury.
Served from Shrewsbury (1).
Canon Stephen Coonan, Rev Christopher Matthews, Cathedral House, 11 Belmont, Shrewsbury SY1 1TE. *Deacon:* **Rev Ron Ball**, 12 Allestree Close, Little Harlescott, Shrewsbury SY1 3RG.
Tel: 01743-465452
M: *Sun 9.30am. Hds As announced.*

■ STALYBRIDGE, Cheshire

1. † St Peter (1839; cons 25 Sept 1946)
Off Castle Hall Close, Stalybridge SK15 2ED
Tel: 0161-338 2575 **Fax:** 0161-338 6077
E-mail: stpetersstalybridge@btinteret.com
Rev Bernard Forshaw.
M *Sat 1st M of Sun 6.30pm. Sun 9.30am, 11am. Hds 9.15am, 7.30pm.*

2. † St Raphael (1958; 1963)
Huddersfield Road, Millbrook, Stalybridge SK15 3JL **Tel:** 0161-338 3260
Also serves Hattersley
Rev Paul Hughes.
M: *Sat 1st M of Sun 6.30pm. Sun 9.30am. Hds 9.30am, 7.30pm.*

■ STOCKPORT

(See also Diocese of Salford)

1. † Our Lady and the Apostles
(1799; 1905; cons 12 Oct 1949)
Shaw Heath, Edgeley, Stockport SK3 8BQ
Tel: 0161-480 2489 **Fax:** 0161-480 0868
E-mail: fr.vin@talk21.com
Rev Vincent Whelan. Also in residence: **Rev Christopher Jenkin.** *Deacon:* **Rev Peter Lafferty**, 24 Beanleach Drive, Offerton, Stockport SK2 5HZ
Tel: 0161-483 8765
M: *Sat 1st M of Sun 7pm. Sun 9.30am, 11am. Hds (vigil 7pm), 10am (term-time only), 12.15pm,*

- ***Sisters of Charity of Our Lady of Evron,*** Evron Centre, 1 Adswood Lane, Cale Green, Stockport SK3 8HT
Tel: 0161-292 7270 **Fax:** 0161-292 7470
E-mail: evroncentre@yahoo.co.uk

2. † St Ambrose (1939)
Adswood Road, Adswood, Stockport.
Tel: 0161-480 3723
E-mail: geoffogrady@talktalk.net
Rev Geoffrey O'Grady. Presbytery, 8 Clover Avenue, Adswood, Stockport SK3 8QA
M: *Sat 1st M of Sun 6.30pm. Sun 10am. Hds 9.30am, 7.30pm.*

3. † St Bernadette (1957; 1961)
22 The Drive, Brinnington, Stockport SK5 8AH
Tel: 0161-480 8065 **Fax:** 0161-406 7551
E-mail: sr.gertrude@btinternet.com
- ***Sisters of Charity of Our Lady of Evron****, Parish Sisters:* **Sr Gertrude Geoghegan, Sr Pauline Briody, Sr Maura Considine.**
M: *Sun 10.30am. Hds 10am.*

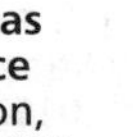

4. † St Joseph
(1853; 1862; cons 10 April 1940)
Tatton Street, St Petersgate, Stockport SK1 1EJ **Tel:** 0161-480 3164
Revv James Matthews SCJ, Thomas McShane SCJ, *Deacon:* **Rev Terence Simms**, 13 Worthing Close, Offerton, Stockport SK2 5RE **Tel:** 0161-483 7672
M: *Sat 1st M of Sun 5pm. Sun 11am, 5pm. (Ukrainian Mass every 3rd & 5th Sun 1.15pm). Hds (vigil 7.30pm), 10am, (in term time) 12noon, 7.30pm.*

5. † St Philip (1967)
Half Moon Lane, Offerton, Stockport SK2 5LB **Tel:** 0161-483 4609
E-mail: stphilipsofferton@ntlworld.com
Website: www.stphilipsofferton.org.uk
Rev Michael Cupit. *Deacon:* **Rev Bernard Barron**, 35 Henley Avenue, Cheadle Hulme, Cheadle SK8 6DE **Tel:** 0161-485 5046
M: *Sat 1st M of Sun 6pm. Sun 10.15am. Hds 9.30am.*

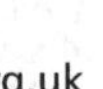

■ TARPORLEY, Cheshire

† St Thomas Becket (1938; 1941; 1971)
3 Nantwich Road, Tarporley CW6 9UN
Tel/Fax: 01829-732511
E-mail: jc4jc@onetel.com
Website: www.saintthomasbecket.org.uk
Also serves Mouldsworth.
Rev Joseph Carney.
M: *Sat 1st M of Sun 5.30pm. Sun 11am. Hds as announced.*

■ TATTENHALL, Chester

See Malpas.

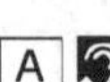

■ TELFORD

1. † The Good Shepherd
Tel/Fax: 01952-586118
E-mail: pp@goodshepherd.telford.org.uk

Website: www.goodshepherd.telford.org.uk
Rev William Dukes. 70 High Street, Madeley, Telford TF7 5AU
Serving the communities and churches of:
St Mary (1760, 1853, 2002)
70 High Street, Madeley TF7 5AU
All Saints (1975, 2002)
Stirchley TF3 1DU - Shared with CoE.
St Paul (1978, 1983, 2002)
Station Road, Dawley TF4 3AH
M: *Sat 1st M of Sun 5pm (Stirchley). Sun 9am (Dawley), 10.30am (Madeley), 6pm. (Madeley). Hds as Announced.*

St Winefride Mass Centre (1869; 1888; 1941)
Church Hall, Barber's Street, Broseley TF12 5NR
M: *Sat 1st M of Sun 6.30pm Hds as announced*

2. † Our Lady of the Rosary (1939; 1967)
Donnington, Telford,
Tel/Fax: 01952-610797
Rev William Fitzgerald. Halcyon, Church Road, Wrockwardine Wood, Telford TF2 7AH
M: *Sat 1st M of Sun 5pm (Meeting Point House, Telford Town Centre), Sat 6.30pm (St Lukes Primary School, Church Road, Donnington TF2 7HG), Sun 10am (Garrison Church, Venning Barracks). Hds as announced.*

3. † St Patrick (1834; 1906; cons 13 June 1950)
King Street, Wellington, Telford TF1 3AP
Tel: 01952-242423 **Rev Alban Greenwood.**
E-mail: admin@stpatrickstelford.com
Website: www.stpatrickstelford.com
M: *Sat 1st M of Sun 6.15pm. Sun 8.45am, 11am. (Pol Community as announced). Hds 9.30am (in School),12.15pm, 7.30pm.*

■ TERN HILL
See Market Drayton.

■ UPTON, Wirral
† St Joseph (1863; 1954; cons 18 Oct 1979)
6 Moreton Road, Upton, Wirral CH49 6LJ

Tel: 0151-677 2185 **Fax:** 0151-677 8426
E-mail: parishpriest@talktalk.net
Website: www.stjosephsupton.org.uk
Rev Peter Robertson. *Deacon:* **Rev Peter Jackson**, 36 Arborn Drive, Upton, Wirral CH49 6JS **Tel:** 0151-677 8598
M: *Sun 9am, 11am. Hds (vigil 7.30pm), 9.30am.*

■ WALLASEY, Wirral
1. † Sacred Heart (1923; 1957, 2003)
The Cross, Moreton, Wirral CH46 9QB
Tel: 0151-677 5220 **Fax:** 0151-677 8817
E-mail: sacredheartmoreton@hotmail.com
Canon Brendan Hoban, Rev Lucas Ngwa (Buéa, Cameroon).
M: *Sat 1st M of Sun 6pm. Sun 10am, 11.30am (Tridentine), 5.30pm. Hds (vigil 7.30pm), 9.30am, 8pm.*

2. † Our Lady Star of the Sea and St Joseph (1860; 1889; cons 8 Sept 1910)
Wheatland Lane, Seacombe, Wallasey CH44 7ED **Tel/Fax:** 0151-638 2873
E-mail: sdvoc@yahoo.com
Rev Jerome Fagan. *Deacon:* **Rev Norman J Carew**, 1 Park Avenue, Wallasey CH44 9DZ **Tel:** 0151-200 1948
M: *Sat 1st M of Sun 6.30pm. Sun 10am, 6.30pm. Hds 7.30am, 9.30am, 7.30pm.*

3. † St Alban (1841; 1853; 1991)
30 Mill Lane, Liscard, Wallasey CH44 5UD
Tel: 0151-638 1520
E-mail: stalbanswallasey@yahoo.co.uk
Website: www.stalbanswallasey.co.uk
Rev David Long. *Deacon:* **Rev David Morriss**, 39 Grosvenor Street, Wallasey CH44 1AW **Tel:** 0151-630 1373
M: *Sat 1st M of Sun 6pm. Sun 8.30am, 10.30am. Hds (vigil 7.30pm), 9.30am, 12noon.*

4. The North Wallasey Catholic Community
1 Gardenside, Leasowe, Wirral CH46 2RR
Tel: 0151-638 3066 **Fax:** 08452-991768
E-mail: jgf@nwallaseyrc.org
Website: nwallaseyrc.org
Rev John G Feeney

† Our Lady of Lourdes (1957; 1962; Church cons 12 June 1987)
Leasowe Road, Leasowe CH46 2RR
M: *Sun: 9.45am Hds:* As announced

† English Martyrs (1902; 1953)
St George's Road, Wallasey Village CH45 6TU
M: *Sun 11am Hds:* As announced

SS Peter & Paul (1879; 1935, 2008)
Services at All Saints, Hoseside Road, New Brighton CH45 0LA
M: *Sat: 1st M of Sun 6pm, Sun 9.45am. Hds:* As announced

■ WARRINGTON
See Appleton, Latchford, and under Archdiocese of Liverpool.

■ WAVERTON, Chester
See Chester (5).

■ WEAVERHAM, Cheshire
† St Bede (1950; 1952; cons 7 June 1961, 2004)
Church Lane, Weaverham, Northwich CW8 3NP Also serves Barnton.

Tel: 01606-853339
Rev James Farrell.
M: *Sat 1st M of Sun 6pm. Sun 11am. Hds (vigil 7.30pm). 9.15am (St Bede's School, Keepers Lane, during term) Otherwise 10am.*

■ **WEM,** Shropshire
Our Lady of Perpetual Succour (1962, 1991)
Drawwell Lane. Served from Ellesmere.
Rev Patrick English, St Michael's, 80 Scotland Street, Ellesmere SY12 0ED
Tel: 01691-853339
M: *Sat 1st M of Sun 5.30pm. Sun 9.30am. Hds 7.30pm.*

■ **WEST KIRBY, Wirral**
† **St Agnes** (1897; cons 8 June 1922)
16 Darmond's Green, West Kirby, Wirral CH48 5DU **Tel:** 0151-625 6367
E-mail: parish@mcagnes.plus.com
Mgr Canon John McManus VG. *Deacon:* **Rev Basil Stephens**, 55 Church Road, West Kirby, Wirral CH48 0RN
Tel: 0151-625 9963
M: *Sun 8.30am, 10.30am, 5.30pm. Hds (vigil 7pm), 12noon.*
• ***Sisters of Notre Dame:*** 5 Marina Court, Hoscote Park, West Kirby CH48 0QR
Tel: 0151-625 2077
E-mail: monicasnd@talktalk.net

■ **WHALEY BRIDGE,** High Peak
† **The Sacred Heart** (1898: 1906)
31 Whaley Lane, Whaley Bridge, High Peak SK23 7AG **Tel:** 01663-732614
E-mail: sacredheartwhaley@btinternet.com
Website:
www.sacredheartwhaleybridge.co.uk
Rev Martin Riley.
Deacon: **Rev Michael Denny,** Glen Lynn, Linglongs Road, Whaley Bridge High Peak SK23 7DS **Tel:** 01663-735492
M: *Sat 1st M of Sun 6pm. Sun 11am. Hds 9.30am, 7pm.*

Disley Mass Centre
Methodist Church, Buxton Road, Disley.
M: *Sun 9.30am.*

■ **WHITCHURCH,** Shropshire
† **St George Protector of England**
(1853; 1878; 1892)
17 Claypit Street, Whitchurch SY13 1LE
Tel: 01948-662935
Rev Gregory Downing.
M: *Sat 1st M of Sun 6pm. Sun 9.30am. Hds (vigil 7.30pm), 10am.*

Shawbury Mass Centre
St Andrew & St Peter, RAF Station.
M: *Sun 11.15am, Hds 7pm.*

■ **WILMSLOW,** Cheshire
† **Sacred Heart and St Teresa** (1871; 1914)
Green Lane, Wilmslow SK9 1LD
Tel: 01625-523584 **Fax:** 01625-533268
Email: stwil@btinternet.com
Rev Anthony Cogliolo.
M: *Sat 1st M of Sun 6.30pm. Sun 9am, 10.30am. Hds 9.30am, 7.30pm.*

■ **WINSFORD,** Cheshire
† **St Joseph** (1948; 1950; 1977)
Woodford Lane, Winsford CW7 2JS
Tel: 01606-592177
Rev Stephen Dwyer.
E-mail: stjosephwinsford@aol.co.uk
M: *Sat 1st M of Sun 5.15pm. Sun 9.30am, 11am. Hds as announced.*
• ***Sisters of St Joseph of the Apparition,*** 73 Swanlow Lane, Winsford CW7 1JD **Tel:** 01606-594443

■ **WISTASTON**
See Crewe.

■ **WYTHENSHAWE,** Manchester
Team Minstry: **Rev Michael Gannon** (*Team Leader*), **Revv Keith Brigham, Sajimon Kuriakose, Michael Murray, Paul Standish.**

1. † **Sacred Heart and St Peter** (1967)
Southmoor Road, Baguley M23 1HP
Tel: 0161-998 5319
E-mail: parishpriest298@btinternet.com
Rev Paul Standish. Presbytery, Floatshall Road, Baguley, Manchester M23 1HP
Deacons: **Revv Gerard Doherty**. 8 Dibden Walk, Baguley M23 1JZ. **Tel:** 0161-945 2542; **Joseph Norbury**, 57 Saville Road, Gatley, Cheadle SK8 4BY
Tel: 0161-286 8965
M: *Sun 9am, (10.30am Wythenshawe Hospital), 11.30am, 5.30pm. Hds 9.30am, (12.30pm Wythenshawe Hospital), 2pm (St Peter's Primary School, term-time only).*

2. † **St Anthony**
(1953; 1960, cons 1998)
Portway, Woodhouse Park.
Tel: 0161-437 2861
Revv Michael Murray, Keith Brigham (*Chaplain to Wythenshawe Hospital*), Presbytery, Dunkery Road, Woodhouse Park, Manchester M22 0WR
Deacon: **Rev Donnan Baron,** 7 Brogden Drive, Gatley, Cheadle SK8 4AS
Tel: 0161-428 3832
M: *Sat 1st M of Sun 6.30pm. Sun 10am. Hds 10am, 7.30pm.*

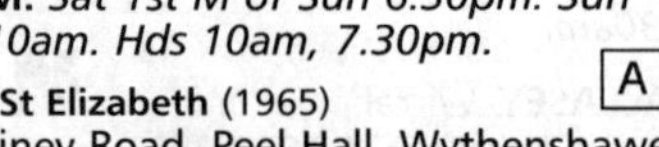

3. † **St Elizabeth** (1965)
Holliney Road, Peel Hall, Wythenshawe.
Tel: 0161-998 2644
Served by Wythenshawe Team Clergy.
M: *Sun 10am. Hds (vigil 7.30pm),*

9.30am term-time only.
- ***Ursuline Sisters,*** 174/6 Crossacres Road, Crossacres, Manchester M22 5BR **Tel:** 0161-499 2923

4. † St Hilda and St Aidan A
(1904; 1970; 2006)
Kenworthy Lane, Northenden M22 4EF
Tel: 0161-998 2895
E-mail: michael.gannon7@ntlworld.com
Rev Michael Gannon, 66 Kenworthy Lane, Northenden, Manchester M22 4EF
M: *Sun 10am. Hds As announced.*

Northern Moor Mass Centre
St Aidan's Centre, 230 Wythenshawe Road, Northern Moor, Manchester M23 0PH
Tel: 0161-613 0209
M: *Sat 1st M of Sun 6pm. Sun 11.30. Hds 10am.*

5. † SS John Fisher and Thomas More A
(1934; 1935; cons 22 June 1995)
133 Woodhouse Lane, Benchill, Manchester M22 9NW **Tel:** 0161-998 2644
Served by Wythenshawe Team Clergy.
Priest in Residence: **Rev Sajimon Kuriakose** (Kottayam, India)
M: *Sat 1st M of Sun 5pm. Sun 11.30am. Hds 11am.*
- ***Sisters of St Joseph of the Apparition,*** 21 Larkhall Rise, Sharston, Manchester M22 4PB **Tel:** 0161-428 7572 **E-mail:** sjaemilie@yahoo.co.uk

■ ORDERS OR CONGREGATIONS, ETC

■ Men

Christian Brothers, Congregation of: Birkenhead (2), Hale Barns.
Franciscans (Capuchin): Chester (3).
Oblates of Mary Immaculate: Birkenhead (4), Crewe (1).
Redemptorists: Hawkstone Hall.
Sacred Heart Fathers: Malpas, Stockport (4).
Salesians: Bollington.
Salvatorians: Runcorn (2, 3).

■ Women

Benedictines: Chester (1).
Carmelites: Birkenhead (2).
Charity, Sisters of: Birkenhead (3), Macclesfield (1).
Charity (of Notre Dame of Evron), Sisters of: Runcorn (4), Stockport (1, 3).
Charity (of St Paul), Sisters of: Oswestry (1).
Cross, Daughters of the: Hawkstone Hall.
Dominican Sisters: Hawkstone Hall.
Faithful Companions of Jesus: Birkenhead (5).
Holy Family of Bordeaux, Sisters of the: Birkenhead (4).
Joseph of the Apparition, Sisters of St: Alderley Edge, Altrincham (3), Winsford (1), Wythenshawe (5).
Loreto, Sisters of: Altrincham (2, 3), Sale (2), Partington.
Medical Missionaries of Mary: Romiley.
Mercy, (Union of Great Britain) Sisters of: Shrewsbury (1).
Nazareth, Sisters of: Birkenhead (3).
Notre Dame, Sisters of: West Kirby.
Our Lady of the Cenacle: Chester (1).
Pallottine Missionary Sisters: Macclesfield (1).
Poor Clares (Colettines): Ellesmere.
Ursuline Sisters: Wythenshawe (3).

■ DIOCESAN INSTITUTIONS, SOCIETIES

For Societies and Organisations without representation in the diocese please see the main Societies and Organisations section.

Aid to the Church in Need: *Northern Appeals' Manager:* **Ralph Ferrigno**, 10 Galtres Park, Bebington, Wirral CH63 8RA **Tel/Fax:** 0151-644 7327 **E-mail:** ralph.ferrigno@ntlworld.com

Archconfraternity of St Stephen for Altar Servers. *Diocesan Director:* **Rev Jonathan Mitchell**, Holy Spirit Runcorn. Enquiries to National Secretary, **Mr D Draycott**, 184 Cheadle Old Road, Edgeley, Stockport.

Associates of the Holy Family of Bordeaux: Enquiries to: **Mr A F Dinsdale**. 33 Barleyfields Road, Wetherby, West Yorkshire, LS22 6PR **Tel:** 01937-583709

Association for the Propagation of the Faith: *Diocesan Secretary:* **Rev Frederick Robinson**, 26 Winstanley Road, Neston, Wirral CH64 0UZ

Association of Inter-Church Families. *Diocesan Contact:* **Mr & Mrs P Mayles**, Five Oaks, Street Hey Lane, Willaston, Neston CH64 1SS **Tel:** 0151-327 7196 **E-mail:** mayles@fsmail.net **Website:** www.interchurchfamilies.org.uk

Beginning Experience: A weekend programme which seeks to help separated, divorced and bereaved people. **Kath Harding**, 11 Walkden Avenue East, Wigan WN1 2DX **Tel:** 01942-246542 **E-mail:** kathharding@blueyonder.co.uk

CAFOD. *Shrewsbury Diocesan Manager:* **Sue Bownas**: 27A Downsfield Road, Chester CH4 8HH **Tel:** 01244 677594 **E-mail:** shrewsbury@cafod.org.uk **Website:** www.cafod.org.uk

Caritas Christi. c/o **J Horsfield**, 11 Lightborne Road, Sale M33 5FG **Website:** ccworldinfo.org

Catenian Association. Information from: **Frank Hinds**, Greystoke, Park Road,

Bowdon, Altrincham WA14 3JG **E-mail:** frank.hinds@btinternet.com *(N&E Cheshire, S Manchester);* **Eric F Smith**, Woodlands, Wethersfield Road, Noctorum, Wirral CH43 9UN **E-mail:** efs99@btinternet.com *(West Cheshire, Wirral)*, or **John Kearns**, 1 Golf Links Lane, Wellington, Shropshire TF1 2DS **E-mail:** jk6229@uwclub.net *(Shropshire, S Cheshire)*.

Catholic Charismatic Renewal Shrewsbury Diocese. *Representative:* **Philip Read-Shaw,** 36 Meadow Drive, Prestbury, Cheshire SK10 4EZ **Tel:** 01625-828152 **E-mail:** philipreadshaw@hotmail.co.uk **Website:** www.charismatic-renewal.co.uk

Catholic Children's Society. **Head Office:** St Paul's House, Farmfield Drive, Beechwood, Prenton CH43 7ZT **Tel:** 0151-652 1281 **Fax:** 0151-652 5002 **E-mail:** info@cathchildsoc.org.uk **Shropshire:** Meeting Point House, South Water Square, Telford TF3 4HS **Tel:** 01952- 292888 **Fax:** 01952-293185 **Runcorn:** The Runcorn Family Advice Service, Holy Spirit Church, Fernhurst, Halton Brook, Runcorn WA7 2NJ **Tel/Fax:** 01928-581459 **Manchester:** Wythenshawe Family Support Project, St Aidan's Centre, 230 Wythenshawe Road, Northern Moor M23 0PH **Tel/Fax:** 0161-998 8802

Catholic Clothing Guild, *Hon Secretary (Shropshire):* **Mrs J Harding**, 2 Ashfield Road, Heath Farm, Shrewsbury SY1 3EE **Tel:** 01743-343117 *Hon Secretary (Cheshire):* **Mrs M Fisher**, 40 Selkirk Road, Curzon Park, Chester CH4 8AH **Tel:** 01244-683812 *Hon Secretary (Cheadle Hulme):* **Mrs R Potter**, 90 Radnormere Drive, Cheadle Hulme Cheshire SK8 5JS **Tel:** 0161 485 8312

Catholic Family History Society. NW *Secretary:* **Mrs J Smith**, 10 Irving Close, Woodsmoor, Stockport SK2 7DX **Website:** www.catholic-history.org.uk

Catholic Guide Guild. *Secretary:* Miss Monica O'Beirne, 125 Thornridge, Stavordale Road, Moreton, Wirral. **Tel:** 0151-678 7133

Catholic Handicapped Fellowship. Diocesan Committee: *Hon Secretary:* **Jane Christley**, 18 Rycroft Road, Meols, Wirral CH47 9RQ

Catholic Women's League: *Diocesan Branch Secretary:* **Mrs Elizabeth Lynch**, 28 Woodside, Knutsford WA16 8BX. **Tel:** 01565 633381 **E-mail:** natsec@cwlhq.org.uk **Website:** www.catholicwomensleague.org

Deaf or Hard of Hearing, Diocesan Pastoral Service to: *Service Co-ordinator:* **Sr Maura Considine SCE**, St Bernadette's Presbytery, 22 The Drive, Brinnington, Stockport SK5 8AH **Voice:** 0161-430 4167 **Minicom:** 0161-406 0418 **Fax:** 0161-406 7551 **E-mail:** considine9@aol.com

Family Housing Association. Regional Office: Mancus House, Mancus Street, Birkenhead CH41 3NY **Tel:** 0151-647 5000 **E-mail:** familyha@btconnect.com

Justice and Peace Groups. *Chairperson:* **Tony Walsh**, 54 Underwood Drive, Ellesmere Port CH65 9BL **Tel:** 0151-355 6419 *Diocesan Co-ordinator:* **Joan Sharples**, 16 Wellington Road, Nantwich CW5 7BH **Tel:** 01270-620584 **E-mail:** joansharples620@btinternet.com

Knights of St Columba. *Greater Manchester Rep:* **Mr Pat Jones**, 2 Appleton Court, Sale M33 3DP **Tel:** 0161 962 4706 **E-mail:** patjones1@ntlworld.com *W. Cheshire & Wirral Rep:* **Mr Ben O'Donnell**, 6 Highfield Road, Little Sutton, Ellesmere Port CH66 4PL **Tel:** 0151 339 5210

Latin Mass Society. *Diocesan Representative:* **Mr Anthony Sibert**, 15 Kings Walk, West Kirby, Wirral CH48 8AE

Leaven Carmelite Secular Institute, The. Contact: **N Green**, 20 Acton Road, Crewe CW2 8TN **Tel:** 01270-213608

Legion of Mary. *President:* **Elizabeth Jackson**, 27 Thornycroft Street, Birkenhead CH41 8EU **Tel:** 0151-653 7113

Lourdes Pilgrimage Association. *Pilgrimage Director:* **Rev Peter Sharrocks**; *Pilgrimage enquiries:* Diocesan Pilgrimage Office, St Peter's, 16 Green Lane, Hazel Grove, Stockport SK7 4EA. **Tel:** 07773-324264 **E-mail:** info@shrewsburypilgrimage.co.uk **Website:** www.shrewsburypilgrimage.co.uk *Lourdes Hospitality President:* **Mr John Campbell**, 84 Midland Road, Bramhall, Stockport SK7 3DT. **E-mail:** hospitality@ shrewsburypilgrimage.co.uk

Marriage and Family Life Ministry. *Diocesan Co-ordinator:* **Mrs Clara Donnelly**, 64 Grosvenor Street, Wallasey CH44 1AQ **Tel/Fax:** 0151-691 2811 **E-mail:** cc.donn@talktalk.net

Marriage Care. Headquarters: Clitherow House, 1 Blythe Mews, Blythe Road, London WW14 0NW **Tel:** 020-7371 1342 **Website:** www.marriagecare.org.uk Diocesan centres in Shrewsbury, South and Mid Cheshire, Stockport, Trafford, and Warrington: **Tel:** 0800 389 3801

Marriage Encounter. Mark & Liz Dutton, 85 Sycamore Crescent, Macclesfield SK11 8LW **E-mail:** lizmark@talktalk.net **Website:** www.wwme.org.uk

National Board of Catholic Women: *Diocesan Link:* **Mrs Hazel Dove**, 14 Edmonton Road, Woodsmoor, Stockport SK2 5BG **Tel:** 0161-483 8200

Newman Association. Manchester and Nth Cheshire Circle. *Secretary:* **Dr Chris Quirke,** 29 Spring Road, Hale, Altrincham WA14 2UQ **Tel:** 0161-941 1707 **E-mail:** dcq@mac.com

Our Lady's Catechists. *Shrewsbury Diocesan Organiser:* **Mrs Joan McCarthy,** 38 Camrose Close, Runcorn WA7 5NS **Tel:** 01928-560198

Pontifical Mission Aid Societies. The Holy Childhood; Society of St Peter Apostle; Association for the Propagation of the Faith. *Diocesan Director:* Appointment Pending

Pontifical Work for Vocations. *Director:* **Rev Jonathan Mitchell**, (Shrewsbury), Holy Spirit & St Martin's, Runcorn

Project 2030 – The Twenty Somethings and The Thirty Somethings. Groups for Catholics in their 20s and 30s, getting together at social and spiritual levels. Walks, meals, evenings out, talks, Masses and retreats. International visits as well as holidays and pilgrimages. Sponsored by the Dehonians (Sacred Heart Fathers). Contact: **Rev Hugh Hanley SCJ,** St John's, 226 Wellington Road North, Stockport SK4 2GR **Tel:** 0161-282 6334 **E-mail:** hugh@project2030.fsnet.co.uk **Website:** www.project2030.co.uk

Secular Franciscan Order. Francisan Friary, 15 Cuppin Street, Chester CH1 2BN **Tel:** 01244-351331 **Website:** www.capuchinfriars.co.uk

Secular Order of Discalced Carmelites. Information from: **Mrs Mary Barton,** 757 Borough Road, Tranmere, Wirral CH42 6QQ. **Tel:** 0151-645 7893 **E-mail:** mary.rose10@ntlworld.com or **Mrs Patricia Belmar**, 43 Cavendish Drive, Rock Ferry, Wirral CH42 6RG **Tel:** 0151-645 8563 **E-mail:** patricia.belmar@ntlworld.com

Serra Club of North Cheshire. *Secretary:* **Dolores Cain.** 88 Nursery Road, Cheadle Hulme SK8 6HL **Tel:** 0161-485 5769

Servitum Christi: Contact: **Frances Cassidy**, 22 Fern Road, Ellesmere Port CH65 6PB **Tel:** 0151-357 1600

Shrewsbury Secular Clergy Fund. *Secretary:* **Rev Michael Hartley**, St Werburgh's and St Laurence's, Birkenhead.

Society for the Protection of Unborn Children. *Diocesan Contact:* **Mr Robin Haig**, 35 Parkway, Wilmslow SK9 1LS **Tel:** 01625-523094

Society of the Holy Childhood. *Diocesan Director:* **Rev Frederick Robinson.**

Society of St Gregory. *Diocesan Representative:* **Judith Hall**, Music Office, Shrewsbury Cathedral, 11 Belmont, Shrewsbury SY1 1TE **Tel:** 01939-210391 **E-mail:** judith.hall@ssg.org.uk **Website:** www.ssg.org.uk

Society of St John Chrysostom. Diocesan Representative: **Mr and Mrs C Aslet.** 56 Panton Road, Hoole, Chester CH2 3HX **Tel:** 01244-345511

Society of St Peter Apostle for Native Clergy. *Diocesan Director:* **Rev F Robinson.**

Society of St Vincent de Paul, Shrewsbury Central Council. *President:* **Mr Roy Sutton**, 10 Pickmere Close, Sandbach CW11 9TR **Tel:** 01270-764763

SPRED. *For information on becoming a helper for children and adults with special needs, contact:* **Mrs Anne Cuffe**, 2 Charlesville, Prenton, Wirral CH43 1TP **Tel:** 0151-652 0039

St Barnabas Society. *Diocesan Representative:* **Jonathan Brown**, 66 Chester Road, Anfield, Liverpool L6 4DZ **Tel:** 0151 260 1186

Survive-Miva. *Head Office:* Survive-Miva, 5 Park Vale Road, Aintree L9 2DG **Tel:** 0151-523 3878 **Fax:** 0151-523 3841 **E-mail:** info@survive-miva.org **Website:** www.survive-miva.org

Union of Catholic Mothers. *Diocesan Secretary:* **Mrs Valerie Ward**, 48 Molvern Road, Wallasey, Wirral CH45 8NW **Tel:** 0151-638 9673 *Diocesan Spiritual Director:* **Rev Michael Murray.**

Volunteer Missionary Movement (VMM). *Diocesan Contacts:* **Sam and Helen Corcoran**, 7 Radbroke Close, Sandbach CW11 1YT **Tel:** 01270-759154 **E-mail:** corcoran@dial.pipex.com

Walsingham Pilgrims. *East Shropshire:* **Mrs C E Jones**, 23 Manchester Drive, Apley Wood, Telford TF1 6XY **Tel:** 01952-253960 *South Manchester:* **Mr Bernard Caine.** 28 Lindwall Close, Northern Moor, Manchester M23 0EH **Tel:** 0161-613 5662

Warrington St Joseph's Family Centre. 9 Museum Street, Warrington WA1 1JA **Tel:** 01925-635448 **Fax:** 01925-657643 **E-mail:** stjosephsfamilycentre@btconnect.com

Website: www.saintjosephsfamilycentre.org.uk

Young Christian Workers & Impact. For young people aged between 13-30. *Contact:* Diocese of Shrewsbury Youth, St Ambrose, Adswood Road, Stockport SK3 8QA *Headquarters:* St Joseph's, off St Joseph's Grove, London NW4 4TY **Tel:** 0208 203 6290 **E-mail:** info@ycwimpact.com **Website:** www.ycwimpact.com

■ HOSPITALS

To contact the Catholic Chaplain of a particular hospital we suggest you contact the hospital reception directly.

■ CATHOLIC SCHOOLS - MAINTAINED

■ CHESHIRE L.E.A.

▲ Primary

St Gabriel's Well Lane ST7 2PG **Tel:** 01270-875770 **Fax:** 01270-882141 *(Alsager)*

St Gregory, Albert Road SK10 5HS **Tel:** 01625-572037 **Fax:** 01625-562015 *(Bollington)*

St Clare, Hawthorn Road, Lache, Chester CH4 8HX **Tel:** 01224-981110 **Fax:** 01244-682294 *(Chester 1)*

St Theresa's, Kipling Road, Blacon CH1 5UU **Tel:** 01244-981070 **Fax:** 01244-370718 *(Chester 4)*.

St Werburgh's & St Columba's, Lighfoot Street, Hoole CH2 3AD **Tel:** 01244-325528 **Fax:** 01244-350540 *(Chester 5)*

St Mary, Belgrave Avenue CW12 1HT. **Tel:** 01260-274690 **Fax:** 01260-297366 *(Congleton)*

St Mary, Danebank Avenue CW2 8AD. **Tel:** 01270-568912 **Fax:** 01270-651175 *(Crewe)*

St Saviour, Seacombe Drive, Great Sutton CH66 2QW **Tel:** 0151-338 2440 **Fax:** 0151-348 1739 *(Ellesmere Port 1)*

Our Lady's Star of the Sea, Capenhurst Lane, CH65 7AQ **Tel:** 0151-357 1004 **Fax:** 0151-356 8669 *(Ellesmere Port 3)*

St Bernard, Sherbourne Road CH65 5EW. **Tel:** 0151-355 2047 **Fax:** 0151-355 3821 *(Ellesmere Port 4)*

St Mary of the Angels, Rossall Grove, Little Sutton CH66 1NN **Tel:** 0151-338 2430 **Fax:** 0151-348 1340 *(Ellesmere Port 2)*

St Luke, The Willows, Off Fluin Lane, WA6 7QP **Tel:** 01928-731721 **Fax:** 01928-739497 *(Frodsham)*

St Benedict, Hall Road, SK9 3AE **Tel:** 01625-520207 **Fax:** 01625-536012 *(Handforth)*

St Vincent, Manor Park South WA16 8AL **Tel:** 01565-633637 **Fax:** 01565-633516 *(Knutsford)*

St Alban, Priory Lane, SK10 3HJ **Tel:** 01625-425905 **Fax:** 01625-511330 *(Macclesfield 1)*

St Edward, Fir Grove, SK11 7SF **Tel:** 01625-427371 **Fax:** 01625-261286 *(Macclesfield 2)*

St Mary, Manor Lane, Middlewich CW10 9DH **Tel:** 01606-832164 **Fax:** 01606-832481 *(Middlewich)*

St Anne, Wellington Road CW5 7DA **Tel:** 01270-625100 **Fax:** 01270-620651 *(Nantwich)*

St Winefride, Mellock Lane CH64 9RW **Tel:** 0151-338 2468 **Fax:** 0151-336 2468 *(Neston)*

St Wilfrid, Greenbank Lane, Hartford CW8 1JW **Tel:** 01606-75669 **Fax:** 01606-784986. *(Northwich)*

St Paul, Marley Road SK12 1LY **Tel:** 01625-871960 **Fax:** 01625-871960 *(Poynton)*.

St Bede, Keeper's Lane CW8 3BY **Tel:** 01606-852149 **Fax:** 01606-851175 *(Weaverham)*

St Joseph, Woodford Lane CW7 2JS **Tel:** 01606-592973 Fax: 01606-863552 *(Winsford)*

▲ Secondary

The Catholic High, Old Wrexham Road, Handbridge CH4 7HS **Tel:** 01244-981600 **Fax:** 01244-681773 *(Chester 5)*

St Thomas More Catholic High School, Danebank Avenue CW2 8AE **Tel:** 01270-568014 **Fax:** 01270-650860 *(Crewe)*

Catholic High School, Capenhurst Lane CH65 7AQ **Tel:** 0151-355 2373 **Fax:** 0151-356 9154 *(Ellesmere Port 2)*

St Nicholas High School, Greenbank Lane CW8 1JW **Tel:** 01606-75420 **Fax:** 01606-784586 *(Hartford)*

All Hallows, Catholic High School Brooklands Avenue, SK11 8LB **Tel:** 01625-426138 **Fax:** 01625-500315 *(Macclesfield)*

▲ Independent

Alderley Edge School for Girls (a Christian Ecumenical School), Wilmslow Road SK9 7QE **Tel:** 01625-583028 **Fax:** 01625-590271 **Infants and Juniors: Tel:** 01625-582532.

■ HALTON L.E.A.

▲ Primary

The Holy Spirit, Cotterill, Halton Brook, WA7 2NL **Tel:** 01928-563148 **Fax:** 01928-566792 *(Runcorn 1)*

Our Lady, Mother of the Saviour, Lapwing

Grove, Palace Fields WA7 2TP
Tel: 01928-711921 **Fax:** 01928-717945 *(Runcorn 2)*

St Augustine, Conwy Court, Castlefields WA7 2JJ **Tel:** 01928-568936 **Fax:** 01928-566892 *(Runcorn 3)*

St Clement, Oxford Road WA7 4NX **Tel:** 01928-572129 **Fax:** 01928-590005 *(Runcorn 4)*

St Edward, Wivern Place WA7 1RZ **Tel:** 01928-572317 **Fax:** 01928-576034 *(Runcorn 4)*

St Martin, St. Martin's Lane, Murdishaw WA7 6HZ **Tel:** 01928-711207 **Fax:** 01928-710673 *(Runcorn 5)*

▲ Secondary

St Chad's, Grangeway, Halton Lodge WA7 5YH **Tel:** 01928-564106 **Fax:** 01928-572902 *(Runcorn 4)*

■ MANCHESTER L.E.A.

▲ Primary

Sacred Heart, Floatshall Road, Baguley, M23 8HP **Tel:** 0161-998 3419 **Fax:** 0161-945 6507 *(Wythenshawe 1)*

St Aidan's, Rackhouse Road, M23 0BW **Tel:** 0161-998 4126 **Fax:** 0161-945 5677 *(Wythenshawe 4)*

St Anthony's, Dunkery Road, Woodhouse Park, M22 0NT **Tel:** 0161-437 3029 **Fax:** 0161-436 5953 (*Wythenshawe 2)*

St Elizabeth's, Calve Croft Road, M22 5EU **Tel:** 0161-437 3890 **Fax:** 0161-490 7024 (*Wythenshawe 3)*

St John's, Woodhouse Lane, Benchill, M22 9NW **Tel:** 0161-998 3422 **Fax:** 0161-945 5616 (*Wythenshawe 5)*

St Peter's, Firbank Road, Newall Green, M23 2YS **Tel:** 0161-437 1495 **Fax:** 0161-437 9337 (*Wythenshawe 1)*

▲ Secondary

St Paul's High School, Firbank Road, M23 2YS **Tel:** 0161-437 5841 **Fax:** 0161-498 2030 (*Wythenshawe 1)*

■ SHROPSHIRE L.E.A

▲ Primary

St John's, Innage Gardens, WV16 4HW. **Tel:** 01746-762061, **Fax:** 01746-768298. *(Bridgnorth)*

Our Lady and St. Oswald, Upper Brook Street, SY11 2TG **Tel:** 01691-652849 **Fax:** 01691-681055 *(Oswestry)*

St Mary's, New Park Road, Castlefields, SH1 2SP **Tel:** 01743-351032 *(Shrewsbury),*

▲ Independent

Moor Park (Preparatory) SY8 4EA **Tel:** 01584-872342 **Fax:** 01584-877311 *(Ludlow)*.

St Winefrid's Convent School, Belmont SY1 1TE **Tel:** 017453-369883 **Fax:** 01743-341650 *(Shrewsbury)*

■ STOCKPORT L.E.A.

▲ Infant

Cheadle RC Infant, Conway Road, SK8 6DB **Tel:** 0161-485 8733 **Fax:** 0161-485 8733 *(Heald Green)*

▲ Junior

Cheadle RC Junior, Conway Road, SK8 6DB **Tel:** 0161-485 3754 **Fax:** 0161-482 8106 *(Heald Green)*

▲ Primary

St Ambrose, Rostrevor Road, SK3 8LQ **Tel:** 0161-480 8466 **Fax:** 0161-480 8466 *(Adswood)*

St Bernadette's, Gorseway, SK5 8AB **Tel:** 0161-430 4601 **Fax:** 0161-406 6235 *(Brinnington)*

Our Lady's, Old Chapel Street, SK3 9HX **Tel:** 0161-480 5345 **Fax:** 0161-480 1086 *(Edgeley, Stockport 1)*

St Peter's, Carisbrooke Avenue SK7 5PL **Tel:** 0161-483 2431 **Fax:** 0161-456 9332 *(Hazel Grove)*

St Simon's, Bosden Avenue SK7 4LH **Tel:** 0161-483 9696 **Fax:** 0161-483 2569 *(Hazel Grove)*

St Philip, Half Moon Lane, SK2 5LB **Tel:** 0161-483 0977 *(Offerton, Stockport 5)*

St Christopher's, Warwick Road, SK6 3AX **Tel:** 0161-430 4473 **Fax:** 0161-285 5717 *(Romiley)*

St Joseph's, Etchells Street, St Petersgate, SK1 1EF **Tel:** 0161-480 5029 **Fax:** 0161-480 5029 *(Stockport 4)*

▲ Secondary

St James Catholic High School, St James' Way, SK8 6PZ **Tel:** 0161-486 9211 **Fax:** 0161-486 6607 *(Cheadle Hulme)*

Harrytown Catholic High, Harrytown Lane, SK6 3BU **Tel:** 0161-430 5277 **Fax:** 0161-430 1700 *(Romiley)*

▲ Sixth Form College

Aquinas College, Nangreave Road, SK2 6TH **Tel:** 0161-483 3237 **Fax:** 0161-487 4072

■ TAMESIDE L.E.A.

▲ Primary

St Mary's, Cheetham Hill Road, SK16 5LD **Tel:** 0161-368 4824 **Fax:** 0161-368 4824 *(Dukinfield)*

St James, Cheriton Close, SK14 3DQ **Tel:** 0161-368 3455 **Fax:** 0161-368 3177 *(Hattersley)*

St Paul's, Turner Lane, SK14 4AG

Tel: 0161-368 2934 Fax: 0161-366 1964 *(Hyde)*

St Raphael's, Huddersfield Road, SK15 3JL **Tel:** 0161-338 4095 **Fax:** 0161-303 9724 *(Millbrook)*

St Peter's, Hough Hill Road SK15 2EO **Tel:** 0161-338 3303 **Fax:** 0161-303 2073 *(Stalybridge)*

▲ Secondary

All Saints Catholic College, Kenyon Avenue, SK16 5AR **Tel:** 0161-338 2120 **Fax:** 0161-338 9750 *(Dukinfield)*

■ TRAFFORD L.E.A.

▲ Infant

St Vincent's Infant, Orchard Road WA15 8EY **Tel:** 0161-928 3440 **Fax:** 0161-929 4881 *(Altrincham)*

▲ Junior

St Vincent's Junior, Osborne Road WA14 8EU **Tel:** 0161-928 1265 **Fax:** 0161-941 2957 *(Altrincham)*

▲ Primary

Our Lady of Lourdes, Lock Lane, M31 4PJ **Tel:** 0161-775 2847 **Fax:** 0161-912 5422 *(Partington)*

St Joseph's, Marlborough Road M33 3AF **Tel:** 0161-973 4938 **Fax:** 0161-973 7028 *(Sale 2)*

All Saints, Cedar Road, Ashton-on-Mersey M33 2JA **Tel:** 0161-912 1288 **Fax:** 0161-962 1887 *(Sale 1)*

Holy Family, Old Hall Road, M33 1HZ **Tel:** 0161-962 5397 **Fax:** 0161-969 9560 *(Sale Moor)*

St Margaret Ward, Cherry Lane M33 4GY **Tel:** 0161-969 9852 **Fax:** 0161-912 3663 *(Sale 3)*

St Hugh's, Park Road WA15 6TQ **Tel:** 0161-962 1852 **Fax:** 0161-905 2380 *(Timperley)*

▲ Secondary

Blessed Thomas Holford College, Urban Road WA15 8HT **Tel:** 0161-911 8090 **Fax:** 0161-911 8049 *(Altrincham)*

St Ambrose College, Wicker Lane, Hale Barns, WA15 0HE **Tel:**0161-980 2711 **Fax:** 0161-980 2323 *(Hale Barns)*

Loreto Convent Grammar, Dunham Road, WA14 4AH **Tel:** 0161-928 3703 **Fax:** 0161-928 7659 *(Altrincham)*

▲ Independent

Loreto Convent Preparatory, Dunham Road WA14 4AH **Tel:** 0161-928 8310 **Fax:** 0161-929 5801 *(Altrincham)*

St Ambrose College (Preparatory), Wicker Lane, Hale Barns WA15 0HE **Tel:** 0161-903 9193 **Fax:** 0161-903 8138 *(Altrincham)*

■ WARRINGTON L.E.A.

▲ Primary

St Monica, St Monica's Close, Stockton Heath WA4 3AG **Tel:** 01925-267609 **Fax:** 01925-268484 *(Appleton)*

Our Lady's, Wash Lane WA4 1JD **Tel:** 01925-633270 **Fax:** 01925-654584 *(Latchford 1)*

St Augustine, Henshall Avenue WA4 1PY **Tel:** 01925-633317 **Fax:** 01925-575119 *(Latchford 2)*

▲ Secondary

Cardinal Newman Catholic High School, Bridgewater Avenue WA4 1RX **Tel:** 01925-635556 **Fax:** 01925-628600 *(Latchford)*

■ WIRRAL L.E.A.

▲ Infant

St John's Infant, Old Chester Road, CH63 7LH **Tel:** 0151-645 5291 **Fax:** 0151-645 6803 *(New Ferry)*

▲ Junior

St John's Junior, Old Chester Road, CH63 7LH **Tel:** 0151-645 9615 **Fax:** 0151-645 6673 *(New Ferry)*

▲ Primary

Holy Cross, Challis Street, CH41 7DH **Tel:** 0151-652 8454 **Fax:** 0151-652 8454 *(Birkenhead 1)*

Our Lady's, Price Street, CH41 8DU **Tel:** 0151-652 3366 **Fax:** 0151-653 7248 *(Birkenhead 3)*

St Anne's, Highfield South, Rock Ferry, CH42 4NE **Tel:** 0151-645 3682 **Fax:** 0151-643 0137 *(Birkenhead 4)*

St Joseph's, Woodchurch Road, Prenton CH43 5UT **Tel:** 0151-652 6781 **Fax:** 0151-670 1843 *(Birkenhead 5)*

St Michael's, New Hey Road, CH49 5LE **Tel:** 0151-677 4088 **Fax:** 0151-677 0885 *(Birkenhead 6)*

St Laurence's Park St, CH41 3JD **Tel:** 0151-647 8409 **Fax:** 0151-647 2623 *(Birkenhead 8)*

St Werburgh's, Park Grove, CH41 2TD **Tel:** 0151-647 8404 **Fax:** 0151-647 7348. *(Birkenhead 8)*

Christ the King, Allport Road CH62 6AE **Tel:** 0151-334 4345 **Fax:** 0151-334 9658 *(Bromborough)*

Our Lady of Pity, Rigby Drive, CH49 1RE **Tel:** 0151-677 6262 **Fax:** 0151-677 5609 *(Greasby)*

Sacred Heart, Danger Lane, CH46 8UG **Tel:** 0151-677 1091 **Fax:** 0151-605 0100 *(Moreton)*

St Peter's, St Peters Way CH43 9QR

Tel: 0151-677 8438 **Fax:** 0151-677 8438 *(Birkenhead 7)*
St Paul's, Farm Fields Drive, Beechwood, Prenton CH43 7TE **Tel:** 0151-652 7828 **Fax:** 0151-652 7828 *(Birkenhead 1)*
Ladymount, Portal Road, CH61 5YD **Tel:** 0151-648 4326 **Fax:** 0151-648 9098 *(Pensby)*
St Joseph's, Moreton Road, CH49 6LL **Tel:** 0151-677 3970 **Fax:** 0151-522 0266 *(Upton)*
St Alban's, Ashburton Road, CH44 5XB **Tel:** 0151-638 6373 **Fax:** 0151-638 2870 *(Wallasey 4)*
St Joseph's, Wheatland Lane, CH44 7ED **Tel:** 0151-638 3919 **Fax:** 0151-638 6104. *(Wallasey 2)*
Our Lady of Lourdes, Gardenside, Leasowe CH46 2RP **Tel:** 0151-638 5180 **Fax:** 0151-638 8700 *(Wallasey 3)*
SS Peter and Paul, Atherton Street, New Brighton, CH45 9JD **Tel:** 0151-639 2991 **Fax:** 0151-638 5232 *(Wallasey 5)*

▲ Secondary
Plessington Technology College, Old Chester Road, Bebington, Wirral CH63 7LF **Tel:** 0151-645 5049 **Fax:** 0151-643 1516
St Mary's College, Wallasey Village, Wirral, CH45 3LN **Tel:** 0151-639 7531 **Fax:** 0151-691 1452 *(Wallasey)*
St Anselm's College, Manor Hill, Prenton CH43 1UF **Tel:** 0151-652 1408 **Fax:** 0151-652 1957 *(Birkenhead 2)*
Upton Hall School (FCJ), Upton Village, CH49 6LJ **Tel:** 0151-677 7696 **Fax:** 0151-677 6868 *(Upton)*

▲ Independent
Redcourt-St Anselm's Christian Brother Day School, 7 Devonshire Place, Prenton CH43 1TX **Tel:** 0151-652 5228 **Fax:** 0151-653 5883

■ WREKIN & TELFORD L.E.A.

▲ Primary
St Luke's, Church Road, Trench TF2 7HG (Serves Donnington) **Tel:** 01952-617355 **Fax:** 01952-270138 *(Telford 2)*
St Mary's, Coronation Crescent, Madeley, TF7 5EJ. Shropshire **Tel:** 01952-580954 **Fax:** 01952-580954 *(Telford 1)*
SS Peter and Paul, Salters Lane, TF10 7HU **Tel:** 01952-811171 **Fax:** 01952-272063 *(Newport)*
St Patrick's, North Road, Wellington, TF1 3ER **Tel:** 01952-242709 **Fax:** 01952-641720 *(Telford 3)*

▲ Secondary
Blessed Robert Johnson Catholic College, Whitchurch Road, Wellington TF1 3DY **Tel:** 01952-417600 **Fax:** 01952-417501*(Wellington Telford)*

ARCHDIOCESE OF SOUTHWARK

Consisting of the London Metropolitan Boroughs (south of the Thames) and the County of Kent

Suffragan Sees:
Arundel and Brighton, Plymouth, Portsmouth

Patrons of the diocese
Our Blessed Lady, Conceived Without Sin, 8 December.
St Thomas of Canterbury, 29 Dec;
St Augustine, Apostle of England, 27 May.

Archbishop
Most Rev Kevin John Patrick McDonald BA, STL, STD, born in Stoke-on-Trent, 18 August 1947; ordained 20 July 1974; cons Bishop of Northampton, 2 May 2001; transfered to the Archdiocese of Southwark 8 December 2003.

Most Rev Kevin McDonald, Archbishop of Southwark

Residence:
Archbishop's House, St George's Road, Southwark, SE1 6HX
Tel: 020-7928 2495 **Fax:** 020-7928 7833
E-mail: aps@rcsouthwark.co.uk

Secretary:
Miss Rachael McKenzie MA

Private Secretary:
Mgr William Saunders BEd(Hons)

Archbishop Emeritus
Most Rev Michael G Bowen STL, PhL. Born Gibraltar, 23 April 1930; ordained 6 July 1958; ordained titular Bishop of Lamsorti, 27 June 1970; succeeded to Diocese of Arundel & Brighton 14 March, 1971; succeeded to the Archdiocese of Southwark 23 April, 1977.

■ AUXILIARY BISHOPS

Rt Rev John Hine PhL, VG, born Tunbridge Wells, 26 July, 1938, ordained priest 28 October 1962, ordained Bishop of the Titular See of Beverley and Auxiliary in Southwark by Archbishop Bowen 27 February 2001. With special responsibilities for the Deaneries of Canterbury, Chatham, Dover, Gravesend, Maidstone, Thanet, Tunbridge Wells. Residence: Bishop's Flat, The Hermitage, More Park, West Maling, Kent ME19 6HN
Tel: 01732-845486 **Fax:** 01732-847888
Email: jhine@absouthwark.org

Rt Rev Patrick Lynch SSCC, MA, VG, born Cork City, 27th April 1947, ordained priest 21st July 1972, ordained Bishop of the Titular See of Castro and Auxiliary in Southwark by Archbishop Kevin Mc Donald 14th February 2006 with special responsibilities for the Deaneries of Bexley, Bromley, Camberwell, Greenwich, Lambeth, Lewisham
Residence: Park House, 6a Cresswell Park, Blackheath London SE3 9RD
Tel: 0208 297 9219
Email: bishoplynch7@btinternet.com

Rt Rev Paul Hendricks MA, PhL, VG, born Beckenham, Kent 19th March 1956, ordained priest 29st July 1984, ordained Bishop of the Titular See of Rosemarkie and Auxiliary in Southwark by Archbishop Kevin Mc Donald 14th February 2006 with special responsibilities for the Deanaries of Balham, Cathedral, Croydon, Kingston, Merton, Mortlake, Sutton.
Residence: 95 Carshalton Road, Sutton, SM1 4LL **Tel:** 0208 643 8007
Email: bishop.hendricks@googlemail.com

■ AUXILIARY BISHOPS EMERITI

Rt Rev John Jukes, OFM Conv, STL, Born in Eltham, London, 7 August 1923; ordained Priest 19 July 1952; ordained Bishop of the Titular See of Strathearn and Auxiliary in Southwark 30 January 1980. Residence: Willowbank, Gladstone Road, Huntly, Aberdeenshire, Scotland AB54 8BD
Tel: 01466-792832.
Email: jjukesofmc@aol.com

Rt Rev Howard George Tripp. Born at Croydon, Surrey, 3 July 1927; ordained

Priest 31 May 1953; ordained Bishop of the Titular See of Newport and Auxiliary in Southwark by Archbishop Bowen 30 January 1980. Residence: 67 Haynt walk, London SW20 9NY **Tel:** 020-8543 4864 **Email:**htripp@tiscali.co.uk

■ ADMINISTRATION

■ Diocesan Curia
Archbishop's House, 150 St George's Road, Southwark, London SE1 6HX
Tel: 020-7928 5592 **Fax:** 020-7401 7383
Email: chancery@rcsouthwark.co.uk

■ Vicar General
Mgr Richard Moth MA, JCL, KCHS, VG
Email: vg@rcsouthwark.co.uk

■ Episcopal Vicar for Religious
Bishop Patrick Lynch SS.CC
Park House, 6a Cresswell Park, Blackheath London SE3 9RD **Tel:** 0208 297 6540

■ Vicars for Religious
For the Cathedral, Lewisham, Camberwell, Greenwich and Bexley Deaneries: **Sr Anne Hoskison FMA**, 14 Streatham Common Northside, Streatham SW16 3HG **Tel:** 0208 677 9569
For Mortlake, Sutton, Kingston, Balham and Merton Deaneries: **Sr Josephine Toal SMR**, Convent of Marie Reparatrice, 115 Ridgeway, Wimbledon SW19 4RB **Tel:** 0208 946 1088
For the Tunbridge Wells, Bromley, Croydon and Lambeth Deaneries: **Sr Sheila Moloney DMT**, Convent of Daughters of Mary and Joseph, 38 Brook Road, Thornton Heath, London CR7 7RB.
For the Maidstone, Dover, Chatham, Thanet, Canterbury and Gravesend Deaneries: **Sr Mary Macnamara RSM**, Sisters of Mercy, Northwood Road, Whitstable, Kent CT5 3EY **Tel:** 01227-280898

■ Chancellor
Mgr Richard Moth.
Vice-Chancellor: **Mgr William Saunders.** *Chancery Admin:* **Rev Michael Kennedy.**
E-mail: mkennedy@rcsouthwark.co.uk
Chancery Secretary: **Mrs Mary Doolan.**
E-mail: mdoolan@rcsouthwark.co.uk

■ The Historic Churches Committee
For the Dioceses of Southwark, Arundel & Brighton, Portsmouth, Plymouth and Clifton: *Chairman:* **Mgr Canon Nicholas Rothon**; *Secretary:* **Mr Mike State**; *Diocescan Representative:* **Rev David Gibbons.**

■ The Diocesan Gift Aid Office
59 Westminster Bridge Road, London SE1 7JE **Tel:** 020-7960 2512 *Organiser:* **Canon Martin Lee**. *Secretary:* Awaiting Appointment.

■ Registrar for Deceased Clergy
Rev Michael Clifton. 15 Camel Grove, Kingston-upon-Thames, Surrey KT2 5GR
Tel: 020-8546 3882

■ Diocesan Communications Officer
Including Press Relations.
Mgr William Saunders. Archbishop's House St George's Road, London SE1 6HX
Tel: 020-7928 2495 **E-mail:** aps@rcsouthwark.co.uk
Website: www.rcsouthwark.co.uk

■ Communications Adviser & Training Officer
Rev Richard Plunkett. The Presbytery, Arbroath Road, Eltham Well Hall, London SE9 6RR **Tel:** 020-8856 4993

■ Diocesan Finance Office
59 Westminister Bridge Road, London SE1 7JE **Tel:** 020-7960 2500
Financial Secretary: **Canon Martin Lee**. *Assistant Financial Secretary (Parish finance):* **Rev John Weatherill**. *Diocesan Accountant:* **Norman Gibbons.** *Schools Grants Administrator:* **Mr Steven Joslin**.

■ Diocesan Finance Committee
Rt Rev Paul Hendricks (*Chairman*), **Mgr Richard Moth, Canon John Kavanagh, Canon Martin Lee, Canon Francis Moran, Revv Matthew Dickens, John Weatherill, Joseph Smith**.

■ Diocesan Seminary Fund
Director: **Canon James Pannett.** 48 Dale Road, Purley, Surrey CR8 2EF
Tel: 020-8660 3815

■ Diocesan Archivist
Rev Charles Briggs, 28 Crown Lane, Chislehurst, Kent BR7 5PL
Tel: 020-8467 3215 *Assistant Diocesan Archivist:* **Rev Michael Clifton.**

■ EDUCATION AND FORMATION

■ Diocesan Schools Commission
Office: St Edward's House, St Paul's Wood Hill, St Paul's Cray, Orpington, Kent BR5 2SR
Tel: 01689-829331 **Fax:** 01689-829255
E-mail: office@rcsouthwark.org.uk
Website: www.rcschools-southwark.org
Director of Education: **Dr Dilys Wadman MA, PhD.** *Buildings Officer:* **Mr Mike Baldwin**

■ Southwark Catholic Youth Service
Director: **John Torryusen**. Castle Road, Whitstable, Kent CT5 2ED

Tel: 01227-272900 **Fax:** 01227-282384
E-mail: info@scys.org.uk
Website: www.scys.org.uk

■ **Diocesan Vocations Director**
Rev Stephen Langridge, 36 Nightingale Square, Balham SW12 8QN
Tel: 020-8355 0211
Permanent Diaconate Director: **Rev Peter Edwards**, 1 Montem Road, New Malden, Surrey KT3 3QW **Tel:** 020-8942 2602
Dean of Studies: **Rev Ashley Beck,** 22 Downs Road, Beckenham, Kent BR3 5JY
Tel: 020-8650 4117

■ **Christian Education Centre**
21 Tooting Bec Road, London SW17 8BS
Tel: 020-8672 7684 and **Tel:** 020-8672 2422 **Fax:** 020-8672 8894
E-mail: office@cectootingbec.org.uk
Website: www.cectootingbec.org.uk
Director: **Rev John O'Toole**. *Co-ordinators Adult Formation, RCIA and Catechesis:* (Kent): **Mrs Molly Styant,** (South London): Awaiting Appointment. Community Development Project for People with Disabilities: **Mrs Christina Gangemi,** *Assistant to Co-ordinator:* **Mr John McCorkell** *Administrative Co-ordinator:* **Dr Frank Keen**. *Centre Administrator:* **Graham Wallis**. *Centre Secretary:* **Mrs Mary Boley**. *Bookshop Supervisor:* **Mr Gary Donaldson.**

■ **Diocesan Theological Adviser**
Rev Canon John Redford. Maryvale Institute, Old Oscott Hill, Kingstanding, Birmingham B44 9AG **Tel:** 0121-360 8118

■ **LITURGY AND ECUMENISM**

■ **Diocesan Liturgical Commission**
Chairman: **Mgr Richard Moth**, Vicar General, Archbishop's House, 150 St George's Road, London SE1 6HX
Tel: 020-7928 5592 *Secretary:* **Mr Paul Moynihan KSG,** 40 Steward Close, Cheshunt, Herts EN8 8UW
Tel: 01922 628840

■ **Diocesan Master of Ceremonies**
Mgr William Saunders, Archbishop's House.

■ **Diocesan Christian Unity Commission**
Chairman: **Rev Mgr Timothy Galligan**.

■ **Area Christian Unity Commissions**
S.E. London Area. *Secretary:* **Mrs Margaret Moloney**. 133a Croydon Road, London SE20 7TT **Tel:** 020-8778 1416
S.W.London Area. *Secretary:* **Barbara Wood**, 6 The Avenue, Kew Gardens, Surrey TW9 2AJ Kent Area. *Secretary:* **Mrs Margaret Jones.** 9 Court Mount, Canterbury Road, Birchington, Kent CT7 0BS **Tel:** 01303-243337

■ **CHRISTIAN RESPONSIBILITY**

■ **Episcopal Vicar for Marriage and Family Life:**
Rev Graham Preston, 72 Paradise Street, Rotherhithe SE16 4HT **Tel:** 020-7237 2969

■ **Safeguarding Commission**
Safeguarding Co-ordinator: **Rev Canon John Kavanagh,** The Presbytery, 79 Moorside Road, Downham, Kent BR1 5EP
Tel: 020-8698 1449
Safeguarding Officer/Advisor: **Mrs Helen Sheppard,** 59 Westminster Bridge Road, London SE1 7JE **Tel:** 020-7960 2504
E-mail: helensheppard@cp-rcdsouthwark.org

■ **Pastoral Care of Travelling People**
Awaiting Appointment
Kent: **Miss Jennifer Austin**, 43 Northwood Road, Whitstable, Kent CT5 2EZ
Tel: 01227 261049

■ **Industrial Mission**
Diocesan Adviser: Awaiting appointment.

■ **Committee for on-going Formation of Priests**
Director of On-going Formation: **Rev Gerald Ewing**. Archbishop's House, 150 St George's Road, London SE1 6HX
Tel: 020-8877 3610

■ **Episcopal Vicar for Retired Priests**
Rev James Nolan. 7 Rosewood Lodge, 79 Wickham Road, Shirley CR0 8TB
Tel: 020-8654 1768

■ **Archbishop's Delegate for Pastoral care of Permanent Deacons**
Deacon Kevin Dunne, 22 Riddlesdale Ave, Tunbridge Wells, Kent TN4 9AB
Tel: 01892 689800 **E-mail:** KevinjeanDunne@btopenworld.com

■ **Co-ordinator for Inter-faith Work**
Rev Canon James Cronin, Cathedral House, Cathedral House, Westminster Bridge Road, London SE1 7HY
Tel: 020-7928 5256

■ **Diocesan Co-ordinator on Aids-Related Matters**
Sr Dorothy Bell (RSCJ). 31 Bute Gardens, London W6 7DR **Tel:** 020-8748 7990

■ **Diocesan Justice, Peace and Integrity of Creation Office**
Cathedral House, Westminster Bridge Road, London SE1 7HY **Tel:** 020-7928 9742
Email: office@southwarkjandp.co.uk
Website: southwarkjandp.co.uk

Chairman: **Rev Michael Scanlon.**
Co-ordinator: Awaiting Appointment.

■ **Advisor on Hospital Chaplaincy**
Rev Paul Mason. Cathedral House, Westminster Bridge Road, London SE1 7HY **Tel:** 020-7188 1187

■ **Chaplain to the Hearing-Impaired**
Rev Edward Perera, 45b Burnt Ash Hill, Lee SE12 0AE **Tel:** 020-8857 5006

■ **Diocesan Laity Commission**
Chairman: **Dr Tony Scott,** 10 Edgehill Road, Mitcham, Surrey CR4 2HU

■ **Black & Ethnic Minority Chaplain's Co-ordinator**
Canon James Cronin, Cathedral House, Westminster Bridge Road, London SE1 7HY **Tel:** 020-7928 5256

■ **Cabrini Children's Society**
Director: Mr Terence Connor, 49 Russell Hill Road, Purley, Surrey CR8 2XB **Tel:** 020-8668 2181/4

■ **CONSULTATIVE BODIES**

■ **Cathedral Chapter**
(erected 2 July 1852) *Provost:* **Canon Joseph Collins**. *Canons:* **Revv James Pannett** (*Secretary*), **Thomas McHugh,** (*Penitentiary*), **Colm Acton, Michael Cooley** (*Theologian*), **Kevin Haggerty, Nicholas Rothon, John Madden, Michael Bunce, James Cronin.**
Canons Emeriti: **Revv Canons John Lennon, John Morris, Charles Walker, John Devane** *(Provost Emeritus)*, **Patrick Pearson.** *Honorary Canons:* **Revv William Clements, Francis Moran, Jeremiah Cronin, Richard Quinlan, Martin Lee, John Naughton, Anthony Ford, John Kavanagh, John Redford, Francis O'Sullivan, John McNamara, Cornelius Beausang, Luke Verhees, John Bailey**.

■ **College of Consultors**
Rt Rev John Hine, Rt Rev Patrick Lynch, Rt Rev Paul Hendricks, Mgr Canon Nicholas Rothon, Mgr Richard Moth, Canons John Madden, Michael Bunce, Martin Lee, Revv John Lavery, Anthony Plummer, John Clark, Geoffrey Pointer, John O'Toole.

■ **Diocesan Council of Priests**
Chairman: Awaiting Appointment.
Secretary: **Rev Kevin Pelham**. The Presbytery, Fir Tree Grove, Carshalton Beeches, Surrey SM5 4NG
Tel: 020-8647 7748 **Fax:** 020-8669 6483
E-mail: cofpsec@rc.net

■ **SOUTHWARK METROPOLITAN TRIBUNAL**
For administrative purposes the Southwark Metropolitan Tribunal, the primary function of which is to deal with applications for nullity of marriage, is divided between two areas – South London and Kent. The Tribunal Office for South London is in Southwark. There is a separate Office for Kent in Chatham.
Judicial Vicar: **Rev Derek Vidler**; *Associate Judicial Vicar:* **Canon James Cronin**; *Secretary to Judicial Vicar:* **Mrs Margaret Hugkulstone**. 59 Westminister Bridge Road, London SE1 7JE **Tel:** 020-7960 2514 **Fax:** 020-7261 1099
Judges: (South London): **Rev Canons James Pannett, Anthony Verhees; Revv William Agley, James Boner OFMCap, Vincent Flynn, Paul Hough, Michael Jones, John Lavery, Michael Leach, Peter Murphy, Peter Ryman, Patrick Zammitt**; *Advocate:* **Mrs Yogi Sutton.**
Kent: *Associate Judicial Vicar:* **Rev Philip Gilbert**. *Co-administrators:* **Mrs Veronica Weaver & Mrs Angela Andriot**. 1a Hills Terrace, Chatham, Kent ME4 6PX
Tel: 01634-830218
E-mail: triboffice@tiscali.co.uk
Judges: (Kent): **Rev Mgr Michael Smith; Revv John Boyle, Paul Fennessy, John Clark, Richard Harvey, Christopher Keen**; *Advocate:* **Rev Philip Yates OFM**.

■ **INTERDIOCESAN TRIBUNAL OF SECOND INSTANCE OF SOUTHWARK**
The Tribunal was established on 26th November 1980 by the Apostolic Signatura to deal with appeals to Second Instance from the Diocesan Tribunals of the Province of Southwark (the dioceses of Southwark, Portsmouth, Arundel and Brighton, Plymouth).
Episcopal Delegate: **Right Rev Paul Hendricks MA, PhL VG**; *Episcopal Delegate Emeritus:* **Right Rev John Jukes OFM Conv**; *President:* **Rev Steven Fisher**; *Administrator:* **Miss June Roberts**. Archbishop's House, 150 St George's Road, London SE1 6HX **Tel:** 020-7928 3754 **Fax:** 020-7928 7833 *Promoter of Justice:* **Rev Mgr Richard Moth VG**. *Judges:* **Rev Mgr Provost Cyril Murtagh** (Portsmouth); **Rev Mgr James Joyce** (Portsmouth); **Rev Canons John Stapleton** (Arundel and Brighton); **Peter Turbitt** (Portsmouth); **Richard Quinlan** (Southwark); **John Naughton** (Southwark); **Revv Anthony Barratt** (Southwark); **Michael Benjamin** (Arundel and Brighton), **Francis Mooney** (Southwark); **Ernest Bonvini** (Southwark), **Edmund Hartley** (Southwark); **Rev Martin**

Edwards (Southwark), **Rev Deacon Fintan Phelan** (Southwark), **Sr Chiara Hatton Hall FMDM** (Southwark), **Mr Paul Barker** (Southwark); *Defenders of the Bond:* **Revv Martin McCarthy, Edward Hill; Rev Deacons James Sheahan, Anthony Ward, Christopher Road; Mrs Eithne D'Auria** (Portsmouth). *Advocates:* **Rev Michael Kennedy** (Southwark); **Rev Robin Sanders** (Portsmouth), **Rev Roy Tablizo** (Southwark), **Rev Dcn Michael Kennedy, Dr Felicity O'Brien** (Southwark).

■ **SOUTHWARK**
Metropolitan Cathedral of St George
(1786-1848; cons 7 Nov 1894, rebuilt 1958)
Lambeth Road, Southwark.
Tel: 020-7928 5256 **Fax:** 020-7202 2189
E-mail: stgeorges@rc.net
Website: southwark-rc-cathedral.org.uk
Canon James Cronin. (*Cathedral Dean*): **Revv Mark Odion MSP, John Eze MSP**. *Deacon:* **Rev James Sheahan**. *Parish Sister:* **Sr Ursula**. Cathedral Clergy House, Westminster Bridge Road SE1 7HY
M: *Sat 1st M of Sun 6pm. Sun 8am, 10am (Family), 11.30am (Sung), 1pm (Spanish) 4.30pm (St Thomas's Hospital) 6pm. Hds 7.30am, 12.30pm, 6pm.*

- ***Franciscan Missionaries of the Divine Motherhood,*** Archbishop's House, St George's Road, SE1 6HY **Tel:** 020-7928 0689
- ***Missionaries of Charity,*** 116 St George's Road, SE1 **Tel:** 020-7620 1504
- ***St Thomas Hospital Chaplaincy:*** Rev Paul Mason **Tel:** 020-7928 9292.

■ **ABBEY WOOD**
1. † St Benet's (1909)
31 Abbey Gr, Abbey Wood SE2 9EU
Tel: 020-8311 2594 **Rev David Camilleri**
M: *Sat 1st M of Sun 6.30pm. Sun 9am, 11.30am. Hds (vigil 8pm), 9am.*

2. † St David's (1964)
Finchale Road, Abbey Wood Estate, Abbey Wood.
Rev Peter Murphy. St Thomas á Becket, School House, Mottisfont Road, Abbey Wood SE2 9LY **Tel:** 020-8311 2727
M: *Sun 9am, 11am, 5.30pm. Hds (vigil 8pm). 9am, 8pm.*

■ **ADDISCOMBE,** Surrey
† Our Lady of the Annunciation
(1925; 1964; 1975)
Bingham Road, Addiscombe, Surrey.
Tel: 020-8654 1709 **Fax:** 020-8662 0843
E-mail: ourlady@addiscombeofs.net.co.uk
Website: addiscombecatholicchurch.com
Revv Joseph O'Connor, Donald Coleman. 147 Bingham Road, Addiscombe, CR0 7EN
M: *Sat 1st M of Sun 7pm. Sun 8.30am, 10am, 11.30am, 6.30pm. Hds (vigil 7pm). 7am, 10am, 8pm.*

- ***Daughters of Mary and Joseph,*** 55 Fitzjames Avenue, CR0 5DN **Tel:** 020-8654 8041 **Fax:** 020-8655 4337

■ **ANERLEY**
† St Anthony of Padua
(1878; 1927; cons 14 June 1950)
2 Genoa Road, Anerley SE20 8ES
Tel: 020-8778 8597
Fax: 020-8778 8597
Website: stantrc.bravehost.com
Rev Sunith Nonis. Also resident **Rev Kerry Barry-Ryan (SJ),** 2 Genoa Road SE20 8ES
M: *Sat 1st M of Sun 6pm. Sun 8.30am, 10am, 11.30am, 5.30pm. Hds 9.30am, 7.30pm.*

■ **ASHFORD,** Kent
† St Theresa of Avila
(1865; New Church 1991; cons 28 April 1991)
Tel: 01233-624771 **Fax:** 01233-665253
E-mail: stteresa.ashford@talk21.com
Website: www.rc.net/southwark/ashford/stteresa
Revv Augustine Kinnane, Joseph Feeley. Priest's House, Maidstone Road TN24 8TX
M: *Sat 1st M of Sun 5.30pm. Sun 8am, 10.30am. Hds 10am, 7.30pm.*

- ***Sisters of Mercy,*** 40 Magazine Road,TN24 8NT **Tel:** 01233-622035

■ **ASHFORD (SOUTH),** Kent
† St Simon Stock (1961; 1987 New Church 1991; cons 31st October 1996)
Brookfield Road, Ashford, Kent TN23 2EU
Tel: 01233-622399
E-mail: parish@stsimon.org.uk
Website: www.stsimon.org.uk
Rev John Boyle. The Priest's House, St Simon's RC Church, Brookfield Road, Ashford, Kent TN23 2EU
M: *Sun 10am, 6pm. Hds 9.30am, 7pm.*

■ **AYLESFORD,** Kent
Shrine of Our Lady and St Simon Stock
(1242, 1247, 1348, 1417, 1949 - Friars Returned; recons 18 July 1965)
The Friars, Aylesford, Kent ME20 7BX
Tel: 01622-717272 **Fax:** 01622-715575
E-mail: enquiry@thefriars.org.uk
Website: www.thefriars.org.uk

- ***Shrine of Our Lady and St Simon Stock, (Carmelites)***: Pilgrimage, Retreat and Conference Centre. **Revv Bernard**

Grady (*Prior*), **Joseph Chalmers** (*Sub-Prior & Novice Director*); **Alphonsus Brennan, Conleth Doyle, Cyril Baxter, Anthony Pelan, David Waite, David Fox; Brs Michael McMullen, Laurence Frost, Paul de Groot.**
M: *Sun 8am, 10.15am.*

- ***Missionary Workers of Donum Dei.*** The Friars, Aylesford, Kent ME20 7BX **Tel:** 01622-710990
- ***The Leaven Secular Institute of Our Lady of Mount Carmel,*** c/o The Friars, Aylesford, Maidstone, Kent ME20 7BX **Tel:** 01622-717272

A

■ **AYLESHAM,** Kent
† **St Finbarr** (1930; 1957)
Aylesham, Kent.
Tel: 01304-840205
Rev Anthony (Jeff) Cridland. Priest's House, Market Square, Aylesham, Kent CT3 3EZ
M: *Sun 10am. Hds 9.30am, 7pm.*

- ***L'Arche Kent***. Little Ewell, Barfrestone, Dover, Kent CT15 7JJ **Tel:** 01304-830930 **Fax:** 01304-832393 **E-mail:** kent@larche.org.uk

A

■ **BALHAM**
1. † **Church of the Holy Ghost**
(1882; 1897; cons 17 May 1934)
Nightingale Square, Balham SW12 8QN
Tel: 020-8355 0211 **Fax:** 020-8355 0212
Revv Stephen Langridge, Augustine Umama MSP 36 Nightingale Square, Balham SW12 8QN
M: *Sat 1st M of Sun 5.30pm. Sun 9am, 10am, 11.30am, 6pm. Hds 6.45pm, 9.30am, 8pm.*

- ***Franciscan Missionaries of the Divine Motherhood,*** 19 West Side, Clapham Common SW4 9AL **Tel:** 020-7228 4695
- ***St Francis Xavier Further Education College,*** Malwood Road, SW12 8EN **Tel:** 020-8772 6000
Chaplain: **Rev Paul Mason.** **Tel:** 020-8675 0563. *Lay Chaplains:* **Hania Lubienska, Francesca Pordage.** **Tel:** 020-8772 6000
- ***Kelston Club,*** (Whose pastoral care is entrusted to the Opus Dei Prelature). 159 Nightingale Lane, SW12 8NQ **Revv Xavier Calduch, Paul Diaper.** **Tel:** 020-8673 2242

2. **Polish Church of Christ the King**
Balham High Road, Balham SW17
Mgr Canon Wladyslaw Wyszowadski, Rev Stanislav Gibzinski. 55 Foxbourne Road, SW17 8EN
Tel: 020-8672 5070 **Fax:** 020-8682 1770

■ **BARMING**
See Maidstone, (4).

■ **BARNES**
† **St Osmund**
(1908; 1926; 1955; cons 26 June 1958)
79 Castelnau, Barnes SW13 9RT
Tel: 020-8748 5833
Rev Dominic Allain.
M: *Sat 1st M of Sun 6.30pm. Sun 8.30am, 10.30am, 6.30pm. Hds 10am, 6.30pm.*

■ **BATTERSEA PARK**
† **Our Lady of Mount Carmel and St Joseph**
(1868; 1879; 10 May 1985)
Battersea Park, SW8 4BH (nr Station)
Tel: 020-7622 4282 **Fax:** 020-7978 1800
Mbl: 07966-206180 (SMS text and urgent)

- **Comboni Missionaries (Verona Fathers): Revv Tesfamichael Debesay Neguse** (Superior and Parish Priest), **John Clarke**. The Presbytery, 8a Battersea Park Road, SW8 4BH
Deacon: **Rev Fidelis Chukwu.**
M: *Sun 10am, 12noon. Hds 9.30am, 7.30pm.*

■ **BATTERSEA (WEST)**
† **The Sacred Heart** (1872; cons 14 Oct 1893)
Trott Street, (off High Street), Battersea SW11 3DS

- ***Salesians of Don Bosco (SDB)*** **Rev Christopher Heaps** (*Parish Priest*). Parish House, 4 Orbel Street, Battersea SW11 3NZ **Tel:** 020-7223 2747
Deacon: **Rev Michael Kennedy**

Email: shbatt@btinternet.com
M: *Sat 1st M of Sun 7pm. Sun 9.30am, 11.30am, Hds 10am, 7.30pm.*

- ***Salesians of Don Bosco (SDB)*** Rinaldi House, 32 Orbel Street, SW11 3NZ **Tel:** 020-7801 9040 **Fax:** 020-7801 9041 **E-mail:** orbelsdb@msn.com
Revv John Dickson (*Rector*), **Ambrose Anene, Joseph Brown, Peter Carr, Sahaya Gnanaselvam, Sergio Haro, Joseph Merriman, Daniel O'Riordan, Martin Poulson, Italo Thomann.**
- ***Salesian Sisters,*** 3 Orbel Street, SW11 3NZ **Tel:** 020-7350 2038
- ***Society of St Paul (SSP)***. 191 Battersea Bridge Road SW11 3AS **Tel:** 020-7228 1656 **Fax:** 020-7228 2656

■ **BEARSTED,** nr Maidstone, Kent
1. † **St Peter** (1978; cons 1984)
Button Lane, Bearsted, ME15 8NJ
Tel: 01622-736100
Email: stpetersbearstead@waitrose.com
Website: www.catholic-bearsted.org.uk
Rev Mgr Timothy Galligan.
Deacon: **Rev Cyril Durbin.**
M: *Sat 1st M of Sun 6pm. Sun 10.30am. Hds 10am, 8pm.*

2. Good Shepherd
Rectory Lane, off East Street, Harriestsham.
Served from Bearsted (1).
M: *Sun 8.45am. Hds 7pm.*

■ BECKENHAM, Kent
† St Edmund of Canterbury
(1891; 1938; cons 24 May 1950).
20 Village Way, Beckenham BR3 3NP
Tel: 020-8650 0970 **Fax:** 020-8650 4124
Canon John Madden. Revv Victor Akongwale, Ashley Beck.
Deacons: **Revv Dennis Barratt, Sean Murphy, Robert Higgs.**
M: *Sat 1st M of Sun 6pm. Sun 8am, 9.30am, 11am, 5.30pm, 7pm. Hds (vigil 7.30pm). 7.30am, 10am, 12noon, 8pm.*
- ***Handmaids of the Sacred Heart,*** 25-27 Village Way BR3 3NA **Tel:** 020-8650 6313
- ***Missionary Sisters of St Peter Claver,*** 89 Shortlands Road, Bromley, Kent BR3 5ES **Tel:** 020-8313 3915 **E-mail:** claver@beck70.fsnet.co.uk

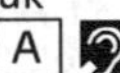

■ BECKENHAM HILL
† The Annunciation and St Augustine
(1928; 1934; cons 26 Aug 1964)
Dunfield Road, Beckenham Hill SE6 3PU
Tel: 020-8695 1092
E-mail: augustine.church@tiscali.co.uk
Rev Tom Creagh-Fuller; *Deacon:* **Rev Jeffrey Singleton.** 88 Beckenham Hill Road, SE6 3PU
M: *Sat 1st M of Sun 6pm. Sun 8.30am, 10.30am. Hds 9.30am.*

■ BENENDEN.
See Cranbrook, (3).

■ BERMONDSEY
1. † The Most Holy Trinity
(1773; 1834-35; cons 28 June 1921; new church cons 24 May 1960)
Dockhead, Bermondsey.
Tel: 020-7237 1641 **Fax:** 020-7394 8548
Rev Alan McLean. Priests' House, Dockhead, SE1 2BS
M: *Sat 1st M of Sun 6pm. Sun 10am, 6pm. Hds 10am, 8pm.*
- ***Sisters of Mercy,*** Convent of Our Lady of Mercy, Parkers Row, SE1 2DG **Tel:** 020-7237 1098.
- ***Sisters of Notre Dame,*** 7 Bushwood Drive, Bermondsey SE1 5RE. **Tel:** 020-7394 6227

2. † Our Lady of La Salette and St Joseph
(1848; 1861; cons 20th March, 1996)
14 Melior Street, Bermondsey SE1 3QP
Tel/Fax: 020-7407 1948
E-mail: lasallete.melior@gmail.com
Website: www.rc.net/southwark/londonbridge-lasallette
Canon Michael Cooley.
M: *Sat 1st M of Sun 6pm. Sun 9.30am, 11am, 6pm. Hds 12.35pm, 8pm.*
- ***Manna Centre:*** Help for single homeless, 6 Melior Street SE1 3QP **Tel:** 020-7403 1931
- ***Jesuit Refuge Service:*** 6 Melior Street SE1 3QP **Tel:** 020-7357 0974 **Fax:** 020-7378 1985 **E-mail:** UK@jrs.net

3. † St Gertrude (1903; cons Sept 21 1980)
1 Debnams Road, Rotherhithe New Road, Bermondsey SE16 2BB
Tel: 020-7237 0355
E-mail: john@stgertrudes.freeserve.co.uk
Rev Addison Okpeh MSP.
M: *Sat 1st M of Sun 6.30pm. Sun 9.15am, 11am. Hds 9am, 7pm.*
- ***Sisters of La Sainte Union,*** 2 Millender Walk, SE16 2BL **Tel:** 020-7231 7117

■ BEXLEY, Kent
† St John Fisher (1935; 1975; cons 31 Oct 1978)
Thanet Road, Bexley, Kent.
Tel: 01322-524813
E-mail: stjfisher@tiscali.co.uk
Rev Francis Hartley. Also in residence: **Rev Geoffrey Winchester,** (Retired). 48 Thanet Road, Bexley, Kent, DA5 1AP
M: *Sat 1st M of Sun 6pm. Sun 8.30am, 10.30am. Hds 9am, 8pm.*

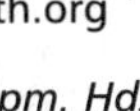

■ BEXLEY HEATH, Kent
† St John Vianney (1932; 1959; 1975)
21 Heathfield Road, Bexleyheath, DA6 8NP
Tel: 020-8303 1957
E-mail: parish@stjv.org.uk
Website: stjohnvianney-bexleyheath.org
Rev Michael Jones.
M: *Sun 8.30am, 10.30am, 5.30pm. Hds 9am, 8pm.*

■ BICKLEY, Kent
See Bromley.

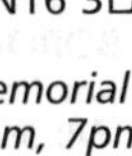

■ BIGGIN HILL, Westerham, Kent
† St Theresa of the Infant Jesus
(1925; 1931; cons. 1 Oct 1985)
1 Haig Road, Biggin Hill, Westerham.
Revv Gerald Flood, David Rhys (non-resident). Presbytery, Haig Road, TN16 3LJ
Tel: 01959-571404
M: *Sat 1st M of Sun 6pm (RAF Memorial Chapel). Sun 9am, 11am. Hds 7am, 7pm.*
- ***Sisters of the Holy Trinity,*** 2b Village Green Avenue, Biggin Hill TN16 3LP **Tel:** 01959-573979

■ BIRCHINGTON, Kent
† Our Lady and St Benedict
(1908; 1958; cons 14 July 1964)
Minnis Road, Birchington CT7 9SP
Tel: 01843-841549
Canon William Clements. The Presbytery, Minnis Road, Birchington CT7 9SF

ARCHDIOCESE OF SOUTHWARK

M: Sat 1st M of Sun 6pm. Sun 8.30am, 10.30am. Hds 8am, 10am, 7.30pm.

■ **BLACKFEN,** Sidcup, Kent
† **Our Lady of the Holy Rosary**
(1937; cons 2 Oct 1986)
330a Burnt Oak Lane, Blackfen, Sidcup, DA15 8LW **Tel:** 020-8300 2697
E-mail: rosary@freeuk.com
Rev Timothy Finigan. *Deacons:* **Revv Braz Menezes, Michael Baldry**.
M: *Sat 1st M of Sun 6pm. Sun 9am, 10.30am, 6pm. Hds 9.30am, 4.15pm, 8pm.*

■ **BLACKHEATH VILLAGE** A
† **Our Lady Help of Christians**
(1873; 1891; cons 3 Sept 1906)
Cresswell Park, Blackheath.
Tel: 020-8852 5420 **Fax:** 020-8852 9298
Website: stmarysblackheath.fslife.co.uk
Canon Nicholas Rothon. St Mary's, 5 Cresswell Park, Blackheath SE3 9RD
Tel: 020-8297 7223
M: *Sat 1st M of Sun 6.30pm. Sun 8am, 9.30am, 11am (Sung), 7.30pm. Hds 7am, 10am, 6.30pm.*
- ***Christ The King Further Education College,*** Belmont Grove, SE13 *Lay Chaplain:* **Mr Javier Elderfield, Mr Christopher Asker**.
- ***Sisters of the Sacred Hearts of Jesus and Mary.*** Sacred Heart Convent, 99 Belmont Hill, SE13 5DY **Tel:** 020-8852 1662/020-8318 0396
- ***Residence of Auxiliary Bishop:*** Park House, 6a Cresswell Park, Blackheath, London SE3 9RD **Tel:** 0208 297 6540 **Rt Rev Patrick Lynch MA VG**

■ **BOROUGH** A
† **The Most Precious Blood** (1892)
O'Meara Street, Borough.
Tel: 020-7407 3951 **Fax:** 020-7407 0201
- ***Salvatorians (SDS):*** **William Harrison, Derek Clark, John Murray (SDS).** 22 Redcross Way SE1 1TA
M: *Sat 1st M of Sun 6pm. Sun 8.30am, 11am. Hds 12.05pm, 1.05pm, 7.30pm.*

■ **BOROUGH GREEN,** Kent
Served from Sevenoaks.
M: *Sun 9.30am. Hds 6pm.*

■ **BOSTALL PARK,** Bexley Heath
† **St Thomas More** (1936, cons 21 July 2000)
420a Long Lane, Bexleyheath DA7 5JW
Tel: 020-8303 2189 **Rev John O'Donoghue**.
M: *Sat 1st M of Sun 6.30pm. Sun 9am, 10.30am. Hds (vigil 8pm). Sun 10am, 8pm.*

■ **BRANDS HATCH**
See Sevenoaks.

■ **BRIXTON** A
† **Our Lady of the Rosary**
(1905; 1953; cons 7 October 1986)
Brixton Road, Brixton SW9
Tel: 020-7274 2367
Rev Bernard Heaphy. 6 Knowle Close, Brixton SW9 0TQ
M: *Sat 1st M of Sun 6.30pm. Sun 8am, 10am, 12noon, 5.30pm. Hds (vigil 7.30pm) 10am, 12.15pm.*

■ **BRIXTON HILL**
† **Corpus Christi**
(1881; 1887; 1904; cons 12 Dec 1984)
11 Trent Road, Brixton Hill SW2 5BJ
Tel: 020-7274 4625
Email: brixtonrc@btinternet.com
Rev Tom Heneghan
M: *Sat 1st M of Sun 6pm. Sun 9am, 10.30am, 12noon, 6pm. Hds (vigil 6pm). 9.30am, 7.30pm.*
- ***51 Horsford Road,*** Brixton Hill SW2 5BP **Tel:** 020-7737 0377
- ***21 Helix Gardens,*** Brixton Hill SW2 2JJ **Tel:** 020-8671 4937 **Rev Andrew Cameron-Mowat** (*Superior*). **E-mail:** andrewcmsj@gmail.com
- ***Franciscan Missionaries of Mary,*** 95 Sudbourne Road, SW2 5AF **Tel:** 020-7274 6082
- ***Contemplative Missionary Movement of Fr de Foucauld:*** 213 Mayall Road, SE24 0PS
- ***Little Brothers of Jesus,*** 97 Sudbourne Road, SW2 5AS **Tel:** 020-7733 7583
- ***Brixton Prison,*** Jebb Avenue, London SW2 5XF. *Chaplain:* **Rev Malachy Keegan**.

■ **BROADSTAIRS,** Kent
† **Our Lady Star of the Sea**
(1878; 1888; 1931; 1961)
Broadstairs Road, Broadstairs, Kent.
Tel: 01843-861627
Rev David Caine. 23 St Peter's Road, Broadstairs CT10 2AP
M: *Sat 1st M of Sun 7pm. Sun 9.30am, 11am. Hds (vigil 7pm). 10am, 7pm.*
- ***Faithful Companions of Jesus,*** Stella Maris Generalate, North Foreland Road, CT10 3NR **Tel:** 01843-602341; Stella Maris Convent , North Foreland Road, CT10 3NR **Tel:** 01843-862109; Redriff Convent, North Foreland Avenue, CT10 3QT **Tel:** 01843-862626
- ***Daughters of the Cross,*** Arusha, Convent Road, CT10 3PT **Tel:** 01843-862561
- ***Canonesses of St Augustine,*** Port Regis Residential Home, Convent Road, Broadstairs CT10 3BE

ARCHDIOCESE OF SOUTHWARK

■ **BROCKLEY**
† **St Mary Magdalen (1895; 1899)**
Howson Road, Brockley, SE4.
Tel: 020-8692 1824 **Fax:** 020-8691 2404
73 Comerford Road, Brockley, SE4 2BA
Rev Michael Lovell.
Deacon: **Rev William Dunphy.**
M: *Sat 1st M of Sun 6.30pm. Sun 8.30am, 10am, 11.30am. Hds 7.30am, 9.30am, 8pm.*
- ***Franciscan Friars of the Immaculate;*** **Rev Agnellus Murphy FI**, 69 Comerford Road, SE4 2BA **Tel:** 0208 691 8997 **E-mail:** ffilondon@talktalk.net

■ **BROMLEY**
† **St Joseph** (1889, 1911; cons 28 Apr 1914)
Plaistow Lane, Bromley, Kent BR1 2PR
Tel: 020-8402 0459 **Fax:** 020-8402 4590
Canon Thomas McHugh, Revv Joseph Karukayil, Reason Mlilo. *Deacon:* **Rev Duncan Aitkins.** *Pastoral Assistants:* **Patricia Carroll, Mary Crosby.**
1 Orchard Road, Bromley, BR1 2PR
M: *Sat 1st M of Sun 6pm. Sun 8am, 9.15am, 11am, 5pm. Hds 7.15am, 10am, 8pm.*
- ***Holy Ghost Fathers (CSSp):*** Hadlow, 6 Woodlands Road, BR1 2AF **E-mail:** spiritans-bickley@tiscali.com **Rev John Kitchen** (*Superior*), **Tel:** 020-8467 3555 **Fax:** 020-8295 4965
- ***Holy Ghost Fathers UK Home for Sick and Retired Missionaries:*** In Residence: **Br John Holme, Revv John Gilroy, Kenneth Martin, Henry Pass, John Beirne, Edward McCann, Francis Bligh, Fr. Vincent Griffin, Fr. Alan Collins, Fr Peter Ward, Fr Seamus Hunter.**
- ***Sisters of the Holy Trinity:*** Holy Trinity Convent, 81 Plaistow Lane BR1 3LL **Tel:** 020-8402 2785
- ***Sisters of the Holy Family,*** Wellsprings, 18 Orchard Road, Bromley BR1 2PS **Tel:** 020-8464 1426

■ **BROMLEY COMMON,** Kent
† **St Swithun** (1910; cons 28 May 1985)
11 Fashoda Road, Bromley Common, Kent BR2 9RE
Tel: 020-8460 5764
Rev Robert Mercer SA.
M: *Sat 1st M of Sun 6pm. Sun 10am, 6pm. Hds 10am, 8pm.*

■ **BUCKLAND AND ST MARGARET'S BAY,** Kent
† **Our Lady of Dover** (1960)
Roosevelt Road, Dover CT16 2BU
Rev John Panario. The Presbytery, 24 Old Park Hill, Dover, Kent CT16 2AW
Tel: 01304-823402 **Fax:** 01304-826412
E-mail: john.panario@tesco.net
M: *Sun 10.30am, 6pm. Hds 10am.*
- ***Sisters of the Christian Retreat,*** Kearsney Manor Convent and Nursing Home, Alkham Valley Road, Dover, Kent CT16 3EQ **Tel:** 01304-822135 Kearsney Manor, Alkham Valley Road, Dover, Kent CT16 3EQ **Tel:** 01304-822254
St Augustine's Chapel. (1913).
Open to the public.
M: *Sun 8.30am.*
- ***Religious of the Eucharist,*** Kearsney Manor Nursing Home Alkham Valley Road, Dover, Kent CT16 3EQ **Tel:** 01304-824178 *Chaplain:* **Rev John Rooney** MHM **Tel:** 01304-822266

St Francis Chapel.
The Droveway, St Margaret's Bay.
M: *Sun 9am. Hds 9am.*

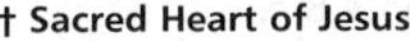

■ **CAMBERWELL**
† **Sacred Heart of Jesus**
(1860; 1863; 1870; 1952; cons 20 June 1974)
Camberwell New Road, Camberwell SE5
Tel: 020-7274 1908 **E-mail:** sacredheart@rccamberwell.freeserve.co.uk
Website:
sacredheartchurchcamberwell.org.uk
Revv David Gibbons, Adolphus Ezeakor, Anthony Edwards.
Deacon: **Rev Samuel Gyepi-Garbrah,** 2 Knatchbull Road, SE5 9QS
M: *Sat 1st M of Sun 6pm. Sun 8.30am, 10am, 11.30am, 6pm. Hds 9am, 10.30am, 12.45pm, 7pm.*
- ***Sisters of Sacred Hearts of Jesus and Mary***, 139 Southampton Way, SE5 7EW. **Tel:** 020-7701 5277
- ***King's College Hospital Chaplain:*** **Revv Luke Marappillil, Adolphus Ezeakor.** **Tel:** 020-3299 3522

■ **CANTERBURY,** Kent
† **St Thomas of Canterbury**
(1750; 1866; 1875; cons 16 Sept 1931)
59 Burgate, Canterbury, Kent CT1 2HJ
Tel: 01227-462896 **Fax:** 01227-450377
Pager: 07923 9722456
E-mail: stthomas.canterbury@talk21.com
Website: www.rc.net/southwark/canterbury
Canon Michael Bunce. Revv George Marsden, Richard Hearn.
Deacon: **Rev David Avery.**
M: *Sat 1st M of Sun 6pm. Sun 8am, 9.30am, 11am (Sung), 6pm. Hds (vigil 6pm). 9.30am, 12noon, 8pm.*
- ***University of Kent Chaplaincy,*** *Chaplain:* **Rev Peter Geldard.** St John Stone House, 41 St Thomas Hill,

CT2 8HW **Tel/Fax:** 01227-462198 Office **Tel:** 01227-823348 **Mbl:** 07970-228762 **E-mail:** chaplain@cathsoc.org **Website:** www.cathsoc.org

- ***Franciscan International Study Centre,*** Giles Lane, CT2 7NA **Tel:** 01227-769349 **Fax:** 01227-786648 **E-mail:** info@franciscans.ac.uk **Website:** franciscans.ac.uk *Principal:* **Rev Philippe Yates OFM.** *Vice-Principal:* **Sr Margaret McGrath FMSJ.**
- ***Franciscans, (OFM),*** **Revv Seamus Mulholland** (*Guardian*), **Philippe Yates** (*Vicar*), **Ninian Arbuckle, Antanas Bluzas, Antony Jukes, Peter Hooper, Alvydas Virbalis, Bro Brendan O'Neill, Christopher Leigh Tel:** 01227-464939
- ***Franciscans, (OFM Conv),*** **Revv Philip Doherty** (*Guardian*), **Joseph Aylekunnell** (*Assistant Vocations' Director*), **Michael Robson.** **Tel:** 01227-454647 /452802
- ***Franciscan Missionary Sisters of Littlehampton,*** Monte Bre, 5 Whitstable Road, Blean, Canterbury CT2 9AA **Tel:** 01227-471293
- **Franciscan Missionaries of St Joseph,** 20 King Street, Canterbury, Kent **Tel:** 01227-464336

■ **CARSHALTON,** Surrey A
† Holy Cross (1914; 1933; cons 9 Nov 1979)
46 North Street, Carshalton, Surrey SM5 2JD **Tel/Fax:** 020-8647 0022
E-mail: holy-cross@catholic.org
Website: rc.net/southwark/carshalton
Rev Paul Sanders.
M: *Sat 1st M of Sun 6.30pm. Sun 8am, 9.30am, 11am, 6.30pm. Hds 7am, 10am, 7.30pm.*

■ **CARSHALTON BEECHES,** Surrey A
† St Margaret (1934; Cons 5 June 1981)
Fir Tree Gr, Carshalton Beeches, Surrey SM5 4NG
Tel: 020-8647 7748 **Fax:** 020-8669 6483
E-mail: stmargarets@rc.net
Website: stmargarets.co.uk
Rev Kevin Pelham.
M: *Sat 1st M of Sun 7.15pm. Sun 9.30am, 11am, 5.30pm. Hds 7.15am, 10am, 8pm.*

■ **CATFORD**
† Holy Cross (1904; cons 6 July 1960)
208 Sangley Road, Catford SE6 2JS
Tel: 020-8698 3672 **Fax:** 020-8697 7590
Rev John Mulligan. *Deacon:* **Rev Roger Chandler-Honnor.**
M: *Sat 1st M of Sun 6.30pm. Sun 10am, 11.30am. Hds (vigil 8pm). 9.15am, 8pm.*

■ **CHARLTON**
† Our Lady of Grace
(1903; 1906; cons 13 Sept 1960)
145 Charlton Road, Charlton SE7 7EZ
Tel: 020-8858 0401 **Rev Michael J Leach**
M: *Sat 1st M of Sun 5.30pm. Sun 10am, 12noon, 6.30pm. Hds 9.30am, 8pm.*

■ **CHATHAM,** Kent
1. † St Michael the Archangel
(1795; 1863; cons 6 June 1951)
1 Hills Tce, Chatham, Kent ME4 6PU
Tel: 01634-842886 **Rev Christopher Baker.**
M: *Sat 1st M of Sun 6.30pm. Sun 9.30am, 11am, 6pm. Hds 7.30am, 10am, 12.30pm, 7pm.*

- ***Sisters of St Joseph,*** 116 Maidstone Road, ME4 6DU **Tel:** 01634-407729

2. St Paulinus
Manor Street, Old Brompton.
Served from Chatham (1).
M: *Sun 9am.*

3. Luton. The Sacred Heart (1949)
Street End Road. Served from Chatham (1).
M: *Sun 10.30am.*

■ **CHEAM,** Surrey
† St Christopher (1937)
Dallas Road, Cheam, Surrey.
Tel: 020-8642 2088, **Fax:** 020-8642 0744.
Rev Bernard Winn. 59 Tabor Gardens, Cheam, SM3 8RU
M: *Sat 1st M of Sun 6pm. Sun 8.30am, 10.30am, 12noon. Hds 7.15am, 9am, 8pm.*

■ **CHERITON**
See Folkestone (West).

■ **CHESSINGTON AND HOOK,** Surrey A
† St Catherine of Siena (1938)
98 Leatherhead Road, Chessington, Surrey KT9 2HY **Tel:** 020-8397 3971
Fax: 020-8391 2242 **E-mail:** office@stcatherineofsiena.org.uk
Website: www.stcatherineofsiena.org.uk
Rev Peter Jenner.
M: *Sun 8am, 10am, 6pm. Hds 10am, 7.30pm.*

■ **CHESTFIELD,** Kent
See Whitstable.

■ **CHISLEHURST,** Kent
† St Mary *(1852; 1854; cons 23 Sept 1943)*
The Common, Crown Lane, Chislehurst.
Tel: 020-8467 3215 **Fax:** 020-8325 9627
E-mail: stmaryrc@waitrose.com
Rev Charles Briggs. *Deacon:* **Rev John Harrison.** 28 Crown Lane, BR7 5PL.
M: *Sun 9.30am, 11am. Hds 9.30am, 8pm.*

ARCHDIOCESE OF SOUTHWARK

• ***Felician Sisters,*** 45 Holbrook Lane, BR7 6PE **Tel:** 020-8467 8103

■ CHISLEHURST WEST, Kent

† **St Patrick** (1961)
Red Hill, Chislehurst West, Kent
Tel: 020-8467 2325 **Fax:** 020-8325 9627
Rev George Webster SSC.
Deacon: **Rev Roger Evans**. 14 Red Hill, Chislehurst West, BR7 6DB
M: *Sun 8.30am, 10am, 5.30pm. Hds 9.30am, 8pm.*

■ CLAPHAM

A

† **Our Immaculate Lady of Victories (known as St Mary's)** (1848; 1851; cons 13 Oct 1852)
Clapham Park Road, Clapham SW4 7AP
Provincial: **Fax:** 020-7627 3153
Community: **Tel:** 020-7622 2793/6410
Fax: 020-7720 8191
Parish: **Tel:** 020-7498 3005
Fax: 020-7627 0767

• ***Redemptorists (CSsR):*** **Rev John Trenchard** (*Rector & Parish Priest*), **Revv John Clancy, Anthony Johnson.**
M: *Sat 1st M of Sun 5.30pm. Sun 8am, 10am, 12noon. Hds 7am, 9.30am, 12.30pm, 7pm.*
• ***Jesuit Community (SJ),*** 4 Windmill Drive, SW4 9DE **Tel:** 020-8673 7647 **Revv Brendan Callaghan** (*Superior*), **Anthony Carroll, William Clark, Simon Wong**.
• ***School Sisters of Notre Dame,*** 12 Hickmore Walk, SW4 6EQ **Tel:** 020-7498 9771
• ***Holy Family Sisters of Bordeaux,*** 40 Netherford Road, Clapham SW4 **Tel:** 020-7720 3295
• ***Focolare Movement,*** 62 Kings Avenue, SW4 8BH **Tel:** 020-8671 8355
• ***Little Way Association,*** 119 Cedars Road, SW4 0PR **Tel:** 020-7622 0466

■ CLAPHAM COMMON

A

† **St Vincent de Paul**
(1903; 1907; cons 17 June 1971)
Clapham Common, SW11
Tel/Fax: 020-7228 2121
E-mail: svpclapham@yahoo.co.uk
Website: web.svpclapham.org
Revv David Standley, Paul Teece.
Also resident: **Christopher O'Brien**
Deacon: **Rev Jon Dal Din**. 36 Altenburg Gardens SW11 1JJ
M: *Sat 1st M of Sun 6pm. Sun 9am, 11am (Sung), 6pm. Hds 9am, 7pm.*
• ***Croatian National Chaplaincy,*** 17 Boutflower Road, SW11 1RE **Tel:** 020-7223 3530 **Rev Ljubomir Simunovic OFM.**
M: *Sun 6pm. Hds 6pm.*

• ***Daughters of Divine Love,*** 46 Latimer House, Beaconsfield Road, London SE17 2EN
Tel: 020-7252 740 **Fax:** 020-7703 8626

■ CLAPHAM PARK

† **St Bede** (1903; 1906; cons 1 July 1969)
58 Thornton Road, Clapham Park SW12 0LF
Revv Christopher Basden, Tomasz Zacharski
Tel: 020-8674 3704 **Fax:** 020-8671 5366
E-mail: cbasden@stbedesclapham.freeserve.co.uk
Also in residence: **Rev Andrew Southwell FSSP. Tel:** 020-8678 5128
M: *Sat 1st M of Sun 6pm. Sun 8am, 9.30am 10.45am (Latin), 12noon, 6pm. Hds 7.15am, 9.30am, 8pm.*
• ***Handmaids of Mary,*** La Retraite Convent, Atkins Road, SW12 0AB **Tel:** 020-8673 1247

■ CLIFTONVILLE, Kent

† **St Anne** (1927)
Eastern Esplanade, Cliftonville, Kent.
Tel: 01843-220720
Rev Eric Mead, St Anne's Presbytery, Devonshire Gardens, CT9 3AF
Deacon: **Rev Neville Gascoigne**
M: *Sat 1st M of Sun 6pm. Sun 8.30am (Oct- May), 8am (June-Sept). 10.30am. Hds 8am, 10.30am, 8pm.*
• ***Institute of St Anselm:*** International Centre for Religious Formation, 26-28 Edgar Road, CT9 2EU
Tel: 01843-234700 **Fax:** 01843-234701
Director: **Rev Leonard Kofler (MHM).**
Students: **Tel:** 01843-224514/292937
Fax: 01843-226629
E-mail: stanselm@adept.co.uk

■ COLLIERS WOOD

A

† **St Joseph** (1966; cons 18 Feb 1980)
63 High Street, Colliers Wood, SW19
Tel: 020-8540 3057 **Fax:** 020-8544 1381
E-mail: stjoes@collywood.freeserve.co.uk
Rev John McGrory. 30 Park Road, Colliers Wood SW19 2HS
Parish Sister: **Sr Veronica Tansey**.
M: *Sat 1st M of Sun 6pm. Sun 9am, 10.45am. Hds 10am, 7.30pm.*

■ COULSDON, Surrey

† **St Aidan** (1907; 1931; 1966; Cons 21 Nov 1986)
Chipstead Valley Road, Coulsdon, Surrey.
Tel: 020-8660 2452
Rev Josef Doetsch. 1 Portnalls Road, Coulsdon CR3 3DD
M: *Sat 1st M of Sun 6pm. Sun 9am, 11am. Hds (vigil 7pm). 10am (9.30am during school term), 8pm.*

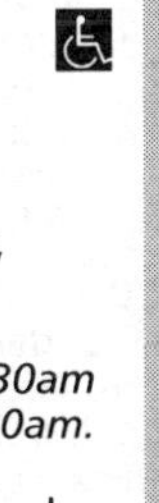

■ **CRANBROOK,** Kent

1. † St Theodore
(1937; 1958. Cons 19 September 1991)
The Priest's House, High Street, Cranbrook, Kent TN17 3DT **Tel:** 01580-713364
Rev Barry Grant *(Parochial Administrator).*
M: *Sat 1st M of Sun 6pm. Sun 10.45am. Hds 9.30am.*

2. Benenden, Catholic Chapel (1928; 1931)
New Pond Road, Cranbrook, Kent.
Served from Cranbrook.
M: *Sun 9am. Hds 7.30pm.*

■ **CRAYFORD,** Dartford

† St Mary of the Crays
(1842; 1973; cons 22 Feb 1987)
111 Old Road, Crayford, Dartford DA1 4DN **Tel:** 01322-523492
Rev John Ryan MBE.
M: *Sat 1st M of Sun 6.30pm. Sun 8.30am, 10.30am. Hds 9.15am, 8pm.*
• ***Sisters of La Sainte Union,*** 83 Watling Street, Bexleyheath DA6 7QJ **Tel:** 01322-528408 85 Watling Street, Bexleyheath, DA6 7QJ **Tel:** 01322-523285/523280

■ **CROYDON (SOUTH),** Surrey

† St Gertrude (1903; cons 25 June 1937)
46 Purley Road, Croydon, Surrey CR2 6EY
Tel: 020-8688 5002
Fax: 020-8760 0855
Email: stgertrude@btconnect.com
Website: stgertrudessouthcroydon.co.uk
Rev Martin McCarthy.
Parish Sister: **Sr Jennie Eldridge DMJ**
M: *Sat 1st M of Sun 6.30pm. Sun 8.30am, 10am, 11.30am (Sung), 6.30pm. (Hungarian Mass, Last Sun of Month, at 3pm). Hds (vigil 8pm). 10am, 8pm.*

■ **CROYDON (WEST),** Surrey

† Our Lady of Reparation
(1838; 1864; cons 27 May 1905)
70 Wellesley Road, Croydon CR0 2AR
Tel: 020-8688 1857 **Fax:** 020-8680 1056
Provost Joseph Collins, Rev Alfred Xureb SJ. Also resident: **Rev David O'Regan.**
Deacons: **Rev Vincent Morrison.**
M: *Sat 1st M of Sun 7pm. Sun 8am, 9.15am, 10.45am (Sung), 12.15pm, 6pm. Hds 8am, 10am, 12.10pm, 7pm.*
• ***Sisters of Mercy,*** 23 Tavistock Road, CR0 2AL **Tel:** 020-8688 8406
• ***Sisters of St Joseph,*** 25 Eden Road, Croydon CR0 1BB **Tel:** 020-8680 6900

■ **DARTFORD,** Kent

1. † St Anselm (1854; 1900; 1975, (cons 30th Oct 2001)
89 West Hill, Dartford, Kent DA1 2HJ
Tel: 01322-220075 **Fax:** 01322-290374
E-mail: stanselm@bigfoot.com
Revv William Scanlan, Jude Okenyi SFB.
Deacon: **Rev Maurice Williams.** *Parish Sister:* **Sr Ursula Hyland RMS.**
M: *Sat 1st M of Sun 6pm. Sun 8.30am, 10.30am, 6.30pm. Hds 7am, 10am, 8pm.*

2. † South Darenth, St George
Devon Road, DA4 9AB
Served from Dartford 1
M: *Sun 9.30am. Hds 6.30pm.*

3. † St Vincent (1982; cons 3 May 1985)
Temple Hill, Dartford, Kent.
Tel: 01322-279955 **Fax:** 01322-279955
Rev Patrick Zammit. The Presbytery, St Vincent's, Temple Hill, Dartford DA1 5HU.
Deacon: **Rev Michael Dale.**
M: *Sat 1st M of Sun 6.30pm. Sun 9am, 11am, 5pm. Hds 10am, 8pm.*
• ***Presentation Brothers:*** 6 The Brent, DA1 1YG. **Tel:** 01322-279106
• ***CAFOD Southwark:*** Hubert House, Holland Close, Temple Hill Square, Dartford DA1 5HU **Tel:** 01322 294924

■ **DEAL,** Kent

† St Thomas of Canterbury
(1842; 1885; cons 8 Aug 1928)
14 Blenheim Road, Deal, Kent CT14 7DB
Tel: 01304-374399 **Fax:** 01304-371191
E-mail: catholicchurchdeal@aol.com
Website: stthomasdeal.co.uk
Rev Duncan Lourensz.
M: *Sat 1st M of Sun 6.30pm. Sun 8.30am, 11am. Hds 9am, 11am, 6.30pm.*

■ **DENTON,** Kent

St Mary (1941)
Rochester Road. Served from Gravesend.
M: *Sun 9.30am.*

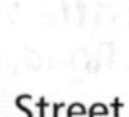

■ **DEPTFORD**

† Our Lady of the Assumption
(1842; 1846; cons 19 May 1890)
The Presbytery, 131 Deptford High Street SE8 4NS **Tel/Fax:** 020-8692 2011
• ***Missionaries of the Saint Paul (MSP):*** **Revv Eustace Durugbo, Gerald Onyejuluwamsp**
M: *Sun 9am, 11am (Sung), 6.30pm. Hds 9.30am, 7.30pm.*
• ***South London Universities,*** 56 Amersham Road, SE14 6QE
Tel: 020-8692 6931
Rev David O'Connell.

■ **DOVER**

† St Paul (1822; 1867; cons 25 Sept 1897)
103 Maison Dieu Road, Dover CT16 1RU
Tel: 01304-206766 **Rev Peter Madden.**
M: *Sat 1st M of Sun 6pm. Sun 9.30am, 11am (Sung). Hds 9.30am, 7pm.*
• ***Ursulines of Jesus,*** 20 Park Avenue, CT16 1HE. **Tel:** 01304-206807

ARCHDIOCESE OF SOUTHWARK

• ***Duke of York Royal Military School.***
M: *Sunday Mass as announced.*

■ **DOWNHAM,** Bromley
† The Good Shepherd
(1928; 1929; cons 25 Nov 1984)
79 Moorside Road, Downham BR1 5EP
Tel/Fax: 020-8698 1449
Rev Canon John Kavanagh.
Parish Sister: **Sr Anne-Marie.**
M: *Sat 1st M of Sun 6pm. Sun 9.15am, 11am. Hds 9.15am, 7.30pm.*

■ **DULWICH (EAST),** London
† St Thomas More
(1879; 1885; 1929; cons 14 Dec 1979)
380 Lordship Lane, Dulwich, London SE22 8ND
Tel: 020-8693 5070 **Fax:** 020-8693 8447
Revv John O'Connor, Roy Tablizo.
M: *Sat 1st M of Sun 6.30pm. Sun 9am, 10.30am, 12noon, 5.30pm. Hds (vigil 7pm). 8am, 10am, 8pm.*
• ***King's College Hospital.*** *Chaplain:* **Rev Luke Marrappillil MST.**
Tel: 020-7274 6179

■ **DULWICH WOOD PARK**
St Margaret Clitherow (1952; 1961; 1974; cons, 20th Oct 2000)
2 Kingswood Drive, Dulwich Wood Park, London SE19 **Tel:** 020-8670 1639
Rev John Hearty. 4 Kingswood Drive, Dulwich Wood Park, London SE19 1UR
M: *Sat 1st M of Sun 6.30pm. Sun 8am, 10.30am. Hds 9am, 7.30pm.*

■ **DYMCHURCH,** Kent
St Monica (1964)
Chapel Road. Served from Hythe.
M: *Sun 8.30am. Hds 8am.*

■ **EARLSFIELD**
† St Gregory
(1904; 1957; cons 23 June 1960)
306 Garratt Lane, Earlsfield SW18 4EH
Tel: 020-8874 5098
Rev John J. Henry. *Deacon:* **Rev Fintan Phelan.**
M: *Sat 1st M of Sun 6pm. Sun 10.30am. Hds 10am.*
• ***Tamil Chaplaincy:*** 304 Garratt Lane SW18 4EH **Tel:** 020-8870 6257
Rev Eugene Francis Saverian.

■ **EAST SHEEN,** Richmond, Surrey
† Our Lady Queen of Peace.
(1938; 1954; cons 15 June 1971)
222 Sheen Road, East Sheen, Richmond, Surrey TW10 5AN.
Tel: 020-8876 6467 **E-mail:** olqp@tesco.net
Rev Michael Boland.
M: *Sat 1st M of Sun 6pm. Sun 8.30am, 10.30am. Hds (vigil 8pm), 10am, 8pm.*
• ***Sisters of Charity of St Louis,***
220 Sheen Road, TW10 5AN
Tel: 020-8876 3300

■ **EDENBRIDGE,** Kent
† St Lawrence M (1931; 1952; cons 3 June 1981)
High Street, Edenbridge, Kent TN8 5AQ
Tel: 01732-862256 **Fax:** 01732-862837
E-mail: stlawrencechurch@btinternet.com
Rev Christopher Keen.
M: *Sat 1st M of Sun 6pm. Sun 9am, 10.30am. Hds 10am, 8pm.*

■ **ELTHAM**
1. † Christ Church
(1870; 1890; 1912; cons 9 Nov 1981)
High Street, Eltham, SE9
Tel: 020-8850 1666 **Fax:** 020-8294 2109
E-mail: office@christchurch.plus.com
Website: christchurcheltham.org.uk
• ***Canons Regular of the Lateran (CRL):*** **Rev John Fricker** (*Parish Priest*).
Community: **Revv Garry Murphy** (*Prior*), **Roy Dunstan, Anthony Maggs, Marcin Kordel**. Christ Church Priory, 229 High Street, Eltham, SE9 1TX
M: *Sat 1st M of Sun 6pm. Sun 9.30am, 11.30am, 6.30pm. Hds 9am, 12noon, 8pm.*
• ***Sisters of Mercy,*** Bethlehem House of Prayer, Convent of Mercy, Glenure Road, SE9 1UF **Tel:** 020-8850 1877

■ **ELTHAM WELL HALL**
† SS John Fisher and Thomas More
(1929; 1936; cons 22 June 1937)
Well Hall Road, Eltham Well Hall.
Tel: 020-8856 4993 **Fax:** 0208-856 5883
Email: richard.plunkett@btinternet.com
Rev Richard Plunkett, Presbytery, Arbroath Road, SE9 6RR
M: *Sun 8am, 10.30am, 6pm. Hds 9am, 8pm.*

■ **ERITH,** Kent
1. † Our Lady of the Angels
(1868, 1870, 1903; 1951; 1963; cons 2002)
Carlton Road, Erith, Kent DA8 1DN
• ***Franciscans (OFMCap):*** **Revv James Boner** (*Provincial Minister*), **John Kavanagh** (*Parish Priest*).
Tel: 01322-402060 **Fax:** 01322-402061
E-mail: ola@btinternet.com
Community: **Revv Michael Hargan** (*Guardian & Post-Novitiate Director*), **James Boner**. **Terence Moore** (*Provincial Secretary*), **Bruno Rowsell, Raymund Hewlett, Bernard Hart, Stephen Innes, Michael Pooley, Jarek Konopko**. **Tel:** 01322-433193 (*Friary*)
Provincial Curia: **Tel:** 01322-433193
Website: www.capuchin-franciscans-gb.org.uk

M: *Sat 1st M of Sun 5.30pm. Sun 8.30am, 10.30am, 6pm. Hds 7.30am, 9am, 8pm.*

■ **EYTHORNE,** Kent
Our Lady of Apostles
Church Hill. Served from Aylesham.
M: *Sat 1st M of Sun 5pm. Hds 11am.*

■ **FARNBOROUGH,** Kent, Orpington, Kent
† St Michael and All Angels
(1964, cons Oct. 2 1998)
Crofton Road, Farnborough, Orpington.
Tel: 01689-851776
Email: info@stmichaelsfarnborough.org.uk
Website: stmichaelsfarnborough.org.uk
Rev Paul Fennessy, 370 Crofton Road, Orpington, Kent BR6 8NN
M: *Sun 9am, 10.30am, 5.30pm. Hds 10am, 7.30pm.*

■ **FAVERSHAM,** Kent
† Our Lady of Mount Carmel
(1899; 1906; 1937)
Tanners Street, Faversham, Kent ME13 7JW
Tel: 01795-532449
E-mail: info@whitefriarsfaversham.org
- ***Carmelites (O Carm):*** **Revv Piet Wijngaard** (*Prior and Shrine Chaplain*), **James Sweeney** (*Parish Priest*) **Wilfrid McGreal** (*Provincial*),
  Whitefriars, Tanners Street ME13 7JW
  Tel: 01795-532449 **Fax:** 01795-539511
  Website: www.whitefriarsfaversham.org
  M: *Sat 1st M of Sun 6pm. Sun 8am, 10.30am, 6pm. Hds 9.30am, 8pm.*
- ***National Shrine of St Jude,*** Tanners Street, Faversham, Kent ME13 7JN
  Tel: 01795-539214
  E-mail: chaplain@stjudesshrine.org.uk
  Website: stjudeshrine.org.uk

■ **FOLKESTONE,** Kent
† Our Lady Help of Christians and St Aloysius
(1863; 1890; cons 21 June 1939)
41 Guildhall Street, Folkestone, CT20 1EF
Tel: 01303-252823
Email: roger.nesbitt@btinternet.com
Website: catholic-folkestone.org.uk
Revv Roger Nesbitt, Francis Capener.
M: *Sat 1st M of Sun 6.30pm. Sun 9.30am, 11am. Hds 10am, 7.30pm.*

■ **FOLKESTONE (WEST),** Kent
† St Joseph (1904; 1913; 1956)
2 Ashley Avenue, Folkestone, CT19 4PX
Tel: 01303-275402
Rev Edmund Hartley, *Deacons*: **Revv John Boughton, Gehad Homsey**.
M: *Sat 1st M of Sun 6pm. Sun 11am. Hds 10am, 7.30pm.*
- ***Society of Our Lady of Fidelity,*** St Mary's Convent, 15/17 Marten Road, CT20 2JR **Tel:** 01303-53713
  M: *Sun 9am. Hds 5pm.*

■ **FOREST HILL,** London
† St William of York
(1905; 1931; cons 5 May 1964)
4 Brockley Park, Forest Hill, SE23 1PS
Tel: 020-8690 4549 **Fax:** 020-8314 5567
E-mail: parish@swoy.org.uk
Website: swoy.org.uk
Rev Roman Kot.
M: *Sat 1st M of Sun 6pm. Sun 9.30am, 11.30am. Hds 10.30am, 8pm.*
- ***Missionary Sisters of the Sacred Heart,*** Honor Oak Park, SE23 3LE
  Tel: 020-8699 2735

■ **GILLINGHAM,** Kent
† Our Lady of Gillingham (1892; 1896)
Railway Street, Gillingham, Kent.
Tel: 01634-852979 **Fax:** 01634-580594
E-mail: gilcathchurch@btinternet.com
Rev Geoffrey Pointer.
Deacon: **Rev Michael Knight.**
Presbytery, 2a Ingram Road, ME7 1YL
M: *Sat 1st M of Sun 6.30pm. Sun 9am, 11am. Hds 11am, 7.30pm.*

■ **GOUDHURST,** Cranbrook, Kent
† Sacred Heart (1882)
Beresford Road, Goudhurst, TN17 1DN
Tel: 01580-211268
Email: vic.mclean@tiscali.co.uk
Rev Victor McLean.
M: *Sat 1st M of Sun 5.30pm. Sun 10.30am. Hds 9.30am, 8pm.*

■ **GRAIN, ISLE OF,** Kent
Holy Child Jesus (1955)
Served from Strood.
M: *Sat 1st M of Sun 5.30pm.*

■ **GRAVESEND,** Kent
1. † St John the Evangelist
(1840; 1851; cons 22 May 1894)
Milton Road, Gravesend, Kent.
Tel: 01474-352415 **Fax:** 01474-334228
E-mail: stjohnschurchgravesend@yahoo.co.uk
Website: www.StJohns.telinco.co.uk
Revv Joseph Smith, Andrew Fernandez.
192 Parrock Street, DA12 1EN
M: *Sat 1st M of Sun 6pm. Sun 8.30am, 10.30am, 6pm. Hds 7.30am, 9am, 12noon, 8pm.*

2. St Katherine's Chapel
Shorne.
M: *Sun 10.30am. Hds 10.30am*
- ***Sons of Divine Providence,*** Pipe's Place, DA12 3DP. St Joseph's Independent Flats for the Elderly. **Tel:** 01474-823930.
  Website: www.sonsofdivineprovidence.org

- *Sisters of Mercy,* St Joseph's Convent, Hillside Drive, DA12 1NZ **Tel:** 01474-569565.

■ **GREENWICH** A

† Our Lady & Star of the Sea
(1792; 1851; cons 16 Sept 1852)
68 Crooms Hill, Greenwich, SE10 8HG
Tel: 020-8858 0662
Rev John Lavery.
M: *Sat 1st M of Sun 6pm. Sun 9am, 11am. Hds 10am, 8pm.*

- *Ursulines,* 66 Croom's Hill, SE10 8HN **Tel:** 020-8858 0779
- *Dominican Missionary Sisters of Zimbabwe,* 38 Hyde Vale, SE10 8QH **Tel:** 020-8692 3382

■ **GREENWICH (EAST)** A

† St Joseph (1792; 1881)
Pelton Road, Greenwich SE10 9AN
Tel: 020-8858 1845 **Fax:** 020-8305 0569
Website: rc.net/southwark/greenwich-east
Rev James Teeling. Commerell Street, Greenwich SE10 0EA
M: *Sun 10am, 5.30pm. Hds 9.30am, 8pm.*

■ **HADLOW,** Kent

St Peter's Chapel
Maidstone Road. Served from Tonbridge.
M: *Sun 10.45am.*

■ **HAM,** Surrey

St Thomas Aquinas
(1953; 1968; 1985; cons 28 Jan 1987)
Ham Common, Ham, Surrey.
Rev Walter Walsh. *Permanent Deacon:* **Rev Peter Simpson**. St Thomas', Ham Street, Ham, TW10 7HT **Tel:** 020-8948 8292
M: *Sat 1st M of Sun 6.30pm. Sun 8.30am, 10am, (German Mass, Suns 11.30am), 6.30pm. Hds 10am, 8pm.*

■ **HARRIETSHAM,** Kent

See Bearsted.

■ **HARTLEY,** Dartford, Kent A

† Oratory of St Francis de Sales
(1913; 1938; cons 18 Oct 1985)
White Friars, Church Road, Hartley, Dartford DA3 8DW
Tel: 01474-705361 **Fax:** 01474-705761
Email: stfrancisdesales@hotmail.co.uk
Rev Alex Saba.
M: *Sat 1st M of Sun 5.30pm. Sun 8.30am, 11am, 5th Sun of the month Mass at New Ash Green Youth Centre at 10.45am. 6.30pm. Hds (vigil 6.30pm), 9.15am, 11am, 7.45pm.*

■ **HAWKHURST**

† St Barnabas (1964)
High Street. Served from Goudhurst.
M: *Sun 8.30am. Hds 11am.*

■ **HAYES,** Kent 

† Our Lady of the Rosary (1977)
Priest's House, West Common Road, Hayes, Bromley BR2 7BX **Tel:** 020-8462 6745
E-mail: rosarychurch@btinternet.com
Rev David Hutton. **Tel:** 020-8462 0192
M: *Sat 1st M of Sun 6pm. Sun 8am, 10am, 5.30pm. Hds 9.30am, 8pm.*

■ **HERNE BAY,** Kent

† Our Lady of the Sacred Heart
(1889; 1890; cons 10 Aug 1897)
Clarence Road, Herne Bay, Kent.
Tel: 01227-375095
Fax: 01227-360941

- *Passionists (CP):* **Revv Mark White** (*Parish Priest*), **Patrick McKeown, James Eamer, Br Francis Welsh**. *Deacons:* **Revv James Foley, Barry Walker**. The Retreat, Sea Street, Herne Bay CT6 8SP
  M: *Sat 1st M of Sun 6pm. Sun 9.30am, 11.30am, 6pm. Hds 9.15am, 11am, 8pm.*
- *Sisters of the Sacred Hearts of Jesus and Mary,* St Peter's Convent, 15 St George's Terrace, CT6 8RQ **Tel:** 01227-375097 (Convent) **Tel:** 01227-362298 (Guests)
- *Daughters of Mary and Joseph,* 90 Central Parade, Herne Bay, Kent CT6 5JJ **Tel:** 01227-373107

■ **HERNE HILL,** SE24

† SS Philip and James
(1906; cons 20 May 1981)
Poplar Walk, Herne Hill SE24 0BS
Tel: 020-7274 4853
Email: ssphilipandjames@yahoo.com
Website: www.ssphilipandjames.org.uk
Rev Casmir Dike MSP.
M: *Sat 1st M of Sun 6pm. Sun 9.30am, 11.30am. Hds 9.30am, 7.30pm.*

- *De La Salle Brothers*, (Postulancy) 26 Half Moon Lane, SE24 9HU **Tel:** 020-7733 2732
- *Chaplain to King's College Hospital:* **Rev Luke Marappillil MST**, 61 Lowden Road, Herne Hill SE24 0BT **Tel:** 020-7274 6179

■ **HERSDEN,** Canterbury, Kent

1. **† St Dunstan** (1935; 1955; 1977)
East View, Hersden, Canterbury
Tel: 01227-710236
Rev Wilfred D'Silva Presbytery, East View, Hersden, Canterbury CT3 4HH
M: *Sun 10am. Hds 7pm.*

Sisters of Our Lady of the Missions. Sturry, Convent of St Anne, Staines Hill, Westbere, Canterbury CT2 0EW **Tel:** 01227-710478

2. St Joseph's Hall, Sturry
River View.
M: *Sun 5.30pm.*

■ **HOO,** Kent
Holy Family (1957)
Served from Strood.
M: *Sun 11.15am.*

■ **HORSMONDEN,** Kent
† **All Saints** (Catholic use 1972)
Served from Goudhurst.
M: *Sun 5.30pm.*

■ **HYTHE,** Kent
† **The Virgin Mother of Good Counsel** (1860; 1891; 1894)
Mill Road, Hythe, Kent.
Tel: 01303-266430
- ***Society of Our Lady of the Most Holy Trinity (SOLT),*** **Revv Frederick Alexander** (*Parish Priest*), **Jon Thomas Kightliner**, Also resident: **Robert Copsey**, 2 Lower Blackhorse Hill, Hythe CT21 5LS **Tel:** 01303-266430. **Fax:** 01303-264773
E-mail: soltuk@hotmail.com

Deacon: **Rev Raymond Partridge**.
M: *Sat 1st M of Sun 6.30pm. Sun 8am, 9.30am, 11.15am, 7pm. Hds 7.30am, 10am, 7.30pm.*
- ***Marist Sisters,*** Villa Maria, 53 & 55 Seabrook Road, CT21 5QE **Tel:** 01303-267870

■ **ITALIAN MISSION**
† (1970; 1974)
20 Brixton Road, London SW9 6BU
Tel: 020-7735 8235 **Fax:** 020-7840 0236
- ***Scalabrini Fathers (CS),*** **Revv Pietro Celotto,** (*Parish Priest*), **Giandomenico Ziliotto, Lucio Bula, Elio Alberti, Jesus Dicto Sumaba.**
M: *Sat 1st M of Sun 7pm. Sun 10.30am, 12noon. Hds 7.30pm.*

■ **KENNINGTON PARK,** London A
† **St Wilfrid** (1904; 1915; cons 14 June 1960)
97 Lorrimore Road, Kennington Park, SE17 3LZ
Tel: 020-7703 4712 **Fax:** 020-7703 1002
Email: wjohngreenwood@aol.com
Rev Gregory Moore.
Deacon: **Rev John Greenwood.**
M: *Sat 1st M of Sun 7pm. Sun 10am, 12noon. Hds 10am, 7pm.*

■ **KEW,** Richmond, Surrey
† **Our Lady of Loreto and St Winefride** (1898; 1906; cons 1979)
1 Leyborne Park, Kew, Richmond TW9 3HB
Tel/Fax: 020-8940 3101
Rev Thomas Scannell.
Deacon: **Rev Patrick Scauflaire.**
M: *Sat 1st M of Sun 6pm. Sun 9.30am, 11am, 6pm. Hds 9am, 7.30pm.*

■ **KIDBROOKE,** London A
† **St John Fisher** (1961; 1964; cons 23 Jan 1987)
141 Kidbrooke Park Road, Kidbrooke SE3 0DZ **Tel:** 020-8856 4536
Rev Eric Nimmo.
M: *Sat 1st M of Sun 6pm. Sun 10am, 6pm. Hds 9.30am, 8pm.*
- ***Sisters of La Sainte Union,*** 43 Lebrun Square, SE3 9NT **Tel:** 020-8856 0274

■ **KINGSTON HILL,** Kingston upon Thames, Surrey
† **St Ann** (1958; 1960; cons 9 Dec 1985)
Kingston Hill, Kingston upon Thames, Surrey **Tel:** 020-8546 8732
Rev Michael Sileshi. St Ann's House, Kingston Hill, Kingston upon Thames, Surrey KT2 7LX
M: *Sun 8am, 10am (Korean Mass, 12noon), 5.30pm. Hds 7.30am, 9.30am, 8pm.*
- ***Religious of the Sacred Heart of Mary (US Province)***, Marymount, George Road, Kingston upon Thames, KT2 7PE **Tel:** 020-8949 0571

■ **KINGSTON UPON THAMES,** Surrey
† **St Agatha** (1894; 1899; cons 25 June 1914)
King's Road, Kingston upon Thames, Surrey **Tel:** 020-8546 4633
Rev Gerard O'Brien. *Deacon:* **Rev Robert Beresford**, 1 Wyndham Road, Kingston upon Thames, Surrey KT2 5JR
M: *Sat 1st M of Sun 6.30pm. Sun 9am, 10.30am, 6.30pm. Hds 7.30am, 9.30am, 7.30pm.*
- ***Kingston University.*** *Chaplain:* **Rev Vincent Flynn**, 4 Westfield Road, Surbiton KT6 4EL **Tel:** 020-8390 6131

■ **KNOCKHOLT,** Kent
St Katherine's (C of E Parish Church)
Served from Orpington.
M: *1st M of Sun 5pm (1st Sat of month).*

■ **LEE,** London
† **Our Lady of Lourdes** (1892, 1939; cons 3 May 1950)
45B Burnt Ash Hill, Lee SE12 0AE
Tel/Fax: 020-8857 5006
Rev Edward Perera.
Also resident: **Manoj Karukayil**
M: *Sat 1st M of Sun 6.30pm. Sun 9am, 11am. Hds (vigil 7.30pm). 9.30am, 11am.*

■ **LEWISHAM,** London A
† **St Saviour and SS John Baptist and Evangelist** (1894; 1909; cons 23 Oct 1917)
175 High Street, Lewisham SE13 6AA

Tel: 020-8852 2490 **Fax:** 020-8852 2262
Revv Christopher Connor, Sean O'Connor, Clive Ross, Hrudawa Raj.
Deacon: **James Friedenthal**
M: *Sat 1st M of Sun 6.30pm. Sun 8.30am, 10am, 11.30am, (for Tamils, 2nd Sun of Month, 4pm), 5.30pm. Hds (vigil 6.30pm). 8.30am, 10am, 1pm, 8pm.*

■ **LEYSDOWN,** Sheppey, Kent
Served from Sheerness.

■ **LITTLESTONE AND NEW ROMNEY,** Kent
St Augustine's Hall (1937)
Queen's Road. Served from Hythe.
M: *Sun 10am. Hds 7pm (Vigil).*

■ **LORDSWOOD**
See Walderslade.

■ **LUTON,** Kent
The Sacred Heart (1949)
Street End Road.
Served from Chatham (1).

■ **LYDD,** Kent
† St Martin of Tours (1892; 1932)
High Street. Served from Hythe.
M: *Sun 11am. Hds 6pm.*

■ **MAIDSTONE,** Kent
1. † St Francis
(1859; 1863; 1880; cons 26 Sept 1982)
126 Week Street, Maidstone, Kent.
Tel: 01622-756217 **Fax:** 01622-690549
Mbl: 07790-363582
E-mail: Johnclark7@hotmail.com
Website:
www.stfrancisparishmaidstone.fsnet.co.uk
Revv John Clark, Maria Alphonse, Anthony Christu. Grove House, 126 Week Street, ME14 1RH *Deacon:* **Rev Joseph Bennett.** *Parish Sister:* **Sr Eileen Keane.**
M: *Sat 1st M of Sun 6pm. Sun 9am, 10.30am, 6pm. Hds (vigil 6pm). 10am, 12.30pm, 8pm.*

2. Preston Hall (1925)
Aylesford, Maidstone, Kent.
British Legion Hospital and Village.
St Luke's Chapel open to public.
M: *Sun 8.30am, 11.30am.*

3. Nettlestead
Maidstone, Kent.
M: *10am (in C of E, St Mary the Virgin).*
- ***Sisters of Providence,*** Fintonagh House, 8 Fintonagh Drive, ME14 2AQ **Tel:** 01622-676033

■ **MAIDSTONE SOUTH,** Kent
1. Holy Family (1969; 1973)
Maidstone South, Maidstone, Kent
Tel: 01622-204563 **Fax:** 01622-662181
Website: maidstonesouthparish.co.uk
Rev Peter Growney (Parish Adminstrator). Presbytery, Bicknor Road, Park Wood, Maidstone ME15 9PS
Deacon: **Rev John Roberts KHS.**
M: *Sat 1st M of Sun 6pm. Sun 8.15am, 10am, 6pm. Hds 9.30am, 8pm.*
- ***Holy Trinity, Coxheath.***
M: *Sun 8.15am.*

2. St Thomas of Canterbury
(1971; cons 25 June 1990)
Station Road, Headcorn, Ashford.
Tel: 07989-457323
M: *Sun 9.45am. Hds 7.30pm.*

■ **MARGATE,** Kent
† SS Austin and Gregory
(1797; 1804, cons 4 Nov 2006)
Victoria Road, Margate, Kent.
Tel: 01843-220825 **Website:**
ssaustinandgregory-margate.org.uk
Rev Luke Smith. *Deacon:* **Rev Neville Gascoigne,** 38 Charlotte Place, Margate, CT9 1LP
M: *Sat 1st M of Sun 5pm. Sun 9.30am, 11.30am. Hds (vigil 8pm). 10am, 8pm.*

■ **MELIOR STREET,** London
See Bermondsey, Melior Street.

■ **MEOPHAM,** Kent
† St Paul (1965; 1987 con 6 May 1988)
Wrotham Road, Meopham, Kent
Tel: 01474-814627 **Fax:** 01474-813764
E-mail: plgilbert@tiscali.co.uk
Rev Philip Gilbert. Presbytery, 46 Hunting Field Road, DA13 0EZ
M: *Sat 1st M of Sun 5.45pm. Sun 10am, Hds 10am, 8pm.*

■ **MERTON,** Surrey
† St John Fisher (1938; 1948; 1962)
207 Cannon Hill Lane, Merton, Surrey SW20 9DB **Tel:** 020-8542 6355
E-mail: st.johnfisher@southwark2000.freeserve.co.uk
Canon Colm Acton, Rev Santiagu Michael. *Deacons:* **Revv Frederick Carter, Thomas Kavanagh.**
M: *Sat 1st M of Sun 6pm. Sun 8am, 9.30am, 11am (Sung), 6.30pm. Hds (vigil 6pm). 9am, 7.30pm.*
- ***Daughters of Our Lady of the Sacred Heart,*** 255 Cannon Hill Lane, SW20 9DB **Tel:** 020-8542 6484
- ***Residence of Auxiliary Bishop:*** **Rt Rev Howard Trapp,** Bishop of Newport, 67 Haynt Walk, London SW20 9NY

■ **MINSTER,** Isle of Sheppey, Kent
† Immaculate Heart of Mary (1958)
Harps Avenue.
Served from Sheerness.
M: *Sun 9am. Hds 12noon.*

■ **MINSTER (THANET),** Kent

† **St Mildred** (1878; cons 26 June 1901)
9 St Mildred's Road, Minster, Kent
CT12 4DE **Tel:** 01843-821340
M: *Sun 10.30am. Hds 7pm.*

- ***Benedictine Nuns,*** Minster Abbey, Church Street, CT12 4HF **Tel:** 01843-821254 Served from St Mildred's, Minster. **M:** *Sun 8.30pm. Hds 8.30am.*

■ **MITCHAM,** Surrey

† **SS Peter and Paul**
(1851; 1889; cons 12 June 1951)
Cranmer Road, Mitcham, Surrey CR4 4LD
Tel: 020-8648 3800

- ***Society of the Missionaries of St Francis Xavier (SFX):*** **Revv Lucas Rodrigues SFX, James Pereira SFX, Oliver Antao SFX.** **M:** *Sat 1st M of Sun 6.30pm. Sun 8am, 9.30am, 11.30am (Sung), 6pm. Hds 9am, 6pm, 8pm.*
- ***Servite Sisters:*** Preshaw Crescent, Lower Green West, CR4 3GA **Tel:** 020-8640 2493 See also Pollards Hill.

■ **MONGEHAM,** Deal, Kent

† **St John the Evangelist** (1933)
St Richard's Road, Mongeham, Deal
CT14 9LF **Tel:** 01304-374870
Parochial Administrator: **Rev Susaimarinatham Mari Anantharaj.**
Presbytery, 149 St Richard's Road, Mongeham, Deal. *Deacon:* **Rev Gerald Watkins.**
M: *Sat 1st M of Sun 6.30pm. Sun 10.30am. Hds 10am, 6.30pm.*

- ***Sisters of Our Lady of the Missions,*** Beech Court, Rectory Road, CT14 9NB **Tel:** 01304-374737

■ **MORDEN,** Surrey

† **St Teresa of the Child Jesus**
(1930; 1965; cons 5 May 1965)
250 Bishopsford Road, Morden, Surrey
SM4 6BZ **Tel:** 020-8648 4113
Revv Brian Coyle, Behruz Raf'at.
Deacon: **Rev John O'Donovan.**
M: *Sat 1st M of Sun 6.30pm. Sun 9am, 11am, 6.30pm. Hds (vigil 7.30pm). 9am, 11am.*

- ***Sisters of St Joseph,*** 15 Pollard Road, SM4 6EG **Tel:** 020-8648 3886
- ***Convent of Our Lady of the Sacred Heart,*** 48 Monkleigh Road, Morden, Surrey SM4 4EW **Tel:** 020 8542 5052

■ **MORTLAKE**

† **St Mary Magdalen**
(1849; 1852; cons 7 Sept 1867)
61 North Worple Way, Mortlake SW14 8PR
Tel: 020-8876 1326 **Fax:** 020-8876 9488
Email: info@stmarymags.org.uk
Website: stmarymags.org.uk

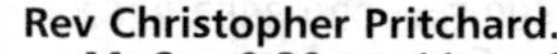

Rev Christopher Pritchard.
M: *Sun 9.30am, 11am, 6.30pm. Hds 9.30am, 8pm.*

■ **MOTTINGHAM**

† **Our Lady Help of Christians**
(1927; 1933; cons 9 May, 1952)
Mottingham Road, Mottingham SE9
Tel: 020-8857 4539
Rev John O'Callaghan, 127 Mottingham Road, Mottingham SE9 4ST
M: *Sat 1st M of Sun 6.30pm. Sun 9am, 11.15am. Hds (vigil 7pm) All Saints, New Eltham, 9.30am, 8pm.*

- ***Sisters of St Joseph,*** 12 Crossway, SE9 4JJ **Tel:** 020-8851 6540

■ **NETTLESTEAD**

See Maidstone (3).

■ **NEW ADDINGTON,** Surrey

† **The Good Shepherd**
(1957; 1962; cons 20 June 1986)
25 Dunley Drive, New Addington,
Surrey CR0 0RG **Tel:** 01689-842644
Rev Stephen Boyle.
M: *Sat 1st M of Sun 6.30pm. Sun 8am, 11am. Hds 9.15am (term time), 10am (outside term time), 8pm.*

- ***Daughters of Mary and Joseph:*** 23 Montacute Road, Croydon, CR0 0JF **Tel:** 01689-841833

■ **NEW CROSS**

South London Chaplaincy:
56 Amersham Road, New Cross, London
SE14 6QE **Tel:** 020-8692 6931
Rev George Webster.
Team members: Responsibility for GKT Medical & Dental School & St George's Medical School: **Miss Claire Connor.**
Responsibility for Greenwich University: **Ms Gabrielle Power.**

■ **NEW ELTHAM**

All Saints. (C of E Parish Church)
Bercta Road, New Eltham SE9.
Served from Mottingham.
M: *Sat 1st M of Sun 5pm. Hds 6.45pm.*

■ **NEW MALDEN,** Surrey

† **St Joseph** (1905; 1922; cons 13 Sept 1951)
1 Montem Road, New Malden, KT3 3QW
Tel: 020-8942 2602 **Fax:** 020-8949 2702
Email: stjoseph.newmalden@btinternet.com
Website: stjoseph-newmalden.org.uk
Revv Peter Edwards, Richard Whinder.
Deacon: **Rev John Sampson**
M: *Sat 1st M of Sun 6pm. Sun 9.30am, 11.30, 5.30pm. Hds 7am, 10am, 8pm.*

- ***Sisters of the Holy Cross,*** Holy Cross Convent, 41 Westbury Road KT3 5AX **Tel:** 020-8942 2703

- ***Marist Sisters (Provincial House)***, 55 Thetford Road, KT3 5DP **Tel:** 020-8949 1355 **Fax:** 020-8336 0193 **E-mail:** grosupsm@signet.co.uk
- ***Teresian Association***, 51 Chestnut Grove, KT3 3JJ **Tel:** 020-8942 6086 **Fax:** 020-8942 7226 **E-mail:** tassoc@supanet.com

■ NORBITON, Surrey

† St Pius X (1956; cons 12 July 1962)
The Triangle, Norbiton, Surrey KT1 3SB
Tel: 020-8942 2178 **Fax:** 020-8287 4626
Rev Geoffrey Munnery, 108 Orme Road, Kingston upon Thames, Surrey KT2 3SB
E-mail: mail@stpiusxchurch.org.uk

M: *Sat 1st M of Sun 6pm. Sun 10am, 5pm. Hds 9.15am, 8pm.*

■ NORBURY

† St Bartholomew
(1908; 1975; cons 6 May 1975)
Hepworth Road, Norbury, SW16
Tel: 020-8679 3545 **Fax:** 020-8679 2151
E-mail:parish&office@rcnorbury.plus.com
Revv Thomas Cooper, Philip Glandfield. *Deacon:* **Rev Paul Milligan**. 159 Ellison Road, SW16 5DE

M: *Sat 1st M of Sun 6.15pm. Sun 8.30am, 10am, 11.30am (Sung), 5pm. Hds 7.30am, 10am, 8pm.*

- ***Daughters of Divine Lore***, 70 Kempshott Road, Streatham Common, London SW16 3LH **Tel:** 0208 264 3632

■ NORTH CHEAM, Surrey

† St Cecilia (1938; 1957)
St Cecilia's Presbytery, 101 Stonecot Road, North Cheam, Sutton, Surrey SM3 9HP
Tel: 020-8641 3141
Rev Robert Sugg.

M: *Sat 1st M of Sun 6.30pm. Sun 8am, 9.30am, 11am, 6.30pm. Hds 10am, 7.30pm.*

- ***Daughters of the Cross***, St Anthony's Hospital, London Road, Sutton SM3 9DW **Tel:** 020-8337 6691

■ NORTHFLEET, Kent

1. † Our Lady of the Assumption
(1865; 1914; cons 5 Dec 1929)
"Stella Maris", 3 The Hill, Northfleet, Kent DA11 9ES **Tel:** 01474-533689
Fax: 01474-532422 **E-mail:** parishpriest@ourladyoftheassumption.eclipse.co.uk
Rev Matthew Dickens.
Deacon: **Rev Thomas Berrie**.

M: *Sat 1st M of Sun 5.30pm. Sun 9am, 10.30am. Hds 9.30am (St Joseph's Catholic School Hall), 8pm.*

■ NORWOOD (SOUTH)

1. † St Chad
(1907; 1932; cons 16 Sept 1950)
5 Whitworth Road, Norwood, SE25 6XN
Tel: 020-8653 2806 **Fax:** 020-8653 4188
Revv William Damah (*Parish Priest*), **Protus Nyatorley, Joseph Akono**.

M: *Sat 1st M of Sun 6.30pm. Sun 8.30am, 10.30am, 6pm. Hds 10am, 7.30pm.*

2. Polish Church of the Merciful Jesus
8 Oliver Grove, Norwood SE25 6EG
Canon Aleksander Ozog. 8 Oliver Grove, Norwood, SE25 6EJ **Tel:** 020-8653 8701

■ NORWOOD (Upper)

† The Faithful Virgin
(1848; 1871; cons 17 June 1931)
Central Hill, Norwood, SE19
Tel: 020-8670 2777
E-mail: virgofidelischurch@hotmail.com
Rev Michael O'Dea. 143 Central Hill, Norwood, SE19 1RT

M: *Sat 1st M of Sun 6pm. Sun 9.30am, 11am, 6pm. Hds 9.30, 7.30pm.*

- ***Society of Our Lady of Fidelity,*** Fidelis Convent, Central Hill, SE19 1RS **Tel:** 020-8670 2506 *Chaplain:* **Rev Joy Alappat**. CMI **Tel:** 0208 670 7827
- ***Society of Christian Doctorine,*** 38 Ryefield Road, Upper Norwood, SE19 3QU **Tel:** 020-8786 5159

■ NORWOOD (West)

† St Matthew (1905; cons 22 Sept 1955)
37 Norwood High Street, Norwood, SE27 9JU **Tel:** 020-8670 1765
Fax: 020-8670 6230 **E-mail:** parish@stmatthews-westnorwood.org.uk
Rev David O'Connell.

M: *Sat 1st M of Sun 6.30pm. Sun 9am, 11am, 6.30pm. Hds 9.30am, 7.30pm.*

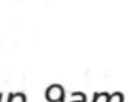

- ***L'Arche, Lambeth***, 15 Norwood High Street, SE27 9JU **Tel:** 020-8670 6714 **Fax:** 020-8670 0818 **E-mail:** lambeth@larche.org.uk

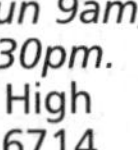

■ NUNHEAD, Peckham

† St Thomas the Apostle
(1905; cons 26 Nov 1989)
Nunhead, Peckham SE15.
Tel: 020-7639 3724
Fax: 020-7635 8215
Website: stthomasnunhead.org.uk
Revv Fergal Maguire (*Parochial Administrator*) **Eddie Higgins, Andrzej Smolka SSCC**. 81 Evelina Road, Nunhead, Peckham SE15 3HL

M: *Sat 1st M of Sun 6.30pm. Sun 9am, 10.30am, 6.30pm. Hds 9.30am, 7.30pm.*

- ***Sisters of Christian Instruction,*** St Gildas, 49 Pepys Road, SE14 5SA **Tel:** 020-7639 8190
- ***Kairos Community Trust:*** 22 Linden Grove, Peckham, SE15 3LF **Tel/Fax:** 020-7277 6264

■ **OLD BROMPTON,** Kent
See Chatham (2).

■ **OLD COULSDON,** Surrey
† **St Mary, Help of Christians**
(1956; 1966; cons 9 May 1979)
Coulsdon Road, Old Coulsdon, Surrey.
Tel: 01737-552420
Rev John Bliss. 372 Coulsdon Road, Old Coulsdon, Surrey CR5 1EF
M: *Sat 1st M of Sun 6.30pm. Sun 8am, 10.45am. Hds 10am, 8pm.*

■ **ORPINGTON,** Kent
† **Holy Innocents**
(1909; 1928, new church cons 1981)
Strickland Way, Orpington, Kent BR6 9UE
Tel: 01689-817537 **Fax:** 01689-817539
E-mail: jwatts@holyinnocents.org.uk
Website: holyinnocents.org.uk
Revv Victor Vella, John Biju.
Deacons: **Revv Austin Martin, Barry Chalkley.**
M: *Sat 1st M of Sun 6pm. Sun 8am, 10am, 6pm. Hds 7am, 10am, 8pm.*
• ***Sisters of Mercy:*** St Anne's Convent, Bishop Butt Close, BR6 9UF
Tel: 01689-832999

■ **OTFORD,** Kent
Holy Trinity (1944; cons 1981)
Pilgrims Way West.
Served from Sevenoaks.
M: *Sun 9.30am. Hds 8pm.*

■ **PADDOCK WOOD,** Kent
† **St Justus**
(1949; 1950; new church 1981, cons 1981)
Mount Pleasant.
Tel: 01892-833699 **Fax:** 01892-838219
Website: stjustusandanselm.org.uk
Rev Liam Gallagher. 11 Alliance Way, TN12 6TY
Email: lgallagher121@btinternet.com
M: *Sat 1st M of Sun 6pm. Sun 9am. Hds 10am, 7.30pm.*

■ **PARKWOOD & WIGMORE,** Kent
† **St Augustine Of Canterbury**
(1973; 1978; 1983; cons 29th May, 1992)
Deanwood Drive, Rainham, Kent, ME8 9PG **Tel:** 01634-377396
Email: st.aug.church@lycos.co.uk
Rev Michael Adams. *Deacon:* **Rev Charles Bianco**
M: *Sat 1st M of Sun 6pm. Sun 9.30am, 11am. Hds 9.30am (9.15am during school term), 8pm.*

■ **PECKHAM**
† **Our Lady of Sorrows**
(1855; 1866; cons July 1966)
Friary Road, Peckham, SE15 1RH
Tel: 020-7639 0947
Website: www.rc.net/southwark/peckham
Rev Anthony Plummer.
M: *Sat 1st M of Sun 6.30pm. Sun 8.30am, 10.30am, 12noon. Hds 7am, 10am, 7.30pm.*

■ **PECKHAM RYE**
† **St James** (1904)
45 Elm Grove, Peckham Rye, SE15 5DD
Tel: 020-7639 1947
Rev Thomas McElhone.
M: *Sat 1st M of Sun 6pm. Sun 8.30am, 10am, 12noon. Hds (vigil 7pm). 10am, 12.30pm, 7pm.*
• ***Canonesses of St Augustine,*** 73 Bellenden Road, SE15 7BH
Tel: 020-7703 8461

■ **PEMBURY,** Paddock Wood, Kent
St Anselm's Chapel and Hall
Served from Paddock Wood.
M: *Sun 10.30am. Hds (vigil 7.30pm)*

■ **PETTS WOOD**, Kent
† **St James the Apostle**
(1937; 1939; 1963; cons 17 July 1988)
Lakeswood Road, Petts Wood, Kent.
Tel: 01689-827100
Website: stjamespettswood.org
Rev Bryan Wells *(Priest-in-Charge)*. 283 Crescent Drive, Petts Wood, BR5 1AY
M: *Sat 1st M of Sun 6pm. Sun 10am, 11.30am. Hds (vigil 8pm). 9.30am.*

■ **PLUMSTEAD**
† **St Patrick**
(1890; 1893; cons 11 Aug 1941; 1969)
Hector Street, Plumstead, SE18
Tel: 020-8854 0960
Rev Michael Branch, 1a Conway Road, SE18 1AQ
Deacon: **Rev David Pease**
M: *Sat 1st M of Sun 6.30pm. Sun 10am, 6pm. Hds 9am, 8pm.*

■ **PLUMSTEAD COMMON**
Holy Cross (1950)
The Slade, Plumstead Common SE18
Tel: 020-8854 7154
Rev Paul Connelly, 27 The Slade, Plumstead Common, London SE18 2NB
M: *Sat 1st M of Sun 6.30pm. Sun 8.30am, 10am, 5.30pm. Hds (vigil 7pm). 9am,7pm, 8pm.*

■ **POLLARDS HILL,** Surrey
† **St Michael** (1964)
Fern Avenue, Pollards Hill, Mitcham, Surrey.
Tel/Fax: 020-8764 1791
Rev John Vallomprayil SDS. 9 Fern Avenue, Pollards Hill, Mitcham, CR4 1LS
M: *Sat 1st M of Sun 6pm. Sun 8.30am, 10.30am, 6pm. Hds 9.30am, 7.30pm.*

■ **PURLEY,** Surrey
† St John the Baptist
(1931; 1939; cons 10 June 1964)
48 Dale Road, Purley, Surrey CR8 2EF
Tel/Fax: 020-8660 3815
Canon James Pannett, Also in residence: **Rev Gregory Verissimo** (*Ljebi-Ode*), 48 Dale Road CR8 2EF **Tel:** 0208-668 1323
Deacon: **Rev Joseph Parsons**.
M: *Sat 1st M of Sun 6.30pm. Sun 8.30am, 10am, 12noon, 6.30pm. Hds (vigil 7.30pm), 7.30am, 10am, 7.30pm.*
- ***The John Fisher School*** (1929; 1931), Peaks Hill, CR2 3YP **Tel:** 020-8660 4555
- ***Hillcrest***, (Pastoral care entrusted to the Prelature of Opus Dei), 33 Plough Lane, Purley, CR8 3QJ **Tel:** 020-8645 2505

■ **PUTNEY**
1. † Our Lady of Pity and St Simon Stock
(1902; 1906; cons 12 Nov 1942)
Hazlewell Road, Putney SW15 6LU
Tel: 020-8788 1131
E-mail: stsimonputney@aol.com
Canon Richard Quinlan. Rev Derek Vidler (also resident). **Tel:** 020-8789 1016
M: *Sun 9.30am (Sung), 11.15am (Sung), 6pm. Hds 10am, 7.30pm.*
- ***Franciscan Missionaries of Mary,*** 36-38 Gwendoline Avenue, Putney SW15 6EJ **Tel:** 020-8780 1828

2. St John the Evangelist
Polish Church. St John's Road, Putney SW15
Revv Roman Werner (SChr), Wojcieh Stachyra, Polish Centre, Ravenna Rd, Putney SW15 6AW
Tel: 020-8788 3933
M: *Sun 9am, 10am, 11.15am, 6pm. Hds 10.30am, 7pm.*

■ **RAINHAM,** Kent
1. † St Thomas of Canterbury
(1934; 1958; cons 11 June 1970)
63 London Road, Rainham, Kent ME8 7RH
Tel: 01634-232972
Rev Douglas Bull. *Deacon:* **Rev Alan Boxall**. The Presbytery, 63 London Road, ME8 7RH
M: *Sat 1st M of Sun 6pm. Sun 9.30am, 6pm. Hds (vigil 8pm). 10am.*

2. St Peter, Prince of Apostles
(1961; 1970; cons 29 June 1990)
110 Beeching Way, Twydall, Rainham.
Served from Rainham, No 1.
M: *Sun 11am. Hds 7pm.*

■ **RAMSGATE,** Kent
1. † St Augustine's Abbey
(1841; 1851; cons 16 July 1884)
St Augustine's Road, Ramsgate, CT11 9PA
Tel: 01843-593045 /850056 *(Parish Office.* **Fax:** 01843-582732.
E-mail: staugabbey@aol.com
- ***Benedictines (OSB):*** **Rt Rev Paulinus Greenwood** (*Abbot*), **Rt Rev Bernard Waldron** (*Abbot-Emeritus*), **Rev Dunstan Keauffling** *(Sub Prior)*, **Rev Benedict Austen** (*Parish Priest*), **Revv Derek Summers, John Seddon, John Bennett, Doms Francis Byrne, Basil Watkins**. *Deacon*: **Rev Peter Brown**.
M: *Sun 9.15am, 10.30am, 6.30pm. Hds 9am, 6.30pm.*

2. † St Benedict (1966)
Whitehall Road, Newington, Ramsgate.
Tel: 01843-593045/850056
- ***Benedictines (OSB):***
Served from Ramsgate (1).
M: *Sat 1st M of Sun 5pm. Sun 8.30am, 10.15am. Hds 7.30pm. Confessions at call.*

3. † SS Ethelbert's and Gertrude (1902)
72 Hereson Road, Ramsgate CT11 7DS
Tel: 01843-592071
E-mail: ethelbert@fastmail.fm
Website: www.rc.net/southwark/ramsgate
Rev Steven Fisher.
Deacon: **Rev Robin Carter**.
M: *Sat 1st M of Sun 6pm. Sun 10.15am. Hds 10.15am, 7.30pm.*

■ **RICHMOND,** Surrey
† St Elizabeth
(1793; 1824; 1902; cons 20 June 1950)
The Vineyard, Richmond, Surrey
TW10 6AQ **Tel:** 020-8940 2439
Rev Philip Mathias.
M: *Sat 1st M of Sun 5.30pm. Sun 9.30am, 11am (Sung), 5.30pm. Hds 7am, 12.30pm, 8pm.*

■ **ROCHESTER,** Kent
† St John Fisher (1953; cons 30 Nov 1979)
Maidstone Road, Rochester, Kent.
Tel: 01634-845430
E-mail: stjohnfisherchurch@btinternet.com
Rev Gary Dyer.
Deacon: **Rev Malcolm Turner**.
M: *Sun 9am, 11am, 6pm. Hds 7.30am, 10am, 8pm.*

■ **ROEHAMPTON**
† St Joseph (1869; 1881; cons 24 July 1883)
218 Roehampton Lane, Roehampton SW15 4LE
Tel: 020-8788 5012 **Fax:** 020-8785 7393
Rev David Gummett.
Also resident: **Rev Paul Naikisi**
M: *Sat 1st M of Sun 6pm. Sun 9am, 11am, 6pm. Hds 6.30pm Vigil, 10am, 6.30pm.*
- ***Society of the Sacred Heart,*** Roehampton Lane, SW15 5PH **Tel:** 020-8876 0380

- ***Society of the Sacred Heart,*** Duchesne House, Aubyn Square, London SW15 5ND **Tel:** 020-8878 8282 **Fax:** 020-8392 3231 *Chaplain:* **Rev Francis Moriasi**
- ***Society of the Sacred Heart,*** New House, Aubyn Square, Roehampton Lane, SW15 5NU **Tel:** 020-8876 0836 Also 10 Rodway Road, SW15 5SD **Tel:** 020-8785 4718
- ***Poor Servants of the Mother of God,*** Maryfield Convent, Mount Angelus Road, Danebury Avenue SW15 4JA **Tel:** 020-8788 4351 (Generalate and Community) **Tel:** 020-8788 4188 (Kairos Centre)
- ***St Mary's Convent,*** High Street, Roehampton SW15 4HJ **Tel:** 020-8788 4188
- ***Digby Stuart College,*** Constituent College of Roehampton University, Roehampton Lane, London SW15 5PH *Chaplain:* **Fr Robert Kaggwa.** **Tel:** 020-8392 3216 **Fax:** 020-8392 3231

■ ROTHERHITHE A

† St Peter and the Guardian Angels (1892; 1902; cons 16th July 2002)
72 Paradise Street, Rotherhithe SE16 4QD
Tel: 020-7237 2969
Email: glpreston@googlemail.com
Rev Graham Preston (*Priest-in-Charge*).
M: *Sat 1st M of Sun 6pm. Sun 9am, 11.30am, 6.30pm. Hds 9am, 7.30pm.*

- ***Salesian Sisters of St John Bosco (FMA),*** 281 Jamaica Road, SE16 4RS **Tel:** 020-7231 2931

■ ST MARGARET'S-AT-CLIFFE, Nr Dover
See under Buckland and St Margaret's Bay.

■ ST MARY AND ST PAUL'S CRAY, Orpington, Kent
† St Joseph
(1873; 1895; 1959; cons 12 July 1985)
High Street, St Mary Cray, Orpington, BR5 4AR **Tel:** 01689-821749
E-mail: stjosephsmc@fastmail.fm
Rev William Agley.
M: *Sat 1st M of Sun 6pm. Sun 9am, 11am. Hds 9.30am, 8pm.*

■ SANDERSTEAD, Surrey A

The Holy Family (1955; 1959)
115 Limpsfield Road, Sanderstead, CR2 9LF
Tel: 020-8657 1728
Rev John Hartley.
M: *Sat 1st M of Sun 6pm. Sun 8am, 10.30am, 7pm. Hds (vigil 7.30pm). 10am, 7.30pm.*

- ***Suore Francescane dell' Immacolata:*** 117 Limesfield Road, Surrey CR2 9LF **Tel/Fax:** 020-8657 8225

■ SANDWICH, Kent
† St Andrew (1929)
St George's Road. *Served from Mongeham.*
M: *Sun 9am. Hds (vigil 7pm).*

■ SELSDON, Surrey
† St Columba
(1927; 1962; cons 14 Sept 1984)
37 Queenhill Road, Selsdon CR2 8DW
Tel: 020-8657 3747
E-mail: mail@st-columba.info
Rev Barry Hughes.
Deacon: **Rev Philip Pond.**
M: *Sat 1st M of Sun 6.30pm. Sun 8am, 10am, 6.30pm. Hds 9.30am, 8pm.*

■ SEVENOAKS, Kent A

† St Thomas of Canterbury
(1880; 1896; cons 16 Sept 1935)
12 Granville Road, Sevenoaks TN13 1ER
Tel: 01732-454177 **Fax:** 01732-458103
Rev Richard Harvey.
M: *Sat 1st M of Sun 6pm. Sun 8am, 9.30am, 11.15am (Sung), 6pm. Hds 7am, 9.30am, 12noon, 8pm.*

- **Franciscan Missionary Sisters for Africa,** Brackley House, 13 South Park, TN13 1EW **Tel:** 01732-451475

■ SHEPPEY, Kent
† SS Henry and Elizabeth (1813; 1864)
Broadway, Sheerness, Kent ME12 1TS
Tel/Fax: 01795-662142
E-mail: frank.moran@tiscali.co.uk
Canon Francis Moran. *Deacon:* **Rev Paul Glock**. The Presbytery, 53 Broadway, Sheerness ME12 1TS
M: *Sat 1st M of Sun 6.30pm. Sun 11.15am. Hds 9.15am (at St Edward's School during term time), 8pm.*

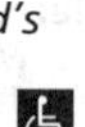

■ SHOOTERS HILL
† St Joseph (1970)
Herbert Road, Shooters Hill SE18 3QE
Tel: 020-8855 7657
E-mail: st_joseph_se18@tiscali.co.uk
Website: stjosephs-rc-shootershill.org
Rev James Kirby. 135 Herbert Road, Shooters Hill SE18 3QE
M: *Sat 1st M of Sun 6.30pm. Sun 10.15am, 12noon. Hds 10am, 7.30pm.*

■ SHORNCLIFFE, Kent
Most Holy Name (1894; 1968)
Military Road.
Served from Folkestone (West).

■ SHORNE
See Gravesend.

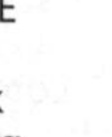

■ SIDCUP, Kent
† St Lawrence of Canterbury
(1902; 1906; cons 6 June 1956)
St Lawrence's Presbytery, 1 Hamilton Road,

Sidcup DA15 7HB
Tel: 020-8300 2480 **Fax:** 020-8308 9880
E-mail: stlawrence@hotmail.co.uk
Website: www.rc.net/uk/southwark/stlawrence

- ***Marist Fathers (SM),*** **Revv Allan Williams** (*Parish Priest*); *Deacon:* **Rev Peter Varnes**. Community: **Ivan Vodopevec** *(Superior)*; **Henry Graystone, Geoffrey Graystone**. 109 Main Road, Sidcup, Kent DA14 6ND **Tel:** 020-8302 6463 **Fax:** 020-8309 7656 **M:** *Sat 1st M of Sun 6.30pm. Sun 8.30am, 10am, 11.30am. Hds (vigil 8pm), 9.30am.*
- ***Marist Fathers Delegation House,*** 3 Hamilton Road, Sidcup DA15 7HB **Tel:** 020-8300 5399 **Fax:** 020-8300 9733 **Rev Alan Williams** (*Delegation Superior*).
- ***Daughters of Jesus,*** 11 Victoria Road. **Tel:** 020-8309 7905 See also Blackfen.

■ **SITTINGBOURNE,** Kent

† **The Sacred Heart** (1892; cons 27 Aug 1902)
63 West Street, Sittingbourne, ME10 1AN
Tel: 01795-472619 **Fax:** 01795-430309
E-mail: frmichael.ryan@gmail.com
Website: www.sacredheartchurch.org.uk
Rev Michael Ryan. Also resident: **Rev Kevin Fitzgerald.** *Deacon:* **Rev Stephen Newman**.
M: *Sat 1st M of Sun 6pm. Sun 9.30am, 11am. Hds 10am, 7.30pm*

- ***Sisters of Christ,*** 11 London Road ME10 1NQ **Tel:** 01795-428744

■ **SLADE GREEN,** Kent

St Joseph (1948)
Bridge Street (Chapel-of-Ease).
Served from Erith (1).
M: *Sun 9.30am. Hds 8pm.*

■ **SNODLAND,** Kent

See West Malling.

■ **SOUTH DARENTH,** Dartford, Kent

St George (1927; 1932)
Served from Dartford.
M: *Sun 9.30am. Hds 6.30pm.*

■ **SOUTHBOROUGH,** Kent

† **St Dunstan**
(1951; 1969; cons 30 Sept 1984)
34a London Road, Southborough TN4 0QA
Tel: 01892-529158 **Rev Francis L Mooney.**
M: *Sun 8am, 10.15am, 5.30pm. Hds 10am, 7.30pm.*

■ **STAPLEHURST,** Kent

See Cranbrook.

■ **STOCKWELL,** Clapham

† **St Francis of Sales and St Gertrude** (1903)
Stockwell, Clapham SW4 6SP
Tel: 020-7622 1621 **Fax:** 020-7720 8084
E-mail: san.fran@btinternet.com
Rev Peter Gee.
M: *Sat 1st M of Sun 6.30pm. Sun 8.30am, 10am, 11.30am, 12.30pm (Spanish), 5 (Portugese at Christ Church, Union Grove), 6.30pm. Hds 10am, 7pm.*

- ***Sisters of St Dorothy,*** 176 Clapham Road, SW9 0LA **Tel:** 020-7735 3058
- ***Sisters of the Holy Family,*** 35/36 Albert Square SW8 1BZ. **Tel:** 020-7735 4751 (Community) **Tel:** 020-7582 2016 (Provincial)
- ***Formation House:*** Albion Villa, Aldebert Terrace, Stockwell SW8 1BJ

■ **STREATHAM**

† **The English Martyrs**
(1888; 1893; cons 16 June 1921)
2 Mitcham Lane, Streatham SW16 6NN
Tel: 020-8769 6268 **Fax:** 020-8769 6714
E-mail: em@emchurch.org.uk
Website: emchurch.org.uk
Rev Gerard Mulvihill. **Tel:** 020-8677 3822
M: *Sat 1st M of Sun 6.30pm. Sun 9.30am (Sung), 11.30am, 5.30pm. Hds 7.30am, 9.30am, 8pm.*

- ***Poor Servants of the Mother of God,*** 29 Fernwood Avenue, Streatham SW16 1RD **Tel:** 0208 769 3348
- ***Salesian Sisters of St John Bosco (FMA),*** Provincialate: 13 Streatham Common North, SW16 3HG **Tel:** 020-8677 9569.

■ **STREATHAM HILL**

† **SS Simon and Jude** (1906; cons 20 July 1990)
5 Hillside Road, Streatham Hill SW2 3HL
Tel: 020-8678 9051 **Fax:** 020-8671 6157
Mbl: 07730-567138
E-mail: info@streathamhillcatholic.co.uk
Website: www.streathamhillcatholic.co.uk
Rev Adrian McKenna-Whyte
M: *Sat 1st M of Sun 6pm. Sun 8.30am, 10.30am, 12.15pm. Hds 9.15am, 7.30pm.*

■ **STROOD,** Kent

† **English Martyrs**
(1904; 1922; cons 19 July 1950)
37 Frindsbury Road, Strood, Kent ME2 4JA
Tel: 01634-717582
E-mail: eng_martyrs_church@totalise.co.uk
Revv William Keogh, Victor Darlington, *Permanent Deacons:* **Revv Antonio Cannavina, John Lettley, Malcolm Turner**. *Parish Sister:* **Sr Augustine Day RSM**.
M: *Sat 1st M of Sun 6pm. Sun 8.30am, 10.30am, 6pm. Hds 10am, 8pm.*

- ***Sisters of Mercy,*** Hillside Avenue, Frindsbury, Strood, ME2 3DB **Tel:** 01634-718386

■ **STURRY**
See Hersden.

■ **SURBITON,** Surrey
† **St Raphael** (1850)
Portsmouth Road, Surbiton, Surrey.
E-mail: straphaelparishoffice@googlemail.com
Website: www.straphael.org.uk
Rev Vincent Flynn, 4 Westfield Road, Surbiton KT6 4EL **Tel:** 020-8390 6131
M: *Sun 9am, 11.30am, 5pm. Hds 10am, 7pm.*

■ **SURREY DOCKS**
1. Our Lady of the Immaculate Conception
(1858; 1987; cons 8 December 1988)
St Elmos Road, Surrey Docks, Surrey.
Tel: 020-7231 9297 **Fax:** 020-7231 9002
Rev Thomas Udie *(Parochial Administrator)*. The Presbytery, 2 St Elmo's Road, Surrey Docks, Surrey SE16 6SJ
M: *Sat 1st M of Sun 5pm. Sun 10.30am, 6pm. Hds 9.15am, 7pm.*

2. Our Lady of the Cenacle
25 Wolfe Crescent, Surrey Quays, London SE16 6SF **Tel:** 0207 252 0892
Email: cenacle.london@btinternet.com

■ **SUTTON,** Surrey
† **Our Lady of the Rosary**
(1881; 1892; cons 5 Oct 1932)
2 St Barnabas Road, Sutton, SM1 4NL
Tel: 020-8642 0275
Website: suttonsurreyrcparish.org.uk
Rev James McGillicuddy.
M: *Sun 8.30am, 10.30am, 5.30pm. Hds 10am, 8pm.*
• ***Residence of Auxiliary Bishop,*** 95 Carshalton Road, Sutton, SM1 4LL
Rt Rev Paul Hendricks MA, PhL, VG
Tel: 0208 643 8007

■ **SUTTON GREEN,** Surrey
† **Holy Family** (1986; cons 5 Mar 1989)
Sorrento Road, Sutton Green, Sutton, Surrey SM1 1QU **Tel:** 020-8641 7458
Rev Julian Shurgold. 9 The Green, Sutton, Surrey, SM1 1QT
M: *Sat 1st M of Sun 6pm. Sun 9am, 11am. Hds 10am, 7.30pm.*

■ **SWANLEY,** Kent
† **The Twelve Apostles** (1930)
Sycamore Drive, Swanley, Kent BR8 7AY
Tel: 01322-662698 **Fax:** 01322-662698
E-mail: twelveapostles@btinternet.com
Rev Michael Doyle.
Deacon: **Rev Michael Gould**.
M: *Sat 1st M of Sun 6pm. Sun 10am, 5.30pm. Hds, 9am, 8pm.*
• ***Good Shepherd Sisters,*** Sycamore Drive, BR8 7AY **Tel:** 01322-664998

■ **SYDENHAM,** London
† **Our Lady and St Philip Neri**
(1870; 1872; 1882; cons 6 July 1964)
208 Sydenham Road, Sydenham, London SE26 5SE **Tel:** 0208-778 9460
E-mail: stphilipneri@btinternet.com
Rev Peter Mansfield.
Parish Sister: **Sr Bridie Clifford DMJ, Sr Deidre Slade DMJ.**
M: *Sat 1st M of Sun 6.30pm. Sun 9.30am, 11am, 5.30pm. Hds 9.30am, 8pm.*
• ***Daughters of Mary and Joseph,*** St Helen's, 37 Addington Gr, SE26 4JX
Tel: 020-8778 6793

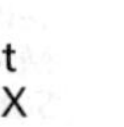

■ **SYDENHAM KIRKDALE,** London
† **Church of the Resurrection of Our Lord**
(1974; cons 24 Sept 1982; 1987)
165-169 Kirkdale, Sydenham Kirkdale SE26 4QL **Tel:** 020-8291 5766
Rev Philip Seed. The Priest's House, Church of the Resurrection, Kirkdale, SE26 4QL
M: *Sat 1st M of Sun 6pm. Sun 9.30am, 11am. Hds 9.30am, 7.30pm.*

■ **TEMPLE FARM,** Rochester, Kent
St Justus (1951)
Clifton Close, Darnley Road.
Served from Strood.
M: *Sun 9.15am. Hds 7pm.*

■ **TENTERDEN,** Kent
1. † St Andrew
(1868; 1934; 1935; cons 18 July 1951)
The Presbytery, 47 Ashford Road, Tenterden, Kent TN30 6LL
Tel: 01580-762785 **Fax:** 01580-764153
E-mail: edward.p.hill@btinternet.com
Rev Mgr Edward Hill.
M: *1st Mass of Sun 6pm (vigil). Sun 8.30am, 10.30am, Hds (vigil 7.30pm). 10am, 7.30pm.*

■ **TEYNHAM,** Kent
Served from Faversham.
M: *Sun in Methodist Church, Lynsted Lane 9am.*

■ **THAMESMEAD CENTRAL**
† **St Paul** (1978)
Bentham Road, London SE28
Tel: 020-8311 4656
Rev Patrick Ryan. 52 Bertrand Way, London SE28 8LN
M: *Sat 1st M of Sun 6pm. Sun 11.15am. Hds 10am, 8pm.*
• ***Sisters of La Sainte Union,*** 19 Titmuss Avenue, SE28 8DH **Tel:** 020-8310 0345
• ***HM Prison Belmarsh***, Western Way SE28 0EB
Chaplain: **Rev Kevin Robinson**.
Tel: 020-8331 4400 Ext 4525

■ **THAMESMEAD SOUTH**

† **St John Fisher** (1972)
7 St Brides Close, Erith, Kent DA18 4DT
Tel: 020-8310 0534 **Rev Gregory Griffiths** *(Parochial Administrator).*
Parish Sister: **Sr Philomena Jordan LSU.**
Tel: 020-8310 0345

M: *(At St John Fisher School) Sun 9am, 10.30am. Hds 10am, 8pm.*

This parish is part of the Thamesmead Christian Community – a Local Ecumenical Project including the Church of England, the Methodist Church and the United Reformed Church.

■ **THORNTON HEATH,** Surrey

† **St Andrew**
(1905; 1969; cons 24 October 1986).
45 Brook Road, Thornton Heath, CR7 7RD
Tel: 020-8684 3013 **Fax:** 020-8684 6626
Email: office@saintandrewschurch.co.uk
Website: saintandrewschurch.co.uk
Revv Francis Moran, Chima Ibekue, Cornelius Boyle. *Deacon:* **Rev Anthony Flavin**.*Parish Sister:* **Sr M Jude DMJ**

M: *Sat 1st M of Sun 6pm. Sun 9.30am, 11.30am, 6pm. Hds (vigil 8pm). 7.30am, 10am, 8pm.*

- ***Daughters of Mary and Joseph,*** 38 Brook Road, Thornton Heath, CR7 7RB **Tel:** 020-8689 0454

■ **TOLWORTH,** Surrey

† **Our Lady Immaculate**
(1934; 1935; 1957; cons 31 May 1963)
401 Ewell Road, Tolworth, KT6 7DG
Tel: 020-8399 9550 **Fax:** 020-8399 3291
E-mail: ourladyimmaculate@ukonline.co.uk
Revv Anthony Charlton, John Diver.
Also Resident: **Rev Desmond Doherty**
Deacon: **Rev Patrick Callan.**

M: *Sat 1st M of Sun 6.30pm. Sun 9am, 11am, 6pm. Hds 9.30am, 8pm.*

■ **TONBRIDGE,** Kent

† **Corpus Christi**
(1894; 1904; cons 6 June 1985)
41 Lyons Crescent, Tonbridge TN9 1EY
Tel/Fax: 01732-353984
Email: corpuschristitonbridge@yahoo.co.uk
Website: corpuschristi-tonbridge.org.uk
Mgr Michael Smith.
Deacon: **James Hayes**

M: *Sat 1st M of Sun 6.30pm. Sun 9am, 6.30pm. Hds 9.30am (at school during term), 12.30pm, 8pm.*

■ **TOOTING (MITCHAM ROAD)**

† **St Boniface** (1896; 1907; cons 22 Sept 1927)
185 Mitcham Road, Tooting SW17 9PG
Tel: 020-8672 2345 **Fax:** 020-8767 4925
Revv Ernest Bonvini, Kuruthakalan Jaraeimir, Michael Britto, Habteghiorghis Ukbay Neghasi OFM Cap.

M: *Sat 1st M of Sun 6.30pm. Sun 9am, 10.30am, 12noon, (2nd Sun of Month 4pm for Ghanaians), 6.30pm. Hds 8am, 9.30am, 12noon, 8pm.*

- ***Vincentians (CM)*** 7a Grenfell Road, Mitcham, Surrey CR4 2BZ **Rev Padraig Regan. Tel:** 020-8685 0974
- ***Sisters of the Holy Family,*** 93 Charlmont Road. SW17 9AF **Tel:** 020-8672 9212

■ **TOOTING (LINKS ROAD)**

† **Our Lady of the Assumption**
(1963; cons 7 Dec 1990)
282 Links Road, Tooting SW17 9ER
Tel: 020-8769 4391
Rev Francis Reid.

M: *Sat 1st M of Sun 6.30pm. Sun 10am (Sung), 12noon, 5pm. Hds (vigil 8pm). 10am.*

■ **TOOTING BEC**

† **St Anselm** (1905; 1933; cons 21 Apr 1980)
Balham High Road, Tooting Bec SW17.
Tel: 020-8672 2179
Website: rc.net/southwark/tootingbec
Rev Dr William Hebborn, Rev Oliver Antao SFX. 9 Tooting Bec Road, Tooting Bec SW17 8BS

M: *Sat 1st M of Sun 6.15pm. Sun 8.30am, 10am (Family), 11.15am (Sung), 6.15pm. Hds 8am, 10am, 6.15pm, 8pm.*

- ***Little Company of Mary,*** (Generalate), 28 Trinity Cres SW17 7AA **Tel:** 020-8682 0928
- ***Focolare Movement,*** 50 Dafforne Road, London SW17 8TZ **Tel:** 020-8767 6092
- ***Religious of St Andrew,*** 28 Upper Tooting Park SW17 7ST

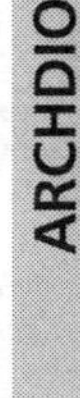

■ **TUNBRIDGE WELLS,** Kent

† **St Augustine**
(1837-1838; 1967; 1975; cons 1980)
Crescent Road, Tunbridge Wells, Kent TN1 2LY
Tel: 01892-522525 **Fax:** 01892-526287
E-mail: office@st-augustine.co.uk
Website: www.st-augustine.co.uk
Revv Peter Stodart, Marcus Holden, Josaphat Ezenwa.
Deacon: **Rev Kevin Dunne.**

M: *Sat 1st M of Sun 5.30pm. Sun 8am, 9.30am, 11.15am (Sung), 5.45pm. Hds 7.30am, 10am, 8pm.*

■ **TWYDALL,** Kent

See Rainham (2).

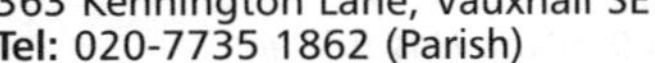

■ **VAUXHALL**

† **St Anne** (1892; 1902; cons 20 March 1911)
363 Kennington Lane, Vauxhall SE11 5QY
Tel: 020-7735 1862 (Parish)

- ***Augustinian Recollects:*** **Rev Mark Powell OAR** (*Prior and Parish Priest*).
  M: *Sat 1st M of Sun 6.30pm. Sun 10am, 12noon, 1.30pm (Spanish) 6.30pm. Hds 9.30am, 12.15pm, 8.30pm.*
- ***Scalabrini Fathers (SC).*** See Italian Mission.
- ***Sons of Divine Providence,*** Vauxhall Project-Impact, Worgan Street, Vauxhall SE11 7DQ **Tel:** 020-7587 1844
- ***Little Sisters of the Poor,*** St Peter's Residence, 2a Meadow Road, SW8 1QH Provincial House: **Tel:** 020-7735 0788 *Chaplain:* **Canon Martin Lee** **Tel:** 020-7735 6246
- ***Augustinian Servants of Jesus and Mary,*** 83 Clapham Road, SW9 0HY **Tel:** 020-7582 0840
- ***Slovenian (Yugoslavia) Chapel***, 62 Offley Road, SW9 0LS **Tel/Fax:** 020-7735 6655
- ***Latin American Chaplaincy:*** **Revv Jesus Gabriel Pérez Recio OAR, Francis Umendia OAR** 363 Kennington Lane, London, SE11 5QY **Tel:** 020-7820 0597

■ WADDON, Croydon

A

† St Dominic (1948; 1961; cons 9 June 1970)
Violet Lane, Waddon, Croydon CR0 4HN
Tel: 020-8686 1634v **Rev Patrick Cannon**.
M: *Sat 1st M of Sun 6pm. Sun 9am, 11am, 5pm. Hds 10am, 8pm.*

■ WALDERSLADE, Chatham, Kent

† St Simon Stock (1955)
Bleakwood Road, Walderslade, Chatham.
Tel: 01634-862910 **Fax:** 01634-311456
E-mail: ppwaldersladekent@btinternet.com
Rev Stephen Wymer. 5 Bleakwood Road, Walderslade, ME5 0NF
M: *Sat 1st M of Sun 6pm. Sun 11am. Hds 9.30am, 8pm.*

- ***St Benedict,*** Lambourn Way, Lordswood. **M:** *Sun 9am. Hds 2.15pm.*

■ WALLINGTON, Surrey

1. **† St Elphege** (1908; 1972; cons 22 May 1980)
Stafford Road, Wallington, Surrey
Tel: 020-8647 5079
Email: stelphegesoffice@yahoo.co.uk
Rev Paul Hough. 120 Stafford Road, Wallington, SM6 9AY
M: *Sat 1st M of Sun 6pm. Sun 9am, 10.30am, 12noon, 5.30pm. Hds 10am, 8pm.*

2. **St Elphege's School**
Mollison Drive.
M: *Sat 1st M of Sun 5.30pm.*

■ WALMER (UPPER), Kent

Sacred Heart Chapel (1875)
318 Dover Road, Walmer, Kent.
Served from Deal.
M: *Sun 9.30am. Hds 9.30am.*

■ WALWORTH

† English Martyrs
(1890; 1903; cons 27 Nov 1919)
142 Rodney Road, Walworth SE17 1RA
Tel: 020-7703 4967 **Fax:** 020-7701 1204
E-mail: office@englishmartyrswalworth.org
Website: englishmartyrswalworth.org

- ***Carmelites (OCarm),*** **Revv Francis Kelmsley** (*Prior and Parish Priest*), **Agostino Sutiono, Thomas Johnston O.Carm**. Also resident: **James Moran.**
  M: *Sat 1st M of Sun 6pm. Sun 8.30am, 10am, 11.30am, 6.30pm. Hds 9.30am, 11am, 7.30pm.*
- ***Daughters of Divine Love,*** 46 Latimer, Beaconsfield Road, Walworth SE17 2EN **Tel:** 020-7252 7402 **Fax:** 020-7703 8626

■ WANDSWORTH EAST HILL

A

† St Mary Magdalen
(1902; 1906; cons 30 July 1981)
East Hill, Wandsworth SW18.
Tel: 020-8874 2724 **Fax:** 020-8870 5254
E-mail: Wandsworthparish@yahoo.co.uk
Revv Martin Edwards, Sylvester Bukenya. 96 North Side, Wandsworth SW18 2QU
M: *Sat 1st M of Sun 6pm. Sun 9.30am, 11am (Sung), 6pm. Hds 10am, 8pm.*

- ***HM Prison (St Peter in Chains)***, Heathfield Road SW18 3HS *Chaplain:* **Rev Dcn Peter Heneghan.** **Tel:** 020-8588 4000 Ext 4240

■ WANDSWORTH WEST HILL

A S

† St Thomas à Becket
(1841; 1895; cons 22 June 1922)
West Hill, Wandsworth SW18.
Tel: 020-8874 1818 **Fax:** 020-8874 0474
E-mail: becket.westhill@btinternet.com
Website: stthomasabecketchurch.co.uk
Rev Gerald Ewing. Becket House, Santos Road, Wandsworth SW18 1NT
Also in residence: **Rev John O'Toole**, **Tel:** 020-8874 3348
M: *Sat 1st M of Sun 5.30pm. Sun 10am. Hds 8pm (Vigil), 10am.*

- ***Society of the Sacred Heart,*** 34 Santos Road, SW18 1NS **Tel:** 020-8874 9640
- ***Handmaids of the Holy Child Jesus,*** 50 Santos Road, SW18. **Tel:** 020-8874 2387
- ***Royal Hospital for Neuro-Disability,*** West Hill. **M:** *Sun 3.30pm*

■ WATERLOO

† Greyfriars (St Patrick) (1897)
26 Cornwall Road, Waterloo SE1 8TW
Tel: 020-7928 8027 **Fax:** 020-7928 2887

- ***Franciscans (Friars Minor Conventual) (OFM Conv)*** **Revv James McCurry** (*Guardian and General Delegate*),

Bede Chaberski, Tel: 020-7633 0997
E-mail: bchaberski@yahoo.co.uk
Jesmond Pawley (*Parish Priest*),
Tel: 020-7928 8897
Rev Grzegorz Wierzowjieki OFM, Conv, E-mail: cmifriar@dircon.co.uk
Bro Matthew Smith.
M: *Sat 1st M of Sun 5pm. Sun 9am, 11am. Hds 8am, 12.30pm.*

■ **WEALD,** Kent
† **St Edward the Confessor** (1956)
Long Barn Road.
Served from Sevenoaks.

■ **WELLING,** Kent
† **St Stephen** (1923; 1936)
26 Deepdene Road, Welling DA16 3QL
Tel: 020-8303 4422
Rev Ranjith Andrade.
M: *Sat 1st M of Sun 6pm. Sun 8.30am, 10am, 11.30am, 6.30pm. Hds (vigil 8pm). 8.15am, 10.30am, 8pm.*

■ **WEST KINGSDOWN,** Kent
St Bernadette's (cons 21 October 1988)
Fawkham Road, West Kingsdown, Kent.
Served from Sevenoaks.
M: *Sun 11am. Hds 11am.*

■ **WEST MALLING,** Kent
1. † **St Thomas More** (1960; 1972; cons Oct 1982)
More Park, West Malling, Kent.
Tel: 01732-843302 **Fax:** 01732-874559
Rev Peter Soper. The Priest's House, The Hermitage, More Park, ME19 6HN
M: *Sun 10am, 5.30pm. Hds 10am, 8pm.*

2. **St Thomas of Canterbury**
Snodland. Holborough Road, West Malling, Kent.
M: *Sat 1st M of Sun 5.30pm. Hds 8pm eve.*
Also resident: **Rt Rev John Hine VG**, Bishop's Flat, The Hermitage, Morre Park, West Mailing, Kent ME19 6HN
Tel: 01732 845486

■ **WEST WICKHAM,** Kent
† **St Mark** (1936; 1948; 1963)
High Street, West Wickham, Kent.
Tel/Fax: 020-8777 6086
E-mail: saintmarks7@btinternet.com
Rev Raymund Brennan. 83 Manor Park Road, BR4 0JY
M: *Sat 1st M of Sun 6.30pm. Sun 9am (Convent, Layhams Road), 10am (Sung) (1st Sun Latin), 11.30am, 6.30pm. Hds (vigil 6.30pm). 9.30am, 8pm.*
• ***Daughters of Mary and Joseph,*** Emmaus Retreat and Conference Centre: Layhams Road, BR4 9QJ **Tel:** 020-8777 2000 Convent: Layhams Road, BR4 9HH **Tel:** 020-8777 5730 Coloma Court Care Home, Layhams Road, BR4 9QJ **Tel:** 020-8776 1129

■ **WESTERHAM,** Kent
† **St John the Baptist**
(1938; 1955; 1976; cons 27 July 1984)
Hosey Hill, Westerham, Kent
Tel: 01959-563226
E-mail: MFC.WEST1@tinyonline.co.uk
Rev James Hurley. Crownest, Hosey Hill, Westerham, TN16 1TB
M: *Sat 1st M of Sun 6pm. Sun 9am, 10.30am. Hds 7.30am, 9.30am, 8pm.*

■ **WESTGATE-ON-SEA,** Kent
† **St Peter** (1966)
Canterbury Road, Westgate-on-Sea, Kent.
Tel: 01843-831593
Rev John Slater (*Priest-in-Charge*).
117 Canterbury Road, Westgate-on-Sea, CT8 8NW
M: *Sat 1st M of Sun 5.30pm. Sun 10am, 5.30pm. Hds 10am, 7.30pm.*
• ***Ursulines,*** 225 Canterbury Road, Westgate-on-Sea. CT8 8LX
Tel: 01843-834431 **Fax:** 01843-832151
• ***The Lourdes Community:***
Tel: 01843-833242 **Fax:** 01843-831290
• ***Daughters of Jesus,*** 63 Sea Road, CT8 8QG **Tel:** 01843-831415

■ **WHITSTABLE,** Kent
1. † **Our Lady Immaculate**
(1900; 1906; cons 3 Sept 1908)
Northwood Road, Whitstable, Kent.
Tel: 01227-272758
Fax: 01227-280841
E-mail: immac.whitstable@btinternet.com
Rev Kevin St Aubyn. 37 Kingsdown Park CT5 2DE Also in residence: **Rev Geoffrey Munnery**. *Deacon:* **Rev Daniel Mulcahy**.
M: *Sat 1st M of Sun 6pm. Sun 10.30am. Hds 9.30am, 8pm.*
• ***Sisters of Mercy,*** Northwood Road CT5 2EY. **Tel:** 01277-272649
Fax: 01227-280841

2. **St Joseph. (1964)**
Chestfield Road, Chestfield CT5 3LD
Served from Whitstable.
M: *Sun 8.30am. Hds (vigil 7pm).*

■ **WIMBLEDON**
† **The Sacred Heart**
(1877; 1887; cons 7 May 1931)
9 Edge Hill, Wimbledon SW19.
Tel: 020-8946 0305 or 020-8947 3184
Fax: 020-8946 9130
E-mail: wimparish@gmail.com
• ***Jesuits (SJ):*** **Revv Gerard Mitchell** (*Parish Priest*), **Michael Ashworth, Keith McMillan, John Fairhurst**. Sacred Heart Presbytery, Edge Hill, London SW19 4LU

M: *Sat 1st M of Sun 6.30pm. Sun 8.15am, 9.45am (Family), 11.15am (Solemn Latin Mass), 12.45pm, 5pm, 8pm. Hds 8am, 10am, 6.30pm, 8pm.*

- ***Sacred Heart School Mass Centre,*** Burlington Road, New Malden. Served from Sacred Heart, Edge Hill. **M:** *Sun 8.30am. Hds 6pm*
- ***Jesuits (SJ),*** 9 Edge Hill, Wimbledon London SW19 4LR **Revv Anthony Nye** (*Superior*), **Adrian Porter, John Grummitt, Patrick Madigan, Luis Caruana, Gerrard Gallen, Gerald O'Collins** Community: **Tel:** 020-8947 4251
- ***Pierre Favre House,*** 19 Belvedere Grove, London SW19 7RQ **Tel:** 0208-947 5237 Wimbledon College: **Tel:** 020-8946 2533 Donhead Prep: **Tel:** 020-8946 7000.
- ***Jesuits Missions Office:*** 11 Edge Hill, Wimbledon, London SW19 4LR **Tel:** 020-8946 0466 **Fax:** 020-8946 2292
- ***Sons of Divine Providence,*** 114 Consfield Avenue, Motspur Park, New Malden KT3 6HE **Tel:** 020-8336 2600
- ***Ursulines,*** 28 Mansel Road, Wimbledon, SW19 4AA **Tel:** 020-8946 4134
- ***Sisters of St Anne,*** Convent, 14 The Downs, Wimbledon, London SW20 8HS **Tel:** 020-8946 8193 (Generalate) **Tel:** 020-8946 4794
- ***St Teresa's Home for the Elderly (Sisters of St Anne)*** 12 Lansdowne Road, SW20 8AN **Tel:** 020-8879 7366
- ***Daughters of the Heart of Mary,*** 41 Murray Road, SW19 4PD **Tel:** 020-8946 3564 **Fax:** 020-8944 6595 Provincial: **Tel:** 020-8944 6168 **E-mail:** admin@dothom.fsnet.co.uk

■ WIMBLEDON COMMON [A]

† Our Lady and St Peter
(1961; 1971; cons 3 October 1986)
15 Victoria Drive, Wimbledon Common SW19 6AD **Tel:** 020-8788 9603 **Fax:** 020-8780 5432 **Rev David Peck.** *Deacon:* **Christopher Rood**

M: *Sat 1st M of Sun 6pm. Sun 10am, 5.30pm. Hds 10am, 8pm.*

- ***Religious of Mary Immaculate,*** Struan House, 44 Augustus Road, SW19 6NB **Tel:** 0208 788 9477 **Fax:** 0208 394 5588 **Email:** struanhouse@maryimmaculate **Website:** religiosademarianmaculada.org
- ***Benedictine Sisters of Our Lady of Grace and Compassion,*** 54 Parkside, SW19 5NF **Tel:** 020-8946 1410

■ WIMBLEDON (SOUTH) [A]

† St Winefride (1905; cons 16 May 1980)
2 Latimer Road, Wimbledon SW19 1EP **Tel:** 020-8542 1600 **E-mail:** winefridechurch@clara.co.uk **Rev Simon Peat.**

M: *Sat 1st M of Sun 6pm. Sun 9am, 11am, 6pm. Hds (vigil 7pm). 9.30am, 12.30pm, 8pm.*

- ***Daughters of the Heart of Mary,*** 32 Latimer Road, SW19 1EP **Tel:** 020-8543 1978
- ***Franciscan Missionaries of Mary,*** 92 Kings Road, Wimbledon SW19 **Tel:** 020-8544 0973

■ WIMBLEDON PARK

† Christ the King
(1913; 1928; cons 25 Sept 1958)
The Crescent, Wimbledon Park SW19. **Tel:** 020-8946 2091 **E-mail:** info@christthekingparish.org.uk **Website:** www.christthekingparish.org.uk **Canon John Naughton**. 9 Crescent Gardens, Wimbledon Park SW19 8AJ

M: *Sat 1st M of Sun 6pm. Sun 8.30am, 10.30am, 12.15pm (Pol), 5.30pm. Hds (vigil 8pm). 7pm.*

■ WINGHAM

Mass Centre in CofE Parish Church. Served from Aylesham.

M: *Sun 8.30am. Hds (vigil 6pm)*

■ WONERSH, Guildford, Surrey

St John's Seminary
(1891; Chapel cons 4 May 1896)
Wonersh, Guildford, Surrey GU5 0QX Rector & Staff: **Tel:** 01483-892217 **Fax:** 01483-894531 Students: **Tel:** 01483-893741/898402. Domestic & Catering: **Tel:** 01483-892520 **E-mails:** Staff: wonersh@dial.pipex.com Students: wonersh@dial.pipex.com *Rector:* rector@wonersh.org **Website:** www.wonersh.org

Rector: **Rev Mgr Canon Jeremy Garratt** Ph B, MA, STL; *Rector's Secretary:* **Ms Melissa Kingdon** BSc **Tel:** 01483 891024 *Bursar:* **Mr Tony Lee; Tel:** 01483 891020 *Finance Assistant:* **Mrs Bernie Minchella; Tel:** 01483 891029; *Bursar's Secretary:* **Mrs Nina Segrove;** *Director of Studies:* **Rev Jonathan How** BSc, BTh, PhL, PGCE(A), ARCS, FHEA, **Tel:** 01483 891023; *Academic's Secretary:* **Mrs Rebecca Teller** BSc **Tel:** 01483 891028; *Director of Spirituality:* **Rev Gerard Bradley,** BMus, BTh, AKC; **Tel:** 01483 891021; *Pastoral Director:* **Sr M Finbarr Coffey** HC, BA, HDipEd, CertTh, **Tel:** 01483 891025; *Human Development Director:* **Rev Paul Lyons** MLitt, MA.
Other Full-time Staff:
Senior Lecturer in Divinity, Librarian: **Rev Stephen Dingley** MA, PhD, STL, **Tel:** 01483 891027; *Spiritual Director:* **Michael Woodgate** BA, **Tel:** 01483 891026.

Part-time Staff:
Sr Maureen Banyard FMDM, Rt Rev Geoffrey Scott OSB, Rev Canon Ken Noakes, Revv John Boyle, Timothy Finigan, Sean Finnegan, Alan Griffiths, John J. Henry, Dylan James, Michael Masterson, Simon Peat, Dominic Rolls, Julian Shurgold, William Wilson, Mr Ged Clapson, Roger Mortimore, Mr Robert Munns, Mrs Lynette Harborne, Frances Henley Lock, Pia Matthews,

■ WOOLWICH

1. † St Peter (1815; 1843; cons 26 Oct 1944)
Woolwich New Road, Woolwich SE18 6EF
Tel: 020-8854 0359 **Fax:** 020-8854 0133
E-mail: frmichael@st-peter-rc-woolwich.co.uk
Revv Michael Scanlon, Shaju Varkey. Also resident: **Rev James Hay, John Masayi**.
103 Woolwich New Road, SE18 6EF
M: *Sat 1st M of Sun 6.30pm. Sun 8.45am, 11.15am, 6.30pm. Hds (vigil 7.30pm). 10am, 12.30pm, 7.30pm.*

2. † St Catherine Labouré (1961)
698 Woolwich Road, Woolwich SE7 8LQ
Served from Woolwich.
M: *Sun 10am.*

■ WORCESTER PARK, Surrey A

† St Matthias (1906; cons 30 May 1977)
201 Cheam Common Road, Worcester Park, KT4 8SX **Tel/Fax:** 020-8337 1782
E-mail: st.matthias@rdplus.net
Web: www.saintmatthias.co.uk
Rev Kevan Hayden.
M: *Sat 1st M of Sun 6.30pm. Sun 9.30am, 11.15am, 5.30pm. Hds 7am, 10am, 7.30pm.*

■ WYE, Kent

† St Ambrose Chapel
Served from Ashford.
M: *Sun 9.30am. Hds (vigil 7pm).*

■ ORDERS OR CONGREGATIONS ETC

The symbol † is used to distinguish Secular Institutes.

■ Men

Benedictines (Congregation of Subiaco): Ramsgate.
Canons Regular of the Lateran: Eltham (1).
Carmelites: Aylesford, Faversham, Walworth.
Comboni Missionaries (Verona Fathers), Battersea Park
Claretian Missionaries, Norbury
De La Salle Brothers: Herne Hill.
Franciscans (Capuchin): Erith.
Franciscans (Friars of the Atonement): Bromley.
Franciscans (Friars Minor Conventual): Canterbury, Waterloo.
Franciscan (Friars Minor): Canterbury.
Holy Ghost Fathers: Bromley, Norwood (South).
Jesuits: Wimbledon.
Jesus, Little Brothers of: West Norwood.
Marists: Sidcup.
Mill Hill Missionaries: Cliftonville.
Missionaries of St Paul (of Nigeria) (MSP), Addiscombe, Bermondsey South, Croydon, Deptford, Tooting.
Passionists: Herne Bay.
Presentation Brothers: Dartford, (2)
Redemptorists: Clapham.
Providence, Sons of Divine: Gravesend, Streatham Hill, Wimbledon.
Sacred Heart Fathers: Norwood (South) Nunhead
Salesians: Battersea (West).
Salvatorians: Borough.
Scalabrini Fathers: Italian Mission, Vauxhall.
Society of Christ: Putney (2).
Society of Christiam Doctorine: Upper Norwood.
Society of Missionaries of St Francis Xavier (Pilar Fathers): Mitcham.
Society of Our Lady of the Most Holy Trinity: Hythe.
Society of St Paul: Battersea West.
Vincentians: Tooting.

■ Women

Andrew, Religious of St: Edenbridge, Tooting Bec.
Anne, Sisters of St: Wimbledon.
Augustinian Servants of Jesus and Mary: Vauxhall.
Benedictine Nuns (Congregation of Subiaco): Minster.
Benedictine Sisters of Our Lady of Grace and Compassion: Wimbledon Common.
Charity (of St Louis), Sisters of: East Sheen, Tolworth.
Charity (Missionaries of): Southwark.
Christ, Sisters of: Sittingbourne.
Christian Instruction, Sisters of: Nunhead.
Christian Retreat, Sisters of the: Buckland.
Contemplative Missionary Movement of Fr de Foucauld: Brixton Hill
Cross, Daughters of the (Liege): Broadstairs, Carshalton, North Cheam.
Daughters of the Heart of Mary: Wimbledon, South Wimbledon.
Divine Love, Daughters of: Clapham Common, Norbury.
Dominican Sisters (Third Order) (Congr of Salisbury, Zimbabwe): Greenwich.
Dorothy, Sisters of St: Stockwell.
Eucharist, Religious of the: Buckland
Faithful Companions of Jesus: Broadstairs.

Felician Sisters: Chislehurst.
Franciscan Missionaries of the Divine Motherhood: Southwark, Balham.
Franciscan Missionaries of Mary: Brixton Hill, Putney, Wimbledon South.
Franciscan Missionary Sisters for Africa: Sevenoaks.
Franciscan Missionary Sisters (of Littlehampton): Canterbury.
Good Shepherd Sisters: Cranbrook, Swanley.
Handmaids of the Holy Child Jesus: Wandsworth, West Hill.
Handmaids of Mary: Clapham Park.
Holy Cross, Teaching Sisters of the: New Malden.
Holy Family (St Emile de Rodat), Sisters of the: Bromley, Stockwell, Tooting, Tooting Bec.
Holy Family of Bordeaux, Sisters of: Clapham.
Holy Trinity, Sisters of the: Biggin Hill, Bromley.
Jesus, Daughters of: Sidcup, Westgate.
Joseph (Annecy), Sisters of St: Chatham, Morden, Mottingham.
Marie Reparatrice, Society of: Wimbledon.
Marist Sisters: Hythe, New Malden.
Mary and Joseph, Daughters of: Addiscombe, Herne Bay, New Addington, Sydenham, Thornton Heath, West Wickham.
Mary, Daughters of the Heart of: Wimbledon.
Mary Immaculate (Madrid), Religious of: Wimbledon Common.
Mary, Little Company of: Tooting Bec.
Mary, Religious of the Sacred Heart of: Kingston Hill.
Medical Mission Sisters: Camberwell.
Mercy, Sisters of: Ashford, Gravesend, Strood.
Mercy Institute, Sisters of: Bermondsey, Croydon West, Eltham, Orpington, Swanley, Whitstable.
Notre Dame, School Sisters of: Clapham.
Notre Dame (de Namur), Sisters of: Bermondsey (Dockhead), Camberwell, Wandsworth, East Hill.
Our Lady of Fidelity, Society of: Folkestone (West), Norwood (Upper).
Our Lady of the Missions, Sisters of: Hersden, Mongeham.
Our Lady of the Sacred Heart (Issoudun), Daughters of: Merton.
Peter Claver, Missionary Sisters of St: Beckenham.
Poor, Little Sisters of the: Vauxhall.
Poor Servants of the Mother of God: Roehampton, Streatham.
Providence (Ruillé-sur-Loir), Sisters of: Maidstone (3).
Retraite Sisters of La: Streatham.
Sacred Heart (Paris), Society of the: Roehampton, Wandsworth, West Hill.
Sacred Heart (Rome), Handmaids of the: Beckenham.
Sacred Heart (Rome), Missionary Sisters of the: Forest Hill.
Sacred Hearts of Jesus and Mary (Chigwell), Sisters of the: Blackheath, Herne Bay.
Sacred Hearts of Jesus and Mary, Congretation of the (Epsom), Sisters of the: Camberwell.
Sacred Heart of Mary (US Province), Religious of: Kingston Hill.
Sainte Union des Sacrés Coeurs, Congregation of the: Bermondsey (3), Crayford, Kidbrooke, Thamesmead Central.
Salesian Sisters of St John Bosco: Battersea West, Rotherhithe, Streatham.
Servite Sisters: Mitcham.
Suore Francescane dell' Immacolata: Sanderstead, Wimbledon Common.
† The Leaven, The Secular Institute of Our Lady of Mount Carmel: Aylesford.
Ursulines of Jesus: Dover.
Ursulines (Roman Union): Greenwich, Westgate-on-Sea, Wimbledon.

■ ASSOCIATIONS AND DIOCESAN SOCIETIES

For Societies and Organisations without representation in the diocese please see the main Societies and Organisations section.

Aid to the Church in Need, 14-16 Benhill Avenue, Sutton SM1 4DA **Tel:** 020-8020 6293 **Fax:** 020-8661 6293 **E-mail:** acn@acnuk.org *UK Director:* **Neville Kyrke-Smith**; *Southwark Area Secretaries:* **Peter Langer**, 28 The Horse Close, Emmer Green, Reading RG4 8TT **Tel:** 0118 947 5259; **John Greig**, 1 Mill Hall Cottages, Whitemans Green, Cuckfield, West Sussex RH17 5HX **Tel:** 01444 451325

Apostleship of the Sea. *Chaplain to the Kent Ports:* **Rev John Slater**. 117 Canterbury Road, Westgate-on-Sea, CT8 8NW **Tel:** 01843-831593

Archconfraternity of St Stephen. *Director:* **Rev S Boyle**, 25 Dunley Drive, New Addington CR0 0RG **Tel:** 01689-842644, **Fax:** 01689-844818 *Chairman:* **John Bonnici**. 43 Brownhill Road, SE6 2HB **Tel:** 020-8698 1107

Ascent, Movement The. For the retired Christian (an active member of Vie Montante Internationale). The Ascent Movement has the special mission of helping retired men & women in their spiritual growth, and of encouraging them to take up their responsibilities as members of the Church as well as they can. *National President:* **Mrs Molly Huckin**. *Local contact:* **Joyce Neill**, 137 Covington Way, London SW16 3JT

Association for Latin Liturgy. *Diocesan Representative:* **Mr E M Barrett**, 14 Connaught Mansions, Prince of Wales Drive, Battersea, London SW11 4SA

Association for the Propagation of the Faith. *Diocesan Director:* **Rev Deacon John O'Donovan**, 16 Culvers Avenue, Carshalton, Surrey SM5 2BS **Tel:** 020-8773 0254

Association of Catholic Clubs. *Chairman:* **Mr T Mulholland**. *Secretary:* **Mrs Eileen Manley**. 2 Hillcrest Road, Crayford, Kent. **Tel:** 01322-2523408

Association of Salesian Co-operators, Third Order of St John Bosco. *Co-ordinator:* **Rev Michael Kennedy**. c/o Parish of the Sacred Heart, Trott Street, Battersea SW11 3NZ.

Association of Seperated and Divorced Catholics. A federation of self help groups to provide mutual help and spiritual support to those who have experienced the pain of marriage breakdown. *Diocesean Contact:* **Tony Finnegan** 020 8767 5293

Beginning Experience. A weekend programme which seeks to help separated, divorced and bereaved people to make a gentle closure on the past and start life afresh. Weekends are held at the Emmaus Centre, West Wickham and All Saints Pastoral Centre, London Colney, April and October. *For further information contact:* **Ruth Kamalagharan**, 11 Baldry Gardens, London SW16 3DL **Tel:** 020-8679 7157

Billings Natural Family Planning Centre (London). *Director:* **Mrs Veronica Pierson**. 58B Vauxhall Grove, London SW8 1TB **Tel:** 020-7793 0026

Catenian Association (For Catholic Professional and Business Men). *Head Office:* 8 Chesham Place, London SW1X 8HP *Grand Secretary:* **T McManus KSG**. 8 Chesham Place SW1X 8HP *Provincial President L7:* **Ignace van Kan**, Solefields Lodge North, Solefields Road, Sevenoaks, Kent TN13 1PF *Provincial Secretary*: **John Rayner**, 96b High Street, Bexley, Kent DA5 1JY *Province President L19:* **Christopher Richards**. The Henley, 1 Broomfield Ride, Oxshott, Surrey KT22 0ZP

Catholic Association of Tamils: To advance the religious life of Tamils. *Secretary:* **Mr S. Bastiampillai (Seelan)**, 104 Melison Road, Tooting. London SW17 9AY **Tel:** 020-8682 4974

Catholic Charismatic Renewal. For information and the location of prayer groups within the Diocese, apply to the National Service Committee. Allen Hall, 28 Beaufort Street, London SW3 5AA **Tel:** 020-7352 5298

Catholic Clothing Guild. *Hon Secretary:* **Mrs B Sayer**, Mayfield, Elm Walk, Farnborough, Orpington, Kent BR6 8LX **Tel:** 01689-855314

Catholic Family History Society meets regularly at the Society of Genealogists, London, EC1M 7BA. *Secretary:* **Mrs Barbara Murray**, 2 Winscombe Crescent, Ealing, London W5 1AZ

Catholic Fund for Overseas Development (CAFOD) *Regional Office:* CAFOD Southwark, Hubert House, Mallard Close, Temple Hill Square, Dartford, Kent DA1 5HU **Tel:** 01322 294924 **Fax:** 01322 279223 *CAFOD Diocesan Manager:* **Mr Paul Whittle**. **Email:** southwark@cafod.org.uk

Catholic Nurses Guild. *Diocesan Representative:* **Mrs Nora McCarthy RGN, RM.** 91 Beverstone Road, Thornton Heath, Surrey. *Chaplain:* **Rev Barry Grant**.

Catholic Police Guild. *National Secretary:* **Geraldine McWilliams**, 18 Chipstead Lane, Lower Kingswood, Surrey KT20 6RS **Tel:** 01737-271017 *National Chaplain:* **Rev William Scanlon**. **Tel:** 01322 220075

Catholic Social Workers' Guild. *Chaplain:* **Rev Theodor Davey**. Heythrop College, London. *Hon Secretary:* **Margaret Bamford**. 10 Foxlea, Findon, West Sussex BN14 0XB

Catholic Youth Hostellers (YHA). A voluntary organisation to help Catholic Youth Hostellers from this country and abroad, and to assist priests in YHA matters. *Southwark Representative:* **Michael J Riley**. 85 Spur Road, Orpington, Kent BR6 0QP **Tel:** 01689-832012

Christian Life Communities. *Representative:* **Rita McManus**. Orchard Drive, Meopham, Kent DA13 OLW **Tel:** 01474-813366

Daughters of St Francis De Sales, A worldwide Lay Society for women, following the spirituality of St Frances De Sales, for the married or single woman who lives in the world and who wishes to consecrate her life to God through 'living' the Gospel by a Rule of Life. *All enquiries:* c/o 1 Haig Road,

Biggin Hill, Westerham, Kent TN16 3LJ **Tel:** 01959-571404

Ecumenical Society of the Blessed Virgin Mary, *London Area Secretary:* **Mr J P Farrelly KSG**. Belmont Road, Wallington, Surrey. **Tel:** 020-8647 5992.

Engaged Encounter. *Contact:* **Paul and Hilary Sabine**, 21 Edmunds Close, Meopham, Kent DA13 0NB **Tel:** 01474-812855 **E-mail:** phsabine@aol.com **Website:** www.wwme.org.uk

Friends of the Holy Father *Diocesan Representative:* **R W Last**. 33 South Road, London, SE3 0RY **Tel:** 020-8852 5803

Grail, The *Diocesan Representative:* **Paul and Ellen Farmer**, 39 Elmbridge Avenue, Tolworth, Surbiton, Surrey KT5 9EZ **Tel:** 020-8399 9039 ***Grail Headquarters:*** The President, The Grail Centre, 125 Waxwell Lane, Pinner, Middlesex MA5 3ER **Tel:** 020-8866 2195 **Fax:** 020-8866 1408

Guild of the Blessed Sacrament. *Diocesan Director:* **Rev Martin Edwards**, 96 North Side, Wandsworth, London SW18 2QU **Tel:** 020-8874 2724 **Fax:** 020-8870 5254

Housing Justice. Formed from the merger of the Catholic Housing Aid Society (CHAS), and Churches National Housing Coalition. Branch in the Diocese of Southwark. *Croydon:* The Old House, 2 Wellesley Court Road, Croydon CR9 1UN **Tel:** 020-8688 7900

Kent Recusant History Society. *Chairman:* **Antony C W Ryan, MA, FRGS.** 83 Roper Road, Canterbury, Kent CT2 7RS **Tel:** 01227-463490

Knights of St Columba. SOUTH LONDON AND KENT (Province 12): *Provincial Grand Knight:* **Mr Henry Brand**, 235 Bedonwell Road, Bexley Heath, Kent DA7 5QA **Tel:** 01322 432918 *Provincial Secretary:* **Mr Ken Smith**, 40 Danson Road, Bexley Heath, Kent DA6 8HB **Tel:** 07860 241196 SURREY (Province 35): *Provincial Grand Knight:* **Michael Steele,** 19 Merrow Woods, Guildford Surrey GU1 2LQ **Tel:** 01483 503875 *Provincial Secretary:* **John Walters**. 9 Highview Road, Woking Surrey GU22 7NH Tel: 01483 730049 *Provincial Youth Officer:* **Mr C Swan**, 86 Haynt Walk West, London SW20 9HX **Tel:** 020-8543 2482 *Chaplain:* **Rev Deacon F Carter**, 331 Common Hill Lane SW20 9HQ **Tel:** 020-8540 6234

Latin Mass Society Urges preservation of Tridentine Rite Mass. *Diocesan Representative:* **Mr Michael Pearce**, 6 Flint Cottages, Grand Hill, Leatherhead, Surrey KT22 7HQ **Tel:** 01322-377169

Legion of Mary, A worldwide organisation living and fulfilling the ideals of the Decree on the Lay Apostolate. Its mission is to be at the disposal of the parish priest for all forms of evangelisation and pastoral care so as to bring all peoples to Christ through Mary. Central information number **Tel:** 020-7234 0125 **Email:** legionofmary@btinternet.com *President:* **Ms Eileen Ruddy**.

Let Live. A comprehensive caring scheme to help any girl or woman who finds herself under pressure to seek an abortion. **Tel:** 020-7828 3824 10am to 10pm daily.

Life and Life Care and Housing Trust. A voluntary organisation helping women with unplanned pregnancies. We offer: free and confidential pregnancy testing and counselling (also post-abortion counselling); free baby/maternity clothes and equipment; advice on welfare benefits; accommodation in nationwide network of 55 LIFE hostels. *Contact:* Croydon LIFE office - 57a London Road, Croydon. **Tel:** 020-8688 1985/6 Life HQ Life House, Newbold Terrace, Leamington Spa, CV32 4EA **Tel:** 01926 421587 / 311667 / 316737 **Fax:** 01926 326497 *National Hotline:* **Tel:** 01926 311511

Little Way Association. 119 Cedars Road, London SW4 0PR **Tel:** 020-7622 0466 To assist Missionaries to spread the Faith by prayer and active work and to promote the message of St Therese of Lisieux.

London Recusant Society. To publish studies of the post-reformation Catholic history of the London District (Dioceses of Westminster and Southwark). *Editor of the London Recusant*: **E S Worrall BA**. 21 Merryhills Drive, Enfield, Middx EN2 7NS **Tel:** 020-8363-5256

Lourdes Pilgrimage (Diocesan). Usually late August, early September, assisted by Catholic Association Pilgrimage Trust. *Director:* **Dcn Michael Kennedy**, 4 Orbel Street, Battersea SW11 3NZ

Manna Society. Working with Homeless People. *Director*: **Mr Paddy Boyle**. 6 Melior Street, London SE1 3QP **Tel:** 020-7403 1931

Marriage and Family Life: *SE Area Office:* The Presbytery, 20 Village Way, Beckenham BR3 3NP **Tel/Fax:** 020 8325 1486

Marriage Care Professionally trained marriage counsellors offer help to those

ARCHDIOCESE OF SOUTHWARK

with marital difficulties, and courses for engaged couples. Resource for teachers and others who are responsible for delivering personal health and social education to young people.
Helpline: 0845 660 6000
Mon - Fri 10am - 4pm.
Website: www.marriagecare.org.uk
E-mail: info@marriagecare.org.uk
Local contacts *Blackheath:* **Tel:** 020 8297 0883, *Croydon, Medway Towns and Wimbledon* **Tel:** 0800 389 3801

Marriage Encounter *Contact:* **Tony and Margaret Hunt**, 21 Chambersbury Lane, Hemel Hempstead, Herts JP3 8BQ
Tel: 01442-293838
E-mail: anthony.hunt2@ntlworld.com
Website: www.wwme.org.uk

Movement of Christian Workers. (Formerly Family and Social Action). To promote on-going Christian formation through small groups and provide a comprehensive service to them. The groups exist to help people relate faith to daily life, build up Christian community on a local level, give positive support to families and equip and sustain Christians for their civic and social responsibilities. The movement has a development worker who is able to encourage and support new groups throughout the country. *National Headquarters:* St Joseph's, Watford Way, London NW4 4TY
Tel: 020-8203 6291 **Fax:** 020-8203 6291
E-mail: mcworkers@aol.com

Myrrh Education and Training. Provides an opportunity by which the disadvantaged can be included in NVQ training programmes of various vocational skills, Myrrh operates from the Training Centres sited in South London. *Chairman:* **Mr Anthony Lester**, Kevin Keohane House, 52 Ossory Road, London SE1 5AN **Tel:** 020-7394 8304
E-mail: headoffice@myrrhltd.co.uk

Newman Association. Rainham Circle: *Chairman:* **Mrs M Casey**. 107 Maidstone Road, Rainham, Kent ME8 0DS
Tel: 01634-389095
Croydon Circle: *Secretary:* **Mr Andy Holton**, 42 Ladygrove, Forestdale, Croydon CR0 1XJ **Tel:** 0208-651 7633
E-mail: andyholton@blueyonder.co.uk

Our Lady's Catechists. *Diocesan Organiser:* **Miss H Cooley**. 7 Alford Court, Bonchurch Close, Sutton, Surrey SM2 6AY **Tel:** 020-8643 4508

Pax Christi International Catholic Movement for Peace. General Secretary: **Patricia Gaffney**, St Jospeh's, Walford Way NW4 4TY **Tel:** 020-8203 4884
Fax: 020-8203 5234
E-mail: paxchristi@gn.apc.org;
Website: www.paxchristi.org.uk

Secular Franciscan Order: Contact: **Paula Pearce**. c/o 27 Prospect Way, Brabourne Lees, Kent TN25 6RL **Tel:** 01303-813095

St Anthony of Padua Foundation for the Disabled: *Secretary:* **Peter McArdle**. Copper Lodge, 11 Clifftown Gardens, Herne Bay, Kent CT6 8DF
Tel: 01227-366862

St Francis of Assisi Catholic Ramblers' Club (London). Rambles organised every Sunday in the countryside around London, also social events and walking week-ends. Please write enclosing sae, with full Christian and surname, to: **Tony Finnegan**, 30 Avarn Road, Tooting, London SW17 9HA **Tel:** 020-8767 5293
E-mail: 30avarn@tfinnegan.org.uk.

Serviam. Ursuline Lay Association. Ursuline Convents at 70 Crooms Hill, London SE10 8HN **Tel:** 020-8858 0779
Canterbury Road, Westgate-on-Sea, Kent CT8 8LX **Tel:** 01843-834431
15 The Downs, London SW20 8HD
Tel: 020-8947 6772

Society of the Friends of St George's. Founded in 1975 to share with the Archbishop the burden of the day to day maintenance and repair of St George's Cathedral. *Chairman:* **David Barlow**. *Secretary:* **Nikki Rutherford**. c/o St George's Cathedral, Lambeth Road, Southwark, London SE1

Society of St Gregory. *Diocesan contacts:* **John and Liz Woodhouse**, 15 Wrights Road, South Norwood SE25 6RY
Tel: 020-8653 2372
E-mail: southwark@ssg.org.uk

Society of St Vincent de Paul, Southwark Central Council. *President:* **Mr Joe Woods**. St Vincent de Paul Society, 5th Floor, 292-299 Borough High Street, London SE1 1JG
Tel: 020-7407 4644 **Fax:** 020-7407 4634
Email: enquiries@svp.org.uk
Website: vp.org.uk

Southwark Brethren Charity. For sick and retired priests. *Secretary and Treasurer:* **Rev Paul Hough**. St Elphege's Presbytery, 120 Stafford Road, Wallington, Surrey, SM6 9AY

Southwark Catholic Association of Widows: *Secretary:* **Mrs C Macklin**.
Tel: 020-8390 2494

Southwark Catholic Guide Guild. *Chairman:* **Miss Kate Chapman**, 2 New Road, Paddock Wood, Kent TN12 6HP
Tel: 01892-832292

Southwark Catholic Youth Service. St Vincent's Centre, Castle Road,

Whitstable, Kent CT5 2ED
Tel: 01227-272900 **Fax:** 01227-282384
E-mail: scys@scys.org.uk
Website: scys.org.uk

Teams of Our Lady. An international Catholic Movement for Christian married couples that aims to deepen the couples' spirituality. A 'Team' consists of four or five couples and a priest or religious as spiritual advisor meeting monthly to share the journey of faith, guided by the Holy Spirit. *Contact couple:* **Peter and Mary Hayes**, 22 Wilton Crescent, Wimbledon, London SW19 3QZ **Tel:** 020-8540 7473 **E-mail:** mary@adidem.demon.co.uk

Teresian Association, International Lay Catholic Association founded in 1911. Aims to promote Christian values in education and culture, through the personal work and witness of members in their professions and through a number of centres throughout the world. 51 Chestnut Grove, New Malden, Surrey KT3 3JJ **Tel:** 020-8942 6086

Third Order of Our Lady of Mount Carmel. For details of monthly meetings in Aylesford, Faversham and Margate, and for information about the spirituality of the Carmelite Family, please contact **Miss Jean Harrigan**, Lay Carmel Central office, The Friars, Aylesford, Kent ME20 7BX

Union of Catholic Mothers. *Spiritual Adviser:* **Rev James Nolan**. *President:* **Mrs Mary Hamblin**, 10 Sunningdale Drive, Rainham ME8 9EE **Tel:** 01634 370907 *Secretary:* **Mrs Josie Honor**, 9 Cowden Street, Catford SE26 3SW *Treasurer:* **Mrs Jo Ruane**, 5 Lonsdale Drive, Sittingbourne, Kent ME10 1TT **Tel:** 01795-476938

Walsingham Association. Erith: **Mrs M Locke**. 65 Edendale Road, Barnehurst, Kent. DA7 6RJ **Tel:** 01322-333506 Sidcup: **Mrs J Hollins**. 231 Hurst Road, Sidcup, Kent DA15 9AL **Tel:** 020-8300 5632

Young Christian Workers & Impact. For young people aged between 13-30. Regional Chaplain: **Fr Geoff Munnery** **Tel:** 01227-272900 **E-mail:** geoff@scys.org.uk Headquarters: St Joseph's, off St Joseph's Grove, London NW4 4TY. **Tel:** 0208 203 6290 **E-mail:** info@ycwimpact.com **Website:** www.ycwimpact.com

■ WELFARE SERVICES

■ Homes for the Elderly

Aylesham: Our Lady's Flats (active elderly).
Cranbrook: Convent of Good Shepherd (women)
Edenbridge: St Andrew's Convent (women).
Gravesend: St Joseph's (flats for active elderly).
Streatham Hill: Fatima House (men and women).
Vauxhall: St Peter's Home (aged poor).
Wimbledon: St Teresa's Home (men and women)
Battersea West, Beckenham, Bickley, Penge, Sevenoaks, Sydenham: Servite Homes, 125 Old Brompton Road, SW7 3RP. **Tel:** 01-370 5466 (flatlets and sheltered housing for elderly).

■ Nursing Homes and Hospitals

Bromley: St Raphael's (elderly men and women).
Buckland: Kearsney Manor (elderly men and women).
Canterbury: East Kent Pilgrim's Hospice (terminally ill).
Clapham: Trinity Hospice (terminally ill).
North Cheam: St Anthony's Hospital (general hospital).
North Cheam: St Raphael's Hospice (terminally ill/day care/home care).
Sydenham Kirkdale: St Christopher's Hospice (terminally ill).
West Wickham: Coloma Court Care Home (elderly men and women).

■ For those with Disabilities

Wimbledon: 114 Consfield Avenue (women with disabilities).
Orpington: Cabrini House (long-stay and respite care).
Roehampton: Maryfield (women with disabilities).
Roehampton: St Mary's (women with disabilities).

■ Holiday Homes

Aylesham: Our Lady's House, (Older men and women).
Herne Bay: St Peter's (Religious Sisters and laywomen).

■ Residential Hostels

Brockley: St Vincent's (young men on probation).
Stockwell: Convent of St Dorothy (young women working/studying).
Streatham: St Edmund's (men on probation).
Vauxhall: Augustinian Sisters (young women, short stay).
Wimbledon: Marian Lodge (young professional women and students).
Wimbledon Common: Struan (working girls and students).

■ CHURCHES IN LONDON POSTAL DISTRICT AREA SOUTH OF THE THAMES
(arranged according to their districts)

■ South-East
1: Bermondsey (Holy Trinity); Bermondsey (Our Lady and St Joseph); Borough; Southwark Cathedral; Waterloo.
2: Abbey Wood - St Benets, Abbey Wood - St Davids.
3: Blackheath; Kidbrooke.
4: Brockley.
5: Camberwell (Sacred Heart).
6: Beckenham Hill; Catford.
7: Charlton.
8: Deptford.
9: Eltham, Eltham Well Hall, Mottingham.
10: Greenwich, Greenwich East.
11: Vauxhall.
12: Lee.
13: Lewisham.
15: Nunhead; Peckham; Peckham Rye.
16: Bermondsey (St Gertrude's); Rotherhithe; Surrey Docks.
17: Newington; Walworth.
18: Plumstead; Plumstead Common; ShootersHill; Woolwich.
19: Dulwich Wood Park; Norwood, Upper.
20: Anerley.
22: Dulwich (East).
23: Forest Hill.
24: Herne Hill.
25: Norwood, South.
26: Sydenham; Sydenham Hill.
27: Norwood, West.
28: Thamesmead Central

■ South-West
2: Brixton; Streatham Hill.
4: Clapham; Larkhall Lane.
8: Battersea Park.
9: Italian Mission, Stockwell.
11: Battersea (West); Clapham Common.
12: Balham; Clapham Park; Earlsfield.
13: Barnes.
14: Mortlake.
15: Putney; Roehampton.
16: Norbury; Streatham.
17: Tooting; Tooting (South East); Tooting Bec.
18: Earlsfield; Wandsworth West Hill; Wandsworth East Hill.
19: Colliers Wood; Wimbledon; Wimbledon (South); Wimbledon Common; Wimbledon Park.
20: Merton.

■ HOSPITALS
To contact the Catholic Chaplain of a particular hospital we suggest you contact the hospital reception directly.

■ DIRECTORY OF CATHOLIC SCHOOLS IN THE DIOCESE
*Schools accommodating boarders

■ LONDON

■ LONDON BOROUGH OF BEXLEY

■ Voluntary Aided

▲ Primary
Our Lady of the Rosary, Holbeach Gardens DA15 8QW **Tel:** 020-8850 4470 *(Blackfen)*

St Thomas More, Sheldon Road DA7 4PH **Tel:** 020-8303 8322 **Fax:** 020-8301 2727 *(Bostall Park)*

St Joseph's, Old Road DA1 4DZ **Tel:** 01322- 524162 *(Crayford)*

St Fidelis, Bexley Road DA8 3HQ **Tel:** 01322-337752 *(Erith)*

St Peter Chanel, Baugh Road DA14 5ED **Tel:** 020-8302 6029 **Fax:** 020-8308 9883 *(Sidcup)*

St John Fisher, Kale Road DA18 4BA **Tel:** 020-8310 7311 *(Thamesmead)*

St Stephen's, Ruskin Avenue, Welling, DA16 3QG **Tel:** 020-8303 9738 *(Welling)*

▲ Secondary
St Catherine's, (G) Watling Street, DA6 7QJ **Tel:** 01322-556333 *(Crayford)*

St Columba's, (B) Halcot Avenue, Bexleyheath, DA6 7QB **Tel:** 01322-553236 **Fax:** 01322-522471 *(Crayford)*

St Mary's & St Joseph's, (M) Chislehurst Road, DA14 6BP **Tel:** 020-8309 7700 **Fax:** 020-8300 6815 *(Sidcup)*

▲ Sixth-Form Colleges
St Luke's Catholic Sixth Form College, Chislehurst Road DA14 6BP. **Tel:** 020-8309 4760, **Fax:** 020-8309 4767 *(Sidcup)*

■ LONDON BOROUGH OF BROMLEY

■ Voluntary Aided

▲ Primary
St Anthony's, Genoa Road SE20 5DE **Tel:** 020-8778 7681 **Fax:** 020-8778 3091 *(Anerley)*

St Mary's, Westgate Road BR3 5DE **Tel:** 020-8650 2355 *(Beckenham)*

St Joseph's, Plaistow Lane BR1 3JQ **Tel:** 020-8460 1976 **Fax:** 020-8466 7508 *(Bromley)*

St Vincent's, Harting Road SE9 4JR **Tel:** 020-8857 5134 *(Mottingham)*

Holy Innocents, Mitchell Road Orpinton BR6 9PT **Tel:** 01689-813040 *(Orpington)*

St James', Maybury Close BR5 1BL **Tel:** 020-8467 8167 *(Petts Wood)*

Fax: 020-8467 8908
St Philomena's, Chelsfield Road BR5 4DR **Tel:** 01689-826550 *(St Mary Cray)*
St Peter and St Paul, St Paul's Wood Hill, Orpington BR5 2SR **Tel:** 01689-828208 *(St Paul's Cray)*

■ **Independent**

▲ **Primary & Secondary**
Bishop Challoner School, (M) Bromley Road BR2 0BS **Tel:** 020-8460 3546 *(Beckenham)*

■ **LONDON BOROUGH OF CROYDON**

■ **Voluntary Aided**

▲ **Infant**
St James the Great, Windsor Road Thornton Heath CR7 8HJ **Tel:** 020-8771 3424 *(Thornton Heath)*
Good Shepherd, Dunley Drive CR0 0RG **Tel:** 01689-841771 *(New Addington)*
St Joseph's, Crown Dale SE19 3NX **Tel:** 020-8670 2385 *(Upper Norwood)*
St Mary's, Bedford Park, CR0 2AQ **Tel:** 020-8688 2891 **Fax:** 020-8688 5955 *(West Croydon)*

▲ **Junior**
St Thomas Becket, Birchanger Road Addiscombe SE25 5BN **Tel:** 020-8654 3006 *(Addiscombe)*
St Aidan's Primary, Portnalls Road CR5 3DE **Tel:** 01737-556036 *(Coulsdon)*
Margaret Roper, Russell Hill CR8 2XP **Tel:** 020-8660 0115 **Fax:** 020-8660 9656 *(Purley)*
Regina Coeli, Kendra Hall Pampisford Road CR2 6DF **Tel:** 020-8688 4582 **Fax:** 020-8688 0225 *(South Croydon)*
St Chad's, Alverston Gardens SE25 6LR **Tel:** 020-8771 3470 *(South Norwood)*
St Joseph's Junior, Woodend, SE19 3NU **Tel:** 020-8653 7195 *(Upper Norwood)*
St Mary's, Junior Sydenham Road CR0 2EW **Tel:** 020-8688 4893 *(West Croydon)*

▲ **Secondary**
Coloma Convent Girls School, (G) Upper Shirley Road CR9 5AS **Tel:** 020-8654 6228 **Fax:** 020-8656 6485 *(Addiscombe)*
St Thomas More, (M) Russell Hill Road CR8 2XP **Tel:** 020-8668 6251 **Fax:** 020-8660 9003. *(Purley)*
St Joseph's College, (B) Beulah Hill SE19 3HL **Tel:** 020-8761 1426 *(Upper Norwood)*
Virgo Fidelis Convent School, (G) Central Hill, SE19 1RS **Tel:** 020-8670 6917 *(Upper Norwood)*
St Mary's High, (M) Woburn Road CR0 2AB **Tel:** 020-8686 3837 **Fax:** 020-8781 1264 *(West Croydon)*

■ **Independent**

▲ **Primary**
Laleham Lea School, Peaks Hill Surrey CR8 3JJ **Tel:** 020-8660 3351 *(Purley)*
Virgo Fidelis Convent Junior School, Central Hill SE19 1RS **Tel:** 020-8653 2169 *(Upper Norwood)*

■ **LONDON BOROUGH OF GREENWICH**

■ **Voluntary Aided and Diocesan Sponsored Academies**

▲ **Primary**
St Thomas a Becket, Mottisfont Road SE2 9LY **Tel:** 020-8310 5394 *(Abbey Wood)*
Our Lady of Grace, 145 Charlton Road SE7 7EZ **Tel:** 020-8858 2262 *(Charlton)*
St Mary's, Glenure Road SE9 1UF **Tel:** 020-8850 7835 **Fax:** 020-8294 2688 *(Eltham)*
St Thomas More, Appleton Road Eltham SE9 6NS **Tel:** 020-8856 9153 **Fax:** 020-8856 6339 *(Eltham Well Hall)*
St Joseph's, Commerell Street SE10 9AN **Tel:** 020-8858 4182 *(Greenwich)*
Holy Family, Tudway Road SE3 9YX **Tel:** 020-8856 2708 **Fax:** 020-8856 1299 *(Kidbrooke)*
St Patrick's, Griffin Road SE18 7QG **Tel:** 020-8854 3881 **Fax:** 020-8855 9288 *(Plumstead)*
Notre Dame, Eglinton Road SE18 3SJ **Tel:** 020-8854 0585 *(Shooter's Hill)*
St Margaret Clitherow, Cole Close SE28 8GB **Tel:** 020-8310 1699 *(Thamesmead)*
St Peter's, Crescent Road SE18 7BN **Tel:** 020-8265 0028 *(Woolwich)*

▲ **Secondary**
St Thomas More, (M) Footscray Road SE9 2SU **Tel:** 020-8850 6700 *(Eltham)*
St Ursula's Convent School, (G) 70 Crooms Hill SE10 8HN **Tel:** 020-8858 4613 **Fax:** 020-8305 0560 *(Greenwich)*
St Paul's Academy, (M) Wickham Lane SE2 0XX **Tel:** 020-8311 3868 **Fax:** 020-8312 1642 *(Plumstead)*

■ **KENT**

■ **Voluntary Aided**

▲ **Primary**
St Simon of England, Noakes Meadow, TN23 4RB **Tel:** 01233 623199 *(Ashford)*
St Teresa's, Quantock Drive, TN24 8QN **Tel:** 01233-622797 *(Ashford)*

St Joseph's, Ackholt Road, CT3 3AS **Tel:** 01304-840370 *(Aylesham)*
St Joseph's School, St Peter's Park Road, CT10 2BA **Tel:** 01843-861738 *(Broadstairs)*
St Thomas School, Old Ruttington Lane, CT1 1NY **Tel:** 01227-462539 *(Canterbury)*
St Anselm's, Littlebrook Manorway, DA1 5EA **Tel:** 01322-225173 *(Dartford)*
Our Lady's, King Edward Avenue, DA1 2HX **Tel:** 01322-222759 **Fax:** 01322-225307 *(Dartford)*
St Mary's, St Richard's Road CT14 9LF **Tel:** 01304-375046 *(Deal)*
St Richard's, Castle Avenue, CT16 1EZ **Tel:** 01304-201118 **Fax:** 01304-242977 *(Dover)*
Stella Maris, Parkfield Road, CT19 5BY **Tel:** 01303 252127 **Fax:** 01303-226085 *(Folkestone)*
St John's, Rochester Road, DA12 2SY **Tel:** 01474-534546 *(Gravesend)*
Our Lady of Hartley, Stack Lane, DA3 8BL **Tel:** 01474-706385. **Fax:** 01474-709757 *(Hartley)*
St Philip Howard, 41-43 Avenue Road, CT6 8TS **Tel:** 01227-362334 *(Herne Bay)*
St Augustine's, St John's Road CT21 4BE **Tel:** 01303-266578 *(Hythe)*
Holy Family, Bicknor Road, Park Wood, ME15 9PS **Tel:** 01622-756778 *(Maidstone)*
St Francis, Queen's Road ME18 5EY. **Tel:** 01622-771540 **Fax:** 01622-771568 *(Maidstone)*
St Gregory's, Nash Road CT9 4BU **Tel:** 01843-221896 *(Margate)*
St Joseph's, Springhead Road, DA11 9QZ **Tel:** 01474-533515 *(Northfleet)*
St Ethelbert's, Dane Park Road, CT11 7LS **Tel:** 01843-585555 *(Ramsgate)*
St Thomas, South Park, TN13 1EH **Tel:** 01732-453921 **Fax:** 01732-460501 *(Sevenoaks)*
St Edward's, New Road, ME12 1BW **Tel:** 01795-662708 *(Sheppey)*
St Peter's, West Ridge, ME10 1UJ **Tel:** 01795-423479 *(Sittingbourne)*
St Bartholomew's, Sycamore Drive BR8 7AY. **Tel:** 01322-663119 *(Swanley)*
St Margaret Clitherow, Trench Road, TN11 9NG **Tel:** 01732-358000 *(Tonbridge)*
St Augustine's, Wilman Road, TN4 9AL **Tel:** 01892-529796 *(Tunbridge Wells)*
More Park, Lucks Hill ME19 6HN **Tel:** 01732-843047 **Fax:** 01732-847706 *(West Malling)*
St Mary's, Northwood Road, CT5 2EY **Tel:** 01227-272692 **Fax:** 01277-770907 *(Whitstable)*

▲ Comprehensive
St Anselm's, Old Dover Road, CT1 3EN **Tel:** 01227-826200 **Fax:** 01227-826201 *(Canterbury)*
St Edmund, Old Charlton Road, CT16 2QB **Tel:** 01304-201551 **Fax:** 01304-202226 *(Dover)*
St John's, Rochester Road, DA12 2JW **Tel:** 01474-534718 **Fax:** 01474-563763 *(Gravesend)*
St Simon Stock, Oakwood Park, ME16 0JP **Tel:** 01622-754551 **Fax:** 01622-691439 *(Maidstone)*
St Gregory's, Reynold's Lane, TN4 9XL **Tel:** 01892-527444 **Fax:** 01892-546621 *(Tunbridge Wells)*
Ursuline College (M), 225 Canterbury Road CT8 8LX **Tel:** 01843-834431 **Fax:** 01843-835365 *(Westgate-on-Sea)*

■ Independent

▲ Primary
St Joseph's Convent Preparatory School, 46 Old Road East DA12 1NR **Tel:** 01474-533012 *(Gravesend)*
St Angela's Junior School, 225 Canterbury Road CT8 8LX **Tel:** 01843-836682 **Fax:** 01843-836685 *(Westgate-on-Sea).*

▲ Primary & Secondary
Combe Bank School, (G) Sundridge, Sevenoaks, TN14 6AE **Tel:** 01959-563720
***Beechwood School - Sacred Heart,** (G) Beechwood, Pembury Road, TN2 3QD **Tel:** 01892-532747 *(Tun. Wells)*

■ LONDON BOROUGH OF KINGSTON-UPON-THAMES

■ Voluntary Aided

▲ Primary
St Agatha, St Agatha's Drive KT2 5TY **Tel:** 020-8546 3879 *(Kingston)*
Corpus Christi, Chestnut Grove KT3 3JU **Tel:** 020-8942 2645 **Fax:** 020-8336 0790 *(New Malden)*
St Joseph's, Fairfield KT1 2UP **Tel:** 020-8546 7178 *(Surbiton)*
Our Lady Immaculate, 399 Ewell Road KT6 7DG **Tel:** 020-8399 9854 *(Tolworth)*

▲ Secondary
Richard Challoner, (B) Manor Drive North KT3 5PE **Tel:** 020-8330 5947 **Fax:** 020-8330 3842 *(Malden Manor)*
Holy Cross, (G) 25 Sandal Road, KT3 5AR **Tel:** 020-8395 4225 **Fax:** 020-8395 4234 *(New Malden)*

■ **Independent**

▲ **Primary**

Holy Cross Preparatory School, Coombe Ridge House George Road KT2 7NU **Tel:** 020-8942 0729 *(Kingston Hill)*

▲ **Secondary**

***Marymount International School,** (G) George Road KT2 7PE **Tel:** 020-8949 0571 *(Kingston Hill)*

■ **LONDON BOROUGH OF LAMBETH**

■ **Voluntary Aided**

▲ **Infants**

St Bede's Infants, Thornton Road, SW12 0LF **Tel:** 020-8674 7292 *(Clapham Park)*

▲ **Primary**

St Helen's, Knowle Close, SW9 0TH **Tel:** 020-7274 4343 *(Brixton)*

Corpus Christi, Trent Road, Brixton, SW2 5BL **Tel:** 020-7274 4722 *(Brixton Hill)*

St Mary's, Crescent Lane, SW4 9QJ **Tel:** 020-7622 5479 *(Clapham)*

St Andrew's, Polworth Road, SW16 2ET **Tel:** 020-8769 4980 *(Streatham)*

St Anne's, 6 Durham Street, SE11 5JA **Tel:** 020-7735 4516 **Fax:** 020-7820 8757 *(Vauxhall)*

▲ **Juniors**

St Bernadette's, Atkins Road, SW12 0AB **Tel:** 020-8673 2061 *(Clapham Park)*

▲ **Secondary**

La Retraite High School, (G) Atkins Road SW12 0AB **Tel:** 020-8673 5644 **Fax:** 020-8675 8577 *(Clapham Park)*

Bishop Thomas Grant, (M) Belltrees Grove, SW16 2HY **Tel:** 020-8769 3294 **Fax:** 020-8769 4917 *(Streatham)*

■ **LONDON BOROUGH OF LEWISHAM**

■ **Voluntary Aided and Diocesan Sponsored Academies**

▲ **Primary**

St Winifred's Infants, 103 Effingham Road, SE12 8NS **Tel:** 020-8852 0187 **Fax:** 020-8297 0089 *(Lee)*

St Augustine's, Dunfield Road, SE6 3RD **Tel:** 020-8698 6083 *(Beckenham Hill)*

Our Lady of Lourdes, *(closes August 2007)* Belmont Hill, SE13 5DZ **Tel:** 020-8852 7337 *(Blackheath)*

St Mary Magdalen's, Howson Road, SE4 2BB **Tel:** 020-8692 5055 *(Brockley)*

Holy Cross, Culverley Road, SE6 2LD **Tel:** 020-8698 2675 *(Catford)*

St Joseph's, Crossfield Street, SE8 3PH **Tel:** 020-8692 4836 **Fax:** 020-8694 6421 *(Deptford)*

St Matthew Academy, St Joseph's Vale, Blackheath SE3 0XX **Tel:** 020-8852 5614 *(Blackheath)*

Good Shepherd, Moorside Road, Downham, BR1 5EP **Tel:** 020-8698 4173 *(Downham)*

St William of York, Brockley Park, SE23 1PS **Tel:** 020-8690 2842 *(Forest Hill)*

St Saviour's, 10 Bonfield Road, SE13 6AL **Tel:** 020-8852 4283 *(Lewisham)*

Our Lady & St Philip Neri, 208 Sydenham Road, SE26 5SE **Tel:** 020-8778 4386 **Fax:** 020-8776 5102 *(Sydenham)*

St Winifred's Junior, Newstead Road, SE12 0SJ **Tel:** 020-8857 8792 *(Lee)*

▲ **Secondary**

St Matthew Academy, St Joseph's Vale, Blackheath SE3 0XX **Tel:** 020-8852 5614*(Blackheath)*

Bonus Pastor, (M) Winlaton Road, BR1 5PZ **Tel:** 020-8695 2100 **Fax:** 020-8695 2105. *Churchdown site:* **Tel:** 020-8695 2110 *(Downham)*

▲ **Sixth-Form College**

Christ the King College, Belmont Grove, SE13 5GE **Tel:** 020-8297 9433 **Fax:** 020-8297 1460 *(Lewisham)*

■ **MEDWAY TOWN UNITARY AUTHORITY**

■ **Voluntary Aided**

▲ **Primary**

St Michael's, Hills Terrace, ME4 6PX **Tel:** 01634-842922 *(Chatham)*

St Mary's, Greenfield Road, ME7 1YH **Tel:** 01634-855783 *(Gillingham)*

St Augustine of Canterbury, Deanwood Drive, ME8 9NP **Tel:** 01634-371892 *(Parkwood & Wigmore)*

St Thomas of Canterbury, Romany Road, ME8 6JH **Tel:** 01634-234677 *(Rainham)*

St William of Perth, Canon Close, Maidstone Road, ME1 3EN **Tel:** 01634-404267 *(Rochester)*

English Martyrs, Frindsbury Road, ME2 4JA **Tel:** 01634-718964 **Fax:** 01634-297811 *(Strood)*

St Thomas More, Bleak Wood, Walderslade, ME5 0NF **Tel:** 01634-864701 *(Walderslade)*

St Benedict's, Lambourn Way, Lordswood, ME5 8PU **Tel:** 01634-669700 *(Walderslade)*

▲ **Comprehensive**

St John Fisher, Ordnance Street, ME4 6SG **Tel:** 01634-842811 *(Chatham)*

■ LONDON BOROUGH OF MERTON

■ Voluntary Aided

▲ Primary

St John Fisher, Grand Drive, SW20 6NA **Tel:** 020-8540 2637 **Fax:** 020-8540 2988 *(Merton)*
Ss. Peter and Paul, Cricket Green, CR4 4LA **Tel:** 020-8648 1459 *(Mitcham)*
St Teresa's, Montacute Road, SM4 6RL **Tel:** 020-8648 1846 *(Morden)*
Sacred Heart, Burlington Road, KT3 4ND **Tel:** 020-80942 0215 *(Wimbledon)*
St Mary's, Russell Road, SW19 1QL **Tel:** 020-8542 4580 **Fax:** 020-8542 5301 *(Wimbledon South)*
St Thomas of Canterbury, Commonside East, CR4 1YG **Tel:** 020-8648 0869 *(Mitcham)*

▲ Comprehensive

Ursuline High School, (G) Crescent Road, SW20 8HA **Tel:** 020-255 2688 **Fax:** 020-8255 2687 *(Wimbledon)*
Wimbledon College, (B) Edge Hill, SW19 4NS **Tel:** 020-8946 2533 **Fax:** 020-8947 6513 *(Wimbledon)*

■ Independent

▲ Primary

The Prep - Ursuline, Wimbledon, 18 The Downs, SW20 8HR **Tel:** 020-8947 0859 *(Wimbledon)*
Wimbledon College Preparatory School, Donhead Lodge, Edge Hill, SW19 4NP **Tel:** 020-8946 7000 *(Wimbledon)*

■ LONDON BOROUGH OF RICHMOND-UPON-THAMES

■ Voluntary Aided

▲ Primary

St Osmund's, 45, Church Road SW13 9HQ **Tel:** 020-8748 3582 *(Barnes)*
St Mary Magdalen's, Worple Street, SW14 8HE **Tel:** 020-8876 6679 *(Mortlake)*
St Elizabeth, Queen's Road, TW10 6HN **Tel:** 020-8940 3015 *(Richmond)*

■ LONDON BOROUGH OF SOUTHWARK

■ Voluntary Aided

▲ Primary

St Joseph's Infants, Pitman Street, SE5 0TS **Tel:** 020-7703 9264 *(Camberwell)*
St Joseph's, 89 George Row, SE16 4UP **Tel:** 020-7237 4267 *(Bermondsey)*
St Joseph's, Little Dorrit Court, Redcross Way SE1 1NJ **Tel:** 020-7407 2642 *(Borough)*
St Anthony's, Etherow Street, SE22 0LA **Tel:** 020-8693 6852 **Fax:** 020-8693 2958 *(Dulwich)*
St Francesca Cabrini, Honor Oak Park, SE23 3LE **Tel:** 020-8699 8862 *(Forest Hill)*
St Francis, Friary Road, SE15 1RQ **Tel:** 020-7639 0187 *(Peckham)*
St James the Great, Peckham Road SE15 5LP **Tel:** 020-7703 5870 **Fax:** 020-7277 1491 *(Peckham Rye)*
St Joseph's, Gomm Road, SE16 2TY **Tel:** 020-7237 4036 *(Rotherhithe)*
St George's Cathedral School, 33 Westminster Bridge Road, SE1 7JB **Tel:** 020-7525 9250 **Fax:** 020-7525 9251 *(Cathedral)*
St John's, St Elmo's Road, SE16 1SA **Tel:** 020-7252 1859 *(Surrey Docks)*
English Martyrs, Flint Street, SE17 1QD **Tel:** 020-7703 4726 **Fax:** 020-7277 1743 *(Walworth)*

▲ Junior

St Joseph's Juniors, Pitman Street, SE5 0TS **Tel:** 020-7703 3455 *(Camberwell)*

▲ Secondary

St Michael's, (M) John Felton Road, SE16 4UN **Tel:** 020-7237 6432 **Fax:** 020-7252 2411 *(Bermondsey)*
Sacred Heart, (M) Camberwell New Road, SE5 0RP **Tel:** 020-7274 6844 **Fax:** 020-7737 1713 *(Camberwell)*
St Thomas the Apostle College, (B) Hollydale Road, SE15 2EB **Tel:** 020-7639 0106 **Fax:** 020-7277 5471 *(Nunhead)*
Notre Dame, (G) 118 St George's Road, SE1 6EX **Tel:** 020-7261 1121 **Fax:** 020-7620 2922 *(Cathedral)*

■ LONDON BOROUGH OF SUTTON

■ Voluntary Aided

▲ Primary

St Mary's, Infants West Street, SM5 2PT **Tel:** 020-8647 5711 *(Carshalton)*
St Elphege's, Mollison Drive, Roundshaw, SM6 9HY **Tel:** 020-8669 6306 *(Wallington)*
St Celilia's, London Road, SM3 9DL **Tel:** 020-8337 4566 *(Cheam)*

▲ Junior

St Mary's Junior, Shorts Road, SM5 2PB **Tel:** 020-8647 4342 *(Carshalton)*
St Elphege's Junior, Mollison Drive, Roundshaw, SM6 9HY **Tel:** 020-8669 4130 *(Wallington)*

▲ Secondary

St Philomena's, (G) Pound Street, SM5

3PS **Tel:** 020-8642 2025 **Fax:** 020-8643 7925 *(Carshalton)*
The John Fisher School, (B) Peaks Hill, CR8 3YP **Tel:** 020-8660 4555 **Fax:** 020-8763 1837 *(Purley)*

■ LONDON BOROUGH OF WANDSWORTH

■ Voluntary Aided

▲ Primary

Holy Ghost, Nightingale Square, SW12 8QJ **Tel:** 020-8673 3080 *(Balham)*
St Mary's, Lockington Road, SW8 4BE **Tel:** 020-7622 5460 *(Battersea)*
Sacred Heart, Este Road, SW11 2TD **Tel:** 020-7223 5611 *(Battersea West)*
Our Lady of Victories, Clarendon Drive, SW15 1AW **Tel:** 020-8788 7957 *(Putney)*
Sacred Heart, Roehampton Lane, SW15 5NX **Tel:** 020-8876 7074 *(Roehampton)*
St Boniface, Undine Street, SW17 8PP **Tel:** 020-8672 5874 *(Tooting)*
St Anselm's, Tooting Bec Road, SW17 8BS **Tel:** 020-8672 9227 *(Tooting Bec)*
St Joseph's, 90 Oakhill Road, Putney, SW15 2QD **Tel:** 020-8874 1888 **Fax:** 020-8870 5900 *(Wandsworth)*
Our Lady, Queen of Heaven, Victoria Drive, SW19 6AD **Tel:** 020-8788 7420 *(Wimbledon Common)*

▲ Comprehensive

Salesian College, (B) Parkham Street, SW11 3PB **Tel:** 020-7228 2857 **Fax:** 020-7223 4921 *(Battersea)*
John Paul II, (M) Princes Way, SW19 6QE **Tel:** 020-8788 8142 **Fax:** 020-8780 1393 *(Wimbledon Common)*

▲ Sixth-Form College

St Francis Xavier College, (M) Malwood Road, SW12 8EN **Tel:** 020-8772 6000 **Fax:** 020-8772 6099 *(Balham)*

DIOCESE OF WREXHAM

(Province of Cardiff)
Established, by a decree of Pope John Paul II on l8 March 1987, from territory taken from the Diocese of Menevia.
Consisting of the Counties of Aberconwy & Colwyn, Anglesey, Denbighshire, Flintshire, Gwynedd, Wrexham & the District of Montgomery in the County of Powys.

Patron of the Diocese
St David, 1 March.

Bishop
Rt Rev Bishop Edwin Regan, Born Port Talbot, West Glam, 31st December 1935; Ordained Priest 5th July 1959; Ordained Bishop by Archbishop John Aloysius Ward, OFM, Cap, 13th December 1994.

Residence:
Bishop's House, Sontley Road, Wrexham, LL13 7EW
Tel: 01978-262726 **Fax:** 01978-354257
E-mail: diowxm@globalnet.co.uk
Website: www.wrexhamdiocese.freeuk.com

Rt Rev Edwin Regan, Bishop of Wrexham

■ ADMINISTRATION

■ Diocesan Curia
Bishop's House, Wrexham.
Tel: 01978-262726 **Fax:** 01978-354257

■ Vicar General
Canon Peter M Brignall VG, Cathedral Church of Our Lady of Sorrows, Regent Street, Wrexham LL11 1RB
Tel: 01978-263943
Fax: 01978-352277
E-mail: office@wrexhamcathedral.fsnet.co.uk

■ Bishop's Secretary
Mrs Cathy Coppack

■ Diocesan Year Book Editor
Counc Jim Kelly KSG.

■ Chancellor
Moderator of the Curia: **Rev James Webb**. St David's Lane, Ffordd Fain, Mold CH7 1LH
Tel: 01352-752087 **Fax:** 01352-700488

■ Diocesan Financial Secretary
Mr Peter Taaffe, c/o Bishop's House,
Tel: 01978-262726 **Fax:** 01978-354257

■ Information Officer
c/o Bishop's House.

■ Registrar for Deceased Clergy
Mrs Cathy Coppack. Bishop's House, Sontley Road, Wrexham, LL13 7EW
Tel: 01978-262726

■ Diocesan Solicitors
Allington Hughes. 10 Grosvenor Road, Wrexham, LL11 1SD **Tel:** 01978-291000

■ Diocesan Finance Committee
Chairman: **Rev Adrian Wilcock; Mr Peter Taaffe** (*Diocesan Financial Secretary*). *Adviser:* **Mr R Thorn** (Quilter & Co), **Mr P Craddock, Mrs Cathy Coppack** (*Secretary*).

■ Diocesan Trustees
Mr Keith McDonogh (*Chairman*), **Revv Bernard Morgan, Adrian Wilcock, Peter Brignall, James Webb, Mrs Kathryn Byrne, Mrs Cathy Coppack** (*Secretary*).

■ Diocesan Accountants
Bresnan, Walsh & Co, 1 Water Street, Liverpool L2 0RD **Tel:** 0151-236 1494

■ Diocesan Insurance
Catholic Church Insurance Association, PO Box 15392, Glasgow G2 2YS
Tel: 0845-603 0337 **Fax:** 0141-221 5409.

■ EDUCATION AND FORMATION

■ Diocesan Education Committee
Director of Education: **Mrs Rita Price,** *Deputy Director:* **Katherine Ransome,** *Chairman:* **Counc Jim Kelly**. Bishop's House, Sontley Road, Wrexham LL13 7EW
Tel: 01978-290344 **Fax:** 01978-354257

■ Diocesan Director of Pontifical Missions Societies
Rev Francis Doyle, 54 High Street, Saltney,

Flintshire CH4 8SF **Tel:** 01244-671581
E-mail: catholicchurch@saltney.fslife.co.uk

■ **Diocesan Director of Religious Education**
Rev Adrian Morrin. 2 Cwrt Brenig, Buckley CH7 2BF

■ **Diocesan Director of Vocations**
Canon D B Lordan, King Edward Street, Barmouth LL42 1PE **Tel:** 01341-280489

■ **Diocesan Admissions Board**
Bishop Regan, Rev B Lordan, Rev Francis Gerrard; Sr Sheila O'Hara, Counc Jim Kelly KSG; Rev Deacon David Joy

■ **Diocesan Vocation Team**
Revv Antony Jones, Bernard Lordon, Mr James Kirkham, Mrs Heidi Roe, Mr Paul Rowlands.

■ **LITURGY AND ECUMENISM**

■ **Diocesan Christian Unity Commission**
Chairperson: Awaiting Appointment

■ **Diocesan Liturgical Commission**
Chairperson: **Canon Peter M Brignall**. Cathedral Church of Our Lady of Sorrows, Regent Street, Wrexham LL11 1RB
Tel: 01978-263943 **Fax:** 01978-352277

■ **Diocesan Archivist**
Mrs K Byrne BA, ALA, Bishop's House, Sontley Road, Wrexham, LL13 7EW

■ **Diocesan Youth Commission**
Chairperson: c/o Bishop's House.

■ **Diocesan Family Life Commission**
Chair: Awaiting appointment.

■ **Child Protection Co-ordinator**
Mr Keith McDonogh, c/o Bishop's House.
Parish Designated Person Co-ordinator: **Mrs Pam Hunt**, Gerddi Beuno, Whitford Street, Holywell, Flintshire CH8 7NJ
Tel: 01352-712392

■ **CONSULTATIVE BODIES**

■ **Cathedral Chapter**
Provost: **Mgr James Feeley.**
Canons: **Leonard Quigley, Bernard Morgan, Peter Brignall, James Webb, Bernard Lordan.**
Canon Emeriti: **Philip B Webb**.

■ **National Council of Priests**
Revv Owen Hardwicke. Terence Carr, Charles Ramsey, Francis Gerrard.

■ **Council of Priests**
Secretary: **Rev Francis Doyle**, 54 High Street, Saltney, Flintshire CH4 8SF
Tel: 01244-671581
E-mail: catholicchurch@saltney.fslife.co.uk

■ **DIOCESAN MATRIMONIAL TRIBUNAL**
Rev Terence Carr (*Judicial Vicar*). **Sr Isabel McPherson SND** (*Defensor Vinculi*); **Rev Paschal Dormer BA(Th), DipTheol; Rev P Hunt, Sr Helen Randle, Mrs P Hunt, Mrs M Joy** (*Auditors*); **Mrs Carole E Philpot** (*Administrator*); ***Judges:*** **Canon Leonard N Quigley, Canon Bernard Morgan.**
Tel: 01978-262726 **Fax:** 01978-354257
E-mail: diowxm@globalnet.co.uk

■ **Bishop's Advisor on Hospital Chaplaincy**
Canon Peter M Brignall, Cathedral Church of Our Lady of Sorrows, Regent Street, Wrexham LL11 1RB
Tel: 01978-263943
Fax: 01978-352277
E-mail: office@wrexham-cathedral.fsnet.co.uk

■ **WREXHAM**
Cathedral Church
of Our Lady of Sorrows
(1828; 1857; cons 7 November 1907)
Regent Street, Wrexham.
Tel: 01978-263943 **Fax:** 01978-352277
Canon Peter M Brignall (*Cathedral Dean & Vicar General*), Cathedral of Our Lady of Sorrows, Regent Street, Wrexham LL11 1RB **Tel: (Voice/Text)** 01978-263943
Revv Christopher Howard, Marious Obalka, St. Therese of Lisieux, Dundonald Avenue, Abergele, Conwy
Tel: 01745 833249
E-mail: office@wrexham-cathedral.fsnet.co.uk
Website: www.wrexhamcathedral.org.uk
Deacons: **Rev Iain Cameron**. 58 Beechley Road, Wrexham. LL13 7BA
Tel: 01978-290287
M: *Sun 10.30am, 7pm.*
Hds 9am, 12noon, 8pm.
Polish Mass Every Sunday 9.30am.

- ***Sisters of the Holy Family of Bordeaux,*** Holy Family Convent, Sontley Road, LL13 7EN **Tel:** 01978-262867 *Chaplain:* **Mgr P Webb**.
- ***Sisters of St Joseph (of Chambery),*** St Joseph's Convent, Derby Road LL13 8EA **Tel:** 01978-291175 **Fax:** 01978-365420
- ***Congregation of La Sainte Union des Sacres Coeurs,*** Peace Studies Centre, 35-37 Kings Mills Road, Wrexham LL13 8NH **Tel:** 01978-356969

■ **ABERDYFI,** Gwynedd
Christ the King (1942; 1975)
Penrhos, Aberdyfi, Gwynedd.
Served from Tywyn
M: *Sat 1st M of Sun 6pm. Hds see notice board.*

■ **ABERGELE,** Denbighshire
† **St Therese of Lisieux** (1934)
Dundonald Avenue, Abergele, Denbigh.
Tel: 01745-833249 **E-mail:** st-theresa-abergele@btopenworld.com
Rev Simon Treloar. 1 Clwyd Avenue LL22 7NF *Deacon:* **Rev John Abbott.** 6 Coed Masarn, Abergele, Conwy.
Tel: 01745-824888 **Fax:** 01745-822760
M: *Sat 1st M of Sun 4.30pm. Sun 9.30am. Hds (vigil 4.30pm), 9.30am.*

■ **ABERSOCH,** Gwynedd
St Garmon (1955)
Tel: 01758-712778 Served from Pwllheli.
M: *Easter to Oct, Sat 6pm, Sun 9.30am.*

■ **AMLWCH,** Anglesey
† **Our Lady of the Sea and St Winefride** (1935)
Bull Bay Road, Amlwch, Anglesey.
Tel: 01407-830361

- ***Oblates of Mary Immaculate (OMI):*** **Revv Declan O'Keefe, Michael Hennessy**. St Joseph's Presbytery, Eryl Mor, Bull Bay Road, Amlwch, LL68 9ED
M: *No Sun Mass. Hds 10am in the Presbytery*

■ **BALA,** Gwynedd
† **Our Lady of Fatima** (1932; 1948)
High Street, Bala, Gwynedd LL40 1LR
Tel: 01341-422805 Served from Dolgellau.
Rev Joshy Thomas Cheruparambil CMI, *Pastoral Assistant:* **Sr Patricia Lane IBVM**.

- ***Institute of the Blessed Virgin Mary, Loreto Sisters:*** 67 High Street, Bala, Gwynedd LL23 7AE **Tel:** 01678-520441
M: *Sun 9am at Parish Church, 5pm at Carmelite Monastry*

■ **BANGOR,** Gwynedd
1. † **Our Lady and St James**
(1827; 1834; New Church 1866; 1996)
Holyhead Road, Bangor, Gwynedd.
Tel: 01248-370421 **Fax:** 01248-372066
E-mail: office@bangorcatholic.fsworld.co.uk
Canon Bernard Morgan. Tyr Offeiriad, 6 Victoria Park, Bangor, Gwynedd LL57 2EW
Tel: 01248-370421 **Fax:** 01248-372066
M: *Sun 10.30am, 6.30pm. Hds 10am, 7.30pm.*

- ***Sisters of Mercy,*** Ty Mair, Menai Avenue, LL57 2HH **Tel:** 01248-353670
- ***Ysbyty Gwynedd Hospital Chaplain:*** **Canon Bernard Morgan,** **Tel:** 01248-384384
M: *Sat 1st M of Sun 4.30pm.*

2. **University Chaplaincy**
Pendyffryn, Menai Avenue, Bangor, Gwynedd. LL57 2HH
Tel: 01248-352522 (Chaplain)
Tel: 01248-352262 (Students)
E-mail: rcchaplainbangor@aol.com
Website: www.bangor.ac.uk/catholic
Lay Chaplain: **Miss Katherine Dunkley**.
M: *Sun (during term time) 6pm.*

■ **BARMOUTH,** Gwynedd
† **St Tudwal** (1885; 1905; cons 14 Aug 1909)
King Edward Street, Barmouth, LL42 1PE
Tel: 01341-280489
Canon Daniel Bernard Lordan.
The Presbytery, St Tudwal, King Edward St, Barmouth, Gwynedd LL4Z 1PE
Tel: 01341 280489
M: *Sat 1st M of Sun 7pm, (Beginning May to end of Sept) Sun 11am. Hds 7.45am, 7pm.*

■ **BEAUMARIS,** Anglesey
† **Our Lady Queen of Martyrs** (1898; 1910)
2 Rating Row, Beaumaris, LL58 8AL
Tel: 01248-810318

- ***Oblates of Mary Immaculate (OMI):*** **Rev Edward McSherry** (*Parish Priest*), *Deacon:* **Tony Griffiths**
  M: *Sun 9am. Hds 9am.*

■ **BEDDGELERT,** Gwynedd
St Mary (Anglican Church in Wales)
Stryd yr Eglwys, Beddgelert, Gwynedd.
Served from Porthmadog.
M: *Sun 4pm. Hds 4pm.*

■ **BENLLECH,** Anglesey
Our Lady of Lourdes (1965)
Beach Road, Benllech, Anglesey.
Served from Amlwch.
M: *Sun 9am. Hds 7.30pm.*
Nearest Mass Centre for Red Wharf Bay, Pentraeth, Llanbedrgoch, Brynteg, Marianglas and Moelfre.

■ **BETHESDA,** Gwynedd
St Pius X and St Richard Gwyn (1963)
Bethesda, Gwynedd.
Served from Bangor.
M: *Sat 1st M of Sun, 6.30pm.*

■ **BETTWS-Y-COED,** Conwy
Served from Llanrwst (2).

■ **BLAENAU FFESTINIOG,** Gwynedd
† **St Mary Magdalene**
(New church 1969; cons 2 Aug 1975)
Tel: 01766-830409
Nearest Church for Roman Bridge
- ***Oblates of Mary Immaculate (OMI):*** **Rev Sean Hynes**. Bethania, 6 Geufron Ter, LL41 3BW
  M: *Sun 11am. Hds 12noon.*

■ **BUCKLEY,** Flintshire
† **Our Lady of the Rosary** (1890; 1893, 1999)
Jubilee Road CH7 2EH
Tel: 01244-550363 **Fax:** 01244-545546
E-mail: olrbuckley@aol.com
Rev Adrian Morrin.
M: *Sun 9.30am, 5pm. Hds 10am, 7.30pm.*

■ **CAERNARFON,** Gwynedd
† **St David and St Helen** (1865; 1890; 1986)
Twthill East, Caernarfon LL55 2PF
Tel: 01286-673129
Rev José Aykaraparampil CMI
M: *Sat 1st M of Sun 6pm. Sun 10.30am. Hds 9am, 7.30pm. Mass in Welsh: Last Sun of month*

■ **CEMAES BAY,** Anglesey
St David (1965)
Athol Street, Cemaes Bay, Anglesey.
Served from Amlwch.
M: *Sat 1st M of Sun 6pm. Hds 6pm.*

■ **CHIRK,** Wrexham
† **Sacred Heart of Jesus** (1928)
Station Road, Chirk, Wrexham.
Served from Ruabon.
M: *Sun 9am. Hds 10am.*

■ **COEDPOETH,** Wrexham
The Holy Family (1991)
Queen's Place, Park Road, (Off High Street), Coedpoeth, Wrexham.
Served from Wrexham (1).
M: *Sun 9.30am. Hds See notices.*

■ **COLWYN BAY,** Conwy
† **St Joseph** (1895; 1900; cons 1975)
63 Conway Road, Colwyn Bay LL29 7LG
Tel: 01492-532670 **Fax:** 01492-534515
- ***Oblates of Mary Immaculate (OMI):*** **Rev Joseph Daly** (*Superior & Parish Priest*), **Rev Fr Brendan O'Sullivan**.
  M: *Sat 1st M of Sun 5.30pm. Sun 9.30am. Hds 9.30am, 12 noon, 7pm. Vigil - when Holy Day falls on Thurs - 7pm Weds.*
- ***Sisters of Mercy,*** 20 Walshaw Avenue, LL29 7UY **Tel:** 01492-532331
- ***Congregation of La Sainte Union des Sacres Coeurs,*** 2 Pwllycrochan Avenue, LL29 7DA **Tel:** 01492-530698

■ **CONNAH'S QUAY,** Deeside, Flintshire
† **Blessed Sacrament** (1910)
High Street, Connah's Quay, Deeside.
Tel: 01244-830358
Rev David Eccleshare. Maude Street, Connah's Quay, CH5 4EQ
M: *Sat 1st M of Sun 5.30pm (Winter time only). Sun 11am. Hds (vigil 7pm). 9am (School), 12noon (Parish).*
- ***Ursulines (Roman Union)***, 2 Beaconsfield Road, Shotton, CH5 1EZ
  Tel: 01244-830692 **Fax:** 01244-816012

■ **CONWY,** Conwy
† **St Michael and All Angels** (1907; 1916)
Rosemary Lane, Conwy, LL32 8HY
Tel: 01492-583048
Mgr James Fealy. 1 Victoria Drive, Llandudno Junction, LL31 9NU
M: *Sun 9am. Hds 7.30pm.*
Nearest church for Roe-Wen, Tal-y-Bontand Tyn-y-Groes, Morfa Camp and Gorse Hill.

■ **CRICCIETH,** Gwynedd
The Holy Spirit (1956)
Caernarfon Road Criccieth, Gwynedd.
Served from Porthmadog.
M: *Sat 1st M of Sun, 6pm.*

■ **DENBIGH,** Denbighshire
† **St Joseph** (1852; 1863; 1968; cons 1976)
Lon Llewelyn, Denbigh, Denbighshire LL16 3NT **Tel:** 01745-812297
E-mail: stjoseph@tiscali.co.uk
Parish Priest: **Rev Ian Dalgleish**
M: *Sun 10am, 4.30pm. Hds 10am, 7pm (may vary, see Notices).*

Nearest Mass Centre for Bodfari, Llandyrnog, Llannefydd, Nantglyn and Trefnant.

- ***Sisters of St Brigid,*** 3 Bron Castell, LL16 3NS **Tel:** 01745-817498

■ **DOLGELLAU,** Gwynedd
† Our Lady of Seven Sorrows
Meyrick Street, Dolgellau, Gwynedd LL40 1LR **Tel:** 01341-422805
Fax: 01341-421040 **E-mail:**olssdolgellau@wrexhamdiocese.fsnet.co.uk
Rev Pius Matthews CMI, St Francis of Assisi, Llay Chain, Llay, Wrexham
Tel: 01978 852297
E-mail: piuscmi@hotmail.com
M: *Sun 9am (Church), 5pm (Monastery). Hds 7pm (Parish Church).*

- ***Carmelites,*** Cader Road, Dolgellau LL40 1SH **Tel:** 01341-422546
M: *Sun 5pm. Hds 9.30am, 7pm.*

■ **FAIRBOURNE,** Gwynedd
St Cynon's
Served from Dolgellau.
M: *See Notice Board in Dolgellau Church.*

■ **FLINT,** Flintshire
† Church of the Immaculate Conception (1854; 1885)
17 Coleshill Street, Flint, CH6 5BQ
Tel: 01352-732245 **Fax:** 01352-731968
Revv Adrian Wilcock, George McLoughlin.
Deacon: **Rev Peter Brownbill.** 5 Maes Alaw, Flint, Clwyd **Tel:** 01352-734227
M: *Sat 1st M of Sun 6pm. Sun 10.30am, 6.30pm. Hds See Bulletin for details.*

■ **GELLILYDAN,** Gwynedd
† Church of the Holy Cross (1952)
Served from Blaenau Ffestiniog.
M: Sat 1st M of Sun 6pm. *Hds Eve 7pm.*

■ **HARLECH,** Gwynedd
St David In Seion
Served from Barmouth.
M: *Sun 9am. Hds (vigil 7pm).*

■ **HAWARDEN,** Deeside, Flintshire
† The Sacred Heart (1922; 1967)
The Highway, Hawarden, Deeside.
E-mail: canon@sacredheart.fsworld.co.uk
Canon Leonard Quigley. 6 Fron Heulog, Hawarden, Deeside **Tel:** 01244 537874
M: *Sun 10.30am. Hds 7.30pm.*

- ***Poor Clares (Colettines),*** Upper Aston Hall Lane, CH5 3EN **Tel:** 01244-531029
M: *Sun 4pm. Hds 8.15am.*

■ **HOLYHEAD,** Anglesey
† St Mary Help of Christians (1855; 1860; 1965)
Longford Road, Holyhead, Anglesey.
Tel: 01407-762102 **Fax:** 01407-765759
E-mail: holyhead@omianglesey.org
Website: www.omianglesey.org

- ***Oblates of Mary Immaculate (OMI):*** **Rev Lorcan O'Reilly** (*Superior & Parish Priest*), St Mary's Presbytery, Longford Road, LL65 1TR
M: *Sat 1st M of Sun 6pm. Sun 11am. Hds 10am, 12 noon.*
- ***Sisters of the Good Saviour,*** Bryn Hyfryd, Longford Road, LL65 1TR
Tel: 01407-762084

■ **HOLYWELL,** Flintshire
† St Winefride (1833)
15 Well Street, Holywell, Flintshire CH8 7PL **Tel:** 01352-713181
Fax: 01352-715231
Deacon: **Rev Peter Hunt.** Gerddi Beuno, Whitford Street, Holywell CH8 7NJ
Tel: 01352-712392 **Fax:** 01352-715231
M: *Sat 1st M of Sun 6pm. Sun 9.30am. Hds 10am (in school), 7pm.*

- ***Vocationalist Fathers,*** **Rev Salvatore Musella** *(Parish Priest).*
- ***Little Sisters of the Assumption,*** Order of the Most Holy Saviour of St Bridget, 20 New Road, Holywell, Flint CH8 7LS
- ***St Winefride's Well, Holywell***, for details contact, The Custodian.
Tel: 01352-713054
- ***Bridgettine Sisters (OSsS),*** Bryn Abbey, Strand Lane, CH8 7AG
Tel: 01352-711890

■ **LLANBERIS,** Gwynedd
† St John Jones (1981)
Charlotte Street, Llanberis, Gwynedd.
Served from Caernarfon
M: *Sun 9am. Hds 4pm. (Mass in Welsh, First Sunday of the month)*

■ **LLANDUDNO,** Conwy
† Our Lady Star of the Sea (1893)
35 Lloyd Street, Llandudno LL30 2YA
Tel: 01492-860546
E-mail: ajserenymor@fsnet.co.uk
Rev Antony Jones.
M: *Sat 1st M of Sun (Welsh) 12 Noon, 2nd M (English) 5.30pm. Sun 9.30am. Hds 12 Noon, 8pm.*

- ***Sisters of Loreto,*** Abbey Road, LL30 2EL
Tel: 01492-876093 Loreto Centre
Tel: 01492-878031 **Fax:** 01492-878031
Provincialate, **Tel:** 01492-879656

■ **LLANDUDNO JUNCTION,** Conwy.
† Most Holy Family.
Bryn Eglwys off Victoria Drive, Llandudno LL31 9NU
Tel: 01492-583048
Mgr Provost James Fealy. 1 Victoria Drive, Llandudno LL31 9NU

M: *Sun 11am. Hds 10am.*

■ **LLANFAIRFECHAN,** Conwy
St Mary of the Angels (1953)
Village Road, Llanfairfechan, Conwy.
M: *Sat 1st M of Sun, 6pm. Hds 7.30pm.*

■ **LLANFECHAIN**
† **St Garmon's** C in Wales Church
Served from Welshpool.
M: *Sun 11.30am. Hds 11.30am.*

■ **LLANGEFNI,** Anglesey [A]
St Joseph (1942; 1951; new church cons May 1971)
30 Lon Tudur, Penmynnydd Road,
Llangefni, LL77 7HP Served from Beaumaris.
M: *Sun 11am. Hds 7.30pm.*
- ***Sisters of Mercy,*** 29, Ty'n Coed Estate, Llangefni, Anglesey. LL77 8YX
Tel: 01248-724175

■ **LLANGOLLEN,** Denbighshire [A]
† **Eglwys y Groes (Holy Cross)** (1948; 1961)
Heol-y-Dderwen, Llangollen, LL20 8NR
Tel: 01978-860639
Rev Joseph Stewart.
M: *Sat 1st M of Sun 6pm. Hds (vigil 7pm). 10am (Feast Day).*

■ **LLANIDLOES,** Powys
† **Our Lady and St Richard Gwyn** (1951; 1959)
Penygreen, Llanidloes, Powys SY18 6AJ
Tel: 01597-810542 Served from Newtown
Rev Peter Wilkie, The Bridgend, Newtown, Powys SY16 2BJ **Tel:** 01686-626423
M: *Sun 11.15am. Hds (vigil 7.30pm).*

■ **LLANRWST,** Conwy
1. Eglwys y Bugail Da (Good Shepherd) (1956)
Llanddoged Road, Llanrwst, LL26 0AU
Tel: 01492-640433
Served from Llandudno Junction.
Mgr Provost James Fealy (*Priest-in-Charge*)
Rev Damien Grimes MHM *(in residence).*
Tel: 01492-5830481
M: *Sun 11am. Hds 12noon.*

2. Eglwys Mair y Coed A Gwenfrewi (1961)
Off Main Road, Bettws-y-Coed.
Tel: 01492-640433
M: *Sun 5.30pm (Summer).*

■ **LLAY,** Near Wrexham
† **St Francis of Assisi** (1922; 1954)
Llay Chain, Llay, Wrexham.
Tel: 01978-852297
Rev Pius Matthew.
E-mails: piuscmi@hotmail.com
M: *Sat 1st M of Sun 6pm. Sun 11am. Hds 7pm.*
Nearest Mass Centre for Hope, Cefn-y-Bedd, Caergwrle, Gwersyllt, Bradley and Gresford, Marford.

■ **MACHYNLLETH,** Powys 

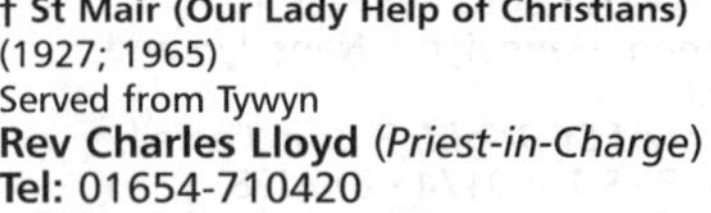
† **St Mair (Our Lady Help of Christians)** (1927; 1965)
Served from Tywyn
Rev Charles Lloyd (*Priest-in-Charge*)
Tel: 01654-710420
M: *Sun 11am. Hds, See notice board.*

■ **MENAI BRIDGE,** Anglesey
† **St Anne** (1956)
Dale Street, Menai Bridge, LL59 5AH
Served from Beaumaris.
- ***Oblates of Mary Immaculate, (OMI).***
M: *Sat 1st M of Sun 5.45pm. Hds (Vigil 11am).*

Nearest Mass Centre for Llandegfan; Llanfair PG; Aberffraw; Brynsiencyn; Dwyran; Llangaffo; Malltraeth; Newborough.

■ **MOLD,** Flintshire [S]
† **St David** (1850-60; 1966)
St David's Lane, Ffordd Fain, Mold CH7 1LH **Tel:** 01352-752087
Canon James F Webb, MA, STL. The Presbytery, St David's Ln, Ffordd Fain, Mold, Flintshire CH7 1LH **Tel:** 01352 752087 **Fax:** 01352 700488
Deacon: **Rev David Joy.** 38 Lon Cae Del, Mold CH7 1QX **Tel:** 01352-754722
Fax: 01352-700488
M: *Sat 1st M of Sun 5.30pm. Sun 10am. Mass for Deaf People: Mass signed in BSL - British sign Language (for details contact Rev Dcn David Joy). Hds (vigil 7pm), 9.15am, 7pm.*
- ***Congregation of La Sainte Union des Sacres Coeurs,*** The Convent, St David's Lane, CH7 1LH **Tel:** 01352-700121

Nearest Mass Centre for Northop, Cilcain, Llanferres, Tryddyn and Leeswood.

■ **MORFA NEFYN,** Gwynedd
The Resurrection of Our Saviour (1968)
Church Road, Morfa Nefyn, Gwynedd.
Served from Pwllheli. **Tel:** 01758-612331
M: *9.30am Summertime only, and as announced.*

■ **NEWTOWN,** Powys
† **God the Holy Spirit** (1902; 1947)
Longbridge Street, Newtown, Powys.
Tel: 01686-626423 **E-mail:** pwilkie5@hotmail.com **Rev Peter Wilkie.** Catholic Presbytery, The Bridgend, SY16 2BJ
M: *Sat 1st M of Sun 6.30pm. Sun 9.30am. Hds 9.30am, 7.30pm.*

■ **OLD COLWYN,** Conwy
† **The Sacred Heart** (1955)
Cliff Road, Old Colwyn. **Tel:** 01492-515091
Rev John Toole. Presbytery, 21 Heenan Road, Old Colwyn, Colwyn Bay LL29 9DP
M: *Sun 9am. Hds 10am.*
- ***Sisters of the Sacred Hearts of Jesus***

and Mary, St Augustine's Priory, Cliff Road. LL29 9RW **Tel:** 01492-514223 **Fax:** 01492-513528
Nearest Mass Centre for Llysfaen and Llanddulas.

■ **OVERTON,** Wrexham
† **Our Lady and the Welsh Martyrs** (1958)
Wrexham Road, Overton, Wrexham LL13 0D. **Tel:** 01978-710439
Mgr Philip Webb.
M: *Sat 1st M of Sun 6.30pm. Sun 10am. Hds 9am, 7.30pm.*
Nearest Mass Centre for Bangor-on-Dee and Worthenbury.

■ **PANTASAPH,** Holywell, Flintshire
† **St David** (1852; cons 1869)
Monastery Avenue, Pantasaph, Holywell, CH8 8PE **Tel:** 01352-711053 *(Friary)*
Fax: 01352-715349.
Tel: 01352-715030 *(Retreat Centre).*
- ***Franciscans (Capuchins) (OFMCap.):*** **Rev Loarne Ferguson** *(Bursar & Retreat Director)*, **Louis Maggiore,** *(Guardian)*, **Simon Denton, Aelred Coleman, Paschal Burlinson, Timothy Dowling, Anthony May, Keith Windsor**.
Franciscan Friary, Monastery Drive CH8 8PE
M: *Sun 10am, 5pm. Hds 10am, 7.30pm.*
- ***Sisters of Charity of Our Lady Mother of Mercy,*** Bryn Mair Convent, Monastery Road, CH8 8PN
Tel: 01352-710030/713728
St Joseph's Villa, Monastery Road, CH8 8PN **Tel:** 01352-712409

■ **PENLEY,** nr Overton, Wrexham
Polish General Hospital.
Penley, nr Overton, Wrexham LL14 0LH
Part-Time Chaplain: **Rev Grezegorz Januszewski (SChr)**. 71 West Street, Crewe. CW1 3HF **Tel:** 01270-256284
M: *Sat 2pm. Hds 2pm, (at the Chapel in Hospital)*

■ **PENMAENMAWR,** Conwy
Religious of The Sacred Heart of Mary.
Noddfa Spirituality Centre, Conwy Old Road, LL34 6YF **Tel:** 01492-623473

■ **PENRHOS,** Gwynedd
Our Lady and St Cynfil (1986)
Penrhos, Gwynedd. LL53 7HN
Rev Stanislaw Leniart (SChr). Penrhos Home, Pwllheli, Gwynedd LL53 7HN
Tel: 01758-613160
M: *Sat 1st M of Sun 4pm, (Summer 6pm). Sun 9.30am, 10.30am (in Extra Care Unit). Hds 9.30am, 10.30pm (in Extra Care Unit)*
Missionary Sisters of Christ the King, **Tel:** 01758-612452

■ **PORTHMADOG,** Gwynedd
† **Most Holy Redeemer** (1933)
Talgraig, Borth Road, Porthmadog, LL49 9BB
Tel: 01766-512348
Fax: 01766-515277
E-mail: catholichurch@porthmadog.fsnet.co.uk
E-bost: eglwysgatholig@portmadog-fsnet.co.uk
Rev Francis J. Gerrard.
M: *Sat 1st M of Sun 6.15pm (1st Sat partly in Welsh) Sun 10am (1st Sun partly in Welsh). Hds 9.15am, 7pm.*
- ***Sisters of Charity of Notre Dame d'Evron***, Bethany, 16 Terrace Road, Porthmadog, Gwynedd LL49 9BA
Tel: 01766-512213 **Fax:** 01766-770310

■ **PRESTATYN,** Denbighshire
† **SS Peter and Frances** (1903)
Plas Avenue, Prestatyn, Denbighshire LL19 9NH
Tel: 01745-854304 **Fax:** 01745-889123
Rev Terence Carr. 6 Plas Avenue, Prestatyn, Denbighshire. LL19 9NH
M: *Sat 1st M of Sun 5pm Sept-June. Sun 10.30am. July-Aug Sat 1st M of Sun 5pm, Sun 10.30, 4pm. Hds 12noon, 6.30pm.*

■ **PWLLHELI,** Gwynedd
† **St Joseph** (1861; 1926; 1982)
Ffordd Mela, South Beach, Pwllheli LL53 5AP **Tel:** 01758-612331
Rev Joseph Henry Clarke.
M: *Sat 1st M of Sun 7pm (Welsh). Sun 11am. Hds 12 Noon, 7pm.*

■ **QUEENSFERRY,** Deeside
† **Blessed Trinity** (1964)
Little Sisters of the Assumption in residence. The Presbytery, 1 Glynne Street, Queensferry, Deeside, CH5 1TA
Tel: 01244-830071 **Fax:** 01244-810914
Served from Connah's Quay.
Tel: 01244-830358.
M: *Sun 9.30am. Hds 8.30am. Weekdays 9.30am Mon; 8.30am Thurs.*
- ***Sisters of Charity of Our Lady Mother of Mercy***, 5 Chester Road West, Queensferry, Deeside CH5 1SA
Tel: 01244-821677

■ **RHOSNEIGR,** Anglesey
St Therese (1957)
Served from Holyhead.
M: *Sun 9am. Hds 7pm.*

■ **RHUDDLAN,** Denbighshire
St Illtyd (1976; cons 24 Oct 1976)
Served from St Asaph.
M: *Sun 9.30am. Hds 9.30am.*

■ **RHYL,** Denbighshire
† Our Lady of the Assumption (1975)
119 Wellington Road, Rhyl, LL18 1LE
Tel: 01745-353395 **Fax:** 01745-330364
E-mail: chas3free@aol.com
Rev Charles Ramsay.
M: *Sat 1st M of Sun 5pm. Sun 10am, 5pm. (except June, July, Aug. 7pm). Hds (vigil 6.30pm), Feast Day 9.30am in School (when in session), 6.30pm.*
- ***Franciscan Missionary Sisters of St Joseph***, 28 Vale Road, Rhyl LL18 2BU **Tel:** 01745-354367

■ **ROSSETT,** Wrexham
Christ the King (1969)
Holt Road, Rossett, Wrexham.
Served from Llay.
M: *Sun 9am. Hds 8am.*

■ **RUABON,** Wrexham
St Mary the Virgin
Ruabon, Wrexham. **Tel:** 01978-821568
3 The Villas, New High Street LL14 6NW
M: *Sun 11am.*

■ **RUTHIN,** Denbighshire
† Our Lady Help of Christians (1860; 1931)
115 Mwrog Street, Ruthin, LL15 1LE
Tel: 01824-702859 **Fax:** 01824-709915
Rev George McLoughlin.
M: *Sat 1st M of Sun 6.15pm. Sun 10.30am. Hds (vigil 7.30pm), 10am.*
Nearest Mass Centre for Llanbedr, Cyffylliog, Clawddnewydd, Glocaenog and Llanfair DC.

■ **ST ASAPH,** Denbighshire
† St Winefride (1854; 1855; cons 8 Dec 1980)
Chester Street, St Asaph, LL17 0RE
Tel: 01745-582213 **Fax:** 01745-585299
Rev J Lochran (*Priest-in-Charge*).
5 Llys Trewithan, St Asaph LL17 0DJ
Tel: 01745-584781
M: *Sat 1st M of Sun 5.45pm. Sun 11am. Hds (Vigil Mass) 7pm.*

■ **ST BEUNO'S,** St Asaph
See Tremeirchion.

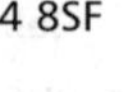

■ **SALTNEY,** Flintshire
† St Anthony of Padua (1862; 1879; 1914)
54 High Street, Saltney, Flintshire. CH4 8SF
Tel: 01244-671581
Rev Francis Doyle.
M: *Sun 11am. Hds 7pm.*

■ **TOWYN,** nr Abergele, Conwy
Eglwys Mair A Gwenfrewi
Christ The King (1974)
Gors Road.
Served from Abergele.
M: *Sun 11am. Hds (vigil) 6.30pm.*

■ **TREMEIRCHION,** St Asaph, Denbighshire
St Beuno's (1848; 1849)
Ignatian Spirituality Centre, Tremeirchion, St Asaph, Denbighshire LL17 0AS
Tel: 01745-583444 **Fax:** 01745-584151
E-mail: stbeunos@aol.com
- ***Jesuits (SJ):*** **Revv David Birchall** (*Director*), **James Chaning-Pearce, Gregory Geoghegan, Damian Jackson, Thomas Shufflebotham** (*Superior*); **Brs David Gornall, Brian McClorry**. *Other Orders represented:* **Rev Stanley Dye MAfr: Srs Louise Swanston SSMM, Renate Düllmann OP, Perpetua Henry RSM, Anne Hewitt RSM, Mary Reidy DJ; Ms Alice Keenleyside**.
M: *Sun 10am.*

■ **TYWYN,** Gwynedd
† St David (1935; 1969)
Corbett Avenue, Tywyn, Gwynedd LL36 0AH
Priest-in-Charge: **Rev Charles Lloyd**.
Tel: 01654-710420
M: *Sun 9am, Hds see Notice Board.*

■ **VALLEY,** Anglesey
Our Lady (1962)
RAF Valley. Served from Holyhead.
M: *Sun 6pm.*

■ **WELSHPOOL,** Powys
† St Winefride (1860; 1963)
2 Raven Street, Welshpool, Powys.
SY21 7LR **Tel:** 01938-552223
Rev Victor Walter.
M: *Sat 1st M of Sun 6.30pm. Sun 9am. Hds 9am, 6.30pm.*

■ **WREXHAM**
1. See start of Parish List.

2. † St Anne (1962)
Prince Charles Road, Wrexham LL13 8TH
Tel: 01978-265879 **Fax:** 01978-351419
Rev James Durkin. *Deacon:* **Rev Clifford Howe**. "Walden", Hugmore Lane, Llan-y-Pwll, Wrexham. LL13 9YE
Tel: 01978-661126
M: *Sat 1st M of Sun 5.30pm. Sun 10.30am. Hds 9.15am, 7pm.*

■ **ORDERS OR CONGREGATIONS, ETC**

■ **Men**
Columban Fathers: Denbigh.
Franciscans (Capuchin): Pantasaph.
Jesuits: Tremeirchion.
Oblates of Mary Immaculate: Amlwch, Beaumaris, Blaenau Ffestiniog, Colwyn Bay, Holyhead.

■ **WOMEN**
Assumption, Little Sisters of the: Queensferry, Holywell.

Brigid, Sisters of St: Denbigh.
Carmelites: Dolgellau.
Charity (of Notre Dame d'Evron), Sisters of: Porthmadog.
Charity (of Our Lady Mother of Mercy), Sisters of: Pantasaph, Queensferry.
Christ the King, Missionary Sisters of: Penrhos.
Cross & Passion, Sisters of: Flint.
Good Saviour, Sisters of the: Holyhead.
Holy Family of Bordeaux, Sisters of the: Wrexham.
Loreto, Sisters of: Llandudno, Bala.
Mercy, Institute of Our Lady of: Colwyn Bay, Llangefni.
Mercy, Sisters of (Union): Bangor, Llangefni.
Poor Clares (Colettines): Hawarden.
St Joseph (of Chambéry), Sisters of: Wrexham, Caernarfon.
St Joseph, Franciscan Missionaries of: Rhyl.
Sacred Heart of Mary (Béziers), Sisters of the: Penmaenmawr.
Sacred Hearts of Jesus and Mary, Sisters of the: Old Colwyn.
Sainte Union des Sacrés Coeurs, Congr of the: Wrexham, Colwyn Bay, Mold.
Ursulines (Roman Union): Connah's Quay.

■ DIOCESAN INSTITUTIONS, SOCIETIES Etc

For Societies and Organisations without representation in the diocese please see the main Societies and Organisations section.

Archconfraternity of St Stephen for Altar Servers. *Diocesan Director:* **Rev Peter Wilkie**. Catholic Presbytery, The Bridgend, Newtown, Powys SY16 2BJ **Tel:** 01686-626423

Association for the Propagation of the Faith. *Diocesan Director:* **Rev Francis Doyle**, St Anthony of Padua, 54 High Street, Saltney, Flintshire CH4 8SF **Tel:** 01244-671581 **E-mail:** catholicchurch@saltney.fslinfe.co.uk

CAFOD in Wales/CAFOD yng Nghymru. Provides speakers & resources in both Welsh & English. If you, your parish or school would like to know how to help or wish to receive any information or support. Please Contact: *Wales:* **Sr Vianney Connolly**, CAFOD Peace and Justice Centre, 35 Kingsmill Road, Wrexham LL13 8NH **Tel:** 01978-356969 *Wales & Hereford:* **Mrs Sue Scanlon**, National Organiser, National Office, 11 Richmond Road, Roath, Cardiff CF24 3AQ **Tel/Fax:** 029-2045 3360 **E-mail:** cafod@wales.cablenet.co.uk

Catenian Association. North Wales Circle (125): *President:* **J B Marginson**, Gleneagles, 20 Earlswood Avenue, Prestatyn LL19 7BB **Tel:** 01745-257738 *Secretary:* **R L Herndlhofer**, 23 East Parade, Rhyl LL18 3AL **Tel:** 01745-350280

Catholic Association of Teachers, Schools and Colleges, (CATSC). Providing quality professional support to Catholic Teachers, Schools and Colleges. *Wrexham CATSC Contact:* **Mr Dominic Tobin**. St Richard Gwyn High School, Flint, Flintshire. **Tel:** 01352-736900 **Fax:** 01352-736914 **E-mail:** srgadmin@richard-gwyn-hs.flintshire.gov.uk

Catholic Centre for Healing in Marriage. A Christian residential centre for couples seeking wholeness in their marriage through prayer, teaching, counselling and healing, in a relaxed and peaceful setting. A variety of courses are available to enrich or rebuild marriages, and are run by married lay couples, qualified in Christian counselling and spiritual direction. Residential marriage preparation courses are also available. Contact: **Tony & Betty Dady**, Oasis of Peace, Penamser Road, Porthmadog, Gwynedd LL49 9NY **Tel:** 01766-514300 **Fax:** 01766-515227 **E-mail:** ccfhim@hotmail.com. **Website:** catholiccentreforhealinginmarriage.org.uk

Catholic Charismatic Renewal, Wales. Information and enquiries: **Mrs Kathryn Byrne**. Chapel House, Selattyn, Oswestry, Shropshire SY10 7DZ

Catholic Deaf Service (Wrexham). Established in October 1999 and with the support of the service at Marian House in Cardiff the Service aims to assist deaf people and their families participate fully in all aspects of the life of the Church in the Diocese. Mass is celebrated on the second Sunday of each month at 3 pm. *Team:* **Fr Peter M Brignall, Dcn David Joy and Angela McDonagh**. c/o Cathedral Clergy House, Regent Street, Wrexham LL11 1RB. **Tel:** (Voice & Text) 01978-263943 **Fax:** 01978-352277

Catholic Nurses' Guild of England and Wales. Wrexham: **Sr Elizabeth Martin** (*Diocesan Representative*), 'Tig Mhuire', 29 Ty'n Coed Estate, Llangefni LL77 8YX **Tel:** 01248-724175

Christian Life Communities. Are small groups of people who meet regularly to help each other deepen their life of prayer. *Diocesan Representative:* **Anne Sherrington**, Llwyn Onn, High Street, Dyserth, Denbighshire LL18 6AB

Handicapped Children's Pilgrimage Trust (HCPT). (Welsh Region). *Local Group Leader:* **E D Ryan**. Glan Aber, The Wern, Bersham, Wrexham LL14 4LT **Tel:** Wrexham 757320

Knights of St Columba. Province No 37. Enquiries: Consult local parish priest. *Provincial Grand Knight:* **J Wilkie**, 24 Pen y Maes, Bistre Heights, Buckley, Flintshire CH7 2QT

Legion of Mary. *President:* **Miss A M Carr**, 4a The Firs, Mold CH7 1JX *Enquiries:* Consult local parish priest.

Marriage Care. (Formerly CMAC). *Wrexham Centre:* 35, Kingsmill Road, Wrexham, LL13 8NH For appointments: **Tel:** 01978-351795 *President:* The Bishop of Wrexham, *Secretary:* 14 The Grove, Marchwiel, Wrexham. **Tel:** 01978-358223

Marriage/Engaged Encounter. Fr John Cavanagh, Franciscan Friary, Pantasaph, Flintshire CH8 8PE *Contact:* **Tony & Win Phillips**. 16 Ty-Isha Terrace, Blackwood, Gwent. NP12 1ER **Tel:** 01495-228125

National Network of Pastoral Musicians. A network of people of all Christian denominations active and interested in liturgy and music who wish to be in touch with others. *President:* **Stephen Dean**. *National Secretary/Treasurer:* **Mrs Kathryn Burke**, 32 Osborne Road, Southport PR8 2RJ **Tel:** 01704-577504 **Fax:** 01704-579790 **E-mail:** kburke32@aol.com *North Wales Area Secretary:* **Tony Warren Tel:** 01244-532341

Natural Family Planning Centre. Dr Pat Walters, Forge Road Surgery, Brynteg Wrexham. **Tel:** 01978-758311

Newman Circle. *Chairman:* **Mr Anthony O'Toole**. 24 Park Avenue, Wrexham. **Tel:** 01978-353815

Our Lady's Catechists. *Diocesan Representative:* **Mrs Ann Ryan**, Greenfield, Station Road, Rhoswiel, Weston Rhyn SY10 7TH **Tel:** 01691-778407

Peace & Justice Centre. 35/37 Kingsmills Road, Wrexham LL13 8NH **Tel:** 01978-356969

St Barnabas Society. *Diocesan Representative:* **Nigel Fisher**, 21 Vernon Road, Chester CH1 4JT **Tel:** 01244-379962

Scouts. *Diocesan Scout & Guide Chaplain:*

Secular Franciscan Order. Information: The National Spiritual Assistant, Franciscan Friary, 15 Cuppin Street, Chester, Cheshire CH1 2BN Fraternities meet at Fransican Friary, Pantasaph, Holywell, Flintshire CH8 8PE. *Diocesan Contact:* **Mrs M McCormick**. The Rosary, 8 Coed Onn Road, Flint, Flintshire CH6 5NE

Serviam. Ursuline Lay Association, Ursuline Convent, 2 Beaconsfield Road, Shotton, Flintshire CH5 1EZ. Contact: **Mrs Ann Richardson**. 2 Church Close, Northop Hall, Flintshire CH7 6HY **Tel:** 01244-815083

Society of St Gregory. The National Society which works to assist priests & people to celebrate the Liturgy worthily. It encourages study & active participation by organising Summer Schools, study days and conferences for all concerned with music and worship. *Chairman:* **Alan Smith**, 7 Larchfield Close, Malvern Link WR14 1RA **E-mail:** alan@ssg-online.demon.co.uk **Website:** http://www.ssg-online.demon.co.uk Diocesan Contact: **Dr Marian Tolley**. Tan y Rhuw, Rhos A Brithdir, Llanfyllin. SY22 5HA **Tel:** 01691-648437 **Fax:** 01691-648155 **E-mail:** maritoll@aol.com

Society of St Peter Apostle for Native Clergy. Rev Francis Doyle. St Anthony of Padua, 54 High Street, Saltney, Flintshire CH4 8SF **Tel:** 01244-671581

Society of St Vincent de Paul. Central Office: 1a Abbey Street, Rhyl LL18 1NT **Tel/Fax:** 01745-355555 **E-mail:** svp@store41freeserve.co.uk

Society of the Holy Childhood. *Contact:* **Rev Jack Cauley** at Bishop's House.

Union of Catholic Mothers. Wrexham Diocesan Branch. *President:* **Mrs Ursula Pickering**, 56 Kings Avenue, Flint CH6 5JR **Tel:** 01352-732163 *Secretary:* **Mrs Jane Bellis**, "Brooklawn", Rossett Road, Commonwood, Holt LL13 9SY **Tel:** 01829-270842

University Catholic Chaplaincy. *Bangor:* Pendyffryn, 1 Menai Avenue, Bangor LL57 2HH **Tel:** 01248-352522 *Lay Chaplain:* **Mrs Roberta Canning**: **Tel:** 01248-352262

Y Cylch Catholig. To help Welsh-speaking Catholics to live a full spiritual life through the medium of their own language, by offering opportunities for worship in Welsh, and by promoting the work of providing books & essential resources to this end. *Chairman:* **Bishop Daniel Mullins of Menevia.** *Secretary:* **Sue Roberts.** Delfryn, Yr Ala, Pwllheli, Gwynedd **Tel:** 01758-614977

■ HOSPITALS

To contact the Catholic Chaplain of a particular hospital we suggest you contact the hospital reception directly.

■ CATHOLIC SCHOOLS - MAINTAINED

■ ANGLESEY

▲ Aided Primary
St Mary's, Longford Road, Holyhead LL65 1TR **Tel:** 01407-763176 *(Holyhead)*

■ CONWY

▲ Junior and Infant
Blessed William Davies Bodnant Crescent Llandudno **Tel:** 01942-875930 *(Llandudno)*
St Joseph's, Brackley Avenue, Colwyn Bay. **Tel:** 01492-532394 *(Colwyn Bay)*

■ DENBIGHSHIRE

▲ Junior and Infant
St Mary's, St Margaret's Drive, Rhyl. **Tel:** 01745-350762 **Fax:** 0745 332479 *(Rhyl)*

▲ Secondary Comprehensive
Blessed Edward Jones, Cefndy Road, Rhyl. LL18 2EU**Tel:** 01745-343433 **Fax:** 01745-344723 *(Rhyl)*

■ FLINTSHIRE

▲ Junior and Infant
St Anthony's, High Street, Saltney, Nr Chester CH4 8SF **Tel:** 01244-680480 *(Saltney)*
St David's, Ffordd Fain, Mold CH7 1LH **Tel:** 01352-752651
St Mary's, Ffordd Llewelyn, Flint CH6 5JZ **Tel:** 01352-733231 *(Flint)*
St Winefride's, Whitford Street, Holywell CH8 7NJ **Tel:** 01352-713182 *(Holywell)*

▲ Junior and Infant
Ven Edward Morgan, Caernarfon Close, Shotton CH5 1EB **Tel:** 01244-830408 *(Shotton)*

▲ Secondary Comprehensive
St Richard Gwyn, Albert Avenue, Flint. CH6 5JZ **Tel:** 01352-732788 **Fax:** 01352-735983 *(Flint)*

■ GWYNEDD

▲ Junior and Infant
Our Lady's Caernarfon Road Bangor. LL57 2UT **Tel:** 01248-352463 *(Bangor)*
St Helen's East Twthill Caernarfon. **Tel:** 01286-4856 *(Caernarvon)*

▲ Primary and Secondary
St Gerard's School Trust, Ffriddoedd Road, Bangor LL57 2EL **Tel:** 01248-351656

■ POWYS

▲ Junior and Infant
St Mary's, Milford Road, Newtown SY16 2EH **Tel:** 01686-625582

■ WREXHAM

▲ Junior and Infant
St Anne's, Prince Charles Road, Wrexham. LL13 8TH **Tel:** 01978-261623 *(Wrexham)*
St Mary's, Lea Road, Wrexham LL13 7NA **Tel:** 01978-352406 *(Wrexham)*

▲ Secondary Comprehensive
St Joseph's RC & Anglican School, Sontley Road, Wrexham LL13 7EN **Tel:** 01978-360310 **Fax:** 01978-262165 *(Wrexham)* *Chaplain:* **Sr Margaret Catlow**

BISHOPRIC OF THE FORCES

Consisting of British Forces' personnel, their spouses, families and other dependants, wherever they are located in the world.

Patrons Of The Diocese
Our Lady of Walsingham, 24 September
St George, 23 April

BISHOP OF THE FORCES

Sede Vacante
Cathedral of St Michael & St George, Queens Avenue, Aldershot GU11 2BY
E-mail: BishopricForces-RtRev@mod.uk

Office:
Wellington House, St Omer Barracks, Thornhill Road, Aldershot, Hants GU11 2BG
Tel: 01252-348234 **Fax:** 01252-348235

Bishop's Secretary:
Major (Retd) Diana Wilson
E-mail: BishopricForces-Secretary@mod.uk

Notary:
Mrs Freda Sheppard.
E-mail: BishopricForces-Notary@mod.uk
Archivist:
Mrs Kay Day. Tel: 01252-683162

Residence:
26 The Crescent, Farnborough, Hants GU14 7AS
Tel: 01252-373699

■ BISHOP EMERITUS
Rt Rev Francis J Walmsley CBE, St John's Convent, Kiln Green, Reading, Berks RG10 9XP **Tel:** 0118-940-2743

■ EPISCOPAL COUNCIL
Mgr Paul Donovan, QHC MBA STL FCMI, FRSA VG RN. Naval Chaplaincy Service, MP1.2, Leach Building, Whale Island, Portsmouth PO2 8BY
Tel: 023-92625193
Email: paul.donovan506@mod.uk
Mgr J Stephen Alker MBE QHC KHS VG. ACG Land Forces/PRCC(A), Erskine Barracks, Wilton, Salisbury SP2 0AG
Tel: 01722-433892
Email: john.alker593@mod.uk
Principal RC Chaplain RAF: **Rev Mgr John Walsh VG RAF**. Chaplaincy Office, RAF Halton, Aylesbury Bucks HP22 5PG
Tel: 01296-656910 **Email:** principalrcchaplain@halton.raf.mod.uk

■ DIOCESAN CURIA
Chancellor: **Rev Ian A Evans**
Tel: 0049-21614722807
E-mail: chancellor_mil_ord@hotmail.com

■ College of Consultors
Bishop, Principal Chaplains, Chancellor and one Chaplain from each service.

■ Ecclesiastical Consultant
The Judicial Vicar. Archbishop's House, Ambrosden Avenue, Westminster, London SW1P 1QJ **Tel:** 020-7828 3255

■ Diocesan Child Protection Officer
Rev Michael Fava. c/o Bishopric Office.

■ Records
Records Office: Bishopric of the Forces, Wellington House, St Omer Barracks, Thornhill Road, Aldershot GU11 2BG
Tel: 01252-348231 **Fax:** 01252-348235
Notary: **Mrs Freda Sheppard**.

E-mail: BishopricForces-Notary@mod.uk

■ **Forces Catholic News Editorial Board**
Revv Paul Owens RAF (*Editor*), **Ricard Blythen RN, David Smith RAChD.**

■ **Liturgy**
Royal Navy: **Rev Mark Cassidy**.
Army: **Rev Nick Gosnell**.
Royal Air Force: **Awaiting Appointment**.

■ **Retreat Group**
Royal Navy: **Rev Mark Cassidy**.
Army: **Rev Ian Evans**.
Royal Air Force: **Rev Bob Halshaw.**

ROYAL NAVY CHAPLAINS

■ **Principal Chaplain & Director Naval Chaplaincy Service (Operations)**
Mgr Paul Donovan QHC MBA, STL, FCMI, FRSA, VG, RN (Northampton), Full Career Commission, 22 April, 1985, Naval Chaplaincy Service, MP1.2, Leach Building, Whale Island, Portsmouth PO2 8BY
Tel: 023-9262 5193
E-mail: paul.donovan506@mod.uk

■ **Chaplains**
Rev Michael Sharkey RN (Glasgow) 1 Oct 1990. **Rev David McLean OP BSc BD RN** (Dominican) 18 Sept 96, **Rev Simon Bradbury RN** (Leeds) 18 Sept 96, **Rev David Yates RN** (Salford) 1 Sept, 1998. **Rev Andrew McFadden PhB STL RN** (Paisley) 1 Sept 98, **Rev Mark Cassidy STL RN** (Dunkeld) 18 Sept 2000, **Rev David Conroy, MA, RN** (Galloway) 18 Sept 2000. **Rev Richard Blythen** (Arundel & Brighton) 6 Sept 05.

NAVAL ESTABLISHMENTS IN PORTSMOUTH & PASTORAL AREA EAST

■ **HMS NELSON,** HM Naval Base
The Chaplaincy Centre, Rodney Block, HMS Nelson HM Naval Base, Portsmouth PO1 3NH
Tel: 023 9272 4233 **Fax:** 023-9272 7851
M: *No Sunday Mass.*

■ **HMS EXCELLENT,** Whale Island Portsmouth. Served from HMS Collingwood

■ **HMS TEMERAIRE,** Portsmouth
Served from HMS Nelson

■ **HMS COLLINGWOOD,**
The Chaplaincy, Newgate Lane, Fareham, Hants PO14 1AS **Tel:** 01329-332236
Fax: 01329-332236
M: *No Sunday Mass.*

■ **HMS SULTAN**
The Chaplaincy, Military Road, Gosport, Hants PO12 3BY
Tel: 023-9254 2327 **Fax:** 023-9254 2437
M: *No Sunday Mass.*

■ **CENTURION BUILDING** –
Served from HMS Sultan

■ **JSU NORTHWOOD**
Served from the Parish of St Matthew.
32 Hallowell Road, Northwood HA6 3HP
Tel: 01923-825639

NAVAL ESTABLISHMENTS IN DEVONPORT & PASTORAL AREA WEST

■ **HMS DRAKE,** HM Naval Base Devonport
The Chaplaincy Centre, Fisher Block, HM Naval Base, Devonport, Devon PL2 2BG
Tel: 01752-555931
M: *No Sunday Mass.*

■ **HMS RALEIGH**
The Chaplaincy, Torpoint, Cornwall PL11 2PD **Tel:** 01752-811259
Fax: 01752-811515
M: *No Sunday Mass.*

■ **BRITANNIA ROYAL NAVAL COLLEGE**
The RC Chaplain, Dartmouth TQ6 0HJ
Tel: 01803-677116 **Fax:** 01803-677015
M: *10am Sun Mass during term time in RC Chapel of St Philip Howard.*

■ **HMS HERON,** RN Air Station Yeovilton
The Chaplaincy, Yeovil, Somerset BA22 8HT
Tel: 01935-455520
M: *No Sunday Mass*

■ **HMS SEAHAWK,** RN Air Station Culdrose
Officiating Chaplain: **Tel:** 01326-572378
M: *No Sunday Mass.*

■ **HMS EAGLET,** RNHQ, Liverpool
Served by **Rev David Gamble** (*Naval Liaison Chaplain*) **Tel:** 0151-929 2149

■ **HQ 3 CDO BRIGADE, RM STONEHOUSE, DEVONPORT.**
Served from HMS Drake
M: *No Sunday Mass.*

■ **40 COMMANDO BRIGADE,**
Royal Marines, Taunton
Served from the Church of St George.
Billet Street, Taunton TA1 3NE
Tel: 01283-272700
M: *No Sunday Mass.*

■ **42 COMMANDO ROYAL MARINES,**
The Chaplaincy: Bickleigh Barracks, Devon PL6 7AJ **Tel:** 01752-727027
M: *No Sunday Mass.*

■ **COMMANDO LOGISTICS REGIMENT**
Royal Marines, Chivenor, Barnstaple EX31 4AS
Served by Officiating Chaplain, **Deacon Philip Waites,** c/o The Chaplaincy.
Tel: 01271-863563/879344

■ **CTC RM LYMPSTONE**
Lympstone, Exmouth, Devon EX8 5AR
Tel: 01392-876953
M: *No Mass on Sunday.*

■ **ROYAL MARINES,** Poole, Dorset
Served from Church of St Mary.
Wimbourne, Poole. **Tel:** 01202-675412

NAVAL ESTABLISHMENTS OVERSEAS

■ **HQBF FALKLAND ISLANDS**
Also Ascension Island, St Helena, South Georgia and Tristan Da Cunha.
The Rt Rev Mgr Michael B McPartland SMA, The Officiating Chaplain British Forces, St Mary's RC Church, Stanley, Falkland Islands. **Tel:** (from UK): 00-500 21204 **Fax:** 00-500 22242

■ **HQBF GIBRALTAR**
Rev Charles Bruzon, Officating Chaplain, c/o The King's Chapel, BFPO 52.
Tel: (from UK) 00-350 55484
Email: revcharl@gibraltar.gi

ARMY CHAPLAINS

■ **PRINCIPAL CHAPLAIN**
Mgr J.S. Alker MBE QHC KHS VG (Liverpool), Assistant Chaplain General Land Forces and Principal RC Chaplain (Army), Erskine Barracks, Wilton, Salisbury SP2 0AG
Tel: 01722-433892, 5 March 1979.
E-mail: john.alker593@mod.uk

REGULAR COMMISSIONS
Chaplains 1st Class:
Rev Anthony B Paris (Westminster) 8 Feb 88. **Rev Francis P A Barber** (Salford) 01 Sep 93.

Chaplains 2nd Class:
Rev Ian A Evans (Dublin) 14 Jun 93. **Rev Andrew P Lloyd MBE** (Shrewsbury) 19 Feb 96. **Rev Stephen Forster** (Hexham and Newcastle) 23 Sep 03.

Chaplains 3rd Class:
Rev Kevin V Prince (Shrewsbury) 04 Sep 84. **Rev Martin P Caddell** (Liverpool) 05 Sep 91. **Rev Thomas Butler** (Lancaster) 12 Jun 95. **Rev Michael P D Fava** (Portsmouth) 27 Jan 97. **Rev Donald J Cumming** (Glasgow) 13 Oct 97. **Rev Nicholas Gosnell** (Westminster) 15 Jun 98. **Rev Nicholas D Farrell** (Leeds) 11 Oct 99. **Rev Daniel F Hernandez** (Gibraltar) 31 Jan 00. **Rev David R J P Campbell** (Westminster) 31 Jan 00. **Rev Alexander E Strachan** (Glasgow) 03 Sep 01. **Rev Ian J Stevenson** (Paisley) 03 Sep 01.**Rev David G S Smith** (East Anglia) 23 Sep 02.

Chaplains 4th Class:
Rev Sean Neylan (Hexham and Newcastle) 22 Sep 03. **Rev Daren G Brown** (Nottingham) 10 Jan 05. **Rev Paschal J Hanrahan** (Killaloe) 26 Sep 05. **Rev Stephen Sharkey** (Galloway). **Rev Mgr Canon Robert Corrigan** (Clifton). **Rev Charles-Edward P Gosnell** (Port Elizabeth).

■ **Military Support Office (MSF) Chaplain**
Rev Terence J Makings MBE (Nottingham). **Rev Timothy J Forbes Turner** (Southwark). **Rev Leonard A Purcell** (Glasgow). **Rev (Deacon) Peter D B Heneghan** (Liverpool).

■ **Officiating Chaplains (Full Time)**
Rev William Boyd SDB MBE.
Rev (Deacon) Jeremy P J D Oliver MBE.

■ **RESERVE CHAPLAINS**

■ **Territorial Army**
Rev Mgr John F Nelson VG (Portsmouth). **Rev Charles A Bruzon** *(Gibraltar).* **Rev Paul McCourt** (Hexham and Newcastle). **Rev Michael C Dunne** (Westminster). **Rev Francis J Lynch** (Wrexham).

■ **Army Cadet Force**
Rev Timothy C R Hutton TD (Westminster). **Rev Stephen P Mulholland** (Dunkeld). **Rev Anthony Cornforth** (Hexham and Newcastle). **Rev Dr Gerard Fieldhouse Byrne** (Salford). **Rev D A Gamble** (Liverpool). **Rev Canon Alfred T Hayes** (Lancaster).

■ **Religious Sisters**
Sr Anne Marie Eden (Sisters of St Joseph of Lyon). **Sr Eileen M Grant MBE** (Religious of Christian Education).

ESTABLISHMENTS IN ENGLAND

■ **ABINGDON,** Oxon
Officiating Chaplain:
St Edmund's, Abingdon OX14 3PL
Tel: 01235 520375

■ **ALDERSHOT,** Hants
Army Chaplain: St Michael's House, Queen's Avenue, Aldershot GU11 2BY
Tel: 01252-347061
Church: SS Michael & George, Queen's Avenue, Aldershot.

■ **ANDOVER,** Hants
Officiating Chaplain: St John Baptist, Alexandra Road, Andover, Hants SP10 3AD **Tel:** 01264-352829

■ **ARBORFIELD,** Berks
Army Chaplain:
Served from Sandhurst.
Church: St Eligius, Garrison Church, Arborfield.

■ **ASHCHURCH,** Tewkesbury
Officiating Chaplain: St Joseph's Church, Chance Street, Tewkesbury GL20 5RF
Tel: 01684-293273

■ **BASSINGBOURN,** Cambs
Army Chaplain:
Church: The RC Chapel, Bassingbourn Barracks, Royston SG8 5LX
Tel: 01223 204320.

■ **BEACONSFIELD,** Bucks
Officiating Chaplain: 40 Warwick Road, Beaconsfield HP9 2PL
Tel: 01494-673018

BICESTER, Oxon
Officiating Chaplain: The Presbytery, The Causeway, Bicester OX26 6AW
Tel: 01869-253277
Church: St Barbara, Bicester Garrison, Ambrosden

■ **BLANDFORD,** Dorset
Officiating Chaplain: 1a Park Place, White Cliff Mill Street, Blandford DT11 7BN
Tel: 01258-452051
Church: All Saints, Blandford Garrison

■ **BORDON,** Hants
Officiating Chaplain: Presbytery, Sacred Heart Church, High Street, Bordon, GU35 OAU **Tel:** 01420- 472415
Church: Sacred Heart, High Street, Bordon

■ **BOVINGTON,** Dorset
Officiating Chaplain: St Joseph's, The Priest's House, The Square, Wool, Dorset BH20 6DU **Tel:** 01929-463334
Church: St Alban, Bovington Camp

■ **BRAMCOTE,** Warwicks
Officiating Chaplain: **Sr Anne Marie Eden**. St Joseph's, Haunton, Nr Tamworth, Staffs B79 9HW **Tel:** 01827-373628
Church: St Barbara, Gamecock Barracks, Bramcote. **Tel:** 01455-222301

■ **BULFORD,** Wilts
Army Chaplain: Kiwi Barracks, Bulford Camp, Salisbury SP4 9HZ
Tel: 01980-672479
Church: Our Lady Queen of Peace, Kandy Road, Bulford Camp

■ **CATTERICK,** North Yorks
Community Chaplain: Baden Powell House, Scotton Road, Catterick Garrison, North Yorks DL9 3JS **Tel:** 01748-872309
Churches: (1) St Joan of Arc, Hipswell Road, Catterick Garrison, (2) St Mary, Catterick

■ **CHEPSTOW,** Monmouthshire
Officiating Chaplain: St Mary's, Bulwark Road, Chepstow NP16 5JE
Tel: 01291-622649

■ **CHESTER,** Dale Barracks
Officiating Chaplain: 1 Elm Rise, Frodsham, Cheshire WA6 6AJ **Tel:** 01928-735765

■ **CHICHESTER,** West Sussex
Officiating Chaplain: The Presbytery, Angel Street, Petworth GU28 0BG
Tel: 01798-342169

■ **CHICKSANDS,** Shefford, Beds
Officiating Chaplain: 25 High Street, Shefford, Beds SG17 5DD
Tel: 01462-813436

■ **CHILWELL,** Notts
Officiating Chaplain: 25 Foster Avenue, Beeston, Notts NG9 1AE
Tel: 0115-925 5324.

■ **COLCHESTER,** Essex
Army Chaplain: Beerchurch Hall Camp, Colchester CO2 9NU
Tel: 01206-783983

■ **CONNAUGHT BARRACKS,** Kent
Officiating Chaplain: 24 Old Park Hill, Dover, Kent CT16 2AW
Tel: 01304-823402

■ **DIDCOT,** Oxford
Officiating Chaplain: 15 Manor Crescent, Didcot, Oxon OX11 7AJ
Tel: 01235-812338

■ **DOVER,** DYMS, Kent
Officiating Chaplain: 103 Maison Dieu Road, Dover, Kent CT16 1RU
Tel: 01304-206766

■ **EMSWORTH,** Hants
Officiating Chaplain: 10 Bristol Road, Southsea, Hants PO4 9QH
Tel: 02392-345521

■ **HARROGATE,** *Army Chaplain:* Army Foundation College, Uniacke Barracks, Penny Pot Lane, Harrogate AFC Harrogate
Tel: 01904-664359

■ **HOUNSLOW,** Middx
Officiating Chaplain:
Church: St Edward, Cavalry Barracks, Hounslow. **Tel:** 020-8570 1693

■ **HOWE BARRACKS,** Canterbury, Kent
Officiating Chaplain: 2 Ashley Avenue, Folkestone CT19 4DX **Tel:** 01303-275402

■ **HULLAVINGTON,** Wilts
Officiating Chaplain: 26 Cross Hayes, Malmesbury, Wilts SN16 9BG
Tel: 01666-822195

■ **KINETON,** Warwicks
Officiating Chaplain: 35 Hammerton Way, Wellesbourne, Warks CV35 9NS
Church: CAD Kineton. **Tel:** 01789 841883

■ **KNELLER HALL,** RMSM, Middlx
Officiating Chaplain: 213 Nelson Road, Whitton, Middlesex TW2 7BB
Tel: 020-8894 9923

■ **LARKHILL,** Wilts
Army Chaplain: Church: St Barbara, Larkhill Camp, Salisbury SP4 8UU **Tel:** 01980-675381

■ **LECONFIELD,** Yorks
Officiating Chaplain: 5 North Bar Without, Beverley, Yorks HU17 7AG
Tel: 01482-882321

■ **LICHFIELD**
Officiating Chaplain: Holy Cross Presbytery, St John Street, Lichfield WS14 9DX
Tel: 01543-263234

■ **MAIDSTONE,** Kent
Officiating Chaplain: 126 Week Street, Maidstone, Kent ME14 1RH
Tel: 01622-756217

■ **MARCHWOOD,** Southampton
Officiating Chaplain: St Bernard's House, Southborne Avenue, Holbury, Hants SO45 2NT **Tel:** 02380-862270

■ **PIRBRIGHT,** Surrey
Army Chaplain: Elizabeth Barracks, Pirbright GU24 2DP **Tel:** 01483 798457

■ **SAIGHTON,** Chester
Officiating Chaplain: 1 Elm Rise, Frodsham, Cheshire WA6 6AJ **Tel:** 01928-735765

■ **SANDHURST,** Berks
Army Chaplain: RMA Sandhurst, Camberley GU15 4PQ **Tel:** 01276 412544
Church: Christ the King, RMA Sandhurst.

■ **SHORNCLIFFE,** Kent
Officiating Chaplain: 2 Ashley Avenue, Folkestone CT19 4PX **Tel:** 01303-275402
Church: Holy Name, Shorncliffe Camp.

■ **SHRIVENHAM,** Oxon
Navy Chaplain: Defence Academy UK/HQ.
Tel: 01793-314488

■ **SWANTON MORLEY,** Norfolk
Officiating Chaplain: 35 London Road, Dereham, Norfolk NR19 1AS
Tel: 01326-694066

■ **TERN HILL,** Salop
Officiating Chaplain: 53 Great Hales Street, Market Drayton, Salop TF9 1JL
Tel: 01630-652568

■ **THORNEY ISLAND**
Served from Emsworth.

■ **TIDWORTH,** Hants
Verger: St Patrick's House, St Patrick's Avenue, Tidworth SP9 7BB
Tel: 01980-602481
Church: SS Patrick & George, St Patrick's Avenue, Tidworth

■ **WARMINSTER,** Wilts
Officiating Chaplain: 31 Boreham Road, Warminster, Wilts BA12 2JP
Tel: 01985-212329

■ **WATERBEACH,** Cambs
Officiating Chaplain: 91 Milton Road, Cambridge CB4 1XB **Tel:** 01223-704640
Church: RC Chapel, RE Barracks, Waterbeach

■ **WATTISHAM,** Suffolk
Officiating Chaplain: HQ 3rd Regt AAC, Wattisham Airfield, Ipswich IP1 7RA
Tel: 01449-728382

■ **WEETON,** Preston
Officiating Chaplain: The Willows Presbytery, Ribby Road, Kirkham, Lancs.
Tel: 01772-683664

■ **WELLINGTON BARRACKS,** London
Officiating Chaplain: 42 Francis Street, London SW1P 1QN **Tel:** 020-7798 9055

■ **WINDSOR,** Berks
Officiating Chaplain: St Edwards Presbytery, 44 Alma Road, Windsor, Berks SL4 3HJ **Tel:** 01753-865163

■ **YORK,** Strensall
Chaplain: St Margaret Clitheroe, 3 Hollytree Lane, Haxby, York YO3 8JY
Tel: 01904-768931

ESTABLISHMENTS IN WALES

■ **BRECON,** Powys
Officiating Chaplain: 11 St Michael's Street, Brecon, LD3 9AB
Tel: 01874-622046
Church: St Michael, St Michael's Street, Brecon

■ **HEREFORD**
Officiating Chaplain: St Christopher, Stirling Lines
Tel: 01981 540051

■ **SENNYBRIDGE, POWYS**
Officiating Chaplain: Served from Brecon.

ROYAL AIR FORCE CHAPLAINS

■ **Principal Chaplain**
Rev Mgr John Walsh CTh VG RAF, *(Liverpool),* 07 Feb 03: Chaplaincy Office, RAF Halton, Aylesbury Bucks HP22 5PG
Tel: 01296-656910
Email:
principalrcchaplain@halton.raf.mod.uk

■ **Chaplains**
Rev Paul Owens *(Leeds)* 21 May 90. **Rev James Caulfield** *(East Anglia)* 7 Aug 97. **Rev Marcus Hodges OP** 7 Aug 97. **Rev Bob Halshaw,** *(Lancaster),* 5 Aug. 99. **Rev Chris Marsden OSA,** 01 Feb 01.

■ **Deacon**
Rev Peter Swindlehurst.

ESTABLISHMENTS IN ENGLAND

■ **BIGGIN HILL,** Surrey
Station Closed, Memorial Chapel still in use.
Officiating Chaplain: Presbytery, 1 Haig Road, Biggin Hill, Westerham, Kent TN16 3LJ
Tel: 01959-571404

■ **BOULMER,** Northumberland
Officiating Chaplain: 3 Prudhoes Villas, Alnwick, Northumberland NE66 1UP
Tel: 01665-602012

■ **BRAMPTON,** Cambs
Officiating Chaplain: Buckden Towers, Buckden, Huntingdon PE18 9TA
Tel: 01480-810344
Church: St Teresa, RAF Brampton, Huntingdon PE18 8QL

■ **BRIZE NORTON,** Oxon
RAF Chaplain: RAF Brize Norton, Carterton, Oxon OX18 3LX
Tel: 01993-842551 ext 7529
Church: sharing St Christopher's, RAF Brize Norton.

■ **CONINGSBY,** Lincs
RAF Chaplain: Served from RAF Cranwell.
Church: Our Lady of Conningsby, RAF Conningsby.

■ **COSFORD,** Shrops
RAF Chaplain: RAF Cosford, Wolverhampton, WV7 3EX
Tel: 01902-377065
Church: Trinity, RAF Cosford

■ **COTTESMORE,** Rutland
Officating Chaplain: Served from Oakham Chaplaincy Centre, RAF Cottesmore, Oakham LE15 7BL **Tel:** 01572-812241

■ **CRANWELL,** Lincs
RAF Chaplain: RAF Cranwell, Sleaford NG34 8HB
Tel: 01400-267025
Church: St Peter, RAFC Cranwell

■ **DIGBY,** Lincs
Served from RAF Cranwell.

■ **HALTON,** Bucks
RAF Chaplain: RAF Halton, Aylesbury. HP22 5PG **Tel:** 01296-656910
Church: Holy Family, RAF Halton.

■ **HEADLEY COURT,** Surrey
Officiating Chaplain: Our Lady & St Peter, Garlands Road, Leatherhead, Surrey KT22 7EA **Tel:** 01372-372278

■ **HENLOW,** Beds
Officiating Chaplain: St Francis of Assisi, 25 High Street, Shefford, Beds. SG17 5DD
Tel: 01462-813436
Church: St Michael, RAF Henlow.

■ **HIGH WYCOMBE,** Bucks
Officiating Chaplain (Deacon): Church: St Teresa, RAF High Wycombe. **Tel:** 01494-496748

■ **HONINGTON,** Suffolk
RAF Chaplain: Served from RAF Marham
Church: St Edmunds, RAF Honington

■ **LEEMING,** North Yorks
Enquiries to Principal Chaplain, Halton.

■ **LINTON-ON-OUSE,** North Yorks
Church: All Saints, RAF Linton-on-Ouse.

■ **LYNEHAM,** Wilts
Served from RAF Brize Norton:
Church: St Joseph, Preston Lane, Lyneham.
Tel: 01249-890381 ext 6453

■ **MANSTON,** Kent
Officiating Chaplain: 9 St Mildreds Road,

Minster, Thanet, Kent CT12 4 DE
Tel: 01843-821340

■ **MARHAM,** Norfolk.
RAF Chaplain: Kings Lynn, Norfolk PE33 9NP **Tel:** 01760-337261 ext 7244
Church: St George, RAF Marham.

■ **NORTHWOOD,** Middlx.
Officiating Chaplain: 32 Hallowell Road, Northwood, Middlesex HA6 1DW
Tel: 01923-825639

■ **ODIHAM,** Hants.
Enquiries to Principal Chaplain, Halton.

■ **SCAMPTON**
Served from Cranwell.

■ **SHAWBURY,** Staffs.
Officiating Chaplain: 17 Claypit Street, Whitchurch SY13 1LE **Tel:** 01948-662935
Church: St Gerard, RAF Shawbury

■ **SHRIVENHAM DEFENCE ACADEMY**
RAF Chaplain: HQ, Greenhill House, Shrivenham SN6 8LA **Tel:** 01793-314488
Church: St Albans

■ **WADDINGTON,** Lincs.
Served from Cranwell.
Church: Our Lady, Waddington

■ **WITTERING**
Served from Cottesmore.

■ **WYTON,** Cambs.
Served from RAF Brampton.

ESTABLISHMENTS IN WALES

■ **ST ATHAN,** South Glam.

■ **VALLEY,** Gwynedd
Officiating Chaplain: St Mary's Church, Longford Road, Holyhead, Gwynedd LL65 1TR
Tel: 01407-762102
Church: Our Lady, RAF Valley.

POLISH CATHOLIC MISSION IN ENGLAND AND WALES

Patron of the Polish Catholic Mission
Blessed Mary of Jesus the Good Shepherd (Frances Siedliska)
25 November

Vicar Delegate for Poles in England and Wales
Mgr Tadeusz Kukla
2 Devonia Road, London N1 8JJ
Tel: 020 7226 3439 **Fax:** 020 7704 7668
E-mail: rector@polishcatholicmission.org.uk

Chancellor of the Polish Catholic Mission
Rev Krzysztof Tyliszczak SChr.
2 Devonia Road, London N1 8JJ **Tel:** 020 7226 3439
E-mail: chancellor@polishcatholicmission.org.uk

Canonical Consultant
Mgr. Ralph Brown Prot. Ap.
Vaughn House, 46 Francis Street, London SW1P 1QN
Tel: 020 7798 9020

Assistant to the Vicar Delegate
Mrs Grazyna Sikora – Sikorski, Tel: 020 7226 3439
E-mail: assistant@polishcatholicmission.org.uk

Website: www.polishcatholicmission.org.uk
E-mail: chancellor@polishcatholicmission.org.uk

■ ADMINISTRATION

■ Council of Deans

Mgr Tadeusz Kukla - Vicar Delegate for Poles in England and Wales, **Mgr Canon Wladyslaw Wyszowadzki** - Deputy Rector, **Rev Krzysztof Tyliszczak SChr** - Chancellor, **Rev Czeslaw Osika SChr**, (South East Deanery), **Mgr Canon Bronislaw Gostomski** (London-North Deanery), **Rev Jerzy Januszkiewicz** (South West Deanery), **Rev Tadeusz Kordys** (Midlands Deanery), **Rev Roman Werner SChr** (London-South Deanery), **Rev Jan Zareba** (Northern Deanery).

■ Child Protection Representative

Mrs. Malgorzata Zajaczkowska
E-mail: chancellor@polishcatholicmission.org.uk

■ Gift Aid Co-ordinator

Mrs. Bozena Junge, 4 Devonia Road, London N1 8JJ **Tel:** 0207 359 8863
E-mail: bozena@polishcatholicmission.org.uk

■ Trustees of the Polish Catholic Mission

Mgr Tadeusz Kukla – Vicar Delegate for Poles in England and Wales - *appointor.*
Mr Janusz Sikora – Sikorski – *chairman*.
Trustees: **Ryszard Gabrielczyk KCSS, Mgr Bronislaw Gostomski, Rev Jerzy Januszkiewicz, Mr Wojciech Tobiasiewicz, Rev Roman Werner SChr, Mgr Wladyslaw Wyszowadzki**

■ Polish Institute of Catholic Action

Coordinates and promotes activities of the lay apostolate among Poles living abroad.
President: **Mr Zenon Handzel**, *Ecclesiastical Assistant:* **Mgr Wladyslaw Wyszowadzki PhD**, *General Secretary:* **Grazyna Bielecka**, 238-246 King Street, London W6 ORF **Tel:** 020 8563 0206

■ Polish Catholic Welfare Bodies

St Albert – Sheltered Accomodation: 180 High Street, Bolton BL3 6P
Tel/Fax: 01204 523 563
St Anthony – Sheltered Accommodation for elderly Poles: 47-49 Foxbourne Road, London SW17 8EN Tel: 020 8672 5106
Laxton Hall – Residential Home for elderly Poles: Laxton Hall, Laxton nr Corby, Northants NN17 3AU **Tel:** 01780 444 292

■ DIOCESE OF WESTMINSTER

■ ACTON

The Holy Family
Vale Lane, Acton W3 0DY
Served from Perivale
M: *Sun 7pm*

■ EALING

Our Lady Mother of the Church
2 Windsor Road, London W5 5PD
• ***Marian Fathers (MIC):*** *Priest in charge:* **Rev Pawel Nawalaniec MIC**, Also in Residence: **Revv Dariusz Kwiatkowski MIC, Antoni Latawiec MIC, Miroslaw Sledzinski MIC, mateusz Turkowski MIC, Tadeusz Wyszomierski MIC**
Tel: 020 8567 1746 **Fax:** 020 8810 0185
E-mail: chris.london@poczta.fm
M: *Sat 1st M of Sun 7.30pm. Sun 9am, 10.15am, 11.30am, 1pm, 5.15pm, 7pm. Hds 8am, 10am, 12.15pm, 7.30pm.*

■ FINCHLEY

St. Philip the Apostle
Regent's Park Road, Finchley N3 3RJ
Rev Krzysztof Kawczynski, The Priest's House, Gravel Hill, Finchley N3 3RJ
Tel: 0780 9412145
E-mail: proboszcz@finchleyparish.co.uk
M: *Sun 6.30pm, Hds 8.30pm*

■ GREENFORD

Our Lady of Visitation
358 Greenford Road, Greenford, Middlesex UB6 9AN **Rev Adam Gliwinski SDB**, 141 Gunnersbury Ave, London W3 8LE
Tel: 020 8993 0097
M: *Sun 5pm*

■ HAMMERSMITH

St. Andrew Bobola
1 Leysfield Road, London W12 9JF
Priest in charge: **Mgr Canon Bronislaw Gostomski**, 18 Greenside Road, London W12 9JG **Tel:** 020 8740 5862
Fax: 020 8733 8848
Also in Residence: **Rev Marek Reczek**, 1 Leysfied Road, London W12 9JF
Tel: 020 8743 8848
E-mail: gostomsk@gotadsl.co.uk
M: *Sat 1st M of Sun 6pm. Sun 9am, 10.30am, 12 noon, 5pm. Hds 10am, 7pm. Mon-Fri 10am, 7pm. Sat 10am.*

■ HESTON

Our Lady Queen of Apostles
15 The Green, Heston Road, Heston, Middlesex TW5 ORLServed from Hammersmith
M: *Sun 7.30pm*

■ HIGHGATE

St. Joseph
Highgate Hill, London N19 5NE
Served from Finchley
M: *Sun 1.30pm, Hds 12 noon.*

■ ISLINGTON

Our Lady of Czestochowa and St Casimir
2 Devonia Road, London N1 8JJ
Tel: 020 7226 9944 **Fax:** 020 7359 8042
E-mail: kciebien@wp.pl
Mgr Tadeusz Kukla, *Vicar Delegate for Poles in England and Wales*; **Revv Krzysztof Ciebien,** *Priest in charge;* **Antoni Prosowicz OFM**
M: *Sat 1st M of Sun 6pm. Sun 9am, 11am, 12.30pm, 3.30pm, 7pm. Hds 9am, 11am, 7pm. Mon-Fri 10.30am, 7pm, Sat 7.30am.*

■ LETCHWORTH

St Hugh of Lincoln
Broadway, Letchworth SG6 3TP
Served from Bedford (Northampton)
M: *Sun 12.30pm*

■ PERIVALE

St. John Fisher
42, Langdale Gardens, Perivale, Middlesex UB6 8DQ **Canon Janusz Gorczyca**
Tel: 020 8997 3682 **E-mail:** gjanusz@onet.eu
M: *Sun 1pm*

■ CHAPLAINCY FOR POLISH STUDENTS

Little Brompton Oratory
Brompton Road, London SW7 2RP
Rev Andrzej Marszewski, 41 Kensington Church Street, Kensington W8 4BB
M: *Sun 12.30pm, 6.30pm*

■ WALTHAM CROSS

The Immaculate Conception and St Joseph
204 High Street, Waltham Cross, Herts EN8 7DP Served from Goodmayes (Brentwood).
M: *Sun 9.30am, Wed 11am*

■ WILLESDEN GREEN

Our Lady of Mercy
182 Walm Lane, London NW2 3AX
Tel: 020 8452 4304 **Fax:** 020 8450 8449
E-mail: parafialondyn@jezuici.vel.pl
Priest in charge: **Rev Jerzy Bialek SJ** *(Superior).* Also in Residence: **Revv Leszek Golebiewski SJ**
M: *Sat 1st M of Sun 7pm, Sun 8am, 11am, 8pm. Hds 7.30am, 9am, 10am, Mon-Fri 7pm.*

St Francis of Assisi
Fleetwood Road, London NW10
M: *Sat 7pm, Sun 9.30am, 12 noon, 7pm*

■ ST ALBANS

SS Alban and Stephen
14 Beaconsfield Road, St Albans, Herts AL1 3RB Served from Dunstable (Northampton)
M: *1st Sun of Month 4pm*

■ DIOCESE OF ARUNDEL & BRIGHTON

■ BOGNOR REGIS
Our Lady of Sorrows
Clarence Road, Bognor Regis, W. Sussex PO21 1JH **Rev Zbigniew Bebenek**, Flat 3B, 148 Aldwick Road, Bognor Regis, W. Sussex PO21 2PA **Tel:** 01243 866 831
E-mail: zbigi_65@onet.eu
M: *Sun 7.15pm*

■ BRIGHTON
St. Mary Magdalen Church
55 Upper North Street, Brighton, E. Sussex BN1 3FH ***Priest in charge:*** **Rev Tadeusz Bialas COr**, Also in Residence: **Rev Waldemar Partyka COr** Flat 1, 30 Sackville Road, Hove, E. Sussex BN3 3FB
Tel: 01273 720 069
E-mail: t.bialas@tiscali.co.uk
M: *Sun 12.30pm, Hds 8pm*

■ CHICHESTER
St Richard
Market Avenue, Chichester, W. Sussex
Served from Bognor Regis
M: *Sun 4pm*

■ CRAWLEY
Our Lady, Queen of Heaven
19 Stagelands, Langley Green, Crawley, West Sussex RH11 7QD Served from Brighton
M: *1st Sun of Month 9.30am, 3rd Sat of Month 7.30pm.*

■ EASTBOURNE
St Agnes
10 Whitley Road, Eastbourne BN22 8NE
Served from Brighton
M: *3rd Sun of month 5pm.*

■ GORING-BY-SEA
English Martyrs
Goring Way, Goring-by-Sea, W. Sussex
Served from Brighton
M: *1st Sun 6pm*

■ GUILDFORD
St. Joseph
12 Eastgate Gardens, Guildford GU1 4AZ
Served from Milford
M: *2nd Sun of month 4pm*

■ HASTINGS
St. Mary Star of the Sea
1 High Street, Hastings, E. Sussex TN34 3EY
Served from Brighton
M: *5pm last Sun of month*

■ HORSHAM
St. John the Evangelist
3 Springfield Road, Horsham, W. Sussex RH12 2PJ Served from Milford
M: *Sun 1pm, Wed 1pm, 1st Fri of month 1pm.*

■ HOVE
Polish Centre
78 Farm Road, Hove BN3 1FD
Served from Brighton
M: *Mon, Wed, Sat 10.30am, Fri 3pm*

■ MILFORD
St Joseph
Portsmouth Road, Milford, Surrey
Rev Miroslaw Slawicki, Ave Maria, Portsmouth Road, Milford, Surrey GU8 5AV
Tel: 01483 420265
E-mail: simir@hotmail.co.uk
M: *1st, 3rd, 4th, 5th of month 8.30am, 6pm, Tue, Fri 11am, Thu 8pm Sat 10am.*

■ REDHILL
St Joseph
122 Ladbrooke Road, Redhill, Surrey RH1 1LF Served from Brighton
M: *2nd Sun 7pm*

■ DIOCESE OF BIRMINGHAM

■ BIRMINGHAM
St Michael
Moor Street, Birmingham B4 7UG
Priest in charge: **Rev Marcin Kordel CRL**, Also in Residence: **Revv Bogdan Lukuc CRL, Apolinary Zawistowski**, 24 Elmbank Grove, Birmingham B20 1JT
Tel: 0121 358 7102 **Fax:** 0121 357 0510
E-mail: marcincrl@hotmail.co.uk
M: *Sat 1st M of Sun 6pm, Sun 11am, 12.15pm, 3pm, Mon-Sat 10.30am, Hds 10.30am, 7pm.*

■ BURTON - ON - TRENT
SS Mary and Mowden
78 Guild Street, Buxton-on-Trent DE14 1NB
Served from Derby (Nottingham)
M: *Sun 2pm.*

■ CANNOCK
St. Mary and St Thomas More
2 Hallcourt Crescent, Walsall Road, Cannock, Staffs WS11 3AB
Served from Wolverhampton
M: *1st Sun of month 12.45pm.*

■ COVENTRY
St Stanislaus Kostka
Springfield Road, Coventry CV1 4GR
Rev Romuald Szczodrowski, The Presbytery, Springfield Road, Coventry CV1 4GR **Tel/Fax:** 024 76222 455
E-mail: romualdsz@gmail.com
M: *Sat 1st M of Sun 5pm. Sun 9am, 11am, Mon-Fri 10.15am.*

■ EVESHAM
St Mary and St Egwin
High Street, Evesham WR11 4EJ
Served from Birmingham
M: *1st Sun of month 3pm.*

■ **GNOSALL,** Nr Stafford
Residential Home, Imstones, Gnosall, Nr Stafford. Served from Stafford.
M: *Sun 3pm.*

■ **KIDDERMINSTER**
Our Lady of Ostra Brama
50 Pitt Street, Kidderminster DY10 2UN
Rev Jan Góra, Tel: 01562 745 914
E-mail: johngora@tiscali.co.uk
M: Sun 10am, 7pm. Mon-Thu 10am, Fri 3pm, Sat 10am; Hds 10am, 7pm.

■ **LEAMINGTON SPA**
Polish Chapel
54 High Street, Leamington Spa CV31 1LW
Served from Redditch.
M: *Sun 11.45am.*

■ **LEEK**
St Mary
Compton, Leek, Staffs ST13 5NH
Served from Stoke-on-Trent.
M: *Sun 8.30am*

■ **OXFORD**
Priory of the Holy Spirit
64 St Giles, Oxford OX1 3LY
Rev Krzysztof Pajak, 59 Carlton Road, Summertown, Oxford OX2 7SB
Tel: 01865 510354
M: *1st Sun of month 12.15am, 11.15am other Suns.*

■ **REDDITCH**
Our Lady of Mount Carmel
Beoley Road West, Redditch, Worcs B98 8LT
Rev Jozef Waclawik, 118 Oakley Road, Redditch B97 4EJ **Tel:** 01527 651131
E-mail: jozef@waclawik.co.uk
M: *Sun 9.45am.*

■ **RUGBY**
St Marie
Dunchurch Road, Rugby CV22 5EL
Served from Coventry.
M: *Sun 12.30pm*

■ **STAFFORD**
St Austin
83 Wolverhampton Road, Stafford ST17 4AW
Rev Wladyslaw Marmol,
70 Wolverhampton Road, Stafford ST17 4AW
Tel: 01785 240 268
M: *Sun 12.15pm.*

■ **STOKE - ON - TRENT**
Our Lady of Czestochowa
1 Battisson Crescent, Stoke on Trent Staffs ST3 4DS
Rev George L. Tyc Tel: 01782 312864
E-mail: george_tyc@hotmail.com
M: *Sun 11.15am, 6pm, Wed, Fri 7pm Hds 7pm.*

■ **STRATFORD-UPON-AVON**
St Gregory the Great
Warwick Road, Stratford-upon-Avon, Warwicks CV37 6UJ Served from Birmingham
M: *Sun 12.30pm.*

■ **WOLVERHAMPTON**
Holy Trinity
Stafford Road, Oxley, Wolverhampton WV10 6DW **Rev Edward Pondel CSSp**, 74 Green Drive, Oxley, Wolverhampton WV10 6DW **Tel/Fax:** 01902 422833
M: *Sat 1st of Sun 6pm, Sun 9.30am, 11.15am, Mon-Fri 10am, Sat 9.30am.*

■ **WORCESTER**
St George
1 Sansome Place, Worcester WR1 1UG
Served from Kidderminster.
M: *2nd and last Sun of month 12.30pm*
St Joseph
Chedworth Drive, Warndon WR4 9PG
M: *2nd, 4th, 5th Sun of month 12.30pm*

■ **DIOCESE OF BRENTWOOD**

■ **BASILDON**
St Basil the Great
Luncies Road, Basildon
Served from Ipswich (East Anglia)
M: *3rd Sun of month 9am*

■ **BRAINTREE**
Our Lady Queen of Peace
The Avenue, Braintree, Essex CM7 3HY
Served from Ipswich (East Anglia)
M: *1st Sun of Month 4pm, 2nd Sun 7pm.*

■ **CHELMSFORD**
Our Lady Immaculate
178 New London Road, Chelmsford CM2 0AR Served from Ipswich (East Anglia)
M: *4th Sun of Month 4pm.*

■ **COLCHESTER**
St James the Less and St Helen
51 Priory Street, Colchester CO1 2QB
Served from Ipswich (East Anglia)
M: *1st Sun of Month 2pm, 3rd Sun 4pm.*

■ **GOODMAYES**
St Cedd
High Road, Goodmayes, Ilford, Essex IG3 8SH
Priest in charge: **Rev Wojciech Rozdzenski SChr**, Also in Residence: **Rev Tomasz Nowak SChr**, 2 Ashgrove Road, Goodmayes, Ilford, Essex IG3 9XE
Tel: 020 8599 1445 **E-mail:** proboszcz@parafialford.co.uk
M: *Sun 12.30pm, Tue 6pm, Thu 9am, Fri 6pm, Sat 9am.*

■ **LEIGH-ON-SEA**
Our Lady of Lourdes and St Joseph
161-181 Leigh Road, Leigh-on-Sea SS9 1NG
Served from Ipswich, East Anglia
M: *1st Sun of month 7pm, 2nd Sun of month 4pm.*

■ **ARCHDIOCESE OF CARDIFF**

■ **BRIDGEND**
St Mary
39 Ewenny Road, Bridgend CF31 3HS
Served from Cardiff
M: *1st Sun of month 7pm.*

■ **CARDIFF**
Nazareth House
Colum Road, Cardiff CF10 3UN
Rev Bogdan Wera, MA, Nazareth House, Colum Road, Cardiff CF10 3UN
Tel: 029 20230427
M: *Sun 11am; 1st Fri of month 7pm.*

■ **CWMBRAN**
Our Lady of Angels
Wesley Street, Cwmbran, Torfaen County Borough NP44 3LT Served from Cardiff.
M: *1st Sun of Month 4pm.*

■ **HEREFORD**
Our Lady Queen of Martyrs
101 Belmont Road, Hereford HR2 7JR
Served from Cardiff
M: *4th Sun of Month 4pm.*

■ **MERTHYR TYDFIL**
St Mary's
St Mary's Priory, Pontmorlais, Merthyr Tydfil CF47 8RG Served from Cardiff.
M: *1st Sat of month 7pm.*

■ **DIOCESE OF CLIFTON**

■ **BATH**
St John the Evangelist
South Parade, Bath BA2 4AF
Served from Trowbridge
M: *1st & 3rd Sun of Month 12.30pm*

■ **BRIDGEWATER**
St Joseph
9 Binford Place TA6 3NJ Served from Bristol
M: *4pm at Christmas and Easter*

■ **BRISTOL**
Our Lady of Ostra Brama
Cheltenham Road, Bristol BS6 5RH
Rev Zygmunt Fraczek
Tel/Fax: 0117 924 3056
M: *Sat 1st M of Sun 7pm., Sun 10am, 7pm. Mon – Sat 8.30am. Fri 8.30am, 7pm. Hds 8.30am, 7pm.*

■ **CHARD**
English Martyrs
2 East Street, Chard TA20 1EP
Served from Taunton
M: *4th Sun of Month 6.30pm*

■ **CHELTENHAM**
Sacred Heart of Jesus and Mary
Moorend Road, Charlton Kings, Cheltenham GL53 9AU
Served from Oxford (Birmingham)
M: *Sun 4pm.*

■ **CIRENCESTER**
St Peter
7 St Peter's Road, Cirencester, Glos GL7 1RE
Served from Swindon
M: *4pm at Christmas and Easter*

■ **DURSLEY**
St Dominic
Jubilee Road, Dursley, Glos. GL11 4ES
Served from Bristol
M: *2nd, 4th and 5th Sun of Month 11am*

■ **GLOUCESTER**
St Peter
London Road, Gloucester GL1 3EX
Served from Oxford (Birmingham)
M: *Sun 2.15pm.*

■ **MINEHEAD**
Chapel at Butlins Served from Taunton
M: *1st Sun of Month 7pm*

■ **SALISBURY**
St Osmund
95 Exeter Street, Salisbury, Wilts SP1 2SF
Served from Trowbridge
M: *2nd Sun of month 4pm.*

■ **SWINDON**
The Sacred Heart of Jesus
Whitbourne Avenue, Swindon, Wilts
Priest in charge: **Rev Witold Maslanka** 27 Groundwell Road, Swindon SN1 2LT
Tel: 01793 531257
E-mail: janusz.paciorek@googlemail.com
M: *Sun 9am, 10.45am; Thu-Sat 9am.*

Holy Rood
2 Groundwell Road, Swindon, Wilts SN1 2LU
M: *Sun 12.30pm, 7pm; Mon-Wed 9am, Thu 10am, 1st Fri of month 10am.*
Served from Taunton
M: *4th Sun of Month 6.30pm*

■ **TAUNTON**
St George
Billet Street, Taunton, Somerset TA1 3NN
Tel: 01823 272700 **Rev Stefan Orzel**
M: *Sat 1st M Sun 6.30pm; Sun 12 noon.*

■ **TROWBRIDGE**
Our Lady of Czestochowa
6 Waterworks Road, Trowbridge, Wilts. BA14 OAL
Rev Andrzej Budzynski, Tel: 01225 752 930

E-mail: andrzej.budzynski@btinternet.com
M: *Sun 10.45am, 7pm, Mon-Sat 9am, Hds 10am, 7pm.*

■ YEOVIL
Holy Ghost
The Avenue, Yeovil Served from Taunton
M: *4th Sun of month 4pm.*

■ WIVELISCOMBE
St Richard
Church Street, Wiveliscombe
Served from Bristol
M: *2nd Sun of Month 11am.*

■ DIOCESE OF EAST ANGLIA

■ BRANDON
St Thomas of Canterbury
Weeting Road, Brandon
Served from Cambridge
M: *Sun 9am.*

■ BURY ST EDMUNDS
St Edmund King and Martyr
21 Westgate Street, Bury St Edmunds, Suffolk IP33 1QG Served from Ipswich
M: *3rd Sat 1st M Sun 4pm.*

■ CAMBRIDGE
Our Lady and the English Martyrs
Hills Road, Cambridge CB2 1JR
Tel/Fax: 01223 368539
Rev Piotr Kisiel,
E-mail: parafia.cambridge@googlemail.com
M: *Sun 12.15pm.*

Polish Centre Chapel
231 Chesterton Road, Cambridge CB4 1RJ
M: *Sun 7.30pm, Mon, Wed 7.30pm, Tue, Thu 10am; Fri 3pm, Sat 9.30am.*

■ HUNTINGDON
St Michael Archangel
82 Hartford Road, Huntingdon Cambs PE29 1XG Served from Cambridge
M: *Sun 4pm.*

■ IPSWICH
St Mary
322 Woodbridge Road, Ipswich, Suffolk IP4 4BD *Priest in charge:* **Rev Krzysztof Kita,** Also in Residence: **Rev Wladyslaw Liptak,** 82 Wellesley Road, Ipswich IP4 1PH
Tel: 01473 217 391
E-mail: atikk@poczta.onet.pl
M: *Mon, Wed, Thu, Fri 10am; Sat 1st M of Sun 7.15pm Sun 12 noon; Hds 12 noon.*

■ KING'S LYNN
Our Lady of Annunciation
London Road, King's Lynn, Norfolk
Served from Boston
M: *Sat 4pm.*

■ NORWICH
Cathedral of St John the Baptist
St Giles Gate, Norwich Served from Ipswich
M: *2nd & 4th Sat of Month 1st M of Sun 4pm.*

■ PETERBOROUGH
St Peter and All Souls
Park Road, Peterborough, Cambs PE1 2RS
Rev Piotr Redlinski SChr, 189 Fletton Avenue, Peterborough PE2 8DE **Tel:** 01733 552726 **E-mail:** predlinski@yahoo.com
M: *Sun 12.30pm, 7.15pm.*

Polish Mission
63 Church Street, Stanground, Peterborough
M: *Sun 10.30am.*

■ SUDBURY
Our Lady and St John the Evangelist
The Croft, Sudbury, Suffolk CO10 1HW
Served from Ipswich
M: *4th Sun of M 7pm.*

■ WISBECH
Our Lady and St Charles Borromeo
69 Queen's Road, Wisbech, Cambs PE13 2P Served from Peterborough.
M: *Sun 4.30pm.*

■ DIOCESE OF HALLAM

■ BARNSLEY
Holy Rood
George Street, Barnsley S70 1AX
Served from Sheffield.
M: *1st & 3rd Sun of Month 4pm.*

■ CHESTERFIELD
St Joseph Convent
Newbold Road, Derbyshire S41 7PL
Served from Doncaster
M: *Sun 9.30am.*

■ DONCASTER
St Peter in Chains
Chequer Road, Doncaster DN1 2AA
Rev Marek Krol
M: *Sun 1.15pm Hds 10am.*

■ RETFORD
St Joseph
Babworth Road, Retford, Notts DN22 7BP
Served from Mansfield (Nottingham)
M: *4th Sun of Month 4pm.*

■ ROTHERHAM
St Bede
Station Road, Rotherham S60 1HF
Served from Sheffield
M: *2nd and 4th Sun of Month 5pm.*

■ SHEFFIELD
Our Lady of Ostra Brama
518–520 Ecclesall Road, Sheffield S11 8PY
Rev Wladyslaw Wlodarczyk, 32 Bristol

Road, Sheffield S11 8RL
Tel: 0114 266 3952
E-mail: wladyslaw-wk@op.pl
M: *Sun 10.30am, Mon, Tue 6.30pm, Thu 9.30am, Fri 10am; Sat 9.30am.*

The Cathedral Church of St Marie
Norfolk Street, Sheffield S1 2JB
M: *Sun 12.30pm.*

■ WORKSOP

St Joseph the Worker and St Mary
Wingfield Avenue, Worksop, Notts S81 0SF
Served from Mansfield (Nottingham)
M: *3rd Sun of month 4pm.*

■ DIOCESE OF HEXHAM AND NEWCASTLE

■ CONSETT

St Patrick
Victoria Road, Consett, Co Durham
DH8 5AX Served from Newcastle-upon-Tyne
M: *1st Sun of Month 3pm.*

■ NEWCASTLE–UPON–TYNE

Our Lady of Czestochowa
2 Maple Terrace, Newcastle–upon–Tyne
NE4 7SF **Rev Robert Mazurowski**, 2 Maple Terrace, Newcastle–upon–Tyne NE4 7SF
Tel: 0191 273 3575
M: *Sat 1st M of Sun 6pm. Sun 10am, 11.15am, 6pm, Mon-Fri 11am.*

■ DIOCESE OF LANCASTER

■ BLACKPOOL

St Kentigern
25a Newton Drive, Blackpool FY3 8BT
Served from Lancaster.
M: *Sun 12.30pm.*

■ CARLISLE

Our Lady and St Joseph
Warwick Square, Carlisle, Cumbria CA1 1LB
Served from Lancaster.
M: *Sun 5.30pm*

■ LANCASTER

Our Lady Queen of Poland
Nelson Street, Lancaster LA1 1PT
Rev Marian Jachym SChr, Polish Centre, Nelson Street, Lancaster LA1 1PT
Tel: 01524 39820 **E-mail:** jachym4@tlen.pl
M: *Sat 1st M of Sun 6pm. Sun 12 noon,* Wed, Thu 7pm, Fri 10am.

■ PRESTON

1. St Ignatius
Meadow Street, Preston PR1 1TT
Rev Krzysztof Góralski, St Ignatius Presbytery, St Ignatius Square, Preston PR1 1TT **Tel:** 01772 821292
M: *Sat 1st M of Sun 6pm; Sun 12 noon; Mon-Fri 10am.*

2. Our Lady Queen of Poland
Served from Blackburn.
M: *10.30am.*

■ DIOCESE OF LEEDS

■ BRADFORD

Our Lady of Czestochowa
29 Edmund Street, Bradford BD5 0BH
Rev Wieslaw Duracz, *(Priest in charge),*
Rev Krzysztof Chaim
Tel/Fax: 01274 720848
E-mail: wieslaw@duracz.freeserve.co.uk
M: *Sat 1st M of Sun 6pm, Sun 10am, 11.15am, Mon-Fri 10am, Hds 10.30am, 7.30pm.*

■ DEWSBURY

Our Lady and St Paulinus
Cemetery Road, Dewsbury, West Yorkshire
WF13 2SE Served from Bradford.
M: *Sun 3pm.*

■ HALIFAX

1. St Marie
Gibbet Street, Halifax, W. Yorks HX1 5DH
Served from Bradford.
M: *Sun 1pm.*

2. Our Lady of Czestochowa
24 Francis Street, Halifax HX1 5JY
Served from Bradford
M: *Tue 12 noon, Hds 12 noon.*

■ HARROGATE

St Aelred of Rievalux
Skipton Road, Harrogate HG1 3HD
Served from Leeds
M: *1st & 4th Sun of month 4.30pm.*

■ HEMSWORTH

The Sacred Heart
Market Street, Hemsworth, Pontefract,
WF9 4LB Served from Mansfield (Nottingham)
Rev Szczepan Bober SAC
Tel: 01623 626470
E-mail: szczepan@szczepan.freeserve.co.uk
M: *2nd Sun of Month 3.15pm.*

■ HUDDERSFIELD

Our Lady of Czestochowa Queen of Poland
88 Fitzwilliam Street, Huddersfield HD1 5BB
Rev Stanislaw Wachala Tel: 01484 420474
E-mail: wujeksz@op.pl
M: *Sun 9.30am, 11.15am. Mon-Thur 9am, Fri 7.30pm.*

- ***Chapel in the Polish Residential Home***
  'Jasna Gora' 52 Fixby Road,
  Huddersfield HD2 2JQ
  M: *Sun 12 noon, Mon-Sat 8.30am.*

■ LEEDS

Our Lady of Czestochowa and St Stanislaus Kostka
Newton Hill Road, Leeds LS7 4JE
Rev Jan Ignacy Zareba, 6A Harehills Lane,

Leeds LS7 4EY **Tel/Fax:** 0113 262 3220
E-mail: janzareba@tiscali.co.uk
M: *Sat 1st M of Sun 6.30pm, Sun 9.30am, 11.00am, Mon, Tue 10am, Wed 11am, Thu, Fri 10am, Sat 9am, Hds 10am, 7pm.*

■ **DIOCESE OF LIVERPOOL**

■ **CHORLEY**
St Mary
Mount Pleasant, Chorley PR7 2SR
Served from Bolton (Salford)
M: *2nd and 4th Sun of Month 1.45pm.*

■ **LEYLAND**
St Mary
Broadfield Drive, Leyland PR5 1PD
Served from Preston
M: *3rd Sun of Month 6pm.*

■ **LIVERPOOL**
Cathedral of Christ the King (CRYPT)
Mount Pleasant, Liverpool L3 5TQ
Served from Northwich (Shrewsbury)
M: *Sun 1pm.*

■ **SOUTHPORT**
St Marie on the Sands
25 Seabank Road, Southport, Merseyside
Served from Preston
M: *1st & 3rd Sun M 2pm.*

■ **WARRINGTON**
St Benedict
Rhodes Street, Warrington WA2 7QE
Served from Northwich (Shrewsbury)
M: *1st & 3rd Sun of month 6pm.*

■ **WIGAN**
St Mary
Standish Gate, Wigan WN1 1XL
Served from Preston
M: *2nd and 4th Sun of Month 2pm.*

■ **DIOCESE OF MENEVIA**

■ **LAMPETER**
Our Lady of Mount Carmel
Pontfaen Road, Lampeter Ceredigion SA48 7BS Served from Cardiff (Cardiff)
M: *2nd Sun of Month 2.30pm.*

■ **SWANSEA**
St Benedict
Llythird Avenue, Sketty Road, Swansea SA2 011 Served from Cardiff (Cardiff)
M: *3rd Sun of Month 1.30pm.*

■ **DIOCESE OF MIDDLESBROUGH**

■ **BRIDLINGTON**
Our Lady and St Peter
Victoria Road, Bridlington YO15 2AT
Served from Hull
M: *1st Sat month 1st M of Sun 7pm.*

■ **HULL**
St Wilfrid
The Boulevard, Hull
Rev Radoslaw Szymoniak. 187 Pickering Road, Hull HU4 6TD **Tel:** 01482 574930
M: *Sun 5pm, Hds 7pm.*

■ **MIDDLESBROUGH**
Sacred Heart and St Patrick
Linthorpe Road, Middlesbrough. Served from Newcastle (Hexham & Newcastle)
M: *Last Sun of Month 3pm.*

■ **SCARBOROUGH**
St Peter
Castle Road, Scarborough
Served from Hull
M: *Sun 9.30am.*

■ **YORK**
English Martyrs
Dalton Terrace, York YO24 4DA
Served from Hull
M: *Sun 1.30pm.*

■ **DIOCESE OF NORTHAMPTON**

■ **AYLESBURY**
Our Lady of Lourdes
69 Camborne Avenue, Bedgrove, Aylesbury HP21 9UE Served from High Wycombe.
M: *Sun 8.30am.*

■ **BEDFORD**
Sacred Heart of Jesus and St Cuthbert
8 Mill Street, Bedford MK40 3EU
Canon Grzegorz Aleksandrowicz,
Tel: 01234 266 901/343 105
E-mail: grzegorz@btinternet.com
M: *Sun 10am, 7pm.*

■ **CORBY**
St Brendan
151 Beanfield Road, Corby, Northants NN18 OAZ Served from Laxton Hall.
Rev Edward Sopala SChr
Tel: 01780 444 242
M: *Sun 4pm.*

■ **DAVENTRY**
St Augustine
32 London Road, Daventry, Northampton NN11 4BZ Served from Northampton
M: *1st & 3rd Sat month 1st M Sun 6.30pm.*

■ **DUNSTABLE**
Our Lady of Czestochowa
17 Victoria Street, Dunstable, Beds LU6 3AZ
Revv Czeslaw Osika SChr, *(Priest in Charge),* **Grzwegorz Kozienski SChr.**
Tel/Fax: 01582 662 807
E-mail: osika@ppld.co.uk
M: *Sun 9am, 11.00am. Hds 11am, 7pm. Wed-Fri 10am. Mon, Tue, Thu 8.30am.*

■ GREAT MISSENDEN
Immaculate Heart of Mary
Damien House, 23 High Street, Great Missenden, Bucks HP16 9AA **Rev Mariusz Gutowski SChr**, 22 Misbourne Drive, Great Missenden HP16 OBL **Tel:** 01494 868 248
E-mail: mariusz11@hotmail.com
M: *Sun 12.30pm.*

■ HENLEY–ON–THAMES
St Anne's
St Joseph's Chapel
Fawley Court, Henley–on–Thames, Oxon RG9 3AE
- ***Marian Fathers (MIC),*** **Rev Wojciech Jasinski MIC** *(Delegate of the Provincial in Great Britain and Superior)*, Also in Residence: **Rev Andrzej Gowkielewicz MIC**
Tel: 01491 574 917/506
Fax: 01491 411 587
M: *Sun 12 noon, 7.30pm, Mon – Thurs 7.30pm (St Joseph's), Fri 7.30pm – St Ann's.*

■ HIGH WYCOMBE
1. St Wulstan
Hollis Road, Totteridge Bucks HP13 7UN
Rev Rafal Jaroslawski, 45 Alexandra Park, Queen Alexander Road, High Wycombe HP11 2HB **Tel:** 01494 462 994
E-mail: rafal.jar@op.pl
M: *Sun 10.45am.*

2. St Augustine
24 Amersham Hill, High Wycombe, Bucks HP13 6NZ
M: *Every Tue and Thu 10.45am.*

■ LAXTON HALL, Nr Corby
Mary Immaculate, Mother of the Church and Her Crusade
Laxton Hall, Laxton nr Corby, Northants NN17 3AU **Rev Edward Sopala SChr**
- ***Sisters of Mary Immaculate:***
Tel: 01780 444 292
- ***Laxton Hall Elderly People's Home:***
Tel: 01780 444 649
M: *Sun 10am, 12 noon. Hds 10am, 7pm.*

■ LEIGHTON BUZZARD
The Sacred Heart
5 Beaudesert, Leighton Buzzard, Beds LU7 8HZ Served from Dunstable.
M: *Last Sun of Month 4.30pm.*

■ LITTLE CHALFONT
St Aidan
Finch Lane, Little Chalfont, Bucks HP7 9NE
Served from Great Missenden.
M: *Sun 9am.*

■ MILTON KEYNES
St Augustine
Langcliffe Drive, Heelands, Milton Keynes, MK13 7PL Served from Dunstable.
M: *1st Sun of Month 1pm*

■ NORTHAMPTON
SS Stanislaus and Lawrence
Duke Street, Northampton NN1 3BA
Revv Bogdan Cisek (*Priest in charge*), **Stanislaw Labuda,** Flat 2, Lawrance House, Duke Street, Northampton NN1 3BA
Tel/Fax: 01604 631623
E-mail: bcisek@hotmail.com
M: *Sun 10.30am, 7pm, Hds.7pm.*

■ RUSHDEN
St Peter
Higham Road, Rushden, Northants.
Served from Northampton.
M: *1st and 3rd Sun of Month 7.50am.*

■ SLOUGH
Divine Mercy and Our Lady Queen of Poland
48 Pitts Road, Slough, Berks SL1 3XH
Tel: 01753 533 861 **E-mail:** darek.kuwaczka@btinternet.com
Revv Dariusz Kuwaczka (*Priest in charge*)
Rev Krzysztof Nowak
M: *Sat 1st M of Sun 6pm. Sun 8.30am, 10am, 11.30am, 6pm. Mon, Tues, Thu, Sat 9.30am, 6pm. Wed, Fri 10.15am, 6pm.*

■ WELLINGBOROUGH
Our Lady of the Sacred Heart
Ranelagh Road, Wellingborough, Northants
Served from Northampton.
M: *Sun 12.30pm Hds 12.30pm 5pm.*

■ DIOCESE OF NOTTINGHAM

■ BOSTON
St Mary
24 Horncastle Road, Boston PE21 9BU
Rev Slawomir Hermanowicz
Tel: 0777 3366120
M: *Sun 7.30am, 6pm; Mon - Wed 6pm.*

■ BUXTON
St Anne
Terrace Road, Buxton SK17 6DU
Served from Stoke on Trent (Birmingham).
M: *2nd & 4th Sun of month 3pm.*

■ DERBY
St Maximilian Kolbe
9 Gordon Road, Derby DE23 6WR
Rev Wlodzimierz Pajak SChr
Tel: 01332 364078 **Fax:** 01332 343950
E-mail: spider.derby@talk.talk.net
M: *Sat 1st M of Sun 5pm, Sun 9.30am, 11am, Mon, Tues, Thu, Fri, Sat 9am, Wed 9.45am, Hds 11am, 7pm.*

■ LOUGHBOROUGH
St Mary
97 Ashby Road, Loughborough LE11 3AB

Served from Melton Mowbray.
M: *Sun 12.45pm.*

■ LEICESTER
Conversion of St Paul
Wakerley Road, Leicester LE5 4WD
Rev Tadeusz Kordys, 58 Bodnant Avenue, Leicester LE5 5RA **Tel/Fax:** 0116 2217 006
E-mail: t.kordys@ntlworld.com
M: *Sat 1st M of Sun 6pm, Sun 8.45am, 11.15am, Mon, Wed, Fri 9.30am, Tue, Thu 10.15am.*

■ LINCOLN
St Hugh
Broadgate, Lincoln LN2 5AQ
Served from Scunthorpe.
M: *Sun 11.45am.*

■ MANSFIELD
Our Lady of Ostra Brama and St Barbara
Windmill Lane, Mansfield NG18 2AL
Rev Szczepan Bober SAC
Tel: 01623 626 470
E-mail: szczepan@szczepan.freeserve.co.uk
M: *Sun 11am, Wed, Fri 7pm, Hds 7pm.*

■ MELTON MOWBRAY
Our Lady of Czestochowa
119 Sandy Lane, Melton Mowbray, Leics. LE13 0AW **Canon Stanislaw Tylka**
Tel: 01664 562101
E-mail: stylka@ntlworld.com
M: *Sat 1st M of Sun 7pm, Sun 11am, Hds 9am, 7pm, Mon- Thu 9am, Fri 7pm.*

■ NOTTINGHAM
Our Lady of Czestochowa
2 Sherwood Rise, Nottingham NG7 6JN
Tel/Fax: 0115 960 4740
Revv Wlodzimierz Skoczen (*Priest in charge*); **Pawel Wlodzimierz**
M: *Sun 9.30, 11.00, 18.30pm, Mon-Fri 9.30am, 11am, Sat 12.15pm, Hds 11am, 6.30pm.*

■ SCUNTHORPE
The Holy Souls
Frodingham Road, Scunthrope DN15 7TA
Rev Grzegorz Czaja SChr, Tel: 01724 855698 **E-mail:** grzegorz@surf3.net
M: *Sun 5pm, Mon, Tue, Thu, Fri, Sat 9.30am, Wed 12 noon.*

■ SKEGNESS
Sacred Heart
22 Grosvenor Road, Skegness, Lincs PE25 2DB Served form Boston
M: *Sun 12.30pm.*

■ SPALDING
The Immaculate Conception and St Norbert
52 St Thomas Rd, Spalding, Lincs PE11 2XX
Served from Peterborough (East Anglia).
M: *Sat 6.30pm.*

■ DIOCESE OF PLYMOUTH

■ CALLINGTON
Our Lady of Victories
Lower Coronation Terrace, Callington
Served from Newton Abbot.
M: *Sat 7pm once a month*

■ NEWTON ABBOT
The Chapel of Christ the King and Our Lady of Ostra Brama
Polish Home, Ilford Park, Stover, Newton Abbot, TQ12 6QH **Rev Edward Stachurski**, **Tel:** 01626 332 043
E-mail: edwardstachurski@yahoo.co.uk
M: *Sun 10.30am.*

■ DIOCESE OF PORTSMOUTH

■ ALTON
St Mary
59 Normandy Street, Alton, Hants GU34 1DN
Served from Milford (Arundel & Brighton).
M: *1st Sat of month 3.15pm*

■ BOURNEMOUTH
The Sacred Heart
Albert Road, Richmond Hill, Bournemouth
Served from Southampton No 1.
M: *Sun 1pm.*

■ EASTLEIGH
The Holy Cross
53 Leigh Road, Eastleigh, Hants SO50 9DD
Served from Southampton No 1.
M: *Sun 9.00am.*

■ ISLE OF WHITE
St Thomas of Canterbury
96 Pyle Street, Newport, Isle of White PO30 1UH Served from Southampton No 1.
M: *3rd Sun of month 7pm.*

■ PORTSMOUTH
St Swithun
Waverly Road, Southsea, Portsmouth
Served from Southampton No 1.
M: *4th Sun of Month 7pm.*

■ READING
Sacred Heart
Watlington Street, Reading RG1 4RF
Priest in charge: **Rev Jerzy Januszkiewicz**, Also in Residence: **Rev Krzysztof Zalewski**, 83 London Road, Reading RG1 4RF **Tel:** 0118 957 3647
E-mail: j.januszkiewicz@btinternet.com
M: *Sat 1st M of Sun 7pm, Sun 9am, 10.30am, 7pm, Mon, Tues, Wed – 10am, Thu 12.30pm, Fri 7pm.*

■ SOUTHAMPTON
1. Our Lady Queen of Poland
507 Portswood Road, Southampton S017 1TH **Revv Wojciech Stachyra SChr**

(Priest in charge); **Mariusz Urbanowski SChr**, 15 Landguard Road, Southampton SO15 5DL **Tel:** 023 8022 4418
E-mail: wstachyra@yahoo.com
M: *Fri 7.30pm, Wed 12.30pm.*

2. St Edmund
The Avenue, Southampton SO15 2EQ
Served from Southamton No 1.
M: *Sat 1st M of Sun 7pm.*

3. Sacred Heart (Convent Chapel)
Bracken Lane, Southampton SO16 6UZ
Served from Southamton No 1.
M: *Sun 10.45am.*

■ DIOCESE OF SALFORD

■ ASHTON–UNDER–LYNE
St Ann
Burlington Street, Ashton-under-Lyne, Lancs OL6 7DG Served from Manchester
Rev Jozef Wozniak SChr
E-mail: wozniakjozef@talktalk.net
M: *Sun 9am, Fri 1.15pm, Hds 1.15pm*

■ BAMBER BRIDGE
St Mary
Brownedge Lane, Bamber Bridge, Preston PR5 6SP Served from Preston
M: *2nd Sun of M 4.30pm*

■ BLACKBURN
Our Lady Queen of Poland
44 Preston New Road, Blackburn BB2 6AH
Tel: 01254 57067
Rev Robert Pytel
E-mail: kspytel@poczta.onet.pl
M: *Sun 10.30am.*

■ BOLTON
The Good Shepherd
180 High Street, Bolton BL3 6PL
Rev Ryszard Zalewski
Tel/Fax: 01204 523 563
E-mail: ryszal@ntlworld.com
M: *Sun 12 noon. Hds 12 noon. Wed 11.30am, Fri 3pm.*

■ BURY
Our Lady Queen of Poland
East Street, Bury BL9 0RU
Served from Bolton.
M: *Sun 10am, Hds 10am, Mon 6.30pm, Thu 11am, First Fri of Month 10am, Sat 10am.*

■ MANCHESTER
Church of Divine Mercy
Moss Lane East, Moss Side, Manchester
Revv Andrzej Zuziak SChr *(Priest in charge)*; **Provincial of the Society of Christ; Artur Stelmach SChr, Pawel Urbanek Schr; Jozef Wozniak SChr; Br Marek Labudda;** 196 Lloyd Street North, Manchester M14 4QB
Tel: 0161 226 1588 **Fax:** 0161 232 0450
E-mail: andrzej@zuziak.me.uk
Rev Jan Wojczynski SChr, 18 Carlton Road, Manchester M16 8BB
Tel: 0161 226 1836
M: *Sat 1st m of Sun 7pm, Sun 10am, 12 noon, 7pm, Hds 8.30am, 12 noon, 7pm, Mon 8.30am, 10am, Tue-Fri 8.30am, 10am, 7pm.*
- ***Polish Centre:*** Cheetham Hill Road, Manchester M8 7PF
  M: *Sun 8.45am, Hds 8.45am.*
- ***Society of Christ Fathers (Soc Chr):*** 18 Carlton Road, Manchester M16 8BB
- ***Albertine Sisters Polish Residential Home:*** Dom Polski, 18 Carlton Road, Manchester M16 8BB

■ OLDHAM
1. Our Lady of Mount Carmel and St Patrick
40 Union Street West, Oldham OL8 1DL
Served from Rochdale.
M: Sun 12.30pm.

2. Our Lady of Czestochowa
Chamber Road, Oldham OA8 4NZ
Served from Rochdale.
M: *Tue, Thu 10am Hds 10am.*

■ ROCHDALE
Our Lady of Czestochowa and Maximilian Kolbe
'Westfield', Manchester Road, Rochdale OL11 4LX Rev **Edward Soska SChr**, 31 Cheltenham Street, Rochdale OL11 3QJ
Tel: 01706 642 649
E-mail: edwardsoska@fsmail.net
M: *Sun 10.45am, Wed, Fri 10am, Hds 7pm.*

■ DIOCESE OF SHREWSBURY

■ CHESTER
St Werburgh
Grosvenor Park Road, Chester CH1 1QJ
Served from Northwich
M: *2nd & 3rd Sun of month 4.30pm.*

■ CREWE
Our Lady of Ostra Brama
71 West Street, Crewe CW1 3HF **Rev Grzegorz Januszewski SChr, Tel:** 01270 256 284 **E-mail:** grzegorz-60@talktalk.net
M: *Sun 12.45am, Hds 10am.*

■ HIGHER HEATH, Nr Whitchurch
Our Lady of Ostra Brama
Higher Heath, Whitchurch SY13 2HP
Served from Crewe.
M: *Sun 11am.*

■ NORTHWICH
Our Lady of Czestochowa
107 London Road, Northwich CW9 8AT
Revv Stanislaw Gladysz SChr *(priest in*

charge), **Pawel Borysiewicz SChr**
E-mail: stanislaw.gladysz@gmail.com
M: *Sat 1st M Sun 7pm, Sun 10am, Mon, Tue, Wed, Fri 10am, Thu 11am, Hds 11am, 7pm.*

■ TELFORD

St Patrick
King Street, Wellington, Telford TF1 3AP
Served from Stafford.
M: *Sun 5pm.*
Rev Leon Ostaszewski *(supply priest)*, 8 Newland Drive, Liscard, Wallasey CH44 2AX **Tel:** 0151 639 0145

■ DIOCESE OF SOUTHWARK

■ BALHAM

1. Christ the King
232-234 Balham High Road, Balham SW17 7AW
Rev Mgr Canon Wladyslaw Wyszowadzki, DD, PhD, *(priest in charge)*
Tel: 020 8672 5070 **Fax:** 020 8682 1770
E-mail: ks.wyszowadzki@btinternet.com
Rev Jan Swietek Tel: 020 8767 5695
M: *Sun 9.30am, 10.45am, 12noon, 6pm, Mon-Sat 8am, 9am.*

2. St Anthony Chapel
47-49 Foxbourne Road, Balham SW17
Served from Balham 1
M: *Sun 8.30am. Tue 9am.*

■ BROCKLEY

St Mary Magdalene Chapel
73 Comerford Road, Brockley, SE4 2BA
Rev Teodor Bartnik SDB, 8A Waldram Park Road **Tel:** 020 8378 5228
M: *Sun 1pm.*

■ CROYDON – CRYSTAL PALACE

Merciful Jesus
6-8 Oliver Grove, London SE25 6EJ
Canon Aleksander Ozog *(Priest in charge)*, **Rev Witold Maslanka**
Tel: 020 8653 8701 **Fax:** 020 8771 0133
E-mail: ozog@aleksander.fsnet.co.uk
M: *Sat 1st M of Sun 6.30pm, Sun 10am, 11.30am.*

■ FOREST HILL

Chapel of St John Bosco
8 Waldram Park Road, London SE23 2PN
Rev Teodor Bartnik SDB,
Tel: 020 8378 5228
M: *2nd Sun of Month 11.30am, (not in July and August). Mon, Fri 7.30pm, Hds 7.30pm.*

■ PUTNEY

St John the Evangelist
St John's Road, Putney SW15
Rev Roman Werner SChr *(Priest in charge)*, **Cezary Kraczkowski SChr**: Polish Centre, Ravenna Road, London, SW15 6AW
Tel: 020 8788 3933 **Fax:** 020 8780 3670
E-mail: romanwerner@yahoo.co.uk
M: *Sat 1st M of Sun 6pm, Sun 9am, 10am, 11.15am, 6pm. Hds 10am, 11.15am, 7pm, Mon – Fri 10.30am, 7pm.*

■ SEVENOAKS

St Thomas of Canterbury
12 Granville Road, Sevenoaks TN13 1ER
Rev Jozef Waclawik CHS
E-mail: jozef@waclawik.freeserve.co.uk
M: *2nd Sun of month 4pm, 3rd & 4th Sun of month 7pm.*

■ WIMBLEDON PARK

Christ the King
The Crescent, Wimbledon Park SW19
Served from Putney.
M: *Sun 12.15pm.*

■ DIOCESE OF WREXHAM

■ PENLEY, Nr Overton

Wrexham Polish Hospital Chapel
Polish General Hospital, Penley nr Overton, Wrexham LL14 OLH
Part-time Chaplain: **Rev Grzegorz Januszewski SChr**
E-mail: grzegorz-60@talktalk.net
M: *Sat 2pm.*

■ PWLLHELI

Our Lady and St Cynfil
Penrhos Home, Pwllheli LL53 7HN
Rev Stanislaw Leniart SChr
Tel: 01758 613160
M: *Sat 1st M of Sun 6pm. Sun 9.30am.*

■ WREXHAM

Cathedral Church
Regent Street, Wrexham
Served from Crewe.
M: *3rd Sun of Month 4.30pm.*

APOSTOLIC EXARCHATE FOR UKRAINIANS IN GREAT BRITAIN

Erected 10 June 1957 for the faithful of the Ukrainian Greek Catholic Rite in England and Wales; extended to Scotland and Great Britain, 12 May 1968.

Apostolic Exarch

Awaiting Appointment

Bishops Emeritus

The Most Rev Michael Kuchmiak, CSsR, DD, titular Bishop of Agathopolis. Born in Obertyn, pov. Horodenka, Ukraine, 5th February 1923; ordained 13th May 1956; consecrated by Metropolitan Stephen Sulyk 27th April 1988 and appointed Auxiliary to Philadelphia; appointed Apostolic Exarch for Ukrainian Catholics in GB 24th June 1989 and installed on 10th October 1989. Retired, 5th April 2002.

Residence:
St John Parish, 719 Sandford Avenue, Newark, NJ 07106, USA. Tel: (973) 371-1356, Fax: (973) 416-0085

The Most Rev Paul Chomnycky OSBM, titular Bishop of Buffada. Born in Vancouver, BC, Canada, 19th May, 1954; ordained 1st October, 1988; consecrated by Cardinal Lubomyr Husar, 11th June, 2002, in Edmonton, AB, Canada; appointed Apostolic Exarch for Ukrainian Catholics in GB, 5th April, 2002, installed on 16th June, 2002 Retired, January 2006

Residence:
14 Peveril Road, Stamford, Connecticut, 06902, USA. Tel: (203-324-7698. Fax: 203-967-9948

■ **ADMINISTRATION**

■ **Apostolic Administrator**
Rev Bohdan-Benjamin Lysykanych
All Saints Presbytery, Chadderton Way, Oldham OL9 6HD **Tel:** 0161-633 5636

■ **CURIA**
22 Binney Street, London W1K 5BQ
Tel: 020-7629 1073

■ **Consultors**
Revv Bohdan-Benjamin Lysykanych, Bohdan-Benjamin Lysykanych, Stephen Wiwcharuk, Andrew Choma.

■ **Vicar General**
Awaiting Appointment

■ **Financial Secretary**
Awaiting Appointment

■ **LONDON**
† Ukrainian Greek Catholic Cathedral of the Holy Family in Exile (Opened 29 June 1968)
Duke Street, Mayfair W1K 5BQ
Rev Irineu Kraiczy (OSBM) (*Administrator*).
Rev Josafat Lescesen, 79 Holland Park, London W11 3SW
Tel: 01207-221 1890 **Fax:** 0207-229 4419

■ **ASHTON-UNDER-LYNE,** Lancs
Services at: **St Paul's**
Stockport Road. Served from Oldham.

■ **BEDFORD**
St Josaphat (1959)
52 York Street. Served from Peterborough.

■ **BLACKBURN**
Services at: **St Alban**
Lingard Terrace. Served from Bolton.

■ **BOLTON**
All Saints Ukrainian Catholic Church
All Saints Street, Bolton
Rev Andrew B Choma. 104 Lonsdale Road, BL1 4PN **Tel:** 01204-840087

■ **BRADFORD,** West Yorks
The Holy Trinity & Our Lady of Pochayey
Wilmer Road, Bradford
Revv Ivo Chomiak (OSBM), Miguel Navochadla (OSBM): 10 Park View Road, Bradford, W. Yorks BA9 9PA
Tel:01274-542307 **Fax:** 01274-409093

■ **BURY**
Services at: **St Marie's**
Manchester Road. Served from Manchester.

■ **CARLISLE**
Ukrainian House, Silloth Street.
M: *Sat 1st M of Sun (eve 6.30pm) First Sun of the Month.*

■ **COVENTRY**
St Vladimir the Great
86 Station Street, Coventry CV6 5FR
Rev Myhaylo Onatsko.
Tel: 024-7663 8598
Rev David Senyk.
34 Dawlish Drive, Styvechale, Coventry CV3 5NB **Tel:** 07870-578883

■ **DERBY**
St Michael Ukrainian Catholic Church
Dairyhouse Road. Served from Nottingham.

DONCASTER, South Yorks
Services at: **Sacred Heart**
Warmsworth Road. Served from Bradford.

■ **DUNDEE**
Services at: **St Andrew's Cathedral**
Nethergate. Served from Edinburgh.
M: *Sun 4pm, fourth Sun of the Month.*

■ **EDINBURGH**
Our Lady of Pochayev and St Andrew (1965)
Dalmeny Street, EH6
Rev Lubomyr Pidluskyj. 6 Mansionhouse Road, EH9 1TZ
Tel: 0131-667 5993 (Office)
Tel: 0131-667 5811 (Home)

■ **FALKIRK**
Services at RC Chapel: **St Martha**
35 Wellside Place.
Served from Edinburgh.
M: *Sun 3pm, second Sun of the Month.*

■ **GALASHIELS,** Selkirkshire
Services at: **Our Lady and St Andrew's Church,**
Market Street. Served from Edinburgh.
M: *Sun 3pm, third Sun of the Month.*

■ **GLASGOW**
Services in: **The Chapel of the Convent of Mercy**
Garnethill. Served from Edinburgh.

■ **GLOSSOP,** Derbys
St Mary Crowned
Sumner Street. Served from Oldham.

■ **GLOUCESTER.**
Good Shepherd (1977)
Ukrainian Catholic Church, Derby Road.
Mitred Archpriest Rev Stephan Wiwcharuk. Derby Road, Gloucester GL1 4AE **Tel:** 01452-529069

■ **HALIFAX,** West Yorks
Our Lady of Perpetual Succour
Lemon Street, Queens Road, HX1 0LN
Served from Bradford.

■ **HUDDERSFIELD,** West Yorks
Services at: **St James the Great**
New Hey Road. Served from Bradford.

■ **HULL,** North Humberside
Services at: **Our Lady of Lourdes and St Peter Chanel**
Cottingham Road. Served from Bradford.

■ **KEIGHLEY,** West Yorks
Services at: **St Anne**
North Street. Served from Bradford.

■ **KIDDERMINSTER,** Worcs
Services at: **St Ambrose**
Birmingham Road. Served from Coventry.

■ **LEEDS**
Services at: **St Augustine**
Harehills Road. Served from Bradford.

■ **LEICESTER**
Ascension of Our Lord (1970)
Ukrainian Catholic Church, Fosse Road South. Served from Peterborough.

■ **LEIGH,** Lancs
Services at: **Sacred Heart**
Walmesley Road. Served from Bolton.

■ **LINCOLN**
Services at: **St Hugh**
Monks Road. Served from Nottingham.

■ **LOCKERBIE,** Dumfriesshire
Services at: **Halmuir Hos**
Served from Edinburgh.

■ **LOUGHBOROUGH,** Leics
Services at: **Sacred Heart**
Park Road, Shelthorpe.
Served from Nottingham.

■ **LUTON**
Services at: **Our Lady**
Castle Street. Served from London.

■ **MANCHESTER**
Our Lady of the Assumption
(cons 29 Aug 1954)

Bury Old Road, Salford.
Rev Jaroslaw Rij. 36 Cardinal Street, Manchester. M8 7PS **Tel:** 0161-205 7050 (Home) **Tel:** 0161-795 9924 (Church)

■ **NORTHAMPTON**
Services at: **St John**
Bridge Street. Served from Coventry.

■ **NOTTINGHAM**
Our Lady of Perpetual Succour and St Alban
Bond Street, Sneinton.
Rev Mykola Martynyuk. Thorneywood House, Carlton Road, NG3 7AF
Tel: 0115-950 5313

■ **OLDHAM,** Lancs
SS Peter and Paul and All Saints (1963; 1986)
Ukrainian Catholic Church, Chadderton Way, Northmoor.
Rev Bohdan-Benjamin Lysykanych.
Syncellus. All Saints Presbytery, Chadderton Way, Oldham OL9 6DH **Tel:** 0161-633 5636

■ **PETERBOROUGH,** Cambs
St Olga's (1964)
Ukrainian Catholic Church, 67 New Road, Woodston, Peterborough PE2 9HD
Rev Nicolau Korczagin. Tel: 01733-568139

■ **PRESTON**
Services at: **St Gregory the Great**
Blackpool Road. Served from Bolton.

■ **READING**
Services at: **St William of York**
Upper Redland Road. Served from London.

■ **ROCHDALE**
St Mary and St James
Ukrainian Catholic Church, 328 Yorkshire Street, Wardleworth OL16 2DS
Served from Oldham.
Tel: 0161-633 5636

■ **RUGBY,** West Midlands
Services at: **St Marie**
Dunchurch Road. Served from Coventry.

■ **SCUNTHORPE,** Lincs
Exaltation of the Cross
High Street East. Served from Nottingham.

■ **SHEFFIELD**
Services at: **St Catherine**
Burngreave Road. Served from Bradford.

■ **STOCKPORT,** Cheshire
Services at: **St Joseph's**
St Petersgate. Served from Manchester.

■ **STOKE-ON-TRENT**
Services at: **Sacred Heart**
Jasper Street, Hanley. Served from Coventry.

■ **SWINDON,** Wilts
Services at: **Holy Rood**
Groundwell Road. Served from London.

■ **TODMORDEN,** Lancs
Services at: **St Joseph**
Wellington Road. Served from Bradford.

■ **WAKEFIELD,** West Yorks
Services at: **St Austin**
6 Wentworth Terrace. Served from Bradford.

■ **WALTHAM CROSS,** Herts
Services at: **The Immaculate Conception and St Joseph**
High Street. Served from London.

■ **WOLVERHAMPTON,** West Midlands
St Volodymyr and St Olga
Merridale Street West. Served from Coventry.

■ **ORDERS AND CONGREGATIONS ETC**

■ **MEN**
Basilian Fathers (OSBM): Bradford

✠ STOKE-ON-TRENT
Services at [illegible]
[illegible] Served from [illegible]

✠ [illegible]
[illegible] Served from [illegible]

✠ TODMORDEN, [illegible]
Services at St Joseph
Wellington Road. Served from Bradford

✠ WAKEFIELD, West Yorks
Services at St [illegible]
[illegible] Street. Served from Bradford

✠ WALSHAM [illegible]
[illegible]
[illegible]
High Street. Served from [illegible]

✠ WOLVERHAMPTON, West Midlands
[illegible] and St Olga
[illegible] Street. Served from Coventry

✠ ORDERS AND CONGREGATIONS ETC

✠ [illegible]
Basilian Fathers (OSBM), Bradford

[illegible]

✠ NOTTINGHAM
Our Lady of Perpetual Succour and St [illegible]
Bond Street, [illegible]
Rev Mykola Matviychuk, [illegible]
[illegible] Road, NG7 7AH
[illegible]

✠ OLDHAM, Lancs
[illegible]
Ukrainian Catholic Church, Chadderton [illegible]
[illegible]
[illegible]
[illegible]

✠ PETERBOROUGH, [illegible]
St Olga's [illegible]
Ukrainian Catholic Church, [illegible] Road
[illegible]
[illegible]

✠ PRESTON
[illegible]

✠ READING
[illegible]

✠ ROCHDALE
St Mary and St [illegible]
Ukrainian Catholic Church, 372 Yorkshire Street, [illegible]
Served from Oldham
Tel: [illegible]

✠ RUGBY, West Midlands
Services at St Marie
Dunchurch Road. Served from Coventry

✠ SCUNTHORPE, Lincs
Exaltation of the Cross
[illegible] Served from [illegible]

✠ SHEFFIELD
Services at St Catherine
Burngreave Road. Served from Bradford

✠ STOCKPORT, Cheshire
Services at St Joseph's
St Petersgate. Served from Manchester

APOSTOLIC EXARCHATE FOR UKRAINIANS

APOSTOLIC PREFECTURE OF THE FALKLAND ISLANDS

Erected 10th January, 1952 for the people of the Falkland Islands. The Independent Mission (Missio sui Iuris) of St Helena, Ascension and Tristan da Cunha was added on 18th August 1986

Prefect Apostolic of the Falkland Islands
Rt Rev Mgr Michael Bernard McPartland SMA
Born in Middlesbrough, 29th Sept 1939;
Ordained 14th May 1978;
appointed Prefect Apostolic 30th July 2002

Residence and Administration:
Apostolic Prefecture
12 Ross Road, Stanley
Falkland Islands
Tel: 00-500 21204 **Fax:** 00-500 22242
E-mail: stmarys@horizon.co.fk

Rt Rev Mgr Michael Bernard McPartland SMA, Prefect Apostolic of the Falkland Islands

■ **STANLEY,** Falkand Islands
St Mary Church
12 Ross Road, Falkand Islands F1QQ 1ZZ
Parish Priest: **Rev Peter Norris** (Southwark)

■ **ASCENSION ISLAND**
The Grotto of Our Lady
Georgetown
Ascension Island ASCN 1ZZ
Administrator: **Mrs Shari Parkhill**

■ **ST HELENA**
Sacred Heart Church
Upper Jamestown,
St Helena STHL 1ZZ

■ **TRISTAN DA CUNHA**
St Joseph Church
Edinburgh of the Seven Seas,
Tristan da Cunha TDCU 1ZZ

ECCLESIAL ORGANISATIONS & CHAPLAINCIES

PERSONAL PRELATURE

Personal Prelatures are juridical structures of a secular character governed by a Prelate and erected by the Holy See to carry out specific pastoral or missionary activities.

The general norms on Personal Prelatures are contained in the Code of Canon Law - canons 294 to 297. Each has its own statutes approved by the Holy See.

PRELATURE OF THE HOLY CROSS AND OPUS DEI

Opus Dei is a personal Prelature, international in its scope, which has as its aim the spreading throughout all sectors of society a deep awareness of the universal call to sanctity and apostolate, in the fulfilment of every day work. It is formed by a Prelate with his own clergy and by lay people, men and women, who in virtue of a divine vocation freely join the Prelature.

• Further -up-to-date information can be found on our Website at: www.opusdei.org.uk

■ **REGIONAL VICAR FOR GREAT BRITAIN:**

Mgr Nicholas Morrish MA, STD. 4 Orme Court, London W2 4RL **Tel:** 020-7229 7574. **Fax:** 020-7243 9400

■ **OTHER PRIESTS OF THE OPUS DEI PRELATURE IN GREAT BRITAIN:**

Rev Peter Bristow, MA, STD. 1 Pine Road, Manchester M20 6UY
Rev Andrew Byrne MA, STD. 1 Leopold Road, London W5 3PB
Rev Xavier Calduch BSc, STD. 159 Nightingale Lane, London SW12 8NQ
Rev Paul Diaper BA, MA, JCD. 159 Nightingale Lane, London SW12 8NQ
Rev Joseph Evans BA, STD. Netherhall House, Nutley Terrace, London NW3 5SA
Rev Robert Farrell BSc, STD. 1 Lower Park Road, Victoria Park, Manchester M14 5RS
Rev Joseph Gabiola PhD, JCD, 4 Orme Court, London W2 4RL
Rev Gonzalo Gonzalez LLB, JCD. 231 Nithsdale Road, Glasgow G41 5HA **Tel:** 0141-427 3236
Rev Peter Haverty BSc, PhD. 1 Pine Road, Manchester M20 6UY
Rev Paul Hayward LLB, JCD. 4 Orme Court, London W2 4RL
Rev Stefan Hnylycia BSc, PGCE, STD. 8 Orme Court, London W2 4RL
Rev Michael Lowenthal BA(Econ), STD, 1 Lower Park Road, Victoria Park, Manchester M14 5RS
Rev Bernard Marsh DIC, STD. 4 Orme Court, London W2 4RL
Rev James Pereiro PhD, STD. Grandpont House, Folly Bridge, Abingdon Road, Oxford OX1 4LD
Rev Stephen Reynolds BLitt, MA, STD. 231 Nithsdale Road, Glasgow G41 5HA
Rev Laurence Richardson BSc, MA, STD. 18 Netherhall Gardens, London NW3 5TH
Rev Gerard Sheehan MA, STD. St Thomas More Presbytery, Maresfield Gardens, London NW3 5TH
Mgr Richard Stork MSc, STD. 18 Netherhall Gardens, London NW3 5TH

Opus Dei Information Office: 6 Orme Court, London W2 4RL
Tel: 020-7221 9176 **Fax:** 020-7243 9400 **E-mail:** info@opusdei.org.uk

ECCLESIAL MOVEMENTS

■ FOCOLARE MOVEMENT

An international movement started by Chiara Lubich in 1943 at Trent in Northern Italy. Its principal aim is to help bring about the fulfilment of the prayer of Jesus "That all may be one".
National Centres, contacts: **Tim King**, 38 Audley Road, London W5 3ET. **Tel:** 0208-991 2022 or **Cathy Grue**, 62 King's Avenue, London SW4 8BM
Tel: 020-8671 8355 **Fax:** 020-8674 1606;
E-mail: info@focolare.org.uk

■ CURSILLOS IN CHRISTIANITY

Cursillo is a Catholic movement to form leaders, who grow through prayer, study and action to evangelise others for Christ. For further information please contact: **Mr Stephen Fox**, National Secretary, Cursillos in Christianity, Clayton House, Newlands Lane, Stoke Row, Henley-on-Thames RG9 5PS. **Tel/Fax:** 01491-681646. **E-mail:** stephen.fox@cursillo.org.uk
Website: www.cursillo.org.uk

■ TERESIAN ASSOCIATION

An International Association of the Faithful for lay Christians, founded by St Pedro Poveda in 1911. Aims to help transform society through education and culture in the light of the Gospel. Its members are men and women who according to their specific calling strive to witness Gospel values in their work, professions, in all they do and through their projects, schools and centres around the world.
Address: 51 Chestnut Grove, New Malden, Surrey KT3 3JJ, **Tel:** 020-8942 6086.
E-mail: tassoc@supanet.com

CENTRES FOR MISSION & EVANGELISATION

■ CATHOLIC AGENCY TO SUPPORT EVANGELISATION (CASE)

Chair of Executive Committee:
Rt Rev Malcolm McMahon OP
Director:
Mgr Keith Barltrop
Team: **Miss Clare Ford, Fr Martin Ganeri OP, Miss Emily Davis, Miss Clare Ward.**

The purpose of the Agency is to support and resource Catholic communities and individuals in England and Wales to proclaim the Gospel; to promote dialogue between gospel and culture; and to offer information on the Catholic faith to enquirers through the Catholic Enquiry Office.
Address: 39 Eccleston Square, London SW1V 1BX **Tel:** 020-0207 901 4863
E-mail: info@caseresources.org.uk
Website: www.caseresources.org.uk
Catholic Enquiry Office:
E-mail: enquiries@lifeseekers.co.uk
Website: www.lifeseekers.co.uk

■ CATHOLIC EVANGELISATION SERVICES

Based at the All Saints Pastoral Centre, produces Catholic teaching resources on DVD to equip parishes, schools and colleges. A wide range of **CaFE** (Catholic Faith Exploration) resources are available for Sacramental preparation, parish renewal, chaplaincy groups and to support the RE curriculum in Secondary schools
Director: **David Payne**, PO Box 333, St Albans, Herts AL2 1EL
Tel/Fax: 01727-822837
E-mail: info@faithcafe.org
Websites: www.faithcafe.org
www.youthcafe.org

■ SION CATHOLIC COMMUNITY FOR EVANGELISM

President:
Rev Gerard Kelly, BSc MTh

We are a community of priests, religious and lay people sharing in life and working together in ministry. We are committed to the spreading of the Gospel and the building up of the Church. We proclaim the Gospel through preaching and teaching; and we train and equip others for the task of evangelisation.
Headquarters:
Sion Community, S.E.N.T., Sawyers Hall Lane, Brentwood, Essex CM15 9BX **Tel:** 01277-215011
Fax: 01277-234401
E-mail: admin@sioncommunity.org.uk
Website: www.sioncommunity.org.uk

■ **SION EVANGELISATION CENTRE FOR NATIONAL TRAINING**
Training and equipping priests, religious and lay people to work together in a collaborative style of Mission helping the Church accomplish its central mission to evangelise. Address: S.E.N.T., Sawyers Hall Lane, Brentwood, Essex CM15 9BX
Tel: 01277-215011 **Fax:** 01277-234401
E-mail: admin@sioncommunity.org.uk
Website: www.sioncommunity.org.uk/sent.htm

CHAPLAINS TO ETHNIC COMMUNITIES (CECS)

■ **AUSTRIAN**
Austrian Catholic Centre: Contact: **Anna Ringler**, 29 Brook Green, London W6 7BL **Tel:** 020-7603 2697
Website: www.acclondon.org.uk

■ **BELARUSIAN**
Belarusian Catholic Mission, Marian House, Holden Avenue, N12 8HY
Tel: 020-8445 5358 **Mitred Archpriest Alexander Nadson** (*Rector*), **Rev Siarhiej Stasievich.**
Services (*Byzantine-Slavonic Rite*).
M: *Sun 10.30am*

■ **CHALDEAN (EASTERN RITE CATHOLIC CHURCH)**
Habib Al-Noufaly; The Holy Family, The Presbytery, Vale Lane, West Acton W3 0DY **Tel/Fax:** 020-8992 1308.
Home: 38 Cavendish Avenue, Ealing, London W13 0JQ
Tel/Fax: 020-8997 6370
E-mail: fr_habib@yahoo.com
Website: www.chaldean,org.uk

■ **CHINESE**
Edward Man-koWoo, MAfr; Our Lady Help of Christians, 4 Lady Margaret Rd, Kentish Town, London NW5 2XT
Tel: 0207-485 4032 **Fax:** 0207-267 3118
Mbl: 07946-383659

■ **CROATIAN**
Fr Ljubomir Simunovic OFM, 17 Boutflower Road, London SW11 1RE
Tel/Fax: 020-7223 3530
E-mail: hrv_kat_misija@yahoo.com

■ **CZECH**
Jozef Vojtek; Velehrad House, 22 Ladbroke Square, London W11 3NA
Tel/Fax: 020-7727 7849
E-mails: info@velehrad.org
Website: www.velehrad.org

■ **FILIPINO**
Claro V Conde; Filipino Missions, PO Box 37976, London SW4 7XU
Tel: 07803-191502
E-mail: cconde8254@aol.com
Columban Sisters: **Sr Amanda V. Martin.** 8 Ridgdale Street, Bow, London E3 2TW **Tel:** 020-8980 3017

■ **GERMAN**
Heinz Medoch; 47 Adler Street, London E1 1EE **Tel:** 020-7247 9529

■ **GOAN**
Francis Rosario SFX; St Thomas of Canterbury, Commonside East, Mitcham, Croydon CR4 1YG
Tel: 0208 665 2176
Available at the Office 11am-3pm (weekdays only)

■ **HUNGARIAN**
Rev Joseph Viragh; Hungarian RC Chaplaincy, 62 Little Ealing Lane, Ealing, London W5 4EA **Tel:** 020 8566 0271
E-mail: hungarian.chaplaincy@btinternet.com
Website: www.magyarkatolikusok.co.uk
Menyhért Fülöp; St John's Presbytery, Dowling Street, Rochdale OL11 1EX
Tel: 01706-645937 **Mbl:** 07785 758090
Mgr George Tüttö, retired; 141 Gunnersbury Avenue, WE3 8EL
Tel/Fax: 020-89922054

■ **ITALIAN**
Carmelo Di Giovanni, SAC; St Peter's Italian Church, 136 Clerkenwell Road, London EC1R 5DL
Tel: 020-7837 1528 **Fax:** 020-7837 9071
E-mails: chiesaitaliana@aol.com
Website: www.chiesaitaliana.org.uk
Parish Office: 4 Back Hill, London EC1R 5EN
M: *Sat 1st M of Sun 7pm. Sun 9.30am,11am, 12.30pm, 7pm. Hds 10am, 12.15pm, 8pm.*
Mgr Agostino Gonella; **Fr Paulo Tornambe,** 197 Durants Road, Enfield, Middx EN3 7DE **Tel:** 020-8804 2307
Ettore Rocchi; 18 Churton Street, London SW1V 2LL **Tel:** 020-7821 5144
E-mails: cetroscalabrini@scalabrini.co.uk
The Members of our Religious Community in London are: **Rev Giandomenico Ziliotto, Jesus S Dicto, Elio Alberti**

■ **LATIN AMERICAN**
Perez Recio, Jesus OAR 363 Kennington Lane, London SE11 5QY **Tel:** 020-75871545; **Mbl:** 07986655138
Frank Umendia OAR Tel: 020-7582 7244

■ **LEBANESE MARONITE (BYZANTINE RITE)**
Augustine Aoun, LMO; (Superior and Parish Priest of the Maronite Community) 6 Dobson Close, Swiss Cottage, NW6 4RS **Tel:** 020-7586 1801 **Fax:** 020-7722 0436 **Mbl:** 0795-7650852
Dany Akiki, LMO; 6 Dobson Close, Swiss Cottage, London NW6 4RS **Tel:** 020-7586 1801 **Fax:** 020-7722 0436

■ **LITHUANIAN**
Aleksandras Geryb, STL; Ashley House, 56 Forest Road, Bordon, Hants GU35 0XT **Tel:** 01420-489877 (now semi-retired)
Canon Valentinas Kamaitis; Nazareth House, Scholes Lane, Prestwich, Manchester M25 0NU **Tel:** 0161-798 4353
Petras Tverijonas; St Casimir's Church, 21 The Oval, Hackney Road, London E2 9DT **Tel:** 020-7739 8735 **Mbl:** 07939 126505 **E-mail:** ptverijonas@btinternet.com **Website:** www.londonas.co.uk

■ **MALTESE**
Stephen Sciberras, OFM, Charles Diacono, OFM; Maltese Mission, Franciscan Friars, 1 Balniel Gate, Pimlico, London SW1V 3SD **Tel:** 020-7834 9512 **Fax:** 020-7233 9755 **E-mail:**maltesemissionuk@yahoo.co.uk **Website:** www.maltesemissionuk.org.uk

■ **MELKITE GREEK CATHOLIC**
(Byzantine Rite)
Rev (Dr) Shafiq Abouzayd, *Parish Priest:* 46 Sunderland Avenue, Oxford OX2 8DU **Tel:** 01865-514041 **Mbl:** 017977-495150 **E-mail:** shafiq.abouzayd@orinst.ox.ac.uk
Rev (Dr) Robert Gibbons, *Assistant Parish Priest:* 40 Nethercote Road, Thackley OX5 3AT **Tel:** 01869-331186 **Mbl:** 07951-817307 **E-mail:** gibbonsr@smuc.ac.uk
Rev John Salter, *Assistant Priest:* 1 St James's Close, Bishop Street, Islington, London N1 8PH **Tel:** 020-7359 0250 **E-mail:** salterexis@aol.com
Rev John Salter, *Assistant Priest:* The Belvedere, Peak Hill Road, Sidmouth, Devon EX10 8RZ **Tel:** 01395 513365 **E-mail:** dwhite4165@aol.com
Dcn Richard Downer; 3 Palmer Close, Redhill, Surrey RH1 4BU **Tel:** 01737-778863 **E-mails:** rhfdowner@talktalk.net

■ **POLISH**
Mgr Tadeusz Kukla; (Vicar Delegate for Poles in England & Wales, & National Director); Polish Catholic Mission, 2 Devonia Road, London N1 8JJ **Tel:** 020-7226 3439 **Fax:** 020-7226 7677 **E-mail:** pbf.pmk@ukonline.co.uk
(See section: Polish Priests)

■ **PORTUGUESE**
Mgr José Vaz Pinto; 6 Minerva Close, London SW9 6NZ **Tel:** 020-7587 0881 **Fax:** 020-7587 0881

■ **SLOVENIAN**
Stanislav Cikanek; 62 Offley Road, London SW9 0LS **Tel:/Fax:** 020-77356655

■ **SPANISH**
P. Ernesto Atanes, CM, (Senior Chaplain), **P. Jose Lopez, P. Jorge Luis Rodriguez**; Delegado Nacional, 47 Palace Court, London W2 4LS **Tel:** 020-7229 8815 **E-mail:** spanish.chaplaincy@virgin.net

■ **TAMIL**
Francis Eugene Saverian; 304 Garratt Lane, London SW18 4EH **Tel:** 020-8870 6257 **E-mail:** frsefrancis@aol.com **Website:** tamil-rcchaplaincy.org.uk

■ **UKRAINIAN GREEK CATHOLIC**
(Byzantine Rite)
See Apostolic Exarchate, Page 605

■ **VIETNAMESE**
Chanh Huynh (Paul); 130 Poplar High Street, Isle of Dogs, London E14 0AG **Tel:** 020-7537 3071 **Fax:** 020-7537 1959
Also The Holy Name and Our Lady of the Sacred Heart, 117 Bow Common Lane E3 4AU **Tel:** 020-7987 3477 **Fax:** 020-7537 3834 **Website:** www.lavang.org.uk
Ly Trong Song (Paul) (Permanent Deacon); 33 Blantyre Walk, World's End Estate, London SW10 0EW **Tel:** 020-7351 0064
Also The Holy Name and Our Lady of the Sacred Heart, 117 Bow Common Lane E3 4AU **Tel/Fax:** 020-7987 3477 **Website:** www.lavang.org.uk
Tien Dac Nguyen, (Peter); Vietnamese Pastoral Centre, 12 Wye Cliff Road, Handsworth, Birmingham B20 3TB **Tel:** 0121-554 8082 **Fax:** 0121-523 6258 **Website:** www.vietmartyrs.org.uk

■ **WEST INDIAN**
Frs Uchenna Njoku CSSp, Ugochukwo Ikwuka CSSp St Philip's Presbytery, Messenger Road, Smethwick B66 3DU **Tel:** 0121-558 1065
Also Chaplaincy: Our Lady of the Caribbean Chapel Centre, Bayswater Road, Birchfield, Birmingham B20 3AE **Tel:** 0121-551 2084

■ **AFRICAN CHAPLAINCY IN BRITAIN**
(Officially recognised by the Bishops' Conference of England and Wales)
Chaplain/Director: **Rev Joseph Baffour-Awuah** St George's Presbytery, 132 Shernall Street, Walthamstow, London E17 9HU
Tel: 020-8521 2359 **Fax:** 020-8520 4805
E-mail: africath@clara.co.uk

PORT CHAPLAINCIES IN ENGLAND AND WALES

Apostleship of the Sea

The (AOS) is the official maritime and welfare mission agency of the Catholic Church in Great Britain, as well as a registered charity wholly reliant on voluntary contributions. Ninety percent of world trade is carried by ship; however seafarers often work in dangerous conditions suffering loneliness, deprivation and even exploitation. AOS deploys chaplains and ship visitors who welcome vulnerable merchant seafarers to our shores and provides for their pastoral and practical needs – regardless of creed or nationality. Catholic seafarers are also given the opportunity to receive the sacraments. AOS also provides chaplains on board cruise ships, works ecumenically to maintain seafarers' centres inside ports, and collaborates with industry bodies to speak up for seafarers' rights. AOS relies on a network of valued parish contacts and volunteers to sustain its development.

National Director:
Captain Paul Quinn OBE. Apostleship of the Sea, Herald House, Lambs Passage, Bunhill Row, London EC1Y 8LE **Tel:** 020-7588 8285 **Fax:** 020-7588 8280
E-mail: londonoffice@apostleshipofthesea.org.uk
Episcopal Agency President / Promoter:
Rt Rev Thomas Burns SM, Bishop in Ordinary to HM Forces

Episcopal Agency Chairman:
Eamonn Delaney, 23 Guildown Avenue, Guildford, Surrey GU2 4HA **Tel:** 07785 234639
Website: www.apostleshipofthesea.org.uk

Registered Charity Number: 1069833 Company Registration: 3320318

■ **BLYTH**
Mr Paul Atkinson
Navigation House, Tyne Dock, South Sheilds, NE34 0AB
Tel: 07906212426
E-mail: paulatkinson@apostleshipofthesea.org.uk

■ **BRISTOL-AVONMOUTH/PORTBURY**
Rev Noel Mullin
Bristol Seafarers Centre, Royal Portbury Dock Road, Portbury BS20 7XS **Tel:** 07758 287856
E-mail: noelmullin@apostleshipofthesea.org.uk

■ **CARDIFF**
Mr Richard Withers
AOS Lay Port Chaplain,
Tel: 07910901936
E-mail: richardwithers@apostleshipofthesea.org.uk

■ **FELIXSTOWE.**
Sr Marian Davey
AOS Lay Port Chaplain, Felixstowe Seafarers' Centre, Dock Road, Felixstowe, Suffolk IP11 3TG
Tel: 07758 356372
E-Mail: mariandavey@apostleshipofthesea.org.uk

■ **IMMINGHAM & GRIMSBY**
Rev Colum Kelly
Immingham Seafarers Centre, Lockside Road, Immingham Dock, Immingham, DN40 2NN
Tel: 07906 855 864
E-mail: columkelly@apostleshipofthesea.org.uk

■ **IPSWICH**
Served from Felixstowe

■ **LIVERPOOL**
Peter Devlin

Seafarers Centre, Colonsay House, 20 Crosby Road South, Liverpool, L20 1RQ
Tel: 07714 219167
E-Mail: peterdevlin@apostleshipofthesea.org.uk

■ **MEDWAY PORTS**
Deacon Daniel Mulcahy
Tel: 07963199924
E-Mail: danielmulcahy@apostleshipofthesea.org.uk

■ **NEWPORT**
Mr Richard Withers
Tel: 07910 901 936
E-Mail: richardwithers@apostleshipofthesea.org.uk

■ **PLYMOUTH**
Mrs Louise Carter
AOS Victoria Wharf, Coxside, Plymouth PL4 0RF **Tel:** 07843 739579
E-Mail: louisecarter@apostleshipofthesea.org.uk

■ **PORTSMOUTH**
Served from Southampton

■ **SOUTHAMPTON**
Fr Jack Padua
Southampton Seafarers Centre, 12 - 14 Queens Terrace, Southampton SO14 3BP
Tel: 07963 345 618
E-mail: jackpadua@apostleshipofthesea.org.uk

■ **TEESPORT (NORTH/SOUTH BANK)**
Tony McAvoy
Tel: 077 1392 4504
E-mail: tonymcavoy@apostleshipofthesea.org.uk

■ **TILBURY**
Rev Patsy Foley SPS,
Tilbury Seafarers Centre, Tenants Row, Tilbury Docks, Tilbury RM18 7EH
Tel: 07986723015
E-Mail: patsyfoley@apostleshipofthesea.org.uk

■ **TYNE**
Paul Atkinson,
Navigation House, Tyne Dock, South Shields NE34 0AB
Tel: 07906212426
E-Mail: paulatkinson@apostleshipofthesea.org.uk

HM PRISONS, YOUNG OFFENDERS INSTITUTIONS AND REMAND CENTRES

AND THE PARISHES FROM WHICH THEY ARE SERVED

Liaison Bishop between the Catholic Hierarchy and HM Prison Service:
Rt Rev Terence Brain, Salford

Principal Roman Catholic Chaplain, HM Prison Service:
Mgr Malachy Keegan
Room 410, Abell House, John Islip Street, London SW1P 4LH
Tel: 020-7217 8714 **Fax:** 020-7217 8980 **Email:** malachy.keegan3@hmps.gsi.gov.uk

CHAPLAINS TO HM PRISON SERVICE

KEY: HMP denotes Her Majesty's Prison, HM YOI denotes HM Young Offenders Institution, HMRC denotes HM Remand Centre

Acklington HMP: Sr Moira Keane, HMP Acklington, Morpeth, Northumberland NE65 9XF, **Tel:** 01670-762300.
Albany HMP: Rev John Stokes, HM Prison, Albany, Newport, Isle of Wight, PO30 5RS **Tel:** 01983-556527
Altcourse HMP. Rev George Hamer, Higher Lane, Fazackerley, Liverpool L9 7LH **Tel:** 0151-522 2000
Ashfield YOI, HMP: Rev Alex Redmond, Shortwood Road, Pucklechurch, Bristol BS16 9QJ **Tel:** 0117-3038000.
Ashwell HMP: Fr P Dooling, Miss L Kidd, Miss Angela Jones. Oakham, Rutland LE15 7LF **Tel:** 01572-884100
Askham Grange HMP: Rev Patrick Smith, Askham Richard, York YO23 3FT **Tel:** 01904-772001
Aylesbury HM YOI: Rev John Fleming, 6 Bierton Road, Aylesbury, Bucks HP20 1EH **Tel:** 01296-444000
Bedford HMP: Rev Seamus Kennan, St Loyes Street, Bedford MK40 1HG **Tel:** 01234-373000
Belmarsh HMP: Sr Teresa & Fr Edward Okon, HM Prison, Western Way,

Thamesmead, London SE28 0EB **Tel:** 020-8317 2436

Birmingham HMP: Rev Peter Allen, HM Prison, Winson Green Road, Birmingham B18 4AS **Tel:** 0121-345 2500

Blakenhurst HMP: See Hewell

Blantyre House HMP: Fr Victor McLean Goudhurst, Kent TN17 1DN **Tel:** 01580-213200

Blundeston HMP: Fr Eric Woodhead Lowestoft, Suffolk NR32 5BG **Tel:** 01502-734500

Brinsford HMYOI: Fr Dominic Chukka and Sr Brendan. HM/YOI Brinsford, New Road, Featherstone, Wolverhampton WV10 7PY **Tel:** 01902-532536/842891

Bristol HMP: Rev Richard McKay, Ms Mary Hopper, 19 Cambridge Road, Horfield, Bristol BS7 8PS **Tel:** 0117-3723100

Brixton HMP: Rev Howard Campbell, HMP Brixton, PO Box 369 Jebb Avenue, London SW2 5XF **Tel:** 020-8588 6053

Brockhill HMP YOI, See Hewell

Bronzefield HMP: Mrs Leonora Gibson, Woodthorpe Road, Ashford Middlx TW15 3JZ **Tel:** 01784-425690

Buckley Hall HMP: Mrs Maria Durcan, Buckley Road, Rochdale, Lancs. OL12 9DP **Tel:** 01706-514472

Bullingdon HMP: Fr Robert Byrne, Euan Henderson, Richard Duffield, Sr Eleanor Boyle, TPO Box 50, Bicester, Oxford OX25 1WD **Tel:** 01869 353100

Bullwood Hall HMP: Fr Martin Joyce, Mrs Helen Ansell High Road, Hockley, Essex SS5 4TE **Tel:** 01702-562800

Camp Hill HMP: Fr John Stokes, Newport, Isle of Wight PO30 5PB **Tel:** 01983-554600

Canterbury HMP: Canon Michael Bunce, 46 Longport, Canterbury, Kent CT1 1PJ **Tel:** 01277-862800

Cardiff HMP: Fr David J Myers, Knox Road, Cardiff CF24 0UG **Tel:** 02920 923100

Castington HM YOI: Sr Moira Keane, HMP.YOI Castington, Morpeth, Northumberland NE65 9XG **Tel:** 01760-382100

Channings Wood HMP: Mrs Zillah Martin, HM Prison, Channing Wood, Denbury, Newton Abbot, Devon TQ12 6DW **Tel:** 01803 814600

Chelmsford HMP: Rev Paul Fox, Kevin Lyons, Sr Philomena, 200 Springfield Road, Chelmsford, Essex CM2 6LQ **Tel/Fax:** 01245-552000

Coldingley HMP: Mrs Rosemary Leclercq, Bisley, Woking GU24 9EX **Tel:** 01483 804300

Cookham Wood HMP: Rev James Clark, Rochester, Kent ME1 3LU **Tel:** 01634-202500

Dartmoor HMP: Rev John Webb, HM Prison Dartmoor, Princetown, Yelverton, Devon PL20 6RR **Tel:** 01822-892000

Deerbolt HMYOI: Rev Patrick Cope, Bowes Road, Barnard Castle, Co. Durham DL12 9BG **Tel:** 01833-633326 **Pager:** 07693-299555 **Mbl:** 078601-08431 **E-mail:** patrick.cope01@hmps.gsi.gov.uk

Doncaster HMP YOI: Mr Harish Massey, Off North Bridge, Marshgate, Doncaster DN5 8UX **Tel:** 01302-760870

Dorchester HMP: Rev Dcn Nicholas Thompson, North Square, Dorchester DT1 1JD **Tel:** 01305-214500

Dover HM YOI: Fr Peter Madden, 13 Heights Terrace, The Citadel, Western Heights, Dover, Kent CT17 9DU **Tel:** 01304-208240

Dovegate HMP: Rev Dcn Tony Rigby, The World Faith Centre, HMP Dovegate, Uttoxeter, Staffordshire ST14 8XR **Tel:** 01283-829525

Downview HMP: Rev Hugh Flower, Sutton Lane, Sutton, Surrey SM2 5PD **Tel:** 020 8929 3300

Drake Hall HMP: Sr Patricia Murphy, Eccleshall, Staffs **Tel:** 01782-774100

Durham HMP: Rev Ernasto Robertson, Sr M Stephen, Old Elvet, Durham DH1 3HU

East Sutton Park HM YOI: Rev Peter Marden, East Sutton Park Prison, Maidstone, Kent ME17 3D7 **Tel:** 01622-845000

Eastwood Park HMP YOI: Rev Alexander McAllister Falfield, Wootton-under-Edge, Gloucs GL12 8DB **Tel:** 01454 382100

Edmunds Hill HMP: Joanna Hornby, Stradishall, Newmarket, Cambs CB8 9YK

Elmley HMP: Rev Steohen Haylett, Chaplaincy HMP Elmley, Church Road Eastchurch, Sheerness, Kent ME12 4AY Tel: 01795-882000

Erlestoke HMP: HM YOI: Fr Eugene Baptiste, Fr Saji Matthew, Devizes, Wilts **Tel:** 01380-814250

Everthorpe HM YOI: Miss Yvonne Lewis (Hessle), Brough, East Yorkshire HU15 1RB **Tel:** 01430 426725

Exeter HMP: Fr Peter Morgan, New Road North, Exeter EX4 4EX **Tel:** 01392-415650

Featherstone HMP: Fr David Standen, New Road, Wolverhampton, WV10 7PU **Tel:** 01902-703000

Feltham HMYOI/RC: Rev Roger Reader, Sr Monica, Bedfont Road, Feltham, Middlesex TW13 4ND **Tel:** 020-8844 5326

Ford HMP: Rev Albert van der Most, Sr Paul Arundel, West Sussex BN18 0BX **Tel:** 01903-663000

Forest Bank HMP, YOI: Mavis Ince and Rev Robert Lasia, Agecroft Road, Pendlebury, Manchester M27 8FB **Tel:** 0161-925 7037,

Foston Hall HMP: Rev Colin Patey, Foston Hall, Foston, Derbyshire DE65 5DN **Tel:** 01283-584325

Frankland HMP: Dr Beth Theobald, HM Prison, Frankland, Finchdale Avenue, Brasside, Durham DH1 5SB **Tel:** 0191-3332 3263/08

Full Sutton HMP: Rev Ged Barry, Full Sutton, York YO41 1PS **Tel:** 01759-375157

Garth HMP: Mr Anthony Wilson, Ulnes Walton Lane, Leyland, Preston, Lancs PR5 3NE **Tel:** 01772-443300 Ext 3407

Gartree HMP: Fr Owen O'Neill, Mr Francis Wison, Gallow Field Road, Market Harbrough, Leics LE16 7RP **Tel:** 01858-436600

Glen Parva HM YOI: Fr Stephen Foster, Sr Theresa Joseph, Tigers Road, Wigston LE8 4TN **Tel:** 0116 228 4100

Gloucester HMP YOI: Rev Bernard Massey, Barrack Square, Gloucester GL1 2JN **Tel:** 01452-453000

Grendon & Springhill HMP: Sr Anne Davey, Grendon Underwood, Aylesbury, Bucks HP18 0TL **Tel:** 01296-443000

Guys Marsh HM YOI: Mr Michael Turnbull, Shaftesbury, Dorset SP7 0AH **Tel:** 01747-856400

Haslar IRC: Fr David Adams, 2 Dolphin Way, Gosport, Hampshire PO12 2AW

Haverigg HMP: Rev Mark Houston, Millom, Cumbria LA18 4NS **Tel:** 01229-713000

Hewell HMP: Rev Fidelis Chukwu, c/o HMP Hewell Grange, Hewell Lane, Redditch, Worcs B97 6QQ **Tel:** 01527-785000

High Down HMP: Revv Hugh Flower, Stephen Coker, Sutton Lane, Sutton, Surrey SM2 5PD **Tel:** 020 8722 6300

High Point HMP, Fr Michael Teader, Sr Carmel, Stradishall, Newmarket, Suffolk CB8 9YG **Tel:** 01440-743100

Hindley HM YOI: Rev Martin Ince, Gibson Street, Bickershaw, Wigan WN2 5TH, **Tel:** 01942-245629

Hollesley Bay HMP: Dcn Mike Vipond, Woodbridge, Suffolk IP12 3JW **Tel:** 01394 412400

Holloway HMP Fr Joe Browne, Sr Kathleen Diamond, Sr Miriam Crowley. Parkhurst Road, London N7 0NU **Tel:** 020-7607 6747

Holme House HMP: Mr Michael Duxbury, Holme House Road, Stockton-on-Tees, Cleveland TS18 2QU **Tel:** 01642-744000

Hull HMP: Rev William Ryan, Martin Pyke, Sr Olive Tuohy, Hedon Road, Hull HU9 5LS **Tel:** 01482-282200

Huntercombe HM YOI: Rev Barry Philips-Delaney, Huntercombe Place, Nuffield, Henley-on-Thames, Oxon RG9 5SB **Tel:** 01491-643100

Kennet HMP: Sr Theresa Clark, Parkbourn, Maghull, Liverpool L31 1HX **Tel:** 0151 527 3500

Kingston HMP: Rev Richard Hind, 122 Milton Road, Portsmouth, Hants PO3 6AS **Tel:** 0239 2953000

Kirkham HMP: Fr Robert Swann: Freckleton Road, Preston, Lancs PR4 2RN **Tel:** 01772-675400

Kirklevington Grange HMP: Br Michael Duxbury, Yarm, Cleveland TS15 9PA **Tel:** 01642-792600

Lancaster Castle HMP, Awaiting Appointment, The Castle, Lancaster LA1 1YL **Tel:** 01524-563450

Lancaster Farms HMP, YOI: Rev David Branford, Far Moor Lane, Stone Row Head, off Quernmore Road, Lancaster LA1 3QZ **Tel:** 01524-563450

Latchmere House HMP: Rev Walter Walsh, Church Road, Ham Common, Richmond, Surrey TW10 5HH **Tel:** 020-8588 6650

Leeds HMP: Sr Kathleen T C O'Brien. HM Prison, Armley, Leeds LS12 2TJ **Tel:** 0113-203 2704

Leicester HMP: Rev Joel Nwalozie, Welford, Leicester LE2 7AJ **Tel:** 0116-228 3000

Lewes HMP YOI: Rev Martin Gosling OPraem. Brighton Road, Lewes, East Sussex BN7 1EA **Tel:** 01273 785100

Leyhill HMP: Fr Aeired Dodson, Wotton-under-Edge, Glos GL12 8HL **Tel:** 01454-264000

Lincoln HMP: Rev Peter Allen, Miss Lorna Palmer, Greetwell Road, Lincoln LN2 4BD **Tel:** 01522-663090

Lindholme HMP: Mr David Palmer, Bawtry Road, Hatfield Woodhouse, DoncasterDN7 6EE **Tel:** 01302-524700

Littlehey HMP: Mrs Jackie Kneeshaw. Fr Pat Cleary RSM, Perry, Huntingdon, Cambs PE28 0SR **Tel:** 01480-333000

Liverpool HMP: Rev Alan Devaney, HM Prison, 68 Hornby Road, Liverpool L9 3DF **Tel:** 0151-525 5971 ext 2795

Long Lartin HMP: Rev Johnny Moore, South Littleton, Evesham, Worcestershire WR11 5TZ **Tel:** 01386-835100

Low Newton HMRC: Dr Beth Theobald, Low Newton, Brasside, Durham DH1

5YV **Tel:** 0191-376 4065/6 Ext: 386

Lowdham Grange HMP: Quentin Jackson OFM, Lowdham, Notts NG14 7DA **Tel:** 0115-966 9200

Maidstone HMP: Fr Anthony Phelan (OCarm), **Fr Terry McCann**, 36 County Road, Maidstone, Kent ME14 1UZ **Tel:** 01622 775300

Manchester HMP: Dcn Ged Doherty, Sr Mary Galvin, HMP Manchester, Southall Street, Manchester M60 9AH **Tel:** 0161-817 5841 General Enquiries **Tel:** 0161-817 5842

Moorland HMP HM YOI: Mr David Palmer, Mrs Laura Goodman, Thorne Road, Hatfield, Doncaster Sth. Yorkshire DN7 6EL

Morton Hall HMP: Fr Michael O'Donoghue, Swinderby, Lincoln LN6 9PT **Tel:** 01522-666700

The Mount HMP: Ms Kim Davey, Molyneaux Ave, Bovingdon, Hemel Hempstead, Herts HP3 0NZ **Tel:** 01442-836300

New Hall HMP HM YOI: Mrs Eileen Shea, Dial Wood, Flockton, Wakefield West Yorkshire WF4 4XX

Northallerton HM YOI: Rev Patrick Cope, 15a East Road, Northallerton, North Yorkshire DL6 1NW **Tel:** 01609-785121, Ext 421

North Sea Camp HMP: Rev Davis Witherick, Freiston, Boston, Lincs PE22 0QX **Tel:** 01205-769300

Norwich HMP: Mr Michael McMahon, Knox Road, Norwich, Norfolk NR1 4LU **Tel:** 01603-414820

Nottingham HMP: Fr John McKay, Perry Road, Sherwood, Nottingham NG5 3AG **Tel:** 0115-872 3000

Onley HM YOI: Mr Charlie Sweeney, Ms Heather Salguero,Willoughby, Rugby, Warks CV23 8AP **Tel:** 01788-523400.

Parc HMP: Rev David O'Keefe, HM Prison Parc, Heol Hopcyn John, Bridgend, South Wales CF35 6AR **Tel:** 01656-300200

Parkhurst HMP: Fr John Stokes, HM Prison, Parkhurst, Newport, Isle of Wight PO30 5NX **Tel:** office: 01983-554055.

Pentonville HMP: Awaiting Appointment, HM Prison, Caledonian Road, Pentonville, London N7 8TT **Tel:** 020-7607 5353 Ext 527

Peterborough HMP: Rev Dale Roberts, Saville Road, Westwood, Peterborough PE3 9TA **Tel:** 01773-217500

Portland HM YOI: Awaiting Appointment, The Presbytery, 1 Stavordale Road, Weymouth, Dorset DT4 0AB

Prescoed HMP: Dcn David O'Keeffe, Coed-y-Paen, Pontypool, Gwent NP14 0TD **Tel:** 01291 671600

Preston HMP: Revv Robert Swann, 2 Ribbleton Lane, Preston PR1 5AB **Tel:** 01772-444550

Ranby HMP: Mr Henry Masterson, Mgr Peter Moran, 19 Wellington Road, Retford, Notts DN22 8EU **Tel:** 01777-706721

Reading HMP YOI: Awaiting Appointment, Forbury Road, Reading, Berks RG1 3HY **Tel:** 0118-9085000

Risley HMP: Rev Aidan Kelly, HMP Risley, Warrington Road, Risley, Warrington, Cheshire WA3 6BP **Tel:** 01925-763871

Rochester HMP HM YOI: Dcn Malcolm Turner 1 Fort Road, Rochester, Kent ME1 3QS **Tel:** 01634-803100.

Rye Hill HMP: Mr Charles Sweeney, Willoughby, Nr. Rugby, Warwickshire CV23 8SZ

Send HMP: Mrs Rosemary Leclerq, Ripley Road, Woking Surrey GU23 7LJ **Tel:** 01483-572605

Shepton Mallet HMP: Sr Anne Martin RSCJ, Ms Mary Shortland-Ball, St Michael, Cornhill, Shepton Mallet, Somerset BA4 5LU **Tel:** 01749-823300

Shrewsbury HMP: Rev Joseph Stefanazzi, The Dana, Shrewsbury SY1 2HR **Tel:** 01743-273000

Spring Hill HMP 31a High Street, Haddenham, Bucks **Tel:** 01844-290178

Stafford HMP: Fr Walter Bance, 54 Gaol Road, Stafford ST16 3AW **Tel:** 01785-773000

Standford Hill HMP: Fr Frank Moran, Catholic Chaplain, Eastchurch, Isle of Sheppey, Kent ME12 4AA **Tel:** 01795-662142

Stocken HMP: Mrs Louise Kidd, Stocken Hall Road, Stretton, Nr Oakham, Rutland LE15 7RD **Tel:** 01780-795100

Stoke Heath HM YOI: Dcn Steve McKenna, Stoke Heath, Market Drayton, Salop. TF9 2JL **Tel:** 01630-636000

Styal HMP: Fr W O'Riordan, Styal, Wilmslow, Cheshire SK9 4HR **Tel:** 01625-553000

Sudbury HMP: Rev Colin Patey, HMP Sudbury, Derby DE6 5HN **Tel:** 01283-584088

Swaleside HMP: Fr Steven Haylett, HMP Swaleside, Brabazon Road, Eastchurch, Isle of Sheppey, Kent ME12 4AX **Tel:** 01795-884045, ext. 4043

Swansea HMP: Rev Dcn Francis McKenna OSB, **Mrs Maureen Clayton,** 200 Oystermouth Road, Swansea, SA1 3SR **Tel:** 01792-485300

Swinfen Hall YOI: Fr David Mellor, Tony Deaville, Swinfen, Lichfield, Staffs WS14 9QS **Tel:** 01543-484000

Thorn Cross YOI: Dcn Stephen McKevitt, Arley Road, Appleton Thorn, Warrington WA4 4RL **Tel:** 01925-805100

Usk HM Prison and YOI: Dcn David

O'Keeffe, 47 Maryport Street, Usk, NP15 1XP **Tel:** 01291-671600

The Verne HMP: Mrs Katrina Thompson, The Verne, Portland, Dorset DT5 1EQ **Tel:** 01305-825000

Wakefield HMP: Fr Alex Redmond. HM Prison Wakefield, 5 Love Lane, Wakefield, West Yorkshire WF 9AG **Tel:** 01924-264053 Ext. 462

Wandsworth HMP: Rev Peter Henneghan, HM Prison, Heathfield Road, Wandsworth, London SW18 3HS **Tel: 020-8874 7292** Ext 326

Warren Hill HMP: Dcn Mike Vipond, Woodbridge, Suffolk IP12 3JW **Tel:** 01394-412400

Wayland HMP: Dcn Martin Sanderson, Griston, Thetford, Norfolk, IP25 6RL **Tel:** 01953 804100

Wealstun HMP: Fr Neil Byrne, Wetherby, W. Yorks **Tel:** 01937-444400

Wellingborough HMP: Awaiting Appointment, Millars Park, Doddington Road, Wellingborough, Northants NN8 2NH **Tel:** 01933-232700

Werrington HM YOI: Fr Brian Wall, St Maria Goretti, 137 Aylesbury Road, Bucknall, Stoke ST2 0LU **Tel:** 01782-281970

Wetherby HM YOI: Fr Simon Winn, Sr Mary O'Kane, York Road, Wetherby, W. Yorks LS22 5ED **Tel:** 01937-544200

Whatton HMP: Rev Anthony Sullivan, Fr Anthony Franey, 14 Cromwell Road, Whatton, Nottingham NG13 9QF **Tel:** 01949 803200

Whitemoor HMP: Fr Kevin Stokes, Mrs Hilary Findlay, HM Prison Whitemoor, Longhill Rd, March, Cambridge PE15 0PR **Tel:** 01345-660653

Winchester HMP: Fr Vincent Convery, Plowmans Park Lane, Milford-on-Sea, Lymington, Hants SO43 0PN

Wolds HMP: Rev William Adlington, Everthorpe, East Yorkshire HU15 2JZ **Tel:** 01430-428000

Woodhill HMP: Rev Austin Mbelu, Tattenhoe Street, Milton Keynes, Bucks MK 4DA. **Tel:** 01908-722000

Wormwood Scrubs HMP: Miss Helen Baly, Rev Gerry McFlynn, Du Cane Road, London W12 0AE **Tel:** 020-8743 0311 **Rev Aelred Connelly OP**

Wymott HMP: Sr Mary Fearne, HMP Wymott, Ulnes Walton, Leyland, Lancs PR5 3LW **Tel:** 01772-421461

PACT – PRISON ADVICE & CARE TRUST
(FORMERLY KNOWN AS THE BOURNE TRUST)

Supports prisoners and their families by running visitors' centres, play areas, first night in custody schemes and resettlement projects at prisons.
Hon President: **Cardinal Cormac Murphy-O'Connor** *Director:* **Andy Keen-Downs**
Address: Suite C5, City Cloisters, 196 Old Street, London EC1V 9FR
Tel: 020-7490 3139 **E-mail:** info@prisonadvice.org.uk
Website: www.prisonadvice.org.uk

HIGH SECURITY PSYCHIATRIC HOSPITALS

Broadmoor Hospital
Crowthorne, Berks RG45 7EG **Tel:** 01344-773111 (Portsmouth Diocese)
Chaplain: **Rev Kevin Jones.** Immaculate Conception, 63-67 Yorktown Road, Sandhurst, Berks GU47 9BS **Tel:** 01252-876820

Rampton Hospital
Retford, Nottingham DN22 0PD
Chaplaincy office **Tel:** 01777-247524 (Hallam Diocese)

Ashworth Hospital
Parkbourn, Maghull, Merseyside L31 1HW **Tel:** 0151-473 0303 (Liverpool Archdiocese)
Chaplain: **Rev Joseph A Robinson** St John's, Lathom, Ormskirk, Lancs L40 7RA
Tel: 01704-892205 **Fax:** 01704-2850

AIRPORT CHAPLAINCIES IN ENGLAND AND WALES

■ Birmingham International Airport
Birmingham B26 3QJ
The Chaplaincy E-mail: airport.chaplain@bhx.co.uk
Chaplains: **Barbara Hayes** (Anglican) **Tel:** 07787-761727
Rev David Lacy (Roman Catholic) **Tel:** 07879-622426
Major Alive Snell (Salvation Army) **Tel:** 07986-387684
Major Brian Snell (Salvation Army) **Tel:** 07941-071272
The Multi-Faith Prayer Room is in the Millennium Link, and the Chaplains may also be contacted via the Information Desk **Tel:** 0121-767 7799

■ Gatwick Airport, London
Gatwick RH6 0NP
Inter-faith chapels are located in the North and South Terminals. Priests taking groups through the Airport are welcome to celebrate Mass in either Prayer Room
Tel: 01273 503851/503857/505775
E-mail: gatwickchaplain@btconnect.com
Catholic Chaplaincy Team:
Dom Richard Wilson OSB, Dcn Chris Dobson, Sr Jo Threfall SND

■ Heathrow Airport, London
Hounslow TW6 1BP
St George's Chapel (opposite Terminal 2 Car Park)
Tel: 020-8745 4261 **E-mail:** chapel-heathrow@baa.com
M: *Sun 10am (Polish), 12.30pm*
Priests and groups who would like to celebrate Mass at Heathrow Airport are asked to contact the chapel office.

■ Manchester Airport
Senior Chaplain: **Rev Kevin Ball** (Anglican)
Chaplains (Part-time): **Dcn Terry Simms** (Roman Catholic) **Rev Kennedy Bedford** (Independent). *Associate Chaplains (all Part-time):* **Moulana Faruk Ali** (Muslim), **Pastor Tony Powell** (Independent).
The Chaplaincy, Manchester Airport, Manchester M90 1QX The Chaplaincy is Ecumenical
Tel: 0161-489 2838/2113/3908 **Fax:** 0161-489 3909
E-mail: thechaplaincy@manairport.co.uk
Website: www.thechaplaincy-manchesterairport.co.uk
There are two Inter-faith Prayer Rooms - For Terminals 1 & 3 – On the corridor between the Terminals, Terminal 2 – In the main Concourse.
For celebrations of the Mass contact the Chaplaincy for details
Priests taking groups through the Airport are most welcome to celebrate Mass in either Prayer Room. To arrange, please contact the Chaplain.

■ Stansted International Airport
Enterprise House, Stansted Airport, Stansted, Essex CM24 1QW
Airport: **Tel:** 0870 0000 303 (Call Centre)
Canon Chris Bishop (Ecumenical Chaplain)
Chaplain's Office, Airport Fire Station, Pincey Road
Stansted Airport, Essex CM24 1QW
Mbl: 07810 851002 **E-mail:** chrismitre@hotmail.com
Industrial Chaplain: **Essex Churches Council for Industry and Commerce**

CLERGY LIFE & FORMATION

IN ENGLAND & WALES

NATIONAL CONFERENCE OF PRIESTS OF ENGLAND AND WALES

First convened by the Hierarchy at Wood Hall, Leeds in June 1970. Constitution accepted by the priests at Liverpool in September 1971, and by the bishops in November of that year; revised at Birmingham, 1978.

'The National Conference of Priests is a representative body, elected by and from the priests engaged in pastoral ministry in the dioceses of England and Wales.

The object of the Conference is primarily to provide an opportunity for the representatives elected by their brethren to discuss the ministry and life of the priests in England and Wales, and to examine the needs of the Church at national and local level, and to make recommendations to the Bishops' Conference and the diocesan Councils or Senates of Priests.
Representatives should bring items of importance and concern to Conference from the deaneries and diocesan meetings for wider discussion and debate, and disseminate good practice' (Constitution: Article 2).

■ OFFICERS

Chairman: **Rev Tom Jordan,** St. Edward the Confessor, 5 Park End Road, Romford Essex RM1 4AT **Tel:** 01708 740308

Vice Chairman: **Rev Tony Sligo,** St. Theresa's, College Road, Upholland, Skelmesdale WN2 0PY **Tel:** 01695 622001

Executive: Secretary **Rev. David Mills,** St Edmund's Presbytery, 65 Oxford Road, Calne SN11 8AQ **Tel:** 01249 813131 **E-mail:** calne@cliftondiocese.com

Treasurer: **Rev Thomas Saunders,** Sacred Heart, 418 Southchurch Road, Southend-on-Sea Essex SS1 2QB **Tel:** 01702 465720

Press Officer: All press enquiries should be directed to Fr Tony Sligo, who is also the Vice-Chairman

Website: www.ncpew.org.uk

■ REGIONAL CO-ORDINATORS

Region A (Brentwood, Southwark, Westminster)
Rev Dan Mason, St Antony's, 56 St Antony's Road, Forest Gate, London E7 9QB **Tel:** 020 8472 0433

Region B (Birmingham, East Anglia, Northampton, Nottingham)
Rev Alan Burbidge, 40 Village Street, Old Normanton, Derbyshire DE23 8SZ **Tel:** 01332 767038

Region C (Arundel & Brighton, Clifton, Plymouth, Portsmouth)
Rev David Mills, St Edmund's Presbytery, 65 Oxford Road, Calne SN11 8AQ **Tel:** 01249 813131 **E-mail:** calne@cliftondiocese.com

Region D (Hallam, Hexham & Newcastle, Leeds, Middlesbrough)
Awaiting Appointment

Region E (Cardiff, Menevia, Shrewsbury, Wrexham)

Rev John Cole, St. Michael's, Clarence Street, Newport NP20 2BZ
Tel: 01633 676876

Region F (Lancaster, Liverpool, Salford)
Rev. Kevan Dorgan, St Margaret Mary's, Scalegate Road, Carlisle CA2 4JX
Tel: 01228 522137

■ **SPECIAL MINISTRIES**

Rev Hugh Sinclair, St Mary's College (Oscott), Chester Road, Sutton Coldfield B73 5AA **Tel:** 0121 321 5000

CONFERENCE OF VOCATIONS DIRECTORS

Websites: www.ukpriest.org **also** www.ukvocation.org

President:
Rt Rev George Stack, Auxiliary Bishop of Westminster

Chairman:
Rev Eddie Clare, Vocations Office, Oscott College, Chester Road, Oscott, Sutton Coldfield, West Midlands B73 5AA **Tel:** 0121-355 4163 **E-mail:** eddie@vocations.org.uk

Vice-Chairman:
Rev Chris Vipers, Priest's House, 247 High Road, Chiswick, London W4 4PU
Tel: 020-7798 9083 **E-mail:** chrisviperws@rcdow.org.uk

Secretary:
Rev Paul Embery, National Office for Vocation, 114 West Heath Road, London NW3 7TX
Tel: 020-8458 6017 **E-mail:** enquiries@ukvocation.org

ARUNDEL
Rev Paul Turner, Priest's House, Haslett Avenue West, Crawley W. Sussex RH10 1HR
Tel: 01293-603773
E-mail: pdturner39@yahoo.com

BIRMINGHAM
Rev Eddie Clare. Vocations Office, Oscott College, Chester Road, Sutton Coldfield, W. Midlands B73 5AA
Tel: 0121-355 4163 **Fax:** 0121-321 1721
E-mail: eddie@vocations.org.uk
Website: www.vocations.org.uk
Vocations Promoter & Publicity Officer:
Chris Smith, Address as above.
E-mail: chris@vocations.org.uk
Mbl: 07730 653787

BRENTWOOD
Rev Joseph Silver. St Vincent's Presbytery, Waldegrave Rd, Dagenham, Essex RM8 2QB **Tel:** 0208 590 7222
E-mail: bdvocations@aol.com
Vocations Promoter:
Fr Dominic Howarth, Walsingham Ho, Lionel Road, Canvey Island, Essex SS8 9DE
Tel: 012696610
E-mail: frdominic@bcys.net

CARDIFF
Rev Paul Millar, The Presbytery, 201 New Road, Porthcawl CF36 5BN
Tel: 01656-782789
E-mail: starofthesea201vocations@yahoo.co.uk
Vocations Promoter: **Rev William Isaac,** St Mary's Presbytery, 39 Ewenny Road, Bridgend LF31 3HS **Tel/Fax:** 01656-652034
E-mail: w.isaac@btconnect.com

CLIFTON
Rev Robert King, University Catholic Chaplaincy, 103 Queens Road, Bristol BS8 1LL **Tel:** 0117-914 0003
E-mail: robert.king@cliftondiocese.com

EAST ANGLIA
Rev David Bagstaff,
4 Norwich Road, North Walsham, Norfolk NR28 9JP **Tel:** 01692 403258
E-mail: david.bagstaff@boltblue.com

HALLAM
Rev Mark McManus,
The Annunciation, 2 Spencer Street, Chesterfield, Derbys S40 4SD
Tel: 01246-232686
E-mail: mgm1988@hotmail.com

Vocations Promotor: **Rev Craig Fitzpatrick**
E-mail: whithergoestthou@hotmail.co.uk

HEXHAM & NEWCASTLE
Rev Andrew Downie, Catholic Chaplaincy, 14 Windsor Terrace, Jesmond, Newcastle NE2 4HE **Tel:** 0191-239 1858
E-mail: andrew.downie@ncl.ac.uk
Vocations Promoter: **Rev Michael McCoy,** Our Lady Queen of Peace, Penshaw, Tyne and Wear DH4 7JZ **Tel:** 0191-385 2434
E-mail: frmccoy@googlemail.com

LANCASTER
Rev Emmanuel Gribben, St Mary's Priory, Cleator, Cumbria CA23 3AB
Tel: 01946-810324 **Fax:** 01946-810614
E-mail: e.gribben@merseymail.com

LEEDS
Rev Paul Grogan, Trinity and All Saints, Brownberrie Lane, Horsforth, Leeds LS18 5HD **Tel:** 0113-283 7199
E-mail: dolvocs@aol.com

LIVERPOOL
Rev Stephen Maloney, All Saint's, 3 Oakfield, Anfield, Liverpool L4 3QG
Tel: 0151 287 8787
E-mail: frstevemaloney@btinternet.com

MENEVIA
Rev Canon Michael Flook, Clergy House, St Joseph's Cathedral, Convent Street, Swansea SA1 2BX **Tel:** 01792-652683
E-mail: michael.flook@ntlworld.com

MIDDLESBROUGH
Rev Gerard Robinson, Sacred Heart, 1 Park Road South, Middlesbrough TS5 6LD
Tel: 01642-850113
E-mail: gerard.paul@btopenworld.com
website: www.yourcalling.org

NORTHAMPTON
Rev Mark Floody, The Presbytery, 24 Freshwater Close, Marsh Farm, Luton Beds LU3 3TA **Tel:** 01582-502400
E-mail: mark.floody@btinternet.com
Vocations Promoter: **Fr Jonathan Hill,** The Presbytery, 366 Leagrave High Street, Luton LU4 0NG **Tel:** 01582 663706
E-mail: frjonhill@ frjonhill.orangehome.co.uk

NOTTINGHAM
Rev David Cain,
St Peter's House, 21 Hinkley Road, Leicester LE3 0TA **Tel:** 0116-251 9370
E-mail: frdavid@nrcdt.org.uk

PLYMOUTH
Rev Paul Cummins, Exeter University Catholic Chaplaincy, Boniface House, Glenthorne Road, Exeter EX4 4QU
Tel/Fax: 01392-271191
E-mail: p.m.cummins@exeter.ac.uk
Vocations Promoter: **Fr Trevor Jordan**. Christ the King, City Centre Church, Armada Way, Plymouth PL1 2EN
Tel: 01752 266523
E-mail: trevorsaintpeter@hotmail.com

PORTSMOUTH
Rev Gerard Flynn, St Saviour's Presbytery, Weston Lane, Totland Bay, Isle of Wight PO30 0HE **Tel:** 01983 752317
E-mail: stsaviour1@btinternet.com

SALFORD
Rev David Featherstone, St Dunstan's Presbytery, 391 Moston Lane, Moston, Manchester M40 9PA
Tel: 0161 681 1410 **Fax:** 0161 681 9045
E-mail: stdunstanmoston@aol.com

SHREWSBURY
Rev Jonathan Mitchell, Holy Spirit & St Martin's Parish Office, Fernhurst, Halton Brook, Runcorn WA7 2NJ
Tel: 01928 591216 **Mbl:** 07590 196795
E-mail: frjonmitchell@cantab.net
Website: www.dioceseofshrewsbury.org

SOUTHWARK
Rev Stephen Langridge, Vocations Office, 36 Nightingale Square, London SW12 8QN
Tel: 020-8355 0211
E-mail: info@southwarkvocations.com
Website: www.southwarkvocations.com

WESTMINSTER
Rev Christopher Vipers, Corpus Christi Catholic Church, 1 Maiden Lane, London WC2E 7NB **Tel:** 020-7798 9083
E-mail: chrisvipers@rcdow.org.uk

WREXHAM
Rev Bernard Lordan, St Tudwal's, King Edward Street, Barmouth, Gwynedd LL42 1PE **Tel:** 01341-280489
E-mail: dlordan@btinternet.com
Vocations Promoter: **Rev Anthony Jones,** Our Lady Star of the Sea, 35 Lloyd Street, Llandudno LL30 2YA
Tel: 01492-860546
E-mail: aj@serenymor.fsnet.co.uk

CONFERENCE OF DIRECTORS OF ON-GOING FORMATION

(or their equivalents)

Chairman:

Canon John Rafferty, St Vincent's, 2 Bentinck Road, Altrincham, Cheshire WA14 2BP
Tel: 0161-928 1689 **Fax:** 0161-929 8972 **E-mail:** johnarafferty@btconnect.com

Secretary:

Rev Gerald Ewing, Archbishop's House, 150 St George's Road, London SE1 6HX
Tel/Fax: 020-8877 3610 **E-mail:** ogf.southwark@btinternet.com

Episcopal Liaison:

Rt Rev Mark Jabalé (OSB), Bishop of Menevia, Curial Offices, 27 Convent Street, Greenhill, Swansea SA1 2BX
Tel: 01792 644017 **Fax:** 01792 458641 **E-mail:** curia@meneviacurialoffice.org

WESTMINSTER
Awaiting Appointment

ARUNDEL AND BRIGHTON
Rev John Healy, 89 St Mary's Close, Littlehampton, West Sussex BN17 5QQ **Tel:** 01903-722250
E-mail: ongoform.clergy@dabnet.org

BIRMINGHAM
Rev Paul McNally, Oscott College, Chester Road, Sutton Coldfield B73 5AA
Tel: 0121 321 5012
E-mail: paul.mcnally@oscott.org

BRENTWOOD
Rev Dr Adrian Graffy, Clergy House, 28 Ingrave Road, Brentwood, Essex CM15 8AT
Tel: 01277-265243 **E-mail:** adriangraffy@dioceseofbrentwood.org

CARDIFF
Awaiting appointment.

CLIFTON
Rev Christopher Whitehead, St Bernadette's, Wells Road, Whitchurch, Bristol BS14 9HU **Tel:** 01275 833699
E-mail: christopherwhitehead@hotmail.com

EAST ANGLIA
Rev David Hennessy, St Felix RC Church, 8 Gainsborough Road, Felixstowe, Suffolk IP11 7HT **Tel:** 01394 282561
E-mail: sacerdotus@googlemail.com

HALLAM
Rev Peter Cullen, University Chaplaincy, Padley House, Wellesley Road, Sheffield S10 2SY **Tel:** 0114-268 1197
E-mail: p.j.cullen@sheffield.ac.uk

HEXHAM AND NEWCASTLE
Rev Anthony Currer, St Cuthbert, Old Elvet, Durham DH1 3HL
Tel: 0191-384 3442
E-mail: a.t.currer@durham.ac.uk

LANCASTER
Rev Adrian Towers, The Presbytery, 114 Hoyles Lane, Cottam, Preston, Lancs PR4 0NB **Tel:** 01772-726166
E-mail: a.j.towers@btinternet.com

LEEDS
Rev Kevin Gleeson, St Thomas Moore Presbytery, Greengates House, 123 Chickenley Lane, Dewsbury WF12 8QD
Tel: 01924 465073

LIVERPOOL
Rev John McLoughlin, Episcopal Vicar for Formation, Liverpool Archdiocesan Centre for Evangelisation, Croxteth Drive, Sefton Park, Liverpool L17 1AA **Tel:** 0151 522 1040 **Fax:** 0151 522 1060
E-mail: j.mcloughlin@rcaol.co.uk

MENEVIA
Rev John Dermody, St Mary Catholic Rectory, Meyrick Street, Pembroke Dock, Pembrokeshire SA72 6AL **Tel:** 01646-682079 **E-mail:** johnd72@aol.com

MIDDLESBROUGH
Awaiting appointment

NORTHAMPTON
Canon John Udris. Cathedral House, Kingsthorpe Road, Northampton NN2 6AG
Tel: 01604 714556
E-mail: office@northamptoncathedral.org

NOTTINGHAM
Rev Michael Moore, *(director)*, **Mrs Karen Foong** *(co-director)*, St Bernadette's Presbytery, Ashby Road, Scunthorpe, N. Lincs DN16 2RS **Tel/Fax:** 0724 844895
E-mail: tmmoore75@hotmail.com or ogf@nrcdiocese.freeserve.co.uk

PLYMOUTH
Canon Kenneth Noakes, The Presbytery, 4 Lewens Lane, Wimborne, Dorset BH21 1LE
Tel: 01202-883312
E-mail: office@stcatherines.plus.com

PORTSMOUTH
Rev Bill Wilson, St Patricks House, S45 Portsmouth Road, Woolston, Southampton SO19 9BD **Tel:** 02380 448671
E-mail: eastside@portsmouth-dio.org.uk

SALFORD
Mgr Canon Mark Davies, Cathedral House, 250 Chapel Street, M3 5LL
Tel: 0161 839 9299
E-mail: vg-office@salforddiocese.org

SHREWSBURY
Canon John Rafferty, St Vincent's, 2 Bentinck Rd, Altrincham, Cheshire WA14 2BP
Tel: 0161-928 1689 **Fax:** 0161-929 8972
E-mail: johnarafferty@btconnect.com

SOUTHWARK
Rev Gerald Ewing. Archbishop's House, St George's Road, London SE1 6HX **Tel/Fax:** 020-8877 3610
E-mail: director@ogfsouthwark.org.uk

WREXHAM
Rev Charles Ramsay, St Mary's Church, 119 Wellington Road, Rhyl, Denbighshire LL18 1LE **Tel:** 01745-353395
E-mail: chas3free@msn.com

BISHOPRIC OF THE FORCES
Rev Bob Halshaw, 3 Plantation Road, Cranwell, Sleaford. Lincs NG34 8DX
Tel: 01400-261089 **Mbl:** 07713-165222
E-mail: roberthalshaw@hotmail.com

CONFERENCE OF DIRECTORS OF THE PERMANENT DIACONATE

Chairman:
Rev Ashley Beck, St Edmund's Catholic Church, 20 Village Way, Beckenham BR3 3NP
Tel: 020-8650 4117 **Fax:** 020-8650 4124 **E-mail:** ashleybeck88@hotmail.com
Administration Secretary:
Rev Deacon Noel Abbott, 15 Haroldene Grove, Prescot, Merseyside L34 1PY
Tel: 0151-449 2212 **E-mail:** abbot@lineone.net
Meetings & Minutes Secretary:
Awaiting appointment

ARUNDEL AND BRIGHTON
Rev Christopher Benyon, Our Lady of Lourdes, 21 Derby Road, Haslemere, Surrey GU27 1BS **Tel:** 01428-643877
E-mail: cmb@linus23.freeserve.co.uk
Assistants: **Revv Dcns Patrick Maloney,** 66 Madeira Avenue, Worthing, W. Sussex BN11 2BA **Tel:** 01903-239276 **Paul Scholey,** 10 Worcester Villas, Hove BN3 5TB **Tel:** 01273-271339

BIRMINGHAM
Rev Paul Chamberlain, St Peter, Abbey Street, Eynsham, Witney, Oxon OX29 4HR
Tel: 01865-881613 **E-mail:** plchamberlain@hotmail.com

BRENTWOOD
Rev Brian O'Shea, 16 East Thurrock Road, Grays, Essex RM17 6SR **Tel:** 01375 372306
E-mail: chelmsfordoli@dioceseofbrentwood.org

CARDIFF
Rev Peter Gwillym Collin, St David's Cathedral, Charles Street, Cardiff CF10 2SF
Tel: 029-2023 1407

CLIFTON
Dcn Tom Douglas, Mrs Fiona Douglas, 25 Kenmore Crescent, Filton Park, Bristol BS7 0TJ **Tel:** 0117-979 1404

EAST ANGLIA
Rev John Shannon, The Catholic Presbytery, Townhouse Road, Costessey, Norwich NR85AA **Tel:** 01603-742812
E-mail: carpe52diem@yahoo.co.uk
Assistants: **Rev Dcn Bill Dimelow.** "Crofthaven", The Croft, Old Costessey, Norwich NR8 5DT **Tel:** 01603-743476
E-mail: bill.dimelow@virgin.net
Rev Dcn Ian Hatfield, 28B, Constitution Hill, Norwich NR3 4BU **Tel:** 01603-491501
E-mail: ian.hatfield2@btopenworld.com

HALLAM
Rev Anthony Hayne, The Immaculate Conception (St Mary's), 238 Herringthorpe Valley Road, Rotherham S65 3BA
Tel: 01709-363753

HEXHAM & NEWCASTLE
Rev Michael Whalen, The Holy Name, 7 North Jesmond Ave, Newcastle NE2 3JX
Tel: 0191 281 0940

E-mail: mwhalen@genie.co.uk
Assistant: **Rev John Gibbons**, St Oswald, Gainsborough Avenue, South Shields NE34 8JN **Tel:** 0191-426 0426
Assistant: **Bill Rooke**, Our Lady St Vincents, Monkchester Road, Newcastle-Upon-Tyne NE6 2TX **Tel:** 0191-265 5217
Assistant: **Mrs P Kennedy**, 42 Southwood Gardens, Kenton, Newcastle-Upon-Tyne NE3 3BU **Tel:** 0191-284 1690

LANCASTER
Rev Adrian Towers (Students), St Wulstan, Poulton Road, Fleetwood FY7 7JY
Tel: 01253-873609
E-mail: stwulstans@supanet.com
Rev Dcn Chris Barwise (Deacons). 16 Fairfield Drive, Preston PR2 1JT
Tel: 01772-760045

LEEDS
Rev Ian Smith, St Bridget's Presbytery, 83 Lowergate, Longwood, Huddersfield HD3 4EP **Tel:** 01484-753225
E-mail: smithim@btinternet.com
Rev Deacon Keith Ballard. 99 Birkby Hall Road, Birkby, Huddersfield HD2 2XE
Tel: 01484 541366

LIVERPOOL
Mgr Austin W Hunt, All Saints, 3 Oakfield, Anfield, Liverpool L4 2QG
Tel: 0151-287 8787 **Fax:** 0151-287 8788
E-mail: austinhunt@diakon.fsnet.co.uk
Assistant: **Rev Dcn Noel Abbott,** 15 Haroldene Grove, Prescot, Merseyside L34 1PY **Tel:** 0151-449 2212
E-mail: abbot@lineone.net

MENEVIA
Rev Michael Lewis, St Michael's Rectory, 11 St Michael Street, Brecon, Powys LD3 9AB **Tel:** 01874-622046
E-mail: mrflewis@aol.com

MIDDLESBROUGH
Rev Gerard Robinson, Sacred Heart Presbytery, 1 Park Road South, Middlesbrough TS5 6LD
Tel: 01642-850113 **Fax:** 01642-852122
E-mail: stpatrickmbro@middlesbrough-diocese.org.uk
Assistant: **Rev Dcn John B Steel,** St Mary's House, High Street, Yarm TS15 9AA
Tel: 01642-781800 **E-mail:** johnsteel@middlesbrough-diocese.org.uk

NORTHAMPTON
Rev Francis Higgins (Training), St Margaret of Scotland, 22a Bolingbroke Road, Luton, Beds LU1 5JD **Tel:** 01582-720966 **E-mail:** stmargaret@freeuk.com
Assistant: **Mrs Joanna Hale,** 1 Cedar Grove, Amersham, Bucks HP7 9BG
Tel: 01494-724 487

NOTTINGHAM
Rev Phillip Scanlan IC VF, St Mary's, Ashby Rd, Loughborough Leic LE11 3AB
Tel: 01509-262123
Assistant: **Rev Dcn Raymond Keogh,** 24 Harewood Close, Langham, Oakham, Rutland PE21 7JZ **Tel:** 0116-275 5360
E-mail: keogh@btopenworld.com

PLYMOUTH
Rev Michael Koppel, The Priests House, Lyne Road, Axminster, Devon EX13 5BE
Tel: 01297-32135
Assistant: **Rev Dcn Nicholas Thompson,** Downwood Lodge, Higher Came, Dorchester, Dorset DT2 8NR
Tel: 01305-812934

PORTSMOUTH
Rev Paul Lyons, 1 Albert Road, Bournmouth, Hants BH1 1BZ **Tel:** 01202-551013 **E-mail:** lennypaullyons@aol.com
Assistant: **Rev Dcn Steve Melhuish,** 33 Hilland Rise, Headley, Hants GU35 8LZ
Tel: 01428-713555
E-mail: steve.melhuish@btinternet.com

SHREWSBURY
Rev Geoffrey O'Grady, St Ambrose, 8 Clover Avenue, Stockport SK3 8QA
Tel: 0161-480 3723
E-mail: geoffogrady@talktalk.net
Rev Dcn Peter Jackson, 36 Arborn Drive, Upton, Wirral CH49 6JS
Tel: 0151 677 8598
E-mail: peter@jackson3636.freeserve.co.uk

SOUTHWARK
Rev Peter Edwards, 1 Montem Road, New Malden KT3 3QW **Tel:** 020-89422602
Assistant (South London): **Rev Deacon Christopher Road,** 50 Coalcroft Road, London SW15 6LP **Tel:** 020-8776 6097
E-mail: christopher.road@virgin.net
Assistant Director (Kent): **Rev Deacon Kevin Dunne.** 22 Riddlesdale Avenue, Tunbridge Wells, Kent TN4 9AB **Tel:** 01892-689800 **E-mail:** kevinjeandunne1@btopenworld.com
Dean of Studies: **Rev Ashley Beck,** St Edmund's, 20 Village Way, Beckenham BR3 3NP **Tel:** 020-8650 4117
Fax: 020-8650 4124
E-mail: ashleybeck88@hotmail.com

WESTMINSTER
Rev Patrick Browne, Holy Apostles, 47 Cumberland Street, Pimlico, London

SW1V 4LY **Tel:** 020-7834 6965
E-mail: patbrowne@rcdow.org.uk

WREXHAM
Rev D Bernard Lordan, St Tudwal, King Edward Street, Barmouth LL42 1PE
Tel: 01341-280489.
Assistant: **Rev Dcn David Joy**, 38 Lon Cae Del, Mold, CH7 1QX **Tel:** 01352-754722
E-mail: margret@joym.freeserve.co.uk

SEMINARIES IN ENGLAND AND WALES

■ ALLEN HALL

(Douai, 1568; Old Hall Green; 1793; Chelsea, 1975.)
28 Beaufort Street, London SW3 5AA
Tel: 020-7349 5600
Fax: 020-7349 5601
E-mail: allenhall@rcdow.org.uk
Website: www.allenhall.org.uk

Rector: **Mgr Mark O'Toole** BSc, BD, MPhil, STL **Tel:** 020-7349 5605;
Vice-Rector: **Fr Roger Taylor**, MA, STB
Tel: 020-7349 5627;
PA to Rector: **Mrs Helena Duckett**
Tel: 020-7349 5786

Formation Team:
Canon Charles Acton STL (Dean of Studies) **Tel:** 020-7349 5611 **Sr Bernadette Hunston** SCJA, BA, MTh *(Formation Advisor)* **Tel:** 020-7349 5622 **Fr John Hemer** MHM STB, MA, LSS *(Formation Advisor)* **Tel:** 020-7349 5600 **Miss Sally McAllister** MA, *(Formation Advisor)* **Tel:** 020-7349 5612 **Rev Dr Dermot Power** BA, BD, STL, STD *(Spiritual Director)* **Tel:** 020-7349 5602 **Rev Dr Stephen Wang** PhL, STL, PhD *(Formation Advisor)* **Tel**: 020-7349 5608**Rev Francesco Donega** STB, SLL *(Formation Advisor)* **Tel:** 020-7724 8643

Academic Staff:
Canon Charles Acton STL (Dean of Theology, Systematic Theology) **Rev Dr Francis Selman** MA, MTh, PhD, PhL *(Dean of Philosophy)* **Rev John Conneely** JCL *(Canon Law)* **Rev Francesco Donega** STB, SLL *(Liturgy, Systematic Theology)* **Rev Peter Harris** BEd, MTh *(Church History)* **Rev John Hemer** MHM, STB, LSS *(Scripture, Biblical Greek)* **Sr Bernadette Hunston** SCJA, BA, MTh *(Spiritual Theology)* **Miss Sally McAllister** *(Pastoral Co-ordinator & Pastoral Theology)*, **Tel:** 020 7349 5612 **Rev Dr Anthony Meredith** SJ, MA, DPhil *(Patristics)* **Miss Letitia Nicoll** LGSM, DipCE, FESB *(Vocal Communications)* **Rev Dr Joseph O'Hanlon** BA, BD, MTh, LSS, PhD *(Scripture)* **Rev Dom Alexander Bevan OSB** *(Latin)* **Rev Dr Dermot Power** BA, BD, STL, STD *Spirituality, Systematic Theology)* **Fr Roger Taylor** MA, STB, MA *(Liturgy)* **Prof Clemens Sedmak** PhD *(Moral Theology)* **Rev Dr Stephen Wang** PhL, STL, PhD *(Philosophy, Systematic Theology)*; **Dr Clare Watkins** *(Pastoral Theology)*; **Sr Petronia Williams** OSM, DipEd *(Pastoral Supervisor)*

Administration:
Administrator: **Mr Gerald Daly** BA, **Tel:** 020-7349 5606; *Receptionist/ Conference Co-ordinator:* **Miss Mary Aldridge Tel:** 020-7349 5600; *Librarian:* **Rev Dr Francis Selman** MA, MTh, PhD, STL

■ ST. CUTHBERT'S COLLEGE,

Ushaw, is the Major Seminary of the Northern Province and Shrewsbury Diocese, originally founded at Douai in 1568 and since 1968 a Licensed Hall of the University of Durham which validates the College's degrees. Degree courses are open to lay students.

Conference Centre: The centre is open throughout the year for residential and day conferences.

President: **Rev John Marsland**, Ushaw College, Durham DH7 9RH
Tel: 0191-373 8501
E-mail: president@ushaw.ac.uk
Vice President: **Rev Philip Gillespie**, PhB, STB, SLL (Liturgy), **Tel:** 0191-373 8524
E-mail: p.gillespie@ushaw.ac.uk
President's Secretary: **Mrs Marjorie Towers Tel:** 0191-373 8510
E-mail: marjorie.towers@ushaw.ac.uk
Director of Teaching and Learning: **Sr Patricia McDonald** SHCJ, BA, PGCE, MA, BD, MPhil, LSS, PhD (Scripture).
Tel: 0191-373 8530
E-mail: p.mcdonald@ushaw.ac.uk
Director of Educational Outreach: **Mrs Ros Stuart-Buttle** BA, MA, PGCE
Tel: 0191-373 855
E-mail: Ros.stuart-buttle@ushaw.ac.uk
Course Administrator: **Mrs Ann Scott**
Tel: 0191-373 8517
E-mail: ann.scott@ushaw.ac.uk
Director of Finance and Communications: **Mrs Kay Wightman Tel:** 0191-373 8511
E-mail: kay.wightman@ushaw.ac.uk

Director of Estates and Facilities: **Mr Peter Seed Tel:** 0191-373 505
E-mail: peter.seed@ushaw.ac.uk
Conference Centre Manager: **Ms Angie George Tel:** 0191-373 588
E-mail: angie.george@ushaw.ac.uk
Finance Manager: **Mr Denis D'Ugo**
Tel: 0191-373 506
E-mail: dendugo@ushaw.ac.uk

Teaching Staff:
Sr Helen Bamber SHCJ, (Assistant to Director of Education Outreach),
Tel: 0191 373 8569
E-mail: helen.bamber@ushaw.ac.uk
Rev Bernard Barlow (OSM) PhB, MA, DRS, MS, STL, PhD, PGCE (Church History)
Tel: 0191 373 8535
E-mail: bernard.barlow@ushaw.ac.uk
Rev Philip Caldwell BA, PGCE, STB, STL, STD, (Systematic Theology)
Tel: 0191 373 8533
E-mail: philip.caldwell@ushaw.ac.uk
Rev Jeremy Corley BA, MA, PhD (Scripture), **Tel:** 0191 373 8521
E-mail: jeremy.corley@ushaw.ac.uk
Peter Cullen, BA, MA, (Spiritual Director),
Tel: 0191 373 8576
E-mail: peter.cullen@ushaw.ac.uk
Bro Brendan Geary (FMS), PhD, (Human Development) **Tel:** 0191-373 8507
E-mail: brendan.geary@ushaw.ac.uk
Mr Timothy Harrison BA, MMus, LTCL, (Director of Music) **Tel:** 0191-373 8607,
E-mail: timothy.harrison@ushaw.ac.uk
Rev Chris Hughes BA, LLB (Pastoral Director), **Tel:** 0191-373 8525
E-mail: chris.hughes@ushaw.ac.uk
Rev Vincent Purcell BA (hons), CPS, (Pastoral Director), **Tel:** 0191-373 8560
E-mail: vincent.purcell@ushaw.ac.uk
Rev Neil Ritchie (Moral Theology),
Tel: 0191-373 8531
E-mail: neil.ritchie@ushaw.ac.uk
Rev Dr Michael Sharratt STL, PhD
Tel: 0191-373 8536
E-mail: michael.sharratt@ushaw.ac.uk
Mgr Peter Verity, (Spiritual Director),
Tel: 0191-373 8528,
E-mail: peter.verity@ushaw.ac.uk

Visiting Lecturers: **Rev Steven Billington** BSc, STB, PhL; **Rev John Farrell** OP, BA, BD, PhD; **Rev Michael McCoy** MA, JCL; **Rev David Potter** MA, STL, PhD

Librarian: **Mr Matthew Watson,**
Tel: 0191-373 8516,
E-mail: matthew.watson@ushaw.ac.uk

Also at Ushaw: *CAFOD North East Regional Office:* **Tel/Fax:** 0191-373 5001 North East Ecumenical Course (NEOC) **Tel:** 0191-373 7600 **The Churches' Regional Commission (CRC): Tel:** 0191-373 5453

■ ST. JOHN'S SEMINARY,

Wonersh, the Major Seminary of the Archdiocese of Southwark and the Diocese of Arundel and Brighton, with degrees validated by the University of Surrey.
St. John's Seminary, Wonersh, Guildford, Surrey GU5 0QX
Tel: 01483-892217 **Fax:** 01483-894531
E-mail: rector@wonersh.org
Website: www.wonersh.org

Rector: **Rev Mgr Canon Jeremy Garratt** Ph B, MA, STL; *Rector's Secretary:* **Ms Melissa Kingdon** BSc **Tel:** 01483 891024
Bursar: **Mr Tony Lee; Tel:** 01483 891020
Finance Assistant: **Mrs Bernie Minchella; Tel:** 01483 891029; *Bursar's Secretary:* **Mrs Nina Segrove;** *Director of Studies:* **Rev Jonathan How** BSc, BTh, PhL, PGCE(A), ARCS, FHEA, **Tel:** 01483 891023; *Academic Secretary:* **Mrs Rebecca Teller** BSc **Tel:** 01483 891028; *Director of Spirituality:* **Rev Gerard Bradley,** BMus, BTh, AKC; **Tel:** 01483 891021; *Pastoral Director:* **Sr M Finbarr Coffey** HC, BA, HDipEd, CertTh, **Tel:** 01483 891025; *Human Development Director:* **Rev Paul Lyons** MLitt, MA, **Tel:** 01483 891028

Other Full-time Staff:
Senior Lecturer in Divinity, Librarian: **Rev Stephen Dingley** MA, PhD, STL, **Tel:** 01483 891027; *Spiritual Director:* **Michael Woodgate** BA, **Tel:** 01483 891026.

Part-time Staff:
Sr Maureen Banyard FMDM, Rt Rev Geoffrey Scott OSB, Rev John Boyle, Dr Victor Darlington, Timothy Finigan, Sean Finnegan, Alan Griffiths, John Henry, Dylan James, Michael Masterson, Simon Peat, Dominic Rolls, Julian Shurgold, Mr Ged Clapson, Roger Mortimore, Mr Robert Munns, Mrs Lynette Harborne, Frances Henley Lock, Pia Matthews.

■ ST. MARY'S COLLEGE

Oscott, and the Major Seminary of the Archdiocese of Birmingham, founded in 1794, with degrees validated by the Catholic University of Leuven and Birmingham University.
St. Mary's College, Oscott, Chester Road, Sutton Coldfield B73 5AA
Tel: 0121-321 5000 **Fax:** 0121-321 5002
E-mail: mark.crisp@oscott.org

Rector: **Rev Mark Crisp** STB
Tel: 0121-321 5035
Vice-Rector: **Rev Richard Walker** LLB, STB,

Tel: 0121-321 5010
Academic Dean: **Rev Harry Curtis** BSc, MEd, STL, **Tel:** 0121-321 5006; *Director of Studies:* **Dr Judith Champ** PhD, **Tel:** 0121-321 5014; *Spiritual Director:* **Rev Hugh Sinclair,** LLB, **Tel:** 0121-321 5024; *Estates Director:* **Rev Paul Fitzpatrick** MA, **Tel:** 0121-321 5017; *Ongoing Formation Director:* **Rev Paul McNally** STL, **Tel:** 0121-321 5012; *New Testament:* **Rev Kenneth Collins, Tel:** 0121-321 5032; **Rev Zbigniew Zieba** MA, LSS, **Tel:** 0121-321 5041; *Programme Manager:* **Mrs Jayne Isaac, Tel:** 0121-321 5004; *Librarian/Schools Outreach:* **Mr Gerard Boylan** BA, PGCE, MEd. **Tel:** 0121-321 5069; *Rector's Secretary:* **Mrs Pat Salter, Tel:** 0121-321 5037; *House Manager:* **Mr Mark Carroll, Tel:** 0121-321 5008; *Financial Manager:* **Mrs Jackie Hall, Tel:** 0121-321 5095; *Cemetery Office/Francis Martyn House:* **Mrs Maggie Wilson Tel:** 0121-321 5026/7 *Visiting Staff:* **Miss Mary Casey,** BEd, MEd, ALAM, LGSM, Fcollp; **Rev Peter Conley** STL, MPhil, PG Cert, ILTM; **Rev Michael Doyle,** PhD, STL, CPsychol; **Rev Eddie Clare,** BSc, STL; **Miss Caroline Farey,** BA, MPhil, MA, STB, PhL; **Rev David Goodill** OP, MA, MPhil; **Rev Julian Green,** BA, STL; **Rev John Hadley,** MA, BSc, STL, PhL; **Rev John Hemer,** MA, STB, LSS; **Miss Mary Holland,** BA; **Dr Don Lynch,** MBCS, MPhil, PhD; **Rev Timothy Menezes,** STB, SLL; **Rev Patrick Mileham,** BD, STB: **Rev Paul Moss,** BA, STB, PhL; **Mr Anthony O'Rourke,** PhB, BA, PGCE.

SEMINARIES ABROAD

■ ROME (PONTIFICAL COLLEGES)

Venerable English College (1579)
Venerabile Collegio Inglese, Via di Monserrato 45, 00186 Roma, Italia
Tel: 0039 06 6868546 or 0039 06 6865808
Fax: 0039 06 6867607
Website: www.englishcollegerome.org

Rector: **Rev Mgr Nicholas Hudson** MA, STL **Tel:** 0039 06 68300278 **Fax:** 0039 06 6864185 **E-mail:** rector.vec@mclink.it
Vice-Rector & Pastoral Tutor: **Rev Andrew Headon** BSc, STL, MBA, **Tel/Fax:** 0039 06 45443600 **E-mail:** vicerector.vec@mclink.it
Spiritual Director: **Mgr Philip Carroll, Tel:** 0039 06 6868546 ext 14. *Philosophy Tutor:* Awaiting Appointment.
Academic Tutor: **Rev Anthony Milner** BSc, STL, **Tel:** 0039 06 6868546

Pastoral Director: **Rev Mark Harold,** BA, STL, PhL, MA, **Tel:** 0039 06 6868546 ext 53
Also in residence: **Rev Mgr Bryan Chestle** STL, PhL, MA. Secretariat of State, Vatican City **Tel:** 0039 06 6868546 ext 24; **Rev Mgr Philip Whitmore, Rev Mark Langham,**
Administrator: **Ms Barbara Donovan. Tel:** 0039 06 6868546 ext 15
E-mail: exec.vec@mclink.it
Rector's PA: **Ms Paoli Caiati. Tel:** 0039 06 6868546 ext 16
E-mail: secrec.vec@mclink.it
Guestmistress: **Sr Mary-Joseph McManamon. Tel:** 0039 06 6868546 ext 18 **E-mail:** maryjosephm@yahoo.com
Archivist: **Ms Iris Jones.**
Tel: 0039 06 6868546 ext 43
E-mail: vecarchive@yahoo.co.uk

Beda College (1852; 1917; 1960)
Pontificio Collegio Beda, Viale di S Paolo 18, 00146 Roma, Italia **Tel:** 0039 06 551271 **Fax:** 0039-06 55127254
Website: www.bedacollege.com

Rector: **Mgr Roderick Strange** DPhil, STL, FRSA (Shrewsbury) **Tel:** 0039 06 55127201 **Fax:** 0039 06 55127219 **E-mail:** r.strange@bedacollege.com
Dean of Studies: **Rev John Breen** BA, MA (Hexham & Newcastle) **Tel:** 0039 06 55127252 **Fax:** 0039 06 551227412
E-mail: j.breen@bedacollege.com
Spiritual Director: **Rev James Brand** MA, STL, PhL (Westminster) **Tel:** 0039 06 55127223
E-mail: JimBrand201@msn.com
Pastoral Director: **Rev Dermot McCaul** SMA BA, Con.(Accredited).
Tel: 0039-06 55127202.
E-mail: d.mccaul@bedacollege.com
Resident Lecturers: **Sr Assumpta Williams** FMDM, STL, BSc **Tel:** 0039 06 55127224
Bursar: **Mrs Susan Marsili Tel:** 0039 06 55127205 **E-mail:** s.marsili@bedacollege.com
Rector's Secretary: Mrs Orietta Mariotti
Tel: 0039 06 55127206 **E-mail:** o.mariotti@bedacollege.com

■ **SPAIN**

St Alban's College (Real Colegio de Ingleses) (1589), Calle Don Sancho 22, 47002 Valladolid, Spain.
Tel: 0034 983 293102
Fax: 0034 983 392300
Country House: **Tel:** 0034 983 554384
Student tel Nos can be found on the
Website: www.valladolid.org

Rector: **Mgr Michael Kujacz**
Tel: 0034 983 392322
Mbl: 0034659999467
Email: mjk@valladolid.org

Vice-Rector: Rev John Pardo
Tel: 0034 983 212896

Spiritual Director: **Rev Kevin McLoughlin**
Tel: 0034 983 295616

Pastoral Director: **Rev Joseph McLoughlin**
Tel: 0034 626 977938

College Secretary: **Senora Rosa Delbarco**

Historian & Archivist: **Senor Javier Burrieza**

Honorary Historian & Archivist: **Rev Peter Harris BEd, MTh**

College Manager: **Senor Javier Serrano**

EDUCATION CHAPLAINCIES AND INSTITUTIONS
IN ENGLAND AND WALES

CONFERENCE OF CATHOLIC CHAPLAINS IN HIGHER EDUCATION IN ENGLAND AND WALES

■ THE COMMITTEE

President:
Rt Rev Peter Doyle
Bishop's House, Marriott Street,
Northampton, NN2 6AW

Chairperson:
Sr Anna O'Connor
Newman House, 29 Harrisons Drive
Birmingham B15 3QS
Tel: 0161 236 6762 **Mbl:** 0783 8374533

Secretary:
Rev Hugh Pollock
Chaplaincy Centre, University of Lancaster,
Lancaster LA1 4XX

Treasurer:
Ms Mia Fox
Catholic Chaplaincy, 14 Windsor Terrace,
Newcastle upon Tyne NE2 4HE

National Co-ordinator:
Sr Teresa Kennedy
167 Fairfield Road, Buxton SK17 7ED
Tel: 01298 77116
Email: t.kennedy@derby.ac.uk

Other Committee Members:
Ms Lousie Walton

CATHOLIC STUDENT TRUST

While the Catholic Student Council remains in abeyance, its Trustees are continuing to pursue the aims of the CSC by making periodic financial grants to Chaplaincies to develop student activities. Details of these grants are publicised direct to all Chaplains.

For information contact Chair of Trustees:
Rev Robert Esdaile The Presbytery, Our Lady of Lourdes RC Church, Hampton Court Way, Thames Ditton, Surrey KT7 0LP **Tel:** 0208-398 6127
The CST is a Registered Charity, no. 328705

OXFORD AND CAMBRIDGE CATHOLIC EDUCATION BOARD

For the maintenance of the Chaplaincies at Oxford and Cambridge

Chairman:
Rt Rev Crispian Hollis, Bishop of Portsmouth.

Secretary and Treasurer:
Rev James Furlong 141 Norfolk Avenue, Palmers Green, London N13 6AL

CATHOLIC CHAPLAINS IN HIGHER EDUCATION

■ **ABERYSTWYTH UNIVERSITY (Menevia Diocese)**
(Awaiting appointment)

■ **ALSAGER: Manchester Metropolitan University, Alsager Campus (Shrewsbury Diocese)**
Rev Anthony Grace
St Gabriel's, 140 Lawton Road, Alsager, Cheshire ST7 2DE **Tel:** 01270 872542

■ **ASTON UNIVERSITY (Birmingham Archdiocese)**
(Awaiting Appointment)
Martin Luther King Chaplaincy Centre, Lawrence Tower, Aston University, Birmingham B4 7ET
Tel: 0121 359 3621 Ext 4076

■ **BANGOR UNIVERITY (Wrexham Diocese)**
(Awaiting Appointment)
Catholic Chaplaincy, Pendyffryn, 1 Menai Avenue, Bangor, Gwynedd LL57 2HH **Tel:** 01248 352522
E-mail: rcchaplainbango@aol.com

■ **BATH UNIVERSITY AND BATH SPA UNIVERSITY COLLEGE (Clifton Diocese)**
Rev William McCoughlin OSM
Ss Peter and Paul, 112 Entry Hill, Combe Down, Bath BA2 5LS
Tel: 01225 832096
E-mail: fatherbill@mcloughlinw.fsnet.co.uk
Website: www.bath-catholics.org.uk
Catholic Chaplaincy House, 5-6 Harley Street, Bath BA1 2SE **Tel:** 01225 465917
Website: www.bath.ac.uk\admin\chaplaincy
Bath Catholic Society:
E-mail: cathsoc@bath.ac.uk or
Website: people.bath.ac.uk/su4csoc
Bath Spa University College Catholic Society: **E-mail:** cathsoc@bathspa.ac.uk

■ **BEDFORD: DE MONFORT UNIVERSITY (Northampton Diocese)**
Ms Elizabeth Ridley
Holy Cross Church, 355 Goldington Road, Bedford MK41 0DP
Tel: 01234 353116 (Church); or 01234 211558 (home)

■ **BIRMINGHAM UNIVERSITY (Birmingham Archdiocese)**
Rev Julian Green
& Sr Anna O'Connor CP
Catholic Chaplaincy, Newman House, 29 Harrisons Road, Edgbaston, Birmingham B15 3QS
Tel: 0121 454 4395
E-mail: a.oconnor@bham.ac.uk
St Francis Hall, University of Birmingham, Edgbaston, B15 2TT
Tel: 0121 414 7000/7001
Fax: 0121 414 7002
Website: www.bham.ac.uk/chaplaincy

■ **BIRMINGHAM; NEWMAN UNIVERSITY COLLEGE (Birmingham Archdiocese)**
Margaret Holland
Newman University College, Genners Lane, Bartley Green, Birmingham B32 3NT **Tel:** 0121 476 1181 x2325
Mbl: 07989 580487
E-mail: m.holland@newman.ac.uk

■ **BIRMINGHAM: UNIVERSITY OF CENTRAL ENGLAND (Birmingham Archdiocese)**
Sr Christina McCann CSJ
103 Anderton Park Road, Moseley, Birmingham B13 9DS
Tel: 0121 449 3854
Mbl: 07974 150365
E-mail: christina.mccann@uce.ac.uk
SR GLADIS PINTO
14 Wye Cliff Road, Handsworth, Birmingham B20 3TB
Ms Jenifer Cummings
1 Bromford Ho, Jockey Rd, Birmingham B73 5XP **Tel:** 0121 355 6889
E-mail: jenifercum@yahoo.co.uk
UCE Ecumenical Chaplaincy, Student Services, Baker Building, Perry Barr, Birmingham B42 2SU
Tel/Fax: 0121 331 5588

■ **BOLTON: INSTITUTE OF HIGHER EDUCATION (Salford Diocese)**
(Awaiting appointment)

■ **BOURNEMOUTH UNIVERSITY (Plymouth Diocese)**
Sr Marion Gormley
Student Centre, Talbot House, University of Bournemouth, Fern Barrow, Poole BH12 5BB
Tel: 01202 595581

■ **BRADFORD UNIVERSITY (Leeds Diocese)**
Rev Dennis Cassidy
The Catholic Chaplaincy, 1 Ashgrove, Bradford, West Yorks BD7 1BN
Tel: 01274 721636
E-mail: catholic-chaplaincy@bradford.ac.uk

■ **BRIGHTON UNIVERSITY [See also Sussex] (Arundel & Brighton Diocese)**
Sr Blanaid McCauley SSL
The Chaplaincy, Steam House, 8 Pelham Place, Lewes Rd, Brighton BN2 4AF
Chaplaincy Office: **Tel:** 01273 642955
Home **Tel:** 01273 693971
Mbl: 07745134626
E-mail: b.m.mccauley@bton.ac.uk

■ **BRISTOL UNIVERSITY (Clifton Diocese)**
Rev Robert King
University Catholic Chaplaincy, 103 Queens Road, Clifton, Bristol BS8 1LL **Tel:** 0117 914 0003
E-mail: Robert.King@bristol.ac.uk
Students' contact: **Tel:** 0117 973 4158
Website: www.bris.ac.uk/Depts/Union/Cassoc

■ **BRISTOL: UNIVERSITY OF THE WEST OF ENGLAND (Clifton Diocese)**
Rev Tom Finnegan
UWE Ecumenical Chaplaincy Centre, The Octagon, Frenchay Campus, Coldharbour Lane, Bristol BSI6 1QY
Tel: 0117 32 83979
Residence: 1b Sydenham Rd Bristol BS6 5SH
E-mail: Robert.Rainbow@uwe.ac.uk
Cathsoc website: www.uwe.ac.uk/cathsoc
Ecumenical chaplaincy website: www.uwe.ac.uk/chaplaincy

■ **BRUNEL UNIVERSITY (Westminster Archdiocese)**
(Awaiting appointment)
See London Central

■ **BUXTON: DERBY UNIVERSITY, BUXTON CAMPUS (Nottingham Diocese)**
Sr Teresa Kennedy PBVM, University of Derby College, Harpur Hill, Buxton SK17 9JZ
Tel: 01298 28376 (office)
Residence: 167 Fairfield Rd, Buxton SK17 7ED **Tel:** 01298 77116

■ **CAMBRIDGE UNIVERSITY (East Anglia Diocese)**
Rev Alban McCoy OFM Conv
Tel: 01223 742190
E-mail: am335@cam.ac.uk
Dom Stephan Ortiger OSB
Tel: 01223 742193
E-mail: so258@cam.ac.uk
Sr Pauline Burling OP
Tel: 01223 742193
E-mail: bpb26@cam.ac.uk
Fisher House, Guildhall Street, Cambridge CB2 3NH
Tel: 01223 742192 **Fax:** 01223 329180

■ **CAMBRIDGE: ANGLIA RUSKIN UNIVERSITY** [See also Chelmsford] **(East Anglia Diocese)**
Rev Rafael Estaban WF
Our Lady and the English Martyrs, Hills Road, Cambridge CB2 1JR
Tel: 01223 350787
rafael@esteban.freeserve.com.uk

■ **CARDIFF UNIVERSITY (Cardiff Archdiocese)**
Rev John Owen
The Catholic Chaplaincy, 62 Park Place, Cardiff CF10 3AS
Tel: 029 2022 9785 **Fax:** 029 2066 8197
E-mail: r-c-chaplaincy@cf.ac.uk
Website: www.cf.ac.uk./suon/catholic/

■ **CENTRAL ENGLAND [See Birmingham]**

■ **CENTRAL LANCASHIRE [See Preston]**

■ **CHELMSFORD: ANGLIA RUSKIN UNIVERSITY [See also Cambridge] (Brentwood Diocese)**
Rev Frank Jackson
The Presbytery, Beardsley Drive, Springfield, Chelmsford, CM1 6GQ
Tel: 01245 465333
E-mail: springfield@dioceseofbrentwood.org.uk

■ **CHESTER UNIVERSITY (Shrewsbury Diocese)**
Rev Paul Shaw
St Werburgh's, Grosvenor Park Road, Chester CH1 1QJ **Tel:** 01244 350236
E-mail: werburgh465@btinternet.com

■ **CRANFIELD UNIVERSITY (Northampton Diocese)** [See also Shrivenham]
Canon Stanislaus Condon
St Mary's, Aspley Hill, Woburn Sands, Beds MK17 8NN **Tel:** 01908 583195

■ **DE MONFORT UNIVERSITY**
[See Bedford and Leicester]

■ **DERBY UNIVERSITY (Nottingham Diocese)**
Ms Ginny Jordan
(Ecumenical Chaplaincy Assistant)
The Chaplaincy, Derby University, Kedleston Road, Derby DE22 1GB
Tel: 01332 591878
Mbl: 07947 134998
E-mail: v.m.jordan@derby.ac.uk
Rev Richard Walsh 5 Derby Rd Homesford Matlock DE4 5HJ
E-mail: r.walsh@derby.ac.uk

■ **DURHAM UNIVERSITY (Hexham & Newcastle Diocese)**
Rev Anthony T Currer
St Cuthbert's Presbytery, Old Elvet, Durham DH1 3HL **Tel:** 0191 384 3442
E-mails: a.t.currer@durham.ac.uk
Catholic.Society@durham.ac.uk
Website: www.dur.ac.uk/cathsoc

■ **EAST ANGLIA UNIVERSITY [see also Ipswich] (East Anglia Diocese)**
Mrs Marion Houssart
Rev John Shannon
The Chaplaincy, University of East Anglia, Norwich NR4 7TJ
Tel: 01603 592168
E-mail: j.shaanon@uea.ac.uk
E-mail: m.houssart@uea.ac.uk
Home Tel: 01603 612143
Website: www.uea.ac.uk/chaplaincy

■ **ESSEX UNIVERSITY (Brentwood Diocese)**
Rev Martin Boland
Catholic Chaplaincy,
University of Essex, Wivenhoe Park, Colchester, Essex C04 3SQ
Tel: 01206 872018
E-mail: mrtnboland@aol.com
Home: 1 Recreation Way, Brightlingsea, Essex CO7 0NJ **Tel:** 01206 302485

■ **EXETER UNIVERSITY (Plymouth Diocese)**
Rev Paul Cummins
Catholic Chaplaincy,
Glenthorne Road, Exeter EX4 4QU
Tel/Fax: 01392 271191
E-mail: p.m.cummins@exeter.ac.uk

■ **GLAMORGAN UNIVERSITY (Cardiff Archdiocese)**
(Awaiting Appointment)
Chaplaincy Centre (Ecumenical),
20 Llantwit Road, Treforest, Pontypridd, Mid Glamorgan CF37 1TR
Tel/Fax: 01443 491514
Website: www.glam.ac.uk/student/chaplaincy/index.php

■ **HALLAM UNIVERSITY**
[See Sheffield: Hallam]

■ **HUDDERFIELD UNIVERSITY (Leeds Diocese)**
Rev Richard Aladics
85 Sheepridge Road, Huddersfield HD2 1HF

■ **HULL UNIVERSITY & LINCOLN UNIVERSITY CAMPUS AT HULL (Middlesbrough Diocese)**
Rev James O'Brien
Catholic Chaplaincy,
113-115 Cottingham Road, Hull HU5 2DH **Tel:** 01482 343216
Fax: 01482 494104
E-mail: j.obrien@hull.ac.uk
Website: www.hull.ac.uk/cathchap

■ **IPSWICH: SUFFOLK COLLEGE, affiliated to UNIVERSITY OF EAST ANGLIA (East Anglia Diocese)**
College Chaplaincy, Rope Walk, Ipswich IP4 1LT **Tel:** 01473 296526

■ **JOHN MOORES UNIVERSITY**
[See Liverpool: John Moores]

■ **KEELE UNIVERSITY (Birmingham Archdiocese)**
Rev Raymund Bayliss
The Cottage, 12 The Village, Keele, Staffs ST5 5AR
Tel: 01782 628352 (house);
Tel: 01782 621111 ext.7162 (chaplaincy)

■ **KENT UNIVERSITY (Southwark Archdiocese)**
Rev Peter Geldard
St John Stone House,41 St Thomas Hill, Canterbury, Kent CT2 8HW
Tel/Fax: 01227 462198
Mbl: 07970 228762
Office: 01227 823348
Website: www.cathsoc.org
E-mail: chaplain@cathsoc.org

■ **KINGSTON UNIVERSITY (Southwark Archdiocese)**
Rev Vincent Flynn
102 Maple Road, Surbiton, Surrey KT6 4AL **Tel:** 020 8399 1574
Mbl: 07931102106

■ **LAMPETER UNIVERSITY (Menevia Diocese)**
Rev Augustine Paikkatt
Our Lady of Mount Carmel, Pontfaen Rd Lampeter SA48 7BS

■ **LANCASTER UNIVERSITY (Lancaster Diocese)**
Rev Hugh Pollock
Chaplaincy Centre,
University of Lancaster, Bailrigg, Lancaster LAl 4XX. **Tel:** 01524 594080
Website: www.chaplancs.org.uk

■ **LANCASTER: ST MARTIN'S COLLEGE (Lancaster Diocese)**
Mavis Lee
St Martin's College, Bowerham Road, Lancaster LA1 4JD
Rev Peter Foulkes
St Bernadette's, Bowerham Road, Lancaster LA1 4HT **Tel:** 01524 63000

■ **LEEDS & LEEDS METROPOLITAN UNIVERSITIES (Leeds Diocese)**
Rev Gerard Kearney
Leeds Universities Catholic Chaplaincy, 5 St Mark's Avenue, Leeds LS2 9BN
Tel: 0113 2438263
E-mail Gerard.Kearney@leeds-diocese.org.uk

■ **LEEDS TRINITY & ALL SAINTS (Leeds Diocese)**
Rev Peter Clark
Trinity & All Saints, Brownberrie Lane, Horsforth, Leeds LS18 5HD
Tel: 0113 283 7201 or 0113 283 7100
Fax: 0113 283 7200 (Reception)
E-mail: p_varey@tasc.ac.uk
E-mail: chaplain@tasc.ac.uk
Mr James Noakes
Tel: 0113 283 7199

■ **LEICESTER UNIVERSITY (Nottingham Diocese)**
Rev Leon Pereira OP
Holy Cross Priory, 45 Wellington Street, Leicester LE1 6HW
Tel: 0116 255 3856 (Priory)
0116 252 1512 (Catholic Chaplaincy)
Fax: 0116 255 5552
The Gatehouse, Leicester University *Chaplaincy:* **Tel:** 0116 285 6493

■ **LEICESTER; DE MONTFORT UNIVERSITY [See also Bedford] Nottingham Diocese)**
Rev Leon Pereira OP
Holy Cross Priory, 45 Wellington Street, Leicester LE1 6HW
Tel: 0116 255 3856 (Priory)
De Montfort University Chaplaincy:
Tel: 0116 255 1551 x8599

■ **LINCOLN UNIVERSITY (Nottingham Diocese)**
Rev Philip O'Dowd
St Hugh's, 34 Broadgate, Lincoln LN2 5AQ **Tel:** 01522 528961
Fax: 01522 537685

■ **LIVERPOOL UNIVERSITY & LIVERPOOL JOHN MOORES (Liverpool Archdiocese)**
Rev Ian McParland
Philip Neri House, 30 Catharine Street, Liverpool L8 7NL **Tel:** 0151 709 3858
Website: www.cathchap.org.uk

■ **LIVERPOOL: HOPE UNIVERSITY (Liverpool Archdiocese)**
Ms Clare Guidi
The Chaplaincy, Hope University College, Hope Park, Liverpool L16 9JD
Tel: 0151 291 3545
E-mail: guidi@hope.ac.uk

■ **LONDON CENTRAL (Westminster Archdiocese)**
Rev Peter Wilson (Senior HE Chaplain, Westminster Diocese)
E-mail: pjw@universitycatholic.net
Rev Mark Barrett OSB *(in residence)*
Mr Christopher Castell
(chaplaincy assistant)
Newman House, 111 Gower Street, London WC1E 6AR
Tel: 020 7387 6370 **Fax:** 020 7388 6431
Newman House Chaplaincy website: www.universitycatholic.net

■ **CENTRAL LONDON: GOODENOUGH COLLEGE (Westminster Archdiocese)**
Rev Casimir Adjoe
Goodenough College, Mecklenburgh Square, London WC1 2AB
Tel: 020 7837 4147

■ **WEST LONDON: MORE HOUSE**
Rev Geoff Wheaton SJ
Rev Nigel Griffen
More House, 53 Cromwell Rd
London SW7 2EH **Tel:** 020 7584 2040
E-mail: rcchaplainmore@aol.com

■ **ST MARY'S UNIVERSITY COLLEGE**
Rev Gerard Devlin
St Marys University College
Strawberry Hill, Twickenham, Middlesex TW1 4SX **Tel:** 020 8240 4006
E-mail: devling@smuc.ac.uk
Chaplaincy office: 020 8240 4331
Website: www.smuc.ac.uk/chaplaincy

■ **LONDON: HEYTHROP (Westminster Archdiocese)**
Bernie Devine SP, Heythrop College, 23 Kensington Square, London W8 5HQ
Tel: 020 7795 4215
E-mail: b.devine@heythrop.ac.uk
Website : www.heythrop.ac.uk

■ **LONDON: MIDDLESEX (Westminster Archdiocese)**
(Awaiting appointment)

■ **LONDON: UNIVERSITY OF EAST LONDON (UEL) (Brentwood Diocese)**
Rev Dcn Thomas Dunton CAJ
79 Barking Road, Canning Town, London E16 4HB **Tel/Fax:** 020 7476 4129
E-mail: canningtown@dioceseofbrentwood.org
Website : www.heythrop.ac.uk

■ **LONDON: SOUTH (Southwark Archdiocese)**
Rev David O'Connell
Chaplaincy House, 56 Amersham Road, New Cross, London SE14 6QE
Tel: 020 8692 6931

E-mail: doconnell@byopenworld.com
Miss Joan Tierney
Chaplain to GKT Medical and Dental School and St George's Medical School
14 Melior Street, Bermondsey, London SE1 3QP. **Tel:** 020 7357 0653

■ **LONDON: UNIVERSITY OF SURREY ROEHAMPTON (Southwark Archdiocese)**
ROBERT KAGGWA
Digby Stuart College, Roehampton Lane, London SW15 5PH
Tel: 020 8392 3005
Website: www.roehampton.ac.uk/dchaplaincy/

■ **LONDON: ROYAL HOLLOWAY (Arundel & Brighton Diocese)**
Rev Vladimir Nikiforov
91a Harvest Road, Englefield Green, Surrey TW20 0QR **Tel:** 01784 437280
Office: 01784 414358
E-mail: vladimir.nikiforov@rhul.ac.uk

■ **LONDON: THAMES VALLEY EALING CAMPUS (Westminster Archdiocese)**
(Awaiting appointment)

■ **LONDON: THAMES VALLEY UNIVERSITY SLOUGH CAMPUS (Northampton Diocese)**
Miss Maria Corcoran
Our Lady Immaculate & St Ethelbert's Church, Wellington Street, Slough, Berks SL1 1XU **Tel:** 01753 523147
E-mail: saintethelberts@ukgateway.net

■ **LOUGHBOROUGH UNIVERSITY (Nottingham Diocese)**
Rev Peter Wade
The Priest's Ho, Sacred Heart, 203 Park Rd, Loughborough, Leics LE11 2HE
Tel: 01509 822646

■ **LUTON UNIVERSITY (Northampton Diocese)**
Rev Kieron Magovern CM
St Mary's, 82 West Street, Dunstable, LU6 1NY **Tel:** 01582 662710
The Ecumenical Chaplaincy, Vicarage Street, Luton LU1 3AG
Tel: 01582 453236 or 565442

■ **MANCHESTER UNIVERSITY (Salford Diocese)**
Rev Ian Kelly
338-339 Oxford Road, Manchester M13 9GB **Tel:** 0161 273 1456
E-mail: info@rc-chaplaincy-um.org.uk
Website: www.rc-chaplaincy-um.org.uk
Sr Kevina Byrne FMSJ, **Monica Zuniga Cobos** MCR, **Karina Bohorquez** MCR.

■ **MANCHESTER METROPOLITAN UNIVERSITY & ROYAL NORTHERN COLLEGE OF MUSIC (Salford Diocese)**
Rev Christopher Gorton
Mr Bernard Burke
Miss Maomi Young MA
St Augustine's, Grosvenor Square, All Saints, Manchester M15 6BW
Tel: 0161 236 6762 (Parish line, 24 hours) 0161 247 3496 (daytime)
Mbl: 07970 977062
E-mail: augustines@eggconnect.net
Website: www.saintaugustines.org.uk

■ **MIDDLESBROUGH: TEESSIDE UNIVERSITY (Middlesbrough Diocese)**
Rev Gerard Robinson
Sacred Heart, 1 Park Road South, Middlesbrough TS5 6LD
Tel: 01642 850113
E-mail: stpatrickmbro@middlesbrough-diocese.org.uk

■ **NEWCASTLE-UPON-TYNE: THE UNIVERSITY OF NEWCASTLE: UNIVERSITY OF NORTHUMBRIA AT NEWCASTLE: NEWCASTLE COLLEGE OF FE (Hexham & Newcastle Diocese)**
Rev Andrew Downie, Ms Mia Fox
Catholic Chaplaincy, 14 Windsor Terrace, Newcastle-upon-Tyne NE2 4HE
Tel: 0191 239 9527
Website: www.catholicchaplaincy.org

■ **NORTHAMPTON: UNIVERSITYCOLLEGE NORTHAMPTON (Northampton Diocese)**
Rev Andrew Behrens
St Gregory's, 22 Park Avenue North, Northampton NN3 2HS
Tel: 01604 713015
E-mail: stgregory@freeuk.com
E-mail: andrew.behrens@btinternet.com

■ **NOTTINGHAM UNIVERSITY (Nottingham Diocese)**
Rev Christopher Thomas
Corpus Christi Presbytery, Listowel Crescent, Nottingham NG11 9BP
Tel: 0115 921 2964
E-mail: christopher.thomas@nottingham.ac.uk
Mr Kurt DeFreitas BA MSc (Hons)
Chaplaincy Office, Portland Building, University Park, Nottingham NG7 2RD
Tel: 0115 951 3929/3930
Cathsoc Website:
www.nottingham.ac.uk./~oczcath
Chaplains Website:
www.nottingham.ac.uk/chaplains

■ **NOTTINGHAM TRENT UNIVERSITY (Nottingham Diocese)**
Rev John Kyne
19 De Ferres Close, East Leeke, Loughborough LE12 6QD
Tel: 01509 852 147
E-mail: john.kyne@ntu.ac.uk
City Site: Dryden Centre, Dryden Street, Nottingham NG1 5EY
Tel: 0115 848 2305
Clifton Site: Student Support Services, Clifton Main Site, Clifton Lane, Nottingham. NG11 8NS
Tel: 0115 848 3279

■ **OXFORD UNIVERSITY (Birmingham Archdiocese)**
Oxford Catholic Chaplaincy, The Old Palace, St Aldate's, Oxford 0X1 1RD
Tel: 01865 276993 **Fax:** 01865 276991
E-mail: jeremy.fairhead@oriel.ox.ac.uk
Sr Nora Coughlan
E-mail: norac@herald.ox.ac.uk

■ **OXFORD: OXFORD BROOKES UNIVERSITY (Birmingham Archdiocese)**
Rev Martin Flatman
62 London Road, Headington, Oxford OX3 7PD **Tel:** 01865 750463
Mbl: 07719 646790
E-mail: meflatman@brookes.ac.uk
Website: www.brookes.ac.uk/student/services/chaplaincy/romancatholic.html
Sr Veronica Ann
St Catherine's, 2 Harberton Mead, Oxford OX3 0DB **Tel:** 01865 764293
E-mail: verann@globalnet.co.uk
Rev Dcn Michael Walsh
2 Gordon Drive. Abingdon, Oxfordshire OX14 3SW **Tel:** 01235 523410
E-mail: mcwalsh@brookes.ac.uk

■ **PLYMOUTH UNIVERSITY (Plymouth Diocese)**
Rev Trevor Jordan
Christ the King Chaplaincy, Armada Way, Plymouth PL1 2EN **Tel:** 01752 266523
Students: 01752 67559

■ **PORTMOUTH UNIVERSITY (Portsmouth Diocese)**
Ms Jordan James
Chaplaincy Student Advice Service
Nuffield Centre. St Michaels Rd
Portsmouth PO1 2ED **Tel:** 023 9284 3167
Fax: 023 9284 3430
Website: www.port.ac.uk/departments/chaplaincy

■ **PRESTON: UNIVERSITY OF CENTRAL LANCASHIRE (Lancaster Diocese)**
Br Mark Elvin OFM, St Walburge's Presbytery, Weston St, Preston PR2 2QE
University of Central Lancashire, Multi-Faith Centre, 33-35 St Peter's Square, Preston PR1 7BX
Tel: 01772 892615
Office: 01772892602
Sr Shelagh Duggan SCMM
Bethany, 4 Mount Street, Preston PR1 8BS **Tel:** 01772 251711
Fax: 01772 881099

■ **READING UNIVERSITY (Portsmouth Diocese)**
Ms Sabine Schwartz
Catholic Chaplaincy, 46 Upper Redlands Road, Reading RG1 5JP
Tel/Fax: 0118 926 8869
Website: www.reading.ac.uk/chaplaincy/cc

■ **SALFORD UNIVERSITY (Salford Diocese)**
Rev Steven Parkinson
Sr Theresa Wild FMSJ
Sr Eithne Donoghue
Catholic Chaplaincy Centre, Chapman Building, University of Salford M5 4WT
Tel: 0161 295 5961 **Fax:** 0161 295 5070
E-Mail: catholic-chaplaincy@salford.ac.uk
St Philip's University Church, Northallerton Road, Lower Kersal, Salford M7 0TP **Tel:** 0161 792 2791

■ **SHEFFIELD UNIVERSITY (Hallam Diocese)**
Rev Peter Cullen
The Catholic Chaplaincy, 7 Wellesley Road, Sheffield S10 2SY
Tel: 0114 266 0178 or 0114 266 0178 (answer phone)
E-mail: P.J.cullen@sheffield.ac.uk
Website: www.shef.ac.uk/uni/union/susoc/ccf

■ **SHEFFIELD: HALLAM UNIVERSITY (Hallam Diocese)**
Sr Anne Lee
Catholic Chaplaincy, 18 Broomhall Road, Sheffield S10 2DR **Tel:** 0114 267 9788

■ **SHRIVENHAM: DEFENCE ACADEMY OF THE UNITED KINGDOM (Portsmouth Diocese)**
Rev Robert C. Jennings
21 Fernham Road, Faringdon, Oxon SN7 7JY
Tel: 01367 242039 **Fax:** 01367 244752
Church Tel: 01793 785507
E-mail: Frbobjennings@aol.com

■ **SOUTHAMPTON UNIVERSITY (Portsmouth Diocese)**
Sr Catherine Cruz
346 Portswood Road, Southampton SO17 3SB **Tel:** 023 8055 9481
E-mail: mjryan_98@yahoo.com
Chaplaincy: 41 University Road, Southampton SO17 1BJ
Tel: 023 8059 4622,
Fax: 023 8059 4625

■ **SOUTHHAMPTON INSTITUTE (Portsmouth Diocese)**
Sr Liliana Gonzalez
Verbum Dei Community, Old All Saints Hall, 425 Winchester Road, Southampton SO16 7DE
Tel/Fax: 023 8039 9301
Chaplaincy: Tel: 023 8031 9819

■ **STAFFORDSHIRE UNIVERSITY (Birmingham Archdiocese)**
Rev Brian Wall SJ
St Maria Goretti, 137 Aylesbury Road, Stoke-on-Trent ST2 0LU
Tel: 01782 281970

■ **STOCKTON: UNIVERSITY COLLEGE (A COLLEGE OF THE UNIVERSITY OF DURHAM) (Hexham & Newcastle Diocese)**
(Awaiting appointment)

■ **SUNDERLAND UNIVERSITY (Hexham & Newcastle Diocese)**
Rev Kevin Dixon
St Anne's, Hylton road, Pennywell, Sunderland SR4 9AA
Tel: 0191 534 2346
University Chaplaincy:
Tel: 0191 515 3482
Website: my.sunderland.ac.uk/web/services/chaplaincy/ahome?ahome

■ **SURREY UNIVERSITY (Arundel & Brighton Diocese)**
John McCarthy
More House, 12 Queen Eleanor's Road, Onslow Village, Guildford, Surrey GU2 7SL **Tel:** 01483 571091
Office: 01483 682755
Website: www.surrey.ac.uk/chaplains/cathsoc
E-mail: j.mccarthy@surrey.ac.uk

■ **SUSSEX UNIVERSITY (Arundel & Brighton Diocese)**
Rev Paul Wilkinson
Howard House. 2 Station Approach, Falmer, Brighton BN1 9SD
Tel: 01273 698032 **Fax:** 01273 672353
Campus Office: Tel: 01273 873879
The Meeting House, Sussex University, Falmer, Brighton BN1 9QF
Tel: 01273 678217 **Fax:** 01273 678918
E-mail: qnfb0@sussex.ac.uk

■ **SWANSEA UNIVERSITY (Menevia Diocese)**
Sr Mary Elizabeth Nash UJ
Catholic Chaplaincy, 12 Uplands Crescent, Uplands, Swansea SA2 0PB
Tel: 01792 472465

■ **THAMES VALLEY [See London: Thames Valley, Ealing and Slough Campuses]**

■ **TRENT [See Nottingham: Nottingham Trent]**

■ **WARWICK UNIVERSITY (Birmingham Archdiocese)**
Rev Prem Fernando
Chaplaincy: Aquinas House, 6 Gibbet Hill Road, Coventry CV4 7AJ
Tel: 024 7641 9369 or 024 7652 3520

■ **WEST OF ENGLAND [See Bristol: University of the West of England]**

■ **WOLVERHAMPTON UNIVERSITY (Birmingham Archdiocese)**
Rev Patrick Daly
SS Peter & Paul, North Street Wolverhampton WV1 1RJ
Tel: 01902 423005
Chaplaincy Centre, University of Wolverhampton, Molineux Street, Wolverhampton WV1 1SB
Tel: 01902 322903 **Fax:** 01902 322914

■ **YORK UNIVERSITY (Middlesbrough Diocese)**
V Rev Antony Lester
Whitefriars, More House, Heslington York YO10 5DX **Tel** 01904 410249
Website: www.york.ac.uk/univ/chap/

■ **YORK: COLLEGE OF FE & HE (Middlesbrough Diocese)**
Mrs Sharon Lusty
York St John College, Lord Mayor's Walk York YO31 7EX **Tel:** 01904 716606
E-mail: s.lusty@yorksj.ac.uk

ASSOCIATION OF CATHOLIC CHAPLAINS IN EDUCATION

A chaplaincy service for Catholic Education in the Primary, Secondary and Sixth Form sectors

National Co-ordinator:
Mrs Maggie Cascioli
ACCE, The Diocesan Centre, Mornington Crescent, Mackworth, Derby IP4 4BD
Tel/Fax: 01622 750504 **Mbl:** 07592 728 683
E-mail: maggiecascioli@hotmail.com

Executive Members:
Mr Michael Collins, E-mail: michaelcollins1949@btinternet.com

Tina Fishwick, St John Fisher and St Thomas More, Gibfield Road, Colne, Lancs BB8 8JT **E-mail:** fishwick.t@fishermore.lancs.sch.uk

Diana Polisano, Blessed Hugh Farringdon Catholic School, Fawley Road, Reading RG30 3EP **E-mail:** admin.hughfarringdon@reading.gov.uk

Treasurer: **Bernard Stuart**
Salford Diocese Religious Education Centre, Plymouth Grove, Longsight, Manchester M13 0AS **E-mail:** btstuart@salforddiocese.org

DIOCESAN CHAPLAINCY CO-ORDINATORS

Since the publication of 'Chaplaincy, The Change and The Challenge' diocesan co-ordinators for school chaplaincy have been appointed by local bishops for most dioceses of England and Wales. The Co-ordinator plans the "provision of appropriate local training for newly-appointed full and part-time school and college chaplains in the diocese, as well as offering support and training for existing chaplains".

(Chaplaincy, The Change and The Challenge, p.24 AA(ii))

Westminster: Rev Vladimir Felzmann, All Saints Pastoral Centre, London Colney, Herts AL2 1AF **Tel:** 01727-828888
E-mail: vladimirf@compuserve.com

Arundel & Brighton:
Rt Rev Paul MacMahon O.Pream, Christian Education Centre, 4 Southgate Drive, Crawley, West Sussex RH10 6RP
Tel: 01293-515666
E-mail: wjdicksonsdb@msn.com

Birmingham: Sr Maria Parcher, 11 Westholme, 160 Oaktree Lane, Bourneville, Birmingham B30 1TP **Tel:** 0121-415 5302
E-mail: mariabparcher@lineone.net

Brentwood: Miss Teresa Carvalho, Cathedral House, Ingrave Road, Brentwood, Essex CM15 8AT
Tel: 01277-265286 **Fax:** 01277-265261
E-mail: teresa@dioceseofbrentwood.org

Cardiff: Rev Robert Coyne, 14 Austin Avenue, Newton, Porthcawl CF36 5RS

Clifton: Ms Ann Fowler, Alexander House, 160 Pennywell Road, Bristol BS5 0TX
Tel: 0117-902 5599 **Fax:** 0117-902 5520
E-mail: ann.fowler@cliftondiocese.com

East Anglia: Awaiting Appointment

Hallam: Mrs Judi Shimmell, The Hallam Pastoral Centre, St Charles Street, Sheffield S9 3WV
Tel: 0114 256 6464 **Fax:** 0114 256 2673
E-mail: jshimmell@hallam-diocese.com

Hexham & Newcastle: Rev Michael McCoy, St Robert of Newminster, Biddick Lane, Washington, Tyne & Wear NE38 8AF
Tel: 0191-219 3810 **Fax:** 0191-219 3815

Lancaster: Rev Michael Docherty, Our Lady Star of the Sea, 2 St Annes Rd East, Lytham St Annes FY1 1UL
Tel: 01253-723661

Leeds: Awaiting appointment

Liverpool: Miss Rosie Woods, Carmel College, Prescott Road, St Helens, Merseyside WA10 3AG
Tel: 01744-45220 **Fax:** 01744-452222

Menevia: Awaiting Appointment

Middlesbrough: Fr John Paul Leonard, St Clare of Assisi, 102 Low Lane, Brookfield, Middlesbrough TS5 8EB
Tel/Fax: 01642-593686

Northampton: Alex Heath, Our Lady of Lourdes Church, 40 Lloyds Coffee Hall, Milton Keynes MK6 5EB

Tel: 01908-233121 **Fax:** 01908-233131

Nottingham: Rev Colin Taylor, The Presbytery, 17 Nottingham Road, Ilkeston, Derbys DE7 5RF **Tel/Fax:** 0115-932 5642

Plymouth: Awaiting Appointment

Portsmouth: Awaiting Appointment

Salford: Mr Bernard Stuart, Salford Diocese Religious Education Centre, Plymouth Grove, Longsight, Manchester M13 0AS
Tel: 0161-256 6207 **Fax:** 0161-256 6201
E-mail: bstuart@salforddiocese.org

Fr Andrew Stringfellow, St Peter's Chaplaincy, 33 Walker Avenue, Bolton BL3 2DY **Tel:** 0161-256 6207
E-mail: andrewjstringfellow@yahoo.co.uk

Shrewsbury: Mr Peter Siney, Ellesmere Port Catholic High School, Capenhurst Lane, Ellesmere Port CH65 7AQ **Tel:** 0151-355 2373

Southwark: Ms Sheila Connolly, 48 Glebe Lane, Maidstone, Kent ME16 9BD
Tel: 01622 729211

Wrexham: Awaiting Appointment

INSTITUTES OF HIGHER EDUCATION

■ **BLACKFRIARS,** Oxford
the house of study of the English Dominicans, orginally founded in 1221; a Dominican Studium and a Permanent Private Hall of the University of Oxford. It offers full ordination courses for clerical students, courses in philosophy and theology for lay people and is able to accept students wishing to read for degrees of the Univerisity. The Regent, Blackfriars, Priory of the Holy Spirit, 64 St Giles, Oxford OX1 3LY **Tel:** 01865-278431
Fax: 01865-278441
E-mail: regent@bfriars.ox.ac.uk
Studies Secretary: Tel: 01865-278441

Resident Tutors and Lecturers:
Regent: **Rev Richard Finn** OP, BA, MA, MPhil, DPhil; *Vice-Regent:* **Rev Richard Conrad** OP, MA, Phil, STL; *Scripture:* **Rev David Sanders** OP, BA, DipTheol, STLic; **Rev Richard Ounsworth** OP, BA; *Theology:* **Revv Benjamin Earl** OP, MA, MSc, JCL; **Simon Gaine** OP, MA, DPhil, STL; **Austin Milner** OP, STLic, SLittPer; **Denis Minns** OP, DPhil; **Rev Vivian Boland** OP, BD, STL, STD; *Philosophy:* **Rev David Goodill** OP, MA, MPLil.

■ **CAMPION HALL,** Oxford
a Permanent Private Hall of the University of Oxford conducted by the Society of Jesus. Campion Hall, Oxford OX1 1QS **Tel:** 01865-286101 **Fax:** 01865-286148
E-mail: postmaster@campion.ox.ac.uk
Master: **Rev Gerard J. Hughes** SJ, MA. PhD, STL **Tel:** 01865-286101 *Home Bursar:* **Rev Clarence Gallagher** SJ, MA, JCD
Librarian: **Rev Peter Edmonds** SJ, STL
Resident Tutors & Lecturers: **Revv Philip Endean** SJ, MA, PhD *(Theology);* **Nicholas King SJ** *(Theology);* **Michael Suarez** SJ (English)

■ **DIGBY STUART COLLEGE,** London
a constituent College of Roehampton University, founded by the Society of the Sacred Heart. *Principal:* **Paul Hodges.** Digby Stuart College, University of Surrey, Roehampton Lane, London SW15 5PH
Tel: 020-8392 3204 **Fax:** 020-8392 3231
E-mail: p.hodges@roehamptonac.uk
College Chaplain: **Robert Kaggwa**

■ **FRANCISCAN INTERNATIONAL STUDY CENTRE,** Canterbury
An institute of theology, spirituality and renewal, operating within the intellectual tradition developed by the Franciscans in this country from 1224. We teach certificate level course in Franciscan Studies and formation, BA Theology, MA Theology and Franciscan Studies, and supervise research degrees in partnership with the University of Wales, Lampeter. We offer an intensive course of training in spiritual direction within the Franciscan tradition and sabbaticals. Franciscan International Study Centre, Giles Lane, Canterbury, Kent CT2 7NA
Tel: 01227 769349 **Fax:** 01227 786648
E-mail: info@franciscans.ac.uk
Website: www.franciscans.ac.uk
The Principal: **Rev Philippe Yates** OFM, BA, MA, MCL, JCD
Vice-Principal: **Sr Margaret McGrath** FMSJ, BA, MA.
Operations Team Leader: **Kathleen Bishop** BA, MBA
Estates Manager: **Dave Palmer**
Senior Accountant: **Tom Robertson** FCA
Librarian: **Lance Housley** TSSF, BA, DipLib, MCLIP
Lecturers
Rev Francis Ninian Arbuckle OFM, STD, LSS *(Spiritual Theology);* **Fr David Blowey** OFMConv, BA, STB, STL, STD *(Systematic Theology);* **Rev Thomas Herbst** *(Systematic*

Theology); **Sr Crispin Jose** SMHC, BA,MA *(Franciscan Studies);* **Sr Margaret McGrath** FMSJ, BA, MA *(Sabbaticals);* **Rev Seamus Mulholland** OFM, BA, PhD *(Philosophy and Biblical Theology);* **Fr Edward Ondrako** OFM Conv, BA, Mth. MA, MSW, PhD *(Systematic Theology);* **Paula Pearce** SFO BA, PGCE, DipTh, MA *(Franciscan Studies);* **Br Philippe Yates** OFM, BA, MA, MCL, JCD *(Canon Law).*

Visiting Lecturers
Rev Andre Cirino OFM *(Franciscan Studies);* **Sr Ilia Delio** OSF, PhD *(Carmalite Spirituality);* **Sr Frances Teresa Downing** OSC *(Franciscan Studies);* **Rev John McCluskey** MHM, MA, PhD *(Psychology);* **Rev Richard Martignetti** OFM *(Franciscan Studies);* **Br Anthony McDowell** OFMCap *(Spiritual Theology);* **Sr Kathleen Moffatt** OSF, MA *(Franciscan Studies);* **Dr Malcolm Pitt** SFO, PhD *(Systematic Theology);* **Sr Ingrid Peterson** OSF *(Franciscan Studies);* **Fr Christopher Shorrock** OFMConv. BA, STL *(Church History);* **Fr Jude Winkler** OFM Conv, SSL.

■ **GREYFRIARS,** Oxford
a Permanent Private Hall of the University of Oxford, conducted by the Capuchin Franciscans whose presence in the University dates back to 1224. *Senior Tutor:* **Dr Richard Lawes.** *Warden:* **Dr Nicholas Richardson.** Greyfriars, Oxford OX4 1SB **Tel:** 01865-243694
E-mail: richard.lawes@greyfriars.ox.ac.uk

■ **HEYTHROP COLLEGE,** London
Originally founded in 1614, this specialist college of theology and philosophy was granted a Royal Charter on 14th May 1971 as a College of the University of London.
Heythrop College, University of London, Kensington Square W8 5HQ
Tel: 020 7795 6600 **Fax:** 020 7795 4200
Website: www.heythrop.ac.uk

President: **Michael Holman** SJ, BA, MDiv, MSc, PGCE
Chair of Governors: **Michael Malone-Lee** CB, DL, MA

Administration
Principal: **John McDade** SJ, BD, MA, PhD
Vice-Principal: **Peter Vardy** FCA, BA, MTh, PhD
Director of Administration:
Elizabeth Thussu
Academic Registrar: **Annabel Clarkson** DipMLBS
Librarian: **Christopher Pedley** SJ, BA(Econ), BA, MTh, ThM, MA
Director of Finance: **Michael Smith**

Fellows:
Dorothy Bell RSCJ, OBE, MA
Theodore Davey CP, DCL
Kevin Donovan SJ, MA, STL, PerSacLit
Patrick Gaynor MA
Sir David Goodall GCMG
David Hamlyn BA, MA
Gerard J Hughes SJ, MA, PhD
Ursula King STL, MA, PhD, HonDD, FRSA
Drummond Leslie MA, FRSA
Joseph Laishley SJ, MA, STD
Kevin Livesey MA, FCA
Jack Mahoney SJ, MA, DTh, CIMgt
Anthony Meredith SJ, MA, STL, DPhil
Robert Murray SJ, MA, STD
Anne Murphy SHCJ, BA, MTh, STD
John Russell SJ, MA, PhD, STL
John Smith CBE, MA
George Vass SJ, LicPhil STD, DD
Michael Walsh MA, STL, DipLib
Graham Zellick MA, PhD, LLD, LHD, AcSS, CCMI, FRSA, Hon FRAM, Hon FSALS

Editor, The Heythrop Journal
Patrick Madigan SJ, BA, STL, MDiv, PhD

Faculty: Theology
Ahmad Achtar, BSc, MA, MA
Michael Barnes SJ, BD, MLitt, DPhil
Rev Anthony Baxter BD, MA, MPhil, PhD
Martin Ganeri OP, MA, MPhil, DPhil
Bridget Gilfillan Upton BAgSci, BA, PhD
Jonathan Gorsky BA, MA
James Hanvey SJ, BA, MTh, DPhil
Rev Ann Jeffers LicTh, PhD
Michael Kirwan SJ, BD, MA, PhD
John McDade SJ, MA, BD, PhD
Anthony Meredith SJ, MA, STL, DPhil
Jonathan Norton BA, MSt, DPhil
Anthony O'Mahony BA, MA, MPhil
Magdalen O'Neill IBVM, BA, MA
Martin Poulsom SDB, BSc, BA, MTh, MPhil, DPhil
Rev Richard Price MA, BD, MTh, DPhil
Oliver Rafferty SJ, BD, MTh, DPhil
Dominic Robinson SJ, MA, BD, MTh, STD

Philosophy:
Elizabeth Burns BD, PhD, PGCE
Louis Caruana SJ, BSc, MA, STL, PhD
Anthony Carroll SJ, BSc, MPhil, BD, PhD
Thomas Crowther BA, MPhil, PhD
Fiona Ellis BA, BPhil, DPhil
Stacie Friend BA, PhD
Peter Gallagher SJ, MA, PhD
Michael Lacewing BA, BPhil, PhD
Stephen Law BSc, BPhil, DPhil
Patrick Riordan SJ, BA, BaccPhil, MA, DPhil
Paul Rout OFM, BA, BPhil(Ed), MTh, PhD
Peter Vardy FCA, BA, MTh, PhD

Pastoral and Social Studies:
Anna Abram MA, MTh, PhD **Brendan Callaghan** SJ, MA, MPhil, MTh, FRSM

EDUCATION CHAPLAINCIES AND INSTITUTIONS

Andrew Cameron-Mowat SJ, MA, MDiv, MTh, STL, PhD
Rev Joanna Collicutt McGrath MA, MPhil, PhD, PG DipTh, CPsychol, AFBPsS
Helen Costigane SHCJ, ACA, MA, MTh, JCL, MA (Canon Law), PhD
Catherine Cowley ra, MA, PhD
Kevin Donovan SJ, MA, STL, PerSacLit
Bernard Hoose BPhil, STB, STL, STD
Edward Howells BA, MSt, PhD
Rev Brendan Killeen BSc, STB, MA, JCL, MCL, PhD
David Lonsdale MA, MTh
Jonathan Loose BSc, PhD
James Sweeney CP, BD, BA, MTh, PhD
Gemma Simmonds CJ, BA MTh, PhD

■ **LIVERPOOL HOPE UNIVERSITY**
Hope is the only ecumenical University of its kind in Europe, providing a wide range of undergraduate and postgraduate programmes in Humanities, Theology & Religious Studies, Education, Science & Social Sciences, Business, Computer Science and Creative & Performing Arts. As a Christian foundation the University consciously seeks to 'educate in the round - educating the whole person in mind, body and spirit'. The University has made significant investments in providing high quality facilities, student support and attracting top academics from around the world. *Vice-Chancellor Rector:* **Professor Gerald J Pillay** BA, BD, DTheol, PhD.
Liverpool Hope University College, Hope Park, Liverpool L16 9JD
Tel: 0151-291 3000 **Fax:** 0151-291 3100
E-mail: kemblep@hope.ac.uk
Liverpool Hope University was awarded full university status in 2005.

■ **MARGARET BEAUFORT INSTITUTE OF THEOLOGY,** Cambridge
Degrees of the University of Cambridge and Anglia Polytechnic University, Cambridge. An Institute of Theology for women, specialising in pastoral theology, founded in 1993. The Institute is the Catholic Member of the Cambridge Theological Federation. **Cardinal Cormac Murphy-O'Connor** and **Archbishop Peter Smith** are among its patrons.
Chair of Board: **Janet Martin Soskice** BA, MA, DPhil(Oxon) *Chair of Directors:* **Susan O'Brien** BA, PhD *Principal:* **Marie Cooke** *Vice Principal/Director of Studies:* **Clare Watkins** MA(Cantab), PhD(Cantab); *Director of Pastoral Studies:* **Dr Oonagh O'Brien**; *Director of Research* **Dr Mary Mills** SHCJ. *Institute/Lecturer:* **Susan Parsons** BA, MA, PhD, Fellow.
Margaret Beaufort Institute of Theology, 12 Grange Road, Cambridge CB3 9DU **Tel:** 01223-741039 **Fax:** 01223-741054
Website: www.margaretbeaufort.cam.ac.uk
Also at the Margaret Beaufort Institute: The Centre for Marian Studies: *Director:* **Dr Sarah Jane Boss. Tel:** 01223-741057

■ **MARYVALE INSTITUTE,** Birmingham
founded by the Diocese of Birmingham in 1980 as a diocesan centre for adult catechesis and religious education, now provides internationally a wide range of distance learning opportunities in Catholic theology, philosophy, religious education, teacher training, catechesis and related subjects. Maryvale offers further education studies, certificates, diplomas and both first and postgraduates degrees as an affiliated Institute of St Patrick's Pontifical University, Maynooth and an accredited Institute of Open University.
Director: **V. Rev Mgr Paul Watson** STL, MA(Ed) (Open), The Maryvale Institute, Maryvale House, Old Oscott Hill, Kingstanding, Birmingham B44 9AG
Tel: 0121-360 8118 **Fax:** 0121-366 6786
E-mail: director@maryvale.ac.uk
President: **The Archbishop of Birmingham**

Permanent Academic Staff
Dr Andrew Beards BA, MA, PhL, PhD; **Mr Gary Buckby,** BA,(Hons); **V Rev Richard Conrad** OP, MA(Oxon), PhD(Oxon), MA(Oxon), STL; **Mrs Francis Etheridge** BA(Hons), MA, PGCBS, PGCHE; **Miss Caroline Farey** BA(Hons), MPhil(Cantab), MA(Theol), STB, PhL, STL; **Mr Michael Hodgetts** MA(Oxon), LicPhil; **Miss Nichola Hurley** OCV, BA(Hons), MA; **Miss Mary Killeen** B.Ed, BD, STL; **Mrs Janet Mellor** BA(Hons), PGCE, MA(Ed); **Rev David Oakley** STL, MEd, PhD; **Mrs Jean Pearson** BA(Hons); **Dr Dudley Plunkett** BA, PhD; **Very Rev Canon John Redford** STL, LSS, ALCD, DD; **Miss Anna Schaeffer** BA; **Rev Peter Weatherby** MA, PGCE, MEd; **Dr Petroc Willey** BA, PhD; **Mr Stephen Yates** BA(Hons), PGCE, MEd; **Mr Tim Kelly** BA Hons, MA, STL, STM; **Mrs Terese Kehoe**, BA, PGCE.
Degrees by distance learning with residential schools: BA Divinity *(Maynooth*);* MA in Theology *(Maynooth*);* MA in Personal, Moral & Spiritual Development *(OU*);* MA in RE & Catechesis *(OUVS*);* MA in Chaplaincy for Catholic Schools *(OUVS*);* BA in Applied Theology (Parish Catechesis) (OUVS*); BA in Applied Theology (Diaconate Ministry) *(OUVS*);* PGCE in Secondary RE *(TDA approved - OUVS*);* PhB - *(OUVS* validation pending)*

Research Degrees: BPhil, MPhil. *(pending)* Also offers Certificates and Diplomas in Evangelization and Ministry for: Youth, the Parish, the Family and the sick, the Apostleship of the Sea; Art, Inspiration and beauty in a Catholic Perspective. Catholic studies for sixth forms; CCRS and courses at other levels.
* Denotes validating institution.

■ **MISSIONARY INSTITUTE LONDON.** A theological institute founded by seven missionary congregations; affiliated to the Catholic University of Leuven and to Middlesex University. *President:* **Danilo Castello** MCCJ, DD, Missionary Institute London, Holcombe House, The Ridgeway, Mill Hill, London NW7 4HY **Tel:** 020-8906 1894 **Fax:** 020-8906 4937. **E-mail:** mil@mdx.ac.uk
Director of Studies: **Richard E Parsons** MA, STL.
Secretary/Treasurer: **Denis Starkey** MA.

Lecturing Staff
Systematic Theology: **David Clark,** STL, STd; **Eamonn Mulcahy** CSSp, BA, STL, STD; *Moral Theology:* **Anna Abram** MA, MTh, PhD; **Ian Linden,** MA, PhD; **John Harwood** BSc, **Terry Burke** MA, STL (Moral); **Richard Parsons** MA, STL; *Scripture:* **Sean Ryan** BD, MTh; **John Hemer** STB, DipTh, LSS; **K Matskevitch** STB, STL.
Church History: **Alan Collins** CSSp, BA.
Canon Law: **John Conneely** JCL.
Liturgy: **Benito de Marchi** MCCJ, STB, STL, STD.
Missiology: **Sally Graham** BEd, PhD; **Eamonn O'Brien** BA, MA, STL; **Ignatius Anipu** MAfr, BA, MA(Ulam), CertPhil, BA(Theol), Lic (Islamic Studies).
Pastoral Studies: **Renzo Marcolongo** IMC, STB, BSc(Ed), MA(Psych); **Valerie Flessati** BA, PhD; **Patricia Gaffney** CertEd, **Aidan Rossiter**, CJ, MA, STB, BSc; **Diana Klein** BA, MA; **Peter Burrows,** MTh, PhD.
Philosophy: **Martin Walsh** SMA, BA, MA, MDiv.
Librarian: **John Harwood** BSc; **Lillian Everitt** BA.

Halls of Residence
Mill Hill Missionaries, St Joseph's College, (Mill Hill); Missionaries of Africa (White Fathers), St Edwards College (Whetstone), Society of African Missions (New Barnet), Comboni Missionaries (Verona Fathers), The Priory (Borehamwood).

■ **NEWMAN UNIVERSITY COLLEGE,** Birmingham
Founded by the Catholic Education Service.

Newman University College, Genners Lane, Bartley Green, Birmingham B32 3NT
Tel: 0121-476 1181 **Fax:** 0121-476 1196
E-mail: p.t.taylor@newman.ac.uk
Principal: **Mrs Pamela Taylor** BA, MA, MPhil, PGCE, DipEd; *Vice-Principal:* **Ms Kathryn Southworth** BA, MPhil; *Registrar and Clerk to the Board of Governors:* **Mrs Heather Somerfield,** BA, MSc, *Director of Finance:* **Mr Tony Sharma** BA.

Initial Teacher Education BA/BSc, Single and Combined Honours degrees, PGCE Primary, Key Stage 2/3 and Secondary courses, Foundation degrees, INSET for Catholic Schools, MEd, MPhil, PhD; Theology related programmes: PGCE RE, BATheol, MATheol, Catholic Certificate in Religious Studies.

Head of School of Science and Humanities: **Dr Stephen Bulman** BA, PhD
Head of School of Education: **Ms Sally Yates** BEd MA.
Head of School of Community & Professional Development: **Prof Stan Tucker** BA, MSocSc, PhD.
Director of Library and Learning Resources: **Miss Christine Porter** BA, MLib.
Director of Quality: **Lysandre de-la-Haye** BA

■ **SARUM COLLEGE,** Salisbury
an ecumenical theological college offering an expanding programme of courses. An MA in Christian Spirituality and other certificate courses. Home of RSCM and STETS. Private Study. Comprehensive facilities for Conferences, Seminars. Groups and Private Guests welcome.

Principal: **Rev Dr Tim Macquiban** MA(Cantab and Bristol), PhD.

Sarum College, 19 The Close, Salisbury, Wiltshire SP1 2EE **Tel:** 01722-424800 **Fax:** 01722 338508 **E-mail:** hospitality@ sarum.ac.uk **Web:** sarum.ac.uk
Short Course Co-ordinator: **Rosie Zaniewski**
Academic Administrator: **Simon Lever**

Centre for Faith and Action in Society (CeFaS)
Social Responsibility Officer: **Ms Fiona Hulbert** BA **Tel:** 01722-424838
Scholars in Residence
New Testament: **Prof David Catchpole** MA, PhD. *Spirituality:* **Br Patrick Moore** PhD, MA, BA. *Theology:* **Dr Mervyn Davies** PhD

■ **ST. BENET'S HALL,** Oxford
a Permanent Private Hall of the University of Oxford, conducted by Ampleforth Abbey. *Master:* **Rev J Felix Stephens OSB,** St. Benet's Hall, 38 St. Giles, Oxford OX1 3LN **Tel:** 01865-280551 **Fax:** 01865-280792 **E-mail:** master@stb.ox.ac.uk

■ **ST. MARY'S UNIVERSITY COLLEGE,**
Strawberry Hill, Twickenham
Principal: **Dr Arthur Naylor**, St. Mary's University College, Waldegrave Road, Strawberry Hill, Twickenham, Middlesex TW1 4SX
Tel: 020-8240 4000 **Fax:** 020-8240 4255
E-mail naylora@smuc.ac.uk
Mass times: Monday, Wednesday, Thursday and Friday 8.30am in the Crypt; Tuesday, 12.15pm in the College Chapel;
Chaplain: **Rev Gerard Devlin Tel:** 020-8240 4006 **E-mail:** devling@smuc.ac.uk
Assistant Chaplain: **Mrs Rebecca Walker, Tel:** 020-8240 4002 **E-mail:** hughesr @smuc.ac.uk
Chaplaincy Administrator: **Mrs Kerry** Anzollitto **Tel:** 020-8240 4331 **E-mail:** anzolitk@smuc.ac.uk **Fax:** 020-8255 6190
Website: www.smuc.ac.uk

■ **LEEDS TRINITY & ALL SAINTS,**
an institution of Higher Education, accredited by the University of Leeds founded by the trusteeship of the Catholic Education Service and the Congregation of the Cross and Passion. *Principal:* **Dr Freda Bridge**, Leeds Trinity and All Saints, Brownberrie Lane, Horsforth, Leeds LS18 5HD **Tel:** 0113-283 7100
Fax: 0113-283 7200.
E-mail: f.a.bridge@leedstrinity.ac.uk

■ **THE VON HÜGEL INSTITUTE**
a multi-disiplinary research institute of St. Edmund's College Cambridge. *Director:* **Professor David Bridges,** Von Hügel Institute, St. Edmund's College, Cambridge CB3 0BN **Tel:** 01223-741844

OTHER EDUCATIONAL CENTRES

■ **INSTITUTE OF ST ANSELM,**
Cliftonville, Margate
(International Centre for Religious Formation)
Founding President: **Cardinal George Basil Hume** OSB, OM. *President:* **Cardinal Cormac Murphy O'Connor** STL, PhL

The Executive
Director: **Rev L Kofler MHM,** DD, DSoc, PhD; (*Registrar*); **Miss C McGuire; Rev J McCluskey MHM,** MA, PhD; **Sr M McMonagle** susc DipCouns, Cert Supervision; **Rev W. Huys MHM**
Residential Diploma Course & Summer Courses for Leaders and Formators, Bishops, Superior Generals, Rectors, Novice Masters/Mistresses, Superiors, Parish Priests, Chaplains and other leadership roles. For those in these positions or destined for them.
Institute of St Anselm, Edgar Road, Cliftonville, Margate, Kent CT9 2EU
Tel: 01843-234700 **Fax:** 01843-234701
E-mail: office@st.anselm.org.uk
Website: www.st.anselm.org.uk
Tel: (students) 01843-234704/234705

■ **AQUINAS COLLEGE,** Stockport
The only sixth form college provided by the Diocese of Shrewsbury. Largest sixth form college in the country 1800+ 16-19 year old students on the roll. Genuinely open-access and non-selective. Strong adult education provision and in partnership with Manchester Metropolitan University for degree courses.
Principal: **Dr Ambrose Smith,**
Principal's PA: **Mrs Janice Aikenhead**
Aquinas College, Nangreave Road, Stockport, Cheshire SK2 6TH
Tel: 0161-483 3237 **Fax:** 0161-487 4072
E-mail: enquiries@aquinas.ac.uk
Website: www.aquinas.ac.uk

■ **CARDINAL NEWMAN COLLEGE,** Preston
A College in the FE sector and in the Diocese of Lancaster. The College serves the needs of over 1600 young people from the Dioceses of Lancaster and Salford, and the Diocese of Liverpool. A full range of courses from Entry (for young people with no formal qualifications) through to Advanced. In addition to "traditional" courses such as GCSEs and A levels, the College offers vocational courses such as GNVQs and VCEs as well as Nursery Nurse courses. The College offers a range of courses for adults, ranging from basic skills, (numeracy, literacy, information technology and ESOL)
Principal: **Mr Stephen Pegg,** Cardinal Newman College, Lark Hill Road, Preston PR14HD **Tel:** 01772-460181 **Fax:** 01772-204671
E-mail: admissions@cnc.hope.ac.uk

■ **CARMEL COLLEGE,** St Helens
A sixth form college provided by the Archdiocese of Liverpool and an associate College of the University of Liverpool.
Principal: **Mr Robert Peacock,**
Carmel Sixth Form College, Prescot Road, St Helens, Merseyside WA10 3AG

Tel: 01744-452200 **Fax:** 01744-452222
Secretary: **Mrs Alison Fishwick**
Tel: 01744-452210
E-mail: info@carmel.ac.uk

■ **HOLY CROSS COLLEGE,** Bury
A Sixth Form college with 1,749 students aged 16-19 and 700 adult part-time students following HE courses in partnership with Liverpool Hope University, Leeds Metropolitan University and St Mary's, Twickenham University. The College Trustees are the Daughters of the Cross of Liege.
Principal: **Mr David Frost,**
Secretary: **Jackie O'Rouke**
Direct Tel: 0161-762 4500
Holy Cross College, Bury BL9 9BB
Tel: 0161-762 4500
Fax: 0161-762 4501
E-mail: information@holycross.ac.uk
Website: www.holycross.ac.uk

■ **ST. BRENDAN'S SIXTH FORM COLLEGE,** Bristol
This College, located in the Diocese of Clifton, provides courses at Levels 1-3 for 1500 students aged 16-19, from the Catholic and wider community.
Principal: **Mr Derek W Bodey.**
Principal's PA: **Mrs Ann Smith**
E-mail: as@stbrn.ac.uk
St Brendan's Sixth Form College, Broomhill Road, Brislington, Bristol BS4 5RQ
Tel: 0117-977 7777 **Fax:** 0117-972 3351
E-mail: info@stbrn.ac.uk
Website: www.stbrn.ac.uk

■ **ST CHARLES CATHOLIC SIXTH FORM COLLEGE,** North Kensington
A beacon college in the Archdiocese of Westminster, providing full time education for 100+ 16-19 year olds. *Principal:* **Mr Paul O'Shea,** St Charles Catholic Sixth Form College, 74 St Charles Square, London W10 6EY
Tel: 020-8968 7755 **Fax:** 020-8968 1061
E-mail: enquiries@stcharles.ac.uk

■ **SAINT DAVID'S CATHOLIC COLLEGE,** Cardiff
An FE college of the Archdiocese of Cardiff, providing a full range of sixth form courses, from Level 1 to Level 3 (A-level available in 40 subjects). Open access and non selective, the college also offers vocational courses including hairdressing, health and social care, hospitality and catering. *Principal:* **Mr Mark Leighfield**, St David's Catholic College, Ty Gwyn Road, Penylan, Cardiff CF23 5QD
Tel: 029-2049 8555 **Fax:** 029-2047 2594
E-mail: marketing@st-davids-coll.ac.uk

■ **ST. DOMINIC'S SIXTH FORM COLLEGE,** Harrow
Provided by the Archdiocese of Westminster; in partnership with the Institute of Education, University of London, for initial teacher training, and the University of Hertfordshire.
Principal: **Mr Patrick Harty,**
Secretary: **Mrs Viju Kale,**
St Dominic's Sixth Form College, Mount Park Avenue, Harrow on the Hill, Middlesex HA1 3HX
Tel: 020-8422 8084 **Fax:** 020-8422 3759.
E-mail: stdoms@stdoms.ac.uk
Website: www.stdoms.ac.uk

■ **ST. FRANCIS XAVIER SIXTH FORM COLLEGE,** Clapham
Originally a foundation of the Xaverian Brothers, now provided by the Archdiocese of Southwark. *Principal:* **Mr Bernie Borland**, St Francis Xavier Sixth Form College, Malwood Road, London SW12 8EN **Tel:** 020-8772 6000 **Fax:** 020-8772 6099
E-mail: enquiries@sfx.ac.uk

■ **ST. JOHN RIGBY CATHOLIC SIXTH FORM COLLEGE,** Orrell, Wigan
A sixth form college under the trusteeship of the Archdiocese of Liverpool.
Principal: **Mr John Crowley,**
PA to the Principal: **Mrs J Okubo**
St John Rigby College, Gathurst Road, Orrell, Wigan WN5 0LJ
Tel: 01942-214797 **Fax:** 01942-216514
Website: www.sjr.ac.uk

■ **ST. MARY'S COLLEGE,** Blackburn
is a Roman Catholic Sixth Form College, operating under the trusteeship of the Marist Fathers.
Principal: **Mr K McMahon**, St Mary's College, Shear Brow, Blackburn BB1 8DX
Tel: 01254-580464 **Fax:** 01254-665991
E-mail: reception@stmarysblackburn.ac.uk
Website: www.stmarysblackburn.ac.uk

■ **ST. MARY'S COLLEGE**, Middlesbrough
A sixth form college under the trusteeship of the Society of Mary. *Principal:* **Mr Donald Lillistone,** BA(hons), NPQH,
Principal's PA: **Miss Carol Owen**
St Mary's College, Saltersgill Avenue, Middlesbrough TS4 3JP
Tel: 01642-814680 **Fax:** 01642-819624
E-mail: carol.owen@stmarys-sfc.ac.uk

■ **XAVERIAN COLLEGE,** Manchester
A sixth form college of 1,400 students + 75 university undergraduates owned by the Diocese of Salford. The College provides a wide range of academic and

vocational courses, level 1-level 4. The College has good links with local schools and the community. It is in a unique partnership with the University of Manchester, providing Foundation Year Courses for Life Sciences, Medicine and Dentistry. The College also offers a pre-University Arts Foundation Course.

Principal: **Mrs Mary Hunter**. Xaverian College, Lower Park Road, Manchester M14 5RB
Tel: 0161-224 1781 **Fax:** 0161-248 9039
E-mail: college@xaverian.ac.uk
Website: www.xaverian.ac.uk

THE CATHOLIC INDEPENDENT SCHOOLS' CONFERENCE

10 Shrewsbury Road, Prenton, Merseyside CH43 1UX
Tel: 0151 652 4326 **E-mail:** p-sweeney@btconnect.com
Website: www.cisc.eteach.com

Chairman: **Mr Adrian Aylward** MA(Oxon); *General Secretary:* **Mr Philip Sweeney** BA; *Vice-Chairman:* **Mr Charles Foulds**
The CISC exists to: promote the work of 140 Catholic Independent Schools throughout the UK. Schools in membership include day and boarding schools, single sex and co-educational, senior and junior schools, and special schools. CISC provides a forum for Catholic Independent Head Teachers; organises an Annual Conference and Study Days; gives advice and support to member schools, and provides a helpline for those seeking a Catholic Independent School for their children.

WELFARE AND CARING SERVICES

IN ENGLAND AND WALES

EPISCOPAL CHAIR FOR HEALTHCARE

Rt Rev Thomas A Williams, Auxiliary Bishop of Liverpool
Address: 14 Hope Place, Liverpool L1 9BG **Tel:** 0151 703 0109 Fax: 0151 703 0267
E-mail: bpwilliams@rcaolp.co.uk

Arundel & Brighton
Rev David Foley Tel: 01273 681587
E-mail: clair.crowley@dabnet.org

Birmingham
Rev Jeremy Howard Tel: 0121 451 3699
E-mail: jeremy.howard@uhb.nhs.uk

Brentwood
Rev Joseph Whisstock Tel: 01206 866317
E-mail: colcester@dioceseofbrentwood.org

Cardiff
Br Brian Butler (IC) Tel: 029 2074 3230
E-mail: brianioc@aol.com

Clifton
Dcn Thomas Douglas Tel: 0117 979 1404
E-mail: thomas.douglas@nbt.nhs.uk
Rev Cavan McElligott Tel: 0117 973 4983
E-mail: cavan@glanyllyn.freeserve.co.uk

East Anglia
Dcn Clive Brooks Tel: 01206 396 319
E-mail: clive.brooks@btopenworld.com
Dcn Pat Limacher Tel: 01603 728935
E-mail: estmanager@stjohncathedral.co.uk

Hallam
Rev Chris Posluszny Tel: 0114 248 6102
E-mail: chrisposluszny@msn.com

Hexham & Newcastle
Rev Mark Millward Tel: 0191 333 2333
E-mail: mark.millward@cddft.nhs.uk

Lancaster
Rev Philip Smith Tel: 01772 719604
E-mail: frsmith@saintclares.co.uk

Leeds
Rev Chris Irving Tel: 01484 866 669
E-mail: christopher.irving@leedsth.nhs.uk

Liverpool
Dcn Graham Appleyard Tel: 01695 422627
E-mail: g-appleyard@tiscali.co.uk

Menevia
Sr Winifred Dwyer Tel: 01792 473453
E-mail: stellacon99@aol.com

Middlesbrough
Dcn Pat Thomas
Tel: 01642 241608
E-mail: eddiegubbins@middlesbrough-diocese.org.uk
Rev Bill Serplus Tel: 01482 835707
E-mail: billserplus@middlesbrough-diocese.org.uk

Northampton
Rev Jonathan Hill Tel: 01582 633706
E-mail: frjonhill@aol.com

Nottingham
Rev Euan Marley (OP) Tel: 0116 252 1513
E-mail: euan.marley@english.op.org

Plymouth
Dcn Declan McConville Tel: 01202 442167
E-mail: declan.mcconville@poole.nhs.uk

Portsmouth
Rev Andrew Chandler Tel: 02392 463854
E-mail: andw.cand@aol.com

Salford
Rev David Glover Tel: 0161 720 9626
E-mail: epvicsocresp@salforddiocese.org.uk

Shrewsbury
Rev Bill Dukes Tel: 01952 586118
E-mail: pp@goodshepherdtelford.org.uk

Southwark
Rev Paul Mason Tel: 0207 928 5256
E-mail: paul.mason@gstt.nhs.uk

Westminster
Rev Peter Scott Tel: 0207 349 5609
E-mail: peterscott@rcdow.org.uk

Wrexham
Rev Peter Brignall Tel: 01978 263 943
E-mail: office@wrexhamcathedral

CATHOLIC DIOCESAN CARE SOCIETIES

(INCLUDING CHILDREN'S SOCIETIES)

AND OTHER CARING SERVICES AND INSTITUTIONS.

■ I. CARITAS – SOCIAL ACTION

Caritas – Social Action is the voice of the Catholic Church on social justice and care in England and Wales. It is an agency of the Bishops' Conference with responsibility for carrying out the social mission of the Church in England and Wales. Together with CAFOD it makes up Caritas England and Wales, part of the Caritas Internationalis federation. Caritas-social action seeks to influence Government policy and advocate for a more just society. It is a federation of organisations and individuals who are involved in the promotion of social justice, the relief of poverty, the care of children, young people and adults in need; and community development for the benefit of people of all faiths and none.
Caritas-social action is the national umbrella body for the Catholic voluntary sector for which there is an estimated turnover of £97 million, 6,500 employed staff, 35.000 volunteers and over one million beneficiaries.

Chair of Trustees: **Bishop Terence Brain**
Vice-Chair: **Mrs Margaret Dight**
Director: **To be appointed**
Address: 39 Eccleston Square, London SW1V 1BX **Tel:** 020-7901 4875
E-mail: caritas@cbcew.org.uk **Website:** www.caritas-socialaction.org.uk

■ II. DIOCESAN CARE SOCIETIES

There are eighteen autonomous Catholic Caring and Children's Societies serving the twenty-two Catholic Dioceses in England and Wales.
These societies vary both in size and in the scope of their activities. Most provide fostering and adoption services. Other work with children and families may include child protection services, school counselling, family centres and casework support.
A number of the societies also provide services for adults including those with learning disabilities, hearing or sight impairment, older people and homeless people. All of these societies offer their services to the whole community, regardless of race or creed.

■ Archdiocese of Westminster
Catholic Children's Society, *Chief Executive:* **Mr Jim Richards,** 73 St Charles Square, London W10 6EJ
Tel: 020-8969 5305 **Fax:** 020-8960 1464
Website: www.cathchild.org.uk

■ Diocese of Arundel and Brighton
Catholic Children's Society.
See Diocese of Southwark.

■ Archdiocese of Birmingham
Father Hudson's Society, Coventry Road, Coleshill, Birmingham B46 3ED
Tel: 01675-434000 **Fax:** 01675-434010
Director: **Mr Kevin Caffrey.**

■ Diocese of Brentwood
Brentwood Catholic Children's Society, Childcare House, Little Wheatley Chase, Rayleigh, Essex SS6 9EH
Tel: 01268-784544 **Fax:** 01268-784540
E-mail: dmadden@childcareuk.org
Director: **Mr Dick Madden**

■ Archdiocese of Cardiff and Dioceses of Menevia and Wrexham
St David's Children Society (formerly Catholic Children and Family Care Society (Wales), Bishop Brown House, Durham Street, Grangetown, Cardiff, CF1 6PB
Tel: 029-2066 7007 **Fax:** 029-2039 4344
Director: **Mr Gerry Cooney** BA, MSc, CQSW

■ Diocese of Clifton
The Catholic Children's Society, 162 Pennywell Road, Eston, Bristol BS35 0TX
Tel: 0845 122 0077 **Fax:** 0117-923 8651

■ Diocese of East Anglia
East Anglia Diocesan Caring Service, 29 Wheatcroft Way, Dereham WR20 3SS
Tel: 01362-699015

■ Diocese of Hallam
Hallam Caring Services, The Pastoral Centre, St Charles Street, Sheffield S9 3WU
Tel: 0114-256 6407 **Fax:** 0114-250 0893
Co-ordinator: **Mr Stuart Hanlon MA**

■ Diocese of Hexham and Newcastle
St Cuthbert's Care, St Cuthbert's House, West Road, Newcastle-upon-Tyne, NE15 7PY
Tel: 0191-228 0111 **Fax:** 0191-228 0177
Director: **Mr A Donohoe**

WELFARE AND CARING SERVICES

■ **Diocese of Lancaster**
Catholic Caring Services, 218 Tulketh Road, Preston PR2 1ES
Tel: 01772-732313/4 **Fax:** 01772-768726
Director: **Mr James Cullen, BA, M.Sc, CQSW, DMS.**

■ **Diocese of Leeds**
Catholic Care (Diocese of Leeds), St Paul's, 11 North Grange Road, Leeds LS6 2BR
Tel: 0113-388 5400 **Fax:** 0113-388 5401
Director: **Mark Wiggin**

■ **Archdiocese of Liverpool**
The Nugent Care Society, 99 Edge Lane, Liverpool L7 2PE **Tel:** 0151-261 2000

■ **Diocese of Middlesbrough**
Catholic Child Care,
Tel: 01642-850505 **Fax:** 01642-851404
E-mail: socialconcern@dioceseofmiddlesbrough.co.uk

■ **Diocese of Northampton**
St. Francis' Children's Society, Collis House, 48 Newport Road, Woolstone, Milton Keynes MK15 0AA
Tel: 01908-572700 **Fax:** 01908-572702
E-mail: enquires@sfcs.org.uk
Director: **Mr Alfred Harrison**

■ **Diocese of Plymouth**
Catholic Children's Society, Plymouth, Rosary House, 27 Fore Street, Exeter EX1 2QJ **Tel:** 01392-255046

■ **Diocese of Portsmouth**
Children's Society.
See Diocese of Southwark.

■ **Diocese of Salford**
Catholic Children's Rescue Society, 390 Parrs Wood Road, Manchester, M20 5NA
Tel: 0161-445 7741 **Fax:** 0161-445 7769

■ **Diocese of Shrewsbury**
Catholic Children's Society, Head Office: St Paul's House, Farm Field Drive, Prenton CH43 7ZT
Tel: 0151-652 1281 **Fax:** 0151-652 5002
E-mail: info@cathchildsoc.org.uk
Director: **Mr Ged Flynn.**

■ **Archdiocese of Southwark and Dioceses of Arundel & Brighton and Portsmouth**
Catholic Children's Society, 49 Russell Hill Road, Purley, Surrey, CR8 2XB
Tel: 020-8668 2181 **Fax:** 020-8763 2274
Director: **Mr Terence Connor, MA.**

■ **III. RELIGIOUS CONGREGATIONS ENGAGED IN CHILD CARE IN ENGLAND AND WALES.**

Daughters of Charity of St Vincent de Paul, Provincial House, The Ridgeway, Mill Hill, London NW7 1EH **Tel:** 020-8959 5898
Franciscan Missionaries of St Joseph, St Joseph's Convent, Greenleach Lane, Worsley, Manchester M28 4TS
Tel: 0161-794 1062
Poor Servants of the Mother of God, Maryfield Convent, Roehampton, London SW15 4JA
Tel: 020-8788 4351
Poor Sisters of Nazareth, Nazareth House, 169-175 Hammersmith Road, Brook Green, London W6 8DB **Tel:** 020-8748 2549
Sisters of Our Lady of Charity, 'Fairlight', The Avenue, North Ascot SL5 7LY
Tel: 01344-626622
Sisters of St Joseph of Peace, 61 Station Road, Rearsby, Leicester LE7 8YW
Tel: 01664-424251
Sisters of the Good Shepherd, Good Shepherd Provincialate, 61 East End Road, East Finchley, London N2 0SF
Tel: 020-8346 8100

■ **IV. RESIDENTIAL CARE FOR CHILDREN**

■ **Diocese of Arundel and Brighton**

Special Schools:
St Joseph's School, Amlets Lane, Cranleigh, Surrey GU6 7DH
Tel: 01483-272449

St Dominic's School, Mount Olivet, Hambledon, Godalming, Surrey GU8 4DX
Tel: 01428-684693

■ **Diocese of Clifton**
Special Schools:
St Rose's Special School, Stratford Lawn, Stroud GL5 4AB **Tel:** 01453-763793
St Edward's School, Melchett Court, Sherfield English, Hants SO51 6ZR
Tel: 01794-884271

■ **Diocese of Hexham and Newcastle**
Children's Homes:
St Vincent's, Auton House, St Vincent's Campus, West Denton, Newcastle-upon-Tyne NE15 7LT **Tel:** 0191-267 4383

Mother and Baby Units:
1/3 Bentinck Road, Newcastle-upon-Tyne NE14 6UT **Tel:** 0191-273 8725
'Tudor House', St Vincent's, The Roman Way, West Road, Newcastle-upon-Tyne NE4 6UT **Tel:** 0191-264 8925

■ **Diocese of Lancaster**
Children's Homes:
Residential Children's Centre, 74 Wellington Road, Ashton, Preston PR2 1BX
Tel: 01772-720654

■ **Diocese of Leeds**
Children's Homes:

29 Moor Road, Headingley, Leeds LS6 4BG
Tel: 0113-278 6562
5 Harrison Crescent, Leeds LS9 6NP
Tel: 0113-249 3973
St Mary's, 41 Church Street, Boston Spa, Wetherby **Tel:** 01937-842138
Redholt, 78 Holly Bank Road, Bradford BD7 4QL **Tel:** 01274-573049
Lanshaw Crescent Children's Home: 44 Lanshaw Crescent, Middleton, Leeds LS10 3NN **Tel:** 0113-271 6669

■ **Archdiocese of Liverpool**
Children's Homes
Clumber Lodge, 88 Victoria Road, Freshfield L37 1LP **Tel:** 01704-872210
St Catherine's Secure Centre, Blackbrook Road, St Helens WA11 0RS
Tel: 01744-22102
Nazareth House, Liverpool Road, Crosby, Liverpool L23 0QT **Tel:** 0151-928 6418

Special Schools:
Nugent House School, Carr Mill Road, Billinge, Nr Wigan WN5 7TT
Tel: 01744-892551

■ **Diocese of Salford**
Children's Homes:
Mount Carmel, 463/465 Parrs Wood Road, Didsbury, Manchester M20 5NA
Tel: 0161-446 2348
Marymount, 56/58 Parrs Wood Avenue, Manchester M20 0NB **Tel:** 0161-445 4237
De Paul Trust, 88 Burnage Lane, Manchester M19 2WL **Tel:** 0161-224 5403

Mother and Baby units:
Maryvale, 8/10 Rydal Road, Blackburn BB1 5NR **Tel:** 01254-670449
Marillac, Laindon Road, Longsight Manchester M14 5YJ **Tel:** 0161-225 1944

■ **Archdiocese of Southwark**
Children's Homes:
Cabrini, 1 Healy Drive, Orpington, Kent BR6 1LP
Tel: 01689-870216
3 Healy Drive, Orpington, Kent BR6 1LP
Tel: 01689-897235

■ V. HOSPITALS

■ **Archdiocese of Westminster**
Hospital of St John and St Elizabeth, 60, Grove End Road, St John's Wood, London, NW8 9NH **Tel:** 020-7586 3179
• ***Sisters of Mercy***
St David's Home, 12 Castlebar Hill, Ealing, London, W5 1TE **Tel:** 020-8997 8850 Ealing
St Joseph's Hospice, Mare Street, Hackney, London, E8 4SA
Tel: 020-8985 0861
• ***Religious Sisters of Charity***

■ **Diocese of Arundel and Brighton**
Holy Cross, Hindhead Road, Haslemere, Surrey, GU27 1NQ. **Tel:** 01428-420586
• ***Daughters of the Cross***
Mount Alvernia Hospital, 46, Harvey Road, Guildford, GU1 3LX
Tel: 01483-570122
• ***Franciscan Missionaries of Divine Motherhood.***

■ **Archdiocese of Cardiff**
St Joseph's Private Hospital, Harding Avenue, Malpas, Newport, Gwent, NP9 6ZE **Tel:** 01633-858203.
• ***Sisters of St Joseph***

■ **Diocese of Clifton**
St Mary's Hospital, Upper Byron Place, Clifton, Bristol, BS8 1JY
Tel: 0117-927 3186/7/8
• ***Poor Servants of the Mother of God.***

■ **Diocese of Leeds.**
St Gemma's Hospice, 329, Harrogate Road, Moortown, Leeds LS17 6QD
Tel: 0113-269 3231/268 9235
• ***Sisters of the Cross and Passion.***

■ **Archdiocese of Liverpool**
Lourdes Hospital, Greenbank Road, Liverpool, L18 1HQ **Tel:** 0151-733 7123
• ***Poor Servants of the Mother of God***

■ **Diocese of Menevia**
Santa Maria Hospital, Ffynone, Swansea, SA16 6DF **Tel:** 01792-472339

■ **Archdiocese of Southwark**
St Anthony's Hospital, London Road, North Cheam, Sutton, Surrey, SM3 9DW
Tel: 020-8337 6691
• ***Daughters of the Cross.***

■ VI. NURSING/CONVALESCENT HOMES

■ **Diocese of Arundel and Brighton**
St Augustine's Home, Firfield House, Addlestone, Surrey, KT15 2AA**Tel:** 01932-842254
• ***Hospitaller Sisters of the Sacred Heart***
St George's Retreat, Burgess Hill, W. Sussex, RH15 0SQ **Tel:** 90444-235874
• ***Augustinian Sisters.***
For Psycho-geriatric and people with learning difficulties.
St Joseph's Nursing Home, East Street, Littlehampton, East Sussex. BN17 6AU
Tel: 903-715589
• ***Franciscan Missionaries.***
St Raphael's, Danehurst, Danehill, Hayward's Heath RH17 7EZ
Tel: 01825-790485
• ***Augustinian Sisters.***

■ **Archdiocese of Birmingham**
St Mary's Home for the Elderly and Sick, Margaret Street, Stone, Staffs ST15 8EJ
Tel: 01785-813894
• ***Dominican Sisters.***
St Mary's Hospice, Raddlebarn Road, Selly Park, Birmingham B29 7DA
Tel: 0121-472 1191

■ **Diocese of Brentwood**
St Michael's, 93 Marine Parade East, Clacton-on-Sea, CO15 6JW
Tel: 01255-423688.
• ***Sisters of Mercy***
The Marillac Nursing Home, Eagle Way, Warley, Brentwood, Essex CM13 3BL
Tel: 01277-220276 Home for the Disabled.
• ***Daughters of Charity***

■ **Archdiocese of Cardiff**
Nazareth House, Colum Road, Cardiff CF10 3UN **Tel:** 029-2022 0943

■ **Diocese of Clifton**
Cedar Park, 27 Oldfield Road, Bath BA2 3NF **Tel:** 01225-312484
St Teresa's Nursing Home, Corston, Nr Bath, BA2 9AG **Tel:** 01225-872643
• ***Poor Servants of the Mother of God.***

■ **Diocese of East Anglia**
Hope House, Residential Nursing Care Home, Brooklands Avenue, Cambridge, CB2 2BQ **Tel:** 01223-359087
• ***Sisters of the Holy Family of Bordeaux***

■ **Diocese of Lancaster**
Boarbank Hall, Grange-over-Sands, Cumbria LA11 7NH **Tel:** 01539-532288
• ***Augustinian Nursing Sisters***
Cross and Passion Convent, 19, East Beach, Lytham St.Annes, FY8 5EU
Tel: 01253-736913
• ***Sisters of the Cross and Passion.***

■ **Archdiocese of Liverpool**
Ince Blundell Hall, Back o'th' Town Lane, Liverpool L38 6JL
Nursing/Convalescent Home.
• ***Augustinian Sisters of the Mercy of Jesus.***

■ **Diocese of Nottingham**
St Mary's Nursing Home, Ednaston Hall, Brailsfold, Nr Ashbourne DE6 3BY
Tel: 01335-60254
• ***Sisters of Mercy***.

■ **Diocese of Plymouth**
St Peter's Nursing Home, Plympton St Maurice, Plymouth, PL7 2LL
Tel: 01752-337202
Psychiatric Nursing Home.
• ***Augustinian Sisters***

■ **Diocese of Salford**
Alexian Brothers Care Centre, St.Mary's Road, Moston, Manchester, M40 OBL
Tel: 0161-681 1929
• ***Alexian Brothers.***

■ **Diocese of Shrewsbury**
Lady of the Vale Nursing Home, Grange Road, Bowdon Vale, Altrincham WA14 3HA
Tel: 0161-928 2567.
• ***Sisters of St Joseph of the Apparition***.
Park Mount Residential Home, 52 Park Mount Drive, Macclesfield SK11 8NT
Tel: 01625-616459 **Fax:** 01625-869080
• ***Pallottine Missionary Sisters.***
Nazareth House, Manor Hill, Prenton CH43 IUG **Tel:** 0151-652 1256
• ***Sisters of Nazareth.***

■ **Archdiocese of Southwark**
Kearsney Manor Nursing Home Alkham Road, Temple Ewell, Dover, Kent CT16 3EQ
Tel: 01304-822135
St. Raphael's Hospice, London Road, North Cheam, Sutton, Surrey, SM3 9DX
Tel: 020-8335 4575
E-mail: enquiries@straphaels.org.uk

■ **Diocese of Wrexham**
Sisters of Mercy Nursing Home, 15, Lansdowne Road, Colwyn Bay LL29 7UY
Tel: 01492-532788.
• ***Sisters of Mercy***

■ VII. HOMES FOR PEOPLE WITH LEARNING DIFFICULTIES

■ **Diocese of Arundel and Brighton**
L'Arche, 51 Alnwick Road, Bognor Regis, W. Sussex. PO21 2NJ **Tel:** 01243 863426
Sundial House, Molesey Venture, Orchard Lane, East Molesey, Surrey KT8 0BN
Tel: 020-8398 8620 Residential home for men with learning disabilities.
Sundial House, Molesey Venture, Orchard Lane, East Molesey, Surrey KT8 0BN
Tel: 020-8398 8620 Residential Home for men with learning disabilities.
Moseley Horticultural Centre, Orchard Lane, East Molesey, Surrey KT8 0BN
Tel: 020-8398 1140 For Training People with Learning Disabilities.

■ **Archdiocese of Birmingham**
St Andrew's Home, 37, Blythe Road, Coleshill, Birmingham, B46 1AF
Tel: 01675-462240
St Catherine's Home, Coventry Road, Coleshill, Birmingham B46 3EA
Tel: 01675-466094

■ **Diocese of Hexham and Newcastle**
'Wingate', 19 Akenside Terrace, Jesmond, Newcastle-upon-Tyne NE2 1TN
Tel: 0191-281 3231

■ **Diocese of Leeds**
Bank House, 113-117, Barkerend Road, Bradford, BD3 9AX **Tel:** 01274-308411
West Haven, 146 Huddersfield Road, Dewsbury, WF13 2RW
Tel: 01924 461720
Craven House, 41 Swadford Street, Skipton BD23 1QY **Tel:** 01756 700099

■ **Archdiocese of Liverpool**
Thingwall Hall, Broadgreen, Liverpool, L14 7NZ **Tel:** 0151-228 4439
Fax: 0151-254 1951
• ***Brothers of Charity.***
Lisieux Hall, Whittle-le-Woods, Chorley, Lancs. PR6 7NZ **Tel:** 01257-266311
Fax: 01257-265671
• ***Brothers of Charity.***
Rosemont, Edge Lane, Liverpool, L7 9LE
Tel: 0151-263 3694.
• ***Poor Servants of the Mother of God.***
Aughton Park Care Centre, Aughton Park Drive, Ormskirk L39 5QE
Tel: 01695-576996
• ***Sisters of Our Lady of Charity***.
L'Arche Community, The Ark, Lockerby Road, Liverpool, L6 0HG
Tel: 0151-260 0933
St Joseph's Nursing Home for Learning Disabilities, Blundell Avenue, Formby L37 1PH **Tel:** 01704-872132
• ***Poor Servants of the Mother of God.***
Margaret Roper House, 447 Liverpool Road, Birkdale, Southport PR8 3BW
Tel: 01704-74348
Geel and Hitchen Court, Woodlands Road, Aigburth, Liverpool L17 0AN
Tel: 0151-729 0117
Gradwell Farm, Moor Road, Croston, Nr Leyland, Lancs PR5 7HP
Tel: 01772-600915
Holiday Home for people with Mental Disabilities and their carers.

■ **Diocese of Plymouth**
St Peter's Private Mental Hospital, Plympton St. Maurice, Plymouth PL7 3LL
Tel: 01752-337202

■ **Diocese of Portsmouth**
Weston Manor, (St Dominic's), Moons Hill Bay, Totland, Isle of Wight. PO39 OHF
Tel: 01983-753031

■ **Archdiocese of Westminister**
The Minims, Hatfield, Hertfordshire, AL10 OAW **Tel:** 01207 257097/8
• ***Brothers of the Hospitaller Order of Saint John of God.*** Two six bedroomed nursing homes for people with learning disabilities.

■ **VIII. REST HOMES FOR ELDERLY**

■ **Archdiocese of Westminster**
Maryland Convent and Residential Home, 29 Townsend Drive, St Albans, Herts AL3 5RF **Tel:** 01727-853601
Nazareth House, Hammersmith Road, London W6 8DB **Tel:** 020-8748 3549
Nazareth House, 162 East End Road, London N2 ORU **Tel:** 020-8883 1104
Orione House, 12 Station Road, Hampton Wick, Kington-upon-Thames KT1 4HG
Tel: 020-8977 0754
St Vincent's Nursing Home, Wiltshire Lane, Eastcote, Pinner, Middlx HA5 2NB
Tel: 020-8872 4900

■ **Diocese of Arundel and Brighton**
Holy Cross Priory, Cross-in-Hand, Heathfield, East Sussex. TN21 OTS
Tel: 01435-863298
• ***Benedictine Sisters.***
St Anne's Convent, 92 Mill Road, Burgess Hill, West Sussex RH15 8EL
Tel: 01444-233179
• ***Franciscan Sisters.***
St Augustine's Home, Firfield House, Simplemarsh Road, Addlestone, Surrey KT15 1QR **Tel:** 01942-842254
St Mary's House, 38 Preston Park Avenue, Brighton, East Sussex BN1 6HG
Tel: 01273-556035.
St Joseph's Albert Road, Bognor Regis, West Sussex. PO21 1NJ **Tel:** 01243-864051
• ***Benedictine Sisters.***

■ **Archdiocese of Birmingham**
Annie Bright Weston House, 6 Norfolk Road, Birmingham B15 3QD
Tel: 0121-454 1289
• ***Sisters of Charity***
Aston Hall, Aston-by-Stone, Staffs ST15 0BJ **Tel:** 01785-812001
Footherley Hall, Footherley Lane, Shenstone, Lichfield, Staffs WS14 OHG
Tel: 01543-480253
• ***Hospitaller Sisters of the Sacred Heart***
St Joseph's Home, 71 Queen's Park Road, Birmingham, B32 2LB **Tel:** 0121-427 2486
• ***Little Sisters of the Poor.***

■ **Diocese of Brentwood**
Nazareth House, 111 London Road, Southend-on-Sea, Essex SS1 1PP
Tel: 01702-345627

■ **Archdiocese of Cardiff**
Nazareth House, Colum Road, Cardiff CF10 3UN **Tel:** 029-2022 0943

WELFARE AND CARING SERVICES

■ Diocese of Clifton
Nazareth House, London Road, Charlton, Kings, Cheltenham, GL22 6YJ
Tel: 01242-516361
St Angela's Convent, 5 Litfield Place, Bristol, BS8 3LU **Tel:** 0117-973 5436.
St Joseph's Home, 66 Cotham Hill, Bristol BS6 6JT **Tel:** 0117-973 3815

■ Diocese of East Anglia
Montana, Great Barton, Bury St.Edmunds, IP31 2RF **Tel:** 01284-787321

■ Diocese of Hallam
St Annes Rest Home, Burghwallis Hall, Grange Lane, Burghwallis, Doncaster DN6 9LJ **Tel:** 01302-700319

■ Diocese of Hexham and Newcastle
Holy Cross Home, Ettrick Grove, High Barnes, Sunderland SR4 8QA
Tel: 0191-567 0862
St Joseph's Home, Westmorland Road, Newcastle-upon-Tyne, NE4 7QA
Tel: 0191-273 1279/3008
St Catherine's Nursing & Residential Home, St Cuthbert's House, West Road, Newcastle NE15 7PY
St Mary's Convent, Ebchester, Consett, DH8 OQD **Tel:** 01207 560288

■ Diocese of Lancaster
Jeanne Jugan Residence, Garstang Road, Fulwood, Preston, PR2 9RB
Tel: 01772-717454
Nazareth House, Ashton Road, Lancaster, LA1 5AQ **Tel:** 01524-32074
Stella Matutina Convent, 16 Clifton Drive, Ansdell, Lytham St Annes FY8 5RQ
Tel: 01253-734834

■ Diocese of Leeds
Mount St Joseph's Home, Shire Oak Road, Leeds LS6 2DE **Tel:** 0113 278 4101
- ***Little Sisters of the Poor***

■ Archdiocese of Liverpool
Nazareth House, Liverpool Road, Crosby, Liverpool, L23 0QT **Tel:** 0151-928 3254.
Cardinal Heenan House, School Lane, Roby Mill, Upholland, Lancs
Tel: 01695-622885
Lime House, Newton Road, Lowton, Wigan WA3 1HF **Tel:** 01942-674135

■ Diocese of Middlesbrough
St Catherine's, Southcoates Lane, Hull HU9 3AJ **Tel:** 01482-375164

■ Diocese of Northampton
Nazareth House, 118 Harlestone Road, Northampton NN5 6AD **Tel:** 01604-751385
St Joseph's Convent, West Street, Olney, Bucks. MK46 5HJ **Tel:** 01234-711267

■ Diocese of Nottingham
Convent of Mercy, Beechwood, Broadway, Derby DE22 1AU Tel: 01332-558043
Mount Carmel House, Highfields, Broadway, Derby DE22 1AU
Tel: 01332-553466
Presentation Sisters Care Centre, Chesterfield Road, Matlock, Derbys DE4 3FT
Tel: 01629-582953 **Fax:** 01629-55140

■ Diocese of Plymouth
Margaret Clitherow House, Prior Road, St Marychurch, Torquay TQ1 4NY
Tel: 01803-326056
Nazareth House, Dunford Street, Plymouth PL1 3QR **Tel:** 01752-660943
Presentation Convent, Medrose, Barwis Hill, Penzance, Cornwall TR18 2AN
Tel: 01736-362618

■ Diocese of Salford
Franciscan Convent, 26 East Park Road, Blackburn, BB1 8BB **Tel:** 01254-53962
Franciscourt, 45 Manor Drive, Chorlton, Manchester M21 7QG **Tel:** 0161-445 9368.
Little Sisters of the Poor, 52 Plymouth Grove West, Longsight, Manchester M13 0AR **Tel:** 0161-273 4147
McCauley Mount, Padiham Road, Burnley, Lancs BB12 6TG **Tel:** 01282-483071
Nazareth House, Preston New Road, Blackburn, BB2 7AJ **Tel:** 01254-530000
Nazareth House, Scholes Lane, Prestwich, Manchester M25 0NU **Tel:** 0161-776 2111

■ Diocese of Shrewsbury
Nazareth House, Manor Hill, Prenton CH43 IUG **Tel:** 0151-652 1256
Park Mount Home for the Elderly, 52 Park Mount Drive, Macclesfield SK11 8NT
Tel: 01625-616459
Lady of the Vale Nursing Home, Grange Road, Bowdon Vale, Altrincham WA14 3HA
Tel: 0161-928 2567

■ Archdiocese of Southwark
Little Sisters of the Poor, St.Peter's Home, 2A Meadow Road South, Lambeth, Vauxhall, London SW8 IQB
Tel: 020-7735 6246
St Mary's, 7-8 Eastbrook Place, Maison Dieu, Dover, Kent CT16 1RP
Tel: 01304-204232
St Teresa's Home, 12 Lansdowne Road, Wimbledon, SW20 8AN
Tel: 020-8879 7366

■ IX. RESIDENTIAL HOMES FOR THE BLIND

■ Archdiocese of Liverpool
Christopher Grange, Youens Way, Prescot Road, Liverpool, L14 2EW
Tel: 0151-220 2525

St Vincent's School for the Blind and Partially Sighted, Yew Tree Lane, West Derby, Liverpool L12 9HN
Tel: 0151-228 9968

■ X. RESIDENTIAL HOMES FOR DEAF PEOPLE

For times and venues of signed Masses in England, Wales, Scotland and Ireland please see www.cda-uk.com under directory

■ Archdiocese of Liverpool
Mary Mount Convent, North Mossley Hill Road, Liverpool L18 8BS
Tel: 0151-724 2203

■ Diocese of Leeds
St John's Residential School for the Deaf, Boston Spa LS23 6DF
Tel: 01937-842334

■ Diocese of Salford
St Joseph's Service to Deaf People, Hollywood House, Sudell Street, Collyhurst, Manchester M4 4JF **Tel:** 0161-834 8828

■ XI. RESIDENTIAL HOSTELS

■ Archdiocese of Westminster
Adoratrices Hostel, 39 Kensington Square, London. W8 5HR **Tel:** 0207-937 4582
Cardinal Hume Centre, 1-7 Arneway Street, Horseferry Road, London SW1P 2BG
Tel: 020-7222 1602
Convent of Religious of Mary Immaculate, 16 Southwell Gardens, London, SW7 4RL **Tel:** 0207-373 3869
Franciscan Missionaries, 9 St George's Drive, London SW1V 4DJ
Irish Centre, 51 Camden Square, London, NW1 9XB **Tel:** 020-7485 0051
More House, 53 Cromwell Road, London SW7 2EH **Tel:** 020-7584 2040
Catholic Chaplaincy to London University, 111 Gower Street, London. WC1E 6AR. **Tel:** 0207-387 6370
Sisters of Providence, Rowland Hill Street, Haverstock Hill, London, NW3 2AD
Tel: 020-7794 4504
St Joseph's Convent, Lichfield Road, Stafford ST17 4LF **Tel:** 01785 251577

■ Archdiocese of Birmingham
Convent of the Assumption, Haberton Mead, Oxford, OX3 0DB
Tel: 01865-764293

■ Diocese of Salford
Allen Hall, Wilmslow Road, Fallowfield, Manchester. M14 6HT **Tel:** 0161-224 6844
St Gabriel's Hall, 1 Oxford Place, Manchester, M14 5RP **Tel:** 0161-224 7061

■ Archdiocese of Southwark
Augustinian Sisters, St Monica's House 83-87 Clapham Road, London, SW9 0HY
Tel: 020-7582 0840
Religious of St Mary Immaculate, 44 Augustus Road, London, SW19 6NB
Tel: 020-8788 9477
Sisters of St Dorothy, 176 Clapham Road, London, SW9 0LA **Tel:** 020-7735 8235

■ XII. COUNSELLING SERVICES

Dympna Centre. Parkside House, 17 East Parade, Harrogate HG1 1LF **Tel:** 01423-817515. The Dympna Centre offers – Pastoral Counselling – Vocation Assessment – Reflective work with groups to Clergy, Religious and those engaged in the ministries of the Church. Founded in 1971, our tradition is in working for the well-being, both spiritual and psychological, of those who minister to others. Contact: *The Director*, **Rev Terry McGrath** at the above address.

■ XIII, CATHOLIC BLIND SERVICES

A service meeting the needs of people who are blind or have a visual impairment. CBS organises various gatherings around the country, provides support groups, workshops and training, resources and produces the Missal in large print.
Contact: The Director, Catholic Blind Services, PO Box 10333, Birmingham B13 8XX
Tel: 0121-441 5577 **Fax:** 0121-441 5599.
Director: **Sean O'Donnell**
Episcopal Adviser: **Most Rev Peter Smith**.

■ XIV, MIGRANT ACCOMMODATION SERVICES

A new accommodation based service for newly arrived migrant workers in Euston, London: Saint John of God Migrant Workers Project, 2-3 Grafton Street, London NW1 1DJ
Contact. **Br John O'Neill**
Tel: 07748 686507

CATHOLIC OFFICE FOR THE PROTECTION OF CHILDREN & VULNERABLE ADULTS (COPCA)

12 St Paul's Square, Bimingham B3 1RB
Tel: 0121-233 1963 **Fax:** 0121-236 3379
E-mail: admin@copca.org.uk

The Catholic Trust for England & Wales Registered Charity 1097482
COPCA is accountable to the Catholic Bishops' Conference and the Conference of Religious through its independent Management Board.

Its purpose is to co-ordinate and monitor the implementation of 'A Progamme for Action' (Lord Nolan, September 2001) within the Catholic Church in England and Wales, with the aim of creating a model of best practice in relation to the protection of children, young people and vulnerable adults. It works with Diocesan and Religious personnel to develop national policies and procedures and to provide advice in relation to best practice. A public Annual Report is issued.

COPCA also acts as the Registered Body for Criminal Records Bureau checks.

Acting Director: **Adrian Child**
Business Manager: **Sally Sanderson**
PA to the Director: **Claire Johnson**

Team Secretary: **Sophie Robbins**
COPCA Management Board
Chair: **The Most Rev Vincent Nichols, Archbishop of Birmingham**
Vice-Chair: **Terry Bamford**
Board Members: **Rt Rev Kevin Dunn, Bishop of Hexham and Newcastle, Enid Hendry, Mgr Jack Kennedy, Helen Kenward, Bernadette Cawley, Prof Peter Gilbert, Rev Jonathan Mitchell, Br Stanislaus Neild OH, Sr Jane Bertelsen FMDM**

Diocesan Child Protection Co-ordinators (CPCs)

Please refer to the relevant Diocesan/Congregational section for details.
Diocesan Child Protection Officers (CPOs)
Please refer to relevant Diocesan section for their details.
For CPCs in Religious Congregations

Please contact the Congregation for information.

DIOCESAN CO-ORDINATORS OF MARRIAGE & FAMILY LIFE MINISTRY

In 1994 the Bishops' Conference accepted the role of the Diocesan Co-ordinator of family Life Ministry as that of:

- Caring for, supporting and promoting all areas of family life; offering pastoral support to all clergy and laity - involved in the work of affirming marriage, family life and the parish family.
- Providing information and resources in family matters for all parishioners and clergy .
- Organising training opportunities and co-ordinating lay involvement.
- Acting as a link with existing diocesan agencies to support families with a particular need.
- Strengthening ecumenical links enabling co-operation with other Christian Churches at appropriate diocesan and parish level and where possible offering joint programmes.

In 2008 diocesan coordinators launched a more formal association for diocesan marriage and family life ministry called FAMILIAS. See www.familias-ew.org.uk

For further information on regional and national meetings of diocesan co-ordinators contact: **Elizabeth Davies**, Marriage and Family Life Project Officer, CBCEW, 39 Eccleston Square, London SW1V 1BX

■ **ARUNDEL AND BRIGHTON**
Liz James, *Specialist Advisor,* Marriage & Family Life Ministry, Christian Education Centre, 4 Southgate Drive, Crawley, West Sussex RH10 6RP **Tel:** 01293 515666
Fax: 01293 616945
E-mail: liz.james@dabnet.org
Website: www.dabnet.org/PastoralTeam/marfam

■ **BIRMINGHAM**
Rev Edward Clare, *Vocations Director*, Oscott College, Chester Road, Sutton Coldfield B73 5AA **Tel:** 0121 355 4163
E-mail: eddie@vocations.org.uk
Website: www.vocations.org.uk/Vocations/Family%20Life.html

■ **BRENTWOOD**
Rev Graham Smith, *Chaplain for Marriage and Family Life*, 96 Ness Road, Shoeburyness, Essex SS3 9DH
Tel: 01702 292726

■ **CARDIFF**
Anne Ballard, *Chair*: Family Life Commission, Pastoral Resources Centre, 910 Newport Road, Rumney, Cardiff CF3 4LL **Tel:** 029 2021 2821
E-mail: annejim98@yahoo.com

■ **EAST ANGLIA**
Diocese Commission on Marriage and Family Life, c/o The White House, 21 Upgate, Poringland Norwich NR14 7SH

■ **HALLAM**
Susan Tym, Family Focus, 524 Queen's Road, Sheffield S2 4DT
Tel/Fax: 0114 255 4790
E-mail: suetym@ukonline.co.uk
Website: www.hallamcaringservices.org.uk/familyfocus/index.html

■ **HEXHAM AND NEWCASTLE**
Peter and Pauline Lavery, *Diocesan Co-ordinators*, 22 Langdale, Vigo, Birtley, Co Durham DH3 2EL
E-mail: laveryp@hotmail.com

■ **LANCASTER**
Rev Keith Armstrong, *Chair,* Diocesan Commission for Marriage and Family Life 'Cornerstones', 4 Archers Meadow, Kendal, Cumbria LA9 7DY **Tel:** 01539 739806
E-mail: p.armstrong1@sky.com

■ **LEEDS**
Breda Theakston, Family Life Ministry Co-ordinator, Hinsley Hall, 62 Headingley Lane, Leeds LS6 2BX
Tel: 0113 261 8050
E-mail: flm@flm.org.uk
Website: www.flm.org.uk

■ **LIVERPOOL**
Veronica Murphy *Assistant Coordinator for Faith Formation:* L.A.C.E., Pastoral Formation Department, Croxteth Drive, Sefton Park, Liverpool L17 1AA
Tel: 0151 522 1048
E-mail: v.murphy@rcaol.co.uk

■ **MENEVIA**
Director: **Rev Tony Lawrence**, Family Life, 88 Main Street, Pembroke SA71 4HH
Tel: 01646 682629
E-mail: anthonylawrence1938@yahoo.co.uk
Swansea Office: Curial Offices, 27 Convent Street, Swansea SA1 2BX
Tel: 01792 403268/651888

■ **MENEVIA**
Director: **Rev Tony Lawrence**, Family Life, 88 Main Street, Pembroke SA71 4HH
Tel: 01646 682629
E-mail: anthonylawrence1938@yaho

■ **NOTTINGHAM**
Rev John Sherrington, *Chair:* Marriage and Family Life Commission, Our Lady of Lourdes Parish, 36 Uttoxeter Road, Mickleover, Derby DE3 9GE
Tel: 01332 514 107
E-mails: family.nottingham@btinternet.com

■ **PLYMOUTH**
Jillian Wilce, *Family Life Project Co-ordinator*, Dept for Formation, Cardinal Newman House, Wonford Road, Exeter EX2 4PF **Tel:** 01392 671320
E-mails: family.nottingham@btinternet.com

■ **PORTSMOUTH**
Keith Chappell, *Advisor for Marriage & Family Life*, Dept for Pastoral Formation, Winchester Road, Wickham, Hants PO17 5HA **Tel:** 01329 835583

■ **SALFORD**
Rev Duncan McVicar, Office of Marriage and the Family, Shoenstatt Shrine and Pastoral Centre, Manchester Road, Kearsley, Bolton BL4 8QQ
Tel: 01204 572077
E-mail: fr.duncan@shoenstatt.org.uk

■ **SHREWSBURY**
Clara Donnelly, *Co-ordinator*, Marriage and Family Life, c/o Curial Offices, 2 Park Road South, Prenton, Wirral CH43 4UX
Tel: 0151 691 2811
E-mail: cc.donn@talktalk.net

■ **SOUTHWALK**
Rev Graham Preston, Episcopal Vicar for Marriage and Family Life, 72 Paradise Street, London SE16 4QD
Tel: 020 7237 2969

E-mail: glpreston@googlemail.com
Kent Area: **Dcn Ray and Elizabeth Partridge**, **Tel:** 01303 873835
E-mail: r.e.partridge@googlemail.com
South-east Area: **Lisette Blanchett Ball**, **Tel:** 020 8325 1486
E-mail: marriagese@tiscali.co.uk

■ **WESTMINSTER**
Edmund Adamus, *Director:* Dept for Pastoral Affairs, Vaughan House, 46 Francis Street, London SW1P 1QN
Tel: 020 7798 9363 Fax: 020 7798 9077
E-mail: edmundadamus@rcdow.org.uk
Catherine MacGillivray, *Administrative Assistant* **Tel:** 020 7931 6064
E-mail: cathmacgillivray@rcdow.org.uk
Website: www.rcdow.org.uk/pastoralaffairs

■ **WREXHAM**
Marriage & Family Life Commission. c/o Bishop's House, Sontley Road, Wrexham LL13 7EW

CATHOLIC MARRIAGE CARE

(FORMERLY CATHOLIC MARRIAGE ADVISORY COUNCIL)
Provides relationship counselling for individuals or couples (married, single, separated, divorced, Catholic or not). Acceptance, respect and complete confidentiality from trained counsellors to help clients to understand and manage difficulties. Marriage Care also provides Relationship and Marriage Education and a Telephone Helpline for those who have difficulty in accessing services.

Chief Executive: **Mr Terry Prendergast**

National Headquarters:
Clitherow House, 1 Blythe Mews, Blythe Road, London W14 0NW
Tel: 020-7371 1341 **Fax:** 020-7371 4921 (Helpline: 0845 660 6000)
E-mail: info@marriagecare.org.uk **Website:** www.marriagecare.org.uk

■ CONTACTS & CENTRES: ENGLAND AND WALES

Diocesan contact and centre addresses/telephone numbers of Appointments Secretary

■ **WESTMINSTER**
Diocese Contact: **Nicole Paice**
Tel: 020-8994-7996
E-mail: nicole@paicefamily.co.uk

Barnet & Enfield
Christ the King, Peace Close, Bramley, Oakwood N14 4HE
Tel: 0800-389 3801

London
46 Notting Hill Gate, London W11 3HZ
Tel: 0800-389 3801

■ **ARUNDEL & BRIGHTON**
Diocese Contact: **Liz James**
Tel: 01293 783098
E-mail: lizandneil@tiscali.co.uk

Brighton, 5 Surrendon Road, Preston Park, Brighton BN1 6PA (Centre)
Tel: 01273-220111

Crawley & Redhill, c/o Christian Education Centre, 4 Southgate Drive, Crawley, West Sussex **Tel:** 0800-389 3801

Eastbourne, c/o 3 Princes Road, Langney, Eastbourne BN23 6HS (Centre & Appts)
Tel: 01323-417460

■ **BIRMINGHAM**
Diocese Contact: **Alicia O'Brien**
Tel: 0121 454 5457
E-mail: alicia_obrien@swissre.com

Birmingham, 37 Victoria Road, Acock's Green, Birmingham B27 7XZ
Tel: 0800 389 3801

Coventry, 13 Stoney Road, Coventry, CV1 2NP (Centre & Appts)
Tel: 0800-389 3801

North Staffs, 3 Eastwood Place, Hanley, Stoke on Trent ST1 3DB
Tel: 0800 389 3801

Oxford, The Priory Annex, 85 Old High Street, Headlington, Oxford OX3 9HT
Tel: 0800-389 3801

Wolverhampton, Walsall & Dudley 23 Glebe Street, Walsall SW1 3NX (Centre & Appts) **Tel:** 0800-389 3801

■ **BRENTWOOD**
Diocese Contact: **Tim Gallagher**
Tel: 01245-353302
E-mail: tim@tangentresourcing.co.uk

Chelmsford, 178 New London Road, Chelmsford, Essex CM1 7PE
Tel: 0800 389 3801

Colchester/Ipswich, The Fletcher Centre, 2 Crescent Road, Ipswich Suffolk IP1 2EX
Tel: 0800 389 3801

Ilford, Kenwood Gardens Health Centre, Cranbrook Road, Ilford IG1 6YG **Tel:** 020-8554 8070

Southend, c/o 64 Keswick Avenue, Hullbridge, Essex SS5 6JW. (Centre & Appts) **Tel:** 01702-233344

■ CARDIFF

Diocese Contact: **Maurice Scanlon**
Tel: 0800 389 3801
E-mail: conorcarter@hotmail.com

Cardiff, Bishop Brown House, Durham Street, Grangetown, Cardiff CF1 7PB (Centre & Appts) **Tel:** 02920-224238

Hereford & Worcester, 21 Old Road, Bromyard, Herefordshire HR7 4BQ **Tel:** 01432-360459

Newport, 9 Stow Hill, Newport, Gwent NP20 1JJ **Tel:** 0800 389 3801

■ CLIFTON

Diocese Contact: **Kay Elliott**
Tel: 0117 962 8732
E-mail: colnkay@talktalk.net

Bristol, 141 Whiteladie Road, Clifton, Bristol BS8 2QB (Centre & Appts) **Tel:** 0800 389 0381

Gloucestershire, 39 Rodney Road, Cheltenham, Gloucester, GL50 1HX (Centre & Appts) **Tel:** 01242 234882

Wiltshire Centre, 2 Groundwell Road, Swindon SN1 2LU **Tel:** 0800-389 3801

■ EAST ANGLIA

Diocese Contact: **Pip Wells**
Tel: 01603 478134
E-mail: apipwells@gmail.com

Newmarket Centre & Cambridge, 14 Exeter Road, Newmarket, Suffolk CB8 8LT (Centre & Appts) **Tel:** 01638-560580

Norfolk, Cathedral House, Unthank Road, Norwich NR2 2PA (Centre & Appts) **Tel:** 0800-389 3801
Tel: 01553-777099 - Kings Lynn

Peterborough, St Luke's Church, 26 Benyon Grove, Orton Malbourne, Peterbrough PE2 5XX (Centre & Appts) **Tel:** 0800-389 3801

■ HALLAM

Diocese Contact: **Jane Perryman**
Tel: 0114 2373301
E-mail: janeandcharles@googlemail.com

Hallam Centre, 524 Queens Road, Sheffield S2 4DT (Centre & Appts) **Tel:** 0800 389 3801

■ HEXHAM & NEWCASTLE

Diocese Contact: **Kath Anderson**
Tel: 0191 413 3402
E-mail: kathleen_tmc@yahoo.co.uk

Tyneside, Third Floor, Mea House, Ellison Place, Newcastle upon Tyne NE1 8XS **Tel:** 0191-232 0342

■ LANCASTER

Diocese Contact: **John Turner**
Tel: 01772 690018
E-mail: jandm.turner@ukgateway.net

Blackpool, Blackpool Centre, 25a Clifton Street, Blackpool FY1 1JD (Centre & Appts) **Tel:** 0800 389 3801

Carlisle, The Rectory, Our Lady & St Josephs Church, Warwick Square, Carlisle CA1 1LB (Centre & Appts) **Tel:** 0800 389 3801

Preston Centre, 218a Tulketh Road, Preston, Lancs PR21ES (Centre & Appts) **Tel:** 01772-731956

■ LEEDS

Diocese Contact: **Tim Lavery**
Tel: 01422 249881
E-mail: timlavery@blueyonder.co.uk

Leeds, Hinsley Hall, 62 Headingley Lane, Leeds LS6 2BX **Tel:** 01132 618045
Huddersfield **Tel:** 01484 422523
York **Tel:** 01904 789115

■ LIVERPOOL

Diocese Contact: **Jo Fenton**
Tel: 01928 733647
E-mail: jo.fenton@btinternet.com

Liverpool, Conference Centre at LACE, Croxteth Drive, Sefton Park, Liverpool. L17 1AA **Tel:** 0800 389 3801

Southport, Parenting 2000, Mornington Road, Southport, Merseyside **Tel:** 01704-567666

Warrington, 9 Museum Street, Warrington, Cheshire. WA1 1JA (Centre & Appts) **Tel:** 01925- 635448

■ MENEVIA

Diocese Contact: **Jean Williams**
Tel: 01792 701189
E-mail: jeancwill@talktalk.net

Swansea, c/o The Presbytery, 9 Promenade Terrace, Mumbles, Swansea SA3 4DS **Tel:** 0800 389 3801

■ MIDDLESBROUGH

Diocese Contact: **Basia Zalewska-Wilson**
Tel: 01287 203846
E-mail: basia_zalewska@hotmail.com

Cleveland, John Paul II Centre, 55 Grange

Road, Middlesbrough TS1 5AU (Centre & Appts) **Tel:** 0191-232 0342

■ **NORTHAMPTON**
Diocese Contact: **Pip Wells**
Tel: 01603 478134
E-mail: apipwells@gmail.com

Milton Keynes, City Counselling Centre, 320 Saxon Gate West, Central Milton Keynes, MK9 2ES (Centre & Appts) **Tel:** 01908-696606

Northampton, 22 Park Avenue North, Northampton NN3 2HS (Centre & Appts) **Tel:** 0800-389 3801

South Bucks, The Priory Centre, 11 Priory Road, High Wycombe HP13 6SL **Tel:** 01494-525875

■ **NOTTINGHAM**
Diocese Contact: **Wendy Edwards**
Tel: 01636 814106
E-mail: cjedwards34@btinternet.com

Nottingham/Derby, 4 Oxford Street, Nottingham, NG1 5BH (Centre & Appts) **Tel:** 0800-389 3801 Also covers Leicestershire, Rutland.

Lincolnshire North, The Presbytery, Laughton Way, Ermine Estate, Lincoln LN2 2HE **Tel:** 0800 389 3801 Covers: Lincoln, Louth, Gainsborough, Brigg, Scunthorpe, Grimsby.

■ **PLYMOUTH**
Diocese Contact: **Paul Henley**
Tel: 01626 872626
E-mail: susanpaul.henley@hotmail.co.uk

South West, The Mount, Teignharvey, Newton Abbot, Devon TQ12 4RS **Tel:** 0800 389 3801

■ **PORTSMOUTH**
Diocese Contact: **Gerry Johnson**
Tel: 02392 463989
E-mail: oakmead@ntlworld.com

Bournemouth, CAB Office, Town Hall, Bournemouth BH2 6DY **Tel:** 0800 389 3801

North East Hants, c/o St Joseph's Parish Centre, Queen Road, Aldershot, Hants (Centre & Appts) **Tel:** 0800-389 3801

Portsmouth, St John's Catholic Church, Edinburgh Road, Portsmouth PO1 3HG **Tel:** 0800-389 3801

Reading, Loddon Vale Practice, Hurricane Way, Woodley, Reading RG5 4UX (Centre & Appts) **Tel:** 0118-946 2529

Southampton, 44 May Tree Close, Winchester, Hants SO22 4JE **Tel:** 0800-389 3801

■ **SALFORD**
Diocese Contact: **Peter Dawson**
Tel: 0161 761 6180
E-mail: pedaw@brandle.demon.co.uk

Greater Manchester, Clitherow House, Lower Chatham Street, All Saints, Manchester M15 6BY (Centre & Appts) **Tel:** 0800-389 3801 Also covers: Bolton, Oldham, Rochdale, Wigan.

■ **SHREWSBURY**
Diocese Contact: **Margaret Kay**
Tel: 01270 626278
E-mail: margaretkay1@aol.com

South & Mid Cheshire, Eaton House, Eaton Street, Crewe, Cheshire CW2 7EG (Centre & Appts) **Tel:** 01270-879911

Stockport, Newbridge House, 28 Tamworth Street, Stockport SK1 2PB **Tel:** 0800-389 3801

Trafford, 305 Manchester Road, West Timperley, Altrincham, WA14 5PH (Centre & Appts) **Tel:** 0800 389 3801

■ **SOUTHWARK**
Diocese Contact: **Patrick Bentham**
Tel: 020 8690 7243
E-mail: jcpb@doctors.org.uk

Blackheath, 5 Cresswell Park, Blackheath, London SE3 9RD (Centre & Appts) **Tel:** 0208-297 0883

Croydon, Purley Cross, 12A Brighton Road, Purley CR8 5BS **Tel:** 0800-389 3801

Medway Towns, The White House, Riverside, Chatham, Kent ME4 4SL (Centre & Appts) **Tel:** 0800 389 3801

Wimbledon, Guild House, Worple Road, London SW19 4EF (Centre & Appts) **Tel:** 0800-389 3801

■ **WREXHAM**
Diocese Contact:

Wrexham, St Joseph of Chamberry Convent, Derby Road, Wrexham, Clwyd, LL13 8EA (Centre & Appts) **Tel:** 01978-351795

■ **GIBRALTAR**

Gibraltar Centre, 215 Main Road, Gibraltar **Tel:** 010 350 71717

WORLDWIDE MARRIAGE ENCOUNTER ENGLAND AND WALES

A movement of couples, priests and religious committed to the renewal of the Church through the sacraments of Matrimony and Holy Orders. We offer weekends for married couples and for priests and religious to help them develop an even deeper appreciation of their vocation. Similar weekends are available for engaged couples giving them the opportunity to evaluate their future lives together.

For more information contact: *National Executive Team:* **Gary and Kay Johnson,** Little Hollies, Tenbury Road, Clee Hill, Nr Ludlow Shropshire SY8 3NE
E-mail: littlehollies@btopenworld.com
Website: www.wwme.org.uk

YOUTH WORK PROVISION

CATHOLIC YOUTH SERVICES

The executive youth work agency of the Bishops' Conference.

Episcopal President: **Bishop Ambrose Griffiths OSB**
Director: **Miss Helen Bardy**
39 Eccleston Square, London SW1V 1BX
Tel: 020-7901 4870 **Fax:** 020-7901 4873 **E-mail:** cys@cbcew.org.uk

CATHOLIC ASSOCIATION OF YOUTH MINISTERS AND ADVISERS

Chair: Rebecca Hughes
Department for Formation, Newman House, Wonford Road, Exeter, EX2 4PF
Tel: 01392-671320 **Fax:** 01392-671319 **E-mail:** rebecca@plymouth-diocesan-office.org.uk

DIOCESAN YOUTH SERVICES

■ ARUNDEL AND BRIGHTON
Ray Mooney (Diocesan Youth Office), Christian Education Centre, 4 Southgate Drive, Crawley, West Sussex RH10 6RP
Tel: 01293-612299 **Fax:** 01293-616945
E-mail: ray.mooney@dabnet.org

■ BIRMINGHAM
Team Manager: **Maria Bracken,** BCYS, Don Bosco House, Coventry Road, Coleshill, West Midlands B46 3ED
Tel: 01675-467887 **Fax:** 01675-466909
E-mail: maria.bracken@bcys.co.uk

■ BRENTWOOD
Director: **Mrs Sarah Beresford,** Walsingham House, Lionel Road, Canvey Island, Essex SS8 9DE **Tel:** 01268-696610
E-mail: sarah@walsinghamhouse.org
Website: www.walsinghamhouse.org
Training and Resources Director:
Mrs Teresa Carvallo
E-mail: teresa@bcys.net
Events Manager: **Mrs Sarah Barber,** The Youth Office, Cathedral House, Ingrave Road, Brentwood, Essex CM15 8AT
Tel: 01277-265286 **Fax:** 01277-265261
E-mail: sarah@bcys.net
Website: www.bcys.net

■ CARDIFF
Rev Martin Donnelly (Chair Youth Task Group). 277 Cowbridge Road West, Ely Cardiff CF5 1JB **Tel:** 029-20-591503
E-mail: davemdon@aol.com

■ CLIFTON
Diocesan Youth Officer, Alexander House, Pennywell Road, Bristol BS5 0TX
Tel: 0117-902 5594 **Fax:** 0117-902 5520
E-mail: clifton.cys@cliftondiocese.com

■ EAST ANGLIA
Hamish McQueen, Director of Youth Service, The White House, 21 Upgate, Poringland, Norwich NR14 7SH
Tel: 01508-494833
E-mail: dys@east-angliadiocese.org.uk

■ HALLAM
Mrs Judi Shimmell (Diocesan Co-ordinator for Ministry to Young People). Hallam CYM, St Charles Street, Sheffield S9 3WU
Tel: 0114-256 6460 **Fax:** 0114-256 2673
Judi Shimmell Tel: 0114-256 6464
E-mail: jshimmell@hallam-diocese.com
Website: www.hallam-diocese.com/youth

■ HEXHAM AND NEWCASTLE
Rev Dermott Donnelly (Director) Diocesan Youth Village, Allensford, Co

Durham DH8 9BA **Tel:** 01207-592244 **Fax:** 01207-592245

■ **LANCASTER**
Sean McMahon (Diocesan Youth Officer) Pastoral Centre, Balmoral Road, Lancaster LA1 3BT **Tel:** 01524-596063 **Fax:** 01524-596064 **E-mail:** sean.mcmahon@lancasterrcdiocese.org.uk **Website:** www.lancastercys.com

■ **LEEDS**
Rev Martin Kelly (Diocesan Youth Chaplain), **Miss Anna Cowell** (Diocesan Youth Officer)
Diocese of Leeds Youth Service, 62 Headingley Lane, Leeds LS6 2BX **Tel:** 0113-261 8058 **Fax:** 0113-261 8035 **E-mail:** dolys@leeds-diocese.org.uk

■ **LIVERPOOL**
Animate Youth Ministries, Lowe House, Crab Street, St Helens WA10 2BE
Tel: 01744 740460
Website: www.animateyouth.org
Rev Stephen Pritchard (*Director*)
Tel: 01744 740465
E-mail: s.pritchard@rcaolp.co.uk
John Biggins (*Adviser for the Formation of Young People*). **Tel:** 01744 740463
E-mail: j.biggins@rcaolp.co.uk
Maria Pleydell (*Team Leader*)
Tel: 01744 740462
E-mail: m.pleydell@rcaolp.co.uk

■ **MENEVIA**
Rev Teyron Williams, Director of Youth Services, The Presbytery, St Benedict, 41 Pontydardawe Road, Clydach, Swansea SA6 5NG **Tel:** 01792-842244

■ **MIDDLESBROUGH**
Rev John Paul Leonard, (Diocesan Youth Officer). The Curial Offices, 50a The Avenue, Linthorpe, Middlesbrough TS5 6QT **Tel/Fax:** 01642-593686 **E-mail:** youthoffice@dioceseofmiddlesbrough.co.uk

■ **NORTHAMPTON**
Avril Baigent (Youth Ministry Co-ordinator)
Liz Clarke (Office Administrator)
Northampton Youth Ministry Office, Ker Anna Centre, Aylesbury Road, Princes Risborough HP27 0JN **Tel:** 01844-273337 **Fax:** 01844-273338 **E-mail:** info@nymo.org **Website:** www.nymo.org

■ **NOTTINGHAM**
Fr Joe Wheat (Diocesan Youth Officer). The Briars Residential Youth Centre, Crich Common, Crich, Matlock, Derbyshire DE4 5BW
Tel: 01773-852044 **Fax:** 01773-852968
E-mail: fr.joe@thebriars.co.uk
Website: www.ndcys.com

■ **PLYMOUTH**
Rebecca Hughes (Co-ordinator for Youth Ministry), Department of Formation, Newman House, Wonford Road, Exeter EX2 4PF **Tel:** 01392-671324 **Fax:** 01392-671319 **E-mail:** rebecca@plymouth-diocesan-office.org.uk

■ **PORTSMOUTH**
Diocesan Advisor for Youth. Dept for Evangelisation and Catechesis, Park Place Pastoral Centre, Winchester Road, Wickham, Hampshire PO17 5HA
Tel: 01329-834677 **Fax:** 01329-833452
E-mails: youth@portsmouth-dio.org.uk smeads@portsmouth-dio.org.uk

■ **SALFORD**
Theresa Davies (Diocesan Youth Officer – Greater Manchester), 5 Gerald Road, Pendleton, Salford M6 6DL
Tel: 0161-736 1421 **Fax:** 0161-745 9708
E-mail: youth@salforddiocese.org
Robert Beardsworth (Diocesan Youth Officer – Lancashire), Mount Carmel High School, Wordsworth Road, Accrington, Lancs BB5 0LU **Tel/Fax:** 01254-395650
E-mail: bobbeardsworth@hotmail.com

■ **SHREWSBURY**
Director: **David Fitton.**
Diocese of Shrewsbury Youth, Saint Ambrose's Church, Clover Avenue, Adswood, Stockport SK3 8QA
Tel: 0161-480 8065 **Mbl:** 07790 509604
E-mail: youth@dioceseofshrewsbury.org
Website: www.dioceseofshrewsbury.org

■ **SOUTHWARK**
Johnny Toryusen (Director of Youth Services); **Tom Hay** (Diocesan Youth Officer – Schools); St Vincent's Residential Centre, Castle Road, Tankerton, Whistable, Kent CT5 2DY **E-mail:** swkcys@aol.com
To be appointed (Diocesan Youth Officer – Parishes). **Website:** www.scys.org.uk

■ **WESTMINSTER**
Mgr Vladimir Felzmann,
(Diocesan Youth Chaplain).
All Saints Pastoral Centre, Shenley Lane, London Colney, Hertfordshire AL2 1AF
Tel: 01727-822010 **Fax:** 01727-822927
E-mail: vladimirf@compuserve.com

■ **WREXHAM**
Sr Helen M Randles LSU
(Chair of Youth Commission).
The Convent, St David's Lane, Mold,

Flintshire, North Wales CH7 1LH
Tel: 01352-700121

RESIDENTIAL YOUTH CENTRES

(By Diocesan location)

■ **BIRMINGHAM**
Alton Castle, Castle Hill, Alton ST10 4TT
Tel/Fax: 01538-703224
Director: **Rev Philip Gay**
Soli House, Mill Lane Stratford-upon-Avon, Warks CV37 6BJ **Tel/Fax:** 01789-267011
Director: **Fr Bill Wilton**

■ **BRENTWOOD**
Walsingham House Residential Youth Centre, Lionel Road, Canvey Island, Essex SS8 9DH **Tel:** 01268-515970
Director: **Mrs Sarah Beresford**
E-mail: sarah@walsinghamhouse.org
Website: www.walsinghamhouse.org

■ **EAST ANGLIA**
St Centre, The Towers, Buckden, St Neots, Cambs PE18 9TA
Tel: 01480-810344 **Fax:** 01480-811918
Director: **Rev Paul Smyth**

■ **LANCASTER**
Castlerigg Manor, Manor Brow, Keswick, Cumbria CA12 4AR
Tel: 01768-772711 **Fax:** 01768-775302
Director: **Rev Peter Stanton.**
E-mail: castleriggmanor@hotmail.com
Website: www.castleriggmanor.co.uk

■ **LEEDS**
Myddelton Grange, Youth Retreat Centre, Langbar Road, Ilkley, West Yorkshire LS29 0EB **Tel:** 01943-607887
Director: **Rev Francis Smith**
Website: info@myddletongrange.org.uk

■ **NOTTINGHAM**
The Briars Residential Youth Centre, Crich Common, Matlock, Derbyshire DE4 5BW
Tel: 01773-852044. **Fax:** 01773-852968
E-mail: bookings@thebriars.co.uk
Director: **Fr Joe Wheat**
Email: fr.joe@thebriars.co.uk
Programme Leaders: **Mrs Claire Butler, Mr Tom Baptist**
Centre Manager: **Mrs Helen Aldridge**

■ **PORTSMOUTH**
Park Place, Winchester Road, Wickham, Fareham, Hampshire PO17 5HA
Tel: 01329-833043
St Cassian Residential Centre, Wallington Road, Kintbury, Hungerford, Berks RG17 9SR **Tel:** 01488-658267
Fax: 01488-657292
E-mail: kintbury@aol.com
Website: www.kintbury.org

■ **SHREWSBURY**
Savio House Residential Centre, Ingersley Road, Bollington, Macclesfield, Cheshire SK10 5RW
Tel: 01625-560724 **Fax:** 01625-560221
E-mail: saviooffice@saviohouse.org.uk
Website: www.salesians.org.uk
Director: **Hugh Preston.**
Retreat Team Leader: **Jessica Wilkinson.**

■ **SOUTHWARK**
St Vincent's Residential Centre, Castle Road, Tankerton, Whistable, Kent CT5 2DY
Tel: 01227-272900 **Fax:** 01227-282384
Catherine Jones (Programme Co-ordinator), assisted by a small team of volunteers **E-mail:** scys@scys.org.uk
Website: www.scys.org.uk

■ **WESTMINSTER**
SPEC Centre, All Saints Pastoral Centre, London Colney, St Albans, Hertfordshire AL2 1AF **Tel:** 01727-828888 **Fax:** 01727-822927 **E-mail:** spec@rcdow.org.uk
Website: www.spec-centre.org.uk
Directors: **Sandra and David Satchell, Ann O'Sullivan, Mike Donohue.**
Southwell House Youth Project, 39 Fitzjohn's Avenue, London NW3 5JT
Tel: 020-7435 8534 **Fax:** 020-7435 9133
Director: **Rev Paul Hamill SJ**
E-mail: shyp@btinternet.com

NATIONAL YOUTH ASSOCIATIONS AND MOVEMENTS

■ **IMPACT!**
Headquarters: St Joseph's, off St Joseph's Grove, London NW4 4TY
Tel: 020-8203 6290 **Fax:** 020-8203 6291
E-mail: ycwworkers@aol.com
Website: www.ycwimpact.com
Young Christian Workers.
Nat. Headquarters: Young Christian Workers, St Joseph's, Watford Way, London NW4 4TY
Tel: 020-8 203 6290 **Fax:** 020-8 203 6291
E-mail: ycwworkers@aol.com

■ **VOCATIONS GROUP**
Chair: **Sr Camilla Oberding**
Tel: 01277-373848
Mbl: 07931-795769
Email: info@vocationsgroup.org.uk
Website: www.vocationsgroup.org.uk

■ **YOUTH 2000**
Managing Director: **Charles Connor**
National Office: 15 Church Street, Wetherby, W. Yorkshire LS22 6LP
Tel: 01937 582200 **Fax:** 01937 582999
E-mail: info@youth2000.org
Website: www.youth2000.org

■ **London:**
Covent Garden: Corpus Christi Church, Maden Lane; Wednesday 7pm
Contact: **Annette, Tel:** 07985 213635
E-mail: youth2000_london@hotmail.com

Croydon: St Mary's Catholic Church, 70 Wellesley Road; Tuesday 7.30pm
Contact: **Alex, Tel 0208 688 1857**
E-mail: Y2Kcroydon@hotmail.co.uk

East Ham: St Michael's Church, 21 Tilbury Road, East Ham; Wednesday 7pm
Contact: **Joel, Tel:** 07944 954 360
E-mail: jam173002@yahoo.co.uk

Kingston/Surbiton: St. Raphael's Catholic Church, Portsmouth Road, Kingston-upon-Thames; Thursday 7pm
Contact: **Chris** or **Maria, Tel:** 020 8390 1174
E-mail: 6byrne@onetel.com
Kennington/Vauxhall: 367 Kennington Lane; Tueday 7.30pm
Contact: **Vincent, Tel:** 07960 103 470
E-mail: kulvchill@yahoo.com

Kew Gardens/Richmond: Our Lady of Loreto and St Winefride Church, Leyborne Park, Richmond; Sunday 7pm
Contact: **Tom, Tel:** 07711 434 176
E-mail: thomas.flintoff@barcap.com

Lewisham: St Saviours Church, 175 Lewisham High Street; Monday 7.30pm
Contact: **Henrietta, Tel:** 07947 194531
E-mail: hionwordi@hotmail.com

Barnet: Mary Immaculate and St Gregory the Great, Union Street, Barnet; Wednesday 7.30pm (except 1st Wed of mth)
Contact: **Tamara, Tel:** 07984 187799
E-mail: youth2000barnett@aol.com

Edmonton: Most Precious Blood and St Edmunds, 115 Hertford Street, Edmonton; Monday 7.30pm
Contact: **Daniel, Tel:** 07707 314793
E-mail: danelcal@yahoo.co.uk

■ **South East**
Guildford: St Joseph's, Eastgate Gardens; Monthly 8pm
Contact: **Dorothy, Tel:** 01428 645265
E-mail: dotty_monkey@hotmail.com

Horley: English Martyr's RC Church, 4 Vicarage Lane; Tuesday 7.30pm
Contact: **Luis, Tel:** 07707 121958
E-mail: fatboyluis@hotmail.com

Brighton: 22 Millcroft, Westdene, Brighton; Wednesday 8pm
Contact: **Chris, Tel:** 0127 355 1577
E-mail: cdrmagpie@ntlworld.com

■ **South West**
Bristol: St Mary-on-the-Quay, Colston Avenue; Wednesday 7pm
Contact: **Merv, Tel:** 07932 111451
E-mail: youth2000bristol@yahoo.com

■ **Midlands:**
Birmingham: Newman House University Catholic Chaplaincy, 29 Harrisons Road, Edgbaston; Thursday 8pm
Contact: **Michael, Tel:** 01213-215082
E-mail: michaelpuljic@hotmail.com

Cambridge: Lady Margaret Beaufort Institute, 12 Grange Road; Fortnightly during term time 7pm
Contact: **Nicole,**
E-mail: nc309@cam.ac.uk@yahoo.co.uk

Coventry: St. Elisabeth's RC Church, Eld Road; Monday 6.30pm
Contact: **Vivien, Tel:** 07792 552960

Northampton: Daughters of the Holy Spirit Convent, 103 Harlestone Road; Weds 8pm
Contact: **Frances, Tel:** 01604-636033
E-mail: franceshooper@btinternet.com

Lincoln: The Sisters of Providence, The Mount, Wragby Road; Wednesday 7pm
Contact: **Emily** or **Ed Tel:** 01437 667125

■ **North West**
Preston: Ladyewell, The Shrine of Our Lady and the Martyrs, Fernyhalgh Lane, Fulwood Weekly - first 3 Suns of each month 7-9pm
Contact: **Fr Philip Connor**
Tel: 01772 725 193
E-mail: philipconner@hotmail.com

■ **North East**
Stockton-on-Tees: St Patrick's, Glenfield Rd, Fairfields; Monthly 7.30pm
Contact: **Lorraine, Tel:** 01642-559466
E-mail: kathleen.clark@stmarys-sfc.ac.uk

Doncaster: St Peter in Chains Parish, Chequer Road; Fornightly 7.30pm
Contact: **Lee, Tel:** 07970 246368
E-mail: lee.marshall@benoy.com

■ **Wales**
Cardiff: Catholic Chaplaincy, Cardiff University, 62 Park Place; Tuesday 7pm
Contact: **Madeleine,**
E-mail: madeleinejeremy@hotmail.com

■ **Jersey**
St Aubin: Sacred Heart Church, La Neuve Route, St Aubin; 1st Wednesday 6.30pm
Contact: **Mary, Tel:** 07797 742767
E-mail: pastoralservices@hotmail.com

VOLUNTARY WORK OPPORTUNITIES FOR YOUNG PEOPLE

■ **Animate Youth Ministries**
(Youth service of the Archdiocese of Liverpool). Lowe House, Crab Street, St Helen WA10 2BE **Tel:** 01744-740460
Website: www.animateyouth.org
Type of Work: Community Living, School Missions, Day Retreats, Residential Work, Peer Training, Pilgrimages, Youth Events, Local Church Communities.
Minimum Age: 18 years.
Average length of service: 1 year (accredited training provided).

■ **ATD Fourth World**
48 Addington Square, London SE5 7LB
E-mail: atd@atd-uk.org
Website: www.atd-uk.org
Type of Work: Community work, family support, residential volunteering in UK and overseas.
Minimum Age: 18 years.
Average length of service: 3months+.

■ **The Briars**
Fr Joe Wheat.
The Briars Residential Youth Centre, Crich Common, Derbyshire DE4 5BW
Tel: 01773 852044
E-mail: fr.joe@thebriars.co.uk
Type of Work: Youth, Retreat Centre, Evangelisation, Community Living. Includes Reach4, Outreach Team working in parishes and schools in the Diocese of Nottingham.
Minimum Age: 18 Years (Outreach 19 yrs)
Average length of service: 1 year.

■ **Castlerigg Manor**
Rev Peter Stanton.
Castlerigg Manor, Manor Brow, Keswick, Cumbria CA12 4AR
Tel: 01768 772711 **Fax:** 01768 775302
E-mail: teamleader@castleriggmanor.co.uk
Website: www.castleriggmanor.co.uk
Type of Work: Residential youth work, Community living, faith sharing.
Minimum Age: 18 Years.
Average length of service: 1 years.

■ **Catholic Institute for International Relations**
Unit 3 Canonbury Yard, 190a New North Road, London SW9 9JF **Tel:** 020-7737 3237
Type of Work: Lay Missionaries.
Minimum Age: 18 Years.
Average length of service: 2 years.

■ **Christians Abroad**
1 Stockwell Green, London SW9 9HP

■ **Claret Centre**
The Towers, High Street, Buckden, St Neots PE19 5TA **Christopher Newman (CMF)**
Type of Work: Youth/retreat centre, community living, overseas missionary experience in Belize, Central America.
Minimum Age: 21.
Average length of service: 1 year.

■ **Columban Lay Missionaries**
28 Reddington Road, London NW3 7RH
Type of Work: Community Living, Faith sharing.
Minimum Age: 23 Years.
Average length of service: 3 years.

■ **Corrymeela Community Volunteering Development Co-ordinator**
Corrymeela Community, Ballycastle, Co Antrim, BT54 6QU
Tel: Ballycastle (028) 2076 2626
Type of Work: Community Living, Residential Centre.
Minimum Age: 18 Years.
Average length of service: Flexible.

■ **Jesuit Volunteer Community**
4th Floor, Swan Buildings, 20 Swan Street, Manchester M4 5JW **Tel:** 0161-832 6888
Fax: 0161 832 6958
E-mail: admin@jesuitvolunteers-uk.org
Website: www.jjvcbritain.org
Ages: Aimed at those 18-35 years.
Type of Work: Offers full time fully funded one year volunteering programme, combining social justice, living in Community and Ignatian spirituality.

■ **Jesuit Volunteer Service**
St Wilfred's Enterprise Centre, Royce Road, Hulme, Manchester M15 5BJ
Tel: 0161-226 6717
Type of Work: Community Living, work in projects for the marginalised in Great Britain
Minimum Age: 18 Years.
Average length of service: 1 year.

■ **L'Arche**
10 Briggate, Silsden, Keighley, West Yorkshire BD20 9JT.
Tel: 01535-656186
Type of Work: Community Living.

■ **Lancaster Diocesan Voluntary Youth Ministry Scheme**
Miss Anne Kennedy. St Joseph's Presbytery, Slyne Road, Lancaster LA1 2HU
Tel/Fax: 01524-848182
E-mail: LancasterDYS@aol.com

■ **Lasallian Developing World Projects**
Br John Deeney FSC.

140 Banbury Road, Oxford OX2 7BP
Tel: 01865 559933
E-mail: ldwpuk@hotmail.com
Type of Work: Team projects overseas. Manual work; work with children
Minimum Age: 18 Years on departure.
Average length of service: 5 weeks

■ **Lay Missionary Volunteer**
Sr Margaret Dobbin.
Sisters of the Sacred Heart of Jesus and Mary, 100 Hassett Road, London E9 5SJ
Tel: 020-8985 3047
Type of Work: Lay Missionary.
Minimum Age: 18 Years.
Average length of service: 1 year.

■ **Leonard Cheshire Foundation**
26/29 Maunsel Street, London NW3 7RH
Tel: 020-7794 8131
Type of Work: Care for sick and disabled.
Minimum Age: 18 Years.
Average length of service: 3 months.

■ **Myddelton Grange Retreat House**
Rev Nigel Polland.
Longbar Road, Ilkley, West Yorkshire LS29 0EB **Tel:** 01943-607887 **Fax:** 01943-885470
Website: myddletongrange@onetel.net.uk
Type of Work: Residential Youth Work, Retreats
Minimum Age: 21 Years.
Average length of service: 2 years.

■ **Order of Malta Volunteers.**
Chairman: **Sebastian Bailey Esq.**
Secretariat: 23 Waldemar Avenue, Fulham, London SW6 5LN **Tel:** 020-7731 3582
Type of Work: promoting pilgrimages and holidays for the handicapped, working with the London homeless and relief work worldwide.
Minimum Age: 17 years.

■ **St Cassian's Centre**
Director: St Cassian's Centre, Kintbury, Hungerford, Berkshire RG17 9SR
Tel: 01488 658267
E-mail: kintbury@aol.com
Website: www.kintbury.org
Type of Work: Youth, Retreat Centre, Community Living.
Minimum Age: 18 Years.
Average length of service: 1 year.

■ **Salesian Volunteers - BOVA**
Rev Martin Coyle
Salesians of Don Bosco, Savio House, Ingersley Road, Bollington,Cheshire SK10 5RW **Tel:** 01625-560724
Email: bova@salesianyouthministry.com
Website: www.boscovolunteeraction.co.uk
Type of Work: Learning through action, serving the young and poor alongside Salesian Communities around the world.
Minimum Age: 18.
Average length of service: 1 month to 2 years.

■ **Savio House**
Rev Martin Coyle
Salesians of Don Bosco, Savio House, Ingersley Road, Bollington,Cheshire SK10 5RW **Tel:** 01625-560405
Email: saviooffice@saviohouse.org.uk
Website: www.saviohouse.org.uk
Type of Work: Youth work, Retreat centre.
Minimum Age: 18.
Average length of service: 1 year.

■ **Youth Discipleship Base**
Sawyers Hall Lane, Brentwood, Essex CM15 9BX
Tel: 01277 215011 **Fax:** 01277 234401
Type of Work: A centre for Youth Evangelisation and Discipleship within a community context.
Email: youthmembers@sioncommunity.org.uk
Website: www.sionyouth.org.uk

■ **Simon Community**
129 Malden Road, London NW5 4HS
Tel: 020-7585 6639/7482 0447
Type of Work: Social work with homeless, Community Living.
Minimum Age: 19 Years.
Average length of service: 6 months.

■ **Soli House Youth Retreat Centre**
Fr Bill Wilton.
Soli House Youth Retreat Centre, Mill Lane, Stratford on Avon CV37 6BJ
Tel: 01789 267011
E-mail: shyrc@hotmail.com
Type of Work: Youth, Retreat Centre, Community Living.
Minimum Age: 18 Years.
Average length of service: 1 year.

■ **Alton Castle Youth Retreat Centre**
Rev Philip Gay, **Tel:** 01583-703224

■ **SPEC**
Sandra and David Satchell.
SPEC Centre, All Saints Pastoral Centre, London Colney, Herts AL2 1AG
Tel: 01727-828888.
Type of Work: Youth, Residential retreat centre for young people and children, Community Living.
Minimum Age: 18 Years.
Average length of service: 1 year.
E-mail: spec@rcdow.org.uk
Website: spec@redow.org.uk

■ **Sue Ryder Care**
1st Floor, King's House, Kings Street, Sudbury, Suffolk CO10 2ED
Tel: 01787-314200
Type of Work: Various volunteering opportunities.
Minimum Age: 18 Years.

■ **Time For God**
2 Chester House, North Bank, 28 Pages Lane, Muswell Hill, London N10 1PP
Tel: 020-8883 1504 **Fax:** 020-8365 2471
E-mail: 100675.2702@compuserve.com
Type of Work: Christian Volunteering in the UK and abroad

■ **Vincentian Volunteers UK**
Director: **Sr Pauline Gaughan, DC,**
39 Marlesford Street, Liverpool, L6 6AX
Tel: 0151-261 0225 **E-mail:** director@vincentianvols.freeserve.co.uk
Website: vincentianvolunteers.org
Type of Work: A gap year in the UK, Young people 18-30 working with people who are poor, while living in small communities, in the spirit of St Vincent de Paul.
Minimum Age: 18 Years.
Average length of service: Programme runs from September to July.
Website: www.vincentianvolunteers.org

■ **Voluntary Service Overseas**
317 Putney Bridge Road, London SW15 2PN
Type of Work: International Development.
Minimum Age: 18 Years.
Average length of service: 2 to 24 months.

■ **Volunteer Missionary Movement**
University Chaplaincy Building, Mount Pleasant, Liverpool L3 5TQ
Tel: 0151-709 7676
E-mail: alice@vmmuk.freeserve.co.uk
Type of Work: Community Service.
Minimum Age: 16 Years.
Average length of service: Flexible.

■ **Walsingham House**
Lionel Road, Canvey Island, Essex SS8 9DE
Tel: 01268-515970
Website: www.walsinghamhouse.org
Type of Work: Youth, Retreat Centre.
Minimum Age: 18 years.
Average length of service: 1 year.

■ **Worth Abbey Lay Community**
The Co-ordinator.
St Bruno's, Worth Abbey, Crawley, West Sussex RH10 4SB
Tel: 01342-710303 **Fax:** 01342-710301
E-mail: worth.abbeylc@ukonline.co.uk

THE CHURCH AND THE MEDIA

■ CATHOLIC COMMUNICATIONS NETWORK

39 Eccleston Square, London SW1V 1BX
Tel: 020-7901 4800 **Fax:** 020-7901 4821
Out of Hours Mobile: 07983 707043
E-mail: ccn@cbcew.org.uk

Director News and Information:
Alexander DesForges
Tel: 020-7901 4807
E-mail: alexander.desforges@cbcew.org.uk

Senior Media Officer:
Maggie Doherty
Tel: 020-7901 4802
E-mail: maggie.doherty@cbcew.org.uk

Webmaster: **James Abbott**
Tel: 020-7901 4804
E-mail: james.abbott@cbcew.org.uk

Office Manager and Media Assistant:
Johanna van den Broeke
Tel: 020-7901 4800 **E-mail:**
johanna@cbcew.org.uk

■ STRATEGIC COMMUNICATIONS COMMITTEE

Chairman:
Rt Rev John Arnold

Vice-Chairman:
Rev Wilfrid McGreal

■ MEDIA ADVISERS IN THE DIOCESES

■ ARUNDEL & BRIGHTON

Bishop's Information Officer:
Refer to: **Mgr T Barry:** DABCEC, 40 Southgate Drive, Crawley, West Sussex
Tel: 01293-55666 **Fax:** 01293-616945

■ BIRMINGHAM

Archbishop's Press Secretary & Press Secretary to the Archdiocese: **Mr Peter Jennings** FRPSL, FRGS, MIPR, 47 Regent Road, Harborne Birmingham B17 9JU
Tel: 0121-427 2780 **Fax:** 01210428 2777
Mbl: 07967-639556
E-mail: imc@peterjennings.co.uk

■ BRENTWOOD

Diocesan Communications Officer:
Rev John Harvey, St Edmund of Canterbury, 9 Trap's Hill, Loughton, Essex IG10 1SZ
Tel: 020-8508 3492 **Fax:** 020-8532 0138
E-mail: jjh152@aol.com

Press Officer: **Mrs Mary Huntington**
Tel: 01245-227518
E-mail: mary@huntingtonhome.plus.com

Radio stations:
Active FM 107.5 (Havering)
Anglia Community Radio (Cable)
BBC Essex FM 95.3 & 103.5
Breeze MW 1359 & 1431
Chelmer FM 107.7 (Chelmsford)
Dream FM100 (Tendring)
Essex FM 102.6, 96.3 & 97.5
SGR FM 96.1 (Colchester)
TEN 17 FM 101.7 (Harlow)
(See also Westminster and Southwark for stations covering SW areas of Brentwood).

■ CARDIFF

Diocesan Information Officer:
Rev John Owen, University Chaplaincy, 62 Park Place, Cardiff CF10 3AS
Tel: 029-2022 9785 **Fax:** 029-2066 8197
E-mail: r-c-chaplincy@cardiff.ac.uk

■ CLIFTON

Diocesan Communication Officer: **Mr Tom Bigwood,** St Ambrose, North Road, Leigh Woods, Bristol BS8 3PW **Tel:** 0117-973 3072
E-mail: tom.bigwood@CliftonDiocese.com
Website: www.cliftondiocese.com

■ EAST ANGLIA

Diocesan Communication Officer:
Awaiting Appointment
For Information contact Bishop's Press Officer: **Rev Mark Hackeson,** The Whitehouse, 21 Upgate, Poringland, Norwich NR14 7SH **Tel:** 01508 492202
E-mail: office@east-angliadiocese.org.uk.uk

■ H M FORCES

Diocesan Communications Officer: **Major (Retd) Diana Wilson**, Bishop's Secretary, Wellington House, St Omer Barracks, Aldershot, Hants GU11 2BG **Tel:** 01252-348234 **E-mail:** BishopricForces-Secretary@mod.uk
Radio Stations: Local chaplains make contact as appropriate.

■ HALLAM

Diocesan Communication Officer: **Fr Mark McManus**. The Annunciation Presbytery, 2 Spencer Street, Chesterfield S40 4SD **Tel:** 01246-232686 **E-mail:** mgm1988@hotmail.com

■ HEXHAM & NEWCASTLE

Enquiries to: *Diocesan Communication officer:* The Bishop's Secretary, East Denton Hall, 800 West Road, Newcastle upon TYne NE5 2BJ **Tel:** 0191-228 0003 **Fax:** 0191-274 0432 **E-mail:** office@rcdhn.org.uk

TV station with adviser:
Tyne Tees TV: **Rev Michael Campion,** St Mary's Presbytery 1 Burn lane, Newton Aycliffe DL5 4HT **Tel:** 01325 313611

■ LANCASTER

Diocesan Communication Officer: **Rev Stephen Shield**, Cathedral House, Balmoral Road, Lancaster LA1 3BT **Tel:** 01524-384820

Radio stations with advisers:
BBC Radio Cumbria (Carlisle) **Mr Anthony Parrini,** Hamethwaite, Rockcliffe, Carlisle CA6 4AA **Tel:** 01288-674553

Independent Radio Stations:
Canon Stephen Shield, Cathedral House, Balmoral Road, Lancaster LA1 3BT **Tel:** 01253-297666
Rock FM (Preston); Magic 999 (Preston); The Wave (Blackpool); The Bay (Morecambe).

TV station with adviser:
BBC North-West: **Canon Stephen Shield,** (Address as above).
Border TV (Carlisle): **Canon Stephen Shield,** (Address as above).

■ LEEDS

Diocesan Communication Officer: **Mr John Grady.** Curial Offices, Hinsley Hall, 62 Headingley Lane, Leeds LS6 2BX **Tel:** 0113-261 8022 **Fax:** 0113-261 8035 **E-mail:** john.grady@dioceseofleeds.org.uk

■ LIVERPOOL

Diocesan Communication Officer: **Mr Peter Heneghan,** Centre for Evangelisation, Croxteth Drive, Sefton Park, Liverpool L17 1AA **Tel:** 0151-522 1007 **Fax:** 0151-522 1008 **E-mail:** p.heneghan@rcaol.co.uk

Radio stations with advisers:
BBC Radio Merseyside, Religious Advisory Panel: **Mgr John Devine.** St Joseph's Upholland, Lancashire WN8 0PZ **Tel:** 01695-625255
This station also has a Shrewsbury diocese adviser. Also Catholic member of religious programme team: **Peter Heneghan** (as above).
Manx Radio (Douglas Isle of Man) **Miss J A Ley.** The Nappin, Lezayre Road, Alen Duff, Ramsey, Isle of Man IM7 2AT **Tel:** 01624-813116

■ MENEVIA

Diocesan Communication Officer: **Rev Michael Burke,** School Rd Morriston, Swansea SA6 6HZ **Tel:** 01792-771053 **E-mail:** michael@w-burke.freeserve.co.uk

■ MIDDLESBROUGH

Diocesan Communication Officers:
Dr James Whiston. Diocesan Curia, 50a The Avenue, Linthorpe, Middlesbrough TS5 6QT **Tel:** 01642-850505 **Tel:** 01325-374870 (Evenings) **E-mail:** jim.whiston@btinternet.com
Rev Derek Turnham. St Joseph, 1 Tanton Road, Stokesley, Middlesbrough TS9 5HN **Tel:** 01642-710239 **E-mail:** stjosephstokesley@dioceseofmiddlesbrough.co.uk

Radio stations with advisers:
BBC Radio Tees (Middlesbrough), **Rev Gerard Robinson,** Sacred Heart Presbytery, 1 Park Road South, Middlesbrough TS5 6LD **Tel:** 01642-850113 **Fax:** 01642-852122 **E-mail:** stpatrickmbro@middlesbrough-diocese.org.uk

BBC Radio Humberside, (Hull), **Mr Tom Timpson,** 41 St Julian's Wells, Kirk Ella, Hull HU10 7AF **Tel:** 01482-653001
BBC Radio North Yorkshire, **Mrs Veronica Walmsley,** 35 Danebury Drive, York YO26 5EQ **Tel:** 01904-791289
Viking Radio, (Hull), **Mr Tom Timpson** (as above) Other local radio stations: DCO (as above)

■ NORTHAMPTON

Diocesan Communication Officer: **Rev David Barrett,** Bishop's House, Marriott Street, Northampton NN2 6AW **Tel:** 01604-715635 **E-mail:** chaplain@northamptondiocese.com

■ NOTTINGHAM

Diocesan Communication Officer:
Awaiting Appointment. c/o Bishop's Ho, 27 Cavendish Road East, The Park, Nottingham NG7 1BB **Fax:** 0115-947 4786

■ PLYMOUTH

Diocesan Communication Officer:
Michael Fay. 106 Steed Close, Paignton, Devon TQ4 7SP **Tel:** 01803-844539

Radio stations with advisers:
BBC Radio Cornwall, (Truro), **Canon Bede Davis**, St Mary's Presbytery, Killigrew Street, Falmouth, Cornwall TR11 3PR
Tel: 01326-312763
Two Counties Radio, (Bournemouth - See under Portsmouth Diocese).

■ PORTSMOUTH

Diocesan Communication Officer:
Mr Barry Hudd. 100 Enborne Road, Newbury RG14 6AN **Tel:** 07770 538693, **Fax:** 01635-44326
E-mail: bhudd@rcdp.org.uk

Radio stations with advisers:
BBC Radio Guernsey, (St Peter Port), **Rev Micheal Hore,** Ampthill House, Cordier Hill, St Peter Port, GY1 1JH
Tel: 01481-720196 **Fax:** 01481-711247
BBC Radio Jersey, (St Helier), **Canon Nicholas France**, 17 Val Plaisant, St Helier JE2 4TA
Tel: 01534-722992 **Fax:** 01534-618227
BBC Radio Solent, (Southampton), **Rev Simon Thomas,** 21 Gladys Avenue, North End, Portsmouth, Hants PO2 9AZ
Tel/Fax: 023-9266 0927
E-mail: raylyons@portsmouth-dio.org.uk
BBC Radio Berkshire/Oxford, **Mr Barry Hudd,** 100 Enborne Road, Newbury RG14 6AN **Tel:** 07770 538693 **Fax:** 01635-44326
E-mail: bhudd@portsmouth-dio.org.uk

TV stations with advisers:
BBC TV South: **Rt Rev Crispian Hollis,** Bishop's House, Edinburgh Road, Portsmouth, Hants PO1 3HG
Tel: 023-9282 0894 **Fax:** 023-9286 3086
E-mail: bishop@portsmouthdiocese.org.uk
Channel Television (Jersey): **Canon Nicholas France,** 17 Val Plaisant, St Helier JE2 4TA
Tel: 01534-722992 **Fax:** 01534-618227
Channel Television (Guernsey): **Rev Michael Hore**, Ampthill House, Cordier Hill, St Peter Port
Tel: 01481-720196 **Fax:** 01481-711247

■ SALFORD

Diocesan Communication Officer:
Rev Michael Walsh, St Paul's, 285 Stockport Road, Guide Bridge, Ashton-under-Lyne, Lancs OL7 0NT
Tel: 0161-330 2777 **Fax:** 0161-343 5595
E-mail: MWalsh1402@aol.com

Radio stations with advisers:
BBC GMR Contact: **Rev Michael Walsh,** (as above).

■ SHREWSBURY

Communications & Press Officer:
Rev John Joyce, St Vincent's, Tatton Street, Knutsford, Cheshire WA16 6HR
Tel: 01565-633040
E-mail: jjoycepat@aol.com

Radio stations with advisers:
BBC Radio Shropshire, (Shrewsbury), BBC Radio Merseyside, (Liverpool), GMR Radio, (Manchester) Signal Cheshire, All c/o DCO **Rev John Joyce.**
WABC Beacon, See Birmingham diocese,

■ SOUTHWARK

Diocesan Communications Officers:
Rev William Saunders, Archbishop's House, St. George's Road, Southwark, London SE1 6HX **Tel:** 020-7928 2495
Fax: 020-7928 7833
E-mail: aps@rcsouthwark.co.uk

Radio stations with advisers:
BBC Radio Kent, (Chatham), **Rev Wilfred McGreal, OCarm**, Whitefriars, Tanner Street, Faversham, Kent ME13 7JN
Tel: 01622- 717272
GLR, Capital Radio, & LBC. See Westminster diocese

■ WREXHAM

Diocesan Communication Officer: **Debbie Riley**, c/o Bishops House, Sontley Road, Wrexham LL13 7EW
E-mail: debbieriley@btinternet.com

CATHOLIC WEEKLY & PERIODICAL NEWSPAPERS

The Universe
Editor: **Joseph Kelly**
Gabriel Communications,
4th Floor, Landmark House, Station Road,
Cheadle Hulme, Cheshire SK8 7JH
Tel: 0161-488 1760 **Fax:** 0161-488 1701
Published by Gabriel Communications Ltd.

Catholic Herald
Editor: **Luke Coppen,**
Herald House, Lamb's Passage,
Bunhill Row, London EC1Y 8TQ
Tel: 020-7588 3101 020-7256 9728
Published by Herald Publishing Co.

The Catholic Times
Editor: **Kevin Flaherty**
Gabriel Communications,
4th Floor, Landmark House, Station Road,
Cheadle Hulme, Cheshire SK8 7JH
Tel: 0161-488 1760 **Fax:** 0161-488 1701
Published by Gabriel Communications Ltd.

Catholic Pictorial
Editor: **Peter Heneghan**
Media House, Mann Island, Pier Head,
Liverpool L3 1DG
Tel: 0151-236 2191 **Fax:** 0151-236 2216
Published by Mersey Mirror.

Catholic Omnibus
(Quarterly newspaper produced by
the National Board of Catholic Women)
Editor: **Mrs Angela Perkins**
12 Worsnall Road, Yarm, Cleveland
TS15 9DF **Tel/Fax:** 01642-791840
Published by Gabriel Communications Ltd.

DIOCESAN PUBLICATIONS

ARUNDEL & BRIGHTON
A & B News
Editor: **Miss Pauline Groves**
Diocesan Christian Education Centre,
4 Southgate Drive, Crawley,
West Sussex RH10 6RP
Tel: 01293-513052 **Fax:** 01293-616945
E-mail: abnews@dabnet.org
Published by Diocese Bellcourt Ltd.

BRENTWOOD
BRENTWOOD NEWS
Editors: **Jean & John Adshead**
Foxfield House, Potash Road, Billericay,
Essex CM11 1DJ
Tel: 01277-623470
E-mail: brentwoodnews@
foxfieldhouse.plus.com
Published by Diocese of Brentwood.

CARDIFF
CATHOLIC PEOPLE
Editor: **Rev John Owen**
Pastoral Resources Centre, 910 Newport
Road, Rumney, Cardiff CF3 4LL
Tel: 029-2036 0044 **Fax:** 029-2079 3172
E-mail: publications@rcadc.org
Published by Mersey Mirror.

EAST ANGLIA
OUR DIOCESAN FAMILY
Editor: **Patrick Byrne**
The White House, 21 Upgate, Poringland,
Norwich, NR14 7SH
Tel: **01508-492202**
Published by Bellcourt Ltd.

FORCES CATHOLIC NEWS
Editor: **Rev Paul Owens RAF**
c/o Principal Chaplain (RAF)
Tel: 01296 656910

HALLAM
HALLAM NEWS
The Editor, Hallam Pastoral Centre,
St Charles Street, Attercliffe, Sheffield
S9 3WU **Tel:** 0114-256 6406
Published by Bellcourt Ltd.

HEXHAM & NEWCASTLE
NORTHERN CROSS
Editor: **John Bailey**
St Joseph's Parish Centre
St Paul's Road, Hartlepool TS26 9EY
Tel: 01429-274305 **Fax:** 01429-274328
Tel: 01429-860660 (Out of Hours)
Email: norcross@btconnect.com

LANCASTER
THE VOICE
Editor: **Edwina Gillett.**
99 Commonside, Ansdell, Lytham St Annes
FY8 4DJ
Tel: 01253 736630 **Mbl:** 07969 967258
E-mail: voicenews@hotmail.co.uk
voiceletters@hotmail.co.uk
Website: www.thevoiceonline.org
Published by Trustees of the Roman
Catholic Diocese of Lancaster.

LEEDS
CATHOLIC POST
Editor: **John Grady,**

Hinsley Hall, 62 Headingley Lane,
Leeds LS6 2BX
Tel: 0113-261 8022 **Fax:** 0113-261 8035
E-Mail: john.grady@dioceseofleeds.org.uk
Published by Mersey Mirror.

■ **MENEVIA**
MENEVIA NEWS
Editor: **Arthur Meredith.**
Diocese of Menevia, Curial Office,
27 Convent Street, Swansea SA1 2BX
Tel: 01792-528213
E-mail: menevianews@ntlworld.com
Published by Bellcourt Ltd.

■ **MIDDLESBROUGH**
MIDDLESBROUGH CATHOLIC VOICE
Editorial Team, Curial Offices, 50a The Avenue, Linthorpe, Middlesbrough TS5 6QT
Tel: 01642-850505 **Fax:** 01642-851404
E-mail: catholicvoice@dioceseofmiddlesbrough.co.uk.
Published by T Snape & Co Ltd.

■ **NORTHAMPTON**
'THE VINE'
Editor: **Rev Paul Hardy**
Church of St Edward, Burchard Crescent, Shenley Church End, Milton Keynes, Buckinghamshire MK5 6DX
Tel/Fax: 01908-504771
News Editor: **Mrs Margaret Busby**
1 Bewcastle Close, Bedford MK41 8BQ
Tel/Fax: 01234-267016
E-mail: vine01@globalnet.co.uk

■ **NOTTINGHAM**
CATHOLIC NEWS
Editor: **John Clawson**
PO Box 8455, Newark, Notts NG23 5WX
Tel: 01636-613341 **Fax:** 01636-640543
E-mail: john@bellcourtltd.co.uk.

■ **PLYMOUTH**
CATHOLIC SOUTH WEST
Editor: **Michael Fay,** Rosary House, 27 Fore Street, Exeter EX1 2QJ
Published by Catholic South West Ltd.
Printed by The Northcliffe Press.

■ **PORTSMOUTH**
PORTSMOUTH PEOPLE
Editor: **Mrs Kathryn Turner**
PO Box 327, Eastleigh SO50 9QS
Tel/Fax: 022-8061 1730
E-mail: editor@portsmouth-dio.org.uk

■ **SHREWSBURY**
THE VOICE
(Shrewsbury Diocesan Catholic Voice)
Editor: **Deacon Basil Stephens.**
55 Church Road, West Kirby, Wirral CH48 0RN **Tel:** 0151-625 9963
E-mail: bms@@pctrain.demon.co.uk
Published by Gemini Print.

■ **WESTMINSTER**
WESTMINSTER RECORD
Editor: **Bishop John Arnold**
Archbishop's House, Ambrosden Avenue, London SW1P 1QJ
Deputy Editor: **Jo Siedlecka**
Tel: 020-7267 3616
E-mail: record@rcdow.org.uk
Published by Gabriel Communications Ltd

■ CATHOLIC MAGAZINES

■ **Catholic Life**
Editor: **Lynda Walker**
Gabriel Communications,
4th Floor, Landmark House, Station Road, Cheadle Hulme, Cheshire SK8 7JH
Tel: 0161-488 1760 **Fax:** 0161-488 1701
E-mail: lynda.walker@totalcatholic.com
Published by Gabriel Communications Ltd.

■ **The Tablet**
Editor: **Catherine Pepinster.**
1 King Street Cloisters, Clifton Walk, London W6 0QZ
Tel: 020-8748 8484 **Fax:** 020-8748 1550
Published by The Tablet Publishing Co. Ltd.

■ **Pastoral Review**
Editor: **Michael Hayes**
1 King Street Cloisters, Clifton Walk, London W6 0QZ
Tel: 020-8748 8484 **Fax:** 020-8748 1550
Published by The Tablet Publishing Co. Ltd.

CATHOLIC SOCIETIES
IN ENGLAND AND WALES

Organisations listed in this section must have the following characteristics:

1. A fundamental commitment to the teaching and practice of the Catholic Church, particularly as expressed by the documents of the Second Vatican Council and the Catechism of the Catholic Church.

2. A membership widely distributed in the area covered by the Catholic Dirctory of England and Wales, or an involvement in work properly described as being of national importance in these countries

Information regarding the criteria for entry in the this section, as laid down by the Bishops' Conference of England and Wales, may be found on the following Website:

www.catholic-ew.org.uk/resource/dir/index.htm

■ **ACHILLE RATTI CLIMBING CLUB**
Under the Patronage of the Bishop of Lancaster and the Bishop of Wrexham, The Achille Ratti Climbing Club is open to all, Catholic and non-Catholic, young and old, who have a genuine love of the hills and would like to go walking, climbing, biking, running, etc, in the company of like-minded people. We have well established properties in the Lake District and Wales. The following huts are maintained by the Club; 1. Dunmail Raise Hut, Raise Cottage, Grasmere, Cumbria *(for school or club parties).*
2. Bishop's Scale, Great Langdale, Cumbria, Chapel of Our Lady of the Snows. Accommodation for seventy.
3. Tyn Twr Bethesda, Caernarvonshire.
Chairman: **Michael Pooler**, Brandwood House, Royds Road, Rakehead, Bacup OL13 0PF *Hon Secretary:* **Ann McGonagle,** 133 Revidge Road, Blackburn BB2 6JB.
For membership forms and information about the huts, contact: **Sue Carter,** 214 Rochdale Road, Shaw, Oldham OL2 7JA
Website:
www.achille-ratti-climbing-club.co.uk

■ **ADVENT**
A support group of priests and religious who have resigned active ministry. ADVENT also provides confidential counselling and support to priests and religious uncertain of the future direction of their ministry.
Website: adventgroup.org.uk

■ **AFRICA-EUROPE FAITH AND JUSTICE NETWORK-UK (AEFJN-UK)**
We are an international group of more than 40 Catholic missionary congregations and societies who are working at grass roots level in Africa and in eleven European countries. Together we work towards the establishment of peace and the conditions required for a dignified livelihood for the people of Africa. Contact the Administrator: 33 Lyonsdown Road, New Barnet, Herts EN5 1JG **Tel/Fax:** 020-8449-9244
E-mail: aefjn.uk@btinternet.com

■ **ARCHCONFRATERNITY OF ST STEPHEN FOR ALTAR SERVERS**
The Archconfraternity of St Stephen exists to promote and encourge high standards of altar serving. Servers can be enrolled into the Guild with permission of their Parish Priest once they have been serving at least six months and made their First Communion. Please contact the Secretary for details on how a parish can be affiliated to the Guild.
National Director: **Rev Dennis Touw**
President: **Mr Michael Chute,**
PO Box 568, London WC1A 1YT.
Secretary: **Mr Michael O'Leary,**
PO Box 568, London WC1A 1YT.
E-mail: secretary@guildofststephen.org
Website: www.guildofststephen.org

■ **ASCENT MOVEMENT**
The ASCENT Movement (Vie Montante Internationale) aims to help Christians in their middle and later years in their spiritual growth, to encourage them to take up their responsibilities as members of the Church through Friendship, Spirituality and Mission. *National*

President: **Miss Margaret Snowdon;** *National Secretary:* **Mrs Marie Ryde,** 63 Dartmouth Road, Hendon, London NW4 3HY **Tel:** 020-8202 4930
E-mail: marieryde@btinternet.com
Website: www.ascentmovement.org.uk

■ **ASSOCIATION FOR THE PROPAGATION OF THE FAITH (APF)**
The APF ensures that every bishop in the new churches has the necessary funds to enable him to build churches and schools, to lead people to learn about Christ and build a better world. The APF 'red boxes' and the World Mission Sunday collection enable every diocese of this country to support the spreading of the Gospel in each of the 1,069 mission dioceses in the world. APF members play a vital role in helping to build up the Church through their prayers and offerings.
Tel: 020-7821 9755
E-mail: apf@missio.org.uk
Website: www.missio.org.uk

■ **ASSOCIATION OF BLIND CATHOLICS**
To enable persons with visual impairment to lead a fuller part in the life of the Church. The ABC offers a monthly Catholic Talking Newspaper and Daisy CD and cassette lending library of religious books for an annual subscription of £1. It also arranges retreats and gatherings. *Chairman:* **David Tinkler.** *Hon Sec:* **Paul Questier,** 58 Oakwood Road, Horley, Surrey RH6 7BU **Tel:** 01293-772104

■ **ASSOCIATION OF CATHOLIC WOMEN**
Under the patronage of Our Lady and St Joseph, the ACW unites women from all parts of the country who find happiness and fulfilment in giving glad assent to the Church's teachings as proclaimed by the magisterium. *Chairman:* **Mrs Josephine Robinson,** *Secretary:* **Mrs Ruth Real,** 22 Surbiton Hill Park, Surbiton, Surrey KT5 8ET **Tel** 0208-399 1459 **Fax:** 0208-715 2316
E-mail: acwreview@aol.com
Website: www.associationofcatholicwomen.co.uk

■ **ASSOCIATION OF DIOCESAN ARCHIVISTS OF ENGLAND AND WALES**
was formed in 1992 to act as a forum for archivists representing the 22 dioceses of England and Wales. *Secretary:* **Rev David Lannon,** St Mary's Presbytery, 3 Todmorden Road, Burnley BB10 4AU **Tel** 01282-42200
E-mail: davelannon@aol.com

■ **ASSOCIATION FOR LATIN LITURGY**
To promote the widespread use of Latin texts and music in the approved rites of the Church. Publishes books and regular newsletter. Regular Masses, meetings and talks. *Secretary:* **Mr Christopher Francis.** 16 Brean Down Avenue, Bristol BS9 4JF
E-mail: Enquiries@Latin-Liturgy.org
Website: www.Latin-Liturgy.org

■ **ASSOCIATION OF CATHOLIC NURSES**
(Formerly Catholic Nurses Guild) To provide spiritual and professional support to members and to inspire practice of of nursing according to Christian principles. *National Chaplain:* **Rev Eric Mead,** St Anne's Presbytery, Devonshire Gardens, Cliftonville CT9 3AF.; *National President:* **Mrs Jacqueline Hall**; *National Vice President:* **Mrs Christine Bentley**; *National Treasurer:* **Mrs Elizabeth Coonay,** 5 Shefford Road, Seabridge, Newcastle-under-Lyme, Staffs ST5 3LE
Tel: 01782 261 7872
Secretary: **Mrs Mary Farnan,** 26 Charnwood Road, Great Barr, Birmingham B42 1JR

■ **ASSOCIATION OF NIGERIAN CATHOLICS**
(Also known as Nigeria Catholic Association). The Association represents the Nigerian Catholic Community in England and Wales. Approved by the Bishops' Conferences of England and Wales and Nigeria. *General Secretary:* **Mrs Vicki Amadi,** 23b Childeric Road, New Cross, London SE14 4DG
Tel: 020-8694 9179 **Mbl:** 07956 206267
Chaplain: **Rev Fidelis Chukwu.** The Presbytery, Our Lady of Mount Carmel & St Joseph, 8a Battersea Park Road, Battersea, London SW8 4BH
Tel: 020-7720 2912 **Mbl:** 07957 108933
E-mail: fchukwu@aol.com

■ **ASSOCIATION OF OUR LADY OF MOUNT CARMEL**
A worldwide lay apostolate dedicated to increasing adoration of Our Eucharistic Lord through Rosary groups, regular vigils of prayer and Holy Hours. *Spiritual Director:* **Rev Brendan Grady OCarm.** *Secretary:* **Dr Ron Atkin,** 9 Clewer Court, Oakfield Rd, Newport Gwent NP20 4LQ
Leader: Awaiting Appointment
Website: www.mtcarmelassociation.org

■ **ASSOCIATION OF PROVINCIAL BURSARS**
Open to Provincial Bursars (or equivalent) of Religious Orders. Its aims are to deepen understanding of Christian

stewardship for religious and to facilitate collaboration and cooperation between members. *General Secretary:* **Mr Michael Barwick,** Green Roofs, Marine Drive, Saltdean, Brighton BN2 8LA **Tel/Fax:** 01273-305183 **E-mail:** apbursars@aol.com **Website:** apbursars.org.uk

■ **ASSOCIATION OF SENIOR RELIGIOUS**
An association for Religious who are retired or are approaching the age of retirement. Its aims are to encourage its members to continue to be outgoing while accepting the challenge which comes with age. *National Secretary:* **Sr Janet Norman,** 55 Kingsdown Avenue, Luton Beds LU2 5BA **Tel:** 01582 897378

■ **ASSOCIATION OF SEPARATED AND DIVORCED CATHOLICS**
A federation of lay support groups, under the episcopal care of the Bishop of Salford. The Association aims to provide mutual help and spiritual support to those who have experienced the pain of marriage failure. Headquarters: ASDC, c/o Cathedral House, 250 Chapel Street, Salford M3 5LL. **Helpline: Tel:** 0113-264 0638 **Media Contact: Tel:** 01225-754320 **Website:** www.asdcengland.org.uk

■ **BANNEUX NOTRE DAME GREAT BRITAIN - INTERNATIONAL UNION OF PRAYER.**
To promulgate the message given by Our Lady at Banneux-Notre Dame under the title of 'The Virgin of the Poor'; to organise pilgrimages to Banneux and raise funds to assist sick pilgrims; to propagate the International Union of Prayer, arrange retreats, all-night vigils, Rosary groups, illustrated lectures, etc. *Hon Secretary:* **Mrs Maria Hare,** 10 Bramble Close, Hillingdon UB8 3QE **Tel:** 01895-420753

■ **CALIX SOCIETY**
To interest members of the fellowship of Alcoholics Anonymous in the spiritual development of total abstinence. *Contact:* **Rev Brian McGinley,** St George's, Sansome Place, Worcester WR1 1UG **Tel:** 01905 22574 or **Rev P Morgan,** Our Lady of Lourdes, 95A Kingsley Road, Liverpool L8 2TY **Tel:** 0151-709 4434

■ **CARMELITE THIRD ORDER (LAY CARMELITES)**
Offers lay people and diocesan clergy the opportunity of deepening their relationship with Jesus Christ, within one of the most ancient traditions of the Church, drawing inspiration from Elijah, the Blessed Virgin and Saints of Carmel. Carmelites form praying communities at the service of God's people. *British Province:* **England, Scotland and Wales.** *Provincial Secretary:* **Miss Sine Cameron-Mowat,** 91 Bellwood Street, Langside, Glasgow G41 3EY **Tel:** 0141-649 1933; Lay Carmel Central Office: The Friars, Aylesford, Kent ME20 7BX **Tel:** 01622-714159; *Lay Carmel Promoter:* **Rev Brendan Grady OCarm.**

■ **CATENIAN ASSOCIATION**
An international brotherhood of Catholic business and professional men who meet together monthly, often with their wives and families, for the purpose of promoting fellowship and mutual support. Founded in Manchester in 1908, it now has a membership of 10,500 throughout the UK and seven other countries across the world. Further information available by request, from: The Grand Secretary, The Catenian Association, 2nd Floor, 1 Copthall House, Station Square, Coventry CU1 2FY

■ **CATHOLIC ARCHIVES SOCIETY**
Promotes the care, management and preservation of the archives of dioceses, religious orders, and other institutions of the Catholic Church in the United Kingdom, but does not store or collect archives. Holds annual conference and occasional seminars; Publishes yearly periodical, Catholic Archives, and circulates a Bulletin. *Chairman:* **Judith Smeaton,** 33 Middlethorpe Drive, Dringhouses, York YO24 1NA *Secretary:* **Margaret Harcourt Williams,** Innyngs House, Hatfield Park, Hatfield, Hertfordshire AL9 5PL

■ **CATHOLIC ASSOCIATION OF TEACHERS, SCHOOLS AND COLLEGES**
The Association was formed, in 1996, from the amalgamation of the Catholic Teachers Federation and the Association of Catholics Schools & Colleges. CATSC provides conferences, advice, representation, support and a helpline for teachers. The journal, *Networking, Catholic Education Today*, is produced five times per year, in addition to *The Vine* newsletter for members *Contact:* **John Lydon**, Salesian School, Guildford, Chertsey, Surrey KT16 9LU **Tel:** 01932-582527

■ **CATHOLIC ASSOCIATION FOR RACIAL JUSTICE (CARJ)**
An Agency of the Catholic Bishops' Conference of England and Wales and a national membership organisation for Catholics of every ethnic identity working for racial justice in Church and society. Charitable, educational and voluntary. Responsible for promoting Racial Justice Sunday (the second Sunday of September) within the Catholic community. Resources and training available.
National Co-ordinator: **Cecilia Taylor-Camara.** *Admin:* **Maureen Corsi,** CARJ, 9 Henry Road, Manor House, London N4 2LH
Tel: 020-8802 8080 **Fax:** 020-8211 0808
E-mail: carj@btconnect.com
Website: www.carj.org

■ **CATHOLIC ASSOCIATION, THE**
The Catholic Association organises and runs the Catholic Association Pilgrimage to Lourdes in each year. The Pilgrimage covers the Dioceses of East Anglia, Portsmouth, Clifton, Northampton, Southwark and Stonyhurst College.
Secretary: **Mr C P Thorpe,** 21 Fargo Road, Larkhill, Salisbury Wiltshire SP4 8LW

■ **CATHOLICS FOR AIDS PREVENTION & SUPPORT (CAPS)**
A registered charity and network of Catholics in Britain and Ireland aiming to be a voice in the Church for people living with HIV/AIDS, and to be a Catholic voice in the HIV pandemic.
Chair of Trustees: **Vincent Manning,** CAPS, PO Box 24632, London E9 6XF
Tel/Fax: 020-8986 0807
E-mail: positivecatholics@btinternet.com
Positve Catholics Support Group
E-mail: positivecatholics@gmail.com
Tel: 07505 608655
Website: http://positivecatholics.googlepages.com

■ **CATHOLIC BIBLICAL ASSOCIATION OF GREAT BRITAIN**
To promote knowledge and love of the Scriptures. *Hon Secretary:* **Sr Marie Therese Roberts MMM.** PO Box 6201, Edgbaston, Birmingham B16 9LB
Tel: 0121-472 3040. *Scripture Bulletin Editor:* **Dr Martin O'Kane.** Department of Theology and Religious Studies, University of Wales Lampeter SA48 7ED
E-mail: m.o.kane@lamp.ac.uk

■ **CATHOLIC CHARISMATIC RENEWAL (CCR)**
The National Service Committee is at the national level the principal co-ordinating organisation of the CCR. Its mission is to serve, communicate and promote the CCR under the Holy Spirit's action and in close contact with the Bishops' Conference through its Episcopal Adviser, The **Rt Rev Ambrose Griffiths.** For further information contact: **Kristina Cooper,** CCR, Allen Hall, 28 Beaufort Street, London SW3 5AA
Tel: 020-7352 5298 **Fax:** 020-7351 4486 **Website:** www.ccr.org.uk

■ **CATHOLIC CLOTHING GUILD**
To supply useful clothing to those who are unable to provide for themselves and their families. *President:* **Countess Charles de Salis.** *Hon. Secretary:* **Mrs F Ripper,** 3 Spring Way, Sible Hedingham, Halstead, Essex CO9 3SB
Tel: 01787-460234

■ **CATHOLIC CONCERN FOR ANIMALS**
To put animal welfare on the agenda of the Church is the aim of this international charity. We also represent Church teaching about the compassionate treatment of all God's creatures, through the media, events and our thrice-yearly journal *The Ark*. For a free copy and details, visit our website: www.catholic-animals.org or write to **Dr Deborah Jones,**
15 Rosehip Way, Bishops Cleeve, Cheltenham GL52 8WP
Tel: 01242-677423
E-mail: deborahjark@aol.com
Website: www.catholic-animals.org
Reg. Charity No: 2312022

■ **CATHOLIC DEAF ASSOCIATION**
An association of Deaf, Hard of Hearing and Hearing People, who support each other and promote services for Deaf People within the community, at local, diocesan and national levels.
Secretary: **Rev P McDonough,** Hollywood House, Sudell Street, Collyhurst, Manchester M4 4JF

■ **CATHOLIC FAMILY HISTORY SOCIETY**
To encourage Catholics and those who have Catholic ancestry to research their family.
General Secretary: **Mrs M Bowery,** 9 Snows Green Road, Shotley Bridge, Co Durham DH8 0HD

■ **CATHOLIC HANDICAPPED FELLOWSHIP**
For the spiritual and material care of the handicapped, working in independent Diocesan Fellowships. Hon *Secretary:* **Mr J Mair,** 15 Woodlands Park Drive, Blaydon, Tyne and Wear NE21 5PQ **Tel:** 0191-414 3221
E-mail: jmair@talk21.com
Website: www.rc.net/uk/national-chf

■ **CATHOLIC MEN'S SOCIETY OF GREAT BRITAIN**
The purpose of the Society is to encourage, help and prepare men to enable them to assume an active and responsible role as laymen in the Church today. *Hon. National Secretary:* **Christopher E Bolger,** 6 Ashlar Road, Liverpool L22 4QP **Tel:** 0151-474 2509

■ **CATHOLIC NETWORK FOR RETREATS & SPIRITUALITY (FORMERLY NATIONAL RETREAT MOVEMENT)**
A Catholic organisation of retreat houses, parishes and individuals promoting retreats. It holds an annual conference, and is a member of the ecumenical Retreat Association, which publishes *Retreats*.
Chair: **Sr Magdalen Lawler SND;** *Secretary:* **Alison MacTier,** The Central Hall, 256 Bermondsey Street, London SE1 3UJ
Tel: 020-7357 7736 **Fax:** 0871 7151917
E-mail: cnrs@retreats.org.uk

■ **CATHOLIC PEOPLE'S WEEKS**
Residential programmes for families and individuals of all ages. Some cater for families whilst others are adults only. Of interest to Catholics and those sympathetic to Catholic ideas, who wish to gain insight into the practice of the Catholic faith and deepen their Christian life in home, parish, workplace and society. Annual programme available January. *Contact:* **Mr Colm Clinton,** 23 Abberley Grove, Stafford, ST17 4FE **Tel:** 01785 224929
E-mail: secretary@ catholicpeoplesweeks.org.uk
Website: www.catholicpeoplesweeks.org.uk

■ **CATHOLIC POLICE GUILD**
An association of serving and retired Catholic police officers, special constables and cadets. *Chaplain:* **Rev Tim Buckley,** St John Vianney, 21 Heathfield Road, Bexley Heath, Kent DA6 8NP. *Secretary:* **Geraldine McWilliams,** 18 Chipstead Lane, Lower Kingswood, Surrey KT20 6RE

■ **CATHOLIC RECORD SOCIETY**
To promote the study of post-Reformation Catholic history in the British Isles (but not genealogy). Publishes volumes of records, monographs and half-yearly journal Recusant History. Holds annual summer conference in July/August.
President: **Rt Rev Daniel Mullins,** Emeritus Bishop of Menevia. Secretary: **Dr L Gooch,** 12 Melbourne Place, Wolsingham, Co Durham DL13 3EH
Tel: 01388-527747
Website: www.catholichistory.org.uk/crs

■ **CATHOLIC STAGE GUILD**
For the spiritual and temporal needs of Catholics in the Theatre, Television, Films, Radio and allied arts. Associate membership open to all. *Chairman:* **Richard O'Callaghan.** *National Chaplain:* **Canon John McDonald.** *Hon Secretary:* **Molly Steele.** "Corpus Christi", 1 Maiden Lane, London WC2E 7NB - All enquiries to the Hon. Sec. by post with SAE.
Email: info@catholicstageguild.org.uk
Website: www.catholicstageguild.org.uk

■ **CATHOLIC TRUTH SOCIETY**
Publisher and Retailer, Publisher to the Holy See. Develops and disseminates publications about the Catholic Church, her faith, practice and teaching, by the publication and distribution of low-priced publications, DVDs and other resources. The Society, founded 140 years ago by **Cardinal Herbert Vaughan,** is a registered Charity and relies on the prayers and support of the Catholic and wider Christian community. *General Secretary:* **Fergal Martin LLB, LLM.** Headquarters: 40-46 Harleyford Road, Vauxhall, London SE11 5AY **Tel:** 020-7640 0042 **Fax:** 020-7640 0046
E-mail: info@cts-online.org.uk
Website: www.cts-online.org.uk
Bookshop: 25a Ashley Place, London,
Tel: 020-7834 1363,
E-mail: bookshop@cts-online.org.uk

■ **CATHOLIC UNION**
Founded in 1871, the Catholic Union is the principle lay forum dedicated to the promotion of Catholic values and the common good in Parliament and public life. The Union draws upon the broad expertise of its members to analyse public policy and provide expertise in cooperation with parliamentarians and the hierarchy. It promotes the role of faith in citizenship, through educational

activities, conferences and the media. *President:* **Lord Brennan QC** Further information from the Secretary, St Maximilian Kolbe House, 63 Jeddo Road, London, W12 9EE
Tel: 020 8749 1321
E-mail: info@catholicunion.org;
Website: www.catholicunion.org

■ **CATHOLIC WOMEN'S LEAGUE**
For promotion of religious, educational, and social welfare, and to represent Catholic women's interests on National and International bodies.
National President: **Mrs Doreen Pooley**
National Secretary: **Mrs Jean Clarke**, CWL HQ, PO Box 70, Ledbury HR8 9AZ
Tel/Fax: 01531 631763
E-mail: natsec@cwlhq.org.uk
Website: catholicwomensleague.org

■ **CATHOLIC WRITERS' GUILD (THE KEYS)**
For Catholics engaged in journalism, writing or publishing. Guild Master: **Sean O'Connor**, Secretary: **Joe Egerton**, 31 Smithbrook Kilns, Cranleigh, Surrey GU6 8JJ
Guild Church: St Mary Moorfields, London EC1.
Website: www.catholicwritersguild.org

■ **CHRISTIAN LIFE COMMUNITY**
A worldwide community composed of small groups. Each group meets regularly, enabling each other to deepen their life of prayer and to support one another in their response to God's love. CCL's special characteristic is the spirituality of St Ignatius, helping members to integrate prayer with daily living. Address: Christian Life Community, St Joseph's, Watford Way, London NW4 4TY

■ **CIEL-UK**
In association with CIEL-France, researches the Church's traditional liturgy in loyalty to the Magisterium. CIEL-UK publishes the annual French conference proceedings in English. There is an annual Solemn Mass and Conference in London. 'Friends' receive CIEL-UK Chronicle. *President:* **Fra' Frederick Crichton-Stuart,** 6 Raeburn Mews, Edinburgh EH4 1RG **Tel/Fax:** 0131-343 3516
Web: www.ciel-uk.org
E-mail: secretariat@ciel-uk.org
Reg. Charity No 1064597

■ **CRUX**
A movement based on prayer, study and action, promoting Christian beliefs and values within the social milieu, employing the Cell techniques of see, judge and act in small groups or as one member. *National Secretary:* **Fred Tippen,** 18 Berwick Avenue, Hayes, Middx UB4 0NF

■ **ECUMENICAL SOCIETY OF THE BLESSED VIRGIN MARY**
To promote ecumenical devotion and the study, at various levels, of the place of the Blessed Virgin Mary in the Church, under Christ. *Secretary:* **Mr Joe Farrelly** KCSG. 11 Belmont Road, Wallington, Surrey SM6 8TE **Tel:** 020-8647 5992 **Website:** esbvm.org.uk/

■ **ENCOURAGE**
A spiritual support group for Catholics who struggle with homosexuality and who wish to live according to the teaching of the Church. Encourage produces a regular newsletter. and also offers confidential group and personal support. Contact: The EnCourage Trust, PO Box 3745, London N2 8LW
Website: www.encouragetrust.org.uk
E-mails: petroc@ntlworld.com
encouragelondon@yahoo.co.uk

■ **ENGLISH CATHOLIC HISTORY ASSOCIATION**
The Association aims to advance the education of the public in English Catholic history including promoting interest and encouraging research in the Catholic History of England and Wales and helping to preserve relevant documents. Regular meetings and visits are arranged and members receive a quarterly newsletter. *Secretary:* **Miss Toni Eccles,** 6 Townside, Church Street, Tisbury, Salisbury, Wiltshire SP3 6AX
Tel: 01747-871070 **E-mail:** toni.eccles@btinternet.com **Website:** www.echa.org.uk

■ **EQUIPES NOTRE DAME**
See 'Teams of Our Lady'

■ **FAITH AND LIGHT**
An international Christian association which brings together mentally handicapped people, their parents and friends in a spirit of Christian community. Faith and Light groups provide various means of support to families with handicapped children and strive to promote the value of handicapped people in the Church.
National Co-ordinator: **Shelagh Hull**, 82 Dereham Road, Norwich NR2 4BU **Tel/Fax:** 01603-471471

■ **FATIMA, FRIENDS OF**
To spread devotion to the Immaculate Heart of Mary, the Rosary and the Scapular of Mount Carmel by means of slide/talk presentations, videos and cassettes. *Promoters:* **Patricia and Eddie Waters,** 'Casimir', 37 Larches Road, Kidderminster, Worcs DY11 7AB **Tel:** 01562-68886

■ **FRIENDS OF CARDINAL NEWMAN**
A society for spreading knowledge of his teaching and for furthering his cause. *Chairman of the Executive Committee:* **Mgr Anthony Stark.** Correspondence to: The Secretary, c/o The Oratory, Hagley Road, Birmingham B16 8UE, from whom Prayer Cards, Relic Cards for the Beatification and a wide range of Newman literature may be obtained **Tel:** 0121-454 0496
Fax: 0121- 455 8160
E-mail: oratory@globalnet.co.uk

■ **FRIENDS OF THE HOLY FATHER**
To pray for His Holiness's intentions, to study his teaching and make it more widely known as well as supporting a fund to assist towards defraying the rising expenses incurred in furthering his Apostolic Ministry. *Chairman:* **John Dean** *Hon. Secretary:* **Dr Michael Straiton KCSG, MBBS**, Archdiocese of Westminster, Vaughan House, 46 Francis Street, London SW1P 1QN

■ **GOOD COUNSEL NETWORK**
National Catholic pregnancy counselling organisation, consecrated to Our Lady, offering information and support to women in crisis pregnancies to enable them to avoid abortion. Faithful to the Church's teaching on contraception and abortion, Good Counsel Network organises post-abortion retreats in conjunction with the Franciscan Friars of the Renewal. *Director:* **Mrs Clare McCullough,** The Good Counsel Network, PO Box 46679, London NW9 8ZT **Tel:** 020-7723 1740

■ **GRAIL**
Grail People quest for the pearl of great price and value all people at whatever point they have reached in their quest. We do this in the awareness of God's presence surrounding us in the living world, in human society and in all we meet. As a community centred on the Eucharist we are committed to sharing the Christian values that inspire us and bring to our lives a spirit of creativity, celebration and joy The Grail offers forms of membership for single women, married couples and young adults. Local groups meet regularly throughout the country.
President: **Miss Claire Davidson,** The Grail Centre, 125 Waxwell Lane, Pinner, Middlesex HA5 3ER
Tel: 020-8866 2195
Website: www.grailsociety.org.uk
E-mails: Community: waxwell@compuserve.com **Business & Centre:** grailcentre@compuserve.com

■ **CATHOLIC MEDICAL ASSOCIATION (UK)**
(formerly Guild of Catholic Doctors of England and Wales).
The CMA is a newly established organisation open to all Catholic healthcare professionals from doctors, nurses, physiotherapists, radiographers, occupational therapists and other qualified therapists and their students to hospital chaplains and health service managers. If you work in a recognised healthcare profession, you are eligible to join the CMA, which exists to allow mutual support, exchanges of clinical experience and ethical expertise across the broadest range of issues in a genuinely multi-disciplinary atmosphere. Whether you are interested in meeting others socially with similar interests, finding mutual support and challenge in confidential online members' discussion fora or contributing to initiatives to raise public awareness of what a Catholic perspective has to offer healthcare in multicultural Britain, you will be made equally welcome.
Chairman: **Dr Stephen Brennan FRCP**.
Hon. Secretary: **Dr Clare Walker,**
Central Office: 38 Circus Road, St. John's Wood, London NW8 9SE
Tel: 020 7266 4246

■ **GUILD OF OUR LADY OF RANSOM**
For the conversion of England and Wales. Principal means: prayer to Our Lady and the Saints of England and Wales, appreciation of our Catholic heritage, financial support for poor parishes in all our dioceses. *Master:* **Mgr Anthony Stark**, KCHS; *Honorary Secretary:* **Prof Brian Ray MSc, PhD,** 31 Southdown Road, Wimbledon, London SW20 8QJ **Tel:** 020-8947 2598
Fax: 020-8944 6355

■ **GUILD OF ST AGATHA, CATHOLIC ASSOCIATION OF BELLRINGERS**
An Association for Catholic bell ringers, seeks to promote the proper use and maintenance of Catholic bells, provides advice and grant aid for belfry projects.

All membership and other enquiries to: *President:* **Patrick Matthews.** 1 Albert Road, Bournemouth, Dorset BH1 1BZ **Website:** www.guildofstagatha.org.uk

■ **HCPT - THE PILGRIMAGE TRUST**
Founded in 1956, The Pilgrimage Trust is a national and international charity taking children and adults with disabilities to Lourdes, and seeking to promote the integration of all peoples, regardless of their disability. HCPT celebrated its 50th Anniversary in 2006. *Chief Executive:* **R A Mills,** HCPT – The Pilgrimage Trust, Oakfield Park, 32 Bilton Road, Rugby, Warwickshire CV22 7HQ
Tel: 01788-564646 **Fax:** 01788-564640
E-mail: hq@hcpt.org.uk
Website: www.hcpt.org.uk

■ **HOUSING JUSTICE (FORMERLY CATHOLIC HOUSING AID SOCIETY – CHAS)**
To support parishes and local groups working with homeless and badly housed people: to provide education and training, liturgy resources and policy guidance to church groups and individuals wanting to learn about and take action on housing. *Chief Executive Officer:* **Alison Gelder**, 209 Old Marylebone Road, London NW1 5QT. Tel:020-7723 7273 **Fax:** 020-7723 5943
E-mail: info@housingjustice.org.uk
Website: www.housingjustice.org.uk

■ **INTERNATIONAL ALLIANCE OF CATHOLIC KNIGHTS**
Founded in Britain in 1979. Promotes co-operation and joint action between fifteen Orders of Catholic Knights in twenty-six countries. Aims: to establish new Orders of Catholic Knights, support the Holy Father, Bishops, Priests and all religious, eliminate injustice and protect all Human life. *Secretary General:* **Tony Rouse KCSG, KHS, OMRI,** 42 Westward Ho, Great Grimsby, Lincolnshire, England. DN34 5AE
Tel/Fax: 01472- **752280 E-mail:** gyiacktonyrouse@adl.com

■ **INTERNATIONAL CENTRE OF NEWMAN FRIENDS C/O THE SPIRITUAL FAMILY THE WORK**
To exercise day to day care of Newman's "College" at Littlemore and – together with the other Int. Centres of Newman Friends and the Friends of Cardinal Newman – to make known the life and work of John Henry Newman and his relevance for the times in which we live.
Contact: The Society of The Work, Ambrose Cottage, 9 College Lane, Littlemore, Oxford OX4 4LQ
Tel: 01865-779743 **Fax:** 01865-773397
E-mail: thework@uk2.net
Website: www.newmanfriendsinternational.org

■ **KNIGHTS OF ST COLUMBA**
A fraternal order of Catholic men. *Supreme Knight:* **J Doran.** *Ecclesiastical Adviser:* **Rt Rev M McMahon OP.** Head Office: 75 Hillington Road South, Glasgow G52 2AE
Tel: 0141-883 5700 **Fax:** 0141-882 5703
E-mail: headoffice@ksc.org.uk
Website: www.ksc.org.uk

■ **LATIN MASS SOCIETY**
The Society promotes the regular and frequent celebration of Holy Mass in the traditional Latin rite. It encourages the study and use of the traditional music of the Church, particularly Gregorian Chant, and works for the wider use of Latin in the Church's worship and administration.
For more information contact: The Latin Mass Society, 11-13 Macklin Street, London WC2B 5NH **Tel:** 020-7404 7284 **Fax:** 020-7831 5585,
E-mail: thelatinmasssociety@snmail.co.uk
Website: www.latin-mass-society.org

■ **LEGION OF MARY**
A worldwide Lay organisation living and fulfilling the ideals of the Decree on the Lay Apostolate. Its objective is the spiritual formation of its members through a life of prayer and apostolic action under ecclestical guidance. Its mission is to be at the disposal of the parish priest for all forms of evangelisation and pastoral care so as to bring all peoples to Christ through Mary. For further information contact: Legion of Mary, Senatus of London, Frank Duff House, 16 Northdown Street, London N1 9BG
Tel: 020-7837 2371

■ **LINACRE CENTRE FOR HEALTHCARE ETHICS**
A national Catholic research and education centre established in 1977, of which the Trustee is the Catholic Trust for England and Wales. *Chairman of the Governors:* **Professor Neil Scolding PhD, FRCP;** *Director:* **Dr Helen Watt PhD.** The Linacre Centre, 38 Circus Road, St John's Wood,

London NW8 9SE
Tel: 020-7266 7410 **Fax:** 020-7266 5424
E-mail: admin@linacre.org
Website: www.linacre.org

■ MARIST WAY

The Marist Way is the name given to the lay branch of the Marist Family. It brings together people who wish to participate in the life and mission of the Church in the 'open spirit of Mary' – a way of living the Gospel envisaged by Jean-Claude Colin, founder of the Marists – Priests, Sisters, Brothers and Laity. For more information please contact: **Mrs Agnes McGrogan,** 15 Daleston Avenue, Linthorpe, Middlesbrough TS5 5PA
Tel: 01642-817504 **E-mail:** ammway.mcgrogan@talktalk.net

■ MISSION TOGETHER (HOLY CHILDHOOD)

Holy Childhood, through its *Mission Together* programme, encourages children to be concerned with mission through prayer, learning activities and fundraising. It is the Church's official overseas charity for children. It's unique motto is 'children helping children'
Tel: 0207 821 9755
E-mail: missiontogether@missio.org.uk

■ MOVEMENT OF CHRISTIAN WORKERS

A Cardijn movement which groups people in order that they are able to relate faith to daily life and build Christian community on a local, regional and national level. This gives positive support to workers and their families and equips and sustains them for their civic and social responsibilities. National Headquarters: St Joseph's, off St Joseph's Grove, London NW4 4TY
Tel: 020-8203 6290 **Fax:** 020-8203 6291 **E-mail:** mcworkers@aol.com
Website: www.mcworkers.org

■ NATIONAL CATHOLIC REFUGEE FORUM

Founded in 2000 the NCRF is a national network of people concerned for asylum seekers and refugees. It aims to: support those working with asylum seekers and refugees; ease the lives of refugees and asylum seekers; educate and inform about asylum issues; share experience. Provides speakers; scriptural and liturgical resources; regular briefings; organises conference days. *Chair:* **Phil Kerton.** *National Co-ordinator:* **Uta Sievers,** 9 Henry Road, London N4 2LH **Tel:** 07871-646224
E-mail: info@refugee-forum.org.uk
Website: www.refugee-forum.org.uk

■ NATIONAL JUSTICE & PEACE NETWORK

To encourage work for Justice and Peace throughout the Church by promoting liaison and communication between Diocesan Justice and Peace Groups. *Chairperson:* **Anne Paecey** *Administrator:* **Maureen Matthews.** 39 Eccleston Square, London SW1V 1BX
Tel: 020 7901 4864 **Fax:** 020-7901 4821
E-mail: justice-and-peace.org.uk

■ NETWORK FOR LAY MINISTRY

Brings together lay people (including religious) working within the Roman Catholic Church and also ecumenically in other organisations. Our aim is to contribute to one another's professional development and on-going faith formation, to share information and resources, and to work towards the clarification of working practices. The Network also offers opportunities to reflect on the nature and theology of lay ministry and invites members to share together in prayer and liturgy. Contact: **Anne Cross** or **Mike Bold,** c/o Westminster House, Watford Way, Hendon NW4 4TY
E-mail: lay_ministry@hotmail.com

■ NEWMAN ASSOCIATION

Membership is open to all Catholics who wish to deepen their knowledge of the faith and place themselves at the service of the Church in the company of others of like mind. Non-Catholic Christians are admitted to associate membership. Regular conferences are held, and there are some 20 local Circles throughout England and Wales. *President:* **Dr Christine Newman.** *Secretary:* **Mr Anthony Baker,** 3 King Harry Lane, St Albans, AL3 4AS
Tel: 01727 835491
E-mail: secretary@newman.org.uk

■ OUR LADY'S CATECHISTS

An association of men and women who are qualified to give religious instruction. Our postal courses include "Sowing the Seed" for training parish catechists, leading to a certificate or as a developmental course; the Diploma course which provides a more academic training, "Catholicism Made Simple", an introduction to the Faith for adults and youth, 'The Children's Section' which will put parents in touch with a qualified Catechist in their area, who may be able to assist their child in the preparation for the Sacraments of Reconciliation, First Holy Communion and Confirmation; the Parents, young people and adults,

including Relgious Brothers and Sisters and Parish Priests are invited to contact: *The Secretary:* **Mrs Carol Taylor,** 36 Ingledene Close, Bedhampton PO9 1DG
Tel: 02392-479846

■ **PAPAL ORDERS IN GREAT BRITAIN OF BLESSED PIUS IX, ST GREGORY THE GREAT & POPE ST SYLVESTER.**
President: **HE Cardinal Cormac Murphy-O'Connor PhL, STL**
Chairman: **Rt Hon Sir Swinton B Thomas PC, KCSG.**
Secretary: **Leo Simmonds KCSG, KCHS,** 5 Sheen Park, Richmond, Surrey TW9 1UN
Website: www.papalknights.org.uk

■ **PAX CHRISTI**
A gospel-based international movement for peace, open to all. Pax Christi strives to help the Church and wider community to proclaim and make peace through its work for reconciliation and the promotion of a culture of peace and non-violence. It provides a wide range of materials for education, reflection and campaigning for peace. Pax Christi produces material for parishes each year to encourage support for Peace Sunday (Pope's World Peace Day message) celebrated on the 2nd Sunday in Ordinary Time. *President:* **Bishop Malcolm McMahon;** *Chairperson:* **Stewart Hemsley.** *General Secretary:* **Ms Pat Gaffney,** St Joseph's, Watford Way, Hendon, London NW4 4TY **Tel:** 020-8203 4884
E-mail: info@paxchristi.org.uk
Website: www.paxchristi.org.uk

■ **PIONEER TOTAL ABSTINENCE ASSOCIATION OF THE SACRED HEART, NATIONAL COUNCIL FOR ENGLAND AND WALES**
A Lay Organisation whose primary aim is the Promotion of Sobriety and Temperance. Its chief means are prayer and self-sacrifice. For further information contact *The Secretary:* **Mrs Mary McGloin,** 20 Parkfield Avenue, Kingsbury NW9 7PE *Contact for Youth Section:* The Youth Officer, 20 Parkfield Avenue, Kingsbury NW9 7PE

■ **PONTIFICAL MISSION SOCIETIES (PMS)**
The Pontifical Mission Societies (PMS) comprise the following societies:
The Association for the Propagation of the Faith (APF) *See page:* 661
Holy Childhood (Mission Together), *See page:* 668
The Society of St Peter the Apostle (SPA), *See page:* 671
Pontifical Missionary Union (PMU), *See below.*
Under the guidance of the Pope, together they form the principal organisation in the Church providing spiritual and financial support for missions overseas.
National Director: **Rev John Dale,** 23 Eccleston Square, London SW1V 1NU
Tel: 020-7821 9755
E-mail: director@missio.org.uk
Website: www.missio.org.uk
Reg Charity No. 1056651

■ **PONTIFICAL MISSIONARY UNION (PMU).**
Through its quarterly theological review *Mission Outlook* (£10.00 pa) encourages the interest of priests, religious and laity in the missionary work of the Church and in developments in the younger churches.
Tel: 020-7821 9755
E-mail: pmu@missio.org.uk

■ **PROJECT 2030**
The Twentysomethings and The Thirtysomethings. To enable Catholics in their 20s and 30s to get together at a social and spiritual level.
National Office: St John's Presbytery, 266 Wellington Road North, Stockport SK4 2QR *Director:* **Rev Hugh Hanley**
Tel: 0161 282 6334 **Mbl:** 07950-202205
E-mail: hugh@project2030.fsnet.co.uk
Website: www.project2030.org.uk

■ **PUERI CANTORES**
is the Church's official organisation for choirs of young people. Originally founded to promote liturgical singing among boys (with or without men), it now also admits choirs with girls. It achieves its aims through choir exchanges, and congresses at diocesan, national and international levels. For information contact: *National President:* **Michael Landers,** 7 Keats Close, Newport NP20 3JU
Tel/Fax: 01633 213049

■ **RADIANT LIGHT**
is a movement within the Roman Catholic Church which seeks to encourage people to grow in holiness by believing and living the Catholic faith in its fullness. It was founded by Elizabeth Wang, and its mission is inspired by her writings, paintings and spirituality. Christ 'is the radiant light of God's glory' (Heb 1:3). Contact: The Secretary, Radiant Light, 25 Rothamsted Avenue, Harpenden, Herts AL5 2DN

E-mail: mail@radiantlight.org.uk
Website: www.radiantlight.org.uk

■ RCIA

Open to anyone working within the RCIA (Right of Christian Initiation of Adults), the Network promotes and assists use of the Rite in the changing Church and Society of today. A national Conference is organised every alternate year and is complemented by regional meetings and study days and by networking between members (supported by a newsletter and web page www.rcia.org.uk). Convenor: **Linda Pennington**
Tel: 0113 261 8043 **E-mail:** linda.pennington@dioceseofleeds.org.uk

■ ST BARNABAS SOCIETY, THE

In co-operation with the Catholic Bishops, to provide pastoral support and financial help to former clergy, ministers and religious of other Churches and their dependants, who have been received into the Catholic Church and who are in need.
Secretary: **Rev Robin Sanders.** 4 First Turn , Wolvercote, Oxford OX2 8AH
Tel: 01865-513377 **Fax:** 01865-516542
E-mail: secretary@stbarnabassociety.org.uk
Website: www.stbarnabassociety.org.uk

■ ST CECILIA'S GUILD

Provides a free audio postal lending library service for the visually impaired under the auspices of the Catholic National Library. Contact: The Librarian, Holy Trinity Monastery, St Mary's Road East Hendred, Wantage OX12 8LF
Tel: 01235 821461
E-mail: guild@benedictinenuns.org.uk

■ ST FRANCIS LEPROSY GUILD

Supporting leprosy hospitals and centres, helping to: find, treat and rehabilitate people with leprosy; provide social care and aid for those affected and their families; provide residential care for those severely disabled by leprosy, particularly the elderly. Hon Secretaries: **Srs Helen McMahon FMM, Anne Curtin MMM,** 73 St Charles Square, London W10 6EJ
Tel: 020-8969 1345 **Fax:** 020-8969 3272

■ ST JOAN'S ALLIANCE

We are a long standing group of Catholic women and men who concern themselves with questions of equality and justice in both the religious and secular spheres. We explore issues arising from God making women equally as men, in God's own image (Gen. 1.27), using gospel values and the insights of Vatican II, acknowledging and accepting the authentic teaching of the Catholic Church. We seek to deepen spiritual insight and Christian response in today's troubled world. *Contact:* **Pam Wearing,** 13 Mildred Avenue, Middx UB5 4LG.

■ ST JOSEPH'S HOSPICE ASSOCIATION

Jospice International, as well as work in South and Central America, has two Hospices for care of chronic and terminally sick patients in beautiful surroundings in Liverpool and Ormskirk. Ince Road, Thornton, Liverpool L23 4UE.
General Manager: **Keith Cawdron Tel:** 0151-924 3812

■ ST THOMAS FUND FOR THE HOMELESS

Founded in 1980 for the care of those made homeless through drugs or alcohol. Today the Fund has one of the most successful programme in the country with three houses in Sussex.
Company Secretary: **Mr David Royce MBA**, 3rd Floor, Tower Point, 44 North Road, Brighton, BN1 1YR
Website: www.cri.org.uk

■ ST VINCENT DE PAUL SOCIETY (ENGLAND AND WALES)

A world-wide Christian voluntary organisation of men and women of all ages, dedicated to alleviating all forms of poverty, through personal contact and friendship. *Director:* **Elizabeth Palmer.** National Office: 5th Floor 291-299 Borough High Street, London SE1 1JG **Tel:** 0207-407 4644
Fax: 0207-407 4634
E-mail: info@svp.org.uk
Website: www.svp.org.uk
Reg. Charity No: 1053992
Co.No. 3174679

■ SERRA INTERNATIONAL GREAT BRITAIN

Purpose and Work: Serra is an association of Catholic laymen and women whose aims are to foster vocations to the priesthood, permanent diaconate and religious life, and to develop their own knowledge and understanding of their Faith. *National Secretary:* **Mr C S Ollieuz,** 23 Mauldeth Close, Heaton Mersey, Stockport SK4 3NP **Tel:** 0161-432 3813
E-mail: sec@serragb.org.uk
Website: www.serragb.org.uk

■ SIGNIS

The World Catholic Association for Communications, representing Catholics involved in broadcasting, film and the Internet. It supports media initiatives throughout the world, facilitates networking at national, regional and international level, and promotes Christian values in all areas of communication. Contact: **Alexander Des Forges,** Director of News and Information, Catholic Communications Network, 39 Eccleston Square, London SW1V 1BX **Tel:** 020-7901 4807 **E-mail:** Alexander.desforges@cbcew.org.uk

■ **SOCIETY OF CATHOLIC ARTISTS**
The purpose of the Society is to support artists practising various forms of Christian and other art and those interested. To make our creativity available to the glory of God and the Church and promote a high standard of Christian Art. *Hon Secretary:* **P J Pike,** 46 Waterlow Road, London N19 5NH **Tel:** 020-7272 5458 **E-mail:** ralderson@ukonline.co.uk.

■ **SOCIETY OF OUR LADY OF LOURDES**
To promote devotion to Our Lady; organise pilgrimages to Lourdes and services in Her honour; to provide financial and other assistance to enable pilgrims who could not afford the cost to go to Lourdes. *Hon Secretary:* **Miranda Villiers** SOLL, Church of the Immaculate Heart of Mary, Botwell Lane, Hayes, Middx UB3 2AB **Tel:** 020-8848 9833 **Fax:** 020-8848 9844 **E-mail:** enquiries@soll-lourdes.com **Website:** www.soll-lourdes.com

■ **SOCIETY OF ST AUGUSTINE OF CANTERBURY**
The society's objective is the promotion and advancement of the Roman Catholic religion in England and Wales, principally through the upkeep and maintenance of Archbishop's House, Westminster. The Society welcomes new members, and bequests from donors sympathetic with its objectives. *Secretary:* **Michael Milbourn**, The River House, St Mary's Lane, Hertingfordbury, Hertford SG14 2LF **Tel:** 01992-551502 **E-mail:** michaelmilbourn@aol.com **Website:** www.staugustineofcanterbury.org.uk

■ **SOCIETY OF ST GREGORY**
National Society which works to assist priests and people to celebrate the liturgy worthily. It encourages study and active participation by organising study days, conferences, and an annual Summer School for all concerned with music and worship. The Society's journal Music and Liturgy, is published quarterly, meetings are arranged for composers. *Chairman:* **John Ainslie,** 76 Great Bushey Drive, London N20 8QL **E-mail:** chairman@ssg.org.uk **Website:** www.ssg.org.uk

■ **SOCIETY OF ST JOHN CHRYSOSTOM**
To encourage a greater appreciation of the spiritual, theological and liturgical traditions of Eastern Christendom; to work and pray for Christian unity and to give support to the Eastern Churches as appropriate. Regular Liturgical Celebrations and meetings in the London area. All welcome. *Secretary:* **Rev Gary Gill CEd(Oxon),** The Rectory, 9 Tooting Bec Road, London SW17 8BS

■ **SOCIETY OF ST PETER THE APOSTLE (SPA)**
The SPA is the Church's official fundraising body for the training of clergy and religious in mission countries. Through prayer and finance SPA supporters help the younger churches provide their own priests and religious. **Tel:** 0207 821 9755 **E-mail:** spa@missio.org.uk **Website:** www.missio.org.uk

■ **SPICMA (SPECIAL PROJECTS IN CHRISTIAN MISSIONARY AREAS)**
Reg No. 270794. Established 1967. A voluntary Catholic organisation engaged in medical assistance, general & emergency aid and projects, via missionary personnel and local priests, overseas. *UK Director:* **Patrick Phelan.** Chequers House, Watton Road, Hertfordshire SG12 0AA **Tel:** 01920-485600 **E-mail:** spicma@tiscali.co.uk

■ **SURVIVE-MIVA (MISSIONARY VEHICLE ASSOCIATION)**
A Catholic organisation which supplies transport to missionaries working in areas of great need. *Director:* **Simon Patrick Foran MA.** Registered with Charity Commission - No 268745. Office: Survive-Miva (Missionary Vehicle Association), 5 Park Vale Road, Aintree, Liverpool L9 2DG **Tel:** 0151-523 3878 **Fax:** 0151-523 3841 **E-mail:** info@survive-miva.org **Website:** www.survive-miva.org

■ **TEAMS OF OUR LADY (EQUIPES NOTRE DAME)**
An international Catholic Movement for Christian married couples that aims to deepen the couples' spirituality. A 'Team' consists of four or more couples and a priest or religious as spiritual

advisor meeting monthly to pray, share a simple meal and deepen their understanding of married spirituality. Teams received its final Decree of Recognition from the Pontifical Council for the Laity in 2002. Contact: **Robert & Mary Jones,** St Peter's Retreat House, Prinknash Abbey, Cranham, Gloucester GL4 8EX Tel: 01452 813 592 **E-mail:** spgprinknash@freeuk.com **Website:** www.teamsofourlady.org.uk

■ **THE RETREAT ASSOCIATION**
Comprises six Christian retreat groups, including Catholic Network for Retreats and Spirituality. Providing resources and information about all aspects of retreats and spiritual direction. It's annual journal 'Retreats' gives details of around 200 retreat houses and their programme for the current year. A publications list, which includes free leaflets about retreats is available on request. *Director:* **Alison MacTier, Tel:** 020-7357 7736 **Fax:** 0871 7151917 **E-mail:** info@retreats.org.uk **Website:** www.retreats.org.uk

■ **THE WORLD APOSTOLATE OF FATIMA**
An association, formally erected as a Public Association of the Faithful by the Pontifical Council for the Laity on 3rd February 2006, to make known and lived the Gospel message of Fatima, through prayer, penance, offering up daily duties in a spirit of sacrifice, daily recitation of the Rosary and the Five First Saturdays Communion of Reparation. National *President:* **Timothy Tindal-Robertson,** 30 Aldrin Road, Exeter EX4 5DN **Tel/Fax:** 01392-433256 **E-mail:** timt-robertson@clara.co.uk **Website:** www.theotokos.org.uk/pages/waof/waof.html

■ **THE UNION OF CATHOLIC MOTHERS**
To uphold the sanctity, responsibilities and permanence of marriage and family life; to ensure for their children Catholic education; to help the family in difficulties; and to foster vocations to the priesthood and religious life. *National President:* **Maureen McVann** *National Secretary:* **Angela Batey,** 27 Beechburn Road, Roby, Liverpool L34 4NE **Tel:** 0151 489 5144 **E-mail:** angela.batey@btinternet.com *National Treasurer:* **Mrs Maureen Jones**

■ **THE UNION OF CATHOLIC MOTHERS – WALES:**
National President: **Mrs Angela Wilkinson,** 25 Overlea Avenue, Deganwy, Conwy LL31 9TA **Tel:** 01492-583122 *National Secretary:* **Mrs Margaret Cleveland,** 11 Mount Pleasant, Gowerton, Swansea SA4 3EN **Tel:** 01792 872048 **Email:** margaret_cleveland@btinternet.com
To promote the following objects in the Roman Catholic Province of Cardiff (the Province) and comprising the Principality of Wales and Part of the County of Hereford and Worcester. To uphold the sanctity, responsibilities and permanence of marriage and family life; to ensure for their children Catholic education; to help the family in difficulties; and to foster vocations to the priesthood and religious life.

■ **WALSINGHAM ASSOCIATION**
Founded in 1933 the Association aims to foster devotion to Our Lady of Walsingham, to promote pilgrimages to Our Lady's National Shrine, and to support prayerfully the growth and development of the Shrine. *Secretary:* **Miss T A Milton,** The Walsingham Association, Pilgrim Bureau, Friday Market, Walsingham, Norfolk NR22 6DB **Tel:** 01328-820217 **Fax:** 01328-821087 **E-mail:** walsinghamassociation@walsingham.org.uk

■ **YOUNG CHRISTIAN WORKERS**
Young people (16-30) and Impact (13-17) meet at local level to plan actions and activities together in order to serve, educate and represent others. YCW helps to develop the confidence, social skills, faith and social awareness of the young people it touches. Resources and training for young adults, teenagers and post confirmation groups are available from YCW National headquarters, St Joseph's, off St Joseph's Grove, London NW4 4TY **Tel:** 020-8203 6290 **Fax:** 020-8203 6291 **E-mail:** info@ycwimpact.com **Website:** www.ycwimpact.com

INTERNATIONAL/THIRD WORLD CATHOLIC AGENCIES

■ AID TO THE CHURCH IN NEED

This international Catholic pastoral relief agency is an official charity of the Church, directly under The Holy See. Wherever the Church is persecuted, oppressed or in need, ACN provides spiritual and material aid – through prayer, information and action. *National Director:* **Neville Kyrke-Smith,** 12-14 Benhill Avenue, Sutton, Surrey SM1 4DA **Tel:** 020 8642 8668
Fax: 020 8661 6293
E-mail: acn@acnuk.org
Web: www.acnuk.org

■ CATHOLIC MISSIONARY UNION OF ENGLAND AND WALES

The national forum and information centre of the missionary societies and other agencies working for the Church overseas. *Secretary:* **Seamus Crowe** 13 Coventry Road, Burlington, Warks CV12 9LY
Website: www.cmu.org.uk

■ CHRISTIANS ABROAD

Is an agency of the Churches Together in Britain and Ireland. Christians Abroad recruits volunteers and professionals with Christian commitment for overseas service. It also provides support services to individuals and groups, from insurance provision to criminal record checks. Several publications are available including the 'Get Practical' as a help to those going overseas with practical information.
Tel: 0870 770 7990
E-mail: recruit@cabroad.org.uk

Christians Abroad also provides through World Service Enquiry practical information and advice about working in mission and development to people of any faith or none. Helpful guides such as 'Working in Development' are available. Development Agency vacancies are available monthly through 'Opportunities Abroad', One to One guidance interviews with an experienced adviser and other advisory and career counselling services are available.
Tel: 0870 770 3274
E-mail: wse@wse.org.uk

■ PROGRESSIO

Progressio is striving for a just world where people can have life in all its fullness, where human rights are respected, where all have their basic needs met and exert control over their lives. Progressio is the working name of the Catholic Institute for International Relations (CIIR). Has partnership programmes with organisations in Latin America, the Caribbean, Africa, the Middle East and Asia. Our areas of work include sustainable environment, HIV and AIDS and civil society participation. *Executive Director:* **Christine Allen,** Unit 3, Canonbury Yard, 190a New North Road, Islington, London N1 7BJ **Tel:** 020-7354 0883
Fax: 020-7359 0017
E-mail: enquiries@progressio.org.uk
Website: www.progressio.org.uk

CATHOLIC LIBRARIES

■ CATHOLIC NATIONAL LIBRARY formerly CATHOLIC CENTRAL LIBRARY

The Catholic National Library is a major theological and historical reference and lending library, containing 70,000 books, pamphlets and periodicals.Formerly known as the Catholic Central Library based in London, we are now in larger premises at St Michael's Abbey, Farmborough. We are able to post books to any part of the British Isles to our members, as well as answering email and phone requests. Full details on our website at www.catholiclibrary.org.uk, or brochure available on request by writing to:

Mrs Joan Bond *(Librarian),* The Catholic National Library, St Michael's Abbey, Farnborough Road, Farnborough, Hants GU14 7NQ
Tel: 01252-543818

E-mail: library@catholic-library.org.uk

Website: www.catholic-library.org.uk

Charity No. 1064460/0.

■ THE TALBOT LIBRARY

The Talbot Library is a major reference library devoted to Catholic theology and history within the wider Christian context. The stock of approximately 60,000 books includes liturgy, spirituality, scripture studies, the lives of the saints and martyrs, and the religious life. There are important collections of works by, and about, J H Newman, G K Chesterton and Hilaire Belloc, and all the major theologians are well represented. An extensive library of books printed before 1800 provides the student of religious controversy and early devotional works with a rich resource, and Church history, particularly of the Catholic heritage of north-west England, is one of the strengths of the library. The Talbot Library, which is maintained by the Diocese of Lancaster, is not a lending library, but is open free of charge to all bona fide students and researchers. It is open each Monday, Wednesday and Friday from 10am to 4pm.

Further details may be obtained from the Librarian.

Librarian: **Rev Michael Dolan MA, FCLIP**.
The Talbot Library, St Walburge's Gardens,
Weston Street, Preston, Lancs PR2 2QE
Tel: 01772-760186
E-mail: talbotlibrary@btconnect.com

SOVEREIGN MILITARY ORDER OF MALTA

(British Association)

Chancellery:

Fortescue House, 58 Grove End Road, London NW8 9NE
Tel: 020-7286 1414

President: **Charles Weld Esq**

Chancellor: **Hugh Van Cutsen Esq**

Principal Chaplain: **The Most Rev Mario Conti**

GRAND PRIORY OF ENGLAND

Grand Prior: **Fra' Fredrik Crichton-Stuart**

Pro-Chancellor: **Duncan Gallie ESO**

Chaplain: **The Rev Antony Conlon**

The Order

World-wide sponsors, runs hospitals and clinics; operates homes for the elderly and handicapped; is active in assistance to refugees; supports the fight against leprosy.

EQUESTRIAN ORDER OF THE HOLY SEPULCHRE OF JERUSALEM

Lieutenancy of England & Wales

Lieutenant: HE Dr Michael F Whelan KSG KGCHS.

Grand Prior: HE The Most Rev Kevin McDonald KC*HS.

Chancellor: Patrick D Burgess MBE KCHS.

Secretary: Patricia M Page DC*HS.

Address: Breach House, 12 High Street, Sandhurst, Berkshire GU47 8DY.

Aims of the Order: To support by prayer and charitable giving, principally through the Latin Patriarch of Jerusalem, the Christian community of the Holy Land.

SACRED MILITARY CONSTANTINIAN ORDER OF SAINT GEORGE

Internationally recognised ancient and charitable Roman Catholic Orders of Knighthood under the custodianship of the Royal House of Bourbon Two Sicilies. Worldwide brotherhood supporting humanitarian, hospitaller and religious initiatives.

Grand Master

HIS ROYAL HIGHNESS PRINCE CARLO OF BOURBON TWO SICILIES
DUKE OF CASTRO
HEAD OF THE ROYAL HOUSE OF BOURBON TWO SICILIES

Grand Prior

His Eminence Albert, Cardinal Vanhoye

DELEGATION OF GREAT BRITAIN AND IRELAND

Delegate

HE THE RIGHT HONOURABLE LORD BRENNAN OF BIBURY, KCSG, KCMCO, QC

Vice-Delegate & Chancellor

JUDGE PATRICK CLYME, KM, KMCO

Prior

HIS EMINENCE CORMAC, CARDINAL MURPHY-O'CONNOR,
Archbishop of Westminster

Sub-Prior

THE RIGHT REVEREND GEORGE STACK, KC*HS, KCGCO,
Auxiliary Bishop of Westminster

Irish Chief Chaplian

HIS EMINENCE DESMOND, CARDINAL CONNELL, KGCHS, GCJCO,
Archbishop Emeritus of Dublin

Council

The Prof The Rt Hon Lord Alton of Liverpool, KCMCO; HE Mr Anthony Bailey OBE, KCSS, KCHS, KCMCO,KCFO; HE Luigi Amaduzzi, GCVO, GCSG, KM, GCMCO; HE Archbishop Luigi Barbarito, GCVO, KCGCO; HMEH Fra Matthew Festing, OBE, KStJ, TD, GCJCO, DL; Norman Gooding, OStJ, KFO; Gen The Rt Hon Lord Guthrie of Craigiebank, GCB, LVO, OBE, KCSG, KM, KCJCO; Mr Dudley Heathcote, KM, KCJCO; Mr John Igoe, KM, KMCO; HE Mr Donal Lydon KCSG, KM, KGCHS, KCMCO, KCFO; Brig Thomas Ogilvie-Graham, MBE, OHBS, OStJ, KMCO,KFO; Dr Colin Smythe, OStJ, KCGCO, KCFO; Sir Conrad Swan, KCVO, KGCN, KM, GCJCO, PhD, FSA.

The Chancery, Sacred Military Constantinian Order of Saint George,
12 Queens Gate Gardens, London SW7 5LY **Tel:** 020 7594 0275 **Fax:** 020 7594 0265
e-mail: info@constantinian.org.uk **Website:** www.constantinian.org.uk

THE ROYAL ORDER OF FRANCIS I

PARLIAMENTARIANS WHO ARE CATHOLIC

We have listed only those who have consented to being included here

MEMBERS OF THE PRIVY COUNCIL WHO ARE CATHOLIC

Duncan Smith, Iain, MP.

Hayhoe of Isleworth, Lord Bernard (Barney).

Kelly, Ruth, MP.

Leonard, Mgr Graham Douglas KCVO.

McAvoy, Thomas, MP.

McFall, John, MP.

Murphy, Paul, KSG, MP.

Murton of Lindisfarne, Lord Henry.

Patten of Wincanton, Lord John.

Pendry of Stalybridge, Lord Thomas.

St John of Fawsley, Lord Norman.

Williams of Crosby, Baroness Shirley.

Members of the Privy Council are 'Right Honourable'

MEMBERS OF THE HOUSE OF LORDS WHO ARE CATHOLIC

Alton of Liverpool, Baron (Life Peer), **David Patrick Alton.**

Brennan, Baron (Life Peer), **Daniel Joseph Brennan.**

Buxton of Alsa, Baron (Life Peer), **Aubrey Leland Oakes Buxton, MC.**

Clarke of Hampstead (Life Peer), **Anthony Clarke CBE, KSG.**

Cumberlege, Baroness, (Life Peer), **Julia Frances Cumberlege, CBE**

Dunn, Baroness, (Life Peer), **Lydia, DBE.**

Gardner of Parkes, Baroness (Life Peer), **Rachel Trixie Anne Gardner.**

Gordon of Strathblane, Baron, (Life Peer), **James Stuart Gordon, CBE.**

Guthrie of Craigiebank (Life Peer), **General Sir Charles Guthrie GCB, LVO, OBE.**

Hayhoe, Baron (Life Peer), **Sir Barney (Bernard) John.**

Hooper, Baroness (Life Peer), **Gloria Dorothy Hooper, CMG.**

Masham of Ilton, Baroness (Life Peer), **Susan Lilian Primrose Cunliffe-Lister, Countess of Swinton.**

McNally, Baron (Life Peer), **Tom, Bt.**

Murton of Lindisfarne, Baron (Life Peer), **Henry Oscar Murton, OBE, TD.**

Patten of Wincanton, Baron (Life Peer), **John Haggitt Charles Patten.**

Pendry, (Life Peer), **Lord Thomas.**

Rees-Mogg, Baron (Life Peer), **Sir William.**

St John of Fawsley, Baron (Life Peer), **Norman Anthony Francis St John-Stevas.**

Tugendhat, Baron (Life Peer), **Sir Christopher Samuel.**

Williams of Crosby, Baroness, (Life Peer), **Shirley Vivian Teresa Brittain Williams.**

MEMBERS OF THE HOUSE OF COMMONS WHO ARE CATHOLIC

Burnham, Andy (Lab), Leigh, Lancs.
Cairns, David (Lab), Inverclyde.
Cooper, Rosie (Lab), West Lancashire.
Cunningham, Jim (Lab), Coventry South.
Dobbin, Jim (Lab), Heywood & Middleton.
Duncan Smith, Rt Hon Iain (Cons), Chingford & Woodford Green.
Durkan, Mark (SDLP), Foyle.
Farrelly, Paul (Lab), Newcastle-under-Lyme.
Goodman, Paul (Cons), Wycombe.
Green, Damian (Cons), Ashford.
Grogan, John (Lab), Selby.
Hoban, Mark (Cons), Fareham.
Irranca-Davies, Huw (Lab), Ogmore.
Kelly, Rt Hon Ruth (Lab), Bolton West
Leigh, Edward (Cons), Gainsborough.
Mackinlay, Andrew (Lab), Thurrock.
McAvoy, Rt Hon Thomas (Lab) Glasgow Rutherglen.
McFall, Rt Hon John (Lab), West Dunbartonshire.
McGovern, Jim (Lab), Dundee West.
McGrady, Eddie (SDLP), South Down.
Mulholland, Gregory (Lib Dem), Leeds North West.
Murphy, Rt Hon Paul, KSG (Lab), Torfaen.
Pope, Greg (Lab), Hyndburn.
Pound, Stephen (Lab), Ealing North.
Prentice, Bridget Theresa (Lab), Lewisham East.
Pugh, Dr John (Lib Dem), Southport.
Vaz, Keith (Lab), East Leicester.
Ward, Claire Margaret (Lab), Watford.
Waterson, Nigel (Cons), Eastbourne.
Younger-Ross, Richard (Lib Dem), Teignbridge.

MEMBERS OF THE NATIONAL ASSEMBLY FOR WALES WHO ARE CATHOLIC

German, Michael OBE (Lib Dem), South Wales East

THE CATHOLIC UNION OF GREAT BRITAIN

President:
The Lord Brennan of Bibury QC

Vice-Presidents: **Professor the Lord Alton of Liverpool, The Baroness Morris of Bolton OBE, The Lord Clarke of Hampstead CBE KSG, Mr Jim Dobbin MP, Edward Leigh MP, Jonathon Evans MEP, Dr Terence J Morris, Professor Maurice Scanlon, Professor John J. Haldane, Mr John Deighan**

Chairman:
Mr Adrian Thacker

Secretary and Development Manager:
Ms Emilia Klepacka
The Catholic Union, St Maximilian Kolbe House, 63 Jeddo Road, London W12 9EE
Tel: 020-8749 1321 **E-mail:** info@catholicunion.org

Episcopal Liaison
Rt Rev John Arnold, Auxiliary Bishop of Westminster

ECCLESIASTICAL INFORMATION

NATIONAL CALENDAR FOR ENGLAND

JANUARY
12 St AELRED OF RIEVAULX, abbot
19 St WULSTAN, bishop

FEBRUARY
14 St CYRIL, monk, and St METHODIUS, bishop, patrons of Europe *(Feast)*

MARCH
1 St DAVID, bishop, patron of Wales *(Feast)*
17 St PATRICK, bishop, patron of Ireland *(Feast)*

APRIL
21 St ANSELM, bishop, doctor of the Church
23 St GEORGE, martyr, patron of England *(Solemnity)*
24 St ADALBERT, bishop and martyr
St FIDELIS OF SIGMARINGEN, priest and martyr
29 St CATHERINE OF SIENA, virgin and doctor of the Church, patron of Europe *(Feast)*

MAY
4 THE ENGLISH MARTYRS* *(Memorial)*
19 St DUNSTAN, bishop,
25 St BEDE THE VENERABLE, priest and Doctor of the Church *(Memorial)*
27 St AUGUSTINE OF CANTERBURY, bishop *(Memorial)*

JUNE
5 St BONIFACE, bishop, martyr *(memorial)*
9 St COLUMBA, abbot
16 St RICHARD OF CHICHESTER, bishop
20 St ALBAN, protomartyr
22 St JOHN FISHER, bishop and St THOMAS MORE, martyrs *(Feast)*
23 St ETHELDREDA, abbess

JULY
1 St OLIVER PLUNKETT, bishop, martyr
11 St BENEDICT, abbot, patron of Europe *(Feast)*
23 St BRIDGET, religious, patron of Europe *(Feast)*

AUGUST
9 St TERESA BENEDICTA OF THE CROSS (EDITH STEIN), virgin, martyr, patron of Europe *(Feast)*
26 Bl. DOMINIC OF THE MOTHER OF GOD BARBERI, priest
30 St MARGARET CLITHEROW, St ANNE LINE, and St MARGARET WARD, virgin, martyrs
31 St AIDAN, bishop, and SAINTS OF LINDISFARNE

SEPTEMBER
3 St GREGORY the Great, Pope and Doctor of the Church *(Memorial)*
4 St CUTHBERT, bishop
19 St THEODORE OF CANTERBURY, bishop
24 OUR LADY of Walsingham *(Memorial)*

OCTOBER
10 St PAULINUS OF YORK, bishop,
12 St WILFRID, bishop
13 St EDWARD THE CONFESSOR
26 St CHAD and St CEDD, bishops,

NOVEMBER
3 St WINEFRIDE, virgin
7 St WILLIBRORD, bishop,
16 St EDMUND OF ABINGDON, bishop
St MARGARET OF SCOTLAND
17 St HILDA, abbess
St HUGH OF LINCOLN, bishop
St ELIZABETH OF HUNGARY religious
30 St ANDREW, apostle, patron of Scotland *(Feast)*

DECEMBER
29 St THOMAS BECKET, bishop martyr

Where no other indication is given the celebration is an optional memorial.

* The English men and women martyred for the Catholic Faith 1535–1680 and beatified or canonised by the Holy See

NATIONAL CALENDAR FOR WALES

FEBRUARY
9 St TEILO, bishop
14 St CYRIL, monk, and St METHODIUS, bishop, patrons of Europe *(Feast)*

MARCH
1 St DAVID, bishop, patron of Wales *(Solemnity)*

APRIL
20 St BEUNO, abbot
28 St CATHERINE OF SIENA, virgin and doctor of the Church, patron of Europe *(Feast)*

MAY
5 St ASAPH, bishop

JUNE
20 St ALBAN, St JULIUS and St AARON, martyrs

JULY
11 St BENEDICT, abbot, patron of Europe *(Feast)*
23 St JOHN JONES, martyr
23 St BRIDGET, patron of Europe
23 St PHILIP EVANS & JOHN LLOYD, martyr

AUGUST
3 St GERMANUS OF AUXERRE, bishop
9 St TERESA BENEDICTA OF THE CROSS (EDITH STEIN), virgin, martyr, patron of Europe *(Feast)*

SEPTEMBER
11 St DEINIOL, bishop

OCTOBER
16 St RICHARD GWYN, martyr
25 SIX WELSH MARTYRS and their COMPANIONS *(Feast)*

NOVEMBER
3 St WINEFRIDE, virgin
6 St ILLTUD, abbot
8 ALL SAINTS of WALES *(Feast)*
14 St DYFRIG, bishop

DECEMBER
10 St JOHN ROBERTS, martyr

HOLYDAYS OF OBLIGATION IN ENGLAND & WALES

From the 1st Sunday of Advent 2006 the Holydays of Obligations for England and Wales have changed. Henceforth they are:

- Every Sunday
- Birth of the Lord (25th December)
- St Peter & St Paul (29 June; 2009 = 28 June)
- Assumption of the Blessed Virgin Mary (15 August; 2009 = 16 August)
- All Saints (November; 2008 = 2 November)

The following celebrations transfer to the nearest Sunday;
• Epiphany of the Lord • Ascension of the Lord • Body and Blood of the Lord

Year	Ss Peter & Paul	Assumption of BVM	All Saints	Christmas Day
2009	28 June	16 Aug	2 Nov	25 Dec
2010	29 June	15 Aug	31 Oct	25 Dec
2011	29 June	14 Aug	1 Nov	25 Dec
2012	29 June	15 Aug	1 Nov	25 Dec
2013	30 June	15 Aug	1 Nov	25 Dec
2014	29 June	15 Aug	2 Nov	25 Dec
2015	28 June	16 Aug	1 Nov	25 Dec
2016	29 June	14 Aug	1 Nov	25 Dec
2017	29 June	15 Aug	1 Nov	25 Dec

TABLE OF PRINCIPAL CELEBRATIONS OF THE LITURGICAL YEAR

Year	Lectionary Cycle Sunday	Lectionary Cycle Weekday	Ash Wednesday	Easter	Ascension Sunday	Pentecost	Body and Blood of Christ
2009	B	I	25 Feb	12 Apr	24 May	31 May	14 June
2010	C	II	17 Feb	4 Apr	16 May	23 May	6 June
2011	A	I	9 Mar	24 Apr	5 June	12 June	26 June
2012	B	II	22 Feb	8 Apr	20 May	27 May	10 June
2013	C	I	13 Feb	31 Mar	12 May	19 May	2 June
2014	A	II	5 Mar	20 Apr	1 June	8 June	22 June
2015	B	I	18 Feb	5 Apr	17 May	24 May	7 June
2016	C	II	10 Feb	27 Mar	8 May	15 May	29 May
2017	A	I	1 Mar	16 Apr	28 May	4 June	18 June
2018	B	II	14 Feb	1 Apr	13 May	20 May	3 June
2019	C	I	6 Mar	21 Apr	2 June	9 June	23 June
2020	A	II	26 Feb	12 Apr	24 May	31 May	14 June
2021	B	I	17 Feb	4 Apr	17 May	23 May	6 June
2022	C	II	2 Mar	17 Apr	29 May	5 June	19 June
2023	A	I	22 Feb	9 Apr	21 May	28 May	11 June
2024	B	II	14 Feb	31 Mar	12 May	19 May	2 June
2025	C	I	5 Mar	20 Apr	1 June	8 June	22 June
2026	A	II	18 Feb	5 Apr	17 May	24 May	7 June
2027	B	I	10 Feb	28 Mar	9 May	16 May	30 May
2028	C	II	1 Mar	16 Apr	28 May	4 June	18 June
2029	A	I	14 Feb	1 Apr	13 May	20 May	3 June
2030	B	II	6 Mar	21 Apr	2 June	9 June	23 June
2031	C	I	26 Feb	13 Apr	25 May	1 June	15 June
2032	A	II	11 Feb	28 Mar	9 May	16 May	30 May
2033	B	I	2 Mar	17 Apr	29 May	5 June	19 June
2034	C	II	22 Feb	9 Apr	21 May	28 May	11 June
2035	A	I	7 Feb	25 Mar	6 May	13 May	27 May
2036	B	II	27 Feb	13 Apr	25 May	1 June	15 June
2037	C	I	18 Feb	5 Apr	17 May	24 May	7 June
2038	A	II	10 Mar	25 Apr	6 June	13 June	27 June
2039	B	I	23 Feb	10 Apr	22 May	29 May	12 June
2040	C	II	15 Feb	1 Apr	13 May	20 May	3 June
2041	A	I	6 Mar	21 Apr	2 June	9 June	23 June
2042	B	II	19 Feb	6 April	18 May	25 May	8 June

WEEKS OF ORDINARY TIME

Year	Lectionary Cycle Sunday	Lectionary Cycle Weekday	Before season of Lent Number of Weeks	Before season of Lent Ending	After season of Easter Beginning	After season of Easter Week Number	First Sunday of Advent
2009	B	I	7	24 Feb	1 June	9	29 Nov
2010	C	II	6	16 Feb	24 May	8	28 Nov
2011	A	I	9	8 Mar	13 June	11	27 Nov
2012	B	II	7	21 Feb	28 May	8	2 Dec
2013	C	I	5	12 Feb	20 May	7	1 Dec
2014	A	II	8	4 Mar	9 June	10	30 Nov
2015	B	I	6	17 Feb	25 May	8	29 Nov
2016	C	II	5	9 Feb	16 May	7	27 Nov
2017	A	I	8	28 Feb	5 June	9	3 Dec
2018	B	II	6	13 Feb	21 May	7	2 Dec
2019	C	I	8	5 Mar	10 June	10	1 Dec
2020	A	II	7	25 Feb	1 June	9	29 Nov
2021	B	I	6	16 Feb	24 May	8	28 Nov
2022	C	II	8	1 Mar	6 June	10	27 Nov
2023	A	I	7	21 Feb	29 May	8	3 Dec
2024	B	II	6	13 Feb	20 May	7	1 Dec
2025	C	I	8	4 Mar	9 June	10	30 Nov
2026	A	II	6	17 Mar	25 May	8	29 Nov
2027	B	I	5	8 Feb	17 May	7	28 Nov
2028	C	II	8	29 Feb	5 June	9	3 Dec
2029	A	I	6	13 Feb	21 May	7	2 Dec
2030	B	II	8	5 Mar	10 June	10	1 Dec
2031	C	I	7	25 Feb	2 June	9	30 Nov
2032	A	II	5	10 Feb	17 May	7	28 Nov
2033	B	I	8	1 Mar	6 June	10	27 Nov
2034	C	II	7	21 Feb	29 May	8	3 Dec
2035	A	I	4	6 Feb	14 May	6	2 Dec
2036	B	II	7	26 Feb	2 June	9	30 Nov
2037	C	I	6	17 Feb	25 May	8	29 Nov
2038	A	II	9	9 Mar	14 June	11	28 Nov
2039	B	I	7	22 Feb	30 May	9	27 Nov
2040	C	II	6	14 Feb	21 May	7	2 Dec
2041	A	I	8	5 Mar	10 June	10	1 Dec

CANON LAW CONCERNING MARRIAGE

1. The Church normally requires for validity that every marriage between Catholics, or between a Catholic and a non-Catholic, be celebrated before a bishop, priest or deacon duly authorised, and two witnesses. Otherwise the parties will not, in the sight of God, be really husband and wife, even though there may be a binding legal contract under civil law. (NB: A marriage between two non-Catholics is not subject to this rule.)

2. In this context, a Catholic means anyone baptised in the Catholic Church; and it also means a baptised person who has become a Catholic.

3. Prior to marriage, so that there may be time for several interviews with the priest for the instruction, collection of documents, publications of banns, etc., it is recommended that the couple should give notice to the parish priest six months before the date proposed for marriage. (When one or both of the parties come from abroad, a considerably longer period of notice may be required.)

4. The Church gives permission for mixed marriages to take place, but only with certain safeguards, between a Catholic and a person baptised into another Christian tradition.

a) The Catholic party undertakes to do all in his/her power within the unity of the marriage to have all the children to be born of the marriage baptised and brought up in the Catholic faith, and the non-Catholic party must be made aware of this undertaking. If for any reason the non-Catholic is opposed to the fulfilment of the Catholic's obligation, the full situation must be explained to the bishop when the application for a dispensation is submitted.

b) The marriage ceremony shall take place in the Catholic Church. For serious reasons, however, the Catholic Church is willing to grant a dispensation enabling the parties of a mixed marriage to have the ceremony in a non-Catholic church.

5 A dispensation is required for marriage between a Catholic and a person who has not been baptised.

FASTING AND ABSTINENCE

Statement from the Bishops of England and Wales on Canons 1249-1253 (24 January 1985)

1. The new code of Canon Law reminds us that all of Christ's faithful are obliged to do penance. The obligation arises in imitation of Christ himself and in response to his call. During his life on earth, not least at the beginning of his public ministry. Our Lord undertook voluntary penance. He invited his followers to do the same. The penance he invited would be a participation in his own suffering, an expression of inner conversion and a form of reparation for sin. It would be a personal sacrifice made out of love for God and our neighbour. It follows that if we are to be true, as Christians, to the spirit of Christ, we must practise some form of penance.

2. So that all may be united with Christ and with one another in a common practice of penance, the Church sets aside certain penitential days. On these days the faithful are to devote themselves in a special way to prayer, self-denial and works of charity. Such days are not designed to confine or isolate penance but to intensify it in the life of the Christian right through the year.

3. Lent is the traditional season of renewal and repentance in Christ. The New Code re-affirms this. It also prescribes that Ash Wednesday and Good Friday are to be observed as days of fast and abstinence. Fasting means that the amount of food we eat is considerably reduced. Abstinence means that we give up a particular kind of food or drink or form of amusement. Those over eighteen are bound by the law of fasting until the beginning of their sixtieth year, while all over fourteen are bound by the law of abstinence. Priests and parents are urged to foster the spirit and practice of penance among those too young to be the subjects of either law.

4. Because each Friday recalls the crucifixion of Our Lord, it too is set aside as a special penitential day. The Church does not prescribe, however, that fish must be eaten on Fridays. It never did. Abstinence always meant the giving up of meat rather than the eating of fish as a substitute. What the Church does require, according to the new Code, is that its members abstain on Fridays from meat or some other food or that they perform some alternative work of penance laid down by the Bishops' Conference.

5. In accordance with the mind of the

universal Church, the Bishops of England and Wales remind their people of the obligation of Friday penance, and instruct them that it may be fulfilled in one or more of the following ways:

a) by abstaining from meat or some other food
b) by abstaining from alcoholic drink, smoking or some form of amusement
c) by making the special effort involved in family prayer, taking part in the Mass, visiting the Blessed Sacrament or praying the Stations of the Cross
d) by fasting from all food for a longer period than usual and perhaps giving what is saved in this way to the needy at home and abroad
e) by making a special effort to help somebody who is poor, sick, old or lonely

6. The form of penance we adopt each Friday is a matter of personal choice and does not have to take the same form every Friday. Failure to undertake this penance on a particular Friday would not constitute a sin. However, penance is part of the life of every Christian and the intention to do penance on Friday is of obligation. We are confident that the faithful of England and Wales will take this obligation to heart in memory of the passion and death of Our Lord.

■ THE EUCHARISTIC FAST

Since November 1964, the Eucharistic fast has been reduced to one hour. This means that food and drink (even alcoholic, in moderation) may always be taken up to one hour before the time of receiving Holy Communion. Water does not break the fast and so may be taken at any time before receiving Holy Communion.

The New Code of Canon Law, Canon 919.3 indicates that no period of fasting is required for those who are sick (not necessarily bedridden or housebound). Persons looking after the sick and aged and wishing to receive Holy Communion with them, whenever they are unable to observe the fast of one hour without inconvenience, are encouraged to receive Holy Communion.

■ RECEPTION OF THE EUCHARIST A SECOND TIME ON THE SAME DAY

In accordance with Canon 917 of the Code of Canon Law it is permitted to receive Holy Communion twice on one day provided this takes place during the celebration of Mass. This provision is to be observed except in the case of Viaticum for the dying.

■ EUCHARISTIC MINISTERS

On the recommendation of their parish priest men and women after study and instruction may be commissioned:

a) to assist with the distribution of Holy Communion under one or both kinds at Mass; and if there is need
b) to take Communion to the sick and housebound and
c) to expose the Blessed Sacrament for periods of Exposition

■ CHRISTIAN BAPTISM

1 A child should be baptised as soon as practicable after birth.

2 Ordinarily a child must be baptised in the parish to which its parents belong; if born in another parish he or she should be taken to the parents' parish.

3 The names given in baptism should be in conformity with the dignity and Christian status conferred by the sacrament.

4 Canon Law requires only one Godparent. In England there is a custom for two and both should be practising Catholics. A baptised non-Catholic may be a witness alongside a Catholic Godparent.

5 Arrangements will be made by the priest for some instructions of the parents and Godparents if practicable.

■ PERMANENT DIACONATE

Authorisation for restoration of the permanent diaconate in the Roman Rite — making it possible for men to become deacons permanently, without going on to the priesthood — was promulgated by Pope Paul VI, 18 June 1967, in a document entitled Sacrum Diaconatus Ordinem ("Sacred Order of the Diaconate").

The Pope's action implemented the desire expressed by the Second Vatican Council for re-establishment of the diaconate as an independent order in its own right not only to supply ministers for carrying on the work of the Church but also to complete the hierarchical structure of the Church of Roman Rite.

Permanent deacons have been traditional in the Eastern Church. The Western Church, however, since the fourth or fifth century, generally followed the practice of conferring the diaconate only as a sacred order preliminary to the priesthood, and of restricting the ministry of deacons to liturgical functions.

The Pope's document, issued on his own initiative provided:

a) Qualified unmarried men 25 years of age or older may be ordained permanent deacons. They cannot marry after ordination.
b) Qualified married men 35 years of age or older may be ordained permanent deacons. The consent of the wife of a prospective deacon is required. A married deacon cannot remarry after the death of his wife.
c) Preparation for the diaconate includes a course of study and formation over a period of at least three years.
d) Candidates who are not religious must be affiliated with a diocese. Re-establishment of the permanent diaconate among religious is reserved to the Holy See.
e) Deacons will practice their ministry under the direction of a bishop and with the priests with whom they will be associated.

'It is the duty of the deacon, to the extent that he has been authorised by competent authority, to administer baptism solemnly, to be custodian and dispenser of the Eucharist, to assist at and bless marriages in the name of the Church, to bring Viaticum to the dying, to read the sacred scripture to the faithful, to instruct and exhort the people, to preside at the worship and prayer of the faithful, to administer sacramentals, and to officiate at funeral and burial services. (Deacons are) dedicated to duties of charity and administration' (Lumen Gentium 29).

ECCLESIASTICAL TITLES AND MODES OF ADDRESS

■ CARDINALS

are addressed in speech as: *Your Eminence* and referred to as: *His Eminence.*
The manner of address in writing is: *Your Eminence, or Dear Cardinal Smith.*
Address on envelope: *His Eminence the Cardinal Archbishop of Oxbridge, or His Eminence Cardinal John Smith, Archbishop of Oxbridge.*

■ ARCHBISHOPS

are addressed in speech as: *Your Grace* and referred to as: *His Grace.*
The manner of address in writing is: *Your Grace, or Dear Archbishop Smith.*
Address on envelope: *His Grace the Archbishop of Oxbridge, or The Most Reverend John Smith, Archbishop of Oxbridge.*

■ BISHOPS

are addressed in speech as: *My Lord* and referred to as: *His Lordship.*
The manner of address in writing is: *Dear Bishop Smith.*
Address on envelope: *The Right Reverend John Smith, Bishop of Oxbridge.*

■ ABBOTS

are addressed in speech as: *Father Abbot.*
The manner of address is: *My Lord Abbot, or Dear Abbot.*
Address on envelope: *Right Reverend the Abbot of Oxbridge * or The Right Reverend Dom John Smith, * Abbot of Oxbridge*

■ PROTONOTARIES APOSTOLIC AND PRELATES OF HONOUR

are addressed in speech as: *Monsignor* and are referred to as: *Monsignor Smith.*
The manner of address in writing is: *Dear Monsignor Smith,*
Address on envelope: *The Reverend Monsignor John Smith (or, if he is also a Canon: The Reverend Monsignor Canon John Smith).*

■ CHAPLAINS OF HIS HOLINESS

As for Prelates. *(See section Protonotaries Apostolic and Prelates of Honour)*

■ PROVOSTS

are addressed in speech as: *Provost* and referred to as *Provost Smith.*
The manner of address in writing is: *Dear Provost Smith.*
Address on envelope: *Reverend Provost John Smith.*

■ CANONS

are addressed in speech as: *Canon* and referred to as *Canon Smith.*
The manner of address in writing is: *Dear Canon Smith.*
Address on envelope: *Reverend Canon John Smith.*

■ PROVINCIALS

are addressed in speech as: *Father Provincial.*
The manner of address in writing is: *Dear Father Provincial.*
Address on envelope: *The Reverend Father Provincial.* *

■ PRIESTS

are addressed in speech as: *Father* and referred to as: *Father Smith.*
The manner of address in writing is: *Dear Father Smith.*
Address on envelope: *The Reverend John Smith.*

■ DEACONS

are addressed in speech as: *Deacon* and referred to as: *Deacon Smith.*
The manner of address in writing is: *Dear Deacon Smith.*
Address on envelope: *The Reverend Deacon John Smith.*

**** Followed by the initials of his Order***

CLERGY

IN ENGLAND AND WALES

CARDINALS, ARCHBISHOPS AND BISHOPS

■ IN ENGLAND AND WALES

Alexander, Mervyn A, former Bishop of Clifton; St Joseph's Presbytery, Camp Road, Weston-super-Mare BS23 2EN
Tel: 01934-629865

Arnold, John, Auxiliary Bishop of Westminster; Flat 1, 8 Morpeth Terr, London SW1P 1EQ **Tel:** 020 7798 9018

Bowen, Michael, Archbishop Emeritus of Southwark; c/o Archbishop's House, St George's Road, Southwark, London SE1 6HX **Tel:** 020-7928 2495
Fax : 020-7928 7833 **E-mail:** aps@southwark.co.uk

Brain, Terence J, Bishop of Salford; Wardley Hall, Worsley, Manchester M28 2ND **Tel:** 0161-794 2825
Fax: 0161-727 8592

Budd, Christopher, Bishop of Plymouth; Bishop's House, 31 Wyndham Street West, Plymouth, Devon PL1 5RZ
Tel: 01752-224414 **Fax:** 01752-223750

Burns, Thomas Matthew SM, Bishop of Menevia, Bryn Rhos, 79 Walter Road, Swansea SA1 4PS
Tel: 01792-650534 **Fax:** 01792-518786

Campbell, Michael OSA, Coadjutor Bishop of Lancaster; Pastoral Centre, Balmoral Road, Lancaster LA1 3BT
Tel: 01524-596050

Chomnysky, Paul OSBM, Apostolic Exarch for Ukrainians in Great Britain, Titular Bishop of Buffada. 22 Binney Street, London W1K 5BQ **Tel:** 020-7629 1073
Fax: 020-7355 3314

Conry, Kieran, Bishop of Arundel & Brighton. St Joseph's Hall, Greyfriars Lane, Storrington, Pulborough RH20 4HE **Tel:** 01903-742172
Fax: 01903-746336

Crowley, John, Bishop Emeritus of Middlesbrough, Our Lady of Lourdes, 51 Cambridge Park, Wanstead, London E11 2PR

Doyle, Peter, Bishop of Northampton, Bishop's House, Marriott Street, Northampton NN2 6AW
Tel: 01604-715635 **Fax:** 01604-792186

Drainey, Terence Patrick, Bishop of Middlesbrough, Bishop's House, 16 Cambridge Rd, Middlebrough TS5 5NN
Tel: 01642 818253 **E-mail:** bishop@dioceseofmiddlebrough.co.uk

Evans, Michael C, Bishop of East Anglia, The White House, 21 Upgate, Poringland, Norwich, Norfolk NR14 7SH
Tel: 01508-492202/493956
Fax: 01508-495358

Gallagher, Paul, Most Rev, STL, JCD, (Liverpool), Titular Archbishop of Hodelm; Apostolic Nuncio to Burundi. Nunciature Apostolique, Chaussée Prince Louis Rwagasore, BP1068 Bujumbura, Burundi
Tel: 00257 22 23 26 **Fax:** 00257 23 31 76
E-mail: nonciat@cbinf.com

Griffiths, Ambrose, OSB, retired Bishop of Hexham and Newcastle; c/o Bishop's House, East Denton Hall, 800 West Road, Newcastle upon Tyne NE5 2BJ
Tel: 0191-228 0003 **Fax:** 0191-274 0432

Hendricks, Paul, MA, PhL, (Southwark), Titular Bishop of Rosemarkie, Auxilliary in Southwark, 95 Carshalton Road, Sutton, Surrey, SM1 4LL
Tel: 020 8643 8007

Hine, John, PhL, VG (Southwark) Titular Bishop of Beverley, Auxiliary in Southwark. Bishop's House, More Park, West Malling, Kent ME19 6HN
Tel: 01732-845486 **Fax:** 01732-847888
E-mail: jhine@rcsouthwark.co.uk

Hollis, Crispian, Bishop of Portsmouth, Bishop's House, Edinburgh Road, Portsmouth, Hants PO1 3HG Tel: 023-9282 0894, Fax: 023-9286 3086.

Hopes, Alan S, BD, AKC, VG, Auxiliary Bishop in Westminster, 16 Abingdon Road, London W8 6AF
Tel: 020-7376 1661

Jabalé, Mark, OSB, Bishop Emeritus of Menevia, c/o Bryn Rhos, 79 Walter Road, Swansea SA1 4PS
Tel: 01792-650534 **Fax:** 01792-518786

Jukes, John, OFMConv, STL, Bishop of Strathearn, former Auxiliary Bishop Emeritus in Southwark; Willowbank, Gladstone Road, Huntly, Aberdeenshire AB54 8DB **Tel:** 01466-792832
E-mail: JJukesOFMC@aol.com

Kelly, Patrick Altham, Archbishop of Liverpool; Archbishop's House, Lowood, Carnatic Road, Liverpool L18 8BY
Tel: 0151-724 6398 **Fax:** 0151-724 6405

Konstant, David, Bishop Emeritus of Leeds; Ashlea, 62 Headingley Lane, Leeds LS6 2BU **Tel/Fax:** 0113-261 8002 **E-mail:** dakons@aol.com

Lang, Declan, Bishop of Clifton. St Ambrose, North Road, Leigh Woods, Bristol BS8 3PW **Tel:** 0117-973 3072

Lindsay, Hugh, former Bishop of Hexham and Newcastle; Convent of Our Lady of Lourdes, Boarbank Hall, Grange-over-Sands, Cumbria LA11 7NH **Tel:** 01539-535591

Longley, Bernard, Titular Bishop of Zarna, Archbishop's House, Ambrosden Avenue, London SW1P 1QJ **Tel:** 020-7931 6061

Lynch, Patrick SSCC, MA, VG, (Southwark), Titular Bishop of Castro, Auxilliary in Southwark, Park House, 6A Cresswell Park, Blackheath, London SE3 9RD **Tel:** 020 8297 9219 **E-mail:** bishoplynch7@btinternet.com

McCartie, Patrick Leo, former Bishop of Northampton, Aston Hall, Aston, Stone, Staffordshire ST15 0BJ **Tel:** 01785-286715

McDonald, Kevin, Archbishop of Southwark, Archbishop's House, 150 St George's Road, London SE1 6HX **Tel:** 020-7928 2495 **Fax:** 020-7928 7833

McGough, David, Auxilliary Bishop of Birmingham, The Rocks, 106 Draycott Road, Tean, Staffs ST10 4JF **Tel/Fax:** 01538 722433

McMahon, Malcolm OP, Bishop of Nottingham; Bishop's House, 27 Cavendish Road East, The Park, Nottingham NG7 1BB **Tel:** 0115-947 4786 **Fax:** 0115-947 5235

McMahon, Thomas, Bishop of Brentwood; Bishop's House, Stock, Ingatestone, Essex CM4 9BU **Tel:** 01277- 840268 **Fax:** 01277-261152

Malone, Vincent, Titular Bishop of Abora, retired Auxiliary BP of Liverpool, 17 West Oakhill Park, Liverpool L13 4BN **Tel:** 0151- 228 7637 **Fax:** 0151-475 0841

Mullins, Daniel J, Bishop Emeritus of Menevia; 8 Rhodfa Gwendraeth, Cydweli, Carmarthenshire SA17 4SR **Tel:** 01554-890142

Munõz, His Excellency Archbishop Faustino Sainz, Apostolic Nuncio, 54 Parkside, London SW19 5NE **Tel:** 020-8944 7189 **Fax:** 020-8947 2494

Murphy-O'Connor, Cormac, Cardinal Archbishop of Westminster. Archbishop's House, Ambrosden Avenue, Westminster London SW1P 1QJ **Tel:** 020-7798 9033 **Fax:** 020-7798 9077

Nichols, Vincent, Archbishop of Birmingham. Archbishop's House, 8 Shadwell Street, Birmingham B4 6EY **Tel:** 0121-236 9090 **Fax:** 0121 212 0171

Noble, Brian Michael, Bishop of Shrewsbury; Laburnum Cottage, 97 Barnston Road, Barnston, Wirral CH61 1BW **Tel:** 0151-648 0623 **Fax:** 0151-648 0624 **E-mail:** bishop@dioceseofshrewsbury.org

O'Donoghue, Patrick, Bishop of Lancaster, Bishop's Apartments, Cathedral House, Balmoral Road, Lancaster LA1 3BT **Tel:** 01254-384830

Pargeter, Philip, Titular Bishop of Valentiniana, Auxilliary in Birmingham; Grove House, College Road, Sutton Coldfield, West Midlands B73 5AH **Tel:** 0121-354 4363

Rawsthorne, John, Bishop of Hallam. 75 Norfolk Road, Sheffield S2 2SZ **Tel/Fax:** 0114-278 7988 **E-mail:** bishopofhallam@btinternet.com.

Regan, Edwin, Bishop of Wrexham, Bishop's House, Sontley Road, Wrexham, LL13 7EW **Tel:** 01978-262726 **Fax:** 01978-354257

Roche, Arthur, Bishop of Leeds. Bishop's House, 13 North Grange Road, Leeds LS6 2BR. Tel: 0113-230 4533 **Fax:** 0113-278 9890 **E-mail:** b.roche@leeds-diocese.org.uk

Smith, Peter, Archbishop of Cardiff, Archbishop's House, 43 Cathedral Road, Cardiff CF11 9HD **Tel:** 029-2022 0411 **Fax:** 029-2037 9036

Stack, George, Auxiliary Bishop of Westminster, 14 Egerton Gardens, London NW4 4BA **Tel:** 020-8202 8024

Tripp, Howard, Auxiliary Bishop Emeritus of Southwark; 67 Haynt Walk, London SW20 9NY **Tel:** 020-8543 4864 **E-mail:** htripp@ukgateway.net

Walmsley, Francis J, Former Bishop-in-Ordinary to Her Majesty's Forces; c/o 26 The Crescent, Farnborough, Hants GU14 7AS **Tel:** 01252-373699 **Fax:** 01252-349006

Williams, Thomas Anthony, Titular Bishop of Mageo, Auxiliary Bishop of Liverpool. Liverpool Archdiocesan Centre for Evangelisation, Croxteth Drive, Liverpool L17 1AA **Tel:** 0151-522 1000

■ IN SCOTLAND

Conti, Mario Joseph, Archbishop of Glasgow; 40 Newlands Road, Glasgow G43 2JD **Tel:** 0141-226 5898

Cunningham, John, Bishop of Galloway; Candida Casa, 8 Corsehill Road, Ayr KA7 2ST **Tel:** 01292-266750

Devine, Joseph, Bishop of Motherwell; 22 Wellhall Road, Hamilton, Lanarkshire ML3 9BG **Tel:** 01698-423058

Logan, Vincent, Bishop of Dunkeld; Bishop's House, 29 Roseangle, Dundee DD1 4LX **Tel:** 01382-24327

Moran, Peter Antony, Bishop of Aberdeen, Bishop's House, 3 Queen's Cross, Aberdeen AB15 4XU **Tel:** 01224 319154

O'Brien, HE Keith Patrick, Cardinal Archbishop of St Andrews and Edinburgh; 42 Greenhill Gardens, Edinburgh EH10 4BJ **Tel:** 0131-447 3337

Tartaglia, Philip, Bishop of Paisley; 107 Corsebar Road, Paisley, Renfrewshire PA2 9PY **Tel:** 0141-889 7200

Toal, Joseph Anthony, Bishop of Argyll and the Isles; Bishop's House, Esplanade, Oban PA34 5AB **Tel:** 01631-571395

■ IN IRELAND

Boyce, Philip, Bishop of Raphoe, Ard Adhamhnain, Letterkenny, Co Donegal **Tel:** 074-21208

Brady, Sean, Cardinal Archbishop of Armagh; Ara Coeli, Armagh BT61 7QY **Tel:** 028-3752 2045

Brennan, Denis, Bishop of Ferns; Bishop's House, Summerhill, Wexford **Tel:** (053) 22177

Brookes, Francis G, DD, former Bishop of Dromore, Drumiller House, 14 Drumiller Road, Jerrettpass, Newry, Co. Down **Tel:** 028-3082 1508

Buckley, John, Bishop of Cork and Ross; Bishop's House, Redemption Road, Cork **Tel:** 021-430 1717

Cassidy, Joseph, Former Archbishop of Tuam, The Presbytery, Moore, Ballydangan, Athlone, Co Roscommon **Tel:** 0905-73539

Clifford, Dermot, Archbishop of Cashel and Emly; Archbishop's House, Thurles, Co Tipperary **Tel:** 0504-21512

Clifford, Gerard, Bishop of Geron, Auxilliary Bishop of Armagh, Annaskeagh, Ravensdale, Dundalk, Co Louth **Tel:** 042-9371012

Comiskey, Brendan, SSCC, former Bishop of Ferns; c/o Bishop's House, Summerhill, Wexford

Connell, Desmond, Emeritus Archbishop of Dublin, Archbishop's House, Drumcondra, Dublin 9 **Tel:** 01-837 3732

Daly, Cahal, former Cardinal Archbishop of Armagh 23 Rosetta Avenue, Ormeau Road, Belfast BT7 3HG **Tel:** 028-9064 2431

Daly, Edward, Former Bishop of Derry; 'Gurteen', 9 Steelstown Road, Derry BT48 8EU **Tel:** 028-7135 9809

Drennan, Martin, Auxiliary Bishop of Dublin, Cluain Mhuaire, Killarney Road, Bray, Co. Wicklow **Tel:** (01) 2760950

Duffy, Joseph, Bishop of Clogher; Bishop's House, Mongahan, Co Monaghan **Tel:** 047-81019

Farquhar, Anthony, Bishop of Ermiana, Auxiliary Bishop of Down and Connor; 73 Somerton Road, Belfast BT15 4DE

Field, Raymond, Auxiliary Bishop of Dublin, 5 The Drive, Temple Manor, Temple Mills, Celbridge, Co. Kildaire **Tel:** (01) 6275051

Finnegan, Thomas A, former Bishop of Killala, Bishop's House, Carramore, Lacken, Ballina, Co Mayo

Fleming, John, Bishop of Killala, Bishop's House, Co Mayo **Tel:** 096-21518

Flynn, Thomas, retired Bishop of Achonry; St Nathy's Ballaghaderreen, Co Roscommon **Tel:** 0907-60021

Forristal, Laurence, Bishop of Ossory; Sion House, Kilkenny **Tel:** 056-62448

Hegarty, Seamus, Bishop of Derry, Bishop's House, St Eugene's Cathedral, Derry City **Tel:** 028-7126 2302

Jones, Christopher, Bishop of Elphin, St Mary's Sligo, **Tel:** 071-62670

Kelly, Brendan, Bishop of Achonry, Bishop's House, Edmonstown, Ballaghaderreen, Co. Roscommon **Tel:** (094) 986 0021

Kirby, John, Bishop of Clonfert, Bishop's House, St Brendan's, Coorheen, Loughrea, Co Galway **Tel:** 091-841560

Lagan, Francis, Bishop of Sidnacestra, Auxilliary Bishop of Derry, 9 Glen Road, Strabane, Co Tyrone BT82 8BX **Tel:** 028-7188 4533

Lee, William, Bishop of Waterford and Lismore, Bishop's House, John's Hill, Waterford City **Tel:** 051-874463

McAreavey, John, Bishop of Dromore Bishop's House, 44 Armagh Road, Newry, **Tel:** 028-3026 2444

McKeown, Donal DD, Bishop of Cell Ausaille and Auxiliary Bishop of Down and Connor, cons 29 April 2001 **Tel:** 028-9077 6185

McKiernan Francis, former Bishop of Kilmore, 5 Brookside, Farnham Road, Cavan **Tel:** 049- 436 1804

McLoughlin, James, Bishop of Galway, Bishop's House, Mount St Mary's, Galway **Tel:** 091-563566

Magee, John, Bishop of Cloyne, Bishop's House, Cobh, Co Cork **Tel:** 021 4811430

Martin, Diarmuid, Archbishop of Dublin, Archbishop's House, Drumcondra, Dublin 9 **Tel:** 01-836 0723

Moriarty, James, Bishop of Kildare and Leighlin, Bishop's House, Carlow, Co Carlow **Tel:** 0503 76725

Murphy, William, Bishop of Kerry, Bishop's House, Killarney, Co Kerry **Tel:** 064-31168

Murray, Donal, Bishop of Limerick, Kilmoyle, North Circular Road, Limerick City **Tel:** 061-451433

Neary, Michael, Archbishop of Tuam, Archbishop's House, Tuam, Co Galway **Tel:** 093-24166

O'Ceallaigh, Fiachra, Bishop of Tres Tabernae and Auxiliary Bishop of Dublin, 19 St Anthony's Road, Rialto, Dublin 8 **Tel:** 01-453 7495

O'Mahony, Dermot, Titular Bishop of Tiava, Former Bishop of Dublin; 19 Longlands, Swords, Co Dublin **Tel:** 01-840 1596

O'Reilly, Colm, Bishop of Ardagh and Clonmacnois; Bishop's House, St Michael's, Longford, Co Longford **Tel:** 043-46432

O'Reilly, Leo, Bishop of Kilmore, Bishop's House, Cullies, Cavan, Co Cavan **Tel:** 049-433 1496

Russell, Michael, Former Bishop of Waterford and Lismore; Woodleigh, 2 Summerville Avenue, Waterford.

Ryan, Laurence, former Bishop of Kildare and Leighlin; "Teach Moling", Oak Park, Carlow **Tel:** 0503-36835

Smith, Michael, Bishop of Meath; Bishop's House, Mullingar, Co Westmeath **Tel:** 044-48841

Treanor, Noel, Bishop of Down and Connor; Lisbreen, 73 Somerton Road, Belfast, Co Antrim BT15 4DE **Tel:** (028) 90776185

Walsh, Eamonn, Bishop of Elmhama, and Apostolic Administrator, Diocese of Ferns, Naomh Brid, Blessington Road, Tallaght, Dublin 24 **Tel:** 01-459 8032

Walsh, Patrick J, retired Bishop of Down and Connor; Lisbreen, 73 Somertown Road, Belfast BT15 4DE **Tel:** 028-9077 6185

Walsh, William, Bishop of Killaloe, Westbourne, Ennis, Co Clare **Tel:** 065-6828638

Williams, Desmond, Former Bishop of Summa. Holy Family Residence, Roebuck Road, Dublin 14 **Tel:** 01-283 2214

A

PRIESTS IN ENGLAND AND WALES

SECULAR AND REGULAR

1. This list is intended to include names and addresses of all priests, secular and regular, living and working in England & Wales.
2. Names of some priests employed or residing abroad, but ecclesiastically connected with England and Wales, are included in this list; it is not possible to include members of missionary orders unless they are stationed in Great Britain.
3. The name of the diocese of priests of England and Wales retired, invalided, or working outside of their diocese is added in brackets where it is known.
4. For priests within a Religious Order the abbreviation is added in brackets where it is known.

Abbreviations:
Ave - Avenue, Cl - Close, Cres - Crescent, Dr - Drive, Ho - House, Ln - Lane, Rd - Road, St - Street, Terr - Terrace.

Abberton, John, BA, (Leeds), Holy Spirit Presbytery, 18 Cemetery Rd, Heckmondwike WF16 9EB **Tel:** 01924-402579 (priest) **Tel/Fax:** 01924-410568 (office)

Abbott, John, LRAM, ARCM, LMus, STCL, (Nottingham, retired), 70 Bramcote Ln, Wollaton, Nottingham NG8 2NG **Tel:** 0115-928 6271

Aboagye-Takiiah, Joseph (Sunyani), 103 Maison Dieu Rd, Dover CT16 1RU **Tel:** 01304-209372

Abbs, Gordon, (Liverpool), St Stephen's Presbytery, 101 Sandy Ln, Orford, Warrington WA2 9HS **Tel:** 01925-632849

Ablewhite, John BA (Westminster), 9 Breakspear, Stevenage, Herts SG2 9SQ **Tel:** 01438-352182

Abonyi, Innocent, (MSP), St Augustine's, 24 Amersham Hill, High Wycombe HP13 6NZ **Tel:** 01753 523147

Abouna, Andreas (Chaldean), 38 Cavendish Ave, Ealing W15 0JQ

Abouzayd, Shafiq, DPhil(Oxon) (Melkite-Greek Catholic Priest), 46 Sunderland Ave, Oxford OX2 8DU

Abuga, Raymond, (MSP), Our Lady and St Ethelbert, Wellington St, Slough, Berks **Tel:** 01753 523147

Acton, Charles, Canon STL, (Westminster), Flat 4, 8 Morpeth Terr, London SW1P 1EQ **Tel:** 020-7798 9021

Acton, Colm, Canon, (Southwark), 207 Cannon Hill Ln, Merton, Surrey SW20 9DB **Tel:** 020-8542 6355

Adam, Richard, (OCSO), Mount Saint Bernard Abbey, Coalville, Leics LE67 5UL **Tel:** 01530-832298/832022

Adams, Brett, BTh(Hons), (Brentwood), 51 Priory St, Colchester, Essex CO1 2QB **Tel:** 01206 866317

Adams, David, (Portsmouth), Maryhouse, 32 High St, Gosport, Hants PO12 1DF **Tel:** 02392-580119 **Fax:** 02392-526954 **E-mail:** gosport@portsmouth-dio.org.uk

Adams, Dunstan, MA, (OSB), Ampleforth Abbey, York YO62 4EN **Tel:** 01439-766714 **Fax:** 01439-766724

Adams, Graham, Mgr, (Northampton), The Presbytery, Aston-le-Walls, Daventry, Northants NN11 6UF **Tel:** 01295-660221

Adams, Juniper, (OFM), The Friary, 120 Niddrie Mains Rd, Edinburgh EH16 4EG **Tel:** 0131-661 2185 **Fax:** 0131-652 0601 **E-mail:** juniper@vodaphone.net

Adams, Leslie, (Portsmouth), Peterhouse, St Peter Street, Winchester, Hants SO23 8BW **Tel:** 01962 852804 **Fax:** 01962 843691 **E-mail:** stpeterswinchester@btopenworld.com

Adams, Michael, (Southwark), English Martyrs, 37 Frindsbury Rd, Strood, Kent ME2 4JA **Tel:** 01634-717582

Adamson, Duncan, (Westminster), 211 Old Marylebone Rd, Marylebone, London NW1 5QT **Tel:** 020-7723 5101

Addison Paul, STB, (OSM), 264 Fulham Rd, London SW10 9EL

Adkins Alex, (Nottingham),St Hughs Rectory, 34 Broadgate, Lincoln LN2 5AQ **Tel:** 01522 5289611 **Fax:** 01522 537685 **Email:** alexad@tiscali.co.uk

Agius, Emmanuel, (Arundel & Brighton), The Holy Family Presbytery, Spinney Oak, Ongar Hill, Addlestone, Surrey KT15 1BP **Tel:** 01932-848616

Agley, William BTh (Southwark) 312 High St, St Mary Cray, Kent BR5 4AR **Tel:** 01689 821749

Ahearn, Beverley M, PhD, (CSSR), Hawkstone Hall, Marchamley, Shrewsbury SY4 5LG **Tel:** 01630-685242 **Fax:** 01630-685565 **E-mail:** hawkhall@aol.com

Ahern, Brian, MA, (MHM, retired), Herbert Ho, 41 Victoria Rd, Freshfield, Liverpool L37 1LW **Tel:** 01704 835851 **E-mail:** brian@bahern.fsbusiness.co.uk

Ahern, John, (Salford), St Mary, Elbow St, Levenshulme M19 3PY **Tel:** 0161-248 8836

Aikens, Patrick, (Southwark), St William of York, 4 Brockley Park, Forest Hill, London SE23 1PS **Tel:** 020-8690 4549

Ainsworth, Jerome, BA, (Lancaster), St Catherine's, Drover Ln, Penrith. Cumbria CA11 9EL **Tel:** 01768-862273

Akoeso, Bernard M, (OSB), Priest in Charge, Monastery of Christ the King, Bramley Rd, Enfield, London N14 4HE **Tel:** 020 8440 7769/6648

Akongwale, Victor (Ogoja), 20 Village Way, Beckenham, Kent BR3 3NP

Aladics, Richard, MA, STL (Leeds) 8-14 Austin Woodbury Place, Old Toongabbie New South Wales 2146, Australia

Alban, Kevin (OCarm), 63 East End Rd, East Finchley, London N2 0SE **Tel:** 020-8346 1458

Aleksandrowicz, Grzegorz, Canon (Lodz, Poland), The Vicarage, Sacred Hear of Jesus and St Cuthbert, Mill St, Bedford MK40 3EU **Tel:** 01234-266901

Alexander, Richard Andrew, (CJ), BSc, St George's College, Weybridge Rd, Addlestone, Weybridge KT15 2QS **Tel:** 01932-839449

Alger, Brendan, Canon, (Liverpool), St Mary, Hill St, Douglas, Isle of Man IM1 1EG **Tel:** 01624-675509 **Fax:** 01624-674359

Alker, J Stephen, Mgr, MBE, QHC, KHS, VG, (Liverpool) (Assistant Chaplain General, Principal RC Chaplain, Army), HQ Land Command, Erskine Barracks, Witton, Salisbury Wilts SP2 0AG **Tel:** 01722 433892 **E-mail:** john.alker593@land.mod.uk

Allan, Hugh BA (OPraem), 178 New London Road, Chelmsford, Essex CM2 0AR **Tel:** 01245 352898

Allain, Dominic, BA, STL (Southwark), 79 Castelnau, Barnes, London SW13 9RT **Tel:** 020-8748 5833

Allen, James Leon, (Lancaster), St Bede's, 120 Wigton Rd, Carlisle CA2 7ES **Tel:** 01228-521704

Allen, John, Mgr, STL, PhL, (Salford), Our Lady of Grace, 11 Fairfax Rd, Prestwich, Manchester M25 1AS **Tel:** 0161-773 2324

Allen, John, (Arundel & Brighton), St Anne's, Sweyn Rd, Thurso, Caithness KW14 7NW **Tel:** 01847-893196

Allen, Philip, (OSM), 264 Fulham Rd, Kensington, London SW10 9EL

Allinson, Francis, (CSsR). St Gerard's Ho, Kiln Green, Reading, Berks RG10 **Tel:** 0181-940 2964

Allman, Andrew, (Lancaster), The Cathedral Ho, Balmoral Rd, Lancaster LA1 3BT **Tel:** 01524 384820 **Fax:** 01524 384831

Allon, Bernard, (Hexham & Newcastle), An Siol, 42 West St, Callan, Co Kilkenny, Eire **Tel:** 00-353 562 5230

Allport, Anthony George, Canon, (Birmingham, retired), 20 Highlands Rd, Finchfield, Wolverhampton WV3 8AG **Tel:** 01902-340646

Al-Noufaly, Habib (Chaldean), The Holy Family Presbytery, Vale Ln, Acton West W3 0DY

Amalados, Michael MA (Birmingham), St Joseph's, Hall St, Burslem, Stoke on Trent ST6 4BB **Tel:** 01782-837602

An, Michael (Andong), 2 Ullswater Cres, Kingston Vale SW15 3RQ

Anandam, Alexander, (SSP), Society of St Paul, 191 Battersea Bridge Rd, SW11 3AS **Tel:** 020 7228 2656

Anders, Gerald, BA (Theol), STL, (Liverpool) Our Lady's Presbytery, 152 Hesketh Lane, Tarleton, Preston PR4 6AS **Tel:** 01772 812242

Anderson, Barry, (Arundel & Brighton), 3 Prince's Rd, Eastbourne, East Sussex BN23 6HT **Tel:** 01323-760048 **E-mail:** banderckhr@aol.com

Anderson, Kieran, BA, DipPT, MA (SDB), Our Lady Help of Christians, 59 Hollow Way, Cowley, Oxford OX4 2ND **Tel:** 01865-770910 **E-mail:** olhoc@aol.com

Anderson, Mark (CSsR), c/o Provincial CSsR, St Mary's, Clapham, London SW4 7AP

Andon, Ephrem (Westminster), Catholic Church, Commonwealth Avenue, London W12 7QR **Tel:** 020-8743 8334

Andrew, Richard, MA, (Westminster), 45 London Rd, Enfield EN2 6DS **Tel:** 020-8363 2569

Anene, Ambrose, (SDB), Rinaldi Ho, 32 Orbel St, Battersea, London SW11 3NZ **Tel:** 020-7801 9040 **Fax:** 020-7801 9041

Anglim, Peter A, Mgr, JCD, STL, (Westminster, retired), Nazareth Ho, 162 East End Rd, London N2 0RU **Tel:** 020-8444 6799

Angel, Christopher (Leeds), St Robert's Presbytery, Robert St, Harrogate HG1 1HP **Tel:** 01423-504988

Angold, Dunstan Paulinus, (OSB), St Mary's Abbey, Buckfast, Buckfastleigh, Devon TQ11 0EE **Tel:** 01364-645500

Angus, Barry, (Southwark, retired), 7 Dawn Court, 16A Chandler Rd, Bexhill-on-Sea, E. Sussex TN39 3QN **Tel:** 01424 223025

Angus, James (Hexham & Newcastle), St Cuthbert's, 130 Stockton Rd, Hartlepool, Cleveland TS25 5AX **Tel:** 01429-272925

Anipu, Ignatius (MAfr), Oak Lodge, 46 Totteridge Common, London N20 8ND **Tel:** 020-8959 1515 **E-mail:** anipustedwards@prontoserve.co.uk

Annear, David, (Plymouth), The Presbytery, Sclerder, Looe, Cornwall PL13 2JD **Tel:** 01503-272627

Ansbro, Stewart, BA, (Salford), St Willibrord, North Rd, Clayton, Manchester M11 4WQ **Tel:** 0161-223 0861

Antao, Oliver (SFX), 9 Tooting Bec Rd, Tooting Bec London SW17 8BS **Tel:** 020 8672 2179

Anthony, Abraham (Berhampur), 89 West Hill, Dartford, Kent DA1 2HJ **Tel:** 01322-220075

Antoba, John (CSSp), 26 Eastbury Avenue, Northwood, Middx HA6 3LN **Tel:** 0208-648 3800

Antwi-Darkwah, Francis A, STB, (Westminster) 337 Harrow Rd, London W9 3RB **Tel:** 020-7286 2170

Anwyl, Bernard Leo, (Birmingham), 8 Weavers Walk, Swynnerton, Staffs ST15 0QZ **Tel:** 01782-796677

Anwyll, Mark, STL, (Westminster), (Chaplain Univ of Hertfordshire), 189 High St, London Colney, Herts AL2 1RP **Tel:** 01727-822218

Aoun, Augustine (Maronite Rite), Our Lady of Lebanon, 6 Dobson Cl, London NW6 4RS

Appleby, Myles Raphael, MA (OSB), Downside Abbey, Stratton on the Fosse, Radstock BA3 4RH **Tel:** 01761-235161

Appleyard, Richard, (CP), 14 Minsteracres Retreat Centre, Consett, Co Durham DH8 9RT **Tel:** 01434-673248

Arbery Price, Justin, BSc, PhL, MEd, (OSB), Ampleforth Abbey, York YO62 4ER **Tel:** 01439 766714 **Fax:** 01439 766724

Arbuckle, Ninian, STD, LSS, DipAD, ED, (OFM), Franciscan International Study Centre, Giles Ln, Canterbury Kent CT2 7NA **Tel:** 01227-464939 **Fax:** 01227-459465 **E-mail:** narbuckle@yahoo.co.uk

Archer, Michael, (Westminster), Cathedral Clergy Ho, 42 Francis St, Westminster SW1P 1QW **Tel:** 020-7798 9055

Ardagh-Walter, David, BA, (Westminster), The Presbytery, St Melitius Church, Tollington Park N4 3AG **Tel:** 020-7272 3415

Areitio, Gabino, (OAR), STL, St Rita's Centre, Ottery Moor Ln, Honiton EX14 8AP **Tel/Fax:** 01404 42601

Arkwright, Leo, BA (OSB) Douai Abbey, Upper Woolhampton, Reading, Berks RG7 5TQ **Tel:** 0118-971 5300 **Fax:** 0118-971 5303

Armitage, John Mgr, VG, (Brentwood), The Presbytery, 1 Berwick Rd, Custom Ho, London E16 3DR **Tel:** 020-7476 2084

Armour, Liam, (MHM), All Souls Presbytery, 622 Liverpool St, Salford M5 5HQ **Tel:** 0161-737 9742 **Mbl:** 07971 627167

Armstrong, Patrick, (Birmingham), The Presbytery, Tower Hill, Witney, Oxon OX8 5YA **Tel:** 01993-702661

Armstrong, Raymond, (CM), St Vincent's Nursing Home, Wiltshire Lane, Eastcote, Pinner, Middx HA5 2NB **Tel:** 020 8872 4900

Arnold, Paul H. MA (Westminster), St Elizabeth's Centre, South End, Much Hadham, Herts SG10 6EW **Tel:** 01279-842145

Arnold, Roger, (SVD), 47 Ashley Ln, Hendon NW4 1PG **Tel:** 020-8203 1432

Arnold, Vincent Gabriel, (OSB), Buckfast Abbey, Buckfastleigh, Devon TQ11 0EE **Tel:** 01364-645500

Arrowsmith, Adrian, Mgr Canon, (Westminster, retired), All Saints Pastoral Centre, Shenley Ln, London Colney, Herts AL2 1AF

Arroyo, Carmello (OAR), Chaplain, Latin American Chaplaincy, 363 Kennington Ln, Vauxhall SE11 5QY **Tel:** 020-7820 0597

Arrilucea, Jesus (OAR), The Presbytery, Chalkhill Rd, Wembley Park, Middx HA9 9EW **Tel:** 020-8904 2306

Arthur, Francis (SDS, retired), Ard Mhuire, Kilmoon, Lisdoonvarna, Co Clare, Eire **Tel:** 00-353 1 65 7074527

Ascante-Kumi, Hubert, 4a Inverness Place, London W2 3JF **Tel:** 020-7229 8153

Ashcroft, B Anthony, DipRE, (Lancaster), 32 Methuen Avenue, Fulwood, Preston, Lancs PR2 9QX **Tel:** 01772-719045

Ashcroft, Martin, STB, MA (CJ), St George's College, Weybridge Rd, Addlestone, Weybridge KT15 2QS **Tel:** 01932-839459 **E-mail:** fr.martin@at-georges-college.co.uk

Ashman, John, (East Anglia), c/o The White Ho, 21 Upgate, Poringland, Norwich NR14 7SH

Ashton, Alan, (Westminster), 112 Carlton Avenue East, Wembley, Middx HA9 8NB **Tel:** 020-8904 6031

Ashton, John K, (Liverpool, retired), Nugent House School, Carr Mill Rd, Billinge, Wigan WN5 7TT

Ashton, John, Dip Ed, (SDB), Our Lady Help of Christians, 59 Hollow Way, Cowley, Oxford OX4 2ND **Tel:** 01865 770 910

Ashton, Richard J, (Brentwood, retired), Evelyn May House, Florence Way, Laindon, Basildon, Essex SS16 6AJ **Tel:** 01268 418683

Ashton, Stephen, (Lancaster), St Mary's, Hall Lane, Great Eccleston, Preston PR3 0XN **Tel:** 01995 670266
Ashworth, Michael, (SJ), Sacred Heart Presbytery, Edge Hill, London SW19 4LU **Tel:** 020-8946 0305 **Fax:** 020-8946 9130 **E-mail:** mashworthsj@yahoo.com
Aspden, Richard, (Salford), (Chaplain: Royal Bolton Hosp.) 33 Walker Avenue, Great Lever, Bolton BL2 3DY 5PB **Tel:** 01204 528080
Atanes, Ernesto, (CM), 47 Palace Court, Bayswater, London W2 4LS **Tel:** 020-7229 8815
Atherton, Richard, Mgr, OBE (Liverpool, retired), 8 Lindley Rd, Elland HX5 0TE **Tel:** 01422-378427
Atkinson, Neville, (Leeds), Sacred Heart Presbytery, 1 Buttfield Rd, Howden, Goole DN14 7DW **Tel:** 01430-430245 **E-mail:** neville@ natkinson.orangehome.co.uk
Atkinson, Philip, (Shrewsbury), St Saviour's, Tarporley Rd, Great Sutton, Ellesmere Port CH66 3JY **Tel:** 0151-339 6588 **E-mail:** parishsts@rcchep.co.uk
Attard, Hugh, (OFM), 22 St George's Dr, London, WIV 4BN **Tel:** 020-7834 9512
Atthill, Thomas R, Canon, MA, STL, (Clifton), Trellis Ho, Station Rd, Tisbury, Salisbury, Wilts SP3 6JR **Tel:** 01747-870228 **E-mail:** stosmund@talk21.com
Attree, Anthony, (Hallam), The Presbytery, West St, Worsbrough, Barnsley S70 5DJ **Tel:** 01226-284961
Auger, Patrick, BSc STB, (Clifton), 2 Court Rd, Kingswood, Bristol BS15 9QB **Tel:** 0117-949 8743
Aust, Michael, (Arundel & Brighton, retired), 6 Oakleigh, Ashley Rd, St Martin's Ave, Epsom, Surrey KT18 5HR **Tel:** 01372-748757 **Email:** aust.michael@yahoo.co.uk
Austen, Benedict, MA, Parish Administrator (OSB), St Augustine's Abbey, Ramsgate, Kent CT11 9PA **Tel:** 01843-593045 **Fax:** 01843-582732
Austen, Philip BA (OSB), The Presbytery, Raddenstile Ln, Exmouth, Devon EX8 2JH **Tel:** 01395 263384
Austin, Alexander, BA, BD (OSB), St Mary's, 103 Alcester Rd, Studley, Warks B80 7NW **Tel:** 01527-852524
Austin, Francis, Chaplain (Salford), Alexian Brothers' Care Centre, 171 St Mary's Rd, Moston, Manchester M40 0BL **Tel:** 0161-681 1929 **Fax:** 0161-947 3609
Austin, James S, MA (Salford), Little Sisters of the Poor, 52 Plymouth Grove West, Manchester M13 0AR
Austin, Nicholas, (SJ), c/o Provincial Offices, 114 Mount St, Mayfair W1K 3AH **Tel:** 0207 499 0285 **E-mail:** n_o_austin@hotmail.com
Aveyard, John, JCL (Leeds), St Mary's Presbytery, Gowthorpe, Selby YO8 4HS **Tel:** 01757-703345 **E-mail:** stmary's.selby@virgin.net
Axe, Anthony (OP), Church of Our Lady of Mercy and St Philip Neri, Church St, Melbourne, Derby DE7 1EJ **Tel:** 01332-862361
Aykaraparampil, Jose (CMI), 3 The Villas, Ruabon, Wrexham LL14 6NW
Aylward, Charles, (Portsmouth, retired), 42 Sunningdale Rd, Porchester, Hants PO16 9BB **Tel:** 023-9237 6886
Aylward, Ronald G, (Westminster, retired), 1 Green Fielde End, Lateham, Staines, Middx TW18 1LZ **Tel:** 01784-450790
Aylward, Terence, (SDB), St Joseph's Ho, 10 Oldhams Ln, Bolton BL1 6PN **Tel:** 01204-590600
Azzi, George (LMO). Our Lady of Lebanon, 6 Dobson Cl, Swiss Cottage NW6 4RS
Azzopardi, Frans, The Presbytery, 68 Rossington Avenue, Borehamwood, Herts, WD6 4LS **Tel:** 020-8953 0715
Babik, Joseph, (Trnava), Chaplaincy for Slovaks, 41 Holden Rd, Finchley North, London, N12 8HS **Tel:** 020-8446 2942
Back, Christopher, MA, (East Anglia, retired), The Catholic Rectory, Hills Rd, Cambridge CB2 1JR **Tel:** 01223-350787
Bacon, Peter Roger, (OSB), Worth Abbey, Crawley, W Sussex RH10 4SB **Tel:** 01342-710310
Baggley, John Samuel, BA (Dunelm) (Birmingham), 88 Wharton Rd, Headington Oxford OX3 8AJ **Tel:** 01865-762433 **Fax:** 01865-742494
Bagstaff, David, (East Anglia), 4 Norwich Rd, North Walsham, Norfolk NR28 9JP **Tel:** 01692-403258 **E-mail:** sacredhtwalsham@go-plus.net
Bailey, Anthony, BSc, STL, MA, (SDB), Thornleigh Ho, Sharples Park, Bolton BL1 6PQ **Tel:** 01204-305125 **Fax:** 01204-308510 **E-mail:** a.bailey@don-bosco-publication.co.uk
Bailey, Bede, (OP), St Dominic's Priory, Southhampton Rd, London NW5 4LB **Tel:** 020 7482 9210
Bailey, John, Canon, (Southwark, retired), Giswil, Fawkham Rd, West Kingsdown, Kent TN15 6JS
Bailey, Patrick, (Northampton), 432 Berkhamsted Rd, Chesham, Bucks HP5 3HQ **Tel:** 01494-785269
Bailey, Philip, (SCJ, retired), c/o Willson Ho, Derby Rd, Nottingham NG1 5AW
Baird, Francis, Rt Rev Abbot, (OSB), Our Lady and St Peter, Prinknash Abbey,

Cranham, Gloucester GL4 8EX **Tel:** 01452-812455 **Fax:** 01452-813305 **E-mail:** abbotfrancis@classicfm.net

Bak, Jan, (SDS), Salvatorian Community, 20 Grove Rd, Newbury, Berks RG14 1UH **Tel:** 01635 826417 **E-mail:** janbaksds@yahoo.co.uk

Baker, Aelred, MA(Oxon) (OSB), Prinknash Abbey, Cranham, Gloucester GL4 8EX **Tel:** 01452-812455 **E-mail:** prinknash@waitrose.com

Baker, Aidan, (CP), St Joseph's Retreat, Highgate Hill, London N19 5NE **Tel:** 020-7281 2274 **Fax:** 020-7281 9433

Baker, Christopher, (Southwark), St Michael the Archangel, 1 Hills Terr, Chatham, Kent ME4 6PU **Tel:** 01634-842886

Baker, David, (East Anglia), Catholic Presbytery, North Everard St, Kings Lynn PE30 5HQ **Tel:** 01553-772220

Baker, Desmond, (Westminster), The Presbytery, Berry Ln, Rickmansworth WD3 7HG **Tel:** 01923-779890

Baker, Thomas, (Salford, retired), Nazareth Ho, Scholes Ln, Prestwich, Manchester M25 8AP

Baldwin, Sean, (Lancaster), c/o Bishop's Ho, Cannon Hill LA1 5NG

Baldwin, Wilfrid, (Portsmouth), 54 High Walton Rd, Walton le Dale, Preston, Lancs PR5 4HB **Tel:** 01420-82030

Bale, John, (Birmingham), The Presbytery, 31 Victoria Rd, Tipton, W. Mids DY4 8SN **Tel:** 0121- 557 1321

Balinnya, Gerard (Uganda), Priest's Ho, Gravel Hill, London N3 3RJ

Ball, Francis, (Liverpool), Sacred Heart, Brooke St, Chorley, Lancs PR6 0NG **Tel:** 01257-410588

Ball, John, MA, (MHM), Poor Clares Monastery, Galley Ln, Arkley, Barnett EN5 4AN **Tel:** 0208 449 8815 **E-mail:** johnball.mnm@virgin.net

Balzi, Aldo, (MCCJ), Comboni Ho, 16 Dawson Place, London W2 4TJ **Tel:** 020-7229 7059

Bamber, Joseph L, (Lancaster), St Mary, Yealand Rd, Yealand Conyers, Nr Carnforth, Lancs LA5 9SF **Tel:** 01524-732943

Bamford, Graham, (Arundel & Brighton), 307 Kingston Rd, Ewell, Surrey KT19 0BW **Tel:** 020-8393 5572

Bance, Walter, (Birmingham), St Patricks, 48 Sandon Rd, Stafford ST16 3HF **Tel:** 01785-252393

Bane, John, BA(Maths), BA(Theol & Phil), (Middlesbrough), St Joseph's Presbytery, 1 Greylands Park Grove, Newby, Scarborough YO12 6HY **Tel/Fax:** 01723 362632

Banks, David Anselm, MA, (OSB), c/o Buckfast Abbey, Buckfastleigh, Devon TQ11 0EE

Banongkur, Fabian, (Damongo, Ghana), St Mary's Presbytery, Elbow St, Levenshulme, Manchester M9 3PY **Tel:** 0161-224 2369

Baptiste, Eugene Philip (MSFS) St Joseph's Presbytery, St Joseph's Place, Devizes, Wiltshire SN10 1DD **Tel:** 01380-723572, **Fax:** 01380-723377 **E-mail:** frphilipmsfs@catholic.org

Barber, Francis, (Salford), Chaplain's Branch, HQ1 (UK) Armd Div, Wentworth Bks BFPO15

Barchiesi, Sandro, (SX), 260 Nether St, Finchley, London N3 1HT

Barker, Anthony, (Hexham & Newcastle, retired), St Thomas Presbytery, Rectory Ln, Wolsingham, Co Durham DL13 3AG **Tel:** 01388-528438

Barlow, Cyril, (Birmingham), 1 Cofton Rd, West Heath, B31 3QT **Tel:** 0121-475 3194

Barltrop, Keith, Mgr, STL, MA, (Westminster), 116 West Heath Rd, London NW3 7TX **Tel:** 020-8731 9796

Barnes, Bruce MA, STL, FRSAS (Portsmouth) 408 Northumberland Avenue, Whitley, Reading, Berks RG2 8NR **Tel:** 0118 931 4469

Barnes, David, BA, (Westminster), 70 Lincoln's Inn Fields, London WC2A 3JA **Tel:** 020-7405 0376

Barnes, John, (East Anglia), 35 London Rd, Dereham, Norfolk NR19 1AS **Tel/Fax:** 01326-694066

Barnes, Kenneth, (SSCC), 372 Uxbridge Rd, W5 3LH **Tel:** 020-8992 5941

Barnes, Michael, (SJ), Superior. De Nobili Ho, 6 Osterley Park Rd, Southall, Middx UB2 4BL **Tel:** 020-8571 1833 **E-mail:** barnesm@heythrop.ac.uk

Baron, John, MA, (Lancaster), The Presbytery, Christ the King, Winton Crescent, Harraby, Carlisle CA1 3JX **Tel:** 01228 525632 **E-mail:** jpbct@ad.com

Barr, Hugh, Canon, (Leeds, retired), 11 Wharfe Grange, Wetherby LS22 6SS

Barr, Justin, (OCSO), Our Lady and St Bernard, Mount St Bernard Abbey, Coalville, Leicester LE67 5UL **Tel:** 01530-832298/832022

Barr, Nigel (Leeds), SS Mary and Walburga Presbytery, Kirkgates, Shipley BD18 3LU **Tel:** 01274-583708

Barralet, Roger, (OFM), 557-559 High Rd, Woodford Green, Essex IG8 0RB **Tel:** 020 8504 1688

Barrass, Alexander, VG, Canon, (Hexham & Newcastle, retired), St Mary's, 27 Bridge St, Sunderland SR1 1TQ **Tel:** 0191-567 5354

Barratt, Anthony, BA, STL, PhD, KCHS, VF, (Southwark), The Rectory, The Church of

Annunciation, 109 West St, Ilion, NY13357 USA **Tel:** 0013158943766

Barrett, Anthony P, (Salford, retired), McAuley Mount, Padiham Rd, Burnley BB12 6TG **Tel:**01254-702525

Barrett, Bernard, (Northampton), 22 Stratford Rd, Wolverton, Milton Keynes MK12 5LJ **Tel:** 01908-313162 **E-mail:** bernard.barrett@diginet.co.uk

Barrett, Francis, (CHS). 464 Chester Rd, Sutton Coldfield, W. Mids B73 5BP **Tel:** 0121-384 4280

Barrett, Illtud, MA, (OSB), The Chaplain's Ho, Holy Cross Priory, Heathfield, E. Sussex. TN21 OTS **Tel:** 01435- 867239

Barrett, Mark, MA, (OSB), Worth Abbey, Crawley, W. Sussex RH10 4SB **Tel:** 01342-710310

Barrett, Philip, BA, MPhil, (Liverpool, retired), 244 Warrington Rd, Spring View, Wigan WN3 4NH

Barrett, Richard, STB, JCD, DCL (Northampton), 108 Limbury Rd, Luton LU3 2PN **Tel:** 01582-519770

Barrett-Lennard, Hugh, (CongOrat), The Oratory, Brompton Rd, SW7 2RP **Tel:** 020-7808 0900

Barrow, Arthur, Mgr, (Brentwood), 16 Clairmont Rd, Lexden, Colchester, Essex CO3 5BE **Tel:** 01206-576898

Barrow, David, BSc, MSc, STB (Westminster), 115 Hertford Rd, London N9 7EN **Tel:** 020-8803 6631

Barrow, Michael, (SJ) Corpus Christi Jesuit Community, 757 Christchurch Rd, Boscombe, Bournemouth BH7 6AN **Tel:** 01202 436730 **Fax:** 01202 436730 **E-mail:** michaelajbarrow@yahoo.co.uk

Barry, Anthony, (Salford), St Joseph's, 71 Horace St, Halliwell, Bolton BL1 3PU **Tel:** 01204-524597

Barry, Anthony, Mgr (Arundel & Brighton), 14 Haslett Avenue West, Crawley, W. Sussex RH10 1HR **Tel:** 01293-524176 **Fax:** 01293-511675 **E-mail:** tony.barry@dabnet.org

Barry, David Jeremiah, (Birmingham), 84 Northfield Rd, Birmingham B30 1LG **Tel:** 0121-458 1236

Barry, Denis, (Southwark, retired), St George's Retreat, Burgess Hill, Sussex RH15 2NP

Barry, Gerard, (Salford), The Garden Cottage, Thicket Priory, York YO19 6DE **Tel:** 01904 448112

Barry, J Anthony, (Middlesbrough, retired), Kirkley Lodge, Dalby Way, Coulby Newham, Middlesbrough TS8 0TW **Tel:** 01642-599080

Barry, Oliver, (OMI), Oblate Retreat Centre, Wistaston Hall, 89 Broughton Ln, Crewe CW2 8JS **Tel:** 01270-568653 **Fax:** 01270-650776 **E-mail:** oblate@wistaston-hall.fsnet.co.uk

Barry, Patrick, Rt Rev Abbot, MA, (OSB, retired), Ampleforth Abbey, York YO6 4EN **Tel:** 01439-766714 **Fax:** 01439-766724

Barry, Robert, (Westminster, retired), St Vincent's Nursing Home, Wiltshire Lane, Pinner, Middx HA5 2NB

Barry, Timothy P, Canon (Clifton, retired), Flat 6, 16 Ellenborough Park South, Weston-super-Mare BS23 1XW **Tel:** 01934-627842

Barry, William Dennis, (Arundel & Brighton), St Joseph's, Albert Rd, Bognor Regis, W. Sussex PO21 1NJ **Tel:** 01243-865680

Barry-Ryan, Kieran, (SJ), 2 Genoa Rd, Anerley, London SE20 8ES **Tel:** 020-8778 8597

Bartlett, Stephen, MA, STh, (Westminster), 17 Cirencester St, London W2 5SR **Tel:** 020-7286 2672 **Fax:** 020-7286 6620

Bartnik, Teodor, (SDB) 8 Waldram Park Road, Forest Hill, London SE23 2PN **Tel:** 020 8378 5228

Barton, Richard J, (Clifton), STB, AKC, St Joseph's Presbytery, Chance St, Tewkesbury GL20 5RF **Tel:** 01684-293273

Basabose, Lambert (WF), The Presbytery, 132 Shernhall Street, Walthamstow, London E17 9HU **Tel:** 020-8520 5877

Basden, Christopher, BA (Southwark), 58 Thornton Rd, Clapham Park, London SW12 0LF **Tel:** 020-8674 3704

Battell, Colin MA (Prior OSB), Ampleforth Abbey, York YO62 4EN **Tel:** 01439-766712 **Fax:** 01439-788132

Batten, George (Clifton), The Presbytery, St Vincent de Paul, Embleton Rd, Southmead, Bristol BS10 6DS **Tel:** 0117-983 3916 **Fax:** 0117-983 3911

Bateman, Michael, (Southwark, retired), c/o Archbishop's Ho, 150 St George's Rd, London SE1 6HX

Batthula, John, MA (Birmingham), c/o Archbishop's Ho, 6 Shadwell St, Birmingham B4 6EY

Battle, Bernard, (Leeds, retired), 2 Hinsley Court, Headingley Ln, Leeds LS6 2HB **Tel:** 0113-2784803

Baxter, Anthony, MA, BD, MPhil, (Westminster), 79 St Charles Square, London W10 6EB **Tel:** 020-8968 6446

Baxter, Anthony, MA, BSc, STL (IC), St Marie's, Oak St, Rugby CV22 5EL **Tel:** 01788-542703

Baxter, Cyril, (OCarm), The Friars, Aylesford, Kent ME20 7BX **Tel:** 01622-717272 **Fax:** 01622-715575

Bayldon, Michael, Canon (Middlesbrough), St Paulinus' Presbytery, 13 Grafton Cl, Guisborough TS14 7BP **Tel:** 01287-638233

Bayliss, David Neil BA (Birmingham), St

Ambrose Barlow, Lakey Ln, Hall Green, Birmingham B28 8QU **Tel:** 0121-777 4524

Bazen, David Peter, MA, (Birmingham), 37 Towers Close, Kenilworth CV8 1FG **Tel:** 01926 857543

Beale, Stephen, 25 Lower Teddington Rd, Hampton Wick KT1 4BH

Beale, Walter, (Portsmouth, retired), 4 Fraser Place, Ullapool, Ross-shire IV26 2UX **Tel:** 01854-612412 **Mbl:** 07751-977056 **E-mail:** wallybeale@hotmail.com

Beasley-Suffolk, Louis, (Clifton), SS Luke and Teresa Presbytery, South St, Wincanton BA9 9DH **Tel:** 01963-34408

Beattie, J Gordon, MCIJ (OSB), Our Lady and All Saints, Lancaster Ln, Parbold, Wigan, Lancs WN8 7HS **Tel:** 01257-463248 **Fax:** 01257-462495

Beattie, Mark, OCD (Liverpool), Holy Name Presbytery, Moss Pits Lane, Fazakerley, Liverpool L10 9LG **Tel:** 0151 476 0289 **Fax:** 0151 476 0285 **E-mail:** holynamechurch@rcal.freeserve.co.uk

Beattie, Michael, (SJ), Corpus Christi Jesuit Community, 757 Christchurch Rd, Boscombe, Bournemouth BH7 6AN **Tel:** 01246-437127

Beatty, John, (ICS), 80 Imperial Cl, North Harrow, Middx HA2 7LW **Tel:** 020-8868 7531 **Fax:** 020-8866 0256

Beatty, Miceál (Arundel & Brighton), St Ann, 4 Brighton Rd, Banstead, Surrey SM7 1BS **Tel:** 01737-353724

Beausang, Cornelius, Canon, (Southwark, Retired), 21 Briar Court, 40 London Rd, North Cheam, Surrey SM3 8JE **Tel:** 020-8641 7883

Becher, Ernest, (Southwark, retired), St Peter's Residence, 2A Meadow Rd Rd, London SW8 1QH **Tel:** 0207 091 4303

Beck, Ashley, MA, (Southwark), 22 Downs Rd, Beckenham, Kent BR3 5JY **Tel:** 020-8776 6087 **E-mail:** ashleybeck88@hotmail.com

Beckett, Luke MA, MPhil (OSB) Ampleforth Abbey, York YO62 4EN **Tel:** 01439-766714 **Fax:** 01439-766724

Bedford, Bernard, (Hallam), St Thomas More Presbytery, 477 Wordsworth Avenue, Sheffield S5 9JE **Tel:** 0114-232 1441

Bedford, John, 5 Garrick Walk, Old Fletion, Peterborough PE2 8DD

Bednar, Dwayne (Lublin), 42 Francis St, London SW1P 1QW **Tel:** 020-7828 4163

Beecroft, Clifford, (Brentwood, retired), 9 Washbury Ho, Andover Rd, Newbury, Berks RG14 6NA

Beer, David Laurence, (OSB), Abbey of St Michael and All Angels, Belmont, Hereford HR2 9RZ **Tel:** 01432-277388

Behrens, Andrew, AKC, (Northampton), The Presbytery, 22 Park Avenue North, Northampton NN3 2HS **Tel:** 01604-713015 **E-mail:** andrew.behrens@ntlworld.com

Beirne, John, (Northampton), 56 High St, Aylesbury, Bucks HP20 1SE **Tel/Fax:** 01296-482267 **E-mail:** jpbeirne.stjoseph@btinternet.com

Beisley, Philip, (Clifton), St Mary's Presbytery, Tovey Rd, Swindon SN2 1LQ **Tel:** 01793-535089

Belevendran, Britto, MA, (Brentwood), The Presbytery, 455 Chingford Rd, Chingford, London E4 8SP **Tel:** 020-8527 3087

Bell, Adrian, STB, JCL, (Brentwood), c/o Cathedral Ho, Ingrave Rd, Brentwood, Essex CM15 8AT

Bell, Alan (CHS), 464 Chester Rd, Sutton Coldfield, W. Mids B73 5BP **Tel:** 0121-384 4280

Bell, Michael J, Canon, (Nottingham), The Presbytery, Jermyn St, Sleaford, Lincs LN34 7RU **Tel:** 01529-302529 **Fax:** 01529 302539

Bellamy, William, (Hexham & Newcastle), 115 Clumber St, Newcastle upon Tyne NE4 7RE **Tel:** 0191-273 3582

Bellenger, Dominic Aidan, MA, PhD, FSA, FRHistS, FRSA, (OSB) Downside Abbey, Stratton on the Fosse, Radstock, Bath BA3 4RH **Tel:** 01761-235119

Bellwood, Robert, (IC), Prieuré St Jean Eudes 14210 Garvus, Caen, Normandy. **Tel:** 0033 231 080385

Belsito, Antonio (IC), Romini Centre, 433 Fosse Way, Ratcliffe-on-the-Wreake LE7 4SJ **Tel:** 01509-813078 **E-mail:** aabelsito@hotmail.com

Benbow, Paul, BA, JCL, (Liverpool), 37 Tithebarn Rd, Knowsley Village, Prescot L34 0EU **Tel:** 0151- 546 4489

Benjamin, Michael, (Arundel & Brighton, retired), 25 Tanbridge Park, Horsham, W. Sussex RH12 1SF **Tel:** 01403-254296

Bennett, George, (Birmingham), St Wilfrid's, Shawsdale Rd, Castle Bromwich B36 8LL **Tel:** 0121-747 2146

Bennett, John, CertEd (SDB), St Joseph's, 10 Oldhams Ln, Bolton BL1 6PN

Bennett, John (OSB), St Augustine's Abbey, St Augustine's Rd, Ramsgate, Kent CT11 9PB **Tel:** 01843-593045 **Fax:** 01843-582732 **E-mail:** staugabbey@aol.com

Bennett, Roy, (Portsmouth, retired), 156 Oakwood Rd, Lordswood, Southampton SO16 8EP **Tel:** 02380-736382 **E-mail:** bennet5@avermail.net

Bentley, John BA, STB (Birmingham), 14 Westhill Rd, Coventry CB6 2AA **Tel:** 024-7659 1618 **Fax:** 024-7659 5547

Bentoglio, Gabriele, Italian Mission, 20 Brixton Rd, London, SW9 6BU **Tel:** 020-7 735 8235

Benyon, Christopher, (Arundel & Brighton), 68 Gratwicke Rd, Worthing, W. Sussex BN11 4BJ **Tel:** 01903 200416

Bergin, Christopher (Arundel & Brighton), 14 Haslett Avenue West, Crawley, W. Sussex RH10 1HR **Tel:** 01293-524176

Bergin, William, (Hallam), The Presbytery, Babworth Rd, Retford, Notts DN22 7BP **Tel:** 01777 703373

Berisic, Drago, 17 Boutflower Rd, London, SW11 1RE **Tel:** 020-7223 3530

Berkeley, Theodore, (OCSO), Our Lady and St Bernard, Mount St Bernard Abbey, Coalville, Leicester LE67 5UL **Tel:** 01530-832298/832022

Bermingham, Edward, (SJ), "Emmaus" 2 Prospect Row, Sunderland, Tyne and Wear, SR1 2BP **Tel:** 0191-514 5384

Bermingham, Francis, (Clifton), Holy Cross Presbytery, Dean Ln, Bristol BS3 1DB **Tel:** 0117-983 3927

Bernal, Florencio, 9 Henry Rd, Manor Ho N4 2LH

Bernardo, Joel, (CM), 2 Flower Lane, London NW7 2JB **Tel:** 020 8959 1021

Berry, John, BA, PhD, (Leeds), St Mary's Cottage, Our Lady of Victories, West Ln, Keighley BD22 6ES **Tel:** 01535-664195

Berry, John A, (Birmingham), 1 Signal Hayes Rd, Walmley, Sutton Coldfield, W. Mids B76 8RS **Tel:** 0121-351 2161

Berry, John E, Canon VF (Nottingham), Our Lady of Good Counsel, 280 Nottingham Rd, Eastwood, Nottingham NG16 2AQ **Tel:** 01773-713532

Berry, Vincent, Canon, (Westminster), St Mary's Rectory, Draycott Terr, Chelsea, London SW3 2QR **Tel:** 020-7589 5487

Bertram, Jerome, (Cong.Orat), St Aloysius, 25 Woodstock Rd, Oxford, OX2 6HA **Tel:** 01865-315800

Bessler, Reginald D, (Hallam, retired), 8 Spencer St, Chesterfield S40 4SD **Tel:** 01246-211785

Bester, Christoper John, (Birmingham), 18 Peppard Rd, Sonning Common, Reading RG4 9SU **Tel:** 0118-972 3418

Bettison, John V, (SVD), 21 Halewood Rd, Gateacre, Liverpool L25 3PH **Tel:** 0151-428286

Bialas, Tadeusz (Cong Orat), 48 Pitts Rd, Slough SL1 3XH **Tel:** 01753-533861

Bialek, Jerzy (SJ) *Superior*, Polish Jesuits, 182 Walm Ln, Willesden Green, London NW2 3AX **Tel:** 0208 452 4304 **Fax:** 0208 450 8449

Bialowas, Dariusz (Krakow, Poland), 2 The Grove, Kettering NN15 7QQ **Tel:** 01536-512497

Bibby, Joseph, (Liverpool) (Lamp) Casilla 1021, Oruro, Bolivia. **E-mail:** parishofparia@yahoo.co.uk

Bickers, Bernard, MA (Leeds), Presbytery, Gowthorpe, Selby YO8 4HS HD3 4XF **Tel:** 01757 703345 **Fax:** 01757 290038

Bickerstaffe, V Rev Anthony, (Middlesbrough, retired), St Catherine's Home, 146 Southcoates Lane, Hull HU9 3AJ

Bidgood, Kevin (Portsmouth), 350 London Rd, Waterlooville, Hants PO7 7SR **Tel/Fax:** 023-9226 2289

Bidzinski, Kazimierz, (Polish), Polonia Ho, 231 Chesterton Rd, Cambridge CB4 1AS **Tel:** 01223-368539

Bielawski, Jonathan, (Plymouth), The Presbytery, Killigrew Street, Falmouth, Cornwall TR11 3PR **Tel:** 01237-472519

Biggerstaff, Richard, (Arundel & Brighton), The Presbytery, Irelands Ln, Lewes, East Sussex BN7 1QX **Tel:** 01273-473309

Billington, Steven (Leeds), Our Lady of Good Counsel Presbytery, Rosgill Dr, Seacroft, Leeds LS14 6QY **Tel:** 0113-273 5917 **Fax:** 0113-265 7274

Bilsborrow, Joseph, (Lancaster, retired), St Winefride's Ho, Low Moor Rd, Bispham, Blackpool FY2 0PA **Tel:** 01253-593828

Bimson, Bernard, (Liverpool, retired), 13 Rock Mount Cl, Vale Rd, Woolton, Liverpool L25 6JN **Tel:** 0151-428 6858

Bingham, David, MBE, MA, (MHM), Mill Hill Missionaries, 17 Tenter Terr, Durham, DH1 4RD **Tel:** 0191 384 5626 **Fax:** 0191 383 0351 **E-mail:** revfdavid@gmail.com

Birch, Clive, (SM), 117 Cottingham Rd, Hull HU5 2DH

Birchall, David (SJ), Director, St Beuno's Ignatian Spirituality Centre, Tremeirchion, St Asaph, Denbighshire LL17 0AS

Birchall, John, (Liverpool), Sacred Heart, Springfield Rd, Wigan WN6 7AT **Tel:** 01942-745689

Bird, David STL (OSB), Monasterio de la Encarnacion, Apartado 8, Sullana, Peru **Tel:** 0051-074-326688

Birmingham, Peter, (Salford, retired), St Mary's, 49 Whalley Rd, Sabden, Clitheroe BB7 9DZ **Tel:** 01282-771517

Blacker, John A, (Clifton), St Gregory's Presbytery, 19 St Jame's Square, Cheltenham GL50 3PR **Tel:** 01242-523737

Blackford, Alan J, (MSFS), 73 Higher Kingston, Yeovil, Somerset, BA21 4AR **Tel:** 01935-423549

Blackledge, Denis, (SJ), Corpus Christi Presbytery, 17/18 St James Sq, Boscombe, Bournemouth BH5 2BX **Tel:** 01202 425286 **Fax:** 01202 417623 **E-mail:** wdb@jesuits.net

Blade, Kevin, (MSC), St Mary, Kennelwood Avenue, Kirkby, Liverpool L33 6UF **Tel:** 0151-546 3838

Blair, Stephen, (East Anglia), 7 St George's, Hospital Rd, Wicklewood, Wymondham, Norfolk NR18 9PD

Blake, Matthew, (OCD), Carmelite Priory, 41 Kensington Church St, London W8 4BB **Tel:** 020-7937 9866 **Fax:** 020-7938 1470 **E-mail:** mblakebhill@yahoo.co.uk

Blake, Raymond, (Arundel & Brighton), 55 Upper North St, Brighton, East Sussex BN1 3FH **Tel:** 01273-326793 **Fax:** 01273-735070

Blakesley, Simon, JCL, MCL (East Anglia), The Presbytery, 7 Fair Green, Diss, Norfolk IP22 4BQ **Tel:** 01379-642914

Blanda, Mgr Giuseppe, (Monreale), 21A Soho Square, W1V 5FJ

Blandford, Philip, LicPhil, BD (CMF), 68 Grange Park Rd, Leyton, London E10 5ES **Tel:** 020-8539 2908 **E-mail:** leyton@dioceseofbrentwood.org

Blaney, Dominic, (OSB), Belmont Abbey, Hereford HR2 9RZ **Tel:** 01432-277388

Blaney, John, (SMM), The Presbytery, Alexandra Rd, Andover, Hants SP10 3AD **Tel:** 01264-352829 **Fax:** 01264-357107 **E-mail:** priest@catholic-andover.org.uk

Blenkinsopp, James, (Middlesbrough), Sacred Heart, 41 Thirsk Rd, Northallerton, Nth Yorks DL6 1PJ **Tel:** 01609-773323

Bligh, Francis, HDipEd (CSSp), 26 Eastbury Avenue, Northwood, Middx HA6 3LN **Tel:** 01923-829655, **Fax:** 01923-836975 **E-mail:** spiritans.uk@virgin.net

Bliss, John, (Southwark), 372 Coulsdon Rd, Old Coulsdon, Surrey CR5 1EF **Tel:** 01737-552420

Bluett, Patrick, (Middlesbrough), Gortboy, Newcastle West, Co Limerick, Ireland **Tel:** 00353-6961881

Blundell, Brendan, Guardian (OFMConv), All Saints Friary, Redclyffe Rd, Dumplington, Urmston, Manchester M41 7LG **Tel:** 0161-202 9896 **Fax:** 0161-749 8238

Blundell, Peter, (Birmingham), The Presbytery, Bleakhouse Rd, Oldbury B68 0TQ **Tel:** 0121-422 2388

Blythen, Richard, (Arundel & Brighton), c/o PRCC(N), MP1.2, Leach Building, Whale Island, Portsmouth PO2 8BY **Tel:** 023-9262 5193

Boagey, Paul (MHM), c/o St Joseph's Missionary Society, PO Box 3608, Maidenhead, Berks SL6 7UX

Boardman, Joseph, (Cardiff), St Joseph's Presbytery, Wordsworth Avenue, Penarth CF64 2RL **Tel:** 029-2070 8247 **Fax:** 029-2070 6014

Boast, Philip, (Salford), St Joseph's, Huttock End Ln, Stacksteads, Bacup OL13 8LD **Tel:** 01706-873299

Boateng, Emmanuel M (OSB), Monastery of Christ the King, Bramley Rd, Enfield, London N14 4HE **Tel:** 020 8440 7769

Bober, Szczepan, SAC, (Polish Priest), 38 Nursery St, Mansfield NG18 2AG **Tel:** 01623-626470

Boerakker, Hans, BA (MHM), Herbert Ho, 41 Victoria Rd, Freshfield, Merseyside L37 1LW **Tel:** 01704 835675 **Tel:** 01704 835837 **E-mail:** mhm.archives@tiscali.co.uk

Boggan, John, 14 Woodland Grove, Rock Ferry, Birkenhead CH42 4NU **Tel:** 0151-645 491 **E-mail:** j.boggan@merseymail.com

Boisseau, Bernard (SM) Marist Fathers, Notre Dame de France, 5 Leicester Place, London WC2H 7BX **Tel:** 020-7437 9363 **Fax:** 020-7437 3857

Boland, John, (Westminster), Sacred Heart Church, Oak Street, Berkhamstead, Herts HP4 1HX **Tel:** 01442 863845

Boland, Martin, MA, STL, (Brentwood), 1 Recreation Way, Brightlingsea, Essex CO7 0NJ **Tel:** 01206-302485

Boland, Michael, (Southwark), 222 Sheen Rd, Richmond, Surrey TW10 5AN **Tel:** 020-8876 6467

Boland, Vivian (OP) Blackfriars, 64 St Giles, Oxford OX1 3LY **Tel:** 01865-278407

Bold, Michael, (CP) 67 Pembury Cl, Pembury Estate, Pembury Rd, London, E5 8JP **Tel:** 0208 986 6335 **E-mail:** mikeboldcp@ukonline.co.uk

Bolger, Kevin, (Hexham & Newcastle), c/o Bishop Ho, East Denton Hall, 800 West Rd, Newcastle upon Tyne NE5 2BJ

Bolland, John, (Plymouth, retired), Flat 4, Notre Dame Ho, Wyndham St West, Plymouth. **Tel:** 01752-662616

Bolton, John, BA, (OSB), c/o Worth Abbey, Crawley, W Sussex RH10 4SB **Tel:** 01342-710310

Bomansaam, Francis (MAfr), St Edwards, 46 Totteridge Common, London N20 8ND

Bonaccorsi, Michael, (Birmingham), St Mary's Presbytery, Compton, Leek ST13 5NH **Tel:** 01538 382385

Boner, James, (OFM Cap), Franciscan Friary, Carlton Rd, Erith, Kent DA8 1DN **Tel:** 01322-402060/433193 **Fax:** 01322-402061 **E-mail:** ola@btinternet.com

Bonvini, Ernest, (Southwark), St Boniface, 185 Mitcham Rd, Tooting, London SW17 9PG **Tel:** 020-8672 2345

Booker, Richard, 10 Ardsley Road, Worsbrough Dale, Barnsley S70 4RJ **Tel:** 01226 282 505

Booth, John, BSc, CertEd (SDB), St James, Chestnut Grove, Bootle L20 4LX **Tel:** 0151-944 1039 **Fax:** 0151-922 3263

Booth, Julian Mark, BA, STB,(Birmingham), English Martyrs, Church Rd, Biddulph, Staffs ST8 6JG **Tel:** 01782-513130

Booth, Michael A, BA, STL, (Westminster), c/o Archbishop's Ho, London SW1P 1QJ

Boothman, Jim, STL (CMF), 68 Grange Park Rd, Leyton, London E10 5ES **Tel:** 020-8539 2908 **E-mail:** leyton@dioceseofbrentwood.org

Bootle, Joseph W, (Lancaster), Presbytery, Mowbreck Ln, Wesham, Kirkham, Preston PR4 3HA **Tel:** 01772-683593

Bord, Andrea, (Cardiff), 67 Talbot St, Canton, Cardiff CF11 9BX **Tel:** 029-20 230492

Boretto, Krzysztoff, (CHS), St Mark's, Woodhill, Kentish Ln, Hatfield, Herts AL9 6EB

Borg, Carmel, (Brentwood), c/o Cathedral Ho, Ingrave Rd, Brentwood, Essex CM15 8AT

Bortolazzo, Giuseppe, (CS), St Frances Cabrini, 10 Woburn Rd, Bedford MK40 1EG **Tel:** 01234-359515

Bossy, Michael (SJ) St Ignatius, 27 High Rd, London N15 6ND **Tel:** 020-8802 5303 **Fax:** 020-8802 8102

Bottigliero, Benito, (PIME), Chinese Catholic Centre, 21A Soho Square, London W1D 4NR **Tel:** 020-7439 1878

Bottoms, Geoffrey, (Lancaster), (On Sabbatical), c/o Pastoral Centre, Balmoral Rd, Lancaster LA1 3BT

Bottrill, David S, Mgr, Provost, (Menevia, retired), "Maes-Gwyn", 63 Margam Rd, Port Talbot, SA13 2HR **Tel:** 01639-883323

Boulter, Rev Stephen, 29 Fern Dr, Middle Rasen, Market Rasen, Lincs LN8 3NU **Tel:** 01673-849566

Boulton, Chad BA, AHSM (OSB), Ampleforth College, York YO62 4ER **Tel:** 01439-766752

Boward, Joseph, (Westminster, retired), 81 Parkway, Welwyn Garden City, Herts AL8 6JF **Tel:** 01707-322579

Bowdren, Daniel M, Canon VF, (Nottingham), St Charles Rectory, The Carriage Dr, Hadfield, Glossop, Derbyshire SK13 1PQ **Tel:** 01457-852351

Bowen, George (Cong Orat), The Oratory, Brompton Rd, London SW7 2RP **Tel:** 020-7808 0900

Bowen, Kenneth, (Northampton), St Mary's Presbytery, Aspley Hill, Woburn Sands MK178NN **Tel:** 01908-583195

Box, Anthony, (SCJ), c/o The Friary, St Bernard's Rd, Solihull, W. Mids B92 7BL **Tel:** 0121-706 0505 **Fax:** 0121-706 8105 **E-mail:** info@oltonfriary.demon.co.uk

Boxall, William, (Cardiff, retired), The Bungalow, St Mary's RC School, Old Bulwark Rd, Chepstow NP16 5JE **Tel:** 01291-627799

Boyd, Patrick, (WF), Vocations Ho, 37 Victoria Parade, Ashton, Preston PR2 1DT **Tel:** 01772-722378

Boyd, William, (SDB), MOD Chaplains (Army), Trenchard Lines, Upavon, Pewsey, Wiltshire SN9 6BE

Boylan, Anthony B, Mgr, JCD, (Leeds), Residence St Boniface Presbytery, 31 Robin Ln, Bentham LA2 7AB **Tel:** 015242-61315

Boylan, Bernard, (Westminster), 110 Station Rd, Hampton-on-Thames, Middx TW12 2AS **Tel:** 020-8979 3596

Boylan, Terence, (Shrewsbury), Our Lady & St John's, 1 Boundry Ln, Heswall, Wirral CH60 5RP **Tel:** 0151-342 6581

Boyle, Brian BA (SCJ), St Joseph, Murcott Rd, Whitnash, Leamington Spa, Warwicks CV31 2JJ **Tel:** 01926-772712

Boyle, Cornelius, BA(Hons), BTh, (Southwark), 45 Brook Rd, Thornton Heath CR7 7RD **Tel:** 020 8684 3013 **Fax:** 020 8684 6626

Boyle, James, (MHM), St Margaret Mary, Middle Rd, Southampton SO31 7GH **Tel/Fax:** 01489-572797 **E-mail:** stmgtmary@parkgate16.fsnet.co.uk

Boyle, John, BSc, MSc, JCL, (Southwark), St Simon's RC Church, Brookfield Rd, Ashford, Kent TN23 2GU **Tel:** 01233-622399

Boyle, Stephen, MSc, STL, (Southwark), Priest's Ho, 25 Dunley Dr, New Addington CR0 0RG **Tel:** 01689-842644 **Fax:** 01689-844818

Boyle, Terence, (Hallam), Holy Rood Rectory, George St, Barnsley S70 1AX **Tel:** 01226-203730

Bradbury, Simon, (Leeds), 8 Tregoning Rd, Torpoint, Cornwall PL11 2NX

Bradley, Gerard, BMus, BTh, KC (Southwark), St John's Seminary, Wonersh, Guildford, Surrey GU5 0QX **Tel:** 01483-892217

Bradley, James, (SDS), Salvatorian Fathers, St Bruno Church, 15740 Citrustree Rd, Whittier, California 90603-2498 **Tel:** 001- 562-947 5637 **Fax:** 001-562-943 3193 **E-mail:** fatherjim@fatherjim.com

Bradley, John P, BEd(Hons) (Liverpool), St Anne's Presbytery, 33 Timms Ln, Freshfield, Merseyside L37 7DW **Tel:** 01704-872467

Bradley, William J, (Arundel & Brighton), 34 Welcheren Cl, Golf Rd, Deal, Kent KT14 62Y

Bradshaw, Brendan, (SM), Queens College, Cambridge CB3 9ET **Tel:** 01223-335571

Brady, John F, (Hexham & Newcastle), Churchland Presbytery, The Shrine of Our Lady of Knock, County Mayo, Ireland **Tel:** 00 353 948 8836

Brady, Kieran (CSsR), The Monastery, Badby Rd West, Daventry, Northants NN11 4NH **Tel:** 01327-702881 **Fax:** 01327-706522

Brady, Owen, (Hallam, retired), 10 St Ronan's Rd, Sheffield S7 1DZ

Brady, Peter, (OSB), Abbey of St Michael the Archangel, Belmont, Hereford HR2 9RZ **Tel:** 01432-374710 **Fax:** 01432-277597

Brady, Philip, (Salford), St Joseph's, Old Ln, Little Hulton, Worsley, Manchester M38 9RU **Tel:** 0161-790 4648

Brady, Vincent, Mgr, (Westminster), 54 Parkside, London SW19 5NE **Tel:** 020-8944 7189

Braiden, Shaun, (Salford), Mother of God and St James, Pendleton Way, Pendleton, Salford M6 5JA **Tel:** 0161-736 1935

Branagan, Patrick, MCL, JCL (Birmingham, retired), 22A Bolingbrooke Rd, Farley Hill, Luton LU1 5JD

Branch, Michael, BTh, (Southwark), 1a Conway Rd, Plumstead SE18 1AQ **Tel:** 020-8854 0960

Brand, James, MA, STL, (Westminster), Pontificio Collegio Beda, Viale di San Paolo 18, 00146 Roma, Italia. **Tel:** 0039-06 5512 7223

Brandon, Jonathan, (Shrewsbury), St Peter's, 16 Green Ln, Hazel Grove, Stockport SK7 4EA **Tel:** 0161-483 3476 **Fax:** 0161-419 9592

Brandon, Michael Charles, MA(Cantab), (Birmingham), All Souls, Kingsland Ave, Coventry CV5 8DX **Tel:** 0247-667 4161

Brandon, Paul D, (Clifton), 4 Lords Croft, Amesbury, Salisbury SP4 7EP **Tel:** 01980-622177

Branford, David, (Lancaster), Sacred Heart, Heys St, Thornton-le-Fylde FY5 4HL **Tel:** 01253-821637

Branson, Joseph, Mgr, (Plymouth, retired), 93 High Rd, Halton-on-Lune, Lancaster LA2 6PS **Tel:** 01524-811286 **E-mail:** joseph.branson@ukonline.co.uk

Brassington, Gary (Clifton) St Augustine's Presbytery, Painswick Rd, Matson, Gloucester GL4 9BS **Tel:** 01452-412702

Brayley, Ian, MA, (SJ), Campion Hall, Brewer St, Oxford OX1 1QS **Tel:** 01865-286100 Personal: **Tel:** 01865-286101

Braz, Cristiano STB (Westminster), Chaplain Royal London/St Barts Hosp, 9 Pekin Street, London **Tel:** 020-7351 6956 (home), 0207-7377385 (Direct)

Brazil, Walter, (Salford, retired), Church St, Ballyporeen, Cahir, Co Tipperary, Ireland **Tel:** 00353 52 67981

Brealey, Peter, BEd, (SDB), St Anne's Presbytery, 10 Highfield Rd, Chertsey KT16 8BU **Tel:** 01932-562375 **E-mail:** pp@st-annes-chertsey.org.uk

Brebner, Terence A, (Hallam), The Presbytery, Wingfield Rd Kimberworth, Rotherham S61 4AZ **Tel:** 01709-562012

Bredin, Joseph F, (Clifton), c/o St Ambrose, North Rd, Leigh Woods, Bristol BS8 3PW

Breen, Gerald, (Birmingham), 69 Lichfield Rd, Sutton Coldfield B74 2NU **Tel:** 0121-354 1211

Breen, John, BA, (Hexham & Newcastle), Pontificio Collegio Beda, Viale di San Paolo 18, 00146 Roma, Italia.

Breen, Martin, (Arundel & Brighton), St John's Presbytery, 59 The Avenue, Adworth, Surrey KT20 5AB **Tel:** 01737-813012

Breen, Patrick J, Canon, (Wrexham), 'Gooton', Kilmallock, Co. Lymerick Ireland **Email:** pjbreen123@gmail.com

Breen, Stephen, (MHM), St Joseph's College, Lawrence St, Mill Hill, London NW7 4JX **Tel:** 020-8959 8254

Breidenback, Joseph, (IC), Sacred Heart Church, 17 Lime Tree Ave, Bilton, Rugby CV22 7QT **Tel:** 01788 813263 **Email:** Fraybee@aol.com

Brennan, Alphonsus (O.Carm), The Friars, Aylesford, Kent ME20 7BX **Tel:** 01622-717272

Brennan, Anthony, (Northampton), 2 Severn Way, Brickhill, Bedford MK41 7BX **Tel:** 01234-352607

Brennan, J Kevin, (Liverpool, retired), 20 St George's Court, Station Rd, Maghull, Liverpool L31 3JD **Tel:** 0151-531 9795

Brennan, John, (Clifton), The Priest's Ho, Lower High St, Chipping Campden, GL55 6DZ **Tel:** 01386-840261

Brennan, Joseph, (Middlesbrough, retired), 4 Mayfield Place, Whitby, Nth Yorks YO21 1UL **Tel:** 01947-600085

Brennan, Patrick, (Birmingham), 2 Hallcourt Cres, Cannock WS11 3AB **Tel:** 01543-503149

Brennan, Raymund, (Southwark), 83 Manor Park Rd, West Wickham BR4 0JX **Tel:** 020-8777 6086

Brenninkmeyer, Andrew, MS, BA, (OSB), c/o Worth Abbey, Crawley, W Sussex RH10 4SB **Tel:** 01342-710310

Brentnall, Mark, (Nottingham), The Presbytery, Hollis St, Derby DE24 8QU. **Tel:** 01332 574474 **Fax:** 01332 571154.

Breslin, Anthony, (Nottingham), Holyrood Ho, Market Rasen, Lincs LN8 3BB **Tel:** 01673 842455

Breslin, Noel, (Birmingham), Presbytery, Frankley Beeches Rd, Northfield B31 5AB **Tel:** 0121-444 1386

Brett, Malachy, VF (Nottingham), The Presbytery, 75 Knighton Rd, Leicester LE3 3HN **Tel:** 0116-221 8385 **Fax:** 0116-221 8514

Brett, Peter (East Anglia), The Priest's House, 20 The Croft, Sudbury, Suffolk C010 1HW **Tel:** 01787-372703

Brewster, George Augustine, (Birmingham, retired), Aston Hall, Aston-by-Stone, Staffs

Bridges, Victor, (Liverpool, retired), Chapel Ho, Copy Ln, Netherton, Bootle L30 7PE **Tel:** 0151-293 0063

Bridson, Tony, (Arundel & Brighton), 46 Hollybush Rd, Northgate, Crawley, W. Sussex RH11 7QD **Tel:** 01293-430321

Brien, Timothy, (Wrexham), Flat 29, 27 Wynnstay Rd, Marford, near Wrexham **Tel:** 01978-851053

Briedenback, Joseph (IC), St Joseph's, New Zealand Rd, Cathays, Cardiff CF14 3BR **Tel:** 029-2041 1819 **Fax:** 029-2041 1820

Briffa, Silvio, (Cardiff), St Aloysius Presbytery, Chestnut Way, Gurnos, Merthyr Tydfil CF47 9SB **Tel:** 01685-722672

Briggs, Charles, BD, STL, HEL, (Southwark), St Mary's, 28 Crown Ln, Chislehurst BR7 5PL **Tel:** 020-8467 3215 **Fax:** 020-8325 9617

Brigham, Keith, (Shrewsbury), St Anthony's, Dunkery Rd, Woodhouse Park, Manchester M22 0WR **Tel:** 0161-992 7070 (day) **Tel:** 0161-437 2861 (evening)

Brignall, Peter M, Canon, (Wrexham), Cathedral of Our Lady of Sorrows, Regent St, Wrexham LL11 1RB **Tel:** 01978-263943 **Fax:** 01978-352277 **E-mail:** office@ wrexhamcathedral.fsnet.co.uk

Brindle, Paul, (Salford), St Vincent de Paul, Caldershaw Rd, Norden, Rochdale OL12 6BU **Tel/Fax:** 01706-645361 **E-mail:** info@stvincentsnorden.org.uk

Briody, James Gerard, MA, BSc, BD, PGCE (SDB), St James' Presbytery, Chesnut Grove, Bootle, Merseyside L20 4LX **Tel:** 0151 944 1039 **E-mail:** briodygerry@hotmail.com

Brisley, Marcus, BD, MTh (Portsmouth), 218 Charminster Rd, Bournemouth, Dorset BH8 9RW **Tel:** 01202-513369, **Fax:** 01202-518192 **E-mail:** mbrisley@portsmouthdio.org.uk

Bristow, Peter, MA, STD (Opus Dei), 1 Pine Rd, Manchester M20 6UY **Tel:** 0161-445 6480

Britt, Gerard, (Liverpool, retired), St Marie's Ho, 27 Seabank Rd, Southport PR9 0EJ **Tel:** 01704-547201

Broadbridge, Nicholas, BA, (OSB), Douai Abbey, Upper Woolhampton, Reading, Berks RG7 5TQ **Tel:** 0118-971 5372 **Fax:** 0118-971 5303

Broadley, Martin J, (Salford), (Chaplain Manchester University), 25 Beech Avenue, Whitefield, Manchester M45 7EN **Tel:** 0161-273 1456

Brockie, Michael Canon, JCL, (Westminster), 7 Cheyne Row, London SW3 5HS **Tel:** 020-7352 0777

Brogan, Cuthbert, (OSB), St Michael's Abbey, Farnborough Rd, Farnborough, Hants GU17 7NQ **Tel:** 01252-546105 **Fax:** 01252-372822 **E-mail:** prior@farnboroughabbey.org

Brogan, Martin, BA, (Salford, retired), Nazareth Ho, Scholes Lane, Prestwich Manchester M25 0NU **Tel:** 0161-773 2111

Brook, Peter, (SJ), John Sinnott Ho, 9 Edge Hill Wimbledon SW19 4LR **Tel:** 020-8947 4251

Brooks, Christopher, Mgr, MA, PsL, (Brentwood), 1 Kings Rd, Chingford, London E4 7HP **Tel:** 020-8529 1804

Brophy, R Paul MA (Westminster), St. Therese's Presbytery, Southdown Road, Port Talbot SA12 7HL **Tel:**01639 884791

Broster, Andrew, (Lancaster), St Joseph, Slyne Rd, Skerton, Lancaster LA1 2HU **Tel:** 01524-32493

Broughton, Simon, (Middlesbrough), St Mary's Cathedral, Dalby Way, Coulby Newham, Middlesbrough TS8 0TW **Tel:** 01642-597750

Broun, Patrick, BA, STB, (Birmingham), St Anne's Presbytery, Lynton Avenue, Weeping Cross, Stafford ST17 0EA **Tel:** 01785-661012

Brown, Alexander, J B, BA, (Birmingham), 18 Charles St, Cheadle, Staffordshire ST10 1ED **Tel:** 01538-753130 **Fax:** 01538-751940

Brown, Andrew, St Mary Magdalane Presbytery, Prospect Street, Cudworth, Barnsley SJ2 8JS **Tel:** 01226 710320

Brown, Darren (Nottingham), c/o Principal RC Chaplain (Army), HQ Land Command, Erskine Barracks, Witton, Salisbury Wilts SP2 0AG **Tel:** 01722 433892

Brown, John (SMA), 61 Blackhorse Rd, Walthamstow London E17 7AS **Tel:** 020 8520 3647

Brown, Joseph, BSc (SDB), Don Bosco Missions, 2 Orbel St, Battersea, London SW11 3NZ **Tel/Fax:** 020-7924 2733 **E-mail:** donbosco@btconnect.com

Brown, Michael, MA, BA, JCL, (Hexham & Newcastle), St Mary's, Clousden Hill, Forest Hall, Newcastle NE12 7AB **Tel:** 0191-268 4222

Brown, Michael, VF (Nottingham), Cathedral Ho, North Circus Street, Nottingham NG1 5AE **Tel:** 0115-953 9839 **Tel:** 0115-953 8112

Brown, Norman, (Westminster, retired), 2a Meadow Rd, London SW8 1QH

Brown, Peter, (East Anglia, retired), 16 Park Road, Wells-Next-The-Sea, Norfolk NR23 1DQ

Brown, Ralph, Mgr, VG, JCD, KHS, ProtAp (Westminster), Flat 3, 8 Morpeth Terrece, SW1P 1EQ **Tel:** 020-7798 9020

Brown, Ronald, Mgr, (Hexham & Newcastle, retired), Seabanks, 73a Lawe Rd, South Shields NE33 **Tel:** 0191-455 8092

Brown, Stephen, JCL, LLB, (Leeds), Catholic Chaplaincy, 1 Ashgrove, Bradford BD7 1BN **Tel:** 01274-726636

Browne, Andrew, (Hallam), The Presbytery, 238 Herringthorpe Valley Rd, Rotherham S65 3BA **Tel:** 01709-363753

Browne, George, (Shrewsbury), St Monica, 38 Dingleway, Appleton, Warrington WA4 3AB **Tel:** 01925-264695 **E-mail:** george@georgebrowne.wanadoo.co.uk

Browne, James BA Post Grad Hons (Nottingham), The Presbytery, Beaumont Leys Ln, Leicester LE4 2BD **Tel:** 0116-235 3329 **Fax:** 0116-235 4399

Browne, Patrick, Canon (Westminster), 47 Cumberland St, London SW1V 4LY **Tel:** 020-7834 6965

Browne, Patrick, Canon (Episcopal Vicar) (Birmingham), St Chad's Cathedral, St Chad's Queensway, Birmingham B4 6EU **Tel:** 0121-236 2251

Browne, Paul, BEd, (OSB), Our Lady Star of the Sea and St Michael, Banklands, Workington CA14 3EP **Tel:** 01900-602114 **Fax:** 01900-871797

Brumwell, Marc Anselm, BA, STB (OSB), Downside Abbey, Stratton on the Fosse, Radstock BA3 4RH

Brunning, Antony, (Westminster), 211 Old Marylebone Rd, London NW1 5QT **Tel:** 020-7723 5101

Bruxby, Paul, JCL, (Brentwood), The Presbytery, Loudoun Avenue, Barkingside, Ilford, Essex IG6 1AU **Tel:** 020-8554 3568

Buckley, David A, MA, FRSA (Portsmouth), The Priest's Ho, Newtown, Uckfield, East Sussex TN22 5DJ **Tel:** 01825-762221

Buckley, Edward, (Plymouth), Gable End, 14 Reeue Cl, New Walk, Totnes, Devon TQ9 5WG

Buckley, John, (Westminster), 729 High Rd, London N17 8AG **Tel:** 020-8808 3554

Buckley, John, (Portsmouth), The Presbytery, Martin St, Bishop's Waltham, Hants SO32 1DN **Tel/Fax:** 01489-895889 **E-mail:** rev.j.buckley@bishopswaltham23.fsnet.co.uk

Buckley, Martin BTh (Brentwood), c/o Cathedral Ho, Ingrave Rd, Brentwood, Essex CM15 8AT

Buckley, Michael (Salford, retired), St Patrick's, 28 Park View, Harpurhey, Manchester M9 5TF **Tel/Fax:** 0161 839 1020

Buckley, Michael J, Mgr, DD, (Leeds, retired), El Shaddai, 9 West Ridings, East Preston, W. Sussex BN16 2TD **Tel:** 01903-772048

Buckley, Timothy, (Southwark) Ardaneanig, Killarney, Co Kerry, Ireland

Buckley, Timothy, (CSsR), Erdington Abbey, SS Thomas & Edmund of Canterbury, Sutton Road, Erdington, Birmingham B23 6QN **Tel:** 01420-83255 **Fax:** 01420-88805

Buckner, John (IC), St Maries, Oak St, Rugby CV22 5EL **Tel:** 07731 503 332 **E-mail:** jfbuck@rosmini.org

Budden, Shaun, (Portsmouth), 42 Exton Rd, Boscombe East, Bournmouth, Dorset BH6 5QG **Tel:** 01202-485588 **E-mail:** seanec@tiscali.co.uk

Budge, Martin, (Plymouth), The Presbytery, Old Mill Ln, Marnhull, Sturminster, Newton, Dorset DT10 1JX **Tel:** 01258-820388

Budzynski, Andrzej, (Gniezno, Poland), The Presbytery, St Stanislaus Kostka, Springfield Rd, Coventry CV1 4GR **Tel:** 024-7622 2455

Buholzer, Josef (MAfr), The Rector, St Edward's, 46 Totteridge Common, London N20 8ND **Tel:** 020-8959 2553 **Fax:** 020-8201 1850 **E-mail:** recstedwards@prontoserve.co.uk

Bukenya, Sylvester, BA, MA, MSC (Masaka), 96 Northside, Wandsworth Common, London SW18 2QU **Tel:** 020-8874 2724 **Mbl:** 07913 201670 **E-mail:** bukenyasilver@yahoo.com

Bula, Lucio (CS), 20 Brixton Rd, London SW9 6BN **Tel:** 020-7735 8235 **Fax:** 020-7840 0236

Bulfin, Austin, (Salford), Presbytery, 1 Chain Rd, Blackley, Manchester M9 2GN **Tel:** 0161-643 2595

Bull, Douglas, BSc, (Southwark), The Presbytery, 63 London Rd, Rainham, Kent ME8 7RH **Tel:** 01634-232972

Bull, Malcolm (Northampton), 27 Cardington Rd, Bedford MK42 0BN **Tel:** 01234-350628

Bullen, Anthony, (Liverpool, retired), The Glade, Aughton, Ormskirk L39 6SY

Bullen, David G, (Liverpool, retired), Ince Blundell Hall, Ince Blundell, Liverpool L38 6JL **Tel:** 0151-929 2596

Bulmer, David, STL MA, (Leeds), St Austin's Presbytery, 6 Wentworth Terr, Wakefield WF1 3QN **Tel:** 01924 372080

Bumstead, Dunstan, (OSB), Prinknash Abbey, Cranham, Gloucester GL4 8EX **Tel:** 01452-812455 **E-mail:** prinknash@waitrose.com

Bunce, Michael, Canon, (Southwark), 59 Burgate, Canterbury, Kent CT1 2HJ **Tel:** 01227-462896

Bunting, Raymond J, (IC), St Patrick's, 151 Cromwell Rd, Newport NP19 0HS **Tel:** 01633-672334

Burbidge, Alan, (Nottingham), St George and All Soldier Saints, 40 Village St, Old Normanton Derby, PE3 8SZ **Tel:** 01332-767038

Burbidge, Bruce, (East Anglia), The Presbytery, 933 Lincoln Road, Walton, Peterborough PE4 6AE **Tel:** 01733-322750

Burgess, Christopher, (AA), 16 Nightingale Rd, Hitchin, Herts SG5 1QS **Tel:** 01462-459126

Burgess, Robin, MA, (Westminster), 20 Willowmead Cl, London W5 1PT **Tel:** 020-8998 4170

Burke, Brendan, (Arundel & Brighton), Priest Ho, Station Rd, Rustington, W. Sussex, BN16 3BE **Tel:** 01903-783973 **Fax:** 01903-779137

Burke, Dermot, (Hexham & Newcastle, retired), c/o Bishop's Ho, 800 West Rd, Newcastle upon Tyne.

Burke, Geoffrey, Canon, BA, (Arundel & Brighton), St Michael's, Church Ln, Danehill, Hayward's Heath, W. Sussex, RH17 7EZ **Tel:** 01825-790268

Burke, Gerard T, (Westminster), St Lawrence's Presbytery, The Green, Feltham, Middx TW13 4AF **Tel:** 020-8890 2367

Burke, James, (Nottingham), St Norberts, 52 St Thomas's Road, Spalding Lincs PE11 2XX **Tel/Fax:** 01775 722056 **E-mail:** fj.jim@btinternet.com

Burke, Michael, JCL, (Menevia), The Presbytery, School Rd, Morriston, Swansea SA6 6HZ **Tel:** 01792-771053

Burke, Peter, (Shrewsbury), St Alban's, 37a Chester Rd, Macclesfield SK11 8DJ **Tel:** 01625-423446, **Fax:** 01625-421867 **E-mail:** stalbanmacc@aol.com

Burke, Raymund, (Shrewsbury), 1 Brook Meadow, Irby, Wirral CH61 4YS **Tel:** 0151-648 6422

Burke, Terence, STL, MA, (MHM), 46 Upper Redlands Rd, Reading, Berkshire RG1 5JJ **Tel/Fax:** 0118-926 8869 **E-mail:** t.l.burke@reading.ac.uk

Burke, Thomas, (Westminster, retired), St Francis, Churchfield, Knock, Co Mayo, Eire

Burke, Thomas, (Northampton, retired), 6 Court Green Cl, Cloughton, Scarborough YO13 0AP

Burke, Thomas, (Hexham & Newcastle), St Mary Magdalen, Harbour Walk, Seaham Harbour, Co Durham SR7 7DS **Tel:** 0191-581 2368

Burke, Timothy Francis, (Birmingham), Holy Cross Presbytery, 40 Hall Green Rd, Stone Cross, West Bromwich B71 3LA **Tel:** 0121-588 2743

Burke, W Anthony, (Hallam), The Rectory, Main Rd, Hathersage, Sheffield S32 1BB **Tel:** 01433-650352

Burlinson, Paschal (OFM Cap), Franciscan Friary, Monastery Dr, Pantasaph, Holywell CH8 8PE **Tel:** 01244-351331

Burns, Andrew (CSsR), The John Paul Centre, 49/55 Grange Road, Middlesborough TS1 5AU **Tel:** 01244-351331

Burns, Anthony John, (Birmingham), The Presbytery, Hardwick Rd, Hethe, Bicester OX6 9AW **Tel:** 01869-277396

Burns, Daniel, (SDS), The Priest's Ho, London Rd, Hook, Hants RG22 9LA **Tel:** 01256-762351 **E-mail:** fatherdanny@burnshook.fsnet.co.uk

Burns, David, St. Wulstan's, Poulton Road, Fleetwood, Lancs FY7 7JY **Tel:** 01253-873609 **Fax:** 01253-772567

Burns, Gerard V, BSc, (SM),117 Cottingham Rd, Hull, Humberside HU5 2DH **Tel:** 01482-444180 **Fax:** 01482-470811

Burns, James, (Lancaster), St Mary's, Cleator, Cumbria CA23 2AB **Tel:** 01946-810324

Burns, Peter Matthew, MA, DipEd, (OSB), Ampleforth Abbey, York YO62 4ER **Tel:** 01439 766714 **Fax:** 01439 766724

Burns, Peter, BA, STB (OSB), Ealing Abbey, Charlbury Grove, London W5 2DY **Tel:** 020-8862 2100

Burns, Peter, BA, Dip Soc, (SDB), Saint Bosco Ho, 121a Reading Rd, Farnborough GU14 6NZ **Tel:** 01252 554 300 **Fax:** 01252 375 395

Burns, Peter (Lancaster), Holy Family, 1 Lytham Road, Warton, Preston PR4 1AD **Tel:** 01772 725193

Burrowes, Vincent R, Canon, (Liverpool, retired), Flat 1, 77 Bath Street North, Southport PR9 0DJ **Tel:** 01704 530572

Burrows, D Peter, MTh, PhD, (Plymouth, retired). 28 Lyonsdown Road, New Barnett, Herts.

Burrows, Neil, (Westminster), 390b Northold Rd, South Harrow HA2 8EX **Tel:** 020-8864 5455

Burrows, Vincent Aelred, MA, (OSB) St Benedict's Monastery, Convent Cl, Duddle Ln, Bamber Bridge, Preston PR5 6US **Tel:** 01772-902201 **Fax:** 01772-902214

Burt, Stanley, (Arundel & Brighton, retired), St Joseph's, Albert Rd, Bognor Regis, W. Sussex PO21 5NJ

Burtoft, William, BSc, STL, (Leeds, retired), 2 Rotherstoke Cl, Moorgate, Rotherham S62 2JU **Tel:** 01709-364159

Burton, Edward, AKC (Westminster), 373 Bowes Rd, London N11 1AA **Tel:** 020-8368 1368

Burton, Gerard, (MAfr, retired), St Mary's Abbey, The Ridgeway, London NW7 4HX **Tel:** 020-8959 1364 **Fax:** 020-8959 4660

Burton, Joseph, (MHM, retired), Herbert Ho, 41 Victoria Rd, Freshfield, Formby, Liverpool L37 1LW **Tel:** 01704-835855

Bushabu, Minga Stanis, (CJ), St George's College, Weybridge Rd, Addlestone, Weybridge KT15 2QS **Tel:** 01932-854811

Bushell, Patrick, (Portsmouth, retired), 39 Observatory St, Oxford OX2 6HU **Tel:** 01865-515708

Busuttil, Anthony, (Westminster, retired), 6 Rockmead Rd, Fairlight, E. Sussex TN35 4DJ **Tel:** 01424-814874

Butchard, John, Mgr, VG, (Liverpool), Holy Rosary Presbytery, Altway, Old Rd, Liverpool L10 2LG **Tel:** 0151-526 8468

Butcher, Gerard, (Brentwood, retired), 5 Goodmayes Ln, Ilford, Essex IG3 3PB **Tel:** 020-8599 7099

Butler, Edward, (Birmingham, retired), c/o Cathedral Ho, St Chad's Queensway, Birmingham B4 6EX

Butler, Michael J, MA, PhL, STB, DipRE, (Brentwood), Church Ho, Mulberry Green, Old Harlow, Essex CM17 0HA **Tel:** 01279-429388

Butler, Thomas, (Lancaster), c/o Principal RC Chaplain (Army), HQ Land Command, Erskine Barracks, Witton, Salisbury Wilts SP2 0AG **Tel:** 01722 433892

Butlin, Mark, MA, (OSB), Ampleforth Abbey, York YO62 4EN **Tel:** 01439-766714 **Fax:** 01439-766724

Butters, John, STD, BA, (Hexham & Newcastle), 2 Grosmont Dr, Sidlaw Rd, Billingham, TS23 2EP **Tel:** 01642- 553118

Butterworth, Keith, (Shrewsbury), Holy Family, 65 Old Hall Rd, Sale M33 2HT **Tel:** 0161-969 7800

Buxton, Wilfrid, Mgr Canon, STL, (Lancaster, retired), Boarbank Hall, Grange-over-Sands, Cumbria LA11 7HN **Tel:** 01539-532288

Byrne, Andrew, MA, STD (Opus Dei), 1 Leopold Rd, London W5 3PB

Byrne, Brendan, (Birmingham), c/o The Archbishop's Ho, 6 Shadwell St, Birmingham B4 6EY

Byrne, Dominic, MA, JCD, STL, (Westminster), 4 Egerton Gardens, Hendon NW4 4BA

Byrne, Garrett Joseph, Canon (Birmingham), The Priory, Barras Ln, Coventry CV1 4AQ **Tel:** 02476-220402

Byrne, Gerard, (Northampton), 2 St Brendan, Beanfield Ave, Corby NN18 0AZ **Tel:** 01536-202879

Byrne, Gerard, STL, DMin, MSW, MA (Salford), St Luke's Centre, Whalley Rd, Whalley Range Manchester M16 8BT **Tel:** 0161-226 4563 **Email:** gerardbyrne@stlukescentre.org.uk

Byrne, James (Westminster), 45 London Rd, Enfield EN2 6DS **Tel:** 020-8363 2569

Byrne, John (Westminster) 186 St John's Rd, Boxmoor, Herts HP1 1NR **Tel:** 01442-391759

Byrne, Mark, (SOLT), Ty Mair, Kings Tunning Rd, Presteigne LD8 2LD **Tel:** 01544-262188

Byrne, Neil (Leeds), St Joseph's Presbytery, 281 Skipton Rd, Harrogate HG1 3HD **Tel:** 01423-504124

Byrne, Paschal, (Shrewsbury), Christ the King, 890 New Chester Rd, Bromborough, Wirral CH62 6AT **Tel:** 0151-334 1657

Byrne, Peter Celestine, (OSB), Buckfast Abbey, Buckfastleigh, Devon TQ11 0EE **Tel:** 01364-643301

Byrne, Robert, (Cong Orat), St Aloysius, 25 Woodstock Rd, Oxford OX2 6HA **Tel:** 01865-315800

Byrne, William, Canon (Salford), St Thomas of Canterbury, 132 Lonsdale Rd, Heaton, Bolton BL1 4PN **Tel/Fax:** 01204-840042

Byrnes, Ian J, BD, (Arundel & Brighton), The Presbytery, Magdelen Rd, St Leonards-on-Sea, E. Sussex TN37 6ET **Tel:** 01424-420815 **E-mail:** ian.byrnes@dabnet.org

Byron, Richard, Canon, (Menevia, retired), Stella Maris Convent, Eaton Cres, Swansea **Tel:** 01792-469651

Byron, Timothy (SJ), St Ignatius Church, 27 High Rd, London N15 6ND **Tel:** 020 8442 5250 **Fax:** 020 8802 8102 **E-mail:** timbyron@jesuits.net

Bywater, Timothy, (Middlesbrough), St Leonard and St Mary, The Presbytery, Church Hill, Malton YO17 7EJ **Tel:** 01653-692128

Caddell, Martin, CF, MCTC (Liverpool), Berechurch Hall Camp, Colchester, Essex CO2 9NU

Caddle, Denis, (OAR), St Rita's Centre, Ottery Moor Ln, Honiton EX14 8AP **Tel/Fax:** 01404 42601 **E-mail:** denisoari@btinternet.com

Cadek, Miroslave (SJ), House of Our Lady of Mercy, 182 Walm Ln, London NW2 3AX **Tel:** 020-8452 4304

Caden, John, (Hexham & Newcastle), Presbytery, West Park Ln, Sedgefield, Stockton, Cleveland TS21 2BX **Tel:** 01740-620405

Cadogan, Daniel, (Liverpool, retired), St Marie's Ho, 27 Seabank Rd, Southport PR9 0EJ

Cadwallader, John Adrian, (CJ), St George's College, Weybridge Rd, Addlestone, Surrey KT15 2QS **Tel:** 01932-839451

Cahill, Charles, (Westminster), 1 Colney Hatch Ln, London N10 1PN **Tel:** 020-8883 5607

Cahill, Daniel, (Middlesbrough, retired), Flat 1, 26 Bagdale, Whitby YO21 1QS **Tel:** 01947-825196

Cahill, James, (Nottingham), Holy Cross, Parsonwood Hill, Whitwick, Leics LE67 5AT **Tel:** 01530-832326 **Fax:** 01530-817515

Cahill, John, VF, STL, (Nottingham), Holy Souls Presbytery, Frodingham Rd, Scunthorpe, N Lincs DN15 7TA **Tel:** 01724-842197

Cahill, Joseph, Canon, (Shrewsbury, retired), 15 Yew Tree Rd, Plumley, Knutsford WA16 0UQ **Tel:** 01565-723265

Cain, Rev David (Nottingham), 21 Hinckley Rd, Leicester LE3 OTA **Tel:** 0116-251 9370 **Email:** frdavid@nrcdt.org.uk

Cain, Edward, (Liverpool), St Ambrose, Heathgate Avenue, Speke, Liverpool L24 7RS **Tel:** 0151-425 3600

Caine, David, MA, (Southwark), Presbytery, 23 St Peters Rd, Broadstairs, Kent CT10 2AP **Tel:** 01843-861627

Cairns, John, (Nottingham), St Mary's Presbytery, Hollins Ln, Marple Bridge, Stockport, Cheshire SK6 5BB **Tel:** 0161-427 2408

Cairns, Malcolm BA, C.Chem, MRSC (Hexham & Newcastle), St Joseph's, Coast Rd, Blackhall, Hartlepool TS27 4HW **Tel:** 0191-586 4319

Calascione, Christopher, BA (OSB), Priest's Ho, Ledbury Rd, Little Malvern, Worcs WR14 4JL **Tel:** 01684-574658

Calcutt, Richard, Bursar (MAfr), Oak Lodge, 48 Totteridge Common, London N20 8NB **Tel:** 020-8959 1968 **E-mail:** richard_calcutt@yahoo.co.uk

Calduch, Xavier, BSc, STD, (Opus Dei), 159 Nightingale Ln, Balham, London SW12 8NQ **Tel:** 020-8673 2242

Caldwell, Justin, MA, (OSB), Ampleforth Abbey, York YO62 4EN **Tel:** 01439-766714 **Fax:** 01439-766724

Caldwell, Philip, STL, (Salford), Ushaw College, Durham DH7 9RH

Callaghan, Brendan, (SJ), Campion Hall, Oxford OX1 1QS **Tel:** 01865 286101

Callaghan, James, (Leeds), St William, Ingleby Rd, Bradford BD8 9AJ **Tel:** 01274-542534

Callaghan, James, MA, PGCE, (OSB), Ampleforth College, Yorks YO62 4ES **Tel:** 01439-766705

Callaghan Joseph, (Lancaster on sabbatical), c/o Pastoral Centre, Balmoral Road, Lancaster LA1 3BT **Tel:** 01253-873609

Callaghan, Kevin, (CSsR), St Mary's, Clapham, London SW4 7AP **Tel:** 020-7622 2793 **Fax:** 020-7627 3153

Callaghan, Kevin, (CSsR), Hawkstone Hall, Marchamley, Shrewsbury SY4 5LG **Tel:** 01630-685242

Callanan, Stanislaus, (OCD), Carmelite Priory, 41 Kensington Church St, London W8 4BB **Tel:** 020-7937 9866 **Fax:** 020-7938 1470

Callon, Frederick J, (Liverpool, retired), Christopher Grange, Youens Way, Liverpool L14 2EW **Tel:** 0151-220 2525

Calnan, Francis, (SCJ), Sacred Heart Presbytery, Pyramid Cl, Northampton NN3 4DP **Tel:** 01604-402301

Cama, Darius S Francis, BSc, (Clifton), St Peter's Presbytery, London Rd, Gloucester GL1 3EX

Cameron, Simon BA, STL, DEI (CMF), The Towers, High St, Buckden, St Neots PE19 5TA **Tel:** 01480-810344 **E-mail:** simon@claret.org.uk

Cameron-Brown, Aldhelm, Rt Rev Abbot Emeritus, MA(Cantab) (OSB), Our Lady & St Peter, Prinknash Abbey, Cranham, Gloucester, GL4 8EX **Tel:** 01452-812455 **Fax:** 01452-813305 **E-mail:** andrewcmsj@gmail.com

Cameron-Mowat, Andrew, Superior (SJ), 21 Helix Gardens, Brixton Hill, London SW2 2JJ **Tel:** 020-8671 4973 **Fax:** 020-8678 9338 **E-mail:** andrewcmsj@gmail.com

Camilleri, Benjamin, (Northampton, retired), 97 St Rita St, Flat 1, Birzebuggia, BBG 09, Malta

Camilleri, David, (Southwark), 31 Abbey Grove, Abbey Wood, London SE2 9EU **Tel:** 020-8311 2594

Camilleri, Victor (OFM), St Boniface, 47 Adler St, London E1 1EE **Tel:** 020-7247 9529

Cammack, Charles Norbert, MA, MEd (MHM). St Peter's Ho, College Ave, Freshfield L37 1LE **Tel:** 01704-831058 **E-mail:** charles.cammack@tesco.net

Campbell, David, (Westminster), c/o Principal RC Chaplain (Army), HQ Land Command, Erskine Barracks, Witton, Salisbury Wilts SP2 0AG **Tel:** 01722 433892

Campbell, Duncan, (OP), Holy Cross Priory, 45 Wellington St, Leicester LE1 6HW **Tel:** 0116-255 6902

Campbell, Eugene, (Clifton), St Lawrence Presbytery, 71 Brd St, Chipping Sodbury, Bristol BS37 6AD **Tel:** 01454-312161

Campbell, Howard (West Indies), Mary Immaculate and St Gregory the Great. 82 Union St, Barnet, Herts EN5 4HZ **Tel:** 020-8449 3338 **Fax:** 020-8449 4761

Campbell, James (SJ), The Immaculate Conception, 114 Mount St, London W1Y 3AH

Campbell, John, (Hexham & Newcastle, retired), St Mary, Swinbourne, Barrasford, Hexham, Northumberland NE48 4DQ

Campbell, Michael G, BA, STL, MA (OSA), Cathedral Ho, Balmoral Rd, Lancaster LA1 3BT

Campion, Michael, BA, (Hexham & Newcastle), St Mary, 1 Burn Lane, Newton, Aycliffe, Co. Durham DL5 4HT **Tel:** 01325 313611

Canavan, Robert, Canon (Lancaster), Greenside, 21 Shay Ln, Hale Barns, Cheshire WA15 8NZ

Canning, Charles E, (Liverpool), St Oswald's, Padgate Ln, Warrington WA1 3LB **Tel:** 01925-813248

Canning, Daniel, (Shrewsbury, retired), 33 Cranlee Park, Culmore, Derry BT48 8NT

Cannon, Owen, (SMM), 27 St Gabriel's Rd, Cricklewood, London NW2 4DS **Tel:** 020-8450 4291

Cannon, Patrick, (Southwark), St Dominic, Violet Ln, Waddon CR0 4HN **Tel:** 020-8686 1634

Cannon, Paul, (Salford) Guardian Angels, Harvey St, Elton, Bury BL8 2RD **Tel/Fax:** 0161-764 1630

Cansse, Stephen, (OPraem), 178 New London Rd, Chelmsford, Essex CM2 0AR **Tel:** 01245 352898

Capener, Francis (Southwark), 41 Guildhall St, Folkestone, Kent CT20 1EF **Tel:** 01303-252823

Caponi, Gismondo, (SX), 130 Holden Rd, Woodside Park, London N12 **Tel:** 020-8445 6430

Carette, Albert, (SDB), 10 Oldhams Ln, Bolton BL1 6PN **Tel:** 01204-590600 **E-mail:** acarette@tiscali.co.uk

Carey, Edmond P, Canon (Lancaster), Sacred Heart, 17 Talbot Rd, Blackpool FY1 1LB **Tel:** 01253-620964

Carey, Francis, PhD, Ed (MAfr), c/o St Edmund's College, Cambridge CB3 0BN **Tel:** 01223-336123 **E-mail:** fc222@cam.ac.uk

Carey, Patrick Dominic, (Hexham & Newcastle), Little Sisters of the Poor, Holy Cross Home, High Barnes, Sunderland SR4 8QA

Carey, Patrick F, Canon, (Northampton, retired), c/o Bridgettine Convent, Fulmer Common Rd, Iver Heath, Bucks SL0 0NR

Carling, James, STB , Our Lady of the Assumption, Bath Rd, Thatcham, Berks RG18 4AG **Tel:** 01635-864416

Carling, James, (Portsmouth), 2 Dean Rd, Bitterne, Southampton, Hants SO18 6AP **Tel:** 023 8044 9088 **Fax:** 023 8042 1531

Carlyle, John, (Birmingham), St Vincent's, Nechells Parkway, Birmingham B7 4JY **Tel:** 0121-359 3305

Carney, Joseph, BSc, Dip Soc Adm, (Shrewsbury), St Thomas Becket, 3 Nantwich Rd, Tarporley CW6 9UN **Tel/Fax:** 01829-732511 **E-mail:** jc4jc@onetel.com

Carney, Matthew, BSc, STB, (OSB), St.Beghs Priory, Coach Rd, Whitehaven, Cumbria CA28 7TE **Tel:** 01946 692342 **Fax:** 01946 591831 **E-mail:** stbeghspriory@tiscali.co.uk

Carolan, Patrick, (OMI), 20 Quex Rd, Kilburn, London NW6 4PS **Tel:** 020-7624 1701

Carpenter, Barry, (Westminster, retired), 4 Merry Hill Rd, Bushey, Watford, Herts WD23 1DY **Tel:** 020-8950 8985

Carpenter, Bernard L, MA, (Clifton, retired), 76 Parkfield Rd, Taunton TA1 4SD

Carr, Colin, (OP), St Dominic's Priory, 41a Red Barns, Newcastle Upon Tyne NE1 2TP **Tel:** 0191-2325939

Carr, Francis, (SCJ, retired), Olton Friary, 140/150 St Bernard's Rd, Solihull, W. Mids B92 7BL **Tel:** 0121-706 0505

Carr, Paul, St Kentigern's, 36 Wilbraham Rd, Fallowfield, Manchester M14 7DW **Tel:** 0161-224 4664 **Fax:** 0161-257 0271 **E-mail:** stkentigern@btinternet.com

Carr, Peter, CertEd, DipRelEd, (SDB), Rinaldi Ho, 32 Orbel St, London SW11 3NZ **Tel:** 020-7801 9040 **Fax:** 020-7801 9041 **E-mail:** pcsdb@aol.com

Carr, Peter, (Hexham & Newcastle), St Cuthbert, Ropery Ln, Chester-le-Street DH3 3PH **Tel:** 0191-388 2302

Carr, Terence, MA. JCL (Wrexham), 6 Plas Avenue, Prestatyn, Denbighshire LL19 9NH **Tel:** 01745 854304 **Fax:** 01745 889123

Carrick, Brendan Joseph, STB (Birmingham), 41 Bee Ln, Fordhouses, Wolverhampton WV10 6LE **Tel:** 01902-782144 **Fax:** 01902-788145

Carrick, George, (Plymouth), The Presbytery, Priory Rd, St Marychurch, Torquay, Devon TQ1 4NY **Tel:** 01803-327612

Carrigg, Noel, (OSCam), St Camillus Hospital, East Park, Hexham NE46 6JY **Tel:** 01434-602869

Carroll, Anthony, (SJ), St Ignatius Church, 27 High Rd, Stamford Hill, London N15 6ND **Tel:** 020 8802 5303 **E-mail:** t.carroll@heythrop.ac.uk

Carroll, Edward, (Westminster, retired), Archbishop's Ho, Ambrosden Avenue, London SW1P 1QJ

Carroll, Francis, (Leeds), St Wilfrid, 2a Whincover Bank, Leeds LS12 5JW **Tel:** 0113-263 9531

Carroll, Gregory, (OSB), Ampleforth Abbey, York YO62 4EN **Tel:** 01439-766714 **Fax:** 01439-766724

Carroll, Mark, (Hexham & Newcastle) St Anne's, 43 Welbeck Avenue, Darlington DL1 2DR **Tel:** 01325-464547

Carroll, Patrick, (Westminster), St Martin de Porres, 4 Church Cl, Cuffley, Herts EN6 4LS **Tel:** 01707-873398

Carroll, Patrick, (SMA), Society of African Missions, Blackrock Rd, Cork, Ireland. **Tel:** 00-353-2154 1069

Carroll, Philip, Mgr, VG (Hexham and Newcastle), Venerabile Collegio Inglese, Via Di Monserrato, 00186 Roma, Italia

Carroll, Sean, (Westminster), 115 Hertford Rd, London N9 7EN **Tel:** 020-8803 6631

Carroll, William MA (SDB), St John Bosco Ho, 121A Reading Rd, Farnborough GU14 6NZ **Tel:** 01252-554300

Carter, Denis (SSC), Director, St Columban's, Widney Manor Rd, Knowle, Solihull, W. Mids B93 9AB **Tel:** 01564-772096/776202 **Fax:** 01564-770500

Carter, John, (Leeds), St Patrick's Presbytery, Torre Rd, Leeds LS9 7QL **Tel:** 0113-248 2852

Carter, Joseph, (Salford), St Antony, Eleventh St, Trafford Park, Manchester M17 1JF **Tel:** 0161-872 0311

Carter, Joseph, (Westminster), The Presbytery, 339 High Rd, Wembley, Middx HA9 6AG **Tel:** 020-8902 0081

Carter, Richard, BA, (Leeds), St Aidan's Presbytery, Baildon Rd, Baildon BD17 6AQ **Tel:** 01274-583032

Carter, Tim (OP), St Dominic's Priory, Southampton Rd, Haverstock Hill, London NW5 4LB **Tel:** 020-7482 9210 **Fax:** 020-7482 9239

Cartwright, Denis, (CSSp), 6 Woodlands Rd, Bickley, Bromley, Kent BR1 2AF **Tel:** 020-8467 3555

Carty, Robert, (SJ), Corpus Christi Jesuit Community, 757 Christchurch Rd, Boscombe, Bournemouth BH7 6AN **Tel:** 01202-436700

Caruana, Louis, (SJ), John Sinnott Ho, 9 Edge Hill, Wimbledon SW19 4LR **Tel:** 020 8947 4251

Carus, James, (Salford, retired), Nazareth Ho, Scholes Ln, Prestwich, Manchester M25 8AP

Carvallo, Carlos, (Leeds), St Mary's Presbytery, 40 Park Ln, Rothwell, Leeds LS26 **Tel:** 0113-282453

Carvill, Francis J, VF, (Nottingham), Holy Cross, Watnall Rd, Hucknall Notts NG15 7NJ **Tel:** 0115 953 9997 **Fax:** 0115 956 8181

Casalucci, Enio (Superior) (SX), 260 Nether St, London N3 1HT **Tel:** 020-8346 0428

Casey, Archbald, (SX), 57 Ewhurst Rd, Jamaica Street E1 3HT

Casey, James (CSsR), The Causeway, Monkwermouth, Tyne & Wear SR6 0BH

Casey, Timothy (CM), Christopher Grange, Youens Way, Liverpool L14 2EW **Tel:** 0141-220-2525

Casinader, Prins (OFMCap), University Chaplain, St Walburge's, Weston St, Preston PR2 2QE **Tel/Fax:** 01772-734499 **Email:** capucin.preston@btinternet.com

Cassidy, Anthony, (CSsR), Erdington Abbey, Sutton Rd, Birmingham B23 6QN **Tel:** 0121-373 0143 **Fax:** 0121-382 6845 **Mbl:** 0956 292839

Cassidy, Damian, Our Lady of Lourdes, 373 Bowes Rd, New Southgate, London N11 1AA **Tel:** 020 8361 3172

Cassidy, Dennis, BA, (Leeds) Corpus Christi Presbytery, 19 Neville Rd, Osmondthorpe, Leeds LS9 0HD **Tel:** 0113 294 7305

Cassidy, Rev Dr James M, STL, PhD, (CRIC), St Augustine's, Langcliffe Dr, Heelands, Milton Keynes MK13 7PL **Tel:** 01908-221228

Cassidy, Michael, Mgr (Lancaster, retired), Moneenbeg, Rooksy, Co Roscommon, Ireland.

Casinader, Prins (OFMCap),University Chaplain, St Walburge's, Weston St, Preston PR2 2QE **Tel:** 01772-734499 **Fax:** 01772-734499 **E-mail:** capucin.preston@btinternet.com

Castelli, John, (Southwark, retired), Obispado, Chachapoyas, Dept: Amazonas. Peru **Email:** jacastelli2@hotmail.com

Castello, Danilo, (MCCJ), DD, MIL Comboni Ho, 16 Dawson Place, London W2 4TJ **Tel:** 020-7229 7059 **Fax:** 020-7229 6123

Caszo, Bernard, (MSFS), St Michael's, 93 Marine Parade East, Clacton-on-Sea, Essex CO15 6JW **Tel:** 01255-423688

Catlin, John, (Portsmouth), The Presbytery, St Mary's Passage, Ryde, Isle of Wight PO33 2RG **Tel:** 01983-562171 **E-mail:** johncatlin@aol.com

Catterall, Louis, (SMM), St Joseph, Abbey Ho Dr, Romsey, Hants SO51 8YB **Tel:** 01794-513646

Catterall, Richard W, BD, BA, (Leeds), St John's Convent, Kiln Green, Reading, RG10 9XP **Tel:** 01734-403870

Caulfield, James, BD, (East Anglia), c/o Principal RC Chaplain (RAF), Chaplaincy Office, RAF Halton, Aylesbury, Bucks HP22 5PG **Tel:** 01296 656910 **E-mail:** jim@cardinal-biggles.demon.co.uk

Causey, John, (Liverpool), St Richard's, 184 Liverpool Rd, Skelmersdale WN8 8BX **Tel:** 01695 724476

Cavanagh, John (OFM Cap), Franciscan Friary, 31 Upper Church Rd, St Leonard's on Sea, E. Sussex TN37 7AS **Tel:** 01424-752665 **E-mail:** fjohn55@aol.com

Cavedon, Christiano MA (OSM), Priory Ho, 25 Woodstock Rd West, Begbroke, Oxon OX5 1RJ **Tel:** 01865-372149

Cavey, Vincent, (Salford), St Mary, Duke St, Denton, Manchester M34 2AN **Tel:** 0161-336 2358

Cawley, Peter Anscar, (OSB), St Mary's Abbey, Buckfast, Buckfastleigh, Devon TQ11 0EE **Tel:** 01364-645500

Cefai, Joseph, MA, (Menevia), St Joseph Presbytery, Water St, Port Talbot, SA12 6LE **Tel:** 01639-882846

Ceglarski, Romano , 19 Val Plaisant, St Helier, Jersey. **Tel:** 01534-767997

Celotto, Petro (CS), The Italian Mission, 20 Brixton Rd, London SW9 6BU **Tel:** 020-7735 8235

Cengel, Martin (SVD), 8 Teignmouth Rd, London NW2 4HN

Cerda, Mario (MCCJ), Comboni Missionaries, Brownberrie Ln, Horsforth, Leeds LS18 5HE **Tel:** 0113-258 2658

Chabanon, Gérard, St Edward's College, 46 Totteridge Common, London N20 8ND **Tel:** 020-8959 2553

Chaberski, Bede, (OFMConv), 26 Cornwall Rd, Waterloo, London SE1 8TW **Tel:** 020-7928 4818

Chadwick, John, (Portsmouth), 64 Riebenrood Rd, Reading, Berks RG30 2EB **Tel:** 0118-957 2149 **Fax:** 0118-957 5214

Chako, Baby Thazhathel, (SSP), 191 Battersea Bridge Rd, London SW11 3AS **Tel:** 020 7228 2656 **Fax:** 020 7228 1656 **E-mail:** thazhathelfrancisco@yahoo.com

Chalmers, Joseph, (OCarm), The Friars, Aylesford, Kent ME20 7BX **Tel:** 01622 717272

Chaloner, John, JCL, (Salford), St Hubert, Trough Rd, Dunsop Bridge, Clitheroe, BB7 3BG **Tel:** 01200-448231

Chamberlain, Leo, MA, (OSB), St John Priory, Long Street, Easingwold, York YO61 3JB **Tel:** 01347 821295 **Fax:** 01347 823542 **E-mail:** leo@ampleforth.org.uk

Chamberlain, Paul L, (Birmingham), 24 Bridle Ln, Streetly, W. Mids **Tel:** 0121-580 7546

Chandler, Andrew (Portsmouth), 43 Portland St, Fareham, Hants PO16 0NQ **E-mail:** andrwchand@aol.com

Chaning-Pearce, James, (SJ), St Beuno's, St Asaph, Denbighshire LL17 0AS **Tel:** 01745-583444 **Fax:** 01745-584151

Chantry, Anthony, MHM (Westminster), 1 Colby Gds, Cookham Rd, Maidenhead, Berkshire SL6 7GZ **Tel:** 01628 588401 **Fax:** 01628 588439 **Mbl:** 0785 297 3733 **E-mail:** gensup@millhillmissionaries.com

Chapman, Michael, (Southwark, retired), Flat 1, Rowena Court, 3 St Mildred's Gardens, Westgate-on-Sea, Kent CT8 8TP **Tel:** 01843-831093

Chappell, Peter, (Lancaster), The Presbytery, Garth Head's Rd, Appleby, Cumbria CA16 6UA **Tel:** 01768-351474

Charles, Bernard (SJ), 27 High Rd, Stamford Hill, London N15 6ND **Tel:** 020 8442 5254 **E-mail:** bcharlessj@yahoo.co.uk

Charles, Rodger, MA (SJ), Corpus Christi Jesuit Community, 757 Christchurch Rd, Boscombe, Bournemouth BH7 6AN **Tel:** 01202 436730

Charles-Roux, Jean-Marie, (IC), Collegio Rosmini, via di Porta Latina 17, Roma 00179, Italia. **Tel:** 00 39 0670 49 17777 **Fax:** 00 39 0677 400025

Charlesworth, Roger David, (OSB), Buckfast Abbey, Buckfastleigh, Devon TQ11 0EE **Tel:** 01364 645500 **Fax:** 01364 643891

Charlton, Anthony, (Southwark), 401 Ewell Rd, Tolworth, Surrey KT6 7DG **Tel:** 020-8399 9550

Charlton, Mgr Canon J Raymond, (Middlesbrough, retired), 1 Springfield Mews, Stokesley, Middlesbrough TS9 5GJ **Tel:** 01642 715711

Charlton, William, BA, LTCL, (Middlesbrough), English Martyrs, Dalton Terr, York YO24 4DA **Tel:** 01904 623783

Charnock, Bernard, (Salford), St Monica, Woodsend Rd South, Flixton, Manchester M41 6QB **Tel:** 0161-748 4590

Charters, David, St Vincent's, 2 Bentinck Road, Altrincham WA14 2BP **Tel:** 0161 928 1689 **Fax:** 0161 929 8972

Chatov, Edward (AA), Assumption Priory, Victoria Park Square, Bethnal Green, London E2 9PB **Tel:** 020-8709 5283

Chatterton, Adrian A, STB, PHL, Dip Rel.Ed. (Nottingham, retired), 61 Station Rd,

Rearsby, Leicestershire LE7 4YY **Tel:** 01664 424251

Chauvel, Charles, BA (SDB), Flat 27, Block D, Les Blancs Bois, Rue Cohu, Castel, Guernsey GY5 7SY **Tel:** 01481-252401

Chavasse, Paul, (CongOrat), STL, The Oratory, Hagley Rd, Birmingham B16 8UE **Tel:** 0121-454 0496

Cheetham, Eric (Leeds), 22 Rosedale, Rothwell, Leeds LS25 0HR **Tel:** 0113-285 5602 **E-mail:** Cova@iria44.freeserve.co.uk

Chestle, Bryan, Mgr, STL, PhL, MA, ProtAp. Venerabile Collegio Inglese, Via di Monserrato 45, 00186 Roma, Italia. **Tel/Fax:** 0039 06 6830 0251

Chidgey, Paul, Canon, (Cardiff, retired), Nazareth Ho, Colum Rd, Cardiff CF10 3UN **Tel:** 01989-562186

Chillman, Gregory, B.Ed (OSB), Ealing Abbey, Charlbury Grove, Ealing, W5 2DY **Tel:** 020-8862 2100

Chilou, Raphaël Jacques, (CFR), St Fidelis Friary, Killip Cl, London E16 1LX **Tel:** 020-7474 0766

Chinnery, David, St Joseph's, Bolton Rd, Darwen, Blackburn BB3 2PG **Tel:** 01254 702026

Chipchase, Paul, (Nottingham), The Presbytery, Laughton Way, Ermine Estate, Lincoln LN2 2HE **Tel:** 01522-522971

Cho, Antony, (OFM), c/c 160 The Grove, Stratford, london E15 1NS

Choi, Jacob BSc, BA, B.Theol, MA (OSA), St Mary, Vivian Rd, Harborne, Birmingham B17 0DN

Cholij, Roman, JCD, DPhil(Oxon), (Ukrainians), c/o Bishop's Ho, 22 Binney St, London W1Y 1YN

Choma, Andrij Bohdan, STB, (Ukrainians), 104 Lonsdale Rd, Heaton, Bolton, Lancs BL1 4PN **Tel:** 01204-840087

Choma, Wolodymyr, SRL, (Ukrainians), c/o Bishop's Ho, 22 Binney St, London W1Y 1YN

Chowaniec, Komelinsz, (OFM) Franciscan Friary, Sample Oak Ln, Chilworth, Guildford, Surrey GU4 8QR **Tel:** 01483 893168 **Fax:** 01483 898071

Choyce, Benjamin, (Nottingham, retired), 29 Thorntondale Dr, Bridlington, E. Yorks YO16 6GW **Tel:** 01262-604593

Chukka, Dominic Savio, MA (Birmingham), 115 Wolverhampton Rd, Codsall WV8 1PF **Tel:** 01902-842891 **E-mail:** dchukka@aol.com

Christiaans, George (CSsR), Our Lady of the Annunciation. Bishop Eton, Woolton Rd, Wavertree, Liverpool L16 8NQ **Tel:** 0151-722 1108 **Fax:** 0151-738 0834

Christiputro, Michael (OCarm), 63 East End Rd, East Finchley N2 0SE **Tel:** 020-8346 1458 **Fax:** 020-8343 0942

Chrystal, Canon Patrick, (Plymouth), The Presbytery, 8 Pinehurst Rd, West Moors, Dorset BH22 0AP **Tel:** 01202-874811

Church, Shaun David, STB, (Westminster), 68 Hazelwood Crescent, Kensal Rd, London W10 5DJ **Tel:** 020-8969 2660

Churchill, Anthony, STL, (Arundel & Brighton), The Parish Centre, Bognor Regis, W. Sussex PO21 1LP **Tel:** 01243 823619

Ciccone, Sebastian Maria (OSB), 6 Shawbury Cl, Winyates, Redditch B98 0PE

Cieleno, Jan, (Northampton), c/o Bishop's Ho, Marriott St, Northampton NN2 6AW

Cikanek, Stanislaw, 62 Offley Rd, London, SW9 0LS **Tel:** 020-7735 6655

Cisek, Bogdan (Przemysl, Poland); St Lawrence Ho, Flat 2, Duke St, Northampton NN1 3BA **Tel:** 01604-631623

Claffey, Pat (SVD), 8 Teignmouth Rd, London NW2 4HN

Clancy, John (CSsR), Our Immaculate Lady of Victories, Clapham Park Rd, Clapham SW4 7AP **Tel:** 020-7622 2793/6410

Clancy, Sean, (Menevia, retired), Tyllymurrihy, Balinaskarthy, Clonakilty, Co. Cork, Ireland

Clare, Edward, BSc, STL (Birmingham), Becket Ho, Market Square, Kineton CV35 0LP **Tel:** 01926-640537 **E-mail:** eddie@vocations.org.uk

Clark, Andrew, (East Anglia), Chaplain, HM Prison Perth, Edinburgh Rd, Perth, Scotland PH2 8AT **Tel:** 01738-622293

Clark, Derek, (SDS), 20 Grove Rd, Newbury, Berkshire RG14 1UH **Tel:** 01635 826417 **Mbl:** 0796 3834061 **E-mail:** derekclarksds@aol.com

Clark, James, BTh (Southwark), 37 Milton Rd, Gillingham, Kent ME7 5LP **Tel:** 01634 854844

Clark, John, BA MA (Southwark), 126 Week St, Maidstone, Kent ME14 1RH **Tel:** 01622-756217 **Fax:** 01622-690549

Clark, John (MCCJ), 8a Battersea Park Road, London SW8 4BH **Tel:** 020-7622 4282

Clark, Kevin (Nottingham), SS Peter & Paul Presbytery, 2a Skellingthorpe Rd, Boulthan, Lincoln LN6 7RB **Tel:** 01522 682278

Clark, Neville Augustine, BA, PhB, STL, DipRSA, (OSB), c/o Downside Abbey, Statton on the Fosse, Radstock, Bath, Somerset BA3 4RH

Clarke, Anthony, (Salford), Holy Family Church, PO Box 17 Koru, Kenya. **Tel:** 00-254-341 51489

Clarke, Bosco, Canon, (Northampton), The

Presbytery, 7 St Peter St, Marlow, Bucks SL7 1NQ **Tel:** 01628-483696

Clarke, Eamon P, MA, DipTh, DipSoc, (Birmingham, retired), St Augustine's, Beehive Hill, Kenilworth CV8 1BW

Clarke, Isidore, (OP), Holy Cross Priory, 45 Wellington St, Leicester LE1 6HW **Tel:** 0116-2556902

Clarke, James, (SX), 179 Ribbleton Ave, Preston, PR2 6AA **Tel:** 01772-792292

Clarke, James, (Salford), St Gregory's Church St, Farnworth, Bolton BL4 8AQ **Tel/Fax:** 01204-573219

Clarke, Joseph Henry (Wrexham), St Joseph's, Ffordd Mela, South Beach, Pwllheli LL53 5AP **Tel:** 01758-612331

Clarke, Paul, (OFMConv), All Saints Friary, Redclyffe Rd, Barton, Urmston, Manchester M41 7LG **Tel:** 0161-748 5416

Clarke, Peter, BA, MTh, (Leeds), Our Lady of Lourdes, 85 Sheepridge Road, Huddersfield HD2 1HF **Tel:** 01484 425084

Clarke, Peter D, STB (Lancaster), Sacred Heart, Heys St, Thornton-le-Fylde FY5 4HL **Tel:** 01253 821637

Clarke, Tony, Canon (Arundel & Brighton), 25 Between Sts, Cobham, Surrey KT11 1AA **Tel:** 01932-862518

Clarke, Trevor, (Nottingham, retired), Presentation Convent, Chesterfield Rd, Matlock, Derbyshire DE4 3FT **Tel:** 01629 582416

Clarkson, James, (Liverpool, retired), Ince Blundell Hall, Back o'the Town Lane, Ince Blundell, Liverpool, L38 6JL **Tel:** 0151-929 2873

Clasby, Raymond, (ODC), St Luke's Priory, Wincanton, BA9 9DH **Tel:** 01963- 32243

Clayton, Martin, (Hallam), St Mary's Presbytery, High Green, Sheffield S35 4HS **Tel:** 0114-284 8344

Cleary, Michael J, BA, (Salford), Our Lady's Presbytery, 275 Plodder Ln, Farnworth, Bolton BL4 0BR **Tel/Fax:** 01204-572340

Cleary, Michael, (SVD), 8 Teignmouth Rd, London NW2 4HN

Cleary, Patrick, (East Anglia), 39 East St, St Neots, Cambridgeshire PE19 1JU **Tel:** 01480-472585

Cleary, Thomas (SCC), St Bede's, Leigh Avenue, Widnes, Cheshire WA8 6EL

Cleevely, Philip MA (CongOrat), The Oratory, Hagley Rd, Birmingham B16 8UE **Tel:** 0121-454 0496

Clemens, David, BPh, STB, STL, (Brentwood), 30 Southend Rd, Stanford-le-Hope, Essex SS17 0PF **Tel:** 01375 672167

Clement, John, (MHM), 6 Bryn Helyg, Abergele, Conwy LL22 8JP **Tel:** 01745-832765 **E-mail:** johndclement@tiscali.co.uk

Clements, Donald T, (Portsmouth, retired), 8 Jeanne Jugan Apartments, New St John's Rd, St Helier, Jersey JE2 3LE **Tel:** 01534-723602

Clements, William, Canon, KHS, (Southwark), The Presbytery, Minnis Rd, Birchington, Kent CT7 9SF **Tel:** 01843-741549

Clifford, Barry, MA (OSA) St Augustine's Priory, 55 Fulham Palace Rd, London W6 8AU **Tel:** 020-8748 3788 **Fax:** 020 8846 9574

Clifford, John, (Brentwood, retired), 387 Ilford Ln, Ilford, Essex IG1 2SL **Tel:** 020-8478 1697

Clifton, Mark, (AA), Our Lady of the Assumption Priory, Victoria Park Square, Bethnal Green, London E2 9PB **Tel:** 020-8980 1968

Clifton, Michael, (Southwark, retired), 15 Camel Grove, Kingston on Thames, Surrey KT2 5GR **Tel:** 020-8546 3882

Clinch, Denis, (Salford), St Mary, 17 Mulberry St, Manchester M2 6LN **Tel:** 0161-834 3547 **Fax:** 0161-834 4207

Clohosey, John, (Hexham), Sacred Heart & St Cuthbert, 37 High St, Amble, Northumberland NE65 0LE **Tel:** 01665 710252

Clothier, Michael, MA, (OSB), Downside Abbey, Stratton on the Fosse, Bath, Somerset BA3 4RH **Tel:** 01761-235111

Clune, Terence, (Plymouth, Retired), Nazareth House, Durnford Street, Stonehouse, Plymouth PL1 3QR **Tel:** 01752-662537

Coakley, Brian, (Liverpool, retired), Flat 3, Woolton Court, Quarry St, Liverpool L25 6HF **Tel:** 0151-428 2411

Coates, Gerald, Canon, (Arundel & Brighton, retired), 57 Arundel Rd, Worthing, W. Sussex BN13 3EN **Tel:** 01903-690088

Cobb, Petroc MA (OSB), St Mary's Abbey, Quarr, Ryde, Isle of Wight PO33 4ES **Tel:** 01983-882420 **Fax:** 01983-884402

Cobham, Gerard, (Liverpool, retired), 22 St George's Court, Station Rd, Maghull, Liverpool L31 3JD **Tel:** 0151 527 1558

Codd, Peter, (Portsmouth),The Presbytery, Alexandra Rd, Andover, Hants, SP10 3AD **Tel:** 01264-352829 **E-mail:** pcodd@ic24.net

Cody, Edward J, (IC), St Joseph's Presbytery, New Zealand Rd, Cardiff CF14 3BR **Tel:** 029-2041 1819 **Fax:** 029-2041 1820

Coe, John, (Salford), c/o Wardley Hall.

Coen, Michael (SCA), 514 Longbridge Rd,

Barking Essex IG11 9BY
Tel: 020-8590 2191
Coffey, John, (OSA), c/o Augustinians, St Ann's Ho, Etterby Scaut, Carlisle CA3 9PD
Coghlan, John, Mgr, (Westminster), Archbishop's Ho, Ambrosden Avenue, London SW1P 1QJ
Cogliolo, Anthony C, BA, MA (Shrewsbury), Sacred Heart & St Teresa, Green Ln, Wilmslow, SK9 1LD
Tel: 01625-523584 **Fax:** 01625-533268
E-mail: stwil@btinternet.com
Coker, Stephen, (Westminster), 24 Holmes Rd, Twickenham, Middx TW1 4RE
Tel: 020-8892 1444 **Mbl:** 0976-400954
Colahan, Noel, (Hexham & Newcastle), St Hilda's Presbytery, The King's Rd, Southwick, Sunderland SR5 2JD
Tel: 0191-548 6839
Cole, Andrew, (Menevia), The Beda College, Pontifico Collegio Beda, Via di S Paulo 18, 00146 Rome
Cole, John (Cardiff), The Immacualte Conception Presbytery, Crossways, Scwrfa, Tredegar NP22 4AT
Tel: 01495-717224
Cole, Michael, (Plymouth), The Presbytery, Dousland Rd, Yelverton, Devon PL20 6AZ **Tel:** 01822-853171
Colebrook, Anthony, (Nottingham), Star of the Sea, Allerton Dr, Immingham, NE Lincs DN40 2HP
Tel: 01469-573503 **Fax:** 01469-573503
Colella, Joseph M, (OSM), 264 Fulham Rd, London SW10 9EL
Coleman, Aelred (OFM Cap), Franciscan Friary, Monastery Dr CH8 8PE
Tel: 01244-351331
Coleman, Donald, MA, FRSA, (Southwark), 147 Bingham Rd, Addiscombe, Surrey CR0 7EN **Tel:** 0208 654 1709
Fax: 0208 662 0843
Coleman, Michael, (SM), Marist Fathers, 119 Cottingham Rd, Hull HU5 2DH
Tel: 01482-446448
Coleman, Paul, (OFM Cap), Iffley Rd, Oxford OX4 1SB **Tel:** 01865 243694
Collier, Raymond, (SSC), c/o St Columban's, Widney Manor Road, Knowle, Solihull, W. Mids B93 9AB
Collin, Denis, (Plymouth, retired), 24 Merrivale View Rd, Dousland, Yelverton, Devon PL20 6NS **Tel:** 01822-854240
Collingwood, Louis J, Canon, (Middlesbrough, retired), 8 Kentra Cl, Redcar TS10 2SL **Tel:** 01642-479630
Collins, Allan, STL, BA, (CSSp), 6 Woodlands Rd, Bickley, Bromley, Kent BR1 2AF
Tel: 020 8467 355 **Fax:** 020 8295 4965
E-mail: allancollins1@yahoo.co.uk
Collins, Anthony, (Arundel & Brighton), The Priest's Ho, 2 Lodge Ln, Keymer Hassocks, W. Sussex BN6 8NA
Tel: 01273-845384 **Fax:** 01273-846874
Collins, Antony, (OFM), The Friary, 120 Niddrie Mains Rd, Edinburgh EH16 4EG
Tel: 0131-661 2185 **Fax:** 0131-661 0601
E-mail: antony@friar.org
Collins, Bernard, (IC), St Mary's, Derryswood, Wonersh, Guildford GU5 0RA **Tel:** 01483-893196
Collins, Gerald, (Nottingham, retired), 22 Gospel Gate, Louth, Lincs
Collins, James, Canon, (Liverpool, retired), Flat 21, St George's Court, Station Rd, Maghull, Liverpool L31 3JD
Tel: 0151-531 9859
Collins, John D G, MA, (Lancaster), English Martyrs, 154 High Cross Road, High Cross, Poulton-le-Fylde PR2 4UD
Tel: 01253 882497
Collins, John (SSC), St Columban's, Widney Manor Rd, Knowle, Solihull B93 9AB
Tel: 01564-772096
Collins, John (SPS), 20 Beauchamp Rd, East Molesey, Surrey KT8 0PA
Tel: 020-8979 1890
Collins, Joseph, Provost, (Southwark), Our Lady of Reparation, 70 Wellesley Rd, Croydon, Surrey CR0 2AR
Tel: 020-8688 1857
Collins, Keith, (Plymouth), The Presbytery, 135 York Rd, Brdstone, Poole, Dorset BH18 8ER **Tel:** 01202-693336
Collins, Kenneth W, STL, LSS, (Birmingham), Oscott College, Chester Rd, Sutton Coldfield, W. Mids B73 5AA
Tel: 0121-312 5000
Collins, Martin, (Salford), Holy Family, Mornington Rd, Kirkholt, Rochdale OL11 2GD **Tel:** 01706-649230
Collins, Peter G, Canon, KHS, STL, (Cardiff), St David's Cathedral, Clergy Ho, Charles St, Cardiff CF10 2SF **Tel:** 029-2023 1407
Collins, Stephen (MAfr), 15 Corfton Rd, London W5 2HP **Tel:** 020-8997 8751
E-mail: stephencollinswf@yahoo.co.uk
Colombo, Siro (Italy), 197 Durants Rd, Enfield, Middx EN3 7DE
Colossi, Domenico, Italian Mission, 20 Brixton Rd, London SW9 6BU
Tel: 020-7 735 8235
Colpman, Robin, (Salford), St Cuthbert's, 3 Palatine Road, Withington, Manchester M20 3LH **Tel/Fax:** 0161-445 1080
Colven, Christopher, (Westminster), 100a Balls Pond Rd, London N1 4AG
Tel: 020-7254 4378
Comerford, Brian (SJ) (Novice Director), Manresa Ho, 10 Albert Rd, Harborne, Birmingham B17 0AN
Tel: 0121-427 4591
Commins, James B, Mgr Canon,

(Liverpool, retired), St Joseph's, Hall Ln, Wrightington, Wigan WN6 9PA **Tel:** 01257-473156

Conaty, Michael, (Hexham), St Anthony of Padua, Church St, Walker, Newcastle upon Tyne NE6 3BT **Tel:** 0191-262 3817

Conaty, Sean P, (Hexham, retired), Our Lady of the Annunciation, Millway, Gateshead, Tyne and Wear NE9 5PQ **Tel:** 0191-487 4237

Concannon, John, (CM), 29 Eversley Cres, Isleworth TW7 4LR **Tel:** 020-8560 7021

Conde, Claro (CSsR), 7 Atherley Rd, Shanklin, Isle of Wight PO37 7AT **Tel:** 01983-862446

Condon, David, (Hexham and Newcastle, retired), Carntyne, Hencotes, Hexham, Northumberland NE46 2EE **Tel:** 01434-603791

Condon, Ian, (OSB), Worth Abbey, Crawley, W Sussex RH10 4SB **Tel:** 01342-710310

Condon, Stanislaus, AD, (Northampton, retired), 2 Westfield Dr, Raunds, Northants NN9 6BZ **Tel:** 01933-461335

Condron, David, P J, (Birmingham), Presbytery, Market Square, Kineton, Warwicks CV35 0LL **Tel:** 01926-640275

Conesa, Augustin, (Westminster), 73 Pembroke Rd, Ruislip HA4 8NN **Tel:** 01895 632739

Coningsby, Mark Raymond, STL, (Westminster), Priests Ho, Laxton Place, Longford St, London NW1 3PT **Tel:** 020-7387 3833

Conley, Peter John, (Birmingham), (Aston University Chaplain) Guardian Angels' Ho, Kitsland Rd, Castle Bromwich, Birmingham B34 7NA **Tel:** 0121-747 2873

Conliss, John (SVD), St Gregory's Ho, 21 Halewood Rd, Gateacre, Liverpool L25 3PH **Tel:** 0151-428 2860

Conlon, Anthony, (School Chaplain) (Westminster), The Oratory School, Woodcote, Nr Reading, Berks RG8 0PJ **Tel:** 01491-681074

Conlon, Benet, (OSB), Buckfast Abbey, Buckfastleigh, Devon TQ11 0EE **Tel:** 01364-645500 **Fax:** 01364-643891

Conlon, James, (AA), The Assumption Priory, Victoria Park Square, Bethnal Green E2 9PB **Tel:** 020-8980 1968

Conlon, Patrick, VF (Plymouth, retired), The Pigeons, Althone, Co. West Meath, Ireland **Tel:** 00353 906485 227

Conneely, John, (Westminster), 165 Arlington Rd, London NW1 7EX **Tel:** 0207-485 2727

Connelly, Aelred, MA (OP), St Dominic's Priory, Southampton Rd, Haverstock Hill, NW5 4LB **Tel:** 020-7482 9210 **Fax:** 020-7482 9230

Connelly, Desmond, STB, MA, (SMM), St Joseph's, Lyndhurst Rd, Ashurst, Hants SO40 7DU **Tel:** 0230-8029 2337 **Fax:** 023-8029 2346

Connelly, Paul, (Southwark), 27 The Slade, Plumstead Common SE18 2NB **Tel:** 020-8854 7154

Connelly, Sean (East Anglia), 1 Norwich Rd, Wymondham, Norfolk NR18 0QE **Tel/Fax:** 01953-603104

Conner, Philip (Lancaster), St Anthony's, Cadley Causeway, Fulwood, Preston PR2 3RX **Tel:** 01772-725193 **Fax:** 01772 732304

Connolly, Bernard, (CP), Nazareth Ho, Hammersmith Rd, London W6 8DB

Connolly, Desmond, STB, MA (SMM), St Joseph's, Lyndhurst Road, Ashurst, Southampton SO40 7DU **Tel:** 023 8029 2337 **Fax:** 023-8029 2346 **E-mail:** fatherdes@andover.co.uk

Connolly, Eugene, BA, H Dip, (SMA), Sacred Heart Presbytery, Stopsley, Luton, Beds LU2 9AY **Tel:** 01582-723099

Connolly, Francis, (Shrewsbury), 45 Derwent Close, Alsager, Stoke-on-Trent STZ 2EL **Tel:** 01270-872542

Connolly, Kevin, (Retired), 1 Albany Rd, Lytham St Annes, Lancs

Connolly, Mark (CCSp), 26 Eastbury Ave, Northwood, Middx HA6 3LN **Tel:** 01923-829655 **Fax:** 01923-836975 **E-mail:** spiritan.bursar-uk@virgin.net

Connolly, Michael (Birmingham, retired), Innisfree, Gregg North, Glendore, Skibbereen, Co Cork, Ireland.

Connolly, Noel (SPS), The Holy Redeemer, Wrexham Rd, Slough SL2 5QR

Connolly, Patrick, BA, HDip, (SMA), St Augustine's, 2 Anson Rd, Victoria Park, Manchester M14 5BG **Tel:** 0161-224 7409

Connolly, Sean, (Brentwood), 146 Little Ilford Ln, Manor Park, London E12 5PJ **Tel:** 020-8478 1895

Connolly, Sean, STD (East Anglia), c/o The White Ho, 21 Upgate, Poringland, Norwich NR14 7SH

Connolly, Thomas, BA (Salford), St Kentigern, 36 Wilbraham Rd, Fallowfield, Manchester M14 7DW **Tel:** 0161-224 4664 **Fax:** 0161-257 0271

Connor, Augustine, (CFR), c/o St Fidelis Friary, Killip Cl, London E16 1LX **Tel:** 020 7474 0766

Connor, Christopher, MA (Westminster), 24 Golden Square, London W1F 9JR **Tel:** 0794-7561414

Connor, Christopher, (Southwark), 175 High St, Lewisham, London SE13 6AA **Tel:** 020-8852 2490 **Fax:** 020-8852 2262

Connor, Dennis J, (OMI), St Mary Help of Christians, Longford Road, Holyhead

Anglesey LL65 1TR
Tel: 01407 762102 **Fax:** 01407 765759

Connor, Michael, (CP), St Joseph's Retreat, Highgate Hill, N19 5NE **Tel:** 020-7272 2320

Connor, Paul, (CJ), The Presbytery, 45 New Rd, Brixham, Devon TQ5 8NB
Tel: 01803-853406
E-mail: frpaulcj@aol.com

Connor, Peter, (Brentwood), The Priest's Ho, 60a Victoria Rd, Maldon, Essex CM9 5HF **Tel:** 01621 852259

Connors, Patrick (SJ), 11 Langsdale St, Liverpool L3 8DT **Tel/Fax:** 0151-207 2271

Conrad, Richard, MA, DPhil, (OP), Blackfriars, Buckingham Rd, Cambridge CB3 0DD **Tel:** 01223-741263

Contreras, Mario Cerda (MCCJ), Vernona Fathers, Brownberrie Ln, Horsforth, Leeds LS18 5HE **Tel:** 0113-258 2658
Fax: 0113-281 8945
E-mail: combonoleeds@supanet.com

Convery, Adrian, MA, EV, (OSB), Ampleforth Abbey, York YO62 4EN
Tel: 01439-766714 **Fax:** 01439-766724

Convery, Anthony, (Westminster), 94 Bath Rd, Hounslow, Middx TW3 3EH
Tel: 020-8570 1693 **Fax:** 020-8570 8059

Convery, Daniel, STD (OFM), 160 The Grove, Stratford, London E15 1NS
Tel: 020-8534 1964
E-mail: decon44@hotmail.com

Convery, John (SX), 179 Ribbleton Avenue, Preston, Lancs PR2 6AA
Tel: 01772-792292

Convery, Vincent, (Portsmouth), 202 Ringmead, Bracknell, Berkshire RG12 7AT
Tel: 01344-423093 **Fax:** 01344-867445

Conway, Brendan, (OSCam), 102 Hassett Rd, London E9 5SJ **Tel:** 020-8986 5181

Conway, Francis (OFM), 160 The Grove, Stratford, London E15 1NS
Tel: 020-8534 1964 **Fax:** 020-8534 1119
Mbl: 07950 878627
E-mail: rfrancisconway@hotmail.com

Conway, James (SJ), St Ignatius Church, 27 High Rd, London N15 6ND
Tel: 020-8442 5251
E-mail: j.conway@jesuits.net

Coogan, Brian, (MHM), St David, 9 Connaught Rd, East Cowes, Isle of Wight PO32 6DP **Tel:** 01983-292726
E-mail: brian.coogan@amserve.net

Cook, Christopher, (MHM, retired), Herbert Ho, 41 Victoria Rd, Freshfield, Merseyside L37 1LE **Tel:** 01704-875849

Cook, Edwin, (OSB), Ampleforth Abbey, York YO62 4EN **Tel:** 01439-766714
Fax: 01439-766724

Cook, Victor, (Arundel & Brighton, retired), 2 Falkland Grove, Dorking, Surrey RH4 3DL **Tel:** 01306-882433

Cooke, John, (Hallam), The Presbytery, Denaby Main, Doncaster DN12 4AQ
Tel: 01709-862177

Cooke, John, (Portsmouth), The Catholic Presbytery, Middle Road, Park Gate, Southampton, Hants SO31 7GH
Tel/Fax: 01489-572797

Cooke, Michael, BA, MPhil (Salford), St Joseph's, Portland Cres, Longsight, Manchester M13 0BU
Tel: 0161-224 4035 **Fax:** 0161-256 1781

Cooke, Russell, (Shrewsbury), St Columba's, 1 Newhall Rd, Plas Newton, Chester CH2 1SA
Tel: 01244-400873 **Fax:** 01244-409407
E-mail: st.columba@btopemworld.com

Cookson, Francis R, Canon, (Lancaster, retired), St. Winefrides' House, Low Moore Road, Bispham, Blackpool FY2 OPA **Tel:** 01253 351142

Cookson, Peter, Mgr Provost, (Liverpool), Cathedral Ho, Mount Pleasant, Liverpool L3 5TQ **Tel:** 0151-709 9222

Cooley, Michael, MA, STL, PhL. (Southwark), Our Lady of La Salette and St Joseph, 14 Melior St, Bermondsey, London SE1 3QP **Tel:** 020-7407 1948

Coonan, Stephen, Canon, STL. (Shrewsbury), Cathedral Ho, 11 Belmont, Shrewsbury SY1 1TE **Tel:** 01743-362366
E-mail: shrewsbury.cathedral@btinternet.com

Cooney, Anselm, (OCD, retired), 41 Kensington Church St, Kensington, W8 4BB **Tel:** 020-7937 9860

Cooper, Dunstan, (Lancaster), St Mary's, Matthias St, Morecambe LA4 5JR
Tel: 01524-410501

Cooper, John, (Hexham and Newcastle), St Robert of Newminster, Oldgate St, Morpeth NE61 1QF **Tel:** 01670- 513410

Cooper, Leo (Liverpool), St Oswald's Presbytery, Chapel Lane, Longton, Preston PR4 5EB **Tel/Fax:** 01772 612136

Cooper, Stephen (Liverpool), St Joseph's Presbytery, Mather Lane Leigh WN7 2PR
Tel: 01942-673517

Cooper, Thomas, (Southwark), 159 Ellison Rd, Norbury SW16 5DE
Tel: 020 8679 3545

Cooper, Vincent, (OSB), Ealing Abbey, Charlbury Grove, Ealing, W5 2DY
Tel: 020-8862 2100

Cooper, Wilfrid (Salford), Nazareth Ho, Preston New Rd, Blackburn BB2 7AL
Tel: 01254-53000

Cope, Patrick, (Middlesbrough), 27 Victoria Rd, Richmond, Nth Yorks DL10 4AS **Tel:** Mobile 07860 108431

Copps, Michael, (OFM), 557 High Rd, Woodford Green, Essex IG8 0RB
Tel: 020-8504 7540 **Fax:** 020-8504 7541
Mbl: 07724 153167

E-mail: michaelcopps@hotmail.com
Copsey, Richard, (OCarm), 63 East End Rd, East Finchley, London N2 0SE **Tel:** 020-8346 1458 **Fax:** 020-8343 0942
Copsey, Robert (SOLT), The Presbytery, 2 Lower Blackhorse Hill, Hythe, Kent CT21 5LS **Tel:** 01303-266430 **Fax:** 01303-264773
Corbett, Michael E, (Hexham & Newcastle), St Andrew, 9 Worswick St, Newcastle-upon-Tyne NE1 6UW **Tel:** 0191-232 1892
Corbett, Raymond, STB, JCL (Birmingham), 69 Lichfield Rd, Sutton Coldfield B74 2NU **Tel:** 0121-354 5849
Corbould, Edward, MA, (OSB), Ampleforth Abbey, York YO62 4EN **Tel:** 01439-766714 **Fax:** 01439-766724
Corcoran, Gregory (OSB), Quarr Abbey, Ryde, Isle of Wight PO33 4ES **Tel:** 01983-882420
Corcoran, John, Mgr, (Salford), SS michael & St John, Lowergate, Clitheroe, Lancs BB7 1AG **Tel/Fax:** 01200 423307 **E-mail:** news@smsjchurch,fsnet.co.uk
Corcoran, Joseph, BSc, BA, DipEd, (Salford), The Presbytery, Astley Rd, Irlam, Manchester M44 6AB **Tel:** 0161-775 2469
Corcoran, Michael, MHM, General Councillor, 4 Colby Gdns, Maidenhead SL6 7GZ **Tel:** 01628 588404 **Fax:** 01628 588439 **Mbl:** 0772 6712190 **E-mail:** counreg@millhillmissionaries.com
Corcoran, Peter, (SM), Newman Ho, 729 Beverley Rd, Hull HU6 7ER **Tel:** 01482 856884
Corduff, Eamon, (Birmingham), St Patrick's Presbytery, Wolverhampton Rd, New Cross, Wolverhampton WV10 0QQ **Tel:** 01902-736440
Cordy, Gordon, (East Anglia, retired), 7 Sandringham Court, Ipswich Rd, Norwich NR2 2LF **Tel:** 01603-766659
Corkery, Patrick (Portsmouth), The Presbytery, Sherborne Rd, Basingstoke, Hants RG21 5TD **Tel:** 01256-465214 **Fax:** 01256-469605
Corley, David Michael, Mgr Canon, STL, JCL, (Brentwood, retired), The Chimes, Weeley Rd, Aingers Green, Great Bentley, Colchester, Essex CO7 8NB **Tel:** 01206-252024
Corley, Jeremy, BA, (Oxon), (Portsmouth), St Cuthbert's College, Ushaw, Co. Durham DH7 9RH **Tel:** 0191-373 8521 **E-mail:** jeremy.corley@ushaw.ac.uk
Cornforth, Anthony, (Hexham & Newcastle), St John Vanney, Hillhead Parkway, West Denton, Newcastle NE5 1DP **Tel:** 0191-267 6063
Cornish, Anthony, (Plymouth), The Presbytery, 19 Fosse Rd, Kingsbridge, Devon TQ7 1NG **Tel:** 01548-852670
Cornwell, Peter, MA, (Clifton), 37 Prior Park Rd, Bath BA2 4NG **Tel:** 01225-331668
Corr, Gerard M, (OSM), 264 Fulham Rd, Kensington SW10 9EL **Tel:** 020-7351 1037
Corradi, Romano, (CS), St Frances Cabrini, 10 Woburn Rd, Bedford MK40 1EG **Tel:** 01234-359515
Correa, Frederick, BA (CMF), St Michael's Presbytery, Esh Laude, Durham DH7 9QN **Tel:** 0191-373 4349
Corrie, George, BA, LLB, (Prior) (OSB), St Mary's, 25 Bond End, Knaresborough HG5 9AW **Tel:** 01423-862388 **Fax:** 01423-869631 **E-mail:** prior@ampleforth.org.uk
Corrigan, Charles, (CSSR), Our Lady of the Annunciation, Bishop Eton, Woolton Rd, Wavertree, Liverpool L16 8NQ
Corrigan, Hugh, (OAR), St Austin's Priory, Cadleigh Park, Ivybridge, Devon PL21 9HW **Tel:** 01752-892606
Corrigan, James, (CSSR), Our Lady of the Annunciation, BIshop Eton, Woolton Rd, Liverpool L16 8NQ **Tel:** 0151-722 1108 **Fax:** 0151-738 0834
Corrigan, Robert, STB, Canon (Clifton), Cathedral Church of SS Peter and Paul, Clifton Cathedral Ho, Clifton Park, Bristol BS8 3BX **Tel:** 0117-973 8411 **Fax:** 0117-974 4897 **E-mail:** robert.corrigan@cliftondiocese.com
Corry, Donal (LC), 22 George St, London W1H 5RB
Cosgrove, Lawrence C, (Lancaster, retired), 11 Wedgewood Way, Cowplain, Portsmouth, Hants PO8 8RW **Tel:** 01705-253193
Cosslett, Ron,(Birmingham), 57 Church St, Darlaston WS10 8DY **Tel:** 0121-5262287
Costello, Hilary, (OCSO), Our Lady and St Bernard, Mount St Bernard Abbey, Coalville, Leicester LE67 5UL **Tel:** 01530-832298/832022 **Fax:** 01530-814608
Costello, Patrick, Canon, (Plymouth), 96 Queen St, Newton Abbot, Devon TQ12 2ET **Tel:** 01626-365231
Cotter, Anthony, Canon, PhL, (Clifton, retired), 40 West Parade, Sea Mills, Bristol BS9 2LA **Tel:** 0117-968 5515
Cotter, Edmond, (Lancaster), c/o Pastoral Centre, Balmoral Rd, Lancaster LA1 3BT
Cotton, Jonathan, (Nottingham), St Joseph's, 120 Langwith Rd, Shirebrook, Derbys NG20 9RP **Tel:** 015623 742349
Cotton, Jonathan, MA, (OSB), St Mary's, Broadfield Dr, Leyland, Preston PR25 1PD **Tel:** 01772-421183 **Fax:** 01772-621183
Cottraill, Mark V, BCL, (Lancaster), c/o

Bishop's Ho, Cannon Hill, Lancaster LA1 5NG

Couch, Paul Benedict, (Plymouth), c/o Bishop's Ho, 31 Wyndham St West, Plymouth PL1 5RZ

Coughlan, Kevin, Mgr Canon, (Middlesbrough, retired), 9 Humber View, Hessle HU13 0PY **Tel:** 01482-644404

Coughlin, Leo, (Hexham & Newcastle), Christ the King Catholic Community, 4925 Torrey Pines, Las Vegas, Nevada, 89118 USA

Coulon Jean-Patrice, (MSFS), 73 Higher Kingston, Yeovil, Somerset BA21 4AR **Tel:** 01935 423549

Coulthard, Joseph, (Salford, retired), Nazareth Ho, Scholes Ln, Prestwich, Mancheseter M25 0NU

Coupe, Robert, STL, BA, (SDB), St Joseph's, 10 Oldhams Ln, Bolton BL1 6PN **Tel:** 01204-590600 **E-mail:** racoupe@tiscali.co.uk

Coupet, Jacques, (OP), St Peter's Residence, 2a Meadow Rd, London SW8 1QH

Courell, Gerald T, (Shrewsbury), St Winefride, 5 Burton Rd, Little Neston, Neston CH64 9RF **Tel:** 0151-336 4189

Courtney, Joseph James, MA, (OSB), Buckfast Abbey, Buckfastleigh, Devon TQ11 0EE **Tel:** 01364-645500 **Fax:** 01364-643891

Cousens, Christopher P, BA, (Lancaster), The Presbytery, St Teresa's Avenue, Cleveleys FY5 3JT **Tel:** 01253-853340

Cousins, David A, Mgr, JCL, (Birmingham), 534 Lichfield Rd, Four Oaks, Sutton Coldfield, W. Mids B74 4EH **Tel:** 0121-308 2560

Couto, Filipe, (IMC), 3 Salisbury Avenue, Finchley, London N3 3RJ **Tel:** 020-8346 2459

Coveney, Francis, BSc, STL, (Brentwood), 7 Grove Cres, South Woodford, London E18 2JR **Tel:** 020-8989 5242

Cowan, Anton, (Westminster), 17 Churchfield Path, Cheshunt, Herts EN8 9EG **Tel:** 01992-629878

Cowins, Aelred (OSB), Belmont Abbey, Hereford HR2 9RZ **Tel:** 01432-277388

Cownley, Edwin, BA, (Birmingham), Presbytery, Three Shires Oak Rd, Bearwood B67 5BT **Tel:** 0121-429 1743 **E-mail:** edwin@cownley.freeserve.co.uk

Cox, Brian (SSCC), 372 Uxbridge Rd, Ealing, London W5 3LH **Tel:** 020-8992 5941

Cox, Gerald, Canon, (Middlesbrough), Our Lady of Perpetual Help, 2 Sancton Rd, Market Weighton YO43 3DB **Tel:** 01430-873202

Cox, Michael (OCarm), 63 East End Rd, East Finchley, London N2 0SE **Tel:** 020 8346 1458

Coxe, Peter, (Plymouth), Cathedral House, 45 Cecil Street, Plymouth PL1 5HW **Tel:** 01752-261899

Coxon, David, (Hexham & Newcastle), St Joseph's, St Paul's Rd, Hartlepool TS26 9EY **Tel:** 01429-272985

Coyle, Brian MA, STL (Southwark), 250 Bishopsford Rd, Morden SM4 6BZ **Tel:** 020-8648 4113

Coyle, John B, VG, (Hexham & Newcastle, retired), c/o Bishop's Ho, 800 West Rd, Newcastle NE5 2BJ

Coyle, Martin, MEd, BA (SDB), Savio Ho, Ingersley Rd, Bollington, Macclesfield SK10 5RW **Tel:** 01625 575405 **Fax:** 01625 560221 **E-mail:** mcoylesdb@tiscali.co.uk

Coyle, Peter, (Nottingham), St Edward's, 633 Aylestone Rd, Leicester LE2 8TF **Tel:** 0116-299 7231

Coyle, Sean (SSC), St Columban's, Widney Manor Rd, Knowle, Solihull B93 9AB **Tel:** 01564-772096

Coyne, Patrick, (Cardiff), c/o Archbishop's House, 41-43 Cathedral Road, Cardiff CF11 9HD

Coyne, Vincent, (OSM), The Priory, 500 Bury New Rd, Salford M7 4WP **Tel:** 0161-792 2152

Crabb, David, (Brentwood, retired), c/o Cathedral Ho, Ingrave Rd, Brentwood, Essex CM15 8AT

Craddy, Peter Claver, (OCSO), Our Lady and St Bernard, Mount St Bernard Abbey, Coalville, Leicester LE67 5UL **Tel:** 01530-832298/832022

Craig, David, (Shrewsbury, retired), 42 Cromwell Court, Beam St, Nantwich CW5 5NZ **Tel:** 01270-627647

Cramaro, Olindo, (East Anglia, retired), c/o 34a Main St, Yaxley, Peterborough **Tel:** 01733-242031

Cramer, Anselm, MA, (OSB), Ampleforth Abbey, York YO62 4EN **Tel:** 01439-766436 **Fax:** 01439-766724

Crampsey, James, (SJ), St Anselm's Rectory, The Green, Southall, Middx UB2 4BE **Tel:** 020-8574-3300 **E-mail:** jcampsey@jesuit.org.uk

Crane, Brian V, (Liverpool, retired), 19 Merrion Cl, Woolton, Liverpool L25 7SY **Tel:** 0151-428 2035

Cravos, Cyril, (Arundel & Brighton), The Priest's Ho, 36 Fort Rd, Newhaven, E. Sussex BN9 9EJ **Tel:** 01273-515254 **Fax:** 01273-515072

Crawford, Charles, (Northampton), The Mount, Spetchley, Worcestershire WR5 1RS

Crawford, Joseph, (Middlesbrough, retired),

c/o Sylphe Peschke, Centro Commercial El Zoco Loal 32, Sitio De Calahonda, 29649 Mijas Costa (Malaga) Spain **Tel:** (Spain) 0034 952939025

Crawley, Mark (Middlesbrough, retired), The Hill, Kilmallock, Co Limerick, Éire.

Creagh, John, BA, MA (MHM), 1029 Oxford Rd, Tilehurst, Reading RG31 6TL **Tel:** 0118 894 1535 **Mbl:** 07815-440512 **E-mail:** jacreagh@hotmail.com

Creagh-Fuller, Tomas MA, FTCL, STB (Southwark), 88 Beckenham Hill Rd, Beckenham, London SE6 3PU **Tel:** 020-8695 1092

Creak, Brian, MA, (Westminster), Newman Ho, 111 Gower St, London WC1E 6AR **Tel:** 0207-387 6370

Crean, Thomas, MA, STL, STLic, (OP) Blackfriars, Buckingham Rd, Cambridge CB3 0DD **Tel:** 01223 741039

Creasey, Gerald A, BA, STL, (Leeds), Mount St Joseph's, Shire Oak Rd, Leeds LS6 2DE **Tel:** 0113-275 6010

Creaton, James, (Salford), 26A Newgrove Avenue, Sandymount, Dublin 4

Cree, James (SMM), 28 Burbo Bank Rd, Blundellsands, L23 6TH 1HS **Tel:** 0151-287 6862 **Fax:** 0151-287 0410

Creech, Michael, (CSsR), The Presbytery, Mutton Hall Ln, Heathfield, E. Sussex TN21 8NX **Tel:** 01435-862191

Creech, Terence, (CSsR), St Benet's, The Causeway, Monkwearmouth, Sunderland, Tyne and Wear SR6 0BH **Tel:** 0191-567 2965

Creighton-Jobe, Ronald, (Cong Orat), The Oratory, Brompton Rd, SW7 2RP **Tel:** 020-7808 0900 or 020-7589 4811

Cremin, Michael, (SCA), 247 High Rd, Chiswick W4 4PU **Tel:** 020-8994 2877

Cremin, Tom, (OSCam), 102 Hassett Rd, London E9 5SJ **Tel:** 020-8986 5181

Crewe, Hilary, (Westminster), St Mary's Rectory, Draycott Terr, London SW3 2QR **Tel:** 020-7589 5487

Crewe, Vincent, (Westminster), Archbishop's Ho, Ambrosden Avenue, London SW1P 1QJ

Cribben, John, (Salford), Our Lady and St Patrick, Higher Walton Rd, Walton-le-Dale, Preston PR5 4HD **Tel/Fax:** 01772-253709

Cridland, Anthony, (Southwark), St Finbarr's, Market Square, Aylesham, Kent CT3 3EZ **Tel:** 01304-840205

Crilly, Michael BA, LLM, (Liverpool), St Basil's Presbytery, Hough Green Rd, Widnes WA8 4SZ **Tel/Fax:** 0151 424 6641

Crisp, Mark, V. Rev, PhB, STB, (Birmingham), Oscott College, Chester Rd, Sutton Coldfield, W. Mids B73 5AA **Tel:** 0121-321 5000

Crocker, Shaun, (Southwark), 25 Thornton Lodge, 24-26 Thornton Hill, Wimbledon SW19 4HS. **Tel:** 020-8974 8314 **E-mail:** shaun.crocker@btinternet.com

Croghan, Eamonn, (Hexham & Newcastle, retired), c/o Bishop's Ho, 800 West Rd, Newcastle-upon-Tyne NE5 2BJ

Cronin, Daniel, LL.M, KCHS, (Westminster), 72 London Rd, Knebworth, Herts SG3 6HB **Tel:** 01438 813303

Cronin, Daniel, Canon, (Northampton, retired), Quarry Cross, Gneeveguilla, Rathmore, Co Kerry, Ireland

Cronin, Denis, (Arundel, retired), 5 Merrywood Ho, Merrywood Ln, Thakeham, Pulborough, W. Sussex RH20 3HD **Tel:** 01903-743005

Cronin, Donal, (Hexham & Newcastle, retired), 1 Norway Avenue, Sunderland, SR4 8QW

Cronin, James, Canon, LCL, MCL, (Southwark), Clergy Ho, Westminster Bridge Rd, SE1 7HY **Tel:** 020-7928 5256

Cronin, James, (MHM), St Bede, Front St, Sacriston, Durham DH7 6AB **Tel:** 0191-371 0257 **Mbl:** 0789-967 6466 **E-mail:** mhmdurham@btconnect.com

Cronin, Jeremiah, Canon, BA, MA (Southwark), "Allington", Barrack Hill, Hythe, Kent CT21 4BY **Tel:** 01303-770509

Cronin, Michael J, (Portsmouth), 418 Coxford Rd, Lordswood, Southampton, Hants SO16 5LL **Tel:** 023-8090 6500 **Fax:** 023-8090 6500

Cronin, Michael, (Cardiff, retired), St Dyfrig's Presbytery, Broadway, Treforest, Pontypridd CF37 1DB **Tel:** 01443-402439

Cronin, Peter, Canon (Liverpool, retired), Ince Blundell Hall, Ince Blundell, Liverpool L38 6JL **Tel:** 0151 929 2596

Crooks, William (SJ), Corpus Christi Jesuit Community, 757 Christchurch Rd, Boscombe, Bournmouth BH7 6AN **Tel:** 01202-436700

Croos, Dushan, (SJ), John Sinnott Ho, 9 Edge Hill, Wimbledon, London SW19 4LR **Tel:** 0208 947 4251 **E-mail:** dcroos@jesuites.com

Cross, John, BA, PGCE (Birmingham), The Presbytery, 32 Vale Rd, Stourport DY13 8YL **Tel/Fax:** 01299-822633

Cross, Philip, Canon (Westminster), 185 Baldwins Ln, Croxley Green, Rickmansworth WD3 3LL **Tel:** 01923-231969

Cross, Stephen, (Lancaster on sabatical), c/o Pastoral Centre, Balmoral Road, Lancaster LA1 3BT

Crossan, Francis, (OCarm), Our Lady of Mount Carmel, Tanners St, Faversham, Kent ME13 7JW **Tel:** 01795-532449

Crossley, Alban, MA, STL, (OSB),

Monastery of Christ the Word, Monte Cassino, Post Bag 902, Macheke, Zimbabwe **Tel/Fax:** 00 263 798 369

Crotty, Fintan, (SSCC), 5 Berrymead Gardens, Acton, London W3 8AA **Tel:** 020-8992 2014 **Fax:** 010-8993 9940 **E-mail:** fintangcrotty@hotmail.com

Croughan, Brian J, BA, MA, MTh, (Portsmouth), 20 Beaumont Rd, Totton, Hants SO40 3AL **Tel:** 023-8086 2270 **Fax:** 023-8057 1363

Crouzet, John Edward, (OSB), STL, MA, Downside Abbey, Stratton on the Fosse, Bath BA3 4RH

Crowe, Bernard, (Westminster, retired), The Lodge, Ware Park, Herts SG12 0DS **Tel:** 01920-460396

Crowe, Jeremiah Joseph, BA, PGCE, (SMA), Society of African Missions, St Augustine's, 2 Anson Rd, Manchester M14 5BG **Tel:** 0161-224 7409

Crowe, Laurence, (Birmingham), 170 Valley Rd, Lillington, Warwicks CV32 8SJ **Tel:** 01926- 423552

Crowley, Liam, (East Anglia, retired), Upper Rathtrout, Ballinadee, Co Cork, Ireland. **Tel:** 00-353 23 44268

Crowther, Peter Charles, (Liverpool), St Joseph's, Bury Ln, Withnell, Chorley PR6 8SD **Tel:** 01254-830229

Crumpton, Michael R (Birmingham), 115 Field Ln, Burton-on-Trent DE13 0NJ **Tel:** 01283 542049 **E-mail:** modwenrc@aol.com

Cryan, Peter, BSc (Shrewsbury), St Edward's, 145 London Rd, Macclesfield SK11 7RL **Tel:** 01625-423576 **Fax:** 01625-424460 **E-mail:** st.edwardmacc@btconnect.com

Cuanam, John, (CssR), The Presbytery, Geneva Street, Peterborough PE1 2RS **Tel:** 01733-562528 **Fax:** 01733-346933

Cukier, Miroslaw MA (Polish Priest), 18 Greenside Rd, Shepherd's Bush, London W12 9JG **Tel:** 020-8743 8848

Cuddihy, Brian, (IC), St Patrick's, 151 Cromwell Rd, Newport NP19 0HS **Tel:** 01633-672334 **E-mail:** b.cuddihy@ntworld.com

Cuff, Paul, (Lancaster), (On Sabbatical) c/o Bishop's Ho, Cannon Hill, Lancaster LA1 5NG

Culhane, Michael, Canon, (Liverpool, retired), Flat 19, St George's Court, Station Rd, Maghull, Liverpool L31 3RH **Tel:** 0151-531 8023

Culkin, James, (Salford, retired), 18 Sharples Hall Fold, Bolton BL1 7EH **Tel:** 01204-300102

Cullen, David (MAfr), St Edward's College, 46 Totteridge Common, London N20 8ND

Cullen, Gerald, (Cardiff, retired), St David, Avondale Rd, Pontnewydd, Cwmbran NP44 1TT **Tel:** 01633-484401

Cullen, John, (Liverpool), St Edmund of Canterbury, 62 Oxford Rd, Waterloo, Liverpool L22 8QF **Tel/Fax:** 0151-928 3629

Cullen, Peter, (Hallam), University Chaplaincy, Padley Ho, Wellesley Rd, Sheffield S10 2SY **Tel:** 0114-268 1197

Cullen, Timothy, (CP), St Joseph's Retreat, Highgate Hill, London N19 5NE **Tel:** 020-7272 2320 **Fax:** 020-7281 9433

Cullinan, Michael, MA, PhD, (Westminster), 36 Chiswick Court, Moss Ln, Pinner HA5 3AP **Tel:** 020-8429 3349

Cullinan, Thomas Anthony MA (Liverpool), Ince Benet, Cross Barn Ln, Ince Blundell, Liverpool L38 6JD

Cummins, Barrie, (Leeds), St Philip's Presbytery, 2 St Philip's Cl, Leeds LS10 3TR **Tel:** 0113-270 5157

Cummins, Kevin, (Hexham & Newcastle), St Oswald's, High St, Wrekenton, Gateshead NE9 7JQ **Tel:** 0191-487 6227

Cummins, Joseph, (MAfr), White Gates, Kingston, Lewes E. Sussex BN7 3LN **Tel:** 01273 483775 **E-mail:** josephcumminsmafr@eircom.net

Cummins, Liam, Formation Staff (MHM), St Joseph's College, Lawrence St, Mill Hill, London NW7 4JX **Tel:** 020-8959 8254

Cummins, Martin, Mgr Canon, BA, (Nottingham, retired), c/o Bishop's Ho, 27 Cavendish Rd East, The Park, Nottingham NG7 1BB

Cummins, Paul, (Plymouth),St Boniface Chaplaincy, Glenthorne Rd, Exeter EX4 4QU **Tel:** 01392-271191

Cummins, Thomas, Superior (MAfr), 129 Lichfield Rd, Sutton Coldfield, W. Mids B74 2SA **Tel:** 0121-308 0226 **Fax:** 0121-323 2476 **E-mail:** suttonlink@dial.pipex.com

Cunliffe, T F Geoffrey, (Lancaster, retired), Wildings Farm, Woodfold Ln, Cabus, Preston, Lancs PR3 1AW

Cunnane, James, Canon, BA, (Menevia, retired), Caermaria, Gwbert Rd, Cardigan SA43 1AF

Cunningham Bryan (SI), Mount Carmel, Wilson Rd, Blackley, Manchester M9 8BG **Tel:** 0161-740 2071 **Fax:** 0161-792 7943

Cunningham, Christopher, MA, VF (OSBl), St Alban's Priory, Bewsey St, Warrington WA2 7JQ **Tel:** 01925-630928 **Fax:** 01925-245256

Cunningham, Christopher, (IC), Collegro Rosmini, Via Per Binda 47, 28838 Stresa (VB), Italia **Tel:** 0039 0323 67011

Cunningham, Denis J, (Liverpool), St Christopher, 47 Stapleton Avenue, Speke, Liverpool L24 0SF

Tel: 0151-486 1874 **Fax:** 0151-486 3963

Cunningham, John, (Liverpool, retired), St Thomas' Ho, Great George's St, Waterloo, Liverpool L221RD

Cunningham, John, (Westminster), 204 High St, Waltham Cross, Herts EN8 7DP **Tel:** 01992-623156

Cunningham, John, (Clifton), St George's Rectory, Billet St, Taunton, Somerset TA1 3NN **Tel:** 01283-272700

Cunningham, Joseph, (Liverpool, retired), Flat 3, The Rectory, School Ln, Formby, Liverpool L37 3LW **Tel:** 01704-831778

Cunningham, Michael, MEd, BA, (SDB), St James' Presbytery, Chesnut Grove, Bootle, Merseyside L20 4LX **Tel:** 0151-944 1039 **Fax:** 0151-922 3263 **E-mail:** mjcsdb@tiscali.co.uk

Cunningham, Seamus, Canon, VG (Hexham & Newcastle), St Mary's Presbytery, Farringdon Rd, Cullercoats, North Shields NE30 3EY **Tel:** 0191-251 3770

Cunningham, Thomas, (Hexham & Newcastle, Retired), Immaculate Heart of Mary, Church Cl, West Monkseaton NE25 2PG **Tel:** 0191-252 7072

Cunningham, Thomas, (CSSp), 63, Somerset Rd, New Barnet, Herts EN5 1RF **Tel:** 020-8449 1961

Cupit, Michael, (Shrewsbury), St Philip's, Half Moon Ln, Offerton, Stockport SK2 5LB **Tel:** 0161-483 4609 **Fax:** 0161 292 3155 **E-mail:** stphilipsofferton@ntlworld.com

Curley, Brendan, MA (Salford), St Cuthbert, 5 Palatine Rd, Withington, Manchester M20 3LH **Tel/Fax:** 0161-445 1080

Curran, Mathew C, (OSA), 10 Waverley Rd, Carlisle CA3 9JU **Tel:** 01228-26765

Curran, William A, (IC), St Joseph's, Westernmoor, Neath SA11 1TP **Tel:** 01693-643323

Currer, Anthony (Hexham and Newcastle), St Cuthbert, Old Elvet, Durham DH1 3HL **Tel:** 0191-384 3442 **Fax:** 0191-375 0442

Currie, Ninian (OFM Cap) c/o Alexian Brothers Care Centre, St Mary's Road, Moston M40 0BL **Tel:** 0161-681 1929 **Tel:** 01244-351331

Curristan, Hugh, (Middlesbrough, retired), St Eunan's Nursing Home, Ramolton Rd, Letterkenny, Co Donegal, Ireland **Tel:** 00353-7491-03860

Curry, Mgr James, STB, (Westminster), The Clergy Ho, 16 Abingdon Rd W8 6AF **Tel:** 020-7937 4778

Curtin, Cornelius, MA, (CM), St Mary, 82 West St, Dunstable, Beds LU6 1NY **Tel:** 01582-662710

Curtis, Henry, BA, STL, MEd, (Birmingham), Oscott College, Chester Rd, Sutton Coldfield, W. Mids B73 5AA **Tel:** 0121-321 5000

Curtis, Timothy (SJ), Pierre Favre Ho, 19 Belvedere Grove, London SW19 7RQ **Tel:** 020-8947 5237 **Fax:** 020-8879 0157 **E-mail:** tim_sj_guy@yahoo.com

Curtis, Vincent, (Clifton), St Dominic's Presbytery, Jubilee Rd, Dursley, Glos GL11 4ES **Tel:** 01453-542039 **Fax:** 01453-548762

Cussen, Anthony E, (SMA), Society of African Missions, 33 Lyonsdown Rd, New Barnet, Herts EN5 1JG **Tel:** 020-8440 4715

Cutts, James, Cert Ed, (OSB), Worth Abbey, Crawley, W. Sussex RH10 4SB **Tel:** 01342-710310

Czaja, Grzegorz (SChr), 117 Buckingham St, Scunthorpe DN15 7JH **Tel:** 01724-855698

Czyz, Ludwik, (Katowice), (Pol 1) 2 Devonia Rd, Islington, London N1 8JJ **Tel:** 020-7226 9944 **Fax:** 020-7226 7677

Da Costa Fernandes, Alexander, BSc, ARCS, BA (OSB), Worth Abbey, Crawley, W. Sussex RH10 4SB **Tel:** 01342-710310

D'Ambrosio, Joseph (CSSp), Rockwell College, Cashel, Co. Tipperary, Ireland. **Tel:** 00 353 62 61444 **Fax:** 00 353 62 61661 **E-mail:** rockwell@iol.ie

D'Arcy, Joseph, Canon, (Liverpool, retired), The School Ho, Victoria St, Rainford, St Helens WA11 8DA **Tel:** 01695-622001

D'Arcy, Paul A, BA, (SMA), 4 Brighton Rd, Banstead, Surrey SM7 1BS **Tel:** 01737-353724 **Fax:** 01737-379910

D'Arcy, Stephen, (CSSp), 111 Portsmouth Rd, Frimley, Camberley, Surrey GU16 5AA **Tel:** 01276-504876 **Fax:** 01276-500070

D'Silva, Wilfrid, (Southwark), The Presbytery, East View, Hersden, Canterbury, Kent CT3 4HH **Tel:** 01227-710236

Da Silva, William (Karwar), 185 Mitcham Rd, Tooting, London SW17 9PG

D'Souza, Frederick (Delhi), 729 High Rd, London N17 8AG **Tel:** 020-8808 3554

Dagens, Emmett, (Salford, retired), 76 Killcoo, Newry, Co Down BT34 5JQ

Dain, Kenneth, BA, (Westminster, retired), 13 Uplands Rd, London N8 9NN **Tel:** 020-8340 0778

Dakin, Gerard, (Lancaster, retired), 21 Freshfields, Lea, Preston PR2 1TH

Dakin, Thomas, Canon, STL, PhL, (Lancaster), St Nicholas Owen, Raikes Ln, Thornton FY5 5LS **Tel:** 01253-850412

Dalfont, Serafino (IMC), 3 Salisbury Avenue, London N3 3AJ

Dale, John, (Liverpool, retired), St Wilfrid's Presbytery, Bolton Rd, Ashton-in-Makerfield WN4 8TH

Dale, John, (Salford), National Director, Pontifical Mission Societies, 23 Eccleston Square, London SW1V 1NU **Tel:** 020-7821 9755 **Fax:** 020-7630 8466 **E-mail:** Director@mission.uk

Daley, Anthony K, (Hexham & Newcastle, retired), Holy Cross Home, Ettrick Grove, High Barnes, Sunderland SR4 8QA **Tel:** 0191-514 5624

Daley, Felix, MA, (Hexham & Newcastle, retired), Holy Cross Home, Ettrick Grove, High Barnes, Sunderland SR4 8QA **Tel:** 0191-514 0562

Daley, James, (MHM, retired), Herbert Ho, 41 Victoria Rd, Freshfiled, Liverpool L37 1LD **Tel:** 01704-835850

Daley, John (IC), 12 Goodwood Rd, Leicester LE5 6SG **Tel:** 0116-241 5159 **Fax:** 0116-243 4565

Daley, Leo Raphael, BA, STL, (OSB), Collegio Sant 'Anselmo, Piazza Cavalieri di Malta 5, 1-00153 Roma, Italia. **Tel:** 0039 06 579 1214

Daley, Michael, BA, BSc, STB, MA, RGN (Westminster), 970 Harrow Rd, Sudbury, Middx HA20 2QE **Tel:** 020-8904 2552

Daley, Roger, Canon, LLB, JCL (Officialis), (Liverpool), 40 Kiln Hey, Eaton Rd, West Derby, Liverpool L12 2AL

Dalgleish, Ian, (Wrexham), Lon Llewelyn, Denbigh, Denbighshire LL11 3NT **Tel:** 01745 812297

Dalton, William, Mgr, (Liverpool), 10 Norris House Dr, Aughton, Ormskirk L39 5AH **Tel:** 01695-422853

Daly, Derl, (Nottingham, retired), The Holy Trinity Presbytery, Boundary Rd, Newark, Nottinghamshire NG24 4AU

Daly, Donal, (Clifton), St Peter's Presbytery, London Rd, Gloucester GL1 3EX

Daly, Eltin (OFMCap). *Director*, Mission to Travelling People, 18 Leopold St, Oxford OX4 1PS **Tel:** 01865-240325

Daly, Frank, (Nottingham), St Peter's, Priory Walk, Leicester Rd, Hinckley, Leicestershire LE10 1LW **Tel:** 01455-634443 **Fax:** 01455-890091

Daly, Gerard (SDS), c/o Provincialate Offices, 129 Spencer Rd, Harrow Weald, Middx HA3 7BJ **Tel:** 0208 426 0495 **Fax:** 0208 426 0927

Daly, Jeremiah (MSC), 14 Beaconsfield Rd, St Albans, Herts AL1 3RB **Tel:** 01727-853585

Daly, John A, Mgr (Salford), St Mary, Catlow Hall Street, Oswaldtwistle, Lancs BB5 3EZ **Tel:** 01254 232433

Daly, John P (Shrewsbury), St Anne, Pillory St, Nantwich CW5 5SS **Tel/Fax:** 01270-625494 **E-mail:** stannesnantwich@btinternet.com

Daly, Joseph (OMI), St Teresa of the Child Jesus, Utting Avenue East, Norris Green, Liverpool L11 3BW **Tel:** 0151 226 1354 **Fax:** 0151 270 2665

Daly, Kevin, MA, (Hexham & Newcastle), 17 North Farm Rd, Hebburn, Tyne and Wear NE31 1LX **Tel:** 0191-384 4009

Daly, Michael, BA, BSc, STB, MA, RGN, (Westminster), 28 Rossington Rd, Borehamwood, Herts WD6 4LA **Tel:** 020 8953 0715

Daly, Marcarten, (CP), Nazareth Ho, Hammersmith Rd, Brook Green, W6 8DB

Daly, Patrick, Canon, (Cardiff), All Hallows, School Rd, Miskin CF72 8PG **Tel:** 01443-228866

Daly, Patrick, (Menevia, retired), Tonevane, Tralee, Co. Kerry, Ireland.

Daly, Patrick, MA, PhD, STL (Birmingham), SS Peter & Paul, North St, Wolverhampton WV1 1RJ **Tel:** 01902-423005

Daly, Paul, STL, (Salford), (Advisor for Adult & Parish Formation) St Joseph's, Mary St, Heywood, OL10 1EG **Tel/Fax:** 01706 369777 **E-mail:** pdaly@salforddicese.org

Daly, Thomas, (SCA), 358 Greenford Rd, Greenford, Middx UB6 9AN **Tel:** 020-8578 1363 **Fax:** 020-8813 2238

Daly, Vincent A, (Wrexham, retired), Little Sisters of the Poor, Sacred Heart Residence, Sybil Hill Rd, Raheny, Dublin 5. **Tel:** 00353 1 8338181

Dalziel, James (MHM), Vice-Rector, Herbert Ho, 41 Victoria Rd, Freshfield, Liverpool L37 1LW **Tel:** 01704-835857

Damah, William, (Westminster) St Chads, 5 Whitworth Rd, South Norwood SE25 6XN **Tel:** 0208 653 2806 **Fax:** 0208 653 4188

Danaher, John Joseph, (Birmingham, retired), Church St, Abbeyfeale, Co. Limerick, Ireland

Danford, John, (Northampton), Sacred Heart Presbytery, 5 Beaudesert, Leighton Buzzard LU7 1HZ **Tel:** 01525-372321 **E-mail:** sacredheart.16@tiscali.co.uk

Dangerfield, Richard G, (Westminster, retired), "Barnacre Gardens", 2 New Peachey Ln, Cowley Peachey, Nr Uxbridge, Middx

Danson, John, MA, (Lancaster, retired), St Winefride's, Low Moor Rd, Bispham, Blackpool FY2 0PA **Tel:** 01253-350185 **Email:** jdanson679@aol.com

Darley, John, (Birmingham), St Mary, High St, Brierley Hill DY5 3AE

Tel: 01384-823445

Darlington, Stephen, (OSB), c/o St Michael's Abbey, Farnborough, Hants GU14 7NQ

Darwen, Robert, (SJ), Manresa Ho, 10 Albert Rd, Harborne, Birmingham B17 0AN **Tel:** 0121 427 2628 **Fax:** 0121 428 1833 **E-mail:** rondarwen@jesuits.net

Dasey, Mgr Canon Gerard, VG, (Middlesbrough), St Bede, 17 Mount Pleasant Avenue, Marske-by-the-Sea, Redcar TS11 7BW **Tel:** 01642-485722 **Fax:** 01642 481362

Davenport, Bernard, (Northampton), Our Lady of Perpetual Succour, 30 Amersham Rd, Chesham Bois, Bucks HP6 5PE **Tel:** 01494-727469 **E-mail:** bdavenport@freenetname.co.uk

Davern, Michael, Canon (Middlesbrough, retired), 53 Kirk Ho, Pryme St, Anlaby, Hull HU10 6EL **Tel:** 01482-657248

Davern, William, BTh, MA, (Arundel & Brighton), 1 St Margaret's Dr, Epsom, Surrey KT18 7LB **Tel:** 01372-723573

Davey, Richard, (Portsmouth, retired), Failte, 69 Castle Rd, Newport, Isle of Wight PO30 1DS **Tel:** 01983-529978 **E-mail:** ricky@failte69.fsnet.co.uk

Davey, Theodore, (CP), St Joseph's Retreat, Highgate Hill, London N19 5NE **Tel:** 020-7281 2274 **E-mail:** Tdaveycp@aol.com

Davidson, Francis LESL, STL (OSB), c/o Ampleforth Abbey, York YO62 4EN **Tel:** 01439 766714

Davies, Anthony John, MA, (Birmingham), c/o St Wulstan's Presbytery, Church Ln, Wolstanton, Newcastle, Staffs ST5 0EF

Davies, Brian, (Hallam), St Michael's Presbytery, Park St, Wombwell, Yorks S73 0HQ **Tel:** 01226-752372

Davies, Carl, BTh(Hons) (Arundel & Brighton), 39 Norton Rd, Hove, E. Sussex BN3 3BF **Tel:** 01273-732843

Davies, Colin, Canon (Westminster), 4 Thurlby Rd, Burnt Oak, Edgeware HA8 8HQ **Tel:** 020-8959 1971

Davies, Jeremy, (Westminster), 52 Castle St, Luton LU1 3AG

Davies, Jeremy M. BTh, LRAM (Westminster) 4 Park Rd, New Barnet, Herts EN4 9QA **Tel:** 020-8449 1207

Davies, Mark, VG (Salford), St Teresa's, 44 Redcar Rd, Little Lever, Bolton BL3 1EN **Tel/Fax:** 0204-571702 **E-mail:** vicargeneral@salforddiocese.org

Davies, Michael, MA (Clifton), St Peter's Presbytery, 7 St Peter's Rd, Cirencester, Glos. GL7 1RE **Tel/Fax:** 01285-652087

Davies, Patrick, Canon, (Westminster), 24 Golden Square, London W1F 9JR **Tel:** 020-7437 1525

Davies, Robert (OCD), Carmelite Centre, 169 Sharoe Green Ln, Fulwood, Preston PR2 8HE **Tel:** 01772 717122 **Fax:** 01772 787674

Davies-Hale, Allan, (Cardiff), St John Lloyd Presbytery, Glan-y-Mor Rd, Cardiff CF3 1RQ **Tel:** 029-2077 8631

Davis, Paul BA (Brentwood, retired), 5 Coltsfoot Court, Braiswick, Colchester, Essex CO4 5UD **Tel:** 01206-852474

Davis, Royston (Plymouth, retired), 32 Bluebell Avenue, Lowman Park, Tiverton, Devon EX16 6SX

Davoren, Hugh (CSSp), All Saints, Hassop, Bakewell, Derbys DE45 1NS **Tel:** 01629 640241

Dawber, Peter (Leeds), St Stephen's Presbytery, Castle View Terr, Skipton BD23 1NV **Tel:** 01756-793000

Dawer, John (SVD), 8 Teignmouth Rd, Highgate Hill, London N19 5NE

Dawson, Christopher, BSc, BA, GRSC (Salford), St Augustine's, Grosvenor Square, All Saints, Manchester M15 6BW **Tel:** 0161 236 6762 **Fax:** 0161 228 1516 **E-mail:** augustines@eggconnect.net

Dawson, Roger, (SJ), Campion Hall, Oxford OX1 1QS **Tel:** 01865 276993 **E-mail:** rogerdawson@jesuits.net

Day, Anthony, (Portsmouth), 10b The Kingsway, Portchester, Hants PO16 8NH **Tel:** 01239-237 0330

Day, Arthur Michael B, (CongOrat), The Oratory, Hagley Rd, Edgbaston, Birmingham B16 8UE **Tel:** 0121-454 0496

Day, Patrick, (Middlesbrough), Holy Cross Presbytery, 3 Carrington Avenue, Cottingham HU16 4DU **Tel:** 01482-847763

Day, Peter, (Westminster, retired), Nazareth Ho, 162 East End Rd, London N2 0AV **Tel:** 020-8442 2502

Day, Stephen Philip, MA(Oxon), (Birmingham), 98 Camp Hill Rd, Chapel End, Nuneaton CV10 0JP **Tel:** 024-7639 2365

Dazeley, Brian, Mgr Provost, (Nottingham), The Presbytery, Halam Rd, Southwell Notts NG25 0AD **Tel:** 01636 812686

de Burca, Brian (OMI), St Teresa of the Child Jesus, Utting Avenue East, Norris Green, Liverpool L11 3BH **Tel:** 0151 226 1354 **Fax:** 0151 270 2665

de Felice, Michael, VF (Liverpool), St Joan's Presbytery, Peel Rd, Bootle, Merseyside L20 4RW **Tel:** 0151-922 1498 **Fax:** 0151-933 4254

de Freitas, Philip, BTh (Southwark), St Michael's Church, Latin Mass Community, 4701 N McMilan, Oklahoma 73008 USA **Tel:** 001405 440 9168

de Gaynesford, Guy, (Plymouth), The Presbytery, St Mary's Parish Centre, St Mary's Rd, Bodmin, Cornwall PL31 1NF **Tel:** 01208-72833

de Lord, Richard, STB, (Westminster), 22 The Crosspath, Radlett, Herts WD7 8HN **Tel:** 01923-856165

de L'Orme, Frederick, MEd (Westminster), Prior Park College, Bath BA2 5AH **Tel:** 01225-835353

de Marchi, Benito, (MCCJ), Comboni Ho, 16 Dawson Place, Bayswater, London W2 4TJ **Tel:** 020-7229 7059.

de Putron, Philip, (Arundel & Brighton, retired), Flat 1, 7 Meads Rd, Easbourne, E. Sussex BN20 7DT **Tel:** 01323-639165

De Smit, Bernard M, (OSB), *Superior*, Monastery of Christ the King, Bramley Rd, Enfield, London N14 4HE **Tel:** 020 8440 7769

de Vere, Anthony G A, MA (Birmingham), 16 St Andrew's Rd, Old Headington, Oxford OX3 9DL **Tel:** 01865-769313

de Wolf, Patrick, (Clifton, retired), St Angela Convent, 5 Litfield Place, Clifton, Bristol, BS8 3LU **Tel:** 0117-983 3926

Dean, Paul, MA, STL, (Birmingham), c/o Cathedral House, St Chad's Queensway, Birmingham B4 6EY

Dean, Timothy, (Westminster) The Clergy Ho, 42 Francis St, London SW1P 1QW **Tel:** 020-7798 9055

Dearman, Richard A, MA, STL, (Salford), St Bede's College, Alexandra Park, Manchester M16 8HX **Tel:** 0161-226 3323

Debesai, Tesfamichael (MCJ), Our Lady of Mt Carmel, 8a Battersea Park Rd, Battersea Park SW8 4BH **Tel:** 020-7622 4282 **Fax:** 020-7978 1800

Dee, William, (Clifton, retired), 21 Albury Avenue, Southways, Dungarvan, Co. Waterford, Ireland

Deegan, Martin, (Hexham & Newcastle), St Mary, Hencotes, Hexham, Northd NE46 2EB **Tel:** 01434-603119

Deegan, Patrick, (Salford), Our Lady's, Plainsfield Cl, Manchester M16 7JQ **Tel:** 0161-226 1730

Deehan, John, MA, STB, LSS, (Westminster), c/o Archbishop's Ho, Ambrosden Avenue, London SW1P 1QJ

Deeney, Edward (SMA), 61 Blackhorse Rd, Walthamstow, London E17 7AS **Tel:** 020-8520 3647

Deeney, Francis, Canon, BA, VG (Salford), SS Peter and Paul, Stydd Lodge, Ribchester, Preston PR3 3YQ **Tel:** 01254-878314

Deeny, John, (Plymouth), Blessed Sacrament Church, 29 Fore St, Heavitree, Exeter Devon EX1 2QJ **Tel:** 01392-272596.

Deiden, Thomas, MA, (IC), St Etheldreda's, Ely Place, London EC1N 6RY **Tel:** 020 7405 1061 **Fax:** 020 7405 7440 **Email:** axsl47@dsl.pipex.com

Deimerly, Georges, (CM), St Vincent, 29, Eversley Cres, Osterley, Middx TW7 4LR **Tel:** 020-8560 7021

Delny, John (OFMCap), University Chaplain, St Walburge's, Weston St, Preston PR2 2QE **Tel:** 01772-734499 **Fax:** 01772-734499

Delny, Kevin, St John's Convent, Kilngreen, Reading, Berks RG10 9XP **Tel:** 0118-940 2964

Delny, Michael Christopher, (OSB), St Mary's, Talbot St, Canton, Cardiff CF11 9BX **Tel:** 02920-230492

Delany, Stephen, (Westminster), 377 Mile End Rd, London E3 4QS **Tel:** 020-9880 1845

Delargy, Joseph, Rt Rev Dom, (OCSO), Mount St Bernard Abbey, Coalville, Leicester, LE67 5UL **Tel:** 01530-832298/832022 **Fax:** 01530-814608 **E-mail:** mountstbernardabbey@btinternet.com

Delepine, Theodore Edward (OSB), St Mary's Abbey, Little Haywood, Colwich, Staffs ST18 0UF **Tel/Fax:** 01889-881173

Dell'Orto, Alessandro, (SX), 130 Holden Rd, N12 7EA

Delsink, Tony (Plymouth), The Presbytery, Tregenna Hill, St Ives, Cornwall TR26 1SE **Tel:** 01736-796412

Dempsey, William, (Westminster, retired), St Camillus Nursing Home, Killucan, Westmeath, Eire. **Tel:** 00353 44937 4196

Denneny, Edward Alan, (Salford), Christ the King, Amos Avenue, Newton Heath, Manchester M40 2RS **Tel:** 0161-681 3055

Dennehy, Michael, B Th, (Portsmouth), 53 Leigh Rd, Eastleigh, Hants SO50 9DD **Tel:** 023-8061 2430

Dennick, Anthony, Mgr, (Liverpool), The Presbytery, 1 West St, Prescot, Merseyside L34 1LE **Tel:** 0151-426 6462

Denton, Edwin, (AA), The Assumption Priory, Victoria Park Square, Bethnal Green, London E2 9PB **Tel:** 020-8709 5286

Denton, Philip, (Brentwood), The Presbytery, Easington Way, South Ockenden, Essex RM15 5EJ **Tel:** 01708-853130

Denton, Simon (OFM Cap), Francisan Friary, Pantasaph, Holywell, Flint CH8 8PE **Tel:** 01352-711053

Denvir, John, (SMA), 148 Ashcroft Rd, Stopsley, Luton, Beds, LU2 9AY **Tel:** 01582-723099

Dermody, John, (Westminster), c/o Curial Offices, 27 Convent Street , Greenhill, Swansea SA1 2B4 **Tel:** 01792 644017

Derrick D'Mello, Michael (Clifton). The Presbytery, Filwood Brdway, Knowle West, Bristol BS4 1JN **Tel:** 0117-966 4843

Desch, Klaus, (Salford), Mount Carmel, Wilson Rd, Blackley, Manchester M9 3PG **Tel:** 0161-740 2071

Desmond, Patrick, (Salford), Sacred Heart, Blackburn Rd, Accrington, Lancs BB5 0AH **Tel:** 01254-232062

Devane, John P, Canon (Southwark, retired), St Peter's Residence, 2A Meadow Road, London SW8 1QH **Tel:** 020 7587 3849

Devaney, Alan, MA (Liverpool), Chaplian HM Prison Liverpool, Hornby Rd, Liverpool L9 3DF **Tel:** 0151-530 4000 ext 4129

Devaney, Paul Dominic Joseph (Birmingham), Corpus Christi, 139 Albert Rd, Stechford B33 8UB **Tel:** 0121-783 2792

Devaney, Robert (Birmingham), 82 Wolverhampton Road, Stafford ST17 4AW **Tel:** 01785 223553

Devany, Lionel, (Salford), St Joseph the Worker, Cutnook Ln, Irlam, Manchester M44 6JX **Tel:** 0161-775 3788

Devany, Mgr Thomas, (Salford), Chaplaincy Services (RAF), RAF Innsworth, Gloucester GL3 1EZ

Devenney, Desmond, (Birminghm), 117 Parkgate Rd, Holbrooks, Coventry CV6 4GF **Tel:** 02476-333128 **E-mail:** desmond.devenney@btinternet.

Dever, Michael Francis, (Salford), St Richard, 10/20 Sutcliffe Avenue, Longsight, Manchester M12 5TN **Tel:** 0161-224 1498

Devine, John, Mgr, (Liverpool), St Benedict's Presbytery, Rhodes St, Warrington WA2 7QE **Tel:** 01925 630127

Devine, Joseph, (SX), 260 Nether St, London N3 1HT **Tel:** 020-8346 0428

Devine, Thomas, (OAR), 68 Hazlewood Cres, Kensal Rd, London W10 5DJ **Tel:** 020-8969 2660

Devriesére, John, (WF), 46 Woodville Gardens, Ealing, London W5 2LQ **Tel:** 020-8998 8552

Dewhirst, Anthony (IC), St Mary's Derryswood, Wonerish, Guildford GU5 0RA **Tel:** 01483-893196 **E-mail:** anthony@rosmini.org

Dewhurst, Robert, (Lancaster), Sacred Heart, 17 Talbot Rd, Blackpool FY1 1LB **Tel:** 01253-620964

Dewis, John Patrick, (Birmingham, retired), Partida Jara 48, Camina Gatera, Pedreguer 03750, Alicante, Spain. **Tel:** 00 34 96 645 6485

Di Giovanni, Carmelo, (SCA), St Peter's Italian Church, 136 Clerkenwell Rd, London EC1M 4LA **Tel:** 020-7837 1528 **Fax:** 020-7837 9071

Diaper, Paul A, BA, MA, JCD (Opus Dei), 159 Nightingale Ln, London SW12 8NQ **Tel:** 020-8673 2242

Dias, Luis Filipe (MCCJ), Verona Fathers, Sunningdale, Ascot, Berkshire SL5 0JY **Tel:** 01344-621328 **Fax:** 01344-874175

Dickens, Matthew, MA, DipLib, BTh, (Southwark), 3 The Hill, Northfleet, Kent DA11 9ES **Tel:** 01474 533689

Dickie, Cassian MA, DipEd (OSB), Prior, St Benedict's Monastery, Convent Cl, Duddle Ln, Bamber Bridge, Preston PR5 6US **Tel:** 01772 602201

Dickie, Ian, (Westminster), 3 Station Rd, Buntingford, Herts SG9 9NT **Tel:** 01763-271471

Dickinson, Francis, (CSSR), Bishop Eton, Woolton Rd, Liverpool L16 8NQ **Tel:** 0151-722 1108 **Fax:** 0151-738 0834

Dickson, Gary, PhD, HGN, Dip.Couns (Hexham & Newcastle), Sacred Heart, Dunelm Rd, Thornley, Co Durham DH6 3HA **Tel:** 01429-820255

Dickson, William John, PhD, MA, BA, DPSE (SDB), Rinaldi Ho, 32 Orbel Street, Battersea, London SW11 3NZ **Tel:** 020 7801 9040 **Fax:** 020 7801 9041 **E-mail:** wjdicksonsdb@msn.com

Diemer, Paul, (OCSO), Our Lady and St Bernard, Mount St Bernard Abbey, Coalville, Leicester LE67 5UL **Tel:** 01530-832298/832022

Digan, Padraig, (SCC), 28 Reddington Rd, London NW7 7RB

Dike, Casmir, (MSP), Presbytery, Poplar Walk, Herne Hill SE24 0BS **Tel:** 0207-274 4853

Dilke, Charles, (CongOrat), The Oratory, Brompton Rd, London SW7 2RP **Tel:** 020-7589 4811

Dillon, John, (Southwark), PO Box 34, Ololunga, Kenya **Tel:** 00254 (0) 305 22954

Dillon, Paschal (OMI), Christopher Ho, 237 Goldhurst Terr, West Hampstead, London NW6 3EP **Tel:** 020-7328 8610

Dillon, S Paul, (Salford), Pipers Hill, Duagh, Listowel, Co Kerry, Eire.

Dingley, Stephen, MA, PhD, STL, (Arundel and Brighton), St John's Seminary, Wonersh, Guildford, Surrey GU5 0QX **Tel:** 01483-892217

Dionne, Nelson (MSC), St Columba's College, 8 King Harry Ln, St Albans AL3 4AW

Diskin, Michael J, (Lancaster), St Mary, Darkinson Ln, Lea Town, Preston PR4 0RJ **Tel:** 01772 726425

Diver, John, (Southwark), 401 Ewell Rd, Tolworth, Surrey KT6 7DG **Tel:** 0208-399 9550 **Tel:** 0208-399 3291

Dixon, Adrian, (Hexham & Newcastle), St Joseph, High St West, Gateshead NE8 1LX **Tel:** 0191-477 1524

Dixon, Kevin T, (Hexham & Newcastle), St Joseph's, 3 Neasham Avenue, Billingham, Cleveland TS23 3NW **Tel:** 01642-560048

Dobson, Aelred, (SDS), 13 Old Town, Wotton-under-Edge, Glos GL17 7DH **Tel/Fax:** 01453-842281 **E-mail:** aelredsds@aol.com

Dobson, Francis, FCA, (OSB), Ampleforth Abbey, York YO62 4EN **Tel:** 01439-766714 **Fax:** 01439-766724

Dobson, John, (Lancaster, retired), 20 Duckworth Dr, Catterall, Garstang, Lancs PR3 1YS

Dobson, William, (CSSp), c/o The White Ho, 21 Upgate, Poringland, Norwich NR14 7SH

Docherty, John (Prior/Parish Priest) (OAR), The Presbytery, Chalkhill Rd, Wembley Park, Middx HA9 9EW **Tel:** 020-8904 2306

Docherty, Michael (Lancaster), Our Lady Star of the Sea, 2 St Annes Rd East, Lytham St Annes FY1 1UL **Tel:** 01253-723661 **Fax:** 01253-780565

Docherty, Vincent, (Middlesbrough, retired) Flat C, 30 South Parade, Southsea, Hants PO4 0SH

Dodd, J Kieran, (Brentwood, retired), 51 Cambridge Park, Wanstead, London E11 2PR **Tel:** 020-8530 0333.

Dodds, Jeffrey, (Hexham & Newcastle), St Patrick's, Victoria Rd, Consett, Co. Durham DH8 5AX **Tel:** 01207-502196

Dodgeon, Terence, MA, Mgr, (Salford, retired), 9 Cottam Cl, Whalley Clitheroe BB7 9RE **Tel:** 01254 822948

Doe, Anthony, BA, STL, (Westminster), Monastery, St Charles Square, London W10 6EA **Tel:** 020-8964 3800

Doetsch, Josef, BA (Southwark), 1 Portnalls Rd, Coulsdon CR3 3DD **Tel:** 020-8660 2452

Doherty, Anthony, (SCA), Prison Chaplain, Wormwood Scrubs Prison, Du Cane Rd, Acton W12 **Tel:** 020-8743 0311

Doherty, Anthony, (OSA), 18 Hoxton Square, London N1 6NT

Doherty, Cornelius, (MSC), 14 Beaconsfield Rd, St Albans, Herts AL1 3RB **Tel:** 01727-53585

Doherty, Daniel, (Raphoe), St Gregory, Three Shires Oak Rd, Smethwick, Warley B67 5BT **Tel:** 0121-429 1743

Doherty, Desmond, (Southwark), 401 Ewell Rd, Toleworth, Surrey KT6 7DG **Tel:** 020 8399 9550

Doherty, Hugh, (Nottingham, retired), The Gatehouse, Our Lady of Bethlehem Abbey, 11 Ballymena Rd, Portglenone, Co Antrim, Northern Ireland BT44 8BL

Doherty, James, (Hexham & Newcastle, retired), St Robert, Oldgate, Morpeth, Northumberland NE61 1QF **Tel:** 01670-513410

Doherty, Michael, (SDS), St Joseph's Presbytery, 191 High Rd, Harrow Weald, Middx, HA3 5EA **Tel:** 020-8427 1955 **Fax:** 020-8427 0543 **E-mail:** michaeldoherty@rcdow.org.uk

Doherty, Philip, Vocations Director (OFMConv), All Saints Friary, Redclyffe Rd, Dumplington, Urmston, Manchester M41 7LG **Tel:** 0161-202 9896 **Fax:** 0161-749 8223

Doherty, Terence, (Hallam), St Hugh of Lincoln, 135 Littlemoor, Newbold, Chesterfield, Derbyshire S41 8QP **Tel:** 01246-277635

Dolan, Anthony P, Canon (Nottingham), The Rectory, 1 North Parade, Grantham, Lincs NG31 8AT **Tel:** 01476-563935

Dolan, Bernard Leo, (Clifton), Paraquia, N Sra A Parecida, Rua Gal Labutat 19, Pira Tininga, Osasco, Sao Paulo, Brazil

Dolan, Eugene, Canon (Salford), St Edward's, Spring Ln, Lees, Oldham OL4 5AJ **Tel:** 0161-624 3762

Dolan, George, (Hexham and Newcastle, retired) Holy Family, Glanmore Rd, Grindon, Sunderland SR4 9PS **Tel:** 0191-534 4212

Dolan, Joseph (SSC), St Columban's, Widney Manor Rd, Knowle, Solihull, W. Mids B93 9AB **Tel:** 01564-772096/776202 **Fax:** 01564-770500

Dolan, Peter, (Lancaster), The Church Ho, Whitby Avenue, Preston PR2 3YP **Tel:** 01772-729992

Dolan, Terence, (Plymouth, retired), Holy Spirit and St Edward, 1 Victoria Avenue, Swanage, Dorset BH19 1AH **Tel:** 01929-422491

Dolman, Michael (Birmingham), Holy Cross Presbytery, 1 Signal Hayes Rd, Walmley B76 2RS **Tel:** 0121 351 2161

Doman, John (IC), Our Lady & St Charles, 69 Queen's Rd, Wisbech, Cambs PE13 2PH **Tel:** 01945-587455 **Mbl:** 07791578615 **E-mail:** doman@mac.com

Domine, Umberto (SX), 179 Ribbleton Ave, Preston PR2 6AA **Tel:** 01772-792292

Dominik, Waclaw (SMA), St Augstine's, 2 Anson Rd, Victoria Park, Manchester M14 5BG **Tel:** 0161-224 7409

Mbl: 0789 1635366
E-mail: waceksma@tiscali.co.uk

Donagher, Daniel, (Plymouth, retired), Nazareth Ho, Durnford St, Stonehouse, Plymouth PL1 3QR **Tel:** 01752-660943

Donaghey, Kevin M, (OSM), St Mary's Priory, 264 Fulham Rd, London, SW10 9EL **Tel:** 020-73526965

Donaghue, Anthony M, (Hexham & Newcastle), St Joseph, High West St, Gateshead, Tyne and Wear NE8 1LX **Tel:** 0191-477 1631

Donaghy, George, (OSA), St Mary's Priory, 111 Vivian Rd, Harbourne B17 0DN **Tel:** 0121 427 2538 **Fax:** 0121 428 3656

Donaghy, Michael, BD, PGCE (Westminster), c/o Archbishop's Ho, Ambrosden Avenue, London SW1P 1QJ

Donlan, Joseph, BEd, (Shrewsbury, retired), 8 Lillehurst, Sheriffhales, Nr Shifnal TF11 8RL **Tel:** 07780 565013 **E-mail:** lillehurst@madasafish.com

Donlon, Aengus G, (Birmingham, retired), 21 Larkspur, Dost Hill, Tamworth B77 1TR **Tel:** 01827-703263

Donlon, Brendan M, (Birmingham, retired), St Joseph's, Queens Park Rd, Harborne, Birmingham B32 2IB

Donnellan, Michael, (Menevia, retired), Taughboy, Ballyforan, Ballinasloe, Roscommon **Tel:** 01792-424107

Donnelly, Andrew, (OCarm), c/o Provincial Office, Morehouse, Heslington, York YO10 5DX

Donnelly, Dermott, (Hexham & Newcastle), Diocesan Youth Village, Allensford, Co Durham DH8 9BA **Tel:** 01207-592244 **Fax:** 01207-592245

Donnelly, Ernest, (Hexham & Newcastle, retired), St Aloysius, 5 Prince Consort Rd, Hebburn, Tyne and Wear NE31 1BE **Tel:** 01207-562304.

Donnelly, Henry, (Portsmouth, retired), c/o St Anthony's Convent, 19 Beatrice Avenue, Shanklin, IOW, PO37 6EP **Tel:** 01983-866555

Donnelly, James, (Cashel), 35 Cricklewood Ln, London NW2 1HR

Donnelly, James, Chaplain's Cottage, The Convent, Ebchester, Consett, Co Durham DH8 0QD **Tel:** 01207-561225

Donnelly, J David, Mgr Canon, STL, (Brentwood, retired), 18 Chancellor Ho, Mount Ephraim, Tunbridge Wells, Kent TN4 8BT **Tel:** 01892-522024

Donnelly, Martin, STB, (Cardiff), The Presbytery, 227 Cowbridge Rd East, Cardiff CF5 1JB **Tel:** 029-2059 1503

Donnelly, Terence, Dip Theol (CSSp), 6 Woodlands Rd, Bickley, Bromley, Kent BR1 2AF **Tel:** 020-8467 3555 **E-mail:** terry@spiritans.co.uk

Donohoe, Daniel, BEd, (SDB), Our Lady Help of Christians, 1a Sherborne Rd, Farnborough GU14 6JS **Tel/Fax:** 01252 545364 **E-mail:** dandonohoe@btinternet.com

Donohoe, Livinus, (OCD), Carmelite Priory, Boars Hill, Oxford,OX1 5HB **Tel:** 01865-735133

Donohoe, Michael, BA, HDE (Nottingham), St Teresa's Presbytery, 8 Kingsbury Dr, Aspley, Nottingham NG8 3EP.

Donohoe, Patrick, (SSC), St Columban's, Widney Manor Rd, Knowle, Solihull, W. Mids, B93 9AA **Tel:** 01564-772096

Donovan, Daniel, (CP), St Joseph's Retreat, Highgate Hill, London N19 5NE **Tel:** 020-7272 2320 **Fax:** 020-7281 9433 **E-mail:** danieldonovan@ukonline.co.uk

Donovan, Paul, MBA, STL, FCMI, RN (Northampton), Principal RC Chaplain (Navy), MP1.2 Leach Building, Whale Island, Portsmouth PO2 8BY **E-mail:** 023 9262 5193

Doolan, Brian, (Birmingham), The Presbytery, Friars Ln, Lower Brailes, Banbury OX15 5HU **Tel:** 01608 685259 **E-mail:** briandoolan@btinternet.com

Dooley, John, (SSC), St Bede's, Leigh Avenue, Widnes, Cheshire WA8 6EL **Tel:** 0151-424 2738

Dooley, Joseph (SJ), Corpus Christi Jesuit Community, 757 Christchurch Rd, Boscombe, Bournmouth BH7 6AN **Tel:** 01202-436700

Dooley, Peter, STL, BA (SDB), St Dominic's, Southdean Rd, Huyton, Liverpool L14 8UL **Tel:** 0151-489 1684 **Fax:** 0151-482 6053 **E-mail:** sdb-huyton@msn.com

Dooley, Terence, (Liverpool), St Mary Immaculate, Blackbrook Rd, St Helens, Merseyside WA11 9RJ **Tel:** 01744-23079

Dooling, Peter, Mgr Canon, (Nottingham), Sacred Heart Presbytery, 20 Grosvenor Rd, Skegness, Lincs PE25 2DB **Tel:** 01754-762528

Doran, John, (Portsmouth), St John's, Kiln Green, Reading, Berks RG10 9XP **Tel:** 0118-940 6766

Doran, John, (MHM), PO Box 204, Sasolburg 9570, Free State, South Africa

Doran, Patrick, Mgr, MA (Liverpool, retired), Ince Blundell Hall, Ince Blundell, Liverpool L38 6JL **Tel:** 0151-929 2596

Dorgan, Kevan, BA (Lancaster) St. John Vianney, Glastonbury Avenue, Marton, Blackpool FY1 6RD **Tel:** 01253-762227

Dormer, Paschal, BA(Theol), (Wrexham), 113 Mwrog St, Ruthin, Denbighshire LL15 1LE

Dorran, Charles A, (Salford), Canon, St Mary's Longsight Rd, Osbaldeston,

Blackburn BB2 7HX **Tel:** 01254-812242
Dorricott, Andrew G, MBE (Brentwood, retired), 25 Homeregal Ho, Bellingham Ln, Rayleigh, Essex SS6 7HN **Tel:** 01268-774552
Dougan, John, (OFM), c/o The Provincialate, 557-559 High Rd, Woodford Green, Essex IG8 0RB
Dougherty, Brian (Liverpool), St Mary of the Isle, Hill St, Douglas, Isle of Man IM1 1EG **Tel:** 01624-675509 **Fax:** 01624-674359
Douglas, Robert, (SMM), Montfort Ho, 28 Burbo Bank Rd, Liverpool L23 6TH **Tel:** 0151-287 6862 **Fax:** 0151-287 0410 **E-mail:** 4@nildram.co.uk
Dowd, Martin, LLB, (Salford), St Charles, St Charles Rd, Rishton, Blackburn, Lancs BB1 4HR **Tel:** 01254 886243
Dowds, William, MBE, (MHM, retired), Herbert Ho, 41 Victoria Rd, Freshfield, Merseyside L37 1LW **Tel:** 01704-835862
Dowling, Adrian, (OP, retired), St Joseph's Ho, Westmorland Rd, Newcastle-upon-Tyne NE4 7QA **Tel:** 0191-272 5640
Dowling, Barnaby, (Clifton), c/o St Ambrose, North Rd, Leigh Woods, Bristol BS8 3PW
Dowling, Liam, (OMI), 30 Prescot St, Tower Hill, London E1 8BB **Tel:** 020-7488 4654
Dowling, Paul, (Middlesbrough), Sacred Heart Presbytery, 1 Park Road South, Middlesbrough TS5 6LD **Tel:** 0642 850113 **Fax:** 01642 852122
Dowling, Timothy (OFM Cap), St Mary's Nursing Home, St Mary's Rd, Moston, Manchester M10 0BL **Tel:** 0161-681 1929
Downey, Michael, STL, (Plymouth, retired), The Studio Flat, Hillside, Gas Hill Road, Sherborne, Dorset D79 6NH **Tel:** 01935-812021
Downie, Andrew (Hexham and Newcastle), Chaplaincy, 14 Windsor Terr, Jesmond, Newcastle NE2 4HE **Tel:** 0191-281 1053
Downing, Gregory, (Shrewsbury), St George's, 17 Claypit St, Whitchurch, Shropshire SY13 1LE **Tel:** 01948-662935
Downs, Francis (MHM), Rector, Herbert Ho, 41 Victoria Rd, Freshfield, Merseyside L37 1LE **Tel:** 01704-835841 **E-mail:** frankdowns2003@yahoo.co.uk
Dowd, Martin (Salford), St Charles' Presbytery, St Charles Rd, Blackburn BB1 4HR **Tel:** 01254-886243
Doyle, Aidan, (OSB), The Presbytery, 2 Queen St, Abertillery NP13 1AN **Tel:** 01495-212339
Doyle, Anthony, (SVD), Presbytery, Balance Rd, London E9 5SR
Doyle, Bernard, Mgr, (Leeds, retired), 5 Hinsley Court, Headingley Ln, Leeds LS6 2HB
Doyle, Conleth, (OCarm), The Friars, Aylesford, Kent ME20 7BX **Tel:** 01622-717272
Doyle, Francis, BA(Hons), BDCertMgnt, HDip, (Wrexham), St Anthony of Padua, 54 High St, Saltney, Flintshire CH4 8SF **Tel:** 01244-671581 **E-mail:** catholicchurch@saltney.fslife.co.uk
Doyle, Gerard, STB, MEd, (Birmigham), Presbytery, Station Rd, Stone, Staffs ST15 8EW **Tel:** 01785-813951
Doyle, Henry, Mgr Canon, (Plymouth), The Presbytery, 25 South St, Exeter, Devon EX1 1EB **Tel:** 01392-272815
Doyle, Ian, BD, GradDipHum, MA, (Arundel & Brighton), PO Box 1601, Rosslyn 0200, South Africa.
Doyle, Michael, BTh, (Southwark), The Presbytery, 2 Sycamore Dr, Swanley, Kent BR8 7AY **Tel/Fax:** 01322-662698
Doyle, Michael J, PhD, STL, CPsychol (Birmingham), The Presbytery, Main Rd, Great Haywood, Stafford ST18 0SW **Tel:** 01889-881324
Doyle, Noel, (Brentwood, retired), 6 Sir William Petre Almshouses, High St, Ingatestone, Essex CM4 9HP **Tel:** 01277-352190 **E-mail:** noel@morxa.org
Doyle, Patrick, (Lancaster, retired), St Winefride's Ho, Low Moor Rd, Bispham, Blackpool, Lancs FY2 0PA **Tel:** 01253-593828
Doyle, Patrick (CongOrat), The Oratory, Brompton Rd, London SW7 2RP **Tel:** 020-7808 0900
Doyle, Seamus, (Hexham & Newcastle), Our Blessed Lady Immaculate, Blackhill, Consett, Co. Durham DH8 8LP **Tel:** 01207-502819
Doyle, Stephen J, (Salford), SS Aidan & Oswald, Vaughan Street, Royton, Oldham OL2 5DL **Tel:** 0161 624 1322 **Email:** ssaidanandoswald@ssao.wanadoo.co.uk
Doyle, Thomas H, (Lancaster), Our Lady and St Michael, Alston Ln, Longridge, Preston, PR3 3BN **Tel:** 01772-782244
Drake-Brockman, David, (Leeds), 112 Beckets Park Dr, Headingley, Leeds LS6 3PL **Tel:** 0113-274 1353
Draper, Peter, (Lancaster), St Mary's, 34 Kemp St, Fleetwood FY7 6JX **Tel:** 01253-873331
Draper, Robert, Mgr Canon, VG, MPhil, STL, (Plymouth), The Priest's Ho, Woodland Rd, St Austell, Cornwall PL25 4RA **Tel:** 01726-73838
Draycott, Christopher, BA (Birmingham), Presbytery, High St, Evesham, Worcs WR11 4EJ **Tel:** 01386-442468
Dring, Kevin, BA, STL (Arundel & Brighton),

D

The Presbytery, 122 Ladbroke Rd, Redhill Surrey RH1 1LF **Tel:** 01737 761017 **Email:** kevin.dring@dabnet.org

Drr, Kevin, (Leeds, retired), Parochial Ho, Golan, Milford PO, Co. Donegal, Ireland

Drozdowski, Stanislaw (MIC), 2 Windsor Rd, London W5 5PD **Tel:** 020-8567 1746 **Fax:** 020-8810 0185

Drumm, Walter, MA, Mgr, (Westminster, retired), Nazareth Ho, 162 East End Rd, London N2 0RU

Drummond, Gerald MA (Brentwood), 'Sweynes', 109 Ashingdon Rd, Rochford, Essex SS4 1RF **Tel:** 01702-544334

Duane, David, (Lancaster), Our Lady of the Wayside, Grasmere, Ambleside, Cumbria LA22 9RX **Tel:** 01539-435469

Duane, Francis J, Canon, (Northampton), The Presbytery, Pope Cl, Flitwick, Beds MK45 1JP **Tel:** 01525-715109 **Fax:** 01525-721752 **E-mail:** frankduane@tiscali.co.uk

Duckett, John, (Brentwood), 56 St Antony's Rd, Forest Gate, London E7 9QB **Tel:** 020-8472 0433

Duckworth, Robin, STL, MA, LSS, (SM), Newman Ho, 729 Beverley Rd, Hull HU6 7ER **Tel:** 01482 856884

Duda, Wladyslaw, (MIC), Marian Fathers, Fawley Court, Henley-on-Thames, Oxon RG9 3AE **Tel:** 01491-571935

Duffield, Richard, MA, STB, (CongrOrat)), St Aloysius, 25 Woodstock Rd, Oxford OX2 7NS **Tel:** 01865-315800

Duffy, Anthony, (Hexham & Newcastle), St Joseph, Birtley Ln, Birtley, Chester-le-Street, Tyne and Wear DH3 1LJ **Tel:** 0191-410 2923

Duffy, Gervase, (IC), St Maries, Oak St, Rugby CV22 5EL **Tel:** 01788-542703

Duffy, Hugh (SJ), Superior, Mount St Jesuit Residence, 114 Mount St, London W1K 3AH **Tel:** 0207 4937811

Duffy, James, (Westminster), St James, 22 George St, London W1U 3QY **Tel:** 020-7935 0943

Duffy, James, MEd (Westminster), 5 Park Rd, Rickmansworth, Herts WD3 1HU **Tel:** 01923-773387

Duffy, Michael, (SCC), St Columban's, 28 Redington Rd, Hampstead, London, NW3 7RB **Tel:** 020-7 794 8131

Duffy, Sean, 28 Highfield Rd, Princes Risborough, Bucks HP27 OHG

Dugdale, John (SCJ), 266 Wellington Rd North, Stockport SK4 2QR **E-mail:** j.dugdale@tesco.net

Duggan, David B, (Birmingham, retired), 5 Grange Park, Albrighton, Wolverhampton WV7 3EN **Tel:** 01902-372983

Duggan, Joseph, (Nottingham, retired), 2 Griffith Place, Waterford, Ireland.

Duggan, Joseph (SJ), St Wilfrid's Presbytery, 1 Winckley Square, Preston PR1 3JJ **Tel:** 01772 555244 **Fax:** 01772 251955

Duggan, Michael, BSc, HDE (SDB), St James' Presbytery, Chesnut Grove, Bootle, Merseyside L20 4LX **Tel:** 0151-944 1039 **Fax:** 0151-922 3236 **E-mail:** mduggo@tiscali.co.uk

Duggan, T Joseph, (Salford), Nazareth Ho, Scholes Ln, Prestwich M25 0NU

Dukes, William, (Shrewsbury), The Good Shepherd, 70 High St, Madeley, Telford TF7 5AU **Tel/Fax:** 01952-586118 **E-mail:** pp@goodshepherdtelford.org.uk

Dumbill, Luke, PhL, STL, MA (Liverpool, retired), St Bartholomew's, Warrington Rd, Rainhill, Prescot L35 6NY **Tel:** 0151-430 8873

Dunkling, Reginald, (Westminster), 262 Kingston Rd, Teddington, Middx TW11 9JQ **Tel:** 020-8977 2986

Dunn, Gerard F, (Lancaster), 4 Ripon Close, Cleveleys FY5 2LQ **Tel:** 01253 822154

Dunn, Michael, (OP), St Dominic's Priory, Southampton Rd, London NW5 4LB **Tel:** 020-7482 9227

Dunne, Christopher, (OMI), St Mary's, 13 Gatefield St, Crewe CW1 2JP **Tel:** 01270-212533 **Fax:** 01270-216407 **E-mail:** oblates@ stmaryscrewe.freeserve.co.uk

Dunne, Gerard, (MHM), Franciscan Convent, 63 Yorkshire St, Burnley Lancs BB11 3BS **Tel:** 01282 831117 **E-mail:** gerry-dunne@wanadoo.co.uk

Dunne, Graeme, (Liverpool), St Anthony's Presbytery, Scotland Rd, Liverpool L5 5BD **Tel:** 0151-207 0177 **Fax:** 0151-298 2112

Dunne, James, BA (Hexham & Newcastle), Sacred Heart, North Road, North Gosforth Newcastle NE3 5EB **Tel:** 0191 236 3182

Dunne, John T, Mgr, (Leeds, retired), 7 Hinsley Court, Headingley Ln, Leeds LS6 2HB **Tel:** 0113-278 4811

Dunne, John, (Portsmouth), 18 Douglas Rd, Bournemouth BH6 3ER **Tel:** 01202-424960

Dunne, Michael (Westminster), 41 Brook Green, London W6 7BL **Tel:** 020-7603 3832

Dunne, Thomas, (Portsmouth, retired), 4 Homewood Cl, New Milton, Hants BH25 2DF

Dunphy, William J, (Portsmouth, retired) Avon Cliff, 50-52 Christchurch Rd, Bournemouth, Dorset BH1 3PE **Tel:** 01202-291640

Dunstan, Roy Michael, (CRL, retired), Christ Church Priory, 229 High St, Eltham SE9 1UF **Tel:** 020-8850 1877

Duracz, Wieslaw, 29 Edmund St, Bradford BD5 0BH **Tel:** 01274-720848

Durand, Michael, MA (Westminster, retired), Cathedral Clergy Ho, 42 Francis St, London SW1P 1QW **Tel:** 020-7798 9055

Durcan, Sean, (Leeds), St Joseph's Presbytery, Pontefract Rd, Castleford WF10 4JB **Tel:** 01977-552753

Durkin, Brendan, (SCJ), 57 Dunstable Rd, Redbourn, Herts AL3 7PN **Tel:** 01582-852270

Durkin, James, (Wrexham), St Anne's, Prince Charles Rd, Wrexham LL13 8TH

Durkin, Thomas, (Hallam), Saint Teresa, 1 Bloomfield Rise, Darton, Barnsley S75 5AB **Tel:** 0114-288 2187

Durrant, Liam, (MHM), Mill Hill Formation Ho, PO Box 29, 5000 Jloilo City, Philippines

Durugbo, Eustace, (MSP), 131 Deptford High St, Deptford SE8 4NS **Tel:** 0208-692 2011

Dutson, Bruce, (Birmingham), Our Lady & St Kenelm, 22 Cobham Rd, Halesowen B63 3JZ **Tel:** 0121-602 1972

Dutton, Anthony, BA, (Salford), St Peter, Jessel Street, Mill Hill, Blackburn BB2 2RQ **Tel:** 01254 51417 **E-mail:** stpetermillhill@talktalk.net

Dutton, Francis, (SCJ), The Friary, Olton, Solihull, W Mids B92 7BN **Tel:** 0121-706 0505

Dutton, Hugh, (Arundel & Brighton), Diocesis de Chulucanas, Cuzco 381, Chulucanas, Piura, Peru. **E-mail:** curdio46@yahoo.es

Dutton, John, (Westminster, retired), St Joseph's Ho, 42 Brook Green, London W6 7BW

Dutton, Peter, ARMCM, (Shrewsbury), St Mary's, 2 New King St, Middlewich CW10 9EB **Tel:** 01606-832359 **E-mail:** pad.st.marys@btinternet.com

Dwyer, Anthony, (Westminster), 247 High Rd, London W4 4PU **Tel:** 020-8994 2877

Dwyer, Christopher, Canon, (Shrewsbury, retired), 14 Haydock Dr, Timperley, Altrincham WA15 7NH **Tel:** 0161-980 7059

Dwyer, Denis P, (Salford, retired), Banemore, Lostowel, Co Kerry, Ireland

Dwyer, Donal, (Shrewsbury), The Spa, Castleconnell, Co. Limerick, Éire. **Tel:** 00-353 61 377126 **E-mail:** djdwyer@eircom.net

Dwyer, John, (Portsmouth, retired), The Palms, Ballykilmurray, Tullamore, Co Offaly, Eire

Dwyer, Matthew, (Leeds, retired), Mount St Joseph's, Shire Oak Rd, Leeds LS6 2DE.

Dwyer, Peter, MA, (Westminster, retired), 47 The Park, St Albans AL1 4RY **Tel:** 01727-856483

Dwyer, Philip, Canon, (Cardiff, retired), The Holmes, 25 Smithies Avenue, Sully, S. Glamorgan

Dwyer, Richard, JCL, AdvDipEd (Clifton), St Thomas More Presbytery, Princess Elizabeth Way, Cheltenham GL51 7RA **Tel:** 01242-516936 **Fax:** 01242-517050

Dwyer, Stephen, MTh, Dip Social & Pastoral Theol. (Shrewsbury), St Joseph's, Woodford Ln, Winsford, Cheshire CW7 2JS **Tel:** 01606-592177 **Email:** stjosephwinsford@aol.co.uk

Dwyer, Timothy, Canon, (Portsmouth Retired), 8 Powis Cl, New Milton, Hants BH25 6AW **Tel:** 01425-612271

Dyckhoff, Christopher, Superior (SJ), St Wilfrid, 1 Winckley Square, Preston PR1 3JJ

Dye, Stanley, (MAfr), Ignatian Spirituality Centre, St Beuno's, St Asaph, Denbigh LL17 0AS **Tel:** 01745-583444

Dye, Stephen (Nottingham), The Presbytery, Broad St, Stamford, Lincs PE9 1FG **Tel:** 01780-762010 **Fax:** 01780-480606

Dyer, Gary, (Southwark), The Presbytery, Canon Cl. Rochester, Kent ME1 3EN **Tel:** 01634-845430

Dyer-Perry, Philip, STB (Westminster), The Presbytery, 1 Stonard Rd, London N13 4DJ **Tel:** 0208 886 9568

Dykes, Anthony, BA, (Birmingham), Presbytery, Church Ln, Wolstanton, Staffs ST5 0EF **Tel:** 01782-626611

Dynan, Paul BA, STB, MA, FIBMS (Brentwood), The Priest's Ho, Luncies Rd, Basildon, Essex SS14 1SD **Tel:** 01268 553425

Dyson, Michael, (Shrewsbury, retired), 47 Brandon Avenue, Heald Green, Cheadle SK8 3SG **Tel:** 0161-436 2147 **E-mail:** dunpreachin@yahoo.co.uk

Dyson, Philip (Plymouth), The Presbytery, Rosevean Road, Penzance, Cornwall TR18 2DX

Eager, Bernard, (Liverpool), St Catherine of Siena Presbytery, Newton Rd, Lowton, Warrington WA3 1LB **Tel:** 01942-206030 **Fax:** 01942-746243

Eagleton, Anthony, (Liverpool), Our Lady of Walsingham, Stand Park Avenue, Netherton, Bootle L30 3SA **Tel:** 0151-525 4812

Ealey, John, (Liverpool), St Aloysius, Twig Ln, Roby, Liverpool L36 2LF **Tel:** 0151-477 0250 **Fax:** 0151-477 0254 **E-mail:** pp@st-aloysius.org.uk

Eamer, James, (Rector), (CP), The Retreat, Sea St, Herne Bay, Kent CT6 8SP **Tel:** 01227-375095 **Fax:** 01227-360941

Earl, Benjamin, MA, MSc, JCL, (OP), Priory

of the Holy Spirit, 64 St Giles, Oxford OX1 3LY **Tel:** 01865 278400

Earley, James, (Nottingham), St Pius X Presbytery, Chelmsford Ave, Grimsby, NE Lincs DN34 5DD **Tel:** 01472-871632 **Fax:** 01472-753543

Earley, J Patrick, (Salford), St Ambrose, Princess Rd, Chorlton, Manchester M21 7QA **Tel:** 0161-445 1653

East, William, (Middlesbrough), St Joseph's Presbytery, 41 Potter Hill, Pickering, N Yorks YO18 8AD **Tel:** 01751-472727

Eastell, Kevin, BA, STh, MEd, PhD (Westminster), L'Aveau 49700 Les Verchers-sur-Layon, Maine et Loire, France **Tel:** 0033-241 599750

Eastman, Patrick, MA, (Tulsa), St Thomas of Canterbury Presbytery, Norcott Rd, Fairford, Glos. GL7 4BX **Tel:** 01285-712586

Eastwood, Michael, (Nottingham), 50 Charnwood Rd, Shepshed, Loughborough, Leics LE12 9QF **Tel:** 01509-502313

Ebo, Richard (Liverpool), St Jospeh's Presbytery, Meeting Ln, Penketh, Warrington WA5 2BB **Tel:** 01925-722105

Ebrahim, Andrew LLB, BD, PGCE (SDB), Salesian Ho, 1 Salesian Gardens, off Eastworth Rd, Chertsey KT16 8SG **Tel:** 01932-579050 **Fax:** 01932-579051 **E-mail:**eebie@tiscali.co.uk

Eccleshare, David, (Wrexham), Blessed Sacrament, Maude St, Connah's Quay, CH5 4WQ **Tel:** 01244-830358

Edgar, Leo (OP), St Dominic's Priory, 41a Red Barns, Newcastle NE1 2TP **Tel:** 0191 232 5939

Edgar, Timothy, MA, BD, AKC, (Westminster), 47 Vesta Avenue, St Albans AL1 2PE **Tel:** 01727 850066

Edmunds, Peter (SJ), Campion Hall, Oxford OX1 1QS **Tel:** 01865-286106 **E-mail:** peter.edmonds@campion.ox.ac.uk

Edwards, Anthony, (Lugano), Flat A15, 216 Kennington Rd, Kennington SE11 6HR

Edwards, Charles, (SJ), Corpus Christi Jesuit Community, 757 Christchurch Rd, Boscombe, Bournmouth BH7 6AN **Tel:** 01202 436700

Edwards, Derek STB (Birmingham), Rectory, Birmingham Rd, Kidderminster DY10 2BY **Tel:** 01562-822839

Edwards, Francis (OSB), Worth Abbey, Paddockshurst Rd, Turners Hill, W Sussex RH10 4SB **Tel:** 01342-710310 **Fax:** 01342-710311

Edwards, John, (SJ), 114 Mount St W1K 3AH **Tel:** 020-7529 4807

Edwards, Martin, MA, STL, (Southwark), 96 North Side, Wandsworth, London SW18 2QU **Tel:** 020-8874 2724

Edwards, Michael, (East Anglia, retired), 12 Unthank Rd, Norwich NR2 2RA **Tel:** 01603- 610349

Edwards, Paul BA, CertEd (Birmingham, retired), St Mary's Presbytery, Leveson St, Willenhall, WV13 1DA **Tel:** 01902-605043

Edwards, Peter, (East Anglia), 42 Kelvin Cl, Cambridge CB1 8DN **Tel:** 01223-240757

Edwards, Peter, (Southwark), 1 Montem Rd, New Malden, Surrey KT3 3QW **Tel:** 020-8942 2602

Edwards, Richard, (Wrexham), Nazareth Ho, Hillbury Rd, Wrexham LL13 7EU

Egan, David, (Salford), Chaplain Central M/cr Hospitals, 16 Kingsway, West Point, Manchester M19 2DD **Tel:** 0161-224 1895 (home) 0161 276 4247 (office).

Egan, Denis M, MA, (Birmingham, retired), 2 Granville Court, Cheyne Ln, Headington, Oxford OX3 0HS **Tel:** 01865-721580

Egan, Gerard, (CSSp), St Edmund Campion, 2 Watcombe Rd, Watlington, Oxon OX9 5QJ **Tel:** 01491-612431 **E-mail:** edcampwatox@cwcom.net

Egan, Patrick, MA, MSc, (Westminster, retired), 24 Frank Lloyd Wright Dr, PO Box 466, Ann Arbor, Michigan, 48106-0466 USA.

Egan, Peter, (Middlesbrough), Sacred Heart Presbytery, 25 Southgate, Hornsea HU18 1RE **Tel:** 01964-532918

Egan, Philip, Our Lady & St Christopher's, 1 Old Bank Close, Bredbury, Romiley, Stockport SK6 1AF **Tel:** 0161-430 2704 **Fax:** 0161-494 6461 **Email:** pegan@nildram.co.uk

Egan, Sean, (CSSp), The Villa, Thornton College, Thornton, Milton Keynes, MK17 0HH **Tel:** 01280-813466

Egan, Thomas, Mgr Canon (Westminster), 373 Bowes Rd, London N11 1AA **Tel:** 020-8368 1638

Eggleshaw, Edmund BA (East Anglia), 17 Howdale Rd, Downham Market, Norfolk PE38 9AB **Tel:** 01366-382353

Eggleston, Edmund Paul, MA (East Anglia), The Presbytery, 17 Howdal Rd, Downham Market, Norfolk PE38 9AB **Tel:** 01366-382353

Ejimofor, Francis (CSSp), 61 Leicester Rd, Higher Broughton, Salford M7 4DA **Tel:** 0161-792 1714 **Fax:** 0161-792 0435

Elder, Anthony, (Shrewsbury), St Winefride's, 18 Booths Hill Road, Lymm WA13 0DL **Tel:** 01925 752224

Elder, David, BSc, Grad Cert Sc Ed, (Lancaster), SS Mary and Michael, Bonds Ln, Garstang, Preston PR3 1ZB

Tel: 01995-602164 **Fax:** 01995-604399
Elders, John, MA, (Leeds), St Brigid's Presbytery, Elland Rd, Churwell, Leeds LS27 7QR **Tel:** 0113-253 4894 **E-mail:** johnelders@tesco.net
Elia, Bartolomeo, (SX), 260 Nether St, Finchley N3 1HT **Tel:** 020-8346 0428
Elias, Harold (SJ), JRS, 64 Southern Avenue, Feltham, Middx TW14 9ND **Tel:** 020-8844 0486 **E-mail:** hjel@btopenworld.com
Elkin, Wilfrid, (Hexham & Newcastle), St Mary's, The Catholic Church, Birch Rd, Barnard Castle, Co Durham DL12 8NR **Tel:** 01833-638133
Elkington, Cyril J, (Southwark, retired), 8 Park Grove, Bromley, Kent BR1 3HR **Tel:** 020-8464 3742
Elliot, James, (SMM), 37 Buckingham Ave, Whitefield, Manchester M45 6DJ **Tel:** 0161-796 6239 **E-mail:** fa66@rapid.co.uk
Elliott, Craig, (Hallam), The Presbytery, 134 Armthorps Rd, Intake, Doncaster DN2 5SF **Tel:** 01302-323936
Elliott, John, (Westminster), 22 The Crosspath, Radlett, Herts WD7 8HN **Tel:** 01923 224085
Elliott, John Mgr, (Southwark, retired), 10 Chesham Avenue, Petts Wood, Orpington BR5 1AA
Elliott, John, (Westminster), Holy Rood House, Exchange Rd, Watford WD18 0PJ **Tel:** 01923 224085
Ellis, Gerard, (SSC), St Bede's, Widnes, Cheshire WA8 6EL **Tel:** 0151-424 2738
Ellis, John Francis, (Birmingham), Aston Hall, Aston by Stone, Staffs ST15 0BJ **Tel:** 01785-811502
Ellis, Robert, BA, MA, (Southwark), c/o Archbishop's Ho, 150 St Geaorge's Rd, London SE1 6HX
Ellwood, Robert, (SMM), Montfort Ho, 28 Burbo Bank Rd, Liverpool L23 6TH **Tel:** 0151-287 6862 **Fax:** 0151-287 0410 **E-mail:** smm3@nildram.co.uk
Ellwood, Robin, CertEd (Portsmouth), c/o Bishop's Ho, Edinburgh Road, Portsmouth, Hants PO1 3HG **Mbl:** 07797-761696
Elvins, Mark MA, GradDipSpir (OFMCap), University Chaplain, St Walburge's, Weston St, Preston PR2 2QE **Tel:** 01352-711053 **Fax:** 01352-715349 **E-mail:** capucin.preston@btinternet.com
Embery, Paul, (Lancaster), Director, Holy Trinity and St George, 33 Blackhall Road, Kendal LA9 4BW **Tel:** 01539 720063 **Tel:** 01539 720063
Emmett, Paul, (Wrexham, retired), "The Chalet", Catholic Church, King's Turning Rd, Presteigne, Powys LD8 2LD
Tel: 01544-260112
Endean, Philip, MA, DPhil (SJ), Campion Hall, Brewer St, Oxford OX1 1QS **Tel:** 01865-286100
English, Barry, (Cardiff), St Mary's, Bulwark Rd, Chepstow NP16 5JE **Tel:** 01291-622649
English, Michael, Canon, (Clifton), St Alphege's Presbytery, Oldfield Ln, Bath BA2 3NR **Tel:** 01225-424894
English, Patrick, (Shrewsbury), St Michael's, 80 Scotland St, Ellesmere SY12 0ED **Tel:** 01691-622283
Enston, Keith George (Birmingham), 1 Sansome Place, Worcester WR1 1UG **Tel:** 01905-22574 **Fax:** 01905-22635
Entwistle, J Paul, (Nottingham, retired), 126 Glossop Rd, Charlesworth, Glossop, Derbyshire SK13 5HB
Esdaile, Robert, BA, STL, (Arundel & Brighton), The Presbytery, Hampton Court Way, Thames Ditton, Surrey KT7 0LD **Tel:** 0208-398 6127
Espinosa, Julio, (OAR), The Presbyery, Chalkhill Rd, Wembley Park HA9 9EW **Tel:** 020 8904 2306
Esteban, Rafaél, Th (MAfr), The Catholic Rectory, Hills Rd, Cambridge CB2 1JR **Tel:** 01223-362213 **E-mail:** rafael@esteban.freeserve.co.uk
Evans, David, PhL, Canon, (Birmingham), 5 Enstone Rd, Charlbury, Oxon OX7 3QR **Tel:** 01608 810576
Evans, David, BSc, BTh (Westminster), 3 King Edward's Rd, London E9 7SF **Tel:** 020-8985 2496
Evans, James (Northampton), The Presbyery, 1 Frithwood Cres, Kents Hill MK7 6HQ **Tel:** 01908-671342 **E-mail:** staugustinedav@aol.com
Evans, Joseph BA, STD (Opus Dei), Netherall Ho, Nutley Terr, London NW3 5SA **Tel:** 020-7435 8888
Evans, Michael, (Cardiff), St Illtyd's Presbytery, Dowlais, Merthyr Tydfil CF48 3BT **Mbl:** 07769 893798
Evans, Michael, BA, FRCA, FRNS (OSB), St Francis Xavier, 19 Brd St, Hereford HR4 9AP **Tel:** 01432-273485
Evans, Neil (Menevia), St Benedicts Presbytery, Llythrid Ave, Swansea SA2 0JJ **Tel:** 01792-298412
Evans, Stephen, BA, (OP), Blackfriars, Oxford OX1 3LY **Tel:** 01865-278400
Everest, Rupert, MA, (OSB), St Benedict's Ho, East End, Ampleforth Village, N Yorks YO62 4DA **Tel:** 01439-788596/766814
Everitt, David, (Nottingham), 13 The Banks, Sileby, Leics LE12 7RE **Tel:** 01509 813834
Everitt, Gabriel, MA, DPhil, (OSB), Ampleforth College, York YO62 4ER

Tel: 01439-766800 **Fax:** 01439-788330

Everson, Simon BA (Westminster), Head & Chaplain, Farleigh School, Red Rice, Andover SP11 7PW **Tel:** 01264-710747

Ewing, Gerald, BTh, MA, (Southwark), Becket Ho, Santos Rd, Wandsworth, London, SW18 1NT **Tel:** 020-8874 1818 **Fax:** 020-8874 0474

Eyles, Cyril, (MCCJ), Presbytery, 1 Coxwell Rd, Buckland, Faringdon SN7 7EB **Tel:** 01367-241474 **Mbl:** 07802 880851

Ezeilo, Laurence, (OCSO), Mount St Bernard Abbey, Coalville, Leics LE67 5UL **Tel:** 01530 839162 **Fax:** 01530 814608 **E-mail:** mountstbernardabbey@btinternet.com

Ezenwa, Josaphat, BD (Onitsha), St Augustine, Cres Rd, Tunbridge Wells, Kent TN1 2LY **Tel:** 01892-522525 **Fax:** 01892-526287

Fabrizio, Gerardo, STB, JCL, Dipluris (Birmingham), 281a Bosworth Dr, Chelmsley Wood, B37 5DP **Tel:** 0121-770 3283

Fagan, Anthony, PhD, MSc, BA, CPsychol, (Portsmouth), c/o Bishop's Ho, Edinburgh Rd, Portsmouth PO1 3HG

Fagan, Jerome, (Shrewsbury), Our Lady and St Joseph's, Wheatland Ln, Seacombe, Wallasey CH44 7ED **Tel/Fax:** 0151-638 2873 **E-mail:** sdvoc@yahoo.com

Fagan, John (SX), 2 Cranwich Rd, London N16 5JX **Tel:** 020-8800 9898.

Fahey, Brendan, (SSC), St Joseph's, Lon Llewelyn, Denbigh LL16 3NT **Tel:** 01745-812297 **E-mail:** stjoseph@tiscali.co.uk

Fahy, John, (Cardiff), St Patrick, Grange Gardens, Grangetown, Cardiff CF24 7LJ **Tel:** 029-2025 3514

Fairhead, Jeremy, MA, BTh, (Westminster), Via Della Serofa 70, 00186 Roma, Italia **Tel:** (39) 0669 861213

Fairhurst, John BSc, STB (Salford), c/o Cathedral Ho, 250 Chapel St, Salford M3 5LL **Tel:** 0161-834 9052

Fairhurst, John BSc, STB (OSB), Ampleforth Abbey, York YO62 4EN **Tel:** 01439-766714 **Fax:** 01439-766724

Fairhurst, John (SJ), Sacred Heart Presbytery, Edge Hill, London SW19 4LU **Tel:** 020-8946 0305 **Fax:** 020-8946 9130

Faix, William STD (OSA), Austin Friars, 15 Dorville Cres, London W6 0HH **Tel:** 020-8741 7586

Faleiro, Braz, (SMA) 378 Upper Brook St, Manchester, M13 0EP **Tel:** 0161-224 4949

Faley, Andrew J, (Hexham and Newcastle), C/O: Bishops' Conference Secretariat 39 Eccleston Square London SW1V 1BX

Fallon, Christopher, MA, (Liverpool), St Philomena's Presbytery, Sparrow Hall Rd, Liverpool L9 6BU **Tel:** 0151 525 6191 **E-mail:** c.a.fallon@dur.ac.uk

Fallon, Joseph Thomas, Mgr MA PhD, (Birmingham), St Francis, 101 Hunters Rd, Handsworth, Birmingham B19 1EB **Tel:** 0121-554 0905

Fallon, Vincent (SSCC),5 Berrymead Gardens, Acton W3 8AA **Tel:** 020-8992 2014 **Fax:** 020-8993 9940

Fallon, William, (Salford), St Stephen, 38 Chappell Rd, Droylsden, Manchester M43 7NA **Tel:** 0161-370 1505

Falloon, Joseph (MSC), Sacred Heart Presbytery, 31 High St, Uppermill, Oldham OL3 6HS **Tel:** 01457-872603 **E-mail:** Joe.falloon@sacredheartparish.org.uk

Faloona, Isidore (OFM), Franciscan Friary, Marine Hill Cleveden BS21 7PP **Tel:** 0275-349001

Falzon, Raymond (OFM), 1 Balniel Gate, London SW1VC 3SD

Fang, Ivan, STB, BAed, (MHM), 7 Colby Gardens, Maidenhead SL6 7GZ **Tel:** 01628 588407 **Fax:** 01628 588439 **E-mail:** navifrog@hotmail.com

Fangoo, Marcel, (CSSp), 15 Peebles Way, Leicester LE4 7ZB **Tel:** 0116-266 1621

Farmer, J Barry, (IC), Holy Family Church, Commercial St, Slaithwaite, Yorks HD7 5JZ **Tel:** 01484-842146

Farrell, Ian, (Salford), (Chaplain to Blackburn Hospitals) 146 Haslingden Rd, Blackburn BB2 3HH **Tel:** 01254 294751(Chaplaincy) **Tel:** 01254 56026 (Home)

Farrell, James, MA (Shrewsbury), St Bede's, Church Ln, Weaverham, Northwich CW8 3NP **Tel:** 01606-853339

Farrell, John, BA, BD, PhD (OP), St Dominic's Priory, Southampton Rd, NW5 4LB **Tel:** 020 7482 9210

Farrell, Joseph, KHS (Brentwood), 240 Alma Avenue, Hornchurch, Essex RM12 6BJ **Tel:** 01708-507020

Farrell, Nicholas, CF (Leeds), c/o Principal RC Chaplain (Army), HQ Land Command, Erskine Barracks, Witton, Salisbury Wilts SP2 0AG **Tel:** 01722 433892

Farrell, Robert, BSc, STD, (Opus Dei), 1 Lower Park Rd, Victoria Park, Manchester M14 5RS **Tel:** 0161 224 2582

Farrell, Thomas, Canon, MA (Birmingham), 14 Westhill Rd, Coventry CV6 2AA **Tel:** 024-7659 1618 **E-mail:** thomas-farrell@beeb.net

Farrell, Valentine, (Lancaster), Holy Family, Links Rd, North Shore Blackpool FY1 2RU **Tel:** 01253-351258

Farrelly, Patrick Henry, (Birmingham), 13 Queen's Avenue, Tunstall, Staffordshire ST6 6EE **Tel:** 01782-838357 **E-mail:** pp-sacredheart-tunstall@btinternet.com

Farrer, Paul, (Middlesbrough), St Thomas More Presbytery, Kirkham Row, Beechwood, Middlesbrough TS4 3EE **Tel:** 01642-814794

Fasnacht, Michael, MB, ChB, (Salford), 4 Norbury Grove, Astley Bridge, Bolton, BL1 8SH **Tel:** 01204-51484

Faughnan, Padraig, (Portsmouth), 105 London Rd, Newbury, Berks RG14 1JP **Tel:** 01635-40167 **Fax:** 01635-30855

Faulkner, Mark, STB, MA, PhD (MHM), Flat 79, Mattock Ln, London W5 5BG **Tel:** 0208 567 8383 **Mbl:** 0798 6465614 **E-mail:** bonimark@hotmail.com

Fava, Michael, MACF (OSB), c/o Principal RC Chaplain (Army), HQ Land Command, Erskine Barracks, Witton, Salisbury Wilts SP2 0AG **Tel:** 01722 433892

Fawcett, Stephen STB (Birmingham), St Werburgh's Presbytery, Seabridge Ln, Clayton, Newcastle, Staffs ST5 4AG **Tel:** 01782-613023

Fawsett, Richard, (Southwark, retired), Wickham Court Nursing Home, West Wickham, Kent BR4 9QJ **Tel:** 020-8776 1129

Fealey, Colin (Liverpool), St Luke's Shaw Ln, Whiston, Prescot L35 5AT **Tel:** 0151-426 6795 **Fax:** 0151-426 5755

Fealey, James, Mgr Provost, (Wrexham), 1 Victoria Dr, Llandudno Junction, Conwy LL31 9NU **Tel:** 01492 583048

Fears, Martin (East Anglia), The Presbytery, 18 Stuart Close, Brandon, Suffolk IP27 OHB **Tel:** 01842812200

Featherstone, David, (Salford), St Dunstan's, Moston Ln, Moston, Manchester M40 9PA **Tel:** 0161-681 1410 **Fax:** 0161-682 9045 **E-mail:** stdunstan@moston92.fsnet.co.uk

Featherstone, Edward, MA (Hexham & Newcastle, retired), 120 Sutherland Avenue, Fenham, Newcastle-upon-Tyne NE4 9NR **Tel:** 0191-273 4481

Feben, Michael S, STL, PhL (Portsmouth, retired), 64 Medina Avenue, Newport, Isle of Wight PO30 1EL

Fedigan, Vincent, (Liverpool), The Parish House, 171 Crow Lane East, Newton-Le-Willows WA12 9UD **Tel:** 01925-226106 **Fax:** 01925-225432

Fee, Terence, (OSA), St Monica's Priory, 19 Hoxton Square, London N1 6NT **Tel:** 020 7739 5006

Feeley, John, (Nottingham), Our Lady of Victories and St Alphonsus, 28 Bitteswell Rd, Lutterworth, Leics LE17 4EY **Tel:** 01455-552523

Feeley, Joseph (Southwark), Priest's Ho, Maidstone Rd, Ashford, Kent TN24 8TX **Tel:** 01233 624771 **Fax:** 01233 665253

Feeley, Joseph, (Salford), 168 Whalley Rd, Langho, Blackburn BB6 8AA

Feely, Timothy P, (Leeds, retired), 2 Park Lea, Bradley, Huddersfield HD2 1QH **Tel:** 01484-540580

Feeney, John G, (Shrewsbury), Our Lady of Lourdes, 1 Gardenside, Leasowe, Wirral CH46 2RR **Tel:** 0151-638 3066 **Fax:** 08700-941047 **E-mail:** jgf@nwallaseyrc.org

Feeney, Patrick (SPS), St Augustine's, 70 Eton Rd, Datchet, Slough SL3 9AY **Tel:** 01782-515836 **E-mail:** pfeeney@spius.org

Fegan, Paul, BA (Liverpool), c/o Centre for Evangelisation, Croxteth Dr, Sefton Park, Liverpool L17 1AA

Feighan, Thomas, (Northampton), St Augustine, Apostle of England, Amersham Hill, High Wycombe, Bucks HP13 6NZ **Tel:** 01494-523969

Fejer, Anthony, (Clifton), The Carmelite Priory, Boars Hill, Oxford OX1 5HB **Tel:** 01793-522062 **Fax:** 01793-432619

Felix, Paul (MCCJ), Verona Fathers, Sunningdale, Berkshire GL5 0JY **Tel:** 01344-621238 **Fax:** 01344-874175 **E-mail:** vernonaf@globalnet.o.uk

Fellows, Terence T, (Nottingham), 7 Melton St, Earl Shilton, Leicester LE9 7FP **Tel:** 01455-842202

Felzmann, Vladimir, Mgr, KCHS, DD, MSc, (Eng), (Westminster), All Saints Pastoral Centre, London Colney, St Albans, Herts AL2 1AF **Tel:** 01727-822010

Fenlon, Benedict, (Shrewsbury, retired), Nazareth Ho, Manor Hill, Prenton, Wirral CH43 1UG **Tel:** 051-652 5282

Fenlon, Dermot, MA, PhD, (CongrOrat, retired), Nazareth Ho, Manor Hill, Prenton CH43 1UG

Fenlon, Thomas, (SMA, retired), St Thomas of Canterbury, 21a St John's St, Woodbridge IP12 1ED **Tel:** 01394-383551 or 0700-3993003

Fennessy, Paul, (Southwark), 370 Crofton Rd, Orpington BR6 8NN **Tel:** 01689-851776

Fenton, Anthony, (Leeds), The Presbytery, Cottingley New Rd, Cottingley, Bingley, W. Yorks BD16 1SA **Tel:** 01274-567639

Ferguson, Duncan, MA (Clifton), 54 Broadmoor Ln, Bath BA1 4LA **Tel:** 01225-445115

Ferkh, Louis, (LMO Maronite Rite), Lebanese Centre, 6 Dobson Cl, Swiss Cottage, NW6 4RS **Tel:** 020-7586 1801

Ferme, Brian Mgr, DPhil, JCL, (Portsmouth), Dean, School of Canon Law, Catholic University of America, 620 Michigan Avenue, Washington CD 20064, USA.

Fernandes, Alexander, da Costa, BSc, ARCS, MA, (OSB), Worth Abbey, Crawley, W. Sussex RH10 4SB **Tel:** 01342-710310

Fernandes, Norbert, BD, (Westminster), 141 Woodhall Lane, Welwyn Garden City AL7 3TP **Tel:** 01707 323234

Fernandez, Andrew, (Southwark), 192 Parrock St, Gravesend, Kent DA12 1EN **Tel:** 01474 352415

Fernando, Prem (Colombo), Catholic Rectory, Hills Rd, Cambridge DB2 1JR

Fernandopulle, Anton (Kingston), St Aidan's Presbytery, Adswood Rd, Huyton, Liverpool L36 7XR **Tel:** 0151-489 3085 **Fax:** 0151-482 6650 **E-mail:** pp@aidans.org.uk

Ferns, Francis, (Liverpool), All Saints, 3 Oakfield, Anfield, Liverpool L4 2QG **Tel:** 0151-4287 8787 **Fax:** 0151-287 8788

Ferrier, Malcolm (Clifton), 44 Woodcock Gdns, Warminster BA12 9JG

Ferry, Manus BA (MSC), Catholic Presbytery, 8 St John's St, Tamworth, Staffs B79 7EX **Tel:** 01827-62161 **Fax:** 01827-313162 **E-mail:** manus@stjohnsrctamworth.org.uk

Fewell, Michael C, STL (CMF), Blessed Sacrament Church, 99 Alexandra Rd, Gorseinon, Swansea SA4 2NX **Tel:** 01792-892722 **E-mail:** mcfewell@claret.org.uk.

ffield, Richard, BSc, ACGI, AMI MechE (OSB), Monastery of Christ the Word, Monte Casino, Post Bag No 902, Macheke, Zimbabwe **Tel/Fax:** 00 263 798 369

ffrench, Barry F, (Westminster, retired), Ballymancy, Gorey, Co Wexford, Ireland.

Finan, Bernard, (SDS), Salvatorian Community, High Rd, Harrow Weald HA3 5DY **Tel:** 0208 427 2808 **E-mail:** bernard@finansds.wannadoo.co.uk

Finan, Joseph, (Leeds), St Columba, Highrd Well Ln, Halifax, W Yorks HX2 0QF **Tel:** 01422-361682

Finbow, Dennis, (East Anglia), c/o The White Ho, 21 Upgate, Poringland, Norwich NR14 7SH

Finch, John BEd (Liverpool), Sacred Heart Presbytery, Walmsley Rd, Leigh WN7 1YE **Tel:** 01942 673753 **E-mail:** shleigh@blueyonder.co.uk

Findlay-Wilson, Christopher, (Plymouth), The Presbytery, Trevu Rd, Camborne, Cornwall TR14 1AE **Tel:** 01209-713143

Finegan, David, (East Anglia), Catholic The Presytery, 29 Lockington Road, Stowmarket, Suffolk IP14 1BQ **Tel:** 01449 612946

Finegan, Peter, BA, (SPS), Our Lady of Pity and St Simon Stock, Hazlewell Rd, Putney, London SW15 6LU **Tel:** 020-8788 1131

Finigan, Timothy, MA, STL, (Southwark), 330a Burnt Oak Ln, Blackfen, Sidcup, Kent DA15 8LW **Tel:** 020-8300 2697 **E-mail:** rosary@freeuk.com

Finley, Alan J, (Clifton), The Presbytery, Sacred Hearts, Charlton Kings, Cheltenham, Glos GL53 9AU **Tel:** 01242-524932

Finn, Cornelius P, (Leeds, retired), Flat 3, 24 Farnley Ln, Otley, LS21 3BA **Tel:** 01943-466110

Finn, John (Cape Coast), 208 Sydenham Rd, London SE23 5SE **Tel:** 020-8778 7343

Finn, John (MSC), St John's Presbytery, 8 St John's St, Tamworth Staffs B79 7EX **Tel:** 01827 62161 **Fax:** 01827 313162 **E-mail:** john@stjohnrctamworth.org.uk

Finn, Kevin, (Liverpool, retired), St Marie's Ho, 27 Seabank Rd, Southport PR9 OEJ

Finn, Richard, MA, M.Phil, DPhil (OP), Blackfriars, 64 St Giles, Oxford OX1 3LY

Finnegan, Sean, MA, BTh, (Arundel & Brighton), 45 John St, Shoreham by Sea, W. Sussex BN43 5DL **Tel:** 01273-452654 **Fax:** 01273-440226

Finnegan, Thomas J, (Clifton), 71 Gloucester Rd North, Filton, Bristol BS34 7PL **Tel:** 0117-983 3938

Finnegan, William, (Leeds), Moorside Rd, Fagley, Bradford BD2 3JE **Tel:** 01274-637438

Finnerty, Liam (OCD), Carmelite Priory, Boars Hill, Oxford OX1 5HB **Tel:** 01865 735133 **Fax:** 01865 326478

Finnigan, James, (Liverpool, retired), Flat 2, 77 Bath Street North, Southport PR9 0DG **Tel:** 0151-424 2827

Firth, Kevin, BA, STL, (Leeds), Sacred Heart & St Patrick Presbytery, Bolton Brow, Sowerby Bridge HX6 2BA **Tel/Fax:** 01422-832085

Firth, Richard, (Liverpool, retired), Flat 7, Devonshire Court, Devonshire Rd, Chorley, Lancs PR7 2BY

Firth, Simon, (Salford), St Anne's, 1 Crumsall Crescent, Manchester M8 5UD **Tel:** 0161-740 2448

Fischer, James, (CMF), Botwell Ho, Botwell Ln, Hayes, Middx UB3 2AB **Tel:** 020-8573 2065 **Fax:** 020-8561 6748

Fisher, Paul, BA (Leeds), St Joseph's Presbytery, 25 Naylor St, Batley Carr, Dewsbury WF13 2DF **Tel:** 01924-465531 **Fax:** 01924-457245

Fisher, Steven MCL, JCL, BSc, BTh (Southwark) 72 Hereson Rd, Ramsgate, Kent CT11 7DS **Tel:** 01843 592071

Fitch, Peter (Brentwood), c/o Cathedral Ho, Ingrave Rd, Brentwood, Essex CM15 8AT

Fitzgerald, Arthur, (Liverpool), 1 Horne St, Liverpool L6 5EH **Tel:** 0151-263 6578

Fitzgerald, Kevin, (Southwark), 63 West St, Sittingbourne, Kent ME10 1AN **Tel:** 01795-472619 **Fax:** 01795-430309

Fitzgerald, Patrick (MAfr), 48 Totteridge Common, London N20 8LZ

Fitzgerald, Philip, (Leeds), St Joseph's Presbytery, Martin St, Brighouse HD6 1DA **Tel:** 01484-712679

Fitzgerald, William, (Shrewsbury), Halcyon, Church Road, Wrockwardine Wood, Telford TF2 7AH

Fitzgerald-Lombard, Michael Charles, Rt Rev Abbot MPhil, (OSB), St Edmunds, Bungay, Suffolk NR35 1AX

Fitzgerald-Lombard, Patrick, (OCarm), Catholic Presbytery, Meyrick Street, Pembroke Dock SA72 6AL **Tel:** 01646 682079

Fitzgibbon, Michael, (MSC) 14 Beaconsfield Rd,St Albans, Herts AL1 3RB **Tel:** 01727-853585

Fitzgibbon, Richard, (Westminster, retired), 141 Woodhall Ln, Welwyn Garden City, Herts AL7 3TP **Tel:** 01707-323234

Fitzpatrick, Craig (Hallam), Cathedral House, Norfolk Street S1 2JB **Tel:** 0114 272 2522

Fitzpatrick, Eugene (Westminster), 216 Dollis Hill lane, London NW2 6HE **Tel:** 020 8452 6158

Fitzpatrick, Christopher Noel, (Birmingham), St Dunstan's Presbytery, Kingsfield Rd, Birmingham B14 7JN **Tel:** 0121-444 1386

Fitzpatrick, David, US Air Force, Base Chapel, Chicksands, Shefford, Beds **Tel:** 01462-812571

Fitzpatrick, Eugene Jude, (Westminster), 216 Dollis Hill Ln, NW2 6HE **Tel:** 020-8452 6158

Fitzpatrick, Francis, (Salford, retired), 51 Greenhill Rd, Bury BL8 2LJ **Tel:** 0161-761 7377

Fitzpatrick, Michael J, Canon (Clifton), St Peter's Presbytery, London Rd, Gloucester GL1 3EX **Tel:** 01452-523603

Fitzpatrick, Neil, BSc, BA, PhL, (Hexham & Newcastle), St Bede's, Catholic Row, Bedlington NE22 6HS **Tel:** 01670-823258

Fitzpatrick, Patrick J, PhD, STL, (Hexham & Newcastle), Little Sisters of the Poor, Holy Cross Home, Ettrick Grove, High Barnes, Sunderland, Tyne and Wear SR4 8QA **Tel:** 0191-567 5688

Fitzpatrick, Paul (Birmingham), Oscott College, Chester Rd, Sutton Coldfield B73 5AA **Tel:** 0121 321 5000

Fitzpatrick, Terence, (OSB), Baydon Road, Lambourn, Berks RG17 8NU **Tel:** 0118-971 5350 **Fax:** 0118-971 5203

Fitzsimmons, Joseph (USA), 19 Hoxton Square, London N1 6NT

Fitzsimmons, Joseph (MHM, retired), Herbert Ho, 41 Victoria Rd, Freshfield, Merseyside L37 1LW **Tel:** 01704 835864

Fitzsimons, Kieran (OFM), 160 The Grove, Stratford, London E15 1NS **Tel:** 020-8534 1964 **Fax:** 020-8534 1119 **E-mail:** kcfbag@yahoo.co.uk

Fitzsimons, Michael, (Liverpool), Christ the King and Our Lady's, 78 Queens Drive, Childwell, Liverpool L15 6YQ **Tel:** 0151 722 2231 **Fax:** 0151 722 2755

Flahive, John Gerard, (Birmingham), c/o Cathedral Ho, St Chad's Queensway, Birmingham B4 6EX

Flanagan, Brian (OMI), The Presbytery, 96 Bradford St, Birmingham B12 0PB

Flanagan, Joseph, (SSC), St Columban's Widney Manor Rd, Knowle, Solihull, W Mids B93 9AB **Tel:** 01564-772096

Flanagan, Vincent, (Portsmouth), 105 London Rd, Twyford, Berks RG10 9EL **Tel:** 0118-934 0854

Flannery, James, (Lancaster), The Presbytery, 9 Harvey Rd, Boscombe, Bournemouth BH5 2AD **Tel:** 01202-425286 **Fax:** 01202 433667

Flannery, Michael (SJ), Corpus Christi Jesuit Community, 757 Christchurch Rd, Boscombe, Bournemouth BH7 6AN **Tel:** 01202 436710

Flannery, Peter, (MHM, retired), Herbert Ho, 41 Victoria Rd, Freshfiled, Liverpool L37 1LW **Tel:** 01704-835854

Flannery, Sean, (OAR), St Rita's Centre, Ottery Moor Ln, Honiton EX14 8AP **Tel/Fax:** 01404 42601

Flatman, Martin, BA(Hull), (Birmingham), St Peter's, Abbey St, Eynsham, Witney, Oxon OX29 4HR **Tel:** 01865-881613

Fleetwood, Jonathan, (OP), St Dominic's Convent, Station Rd, Stone, Staffs ST15 8EN **Tel:** 01785-811035

Fleetwood, Paul, BA, (OSB), Worth Abbey, Crawley, W Sussex RH10 4SB **Tel:** 01342-710310

Fleetwood, Peter, Mgr, STB, PhL, (Liverpool), St Joseph's Presbytery, 40 Warren Rd, Blundellsands, Liverpool L23 6UE **Tel:** 0151 924 2101

Fleming, Alexander, BEd (Liverpool, retired), Flat 2, The Rectory, School Ln, Formby, Liverpool L37 3LW

Fleming, Anthony, (Liverpool), St Michael's Presbytery, St Michael's Rd, Ditton, Widnes WA8 8TF **Tel:** 0151-424 2827 **Fax:** 0151-424 2837

F

Fleming, Jim (SSC), c/o St Columba's, Widney Manor Rd, Knowle B93 9AA

Fleming, John, (Northampton), The Guardian Angels, Presbytery, 6 Chaloner Rd, Southcourt, Aylesbury, Bucks HP21 8NN **Tel:** 01296-421826

Fleming, Michael, BA (Salford), St Joseph's, 24 Curzon St, Mossley, Ashton-under-Lyne OL5 0HB **Tel:** 01457-832505

Fleming, Terence, (Plymouth), The Presbytery, 20 Radford Park Rd, Plymstock, Plymouth PL9 9DW **Tel:** 01752-401281

Fletcher, Martin, BA, (Brentwood), c/o Cathedral Ho, Ingrave Rd, Brentwood, Essex CM15 8AT

Fletcher, Paul, Superior (SJ), St Ignatius, 27 High Rd, Stamford Hill, London N15 6ND **E-mail:** pmf@jesuits.net

Flood, Edmund, MA, PhL (OSB), Ealing Abbey, Charlbury Grove, Ealing W5 2DY **Tel:** 020-8862 2107/2100 **E-mail:** edmund.flood@ukgateway.net

Flood, Eric, Canon, (Arundel & Brighton, retired), 187 Tanbridge Park, Horsham, W. Sussex RH12 1SU **Tel:** 01403-253168

Flood, Gerald, BTh (Southwark), The Presbytery, 1 Haig Rd, Biggin Hill, Westerham, Kent TN16 3LJ **Tel:** 01959-571404

Floody, Mark, (Northampton), 24 Freshwater Cl, Marsh Farm, Luton LU3 3TA **Tel:** 01582-502400 **E-mail:** mark.floody@btinternet.com

Flook, Michael, Canon (Menevia), The Presbytery, Convent St, Greenhill, Swansea SA1 2BX **Tel:** 01792-652683

Flower, Hugh, DipHort, (Arundel & Brighton), The Holy Spirit, 5 Bell Ln, Fetcham, Surrey KT22 9ND **Tel:** 01372-373387

Fludder, Patrick, BSc, BD, MA, (OSB), Co-ordinator, The Open Cloister, Worth Abbey, Crawley, W. Sussex RH10 4SB **Tel:** 01342-710316 **Fax:** 01342-710311 **E-mail:** worth.abbey@ukonline.co.uk

Flynn, Francis Paul, (Hallam), The Holy Family, Derby Rd Chesterfield, Derbys S40 2EP **Tel:** 01246-273753

Flynn, Francis, (Lancaster), St Peter's, 4 Clifton St, Lytham, Lancs FY8 5EP **Tel:** 01253-736721

Flynn, Gerard BA, PGCE, MA(Ed), STB (Portsmouth), The Presbytery, 96 Pyle Street, Newport, Isle of Wight PO30 1UH **Tel/Fax:** 018983 522027

Flynn, John, (Birmingham, retired), Aston Hall, Aston, Stone, Staffs ST15 0BJ

Flynn, John, (Salford), St Kentigern, 36 Wilbraham Rd, Fallowfield, Manchester M14 7DW **Tel:** 0161 224 4664 **Fax:** 0161 257 0271

Flynn, Maurice, (OCD), St Joseph's Priory, Austenwood Common, Gerrards Cross, Buckinghamshire SL9 8RY **Tel:** 01753-886581 **Fax:** 01753-892371

Flynn, Nicholas, (Kerry), 14 Melior St, Bermondsey, London SE1 3QP **Tel:** 020-7407 1948

Flynn, Seamus, Canon (Plymouth), The Presbytery, 24 Cecil St, Paignton, Devon TQ3 2SH **Tel:** 01803-557518

Flynn, Vincent, MA, MCL, JCL, (Southwark), 4 Westfield, Surbiton, Surrey KT6 4EL **Tel:** 0208 390 6131

Flynn, Wilfrid, (Liverpool, retired), Flat 2, Springfield Ho, 35a Church Rd, Formby, Liverpool L37 8BQ **Tel:** 01704-830707

Fogarty, Dermod, Canon, DD, LCL, (Arundel and Brighton, retired), St Joseph's, Albert Rd, Bognor Regis, W Sussex PO21 1NJ **Tel:** 01243-840689

Folan, Nicholas, (OP), Plater College, Pullen's Ln, Oxford OX3 0DT **Tel:** 01865-67626

Foley, David, (Arundel & Brighton), 2 Bristol Rd, Brighton BN2 1AP **Tel:** 01273-681587

Foley, Con, (Arundel & Brighton), c/o Bishop's Ho, The Upper Drive, Hove, E Sussex BN3 6NB

Foley, Francis P, (OMI), St Mary's College, Abbey Rd, Rhos-on-Sea, Colwyn Bay, Clwyd LL28 4NR **Tel:** 01492-4477

Foley, John, (CSsR), The John Paul Centre, 55 Grange Rd, Middlesbrough TS1 5AU **Tel:** 01642-251800 **Fax:** 01642-221003

Foley, John, (Hexham & Newcastle), c/o Bishop's Ho, 800 West Rd, Newcastle-upon-Tyne NE5 2BJ

Foley, Michael (SSCC), Sacred Heart Community, 372 Uxbridge Rd, Ealing, London W5 3LH **Tel:** 020-8993 6040/8992 5941 **Mbl:** 00353 872 391888

Foley, Patrick, (SPS), 96 Dock Rd, Tilbury, Essex RM18 7BT **Tel:** 01375 842309

Foley, Patrick, (Westminster), Church of St Helen, The Harebreaks, Watford, Herts WD2 5NJ **Tel:** 01923-223175

Foley, Thomas, (Portsmouth, retired), Springville, Kanturk, Co Cork, Eire.

Foley, William, (Salford), St Winifred, Mauldeth Rd, Heaton Mersey, Stockport SK4 3NB **Tel:** 0161 432 4412 **Fax:** 0161 975 0120.

Foley, W Brian, (Liverpool, retired), Nazareth Ho, Liverpool Rd, Crosby, Liverpool L23 0QT

Forbes Turner, Timothy J, CF, (RC), (Southwark), c/o Principal RC Chaplain (Army), HQ Land Command, Erskine Barracks, Witton, Salisbury Wilts

SP2 0AG **Tel:** 01722 433892

Ford, Anthony, MA, (Southwark), 73 Sandown Lodge, Avenue Rd, Epsom KT18 7QU

Ford, Eugene (OMI), New Priory, Sacred Heart Chuch, Quex Rd, Kilburn, London NW6 4PS **Tel:** 020-7624 1701 **Fax:** 020-7328 8176 **E-mail:** parish@omiquex.org.uk

Ford, Timothy, BSc, PhD, PGCE, (Birmingham), Jockey Rd, Boldmere, Sutton Coldfield **Tel:** 0121-354 1763

Forde, David, Mgr Canon, (Nottingham, retired), c/o Willson Ho, Derby Rd, Nottingham NG1 5AW

Forde, Sean (OCarm), 63 East End Rd, East Finchley, London N2 0SE **Tel:** 020-8346 1458

Forde, Thomas (Westminster), 4 Lady Margaret Rd, London NW5 2XT **Tel:** 020-7485 4023

Forde, Martin, (Leeds), SS Peter & Paul Presbytery, 23 New Rd, Yeadon, Leeds LS19 7HW **Tel:** 0113-250 2192

Forde, Thomas, (Lancaster), c/o Bishop's Ho, Cannon Hill, Lancaster LA1 5NG

Fordham, John, (Cong Orat), The Oratory, Brompton Rd, London SW7 2RP **Tel:** 020-7589 4811

Foreman, Anthony, (East Anglia), Wheelwrights, Lidgate, Newmarket, Suffolk CB8 9PR **Tel:** 01638 500078

Formby, John, Canon (Westminster, retired), 81 St Charles Square, London

Forrester, David, MA, DPhil, STL, DipEd (Portsmouth, retired), Woldingham School, Marden Park, Woldingham, Surrey CR3 7YA **Mbl:** 01883-654484 **E-mail:** forresterd@woldingham.surrey.sch.uk

Forristalle, Graham, MA, BA, PGCE, (SDB), Savio Ho, Ingersley Rd, Bollington, Macclesfield SK10 5RW **Tel:** 01625-575405 **Fax:** 01625-560221 **E-mail:** gforristalle@tiscali.co.uk

Forshaw, Bernard, (Shrewsbury), St Peter's, off Castle Hall Cl, Stalybridge SK15 2ED **Tel:** 0161-338 2575 **Fax:** 0161-338 6077 **E-mail:** stpetersstalybridge@btinternet.com

Forster, Steven, (Hexham & Newcastle), c/o Principal RC Chaplain (Army), HQ Land Command, Erskine Barracks, Witton, Salisbury Wilts SP2 0AG **Tel:** 01722 433892

Forster, Thomas Paul, DipRE, KHS, (Lancaster, retired), Jeanne Jugan Residence, 228 Garstang Rd, Preston PR2 9RB

Fortune, Colin, BA, (SCJ), Holy Name, 9 Cross Ln, Great Barr, Birmingham B43 6LN **Tel:** 0121-357 1351

Forys, Andrzej, (MS), The Presbytery, Howard Way, Harlow, Essex CM20 2NS **Tel:** 01279-426017

Foster, A E John, (Clifton), 18 Trafalgar Rd, Weston, Bath BA1 4EW **Tel:** 01225-447117

Foster, Andrew James (Birmingham), The Presbytery, Arkell Ave, Carterton, Oxon OX18 3BS **Tel:** 01993 842463

Foster, David, MA, STL (OSB), Downside Abbey, Stratton on the Fosse, Radstock, Bath, Somerset, BA3 4RH **Tel:** 01761-235162

Foster, David, BSc, (Salford), St Edmund & St Patrick, 14 St Edmund St, Bolton BL1 2JR **Tel:** 01204 525716 **Fax:** 01204 532338 **Email:** stedmund.bolton@btconnect.com

Foster, Stephan, (Nottingham), St Mary's, Countesthorpe Rd, South Wigston, Leicester LE18 2PG **Tel:** 0116-278 3863

Foster, Stewart M, BA, PhD, DipH.ED, FRHistS, FRSA, (Brentwood), 56 St Antony's Rd, Forest Gate, London E7 9QB **Tel:** 020-8472 0433

Foulkes, John C, (Lancaster), St Kentigern, 25a Newton Dr, Blackpool FY3 8BT **Tel:** 01253-393439 **Fax:** 01253-396131 **E-mail:** JohnCFoulkes@aol.com

Foulkes, Kevin, MEd, (Salford), Our Lady's, Haigh Rd, Wigan WN2 1YA **Tel:** 01942-516732

Foulkes, Peter, (Lancaster), St Bernadette's, Bowerham Rd, Lancaster LA1 4HT **Tel:** 01524-63000

Fountaine, Michael, MA, (Clifton), 20a Bristol Rd, Keynsham, Bristol BS31 2BQ **Tel:** 0117-983 3930

Fowler, John (East Anglia, retired), 21 Painters Ln, Sutton, Cambridgeshire CB6 2NS

Fox, David, (OCarm), The Friars, Aylesford, Kent ME20 7BX **Tel:** 01622 717272

Fox, Frederick, (SVD, retired), St Gregory's Ho, 21 Halewood Rd, Gateacre, Liverpool L25 3PH **Tel:** 0151-428 2860

Fox, Kevin, (SJ), St Ignatius, 27 High Road, Stamford Hill N15 6ND **Tel:** 020-8802 5303 **E-mail:** kfox@gbsj.org

Fox, Paul AE, MSc, CertEd, STL (Brentwood), 36 Inchbonnnie Rd, South Woodham Ferrers, Essex CM3 5FG **Tel:** 01245-324138

Fox, Peter, (Liverpool), 55 Moorfield Rd, Widnes WA8 3JA **Tel/Fax:** 0151-424 3841

Foxwell, Eric E, (Clifton), St Joseph, 232 Forest Rd, Fishponds, Bristol BS16 3QT **Tel:** 0117-983 3912

Foy, Anthony, (CSSR), Bishop Eton, Woolton Rd, Liverpool L16 8NQ **Tel:** 0151-722 1108 **Fax:** 0151-738 0834

Fraczek, Zygmunt (Tarnow, Poland), Sherwood Rise, Nottingham NG7 6JN **Tel:** 0115-960 8831

Fraher, Michael, (Salford, retired), St Philip's Presbytery, Slade Lane, Padiham, Burnley BB12 8NS **Tel:** 01282-771494

Fraile, Benito, (CM), 47 Palace Court, Bayswater, London W2 4LS **Tel:** 020-7229 8815

Frain, Anthony, Cert Ed, DipCS, (SDB), St Dominic's, Southdean Rd, Huyton, Liverpool L14 8UL **Tel:** 0151 489 1684 **Fax:** 0151 482 6053

France, Nicholas, (Portsmouth), Canon, 17 Val Plaisant, St Helier, Jersey C.I. JE2 4TA **Tel:** 01534-722992 **Fax:** 01534-720235 **Fax:** 01534-607991 **E-mail:** centreparish@jerseymail.co.uk

Frances, Jesus, (OAR), St John Stone, 18 Cheniston Gardens, Kensington, London W8 6QT **Tel:** 020 7937 7681

Franey, Anthony, (Nottingham), St Anne, 6 New Rd, Radcliffe-on-Trent, Notts NG12 2AJ **Tel:** 0115-933 2738

Franklyn, David, (Northampton), 20 Oriel Rd, Daventry NN11 4SP **Tel:** 01327 878897

Frankowski, Zbigniew (Order of St Paul the First Hermit), SS Mary & John, Snow Hill, Wolverhampton WV2 4AD **Tel:** 01902-421676

Franz, Simon (Iranian Priest). St Cuthbert's, Ropery Ln, Chester-le-Street DH3 3PH **Tel:** 0191-388 2302

Fraser, Andrew, (Guardian) (OFMConv), "Kolbe" Franciscan Study Centre, Giles Ln, Canterbury CT2 7NA **Tel:** 01227-452802

Fraser, Alexander, (Southwark, retired), 16 Hall's Dr, Faygate, Horsham, W. Sussex RH12 4QN **Tel:** 01293-851503 **E-mail:** valalec@ukf.net

Freely, Gerald KCHS (Westminster), 22 Roxborough Park, Harrow-on-the-Hill, Middx HA1 3BE **Tel:** 020-8869 6892

Freeman, David, (Portsmouth, retired), 14 Grebe Cl, Portchester, Fareham Hants PO16 8QN

Freeman, Kenneth, (Arundel & Brighton), Christ the Redeemer of Mankind, The Presbytery, 2 St Nicolas Avenue, Cranleigh, Surrey GU6 7AQ **Tel:** 01483-272075

Freeman, Laurence M, (OSB), Monastery of Christ the King, 29 Bramley Rd N14 4HE **Tel:** 020-8440 7769

Fricker, John, (CRL), 229 Eltham High St, Eltham SE9 1TX **Tel:** 020-8850 1666

Friel, Desmond, (Shrewsbury, retired), Mater Dei, Church Rd, Crowborough, E Sussex TN6 1ED

Frigerio, Enrico (SCJ), St Joseph's Presbytery, Mather Ln, Leigh WN7 2PR **Tel:** 01942-673517 **Fax:** 01942-269094

Frisby, Keith, (Nottingham, retired), c/o Willson Ho, Derby Rd, Nottingham NG1 5AW

Frith, Simon, (Salford), St John's, Bracewell St, Burnley BB10 1TB **Tel:** 01282 423824

Frost, Brian, Canon, (Northampton, retired), 32 Dukes Dr, Halesworth, Suffolk IP19 8DS

Frost, Francis, Professor, DD, L-és-L, (Salford), Foyer Sacerdotal Internationale, 01480 Ars- sur-Forman, France. **Tel:** 00-33 4 74 08 19 11

Frost, Russell, (East Anglia), 48 Norwich Rd, Ipswich IP1 6JS **Tel:** 01473-751975

Fudge, Alan J, (Westminster), 8 Ogle St, W1P 7LG **Tel:** 020-7636 2883

Fuentes, Albert, (OAR), Church of English Martyrs, Chalkhill Rd, Wembley Park, Middx HA9 9EW **Tel:** 020-8904 2306

Fullam, Seamus, (Westminster, retired), Abbeylara Rd, Granard, Co Longford Eire

Fuller, Reginald, Canon, DD, LSS, PhD (Westminster, retired), Nazareth Ho, 162 East End Rd, London N2 0RU

Funnell, Bernard, (Leeds, retired), 2 Stella Gardens, Pontefract WF8 2SR

Fura, Mariusz (MS), 1 Rainham Rd, Rainham, Essex RM13 8SP **Tel:** 01708-552897

Furlong, Aidan, (AA), Assumption Priory, Victoria Park Square, Bethnal Green E2 9PB **Tel:** 020-8980 1968

Furlong, Anthony, (IC), Collegio Rosmini, Via di Porta Latina 17, 00179 Roma, Italia. **Tel:** 0039-0677 400020. **E-mail:** furlong39@hotmail.com

Furnival, John, Mgr, (Liverpool), St Peter and St Paul, 161 Liverpool Rd, Crosby, Liverpool L23 5TE **Tel:** 0151-928 3456 **Fax:** 0151-949 1930

Furtado, Anthony, (SVD), 8 Teignmouth Rd, Willesden Green NW2 4HN **Tel:** 020-8452 9756

Fuse, Christopher, (IC), St Joseph's, New Zealand Rd, Cathays, Cardiff CF14 3BR **Tel:** 029-2041 1819 **E-mail:** chrisfuse@mac.com

Fyfe, James (East Anglia), 81 Mountbatten Road, Dersingham, King's Lynn, Norfolk PE31 6YE **Tel:** 01485-543818

Gabiola, Joseph, PhD, JCD (Opus Dei), 4 Orme Court, London W2 4RL **Tel:** 020 7229 7574

Gadie, Paul, (Liverpool), University of Wales, Lampeter, Department of Theology and Religious Studies, Lampeter, Ceredigion SA48 7ED

Gagie, Thomas, (Liverpool), St Thomas of Canterbury, Dentons Green Ln, Windleshaw, St Helens WA10 6SE

Tel: 01744-23973

Gaine, John J, Canon, PhL (Liverpool), St Teresa, 27 Everton Rd, Southport PR8 4BT **Tel:** 01704-566865

Gaine, Michael B, BA, (Liverpool, retired), 40 Westbourne Rd, West Kirby, Wirral CH48 4DH **Tel:** 0151-625 7311

Gaine, Simon Francis, STL, MA, DPhil (OP), Blackfriars, 64 St Giles, Oxford OX1 3LY **Tel:** 01865-278405

Gaisford, Philip, MA, SThB, ARCMA. (OSB), Worth Abbey, Crawley, W Sussex RH10 4SB **Tel:** 01342-710310

Gajecki, Walerian, Mgr Canon, (Southwark, retired), 26 Queensthorpe Rd, London SE26 4PH **Tel:** 0208-778 5592

Gallagher, Anthony, (Salford), The Presbytery, Wellington Road, Todmorden, Lancs OL14 5HL **Tel:** 01706-813676 **Fax:** 01706-810423 **E-mail:** stjosephintod@aol.com

Gallagher, Cahal, (SCC), 26 Larkhall Ln, London SW4 6SP **Tel:** 020-7622 1621

Gallagher, Clarence, MA, JCD (SJ), Campion Hall, Brewer St, Oxford OX1 1QS **Tel:** 01865-286115 **E-mail:** clarence.gallagher@campion.ox.ac.uk

Gallagher, Declan, (Salford), The Presbytery, 1 Stillgoran Rd, Donnybrook, Dublin 1. **Tel:** 00-353 1 842 1486

Gallagher, Francis, (Middlesbrough), SS Mary & Joseph, 48 Union St, Pocklington, York YO42 2JN **Tel:** 01759-303126

Gallagher, J Michael, (O Praem), 178 New London Road, Chelmsford, Essex CM2 0AR **Tel:** 01245 352898

Gallagher, James, BA (SDB), St Dominic's, Southdean Rd, Huyton, Liverpool L14 8UL **Tel:** 0151-482 1117 **Fax:** 0151-482 6053 **E-mail:** jimgsdb@tiscali.co.uk

Gallagher, John F, (SJ), Nazareth Ho, Hammersmith Rd, London W6 8DB **Tel:** 020-8748 3549

Gallagher, John J, (Brentwood, retired), Nazareth Ho, 1647 Paisley Rd West, Glasgow G52 3QT **Tel:** 0141-882 1741

Gallagher, Kevin, BA, STL, (Hexham & Newcastle), Our Lady Star of the Sea, South Terr, Horden, Co Durham SR8 4NQ **Tel:** 0191-586 4221

Gallagher, Liam (Southwark), 11 Alliance Way, Paddock Wood, Tonbridge, Kent TN12 6TY **Tel:** 01892-833699

Gallagher, Michael (Nottingham), St Teresa's, 8 Kingsbury Dr, Aspley, Nottingham NG8 3ED **Tel:** 0115-929 2022

Gallagher, Padraig, BA, (CSsR), c/o Redemptorist Superior, St Mary's, Clapham, London SW4 7AP

Gallagher, Peter, St Benedict, (Birmingham), Owen St, Atherstone, Warwicks CV9 1DG **Tel:** 01827-713177

Gallagher, Peter, Superior (SJ), Favre Ho, 19 Belvedere Grove, Wimbledon SW19 7RQ **Tel:** 020-8947 5237 **Fax:** 020-8879 0157 **E-mail:** p.gallagher@heythrop.ac.uk

Gallanagh, Neil, (Leeds, retired), c/o Bishop's Ho, 13 North Grange Rd, Leeds LS6 2BR **Tel:** 0113-230 4533 **Fax:** 0113-278 9890

Gallen, Gerard (SJ), St Winifreds, 1 Winckley Square, Preston PR1 3JJ **Tel:** 01772 255244 **Fax:** 01772 251955 **E-mail:** gallensj@jesuits.org.uk

Galligan, Timothy, Mgr, MA, STL, (Southwark), The Presbytery, Button Ln, Bearstead, ME15 8NJ **Tel/Fax:** 01622 736100

Gallogly, Vincent, (OFM), 52 Uxbridge Rd, Hanwell W7 3SU **Tel:** 020-8567 4056

Gallon, Michael L, (Leeds, retired), 4 Hinsley Court, Headingley Ln, Leeds LS6 2HB **Tel:** 0113-278 4805

Galvin, Aidan, (CM), 29 Eversley Cres, Isleworth TW7 4LR

Galvin, John, (Westminster, retired), Flat 17, St Joseph's Home, 4 Brook Green, London W6 7BW **Tel:** 020-7603 0450

Galvin, John, (Leeds), Westfield Rd, Morley, Leeds LS27 9NF **Tel:** 0113-253 4881 **E-mail:** parish@st-francis.fsnet.co.uk

Gamble, David, (Liverpool), Our Lady of Victories, Sandy Ln, Hightown, Liverpool L38 3RP **Tel:** 0151-929 2149

Gamble, Michael, STD (Birmingham), The Presbytery, Weston Ln, Bulkington, Nuneaton CV12 9RU **Tel:** 012476-312293

Gamracy, Leszek, (MS) 52 Goresbrook Rd, Dagenham, Essex RM9 6UR **Tel:** 020-8595 1227

Ganeri, Martin Robindra, MA, MPhil, DPhil, (OP), Blackfriars, Buckingham Rd, Cambridge CB3 0DD **Tel:** 01223 741039

Gannon, Austin, (Lancaster, retired), Little Sisters of the Poor, 228 Garstang Rd, Fulwood, Preston PR2 4RB **Tel:** 01772-712368 **Fax:** 01772-712368

Gannon, Edward F, (Lancaster), St Kentigern's, 25A Newton Drive, Blackpool FY3 8BT **Tel:** 01253 303439 **Fax:** 01253 396131

Gannon, Michael, (Shrewsbury), St Aidan's and St Hilda's, 66 Kenworthy Ln, Northenden, Manchester M22 4EH **Tel:** 0161-998 2895 **Email:** michaelgannon7@ntlworld.com

Gardiner, Kieron, (Arundel & Brighton), The Priests Ho, 37 Whyteleafe Rd, Caterham, Surrey CR3 5EG **Tel:** 01883 343241

Gardner, James Robert BA, PG Cert in Management (SDB), Savio Ho, Ingersley Rd, Bollington, Macclesfield SK10 5RW

Tel: 01625-560724
E-mail: bobbybosco21@hotmail.com

Gardner, Timothy (OP), St Dominic's Priory, Southampton Rd, London NW5 4LB.

Gardon, Piotr MA, (Polish Priest) (SChr), 22 Misbourne Dr, Great Missenden HP16 0BL **Tel:** 01494-868248

Garnett, Michael, MA, PhL, (Westminster), Apartado 319, Cajamarca, Peru, South America. **Tel:** 0051 44 853517 **E-mail:** imprentaomc@mixmail.com

Garratt, Jeremy Mgr Canon, MA, STL, (Portsmouth), St John's Seminary, Wonersh, Guildford GU5 0QX **E-mail:** jgarratt@wonerish.org

Garrett, Anthony, (Liverpool, retired), "Quinnels", Bendover Rd, Yalding, Kent ME18 6EY

Garrett, Bernard, (Brentwood), Henley Ho, Causeway, Bicester OX26 6AW **Tel:** 01869 253277

Garrett, John, (Brentwood), The Presbytery, Castle St, Saffron Walden, Essex CB10 1BP **Tel:** 01799-527011

Garrett, Michael (Westminster), Santa Apolonia 146, Apartado 319, Cajamarca, Peru **Tel:** 0051 76 823517

Garvey, Austin, MA, (Westminster, retired), 211 Old Marylebone Rd, London NW1 5QT **Tel:** 020-7723 7757

Garvey, James Patrick, (Westminster), 160 Long Ln, Hillingdon, Middx UB10 0EH **Tel:** 01895-234577

Garvey, Joseph Michael, (Liverpool, retired), 4 Scape Lane, Crosby, Liverpool L23 2SJ **Tel:** 0151-924 0366 **E-mail:** michael.garvey4@btinternet.com

Gaskin, Anthony BA, (Lancaster), Mater Amabilis, Wansfell Rd, Ambleside LA22 0EG **Tel:** 015394 32283 **Fax:** 015394 34412

Gaskin, Kevin, (Arundel & Brighton), The Priest's Cottage, Mayfield Ln, Wadhurst, E Sussex TN5 6DQ **Tel:** 01892-782470

Gassor, A David, JCL, STB, (Plymouth), 21 Mayne Cl, St Stephen's Hill, Launceston, Cornwall PL15 8XQ **Tel:** 01566-773166

Gates, Adrian, MA, STB (Louvain) (East Anglia), St James, 482 Landseer Rd, Ipswich, Suffolk IP3 9LU **Tel:** 01470-726701

Gates, Robert, MA, (Westminster, retired), 205 Nelson Rd, Whitton, Middx TW2 7BB **Tel:** 020-8898 3768

Gatt, Anthony, MA (Portsmouth), 18 Cherry Avenue, Larchmont 10538, New York, USA, **E-mail:** saheillum@aol.com

Gaughran, Michael, (SSC), 'Lyndhurst', Park Rd, Waterloo, Liverpool L22 3XB **Tel:** 0151-928 0137

Gaul, John, (SCJ), St Joseph's Presbytery, Tilston Rd, Malpas, Cheshire SY14 7DD **Tel:** 01948-861327

Gavin, Frank, (Nottingham, retired), Sacred Heart Residence, Sybil Hill Road, Raheny, Dublin 5 Ireland

Gavin, Thomas Joseph, Mgr, MA, (Birmingham, retired), St Wilfred's, 40 Pevril Dr, Stivichall, Coventry CV3 6NQ

Gawecki, Christopher, (Westminster, retired), 130 St Margaret's Rd, East Twickenham TW1 1RL **Tel:** 020-8892 3902

Gay, Philip, (Birmingham), Alton Castle, Castle Hill Rd, Alton, Staffs ST10 4TT **Tel:** 01538-703224 **E-mail:** office@altoncastle.co.uk

Geddes, Stephen, (Plymouth), The Presbytery, 38 Dorchester Road, Weymouth, Dorset D74 7JX **Tel:** 01305-786886

Gee, Peter (Southwark) 26 Larkhall Ln, Stockwell, London SW4 6PS **Tel:** 020-7622 1621 **Fax:** 020-7720 8084

Geldard, Peter, (Southwark), St John Stone Ho, 41 St Thomas Hill, Canterbury, Kent CT2 8HW **Tel/Fax:** 01227-462198 **E-mail:** chaplain@cathsoc.org

Geoghegan, Denis, (OCSO), Mount Saint Bernard Abbey, Coalville, Leicester LE67 5UL **Tel:** 01530-832298/832022 **Fax:** 01530-814608

Geoghegan, Gregory, (SJ), St Beuno's Ignatian Spirituality Centre, St Asaph, Denbighshire LL17 0AS **Tel:** 01745-583444 **Fax:** 01745-584151

Geoghegan, Joseph (MHM, retired), Herbert Ho, 41 Victoria Rd, Freshfield, Liverpool L37 1LW **Tel:** 01704-835858 **E-mail:** arakajoe@herberthouse.plus.net

George, Daryl, JCL, (Arundel & Brighton), St Charles Presbytery, Chesswood Rd, Worthing W. Sussex BN11 2AE **Tel:** 01903 239611

George, Mathew, 73 Newtown, Thetford, Norfolk IP24 3AU **Tel:** 01842-752266

George, Peter Alexander, MA, BCL, LLB, BD, (OSB), Downside Abbey, Stratton on the Fosse, Bath, Somerset BA3 4RH **Tel:** 01761-235114

Geraghty, Denis, BA, (OP), St Dominic's Priory, Southampton Rd, London NW5 4LB **Tel:** 020-7485 5491 **Fax:** 020-7485 2948

Gerrard, Francis Joseph, (Wrexham), 6 Plas Ave, Prestatyn, Denbighshire LL19 9NH

Gerrard, John, Provincial Superior, (MAfr), 42 Stormont Rd, London N6 4NP **Tel:** 020 8348 7799 **E-mail:** mafrgb@blueyonder.co.uk

Gerry, George, (Plymouth), The Presbytery, 20 Clinton Terr, Budleigh Salterton, Devon EX9 6RZ **Tel:** 01395-443339

Gibb, Joseph, Mgr, (Liverpool, retired),

Christopher Grange, Youens Way, Liverpool L14 2EW **Tel:** 0151-220 2525

Gibbins, Guy, (Clifton, retired), Nazareth Ho, London Rd, Charlton Kings, Cheltenham GL52 6YJ **Tel:** 01242-510038

Gibbons, David, MA (Southwark), 2 Knatchbull Rd, Camberwell, London SE5 9QS **Tel:** 020-7274 1908

Gibbons, Edward, (Hexham & Newcastle), Our Lady & St Cuthbert's, Church Hill, Crook, Co Durham **Tel:** 01388-762724

Gibbons, John, (Hexham & Newcastle), St Oswald, Gainsborough Avenue, Whiteleas, South Shields NE34 8JN **Tel:** 0191-426 0426

Gibbons, Michael, (Southwark, retired), 68 Cedar Cl, Dulwich, London SE21 8JF **Tel:** 020 8766 0308

Gibbons, Robert BA, MTh, Mst(Cantab), PhD (Melkite-Greek Catholic Priest, Westminster), 40 Nethercote Rd, Tackley, Oxford OX5 3AT

Gibson, John X, (Lancaster), Our Lady of Lourdes, Kellet Rd, Carnforth LA5 9LR **Tel:** 01524 732940

Gilbert, Ceiron, (Menevia) St David's Priory, St David's Place, Swansea SA1 3NG **Tel:** 01792 653 343

Gigli, Paul, (WF), Oak Lodge, 48 Totteridge Common, Whetstone, London N20 8NB **Tel:** 020-8959 1515 **E-mail:** paul.gigli@ukonline.co.uk

Gilbert, John, (Birmingham), HMP Blackenhurst, Hewell Ln, Redditch B97 6QS **Tel:** 01527-591295

Gilbert, Philip, (Southwark), Presbytery, 46 Hunting Field Rd, Meopham, Kent DA13 0EZ **Tel:** 01474-814627

Gilbride, Francis, Retired, (Northampton), 93 Forfey Lisnaskea, Co Fermanah, N Ireland BT92 OHS

Gilburt, Peter, Canon, (Westminster, retired), 56 Thornton Avenue, London W4 1QQ **Tel:** 020-8400 1677

Gilby, Anthony, Mgr, (Plymouth, retired), The Presbytery, 27 Exeter Road, Dawlish, Devon EX7 OBG

Gildea, John, (Liverpool), St Peter's, Weir Ln, Woolston, Warrington WA1 4QQ **Tel:** 01925-812443

Giles, Simon (IC), 369 Fosse Way, Radcliffe -on-the-Wreake, Leics LE7 4SJ **Tel:** 01509 816721 **E-mail:** simon@rosmini.org

Gilheney, John, MSc, Dip (Ed), (SDB), Saint John Bosc Ho, 121a Reading Rd, Farnborough GU14 6NZ **Tel:** 01252 554 300 **Fax:** 01252 375 395 **E-mail:** johngil@tiscali.co.uk

Gili-Hammett, Emmanuel, (CHS), The Presbytery, Arkell Avenue, Carterton, Oxon OX18 3BS **Tel:** 01993-842463

Gill, Gary (Southwark), 9 Tooting Beck Rd, Tooting, London SW17 8BS **Tel:** 020-8672 2179

Gillen, Patrick, CertEd, (SDB), The Holy Trinity, Aldershot Rd, Church Crookham, Hants GU13 0JU **Tel:** 01252-617811 **Fax:** 01252-625806 **Mbl:** 07767 607933 **E-mail:** p.gillen@btinternet.com

Gillespie Donal B, BEd, BD, (Cardiff, retired), Presbytery, Pisgah St, Kenfig Hill, Pyle, Bridgend CF33 6DA **Tel:** 01656-740389 **Fax:** 01656-749151

Gillespie, Philip, (Liverpool), *Term time:* Ushaw College, Durham DH7 9RH; *residence out of term:* Christ the King Presbytery, 78 Queen's Dr, Childwall, Liverpool L15 6YQ **Tel:** 0151-722 2231 **Fax:** 0151-722 2755

Gilligan, Michael, (Nottingham), c/o Cathedral Ho, North Circus St, Nottingham NG1 5AE **Tel:** 01115 953 9839

Gilligan, Sean, (Leeds), St Anne's Presbytery, North St, Keighley BD21 3AD **Tel:** 01535-603356

Gillman, Graham, BA, (Clifton), 16 Vine Tree Cres, St Peter's Cl, Rickmansworth, Hertfordshire WD3 8QY

Gilman, Aidan, MA, (OSB), Ampleforth Abbey, York YO62 4EN **Tel:** 01439-766714 **Fax:** 01439-766724

Gilmore, Brian, (SVD, retired), Divine Word Missionaries, 1 Blackwood Avenue, Liverpool L25 4RW

Gilmore, John, (SSC), 28 Redington Rd, Hampstead, London NW3 7RH **Tel:** 020-7794 8131

Gilroy, John, (CSSp, retired), 6 Woodlands Rd, Bickley, Bromley, Kent BR1 2AF **Tel:** 020-8467 3555

Gilsenan, Patrick, (Birmingham), Evelyn Rd, Sparkhill, Birmingham B11 3JN **Tel:** 0121-722 1272 **Fax:** 0121-722 5816

Gilsenan, Peter, Canon (Birmingham), 130 Horseshoe Ln, Sheldon, Birmingham B26 3HU **Tel:** 0121-743 2367

Giovanni, Meneghetti, (Scalabrini Fathers [CS]), 10 Woburn Rd, Bedford MK40 1EG **Tel:** 01234 359515 **Fax:** 01234 340626 **E-mail:** info@italianmission.co.uk

Glandfield, Philip BTh (Southwark), 159 Ellison Rd, Norbury SW16 5DE **Tel:** 020-8679 3545 **Fax:** 020-8679 2151

Glas, Piotr, MA, (SChr) (Polish Priest), St Matthew's Presbytery, Coin Varin, St Peter, Jersey JE3 7EW **Tel:** 01534-863149 **E-mail:** westparish@jerseymail.co.uk

Glasswell, William, (Lancaster), Our Lady of the Rosary, 101 Ulverston Rd, DAlton in Furness LA16 8EY **Tel:** 01229 462513 **E-mail:** wglass@tiscali.co.uk

Glaysher, Anthony (Portsmouth), Ampthill Ho, Cordier Hill, St Peter Port, Guernsey GY1 1JH

Glaze, Malcolm, BA, (Birmingham), 30 High St, Hilmorton, Rugby CV21 4EE **Tel:** 01788-565016

Gleeson, Kevin, BA(hons) (Leeds), St Thomas More Presbytery, Greengates Ho, 123 Chickenley Ln, Dewsbury WF12 8QD **Tel:** 01924-465073 **Mbl:** 0410 434653

Gliwinski, Adam, (SDB), Salesian Ho, 1 Salesian Gardens, off Eastworth Road, Chertsey KT16 8SG **Tel:** 01932 579 050 **Fax:** 01932 579 051

Glover, David, (Salford), Chaplain North Manchester Hospital, 67 Kearsley Rd, Higher Crumpsall, Manchester M8 4QJ **Tel:** 0161-720 9626

Glover, Paul, (Liverpool), Holy Cross Presbytery, Corporation St, St Helens WA10 1EF **Tel:** 01744-22077

Glowczyk, Jan, Canon (Birmingham, retired), 48 Maple Grove, Stafford ST17 9EQ **Tel:** 01785 245946

Glynn, Cronan, (OCD), Carmelite Centre, 169 Sharoe Green Ln, Fulwood, Preston PR2 8HE **Tel:** 01772-717122

Glynn, John, (Brentwood), 61 London Rd, Wickford, Essex SS12 0AW **Tel:** 01268-733219

Gnanaselvam, Sahaya, (SDB), Rinaldi Ho, 32 Orbel St, Battersea, London SW11 3NZ **Tel:** 020-7801 9040 **Fax:** 020-7801 9041

Gnosill, David BD, STL (Birmingham), St Joseph's, Edmunds Rd, Banbury Oxon OX16 0PP **Tel:** 01295 264661

Goddard, David, BMus, FTCL, LRAM, ARCO, (Arundel and Brighton), The Priest's Ho, Park Ln, West Grinstead, Horsham, W. Sussex RH13 8LT **Tel:** 01403-710273 **Fax:** 01403-712512

Godden, Brian T V, BA, (Northampton, retired), 3 Abbeyfield (Burnham) Society, 3 Church St, Burnham, Bucks SL1 7HX **Tel:** 01628-602828 **Mbl:** 07821 163860

Godilano, Celso, (SSP), 191 Battersea Bridge Rd, London SW11 3AS **Tel:** 020 7228 2656 **Fax:** 020 7228 1656 **E-mail:** cgodilano@stpauls.ph

Goergen, David, Provincial Treasurer (MAfr), 42 Stormont Rd, Highgate, London N6 4NP **Tel:** 020-8348 6796 **Fax:** 020-8347 8147 **E-mail:** mafrukpt@blueyonder.co.uk

Golding, Dominic, JV, JCL, KHS (Portsmouth), St James Presbytery, Abbey Ruins, Forbury Rd, Reading, Berks RG1 3HW **Tel:** 0118-957 4171 **Fax:** 0118-956 1171 **E-mail:** parishpriest@jameswilliam-reading.org.uk

Gonella, Agostino, Mgr, (Alba), 197 Durants Rd, Enfield, Middx EN3 7DE **Tel:** 020-8804 2307

Gonella, Giorgio, Italian Catholic Mission, 68 Little Horton Ln, Bradford BD5 0HU **Tel:** 01274-721612

Good, Kevin James, Canon, (Birmingham, retired), St Anne, Lynton Avenue, Weeping Cross, Baswich, Stafford ST17 0EA **Tel:** 01785-661012

Goodall, Francis (CSsR), Our Lady's, Bishop Elton, Woolton Rd, Liverpool L16 8NQ **Tel:** 0151-722 1108 **Fax:** 0151-738 0834

Gooden, Peter, (Salford), St John Fisher, Mancunian Rd, Haughton Green, Denton, Manchester M34 7WN **Tel:** 0161-336 2625 **Fax:** 0161-336 2964

Goodill, David (OP), Priory of the Holy Spirit, 64 St Giles, Oxford OX1 3LY **Tel:** 01865 278400

Goodman, Andrew D, STB, (Clifton), 44 St Gregory's Avenue, Salisbury SP2 7JP **Tel:** 01722 334496

Goodman, Stephen John BSc (Dunelm) (Birmingham), The Island, Willenhall Rd, Wolverhampton WV1 2QN **Tel:** 01902-452841

Goodwin, David, Canon, BEd, ACP, (Birmingham, retired), St John's Presbytery, Loomer Rd, Chesterton, Staffordshire ST5 7JS **Tel:** 01782-561600

Goonan, Thomas, BA, (SM), St Oswald's Church, 126 Southend Rd, Wybourn, Sheffield, S2 5FT **Tel:** 0114-272 3881 **Fax:** 0114-272 5760

Gora, John, "Ave Maria", Portsmouth Rd, Milford, Godalming, Surrey GU8 5AU **Tel:** 01483-420265

Gordon, Donald J, (Liverpool, retired), Flat 5, Alston Court, 483 Liverpool Rd, Ainsdale, Southport PR8 3PB **Tel:** 01704-570383

Gordon, Edwin, LLB, (Clifton, retired), c/o St Ambrose, North Rd, Leigh Woods, Bristol BS8 3PW

Gordon, John F, Canon, (Shrewsbury), St Chad's, Stockport Rd, Cheadle SK8 2AF **Tel:** 0161-428 2480

Gordon, Maurice, (Brentwood), The Presbytery, 132 Shernhall St, Walthamstow, London E17 9HU **Tel:** 020-8520 5877

Gore, Simon, (Liverpool), St Judes Presbytery, Poolstock Ln, Worsley Mesnes, Wigan WN3 5JE **Tel:** 01842 244864

Gorham, Timothy, STB (OSB), Ealing Abbey, Charlbury Grove, London W5 2DY **Tel:** 020-8862 2100

Gorman, Brendan, (Northampton), The Presbytery, Harrowden Rd, Bedford

MK42 0SP **Tel:** 01234-267714 **E-mail:** BrendanG@btinternet.com

Gorman, John (Liverpool), Chaplain Broadgreen Hosp. Our Lady's Parish House, Chestnut Grove, Wavertree, Liverpool L15 8HS **Tel:** 0151-522 9276

Gornall, Edmund, (Lancaster), St Gregory's, Furness Rd, Workington CA14 3PD **Tel:** 01900 603800 **E-mail:** Ed@etgo.freeserve.co.uk

Gormley, Francis (OMI), St Teresa of the Child Jesus, Sedgemoor Rd, Norris Green, Liverpool L11 3BW **Tel:** 0151-226 1354 **Fax:** 0151-270 2665 **E-mail:** oblate@norris3.freeserve.co.uk

Gorst, Christopher BA (OSB), Ampleforth Abbey, York YO62 4EN **Tel:** 01439 766714 **Fax:** 01439 766724

Gorton, Christopher, B.Mus, BA, PGCE, Chaplain to Manchester Metropolitan University and Royal Northern College of Music (Salford), St Augustine's, Grosvenor Square, All Saints, Manchester M15 6BW **Tel:** 0161-236 6762 **Fax:** 0161-228 1516 **E-mail:** augustines@eggconnect.net

Gosling, Martin P, MA, (OPraem), Our Lady of England Priory, School Ln, Storrington, W. Sussex **Tel:** 01903-742150 **Fax:** 01903-740821 **E-mail:** norbertines@pavilion.co.uk

Gosnell, Nicholas, BTh, MA (Westminster), 8 Keogh Cl, Mytchett, Hants GU12 5RJ

Gosselin, Lawrence (US Forces), Major USAF, 100 ARW/HC, RAF Mildenhall, Bury St Edmunds, Suffolk IP28 8NF

Gostling, Gerald, BA, CertEd, (Brentwood), c/o The Bishop of Dundee, PO Box 83, Dundee 3000, Natal, South Africa **Mbl:** (for text messages only) 0027 7778-158965 **E-mail:** catholic.church@secunda.co.za

Gostomski, Bronislaw, Mgr Canon (Polish Priest), 1 Lyesfield Rd, Shepherd's Bush, London W12 9JF **Tel:** 020-8743 8848

Gott, John J, (Leeds), Good Shepherd Presbytery, Royal Fold, New Rd, Mytholmroyd HX7 5EA **Tel:** 01422-886189 **E-mail:** goodshepherd@iclways.co.uk

Goulbourn, Francis, (Liverpool, retired), Ince Blundell Hall, Ince Blundell, Liverpool L38 6JL **Tel:** 0151 929 2596

Gould, Robert D, (Southwark), 15 Up, The Quadrangle, Morden College, London SE3 0PW **Tel:** 020-8293 4970

Goward, Giles C, BSc, MA, (Birmingham), The Presbytery, 2 South View Avenue, Caversham RG4 0AB **Tel:** 0118-947 1787 **E-mail:** st.anne@virgin.net

Gowers, Stephen, (OCSO), Our Lady and St Bernard, Mount St Bernard Abbey, Coalville, Leicester LE67 5UL **Tel:** 01530-832298/832022

Gowkielewicz, Andrzej, (MIC), (Pol 3) 2 Windsor Rd, London W5 5PD **Tel:** 020-8567 1746 **Fax:** 020-8810 0185

Gowman, Martin R, MA, ARCO (OSB), Downside Abbey, Stratton on the Fosse, Radstock BA3 4RH

Grace, Anthony (MSC), St Gabriel's, 140 Lawton Road, Alsager, Cheshire ST7 2DE **Tel:** 01270-872542 **E-mail:** stvincentdepaul@btconnect.com

Grady, Brendan, (OCarm), The Friars, Aylesford, Kent ME20 7BX **Tel:** 01622 717272

Grady, Francis, MA (Birmingham, retired), 6 Thyme Grove, Meir Park, Stoke-on-Trent ST3 7YF **Tel:** 01782-393721

Grady, John, (Liverpool, retired), 62 Swinley Ln, Wigan WN1 2EB **Tel:** 01942-494163

Grady, Sean, (Birmingham), Our Lady of Lourdes, 222 Trittiford Rd, Yardley Wood, Birmingham B13 0EU **Tel:** 0121-444 5106 **Fax:** 0121-444 0662

Graffy, Adrian, DSS, STB, PhL, (Brentwood), Clergy Ho, 28 Ingrave Rd, Brentwood, Essex CM15 8AT **Tel:** 01277-265243

Graham, David, (Liverpool), Lower Strenaby, Abbeylands, Isle of Man IM4 5EF **Tel:** 01624-626091

Graham, Donald, (Westminster), 177 Bow Rd, London E3 2SG **Tel:** 020-8980 3961

Graham, Francis (MHM), Tenter Ho, 17 Tenter Terr, Durham City DH1 4RD **Tel:** 0191-384 5626

Graham, Paul, STB, MA, (OSA), St Monica's Priory, 19 Hoxton Square, London N1 6NT **Tel:** 020-7739 5006 **Fax:** 020-7613 0394 **E-mail:** pvgraham@gmail.com

Grant, Barry, Parochial Administrator (Southwark), The Priest's Ho, High St, Cranbrook, Kent TN17 3DT **Tel:** 01580 713364

Grant, David, (Middlesbrough), Our Lady & St Peter, 32 Victoria Rd, Bridlington YO15 2AT **Tel:** 01262-673696

Grant, Gregory A, (Clifton), St Patrick's Presbytery, Dillon Court, Redfield, Bristol BS5 9PF **Tel:** 0117-955 7662 **Fax:** 0117-941 4156 **E-mail:** stpatricks@mail.com

Grant, Owen (MHM), Herbert Ho, 41 Victoria Rd, Freshfield, Merseyside L37 1LW **Tel:** 01704-835677

Grant, Patrick, (Middlesbrough, retired), 15 Well Field, Kilkee, Co Clare, Éire

Grant, Peter John, Mgr (Leeds, retired), 2 Hinsley Court Leeds LS6 2HB

Grant, Peter, (Westminster), Sacred Heart Church, Park St, Berkhamsted HP4 1HX **Tel:** 01442-863845

G

Grant-Ferris, Piers, DipEd(OSB), c/o Ampleforth Abbey, York YO62 4EN **Tel:** 01439 766714

Gray, Brian, (Cardiff), St Cadoc's Presbytery, Parracombe Cres, Llanrumney, Cardiff CF3 5LT **Tel:** 029-2077 8038 **E-mail:** pp@stcadocs.org

Gray, John, (Westminster), The Presbytery, King Edward's Rd, Ware SG12 7EJ **Tel:** 020-8902 0081

Gray, Reginald, (OFM), Franciscan Friary, Marine Hill, Clevedon, N Somerset BS21 7PP **Tel:** 01275-873205 **Fax:** 01275-349001 **E-mail:** reg@friar.org

Graydon, Andrew, (Hallam), The Presbytery, 1 Swinston Hill Road, Dinnington, Sheffield S25 7RX **Tel:** 01909 562664 **E-mail:** andyaj_98@yahoo.com

Graystone, Geoffrey, DSS (SM), Marist Fathers, 109 Main Rd, Sidcup, Kent DA14 6ND **Tel:** 020-8302 6463 **Fax:** 020-8309 7656

Graystone, Henry, MA, BA, (SM), St Mary's Retreat, Union St, Carmarthen **Tel:** 01267-237205

Graystone, Philip, MA, (SM), Marist Fathers, Half Moon Ho, 12 Hindringham Rd, Great Walsingham, Norfolk NR22 6DR **Tel:** 01328-820588

Greaney, Christopher, BA, STB (Birmingham), The Presbytery, 142 Oxford Rd, Kidlington, Oxon OX5 1DZ **Tel:** 01865-377093 **Fax:** 01865-842265

Greasley, Patrick, (Salford), St Anne's, 1043 Chester Rd, Stretford, Manchester M32 8LF **Tel:** 0161-865 2079

Grech, Saviour (Westminster), 59 Gresham Rd, Staines, Middx TW18 2BD **Tel:** 01784-452381

Green, Bernard, MA, MPhil, (OSB), St Benet's Hall, Oxford, 38 St Giles, Oxford OX1 3LN **Tel/Fax:** 01865-280556

Green, Brian, (Hallam), 1 Swinston Hill Rd, Dinnington, Sheffield S31 7RX **Tel:** 01909-562664

Green, Julian, (Birmingham), 29 Harrisons Rd, Edgbaston B15 3QR **Tel:** 0121-454 4395 **E-mail:** julian.green@blueyonder.co.uk

Greener, Christopher BA (OSB), Douai Abbey, Upper Woolhampton, Reading, Berks RG7 5TQ **Tel:** 0118-971 5300 **Fax:** 0118-971 5303

Greenwood, Alban, BA, (Shrewsbury), St Patrick, King St, Wellington, Telford TF1 3AP **Tel:** 01952-242423 **E-mail:** admin@stpatrickstelford.com

Greenwood, Paulinus, BA, PGCE, MIL, SMIC (OSB), St Augustine's Abbey, Ramsgate, Kent CT11 9PA **Tel:** 01843-593045 **Fax:** 01843-582732

Grenfell, Julian BA (OSB), c/o Buckfast Abbey, Buckfastleigh, Devon TQ11 0EE **Tel:** 01364-645500 **Fax:** 01364-643891

Gregory, Philip (Liverpool), Holy Family Presbytery, 1 Brompton Rd, Southport PR8 6AS **Tel:** 01704-532613

Gribben, Emmanuel J, BA, (Lancaster), St Mary's, Cleator CA23 3AB **Tel:** 01946-810324

Gribbin, Hugh, MA, (SM), Marist Fathers, 76 Newland Park, Hull HU5 2DS **Tel:** 01482-444180

Griffin, Austin, (Liverpool), St Teresa, 34 Queensway, Penwortham, Preston, Lancs PR1 0DS **Tel/Fax:** 01772-743337

Griffin, J M (Provincial) (MSFS), St Joseph's Presbytery, St Joseph's Place, Devizes, Wiltshire SN10 1DD **Tel:** 01380-723572 **Fax:** 01380-723377 **E-mail:** coladh@yahoo.com

Griffin, James, 13/19 Portland Gardens, Edinburgh EH6 6NY **Tel:** 0131 553 1216

Griffin, Kevin, STB (Salford), St John Vianney, 355 Livesey Branch Rd, Blackburn, BB2 4QJ **Tel:** 01254-201430

Griffin, Kevin, (Arundel & Brighton), Priest's Cottage, Queen's Rd, Chapel Green, Crowborough, E Sussex TN6 2LB **Tel:** 01892-654608

Griffin, Martin, (MSFS), St Francis de Sales, 16 Wellington Rd, Hampton Hill, Middx TW12 1JR **Tel:** 020-8977 1415 **Fax:** 020-8943 9593 **E-mail:** msfs@globalnet.co.uk

Griffin, Michael, (East Anglia), The Presbytery, Newmarket Rd, Kirtling, Cambridgeshire CB8 9PA **Tel/Fax:** 01638-730603

Griffin, Nigel, BSc, FRSA (Westminster), 207 Nelson Rd, Whitton, Twickenham TW2 7BB **Tel:** 020-8241 2941

Griffin, Philip J, MA(Oxon), (Birmingham), Holy Trinity Presbytery, London Rd, Newcastle-under-Lyme ST5 1LQ **Tel:** 01782-616483

Griffin, Vincent, (CSSp, retired), 6 Woodlands Rd, Bickley, Bromley, Kent **Tel:** 020-8467 3555

Griffiths, Alan, Canon (Portsmouth), 1 Grange Road, Alresford, Hants PO30 1UH **E-mail:** alngriffiths@aol.com

Griffiths, Antony, Canon, (Northampton, retired), 5a Pugin Ho, St Peter St, Marlow, Bucks SL7 1NQ **Tel:** 01628-483696

Griffiths, Benjamin, (Leeds), Priest's Ho, Ebor Ln, Haworth, Keighley BD22 2HR **Tel:** 01535-643240

Griffiths, Brian (OSCarm) 102 Hassell Rd E9 5SJ; also St Joseph's Hospice, Mare St, London E8 4SA **Tel:** 020-8985 0861

Griffiths, Gregory, (Southwark), 7 St Bride's Cl, Erith DA18 4DT **Tel:** 020-8310 0534

Griffiths, Iain (Shrewsbury), St John's, 13 Northgate, Bridgnorth WV16 4ER **Tel:** 01746-762348 **Fax:** 01928-580800 **E-mail:** iaingriffiths@hotmail.com

Griffiths, John G, (Cardiff), St Helen's Church, Nantgarw Rd, Caerphilly CF83 3FB **Tel:** 02920-883192

Griffiths, Liam, (SSC), St Columban's, Widney Manor Rd, Knowle, Solihull, W Mids B93 9AB **Tel:** 01564-772096

Griffiths, Michael, (Northampton), Our Lady's Presbytery, 52 Castle St, Luton LU1 3AG **Tel:** 01582-723254 **Fax:** 01582-451840

Griffiths, Michael J, (Hexham & Newcastle), St Joseph. Durham Rd, Ushaw Moor, Durham DH7 7LF **Tel:** 0191-373 0219

Grimes, Damian MA, EdBDip, MBE (MHM), 1 Eglwys y Bugail Da (Good Shepherd), Talybont Rd, Llanrwst LL26 0AU **Tel:** 01492-642677 **Mbl:** 07766 962467 **E-mail:** damian@goodshepherd.freeserve.co.uk

Grimshaw, Anthony J, (Salford), St Mary, Longridge Rd, Chipping, Preston PR3 2QD **Tel:** 01995 61238

Grogan, Bernard, (SDB), Salesiani, Via della Pisana 1111, CP 18333, 00163 Rome Italy **Tel:** 00-396 656121 **Fax:** 00-396 65612 556

Grogan, Paul, STL (Leeds), All Saints College, Brownberrie Ln, Horsforth, Leeds LS18 5HD **Tel:** 0113-283 7201 **E-mail:** paul.grogan4@btinternet.com

Groody, Peter, (Lancaster), c/o Pastoral Centre, Balmoral Road, Lancaster LA1 3BT

Growney, Bernard, (Liverpool), Poor Sisters of Nazareth, Nazareth Ho, Liverpool Rd, Liverpool L23 0QT **Tel:** 0151 928 2896

Growney, Peter, (Perth), The Presbytery, Bicknor Road, Maidstone Kent ME15 9PS

Grufferty, Thomas, (Portsmouth), The Presbytery, 134 West St, Havant, Hants PO9 1LP **Tel:** 023-9248 4520 **Fax:** 023-9278 7774 **E-mail:** tom.grufferty@ntlworld.com

Grugan, Aelred (OSB). St Mary's, High Rd, Whitehaven, Cumbria CA28 9PG **Tel:** 01946-692757

Grumitt, John (SJ), Corpus Christi, 757 Christchurch Rd, Boscombe, Bournemouth BH7 6AN **Tel:** 01202 436700

Grundy, Thomas, (Portsmouth, retired), McAuley Mount, Park Hill, Padiham Rd, Burnley, Lancs BB12 6TG

Gruszkiewicz, Josef, (Warmia), 83 Bramsdean Dr, Havant, Hants PO9 4RR **Mbl:** 07880-541377 **E-mail:** frjoe@btopenworld.com

Grzymala, Kazimierz, (MIC), Fawley Court, Henley-on-Thames, Oxon RG9 3AE **Tel:** 01491-574917

Gubbins, Edmond, Canon, DipTheol, (Middlesbrough), St Andrew, 1 Bondfield Rd, Teesville, Middlesbrough TS6 9BA **Tel:** 01642-453556 **Fax:** 01642 455441 **Email:** eddiegubbins@middlesbrough-diocese.org.uk

Guest, Bernard (CMF), 99 Alexandra Rd, Gorseinon, Swansea SA4 4NX **Tel:** 01792-892722

Guest, John, BA, STL, PHL, VG (Nottingham), 23 Belle Vue Rd, Ashbourne, Derbyshire DE6 1AT **Tel:** 01335-342236

Guiver, Roger (Middlesbrough), St Alban, 3 Yew Tree Avenue, Redcar TS10 4QN **Tel:** 01642-485901

Gula, Józef, PhD (SChr), (Southwork, retired), St John's Hall, Ravenna Road, London SW15 6AW

Gullan-Steel, Stuart, BD, (Westminster), 21 Main St, Ravene, New York 12143 **Tel:** 581 756 3145

Gummett, David, (Southwark), 218 Roehampton Ln, Roehampton SW15 4LE **Tel:** 020-8788 5012

Gunn, John, (Birmingham), St Ambrose Barlow, Lakey Ln, Hall Green, Birmingham B28 8QU **Tel:** 0121-777 4524 **E-mail:** sjoeroe@aol.com

Gunn, Timothy, (Salford, retired), Lyre, Lisselton, Co. Kerry, Eire **Tel:** 0161-748 4844

Gunning, Thomas K, (Clifton), St John's Presbytery, South Parade, Bath BA2 4AF **Tel:** 01225-464471 **Fax:** 01225-462614

Gurr, P Austin, MA, (OSB), St Gregory's Priory, Welcombe Rd, Stratford-upon-Avon CV37 6UJ **Tel:** 01789-292439 **Fax:** 01789-267852

Gutowski, Mariusz, MA (SChr) (Polish Priest), 1 Battisson Cres, Longton, Stoke-on-Trent ST3 4DS **Tel:** 01782-343455

Guziel, Anton, STB, (Birmingham), Presbytery, Watkin St, Fenton, Stoke-on-Trent ST4 4PF **Tel:** 01785-414071

Gwinnell, Michael, (Southwark, retired), 1 Chestnut Grove, New Malden, Surrey KT3 3JS **Tel:** 020-8949 3618

Gwinnett, Francis, BA, (Birmingham, retired), 1a Castlecroft Ln, Wightwick, Wolverhampton WV3 8JX **Tel:** 01902-765269

Gynn, Thomas, (SSP), 6 Woodlands Rd, Hadlow, BR1 2AF **Tel:** 020-8467 3555

Habron, Matthew, (Leeds) St Austin's Presbytery, 6 Wentworth Terr, Wakefield WF1 3QN **Tel:** 01924-372080 **Fax:** 01924-215723

Hackeson, Mark, LLB(Hons), STB (East Anglia), The Lodge, 17 Upgate, Poringland, Norwich NR14 7SH **Tel:** 01508-493919/492202

Fax: 01508-495358
E-mail: mhackeson@east-angliadiocese.org.uk

Hackett, Peter (SJ), Corpus Christi, 757 Christchurch Rd, Boscombe, Bournemouth, Dorset BH7 6AN **Tel:** 01202-436700 **Fax:** 01202-436730 **E-mail:** hackpete2001@yahoo.co.uk

Hadley, John, MA, BSc, STL VF (Nottingham), St Pius X Presbytery, 52 Leicester Rd, Narborough, Leics LE9 5DF **Tel:** 0116-286 3676 **Fax:** 0116-284 9021

Haffner, Paul, PhB, MA, STD (Portsmouth), Salita di Monte del Gallo 23, 00165 Roma, Italia **Tel:** 0039 06 635 643 **E-mail:** haffner@unigle.it

Hagan, Kentigern BA (OSB), Ampleforth Abbey, York YO62 4EN **Tel:** 01439-766714 **Fax:** 01439-766724

Hagen, Richard (CSSR), The Redemptorist Mission Team, The Monastery, Badby Rd West, Daventry, Northants NN11 4NH

Hagerty, Michael, (Cardiff), All Saints, Tredegar Rd, Ebbw Vale NP23 6JQ **Tel:** 01495-302243

Haggerty, Kevin Canon, PhB, MA, STL, PGCE(A), (Southwark), 11 Flaxman Dr, Maidstone, Kent, ME16 0RU **Tel:** 07958 310210

Hahesy, Bernard, (Plymouth), The Presbytery, Home Park Avenue, Peverell, Plymouth PL3 4PG **Tel:** 01752-665406

Haigh, Martin, MA, TD, (OSB), St Mary's, Brdfield Dr, Leyland, Preston PR25 1PD **Tel:** 01772-421183 **Fax:** 01772-621183

Hain, Antony BA (OSB), Ampleforth Abbey, York YO62 4EN **Tel:** 01439-766714 **Fax:** 01439-766724

Hale, Anthony, (CP), Our Lady Help of Christians, Madeira Rd, West Byfleet, Surrey KT14 6DH **Tel:** 01932-342892 **Fax:** 01932-354523

Hale, Kevin, (Brentwood), 1 Cliffsea Grove, Leigh-on-Sea, Essex SS9 1NG **Tel:** 01702-478078

Hall, Denis J, (Brentwood), 56 St Antony's Rd, Forest Gate, London E7 9QB **Tel:** 020-8472 0433

Hall, Michael (Leeds), 12 Smith Ho Ln, Brighouse HD6 2JY **Tel:** 01484-711713

Hall, Peter (OFM), The Friary, Sample Oak Ln, Chilworth, Guildford GU4 8QR **Tel:** 01483-893168 **Fax:** 01483-898071

Hall, Sean, BA, MA, PhD, (Hexham & Newcastle), St Bede's New Rd, Coach Rd Estate, Washington, Tyne & Wear NE37 2HE **Tel:** 0191-416 3805

Hall, Simon (Arundel & Brighton), 14 Haslett Avenue West, Crawley, W Sussex RH10 1HR **Tel:** 01293-524176

Hall, Simon, STB (Birmingham), The Presbytery, 273 Wellington Rd, Perry Barr, Birmingham B20 2QQ **Tel:** 0121-356 4402 **Fax:** 0121-356 4199

Hallett, Barry, (Plymouth), The Presbytery, 2a Archway Rd, Parkstone, Poole, Dorset BH14 9AZ **Tel:** 01202-746539

Hallinan, Charles, MA, (OSB), Worth Abbey, Crawley, W Sussex RH10 4SB **Tel:** 01342-710310

Halpenny, James, (Hallam), 44 Warmsworth Rd, Balby, Doncaster DN4 0RR **Tel:** 01302-853937

Halshaw, Robert T, (Lancaster), c/o Principal RC Chaplain (RAF), Chaplaincy Office, RAF Halton, Aylesbury, Bucks HP22 5PG **Tel:** 01296 656910

Halton, Edward (Middlesbrough), The Monastery of Our Lady of Mount Grace, 18 North End, Osmotherley, Northallerton, N Yorks DL6 3BB **Tel:** 01609-883308 **Fax:** 01609-883740

Hamielec, Augustyn, (MS), 52 Goresbrook Rd, Dagenham, Essex RM9 6UR **Tel:** 020-8595 1227

Hamill, Bob, (Brentwood), 1 Ullswater Way, Elm Park, Hornchurch, Essex RM12 5JX **Tel:** 01708-451449

Hamill, Gerard, (MHM), All Saints Presbytery, 622 Liverpool St, Salford M5 5HQ **Tel:** 0161 737 9742 **Mbl:** 07867 895888 **E-mail:** gerardhamill@msn.com

Hamill, Harold E, (Westminster, retired), 3 Copper Beeches, Witham Rd, Osterley, Middx TW7 4AW **Tel:** 020-8568 6581

Hamill, Paul, (SJ), *Asst to the Provincial,* 221 Goldhurst Terr, Hampstead, London NW6 3EP **E-mail:** socius@gbsj.org

Hamilton, Robert Douglas, (CJ), Our Lady Immaculate, 636 Commercial Rd, Limehouse, London E14 7HS **Tel:** 020-7987 3563 **Fax:** 020-7536 9043

Hamilton-Gray, Christopher, BA, BSc, DipTh, (Westminster), Chaplain Whittington Hosp, Catholic Church, Crown Rise, Garston, Watford, Herts WD2 6NE **Tel:** 01923-673239

Hancock, Christpher, (MHM), Procura Generale dei Missionari di Mill Hill, Via Innoceazo X, 16 00152 Roma Italy **Tel:** 0039 06 5810330

Hancock, John, (Birmingham), Blessed Dominic Barberi. The Barbieri Rectory, 2 St Mary's Cl, Littlemore, Oxford OX4 4PJ **Tel/Fax:** 01865-778454 Office **Tel:** 01865-775591

Handforth, Christopher Thomas, (Birmingham), 297 Oldbury Rd, Rowley Regis, Blackheath B65 0PR **Tel:** 0121-559 1677

Handing, John, Canon (Clifton), Flat D, St John's Flats, South Parade, Bath BA2 4AF

Hanley, Hugh, (SCJ), c/o Provincial House,

266 Wellington Road North, Stockport, SK4 2QR
Hanlon, Gerard John, Canon (Birmingham), 39 Whetstone Ln, Aldridge WS9 0JDG **Tel:** 01922-452316
Hanlon, G E, (Leeds), Vicariato Apostolico, de Iquitos, Celle Putamayo 324, Aportado 108, Iquitos, Peru **Tel:** 00-51- 234 465
Hanly, William (SCA), 358 Greenford Rd, Greenford, Middx UB6 9AN **Tel:** 020-8578 1363
Hannah, Peter, (Liverpool), The Parish Ho, 179 Derbyshire Hill Rd, St Helens WA9 2LS **Tel:** 01744-22972 **Fax:** 01744-26377
Hannigan, James, (Nottingham, retired), The Sycamores, Mullagh Rd, Virginia, Co Cavan, Ireland
Hannigan, Neil, (Westminster), 131 Glenarm Rd, London E5 0NB **Tel:** 020-8525 1929
Hanrahan, Desmond, BSc (SM), St Mark's Retreat, Union St, Carmarthen SA31 3DE **Tel:** 01267-237205 **E-mail:** stmarys.retreat@virgin.net
Hanratty, Sean (Nottingham), St Francis of Assisi Presbytery, 199 Tamworth Road, Long Eaton, Derbys NG10 1DH **Tel:** 0115-973 4816 **Fax:** 0115-946 2483
Hanvey, James (SJ), Copleston Ho, 221 Goldhurst Terr, London NW6 3EP **Tel:** 020 7795 4231 **Fax:** 020 7604 5850 **E-mail:** james.hanvey@lineone.net
Haran, Patrick, (Southwark, retired), Churchfield Rd, Knock, Claremorris, Co Mayo, Ireland
Harbert, Bruce, MA, STL, MPhil, (Birmingham), ICEL, 1522 K St NW Suite 1000, Washington DC 20005, USA
Hardaker, Stephen (Arundel & Brighton), 21 Derby Rd, Haslemere, Surrey GU27 1BS **Tel:** 01428 643877
Harden, Andrzej (SJ), 182 Walm Ln, London NW2 3AX **Tel:** 020-8452 4304 **Fax:** 020-8450 8449
Harding, John Anthony, MLitt, PhD, (Clifton), St Bernadette's Presbytery, Wells Rd, Bristol BS14 9HU **Tel:** 01275-833699
Harding Rees, D (Menevia), St Michael's Rectory, 11 St Michael St, Brecon, Powys LD3 9AB **Tel:** 01874-622046
Hardstaff, Rev Richard (Nottingham), St Mary's, Countesthorpe Rd, South Wigton, Leicestershire LE18 4PG **Tel:** 0116-278 3863 **Fax:** 0116-278 5546
Hardwicke, J Owen, (Wrexham, retired), 1 Bury St, Wrexham LL13 8NS **Tel/Fax:** 01978- 312375
Hardy, Martin, (East Anglia), c/o The White Ho, 21 Upgate, Poringland, Norwich NR14 7SH
Hardy, Paul, (Northampton), St Edward, Burchard Cres, Shenley Church End, Milton Keynes MK5 6DX **Tel/Fax:** 01908-504771 **E-mail:** vine01@btopenworld.com
Hare, Dennis, P, (IC), Grace Dieu Manor School, Coalville, Leicestershire LE67 5UG. **Tel/Fax:** 01530-224140 **E-mail:** dennis.ic@btinternet.com
Hare, Michael, MA, (IC), 3 Gray St, Loughborough LE11 2DZ **Tel:** 01509 260304 **Fax:** 01509 267059
Hargan, Michael (OFM Cap), Franciscan Friary, Carlton Rd, Erith, Kent DA8 1DN **Tel:** 01322-433193
Hargreaves, Geoffrey, (CHS), Holy Trinity Presbytery, Oxford St, Bilston WV14 7EL **Tel:** 01902-493549
Hargreaves, Gerald, (Leeds, retired), 6 Hinsley Court, 62 Headingley Ln, Leeds
Hargreaves, Mark, Rt Rev (Abbot Emeritus) (OSB), Prinknash Abbey, Cranham, Gloucester GL4 8EX **Tel:** 01452-812455 **Fax:** 01452-813305 **E-mail:** prinknash@waitrose.com
Harkness, Eugene, Mgr, (East Anglia), St Philip Howard, Walpole Rd, Cambridge CB1 3TH **Tel/Fax:** 01223-211235
Harkness, James (SJ), Corpus Christi Jesuit Community, 757 Christchurch Rd, Boscombe, Bournmouth BH7 6AN **Tel:** 01202 436700 **E-mail:** james_harkness_sj@yahoo.com
Harnan, Nick, (MSC), St Mary Mother of God, Kennelwood Avenue, Northwood, Kirkby, Liverpool L33 6UF **Tel:** 0151-546 3838 **Fax:** 0151-548 6509 **E-mail:** materdei_uk@yahoo.co.uk
Harnett, Patrick, (SCJ), St Robert Bellarmine, 52 Orrell Rd, Bootle L20 6DZ **Tel/Fax:** 0151-922 1352
Harney, Gerard, (Hallam), St Ann's Presbytery, Deepcar, Sheffield S36 2QQ **Tel:** 0114-288 2187
Harney, V Rev Patrick, (Middlesbrough retired), Comeragh, 106 Lawrence St, York YO10 3EB **Tel:** 01904 422387
Haro, Sergio, (SDB), Rinaldi Ho, 32 Orbel St, Battersea, London SW11 3NZ **Tel:** 020-7801 9040 **Fax:** 020-7801 9041
Harold, Mark, BA, STL (Salford), Ven Collegio Inglese, via di Monserrato 45, 00186 Roma, Italia. **Tel:** 06 686 4185
Harries, Peter, (OP), St Dominic's Priory, Southampton Rd, London, NW5 4LB **Tel:** 020-7482 9216
Harrington, Dunstan, FCII (Liverpool) The Presbytery, 74 Edge Ln, Thornton, Liverpool L23 4TG **Tel:** 0151-931 4993 **Fax:** 0151-932 0413
Harrington, Francis, (Arundel & Brighton), The Priest's Ho, St Paul's Rd, Woking GU22 7DZ **Tel:** 01483-760652

Harrington, John Basil, (Birmingham), St Patrick's, Blue Ln East, Walsall, WS2 8HN **Tel:** 01922-623823

Harrington, Niall, (Brentwood), 116 Melbourne Avenue, Chelmsford, Essex CM1 2DU **Tel:** 01245-354256

Harrington, Thomas, (Westminster, retired), Marian Ho, 100 Kingston Ln, Uxbridge UB8 3PW

Harrington, Timothy, Canon (Shrewsbury, retired), Ballygriffin, Kenmare, Co Kerry, Éire **Tel:** 00353 64 41264

Harriott, Richard B, (Hexham & Newcastle), St John the Baptist, Annitsford, Cramlington, Northumberland NE23 7QR **Tel:** 0191-250 0200

Harris, Anthony (Northampton, retired), 3 Woburn Court, Vincent Rd, Luton LU4 9BB **Tel:** 01582 507778

Harris, Anthony J, Mgr, (SCA), 514 Longbridge Rd, Barking, Essex IG11 9BY **Tel:** 020-8590 2191

Harris, Dyfrig, (OSB), Belmont Abbey, Hereford HR2 9RXZ **Tel:** 01432-277388

Harris, Frank, (Plymouth), 4 Gwel Marten, Headland Rd, Carbis Bay, St Ives, Cornwall TR26 2PB **Tel:** 01736 793280

Harris, Jack, (CM), 2 Flower Lane, London NW7 2JB **Tel:** 020 8959 1021

Harris, John, (FCA), Holy Spirit, 66/68 Sterrix Ln, Litherland, Liverpool L21 0DA **Tel:** 0151-928 0040 **Fax:** 0151 928 0040

Harris, John D, (Northampton, retired), 7 Lumbertubs Rise, Bouthville, Northants NN3 6AJ **Tel:** 01604-492899

Harris, Luke, (OCSO), Our Lady and St Bernard, Mount St Bernard Abbey, Coalville, Leicester LE67 5UL **Tel:** 01530-832298/832022

Harris, Peter, BEd, MTh (Westminster), 297 Westferry Rd, London E14 3RS **Tel:** 020-7987 4114

Harris, Phillip, The Persbytery, Queen's Road, Aberystwyth, Ceredigion SY23 2HS **Tel:** 01970 612549 **Email:** parishofaberystwyth@btinternet.com

Harrison, Alfred, (WF), 37 Victoria Parade, Ashton, Preston PR2 1DT **Tel:** 01772-722378

Harrison, Daniel, (Leeds), St Mary's Presbytery, Brdgate Ln, Horsforth, Leeds LS18 4AG **Tel:** 0113-258 2607

Harrison, Ignatius, (Cong Orat), The Oratory, Brompton Rd, London SW7 2RP **Tel:** 020-7589 4811

Harrison, Jude, Canon, (Salford), St Alban's, Larkhill, Blackburn BB1 6HY **Tel:** 01254-59331, **Fax:** 01254-668102.

Harrison, Michael, (Northampton), St Thomas Aquinas Presbytery, 1 Sycamore Avenue, Bletchley, Milton Keynes MK2 2JE **Tel:** 01908-372315 **E-mail:** michael@staq.freeserve.co.uk

Harrison, Paul, MA, (Lancaster), The Presbytery, 13 Margate Street, Walney, LA14 3AF. **Tel:** 01229 471405

Harrison, William (SDS), Our Lady's, Lapwing Grove, Palace Fields, Runcorn WA7 2TP **Tel:** 01928 717114 **E-mail:** w.harrison@talk21.com

Harrity, Patrick, Superior (MAfr), 37 Victoria Parade, Ashton-on-Ribble, Preston PR2 1DT **Tel:** 01722-722378 **Fax:** 01722-729414 **E-mail:** mafr@preston39.freeserve.co.uk

Harrop, Philip, BEd (Birmingham), Our Lady of the Angels, Coton Rd, Nuneaton, Warwickshire CV22 5UA **Tel:** 024-7638 2139

Harrow, Reg. c/o Bishop's Ho, Marriott St, Northampton NN2 6AW

Hart, Austin, (Westminster, retired), Nazareth Ho, 162 East End Rd, London N2 0RU **Tel:** 020-8883 1104

Hart, David, (Brentwood) c/o Cathedral Ho, Ingrave Rd, Brentwood, Essex CM15 8AT

Hart, Jean (SOLT), 2 Lower Blackhorse Hill, Hythe CT21 5LS **Tel:** 01303-26430 **Fax:** 01303-264773

Hart, Jonathan, (Leeds), St Peter's Presbytery, 651 Leeds Rd, Bradford BD3 8EL **Tel:** 01274-664380 **E-mail:** jonathan@hartone.freeserve.co.uk

Hart, Karl, (Liverpool), c/o Liverpool Archdiocesan Centre for Evengelisation, Croxteth Dr, Liverpool L17 1AA

Hart, Peter, (Lancaster), St Cuthbert, Burnfoot, Wigton CA7 9HU **Tel:** 01697-342379

Hart, Peter, (Portsmouth), 59 Normandy St, Alton GU34 1DN **Tel:** 01420-82020 **Fax:** 01420-85821 **E-mail:** pghart@onetel.net

Hartcher, Allan, Franciscan Study Centre, Giles Ln, Canterbury CT2 7NA **Tel:** 01227 452822/459465

Hartford, James, (OMI), Rushmere, 32 Allanson Rd, Rhos-on-Sea, Conwy, North Wales LL28 4HL **Tel:** 01492-545241

Hartley, David Michael, BA (Birmingham), 20 Bickerton Rd, Headington, Oxford OX3 7LS **Tel:** 01865-434480

Hartley, Edmund, (Southwark), St Joseph, 2 Ashley Avenue, Folkestone, Kent CT19 4PX **Tel:** 01303-275402

Hartley, Francis, (Southwark), 48 Thanet Rd, Bexley, Kent DA5 1AP **Tel:** 01322-524813

Hartley, John, (Southwark), The Holy Family, 115 Limpsfield Rd, Sanderstead, Surrey CR2 9LF **Tel:** 020-8657 1728

Hartley, Mark, (OCSO), Our Lady and St Bernard, Mount St Bernard Abbey,

Coalville, Leicester LE67 5UL **Tel:** 01530-832298/832022 **Fax:** 01530-814608

Hartley, Michael, (Salford), c/o Wardley Hall, Worsley, Manchester M28 2ND

Hartley, Michael, (Shrewsbury), St Werburgh's & St Laurence's, 5 Werburgh's Square, Birkenhead CH41 2XZ **Tel:** 0151-647 9124 **Fax:** 0151-647 9125 **Email:** werlau@btinternet.com

Hartnett, Patrick, (Middlesbrough), St George's Rectory, 7 Peel St, York YO1 1PZ **Tel:** 01904-623728

Harvey, John J, BA(Div), JCL, MCL, (Brentwood), 9 Trap's Hill, Loughton, Essex IG10 1SZ **Tel:** 020-8508 3492

Harvey, Peter, STL, (Nottingham), The Presbytery, 53 London Rd, Coalville LE67 3JB **Tel:** 01530-832098

Harvey, Richard, (Southwark), 12 Glanville Rd, Sevenoaks, Kent TN13 1ER **Tel:** 01732-454177

Harvey, Vincent, (Portsmouth), Holy Ghost Presbytery, Sherborne Rd, Basingstoke RG21 5TD **Tel:** 01256-465214 **Fax:** 01256-469605 **E-mail:** vharvey@nildram.co.uk

Hasker, Stewart P, BA, CQSW, (Westminster), 112 Twickenham Rd, Isleworth, Middx TW7 6DL **Tel:** 020-8560 1431

Hassay, Gerard (SJ), St Anselm's Rectory, The Green, Southall, Middx UB2 4BE **Tel:** 020-8574 3300 **Fax:** 020-8813 8784

Hastie, Anthony M, (Hexham & Newcastle), St Cuthbert, Mill Rd, New Seaham, Co Durham SR7 0HW **Tel:** 0191-581 2221

Hatton, Edmund MA (OSB), Monastery of Our Lady of Mount Grace, 18 North End, Osmotherley, N Yorks DL6 3BB **Tel:** 01609-883308 **Fax:** 01609-883740

Haugh, Gerard, (Salford, retired), Holy Family, 24 Cale Lane, New Springs, Wigan WN2 1HA **Tel:** 01942 242542 **Email:** holy.fam@btconnect.com

Hauser, Hermann, ES, Th (MAfr), Oak Lodge, 48 Totteridge Common, London N20 8NB **Tel:** 020-8595 1515 **Fax:** 020-8959 7421 **E-mail:** mafr@oaklodge.debsol.co.uk

Havard-Brown, Mervin, (Clifton), Kings Farm, Livery Rd, West Winterslow, Salisbury, SP5 1RG

Haverty, Peter, PhD, BSc,(Opus Dei), 1 Pine Rd, Manchester M20 6UY **Tel:** 0161-445 6480

Hawe, Vincent, (SJ), Farm St Church, 114 Mount St, London W1K 3AH **Tel:** 020-7493 7811 **Fax:** 020-7495 6685

Hawes, James C, STL, (Brentwood), 11 Church Hill, Epping, Essex CM16 4RA **Tel:** 01992-572516

Hawkins, John, (Lancaster), St Pius X, Schneider Rd, Barrow-in-Furness LA14 4AA **Tel:** 01229-820283

Hawkins, Peter Edward, BA, (Clifton), 15 St Andrew's Rd, Stogursey, Somerset TA5 1TE **Tel/Fax:** 01278-733635

Hawksworth, Simon, (Lancaster), 64 Larches Ln, Preston PR2 1PP **Tel:** 01772-726336 **Fax:** 01772-760910 **E-mail:** simon@shawksworth.freeserve.co.uk

Hawley, Kenneth, (Leeds), St Winefride's Presbytery, 54 St Pauls Ave, Wibsey BD6 1ST **Tel:** 01274 677992

Haworth, Michael, (Salford), St Mary Magdalene, Gawthorpe Rd, Burnley BB12 0JP **Tel/Fax:** 01282-422502

Hay, George, Mgr Provost, MA, (Plymouth), The Presbytery, Ashburton Rd, Bovey Tracey, Devon TQ13 9BY **Tel:** 01626-833432

Hay, James, (Southwark), 103 Woolwich New Rd, Woolwich, London SE18 6EF **Tel:** 020-8854 0359

Hay-Will, Raglan, MA, STL, (Arundel & Brighton), The Presbytery, 3 Springfield Rd, Horsham, W. Sussex RH12 2PJ **Tel:** 01403-253667 **Fax:** 01403-271509

Hayden, Colm, (Hexham & Newcastle), St Joseph, Mill Ln, Gilesgate, Durham City DH1 2JG **Tel:** 0191-384 3810

Hayden, Kevin, BA, MA. (Southwark), The Priest's Ho, 201 Cheam Common Rd, Worcester Park, Surrey KT4 8SX **Tel:** 020-8337 1782

Hayes, Alfred T, STB, Canon (Lancaster), Christ the King, 15 Haverflatts Ln, Milnthorpe LA7 7PS **Tel:** 01539 562387 **E-mail:** alfhayes@hotmail.com

Hayes, Denis, (Arundel and Brighton, retired), Eastridge Manor, Wineham Lane, Bolney, Haywards Heath, W Sussex RH17 5SD

Hayes, James (SJ), Christopher Grange, Youens Way, East Prescot Rd, Liverpool L14 2EW **Tel:** 0151-220 2525

Hayes, John F, (Brentwood), 213 Hornchurch Rd, Hornchurch, Essex RM12 4TL **Tel:** 01708- 447761

Hayes, Liam, BA(Hons), BTh(Hons), (Brentwood), c/o Cathedral Ho, Ingrave Rd, Brentwood, Essex CM15 8AT

Hayes, Martin, BA, BD, (Westminster), Private Secretary to Cardinal, c/o Archbishop's Ho, London SW1P 1QJ

Hayes, Matthew, Canon (Clifton, retired), Flat 2, St John's Flats, South Parade, Bath BA2 4AF **Tel:** 01225-311864

Hayes, Michael A, Rev, Dr, BD, MA, PhD DipPsych, (Southwark), 34 Clive Rd, Strawberry Hill, Twickenham TW1 4SG **Tel:** 020-8255 0012 **Mbl:** 07740-619080

Haylett, Stephen, BA(Hons) (Southwark),

HM Prison, Elmley, Brabazon Rd, Eastchurch, Sheppey, Kent ME12 4DA **Tel:** 01795 882131

Hayman, David, (Cardiff), The Priest's Ho, Conway Rd, Pontypool NP4 6HL **Tel:** 01495-762280

Hayne, Antony, (Hallam), The Presbytery, Morrell St, Rotherham S66 7LH **Tel:** 01709-812883 **E-mail:** hayne@priory9.fsnet.co,.uk

Hayne, Raymond Guy, (Clifton), 6 Wool Ho Gardens, Codford, Warminster, Wilts BA12 0PS **Tel:** 01985-850942

Haynes, Thomas, FCMA (OSB). Worth Abbey, Crawley, W. Sussex, RH10 4SB **Tel:** 01342-710228

Hayward, Paul, LLB, JCD, (Opus Dei), 4 Orme Court, London, W2 4RL **Tel:** 020-7229 7574

Hazell, Michael, Canon, (Northampton, retired), 3 Veronica Ho, St William Court, Kesgrave, Ipswich, Suffolk IP5 2QP **Tel:** 01473 612819 **E-mail:** mhazell@supanet.com

Hazlewood, Cyril, (SCJ), The Holy Ghost and Mary Immaculate, St Bernard's Rd, Olton, Solihull, W Mids B92 7BL **Tel:** 0121-706 0505 **Fax:** 0121-706 8105

Headon, Andrew M J, BSc, STL, (Brentwood), Venerabile Collegio Inglese, Via di Monserrato 45, 00186 Roma, Italia **Tel:** 003906-6868546, **E-mail:** vicerector.vec@mclink.it

Heakin, Dermot P, (Salford), Corpus Christi, Derby St, Hollinwood, Oldham OL9 7HX **Tel:** 0161-624 2008

Heakin, Leo, (Salford), St Edmund's, Bridgewater St, Little Hulton, Worsley, Manchester M38 9ND **Tel:** 0161-790 2104

Heal, Martin, (Westminster, retired), Charterhouse, London EC1M 6AN **Tel:** 020-7251 3943

Healey, Patrick, Canon, (Shrewsbury, retired), 106 Mount Pleasant Rd, Davenham, Northwich CW9

Healey, Richard, (East Anglia), Catholic Presbytery, Hills Rd, Cambridge CB2 1JR **Tel:** 01223-350787 **Fax:** 01223-224860

Healy, Bruno J, (Westminster), St Joseph's Presbytery, Lamb's Passage, Bunhill Row, London EC1Y 8LE **Tel:** 020-7628 0326

Healy, John, (Arundel & Brighton), 89 St Mary's Cl, Littlehampton, W. Sussex BN17 5QQ **Tel:** 01903-722250

Healy, Michael, STL, (Clifton), St Bonaventure, Egerton Rd, Bishopston, Bristol BS7 8HP **Tel:** 0117-942 4448

Healy, Sean, Mgr (Northampton), 32 London Rd, Daventry, Northants NN11 4BZ **Tel:** 01327-300428 **E-mail:** Sean.Healy@virgin.net

Healy, Terence V, Canon (Portsmouth), 5 Orchard Cl, Horndean, Hants PO8 9LL **Tel:** 023-9259 3010 **E-mail:** terence_healy@msn.com

Heaney, Brian, (Westminster, retired), Nazareth Ho, 162 East End Rd, London N2 0RU

Heaney, John, (Lancaster), 25 Harrel Ln, Barrow in Furness LA13 9LN **Tel:** 01229-824429

Heaney, William Oliver, (Arundel & Brighton), Priest's Ho, 5 Surrenden Rd, Brighton, E Sussex BN1 6PA **Tel:** 01273-554509

Heap, Nicholas, BA, DPhil (Portsmouth), Eton College, Windsor, Berks SL4 7DW **Tel:** 01753-671409

Heaphy, Bernard, (Southwark), 6 Knowle Cl, Brixton, London SW9 0TQ **Tel:** 020-7274 2367

Heaps, Christopher MA, BA, (SDB), Sacred Heart Parish, 4 Orbel St, Battersea, London SW11 3NZ **Tel:** 0207 223 2747 **Fax:** 0207 223 2756 **E-mail:** christopherheaps@hotmail.com

Hearn, Richard, (Southwark), 59 Burgate, Canterbury, Kent CT1 2HJ **Tel:** 01227 462896

Hearty, Bernard, (Lancaster), St Joseph, Yeathouse Rd, Frizington, Cumbria CA26 3PX **Tel:** 01946-810284

Hearty, John, (Southwark), 4 Kingswood Dr, Dulwich Wood Park, London SE19 1UR **Tel:** 020-8670 1639

Heath, Bernard, (East Anglia, retired), 23 Ship Rd, Pakefield, Lowestoft, Suffolk NR33 7DN

Heath, James, "Annan", Norfolk Rd, Turvey MK43 8DU **Tel:** 01234 888858

Hebborn, William, (Southwark), 9 Tooting Bec Rd, London SW17 8BS **Tel:** 020-8672 2179

Heffernan, Fionan (OSA), Austin Friars, 15 Dorville Cres, London W6 0HH **Tel:** 020-8741 7586

Hegarty, Eamonn BA, (Leeds), First Martyrs Presbytery, Heights Ln, Heaton, Bradford BD9 6HZ **Tel:** 01274 543789 **Email:** eamonnh1@tiscali.co.uk

Hegarty, James (SSS), Blessed Sacrament Shrine, 4 Dawson St, Liverpool L1 1LE **Tel:** 0151-709 5528 **Fax:** 0151-709 5977

Heiberg, Philip (Shrewsbury), c/o Curial Office, 2 Park Rd South, Prenton CH43 4UX **Tel:** 0151-652 9855

Heley, John, (East Anglia, retired), 24 Kestral, Burnham Market, Norfolk PE31 8EF **Tel:** 01328 730036

Helm, John, (Westminster), 700 Finchley Rd, Golders Green, London NW11 7NE **Tel:** 020-8455 1300

Hemer, John STB, LSS (MHM), Allen Hall,

28 Beaufort St, Chelsea SW3 5AA **Tel:** 0207 349 5613 **E-mail:** johnhemer@googlemail.com

Hemy, Gregory, (Cong Orat), The Oratory, Brompton Rd, London SW7 2RP **Tel:** 020-7589 4811

Henderson, Euan, (Birmingham), The Old Forge, Stonor, Henley-on-Thames RG9 6HE 1RH **Tel:** 01491-638865

Heneghan, John, (Liverpool), St Marie's Presbytery, 25 Seabank Rd, Southport PR9 0EJ **Tel:** 01704-531229 **Fax:** 01704-512590

Heneghan, Kieran, (SSC), 18 Gunnersby Cres, London W3 9AA **Tel:** 020-8992 9347

Heneghan, Paul, (Leeds), c/o Bishop's Ho, 13 North Grange Rd, Leeds LS6 2BR

Heneghan, Thomas, (Southwark), 11 Trent Rd, Brixton, SW2 5BJ **Tel:** 020-7274 1621

Hennessey, Kevin, (Clifton), The Presbytery, Cheltenham Rd East, Churchdown, Gloucester GL3 1HU **Tel:** 01452-713254

Hennessey, Thomas, (SDS, retired), Salvatorian Community, High Rd, Harrow Weald, Middx HA3 5DY **Tel:** 020-8427 2808

Hennessy, David (East Anglia), 8 Gainborough Rd, Felixstowe, Suffolk IP11 7HT **Tel:** 01394 282561 **E-mail:** brendamoffatt@yahoo.co.uk

Hennessy, Liam, MA, (Cardiff), Sacred Heart Presbytery, 160 Brd St, Leckwith, Cardiff CF11 8BY **Tel:** 029-2038-3187

Hennessy, Patrick, Mgr, (Leeds), The Lodge, 35 Oatlands Dr, Harrogate HG2 8PU **Tel:** 01423-819598

Henry, John J., MTh, LSS, PhD, (Southwark), 306 Garrett Ln, Earlsfield, London SW18 4EH **Tel:** 020-8874 5098

Henry, Simon, ChLJ, BA, MA, (Liverpool), c/o Liverpool Archdiocesan Centre for Evangelisation, Croxteth drive, Liverpool L17 1AA

Henshaw, Robert, (AA), 16 Nightingale Rd, Hitchin, Herts SG5 1QS **Tel:** 01462-457673

Henson, Andrew, (OCSO), Our Lady and St Bernard, Mount St Bernard Abbey, Coalville, Leicester LE67 5UL **Tel:** 01530-832298/832022 **Fax:** 01530-814608

Henwood, George R J, STB, (Clifton), St Gerard's Presbytery, 69 Talbot Rd, Bristol BS4 2NP **Tel:** 0117-983 3924

Heptonstall, Frederick (MHM), St Alban, Larkhill, Blackburn, Lancs BB1 6HY **Tel:** 01254-59331

Herlihy, Denis, (Shrewsbury), 8 Kenilworth Avenue, Knutsford WA16 8JT

Hermanowicz, Slawomir, St Anthony's, Farnham Rd, Slough SL2 3AE

Heron, Benedict M, (OSB), Monastery of Christ the King, 29 Bramley Rd, Cockfosters, London N14 4HE **Tel:** 020-8447 7726

Hersey, Peter, (SMA), 14 Swifts, Langford Budville, Somerset TA21 0RA **Tel:** 01823-400692

Heskett, Ralph (CSsR), Our Lady of the Annunciation, Bishop Eton, Woolton Rd, Wavertree, Liverpool L16 8NQ

Heskin, Kieran, Mgr, BA, PhD, VG, (Leeds), Stockeld Rd, Ilkley LS29 9HD **Tel:** 01943 607690

Heslin, John E, Mgr, (Birmingham, retired), 35 Garnet St, Saltburn-by-the-Sea, Cleveland TS12 1EQ

Heslin, Matthew John, BA, HDipEd, STB (Westminster). Presbytery, Osborn Rd, Uxbridge, Middx UB8 1UE **Tel:** 01895-233193

Hester, Seamus, Canon, (Arundel & Brighton), 2-4 Grange Rd, Eastbourne, E. Sussex BN21 4EU **Tel:** 01323-723222 **Fax:** 01323-645605 **E-mail:** ransomeagnes@mistral.co.uk

Hetherington, Gerard, Provost, (Portsmouth), 12 Station Rd, Petersfield, Hants GU32 2ED **Tel:** 01730 262290 **E-mail:** office@petersfieldparish.org.uk

Hetherton, Seamus, (Southwark), The Presbytery, 23 Upper Meadow Rd, Quinton, Birmingham B32 1NT **Tel:** 0121-422 4865 **E-mail:** fatimaquinton@aol.com

Hewett, William, MA (SJ), Campion Hall, Brewer St, Oxford OX1 1QS **Tel:** 01865-286118 **Fax:** 01865-286148

Hewitt, David, (Hexham and Newcastle), RC Chaplain's Office, Chaplaincy Centre, RAF Halton, Aylesbury, Bucks HP22 5PG **Tel:** 01296-623535 ext 6414

Hewitt, Thomas, (MSC), Catholic Presbytery, 14 Beaconsfield Rd, St Albans, Herts AL1 3RB **Tel:** 01727 853585 **Fax:** 01727 855410

Hewlett, Raymund (OFM Cap), Franciscan Friary, Carlton Rd, Erith, Kent DA8 1DN **Tel:** 01322-433193

Heyes, Harold, (WF), 15 Corfton Rd, Ealing, W5 2HP **Tel:** 020-8998 8552

Heywood, David Paul, (Liverpool), Holy Family Presbytery, 208 Chaddock Ln, Boothstown, Worsley, Manchester M28 1DN **Tel:** 0161-790 2390 **Fax:** 0161-799 0417

Hibberd, Wulstan, (OSB), St Michael's Abbey, Farnborough Rd, Farnborough, Hants GU14 7NQ RIP **Tel:** 01252-546105 **Fax:** 01252-372822

Hibbert, Giles, MA, STL, PhD, (OP, retired), 13 Laneside Cl, Chapel-en-le-Frith, High Peak SK23 0TS **Tel:** 01298-813958

Hibbert, Patrick, (Lancaster), St Alban's, 64 Kilnhouse Ln, St Annes-on-Sea FY8 3AA **Tel:** 01253-725557

Hickey, Ambrose, (Liverpool, retired), Clare Abbey, Clare Castle, Co Clare, Éire **Tel:** 00 353 6865 2328

Hickey, Christopher W, MBIM, (Clifton), St Patrick's Presbytery, 24 Ermin St, Brockworth, Glos GL3 4HL **Tel:** 01452-862709 **Fax:** 01452-863794

Hickey, Michael, MA, (Hexham & Newcastle), St Robert's, Cedar Rd, Fenham, Newcastle-upon-Tyne NE4 9PH **Tel:** 0191-273 3903 **E-mail:** strobertsfenham@btconnect.com

Hickford, Peter, (SMA), Society of African Missions, 378 Upper Brook St, Manchester M13 0EP **Tel:** 0161-224 4949

Hickman, Frank (OFM Cap, retired), 36 New St, Pontnewydd, Cwmbran NP44 1EF **Tel:** 01633-860853

Hicks, Gerald STL DIP, C.E. (OFM Conv), Greyfriars, 1 Elmsley Rd, Mossley Hill L18 8AY **Tel:** 0151-724 2109 **Fax:** 0151-724 2553 **E-mail:** anthonyofpadua@aol.com

Hicks, Robert, (MCCJ), Verona Fathers, London Rd, Sunningdale, Ascot, Berks SL5 0JY **Tel:** 01344-621238 **Fax:** 01344-621351

Higginbottom, Michael, (Hexham & Newcastle), St Augustine's, Coniscliffe Rd, Darlington DL3 7RG **Tel:** 01325-266602 **Fax:** 01325-253363

Higgins, Bernard, DipEd, (SDB), St Joseph's, 10 Oldhams Ln, Bolton BL1 6PN **Tel:** 01204-590600 **E-mail:** mdelmer@msn.com

Higgins, Dennis, (Nottingham), St Anne, Terrace Rd, Buxton, Derbys SK17 6DU **Tel:** 01298-23777

Higgins, Edmund BA (SSCC), 81 Evelina Rd, Nunhead, London SE15 3HL **Tel:** 020-7639 3724 **Fax:** 020-7635 8215 **Mbl:** 077 8774 2699 **E-mail:** edhggns@aol.com

Higgins, Francis, (Nottingham), The Presbytery, School St, Kirkby-in-Ashfield, Notts NG17 7BT **Tel:** 01623-754495

Higgins, Francis, (Northampton), St Teresa's Presbytery, 40 Warwick Rd, Beconsfield HP9 2PL **Tel:** 01494-673018 **E-mail:** office@littleflower.co.uk

Higham, Bernard, STB (Liverpool), Our Lady of Compassion, The Rectory, School Ln, Formby, Liverpool L37 3LW **Tel/Fax:** 01704-873230

Higham, Charles, (SJ), St Wilfrid's Presbytery, 1 Winkley Sq, Preston, Lancs PR1 3JJ **Tel:** 01772 555244 **Fax:** 01772 251955

Higham, David Anthony, (Birmingham), St Mary's, Harvington Hall Ln, Kidderminster, Worcs DY10 4LR **Tel:** 01562-777319

Highton, Edmund, (OFM), The Friary, 270 Ballatar St, Glasgow G5 0YT **Tel:** 0141-429 0740 **Fax:** 0141-440 1039 **E-mail:** edhighton@yahoo.com

Hill, Bede, (OSB), Worth Abbey, Crawley, W Sussex RH10 4SB **Tel:** 01342-7103310

Hill, Christopher Boniface, (OSB), Downside Abbey, Stratton on the Fosse, Radstock, Bath, Somerset BA3 4RH

Hill, Edmund, (OP), Priory of St Michael, Buckingham Rd, Cambridge CB3 0DD **Tel:** 01223-741251 **Fax:** 01223-741252

Hill, Edward P, Mgr, (Southwark), The Presbytery, 47 Ashford Road, Tenterden, Kent TN30 6LL **Tel:** 01580 762785 **E-mail:** edward@ehill.freeserve.co.uk

Hill, Jonathan, (Northampton), 366 Leagrave High St, Luton, Beds LU4 0NG **Tel:** 01582-663706 **E-mail:** FrJonHill@aol.com

Hilton, Christopher BA(Hons), STB (Salford), Holy Name, Oxford Rd, Chorlton-on-Medlock, Manchester M13 9PG **Tel/Fax:** 0161-273 2873 **E-mail:** christopherhilton@hotmail.com

Hilton, Geoffrey, (Salford), St Augustine's Presbytery, 55a Lowerhouse Ln, Burnley BB12 6HZ **Tel:** 01282-425631

Hind, Kenneth, (Lancaster), c/o Bishop's Ho, Cannon Hill, Lancs LA1 5NG.

Hind, Richard Q, (Portsmouth), 38 Hartlands Rd, Fareham, Hants PO16 0NL **Tel:** 01329-239584

Hindley, John (Liverpool) St Bernadette's Presbytery, 1 Elnup Ave, Shelvington, Wigan WN6 8AT **Tel:** 01257 423675

Hipkins, John (Wrexham, retired), Two Gates, 124 Lon Penrhyn, Benlech, Anglesey LL74 4RW **Tel:** 01248-852344

Hird, Nicholas, (Leeds), St Paulinus' Presbytery, Cemetery Rd, Dewsbury WF13 2SE **Tel:** 01924-465638

Hishon, Ronald, Mgr, BA, DipSp (Portsmouth), 2 Short Cl, Bournemouth BH12 5DX **Mbl:** 07831-694168 **E-mail:** ronhishon.personal@tesco.net

Hitchen, John, (Salford), St Ann's, Chester Rd, Stretford, Manchester M32 8LF **Tel:** 0161-865 2079

Hnylycia, Stefan BSc, PGCE (Opus Dei), 8 Orme Court, London W2 4RL

Ho-Huu-Nghia, Michael, JCL, STB (Birmingham), 650 Tile Hill Ln, Coventry CV4 9TA **Tel:** 024-7646 6834

Ho Dinh (Xavier) RGN (OSB), St Benedict's Monastery, Convent Cl, Duddle Ln, Bamber Bridge, Preston PR5 6US **Tel:** 01772-902201 **Fax:** 01772902214

Hoare, Liam MA, CADAC, LPCC(sP), Our

Lady of Victory, Brownshill, Glos GL6 8AL **Tel:** 01453-883084 **Fax:** 01453-731888 **E-mail:** post@olvt.org

Hoare, Michael, (Salford), 54 Bedford Rd, Firswood, Manchester M16 0JA

Hoban, Brendan, Canon, (Shrewsbury), Sacred Heart, The Cross, Moreton, Wirral CH46 9QB **Tel:** 0151-677 5220 **Fax:** 0151-677 8817 **E-mail:** sacredheartmoreton@hotmail.com

Hobbs, Stanislaus, STL, (OSB), Ealing Abbey, Charlbury Grove, Ealing W5 2DY **Tel:** 020-8862 2100 **Fax:** 020-8862 2166 **E-mail:** stanEa@ukf.net

Hobson, Walter, (OFM), The Friary, 557/559 High Rd, Woodford Green, Essex IG8 0RB **Tel:** 020-8504 1686/1688 **Fax:** 020-8498 1844

Hocken, Peter, Mgr, STL, PhD, (Northampton, retired), Missionsschwestern Konigina-posteln, Kreuzwiesengasse 9 A-1170 Wien, Austria. **E-mail:** p.hocken@inode.at

Hodges, Anthony Wayne, (Cardiff), The Presbytery, Llanedeyrn Dr, Llanedeyrn, Cardiff CF23 9UL **Tel:** 029-2073 1061

Hodges, Marcus, BD, (OP), c/o Principal RC Chaplain (RAF), Chaplaincy Office, RAF Halton, Aylesbury, Bucks HP22 5PG **Tel:** 01296 656910

Hodgson, Brendan, (OP), Dominican Sisters, Rosary Priory, Elstree Rd, Bushey, Watford, Herts WD2 3RJ **Tel:** 020-8950 1148

Hodkinson, Jerome, Rt Rev Abbot, MA (OSB), Abbey of St Michael and All Angels, Belmont, Hereford HR2 9RZ **Tel:** 01432-277388

Hoey, Augustine, MA (OSB, retired), 2a Meadow Rd, London SW8 1QH **Tel:** 020-7582 5383

Hogan, Rev Christopher (Nottingham), St Mary's Presbytery, Horncastle Rd, Boston, Lincs PE21 9BU **Tel:** 01205-362056 **Fax:** 01205-362205

Hogan, Daniel, (SMM), Montford Ho, 28 Burbo Bank Rd, Liverpool L23 6TH **Tel:** 0151-287 6862 **Fax:** 0151-287 0410

Hogan, David, Mgr, JCL, (Middlesbrough), St Bernadette, Gypsy Ln, Nunthorpe, Middlesbrough, Cleveland TS7 0EB **Tel:** 01642-316171

Hogan, Gregory STB (Birmingham), c/o Cathedral House, St Chad's Queensway, Birmingham B4 6EY

Hogan, Lawrence, (IC, retired), St Mary's, Derrys Wood, Wonersh, Guildford, Surrey GU5 0RA **Tel:** 01483-893196

Hogan, Mark, (Portsmouth), St Joseph's Presbytery, 171A St Michael's Road, Basingstoke, Hants RG22 6TY **Tel:** 01256 323595 **Fax:** 01256 814569

Hogarth, Anthony, (Northampton), c/o Bishop's Ho, Marriott St, Northampton NN2 6AW **Tel:** 01604-715635

Hogg, William, (Southwark, retired), 2 Wellington Rd, Deal, Kent CT14 7AL **Tel:** 01304-367603

Hoiles, Kevin, (Portsmouth), 36 Cookham Road, Maidenhead, Berks SL6 7EG **Tel:** 01628 783988 **Fax:** 01628 776863 **E-mail:** presbytery@stjosephs-mh.freeserve.co.uk

Holbrook, Angelo, (CP), The Retreat Centre, Sea St, Herne Bay, Kent CT6 8SP **Tel:** 01227-375095 **Fax:** 01227-360941

Holdaway, Gervase, MA (OSB), Douai Abbey, Upper Woolhampton, Reading Berks RG7 5TQ **Tel:** 0118-971 5333 **E-mail:** douaiabbey@aol.com

Holden, Henry N, (Lancaster), St Joseph's, Woodlands Rd, Ansdell, Lytham St Annes FY8 4EP **Tel:** 01253-737037 **Fax:** 01253-737034

Holden, John Forest, (OFM), The Friary, Gordon Rd, Nottingham NG3 2LG **Tel:** 0115-950 1064

Holden, Marcus P, MA(Oxon), STL (Southwark), St Augustine's, Cresent Rd, Tunbridge Wells, Kent TN1 2LY **Tel:** 01892 522525 **Fax:** 01892 526287

Holdsworth, Stephen, DipEd (OSB), The Presbytery, Kington Rd, Weobley, Hereford HR4 8QS **Tel:** 01544-318325

Holland, Philip-Mary M, BA, (Nottingham), St Patricks Prestbytery, Clipstone Rd West, Forrest Town, Mansfield, Notts NG19 0BU

Hollins, Peter, (Portsmouth), 105 Waverley Rd, Southsea, Portsmouth, Hants PO5 2PL **Tel:** 023-9282 8305 **Fax:** 023-9264 8498 **E-mail:** stswithuns@lineone.net

Holman, Michael, Provincial, (SJ), c/o 114 Mount St, London W1K 3AH

Holmes, Barrie, (Leeds, retired), St Robert's Presbytery, Robert St, Harrowgate HG1 1HP **Tel:** 01423-504988

Holmes, Charles, (Leeds, retired), 22 Carleton Crest, Pontefract WF8 2QP **Tel:** 01977-702987

Holmes, Oliver BA (OSB), c/o Ampleforth Abbey, York YO62 4EN

Holmes-Walker, Robert, BSc, C.Chem, MRSC, (Westminster, retired), 15 Riddell Gardens, Baldock, Herts SG7 6JR **Tel:** 01462-894968

Holroyd, Philip, Mgr, STL, DPhil, (Leeds), St Theresa's Presbytery, Station Rd, Cross Gates, Leeds LS15 7JY **Tel:** 0113-264 5260 **Fax:** 0113-260 9133 **E-mail:** pholroyd@hinsley-hall.co.uk

Holt, Geoffrey, (SJ), Corpus Christi Jesuit

Community, 757 Christchurch Rd, Boscombe, Bournemouth BH7 6AN **Tel:** 01202 436700

Holt, Oliver, MA (OSB), Douai Abbey, Upper Woolhampton, Reading, Berks, RG7 5TQ **Tel:** 0118-971 5319 **Fax:** 0118-971 5303

Holtham, Alan Leslie, (Birmingham, retired), Aston Hall, Aston-by-Stone, Stone ST15 0BJ

Holwell, Harry, (Menevia), c/o Curial Offices, 27 Convent St, Greenhill, Swansea SA1 2BX

Hone, Edward, (CSsR), St Benet, The Causeway, Monkwearmouth, SR6 0BH **Tel:** 0191-567 2965

Hood, Alban, MA, PhD, Adv Dip Couns, Novice Master (OSB), Douai Abbey, Upper Woolhampton, Reading, Berks RG7 5TQ **Tel:** 0118-971 5300 **Fax:** 0118-971 5303 **E-mail:** albanhood@hotmail.com

Hood, Martin James, (OSB), Downside Abbey, Stratton on the Fosse, Radstock, Bath, Somerset BA3 4RH **Tel:** 01761-235161

Hook, James, Mgr, (Lancaster, retired), 6 Greenacres, off School Ln, Freckleton, Preston, Lancs PR4 1PS **Tel:** 01772-634894

Hoole, Thomas (Lancaster), St Mary's, Fernyhalgh Ln, Fulwood, Preston PR2 5RR **Tel:** 01772-862231

Hooper, Kevin, MA, Cantab, (Birmingham), 110 Warwick Rd, Kenilworth, Warks CV8 1HL **Tel:** 01926-855224

Hooper, Peter, (Shrewsbury), St Luke, 76 Church Rd, Bebington, Wirral CH63 3EB **Tel:** 0151-644 7530

Hooper, Peter, BA, DipSlit, MA, (OFM), Franciscan Inernational Study Centre, Giles Ln, Canterbury, Kent CT2 7NA **Tel:** 01227-464939 **Fax:** 01227-470496

Hopgood, David, Canon, (Portsmouth), Bishop's Ho, Edinburgh Rd, Portsmouth PO1 3HG **Tel:** 023-9282-6613 **Fax:** 023-9283 9143 **E-mail:** dchopgood@btopenworld.com

Hopkins, Timothy, (Salford), St Anne & St Brigid, Carruthers St, Ancoats, Manchester M4 7EQ **Tel/Fax:** 0161-273 2873 **E-mail:** tim@vincents.fslife.org.uk

Hopkinson, Peter, (Salford), St John the Baptist, St John's Rd, Padiham, Burnley BB12 7BN **Tel:** 01282-772200 **Fax:** 01282-680608

Hopley, Michael, (OSB), Ealing Abbey, Charlbury Grove, Ealing, W5 2DY **Tel:** 020-8862 2100

Horan, Anthony, (SJ), Mount St Jesuit Residence, 114 Mount St, W1K 3AH **Tel:** 0207-493 7811 **Fax:** 0207-495 6685 **E-mail:** tony.horan@btinternet.com

Horan, Cornelius, (Hexham & Newcastle, retired), 3 Lower Artane Cottages, Malahide Rd, Dublin 5, Ireland. **Tel:** 00353 1 831 0044

Horan, Danny (Westminster), 18 St John's Villas, London N19 3EE **Tel:** 020-7272 8195

Horan, John, (Hallam, retired), Knockeenahone, Killarney, Scarfaglen, Co Kerry, Èire

Hore, Michael, (Portsmouth), Ampthill Ho, Cordier Hill, St Peter Port, Guernsey GY1 1JH **Tel:** 01481-720196 **Fax:** 01481-711247 **E-mail:** sjoss.guernsey@virgin.net

Horgan, Sean, (Salford), St Mary's Presbytery, York Ln, Langho, Blackburn BB6 8DW **Tel/Fax:** 01254-248186

Horkin, Edward, (Leeds, retired), The Bungalow, 6 Harker Terr, Stanningley, Leeds LS28 6BL **Tel:** 0113-257 2342

Horn, John, (Arundel & Brighton), The Prestbytery, 157 Aldershot Rd, Guildford, Surrey GU2 8BP **Tel:** 01483 573279

Horn, Robert, (Lancaster), Christ the King Presbytery, Gateside Dr, Grange Park, Blackpool FY3 7PL **Tel/Fax:** 01253-391002

Horrax, Michael, STL, (Nottingham, retired), Flat 83, Coningsby Ho, Sandygate Grove, Sheffield S10 5TG **Tel:** 0114-230 9392

Horsey, Kevin, (OSB), Ealing Abbey, Charlbury Grove, Ealing W5 2DY **Tel:** 020-8862 2100

Horsley, Austin, MA, (SM), Newman Ho, 729 Beverley Rd, Hull HU6 7ER **Tel:** 01482 856884

Horton, Stephen, Prior/Novice Master (OSB), Prinknash Abbey, Cranham, Gloucester GL4 8EX **Tel:** 01452-812455 **E-mail:** prinknash@waitrose.com

Hosford, Horatio, (Westminster, retired) Flat 2, 8 Morpeth Terr SW1P 1EQ **Tel:** 020-7798 9019

Hoskins, Ian, MA, (Hexham & Newcastle), St Thomas of Canterbury, Longhorsley Northumberland NE65 8UY **Tel:** 01670-788344

Hothersall, Joseph L, (Lancaster), c/o Pastoral Centre, Balmoral Road, Lancaster LA1 3BT

Hough, Denis, (AA), The Persbytery, New Street, Oadby, Leicester LE2 4LJ **Tel:** 0116-271 5139

Hough, Paul, (Southwark), 120 Stafford Rd, Wallington, Surrey SM6 9AY **Tel:** 020-8647 5079

Houghton, Edward, (Westminster), 247 High Road, London W4 4PU **Tel:** 020 8994 2877 **Fax:** 020 8987 8332

Houghton, Peter, STL, LSS, (Lancaster), Sacred Heart, Haws Bank, Torver Rd, Coniston LA211 8AW **Tel:** 01539-441351

Houle, Angelus (CFR), St Fidelis Friary, Killip Cl, London E16 1LX **Tel:** 020 7474 0766

Houlihan, Liam, Episcopal Vicar for Religious (Salford), St Sebastian, Gerald Rd, Pendleton, Salford M6 6DW **Tel:** 0161-736 1774

House, Michael C C, (Clifton, retired), Mirthios, Finikas 74060, Rethymnon, Crete, Greece

Houston, Mark, BEng(Hons), (Lancaster), The Presbytery, Lonsdale Rd, Millom LA18 4AS **Tel:** 01229-772479

Hovington, John, (Shrewsbury), Holy Name & St Peter's, 60 Beresford Road, Oxton, Prenton, Wirral CH43 2JD **Tel:** 0151-652 3034 **E-mail:** oxtonholyname@tiscali.co.uk

How, Jonathan, BSc, ARCS, BTh, (Arundel & Brighton), St John's Seminary, Wonersh, Guildford, Surrey GU5 0QX **Tel:** 01483-892217 **Fax:** 01483 894531

Howard, Damian, (SJ), Manresa Ho, 10 Albert Rd, Harborne, Birmingham B17 0AN **Tel:** 0121 427 2628 **Fax:** 0121 428 1833 **E-mail:** damian@jesuits.net

Howard, Jeremy, BA, Oxon, (Birmingham), 17 Kidderminster Rd, Bromsgrove, B61 7JP **Tel:** 01527-835712

Howard, Michael, Canon (Plymouth, retired), The Presbytery, 42 Fore Street, Shaldon, Devon TQ14 0EA **Tel:** 01626-873410.

Howarth, Dominic (Brentwood), 21 Eastfield Rd, Brentwood, Essex CM14 4HB **Tel:** 01277 201427

Howe, Antony, Mgr, (Westminster, retired), 212 Crescent Ho, London EC1Y 0SL **Tel:** 020-7 608 0911

Howell, Adrian, (SJ), Stonyhurst College, Stonyhurst, Clitheroe, Lancs BB7 9PZ **Tel:** 01254-826345 **Fax:** 01254-827059 **E-mail:** a.howell.sj@stonyhurst.ac.uk

Howell, Charles BA(Cantab), BTh (Arundel & Brighton), St Teresa's Presbytery, Weldon Way, Merstham, Surrey RH1 3QA **Tel:** 01737-643399

Howell, Petroc, (Birmingham, retired), St Joseph's Home, Lichfield Rd, Stafford ST17 4LC

Hudson, Nicholas, Mgr, MA, STL (Southwark), Venerabile Collegio Inglese, Via di Monserrato 45, 00186, Roma, Italia, **Tel/Fax:** 0039 06 6830 0278 **E-mail:** rector.vec@mclink.it

Hughes, Andrew, (OSB), Ealing Abbey, Charlbury Grove, Ealing W5 2DY **Tel:** 020-8862 2100

Hughes, Anthony (Portsmouth), St Peter the Apostle Parish Office, 204 S Boulder Highway, Henderson, Nevada NV 89015, USA **E-mail:** tonyhughes@tews69.freeserve.co.uk

Hughes, F Austin, BD, Provincial (SCJ), The Friary, St Bernard's Rd, Solihull, W Mids B92 7BL **Tel:** 0121-706 0505 **Fax:** 0121-706 8105 **E-mail:** info@oltonfriary.demon.co.uk

Hughes, Barry, BA, MA (Southwark), c/o 37 Queenhill Rd, Selsdon CR2 8DW **Tel:** 020 8657 3747

Hughes, Bernard, (Northampton), 16 Bedford Rd, Wilstead MK45 3HW **Tel:** 01234-743748 **Mbl:** 0701 5474913

Hughes, Christopher, LLB, BA, (Hexham & Newcastle), Ushaw College, Durham DH7 9RH **Tel:** 0191-373 8525

Hughes, Francis BSc, MA, (OSB), St Benet's Presbytery, Evesham Rd, Kemerton, Tewkesbury, Glos GL20 7JE **Tel:** 01386-725286

Hughes, Gerald, (OSB), St Austin, 561 Aigburth Rd, Grassendale, Liverpool, L19 0NU **Tel:** 0151-427 3033 **Fax:** 0151-494 0600

Hughes, Gerard J, (Brentwood), 410 Brentwood Rd, Gidea Park, Romford, Essex RM2 6DH **Tel:** 01708-449914

Hughes, Gerard J, (SJ), Campion Hall, Oxford OX1 1QS **Tel:** 01865 286111 **E-mail:** gerard.hughes@campion.ox.ac.uk

Hughes, Gerard W, (SJ), Manresa Ho, 10 Albert Rd, Harborne B17 0AN **Tel:** 0121-428 3650

Hughes, John (OCD, retired), c/o Carmelite Priory, 41 Kensington Church Street, London W8 4BB

Hughes, Michael (Leeds), Our Lady of Lourdes Presbytery, 130 Cardigan Rd, Leeds LS6 3BJ **Tel/Fax:** 0113-275 2093

Hughes, Michael, (SCJ), St Raphael's, Huddersfield Road, Millbrook SK15 3JL **Tel:** 0161-338 3260

Hughes, Paul, (Shrewsbury), St James, 40 Underwood Rd, Hattersley, Hyde SK14 3DH **Tel:** 0161-368 3618

Hughes, Tony, (Portsmouth),St Patrick's Ho, 45 Portsmouth Rd, Woolston, Southampton SO19 9BD **Tel:** 02380-448671

Hull, Francis, (SJ), St Wilfrid's Presbytery, 1 Winckley Sq, Preston PR1 3JJ **Tel:** 01772 555244 **Fax:** 01772 251955

Hull, John, Mgr Canon, (Arundel & Brighton), 14 Church Cl, Patcham, Brighton, E Sussex BN1 8HS **Tel:** 01273-563017/506387

Hull, Ronald, (SJ), Stonyhurst, Clitheroe, Lancs BB7 9PZ **Tel:** 01254-827066

Hulme, Lawrence R, V. Rev Canon (Leeds),

St Joseph's Presbytery, Back St, Pontefract WF8 1HL **Tel:** 01977-702297 **Fax:** 01977-599050

Humble, Michael, (Hexham & Newcastle), Immaculate Heart of Mary, Malvern Gardens, Lobley Hill, Gateshead, Tyne & Wear NE11 9LL **Tel:** 0191-460 4274

Humfrey, Peter, Canon, MA, DipEd, STL, (Arundel & Brighton), 22 Wyeths Rd, Epsom, Surrey KT17 4EB **Tel:** 01372-500229

Humphrey, Colin Luke, (OSB), Buckfast Abbey, Buckfastleigh, Devon TQ11 0EE **Tel:** 01364-645500 **Fax:** 01364-643891

Humphreys, John, (Portsmouth), The Presbytery, Immaculate Conception, Bells Ln, Stubbington, Hants PO14 2PL **Tel:** 01329-663435 **Fax:** 01329-663435 **E-mail:** fatherjohn@onetel.net.uk

Humphries, Damian (Prior) MA, BD (OSB), The Monastery of Our Lady of Mount Grace, 18 North End, Osmotherley, Northallerton, Nth Yorks DL6 3BB **Tel:** 01609-883308

Hunt, Austin W Mgr, (Liverpool, retired), 9 Grinstead Cl, Southport PR8 4RP **Tel:** 01704 567072 **Fax:** 01704 567428 **E-mail:** a.hunt@talktalk.net

Hunt, Desmond (SM) Marist Fathers, Notre Dame de France, Leicester Place, London WC2H 7BP **Tel:** 020-7437 9363 **Fax:** 020-7437 3857

Hunt, William, STL, (Salford, retired), 1 Ketton Cl, Openshaw, Manchester M11 1NA **Tel:** 0161-231 2585

Hunter, James (CSSp, retired), St Felix Convent for Retired Sisters, 63 Orwell Rd, Felixstowe IP11 7PP **Tel:** 01394 277289

Hunter, Peter (OP), Holy Cross Priory, 45 Wellington St, Leicester LE1 6HW **Tel:** 0116 255 3856

Hunting, Daniel Christopher, MA (CJ), St George's College, Weybridge Rd, Addlestone, Weybridge KT15 2QS **Tel:** 01932-839458

Hunting, Tim (Arundel & Brighton), 2/4 Grange Rd, Eastbourne E Sussex **Tel:** 01323 723222 **Fax:** 01323 645605 **Email:** tim.hunting@dabnet.org

Hunton, Geoffrey (Nottingham), Bishop's Ho, 27 Cavendish Road East, The Park, Nottingham NG7 1BB **Tel:** 0115-947 4786 **Fax:** 0115-947 5235

Hurley, Andrew, PhL, STL, (Brentwood), 87 High St, Ongar, Essex CM5 9DX **Tel:** 01277-362645

Hurley, James, (Southwark), Crowsnest, Hosey Hill, Westerham, Kent TN16 1TB **Tel:** 01959-563226

Hurley, Peter, (Hallam), St Patrick's Presbytery, Barnsley Rd, Sheffield S5 0QF **Tel:** 0114-245 6160

Hurst, Geoffrey, (Hallam), 80 Sunnyvale Rd, Totley, Sheffield S17 4FB **Tel:** 0114-236 1407

Hurst, Gerald, (Liverpool), St Mary's 24 Bowling Green Rd, Castletown, IOM IM9 1EB **Tel:** 01624-822272

Hutchinson, Keith, (Middlesbrough, retired), Littlemore, Station Rd, Ampleforth, York YO62 4DG **Tel:** 01439-788127 **Fax:** 01439-788034

Hutt, David Walter, (Birmingham, retired) Priest's Ho, 40 Brockhurst Rd, Monks Kirby, Rugby, CV23 0RA **Tel:** 01788- 832471

Hutton, David, BA(Hons), (Southwark), Priest's Ho, West Common Rd, Hayes, Bromley BR2 7BX **Tel:** 020-8462 6745 **E-mail:** d.p.hutton@talk21.com

Hutton, Timothy, TD, FCII, (Westminster), 32 Hallowell Rd, Northwood, Middx HA6 1DW **Tel:** 01923-825639

Hyde, Kenneth, (Liverpool), Our Lady, Queen of Martyrs and St Swithin, Stonebridge lane, Liverpool L11 9AZ **Tel:** 0151-546 3574 **Fax:** 0151-546 7316

Huynh Chanh (Paul), (Birmingham), 130 Poplar High St, Isle of Dogs, London E14 0AG **Tel:** 020-7537 3071 **Fax:** 020-7537 1959 also The Holy Name and Our Lady of the Sacred Heart, 117 Bow Common Ln, London E3 4AU **Tel:** 020-7987 3477 **Fax:** 030-7537 3834

Hynes, David, (Middlesbrough), Our Lady and St Edward, Westgate, Driffield YO25 6TD **Tel:** 01377-253362

Hynes, Michael, CertEd (SDB), Salesian Ho, 1 Salesian Gardens, Chertsey KT16 8SG **Tel:** 01932 579050 **E-mail:** Michael@Hynessdb.fsnet.co.uk

Hypher, Paul, Mgr, (East Anglia, retired), Moon's Acre Ho, 14 Moon's Acre, Low Bentham Rd, Bentham, Lancs LA2 7BP **Tel:** 01524-262541

Igo, Robert MA, BA, MTh (OSB) (Prior), Monastery of Christ the Word, Monte Cassino, Post Bag 902, Macheke, Zimbabwe, **Tel/Fax:** 00 263 798 369

Igoa, Vincent, (OMI), St Thomas, 17 Val Plaisant, St Helier, Jersey, Channel Isles JE2 4TA **Tel:** 01534-20235

Ikirodah, Cosmas (MSP), St Nicholas of Tolentino, Lawford's Gate, Bristol BS5 0RE **Tel:** 0117-983 3920 **Fax:** 0117-935 1555 **E-mail:** Ikirodah@hotmail.com

Ilunga, Jean Paul, STB, PhL, (Liverpool), Christ the King Presbytery, 78 Queens Drive, Childwall, Liverpool L15 6YQ **Tel:** 0151 722 2231 **Fax:** 0151 722 2755

Inch, Philip, (Liverpool), St John Arnold,

Hedgefield, Gateacre, Liverpool L25 2RW **Tel:** 0151-487 9372 **Fax:** 0151-283 4735

Incledon, Richard, MA, STL, Canon, (Arundel & Brighton), West Flexford Farm, Wansborough, Guildford, Surrey GU3 2JW **Tel:** 01483-810124

Ingham, Peter, (Nottingham), St Mary's Rectory, Bridge Gate, Derby DE1 3AU **Tel:** 01332 346126

Ingle, Christopher, (Arundel & Brighton), 19 Hayling Rise, High Salvington, Worthington BN13 3AL **Tel:** 01903-264770

Inglis, John, (Arundel & Brighton), 6 Wellington Rd, Brighton, E Sussex BN2 3AA **Tel:** 01273-386159

Ingman, Peter, (Nottingham), St Mary's, Countesthorpe Rd, South Wigston, Leicester LE18 2PG **Tel:** 0116-278 3863

Ingwell, Michael, (Leeds), St Edward's Presbytery, 2 Chapel Ln, Clifford LS23 6HU **Tel:** 01937-842318

Innamorati, Dominic, BA, (SCJ), St John the Evangelist and St Martin, 31 George St, Balsall Heath, B12 9RG **Tel:** 0121-440 3025

Innes, Stephen (OFM Cap), Franciscan Friary, Carlton Rd, Erith, Kent DA8 1DN **Tel:** 01322-433193

Irving, Bryan, (Lancaster), Our Lady of the Lakes & St Charles, High Hill, Keswick, Cumbria CA12 5PB **Tel:** 01768-772928

Irving, Christopher (Leeds), 69 Ings Mill Dr, Clayton West, Huddersfield HD8 9PW **Tel:** 01484-866669 **E-mail:** 113135.3047@compuserve.com

Irwin, David, AKC, (Westminster), 12 Womersley Rd, London N8 9AE **Tel:** 020-8340 3394

Isaac, William, (Cardiff), St Mary's Presbytery, 39 Ewenny Rd, Bridgend, CF31 3HS **Tel:** 01656-652034

Jachym, Marian, MA, STL, Vice-Provincial (SChr), Queen of Poland, Nelson St, Lancaster LA1 1PY **Tel:** 01524-39820 **E-mail:** jachym@dompolski.freeserve.co.uk

Jackson, Anthony, (Leeds), Our Lady of Lourdes Presbytery, 130 Cardigan Rd, Leeds LS6 3BJ **Tel/Fax:** 0113 275 2093 **E-mail:** revjackson@hotmail.com

Jackson, Bernard, (Liverpool), St Mary, Birchley Rd, Birchley, Billinge, Wigan WN5 7QJ **Tel:** 01744-892227

Jackson, Christopher W, MA, (Hexham & Newcastle), St Mary's, 27 Bridge St, Sunderland SR1 1TQ **Tel:** 0191-567 5354

Jackson, Damian (SJ), St Beuno's, St Asaph, Denbighshire LL17 0AS **Tel:** 01745-583444 **Fax:** 01745-584151 **E-mail:** damianjack@aol.com

Jackson, Frank J, BA(Econ)(Hons), MA(Theol), ACIS, (Brentwood), The Presbytery, Beardsley Dr, Springfield, Chelmsford, Essex CM1 6GQ **Tel:** 01245-465333

Jackson, Frederick, BA, (Westminster), 16 Abingdon Rd, London W8 6AF **Tel:** 020-7937 4778

Jackson, Ian, (Hexham & Newcastle), St Aidan's, Station Rd, Ashington, Northumberland NE63 8AD **Tel:** 01670-812200

Jackson, Michael, Mgr, STL, (Arundel & Brighton), 39 Norton Rd, Hove, E Sussex BN3 3BF **Tel:** 01273-732843

Jackson, Peter, (OSB), Prinknash Abbey, Cranham, Gloucester GL4 8EX **Tel:** 01452-812455 **Fax:** 01452-813305

Jackson, Quentin, PhD, (OFM), The Friary, Gordon Rd, Nottingham NG3 2LG **Tel:** 0115-950 1064 **E-mail:** quentin@nottfriary.freeserve.co.uk

Jackson, William, (IC), St Mary's Derryswood, Wonersh, Guildford GU5 0RA **Tel:** 01483-893196 **E-mail:** bill @rosmini.org

Jacob, Nicholas Dominic, (Cong Orat), St Aloysius, 25 Woodstock Rd, Oxford OX2 6HA **Tel:** 01865-315800

Jacobson, Norman, (Middlesbrough), St Anthony & Our Lady of Mercy, 28 Inglemire Lane, Hull HU6 7TA **Tel:** 01482 850767 **Fax:** 01482 801253

Jaffa, Bernard, Canon, (Plymouth, retired), St Augustine, Manor Rd, Seaton, Devon, EX12 2AJ **Tel:** 01297-20476

Jakes, Matthew (Nottingham), 125 Alexandra Rd, Burton-on-Trent, Staffs DE15 0JD **Tel:** 01283 564814

Jakobsson, Bengt-Ove, (CHS), The Presbytery, Arkell Avenue, Carterton, Oxon **Tel:** 01992-842463

Jakubas, Martin, MA, GRSM, LRAM, ARCM, ARCO, (Arundel & Brighton), The Presbytery, Hazelgrove Rd, Haywards Heath, W. Sussex RH16 3PQ **Tel:** 01444-450139 **Fax:** 01444-441439

Jakubiak, Michael, (Ukrainians), 12 Ashbourne Dr, Bradford, W Yorks BD2 4AQ **Tel:** 01274-403041

Jakubiec, Slawomir (Poland), 58 Bodnant Avenue, Leicester LE5 5RA **Tel:** 0116-273 0861

James, Dylan (Plymouth), BSc STD, St John's Seminary, Wonersh, Guildford, Surrey GU5 0QX

James, Howard, MA, BSc, STB, (Westminster), Holy Family Cathedral, PO Box 16, St Johns, Antigua, West Indies **Tel:** 001 268 461 1127

James, John, BA, (Hexham & Newcastle), SS Peter & Paul, Belle Vue Cres, South

Shields, Tyne & Wear NE33 4RE
Tel: 0171-456 1858
James, Nicholas, BA, (Cardiff), 3 Chartist Rise, Monmouth NP25 SGA
Tel: 01600 712029
James, Peter, BEd, (OSB), Ampleforth Abbey, York YO62 4EN
Tel: 01439-766714 **Fax:** 01439-766724
Jamison, Christopher, Rt Rev Dom, MA, BA (OSB), Worth Abbey, Crawley, W Sussex RH10 4SB **Tel:** 01342-710320
Janes, William, (Arundel and Brighton, retired), Flat 15 Eaton Hall, 15 Eaton Gardens, Hove, E Sussex BN3 3TZ
Tel: 01273-207491
Janicki, Andrzej, (MIC) (Northampton, retired), Marian Fathers, Fawley Court, Henley-on-Thames, Oxon RG9 3AE
Tel: 01491-574917
Jankiewicz, Kazimierz (MIC) *(Superior)*, 2 Windsor Rd, London W5 5PD
Tel: 020-8567 1746 (Pol 3)
Januszewski, Grzegorz, (SChr) (Polish Priest), Polish Catholic Centre, 71 West St, Crewe CW1 3HF
Tel: 01270-256284
Januszkiewicz, Jerzy, 83 London Rd, Reading RG1 5BY. **Tel:** 0118-957 3647
E-mail: pbf.wacpan@ukonline.co.uk
Jarosz, Edward, Canon (Nottingham), St Peter's Presbytery, 21 Hinckley Rd, Leicester LE3 0TA **Tel:** 0116-251 9802
E-mail: eddy.jarosz@nottinghamdiocese.org.uk
Jarvis, Geoffrey, (East Anglia, retired), 13 Cleaves Dr, Little Walsingham, Norfolk NR22 6EQ **Tel:** 01328-820957
Jarzabek, Mariusz (MIC). 2 Windsor Rd, London W5 5PD **Tel:** 020-8810 0185
Jasinski, Pawel, DD, (MIC, retired), Fawley Court, Henley-on-Thames, Oxon RG9 3AE **Tel:** 01491-574917
Jasinski, Wojciech (MIC), Fawley Court, Henley-on-Thames, Oxon RG9 3AE
Tel: 01491-571935 **Fax:** 01491-411587
E-mail: wojtj@aol.com
Jebb, Anthony Philip, MA, Guestmaster (OSB), Downside Abbey, Stratton on the Fosse, Radstock, Bath, Somerset BA3 4RH **Tel:** 01761-235148
Jedrych, Slawomir (MS), The Presbytery, Howard Way, Harlow, Essex CM20 2NS
Tel: 01279 426017
Jeffries, Charles, (Arundel & Brighton, retired), 4 The Old Village Hall, High St, Billingshurst, W. Sussex RH14 9PL
Tel: 01403-784067
Jelf, Timothy, (Arundel & Brighton, retired), 23 Barncroft, Farnham, Surrey GU9 8RU **Tel:** 01252-727631
Jenkins, Christopher (OSB), Our Lady of the Assumption, 8 Weaver's Walk, Swynnerton, Staffs ST15 0QZ
Tel: 01782-796677
Jenkins, Christopher, (SCJ) (Adscripti), 266 Wellington Rd North, Stockport, SK4 2QR
E-mail: scj@malpas2000.freeserve.co.uk
Jenkins, Nicholas, Canon, BA(hons), MEd, (Menevia, retired), 7 Chapel Rd, Llanharan, Cardiff CF72 9QA
Jenner, Peter, BTh, (Southwark), 98 Leatherhead Rd, Chessington, Surrey KT9 2HY **Tel:** 020-8397 3971 **Fax:** 020 8391 2242 **Mbl:** 07966 206180
E-mail: office@stcatherineofsiena.org.uk
Jennings, David, (East Anglia), Catholic Presbytery, Geneva St, Peterborough PE1 2RS **Tel:** 01733-562528 **Fax:** 01733-346933 **E-mail:** parishoffice@stpeterandallsouls-peterborough.org.uk
Jennings, Francis, (Salford), 10 Slade Ln, Padiham BB12 9AA **Tel:** 01282-770412
Jennings, Nicholas, (Hexham & Newcastle), St Patrick's Presbytery, Glenfield Rd, Fairfield, Stockton-on-Tees TS19 7PJ **Tel/Fax:** 01642-580171
Jennings, Paul, LCL, MCL (Arundel & Brighton), 4 Vicarage Ln, Horley, Surrey RH6 8AR **Tel:** 01293-431703
Jennings, Robert BA, KHS (Portsmouth), 21 Fernham Rd, Faringdon, Oxon SN7 7JY **Tel:** 01367-242039
Fax: 01367 244752
E-mail: frbobjennings@aol.com
John, David, (Plymouth), Box 116, Chetwynd, British Columbia, Voc 150, Canada
Johnson, Anthony, (CSsR), St Mary's, Clapham, London SW4 7AP
Tel: 020-7622 2793 **Fax:** 020-7720 8191
Johnson, Clyde Hughes, Canon, PhB, STL, VF (Menevia), The Presbytery, Vergam Terr, Fishguard, Pembrokeshire SA65 9DF **Tel/Fax:** 01348-873865
Johnson, Cuthbert, STD (Abbot) (OSB), St Mary's Abbey, Quarr, Ryde, Isle of Wight PO33 4ES
Tel: 01983-882420 **Fax:** 01983-884402
E-mail: quarr@portsmouth.dio.org.uk
Johnson, Francis (Liverpool), (Focolare Movement) 14 Sinclair Drive, Liverpool L18 0HN
Tel: 0151 722 3981 **Fax:** 0151 475 1033
E-mail: frankjohnson@btconnect.com
Johnson, Frank (Nottingham) 14 Sinclair Drive, Liverpool L18 0HN
Tel: 0151-722 3981 **Fax:** 0151-475 1033
Johnson, Gerard M, (Wrexham), 17 Coleshill St, Flint, Flintshire CH6 5BQ
Tel: 01352-673245
Johnson, John, (Liverpool), St Mary's, Standishgate, Wigan, Lancs WN1 1XL
Tel: 01942-242066

Johnson, Paul (Clifton), Wellsprings, Glasshouse Ln, Taynton, Glos GL19 3HJ **Tel:** 01452-831205

Johnson, Peter W, (Leeds, retired), 27 Hollyshaw Ln, Church View Court, Leeds LS15 7BA **Tel:** 0113-264 2416

Johnson, Ronald (Liverpool), St Francis of Assisi, Earp St, Garston, Liverpool L19 1RT **Tel:** 0151-427 4015

Johnson, Stephen, (Hexham & Newcastle, Retired), 9 Greenside, Greatham, Hartlepool TS25 2HQ **Tel:** 01429 870890

Johnston, Michael, (Westminster), 73 Pembroke Rd, Ruislip, Middx HA4 8NN **Tel:** 01895-632739

Johnston, Norman, (Lancaster), Blessed Sacrament, Farrington Ln, Ribbleton, Preston PR2 6LX **Tel:** 01772-791782

Johnston, Sean, (CM), Damascus Ho, The Ridgeway, Mill Hill, London NW7 1HH **Tel:** 020-8959 8971 **Fax:** 020-8906 4573

Johnstone, Michael, (East Anglia), Catholic Presbytery, 31 Station St, Swaffham, Norfolk PE37 7HP **Tel:** 01760-721418

Johnstone, Paul, (Lancaster), The Willows, Ribby Rd, Kirkham PR4 2BE **Tel/Fax:** 011772-683664

Johnstone, Peter (Arundel & Brighton), St Mary's Presbytery, Bepton Rd, Midhurst, W. Sussex GU29 9HD

Johonnett, Michael, (Salford), English Martyrs Presbytery, Alexandra Rd South, Whalley Range, Manchester M16 8GF **Tel:** 0161-226 1980 **Fax:** 0161-227 8788

Jolly, Andrew (Liverpool), Sacred Heart Presbytery, Springfield Rd, Wigan WN6 7AT **Tel:** 01942-745689

Jolly, Luke, BA, (OSB), Worth Abbey, Crawley, W Sussex RH10 4SB **Tel:** 01342-710310

Jones, Anthony, (Birmingham), c/o Archbishop's Ho, Shadwell St, Birmingham B4 6EY

Jones, Antony, STL, (Wrexham), Our Lady Star of the Sea, 35 Lloyd St, Llandudno LL30 2YA **Tel:** 01492-850456 **Fax:** 01492-879808 **E-mail:** aj@serenymor.fsnet.co.uk

Jones, Bernard, (OCarm), Nazareth Ho, London Rd, Cheltenham GL52 6YT **Tel:** 01242 580308

Jones, Brian, (Wrexham, retired), 'College', Llansadwrm, Anglesey, Gwynedd LL59 5SN **Tel:** 01248-810287

Jones, Gareth Adrian, (Cardiff), Catholic The Oratory, 141 Hagley Road, Edgbaston, Birmingham B16 8UE **Tel:** 0121 454 0496 **Email:** oratory@globalnet.co.uk

Jones, Henry, (Salford), St Mary, 86 Chorley New Rd, Horwich, Bolton BL6 5QJ **Tel:** 01204-468209

Jones, Ieuan Wyn, (Cardiff), 39 Dorset St, Cardiff CF11 7PS

Jones, James, (SCJ, retired), St Johns, 266 Wellington Rd North, Stockport **Tel:** 0161-442 4117

Jones, Jason, (Menevia), North Rd, Cardigan SA43 1LT **Tel:** 01239-612615

Jones, Kevin, (Portsmouth), Priest's Ho, Church of Immaculate Conception, 63-67 Yorktown Rd, Sandhurst, Berks GU47 9BS **Tel:** 01252 876820 **E-mail:** crowsand@btinternet.com

Jones, Lawrence, (Hexham & Newcastle), English Martyrs, Hardwick Rd, Stockton-on-Tees, TS19 8JX **Tel:** 01642- 673032

Jones, Matthew, JCL, (Cardiff), St Brigid's Presbytery, Crystal Glen, Heath, Cardiff CF14 5QN **Tel:** 029-2075 2389

Jones, Michael, STB (Salford), (Chaplain to Pendleton College; Part-time Asst Chaplain to HMP Manchester; English Martyrs Presbytery, 5 Roseneath Road, Urmston, Manchester M41 5AX **Tel:** 0161-748 2328 **Fax:** 0161 755 3473

Jones, Michael, BA (Southwark), 21 Heathfield Rd, Bexley Heath, London DA6 8NP **Tel:** 020 8303 1957

Jones, Peter, (Birmingham), 85 Prestbury Rd, Aston B6 6EG **Tel:** 0121-327 0505

Jones, Philip, (CSsR), 49 Sutton Rd, Erdington, Birmingham B23 6QN **Tel:** 0121-373 0143

Jones, Pius (SM), St Mary's Retreat, Union St, Carmarthen SA31 3DE **Tel/Fax:** 01267-237205 **E-mail:** carmarthenpp@marist.org.uk

Jones, Raphael, STB, (OSB), St Benedict's Monastery, Convent Cl, Duddle Ln, Bamber Bridge, Preston PR5 6US **Tel:** 01772-902201 **Fax:** 01772-902214

Jones, Richard, MA (OSB), Our Lady and St Joseph, Priory Rd, Alcester, Warks B49 5DY **Tel:** 01789-762573

Jones, Roderick, (OSB), BA, Dip Arch, Parish Priest, Worth Abbey, Crawley, W Sussex RH10 4SB **Tel:** 01342-710310

Jones, William, (Salford, retired), Nazareth Ho, Preston New Rd, Blackburn BB2 7AL **Tel:** 01254-691774

Jónsson, Atli, STB (Reykjavik) St Joseph's Rectory, 40 York Rd, Birkdale, Southport PR8 2AY **Tel:** 01704-568313

Jonsson, Atli G, STL (Reykjavik), Priest's Ho, 184 Liverpool Rd, Skelmersdale WN8 8BX **Tel:** 01695-724476

Jordan, Gerard, (SCJ, retired), St Johns, 266 Wellington Rd North, Stockport **Tel:** 0161-442 4117

Jordan, Kevin (Westminster), 80 Imperial Cl, North Harrow, HA2 7LW **Tel:** 0208-868 7531

Jordan, Michael F, (Birmingham), 1 De

Montfort Way, Coventry CV4 7DU
Tel: 024-7641 9111

Jordan, Thomas, (Brentwood), 5 Park End Rd, Romford, Essex RM1 4AT
Tel: 01708-740308

Jordan, Trevor, (Plymouth), Christ the King, Armada Way, Plymouth PL1 2EW
Tel: 01752-266523

Jordan, William, (Brentwood), c/o Cathedral Ho, Ingrave Rd, Brentwood, Essex CM15 8AT

Joseph, Benny (MSFS), Cathedral Ho, Kingthorpe Rd, Northampton NN2 6AG **Tel:** 01604-714556

Joyce, Anthony, STB, (Birmingham), The Presbytery, Beoley Rd, Redditch, Worcester B98 8LT **Tel:** 01527-63096
E-mail: office@mtcarmel.fsnet.co.uk

Joyce, Cornelius J, (Brentwood, retired), 11A Woodfield Park Dr, Leigh-on-Sea, Essex SS9 1LN **Tel:** 01702-712562

Joyce, James, Mgr, LIB, STD (Portsmouth), 60 Sturges Rd, Wokingham, Berks RG40 2HE **Tel:** 0118-978 0348
Fax: 0118-979 5825 **Mbl:** 07730-127908
E-mail: james.joyce@networld.com

Joyce, John, (Shrewsbury), St Vincent de Paul, Tatton St, Knutsford WA16 6HR
Tel: 01565-633040
E-mail: jjoycespat@aol.com

Joyce, John T, (Liverpool) All Saints, High St, Golborne, Warrington WA3 3BG
Tel: 01942-728962

Joyce, Martin, BA, DipCouns, (Brentwood), 50 London Hill, Rayleigh, Essex SS6 7HP
Tel: 01268-742229

Joyce, Michael, (Superior) (SVD), 8 Teignmouth Rd, London NW2 4HN
Tel: 020-8452 8430

Joyce, Patrick, (Birmingham), SS Mary & John, 20 Gravelly Hill, North Erdington, Birmingham B23 6BQ **Tel:** 0121-373 0263

Joye, George, (OPraem), St Mary Magdalen's Priory, 55 Upper North St, Brighton BN1 3FH **Tel:** 01273-326793

Juszczyk, Marian (STB) (Kielce, retired), 39 Edinburgh Dr, Pemberton, Wigan WN5 9ET **Tel:** 01942-211678

Kaczharczyk, Darius (OFM), 557-559 High Rd, Woodford Green, Essex IG8 0RB
Tel: 020-8504 1688

Kaggwa, Robert, BA, MA, STL, STD (MAfr), Digby Stuart Chaplaincy, Roehampton University, Roehampton Ln, Roehampton London SW15 5PH
Tel: 020 8392 3231

Kalinda, Floribert Mulikita (SDS), Novice Director, 25 Church Rd, Thornbury, S Glos BS35 1EL

Kalski, Remigiusz (SJ), House of Our Lady of Mercy, 182 Walm Ln, London NW2 3AX **Tel/Fax:** 020-8452 4304

Kamaitis, Valentinas, Canon, (Salford, retired), Nazareth Ho, Scholes Ln, Prestwich, Manchester M25 0NU
Tel: 0161-798 4353

Kane, Gerry (SM), Notre Dame de France, 5 Leicester Square, London WC2H 7BP
Tel: 020-7437 9363 **Fax:** 020-7437 9364

Kane, Ian, (CSsR), The Redemptorist Mission Team, The Monastery, Badby Rd West, Daventry, Northants NN11 4NH

Kapuscinski, Antoni, KHS, (Polish Priest), 118 Oakley Rd, Redditch B97 4EJ
Tel: 01527-591391

Karamvelil, Sebastian, MA, LPh, LTh, (SSP), Society of St Paul, 191 Battersea Bridge Rd, London SW11 3AS
Tel: 020-7228 2656 **Fax:** 020-7228 1656

Karpinski, Aleksander, (MIC), (Northampton, retired), Fawley Court, Henley-on-Thames RG9 3AE
Tel: 01491 574 917

Kavanagh, Dominic, (Birmingham), 1 Herbert Rd, Solihull, B91 3QE
Tel: 0121-705 0228

Kavanagh, John, (Southwark), The Presbytery, 79 Moorside Rd, Downham, Bromley BR1 5EP **Tel:** 020-8698 1449

Kavanagh, Kevin, (Birmingham), Presbytery, Chedworth Dr, Worcester WR4 9PG **Tel:** 01905- 454352

Kavanagh, Nichoas J. MA, BD (Westminster), 22 George St, London W1U 3QY **Tel:** 020-7935 0943

Kay, Anthony, BD (Salford) 106 Crowhill South, Alkrington, Middleton, Manchester M24 1JU
Tel: 0161-794 2825 **Fax:** 0161-727 8592
E-mail: revsec@wardleyhall.org.uk

Kealey, Brian, (Salford), Christ the King, 9 Healey Court, Burnley, Lancs BB11 2QJ
Tel: 01282-423270

Kealy, Rt Rev Dom Finbar, BSc, MA (OSB), St. Mary's Abbey, Quarr, Ryde, Isle-of-Wight PO33 4ES **Tel:** 01983-882420
Email: prior@quarrabbey.co.uk

Keane, A Thomas, Canon, (Cardiff, retired), 6 Harvey Rd, Hamilton Dean, Hereford HR1 1XB **Tel:** 01432 279909

Keane, James, (Hexham & Newcastle), St George, Bells Cl, Newcastle upon Tyne NE15 6XX **Tel:** 0191-267 4120

Keane, Liam, (Salford, retired), 56 Old Croft Bank, Davyhulme, Manchester M41 7AB **Tel:** 0161-370 1615
E-mail: lkeane@stannes.plus.com

Keane, Manus, (SJ), St Wilfrid's Presbytery, 1 Winckley Sq, Preston PR1 3JJ
E-mail: m.patrickkeane@btinternet.com

Keane, Noel, (SDS), Salvatorian Community, High Rd, Harrow Weald, Middx HA3 5DY **Tel:** 020-8427 2808 (Community) 020-8427 1955 (Parish)

E-mail: noelsds@btconnect.com

Keane, Patrick, Canon, (Salford, retired), c/o Wardley hall, Worsley, Manchester M28 2ND

Keane, Paul, MA(Cantab), STL (Brentwood), Clergy Ho, 28 Ingrave Rd, Brentwood, Essex CM15 8AT **Tel:** 01277 265235

Keaney, Kevin, (Birmingham, retired) Parochial Ho, Graughwell, Co Galway, Ireland **Tel:** 00 353 91 46124

Kearney, Francis, Canon, STL (Hexham & Newcastle), St Agnes, Westburn, Crawcrook, Ryton, Tyne and Wear NE40 4ET **Tel:** 0191-413 2766

Kearney, Gerard, (Leeds), St Benedict's Presbytery, Aberford Rd, Garforth LS25 1PX **Tel:** 0113-286 3224 **Fax:** 0113 287 7286 **E-mail:** gerard.kearney@dioceseofleeds.org.uk

Kearney, John, (FDP), 25 Lower Teddington Rd, Hampton Wick, Kingston-upon-Thames KT1 4HB **Tel:** 020-8977 5130

Kearney, Nicholas, MA, Mag Theol Lic Phil, (East Anglia), 82 Hartford Rd, Huntingdon PE29 1XG **Tel:** 01480-453257

Kearney, Sean M, Canon, (Cardiff, retired), Gleann Mhuire, Dromillihy, Leap, Co Cork, Eire

Kearney, William, (Portsmouth, retired), Glaunthorn, Co Cork, Ireland

Kearns, John, (CP), St John's Presbytery, 13 Powell St, Wigan WN1 1XD **Tel:** 01942-245625

Keating, Denis, (OP), STL, MA, c/o The Provincial, St Dominic's Priory, Southampton Rd, London NW5 4LB

Keauffling, Dunstan, BA, (OSB), (Novice Master/Bursar), St Augustine's Abbey, Ramsgate, Kent CT11 9PA **Tel:** 01843-593045 **Fax:** 01843-582732 **E-mail:** frdunstan@aol.com

Keaveny, Patrick, Mgr, (Southwark), St Mary's, 5 Cresswell Park, Blackheath SE3 9RD **Tel:** 020-8852 5420 **Fax:** 020-8852 9298

Keefe, Anthony, MA, (Lancaster), St. Thomas the Apostle, Rectory, Smithy Lane, Claughton-on-Brock, Preston PR3 0PN **Tel:** 01995 640208

Keegan, Arthur, Monsignor (Salford, retired), 76 Temple Rd, Sale, Manchester M33 2FG

Keegan, Desmond, (CSsR) St Mary's, Clapham, London SW4 7AP. (Parish): **Tel:** 020-7622 2793 **Fax:** 020-7720 8191

Keegan, Jack (Wrexham), St Francis of Assisi, Llay Chain, Llay, Wrexham LL12 0NT **Tel:** 01978-852297 **Fax:** 01978-852932

Keegan, Malachy, Prison Chaplain, (Wrexham), 2 Lynne Cl, Selsdon, South Croydon CR2 8QA **Tel:** 020-8657 8645 **Mbl:** 07801 701763 and also RC Chaplain, HM Prisons, Room 410, Abell House, John Islip Street, London SW1P 4LH **Tel:** 0207 217 8714 **E-mail:** mal.keegan@blueyonder.co.uk

Keeling, Peter, (Middlesbrough), St Francis of Assisi Presbytery, 5 Levick Cres, Acklam, Middlesbrough TS5 4RL **Tel:** 01642-818190

Keely, Patrick, (OCD), Carmelite Priory, 41 Kensington Church St, London W8 4BB **Tel:** 020-7937 9866 **Fax:** 020-7938 1470

Keen, Christopher, (Southwark), St Lawrence, High St, Edenbridge, Kent TN5 5AQ **Tel/Fax:** 01732-862256

Keenan, Enda, (Brentwood, retired), 20 Sue Ryder Homes, Holycross, Thurles, Co. Tipperary, Ireland

Keenan, Francis, (SJ), St Beuno's, St Asaph, Denbighshire LL17 0AS **Tel:** 01745-583444 **Fax:** 01745-584151 **E-mail:** civuna@aol.com

Keenan, James, (Portsmouth, retired), c/o Bishop's Ho, Edinburgh Rd, Portsmouth PO1 3HG

Keenan, Seamus, (Northampton), 2 Brereton Rd, Bedford MK40 1HU **Tel/Fax:** 01234-352569 **E-mail:** stjosephsbedford@yahoo.co.uk

Keevins, Frank, (CP), Monastery, Minsteracres, Consett, Co Durham DH8 9RT

Kehoe, Philip, Regional Superior (SDP), 13 Lower Teddington Rd, Hampton Wick, Kingston-on-Thames, Surrey KT1 4EU **Tel:** 020-8977 5130/9182 **Fax:** 020-8977 0105

Kelleher, Colm, (Portsmouth, retired), 17 Claude Rd, Drumcondra, Dublin 9, Eire

Kelleher, Patrick, (SPS), 20 Beauchamp Rd, East Molesey, Surrey KT8 0PA **Tel:** 020 8979 1890 **E-mail:** pkeller@iol.ie

Keller, Joseph, (Liverpool), St Bernadette's, Heath Rd, Liverpool L19 4TW **Tel:** 0151-427 7648 **Fax:** 0151-427 6199 **Mbl:** 07979 471378

Kellett, Denis, (Hexham & Newcastle), St Teresa of the Child Jesus, Heaton Rd, Newcastle upon Tyne NE6 5HN **Tel:** 0191-265 5290 **Fax:** 0191-265 5380

Kelliher, Alexander, (SA), 47 Francis St, Westminster, SW1P 1QR **Tel:** 020-7828 4163

Kelly, Aidan, (Liverpool), Catholic Chaplain, HM Prison Risley, Warrington WA3 6BP **Tel:** 01925-763871 Ext 326

Kelly, Aloysius, (OFM), PO Box 1621, Ladysmith, Natal, South Africa 3370

Kelly, Bernard (CHS), 141 Parkfield Rd, Saltley, Birmingham B8 3BB **Tel:** 0121-327 0585

E-mail: rosary@saltley.ukf.net

Kelly, Brendan, (Hexham & Newcastle), Our Lady and St Cuthbert, 64 Ravensdowne, Berwick-upon-Tweed TD15 1DQ **Tel:** 01289-307297

Kelly, Christopher, (CP), St Joseph's Retreat, Highgate Hill, London N19 5NE **Tel:** 020-7272 2320

Kelly, David, CF(RC), (Westminster), c/o MOD Chaplains (Army), Trenchard Lines, Upavon, Pewsey, Wiltshire SN9 6BE

Kelly, Edward, (CRL), Christ Church, 229 High St, Eltham, London SE9 1TX **Tel:** 020-8850 1666

Kelly, Fergus, BA, (CM), 2 Flower Ln NW7 2JB **Tel:** 020-8959 1021

Kelly, Gerard, BSc, MTh (Liverpool), Sion Community, Sawyers Hall Ln, Brentwood, Essex CM15 9BX **Tel:** 01227-215011 **Fax:** 01227 234401 **E-mail:** gerard.kelly@sioncommunity.org.uk

Kelly, Gerard, BA (Birmingham), Our Lady of Perpetual Succour Presbytery, Cannock Rd, Old Fallings, Wolverhampton WV10 8PG **Tel/Fax:** 01902-731189

Kelly, Ian G, MPhil, (Salford), (Chaplain, Manchester University), Avila Ho, 337 Oxford Rd, Manchester M13 9PG **Tel:** 0161-273 1456

Kelly, Ignatius, (OFM), The Friary, Sample Oak Ln, Chilworth, Guildford, Surrey GU4 8QR **Tel:** 01483-893168 **Fax:** 01483-898071

Kelly, John, (Cardiff), The Presbytery, Stow Hill, Newport NP20 1TP **Tel:** 01633-265533

Kelly, John, Canon, (Leeds, retired), Mount St Joseph's, Shire Oak Rd, Leeds LS6 2DE **Tel:** 0113-275 4685

Kelly, John A, (Leeds), St Gregory's Presbytery, Swarcliffe Dr, Leeds LS14 5AW **Tel:** 0113-293 0288 **Fax:** 0113-232 8101 **E-mail:** stcolumbas.bradford@lincome.net

Kelly, Joseph, (OCarm), Nazareth Ho, Hammersmith Rd, London W6 8DB **Tel:** 020 8748 3549

Kelly, Joseph, (SMM), Nazareth Ho, Liverpool Rd, Blundellsands, Liverpool L23 0QT **Tel:** 0151-928 3254

Kelly, Joseph, (Liverpool), St George, Station Rd, Maghull, Liverpool L31 3DF **Tel:** 0151-526 1071 **Fax:** 0151-526 9660

Kelly, Joseph, Chaplain (OCarm), Nazareth Ho, London Rd, Charlton Kings, Cheltenham GL52 6YJ **Tel:** 01242-516361

Kelly, Kevin, DD, JCL (Liverpool, retired), 31 Arch View Crescent, Liverpool L1 7BA **Tel/Fax:** 0151-707 3565 **E-mail:** rkklrkk@aol.com

Kelly, Leo J, (Lancaster, retired), 21 Old Hall Cl, Torrisholme, Morecambe LA4 6NL **Tel:** 01524-400231

Kelly, Martin, (Leeds), Bishops Ho, 13 North Grange Rd, Leeds LS6 2BR **Tel:** 0113-230 4533 **Fax:** 0113 278 9890

Kelly, Michael, (Leeds), St Augustine's Presbytery, Harehills Rd, Leeds LS8 5HR **Tel:** 0113-249 0762

Kelly, Patrick A, (Liverpool), St Sebastian 18 Lilley Rd, Fairfield, Liverpool L7 0LR **Tel:** 0151-263 1755

Kelly, Patrick J, (Plymouth), 44 Popham Close, Tiverton, Devon EX16 4GA **Tel:** 01884-251730

Kelly, Patrick Laurence, MA, (OSB), Downside Abbey, Stratton on the Fosse, Radstock, Bath BA3 4RH **Tel:** 01761-235161

Kelly, Peter, (Hexham & Newcastle), Victoria Ln, Coudon, Bishop's Auckland, Co Durham DL14 8NL **Tel:** 01388 602030

Kelly, Peter, (Liverpool, retired), Alston Court, 483 Liverpool Rd, Ainsdale, Southport PR8 3BP

Kelly, Peter, (Menevia), St Joachim and St Anne, Llysteg, Dunvant, Swansea SA2 7QQ **Tel:** 01792-201046

Kelly, Peter, (MAfr), 129 Lichfield Rd, Sutton Coldfield, W. Mids B74 2SA

Kelly, Rory, (Arundel & Brighton), St Wilfrid's, South Rd, Hailsham E. Sussex BN27 3JG **Tel:** 01323-841504

Kelly, T, BA, (SCJ), Sacred Heart and St Catherine of Alexandria, Worcester Rd, Droitwich, Worcestershire WR9 8UT **Tel:** 01905-773258

Kelly, Thomas Patrick, (Clifton), 9 Binford Place, Bridgwater, TA6 3NJ **Tel:** 01278-422703

Kemball, Eric, MA, (Birmingham), 22 Ronson Avenue, Trent Vale, Stoke-on-Trent ST4 6PX **Tel:** 01782-411836

Kemp, Oliver Plunket, (Birmingham), c/o Archbishop's Ho, 8 Shadwell St, Birmingham B4 6EY

Kemsley, Francis, (OCarm), 142 Rodney Rd, London SE17 1RA **Tel:** 020 7703 4967

Keniry, David Francis, (Birmingham), 110 Potters Green Rd, Coventry CV2 2AN **Tel:** 02476-604144

Kennedy, Jack, (Leeds), St Clare's Presbytery, Moorside Rd, Fagley, Bradford BD2 3JE **Tel:** 01274-637438

Kennedy, James, (CMF), The Towers, High St, Buckden, St Neots PE19 5TA **Tel:** 01480 810344 **E-mail:** leyton@dioceseofbrentwood.org

Kennedy, James R, (Hallam), Our Lady of Perpetual Help, 54 High St, Bentley,

Doncaster DN5 0AT **Tel:** 01302-874337

Kennedy, Jim (Westminster), 157 Copenhagen St, London N1 0SR **Tel:** 020-7837 4841

Kennedy, John, Mgr, MPhil, STL, (Liverpool), 1 Brompton Rd, Southport, Merseyside PR8 6AS **Tel:** 01704-532613

Kennedy, John, (Hexham & Newcastle), Presbytery, Braemar Rd, Owton Manor, Hartlepool, Cleveland TS25 3AS **Tel:** 01429-274557

Kennedy, Michael, (Westminster), c/o Archbishop's Ho, London SW1 1QJ **Tel:** 020-8452 2475

Kennedy, Patrick J, (Hexham & Newcastle, retired), St Gregory, 20 St Gregory's Court, South Shields NE34 6NR **Tel:** 0191-456 0724

Kennedy, Thomas J, (Liverpool), The Blessed English Martyrs, Piele Rd, Haydock, St Helens WA11 0JY **Tel:** 01942-727005

Kennedy, Vincent, Greyfriars, 1 Elmsley Rd, Mossley Hill L18 8AY **Tel:** 0151-724 2109 **Fax:** 0151-724 2553

Kennedy-Thomas, Thomas STB (Westminster), c/o Archbishop's Ho, Ambrosden Avenue, London SW1P 1QJ

Kenny, Andrew, (Birmingham), The Lodge, 94 Selly Park Rd, Birmingham B29 7LL **Tel:** 0121 415 6110.

Kenny, James V, (Shrewsbury), St Theresa's, 128 Blacon Avenue, Blacon, Chester CH1 5BU **Tel:** 01244-371660 **Fax:** 01244-390976 **E-mail:** st.theresas@tiscali.co.uk

Kenny, John Kevin, KCHS, (Salford), Priory Cottage, Sandy Ln, Pleasington, Blackburn BB2 6RF **Tel:** 01254-201173

Kenny, John, (Southwark, retired) Levalley, Rathdowney, Co Laois, Ireland **Tel:** 00 353 505 46663

Kenny, Patrick, (Arundel & Brighton, retired), 30 Arlington Rd, Easthouse, E Sussex BN21 1DL **Tel:** 01323-639929

Kenny, Thomas A, (Northampton, retired), Bloomhill, Ballynahown, Athlone, Co Westmeath Ireland **E-mail:** kenny.tom@gmail.com

Kenny, Thomas J, (Leeds, retired), 313 Dewsbury Rd, Lupset, Wakefield WF2 9DD **E-mail:** tomkenny@blueyonder.co.uk

Kenrick, John Patrick BA, MA (OP) Blackfriars, Buckingham Rd, Cambridge CB3 0DD **Tel:** 01223-741251

Kenwrick, Brian, (Plymouth), The Presbytery, 76 Abbey Rd, Torquay, Devon TQ2 5NJ **Tel:** 01803-294142

Kenyon, Alexander, (OSB), c/o Belmont Abbey, Hereford HR2 9RZ **Tel:** 01432-374710

Keogh, Joseph, (Nottingham), 94 Butterley Hill, Ripley, Derbyshire DE5 3LW **Tel:** 01773-743336

Keogh, Michael, (Middlesbrough), St Patrick's Rectory, 39 Westbury St, Thornaby, Stockton on Tees TS17 6NW **Tel:** 01642-674140

Keogh, Patrick, (Middlesbrough), St Joseph's, Park Rd South, Grove Hill, Middlesbrough TS4 2RB **Tel:** 01642-818203

Keogh, William, MDiv (Jefferson City), 37 Frindsbury Rd, Strood, Kent ME2 4JA **Tel:** 01634 717582

Keoghan, Michael, (Hexham & Newcastle), Our Blessed Lady and St Joseph, Brooms, Leadgate,Co Durham DH8 6RS **Tel:** 01207-503550

Ker, Ian, (Portsmouth), 171 The Hill, Burford, Oxon, OX18 4RE **Tel:** 01993-823219

Kerby, Raymond, MA, (East Anglia, retired), 34 The Elms, Chatteris, Cambs PE16 6JN **Tel:** 01354-693123

Kern, Nicholas, (Shrewsbury), St Joseph's, 10 Willowbank Rd, Birkenhead CH42 7JY **Tel:** 0151-652 5767 **Fax:** 0151-201 7956 **Email:** nick.kern@btinternet.com

Kernan, Lawrence, (Lancaster), c/o Pastoral Centre, Cathedral Ho, Balmoral Rd, Lancaster LA1 3BT

Kerrisk, Patrick, (Cardiff), The Holy Family, Carter Pl, Fairwater, Cardiff CF5 3NP **Tel:** 02920-563871

Kershaw, Martin, (Liverpool), St Austin's, Heath St, Thatto Heath, St Helens WA9 5NN **Tel:** 01744-812115

Keville, James, (Lancaster), Presbytery, Darkinson Ln, Lea Town, Preston PR4 0RJ **Tel:** 01772-726425

Keyworth, Thomas, (Salford), Lilac Cottage, Market Hill, Glass, Huntley, Aberdeenshire AB54 4XE **Tel:** 078-668 68888 and 01343-812121 ext 7180 **E-mail:** thosbeckete@supanet.com

Kiely, Benedict, (OFM Cap), Franciscan Friary, Carlton Rd, Erith, Kent DA8 1DN **Tel:** 01322-433193/402060 **Fax:** 01322-402061

Kiely, Daniel, Canon, (Northampton), St Bernardine, Chandos Rd, Buckingham MK18 1AL **Tel:** 01280-813105 **E-mail:** dankiely@freeuk.com

Kiely, Michael, (SCA), The Presbytery, 5 Amwell St, Rosebery Avenue, Clerkenwell EC1R 1UL **Tel:** 020-7837 2094

Kiely, William, BA (Plymouth), The Presbytery, Shortlands, Cullompton, Devon EX15 1EW **Tel:** 01884-32253

Kiernan, Thomas, (Westminster, retired), 33 Coolamber Court, Templeogue,

Dublin 6 **Tel:** 00-3531 494 5204

Kilbane Seamus, Mgr, (Middlesbrough, retired), St Agnes, 58 Cemetery Rd, York YO10 5AJ **Tel:** 01904-628677

Kilgannon, William, Mgr, VG, (Hallam), St Wilfrid's Presbytery, St Ronan's Rd, Sheffield S7 1DX **Tel:** 0114-255 0827

Kilgarriff, Patrick, (Plymouth, retired), Flat 2, Balfours Court, 53 Balfours, Sidmouth, Devon EX10 9EG

Kilgarriff, Patrick Michael, Mgr (Birmingham), 125 Newton Rd, Malvern, Worcestershire WR14 1PF **Tel:** 01684-574250

Kilkenny, William, (Shrewsbury), St Mary, 30 West Rd, Congleton, CW12 4ES **Tel:** 01260-273314 **E-mail:** stmaryscongleton@btinternet.com

Killeen, Brendan, BSc, PhD, STB, MA, JCL, MCL, PhD (Northampton), Ss Francis and Therese, Overslade Cl, Clannell Rd, East Hunsbury, Northampton NN4 0RZ **Tel:** 01604-768483 **Fax:** 01614 677655

Killeen, Michael, STL, (Hallam, retired), Mount St Joseph's, Shire Oak Ln, Leeds LS6 2DE

Kinane, James BA, PGCCE, MADiv, PhD, (Nottingham), Ceili Community, Harbour Rd, Kilbeggan, Co Westmeath, Ireland. **Tel:** 00 353-579 333 322

King, Gerard, (Westminster), 26 Salisbury Square, Old Hatfield, Herts AL9 5JD **Tel:** 01707-262439

King, John, (Brentwood), Our Lady of Compassion, Green St, Upton Park, London E13 9AX **Tel:** 020-8472 1181

King, Lawrence, FRICS (Birmingham), 534 Lichfield Rd, Four Oaks, Sutton Coldfield B74 4EH **Tel:** 0121 308 2560

King, Malcolm, (Arundel & Brighton), Cathedral Ho, Parson's Hill, Arundel, W Sussex BN18 9AY **Tel:** 01903 882297 **Fax:** 01903 885335 **Email:** aruncath1@aol.com

King, Nicholas (SJ), Campion Hall, Brewer St, Oxford OX1 1QS **Tel:** 01865-286119 **E-mail:** nicholas.king@campion.ox.ac.uk

King, Paul, (Portsmouth), 60 Abingdon Rd, Oxford OX1 4PE **Tel/Fax:** 01865-437066 **E-mail:** paulking@ portsmouth-dio.org.uk

King, Robert STB (Clifton), 103 Queens Rd, Clifton, Bristol BS8 1LL **Tel:** 0117-914 0003 **Email:** robert.king@cliftondiocese.com

Kinlen, Richard, ThEd (MAfr), St Anthony's Presbytery, Cadley Causeway, Fulwood, Preston PR2 3RX **Tel:** 01772-725193 **Fax:** 01772-732304

Kinlen, Robert, (Hexham & Newcastle), St Cuthbert's, 292 Cowpen Rd, Cowpen, Blyth, Northumberland NE24 5JN **Tel:** 01670 363458

Kinane, Rev James, c/o Cathedral Ho, North Circus St, Nottingham NG1 5AE

Kinnane, Augustine, (Southwark), Priests' Ho, Ashford Kent TN24 8TX **Tel:** 01233-0624771

Kinrade, Brian, Mgr Canon, VG, MA (Menevia), The Presbytery, 9 Promenade Ter. Mumbles, Swansea SA3 4DS **Tel:** 01792 366305

Kinsella, Austin, BA (OFM), 557-559 High Rd, Woodford Green, Essex IG8 0RB **Tel:** 020-8504 1688 **E-mail:** kinsella@friar.org

Kinsella, Peter, (Salford), St Boniface's, St Boniface Rd, Salford M7 2GE **Tel:** 0161-708 9456

Kirby, James, (Southwark), 135 Herbert Rd, London SE18 3QE **Tel:** 020-8855 7657

Kirby, Kieran (Plymouth), Our Lady Star of the Sea, Runacleare Road, Ilfracombe, Devon EX34 8AQ **Tel:** 01271-863563

Kirinich, Roger, (Westminster), 2 Tynemouth St, London SW6 2QT **Tel:** 020-7736 4864

Kirkham, Michael J, Mgr, STL, (Lancaster), 42 Oxford Court, Oxford Rd, Ansdell, Lytham St Annes FY8 4EB **Tel:** 01253-737038

Kirkham, Michael (Nottingham), 12 Gibfield Ln, Belper, Derbys DE56 1WA **Tel:** 01773-822182

Kirkham, Peter, (Hallam), St Joseph's Presbytery, Wingfield Avenue, Worksop, Notts S81 0SF **Tel:** 01909-473373

Kirkpatrick, J Michael BA(Div) (Plymouth), Cathedral Ho, 45 Cecil St, Plymouth, Devon PL1 5HW **Tel:** 01752-662537 **Fax:** 01752-223750 **Mbl:** 07714-231830

Kirkwood, David, Mgr, (Hallam), The Presbytery, St Joseph's Rd, Handsworth, Sheffield S13 9AT **Tel:** 0114-269 3175

Kirwan, Michael, (SJ), Superior, Garnett Ho, 4 Windmill Dr, London SW4 9DE **Tel:** 0208 6754710 **Fax:** 0208 6737647 **E-mail:** m.kirwan@heythrop.ac.uk

Kirwin, Sean, (Liverpool), St Paul's Presbytery, Spring Grove, West Derby, Liverpool L12 8SJ **Tel:** 0151-228 3405 **Fax:** 0151-230 0893

Kita, Krzysztof, MA (Polish Priest), 18 Greenside Rd, Shepherd's Bush, London W12 9JG **Tel:** 020-8743 8848

Kitchen, John, (CSSp), c/o 18 Limesdale Gdns, Burnt Oak, Edgeware, Middlx HA8 5JA

Klaver, Jan, (MHM), All Souls Presbytery, 622 Liverpool St, Salford M5 5HQ **Tel:** 0161-737 9742 **Mbl:** 07711 542715 **E-mail:** j.klaver@btinternet.com

Klyberg, John, Mgr, (Westminster, retired),

44 Naildown Cl, Hythe, Kent CT21 5TB
Tel: 01303-239445

Klymczuk, Vidal Adrian, (OSBM), 10 Park View, Rd, Bradford BD9 4PA
Tel: 01274-481540

Knight, Eric (Oriental Rite), c/o St Edmund's Presbytery, 95 Exeter St, Salisbury, Wiltshire SP1 2SF
Tel/Fax: 01722-333581.

Knight, H Albert, DD, (Shrewsbury, retired), 36 Rostherne Court, Brown St, Hale, Altrincham WA14 2EU

Knight, Leslie, (Brentwood), 17 Highview Cres, Hutton, Brentwood, Essex CM13 1BJ **Tel:** 01277-221917

Knight, Michael G, (Birmingham), St Gerard's Presbytery, Renfrew Square, Castle Vale, Birmingham B35 6JT
Tel: 0121-747 7390

Knights, Philip, MA(Oxon), BA, PhD (Westminster), 114 West Heath Rd, London NW3 7TX **Tel:** 020-8458 3316

Knollys, Bonaventure, STL, (OSB), Ampleforth Abbey, York YO62 4EN
Tel: 01439-766714 **Fax:** 01439-766724

Knott, Peter, (SJ), Corpus Christi Jesuit Community, 757 Christchurch Rd, Boscombe, Bournemouth BH7 6AN
Tel: 01246-437127

Knowles, Gregory (Leeds), St Aidan, 33 Fenton St, Mirfield WF14 8DG
Tel/Fax: 01942-492950

Knowles, John, (OSM), Servite Priory, 500 Bury New Rd, Salford, Lancs M7 4WP
Tel: 0161-792 2152 **Fax:** 0161-792 7943

Knowles, Mark, (Leeds, retired), St Aiden's Presbytery, Baildon Rd, Baildon BD17 6AQ **Tel:** 01274-583032

Knowles, John M, (OSM), Servite Priory, 500 Bury New Rd, Salford, Lancs M7 4WP
Tel: 0161-792 2152 **Fax:** 0161-792 7943

Knowles, Peter G, (Salford), (Diocesan Ecumenical Officer, Lancashire Churches Together), Holy Souls Presbytery, Whalley New Rd, Brownhill, Blackburn BB1 9BE **Tel:** 01254-248047
E-mail: theparish@holysouls.freeserve.co.uk

Knox-Lecky, P J Kevin, BA, (Clifton), St Mary's Presbytery, Magdalene St, Glastonbury, Somerset BA6 9EJ
Tel: 01458-832203

Kochalumchuvattil, Thomas, MSFS, (Menevia), Sacred Heart Church, Pantyffynon Rd, Ystradgynlais, Swansea
Tel: 01639-842202

Koenig, John, Canon, (Northampton), 2 The Grove, Kettering, Northants NN15 7QQ **Tel:** 01536-512497

Kofler, Leonard, DD, DSoc, PhD, (MHM), Institute of St Anselm, 26-28 Edgar Rd, Cliftonville, Kent CT9 2EU
Tel: 01843-234700 **Fax:** 01843-234701

Kolodziejski, Leon, CSSp, (Birmingham, retired), 146 Leverton Rise, Oxley, Wolverhampton WV10 6HU
Tel: 01902 716749

Koppel, Michael, (Plymouth), The Priest's Ho, Lyme Rd, Axminster, Devon EX13 5BE **Tel:** 01297-32135

Korczagin, Nicolau, (Ukrainian), 22 Binney St, London W1K 5BQ **Tel:** 020-7629 1534

Kordel, Mardin, (CRL), 229 Eltham High St, Eltham SE9 1TX
Tel: 0208 850 166 **Fax:** 0208 294 2109

Kordys, Tadeusz, 58 Bodnant Avenue, Evington, Leicester LE5 5RA
Tel: 0116-221 7006

Kosciolek, Krzysztof, MA (SChr) (Polish Priest), 15 Landguard Rd, Southampton SO15 5DL **Tel:** 023-8022 4418

Kot, Boguslaw, (MS), The Presbytery, Howard Way, Harlow, Essex CM20 2NS
Tel: 01279-426017

Kot, Roman, BA, MA, (Southwark), 4 Brockley Park, Forest Hill SE23 1PS
Tel: 0208 690 4549 **Fax:** 0208 314 5567

Kotik, Thaddeus, (OCSO), Abbey of Our Lady and St Samson, Caldey Island, off Tenby, SA70 7UH
Tel: 01834-2632 and 01834-2879

Kozakiewicz, Krzysztof, BA, PGCE (Arundel & Brighton, retired), 48 Worcester Villas, Hove BN3 5TB **Tel:** 01273 416 261

Kravos, Peter, JCL (Leeds), Leeds Universities Catholic Chaplaincy, 5 St Marks Ave, Leeds LS2 9BH
Tel/Fax: 0113-243 8263
E-mail: pmkravos@clara-net

Kruger, Boniface, PhD, (OFM), 557-559 High Rd, Woodford Green, Essex IG8 0RB **Tel:** 020-8504 7540
E-mail: bkruger@friar.org

Krupa, Sylwester (SChr, retired), 16 Carlton Road, Manchester M16 8BB

Krychiwskyj, Michael, (Leeds), The Presbytery, 2 Moor Park Drive, Leeds LS6 4BX **Tel:** 01924 471958
Email: mick@krickers.com

Kubiak, Adam, (SChr) 2 Ashgrove Rd, Goodmayes, Ilford IG3 9XE
Tel: 020-8599 1445

Kujacz, Michael, (Salford), Rector, St Alban's College, Calle Don Sancho 22, 47005 Valladolid, Spain
E-mail: michaelkujacz@hotmail.com

Kukla, Tadeusz, Mgr, Vicar Delegate & Rector, Polish Catholic Mission, 2 Devonia Rd, London N1 8JJ

Kulak, Wojciech, (SDB), Lisieux Hall, Dawson Ln, Whittle-le-Woods Chorley PR6 7DX **Tel:** 01257 248 865

Kullu, Marianus (Dibrugarh), Holy Sprirt, Leigh Avenue, Marple, Stockport

SK6 6DF **Tel:** 0161-427 4922

Kuriakose, Sajimon, (Kottayam), St Anthony's, Dunkery Rd, Woodhouse Park, Manchester M22 0WR **Tel:** 0161-973 1694

Kuwaczka, Dariusz, (Katowice, Poland), 48 Pitts Rd, Slough SL1 3XH **Tel:** 01753-533861

Kyne, John (Nottingham), St Hugh's Rectory, 34 Broadgate, Lincoln LN2 5AQ **Tel:** 01522 528961 **Fax:** 01522 537685

Labartette, Denis, (IC), St Etheldreda's, Ely Place, London EC1N 6RY **Tel:** 020 7405 1061 **E-mail:** Denis@labartette.freeserve.co.uk

Lacy, David A, BA, (Birmingham), Chaplain for: Birmingham International Airport and Solihull Hospital. The Presbytery, 57 East Meadway, Kitts Green, Birmingham B33 0AU **Tel:** 9121-783 3537 **Fax:** 0121-783 6969 **E-mail:** olhoc783537@btconnect.com

Lagan, Hugh, (Southwark, retired), 79 Langley Way, West Wickham, Kent

Lagorio, Mark, (Birmingham), St Joseph, Brook Ln, Thame, Oxon OX9 2AB **Tel:** 01844-212860 **E-mail:** mail@stjosephsthame.org

Laide, John, (Salford, retired), Ballydwyer, Ballymacelligot, Tralee, Co. Kerry. **Tel:** 00 353 6637076

Laishley, Francis, (SJ), 114 Mount St, London, W1K 3AH **Tel:** 020-7493 7811

Lakatos, Denes, (Hungarian Chaplain), c/o St Mary's, East Parade, Bradford BD1 5EE **Tel:** 01274-721248

Lakeland, Michael, (Lancaster), St. Francis' Horns Lane, Goosnargh, Preston PR3 2FJ **Tel:** 01772 865229

Lakeland, Thomas, (SJ), St Wilfrid's Presbytery, 1 Winckley Square, Preston PR1 3JJ **Tel:** 01772-555244 **Fax:** 01772-251955

Laker, Martin G, (Portsmouth), The Presbytery, Braye Rd, St Anne's, Alderney, C.I., GY9 3XJ **Tel:** 01481-822105

Lally, Rev Mgr John, (Nottingham), 25 Mere Rd, Leicester LE5 2HS **Tel:** 0116-262 4645, **Fax:** 0116-251 1437

Lally, Michael, (SVD), St Francis de Sales, 729 High Rd, Tottenham, London N17 8AG

Lamb, Douglas, BA, (Birmingham), St Ambrose, Birmingham Rd, Kidderminster, Worcs DY10 2BY **Tel:** 01562-822839

Lambe, Michael, (Middlesbrough, retired), Christopher Grange, Youens Way, East Prescott Rd, Liverpool L14 2EW **Tel:** 0151 220 2525

Lambert, Michael Ambrose, MA, (OSB) Downside Abbey, Stratton on the Fosse, Radstock, Bath, Somerset BA3 4RH **Tel:** 01761-235170

Lambert, Michael, (AA), 16 Nightingale Rd, Hitchin, Herts SG5 1QS **Tel:** 01462-459126 **Fax:** 01462-432043 **Mbl:** 07958-575442

Lance, Derek, MA, DipEd, (Northampton, retired), 60 Spinney Hill Rd, Northampton, NN3 6DN **Tel:** 01604-491759

Lane, Frederick, (SJ), St Wilfrid's Presbytery, 1 Winckley Sq, Preston PR1 3JJ **Tel:** 01772 555244 **Fax:** 01772 251955

Lane, John, (Brentwood, retired), Fishermore, 41 Turpins Ride, Welwyn, Herts AL6 0QX **Tel:** 01438-717481

Lane, Thomas, (Clifton, retired), Shravokee, Clonlara, Limerick, Ireland

Langan, James, (SJ), St Wilfrid's Presbytery, 1 Winckley Square, Preston PR1 3JJ **Tel:** 01772-555244

Langham, Mark, Mgr, MA, STL, (Westminster), Ven Collegio Inglese, via di Monserrato 45, 00186 Roma, Italia

Langridge, Stephen, MA, (Southwark), 36 Nightingale Square, Balham, London SW12 8QN **Tel:** 020-8355 0211

Lannon, David, Diocesan Archivist (Salford), St Mary's, 3 Todmorden Rd, Burnley, Lancs BB10 4AU **Tel:** 01282-42007 **Fax:** 01282-422007 **E-mail:** davelannon@aol.com

Larkin, Malachy, (Leeds), Our Lady of Mount Carmel Presbytery, 7 Wesley Place, Silsden BD20 0PH **Tel:** 01535-653153 **E-mail:** malachy@st-edmunds.org.uk

Larkin, Michael T, (Clifton, retired), c/o St Ambrose, North Rd, Leigh Woods, Bristol BS8 3PW

Lasia, Robert, STL, JCL, Judicial Vicar (Salford), St Mark, Station Rd, Pendlebury, Manchester M27 6BY **Tel:** 0161-794 1099 **Fax:** 0161-281 1268 **E-mail:** stmark@pendlebury184.freeserve.co.uk

Laszczyk, Stefan, STB, BSc (Louvain), (Birmingham), St Paul, Sisefield Rd, Kings Norton, B38 9JB **Tel:** 0121-458 1139

Latham, John Nicholas Leeming, BA, FSA(Sc) (Birmingham), 1 Quarry Walk, Leach Green Rd, Rednal, Birmingham B45 9BQ **Tel:** 0121-453 3452 **E-mail:** john.latham@virgin.net

Lavender, Gerard, Mgr, RN, (Hexham & Newcastle), 60 Cockerton Green, Darlington, Durham DL3 9EU **Tel:** 01325-464848 **Fax:** 01325-382534

Laverty, Derek, BD, MA, (SSCC), 372 Uxbridge Rd, Ealing, London W5 3LH **Tel:** 020-8993 6040

E-mail: dereklaverty2005@yahoo.co.uk
Lavery, John, (Southwark), 68 Crooms Hill, Greenwich, London SE10 8HG **Tel:** 020-8858 0662
Lavery, William, (CSsR), St Benet, The Causeway, Monwearmouth, Sunderland SR6 0BH **Tel:** 0191-567 2965
Lavery, William, (CSsR), Hawkstone Hall, Marchamley, Shrewsbury SY4 5LG
Lavin, Michael, (Salford), Sacred Heart, 313 Preston New Rd, Blackburn BB2 6PL **Tel:** 01254-51808
Lavin, Thomas, (Brentwood), 342 High Rd, Ilford, Essex IG1 1QP **Tel:** 020-8478 0583
Law, Philip, (Westminster), 6 Athenaeum Rd, London N20 9AE **Tel:** 020-8445 0838
Lawler, Mark, (Leeds), St John the Evangelist Presbytery, 40 Preston Ln, Allerton Bywater, Castleford WF10 2HL **Tel:** 0113-286 2118 **E-mail:** mame@mcmail.com
Lawlor, Brian Ambrose, BD, (OSA), (Parish Priest & Prior), St John Stone, Sandbrook Way, Woodvale, Southport, Merseyside PR8 3RN **Tel:** 01704-577722 **Fax:** 01704-570647
Lawrence, George, (Portsmouth), c/o Bishop's Ho, Edinburgh Rd, Portsmouth, Hants PO1 3HG
Lawrence, John, (Southwark, retired), 26 St Anne's Court, Maidstone, Kent ME16 0UQ **Tel:** 01304 814271
Lawton, Anthony, (Salford), St Marie, Manchester Rd, Bury BL9 0DR **Tel:** 0161-764 1048 **E-mail:** stmarie@bury34.freeserve.co.uk
Laybourn, John, (Birmingham), The Presbytery, Wood St, Southam, Warwickshire CV47 1PP **Tel:** 01926-812351
Laydon, Patrick, J C, (Hexham & Newcastle, retired), St Cuthbert, Hexham Rd, Throckley, Newcastle upon Tyne NE15 7DZ **Tel:** 0191-267 4389
Le-Van-Hong (Louis), (Birmingham), 260 High St, West Bromwich B70 8AQ **Tel:** 0121-553 0034
Leach, Francis Bede, ARICS, MCIOB, MCIArb, (OSB), Ampleforth Abbey, York YO62 4EN **Tel:** 01439-766714 **Fax:** 01439-766724
Leach, Michael, (Southwark), 145 Charlton Rd, Charlton, London SE7 7EZ **Tel:** 020-8858 0401
Leachman, James, BSc MA, MTh, SLD (OSB), Ealing Abbey, Charlbury Grove, Ealing W5 2DY **Tel:** 020-8862 2100
Leadbeater, Michael J, MEd, BTh (Birmingham, retired). St Mary's Presbytery, Vicarage Walk, Walsall WS1 3NF **Tel:** 01922-622633
Leafe, Maurice, (Northampton), 89 Highfields, Towcester, Northants NN12 6EA
Leahy, John, (SSCC), 5 Berrymead Gardens, Acton, London W3 8AA **Tel:** 020-8992 2014 **Fax:** 020-8993 9940
Lear, Richard, MA (CJ), St George's College, Weybridge Rd, Addlestone, Surrey KT15 2QS **Tel:** 01932-839454
Leatham, Andrew, (Salford), Sacred Heart, Levenshulme Rd, Gorton, Manchester M18 7WJ **Tel:** 0161-223 0338
Leathem, Michael, (Westminster), c/o Archbishop's Ho, Ambrosden Avenue, London SW1P 1QJ
Leatherland, Brian, (Northampton), The Presbytery, 2 Sackville St, Thrapston, Northants NN14 4NZ **Tel/Fax:** 01832-732772
Leavy, James P, (Leeds), St Aelred, 71 Woodlands Dr, Harrowgate HG2 7BE **Tel:** 01423-889442
Lebasi, Kidane, STL, (Westminster), 24 Golden Square, London W1F 9JR **Tel:** 020-7025 1594
Leczuk, Moacyr (OSBM), 22 Binney St, London W1K 5BQ **Tel:** 020-7629 1534 **Fax:** 020-7355 3314 **E-mail:** mleczuk@hotmail.com
Leddy, Patrick, MA, STL, (CSSp), The Presbytery, Church Ho, East Wittering, W. Sussex PO20 8PS **Tel:** 01243-673194 **E-mail:** pjleddy@aol.com
Lee, Clive J. F. BA, AKC, TEFEL, OND (Westminster), 9 Henry Rd, London N4 2LH **Tel:** 020-8802 9910
Lee, Gerard, BA, (Hexham & Newcastle), Our Lady and St Edmund, Station Rd, Backworth, Newcastle Upon Tyne NE27 0RU **Tel:** 0191-268 4332
Lee, Gerard, BA (Liverpool, retired), Flat 4, Redcroft, Well Ln, Greasby, Wirral CH49 3GS **Tel:** 0151-606 8165
Lee, John, St Joseph, (Clifton), St Angela's Convent, 5 Litfield Place, Clifton, Bristol BS8 3LU
Lee, John (OMI) 67 Purewell, Christchurch, Dorset BH23 1EH **Tel:** 01202-483340 **E-mail:** priest@stjosephs.christchurch.org.uk
Lee, Ka Fai, (Nottingham), c/o Willson Ho, 25 Derby Rd, Nottingham, NG1 5AW **Tel:** 0115-953 9800
Lee, Martin, Canon, MA, (Southwark), 4 Meadow Rd, Vauxhall, London SW8 1QB **Tel:** 020-7735 6246
Lee, Michael, (Liverpool), St Columba, Primsrose Dr, Huyton, Liverpool L36 8DL **Tel/Fax:** 0151-489 1802
Leeder, Francis, (East Anglia), St Pancras, 1 Orwell Place, Ipswich, Suffolk IP4 1BD **Tel:** 01473-252596
Leeming, Peter, Mgr, (East Anglia), 322

Woodbridge Rd, Ipswich, Suffolk IP4 4BD **Tel:** 01473-274530 **Fax:** 01473-274529

Leenane, Mark BSc, BA (Westminster), 2 Witham Rd, Osterley, Isleworth TW7 4AJ **Tel:** 020-8560 4737

Legg, Bryan, (Plymouth, retired), Cathedral Ho, 45 Cecil St, Plymouth PL1 5HW **Tel:** 01752-662537

Legge, Raymond, (Westminster), The Presbytery, Rant Meadow, Hemel Hempstead, Herts HP3 8PG **Tel:** 01442-255471

Leigh, David, (MAfr), c/o Provincial Ho, 42 Stormont Rd, London N6 4NP

Leigh, Thomas, (Liverpool), St Patrick, 35 Marshside Rd, Churchtown, Southport, Merseyside PR9 9TJ **Tel:** 01704-228943 **Fax:** 01704-233386

Leighton, Cadoc D, BD, PhD, (OPraem), 178 New London Rd, Chelmsford, Essex CM2 0AR **Tel:** 01245 352898

Leighton, Peter, (Hexham & Newcastle), St Mary's Cathedral, Clayton St West, Newcastle upon Tyne NE1 5HH **Tel:** 0191-232 6953 **Fax:** 0191-239 5708 **E-mail:** office@stmaryscathrdral.org.uk

Lekule, Arbogast (MAfric), c/o Bishop's House, 150 St Georges Road, London SE1 6HX

Leniart, Stanislaw, (SChr), Penrhos Home, Pwllheli, Gwynedd LL53 7HN **Tel:** 01758-613160

Lennard, Shaun, BSc, STB, (Westminster), The Presbytery, 1 Stonard Rd, London N13 4DJ **Tel:** 020-8886 9568

Lennon, Gerard, (Birmingham), 85 Prestbury Rd, Aston, Birmingham B6 6EG **Tel:** 0121-327 0505

Lennon, James, (Hexham & Newcastle, retired), Church of All Saints, Castledockrell, Enniscorthy, Co Wexford, Éire **Tel:** 00 353 5488569

Lennon, John, Canon, (Southwark, retired), St Peter's Residence, Meadow Rd, Vauxhall, London SW8 1QH **Tel:** 020-7582 6794

Lennon, Kevin, (Birmingham), c/o Cathedral Ho, St Chad's Queensway, Birmingham B4 6EX

Leonard, Ciaran, (OMI), Utting Ave East, Liverpool L11 3BW **Tel:** 0151-270 2817

Leonard, Daniel, Mgr Canon, (Birmingham, retired), St Joseph's, Queens Park Rd, Harborne, Birmingham B3L 2IB

Leonard, Desmond, (OSB), St Anne, 23 Prescot Rd, Ormskirk, Lancs L39 4TG **Tel:** 01695-572168

Leonard, Francis, (Westminster), 4 Basils Rd, Stevenage, Herts SG1 3PX **Tel:** 01438-226857

Leonard, Graham Douglas, Mgr, KCVO, PC, MA, STD, (Westminster, retired), 25 Woodlands Rd, Witney, Oxon OX8 6DR **Fax:** 01993-773472

Leonard, John Paul, BSc, STL, (Middlesbrough), St Clare of Assisi, 102 Low Ln, Brookfield, Middlesbrough TS5 8EB **Tel/Fax:** 01642-593686

Leonard, Sean, (Leeds), St Patrick's, Victoria Rd, Elland, W Yorks HX5 0PU **Tel:** 01422-373734

Lerche, Simon, (Hexham and Newcastle), St Paul, Dewley, Cramlington, Northumberland NE23 6EF **Tel:** 01670 712476

Lester, Antony, (OCarm), Whitefriars, More Ho, Heslington, York YO10 5DX **Tel:** 01904 410 249

Lester, Michael, (Shrewsbury), Our Lady of Pity, 24 Mill Ln, Greasby, Wirral CH49 3NN **Tel:** 0151-677 2585 **E-mail:** father.lester@virgin.net

Letellier, Robert Ignatius, MA, MLitt, PhD, SSL, STD, (Westminster: Further studies) c/o 7 Parker St, Cambridge CB1 1JL.

Levins, Joseph, (Southwark, retired), 2 Wellington Rd, Deal, Kent CT14 7AL **Tel:** 01304-367603

Lewis, Denis J (OSB), Prinknash Abbey, Cranham, Gloucester GL4 8EX **Tel:** 01452-812455 **Fax:** 01452-813305

Lewis, Jacob Brian BA(Wales), MA(Cantab) (Birmingham), The Beeches, Downs Rd, Compton, Newbury, Berks RG20 6RE **Tel:** 01635-578714 **E-mail:** jacob.lewis@btinternet.com

Lewis, Michael, Canon, BA, (Menevia), The Presbytery, Ithon Rd, Llandidrod Wells, Powys LD1 6AS **Tel:** 01597-822353 **Fax:** 01597-824380

Lewis, Michael, BA, (Clifton), Coombe Corner, Adsborough, Taunton, Somerset TA2 8RF **Tel:** 01823-413560

Lewis, Timothy, (Plymouth), St Paul's, 6 Pemros Rd, St Budeaux, Plymouth PL5 1NE **Tel:** 01752-361161

Lewis-Vivas, Hugh, MA, CertEd, STB, (OSB), Ampleforth Abbey, York YO62 4EN **Tel:** 01439-766714 **Fax:** 01439-766724

Leyden, Denis, (MCCJ) (Salford), Chaplain, HM Prison Walton, Hornby Rd, Liverpool L9 3DDF **Tel:** 0151-525 5971 ext 2795

Leyden, Gervase, (OFM), 557-559 High Rd, Woodford Green, Essex IG8 0RB **Tel:** 020-8504 1688 **Fax:** 020-8504 1844

Leyden, Patrick Gabriel, Mgr Canon, VG (Clifton), Corpus Christi Presbytery, 14 Ellenborough Park South, Weston-super-Mare BS23 1XW **Tel:** 01934-621929 **Fax:** 01934-642415

Leyshon, Gareth J, PhD, MA, BTh, MInstP, (Cardiff), St Dyfrig's Presbytery,

Broadway Treforest, Pontypridd CF37 1DB **Tel:** 01443 402439

Liddle, Gladstone, BA, (Westminster), The Immaculate Conception, 23 St John's St, Hertford, Herts SG14 1RX **Tel:** 01992-582109

Lightbound, Christopher, Mgr Canon, (Shrewsbury, retired), 3 Meadow Cl, Willaston, Wirral CH64 2TS **Tel:** 0151-328 1868 **E-mail:** chrislightbound@hotmail.com

Lim, Joseph (US Forces), Catholic Chaplain, Base Chapel Building 990, RAF Lakenheath, Brandon, Suffolk IP27 9PN

Lindsay, Michael, BA, CGLI, (SDB), St Joseph's, 10 Oldhams Ln, Bolton BL1 6PN **Tel:** 01204-590600 **E-mail:** mjdelmer@tiscali.co.uk

Linley, Piers, BSc, (OP), St Mary's Hill Ho, St Mary's Hill, Inchbrook, Woodchester, Stroud GL5 5HP **Tel:** 01453-832120

Lister, Lawrence (Leeds, retired),The Presbytery, 2 Clarence St, Halifax HX1 5DH **Tel:** 01422-352141. **E-mail:** lister@leeds-diocese.org.uk

Livesey, Robert, (Salford), St Mary, Oxford St, Eccles, Manchester M30 0LU **Tel:** 016789 3236 **Fax:** 0161-7075044 **E-mail:** stmaryeccles@cwcom.net

Livingstone, Benedict MB, ChB, DPM (sP), Our Lady of Victory, Brownshill, Stroud, Gloucester GL6 8AL **Tel:** 01453-883084 **Fax:** 01453-731888 **E-mail:** blsp@freeuk.com

Lizinczyk, Tadeusz (OSPPE), Our Lady of Victory, Brownshill, Stroud, Gloucester GL6 8AL **Tel:** 01453-883084 **Fax:** 01453-731888

Llywelyn, Dorian, MA, STL, (Menevia), c/o Curial Offices, 27 Convent St, Greenhill, Swansea SA1 2BX

Lloyd, Andrew (Shrewsbury), c/o Principal HQ 43 (Wessex) BDE, Picton BKS, Bulford Camp, Wilts SP4 9NY **Tel:** 01980 672871

Lloyd, Charles, (Wrexham) Dolobran Isaf, Pont Robert, Meifod, Powys, SY22 6HU **Tel:** 01938-500 525

Lloyd, David J, (Birmingham), St Peter and the English Martyrs, Temple St, Lower Gornal, W Mids DY3 2PE **Tel:** 01384-452254

Lloyd, Denys, (East Anglia), The Presbytery, St Joseph's Catholic Church, Cromer Road, Sheringham, Norfolk NR26 8RT **Tel:** 01263-822036

Lloyd, Gwilym Wyn BA, LLB, MSc, MA, PGCE (Birmingham), 24 Grosvenor Ave, Streetly, Sutton Coldfield B74 3PE **Tel:** 0121-353 4493

Lloyd, Joseph, (Lancaster), Catholic Youth Service Training Officer, c/o Newman College, Genners Ln, Bartley Green, Birmingham B32 3NT **Tel:** 0121-476 1181

Lloyd, Paul (Nottingham), St Mary's, 69 Upgate, Louth, Lincs LN11 9HD **Tel/Fax:** 01507 603277

Lloyd, Vaughan John, STL, (Birmingham, retired), 19 Blackthorne Rd, Lichfield, Staffs WS14 9YJ **Tel:** 01543-262661

Llywelyn, Dorian, MA, Cantab, STL, (Menevia), c/o Curial Offices, 27 Convent St, Greenhill, Swansea SA1 2BX

Lobb, Ronald, (Portsmouth), Jeanne Jugan Residence, New St John's Rd, St Helier, Jersey JE2 3LE **Tel:** 01534-875960

Lobo, C Bosco (MSFS), c/o 16 Wellington Rd, Hampton Hill, Middx TW12 1JR

Lochran, J (Wrexham), St Winefride's, Chester St, St Asaph, Denbighshire LL17 0RE **Tel:** 01745-582213 **E-mail:** info@stasaphrc.freeserve.co.uk

Lock, Michael, (Plymouth), The Presbytery, West St, Liskeard, Cornwall PL14 6BW **Tel:** 01572-344906

Locke, Laurie, (East Anglia), Cathedral Ho, Unthank Rd, Norwich NR2 2PA **Tel:** 01603-624615 **Fax:** 01603-762512

Lodge, Benedict, (CP), The Retreat, Sea St, Herne Bay, Kent CT6 8SP **Tel:** 01227-375095 **Fax:** 01227-360941 **E-mail:** ben.lodge@ priest0.demon.co.uk

Lodge, Simon (Leeds), Myddelton Grange, Langbar Rd, Ilkley LS29 0EB **Tel:** 01943-607887 **Fax:** 01943-885470 **E-mail:** simonlodge@hotmail.com

Loewenstein, Rudolf (OP), St Dominic's Priory, Southampton Rd, London NW5 4LB **Tel:** 020-7482 9210

Loftus, Basil, Mgr, JCD, STL, PhL, (Leeds, retired), 'Braeval', Helmsdale, Sutherland KW8 6HH **Tel:** 01431-821360

Loftus, Joseph, (CM), Damascus Ho, The Ridgeway, Mill Hill, London NW7 1HH **Tel:** 020-8959 8971

Logan, Anthony, (Southwark, retired), 93 Lichfield Court, Sheen Road, Richmond, Surrey TW9 1AX

Logue, Peter, (OCSO), Our Lady and St Bernard, Mount St Bernard Abbey, Coalville, Leicester LE67 5UL **Tel:** 01530-832298/832022

Lomas, Paul (Shrewsbury), Christ Church, Finney Lane, Heald Green, Cheadle SK8 3DY **Tel:** 0161-437 5042 **E-mail:** paul.lomas54@ntlworld.com

Lomax, Barry, DipFD, MBIE (Salford), St Gabriel, Smalley Street, Castleton, Rochdale OL11 3EB **Tel:** 01706 631973 **Fax:** 01706 861101 **Email:** stgabriels@btinternet.com

Lomlem, Tesfay, (Ethiopia), St Ann, 1043 Chester Rd, Stretford, Manchester

M32 8LD **Tel:** 0161-865 2079

Long, David, MTheol, STL, (Shrewsbury), St Alban's, 30 Mill Ln, Liscard, Wallasey CH44 5UD **Tel:** 0151-638 1520 **Fax:** 0151-630 5540 **E-mail:** stalbanswallasey@yahoo.co.uk

Longland, Daniel, (Plymouth), The Friary, Sample Oak Ln, Chilworth, Guildford, Surrey GY4 8QR **Tel:** 01483-893168 **Fax:** 01483-898071 **E-mail:** patrick@friar.org

Lonsdale, Patrick, BA, (OFM), Franciscan Friary, Graiglwydd Rd, Penmaenmawr, Conwy LL34 6YG **Tel:** 01492-622353

Lordan, Daniel Bernard, Canon, (Wrexham), The Presbytery, St Tudwal, King Edward St, Barmouth, Gwynedd LL4Z 1PE **Tel:** 01341-280489

Lorenc, Marisz, (OSPPE), SS Mary & John's Presbytery, Snow Hill, Wolverhampton WV2 4AD **Tel:** 01902-421676

Loring, Ulrick, MA, BD, (Westminster), 61 Pope's Grove, Twickenham, Middx TW1 4JZ **Tel:** 020-8892 4578

Louden, Stephen H, Mgr, BA, MTh, PhD, (Liverpool), 3 Ridgefield Rd, Pensby Wirral CH61 8RS

Lough, Christopher, (Salford), St Bernadette's, 436 Bury New Rd, Whitefield, Manchester M45 7SX **Tel:** 0161-766 2356 **Fax:** 0161-796 7877

Loughlin, V Rev John, STB, (Middlesbrough), St Peter's Presbytery, Castle Road, Scarborough YO11 1TH **Tel:** 01723-360358

Loughlin, Michael, Canon, (Middlesbrough), St Charles Borromeo, 12 Jarratt St, Hull HU1 3HB **Tel:** 01482-329100

Loughran, Christopher, (Lancaster), St. Clare's, Sharoe Green Lane North, Fulwood, Preston PR2 9HH **Tel:** 01772 719604

Loughran, Malachy (OSA), 55 Fulham Rd, London W6 8AU

Lourensz, Duncan, BA, LLB (Southwark), 14 Blenheim Rd, Deal, Kent CT13 7DB **Tel:** 01304 374399 **Fax:** 01304 371191

Lovatt, Roy, (Middlesbrough), St John of Beverley, 5 North Bar Without, Beverley HU17 7AG **Tel:** 01482-882321

Lovegrove, Anthony, MUniv, LesPh (Arundel & Brighton, retired), The Towers Convent, Upper Beeding, W Sussex BN44 3TF **Tel:** 01903 813259 **Email:** tony.lovegrove@dabnet.org

Lovell, Michael, BA STB (Southwark), 73 Comerford Rd, London SE4 2BA **Tel:** 0208 692 1824 **Fax:** 0208 691 2404

Lowden, Brian, (Arundel & Brighton), The Priests Ho, The Marld, Ashtead, Surrey KT21 1RS **Tel:** 01372-272267

Lowenthal, Michael BA(Econ), STD (Opus Dei), 1 Lower Park Rd, Victoria Park, Manchester M14 5RS **Tel:** 0161-224 2582

Lowry, Conrad, (Clifton), St Thomas More, 3 Market St, Bradford-on-Avon BA15 1LH **Tel/Fax:** 01225-862739

Lowry, Kevin, STB (Lancaster), St Benedict, Whinlatter Rd, Whitehaven CA28 8BN **Tel:** 01946-692083

Lowry, Mehal, (Westminster), 22 Cortayne Rd, London SW6 3QA **Tel:** 020 736 1068

Lucey, Donal, Mgr MA, (Leeds), St Robert's Presbytery, Robert Street, Harrogate, HG1 1HP **Tel:** 01423 504988 **Email:** gsymes@tiscali.co.uk

Lucie-Smith, Alexander, MA, BTh, PGSA, (IC), c/o Fisher House, Guildhall St, Cambridge CB2 3NH **Email:** d40mclaurin@hotmail.com

Ludden, Liam (MAfr, retired), Nazareth Ho, Preston New Rd, Blackburn BB2 7AL **Tel:** 0111254-51808

Lukuc, Bogdan (CRL), Polish Centre, 1 Battison Cres, Longton, Stoke-on-Trent ST3 4DS **Tel:** 01782-312864

Lumley, John, MTh, BA, BD, PGCE, (Middlesbrough), St Augustine, 10 Warwick Road, Redcar TS10 2ER **Tel:** 01642-482738

Lupton, David, (Salford), St James the Less, Burnley Rd, Rawtenstall, Rossendale BB4 8HH **Tel:** 01706-215634 **E-mail:** stjamestheless@freeserve.co.uk

Lynch, Bartholomew, (Brentwood, retired), Nazareth Ho, 111 London Rd, Southend-on-Sea, Essex SS1 1PP **Tel:** 01702-340855

Lynch, Denis, (OCarm), Flat 41, Andorra Court, 155 Widmore Rd, Bromley BR1 3AD **Tel:** 0798 0492957

Lynch, Francis, (Cardiff), The Presbytery, 5 Porth-y-Carne St, Usk NP15 1RY **Tel:** 01291-672594

Lynch, Geoffrey, MA (OSB), Ampleforth Abbey, York YO62 4EN **Tel:** 01439-766714 **Fax:** 01439-766724

Lynch, George Leo, (Liverpool, retired), Flat 3, Springfield House, 35a Church Rd, Formby, Liverpool L37 8BQ

Lynch, James, (Nottingham), 2 Newstead Rd, Mablethorpe, Lincs LN12 2AW **Tel:** 01507-472300

Lynch, Michael, (Leeds), c/o Bishop's Ho, 13 North Grange Rd, Leeds LS6 2BR

Lynch, Michael, (Nottingham, retired), St Colmcille's, 70 Malham Dr, Lincoln LN60 0XD

Lynch, Patrick, Mgr Provost, (Clifton), c/o St Teresa of Lisieux, Eastwick Rd, Taunton TA2 7HF

Lynch, Patrick, Mgr, BD, MA, (Nottingham), Ceili Community, Harbour Rd, Kilbeggen, Co Westmeath, Ireland **Tel:** 00353 579 333222

Fax: 00353 868 172973
Lyness, Peter, MA, (Westminster), 291 Shenley Rd, Borehamwood, Herts WD6 1TG **Tel:** 020-8953 1294
Lyons, George, (Portsmouth), The Parish Office, 26 Abbey Water, Romsey SP51 8EJ **Tel:** 01794 513646
Lyons, George, BTh (Westminster), c/o Archbishop's Ho, Ambrosden Ave, London SW1P 1QJ
Lyons, Patrick, BSc, (Westminster, retired), Garden Flat, 19/21 Lower Teddington Rd, Hampton Wick, Kingston-upon-Thames, Surrey KT1 4EU **Tel:** 020-8943 3232
Lyons, Paul MLitt, MA (SP), Head of Dept for Human Development, St John's Seminary, Wonerish, Guildford Surrey GU5 0QX **Tel:** 01483 892217 **Fax:** 01483 894531
Lyons, Raymond, BTh, MBII (Portsmouth), The Beacons, 18 Shelley Rd, Worthing, W Sussex BN11 1TU **Mbl:** 07973-740195 **E-mail:** raymlyons@aol.com
Lysaght, Gary, BA, STL, DPhil, AKC, KHS (Southwark), c/o Bishop's Ho, 150 St George's Rd, London SE1 6HX
Lysykanych, Benjamin B, DLitt, VG, All Saints Presbytery, Chadderton Way, Oldham, Lancs OL9 6DH **Tel:** 0161-633 5636 **Fax:** 0161-627 0250
MacAuley, John Charles, (OSB), St John's, Long St, Easingwold, York YO61 3JB **Tel:** 01347-821295 **Fax:** 01347-823524
MacCarthy, Brendan, MA, (Arundel & Brighton), 13 Queen's Rd, Hersham, Walton-on-Thames, Surrey KT12 5LU **Tel:** 01932-221007
MacCarthy, Henry, (East Anglia), 17a Sussex Rd, Gorleston, Great Yarmouth, Norfolk NR31 6PF **Tel:** 01493-662239
MacCurtain, William, (SJ), Mount St Jesuit, Residence, 114 Mount St, London W1K 3AH **Tel:** 020 7493 7811 **E-mail:** curtin@ukonline.co.uk
MacDermot-Roe, Dermot, Canon, (Portsmouth, retired), 75a Anglesea Rd, Shirley, Southampton SO15 5QR **Tel:** 023-8052 9354
MacDonald, Bosco, (Clifton), Holy Family Presbytery, Southsea Rd, Patchway, Bristol BS34 5DP **Tel:** 0117-908 1247
MacDonald, Donald, (SMM), Montfort Ho, Darnley Rd, Barrhead, Glasgow G78 1TA **Tel:** 0141-881 1440
MacDonald, Ian, (MHM), Institute of St Anselm, 26-28 Edgar Rd, Cliftonville, Kent CT9 2EU **Tel:** 01843 234700 **Mbl:** 07743 099911
MacFarln, David, (Salford), St Thomas of Canterbury, 327 Cheetham St East, Higher Broughton, Salford M7 4UE **Tel/Fax:** 0161-792 2108 **E-mail:** drjmac@skynow.net
MacKenzie, Hugh, MSc, PhL (Westminster), Clergy Ho, Peter Ave, London NW10 2DD **Tel:** 020-8451 4677
MacKnight, Alan, (Hexham & Newcastle), St Patrick, Goatbeck Terr, Langley Moor, Co Durham DH7 8JJ
MacLaifeartaigh Michael, (OCD), Carmelite Priory, Youlbury, Boars Hill, Oxford OX1 5HB **Tel:** 01865 735133 **Fax:** 01865 326478
MacLeod Donald, (WF), 42 Stormort Rd, London N6 4NP **Tel:** 020-8348 7799
MacMahon, John A, (Leeds), 1st Floor Flat, 7 Oakwell Mount, Oakwood, Leeds LS8 1RS
MacMahon, Paul (OPraem), Our Lady of England Priory, School Ln, Storrington, W. Sussex RH20 4LN **Tel:** 01903-742150 **Fax:** 01903-740821 **E-mail:** norbertines@pavilion.co.uk
MacNally, Patrick J, (Liverpool), St Jude, Poolstock Ln, Worsley Mesnes, Wigan WN3 5JE **Tel:** 01942-244864
MacNamara, Adrian, (Birmingham), The Presbytery, Langbank Ave, Ernesford Grange, Coventry CV3 2QP **Tel:** 024-7644 8170
MacRory, Vincent, (Northampton), 7 Keemore Heights, Dunamore, Cookstown, Co. Tyrone, N. Ireland BT80 9NA
Mbannor, John MSP (Leeds) Immaculate Heart of Mary Presbytery, 294 Harrogate Rd, Leeds LS17 6LE **Tel:** 0113-268 1371 **E-mail:** hawkhall@aol.com
McAleenan, Patrick, Mgr Canon, (Northampton), Our Lady of Walsingham, Occupation Rd, Corby, Northants NN17 1EE **Tel/Fax:** 01536-203121 **E-mail:** ourlady.corby@virgin.net
McAleenan, Paul, (Westminster), Holy Rd Ho, Exchange Rd, Watford, Herts WD1 7AJ. **Tel:** 01923-224085
McAlinden, Francis, (Portsmouth), Morestead, 53 Stoney Ln, Weeke, Winchester, Hants SO22 6DR **Tel:** 01962-882711
McAllister, Alex, (SDS), Christ the King Presbytery, 11 Castle St, Thornbury, South Gloucestershire BS35 1HA **Tel:** 01454-412223 (Parish) 01454-854586 (house) **Fax:** 01454-412427 **E-mail:** amcallister@blueyonder.co.uk
McAllister, Barry, BA, (Liverpool), St Elizabeth of Hungary, Webster St, Litherland, Liverpool L21 8JH **Tel:** 0151-922 3820 **Fax:** 0151-933 7941
McAllister, Joseph, (Portsmouth, retired), 9 Innishmaan Rd, Whitehall, Dublin 9,

McAndrew, Michael, (Clifton), St Francis Presbytery, Ash Hayes Rd, Nailsea Bristol BS48 2LP **Tel:** 01275-851530

McAneny, Christopher, (SSCC), 372 Uxbridge Road, Ealing, London W5 3LH **Tel:** 020-8993 6040

McAneny, Martin (SM), Notre Dame de France, 5 Leicester Place, London WC2H 7BP **Tel:** 020-7437 9363 **Fax:** 020-7437 3857

McArdle, Francis Gerard, (Birmingham), 182 Thimblemill Ln, Nechells, B7 5HT **Tel:** 0121-327 0235 **E-mail:** frgerry@stjosephs11.freeserve.co.uk

McArdle, John, STB (Northampton), St Joseph's Presbytery, 68 Gardenia Ave, Limbury, Luton LU3 2NS **Tel:** 01582-571187 **E-mail:** stjosephsluton@fsmail.net

McArdle, Nicholas, Canon, (Lancaster, retired), St Bernadette's, Bowerham Rd, Lancaster LA1 4HT **Tel:** 01524-848009

McArdle, Patrick, (OMI), English Martyrs, 30 Prescot St, London E1 BB **Tel:** 020-7488 3462

McAuley, Michael, LLB, DPA, MCL, JCL, (Clifton), St Teresa's Nursing Home, Corston, Bath BA2 9AG **Tel:** 01225-872759

McAuliffe, James, BA, BMus, (SPS), Church of Our Lady Immaculate, 52 Alum Chine Rd, Westbourne, Bournemouth BH4 8DZ **Tel:** 01202-764027 **E-mail:** j.mcaul@btopenworld.com

McAvoy, Daniel, JTB, MA, (SMM), St Joseph's, Lyndhurst Rd, Ashurst, Hants SO40 7DU **Tel:** 023-8029 2337 **Fax:** 023-8029 2346 **E-mail:** smm-dw@refuge-arc.freeserve.co.uk

McBride, Denis, MA, STM, (CSsR), St Clements, Wolf Lane, Chawton, Alton Hants GU34 3HG **Tel:** 01420 807310

McBride, Edward, Mgr Canon (East Anglia, retired), 2 Burlington Court, 3 The Esplanade, Sheringham Norfolk NR26 8LG **Tel:** 01263-825122

McBride, Malachy (OSB), St Gerard's, Mitchell St, Thurles, Co Tipperary, Eiré **Tel:** 00353-504 21912

McBride, Oswald BSc, MB, CHB, BA (OSB), Ampleforth College, York YO62 4ER **Tel:** 01439-766758

McBride, T Anthony, (Salford), St John's Cathedral, 250 Chapel St, Salford M3 5LL **Tel:** 0161-834 0333 **Fax:** 0161-834 9596

McBrien, Philip, BSc, BD, (Nottingham), The Prestbytery, New Street, Oadby, Leics LE2 4LJ **Tel:** 0116 - 271 5139

McCabe, Alexander, MA, CertEd, (OSB), Ampleforth Abbey, York YO62 4EN **Tel:** 01439-766714 **Fax:** 01439-766724

McCabe, John, (SJ), Manresa Ho, 10 Albert Rd, Harborne, Birmingham B17 0AN **Tel:** 0121 427 2628

McCabe, Kenneth, (Westminster), More Ho, 28 The Grove, Isleworth, Middx TW7 4JU **Tel:** 020-8568 9487

McCaffery, Anthony, BD, JCL (Liverpool), c/o Liverpool Archdiocesan Centre for Evangelisation, Croxteth Dr, Sefton Park, Liverpool L17 1AA

McCaffery, John, (OFM), Franciscan Friary, Gordon Rd, Nottingham NG3 2LG **Tel:** 0115-950 6549 **E-mail:** johnaloysius@onetel.com

McCaffery, Terence, (Plymouth, retired), 5 Mallett Rd, Laira, Plymouth PL3 6TD **Tel:** 01752-674802

McCaffrey, Andrew, MA, BD, MPhil, MEd, LSS, (OSB), Ampleforth Abbey, York YO62 4EN **Tel:** 01439-766714 **Fax:** 01439-766724

McCaffrey, Benedict, (CP, retired), Kearnsey Manor Nursing Home, Alkham Valley Rd, Dover, Kent CT16 3EQ **Tel:** 01304-822254

McCaffrey, Eugene (OCD), Tabor, 169 Sharoe Green Lane, Fulwood, Preston PR2 8HE **Tel:** 01772-717122 **Fax:** 01772-787674 **E-mail:** emccaffrey17@hotmail.com

McCaffrey, James (OCD), Carmelite Priory, Boars Hill, Oxford OX1 5HB **Tel:** 01865-735133 **Fax:** 01865-326478

McCaffrey, Patrick (SSC), Columba Ho, 163 Horton Grange Rd, Bradford BD7 2DN **Tel:** 01274-571975 **E-mail:** PatMcCaffrey@lineone.net

McCanalogue, William (Westminster), 194 Knightsfield, Welwyn Garden City, Herts AL8 7RQ **Tel:** 01707-327434

McCann, Andrew, (Birmingham), 1 Herbert Rd, Solihull B91 3QE **Tel:** 0121 705 0228

McCann, Edward, (CSSp), 6 Woodland Rd, Bickley, Bromley BR1 2AF **Tel:** 020-8467 3555 **Fax:** 020-8295 4965 **E-mail:** spiritansbickley@btconnect.com

McCann, George, (Northampton, retired), 181 St John's Rd, Kettering, Northants NN15 5AW **Tel:** 01536-502090

McCann, Gerard, (OFM Conv), Franciscan Study Centre, Giles Lane, Canterbury CT2 7NA **Tel:** 01227-454647

McCann, Hugh, (Hexham & Newcastle), St Thomas More, Easington Rd, Hartlepool, Cleveland TS24 8JZ **Tel:** 01429-274775

McCann, Terence, (Salford), Chaplain, Buckley Hall Prison. 3 Highfield Ave, Mosley Common, Worsley, Manchester M28 1AL **Tel:** 0161-799 0144

McCartan, Edmund, (Lancaster, retired), Hesketh Hall, Broughton Mills, Broughton in Furness, Cumbria LA20 6AY

McCarthy, Francis, (MHM, retired), Herbert Ho, 41 Victoria Rd, Freshfield, Liverpool L37 1LW **Tel:** 01704-835856
E-mail: romanusipsc@yahoo.com

McCarthy, Ian, (Clifton), Our Lady and St Kenelm, Back Walls, Stow-on-the-Wold, Glos GL54 1DR **Tel:** 01451-830431
Mbl: 07941-232246

McCarthy, Kenneth, (Arundel & Brighton, retired), 1 Queen's Cl, Walton-on-the-Hill, Tadworth, Surrey KT20 7SU
Tel: 01737-813016

McCarthy, Martin, BA (Southwark), 46 Purley Road, Croydon, Surrey CR2 6EY
Tel: 020-8641 3141

McCarthy, Michael, (IC), St Peter's, St Peter's St, Roath, Cardiff CF24 3BA
Tel: 029 2048 3394
E-mail: mikemac@beeb.net

McCarthy, Michael, (Leeds), St Joseph's Presbytery, Church View, Low St, Sherburn-in-Elmet, LS25 6HL
Tel: 01977-685226

McCarthy, Timothy, (Westminster), 599 Keith Rd West, Vancouver BC, Canada V7T 1L8

McCartney, James, Director, T.H.O.M.A.S. (Salford), St Anne's Presbytery, France St, Blackburn, Lancs BB2 1LX
Tel: 01254-59240 **Fax:** 01254-56884
E-mail: edges@globalnet.co.uk

McCaul, Dermot, (SMA), Pontificio Collegio Beda, Viale di San Paolo 18, 00146 Roma, Italia **Tel:** 0039 06 5512 7202 **Fax:** 0039 06 5512 7254
E-mail: mccaulda@hotmail.com

McCauley, Francis, (Salford), St Columba, Ripley St, Tonge Moor, Bolton BL2 3AR
Tel: 01204-303232

McCay, John, (Nottingham), St Paul's, Lenton Boulevard, Nottingham NG7 2BY **Tel:** 0115-978 6236

McClarey, Liam (SCA), 358 Greenford Rd, Greenford, Middx UB6 9AN

McClean, Ian (OPraem), Parish Ho, 2 Fern Rd, Storrington, Pulborough RH20 4LW *(Priory and Parish)*
Tel: 01903-742150 **Fax:** 01903-740821
E-mail: norbertines@pavilion.co.uk

McClean, Victor, (Southwark), Sacred Heart, Beresford Rd, Goudhurst, Cranbrook TN17 1DN **Tel:** 01580-211268

McClement, Neville, (Northampton, retired), 12 The Pightle, North Cove, Beccles, Suffolk NR34 7PR
Tel: 01502-476702

McClorey, John BA (MHM), Herbert Ho, 41 Victoria Rd, Freshfield, Merseyside L37 1LW **Tel:** 01704-835842
E-mail: jmaklori@herberthouse.freeserve.plus.com

McClorry, Brian (SJ), St Beuno's, St Asaph, Denbigh LL17 0AS **Tel:** 01745 586718
E-mail: b.mcclorry@yahoo.com

McCloskey, Charles, (Portsmouth), The Friary, Coronation Rd, Ascot, Berkshire SL5 9HG **Tel:** 01344-620591
Fax: 01344-620591

McCluskey, John, MA, PhD, (MHM), 38 Maderia Rd, Cliftonville, Kent CT9 2QQ
Tel: 01843 293280 **E-mail:** johnmccluskeymhm@lineone.net

McCollough, John, (Brentwood), c/o Cathedral Ho, Ingrave Rd, Brentwood, Essex CM15 8AT

McConalogue, William, (Westminster), 194 Knightsfield, Welwyn Garden City, Herts AL8 7RQ **Tel:** 01707-327434

McConnell, Lawrence, (MHM), St John the Evangelist, 39 Duncan Terr, Islington N1 8AL **Tel:** 027 359 3199
Mbl: 07999 625453
E-mail: larry@mcconnell.net

McConnell, Wilfrid, BA, STL (Hexham & Newcastle), c/o Bishop's Ho, 800 West Rd, Newcastle-upon-Tyne

McConnon, Michael, Mgr, STL, PhL, (Salford), Nazareth Ho, Scholes Lane, Prestwich, Manchetser M25 0NU

McCoog, Thomas, (SJ), Farm St Church, 114 Mount St, London W1Y 6AH
Tel: 020 7629 4202 **Fax:** 020-7495 6685 **E-mail:** 101543.3244772@compuserve.com

McCormack, Austin Linus, (OFM), Franciscan Friary, Sample Oak Lane, Chilworth, Guildford, Surrey GU4 8QR
Tel: 01483-893168 **Fax:** 01483-898071
Mbl: 07940 178108
E-mail: patrick@friar.org

McCormack, James (Brentwood), 1 Church Rd, Clackton-on-Sea, Essex CO15 6AG
Tel: 01255-423319

McCormack, John, (Southwark, retired), The Parish Ho, St Vincent's, Mallard Cl, Temple Hill, Dartford, Kent DA1 5HU **Tel:** 01322-272566

McCormack, Thomas, (Hexham & Newcastle, retired), Stichell House, Hospital of God, Greatham, Hartlepool TS25 2HS **Tel:** 07982001435

McCormick, Fabian (OCD), Carmelite Priory, 41 Kensington Church St, London W8 4BB **Tel:** 020-7937 9866,
Fax: 020-7938 1470

McCormick, James, (Westminster, retired), The Villa, Thornton College, Thornton, Bucks MK17 0HJ **Tel:** 01280-813466

McCormick, Michael J, (Liverpool), St Leo's Presbytery, Lickers Lane, Whiston, Prescot L35 3PN **Tel:** 0151 426 6482

McCormick, Robert, (East Anglia, retired), c/o The Presbytery, 6 Fair Green, Diss, Norfolk IP22 4BQ **Tel:** 01379-640637

McCourt, Paul, (Hexham & Newcastle), English Martyrs, 176 Stamfordham Rd, Newcastle NE5 3JR **Tel:** 0191 286 9246

McCoy, Alban, (OFM Conv), Catholic Chaplaincy, Fisher Ho, Guildhall St, Cambridge CB2 3NH **Tel:** 01223-742192

McCoy Christopher, MA, (Liverpool), International HE Chaplaincy, IMCS, 7 Impasse Reille, 75014 Paris, France **Tel:** 0033 145 447 075 **E-mail:** cmcoy@imcs-miec.org

McCoy, John, (Westminster, retired), 41 Parkside, Welwyn, Herts AL6 9DQ **Tel:** 01438-718524

McCoy, Michael, JCL, (Hexham & Newcastle), Our Lady Queen of Peace, Penshaw, Tyne and Wear DH4 7JZ **Tel:** 0191-385 2434

McCreadie, Michael V.Rev Canon, (Leeds), St Paul's Presbytery, 1 Buckstone Cres, Leeds LS17 5ES **Tel/Fax:** 0113-268 2942

McCready, David, (Clifton), c/o St Ambrose, North Rd, Leigh Woods, Bristol BS8 3PW

McCue, Gerard Matthew, (OSB), St Mary's Abbey, Buckfast, Buckfastleigh, Devon TQ11 OEE **Tel:** 01368-443301

McCullagh, Francis, BA, (Hexham & Newcastle), Our Lady of the Rosary, Passfield Way, Peterlee SR8 1DE **Tel/Fax:** 0191-586 2526

McCulloch, David Benedict BA (OSB), St Mary's Abbey, Quarr, Ryde, Isle of Wight PO33 4ES **Tel:** 01983-882420 **Fax:** 01983-884402

McCulloch, Gordon, (Liverpool), Liverpool Archdiocesan Centre for Evangelisation, Croxteth Dr, Sefton Park, Liverpool L17 1AA

McCullough, Kieran (MCS), Princethorpe College, Leamington Rd, Princethorpe, Rugby CV23 9PX **Tel:** 01926-632147

McCumiskey, Bernard, MA, BSc, STL, JCL, (Westminster), 51 Nether St, London N12 7NN **Tel:** 020-8446 0224

McCurry, Christopher, (Shrewsbury), St Ann's, 29 Vicarage Ave, Cheadle Hulme, Cheadle SK8 7JW **Tel:** 0161-485 1685 **E-mail:** chris.mccurry@virgin.net

McCusker, Gerald, (Liverpool), St Mary's Presbytery, Wigan Rd, Euxton, Chorley PR7 6JW **Tel:** 01257 262665

McDade, John, (SJ), Principal, Heythrop College, Kensington Square, London W8 5HQ **Tel:** 020-7795 6600 **Fax:** 020-7795 4200

McDermott, Anthony, Mgr, (Northampton), Manor Ho, 10 Manor Rd, Kingsthorpe, Northampton NN2 6QJ **Tel:** 01604-715661 **Fax:** 01604-713590 **E-mail:** tonymcdstaidan@tinyworld.co.uk

McDermott, Bernard, (SSC), St Columban's, Widney Manor Rd, Knowle, Solihull B93 9AB **Tel:** 01564-772096 **Fax:** 01564-700500

McDermott, Francis, (Northampton), c/o Bishop's Ho, Marriott St, Northampton NN2 6AW

McDermott, Gilmour, (Arundel & Brighton), Our Lady of the Portal and St Piran, St Austell St, Truro, Cornwall TR1 1SE **Tel:** 01872-273391

McDermott, Hugh, (SCJ), Sacred Heart and St Catherine of Alexandria, Worcester Rd, Droitwich. **Tel:** 01905-773258

McDermott, John, (MHM), Herbert Ho, 41 Victoria Rd, Freshfield, Liverpool L37 1LW **Tel:** 01704-875833

McDermott, Louis, (OMI), The Presbytery, Redbridge Hill, Southampton, Hants SO16 4PL **Tel:** 023-8077 5199 **Fax:** 023-8077 8203 **Mbl:** 07803-901570 **E-mail:** louis.mcdermott@btopenworld.com

McDermott, Paul (Westminster), 35 Cricklewood, London NW2 1HR **Tel:** 020-8208 3924

McDermott, Sean, (OMI), Rushmere, 32 Allanson Rd, Rhos-on-Sea, Conwy, North Wales LL28 4HL **Tel:** 01492-545241

McDevitt, Kevin, (Westminster), 15 St John's Villas, London N19 3EE **Tel:** 020-7272 8195

McDonagh, Aloysius (SDS), 20 Grove Rd, Newbury, Berkshire RG14 1UH **Tel:** 01635 826417 **E-mail:** frpmcd@yahoo.co.uk

McDonagh, Francis Gabriel, (OSA), Clare Priory, Clare, Sudbury, Suffolk CO10 8NX **Tel:** 01787-277326 **Fax:** 01787-278688

McDonald, John D, Canon (Westminster), 54 Lodge Rd, London NW8 8LA **Tel:** 0207-286 3214

McDonald, Martin (OCD), St Joseph's Priory, Austenwood Common, Gerrards Cross, Bucks SL9 8RY **Tel:** 01753-886581 **Fax:** 01753-892371

McDonald, Stephen, MBA MAAT ACMI (Nottingham), c/o Bishop's Ho, 27 Cavendish Road East, The Park, Nottingham NG7 1BB

McDonnell, Ciaran, (Hexham & Newcastle), St Augustine, Wealcroft, Leam Lane, Fetting, Gateshead NE10 8QS **Tel:** 0191-469 0375

McDonough, Peter, DipTD, MA (Salford), Henesy Ho, Sudell St, Collyhurst, Manchester M4 4JF **Tel:** 0161-834 8828 **Fax:** 0161-833 3674 **E-mail:** peter.mcdonough@btinternet.com

McDowell, Anthony (OFM Cap) Franciscan Friary, Carlton Rd, Erith, Kent DA8 1DN

Tel: 01322-433193
McElhinney, Brian, (Leeds), St Mary's, Castlerahan, Ballyjamesduff, Co Cavan, Ireland
McElhinney, Joseph, (Portsmouth), c/o Bishop's Ho, Edinburgh Rd, Portsmouth PO1 3HG
McElhinney, Kevin, BTh, (Southwark), c/o Archbishop's Ho, 150 St George's Rd, London SE1 6HX **Tel:** 020-7928 2495 **E-mail:** mailto.kevinmcesja@hotmail.com
McElhone, John, (Hexham & Newcastle), Holy Cross, Coniston Rd, Willington Quay, Wallsend NE28 0EP **Tel:** 0191-262 3820
McElhone, Thomas, (Southwark), 45 Elm Grove, London SE15 5DD **Tel:** 020-7639 1947
McElligott, Cavan (Clifton), 5 Hampton Rd, Bristol BS6 6HW **Tel:** 0117-973 4983
McElroy, James, (Lancaster), St Joseph, Crown St, Cockermouth, Cumbria CA13 0EJ **Tel:** 01900-822121
McEvoy, Brian, Canon, STL, PhL, (Clifton), St Mary's Rectory, 4 Harley St, Bath BA1 2SF **Tel:** 01225-311725
McEwan, Kevin, (CSsR), 24b Morley Rd, Lewisham, London SE13 6DF
McFadden, John (OMI), St Theresa of the Child Jesus, Utting Ave East, Liverpool L11 3BW **Tel:** 0151-226 1354 **Fax:** 0151-270 2665
McFadden, John (CSSp), c/o 18 Limesdale Gdns, Burnt Oak, Edgeware, Middlx HA8 5JA
McGann, Andrew, (MHM), St Bernadette, 9 Rennison Drive, Womborne, Wolverhampton WV5 9HW **Tel:** 01902 893434
McGarry, Bernard, MA, (Salford), St Chad, Cheetham Hill Rd, Manchester M8 8GG **Tel:** 0161-834 4699
McGarry, David, PhL, STB, (Salford), St Catherine, School Lane, Didsbury, Manchester M20 6HS **Tel:** 0161-445 2079 **Fax:** 9161-613 2852 **E-mail:** parish@stcaths.org.uk
McGeady, Joseph, 5 Whitworth Rd, Norwood. London SE25 6XN **Tel:** 020-8653 2806 **Fax:** 020-8653 4188
McGee, Martin, BA, MA, MSTh, (OSB) Worth Abbey, Crawley, W Sussex RH10 4SB **Tel:** 01342-710310
McGeoghan, Seamus, (Westminster), 6 Melbourne Rd, Royston, Herts SG8 7DB **Tel:** 01763-243117
McGeough, Eamon (Leeds), St Peter with St Joseph, Presbytery, Petersfield Ave, Belle Isle, Leeds LS10 3QN **Tel:** 0113-271 2378
McGettigan, Oliver, (OCD), Carmelite Priory, 41 Kensington Church St, London W8 4BB **Tel:** 020-7937 9866, **Fax:** 020-7938 1470
McGhee, Michael, (OMI), Rushmere, 32 Allanson Rd, Rhos-on-Sea, Conwy LL28 4HL **Tel:** 01492 545241
McGillicuddy, Denis, (Birmingham), 93 Raddlebarn Rd, Selly Park, Birmingham B29 7DB **Tel:** 0121-472 0190
McGillicuddy, Des, BA, Dr Theol, (MHM), St Joseph's College, Lawrence St, Mill Hill, London NW7 4JX **Tel:** 020-8906 7587 **E-mail:** dmcgillicuddy@lineone.net
McGillicuddy, James, MA (Southwark), 2 St Barnabas Rd, Sutton, Surrey SM1 4NL **Tel:** 020-8642 0275
McGilloway, Bernard (Brian), (Brentwood), 18 Ken Cooke Court, Colchester, Essex CO1 1FF **Tel:** 01206-542708 **Mbl:** 07766-172822
McGillycuddy, Eugene, (Leeds), Oakwood Ln, Gipton, Leeds LS9 6QY **Tel:** 0113 249 5131 **Fax:** 0113 216 1934 **E-mail:** dmcgillycuddy@hotmail.com
McGinley, Brian, (Birmingham), 1 Sansome Place, Worcester WR1 1UG **Tel:** 01905 22574
McGinn, Canice, (Leeds), The Presbytery, Saffron Dr, Allerton, Bradford BD15 7NQ **Tel:** 01274-542431
McGinn, Paul, Mgr Canon (Westminster), 60 Rylston Rd, London SW6 7HW **Tel:** 020-7385 4040
McGinnell, Kevin, Mgr, (Northampton), Holy Ghost Presbytery, 33 Westbourne Rd, Luton LU4 8JD **Tel:** 01582-728849 **Mbl:** 07889-762005 **E-mail:** mcginnell.nores@btconnect.com
McGivern, Desmond, (Hexham & Newcastle), St Paul's Church, 3 Prudhoe Villas, Alnwick NE66 1UP **Tel:** 01665-602012
McGivern, Dominic J, (Hexham & Newcastle, retired), 72 Oswald Court, New Elvet, Durham City DH1 3DJ **Tel:** 0191-386 0372
McGivern, Ronald, (Liverpool), St William's, Ince Green Lane, Ince, Wigan WN2 2DG **Tel:** 01942-512815 **Fax:** 01942-517914
McGivern, Seamus, (Hexham & Newcastle Retired), 20, The Cliff, Seaton Carew, Hartlepool
McGiveron, Peter, (Salford), St Thomas More, 102 Mainway, Alkrington, Middleton, Manchester M24 1PP **Tel:** 0161-643 3847 **Fax:** 0161-655 3022
McGloin, James, (Birmingham, retired), Priest's Ho, Main St, Manorhamilton, Co Leitrim, Ireland **Tel:** 00 353 7255086
McGoldrick, Michael, (OCD), Carmelite Priory, 41 Kensington Church St,

London W8 4BB **Tel:** 0207 937 9866 **E-mail:** mcgoldocd@gmail.com

McGonagle, Cathal, BA, (Westminster, retired), 87 Blue Cedars, Cappry, Ballybofey, Co Donegal, Ireland **Tel:** 00353 749 189372

McGovern, Joseph (Nottingham, retired) 5 Trevor Close, Tile Hill Village, Coventry CV4 9HP. **Tel:** 024 7642 15854

McGovern, Philip, (Shrewsbury), Our Lady and St Oswald's, Upper Brook St, Oswestry SY11 2TG **Tel:** 01691-652248 **E-mail:** philip.mcgovern2@btinternet.com

McGovern, Thomas, Mgr Canon VG, (Nottingham), St Joseph's Presbytery, Station Rd, Oakham, Rutland LE15 6QU **Tel:** 01572 722308

McGowan, Phelim (SJ), Holy Cross Hospital, Hindhead Rd, Haslemere GU27 1BS **Tel:** 01428-643311

McGrail, Peter, BA SLL (Liverpool), Carmelite Lodge, Eccleston, St Helens WA10 5HH

McGrane, Christopher, BD (Hons), (Salford), St Michael's, Albert Rd, Whitefield, Manchester M45 8NH **Tel:** 0161-766 5961

McGrath, Brian (OFM), 557-559 High Rd, Woodford Green, Essex IG8 0RB **Tel:** 020-8505 3624 **Fax:** 020-8504 7541 **Mbl:** 07939-107674 **E-mail:** brian@friar.org

McGrath, Dermot, (Westminster, retired), 50 McClure Meadows, Newline Rd, Wexford, Ireland **Tel:** 00 353 53 21116

McGrath, Francis M, (Leeds), Holy Family Presbytery, 12 Green Lane, Leeds LS12 1HU **Tel:** 0113-263 7484

McGrath, James, (Shrewsbury, retired), 26 Riverside Crescent, Holmes Chapel, Crewe CW4 7NR Tel: 01477 537297 **E-mail:** jimmcgrathholmeschapel@yahoo.co.uk

McGrath, James, STB, MA (Portsmouth), 132 High St, Lymington, Hants SO41 9AQ **Tel:** 01590-672462 **Mbl:** 07947-890970 **E-mail:** jamiemcgrath@ukgateway.net

McGrath, John, (Brentwood), 21 Laindon Rd, Billericay, Essex CM12 9LL. **Tel:** 01277-624891

McGrath, Michael Francis, (Birmingham, retired), St Michael's, 34 Kill Ave, Dun Laoghaire, Co Dublin, Ireland **Tel:** 00 353 2 805129

McGrath, Rick BA(Phil) BTh(Hons) MEd (Arundel & Brighton), The Priest's Ho, Station Rd, Burgess Hill, W. Sussex RH15 9EN **Tel:** 01444-232358

McGrath, Terry (MSFS), Dympna Centre, Parkside Ho, 17 East Parade, Harrogate HG1 1LF **Tel:** 01423-817515 **E-mail:** thedympnacentre@hotmail.com

McGrath, Thomas, (Portsmouth), 36 Cookham Rd, Maidenhead, Berks SL6 7EG **Tel:** 01628-783988 **Fax:** 01628-776863

McGrath, Timothy, (Cardiff), St Mary's Presbytery, 39 Ewenny Rod, Bridgend CF31 3HS **Tel:** 01656-652034

McGraw, Brian BEd (SDB), St John Bosco Ho, 121A Reading Rd, Farnborough GU14 6NZ **Tel:** 01252-554310 **Fax:** 01252-375395 **E-mail:** bmbriansdb@aol.com

McGreal, Owen, BA (Menevia), The Presbytery, St. Florence Parade, Tenby, Penbrokeshire SA70 7DT **Tel:** 01884 942692

McGreal, Wilfrid, (OCarm), Prior Provincial, Whitefriars, 35 Tanners St, Faversham, Kent ME13 7JW **Tel:** 01795-532449 **E-mail:** provincial@carmelite.org

McGreevy, Michael, STD, BA, (CSsR), Alphonsus Ho, Wolf Lane, Chawton, Alton, Hants GU34 3HQ **Tel:** 01420-88222 **Fax:** 01420-88805

McGrory, John, (Southwark), 30 Park Rd, Colliers Wood SW19 2HS **Tel:** 020-8540 3057 **Fax:** 020-8544 1230

McGuckin, Terence, STD, STL, MLitt, BD, BA, (Westminster), 4a Inverness Place, London W2 3JF **Tel:** 020-7229 8153

McGuiness, Ciaran, (MAfr), Our Lady of Lourdes and Saint Felicia Presbytery, White Cliff Mill Street, Blanford, Dorset DT11 7BN **Tel:** 01747-852125

McGuiness, Gerard I, ALAM, MA, LGSM, (Shrewsbury, retired), 37 St James Road, Belvidere, Shrewsbury SY2 5YJ **Tel:** 01743 344 141

McGuinness, Brendan, DipMus, DPA, DMus, (SDB), St John Bosco Ho, 121a Reading Rd, Farnborough GU14 6NZ **Tel:** 01252-554300 **Fax:** 01252-375395 **E-mail:** sdb_farnborough@msn.com

McGuinness, Stephen, (Northampton), St Wulstan, Hollis Rd, Totteridge, High Wycombe, Bucks HP13 7UN **Tel/Fax:** 01494-438300 **E-mail:** stwulstans@clara.co.uk

McGuire, Derek, STB (OSA), Clare Priory, Clare, Suffolk CO10 8NX **Tel:** 01787-277326 **Fax:** 01787-278688

McGuire, James, (SDB), Nazareth Ho, Hammersmith Rd, London W6 8DB **Tel:** 020-8563 9728

McGuire, Mgr Canon, ProtAp (Leeds), 7 Lancaster Court, Lancaster Lane, Parbold WN8 7HS **Tel:** 01257-465017

McGuire, Peter Damien, (Hallam), 28 College Rd, Spinkhill, Sheffield S21 3YB. **Tel/Fax:** 01246-432289

McGurk, Simon, (OSB), St Francis Xavier, 19 Brd St, Hereford HR4 9AP **Tel:** 01432-273485

McHugh, Francis R, Phd, MA, Dip Econ; (Arundel & Brighton, retired), 56 Hampton Rd, Twickenham TW2 5QB **Tel:** 0208 893 3588

McHugh, J Daniel, Mgr Canon, PhL, MSc, STD, DUniv (Birmingham), 227 Station Rd, Dorridge B93 8EY **Tel:** 01564-772098

McHugh, Thomas, Canon, (Southwark), 1 Orchard Rd, Bromley, Kent BR1 2PR **Tel:** 0208 402 0459 **Fax:** 0208 402 4590 **Email:** stjosephsbromley@aol.com

McHugo, Peter Jude, (CJ), The Presbytery, 46 Durdells Rd, Kinson, Bournemouth BH11 9EH **Tel:** 01202-572939.

McIlroy, Stephen, (SDS), c/o Provincialate Offices, 129 Spencer Rd, Harrow Weald, Middx HA3 7BJ **Tel:** 0208 426 0495 **Fax:** 0208 426 0927

McInerney, James Edward, (Birmingham), St Filumena, Caverswall, Stoke-on-Trent ST11 9EA **Tel:** 01782-393161

McInerney, Matthew, BA(Hons), DipSacLit, (Arundel & Brighton), Dul Siar, Leckenagh, Burtonport, Co Donegal, Republic of Ireland **Tel:** 074-95 42935.

McIntyre, Patrick, (Salford), Padres de Santiago Apostol, Casilla 17-11-6015, Quito, Ecuador

McInulty, Bernard (OSB), Ampleforth Abbey, York YO62 4EN **Tel:** 01439 766714 **Fax:** 01439 766724

McIver, Daniel, (Middlesbrough, retired), Calpe, Main St, Ballyhahill, Co Limerick, Eire **Tel:** 00353 69 82326

McKay, John, (Arundel & Brighton, retired), 1 Downies, Downings, Co Donegal, Republic of Ireland **Tel:** 074 915 4641

McKay, Richard, DipCCD, (Clifton), St Nicholas' Presbytery, Lawford's Gate, Bristol BS5 0RE **Tel:** 0117-983 3920 **Fax** 0117-935 1555

McKee, Kevin (MHM) St Joseph's College, Lawrence St, London NW7 1RG

McKee, Raymond, (Salford), Our Lady, Turf Pit Lane, Oldham OL4 2NE **Tel/Fax:** 0161-624 9039

McKeever, John, (Middlesbrough), The Presbytery, 39 High St, Loftus, Saltburn-by-the-Sea TS13 4HA **Tel:** 01287-640278

McKenna, Christopher B, OBE, TD, (Westminster, retired), St John's Convent, Kiln Green, Reading RG10 9XP

McKenna, Dominic, (Westminster), 165 Arlington Rd, London NW1 7EX **Tel:** 020 7485 2727

McKenna, Francis, DipEd (OSB), St David's Priory, St David's Place Swansea SA1 3NG **Tel:** 01792-653343

McKenna, John, BA, STB, MTh, (Westminster), 22 Bradley Rd, London N22 7SZ **Tel:** 020 8888 2390

McKenna, Joseph, (Birmingham, retired), The Priest's Ho, Villa 1, Church Rd, Bundoran, Co Donegal, Ireland **Tel:** 001 353 724 1756

McKenna, Michael, Mgr, (Liverpool), St Gregory's Presbytery, Weldbank Lane, Chorley, Lancs PR7 3NW **Tel/Fax:** 01257-262462

McKenna, Michael F, (Hexham & Newcastle), St Oswald, Bellingham, Northumberland NE48 2JT **Tel:** 01434 220262

McKenna, Michael, LCL, (MHM), Monastery of Our Lady of Hyning, Warton, Carnforth, Lancs LA5 9SE **Tel:** 01524-733383

McKenna, Patrick, (Hexham & Newcastle), St Bede's, Bishopton Rd, Stockton-on-Tees, Cleveland TS18 4PA **Tel:** 01642-676164

McKenna-Whyte, Adrian RN, BTh, MSc (Southwark), 5 Hillside Rd, Streatham, London SW2 3HL **Tel:** 020 8678 9051 **Fax:** 020 8671 6157 **Email:** info@streathamhillcatholic.co.uk

McKentey, Anthony, (Brentwood), The Presbytery, The Ave, Braintree, Essex CM7 3HY **Tel:** 01376-326779

McKenzie, Barrie, (Hexham & Newcastle, Retired), St Williams, Front Street, Trimdon Village, Co Durham TS29 6LZ

McKeon, John, (Brentwood, retired), The Presbytery, Oxlow Ln, Dagenham, Essex RM9 5XJ **Tel:** 020 8592 1634

McKeown, John, BA, (SM), Marist Fathers, 76 Newland Park, Hull HU5 2DS **Tel:** 01482-444180

McKeown, Maximilian, (OFMConv), St Anthony of Padua, Greyfriars, 1 Elmsley Rd, Liverpool L18 8AY **Tel:** 0151-724 2109

McKeown, Patrick, BA, (Salford), St Mary's, Clive Rd, Failsworth, Manchester M35 0NN **Tel:** 0161-681 1835

McKeown, Patrick (CP), The Retreat, Sea St, Herne Bay, Kent CT6 8SP **Tel:** 01227-375095 **Fax:** 01227-360941

McKie, Peter, (Salford), St Herbert's, 148 Broadway, Chadderton, Oldham OL9 0JY **Tel:** 0161-624 2258

McKinney, Patrick, Mgr Canon, STL, (Birmingham), 13 New Rd, Stourbridge, W. Mids DY8 1PG **Tel:** 01384-395308

McKivergan, Richard, (OFM Conv), Franciscan Study Centre, Giles Lane, Canterbury CT2 7NA **Tel:** 01227-454647

McKnight, James, (IC), St Peter's Presbytery, St Peter's St, Roath, Cardiff CF24 3BA **Tel:** 029-2048 3394

E-mail: JimMcknight@freenet.co.uk
McLaughlin, Anthony, (Salford), 29 Beardwood Park, Blackburn BB2 7BW
McLaughlin, Daniel (SMM), 94 Whinney Hill, Durham DH1 3BQ **Tel/Fax:** 0191-386 8523
McLaughlin, Francis, (Nottingham), 3 Thackeray's Lane, Woodthorpe, Nottingham NG5 4HT **Tel:** 0115-926 8288
McLaughlin, Martin, MA(Oxon), Bursar (OSB), Prinknash Abbey, Cranham, Gloucester GL4 8EX **Tel:** 01452-812455 **Fax:** 01455-813305 **E-mail:** prinknash@waitrose.com
McLaughlin, Michael (Leeds), Cathedral Ho, Great George St, Leeds LS2 8BE **Tel:** 0113-245 4545 **Fax:** 0113-245 3626
McLaughlin, Neil, (Nottingham, retired), Glacknabrad, Malin, Co. Donegal, Éire
McLauglin, Kevin, (OMI), New Priory, Quex Rd, Kilburn, London NW6 4PS **Tel:** 020-7624 1701
McLean, Alan, (Southwark), Priest's Ho, Dockhead, Bermondsey SE1 2BS **Tel:** 020-7237 1641
McLean, Colin, (Westminster, retired), 165 Arlington Rd, London NW1P 7EX **Tel:** 020-7267 0214
McLean, David, MA, (OP), c/o PRCC(N), MP1.2, Leach Building, Whale Island, Portsmouth PO2 8BY **Tel:** 023-9262 5193
McLean, John, (WF), 42 Stormont Rd, London N6 4NP **Tel:** 020-8340 5036
McLean, Ian (OPream), Cuan Mhuire, Bruree, Co Limerick, Éire
McLean-Wilson, Terence, (Arundel & Brighton, retired), Marian Ho, 33 Battle Gates, Battle, E. Sussex TN33 0JD
McLeish, John, (Shrewsbury), SS Thomas Aquinas & Stephen Harding, 53 Great Hales St, Market Drayton TF9 1JL **Tel:** 01630-652568 **Fax:** 01630-656351 **E-mail:** priest.greathales@btinternet.com
McLeod, Donald, (WF), 46, Woodville Gardens, Ealing W5 2HP **Tel:** 020-8998 8552
McLoughlin, George, BA, (Wrexham), University Chaplaincy, Pendyffryn, Menai Ave, Bangor Gwynedd LL57 2HH **Tel:** 01248-352522
McLoughlin, John, STB SLL (Liverpool) Episcopal Vicar for Formation, St Agnes Parish House, 89 St Mary's Rd, Huyton, Liverpool L36 5SR **Tel:** 0151 489 1296
McLoughlin, Joseph Peter, BA, STB (Birmingham), Collegio de Ingleses, Calle Don Sancho 22, 47002, Valladolid, Spain
McLoughlin, Kevin, (Liverpool), Spiritual Director, St Alban's College, Valladolid (1589), Calle Don Sancho 22, 47002, Valladolid, Spain
McLoughlin, Patrick A, BA, (Southwark, retired), Baunahas, Glenavoo, Aclare, Co Sligo, Ireland **Tel:** 00-353 718 1257
McLoughlin, Patrick, (Westminster), The Presbytery, Hardie Close, London NW10 0VH
McLoughlin, William PhL, BD, MTh (OSM), Ss Peter & Paul, 112 Entry Hill, Coombe Down, Bath BA2 5LS **Tel:** 01225-832096
McMahon, Andrew, MBE, MA (OFM), Park Place Pastoral Centre, Winchester Rd, Wickham, Hants PO17 5HA **Tel:** 01329-833805 **E-mail:** parkplace1@hotmail.co.uk
McMahon, Brian, (Lancaster), c/o Our Lady and St Edward's, Marlborough Dr, Fulwood, Preston PR2 4UE
McMahon, Edward, (OMI), St Anne's, 96 Bradford St, Birmingham B12 0PB **Tel:** 0121-772 2780 **Fax:** 0121-773 6023
McMahon, Hugh, (CM), 2 Flower Lane, London NW7 2JB **Tel:** 020-8959 1021
McMahon, Patrick, (Salford), Our Lady & St John, High Lane, Chorlton-cum-Hardy, Manchester M21 1EE **Tel:** 0161-881 3558 **Fax:** 0161-860 1058
McMahon, Patrick, (Lancaster), Our Lady and St Edward, Marlborough Dr, Fulwood, Preston PR2 4UE **Tel:** 01772-862437
McMahon, Patrick, (Hexham & Newcastle), St Teresa's, Heaton Rd, Newcastle upon Tyne NE6 5HN **Tel:** 0191 265 5290
McMahon, Thomas, (Nottingham, retired), Kilmorna, Listowel, Co. Kerry, Ireland **Tel:** 00 343 6845992
McMahon, Paul, CertEd, House Superior (O Praem), Parish Ho, 2 Fern Rd, Storrington, Pulborough RH20 4LW *(Priory and Parish)* **Tel:** 01903-742150 **Fax:** 01903-740821 **E-mail:** norbertines@pavilion.co.uk
McManus, Francis, STL, PhL, (Shrewsbury, retired), 4 Adelaide Rd, Bramhall, Stockport SK7 1LT **Tel:** 0161-439 9749
McManus, Gregory, (SPS), Our Lady, College View, Llandovery SA20 0BD **Tel:** 01550-20474
McManus, James, (CSSR), Our Immaculate Lady of Victories, Clapham Park Rd, Clapham SW4 7AP **Tel:** 020-7622 2793
McManus, John, Mgr Canon VG, (Shrewsbury), St Agnes, 16 Darmond's Green, West Kirby, Wirral CH48 5DU **Tel:** 0151-625 6367 **Fax:** 0151-625 0453 **E-mail:** parish@mcagnes.plus.com
McManus, Mark, (Hallam), The Presbytery, 2 Spencer St, Chesterfield S40 4SD **Tel:** 01246-323686
McMillan, Keith (SJ), Sacred Heart

Presbytery, Edge Hill, London SW19 4LU **Tel:** 020-8946 0305

McMorrow, Desmond (CM), 110 Station Rd, Hampton-on-Thames, Middx TW12 2AS **Tel:** 020-8979 3596 **Fax:** 020-8979 8854

McNally, Bernard, (Southwark), Our Lady and St Joseph, 14 Melior St, Bermondsey, London SE1 3QP **Tel:** 020-7407 1908

McNally, Paul, STL (Birmingham), Oscott College, Chester Rd, Sutton Coldfield W. Mids B73 5AA **Tel:** 0121-321 5000

McNamara, Denis, (Liverpool), c/o Liverpool Archdiocesan Centre for Evangelisation, Croxteth Dr, Sefton Park, Liverpool L17 1AA

McNamara, Hubert, (Hallam, retired), 71 Doncaster Rd, Thrybergh, Rotherham S65 4AD **Tel:** 01709-850756

McNamara, John F, (Salford), SS Peter and Paul, 61 Pilkington St, Bolton BL3 6HP **Tel:** 01204-522744

McNamara, John, Canon, PhL (Southwark), 85 Avalon Rd, Orpington, Kent BR6 9AZ **Tel:** 01689-897975,

McNamara, Joseph Brian, STL, PhL, (Hexham & Newcastle, retired), c/o Bishop's Ho, 800 West Rd, Newcastle NE5 2BJ

McNamara, Paul, (Brentwood), c/o Cathedral Ho, Ingrave Rd, Brentwood, Essex CM15 8AT

McNamara, Thomas (SMA) c/o Provincial Office, Abbey Ho, Claredon Place, Dunblane, Perthshire FK15 9HB

McNamee, John, (Hallam), Christ the King, Skipwith Gdns, New Rossington, Doncaster D11 0TU **Tel:** 01302-868231 **Fax:** 01302-867398

McNeill, Anthony, (OFM), 557-559 High Rd, Woodford Green, Essex IG8 0RB **Tel:** 020-8504 1688

McNerney, Joseph, (Portsmouth), 43 Portland St, Fareham PO16 0NQ **Tel:** 01329-318869 **Fax:** 01329-318868 **E-mail:** joemcnerney@hotmail.com

McNicholas, James, BD, MTh, (Westminster), 20 Phoenix Rd, Euston, London NW1 1TA **Tel:** 020-7387 1971

McNicholas, Neil, (Middlesbrough), St Hilda's Presbytery, 1 Walker St, Whitby YO21 1QT **Tel:** 01947-602476

McNulty, John, (Liverpool),Liverpool Archdiocesan Centre for Evangelisation, Croxteth Drive, Sefton Park, Liverpool L17 1AA

McNulty, Thomas, (CSsR), Hawkstone Hall, Marchamley, Shrewsbury SY4 5LG **Tel:** 01630-685242 **Fax:** 01630-685565 **E-mail:** hawkhall@aol.com

McPake, Martin (SVD), St Gregory's Ho, 31 Halewood Rd, Gateacre, Liverpool L25 3PH **Tel:** 0161-428 2860

McPake, Michael, (SVD), Assumption Priory, Victoria Park Square, London E2 9PB **Tel:** 020-8980 1968 **Fax:** 020-8983 7713

McParland, Ian, MA (Liverpool), University Church of St Philip Neri, Philip Neri Ho, 30 Catharine St, Liverpool L8 7NL **Tel:** 0151-709 3858

McPartland, Paul, MA, STL, DPhil, (Westminster), School of Theology, Catholic University of America, 620 Michigan Ave NE, Washington DC 20064 **Tel:** (001) 1020-319 6515 **E-mail:** mcpartland@cua.edu

McPartland, Michael B, (SMA), c/c MOD Chaplains (Army), Trenchard Lines, Upavon, Pewsey, Wiltshire SN9 6BE

McQuillan, Brendan, BSS, BTh (Southwark), 37 Kingsdown Pk, Whitstable Kent CT5 2DE

McQuillan, William (OCarm), 63 East End Rd, East Finchley, London N2 0SE **Tel:** 020-8346 1458

McQuinn, Michael, VG, BA(hons) (Leeds), Cathedral Ho, Great George St, Leeds LS2 8BE **Tel:** 0113-245 4545

McRaye, Louis D, Mgr, MA, LLB, (Birmingham), 566 Stratford Rd, Shirley, Solihull B90 4AY **Tel:** 0121-744 1967

McShane, James, (Brentwood), 96 Dock Rd, Tilbury, Essex RM18 7BT **Tel:** 01375-842309

McShane, Thomas, (SCJ), St Joseph, Tatton St, St Petersgate, Stockport SK1 1EJ **Tel:** 0161-480 3164

McShane, Vincent, (Liverpool), Presbytery and Parish Office, Penmann Crescent, Halewood, Liverpool L26 0UG **Tel:** 0151-486 9883 **Fax:** 0151-486 9885 **E-mail:** vianney.halewood@ btinternet.com

McSherry, Edward (OMI), Our Lady Queen of Martyrs, 2 Rating Row, Beaumaris, Anglesey, North Wales LL58 8AL **Tel:** 01248-810318 **Fax:** 01248-810942

McSweeney, Anthony (East Anglia), St George's Presbytery, 223 Sprowston Rd, Norwich NR3 4HZ **Tel:** 01603-426971

McSweeney, Denis, Canon, (Northampton), The Presbytery, Pope Cl, Flitwick, Beds MK45 1JP **Tel:** 01525-715109

McSweeney, Edward, Canon, (Leeds, retired), Dun Na Ri, Kiskean, Mallow, Co. Cork, Éire

McSweeney, Terence, (Liverpool), St John's Presbytery, 70 Fountains Rd, Kirkdale, Liverpool L4 1QL **Tel:** 0151-922 3604 **E-mail:** palazzola@palazzola.it

McTaggart, Laurence MA (OSB),

Ampleforth Abbey, York YO62 4EN **Tel:** 01439-766714 **Fax:** 01439-766724

McTernan, Sean Patrick, Canon, (Birmingham), Retired, St Augustine's, Station Rd, Solihull B91 3TG **Tel:** 0121-705 0228

McVicar Duncan, (SI), Our Lady of Mount Carmel Presbytery, Wilson Rd, Manchester M9 3BG **Tel:** 0161-740 2071

McWeeney, Sean, (Westminster, retired), 13 Mill Way, Feltham, Middx TW14 0JX **Tel:** 020-8890 2863

McWilliams, Brian, (Brentwood, retired), Nazareth Ho, 111 London Rd, Southend-on-Sea, Essex SS1 1PP **Tel:** 01702-345627

Maciuszek, Stanislaus (Polish Priest). 226 Trelawney Ave, Langley, Slough SL3 7UD **Tel:** 01753-543770

Mack, John, (Nottingham), 68 Derby Rd, Borrowash, Derby DE7 3HB **Tel:** 01332-673562

Mackie, John, (Salford), St William's, 76a Lever Edge Lane, Great Lever, Bolton, BL3 3EN **Tel:** 01204-62316

Mackrell, Gerard BA, MPhil, (SMM, retired), Nazareth Ho, Colum Rd, Cardiff CF10 3UN **Tel:** 029-2022 0943

Madden, Cuthbert, MB, BS, MRCP, (OSB), Rt Rev Abbot, Ampleforth Abbey, York YO62 4EN **Tel:** 01439-766700 **Fax:** 01439-788132

Madden, John, Canon, (Southwark), 20 Village Way, Beckenham, Kent BR3 3NP **Tel:** 020-8650 0970 **Fax:** 020-8249 3316

Madden, Mark, (Liverpool), St Cecilia's Presbytery, 21-23 Green Lane, Tuebrook, Liverpool L13 7DT **Tel:** 0151-228 1310

Madden, Peter, (Southwark), 103 Maison Dieu Rd, Dover, Kent CT16 1RU **Tel:** 01304-206766 **Fax:** 01304-209372

Madden, Peter BA(Cant), STB (Birmingham). The Presbytery, St Mary's Rd, Wednesbury WS10 9DL **Tel:** 0121 556 0414

Madden, William, Canon, (Middlesbrough), Our Lady of Lourdes Presbytery, Milton St, Saltburn-by-the-Sea TS12 1DE **Tel:** 01287-623619

Madden, Peter (OSB), Belmont Abbey, Herefordshire HR2 9RZ **Tel:** 01432-374710

Madders, Richard, Mgr, MBE, (Arundel and Brighton), 1 Caesar's Camp Rd, Camberley, Surrey GU15 4ED **Tel:** 01276 476678

Maddison, Paul, (East Anglia), Sacred Heart, 19 Needingsworth Rd, St Ives, Cambs PE27 5JT **Tel:** 01480-462192

Maddock, Grant, (Liverpool), Christ the King Presbytery, 78 Queens Dr, Liverpool L15 6YQ **Tel:** 0151-722 2231 **Fax:** 0151-722 2755

Maddox, Bernard Thomas (Birmingham), St Bede's, 1 Hayworth Rd, Lichfield, Staffs WS13 6AL **Tel:** 01543-418184

Madej, Anton, BEd(Hons), (SCJ), St Joseph's Mather Lane, Leigh, Lancs WN7 2PR **Tel:** 01942-673517 **Fax:** 01942-269094

Madeley, Timothy, Canon, B.Th (Arundel & Brighton), Cathedral Ho, Parsons Hill, Arundel, W. Sussex BN18 9AY **Tel:** 01903-882297

Madigan, Patrick, (SJ), John Sinnott Ho, 9 Edge Hill, Wimbledon SW19 4LR **Tel:** 020-8947 4251

Magbanu, Sergio, (SSP), The Presbytery, 132 Shernhall St, Walthamstow, London E17 9HU **Tel:** 020-8520 5877

Magee, Luke, (CP), Minsteracres Retreat Centre, Consett, Co Durham DH8 9RT **Tel:** 01434-673248

Magee, Martin, JCL (Salford), SS Peter and Paul, 3 Barleydale Rd, Barrowford, Nelson, Lancs BB9 6AD **Tel:** 01282-613023.

Mageean, James Francis (SDB), St Gregory's, 38 Wellington Rd, Bollington, Macclesfield SK10 5JR **Tel:** 01625-572108 **E-mail:** jfmsdb@gmail.com

Maggiore, Louis (OFM Cap), Franciscan Friary, Carlton Rd, Erith, Kent DA8 1DN **Tel:** 01322-433193

Maggs, Anthony, (CRL), Christ Church Priory, 229 Eltham High St, Eltham, London SE9 1TX **Tel:** 020-8850 1666

Magill, Daniel (MAfr), 270 March Rd, Coates, Peterborough PE7 2DL **Tel:** 01733-840677

Magnante, Antonio, (IMC), 3 Salisbury Ave, Finchley N3 3AJ **Tel:** 020-8346 5498

Magner, Patrick, (Hexham and Newcastle, retired), 38 Sue Ryder Ho, Owning, Piltown, Co Kilkenny, Ireland.

Magnier, Daniel, (Westminster), 1 Du Cross Dr, Stanmore, Middx HA7 4TJ **Tel:** 020-8954 1299.

Magovern, Kieran BA, BD, HDE, LRSM, STL (CM), 82 West St, Dunstable, Beds LU6 1NY **Tel:** 01582-662710 **Fax:** 01582-670968 **E-mail:** kierancm54@aol.com

Magrath, Eamonn, (Brentwood, retired), Nazareth Ho, 111 London Rd, Southend-on-Sea, Essex SS1 1PP **Tel:** 01702 340855 **Mbl:** 07710-402098

Maguire, Derek (OSA), St Monica's Priory, 19 Hoxton Square, Hoxton N1 6NT **Tel:** 020-7739 5006 **Fax:** 020-8570 8059

Maguire, Edmund, (Salford), c/o Bishop's Ho, Monaghan, Ireland

Maguire, Fergal (SSCC), 81 Evelina Rd, Nunhead, Peckham, London SE15 3HL **Tel:** 020-7639 3724 **Fax:** 020-7635 8215

E-mail: fergal_maguire@hotmail.com
Maguire, Gabriel (CSsR), 49 Sutton Rd, Eardington, Birmingham B23 6QN **Tel:** 0121-373 0143 **E-mail:** ppabbeyerdington@aol.com
Maguire, James, (Arundel & Brighton), 25 Between Streets, Cobham, Surrey KT11 1AA **Tel:** 01932 862518
Maguire, John, Mng (Cardiff), St Mary of the Angels, 67, Talbot St, Canton, Cardiff CF11 9BX **Tel:** 02920-230492
Maguire, Patrick, (SCC), Presbytery, Old Oak Common Lane, London, W3 7DD **Tel:** 020-8743 5732
Maguire, Peter, Canon, (Leeds), St John the Baptist Presbytery, Newland Lane, Normanton WF6 1BA **Tel:** 01924-892172
Mahady, Michael J, (Leeds), Highroad Well Ln, Pellon, Halifax HX2 0QF LS27 9NF **Tel:** 01422 361682
Maher, David, St Paul, (Southwark, retired), 14 Seamus Quirke Park, Ballinlough, Cork, Ireland **Tel:** 00-353 21 291167
Maher, Denis, (Shrewsbury), St Paul's, St Paul's St, Newton, Hyde, SK14 2JU **Tel/Fax:** 0161-367 8326 **E-mail:** dionysios2003@yahoo.co.uk
Maher, Peter, (Westminster), 141 Woodhall Lane, Welwyn Garden City, Herts AL7 3TP **Tel:** 01707-323234
Maher, Pierce, (Cardiff), The Catholic Presbytery, Ham Lane East, Llantwit Major CF61 1TQ **Tel:** 01446-792381
Maher, Roger, Canon, (Nottingham, retired), Fort Villa, Ballyhane, Cappawhite, Co Tipperary, Ireland
Mahony, Senan, Prior & Guestmaster (OCSO), Abbey of Our Lady and St Samson, Caldey Island, Tenby SA70 7UH **Tel:** 01834-842632
Mahy, David, Canon, (Portsmouth), The Presbytery, Queen's Rd, Aldershot, Hants GU11 3JB **Tel:** 01252-320956 **Fax:** 01252-323030 **Mbl:** 07720 058215 **Email:** dmahy@stjosephs.datanet.co.uk
Maidlow Davis, Richard Leo, MA, BD, STL, (OSB), Downside Abbey, Stratton on the Fosse, Radstock, Bath BA3 4RH **Tel:** 01761-235101 (Secretary)
Maitland, Derrick (SJ), Corpus Christi Jesuit Community, 757 Christchurch Rd, Boscombe, Bournemouth BH7 6AN **Tel:** 01202-436700
Maitland, Keith Bede, MA, (OSB), Downside Abbey, Stratton on the Fosse, Radstock, Bath BA3 4RH **Tel:** 01761-235161
Makings, Terence, MBE, (Nottingham), Stirling Walk 4, 41179 Monchengladbach, Germany
Makulski, Aleksander, 44 Preston New Rd, Blackburn BB2 6AH **Tel:** 01254-57067
Malecki, George, (SDS), St Augustine's Presbytery, Castlefields Ave North, Castlefields, Runcorn WA7 2HT **Tel:** 01928-566068 **E-mail:** staugustines@sdsruncorn.fsnet.co.uk
Maley, Joseph, (Lancaster), St Gregory's, Blackpool Rd, Deepdale, Preston PR1 6HQ **Tel:** 01772 795328
Malia, J Brian, (Hexham and Newcastle, retired), Our Lady and St Joseph, New Hartley, Whitley Bay, Tyne & Wear NE25 0RT **Tel:** 0191 237-0455
Maliekal, Jose, (MSFS), 16 Wellington Rd, Hampton Hill, Middx TW12 1JR **Tel:** 020-8977 1415
Mallaley, Vincent, (Hexham & Newcastle, retired). 21 Thistle Cl, Whitworth Manor, Middlestone Moor, Co. Durham DL16 7YD **Tel:** 01388-818562
Mallavarappu, Selva Raj (SDS), parish Priest, Sacred Heart Church, Pantyffynon Road, Ystradgyanlais, Swansea SA9 1EU **Tel:** 01639 842202
Mallon, James, (Westminster), Archbishop's Ho, Ambrosden Ave, London SW1P 1QJ
Malloy, Austin, BA, (SDB), St Joseph's, 10 Oldhams Lane, Bolton BL1 6PN **Tel:** 01204-590600
Maloney, John J, (Nottingham), Blessed Sacrament, Gooding Ave, Leicester LE3 1JS **Tel:** 0116-285 8795
Maloney, Peter, (Salford, retired), 4 Merinall Cl, Kingsway, Rochdale OL16 5BY
Maloney, Stephen, (Liverpool), Vocations Director, All Saints Presbytery, 3 Oakfield, Anfield, Liverpool L4 2QH **Tel:** 0151 287 8787 **Fax:** 0151 287 8788
Maloney, Timothy, (IC), The Presbytery, 4 Belmont Rd, Hay-on-Wye, Hereford HR3 5DA **Tel:** 01497-820452
Manahan, William Philip, JCL, (OSB), c/o Buckfast Abbey, Buckfastleigh, Devon TQ11 0EE **Tel:** 01364-645500 **Fax:** 01364-643891
Mangnall, Anthony, (Liverpool), Holy Family Presbytery, Lily Ln, Platt Bridge, Wigan WN2 5LL **Tel:** 01942 866102 **E-mail:** amangnall@aol.com
Maniak, Richard J, (Portsmouth), 54 Amblecote Rd, Tilehurst, Reading, Berks RG3 4BP **Tel:** 07835 496692 **E-mail:** richardmaniak@lycos.com
Manimala, Bosco (SVD), 8 Teignmouth Rd, London NW2 4HN
Manley-Harris, Eric (Northampton), The Presbytery, Long Crendon, Bucks HP18 9BS **Tel:** 01844-208754.
Mann, Thomas More (OFM Cap) Greyfriars, Iffley Rd, Oxford, OX4 1SB **Tel:** 01865-423694

Manning, Michael, Parish Priest (OCarm), The Presbytery, Waun-lan-yr-afan Rd, Llanelli, Carmarthenshire SA15 3AB **Tel:** 01554-774070 **E-mail:** olqpllanelli@btinternet.com

Mannion, Michael, (Westminster), The Presbytery, Bouverie Rd, London N16 0AJ **Tel:** 020-8800 5250

Manock, James, PhB, STB, (Salford), St Mary, 129 Spring Lane, Radcliffe, Manchester M26 2QZ **Tel:** 0161-723 2340 **Fax:** 0161-724 6376 **E-mail:** salfordliturgy@hotmail.com

Mansfield, Dermot, (SJ), Manresa Ho, 10 Albert Rd, Harborne, Birmingham B17 0AN **Tel:** 0121 427 2628 **Fax:** 0121 428 1833

Mansfield, Peter, (Southwark), 208 Sydenham Rd, Sydenham, Kent SE26 5SE **Tel:** 020 8778 9460

Mansford, Emmanuel, (CFR), St Fidelis Friary, Killip Cl, London E16 1LX **Tel:** 020 7474 0766

Mansi, Ronald Dominic, (OSB), Downside Abbey, Stratton on the Fosse, Bath BA3 4RH

Manson, David Mgr, SLL, LLB, VG, (Brentwood), St John's Presbytery, Roman Rd, Ingatestone, Essex CM4 9AA **Tel:** 01277-353193

Maple, Francis MBE (OFM Cap), **E-mail:** francis@francismaple.co.uk

Maram, William (CSsR), Our Lady's, Bishop Eton, Woolton Rd, Liverpool L16 8NQ **Tel:** 0151-722 1108 **Fax:** 0151-738 0834

Marcak, Andrzej (Polish Priest), 29 Edmund St, Bradford BD5 0BH **Tel:** 01274-720848.

Marcolongo Renzo (IMC), The Missionary Institute, The Ridgeway, London NW7 4HY

Marden, Peter, MA, (Southwark), 18 Colwill Road, Gabalfa, Cardiff CF14 2QQ **Tel:** 029 2062 3622

Marett-Crosby, Anthony MA (OSB), c/o Bishops Ho, Edinburgh Road, Portsmouth PO1 3HG

Marie, Jean-Laurent, (Brentwood), 27 Milton Rd, Westcliff-on-Sea, Essex SS0 7JP **Tel:** 01702-342324

Markey, Michael, (Westminster), The Presbytery, London Rd, Bushey, Watford WD23 1BH **Tel:** 020-8950 2077

Marley, Euan (OP), Holy Cross Priory, 45 Wellington St, Leicester LE1 6HW **Tel:** 0116-255 3856 **Fax:** 0116-255 5552

Marlor, Geoffrey, (Salford), English Martyrs, Ralph Sherwin Ho, 68 Alexandra Rd South, Whalley Range, Manchester M16 8QT **Tel:** 0161-624 7925

Marmion, Denis, STL, PhL, (Shrewsbury, retired), 2 Allans Meadow, Neston, CH64 9SG **Tel:** 0151-336 2877

Marmion, John P, Canon, MA, MEd, PhD, (Shrewsbury, retired), 32 Larkhall Ave, Upton, Wirral CH49 4PN **Tel:** 0151-677 5689

Marmol, Wladyslaw, (Polish Priest), 70 Wolverhampton Rd, Stafford ST17 4AW **Tel:** 01785-240268

Marr, Michael R, MTh, (Hexham and Newcastle, retired), 10 Sandringham Court, Blackfriars Way, Longbenton, Newcastle NE 12 **Tel:** 0191 2668262

Marrapillil, Luke (MST), 61 Lowden Rd, Herne Hill SE24 0BT **Tel:** 020-7274 6179

Marriott, Richard, MA, Canon (Westminster, retired), c/o Archbishop's Ho, Ambrosden Ave, London SW1P 1QJ

Marrison, Cenydd, STB, (OSB), Our Lady Queen of Martyrs, 101 Belmont Rd, Hereford HR2 7JR **Tel:** 01432-265177

Marsden, Christopher (OSA). c/o Principal RC Chaplain (RAF), Chaplaincy Office, RAF Halton, Aylesbury, Bucks HP22 5PG **Tel:** 01296 656910

Marsden, David (SCJ). c/o Provincial Office, St Joseph's Centre, Malpas, Cheshire SY14 7DD **Tel:** 01948-860619

Marsden, Francis, MA, PhD, STL, (Liverpool), St Mary's Presbytery, Mount Pleasant, Chorley PR7 2SR **Tel:** 01257-262537 **E-mail:** stmaryschorley@fsmail.net

Marsden, George, MA (Southwark), 43 Castle St, Canterbury, Kent CT1 2PY. **Tel/Fax:** 01227-462896

Marsden, Gerard (SJ), St Wilfrid's Presbytery, 1 Winckley Square, Preston, PR1 3JJ **Tel:** 01772 554382

Marsden, Michael, (Middlesbrough), Our Lady of Lourdes, 56 Swanland Rd, Hessle HU13 0LY **Tel:** 01482-648802

Marsh, Adrian (OFM Cap), Franciscan Friary, 15 Cuppin St, Chester CH1 2BN **Tel:** 01865-243694 **Fax:** 01865-256750

Marsh, Bernard, MSc, DIC, STD, (Opus Dei), 4 Orme Court, London W2 4RL **Tel:** 020-7229 7574

Marsh, John J, STL, LSS, (Lancaster), St Mary, Station Lane, Newhouse, Barton, Preston PR3 5DY **Tel:** 01772-862831

Marsh, Peter (East Anglia, retired), 12 Unthank Rd, Norwich NR2 2RA **Tel:** 01603-610349

Marsh, Philip, (CSSp), 18 Limesdale Gdns, Edgeware, Middx HA8 5JA **Tel:** 0208 200 5091 **Fax:** 0208 200 3486

Marsh, Robert STB (OSA) Collegio S. Monica, Via Paolo VI, 25 00193 Rome Italy

Marsh, Robert (SJ), Loyola Hall, Warrington Rd, Prescot, Merseyside L35 6NZ **Tel:** 0151-426 4137 **Fax:** 0151-431 0115 **E-mail:** rob@rmarsh.com

Marsh, Stephen, (Wrexham), c/o Bishop's

Ho, Sontley Rd, Wrexham LL13 7EW

Marshall, Clement, (Portsmouth, retired), Flat 6, Grosvenor Court, Montfort Close, Romsey, Hants SO51 5AH **Tel:** 01794 518118

Marshall, Jeba, (Brentwood), 1 Stoneleigh Rd, Clayhall, Ilford, Essex IG5 0JB **Tel:** 020-8550 4540

Marshall, Peter, Prospect House, Madam Lane, Barnby Dun, Doncaster DN3 1EW **Tel:** 01302 885 358

Marsland, John C, STL, (Salford), President, Ushaw College, Durham DN7 9RH **Tel:** 0191 373 8501

Marszewski, Andrezej, STL, BA (hons), (MSFS), 16 Wellington Rd, Hampton Hill, Middx TW12 1JR **Tel:** 020 8977 1415

Martin, Gerard, (Hexham & Newcastle, retired), 76 Wood Terr, Monkton, Jarrow, Tyne and Wear NE32 5LU **Tel:** 0191-489 7496

Martin, Jonathan, (Arundel & Brighton), Domus Internationalis Paulus VI, Via Della Serofa 70, 00186 Roma, Italia **Tel:** (39) 06 698 619

Martin, Kenneth, CI (CSSp), 6 Woodlands Rd, Bickley, Bromley, Kent BR1 2AF **Tel:** 020-8467 3555

Martin, Laurence, BA, (SDB), St John Bosco Ho, 121a Reading Rd, Farnborough GU14 6NZ **Tel:** 01252-554300 **Fax:** 01252-375395 **E-mail:** sdb_farnborough@msn.com

Martin, Nicholas, (OSM), St Mary's Priory, 264 Fulham Rd, Kensington SW10 9EL. **Tel:** 020-7351 1037.

Martin, Paul, BA (Birmingham), Henley Ho, Causeway, Bicester, Oxon OX26 6AW. **Tel:** 01869-253277 **Fax:** 01869-249830

Martin, Paul, (SJ), Loyola Hall, Warrington Rd, Prescott, Merseyside L35 6NZ **Tel:** 0151 426 4137 **E-mail:** pmartins@yahoo.co.uk

Martin, Peter V, (Hexham & Newcastle), St Matthew's, York Ave, Jarrow, Tyne & Wear NE32 5LP **Tel:** 0191-489 7925.

Martin, Richard, (SSC), c/o 28 Redington Rd, London NW3 7RB

Martin, Terry (Arundel & Brighton), The Prestbytery, 3 Springfield Rd, Horsham, W. Sussex RH12 2PJ **Tel:** 01403 253667 **Tel:** 01403 271509 **Email:** terry.martin@dabnet.org

Martynyuk, Mykola (Ukrainian), Thorneywood Ho, 575 Carlton Road, Nottingham NG3 7AF **Tel:** 0115 950 5313

Masarira, Constantine (OCarm), 63 East End Rd, East Finchley N2 0SE **Tel:** 020-8346 1458 **Fax:** 020-8343 0942

Maskell, David, (Arundel & Brighton), 91 Harvest Rd, Englefield Green, Surrey TW20 0QR **Tel:** 01784-434280

Mason, Daniel, BA(Hons) (Brentwood), 56 St Antony's Rd, Forest Gate, London E7 9QB **Tel:** 020 8472 0433.

Mason, David, Ven Collegio Inglese, Via di Monserrato 45, 00186 Roma, Italy

Mason, Michael, (Nottingham), 5 Boundary Court, Newark, Nottinghamshire NG24

Mason, Paul BA, STL (Southwark), Cathedral Ho, Westminster Bridgerd, London SE1 7HY **Tel:** 020-7928 5256 **Fax:** 020-7202 2189

Mason, Stuart, (Lancaster), c/o Bishop's Ho, Cannon Hill, Lancaster LA1 5NT

Mason, William, (East Anglia, retired), 4 Cardinal Cl, Bury St Edmunds, Suffolk IP32 7LR **Tel:** 01284-750671

Massey, Harish, 94 Sandringham Road, Intake, Doncaster DN3 1EW **Tel:** 01302 326 408

Massey, J Bernard, (Clifton), St Augustine's Presbytery, Boscombe Cres, Downend, Bristol BS16 6QR **Tel:** 0117-983 3939

Massie, William, MA, STL, (Middlesbrough), West Hull Parishes, 187 Pickering Rd, Hull HU4 6TD **Tel/Fax:** 01482-351012 **E-mail:** westhull.parishes@virgin.net

Masterson, Michael, OBE, MTh, BD, BA, HDipEd, (Arundel and Brighton), 2 Garlands Rd, Leatherhead, Surrey KT22 7EZ **Tel:** 01372-372278

Mastromauro, Franco STL (MCCJ), Comboni Ho, 16 Dawson Place, London W2 4TJ **Tel:** 020 7229 7059 **E-mail:** combonileeds@supanet.com

Mathew, Saji, (MSFS), St Joseph Presbytery, Devizes, Wilts SN10 1DD **Tel:** 01380 723572

Mathias, Philip, (Southwark), St Elizabeth, The Vineyard, Richmond, Surrey TW10 6AQ **Tel:** 020-8940 2439

Matthew, Iain, (OCD), Carmelite Priory, 41 Kensington Church St, London W8 4BB **Tel:** 020-7937 9866 **Fax:** 020-7938 1470 **E-mail:** iainmatthew@yahoo.com

Matthew, Pius (CMI), St Francis of Assisi, Llay Chain, Llay, Wrexham **Tel:** 01978 852297 **E-mail:** piuscmi@hotmail.com

Matthews, Christopher, (Shrewsbury), Cathedral House, 11 Belmont Shrewsbury SY1 1TE **Tel:** 01743 362366 **Email:** fatherchristophermatthews@hotmail.co.uk

Matthews, Edward, LTL, Canon (Westminster), 3 Windhill, Bishops Stortford, Hertfordshire CM23 2ND **Tel:** 01279-654063

Matthews, Frederick, BA, DipCouns (SMM), St Jerome's Presbytery, Greenloons Dr, Formby, Liverpool

L37 2LX **Tel:** 01704-830784

Matthews, James, (SCJ), St Josephs, Tatton Street, St Petersgate, Stockport SK1 1ET **Tel:** 0161 480 3164

Matus, Gregory (MIC), The Presbytery, Cardiff Rd, Abercynon CF45 4RR **Tel:** 01443-740353 **E-mail:** stpeters.bargoed@btopenworld.com

Matus, Raymond (Clifton), BA, STB, PhB, Holy Name Church, Oxford Rd, Chorlton-on-Medlock, Manchester M13 9PG **Tel:** 0161-273-2435

Matuszynski, Joseph (Przemysl), 126 Week St, Maidstone, Kent ME14 1RH **Tel:** 01622-756217 **Fax:** 01622-690549

Matysik, Jozef, Mgr (Leeds, retired) 65 Harehills Lane, Leeds LS7 4EZ **Tel:** 0113 262 0334

Maughan, Stephen, (Middlesbrough), St Charles Borromeo, 12 Jarratt St, Hull HU1 3HB **Tel:** 01482-329100 **Fax:** 01482-219671

Mauri, Giuseppe, (SX), 260 Nether St, Finchley, London N3 1HT **Tel:** 020-8346 0428

Maxwell, Blane, DipTh (OSB), c/o Worth Abbey, Paddockhurst Rd, Turners Hill, W. Sussex RH10 4SB **Tel:** 01342-710310

Maxwell, Brian, (Southwark, retired), 67 Thetford Rd, New Malden KT 5 8LW

Maxwell, Stanley, (SJ), Corpus Christi, 757 Christchurch Rd, Boscombe, Bournemouth BH7 6AN **Tel:** 01202 436700

May, Ambrose (OFM Cap), Greyfriars, Iffley Rd, Oxford OX4 1SB **Tel:** 01865-243694 **Fax:** 01865-256750

May, Leonard, (Hallam, retired), 13 Stag Lane, Rotherham S60 3NR **Tel:** 01709-305891

May, Peter Dominic, (OSB), Buckfast Abbey, Buckfastleigh, Devon TQ11 0EE **Tel:** 01364-645500 **Fax:** 01364-643891

Mayhead, John (OSB), Monastery of Christ Our Saviour, Turvey Mews, Turvey, Beds MK43 8DH **Tel:** 01234-881211

Mayne, Laurence J, (Liverpool), St Oswald, 20a Tansley Ave, Coppull, Chorley, Lancs PR7 5DJ **Tel:** 01257-791208

Mayor, Marcelino, (OAR), St Rita's Centre, Ottery Moor Ln, Honiton EX14 8AP **Tel/Fax:** 01404 42601

Mazzotta, Carlo, (FDP), Don Orione Centre, Cardinal Heenan Ho, Roby Mill, Upholland WN8 0QR **Tel:/Fax:** 01695-622885

Mazurouski, Robert 2 Maple Terrace, Newcastle NE4 7SF **Tel:** 0191-273 3575

Mbelu, Austin (CM), 29 Eversley Crescent, Isleworth TW7 4RL **Tel:** 020 8560 7021

Mead, David Jeffrey, (Birmingham), The Retreat, Higher Menadue, Bugle, St Austell, Cornwall PL26 8QW **Tel:** 01726-851404

Mead, T Eric, BA, FSA (Scot), (Southwark), St Anne's Presbytery, Devonshire Gardens, Cliftonville, Kent CT9 3AF **Tel:** 01843-220720

Meagher, Desmond, (Hexham & Newcastle, retired), Our Lady of Lourdes, Fleming Field, Shotton Colliery, Shotton, Co. Durham DH6 2JQ **Tel:** 0191-526 1150

Meagher, Thomas Norbert, (Birmingham, retired), Peterhouse, 10 St Peter's St, Winchester SO23 8BW **Tel:** 01962-867479

Mealey, James BA, STB (Birmingham), The Island, Willenhall Rd, Wolverhampton WV1 2QN **Tel:** 01902 452841

Meaney, Gerard, (Westminster, retired), Nazereth Ho, East End Rd, London N2 8RU **Tel:** 0208-444 3691

Measures, Anthony Augustine, MA, (OSB), St Benedict's Monastery, Convent Cl, Duddle Lane, Bamber Bridge, Preston PR5 6US **Tel:** 01772-902201 **Fax:** 01772-902214

Meehan, John D, (Brentwood), 224 Long Rd, Canvey Island, Essex SS8 0JS **Tel:** 01268-696908

Melham, Boulos, (LMO), Our Lady of Lebanon, 6 Dobson Cl, Swiss Cottage, NW6 4RS **Tel:** 020-7586 1801

Melia, Michael, (Hexham & Newcastle), St Osmund's Church, Gainford, Darlington DL2 3DE **Tel:** 01325-730191

Melia, Vincent, (Hexham & Newcastle), St Matthew, West Rd, Ponteland, Newcastle upon Tyne NE20 9SX **Tel:** 01661-822767

Mellor, David John BTh(Notts) (Birmingham), The Presbytery, 40 Warren Place, Brownhills, Walsall WS8 6BY **Tel:** 01543-372759

Mellor, Steven, (Birmingham), c/o Archbishop's Ho, Shadwell St, Birmingham B6 6EY

Melly, David, (Liverpool), Our Lady Help of Christians, Portico Lane, Portico, Prescot L34 2QT **Tel:** 0151-426 6251 **Fax:** 0151-430 0882

Melnicki, Carlos (OSBM), 10 Park Rd, Bradford BD9 4PA **Tel:** 01274-542307 **Fax:** 01274-409093

Melody, Kevin (OCarm), c/o Provincial Office, Whitefriars, Tanners St, Faversham ME13 7JW

Mendes, Joseph, (MSFS), 267 Hale Lane, Edgeware, Middx HA8 8NW **Tel:** 020-8958 5622

Meneghini, Renzo, (IMC), 3 Salisbury Ave, London, N3 3AJ **Tel:** 020-8346 5498

Menezes, Timothy, (Birmingham), St Thomas More Presbytery, 112 Knoll Dr, Stivichale, Coventry CV3 5DE **Tel:** 024-7641 1900 **Fax:** 024-7641 7935

Mercer, Joseph W, (Liverpool, retired), Flat 4, Springfield Ho, 35a Church Rd, Formby, L37 8BQ

Mercer, Paul (East Anglia, retired), 26 Bury Park Dr, Bury St Edmunds, Suffolk IP33 2DA **Tel:** 01284-753982

Mercer, Robert, (SA), 11 Fashoda Rd, Bromley, Kent BR2 9RE **Tel:** 020-8460 5764

Meredith, Anthony, (SJ), 114 Mount St, London W1K 3AH **Tel:** 020-7493 7811 **Fax:** 020-7495 6685

Meredith, Anthony D (IC), 383 Fosse Way, Leicester LE7 4SJ **Tel:** 01509-817048 **E-mail:** anthonyic@btinernet.com

Meredith, John, (Cardiff), Our Lady of the Angels, Oak St, Cwmbran, Gwent NP44 3LT **Tel/Fax:** 01633-482346

Merriman, Joseph BSc, Dip Adv Div Studies, MLC (SDB), Rinaldi Ho, 32 Orbel St, London SW11 3NZ **Tel:** 020-7801 9040 **Fax:** 020-7801 9041 **E-mail:** jmmsdborb@hotmail.com

Merron, Bernard (Southwark, retired), Colinvale Court, Shaws Rd, Belfast BT11 8BU

Metcalfe, John, (Hallam), Our Lady of Beauchief & St Thomas of Canterbury, 34 Meadowhead, Sheffield S8 7UD **Tel:** 0114-274 7257

Meyer, Conrad J, MA, Canon, (Plymouth, retired), Hawk's Cliff, 38 Praze Rd, Newquay, Cornwall TR7 3AF **Tel:** 01637-873003

Meyer, Richard (Plymouth), St Anthony's Leweston School, Sherborne, Dorset DT9 6EN **Tel:** 01963-210691

Mgungwe, Nazarius (Malawi), SS George & Martin, Gibbins St, Birches Head, Stoke-on-Trent ST1 2LS **Tel:** 10782 212217

Michael, Santiago (Sivangal), 207 Cannon Hill Lane, Merton SW20 9DB **Tel:** 020 8542 6355

Middleton, David Bernard, BA, STL, (Provincial) (OSA), Clare Priory, Clare, Sudbury, Suffolk CO10 8NX **Tel:** 01787-277326 **Fax:** 017870278688

Middleton, Shaun, (Westminster), The Presbytery, Pottery Lane, London W11 4NQ. **Tel:** 020-7727 7968

Mignolli, Natalino, (CSS), 5 Hanover Rd, Kensal Rise, London NW10 3DJ **Tel:** 020-8451 1408

Milburn, David, DSH (Hexham & Newcastle, retired), SS Peter & Paul, Benton Lane, Longbenton, Newcastle-upon-Tyne NE12 8PB **Tel:** 0191-266 1533

Milcz, Jan, (CSSR), St Benet's, The Causeway, Monkwearmouth, Sunderland, Tyne and Wear SR6 0BH **Tel:** 0191-567 2965

Mileham, Patrick BD, STL (Birmingham), St Joseph's Presbytery, Cannock Rd, Burntwood WS7 6XY **Tel:** 01543 686266

Miles, Frederick A, ProtAp, Mgr Canon, MA, (Westminster, retired), St Peter's Residence, 2a Meadow Rd, London SW8 1QH **Tel:** 020-7793 1338

Miles, Keith, LicCIPD (Clifton), English Martyrs Presbytery, Tuffley Lane, Tuffley, Gloucester GL4 0NX **Tel:** 01452-504997

Millane, John, Superior (MAfr), 15 Corfton Rd, Ealing, London W5 2HP **Tel:** 020-8997 8751 **Fax:** 020-8998 2920 **E-mail:** wfslondon@btinternet.com

Meredith, Edward 17 Heath Avenue, Rode Heath, Stoke-on-Trent STY 3RY **Tel:** 01270-876814 **E-mail:** miller@heathavenue.fslife.co.uk

Millar, Paul, (Cardiff), 201 New Rd, Porthcawl CF36 5NN **Tel:** 01656-782789

Millard, Norman John, (Birmingham, retired), 8 Priory Ave, Caversham, Reading RG4 7SE

Miller, Christopher, (Birmingham), The Presbytery, Dormer Place, Leamington Spa, CV32 5AA **Tel:** 01926 420366

Miller, Edgar, (OSB), Ampleforth Abbey, York YO62 4EN **Tel:** 01439-766714 **Fax:** 01439-766724

Miller, John M, (Westminster, retired), 13 Highlands, 131 Oakleigh Rd North, London N20 9HA **Tel:** 020-8445 8896

Miller, Philip MA, PhD, STL (Westminster), The Presbytery, High Street, Hoddesden EN11 8DS **Tel:** 01992 440244

Miller, Robert, AKC, MA, Mth, PhD, MCIPD, (Clifton), Bridge Ho, 2 High St, Dulverton, Somerset TA22 9HB **Tel:** 01398-324217

Millett, Desmond, Canon, BA, HDipEd, FRSA (Clifton), 20 Station Hill, Chippenham, Wilts SN15 1EG **Tel:** 01249-652404

Mills, Alexander M, (OSB), 54 Lodge Rd, St John's Wood, London NW8 8LA **Tel:** 020-7286 3214

Mills, David (Clifton). 65 Oxford Rd, Calne SN11 8AQ **Tel:** 01249-813131

Mills, Donald, BSc, (Brentwood, retired), Nazareth Ho, 111 London Rd, Southend-on-Sea, Essex SS1 1PP **Tel:** 01702-340855

Mills, John Orme, (OP), Blackfriars, Buckingham Rd, Cambridge CB3 0DD **Tel:** 01223-741251 **Fax:** 01223-741252

Mills, Philip (Leeds) 151 Healey Wood Rd, Brighouse HD6 3RR **Tel:** 01484-400410

Millward, Mark (Hexham & Newcastle) Our

Lady, Village Lane, Washington, Tyne & Wear NE38 7HS
Tel: 0191-416 3583

Milner, Austin John, (OP), Dominican House, 61 Deanery Road, Kingston 3, Jamaica

Milroy, Dominic, MA, (OSB), Ampleforth Abbey, York, YO62 4EN
Tel: 01439-766714 **Fax:** 01439-766724

Miners, Michael, (Birmingham), St Mary's Presbytery, Kiddemore Green Rd, Brewood ST19 9BG **Tel:** 01902 850394

Minihane, Mark (OSA), St Monica's Priory, 19 Hoxton Square, London N1 6NT
Tel: 020-7739 5006 **Fax:** 020-7613 0394

Minguez, Epifaio Puertas, (FDP), 25 Lower Teddington Rd, Hampton Wick, Kingston upon Thames KT1 4HB
Tel: 020-8977 5130

Minskip, Dominique, BA, (Middlesbrough), English Martyrs, Dalton Terr, York YO24 4DA **Tel:** 01904-623783

Miranda, Huebert, STL, (MSFS), 16 Wellington Rd, Hampton Hill, Middx TW12 1JR **Tel:** 020-8977 1415
Fax: 020-8943 9593
E-mail: fathermiranda@yahoo.co.uk

Miros, Peter, (MIC, retired), 48 Pitts Rd, Slough, Berks SL1 3XH
Tel: 01753-533861

Miscampbell, Patrick, (OSB), Nazareth Ho, 162 East End Rd, London, N2 0RU **Tel:** 020-8444 1651

Mitchell, Gerard, (SJ), Sacred Heart Presbytery, Edge Hill, London SW19 4LU
Tel: 020-8946 0305 **Fax:** 020-8946 9130
E-mail: wimparish@btconnect.com

Mitchell, Gregory, BSc, BA, (OSB), Worth Abbey, Paddockhurst Rd, Turners Hill, Crawley, W. Sussex RH10 4SB
Tel: 01342-710310

Mitchell, Jonathan (Shrewsbury), 9 Summer ln, Runcorn WA7 2AE
Tel: 01928 564492 **Mbl:** 07590 196795
E-mail: frjonmitchell@cantab.net

Mitchell, Keith, Canon (Plymouth), St Peter's, Tavistock Rd, Crownhill, Plymouth PL5 3AX **Tel:** 01752-701660

Mitchell, Ronald (SMM), Montfort Ho, 28 Burbo Bank Rd, Blundellsands, Liverpool L23 6TH **Tel:** 0151-287 0410

Mitchell, William, Mgr Canon, MA, JCL, JV (Clifton), St Michael's, 31 Silver St, Tetbury, Gloucestershire GL8 8DH
Tel: 01666-502367.

Mitcheson, Paul, (Salford), St Wilfrid, 44 Derby Rd, Longridge, Preston PR3 3JT
Tel/Fax: 01772-782641

Mlilo, Reason, (Bulawayo), 1 Orchard Rd, Bromley BR1 2PR **Tel:** 020 8402 0459

Moakler, John, (OCSO), Holy Cross Abbey, Whitland, Camarthenshire SA34 0QX
Tel: 01994-240725 **Fax:** 01994-240725

Mocciaro, Nunzio, St Francis, 101 Hunters Rd, Handsworth B19 1EB
Tel: 0121-554 0905

Moffatt, Brendan, (East Anglia), The Catholic Presbytery, Gordon Rd, Lowestoft, Suffolk NR32 1NL
Tel/Fax: 01502 572453
E-mail: brendanmoffatt@yahoo.co.uk

Moffatt, John (SJ), Campion Hall, Oxford OX1 1QS **Tel:** 01865 276993
Fax: 01865286148
E-mail: moffsj@yahoo.com

Moger, Philip, Mgr (Leeds), Dean, Cathedral Ho, Great George St, Leeds LS2 8BE **Tel:** 0113 245 4545
Fax: 0113 245 3626.

Mol, Jan (MAfr), St Edwards, 46 Totteridge Common, London N20 8ND
Tel: (Staff) 020-8959 2553; (College) 020-8959 4477 **Fax:** 020-8201 1850

Molloy, Sean, (Leeds), St Mary & St Monica's Presbytery, Cottingley New Rd, Cottingley, Bingley BD16 1SA
Tel: 01274-567639

Molloy, Thomas, (CSsR), 49 Sutton Rd, Erdington, Birmingham B23 6QN
Tel: Home 0121-373 2073
Office 0121-373 0143

Molloy, William, (Salford), Holy Rosary, Fir Tree Avenue, Fitton Hill, Oldham OL8 2SR **Tel:** 0161 624 7925

Moloney, Kieran, (SSC), St Columba's, 28 Redington Rd, Hampstead, London NW3 7RB **Tel:** 020-7794 8131
Fax: 020-7794 7074

Moloney, Patrick, (Southwark), 222 Bellegrove Rd, Welling, Kent DA16 3RT
Tel: 020-8319 0993

Monaghan, Brendan, BA, (Lancaster, retired), 26 Glastonbury Ave, Marton, Blackpool FY1 6RD **Tel:** 01253-762227

Monaghan, Eugene, (IC), The Presbytery, Westernmoor, Neath.

Monaghan, Gerard J, (Hexham & Newcastle, retired), 9 Roseberry Rd, Hartlepool TS26 8JZ

Monaghan, Shaun, Mgr Canon, DCL (Lancaster, retired), Brooklands Ho Rest Home, 3 Woodville Terr, Lytham St Annes FY8 5QB

Monahan, Keiran BTh (OSB), Ampleforth Abbey, York YO62 4EN
Tel: 01439-766714 **Fax:** 01439-766724

Montgomery, John, (Clifton), 39 Church St, Tutbury, Burton upon Trent DE13 9JE

Montgomery, Peter, LCL, (Shrewsbury), Our Lady and St Augustine's, 26 St Mary St, Latchford, Warrington WA4 1BN **Tel:** 01925-634849
E-mail: olsa@amionline.co.uk

Mooney, Francis, PhL, STL, (Southwark),

34a London Rd, Southborough, Kent TN4 0QA **Tel:** 01892-529158

Mooney, George J, Mgr, (Liverpool, retired), 8 Alexander Dr, Lydiate, Liverpool L31 2NJ **Tel:** 0151-526 3595

Mooney, Paul, (MHM), 56 Cookham Rd, Maidenhead SL6 7HT **Tel:** 01628 588411 **Mbl:** 07707 692544 **E-mail:** pfmmhm@yahoo.com

Moor, Philip, (Shrewsbury), 12 Oakwood Dr, Claughton, Prenton CH43 7NX **Tel:** 0151-652 2398 **E-mail:** pp@holy-x.org.uk

Moorcraft, Gerald, Mgr, MA, (Northampton), St Teresa of the Child Jesus, New Rd, Princes Risborough, HP27 0JN **Tel:** 01844-345578 **Fax:** 01844-274503 **E-mail:** geraldmoorcrat85@ hotmail.com

Moore, Andrew MA, GRSM, (Portsmouth), Prentice Cottage, 40 Prentice St, Lavenham, Suffolk CO10 9RD

Moore, Anthony (Hexham & Newcastle), c/o Bishop's Ho, East Denton Hall, 800 West Rd, Newcastle upon Tyne NE5 2BJ **Tel:** 0191-228 0003/0004

Moore, Bede, (OSB), St Mary, 22 Church Rd, Harrington, Cumbria CA14 5QA **Tel/Fax:** 01946-830234

Moore, Charles Sebastian, MA, STD, (OSB), Downside Abbey, Stratton on the Fosse, Radstock, Bath, Somerset BA3 4RH **Tel:** 01761-235161

Moore, Eric Joseph, (Liverpool), 21 Sweau Whallian Park, St John, Isle of Man **Tel:** 01624-801070

Moore, Gareth, BA, BLitt, STL, (OP), Blackfriars, 64 St Giles, Oxford OX1 3LY **Tel:** 01865-278400

Moore, Gregory F, (Southwark), 97 Lorrimore Rd, London SE17 3LZ **Tel:** 020-7703 4712

Moore, James G, (Liverpool, retired), Flat 6, Alston Court, 483a Liverpool Rd, Southport PR8 3BP **Tel:** 01704-571305

Moore, Jonathan, Mgr, FFA FIAB (Nottingham), Royle Ho, Church St, Old Glossop, Derbys SK13 7RJ **Tel/Fax:** 01457-853113

Moore, John (Birmingham), St Joseph's Presbytery, Quinney's Lane, Bidford-on-Avon, Warks B50 4JL **Tel:** 01789-773291

Moore, Michael, (Nottingham), The Presbytery, Ashby Rd, Scunthorpe, South Humberside DN16 2RS **Tel:** 01724-844895

Moore, Robert, (OH), 78 Abbey Rd, Darlington DL3 8NN **Tel:** 01325 461753

Moore, Terry (OFM Cap), Franciscan Friary, Carlton Rd, Erith, Kent DA8 1DN **Tel:** 01322-402116 **Fax:** 01322-402061

Moraes, Arthur, (Westminster, retired), 25 Lower Teddington Rd, Hampton Wick, Kingston-upon-Thames KT1 4HB **Tel:** 020-8977 5130

Moran, Boniface, MA, (OSB), Douai Abbey, Upper Woolhampton, Reading, Berkshire RG7 5TQ **Tel:** 0118-971 5310 **Fax:** 0118-971 5303 **E-mail:** boniface@douaiabbey.org.uk

Moran, Francis, Canon (Southwark), 53 The Broadway, Sheerness, Kent ME12 1TS. **Tel:** 01795-662142.

Moran, Francis, MA (Southwark), 45 Brook Road, Thornton Heath, Surrey CR7 7RD **Tel:** 020-8684 3013

Moran, James (OCarm), 63 East End Rd, East Finchley, London N2 0SE **Tel:** 020-8346 1458

Moran, John M, Mgr Canon VG, (Birmingham), 14 Spring Rd, Edgbaston B15 2HG **Tel:** 0121-440 3487

Moran, John, Mgr, CBE, (Leeds, retired), Im Ends 43, 41844 Wegberg, Germany

Moran, Mark, (Liverpool), St Margaret's Parish Ho, Pilch Lane, Liverpool L14 0JG **Tel:** 0151-228 1332 **Fax:** 0151-259 6019

Moran, Mark, (Clifton), Holy Rood Presbytery, 2 Groundwell Rd, Swindon SN1 2LU **Tel:** 01793-522062

Moran, Peter, Mgr, (Hallam Retired), The Presbytery, Eccleston Road, Sandall, Doncaster DN3 1NX

Moran, William (OCD), 169 Sharoe Green Ln, Fulwood, Preston PR2 8HE **Tel:** 01772-717122 **Fax:** 01772-787674

Moreno, Antonio (SJ), Copplestone Ho, 221 Goldhurst Terr, London NW6 3EP **Tel:** 020-7604 5862 **Fax:** 020-7604 5860

Morgan, Bernard, Canon (Wrexham), Tyr Offeiriad, 6 Victoria Park, Bangor, Gwynedd LL57 2EW **Tel:** 01248-370421 **Fax:** 01248-372066

Morgan, Francis (Frank) (SPS), St Patrick's Missionary Society (Kiltegan Fathers). 20 Beauchamp Rd, East Molesey, Surrey KT8 0PA **Tel:** 020-8979 1890 **Fax:** 020-8941 8221 **E-mail:** spsuk@aol.com

Morgan, Paul Peter, BA (OSB), St Boniface, 95 Station Rd, Okehampton, Devon EX20 1ED **Tel:** 01837-52229

Morgan, Peter, MA, (Liverpool), Our Lady of Lourdes and St Bernard, 95a Kingsley Rd, Liverpool L8 2TY **Tel:** 0151-709 4434 **Fax:** 0151-708 5873

Morgan, Ricardo, Mgr, (Middlesbrough), St Mary's Cathedral, Dalby Way, Coulby Newham, Middlesbrough TS8 0TW **Tel:** 01642-597750

Morgan, Vaughan, Mgr, (Birmingham), St

Teresa, 5 Enstone Rd, Charlbury, Oxon OX7 3QR **Tel:** 01608-810576

Moriarty, Myles, BA, (SM), Marist Fathers, 36 Shear Bank Rd, Blackburn, Lancs BB1 8AZ **Tel:** 01254-53074 **Fax:** 01254-676537

Morland, David, MA, STL, (OSB), St Austin, 561 Aigburth Rd, Grassendale, Liverpool L19 0NU **Tel:** 0151-728 5802

Morland, Robert, (SMA), 33 Lyondown Rd, New Barnet EN5 1JG, **E-mail:** robmorland@btconnect.com

Moroney, Richard, (Northampton), Presbytery, Farnham Rd, Slough, Berks SL2 3AE **Tel/Fax:** 01753-643320 **E-mail:** rich.mor@btopenworld.com

Morrin, Adrian, (Wrexham), Our Lady of the Rosary, 2 Cwrt Brenig, Buckley CH7 2BF **Tel:** 01244-545546 **E-mail:** olrbuckley@aol.com

Morrin, Dermot, BA, BE, STB, (OP), St Dominic's Priory, Southampton Rd, London NW5 4LB **Tel:** 020-7482 9224

Morris, Allen, MA, BA, BD, (Westminster), 54 Lodge Rd, London NW8 8LA **Tel:** 0207 286 3214

Morris, John, Canon, (Southwark, retired), St George's Retreat, Burgess Hill Sussex RH15 2NP

Morris, Martin, (Hexham & Newcastle), St Aloysius, 5 Prince Consort Rd, Hebburn, Tyne and Wear NE31 1BE **Tel:** 0191-483 2165

Morris, Peter, BA M.Ed (Arundel & Brighton, retired), 12 St Catherine's Court, Garland Road, East Grinstead W. Sussex RH19 1NJ **Tel:** 01435-863547

Morris, Peter, (Liverpool, retired), 3 Osbourne Court, St Matthew's Grove, Grange Park, St Helens, WA10 3SP **Tel:** 01744-730647

Morris, Thomas, (SVD), St Joseph's, Hall St, Burslem, Stoke-on-Trent ST6 4BB **Tel:** 01782-837602

Morrish, Nicholas, Mgr (Opus Dei), 4 Orme Court, Bayswater London W2 4RL **Tel:** 020-7229 7574

Morrissey, Edward, (Salford, retired), Killarney Rd, Abbeyfeale, Co. Limerick, Ireland **Tel:** 00353 6831784

Morrissey, James, Canon, (Menevia, , retired), 16 Cwrt Llwyn Fedwen, Lon Arian, Morriston, Swansea SA6 6HW

Morrissey, Michael, (Portsmouth), 44 Alma Rd, Windsor, Berks SL4 3HJ **Tel:** 01753-865163 **Fax:** 01753-730018 **E-mail:** mnmorrissey@windsor3.fsnet.co.uk

Morrison, Hugh, (OMI), St Luke's, College Ave, Rhos-on-Sea, Clwyd LL28 4NR **Tel:** 01492-548035

Morrow, Robert, (Salford), St Joseph, Peter St, Bury BL9 6AB **Tel:** 0161-764 4240 **E-mail:** romorrow@btinernet.com

Mortimer, Kevin C, DipPT (Clifton), Sacred Heart Presbytery, Grange Court Rd, Westbury on Trym, Bristol BS9 4DR **Tel:** 0117-983 3926

Mortimer-Anderson, Robert (Brentwood), 59 Eastwood Rd North, Eastwood, Leigh-on-Sea, Essex SS9 4BX **Tel:** 01702-522879

Morton, Michael G, STL, MPhil, (Shrewsbury), St Winefride, Middlewich Rd, Sandbach CW11 1HU **Tel:** 01270-762198 **E-mail:** stw_sandbach@btinternet.com

Moscinski, Fidelis (CFR), c/o St Fidelis Friary, Killip Cl, London E16 1LX **Tel:** 020-7474 0766

Moss, Frederick, (MHM, retired), Herbert Ho, 41 Victoria Rd, Freshfield, Merseyside L37 1LW **Tel:** 01704-835846

Moss, Paul, (Birmingham), St Patrick's, Deedmore Rd, Bell Green, Coventry CV2 1EQ **Tel:** 024-7661 2193

Moth, Richard, Mgr, MA, JCL, VG, KCHS, (Southwark), Archbishop's Ho, 150 St George's Rd, Southwark, London SE1 6HX **Tel:** 020-7928 2495 **Fax:** 020-7928 7833 **E-mail:** rmoth@rcsouthwark.co.uk

Motherway, Edmund, (Birmingham, retired), Ashling, Kilclough, Co. Cork, Ireland **Tel:** 001 353 252 7482

Mountford, Robin, (Arundel & Brighton), Holy Cross Hospital, Shottermill Hall, Hind Head Rd, Haslemere, Surrey GU27 1NQ **Tel:** 01428-643311

Mowe, Aloysius, (SJ), Campion Hall, Oxford OX1 1QS **Tel:** 01865-286129

Moxon, Paul F, MA, Theol, (Leeds), St Wilfrid's Presbytery, Coltsgate Hill, Ripon, HG4 2AB **Tel:** 01765-603614

Moynihan, Cornelius, (Nottingham), Christ the King Presbytery, 104 Nottingham Rd, Alfreton, Derbys DE55 7GL **Tel:** 01773-833174 **Fax:** 01773-520844

Mpanda, Appolinan (CJ). 2 Knatchbull Rd, Camberwell, London SE5 9QS **Tel:** 020-7274 1908

Muir, Faustyn Steven (OSP), SS Mary & John, Snow Hill, Wolverhampton WV2 4AD **Tel:** 01902-421676

Muir, Gerald, (AC), (Lancaster), St John the Evangelist, Breck Rd, Poulton-le-Fylde FY6 7HT **Tel:** 01253-883110

Muir, Neil (Cairns), 218 Roehampton Lane, London SW15 4LE

Muir, William, (CJ), 46 Draycott Rd, Ensbury Park, Bournemouth BH10 5AR **Tel:** 01202-529384

Mulcahey, Arthur, (Liverpool, retired), Homechase Ho, Chase Cl, York Rd, Birkdale, Southport PR8 2DG.

Mulcahy, Eamon, (CSsp), 263 Somerset Rd, New Barnet EN5 1RF **E-mail:** mulcahy@mdx.ac.uk

Mulhall, Brendan, MHM, (Westminster), Vicar General, 3 Colby gardens, Maidenhead Berks SL6 7GZ **Tel:** 01628 588403 **Fax:** 01628 588439 **Mbl:** 07784 278930 **E-mail:** vicgen@millhillmissionaries.com

Mulhearn, Kevin, (Liverpool), St Joseph, High Moor, Wrightington, Wigan WN6 9PA **Tel:** 01257-422879

Mulheran, Thomas, VG (Salford), (Financial Secretary/Secretary to the Trustees), 39 Wingate Dr, Didsbury, Manchester M20 8RT **Tel:** 0161-736 1421 **E-mail:** finsec@salforddiocese.org

Mulholland, Peter, (Middlesbrough), Our Lady Star of the Sea, 32 Staithes Lane, Staithes, Saltburn TS13 5AD **Tel:** 01947-840218

Mulholland, Seamus, BA(Hons), (OFM), Franciscan International Study Centre, Canterbury, Kent CT2 7NA **Tel:** 01227 464939 **Fax:** 01227 459465 **Mbl:** 07984 731669 **E-mail:** semulholland@yahoo.com

Mullaley, Niall, (Shrewsbury), Our Lady of the Sea, 2a Enfield Rd, Ellesmere Port, CH65 8BY **Tel:** 0151-355 1255 **E-mail:** priest@stsaviours.wanadoo.co.uk

Mullarkey, Kieran (Salford), St Peter, Taylor Street, Middleton, Manchester M24 1BL **Tel:** 0161-643 2168 **E-mail:** cathedral@salforddiocese.org

Mullan, James Brian, Canon, DCL (Liverpool, retired), 14 Rockmount Cl, Liverpool L25 6JN **Tel:** 0151-428 8437

Mullen, Joseph, (WF), 42 Stormont Rd, Highgate, London N6 4NP

Mullen, Joseph (IC), St Mary's, Ashby Rd, loughborough LE11 3AB **Tel:** 01509 262123 **E-mail:** joemullen@mac.com

Mullen, Kevin, Canon, (Liverpool, retired), The Lodge, Weldbank Lane, Chorley PR7 3NW **Tel:** 01257-469352

Mullen, Noel, Mgr, QHC, now resident at Plater College, Pullens Lane, Oxford OX3 0DT **Tel:** 01865 740500

Mullen, Pearse (SSCC), 28 Barkers Lane, Bedford MK41 9SJ **Tel:** 01234-535116

Mullen, Peter, STB (IC), Sacred Heart Church, 17 Lime Tree Ave, Bilton, Rugby CV22 7QT **Tel:** 01788-814197 **Mbl:** 0797 337 0620 **E-mail:** ted@mulls.freeserve.co.uk

Mullen, Thomas, (SSCC), 28 Barkers Lane, Bedford MK41 9SJ **Tel:** 01234-353116

Mulligan, Gerard, STL, LSS, (CSsR), The John Paul Centre, 55 Grange Rd, Middlesbrough, Cleveland TS1 5AU **Tel:** 01642-251800 **Fax:** 01642-221003

Mulligan, James, (Westminster), 2 Lukin St, Commercial Rd, London E1 0AA **Tel:** 020-7790 5911

Mulligan, John, MA (Southwark), Holy Cross, 208 Sangley Rd, Catford, London SE6 2JS **Tel:** 020-8698 3672

Mullin, Noel Mgr, MA (Lancaster), Plater College, Pullens Lane, Oxford OX3 0DT **Tel:** 01865-740500

Mullin, Thomas F, (Salford), Bree, Malin Head, Co Donegal, Ireland

Mullins, Edmund J, Canon, (Menevia, retired), 2 Heol Emrys, Fishguard SA65 9EE **Mbl:** 07973-150258

Mullins, Kevin, (SSC), 23 Redington Rd, Hampstead, London NW3 7RB

Mullins, Tadgh, (Salford), Our Lady, Bowness Rd, Langley, Middleton M24 4HN **Tel:** 0161-643 4210 **E-mail:** tmullins@ ourlady.fsbusiness.co.uk

Mulumba, Kizito (Kampala), 103 Woolwich New Rd, Woolwich SE18 6EF **Tel:** 020 8854 0359

Mulvany, Patrick, Canon (Lancaster), St Patrick's, 22 St John's Rd, Morecambe LA3 1EX **Tel:** 01524-410322

Mulvey, Francis, (Cardiff), 151 Wentloog Rd, Rumney, Cardiff CF3 8HE **Tel:** 029-2079 7872

Mulvey, Thomas, (Arundel & Brighton, retired), St Sharbel, 6 New Glenview, Castlepollard, Co. Westmeath, Eire **Tel:** 00 353 44 61791 **E-mail:** mulveytom@mistral.co.uk

Mulvihill, Gerard MPS, (Southwark), 2 Mitcham Lane, London SW16 6NN **Tel:** 020-8769 6268

Mulvihill, James, Canon, (Cardiff, retired), Nazareth Ho, Colum Rd, Cardiff CF10 1DQ

Mulvihill, Michael, (CSSp), Tyburn Convent, 8, Hyde Park Place, London, W2 2LJ **Tel:** 020-7706 2842

Mundackal, Sebastian BPh, BTh, MA, MTh (OSB) (Indian priest), The Presbtyery, Upper King's Head Rd, Gendros, Swansea SA5 8BR **Tel:** 01792-586454

Mundy, Charles, (Hexham and Newcastle, retired), 8 West Farm Rd, Newcastle upon Tyne NE6 4JA

Mungovin, Patrick, (Leeds), Our Lady of Victories, West Lane, Keighley BD22 6ES **Tel:** 01535-603819

Munitiz, Joseph, (SJ), Manresa Ho, 10 Albert Rd, Harborne, Birmingham B17 0AN **Tel:** 0121-427 2628 **Fax:** 0121-428 1833

E-mail: jmunitz@arrupe.demon.co.uk

Munnelly, Michael, BD, MA, Canon (Westminster), 22 Bradley Rd, London N22 7NZ **Tel:** 020-8888 2390

Munnery, Geoffrey, BTh, (Southwark), 108 Orme Rd, Kingston-upon-Thames, Surrey KT1 3SB **Tel:** 020 8942 2178 **Fax:** 020 8287 4626

Munroe, Patrick,(Shrewsbury), St Winifred's, Witton St, Northwich CW9 5NP **Tel:** 01606-42460

Murnaghan, Hugh, (CM), Sacred Heart Residence, Sybil Hill, Raheny, Dublin 5 **Tel:** 01-831 8113

Murphy, Billy, (Kildare & Leighlin), 175 High St, Lewisham, London SE13 6AA **Tel:** 081 852 2490

Murphy, Brian, (Hexham & Newcastle), All Saints, Dean Rd, Ferryhill, Co. Durham DL17 9ET **Tel:** 01740-651343

Murphy, Brian, (Salford), St Mary, Park St, Swinton, Manchester M27 4UR **Tel:** 0161-281 1818

Murphy, Brian B, BA JCL, MCL (Liverpool), Augustinian Convent, Park Ho, Waterloo, Liverpool L22 3XS **Tel:** 0151-928 4343

Murphy, Colin, (Southwark), c/o Bishop's Ho, 150 St George's Rd, London SE1 6HX

Murphy, Columcille, (OFM Conv), Greyfriars, 1 Elmsley Rd, Liverpool L18 8AY **Tel:** 0151-724 2109 **Fax:** 0151-724 2553

Murphy, Conor, (OMI), St Anne's Presbytery, 96 Bradford St, Birmingham B12 0PB **Tel:** 0121 772 2780 **Fax:** 0121 773 6023

Murphy, Eddie, BSc, (IC), The Presbytery, Westernmoor, Neath SA11 1TP **Tel:** 01639 643323 **E-mail:** eddie@rosmini.org

Murphy, Edmond P, Canon (Clifton, retired), The Penthouse, 2 North End, Batheaston, Bath BA1 7EN **Tel:** 01225-858271

Murphy, Garry, Provincial (CRL), Christ Church Priory, 229 Eltham High St, Eltham, SE9 1TX

Murphy, Gerald, (Salford), Our Lady's, 275 Plodder Lane, Farnworth, Bolton, BL4 0BR **Tel:** 01204-572380 **E-mail:** olofl.stgreg@btinternet.com

Murphy, Gerald, (Nottingham), St Alban's Presbytery, Roe Farm lane, Chaddesden, Derbys DE21 6ET **Tel:** 01332-672914

Murphy, Gerard, BA, (Brentwood), Nazareth Ho, 111 London Rd, Southend-on-Sea, Essex SS1 1PP **Tel:** 01702-340855

Murphy, Henry, (Portsmouth), 2 Valley Cl, St Catherine's Hill, Christchurch, Dorset BH23 2RX **Tel:** 01202-484749

Murphy, James, (Lancaster), St Patrick's, 51 St John's Rd, Morecambe LA3 1EX **Tel:** 01524-410322

Murphy, Jeremiah, (Leeds), St Patrick, Sedgefield Terr, Bradford BD1 2RU **Tel:** 01274-724941

Murphy, John, (OMI), The Presbytery, Sicklinghall, Wetherby, Yorks LS22 4BE **Tel:** 01937-580547

Murphy, John V (Shrewsbury, retired), 123 Woodhouse Lane, Sale M33 4LW **Tel:** 0161-962 9281

Murphy, John, Mgr, (Leeds, retired), 1 Hinsley Court, Headingley Lane, Leeds LS6 2HB **E-mail:** johnmurphy@hinsleycourt.freeserve.co.uk

Murphy, John A, (OSA), 55 Fulham, Palace Rd, Hammersmith, W6 8AU **Tel:** 020-8748 3788

Murphy, John B, (Leeds, retired), "Rosnaree", Royal Chase, Tadcaster Rd, York YO24 1LN

Murphy, John J, (Westminster, retired), c/o Nazareth Ho, Hammersmith Rd, London W6 8DB **Tel:** 020-8748 3545

Murphy, John K, (Liverpool, retired), 18 St Geroge's Court, Station Rd, Maghull, Liverpool L31 3JD **Tel:** 0151-520 0447

Murphy, John M, (Salford, retired), McAuley Mount, Padiham Rd, Burnley BB12 6TG **Tel:** 01282-38071

Murphy, John M, (Westminster), c/o Archbishop's Ho SW1P 1QJ

Murphy, Martin, (Southwark, retired), The Little Sisters, Sacred Heart Residence, Sybil Hill Rd, Raheny, Dublin 5 **Tel:** 00 353 1 8338814

Murphy, Maurice, (Pastor Emeritus) (Salford, retired), St Joseph's Home, Little Sisters of hte Poor, Plymouth Grove West, Manchester M13 0AR **Tel:** 0161-273 4147

Murphy, Michael, (Lancaster), St Augustine of Canterbury, St Austin's Place, Preston PR1 3YJ **Tel:** 01772-555547

Murphy, Michael G, (Plymouth, retired), St Michael's, 81 Uam-Var Ave, Bishopstown, Cork, Ireland **Tel:** 021-4341560

Murphy, Michael, DD, PHL, (Southwark, retired), 49 Carpenter Grove, Long Barn Cheshire WA2 0QR **Tel:** 07730 567138 **Email:** m_murphy@tiscali.co.uk

Murphy, Nicholas, (CJ), St George's College, Weybridge Rd, Addlestone, Weybridge KT15 2QS **Tel:** 01932-839463

Murphy, Patrick R, (Hallam, retired), 4 Oakwood Dr, Branton, Doncaster DN3 3NU **Tel:** 01302-530668 **Mbl:** 077698 37519

Murphy, Peter, BTh (Southwark), School Ho, Mottisfont Rd, London SE2 9LY **Tel:** 020-8311 2727 **Fax:** 020-8311 8772

Murphy, Robert Timothy, (Birmingham), 208 High St, Bloxwich WS3 3LA **Tel:** 01922 476765

Murphy, Robert David, MA, LTh, STL (Birmingham), Nunciature Apostolica Carrera 15, N36-33 Apartado Aerreo 3740 Bogota DC Colombia **Tel:** +57-1 3200-289 **Email:** rdm80@hotmail.com

Murphy, Seamus, (Westminster), 84 Pixmore Way, Letchworth, Herts SG6 3TP **Tel:** 01362-683504

Murphy, Sean (CM), Marrillac Hospital, Eagle Way, Warley, Brentwood, Essex CM13 3BL **Tel:** 01277-220276

Murphy, William A, (Salford), St Caimin, Mountshannon, Col, Clare, Eire

Murphy, William, (Liverpool), Blessed Sacrement Presbytery, 9 Park Vale Road, Aintree, Liverpool L9 2DG **Tel:** 0151-474 2682 **Fax:** 0151-474 2569 **E-mail:** blessed@locall.net

Murphy-O'Connor, Brian G, Canon (Portsmouth, retired), 171a St Michael's Rd, Basingstoke, Hants RG22 6TY **Tel:** 01256-224195

Murray, Aidan, BSc, PhD, BA (OSB), Subprior and Bursar, Worth Abbey, Crawley, W Sussex RH10 4SB **Tel:** 01342-710303

Murray, Aidan, (SDB), Our Lady of Lourdes, Drumlanrig, Ross Rd, Newent GL18 1BG **Tel:** 01531-821647 **E-mail:** aidansdb@newentbb,co,uk

Murray, Eamon (Northampton), St Margaret's Presbytery, 22a Bolingbroke Rd, Farley Hill, Luton LU1 5JD **Tel:** 01582-720966 **E-mail:** stmargaret@freeuk.com

Murray, Francis, (SCJ), Stella Maris, New Strand, Bootle, Merseyside, L20 4TQ **Tel:** 0151-922 6161

Murray, Francis, (OMI), St Anne's Presbytery, 96 Bradford St, Birmingham B12 0PB **Tel:** 0121-772 2780 **Fax:** 0121-773 6023 **E-mail:** sabham@btopenworld.com

Murray, Gerard Paul, STL, (Birmingham), 566 Stratford Rd, Shirley, Solihull B90 4AY **Tel:** 0121-744 1967

Murray, James, (SMM), The Presbytery, Ballance Rd, Homerton, London E9 5SR **Tel:** 020-8985 1495

Murray, John (SCA), 514 Longbridge Rd, Barking, Essex IG11 9BY **Tel:** 020-8590 2191

Murray, John A, (SDS), Salvatorian Community, High Rd, Harrow Weald, Middx HA3 5DY **Tel:** 020-8427 2808

Murray, John Sean, CertEd, Dip Rem Teaching, (SDB), St James' Presbytery, Chesnut Grove, Bootle, Merseyside L20 4LX **Tel:** 0151-944 1039 **Fax:** 0151-922 3263 **E-mail:** johnseanmurray@tiscali.co.uk

Murray, Michael, (Shrewsbury), St Anthony, Dunkery Rd, Woodhouse Park, Manchester M22 0WR **Tel:** 0161-437 2861

Murray, Michael, (Middlesbrough, retired), 38 Edgehill Rd, Carlisle, Cumbria CA1 3PE **Tel:** 01228-523598

Murray, Peter, (SM), Marist Fathers, Half Moon Ho, 12 Hindringham Rd, Great Walsingham, Norfolk NR22 6DR **Tel:** 01328-820588

Murray, Robert, (SJ), Copleston Ho, 221 Goldhurst Terr, London NW6 3EP **Tel:** 020-7604 5850 **Fax:** 020-7604 5860 **E-mail:** rprmurray@hotmail.com

Murray, Sandy, (MSC), 14, Beaconsfield Rd, St Albans Herts AL1 3RB **Tel:** 01727-853585 **Fax:** 01727 855410

Murray-Bligh, Geoffrey Gervase, BA, (OSB), Downside Abbey, Stratton on the Fosse, Radstock, Bath, Somerset, BA3 4RH **Tel:** 01761-235144

Murtagh, Cyril J, Mgr Provost, MA, STL (Portsmouth), 108 Headley Rd, Liphook, Hants GU30 7PT **Tel:** 01428-722151 **E-mail:** cmurtagh@portsmouth-dio.org.uk

Murtagh, Patrick, (Southwark), 20 Sanderstead Heights, 2 Addington Rd, Sandstead CR2 8RE

Murtha, Kieran (SSCC), 5 Berrymead Gardens, Acton, London W3 8AA **Tel:** 020-8992 2014 **Fax:** 020-8993 9940 **Mbl:** 078-3356 1919 **E-mail:** kieran@ealing-sscc.demon.co.uk

Musaala, Anthony, STB, St Charles Lwanga, PO Box 9415, Kampala, Uganda

Muscat, John, (OFM), 1 Balniel Gate, Lindsay Square, London SW1V 2HN **Tel:** 020-7834 9512

Myers, David J, (IC), St Peter's Presbytery, St Peters St, Cardiff CF24 3BA **Tel:** 029-2048 3394 **Fax:** 029-2045 1535 **E-mail:** DJM@rosmini.org

Myers, Stephen, BSc(Hons), CertEd, CertTheo, (Brentwood), The Presbytery, Oxlow Lane, Dagenham, Essex RM9 5XJ **Tel:** 020-8592 1634

Myers, T Anthony, LCL, (Shrewsbury), St Hugh of Lincoln, 314 Manchester Rd, West Timperley, Altrincham WA14 5NB **Tel:** 0161-973 1694 **E-mail:** shol.westtimp@talktalk.net

Nadson, Alexander, Archpriest (Byelorussian), Marian Ho, Holden Ave, Finchley North, N12 8HY **Tel:** 020-8445 5358

Nally, Frank, (SSC), 28 Redington Rd, Hampstead, London N15 6ND

Nam, Lawrence, (SJ), Sacred Heart

Presbytery, Edge Hill, Wimbledon SW19 4LU **Tel:** 020-8946 0305

Nannery, Bartholomew, Canon, BA, (Plymouth), The Cathedral Ho, 45 Cecil St, Plymouth PL1 5HW **Tel:** 01752-662537

Napier, Charles, (SPS), St Augustine's, 70 Eton Rd, Datchet, Slough, Berks SL3 9AY **Tel:** 01753-542862

Napier, Michael Scott, (Cong Orat), The Oratory Brompton Rd, SW7 2RP **Tel:** 020-7589 4811

Narikuzhi, Joseph, (Raipur), The Presbytery, 2 Catholic Lane, Sedgley DY3 3UE **Tel:** 01902-882215 **E-mail:** jnarikuzhi@yahoo.co.uk

Nash, Brian, STL, PhL, (Westminster, retired), 377 Mile End Rd, London E3 4QS **Tel:** 020-8980 1845

Nathaniel, Philip, (Salford), Revendisimo Senor Rector, Seminario Mayor Diocesano Malecon, Maldonado 219, Apartado 108, Iquitos, Peru, S. America **E-mail:** felipeiquitos@terra.com.pe

Naughton, Enda B, PhD, FRSA (Arundel & Brighton), Runnamoat, Roscommon, Éire

Naughton, John, Canon (Southwark), 9 Crescent Gardens, London SW19 8AJ **Tel:** 020-8946 2091

Naughton, Mark, (Leeds), St Joseph's Presbytery, 281 Skipton Rd, Harrogate HG1 3HD **Tel:** 01423-504124 **E-mail:** ParishPriest@st-josephs-church.org.uk

Naughton, Stephen (OSM) 264 Fulham Rd, London NW3 7RB

Naylan, Sean (Hexham & Newcastle, retired), St Joseph, Paxton Terr, Millfield, Sunderland SR4 6HP **Tel:** 0191-567 4574

Naylor, Vincent, (Salford, retired), 96 Hopefold Rd, Worsley, Manchester M28 3PW

Naylor, William, STB (Nottingham), St Joseph's Rectory, Burton Rd, Derby DE1 1TJ **Tel:** 01332-343777

Nealon, Michael, (Leeds), Russell Rd, Queensbury, Bradford BD13 2AN **Tel:** 01274-880119

Nealon, Peter, BSc, (Leeds), Our Lady & St Malachy's Presbytery, Nursery Lane, Ovenden, Halifax HX3 5NS **Tel:** 01422-352382

Nearey, Arthur C, (Salford), St Mary, 40 Featherstall Rd, Littleborough OL15 8DW **Tel:** 01706-3 78261

Neath, Gerard, MA, (OP), St Dominic's Convent, Stone, Staffs ST15 8EN **Tel:** 01785-811035

Nee, Eugene O, Canon, (Military Chaplain, retired), Lt Col USAF c/o San Antone Ho, 14 Shakespeare St, Coventry CV2 4JZ **Tel:** 02476-448189

Needham, Bernard, Canon, VF STL, PhL, (Nottingham), 1 St Joseph's St, Matlock, Derbys DE4 3NG **Tel:** 01629-582804

Neendoor, Saji, (MSFS), c/o St Joseph's Presbytery, Devizes, Wilts SN10 1DD **Tel:** 01629-582804

Negary, Girma (Ethiopian Catholic Church) St Mary's Rectory, Draycott Terr, London SW3 2QR **Tel:** 020-7589 5487

Neguse, Tesfamichael (MCCJ) 8a Battersea Park Road, London SW8 4BH **Tel:** 020-7622 4282

Nellikulam, Paul (IC), Mother of God, Greencoat Rd, Leicester LE3 6NZ **Tel:** 0116 287 5232 **E-mail:** nellikulamp@hotmail.com

Nelson, John, Mgr VG, STL, JCL (Portsmouth), 64 Liebenrood Rd, Reading, Berks RG30 2EB **Tel:** 0118-957 2149 **Fax:** 0118-957 5241 **Mbl:** 07776-250914 **E-mail:** nelsonjohn@aol.com

Nelson, Phillip, MA, B.Th, (Southwark), 71 Comerford Rd, Brockley SE4 2BA

Nemer, Larry BA, LMiss, MA, PhD. 8 Teignmough Rd, London NW2 4HN

Nesbitt, Richard, (Westminster), 52 Uxbridge Rd, London W7 3SU

Nesbitt, Roger, MSc, DIC, ACGI (Southwark), Our Lady Help of Christians and St Aloysius, 41 Guildhall St, Folkestone, Kent CT20 1EF **Tel:** 01303-252823

Netto, Ivor, BSc, BD, JCL (SDB), Thornleigh Ho, Sharples Park, Bolton BL1 6PQ **Tel:** 01204-591144 **Fax:** 01204-308510 **E-mail:** jivor1sdb@yahoo.co.uk

Neville, John, (Salford, retired), 7 Grange Dr, Hoghton Preston PR5 0LP **Tel:** 01254-853377

Nevin, Henry (SDS), Saint Saviour's Presbytery, 96 The Crescent, Abbots Langley, Hertfordshire WD5 0DS **Tel:** 01923-265646 **Fax:** 01923-281146 **E-mail:** henrynevinsds@hotmail.com

Newbold, Philip, (Birmingham), The Presbytery, Uxbridge St, Hednesford, Staffs WS12 5DB **Tel:** 01543 422576

Newbound, Eric, (Hallam, retired), 12 St Ronan's Rd, Sheffield S7 1DZ.

Newby, Peter, MA PhL, (Westminster), 4/5 Eldon St London EC2M 7LS **Tel:** 020-7247 8390

Newell, David, (Birmingham), St Joseph's, High St, Goldenhill, Stoke-on-Trent ST6 5RD **Tel:** 01782-782121

Newell, Martin, (CP), 16 De Beauvoir Rd, De Beauvoir Town, London N1 5SU **Tel:** 020-7249 0041 **Mbl:** 077 26 997 638 **E-mail:** martin_newell1967@yahoo.co.uk

Newman, Christopher (CMF), Claret Centre Director; The Towers, High St,

Buckden, St Neots PE19 5TA
Tel: 01480 810344
E-mail: chrisnewman@claret.org.uk

Newman, John, (Leeds), St Joseph's Presbytery, 40 Pakington St, Bradford BD5 7LD **Tel/Fax:** 01274-720299

Newman, Paul, (Nottingham), The Presbytery, Brooklyn Road, Bulwell, Nottingham, NG6 9ES
Tel: 0115-927 8403 **Faz:** 0115-927 0883

Newns, Brian, (Liverpool), St Oswald & St Edmund Arrowsmith, Liverpool Rd, Ashton-in-Makerfield, Wigan, Lancs WN4 9NP **Tel/Fax:** 01942-727249

Newrer, Larry (SVD), 8 Teignmouth Rd, London NW2 4HN **Tel:** 020-8452 8430

Newsam, Peter (Arundel & Brighton), The Presbytery, Angel St, Petworth, W. Sussex GU28 0BG **Tel:** 01798-342169

Newton, William, (Brentwood), 661 High Rd, South Benfleet, Essex SS7 5SF
Tel: 01268-792082 **Fax:** 01268-799649

Neylon, Michael, (Birmingham), 82 Wolverhampton Rd, Stafford ST17 4AW
Tel: 01785-223553

Neylon, Thomas, (Liverpool), St Julie's Presbytery, Howards Lane, Eccleston, St Helens WA10 5HJ **Tel:** 01744-28196

Nguyen Duc Tang, Simon (Westminster). 54 Lodge Rd, London NW8 8LA
Tel: 020-7286 3214

Nguyen Minh Hoan (John Minh) STB (East Anglia). Catholic Presbytery, Geneva St, Peterborough PE1 2RS
Tel: 01733-562528 **Fax:** 01733-346933
E-mail: johnminh@mail.com

Nguyen Tien Dac, (Peter), (Birmingham), Vietnamese Pastoral Centre, 12 Wye Cliff Rd, Handsworth, Birmingham B20 3TB
Tel: 0121-554 8082 **Fax:** 0121-523 6258

Nguyen The-Quang (Joseph), STB, (Birmingham), 106 Hartshill Rd, Stoke-on-Trent ST4 7LZ **Tel:** 01782-844308
E-mail: ppourlady.stoke@tiscali.co.uk

Nguyen Van Tien (Joseph), (Birmingham), Our Lady of Mt Carmel, Beoley Rd West, Redditch **Tel:** 01527 63096

Ngwa, Lucas (Buéa, Cameroon), Sacred Heart, The Cross, Moreton, Wirral CH46 9QB **Tel:** 0151 677 5220
E-mail: ngwalucas@yahoo.com

Njoku, Bede (OSA), St Monica's Priory, 19 Hoxton Square, Hoxton, London N1 6NT
Tel: 020-7739 5006 **Fax:** 0207-613 0394

Njoku, Uche (CSSp), 18 Limesdale Gdns, Edgeware, Middx **Tel:** 0208 200 5091
Fax: 0208 200 3486

Nichols, Aidan, STL, MA, PhD, DipTheol, (OP), Blackfriars, Buckingham Rd, Cambridge CB3 0DD **Tel:** 01223-741251

Nicholls, Guy Paul, MA, STL, (CongOrat), The Oratory, 141 Hagley Rd, Edgbaston, Birmingham B16 8UE
Tel: 0121-454 0496

Nicholson, Ambrose J, (Shrewsbury), St Milburga, Watling St North, Church Stretton SY6 7AR **Tel/Fax:** 01694 722897

Nicholson, Brian, (Middlesbrough, retired), 15a Church Street, Whitby, Nth Yorks YO22 4AE

Nicholson, Herbert, (Hexham & Newcastle retired), 11 Sedgemoor Gardens, Billingham, Cleveland TS23 3QP

Nicholson, Paul, (SJ) Superior & Novice Director, Manresa Ho, 10 Albert Rd, Birmingham B17 0AN
Tel: 0121-427 2628
E-mail: pauln@jesuits.net

Nieweglowski, Zygmunt (Warsaw, Poland), 55 Foxbourne Rd, London SW17 8EN **Tel:** 020-8767 5695 or 020-8672 5070

Nightingale, John Henry Stuart, BA(Lond) Barrister (Birmingham), 20 Beaumont Buildings, Oxford OX1 2LL
Tel: 01865-553536

Nimmo, Eric, (Southwark), 141 Kidbrooke Park Rd, London SE3 0DZ
Tel: 020-8856 4536

Nix, William, Mgr, (Brentwood), Clergy Ho, 28 Ingrave Rd, Brentwood, Essex CM15 8AT **Tel:** 01277-265235

Nixon, David, BD, (MSC), St Albert's Presbytery, 31 Hollow Croft, Stockbridge Village, Liverpool
Tel: 0151 228 7126 **Fax:** 0151 259 6743
E-mail: dnixon@mscvocations.com

Nixon, Geoffrey, (Arundel & Brighton, retired), St Theresa, 8 New St, Ottery St Mary, Devon EX11 1EA
Tel: 01404 812423

Nkumu, Emile, (Kinshasa), 253 Lavender Place, Ilford, Essex IG1 2BE
Tel: 020-8478 0027

Noakes, Kenneth, Canon (Plymouth), The Presbytery, 4 Lewens Lane, Wimborne, Dorset BH21 1LE **Tel:** 01202-883312

Noctor, James, (Westminster), 49 Mattison Rd, Harringay, London N4 1BG
Tel: 020-8348 1378

Noel, Dominic (OP), St Dominic's Priory, Southampton Rd, London NW5 4LB
Tel: 020-7482 9210

Nolan, Francis, (MAfr), 129 Lichfield Rd, Sutton Coldfield, W. Mids B74 2SA

Nolan, James, (Southwark, retired), 7 Rosewood Lodge, 79 Wickham Rd, Shirley, Surrey CR0 8TB
Tel: 020-8654 1768

Nolan, John, MA, (Birmingham), c/o Archbishops Ho, St Chad's Queensway B4 6EX

Nolan, Patrick, (Westminster, retired), Flat 3, 165 Arlington Rd, London NW1 7EX

Tel: 020-7428 6807

Nolan, Timothy, (Southwark, retired), 26 Sherwood Court, High St, West Wickham BR4 0NB **Tel:** 020-8777 7208

Nolan, Tony (MSC), Gem Cottage, Tyla Lane, Old St Mellows, Cardiff CF3 6XG **Tel:** 01446 781361 **E-mail:** tony_nolan@btinternet.com

Nonis, Sunith (Southwark), 2 Genoa Rd, Anerley SE20 8ES **Tel:** 020 8778 8597

Noonan, Benjamin, (Northampton), 25 High St, Shefford, Beds SG17 5DD **Tel:** 01462-813436 **E-mail:** fatherbennie@members-v21.co.uk

Norbury, Francis, (Clifton), 8 Townsend Rd, Minehead, Som, TA24 5RG **Tel:** 01643-702201

Norman, Denis, (Hallam), Saint Joseph & St Teresa, The Presbytery, Welfare Rd, Woodlands, Doncaster DN6 7QG **Tel:** 01302-330205

Norris, Bernard, (Menevia, retired), 25 Pentre-Afan, Baglan Moors, Port Talbot SA12 7RL

Norris, David J, Mgr, Prot Ap, VG, MA, (Westminster, retired), Cathedral Clergy Ho, 42 Francis St, London SW1P 1QW **Tel:** 020-7798 9055

Norris, James, (OSB), St Joseph's, 21 Old Rd, Bromyard, Herefordshire HR7 4BQ **Tel:** 01885 482446

Norris, Peter, DipHum (Southwark), The Officiating Chaplain, British Forces, Port Stanley, Falkland Islands **Tel:** 00500 21204 **Fax:** 0050022242

Northey, Richard, (Clifton), 22 West End, Melksham SN12 6HJ **Tel:** 01225-702128

Norton, Anthony, (Birmingham), Sacred Heart, Harefield Rd, Coventry CV2 4BT **Tel:** 024-7645 6214 **Fax:** 024-7665 1308

Nott, Martin, (Brentwood), 13a Mill Ln, Dunmow, Essex CM6 1BG **Tel:** 01371-872550

Notarianni, Gianni, (OSA), St Augustine's Priory, 55 Fulham Palace Rd, Hammersmith, London W6 8AU **Tel:** 0208 748 3788

Nowotnik, Jan (STB) (Birmingham), St Augustine, Sandon Rd, Meir, Stoke-on-Trent ST3 7DF **Tel:** 01782-313743 **Fax:** 01782-315034

Ntuwa, J K, St John's, Breck Rd, Poulton-Le-Fylde, Lancaster FY6 7HT **Tel:** 01253-883110

Nunan, Dermot, (Middlesbrough), Sacred Heart Presbytery, 7 Lobster Rd, Redcar, Cleveland TS10 1SH **Tel:** 01642-484047

Nunan, John, (Leeds), St Joseph's Presbytery, 20 West Gate, Wetherby, W. Yorks LS22 6LL **Tel/Fax:** 01937 582283

Nunes, Matthew (Liverpool), St Bede's Presbytery, Appleton Village, Widnes WA8 6EL **Tel:** 0151-424 2738 **Fax:** 0151-423 2299

Nunn, Alban, MMus (OSB), Ealing Abbey, Charlbury Grove, London W5 2DY **Tel** 020-862 2100 **E-mail:** alban@philip-nunn.freeserve.co.uk

Nurse, Timothy T, (Clifton), Our Lady of the Rosary, 12 Kingsweston Lane, Lawrence Weston, Bristol BS11 0QU **Tel:** 0117-982 3380

Nuttall, John, MA (Arundel & Brighton), The Priest's Ho, 63-67 Yorktown Rd, Sandhurst, Berks GU47 9BS **Tel/Fax:** 01252-876820 **E-mail:** virtualwire@lineone.net

Nyatorley, Protus, (CSSp), St Chads, 5 Whitworth Rd, South Norwood SE25 6XN **Tel:** 0208 653 2806 **Fax:** 0208 653 4188

Nye, Anthony, (SJ), John Sinnott Ho, 9 Edge Hill, Wimbledon, London SW19 4LR **Tel:** 020 8947 4251 **E-mail:** tonynyesj@jesuits.net

O'Boy, Michael BA, PhD, STB (Westminster), Flat 5, 8 Morpeth Terr, London SW1P 1EQ **Tel:** 020-7798 9022

O'Boyle, Patrick James, (OMI), St Mary's, Abbey Rd, Rhos-on-Sea, Colwyn Bay LL28 4NR **Tel:** 01492-544777

O'Boyle, Seamus, Mgr, STL, VG (Westminster), 24 Golden Square, London W1F 9JR **Tel:** 020-7931 6076

O'Brien, Anthony, (Liverpool), Cathedral Dean, Cathedral House, Mount Pleasant, Liverpool L3 5TQ **Tel:** 0151-709 9222 **Fax:** 0151 708 7274 **E-mail:** a.obrien@metcathedral.org.uk

O'Brien, Bernard, (Hallam), St Paul's Presbytery, Goodison Boulevard, Cantley, Doncaster DN4 6BT **Tel:** 01302-353800

O'Brien, Christopher, (Southwark, retired), 36 Altenberg Gardens, Clapham Common, London SW11 1JJ **Tel:** 020 7228 2121

O'Brien, Christopher (OSM), 264 Fulham Rd, London SW10 9EL

O'Brien, Con (New Zealand), 43 Folly Rd, Wymondham, Norfolk NR18 0QT.

O'Brien, David Herbert, (OSB), St Benedict's Monastery, Convent Cl, Duddle lane, Bamber Bridge, Preston PR5 6US **Tel:** 01772-902201 **Fax:** 01772-902214 **E-mail:** donalobrien@supanet.com

O'Brien, Donal, (Portsmouth, retired), 3 Ashburton Park, Gardiner's Hill, Cork Eire.

O'Brien, Eamonn (SSC), 28 Redington Rd, London NW3 7RB

O'Brien, Eamonn, DipRE (Westminster), St Christopher's Catholic Church, 2278 Booksin Ave, San Jose CA 95125 4701

Tel: 408 978 8980
E-mail: eamonnobrien00@hotmail.com

O'Brien, Edward, (MSC), 12 Range Rd, Eastchurch, Isle of Sheppey, Kent ME12 4DU **Tel:** 01795-880423

O'Brien, Gerard, (Southwark), 1 Wyndham Rd, Kingston upon Thames, KT2 5JR **Tel:** 020-8546 4633

O'Brien, James, MA, BD, HDipEd, (Middlesbrough), Hull University Catholic Chaplaincy, 115 Cottingham Rd, Hull HU5 2DH **Tel:** 01482-343216

O'Brien, James F, (Clifton), Canon, 2 East St, Chard, Som TA20 1EP **Tel:** 01460-62197

O'Brien, Jeremiah, (Arundel & Brighton), The Presbytery, Shelley Rd, Hove, E. Sussex BN3 5GD **Tel:** 01273-733840

O'Brien, John, BEd, STL, (Birmingham), St Michael's Presbytery, Moor St, Birmingham B4 7UG **Tel:** 0121-643 0940

O'Brien, John, (SCA), 1 High St, Hastings, E. Sussex TN34 3EY **Tel:** 01424-421263 **Fax:** 01424-460893

O'Brien, John, (CMF), Blessed Sacrament, 99 Alexandra Rd, Gorseinon, Swansea, W. Glam SA4 2NX **Tel:** 01792-892722

O'Brien, John (SPS), St Patrick's, 30 Park Lane, Corsham, Wiltshire SN13 9LG **Tel:** 01249-712136

O'Brien, Joseph, (Middlesbrough, retired), St Catherine's, Southcoates Lane, Hull HU9 3AJ **Tel:** 01482-703443

O'Brien, Joseph, (Clifton), St Catherine's Presbytery, 4 Park Rd, Frome, Somerset BA11 1EU **Tel:** 01373-462705

O'Brien, Kevan, STB (Liverpool), St Peter and Paul, 89 Woodlands Rd, Haresfinch, St Helens WA11 5AQ **Tel:** 01744-23837

O'Brien, Kevin, (Portsmouth), St John's Presbytery, Wood St, Wallingford, Oxon OX10 0BD **Tel:** 01491-836814
E-mail: donalobrien@supanet.com

O'Brien, Kieran, BSc, (OSA), Curia Generalizia Agostiniana, Via Padlovi 25, 00193 Roma, Italia

O'Brien, Kieron, BTh, STL, (Arundel & Brighton), The Presbytery, Cawley Rd, Chichester, W. Sussex PO19 1XB **Tel:** 01243-782343 **Fax:** 01243-782332

O'Brien, Morrough, (Salford), St John the Baptist, Bracewell St, Burnley BB10 1TB **Tel:** 01282-423824

O'Brien, Patrick, (Shrewsbury), Holy Family, 74 Kylemore Drive, Pensby, Wirral CH61 6XZ **Tel:** 0151-648 0137

O'Brien, Patrick, (Liverpool), St Mary's, Church Rd, Woolton, Liverpool L25 5JF **Tel:** 0151-428 2256 **Fax:** 0151-428 9936

O'Brien, Pearse, (SDB), Salesian College, 119 Reading Rd, Farnborough, Hants GU14 6PA **Tel:** 01252-545035

O'Brien, Philip, (Hexham & Newcastle), Immaculate Heart of Mary, Durham Rd, Springwell, Sunderland SR3 4DF **Tel:** 0191-528 3779

O'Brien, Robert, (OCSO), Abbey of Our Lady and St Samson, Caldey Island, Tenby SA70 7UH **Tel:** 01834-842632

O'Brien, Teddy, (MSC), St Anne's Church, Wappenbury, Leamington Spa, Warks CV33 9DW **Tel:** 01926 632214
E-mail: obrien633@btinternet.com

O'Brien, Thomas, (AA), Assumption Priory, Victoria Park Square, Bethnal Green, London E2 9PB, **Tel:** 020-8709 5280
E-mail: tomobrien@freeuk.com

O'Brien, Thomas BD, PhL (MHM), Franciscan Sisters of Mill Hill, St Mary's Cottage, The Ridgeway, London NW7 4ER **Tel:** 020-8959 1433
E-mail: frtob@hotmail.com

O'Brien, Timothy, (MSC), St Anne's Presbytery, Wappenbury, Leamington Spa, CV33 9DW **Tel:** 01926-632214

O'Byrne, John, (CMF), Botwell Ho, Botwell Ln, Hayes, Middx UB3 2AB **Tel:** 020 8573 2065 **Fax:** 020 8561 6748
E-mail: botwell@claret.org.uk

O'Callaghan, Brendan, (Nottingham, retired), Knockanure, Moyvane, Co Kerry, Ireland

O'Callaghan, John, (Southwark), 127 Mottingham Rd, Mottingham, London SE9 4ST **Tel:** 020-8857 4539

O'Callaghan, Matthew, (Liverpool, retired), 56 Arundel Rd, Birkdale, Southport PR8 3DA

O'Callaghan, Robert, (Nottingham), Cathedral Ho, North Circus St, Nottingham NG1 5AE **Tel:** 0115 953 9839
E-mail: stbarnabas@tiscali.co.uk

O'Carroll, Joseph B, MA, (Salford), St Alban, Larkhill, Blackburn BB1 6HY **Tel:** 01254-59331 **Fax:** 01254-668102

O'Collins, Gerard (SJ), John Sinnott Ho, 9 Edge Hill, Winbledon, London SW19 4LR **Tel:** 020-8947 4251 **Fax:** 020 8944 6571
E-mail: ocollins@unigre.it

O'Connell, Andrew (Westminster), The Presbytery, Brentfield Rd NW10 8ER **Tel:** 020-8965 3313

O'Connell, Con (OFM), The Friary, 270 Ballater St, Glasgow G5 0YT **Tel:** 0141-429 0740 **Fax:** 0141-418 0413
E-mail: conocon@friar.org

O'Connell, Daniel, BA, (MHM), 58 Cookham Rd, Maidenhead SL6 7HT **Tel:** 01628 588410 **Mbl:** 07761465363
E-mail: fatherdanmhm@yahoo.co.uk

O'Connell, David, (Southwark), 37 Norwood High Street, Norwood SE27 9JU **Tel:** 020-8670 1765

O'Connell, Edward, (SSC), St Columban's, Widney Manor Rd, Knowle, Solihull, W. Mids B93 9AB **Tel:** 01564-772096

O'Connell, Edward, (Cardiff), St Teilo's Presbytery, Old Church Rd, Cardiff CF14 1AD **Tel:** 029-2062 3444

O'Connell, Joseph, (CSsR), The Redemptorist Mission Team, The Monastery, Badby Rd West, Daventry, Northants NN11 4NH

O'Connell, Kevin, (Northampton), St Alban's, Sheep St, Winslow, Bucks MK18 3HL **Tel:** 01296-712615

O'Connell, Kieran, (Hallam), St Joseph's Presbytery, Green Lane, Rawmarsh, Yorks S62 6JY **Tel:** 01709-522537

O'Connell, Maurice, Canon, (Salford), St Joseph's, 23, Gorton Rd, Reddish, Stockport SK5 6AZ **Tel:** 0161-432 2168

O'Connell, Michael, (MSC), Sacred Heart, Briery Hey Ave, Northwood, Kirkby, Liverpool L33 0YF **Tel:** 0151-546 3686

O'Connell, Patrick, (Hexham & Newcastle, retired), St Bernadettes, Station Rd, North Wallsend, Tyne & Wear NE28 8AE **Tel:** 0191-262 8488

O'Connell, Raphael, (OCD), Carmelite Priory, Boars Hill, Oxford OX1 5HB **Tel:** 01865-735133 **Fax:** 01865-326478

O'Connell, Thomas, (Middlesbrough, retired), St George, Link Walk, Eastfield, Scarborough YO11 3LR **Tel:** 01723-582205

O'Connor, Bernard (SSC), St Columban's, Widney Manor Rd, Knowle, Solihull B93 9AB **Tel:** 01564-772096

O'Connor, Bernard (OSA), St Mary's Priory, Vivian Rd, Harborne, Birmingham B17 0DN **Tel:** 0121-427 2538 **Fax:** 0121-428 3656

O'Connor, Christopher, (Nottingham), The Presbytery, Cross St, Gainsborough, Lincs DN21 2AX **Tel:** 01427 612427 **Fax:** 01427-612427

O'Connor, Cornelius C, (Hexham & Newcastle), St Charles, Church Rd, Gosforth, Newcastle NE3 1TX **Tel:** 0191-285 1370

O'Connor, Denis, (MHM), St Peter's, 42 Adam's Hill, Bartley Green, Birmingham B32 3QG **Tel:** 0191-476 1799

O'Connor, Dominic, (OP), St Mary's Presbytery, 12 Barnard Avenue, Brigg, N. Lincs DN20 8AS **Tel:** 01652 652221

O'Connor, Donal M, MA(Cantab), MEd, CTS, (SMA, retired), 13a West Avenue Rd, Walthamstow, London E17 9SE **Tel:** 020-8520 0430

O'Connor, John, Mgr, PhL, STL, DCL, MA, (Salford, retired), 106 Crow Hill South, Alkrington, Middleton, Manchester M24 1JU **Tel:** 0161-654 9023

O'Connor, John, (Southwark), St Thomas More, 380 Lordship Lane, Dulwich, London SE22 8ND **Tel:** 020-8693 5070

O'Connor, Joseph, (Southwark), 147 Bingham Rd, Addiscombe CR0 7EN **Tel:** 020-8654 1709 **Fax:** 020-8662 0843 **E-mail:** ourlady@addiscombe.fsnet.co.uk

O'Connor, Joseph, (Lancaster), St. John Vianney, Glastonbury Avenue, Marton, Blackpool FY1 6RD **Tel:** 01253 762227 **Email:** frjoe@btinternet.com

O'Connor, Kevin, Canon, (Salford), St Margaret Mary, St Margaret's Rd, New Moston, Manchester M40 0JE **Tel:** 0161-681 1651

O'Connor, Liam Peter, (Birmingham), c/o Cathedral Ho, St Chad's Queensway, Birmingham B4 6EX

O'Connor, Liam, (Arundel & Brighton), 37 Compton Ave, Goring-by-Sea, W. Sussex, BN12 4UE **Tel:** 01903-242624

O'Connor, Martin, (Brentwood), The Presbytery, Bishop's Ave, Chadwell Heath, Romford, Essex RM6 5RS **Tel:** 020-8590 8818

O'Connor, Michael, (Hallam), c/o Bishop's Ho, 75 Norfolk Rd, Sheffield S2 2SZ

O'Connor, Michael, (Middlesbrough, retired), 23 Clough Garth, Hedon, Hull HU12 8LS **Tel:** 01482-891297

O'Connor, Michael, Canon, (Liverpool, retired), The Bungalow, Moulagow, Rathmore, County Kerry, Ireland **Tel:** 00-353 87 670 3181

O'Connor, Oliver (SVD, retired), St Gregory's Ho, 21 Halewood Rd, Gateacre, Liverpool L25 3PH **Tel:** 0151-428 2860

O'Connor, Patrick, (Hallam), The Presbytery, 44 Warmsworth Rd, Balby, Doncaster DN4 0RR **Tel:** 013402-853937

O'Connor, Richard, (Salford), Immaculate Conception, Bury Rd, Haslingden BB4 5PG **Tel:** 01706-215642

O'Connor, Sean, BTh (Southwark), 175 Lewisham High St, Lewisham SE13 6AA **Tel:** 0208 852 2490

O'Connor, Sean, (Liverpool), St Benet's Presbytery, Copy Lane, Netherton, Bootle L30 7PE **Tel:** 0151-520 2600 **Fax:** 0151-531 8836

O'Connor, Simon, (Shrewsbury), St Michael & All Angels, New Hey Road, woodchurch, Wirral CH49 5LE **Tel:** 0151-677 4915

O'Connor, Thomas B, (Leeds), Our Lady & All Saints Presbytery, 4 Bridge St, Otley LS21 3AZ **Tel/Fax:** 01943-462148 **E-mail:** OLAS@otleyyorks.freeserve.co.uk

O'Connor, Thomas William, (Birmingham, retired), 16 Gardenrath Rd, Kells, Co. Meath, Eire

O'Connor, Thomas, (OSCam), 102 Hassett Rd, Homerton, London E9 5SJ

O'Connor, Timothy, BA, DipRelEd (Westminster),243 Mutton Lane, Potters Bar, Herts EN6 2AT **Tel:** 01707-654359

O'Conor, Patrick A, (SSC), 28, Redington Rd, Hampstead, London NW3 7RB **Tel:** 020-7794 8131/2

O'Dea, Michael, MA, STL, (Southwark), The Presbytery, 143 Central Hill, Norwood, London SE19 1RT **Tel:** 020-8670 2777

O'Dea, Patrick, Mgr Canon, P, (Lancaster), Chaplain Nanareth Ho, Ashton Rd, Lancaster LA1 5AQ **Tel:** 01524-32074 **Fax:** 01524-66369

O'Dell, Andrew, (AA), Assumption Priory, Victoria Park Square, Bethnal Green, London E2 9PB **Tel:** 020-8980 1968, **Fax:** 020-8983 7713

O'Doherty, James Oliver, (Shrewsbury), St Mary's, 29 Zetland St, Dukinfield SK16 4EJ **Tel:** 0161-330 2424 **E-mail:** o.odoherty@ntlworld.com

O'Doherty, Michael, (Westminster), 216 Dollis Hill lane, London NW2 6HE **Tel:** 020-8452 6158

O'Doherty, Patrick, (Nottingham, retired), 18 Rosehip Rd, Morton, Bourne, Lincs PE10 OPD

O'Donnell, Anthony S, Canon, (Menevia), 'Maes-Gwyn', 63 Margam Rd, Margam, Port Talbot SA13 2HR **Tel:** 01639-883323

O'Donnell, David, (Cardiff), The Presbytery, Trinity Road, Tonypandy CF40 1DQ **Tel:** 01443-432142

O'Donnell, Francis, (Cardiff, retired), 212 Llantarnam Rd, Cwmbran Torfaen NP44 3BH **Tel:** 01633-873635

O'Donnell, John, (Nottingham), 15 Cromwell Ave, Woodhall Spa, Lincs LN10 6TH **Tel:** 01526-352245

O'Donnell, Patrick, (Portsmouth, retired), St Joseph's Presbytery, Headley Rd, Grayshott, Hindhead, Surrey GU26 6DP **Tel/Fax:** 01428-608223 **Mbl:** 07900-973634 **E-mail:** odonpja@aol.com

O'Donnell, Sean, (SSC), St Columban's, Widney Manor Rd, Knowle, Solihull, W. Mids B93 9AA **Tel:** 01564-772096

O'Donnell, Sean, (Middlesbrough), St Mary's Presbytery, 23 Brooklands, Filey, N. Yorks YO14 9BA **Tel:** 01723-513139

O'Donoghue, Dermot, (Liverpool, retired), 16 Mere Park, Cambridge Rd, Crosby, Liverpool, L23 7TF **Tel:** 0151-924 0941

O'Donoghue, Gabriel, (Salford), St Hilda's, Turton Rd, Tottington BL8 4AW **Tel:** 01204-882908 **Fax:** 01024-880360 **E-mail:** sthildas@tottingtonlancs. freeserve.co.uk

O'Donoghue, John, (Southwark), 420a Long Lane, Bexleyheath, Kent DA7 5JW **Tel:** 020-8303 2189

O'Donoghue, Michael VF, (Nottingham), Holy Trinity Presbytery, Boundry Rd, Newark, Notts NG24 4AU **Tel/Fax:** 01636 704936

O'Donohue, John (MAfr), Oak Lodge, 48 Totteridge Common, London N20 8NB **Tel:** 020-8959 1515

O'Donovan, Andrew, (OCarm), 56 Holland Park Rd, London W14

O'Donovan, Bernard, (OCart), St Hugh's Charterhouse, Henfield Rd, Parkminster RH13 8EB **Tel:** 01403-864231

O'Donovan, John A, (Wrexham), Canon, Our Lady Help of Christians, 115 Mwrog St, Ruthin, Clwyd LL15 1LE **Tel:** 01824-702859

O'Donovan, Michael, Canon, (Menevia, retired), 2 Camrose Dr, Waunarlwyd, Swansea SA5 4QE **Tel:** 01792-874531

O'Donovan, Patrick, (Clifton), St Nicholas Presbytery, Chandos St, Winchcombe, Glos GL54 5HX **Tel:** 01242-602412 **E-mail:** PODGE@WInch35.fsnet.co.uk

O'Donovan, Richard, (OMI, retired), 7 College Ave, Colwyn Bay, Conwy, North Wales LL28 4NT

O'Donovan, Terence, (Plymouth), The Presbytery, 45 Lee Rd, Lynton, Devon EX35 6BS **Tel:** 01598-753255

O'Donovan, William, (Cloyne), 247, High Rd, Chiswick, London W4 4PU **Tel:** 020-8994 2877

O'Dowd, Anthony, (Nottingham, retired), St Philomena's Convent, 312 Highfield Park Drive, Derby DE22 1AU **Tel:** 01332 550122

O'Dowd, Michael, STL, (Liverpool), St Agnes, The Green, Eccleston, Chorley, Lancs PR7 5PH **Tel:** 01257-451337 **Fax:** 01257-452150 **E-mail:** odowdm@btinternet.com

O'Dowd, Philip, (Nottingham), Corpus Christi Presbytery, Listowel Cres, Clifton Nottingham NG11 9BP **Tel:** 0115 921 2964

O'Driscoll, Desmond, (Salford), The Presbytery, Astley Rd, Irlam, Manchester M44 6AB **Tel:** 0161-775 2469

O'Driscoll, Fintan, (MSC), St Albert, 31 Hollow Croft, Stockbridge Village, Liverpool L28 4EA **Tel:** 0151-228 7126 **Fax:** 0151-259- 6743

O'Driscoll, Kevin, (Northampton), 226 Trelawney Ave, Langley, Slough SL3 7UD **Tel:** 01753-543770 **E-mail:** holyfamily@freeuk.com

O'Driscoll, Liam, Canon (Clifton), St John the Baptist, 2 Wingfield Rd, Trowbridge, Wilts BA14 9EA **Tel:** 01225-752152

O'Driscoll, Patrick, (Westminster, retired), 14 Johnson's Courtyard, South St, Sherborne DT9 3TD **Tel:** 01935-817979

O'Driscoll, Peter, (Plymouth), Basildon and Thurrock University Hospitals Co-ordinating Chaplain, Nethermayne, Basildon, Essex SS16 5NL. **Tel:** 01268-593503

O'Duill, Seamus (SDS), Teach an tsagairt cill Chiaráin, Conamara, Co na Gaillimhe Éire **Tel:** 00356 95 33403 **E-mail:** seamusoduill@eircomm.net

O'Dwyer, Louis, MA, LPh, (OSB), Douai Abbey, Upper Woolhampton, Reading, Berks RG7 5TQ **Tel:** 0118 971 5300

O'Flynn, Michael, (CSSR), Alphonsus Ho, Wolf Lane, Chawton, Hampshire GU34 3HQ **Tel:** 01420-83255 **Fax:** 01420-88805

O'Gara, John, (SM), Marist Fathers, 109 Main Rd, Sidcup, Kent DA14 6ND **Tel:** 020-8302 6463

O'Gorman, Ambrose, (Brentwood, retired), Shannagh Private Nurisng Home, Bellcare Ltd, Commons, Balleek, Co Fermanagh BT93 3EP **Tel:** 02868 659128

O'Gorman, Anthony, (Westminster), 60 Rylston Rd, London SW6 7HW **Tel:** 020-7385 4040

O'Gorman, Denis, (CRL), The Presbytery, Bencoolen Rd, Bude, Cornwall EX23 8PJ **Tel:** 01288-353415

O'Gorman, John, (Hexham & Newcastle), 31 Turnpike Walk, Sedgefield, Co Durham TS21 3NP

O'Gorman, Patrick, Canon (Cardiff), St Helen's, The Presbytery, Court Rd, Barry CF63 4ET **Tel:** 01446-735051 **Fax:** 01446-740133

O'Gorman, William VG, (Hexham & Newcastle), St Michael, Durham Rd, Houghton-Le-Spring, Tyne and Wear DH5 8NF **Tel:** 0191-5842142

O'Grady, Geoffrey, LSS, (Shrewsbury), St Ambrose, 8 Clover Ave, Adswood, Stockport SK3 8QA **Tel:** 0161-480 3723 **E-mail:** geoffogrady@talktalk.net

O'Grady, Kieran (Liverpool), St Paul's Presbytery, 10 Spring Grove, West Derby, Liverpool L12 8SJ **Tel:** 0151-228 3405 **Fax:** 0151-230 0839

O'Grady, Paul, (Shrewsbury), 44 Chester Rd, Childer Thornton, Ellesmere Port CH66 1QJ

O'Grady, Thomas (SSC), 28 Redington Rd, London NW3 7RB

O'Hagan, Patrick, (OAR), 18 Cheniston Gardens, Kensington, London W8 6TQ **Tel/Fax:** 020-7937 7681

O'Halloran, John, MA, (Westminster, retired), 16 Hartley Ho, Ballards Lane, N3 1NF **Tel:** 020-8346 1768

O'Halloran, Michael, (SJ), St Wilfrid's Presbytery, 1 Winckley Square, Preston, Lancs PR1 3JJ **Tel:** 01772-555244

O'Halpin, Aodh, (SSC), c/o St Columban's, Widney Manor Road, Knowle, Solihull, W. Mids B93 9AB

O'Hanlon, James, (Nottingham), 77 Welby Lane, Melton Mowbray, Leicestershire LE13 0ST **Tel:** 01664-62274

O'Hanlon, Joseph, (Nottingham), 25 Westfield, Blean, Canterbury, Kent CT2 9ER

O'Hara, Conleth, (CP) St Joseph's Retreat, Highgate Hill, London N19 5NE **Tel:** 020-7272 2320 **Fax:** 020-7281 9433 **E-mail:**conoh@ohara39.freeserve.co.uk

O'Hara, Dominic, (Arundel & Brighton), The Parish Centre, Hislop Walk, Bognor Regis, W. Sussex PO21 1LP **Tel:** 01243 823619 **Fax:** 01243 842718 **Email:** domohara1563@yahoo.com

O'Hara, Eamonn, (Nottingham), The Sacred Heart of Jesus, 99 Carlton Hill, Nottingham NG4 1FP **Tel:** 0115-911 8266 **Fax:** 0115-910 0684

O'Hara, Paul, (Hallam), Our Lady of Lourdes Presbytery, Springwater Avenue, Hackenthorpe, Sheffield S12 4HU **Tel:** 0114 248 6102

O'Hara, Vincent, (Leeds), Our Lady Immaculate Presbytery, Panorama Way, Ripon Rd, Pateley Bridge HG3 5NJ **Tel:** 01423-711277

O'Hara, Vincent, (OCD), Carmelite Priory, Youlbury, Boars Hill, Oxford OX1 5HB **Tel:** 01865 735133 **Fax:** 01865 326478 **E-mail:** vincent.ohara@gmail.com

O'Higgins, Brian, BA, DD, (Brentwood), 21 Tilbury Rd, East Ham, London E6 6ED **Tel:** 020-8472 2557

O'Kane, David, (Salford), Sacred Heart, Kingsway, Rochdale OL16 5BX **Tel:** 01706 645603 **Fax:** 01706-340150

O'Kane, Michael, (OFM), BA, The Friary, Sample Oak Lane, Chilworth, Guildford, Surrey GU4 8QR **Tel:** 01483-893168 **Fax:** 01483-898071

O'Kane, Seamus, (Hexham & Newcastle), St Mark's, Trevelyan Dr, Newbiggin Lane, Westerhope, Newcastle upon Tyne NE5 4BT **Tel:** 0191-286 0596

O'Keefe, James, (Hexham & Newcastle),

O'Keeffe, Daniel J, (Leeds, retired), Hinsley Court, 62 Headingley Lane, Leeds LS6

O'Keeffe, Declan (OMI), St Joseph's Presbytery, 63 Conway Rd, Colwyn Bay, Conwy, North Wales LL29 7LG **Tel:** 01492 532670 **Fax:** 01492 534515

O'Keeffe, Desmond Dunstan, MA, STL (OSB), c/o Downside Abbey, Stratton on the Fosse, Radstock, Bath BA3 4RH

O'Keeffe, John B, (Leeds), St Joseph, Queens Rd, Ingrow, Keighley, W. Yorks BD21 1AT **Tel:** 01535-603931

O'Keeffe, Laurence, LSS, Rt Rev Abbot, (OSB), St Augustine's Abbey, Ramsgate, Kent CT11 9PA **Tel:** 01843-593045 **Fax:** 01843-582732 **E-mail:** ablaurence@aol.com

O'Keeffe, Mark, (Plymouth), Most Holy Trinity, Presbytery, 3 Tower Road, Newquay, Cornwall TR7 1LS **Tel/Fax:** 01204-306409 **Email:** holytrinitynewquay@tiscali.co.uk

O'Keeffe, Patrick, (OCarm), Whitefriars, More Ho, Heslington, York YO10 5DX **Tel:** 01904 410 446

O'Kelly, Patrick, (Portsmouth), c/o Bishop's Ho, Edinburgh Rd, Portsmouth PO1 3HG

O'Leary, John, STB, PhL, (Westminster), 70 Lincolns Inn Fields, London WC2A 3JA **Tel:** 0208-405 0376

O'Leary, Michael (Salford, retired), Flat 1, Springfield Ho, 35A Church Rd, Formby L37 8BQ

O'Leary, Patrick, (Southwark, retired), Giswil, Fawkham Rd, West Kingsdown, Kent TN15 6JS

O'Loughlin, Thomas, BA, STB, (Arundel & Brighton, retired), The University of Wales Lampeter, Ceredigion SA48 7ED **Tel:** 01570-424708

O'Mahoney, Killian, MA, STL (OSA), St John Stone, 7 Sandbrook Way, Woodvale, Southport PR8 3RN **Tel:** 01704-577722, **Fax:** 01704-570647

O'Mahony, Brian, (CSSp), Our Lady, Star of the Sea, Queens Promenade, Ramsey, Isle of Man IM8 1BH **Tel:** 01624-813181

O'Mahony, Denis, (Hexham & Newcastle), St Cecilia and St Patrick, Ryhope Rd, Sunderland SR2 7TG **Tel:** 0191-567 2718

O'Mahony, Gerald, (SJ), Loyola Hall, Warrington Rd, Prescot, Merseyside L35 6NZ **Tel:** 0151-426 4137 **Fax:** 0151-431 0115 **E-mail:** gerry@loyolahall.f2s.com

O'Mahony, Jeremiah, (Leeds), The Presbytery, Bolton Rd, Addingham, Ilkley LS29 0NQ **Tel:** 01943-830259

O'Mahony, Maurice (CSsR), Hawkstone Hall, Marchamley, Shrewsbury SY4 5LG **Tel:** 01630-685242 **Fax:** 01630-685565

O'Malley, Brendan Noel, (Birmingham, retired), 17 Appletree Lane, Redditch, Worcs, B97 6SE **Tel:** 01527-591295

O'Malley, Brendan, (AA), Assumption Priory, Victoria Park Square, Bethnal Green, London E2 9PB **Tel:** 020-8709 5284

O'Malley, David, MA, CertEd, Certs in Spirituality & Counselling (SDB), Thornleigh Ho, Sharples Park, Bolton BL1 6PQ **Tel:** 01204-306409 **Fax:** 01204-308510 **E-mail:** davidomalley@lineone.net

O'Malley, Martin William, STB, MA (Birmingham), c/o Archbishop's Ho, 8 Shadwell St, Birmingham B4 6EY

Omana, Max (US Forces), US Air Force Base, Alconbury, Huntingdon, Cambridgeshire PE17 5DA

Ommer, Gilmour. MRCVS, (Galloway, retired), 464 Downall Green Rd, Bryn, Wigan WN4 0NA **Tel:** 01942-721712

O'Meara, Aloysius Terence, (CSS), Henesy Ho, Sudell St, Collyhurst, Manchester M4 4JF **Tel:** 0161-834-8828

O'Murchú, Diarmuid, (MSC), 38 Cambourne Ave, London W13 9QZ **Tel:** 0208 567 5421 **E-mail:** diarmuid.13@gmail.com

O'Neill, Austin, (Middlesbrough, retired), 1 Bolton Ho, Nicholas Gardens, York YO10 3FE

O'Neill, Daniel, (Middlesbrough), SS Joseph and Francis Xavier, Loyola Lodge, 25 Victoria Rd, Richmond, N. Yorks DL10 4AS **Tel:** 01748-822175

O'Neill, Dermot, (Westminster), 2a Salehurst Cl, Kenton HA3 0UG **Tel:** 020-8204 3550

O'Neill, John D, (Westminster, retired), Appletree Court Care Home, 158 Burnt Oak, Broadway HA8 0AX **Tel:** 0208 381 3243

O'Neill, Kevin, MA, (SM), Marist Fathers, 109 Main Rd, Sidcup, Kent DA14 6ND **Tel:** 020-8302 6463

O'Neill, Michael, (MHM), St Bede's, 598 Preston Rd, Clayton-le-Woods, Chorley PR6 7EB **Tel:** 01772-335209 **E-mail:** maoneill@mara.freeserve.co.uk

O'Neill, Owen, Canon, (Nottingham), The Priest's Ho, 1 Fairfield Rd, Market Harborough, Leicestershire LE16 9QQ **Tel:** 01858-462359

O'Neill, Patrick, (Middlesbrough), SS Peter and Paul, Richmond Rd, Leyburn, N. Yorks DL8 5DL **Tel:** 01969-623141

O'Neill, Peter, Mgr Canon, MA, (Shrewsbury), St Luke's, 61 High St, Frodsham WA6 7AN **Tel/Fax:** 01928-733127 **E-mail:** frpeter@gmail.com

O'Neill, Shaun, (Hexham & Newcastle), SS Peter and Paul, Redhill Rd, Stockton-on -Tees TS 9BY **Tel/Fax:** 01642-676799

O'Neill, Thomas, (Middlesbrough), St Gabriel's, Allendale Rd, Ormesby, Middlesbrough TS7 9LF **Tel:** 01642-314501

O'Regan, David, (Southwark, retired), 22 Avoca Rd, London SW17 8SL **Tel:** 020-8672 3669

O'Regan, David, (Southwark), Our Lady of

Reparation, 70 Wellesley Rd, Croydon Surrey CR0 2AR **Tel:** 020-8688 1857

O'Regan, John, Canon, (Cardiff), Presbytery, Turberville Rd, Ynyshir, Porth, Mid Glam CF39 0NF **Tel:** 01443-682689

O'Reilly, Aidan, (Salford, retired), 'Regina Coeli', 70 Pole Lane, Unsworth, Bury BL9 8PX **Tel:** 0161-766 3310

O'Reilly, Augustine, (Hallam), St Peter in Chains, Chequer Rd, Doncaster DN1 2AA **Tel:** 01302-342068

O'Reilly, Bernard, (CSSp), 6 Woodlands Rd, Bickley, Bromley, Kent BR1 2AF **Tel:** 020-8467 3555

O'Reilly, Henry, (Hexham & Newcastle), St Charles, St Charles Rd, Tudhoe, Spennymoor, Co Durham DL16 9JY **Tel:** 01388-814713

O'Reilly, John, BSc, LCL, (Shrewsbury), Our Lady and St Christopher, 52 Barrack Hill, Romiley, Stockport SK6 3BA **Tel:** 0161-430 2704 **Fax:** 0161-494 6461 **E-mail:** stchrisromiley@aol.com

O'Reilly, Matthew, (SSC), St Columban's, Widney Manor Rd, Knowle, Solihull, W. Mids B93 9AA **Tel:** 01564-772096

O'Reilly, Michael, BEng, DipEd, (Leeds), St Joseph's Presbytery, Mount Pleasant Rd, Pudsey LS28 7AZ **Tel:** 0113-257 0803

O'Reilly, Paul, (SJ), 114 Mount Street, London W1K 3AH **Tel:** 020 7529 4818 **Fax:** 020 7495 6685 **E-mail:** fatbaldnproud@yahoo.co.uk

O'Reilly, Thomas, (Leeds, retired), Our Lady's Nursing Home, Edgeworthstown, Co Longford, Ireland

O'Riain, Colm, (OMI), Mercy Nursing Home, 15 Lansdowne Rd, Colwyn Bay LL29 7UY

O'Riordan, Daniel, BA, BacSTh, DipEd (SDB), Rinaldi Ho, 32 Orbel St, Battersea, London SW11 3NZ **Tel:** 020-7801 9040 **Fax:** 020-7801 9041 **E-mail:** orbelsdb@msn.com

O'Riordan, Kenneth, (Nottingham), 103 Portreath Dirve, Allestree, Derby DE22 2RS

O'Riordan, William, (Shrewsbury), St Benedict's, 10 Hall Rd, Handforth, Wilmslow SK9 3AD **Tel:** 01625-522776

O'Rourke, Benignus, BA, STL (OSA), Clare Priory, Clare, Sudbury, Suffolk CO10 8NX **Tel:** 01787-277326 **Fax:** 01787-278688

O'Rourke, Patrick, (CMF), Blessed Sacrament, 99 Alexandra Rd, Gorseinon, Swansea SA4 2NX **Tel:** 01792-892722

O'Shaughnessy, Gerard, BEd, Farmington Fellowship in RE (Oxford), (SDB), St James' Presbytery, Chesnut Grove, Bootle, Merseyside L20 4LX **Tel:** 0151-944 1039 **Fax:** 0151-922 3263 **E-mail:** gerryosdb@aol.com

O'Shea, Benedict, Mgr, VG, (Arundel & Brighton), 42 Arbrook Ln, Esher, Surrey KT10 9EE **Tel:** 01372 462451

O'Shea, Brian, BA(Hons), MA, (Brentwood), 16 East Thurrock Rd, Grays, Essex RM17 6SR **Tel:** 01375 372306

O'Shea, Ian, (Liverpool), Chaplain Royal Liverpool Hosp., Cathedral House, Mount Pleasant, Liverpool L3 5TQ **Tel:** 0151 709 9222 **Fax:** 0151 708 7274

O'Shea, John, Canon, MRE (Portsmouth), 14 Rockstone Place, Southampton SO15 2EQ **Tel:** 023 8033 3589 **Fax:** 023-8063 5153 **Mbl:** 07887-771155 **E-mail:** jjoshea@yahoo.co.uk

O'Shea, Kevin, (CM), 2 Flower Lane, London NW7 2JB **Tel:** 020 8959 1021

O'Shea, Morty (SOLT), St Mary's Retreat, Union St, Carmarthen SA31 3DE **Tel:** 01267 237205

O'Shea, Raymond, (Cardiff, retired), St David's Cathedral Clergy Ho, Charles St, Cardiff CF10 2SF **Tel:** 029-2023 3722

O'Sullivan, Andrew, (CSSp), 117 Newarthill Rd, Carfin, Motherwell ML1 5AL **E-mail:** spiritans.uk@virgin.net

O'Sullivan, B, (OMI), St Mary's College, Abbey Rd, Rhos on Sea LL28 4NF **Tel:** 01422-4477

O'Sullivan, Barry, MA (Salford), 36 Dundee Lane, Ramsbottom, BL0 9HL **E-mail:** bosullibe@aol.com

O'Sullivan, Brendan, Canon (Nottingham, retired), 16 Buckingham Cl, Boston, Lincs PE21 9QB **Tel:** 01205 366347 **E-mail:** brendan.os@btinternet.com

O'Sullivan, Brendan, (Liverpool, retired), 10 Waterfoot Ave, Ainsdale, Southport PR8 3TE **Tel:** 01704 575508

O'Sullivan, Brendan, (OMI), St Joseph's Presbytery, 63 Conway Rd, Colwyn Bay, Conwy, North Wales LL29 7LG **Tel:** 01492-532670 **Fax:** 01492-534515

O'Sullivan, Brian, Canon, (Arundel & Brighton), The Priest's Ho, Penlands Way, Steyning, W. Sussex BN44 3AN **Tel:** 01903-813199

O'Sullivan, Daniel J, MA, (Clifton), Mision Catolica, San Antonio – San Francisco, Apartado 136, Moquegua, Peru

O'Sullivan, David (Portsmouth), 15 Manor Cres, Didcot, Oxon OX11 7AJ **Tel:** 01235-812388

O'Sullivan, Denis, (Shrewsbury, retired), c/o Curial Offices, 2 Park Road South, Prenton CH43 4UX

O'Sullivan, Francis, Canon, (Southwark), The Lodge, 47 Russell Hill Rd, Purley, Surrey CR8 2XB

O'Sullivan, George, (MSFS), 26 Cross Hayes, Malmesbury, Wilts SN16 9BG **Tel:** 01666-822195

O'Sullivan, Hugh, DipTh, CertEd, (SDB), Grace and Compassion Benedictines, St Mary's Ho, 38/39 Preston Park Ave, Brighton BN1 6HG **Tel:** 01273-501891

O'Sullivan, James Mgr, CBE (Sandhurst), 'Osgil' Vicarage Lane, Ropley, Alresford, Hants SO24 0DU

O'Sullivan, John (Arundel & Brighton), 111 Portsmouth Rd, Frimley, Camberley. GU16 5AA **Tel:** 01276-504876 **Fax:** 01276-500070

O'Sullivan, Michael Francis, (Clifton, retired), Shamrock Ho, Main St, Boherbue, Mallow, Co Cork, Ireland.

O'Sullivan, Patrick Joseph, (Birmingham, retired), The Presbytery, St Mary's Rd, Wednesbury, W. Mids WS10 9DL **Tel:** 0121-556 0414

O'Sullivan, Timothy, Canon VF (Nottingham), St Mary, Bridge Gate, Derby DE1 3AU **Tel:** 01332-346126

O'Sullivan, William, Canon, (Liverpool, retired), Flat 16, St George's Court, Station Rd, Maghull, Liverpool L31 3JD **Tel:** 0151-520 0066

O'Toole, Barrie, (CSsR), The John Paul Centre, 55 Grange Rd, Middlesbrough TS1 5AU **Tel:** 01642-251800 **Fax:** 01642-221003

O'Toole, Edward (Liverpool), St Edward's Presbytery, Scot Lane, Newtown, Wigan WN5 0UA **Tel:** 01942-244175 **Fax:** 01942-231181

O'Toole, John, MA, AKC, CertEd (Southwark). Beckett Ho, Santos Rd, Wandsworth SW18 1NT **Tel:** 020-88743348

O'Toole, Laurence, (East Anglia, retired), 23 Risbridge Dr, off Mill Lane, Kedington, Haverhill, Suffolk CB9 7ZE

O'Toole, Mark, Mgr, BSc, BD, MPhil, STL (Westminster), Archbishop's Ho, Ambrosden Ave, London SW1P 1QJ **Tel:** 020-7798 9033

O'Toole, Sean P. STL, BEd (Westminster), *Chaplain Whittington Hosp*, St Raphael's House, Morrison Road, Yeading UB4 9JD **Tel:** 020-8969 2660

Oakley, David, MEd, PhD (Birmingham), 82 Old Oscott Hill, Kingstanding, Birmimgham B44 9SP **Tel:** 0121-360 7141

Oates, Vincent (MHM). Mill Hill Formation Ho, Peddafoerdiyal PO, Karunapuram, Warangal St 506151 AP India

Obasi, Cletus, 52a Raglan St, Coventry CV1 5QF **Tel:** 02476-258901

Odion, Mark, (MSP) Cathedral Ho, Wesstminster Bridge Rd, London, SE1 6HX **Tel:** 0207-928 5256

Okon, Edward, (OCarm), STL, MTh, PGCE, c/o Provincial Office, Whitefriars, Tanners St, Faversham ME13 7JW

Okoye, Gabriel, (CMF), 1 Debnams Rd, Rotherhithe New Rd, Bermondsey SE16 2BB **Tel:** 020-7237 0355

Okoye, Patrick, (Awka, Nigeria), 342 High Rd, Ilford, Essex IG1 1QP **Tel:** 020 8478 0583

Okpeh, Addison (MSP), 1 Debnams Road, Rotherhithe New Road SE16 2BB **Tel:** 020 7237 0355

Oliver, Edward, (CSSp), 63 Somerset Rd, New Barnet, Herts EN5 1RF **Tel:** 020-8449 1961

Ollard, Andrew (Northampton), Our Lady of Lourdes, 40 Lloyds, Coffee Hall, Milton Keynes MK6 5EB **Tel/Fax:** 01908-670850 **E-mail:** andyollard@yahoo.co.uk

Olliver, John (Arundel & Brighton), 17 Bluehouse Ln, Oxted, Surrey, RH8 0AA

Onatsko, Myhaylo (Ukrainian), 186 Station St, Coventry CV6 5FR **Tel:** 024-7663 8598

Onuoha, Anthony, (Orlu, Nigeria), The Presbytery, 5 Monkswood Ave, Waltham Abbey, Essex EN9 1LA **Tel:** 01992 711051

Onyejuluwa, Gerald (MSP), The Presbytery, 131 Deptford High St, London SE8 4NS **Tel:** 020-8692 2011

Orchard, Bernard, MA, DLit(Hon) (OSB), Ealing Abbey, Charlbury Grove, Ealing W5 2DY **Tel:** 020-8862 2100

Orme, Martin, (East Anglia), 468 Norwich Rd, Ipswich, Suffolk IP1 6JS **Tel:** 01473-741975

Orr, Peter, (SJ), St Wilfrid's Presbytery, 1 Winckley Sq, Preston PR1 3JJ **Tel:** 01772 555244 **Fax:** 01772 251955

Ortiger, Stephen, Rt Rev Dom, MA, STB (OSB), Worth Abbey, Crawley, W Sussex RH10 4SB **Tel:** 01342-710310

Orzel, Stefan, (Lublin, Polish Priest), 27 Groundwell Rd, Swindon, Wilts SN1 2LT **Tel:** 01793-531257

Osborne, John, (Northampton), Catholic Presbytery, Millais Rd, Corby NN18 0SP **Tel:** 01536-202323

Osborne, David (Arundel & Brighton), 65 Ash Church Rd, Ash, Aldershot, Hampshire GU12 6LU **Tel:** 01252-321422

Osika, Czeslaw, MA, STL (SChr), (Polish Priest), 17 Victoria St, Dunstable LU6 3AZ **Tel:** 01582-662807

Osman, Francis, (Lancaster), The Presbytery, Pottery St, Barrow-in-Furness LA14 2AX **Tel:** 01229 821498

Osman, John, MA, STL (Birmingham), Bridge Ho, Dorchester-on-Thames, Oxon OX10 7JR

Ospina, Jose (IMC), Consolata Missionary College, Totteridge Green, London N20 8PL

Ostaszewski, Leon A J, (Warsaw, retired), 8 Newland Dr, Liscard, Wallasey, Merseyside CH44 2AX **Tel:** 0151-639 0145

Oswald, Brian, BA, STB, MPS, (MHM), 56A Cookham Rd, Maidenhead SL6 7HT **Tel:** 01628-588412 **Mbl:** 07876 208616 **E-mail:** mhmbrianos@hotmail.com

Otieno, John (AI), 103 Maison Dieu Rd, Dover, Kent CT16 1RU **Tel:** 01304-206766

Ouard, Andrew (Northampton), St Thomas Aquinas, 1 Sycamore Ave, Bletchley MK2 2JE **Tel:** 01908-372315 **Fax:** 01908-645163

Ounsworth, Richard (OP), Priory of the Holy Spirit, 64 St Giles, Oxford OX1 3LY **Tel:** 01865 278400

Overton, James, Mgr, MA, STL, BD, (Westminster), 112 Clarendon Rd, Ashford TW15 2QD **Tel:** 01784-252230

Owen, Charles, (CP), St Joseph's Retreat, Highgate Hill, London N19 5NE **Tel:** 020-7272 2320

Owen, Francis C J, St George's College, Weybridge Rd, Addlestone, Surrey, KT15 2QS **Tel:** 01932-839450 **E-mail:** aowen74753@aol.com

Owen, John, BSc(Econ), MTh, (Cardiff), University Chaplaincy, 62 Park Place, Cardiff CF10 3AS **Tel:** 029-2022 9785 **Fax:** 079-2066 8197

Owens, Anthony, (Hexham & Newcastle), St Aiden, 18 King St, Seahouses, Northumberland NE68 7XP **Tel:** 01665-720427

Owens, Paul, (Leeds), RAF Chaplain, Defence College of Aeronautical Engineering, Cosford, Wolverhampton WV7 3EX 5PG **Tel:** 01902-377 065

Owens, Robert A, (Leeds), St Anthony, 19 Old Lane, Beeston, Leeds LS11 7AA **Tel:** 0113-271 6597 **Fax:** 0113-277 4998

Owiredu, John Kwame, (SJ), Campion Hall, Oxford OX1 1QS **Tel:** 01865-286128

Ozog, Aleksander, Canon, (Lublin, Poland), 8 Oliver Grove, London SE25 6EJ **Tel:** 020-8653 8701 **Fax:** 020-8771 0133

Padua, Jacinto Rey (Jack) (Menevia), 35 Margaret St, Ammanford, Carmarthenshire SA18 2NP **Tel:** 01269-592533

Page, Barnabas, (Clifton), St Luke and St Teresa's Presbytery, South St, Wincanton, Somerset BA9 9DH **Tel:** 01963-34408

Paikkatt, Augustine (MCBS), "Carmel", Pontfaen Rd, Lampeter **Tel:** 01570-422437

Paine, Kevin, (Cardiff), Our Lady of Peace, Ashfield Rd, Newbridge, Gwent NP11 4RB **Tel:** 01495-243304

Pajak, Wlodzimierz, MA, STL (SChr) (Polish Priest), 9 Gordon Rd, Derby DE23 6WR **Tel:** 01332 343950 **E-mail:** pbf@ukonline.co.uk

Pak, Philip, BA, DipTh (Southwark), Chaplain to St George's Hospital, 147 Church Ln, Tooting, London SW17 9PD **Tel:** 020 8682 3723

Palmer, David H, BA, (Westminster), 29 Manor House Way, Isleworth, Middx TW7 6BJ **Tel:** 020-8847 4632

Panario, John, MA, (Southwark), The Presbytery, 24 Old Park Hill, Dover, Kent CT16 2AW **Tel:** 01304-823402

Panathara, Chako (CM), 29 Eversley Cres, Isleworth TW7 4RL **Tel:** 020 8560 7021

Panato, Pasquino, STL (MCCJ), Verona Fathers, Brownberries Ln, Horsforth, Leeds LS18 5HE **Tel:** 0113 258 2658

Panda Koten, Philip (SVD), 8 Teignmouth Rd, London NW2 4HN

Pannell, Roy (Hallam), Bloomhill Rd, Moorends, Doncaster DN8 4SS **Tel/Fax:** 01405-812248

Pannett, James, Canon, KCHS, (Southwark), 48 Dale Rd, Purley, Surrey CR8 2EF **Tel:** 020-8660 3815 **E-mail:** jimpannett@hotmail.com

Papworth, David, STL, (Brentwood), 281 Straight Rd, Harold Hill, Romford, Essex RM3 7JS **Tel:** 01708-342127

Parfitt, Geoffrey M, (Leeds), The Manse, Broughton Hall, Skipton BD23 3AE **Tel:** 01756-793794

Paris, Anthony, STC, (Westminster), c/o Principal RC Chaplain (Army), HQ Land Command, Erskine Barracks, Wilton, Salisbury SP2 0AG **Tel:** 01722 433892

Parish, Anthony, (SJ), Corpus Christi Jesuit Community, 757 Christchurch Rd, Boscombe, Bournemouth BH7 6AN **Tel:** 01202-436700

Park, Joseph, (Hexham & Newcastle), St Joseph, Thorneyholme Tce, Stanley, Co Durham DH9 0BL **Tel:** 01207-232034

Park, Stefan, (OSA), St Augustines, 55 Fulham Palace Road, Hammersmith W6 8AU

Parker, Henry, (CSsR), Our Immaculate Lady of Victories, Clapham Park Rd, Clapham, London SW4 7AP **Tel:** 020-7622 2793

Parker, W Alfred, (Lancaster), Presbytery, Kents Bank Rd, Grange-over-Sands LA11 7EY **Tel:** 01539-532731

Parkes, Bernard, BA, CQSW (SDB), Savio Ho, Ingersley Rd, Bollington, Macclesfield SK10 5RW **Tel:** 01625-575405 **Fax:** 01625-560221 **E-mail:** bernard@saviohouse.org.uk

Parkin, Bernard, (SJ), St Ignatius, 27 High Rd, London N15 6ND **Tel:** 020-8442 5234 **E-mail:** bernardparkin@jesuits.net

Parkinson, Francis, BA(Hons), STL, PGCE (Salford), St Joseph, 99 Audley Range, Blackburn BB1 1TG **Tel:** 01254 675534 **Fax:** 01254 279581

Parkinson, Steven, PGCE, MA (Salford), (Chaplain to Salford University), SS Peter and Paul, Park Rd, Pendleton, Salford M6 8JR **Tel:** 0161-789 455 **E-mail:** s.f.parkinson@salforddiocese.ac.uk

Parmiter, David (Arundel and Brighton), The Priests Ho, St Pauls Rd, Woking Surrey GU22 7DZ **Tel:** 01483 760652

Parolin, Gaetano, (CS), 20 Brixton Rd, London, Italian Mission SW9 6BU **Tel:** 020-7735 8235

Parrish, Ivor (Northampton), c/o Bishops Ho, Marriott St, Northampton NN2 6AW **Tel:** 01604-715635 **Fax:** 01604-715339 **E-mail:** holyfamily@freeuk.com

Parry, Denis, (Liverpool), Apartado 18-1025, Lima, Peru **Tel:** 0051 1467 1153 **E-mail:** padredenis@webhouse.com.pe

Parsons, Anthony (OCD), St Joseph's Priory, Austenwood Common, Gerrard's Cross, Bucks SL9 8RY **Tel:** 01753-886581 **Fax:** 01753-892371

Parsons, Richard E. BD, MTh, MPhil, AKC, STL (Westminster), 22 Boniface Walk, Harrow, Middx HA3 6PU **Tel:** 020-8428 3260

Parsons, Sean, (Leeds), c/o Bishop's Ho, 13 North Grange Rd, Leeds LS6 2BR **Tel:** 0113-230 4533 **Fax:** 0113-278 9890

Partington, Bernard, (Lancaster), The Presbytery, Garstang Rd, Pilling, Preston PR3 6AL **Tel:** 01253 790264

Paryono, Agostino, Carmelite Friars, 63 East End Rd, East Finchley, London N2 OSE **Tel:** 020-8346-1458

Pascoe, John, BA, DipTh (Shrewsbury), "Rosa Mystica", 33 Beech Dr, Shifnal TF11 8HJ **Tel:** 01952-461626 **E-mail:** stmarys@fatherjohnpascoe.co.uk

Pass, Henry BA (Archivist) (CSSp) 6 Woodland Rd, Bickley, Bromley, Kent BR1 2AF **Tel:** 020-8467 3555 **Fax:** 020-8295 4965 **E-mail:** spiritansbickley@btconnect.com

Pastore, Andrew, (SI), Our Lady of Mount Carmel, Wilson Rd, Blackley M9 8BG **Tel:** 0161-740 2071

Pateman, Anthony (Nottingham), 63 Broad St, Syston, Leicestershire LE7 1GH **Tel:** 0115-260 8476

Patey, Colin, (Nottingham), 56 Huntingdon Rd, Ashby-de-la-Zouch, Leics LE65 2NH **Tel/Fax:** 01530-413270

Pathe, Eugene, MA (Leeds, retired), St Mary's Catholic Church, 110 St Mary Ave S. W. Fort Walton Beach, Florida 32548, USA **Tel:** 00 850 478 2797

Patterson, Ian, (Hexham & Newcastle), 9 High St, Felling, Gateshead, Tyne and Wear NE10 9LT **Tel:** 0191-495 2277

Patterson, Ross, STL, BD, DipTheol (Menevia), St Michael's Rectory, 11 St Michael's St, Brecon, Powys LD3 9AB **Tel:** 01874-622046

Paul, David, (East Anglia), Catholic Presbytery, 91 Milton Rd, Cambridge CB4 1XB **Tel:** 01223-354788

Paul, Denis, (Southwark, retired), The Coach Ho, 92 Upper Shirley Rd, Croydon, Surrey CR0 5HA **Tel:** 020-8656 3550

Paul, Sunny, (MSFS), 73 Higher Kingston BA21 4AR, **Tel:** 01935-423549.

Paulena, Pedro, OSBM, (Ukrainians), 10 Park View Rd, Bradford, W. Yorks BD9 49A **Tel:** 01274-542307

Paulose, Joseph (CMF), Botwell Ho, Botwell Lane, Hayes, Middx UB3 2AB **Tel:** 020-8573 2065 **Fax:** 020-8561 6748 **E-mail:** paulusjoe@claret.org.uk

Paulson, Robin (IC), St Mary's, Derryswood, Wonersh, Guildford GU5 0RA **Tel:** 01483-893196 **Fax:** 01483-890700 **E-mail:** derryswood@rosmini.org

Paver, Kristian, (CRL), The Presbytery, 61 Fore St, Totnes, Devon TQ9 5NJ **Tel:** 01803 862126

Paxman, Denis, (Lancaster), Corriegills, Brough Sowerby, Kirkby Stephen, Cumbria CA17 4EG **Tel:** 01783-41427

Paxton, Nicholas, STB, PhD, BD, MPhil, (Salford), 22 Ballbrook Court, Wilmslow Rd, Manchester M20 3GU **Tel:** 0161-448 2230 **E-mail:** nicholas.paxton@btopenworld.com

Payne, Kenneth J, BSc, DipEd (Northampton), St Aidan, Finch Lane, Little Chalfont, Bucks HP7 9NE **Tel:** 01494-763518 **E-mail:** kenpayne@post.com

Peach, Eduard V, (Clifton), c/o St Ambrose, North Rd, Leigh Woods, Bristol BS8 3PW

Pearce, David, BD, MTh, MPhil, LDSRCSEng, KHS (OSB), Ealing Abbey, Charlbury Grove, Ealing W5 2DY **Tel:** 020-8862 2100 **E-mail:** dpearcew5@aol.com

Pearce, Maurice, (Leeds), Our Lady of Victories Presbytery, West Lane, Keighley BD22 6ES **Tel:** 01535-603819

Pearsall, William (SJ), The Immaculate Conception, 114 Mount St, London W1Y 3AH

Pearson, Basil, (Brentwood, retired), c/o 1 Cliffsea Grove, Leigh -on-Sea, Essex SS9 1NG.

E-mail: basilpearson64@hotmail.com

Pearson, E Antony, BSc, BA, (Leeds), Stockeld Rd, Ilkley, LS29 9HD **Tel:** 01943-607690

Pearson, John, MA, (Arundel & Brighton), 22 Esher Ave, Walton-on-Thames, Surrey KT12 2TA **Tel:** 07932-221101

Pearson, Patrick, Canon (Southwark, retired), 274 Imperial Court, 225 Kennington Lane, London SE1 5QN **Tel:** 020 7793 7693

Pearson, Stephen, MA, (Lancaster), St Bernadette's, 26 All Hallows Rd, Bispham, Blackpool FY2 0AS **Tel:** 01253-352587

Peat, Simon, BSc, STL, (Southwark), 2 Latimer Rd, Wimbledon, London SW19 1EP **Tel:** 020-8542 1600

Peate, Stephen, (OCSO), Abbey of Our Lady and St Samson, Caldey Island, off Tenby, SA70 7UH **Tel:** 01834-842632 and 842879

Pedley, Christopher, (SJ), Southwell Ho, 39 Fitzjohn's Ave, London NW3 5JT **Tel:** 020-7472 5152 **Fax:** 020-7435 9133 **E-mail:** c.pedley@heythrop.ac.uk

Peel, Derek (Hexham & Newcastle), St Joseph's Presbytery, Highfield, Rowlands Gill, Tyne & Wear NE39 2DB **Tel:** 01207-542339

Pegley, Royston (Arundel and Brighton), The Presbytery, Cawley Rd, Chichester, W. Sussex PO19 1XB **Tel:** 01243-782343

Pelan, Anthony (OCarm), The Friars, Aylesford, Kent ME20 7BX **Tel:** 01622-717272

Pelham, Kevin, (Southwark), St Margaret, Fir Tree Gr, Carshalton Beeches, Surrey SM5 4NG **Tel:** 020-8647 7748

Pellegrini, Anthony KSG, BA, BTH, ARCO (Westminster), 279 High Rd, London N2 8HQ **Tel:** 0208-883 4234

Pelosi, Laurence, Canon, (Wrexham), 40 Heol Awstin, Ravenhill, Swansea SA5 5EE

Pelucchi Alberto, (MCCJ), Comboni Ho, 16 Dawson Place, Bayswater, London W2 4TJ

Penhalagan, Simon, Cathederal House, Kingsthorpe Road, Northhampton NN2 6AG **Tel:** 01604 714556

Pennicott, Anthony, (Portsmouth), 1 Albert Rd, Bournemouth, Dorset BH1 1BZ **Tel:** 01202-551013 **Fax:** 01202-557991 **E-mail:** ajpennicott@tiscali.co.uk

Pennington, George A, (Lancaster), St Winefride's House, Low Moor Road, Bispham, Blackpool FL2 OPA **Tel:** 01253-351142

Pennington, Paschal M, (OSB), Monastery of Christ the King, 29 Bramley Rd, London N14 4HE **Tel:** 020-8440 7769 **Fax:** 020-8449 2338

Peoples, Aloysius (OSM), Priory Ho, 25 Woodstock Rd West, Begbroke, Oxon OX5 1RJ **Tel:** 01865-372149

Perceval, Benet, MA, (OSB), Ampleforth Abbey, York YO62 4EN **Tel:** 01439-766714 **Fax:** 01439-766724

Pereira, James (SFX), SS Peter and Paul, Cranmer Rd, Mitcham CR4 4LD **Tel:** 0208-648 3800

Pereira, Leon Kuriakos (OP), Holy Cross Priory, 45 Wellington St, Leicester LE1 6HW **Tel:** 0116-255 5552

Pereiro, James, (Opus Dei), Grandpont Ho, Abingdon Rd, Oxford OX1 4LD **Tel:** 01865-244150

Perera, Edward, (Southwark), 45b Burnt Ash Hill, Lee SE12 0AE **Tel/Fax:** 020-8857 5006

Perez, Jesús, (OAR), The Presbytery, Chalkhill Rd, Wembley Park, Middx HA9 9EW **Tel:** 020-8904 2306

Peries, Ignatius, (CHS), St Mark, Woodhill, Kentish Lane, Hatfield, Herts Al9 6EB

Perkins, Douglas, (Arundel & Brighton, retired), 14 Great College St, Brighton, E. Sussex BN2 1HL **Tel:** 01273-694619

Perkins, Terence, (Plymouth, retired), The Presbytery, Grove Hill, St Mawes, Cornwall TR2 5BJ **Tel:** 01326-270457.

Perrotta, John Carmel, Superior (FDP), 25 Lower Teddington Rd, Hampton Wick KT1 4HB

Perry, James (SVD), St Gregory's Ho, 21 Halewood Rd, Gateacre, L25 3PH **Tel:** 0151-428 2860

Perry, Michael J, (Arundel & Brighton), 19 Croft Rd, Godalming, Surrey GU7 1DB **Tel:** 01483-416880

Pesterfield, Gordon (OFM Cap), Franciscan Friary, 15 Cuppin St, Chester CH1 2BN **Tel:** 01244-351331

Peterburs, Wulstan BA, PhD, PGCE, (OSM) Ampleforth College, York YO62 4ER **Tel:** 01439-766751

Peters, David, (Shrewsbury), St Pius X, Stamford Ho, Stamford Rd, Alderley Edge SK9 7NS **Tel:** 01625-582386 **E-mail:** stpius@tiscali.co.uk

Peters, Eugene Michael, (Portsmouth), St Mary's College, 106 Cobden Ave, Southampton, Hants SO18 1FS **Tel:** 023-8055 8497 Mbl: 07071 201200 **E-mail:** eugenepeters@compuserve.com

Petty, Anthony, (Salford), Holy Family Presbytery, Thornley Lane, North, Reddish, Stockport SK5 6QR **Tel:** 0161-223 2930

Peyton, John, (Birmingham), 106 Dudley Rd, Birmingham B18 7QN **Tel:** 0121 454 2618

Peyton, Martin, (Salford), St James, 2607

27th St, Vernon, BC V1T 4W1, Canada
Tel: 1-250-542 1276
Fax: 1-250-542 1270
E-mail: stjameschurch@home.com

Pfleger, Alphonse, (SM), 92 Castle Rd, Scarborough, N. Yorks YO11 1TG **Tel:** 01723-371611

Pham, Ngoc Dung (Joseph), (Northampton), Cathedral Ho, Kingsthorpe Rd, Northampton NN2 6AG **Tel:** 01604-714556 **Fax:** 01604-715339 **E-mail:** info@northamptoncathedral.org

Pham-Tri-Van, Anthony, (Birmingham), Our Lady of Lourdes, 224 Halesowen Rd, Old Hill, Cradley Heath, Warley, W. Mids B64 6HN **Tel:** 01384-410516

Pham Huu Hai (John) STB (Westminster), Presbytery, Everglade Strand, London NW9 5PX **Tel:** 0208-205 6830

Pham, Nam Xuan (Barnabas) BA (OSB), Monastery of Christ the Word, Monte Cassino, PB No. 902, Macheke, Zimbabwe **Tel/Fax:** 00 263 798 369

Phelan, Joseph F, Mgr Canon, (Nottingham), St Anne's Prestbytery, Highfield Road, Rock Ferry, Birkenhead CH42 2BY **Tel:** 0151 645 3996 **Fax:** 0151 654 0419

Phelan, Michael, (OMI), St Anne's Presbytery, Highfield Road, Rockferry, Birkenhead CH42 2BY **Tel:** 0151 645 3996 **Fax:** 0151 645 0419 **E-mail:** stanne.rf@ntlworld.com

Phelan, Michael D, Ennerdale Ho, 41 Penn Rd, Beaconsfield HP9 2LN **Tel:** 0151-226 1354 **Fax:** 0151-270 2665

Phelps, Sandy (East Anglia, retired), 24 Brandon Court, Prospect Row, Cambridge CB1 1DZ **Tel:** 01223-303811

Philips, Angelo, (Leeds, retired), 2Majestic Court, Harrogate HG1 2HT

Phillips, David, (Hexham & Newcastle), SS Mary and Thomas Aquinas, Stella Rd, Blaydon-on-Tyne NE21 4LR **Tel:** 0191-414 2749

Phillips, John, (LBN), c/o St Ambrose, North Rd, Leigh Woods, Bristol BS8 3PW

Phillips, Lamont (Westminster), 729 High Rd, London N17 8AG **Tel:** 020-8808 3554

Phillips, Michael, MA, (OSB), Our Lady Star of the Sea & St Michael, The Priory, Banklands, Workington, Cumbria, CA14 3EP **Tel:** 01900-602114 **Fax:** 01900-871797

Phillips, Peter, BA, MTh, PhD, (Shrewsbury), St Mary of the Angels, Chester Rd, Childer Thornton, Ellesmere Port CH66 1QJ **Tel:** 0151-327 6158 **E-mail:** pw.phillips3@btinternet.com

Phillips, Peter B, MA, Canon, (Westminster, retired), The Presbytery, Maresfield Gardens, Swiss Cottage NW3 5SU

Tel: 020-7431 6192

Philpot, Anthony, Mgr, STL, (East Anglia, retired), 48 Tollgate, Bretton, Peterborough PE3 9XA **Tel:** 01733 331990

Phipps, Terence, MA, STL, (Westminster), 22 George St, London W1H 5RB **Tel:** 020-7935 0943

Phiri, Felix (MAfr), 46 Woodville Gardens, Ealing, London W5 1LQ **Tel:** 020-8998 8552

Piccolomini, Charis, (Westminster), c/o Archbishop's Ho, Ambrosden Ave, London SW1P 1QJ

Pidluskyj, Lubomyr (Ukrainian), 6 Mansionhouse Rd, Edinburgh, Scotland EH9 1TZ **Tel:** 0131-667 5993

Piercy, Anthony P, Canon, (Birmingham, retired), St Joseph's Home, Queens Park Rd, Harborne B32 2LB **Tel:** 0121-427 2486

Pietros, Midele, OFM, Cap, BA, c/o Franciscan Friary, Cuppin St, Chester CH1 2BN **Tel:** 01244-351331

Pilak, Henryk, (Northampton, retired), 32 New Court, Liston Road, Marlow SL7 1AS **Tel:** 01494-462994

Pilsner, Joseph, (CSB), Campion Hall, Oxford OX1 1QS **Tel:** 01865-286112

Pimlott, Stephen, (Birmingham), 32 Vale Rd, Stourport, Worcs DY13 8YL **Tel:** 01299-822633

Pinot de Moira, Michael, (Westminster), St Edmund's College, Old Hall Green, Ware, Herts **Tel:** 01920-821334

Pinsent, Andrew (Arundel & Brighton), c/o The Presbytery, Irelands Way, Lewes, E. Sussex BN7 1QX

Pisiak, Czeslaw (MIC), Fawley Court, Henley-on-Thames, Oxon RG9 3AE **Tel:** 01491-574917

Pitre, Peter, (CSJ), 79 Barking Rd, Canning Town, London E16 4HB **Tel:** 020 7476 4129

Pitt, Bernard, (Hexham & Newcastle), St Teresa's, James St, Annfield Plain, Stanley, Co Durham DH9 7SL **Tel:** 01207-234388 **Fax:** 01207-237947 **E-mail:** bernard-pitt@msn.com

Pitya, Moses (AJ), The Presbytery, St Elizabeth's Rd, Foleshill, Coventry CV6 5BX **Tel:** 024-7668 8536

Plant, Robert, (Plymouth), Holy Cross, Station Rd, Topsham, Exeter EX3 0EE **Tel:** 01392-873898

Platts, Michael (OP), Rosary Priory, Elstree Rd, Bushey, Watford WD23 4EE **Tel:** 020-8950 4315

Plona, Pietro, (IMC), Consolata Missionary College, Totteridge Green, London N20 8PL

Plourde, Robert, Canon (Westminster), 28

Love Lane, Pinner, Middx HA5 3EX **Tel:** 020-8866 0098

Plumb, Joseph, (Hexham & Newcastle), Vicariato Apostolico de Iquitos, Apartado 108, Iquitos, Peru, S. America

Plummer, Anthony, (Southwark), Our Lady of Sorrows, Friary Rd, Peckham SE15 1RH **Tel:** 0207 639 0947

Plunkett, Richard, (Southwark), The Presbytery, Arbroath Rd, Eltham, London SE9 6RR **Tel:** 020-8856 4993

Pointer, Geoffrey, (Southwark), The Presbytery, 2a Ingram Rd, Gillingham, Kent ME7 1YL **Tel/Fax:** 01634-852979

Polland, Nigel, BA (Hons) BD (Hons) D.P. Sch. Phil (Leeds), Immaculate Heart Presbytery, 294 Harrogate Rd, Leeds LS17 6LE **Tel/Fax:** 0113-2681373

Pollock, Hugh, STL, (Lancaster), Lancaster University Chaplaincy, Bailrigg, Lancaster LA1 4XX **Tel:** 01524-594080

Pondel, Edward, (CSSp), 74 Green Dr, Oxley, Wolverhampton WV10 6DW **Tel:** 01902-422833

Pooavathumkal, Joe, (IC), Mother of God, Greencoat Rd, Leicester LE3 6NZ **Tel:** 0116 287 5232 **E-mail:** joepvH@hotmail.com

Poole, John (OMI), St Mary of the Immaculate Conception, 13 Gatefield St, Crewe CW1 2JP **Tel:** 01270-212533 **Fax:** 01270-216407

Poole, Robert, (Westminster), PO Box 7111, Ottawa, Ontario, Canada K1L 8EZ

Pooley, Michael, (OFM Cap), Our Lady of Angels, Carleton Rd, Erith, Kent DA8 1DN **Tel:** 01322 433193

Popoleski, Frank, X, RAF Station, Croughton, Northants **Tel:** 08692-34471

Porter, Adrian (SJ), John Sinnott Ho, 9 Edge Hill, Wimbledon, London SW19 4LR **Tel:** 020 8947 4251

Posluszny, Christopher, (Hallam), Cathedral House, Norfolk Street, Sheffield S1 2JB **Tel:** 0114 272 2522 **Fax:** 0114 276 3861

Postlethwaite, Nicholas, Provincial (CP), 12 Belgrave Rd, Aigburth, Liverpool L17 7AG **Tel:** 0151-727 2024 **Mbl:** 07720-577324 **E-mail:** npostlethwaite@ukonline.co.uk

Potrido Gomilao, Cirino (CM), 29 Eversley Crescent, Isleworth TW7 4RL **Tel:** 020 8560 7021

Potter, David STL, MA, PhD (Liverpool), Chaplain University Hosp. Aintree, 2 Sunloch Cl, Aintree, Liverpool L9 0PA **Tel:** 0151-523 7261

Poulsom, Martin, BSc, BA, MTh, MPhil, DPhil, (SDB), Rinaldi Ho, 32 Orbel St, Battersea, London SW11 3NZ **Tel:** 0207 801 9040 **Tel:** 0207 801 9041 **E-mail:** martinpsdb@hotmail.com

Pound, Rufus, (OCSO), Our Lady and St Bernard, Mount St Bernard Abbey, Coalville, Leicester LE67 5UL **Tel:** 01530-832298/832022 **Fax:** 01530-814608

Powell, Eric (SDS), Our Lady of Victories Presbytery, Pearse St, Sallynoggin, Dun Laoghaire, Co Dublin, Eire **Tel:** 00-353 1 2854667 **Fax:** 00-353 1 2847024

Powell, Mark (Prior and Parish Priest) (OAR), 363 Kennington Lane, Vauxhall, London SE11 5QY **Tel:** 020-7735 1862

Powell, Michael, (Leeds, retired), 17 Kendal Garth, Townville, Castleford WF10 3TA **Tel:** 01977-510266 **E-mail:** michaelpowellm49@hotmail.com

Power, Dermot, BA, BD, STL, STD (Westminster), 28 Beaufort St, London SW3 5AA **Tel:** 020-7349 5628

Power, Desmond, (Liverpool, retired), 5 Charnley Place, Liverpool L15 6WA

Power, Eamonn, BSc(Hons), MA (Brentwood), The Presbytery, Brook Rd, Newbury Park, Ilford, Essex IG2 7JA **Tel:** 020-8590 2414

Power, Joseph P, (Salford, retired), Ardnagaoithe, Bantry, Co. Cork, Eire

Power, Matthew, (SJ), Loyola Hall, Warrington Rd, Prescot, Merseyside L35 6NZ **Tel:** 0151-426 4137 **Fax:** 0151-431 0115

Power, Michael Aidan, (OSA), St John Stone, Sandbrook Way, Woodvale, Southport PR8 3RN **Tel:** 01704 577722 **Fax:** 01704 570647

Power, Thomas, (Birmingham, retired), 21 Aisling Dr, Clareview, Limerick

Powney, Derek (Brentwood, retired), 1 Eastview Dr, Rayleigh, Essex SS6 9NY **Tel:** 01268-780622

Pozzuoli, Lawrence (OFM Cap) Franciscan Friary, 15 Cuppin St, Chester CH1 2BN **Tel:** 01244-351331

Praeger, Charles (SJ), Corpus Christi, 757 Christchurch Rd, Boscombe, Bournemouth BH7 6AN **Tel:** 01202 436700

Pratt, Martin, Archbishop's Secretary (Birmingham), Archbishop's Ho, 8 Shadwell St, Birmingham B4 6EY **Tel:** 0121-236 9090 **Fax:** 0121-212 0171

Preece, Robert, (Northampton), Our Lady of Walsingham, Occupation Rd, Corby, Northants NN17 1EE **Tel/Fax:** 01536-203121 **E-mail:** ourlady.corby@virgin.net

Prescott, Aidan, BSc, (Liverpool), St Clare's, Arundel Ave, Liverpool L17 2AU **Tel:** 0151-733 2374 **Fax:** 0151-280 6062

Press, Francis, (Westminster), 4 Egerton Gardens, London NW4 4BA

Tel: 020-8202 0560
Preston, Francis, BD, BA, (SDB) Ratisbonne Monastery, 26 Rehov Shemuel Hanagid, PO Box 7336, 91702 Jerusalem **Tel:** 00972 026258677 **Fax:** 00972 026259172 **E-mail:** fprestonsdb@hotmail.com
Preston, Graham, (Southwark), 72 Paradise St, Rotherhithe SE16 4HT **Tel:** 020-7237 2969
Preston, Hugh, BD, BA, (SDB), Thornleigh Ho, Sharples Park, Bolton BL1 6PQ **Tel:** 01204 591 144 **E-mail:** hughpreston@tiscali.co.uk
Preston, James (Liverpool), St Bedes Presbytery, Appleton Village, Widnes WA8 6EL **Tel:** 0151 424 2738 **Fax:** 0151 423 2299
Preston, Peter (SDS), Provincial Superior, 129 Spencer Rd, Harrow Weald, Middx HA3 7BJ **Tel:** 020-8426 0495 **Email:** gbprovsds@btconnect.com
Price, Greg STL (Hexham & Newcastle), St Joseph, Wallsend Rd, North Shields, Tyne and Wear NE29 7AA **Tel:** 0191-257 5801
Price, John, (Salford), St John Southworth, 5 Park Dr, Nelson BB9 0TY **Tel/Fax:** 01282-614859 **E-mail** johnpr@fish.co.uk
Price, Justin Arbery, BSc, PhL, MEd, (OSB), St Austin, 561 Aigburth Rd, Grassendale, Liverpool L19 0NU **Tel:** 0151-427 3033 **Fax:** 0151-494 0600
Price, Philip, (Salford), English Martyrs, The Sands, Whalley, Lancs BB7 9TN **Tel:** 01254-823283
Price, Richard, (Westminster), Heythrop College, University of London, Kensington Square W8 5HQ **Tel:** 020-7795 4209
Prieto, Francisco, (CM), 47 Palace Court, Bayswater, London W2 4LS **Tel:** 020-7229 8815
Primavesi, Anthony DSc, FIS, MIBiol (IC), St Marie's Presbytery, Oak St, Rugby CV22 5EL **Tel:** 01788-542703
Prince, Kevin, BD, Chaplain JSSU (AN) c/o Principal RC Chaplain (Army), HQ Land Command, Erskine Barracks, Wilton, Salisbury SP2 0AG **Tel:** 01722 433892
Prince, Malcolm, BA, DipRE (Liverpool), St Luke's Presbytery, Shaw Lane, Whiston, Prescot L35 5AT **Tel:** 0151-426 6795 **Fax:** 0151-426 5755
Prior, Basil, (OSM), The Priory, 500 Bury New Rd, Salford M7 4WP **Tel:** 0161-792 2152
Prior, David H, MA (Brentwood), The Presbytery, 14 Guithavon St, Witham, Essex CM8 1BN **Tel:** 01376-512219
Pritchard, Christopher, (Southwark), St Mary Magdalen's, 61 North Worple Way, Mortlake, London SW14 8PR **Tel:** 020-8876 1326
Pritchard, Stephen, (Liverpool), Archdiocesan Youth Chaplain, St Mary, Lowe Ho, Crab St, St Helens WA10 2BE **Tel:** 01744-22167 **Fax:** 01744-739154
Probert, Wulstan, Very Rev, (OSB), Belmont Abbey, Hereford HR2 9RZ **Tel:** 01432-277388
Proctor, Gerald, BA (Liverpool), Liverpool Archdiocesan Centre for Evangelisation, Croxteth Dr, Liverpool L17 1AA
Przybylski, Pawel, Mgr, DD, (Westminster, retired), 45 Twyford Ave, London W3 9QB **Tel:** 020-8993 7431
Przybysz, Jan, (MIC), (Northampton, retired), Fawley Court, Henley-on-Thames, Oxon RG9 3AE **Tel:** 01491-574917
Przyjalkowski, Voytek, BD, MTh, (Westminster), 60 Highbury Park, London N5 2XH **Tel:** 020-7226 0257
Psaila, Anthony, (Westminster), 94 Bath Rd, Hounslow, Middx TW3 3EH **Tel:** 020-8570 1693
Pugh, Philip, (SJ), 66 Westoning Rd, Harlington, Beds LU5 6PD **Tel:** 01525-875445 **E-mail:** graham.pugin@campion.ox.ac.uk
Pugin, Graham, (SJ), Campion Hall, Oxford OX1 1QS **Tel:** 01865-286113 **E-mail:** graham.pugin@campion.ox.ac.uk
Purakkal, Dominic Joseph K, BA, BPh, DipSpirituality (OSB), The Presbytery, 128 Priory Rd, Milford Haven SA73 2EE **Tel:** 01646-693371
Purbrick, Michael, (Portsmouth), St Thomas of Canterbury, 22 Terminus Rd, Cowes, Isle of Wight PO31 7TJ **Tel:** 01983-292739 **Mbl:** 07960-360210
Purcell, James, (Middlesbrough, retired), Marie Goretti Nursing Home, Co Limerick, Éire
Purcell, Louis, (MHM), All Soul's Presbytery, 622 Liverpool St, Salford M5 5HQ **Tel:** 0161 737 9742
Purnell, Patrick, (SJ), Corpus Christi Jesuit Community, 757 Christchurch Rd, Boscombe, Bournemouth BH7 6AN **Tel:** 01202-436700 **E-mail:** patrickpurnell@fish.co.uk
Purnell, Steven, (Arundel & Brighton), 17 St James' Rd, East Grinstead, W. Sussex RH19 1DL **Tel:** 01342-325705
Purtill, Michael, (Hexham & Newcastle), Corpus Christi, Kelvin Grove, Gateshead, Tyne and Wear NE8 4QP **Tel:** 0191-477 1428
Puthussery, Robert (OCarm), 63 East End Rd, East Finchley N2 0SE

Tel: 020-8346 1458 **Fax:** 020-8343 0942

Pyle, Anthony, (Southwark, retired), 149a St Richard's Rd, Deal, Kent CT14 9LD **Tel:** 01304-360260 **E-mail:** tonypyle@hotmail.com

Pyle, Leo, (Hexham & Newcastle), St John's North Bank, Haydon Bridge, Hexham NE47 6LP **Tel:** 01434-684265

Pyster, Andrzej, (Wloclawek, Polish Priest), 32 Bristol Rd, Sheffield S11 8RL **Tel:** 0114-266 3952

Quadri, Giancarlo, 22 Portland Rd, Birmingham B16 9HS

Quarmby, David, (Portsmouth), 15 Kilmington Way, Highcliffe, Christchurch, Dorset BH23 5BL **Tel/Fax:** 01425-274838 **E-mail:** djquarmby@hotmail.com

Queenan, Martin (Clifton), 28 Baytree Rd, Milton, Weston-super-Mare BS22 8HQ **Tel:** 01934-627137

Quigley, Gerard, (East Anglia), Coldham Cottage, Bury Rd, Lawshall, Bury St Edmunds, Suffolk IP29 4PL **Tel/Fax:** 01284-830393 **E-mail:** kwakarider@lineone.net

Quigley Joseph,BA, PhB, STB (Birmingham), St Charles Borromeo, Hampton-on-the-Hill, Warks CV35 8QR

Quigley, Leonard N, Canon, (Wrexham), 6 Fron Heulog, Hawarden Deeside, Flintshire **Tel:** 01244-537874

Quigley, Seamus, (Salford), St Anne, Cobham Rd, Accrington BB5 2AD **Tel:** 01254-232920

Quiligotti, David, Chaplain (Salford), 53 Brook Rd, Urmston, Manchester M41 5RY. **Tel:** 0161-755 3468

Quin-Morris, Laurence, (Arundel & Brighton), The Presbytery, 122 Ladbrooke Rd, Redhill, Surrey RH1 1LF **Tel:** 01737-761017 **Fax:** 01737-763061 **E-mail:** iqunmorris@btopenworld.com.

Quinlan, Michael, Mgr Canon, DCL (Salford), St Winifred's, Mauldeth Rd, Heaton Mersey, Stockport SK4 3NB **Tel:** 0161-432 4412 **Fax:** 0161-975 0120

Quinlan, Michael, Canon, (Arundel & Brighton), St Joseph's Nursing Home, East St, Littlehampton, W. Sussex BN17 6AU **Tel:** 01903-721053

Quinlan, Patrick, (Salford, retired), 13 Caldbeck Ave, Heaton, Bolton BL1 5PR **Tel:** 01204-492533

Quinlan, Richard, Canon, (Southwark), Our Lady of Pity and St Simon Stock, Hazlewell Rd, Putney, London SW15 6LU **Tel:** 020-8788 1131

Quinn, Anthony, (Arundel & Brighton, retired), 11 Cullycapple Rd, Aghadowey, Co Derry, N Ireland BT51 4AR

Quinn, Edward, (OMI), St Anne's Presbytery, Highfield Rd, Rock Ferry, Birkenhead, Merseyside CH42 2BY **Tel:** 0151-645 3996 **Fax:** 0151-645 0419 **E-mail:** stanne.rf@ntlworld.com

Quinn, Gerard, BA, STL, (Westminster), 44 Boston Park Rd, Brentford, Middx **Tel:** 0208-560 1671

Quinn, John, (Clifton), 25 Countess Court, London Rd, Amesbury, Salisbury SP4 7EP **Tel:** 01980-622177

Quinn, Peter, MA (SDB), Saint John Ho, 121A Reading Rd, Farnborough GU14 6NZ **Tel:** 01252 554 300

Quinn, Philip, (Hexham & Newcastle), St Wilfrid's, 128 Bondicar Terr, Blyth, Northumberland NE24 2JZ **Tel:** 01670-2352513

Quinn, Thomas, (Westminster), 38 Camborne Ave, Northfields, Middx W13 9QZ **Tel:** 020-8567 5421

Quirke, John, (Leeds, retired), Mount St Joseph's, Shire Oak Rd, Leeds LS6 2DE **Tel:** 0113-278 4101

Quirke, Thomas, BSc, HDipEd, (Lancaster, retired), St Winefride's Ho, Low Moor Rd, Bispham, Blackpool, Lancs FY2 0PA **Tel:** 01253-592850

Radcliffe, Fabian, (OP), Holy Cross Priory, Wellington St, Leicester LE1 6HW **Tel:** 0116-255 6902

Radcliffe, Timothy MA, Hon DD, Hon DHumLit, Hon STD, HonLLD (OP), Blackfriars, St Giles, Oxford OX1 3LY **Tel:** 01865-278422

Raf'at, Behruz, BTh(Southwark), c/o Archbishop's Ho, 150 St George's Rd, London SE1 6HX

Rafferty, Dominic, (Northampton, retired), Earlsquarter, Riverstown, Dundalk, Co. Louth, Ireland

Rafferty, James BA, DCV (CM), Sacred Heart Presbytery, 2 Flower Lane, Mill Hill, London NW7 2JB **Tel:** 020-8959 1021

Rafferty, John, STL, PhL (Shrewsbury), St Vincent's, 2 Bentinck Rd, Altrincham, WA14 2BP **Tel:** 0161-928 1689 **Fax:** 0161-929 8972 **E-mail:** johnarafferty@btconnect.com

Rafferty, Oliver, (SJ), Mount St Jesuits 114 Mount St, London W1K 3AH **Tel:** 020 7493 7811 **Fax:** 0020 7495 6685

Raftery, Eamon (CM), 82 West Street, Dunstable, Beds LU6 1NY **Tel:** 01582 662710

Rainbow, Robert A, AMIMechE, (Clifton), 57 Mantle St, Wellington TA21 8AX **Tel:** 01823-662283

Rainey, Sean (SSC), Columba Ho, 163 Horton Grange Rd, Bradford BD7 2DN **Tel:** 01274-571975

Ramsay, Charles, (Wrexham), 119 Wellington Rd, Rhyl, Denbighshire

LL18 1LE **Tel:** 01745 353395
Fax: 01745 330364
E-mail: chas3free@aol.com

Ramsay, Hayden, MA, PhD, (OP), Priory of the Holy Spirit, 64 St Giles, Blackfriars OX1 3LY **Tel:** 01865-278400

Ranahan, George, Provincial Delegate (SCA), 35 Amwell St, Clerkenwell EC1R 1UL **Tel:** 020-7837 2094 **Fax:** 020-7837 2724 **E-mail:** seoirse@aol.com

Randall, Peter, (SJ) St Ignatius, 27 High Rd, London N15 6ND **Tel:** 020-8800 2121 **E-mail:** peterarandall@googlemail.com

Randolph, Hugh (OCSO) Abbey of Our Lady and St Samson, Caldey Island, off Tenby SA70 7UH **Tel:** 01834-842632 and 842879

Randolph, Richard, MA (SJ), Campion Hall, Brewer St, Oxford OX1 1QS **Tel:** 01865-286129

Raniey, Sean (SCC), Columba Ho, 163 Horton Grange Rd, Bradford BD7 2DN **Tel:** 01274-571194

Rataj, Alfons, Canon, (Northampton, retired), Laxton Hall, Nr Corby, Northants NN17 3AU **Tel:** 01780-444 242

Ratcliffe, Gerard, (CSSR), St Benet's, Monkwearmouth, Sunderland SR6 0BH **Tel:** 0191-567 2965 **Fax:** 0191-565 4054

Rathappillil, Thomas, (Leeds), Anagari Estate, Perumal Malai PO, Kodaikanal 624104, Tamil Nadu, India

Rathe, Thomas, (WF), Oak Lodge, 48 Totteridge Rd, London N20 8LZ **Tel:** 020-8959 1515

Ratlidge, Bernard, (Leeds, retired), 25 Garden Cl,Ossett, WF5 0SQ

Rattigan, Anthony BA, CQSW (OP), St Dominic's Priory, Southampton Rd, NW5 4LB **Tel:** 020 7482 9210

Raybould, Joseph, (SJ), 114 Mount St, London W1K 3AH **Tel:** 020-7493 7811

Rayner, Douglas, (IC, retired), The Presbytery, 151, Cromwell Rd, Newport NP19 0HS **Tel:** 01633-277440

Rea, Christopher, (CRL), Christ Church, 229 High St, Eltham, London SE9 1TX **Tel:** 020-8850 1666

Rea, David, (Arundel & Brighton), Priests Ho, Vermont Dr, East Preston, Littlehampton, W. Sussex BN16 1JU **Tel:** 01903-785091

Rea, Kevin, Canon, (Plymouth, retired), The Presbytery, 1a Moor View, Torpoint, Cornwall PL11 2LH **Tel:** 01752-812347

Rea, Paul, (CRL), St James, Old Rd (off Canal Hill), Tiverton, Devon **Tel:** 01664-252292

Read, Gordon, Mgr, MA, BD, JCL, (Brentwood), The Presbytery, Church St, Kelvedon, Colchester, Essex CO5 9AH **Tel:** 01376-570348

Reader, Roger, BA (Westminster), Chaplain, HM Young Offenders Institution, Bedfont Rd, Feltham, Middx TW13 4ND **Tel:** 020-8844 5326

Reading, Paul, (Southwark), c/o Archbishop's Ho, St George's Rd, London SE1 6HX

Rear, Michael, (East Anglia, retired), The Presbytery, 29 Wells Rd, Fakenham, Norfolk NR21 9EG **Tel:** 01328-862110 **E-mail:** rearmj@aol.com

Reardon, Richard (Cardiff), The Presbytery, St Michael St, Newport NP20 2BZ **Tel:** 01633 676876

Reardon, Robert, Mng, (Cardiff), Archbishop's Ho, 41-43 Cathedral Rd, Cardiff CF11 9HD **Tel** 029-2037 9494 **Fax:** 029-2037 9036

Rebello, Alex Mgr (Bombay), Church of Our Lady of Sorrows, Meyrick St, Dolgellau, Gwynedd LL40 1LR **Tel:** 01342-422805 **E-mail:** olssdolgellau@ wrexhamdiocese.fsnet.co.uk

Recio, Jesus Gabriel, (OAR), The Latin American Chaplaincy, 363 Kennington Ln, Vauxhall, London SE11 5QY

Reddan, Michael Charles, (SDS), 26 Castle St, Thornbury, Bristol BS35 1HA **Tel:** 01454-854586

Redford, John, STL, LSS, DD, (Southwark), Maryvale Institute, Old Oscott Hill, Kingstanding, Birmingham B44 9AG

Redlinski, Piotr, MA (SChr), Polish Centre, Ravenna Rd, London SW15 6AW **Tel:** 020-8788 3933

Redman, Alexander, BA, STB (Clifton), 95 Exeter St, Salisbury SP1 2SF **Tel:** 01722-333581

Redmond, Paul, STL, (Leeds), Christ the King Presbytery, Houghley Ln, Bramley Leeds LS13 2DX **Tel/Fax:** 0113 257 4740

Redmond, Paulinus, BA, (Hermit) The Hermitage, 3 Horton Dr, Rhos-on-Sea, Colwyn Bay LL28 2AG

Redmond, William, MA, LSS (Liverpool), Our Lady of Perpetual Succour Presbytery, Mayfield Ave, Hough Green, Widnes WA8 8PR **Tel:** 0151-424 4021 **Fax:** 0151-424 2531

Reece, Philip (Liverpool), St Bede's Presbytery, Appleton Village, Widnes WA8 6EL **Tel/Fax:** 0151-424 3841

Rees, David, Harding, (Menevia, retired), 7 Gerddi Rheidol, Aberystwyth SY23 1DB

Reeve, Derek, BTh (Portsmouth), 12 Riverhead Cl, Portsmouth PO4 8SN **Tel:** 023-9282 7881 **E-mail:** derek@jwis.fsnet.co.uk

Reeves, Brian, (Plymouth, Retired), The Presbytery, 55 Salisbury St, Shaftesbury, Dorset SP7 8EL **Tel:** 01747-852125

Regan, Frank, (SSC), 28 Redington Rd, Hampstead, London NW3 7RB

Regan, Padraig, (CM), 7a Grenfell Rd, Mitcham CR4 2BZ **Tel:** 020 8685 0974

Regan, Thomas BA (OSB), Priory of Our Lady & St Michael, 10 Pen-y-Pound, Abergavenny, Gwent NP7 5UD **Tel:** 01873-856660

Reid, Darren, (Hallam), The Presbytery. Mere Lane, Arnthorpe, Doncaster DN3 2DB **Tel:** 01302 831 395

Reid, Francis, (Southwark), Our Lady of the Assumption, 282 Links Rd, Tooting, London SW17 9ER **Tel:** 020-8769 4391

Reid, John, (Hexham & Newcastle), Cumberland Terr, Willington, Co Durham DL15 0PB **Tel:** 01388-746220

Reid, Paul, (Leeds, retired), 11 Avondale Court, Leeds LS17 6DT **Tel:** 0113-226 5809

Reid, Richard (CSsR), The Redemptorist Team, Badby Rd West, Daventry, Northants NN11 4NH

Reidy, Raymond, (SPS), Holy Redeemer, Wrexham Rd, Slough SL2 5QR

Reilly, Duane, (Leeds), English Martyrs Presbytery, Teddington Ave, Dalton, Huddersfield HD5 9HS **Tel:** 01484 327007

Reilly, Michael, (Liverpool), Ince Blundell Hall, Ince Blundell, Liverpool L38 6JL **Tel:** 0151-929 2596

Reilly, Peter J, Canon, (Birmingham, retired), 84 Blackford Rd, Shirley, Solihull B90 4BX **Tel:** 0121-472 0190

Reith, Stephen, (Northampton, retired), 2 Norwich Rd, North Walsham, Norfolk NR28 9JP **Tel:** 01692-403567

Reney, Benedict (OCarm), 63 East End Rd, East Finchley, London N2 0SE **Tel:** 020-8346 1458

Restori, Steven, BTh (Portsmouth), Bishop's Ho, Edinburgh Rd, Portsmouth PO1 3HG

Reville, John, BA(Hons), CertEd, DipCat (Clifton), 8 Folkestone Rd, Swindon, Wilts SN1 3NH **Tel:** 01793-526933

Reyes, Carlito, 35 Margaret Street, Ammanford, Carmarthenhsire SA18 2NP **Tel:** 01269 592 533

Reynell, Michael, Canon (Arundel & Brighton), 12 Church Rd, Selsey, W Sussex PO20 0LS **Tel:** 01243-602312

Reynolds, Anthony, KHS (Liverpool), Our Lady's Presbytery, Downall Green Rd, Bryn, Ashton-in-Makerfield, Wigan WN4 0LZ **Tel:** 01942-727271

Reynolds, Brian, (Westminster), 7 Marford Rd, Wheathampstead, Herts AL4 8AY **Tel:** 01582-832114

Reynolds, Henry, (Southwark, retired) St Peter's Residence, Meadow Road, Vauxhall, London SW8 1QH

Reynolds, John M, KCHS, (Salford, retired), School Cottage, Kells, Co Kilkenny Eire

Reynolds, Neil Francis, BEd, (Westminster), 1 Peppard Cl, Redbourne, St Albans AL3 7EB **Tel:** 01582-792270

Reynolds, Peter A, (IC), St Peter's, St Peter's St, Roath, Cardiff CF24 3BA **Tel:** 029-2048 3394 **Fax:** 029-2045 1535

Reynolds, Stephen, (Opus Dei), 231 Nithsdale Rd, Glasgow G41 5HA

Rhys, David MA, (Southwark), Presbytery, Haig Rd, TN16 3LJ **Tel:** 01959-571404

Rice, Brendan, (Liverpool), St Mary's, Lowe House, Crab St, St Helen's WA10 2BE **Tel:** 01744 740467 **E-mail:** brendan.rice@rcadolp.co.uk

Rice, Francis, STL, PhL, (Shrewsbury), St John's, 128 Bebington Rd, New Ferry, Wirral CH62 5BJ **Tel:** 0151-645 3314 **E-mail:** stjohntheevangelist@gmail.com

Rice, John, MA, (Plymouth), The Presbytery, Holy Trinity Parish Centre, Culliford Road North, Dorchester DT1 1QG **Tel:** 01305-251976

Richardson, Andrew, 2, The Grove, Kettering NN15 7QQ **Tel:** 01536 512497

Richardson, Charles, (Plymouth), John's Ho, 7 Wokefield Way, Ecclestone, St Helens WA10 4QP **Tel:** 021-903 6961

Richardson, John (Plymouth, Retired), The Presbytery, Clodgey Lane, Helston, Cornwall TR13 8PT **Tel:** 01326-572378

Richardson, Laurence BSc, MA, STD, (Opus Dei), 18 Netherhall Gardens, London NW3 5TH **Tel:** 020-7472-5730

Richardson, Niven (Arundel & Brighton), 54 Sutton Rd, Seaford, E. Sussex **Tel:** 01323 892427

Richardson, Robert, (OSB), Douai Abbey, Upper Woolhampton, Reading Berks, RG7 5TQ **Tel:** 0118-971 5300

Richardson, Terence, BSc, MDiv, VF (OSB), St Benedict's Monastery, Convent Cl, Duddle Lane, Bamber Bridge PR5 6US **Tel:** 01772 902201 **Fax:** 01772 902214

Richer, Edward, DipJur (Portsmouth), Sacred Heart Presbytery, High St, Bordon, Hants GU35 0AD **Tel:** 01420-472415 **Fax:** 01420-475672

Richins, Anthony, BA, FCP, (Southwark), 26 Balham Park Rd, London SW12 8DU **Tel:** 020-8673 2048

Richmond, Ronald, MEd, (Hexham & Newcastle, retired), St Joseph's, Church Lane, Murton, Co. Durham SR7 9RD **Tel:** 0191-526 1116

Ricketts, Graham (Arundel & Brighton), Eastfield, Steyning Rd, Rottingdean, E. Sussex BN2 7GA **Tel:** 01273-302903 **E-mail:** graham.ricketts@dabnet.org

Riezu, Robert, STL, JCL, (OAR), 18 Cheniston Gardens, London W8 6TQ

Tel/Fax: 020-7937 7681

Rigby, John, VG (Salford), St Vincent's Presbytery, 40 Newbrook Rd, Over Hulton, Bolton BL5 1ER **Tel:** 01204-651695

Rigden, Jeremy Harry, Mgr Canon VG, MA, STB, (Clifton), Holy Family Presbytery, Marlow Ave, Swindon SN3 2PT **Tel:** 01793-527931

Rij, Jaroslaw, (Ukrainian), 36 Cardinal St, Chedham, Manchester M8 7PS **Tel:** 0161-205 7050 (Home) **Tel:** 0161-795 9924 (Church)

Riley, Martin, (Shrewsbury), Sacred Heart, 31 Whaley Lane, Whaley Bridge, High Peak SK23 7AG **Tel:** 01663-732614, **E-mail:** sacredheartwhaley@btinternet.com

Riley, Reginald MA, (SM), Marist Fathers, 36 Shear Bank Rd, Blackburn, Lancs BB1 8AZ **Tel:** 01254-52074

Riley, Sean, (SM), (Liverpool), St Luke the Evangelist, Shaw Lane, Prescot L35 5AT **Tel:** 0151 426 6795 **Fax:** 0151 426 5755 **E-mail:** stlukeswhiston@lineone.net

Riley, Sidney, (Hexham & Newcastle, Retired), 12 Croxdale Road, Billingham, Cleveland TS23 3DD **Tel:** 01642 561207

Rimini, Kenneth M. MISM, AIM (Westminster), St David's, Everest Rd, Stanwell, Staines TW19 7EE **Tel:** 01784-255973

Riordan, John (Leeds, retired), Kyle Ho, Herbertstown, Co. Limerick, Ireland **Tel:** 00-353-61-85115

Riordan, Patrick (SJ), Superior, Copleston Ho, 221 Goldhurst Terr, London NW6 3EP **Tel:** 020 7604 5857 **Fax:** 020 7604 5850 **E-mail:** p.riordan@heythrop.ac.uk

Ritaccio, Antonio, STB (Westminster), Corpus Christi Presbytery, c/o Archbishop's Ho, SW1P 1QJ **Tel:** 0207-836 4700

Ritchie, Neil, BA(Hons), DipHE, MBACP, (Liverpool), Ushaw College, Durham DH7 9RH **Tel:** 0191 373 8531 **E-mail:** neil.ritchie@ushaw.ac.uk

Roach, John T, (Leeds, retired), 13 D'Arcy Rd, Selby, Yorks YO8 8BS **Tel:** 01757-707567

Roban, Myles, (SSC), St Columban's Widney Manor Rd, Knowle, Solihull, W. Mids B93 9AB **Tel:** 01564-772096

Roberts, David, (Shrewsbury), Holy Angels, Wicker Lane, Hale Barns, Altrincham WA15 0HF **Tel:** 0161-980 4784 **E-mail:** robertdm@talk21.com

Roberts, Leslie, (OFM), Kingshurst Court, Kingshurst Dr, Paignton, Devon TQ3 2TL

Robertson, Michael, (Clifton), St Bonaventure's Presbytery, Egerton Rd, Bishopston, Bristol BS7 8HP **Tel:** 01117-942 4448 **E-mail:** mjdrobertson@btinernet.com

Robertson, Peter, (Shrewsbury), St Joseph's, 6 Moreton Rd, Upton, Wirral CH49 6LJ **Tel:** 0151-677 2185 **Fax:** 0151-677 8426 **E-mail:** parishpriest@talktalk.net

Robinson, Alan (Westminster), The Parish Ho, Moorhouse Rd, Bayswater W2 5DJ. **Tel:** 020-7229 0487 **Fax:** 020-7229 3223

Robinson, Andrew, STB, MA (Liverpool), Metropolitan Cathedral of Christ the King, Mount Pleasant, Liverpool L3 5TQ **Tel:** 0151 709 9222 **Fax:** 0151 708 7274

Robinson, Dominic, (SJ), Mount St Jesuits, 114 Mount Street, London W1K 3AH **Tel:** 0020 7493 7811

Robinson, Francis, Mgr, BA, (Leeds), St Francis of Assisi, Bismarck St, Leeds LS11 6TN **Tel:** 0113-270 6962 **E-mail:** frobinson@holbeckleeds.fs.co.uk

Robinson, Frederick, ALAM, (Shrewsbury, retired), 26 Winstanley Rd, Little Neston, Neston CH64 0UZ **Tel:** 0151-336 4051

Robinson, Gerard MBA, MTh, MA Lit, (Middlesbrough), Sacred Heart Presbytery, 1 Park Rd South, Middlesbrough TS5 6LD **Tel:** 01642-850113 **Fax:** 01642-852122 **E-mail:** gerard.paul@btopenworld.com

Robinson, James, PhL, (Shrewsbury), St Peter's, Henley Rd, Ludlow SY8 1QZ **Tel:** 01584-872906

Robinson, Joseph A, (Liverpool), Burscough Hall, Lathom, Ormskirk, Lancs L40 7RA **Tel:** 01704-892205 **Fax:** 01704-892850

Robinson, Kevin, (Southwark), c/o Archbishop's Ho, 150 St George's Rd, London SE1 6HX

Robinson, Thomas M, (OSM), St Mary's Priory, 264 Fulham Rd, London SW10 9EL **Tel:** 020-73526965

Robson, George, BSc, (SDB), St Dominic, Southdean Rd, Huyton, Liverpool L14 8UL **Tel:** 0151-489 1684 **Fax:** 0151-482 6053

Robson, Michael, (OFM Conv), St Edmund's College, Mount Pleasant, Cambridge CB3 0BN **Tel:** 01223-350398

Robson, Simon-Sebastian (OP), Holy Cross Priory, 45 Wellington St, Leicester LE1 6HW **Tel:** 0116-255 3956 **Fax:** 0116-255 5552

Rocca, Anacleto, (SC), 271 Gladstone St, Peterborough, Cambs PE1 2BV **Tel:** 01733-65527

Roche, Jeremiah, (SPS), Holy Redeemer, Wrexham Rd, Slough, Berks SL2 5QR **Tel:** 01753-520621

Roche, Michael, BA (OSA), (Prior), St Mary's Priory, 111 Vivian Rd, Harborne, Birmingham B17 0DN **Tel:** 0121-427 2538 **Fax:** 0121-428 3656

Roche, William, Canon, (Clifton, retired), Flat 3, St John's Flats, South Parade, Bath BA2 4AF **Tel:** 01225-464147

Rock, Thomas J, MA, (Birmingham, retired), 4 Hunter's Gate, Much Wenlock, Salop TF13 6BW **Tel:** 01952-728012

Roddy, Austin (Leeds, retired), Mount St Joseph's Home, Shire Oak Rd, Leeds LS6 2DE

Rodgers, Gerald, Canon (Clifton, retired), 137 Gloucester Rd, Patchway, Bristol BS34 5JG **Tel:** 0117-908 6088

Rodgers, Terence, STL, MA, (Lancaster), St Monica's, 2 St Monica's Way, Blackpool FY4 4FA **Tel:** 01253 761623

Rodrigues, Lucas, (SFX), SS Peter and Paul, Cranmer Rd, Mitcham CR4 4LD **Tel:** 0208-648 3800

Rogers, Anthony, Mgr (East Anglia), Hills Rd, Cambridge, CB2 1JR **Tel:** 01223-350787

Rogers, Michael, (OSM), Servite Priory, 500 Bury New Rd, Salford, Lancs, M7 4WP **Tel:** 0161-792 2152

Rogers, Peter, BA (Arundel & Brighton, retired), 10 Westbury Lodge, Queen's Lane, Arundel, W. Sussex BN18 9RZ

Rogers, Peter John, (Birmingham), 26 Leamington Rd, Broadway, Worcester WR12 7EA **Tel:** 01386-853753

Rogers, Stephen, (MSC), St Albert, 31 Hollow Croft, Stockbridge Village, Liverpool L28 4EA **Tel:** 0151-228 7126

Rogerson, Cecil, (Birmingham), 46 Vicarage Rd, Wollaston, Stourbridge DY8 4NP **Tel:** 01384 395674

Rohan, Anthony, (Birmingham), Holy Family, 763 Coventry Rd, Small Heath, Birmingham B10 0HT **Tel:** 0121-772 0059 **Fax:** 0121-773 1485

Rollings, Peter, (East Anglia), The Presbytery, North Everard Street, King's Lynn, Norfolk PE30 5HQ **Tel:** 01553-772220

Rolls, Bernard Martin, (OSA), BA, STL, Clare Priory, Clare, Suffolk CO10 8NX **Tel:** 01787 277326

Rolls, Dominic, MA(Hon), STL, (Arundel & Brighton), 2 Falkland Grove, Dorking, Surrey RH4 3DL **Tel:** 01306-882433

Rolph, Edward, (sP), Our Lady of Victory, Brownshill, Stroud, Glos GL6 8AL **Tel:** 01453-883084 **Fax:** 01453-731888

Rolph, W Alan, (Brentwood), c/o Cathedral Ho, Ingrave Rd, Brentwood, Essex CM15 8AT

Ronan, Michael, (Cardiff), St Gabriel's Presbytery, 141 Ringland Circle, Newport NP19 9PQ **Tel:** 01633-272144

Rooke, William, (Hexham & Newcastle), Our Lady and St Vincent, Monkchester Rd, Newcastle-upon-Tyne NE6 2TX **Tel:** 0191-265 5217.

Rooney, James, (Northampton, retired), 68 The Farthings, Astley Village, Chorley PR7 1SH **Tel:** 01257-270814

Rooney, John, MA, MSc, PhD, (MHM), Kearsney Manor Nursing Home, Alkham Valley Rd, Kearsney, Dover Kent CT16 3EQ **Tel:** 01304 822266

Rooney, Joseph (SM), Marist Fathers, Notre Dame de France, 5 Leicester Place, London WC2H 7BP **Tel:** 020-7437 9363 **Fax:** 020-7437 3857

Rose, Frederick, (Liverpool), 27 Silvester St, Liverpool L5 8SE **Tel:** 0151-207 0161 **Fax:** 0151-298 2626

Rose, Jonathan BA, (Hexham & Newcastle), St Marys, Vart Rd, Woodhouse Close Estate, Bishop Auckland DL14 6PQ **Tel:** 01388-603431

Rose, William, (OS Cam), 102 Hassett Rd, Hackney, London E9 5SJ **Tel:** 020-8986 5181

Ross, Clive ACII (Southwark), St Saviour and St John Baptist and Evangelist. High St, Lewisham SE13 6AA **Tel:** 020-8852 2490 **Fax:** 020-8852 2262

Rosser, Peter, (Leeds), St Augustine's Presbytery, Harehills Rd, Leeds LS8 5HR **Tel:** 0113-249 0762 **E-mail:** prosser@leeds-diocese.org.uk

Rossiter, Aidan Peter, BSc, STB, MA, (CJ), 1 Island Row, 636 Commercial Rd, London E14 7HS **Tel:** 020-7987 3563

Rossiter, Francis, Rt Rev Abbot, JCL, DD(Hon) (OSB), Ealing Abbey, Charlbury Grove, Ealing W5 2DY **Tel:** 020-8862 2100

Rossman, Martin, Fr, The Presbytery, 17 Vickarage Road, Plympton, Plymouth, Devon PL7 4JX **Tel:** 01752-331288

Rothon, Nicholas, Mgr Canon, MA (Southwark), St Mary's, 5 Cresswell Park, Blackheath SE3 9RD **Tel:** 020-8852 5420

Rotter, Paul Richard, (OSB), Buckfast Abbey, Buckfastleigh, Devon TQ11 0EE **Tel:** 01364-645500

Rouco Gutierrez, Hector, BA, BATS (Westminster), 17 Kenninghall Rd, London E5 8BS **Tel:** 020-8985 2178

Round, W A Dominic, MA, PhL, STB (Birmingham), 9 School Lane, Upton-on-Severn, Worcestershire WR8 0LA **Tel:** 01684-592602

Rout, Paul (OFM), Heythrop College, Kesington Gardens, London W8 5HQ

Rowan, John, (Salford, retired), 33 Sergeants Ln, Whitefield, Manchester M45 8NH **Tel:** 0161-766 5961

Rowan, Paul, PhL, STL, (Liverpool), Liverpool Archdiocesan Centre for

Evangelisation, Croxteth Dr, Liverpool L17 1AA

Rowe, Bede, MA(Oxon), MPhil, STB (Clifton), 31 Boreham Rd, Warminster BA12 9JP **Tel:** 01935-212329

Rowe, D Francis, CF, (Birmingham), St Jude's Cl, Maypole, Birmingham B14 5PD **Tel:** 0121-430 6932

Rowe, Richard, (Brentwood, retired), 5 Newbiggen St, Thaxted, Essex CM6 2QS **Tel:** 01371 830808

Rowland, Phelim, Mgr, RAChD (Westminster), Ministry of Defence (Chaplains), Trenchard Lines, Upavon, Pewsey, Wilts SN9 6BE **Tel:** 01980-615803

Rowlands, Andrew, (Liverpool), St Michael's, Oatlands Rd, Westvale, Kirkby L32 4UH **Tel:** 0151-546 9687 **Fax:** 0151-549 2399

Rowles, Mark Joseph, (Cardiff), The Presbytery, Miskin Rd, Mountain Ash CF45 3UA. **Tel:** 01443-473710 **E-mail:** markjrowles@hotmail.com

Rowswell, Bruno (OFM Cap), Franciscan Friary, Carlton Rd, Erith, Kent DA8 1DN **Tel:** 01322-433193

Royles, Vincent, (Birmingham, retired), Presbytery, Hall Rd, Marchington, Uttoxeter, Staffs ST14 8LG **Tel:** 01283-820323

Rozdzenski, Wojciech, MA (SChr) (Polish Priest), 9 Gordon Rd, Derby DE23 6WR. **Tel/Fax:** 01332-343950

Rozzo, Karl, (Salford), Venerabile Collegio Inglese, Via di Monserrato 45, 00186 Roma, Italia **E-mail:** karl.rozzo@virgin.net

Rubaya, Regis, (Gweru), St Saviour, 175 High St, Lewisham, London SE13 6AA **Tel:** 020-8852 2490

Ruddy, Michael, Provincial (SSCC), 372 Uxbridge Rd, Ealing, London W5 3LH **Tel:** 020-8993 6040/8992 5941 **Mbl:** 00353 868 358 145 **E-mail:** mikeruddy@eircom.net

Rudkin, Ivan, (East Anglia), The Presbytery, 21a, St John Steret, Woodbridge, Suffolk IP12 1ED **Tel:** 01394-383551

Ruiz, Javier, STB (Westminster), c/o Archbishop's Ho, Ambrosden Ave, London SW1P 1QJ **Tel:** 020-7937 4778

Ruscillo, Benedict, MA, (Lancaster), 1 Haighton Top Cottages, Haighton Green Lane, Fernyhalgh, Preston PR2 5FR

Ruscillo, Luiz, (Lancaster), St Mary's, 59 Main St, Hornby, Lancaster LA2 8JT **Tel:** 01524-221246

Russ, Timothy, Canon, MA, (Northampton), Damian Ho, 23 High St, Great Missenden, Bucks HP16 9AA **Tel:** 01494-862049

Russell, Brian, (CSsR), St Leonard, Tunstall Village, Silksworth, Sunderland SR3 2BB **Tel:** 0101-521 0355

Russell, David, (Arundel & Brighton), 18 Parker Court, Portslade, East Sussex BN41 2FT **Tel:** 01273-415799

Russell, David, (Hexham & Newcastle), St Edward, Coquet Ave, Whitley Bay NE26 1EE **Tel:** 0191-252 8021

Russell, George, (Liverpool), St Charles Borromeo, 224 Aigburth Rd, Liverpool L17 9PG **Tel:** 0151-727 2493 **Fax:** 0151-726 1987

Russell, Paul, (Birmingham), 4 Innage Rd, Northfield, Birmingham B31 2DX

Russo, Roberto, (Superior) (SCA), St Peter's Italian Church, 4 Back Hill, Clerkenwell Rd EC1R 5EN **Tel:** 020-7837 1528 **Fax:** 020-7837 9071

Rutledge, Christopher, (Portsmouth), St Joseph's Presbytery, Stanley Walk, Town Centre, Bracknell, Berks RG12 1HA **Tel/Fax:** 01344-425729 **Mbl:** 07802-880860

Rutledge, Robert, (Nottingham, retired), Newton-Cloghans, Ballina, Co Mayo

Rutt, Richard, MA, Canon, (Plymouth, retired), 3 Marlborough Court, Falmouth, Cornwall TR11 2QU **Tel:** 01326-312276

Ryall, Patrick, M, (OSM), St Mary's Priory, 264 Fulham Rd, London SW10 9EL **Tel:** 020-7352 6965 **Fax:** 020-7351 1475

Ryan, Colman, (Middlesbrough), All Saints Presbytery, 5 Castlegate, Thirsk, N. Yorks YO7 1HL **Tel:** 01845-523113

Ryan, Columba, (OP), St Dominic's Priory, Southampton Rd, Haverstock Hill, NW5 4LB **Tel:** 020-7482 9210 **Fax:** 020-7482 9239

Ryan, David, (Clifton), The Immaculate Conception, Beeches Green, Stroud, Glos GL5 4AA **Tel:** 01453-762442

Ryan, Francis (OMI), New Priory, Sacred Heart Church, Quex Rd, Kilburn, London NW6 4PS **Tel:** 020-7624 1701 **Fax:** 020-7328 8176

Ryan, Gerard, (Northampton, retired), Nazareth Ho, 116-120 Harlestone Rd Northampton NN5 6AD **Tel:** 01604 756192

Ryan, Gordon MA, BD (Hexham & Newcastle), St Joseph, Paxton Terr, Millfield, Sunderland SR4 6HP **Tel:** 0191-567 4574

Ryan, Henry, (Hexham & Newcastle), St Paulinus, Manor Rd, St Helen Auckland, Bishop Auckland, Co. Durham DL14 9ER **Tel:** 01388-604169

Ryan, James, (Salford), Our Lady and St Paul, Argyle St, Heywood OL10 3PB **Tel:** 01706-360774

Ryan, John, MBE, (Southwark), 111 Old Rd, Crayford DA1 4DN **Tel:** 01322-523492

Ryan, John, Mgr Canon, (Northampton, retired) Nazareth Ho, 116-120 Harlestone Rd Northampton NN5 6AD **Tel:** 01604 756192

Ryan, John, Mgr, (Hallam), St Bede's Presbytery, Station Rd, Rotherham S60 1HF **Tel:** 01709-562012

Ryan, Joseph, (Westminster), 4 Vincent Rd, West Green, London N15 3QH **Tel:** 020-8888 5518

Ryan, Maurice, (OFM), The Friary, Marine Hill, Clevedon, Somerset BS21 7PP **Tel:** 01275-873205

Ryan, M Gordon, MA, BD, (Hexham & Newcastle), St Joseph's, Paxton Terr, Millfield, Sunderland SR4 6HP **Tel:** 0191-567 4574

Ryan, Michael, Canon (Middlesbrough), St Wilfrid's Rectory, 11 High Petergate, York YO1 7EN **Tel:** 01904-624767

Ryan, Michael, (OMI), St Mary Help of Christians, Longford Rd, Holyhead Anglesey LL65 1TR **Tel:** 01407 762102 **Fax:** 01407 765759

Ryan, Michael, (East Anglia), St Mark's Presbytery, 180 Hawthorne Dr, Ipswich IP2 0QQ **Tel:** 01473-691187

Ryan, Michael, (Salford), Henesy Ho, Sudell St, Collyhurst, Manchester M4 4JF **Tel:** 0161-834 8828

Ryan, Michael, BTh, (Southwark), 63 West St, Sittingborne Kent ME10 1AN **Tel:** 01795 472619

Ryan, Michael, (SM), c/o French Church, 5 Leicester Place, London WC2H 7BP **Tel:** 020-7437 9363

Ryan, Paschal, (Westminster), 32 High St, Cranford, Hounslow, Middx TW5 9RG **Tel:** 020-8759 2160

Ryan, Patrick, (Southwark), 52 Bertrand Way, Thamesmead, SE28 8LN **Tel:** 020-8311 4656

Ryan, Peter, (Middlesbrough), Island Cottage, Lealholm, Whitby, N. Yorks YO21 2AQ **Tel:** 01947-897937

Ryan, Peter W, Mgr, (Liverpool, retired), Stile Cottage, Daniell's Walk, Lymington, Hants SO41 3PN **Tel:** 01590-674331

Ryan, Thomas, (SPS), 218 Arundel Rd Central, Peacehaven, E. Sussex BN10 8JA **Tel:** 01273-583046 **E-mail:** tryan@spms.org

Ryan, Thomas (SSC), 28 Redington Rd, London NW3 7RB

Ryan, Thomas J, (SMA), Society of African Missions, St Augustine's, 378 Upper Brook St, Manchester M13 0EP **Tel:** 0161-224 4949 **Fax:** 0161-248 0241 **Mbl:** 0385-254102 **E-mail:** thomasjryan@btconnect.com

Ryan, Thomas, (Middlesbrough, retired), Bawnbee, Caherconlish, Co. Limerick, Eire

Ryan, Vincent J, (Clifton), St Bernard's Presbytery, 43 Station Rd, Shirehampton, Bristol BS11 9TU **Tel:** 0117-983 3929

Ryan, William, (Middlesbrough), SS Mary and Joseph, Baxtergate, Hedon HU12 8JN **Tel:** 01482-898338

Ryder, Andrew, SCJ. c/o 266 Wellington Rd North, Stockport, SK4 2QR **E-mail:** andrewryder@eircom.net

Ryder, David, (Salford), (Chaplain, North Manchester Hosp.), 9 Crumpsall Lane, Higher Crumpsall, Manchester M8 4ED **Tel/Fax:** 0161-740 8598. **E-mail:** dcryder@tiscali.co.uk

Ryman, Peter, PhD, BSc, FCS, LRIC, ACP, (Southwark, retired), 1 Ethnard Rd, London SE15 1RY **Tel/Fax:** 020-7732 2042

Rynn, Sean (SPS), St Augustine's, 70 Eton Rd, Datchet, Slough, Berks SL3 9AY **Tel:** 01753-542862

Saba, Alex Rex Cletus, Christus Rex (Southwark), Whitefriars, Church Road, Hartley, Dartford kent DA3 8DW **Tel:** 01474 705361

Sabathé, Martin, (CSJ), 79 Barking Rd, Canning Town, London E16 4HB **Tel:** 020 7476 4129

Sacco, Paul, (SM), Newman Ho, 729 Beverley Rd, Hull HU6 7ER **Tel/Fax:** 01482 856884

Sacré, Anthony, (Westminster), 377 Mile End Rd, E3 4QS **Tel:** 020-8980 1845

St Aubyn, Kevin, (Southwark), 37 Kingsdown Park, Whitstable, Kent CT5 2DE **Tel:** 01227-272758

St Clair, Michael, (Cardiff), St Mary's Priory, Merthyr Tydfil CF47 8RG **Tel:** 01685-723336

Sainter, Philip, BSc, BPhil, MA, STL (IC), St Marie's, Oak St, Rugby CV22 5EL **Tel:** 01788-542703 **E-mail:** Philip.Sainter@virgin.net

Salter, John, TD, AKC, JCLJ(J) (Melkite Greek Catholic), 1 St James Cl, Bishop St, Islington, London N1 8PH **Tel:** 020-7359 0250

Saksons, Richard R, BA(Hons) (O Praem) 178 New London Rd, Chelmsford, Essex CM2 0AR **Tel:** 01245 352898

Salcedo, Jorge Entigue (SJ), Copleston House, 221 Goldhurst Terr, London NW6 3EP **Tel:** 020-7604 5860 **Fax:** 020-7604 5850

Saluma, Raymond (SM), Notre Dame de France, 5 Leicester Place, Leicester Sqare, London WC2H 7BP **Tel:** 020-7437 9363 **Fax:** 020-7437 9364

Salvans, Albert, MTh, (Westminster), c/o

Archbishop's Ho, Ambrosden Ave, London SW1P 1QJ

Sammarco, Anthony (Westminster), 42 Langdale Gardens, Perivale, Greenford, Middx UB6 8DQ **Tel:** 0208-997 3164

Sammon, Patrick J, (Brentwood), 51 Cambridge Park, Wanstead, London E11 2PR **Tel:** 020-8989 2074

Sammon, Patrick, (Westminster), 5 Garratt Rd, Edgware, Middx HA8 9AN **Tel:** 020-8952 0663

Samuels, Digby, Canon (Westminster), The Presbytery, Dundee St, Green Bank, London E1 9PH **Tel:** 020-7481 2202

Samuels, Peter, (Salford), 34 Shirley Ave, Denton, Manchester M34 2LN **Tel:** 0161-223 1265

Samy, Arul MA, BEd, BTh (Birmingham), 16 Wales Ln, Barton under Needwood, Burton DE13 8JF **Tel:** 01283 713104

Sandeman, Brian, (Portsmouth), 26 St Clement Gdns, La Grande Route de St Clement, Jersey CI, JE2 6QT **Tel:** 01534-722909

Sanders, David, (OP), BA, STL, DipTheol, Blackfriars, 64 St Giles, Oxford OX1 3LY **Tel:** 01865-278400

Sanders, Paul, BA, (Southwark), 46 North St, Carshalton, Surrey SM5 2JD **Tel:** 020 8647 0022

Sanders, Robin, MA (Portsmouth), 52 Arthray Rd, Oxford OX2 9AB **Tel:** 01865-250524 **Mbl:** 07775-733494 **E-mail:** robinsanders@amserve.net

Sanderson, John Paul (OCSO), Mount Saint Bernard Abbey, Coalville, Leicestershire LE67 5UL **Tel:** 01530-832298 **Fax:** 01530-814608

Sanderson, Mario, BA(Hons), BEd, (Arundel & Brighton), Priest's Ho, Station Rd, Mayfield, E. Sussex TN20 6BU **Tel:** 01435-872381

Sankey, Paul, MA, (Clifton, retired), c/o St Ambrose, North Rd, Leigh Woods, Bristol BS8 3PW

Sarsfield, Denis (Westminster), 42 Francis St, London SW1P 1QW **Tel:** 020-7798 9055

Sauge, Jean-Pierre (MAfr), St Edward's College, 46 Totteridge Common, London N20 8ND **Tel:** 020-8959 2553 **Fax:** 020-8201 1850 **E-mail:** mafr@mdx.ac.uk

Saunders, Laurence, (Nottingham, retired), The Bungalow, Brooklyn Road, Bulwell, Nottingham NG6 9ES

Saunders, Martin, BA(Hons), BD, Dip.Psyth (Salford), St Joseph's, Belgarth Rd, Accrington BB5 6AH **Tel:** 01254-213754 **E-mail:** joseph@martinsaunders.org.uk

Saunders, Michael P, PhD, JCD, MA, BD (Clifton), St Peter's Presbytery, Carronbridge Rd, East Leaze, Swindon SN5 7ES **Tel:** 01793-874400

Saunders, Thomas (Brentwood), 418 Southchurch Rd, Southend-on-Sea, Essex SS1 2QB **Tel:** 01702-465720

Saunders, William, Mgr, B.Ed(Hons), Diocesan Communications Officer (Southwark), Archbishop's Ho, 150 St George's Rd, London SE1 6HX **Tel:** 020-7928 2495 **E-mail:** aps@rcsouthwark.co.uk

Savaille Albert (Hallam), St Catherine's Presbytery, 23 Melrose Rd, Sheffield S9 3DN **Tel:** 0114-249 8225

Saverian, Francis Eugene (Southwark) (Tamil Chaplain), 304 Garratt Lane, London SW18 4EH **Tel:** 020-8870 6257

Saward, John (Birmingham), c/o 322 Woodstock Rd, Oxford OX2 7NS

Sawyer, Guy, (Westminster), 22 Roxborough Park, Harrow-on-the-Hill, Middx HA1 3BE **Tel:** 020-8422 2513

Sawyer, Keith, MA, (Northampton), 29 Fieldgate Rd, Luton, Beds LU4 9TA **Mbl:** 07773-591554

Sayer, Peter, (Lancaster), St Mary, St Bridget's Lane, Egremont CA22 2BD

Sayles, Patrick, (SSC), Our Lady and St Benedict. Alcester Rd, Wootton Wawen, Warwicks B95 6BQ **Tel:** 01564-792647

Scally, Peter (SJ), St Ignatius, 27 High Rd, London N15 6ND **Tel:** 020-8802 5303 **Fax:** 020-8802 8102 **E-mail:** peter.scally@jesuits.net

Scanlan, John, (Salford), St Joseph, Oldham Rd, Shaw, Oldham OL2 8SZ **Tel:** 01706-847489

Scanlan, Philip, (IC), St Mary, Ashby Rd, Loughborough LE11 3AB **Tel:** 01509-262123

Scanlan, William (Southwark), 89 West Hill, Dartford, Kent DA1 2HJ **Tel:** 01322-220075 **Fax:** 01322-290374

Scanlon, Michael, (Southwark), 103 Woolwich New Rd, Woolwich, London SE18 6EF **Tel:** 020-8854 0359

Scannell, Thomas, (Southwark), 1 Leyborne Park, Kew, Richmond, Surrey TW9 3HB **Tel:** 020-8940 3101

Scantlebury, Brian C, Canon, (Portsmouth, retired), 29/1 South Parade, Southsea, Hants PO4 0SH **Tel:** 02392-818046

Schlatmann, Willibrord M, (OSB), Monastery of Christ the King, 29 Bramley Rd, Cockfosters, London N14 4HE **Tel:** 020-8440 7769

Schofield, John, BA, (Liverpool), St Paul of the Cross, Clay Lane, Burtonwood, Warrington WA5 4HW **Tel:** 01935-226184

Schofield, Nicholas (Westminster), 100a Balls Pond Rd, London N1 4AG **Tel:** 020-7254 4378

S

Schofield, Rodney (Plymouth), 15 Johnson's Courtyard, South Street, Sherbourne Dorset DT9 3TD **Tel:** 01935 814932

Schofield, Terence, (Salford), 91 Higher Reedley Rd, Brierfield, Nelson BB9 5EY **Tel:** 01282-615850 **Fax:** 01282 697615

Scholes, Bernard, Canon, MA, (Westminster), 52 Uxbridge Rd, Hanwell W7 3SU **Tel:** 020-8567 4056 **Fax:** 020-8810 0219

Schrenk, Hans, ThEd, Superior (MAfr) Oak Lodge, 48 Totteridge Common, London N20 8ND **Tel:** 020-8959 1515

Sciberras, Stephen (OFM) The Maltese Mission, 1 Balniel Gate, Lindsay Square, London SW1V 3SD **Tel/Fax:** 020-7834 9512

Scott, Geoffrey, (OSB) Abbot, MA, PhD, FSA, FRHistS, (OSB), Douai Abbey, Upper Woolhampton, Reading RG7 5TQ **Tel:** 0118-971 5300 **Fax:** 0118-971 5303 **E-mail:** info@douaiabbey.org.uk

Scott, Jeffrey Haydn, Mgr Canon, LCL, MCL, (Arundel & Brighton), 95 Victoria Rd, Knaphill, Woking, Surrey GU21 2AA **Tel:** 01483-472404

Scott, Peter Michael, STB, (Westminster), 15 Wood Rd, Shepperton TW17 0DH **Tel:** 020 7385 4040

Scott, Richard, (Birmingham), c/o Archbishop's House, Shadwell Street, Birmingham B4 6XY

Scragg, Frederick (SMM), Montford Ho, 28 Burbo Bank Rd, Liverpool L23 6TH **Tel:** 0151-287 6862 **Fax:** 0151-287 0410 **E-mail:** smm1@nildram.co.uk

Scerri, Louis (Portsmouth), Sacred Heart Presbytery, Albert Rd, Richmond Hill, Bournemouth.

Scudiero, Giovanni, MTh, MPhil, (IMC), Consolata Missionary College, Totteridge Green, London N20 8PL

Scurlock, Anthony, (Westminster), c/o Archbishop's Ho, Ambrosden Ave, London SW1P 1QJ

Seabrook, John, (Westminster), 1 Bolton Rd, London W4 3TE **Tel:** 020-8994 6861

Seale, Brian, (Salford), St John Vianney, Poynter St, Moston, Manchester M40 0DH **Tel:** 0161-681 6844

Seasman, Terence, MA BACP (Westminster), 79a Berkeley Rd, Kingsbury NW9 9DH

Seddon, Desmond, (Liverpool), St Mary's Presbytery, Prescot Rd, Aughton, Ormskirk L39 6TA **Tel:** 01695 422146 **E-mail:** desmond.seddon@btinternet.com

Seddon, John, (Liverpool), National Chaplain to the Scout Movement, St Peter and St Paul, 165 Liverpool Rd, Crosby, Liverpool L23 0QN **Tel:** 0151-949 1782 **Fax:** 0151-949 1782

Seddon, John, BA, DipLib (OSB), St Augustine's Abbey, Ramsgate, Kent CT11 9PA **Tel:** 01843-593045 **Fax:** 01843-582732

Seddon, Paul, MA (Liverpool), St Richard's Presbytery, Mayfield St, Atherton, Manchester M46 0AQ **Tel:** 01942-883395 **Fax:** 01942 871163

Seed, Michael, PhD, STD, (SA), St Francis Friary, 47 Francis St, Westminster SW1P 1QR **Tel:** 020-7828 4163

Seed, Philip, BA, BTh, MLitt (Southwark), The Priest's Ho, Church of the Resurrection, 165-169 Kirkdale, Sydenham SE26 4PL **Tel:** 01227-462896 **Fax:** 01227-450377

Seeldrayers, Anthony, (Westminster), 970 Harrow Rd, Sudbury, Wembley, Middx HA0 2QE **Tel:** 020-8904 2552

Seely, Anthony, (East Anglia), Cathedral Ho, Unthank Rd, Norwich NR2 2PA **Tel:** 01328-823456

Sellers, Michael, BA, (Middlesbrough), St Bede's Presbytery, 94 Staveley Rd, Bilton Grange, Hull HU9 4SJ **Tel:** 01482-781897

Selman, Francis, MA, MTh PhD (East Anglia), Allen Hall, 28 Beaufort St, London SW3 5AA **Tel:** 020 7351 1296

Selvini, Jean-Claude, (Brentwood), The Presbytery, 98 Manford Way, Chigwell, Essex IG7 4DF **Tel:** 020-8500 3953

Selway, Michael D, BA, STL, (Clifton), c/o St Ambrose, North Rd, Leigh Woods, Bristol BS8 3PW

Senior, Barrie, (Leeds), SS Peter & Paul Presbytery, St Geroge's Walk, Kettlethorpe, Wakefield WF2 7NR **Tel:** 01924-240240 **E-mail:** mail@peterpaul.org.uk

Senno, Tony (XM), 2 Cranwich Rd, Stamford Hill N16 5JX **Tel:** 020-8800 9898

Senyz, David (Ukrainian), 34 Dawlish Dr, Styvechale, Coventry CV3 5NB **Mbl:** 07870-578883

Serignat, Charles (OFM Cap), Greyfriars, Iffley Rd, Oxford OX4 1SB **Tel:** 0039 06 46201 220

Serplus, William (Middlesbrough), St Mary's Presbytery, 200 Nidderdale, Bransholme, Hull HU7 4BS **Tel/Fax:** 01482-835707

Severs, Geoffrey, (Lancaster, retired), 1a Kirkgate Rd, Linthorpe, Middlesbrough, Teesside TS5 5LS **Tel:** 01642-286135 **E-mail:** geoff.severs@ntlworld.co.uk

Sexton, Christopher, (Arundel & Brighton, retired), Lapwater, Marsh, Yarcombe, Honiton, Devon EX14 9AL

Sexton, Desmond, (Hallam), St Mary's Presbytery, 238 Herringthorpe Valley Road, Rotherham S65 3BA

Tel: 01709 363 753
Sexton, Patrick, (Liverpool), St Monica's, Fernhill Rd, Bootle L20 9GA **Tel:** 0151-922 4819 **Fax:** 0151-284 3856
Shackleton, Bernard, BA, BD, (Clifton), St John Fisher, 57 Mantle St, Wellington, Somerset TA21 8AX **Tel:** 01823-662283
Shaddock, Jonathan, (Plymouth), St John, Shortmoor, Beaminster, Dorset DT8 3EL **Tel:** 01308-862741
Shanahan, Kevin, (MSC), St John Baptist, 8 St John's St, Tamworth, Staffs B79 7EX **Tel:** 01827-62161
Shanahan, Patrick (MAfr), Oak Lodge, 48 Totteridge Common, London N20 8NB **Tel:** 020-8959 1515
Shannon, John, (East Anglia), The White House, 21 Upgate, Poringland, Norwich NR14 7SH **Tel:** 01603-742812
Shannon, Plunkett Joseph, (Birmingham, retired), St Mary's Home, Stone, Staffs ST15 8EJ
Sharkey, Michael, STD, Mgr, (Birmingham), The Presbytery, St John St, Lichfield WS14 9DX **Tel:** 01543-263234
Sharp, J Bryan, Mgr Canon, JCL, (Leeds, retired), Flat 3, 33A Shire Oak Rd, Leeds LS6 2DD
Sharp, John, BA, MTh, PhD (Hallam), St Francis of Assisi, Rising Lane, Baddesley Clinton, Knowle, Solihull, W Mids B93 0DD **Tel:** 01564-782498
Sharp, Peter, (Westminster, retired), 25 Albert St, Lytham, Lancs FY8 5EB **Tel:** 01253-732524
Sharples, Richard, (Birmingham), Church Ho, 59 Perry Common Rd B23 7AB **Tel:** 0121-373 0069
Sharratt, Aidan, BA, STL, (Westminster), St Joseph's Church, Oxhey Dr, South Oxhey, Watford WD19 7SW **Tel:** 020-8428 2774
Sharratt, Michael, PhD, STL, (Hexham & Newcastle), Ushaw College, Ushaw, Durham DH7 9RH **Tel:** 0191-3733966
Sharrock, Peter, (Lancaster), Our Lady of the Lakes and St Charles, High Hill, Keswick CA12 5PB **Tel:** 01768-772928
Sharrocks, Peter, (Shrewsbury), St Peter's, Green Lane, Hazel Grove, Stockport SK7 4EA **Tel:** 0161-483 3476 **Tel:** 0161-419 9592 **E-mail:** petersharrocks@stpetershazelgrove.org.uk
Shaw, Albert, Canon, (Liverpool, retired), Flat 2, Alston Court, 483a Liverpool Rd, Southport PR8 3BP
Shaw, Andrew, St Joseph, Mill Lane, Gilesgate, Durham City DH1 4NE **Tel:** 0191 3843810
Shaw, John, (Nottingham, retired), 21 Knighton Court, Knighton Park Rd, Leicester LE2 1ZB
Shaw, Paul, (Chester), St Werburgh's, Grosvenor Park Rd, Chester CH1 1QJ **Tel:** 01244-350236 **Fax:** 01244-347684 **E-mail:** werburgh465@btinternet.com
Shayo, Polycarp, (IC), St Alban's, Cameron St, Splott, Cardiff CF24 2NX **Tel:** 02920 46 3219 **Fax:** 02920 48 8308 **E-mail:** polycarpshayo@yahoo.ie
Sheahan, Denis, (Salford), 4 Sharples Hall Fold, Sharples, Bolton BL1 7EH
Sheahan, Myles, (Salford), St Christopher's, Lees Rd, Hurst Cross, Ashton-under-Lyne OL6 8BA **Tel:** 0161-330 3262
Sheahan, Peter, (Salford), St Mary's Presbytery, 2 Ruth St, Oldham OL1 3EZ **Tel:** 0161-624 2622
Sheehan, Gerard, MA, STD (Opus Dei), St Thomas More Presbytery, Maresfield Gardens, London NW3 5SU **Tel:** 020-7435 1388
Sheehy, James, (Salford, retired), c/o Wardley Hall, Worsley, Manchester M28 2ND
Sheehy, John I, (Arundel & Brighton, retired), 14 Westbrooke, Worthing, W. Sussex, BN11 1RF
Sheeky, Joshua J, BA, STB, (Salford, retired), McAuley Mount, Padiham Rd, Burnley BB12 6TG **Tel:** 01282-438071
Sheil, James V, (CM), 82 West St, Dunstable, Beds LU6 1NY **Tel:** 01582-662710 **Fax:** 01582-670968
Sheils, Sean F, (Brentwood), The Presbytery, Lowshoe Lane, Collier Row, Romford, Essex RM5 2AP **Tel:** 01708-749050
Sheldon, Frederick, (Birmingham), St Mary's Presbytery, 11 Balance St, Uttoxeter, Staffs ST14 8JB **Tel:** 01889-562082
Shelley, Anthony, (Arundel & Brighton, retired), 13 Church Rd, East Wittering W. Sussex PO20 8PS **Tel:** 01243-670034
Shelton, Angus, (MAfr), 129 Lichfield Rd, Sutton Coldfield, W. Mids B74 2SA **Tel:** 0121-308 0226 **E-mail:** suttonlink@dialpipex.com
Sherbrooke, Alexander, (Westminster), 21a Soho Square, London W1D 4NR **Tel:** 020-7437 2010
Sheridan, Alan, JCL, BA, Canon, (Middlesbrough), St Thérèse of Lisieux, 9 Holystone Dr, Ingleby Barwick, Stockton on Tees TS17 0PW **Tel/Fax:** 01642-750480
Sheridan, Peter, (Leeds), 4 Boake Place, Garran ACT 2605, Australia
Sheridan, Terence (SCJ) The Friary, St Bernard's Rd, Olton, Solihull, W. Mids B92 7BL **Tel:** 0121-706 0505

Sherlock, Patrick, BSc, BA, PGCE, DPSE, (SDB), Thornleigh Ho, Sharples Park, Bolton BL1 6PQ **Tel:** 01204-591144 **E-mail:** secretary@salesians.org.uk

Sherrington, John, (CP), 10 Jubilee Terr, Byker, Newcastle on Tyne NE6 2QW **Tel:** 0191-276 0841 **Mbl:** 0790 400 6824 **E-mail:** johnsherringtoncp@ukonline.co.uk

Sherrington, John, STL, (Nottingham), 36 Uttoxeter Rd, Mickleover, Derby DE3 9GE **Tel:** 01332-514107.

Shewring, John, (Westminster), 192 Nags Head Rd, Ponders End, Enfield, Middx EN3 7AR **Tel:** 020-8804 2149

Shield, Stephen, Canon, STL,(Lancaster), Cathedral Ho, Balmoral Rd, Lancaster LA1 3BT **Tel:** 01524-384820 **Fax:** 01524-384831

Shilstone, John, (Limerick), Flat 1, St John's Flats, South Parade, Bath BA2 4AF **Tel:** 01225-444890

Shipperlee, Martin, Rt Rev Abbot, BA, BD (OSB), Ealing Abbey, Charlbury Grove, Ealing W5 2DY **Tel:** 020-8862 2100

Shirrat, James (Clifton), c/o St Ambrose, North Rd, Leigh Woods, Bristol BS8 3PW

Shonibare, Joseph BA (Parish Priest of Honiton and Ottery St Mary) (OAR), St Rita's Centre, Ottery Moor Lane, Honiton, Devon EX14 1AP **Tel:** 01404-45349

Shore, Christian, BSc, AKC, (OSB), Ampleforth Abbey, York YO62 4EN **Tel:** 01439-766750

Shore, Liam J, (Cardiff, retired), Kiltown, Castlecomer, Kilkenny, Ireland

Shorter, Aylward, (MAfr), Oak Lodge, 48 Totteridge Common, London N20 8NB **Tel:** 020-8959 1515 **Fax:** 020-8959 7421 **E-mail:** mail@aylwardshorter.com

Shyrane, Anthony, (East Anglia), Catholic Presbytery, 19 Egremont St, Ely, Cambs CB6 1AE **Tel/Fax:** 01353-662759

Shyrane, James (Hallam, retired), Holy Rood Rectory, George St, Barnsley S70 1AX **Tel:** 01226-203730

Shryane, Philip, Mgr (East Anglia), St Edmund, 21 Westgate St, Bury St Edmunds, Suffolk IP33 1QG **Tel:** 01284-754358 **Fax:** 01284-700198

Shufflebotham, Thomas, Superior (SJ), St Beuno's, St Asaph, Denbighshire LL17 0AS **Tel:** 01745-583444

Shurgold, Julian, BA, STB (Southwark), 9 The Green, Sutton, Surrey SM1 1QT **Tel:** 0208-641 7458

Shuttleworth, Bernard, (Lancaster), c/o Bishop's Ho, Cannon Hill, Lancaster LA1 5NG

Siebers, Erwin, (SCA), 47 Adler St, London E1 1EE **Tel:** 020-7247 9529

Sierla, Jeremy, MA Sub-Prior, (OSB), Ampleforth Abbey, York YO62 4EN **Tel:** 01439-766714 **Fax:** 01439-766724

Sileshi, Michael, (Southwark), St Ann's House, Kingston Hill, Kingston upon Thames KT2 7LX **Tel:** 020-8546 8732

Siletti, Vincent R, (SSP), St Paul's Ho, Middle Green, Slough SL3 6BT **Tel:** 01753-520621

Silke, Leo, (SMA), St Matthew's Presbytery, 32 Hallowell Rd, Northwood, Middx HA6 1DW **Tel:** 01923-825639

Sillince, David, (Portsmouth), The Priest's Ho, 413 Shirley Rd, Southampton, Hants SO15 3JD **Tel:** 023-8077 1231 **Fax:** 023-8052 8236 **E-mail:** davidsillince@yahoo.co.uk

Silva, Christopher, BSc, (Westminster), 970 Harrow Rd, Sudbury, Middx HA0 2QE **Tel:** 020-8904 2552

Silver, Joseph, BD, MA, STL, (Brentwood), St Vincent's Presbytery, Waldergrave Rd, Dagenham, Essex RM8 2QB **Tel:** 020 8590 7222

Simionato, Joseph (FDP), House of Our Lady of Westminster, 25 Lower Teddington Rd, Hampton Wick, Kingston-upon-Thames, Surrey KT1 4HB **Tel:** 0208-977 5130 **Fax:** 0208-977 5130

Simison, Michael, BA, (SM), Marist Fathers, 12 Hindringham Rd, Great Walsingham, Norfolk NR22 6DR **Tel:** 01328-820588 **Fax:** 01328-820331

Simmonds, Simon, (OFM), 160 The Grove, Stratford, London E15 1NS **Tel:** 020-8534 1964

Simmons, Alistair, BA(Hons), (Arundel & Brighton), The Priest's Ho, 92 Downland Ave, Southwick, W. Sussex BN42 4RY **Tel:** 01273-708227

Simmons, Gordon, (Arundel & Brighton, retired), 2 Poels Court, Moat Rd, East Grinstead, W. Sussex RH19 2AS

Simmons, Paul (Shrewsbury), c/o Curial Office, 2 Park Road South, Prenton Wirral CH43 4UX **Tel:** 0151 652 9855

Simon, Jonathan, (Plymouth), Cary Ho, South Cary Lane, Castle Cary, Somerset BA7 7ER **Tel:** 01963 350276

Simon, Lawrence (OFM), c/o 557-559 High Road, Woodford Green, Essex IG8 0RB

Simons, Richard BA (OSB), The Presbytery, New St, Ledbury, Herefordshire HR8 2EE **Tel:** 01531-635354

Simpson, Edward, (SCJ), The Friary, Olton, Solihull, W Mids B92 7BL **Tel:** 0121-706 0505

Simpson, Francis William, (Liverpool), Our Lady, Queen of Peace, 74 Kirkstone Rd West, Litherland, Liverpool L21 0EQ **Tel/Fax:** 0151-928 3697

Simpson, Romuald, (OSB), Douai Abbey,

Upper Woolhampton, Reading RG7 5TQ **Tel:** 0118-971 5300 **Fax:** 0118-971 5303

Sims, Anthony G, BA, (Birmingham), St Philip, Crabmill Lane, Ilmington, Shipston-on-Stour CV36 4LE **Tel:** 01608-682241

Sinclair, Hugh, (Birmingham), Oscott College, Chester Rd, Sutton Coldfield, W. Mids B73 5AA

Singleton, Thomas, (Lancaster), English Martyrs, 18 Garstang Rd, Preston PR1 1NB **Tel:** 01772-257878 **Fax:** 01772-252578.

Sinnott, Patrick, (Wrexham), The Presbytery, King Edward St, Barmouth, Gwynedd LL42 1PE **Tel:** 01341-280489

Sinnott, Thomas, BA, STL, (MHM), St Joseph's College, Lawrence St, Mill Hill, London NW7 4JX **Tel:** 020-8959 8254 **E-mail:** tomgsinnott@netscapeonline.co.uk

Skehan, William, (Westminster), 60 Highbury Park, London N5 2XH **Tel:** 020-7226 0257

Skelton, Mark, (Plymouth), The Presbytery, 211b Wimborne Rd, Poole, Dorset BH15 2EG **Tel:** 01202-675412 **Fax:** 01202-668901 **E-mail:** stmaryspoole@onetel.net.uk.

Sketch, Anthony, (East Anglia, retired), 13 Victoria Court, Kirkley Cliff Rd, Lowestoft, Suffolk NR33 0DE **Tel:** 01502-567430 **Fax:** 01502-567490 **E-mail:** a.e.sketch@btinernet.com

Skillen, Anthony, MSc, (SM), Emmaus Retreat Centre, Layhams Rd, West Wickham, Kent BR4 9HH **Tel:** 020-8777 8455 **E-mail:** tskillen@aol.com

Skinner, Gerard, GRSM, LRAM, PhB, STL, FRSA (Westminster), 390a Northholt Rd, South Harrow HA2 8EX **Tel:** 020 8864 5455

Skivington, John J, MDiv (Hexham & Newcastle), 20 Clarendon Ho, Clayton St West, Newcastle-upon-Tyne NE1 5EE **Tel/Fax:** 0191-222 1916

Skoczen, Wlodzimierz, 2 Sherwood Rise, Nottingham NG7 6JN **Tel:** 0115 960 4740

Slack, Anthony, BSc (IC), St Jude the Apostle, 3 Station Rd, Whittlesey PE7 1SA **Tel:** 01733-203411

Slater, Francis X, (Cardiff), St Ethelbert, 86 The Bargates, Leominster HR6 8QS **Tel:** 01568-612238

Slater, John, (Southwark), 117 Canterbury Rd, Westgate-on-Sea, Kent CT8 8NW **Tel:** 01843-831593

Slattery, Francis, Mgr Provost, MA, (Lancaster), Our Lady and St Herbert, Lake Rd, Windermere LA23 2EQ **Tel:** 01539-443402

Slattery, Liam, (Clifton), St Mary's Presbytery, Tovey Rd, Swindon, SN2 1LQ **Tel:** 01793-535089 **Fax:** 01793-480560 **E-mail:** toveyrd@aol.com

Slaughter, Charles, STL, MA (Arundel & Brighton, retired), Dalling Ho, Croft Rd, Crowborough, E. Sussex TN6 1HA **Tel:** 01892 662917

Slawicki, Miroslaw (Katowice, Poland), 29 Edmund St, Bradford BD5 0BH **Tel:** 01274-720848.

Slepokura, Maria Olaf, (OFMConv), Laxton Hall, near Corby, Northants NN17 3AU **Tel:** 01780-444242 **Fax:** 01780-444574

Slinger, John, (WF), 42 Stormont Rd, Highgate, London N6 4NP **Tel:** 020-8348 7799

Slingo, Anthony, (Liverpool), St Teresa's Presbytery, College Rd, Upholland, Skelmersdale WN8 0PY **Tel:** 01695 622001

Sloan, Richard, (Liverpool), 65 Avenell Road, London N5 1BT

Slocombe, Peter, (Clifton), 12 Highbridge Rd, Burnham-on-Sea, Somerset TA8 1LL **Tel:** 01278 783832 **E-mail:** BurnhamOnSeaPP@aol.com

Slowey, Edmund, (MHM, retired). Herbert Ho, 41 Victoria Rd, Freshfield, Merseyside L37 1LW **Tel:** 01704-835845

Smale, James (CScR) Our Lady's, Bishop Eton, Woolton Rd, Liverpool L16 8NQ **Tel:** 0151-722 1108 **Fax:** 0151-738 0834

Smeaton, Malcolm, BSc (Southwark), Prior Park College, Ralph Allen Dr, Combe Down, Bath BA2 5AH **Tel:** 01225 831007

Smethurst, John M B, MA(Oxon) (Plymouth). St Antony Ho, 11 Seaton Cl, Torquay, Devon TQ1 3UH **Tel:** 01803-402357

Smialek, Waldemar (MS), 1 Rainham Rd, Rainham, Essex RM13 8SP **Tel:** 01708 552897

Smith, Adrian, (MAfr, retired), MA, 27 Aldersgate, Rose Lane, Nuneaton CV11 5TR **Tel/Fax:** 02476-344983 **E-mail:** adriansmith@onetel.net.uk

Smith, Alfred, MA, (Salford, retired), Little Sisters of the Poor, St Joseph's Home, 52 Plymouth Grove West, Manchester M13 0AR **Tel:** 0161-273 5021 **E-mail:** xjz30@dial.pipex.com

Smith, Andrew H, Parish Priest (OPraem), Our Lady of England Priory, School Lane, Storrington, W. Sussex RH20 4LN **Tel:** 01903-742150 **Fax:** 01903-740821 **E-mail:** norbertines@pavilion.co.uk

Smith, Anthony, (Liverpool), c/o Liverpool Archdiocesan Centre for Evangelisation, Croxteth Dr, Sefton Park, Liverpool L17 1AA

Smith, Austin, (CP), 9 Steve Biko Cl, Magdala St, Liverpool L8 0QB **Tel:** 0151-734 4308 **E-mail:** austinsmithcp@ukonline.co.uk

Smith, Brian, SLit, Dip, (Westminster), 20 The Green, West Drayton, Middx UB7 7PJ **Tel:** 01895-442777

Smith, Charles, David, MA, (Birmingham, retired), Manor Nursing Home, Meron, Bicester, Oxon

Smith, Christopher, (East Anglia), 15 The Terr, Aldeburgh, Suffolk IP15 5HJ **Tel:** 01728-452782

Smith, Christopher, (IC, retired), Nazareth Ho, Colum Rd, Cardiff CF10 3UN

Smith, Conrad, (Brentwood), 21 Blackthorn Ave, Greenstead, Colchester, Essex CO4 3QD **Tel:** 01206-870460

Smith, Cyprian, MA, (OSB), Ampleforth Abbey, York YO62 4EN **Tel:** 01439-766714 **Fax:** 01439-766724

Smith, David, BD, AKC, MTh, RGN (East Anglia), c/o Principal RC Chaplain (Army), HQ Land Command, Erskine Barracks, Wilton, Salisbury SP2 0AG **Tel:** 01722 433892

Smith, David J, (Leeds), St Alban's Presbytery, St Alban's Croft, Abbey Walk South, Halifax HX3 0AP **Tel:** 01422-365384

Smith, David L, (Cardiff), The Presbytery, Commercial St, Maesteg CF34 9AY **Tel:** 01656-733282 **Mbl:** 07811 214478

Smith, Francis (Leeds), St Columba's Presbytery, 229 Tong St, Dudley Hill, Bradford BD4 9PY **Tel/Fax:** 01274-682284

Smith, Francis, (Liverpool), St Patrick, 111 Common Rd, Newton-le-Willows, Merseyside WA12 9JH **Tel:** 01925-225884. **Fax:** 01925-290625

Smith, Geoffrey (Southwark), 7 Hollybank, 123 Bedford Hill, London SW12 9HE **Tel:** 020-8675 0115

Smith, George, Superior (MAfr), 46 Woodville Gardens, Ealing, London W5 1LQ **Tel:** (House) 020-8998 8552 (Visitors), 020-8997 8792

Smith, George, (Birmingham, retired), 11 Perryfield Court, Landsdown, Bourton-on-the-Water, Gloucestershire GL54 2BH

Smith, Graham, (Brentwood), 96 Ness Rd, Shoeburyness, Essex SS3 9DH **Tel:** 01702 292726

Smith, Ian, BA (Leeds), S34 New North Rd, Huddersfield HD1 5JY **Tel:** 01484-531483 **Fax:** 01484 531504 **E-mail:** smithim@talk21.com

Smith, James, (East Anglia, retired), Sue Ryder Ho, Ballyroan, nr Portlaoise, Co. Laois, Eire

Smith, John P, (Liverpool), St Gregory the Great, 94 Liverpool Rd, Lydiate L31 2NA **Tel:** 0151-526 3843 **Fax:** 0151-520 0602

Smith, Joseph, (Southwark), 192 Parrock St, Gravesend, Kent DA12 1EN **Tel:** 01474-352415

Smith, Joseph, (Leeds), SS John Fisher & Thomas More Presbytery, Bradford Rd, Burley-in-Wharfedale, Ilkley LS29 0LE **Tel:** 01934-863179 **Fax:** 01943-864789 **E-mail:** jassacredheart@aol.com

Smith, Kenneth, (Liverpool, retired), Hollymount, Rufford Rd, Mawdesley, Lancs L40 3SA **Tel:** 01704-821150

Smith, Liam, (Hallam, retired), 93 The Grove, Wheatley Hills, Doncaster DN2 5SF

Smith, Luke (Darren) C, BTh, (Southwark), 38 Charlotte Place, Margate, Kent CT9 1LP **Tel:** 01843-220825

Smith, Michael, (SJ), Southwell Ho. 39 Fitzjohn's Ave, London NW3 5JT **Tel:** 020-7472 5150 **E-mail:** michael.smith@southwellhouse.com

Smith, Michael, Mgr, MA, (Southwark), Corpus Christi, 41 Lyons Cres, Tonbridge, Kent TN9 1EY **Tel:** 01732-353984

Smith, Michael, (Lancaster), 11 Low Saintagnesgate, Ripon, N. Yorks HG4 1NA

Smith, Norman, Canon, (Northampton, retired), Flat 1, Collingwood Ho, Collingwood Rd, Northampton NN1 4RX **Tel:** 01604-710937

Smith, Patrick, (Middlesbrough), Our Lady's, Gale Lane, Acomb, York YO24 3AE **Tel:** 01904-791242

Smith, Paul F, Mgr, STL, (*Diocesan Ecumenical Officer, Greater Manchester Churches Together*) (Salford), St Charles Presbytery, Moorside Rd, Swinton, Manchester M27 3PD **Tel:** 0161-794 1089 **Fax:** 0161-727 8077 **E-mail:** paulsmith@saintcharles.freeserve.co.uk

Smith, Paul J, (Portsmouth), 14 Rockstone Place, Southampton, Hants SO15 2EQ **Tel:** 023-8033 3589 **Fax:** 023-8063 5153

Smith, Paul, (Birmingham), The Presbytery, Bedley Rd, Redditch B98 8LT **Tel:** 01527 63096

Smith, Peter, (Hexham & Newcastle, retired), 5 Middle Street, Tynemouth NE30 4ED **Tel:** 0191 2574318

Smith, Peter, JCL (Birmingham), St Augustine's Presbytery, Ave Rd, Handsworth, Birmingham B21 8ED **Tel:** 0121-524 2662

Smith, Peter (Leeds), St Paul's Presbytery, 57 Dewsbury Rd, Cleckheaton BD19 5BT **Tel:** 01274-872984

Smith, Philip, (Lancaster), St Clare's, Sharoe Green Ln North, Fulwood, Preston,

Lancs PR2 9HH **Tel:** 01772-719604
Smith, Robert, (Liverpool), 45 Carr Lane, Wigan WN3 5NL **Tel:** 01942-231459
Smith, Shaun, (Hallam), Sacred Heart Presbytery, 479 Langsett Rd, Sheffield S6 2LN **Tel:** 0114-234 3580
Smith, Tom, (Clifton), St Gregory's Presbytery, 10 St James Square, Cheltenham GL50 3PR **Tel:** 0242-523737
Smith, William, (IC), Te Hira, 21 Moultrie Rd, Rugby CV21 3BD
Smithwick, Anthony M, (OSB), Monastery of Christ the King, 29 Bramley Rd, N14 4HE **Tel:** 020-8440 7769
Smulski, George, (OFM), Franciscan Community, 270 Ballater St, Glasgow G5 0YT **Tel:** 0141-429 0740 **Fax:** 0141-418 0413 **Mbl:** 07957-457736 **E-mail:** geological55@yahoo.co.uk
Smyth, Edmund, (OCD), Carmelite Priory, Youlbury, Boars Hill, Oxford OX1 5HB **Tel:** 01865 735133 **Fax:** 01865 326478 **E-mail:** edmundsmyth@hotmail.com
Smyth, Paul, BA, MA, MSc (CMF), Botwell Ho, Botwell Ln, Hayes, Middx UB3 2AB **Tel:** 020 8573 2065 **Fax:** 020 8561 6748 **E-mail:** provincial@claret.org.uk
Smyth, Philip, BA(Hons), MA, DD, STL, (Clifton), c/o St Ambrose, North Rd, Leigh Woods, Bristol BS8 3PW
Smythe, Patrick, MA (Leeds), Holy name Presbytery, 52 Otley Old Rd, Leeds LS16 6HW **Tel:** 0113-267 8257 **E-mail:** psmythe@globalnet.co.uk
Snape, Kevin, (Liverpool, retired), 47 Almond Brook Rd, Standish, Wigan WN6 0TB **Tel:** 01257-42321
Snee, Patrick J, Canon, (Nottingham, retired), Clounturk, Kilkelly, Co, Mayo, Ireland
Snell, Archibald, (Birmingham, retired), 38 Blackwood Rd, Stly BT4 3PL **Tel:** 0121-580 8244
Soars, Kevin (Salford). c/o Wardley Hall, Worsley, Manchester M28 2ND
Socco, Paul (SM), 109 Main Rd, Sidcup, Kent DA14 6ND
Soley, Bernard, BTh, (Brentwood), The Presbytery, Tracyes Rd, Harlow, Essex CM18 6JJ **Tel:** 01279-425776
Soltys, Stephan, STB, (Ukrainian), c/o Bishop's Ho, 22 Binney St, London W1Y 1YN
Somerville-Knapman, Hugh, BA, MA (Theol), STB, Douai Abbey, Upper Woolhampton, Reading, Berks RG7 5TQ **Tel:** 0118 9715339 **Email:** hughosb@googlemail.com
Sonek, Krzystof, ThM, STL, SSL (OP), Blackfriars, St Giles Oxford OX1 3LY **Tel:** 01865-278400
Sopala, Edward, MA (SChr) Nazareth Ho, Colum Rd, Cardiff CF10 3UN **Tel:** 029-2023 0427
Soper, Laurence, Rt Rev Abbot, STD (OSB), Collegio Sant' Anselmo, Piazza Cavalieri di Malta 5, I-00153, Roma, Italy **Tel:** +39 06 579 1336
Soper, Peter, (Southwark), The Hermitage, More Park, West Malling, Kent ME19 6HN **Tel:** 01732-843302
Sorenti, Carlo, (Parma), 197 Durants Rd, Enfield, Middx EN3 7DE **Tel:** 020-8804 2307
Sormany, Charles, MA, (IC), St Mary's, Ashby Rd, Loughborough LE11 3AB **Tel:** 01509-212754
Soska, Edward, MA (SChr) (Polish Priest), Our Lady of Czesochowa, 107 London Rd, Northwich CW9 8AT **Tel:** 01606-42877
Soule, Becket, (OP), Blackfriars, Buckingham Rd, Cambridge CB3 0DD **Tel:** 01223-352461
Southey, Ambrose, Rt Rev Dom, (OCSO), Our Lady and St Bernard, Mount Saint Bernard Abbey, Coalville, Leics LE67 5UL **Tel:** 01530-832298/832022
Southwell, Andrew (OSB), 58 Thornton Rd, London SW12 0LF **Tel:** 020 8674 3704
Southworth, John, (Liverpool), Our Lady's Presbytery, 27 High Park St, Liverpool L8 8DX **Tel:** 0151-727 1463 **Fax:** 0151-281 7108
Sowa, Adam, (MS), 4 Blythswood Rd, Goodmayes, Ilford, Essex IG3 8SH **Tel:** 020-8590 9026
Spaight, Daniel, Canon (Middlesbrough), Christ the King, Trenchard Ave, Thornaby, Cleveland TS17 0EG **Tel:** 01642-659008
Spain, Christopher, BTh, (Arundel & Brighton), St Mary Magdalene's Presbytery, Sea Rd, Bexhill-on-Sea, E. Sussex TN40 1RH **Tel:** 01424-210263 **E-mail:** chris.spain@dabnet.org
Sparks, Bernard, (Salford, retired), 35 Brookside, Palatine Rd, Didsbury, Manchester M20 2UE **E-mail:** b.sparks@cwctv.net
Spellman, Paul, MA (Portsmouth), 346 Portswood Rd, Southampton, Hants SO17 3SB **Tel:** 023-8055 5470 **Mbl:** 07751 662741 **E-mail:** portswood@portsmouth-dio.org.uk
Spelman, Michael, Canon (Arundel & Brighton, retired), Lake View Cottage, Woodfield, Aghamore, Ballyhaunis, Co Mayo, Ireland
Spence, Robert A, Canon, VG, STL, BA (Hexham & Newcastle), All Saints, Kitswell Rd, Lanchester, Co. Durham DH7 0JQ **Tel:** 01207-520374

Spencer, Eric, DCL, (Portsmouth, retired), 43 Homeyork Ho, Danesmead Cl, Fulord, York YO10 4QX

Spencer, James, BA, BTh, (Southwark), 26 Deepdene Rd, Welling DA16 3QL **Tel:** 0208 303 4422

Spencer, Nicholas BD (OSB) Quarr Abbey, Ryde, Isle of Wight PO33 4ES **Tel:** 01983-882420

Spencer, Roger (East Anglia), The Presbytery, The Common, Southwold IP18 6AH **Tel:** 01502-723207

Spinelli, Aaron (Arundel & Brighton), 12 Eastgate Gdns, Guildford Surrey GU1 4AZ **Tel:** 01483 562704 **Fax:** 01483 452206 **Email:** admin@stjo-guildford.co.uk

Spirik, Cyril (Ukrainian), 10 Park View Rd, Bradford BD9 4PA **Tel:** 01274-542307

Sporny, Tadeusz, (SJ (Westminster, retired), 182 Walm Lane, Willesden Green London NW2 3AX **Tel:** 0208-452 4304

Sprague, Peter, (Portsmouth), c/o Bishop's Ho, Edinburgh Road, Portsmouth PO1 3HG

Spring, John J, BA, (Salford), All Hallows College, Gracepark Rd, Drumcondra, Dublin 9, Eire

Squires, Stephen, (Birmingham), 173 Coalway Rd, Merry Hill, Wolverhampton WV3 7ND **Tel:** 01902 341343 **E-mail:** stjosephschurch@hotmail.com

Stachurski, Edward, (Polish, Opole), 50 Pitt St, Kidderminster DY10 2UN **Tel:** 01562-745914

Stack, Michael, (Birmingham), St Osburg's, Barras Ln, Coventry CV1 4AQ **Tel:** 024 76 220402

Stacpoole, Alberic, MC, MA, DPhil, FRHistS, (OSB), Ampleforth Abbey, York YO62 4EN **Tel:** 01439-766714 **Fax:** 01439-766724

Stainton-Polland, Conor, MA, BD (Liverpool), St Matthew's Presbytery, 19 Townsend Ave, Liverpool L13 9DL **Tel/Fax:** 0151 226 1828 **E-mail:** stmatts@blueyonder.co.uk

Stamp, Simon, (Salford), Wardley Hall, Worsley, Manchester M28 2ND **Tel:** 0161-794 2825 **Tel:** 0161-727 8592 **Email:** revsec@wardleyhall.org.uk

Standen, David, BD, (Birmingham), The Presbytery, Gregory Ave, Weoley Castle B29 5DY **Tel:** 0121 475 1634

Standish, Benjamin (OSB), St Anne's Priory, 23 Prescot Rd, Ormskirk, Lancs L39 4TG **Tel:** 01695-572168 **Fax:** 01695-571136

Standish, Paul, (Shrewsbury), Sacred Heart, St Peter's, Wythenshawe **Tel:** 0161-998 5319 **E-mail:** parishpriest@298@btinternet.com

Standley, David, (Southwark), 36 Altenburg Gardens, London SW11 1JJ **Tel:** 020-7228 2121

Stanier, Michael, MA (Portsmouth), The Presbytery, 2 Connaught Rd, Fleet, Hants GU51 3RA **Tel:** 01252-616963 **Fax:** 01252-815882 **E-mail:** mstanier@portsmouth-dio.org.uk

Stanley, Cedric, (Westminster), 1 Dunster Cl, Park Lane, Harefield, Middx UB9 6BS **Tel:** 01895-822365

Stanley, Mortimer, Canon, (Salford, retired), Stella Maris, Doon Rd, Ballybunnion, Co Kerry, Ireland.

Stanley, Peter, (Liverpool), St Joseph's Presbytery, Harpers Lane, Chorley, Lancs PR6 0HR **Tel:** 01257-262713 **Fax:** 01257-270749

Stanley, Thomas (SCJ), Dehon Vidya Sadhan, U.C. College, Alwaye 683102, Kerala, India

Stanton, Peter J, BSc, BA, (Lancaster), Castlerigg Manor, Keswick CA12 4AR **Tel:** 01768-772711 **Fax:** 01768-775302

Stapleford, Thomas, BA (OSB), Ealing Abbey, Charlbury Grove, Ealing W5 2DY **Tel:** 020-8862 2100

Staples, David, (MHM, retired), Herbert Ho, 41 Victoria Rd, Freshfield, Merseyside L37 1LW **Tel:** 01704-835843

Stapleton, Ciaran, (Salford), Parroquia Los Santos Martires, Apartado 355, Miraflores, Alto Chimbote, Peru, South America

Stapleton, John, Canon, BA, JCL, FRGS; (Arundel and Brighton, retired), 14 Westbrooke, Worthing, W. Sussex BN11 1RF **Tel:** 01903 206969

Stappard, Michael, (Nottingham, retired), 4 Greenacre, Stanton Hill, Sutton-in-Ashfield, Notts NG17 3HZ **Tel:** 01623-442837

Stark, Anselm, (OCSO), Our Lady and St Bernard, Mount St Bernard Abbey, Coalville, Leicester LE67 5UL **Tel:** 01530-832298/832022

Stark, Anthony G, Mgr, KCHS (Westminster), 31 Southdown Rd, Wimbledon SW20 8QJ **Tel:** 020-8947 2598

Starkey, Denis, ThCC (MAfr), Missionary Institute of London, Holcombe Ho, The Ridgeway, London NW7 4HY **Tel:** 01772-722378 **E-mail:** mafr@preston39.freeserve.co.uk

Starrs, Peter, (Hexham & Newcastle, retired), 445 Ballyoran Park, Portadown, Co. Armagh, Northern Ireland **Tel:** 028-3839 4464

Stebakunzi, Justin (MAfr), 46 Woodville Gardens, London W5 1LQ **Tel:** 020-8998 8552 **Fax:** 020-8997 8792

Stebbens, Alphege, Sub-prior (OSB),

Prinknash Abbey, Cranham, Gloucester, GL4 8EX **Tel:** 01452-812455 **E-mail:** prinknash@waitrose.com

Steel, Geoffrey, BA, MTh, (Lancaster), St Augustine, 10 Waverley Rd, Carlisle CA3 9JU **Tel:** 01228-526765

Steele, Joseph, (CSSp), Saint Bede, Station Rd, Rotherham S60 1HF **Tel:** 01709-562012

Steele, William, Mgr, MA, PhL, STL, (Leeds, Retired), Ashlea, 62 Headingley Lane, Leeds LS6 2BU **Tel:** 0113-261 8048/49 **E-mail:** william.steele@dioceseofleeds.org.uk

Steen, Kevin, (Arundel & Brighton, retired), St Joseph's Nursing Home, East St, Littlehampton, W. Sussex BH17 6AU **Tel:** 01903-715590

Steenson, Malachy, (CP), St Joseph's Retreat, Highgate Hill, London N19 5NE **Tel:** 020-7272 2320 **Fax:** 020-272 2320

Stefek, Kazimierz, (OSPPE), SS St Mary & John's Presbytery, Snow Hill, Wolverhampton WV2 4AD **Tel:** 01902-421676

Stempczyk, Martin, (Hexham & Newcastle), St Bede, Chapel Rd, Jarrow, Tyne & Wear NE32 3LX **Tel:** 0191-489 7364 **Fax:** 0191-430 1351

Stenger, Friedrich, (MAfr), Oak Lodge, 48 Totteridge Common, Whetstone, London N20 8LZ

Stenico, Joseph, (MCCJ, retired), Sacred Heart London Rd, Sunningdale, Berks SL5 0JX **Tel:** 01990-21238

Stephen, Francis, MSFS, St Dunstan's Presbytery, Langport Rd, Somerton, Somerset TA11 6RS **Tel:** 01458-272824

Stephens, Felix, MA, (OSB), St Mary's, Smith St, Warrington WA1 2NS **Tel:** 01925-635664 **Fax:** 01925-411830

Stephens, Simon James BD, MTh (Birmingham), St Mary's Presbytery, Ford Green Rd, Northon-le-Moors, Stoke ST6 8LT **Tel:** 01782-257371

Stevens, Brian PhD, MA, LLM, LLB (Plymouth), 22 Hillgrove, Newquay, Cornwall TR7 2QZ **Tel:** 01637-874188

Stevens, Michael, (Westminster, retired), 39 Barum Court, Litchdon St, Barnstable EX32 8QL

Stevens, Peter Francis, (Westminster), Flat 1, Croft Court, Brickwall Lane, Ruislip HA4 8JT **Tel:** 01895 677908

Steward, John, BSc, PGCE, DipEd, Tech, (Birmingham, retired), St Mary's, Harbourne, Birmingham B17 0DN

Stewart, David (SJ), Garnett Ho, 4 Windmill Dr, London SW4 9DE **Tel:** 0208 6754710 **Fax:** 0208 6737647 **E-mail:** dave@fsplus.info

Stewart, Edward, STL, MA, Canon, (Birmingham), St Mary, 45 West St, Warwick CV34 6AB **Tel:** 01926-492913

Stewart, Jonathan (Plymouth), The Presbytery, Glendaragh Rd, Teignmouth, Devon TQ14 8PH **Tel:** 01626-774640

Stewart, Joseph, (Wrexham), Church of St Mary the Virgin, 3 The Villas, New High St, Ruabon, Wrexham LL14 6NW **Tel:** 01978-821568

Stewart, Michael, (Westminster, retired), 50 Bull Stag Green, Hatfield, Herts AL9 5DE **Tel:** 01707-264213

Stewart, Rory, (Northampton), 39 Bush Hill, Northampton NN3 2PD **Tel:** 01604-408407

Stibbles, George, STL (OSA), St Augustine's Priory, 55 Fulham Palace Rd, Hammersmith, London W6 8AU **Tel:** 020-8748 3788 **Fax:** 020-8846 9574

Stickland, Augustine, MA, (OSB, retired), Douai Abbey, Upper Woolhampton, Reading, Berks RG7 5TQ

Stirrat, James, (Clifton, retired), 186 Killala Rd, Cabra West, Dublin 7 Ireland

Stoakes, Keith, (Westminster), Catholic Church, Commonwealth Ave, London W12 7QR **Tel:** 020-8743 8334

Stock, Marcus, MA, STL (Birmingham), Sacred Heart & St Theresa's, 67 Coventry Rd, Coleshill, Birmingham B46 3EE **Tel:** 01675-463939 **Fax:** 01675-430325 **E-mail:** mstock@btconnect.com

Stockford, Donovan Cyprian, BSc, ARCO, (OSB), Downside Abbey, Stratton on the Fosse, Radstock, Bath, Somerset BA3 4RH **Tel:** 01761-235161

Stocks, Brian, (Hallam), 3 Coldwell Lane, Sheffield S10 5TJ **Tel:** 0114-230 8540

Stodart, Peter, (Southwark), St Augustine, Crescent Rd, Tunbridge Wells TN1 2LY **Tel:** 01892-522525 **Fax:** 01892-526287

Stoker, Donald, (Hallam, retired), 31 Orange Croft, Tickhill, Doncaster DN11 9EW **Tel:** 01302-744655

Stoker, Leo, Canon, (Liverpool), Ince Blundell Hall, Ince Blundell, Liverpool L38 6JL **Tel:** 0151 929 2596

Stokes, George, Mgr, (Brentwood), 16 East Thurrock Rd, Grays, Essex RM17 6SR **Tel:** 01375 372306

Stokes, John (Westminster), HM Prison Whitemoor, Longhill Rd, March, Cambs PE15 0PR **Tel:** 01345-660653

Stokes, Kevin BTh (Southwark), St Laurence's 1 Milton Rd, Cambridge, Cambs CB4 1XB

Stokes, Michael W, (Brentwood), 114 Connaught Ave, Frinton-on-Sea, Essex CO13 9AD **Tel:** 01255-674475

Stone, Martin, (CMF), Botwell Ho, Botwell Lane, Hayes, Middx UB3 2AB

Tel: 020-8573 2065 **Fax:** 020-8561 6748 **E-mail:** Botwell@claret.org.uk

Stone, Peter, (Plymouth, retired), 3 Trescobeas Rd, Falmouth, Cornwall TR11 2JB **Tel:** 01326-313156

Stonehill, Terence T, Mgr Provost Emeritus (Arundel & Brighton, retired), St Mary's Ho, 38 Preston Park Ave, Brighton E. Sussex **Tel:** 01273-507480

Stones, Gerald, STL, LSS, (MAfr), Oak Lodge, 48 Totteridge Common, London N20 8NB **Tel:** 020-8959 1515 **Fax:** 020-8959 7421 **E-mail:** gerry@gerston.freeserve.co.uk

Stonham, Paul, Abbot, BA, STB (OSB), Belmont Abbey, Hereford HR2 9RZ **Tel:** 01432-374718 **E-mail:** abbotofbelmont@aol.com

Stonier, Peter J, BA(Dunelm), (Birmingham), 34 Heron St, Rugeley WS15 2DZ **Tel/Fax:** 01889-582586

Stonier, Peter William, Mgr, (Birmingham, retired), 71 Queen's Park Rd, Harborne, Birmingham B32 2LB

Storey, Bryan, (Arundel and Brighton), Chy an Pronter, Bossinet Rd, Tintagel, Cornwall PL34 0AQ **Tel:** 01840-770663

Stork, Richard Mgr, MSc, STD, (Opus Dei), 18 Netherhall Gardens, London NW3 5TH **Tel:** 020-7472 5730

Stott, Peter J, (Hexham & Newcastle), St Bede's, 233 Whickham View, Newcastle upon Tyne NE15 7HP **Tel:** 0191-274 6147

Stoyle, Peter, (Portsmouth, retired), Floreat, Manor Rd, Hayling Island, Hants PO11 0QX **Tel:** 02392-468002

Strain, William, (Northampton), St Augustine's Presbytery, 24 Amersham Hill, High Wycombe, Bucks HP13 6NZ **Tel:** 01494-523969

Strange, C Roderick, Mgr, PhD (Shrewsbury), Pontificio Collegio Beda, Viale di San Paolo 18, 00146 Roma, Italia **Tel:** 00 3906 5512 7201 **Fax:** 00 3906 5512 7219 **E-mail:** r.strange@bedacollege.com

Stratton, Joseph Henry, MA, MEd, MIBiol, Provost, (Shrewsbury), St Paul's, 33 Bulkeley Rd, Poynton, Stockport SK12 1NR **Tel/Fax:** 01625-872606 **E-mail:** jhstratton@aol.com

Straw, Francis Gavin, MA, BSc, Novice Master (OSB), St Mary's Abbey, Buckfast, Buckfastleigh, Devon TQ11 0EE **Tel:** 01364-645500

Stickland, Augustine MA (OSB), Our Lady and St Joseph, Priory Rd, Alcester, Warwicks B49 5DY **Tel:** 01789-762573

Stringfellow, Andrew, PhB, SDB, STL, (Salford), St Winifred's, Mauldeth Rd, Heaton Mersey, Stockport SK4 3NB **Tel:** 0161-432 4412 **Fax:** 0161-975 0120

Stringfellow, Anthony, Mgr, (Liverpool, retired), Flat 2, St Marie's Ho, 27 Seabank Rd, Southport PR9 0EJ **Tel:** 01704 537783

Strowbridge, John H, (Liverpool, retired), 3 Harlech Ave, Hindley Green, Wigan WN2 4RA

Stuart, Kentigern, (OFM), St Mary's Nursing Home, St Mary's Rd, Moston M40 0BL **Tel:** 0161-681 1929

Sturdy, Damian, (OSB), Prinknash Abbey, Cranham, Gloucester GL4 8EX **Tel:** 01452-812455 **E-mail:** prinknash@waitrose.com

Styles, Robert, (SJ), The Priest's Ho, Holy Cross, Ash Meadow, Much Hadham, Hertfordshire SG10 6AW **Tel/Fax:** 01279-842354 **E-mail:** bstylessj@aol.com

Suarez, Michael, (SJ), Campion Hall, Oxford OX1 1QS **Tel:** 01865-286131

Sugg, Robert, BTh, (Southwark), St Cecilia's Presbyery, 101 Stonecot Hill, Sutton, Surrey SM3 9HP **Tel:** 020 8641 3141

Suhartana, Paul (SVD), 8 Teignmouth Rd, London NW2 4HN **Tel:** 020-8452 8430

Sullivan, Brendan, (MHM, retired), Herbert Ho, 41 Victoria Rd, Freshfield, Liverpool L37 1LW **Tel:** 01704-835848

Sullivan, Emmanuel, (Arundel & Brighton), 2 Falkland Grove, Dorking, Surrey RH4 3DL

Sullivan, John, (Director, Overseas Missions) (Salford), St Joseph, 81 Bolton St, Ramsbottom BL0 9HY **Tel/Fax:** 01706-823200

Sullivan, John J, (Nottingham, retired), 22 Alderdale Dr, High Lane, Stockport, Cheshire SK6 8BX **Tel:** 01663-763904

Sullivan, Michael A, (Clifton), Flat A, St John's Flats, South Parade, Bath BA2 4AF **Tel:** 01255-460112

Sullivan, Michael C, (Leeds), St Mary's Presbytery, 142 East Parade, Bradford BD1 5EE **Tel:** 01274-721248

Sullivan, Timothy, (Lancaster), St Maria Goretti, Gamull Lane, Ribbleton, Preston PR2 6SJ **Tel:** 01772-700231

Sultana, Anthony, (SDB), Our Lady of Lourdes, 71 High View Rd, Farnborough GU14 7PT **Tel:** 01252-546897 **Fax:** 01252-514578 **Mbl:** 07818-604848 **E-mail:** tsultana@portsmouth-dio.org.uk

Summers, Derek, (Prior and Bursar), (OSB), St Augustine's Abbey, Ramsgate, Kent CT11 9PA **Tel:** 01843-593045 **Fax:** 01843-582732 **E-mail:** ablaurence@aol.com

Summers, Richard Gwyn, (OCSO), Abbey of Our Lady and St Samson, Caldey Island, Tenby SA70 7UH **Tel:** 01834-842632.

Summersgill, Mgr Andrew, JCL, (Leeds),

General Secretary, The Bishop's Conference of England and Wales, 39 Eccleston Square, London SW1V 1BX **Tel:** 020-7630 8220 **E-mail:** gensec@cbcew.org.uk

Sumner, Philip, MCL, LCL (Salford), Our Lady and St Patrick, 40 Union St West, Oldham OL8 1DL **Tel:** 0161-624 4834 **Mbl:** 07976-230919 **E-mail:** phil.sumner@telinco.com

Sunny, Paul, (Plymouth, retired) (MSFS), 73 Higher Kingston, Yeovil, Somerset, BA21 4AR **Tel:** 01935-423549

Supple, John A, Canon, (Clifton, retired), Nazareth Ho, London Rd, Charlton Kings, Cheltenham GL52 6YJ

Sutch, Timothy Antony, MA, (OSB), St Benet, St Mary's Rd, Beccles, Suffolk NR34 9NR **Tel:** 01502-713179

Sutcliffe, David, (Arundel and Brighton, retired) 33 Keld Dr, Uckfield, E. Sussex TN22 5BT **Tel:** 01825-764435

Sutherland, Francis, CertEd, (SDB), St John Bosco Ho, 121a Reading Rd, Farnborough GU14 6NZ **Tel:** 01252-554300 **Fax:** 01252-375395 **E-mail:** hifibosco@aol.com

Sutiono, Agostinus, (OCarm), 142 Rodney Rd, London SE17 1RA **Tel:** 020-7703 4967

Sutton, Robin I. R., (Shrewsbury, retired), 9 Sherbourne rd, Wallasey CH44 2EY **Tel:** 0151-639 4645 **E-mail:** sutty@psutton.fsworld.co.uk

Swaffer, Thomas C (OPraem), Our Lady of England, Priory School Lane, Storrington, W. Sussex RH20 4LN **Tel:** 01903 742180

Swagemakers, Jan, LCL (MHM). Our Lady of Muswell, Colney Hatch Lane, Muswell Hill, London N10 1PN **Tel:** 020-8883 5607 **Fax:** 020-8444 3463 **E-mail:** janswage@hotmail.com

Swales, Shaun (Hexham & Newcastle), SS Joseph, Patrick & Cuthbert, Church St, Coxhoe Durham DH6 4DA **Tel:** 0191-377 0542

Swann, Robert, (Lancaster), St Robert of Newminster, Benson Lane, Catforth, Preston PR4 0HY **Tel:** 01772-690425

Swanson, Philip, (Liverpool), St Theresa's Presbytery, Gartons Lane, Sutton Manor, St Helens WA9 4RR **Tel:** 01744-812127 **Fax:** 01744-812327

Swarbrick, Paul, (Lancaster), Sacred Heart, 44 Beech Grove, Ashton-on-Ribble, Preston PR2 1AU **Tel:** 01772 726674

Sweeney, Charles J, (MSC), Catholic Presbytery, 14 Beaconsfield Rd, St Albans, Herts AL1 3RB **Tel:** 01727 853585 **Fax:** 01727 855410 **E-mail:** charles.sweeney@tiscali.co.uk

Sweeney, Geoffrey, (MAfr), Nazareth Ho, Hammersmith Rd, London W6 8DB.

Sweeney, James, (OCarm), Whitefriars, 35 Tanners St, Faversham, Kent ME13 7JW **Tel:** 01795-532449

Sweeney, John (CSSp) 22 Linden Grove, Peckham SE15 3LF **Tel/Fax:** 020-7277 6264

Sweeney, Joseph F, MEd, MA, (Salford), St Patrick, 2 Watts St, Rochdale OL12 OHE **Tel:** 01706-645710 **Fax:** 01706-640424 **E-mail:** stpatricksrc@btinternet.com

Sweeney, Liam, (SCA), 90 Colchester Rd, Halstead, Essex CO9 2EW **Tel:** 01787-472477

Sweeney, Martin, (MHM, retired), Herbert Ho, 41 Victoria Rd, Freshfields, Merseyside L37 1LW **Tel:** 01704 835844

Sweeney, Michael F, (Hexham & Newcastle, retired), Aughrim Ho, Ballyliffin, Co Donegal, Ireland **Mbl:** 07711 469730

Swift, Allan, (Salford), St Ethelbert's Presbytery, 67 Wigan Rd, Deane, Bolton BL3 5QJ **Tel:** 01204-62653

Swindlehurst, Peter, (Northampton), RAF Halton, 181b Aylesbury Rd, Wendover, Aylesbury HP22 6AA

Swinglehurst, Timothy, SSL (Leeds), St Austin's Presbytery, 6 Wentworth Terr, Wakefield WF1 3QN **Tel:** 01924-215723

Swingler, Phillip, (Northampton), The Presbytery, 28 Peveril Rd, Duston, Northampton NN5 6JW **Tel:** 01604-751071

Swinhoe, Bernard, MA, (OSB), Douai Abbey, Upper Woolhampton, Reading Berks RG7 5TQ **Tel:** 0118-971 5300

Swires, Mark, (Brentwood), 213 Hornchurch Rd, Hornchurch, Essex RM12 4TL **Tel:** 01708-447761

Sykes, Perry, (Westminster), 16 Abingdon Rd, London W8 6AF **Tel:** 020-7937 4778

Sylvester, Martin, (Nottingham), The Presbytery, 70 Newhall Rd, Swadlincote DE11 0BD **Tel:** 01283-217169

Symondson, Anthony (SJ), 114 Mount St, London W1K 3AH **Tel:** 020 7529 4809 **E-mail:** symondson@googlemail.com

Szczepaniak, Andrzej, MA (SChr), 189 Fletton Ave, Peterborough PE2 8DE **Tel:** 01733-552726

Szende, Tibor (OSB), c/o Quarr Abbey, Ryde, Isle of Wight PO37 7AT **E-mail:** szendetib@hotmail.com

Szponar, Jan, Mgr, (Salford, retired), Albert Ho, Flat 7, 180 High St, Bolton BL3 6PL **Tel:** 01204-399758

Taaffe, Thomas, EpV, BA, MA, (Portsmouth), 1 Radley Rd, Abingdon, Oxon OX14 3PL **Tel:** 01235-520375 **E-mail:** tomtaaffe@aol.com

Tablizo, Roy (Virac), 380 Lordship Ln,

Dulwich SE22 8ND **Tel:** 020-8693 5070 **Fax:** 020-8693 8447

Taggart, John, (Hexham & Newcastle), Sacred Heart, Byermoor, Burnopfield, Newcastle upon Tyne NE16 6NU **Tel:** 01207-270226

Taggart, Kevin, MA, Prior (OSB), Worth Abbey, Crawley, W Sussex RH10 4SB **Tel:** 01342-710310

Talbot, Anthony, (Birmingham), Monastery of Notre Dame , 36220 Fontgombault, France

Talbot, Liam, (SDS), Our Lady of Victories Presbytery, Pearse St, Sallyn Oggim, Dun Laoghaire, Co Dublin Eiré **Tel:** 00353 1 2854667 **Fax:** 00353 1 2847024 **E-mail:** liamsds@gmail.com

Tams, David, (Birmingham), 1151 Warwick Rd, Acocks Green, Birmingham B27 6RG **Tel:** 0121-706 0800 **Fax:** 0121-707 5734

Tan, Joseph, (Brentwood), The Presbytery, Petersfield Ave, Harold Hill, Romford, Essex RM3 9PB **Tel:** 01708-343492

Tangney, Denis, Canon, (Leeds, retired), Mount St Joseph's Home, Flat 1E1, Shire Oak Rd, Leeds LS6 2DE **Tel:** 0113-275 4611

Tanner, David, LCL, (Hexham & Newcastle), Our Lady Immaculate, Whittingham, Alnwick, Northumberland NE66 4SY **Tel:** 01665-574240

Tanner, Norman, (SJ), Campion Hall, Oxford OX1 1QS **Tel:** 01865-286104 **E-mail:** norman.tanner@campion.ox.ac.uk

Tansey, Patrick, (Salford), St James, 58 Bowland Dr, Montserrat, Bolton BL1 5TX **Tel:** 01204-840030 **E-mail:** frpattansey@aol.com

Tansey, Patrick, BA, PGCE, CertTheol (Portsmouth), 1 Coxwell Rd, Faringdon, Oxon SN7 7EB **Tel:** 01367-241474 **Fax:** 01367-241474

Tapparo, Aldo Luigi MA (Birmingham), 115 Headley Way, Oxford OX3 7SS **Tel:** 01865-762964

Tarbuck, Benedict, Canon, (Birmingham, retired), St Joseph's Home, Coventry Rd, Coleshill B46 3ED

Targett, Leo, (Portsmouth, retired), 1 Hughes Cres, Longcot, Oxon SN7 7SU **Tel:** 01793-784126

Tastard, Terry, BA, BD, AKC, MPhil, (Westminster), 41 Brook Green, London W6 7BL **Tel:** 020-7603 3832

Taunton, Clifford, (SJ), Corpus Christi Jesuit Community, 757 Christchurch Rd, Boscombe, Bournemouth BH7 6AN **Tel:** 01202-436700

Tavares, John, (Nottingham), The Priests Ho, Sherwood Dr, New Ollerton, Notts NG22 9PP **Tel:** 01623-860238

Tavera, Giuseppe (SX) 260 Nether St, London N3 1HT **Tel:** 020-8346 0428

Taylerson, Robert, BSc, STL, (Birmingham), The Presbytery, Stone Rd, Trent Vale ST4 6SP **Tel:** 01782 658063

Taylor, Anthony, (Birmingham, retired), 22 Hunter's Court, 196 Chester Rd, Streetly B74 3QX **Tel:** 0121-357 1583

Taylor, Augustine, BA, (OSB), St Mary's Abbey, Buckfast, Buckfastleigh, Devon TQ11 0EE **Tel:** 01364-43301

Taylor, Bertram, (Lancaster, retired), 15 Hall Rd, Fulwood, Preston PR2 9QD **Tel:** 01772-715504

Taylor, Brian, MA, MTh, FSA, FRHistS (Arundel & Brighton), Vine Cottage, St Edward's, Sutton Park, Guildford, Surrey GU4 7QN **Tel:** 01483-504630

Taylor, Colin, (Nottingham), The Presbytery, 17 Nottingham Rd, Ilkeston, Derbys DE7 5RF **Tel:** 0115-9325642

Taylor, David, (Hexham & Newcastle), St Peter's, Kells Ln, Low Fell, Gateshead NE9 5HY **Tel:** 0191-487 6505 **Fax:** 0191-487 4190

Taylor, John, (Brentwood), The Presbytery, Champion Rd, Upminster, Essex RM14 2SY **Tel:** 01708-222432

Taylor, John, PhD (Plymouth, retired), Rock Croft, 2 Buckfast Cl, Buckfastleigh, Devon TQ11 0EW **Tel:** 01364-643555

Taylor, Joseph (Portsmouth, retired), McCauley Mount, Padiham Rd, Burnley, Lancs BB12 6TG

Taylor, Joseph M, (Leeds), St Bernard's Presbytery, Range Ln, Halifax HX3 6DL **Tel:** 01422-353690 **Fax:** 01422-254684

Taylor, Leonard, (Southwark, retired), Curraghnagh, Easkey, Co Sligo, Ireland **Tel:** 00353 (0) 9649959

Taylor, Paul, (OMI), St Theresa's Presbytery, Bentley St, Blackburn, Lancs BB1 3JT **Tel:** 01254-55888

Taylor, Peter, Canon, (Birmingham), St Mary's, The Mount, Walsall, W. Mids WS1 3NF **Tel:** 01922-622633

Taylor, Philip (SP), Our Lady of Victory, Brownshill, Gloucestershire GL6 8AL **Tel:** 01453-333084 **Fax:** 01453-731888

Taylor, Richard, (Salford), San Tommaso d'Aquino (Convitto Internazionale), Via Degli Ibernesi 20, 00184 Roma, Italia.

Taylor, Roger, MA, STB, (Westminster), The Presbytery, Stonard Rd, Green Lns, London N13 4DJ **Tel:** 020-8886 9568

Tchang, Louis, 21a Soho Square, London W1V 5FJ **Tel:** 020-7437 0892

Teader, Michael (East Anglia), 112 Withersfield Rd, Haverhill, Suffolk CB9 9HE **Tel:** 01440-704923

Teece, Paul, (Southwark), 36 Altenburg

Gardens, Clapham Common, London SW11 1JJ **Tel:** 020-7228 2121**E-mail:** stvincentdepaul@compuserve.com.

Teeling, James, (Southwark), Priest's Ho, 2 Commerell St, Greenwich, London SE10 0EA **Tel:** 020-8858 1845 **Fax:** 020-8305 0569

Temple, Philip-Herluin, M, (OSB), Monastery of Christ the King, 29 Bramley Rd, London N14 4HE **Tel:** 020-8440 7769

Tetlow, Francis, MA, (Salford, retired), McAuley Mount, Padiham Rd, Burnley, Lancs BB12 6TG

Thacker, Robert, (Nottingham),The Presbytery, 2 Horderns Rd, Chapel-en-le-Frith Derbys SK23 9ST **Tel:** 01298-813491

Thadathil, Cyril, BA, BPh, BTh, MTh, (OSB), Upper King's Head Rd, Gendros, Swansea SA5 8BR **Tel:** 01792 586454

Thankachan, Valomchalil Augusty, (Menevia), St David's Priory, St David's Place, Swansea SA1 3NG **Tel:** 01792 653 343

Theverajan, E, (Tamil Chaplain), 304 Garratt Ln, Earlsfield, London SW18 4EH **Tel:** 020-8870 6257

Thom, Bernard, Canon, (Arundel & Brighton, retired), 30 Downsview Dr, Midhurst, W. Sussex GU29 9LW **Tel:** 01730-810332

Thomann, Italo, (SDB), 32 Orbel St, Battersea, London SW11 3NZ **Tel:** 020-7801 9040 **Fax:** 020-7801 9041

Thomas, Brendan, BA, STL, (OSB), Belmont Abbey, Belmont, Hereford HR2 9RZ **Tel:** 01432-277388 Ext 223 **E-mail:** dombrendan@aol.com

Thomas, Christopher, (Liverpool), "Irenaeus", 31 Rosemary Ln, Formby L37 3HA **Tel:** 01704-834271 **E-mail:** chris@irenaeus.freeserve.co.uk

Thomas, Christopher A, (Birmingham), 29 Charnwood Grove, West Bridgeford Nottingham NG2 7NT **Tel/Fax:** 0115-981 4271 **E-mail:** holyspirit.wb@lineone.net

Thomas, Christopher P, (Nottingham), Corpus Christi Presbytery, Listowel Cres, Clifton Estate, Nottingham NG11 9BP **Tel/Fax:** 0115-921 2964

Thomas, Hilary, (SJ), St Wilfrid's Presbytery, 1 Winckley Square, Preston PR1 3JJ **Tel:** 01772 555244 **Fax:** 01772 251955

Thomas, John James, (Cardiff, retired), 317 Malpas Rd, Newport NP20 6DX

Thomas, John Patrick, (Menevia), The Presbytery, 9 Fountain Row, Haverfordwest, Pembrokeshire SA61 15X **Tel:** 01437 762284 **E-mail:** ourladystowhill@aol.com

Thomas, Louis, Canon, (Westminster, retired), 22 Sherwood Hall, East End Rd, Finchley, London N2 0TA **Tel:** 020-8444 6141

Thomas, Michael (Clifton). St George's Rectory, Billet St, Taunton TA1 3NE **Tel:** 01823-272700

Thomas, Philip, BA, (Clifton), Priests Ho, 3 Priorsfield, Marlborough, Wilts SN8 4AQ **Tel:** 01672-513267

Thomas, Thomas Kennedy, STB (Westminster), c/o Archbishop's Ho, Ambrosden Ave, London SW1P 1QJ

Thompson, Benedict, ARCM, LTCL, CertCouns (OSB), Douai Abbey, Upper Woolhampton, Reading RG17 5TQ **Tel:** 0118-971 5350 **Fax:** 0118-971 5303 **E-mail:** parish@douaiabbey.org.uk

Thompson, Francis, (MHM), 9 Northridge Way, Boxmoor, Hemel Hempstead, Herts HP1 2AE **Tel:** 01442 217907 **E-mail:** frank-kaziu@khotmail.co.uk

Thompson, Gordon, (Southwark), 10 Woodland Court, Grove Rd, Sutton, Surrey SM1 2DB **Tel:** 020-8643 7200

Thompson, John, JCL, (Liverpool), St Francis de Sales, 75 Hale Rd, Walton, Liverpol L4 3RL **Tel:** 0151-525 3483 **Fax:** 0151-525 2449

Thompson, Martin, BTh, STL, (Arundel & Brighton), **E-mail:** frmwjt@hotmail.com

Thompson, Michael, MA (Liverpool), Priest's House, 184 Liverpool Rd, Skelmersdale WN8 8BX **Tel/Fax:** 01695 724476 **E-mail:** strichards_skem@tiscali.co.uk

Thompson, Ross, (Middlesbrough), St Joseph, 169 Burdyke Ave, York YO30 6JX **Tel/Fax:** 01904-622448

Thomson, Simon, (Portsmouth), 21 Gladys Ave, North End, Portsmouth, Hants PO2 9AZ **Tel/Fax:** 023-9266 0927 **E-mail:** ccsj@rcdp.org.uk

Thoppil, Joseph (Verapoly, India), 2 Brereton Rd, Bedford MK40 1HU **Tel:** 01234-352569

Thora, Jack (MAfr), 42 Stormont Rd, London N6 4NP **Tel:** 020-8342 8447

Thorne, Selwyn Columba, MA, (OSB), Downside Abbey, Stratton on the Fosse, Bath BA3 4RH **Tel:** 01761-235161

Thornton, Gerald, (Leeds), Holy Rosary Presbytery, 3 Cross Francis St, Leeds LS7 4BZ **Tel:** 0113-262 3624

Thornton, Kevin, (Hallam), St Francis Presbytery, 277 Sandygate Rd, Sheffield S10 5SD **Tel:** 0114-263 0383

Thornton, Niall, (Southwark, retired), Shanaleigh, Mageney Athy, Co. Kildare, Eire **Tel:** 00353(0) 599145140

Thornton, Sean, (Westminster), 1 Wrentham Ave, London NW10 3HT **Tel:** 020-8964 4040

Thorpe, Francis MA, (Salford), All Souls and St John Vianney, Liverpool St, Salford M5 2HQ **Tel:** 0161-736 5432

Thwaites, Hugh (SJ), Corpus Christi, 757 Christchurch Rd, Boscombe, Bournemouth BH7 6AN **Tel:** 01202 436700

Tierney, Kevin, (Salford), St Cuthbert's, 3 Palatine Rd, Withington, Manchester M20 3LH **Tel/Fax:** 0161-445 1080

Tierney, Paul, (SSC), St Columban's, 28 Redington Rd, Hampstead, London NW3 7RB **Tel:** 020-7794 8131 **Fax:** 020-7794 7074

Tierney, Peter, (Salford), St Mary's Hospital Chaplaincy, 146 Haslingden Rd, Blackburn, Lancs BB2 3HJ **Tel:** 01254-56026

Tighe, Wilfrid, (CongOrat), The Oratory, Brompton Rd, London SW7 2RP **Tel:** 020-7589 4811

Tilley, David, (FDP), Westminster Ho, 25 Lower Teddington Rd, Hampton Wick, Kingston upon Thames KT1 4HB **Tel:** 020-8977 5130/3434 **Fax:** 020-8977 0105

Tillotson, Francis W, (Liverpool), St Aidan's Presbytery, Holmes House Ave, Winstanley, Wigan WN3 6EE **Tel:** 01942-511630

Timlin, Anthony, (Birmingham, retired), Aston Hall, Aston, Stone, Staffordshire ST15 0BJ **Tel:** 01785-811844

Timmins, John, (Brentwood), Church Ho, Braintree Rd, Great Bardfield, Essex CM7 4RN **Tel:** 01371-810428

Timney, Godric, CertEd (OSB), St Anne's Priory, 23 Prescot Rd, Ormskirk L39 4TG **Tel:** 01695-572168 **Fax:** 01695-571136

Tindall, Dennis, (Hexham & Newcastle), St Mary's, South Moor, Stanley, Co Durham DH9 6NR **Tel:** 01207-232798

Tingay, Alexander MA(Cantab) (OSB), St Mary's Abbey, Quarr, Ryde, Isle of Wight PO33 4ES **Tel:** 01983-882420 **Fax:** 01983-884402

Tirello, Joseph, (FDP), 25 Lower Teddington Rd, Hampton Wick KT1 4BH

Tobin, David (IC), Collegio Rosmini, via di Porta Latina 17, Roma 00179 **Tel:** 0039 0670 495601 **Fax:** 0039 0677 400003 **E-mail:** David.ic@btinternet.com

Tobin, Gregory, (Nottingham), The Presbytery, 29 Charnwood Grove, West Bridgford, Nottingham NG2 7NT **Tel:** 0115-981 4271

Tobin, Sean, STB (Portsmouth), The Presbytery, St Colman's Ave, Portsmouth PO6 2JJ **Tel:** 023-9237 6151 **Fax:** 023-9238 4363 **E-mail:** seantobin@aol.com

Toffolo, Adrian, Mgr PhL, STL, (Plymouth), The Presbytery, Higher Church St, Barnstaple, Devon EX32 8JE **Tel:** 01271-343312

Tolan, Terence, (Hallam), St William's Presbytery, Ecclesall Rd, Sheffield S11 8TL **Tel:** 0114-266 2034

Tolhurst, Joseph DD, (Cong Orat), The Oratory, Hagley Rd, Birmingham B16 8UE **Tel:** 0121-454 0496

Tomaney, Austin, (Hexham & Newcastle, retired), 3 Flagg Ho, Westoe Village, South Shields NE33 3EB **Tel:** 0191-425 2776

Tomblin, John, (Hallam, retired), 74 Sandygate Rd, Sheffield S10 5RZ **Tel:** 0114 284 8344

Tomlinson, Adrian (Hallam), 21 Ashleigh Ave, Gleadless, Sheffield S12 5RZ **Tel:** 0114-239 7191

Tomlinson, Ian, Superior (SJ), Loyola Hall, Warrington Rd, Rainhill, Merseyside L35 6NZ **Tel:** 0151-426 4137 **Fax:** 0151-431 0115

Tomlinson, Keith (IC), St Teresa of Lisieux, 53 Front St, Birstall, Leicester LE4 4DQ **Tel:** 01662-929939 **E-mail:** kat444@arsenalfc.net

Tonge, Ivan, (Dublin), 24 Golden Square, W1R 3PA **Tel:** 020-7437 1525

Tonna, Charles, (OFM), 22 St George's Dr, Pimlico, London SW1V 4BN **Tel:** 020-7834 9512

Toole, John, (Wrexham), Presbytery, 21 Heenan Rd, Old Colwyn, Clwyd LL29 9DP **Tel:** 01492-515091

Torrens, Alberic (OFM), Franciscan Friary, Sample Oak Ln, Chilworth GU4 8QR

Tosolino, Tiziano, (SX), 130 Holden Rd, Woodside Park, London N12 7EA

Touw, Dennis, (Westminster), 447 Victoria Rd, South Ruislip, Middx HA4 0EG **Tel:** 020-8845 2186

Tower, Mervyn, MA, LSS, (Birmingham), 25 South Bar St, Banbury, Oxon OX16 9AE **Tel:** 01295-262073

Towers, Adrian J, BA, STL, (Lancaster), St Andrew and Blessed George Haydock, 114 Hoyles Ln, Cottam, Preston PR4 1NB **Tel:** 01772-726166

Towey, Anthony, STL, (Hallam), c/o Bishop's Ho, 75 Norfolk Rd, Sheffield S2 2SZ

Towler, George, BSc(Econ), (Brentwood, retired), Appledore, Stock Rd, Stock, Ingatestone, Essex CM4 9PN **Tel:** 01277-829915 **E-mail:** gtowruss@hotmail.co.uk

Townend, H, (Leeds, retired), c/o Mr & Mrs Travis, 75 Chevet Ln, Sandal, Wakefield WF2 6JE **Tel:** 01924-256941

Townsend, Paul, (Portsmouth), Peter Ho, St Peter St, Winchester, Hants SO23 8BW **Tel/Fax:** 01962-852804

E-mail: paul-townsend@tregalic.co.uk
Trafford, Anthony David, BA, (Clifton), 64 Forbes St, Croydon Park, Sydney, Australia NSW 2133
Tran, Paschal (OSB) Our Lady Star of the Sea and St Michael, Banklands, Workington CA14 3EP **Tel:** 01900-602114 **Fax:** 01900 871797
Tran Van Khug, Peter (AA) Assumption Priory, Victoria Park Square, London E2 9PB **Tel:** 0208 980 1968
Tranter, Carl R, BD, MEd (MSC), Cordate Community, 157 Ettington Rd, Aston, Birmingham B6 6ED **E-mail:** carl@msceurope.co.uk
Tranter, Nicholas J, STL, DipAc, (Clifton), St Joseph's Presbytery, Devizes Rd, Wroughton SN4 0RZ **Tel:** 01793-812330
Trask, Martin, (Hallam), St Thomas More, 477 Wordsworth Ave, Sheffield S5 9JE **Tel:** 0114-232 1441
Travers, Joseph, (Hexham & Newcastle, Retired), St Mary, Dockendale Lane, Whickham NE16 4EN
Travers, Noel, (CM), 29 Eversley Cres, Isleworth TW7 4LR **Tel:** 020-8560 7021
Tredget, Dermot, MSc, MA (OSB), Douai Abbey, Upper Woolhampton, Reading, Berks RG7 5TQ **Tel:** 0118-971 5300 **Fax:** 0118-971 5303
Tredota, Edward, (MS), 4 Blythswood Rd, Goodmayes, Ilford, Essex IG3 8SH **Tel:** 020-8590 9026
Treherne, Thomas, (Arundel & Brighton), Priest's Ho, Portmore Way, Weybridge, Surrey KT13 8JD
Trehy, Kevin, (Middlesbrough), St Margaret Clitherow Presbytery, 3 Holly Tree Ln, Haxby, York YO32 3YJ Tel 01904-768931
Treloar, Simon, (Wrexham) St. Therese of Lisieux, Dundonald Avenue, Abergele, Conwy **Tel:** 01745 833249
Trenchard, John, (CSsR), Rector, St Mary's, Clapham Park Rd, Clapham, London SW4 7AP
Trevillion, Peter, (Brentwood), c/o Cathedral Ho, Ingrave Rd, Brentwood, Essex CM15 8AT
Trinder, Paul A, (Hexham & Newcastle, retired), The Slipper Chapel Cottage, Gray's Ln, Houghton St Giles, Walsingham, Norfolk NR22 6AL
Trojnar, Eugeniusz, (Polish), 88 Fitzwilliam St, Huddersfield HD1 5BB **Tel:** 01484-420474
Trood, Jeremy MA, ACA, STB (Westminster), 130 St Margaret's Road, East Twickenham TW1 1RL **Tel:** 020 8607 9001
Troop, Herbert, (IC), Ker-Maria, Aylesbury Rd, Princes Risborough HP17 0JW **Tel:** 01844-345474
Troy, John Martin STL (MCCJ), Verona Fathers, London Road, Sunningdale, Berks SL5 0JY **Tel:** 01344 621267 **E-mail:** johntroy@yahoo.com
Tubman, James, (Salford), The Sacred Heart, Queen St, Colne BB8 9NB **Tel:** 01282-863135
Tuck, Michael, (Westminster), Catholic Rectory, Green St, Sunbury-on-Thames TW16 6QB **Tel:** 01932-783507
Tucker, Lawrence (SOLT), 2 Lower Blackhorse Hill, Hythe CT21 5LS **Tel:** 01303-266430 **Fax:** 01303-264773
Tuckwell, Adrian, (Hexham & Newcastle), St Patrick's, Owton Manor Ln, Hartlepool TS25 3QG **Tel:** 01429-266734
Tuckwell, Christopher, Canon (Westminster), Clergy Ho, 42 Francis St, London SW1P 1QW **Tel:** 020-7798 9055
Tuite, Gerard (FDP), Don Orione Fathers, Our Lady's Missionary Ho, 2 Walthew Green, Roby Mill, Upholland, Skelmersdale WN8 0QT **Tel/Fax:** 01695-622516
Tuite, Patrick (SDS, retired), Our Lady of Victories Presbytery, Pearse St, Sallynoggin, Dun Laoghaire, Co Dublin, Éire **Tel:** 00353-1 285 4667 **Fax:** 00353-1 284 7024
Tully, Michael J, PhL, STL, (Lancaster), SS Mary and James, Snow Hill, Scorton, Preston, Lancs PR3 1AY **Tel:** 01524-791268
Tully, Paul, (Hexham & Newcastle), St Mary's Presbytery, South Hetton Rd, Easington Lane, Tyne & Wear DH5 0LG **Tel:** 0191-526 2136
Tumelty, Antony, MOC (OSB), The Chaplain's Flat, Poor Clare Convent, Much Birch, Hereford HR2 8PS **Tel:** 01981-540051
Tuohy, John, (Brentwood), 349 Wanstead Park Rd, Cranbrook, Ilford, Essex IG1 3TS **Tel:** 020-8554 3763
Turbitt, Peter, (Portsmouth), St John Vianney, Charlton Rd, Wantage OX12 8ER **Tel:** 01235-762374 **Fax:** 01235-772881 **E-mail:** peterturbitt@aol.com
Turley, Sean BA, MDiv (Wilmington, USA), SS Michael & James, Haunton, Tamworth B79 9HL **Tel:** 01827-373241 **Fax:** 01827-373628 **E-mail:** sean@home4u83.freeserve.co.uk
Turner, Aidan J, MA, (Lancaster), Our Lady Star of the Sea, 2 St Annes Rd East, St Annes on the Sea, Lytham St Annes FY8 1UL Tel: 01253-723661 Fax: 01253-780565
Turner, Gregory, Mgr Canon, VG, (Lancaster), The Rectory, Warwick Square, Carlisle, Cumbria CA1 1LB **Tel:** 01228-521509

Turner, Henry, Mgr Canon, (Westminster), 1 Kirkwick Ave, Harpenden, Herts AL5 2QH **Tel:** 01582-712245

Turner, John, (Westminster, retired), St George's Retreat, Burgess Hill, Sussex RH15 0SQ **Tel:** 01444-232669

Turner, John T, MA, (Lancaster, retired), St Winefride's Ho, Low Moor Rd, Bispham, Blackpool FY2 0PA **Tel:** 01253 590162

Turner, Leonard, (Arundel & Brighton, retired), Flat 7, Cranfield Lodge, Maypole Rd, East Grinstead, W. Sussex RH19 1HW **Tel:** 01342 313332

Turner, Michael, (Northampton), Our Lady of Peace, Lower Britwell Rd, Burnham, Slough SL2 2NL **Tel:** 01628-605764 **E-mail:** fathermichael@beeb.net

Turner, Paul, BA, BTh, (Arundel & Brighton), 14 Haslett Ave West, Crawley, W. Sussex RH10 1HR **Tel:** 01293 603773

Turnham, Derek, (Middlesbrough), St Joseph, 1 Tanton Rd, Stokesley, Middlesbrough TS9 5HN **Tel:** 01642-710239

Turnham Elvins, Mark, MA, GradDipSp (OFMCap), The Franciscan Friary, 15 Cuppin St, Chester CH1 2BN **Tel:** 01244-351331

Tutcher, Michael, BTh, MTh, MPhil, (Nottingham, retired), Presentation Sisters Care Centre, Presentation Convent, Chesterfield Rd, Matlock DE4 3FT

Tütto, George, Mgr, (Nottingham, retired), Hungarian Chaplaincy, 141 Gunnersbury Ave, W3 8LG **Tel:** 020-8992 2054

Tverijonas, Petras (Lithuanian), 21 The Oval, Hackney Rd, London E2 9DT

Twist, Gordon, (SDS), c/o Provincialate Offices, 129 Spencer Rd, Harrow Weald, Middx HA3 7BJ

Twist, John, (SJ), *Chaplain,* Stonyhurst College, Stonyhurst, Clitheroe, Lancs BB7 9PZ **Tel:** 01254-826345 **Fax:** 01254 827059 **E-mail:** johntwist100@yahoo.co.uk

Twohig, Henry, (MSC), Clayton Court, Rogate Rd, Hill Brow, Liss, Hampshire GU33 7QS **Tel:** 01730-829986 **Fax:** 01730-895076

Twomey, Jeremiah, Canon (Middlesbrough), St Aelred, 216 Fifth Ave, Tang Hall, York YO31 0PN **Tel:** 01904-426446

Twomey, Maurice, (Portsmouth, retired), c/o Bishop's Ho, Edinburgh Rd, Porstmouth PO1 3HG

Twomey, Michael, (Salford), St Mary, Dales St, Bacup OL13 8HG **Tel:** 01706-873243

Twomey, Richard J, Mgr (Clifton), Holy Rood, 2 Groundwell Rd, Swindon, Wilts SN1 2LU **Tel:** 01793-522062 **Fax:** 01793-432619

Tworek, Janusz, Mgr, (Westminster, on sabatical), c/o 2 Devonia Rd, Islington N1 8JJ **Tel:** 0207-226 3439 **E-mail:** pbf.pmk@ukonline.co.uk

Tylor, Matthew, BA, (OSB), Pluscarden Abbey, Elgin, Moray, Scotland IV30 8UA **Tel:** 01343 890257

Tyliszczak, Krzysztof, MA, Provincial (SChr), Provincial Ho, 16 Carlton Rd, Manchester M16 8BB **Tel:** 0161-227 1997

Tylka, Stanislaw, Canon,(Polish, Wroclaw), 119 Sandy Ln, Melton Mowbray, Leics LE13 5RA **Tel:** 01664-622101

Tynan, Joseph V, (Birmingham, retired), 43 Rugby Dr, Dresden, Longton, Stoke ST3 6PA **Tel:** 01782-312704

Tyrakowski, Marek (SVD), 8 Teignmouth Rd, London NW2 4HN **Tel:** 020-8452 8430

Uba, Livinus C (Nnewi), 418 Coxford Rd, Southampton SO16 5LL **Tel:** 023-8077 6537 **E-mail:** lcu100@socsci.soton.ac.uk

Udie, Thomas, (Ogoj a), 2 St Elmos Rd, Surrey Docks SE16 6SJ **Tel:** 020 7231 9297

Udris, John, (Dean) (Northampton), Cathedral Ho, Kingsthorpe Rd, Northampton NN2 6AG **Tel:** 01604-714556 **Fax:** 01604-715339 **E-mail:** office@ northamptoncathedral.org

Udoma, Patrick, (Ikot Ekpene), 524 Griffiths Dr, Ashmore Park, Wolverhampton WV11 2LH **Tel:** 01902-732713

Umama, Augustine, (MSP), 36 Nightingale Sq, Balham SW12 8QN **Tel:** 020 8355 0211

Umendia, Francis (Chaplain) (OAR), The Latin American Chaplaincy, 363 Kennington Ln, Vauxhall, London SE11 5QY

Unsworth, Andrew (Liverpool), Our Lady Queen of Martyrs, Stonebridge Lane, Liverpool L11 9AZ **Tel:** 0151 546 3574 **Fax:** 0151 546 7316

Usher, Thomas BA (Westminster), c/o Archbishop's Ho, Ambrosden Ave, London SW1P 1QJ

Valliamthadathil MSFS, St Nicholas Presbytery, Lawford's Gate, Easton, Bristol BS5 0RE **Tel:** 0117 983 3920

Vallomprayil, John (SDS), St Michael's Church, 9 Fern Ave, Pollards Hill, Mitcham, Surrey CR4 1LS **Tel:** 020-8764 1791 **E-mail:** johnvsds@googlemail.com

Van Beeumen, Mark (MSC) Cordate Community, 157 Ettington Rd, Aston, Birmingham B6 6ED **E-mail:** mark@msceurope.co.uk

Van der Kleij, Gregory (OSB), Monastery of Christ Our Saviour, Turvey Mews, Turvey, Bedford MK43 8DH

Tel: 01234-881211
Van der Most, Albert, (Arundel & Brighton), St Catherine's, Beach Rd, Littlehampton, W Sussex BN17 5JH **Tel:** 01903-731171
Van Santvoort, Daniel, (OCSO), Abbey of Our Lady and St Samson, Caldey Island, Tenby SA70 7UH **Tel:** 01834-842632
van Son, Francis, (Westminster), c/o Archbishop's Ho, Ambrosden Ave, London SW1P 1QJ
van Straelen, Henry, (SVD), c/o Divine Word Missionaries, 20 Oakfield Rd, Selly Park, Birmingham B29 7EJ
Vane, Ian, (Arundel & Brighton), 37 St Leonards Rd, Hove, E.Sussex BN3 4QP
Vann, Gerald, (Arundel & Brighton, retired), 30 Potters Place, Horsham, W. Sussex RH12 2PL
Varey, Paul, (Leeds), c/o Bishop's Ho 13 North Grange Rd Leeds LS6 2BR
Varkey, Shaju, (Southwark), 103 Woolwich New Rd, Woolwich SE18 6EF **Tel:** 020 8854 0359 **Mbl:** 07854560637 **Email:** shajufs@yahoo.co.uk
Vaughan, Michael (Birmingham), The Presbytery, Abbey Lane, Abbey Hulton, Stoke ST2 8AU **Tel:** 01782 534545 **Fax:** 01782 545052 **E-mail:** revmichaelvaughan@supanet.com
Vaz Pinto, Jose, (Portuguese), 165 Arlington Rd, Camden Town, London NW1 7EX **Tel:** 020-7267 9612
Veal, Herbert, Canon, DSC (Westminster , retired), Nazareth Ho, Hammersmith Rd, London W6 8DB
Veal, Richard (Arundel & Brighton, retired), 19 Charles Keighley Court, Hardy Crescent, Wimbourne, Dorset BH21 2TR
Veasey, Jonathan, STL, (Birmingham), The Bungalow, St John Vianney School, Mount Nod Way, Coventry CV5 7GX **Tel:** 024-7646 6332
Vella, John, (Gozo), Our Lady Queen of Heaven, 4a Inverness Place, London W2 3JF **Tel:** 020-7229 8153
Vella, Victor, PhB, CertPol, MA, (Southwark), Holy Innocents Presbytery, Stricklandway, Orpington BR 9UE **Tel:** 01689 817537 **Fax:** 01689 817539
Vellacott, Peter (Nottingham), 19 De Ferrer's Cl, east Leake, Loughborough Leics LE12 6LB **Tel:** 01509 852147
Venn, Graham, (IC), St Alban's, Cameron St, Splott, Cardiff CF24 2NX **Tel:** 029-2046 3219 **Mbl:** 07951-112987 **E-mail:** graham@rosmini.org
Verborg, Rainer SEM, FRCS, RCPS, (OSB), Ampleforth Abbey, York YO62 4EN **Tel:** 01439-766714 **Fax:** 01439 766724
Verhees, Anthony, Canon, BA, (Southwark, retired), The Lodge, Pound Street, Carshalton, Surrey SM5 3PN **Tel:** 020-8642 3863 **E-mail:** fatherluke@btinternet.com
Verrissimo, Gregory, (Ljebu-Ode), 48 Dale Rd, Purley CR8 2EF **Tel:** 020 8660 3815
Verity, Ushaw College, Durham DH7 9RH
Vervenne, Gerrit, (Portsmouth), The Presbytery, 15 Mount Ave, New Milton, Hants BH25 6NT **Tel:** 01425-614968, **E-mail:** gvervenne@aol.com
Viaguladasan, Manickam, (SJ), St Henry Walpole, The Green, Burnham Market, Norfolk PE31 8HD **Tel:** 01328-738386
Vickers, Mark, BA, STB (Westminster), St Peter's Presbytery, Bishop's Rise, Hatfield, Herts AL10 9HN **Tel:** 01707-262121
Vidler, Derek, (Southwark), Our Lady of Pity and St Simon Stock, Hazlewell Rd, Putney, London SW15 6LU **Tel:** 020-8789 1016
Vincent, Irenaeus (OP), Blackfriars, 64 St Giles, Oxford OX1 3LY **Tel:** 01865-278418
Vincent, Neil Marthirupan (Southwark), 70 Wellesley Rd, Croydon CR0 2AR **Tel:** 020-8688 1857 **Fax:** 020-8680 1056
Vipers, Christopher J, BA, (Westminster), Corpus Christi Presbytery, Maiden Lane WC2E 7NE **Tel:** 020-7836 4700
Viray, Primitivo, (SJ), Cathedral Ho, Unthank Rd, Norwich NR2 2PA **Tel:** 01603-624615
Vodopivec, Ivan, (SM), St Oswald's, 126 Southend Rd, Sheffield S2 5FT **Tel:** 0114-272 3881
von Wernich, Christian (on loan from Argentina), St Mary's, High Rd, Kells, Whitehaven, Cumbria CA28 9PG **Tel:** 01946-692757
Vu-Duc-Yen, Joseph, STL (Birmingham), 2 Dunsmore Ave, Willenhall, Coventry CV3 3HJ **Tel/Fax:** 02476-303389
Vulliamy, Michael, (East Anglia), Catholic Presbytery, Long Bessels, Hadleigh IP7 5DB **Tel:** 01473-823989 **Fax:** 01473-810095
Waclawik Josef, (CHS), Flat 8, Albert Ho, 180 High St, Bolton BL3 6PL **Tel:** 01204-523563
Wade, Peter, (Nottingham), 203 Park Rd, Loughborough, LE11 2HE **Tel:** 01509-212534
Wadsworth, Andrew, BA, GTCL, LTCL, LRAM (Westminster), 41a Peterborough Rd, Harrow-on-the-Hill HA1 3DY **Tel:** 020-8422 3783
Wadsworth, Francis (OFM Conv) St Ann, Burlington St, Ashton-under-Lyne OL6 7DG **Tel:** 0161-330 2141
Wagay, Gideon, BA, MA, STB, (Westminster), 62 Eden Grove, London

N7 8EN **Tel:** 020-7607 3594

Wahle, Francis, STL, BSc, (Westminster, retired), 17 Chiltern Court, Baker St, London NW1 5TD **Tel:** 020-7487 5956

Wairagu, John (AJ), The Presbytery, St Elizabeth's Rd, Foleshill, Coventry CV6 5BX **Tel:** 024-7668 8536

Waite, David, (OCarm), The Friars, Aylesford, Kent ME20 7BX **Tel:** 01622-717272

Waldron, Bernard, Rt Rev Abbot, (OSB), St Augustine's Abbey, Ramsgate, Kent CT11 9PA **Tel:** 01843-593045 **Fax:** 01843-582732

Waldron, Patrick, (Leeds), Our Lady of Mount Carmel, 7 Wesley Place, Keighley, Silsden BD20 0PH **Tel:** 01535-653153

Walford, David, (Plymouth, retired), Sibford, Church Hill, Marnhull, Sturminster Newton, Dorset DT10 1PU **Tel:** 01258-820201

Walker, Adrian, (Westminster, retired), 42 Bell St, Maidenhead, SL6 1BR **Tel:** 01628-637796

Walker, Alban, (Hexham & Newcastle, retired), St Patricks, Smith Street, Ryhope, Sunderland SR2 0RG **Tel:** 0191-521 0340

Walker, Basil, (Liverpool, retired), Flat 1, The Rectory, School Lane, Formby, Liverpool L37 3LW **Tel:** 01704 832170

Walker, Charles, MA, Canon, (Southwark, retired), 69 North Salts, Rye, E. Sussex TN31 7NU **Tel:** 01797-227871

Walker, Edward, Mgr, (Nottingham), St Hugh of Lincoln, 90 Staverton Rd, Bilborough, Nottingham NG8 4EX **Tel:** 0115-929 3633

Walker, Keiron, BD (Leeds), St Winefride's Presbytery, 54 St Paul's Ave, Wibsey, Bradford BD6 1ST **Tel/Fax:** 01274-677992

Walker, Keith, BA, (Hexham & Newcastle), St Joseph's, Shibdon Rd, Blaydon-on-Tyne, Tyne and Wear NE21 5AE **Tel:** 0191-414 3115

Walker, Raymond, (Liverpool, retired), Flat 4, The Rectory, School Ln, Formby, Liverpool L37 3LW **Tel:** 01704-832170

Walker, Richard LLB, STL (Birmingham), Oscott College, Chester Rd, New Oscott B73 5AA **Tel:** 0121-321 5000

Walker, W, (IC), St Mary's Derryswood, Wonersh, Guildford, Surrey GU5 0RA **Tel:** 01483-893196

Wall, Brian, MA (SJ), St Maria Gorretti Aylesbury Rd, Bucknall, Stoke-on-Trent ST2 0LU **Tel:** 01782-281970

Wall, Edward, (Shrewsbury), All Saints, 164 Carrington Lane, Ashton in Mersey, Sale M33 5WL **Tel:** 0161 962 4444

Walls, Jonathan, Christ The King, 1 Frithwood Crecsent, Kents Hill, Milton Keynes MK7 6HQ **Tel:** 01908 671342

Wall, Patrick, (Leeds), St Francis Presbytery, 144 Norman Ln, Eccleshill, Bradford BD2 2JU **Tel:** 01274 637937 **E-mail:** pdwalls@wallspace.fsnet.co.uk

Wallace, James, (Northampton), St Thomas's Church, Arbroath, Co Angus

Wallbank, Christopher, (MAFR), 15 Corton Rd, Ealing, London W5 2HP **Tel:** 0208 8354 3104 **Email:** wfcorfton@blueyonder.co.uk

Waller, Andrew, MA, BA, BD, PGCE (SDB), Thornleigh Ho, Sharples Park, Bolton BL1 6PQ **Tel:** 01204-591144 **Fax:** 01204-308510 **E-mail:** awallersdb@tiscali.co.uk

Walne, Damien, (Northampton), 1 Elwes Way, Great Billing, Northampton NN3 4EA **Tel/Fax:** 01604-406410 **E-mail:** ourladysparish@aol.com

Walsh, Aidan, (OFMConv), c/o St Patrick's Friary, 26 Cornwall Road, Waterloo, London SE1 8TW

Walsh, Ambrose, (Cardiff, retired), 2 Dorchester Court, Brandreth Rd, Cardiff CF12 5LU

Walsh, Anthony, (Lancaster), Presbytery, Caroline Street, Preston PR1 5UY **Tel:** 01772 796053

Walsh, Bede (Birmingham), 25 South Bar St, Banbury, Oxon OX16 9AE **Tel:** 01295-262073

Walsh, Christopher J, BSc, STL, PSL, Canon (Shrewsbury), SS Catherine & Martina, Birkenhead Rd, Hoylake, Wirral CH47 5AF **Tel:** 0151-632 4388 **Fax:** 0151-633 2613

Walsh, Eamon, (Portsmouth), Warren Lodge, Warren Road, Wash Common, Newbury, Berks RG14 6NH **Tel:** 01623 40332

Walsh, Gary Patrick, STB, MA (SSS), Blessed Sacrament Shrine, 4 Dawson St, Liverpool L1 1LE **Tel:** 0151-709 5528 **Fax:** 0151-709 5977 **E-mail:** peterеymard@aol.com

Walsh, Gerard, (Clifton), 87 West Hill, Portishead, Bristol BS20 6LN **Tel:** 01275-842912

Walsh, James C, CertEd, GeogDip (SDB), More Hall Convent, Randwick, Stroud GL6 6EP **Tel:** 01453 764486

Walsh, James, (East Anglia), Cathedral Ho, Unthank Rd, Norwich NR2 2PA **Tel:** 01603-624615

Walsh, James, (Galway), 79 St Charles Square, London W10 6EB

Walsh, James, (WF), 129 Lichfield Rd, Sutton Coldfield, W. Mids B74 2SA **Tel:** 0121-308 0226

Walsh, John, (Lancaster), St Margaret

Mary's, Scalegate Rd, Carlisle CA2 4JX **Tel:** 01228 522137 **Fax:** 01228 599052

Walsh, John Michael, CTh, VG, RAF, (Liverpool), Principal RC Chaplain (RAF). The Chaplaincy Centre, RAF Halton, Aylesbury, Bucks. HP22 5PG **Tel:** 01296 656910

Walsh, John Anthony, BA (Birmingham), 14 Priest Ln, Pershore, Worcestershire WR10 1EB **Tel:** 01386-552737

Walsh, Joseph, (OCSO), Abbey of Our Lady and St Samson, Caldey Island, off Tenby, SA70 7UH **Tel:** 01834-842632/842879

Walsh, Joseph, (Northampton), St Peter's Presbytery, 1 Hayway, Rushden, Northants NN10 6AG **Tel:** 01933-353649 **E-mail:** fjw.stpeters@ukonline.co.uk

Walsh, Joseph, (SSC), St Columban's Widney Manor Rd, Knowle, Solihull, W. Mids B93 9AB **Tel:** 01564-772096

Walsh, Martin, MA, M Div, (SMA), Society of African Missions, 33 Lyonsdown Rd, New Barnet, Herts EN5 1JG **Tel:** 020-8440 4715

Walsh, Michael D, DipCounsel (Clifton), St Anthony's Presbytery, Satchfield Cres, Henbury, Bristol BS10 7BE **Tel:** 0117-983 3906 **Fax:** 0117-983 3934

Walsh, Michael, Rural Dean and Diocesan Communications Officer (Salford), St Paul's, 285 Stockport Rd, Guide Bridge, Ashton-under-Lyne OL7 0NT **Tel:** 0161-330 2777 **Fax:** 0161-343 5595 **E-mail:** mwalsh1402@aol.com

Walsh, Michael, (Leeds), St Joseph's Presbytery, St Joseph's St, Tadcaster LS24 9HA **Tel:** 01937 833105

Walsh, Michael, (OFM Cap),Franciscan Friary, 15 Cuppin St, Chester CH1 2BN

Walsh, Patrick, (SCJ), c/o St Joseph's, Tilston Rd, Malpas, Cheshire SY14 7DD

Walsh, Patrick, (Hallam), Saint Vincent's Presbytery, 40 Pickmere Rd, Crookes, Sheffield S10 1GY **Tel:** 0114-268 9716 **Tel:** 0114-233 3971

Walsh, Patrick, (MSC), Clayton Court, Rogate Rd, Hillbrow, Liss, Hampshire GU33 7QS **Tel:** 01730-893130

Walsh, Patrick (SSS), Blessed Sacrament Shrine, 4 Dawson St, Liverpool L1 1LE **Tel:** 0151-709 5528 **Fax:** 0151-709 5977

Walsh, Paul (SM), 5 Leicester Place, London WC2H 7BP

Walsh, Terence, Canon, STL, JCD, (Portsmouth, retired), 9 Janson Rd, Shirley, Southampton SO15 5FU **Tel:** 02380-778502 **E-mail:** cantkw@aol.com

Walsh, Walter, (Southwark), St Thomas's, Ham St, Ham, Richmond TW10 7HT **Tel:** 020-8948 8292

Walshe, Michael (SCJ), 266 Wellington Rd North, Stockport SK4 2QR **E-mail:** prov@heartscj.fsnet.co.uk

Walshe, Philip, MA, M.Phil(Ecum) (CM), Marillac Hospital, Eagle Way, Warley, Brentwood, Essex CM13 3BL **Tel:** 01277 220276 **E-mail:** philwalshe@aol.com

Walter, Bruno, (OCSO), Garson Ho, 7 Lee Rd, Lynton, Devon EX35 6HU **Tel:** 015985-3202

Walter, Victor, (Wrexham), The Presbytery, 2 Ravan St, Welshpool, Powys SY21 7LR **Tel:** 01938-552223

Walters, Hugh, BA, (OP), House of Theology, 64, St Giles, Blackfriars, Oxford OX1 3LY **Tel:** 01865-278400

Walton, Peter, Mgr Canon, BA, (Shrewsbury, retired), 1 Lymington Road, Wallasey CH44 3AA **Tel:** 0151-639 1541

Walton, Thomas, (Birmingham), The Presbytery, Mill Rd, Shelfield, W. Mids WS4 1ZH **Tel:** 01922-685542

Wang, Stephen, MA, ThL (Westminster), Allen Hall, 28 Beaufort St, Chelsea, London SW3 5AA **Tel:** 020-7349 5608 **E-mail:** cd@wjw2.sent.com

Wansbrough, Henry, MA, STL, LSS, (OSB), Ampleforth Abbey, York YO62 4EN **Tel:** 01439 766714 **Fax:** 01439 766724

Ward, Bernard (MCCJ), Camboni Missionaries, Brownberrie Ln, Horsforth, Leeds LS18 5HE **Tel:** 0113-258 2658

Ward, Brian, (Westminster, retired), 2 Evergreen Park, Tanderagee, Binion, Clonmany, Co Donegal. **Tel:** 00353 7493 78659

Ward, Colin, (Portsmouth), 14 Jeanne Jugan Apartments, New St John's Rd, St Helier, Jersey JE2 3LE **Tel:** 01534-744490

Ward, David, (East Anglia), Cathedral Ho, Unthank Rd, Norwich NR2 2PA **Tel:** 01603-624615

Ward, James F, JCL, (Birmingham), The Presbytery, Summerhill, Kingswinford DY6 9JG **Tel:** 01384-274520

Ward, John, BA, (Glasgow), Chaplaincy Services, (Army), Bagshot Park, Bagshot, Surrey GU19 5PL

Ward, Joseph, (CP), Bursar, St Joseph's Retreat, Highgate Hill, London N19 5NE **Tel:** 020-7272 2320

Ward, Kevin, (SCA), 358 Greenford Rd, Greenford, Middx UB6 9AN **Tel:** 020-8578 1363

Ward, Peter, (CSSp, retired), 6 Woodlands Rd, Bickley, Bromley, Kent BR1 2AF **Tel:** 020 8467 355

Ward, Thomas G, (Lancaster, retired), 85

Kingsway, Ansdell, Lytham, St Annes FY8 1AD **Tel:** 01253-732381

Wardle, Terence L, (Westminster, retired), 7 Hutchings Lodge, High St, Rickmansworth. **Tel:** 01923-710031

Ware, Joseph, (Arundel & Brighton, retired), 'San Antonio', 32 Prideaux Rd, Eastbourne, E. Sussex BN21 2NB **Tel:** 01323-645928

Wareing, Peter F, (CMF), The Towers, High Street, Buckden, St Neots PE19 5TA **Tel:** 01480-810344

Wareing, Joseph, (SJ), Stonyhurst College, Stonyhurst, Clitheroe, Lancs BB7 9PZ **Tel:** 01254 827118 **E-mail:** smjchurch@hotmail.co.uk

Waring, Luke, STL, V Rev, (OSB), St Mary's, Colwich, ST18 0UF

Warnock, John, (Shrewsbury, retired), St Catherine Nursing Home, Barnoy Rd, Nantwich **Tel:** 01270-610881

Warren, Christopher, (Hexham & Newcastle), St Mary's Cathedral, Clayton St West, Newcastle NE1 5HH **Tel:** 0191 232 6953

Warren, Raymond, (OMI), New Priory, Sacred Heart Church, Quex Rd, Kilburn, London NW6 4PS **Tel:** 020-7624 1701 **Fax:** 020-7328 8176 **E-mail:** parish@omiquex.org.uk

Warrington, John, (East Anglia), 14 Sellers Grange, Orton Goldhay, Peterborough PE2 5XX **Tel:** 01733-370877 **Mbl:** 0777 3478835. **E-mail:** saintlukesparish@yahoo.co.uk

Was, Adam (SVD), 8 Teignmouth Rd, London NW2 4HN

Wastell, Eric (Menevia), 18 Belgrave Court, Walter Rd, Swansea SA1 4PY **Tel:** 01792-466709

Waters, Francis, BA, (SDS), St Joseph's Presbytery, 191-193 High Rd, Harrow Weald, Middx HA3 5EA **Tel:** 0208 427 1955 **Fax:** 0208 427 0543 **E-mail:** ciscus191@btconnect.com

Waters, Michael, BSc (Salford), St John the Baptist, Ivy St, Burnley, Lancs BB11 4SB **Tel:** 01282-423824

Waterworth, Francis, Chaplain to Hope Hospital (Salford), 15 Wilton Rd, Salford M6 8FT **Tel:** 0161-789-4470

Watine, Damien (MAfr), 46 Woodville Gardens, London W5 2LQ **Tel:** 020-8998 8552

Watkins, Dunstan, (OSB), Ealing Abbey, Charlbury Grove, Ealing W5 2DY **Tel:** 020-8862 2100

Watkins, John (Plymouth), 3 Matford Ave, Exeter, Devon EX2 4PP.

Watson, David, (Portsmouth), De Aston School, Willingham Rd, Market Rasen, Lincs LN8 3RF

Watson, Frederick (Salford), St Mary and St John Southworth, Preston New Rd, Samlesbury, Preston PR5 0UL **Tel:** 01772-877241

Watson, John, STL, (Lancaster), St Mary of Furness, Duke St, Barrow in Furness LA14 1XW **Tel:** 01229-820210

Watson, Keith F, (Northampton), 17 Rushton Rd, Rothwell, Kettering NN14 6HG **Tel:** 01229-820210

Watson, Lawrence, (Shrewsbury), Christ the King, 890 New Chester Rd, Bromborough, Wirral CH62 6AT **Tel:** 0151-334 1657

Watson, Paul, MTh, DPT, (Menevia), The Presbytery, Queen's Rd, Aberystwyth, Ceredigion SY23 2HS **Tel:** 01970-612549

Watson, Paul Joseph, V. Rev, STL (Birmingham), Director, The Maryvale Institute, Maryvale Ho, Old Oscott Hill, Kingstanding, Birmingham B44 9AG. **Tel:** 0121-360 8118 **Fax:** 0121-366 6786

Watson, Stephen (Hexham & Newcastle), Holy Rosary, Arbroath Rd, Sunderland SR3 3LD **Tel:** 0191-528 1992

Watson, Terence, (IC), Rosmini Ho, Woodbine Rd, Pity Me, Durham DH1 5DR **Tel:** 01913-849268 **E-mail:**tpdurham@ rosmini-in-english.org

Watson, William T P, (Clifton), St Joseph's Presbytery, Oldends Ln, Stonehouse, Gloucestershire GL10 2DG

Watters, Denis, (Westminster), St Joseph's Presbytery, Bedwell Cres, Stevenage SG1 1NJ **Tel:** 01438-351243

Watts, Geoffrey, (Plymouth), St Joseph's. The Square, Wool, Dorset BH20 6DS **Tel:** 01929-463334.

Watts, John, Canon, BA, STL, CertEd (Southwark), c/o Archbishop's House, 150 St George's Rd, London SE1 6HX

Weatherby, Peter, MA, MEd, PGCE (Birmingham), Sacred Heart Presbytery, 1 Eastwood Place, Hanley, Stone-on-Trent ST1 3DB **Tel:** 01782-215217

Weatherill, John MA, STB (Southwark), 28 Queens Court, Queens Rd, Richmond, Surrey TW10 6LA

Webb, Anthony, (East Anglia), 29 Wells Rd, Fakenham, Norfolk NR21 9EG **Tel:** 01328-862110

Webb, Benedict, MA, MRCS, LRCP, (OSB), Ampleforth Abbey, York YO62 4EN **Tel:** 01439-766714 **Fax:** 01439-766724

Webb, Christopher, RAF, (Westminster), c/o Principal RC Chaplain (RAF), Chaplaincy Office, RAF Halton, Aylesbury, Bucks HP22 5PG **Tel:** 01296 656910

Webb, Geoffrey (Westminster, retired), 93 Cowley Hill, Borehamwood, Herts

Webb, James F, (Wrexham), The Presbytery,

St David's Ln, Ffordd Fain, Mold, Flintshire CH7 1LH **Tel:** 01352 752087 **Fax:** 01352 700488

Webb, John, (Plymouth), RC Prison Chaplain, HM Prison Princetown, Yelverton, Devon **Tel:** 01822-892000

Webb, Peter, Canon, (Plymouth), The Presbytery, 35 Brixey Rd, Upper Parkstone, Poole, Dorset BH12 3PB **Tel:** 01202-748166 **E-mail:** parish@ourladyfatima.fsnet.co.uk

Webb, Philip, Mgr Provost, (Wrexham), Our Lady and the Welsh Martyrs, Wrexham Rd, Overton, Wrexham, Clwyd LL13 0HF **Tel:** 01978-710439

Webb, Stephen, (Leeds), 294 Harrogate Rd, Leeds LS17 6LE **Tel:** 01113 268 1373

Webster, Frank, STB, MA, (MHM), SS Aidan and Oswald, Vaughan St, Royton, Oldham OL2 5DL **Tel:** 0161-624 1322 **E-mail:** frankwebster@zinzade.com

Webster, George (SSC), 56 Amersham Rd, London SE14 6QE (South London Universities Chaplaincy)

Webster, George (CSsR), St Clement's, Wolf lane, Chawton, Alton, Hants GU34 3HG **Tel:** 01420 807310

Weinandy, Thomas, (OFM), SS Edmund & Fridewide, Iffley Rd, Oxford OX4 1SB **Tel:** 01865-248455

Weiss, Wolfgang, (SCA), St Boniface's, 47 Adler St, London E1 1EE **Tel:** 020-7247 9529

Wells, Bryan MA, BMus, DipEd, LRAM, LTCL (Southwark), 283 Crescent Dr, Petts Wood, Kent BR5 1AY **Tel:** 01689-827100

Wells, William A J, BTh(Oxon), LLM, ThL (East Anglia, retired). St Peter's Presbytery, Back Ln, Blakeney, Norfolk NR25 7NP **Tel:** 01263-741519

Welsh, Alexander, (SJ), 1 Winckley Square, Preston PR1 3JJ **Tel:** 01772-554388

Welsh, Brian, (Nottingham, retired), 9 Fell Croft, Farndon, Newark Notts NG24 3TB **Tel:** 01636-676765.

Welsh, John, (Westminster), St Raphael's Ho, Morrison Rd, Yeading, Middx UB4 9JP **Tel:** 020-8845 1919

Welsh, Peter, (MAfr), Sector Superior, 42 Stormont Rd, London N6 4NP **Tel:** 020-8348 7799 **E-mail:** mafrgb@blueyonder.co.uk

Welsh, Thomas, (SX), 130 Holden Rd, London N12 7EA

Welsh, Thomas, Xaverian Missionaries, 179 Ribbleton Ave, Preston PR2 6AA **Tel:** 01772-792 292

Wentworth, Michael, (Shrewsbury, retired), Flat 4, York Ho, York Ave, West Kirby CH48 3JF **Tel:** 0151-625 2444

Werner, Roman, (SChr), Polish Centre, Ravenna Rd, London SW15 6AW **Tel:** 020-8788 3933 **Fax:** 020-8780 3670

Weston, David, (Arundel & Brighton), The Chantry, 13 Court Farm Rd, Hove, Sussex BN3 7QR **Tel:** 01273-503647

Weston, Joseph, (Liverpool), St Benedict, 109 Market St, Hindley, Wigan WN2 3AA **Tel:** 01942-255306

Wesolowski, Jacek MA (SChr) 197 Lloyd St North, Manchester M14 4QB **Tel:** 0161-226 1588

Wetherall, Stephen, (CSSR), Little Sisters of the Poor, Holy Cross Home, Ettrick Grove, High Barnes Sunderland SR4 8QA **Tel:** 0191-567 0862

Wetz, Nicholas, BA, STB, (OSB), Belmont Abbey, Belmont, Hereford HR2 9RZ **Tel:** 01432-277388 **E-mail:** nickwetz@aol.com

Weymes, Michael, (Hexham & Newcastle), St Bede, Westoe Rd, South Shields, Tyne & Wear NE33 4LZ **Tel:** 0191 456 3536

Weymes, Simon, (Hexham & Newcastle), St Cuthberts, Spring St, Stockton, TS18 3NR **Tel:** 01642 674321

Whale, Anthony, Canon, (Arundel & Brighton), 19 Tilford Rd, Farnham, Surrey GU9 8DJ **Tel:** 01252-716711 **Fax:** 01252-716733

Whalen, Michael, BA, (Hexham & Newcastle), The Holy Name, 7 North Jesmond Ave, Jesmond, Newcastle-upon-Tyne, Co Durham NE2 3JX **Tel:** 0191-281 0940 **Fax:** 0191-281 0905

Wharton, Gerard, Canon, (Liverpool), 32 Great George's Rd, Waterloo, Liverpool L22 1RD

Whatling, Colin, (Westminster, retired), 2b Eaton Ave, Heston, Middx TW5 0HB **Tel:** 0208-606 9544

Whatmore, T J Brian (Birmingham), 26 Knightly Way, Gnosall, Stafford ST20 0HX **Tel:** 01785-823726

Wheat, Rev Joseph (Nottingham), The Briars Residential Centre, Crich Common, Matlock, Derbys DE4 5BW **Tel:** 01773-852044 **Fax:** 01773-852968

Wheaton, Geoffrey (SJ), More Ho, 53 Cromwell Rd, London SW7 2EH **Tel:** 020-7584 2040 **Fax:** 020-7581 5748 **E-mail:** geoff.wheaton@talk21.com

Wheaton, Michael (Plymouth), The Presbytery, 25 South St, Exeter EX1 1EB **Tel:** 01392-272815

Whelan, Alan R, (MSC), BA, Princethorpe College, Leamington Rd, Princethorpe, Rugby CV23 9PX **Tel:** 01926-634240 **Fax:** 01926-634228 **E-mail:** arw@princethorpe.co.uk

Whelan, Christopher, BTh (Portsmouth), 58 Western Ave, Woodley, Berkshire

RG5 3BH **Tel/Fax:** 0118-969 3423

Whelan, Eamonn, (Southwark, retired), 'Emmanuel', 64 Queens Rd, Ash, Kent CT3 2BA **Tel:** 01304-814271 **Email:** efwdeal@aol.com

Whelan, Edmund Joseph, (Birmingham, retired), 7 The Hermitage, Castleconnel, County Limerick, Ireland

Whelan, Patrick, (Parish Priest) (OSB), St Augustine's Abbey, Ramsgate, Kent CT11 9PA **Tel:** 01843-593045 **Fax:** 01843-582732

Whelan, Vincent, Canon (Shrewsbury), Our Lady and the Apostles, Shaw Heath, Stockport SK3 8BQ **Tel:** 0161-480 2489 **Fax:** 0161-480 0868 **E-mail:** fr.vin@talk21.com

Whelehan, Mark, (CP), Passionist Community, Minsteracres,Nr Consett, Co Durham DH8 9RT **Tel:** 01434-673248

Whelton, John (IC) Grace Dieu Manor School, Whitwick, Coalville, Leics LE67 5UG **Tel:** 01530-223450

Whieldon, Paul Alan, BA, STB (Birmingham), 10 Bransford Rd, St John's, Worcs WR2 4EN

Whinder, Richard, BA(Hons), STL (Southwark), 1 Montem Rd, New Malden, Surrey KT3 3QW **Tel:** 0208 942 2602 **Fax:** 0208 949 2702

Whisstock, Joseph, BSc(Hons), BA(Hons), (Brentwood), 51 Priory St, Colchester, Essex CO1 2QB **Tel:** 01206-866317

White, Anthony, (Arundel & Brighton), 14 Mount St, Battle, E. Sussex TN33 0EG **Tel:** 01424-773125

White, Augustine, (Nottingham, retired), Castlepollard, Co Westmeath, Eire

White, David J, ECLJ, OMLJ, MSM, FILFRSA (Melkite-Greek Catholic Priest), The Belvedere, Peak Hill, Sidmouth, Devon EX10 0NW **Tel/Fax:** 01395-513365

White, David Nicholas, (Middlesbrough), St Alphonsus Presbytery, 95 Westbourne Grove, North Ormesby, Middlesbrough TS3 6EW **Tel:** 01642-243043

White, Dominic, MA, PhD, (OP), St Dominic's Priory, Southhampton Rd, London NW5 4LB **Tel:** 020 7482 9210

White, Jerry, (SSCC), Holy Cross, 355 Goldington Rd, Bedford MK41 0DP **Tel:** 01234-353116 **E-mail:** 114563.14560@compuserve

White, John, (Westminster), 167 Broadway, London NW9 7ER **Tel:** 0208-202 5143

White, John, (SPS), 66a Gowan Ave, Fulham, London SW6 6AF **Tel:** 020-7384 1354

White, Joseph, (Brentwood) The Presbytery, High Ln, Stansted, Essex CM24 8LQ **Tel:** 01279-814349

White, Leo, Mgr, (Brooklyn), 14 Bourdon Rd, Penge, London SE20 7SR

White, Mark, (CP), Minsteracres Retreat Centre, Consett, Co. Durham DH8 9RT **Tel:** 01434-673518 **Fax:** 01434-673540 **E-mail:** mwhite8684@aol.com

White, Michael, (Middlesbrough), St Vincent de Paul, 2 Victoria Ave, Hull HU5 3DR **Tel:** 01482-343017

White, Michael, MA (Birmingham), 124 Warren Farm Rd, Kingstanding B44 0QN **Tel:**0121-373 0988

White, Paul (OP), Blackfriars, Buckingham Rd, Cambridge CB3 0DD **Tel:** 01223 741039

White, Richard Nicholas, (OSB), c/o Downside Abbey, Stratton on the Fosse, BA3 4RH **Tel:** 01761-235161

White, Richard (East Anglia), 1 Norwich Rd, Wymondham, Norfolk NR18 0QE **Tel:** 01953-603104

White, Thomas Gerald, (Hallam), St Helen's Rectory, Main St, Oldcotes, Worksop, Notts S81 8JF **Tel:** 01909-730316

Whitehead, Ambrose, (CRL), Christchurch Priory, 229 Eltham High St, London SE9 ITX **Tel:** 020-8850 1666

Whitehead, Burton, (Portsmouth, retired), 33 Saxon Court, Wessex Way, Bicester, Oxon OX26 6AX

Whitehead, Christopher J, STB, (Clifton), St Bernadette's Presbytery, Wells Rd, Bristol BS14 9NU **Tel:** 01275-833699

Whitehead, David, (Portsmouth, retired), 195 Winchester Rd, Chandlers Fort, Hants SO53 2DU **Tel:** 023-8026 0824

Whitehouse, Christopher, (Northampton), 148 Ashcroft Rd, Stopsley, Luton LU2 9AY **Tel/Fax:** 01582 723099

Whiteside, R, (Leeds), All Hallows College, Drumcondra, Dublin 9, Eire **Tel:** 00 353 1 373745

Whitfield, Tony, (Northampton), Priest's Ho,10 Stoke Hill, Oundle, Peterborough PE8 4BH **Tel:** 01832-272615 **E-mail:** tony@ oundlechurch.freeserve.co.uk

Whitmore, Philip, Mgr, MA, DPhil, STL (Westminster), Via di Monserrato 48/2 00186 Roma, Italia **Tel:** 00 3906 687 2975 **E-mail:** philipwhitmore@lineone.net

Whitney, Robin C, (Westminster, retired), Nazareth Ho, 162 East End Rd, London N2 0RU

Whooley, John, (Westminster), 44 Ashchurch Grove, London W12 9BU **Tel:** 0208-743 5196

Whooley, Joseph, ACP, FCollP, (Southwark), 92 Poplar Grove, Maidstone, Kent ME16 0AL

Wickman, Charles, (OFM), 1 Balmiel Gate,

Lindsay Square, London SW1V 3SD

Wiener, Julian F, (Brentwood), The Priests' Ho, Luncies Rd, Basildon, Essex SS14 1SD **Tel:** 01268-553425

Wijngaard, Piet, (OCarm), c/o Provincial Office, Whitefriars, Tanners St, Faversham ME13 7JW

Wilberforce, Gerard, (Plymouth), Dutch Court, Topsham, Exeter EX3 0JD **Tel:** 01392-876593

Wilby, William, (Westminster), St Winifrid's Convent, 29 Tite St, London SW3 4JX **Tel:** 020-7351 5339

Wilcock, Adrian, (Wrexham), Church of the Immaculate Conception, 17 Coleshill St, Flint CH6 5BQ **Tel:** 01352-732245 **Fax:** 01352-731968

Wilcox, Anthony, MEd, (Birmingham), The Sacred Heart, 31 Vicarage Rd, Henley-on-Thames, Oxon RG9 1HT **Tel:** 01491-573258 **E-mail:** anthony.wilcox@ukonline.co.uk

Wilczak, Jaromir (SCJ), Polish Home, Ilford Park, Stover, Newton Abbot **Tel:** 01626-323043

Wild, Anthony, BA, LCL (Shrewsbury), SS Peter and Paul, Salters's Ln, Newport, Shropshire TF10 7LB **Tel:** 01952-811299

Wilde, Nicholas, (Liverpool), St Laurence, Lydbury Cres, Kirkby, Liverpool L32 9RH **Tel:** 0151-546 4247 **Fax:** 0151-548 0900

Wiley, John, KSJ, MA, BD (Westminster), The Presbytery, Vale Ln, London W3 0DY **Tel:** 020-8992 1308

Wiley, Timothy, (Leeds), St Mary's Presbytery, Cross Bank Rd, Batley WF17 8PQ **Tel:** 01924-474650

Wilkie, Peter, (Wrexham), Catholic Presbytery, The Bridgend, Newtown, Powys SY16 2BJ **Tel:** 01686-626423

Wilkie, Peter, Canon, (Portsmouth, retired), Ploughman's Park Ln, Milford-on-Sea, Hants SO41 0PN **Tel:** 01590-643276

Wilkinson, Anthony, (Leeds, Retired), Address available shortly.

Wilkinson, Edward V, (Hexham & Newcastle, retired), St Mary Magdalen, Harbour Walk, Seaham Harbour SR7 7DS **Tel:** 0191-581 2368

Wilkinson, Graham Mgr, (Birmingham), St Peter's Presbytery, 2A Charford Rd, Bromsgrove B60 3LU **Tel:** 01527 832530

Wilkinson, Paul (Arundel & Brighton), Howard Ho, 2 Station Approach, Falmer, Brighton, E. Sussex BN1 9SB **Tel:** 01273-698032

Wilkinson, Patrick, (MCCJ), Verona Fathers, Brownberrie Manor, Horsforth, Leeds LS18 5HE **Tel/Fax:** 0113-258 2658

Wilkinson, Peter, Mgr, (Salford, retired), St Joseph's, 149 Bolton Rd, Darwen, Lancs BB3 2PG **Tel:** 01254 702026 **E-mail:** stjosephdarwen@btinternet.co.uk

Willcocks, Peter, (SJ) Corpus Christi Presbytery, 17/18 St James Sq, Boscombe, Bournemouth BH5 2BX **Tel:** 01202 425286 **Fax:** 01202 417623

Willenbrock, Philip, MA, BMBCh (Brentwood), 13 Woodland Way, Wivenhoe, Colchester, Essex CO7 9AP **Tel:** 01206-823812

Willett, Eric, STL, (IC),The Presbytery, 8 St John's Rd, March, Cambs PE15 8RJ **Tel:** 01354-653268. **E-mail:** eric.willet@btinternet.com

Williams, Alan, MA, PhD, Major Provincial (SM), St Lawrence's Presbytery, 1 Hamilton Rd, Sidcup DA15 7HB **Tel:** 0208 300 2480

Williams, Cadfan (OSB), Belmont Abbey, Hereford HR2 9RZ

Williams, Cyril, (Southwark, retired), 15 Castle Rd, Whitstable, Kent CT5 2DY **Tel:** 01227-277674

Williams, David (Plymouth), c/o The Presbytery, 25 South St, Exeter EX1 1EB **Tel:** 01392-272815

Williams, David, PhD (CP), 62 Cambridge Rd, Otley, Yorks LS21 1DD **Tel:** 01943-466359 **E-mail:** davidcp@compuserve.com

Williams, Daniel, BA, BD, (Menevia, retired), 46 Llythrid Ave, Sketty Swansea SA2 0JJ **Tel:** 01792-296535

Williams, David (CP), 9 Riverdale Gardens, Otley LS21 1SX, **E-mail:** daicp@aol.com

Williams, George, PhD (SDB), St Joseph's, 10 Oldhams Ln, Bolton BL1 6PN **Tel:** 01204-590600 **E-mail:** gwilliamssdb@merseymail.com

Williams, Graham, (Hexham and Newcastle), St Anne, Rokeby View, Low Fell, Gateshead NE9 7UD **Tel:** 0191-482 1234

Williams, Gordon (East Anglia), Catholic Rectory, Regent Rd, Great Yarmouth, Norfolk NR30 2AJ **Tel:** 01493-842001, **Fax:** 01493-844968

Williams, James Gerard, (Clifton), SS Joseph & Teresa, 16 Chamberlain St, Wells, Somerset BA5 2PF **Tel:** 01749-673183

Williams, John, (Salford), St Luke, Swinton Park Rd, Irlams-o'th'-Height, Salford M6 7WR **Tel:** 0161-736 2696

Williams, John Martin, (Hallam), Holy Spirit Presbytery, 4 Stonelow Rd, Dronfield, Derbys S18 6EP **Tel:** 01246-413094

Williams, John N, Mgr, (Shrewsbury, retired), 15 Oxford Dr, Thornton Hough, Wirral, CH63 1JG

Williams, Joseph (Northampton), 7a Station Rd, Biggleswade SG18 8AL **Tel:** 01767-312013

Williams, Mervyn, BD, BSc, MA, (SDB), Thornleigh Ho, Sharples Park, Bolton BL1 6PQ **Tel:** 01204-591144 **Fax:** 01204 308510 **E-mail:** economer@salesians.org.uk

Williams, Michael E, Mgr DD, (Birmingham), Aston Hall, Aston, Stone Staffs ST1 0BJ **Tel:** 01785 817151

Williams, Michael (Liverpool), Metropolitan Cathedral of Christ the King, Mount Pleasant, Liverpool L3 5TQ **Tel:** 0151-709 9222 **Fax:** 0151-708 7274

Williams, Peter, (OSB), Worth Abbey, Paddockhurst Rd, Turners Hill, Crawley, W. Sussex RH10 4SB **Tel:** 01342-710310

Williams, Teyrnon, BA, BD, (Menevia), The Presbytery, 41 Pontardawe Rd, Clydach, Swansea SA6 5NS **Tel:** 01792-842244

Williams, Thomas, CGLI, CQSW, (SDB), St James, Chesnut Grove, Bootle L20 4LX **Tel:** 0151-944 1039 **E-mail:** tsrwills@tiscali.co.uk

Williams, Thomas Edward, (Birmingham), Our Lady and St John, Ferry Ln, Goring-on-Thames, Reading RG8 9DX **Tel:** 01491-872181

Williams-Keogh, Terence, (OMI), Presbytery of the English Martyrs, 30 Prescot St, London E1 8BB **Tel:** 0207 488 4654 **Fax:** 0207 488 1418

Williamson, David, STD, (Westminster), The Presbytery, Hay Ln, London NW9 0NG **Tel:** 020-8204 2834

Williamson, John, (Nottingham), Holy Rood Ho, Exchange Rd, Watford, Herts WD1 7AJ **Tel:** 01923-224085

Williamson, John, (OCD), Carmelite Priory, Kensington Curch Street, London W8 4BB **Tel:** 020 7937 9866 **Fax:** 020 7938 1470 **E-mail:** jwilliamsonocd@yahoo.com

Williment, Paul (Leeds), 148 Coal Rd, Leeds LS14 2DQ **Tel:** 0113-2733957 **E-mail:** paul@stgemma.co.uk

Willis, Christopher, (Leeds), Venerabile Collegio Inglese, Via di Monserrato 45, 00186 Roma, Italia

Willis, Stephen A, BA, (Westminster), The Presbytery, Nicoll Rd, London NW10 9AX **Tel:** 020-8965 4935

Willoughby, Edmund, (SJ), Our Lady of Perpetual Succour, Pilmuir Rd, Longshaw, Blackburn BB2 3JB **Tel:** 01254-54900

Wilson, Anthony, (Leeds), St Patrick's Presbytery, Low Ln, Birstall, Batley WF17 9HD **Tel:** 01924-472257. **E-mail:** awilson@leeds-diocese.org.uk

Wilson, Bernard, (Salford), 287b Didsbury Rd, Heaton Mersey, Stockport SK4 3HE **Tel:** 0161-432-0762

Wilson, Colin Myles, (Shrewsbury, retired), 1 Elm Rise, Frodsham WA6 6AJ **Tel:** 01928-735765 **E-mail:** colin@wilson731.fsnet.co.uk

Wilson, David, (Westminster), Les Trois Fontaines, 6 rue de l'Ecluse, Ambleteuse 62164, France **Tel:** 00-33321 99298 **E-mail:** davidwilson@wanadoo.fr

Wilson, Francis, (Portsmouth, retired), San Jose, Miltown Malbay Rd, Lahinch, Co Clare, Eire **Tel:** 065-81673 **E-mail:** frfrankwilson@eircom.net

Wilson, Gerald, (Prior and Director of Pastoral Centre) (OAR), St Rita's Centre, Ottery Moor Ln, Honiton, Devon EX14 1AP **Tel/Fax:** 01404-42601 **E-mail:** gerald.wilson1@btinternet

Wilson, Ian, (OSA), Convento S. Agostino, Piazza S. Agostino 10, 53037 San Gimignano SI, Italy **Tel:** 0577 90 70 12

Wilson, John, BA STL (Leeds), 13 North Grange Rd, Leeds LS6 2BR **Tel:** 0113-261 8782

Wilson, Magnus, (OSB), St Michael's Abbey, Farnborough Rd, Farnborough, Hants GU14 7NQ **Tel:** 01252-546105 **Fax:** 01252-372822

Wilson, Martin, (Cardiff), c/o Archbishop's Ho, 43 Cathedral Rd, Cardiff CF11 9HD

Wilson, Peter, MA, FCA, (Northampton), 10 Stoke Hill, Oundle, Peterborough, PE8 4BH **Tel:** 01832 272615

Wilson, Peter J, BA, HDipEd, (Westminster), Newman Ho, 111 Gower St, London WC1E 6AR **Tel:** 020-7387 6370

Wilson, Richard (OSB), Worth Abbey, Crawley RH10 4SB **Tel:** 01342-710310

Wilson, Richard, (East Anglia, retired), 47 Gilman Rd, Norwich NR3 4JB

Wilson, Stuart M P, MA, BSc, (Westminster), 16 Abingdon Rd, London W8 6AF **Tel:** 020-7937 9165

Wilson, Terence, (OCSO), Our Lady and St Bernard, Mount St Bernard Abbey, Coalville, Leicester LE67 5UL **Tel:** 01530-832298/832022

Wilson, Terence McLean (Arundel & Brighton), Our Lady Immaculate & St Michael, 14 Mount St, Battle, E. Sussex TN33 0EG **Tel:** 01424-773125

Wilson, William, BSc, BA (Portsmouth), St Patrick's Ho, 45 Portsmouth Rd, Woolston, Southampton SO19 9BD **Tel:** 023-8044 8671**E-mail:** eastside@portsmouth-dio.org.uk

Wilton, William Patrick (Birmingham), St Joseph's, Avon Dassett, Leamington CV33 0AR **Tel:** 01295-690395

Wiltshire, Adrian (Cardiff), The Presbytery, St Michael Street, Newport NP20 2PZ **Tel:** 01633 676876

Winchester, Geoffrey, (Southwark), 48 Thanet Rd, Bexley, Kent DA5 1AP **Tel:** 01322 524813

Wingfield, John C, FRGS, FR MetS, MRIN, MIITTed (Southwark), c/o Archbishop's Ho, 150 St George's Rd, London SE1 6HX

Wijngaard, Piet H (OCarm), Whitefriars, More Ho, Heslington, York YO10 5DX **Tel:** 01904-410446

Windsor, Francis, (OFMcap), Franciscian Friary, 15 Cuppin St, Chester CH1 2BN **Tel:** 01244-351331

Windsor, Keith, (OFMcap), St David's, Monastery Ave, Pantasaph, Holywell CH8 8PE **Tel:** 01352-711053

Winn, Bernard, MA (Southwark), 59 Tabor Gardens, Cheam, Surrey SM3 8RU **Tel:** 020-8642 2088

Winn, Simon STL (Leeds). St Joseph's Presbytery, 22 Gisburn Rd, Barnoldswick, Lancs BB8 5HA **Tel:** 01282 812204

Winstanley, John BA (Lancaster), Sacred Heart, 17 Talbot Rd, Blackpool FY1 1LB **Tel:** 01253-620964

Winstanley, Michael, MTh, STL, BA, (SDB), Thornleigh Ho, Sharples Park, Bolton BL1 6PQ **Tel:** 01204 591144 **E-mail:** provincial@salesians.org.uk

Winter, Marcus, (Westminster), 79 St Charles' Square, London W10 6EB **Tel:** 020-8969 6844

Winterton, Gregory Cecil John, (CongOrat), The Oratory, Hagley Rd, Birmingham B16 8UE **Tel:** 0121-454 0496

Wisdom, John, (OPaem), 178 New London Road, Chelmsford, Essex CM2 0AR **Tel:** 01245 352898

Wisniewski, Leszek, (Northampton), 45 The Croft, Haddenham, Bucks HP17 8AS **Tel:** 01844-290178

Witchalls, Bruno (Arundel & Brighton), 1 St Margaret Drive, Epsom, Surrey KT18 7LB **Tel:** 01372 723573

Witon, Slawomir, STB (Westminster), Clergy Ho, 42 Francis St, London SW1P 1QW **Tel:** 020-7798 9055

Wiwcharuk, Stephan, STD, Mitrat, (Ukrainian) Ukrainian Catholic Church, Derby Rd, Gloucester GL1 4AE **Tel:** 01452-529069

Wizeman, William (SJ), Campion Hall, Oxford OX1 1QS **Tel:** 01865-286133

Wlodarczyk, Wladyslaw, 2 Sherwood Rise, Nottingham NG7 6JN **Tel:** 0115-962 3713

Wojcieszak, Krzysztof (MIC), 2 WIndsor Rd, London W5 5PD **Tel:** 020-8567 1746

Wojczynski, Jan, (SChr), Dom Polski, 18 Carlton Rd, Whalley Range, Manchester M16 8BB **Tel:** 0161-226 1836 **Fax:** 0161-226 6221

Wolczak, Colin, (Arundel & Brighton), 12 Eastgate Gardens, Guildford, Surrey GU1 4AZ **Tel:** 01483-562704

Woldeghebriel, Tekié (MCCJ), Comboni Missionaries, The Priory, Barnet Ln, Elstree, Herts WD6 3QU **Tel:** 020-8953 8065

Wolf, Alex (MHM), Red Gables, 41 Victoria Rd, Freshfield, Liverpool L37 1LW **Tel:** 01704 835 679

Wolff, Franz Sebastian, Very Rev, FRCO, (OSB), Buckfast Abbey, Buckfastleigh, Devon TQ11 0EE **Tel:** 01364-645500, **Fax:** 01364-643891

Woo Edward Man-ko (MAfr), Our Lady Help of Christians, 4 Lady Margaret Rd, Kentish Town, London NW5 2XT **Tel:** 07946-383659

Wood, Bernard, JCL, (Salford, retired), 14 Taylor St, Clitheroe BB7 1NL

Wood, P Damian, (Portsmouth), St John's Convent, Kiln Green, Reading, Berks RG10 9XP **Tel:** 0118-940 2964

Wood, Deryck, (IC), 189 Balloan Rd, Inverness IV2 4PW **Tel:** 01463-239358

Wood, John, BA, (Middlesbrough), SS Peter & John Fisher, 91 Bannister St, Withernsea HU19 2DT **Tel/Fax:** 01964-612204

Wood, Thomas, JCL, STB, PhB (Liverpool), Our Lady Star of the Sea, 1 Crescent Rd, Seaforth Village, Liverpool L21 4LJ **Tel:** 0151-928 2338 **Fax:** 0151-949 1186

Woodall, George J, Canon, MA, PGCE, STD, JCL (Nottingham), Casa Madre Teresa Casini, Via Del Casaletto, 128 00151 Roma,Italia **Tel:** 0039-06 5327 3857

Woodgate, Michael, BA, (Southwark), Oak Cottage, Church Walk, Headcorn, Kent TN27 9NP

Woodhead, Eric (East Anglia), c/o The White House, 21 Upgate, Poringland, Norwich NR14 7SH

Woodhead, J Derek, (Salford), c/o The White House, 21 Upgate, Poringland, Norwich NR14 7SH

Woodman, Henry Benet, (CJ), 46 Durdells Ave, Kinson, Bournemouth BH11 9EH **Tel:** 01202-572939

Woodruff, Mark, (Westminster), The Sainsbury Family Trust, Allington Ho, Victoria St, London SW1E 5AE **Tel:** 0207-410 7049

Woods, Bernard, (Lancaster), St Cuthbert, 53 Crystal Rd, Blackpool FY1 6BS **Tel:** 01253-346471

Woods, John L, (Shrewsbury, retired), Park Mount, 52 Park Mount Drive, Macclesfield SK11 8NT **Tel:** 01625 420075

Woolley, Stephen, (Shrewsbury), St Joseph's, Hope Rd, Sale M33 3BF **Tel:** 0161-973 1615 **Fax:** 0161-976 4058 **E-mail:** stjoseph.sale.uk@ btinternet.com

Worthy, Edmund, (Northampton), 82 Knox

Rd, Wellingborough, Northants NN8 1JA **Tel/Fax:** 01933-222780 **E-mail:** edmundworthy@yahoo.co.uk

Wozniak, Jozef, PhD (SChr) (Polish Priest) 31 Cheltenham St, Rochdale OL11 3QJ **Tel:** 01706-642649

Wratherill, John, MA, STB, (Southwark), 103 Maison Diru Rd, Dover, Kent CT16 1RU **Tel:** 01304-206766

Wright, Alan, (Southwark, retired), Flat 2, St Peters' Residence, 2A Meadow Rd, Vauxhall SW8 1QH **Tel:** 020-7587 5346

Wright, Eric, (Southwark, retired), No 214, cpl, Ward 12, The Royal Hospital, Royal Hospital Rd, Chelsea, London SW3 4SR

Wright, J Colin, (Salford), Holy Infant, Baxendale St, Astley Bridge, Bolton BL1 6QH **Tel:** 01204-303871

Wright, John, MA, (Shrewsbury), Danesford, High St, Albrighton, Wolverhampton WV7 3LA **Tel:** 01902-374109

Wright, Melville, (SSS), Blessed Sacrament Shrine, 4 Dawson St, Liverpool L1 1LE **Tel:** 0151-709 5528 **Fax:** 0151-709 5977 **E-mail:** petereymard@aol.com

Wright, Peter, (Shrewsbury), St Edward's, Ivy St, Runcorn, WA7 5NZ **Tel:** 01928-577755 **Fax:** 01928-580800 **E-mail:** saintedwardsrun@msn.co.uk

Wright, Robert J, (Birmingham), St John Fisher, Tiverton Rd, Wyken, Coventry CV2 3DL **Tel:**024-7644 3459

Wright, Russell, LLB STL (Leeds), Church of the Ascension, 6025 Estero Boulevard, Fort Myers Beach, Florida 33931 **Tel:** (941) 463 6754

Wright, Stephen, MA, (OSB), The Priory, Banklands, Workington CA14 3EP **Tel:** 01900 602114

Wright, Stephen (Birmingham), 78a Guild St, Burton-on-Trent DE14 1NB **Tel:** 01283 63246

Wright, Timothy, Rt Rev, MA, BD, (OSB), Monastery of Our Lady of Mount Grace, 18 North End, Osmotherley, Northallerton DL6 3BB **Tel:** 01609-883271

Wright, William, BSc, (OSB), Ampleforth Abbey, York YO62 4EN **Tel:** 01439-766714 **Fax:** 01439-766724

Wrightson, Arthur, (Hallam, retired), c/o Bishop's Ho, 75 Norfolk Rd, Sheffield S2 2SZ

Wymer, Stephen, BTh (Southwark), 5 Bleakwood Rd, Walderslade, Kent ME5 0NF **Tel:** 01634-862910 **Fax:** 01634-311456 **Email:** pp-walderslade@amserve,com

Wymes, Barry, Mgr, (Arundel & Brighton, retired), 16 Cobham Grange, Between Streets, Cobham, KT11 1DH **Tel:** 01932-588382 **Mbl:** 07740 825836

Wynekus, Peter, (East Anglia, retired), Flat 3 Seckford Almshouse, Seckford St, Woodbridge, Suffolk IP12 4ND **Tel:** 01394 388787

Wynn, Noel, MA, (SM), Marist Fathers, 12 Hindringham Rd, Great Walsingham, Norfolk NR22 6DR **Tel:** 01328-820588 **Fax:** 01328-820331

Wyszomierski, Tadeusz, (MIC) 2 Windsor Rd, London W5 5PD **Tel:** 020-8567 1746

Wyszowadzki, Wladyslaw, Mgr Canon, DD PhD, 55 Foxbourne Rd, Balham, London SW17 8EN **Tel:** 020-8672 5070 **Fax:** 020-8682 1770

Yap, Roberto, (SJ), Copleston Ho, 221 Goldhurst Terr, London NW6 3EP **Tel:** 020-7604 5854 **E-mail:** r.yap@aol.ac.uk

Yasinto, Julius (SVD), 8 Teignmouth Rd, London NW2 4HN. **Tel:** 020-8452 8430.

Yates, David, (Salford), c/o PRCC(N), MP1.2, Leach Building, Whale Island, Portsmouth PO2 8BY **Tel:** 023-9262 5193

Yates, Philippe, MA(Cantab), BA(Theo), MCL (OFM). Franciscan International Study Centre, Giles Ln, Canterbury, Kent CT2 7NA **Tel:** 01227-464939/769349 **Fax:** 01227-459465/786648 **E-mail:**phillippe.yates@franciscans.ac.uk

Yeo, Christopher Richard, MA, JCD, (OSB), Abbot President, English Benedictine Congregation. Buckfast Abbey, Buckfastleigh, Devon TQ11 0EE **Tel:** 01364 645500 **Fax:** 01364 643891

Youell, Michael, (Liverpool, retired), Flat 17, St George's Court, Station Rd, Maghull, Liverpool L31 3RH **Tel:** 0151-527 1521

Younes Habib, (LMO Maronite Rite), Lebanese Centre, 6 Dobson Cl, Swiss Cottage, London NW6 4RS

Young, David STL, Guardian (OFMConv), St Clare's Friary, Victoria Ave, Higher Blackley, Manchester M9 0RR **Tel:** 0161-740 4161 **Fax:** 0161-740 1261

Young, Henry, MA, (Westminster, retired), 63 Heathfield Court, Heathfield Terr, London W4 4LS

Young, Theodore, (OSB), St Austin's, 561 Aigburth Rd, Grassendale, Liverpool L19 0NU **Tel:** 0151-427 3033 **Fax:** 0151-494 0600

Young, William, MA, PhB, STL, (Brentwood), The Presbytery, 41 Linton Rd, Barking, Essex IG11 8HG **Tel:** 020-8594 2849

Younger, John, (Nottingham), St Mary's Rectory, Heneage Rd, Grimsby, N. E. Lincs DN32 9DZ **Tel:** 01472-342301 **Fax:** 01472-251894.

Zalewski, Ryszard (Katowice, Poland), 82 Wellesley Rd, Ipswich IP4 1PH **Tel:** 01473-217391

Zammit, James, (OFM), 1 Balniel Gate, Lindsay Square, London SW1V 3SD

Zammit, Patrick, (Southwark), The Presbytery, St Vincent's, Temple Hill, Dartford DA1 5HU **Tel:** 01322-279955

Zampese, John (XM), 2 Cranwich Rd, Stamford Hill N16 5JX **Tel:** 020-8800 9898

Zanchi, Alessandro (SX), 260 Nether St, London N3 1HT

Zang, Richard, Chaplain (East Anglia), Chaplain's Residence, Carmelite Monastery, Quidenham, Norfolk NR16 2PG **Tel:** 01953-887302

Zareba, Jan, (Katowice, Poland), 2 Sherwood Rise, Nottingham NG7 6JN **Tel:** 0115-960 8831

Zastocki, Zygfryd, (CRL), Polish Catholic Centre, Millennium Ho, Bordesley St, Birmingham B5 5PH **Tel:** 0121-643 3577/358 7102 (B37)

Zawistowski, Apolinary, (CRL), Polish Catholic Centre, Millennium Ho, Bordesley St, Birmingham B5 5PH **Tel:** 0121-643 3577/358 7102 (B37)

Zentile, Ettore, (CS), St Frances Cabrini, 10 Woburn Rd, Bedford MK40 1EG **Tel:** 01234-359515

Zernoff, Raphael, (OSA), St Augusines, 55 Fulham Palace Rd, Hammersmith W6 8AU **Tel:** 0208 748788

Zhuwakia, Antonio (Bulawayo), St Mary's Rectory, Draycott Terr, London SW3 2QR

Zielinski, Paul, BD JCL. (Hexham & Newcastle), Our Lady and St Cuthbert, Highfield Ln, Prudhoe, Northumberland NE42 6EY **Tel:** 01661-832298

Ziliotto, Gian Domenico, Italian Mission, 20 Brixton Rd, London SW9 6BU **Tel:** 020-7735 8235

Ziomek, Philip, BD, BA (Nottingham), The Priest's Ho, 3 Chesterfield Rd South, Mansfield, Notts NG19 7AB **Tel:** 01623-623458 **Fax:** 01623-423363

Zsidi, Gabriel, (Westminster), c/o Archbishop's Ho, Ambrosden Ave, London SW1P 1QJ

Zuzlak, Andrzej, MA (SChr), (Polish Priest), 196 Lloyd St North, Manchester M14 4QB **Tel:** 0161-226 1588 **Fax:** 0161-232 0450

Zwart, Ton, (MSC), Cordate Community, 157 Ettington Rd, Aston, Birmingham B6 6ED **E-mail:** ton@msceurope.co.uk

PRIESTS OF ENGLAND AND WALES WORKING ABROAD

Priests of Religious Congregations as listed by the Catholic Missionary Union Secretariat, Watling House, 8 King Harry Lane, St Albans, Herts AL3 4AW. April 2005.
Where known, their home diocese is shown in brackets.
Some addresses are not given in full, but may be obtained from their Provincial House.

Alessi, Giovanni, (SC, retired), 3 Fairfield Rd, Fletton, Peterborough PE2 8BD **Tel:** 01733-565527 **Fax:** 01733-348346

Anderson, Don, MAfr, (Arundel and Brighton), PO Box 12059, Arusha, Tanzania

Annis, Paul, MCCJ, (Westminster), Sudan

Arkwright, Norman, SM, (Salford), Solomon Islands, Oceania

Armstrong, Raymond, SJ, (Brentwood), c/o Garnet House, 52 Mount Pleasant Drive, Harare, Zimbabwe

Barnes, Francis, MAfr, (Salford), Spiritual Formatin Centre, PO Box 410777, Kasma, Zambia

Barrett, David, Pontifical North American College CASA Santa Maria Vin Dell Umita 30, 00187 Roma Italy
Tel: 0039066900l226
Email: david.barrett15@btopenworld.com

Barrow, Robert, SJ, (Brentwood), c/o 29 Brickdam, PO Box 10720, Georgetown, Guyana

Baye, Antoine OFM, The Franciscans, PO Box 612, 00606 Sarit Centre, Westlands, Nairobi, Kenya

Beirne, Charles, SMM, (Leeds), Montfort Missionaries, PO Box 830, Mbarara, Uganda

Bex, Anthony, SJ, (Westminster), The Seminary, PO Box 970, PO Chisipite, Harare, Zimbabwe

Bird, Dom David OSB (Cardiff), Monasterio de la Encarnacion, Apartado 8, Sullana, Peru

Boles, John, SSC, (Shrewsbury), Padre de St Columbano, Apartado 262, Lima 100, Peru

Bonsall, Leo, OSB (Cardiff), Monasterio Trapense, Nuestra Señora de Coromoto Humocaro Alto, Ed Lara, Venezuela

Booth, Edward, (OP), Fransiskussystur, Austurgata7, IS-340 Stkkisholmur, Iceland

Botto, Stephen, MHM, PO Box 5058, Nkwen-Bamenda, North-West Province, Cameroon
E-mail: estefano-ib@yahoo.co.uk

Bowe, Rev Dom Peter, MA, STL, Maisin St. Benoit, 94 Rue Des Blancs Mouchons 59500-Douai, France
Tel: +33 (0) 327-97-17-02
E-mail: msb94@wanadoo.fr

Brandon, William, SMA, (Liverpool), St John's Catholic Church, PO Box 211, Kaltungo, Gombe State, Nigeria

Brennan, Joseph, SMA, (Hexham & Newcastle), St Joseph's, Wilton, Cork, Ireland

Britt-Compton, Peter, SJ, (Portsmouth), St Ignatius, Lethem, Rupununi, Guyana

Burke, Kevin, SM, (Salford), Tonga

Byrne, Dermot, MHM, (Shrewsbury), Mill Hill Formation House, PO Box 2130, Jinja, Uganda

Campbell-Johnston, Michael, SJ, (Westminster), St Francis of Assisi Church, Mount Standfast, St James, Barbados, West Indies

Cantwell, Terence, (SDS), Catholic Mission, Chingulungulu, PO Box 43, Masasi, Mkoa Mtwara, Tanzania, East Africa
Tel: 00255-23 2510028
E-mail: sdsmasasi@sds-ch.ch

Carroll, Patrick, SMA, (Liverpool), African Missions, Wilton, Cork City, Ireland
Tel: 00353 21 454 1069
Fax: 00353 21 493 3462

Carey, Francis, MAfr (Liverpool), Woodlands, PO Box 320076, Lusaka, Zambia

Casey, Terence, CSSP, (Salford), Catholic Mission, Yadim, PO Box 1422, Yola, Adamawa State, Nigeria

Cashin, Patrick, (Cardiff), Lourdes Catholic Church, Lusaka Road, PO BOX 91100 Mongu Western Province Zambia.

Castelli, John, (Southwark, retired), obispado, Chachapoyas, Dept De Amazonas, Peru

Centis, Felix, MCCJ, (Westminster), Uganda

Chadwick, Robert, SJ, (Clifton), 29 Brickdam, PO Box 10720, Georgetown, Guyana

Chambers, James, (MHM), 10 Las Vegas, Merville, Paranaque, 1700 Manila, The Philippines **Tel:** +63 910770767
E-mail: jpchmbrs@yahoo.co.uk

Clark, John, MCCJ, (Hexham and Newcastle), Missionarios Combonianos Rue Jose Rubens 15, Previdencia, 05515-000 Sao Paulo, Brazil

Clarke, Peter Thomas, OP, (Birmingham), Rosary Priory, Roxborough, St Paul's, Grenada, West Indies.

Clarke, Roger, (Shrewsbury), c/o Padres de

Santiago Apostol, Casilla 919, Santa Cruz Bolivia **Tel:** 00591 3 345 9040

Coleman, John, SDB, (Southampton), St John Bosco House, PO Box 25, Randvaal 1873, South Africa

Connolly, Mark, CSSP, PO Box 3 Wyndham, West Australia, Australia

Conroy, John BSc, STB (MHM), No7 Weixing Rd, Chenchung, 130022, Jilin Province P.R. China **Tel:** 086 431 85303278 **E-mail:** conroy9375@yahoo.co.uk

Coxhead, Gilbert, OP, Rosary Priory, St Paul's, Grenada, West Indies

Croft, George, SJ, (Westminster), St Augustine's Regional Seminary, PO Box 3800, Bulaway, Zimbabwe

Crombie, William (MAfr), (Salford), Makokola Parish, PO Box 13, Tabora, Tanzania

Cullen, David, MAfri, (Westminster), Kabwata Parish, PO Box 50164, Lusaka, Zambia

Cushlow, Gerard, MHM, (Hexham and Newcastle), Papatoetoe, Auckland 1701, New Zealand **Tel:** 00-64 9 279 3103

Dalton, Desmond, (Cardiff), Parroquia San Pablo Casilla 09-01-5825 Guayaquil, Ecuador

Davies, Rt Rev Bishop Colin, MHM, c/o Assumbi Sisters, PO Box 669, Kisii-40200, Kenya **Tel:** 00254-20891119, **E-mail:** ccdraf@yahoo.com

Davoren, Hugh, CSSp, (Shrewsbury), Pope John XXIII Parish, 35 chemin Dr A Pasteur, 1209, Geneva, Switzerland **Tel:** 00 41 22 734 6826 **E-mail:** hjdav@freeserve.ch

Dooley, Canice, SDB, (Shrewsbury), Salesian Church, 18 Dorchester Street, Robertsham, Johannesburg 2091, South Africa

Doran, John, MHM, PO Box 204, Sasolburg 9570, Free State, South Africa

Dore, Patrick, SSC, (Westminster), Padres de San Columbano, Casilla, 4263 Correo 2, Valparaiso, Chile

Dove, John, SJ, (Westminster), Silveira House, Box 545, Harare, Zimbabwe

Doyle, Ian, BD, BSc, RGN, (Arundel & Brighton), PO Box 1601, Rosslyn 0200, South Africa.

Duffy, Kevin, SM (Hexham and Newcastle), Scholasticat St Pierre Chanel, BP185 Yaounde, Cameroon

Durrant, Liam, MHM, Mill Hill Formation House, PO Box 29 5000 Iloilo City, The Philippines Tel: +63 33 321 0309 **E-mail:** liamdurrant@yahoo.co.uk

Edmonds, Peter, SJ, (Salford), Hekima College, PO Box 21215, Nairobi, Kenya

Edney, Mark, BA, MPhil, (OP), Convento santa Sabina, Piazza Pietro d'Illiria 1, Aventino, 00153 Roma, Italia

Edwards, Adrian CSSP (Lancaster), Spiritan Institute of Philosophy, PO Box 11, Ejisu, Ashanti Region, Ghana

Edwards, Paul, SJ, (Southampton), St George's College, Bag 7727, Causeway, Harare, Zimbabwe

Enright, Brian, SJ, (Westminster), St Igantius' College, Box CH80, Chisipite, Harare, Zimbabwe

Evans, Michael, SMA, (Southwark), Parish of Christ the King Parish, 61 Lefroy Road, Beaconsfield 6162, West Australia

Ezekwere, Gerald, (CMF), Sacred Heart Parish, PO Box 28, Dangriga, Stann Creek District, Belize, Central America **Tel:** 0044 501 522025

Fanning, James, (MHM), (Westminster), Promotion Office of the EAR, PO Box 60, Tororo, Uganda **Mbl:** 00256-77469544

Felix, Paul MCCJ (Southwark). Comboni Missionaries, PO Box 191, Asmara, Eritrea

Fitzgerald, Rt Rev Michael, MAfr, (Birmingham), Apostolic Nuncio to Egyot, 5 Mohamed Mazhar St, 11211-Zamalek Cairo

Fitzsimons, James, SJ, (Liverpool), 493 Marshall Street, Belgravia, Johannesburg, South Africa

Flannagan, Finbarr OFM, PO Box 141, Dundee 3000, South Africa **Tel:** 0027 34 212 2241

Ford, Vincent, SDB, (Salford), Catholic Church, 310 Lansdowne Road, 7780 Lansdowne, South Africa

Fosker, Roy, SDB, (East Anglia), Salesians of Don Bosco, Provincial Ho. PO Box 776, Ashaiman, Ghana

Franklin, Frederick, (MHM), 23 Chemin de Mouchairas Sud 11590 Cuxac d'Aude France **Tel:** (0033) 468335142 **E-mail:** z-fjf2323@yahoo.co.uk

Garman, Anthony, SDB, (Southampton), Catholic Church, 310 Lansdowne Road, Lansdowne C.P. 7785, South Africa

Giles, Stephen, MHM, (Nottingham), PO Box 17128, Gruenkloof 0027, Pretoria, South Africa **Tel:** +27 12 4602039 **E-mail:** stephengiles@johnvianney.co.za

Gillick, John, SJ, (Liverpool), 8 The Elms, York Road, Rosebank, Cape Town, South Africa

Gittins, Anthony, CSSp, (Salford), 4740 North Malden St, Chicago, IL USA **Tel:** 001 773 753 5343 (office) **Fax:** 001 773 324 4360 **Tel:** 001 773 728 9466 (home) **E-mail:** tgittins@ctu.edu.us

Gornall, David, SJ, (Salford), Archbishop's House, PO Box CY330, Causeway, Harare, Zimbabwe

Gould, John MAfr (Cardiff), Lavigerie House, PO Box 532, Jinja, Uganda

Greenway, Francis, MHM (Salford), St Joseph's House, Ramanthapur, Amberget PO, Hyderabad 500 013, Andhra Pradesh, India
Tel/Fax: +91 4412222584
E-mail: fgreenway@yahoo.com

Gunter, Paul, BD, SLD, (OSB), Collegio Sant'Anselmo, Piazza Cavalieri di Malta 5, I-00153 Roma, Italia
Tel: 0039 06 579 1263
E-mail: pcfgunter@libero.it

Hackett, Mark, SJ, (Portsmouth), Catholic Church, 21 Pendennis Road, Mount Pleasant, Harare, Zimbabwe

Hannon, Paul, MAfr, (Hexham and Newcastle), St Stephen's Church, PO Box 13081, Khartoum, Sudan

Harold-Barry, David, SJ, (Middlesbrough), Garnet House, 52 Mount Pleasant Drive, Mount Pleasant, Harare, Zimbabwe

Heap, Michael, MAfr, (Salford), Ghana

Henze, John, MAfr, (Nottingham), Zambia

Higgins, Dennis, SDB (Salford), Salesians of Dom Bosco, PO Box 15, Rundu, Namibia **Tel:** 00264 66 255 053
E-mail: sdbrundu@africaonline.com.na

Hopper, Paul, CSSP, (Hexham and Newcastle), St Joseph's Catholic Church, PO Box 39, Kingswood, NSW 2747, Australia

Hunter, James CSSP (Liverpool), PO Box 21, Makurdi, Nigeria

Jackson, Thomas, SJ, (Leeds), St Paul's Musami Mission, Box CH650, Harare, Zimbabwe

Jenkins, Gareth, SMA, (Portsmouth), St Dominic's Catholic Mission, PO Box 297, Monrovia, Liberia

Jerstice, *Brian,* SDB, (Salford), Salesians of Don Bosco, PO Box 220, Mafinga, Tanzania **Tel:** 00255 26 2772 104
E-mail: bjerstice@yahoo.co.uk

Johnson, Nigel, SJ, (Lancaster), 45 Moffat Avenue, Hillside, Bulawayo, Zimbabwe

Keaney, Patrick, SDS. Pugu Road, PO Box 39936, Dar Es Salaam, Tanzania, East Africa. **Mbl:** 00255 744884576
E-mail: sdsmasasi@sds-ch.ch

Kearney, Leslie, SJ, (Nottingham), Catholic Church, Mabaruma, Hosororo, Guyana

Kelleher, Brendan, SVD, (Southwark), Japan

Kelleher, Maurice, SMA, (Southwark), St Joseph's Church, Wilton, Cork, Ireland

Kirwan, John, STL, (MHM), (Shrewsbury), BP1800, Kinshasa, Democratic Republic of Congo **Tel:** +24 397647053
E-mail: mhmbasankusu@gb-solution.cd

Littlewood, Patrick, MHM, (Leeds), c/o St Joseph's Parish, 23A Dominion Rd, PO Box 148, Kaitaia, New Zealand
Tel: +64 94080289

Lorriman, Gerard, SJ, (Hexham and Newcastle), St Mary's, Nyanga, PO Box 32050, Ottery 7808, Cape Town, S. Africa

Loughran, Francis, SMM, (Liverpool), Nametembo Parish, PO Box 11, Chingale, Malawi

Lucie-Smith, Alexander IC, Kenya

MacGarry, Brian, SJ, Zambuko House, 12 Fern Road, PO Hatfield, Harare, Zimbabwe

MacWilliam, John, MAfr, (Southwark), Algeria

McClory, Brian SJ, 8 The Elms, York Road, Rosebank, Cape Town 7700, South Africa

McDonagh, Dominic BSc, BA (CMF), Sacred Heart Parish, PO Box 28, Dangriga, Stann Creek District, Belize, Central America **Tel:** 0044-501 522 025
E-mail: dominic@claret.org.uk

McElhatton, Kevin, SJ, St Martin de Porres, PO Box 103, Orlando, Ganteng 1803 2017, South Africa

McGuiness, Dominic, OFMCap, (Westminster), St Fidelis College, PO Box 827, Madang, Papua, New Guinea

McGurk, Very Rev Dom Simon OSB (Cardiff), *(Monk of Belmont)* St Anselm's Abbey, 4501 South Dakota Avenue NE, Washington DC, USA 20017
E-mail: ssm72@verizon.net

McHugh, Peter, SVD, (Liverpool), Italy

McKeown, Maximilian, OFMConv, Sacred Heart Mission, PO Box 160040, Ikelenge, Zambia

McPartland, Michael SMA (Middlesbrough), St Mary's Church, Port Stanley, Falkland Islands

Madden, Terry, MAfr, (Middlesbrough), Burkina Faso

Maitland, D, SJ, (Southwark), St Francis Xavier Church, Port Mourant, Corentyne, Guyana

Martin, Paul, SJ, (Liverpool), Catholic Church, Kato, Pakaraima Mountains, Guyana

Mehers, John, SDB, (Salford), St John Bosco House, PO Box 25, Randvaal 1873, South Africa

Meiring, Peter, SJ, (Salford), Campion House, PO BOx 54, Harare, Zimbabwe

Melhuish, John, MHM, (Arundel and Brighton), c/o PO Box 1933, Phokeng 0335, North West Province, South Africa **Tel:** +27 145733731
E-mail: jonrdmel@mweb.co.za

Meredith, Anthony IC, Rosmini Ashram, T M Palayam PO Coimbatose 695315, Kerala, India
E-mail: anthonymeredith@mac.com

Milner, Anthony, BSc, STL, (Arundel & Brighton), Venerabile Collegio Inglese, Via di Houserrato 45, 00186 Roma, Italia **Tel:** 05 6868546
Milward, Peter, SJ, (Southwark), Sophia University, Kioicho 7, Tokyo, Japan
Moloney, Patrick, SJ, (Westminster), Prestage House, 50 Mount Pleasant Drive, Mount Pleasant, Harare, Zimbabwe
Monaghan, Augustine MHM (Hexham & Newastle), Nazareth House, 13 Millhead, Lasswade, Midlothian, Scotland
Murphy, Gerard IMC (Northampton), Franciscan Centre Friary, PO Box 70992, Ndola, Zambia
Murphy, Laurence SDS, Our Lady of Lourdes, 28 Marda Way, Nollamara, Western Australia WA6062 **Tel:** 0061-8 9349 8361 **Fax:** 00611-8 9345 5581 **E-mail:** shaym@iinet.au
Newbury, Peter, SDB, (Shrewsbury), Saint Louis School, 179 Third Street, West Point, Hong Kong
Oates, Vincent, MHM, St Joseph's House, Ramanthapur Amberpet PO, Hyderabad 500013, Andhra Pradesh, India **Tel:** +91 4027202934 **Tel:** +91 4027207802 **E-mail:** voates26@yahoo.co.uk
O'Connell, Edward SSC (Southwark), Padres de San Columbano, Apartado 262, Lima 100, Peru
O'Donohue, John, St Anne's Convent, Windsor Gardens, Musselburgh, Scotland
O'Gorman, Maurice, OSM, (Salford), Good Shepherd Mission, PO Box 7, Siteki, Swaziland
O'Kelly, Fritz, OFM Conv, Franciscan Centre Friary, PO Box 70992, Ndola, Zambia
O'Leary Finbarr, Monsignor, M.Sc, GQ,S,W (Cardiff) The Society of St James The Apostle, 24 Clark Street, Boston MA 02109 USA
O'Neill, Edmund, SDB, (Salford), Salesian Institute, PO Box 870, Capetown 8000, S. Africa
O'Reilly, Paul SJ, (Southwark), St Ignatius, Lethem PO, Rupununi, Guyana
O'Sullivan, Andrew, CSSP, 117 Newarthill Road, Carfin, Motherwell, Scotland
O'Toole, Austin, SDB, (Salford), Casa Salesiana, AV Brasil 210, Lima 5, Peru
O'Toole, Kevin, SVD, (Salford), West Indies
Parkinson, Rev Dom Joseph, OSB, (Cardiff), Parish of San Lorenzo, **Tel:** +51 739977479 **E-mail:** parkinsonkerr@hotmail.com
Pathe, Anthony, CSsR, (Hallam), PO Box 107, Rustenburg 0300, Transvaal, South Africa
Penhallurick, Robert (East Anglia), St Francis de Salles, 66 Granville Street, Newark, Ohio 43055, USA
Pereira, Max, MHM, (Westminster), Procure of Mill Hill Missionaries, 10 Las Vegas, Merville Park, Parañaque, 1700 metro Manila, The Philippines **Tel:** 0063-916 421 7186
Perry, James, SVD, Moyglare Road, Maynooth, Co. Kildare, Ireland
Pham, Xuan Nam (Barnabas), BA (OSB), Monastery of Christ the Word, Monte Cassino, Post Bag 902 Macheke, Zimbabwe
Phelan, Bernard DipRel Ed, MPS (MHM), Paryangara Catholic Church, PO Box 92, Kotido Uganda **Tel:** 00256 772410641 **E-mail:** bcphelanuganda@yahoo.co.uk
Pierce, Roy (MHM), Caritas Drug Abuse Treatment Prog, PO Box 1311, Peshawar, Pakistan **Tel:** +92 91 2261181 **E-mail:** rdpdove@yahoo.com
Platt, Graham (Northampton), 1 bis Rue de la Rouqueille, Aiat les Bains 1150 France **Tel:** 00334 68691433
Porter, Brian, SJ, (Brentwood), 52 Mt Pleasant Drive, Mount Pleasant, Harare, Zimbabwe
Power, Edmund, (OSB), Abbot, BD PhD, Abbazia di San Paulo Fuori le Mura, Via Ostiense 186, 1-00146 Roma, Italy **Tel:** +39 064 547 7849
Power, Michael, SDB (Liverpool), Salesian Ho, 18 Dorchester Street, Robertsham, Johannesburg, 2091 South Africa **Tel:** 0027 11 680 3900 **E-mail:** boscorob@xsinet.coza
Prior, John, SVD, (East Anglia), Indonesia
Preston, Francis, SDB (Birmingham), Ratisbonne Monastery, 26 Rehov Shemuael Hanagid, PO Box 7336, 91702 Jerusalem **Tel:** 00972 026258677 **E-mail:** salesians@sdbratisbonne.com
Quigley, Joseph, MHM, c/o P&J Paulus, Trillik, Buncrana, Donegal, Ireland
Redmond, Tim SPS (Liverpool), St Patrick's, PO Box 25084, Nairobi, Kenya
Riddle, Geoffrey, MAfr, (Westminster), Tanzania
Roden, Martin, OP, (Birmingham), Blackfriars, 46 Derby Avenue, PO Box 815, Springs 1560, South Africa
Rogers, Edward, SJ, (Liverpool), Canisus House, 37 Admiral Tait Road, Marlborough, Harare, Zimbabwe
Ross, Hugh, SJ, St.George's College, PO Box 7727, Causeway, Harare, Zimbabwe
Ryan, Peter, MHM, (Shrewsbury), Tamaki Maori Mission, 7 Westminster Road, Balmoral, Auckland, New Zealand **Tel:** +64 9 630 9554 **E-mail:** paryan@clear.net.nz

Scott, Joseph Patrick, SVD, (Nottingham), USA
Sheehy, Jeremiah, SCJ
Sherry, Edward, SSC, (Liverpool), Australia
Shevlin, John, SVD, (Salford), USA
Simons, Derek, SVD, (Cardiff), USA
Slinger, John, MAfr, (Shrewsbury), Tanzania
Smith, Francis, MHM, (Salford), Misioneros San José de Mill Hill, Casilla 8802, Guayaquil, Ecuador
Tel: +59 3042426813
E-mail: franksmithmhm@yahoo.com
Smith, John, CSsR, (Shrewsbury), The Monastery, Bergvliet Road, Bergvliet 7800, S. Africa
Smith, Peter, MAfr, (Middlesborough), Tanzania
Starkey, Denis, MAfr, (Salford), Washington, USA
Targett, Michael, MAfr, (Westminster), Ghana
Taylor, John, MHM, STL, LTL,(Salford), Mill Hill Formation House, Peddapendiyal, PO Karurapuram, Warangal Dt 506 151, AP, India **Tel:** 0091-8711 223371
E-mail: jtmhm@rediffmail.com
Taylor, Theodore, c/o Rosary Priory, Roxborough St Paul's, Grenada, West Indies
Tinneney, Joachim, OFM, St Francis of Assisi Church, Jawalgira 584 143, Raichur Dt, Karnataka, India
Tierney, Paul SSC (Clifton), Columban Fathers, PO Box 2364, Government Buildings, Suba, Fiji
Toner, Gerald, MA (SMA), Christ the King Catholic Church, 1a Milton Place, Pittenweem, Anstruther, Fife KY10 2LR
Tel: 0133-311262
E-mail: gerry.toner@tiscali.co.uk
Torri, Charles MCCJ (Birmingham), Comboni Missionaries-Angal, PO Box 3872, Kampala, Uganda.
Tulloch, Keith, SM, (Middlesbrough), Japan
E-mail: maristna@maharoba.ne.jp
Turnbull, William, MAfr, (Salford), Malawi
Ward, Peter CSSP, PO Box 1219, Bethlehem, F.S. 9700, South Africa
Watsham, Anthony, SJ, (Westminster), C.P.S. Novitiate, PO Box 51, Macheke, Harare, Zimbabwe
Watson, Peter, MHM, (Hexham and Newcastle), St Aloysius Minor Seminary, PO Box 115, Kumbo, Bui Division, North West Province, Cameroon
Webster, George CSsR (Westminster), St Gerard's House, Stonechat Lane, PO Borrowdale, Harare, Zimbabwe
Whelan, David, MHM, (Liverpool), 13A Fenwick Avenue, Milford, Auckland 1309, New Zealand **Tel:** +64-9489 6543
E-mail: dgwhelan@xtra.co.nz
White, Allan, MA, STL, PhD, (OP), Convento santa Sabina, Piazza Pietro d'Illiria 1, Aventino, 00153 Roma, Italia
Wild, Julian, MHM, (Hexham and Newcastle), Lwak Sisters, PO Box 2021, Kisumu 40100, Kenya **Tel:** 00254 733 627060
Wilkinson, Denis, MCCJ, (Birmingham), Dublin, Ireland
Wilkinson, Patrick MCCJ (Birmingham), Comboni Missionaries, 8 Clontarf Road, Clontarf, Dublin 3, Ireland
Wilson, *Edmund, SJ*, (Salford), Monte Cassino Mission, Bag 902, Macheke, Zimbabwe
Wolstenholme, Anthony, MCCJ, (Hallam), Scotland

PERMANENT DEACONS IN ENGLAND AND WALES

Abbot, John, (Wrexham), 6 Coed Masarn, Abergele, Conwy **Tel:** 01745-824888

Abbott, Noel, (Liverpool), 15 Haroldene Grove, Prescot L34 1PY **Tel:** 0151-449 2212

Adams, Eugene, (Arundel & Brighton), Penhams, 39 Raffle Rd, Westham, Eastbourne E. Sussex BN24 5DG **Tel:** 01323 762252

Adams, William, (Lancaster), 8 Winckley Rd, Broadgate, Preston PR1 8EL **Tel:** 01772 259795

Adlington, Neil, (Birmingham), 1 High St, Silverdale ST5 6NG **Tel:** 01782-624325

Adlington, Stuart, (Shrewsbury), 36 Hogarth Rd, Marple Bridge, Stockport SK6 5BP **Tel:** 0161-449 8427

Adlington, William, (Middlesbrough), 1 Sandfield Close, Market Weighton, York YO43 3ET **Tel:** 01430-873362

Ainsworth, Michael H, (Birmingham), 9 Gadsby Ave, Wolverhampton, W. Mids WV11 3EH **Tel:** 01902-730105

Aitkins, Duncan, (Southwark), 22 Beaconfield Rd, Bickley, Kent BR1 2BP **Tel:** 020-8460 4189

Alcock, Terence, (Liverpool), 36 Budworth Ave, Sutton Manor, St Helens WA9 **Tel:** 01744 819037

Alger, Desmond P L, (Liverpool), 45 Larkhill, Ashurst, Skelmersdale WN8 6TE **Tel:** 01695-559271

Allen, Henry, (Birmingham), 5 The Green, Shutford, Banbury, Oxon OX15 6PJ **Tel:** 01295-780642

Allen, Michael, (Plymouth, retired), St Catherine's Church, 4 Lewens Lane, Wimborne, Dorset BH21 1LE

Allen, Peter, (Nottingham), Apartment 14, Venables Court, Ross Cl, Lincoln LN2 4QW **Tel:** 01522-808177

Anderson, Vincent A, (Liverpool), 6 Willoughby Dr, Eccleston Hill, St Helens, WA10 3AY **Tel:** 01744- 758088

Andrews, Robert, (Arundel & Brighton), Flat 3, The Gatehouse, The Old Palace, High St, Mayfield, East Sussex TN20 6PH

Andrews, Francis M, Dr, (Birmingham), 2a Woodlands Rd, Sonning Common, Reading, RG4 9TE **Tel:** 01734-722354

Anscombe, Hugh, (Clifton), 21 Marigold Close, Woodhall Park, Swindon, Wilts SN2 2SY **Tel:** 01793-727345

Anthony, Rev James, (Nottingham), 16 Nightingale Ho, Oak Brook Dr, Mapperley, Nottingham NG3 6AT **Tel:** 0115-962 0409

Anwyl, Gerard H, (Liverpool), Christ the King, 81 Score Ln, Childwall, Liverpool, L16 5EB **Tel:** 0151-722 6550

Appleyard, J Grahame, (Liverpool), 58 Westhaven Cres, Aughton, Ormstirk. L39 5BW **Tel:** 01695-422627

Arblaster, David, (Leeds), 20 Christ Church Oval, Harrogate HG1 5AJ **Tel:** 01423-560279

Arch, Leslie, (Shrewsbury), 106 Woodchurch Ln, Prenton CH42 9PD **Tel:** 0151 608 7585 **Email:** les.arch@btinternet

Armstrong, James, (Liverpool), 32 Denebank Rd, Anfield, Liverpool L4 2SY **Tel:** 0151-263 8335

Armstrong, Keith, (Lancaster), Cornerstones, 4 Arches Meadow, Kendal **Tel:** 01539-739806

Arrowsmith, Anthony, (Liverpool), 15 Romford Ave, Leigh WN7 1QB **Tel:** 01942-606329

Ashcroft, Thomas, (Birmingham), 4 Chaddesley Rd, Kidderminster, Worcs DY10 3AD **Tel:** 01562-823573

Atkinson, Henry, (Birmingham), 1 The Drive, Rolleston Rd, Burton-on-Trent, Staffs DE12 0JT **Tel:** 01283-530891

Avery, David, (Southwark), 42, Sleigh Rd, Sturry, Canterbury, Kent CT2 0HT **Tel:** 01227-712129

Baccas, David, (Nottingham), 33 St Margaret's Dr, Sibsey, Boston, Linconlshire PE22 0ST **Tel:** 01205-750477

Baffour-Awuah, Joseph, (Brentwood), 53 Netley Rd, Walthamstow, London E17 7QD **Tel:** 020-8521 2359

Baggio, Nick, MA, CertEd, (Leeds), Ivy Ho, 16 Russell St, Bradford, W. Yorks. BD5 0JB **Tel:** 01274-740292 **Fax:** 01274-306347 **Mob:** 0421-509207 **E-mail:** 101524.3725@compuserve.com

Baines, William, (Birmingham), Flat 1, 98 Princethorpe Rd, Weoley Castle, Birmingham B29 5QA **Tel:** 0121-411 1344

Baker, Michael, (Nottingham), 57 Ridgeway Nettleham, Lincoln LN2 2TL **Tel:** 01522-752718

Baldry, Michael, (Southwark), 93 Raeburn Rd, Blackfen, Sidcup, Kent DA15 8RE **Tel:** 020-8850 0566

Ball, Ron, (Shrewsbury), 12 Allestree Close, Little Harlescott, Shrewsbury SY1 3RG **Tel:** 01743-465452 **Email:** ron@rjball.fsnet.co.uk

Ball, William, (Liverpool), 76 Dunbar Rd, Southport PR8 4RL **Tel:** 01704-567788

Ballard, Keith, (Leeds), 99 Birkby Hall Rd, Birkby, Huddersfield HD2 2XE **Tel:** 01484-541366

Balmer, David, (Brentwood), 9 Nutter Ln, Wanstead E11 2HY **Tel:** 020-8989 4640

Baron, Donnan P, (Shrewsbury), 7 Brogden Dr, Gatley, Cheadle SK8 4AS **Tel:** 0161-428 3832

Barr, Peter, (Liverpool), 2 Pimblett Rd, Haydock, St Helens WA11 0PZ **Tel:** 01942-715298

Barratt, Dennis, (Southwark), 182 Langley Way, West Wickham, Kent BR4 ODT **Tel:** 020-8777 3472

Barron, Bernard, (Shrewsbury), 35 Henley Ave, Cheadle Hulme, Cheshire SK8 6DE **Tel:** 0161-485 5046

Barton, Leonard, (Liverpool, retired), Flat 41, Mayhall Court, Westway, Maghull, Liverpool L31 0EB **Tel:** 0151-520 3115

Barwise, Christopher, (Lancaster), 16 Fairfield Dr, Ashton-on-Ribble, Preston PR2 1JJ **Tel:** 01772-760045

Bavidge, Nigel, (Leeds), 22 Savile Park, Halifax HX1 3EW **Tel:** 01422-353955

Bayes, Andrew, (Arundel and Brighton), 38 Redgrave Rd, Maidenbower, Crawley, W. Sussex RH10 7WK **Tel:** 01293-88706

Beach, Geoffrey, (Cardiff), 97 Van Road, Caerphilly CF83 1FA **Tel:** 029-2086 1850 **Email:** geoff@beachfamily.plus.com

Beddow, Frederick J, (Shrewsbury), 84 Corndon Cres, Harlescott, Shrewsbury SY1 4LQ **Tel:** 01743-462510

Belfield, John, (East Anglia), 3 John St, Kings Lynn, Norfolk PE30 5HH **Tel:** 01552-774303

Bell, Frank, (Lancaster), Castle Cottage, Beaumont, Carlisle CA5 6ED **Tel:** 01228-576561 **Mbl:** 07890-359836

Belt, Michael, (Clifton), 148 Northcote Rd, Downend, Bristol BS16 6AR **Tel:** 0117-940 0799.

Bennett, David, (Liverpool), 4 Brookfield, Parbold, Lancs WN8 7JJ **Tel:** 01257-462998

Bennett, Joseph, (Southwark), Flat 7 Oakapple Ho, Oakapple Ln, Maidstone, Kent ME16 9NW **Tel:** 01622-728850

Bentley, Stephen, DipSM, MICRSM (Clifton), 70 Langtoft Rd, Stroud, Glos GL5 1NJ **Tel:** 01453-751101

Beresford, Robert, (Southwark), 46 Cardinal Ave, Kingston-upon-Thames, Surrey KT2 5SB **Tel:** 020-8546 8684

Berrie, Thomas, (Southwark), 165 Saint Hilda's Way, Gravesend, Kent DA12 4AZ **Tel:** 01474-351666

Bianco, Charlie, (Southwark), San Martin, 20 Burleigh Cl, Strood, Kent ME2 3TQ **Tel:** 01634-726714

Bill, Desmond, (Liverpool), c/o Centre for Evangelisation, Croxteth Dr, Liverpool L17 1AA **Tel:** 0151-522 1043

Birtles, Robert, (Portsmouth), 3 Shorts Rd, Fair Oak, Eastleigh, Hants SO50 7EJ **Tel:** 023-8069 2416 **Mbl:** 07092-168127 **E-mail:** bob@mbsc.clara.net

Black, Philip, (Middlesbrough), 3 Broome Cl, Huntington, York YO32 9RH **Tel:** 01904-764020

Blackman, Christopher, (Birmingham), 10 Foxburrow Cl, Sutton, Witney OX29 5SH

Bland, Thomas, (Lancaster), 64 Cherry Tree Rd, Blackpool FY4 4PF **Tel:** 01253-762495

Blinston, Paul Anthony (Liverpool), 7 Argyll St, Wigan WN5 9BG **Tel:** 01942-321146

Body, John, (Arundel and Brighton), 17 Penhill Road, Lancing, W. Sussex BN15 8HA **Tel:** 01903-536319

Bond, Alan, (Southwark), 167 Waller Rd, New Cross, SE14 5LX **Tel:** 020-7732 8379 **E-mail:** alanbond@btopenworld.com

Borthwick, Trevor David, (Birmingham), 358 Sandon Rd, Meir Heath, Stoke on Trent ST3 7EB **Tel:** 01782-388416

Boshell, Paul, (Nottingham), 10 Cheriborough Rd, Castle Donnington, Leics LE74 2RY **Tel:** 01332-850447

Boughton, John, (Southwark), 24 Marler Rd, Folkestone, Kent CT19 4DA **Tel:** 01303-275104 **E-mail:** johnboughton@btinternet.com

Boulter, Stephen, (Nottingham), 29 Fern Dr, Middle Rasen, Market Rasen, Lincs LN8 3NU **Tel:** 01673-849566

Bower, Delian, (Plymouth), Sacred Heart Church, 25 South St, Exeter, Devon EX1 1EB

Bowgett, Vincent, (Southwark, retired), 45 Dale Walk, Dartford, Kent DA2 6JA **Tel:** 01322-224356

Bowler, Steven, (Portsmouth), 19 Windrush Way, Hythe, Hants SO45 6JF **Tel:** 023 8020 7449

Bowman, Francis, (Liverpool), 20 Calderstones Rd, Liverpool L18 6HS **Tel:** 0151-724 4937

Bowyer, Peter William, (Birmingham), 17 School Cl, Dilhorne, Stoke-on-Trent ST10 2QB **Tel:** 01782-393892

Boxall, Alan, (Southwark), 51 Hickory Dell, Hempstead, Nr Gillingham, Kent **Tel:** 01634- 360637

Boyd, William, (Southwark), 3 Minster Dr, Croydon, Surrey CR0 5UP **Tel:** 0208681 0905

Boyle, Cornelius Gerard Joseph, BA, (Southwark), 103 Woolwich New Road, Woolwich SE18 6EF **Tel:** 020 8854 0359

Boyle, Gerard, (Shrewsbury), 9 Elm Rd, Prenton, Wirral CH42 9NY **Tel:** 0151-608 1214

Bradley, James, (Clifton), 17 Talboys Walk, Tetbury, Glos, GL8 8YU **Tel:** 01666- 502981

Bradshaw, Anthony T, (Birmingham), 38

Queens Rd, Hartshill, Stoke-on-Trent ST4 7LJ **Tel:** 01782-614749

Braithwaite, Francis, (Liverpool), 28 Ruddington Rd, Kew, Southport PR8 6XD **Tel:** 01704- 532960

Bravey, Peter, (Shrewsbury) 3 Blake Cl, Crewe CW2 8EB **Tel:** 01270-569957 **E-mail:** pm.bravery@btinternet.com

Brannigan, Jack R, (Clifton), 1a Warren Rd, Filton, Bristol BS34 7EH **Tel:** 01179-755365

Breen, Kenneth, (Liverpool), 20 Gower Gardens, Burscough, Ormskirk L40 5SP **Tel:** 01704-893709

Breslin, Thomas, (Nottingham), 6 Hornbeam Cl, Oakwood, Derby DE21 2DJ **Tel:** 01332-601709

Bright, Patrick, (East Anglia), 2 Cage Ln, Stretham, Cambs CB6 3LB

Brighten, Christopher, (East Anglia), 4 Godbold Close, Kesgrave, Ipswich IP5 2FE

Brindley, John, (Birmingham), 146 Barnett Ln, Kingswinford, Dudley DY6 9QA **Tel:** 01384-271012

Brinn, David, (Clifton), 7 Littlewood, Witham Friary, Frome BA11 5HE

Broadbent, Paul, (Lancaster), Bridge Ho, Kearstwick, Kirby Lonsdale LA6 2GB **Tel:** 01524-273737

Brockman, John, CB, MA, LLB, (Arundel & Brighton), 3 Homewell Ho, The Moors, Kidlington, Oxon 0X5 2XT RIP 2009 **Tel:** 01865-841662

Brogan, Peter, (Nottingham), 6 Wentworth Close, Heighington, Lincoln LN4 1SU **Tel:** 01522-828587

Brooker, George, (Northampton), 56 Lower Chippenham Ln, Slough SL1 5DF **Tel:** 01753-524100

Brooks, Clive, (East Anglia), 76 Broom Knoll, East End, East Bergholt, Suffolk CO7 6XN **Tel:** 01206-396319

Brown, Peter Radnor, (Southwark), Canterbury Rd, St Nicholas-at-Wade, Kent CT7 0PG

Brownbill, Peter, (Wrexham), 10 Monza Close, Buckley, Flintshire CH7 2QH **Tel:** 01244-545913

Bryan, Alan, (Southwark), 20 Pleasant Rd, Southend on Sea, Essex SS1 2HJ **Tel:** 01702 462903

Budgen, Richard, (Portsmouth), 16 Pottle Close, Botley, Oxford OX2 9SN **Tel:** 01865-864191 **E-mail:** richardbudgen50@hotmail.com

Bulmer, David, (Brentwood), 9 Nutter Ln, Wanstead, London E11 2NY **Tel:** 020-8989 4640

Burleigh, Bill, (Hallam), 42 Housley Park, Chapeltown, Sheffield S35 2UE

Burleigh, James, (Southwark), Flat 4, 6 Birchhill Court, Birchhill Park, Birchington-on-Sea CT7 9UQ **Tel:** 01843 841579

Burns, Brian, (Lancaster), 25a Deanpoint, Westgate, Morecambe LA3 3DJ **Tel:** 01524-401894

Burrows, John, (Birmingham), 13 Conrad Close, Rugby CV22 5RX **Tel:** 01788-334957

Butler, Thomas, (Lancaster), 18 Pineway, Fulwood, Preston PR2 3SH **Tel:** 07812-383020

Byrne, Patrick, (Wrexham), Chapel House, Selattyn, Oswestry, Shropshire SY10 7DZ **Tel:** 01691-680328

Cafferata, Michael, (Shrewsbury, on Sabbatical), Merrywood, Brereton Heath Ln, Somerford, Congleton CW12 4SZ **Tel:** 01477-533094 **Email:** mike@merrywood.org

Caffrey, Anthony, (Shrewsbury), 26 Avonlea Rd, Sale M33 4HZ **Tel:** 0161-973 3606

Cairns, Anthony, (Portsmouth), 8 St Clement Close, Lower Earley, Reading, Berks RG6 4BT **Tel:** 07768-214033 **E-mail:** cairns@totalserve.co.uk

Calder, Vincent, (Clifton), 9 Mallard Close, Chipping Sodbury, Bristol BS37 6JA **Tel:** 01454-311717

Caldwell, David P, (Liverpool), 32 Abberley Close, St Helens WA10 2AZ **Tel:** 01744-733587

Callan, Patrick, (Southwark), 59 Princes Avenue, Tolworth, Surrey **Tel:** 020-8399 9862

Callaghan, Anthony, (Liverpool, retired), 43 Salisbury Rd, Liverpool L5 6RE **Tel:** 0151-263 2205

Callaghan, Anthony Thomas, (Liverpool), 184 Liverpool Rd, Skelmersdale WN8 8BX **Tel:** 01695 724476

Cameron, Iain, (Wrexham), The Haven, Tudor Rd, Wrexham LL13 7HF **Tel:** 01978-290287

Campbell, Brendan, (Nottingham), 10 Lanes Close, Sileby, Loughborough, Leicestershire LE12 7PD **Tel:** 01509-813540

Campbell, Peter, MBBS (Lancaster, Retired), Briarwood, Highfield Rd, Sedbergh LA10 5DH **Tel:** 015396-20918

Campion, Donald, (Liverpool), 267 Walton Ln, Walton, Liverpool L4 5RQ **Tel:** 0151-525 3029

Cannavina, Antonio, (Southwark), 89 Jersey Rd, Strood, Rochester, Kent ME2 3PG **Tel:** 01634-719445

Cardy, James C, (Liverpool), 56 Melrose Dr, Winstanley, Wigan WN3 6EG **Tel:** 01942- 214818

Carew, Norman, (Shewsbury), 1 Park Avenue, Wallasey CH44 9DZ **Tel:** 0151-200 1948

Carey, Geoffrey, (Plymouth), St Augustine's Church, 38 Dorchester Rd, Weymouth, Dorset DT4 7JZ

C

Carpen, Allan, (Liverpool), 6 Ashfield Crescent, Billinge, Wigan WN5 7TE **Tel:** 01744-895173

Carr, Richard, (Northampton), 20 Highfield Rd, Princes Risborough, Bucks HP27 0HG **Tel:** 01844-347623

Carter, Andrew, (Portsmouth), 41 Birchnott Rd, Liphook, Hants GU30 7PQ **Tel:** 01428-724171

Carter, Frederick, (Southwark), 331 Cannon Hill Ln, London SW20 9HQ **Tel:** 020-8540 6234

Carter, Mark, (Birmingham), Brookhouse Farm, Pershall, Eccleshall, Staffs ST21 6NE **Tel:** 01785-850151

Carter, Robin, (Southwark), Ty Canol, 82 Gladstone Rd, Broadstairs, Kent CT10 2JB **Tel:** 01843-604795

Carter, Thomas Mark, FRICS, JP, (Birmingham), Brookhouse Farm, Eccleshall, Staffs ST21 6NE **Tel:** 01785-850151

Cary, Geoffrey, (Plymouth), 63 Goldcroft Avenue, Weymouth, Dorset DT4 0ES

Cassidy, Christopher, (Southwark), 74 The Avenue, Aylesford, Maidstone, Kent ME20 7LE **Tel:** 01622-718497

Cassidy, Francis, (Liverpool), 56 Wensley Rd, Aintree, Liverpool, L9 8DW **Tel:** 0151-476 7152

Chalkley, Barry, (Southwark), 16 Cathcart Dr, Orpington, Kent BR6 8BX **Tel:** 01689-603294

Chandler-Honnor, Roger, (Southwark, retired), St Mary's Home for the Elderly, Tooting Bec Gardens, Streatham SW16 1QY **Tel:** 020 8677 9677

Channing, Edward, Rev (Plymouth), Coombe Cottage, Woodbury, Oakfield, Willand, Cullumpton, Devon EX15 2VA

Channing, John, (Lancaster), 9 St Anne's Close, Ambleside, Cumbria LA22 9HB

Chappinelli, Claudio, (East Anglia), 202 The Broadway, Peterborough PE1 4DT

Charles, Terence, (Birmingham), 56 Carter Rd, Great Barr, Birmingham B43 6JP **Tel:** 0121-358 3929

Chegwin, John, (Liverpool), 51 Vaux Cresent, Bootle, Merseyside L20 OAP **Tel:** 0151-922 4917

Child, David, MRCS, LRCP (Birmingham), 2 Pennine Way, Biddulph ST8 7EJ **Tel:** 01782-513590

Chilton, Desmond, (Birmingham), 7 Barford Close, Matchborough, East Redditch B98 0BA **Tel:** 01527-516711

Choppen, Michael, (Southwark), 185 Mitcham Rd, Tooting, London SW17 9PG

Chrisp, Thomas, (Shrewsbury), 41 Windermere Rd, Handforth, Wilmslow SK9 3NJ **Tel:** 01625 251047 **Tel:** tomchrisp@hotmail.co.uk

Chukwu, Fidelis, (Southwark), 51 Elmwood Court, 38 Battersea Park Rd, London SW11 4JE **Tel:** 020-7720 2912 **E-mail:** Fchukwu@aol.com

Clark, Anthony, (Westminster), 700 Finchley Rd, London NW11 7NE

Clifton, David, (Arundel & Brighton), 33 Tarrant Street, Arundel, W. Sussex BN18 9DG **Tel:** 01903-882968

Clowes, John, (Shrewsbury), 51 Higher Ln, Lymm, Cheshire WA13 0BE **Tel:** 01925-752193

Coates, Peter, (Moldova), 46 Greenways, Sutton Heath, Woodbridge, Suffolk IP12 3TR **Tel:** 01394 420859

Cobb, Petroc, MA (OSB), Quarr Abbey, Ryde, Isle of Wight PO33 4ES **Tel:** 01983-882420 **Fax:** 01983-884402

Cockshutt, Simon, (Southwark), 12 Gibson Ho, 37 Haling Park Rd, South Croydon Surrey CR2 6NJ **Email:** simoncokshutt@yahoo.com

Colby, Anthony, (Birmingham), 99 Ivy Bridge Rd, Coventry CV3 5PG **Tel:** 024-7641 1057

Cole, Francis, (Lancaster), 2 Empress Avenue, Fulwood, Preston PR2 8JT **Tel:** 01772-716481

Coleman, Donald, MA, FRSA, (Southwark), 3 Farnham Close, Langton Green, Tonbridge Wells, Kent TN3 0DL **Tel:** 01892-864281

Collier, John, (Lancaster), 83 Anchorsholme Ln East, Thornton Cleveleys FY5 3PE **Tel:** 01253-864704

Colling, John, (Clifton), Flat K, Coat Drive, Westbury on Trym, Bristol BS9 3UP **Tel:** 0117-962 5288

Collings, Len, MA (Middlesbrough), 28 Spaunton Close, Milton Grange, Hemlington, Middlesbrough TS8 9RE **Tel:** 01642-599564

Collins, Paul R, (Liverpool), 1 Kensington Rd, Formby, Merseyside L37 6EL **Tel:** 01704-875183

Connelly, Edward, (Northampton Retired), 54 Hogfair Ln, Burnham, Bucks SL1 7HQ **Tel:** 01628 661615

Conner, Charles, (Leeds), 11 Northgates, Wetherby LS22 6HX **Mbl:** 07711 345176

Connors, John, (Plymouth), St Mary's Church, Higher Church Street, Barnstaple, Devon EX32 8JE

Conrad, Paul N, (Brentwood), 2 Grange Close, Ingrave, Brentwood, Essex CM13 3QP **Tel:** 01277- 810321

Constable, John, (Lancaster), 206 Greystone Rd, Carlisle CA1 2BY **Tel:** 01228- 593699

Conway, John, (Shrewsbury), 58 Norris Rd, Sale, Chestire M33 3QR **Tel:** 0161-962 6983

Conyngham, Vincent J, (Liverpool Retired),

12 Fairway, Huyton L36 1UD
Tel: 0151-480 7173

Cook, Geoffrey, (East Anglia), 20 Brierley Walk, Cambridge, CB4 3NH
Tel: 01223-351650

Cooke, Fred J, (Liverpool), Our Lady, 83 Duke Street, Formby, Liverpool L37 4AR
Tel: 01704-877403

Cooper, Paul, (Liverpool), 71 Newbridge Close, Warrington WA5 9EA
Tel: 01925-232257

Copeman, Peter, (Wrexham), 5 Llys Trewithan, St Asaph, Denbighshire LL17 0DJ **Tel:** 01745-584781

Cordes, Anthony, (Nottingham), Newman House, 339 Wollaton Rd, Nottingham NG8 1FQ **Tel:** 0115-928 0574

Cornell, Robert, (Clifton), 7 Elm Wood Avenue, Bridgewater, Somerset TA6 6AQ **Tel:** 01278 451443

Cox, Brian, (Birmingham), The Sacred Heart, Silver Link Heath, Glascote Heath, Tamworth B77 2EA **Tel:** 01827-288226

Coyne, Robert, (Cardiff), 14 Austin Avenue, Newton, Porthcawl CF36 5RS
Tel: 01656-783540
Email: robert@thecoynes.plus.com

Cramer-Barnicoat, Donald, (Clifton), 50 Beaufort Crescent, Stoke Gifford BS34 8QY

Crane, Harry Joseph, (Arundel & Brighton, retired), 49 Greenmeads, Westfield, Woking, Surrey, GU22 9QJ
Tel: 01483- 766661

Crisp, Anthony, (Shrewsbury), 126 Birkenhead Rd, Meols, Wirral CH47 0LE **Tel:** 0151-632 6617

Crocker, Keith, (Portsmouth), 12 Birch Tree Dr, Emsworth PO10 7RT
Tel: 01243- 374455
E-mail: keith.crocker@tesco.net

Crocker, Shaun, (Southwark), 38 Vale Rd, Ramsgate, Kent CT11 9LT
Tel: 01843-594760

Croft, Bernard, (Nottingham), 26 York Ave, Bottesford, Scunthorpe DN16 3SD
Tel: 01724-862567

Crooks, A John, (Liverpool), 18 Brooks Rd, Formby L37 2JL

Croucher, David, (Portsmouth), Chalkhills, Whitwell Rd, Ventnor, Isle of Wight PO38 1LJ **Tel:** 01983-853029.

Crowley, Andrew, (Hallam), 219 Abbeyfield Rd, Sheffield S4 7AW

Crowshaw, John, (Northampton, Retired), Hammerswood, 64 Long Park, Chesham Bois, Amersham, Bucks HP6 5LF
Tel: 01494-726931 **Fax:** 01494-434209

Crowther, Stephen, (Liverpool), 6 Sefton Dr, Maghull, Merseyside L31 8AQ
Tel: 0151 526 6434

Cummings, William, (Liverpool), 28 Merton Dr, Huyton, Liverpool L36 4NS
Tel: 0151-289 3586

Cumpsty, John, (Portsmouth), 17 Ridgeway Parade, The Verne, Church Crookham, Hants GU52 6NY
Tel: 01252-683606 **Mbl:** 07715-633250
E-mail: deacon.john@ntlworld.com

Cunliffe, Malcolm, (Liverpool), 1 Cranbrook Avenue, Ashton-in-Makerfield, Wigan WN4 9QX **Tel:** 01942-725522

Cunningham, Anthony, (Portsmouth), 21 Qualitas, Roman Hill, Bracknell, Berks RG12 7QG **Tel:** 01344-482652

Cunningham, Terence, (Liverpool), 8 Hazelhurst Close, Formby, Liverpool L37 2LJ **Tel:** 01704-874854

Curtin, Bernard, (Birmingham), 68 Richens Dr, Carterton OX18 3XU
Tel: 01993-843231

Dal Din, Jon, (Southwark), 112 Kelmscott Rd, London SW11 6PT
Tel: 020-7228 2795

Dale, Michael, (Southwark), 19 Fairview Gardens, Meopham, Kent DA13 0NG
Tel: 01474-814935

Daly, John, (Leeds, retired), 15 High Street, Carlton, Goole, N. Humberside DN14
Tel: 01405-862194

Darlison, E, (Arundel and Brighton), No4 Chetnole, Off Lingfield Rd, East Grinstead, W Sussex RH19 2HA
Tel: 01342-322562

Davies, Adrian, (Birmingham), 67 Newman Rd, Erdington, Birmingham B24 9AG
Tel: 0121-373 7514

Davies, William A, (Birmingham), The School House, Longton Hall Rd, Stoke-on-Trent ST3 2NJ **Tel:** 01782-328583

Davy, Thomas, (Lancaster), Thorn How, St Bridget's Ln, Egremont, CA22 2BB
Tel: 01946-820247

Dawson, Robert S, (Nottingham), Oak Ho, Lounde, Bourne, Lincs PE10 0LJ
Tel: 01778-590650

da Gama, Joe, (Forces), Lasenia, Water Ln, Somerton, Somerset TA11 6RE

Deary, Peter, (Liverpool), 11 Sherwood Rd, Crosby, Liverpool L23 7UE
Tel: 0151-932 0835

Deaville, Thomas, (Birmingham), 21 Union Street, Chasetown, Burntwood, Staffs WS7 8XX **Tel:** 01543-686901

Denny, Douglas, (Northampton), Ladysgate, Poyle Ln, Burnham, Slough SL1 8LA
Tel: 01628-602123

Denny, Michael, (Shrewsbury), Glen Lynn, Linglongs Rd, Whaley Bridge, High Peak SK23 7DS **Tel:** 01663 735492
Email: mike.denny@hotmail.co.uk

Derbyshire, John, (Northampton), 296 Sundon Park Rd, Luton LU3 3AL
Tel: 01582-582032
E-mail: revd.john@byopenworld.com

D
E

Detain, John, (Clifton), 105 Roman Rd, Salisbury SP2 9BZ **Tel:** 01722-339163

Dickinson, Adrian, (Liverpool), 9 Sylvan Court, Woolton, Liverpool L25 7AJ **Tel:** 0151-421 0148

Dickinson, Rev Barry, (Nottingham), 6 Harlow Avenue, Mansfield, Notts NG18 4SJ **Tel:** 01623 626366

Diggory, Ernest Cyril Paul, (Liverpool), 'Rannoch', 72 Seafield Avenue, Great Crosby, Liverpool L23 **Tel:** 0151-924 1854

D'Mello, Anthony, (Portsmouth), 3 Pool Rd, Aldershot, Hants GU11 3SN **Tel:** 01252-651747

Dimelow, William, (East Anglia), Crofthaven, The Croft, Old Costessey, Norwich, Norfolk NR8 5DT **Tel:** 01603-743476 bill.dimelow@tiscali.co.uk

Dobson, Christopher, (Arundel & Brighton), Soper's Ride, Slesfield Rd, Turner's Hill, Crawley, West Sussex RH10 4PP **Tel:** 01342-715345

Dockerty, Brian, (Birmingham), 7 Marlborough Gardens, Wolverhampton WV6 0LU **Tel:** 01902-756573

Doherty, Gerard, (Shrewsbury), 8 Dibden Walk, Baguley, Manchester M23 1JZ **Tel:** 0161-945 2542

Dolan, Michael, (Lancaster), The Rectory, Farringdon Ln, Ribbleton, Preston PR2 6LX **Tel:** 01772-791782 **Fax:** 01772-798091

Dolan, Terence, (Liverpool), 7 Charminster Close, Warrington WA5 1JY **Tel:** 01925-492857

Done, David, (Lancaster), St Anne's Presbytery, Westby Mills, Westby, Preston PR4 3PL **Tel:** 01772-682332 **E-mail:** davidmichaeldone@hotmail.com

Donnelly, Graham, BSc (Econ), (Brentwood), c/o Cathedral Ho, Ingrave Rd, Brentwood, Essex CM15 8AT

Donnelly, Nick, (Lancaster), 3 Croft Grove, Barrow in Furness LA13 9NJ **Tel:** 01229-821866

Doona, Rev Stephen, (Nottingham), 52a Derby Rd, Eastwood, Nottingham NG16 3NX **Tel:** 01773-785196

Doran, Peter A W, BA(Hons), (Clifton), High Trees, Undercliff Dr, St Lawrence, Isle of Wight PO38 1XY

Douglas, Tom, (Clifton), 25 Kenmore Crescent, Fulton Park, Bristol BS7 0TJ **Tel:** 0117-979 1404

Douglas, William Edward, (Liverpool), 2 Roehampton Dr, Blundellsands, Liverpool L23 7XD **Tel:** 0151-924 4609

Downer, Richard, (Melkite-Greek Catholic), 3 Palmer Close, Redhill, Surrey RH1 4BU **Tel:** 01737-778863

Doyle, Christopher, (Liverpool, retired), 76 Cranwell Rd, Liverpool L25 1NY **Tel:** 0151-488 6504

Driscoll, James, (Plymouth), Sacred Heart Church, North Rd, Bideford, North Devon EX39 2NW

Duckett, Clifford, (Birmingham),9 Overdale Rd, Whoberley, Coventry CV5 8AJ

Duffy, Patrick Owen, (Birmingham), 18 Sabrina Dr, Bewdley, Worcs DY12 2RJ **Tel:** 01299-400681

Duffy, Sean, (Northampton), Lavender Cottage, Askett, Princes Risborough HP27 9LT **Tel:** 01844-343705

Dunne, Kevin, (Southwark), 22 Riddlesdale Avenue, Tunbridge Wells, Kent TN4 9AB **Tel:** 01892-689800 **E-mail:** kevinjeandunne1@tinyworld.co.uk

Dunn, Kevin, (Liverpool), 8 Westbrook Avenue, Prescot L34 1NU **Tel:** 0151-426 3903

Dunphy, William, (Southwark), 294 Brockley Rd, Brockley, London SE4 2RA **Tel:** 020-8691 7943

Durbin, Cyril, (Southwark), 15 Saddlers Close, Weavering, Maidstone, Kent ME14 5TF **Tel:** 01622- 630055

Dyczek, Christopher, (OFM), 160 The Grove, Stratford, London E15 1NS **Tel:** 020-8534 1964

Dyer, Adrian, (Plymouth) Church of St John the Baptist, 15 Trevu Rd, Camborne, Cornwall TR14 7AE

Eason, William, (Southwark), 8 Hastings Rd, Pembury, Kent TN2 4PD **Tel:** 01892- 824113

Edwards, Anthony, (Lancaster), 221 Fleetwood Rd North, Thornton Cleveleys FY3 4LB **Tel:** 01253-852141 **Mbl:** 07909-756233 **E-mail:** tongy-margaret@tinyworld.co.uk

Edwards, John, (Arundel & Brighton), The Priest's House, Alma Ln, Heath End, Farnham, Surrey GU9 0LH **Tel:** 01252-321383

Edwards, Lloyd, (Hallam), Avalon, 18 Whin Hill Rd, Doncaster DN4 7AE **Tel:** 01302-534325

Edwards, Richard, (Arundel & Brighton), 36 Penfold Way, Steyning, West Sussex BN44 3PG **Tel:** 01903-815351

Elliot, Tom, (Leeds), 22 Spencer Way, Harrogate HG1 3DN **Tel:** 01423-565076

Enright, Terrence, (Plymouth), Church of the Holy Ghost, 11 Raddenstile Ln, Exmouth, Devon EX8 2JH

Erhardt, Andreas, (Cardiff), 226 Underhill Crescent, Abergavenny NP7 6DU **Tel:** 01873-855078 **Email:** erhardt.andreas @rcadc.org

Evans, Paul, (Portsmouth), Glebe House, 7 The Birches, Cove, Farnborough, Hants GU14 9RP

Evans, Roger, (Southwark), 38 Sandy Ridge, Chislehurst, Kent BR7 5DR

Tel: 020-8325 2673
Everall, Brian, (Plymouth), Holy Trinity Church, 3 Tower Road, Newquay, Cornwall TR7 1LS
Fagan, Terence, (Lancaster), 12 Tarnbrook Court, Euston Rd, Morecambe LA4 5LA **Tel:** 01524-421070
Faghy, Ray, (Nottingham), 22 Hayworth Rd, Sandiacre, Derbyshire NG10 5LL
Fantham, James, (Birmingham), 238 The Broadway, Dudley, W Midlands DY1 3DN **Tel:** 01384- 254916
Farnworth, George, (Lancaster), "Cragneish", Highfield Rd, Grange-over-Sands LA11 7JA **Tel:** 015395-33214
Farrell, Paul G, (Liverpool), 12 Winchfield Rd, Wavertree, Liverpool L15 5BJ **Tel:** 0151-475 0219
Fehrenbach, P, (Liverpool), 4a St Paul's Street, Southport, PR8 1NG **Tel:** 01704-500200
Felton, Tony, (East Anglia), 6 Borough End, Beccles, Suffolk NR34 9YW **Tel:** 01502-715744
Ferriere, Yves, (Southwark), 76 Earlshall Rd, Eltham, London SE9 1PR **Tel:** 020-8850 9573
Fitzpatrick, Gerard, (Liverpool), 21 Barnfield Close, Netherton, Merseyside, L30 3UA **Tel:** 0151-523 3939
Fishwick, Gerard, (Liverpool), Cobweb Cottage, Pincock, Euxton, Chorley PR7 6LR **Tel:** 01257-261711
Flanagan, Ken, (Middlesbrough), 40 Easson Rd, Redcar TS10 1HJ **Tel:** 01642-484457
Flanagan, Patrick, (Birmingham), 106 Rosslyn Avenue, Coventry CV6 1GN **Tel:** 024-7633 5383
Flavin, Anthony, (Southwark), 32 Wharfedale Gardens, Thornton Heath CR7 6LA **Tel:** 020-8684 9338
Fleming, Michael, (Northampton), 22 Lavant Walk, Parklands, Northampton NN3 6EL **Tel:** 01604- 647750 **E-mail:** mvf@btinternet.com
Fletcher, Michael, (Liverpool), 7 The Greenway, Knotty Ash, Liverpool L12 3HP **Tel:** 0151-259 4875
Foley, James, (Southwark), 30 Bognor Dr, Herne Bay, Kent CT6 8QP **Tel:** 01227-366841
Foley, John, (Portsmouth), 70 West End Rd, Mortimer Common, Berks RG6 3TS
Ford, Anthony, (Shrewsbury), 23 Hadrian Way, Middlewich CW10 9RB **Tel:** 01606-837875
Forge, Mark, (Clifton), 28 Barrow Ln, Winford, Bristol BS40 8AG **Tel:** 01275-472391
Forsyth, George, (Plymouth, retired), The Cathedral, 45 Cecil Street, Plymouth PL1 5HW **Tel:** 01752-662537
Fothergill, John, (Clifton), 1 Hill View, All Alone, Northleach, Glos GL54 3HJ **Tel:** 01451 860609
Found, Peter, (Northampton), 123 Bouverie Rd, Hardingstone, Northampton NN4 6EG **Tel:** 01604-709914
Fowler, Kenneth, (Clifton), Maryvale, 17 Highfield, Ilminster TA19 9SR **Tel:** 01460-54596
Fox, Terence (Liverpool), 22 Barrows Green Lane, Widnes, Cheshire WA3 3JR **Tel:** 0151-424 0277
Franklyn, David, (Northampton), 20 Oriel Rd, Daventry NN11 4SP **Tel:** 01327-878897
Friedenthal, James, BA, MA, BTh, PGCE, (Southwark), 7 Cliffview Rd, Lewisham, London SE13 7DB **Tel:** 0208 244 6281
Fulbrook, Kingsley, (Clifton), 1 Ellesmere, Thornbury, Bristol BS35 2ER **Tel:** 01454-412772
Gahan, Peter, (Plymouth), Church of St John the Baptist, 15 Trevu Rd, Camborne, Cornwall TR14 7AE
Gascoigne, Neville, (Southwark), 31 Magnolia Avenue, Cliftonville, Margate, Kent CT9 3DX **Tel:** 01843-324880 **E-mail:** nevgasco@btinternet.com
Geary, Stuart, (Arundel & Brighton), Tulp Cottage, Old Lane, Tatsfield, near Westerham, Kent TN16 2LJ **Tel:** 01959-577377
Gee, Stephen, (Birmingham), 122 Court Rd, Wolverhampton WV6 0JJ
Gilbertson, Simon, (Liverpool), 12 Hartington Rd, Brinscall, Chorley PR6 8RG **Tel:** 01254-832031
Gillan, William, (Lancaster), 19 Salcombe Rd, Lytham St Annes FY8 2RD **Tel:** 01253-725997.
Gilligan, James, (Southwark), 13 Loughmill Rd, Pershore, Worcs WR10 1QB **Tel:** 01386-555268
Gilvin, Terence,(Liverpool, retired), 216 East Lancs Rd, Liverpool L11 3DS **Tel:** 0151-226 2680
Glanville, Peter, (East Anglia), White Lilacs, Station Rd, Cantley, Norfolk NR13 3SQ **Tel:** 01493-701341
Glock, Paul, (Southwark), 62 Sunnyfields Dr, Halfway, Sheppey, Kent ME12 3DH **Tel:** 01795-667148 **E-mail:** paulglock@medwaysports.com
Godwin, Stephen, (Clifton), 116 Alexandra Rd, Salisbury SP2 9JY **Tel:** 01722-501854
Gould, Michael, (Southwark), Flat 1, 2 Sycamore Dr, Swanley, Kent BR8 7AY **Tel:** 01322-667814
Graney, Michael, (Northampton), 16 Ledaig Way, Northampton NN3 6DA **Tel:** 01604-452327
Grayston, Anthony, (Liverpool), 48 Bull

Bridge Ln, Aintree, Liverpool L10 6LZ **Tel:** 0151-526 7845

Greaves, Hubert, (Lancaster), 24 Dorchester Rd, Blackpool, Lancs FY1 2LU **Tel:** 01253-356216

Greef, Nicholas, (East Anglia), 18 Levine Cl, Brundall, Norwich NR13 5RH

Green, Harold Anthony, (Liverpool), 36 Cross Ln, Prescot L35 3QJ **Tel:** 0151-289 1036

Green, John, (Birmingham), 2 Farcroft Avenue, Handsworth, Birmingham B21 8AA **Tel:** 0121-523 7559

Green, Malcolm, (Lancaster), 19 Judd House, South Meadow Ln, Broadgate, Preston PR1 8LA **Tel:** 01772-880231

Greenwood, John BA, BPhil (Southwark), 22 Alberta Street, London SE17 3SD **Tel:** 020-7735 8787 **Mbl:** 07710-145780

Gregory, Peter, (Clifton), 16 Nithsdale Rd, Weston-super-Mare BS23 4JR **Tel:** 01934-629326

Grennell, James, (Northampton), 39 Blandford Avenue, Luton, Beds LU2 7AY **Tel:** 01582-580877

Griffin, James (Northampton), Elmsdale, Martinsend Ln, Great Missenden, Bucks HP16 9HR **Tel:** 01494-862275

Griffin, Peter, (Northampton), 178 London Rd, Woolaston, Northants NN9 2QS **Tel:** 01933-664611

Griffiths, Peter, (Birmingham), 1 St Mary's Rd, WKinwarton Park, Alcester B49 6HQ **Tel:** 01789-763877

Grynowski, George, (Birmingham), c/o 18 Charles Street, Cheadle ST10 1ED.

Guilfoyle, Anthony A, (Clifton), 10 Shakespeare Rd, Wootton Bassett, Wiltshire, SN4 8HB **Tel:** 01793- 853545

Guina, Noel, (Northampton), 3 Penina Cl, Bletchley, Milton Keynes MK3 7TL **Tel:** 01908-649356

Gummett, Phillip, (Southwark), 11 Glynmarch Street, Deri, Bargoed, Mid-Glamorgan, Wales CF81 9HZ **Tel:** 01443-831488 **E-mail:** papagumme@aol.com

Gyepi-Garbrah, Samuel Hilton, (Southwark), 14 Claribel Rd, Stockwell SW9 6TH **Tel:** 020-7733 0648

Hagg, Paul, (Portsmouth), Beulah, Le Chemin des Moulins, St Lawrence, Jersey JE3 1HQ **Tel:** 01534-618543 **Fax:** 01534-860723 **E-mail:** paulhagg@jerseymail.co.uk

Hague, John, (Nottingham), Dale End Farm, Gratton Youlgreave, Bakewell, Derbyshire DE45 1LN **Tel:** 01629-650453

Hall, Richard, (Middlesbrough), 34 Beningborough Gdns, Ingleby Barwick, Stockton TS17 0TY **Tel:** 01642-864597

Hamer, George, (Liverpool), 137 Sherwoods Ln, Fazakerley, Liverpool L10 1ND **Tel:** 0151-521 8981

Hanley, Francis, (East Anglia), 30 Churchfield Green, Thorpe St Andrew, Norwich NR7 0HN **Tel:** 01603-431929

Hanly, Rory, (SCA), 1 High Street, Hastings, East Sussex TN34 3EY **Tel:** 02424-421263 **Fax:** 01424-460893

Hartshorn, Anthony, (Birmingham), 8 Bilford Ave, Worcester WR3 8PJ

Harvey, Richard, (Arundel and Brighton), 38 Broad Rig Ave, Hove, E. Sussex BN3 8EW **Tel:** 01273-418770

Harwood, Melvyn, (Nottingham), 17 Orchard Cl, Coven, Wolverhampton **Tel:** WV9 5AS **Tel:** 01902 798489

Harrison, David, (Shrewsbury), 31 Dane Bank Rd, Witton Park, Northwich CW9 5PL **Tel:** 01606-41518 **Email:** davidharrison@lineone.net

Harrison, Gibson, (Lancaster), 5 The Old Tannery, Scotby, Carlisle CA4 8LD **Tel:** 01228-631471

Harrison, John, (Southwark), 1 Arnside, Willow Grove, Chislehurst, Kent BR7 5BU **Tel:** 020-8467 9610

Hatfield, Ian, (East Anglia), Flat B, 28 Constitution Hill, Norwich NR3 4BU **Tel:** 01603-491501 **E-mail:** ianhatfield@pastor.co.uk

Hayes, James, (Southwark), 1 Maltings Close, Hadlow, Tonbridge, Kent TN11 0DY **Tel:** 020-8851 4491

Hayter, Dwight N, (Brentwood, retired), 7 The Cobbles, Brentwood, Essex CM15 8BP **Tel:** 01277- 225812

Hayward, Joe, (Portsmouth), Purbrook, Park Rd, Winchester, Hants, SO22 6AA **Tel:** 01962- 861367

Hayward, Richard, (Clifton, retired), Saffron Lodge, Weston Ln, Bath BA1 4AG **Tel:** 01225-422142

Heath, Chris, (East Anglia), 8 Castle Rd, Bury St Edmunds, Suffolk IP33 3NL **Tel:** 01284-752495

Heath, James, (Northampton), "Shalom", 15 Canberra Gardens, Luton, Beds LU3 2EU **Tel:** 01582-653949

Hegarty, Charles, (Liverpool), 5 Montgomery Rd, Liverpool L9 8DG **Tel:** 0151-525 0069

Hemming, Laurence Paul MA, MPhil (Westminster), Heythrop College, Kensington Square, London W8 5HQ **Tel:** 020-7795 6600

Hender, Paul, (Birmingham), 5 Fennel Close, Cheslyn Hay, Walsall WS5 7DZ **Tel:** 01922- 416275

Heneghan, Peter D B, (Liverpool), HMP Wandsworth, Heathfield Rd, Wandsworth, London SW18 3HX **Tel:** 020-8874 7292 Ext 326

Hesketh, Peter, BSc (Birmingham), The Presbytery, Shrewsbury Rd,

Kidderminster DY11 6DR
Tel: 01562-748474

Hewertson, Robert, (Liverpool), 79 Green Ln, Astley, Manchester M29 7FF **Tel:** 01942-747173 (St Ambrose Barlow, Astley).

Hewitt, Tony, (Birmingham), 118 West Ave, Handsworth Wood, Birmingham B20 2LY **Tel:** 0121-554 8898

Hewson, Paul, (Plymouth), St Joseph's Presbytery, 96 Queen Street, Newton Abbot, Devon TQ12 2ET

Hickey, Kevin J, (Lancaster), 33 Raven St, Carlisle, CA1 2DQ **Tel:** 01228- 520433

Higgins, John William, (Birmingham), 15 Longwood Rd, Aldridge, Walsall WS9 0TA **Tel:** 01922-58969

Higgs, Robert Anthony, (Southwark), 21 Forster Road, Beckenham, Kent BR3 4NQ **Tel:** 020 8663 6906

Hill, G Stuart, (Birmingham), 5 Holly Lodge Walk, Chelmsley Wood, Birmingham B37 5HG **Tel:** 0121-770 5494

Hill, T Alan, (Liverpool, retired), 29 Runnells Ln, Sefton, Merseyside L23 1TR **Tel:** 0151-284 6443

Hilton, David, (Wrexham), "Brentwood" Allt Goch, Flint CH6 5NF **Tel:** 01352- 735815

Hinchey, Peter, (Clifton), 51 Westerleigh Rd, Downend, Bristol, BS16 6UU **Tel:** 0117-956 2824

Hirons, Paul, (East Anglia), 123 Houghton St Giles, Walsingham, Norfolk NR22 6AQ **Tel:** 01328-821523

Hogan, Edward, (Portsmouth), 10 Sutton Gardens, St Peter St, Winchester, Hants SO23 8HP **Tel:** 01962- 864340

Hogan, John, (Livcerpool), 2 Fellstone Vale, Withnell, Chorley PR6 8UE **Tel:** 01254-8319446

Holder, Stephen, (Middlesbrough), St George's Rectory, 7 Peel St, York YO1 1PZ

Holding, Kenneth A, (Liverpool), 3 Greenbank, Hindley Green, Wigan WN2 4SN **Tel:** 01942-253944

Homsey, Gehad, MB, BCh, (Southwark), 105 Lynwood, Folkestone, Kent CT19 5DD **Tel:** 01303-253601 **E-mail:** gehadhomsey@hotmail.com

Hordley, Lawrence, (Shrewsbury), 23 Chatsworth Dr, Newton, Chester CH2 2NB **Tel:** 01244-342048

Horn, John, (Lancaster), 13 Graham Rd, Cabus, Garstang PR3 1LB **Tel:** 01995-602341 **E-mail:** john.horn3@btopenworld.com

Hounslow, Peter, (Menevia), 10 Heol y Drudwen, Gwernfadog, Morriston Swansea **Tel:** 01792 701711

Howard, Christopher, (Wrexham), Oscott College, Chester Rd, Sutton Coldfield West Mids B73 5AA

Howard, Shaun, (Northampton), 17 St Dunstan's Close, Kettering, Northants NN15 5JE **Tel:** 01536-516005

Howe, Clifford, (Wrexham), "Walden" Hugmore Ln, Llan-Y-Pwll,Wrexham, Clwyd. LL13 9YE **Tel:** 01978-661126

Howlings, Raymond, (East Anglia), 10 Gilman Rd, Norwich NR3 4JB **Tel:** 01603-426918

Hughes, Michael, (Plymouth), Holy Name of Jesus and St Edward, Salisbury Street, Shaftesbury, Dorset SP7 8EL

Hughes, Robert, (Birmingham), 11 Lawrence Leys, Bloxham, Banbury Oxon OX16 9AE **Tel:** 01295-720869

Hum, Terry, (Birmingham), 65 St Wulstan Way, Southam CV33 1TV **Tel:** 01926-817932

Hunt, Anthony, (Shrewsbury), 1 Skipton Dr, Little Sutton, Ellesmere Port CH66 4SP **Tel:** 0151-339 9684

Hunt, Peter, (Wrexham), Gerddi Beuno, Whitford St, Holywell CH8 7NJ **Tel:** 01352-712392

Hunt, Peter, (Hallam), 35 Wingfield Ave, Worksop, Notts S81 0SY **Tel:** 01909-487368

Hutchinson, William, (Nottingham), 59 Garenden Rd, Shepshed, Loughborough LE12 9NU **Tel:** 01509-505260

Hyde, Peter, (Northampton), 63 Hillfoot Rd, Shillington, Hitchen, Herts SG5 3NS **Tel:** 01462-711702

Hyland, Dominic, BA, MEd (Lancaster), 105 Victoria Rd East, Thornton, Blackpool FY5 5HQ **Tel:** 01253-826188 **E-mail:** dominic@hyland1.fsnet.co.uk

Irwin, Anthony, (Plymouth), Sacred Heart Church, Fore St, Kingsbridge, Devon

Irwin, Gerard, (Arundel & Brighton), 16 Finches Park Rd, Lindfield, West Sussex RH16 2DN **Tel:** 01444-483635

Jackson, Michael, (Portsmouth), 4 Brdwater Rd, Twyford, Reading, Berks RG10 0EX

Jackson, Peter, (Shewsbury), 36 Arborn Dr, Upton, Wirral CH49 6JS **Tel:** 0151-677 8598

James, Robert G, (Clifton), 31 Heron Gardens, Portishead, BS20 9DH **Tel:** 01275-844988

Jeary, Patrick Joseph, (Birmingham), 21 Modbury Close, Stivichall, Coventry, CV3 5AL **Tel:** 024-7641 2564

Jenkinson, James, (Clifton), 49 Cheltenham Rd, Gloucester GL2 0JG **Tel:** 01452-418287

Jennings, Barry, (Portsmouth), "Squirrels Leap", 60a Queens Park Ave, Queens Park, Bournemouth BH8 9EZ **Tel:** 01202-251163 **E-mail:** barry.jennings@ntlworld.com

Johnson, Anthony R, (Liverpool), 33 Princes Ave, Crosby, Liverpool L23 5RR **Tel:** 0151-924 3543

Jones, Elfed, (Cardiff), St Joseph's, 179 Stanwell Road, Penarth, CF64 3LN **Tel:** 0290-2021 5158 **Email:** elfed179@ntlworld.com

Jones, Peter, (Hexham & Newcastle), 26 Victoria Rd East, Hebburn, NE31 1XQ **Tel:** 0191-483 4781

Jones, Robert Vincent, (Portsmouth), 50 Bellecroft Dr, Newport, Isle of Wight PO30 2JH **Tel:** 01983-524694

Jones, Trevor, BA, MEd, MInstAM (Clifton), 21 Burton Place, Taunton, Som TA1 4HE **Tel:** 01823-270935

Jordon, Michael, (East Anglia), 19 Cambridge Dr, Wisbech, Norfolk PE13 1SE

Joy, David, BA, BEd (Wrexham), 38 Lon Cae Del, Mold, Flintshire CH7 1QX **Tel:** 01352- 754722

Joyce, Robert, (East Anglia), 'Otter Bank', 72 Green End, Comberton, Cambridge CB3 7DA **Tel:** 01223-262964

Kane, Edward, (Liverpool), 1 Thatchers Mount, Collins Green, Warrington WA5 4EH **Tel:** 01925-221720

Kavanagh, Thomas, (Southwark), 104 Grand Dr, Merton SW20 9DX **Tel:** 0208-395 6387

Keeley, John, (Liverpool), 18 Gipsy Ln, Liverpool L18 3HL **Tel:** 0151-737 1588

Kelly, Louis P, (Birmingham), 4 Albert Park Mews, off Albert Park Rd, Malvern WR1 4HN **Tel:** 01684-569988

Kelly, Patrick, (Leeds), 77 Bywell Close, Dewsbury, West Yorkshire WF12 7LP **Tel:** 01924-462948

Kelly, Vincent, (Nottingham), 28 James Gavin Way, Oadby, Leicester **Tel:** 0116-271-9609

Kennedy, John, (Lancaster), 2 The Priory, Foxholes Rd, Whitehaven, CA28 8AE **Tel:** 01946- 692369 **Mbl:** 07811-092364

Kennedy, Michael, (Southwark), 21 Coleridge Cl, Battersea, London SW8 3EY

Kenny, Patrick, (Leeds), 35 Cleasby Rd, Menston, Ilkley LS29 6HZ **Tel:** 01943-876545

Keogh, Raymond, (Nottingham), 24 Harewood Close, Langham, Oakham, Rutland LE13 7JZ **Tel:** 01572-755360

Kerrigan, Anthony Thomas, (Liverpool), 61 Anderson Close, Padgate, Warrington WA2 1PG **Tel:** 01925-811446.

Kilgallon, Peter, (Birmingham), 215 Cemetery Rd, Cannock, Staffs **Tel:** 01543- 503593

Kilshaw, John, (Lancaster), St Anthony of Padua, Cadley Causeway. Preston PR2 3RX **Tel:** 01772 725193

Kinal, Tony, (Arundel & Brighton), Berkeley Ho, 18 Horsham Rd, Dorking, Surrey RH4 2JD **Tel:** 01306 889199 **Tel:** 0151 928 3414

Kindelan, Paul P, (Liverpool), 76 Endbutt Ln, Crosby, Merseyside L23 0TZ **Tel:** 0151 928 3414

King, Malcolm, (Leeds), 33 Water St, Earby, Colne BB8 6QS **Tel:** 01282-843005

Kirkley, William, (Lancaster) Strandline Lees Hill, Brampton, Cumbria CA8 2BB **Tel/Fax:** 01697-72669 **E-mail:** bill.kirkley@totalise.co.uk

Knight, Michael David, (Southwark) 46 Holmside, Gillingham, Kent ME7 4BD **Tel:** 01634 574404

Lafferty, Peter, (Shrewsbury), 24 Beanleach Dr, Offerton, Stockport SK2 5HZ **Tel:** 0161-483 8765

Lamb, John Anthony, (Arundel & Brighton), Dunreyh, Heath Mill Ln, Fox Corner, Guildford, Surrey GU3 3PR **Tel:** 01483-232112

Larwood, Chris, (Middlesbrough), 14 Fountain Close, Hessle, East Yorks HU13 0LB **Tel:** 01482-645368

Lavery, Peter, (Hexham & Newcastle), 22 Langdale, Birtley, Chester-le-St DH3 2EL **Tel:** 0191- 410 2530

Lattey, Peter, (Portsmouth), 38a Elms Rd, Fleet, Hants GU51 3EQ **Tel:** 01252-621295 **Fax:** 01252-815882 **E-mail:** peter.lattey@which.net

Lavery, Graham, (Lancaster), 66 YewTree Ave, Ribbleton, Preston PR2 6QA **Tel:** 01772- 792885

Lawrence, Anthony, (Menevia), 88 Main St, Pembroke SA71 4HH **Tel:** 01646-682629

Leach, John, (Birmingham), 160 Knightlow Rd, Harborne, Birmingham B17 8QA **Tel:** 0121-684 1469

Leadley, Lawrence, (Liverpool), 5 Westlands, Peel, Isle of Man IM5 1JT **Tel:** 01624-842856

Leahy, Michael, (Leeds), 42 West Park Grove, Leeds LS8 2DY **Tel:** 0113-266 1830

Leahy, Raymond, (Middlesbrough), 124 Stanbury Rd, Haworth Park, Hull HU6 7BX **Tel:** 01482-850125

Lee, Gerard, (Northampton), 5 Chestnut Ave, Corby, Northants NN17 2ER **Tel:** 01536-399421

Leeder, Stephen, (East Anglia), 75 Langham Rd, Field Dalling, Holt, Norfolk NR25 7LG **Tel:** 01328-830712

Lemon, Les, (Nottingham), 50 Thanet St, Clay Cross, Chesterfield S45 9JJ **Tel:** 01246-866139

Letley, John, (Southwark), 1 Cooling Rd, Frindsbury, Rochester, Kent ME2 4RE **Tel:** 01634-715151

Levett, Robert, (Westminster), St George's

Chapel, Heathrow Airport, Houslow, Middlx TW6 1BP **Tel:** 0208-745 4261

Lewis, Reginald, (Birmingham), 35 The Hill Ave, Worcester WR5 2AW **Tel:** 01905-353163

Limacher, Patrick, (East Anglia), c/o Cathedral Ho, Unthank Rd, Norwich NR2 2PA **Tel:** 01603 624615

Linthwaite, Patrick, (Birmingham), Maryknoll, 20 Hagley Park Dr, Rednal B45 9JZ **Tel:** 0121-453 2763

Lipscomb, Paul, FCA (Northampton), Crane Ho, Rowanhurst Dr, Farnham Common, Slough SL2 3HG **Tel:** 01753-645349 **Fax:** 01753-645890 **E-mail:**paullipscomb@btinternet.com

Littlewood, Robin, (Clifton), 3 St James' Square, Cheltenham, Gloucester GL50 3PR **Tel:** 01242-244844

Livesey, Louis J, (Birmingham), The Willows, Audmore, Gnosall, Staffs ST20 0HF **Tel:** 01785-822552

Lloyd, F. Joseph, (Liverpool), 54 Sandbrook Rd, Orrel, Wigan WN5 8UB **Tel:** 01695-632646

Lockett, Frank, (Birmingham), 10 Eaton Rise, Willenhall, Walsall WV12 4SH **Tel:** 01902-417584

Lomas, John (Shrewsbury), 49 Cedarway, Bollington, Macclesfield SK10 5HR **Tel:** 01625-572876

Loone, Sean, (Birmingham), 182 Widney Manor Rd, Solihull B91 3JW **Tel:** 0121-703 0712

Loveland, Bernard, BA, MA(Ed) (Lancaster), 18 Hillcrest Dr, Slackhead, Milnthorpe LA7 7BB **Tel:** 01539-563391 **E-mail:** Bernard@medjugorje.freeserve.co.uk

Lovelock, John E, (Northampton), 40 Gilbert Scott Rd, Buckingham MK18 1PS **Tel:** 01280-812997

Ly Trong Song (Paul), (Southwark), 33 Blantyre Walk, World's End Estate, London SW10 0EW. Office: The Holy Name and Our Lady of the Sacred Heart, 117 Bow Common Ln, London E3 4AU **Tel/Fax:** 020-7987 3477

Lynch, Aidan, (Arundel & Brighton), 270 Chertsey Rd, Staines, Middlesex **Mbl:** 07713 149424 **E-mail:** aidanlynch@btconnect.com

Lyons, J Kevin, (Brentwood), 76 Beardsley Dr, Springfield, Chelmsford, Essex CM1 5ZG **Tel:** 01245-460783 **E-mail:** KevinLyons@Supanet.com

Lythe, John, 52 Wensley Rd, Leeds LS7 2LS **Tel:** 0113-269 0006

Macdougall, Dugald. 1 Dearne Croft, Wetherby LS22 7UP **Tel:** 01957-588430

MacFirbhisigh, Iain, (Portsmouth), Vimeira Ho, 47 Stopford Rd, St Helier, Jersey, Channel Isles JE2 4LB **Tel:** 01534-725963 **Fax:** 01534-725823 **Mbl:** 07797-723825 **E-mail:** blessings@jerseymail.co.uk

McCann, John, (Lancaster), 15 Stuart Ave, Morecambe LA4 6E **Tel:** 01524-421795

McCarroll, David, (Birmingham), 3 Broadmeadow Croft, Doxey, Stafford ST16 1DG **Tel:** 01785-225832

McCarthy, Lawrence, (Clifton), 43 Jubilee Dr, Thornbury, Bristol BS35 2YQ **Tel:** 01454-419711

McClure, John, (Liverpool), 8 Roby Grove, Great Sankey, Warrington WA5 1RW **Tel:** 01925-726785

McConnell, Bernard, (Shrewsbury), Flat 2, 'Intabene', 192 Upton Rd, Bidston, Prenton CH43 7QQ **Tel:** 0151-653 2257

McConville, Declan, (Plymouth), St Mary's Church, 211a Wimborne Rd, Poole, Dorset BH15 2RG

McCormack, Michael, (Birmingham), 17 Sunningdale, Walton, Stone ST15 0LZ **Tel:** 01785-816018

McDermott, Philip, (Liverpool), 103 Marians Dr, Ormskirk L39 1LG **Tel:** 01695-577325

McDonagh, Dominic, BSc, BA (CMF), Buckden Towers, Buckden, St Neots, Cambs PE18 9TA **Tel:** 01480-810344 **E-mail:** dominic@claret.org.uk

McDonald, David, (Clifton), 10 Clarence Square, Cheltenham, Glos GL50 4JN **Tel:** 01242-233894

McGeoch, John, (Liverpool), 26 Church Rd, Liverpool L13 2BA **Tel:** 0151-220 2129

McGlynn, Michael T, (Liverpool), 73 Victoria Rd, Garswood WN4 0SZ **Tel:** 01942-716705

McGrail, Michael, (Birmingham), The Presbytery, St Thomas of Canterbury, Dartmouth Ave, Walsall WS3 1SP **Tel:** 01922-626923

McGraw, James, (Liverpool), 149 Hillock Lane, Woolston, Warrington WA1 4PJ

McGunigle, Joseph, (Liverpool), 31 Zigzag Rd, West Derby, Liverpool L12 9EQ **Tel:** 0151-280 9414

McKenna, Stephen, (Shrewsbury), 23 Thornhurst Ave, Oswestry SY11 1NF **Tel:** 01691-654983

McKevitt, Kevin, (Portsmouth), 3 Hawthorn Cres, Grove, Wantage OX12 7JB **Tel:** 01235-764168 **E-mail:** kjmck@freeuk.com

McKevitt, Stephen, (Shrewsbury), 25 Meakin Close, Congleton, Cheshire CW12 3TG **Tel:** 01260-271362 **E-mail:** steve.mckevitt@tesco.net

McKillop, Donagh, (Liverpool), 10 Birchtree Court, West Derby, Liverpool L12 7LW **Tel:** 0151-526 1174

McLaren, Peter, (Cardiff), 1 Winston Path, Fairwater, Cwmbran NP44 4PZ

Tel: 01633-770754 **Email:** peter.mclaren1 @ntlworld.com

McLaughlin, Thomas, (Hexham & Newcastle), 8 Tilbury Grove, Marden, North Shields NE30 3HL **Tel:** 0191-251 4591

McLoughlin, John Philip, (Liverpool), St Anne and Blessed Dominic, 179 Derbyshire Hill Road, St Helens WA9 2LS **Tel:** 01744 811935

McMahon, Alan, (East Anglia), 42 College St, Bury St. Edmunds, Suffolk IP33 1NL **Tel:** 01284 756324

McNicholas, Leo, (Liverpool), 'The Larches', Gill Ln, Longton, Nr Preston PR4 4SS **Tel:** 01772-612838

McNicholl, Paul, (Liverpool), 1 Alston Rd, Liverpool L17 6BA **Tel:** 0151-427 2850

Macardle, James E, (Liverpool), 109 Town Row, Liverpool L12 8RJ

Macpherson, Duncan M, KHS, MA, D.Min, (Westminster), 16 Ormond Dr, Hampton, Middx TW12 2TN **Tel:** 020-8274 0210 **E-mail:** duncan@deaconduncan.com

Maguire, James, (Lancaster), 182 Roundhay Down, Fulwood, Preston PR2 3NE **Tel:** 01772-860980

Mahon, Seamus, (Arundel & Brighton), 1 Tollgate Cottages, Lower Beeding, West Sussex RH13 6NJ **Tel:** 01403-891939

Mahoney, Peter, (East Anglia), 3 White Villas, Silfield Rd, Wymondham, Norfolk NR18 9AT **Tel:** 01953-603025

Maloney, Patrick, (Southwark, retired), Flat 1, Pipes Place, Forge Ln, Shorne, Gravesham, Kent DA12 3DP

Maloney, Patrick, (Cardiff), F87 Golf Road, New Inn, Pontypool, Torfaen NP4 0QW **Tel:** 01495 756695 **Email:** mrpatmaloney87@yahoo.co.uk

Manghan, Philip, (Cardiff), 25 Lark Rise, Brackla, Bridgend CF31 2NU **Tel:** 01656-652034 **Email:** philipmanghan @lineone.net

Mannings, Paul, (Liverpool), 32 North Sudley Rd, Liverpool L17 0BG

Marley, Paul, (Lancaster), 7 Dunes Ave, Blackpool FY4 1PU **Tel:** 01253-318171 **Mbl:** 0774-8002818 **E-mail:** pnjmarley@aol.com

Marsh, Gerald, (Liverpool, retired), 37 Forest Grove, Eccleston Park, Prescot, Merseyside, L34 2RY **Tel:** 0151-426 7490

Marshall, Thomas, (Leeds), 24 Elm Royds Ln, Leeds LS26 0BW **Tel:** 0113-282 6947

Martin, Anthony, (Cardiff), 27 Wellfield Avenue, Porthcawl CF36 5TP **Tel:** 01565-772270 **Email:** anthony@smartin27.fsnet.co.uk

Martin, Austin, (Southwark), 8 Standard Rd, Downe, Orpington BR6 7HL **E-mail:** amartin@rc.net

Martin, James, (Arundel & Brighton), 65 Ash Church Rd, Ash, Aldershot, Hampshire GU12 6LU

Mason, Peter, PhD, (Birmingham), 21 New Rd, Stourbridge, West Midlands DY8 1PQ **Tel:** 01384-370229

Mason, Robert, MSc, ARIBA, FRTPI, (Arundel & Brighton, retired), 16 Hall Ave, Offington, Worthing, W. Sussex BN14 9BA **Tel:** 01903-691663

Mascarenhas, Peter, (Shrewsbury), 26 Delamere Rd, Nantwich CW5 7DL **Tel:** 01270-624865

Matthews, Leonard, (East Anglia, retired), 82 Mountbatten Rd, Dersingham, PE31 6YE

Mayland, Paul, (Birmingham), Thorney Edge Farm, Bagnall, Stoke-on-Trent ST9 9LD **Tel:** 01782-502084

Meadows, Timothy, (Clifton), 25 Holland Court, Denmark St, Gloucester GL1 3LB

Meahan, Henry, (Hallam), 20 Greenland Ave, Rossington, Doncaster DN11 0EL

Meaney, Patrick H, (Liverpool), 19 Westbrook Ave, Prescot L34 1NW **Tel:** 0151-426 6947

Mee, Alan, (Liverpool), 402 Warrington Rd, Glazebury, Warrington WA3 5NX **Tel:** 01942-674529

Melhuish, Steven, BA (Portsmouth), 33 Hilland Rise, Headley, Hants GU35 8LZ **Tel:** 01428-713555 **E-mail:** steve-melhuish@btinternet.com

Melia, James, (Liverpool, retired), 56 Vicars Hall Gardens, Boothstown M28 4HU **Tel:** 0161 799 8884

Menezes, Braz, (Southwark), 76 Willersley Ave, Sidcup, Kent DA15 9EN **Tel:** 020-8302 4396

Milligan, Paul, (Southwark), 1 Gibsons Hill, Norbury London SW16 3JL **Tel:** 020-8764 4030 **Email:** paul_t_milligan@yahoo.co.uk

Milton, Bill, (Lancaster), St John's, Breck Rd, Poulton-le-Fylde FY6 7HT **Tel:** 012563 883110 **Fax:** 01253 880273

Mitchinson, Jeremy, (Liverpool), St Charles, 224 Aigburth Rd, Aigburth, Liverpool L17 9PG **Tel:** 0151-727 2493

Mkpadi, Michael C (Leeds), 1 Deanswood Gardens, Leeds LS17 **Tel:** 0113-295 9718

Moffatt, Thomas, (Clifton), The New Ho, Shrubbery Rd, Weston-super-Mare BS23 2JH

Moloney, Kevin, (Cifton), 46 Wellington HIll, Horfield, Bristol BS7 8SR **Tel:** 0117-908 9741

Moloney, Patrick, (Arundel & Brighton), 66 Madiera Ave, Worthing, West Sussex, BN11 2BA **Tel:** 01903-239276

Monk, John, (Lancaster), 27 Margate Rd, Ingol, Preston PR2 3TB **Tel:** 01772- 724235

Moore, Eric, (Liverpool), 21 Westlands, Peel,

Isle of Man IM5 1JT **Tel:** 01624-843021
Moore, Roy, (Liverpool), 11 Ennerdale Ave, Ashton-in-Makerfield, Wigan WN4 8BA **Tel:** 01942-201693
Moreland, Joseph P, (Liverpool), 5 Greenloons Walk, Formby, Liverpool L37 2LE **Tel:** 01704-832064
Morgan, Brian, (Middlesbrough), 15 Swift Close, Hornsea, East Yorkshire HU18 1LD **Tel:** 01964-532002 **E-mail:** brianmorgan1947@hotmail.com
Morgan, David, (Portsmouth), 63 Maple Gardens, Yateley, Hants GU46 6JQ
Morgan, Stephen David, (Portsmouth), 14 Empress Lyndhurst, Hants SO43 7AE **Tel:** 023 8028 2612
Morland, Jerome, (Portsmouth), 11 Wetherby Close, Emmer Green, Reading RG4 8UD **Tel:** 0118-947 7467
Morrill, John, (East Anglia), 1 Bradford's Close, Bottisham, Cambridge CB5 9DW **Tel:** 01223-811822/813499
Morris, Alan, (Shrewsbury), 35 Rivington Rd, Hale, Cheshire WA15 9PJ **Tel:** 0161- 941 1422 **E-mail:** arm@holyangels.fsnet.co.uk
Morris, Derek, (Liverpool), 14 Chestnut Dr, Leigh, Lancs WN7 3JW **Tel:** 01942-206030
Morris, Keith,(Southwark), "Constantia", 15b Harvey Rd, Rainham, Kent ME8 0BA **Tel:** 01634-234524
Morrison, Vincent, (Southwark), 52 Devonshire Way, Shirley, Croydon, Surrey CR0 8BR **Tel:** 020-8777 5755 **E-mail:** marycrmorrison@yahoo.co.uk
Morriss, David, (Shrewsbury), 39 Grosvenor St, Wallasey, Wirral CH44 1AW **Tel:** 0151-630 1373
Morrissey, Melvyn, (Cardiff), 'Carmel', Corbetts Lane, Caerphilly CF83 3HX **Tel:** 029-2086 4960 **Email:** mel_morrisey@tiscali.co.uk
Morton, Andrew, (East Anglia), 11 Maple Way, Leaven Heath, Nr Colchester CO6 4PQ
Moss, David, (Middlesbrough), 3a Selstone Cres, Sleights, Whitby YO22 5DJ **Tel:** 01947-811142
Moss, Laurence,(Clifton), 65 Priors Hill, Wroughton, Swindon, SN4 0RL **Tel:** 01793- 813318
Mulcahy, Daniel, (Southwark), Willow Cottage, Ridgeway, Chestfield, Whitstable, Kent CT5 3JT **Tel:** 01227-792660 **E-mail:** mulcahy 776@compuserve.com
Munday, Stephen, (Clifton), 25 Southend Rd, Weston-super-Mare, Somerset BS23 4JY **Tel:** 01934-622989
Munro, Neil, (Hexham, retired), St Cuthbert's, Hillsview Ave, North Kenton Newcastle NE3 3QR
Murphy, Edwin, (Leeds), 15 Thorp Arch Park, Thorp Arch, Wetherby LS23 7AP **Tel:** 01937-843865
Murphy, James, (Lancaster), 15 Jevington Way, Heysham LA3 2HQ **Tel:** 01524-855895
Murphy, John M, MBE (Liverpool), 33 Galloway Rd, Waterloo L22 4QX **Tel:** 0151-920 678114
Murphy, Shaun, (Clifton), 28 Harber Court, May Close, Gorse Hill, Swindon, SN2 1XD **Tel:** 01793-612607
Murray, Francis J, (Liverpool, retired), 8 Tulip Rd, Haydock, St Helens WA11 0NH **Tel:** 01744-604632
Murray, Sean, BA, (Southwark), 37 The Drive, Beckenham, Kent BR3 1EE **Tel:** 0208 289 3043
Murray, Tom, (Arundel & Brighton), 178 St Leonard's Rd, Horsham, West Sussex RH13 6BA **Tel:** 01403-261285
Murrill, Tim, (Arundel & Brighton), 20 Batts Hill, Redhill, Surrey RH1 2DH **Tel:** 01737 761017 **Fax:** 01737 763061 **Email:** stjoe@btinternet.com
Navarro, Luis, (Clifton), 102 Moselle Dr, Churchdown, Glos. GL3 2TA **Tel:** 01452-855605
Neal, James, (Westminster), Venerable English College, Via De Monserrato 45, 00186 Roma, Italia
Neate, Andrew, (East Anglia), 3 Ashtead Court, Hill Rd, Cambridge CB1 3UG **Tel:** 01223 241497
Newman, John, (Southwark), 1 Archer Rd, Chatham, Kent ME5 8LH **E-mail:** john.newman@btinternet.com
Newman, Stephen, (Southwark), 11 Genesta Close, Milton Regis, Sittingbourne, Kent ME10 2HL **Tel:** 01795-427195 **E-mail:** mailto.stephenpha@tiscali.co.uk
Newton, Francis J, (Shrewsbury), 2 Telford Place, Welsh Row, Nantwich CW5 5HX **Tel:** 01270-619367
Newton, Jude, (Hexham, retired), 36 Crookham, Cornhill on Tweed, Northumberland TD12 4TA **Tel:** 01942-605703
Norbury, Joseph, (Shrewsbury), 57 Saville Rd, Gatley, Cheadle, Cheshire SK8 4BY **Tel:** 0161-286 8965
Norman, Brian J, (Liverpool), 1 Ranleigh Dr, Newburgh, Wigan, Lancs WN8 7NA **Tel:** 01257-462735
Northrop, Anthony, (East Anglia), 7 Keynes Rd, Cambridge CB5 8PP **Tel:** 01223-293677
Noughton, Edward, (Westminster), Clergy Ho, 42 Francis Street, London SW1P 1QW **Tel:** 020 7798 9055
Nunn, Gordon, (Westminster), Ealing Abbey, Charlbury Grove W5 2DY **Tel:** 020 8862 2160

O'Beirne, Kevin, (Liverpool, retired), 1 Nutgrove Hall Dr, Thatto Heath, St Helens WA9 5PT **Tel:** 01744- 813591

O'Brien, John J, (Liverpool), 51 Ashton Heath, Ashton-in-Makerfield, Wigan, WN4 9JL **Tel:** 01942 725 752

O'Brien, John Michael, (Birmingham), Severn Bank Ho, Severn Side South, Bewdley, DY12 2DU **Tel:** 02785-826018

O'Brien, Kevin, (Arundel & Brighton), 16 Fairlawn Rd, Carshalton, Surrey SM5 4HT **Tel:** 020-864 3482

O'Connell, John, (Lancaster), 71 St David's Rd South, St Annes-on-the-Sea, Lytham St Annes FY8 1TY **Tel:** 01253-726253

O'Connell, Patrick, (Portsmouth), 33 Beachway, Basingstoke, Hants RG23 8LR **Tel:** 01256 420048

O'Connell, William, (Portsmouth), 7 Birchdale, Hythe, Hants SO45 3HX **Tel:** 023-8079 8517

O'Connor, Andrew, (Hexham & Newcastle), "Hillview", Lanchester DH7 0HY

O'Connor, Kevin, (Nottingham), 9 Court Rd, Glen Parva, Leicester LE2 9JB **Tel:** 0116-278 7441

O'Donnell, Patrick, BSEC, MBA (Portsmouth, Retired), Aldebaran, Long Hill Rd, Chavey Down, Ascot, Berks SL5 8RD **Tel/Fax:** 01344-893850 **E-mail:** odonpj@aol.com

O'Donovan, John, (Southwark), 16 Culvers Ave, Carshalton, Surrey SM5 2BS **Tel:** 020-8773 0254

O'Keefe, David, (Cardiff), 17 Gwendoline Street, Merthyr Tydfil, CF47 9AD **Tel:** 01685-375761 **Email:** dave@okeefemerthyr.fsnet.co.uk

O'Neill, Frank, (Hexham & Newcastle), Helmdon Ho, Glebe Cres, Washington NE38 7AW **Tel:** 0191-417 5260

O'Reilly, Gerard, (Birmingham), 30 Branksome Rd, Coundon, Coventry CV6 1FX **Tel:** 024-7633 3881

O'Toole, Ron, (East Anglia), 23 Margaret Lilly Way, Aldborough, Norfolk NR11 7PA **Tel:** 01263-768053

Oldman, Patrick, (Birmingham), 8 Glentworth Ave, Coventry CV6 2HW **Tel:** 024-4763 32869

Oliver, Jeremy, MBE, B.Th(hons), MA, (Arundel & Brighton), St Michael & St George, Queens Ave, Aldershot, Hants GU11 2BY **Tel:** 01252 347464 **Fax:** 01252 319203

Omer, Louis, (Portsmouth), Leyton, Green St, St Helier, Jersey JE2 4UH **Tel:** 01534-738592

Owen, Joseph, (Plymouth), Sacred Heart Church, Cecil Rd, Paignton, Devon TQ3 2SH

Owen, Paul, (Portsmouth), Sacred Heart Church, Cecil Rd, Paignton, Devon TR3 2SH

Oxley, Michael, (Liverpool), 40 Fairfield Gdns, Stockton Heath, Warrington WA4 2BX

Park, John, (Plymouth), Holy Family Church, Exeter Rd, Honiton, Devon.

Parker, Charles, (Arundel & Brighton), 2a West Meads, Onslow Village, Guildford, Surrey GU2 7SJ **Tel:** 01483 539615

Parker, John, (Nottingham), 44 Park Hill Dr, Aylestone, Leicester LE2 8PG **Tel:** 0116-291 0281

Parr, William, (Liverpool), 53 Buck St, Leigh, Gtr Manchester WN7 4HE **Tel:** 01942-746443

Parsons, Hilary, BA, DipAdEd (Arundel & Brighton, retired), Forest Oaks, The Rise, Brockenhurst, Hants SO42 7SJ **Tel:** 01590-624702 **E-mail:** parsons@francishilary.freeserve.co.uk

Parsons, Joseph, (Southwark), 24 Old Oak Ave, Chipstead, Surrey CR5 3PG **Tel:** 01737-554883

Partridge, Raymond, (Southwark), 11 Orchard Rd, St Mary's Bay, New Romney, Kent TN29 0RB **Tel:** 01303-873835

Pearce, Maurice, (Leeds, retired), 14 Whinwood Grange, Whinmore, Leeds LS14 2EU **Tel:** 0113-265 4234

Pearson, Christopher, (Liverpool), 479 Liverpool Rd, Huyton, Merseyside L36 8HT **Tel:** 0151-480 5310

Pease, David, (Southwark), 5 Hoveton Rd, London SE28 8LW **Tel:** 020-8311 4415

Pelling, Ivor, (Arundel & Brighton, retired), 1 Ladies Mile Court, Ladies Mile Rd, Brighton, East Sussex BN1 8QN **Tel:** 01273-507956

Pemberton, Richard, (Birmingham), 6 Spring View, Brown Edge, Stoke-on-Trent ST6 8PZ **Tel:** 01782-505196

Pendlebury, Stephen IS, GDBM, PGCE, PGDipGd (Lancaster), 2 Dunsop Gardens, Grosvenor Park, Morecambe LA3 3SL **Tel:** 01524-849412

Penny, John, (Shrewsbury), 25 West Vale Rd, Timperley, Altrincham WA15 7RL **Tel:** 0161-941 1411

Phelan, Fintan, (Southwark), 5 Gambole Rd, Tooting, London SW17 0QJ **Tel:** 020-8672 1615 **E-mail:** jfintan@ic24.net

Phelan, Michael D, (Northampton), Ennerdale Ho, 41 Penn Rd, Beaconsfield HP9 2LN

Phelan, Peter, (Birmingham), 4 Rushmore Grove, Meir Park, Stoke-on-Trent ST3 7SY **Tel:** 01782-396799

Philpott, Andrew, (Portsmouth), 31 Filton Close, Calmore, Southampton, Hants

SO40 2UW **Tel:** 023-80869853

Pilley, Leo, (Plymouth), Sacred Heart Church, Tregenna Hill, St Ives, Cornwall TR26 1SE

Pole-Baker, Paul, BTh, CEng, MIEE (Portsmouth), 2 Delville Close, Southwood, Farnborough, Hants GU14 0PY **Tel:** 01252- 544152 **E-mail:** paul.pole-baker@ntlworld.com

Pollard, Robin, (Nottingham), 76 Coventry Rd, Burbage, Hinckley, Leicestershire LE10 2HR **Tel:** 01455-616718

Pomeroy, Stephen, (Portsmouth), 78 Bramhall Ln South, Bramhall, Stockport SK7 2EA **Tel:** 0161-440 0680

Pond, Philip, (Southwark), 15 Ravenshead Close, Selsdon, South Croydon CR2 8RL **Tel:** 020-8651 4653 **E-mail:** philippond@blueyonder.co.uk

Potts, Harry, (Clifton, retired), Orchard Close, Ashill, Ilminster, Somerset TA19 9ND **Tel:** 01823-480475

Proctor, John, (Clifton), Alabare House of Prayer, 15 Tollgate Rd, Salisbury SP1 2JA

Pugh, Philip, (Northampton), 66 Westoning Rd, Harlington, Beds LU5 6PD **Tel:** 01525-875445

Pukacz, Czeslaw, (Leeds), 48 Larch Rd, Paddock, Huddersfield. HD1 4JG **Tel:** 01484-301191

Purcell, Vincent, (Hexham & Newcastle), 35 Browning Hill, Coxhoe, Co Durham DH6 4HB **Tel:** 01484-301191

Quirk, Cornelius, (Southwark), Rivendell, 8 Trewyn Park, Holsworthy, Devon EX22 6LS **Tel:** 01409-259027 **E-mail:** neil.quirk@btinternet.com

Ranzetta, Anthony R, (East Anglia), Frogs Hall, Frogs Hall Rd, Laveham, Suffolk CO10 9QH **Tel:** 01787-248042

Ratcliffe, Rev Brian, (Nottingham), 101 Cotes Rd, Barrow-on-Soar, Leicestershire LE12 8JP **Tel:** 01509 412505

Regan, Patrick, (Shrewsbury), 8 Ledbury Cl, Prenton CH43 0UJ **Tel:** 0151 608 6146

Reddington, Paul, 37 Tetbury Gardens, Nailsea, Bristol BS48 2TL **Tel:** 01275-858485 **E-mail:** Reddington@btinternet.com

Reed, Henry, (Northampton Retired), 3 Buttermere Way, Barrow-upon-Soar, Loughborough LE12 8PG

Reeves, Peter, (Plymouth), St Mary's Church, 211 Wimborne Rd, Poole, Dorset BH15 2RG

Reynolds, Ivan, BSc(Hon), PhD (Clifton), 9 Valley Close, Nailsea BS48 7JE **Tel:** 01275-858639

Reynolds, Nick, (Portsmouth), Hall Place Cottage, Petersfield Rd, Ropley, Hants SO24 0EJ **Tel:** 01962-772393 **Fax:** 01962-772098 **E-mail:** nickreynolds@freeuk.com

Rider, Ted, (Arundel & Brighton), Clarendon, Claridge Gardens, Dormansland, Surrey RH7 6HZ **Tel:** 01342-835110

Rigby, Anthony, (Birmingham), 11 Firtree Close, Coton Green, Tamworth, Staffs B79 8NL **Tel:** 01827-700241

Rigby, Bernard, (Liverpool), 3 Seagram Cl, Aintree, Liverpool L9 0NA

Riley, William, LLB (Lancaster), Mossfield Ho, Talbot Rd, Lytham FY8 4JJ **Tel:** 01253-737985

Rimmer, Terence, (Liverpool), 12 Esplen Ave, Crosby, Liverpool L23 2SS

Road, Christopher, (Southwark), 51 Sefton St, London SW15 1NA **Tel:** 020-8788 5601

Roberts, Andrew, (Wrexham), St Mary's Cathedral, Regent St, Wrexham LL11 1RB

Roberts, Dale, (Birmingham), c/o Chaplaincy, Hunter Combe Young Offenders, Nuffield, Henley-on-Thames

Roberts, John, KHS (Southwark), 16 Knaves Acre, Headcorn, Ashford, Kent TN27 9JJ **Tel:** 01622-890690 **E-mail:** john@headcorn.fsworld.co.uk

Roberts, Michael, (Clifton), 7 Logan Rd, Bishopston, Bristol BS7 8DU **Tel:** 0117-942 4362

Robertson, Ernesto, (Hallam), HMP Durham, Old Elvet, Durham DN1 3HU

Robinson, Colm, (Clifton), 27 Midsummer Walk, Hempsted, Glos. GL2 5EF

Robinson, Hugh, (Birmingham, retired), 50 Glentworth Gardens, Dunstall, Wolverhampton WV6 0SG **Tel:** 01902-712795

Rogan, Rev Joseph, (Nottingham), 15 Southfields, Bourne, Lincolnshire PE10 9TZ **Tel:** 01778 422857

Rooke, Thomas George, (Hexham & Newcastle), St John Vianney, King Oswy Dr, Hartlepool TS24 9LX **Tel:** 01429 267457

Rorke, Kevin, (Lancaster), The Hedges, 11 Park Rd, Wigton, Cumbria CA7 9RA **Tel:** 01697-342154

Rose, Peter, (Clifton), 6 Bedwin Close, Portishead, Bristol BS20 8BY **Tel:** 01275-844647

Ross, Clive, (Southwark), Lynton, 114 Manwood Rd, London SE4 1SE **Tel:** 020-8690 4623

Rossmann, Martin, (Plymouth), The Presbytery, 70 Westeria Tr, Beacon Park, Plymouth PL2 3LR **Tel:** 01752-772181

Rowan, Henry, (Leeds), 104 Main St, Cononley, Keighley BD20 8NR **Tel:** 01535-633175

Russell, Paul, (Birmingham), 4 Innage Rd, Northfield, Birmingham B31 2DX **Tel:** 0121-475 5532

Ryan, D'Arcy, (Lancaster), 19 Hillview Rd, Garstang PR3 1JU **Tel:** 01995-603090

Ryan, O Francis, (Birmingham), 40 South Lawns, Witney, Oxon OX13 7HX **Tel:** 01993-201080

Salter, Brian, (Birmingham), 15 Newhouse Farm Close, Walmley, Sutton Coldfied, W. Midlands B76 8TJ **Tel:** 0121 351 3265

Sampson, John, LLB, (Southwark), 5 The Glebe, Worcester Park, Surrey KT4 7PG **Tel:** 0208 715 3431

Sanders, John, (Plymouth), St Augustine's Church, Woodland Rd, St Austell, Cornwall PL25 4RA

Sanderson, Frederick, (Lancaster), St Clare's, Sharoe Green Ln, Fulwood, Preston PR2 9HH **Tel/Fax:** 01772-719604

Sanderson, Martin Scott, (Liverpool), Homestead, Daffy Green, Shipdham, Thetford, Norfolk IP25 7QQ **Tel:** 01362-822590

Sankey, Deryck, (Shrewsbury), 50 Acton Ave, Appleton, Warrington WA4 5PT **Tel:** 01925-266459

Scanlon, Prof Maurice, (Cardiff), 117 Pencisely Rd, Llandaff, Cardiff CF5 1DL **Tel:** 029 2021 2651 **Email:** conorcarter@hotmail.com

Scholey, Paul, (Arundel and Brighton), 10 Worcester Villas, Hove, East Sussex BN3 5TB **Tel:** 01273-271339

Seeney, Peter, (Birmingham), 16 Sandaway Grove, Billesley, Birmingham B13 0HU **Tel:** 0121-441 5039

Selby, John, (Lancaster), Selwyns, 21 Birkdale Close, Kendal LA9 7PW **Tel:** 01539-720038

Senior, Ken, (Middlesbrough), 15 Amesbury Cres, Hemlington, Middlesbrough TS8 9HR **Tel:** 01642-270201

Senyk, David, (Ukrainian), 34 Dawlish Dr, Styvechale, Coventry CV3 5NB **Tel:** 024-7641 3725

Sheahan, James, (Southwark), Cathedral Clergy Ho, Westminster Bridge Rd, Southwark, London, SE1 4HY **Tel:** 020-7928 5256

Sheehan, Michael, (Southwark), 44 Kings Ave, Bromley, Kent BR1 4HW **Tel:** 020-8249 2497

Shepherd, Frank, (Northampton), Broom Ho, Stoke Poges Ln, Stoke Poges, Slough SL2 4NP **Tel:**01753- 529456

Shepherd, Keith CH, (Brentwood), c/o Cathedral Ho, Ingrave Rd, Brentwood, Essex CM15 8AT

Shields, Nicholas, (Leeds), The Lodge, 42 Blenheim Rd, St John's, Wakefield WF1 3JZ **Tel:** 01924-377921

Shute, Andrew, (Plymouth), O.L. of the Portal and St Piran, St Austel Street, Truro, Cornwall 7R1 1SE

Short, Michael, (Portsmouth), 37 Corunna Main, Andover, Hants SP10 1SD

Short, Stephen, (Southwark), Furzey Lawn, Romsey Rd, Lyndhurst, Hants SO43 7FL **Tel:** 023-8028-2011 **E-mail:** stephen.short@btinternet.com

Simms, Terence, (Shrewsbury), 13 Worthing Close, Offerton, Stockport SK2 5RE **Tel:** 0161-483 7672

Simon, Jonathan, (Plymouth), Sacred Heart Church, Westbury, Sherborne, Dorset DT9 3EL

Simpson, Peter, (Southwark), 9 Langham Ho Close, Itam Common, Richmond, Surrey TW10 7JE **Tel:** 020-8948 8531

Singleton, Jeffrey, (Southwark), 9 Daneswood Ave, Catford, London SE1 7RS **Tel:** 020-8698 5097

Sinnott, Anthony W, (Liverpool), 21 Somerset Rd, Bootle L20 9BS **Tel:** 0151-922 5890

Skidmore, Michael, (Birmingham), 270 Lutterworth Rd, Nuneaton, Warks CV11 6PQ **Tel:** 02476-384406

Skoyles, Peter, (Nottingham, retired), Hillside, Minions, Liskeard, Cornwall PL13 2PG **Tel:** 01579-362936

Slater, James, (Lancaster), 89 West Park Ave, Ashton, Preston PR2 1UJ **Tel:** 01772-732652 **Mbl:** 07866-081045

Slim, John, (Port Elizabeth, South Africa), 9 Stokes Dr, Holdingham, Sleaford, Lincolnshire NG34 8BA

Smith, Bernard T, (Liverpool), 2 Fawley Rd, Rainhill, Prescot L35 6PL **Tel:** 0151-426 7925

Smith, Robert, (Liverpool), 45 Carr Ln, Wigan WN3 5NL **Tel:** 01942-231459

Smith, Trevor, (Birmingham), Railway Tavern, Bond St, Nuneaton, Warwickshire CV11 4BX **Tel:** 02476-382015

Spark, Geoffrey, (Hallam), St Mary Magdalene, Morrell St, Maltby, Rotherham S66 7LH **Tel:** 01709-812883

Sparks, Roger, (East Anglia), Winton Ho, 34 Theatre St, Swaffham, Norfolk PE37 7HA **Tel:** 01760 724113

Stafanazzi, Joseph, (Shrewsbury), 5 Moors Bank, St Martins, Oswestry SY10 7BE **Tel:** 01691 770158

Stanning, John, (Lancaster), 46 Cleveland Rd, Lytham, Lancs FY8 5JH **Tel:** 01253-733810 **Fax:** 01253-733815

Stark, John, (Birmingham), 11 Wycombe Rd, Hall Green, Birmingham B28 9EN **Tel:** 0121-777 2539

Steel, John B, (Middlesbrough), St Mary's Ho, High St, Yarm TS15 9AA **Tel:** 01642-781800 **E-mail:** johnbsteel@btinternet.com

Stephens, Basil, (Shrewsbury), 55 Church Rd, West Kirby, Wirral CH48 0RN **Tel:** 0151-625 9963 **E-mail:** basil.stephens@catholic.org.uk

Stevenson, Michael, (Northampton), 'Ticehurst', West St, East Sussex BN26 5UX **Tel:** 01232-870418

Stewart, Rory, (Northampton), 39 Bush Hill, Abington, Northampton NN3 2PD **Tel:** 01604-408407

Stoessel, Edward, (Galveston - Houston); The Coach Ho, 4 Putney Park Ave, London SW15 5QN **Tel:** 020-8876 8899

Stoker, Brian, (Northampton), Closefield, 31 Townside, Haddenham HP17 8BQ **Tel:** 01844-290553

Stone, Roger, (Arundel & Brighton), 5 Ryecroft Ln, Storrington, West Sussex RH20 4PA **Tel:** 01903-740164

Strickland, Paul, (Plymouth), The Presbytery, Silver St, Lyme Regis, Devon DT7 3HS

Strickland, Ronald, (Liverpool), 33 Princess Way, Euxton, Chorley PR7 6PL **Tel:** 01257-276866

Strike, Anthony, (Portsmouth), 46 Trevor Way, Fareham, Hants PO14 4NQ **Tel:** 01489-583602

Strype, William, (Liverpool), 7 Manor Way, Liverpool, L25 8QY **Tel:** 0151 428 3131

Sullivan, Rev Anthony, (Nottingham), c/o Willson Ho, Derby Rd, Nottingham NG1 5AW

Sullivan, Keith, (Clifton), 57 Sedgemoor Rd, Bridgwater, Somerset TA6 5NP **Tel:** 01278-423165

Sutton, Anthony, (East Anglia), 85 Hollytrees, Bar Hill, Cambridge CB3 8SG **Tel:** 01954-781443

Sutton, Dennis, BA(Hons), (Clifton), 4 Wardour Close, The Lawns, Swindon, Wilts SN3 1JZ **Tel:** 01793-520753

Sutton, Paul, (Shrewsbury), 32 Underwood Dr, Ellesmere Port CH65 9BL **Tel:** 0151-355 1686 **E-mail:** sutty@psutton.fsworld.co.uk

Swarbrick, Peter, (Nottingham), 43 Brookview, Keyworth, Nottinghamshire NG12 5RA **Tel:** 0115-914 3973

Swift, Michael, (Liverpool), 2 Hawes Crescent, Ashton-in-Makerfield, Wigan WN4 8BW

Swindlehurst, Peter, (Northampton),RAF Halton, 181b Aylesbury Rd, Wendover, Aylesbury HP22 6AA

Tarbrook, John, (Wrexham), 21 Osborne St, Rhos, Wrexham LL14 2HU **Tel:** 01978-840665

Tarode, Clifford, (Portsmouth), Westview, Belmont Estate, King's Rd, St Peter Port, Guernsey, C.I. **Tel:** 01481-720233

Tasker, Gareth, (Cardiff), 63 Penybryn Estate, Pennydarren, Merthyr Tydfil CF47 9YY **Email:** Garth.tasker@tiscali.co.uk

Taylor, Barry, (Clifton),Holmleigh, Hill End, Twyning, Glos GL20 6DW

Taylor, Patrick, (Portsmouth), 4 Foyle Park, Basingstoke, Hants RG21 3HD **Tel:** 01256- 326726 **Mbl:** 07778-505693

Taylor, Richard, (Salford, retired), Boarbank Hall, Allithwaite, Grange-over-Sands, Cumbria LA11 7NH **Tel:** 01539 532288

Taylor, William, (Hallam), 18 Silverdale Close, Branton, Doncaster, DN3 3PS **Tel:** 01302-537021

Telford, Jeffrey, (Shrewsbury), 69 Nelson Dr, Pensby, Wirral CH61 5UP **Tel:** 0151-342 3859 **Email:** telford.jeff@yahoo.co.uk

Thomas, Pat, (Middlesbrough), 11 Trenholme Road, Longlands, Middlesbrough, TS4 2JX **Tel:** 01642 241608

Thompson, John, (Northampton), 2 Beckham Close, Warden Hill, Luton, Beds, LU2 7BX **Tel:** 01582-654942

Thompson, Nicholas, (Plymouth), Holy Trinity Church, High West St, Dorchester, Dorset

Thoms, Michael, (Arundel & Brighton), Harrock Barn, Buxted, E. Sussex TN22 4BA **Tel:** 07887 506592

Tibke, Peter, (Birmingham), 3 Grosvenor Way, Droitwich, Worcs WR9 7SR **Tel:** 01905-776224

Timson, John, (Nottingham), Hill Top Farm, Copt Oak Rd. Charley, Nr. Loughborough, Leics LE12 9XL **Tel:** 01530-243477

Tingay, Alexander, MA (OSB), Quarr Abbey, Ryde, Isle of Wight PO33 4ES **Tel:** 01983-882420 **Fax:** 01983-884402

Titchmarsh, Ernest John, (Birmingham), 10 Waverley Grove, Solihull, West Midlands B91 1NP **Tel:** 0121-704 1875

Tobin, Ian, (Portstmouth), Trolls End, The Lane, Fawley, Hants SO45 1EY **Tel:** 023-8089 7354 **E-mail:** I.tobin@btinternet.com

Tomney, Bernard, (Shrewsbury), 71 White Lodge Park, Shawbury, Shropshire SY4 4NU **Tel:** 01939 250031

Tompkinson, Harry, (Nottingham), 10 Holme Hall Ave, Bottesford, Scunthorpe DN16 3PY **Tel:** 01724-866044

Torr, John, (Clifton), Narnia, 56 Kingston Rd, Tewkesbury GL20 8QJ **Tel:** 01684-294333

Traynor, John, (Liverpool), 73 Warrington Rd, Penketh, Warrington WA5 2DG **Tel:** 01925-725704

Trong Song Ly, Paul, (Southwark), 33 Blantyre Walk, World's End Estate, London SW10 0EQ **Tel:** 020-7351 0064

Truman, John, (Arundel & Brighton), 3 Broad Rd, Lower Willingdon, Eastbourne, East Sussex BN20 9QS **Tel:** 01323-486280

Tuck, Steven Ralph Joseph, (Birmingham), 255 Linthouse Ln, Wednesfield, Wolverhampton WV11 3TT **Tel:** 01902-724386

Turnbull, Gerard, (Shrewsbury), 135 Vernon

Rd, Poynton, Stockport SK12 1YS **Tel:** 01625-879932 **E-mail:** gerardt135@yahoo.co.uk

Turner, Malcolm, (Southwark), 34 Cranmere Court, Strood, Rochester, Kent ME2 4SF **Tel:** 01634-294871

Tutt, David, (Arundel & Brighton), 35 Christie Ave, Ringmer, Lewes BN8 5JT **Tel:** 01273-812894

Ullmann, Michael, (Shrewsbury), 34 Ivy Rd, Macclesfield SK11 8QB **Tel:** 01625-425651

Varnes, Peter, (Southwark), 33a Priestlands Park Rd, Sidcup, Kent DA15 7HJ **Tel:** 020-8300 5074

Vaughan-Spruce, Brendan, (Clifton), 39 Mayfield Dr, Hucclecote Gloucester GL3 3DS

Venes, Peter, (Northampton), 21 Clarence Ave, Northampton, NN2 6XN **Tel:** 01604- 711937

Vincent, Langford, BSc (Portsmouth), 29 Park Ln, Fareham, Hants PO16 7LE **Tel:** 01329- 280058 **E-mail:** langford.vincent@ntlworld.com

Vint, Dennis, (Liverpool), 33 Urmston St, Leigh WN7 4SW **Tel:** 01942-746217

Vlpond, Michael, (East Anglia), 8 The Scrum, Danforth Dr, Framlingham, Suffolk IP13 9HH **Tel:** 01728-724646

Waites, Philip, (Plymouth), 11 Trinity Gardens, Ilfracombe, Devon EX34 8ED

Wakefield, David, (Clifton), 68 Eastleigh Rd, Devizes, Wilts SN10 3EH **Tel:** 01380-720916

Wakeling, Rev John, (Nottingham), 11 Aylesham Ave, Arnold, Nottingham NG5 6PX

Walker, Barry, (Southwark), 7 Alma Rd, Herne Bay, Kent CT6 6JJ **Tel:** 01227-368685 **E-mail:** barrywalker@kent69.fsnet.co.uk

Walker, Michael, (Birmingham), 16 Greystoke Rd, Caversham, Reading RG4 5EL **Tel:** 0118-947 1366

Walsh, Michael, (Birmingham), 37 Windmill Ln, Wheatley, Oxford OX3 1TA

Walsh, Richard, (Nottingham), 5 Derby Rd, Homesford, Matlock, Derbyshire DE4 5HL **Tel:** 01629-822535

Walton, John, (Lancaster), 53 Headroomgate Rd, St Annes-on-Sea, Lancs, FY8 3BD **Tel:** 01253-726878 **Fax:** 01253-780565

Ward, Anthony, (Portsmouth), Le Perchoir, Le Bourg, St Clement, Jersey CI JE2 6SQ **Tel:** 01534-853804 **E-mail:** deacontony@surefish.co.uk

Ward, Anthony, (Southwark), 9 Badgers Croft, London SE9 3DA **Tel:** 020-8857 4762 **E-mail:** tony@indamac.org

Ward, Bernard C, (Lancaster) 4 Willowdene, Thornton Cleveleys FY5 1QC **Tel:** 01253-821306 **Mbl:** 07786-521471

Warriner, Frederick G, (Liverpool), 61 Caldy Rd, Aintree, Liverpool L9 4RZ **Tel:** 0151-525 9916

Washington, Thomas, (Liverpool),10 Greymist Ave, Woolston, Warrington WA1 4AR **Tel:** 01925- 491359

Waters, Roy, (Arundel & Brighton), 1 Malthouse Cottages, Goose Green, Gomshall, Guildford GU5 9LW **Tel:** 01483-202913

Watkins, Gerald, (Southwark), 25 Court Rd, Walmer, Deal, Kent CT14 7RG **Tel:** 01304-374889

Watkins, Ralph, (Birmingham), 35 Hammerton Way, Wellesbourne, Warwickshire CV35 9NS **Tel:** 01789-841883

Watson, John, (OP), St Dominic's, 41A Red Barnes, Newcastle NE1 2TP **Tel:** 0191-232 5939

Watson, Keith F (Northampton), 17 Rushton Rd, Rothwell, Kettering NN14 6HG

Wawszczyk, Paul, MA, MTh, PGCE (Lancaster), 36 Bay Horse Dr, Lancaster LA1 4LA **Tel:** 01524-848009 **E-mail:** paul@wawszczk.fsnet.co.uk

Welch, Michael, (Portsmouth), 5 Grove Gardens, Barton on Sea, New Milton, Hants BH25 7HJ **Tel:** 01425-614706 **Mbl:** 07092-383791 **E-mail:** revmwelch@onetel.net.uk

Wells, Ian, (Arundel & Brighton), Harvest, 22 Pelham Way, Great Bookham, Surrey KT23 4PR

Wells, Martin, (East Anglia), Glencar, 39 Meadowvale Cl, Beccles, Suffolk NR34 9EP **Tel:** 01502 715163

Wells, Michael, (East Anglia), 35 Fair Close, Beccles, Suffolk NR34 9QR **Tel:** 01502-715163

Westlake, Wilfred, (Plymouth, Retired), Holy Trinity Parish Centre, Culliford Rd, Dorchester, Dorset DT1 1QG

Whelan, Anthony, (Liverpool), 72 Mossbrow Rd, Huyton, Liverpool L36 7SW **Tel:** 0151-480 0736

Whelan, Michael J, (Liverpool), 5 Adswood Rd, Huyton, Liverpool L36 7XN **Tel:** 0151-289 0502

White, Philip, (Liverpool), Larlaith, 19 Templemore Rd, Oxton, Prenton CH43 2HB **Tel:** 0151-652 2330 **E-mail:** philip.white@tesco.net

Whitehead, Paul, (Liverpool), 2 Grassendale Rd, Liverpool L19 0NA **Tel:** 0151-427 3387

Whitehouse, Duncan J, (Brentwood), 3 Lynceley Grange, Epping, Essex CM16 6RA **Tel:** 01992- 577173 **E-mail:** duncanwhitehouse@btinternet.com

Wilford, John, (Nottingham), 33 Westcliffe St, Lincoln LN1 3TZ **Tel:** 01522-800114

Wilson, Rev Paul, (Nottingham), 1 Hawthorne Close, Stanton Hill, Sutton-in-Ashfield, Nottinghamshire NG17 3NQ **Tel:** 01623-489479

Willcock, A, (Liverpool), 126 Hardshaw St, St Helens, WA10 IJR **Tel:** 01744-731118

Williams, John, (Liverpool), 15 Belmont Rd, Widnes, Cheshire WA5 0JB **Tel:** 0151-424 1839

Williams, J Peter, BSc, DipEd (Lancaster), 47 Lightfoot Ln, Fulwood, Preston PR2 3LQ **Tel:** 01772-863444 **E-mail:** peter.williams@ukzone.org

Williams, Maurice, (Southwark), 34 Paddock Close, South Darenth, Kent DA4 9AD **Tel:** 01322-863286

Williams, Noel, (Cardiff), 8 Llanwern Street, Newport NP19 OBX **Tel:** 01633-665428 **Email:** mrnoelwiliams@yahoo.co.uk

Winder, Bill, (Lancaster), St Walburge's, Weston St, Preston PR2 2QE **Tel:** 01772-726370 **Mbl:** 01772-734499

Windle, John (Hexham & Newcastle), All Saints Presbytery, Thropton, Morpeth, Northumberland NE65 7ND **Tel:** 01669 620288

Winn, Anthony, (Leeds Retired), 26 Mayor's Walk, Pontefract, West Yorkshire WF8 2RR **Tel:** 01977-707341

Witherick, David, (Nottingham), 4 Forge Close, Frieston, Boston, Lincolnshire PE22 0PL **Tel:** 01205-760298

Woodcock, John, (Clifton), 16 West Way, Clevedon BS21 7XN. **Tel:** 01275-877583

Woodruff, John, (Liverpool), 22 Cyprus St, Prescot L34 5RY **Tel:** 0151-426 2164

Woods, Charles, (Shrewsbury), 36 Dyserth Rd, Blacon, Chester CH1 5QF **Tel:** 01244- 375634

Wood, James, (Lancaster), 3 Winmarleigh Rd, Lancaster LA11 4LE

Woods, Mark, (Arundel & Brighton), 43 Cissbury Gardens, Worthing, West Sussex BN14 0DZ **Tel:** 01903-877801

Woods, Vincent, (Clifton), Visions, 18 Cherry Tree Way, Doniford, Watchet, Somerset TA23 0UB **Tel:** 01984-634681

Wooff, Eric, (Lancaster), 14 Mill Hill, Appleby, Cumbria **Tel:** 017683-52317

Worden, Bernard H, (Liverpool), 112 Holden Rd, Leigh WN7 1EX **Tel:** 01942- 706768

Wordsworth, Robert, (Lancaster), 56 Seedfield, Staveley, Kendal LA8 9JN **Tel:** 01539-821985 **E-mail:** wordsworth@pgen.net

Wright, F Herbert, (Liverpool), 337 Walkers Ln, Sutton Manor, St Helens WA9 4AQ **Tel:** 01744-812491

Wright, Simon, (Westminster), 186 St John's Rd, Boxmorr, Herts HP1 1NR

Wright, William C, (Lancaster), 15 Ash St, Fleetwood FY7 6TH **Tel:** 01253-779301 **E-mail:** williamcwright@compuserve.com

Wyman, Eddie, (Cardiff), 1 Bridle Rd, Hereford HR4 0PP **Tel:** 01432-263575 **Email:** redjag@tiscali.co.uk

Young, George, (Portsmouth), 2 Carter Close, Windsor, Berks SL4 4QX **Tel:** 01753-842343

Young, Russell, (Arundel & Brighton), 29 Martinsyde, Woking, Surrey GU22 5HT **Tel:** 01483 763206

ORDINATIONS
(INCLUDING PERMANENT DEACONS)

Arundel & Brighton
Deacons:
Lynch, Aidan 28th Jun 2008
Murrill, Tim 29th Jun 2008
Wells, Ian 7th Jun 2008
Priests:
King, Malcolm 24th Jan 2008
O'Hara, Dominic 1st June 2008
Spinelli, Aaron 30th Aug 2008

Birmingham
Priests:
Miller, Christopher 28th June 2008
Rogerson, Cecil 7th June 2008
Smith, Paul 5th July 2008
McCann, Andrew 6th July 2008
Garrett, Bernard 12th July 2008
Devaney, Robert 12th July 2008
Peyton, John 19th July 2008

Clifton
Deacons:
Brinn, David 5th July 2008
Taylor, Barry 5th July 2008
Vaughan-Spruce, Brendan 5th July 2008
Priests:
Ferrier, Malcolm 11th July 2008

East Anglia
Deacons:
Bedford, John 28th Jun 2008
Priests:
Burbidge, Bruce 2008
Cuanam, John (CssR) 2008

Hallam
Priests:
Marshall, Peter 1st Dec 2007
Massey, Harish 1st Dec 2007

Hexham and Newcastle
Priests:
Shaw, Andrew 6th Jun 2008

Lancaster
Priests:
Howard, Christopher 28th Jun 2008
Dawson, Andrew 22nd Nov 2008

Liverpool
Deacons:
McGraw, James 6th July 2008
Mannings, Paul 6th July 2008
Oxley, Michael 6th July 2008
Rigby, Bernard 6th July 2008
Rimmer, Terence 6th July 2008
Swift, Michael 6th July 2008
Priest:
Riley, Sean 11th July 2008

Leeds
Deacon:
Conner, Charles 18th May 2008

Minevia
Priests:
Harris, Phillip 31st May 2008

Northampton
Priests:
Richardson, Andrew 21st Jun 2008
Penhalagan, Simon 28th Jun 2008
Deacons:
Walls, Jonathan 12st July 2008

Nottingham
Priests:
Breslin, Thomas 5th July 2008
O'Callaghan, Robert 26th July 2008

Plymouth
Deacons:
Everall, Brian 2nd Dec 2005
Hughes, Michael 2nd Dec 2005
Shute, Andrew 2nd Dec 2005
Hewson, Paul 13th July 2007
Priests:
Rossman, Martin 6th May 2005

Shrewsbury
Priests:
Charters, David 6th Sept 2008

Southwark
Priests:
Boyle, Cornelius 14th June 2008
Varkey, Shaju 12th July 2008

Westminster
Deacons:
Nunn, Gordon 2008
Clark, Anthony 2008
Wright, Simon 2008

■ ORDINATIONS

(RELIGIOUS ORDERS)

Cistercians (OCSO)

Ezeilo, Laurence 8th Mar 2008

■ NECROLOGY

(INCLUDING PERMANENT DEACONS)

■ 2006

January

14th Friend, Julian

June

7th Davis, A. Bede

September

27th Symons, Peter

October

14th Reid, Michael

November

13th O'Leary, Patrick

■ 2007

January

18th Jeanneau, Ernest
26th Smith, Christopher

May

8th Oddy, William

September

29th Capitanio, Joseph

October

11th Hughes, Gordon
13th Gough, John
15th Flanagan, Peter
15th Moverley, Cyril
17th Bulbeck, Robert
20th Higgins, Patrick
25th McCormack, Michael
25th Kearney, John
31st Mallon, Joseph

November

1st Grosvenor, Paul
6th Menken, Hugh
8th McGrath, Patrick
9th Duggan, Ronald
14th Tait, Adrian
15th Boyle, William
20th Linburgh, James H
26th Cooke, Anthony J
28th Fitzgerald, John

December

1st Davies, Dewi
2nd Bateman, Richard
8th Boswell, Wilbur J
8th Vaughan, Sidney Keiran
8th Mendel, G Raymund
9th Molloy, Hugh
10th Cutler, Christopher
15th Flanagan, Peter
15th Tokarski, Tadeusz
16th Earlam, Kenneth
23rd Elliott, Robert
25th Torney, Dennis J
30th Treacy, Daniel

■ 2008

January

1st FitzGibbon, Gerald
4th Connolly, Francis
5th Garrett, Philip
16th O'Shea, John
19th Pennington, John
21st Collier, John

February

3rd Corcoran, John
7th Groarke, Michael
10th O'Sullivan, Dominic
15th Chick, Patrick
21st Farrell, Sean
29th McKenna, Hugh

March

16th Sermin, Vincent
22nd Ward, Peter
24th Odlum, Peter
26th Power, Thomas
27th Bourke, Patrick
29th McAtamney, Vincent
31st Fox, Patrick

April

3rd Kitchen, Peter
7th Sheehan, Malachy
13th Tester, Francis
17th McHugh, Kevin
18th Cantwell, Desmond
27th Fahy, Denis

May

4th Brown, Tony
7th Nolan, Patrick
10th Eastwell, Ralph
16th Bradley, George

18th Brady, John
18th Ward Louis
18th Snape, Gerard
23rd Fraser, Donald
23rd Howell, William
25th Cloonan, Andrew
31st Robson, Francis
31st Boyd, David

June
5th O'Connor, William
7th Murphy, Edward
9th Cunningham, Vincent
12th Delaney, Patrick
13th Lanny, Joseph
17th Birdwhistle, Hugh
17th Macauley, Charles
18th Buckley, Gerard
19th Flanagan, Peter
25th Hennessy, Michael
29th Byrne, James
30th Bedford, Christopher

July
7th Gould, Edward
9th Bateman, Anthony
17th Budworth, Austin

August
5th Beer, Andrew
18th Carney, Godfrey
21st Donovan, Kevin
25th Coleman, Peter

Date Unknown
Houlihan, Patrick
Saunders, Ronald

RELIGIOUS ORDERS, CONGREGATIONS, INSTITUTES & SOCIETIES

IN ENGLAND AND WALES

ABBREVIATIONS FOR RELIGIOUS ORDERS REPRESENTED IN ENGLAND AND WALES

■ RELIGIOUS ORDERS OF MEN

AA	Augustinians of the Assumption.
BGS	Little Brothers of the Good Shepherd.
CFA	Alexian Brothers.
CFC	Congregation of Christian Brothers.
CFR	Franciscan Friars of the Renewal
CFX	Congregation of the Brothers of St Francis Xavier (Xaverian Brothers).
CHS	Crusade of the Holy Spirit.
CJ	Josephites.
CM	Congregation of the Mission - Vincentians.
CMF	Claretian Missionaries.
Cong Orat	Congregation of the Oratory - Oratorians
CP	Congregation of the Passion of Jesus Christ - Passionists.
CRIC	Canons Regular of the Immaculate Conception.
CRL	Canons Regular of the Lateran.
CS	Scalabrini Fathers.
CSJ	Community of St John.
CSS	Stimmatini Fathers.
CSSp	Holy Ghost Fathers.
CSsR	Congregation of the Most Holy Redeemer - Redemptorists.
FC	Brothers of Charity.
FCJ	Faithful Companions of Jesus
FIC	Brothers of Christian Instruction.
FMI	Sons of Mary Immaculate.
FPM	Presentation Brothers.
FSC	De La Salle Brothers.
IC	Institute of Charity - Rosminians.
IMC	Consolata Missionaries.
LBN	Little Brothers of Nazareth.
LMO	Lebanese Maronite Order
MAfr	Missionaries of Africa.
MCCJ	Comboni Missionaries of the Heart of Jesus - Verona Fathers.
MIC	Marian Fathers.
MS	Missionaries of La Salette.
MSC	Missionaries of the Sacred Heart - Issoudum.
MSFS	Missionaries of St Francis de Sales - Fransalians.
O Carm	Order of Carmelites.
O Cart	Carthusians.
O Praem	Canons Regular of Premontre - Ordo Praemonstratensis (Norbertines).
OAR	Augustinian Recollects.
OCD	Order of Carmelites - Discalced.
OCSO	Cistercians of the Strict Observance.
OFM Conv	Order of Friars Minor - Conventual.
OFM Cap	Order of Friars Minor - Capuchin.
OFM	Order of Friars Minor.
OH	Hospitaller Order of St John of God.
OMI	Missionary Oblates of Mary Immaculate.
OP	Order of Preachers - Dominicans.
OSA	Order of St Augustine (Augustinians).
OSB	Benedictines, English Congregation.
OSB	Benedictines, Solemnes Congregation.
OSB	Benedictines, Subiaco Congregation.
OS Cam	Order of St Camillus.
OSM	Friar Servants of Mary - Servites.
SA	Franciscan Friars of the Atonement.
SC	Brothers of the Sacred Heart.
SCA	Society of the Catholic Apostolate - Pallottine Fathers.
SChr	Society of Christ.
scj	Sacred Heart Fathers (Dehonians).
SCJ	Priests and Brothers of the Sacred Heart (Betharram).
SDB	Salesians of Don Bosco.
SDP	Sons of Divine Providence.
SDS	Society of the Divine Saviour - Salvatorians.
SG	Congregation of the Brothers of St Gabriel.
SJ	Society of Jesus - Jesuits.
SM	Society of Mary - Marists.
SMA	Society of African Missions.
SMM	Company of Mary – Montfort Missionary Fathers.
SPS	Missionary Society of St Patrick - Kiltegan Fathers.
SSCC	Congregation of the Sacred Hearts of Jesus and Mary - Picpus
SSC	Missionary Society of St Columban.
SSP	Society of St Paul.
SSS	Congregation of the Blessed Sacrament.
SVD	Society of the Divine Word.
SX	Xaverian Missionaries.

■ RELIGIOUS ORDERS OF WOMEN

AASC Handmaids of the Blessed Sacrament and of Charity.
ACI Handmaids of the Sacred Heart of Jesus.
BPS Sisters of Charity of Our Lady of Good and Perpetual Succour.
BS Sisters of the Good Saviour *(Bon Sauveur)*.
CBS Sisters of Bon Secours de Paris.
CJC Sisters of Jesus Crucified.
CLP Congregation of Our Lady of Pity.
CM Carmelite Missionaries.
CMMC Congregation of Mary Mother of the Church.
CMS Comboni Missionary Sisters.
CP Congregation of the Passion of Jesus Christ *(Passionist Contemplative Nuns)*.
CP Sisters of the Cross and Passion.
CR Sisters of Christian Retreat
CR Sisters of the Resurrection.
CRL Canonesses Regular of the Lateran.
CRSF Sisters of St Francis.
CROSA Augustinian Canonesses of the Order of St Augustine
CRSS Canonesses of the Holy Sepulchre.
CS Capitanio Sisters.
CSA Congregation of Our Lady - Canonesses of St Augustine.
CSB Sisters of St Brigid.
CSBV Sisters of the Saviour and the Blessed Virgin Mary.
CSFN Sisters of the Holy Family of Nazareth.
CSI Sisters of St Joseph of Chamberey
CSJL Sisters of St Joseph of Lyon
CSJP Sisters of St Joseph of Peace.
CSN Sisters of Nazareth.
CSST Sisters of the Holy Trinity.
CRW Canonesses Regular of Saint Augustine.
DC Sisters of Charity of St Vincent de Paul.
DDL Daughters of Divine Love.
DHM Daughters of the Heart of Mary.
DHS Daughters of the Holy Spirit.
DJ Daughters of Jesus.
DMJ Daughters of Mary and Joseph *(Formerly Ladies of Mary)*.
DoP Daughters of Providence - St Brieuc.
DW Daughters of Wisdom.
FC Daughters of the Cross of Liege.
FCJ Faithful Companions of Jesus.
FCJ Franciscan Sisters, of the Heart of Jesus (Malta).
FDC Daughters of Divine Charity.
FDCC Canossian Daughters of Charity.
FDLC Daughters of the Cross (of Torquay).
FDNSC Daughters of Our Lady of the Sacred Heart.
FMA Daughters of Mary Help of Christians - Salesian Sisters.
FMDM Franciscan Missionaries of the Divine Motherhood.
FMM Franciscan Missionaries of Mary.
FMSA Franciscan Missionary Sisters for Africa
FMSJ Franciscan Missionaries of St Joseph.
FMSL Franciscan Missionary Sisters of Littlehampton.
FSM Franciscan Sisters Minoress.
FSMA Franciscan Sisters of St Mary of the Angels.
FSP Daughters of St Paul.
HC Sisters of the Holy Cross.
HFB Sisters of the Holy Family of Bordeaux.
HHCJ Handmaids of the Holy Child Jesus.
HHS Helpers of the Holy Souls.
HSC Hospitaller Sisters of the Sacred Heart of Jesus.
IBVM Institute of the Blessed Virgin Mary.
IBVM (L) Institute of the Blessed Virgin Mary *(Loreto)*.
IC Institute of Charity, Rosminians.
IHM Daughters of Immaculate Heart of Mary (Blon).
IM Sisters of St Marcellina.
IMC Sisters of the Immaculate Conception.
IJS Infant Jesus Sisters
IUU The Union of Ursuline Sisters in Ireland.
JT Sisters of Jesus in the Temple.
LCM Little Company of Mary.
LS The Fraternity of the Little Sisters of Jesus.
LSA Little Sisters of the Assumption.
LSP Little Sisters of the Poor.
LSU Congregation of La Sainte Union.
M Ch Missionaries of Charity.
MC Consolata Missionary Sisters.
MFIC Missionary Franciscans of the Immaculate Conception
MMM Medical Missionaries of Mary.
MMS Medical Mission Sisters.
MPF Pontifical Institute of the Religious Teachers Filipini - Sisters of St Lucy.
MSC Missionary Sisters of the Sacred Heart - Cabrini.
MSHR Missionary Sisters of the Holy Rosary.
MSI Missionary Sisters of the Immaculate (PIME).
MSOLA Missionary Sisters of Our Lady of Africa *(White Sisters)*.
MSP Missionaries of St Paul
MSSPC Missionary Sisters of St Peter Claver.
NDS Our Lady of Sion, Congregation of.
OA Oblates of the Assumption.
OC Bernardine Cistercians - Esquermes
OCSO Cistercians of the Strict Observance
O Carm Corpus Christi Carmelites, Congregation of.
O SS S Order of the Most Holy Saviour and St Bridget.

ODN	Company of Mary Our Lady.
OLA	Sisters of Our Lady of the Apostles.
OLC	Sisters of Our Lady of Charity.
OLF	Sisters of Our Lady of Fidelity.
OP	Dominican Sisters of Charity of the Presentation of Our Lady.
OP	Dominican Sisters of the Eng Congregation of St Catherine of Siena.
OP	Congregation of St Catherine of Siena, Newcastle, Natal.
OP	Dominican Sisters of St Catherine of Siena of King Williams Town
OP	Dominican Missionary Sisters of the Most Sacred Heart - Zimbabwe.
OP	Congregation of Dominican Sisters of the Presentation of Tours.
OP	Dominican Sisters - Oakford.
OSA	Augustinian Canonesses of the Mercy of Jesus - Bruges.
OSA	Sisters of St Augustine of the Mercy of Jesus.
OSA	Augustinian Sisters of Meaux.
OSA	Augustinian Sisters of the Mercy of Jesus - Liverpool.
OSB	Benedictine Sisters of the Holy Child.
OSB	Benedictine Sisters of Our Lady of Grace and Compassion.
OSB	Order of St Benedict (Olivetan Congregation).
OSC	Sisters of St Clare. (Poor Clares)
OSF	Franciscan Missionary Sisters for Africa.
OSF	Franciscan Missionary Sisters.
OSF	Franciscan Sisters of the Immaculate Conception.
OSF	Franciscan Sisters of Mill Hill.
OSFS	Oblate Sisters of St Francis De Sales.
OSM	Servants of Mary - Servite Sisters.
OSsS	Order of the Most Holy Saviour (Bridgettines).
OSU	Ursulines of the Roman Union.
OSU	Ursulines of Brentwood.
PBVM	Union of the Sisters of the Presentation of the Blessed virgin Mary.
PCJ	Sisters of the Poor Child Jesus.
PHJC	Poor Handmaids of Jesus Christ.
pm	Sisters of the Presentation of Mary.
PRE	Religious of the Eucharist.
ra	Religious of the Assumption.
rc	Sisters of Our Lady of the Cenacle.
RCE	Institute of the Religious of Christian Education.
RCI	Religious of Christian Instruction.
RGS	Congregation of Our Lady of Charity of the Good Shepherd.
RHF	Sisters of the Holy Family - St Emilie De Rodat.
RJM	Religious of Jesus and Mary.
RLR	Sisters of La Retraite.
RMA	Sisters of Marie Auxiliatrice.
RMI	Religious of Mary Immaculate.
RNDM	Sisters of Our Lady of the Missions.
RSA	Religious of St Andrew.
RSC	Religious Sisters of Charity.
rscJ	Society of the Sacred Heart.
RSHM	Religious of the Sacred Heart of Mary - Beziers.
RSJT	Sisters of St Joseph of Tarbes.
RSM	The Union of the Sisters of Mercy.
RSM	Sisters of Mercy of the English Federation.
RSM	Institute of Our Lady of Mercy.
RSM	Sisters of St Martha.
RSS	Blessed Sacrament Sisters.
S de M	Handmaids of Mary.
SAC	Sisters of the Catholic Apostolate - Pallotine Missionary Sisters.
SCE	Sisters of Charity of Our Lady of Evron.
SCI	Sisters of Christian Instruction - St Gildas.
SCJA	Sisters of Charity of St Jeanne Antide Thouret.
SCJM	Sisters of Charity of Jesus and Mary.
SCMM	Sisters of Charity of Our Lady Mother of Mercy.
SCMM	Medical Mission Sisters
SCN	Sisters of Charity of Nevers.
SCSL	Sisters of Charity of St Louis.
SDS	Sisters of the Divine Saviour - Salvatorians.
SHCJ	Society of the Holy Child Jesus.
SJA	Sisters of St Joseph of the Apparition.
SJC	Sisters of St Joseph of Cluny.
SJG	Sisters of St John of God
SJL	Sisters of St Joseph of Lyon.
SLO	Sisters of the Little Ones.
SM	Congregation of Mary - Marist Sisters.
SMG	Poor Servants of the Mother of God.
SMP	Sisters of St Marie de la Providence.
SMR	Society of Marie Reparatrice.
SND	Sisters of Notre Dame de Namur.
SND	Sisters of Our Lady.
SOP	Sisters of Providence (Rouen).
SP	Sisters of Charity of St Paul the Apostle (Selly Park Sisters).
SP	Sisters of Providence - Ruille sur Loir.
SPC	Sisters of St Paul de Chartres.
SPIC	Sisters of Providence and of the Immaculate Conception.
SPR	Sisters of Providence - Rosminians.
SSA	Congregation of the Sisters of St Anne.
SSC	Missionary Sisters of St Columban.
SS CC	Congregation of the Sacred Hearts of Jesus and Mary - Picpus
SSCJ	Sisters of the Sacred Heart - St Jacut.
SSD	Sisters of St Dorothy.
SSHJ	Sisters of the Sacred Heart of Jesus - St Aubin.
SSHJM	Sisters of the Sacred Hearts of Jesus and Mary - Chigwell.
SSJ	Sisters of St Joseph of Chambery.
SSJA	Sisters of St Joseph of Annecy.
SSJB	Sisters of St Joseph of Bordeaux.
SSL	Sisters of St Louis.
SSMMP	Sisters of St Marie Madeleine Postel.
SSMN	Sisters of St Mary of Namur.
SSND	School Sisters of Notre Dame.

S Sp S	Missionary Sister Servants of the Holy Spirit.
UJ	Ursulines of Jesus.
USAM	Ursuline Sisters of St Angela Merici.
VBVM	Sisters of the Visitation of the Blessed Virgin Mary.
VHM	Visitation of Holy Mary
VS	Vocation Sisters - Daughters of Our Lady of Good Counsel, and St Paul of the Cross.

CONFERENCE OF RELIGIOUS IN ENGLAND AND WALES

(Conference of Major Religious Trust Reg Charity Number 277024)

The Conference of Religious, 3 Montpelier Avenue, Ealing, London W5 2XP
Tel: 020-3255 1085
Website: www.corew.org

President:
Sr Kathleen McGhee SND

Vice-President:
Abbot Martin Shipperlee OSB

General Secretary:
Ms Connie Burke
3 Montpelier Avenue, Ealing London W5 2XP
E-mail: gebsec@corew.org

Office Administator:
Patricia Geraerts
E-mail: admin@corew.org

■ **CoR/COPCA Counter Signatory Office**
Mrs Caroline Power and Mr Ray Wilson
Tel: 020-8959 8578 **E-mail:** cso@corew.org

■ **Safeguarding Advisor**
Eileen Campling
Tels: 020-3255 1085, 01702 301275
E-mail: safeguarding@corew.org

■ **Association of Provincial Bursars**
Secretary: **Mr Michael Barwick**
Green Roofs, Marine Drive, Saltdean, Brighton BN2 8LA
Tel/Fax: 01273-305183 **Email:** apbursars@aol.com
Website: www.apbursars.org.uk

LEADERS, OR THEIR DELEGATES, OF RELIGIOUS ORDERS, IN ENGLAND AND WALES

All Religious Orders included in this section are members of the Conference of Religious, with the exception of those marked with an*.

■ PRIESTS

Africa, Society of Missionaries of (MAfr): Fr Peter Walsh, *Provincial*, The White Fathers, 42 Stormont Road, Highgate, London N6 4NP **Tel:** 020-8348 7799 **Fax:** 020-8347 8147 **E-mail:** mafrgb@blueyonder.co.uk

African Missions, Society of (SMA): Fr Patrick N McGuire *Provincial Superior*, Abbey Ho, Claredon Place, Dunblane, Perthshire FK15 9HB **Tel:** 01786 824 002 **Fax:** 01786 825 997 **E-mail:** pmcguire@smafathers.org.uk

Assumptionists (AA): Fr Tom O'Brien, Assumption Priory, Victoria Park Square, Bethnal Green, London E2 9PB **Tel:** 020 8980 1968 **E-mail:** tomobrien@freeuk.com

Augustinian Recollects (OAR): Rev Gerald Wilson *Vicar Provincial*. St Rita's Centre, Ottery Moor Lane, Honiton, Devon EX14 1AP **E-mail:** vicar.uk@agustinosrecoletos.org

Augustinians (OSA): Rev David Middleton, *Provincial*, Provincial Office, 15 Dorville Crescent, London W6 0HH **Tel/Fax:** 020-8748 1529 **E-mail:** augprov.engscot@btinternet.com

Benedictines (OSB) (English Cong):

Ampleforth: **Rt Rev Abbot Cuthbert Madden.** Ampleforth Abbey, York YO62 4EN **Tel:** 01439-766700 **Fax:** 01439-788132 **E-mail:** abbot@ampleforth.org.uk

Belmont: **Rt Rev Abbot Paul Stonham OSB**, Belmont Abbey, Hereford HR2 9RZ. **Tel:** 01432-374718 **Fax:** 01432-374711 **E-mail:** AbbotofBelmont@aol.com

Buckfast: **Rt Rev Richard Yeo**, Buckfast Abbey, Buckfastleigh, Devon TQ11 0EE **Tel:** 01364-645555 **Fax:** 01364-643891

Douai: **Rt Rev Abbot Geoffrey Scott OSB**, Douai Abbey, Upper Woolhampton, Reading RG7 5TQ **Tel:** 0118-971 5300 **Fax:** 0118- 971 5203 **E-mail:** info@douaiabbey.org.uk

Downside: **Rt Rev Aidan Bellenger**, Downside Abbey, Stratton-on-the-Fosse, Radstock Bath BA3 4RH **Tel:** 01761-235121 **Fax:** 01761-235156 **E-mail:** abbotyeo@aol.com

Ealing: **Rt Rev Martin Shipperlee** *(Rt Rev Abbot)* **Anthony Francis Rossiter JCL**, *(Abbot President)*, Ealing Abbey, Charlbury Grove, London W5 2DY **Tel:** 020-8862 2100 **Fax:** 020-8862 2206

Worth: **Rt Rev Abbot Christopher Jamison OSB**, Worth Abbey, Paddockhurst Road, Turners Hill, Crawley, W Sussex RH10 4SB **Tel:** 01342-710320 **Fax:** 01342-710321 **E-mail:** cjamison@worth.org.uk

Benedictines (OSB) (Solesmes Cong);

*Quarr: **Rt Rev Cuthbert Johnson OSB**, Quarr Abbey, Ryde, Isle of Wight, PO33 4ES **Tel:** 01983 882420

Benedictines (Cong of Subiaco);

*Ramsgate: **The Right Reverend Laurence O'Keefe OSB**, St Augustine's Abbey, Ramsgate, Kent CT11 9PA **Tel:** 01843 593045 **Fax:** 01843 582732

*Prinknash: *Prior Administrator* **Rev Francis Baird OSB**, Prinknash Abbey, Cranham, Gloucester GL4 8EX **Tel:** 01452 812455 **Fax:** 01452 812529

*Farnborough: **Very Rev Cuthbert Brogan OSB**, *Conventual Prior*, St Michael's Abbey, Farnborough, Hants GU14 7NQ **Tel:** 01252-546105 **Fax:** 01252 372822 **E-mail:** prior@farnbroughabbey.org

Benedictines (Olivetan Cong):

*Cockfosters: **Rt Rev Prior Constanzo M Scaglia OSB**, Priory of Christ the King, Bramley Road, Oakwood, Cockfosters, London, N14 4HE **Tel:** 020-8449 6648 **Fax:** 0020-8449 2338

Blessed Sacrament, Congregation of the, Rev Patrick Costello SSS *(Provincial)*, Blessed Sacrament Chapel, 20 Bachelors Walk, Dublin **Tel:** 01-872 4597 **E-mail:** pjcostello@aol.com

Canons Regular of the Lateran*:* **Rev Garry Murphy CRL**, Christ Church Priory, 229 Eltham High Street, Eltham SE19 1TX **Tel:** 020-8850 1666 **Fax:** 020-8294 2109

Carmelites (OCarm): Rev Wilfrid McGreal. *Prior Provincial.* Carmelite Provincial Office, Whitefriars, Tanners Street, Faversham ME13 7JW **Tel:** 01795 532449 **E-mail:** provincial@carmelite.org

Carmelites, Discalced (OCD): Fr Michael McGoldrick OCD, Carmelite Priory, 41 Kensington Church St, London W8 4BB **Tel:** 0207-937 9866 **E-mail:** mcgoldocd@gmail.com

Charity, Institute of (Rosminians) (IC): Rev David Myers IC, St Peter's, St Peters Street, Cardiff CF24 3BA **Tel:** 02920 483394

Cistercians (Strict Observance) (OCSO): Rt Rev Dom Joseph Delargy, *Abbot,*

Mount St. Bernard Abbey, Coalville, Leicester LE67 5UL **Tel:** 01530-832298/832022 **Fax:** 01530-814608 **E-mail:** mtstbernardabbey@btinternet.com

Rt Rev Dom Daniel Santvoort *(Abbot)*, Abbey of Our Lady and St Samson, Caldey Island, off Tenby, SA70 7UH **Tel:** 01834-842632 **Fax:** 01834-845942 **E-mail:** abbotcaldey@beeb.net

Claretian Missionaries (CMF): Rev Paul Smyth, Botwell House, Botwell Lane, Hayes, Middlesex UB3 2AB **Tel:** 020-8573 2065 **Fax:** 020-8561 6748 **E-mail:** provincial@claret.org.uk **Website:** www.claret.org.uk

Columban Fathers (SSC): Rev Denis Carter, *Director,* St Columban's, Widney Manor Road, Knowle, Solihull, West Midlands B93 9AB **Tel:** 01564-772096 **Fax:** 01564-770500 **E-mail:** director.columbans@btinternet.com

Crusade of the Holy Spirit, (CHS)*:* **Rev. Bernard Kelly**, *Regional Director,* 464 Chester Road, Sutton Coldfield, West Midlands B73 5BP **Tel:** 0121-384 4280 **Fax:** 0121-328 8148

Divine Providence, Sons of (FDP): Rev Stephen Beale, *Regional Superior,* 25 Lower Teddington Road, Hampton Wick, Kingston-upon-Thames, Surrey KT1 4HB **Tel:** 020-8977 5130 **Fax:** 020-8977 0105 www.sonsofdivineprovidence.org

Divine Word Missionaries (SVD): Rev Michael Egan SVD, 8 Teighmouth Rd, London NW2 4HN **Tel:** 020 8452 8430 **Fax:** 020 8452 9756 **E-mail:** lonpraesis@yahoo.co.uk

***Dominicans (Order of Preachers) (OP): Very Rev Allan White** *(Provincial)*, St Dominic's Priory, Southampton Road, London NW5 4LB **Tel:** 0207 485 2760 **Fax:** 0207 482 3976 **E-mail:** provincial@english.op.org

Franciscans (Friars Minor) (OFM): Rev Austin Linus McCormack, Provincial, 557-559 High Road, Woodford Green, Essex IG8 0RB **Tel:** 020-8504 7540

Franciscans (Capuchin Friars Minor) (OFM Cap): Rev James Boner, *Provincial Curia*, Franciscan Friary, Carlton Road, Erith, Kent DA8 1DN **Tel:** 01322-444960 **Fax:** 01322-402061 **E-mail:** jab@btconnect.com

Franciscans (Friars Minor Conventual) (OFMConv): Rev James McCurry *(Provincial),* St Patrick's Friary, 26 Cornwall Road, Waterloo, London SE1 8TW **Tel:** 020-7928 8897 **Fax:** 020-7928 2887 **E-mail:** greyfriarjames@btconnect.com

Franciscan Friars of the Atonement (SA): Rev Michael Seed SA. St Francis Friary, 47 Francis Street, London SW1P 1QR **Tel:** 020-7828 0543

Fransalians (Missionaries of St Francis de Sales) (MSFS): Rev J M Griffin, *Provincial*, 16 Wellington Road, Hampton Hill, Middlesex TW12 1JR **Tel:** 020-8977 1415 **Fax:** 020-8943 9593 **E-mail:** coladh@yahoo.com/devizes@catholic.org

Holy Ghost Fathers (CSSp): Rev Philip Marsh CCSp, *(Provincial)*, 18 Limesdale Gardens, Edgware, Middlesex HA8 5JA **Tel:** 020-8200 5091 **E-mail:** provincial@spiritans.co.uk

Immaculate Conception, Canons Regular of the, (CRIC): Rev James Cassidy CRIC, St Augustine's Church, 30 Langcliffe Drive, Heelands, Milton Keynes MK13 7PL **Tel/Fax:** 01908-221228 **E-mail:** james.cassidy@zetnet.co.uk

Institute of Charity, Rosminians, (IC): Rev David Myers IC, *Provincial Superior* St Peters, St Peter's Street, Roath, Cardiff CF24 3BA **Tel:** 029 2048 3394 **E-mail:** dm@ic-uk.org

Jesuits (SJ): Rev Michael Holman SJ, *Provincial*. 114 Mount Street, London W1K 3AH **Tel:** 020-7499 0285 **Fax:** 020-7408 7111 **E-mail:** prov@gbsj.org

Josephites (CJ): *Provincial Leader:* **Rev William Muir**, 42 Durdells Avenue, Kinson, Bournemouth BH11 9EH **Tel:** -01202-577821 **E-mail:** bmuircity@aol.com

Marian Fathers (MIC): Rev Wojtek Jasinski MIC (Provincial), Fawley Court, Marlow Road, Henley-on-Thames, Oxon RG9 3AE **Tel:** 01491-574917/571935 **Fax:** 01491-411587 **E-mail:** marian-f@dircon.co.uk

Marists Fathers (SM): Rev Alan Williams SM (*Major Superior*), Provincial Office, Marist Fathers, 3 Hamilton Road, Sidcup, Kent DA15 7HB **Tel:** 020-8300 5339 **Fax:** 020-8300 9733 **E-mail:** alanwilliamssm@hotmail.com

Mary Immaculate, Oblates of (OMI), Rev Raymund Warren *(Delegate),* New Priory, Quex Road, Kilburn, London NW6 4PS **Tel:** 020-7624 1701

Mill Hill Missionaries (MHM): Rev Anthony Chantry MHM St Joseph's Missionary Society, PO Box 3608, Maidenhead, Berks SL6 7UX **Tel:** 01628 588 406 **E-mail:** gensup@millhillmissionaries.com

Missionaries of Africa (MAfr): Rev Peter Welsh *(Sector Superior),* 42 Storment Rd, London N6 4NP **Tel:** 020-8348 7799 **E-mail:** mafrgb@blueyonder

Missionary of Charity Brothers (MCB):

Br Marc-Daniel Delapeyre, St Malachy's House, Eggington St, Manchester M40 7RN **Tel:** 0161-205 2055

Missionaries of St Paul (of Nigeria) (MSP): Fr Eustace Durugbo *(Local Superior, UK Mission)*, Our Lady of Assumption Parish, 131 Deptford High Street, London SE8 4NS **Tel:** 020-8692 2011 **E-mail:** iykjud@yahoo.com

Montfort Missionaries (Company of Mary) (SMM): Rev Frederick Scragg, *Provincial*, Montfort House, 28 Burbo Bank Road, Liverpool L23 6TH **Tel:** 0151-287 6865 **Fax:** 0151-287 0410 **E-mail:** smm1@montfort.org.uk

Norbertine Canons (OPraem): Rev Paul McMahon, OPraem, Our Lady of England Priory, School Lane, Storrington, West Sussex RH20 4LN **Tel:** 01903-742150 **E-mail:** norbertines@pavilion.co.uk

Pallottine Fathers (SCA): Rev Tom Daly SCA, *Provincial Delegate*. 358 Greenford Road, Greenford, Middlesex UB6 9AN **Tel:** 020-8578 1363

Passionists (CP): Rev Nicholas Postlethwaite. 12 Belgrave Road, Liverpool L17 7AG **Tel:** 0151-727 2024 **Fax:** 0151-222 1207 **E-mail:** nicholas.postlewaite@sky.com

Redemptorists (Congregation of the Most Holy Redeemer) (CSsR): Rev Ronald McAinsh, *Provincial*, St Mary's, Kinnoull, Perth PH2 7BP **Tel:** 01738 624075 **Fax:** 01738 442071 **E-mail:** rmcainsh@yahoo.com

Sacred Heart Fathers (SCJ): *Provincial*, **Rev Hugh Hanley**, 266 Wellington Road North, Stockport, SK4 2QR **E-mail:** prov@heartscj.fsnet.co.uk

Sacred Heart (Betharram), Priests and Brothers of the (SCJ): Rev Austin Hughes SCJ *Provincial.* The Friary, 140/150 St Bernard's Road, Solihull, West Midlands B92 7BL **Tel:** 0121-706 0505 **Fax:** 0121-706 8105 **E-mail:** a.hughes@attglobal.net

Sacred Heart, Missionaries of (MSC): Rev Joseph McGee MSC *(Delegate)*, 65 Terenure Road West, Terenure, Dublin 6W, Ireland **Tel:** 00 353 1 4906622 **E-mail:** joem@misacorirl.com

Sacred Hearts, Congretation of the – Picpus Fathers (SSCC), Fr Derek Laverty SSCC *(Delegate)*, 372 Uxbridge Road, London W5 3LH **Tel:** 020-8992 5941 **E-mail:** dereklaverty2005@yahoo.co.uk

Salesians (SDB): Rev Michael Winstanley, *Provincial*, Salesian Provincial House, Thornleigh Ho, Sharples Park, Bolton BL1 6PQ **Tel:** 01204 600720 **Fax:** 0161-443 2378 **E-mail:** provincial@salesians.org.uk

Salvatorians (SDS): Rev Peter Preston SDS, *Province Superior*, Salvatorian Fathers, 129 Spencer Road, Harrow Weald, Middx HA3 7BJ **Tel:** 020-8426 0495 **Fax:** 020 8426 0927 **E-mail:** gbprovsds@btconnect.com

***Scalabrini Fathers (CS): Rev Alberto Vico**, Villa Scalabrini, Green Street, Shenley, Herts **Tel:** 020-8207 5713

Servites, (Friar Servants of Mary), (OSM): Rev Patrick Ryall OSM. St Mary's Priory, 264 Fulham Road, London SW10 9EL **Tel:** 020-7795 2181 **Fax:** 020-7352 8440 **E-mail:** patryalosm@aol.com

Society of Christ (SChr) (Sacred Heart Province)*:* **Rev Krzysztof Tyliszczak MA** *(Provincial)*, Provincial House, 16 Carlton Road, Manchester M16 8BB **Tel:** 0161-227 1997

Society of St Paul (SSP): Rev Celso Godiland SSP, *Regional Superior,* 191 Battersea Bridge Road, London SW11 3AS **Tel:** 020-7228 2656 **Fax:** 020-7228 1656 **E-mail:** cgodilano@stpauls.ph

St Patrick's Missionary Society (SPS): Rev Edward McGettrick *Local Superior*. 20 Beauchamp Road, East Molesey, Surrey KT8 0PA **Tel:** 020-8979 1890 **Fax:** 020-8941 8221 **E-mail:** spsuk@aol.com

Verona Fathers (Comboni Missionaries of the Heart of Jesus) (MCCJ): Rev Paul Felix MCCJ, Verona Fathers, London Road, Ascot, Sunningdale, Berks. SL5 0JY **Tel:** 01344-621238 **Fax:** 01344-621351 **E-mail:** veronaf@globalnet.co.uk

Vincentians (Congregation of the Mission (CM): Rev Kieran MaGovern CM *(Regional Superior),* St Mary;s Presbytery, 82 West Street, Dunstable LU6 1NY **Tel:** 01582-662710 **Fax:** 01582-670968 **E-mail:** kierancm54@aol.com

Xaverian Missionaries (SX): Rev John Convery *Provincial,* Xaverian Missionaries, Calder Avenue, Coatbridge, Lanarkshire ML5 4JS **Tel:** 01236-606364 **Fax:** 01236-606365 **E-mail:** coatbridge@xavs.org

■ BROTHERS

Alexian Brothers (CFA): Br Barry Butler, 47, Upper Drumcondra Road, Dublin 9, Ireland. **Tel:** 00 353 1 837 5973 **Fax:** 00 353 1 836 8324 **E-mail:** alexianbros@eircom.net

Brothers of Christian Introduction (FIC), BR Francis Patterson, St Mary's College, Bitterne Park, Southampton SO18 4DJ **Tel:** 02380 558425 **Fax:** 02380 671268

Brothers of the Good Shepherd (BGS): Rev Br William Cahill. Montini House, 2

Richmond Road, Wolverhampton WV3 9HJ **Tel:** 01902-422218 **Fax:** 01902-426096

Charity, Brothers of (FC): Rev Br Denis Kerins, *(Delegate)*, Lisieux Hall, Whittle-le-Woods, Chorley, Lancs PR6 7DX **Tel:** 01257-266311 **Fax:** 01257-260993 **E-mail:** trustees@lisieuxhall.f9.co.uk

Christian Brothers, Congregation of (CFC): Br John Kevin Mullan. 274 North Circular Road, Dublin 7 **Tel:** 00 353 1 8680247 **E-mail:**jkmcfc@aol.co.uk

De La Salle Brothers (FSC): Rev Bro Aidan Kilty *Provincial.* 140 Banbury Road, Oxford OX2 7BP **Tel:** 01865-311332 **Fax:** 01865-554356 **E-mail:** akilty@yahoo.com

Gabriel, Brothers of (SG): Rev Br John Hegarty, 11 Longfield Road, Ealing, London W5 2DH **Tel:** 020-8998 9182

Brothers of the Hospitaller Order of Saint John of God *(OH)*: **Rev Br John Martin** OH *(Provincial)*, St Bedes House, Morton Park Way, Darlington, Co Durham DL1 4XZ **Tel:** 01325-373701 **Fax:** 01325-373707 **E-mail:** johnmartin@ sjogcareservices.org.uk

Presentation Brothers (FPM): Br Walter Hurley, *(Provincial)*, 3 Heatherton Park, South Douglas Road, Cork, Ireland. **Tel:** 00 353 21 4361308 **Fax:** 00353 021 4364043 **Br Richard English FPM** 6 The Brent, Dartford, Kent DA1 1YG **Tel:** 01322-279106

Sacred Heart, Brothers of the (SC): Br Raymond Hetu, Watling House, 8 King Harry Lane, St Albans, Herts AL3 4AW. **Tel:** 01727-861969. **Fax:** 01727-861969

Xaverian Brothers (CFX): Rev Br John T Hart, 58 Bonser Road, Twickenham TW1 4RG **Tel:** 020-8287 3008 **E-mail:** cfxuk@onetel.net.uk

■ SISTERS

Andrew, Religious of St (RSA): Souer Clara Pavanello, Soeurs de Saint Andre, Avenue Lambeau, 108, B-1200 Bruxelles **Tel:** 0032 2735 09 08 **E-mail:** clara.pavanello@saint-andre.be

Anne, Congregation of Sisters of St (SSA): Sr Barbara O'Mahony SSA, *Superior General*. St Agnes Lodge, 14a The Downs, London SW20 8HS **Tel:** 020-8946 1094 **Fax:** 020-8947 7602

Assumption, Little Sisters of the (LSA): Sr Mary Keenan *(Provincial)*, Provincial House, 42 Rathfarnham Road, Terenure, Dublin 6W **Tel:** 00353 31 4909850 **Fax:** 00353 31 4925740

Assumption, Oblates of the (OA): Sr Josephine Canny OA, Assumption Convent, 20 Higham Station Avenue, South Chingford, London E4 9AZ **Tel/Fax:** 020-8531 0466

Assumption, Religious of the (RA): Sr Christine Charlwood, *Provincial*, Convent of the Assumption, 23 Kensington Square, London W8 5HN **Tel:** 020-7361 4700 **Fax:** 020-7361 4757 **E-mail:** raproveng@aol.com

Augustinian Sisters of Bruges (OSA): Sr Elizabeth (Monica) OSA, *Superior General*, St George's Retreat, Ditchling Common, Ditchling, E. Sussex RH15 0SF **Tel:** 01444-235874 **Fax:** 01444-248411 **E-mail:** patf@ank.org.uk

Augustinian Sisters of Meaux (OSA): Sr Christopher Billington, Bethanie Convent, 54 Highgate Hill, Highgate, London N19 5NQ **Tel:** 020-7272 3696

Augustinian Sisters of the Mercy of Jesus (OSA): Sr Marie Laura Hughes. Augustinian Convent, Ince Blundell Hall, Ince Blundell, Liverpool L38 6JL **Tel:** 0151-929 2596 **Fax:** 0151-929 2188 **E-mail:** enquiries@ithnursinghome,org

Benedict (Olivetan Cong.), Order of St (OSB): Sr Zoë Davis *Prioress*, Our Lady of Peace Priory, Turvey Abbey, Turvey, Bedford MK43 8DE **Tel:** 01234-881432 **Fax:** 01234-881538 **E-mail:** turveyabbey@btinternet.com

Benedictines (OSB): Abbess Andrea Savage, Stanbrook Abbey, Callow End, Worcester WR2 4TD **Tel:** 01905-831727 **E-mail:** abbess@stanbrookabbey.org.uk

Benedictines of The Holy Child (OSB): Sr Maura Fewtrell, St Benedict's Convent, Penton Lodge, Andover, Hants SP11 0RD **Tel:** 01264-771692

Benedictine Sisters of Our Lady of Grace and Compassion (OSB): Sr Kathy Yeeles *Prioress General*, Grace and Compassion Convent, 57 Surrenden Rd, Brighton, East Sussex BN1 6PQ **Tel:** 01273-502129 **Fax:** 01273-552440 **E-mail:** osb@graceandcompassion.co.uk

Bernardine Cistercians (OC): Sr Mary Helen Jackson OC, Monastery of Our Lady of Hyning, Hyning Hall, Carnforth, Lancs LA5 9SE **Tel:** 01524 732684 **Fax:** 01524 720287 **E-mail:** sistermaryhelen@hotmail.com

Blessed Sacrament and of Charity, Handmaids of the (AASC): Sr Ancy Mathew AASC, 38-39 Kensington Square, London W8 5HP **Tel:** 020-7937 5237

Blessed Sacrament Sisters (CBS): Sr Mary Patrick Forristal. The Towers, Upper Beeding, Steyning, W. Sussex BN44 3TF **Tel:** 01903-812185 **Fax:** 01903-813858 **E-mail:** spatrick@towers.w-sussex.sch.uk

Blessed Virgin Mary (Loreto), Institute of the (IBVM(L)): Sr Eileen McConnon IBVM *Provincial Superior,* Loreto Provincial

Offices, 30 Maher Gardens, Hulme, Manchester M15 5PW **Tel:** 0161-227 0228 **Fax:** 0161-227 0229 **E-mail:** eileenmcc@ibvm.org.uk

Bon Secours de Paris, Sisters of (CBS): Sr Anne Campbell CBS, St Dunstan's Presbytery, Cores End Road, Bourne End, Bucks SL8 5AR **Tel:** 01628-522956 **Fax:** 01628-520462 **E-mail:** sranne@littleflower.co.uk

Brigid, Congregation of (CSB): Sr Brenda McEveney CSB, 81 Castle Street, Saffrons Walden, Essex CB10 1BQ **Tel:** 01799-503542

Bridget, Order of the Most Holy Saviour (Sweden) (OSsS): Rev Mother Mary Joseph Puthempurakal OSsS, Bridgettine Convent, Fulmer Common Road, Iver Heath, Bucks SL0 0NR **Tel:** 01753-662645

Canonesses of St Augustine of the Mercy of Jesus (CROSA): Sr Eileen Pollard. Convent of Our Lady of Lourdes, Boarbank Hall, Grange-Over-Sands, Cumbria LA11 7NH **Tel:** 01539-532288 **Fax:** 01539-535386 **E-mail:** mail@boarbankhall.org.uk

Canonesses of St Augustine of the Mercy of Jesus (CROSA): Sr Eileen Pollard (CROSA): Sr Mary Gill. Park House, Haigh Road, Waterloo, Liverpool L22 3XS **Tel:** 0151-928 4343 **Fax:** 0151-949 0947

Canossian Daughters of Charity (FdCC): Sr Teresa Bonavetura *(Superior)*, Canossian Sisters, 2 Longland Close, Cheshunt, Walthamcross, Herts EN8 8LW **Tel:** 01992-621168

Capitanio Sisters (Sisters of Charity of Ss Bartolomea Capitanio and Vincenza Gerosa) (CS): Sr Maria Grazia Bianchi *Superior,* Nile Lodge, Queen's Walk, Ealing, London W5 1TJ **Tel/Fax:** 020-8997 3933 **E-mail:** stbcsisters@virgin.net

Carmelite Sisters of Corpus Christi (OCarm): Sr Teresa Joseph Pegus *Regional Superior,* 15 Southernhay Close, Knighton, Leicester LE2 3TW **Tel:** 0116-2704564

Carmelite Missionaries, (CM): Sr Isabel Hualde CM *(Superior)*, 189, Gloucester Place, London NW1 6BU **Tel:** 020-7262 4737 **Fax:** 020-7262 4737 **E-mail:** cmldn@yahoo.com

Charity of Nevers, Sisters of, (SCN): Sr Eileen Butler SCN, *Delegate and Area Leader,* 19 Oakengate, Fulwood, Preston, Lancs PR2 6RB **Tel:** 01772-793519 **Fax:** 01772-793494

Charity of Jesus and Mary, Sisters of (SCJM): Sr Helen O'Brien SCJM, *Provincial Superior*, Provincial House, 108 Spring Road, Letchworth, Herts SG6 3SL **Tel:** 01462-682153 **Fax:** 01462-623862 **E-mail:** helen@scjm.org

Charity of Our Lady Mother of Mercy, Sisters of (SCMM): Sr Sarah Mooney SCMM, *Provincial,* 16 Willsbrook Terrace, Raheen, Limerick, Ireland **Tel:** 0035 36 122 9984 **Fax:** 0035 36 122 9917 **E-mail:** willsbrook@eircom.net

Charity of Our Lady of Evron, Sisters of (SCE): Sr Clare Kelly SCE *Provincial Superior,* 'Shalom', 1 Adswood Lane West, Stockport SK3 8HT **Tel:** 0161 429 0260 **E-mail:** clarekelly234@yahoo.co.uk

Charity of St Jeanne Antide Thouret, Sisters of (SCJA): Sr Mary Bernadette Hunston. 'Bethany', 53 Bethune Road, Stoke Newington, London N16 5EE **Tel:** 020-8802 3430 **Fax:** 020-8800 5182

Charity of St Louis, Sisters of (SCSL): Sr Maria Goretti Grimes SCSL, *Delegate*, 220 Sheen Road, Richmond, Surrey TW10 5AN **Tel:** 020-8876 3300 **Fax:** 020-8392 6945 **E-mail:** scsl@blueyonder.co.uk

Charity of St Paul The Apostle, Sisters of (SP): Sr Thérèse Browne SP, *Superior General.* St Paul's Convent, 94 Selly Park Road, Selly Park, Birmingham B29 7LL. **Tel:** 0121-415 6101 **Fax:** 0121-414 1063 **E-mail:** theresebrowne@sellypark.org

Charity (of St Vincent de Paul) Daughters of (DC); also known as **Sisters of Charity: Sr Sarah King-Turner**, Provincial House, The Ridgeway, Mill Hill, London NW7 1EH **Tel:** 020-8906 3777 **Fax:** 020-8201 0542 **E-mail:** skingturner@aol.com

Charity, Missionaries of *(MC)*: UK Provincialate, 177 Bravington Road London W9 3AR **Tel:** 020 8960 2644

Charity, Religious Sisters of (RSC): Sr Jacinta Boland *(Superior)*, The Sisters of Charity, "Caritas", 55 Barrowgate Road, Chiswick, London W4 4QT **Tel:** 020-8995 1963 **Fax:** 020-8742 2175 **E-mail:** jboland@pobox.com

Christ, Sisters of: Sr Joyce Bone *Provincial Superior*, 11 London Road, Sittingbourne, Kent ME10 1NQ **Tel:** 01795 428744 **E-mail:** joycebone@iname,com

Christian Education, Institute of the Religious of (RCE): Sr Rosemary O'Looney *Provincial,* 3 Bushey Park House, Templeogue, Dublin 6W, Ireland **Tel:** 00-353 1 490 1668 **Fax:** 00-353 1 490 1101

Christian Instruction (St Gilda's), Sisters of (SCI): Sr Paula O'Leary, "Summerhill", Leecroft Road, Barnet, Herts EN5 2TH **Tel:**020-8449 2690 **E-mail:** paulaoleary@talk21.com

Christian Instruction, Religious of (RCI): Sr John Bosco Lloyd RCI *Provincial,* St Teresa's Convent, Effingham Hill, Dorking, Surrey RH5 6ST **Tel:** 01372-453810 **E-mail:** stcommunity6@yahoo.co.uk

Christian Retreat, Sisters of (CR): Sr Melanie Kingston *Regional Superior,* House of Prayer, 35 Seymour Road, East Molesey, Surrey KT8 0PB **Tel:** 020-8941 2313 **Fax:** 020-8941 2313 **E-mail:** houseofprayer@aol.com

Cistercians (Strict Observance) (OCSO): Mother Christine Wood, *(Abbess)* Holy Cross Abbey, Whitland, Wales SA34 0QX **Tel:** 01994-240725 **Fax:** 01994-241183 **E-mail:** hcawhit@tiscali.co.uk

Clare, Sisters of St (OSC): Sr Christine Ormsby, *Regional Superior.* St Clare's Convent, 197 Green Lane, Maghull, Liverpool L31 8BD **Tel:** 0151 531 6675 **E-mail:** claraanam@yahoo.co.uk

Columban, Missionary Sisters of (SSC): Sr Maura Lyden SSC, *Congregational Leader,* 55 Thornhill Road, Handsworth, Birmingham B21 9BT **Tel:** 0121 523 6090 **Fax:** 0121-551 2896 **E-mail:** mauralyden1@yahoo.com

Comboni Missionary Sisters (CMS): Sr Mariateresa Goffi CMS, *Provincial Leader,* 26 Black Boy Lane, London N15 3AR **Tel/Fax:** 020-8809 2893 **E-mail:** provlondon@combonisisters.co.uk

Community of Our Lady of Walsingham (COLW): Sr Camilla Oberding, *Community Servant,* Diocesan House of Prayer, Abbotswick, Navestock Side, Brentwood CM14 5SH **Tel:** 01277-373848 **Email:** comolw@hotmail.com **Website:** vocationsgroup.org.uk/colw

Consolata Missionary Sisters (MC): Sr Celestia Quaranta *Delegate Superior.* 13 The Avenue, Wanstead, London E11 2EE **Tel:** 020-8989 6186 **Fax:** 020-7837 2256

Cross, Daughters of the (FDLC): Sr Perpetua Foskin *Superior General.* Stoodley Knowle Convent, Ansteys Cove Road, Torquay, Devon TQ1 2JB **Tel/Fax:** 01803-290880 **E-mail:** perpetua@stoodleyknowle.devon.sch.uk

Cross of Liege, Daughters of the (FC): Sr Veronica Hagen FC, *Provincial,* St Wilfred's Convent, 29 Tite Street, Chelsea, London SW3 4JX **Tel:** 020-7351 2117 **Fax:** 020-7351 4634 **E-mail:** veronicahagen@ducross.org.uk

Cross and Passion, Sisters of the (CP): Sr Anne Cunningham CP, *Superior General.* The Generalate, Parkmount, 458 Bury New Road, Salford M7 4LH **Tel:** 0161-792 0333 **Fax:** 0161-792 0760 **E-mail:** anne@generalate.fhbnet.co.uk

Sr Francis Cullen CP, *Provincial,* Cross and Passion Convent, 299 Boarshaw Road, Middleton, Manchester M24 2PF **Tel:** 0161-655 3184 **Fax:** 0161-654 7380 **E-mail:** francis@crossandpassion.plus.com

Divine Charity, Daughters of (FDC): Sr Thomas More Prentice FDC, *Provincial,* Convent of the Sacred Heart, 17 Mangate Street, Swaffham, Norfolk PE37 7QW **Tel:** 01760 724577 **E-mail:** sisterthomasmore@yahoo.co.uk

Daughters of Divine Love: Sr Eunice Offor, Regional House, 70 Kempshott Road, London SW16 5LH **Tel:** 020-8765 8060 **Fax:** 020-8764 3623

Daughters of Mary, Mother of Mercy (DMMM): Sr Mary Stella Okeadu, 16 St Margaret's Road, Edgware, Middlesex HA8 9UP **Tel:** 020-8958 6691

Divine Saviour (Salvatorians), Sisters of the (SDS): Sr. Maria Gorreti Comerford SDS, *Regional Superior,* Divine Saviour Convent, Dillon Court, Nethan Road, Redfield, Bristol BS5 9PF **Tel:** 0117-941 3774

Dominican Missionary Sisters of The Sacred Heart of Jesus (OP): Sr Reingard Berger, 4 Gossops Green Lane, Gossops Green, Crawley, W. Sussex RH11 8BJ **Tel:** 01293-524067 **Fax:** 01293-527140 **E-mail:** reingard@domgen,uk.net

Dominican Sisters (King William's Town), of St Catherine of Siena (OP): St Martin's Convent, Stoke Golding, near Nuneaton, Warks CV13 6HT **Tel:** 01455-212207 **Fax:** 01455-213476 **E-mail:** stmartinop@aol.com

Dominican Sisters (Newcastle) (OP): Sr Ann Cunningham OP, *Superior General,* Rosary Priory, 93 Elstree Road, Bushey Heath, Bushey WD23 4EE **Tel:** 020-8950 3629 **Fax:** 020-8950 7991 **E-mail:** anncunningham@rosarypriory.co.uk

Dominican Sisters (Oakford) (OP): Sr Carol Mouat OP (*District Leader),* Hawkstone Hall, Marchamley, Shrewsbury SY4 5LG **Tel:** 01630-685242 **E-mail:** junemouat65@hotmail.com

Dominican Sisters (Stone), of St Catherine of Siena (English) (OP): Sr Mary Pauline Burling, *Prioress General.* The Generalate, 21 Station Road, Stone, Staffs ST15 8EN **Tel:** 01785-812091 **Fax:** 01785-819269 **E-mail:** bpburling@googlemail.com

Dominican Sisters, of the Presentation of Our Lady (Tours) (OP): Sr Veronica Mary Jackson, Presentation Convent, 73 Easthampstead Road, Wokingham, Berks RG40 2ED

Tel: 0118-978 2553 **Fax:** 0118-989 3822
E-mail: poussepin@aol.com

Dominican Sisters, of St Joseph (OP): Sr Rosaleen M.S. Shaw OP, St Dominic's Priory, Shirley Holms, Lymington, Hants SO41 8NH
Tel: 01590 68 1874 **Fax:** 01590 68 1875
E-mail: dominican.sisters@talk21.com

Dorothy, Sisters of St (SSD): Sr Pauline Taylor, St Dorothy's Convent, Frognal House, 99 Frognal, Hampstead, London NW3 6XR
Tel: 020-7794 6893 **Fax:** 020-7435 0724
E-mail: st.dorothy@talktalk.net

Faithful Companions of Jesus (fcJ): Sr Margarita Byron, Provincialate, 24 Singleton Road, Salford, Lancs M7 4WL
Tel: 0161-792 2267 **Fax:** 0161-708 9683

Francis, Sisters of St: Sr Kathleen Harmon St Francis House, 20 Leslie Road, Forest Fields, Nottingham NG7 6PD
Tel: 0115-978 3889 **Fax:** 0115-979 4772
E-mail: sof@stfrschool.freeserve.co.uk

Franciscan Sisters Minoress (FSM): Sr Columba Redmond, *Superior General.* St Clare's Franciscan Convent, 52 Dalby Road, Melton Mowbray, Leics LE13 0BP
Tel: 01664-562422 **Fax:** 01664-565131
E-mail: srcolumba@columba52.plus.com

Franciscan Missionaries of Mary (FMM): Sr Joan Doyle FMM. 5 Vaughan Avenue, Shepherds Bush, London, W6 0XS
Tel: 020-8748 4077 **Fax:** 020-8741 9618
E-mail: provsecuk@aol.com

Franciscan Missionaries of St Joseph (FMSJ): Sr Joan O'Gorman *Superior General,* St Joseph's Convent, 150 Greenleach Lane, Worsley, Manchester M28 2TS **Tel:** 0161-794 1062
Fax: 0161-794 6420 **E-mail:** fmsj@aol.com

Franciscan Missionaries of the Divine Motherhood (FMDM): Sr Teresa Mitchell SC, *Congregational Leader,* Ladywell Convent, Ashstead Lane, Godalming, Surrey GU7 1ST
Tel: 01483-425775 **Fax:** 01483-426244
E-mail: teresamitchell@ladywell.org.uk
Sr Philomena Hynes FMDM, St Clares, 19 West Side, Clapham Common, London SW4 9AL **Tel:** 020 7350 1790

*__Franciscan Missionary Sisters of the Immaculate Conception (MFIC): Sr M Agatha McEvoy (MFIC)__, *Regional Superior,* Missionary Franciscan Sisters, Diocesan House of Prayer, Abbotswick, Navestock Side, Brentwood, Essex CM14 5SH **Tel:** 01277-373959
Fax: 01277-375327
E-mail: Braintreesisters@aol.com

Franciscan Missionary Sisters for Africa (FMSA): Sr Annetta Heeran *(Delegate),* 52 Madeira Park, Tunbridge Wells, Kent TN2 5SY **Tel:** 01892-539789
E-mail: aheeran38@talktalk.net

Franciscan Missionary Sisters of Littlehampton (FMSL): Sr Anastasia McGonagle, *Superior General.* St Joseph's Franciscan Convent, East Street, Littlehampton, W Sussex, BN17 6AU
Tel: 01903-714039 **Fax:** 01903-731097
E-mail: anastasia@franciscan.co.uk

Franciscan Sisters of Mill Hill (OSF): Sr Catherine McGovern OSF, *Superior General.* St Francis Cottage, The Ridgeway, Mill Hill, London NW7 4ER
Tel: 020-8959 1364 **Fax:** 020-8906 4660

Franciscan Sisters of St Mary of the Angels (FSMA): Sr Evelyn Cardoz *(Superior General)* Park Place Pastoral Centre, Winchester Road, Wickham, Fareham, Hants PO17 5HA
Tel: 01329-833043 **Fax:** 01329-832226
E-mail: evelyncardoz@aol.com

Franciscan Sisters of the Immaculate Conception (OSF): Sr Celestine McKenna OSF, St Anthony's Convent, 93 Belle Vue Road, Cinderford, Glos G14 2AA
Tel: 01594-822310 **Fax:** 01594-824799
E-mail: sister@gl142aa.fsnet.com.uk

Fraternidad Missionera Verbum Dei: Sr Maria De La Portilla FMVD, Verbum Dei Centre, Nunnery Lane, Carrisbrooke, Isle of Wight PO30 1YR **Tel:** 01983-529554
E-mail: vdeicentre@islewight.co.uk

Good Shepherd, Congregation of Our Lady of Charity of the (RGS): Sr Anne Josephine Carr *Provincial Leader,* Good Shepherd Provincialate, 61 East End Road, East Finchley, London N2 0SF
Tel: 020-8346 8100 **Fax:** 020-8343 0970
E-mail: rgslondon@lineone.net

Handmaids of the Holy Child Jesus (HHCJ): Sr Josephine Udie. 50 Santos Road, Wandsworth, London SW18 1NS
Tel: 020-8874 2387

Heart of Mary, Daughters of the (DHM): The Sisters *Provincial Superior,* 41 Murray Road, Wimbledon, London SW19 4PD
Tel: 020-8946 3564 **Fax:** 020-8944 6595

Helpers of the Holy Souls (HHS): Sr Elizabeth Kelly *(Provincial),* 32 St Agnes Road, Huyton, Liverpool L36 5TA
Tel/Fax: 0151-480 7904
E-mail: hhselizabeth@aol.com

Holy Child Jesus, Society of the (SHCJ): Sr Pauline Darby, 10 Holland Villas Road, London W14 8BP **Tel:** 020-7603 2133
Fax: 020-7602 7304
E-mail: pmdarbymk@btinternet.com

Holy Cross, Sisters of the (HC): Sr Imelda Fleming *(Superior)*, Holy Cross Provincialate, 'Assisi', 82 The Avenue, Ealing, London W13 8LB
Tel/Fax: 020-8991 0153

E-mail: holycross@hcengland.co.uk
Holy Family (St Emilie de Rodat), Sisters of the (RHF): Sr Irena Madej *Provincial,* Convent of the Holy Family, 35/36 Albert Square, Stockwell, London SW8 1BZ **Tel:** 020-7582 2016 **Fax:** 020-7735 6568 **E-mail:** irena.hfe@btinternet.com
Holy Family of Bordeaux, Sisters of the (HFB): Sr Aine Hayde HFB *Provincial Leader,* Holy Family Provincial House, 2 Aberdare Gardens, London NW6 3PX **Tel:** 020-7624 7573 **Fax:** 020-7625 8984 **E-mail:** ainehayde@virgin.net
Holy Family of Nazareth, Sisters of the (CSFN): Sr Mary James O'Hora MSHR, *(Delegate).* Holy Family Convent, 52 London Road, Enfield, Middlesex EN2 6EN **Tel:** 020-8363 4483 **Fax:** 020-8363 2583 **E-mail:** maryoh@fsmail.net
Holy Rosary, Missionary Sisters of (MSHR): Sr Mary Coleman MSHR *(Major Superior),* 42 Westpark, Artane, Dublin 5, Ireland **Tel:** 00353-1 851 0010 **Fax:** 00353-1 818 7494 **Sr Ruth Kidson** 44 Graveston Road, Coventry CV6 1GZ **Tel:** 02476 335319 **Conchita McDonnell MSHR (MS)**, 42 Westpark, Artane, Dublin 5 Ireland **Tel:** 003531 851 0010 **Fax:** 003531 818 7494
Holy Sepulchre, Canonesses of the (CRSS): Sr Teresa Lenahan CRSS, 48 Priory Street, Colchester, Essex CO1 2QB **Tel:** 01206-869479 **Fax:** 01206-869479 **E-mail:** teresalenahan@hotmail.com
Holy Spirit, Daughters of the (DHS): Sr Dympna Connolly *Provincial Superior,* 22 Holyrood Rd, Northampton NN5 7AH **Tel/Fax:** 01604-587423 **E-mail:** provincial.office@virgin.net
Holy Spirit, Missionary Sisters Servants of the (SSpS): Sr Carmen Lee, 143 Philipsburgh Avenue, Fairview, Dublin 3 **Tel:** 00353 (0) 836 9383
Holy Trinity, Sisters of the (CSST): Sr Jeanne Madeleine Timmins, Holy Trinity Convent, 81 Plaistow Lane, Bromley, Kent BR1 3LL **Tel:** 020-8402 2785 **Fax:** 020-8466 6018 **E-mail:** sisterjmt@tiscali.co.uk
Immaculate Conception, Sisters of the (IMC): Sr Marie-Elisabeth Pronost IMC *(Superior),* Straven Platdouet Road, St Clements, Jersey, Channel Islands JE2 6PN **Tel/Fax:** 01534-734997
Infant Jesus Sisters (IJS): Sr Marie Pitcher *(Superior General)*, 22 Hexham Close, Worth, Crawley, West Sussex R10 7TZ **Tel:** 01293-881874 **Fax:** 01293-881875 **Sr Rosemary Barter** *(Provincial),* 56 St Lawrence Road, Clontarf, Dublin 3, Ireland **Tel:** 00353 1 833 8930 **Fax:** 00353 1 853 0857
Jesus and Mary, Religious of (RJM): Sr Judith Mary Cuff *Provincialate*, 63 Orwell Road, Felixstowe, Suffolk IP11 7PP **Tel:** 01394 282386 **Fax:** 01394-279886
Jesus, Congregation of (CJ): Sr Jane Livesey CJ *Provincial Superior,* 8 Brookside, Cambridge CB2 1JE **Tel/Fax:** 01223-302449 **E-mail:** jflcj@virgin.net
Jesus, Daughters of (DJ): Sr Anne Thompson *Provincial*, The Provincial Office, Blakenhall, 55 Nightingale Road, Rickmansworth, Herts WD3 7BU **Tel:** 01923-897386 **Fax:** 01923-897412 **E-mail:** Thompsona@ukonline.co.uk
Jesus, Little Sisters of (LS): Sr Deidre Dowling *Regional Superior*, 18 Donard View, Bishop's Court, Downpatrick, Co. Down BT30 7BN **Tel:** 02844-841085 **E-mail:** deidre30@btopenworld.com
John of God, Sisters of St (SJG): Sr Agnes Miller. Convent of St John of God, 103 Black Boy Lane, London N15 3AS **Tel/Fax:** 020-8374 1693 **E-mail:** amillersjg@blueyonder.co.uk
Joseph of Annecy, Sisters of St (SSJA): Sr Alice Brennan *(Province Leader),* Provincialate SSJA, 173 Chepstow Road, Newport NP19 8GH **Tel:** 01633-245075 **Fax:** 01633-245085 **E-mail:** alice@sistersofstjoseph.co.uk
Joseph of Lyon, Sisters of St (SSJL): Sr Anne Tynan, St Joseph's Convent, Haunton, Nr Tamworth, Staffs B79 9HL **Tel:** 01827-373453 **Fax:** 01827-373628 **E-mail:** anne.tynan@tiscali.co.uk
Joseph of Cluny, Sisters of St (SJC): Sr Clare Little, St Joseph's Convent, Lichfield Road, Stafford ST17 4LG **Tel/Fax:** 01785-223836
Joseph of Peace, Sisters of St (CSJP): Sr Laurett Bergin *(Superior),* Sacred Heart Provincial House, 61 Station Road, Rearsby, Leicester LE7 4YY **Tel:** 01644-424563 **Fax:** 01664-423819 **E-mail:** provleader@csjpuk.wanadoo.co.uk
Joseph of Tarbes, Sisters of St (RSJT): Sr Andrea Burrows SJT *Sector Superior,* St Joseph's Convent, 33 Almada Gdns, Tettenhall, Wolverhampton WV6 9EX **Tel:** 01902-751614 **Fax:** 01902-744532 **E-mail:** stjosephsconvent2@btinternet.com
Joseph of the Apparition, Sister of St (SJA): Sr. Patricia Hughes, Provincial House, Ryley's Lane, Alderley Edge, Cheshire SK9 7UU **Tel/Fax:** 01625-585655 **E-mail:** prov@sjoa.fsnet.co.uk
La Retraite, Sisters of (RLR): Sr Barbara Stafford, 722 Bristol South End, Bedminster BS3 5BH **Tel:** 0117 953 3544 **E-mail:** barbarastaffordrlr@eirecom.net

La Sagesse, Sisters of (Congregation of the Daughers of Wisdom): Sr Jean Quinn *Provincial Administration,* Wisdom House, Romsey, Hampshire SO51 8EL **Tel:** 01794-830206 **Fax:** 01794-830614 **E-mail:** jquinn@wisdomhouseromsey.co.uk

La Sainte Union Des Sacres Coeurs, Congregation of (LSU): Sr Una Burke. LSU Provincialate, 53 Croftdown Road, London NW5 1EL **Tel:** 020-7482 7225 **Fax:** 020-7485 4760 **E-mail:** lsu@ahtprovince.f2s.com

Little Ones, Sisters of the (SLO): Sr Agnes Vernon SLO, *Sister Superior,* 14 Holly Road, Fairfield, Liverpool L7 0LH **Tel:** 0151-260 4431 **E-mail:** dorothyhindle@btinternet.com

Lucy, Sisters of St (Pontifical Institute Religious Teachers Filippini) (MPF): Sr Dorothy Di Cristofaro, Convent of St Lucy, Medstead, Alton, Hants GU34 5LL **Tel:** 01420-563562 **Fax:** 01420-561341 **E-mail:** stlucysconvent@ukonline.co.uk

Marcellina, Sisters of St (IM): Sr Giuliana Carrara IM, Hampstead Towers, 6 Ellerdale Road, London NW3 6BD **Tel:** 020-7435 0181 **Fax:** 020-7433 3459 **E-mail:** stmarcellina@btconnect.com

Marie Auxiliatrice, Sisters of (RMA), Sr Anne-Marie Farrell 20 Elgin Road, London N22 7UE **Tel:** 020-8888 0094 **Fax:** 020-8881 5496 **E-mail:** annemarie@marieauux.org

Marie de la Providence Sisters of St (SMP): Sr Mary Patrick Webb *Regional Delegate,* 15 Burgess Road, Basingstoke, Hants RG21 5NP **Tel:** 01256-321276 **Fax:** 01256-323348 **E-mail:** avery.webb@btopenworld.com

Marie Reparatrice, Society of (SMR): Sr Maureen Peart (Delegate), Marie Reparatrice, 115 Ridgway, London SW19 4RB **Tel/Fax:** 020-8946 1088 **Fax:** 020-8947 9820 **E-mail:** maureen.peart@smr.org

Marist Sisters (SM): Sr Mary Frances Boyle SM, *Provincial Superior,* Provincial House, 55 Thetford Road, New Malden, Surrey KT3 5OP **Tel:** 020-8336 2858 **Fax:** 020-8336 0193 **Email:** prosupsm@sagnet.co.uk

Martha, Sisters of St: Cécile Archer RSM, St Martha's Convent, The Green, Rottingdean, East Sussex BN2 7HA **Tel:** 01273-302354

Mary and Joseph, Daughters of (DMJ): Sr Margaret Eason. 55 Fitzjames Avenue, Croydon, Surrey CR0 5DN **Tel:** 020-8654 8041 **Fax:** 020-8655 4337 **E-mail:** dmjregional@yahoo.couk

Mary Help of Christians (Salesians), Daughters of (FMA): Sr Elizabeth Purcell. *Provincial,* 13 Streatham Common North, London SW16 3HG **Tel:** 020-8677 4573 **Fax:** 020-8677 4523 **E-mail:** fmaprovincial@ukonline.co.uk

Mary Immaculate, Religious of (RMI): Sr Marysa Gomez, 15/16 Southwell Gardens, London, SW7 4RL **Tel:** 020-7373 3869 **E-mail:** rmilondon@btconnect.com

Mary of Namur, Sisters of St (SSMN): Sr Margaret Young SSMN 25 Newsham Drive, Liverpool L6 7UG **Tel:** 0151-263 1492 **E-mail:** margaret954@btinternet.com

Mary, Little Company of (LCM): Sr Margaret Watson *(Province Leader),* LCM, 93 Gunnersby Avenue, Ealing, London W5 4LR **Tel:** 020-8752 1373 **Fax:** 020-8752 0449 **E-mail:** sisterm@btinternet.com **Sr Jeannette Connell** *Congregational Leader,* The Generalate, 28 Trinity Crescent, London SW17 7AE **Tel:** 020-8682 0928 **Fax:** 020-8682 0552 **E-mail:** jconnell@lcmgeneralate.org

Mary, Mother of the Church, Congregation of: Sr Margaret Rose McHale CMMC, Mater Ecclesiase Convent, Street Ashton, Stretton-under-Fosse, Rugby CV23 0PJ **Tel:** 01788 833825

Mary, Servants of (OSM): Sr Rachel O'Riordan OSM *(Superior General).* St Joseph's Priory, Harrow Road West, Dorking, Surrey RH4 3BE **Tel:** 01306-888935 **Fax:** 01306-742720 **E-mail:** rachelosm@ntlworld.com **Sr Catherine Ryan OSM, Tel:** 01306-889821 **Fax:** 01306-640125

Mary, The Handmaids of (SdeM): Sr Lourdes Susaeta. 2 Atkins Road, Clapham Park, London SW5 0AB **Tel:** 020-8673 1247 **Fax:** 020-8673 5223

Medical Missionaries of Mary (MMM): Sr Mary Howard *Area Leader,* 2 Denbigh Road, Ealing, London W13 8PX **Tel:** 020-8998 1725 **E-mail:** mmmealing37@yahoo.co.uk

Medical Mission Sisters (MMS): Medical Mission Sisters, 41 Chatsworth Gardens, Acton, London W3 9LP **Tel:** 020-8992 6444 **Fax:** 020-8896 2397 **Sr Josephine Brannigan** *(Sector Co-ordinator).* Medical Mission Sisters, 109 Clitherow Avenue, Hanwell, London W7 2BL **Tel:** 020-8567 1504 **E-mail:** districtengland@btinternet.com

Mercy, Institute of Our Lady of (RSM): Sr Patricia Bell, *Institute Leader,* Convent of Mercy Generalate, Cemetery Road, Yeadon, Leeds LS19 7UR **Tel:** 0113-250 0253 **Fax:** 0113-250 0241 **E-mail:** patricia.bell@ ourladyofmercy.org.uk

Mercy, (English Federation) Sisters of (RSM): Gravesend: **Sr Elizabeth O'Hara** *Superior,* Convent of Mercy, Hillside Drive, Gravesend, Kent DA12 1NY **Tel:** 01474-569565 **E-mail:** sisterelizabethohara@yahoo.co.uk Midhurst: **Sr Patricia McGovern RSM**. Convent of Mercy, Petersfield Road, Midhurst, W. Sussex GU29 9JN **Tel:** 01730-816600 **Fax:** 01730-810788 **E-mail:** mcgovernpatricia@hotmail.com Sunderland: **Sr Dolores Magee**, 'Oak Lea', Tunstall Road, Sunderland, Tyne and Wear SR2 7JR **Tel/Fax:** 0191-514 1502

Mercy (the Union), Sisters of (RSM): Sr Phillomena Bowers *Congregational Leader,* The Generalate, St Edward's Convent, 11 Harewood Avenue, London NW1 6LD **Tel:** 020-7402 7785 **Fax:** 020-7224 8551 **E-mail:** pbowers31@aol.com

Missionary Sisters of the Immaculate (PIME): Sr Angelinia Marchesi PIME (*Local Superior)*, Regina Pacis Convent, 10 Chiswick Lane, London W4 2JE **Tel:** 020-8994 2053 **Fax:** 020-8747 9354 **E-mail:** mislondon@srs1234.co.uk

Nazareth, Sisters of (CSN): Sr Mary Anne Monaghan, Nazareth House, Hammersmith Road, London W6 8DB **Tel:** 020-8748 3549 **Fax:** 020-8741 4287 **E-mail:** generalate@nazhammersmith.org.uk

Notre Dame de Namur, Sisters of (SND): Sr Kathleen McGhee *Provincial Moderator,* 4 Lancaster Court, Lancaster Lane, Parbold, Lancashire WN8 7HS **Tel:** 01257-465000 **Fax:** 01257-464544 **E-mail:**kmcgheepar@aol.com

Notre Dame, School Sisters of (SSND): Sr Eileen Donohoe *(Delegate)*, St Aidan's Convent, 92 Adswood Convent, Huyton, Liverpool L36 7XR **Tel:** 0151-481 0324 **Fax:** 0151-489 0125 **E-mail:** eileen_donohoe@yahoo.co.uk

Our Lady (Canonesses of St Augustine), Congregation of (CSA): Sr Martina Adyeri Boylan CSA *(Provincial),* New Horizons, 18/19 Stewarton Terrace, Wishaw, Lanarkshire ML2 8AJ **Tel:** 01698 372278 **E-mail:** martina@wishaw101.freeserve.co.uk

Our Lady, Sisters of (SND): Sr Marion Connaughty *Area Leader,* Convent of 'The Crossways', 131 Hawthorn Road, Kettering, Northants NN15 7HU **Tel:** 01536-513711 **Fax:** 01536-392599 **E-mail:** marionconnaughty@hotmail.com

Our Lady of Africa, Missionary Sisters of Sr Catherine Booth (MSOLA) *Regional Superior*. 5 Charlebury Grove, Ealing, London W5 2DY **Tel:** 020-8998 5017 **E-mail:** regmsolauk@aol.com

Our Lady of the Apostles, Sisters of (OLA). Sr Mary Crowley OLA, *(Provincial Leader),* 10 Vincent Road, Westgreen, Tottenham N15 3QH **Tel:** 020-8888 9036

Our Lady of Charity, Sisters of (OLC): Sr Charlotte Cassidy. 'Fairlight', The Avenue, North Ascot, Berks SL5 7LY **Tel:** 01344-626622 **E-mail:** charlotte@fairlightolc.plus.com

Our Lady of Fidelity, Sisters of (OLF): Sr Betty-Mary Hampson OLF *(Superior),* 15-17 Marten Road, Folkestone, Kent CT20 2JR **Tel:** 01303-253713 **Fax:** 01303-247553

Our Lady of Pity, Sisters of (CLP): Sr Veronica Thompson, St John's Convent, Linden Hill Lane, Kiln Green, Reading, Berks RG10 9XP **Tel:** 0118-949 2964

Our Lady of Sion, Sisters of (NDS): Sr Brenda McCole, 49 St Peter's Road, Harbourne, Birmingham B17 0AU **Tel:** 0121 426 6679 **E-mail:** brendamccole@btinternet.com

Our Lady of the Cenacle, Sisters of (rc): Sr Christine Warrington rc, *(Provincial),* Cenacle Provincialate, Tithebarn Grove, Lance Lane, Liverpool L15 6TW **Tel:** 0151-738 0099 **Fax:** 0151-738 0044 **E-mail:** provcenacle@btconnect.com

Our Lady of the Missions, Congregation of (RNDM): Sr Louise Shields, *Province Leader,* 108 Spencer Road, Wealdstone, Middlesex HA3 7AR **Tel:** 020 8861 4174 **Fax:** 020-8424 2133

Our Lady of the Sacred Heart, Daughters of (FDNSC): Sr Catherine Mulcahy, 255 Canon Hill Lane, London SW20 9DB **Tel:** 020-8542 5052 **Fax:** 020-8543 3613

Pallottine Missionary Sisters (SAC): Sr Marie Keegan *Provincial Superior,* 52 Park Mount Drive, Macclesfield, Cheshire SK11 8NT **Tel:** 01625-616459 **Fax:** 01625-869080

Paul de Chartres, Sisters of St (SPC): Sr Rose Mary Clifford. 30 Aberdeen Park, London N5 2BL **Tel:** 020-7359 1712 **Fax:** 020-7704 2555

Paul, Daughters of St (FSP): Sr Catherine Skelton. Daughters of St Paul, Middle Green, Slough SL3 6BS **Tel:** 01753-577629 **Fax:** 01753-511809 **E-mail:** catherine@pauline-uk.org **Website:** www.pauline-uk.org

Peter Claver, Missionary Sisters of St (MSSPC): Sr Assumpta Giertych, 89 Shortlands Road, Bromley, Kent BR2 0JL **Tel:** 020-8313 3915 **Fax:** 020-8313 3915 **E-mail:** claversisters@catholic.org

Poor Child Jesus, Sisters of the (PCJ):

Sr Maire Morris *(Provincial Administration)*, 7 The Cloisters, Daventry Road, Southam, Warwickshire CV47 1FE **Tel/Fax:** 01926-812338 **E-mail:** maire@manete-in-me.org

***Poor Clares (Colettines) (OSC): Sr Stephanie Davidson**, St Clare's Convent, 15 Glyndebourne Gardens, Corby, Northants NN18 0QA **Tel:** 01536-741425 **Fax:** 01536-743573

Poor Handmaids of Jesus Christ (PHJC): Sr Anthony O'Rourke, St Joseph's Convent, Westminster House, Watford Way, Hendon, London NW4 4TY **Tel/Fax:** 020-8202 7626 **E-mail:** winifred.orourke@btinternet.com

Poor, Little Sisters of the (LSP): Sr Stephen Henry *Provincial*, St Peter's, 2a Meadow Road, London SW8 1QH **Tel:** 020-7735 0788 **Fax:** 020-7582 0973 **E-mail:** mplond@aol.com

Poor Servants of the Mother of God (SMG): Sr Mary Whelan *Superior General*, Maryfield Convent, Mount Angelus Road, Roehampton, London SW15 4JA **Tel:** 020-8788 4351 **Fax:** 020-8789 9281 **E-mail:** mary.whelan@psmgs.com **Sr Margaret O'Shea** *Regional Leader*, Taylor House, 2-4 The Butts, Brentford, Middx TW8 8BQ **Tel:** 020-8568 6306 **E-mail:** margaret.oshea@psmgs.org

Poor Sisters of Nazareth (CSN): Sr Mary Anne Monaghan *Nazareth House*, 173-175, Hammersmith, London W6 8DB **Tel:** 020-8748 3549 **Fax:** 0208-741 4287

***Presentation of Mary (Castelgandolfo), Sisters of the (PM): Sr Guy-Marie Lamontagne**, Mount St Mary's Convent, Wonford Road, Exeter, Devon EX2 4PF **Tel:** 01392-433301 **Fax:** 01392-490859

Presentation Sisters (Union) (PBVM): Sr Susan Richert *Provincial Leader*, Provincial House, 27 Bushey Close, Woodrow North, Redditch B98 7TU **Tel:** 01527 501568 **E-mail:** eprov@pbvmengland.co.uk

Providence (Rosminians), Sisters of (SPR): Sr Bernadette Larkin *Mother Provincial*, 45 Kerr Place, Old Brewery Close, Walton Street, Aylesbury HP21 7BB **Tel:** 01296 487368

Providence (Rouen), Sisters of (SOP): Sr Patricia McCaffrey IJPR, Convent of Providence, 10 Sutton Avenue, Seaford, E Sussex BH25 4LA **Tel:** 01323-896954 **E-mail:** srpatmcc@yahoo.co.uk

Providence (Ruille-Sur-Loir), Sisters of (SP): Sr Martine Meuwissen, *Provincial*. c/o Sr Mary Agnes Crick SP, The Mount Wragby Road, Lincoln LN2 5SL **Tel:** 01522-540894 **Sr Ann Heaney** *(Delegate)*. 78 Oakfield, Road, Stroud Green, London N4 4LB **Tel/Fax:** 020-8340 1088

Providence and of the Immaculate Conception, Sisters of (SPIC): Sr Marie Catherine Flannigan, Bartrams Convent, Rowland Hill Street, Hampstead, London NW3 2AD **Tel:** 020-7794 4504 **Fax:** 020-7794 8644

Resurrection, Sisters of the (CR): Sr Mary Pauline Hebron *Delegate*, 18 Carlton Road, London W5 2AW **Tel:** 020-8810 6241 **Fax:** 020-8998 9804 **E-mail:** ealingcrsisters@fsnet.co.uk

Sacred Heart (Cabrini), Missionary Sisters of the (MSC): Sr Benedict O'Donnell, Convent of the Sacred Heart, Honor Oak, Forest Hill Road, London SE23 3LE **Tel:** 020-8699 2735 **Fax:** 020-8699 1930

Sacred Heart of Jesus (St Aubin), Sisters of the (SSHJ): Sr Mary Ann Bear. The Priory, 85 Old High Street, Headington, Oxford OX3 9HT **Tel:** 01865-761389 **E-mail:** mapriory@yahoo.co.uk

Sacred Heart of Jesus (St Jacut), Sisters of the (SSCJ): Sr Mary Paul Ewen, *Provincial*, Provincial House, 6 Oakleigh Park South, Whetstone, London N20 9JU **Tel/Fax:** 020-8445 9299 **E-mail:** avewen@fsmail.net

Sacred Heart of Jesus, Handmaids Of the (ACI): Sr Patricia Lynch *Provincial Superior*, 25 St Edmund's Terrace, London NW8 7PY **Tel:** 020-7722 2756 **Fax:** 020-7586 3454 **E-mail:** trishaci@yahoo.com

Sacred Heart of Jesus, Hospitaller Sisters of the (HSC): Sr Maria Lourdes Sanz *Provincial Superior*, 42 Roland Gardens, London SW7 3PW **Tel:** 020-7373 3054 **Fax:** 020-7259 2446 **E-mail:** provincial@hsc-uk.org

Sacred Heart, Society of the (RScJ): Sr Margaret Wilson, 3 Bute Gardens, Hammersmith, London W6 7DR **Tel:** 020-8748-9353 **Fax:** 020-8748 6814 **E-mail:** margaretwilsonrscj@hotmail.com

Sacred Hearts of Jesus and Mary (Chigwell), Sisters of the (SSHJM): Sr Catherine Collins *(Superior General)*, Chigwell Convent, 803 Chigwell Road, Woodford Bridge, Essex IG8 8AU **Tel:** 020-8504 1624 **Fax:** 020-8559 2149 **E-mail:** shjmleader@shjm.org.uk

Sacred Hearts of Jesus and Mary, Congregation of the (SSCC): Sr Aileen Kennedy *Provincial Superior*, 139 Southampton Way, London SE5 7EW **Tel:** 020 7701 5277 **E-mail:** aileenkennedysscc@hotmail.com

Sacred Heart of Mary (Beziers), Religious of the (RSHM): Sr Barbara Bailey Provincial House. 64 Little Ealing Lane,

London W5 4XF **Tel:** 020-8567 3148 **Fax:** 020-8579 8072 **E-mail:** provincial@rshmloondon.org

Salesian Sisters of St John Bosco (Daughters of Mary Help of Christians) (FMA): Sr Elizabeth Purcell FMA (Provincial), 13 Streatham Common North, London SW16 3HG **Tel:** 020-86774573 **E-mail:** fmaprovincial@ukonline.co.uk

Saviour and the Blessed Virgin, Sisters of the (CSBV): Sr Jacqueline Brain *Area Leader,* 61 New Road, Chiseldon, Swindon, SN4 0PE **Tel:** 01793-740606

St Louis, Sisters of (SSL): Sr Margaret Healy SSL, 16 Chaucer Close, New Southgate, London N11 1AU **Tel:** 020-8361 1935 **E-mail:** margarethg7@btinternet.com

Temple, Sisters of the (JT): Sr Marie-Louise Le Vern, St Angela's Convent, 5 Litfield Place, Clifton, Bristol BS8 3UL **Tel:** 0117-973 5436 **Fax:** 0117-970 6844 **E-mail:** stangelas1@btconnect.com

Ursulines of Brentwood (OSU), Sr Margaret Soper *(Superior General),* Ursuline Generalate, 93 Queens Road, Brentwood, Essex CM14 4EY **Tel:** 01277-260156 **Fax:** 01277-263618

Ursulines of Jesus (UJ): Sr Hilary Brown *Provincial Superior,* The Provincialate, 11 Amhurst Park, Stamford Hill, London N16 5DH **Tel:** 020-8802 0256 **Fax:** 020-8809 7261 **E-mail:** hilaryuj@tiscali.couk

Ursulines of the Roman Union (OSU): Sr Maureen Maloney *Provincial,* Ursuline Provincialate, 66 Crooms Hill, Greenwich, London SE10 8HG **Tel:** 020-8293 0044 **Fax:** 020-8269 2450

Union of Irish Ursulines (UIU): Sr Aloysius Hourigan *(Superior)*, Ursuline Convent, 1 Glamorgan Street, Brecon, Powys LD3 7DN **Tel:** 01874-622080 **E-mail:** havard1556@btopenworld.com

Vocations Sisters (VS): 'Meristem', 25 Coltsfood Drive, Guildford, Surrey GU1 1YH **Tel:** 01483-570413

RELIGIOUS ORDERS, CONGREGATIONS, SOCIETIES, etc. REPRESENTED IN ENGLAND AND WALES

(The references are to dioceses. The list of Congregations given at the end of each diocese contains the parishes in which individual monasteries or convents are situated. For full addresses see the parishes concerned.)

■ MEN

Africa, Society of Missionaries of (MAfr): Westminster, Birmingham, Lancaster.

African Missions, Society of (of Lyons, SMA): Westminster, Brentwood, Liverpool, Salford.

Alexian Brothers (CFA): Westminster, Salford.

Assumptionists (Augustinians of the Assumption AA): Westminster, Northampton.

Augustinian Recollects (OAR): Westminster, Plymouth.

Augustinians (OSA): Westminster, Birmingham, East Anglia, Liverpool.

Benedictines Confederated (OSB):
English Congregation: Westminster, Arundel & Brighton, Birmingham, Cardiff, Clifton, East Anglia, Hexham & Newcastle, Lancaster, Leeds, Liverpool, Menevia, Middlesbrough, Plymouth, Portsmouth, Salford.
Congregation of Solesmes: Portsmouth.
Congregation of Subiaco: Clifton, Southwark, Portsmouth.
Olivetan Congregation: Westminster, Northampton.

Blessed Sacrament Congregation (SSS): Liverpool.

Camillians (Order of St Camillus, OS Cam): Westminster, Hexham & Newcastle.

Canons Regular of the Immaculate Conception (CRIC): Northampton.

Canons Regular of the Lateran (CRL): Southwark.

Carmelites (OCarm): Clifton, Menevia, Middlesbrough, Southwark, Westminster.

Carmelites, Discalced (OCD): Westminster, Lancaster, Northampton, Portsmouth.

Carthusians (OCart): Arundel & Brighton.

Charity, Brothers of (FC): Liverpool.

Charity, Brother Missionaries of: Salford.

Charity, Institute of (Rosminians, IC): Westminster, Arundel & Brighton, Birmingham, Cardiff, East Anglia, Hexham & Newcastle, Leeds, Menevia, Nottingham.

Christian Brothers, Congregation of (CFC): Westminster, Hexham & Newcastle, Liverpool, Salford, Shrewsbury.

Cistercians (of the Strict Observance, OCSO): Menevia, Nottingham.

Claretian Missionaries (Missionary Sons of the Immaculate Heart of Mary, CMF): Westminster, Brentwood, East Anglia, Hexham & Newcastle, Menevia.

Columban Fathers (SSC): Westminster, Birmingham, Leeds, Liverpool, Southwark.

Comboni Missionaries (MCCJ) see Verona Fathers.
Community of St John (CSJ): Brentwood.
Consolata Fathers (IMC): Westminster.
De La Mennais Brothers (Brothers of Christian Instruction, FIC): Liverpool, Portsmouth.
De La Salle Brothers (Brothers of the Christian Schools, FSC): Arundel & Brighton, Birmingham, Hexham, Liverpool, Portsmouth, Salford, Southwark.
Divine Providence, Sons of (SDP): Westminster, Liverpool.
Divine Word Missionaries (SVD): Westminster, Birmingham, Clifton, Liverpool.
Dominicans (Order of Preachers, OP): Westminster, Birmingham, East Anglia, Hexham & Newcastle, Nottingham.
Franciscan Friars of the Atonement (SA): Westminster, Southwark.
Franciscans (Friars Minor, OFM): Westminster, Arundel, Brentwood, Clifton, Nottingham, Portsmouth, Southwark.
Franciscans, Capuchin (Capuchin Friars Minor, OFMCap): Cardiff, Birmingham, Shrewsbury, Southwark, Wrexham.
Franciscans Conventual (Friars Minor Conventual, OFM. Conv): Arundel & Brighton, Liverpool, Salford, Southwark.
Fransalians (Missionaries of St Francis de Sales, MFS): Westminster, Clifton, Leeds, Plymouth.
Franciscan Friars of the Renewal (CFR): Brentwood.
Gabriel, Brothers of St (SG): Westminster.
Good Shepherd, Little Brothers of the (BGS): Birmingham.
Holy Ghost Fathers (CSSp): Westminster, Arundel & Brighton, Birmingham, East Anglia, Hallam, Middlesbrough, Nottingham, Portsmouth, Salford, Southwark.
Holy Spirit, Crusade of (CHS): Birmingham, Clifton.
Institute of Charity, Rosminians (IC): Westminster, Birmingham, Cardiff, Hexham & Newcastle, Leeds, Nottingham.
Jesuits (Society of Jesus, SJ): Westminster, Arundel, Birmingham, Cardiff, Clifton, Hallam, Lancaster, Liverpool, Menevia, Portsmouth, Salford, Southwark, Wrexham.
Jesus, Little Brothers of: Leeds, Southwark.
Order of Saint John of God: Brothers of the (OH): Westminster, Leeds, Hexham & Newcastle.
Josephites (CJ): Westminster, Arundel, Plymouth.
Lebanese Maronite Order (LMO): Westminster.
Little Brothers of Nazareth (LBN): Clifton.
Marian Fathers (MIC): Westminster, Cardiff, Northampton.
Marists (SM): Westminster, East Anglia, Hallam, Middlesbrough, Menevia, Portsmouth, Salford.
Mill Hill Missionaries (St Joseph's Missonary Society of Mill Hill, MHM): Westminster, Arundel & Brighton, Birmingham, East Anglia, Hexham & Newcastle, Lancaster, Liverpool, Portsmouth, Salford, Southwark.
Missionaries of La Salette: Brentwood.
Missionaries of St Paul (of Nigeria): Clifton, Southwark.
Montfort Missionaries (Company of Mary, SMM): Westminster, Hexham & Newcastle, Liverpool, Portsmouth.
Norbertine Canons (Canons Regular of Prémontre, O Praem): Arundel & Brighton, Brentwood, Nottingham, Salford.
Oblates of Mary Immaculate (OMI): Westminster, Birmingham, Clifton, Leeds, Liverpool, Portsmouth, Shrewsbury, Wrexham.
Oratorians (Congregation of the Oratory, Cong Orat): Westminster, Birmingham.
Pallottine Fathers (Society of Catholic Apostolate, SCA): Westminster, Arundel & Brighton, Brentwood.
Paraclete, Servants of the (sP): Clifton.
Passionists (Congregation of the Passion of Jesus Christ, CP): Westminster, Hexham & Newcastle, Liverpool, Menevia, Southwark.
Patrick's (St) Missionary Society (SPS) (Kiltegan Fathers): Arundel & Brighton, Clifton, Northampton, Nottingham, Portsmouth.
Picpus Fathers (SSCC): Westminster, Northampton, Southwark.
Presentation Brothers: Westminster, Portsmouth, Southwark.
Redemptorists (Congregation of the Most Holy Redeemer, CSSR): Birmingham, Hexham & Newcastle, Liverpool, Middlesbrough, Northampton, Portsmouth, Shrewsbury, Southwark.
Sacred Heart, Brothers of the: Westminster.
Sacred Heart, Missionaries of the (MSC): Westminster, Birmingham, Leeds, Liverpool, Shrewsbury.
Sacred Heart Fathers (SCJ): Liverpool, Northampton, Nottingham, Shrewsbury.
Sacred Heart (Betharram), Priests and Brothers of the (SCJ): Birmingham, Liverpool.
Salesians (of Don Bosco, SDB): Birmingham, Arundel & Brighton, Clifton, Hexham & Newcastle, Liverpool, Portsmouth, Salford, Shrewsbury, Southwark.
Salvatorians (Society of the Divine Saviour,

SDS): Westminster, Clifton, Hexham & Newcastle, Menevia, Middlesbrough, Shrewsbury, Southwark.
Scalabrini Fathers (CS): Arundel, Northampton, Southwark, Westminster.
Servites (Servants of Mary, OSM): Westminster, Salford, Southwark.
Society of Christ: Westminster, Arundel & Brighton, Brentwood, East Anglia, Lancaster, Leeds, Northampton, Salford, Southwark.
Society of St Paul (SSP): Southwark.
Stigmatine Fathers (CSS): Westminster.
Verona Fathers (Comboni Missionaries of the Heart of Jesus, MCCJ): Westminster, Arundel & Brighton, Leeds.
Vincentians (Congregation of the Mission, CM): Westminster, Northampton.
Xaverian Brothers (CFX): Westminster, Salford.
Xaverian Missionaries (SX): Westminster, Lancaster.

■ WOMEN

Adoratrices, Handmaids of the Blessed Sacrament and of Charity: Westminster.
Adorers of the Sacred Heart, Benedictine: Westminster, Arundel & Brighton.
Andrew, Religious of St: Southwark.
Anne, Sisters of St: Plymouth, Southwark.
Assumption, Little Sisters of the: Westminster, Birmingham, East Anglia, Hexham & Newcastle, Liverpool, Menevia, Wrexham.
Assumption, Oblates of the: Brentwood, Portsmouth.
Assumption, Religious of the: Westminster, Birmingham, East Anglia.
Augustinian Canonesses of the Order of St Augustine: Liverpool.
Augustinian Servants of Jesus and Mary: Westminster, Southwark.
Augustinian Sisters (Bruges): Arundel & Brighton, Northampton, Plymouth,
Augustinian Sisters (Meaux): Westminster.
Benedictine Nuns:
English Congr: Birmingham, Shrewsbury.
of Perpetual Adoration: Plymouth.
Olivetan: Northampton
Solesmes Congr: Portsmouth.
Independent Communities: Birmingham, Portsmouth, Southwark.
Benedictine Sisters of the Holy Child: Portsmouth.
Bernardines: Lancaster, Northampton.
Blessed Sacrament, Sisters of the: Arundel & Brighton.
Bon Secours Sisters (Paris): Westminster, Northampton, Southwark.
Bridgettine Nuns: Plymouth.
Bridgettine Sisters (Rome): Birmingham, Northampton.
Brigid, Sisters of St: Leeds, Menevia, Northampton, Portsmouth, Wrexham.
Canonesses of St Augustine, Congr of Our Lady: Westminster, Arundel & Brighton, Brentwood, East Anglia, Middlesbrough, Southwark.
of Windeshelm: Arundel & Brighton.
Canonesses of St Augustine of the Mercy of Jesus: Lancaster, Liverpool.
Canossian Daughters of Charity: Westminster.
Capitanio Sisters: Westminster.
Carmelite Missionaries: Westminster.
Carmelites: East Anglia, Salford.
Carmelites Corpus Christi: Hallam, Middlesbrough, Nottingham.
Carmelites (Discalced): Westminster, Arundel & Brighton, Birmingham, Hallam, Hexham & Newcastle, Lancaster, Leeds, Liverpool, Middlesbrough, Plymouth, Portsmouth, Salford, Shrewsbury, Wrexham.
Catholic Apostolate, Sisters of the: See Pallotine Missionary Sisters.
Cenacle, Sisters of Our Lady of the: Westminster, Liverpool, Portsmouth, Salford, Shrewsbury.
Charity, Missionaries of: Westminster, Birmingham, Liverpool.
Charity, Religious Sisters of: Westminster, Birmingham, Brentwood, Clifton, Leeds, Shrewsbury.
Charity of Jesus and Mary, Sisters of: Westminster, Arundel & Brighton, Birmingham, Lancaster, Plymouth .
Charity of Our Lady Mother of Mercy, Sisters of: Lancaster, Wrexham.
Charity of St Jeanne Antide, Sisters of: Westminster.
Charity of St Louis, Sisters of: Southwark.
Charity of St Paul, Selly Park, Sisters of: Westminster, Birmingham, Clifton, Hexham & Newcastle, Lancaster, Leeds, Liverpool, Plymouth, Portsmouth, Salford, Shrewsbury, Wrexham.
Charity of St Vincent de Paul, Daughters of: Westminster, Birmingham, Brentwood, Cardiff, Clifton, East Anglia, Hallam, Hexham & Newcastle, Liverpool, Menevia, Middlesbrough, Salford, Southwark.
Charity of Nevers, Sisters of: Arundel & Brighton, Lancaster.
Charles de Foucald, Contemplative Missionary Movement of: Southwark.
Christ, Sisters of: Westminster, Portsmouth, Southwark.
Christian Education, Institute of the Religious of (RCE): Portsmouth.
Christian Instruction (St Gildas), Sisters of: Westminster, Birmingham, Clifton, Southwark.
Christian Instruction, Religious of (RCI): Arundel & Brighton, Plymouth.
Christian Retreat, Sisters of the: Arundel

& Brighton, Southwark.
Cistercians: Menevia.
Clare, Sisters of St: Cardiff, Liverpool, Menevia, Nottingham, Northampton.
Columban Sisters: Westminster, Birmingham.
Comboni Missionary Sisters: Westminster.
Consolata Missionary Sisters: Westminster, Brentwood.
Cross (Liege), Daughter of the: Westminster, Arundel & Brighton, Hexham & Newcastle, Plymouth, Salford, Southwark.
Cross (Torquay), Daughters of the: Plymouth.
Cross and Passion, Sisters of the: Westminster, Birmingham, Hexham & Newcastle, Lancaster, Leeds, Menevia, Liverpool, Salford.
Dominicans: Congr of Malta: Portsmouth
Congr of Newcastle, Natal: Westminster, Arundel & Brighton.
Congr of Oakford: Westminster, Brentwood, Hallam, Lancaster, Portsmouth, Westminster.
Congr of Salisbury, Zimbabwe: Southwark.
Congr of Stone (St Catherine of Siena): Westminster, Birmingham, Clifton, Hexham & Newcastle, Nottingham.
Cong of Tours (Presentation of Our Lady): Portsmouth.
Divine Charity, Daughters of: East Anglia, Hallam.
Divine Love, Daughters of: Southwark.
Dorothy, Sisters of St: Westminster, Arundel & Brighton.
Eucharist, Religious of the: Southwark.
Faithful Companions of Jesus: Westminster, Hexham & Newcastle, Lancaster, Liverpool, Middlesbrough, Northampton, Portsmouth, Salford, Shrewsbury, Southwark.
Felician Sisters: Clifton, Southwark.
Francis, Sisters of St: Nottingham.
Franciscan Sisters Minoress: Brentwood Nottingham.
Franciscan Missionary Sisters for Africa (FMSA): Southwark.
Franciscan Missionaries of Mary: Westminster, Birmingham, Brentwood, East Anglia, Hexham & Newcastle, Liverpool, Menevia, Portsmouth, Southwark.
Franciscan Missionaries of St Joseph: Liverpool, Salford, Southwark, Wrexham.
Franciscan Missionaries of the Divine Motherhood: Arundel & Brighton, Birmingham, Brentwood, Leeds, Portsmouth, Southwark.
Franciscan Missionary Sisters (Littlehampton) (FMSL): Arundel & Brighton, Leeds, Southwark.
Franciscan Sisters of the Immaculate Conception (OSF): Clifton.
Franciscan Sisters of Mill Hill: Westminster, Clifton, Liverpool.
Franciscan Sisters (of St Mary of the Angels): Portsmouth.
Franciscan Sisters (of Our Lady of Victories): Westminster.
Good Saviour, Sisters of the: Wrexham.
Good Shepherd, Sisters of the (RGS): Westminster, Northampton, Salford.
Grace and Compassion, Benedictine Sisters of Our Lady of: Arundel & Brighton, Clifton, East Anglia, Southwark
Handmaids of the Holy Child Jesus (HHCJ): Southwark.
Holy Child Jesus, Society of the (SHCJ): Westminster, Arundel & Brighton, Birmingham, Lancaster, Leeds, Northampton, Salford.
Holy Cross, Sisters of the (HC): Westminster, Hallam, Northampton, Southwark.
Holy Family of Bordeaux, Sisters of the: Westminster, Brentwood, East Anglia, Leeds, Liverpool, Northampton, Shrewsbury, Southwark, Wrexham.
Holy Family (Ste Emilie de Rodat), Sisters of the (RHF): Arundel & Brighton, Plymouth, Salford, Southwark.
Holy Family of Nazareth, Sisters of the: Westminster, Northampton.
Holy House of Nazareth, Sisters of the: East Anglia, Northampton.
Holy Name, Sisters of: Westminster.
Holy Sepulchre, Canonesses of the: Brentwood.
Holy Souls, Helpers of the: Westminster, Liverpool, Portsmouth.
Holy Spirit, Daughters of the (DHS): Birmingham, Cardiff, Menevia, Northampton, Plymouth.
Holy Spirit, Missionary Sisters Servants of the: Arundel & Brighton, Birmingham, Clifton.
Holy Trinity, Sisters of the: Birmingham, Southwark.
Immaculate Conception, Sisters of: Arundel & Brighton, Portsmouth.
Infant Jesus, Sisters of the: Westminster, Arundel & Brighton, Birmingham, Liverpool, Portsmouth.
Institute of the Blessed Virgin Mary: Westminster, Clifton, East Anglia, Middlesbrough, Plymouth, Portsmouth.
Jesus Daughters of (DJ): Westminster, East Anglia, Hexham & Newcasle, Salford, Southwark.
Jesus (Aix en Provence), Little Sisters of: Westminster, Birmingham, East Anglia.
Jesus and Mary, Religious of: Westminster, East Anglia, Northampton.
Jesus, Little Sisters of: Westminster, East Anglia.

John of God, Sisters of St: Westminster, Cardiff, Clifton, Plymouth.
Joseph (Annecy), Sisters of St: Cardiff, Clifton, Menevia, Portsmouth, Plymouth, Southwark.
Joseph (of Lyon), Sisters of St: Birmingham, Wrexham.
Joseph (Chambéry), Sisters of St: Wrexham.
Joseph (Cluny), Sisters of St: Birmingham
Joseph of Peace: Sisters of St: Westminster, Leeds, Nottingham .
Joseph (of the Apparition), Sisters of St: Liverpool, Salford, Shrewsbury.
Joseph (of Tarbes), Sisters of St: Birmingham, Brentwood.
La Sagesse, Congregation of, Westminster, Hexham & Newcastle, Lancaster, Liverpool, Portsmouth.
La Sainte Union Sisters: Westminster, Brentwood, Clifton, Liverpool, Portsmouth, Southwark, Wrexham.
Life, Sisters of: Nottingham.
Little Ones, Sisters of the: Liverpool.
Loreto, Sisters of (Irish Branch of Inst of the BVM): Westminster, Brentwood, Liverpool, Middlesbrough, Nottingham, Salford, Shrewsbury,Wrexham.
Louis, Sisters of St: East Anglia, Salford, Shrewsbury.
Lucy, Sisters of St: Portsmouth.
Marcellina, Sisters of St: Westminster.
Marian Missionary Sisters of the Poor: Brentwood.
Marie Auxiliatrice, Society of: Westminster, Leeds, Liverpool.
Marie Madeleine Postel, Sisters of St: Birmingham, Portsmouth.
Marie de la Providence, Sisters of St: Portsmouth.
Marie Reparatrice, Society of: Hexham & Newcastle, Southwark.
Marist Sisters: Westminster, Arundel & Brighton, Birmingham, Clifton, East Anglia, Hallam, Menevia, Plymouth, Portsmouth, Salford, Southwark.
Martha, Sisters of St: Westminster, Arundel & Brighton.
Mary and Joseph, Daughters of: East Anglia, Hexham & Newcastle, Middlesbrough, Plymouth, Portsmouth, Southwark.
Mary, Daughters of the Heart of: Liverpool, Southwark.
Mary, Help of Christians, Daughters of: Birmingham, Lancaster, Liverpool, Southwark.
Mary Immaculate, Religious of: Westminster, Southwark.
Mary, Immaculate, Sister Servants of: Westminster, Leeds.
Mary, Inst of the Blessed Virgin: Westminster, Clifton, East Anglia, Hexham & Newcastle, Middlesbrough, Plymouth, Portsmouth.
Mary, Little Company of: Westminster, Brentwood, Cardiff, Liverpool, Nottingham, Southwark.
Mary, Mother of the Church, Congregation of: Birmingham, Clifton.
Mary, Religious of the Sacred Heart of: Southwark.
St Mary of Namur, Sisters of: Westminster, Liverpool.
Mary and Joseph, Sisters of: Westminster.
Mary Immaculate (Madrid), Daughters of: Westminster.
Mary Mother of Mercy, Daughters of: Brentwood.
Mary, Immaculate, Missionary Sisters of: (PIME): Westminster.
Mary, Sisters of the Company of: Arundel & Brighton.
Medical Mission Sisters: Westminster, Southwark.
Medical Missionaries of Mary: Westminster, Birmingham, Shrewsbury.
Mercy, English Federation of the Sisters of: Arundel & Brighton, Hexham & Newcastle, Portsmouth, Southwark.
Mercy, Institute of Our Lady of (RSM): Westminster, Arundel & Brighton, Birmingham, Brentwood, East Anglia, Hallam, Hexham & Newcastle, Lancaster, Leeds, Liverpool, Middlesbrough, Nottingham, Plymouth, Portsmouth, Salford, Southwark, Wrexham.
Mercy, Sisters of Mercy of the Union: Westminster, Birmingham, Brentwood, Clifton, Hallam, Hexham & Newcastle, Lancaster, Menevia, Nottingham, Plymouth, Shrewsbury, Wrexham.
Nazareth, Poor Sisters of: Westminster, Brentwood, Cardiff, Clifton, Lancaster, Liverpool, Middlesbrough, Northampton, Nottingham, Plymouth, Salford, Shrewsbury, Wrexham.
Notre Dame (Namur), Sisters of: Westminster, Arundel & Brighton, Leeds, Liverpool, Plymouth, Southwark.
Notre Dame (Rome), Sisters of: Southwark.
Notre Dames des Missions: Southwark.
Notre Dame, School Sisters of: Hallam, Liverpool, Southwark.
Our Lady, Sisters of: Westminster, Northampton.
Our Lady of Africa, Missionary Sisters of: Westminster.
Our Lady of Charity, Sisters of: Westminster, Birmingham, Liverpool, Portsmouth.
Our Lady of Evron, Sisters of Charity of: Liverpool, Salford, Shrewsbury, Wrexham.
Our Lady of Fidelity, Society of:

Southwark.
Our Lady of Good and Perpetual Succour, Sisters of: Hexham & Newcastle.
Our Lady of Good Counsel and St Paul of the Cross, Daughters of: See Vocation Sisters.
Our Lady of Africa, Missionary Sisters of: Westminster, Arundel & Brighton.
Our Lady of Pity, Sisters of: Portsmouth.
Our Lady of the Apostles, Sisters of: Westminster, Lancaster.
Our Lady of the Holy Rosary, Missionary Sisters of: Clifton.
Our Lady of the Immaculate Conception (Briouze), Sisters of: Southwark.
Our Lady of the Missions, Sisters of: Westminster, Arundel & Brighton, Clifton, Liverpool, Salford, Southwark, Wrexham.
Our Lady of the Sacred Heart (Issoudun), Daughters of: Birmingham, Southwark.
Pallottine Missionary Sisters: Westminster, Salford, Shrewsbury.
Parish Mission Sisters: Ince Blundell
Passionist Nuns: Cardiff, Northampton.
Paul, Daughters of St: Westminster, Liverpool, Northampton.
Paul of Chartres, Sisters of St: Westminster
Peter Claver, Missionary Sisters of St: Southwark.
Poor, Little Sisters of the: Westminster, Birmingham, Clifton, Hexham & Newcastle, Leeds, Portsmouth, Salford, Southwark.
Poor Child Jesus, Sisters of the: Westminster, Birmingham, Hallam.
Poor Clares Colettines: Westminster, Arundel & Brighton, Birmingham, Cardiff, Clifton, Liverpool, Menevia, Middlesbrough, Nottingham, Plymouth, Portsmouth, Shrewsbury, Wrexham.
Congr of Newry: Cardiff, Liverpool, Menevia, Nottingham.
Poor Handmaids of Jesus Christ: Westminster, Northampton, Plymouth.
Poor Servants of the Mother of God: Westminster, Arundel & Brighton, Clifton, East Anglia, Liverpool, Southwark.
Presentation of the Blessed Virgin Mary, Union of Sisters of The: Birmingham, Clifton, Hallam, Leeds, Nottingham, Portsmouth, Salford.
Presentation of Mary, Sisters of the (Castelgandolfo): Plymouth.
Providence, Sisters of (Rosminians): Westminster, Arundel & Brighton, Birmingham, Cardiff, Nottingham.
Providence (Rouen), Sisters of: Arundel & Brighton.
Providence (Ruille-sur-Loire), Sisters of: Westminster, Birmingham, Nottingham, Southwark.
Providence (St Brieuc), Daughters of: Westminster, Birmingham, Northampton.
Providence (Saintes), Sisters of Our Lady of: Portsmouth.
Providence, of the Immaculate Conception (Sisters of): Westminster, Nottingham.
Redemptoristines (Order of the Most Holy Redeemer): Liverpool.
Religious Teachers Filippini: Portsmouth.
Resurrection, Sisters of the: Westminster.
Retraite, Sisters of La: Birmingham, Clifton, Southwark.
Sacra Famiglia, Suore Collegina della: Westminster.
Sacred Heart (Madrid), Sisters Hospitallers of the: Westminster, Arundel & Brighton, Birmingham.
Sacred Heart (Paris), Society of the: Westminster, Arundel & Brighton, Brentwood, Birmingham, Hexham & Newcastle, Leeds, Menevia, Northampton, Portsmouth, Southwark.
Sacred Heart (Rome), Handmaids of the: Westminster, Portsmouth, Southwark.
Sacred Heart (Rome), Missionary Sisters of the: Southwark.
Sacred Heart (St Aubin), Sisters of the: Birmingham.
Sacred Heart (St Jacut), Sisters of the: Westminster, Northampton.
Sacred Heart of Jesus: Liverpool.
Sacred Heart of Mary (Béziers), Religious of the: Westminster, Brentwood, Lancaster, Leeds, Liverpool, Wrexham.
Sacred Heart of Mary, Religious of (US Province): Westminster, Southwark.
Sacred Hearts of Jesus and Mary (Chigwell), Sisters of the: Westminster, Brentwood, East Anglia, Lancaster, Liverpool, Menevia, Southwark, Wrexham
Sacred Hearts of Jesus and Mary (Epsom): Arundel & Brighton, Southwark.
Sacred Hearts (Picpus), Sisters of the: Arundel & Brighton, Westminster.
Saints Coeurs de Jésus et de Marie, Congr des: Portsmouth.
Salesian Sisters of St John Bosco (Daughters of Mary Help of Christians), FMA: Arundel & Brighton, Birmingham, Lancaster, Liverpool, Southwark.
Salvatorian Sisters, Sisters of the Divine Saviour: Clifton.
Santa Ana, Spanish Sisters of: Westminster.
Saviour and Blessed Virgin, Sisters of the: Clifton.
Servite Sisters (Servants of Mary): Westminster, Arundel & Brighton, Birmingham, Brentwood, Hallam, Southwark.
Sion, Congregation of Our Lady of: Westminster, Arundel & Brighton,

Birmingham, Leeds, Salford.
Suore Francescane dell' Immacolata: Southwark.
Temple, Sisters of the: Clifton.
Ursula, Congregation of the Sisters of the Order of St: Brentwood.
Ursuline Sisters of St Angela Merici: Westminster.
Ursulines (Roman Union): Brentwood, Lancaster, Shrewsbury, Southwark.
Ursulines of Jesus: Westminster, Menevia, Portsmouth, Southwark.
Ursulines (Thurles) Irish Union: Menevia.
Verbum Dei Community: Portsmouth.
Visitation, Order of the: Arundel & Brighton.
Visitation (Mt St Amand), Sisters of the: Birmingham.
Vocation Sisters: Arundel & Brighton, Birmingham, Northampton.
Walsingham, Community of Our Lady of: Brentwood.
Wisdom, Daughters of (La Sagesse): Westminster, Hexham & Newcastle, Lancaster, Liverpool, Portsmouth.

■ OTHER FORMS OF CONSECRATED LIFE

Order of Consecrated Virgins Living in the World (cf canon 604): *Contact:* **Sr Elizabeth Rees OCV**. **Tel:** 01458-8515611.
Consecrated Widows/Widowers: Southwark.
Consecrated Hermits (cf canon 603): Westminster

■ NEW FORMS OF CONSECRATED LIFE

The Spiritual Family The Work (Rome): Birmingham.

ASSOCIATION OF BRITISH CONTEMPLATIVES

The Association was formed in 1992 and represents the 19 contemplative orders for women living in 70 convents – both Catholic and Anglican – in the United Kingdom.

Press Officer: **Sister Mary Bernadette OssR**
Association of British Contemplatives, Redemptoristine Convent, Back Gillmoss Lane, Liverpool L11 0AY **Tel:** 0151-546 3968 **E-mail:** bernie.ossr@btinternet.com

■ Executive Committee

Sister Mary of the Holy Spirit ODC – Dumbarton *(Chairwoman)*
Dame Joanna Jamieson OSB – Stanbrook *(Deputy Chairwoman)*
Sister Anne Marie OSC – Lynton
Sister Mary Thomas CRW – Sayers Common
Sister Elizabeth Mary SPB – Burnham Abbey
Sister Mary of St Philip ODC – Notting Hill
Sister Zoe OSB – Turvey Abbey
Treasurer: **Sister Mary Colette** – Hyning
Secretary: **Sister Dorothy ODC** – Langside

■ Orders Represented

Adoration Sisters, Benedictines *(Roman Catholic & Anglican)*, Bernardine Cistercians, Bridgettines, Canonesses of St Augustine, Carmelites, Cistercians, Contemplatives of the Good Shepherd, Dominicans, Passionists, Poor Clares *(Roman Catholic & Anglican)*, Redemptoristines, Visitandines.

Anglican: Sisters of the Love of God, Society of the Holy Cross, Society of the Precious Blood, Society of the Sacred Cross

The Association of British Contemplatives Directory is now available from the Press Office. To obtain a copy please telephone Sr Bernadette OssR on 0151-546 3968 or E-mail: bernie.ossr@btinternet.com

The Directory is also now available on the web at www.abc.mydom.co.uk

THE UNION OF MONASTIC SUPERIORS

The association of Benedictine and Cistercian houses in the British Isles, founded in 1973 to promote co-operation and support among the monastic communities. The Union includes a Commission for Benedictine Women and the Anglican monastic houses. It is recognised by the Secretariat of the Bishops' Conference as the official body representing monastic houses in England and Wales in relationships with the bishops and it has, as such, been affiliated to the Conference of Religious since May 1991

Chairperson:
Abbot Joseph Delargy (Mount St Bernard)

Assistant Chairperson:
Prioress Nikola Proksch (Minister)

Second Assistant:
Abbot Stuart Burns (Burford)

Council:
Abbot Aidan Bellanger (Downside)
Abbot Hugh Gilbert (Pluscarden)
Dr Elizabeth Mary Mann (Brownshill)
Mother Mary Luke Wise (Rempstone)

Treasurer:
Abbot Charles Fitzgerald-Lombard (Downside)

General Secretary:
Sr Carmel Murtagh (Grace & Compassion)

Members

Abbot Giles Hill (Alton)
Abbot Cuthbert Madden (Ampleforth)
Sister Scholastica Grundy Parkers (Andover)
Abbot Paul Stonham (Belmont)
Abbot Peter Garvey (Bolton)
Abbot Philip Manahan (Buckfast)
Dame Christine Lowings (Buckfast Convent)
Prioress Mildred Murray-Sinclair (Buckfast)
Abbot Stuart Burns (Burford)
Abbot Daniel Van Santwoort (Caldey)
Abbess Paula Fairlie (Chester)
Prior Constanzo Scaglia (Cockfosters)
Abbess Gertrude Baker (Colwich)
Abbot Geoffrey Scott (Douai)
Abbot Aidan Bellenger (Downside)
Abbot Martin Shipperlee (Ealing)
Abbess Mary Therese Zelent (Edgware)
Abbot Simon Jarratt (Elmore Abbey)
Abbot Cuthbert Brogan (Farnborough)
Mother Mary Fahy (Glencairn)
Abbot Christopher Dillon (Glenstal)
Mother Kathy Yeeles (Grace & Compassion)
Prioress Elizabeth Mary Mann (Brownshill)
Sr Mary Margaret Funk (Kylemore)
Mother John Paul Spackman (Largs)
Abbot Augustine McGregor (Mellifont)
Prioress Nikola Proksch (Minster)
Fr George Guiver (Mirfield)
Abbot Eamon Fitzgerald (Mount Melleray)
Abbot Joseph Delargy (Mount Saint Bernard)
Abbot Raymond Jaconelli (Nunraw)
Dame Benedicta Scott, Prioress Admin. (Oulton)
Abbot Hugh Gilbert (Pluscarden)
Abbot Celsus Kelly (Portglenone)
Abbot Francis Baird (Prinknash)
Dom Finbar Kealy (Quarr)
Abbot Paulinus Greenwood (Ramsgate)
Mother Mary Luke Wise (Rempstone)
Abbot Kevin Daly (Roscrea)
Dom Mark Ephrem M Nolan (Rostrevor)
Abbess Ninian Eaglesham (Ryde)
Prioress Mary Helen Jackson (Hyning)
Helen Leith (St Boniface Lay Institute)
Abbess Joanna Jamieson (Stanbrook)
Prioress Zoë Davis (Turvey)
Abbot Christopher Jamison (Worth)
Mother Mary Xavier McMonagle (Tyburn)
Abbess Mary John Marshall (West Malling)
Sister Judith (Whitby)
Abbess M. Christine Wood (Whitland)
Dom John Mayhead (Turvey)

Abbot President, English Congregation:
Abbot Richard Yeo

Prioress General, Bernardines:
Mother Josephine Mary Miller

CENTRES FOR RETREATS & FORMATION

■ HOUSES CONDUCTING RETREATS ALL YEAR ROUND

■ Berkshire

Douai Abbey, Upper Woolhampton, Reading, Berks RG7 5TQ
Tel: 0118-971 5399
E-mail: guestmaster@douaiabbey.org.uk
Contact: The Guestmaster

■ Bristol

Emmaus House, Retreat & Conference Centre, Clifton Hill, Clifton, Bristol BS8 1BN (Congregation of La Retraite). Retreat and Conference Centre offering in-house workshops, retreats and professional training courses, along with corporate lettings: 4 meeting rooms for hire, 23 single bedrooms available, some convertible to twin beds, 7 en-suite. Restaurant *Chez La Retraite* seating up to 40, larger numbers by arrangement. Extensive, award-winning gardens. Contact the Administration Manager to discuss your requirements or arrange a visit to view our facilities.
Administrators: **Angela Groves and Fiona McDonald.**
Office Hours: Mon-Fri, 9.30am-3.30pm
Tel: 0117-907 9950,
Restaurant: 0117-907 9954
E-mail: administration@emmaushouse.org.uk
Web: www.emmaushouse.co.uk

■ Cambridgeshire

Claret Centre, The Towers, High Street, Buckden, St Neots, Cambs PE19 5TA
Tel: 01480-810344
Website: www.centre.claret.org.uk
Youth and Adult Residential Facilities

■ Cheshire

Oblate Retreat Centre, Wistaston Hall, 89 Broughton Lane, Crewe CW2 8JS **Tel:** 01270-568653 **Fax:** 01270-650776 (OMI) Contact: **Oliver Barry**
E-mail: Director@oblateretreatcentre.org.uk
Website: www.oblateretreatcentre.org.uk
27 rooms/43 beds available, Retreats & Conferences. Newly refurbished with more single rooms, 22 en-suite and three rooms on the ground level for those with disabilities. Contact the Director to discuss your requirements.

Savio House, Ingersley Road, Bollington, Macclesfield, SK10 5RW
Tel: 01625- 573256 **Fax:** 01625-560221
E-mail: saviooffice@saviohouse.org.uk
Website: www.saviohouse.org.uk
Retreat Team Leader: **Jessica Wilkinson.**

■ Cumbria

Time Out Project – Brettargh Holt, Kendal, Cumbria LA8 8EA **Tel/Fax:** 01539-561322 (Salesian Sisters) Youth Pastoral and Retreat/Conference Centre. Contact bookings secretary

■ Durham

Ushaw College Conference Centre, Ushaw College, Durham DH7 9RH. Provides facilities for conferences – residential up to 150, non-residential up to 250 people. Also available for Parish Groups wishing to visit the area. Further information can be obtained by contacting **Angie George**, *Conference Centre Manager*, **Tel:** 0191-373 8588, or the Conference Office
Tel: 0191 373 8502
E-mail: bookings@ushaw.ac.uk

■ Flintshire

Franciscan Retreat Centre. (Capuchin Franciscans) Contact: The Retreat Director, Monastery Avenue, Pantasaph, Holywell, Flintshire CH8 8PE
Tel: 01352-711053
E-mail: pantasaph@gmail.com
Website: www.pantasaph.org.uk

■ Hertfordshire (Westminster Diocese)

All Saints Pastoral Centre, Shenley Lane, London Colney, Hertfordshire AL2 1AF
Tel: 01727-829306 **Fax:** 01727 822880
E-mail: conf.office@allsaintspc.org.uk
Director: **Mgr Vladimir Felzmann** KCHS, DD, MSc(Eng). *Administrator:* **Alan Johnstone.** *In residence:* **Mgr Canon Adrian Arrowsmith.**
SPEC and The Loft at SPEC; *Co-directors:* **David and Sandra Satchell**
Tel: 01727-829222 **Fax:** 01727-822927
E-mail: spec@rcdow.org.uk

■ Herefordshire

Belmont Abbey, Hereford HR2 9RZ
Contact: Retreats Office
Tel: 07799 811646
E-mail: retreats@belmontabbey.org.uk
Web: www.belmontabbey.org.uk

■ **Kent**

The Friars Retreat House, Aylesford Priory, Aylesford, Maidstone, Kent ME20 7BX
Tel: 01622-717272 **Fax:** 01622-715575
E-mail: retreat@thefriars.org.uk
Web: thefriars.org.uk

Emmaus Retreat and Conference Centre, Layhams Road, West Wickham, Kent BR4 9HH
Tel: 020-8777 2000 **Fax:** 020-8776 2022
E-mail: enquiries@emmauscentre.org
Website: www.emmauscentre.org
(Daughters of Mary and Joseph).
Chaplain: **Rev Anthony Skillen** SM
Tel: 020-8777 8455

■ **Lancashire**

Tabor Carmelite Retreat Centre, 169 Sharoe Green Lane, Fulwood, Preston PR2 8HE **Tel:** 01772-717122
E-mail: tabor@carmelite.net
Website: www.tabor-preston.org

Monastery of Our Lady of Hyning. Warton, Carnforth, Lancashire LA5 9SE
Tel: 01524-732684 **Fax:** 01524-720287
Contact: Bookings Secretary.
E-mail: hyningbookings@yahoo.co.uk

■ **Liverpool**

Cenacle, Tithebarn Grove, off Lance Lane, Liverpool L15 6TW **Tel:** 0151-722 2271
E-mail: cenacleliverpool@btconnect.com

Loyola Hall Jesuit Spirituality Centre. 43 en-suite rooms. *Superior:* **Rev Ian Tomlinson** SJ, *Director:* **Ruth Holgate**. Warrington Road, Rainhill, Prescot, Merseyside L35 6NZ **Tel:** 0151-426 4137
Fax: 0151-431 0115 **E-mail:** mail@loyolahall.co.uk
Website: www.loyolahall.co.uk

■ **Manchester**

The Cenacle, 4 Old Birley Street, Hulme, Manchester M15 5RG **Tel:** 0161-226 1241 (Religious of the Cenacle)

■ **Middlesex**

The Grail Centre, 125 Waxwell Lane, Pinner, Middlesex HA5 3ER **Tel:** 020-8866 2195
E-mail: waxwell@compuserve.com
Website: www.grailsociety.org.uk

Osterley Retreats, 112 Thornbury Road, Osterley, Middlesex TW7 4NN **Tel:** 020-8568 3821 (Loreto Sisters & Jesuits)

■ **Northumberland**

Minsteracres Retreat Centre, Minsteracres, Nr Consett, Co Durham DH8 9RT **Tel:** 01434-673248
Residential and day retreats and events. Individual guided retreats, themed retreats. Workshops, Spiritual Accompaniment, parish and ministry support, also offering conference spaces for hire. Facilities also include a poustina and a fully self-contained youth centre - **Tel:** 01434-682575 (Staffed under the auspices of the Passionists).
E-mail: info@minsteracres.co.uk
Web: www.minsteracres.co.uk

■ **Oxfordshire**

Marian Fathers Retreat and Conference Centre, Fawley Court, Marlow Road, Henley-on-Thames RG9 3AE
Tel: 01491-574917 **Fax:** 01491-411587
Website: www.fawleycourt.com
E-mails: marian-f@dircon.co.uk
fcoffice@dircon.co.uk

■ **Shropshire**

Hawkstone Hall Redemptorist International Pastoral Centre, Marchamley, Shrewsbury SY4 5LG
Tel: 01630-685242 **Fax:** 01630-685565
E-mail: hawkhall@aol.com
Website: hawkstone-hall.com
Redemptorists: **Rev Maurice P O'Mahony** BA(Hons) CertEd *(Rector and Course Director);* **Frs Kevin Callaghan, William Lavery, Br Richard Golding**; **Srs Carol Mouat** OP, **Laurice McMullan** CSN, **Jacqueline Smith** SP, **Mr David Minney** (*Bursar*), **Mrs Lindsay Swatman** (*Secretary*). Apply to: The Secretary for three-month courses, short courses, retreats, private groups.

■ **Somerset**

Ammerdown Centre, Radstock, Bath BA3 5SW **Tel:** 01761-433709
Fax: 01761-433094.
Ammerdown offers a wide range of retreats and courses. Adrian Smith and Margaret Silf are just some of the speakers used. Full programme includes individual guided retreats, arts courses and parish musicians' weekends. There are also opportunities for personal development in a Christian context. Private stays and bookings for groups are also welcome. Ammerdown is set in beautiful countryside. Bedrooms are ensuite, conference rooms are modern and well equipped.
E-mail: centre@ammerdown.org
Website: www.ammerdown.org

Bainesbury House, Downside Abbey, Stratton-on-the-Fosse, Bath BA3 4RH
Tel: 01761-235114 **Fax:** 01761-235124
Self Catering; Suitable for groups of up

to 20 young people. Contact the Warden at the above address
Web: www.downside.co.uk

■ **Southampton**
The Cenacle, (The Sisters of the Cenacle). 48 Victoria Road, Netley Abbey, Southampton SO31 5DQ
Tel/Fax: 023-8045 3718
E-mail: cenaclenetley@btinternet.com
(Open throughout the year)

■ **Yorkshire**
Ampleforth Abbey: Hospitality and Pastoral Office, Ampleforth Abbey, York YO62 4EN (Benedictine). *Director:* **Mrs Jan Fitzalan Howard.**
Tel: 01439-766889 and 01439-766486
Fax: 01439-766755
E-mail: pastoral@ampleforth.org.uk
Monastic Pastoral Team: **Revv Peter James, Bede Leach, Christopher Gorst, Kieran Monahan.**
Lay Pastoral Team: **Kit and Caroline Dollard. Tel:** 01439-766874
E-mail: kcd@ampleforth.org.uk

The Briery Retreat Centre, 38 Victoria Avenue, Ilkley, West Yorkshire LS29 9BW
Tel: 01943-607287 **Fax:** 01943-604449
(Sisters of Cross and Passion)
E-mail: srscp@aol.com
Website: www.briery.org.uk

■ **Wales**
St Beuno's Ignatian Spirituality Centre, Tremeirchion, St Asaph, Denbighshire, North Wales LL17 0AS
Individual guided, silent retreats and sabbatical programmes in Ignatian Spirituality. *Director:* **Rev David Birchall** SJ, *Superior:* **Rev Thomas Shufflebotham** SJ
E-mail: secretary@beunos.com
Website: www.beunos.com

■ **Warwickshire**
Soli House (Youth Retreat Centre) Mill Lane, Stratford-on-Avon CV37 6BJ
Tel/Fax: 01789 267011
Director: **Rev Bill Wilton.**

■ **OCCASIONAL AND DAY RETREATS**

■ **Berkshire**
Cold Ash Retreat and Conference Centre, The Ridge, Cold Ash, Thatcham, Berks RG18 9HU **Tel:** 01635-865353
Fax: 01635-866621. (Franciscan Missionaries of Mary)

■ **Derbyshire** (Nottingham Diocese)
The Briars Residential Youth Centre, Crich, Matlock, Derbys DE4 5BW **Office: Tel:** 01773-852044 **Fax:** 01773-852968
E-mail: bookings@thebriars.co.uk

■ **Cheshire**
Evron Centre, 1 Adswood Lane West, Cale Green, Stockport SK3 8HT **Tel:** 0161-292 7270 **Fax:** 0161-292 7470
E-mail: evroncentre@yahoo.co.uk

■ **Essex**
Diocesan House of Prayer, 'Abbotswick', Navestock Side, Brentwood, Essex CM14 5SH **Tel:** 01277-373959
E-mail: info@abbotswick.org
Website: www.abbotswick.org
Open to individuals and groups wanting a quiet space. 16 beds, extensive grounds and daily Exposition when possible, closed Mondays. (Brentwood Diocese)

Domus Mariae Conference & Retreat Centre, Chigwell Convent, 803 Chigwell Road, Woodford Green, Essex IG8 8AU
Tel: 020-8505 8180 **Fax:** 020-8559 2149. (Sisters of the Sacred Hearts of Jesus and Mary)

■ **Hampshire**
Franciscan Sisters of St Mary of the Angels, Park Place Pastoral Centre, Winchester Road, Wickham, Fareham, Hants PO17 5HA Contact: **Sr Juliette D'Souza** FSMA (Administrator)
Tel: 01329-833043
Email (Centre): pastoralcentre@aol.com
Superior General: **Sr M Evelyn Cardoz**
Tel: 01329-833043
E-mail: evelyncardoz@aol.com

■ **Kent**
Minster Abbey Guest House, Minster, Nr Ramsgate, Kent **Tel:** 01843-821254 (Benedictine Nuns) Closed Oct -Jan. Contact: **Sr Aelred.**

■ **Liverpool**
Sandymount House of Prayer, 16 Burbo Bank Road, Blundellsands, Liverpool L23 6TH **Tel:** 0151-924 4850
Open for day and weekend retreats, please contact the Booking Secretary.

■ **London**
Southwell House Youth Project, 39 Fitzjohns Avenue, London NW3 5JT
Tel: 020-7435 8534 **Fax:** 020-7435 9133 (Jesuits)
Retreats and other programmes for young people and those who work

with them.
Director: **Rev Michael Smith** SJ
E-mail: director@southwellhouse.com
Website: www.southwellhouse.com

■ Suffolk

Clare Priory, Ashen Road, Clare, Suffolk, CO10 8NX
Tel: 01787-277326 **Fax:** 01787-278688
E-mail: clare.priory@virgin.net
Website: www.clarepriory.org.uk
Contact: The Secretary (9.30-14.30 Mon-Fri)

■ Sussex

Priory of Our Lady, Dove Cottage, Kingston Ridge, Kingston-near-Lewes, E. Sussex BN7 3JX Contact: The Secretary
Tel: 01273-486677 (Canonesses Regular of St Augustine)

St Cuthman's, Coolham, Horsham West Sussex RH13 8QL
Director: **Mrs Denise Mitchell**
Tel: 01403-741220
E-mail: stcuthmans@dabnet.org
Website: www.stcuthmans.com

■ PRIVATE RETREATS

(a) Open to all

St Cuthman's, Coolham, Horsham West Sussex RH13 8QL.
Director: **Mrs Denise Mitchell**
Tel: 01403-741220
E-mail: stcuthmans@dabnet.org
Website: www.stcuthmans.com

(b) Sisters and laywomen

Bridgettine Convent, Fulmer Common Road, Iver Heath, Bucks SL0 0NR
Tel: 01753-662073/662645

Visitation Monastery, Fox Hunt Green, Waldron, Heathfield, East Sussex TN21 0RX **Tel:** 01435-812619
E-mail: vis1610@uk2.net

(c) Priests and laymen

Caldey Abbey, Our Lady and St Samson, Caldey Island, off Tenby, Pembrokeshire SA70 7UH **Tel:** 01834-842632
Fax: 01834-845942
E-mail: brotherdaniel@tiscali.co.uk
Abbot: **Rt Rev Daniel van Santvoort**, *Prior:* **Rev Gildas Gage**, *Subprior:* **Br Luca Cestro**; *Novice Director:* **Br David Hodges**

Douai Abbey. Contact: The Guestmaster, Upper Woolhampton, Reading, Berks RG7 5TQ
Tel: 0118-971 5399 **Fax:** 0118-971 5399
E-mail: guestmaster@douaiabbey.org.uk

Prinknash Abbey, The retreat house known as St Peter's Grange is now closed. It is planned to open an alternative retreat house in 2010. For further details:
Tel: 01452-813592
E-mail: spgprinknash@freeuk.com
Web: Google: Prinknash Abbey

Quarr Abbey, Ryde, Isle of Wight PO33 4ES Contact: **Bro Francis Verry**
Tel: 01983-882420

(d) Sisters and laywomen, priests and laymen

Clare Priory, Ashen Road, Clare, Suffolk, CO10 8NX
Tel: 01787-277326 **Fax:** 01787-278688
Contact: The Secretary. (09.30 - 14.30 Mon - Fri). **E-mail:** clarepriory@virgin.net

(e) Sisters, laywomen and married couples

St Cecilia's Abbey, Ryde, Isle of Wight PO33 1LH **Tel:** 01983-562602
Fax: 01983-810735
E-mail: info@stceciliasabbey.org.uk
Website: www.stceciliasabbey.org.uk
www.abbeyscribes.org.uk
Contact: The Guest Mistress

■ ITALY

Villa Palazzola. Venerable English College Retreat and Pilgrim Centre, Via dei Laghi Km 10,800, 00040 Rocca di Papa (RM), Italia **Tel:** 0039 0694 749178 **Fax:** 0039 0694 749166
E-mail: palazzola@palazzola.it
Website: www.palazzola.it
Director: **Mrs Joyce Hunter**

RECAPITULATION OF STATISTICS
OF ENGLAND AND WALES

■ GENERAL STATISTICS

1. In the following table of general statistics, it should be noted that the estimated Catholic population in each diocese, and, consequently, throughout England and Wales, is based on figures supplied by the parish clergy who give an estimate of Catholics known to them in their parish. It is generally agreed that the resultant figures underestimate the Catholic population and should not be regarded as a reliable guide to the size of the total Catholic community which is thought to be approximately 12% of the national population. It should also be noted that the figures take no account of the sizeable ethnic Catholic communities served by the chaplains to foreign immigrants.
2. The figures of clergy, churches and convents are supplied by the ecclesiastical authorities listed in the first column of the statistics.
3. The figures of infant baptisms, marriages and reception into full communion are taken from records kept by each parish.
4. The marriage total comprises both marriages between two Catholics and mixed marriages.
5. The weekly Mass attendance throughout England and Wales, compiled from an annual count taken on one typical Sunday in 2007, does not include those who attended Service churches or the churches and chapels of the ethnic Catholic communities.

Diocese	Diocesan Priests *(1)*	Diocesan Priests Retired	Religious Priests	Permanent Deacons
WESTMINSTER	387	86	304	8
ARUNDEL & BRIGHTON	178	50	62	30
BIRMINGHAM	273	52	106	75
BRENTWOOD	114	24	43	8
CARDIFF	66	14	41	15
CLIFTON	138	20	0	49
EAST ANGLIA	90	28	32	36
HALLAM	63	13	3	11
HEXHAM & NEWCASTLE	192	55	16	15
LANCASTER	140	27	27	52
LEEDS	180	39	12	26
LIVERPOOL	249	72	94	107
MENEVIA	32	11	19	2
MIDDLESBROUGH	91	24	62	12
NORTHAMPTON	94	24	17	37
NOTTINGHAM	131	32	48	37
PLYMOUTH	93	27	30	27
PORTSMOUTH	132	40	83	41
SALFORD	242	43	79	0
SHREWSBURY	125	27	25	45
SOUTHWARK	286	58	178	78
WREXHAM	45	11	26	9
EXARCHATE FOR UKRANIANS	10	1	5	1
POLISH PRIESTS	114	3	0	0
CHAPLAINS TO FOREIGN IMMIGRANTS	41	0	0	0
TOTAL	**3506**	**781**	**1312**	**721**

(1) Figure includes retired

RECAPULATION OF STATISTICS

2007 STATISTICS OF DIOCESES OF ENGLAND AND WALES

Diocese	Churches and Chapels		Conventso (Women)	Estimated Catholic Population of Diocese	Estimated Weekly Mass Attendance	Baptisms (up to 7 yrs)	Marriages	Receptions
	Parish Churches	Others open to the Public						
WESTMINSTER	216	40	216	500,000	156,513	5,899	795	484
ARUNDEL & BRIGHTON	110	24	58	183,484	41,772	2,280	476	214
BIRMINGHAM	225	46	102	278,741	74,742	5,437	821	476
BRENTWOOD	93	28	62	225.000	49,000	3,441	424	260
CARDIFF	64	20	16	144,000	18,484	1.053	251	88
CLIFTON	104			137,783	33,264	1,683	401	155
EAST ANGLIA	55	37	22	97,471	21,147	1,145	229	92
HALLAM	66	7	28	65,777	14,438	778	167	104
HEXHAM & NEWCASTLE	182		36	196,947	43,820	3,213	564	331
LANCASTER	109	29	25	108,137	24,639	1500	369	87
LEEDS	109	7	35	150,933	35,671	2,536	427	181
LIVERPOOL	212	10	75	500,616	61,527	6,156	958	157
MENEVIA	33	24	24	27,561	7,797	373	75	78
MIDDLESBROUGH	70	17	24	82,849	18,071	1,146	257	60
NORTHAMPTON	70	33	30	174,956	31,213	2,033	401	113
NOTTINGHAM	115	43	29	124,293	32,981	1,947	402	231
PLYMOUTH	108	2	33	58,608	15,391	681	188	93
PORTSMOUTH	153	6	43	177,082	37,748	2,227	480	199
SALFORD	194	11	65	288,000	59,242	4.860	707	223
SHREWSBURY	111	17	31	198,405	35,348	2,982	557	154
SOUTHWARK	183		112	393,553	93,685	7,028	785	417
WREXHAM	77		18	35,900	7,700	401	129	42
HM FORCES				6448	1363	192	87	
TOTAL	**2659**	**401**	**1084**	**4,156,544**	**915,556**	**58,991**	**9,950**	**4239**

Education Statistics for 2006/7 are currently unavailable. For statistics from 2004 please refer to the 2007 edition of the Directory

INFORMATION OF HISTORICAL INTEREST

HISTORICAL LIST OF THE ROMAN PONTIFFS

Information includes the name of the pope, in many cases his name before becoming pope, his birthplace or country of origin, the date of accession to the papacy, and the date of the end of reign which, in all but a few cases, was the date of death. Double dates record the day of election and coronation. Source: 'Annuario Pontificio'.

St. Peter, (Simon Bar-Jona): of Bethsaida, in Galilee, Prince of the Apostles, who received from Jesus Christ supreme pontifical power to be transmitted to his successors, resided first at Antioch, then at Rome, where he was martyred in the year 64 or 67, having governed the Church from that city for twenty-five years.

St Linus: Tuscany; 67-76.
St Anacletus (Cletus): Råoååme; 76-88.
St Clement: Rome; 88-97.
St Evaristus: Greece; 97-105.
St Alexander I: Rome; 105-115.
St Sixtus I: Rome; 115-125.
St Telesphorus: Greece; 125-136.
St Hyginus: Greece; 136-140.
St Pius I: Aquileia; 140-155.
St Anicetus: Syria; 155-166.
St Soter: Campania; 166-175.
St Eleutherius: Nicopolis in Epirus; 175-189.
Up to the time of St Eleutherius, the years indicated for the beginning and end of pontificates are not absolutely certain. Also, up to the middle of the 11th century, there are some doubts about the exact days and months given in chronological tables.
St Victor I: Africa; 189-199.
St Zephyrinus: Rome; 199-217.
St Callistus I: Rome; 217-222.
St Urban I: Rome; 222-230.
St Pontian: Rome; 21 Jul 230 to 28 Sep 235.
St Anterus: Greece; 21 Nov 235 to 3 Jan 236.
St Fabian: Rome; 10 Jan 236 to 20 Jan 250.
St Cornelius: Rome; Mar 251 to Jun 253.
St Lucius I: Rome; 25 Jun 253 to 5 Mar 254.
St Stephen I: Rome; 12 May 254 to 2 Aug 257.
St Sixtus II: Greece; 30 Aug 257 to 6 Aug 258.
St Dionysius: 22 Jul 259 to 26 Dec 268.
St Felix I: Rome 5 Jan 269 to 30 Dec 274.
St Eutychian: Luni; 4 Jan 275 to 7 Dec 283.
St Caius: Dalmatia; 17 Dec 283 to 22 Apr 296.
St Marcellinus: Rome; 30 Jun 296 to 25 Oct 304.
St Marcellus I: Rome; 27 May 308 or 26 Jun 308 to 16 Jan 309.
St Eusebius: Greece; 18 Apr 309 or 310 to 17 Aug 309 or 310.
St Melchiades (Miltiades): Africa; 2 Jul 311 to 11 Jan 314.
St Sylvester I: Rome; 31 Jan 314 to 31 Dec 335.
Most of the popes before St Sylvester I were martyrs.
St Marcus: Rome; 18 Jan 336 to 7 Oct 336.
St Julius I: Rome; 6 Feb 337 to 12 Apr 352.
Liberius: Rome; 17 May 352 to 24 Sep 366.
St Damasus I: Spain; 1 Oct 366 to 11 Dec 384.
St Siricius: Rome; 15 or 22 or 29 Dec 384 to 26 Nov 399.
St Anastasius I: Rome; 27 Nov 399 to 19 Dec 401.
St Innocent I: Albano; 22 Dec 401 to 12 Mar 417.
St Zozimus: Greece; 18 Mar 417 to 26 Dec 418.
St Boniface I: Rome; 28 or 29 Dec 418 to 4 Sep 422.
St Celestine I: Campania; 10 Sep 422 to 27 Jul 432.
St Sixtus III: Rome; 31 Jul 432 to 19 Aug 440.
St Leo I (the Great): Tuscany; 29 Sep 440 to 10 Nov 461.
St Hilary: Sardinia; 19 Nov 461 to 29 Feb 468.
St Simplicius: Tivoli; 3 Mar 468 to

10 Mar 483.

St Felix III (II); Rome; 13 Mar 483 to 1 Mar 492.
He should be called Felix II, and his successors of the same name should be numbered accordingly. The discrepancy in the numerical designation of popes named Felix was caused by the erroneous insertion in some lists of the name of St Felix of Rome, a martyr.

St Gelasius I: Africa; 1 Mar 492 to 21 Nov 496.

Anastasius II: Rome; 24 Nov 496 to 19 Nov 498.

St Symmachus: Sardinia; 22 Nov 498 to 19 Jul 514.

St Hormisdas: Frosinone; 20 Jul 514 to 6 Aug 523.

St John I, Martyr: Tuscany; 13 Aug 523 to 18 May 526.

St Felix IV (III): Samnium; 12 Jul 526 to 22 Sep 530.

Boniface II: Rome; 22 Sep 530 to 17 Oct 532.

John II: Rome; 2 Jan 533 to 8 May 535.
John II was the first pope to change his name. His given name was Mercury.

St Agapitus I: Rome; 13 May 535 to 22 Apr 536.

St Silverius, Martyr: Campania; 1 or 8 Jun 536 to 11 Nov 537 (d. 2 Dec 537).
St Silverius was violently deposed in March 537 and abdicated 11 Nov 537. His successor, Vigilius, was not recognised as pope by all the Roman clergy until his abdication.

Vigilius: Rome; 29 Mar 537 to 7 Jun 555.

Pelagius I: Rome; 16 Apr 556 to 4 Mar 561.

John III: Rome; 17 Jul 561 to 13 Jul 574.

Benedict I: Rome; 2 Jun 575 to 30 Jul 579.

Pelagius II: Rome; 26 Nov 579 to 7 Feb 590.

St Gregory I (the Great): Rome; 3 Sep 590 to 12 Mar 604.

Sabinian: Blera in Tuscany; 13 Sep 604 to 22 Feb 606.

Boniface III: Rome; 19 Feb 607 to 12 Nov 607.

St Boniface IV: Abruzzi; 25 Aug 608 to 8 May 615.

St Deusdedit (Adeodatus I): Rome; 19 Oct 615 to 8 Nov 618.

Boniface V: Naples; 23 Dec 619 to 25 Oct 625.

Honorius I: Campania; 27 Oct 625 to 12 Oct 638.

Severinus: Rome; 28 May 640 to 2 Aug 640.

John IV: Dalmatia; 24 Dec 640 to 12 Oct 642.

Theodore I: Greece; 24 Nov 642 to 14 May 649.

St Martin I, Martyr: Todi; Jul 649 to 16 Sep 655 (in exile from 17 Jun 653).

St Eugene I: Rome; 10 Aug 654 to 2 June 657.
St Eugene I was elected during the exile of St Martin I, who is believed to have endorsed him as pope.

St Vitalian: Segni; 30 Jul 657 to 27 Jan 672.

Adeodatus II: Rome; 11 Apr 672 to 17 Jun 676.

Donus: Rome; 2 Nov 676 to 11 Apr 678.

St Agatho: Sicily; 27 June 678 to 10 Jan 681.

St Leo II: Sicily; 17 Aug 682 to 3 Jul 683.

St Benedict II: Rome; 26 June 684 to 8 May 685.

John V: Syria; 23 Jul 685 to 2 Aug 686.

Conon: birthplace unknown; 21 Oct 686 to 21 Sep 687.

St Sergius I: Syria; 15 Dec 687 to 8 Sep 701.

John VI: Greece; 30 Oct 701 to 11 Jan 705.

John VII: Greece; 1 Mar 605 to 18 Oct 707.

Sisinnius: Syria; 15 Jan 708 to 4 Feb 708.

Constantine: Syria; 25 Mar 708 to 9 Apr 715.

St Gregory II: Rome; 19 May 715 to 11 Feb 731.

St Gregory III: Syria; 18 May 731 to Nov 741.

St Zachary: Greece; 10 Dec 741 to 22 Mar 752.

Stephen II (III): Rome; 26 Mar 752 to 26 April 757.
After the death of St Zachary, a Roman priest named Stephen was elected but died (four days later) before his consecration as bishop of Rome, which would have marked the beginning of his pontificate. Another Stephen was elected to succeed Zachary as Stephen II. (The first pope with this name was St Stephen, 254-57.) The ordinal III appears in parentheses after the name of Stephen II because the name of the earlier elected but deceased priest was included in some lists. Other Stephens have double numbers.

St Paul I: Rome; Apr (29 May) 757 to 28 Jun 767.

Stephen III (IV): Sicily; 1 (7) Aug 768 to 24 Jan 772.

Adrian I: Rome; 1 (9) Feb 772 to 25 Dec 795.

St Leo III: Rome; 26 (27) Dec 795 to 12 Jun 816.

Stephen IV (V): Rome; 22 Jun 816 to 24 Jan 817.
St Paschal I: Rome: 25 Jan 817 to 11 Feb 824.
Eugene II: Rome; Feb (May) 824 to Aug 827.
Valentine: Rome; Aug 827 to Sep 827.
Gregory IV: Rome; 827 to Jan 844.
Sergius II: Rome; Jan 844 to 27 Jan 847.
St Leo IV: Rome; Jan (10 Apr) 847 to 17 Jul 855.
Benedict III: Rome; Jul (29 Sep), 855 to 17 Apr 858.
St Nicholas I (the Great): Rome; 24 Apr 858 to 13 Nov 867.
Adrian II: Rome; 14 Dec 867 to 14 Dec 872.
John VIII: Rome; 14 Dec 872 to 16 Dec 882.
Marinus I: Gallese; 16 Dec 882 to 15 May 884.
St Adrian III: Rome; 17 May 884 to Sep 885.
Stephen V (VI): Rome; Sep 885 to 14 Sep 891.
Formosus: Portus; 6 Oct 891 to 4 Apr 896.
Boniface VI: Rome; Apr 896 to Apr 896.
Stephen VI (VII): Rome; May 896 to Aug 897.
Romanus: Gallese: Aug 897 to Nov 897.
Theodore II: Rome; Dec 897 to Dec 897.
John IX: Tivoli; Jan 898 to Jan 900.
Benedict IV: Rome; Jan (Feb) 900 to Jul 903.
Leo V: Ardea; Jul 903 to Sep 903.
Sergius III: Rome; 29 Jan 904 to 14 Apr 911.
Anastasius III: Rome; Apr 911 to Jun 913.
Landus: Sabina; Jul 913 to Feb 914.
John X: Tossignano (Imola); Mar 914 to May 928.
Leo VI: Rome; May 928 to Dec 928.
Stephen VII (VIII): Rome; Dec 928 to Feb 931.
John XI: Rome; Feb (Mar) 931 to Dec 935.
Leo VII: Rome; 3 Jan 936 to 13 Jul 939.
Stephen VIII (IX): Rome; 14 Jul 939 to Oct 942.
Marinus II: Rome; 30 Oct 942 to May 946.
Agapitus II: Rome; 10 May 946 to Dec 955.
John XII (Octavius): Tusculum; 16 Dec 955 to 14 May 964 (date of his death).
Leo VIII: Rome; 4 (6) Dec 963 to 1 Mar 965.
Benedict V: Rome; 22 May 964 to 4 Jul 966.

Confusion exists concerning the legitimacy of claims to the pontificate by Leo VIII and Benedict V. John XII was deposed 4 Dec 963 by a Roman council. If this deposition was invalid, Leo was an antipope. If the deposition of John was valid, Leo was the legitimate pope and Benedict was an antipope.

John XIII: Rome; 1 Oct 965 to 6 Sep 972.
Benedict VI: Rome; 19 Jan 973 to Jun 974.
Benedict VII: Rome; Oct 974 to 10 Jul 983.
John XIV (Peter Campenora): Pavia; Dec 983 to 20 Aug 984.
John XV: Rome; Aug 985 to Mar 996.
Gregory V (Bruno of Carinthia): Saxony; 3 May 996 to 18 Feb 999.
Sylvester II (Gerbert): Auvergne; 2 Apr 999 to 12 May 1003.
John XVII (Siccone): Rome; Jun 1003 to Dec 1003.
John XVIII (Phasianus): Rome; Jan 1004 to Jul 1009.
Sergius IV (Peter): Rome; 31 Jul 1009 to 12 May 1012.

The custom of changing one's name on election to the papacy is generally considered to date from the time of Sergius IV. Before his time, several popes had changed their names. After his time, this became a regular practice, with few exceptions; e.g., Adrian VI and Marcellus II.

Benedict VIII (Theophylactus): Tusculum; 18 May 1012 to 9 Apr 1024.
John XIX (Romanus): Tusculum; Apr (May) 1024 to 1032.
Benedict IX (Theophylactus): Tusculum; 1032 to 1044.
Sylvester III (John): Rome; 20 Jan 1045 to 10 Feb 1045.

Sylvester III was an antipope if the forcible removal of Benedict IX in 1044 was not legitimate.

Benedict IX (second time): 10 Apr 1045 to 1 May 1045.
Gregory VI (John Gratian): Rome; 5 May 1045 to 20 Dec 1046.
Clement II (Suitger, Lord of Morsleben and Hornburg): Saxony; 24 (25) Dec 1046 to 9 Oct 1047.

If the resignation of Benedict IX in 1045 and his removal at the December 1046 synod were not legitimate, Gregory VI and Clement II were antipopes.

Benedict IX (third time): 8 Nov 1047 to 17 July 1048 (d. c. 1055).
Damasus II (Poppo): Bavaria; 17 Jul 1048 to 9 Aug 1048.
St Leo IX (Bruno): Alsace; 12 Feb 1049 to 19 Apr 1054.
Victor II (Gebhard): Swabia; 16 Apr 1055 to 28 Jul 1057.
Stephen IX (X) (Frederick): Lorraine; 3 Aug

1057 to 29 Mar 1058.
Nicholas II (Gerard): Burgundy; 24 Jan 1059 to 27 Jul 1061.
Alexander II (Anselmo da Baggio): Milan; 1 Oct 1061 to 21 Apr 1073.
St Gregory VII (Hildebrand): Tuscany; 22 Apr (30 Jun) 1073 to 25 May 1085.
Bl Victor III (Dauferius; Desiderius): Benevento; 24 May 1086 to 16 Sep 1087.
Bl Urban II (Otto di Lagery): France; 12 Mar 1088 to 29 Jul 1099.
Paschal II (Raniero): Ravenna; 13 (14) Aug 1099 to 21 Jan 1118.
Gelasius II (Giovanni Caetani): Gaeta; 24 Jan (10 Mar) 1118 to 28 Jan 1119.
Callistus II (Guido of Burgundy): Burgundy; 2 (9) Feb 1119 to 13 Dec 1124.
Honorius II (Lamberto): Fiagnano (Imola); 15 (21) Dec 1124 to 13 Feb 1130.
Innocent II (Gregorio Papareschi): Rome; 14 (23) Feb 1130 to 24 Sep 1143.
Celestine II (Guido): Citta di Castello; 26 Sep (3 Oct) 1143 to 8 Mar 1144.
Lucius II (Gerardo Caccianemici): Bologna: 12 Mar 1144 to 15 Feb 1145.
Bl Eugene III (Bernardo Paganelli di Montemagno): Pisa; 15 (18) Feb 1145 to 8 Jul 1153.
Anastasius IV (Corrado): Rome; 12 Jul 1153 to 3 Dec 1154.
Adrian IV (Nicholas Breakspear): England; 4 (5) Dec 1154 to 1 Sep 1159.
Alexander III (Rolando Bandinelli): Siena; 7 (20) Sep 1159 to 30 Aug 1181.
Lucius III (Ubaldo Allucingoli): Lucca; 1 (6) Sep 1181 to 25 Sep 1185.
Urban III (Uberto Crivelli): Milan; 25 Nov (1 Dec) 1185 to 20 Oct 1187.
Gregory VIII (Alberto de Morra): Benevento; 21 (25) Oct 1187 to 17 Dec 1187
Clement III (Paolo Scolari): Rome; 19 (20) Dec 1187 to Mar 1191.
Celestine III (Giacinto Bobone): Rome; 30 Mar (14 Apr) 1191 to 8 Jan 1198.
Innocent III (Lotario dei Conti di Segni); Anagni; 8 Jan (22 Feb) 1198 to 16 Jul 1216.
Honorius III (Cencio Savelli): Rome; 18 (24) Jul 1216 to 18 Mar 1227.
Gregory IX (Ugolino, Count of Segni): Anagni; 19 (21) Mar 1227 to 22 Aug 1241.
Celestine IV (Goffredo Castiglioni): Milan; 25 (28) Oct 1241 to 10 Nov 1241.
Innocent IV (Sinibaldo Fieschi): Genoa; 25 (28) Jun 1243 to 7 Dec 1254.
Alexander IV (Rinaldo, Count of Segni): Anagni; 12 (20) Dec 1254 to 25 May 1261.
Urban IV (Jacques Pantaléon): Troyes; 29 Aug (4 Sep) 1261 to 2 Oct 1264.
Clement IV (Guy Foulques or Guido le Gros): France; 5 (15) Feb 1265 to 29 Nov 1268.
Bl Gregory X (Teobaldo Visconti): Piacenza; 1 Sep 1271 (27 Mar 1272) to 10 Jan 1276.
Bl Innocent V (Peter of Tarentaise): Savoy; 21 Jan (22 Feb) 1276 to 22 Jun 1276.
Adrian V (Ottobono Fieschi): Genoa; 11 Jul 1276 to 18 Aug 1276.
John XXI (Petrus Juliani or Petrus Hispanus): Portugal; 8 (20) Sep 1276 to 20 May 1277.

Elimination was made of the name of John XX in an effort to rectify the numerical designation of popes named John. The error dates back to the time of John XV.

Nicholas III (Giovanni Gaetano Orsini): Rome; 25 Nov (26 Dec) 1277 to 22 Aug 1280.
Martin IV (Simon de Brie): France; 22 Feb (23 Mar) 1281 to 28 Mar 1285.

The names of Marinus I (882-84) and Marinus II (942-46) were construed as Martin. In view of these two pontificates and the earlier reign of St Martin I (649-55), this pope was called Martin IV.

Honorius IV (Giacomo Savelli): Rome; 2 Apr (20 May) 1285 to 3 Apr 1287.
Nicholas IV (Girolamo Masci): Ascoli; 22 Feb 1288 to 4 Apr 1292.
St Celestine V (Pietro del Murrone); Isernia; 5 July (29 Aug) 1294 to 13 Dec 1294; d. 1296. Canonised 5 May 1313.
Boniface VIII (Benedetto Caetani); Anagni; 24 Dec 1294 (23 Jan 1295) to 11 Oct 1303.
Bl Benedict XI (Niccolo Boccasini): Treviso; 22 (27) Oct 1303 to 7 Jul 1304.
Clement V (Bertrand de Got): France; 5 June (14 Nov) 1305 to 20 Apr 1314. (First of Avignon popes.)

From 1309-77 Avignon was the residence of a series of French popes during a period of power struggles between the rulers of France, Bavaria and England and the Church. Despite some positive achievements it was the prologue to the Western Schism which began in 1378.

John XXII (Jacques d'Euse): Cahors; 7 Aug (5 Sep) 1316 to 4 Dec 1334.
Benedict XII (Jacques Fournier): France; 20 Dec 1334 (8 Jan 1335) to 25 Apr 1342.
Clement VI (Pierre Roger): France; 7 (19)

May 1342 to 6 Dec 1352.

Innocent VI (Etienne Aubert): France; 18 (30) Dec 1352 to 12 Sep 1362.

Bl Urban V (Guillaume de Grimoard): France; 28 Sept (6 Nov 1362 to 19 Dec 1370.

Gregory XI (Pierre Roger de Beaufort): France; 30 Dec 1370 (5 Jan 1371) to 26 Mar 1378. (Last of Avignon popes.)

Urban VI (Bartolomeo Prignano): Naples; 8 (18) Apr 1378 to 15 Oct 1389.

Boniface IX (Pietro Tomacelli): Naples; 2 (9) Nov 1389 to 1 Oct 1404.

Innocent VII (Cosma Migliorati): Sulmona; 17 Oct (11 Nov) 1404 to 6 Nov 1406.

Gregory XII (Angelo Correr): Venice; 30 Nov (19 Dec) 1406 to 4 July 1415 *when he voluntarily resigned from the papacy to permit the election of his successor. This brought to an end in the Council of Constance the Western Schism which had divided Christendom into two and then three papal obediences from 1378 to 1417. Gregory XII died 18 Oct 1417.*

Martin V (Oddone Colonna): Rome; 11 (21) Nov 1417 to 20 Feb 1431.

Eugene IV (Gabriele Condulmer): Venice; 3 (11) Mar 1431 to 23 Feb 1447.

Nicholas V (Tommaso Parentucelli): Sarzana; 6 (19) Mar 1447 to 24 Mar 1455.

Callistus III (Alfonso Borgia); Jativa (Valencia); 8 (20) Apr 1455 to 6 Aug 1458.

Pius II (Enea Silvio Piccolomini): Siena; 19 Aug (3 Sep) 1458 to 14 Aug 1464.

Paul II (Pietro Barbo): Venice; 30 Aug (16 Sep) 1464 to 26 Jul 1471.

Sixtus IV (Francesco della Rovere): Savona; 9 (25) Aug 1471 to 12 Aug 1484.

Innocent VIII (Giovanni Battista Cibo): Genoa; 29 Aug (12 Sep) 1484 to 25 Jul 1492.

Alexander VI (Rodrigo Borgia): Jativa (Valencia); 11 (26) Aug 1492 to 18 Aug 1503.

Pius III (Francesco Todeschini-Piccolomini): Siena; 22 Sep (1, 8 Oct) 1503 to 18 Oct 1503.

Julius II (Giuliano della Rovere): Savona; 31 Oct (26 Nov) 1503 to 21 Feb 1513.

Leo X (Giovanni de' Medici): Florence; 9 (19) Mar 1513 to 1 Dec 1521.

Adrian VI (Adrian Florensz): Utrecht; 9 Jan (31 Aug) 1522 to 14 Sep 1523.

Clement VII (Giulio de' Medici): Florence; 19 (26) Nov 1523 to 25 Sep 1534.

Paul III (Alessandro Farnese): Rome; 13 Oct (3 Nov) 1534 to 10 Nov 1549.

Julius III (Giovanni Maria Ciocchi del Monte): Rome; 7 (22) Feb 1550 to 23 Mar 1555.

Marcellus II (Marcello Cervini): Montepulciano; 9 (10) Apr 1555 to 1 May 1555.

Paul IV (Gian Pietro Carafa): Naples; 23 (26) May 1555 to 18 Aug 1559.

Pius IV (Giovan Angelo de' Medici): Milan; 25 Dec 1559 (6 Jan 1560) to 9 Dec 1565.

St Pius V (Antonio-Michele Ghislieri): Bosco (Alexandria); 7 (17) Jan 1566 to 1 May 1572. Canonised 22 May 1712.

Gregory XIII (Ugo Buoncompagni): Bologna; 13 (25) May 1572 to 10 Apr 1585.

Sixtus V (Felice Peretti): Grottammare (Ripatransone); 24 Apr (1 May) 1585 to 27 Aug 1590.

Urban VII (Giovanni Battista Castagna): Rome; 15 Sep 1590 to 27 Sep 1590.

Gregory XIV (Niccolo Sfondrati): Cremona; 5 (8) Dec 1590 to 16 Oct 1591.

Innocent IX (Giovanni Antonio Facchinetti): Bologna; 29 Oct (3 Nov) 1591 to 30 Dec 1591.

Clement VIII (Ippolito Aldobrandini): Florence; 30 Jan (9 Feb) 1592 to 3 Mar 1605.

Leo XI (Alessandro de' Medici): Florence; 1 (10) Apr 1605 to 27 Apr 1605.

Paul V (Camillo Borghese): Rome; 16 (29) May 1605 to 28 Jan 1621.

Gregory XV (Alessandro Ludovisi): Bologna; 9 (14) Feb 1621 to 8 July 1623.

Urban VIII (Maffeo Barberini): Florence; 6 Aug (29 Sep) 1623 to 29 Jul 1644.

Innocent X (Giovanni Battista Pamfili): Rome; 15 Sep (4 Oct) 1644 to 7 Jan 1655.

Alexander VII (Fabio Chigi): Siena; 7 (18) Apr 1655 to 22 May 1667.

Clement IX (Giulio Rospigliosi): Pistoia; 20 (26) Jun 1667 to 9 Dec 1669.

Clement X (Emilio Altieri): Rome; 29 Apr (11 May) 1670 to 22 Jul 1676.

Bl Innocent XI (Benedetto Odescalchi): Como; 21 Sep (4 Oct) 1676 to 12 Aug 1689. Beatified 7 Oct 1956.

Alexander VIII (Pietro Ottoboni): Venice; 6 (16) Oct 1689 to 1 Feb 1691.

Innocent XII (Antonio Pignatelli): Spinazzola; 12 (15) Jul 1691 to 27 Sep 1700.

Clement XI (Giovanni Francesco Albani): Urbino; 23, 30 Nov (8 Dec) 1700 to19 March 1721.

Innocent XIII (Michelangelo dei Conti): Rome; 8 (18) May 1721 to 7 Mar 1724.

Benedict XIII (Pietro Francesco [in religion Vincenzo Maria] Orsini); Gravina (Bari);

29 May (4 Jun) 1724 to 21 Feb 1730.
Clement XII (Lorenzo Corsini): Florence; 12 (16) Jul 1730 to 6 Feb 1740.
Benedict XIV (Prospero Lambertini): Bologna; 17 (22) Aug 1740 to 3 May 1758.
Clement XIII (Carlo Rezzonico): Venice; 6 (16) Jul 1758 to 2 Feb 1769.
Clement XIV (Giovanni Vincenzo Antonio [in religion Lorenzo] Gaganelli): Rimini; 19, 28 May (4 Jun) 1769 to 22 Sep 1774.
Pius VI (Giovanni Angelo Braschi): Cesena; 15 (22 Feb) 1775 to 29 Aug 1799.
Pius VII (Barnabà [in religion Gregorio] Chiaramonti): Cesena; 14 (21) Mar 1800 to 20 Aug 1823.
Leo XII (Annibale della Genga); Genga (Fabriano); 28 Sep (5 Oct) 1823 to 10 Feb 1829.
Pius VIII (Francesco Saverio Castiglioni): Cingoli; 31 Mar (5 Apr) 1829 to 30 Nov 1830.
Gregory XVI (Bartolomeo Alberto [in religion Mauro] Cappellari): Belluno; 2 (6) Feb 1831 to 1 Jun 1846.
Pius IX (Giovanni M. Mastai-Ferretti): Senigallia; 16 (21) June 1846 to 7 Feb 1878.
Leo XIII (Gioacchino Pecci): Carpineto (Anagni); 20 Feb (3 Mar) 1878 to 20 Jul 1903.
St Pius X (Giuseppe Sarto): Riese (Treviso); 4 (9) Aug 1903 to 20 Aug 1914. Canonised 29 May 1954.
Benedict XV (Giacomo della Chiesa): Genoa; 3 (6) Sep 1914 to 22 Jan 1922.
Pius XI (Achille Ratti): Desio (Milan); 6 (12) Feb 1922 to 10 Feb 1939.
Pius XII (Eugenio Pacelli): Rome; 2 (12) Mar 1939 to 9 Oct 1958.
John XXIII (Angelo Giuseppe Roncalli): Sotto il Monte (Bergamo); 28 Oct (4 Nov) 1958 to 3 Jun 1963 (beatified).
Paul VI (Giovanni Battista Montini): Concessio (Brescia); 21 (30) Jun 1963 to 6 Aug 1978.
John Paul I (Albino Luciani): Forno di Canale (Belluno); 26 Aug (3 Sep) 1978 to 28 Sep 1978.
John Paul II (Karol Wojtyla): Wadowice (Poland); 16 Oct (22 Oct) 1978 to 2 April 2005.

VICARS APOSTOLIC

After the Elizabethan Religious Settlement of 1559 the Catholics who refused to conform (known as recusants) were left without any formal ecclesiastical organisation until in 1581 the Pope appointed William Allen, resident on the Continent, as Prefect of the English Mission. Then from 1599 until 1621 the English secular clergy were placed under the authority of archpriests resident in England, while the regular clergy had their own superiors.

Prefect of the English Mission
William Allen (created cardinal 1587 and took up residence in Rome; appointed Archbishop of Malines 1589 though never resident) 1581-94

Archpriests
George Blackwell 1599-1608
George Birkhead 1608-14
William Harrison 1615-21

In 1623 the Pope appointed a bishop (with a titular see) as vicar apostolic in England and Wales. The first vicar apostolic William Bishop died the year after his appointment but not before he had organised the mission into districts and appointed a chapter. His successor Richard Smith was driven by internal opposition into exile in 1631. The brief reign of the Catholic King James II allowed the appointment of another vicar apostolic, and then the mission was divided into four districts each with its own vicar apostolic.

Vicars Apostolic Of England
William Bishop (Chalcedon) 1623-24
Richard Smith (Chalcedon) 1623-55
John Leyburn (Adrumetum) 1685-88

Vicars Apostolic Of The London District
John Leyburn (Adrumetum) 1688-1702
Bonaventure Giffard (Madaura) 1703-34
Benjamin Petre (Prusa) 1734-58
Richard Challoner (Debra) 1758-81
James Talbot (Birtha)1781-90
John Douglass (Centuriae) 1790-1812
William Poynter (Halia) 1812-27
James Yorke Bramston (Usulae) 1827-36
Thomas Griffiths (Oleno) 1836-47

Vicars Apostolic Of The Midland District
Bonaventure Giffard (Madaura) 1687-1703
George Witham (Marcopolis) 1703-15
John Talbot Stoner (Thespiae) 1716-56
John Hornyold (Philomenlia) 1756-78
James Talbot (Acone) 1778-95
Charles Berington (Hierocaesarea) 1795-98
Gregory Stapleton (Hierocaesarea) 1801-02
John Milner (Castabala) 1803-26
Thomas Walsh (Cambysopolis) 1826-40

Vicars Apostolic Of The Northern District
James Smith (Callipolis) 1688-1711
George Witham (Marcopolis) 1715-25
Thomas Dominic Williams, OP., (Tiberiopolis) 1725-40
Edward Dicconson (Mallus) 1741-52
Francis Petre (Amorius) 1752-75
William Walton (Trachonitis) 1775-80
Matthew Gibson (Comana) 1780-90
William Walton (Acanthus) 1790-1821
Thomas Smith (Bolina) 1821-31
Thomas Penswick (Europus) 1831-36
John Briggs (Trachis) 1836-40

Vicars Apostolic Of The Western District
Philip Michael Ellis, OSB, (Aurelipolis) 1688-1705
Matthew Prichard, OSF, (Myra) 1715-50
Lawrence William York, OSB, (Nisibis) 1750-70
Charles Walmsley, OSB, (Ramatha) 1770-97
William Gregory Sharrock, OSB, (Telmessus) 1797-1809
Peter Bernardine Collingridge, OSF, (Thespiae) 1809-29
Peter Augustine Baines, OSB, (Siga) 1829-43

IN 1840 THE FOUR DISTRICTS WERE DIVIDED INTO EIGHT

Vicars Apostolic Of The London District
Thomas Griffiths (Oleno) 1833-47
Thomas Walsh (Cambysopolis) 1847-49
Nicholas Wiseman (Melipotamus) 1849-50

Vicars Apostolic Of The Western District
Peter Augustine Baines, OSB, (Siga) 1829-43
Charles Michae Baggs (Pella) 1844-45
William Bernard Ullathorne, OSB, (Hetalonia) 1846-48
Joseph William Hendren, OSF, (Uranaopolis) 1848-50

Vicars Apostolic Of The Eastern District
William Wareing (Areopolis) 1840-50

Vicars Apostolic Of The Central District
Thomas Walsh (Cambysopolis) 1840-48
William Bernard Ullathorne, OSB, (Hetalonia) 1848-50

Vicars Apostolic Of The Welsh District
Thomas Joseph Brown, OSB, (Apollonia) 1840-50

Vicars Apostolic Of The Lancashire District
George Hilary Brown (Tloa) 1840-50

Vicars Apostolic Of The Yorkshire District
John Briggs (Trachis) 1840-50

Vicars Apostolic Of The Northern District
Francis George Mostyn (Abydus) 1840-47

William Riddell (Longona)
Aug 1847 - Nov 47
William Hogarth (Samosata) 1848-50

In 1850 the English Hierarchy, that is a structure of bishops-in-ordinary of dioceses, was restored.

FORMER APOSTOLIC DELEGATES AND APOSTOLIC NUNCIOS TO GREAT BRITAIN

APOSTOLIC DELEGATES

(The Apostolic Delegation was established in Great Britain on 21 November 1938)

Archbishop (later Cardinal) William Godfrey. Born 25 Sept 1889; ordained priest for the Archdiocese of Liverpool, 28 Oct 1916; ordained Titular Archbishop of Cius, 21 Nov 1938; appointed Apostolic Delegate to Great Britain, 21 Nov 1938-1954; Official to Poland, 1943; appointed Archbishop of Liverpool, 10 Nov 1953; appointed Archbishop of Westminster, 3 Dec 1966; elevated to Cardinal-Priest, of the title Ss Nereo ed Achilleo, 15 Dec 1958. Died 22 Jan 1963.

Archbishop Gerald Patrick Aloysius O'Hara. Born 4 May 1895; ordained priest for the Diocese of Philadelphia, USA; ordained Auxiliary Bishop of Philadelphia, 21 May 1929; installed as Bishop of Savannah, Georgia, USA, 15 Jan 1936; secondary appointment as Official to Romania 19 Feb 1947-5 July 1950; appointed Archbishop of Savannah-Atlanta, Georgia, USA, 12 July 1950; appointed Apostolic Nuncio to Ireland, 27 Nov 1951-8 June 1954; appointed Apostolic Delegate to Great Britain, 8 June 1954; resigned as Bishop of Savannah, 12 Nov 1959. Died 16 June 1963.

Archbishop Igino Eugenio Cardinale. Born 14 Oct 1916; ordained priest 13 July 1941; appointed Apostolic Delegate to Great Britain 4 Oct 1963-19 April 1969; ordained Titular Archbishop of Nepte, 20 Oct 1963; Apostolic Nuncio to Belgium, 19 April 1969; Apostolic Nuncio to Luxembourg, 9 May 1969; Apostolic Nuncio to European Community, 10 May 1970. Died 24 March 1983.

Archbishop Domenico Enrici. Born 9 April 1909, Cervasca, Italy; ordained priest 29 June 1933; ordained Titular Archbishop of Ancusa, 17 Sept 1955; appointed Apostolic Internuncio to Indonesia, 17 Sept, 1955; Apostolic Nuncio to Haiti, 1958; Apostolic Internuncio to Japan, 1959; Apostolic Delegate to Australia, 1 Oct 1962; Apostolic Delegate to Great Britain, 26 Oct 1969; appointed Official of the Roman Curia, 1973; resigned 1979. Died 3 Dec 1997.

Archbishop Bruno Bernard Heim. Born 5 March 1911; ordained priest of Basel, Switzerland, 29 June 1938; ordained Titular Archbishop of Xanthus, 10 Dec 1961; Apostolic Pro-Nuncio to Finland, 1966; Apostolic Pro-Nuncio to Egypt, 7 May 1969; appointed Apostolic Delegate to Great Britain, 16 July, 1973; Apostolic Pro-Nuncio to Great Britain (see entry below), 1982, resigned 1985. Died 18 March 2003.

APOSTOLIC PRO-NUNCIOS AND NUNCIOS

(The Apostolic Nunciature was established 17 January, 1982)

Archbishop Bruno Bernard Heim. Appointed first Apostolic Pro-Nuncio to Great Britain 1982, resigned 1985.

Archbishop Luigi Barbarito. Born Atripaldi, Italy, 19 April 1922; ordained priest, 20 Aug 1944; appointed Apostolic Nuncio to Haiti, 11 June, 1969; ordained Titular Archbishop of Fiorentino, 10 Aug 1969; appointed Apostolic Pro-Nuncio to Niger, Apostolic Nuncio to Senegal, and Apostolic Delegate to Guinea-Bissau, Mali, Mauritania, 5 April, 1975; appointed Apostolic Pro-Nuncio to Australia, 10 June, 1978; Apostolic Pro-Nuncio to Great Britain, 21 Jan, 1986 and Nuncio 13 April 1993. Retired – Apostolic Nuncio Emeritus, 31 July 1997.

Archbishop Pablo Puente Buces. Born Colindres, Spain, 16 June, 1931; ordained priest 2 April, 1956; appointed Apostolic Pro-Nuncio to Indonesia, 19 March, 1980; ordained Titular Archbishop of Macri; appointed Apostolic Pro-Nuncio to Capo Verde and Senegal, 15 March 1986; appointed Apostolic Delegate to Guinea-Bissau, Mauritania, 15 March, 1986; Apostolic Pro-Nuncio to Mali, 12 May, 1986; Apostolic Pro-Nuncio to Guinea-Bissau, 29 May, 1987; appointed Apostolic Nuncio to Lebanon, 31 July, 1989; Apostolic Nuncio to Kuwait, 25 May 1993; appointed Apostolic Nuncio to Great Britain, 31 July, 1997; resigned – Apostolic Nuncio Emeritus, 23 Oct, 2004.

SEES IN GREAT BRITAIN AND IRELAND

I. ENGLAND AND WALES

By Letters Apostolic *(Universalis Ecclesiae)* of Pope Pius IX, dated 29 Sept 1850, the English Hierarchy was restored, and the Metropolitan See fixed at Westminster. There were at first twelve Suffragan Sees: Beverley, Birmingham, Clifton, Hexham, Liverpool, Newport and Menevia, Northampton, Nottingham, Plymouth, Salford, Shrewsbury and Southwark. On 23 May 1861, the title of Hexham was changed to Hexham and Newcastle. On 20 Dec 1878, the diocese of Beverley was divided by Leo XIII into two, Leeds and Middlesbrough. On 19 May 1882, the diocese of Portsmouth was formed out of Southwark. By an Apostolic Brief *(De animarum salute)* of 4 March 1895, the Principality of Wales (except Glamorganshire) was made a separate Vicariate, with a Bishop as Vicar-Apostolic. The Vicariate, which had remained attached to the Province of Westminster, was changed on 12 May 1898 to the diocese of Menevia, and became a Suffragan See, the title of Newport and Menevia having been changed in 1896 to that of Newport only. Thus the Province of Westminster had at that time fifteen Suffragan Sees.

By Letters Apostolic *(Si qua est)* of 28 Oct 1911, Pius X divided the Province of Westminster into three new Provinces, viz, Westminister, Liverpool and Birmingham, reserving certain special privileges to the Archbishop of Westminister. The other dioceses were rearranged as follows:

With Westminster remained Northampton, Nottingham, Portsmouth and Southwark. To Birmingham were assigned the dioceses of Clifton, Newport, Plymouth, Shrewsbury and Menevia; the remaining sees of Hexham and Newcastle, Leeds, Middlesbrough and Salford were assigned to Liverpool.

By Letters Apostolic *(Cambria Celtica)* of 7 Feb 1916. Benedict XV raised Newport to Archiepiscopal rank, under the title of Cardiff; and Menevia became a Suffragan See of this new Province.

On 22 March 1917, the county of Essex, which had formerly formed part of the Archdiocese of Westminster, was made by Benedict XV into a separate diocese, and by a Bull *(Universalis Ecclesiae procuratio)* dated 20 July 1917, the Episcopal See was fixed at Brentwood, which accordingly became an additional Suffragan See of Westminster.

On 22 Nov 1924, by Apostolic Constitution *(Universalis Ecclesiae solicitudo)* a new Diocese of Lancaster was formed of the Counties of Cumberland and Westmorland, taken from the Diocese of Hexham and Newcastle, and Lancashire, north of the river Ribble, taken from the Archdiocese of Liverpool, of which this new diocese became an additional Suffragan See.

On 28 May 1965, by Letters Apostolic *(Romanorum Pontificum)*, Pope Paul VI decreed the formation of the new Province of Southwark to include the dioceses of Southwark, Portsmouth, Plymouth and Arundel and Brighton. By the same Letters the new Diocese of Arundel and Brighton was formed of the county of Sussex and the County of Surrey, south of the river Thames and outside the new Greater London Boroughs, taken from the Diocese of Southwark. Plymouth was taken from the Province of Birmingham: Southwark and Portsmouth were taken from the Province of Westminster.

On 13 March 1976 by the decree *Quod Ecumenicum* Pope Paul VI formed the diocese of East Anglia for the counties of Cambridge, Norfolk and Suffolk, which were formerly part of Northampton diocese.

By a Bull *Qui Arcano Dei* dated 30 May 1980, the Holy See announced the creation of the diocese of Hallam with its seat at Sheffield and formed from parts of the Leeds and Nottingham dioceses.

By a decree of Pope John Paul II, dated 18 March 1987, the Diocese of Wrexham was formed from territory taken from the Diocese of Menevia, consisting of the counties of Gwynedd and Clwyd, and the District of Montgomery in the County of Powys. By the same decree the County of West Glamorgan was transferred from the Archdiocese of Cardiff to the Diocese of Menevia.

ARCHBISHOPS, BISHOPS & AUXILIARIES SINCE THE RESTORATION OF THE HIERARCHY (1850)

■ ARCHDIOCESE OF WESTMINSTER

I Cardinal Nicholas Wiseman: born 3 Aug 1802; cons 8 June 1840, as Coadj for the Midland District; trans from the London District to Westminster, 29 Sept 1850; created Cardinal Priest, 30 Sept 1850; died 15 Feb 1865.

II Cardinal Henry Edward Manning: born 15 July 1808; cons 8 June 1865; created Cardinal Priest, 15 Mar 1875; died 14 Jan 1892.

III Cardinal Herbert Vaughan: born 15 April 1832; cons Bishop of Salford, 28 Oct 1872; trans to Westminster, 8 April 1892; created Cardinal Priest, 16 Jan 1893; died 19 June 1903.

IV Cardinal Francis Bourne: born 23 Mar 1861; cons as Coadj for Southwark, 1 May 1896; succ 9 April 1897; trans to Westminster, 11 Sept 1903; created Cardinal Priest, 27 Nov 1911; died 1 Jan 1935.

V Cardinal Arthur Hinsley: born 25 Aug 1865; cons Bp of Sebastopolis, 30 Nov 1926; Abp of Sardis, May 1930; trans to Westminster, 25 Mar 1935; created Cardinal Priest 13 Dec1937; died 17 Mar 1943.

VI Cardinal Bernard William Griffin: born 21 Feb 1899; cons Bp of Abya, and Aux for Birmingham, 30 June 1938; trans to Westminster, 18 Dec 1943; created Cardinal Priest, 18 Feb 1946; died 20 Aug 1956.

VII Cardinal William Godfrey: born 25 Sept 1889; cons Abp of Cius, 21 Dec 1938; Apostolic Delegate to Great Britain, 21 Nov 1938; trans to Liverpool, 14 Nov 1953; trans to Westminster, 3 Dec 1956; created Cardinal Priest, 15 Dec 1958; died 22 Jan 1963.

VIII Cardinal John Carmel Heenan: born 26 Jan 1905, cons Bp of Leeds 12 Mar 1951; trans to Liverpool as Abp 2 May 1957; trans to Westminster 2 Sept 1963; created Cardinal Priest 22 Feb 1965; died 7 Nov 1975.

IX Cardinal George Basil Hume: born 2 Mar 1923; ord Archbishop of Westminster 25 Mar 1976, created Cardinal Priest 24th May 1976 Died 17 June 1999.

X Archbishop Cormac Murphy-O'Connor: born 24 Aug 1932; ord. Bp of Arundel and Brighton 21 Dec 1977; trans. to Westminster 22 March 2000; created Cardinal (Titular church, Santa Maria Sopra Minerva), 21 Feb 2001.

■ DIOCESE OF ARUNDEL AND BRIGHTON

I David J Cashman: born 27 Dec 1912; cons Bp of Cantano and Aux of Westminster 27 May 1958; trans 14 June 1965; died 14 Mar 1971.

II Michael Bowen: born 23 April 1930; cons as Coadj 27 June 1970; succ 14 Mar 1971; trans to Southwark 23 April 1977.

III Cormac Murphy O'Connor: born 24 Aug 1932; ord Bishop of Arundel & Brighton 21 Dec 1977. Trans to Westminster 22 March 2000. Created Cardinal Priest Feb 21, 2001.

IV Kieran Thomas Conry, born 1 Feb 1951, ord Bishop of Arundel and Brighton 9 June 2001.

■ ARCHDIOCESE OF BIRMINGHAM

I William Bernard Ullathorne, OSB: cons 21 June 1846; Vicar-Apostolic of Western District; trans from Central District to Birmingham, 29 Sept 1850; to Archiepiscopal See of Cabasa, 27 April 1888; died 21 Mar 1889.

II Edward Ilsley: cons 4 Dec 1879, as Bishop-Auxiliary; trans to Birmingham, 17 Feb 1888; named Archbishop and Metropolitan, 28 Oct 1911; resigned 15 Jan 1921; appointed Abp of Macre, 13 June 1921; died 1 Dec 1926.

III John McIntyre: born 1 Jan 1855; cons Bp of Lamus and Auxiliary, 30 July 1912; reappointed Auxiliary and named Abp of Oxyrhnchus, 24 Aug 1917; succ 16 June 1921; resigned and appointed Abp of Odesso, 16 Nov 1928; died 21 Nov 1934.

IV Thomas Leighton Williams: born 20 Mar 1877; cons 25 July 1929; died 1 April 1946.

V Joseph Masterson: born 29 Jan 1899; cons 19 Mar 1947; died 30 Nov 1953.

VI Francis Joseph Grimshaw: born 6 Oct 1901; cons Bp of Plymouth 25 July 1947; trans to Birmingham as Archbishop 11 May 1954; died 22 Mar 1965.

VII George Patrick Dwyer: born 22 Sept 1908; cons 24 Sept 1957; trs to Birmingham 7 Oct 1965; resigned 1 Sept 1981; Apostolic Administrator 1 Sept 1981; retired March 1982; Died 17 Sept 1987.

VIII Maurice Couve de Murville: born 27 June 1929; ord Archbishop of Birmingham 25 Mar 1982, retired 29 June 1999, died 3 Nov 2007.

IX Vincent Nichols; born 8th Nov 1945; ord. titular Bp of Othona on appnt as Aux. Bp of Westminster 24 Jan 1992; trans. to Archdiocese of Birmingham 22 March 2000.

■ **DIOCESE OF BRENTWOOD**

I Bernard Nicholas Ward: born 4 Feb 1857; cons Bishop of Lydda (and Administrator Apostolic of the new diocese) 10 April 1917; trans to Brentwood 20 July 1917; died 21 Jan 1920.
II Arthur Doubleday: born 17 Oct 1865; cons 23 June 1920; died 23 Jan 1951.
III George Andrew Beck, AA: born 28 May 1904; cons Bishop of Tigia and Coadjutor, 21 Sept 1948; succ 23 Jan 1951; trans to Salford 28 Nov 1955, trans to Liverpool 29 jan 1964, retired 11 Feb 1976, died 13 Sept 1978.
IV Bernard Patrick Wall: born 15 Mar 1894; cons 18 Jan 1956; resigned and apptd. Bishop of Othona, 14 April 1969; died 18 June 1976.
V Patrick Joseph Casey: born 20 Nov 1913; cons Bishop of Sufar and Auxiliary of Westminster, 2 Feb 1966; trans 28 Nov 1969; resigned 11 Dec 1979, died 26 Jan 1999.
VI Thomas McMahon: born 17 June 1936; ord Bishop of Brentwood 17 July 1980.

■ **ARCHDIOCESE OF CARDIFF**

I Thomas Joseph Brown, OSB: born 2 May 1798; cons 28 Oct 1840, as Vicar-Apostolic of the Welsh District; trans to Newport and Menevia, 29 Sept 1850; died 12 April 1880.
II John Cuthbert Hedley, OSB: born 15 April 1837; cons 29 Sept 1873, as Bishop Auxiliary; trans to Newport and Menevia, 18 Feb 1881; died 11 Nov 1915.
III James Romanus Bilsborrow, OSB; born 27 Aug 1862; cons as Bishop of Port Louis, 24 Feb 1911; trans to Cardiff, 7 Feb 1916, as Archbishop and Metropolitan; resigned 1 Sept 1920; apptd Abp of Cius, 16 Dec 1920; died 19 June 1931.
IV Francis Mostyn: born 6 Aug 1860; cons as Vicar-Apostolic of Wales, 14 Sept 1895; trans to Menevia, 14 May 1898; trans to Cardiff as Archbishop and Metropolitan, 7 Mar 1921; died 25 Oct 1939.
V Michael McGrath: born 24 March 1882; cons Bishop of Menevia 24 Sept 1935; trans to Cardiff 20 June 1940; died 28 Feb 1961.
VI John A Murphy: born 21 Dec 1905; cons as Coadj Bishop of Shrewsbury 25 Feb 1948; succ 3 June 1949; trans 26 Aug 1961; retired 25 Mar 1983; died 18 November 1995.
VII John Aloysius Ward: born 24 Jan 1929; ord Coadjutor Bishop of Menevia 1 Oct 1980; succd 5 Feb 1981; trans to Cardiff 25 Mar 1983; retired 2001, died 27 Mar 2007
VIII Peter D Smith: b 21 Oct 1943; cons Bishop of East Anglia 27 May 1995; trans to Cardiff as Archbishop and Metropolitan 4 Dec 2001.

■ **DIOCESE OF CLIFTON**

I Joseph William Hendren, OSF: born 19 Oct 1791; cons 10 Sept 1848; as Vicar-Apostolic of the Western District; trans to Clifton, 29 Sept 1850, to Nottingham, 22 June 1851, to Martyropolis, 23 Feb 1853; died 14 Nov 1866.
II Thomas Burgess; born 1 Oct 1791; cons 27 July 1851; died 27 Nov 1854.
III William Joseph Hugh Clifford: born 24 Dec 1823; cons 15 Feb 1857; died 14 Aug 1893.
IV William Robert Brownlow: born 4 July 1830; cons 1 May 1894; died 9 Nov 1901.
V George Ambrose Burton: born 28 April 1852; cons 1 May 1902; died 8 Feb 1931.
VI William Lee: born 27 Sept 1875; cons 26 Jan 1932; died 21 Sept 1948.
VII Joseph E Rudderham: born 17 June 1899; cons 26 July 1949; resigned 31 Aug 1974; died 24 Feb, 1979.
VIII Mervyn A. Alexander: born 29th June 1925; ord Coadjutor Bishop 25 April 1972; succd 20th Dec 1974.
IX Declan R Lang, born 15 April 1950, ord Bishop of Clifton 28 March 2001.

■ **DIOCESE OF EAST ANGLIA**

I Alan Charles Clark: born 9 Aug 1919; cons Bishop of Elmham 13 May 1969 on appointment as Auxiliary in Northampton; trs to newly-erected see of East Anglia 2 June 1976; retired 25 May 1995.
II Peter Smith: born 21 Oct 1943; ord Bishop 27 May 1995; trans to Cardiff 26 Oct 2001.
III Michael Charles Evans: b 10 Aug 1951; cons Bishop of East Anglia, 19 March 2003.

■ **DIOCESE OF HALLAM**

I Gerald Moverley: born 19 April 1922; cons Bishop of Tinisa in Proconsulari 25 Jan 1968; trs in May 1980 to newly-erected See of Hallam; retired 8 July 1996; died 14 Dec 1996.
II John Rawsthorne: born 12 Nov 1936; ord titular Bishop of Rotdon 16 Dec 1981; trans 3 July 1997.

■ **DIOCESE OF HEXHAM & NEWCASTLE**

I William Hogarth: born 25 March 1786; cons 24 Aug 1848, as Vicar-Apostolic of the Northern District; trans to Hexham, 29 Sept 1840; died 29 Jan 1866.
II James Chadwick: born 24 April 1813; cons 28 Oct 1866; died 14 May 1882.
III John William Bewick: born 20 April 1824; cons 18 Oct 1882; died 29 Oct 1886.
IV Henry O'Callaghan; born 29 Mar 1827; cons 18 Jan 1888; resigned 1889; trans to

Archiepiscopal See of Nicosia, 1 Oct 1889; died 11 Oct 1904.
V Thomas W Wilkinson: born 5 April 1825; cons 25 July 1888, as Bishop-Auxiliary; trans to Hexham and Newcastle, 28 Dec 1889; died 17 April 1909.
VI Richard Collins: born 5 April 1857; cons as Bishop- Auxilliary, 29 June 1905; trans to Hexham and Newcastle, 21 June 1909; died 9 Feb 1924.
VII Joseph Thorman: born 6 Aug 1871; cons 27 Jan 1925; died 7 Oct 1936.
VIII Joseph McCormack: born 17 May 1887; cons 4 Feb 1937; died 2 Mar 1958.
IX James Cunningham: born 15 Aug 1910; cons as Bishop-Auxiliary 12 Nov 1957; trans to Hexham and Newcastle, 1 July 1958; resigned 16 May 1974; died 10 July 1974.
X Hugh Lindsay: born 20 June 1927; ord Bishop of Chester-le-Street 11 Dec 1969, trans 12 Dec 1974. Resigned 20th March 1992.
X1 Ambrose Griffiths: born 4 Dec 1928; ord 20 Mar 1992; rtd 24 May 2004.
XII Kevin Dunn, b, July 9, 1950, cons 25 May, 2004, died 1 mar 2008.

■ DIOCESE OF LANCASTER

I Thomas Wulstan Pearson, OSB: born 4 Jan 1870; cons 24 Feb 1925; died 1 Dec 1938.
II Thomas E Flynn: born 6 Jan 1880; cons 24 July 1939; died 4 Nov 1961.
III Brian C Foley: born 25 May 1910; cons 13 June 1962; retired 22 May, 1985. Died 23 Dec 1999.
IV John Brewer: born 24 Nov 1929; ord Auxiliary Bishop of Shrewsbury 28 July 1971; trans Coadjutor Bishop of Lancaster 15 Nov 1983; succd 22 May 1985. Died 20 June 2000.
V Patrick O'Donoghue, born 4 May 1934, ord Auxiliary Bishop of Westminster 29 June 1993; trans to Lancaster 4 July 2001.

■ DIOCESE OF LEEDS

I John Briggs: Cons as Coadjutor for the Northern District, 29 June 1833; trans from the Yorkshire District to Beverley, 29 Sept 1850; resigned 7 Nov 1860; died 4 Jan 1861.
II Robert Cornthwaite: born 9 May 1818; cons 10 Nov 1861, as Bishop of Beverley; trans to Leeds 20 Dec 1878; died 16 June 1890.
III William Gordon: born 24 Sept 1831; cons 24 Feb 1890, as Coadjutor; succ 16 June 1890; died 7 June 1911.
IV Joseph Robert Cowgill: born 23 Feb 1860; cons 30 Nov 1905, as Coadjutor; succ 7 June 1911; died 12 May 1936.
V Henry John Poskitt: born 6 Sept 1888; cons 21 Sept 1936; died 19 Feb 1950.
VI John Carmel Heenan: born 26 Jan 1905; cons 12 Mar 1951; trans to Liverpool as Abp 2 May 1957; trans to Westminster 2 Sept 1963; died 7 Nov 1975.
VII George Patrick Dwyer: born 25 Sept 1908; cons 24 Sept 1957; trans to Birmingham as Abp, 5 Oct 1965, died 1987.
VIII William Gordon Wheeler; born 5 May 1910; cons Bishop of Tendali and Coadjutor Bishop of Middlesbrough 19 Mar 1964; trans to Leeds 3 May 1966; retired 10 Sept 1985 died 20th Feb 1998.
IX David Konstant: born 16 June 1930; ord Auxiliary Bishop of Westminster 25 Apr 1977; trans to Leeds 23 July 1985.
X Arthur Roche; b 6 March, 1950, Bishop of Rusticania 10 may 2001, Coadj Bishop of Leeds 16 Jul 2002, succ 7 Apr 2004.

■ ARCHDIOCESE OF LIVERPOOL

I George Brown: born 13 Jan 1786; cons 24 Aug 1840, as Vicar-Apostolic of the Lancashire District; trans to Liverpool, 29 Sept 1850; died 25 Jan 1856.
II Alexander Goss: born 5 July 1814; cons 25 Sept 1853, as Coadj; succ 25 Jan 1856; died 3 Oct 1872.
III Bernard O'Reilly: born 10 Jan 1824; cons 19 Mar 1873; died 9 April 1894.
IV Thomas Whiteside: born 17 April 1857; cons 15 Aug 1894; Archbishop and Metropolitan, 28 Oct 1911; died 28 Jan 1921.
V Frederick William Keating: born 13 June 1859; cons Bishop of Northampton, 25 Feb 1908; trans to Liverpool as Abp, 14 June 1921; died 7 Feb 1928.
VI Richard Downey: born 6 May 1881; cons 21 Sept 1928; died 16 June 1953.
VII William Godfrey: born 25 Sept 1889; cons Archbishop of Cius, 21 Dec 1938; apptd Apostolic Delegate to Great Britain, 21 Nov 1938; trans to Liverpool, 14 Nov 1953; trans to Westminster, 3 Dec 1956; died 22 Jan 1963.
VIII John Carmel Heenan: born 26 Jan 1905; cons Bishop of Leeds 12 Mar 1951; trans to Liverpool as Abp 2 May 1957; trans to Westminster, 2 Sept 1963; died 7 Nov 1975.
IX George Andrew Beck, AA: born 28 May 1904; cons Bishop of Tigia and Coadj of Brentwood 21 Sept 1948; succ 23 Jan 1951; trans to Salford 28 Nov 1955; trans to Liverpool 29 Jan 1964; retired 11 Feb 1976; died 13 Sept 1978.
X Derek Worlock: born 4 Feb 1920; ord Bishop of Portsmouth 21 Dec 1965; trans 7 Feb 1976; died 8 Feb 1996.
XI Patrick Altham Kelly: born 23 Nov 1938; ord Bishop of Salford 3 Apr 1984, trans to Liverpool 3 July 1996

■ DIOCESE OF MENEVIA

I Francis Mostyn: born 6 Aug 1860; cons as Vicar-Apostolic of Wales, 14 Sept 1895; trans to Menevia 14 May 1898; trans to Cardiff as Archbishop and Metropolitan, 7 Mar 1921, and was Apostolic-Administrator of Menevia till appointment of Bishop Vaughan; died 25 Oct 1939.
II Francis Vaughan: born 5 May 1877; cons 8 Sept 1926; died 13 Mar 1935.
III Michael McGrath: born 25 Mar 1882; cons 24 Sept 1935; trans to Cardiff, 20 June 1940; died 28 Feb 1961.
IV Daniel Joseph Hannon: born 12 June 1884; cons 1 May 1941; died 26 April 1946.
V John E Petit: born 22 June 1895; Cons 25 Mar 1947; resigned 19 July 1972; died 3 June 1973.
VI Langton D Fox: born 21 Feb 1917; cons 16 Dec 1965; resigned 5 Feb 1981; died 26 July 1997.
VII John Aloysius Ward, OFM.Cap: born 24 Jan 1929; cons Coadjutor Bishop of Menevia 1 Oct 1980; succ 5 Feb 1981; trans to Cardiff 11 July 1983, died 27 Mar 2007.
VIII James Hannigan: born 15 July 1928; cons 23 Nov 1983; trans to newly erected see of Wrexham 24 Mar 1987; died 6 March 1994.
IX Daniel Joseph Mullins: born 10 July 1929; ord Titular Bishop of Sidnacestre 1 April 1970; trans to Menevia as Bishop 17 Feb 1987.
X Mark Jabalé OSB, born 16 Oct 1933, ordained Co-adjutor Bishop of Menevia 7 Dec 2000, installed as Bishop 12 June 2001.

■ DIOCESE OF MIDDLESBROUGH

I Richard Lacy: born 16 Jan 1841; cons 18 Dec 1879; died 11 April 1929.
II Thomas Shine: born 11 Feb 1872; cons Bishop of Lamus and Coadjutor, 29 June 1921; succ 11 April 1929; named Archbishop ad personam 19 Jan 1955; died 22 Nov 1955.
III George Brunner: born 21 Aug 1889; cons Bishop of Elide and Auxiliary 25 July 1946; trans 7 June 1956; resigned 13 June 1967; died 21 Mar 1969.
IV John Gerard McClean: born 24 Sept 1914; cons as Coadjutor 24 Feb 1967; succ 13 June 1967; died 27 August 1978.
V Augustine Harris: born 27 Oct 1917; ord Bishop of Socia 11 Feb 1966, transl 20 Nov 1978; retired December 1992; died 30 August 2007.
VI John Crowley: born 23 June 1941; ord Bishop of Tala 8 Dec 1986, transl 18 Jan 1993; resigned 3 May 2007
VII Terence Patrick Drainey: born 1 Aug 1949; cons Bishop of Middlesbrough 25 Jan 2008.

■ DIOCESE OF NORTHAMPTON

I William Wareing: born 16 Feb 1791; cons 12 Sept 1840 as Vicar-Apostolic of the Eastern District; trans to Northampton, 29 Sept 1850; resigned 11 Feb 1858; apptd Bp of Retimo, 23 Dec 1858; died 26 Dec 1865.
II Francis Kerril Amherst: born 21 Mar 1819; cons 4 July 1858; resigned 1879; apptd Bp of Szusa, 1880; died 21 Aug 1883.
III Arthur Riddell: born 15 Sept 1836; cons 9 June 1880; died 15 Sept 1907.
IV Frederick William Keating: born 13 June 1859; cons 25 Feb 1908; trans to Liverpool as Archbishop and Metropolitan, 13 June 1921.
V Dudley Charles Cary-Elwes: born 5 Feb 1868; cons 15 Dec 1921; died 1 May 1932.
VI Laurence Youens: born 14 Dec 1873; cons 25 July 1933; died 14 Nov 1939.
VII Thomas Leo Parker: born 21 Dec 1887; cons 11 Feb 1941; resigned 14 Feb 1967; died 25 Mar 1975.
VIII Charles Alexander Grant: born 25 Oct 1906; cons 25 April 1961; resigned 1982.
IX Francis Gerard Thomas: born 29 May 1930, cons 29 Sept 1982, died 25 Dec 1988.
X Patrick Leo McCartie: born 5 Sept 1925; ord Bishop of Elmham and Auxiliary Bishop of Birmingham 20 May 1977; transl 19 Mar 1990.
XI Kevin John Patrick McDonald, born 18 Aug 1947, ord Bishop of Northampton 2 May 2001; trans to Metropolitan See of Southwark 8 Dec 2003.
XII Peter John Haworth Doyle, born 3 May 1944, ord Bishop of Northampton 28 June 2005.

■ DIOCESE OF NOTTINGHAM

I Joseph W Hendren, OSF: born 19 Oct 1791; cons 10 Sept 1848, as Vicar-Apostolic of the Western District; trans to Clifton, 29 Sept 1850; to Nottingham, 22 June 1851; to Martyropolis 23 Feb 1853; died 14 Nov 1866.
II Richard Roskell: born 15 Aug 1817; cons 21 Sept 1853; resigned 1874; trans to Abdera, 5 July 1875; died 27 Jan 1883.
III Edward G Bagshawe: born 12 Jan 1829; cons 12 Nov 1874; resigned 1901; trans to Hypoepa 1902; to Archiepiscopal See of Seleucia, 1904; died 6 Feb 1915.
IV Robert Brindle: born 4 Nov 1837; cons 12 Mar 1899 as Bishop-Auxiliary for Westminster; trans to Nottingham, 6 Dec 1901; to Tacape, 1 June 1915; died 27 June 1916.

V Thomas Dunn: born 28 July 1870; cons 25 Feb 1916; died 21 Sept 1931.
VI John Francis McNulty: born 11 Aug 1879; cons 11 June 1932; died 8 June 1943.
VII Edward Ellis: born 30 June 1899; cons 1 May 1944; retired 31 Oct 1974; died 6 July, 1979.
VIII James J. McGuinness: born 2 Oct 1925; ord Coajutor Bishop 23 Mar 1972; succd 31 Oct 1974, died 6 Apr 2007
IX Malcolm McMahon OP, born 14 June 1949, ord Bishop of Nottingham 8 Dec 2000.

■ DIOCESE OF PLYMOUTH

I George Errington: born Sept 1804; cons 25 July 1851; trans to Archiepiscopal See of Trebizond, April 1855; died 19 Jan 1886.
II William Vaughan: born 14 Feb 1814; cons 16 Sept 1855; died 25 Oct 1902.
III Charles Graham: born 5 April 1834; cons as Coadjutor 28 Oct 1891; succ 25 Oct 1902; trans to Episcopal See of Tiberias, Feb 1911; died 2 Sept 1912.
IV John Keily: born 23 June 1854; cons 13 June 1911; died 23 Sept 1928.
V John P Barrett: born 31 Oct 1878; cons as Aux for Birmingham 22 Feb 1927; trans 7 June 1929; died 2 Nov 1946.
VI Francis Joseph Grimshaw: born 6 Oct 1901; cons 25 July 1947; trans to Birmingham, 11 May 1954; died 22 Mar 1965.
VII Cyril Edward Restieaux: born 25 Feb 1910; cons 14 June 1955; retired 13 Jan 1986, died 26th Feb 1996.
V111 Christopher Budd: born 27 May 1937; ord Bishop of Plymouth 15 Jan 1986.

■ DIOCESE OF PORTSMOUTH

I John Vertue: born 28 April 1826; cons 25 July 1882; died 23 May 1900.
II John Baptist Cahill: born 2 Sept 1841; cons 1 May 1900; died 2 Aug 1910.
III William T Cotter: born 21 Dec 1866; cons Bishop Auxiliary, 19 Mar 1905; trans to Portsmouth, 24 Nov 1910; died 24 Oct 1940.
IV John Henry King: born 16 Sept 1880; cons Bishop of Opus and Auxiliary, 15 July 1938; trans 4 June 1941; named Archbishop ad personam 6 June 1954; died 23 Mar 1965.
V Derek Worlock: born 4 Feb 1920; cons 21 Dec 1965; trans to Liverpool, 16 Mar 1976, died 8 Feb 1996
V1 Anthony Joseph Emery: born 17 May 1918; ord Bishop of Tamallula and Auxiliary of Birmingham 4 Mar 1968; transl 13 Sept 1976; died 5th April 1988.
VII Crispian Hollis: born 17 Nov 1936; ord Bishop of Cincarr and Auxiliary in Birmingham 5 May 1987, transl 6 Dec 1988.

■ DIOCESE OF SALFORD

I William Turner: born 25 Sept 1799; cons 25 July 1851; died 12 July 1872.
II Cardinal Herbert Vaughan: born 15 April 1832; cons 28 Oct 1872; trans to Westminster, 8 April 1892; died 19 June 1903.
III John Bilsborrow: born 30 Mar 1836; cons 24 Aug 1892; died 5 Mar 1903.
IV Louis Charles Casartelli: born 14 Nov 1852; cons 21 Sept 1903; died 18 Jan 1925.
V Thomas Henshaw: born 2 Feb 1873; cons 31 Dec 1925; died 23 Sept 1938.
VI Henry Vincent Marshall: born 19 July 1884; cons 21 Sept 1939; died 14 April 1955.
VII George Andrew Beck, AA: born 28 May 1904; cons Bishop of Tigia and Coadjutor to Brentwood, 21 Sept 1948; succ 23 Jan 1951; trans to Salford, 28 Nov 1955; trans to Liverpool as Abp 29 Jan 1964; died 13 Sept 1978.
VIII Thomas Holland; born 11 June 1908; cons Bishop of Etenna and Coadjutor to Portsmouth 21 Dec 1960; trans 3 Sept 1964; retired 21 June 1983, died 30 Sept 1999.
IX Patrick Altham Kelly: born 23 Nov 1938; ord Bishop of Salford 3 Apr 1984; trans to Liverpool 3 July 1996.
X Terence J Brain: born 19th Dec. 1938; ord. titular Bishop of Amudarsa 25th April 1991; trans to Salford 7th Oct 1997.

■ DIOCESE OF SHREWSBURY

I James Brown: born 11 Jan 1812; cons 27 July 1851; died 14 Oct 1881.
II Edmund Knight: born 27 Aug 1827; cons 25 July 1879; as Bishop-Auxiliary; trans to Shrewsbury, 25 April 1882; resigned 11 May 1895; trans to Flavias, 28 May 1895; died 9 June 1905.
III John Carroll: born 1838; cons 28 Oct 1893 as Bishop-Coadjutor; succ 1 May 1895; died 14 Jan 1897.
IV Samuel W Allen: born 23 Mar 1844; cons 16 June 1897; died 13 May 1908.
V Hugh Singleton: born 30 July 1851; cons 21 Sept 1908; died 17 Dec 1934.
VI Ambrose J Moriarty: born 7 Aug 1870; cons 28 Jan 1932; as Bishop-Coadjutor; succ 17 Dec 1934; died 3 June 1949.
VII John A Murphy: born 21 Dec 1905; cons Bishop-Coadjutor, 25 Feb 1948; succ 3 June 1949; trans to Cardiff, 26 Aug 1961.
VIII William E Grasar: born 18 May 1913; cons 27 June 1962; retired 30 Aug 1980; died 28 Dec 1982.
IX Joseph Gray: born 20 Oct 1919; ord Auxiliary Bishop of Liverpool 16 Feb 1979;

transl 30 Sept 1980; retired 30 Aug 1995. Died 7 May 1999.
X Brian Michael Noble: born 11 April 1936; ord Bishop 30 Aug 1995.

■ ARCHDIOCESE OF SOUTHWARK

I Thomas Grant: born 25 Nov 1816; cons 6 July 1851; died 1 June 1870.
II James Danell: born 14 July 1821; cons 24 Mar 1871; died 14 June 1881.
III Robert A Coffin, CSSR: born 19 July 1819; cons 11 June 1882; died 6 April 1885.
IV John Butt: born 20 April 1826; cons as Auxiliary, 29 Jan 1885; trans to Southwark, 26 June 1885; resigned 9 April 1897; died 1 Nov 1899.
V Francis Bourne: born 23 Mar 1861: cons as Coadjutor, 1 May 1896; succ 9 April 1897; trans to Westminster, 11 Sept 1903; died 1 Jan 1935.
VI Peter E Amigo: born 26 May 1864; cons 25 Mar 1904; named Archbishop ad personam 18 Dec 1937; died 1 Oct 1949.
VII Cyril Cowderoy: born 5 May 1905; cons 21 Dec 1949; named Archbishop and Metropolitan 28 May 1965; died 10 Oct 1976.
VIII Michael G. Bowen: born 23 Apr 1930; ord Bishop of Lamsorti and Cadjutor Bishop of Arundel and Brighton 17 June 1970; succd 14 Mar 1971; transl 23 Apr 1977.
IX John Patrick McDonald: born 18 Aug 1947; cons Bishop of Northampton 2 May 2001; trans as Archbishop of Southwark 8 Dec 2003.

■ DIOCESE OF WREXHAM

I James Hannigan: born 15 July 1928; cons Bishop of Menevia 23 Nov 1983; trans to newly-erected See of Wrexham 24 Mar 1987; died 6th March 1994.
II Edwin Regan: born 31 Dec 1935; ord Bishop 13 Dec 1994.

■ BISHOPRIC OF THE FORCES

Prior to Nov 1917 the Archbishop of Westminster was Vicar Delegate to the Navy and Army; he remained Vicar Delegate to the Navy until April 1954.
I William Keatinge: born 1 Aug 1869; cons Bishop of Metellopolitano and first Ordinary to the Army 17 Nov 1917; apptd first Ordinary to the Air Force on its formation in 1918; died 21 Feb 1934.
II James Dey: born 14 Oct 1869; cons Bishop of Sebastopolis and second Ordinary to the Army and Air Force 2 June 1935; died 8 June 1946. Between June 1946-April 1954, Apostolic Administrators were appointed for the Army and Air Force. The Vicariate of the Forces was established by SCC Decree Inexhausta Caritate of 2l Nov 1953.
III David Mathew: born 15 Jan 1902; cons Bishop of Aeliae and Auxiliary of Westminster, 21 Dec 1938; created Abp of Apamea in Bithynia and apptd Apostolic Delegate to British East and West Africa 10 May 1946; apptd first Vicar of the Forces 23 April 1954; retired 30 Nov 1963; died 12 Dec 1975.
IV Gerard Tickle: born 2 Nov 1909; cons Bishop of Bela and second Vicar of the Forces 30 Nov 1963; retired 22 Feb 1979; died 14 Sept 1994.
V Francis J Walmsley: born 9 Nov 1928; ord Bishop of Tamalluna and third Military Vicar 22 Feb 1979; became first Military Ordinary 21 July 1987; Bishop-in-Ordinary to Her Majesty's Forces 20 Nov 1997.
VI Thomas Matthew Burns, born 3 June, 1944; cons Bishop-in-Ordinary to HM Forces, 18 June, 2002.

■ AUXILIARY BISHOPS.

ARCHDIOCESE OF WESTMINSTER.

William Weathers: born 6 May 1814; ord. titular Bishop of Amclea 28 Oct. 1872; died 4th March 1895.
James Paterson: born16 Nov. 1822; ord. titular Bishop of Emmaus 9 May 1890; died 3rd Dec. 1901.
Robert Brindle: born 4 Nov. 1837; ord. titular Bishop of Ermopolis 12 Mar. 1899; trans. to Nottingham 6 Dec. 1901; died 27 June 1916.
Charles Algernon Stanley: born 16 Sept. 1843; ord. titular Bishop of Emmaus 15 Mar. 1903; died 23 April 1928.
William Anthony Johnson: born 20 Aug. 1832; ord. titular Bishop of Arindela 1 May 1906; died 27 Mar. 1909.
Joseph Butt: born 27 March 1869; ord. titular Bishop of Cambysopolis 24 Feb. 1911; died 23 Aug. 1944.
Bernard Nicholas Ward: born 4 Feb. 1857; ord. titular Bishop of Lydda 10 April. 1917; tran. to Brentwood 20 July 1917; died 21 Jan 1920.
Emmanuel Bidwell: born 29 June 1872; ord. titular Bishop of Miletopolis 1 Dec. 1917; died 11 July 1930.
Edward Myers: born 8 Sept. 1875; ord. titular Bishop of Lamus 25 July 1932; trans to titular Archbishop of Beroea and coadjutor 20 Jan. 1951; died 13 Sept. 1956.
David Mathew: born 15 Jan. 1902; ord. titular Bishop of Alia 21 Dec. 1938; trans. to titular Archbishop of Apamea in Bythinia and Apostolic Delegate to East Africa 20 Feb. 1946; apptd first Vicar of the Forces 23 April 1954; died 12 Dec. 1975.

George Craven: born 1 Feb. 1884; ord. titular Bishop of Sebastopilis 25 1947; died 15th March 1967.
David John Cashman: born 27 Dec. 1912; ord. titular Bishop of Cantanus 27 May 1958; trans. to Arundel and Brighton 14 June 1965, died 14 March 1971.
Patrick Joseph Casey: born 20 Nov. 1913; ord. titular Bishop of Sufar 2 Feb. 1966; trans to Brentwood 28 Nov 1969; resigned 11 Dec. 1979, died 26 Jan. 1999.
Basil Christopher Butler OSB: born 7 May 1902; ord. titular Bishop of Nova Barbara 21Dec. 1966; died 20 Sept. 1986.
Gerald Mahon MHM: born 4 May 1922; ord. titular Bishop of Eanach Duin 23 May 1970; died 29 Jan. 1992.
Victor Guazelli: born 19 March 1920; ord. titular Bishop of Lindisfarne 23 May 1970, retired. Died 2004.
Philip Harvey: born 6 March 1915; ord. titular Bishop of Baanna 25 April 1977; retired, died 2 Feb 2003.
David Konstant: born 16 June 1930; ord. titular Bishop of Betagbara 25 April 1977; trans. to Leeds 25 Sept. 1985.
James O'Brien: born 5 Aug. 1930. titular Bishop of Manaccenser 21 Sept. 1977.
John Crowley: born 23 June 1941; ord. titular Bishop of Tala 8 Dec. 1986; trans to Middlesbrough 18th Jan 1993.
Vincent Nichols: born 8 Nov. 1945; ord. titular Bishop of Othona 24 Jan. 1992, trns to Birmingham 29 March 2000.
Patrick O'Donoghue: born 4 May 1934; ord titular Bishop of Tulana 29 June 1993; trans. to Lancaster 4 July 2001.
Arthur Roche, born 6 March 1950, ord titular Bishop of Rusticana 10 May 2001; appointed Bishop of Leeds 7 April 2004.
George Stack, born 9 May 1946, ord titular Bishop of Gemallae 10th May 2001.
Alan Hopes, born 14 March, 1944, ord titular Bishop of Cuncacestre, 24 January 2003.
Bernard Longley, born 5 April, 1955, ord titular Bishop of Zarna, 24 January 2003.
James O'Brien, born 5 Aug, 1930, ord titular Bishop of Manaccenser 21st Sept 1977.

■ DIOCESE OF ARUNDEL AND BRIGHTON

Michael George Bowen: born 23 April 1930; ord. titular Bishop of Lamsorti and coadjutor 27 June 1970; succeded to See 14 March 1971; trans to Southwark as Archbishop 23 April. 1977.

■ ARCHDIOCESE OF BIRMINGHAM.

Edward Ilsley: born 11 May 1838; ord. titular Bishop of Fessei 4 Dec. 1879; succeeded as Bishop 17 Feb. 1888.
Michael Francis Glancey: born 25 Oct. 1854; ord. titular Bishop of Flaviopolis 29 Sept. 1924; died 16 Oct. 1925.
John Patrick Barrett: born 31 Oct. 1878; ord. titular Bishop of Assus 22 Feb. 1927; trans. to Plymouth as Bishop 7 June 1929.
Bernard William Griffin: born 21Feb. 1899; ord. titular Bishop of Appia 30 June 1938; trans to Westminster as Archbishop 18 Dec. 1943.
Humphrey Bright: born 27 Jan 1903; ord. titular Bishop of Soli 28 Oct. 1944; died 26 March 1964.
Joseph Francis Cleary: born 4 Sept. 1912; ord. titular Bishop of Cresima 25 Jan. 1965 died 25 Feb. 1991.
Anthony Emery: born 17 May 1918; ord. titular Bishop of Tamallula 8 March 1968; trans to Portsmouth 13 Sept. 1976.
Patrick Leo McCartie: born 5 Sept. 1925; ord. titular Bishop of Elmham 30 May 1977; trans. to Northampton 19 March 1990.
Crispian Hollis: born 11 Nov. 1936; ord. titular Bishop of Cincari 5 May 1987; trans. to Portsmouth 6 Dec. 1988.
Terence J Brain: born 19 Dec 1938; ord. titular Bishop of Amudarsa 22 May 1991; trans. to Salford 8 Oct 1997.
Philip Pargeter: born 13 June 1933; ord. titular Bishop of Valentiniana 21 Feb. 1990.

■ DIOCESE OF BRENTWOOD.

George Andrew Beck, AA: born 28 May 1904; ord. titular Bishop of Tigia and Coadjutor 21 Sept. 1948; succeeded to See 23 Jan. 1951.

■ ARCHDIOCESE OF CARDIFF.

Daniel Joseph Mullins: born 10 July 1929; ord. titular Bishop of Sidnacestre 1 April 1970. trans. to Menevia as Bishop 17 Feb. 1987.

■ DIOCESE OF CLIFTON

Mervyn Alban Alexander: born 29 June 1925; ord. titular Bishop of Pinhel 25 April 1972; succeeded to See 20 Dec. 1974.

■ DIOCESE OF ARUNDEL AND BRIGHTON

Thomas William Wilkinson: born 5 April 1825; ord. titular Bishop of Cisamus 25 July 1888; succeeded to the See 28 Dec. 1889.
Richard Preston: born 12 Dec 1858; ord. titular Bishop of Rhocea 25 July 1900; died 9 Feb. 1905.
Richard Collins: born 5 April 1857; ord. titular Bishop of Selinonte 29 June 1905; succeeded to the See 21 June 1909.
James Cunningham: born 15 Aug 1910; ord. titular Bishop of Jos 12 Nov. 1957: succeeded to the See 1 June 1958.

Hugh Lindsay: born 20 June 1927; ord. titular Bishop of Cunccestre 11 Dec. 1969; succeeded to the See 12 Dec. 1974; resigned 20 March 1992.
Owen Swindlehurst: born 10 May 1928; ord. titular Bishop of Cuncecestre 25 July 1977; died 28 Aug 1995.

■ DIOCESE OF LANCASTER
Thomas Bernard Pearson: born 18 Jan 1907; ord. titular Bishop of Sinda 25 July 1948; died 17 Nov. 1987.

■ DIOCESE OF LEEDS.
William Gordon: born 24 Sept. 1831; ord. titular Bishop of Arcadiopolis and coadjutor 24 Feb. 1890; succeeded to the See 16 June 1890.
Robert Joseph Cowgill: born 23 Feb. 1860; ord. titular Bishop of Olena 30 Nov. 1905; succeeded to the See 7 June 1911.
Gerald Moverley: born 9 April 1922; ord. titular Bishop of Proconsularia 25 Jan 1968; trans. to Hallam 30 May 1980.
Arthur Roche, born 6 March 1950, ord titular Bishop of Rusticana 10 May 2001; trans to Leeds (coadjutor Bishop)

■ ARCHDIOCESE OF LIVERPOOL
Alexander Goss: born 5 July 1814; ord. titular Bishop of Gerra and Coadjutor 25 Sept. 1853; succeeded to the See 25 Jan. 1856.
Robert Dobson: born 20 Jan. 1867; ord. titular Bishop of Cynopolis 30 Nov. 1922; died 6 Jan 1942.
Joseph Halsall: born 15 Feb. 1902; ord. titular Bishop of Aabi 21 Sept. 1945; died 13 March 1958.
Augustine Harris: born 27 Oct. 1917; ord. titular Bishop of Socia 11 Feb. 1966; trans. to Middlesbrough 10 Nov. 1978.
Joseph Gray: born 20 Oct. 1919; ord. titular Bishop of Mercia 16 Feb. 1969; trans to Shrewsbury 19 Aug. 1980.
Kevin O'Connor: born 20 May 1929; ord. titular Bishop of Glastonia 3. July 1979; died 5 May 1993.
Anthony Hitchen: born 23 May 1930; ord. titular Bishop of Othona 3 July 1979; died 10 April 1988.
John Rawsthorne: born 12 Nov 1936; ord. titular Bishop of Rotdon; 16 Dec 1981; trans to Hallam 3 July 1997.
Vincent Malone: born 11 Sept 1931; ord. titular Bishop of Abora 3 July 1989.
Thomas Williams:

■ DIOCESE OF MENEVIA.
John Cuthbert Hedley: born 15 April 1837; ord. titular Bishop of Caesaropolis and Coadjutor 29 Sept. 1873; succeeded to the See 18 Feb. 1881.

Langton Fox: born 21 Jan. 1917; ord. titular Bishop of Maura 16 Dec. 1965; succeeded to the See 16 June 1972; resigned 5 Feb 1981.
John Aloysius Ward OFMCap: born 24 Jan 1929; ord. titular Bishop and Coadjutor 1 October 1980; succeded to the See 5 Feb. 1981; trans. as Archbishop to Cardiff 23 March 1983.

■ DIOCESE OF MIDDLESBROUGH
Thomas Shine: born 11 Feb 1872; ord. titular Bishop of Lamus and Coadjutor 29 June 1921; succeeded to the See 11 April 1929.
George Brunner: born 21 Aug. 1889; ord. titular Bishop of Ellis 25 July 1946; succeeded to the See 11 April 1956.
William Gordon Wheeler: born 5 May 1910; ord. titular Bishop of Theudalis and Coadjutor 19 March 1964; trans to Leeds as Bishop 25 April 1966.
John Gerard McClean: born 24 Sept. 1914; ord. titular Bishop of Maxita and Coadjutor 24 Feb. 1967; succeeded to the See 13 June 1967.
Thomas Kevin O'Brien: born 18 Feb. 1923; ord. titular Bishop of Ard Carna 8 Dec. 1981. Rtd 1998; died 27 Dec. 2004.

■ DIOCESE OF NORTHAMPTON
Alan Charles Clark: born 9 August 1919; ord, titular Bishop of Elmham and Auxiliary Bishop 13 May 1969; translated to newly erected see of East Anglia 2 June 1976.

■ DIOCESE OF NOTTINGHAM.
James McGuinness: born 2 Oct. 1925; ord. titular Bishop of St. Germans and Coadjutor 23 March 1972; succeeded to the See 31 Oct. 1974.

■ DIOCESE OF PLYMOUTH.
Charles Maurice Graham: born 5 April 1834; ord. titular Bishop of Cisamus and Coadjutor 28 Oct 1891; succeeded to the See 25 Oct. 1902.

■ DIOCESE OF PORTSMOUTH.
John Baptist Cahill: born 2 Sept. 1841; ord. titular Bishop of Thagora 1 May 1900; succeeded to the See 30 Aug. 1900.
William Timothy Cotter: born 21 Dec. 1866; ord. titular Bishop of Clazomenae 19 March 1905; succeeded to the See 24 Nov. 1910.
John Henry King: born 16 Sept. 1880; ord. titular Bishop of Opus 15 July 1938; succeeded to the See 4 June 1941.
Thomas Holland: born 11 June 1908; ord. titular Bishop of Etenna and Coadjutor 21 Dec. 1960; trans. to Salford as Bishop 28 Aug. 1964.

■ **DIOCESE OF SALFORD.**
John Francis Vaughan: born 24 Jan. 1853; ord. titular Bishop of Sebastopolis 15 Aug. 1909; died 4 Dec. 1925.
Geoffrey Burke: born 31 July 1913; ord. titular Bishop of Vaugrata 29 June 1967; retired 31 July 1988.

■ **DIOCESE OF SHREWSBURY**
Edmund Knight: born 27 Aug. 1827; ord. titular Bishop of Carycys 27 July 1879; succeeded to the See 25 April 1882.
John Carroll: born 17 May 1838; ord. titular Bishop of Acmonia and Coadjutor 28 Oct 1893; succeeded to the See 17 Dec. 1934.
Ambrose James Moriarty: born 9 Aug. 1870; ord. titular Bishop of Miletopolis and Coadjutor 28 Jan. 1932; succeeded to the See 17 Dec. 1934.
John Aloysius Murphy: born 21 Dec. 1905; ord. titular Bishop of Appia and Coadjutor 25 Feb. 1948; succeeded to the See 3 June 1949.
John Brewer: born 24 Nov. 1929; ord. titular Bishop of Britonia 28 July 1971; trans to Lancaster as Coadjutor 15 Nov. 1983.

■ **ARCHDIOCESE OF SOUTHWARK**
John Baptist Butt: born 20 April 1826; ord. titular Bishop of Melos 29 Jan. 1885; succeeded to the See 26 June 1885.
Francis Alphonsus Bourne: born 23 March 1861;ord. titular Bishop of Epiphania and Coadjutor 1 May 1896; succeeded to the See 9 April 1897; trans. to Westminster as Archbishop 11 Sept. 1903.
William Brown: born 3 May 1862; ord. titular Bishop of Pella 12 March 1924; died 16 Dec. 1951.
Charles Joseph Henderson: born 14 April 1924; ord. titular Bishop of Tricala 8 Dec. 1972.
John Jukes OFMConv: born 7 Aug. 1923; ord. titular Bishop of Strathearn 30 Jan. 1980.
Howard Tripp: born 3 July 1927; ord. titular Bishop of Newport 30 Jan. 1980.
John Hine, born 26 July 1938; ord titular Bishop of Beverley, 27 Feb 2001.

INDEX OF PLACES

INDEX OF PLACES

INDEX OF PLACES

GENERAL INDEX

from traditional ... to contemporary
ECCLESIASTICAL ART
Wood carved
Bronze
Fiberglass
KEVIN KEARNEY
RELIGIOUS ARTICLES
Telephone: (028) 3086 1522
From R.O.I.: +48 3086 1522
Fax: (028) 3086 8352
ail: kevinkearney@religiousarticles.co.uk
Web: www.religiousarticles.co.uk
Cullyhanna
County Armagh
Northern Ireland BT35 0JG
KEVIN KEARNEY RELIGIOUS ARTICLES
CHURCH VESTMENTS
APOSTOLIC GOODS
MASS KITS
CANDLES
STATIONS OF THE CROSS
CHURCH ENVELOPES
ALTAR WINE
DEVOTIONAL ITEMS
CRIB SETS
VDF
©
DEMETZ
STUDIO